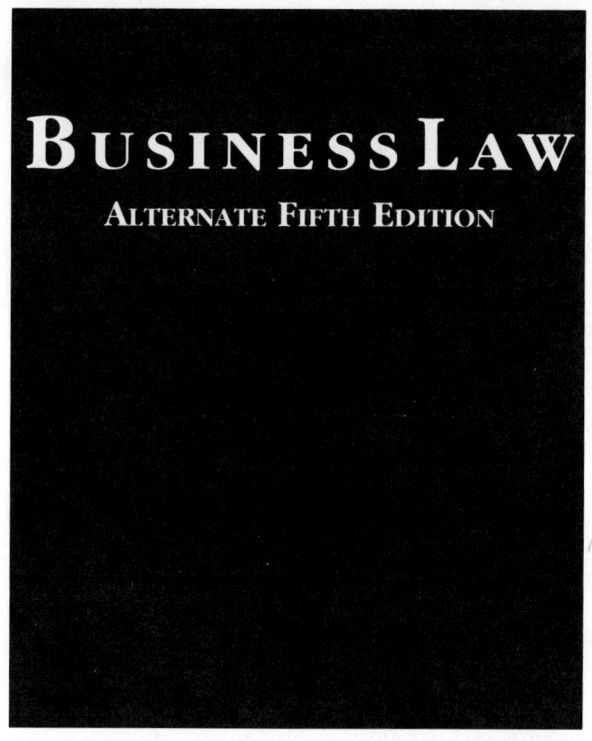

# BUSINESS LAW
## ALTERNATE FIFTH EDITION

John R. Allison
*University of Texas at Austin*

Robert A. Prentice
*University of Texas at Austin*

Rate A. Howell
*The Ohio State University*

The Dryden Press
A Harcourt Brace Jovanovich College Publisher
Fort Worth  Philadelphia  San Diego
New York  Orlando  Austin  San Antonio
Toronto  Montreal  London  Sydney  Tokyo

Developmental Editor:   Kathryn Erley
Project Editor:   Karen Shaw
Cover Design:   Annette Spadoni
Production Manager:   Barb Bahnsen
Director of Editing, Design, and Production:   Jane Perkins

Copy Editor:   Charlene Posner
Indexer:   Leoni McVey
Compositor:   G&S Typesetters, Inc.
Text Type:   10/12 ITC Garamond Book

**Library of Congress Cataloging-in-Publication Data**
Allison, John Robert, 1948–
    Business law / John R. Allison, Robert A. Prentice, Rate A. Howell.—Alternate 5th ed.
        p.    cm.
    ISBN 0-03-073153-4
    1. Commercial law—United States—Cases.   I. Prentice, Robert A., 1950–  .  II. Howell, Rate A.  III. Title.
KF888.A38   1992
346.73'07—dc20
[347.3067]                                                       90-28281

Printed in the United States of America
    2-041-98765432
Copyright © 1992, 1989, 1986, 1982, 1979 by The Dryden Press.

All rights reserved. No part of this publication may be reproduced or transmitted in any form or by any means, electronic or mechanical, including photocopy, recording, or any information storage and retrieval system, without permission in writing from the publisher.

Requests for permission to make copies of any part of the work should be mailed to: Permissions Department, Harcourt Brace Jovanovich, Publishers, 8th Floor, Orlando, FL 32887.

Address orders:
The Dryden Press
Orlando, FL 32887

Address editorial correspondence:
The Dryden Press
301 Commerce Street, Suite 3700
Fort Worth, TX 76102

The Dryden Press
Harcourt Brace Jovanovich

# PREFACE

We have had but one goal in preparing *Alternate Fifth Edition: Business Law*: to make the text a more useful vehicle for the study of Business Law by future business managers at both graduate and undergraduate levels in our colleges and universities. In striving to attain this goal, we rejected the temptation merely to fine-tune the prior edition and have developed a number of new features that will be highlighted later in the preface.

This edition, nonetheless, retains the basic strengths of earlier editions, which can be described as follows:

First, we have continued to use a lucid, conversational writing style. In addition, we have tried to illuminate legal principles by frequent use of examples to show how these rules apply to "real world" situations.

Second, illustrative court cases are interspersed throughout the text materials, rather than relegated to chapter ends. As in previous editions, this text's alternate format presents the cases in an abbreviated form. Both the fact presentations and case decisions are summarized in the authors' own words, thus meeting the needs of instructors and students who are required to move through the material at a pace that does not permit detailed analysis of the reasoning of each court decision.

Third, the text continues to be essentially a traditional one, rather than an environmental one. In other words, despite a rather full discussion of the legal system in Part I and of several regulatory topics in Part VII, most of the text is again devoted to such subjects as contracts, agency, sales, commercial paper, property, and business organizations.

## CHANGES IN THIS EDITION

- A new chapter on Criminal Law and Business, providing coverage of fundamental concepts and an extensive treatment of white-collar and computer crime (Chapter 7)
- A new chapter on Contract Interpretation and Remedies for Breach of Contract (Chapter 19)
- A new chapter on The Legal Environment of International Business (Chapter 51)
- The chapter on Business Ethics, Corporate Social Responsiveness, and the Law completely rewritten (Chapter 10)
- Material on alternative dispute resolution completely rewritten (in Chapter 3)
- Coverage of new Article 2A of the Uniform Commercial Code—Leases—in several different chapters, including Sales: Introduction to the Law of Sales (Chapter 20), Sales: Warranties and Products Liability (Chapter 22), Secured Transactions (Chapter 29), and Personal Property and Bailments (Chapter 45)
- A substantial new section on increasing federal control over checks and the bank–depositor relationship, especially Federal Reserve Board Regulation CC (in Chapter 28)
- A substantial new section on new Article 4A of the Uniform Commercial Code—Commercial Electronic Funds Transfers (in Chapter 28)
- Expanded coverage of Business (Competitive) Torts (Chapter 9)
- Increased integration of sales contract principles from the UCC with material on contracts (in Chapters 11–19)
- Material on employment discrimination completely rewritten, with coverage of recent dramatic changes in the area of employment law (in Chapter 49)
- A new section on the employer's right to discharge employees, including exceptions to employment-at-will (in Chapter 49)
- A new section on employee privacy, including employer use of lie detectors and drug tests (in Chapter 49)
- A new chapter on Antitrust Law (Chapter 48)
- Substantial rewriting of the remaining text
- Many new cases

## ANCILLARY MATERIALS

*Business Law: Alternate Fifth Edition* is supported by a comprehensive ancillary package which includes an *Instructor's Manual and Transparency Masters*, a *Test Bank*, a set of preprinted tests, a *Computerized Test Bank*, and a *Study Guide*.

Each instructor has his or her own unique approach to the teaching of Business Law. Our *Instructor's Manual* is a tool that assists the instructor in integrating his or her style with the approach taken by the book. Each chapter includes helpful authors' suggestions for teaching the chapter. Chapter outlines have been added to assist the instructor in organizing lecture notes. Succinct case briefs are included for each case in the book. We have also added an annotated list of additional cases so that the instructor can easily supplement the cases found in the text. Each chapter in the *Instructor's Manual* ends with answers to end-of-chapter questions and problems.

The *Test Bank* contains over 2,000 multiple-choice and true-false questions. We have added numerous essay questions for the instructor to choose from.

A *Computerized Test Bank* is also available for this edition for use on the IBM PC®.

A comprehensive *Study Guide* provides additional review and reinforcement of all topics covered in the text. Each chapter of the guide, which has traditionally been well received by students and instructors, begins with a chapter summary. The key term and matching exercises also provide an excellent review for students. The purpose of these two sections is to test the student's basic mastery of the concepts, laws, and rulings discussed in the text. Multiple-choice and true-false questions are provided, as well as case analysis problems which provide fact-patterns to which the student is asked to respond. All three types of questions will test the student's comprehension of the material in an examination setting. The questions are similar in format and type to those included in the *Test Bank*.

Another feature of the *Study Guide* is the inclusion of legal forms. We include these forms to give the student a good idea of how legal concepts are employed in the business world.

## ACKNOWLEDGMENTS

As with any major undertaking, this text owes its existence to the efforts of many individuals. We owe a special debt to bankruptcy attorney Leslie K. Prentice for her substantial assistance in the revision and updating of Chapter 30. We wish to thank John McGee at Southwest Texas State University for his preparation of the *Test Bank* and help with the *Instructor's Manual*, Carol Rasnic at Virginia Commonwealth University for the *Study Guide*, and the many reviewers who read the manuscript for this and previous editions and provided valuable suggestions. They are Anita Cava *University of Miami*, Frank Cavilere *Lamar University*, Renee Culverhouse *Auburn University*, Bob Ek *Seminole Community College*, Bradley Lutz *Hillborough Community College*, W. Albert Martin *Johnson and Wales College*, Roy Smith *University of Arkansas*, Charles Stowe *Sam Houston State University*, Marleen Swerdlow *Lamar University*, Andy Vanderplatt *Linn-Benton Community College*, and James Walsh *Tidewater Community College*.

We also wish to thank our editors at The Dryden Press, Kathi Erley, Karen Shaw, and Charlene Posner, for their commitment to excellence.

In addition, we are grateful to our students for keeping us fresh and fully challenged, and to our families for their continued support.

Finally, we would be terribly remiss not to acknowledge the fundamental contributions of Professor Rate A. Howell, who was the lead author on the first four editions but who has now retired to engage in kinder and gentler pursuits. We not only express our sincere gratitude to Professor Howell, but also wish him the very best in his future endeavors.

John R. Allison, *Austin, Texas*
Robert A. Prentice, *Austin, Texas*

# Contents

## PART I
## THE LEGAL ENVIRONMENT OF BUSINESS  1

**CHAPTER 1  Nature and Sources of Law**  3
Law as a Subject of Study  3
What is Law?  3
Rules and Processes  4
Requisites of a Legal System  4
Some Classifications of Law  6
Legal Misconceptions  8
Law, Justice, and Morals  9
Selecting and Using Attorneys  11
Summary  12
Key Terms  13
Questions and Problems  13

**CHAPTER 2  Court Systems, Jurisdiction, and Functions**  15
Court Systems  15
Problems of Jurisdiction  18
Law, Equity, and Remedies  23
Summary  25
Key Terms  25
Questions and Problems  25

**CHAPTER 3  Dispute Resolution**  27
Litigation: Pretrial Proceedings  27
Litigation: Trial Proceedings  30
Litigation: The Appellate Courts  32
Analysis of the Adjudicative Process  35
Alternative Methods of Dispute Resolution  36
Summary  38
Key Terms  39
Questions and Problems  39

**CHAPTER 4  Common and Statutory Law**  41
Origin of Common Law  41
Common Law—The Doctrine of *Stare Decisis*  43
A Profile of Our Federal and State Statutory Law  45
Statutory Law—The Rationale  45
Limitations on Legislative Bodies  46
Statutory Law and Common Law—A Contrast  47
Statutory Interpretation  48
Selected State Statutes  51
Summary  52
Key Terms  52
Questions and Problems  52

**CHAPTER 5  Constitutional Law**  55
Organization and Jurisdiction  55
Legislative, Executive, and Judicial Authority  59
Basic Rights  61
Summary  71
Key Terms  72
Questions and Problems  72

**CHAPTER 6  Lawmaking by Administrative Agencies**  75
Rise of the Administrative Agency  75
The Agency—An Overview  76
Legislative Delegation of Lawmaking Power  76
Function and Powers  76
Procedural Due Process  82
Estoppel  83
Recent Developments  84
Summary  86
Key Terms  86
Questions and Problems  86

**CHAPTER 7  Criminal Law and Business**  89
Nature of Criminal Law  89
Constitutional Protections  91

| | |
|---|---|
| General Elements of Criminal Responsibility | 94 |
| General Criminal Defenses | 95 |
| State Crimes Affecting Business | 96 |
| Federal Crimes Affecting Business | 99 |
| Computer Crime | 101 |
| White Collar Crime | 102 |
| Summary | 103 |
| Key Terms | 103 |
| Questions and Problems | 103 |

### CHAPTER 8  TORTS  107
| | |
|---|---|
| A Preface | 107 |
| Scope and Complexity of Tort Law | 107 |
| Negligence | 108 |
| Major Intentional Torts | 114 |
| Other Intentional Torts | 121 |
| Special Problems | 123 |
| Summary | 124 |
| Key Terms | 124 |
| Questions and Problems | 124 |

### CHAPTER 9  BUSINESS TORTS  127
| | |
|---|---|
| Interference with Business Conduct | 127 |
| Trademark Infringement | 129 |
| Misuse of Trade Secrets | 132 |
| Patent Infringement | 134 |
| Copyright Infringement | 136 |
| Unfair Competition | 139 |
| Summary | 141 |
| Key Terms | 141 |
| Questions and Problems | 141 |

### CHAPTER 10  BUSINESS ETHICS, CORPORATE SOCIAL RESPONSIVENESS, AND THE LAW  143
| | |
|---|---|
| What is Ethics? | 143 |
| The Relationship between Law and Ethics | 144 |
| Are There Any Moral Standards? | 146 |
| The "Moral Minimum" | 146 |
| Is There a Duty to "Do Good"? | 149 |
| Excusing Conditions | 150 |
| Moral Dilemmas | 150 |
| Moral Reasoning and Decision Making | 151 |
| Are Corporations Moral Agents? | 155 |
| Does Ethics Pay? | 157 |
| Corporate Social Responsiveness | 158 |
| Summary | 160 |
| Key Terms | 161 |
| Questions and Problems | 161 |

## PART II
## PRINCIPLES OF CONTRACT LAW  163

### CHAPTER 11  NATURE AND CLASSIFICATION OF CONTRACTS  165
| | |
|---|---|
| A Perspective | 165 |
| Nature of a Contract | 165 |
| Classification of Contracts | 165 |
| Contract Law and Sales Law—A Special Relationship | 171 |
| Summary | 172 |
| Key Terms | 172 |
| Questions and Problems | 172 |

### CHAPTER 12  THE AGREEMENT  175
| | |
|---|---|
| Intention of the Parties | 175 |
| Requirements of the Offer | 176 |
| Termination of the Offer | 184 |
| Preliminary Considerations of the Acceptance | 186 |
| Requirements of the Acceptance | 186 |
| Summary | 196 |
| Key Terms | 197 |
| Questions and Problems | 197 |

### CHAPTER 13  CONSIDERATION  199
| | |
|---|---|
| Historical Note | 199 |
| The Basic Concept of Consideration | 199 |
| Special Situations | 209 |
| Summary | 212 |
| Key Terms | 212 |
| Questions and Problems | 213 |

### CHAPTER 14  ILLEGALITY  215
| | |
|---|---|
| Contracts Contrary to Statute | 215 |
| Contracts Contrary to Public Policy | 218 |
| Effects of Illegal Contracts | 224 |
| Summary | 225 |
| Key Terms | 225 |
| Questions and Problems | 225 |

### CHAPTER 15  VOIDABLE CONTRACTS  229
| | |
|---|---|
| Capacity | 229 |
| Minors | 229 |
| Mentally Impaired and Intoxicated Persons | 235 |
| Reality of Consent | 236 |
| Fraud | 236 |
| Innocent Misrepresentation | 242 |
| Mistake | 242 |
| Duress | 245 |

| | |
|---|---|
| Undue Influence | 246 |
| Summary | 247 |
| Key Terms | 247 |
| Questions and Problems | 248 |

### CHAPTER 16  CONTRACTS IN WRITING  251
| | |
|---|---|
| The Statute of Frauds | 251 |
| Contracts That Must Be in Writing | 252 |
| Contracts Calling for Sale of Goods | 256 |
| When Is the Writing Sufficient? | 259 |
| The Parol Evidence Rule | 259 |
| Summary | 260 |
| Key Terms | 261 |
| Questions and Problems | 261 |

### CHAPTER 17  RIGHTS OF THIRD PARTIES  263
| | |
|---|---|
| Third-Party Beneficiaries | 263 |
| Assignments | 264 |
| Delegation of Duties | 267 |
| Summary | 269 |
| Key Terms | 269 |
| Questions and Problems | 269 |

### CHAPTER 18  DISCHARGE OF CONTRACTS  271
| | |
|---|---|
| Discharge by Operation of Conditions | 271 |
| Discharge by Performance | 274 |
| Discharge by Breach | 278 |
| Discharge by Legal Impossibility | 278 |
| Discharge by Commercial Impracticability | 281 |
| Discharge by Frustration of Purpose | 282 |
| Discharge by Parties' Agreement | 283 |
| Discharge by Operation of Law | 283 |
| Summary | 284 |
| Key Terms | 284 |
| Questions and Problems | 285 |

### CHAPTER 19  CONTRACT INTERPRETATION AND REMEDIES FOR BREACH OF CONTRACT  287
| | |
|---|---|
| Contract Interpretation | 287 |
| Remedies for Breach of Contract | 291 |
| Summary | 301 |
| Key Terms | 301 |
| Questions and Problems | 301 |

## PART III  SALES, COMMERCIAL TRANSACTIONS, AND BANKRUPTCY  305

### CHAPTER 20  SALES: INTRODUCTION TO THE LAW OF SALES  307
| | |
|---|---|
| Scope of Article 2 of the UCC | 307 |
| Review of Basic Principles of Sales Contracts | 311 |
| Documents of Title | 313 |
| Summary | 314 |
| Key Terms | 314 |
| Questions and Problems | 314 |

### CHAPTER 21  SALES: TITLE, RISK OF LOSS, AND INSURABLE INTEREST  317
| | |
|---|---|
| Title to Goods | 317 |
| Risk of Loss | 322 |
| Insurable Interest | 327 |
| Sale on Approval and Sale or Return | 327 |
| Summary | 329 |
| Key Terms | 330 |
| Questions and Problems | 330 |

### CHAPTER 22  SALES: WARRANTIES AND PRODUCTS LIABILITY  333
| | |
|---|---|
| Warranty | 333 |
| Negligence | 343 |
| Strict Liability | 344 |
| Federal Consumer Legislation | 348 |
| Legislative Limitations on Products Liability Revolution | 350 |
| Summary | 350 |
| Key Terms | 351 |
| Questions and Problems | 351 |

### CHAPTER 23  SALES: PERFORMANCE AND REMEDIES  353
| | |
|---|---|
| Performance of the Sale Contract | 353 |
| Introduction to Remedies | 360 |
| Seller's Remedies | 360 |
| Buyer's Remedies | 362 |
| Lemon Laws | 366 |
| Summary | 366 |
| Key Terms | 367 |
| Questions and Problems | 367 |

### CHAPTER 24  COMMERCIAL PAPER: TYPES, PARTIES, AND BASIC CONCEPTS  369
| | |
|---|---|
| Development of the Law | 369 |
| Purposes of Commercial Paper | 370 |

| | |
|---|---|
| Types of Commercial Paper | 370 |
| Assignee versus Holder in Due Course | 374 |
| Parties to Commercial Paper | 374 |
| Summary | 375 |
| Key Terms | 376 |
| Questions and Problems | 376 |

## CHAPTER 25  COMMERCIAL PAPER: NEGOTIABILITY AND TRANSFER 377

| | |
|---|---|
| Requirements of Negotiability | 377 |
| Transfer | 385 |
| Assignment and Negotiation | 385 |
| Blank, Special, Qualified, and Restrictive Indorsements | 386 |
| Miscellaneous Negotiation Problems | 391 |
| Summary | 393 |
| Key Terms | 394 |
| Questions and Problems | 394 |

## CHAPTER 26  COMMERCIAL PAPER: HOLDERS IN DUE COURSE AND DEFENSES 397

| | |
|---|---|
| Holders in Due Course | 397 |
| Defenses | 403 |
| Limitations on Holder in Due Course Doctrine | 408 |
| Summary | 409 |
| Key Terms | 410 |
| Questions and Problems | 410 |

## CHAPTER 27  COMMERCIAL PAPER: LIABILITY OF THE PARTIES 413

| | |
|---|---|
| The Signing Requirement | 413 |
| Liability of Primary Parties | 414 |
| Promissory Liability of Secondary Parties, Generally | 416 |
| Promissory Liability of Drawers | 416 |
| Promissory (Conditional) Liability of Indorsers | 417 |
| Warranty Liability of Indorsers | 420 |
| Selected Transferor-Indorser Problems | 422 |
| Discharge of the Parties | 423 |
| Summary | 424 |
| Key Terms | 424 |
| Questions and Problems | 424 |

## CHAPTER 28  COMMERCIAL PAPER: CHECKS AND THE BANK–DEPOSITOR RELATIONSHIP 427

| | |
|---|---|
| Checks | 427 |
| The Bank-Depositor Relationship | 428 |
| Selected Bank-Depositor Problems | 431 |

| | |
|---|---|
| Increased Federal Control over Checks and the Bank-Depositor Relationship | 435 |
| Electronic Banking | 437 |
| Summary | 440 |
| Key Terms | 441 |
| Questions and Problems | 441 |

## CHAPTER 29  SECURED TRANSACTIONS 443

| | |
|---|---|
| Secured Credit Transactions | 443 |
| Article 9 Terminology | 444 |
| Scope of Article 9 | 445 |
| Attachment (Creation) of a Security Interest | 447 |
| Perfection of the Security Interest | 448 |
| Limitations on Perfection | 453 |
| Perfection and the Floating Lien Concept | 455 |
| Proceeds and Commingling | 456 |
| Priorities between Creditors | 456 |
| Special Rules Applicable to Purchase Money Security Interests | 457 |
| Rights and Duties Prior to Termination | 458 |
| Default of the Debtor | 460 |
| Termination | 462 |
| Summary | 462 |
| Key Terms | 463 |
| Questions and Problems | 463 |

## CHAPTER 30  BANKRUPTCY 465

| | |
|---|---|
| Overview of Debtor-Creditor Relations | 465 |
| Bankruptcy Proceedings | 468 |
| Liquidation Proceedings | 468 |
| Business Reorganization | 477 |
| Adjustment of Debts | 480 |
| Summary | 482 |
| Key Terms | 482 |
| Questions and Problems | 483 |

# PART IV
# AGENCY AND PARTNERSHIP 485

## CHAPTER 31  AGENCY: NATURE, CREATION, DUTIES, AND TERMINATION 487

| | |
|---|---|
| Nature of the Agency Relationship | 487 |
| Creation of the Agency Relationship | 488 |
| Duties of Principal and Agent | 490 |
| Termination of the Agency Relationship | 492 |
| Summary | 495 |
| Key Terms | 495 |
| Questions and Problems | 495 |

## CHAPTER 32  AGENCY: LIABILITY OF THE PARTIES — 497
- Liability of the Principal — 497
- Liability of the Agent — 503
- Liability of the Third Party — 503
- Nonexistent, Partially Disclosed, and Undisclosed Principals — 503
- Tort Liability — 505
- Criminal Liability — 510
- Summary — 511
- Key Terms — 511
- Questions and Problems — 511

## CHAPTER 33  PARTNERSHIPS: NATURE, FORMATION, AND PROPERTY — 513
- The Nature and History of Partnerships — 513
- Formation of a Partnership — 514
- Partnership Property — 520
- Summary — 523
- Key Terms — 523
- Questions and Problems — 523

## CHAPTER 34  PARTNERSHIPS: OPERATING THE BUSINESS — 525
- Relations among Partners — 525
- Relations with Third Parties — 530
- Summary — 536
- Key Terms — 537
- Questions and Problems — 537

## CHAPTER 35  PARTNERSHIPS: TERMINATION — 539
- Dissolution — 539
- Winding Up Partnership Affairs — 544
- Summary — 549
- Key Terms — 549
- Questions and Problems — 549

## CHAPTER 36  LIMITED PARTNERSHIPS — 551
- The Nature and History of Limited Partnerships — 551
- Forming the Limited Partnership — 552
- Financing the Limited Partnership — 554
- Rights and Duties of General Partners — 554
- Rights and Duties of Limited Partners — 554
- Assignment of an Interest in a Limited Partnership — 557
- Dissolution and Winding Up of the Limited Partnership — 557
- Summary — 559
- Key Terms — 560
- Questions and Problems — 560

# PART V  CORPORATIONS AND SECURITIES REGULATION — 563

## CHAPTER 37  CORPORATIONS: NATURE AND FORMATION — 565
- The Nature and History of Corporations — 565
- The Corporation as a Legal Entity — 567
- Formation of the Corporation — 570
- Summary — 576
- Key Terms — 576
- Questions and Problems — 577

## CHAPTER 38  CORPORATIONS: CORPORATE POWERS AND MANAGEMENT — 579
- Corporate Powers — 579
- Corporate Management — 580
- Management of Close Corporations — 589
- Summary — 591
- Key Terms — 591
- Questions and Problems — 591

## CHAPTER 39  CORPORATIONS: RIGHTS AND LIABILITIES OF SHAREHOLDERS AND MANAGERS — 593
- Rights of Shareholders — 593
- Liabilities of Shareholders — 598
- Rights of Corporate Managers — 599
- Liabilities of Corporate Managers — 600
- Summary — 607
- Key Terms — 608
- Questions and Problems — 608

## CHAPTER 40  CORPORATIONS: MERGER, CONSOLIDATION, AND TERMINATION — 611
- Mergers and Consolidations — 611
- Termination — 622
- Summary — 624
- Key Terms — 625
- Questions and Problems — 625

## CHAPTER 41  SECURITIES REGULATION — 627
- Introduction to Securities Regulation — 627
- 1933 Act: Regulating the Issuance of Securities — 629
- 1934 Act: Regulating the Trading of Securities — 635
- State Regulation — 643
- RICO — 644
- Summary — 645
- Key Terms — 645
- Questions and Problems — 645

## CHAPTER 42 LEGAL LIABILITY OF ACCOUNTANTS  647
Common-Law Liability to Clients  647
Common-Law Liability to Third Parties  650
Management Advisory Services  652
Tax Practice  652
Accountants and the Federal Securities Laws  653
RICO  657
Criminal Liability of Accountants  657
Accountants' Privilege and Confidentiality  658
Summary  659
Key Terms  660
Questions and Problems  660

# PART VI
# PROPERTY: OWNERSHIP, CONTROL, AND PROTECTION  663

## CHAPTER 43 REAL PROPERTY  665
The Nature of Real Property  665
Interests in Real Property  667
Concurrent Ownership  671
Sales of Real Property  673
Adverse Possession  679
Regulation of Real Property Ownership, Use, and Sale  680
Summary  682
Key Terms  682
Questions and Problems  683

## CHAPTER 44 LANDLORD AND TENANT  685
The Nature of the Landlord–Tenant Relationship  685
Creation and Termination of the Landlord–Tenant Relationship  685
Possession of the Premises  687
Use of the Premises by the Tenant  688
The Duty to Maintain the Premises  689
Injuries on the Premises  693
Landlord's Responsibility to Protect Tenants from Crimes  695
Rent and Other Financial Obligations of the Tenant  696
The Landlord's Remedies  696
Assignments and Subleases  697
Summary  698
Key Terms  698
Questions and Problems  699

## CHAPTER 45 PERSONAL PROPERTY AND BAILMENTS  701
Ownership of Personal Property  701
Gifts of Personal Property  701
Other Methods of Acquiring Ownership  704
Bailments of Personal Property  708
Special Bailments  715
Summary  717
Key Terms  717
Questions and Problems  718

## CHAPTER 46 WILLS, TRUSTS, AND ESTATE PLANNING  721
Wills  721
Intestacy—Statutes of Descent and Distribution  725
Administration of the Estate  726
Trusts  728
Estate Planning  731
Summary  732
Key Terms  733
Questions and Problems  733

## CHAPTER 47 INSURANCE LAW  735
Nature and Functions of Insurance  735
Types of Insurance  739
Summary  747
Key Terms  748
Questions and Problems  748

# PART VII
# GOVERNMENT REGULATION OF BUSINESS  751

## CHAPTER 48 ANTITRUST LAW  753
Introduction  753
Monopolization  755
Mergers  759
Horizontal Restraints of Trade  763
Vertical Restraints of Trade  768
Summary  774
Key Terms  774
Questions and Problems  775

## CHAPTER 49 EMPLOYMENT LAW  777
Labor Relations Law  777
Employment Discrimination Law  780
Protection of Safety and Welfare  789
Employer's Right to Discharge Employees  790

| | |
|---|---|
| Protection of Employee Privacy | 793 |
| Summary | 794 |
| Key Terms | 795 |
| Questions and Problems | 795 |

## CHAPTER 50  CONSUMER TRANSACTIONS AND THE LAW — 797

| | |
|---|---|
| Deceptive Trade Practices | 797 |
| The Consumer Credit Protection Act | 800 |
| The Uniform Consumer Credit Code | 807 |
| The Real Estate Settlement Procedures Act | 809 |
| Additional Consumer Protection Measures | 810 |
| Summary | 810 |
| Key Terms | 811 |
| Questions and Problems | 811 |

## CHAPTER 51  THE LEGAL ENVIRONMENT OF INTERNATIONAL BUSINESS — 813

| | |
|---|---|
| Introduction | 813 |
| The International Sales Contract | 814 |
| Resolving International Trade Disputes | 817 |
| National Regulation of the Export/Import Process | 823 |
| Organizing for International Trade | 826 |
| Other Ways of Doing Business | 829 |
| Regulating the Transnational Corporation | 830 |
| Summary | 831 |
| Key Terms | 832 |
| Questions and Problems | 832 |

## APPENDIX A  THE UNIFORM COMMERCIAL CODE — 835

## APPENDIX B  THE UNIFORM PARTNERSHIP ACT — 938

## APPENDIX C  UNIFORM LIMITED PARTNERSHIP ACT — 946

## APPENDIX D  REVISED UNIFORM LIMITED PARTNERSHIP ACT — 951

## APPENDIX E  THE MODEL BUSINESS CORPORATION ACT — 960

## APPENDIX F  THE CONSTITUTION OF THE UNITED STATES OF AMERICA — 992

## GLOSSARY — 1001

## CASE INDEX — 1027

## SUBJECT INDEX — 1031

# PART I

# THE LEGAL ENVIRONMENT OF BUSINESS

■ Part I of this text consists of ten chapters that are devoted to matters that cut across or substantially affect all areas of law. Its purpose is to lay the groundwork for an understanding of the somewhat narrower substantive bodies of law, such as the law of contracts and corporation law, that are covered in the parts of the text that follow.

These introductory matters are largely concerned with structures, processes, and analyses—the structure of our existing laws and court systems, the legal processes by which laws are made and applied to actual controversies, and analysis of the historical reasons responsible for these structures and processes.

Chapter 1 examines the nature and purpose of legal rules—the special characteristics that set these rules apart from other societal rules and the characteristics which these rules must possess if they are to remain an effective part of the legal system.

Chapter 2 provides familiarity with the structure and jurisdiction of the federal and state courts, while Chapter 3 examines the roles of the trial and appellate courts in the resolution of real controversies. We examine these "adjudicatory processes" of the law in these chapters so that actual court cases can be utilized in the text as early and effectively as possible. Chapter 3 also discusses alternative dispute resolution—means by which disputes are resolved without court litigation.

Chapters 4 through 6 deal with the most important *sources* of legal principles and processes. Chapter 4 explains the difference between "common law"—law that is made by judges in the courts, and statutory law—law that originates in the legislatures. In Chapter 5, our paramount source of law—the Constitution—is explored; particular attention is paid to the role played by the Constitution in empowering and limiting the actions of government in regulating business activities. Chapter 6 discusses the role of federal and state administrative agencies as makers, interpreters, and enforcers of law through rule-making and decision-making activities.

Chapters 7 through 9 examine the various kinds of "wrongs" that our legal system must deal with. Chapter 7 briefly looks at the basic nature of criminal law and procedure, and then devotes most of its attention to "white collar crime"—that is, crime in business. Chapter 8 provides a broad overview of the law of torts, or civil wrongs, which are those kinds of wrongful conduct (such as negligence or defamation) that may be encountered in both business and nonbusiness settings. Chapter 9 then looks at "competitive torts," a term we use to describe torts that occur almost exclusively in the course of competition among business firms. Tort actions arising out of the sale of defective products, however, are reserved for later discussion in Chapter 22 when we study the law of sales transactions.

Chapter 10 concludes Part I with an examination of the ethical questions and moral obligations that permeate business life. The chapter pays special attention to the relationship between law and ethics, and the ethical problems that often run as undercurrents beneath legal problems. ■

# CHAPTER 1

# Nature and Sources of Law

## LAW AS A SUBJECT OF STUDY

A. P. Herbert once wrote: "The general mass, if they consider the law at all, regard it as they regard some monster in the zoo. It is odd, it is extraordinary; but there it is, they have known it all their lives, they suppose that there must be some good reason for it, and accept it as inevitable and natural."[1]

While the law is not nearly as odd or extraordinary as many persons believe, it is undeniably "there"—an integral part of the environment that has been a source of great interest, even fascination, for centuries.

Considering the pervasiveness of the law, this is hardly surprising. Almost all human activity is affected by it in one manner or another, and this alone is adequate explanation for such widespread interest. Certainly, anyone contemplating a business transaction of any magnitude today realizes that he or she must consider not only the physical and financial effort it will entail but—to some extent, at least—the legal ramifications as well. And beyond the practical effect law has on individual conduct in specific situations, it possesses additional characteristics that make its study uniquely rewarding.

First, while the law is by no means an occult language understood only by lawyers, it clearly is a subject that is *academically stimulating*. For students to get any real benefit from a course in law, they must at the very least learn to recognize precise legal issues, understand the reasoning of the courts as set forth in their decisions, and subject this reasoning to critical analysis. These activities involve varying degrees of mental exercise; and while this is not always pleasurable, it fosters a degree of mental discipline that is not easily acquired elsewhere.

Second, students should have the opportunity to consider the law as a *societal institution*—to see how it has affected conduct and thought and how it has been influenced by them in return. Whatever the law is, it certainly is not static, and it certainly does not exist in a vacuum.

This approach, which emphasizes the impact of social and economic changes on the law, gives the subject a liberal arts flavor. When viewed in this light, the law and its processes become rewarding to anyone having even a passing interest in economics, sociology, and political science.

## WHAT IS LAW?

Ever since the law began to take form, scholars have spent impressive amounts of time and thought analyzing its purposes and defining what it is and what it ought to be—in short, fitting it into a philosophical scheme of one form or another. While space does not permit inclusion of even the major essays in which these philosophers defend their respective views, their conclusions provide us with useful observations about the nature of law. Consider, for example, the following:

> We have been told by Plato that law is a form of social control, an instrument of the good life, the way to the discovery of reality, the true reality of the social structure; by Aristotle that it is a rule of conduct, a contract, an ideal of reason, a rule of decision, a form of order; by Cicero that it is the agreement of reason and nature, the distinction between the just and the unjust, a command or prohibition; by Aquinas that it is an ordinance of reason for the common good, made by him who has care of the community, and promulgated [thereby]; by Bacon that certainty is the prime

[1] *Uncommon Law,* 1936.

necessity of law; by Hobbes that law is the command of the sovereign; by Spinoza that it is a plan of life; by Leibniz that its character is determined by the structure of society; by Locke that it is a norm established by the commonwealth; by Hume that it is a body of precepts; by Kant that it is a harmonizing of wills by means of universal rules in the interests of freedom; by Fichte that it is a relation between human beings; by Hegel that it is an unfolding or realizing of the idea of right.[2]

While these early writers substantially agree as to the general *purpose* of law—the insuring of orderliness to all human activity—their *definitions* of the term vary considerably. Today there is still no definition of *law* that has universal approval, even in legal circles—a fact that is no doubt attributable to its inherent breadth. One can understand how very broad the law is by considering just these few widely varying matters with which the law must deal: (1) the standards of care required of a surgeon in the operating room, (2) the determination of whether an "exclusive-dealing" provision in a motion picture distributor's contracts constitutes an unfair method of competition under federal law, and (3) the propriety of a witness's testimony when it is challenged as constituting "hearsay" under the rules of evidence.

## RULES AND PROCESSES

At the risk of oversimplification, it can be said that two major approaches to the teaching and study of law exist today. The *rule-oriented approach* views the law as consisting of the rules that are in effect within a state or nation at a given time. This is very likely what practicing attorneys have in mind when they speak about the law, and it is a perfectly respectable view. Witness the following definition adopted by the American Law Institute: "[Law] is the body of principles, standards and rules which the courts . . . apply in the decision of controversies brought before them."[3]

The *process-oriented approach* sees the law in a broader light: the *processes by which the rules and principles are formulated* (rather than the rules and principles themselves) constitute the major element of law. Because law is necessitated solely by human activity, those who emphasize process contend that the ever-changing problems resulting from this activity and *the ways in which the law attempts to solve them* must receive primary emphasis if one is to gain a proper insight into the subject. The following definition expresses this view: "Law is a dynamic process, a system of regularized, institutionalized procedures for the orderly decision of social questions, including the settlement of disputes."[4]

Obviously, the law is both rule and process. Each approach to the teaching and study of law is legitimate; indeed, each is essential and inevitable. The only difference is in emphasis. In this text, process is emphasized in the first few chapters, and rules in many of the later chapters. Our discussion of rules and principles, however, always includes related legal processes.

## REQUISITES OF A LEGAL SYSTEM

In order for a legal system to function properly, particularly within a democratic government such as ours, it must command the respect of the great majority of people governed by it. In order to do so, the legal rules which compose it must, as a practical matter, possess certain characteristics. They must be (1) relatively certain, (2) relatively flexible, (3) known or knowable, and (4) apparently reasonable.

In the following chapters we consider these requirements more fully and determine the extent to which our legal system satisfies them. For the moment, we give brief descriptions of each of the four.

### Certainty

One essential element of a stable society is reasonable certainty about its laws, not only at a given moment but over long periods of time. Many of our activities, particularly business activities, are based on the assumption that legal principles will remain stable into the foreseeable future. If this were not so, chaos would result. For example, no television network would enter into a contract with a professional football league, under which it is to pay millions of

---

[2] Huntington Cairns, *Legal Philosophy from Plato to Hegel* (Baltimore: Johns Hopkins University Press, 1949).

[3] *Restatement, Conflict of Laws 2d,* §4. The American Law Institute, 1971.

[4] James L. Houghteling, Jr., *The Dynamics of Law* (New York: Harcourt Brace Jovanovich, 1963).

dollars for the right to televise league games, if it were not reasonably sure that the law would compel the league to live up to its contractual obligations or to pay damages if it did not. And no lawyer would advise a client on a contemplated course of action without similar assurances.

Because of these considerations, the courts (and to a lesser extent the legislatures) are generally reluctant to overturn principles that have been part of the law for any appreciable length of time. This is not to say, of course, that the law is static. Many areas of American law are dramatically different than they were fifty, or even twenty-five years ago. However, most of these changes resulted from a series of modifications of existing principles rather than from an abrupt reversal of them. The *Soldano v. O'Daniels* case later in this chapter illustrates one such modification.

## *Flexibility*

In any nation, particularly a highly industrialized one such as the United States, societal changes occur with accelerating (almost dismaying) rapidity. Each change presents new legal problems that must be resolved without undue delay. This necessity was recognized by Justice Cardozo when he wrote that "the law, like the traveler, must be ready for the morrow."[5]

Some problems are simply the result of scientific and technological advances. Prior to Orville and Wilbur Wright's day, for example, it was a well-established principle that landowners had unlimited rights to the airspace above their property, any invasion of which constituted a *trespass*—a wrongful entry. But when the courts became convinced that the flying machine was here to stay, the utter impracticality of this view became apparent and owners' rights were subsequently limited to a "reasonable use" of their airspace.

Other novel problems result from changing methods of doing business or from shifting attitudes and moral views. Recent examples of the former are the proliferating use of the business franchise and of the general credit card. Attitudinal changes involve such questions as the proper ends of government, the propriety of Sunday sales, and the circumstances in which abortions should be permitted.

Some of these problems, of course, require solutions that are more political than legal in nature. This is particularly true where large numbers of the citizenry are faced with a common problem, such as the inability of many elderly persons to pay for proper health care, and where the alleviation of the problem may well be thought to constitute a legitimate function of either the state or federal government. The passage by Congress of the so-called Medicare Act of 1964 is an example of an attempted solution at the federal level of this particular problem.

Regardless of political considerations, however, the fact remains that there are many problems (particularly those involving disputes between individuals) which can be settled only through the judicial processes—that is, by one of the parties instituting legal action against the other. The duty to arrive at a final solution in all such cases falls squarely upon the courts, no matter how novel or varied the issues. It is to their credit, but it is also their curse, that Americans increasingly turn to them for dispute resolution, and not to the churches, schools, or other institutions that are available.

## *Knowability*

One of the basic assumptions underlying a democracy—and, in fact, almost every form of government—is that the great majority of its citizens are going to obey its laws voluntarily. It hardly need be said that obedience requires a certain knowledge of the rules, or at least a reasonable means of acquiring this knowledge, on the part of the governed. No one, not even a lawyer, "knows" all the law or all the rules that make up a single branch of law; that could never be required. But it is necessary for persons who need legal advice to have access to experts on the rules—lawyers. It is equally necessary that the law be in such form that lawyers can determine their clients' positions with reasonable certainty in order to recommend the most advantageous courses of action.

## *Reasonableness*

Most citizens abide by the law. Many do so even when they are not in sympathy with a particular rule, out of a sense of responsibility, a feeling that it is their civic duty, like it or not; others, no doubt, do so simply through fear of getting caught if they don't. But by and large the rules have to appear reasonable to the great majority of the people if they are going to

---

[5] Benjamin N. Cardozo, *The Growth of the Law* (New Haven: Yale University Press, 1924), pp. 19–20.

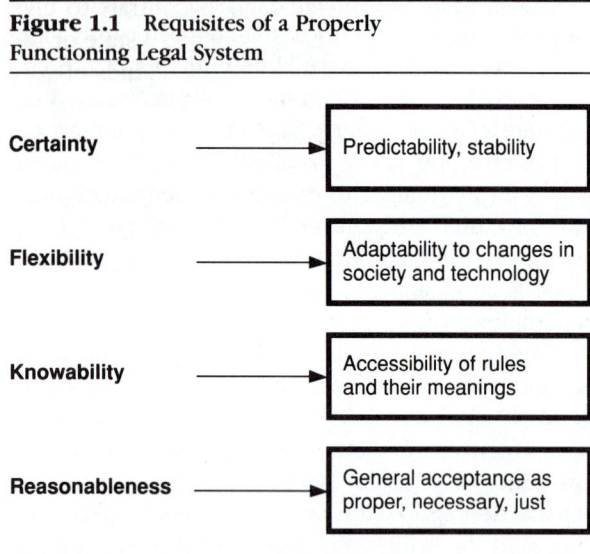

**Figure 1.1** Requisites of a Properly Functioning Legal System

be obeyed for long. The so-called Prohibition Amendment, which met with such wholesale violation that it was repealed in 1933, is the classic example of a rule lacking widespread acceptance. Closely allied with the idea of reasonableness is the requirement that the rules reflect, and adapt to, changing views of morality and justice. Figure 1.1 summarizes the qualities a legal system must possess to function properly.

## SOME CLASSIFICATIONS OF LAW

While the lawmaking and adjudicatory processes are the major concern in Part I, the products that result from the law-making process—the rules themselves and the bodies of law which they make up—must not be overlooked. At the outset, particularly, it is useful to recognize some of the more important *classifications of law*.

### Subject-matter Classification

One way of classifying all the law in the United States is on the basis of the *subject matter* to which it relates. Fifteen or twenty branches or subjects are of particular importance, among them:

- Administrative law
- Agency
- Commercial paper
- Constitutional law
- Contracts
- Corporation law
- Criminal law
- Domestic relations
- Evidence
- Partnerships
- Personal property
- Real property
- Sales
- Taxation
- Torts
- Wills and estates

Two observations can be made about this classification.

1. The subjects of agency, contracts, and torts are essentially *common law* in nature, while the subjects of corporation law, criminal law, sales, and taxation are governed by *statute*. Most of the remaining subjects, particularly evidence and property, are mixed in nature.

2. Several of these subjects obviously have a much closer relationship to the world of business than the others; these are the topics that fall within the usual business law or legal environment courses of a business school curriculum. Agency, contracts, corporation law, and sales are typical examples.

### Federal and State Law

Another way of categorizing all law in this country is on the basis of the governmental unit from which it arises. On this basis, all law may be said to be either *federal law* or *state law*. While there are some very important areas of federal law, as we shall see later, the great bulk of our law is state (or "local") law. Virtually all the subjects in the preceding list, for example, are within the jurisdiction of the individual states. Thus it is correct to say that there are fifty bodies of contract law in the United States, fifty bodies of corporation law, and so on. But this is not as bewildering as it appears, because the rules that constitute a given branch of law in each state substantially parallel those that exist in the other states—particularly in regard to common-law subjects.

## Common Law (Case Law) and Statutory Law

The term **common law** has several different meanings. It sometimes is used to refer only to the judge-made rules in effect in England at an early time—the "ancient unwritten law of England." It sometimes is also used to refer only to those judge-made rules of England that were subsequently adopted by the states in this country. In this text, however, we define the term more broadly to mean *all the rules and principles currently existing in any state, regardless of their historical origin, that result from judicial decisions in those areas of law where legislatures have not enacted comprehensive statutes.* This type of law, examined further in Chapter 4, is frequently referred to as case law, judge-made law, or unwritten law.

The term **statutory law**, by contrast, is generally used to refer to the state and federal *statutes* in effect at a given time—that is, rules which have been formally adopted by legislative bodies rather than by the courts. When *statutory law* is used in contrast to *common law*, it also comprises state and federal constitutions, municipal ordinances, and even treaties. Statutory law is frequently referred to as written law in the sense that once a statute or constitutional provision is adopted, its exact wording is set forth in the final text as passed—though the precise meaning, we should recall, is still subject to interpretation by the courts. The subjects of statutory law and judicial interpretation are also covered in Chapter 4.

## Civil and Criminal Law

**Civil Law:** The most common types of controversies are civil actions—that is, actions in which the parties bringing the suits (the **plaintiffs**) are seeking to enforce private obligations or duties against the other parties (the **defendants**). **Civil laws,** then, are all those laws which spell out the rights and duties existing among individuals, business firms, and sometimes even government agencies. Contract law, tort law, and sales law all fall within the civil category.

The usual remedy which the plaintiff is seeking in a civil suit is *damages*—a sum of money roughly equivalent to the loss which he or she has suffered as a result of the defendant's wrong. Another civil remedy is the *injunction,* a court decree ordering the defendant to do or not to do some particular thing.

**Criminal Law:** **Criminal law,** in contrast to civil law, comprises those statutes by which a state or the federal government prohibits specified kinds of conduct, and which additionally provide for the imposition of *fines or imprisonment* upon persons convicted of violating them. Criminal suits are always brought by the government whose law has allegedly been violated. In enacting criminal statutes, a legislature is saying that there are certain activities so inherently inimical to the public good that they constitute wrongs against organized society as a whole.

In addition to the nature of the liability that is imposed, criminal suits also differ from civil suits in another significant respect. In a criminal action it is necessary that the government's case be proved "beyond a reasonable doubt," whereas in civil actions the plaintiff—the person bringing the suit—need prove his or her allegations only by "a preponderance of the evidence."

Crimes are either *felonies* or *misdemeanors,* depending upon the severity of the penalty which the statute prescribes. A **felony** is the most serious of the two, and is usually defined as a crime for which the legislature has provided a maximum penalty of either imprisonment for more than one year or death, as in the cases of murder, arson, or rape. **Misdemeanors** are all crimes carrying lesser penalties, most traffic offenses, for example.

Finally, it should be noted that some wrongful acts are of a dual nature, subjecting the wrongdoer to both criminal and civil penalties. For example, if X steals Y's car, the state could bring a criminal action against X, and Y could also bring a civil action to recover damages arising from the theft.

## Public and Private Law

Some branches of law deal more directly with the relationship that exists between the government and the individual than do others. On the basis of the degree to which this relationship is involved, law is occasionally classified as public law or private law.

When an area of law is directly concerned with the government-individual relationship, it falls within the *public law* designation. Subjects that are most clearly of this nature are criminal law, constitutional law, and administrative law. Since *criminal laws* consist of acts that are prohibited by a government itself, the violation of which is a "wrong against the state," such laws more directly affect the government-individual relationship than do any of the other laws. To the extent that our federal Constitution contains provisions substantially guaranteeing that certain rights of the individual cannot be invaded by federal and state government activities, the subject of *constitutional law* falls within the same category. *Administrative law*—comprising the principles that govern the procedures and activities of government boards and commissions—is of similar nature, in that such agencies are also concerned with the enforcement of certain state and federal statutes (and regulations promulgated thereunder) against individual citizens.

Other areas of law, which are primarily concerned with the creation and enforcement of the rights of one individual against another, fall within the *private law* category. While a state is indeed concerned that all its laws be properly enforced, even when individuals' rights alone are being adjudicated, the concern in these areas is distinctly secondary to the interests of the litigants themselves.

## LEGAL MISCONCEPTIONS

Before proceeding to the more substantive areas of law, we will reflect briefly on two widely held misconceptions about our legal system.

### The Myth of the One Right Answer

It is widely believed that there is one "correct" legal answer to any legal controversy. This is true in a good many situations but certainly not as often as many persons believe. The chief reasons for divergent legal opinions are quite explainable.

**1.** Many rules are expressed in rather general terms so as to fit varying situations. Consequently, they afford the courts considerable latitude in deciding how they should be applied to specific situations.

**2.** The ultimate legal processes are in the hands of people, the judges, whose application of rules is always subject, to some extent, to their individual economic and political philosophies and personal moral beliefs. The law, therefore, is not an exact science and never will be.

**3.** The nature of most legal problems is such that something can be said in behalf of both litigants. The ordinary controversy does not present a clear-cut case of a "good" person suing a "bad" one. In some cases, each party has acted in good faith; in others,

each is guilty of some degree of wrong. Additionally, there are some "legal collision" situations, where one general principle of law may lead to one result while a second will lead to a different result. In such instances each principle will probably have to undergo some modification when applied to particular cases, with results that are not always harmonious.

### The Myth of Judicial Eccentricity

The feeling is sometimes expressed that the law is not based on common sense—that its rules are so esoteric and arbitrary, and the judges and lawyers so preoccupied with them, that the results are not in keeping with reality or with what a reasonable person would expect. This indictment, in very large measure, is false. Cases invariably present practical problems for the courts, and the courts keep the practical considerations in mind in choosing the rules that apply.

Take, for example, this situation. C, a contractor, agrees to build a house according to certain specifications for O, the owner, for $60,000. When the house is completed, by which time O has paid $36,000, O discovers that the family room is 10 inches shorter than the plans specified. O refuses to make further payments for this reason, whereupon C brings suit to recover the balance of $24,000.

Now, as far as contract law is concerned, the principle is well established that a person who breaches a contract is not permitted to recover anything from the other party. The question here is: Should that rule be applicable to this specific situation, where that would mean that C would not recover any of the balance? The practical person might well say, "I wouldn't think so—where the defect is so slight, it would seem unfair for C to suffer a loss of $24,000." The law reaches the same conclusion; under a view known as the *doctrine of substantial performance,* a person in C's position is usually permitted to recover most of the unpaid balance (even though he did, technically, breach the contract).

The foregoing does not mean, of course, that the law is perfect or that startling or unfair decisions never occur. They do. But by and large the unreasonable result occurs with much less frequency than reports in the news media would indicate; and even in such cases, the possibility usually exists that an appellate court will subsequently repair much of the damage.

# LAW, JUSTICE, AND MORALS
## Law and Justice

There is a close relationship between law and justice, but the terms are not equivalent. Most results of the application of legal rules are "just"—fair and reasonable. Where this is not so to any degree, the rules are usually changed. Yet it must be recognized that results occasionally "aren't fair." Without attempting to defend the law in all such instances, some cautions should nevertheless be voiced.

First, there is never complete agreement as to what is just; there are always some decisions that are just to some people but not to others. And even if there were unanimity of opinion—a perfect justice, so to speak—the facts in many cases are such that it is simply impossible to attain this end.

In some situations, for example, a legal controversy may arise between two honest persons who dealt with each other in good faith, as sometimes occurs in the area of "mutual mistake." Take this case: P contracts to sell land to G for $40,000, both parties mistakenly believing that a General Motors plant will be built on adjoining land. When G learns that the plant will not be built, he refuses to go through with the deal. If a court rules that the mistake frees G of his contractual obligations, the result might be quite unjust as far as P is concerned. And if it rules otherwise, the decision might seem quite unfair to G. Yet a decision must be made, one way or the other.

Second, in some instances it is fairly clear who is right and who is wrong, but the situation has progressed to the point where it is impossible, either physically or legally, to put the "good" person back into the original position. These "bad check" cases will illustrate: A buys a TV set from Z, giving Z her personal check in payment. If the check bounces, it is clear that Z should be allowed to recover the set. But what if the TV has been destroyed by fire while in A's hands? Here the most the law can do is give Z a *judgment* against A—an order requiring A to pay a sum of money to Z equal to the amount of the check, which A may or may not be financially able to do. Or suppose that A had resold the TV to X before Z learned that the check had bounced. Would it not be unfair to permit Z to retake the set from X, an innocent third party?

Because of these considerations, and others to be discussed later, the most the law can seek to accomplish is *substantial* justice in the greatest possible number of cases that come before it.

## Law and Morals

Although the terms *law* and *morals* are not synonymous, legal standards and moral standards parallel one another more closely than many people believe. For example, criminal statutes prohibit certain kinds of conduct that are clearly "morally wrong"—murder, theft, arson, and the like. And other rules of law impose civil liability for similar kinds of conduct which, though not crimes, are also generally felt to be wrongful in nature—such as negligence, breach of contract, and fraud. To illustrate: S, in negotiating the sale of a race horse to B, tells B that the horse has run an eighth of a mile in fifteen seconds on several occasions within the past month. In fact, the animal has never been clocked under eighteen seconds, and S knows this. B, believing the statement to be true, purchases the horse. In such a case S's intentional misstatement constitutes the tort of *fraud,* and B—assuming he can prove these facts in a legal action brought against S—has the right to set aside the transaction, returning the horse and recovering the price he has paid.

Why, then, are the terms *law* and *morals* not precisely synonymous? First, there are some situations where moral standards are higher than those imposed by law. For example, a person who has promised to keep an offer open for a stated period of time generally has the legal right to withdraw the offer before the given time has elapsed (for reasons appearing in a later chapter). Yet many persons who make such offers feel morally compelled to keep their offers open as promised, even though the law does not require this. Second, sometimes the law imposes higher standards than do our morals. For example, no religions or philosophies feature the 65-mile-per-hour speed limit as a major tenet, yet it is illegal to drive faster. Third, many rules of law and court decisions are based upon statutory or practical requirements that have little or no relationship to moral considerations. For example, in the area of minors' contracts, we see later that most courts feel, on balance, that it is sound public policy to permit minors to disaffirm (cancel) their contracts until they reach the age of majority, even though the contracts were otherwise perfectly valid and even though the persons with whom they dealt did not overreach or take advantage of them in any way. These observations notwithstanding, a society's moral standards will always heavily influence its legal standards. The relationship between legal standards and moral standards, as well as many related questions, is explored thoroughly in Chapter 10.

The interplay between law and morality is illustrated in the following case. Because the study of law involves to a very great extent the ability to reason from cases, students must have some familiarity with court procedures and jurisdiction. For this reason, major emphasis on cases will begin in the following chapter. The case below is our first, and therefore requires a few prefatory comments:

**1.** This is a *wrongful death* action authorized by statute to allow close relatives of deceased persons to sue those whose wrongful acts have caused a death. Absent such statutes, we could be held liable for carelessly or intentionally injuring someone, but could escape civil liability if we killed them.

**2.** In a civil case, the jury is normally the "judge of the *facts*." The trial judge decides the *law*. However, a judge, for reasons of judicial efficiency, can grant a summary judgment, terminating the case before it is ever tried. This can happen in two instances. First, summary judgment can be granted a defendant when plaintiff's legal theory is so defective that even if plaintiff proves all facts alleged, recovery should still be denied. Second, summary judgment is appropriately granted if the evidence in the case so clearly indicates that factually one side or the other is entitled to prevail that a trial would be a waste of time. Only if the judge can conclude that there is "no genuine issue of material fact" should a summary judgment be granted on this ground. The following case involves a summary judgment granted on the former basis.

**3.** If a trial court does grant a summary judgment motion, the losing party can always seek review in an appellate court. If the appellate court finds that the ruling was in error, the case will be returned to the trial court with instructions for a jury trial on the issue.

### Soldano v. O'Daniels
California Court of Appeal, 190 Cal. Rptr. 310 (1983)

On August 9, 1977, Villanueva pulled a gun and threatened the life of Soldano at Happy Jack's Saloon. A patron of Happy Jack's ran across the street to the Circle Inn and informed the bartender of the threat, asking the bartender either to call the police or allow him to use the phone to call the police. The bartender refused both requests. Soon thereafter, Villanueva shot Soldano to death. The plaintiff in this wrongful death action is Soldano's child. Defendants are the bartender and his employer. The trial judge dismissed the claim upon defendants' motion for summary judgment. Plaintiff appeals.

**Decision:** "Does a business establishment incur liability for wrongful death if it denies use of its telephone to a good samaritan who explains an emergency situation occurring without and wishes to call the police?" The court of appeal answered "yes" to this narrowly-framed question and therefore reversed the trial court's grant of summary judgment to the defendants.

Although it has been criticized, the general rule is that citizens have no *legal* duty to help their fellow man. However, for public policy reasons the courts have created various exceptions to the general rule. For example, where special relationships exist (*e.g.*, parent-child, psychiatrist-patient, common carrier-passenger), some courts have created a "duty to rescue." Although the traditional exceptions do not apply here, public policy interests in crime prevention support creation of a new, limited exception to the "no duty" rule. The court stressed that it was not creating a duty to aid another, but merely a duty not to interfere with another's attempt to render aid in these narrow circumstances. ■

**Comment:**

1. As noted in the preface, all decisions following the statement of facts for the cases are brief summaries of the higher courts' decisions. In other words, the authors have selected and paraphrased the major points made by the appellate courts in their decision.

2. In regard to substantive matters presented by this case, the following can be noted.

   a. If a trial jury finds the bartender to have refused to act, as alleged, then he will be liable to plaintiff and so will his employer under *agency law*. While that subject is essentially outside the scope of this chapter, one of its principles imposes liability on an employer for the torts (wrongs) committed by employees if they were "carrying on the employer's business at the time." (This specific question is considered in detail in Chapter 32).

   b. If the jury finds the bartender liable and the employer pays the entire judgment to the plaintiff, the employer will have the legal right to seek reimbursement from the bartender. As a practical matter, however, employers seldom exercise this right.

3. A word of caution: It is imperative for readers to acquire the ability *to determine the precise issue of a case,* so they will not leap to unwarranted general conclusions. Could we say, for example, that the instant case establishes the principle that upon seeing one person attack another with a knife a bystander has the legal duty to personally intervene to save the victim? Not at all. This court was very careful in stating the issue narrowly, and emphasizing that it was only creating a small exception to the traditional rule.

## SELECTING AND USING ATTORNEYS

Choosing an attorney can be as important as choosing one's clergyman, banker, or doctor . . . and more difficult.

### *Individuals*

Individuals frequently require an attorney's services for their business matters as well as for their personal affairs. As sole proprietors of, or partners in a business enterprise, individuals facing (or seeking to avoid) legal problems must select an attorney. This is no easy task.

Now that the Supreme Court has made advertising by attorneys permissible,[6] at least a little more information about attorneys is publicly available than was formerly the case. Still, much investigation and consultation may be required before a selection is made, in part because most attorneys (especially successful ones) choose not to advertise. In addition, much attorney advertising is not very informational.

If friends or business associates have had similar problems in the past, their advice may be particularly helpful. If their experience with a specific attorney was quite favorable, that attorney can be contacted. Professionals in the area of concern are also valuable resources. For example, if the legal problem is financial in nature, an individual's banker might provide valuable insight regarding attorneys with experience in that type of case. A call to a nearby law school permits consultation with a professor who specializes in the problem area and will probably know local attorneys who practice that type of law. A trip to a library to consult the *Martindale-Hubbell Law Directory,* which gives significant background information on attorneys and their specialties (and even rates them), can be beneficial. Finally, the Yellow Pages will list the local attorneys and contain the number of a lawyers' referral service sponsored by the local bar association.

An individual consulting an attorney must not be hesitant to ask questions, including: How much will I be charged for an initial consultation? Do you frequently handle this type of case? Will my case receive the attention of an experienced attorney in the firm? How will the fee be structured? How much is your representation likely to cost for the total case?

The matter of fees is a delicate subject, but the client should demand that all specifics be spelled out before hiring an attorney. For many types of cases, lawyers work for an *hourly fee.* The rate charged varies with the geographic area, type of firm, and type of case. Unless the client investigates thoroughly, "comparison shopping" will be impossible. Some types of cases, particularly plaintiffs' personal injury cases, are handled on a *contingency fee* basis. That is, the attorney's compensation is a percentage of the plaintiff's recovery, *if any.* No recovery usually means no fee for the attorney. Sometimes contingency fees are set on a sliding scale where the attorney receives an

---

[6]*Bates v. State Bar of Ariz.,* 433 U.S. 350 (1977).

agreed percentage if the case is settled out of court, a larger percentage if the case is settled after suit is filed, and a still larger percentage (sometimes as high as 50 percent) if the case must be tried.

Once a relationship is established, clients must be completely open with their attorneys. Only if attorneys are given all relevant information by their clients can they provide effective counsel. Clients should trust their attorneys absent specific evidence of unethical practices, overbilling, or the like. The attorneys are being paid to provide advice, and that advice should normally be trusted just as a patient trusts a surgeon's advice. However, clients should always remember that it is *their case* that is the basis of the relationship. The attorney works for and is paid by the client, not vice versa. Matters of strategy are in the attorney's discretion, but the client has the ultimate choice of whether to file suit, whether to accept a settlement offer, and whether to take an appeal. An attorney who refuses to follow a client's instructions should be discharged.

## *Corporations*

Corporations are even more dependent on attorneys than individual businesspersons. As fictional entities, corporations must appear in court through a licensed attorney. That is, while individuals have the right (although it is not usually the sensible thing to do) to represent themselves in court, corporations do not. Not even the president of the corporation can represent it in court if the president is not an attorney. Much of what was said about selection and use of attorneys by individuals is also applicable to corporations.

Many corporations have "in-house" counsel—lawyers who work for the corporation full time. Other corporations farm out all their legal work to law firms which represent a number of other clients as well. Many larger corporations combine these approaches, with routine matters handled by in-house counsel and litigation and specialty matters handled by outside counsel.

The high cost of litigation, particularly attorneys' fees, is a major concern for corporations. The average manufacturing company spends about 1 percent of its revenues on legal services. Some corporations have reacted to this problem by increasing their reliance on in-house counsel. Others have put their legal business up for competitive bid by local law firms. Still others have instituted "legal audits" in which experienced attorneys evaluate a company's practices in order to detect potential legal troublespots. These troublespots might not be illegal practices, only activities which might invite litigation or inhibit success should litigation ensue. Such "preventive law" is being hailed, much as is preventive medicine. An attorney who can keep the client out of court altogether is at least as valuable as one who can win a case in court.

Corporations, like individuals, must cooperate with their attorneys. Obviously corporations can act only through their employees. Those employees must also be open and cooperative. The Supreme Court has recognized this, holding that the attorney-client privilege applies to communications made by corporate employees to the corporation's attorneys.[7]

## SUMMARY

The law pervades our lives, both business and personal. Philosophers have characterized the law in an endless variety of ways, but two major approaches are the "rule-oriented" and the "process-oriented." The former sees the law as a set of rules and standards which the courts use to resolve cases; the latter views the law more as a dynamic process for resolution of social questions.

An effective legal system must provide certainty, yet be flexible so it can adjust to changed circumstances. It must be knowable so that people realize what is generally expected of them, and it must generally be considered reasonable.

Our multifaceted law can be classified in many ways. Each law will fit into a particular subject-matter category—contract law, corporate law, tax law, and the like. At the same time it will be either a federal or a state law, a court-made rule or a statute, a civil or a criminal law, and a public or a private law. As in any field of study, mastery of the proper labels for concepts can facilitate understanding.

The untutored are likely to have various misconceptions about how the legal system operates. Because the law has so many human factors, there is no one right answer to legal questions. Witnesses perceive "facts" in different ways. Attorneys will view

---

[7] *Upjohn Co. v. United States,* 449 U.S. 383 (1981).

"the law" in various ways, depending on policy considerations and their own feelings of justice. You cannot simply feed the facts and the law into a computer and produce *the* right answer. Although it is generally helpful to have as much money as possible when facing a legal struggle, the ability to hire the best attorney does not guarantee anyone absolute immunity from the restraints and punishments of the law. Finally, although judges do not always make the best decisions, their conclusions are seldom based on pure whim. Many judicial actions which seem ludicrous when summarized in the newspaper, are really quite reasonable when understood in context.

One important purpose of law is to produce justice. Unfortunately, this is an amorphous concept. Because not all people can agree on what is just, not everyone will be able to agree on whether our law is producing justice. The law is heavily influenced by society's moral convictions, though practical considerations cannot be ignored in making legal rules.

Finally, hiring an attorney is likely to be a difficult task for individuals and corporations alike. Substantial investigation and careful reflection are advised.

## KEY TERMS

**Common law**
**Statutory law**
**Plaintiff**
**Defendant**
**Civil law**
**Criminal law**
**Felony**
**Misdemeanor**

## QUESTIONS AND PROBLEMS

1. In two cases reaching the U.S. Supreme Court in 1985, the United States—through action by the Solicitor General—asked the court to overrule its controversial 1973 decision in *Roe v. Wade*, 410 U.S. 113. (In that case the court held that a Texas statute making it a crime for anyone to have an abortion within the state except where the abortion was done "upon medical advice for the purpose of saving the mother's life" violated the Due Process clause of the U.S. Constitution). In effect, this controversial ruling "legalized" abortion to the extent that it gave pregnant women the absolute right to an abortion during the first trimester of their pregnancies, if they so desired.

Leaving aside the precise constitutional question that is raised, do you generally agree with the 1985 position of the United States? In other words, do you feel—because of religious beliefs or moral principles—that a duly-enacted state "anti-abortion" statute (such as the Texas statute), ought not be set aside by the federal courts in the absence of a federal statute mandating such a result? Discuss.

2. While there is no universal agreement as to what law is when viewed in the abstract, there seems to be substantial agreement among philosophers as to what the *primary purpose* of law is.
   a. How would you describe this purpose?
   b. Identify the specific passage or clause in each of the philosophers' quoted observations that substantiates your conclusion.

3. Briefly summarize the main factors that require a nation's legal rules to be flexible and somewhat changing.

4. If X and Y make a contract and X later refuses to go through with the deal, having no reason to do so, we say that X's conduct is a *wrong* but it is not a *crime*. Why is it not a crime?

5. For some years the Washington Interscholastic Activities Association had a rule that prohibited girls from participating on high school football teams in the state. When this rule was challenged by parents of two girls who wanted to go out for football, the Supreme Court of Washington had to decide whether the rule violated the state constitution (*Darrin v. Gould,* 540 P.2d 882, 1975). Leaving aside the precise legal question that was posed, do you think that such a rule is a good one? Discuss.

6. In 1884 a ship sank 1600 miles from shore. Dudley, Stephens, Brooks, and a 17-year-old boy, Richard Parker, scrambled into a life boat with only two pounds of turnips to eat and no fresh water. They caught a turtle, but by their 12th day in the raft the provisions were completely consumed. Soon thereafter Dudley and Stephens proposed killing the boy for food, but Brooks resisted the idea. Finally, on the 20th day following the shipwreck as the boy lay almost dead, Dudley and Stephens slit his throat and Brooks then joined them in eating him. Four days later a passing ship picked up the three survivors. They were returned to England where Dudley and Stephens were charged with murder. Assume that you are the judge in this case. Assume further that the evidence shows (a) all four men would have been dead by the 24th day had Parker not been eaten and (b) the mandatory penalty for murder is death. What will you do? (*Regina v. Dudley & Stephens,* [1884] L.R., Q.B. 61.)

7. A minor child and its mother brought a paternity action against defendant. Defendant admitted that he was the father of the child and agreed to pay child support, but filed a counterclaim against the mother claiming (a) she had falsely represented that she was taking birth control pills,

(b) defendant had engaged in sexual intercourse with her in reliance upon the misrepresentation, and (c) as a direct result of the birth he had been injured in the form of mental agony and distress and creation of an obligation to support the child financially. The mother moved to dismiss the counterclaim, arguing that even if the facts alleged by defendant were true, he should not be allowed to recover money damages. Discuss. (*Lasher v. Kleinberg,* 164 Cal. Rptr. 618, Cal. App. 1980.)

8. A wooden bridge crossing a canal ditch was destroyed by a fire of unknown origin one afternoon. McCarthy soon learned of the fire; he attempted to contact the County Commissioners but failed. Simpson also learned of the fire and told another traveler, Ramos, that he would notify somebody about the fire, but he did not do so. At 6:30 the next morning Roberson drove off the bridge in the dark and was killed. There were no barricades or any type of warning devices at the site of the burned-out bridge. Roberson's wife brought a wrongful death action against McCarthy and Simpson. Should she prevail? Discuss. (*Roberson v. McCarthy,* 620 S.W.2d 912, Tex. Civ. App. 1981.)

CHAPTER 2

# COURT SYSTEMS, JURISDICTION, AND FUNCTIONS

Legal rules and principles take on vitality and meaning only when they are applied to real-life controversies between real persons, when the rules are *applied to facts*—when, for example, a particular plaintiff is successful or unsuccessful in his or her attempt to recover a specific piece of land from a particular defendant, or where one company is successful or unsuccessful in recovering damages from another company as a result of an alleged breach of contract on the latter company's part. But the fitting of rules to facts—the settling of legal controversies—does not occur automatically. This process, which we call the process of **adjudication,** has to be in somebody's hands; that "somebody" is the state and federal courts that hear the thousands of cases that arise every year.[1] As Figure 2.1 indicates, rules and facts come together in the adjudication process, leading to a decision.

The primary reason, then, for looking at the courts and the work that they do is to gain an overall awareness of this important legal process. There is, however, another reason for doing so. In the following chapters many actual cases are presented. The reader is given the basic facts of a particular controversy, the judgment entered by the trial court on the basis of those facts, and excerpts of the appellate court's decision in affirming or reversing the trial court's judgment. Obviously, some familiarity with court systems and the judicial process will facilitate one's understanding of the legal significance of each step in these proceedings.

In this chapter, then, we take a brief look at the state and federal court systems, and at some problems of jurisdiction arising thereunder. In Chapter 3, we will examine the litigation process, focusing on the functions of the trial and appellate courts, and then we will discuss some alternative methods of dispute resolution.

## COURT SYSTEMS

As a result of our federal system of government, we live under two distinct, and essentially separate, sovereign types of government—the state governments and the federal government. Each has its own laws and its own court system. For this reason, it is necessary to examine both systems in order to acquire an adequate knowledge of the court structures within which controversies are settled.

### *The Typical State System*

While court systems vary somewhat from state to state, most state courts fall into three general categories. In ascending order, they are (1) courts of limited jurisdiction, (2) general trial courts, and (3) appellate courts (which frequently exist at two levels).

**Courts of Limited Jurisdiction:** Every state has trial courts which are limited as to the kinds of cases they can hear [2] and are thus called **courts of limited jurisdiction.** Examples include justice of the peace courts, municipal courts, traffic courts, probate courts (hearing matters of wills and decedents' estates), and domestic relations courts (handling divorce, custody,

---

[1] In addition to the state and federal trial courts, many administrative agencies (such as the Federal Trade Commission) also hear certain kinds of controversies—usually those in which the agency is contending that a company has violated the agency's own rules or regulations. (The general subject of administrative agencies, including the role that they play in the adjudicatory process, is covered in Chapter 6.)

[2] *Jurisdiction* means the legal power to act; *jurisdiction of a court* refers to the types of disputes that a particular court is empowered to hear and decide.

15

**Figure 2.1** The Process of Adjudication

Controversy → Facts ← Rules ← Law → Court → Decision

and child support cases). Numerically speaking, these courts hear the majority of cases that come to trial. However, they need not be discussed in detail here because many of the matters they hear are relatively minor in nature (such as traffic violations) and others involve very specialized subject matter (such as a dispute over a large estate).

**General Trial Courts:** The most important cases involving state law, and the ones we will be most concerned with hereafter, commence in the **general trial courts.** These are courts of "general jurisdiction"; they are empowered to hear all cases except those expressly assigned by statute to the "minor" courts discussed above. Virtually all important cases involving contract law, criminal law, and corporation law, for example, originate in the general trial courts.[3] In some states these courts are called "district courts," in others "common pleas courts," and in still others "superior courts." Whatever the specific name, such a court normally exists in every county of every state. It is in these courts that trial by jury is generally available.

**Appellate Courts:** All states have one or more **appellate courts,** which hear appeals from judgments entered by the courts below. In many states there is only one such court, usually called the "supreme court," but in the more populous states there is a layer of appellate courts interposed between the trial

courts and the supreme court. Such courts decide legal questions; they do not hear testimony of witnesses or otherwise entertain new evidence.

## The Federal Court System

Article III, Section 1 of the U.S. Constitution provides that "the judicial power of the United States shall be vested in one Supreme Court, and in such inferior courts as the Congress may from time to time ordain and establish." The numerous federal courts that exist today by virtue of this section can, at the risk of oversimplification, be placed into three main categories similar to those of the state courts: (1) specialized courts, (2) general trial courts (district courts), and (3) appellate courts—the courts of appeal and the Supreme Court.

**Specialized U.S. Courts:** Some federal courts have limited jurisdiction, such as the U.S. Tax Court, the U.S. Court of Military Appeals, and the recently created U.S. Claims Court. While these courts frequently deal with important matters, we are eliminating them from further consideration (as we did the similar state courts) because of their specialized nature.

**General Trial Courts:** The basic courts having general jurisdiction within the federal system are the *U.S. district courts,* sometimes called federal trial courts. Most federal cases originate in these courts.

Congress has created about ninety-four judicial districts. The federal districts, with the exceptions noted above, essentially are based upon state lines. The less populated states have only one federal district court within their boundaries, while most of the remaining states have two. Every square foot of land in this country and its territories is, geographically speaking, within the jurisdiction of one U.S. district court.

**The Appellate Courts:** Above the district courts are two levels of *federal appellate courts*—the U.S. courts of appeal and, above them, the U.S. Supreme Court. There are thirteen U.S. courts of appeal. Eleven of these, located in "circuits" across the country, have jurisdiction to hear appeals from the district courts located in the states within their respective boundaries. For example, the U.S. Court of Appeals for the Ninth Circuit in San Francisco hears appeals from decisions of district courts within the states of Alaska, Arizona, California, Hawaii, Idaho, Montana,

---

[3] These courts may occasionally be referred to hereafter simply as *state trial courts,* to distinguish them from federal trial courts. When this is done, reference is being made to the trial courts of *general jurisdiction* rather than to the minor trial courts.

Nevada, Oregon, and Washington. Each of these eleven appellate courts also hears appeals from the rulings of federal administrative agencies.

The jurisdiction of the remaining two appellate courts is somewhat different from that of the others. The U.S. Court of Appeals for the District of Columbia hears appeals from the federal district court located in the District, as well as appeals from rulings of federal agencies that are issued there. The other appellate court is the U.S. Court of Appeals for the Federal Circuit, which hears all patent appeals from Patent and Trademark Office boards throughout the country and appeals from decisions of the new U.S. Claims Court, which is the trial court in which most contractual claims against the federal government originate.

Appeals from judgments of the U.S. courts of appeal, like appeals from judgments of the state supreme courts that present federal questions, can be taken to the U.S. Supreme Court. In virtually all cases, however, these appeals are not a matter of right. Rather, the parties who seek review must petition the Supreme Court for a *writ of certiorari,* and the Court has absolute discretion in deciding which of these cases are sufficiently important to warrant the granting of certiorari.[4] In a typical year the Court can hear only 150 or so of the 4,500 appeals that are made.

## *Some Observations*

The typical state court system and the federal system can be diagrammed as in Figure 2.2. Several general comments can be made about this diagram.

**1.** The basic trial courts are the U.S. district courts and the state general trial courts; all courts above this level are appellate courts.

---

[4] A *writ of certiorari* is an order of a higher court requiring a lower court to forward to it the records and proceedings of a particular case.

**Figure 2.2** The Federal and State Court Systems

2. Trial courts must settle questions of both *fact* and *law*, while appellate courts rule on questions of law only. Questions of fact are "what happened" questions: for instance, did the defendant corporations expressly or implicitly agree not to sell goods to the plaintiff? Questions of law, by contrast, are "what is the rule applicable to the facts?" (Much more is said about the fact/law distinction in the next chapter.)

3. While a majority of the decisions of the trial courts are not appealed, a good many are. Hereafter we are concerned primarily with the *decisions of the appellate courts*. There are several basic reasons for this. First, state trial courts usually enter a judgment without writing a formal opinion as to their reasoning; and, even if there is such an opinion, it is normally not reported (published). Appellate courts, on the other hand, normally do write opinions which are reported, and access to them is available to anyone wishing to look up the rulings of law involved. Second, appellate courts have more opportunity to delineate the legal issues in their opinions for the benefit of lawyers and others who may read them. Third, if the appellate court disagrees with the result reached by the trial court, the appellate court's decision is, of course, controlling.

4. Once a case is initiated within a given court system, it will normally stay within that system until a final judgment is reached. Thus, if a case is properly commenced in a state court of general jurisdiction, any appeal from the trial court's judgment must be made to the next higher state court rather than to a federal appellate court. And if a case reaches the highest court in the state, its judgment is final. In other words, on matters of state law, state supreme courts are indeed supreme.[5] However, should a state supreme court rule on a case that turns on interpretation of a federal statute or a provision of the U.S. Constitution, an appeal could be taken to the U.S. Supreme Court which has the final word on matters of *federal* law.

5. With regard to the "title" of an appealed case, the state and federal courts follow somewhat different rules. In most state courts, the original plaintiff's name appears first—just as it did in the trial court. Suppose, for example, that Pink (plaintiff) sues Doe (defendant) in a state trial court, where the case is obviously *Pink v. Doe*. If the judgment of the trial court is appealed, the rule followed by most state courts is that the title of the case remains *Pink v. Doe* in the appellate courts, no matter which party is the *appellant* (the one bringing the appeal). In the federal courts, on the other hand, the appellant's name appears first. Under this rule, if Doe (defendant) loses in a U.S. district court and appeals to a U.S. court of appeals, the title of the case will be *Doe v. Pink* in the higher court. For this reason, when one sees a case in a federal appellate court so entitled, one cannot assume that Doe was the party who originated the action in the trial court. That determination must be made by referring to the facts of the case as set forth in the decision of the appellate court.

## PROBLEMS OF JURISDICTION

In order for a court to settle a particular controversy, it is necessary for it to have "jurisdiction over the case."[6] This means that it must have **jurisdiction** of both the *subject matter* involved in the suit and, in most cases, jurisdiction of the *person* (the individual or company) against whom the suit is being brought. If a trial court should enter a judgment in a particular case and, on appeal, the higher court finds that either of these kinds of jurisdiction was lacking, the judgment of the trial court is void—of no effect whatever.

### Subject Matter Jurisdiction

As we have already seen, some courts—such as a state probate court or the U.S. Tax Court—are considerably limited as to the type of cases they can hear. Within a given court system, then, the subject matter jurisdiction of the several courts is essentially clear. Lines of demarcation between the general trial courts of the state systems and those of the federal system are less clear and require some explanation.

### Subject Matter: State versus Federal Jurisdiction

Federal courts' subject matter jurisdiction is limited to the types of cases the Constitution provides they can hear. Most of the 250,000 or so cases filed each

---

[5] The normal terminology is being used here. In a few states, however, the "supreme court" label is given to an intermediate appellate court, with the highest court in the state bearing some other name. The court of last resort in the state of New York, for example, is the Court of Appeals of New York.

[6] As stated earlier, *jurisdiction* means the legal power to act, especially to hear and decide controversies.

year in federal district court fall into one of two categories, "federal question" and "diversity of citizenship."

**Federal Questions:** A **federal question** exists in any suit where the plaintiff's claim is based in whole or in essential part upon a *federal statute* or upon a provision of the *U.S. Constitution* or a *U.S. treaty*. Thus, if a group of environmentally concerned citizens sued a corporation alleging that it was polluting in violation of the federal Clean Water Act, federal subject matter jurisdiction would exist, regardless of the amount in dispute.

**Diversity of Citizenship:** A federal court may hear a case based on *state* law if (a) plaintiff and defendant are citizens of different states,[7] and (b) the amount in controversy exceeds $50,000. A suit between citizens of different states involving less than $50,000 must be filed in a state trial court. Diversity jurisdiction was originally created to protect out-of-state litigants from the bias of local state courts on the theory that the federal judge in that state, as a representative of the government of the entire country, would more likely be impartial.

Whether or not fears of local bias are well founded today, federal courts continue to hear many diversity cases (though fewer than before the "amount in controversy" requirement was raised from $10,000 in 1989). Many cases are as simple as, for example, an Oklahoma citizen injured in an auto accident caused by a Colorado citizen suing for $65,000 to cover medical bills and pain and suffering. Whether Colorado or Oklahoma state law should apply is a matter we will address presently, but in diversity cases federal courts must apply *state* substantive law (the law governing the rights of the parties) and *federal* procedural law (the law governing the manner in which the rights are enforced).

**Concurrent State Jurisdiction:** A basic state trial court is a court of general jurisdiction which is *presumed* to have subject matter jurisdiction over the cases filed in it until the defendant can overcome the presumption. Most of the 30 million or so nontraffic cases filed in state courts each year could not have been filed in federal courts. However, many of them could have been because state courts have **concurrent jurisdiction** over most federal cases. That is to say, state courts can hear diversity cases involving more than $50,000 and can even hear federal question cases involving federal laws and the U.S. Constitution. There are, however, a few exceptions to this general rule—cases where the Constitution or federal statutes have given **exclusive jurisdiction** to the federal courts. Examples of this exclusive federal jurisdiction include federal criminal cases, patent, trademark, and copyright cases, bankruptcy cases, and certain federal securities law cases.

**Removal:** Because of concurrent jurisdiction, a plaintiff with a federal question or diversity case involving more than $50,000 may choose between filing it in federal court or in state court. Usually federal court is chosen, but considerations of court congestion, familiarity with procedures, or judges' philosophies might lead a plaintiff's lawyer to choose state court.

The fact that a case with federal court potential is filed in state court does not mean that it will stay there, because defendants usually have the **right of removal;** that is to say, they have the right to have a case with federal subject matter jurisdiction transferred from the state court in which it was filed to the federal district court having jurisdiction over that geographic area.

The right of removal exists in every federal question case. Part of the rationale is that the defendant is entitled to have a federal question determined by a federal court, which presumably is more expert in such matters. A defendant in a diversity case who is sued in state court in the plaintiff's state has the right to remove the suit to federal court in the plaintiff's state on the theory that a federal court is less likely to be biased against an out-of-state defendant than is a state court. On the other hand, a defendant sued in diversity in a state court in his own state cannot remove to federal district court because that defendant need not worry about being discriminated against by his own state's judge.

## *Jurisdiction of the Person*

A court does not have the power to hear a case simply because its subject matter, the general nature of the proceeding, falls within its jurisdiction. A second type of jurisdiction—jurisdiction over *the person of the defendant* (or, in some cases, property of the de-

---

[7] For diversity of citizenship purposes, a corporation is a citizen of both the state in which it is incorporated and, if different, the state in which it has its principal place of business.

fendant)—must also be present. In other words, while subject matter rules determine the court system that may hear a case, jurisdiction of person rules determine the *particular trial court* within that system where the case must be commenced. In this regard, a distinction between actions *in personam* and actions *in rem* must be noted.

**Actions *in Rem*:** In some actions the plaintiff is seeking merely to enforce a right against certain *property* that is owned by the defendant or in which the defendant claims an interest. Such suits are **actions *in rem*,** and can be brought in any court within whose territorial jurisdiction the property—the *res,* or thing—is located.

The typical case is the mortgage foreclosure action, which can be illustrated as follows. X, a Missouri resident, owns an apartment building in Iowa with a $35,000 mortgage on it held by an Iowa bank. If X defaults on the mortgage payments, the bank can bring a mortgage foreclosure action in Iowa in the state district court of the county where the building is located.

The general notion in an *in rem* case is that if a defendant is going to claim an interest in a certain parcel of real estate, it is not unfair to make that defendant go where the real estate is located to defend a lawsuit. This is fairly straightforward. The more difficult questions tend to involve *in personam* actions.

**Actions *in Personam*:** The great majority of civil actions are *in personam*—that is, actions in which the plaintiff is seeking to hold the defendant liable on a personal obligation. Three common examples would be: P sues D to recover damages (that is, a sum of money) arising out of a breach of contract by D; P sues to recover damages for personal injuries sustained in an accident caused by D; and P sues to recover a debt owed by D's company.

Assume that plaintiff lives in Wisconsin and wishes to file suit there. For purposes of discussion we shall concentrate on state court, although the rules are basically the same for federal court. Traditionally, plaintiff could establish personal jurisdiction in one of three ways. First, if plaintiff can demonstrate that defendant is also a citizen of Wisconsin, then personal jurisdiction over defendant exists as soon as plaintiff serves a *summons* (to be explained in the next chapter) upon defendant. Surely it cannot be unfair to ask defendant to appear in court in his home state.

But assume that defendant lives in Tennessee, and the lawsuit arises out of an accident that defendant caused while driving through Wisconsin on a vacation. Defendant is now back in Tennessee. A second method of establishing personal jurisdiction in Wisconsin is to serve defendant with a summons when defendant returns to Wisconsin. However, a defendant who knows that a potential lawsuit awaits in Wisconsin is likely to avoid the state altogether. The third traditional method to establish personal jurisdiction is to induce the defendant to consent to appear in the Wisconsin court. Obviously, few out-of-state defendants are so cooperative.

Thus, under these traditional methods of securing personal jurisdiction, our plaintiff was usually forced to go to Tennessee to file suit. This scarcely seems fair since the accident did take place in Wisconsin. The legislatures of Wisconsin and all other states decided they were not adequately protecting the interests of their citizens against wrongs done by citizens of foreign states. Therefore, they passed **long-arm statutes** that authorize the "long arm of the law" emanating from the courts of Wisconsin to reach out to Tennessee to bring defendant back to Wisconsin to defend the suit. Most long-arm statutes provide that if a person does certain acts in a state, such as conduct business, enter into a contract, own real estate, drive a car, or actively solicit sales, the law presumes that such person consents to be sued in the state in litigation arising out of those actions. Because our Tennessee defendant used Wisconsin roads and arguably committed a tortious act (negligent driving) in Wisconsin, the long-arm statute is satisfied.

However, in every instance in which a plaintiff attempts to invoke a long-arm statute to secure personal jurisdiction over an out-of-state citizen, two requirements must be met. First, plaintiff must demonstrate that defendant committed one of the acts listed in the long-arm statute.[8] Second, plaintiff must demonstrate that it is constitutional—i.e., consistent with our due process notions of fair play and justice—to make defendant come to plaintiff's jurisdiction to defend.

The following case illustrates the Supreme Court's view of how many contacts a defendant must have with a particular state before it is fair to make the defendant appear in that state to defend a lawsuit.

---

[8] Some states have omitted a listing of specific acts and simply make clear their intent to exercise personal jurisdiction over foreign citizens whenever it is constitutional to do so.

### Helicopteros Nacionales de Colombia v. Hall
United States Supreme Court, 466 U.S. 408 (1984)

Petitioner "Helicol," a Colombian corporation, entered into a contract to provide helicopter transportation for Consorcio/WSH, a Peruvian company closely connected to a joint venture headquartered in Houston, Texas, during the company's construction of a pipeline in Peru. One of the helicopters crashed in Peru, killing four United States citizens. Respondents, survivors and representatives of the four decedents, filed this suit in Texas state court in Houston.

At the request of Consorcio/WSH, Helicol's chief executive officer had flown to Houston to negotiate the contract; the agreement was signed in Peru. During the years 1970–77, Helicol also purchased helicopters, spare parts, and accessories for more than $4,000,000 from a Fort Worth company. Helicol had sent prospective pilots to Fort Worth for training and to ferry the helicopters back to South America, and also sent some management and maintenance personnel there for technical consultation. Helicol received into its New York and Florida bank accounts over $5,000,000 in payments from Consorcio/WSH drawn on a Houston bank.

On the other hand, Helicol has never been authorized to do business in Texas, and never had an agent for service of process there. Nor has it ever performed helicopter operations, sold products, solicited business, signed contracts, based employees, recruited employees, owned property, maintained an office or records, or had shareholders in Texas.

Helicol filed a special appearance[a] in the trial court and moved to dismiss for lack of personal jurisdiction. The trial court denied the motion and, after a jury trial, entered a $1,141,200 judgment against Helicol. The Texas Court of Civil Appeals reversed for lack of personal jurisdiction, but the Texas Supreme Court later reinstated the verdict. Helicol then appealed to the U.S. Supreme Court.

**Decision:** The Supreme Court reversed, holding that Texas could not constitutionally exercise personal jurisdiction over the defendant. The Due Process Clause of the Fourteenth Amendment prohibits a state from exercising personal jurisdiction over a nonresident corporate defendant unless that defendant has "certain minimum contacts with the forum such that maintenance of the suit does not offend traditional notions of fair play and substantial justice." Fewer contacts may be required where the lawsuit arises directly out of defendant's contacts with the forum. But where, as here, the suit arises out of actions that occurred outside the forum (i.e., a crash in Peru), personal jurisdiction can be exercised only if defendant had "continuous and systematic general business contacts" with the forum.

The Court held that purchasing helicopters in Texas and related activities did not constitute "continuous and systematic general business contacts." Defendant had no place of business in Texas and no employees permanently located there. ∎

[a] In a special appearance, defendant comes into the state only to contest existence of personal jurisdiction in the litigation and while there cannot be served summons in the traditional way.

**Comment:** To reiterate, the concept of *in personam* jurisdiction is geographical in nature, and in the United States is inevitably linked to state boundaries. The court asks: Is it fair to make this defendant come to this state to defend? The result in *Hall* would probably have been the same had Helicol been from Oklahoma rather than Colombia. Also, the result would have been the same had the case been filed in *federal* district court in Houston rather than in state district court. Geographically, it is no less burdensome for Helicol to come to Houston to defend in federal court than in state court. A federal court usually uses the long-arm statute of the state in which it sits to determine personal jurisdiction.

Also note that plaintiffs were attempting to sue in Texas for an accident *that occurred elsewhere*. In order to do so, plaintiffs needed to prove that defendant had "systematic and continuous" contacts with Texas, often called "general jurisdiction." However, had the president of Helicol caused an auto accident while in Houston negotiating the contract, he would have been subject to personal jurisdiction in a subsequent lawsuit by the injured party because the suit *arose out of his contact with Texas*. This is often called "specific jurisdiction." For specific jurisdiction to exist, many courts hold that the nonresident defendant must either purposefully direct his activities or consummate some transaction within the forum, or must perform some act by which he purposefully avails himself of the privilege of conducting activities in the forum, thereby invoking the benefits and protections of the law. For example, a manufacturer that sends its products into Maine and wants to use the courts of Maine to sue for breach of contract should a buyer not pay, will likely be subjected to personal jurisdiction in Maine in any suits arising out of injuries caused there by the product.

To make one last point, return to our hypothetical of the Tennesseean who caused an accident in Wisconsin. The statutory and constitutional prerequisites for assertion of long-arm jurisdiction by the Wisconsin courts appear to be met. What happens if defendant simply ignores the lawsuit, assuming that the Wisconsin courts cannot touch him? Defendant is wrong. Defendant's failure to appear will lead to a default judgment being rendered against him. In most instances, plaintiff can take that Wisconsin judgment and have it enforced by Tennessee courts just as though it had been rendered by them. Under the Full Faith and Credit Clause of the Constitution, Tennessee courts will honor and enforce most judgments from Wisconsin and other states.

## Additional Concerns

**Venue:** That a court has subject matter and personal jurisdiction does not always end the inquiry. In our Wisconsin accident hypothetical, for example, every trial court in every county in Wisconsin would have had subject matter and personal jurisdiction over the defendant. But should the case be filed in southern Wisconsin or northern Wisconsin? **Venue** statutes answer this question by specifying geographically the particular court that should hear a case. Typically, venue is available in the county where the defendant resides or where the cause of action arose. In our hypothetical, a plaintiff filing in Wisconsin state court should file in the county where the accident occurred.

***Forum Non Conveniens:*** A court with both subject matter and personal jurisdiction may decline to exercise them if another court, more conveniently connected to the suit, also has both types of jurisdiction. Under the doctrine of ***forum non conveniens,*** the court may choose to transfer the suit or even dismiss it, forcing plaintiff to file in the more convenient court.

For example, in one case arising out of a defendant's agent carelessly causing a fire in the plaintiff's warehouse in Virginia, plaintiff sued 400 miles away in New York City where the state court had subject matter jurisdiction over the simple tort case and personal jurisdiction because of defendant corporation's many business contacts in New York. However, the New York court declined to exercise its jurisdiction on grounds that the suit was more conveniently brought in Virginia where plaintiff and all witnesses were located and where the accident had occurred. The only justification plaintiff gave for filing in New York—that a New York jury was likely to give a bigger verdict—was inadequate.[9]

In determining the most convenient forum, courts will consider private interest factors such as ease of access to sources of proof, costs of obtaining witnesses' attendance, the possibility of a view of the site of the accident, and the convenience of the parties. Public factors to be considered include the imposition of jury service on residents of the community, the congestion of court dockets, and the interest in having local controversies decided at home.

A U.S. court of appeals recently affirmed, on *forum non conveniens* grounds, the transfer of litigation against Union Carbide arising out of the Bhopal tragedy in India from a federal district court in New York to India. It did so only after the trial judge convinced himself that Indian courts could provide substantial justice. The transfer was conditioned on Union Carbide's consent to the jurisdiction of the Indian courts and waiver of any statute of limitations defense.[10]

**Conflict of Laws:** Assume D Corporation, formed in Delaware with its principal place of business in Colorado, hires P from California to do subcontracting work on D's condominiums in New Mexico. The contract is negotiated in California, Colorado, and New Mexico before being signed in Colorado. When New Mexico officials ordered P to stop work because he did not have a license to do such work in New Mexico, D fired him. P sued in Colorado to recover for the work he had done before being stopped. Several states' laws are potentially applicable to this case. If they all lead to the same result, it does not matter which state's rules are applied. However, in this case, New Mexico law bars P from recovery because he

---

[9] *Gulf Oil Corp. v. Gilbert,* 330 U.S. 401 (1947).

[10] *In re Union Carbide Corp. Gas Plant Disaster at Bhopal, India in Dec. 1984,* 809 F.2d 195 (2d. Cir. 1987).

had no license. Colorado and California law would allow him to recover despite the lack of a license. There is a "conflict of laws." To determine which state's laws to apply, we must resort to "choice of law" rules which are designed to prevent a plaintiff with multiple jurisdictions from which to choose (because all have subject matter and personal jurisdiction) from "forum shopping" for the jurisdiction with the laws most favorable to him or her.

*Contract cases:* If the parties stipulate in the contract that, for example, "California law will govern any disputes arising out of this contract," the courts will normally respect that choice if it was fairly bargained and California has at least a passing connection to the parties or the transaction.

Absent a choice by the parties, the traditional view was to apply the law of the state in which the contract was made to any litigation about the validity of the contract, and to apply the law of the state in which the contract was to be performed to any litigation about the performance of the contract. The strong modern trend, however, is to use an "interest" analysis.

Using an interest analysis to determine which state's law to apply, courts would consider such factors as the relevant policies of the forum (Colorado) and of other interested states, the protection of justified expectations (i.e., which state's laws did the parties assume would apply), certainty, predictability, ease of determination of the law to be applied, and uniformity of result.

In contract cases specifically, most modern courts attempt to determine the state with the "most significant relationship" to the parties and the transaction, considering such factors as (1) the place of contracting, (2) the place of negotiation, (3) the place of performance, (4) the location of the subject matter of the contract, and (5) the domicile, residence, nationality, place of incorporation, and place of business of the parties.

In the factual situation outlined above, the Colorado Supreme Court applied New Mexico's law, reasoning that New Mexico's interest in protecting its citizens from substandard construction by unlicensed subcontractors outweighed Colorado's interest in validating agreements and protecting parties' expectations.[11]

*Tort cases:* Assume that a husband and wife from New Mexico are killed when a plane the husband is piloting crashes in Texas. The parties intended to return to New Mexico and had no other contacts with Texas. The estate of the wife filed suit against the husband's estate in state court in Texas. Texas' doctrine of interspousal immunity would not allow the suit. New Mexico has no such doctrine; its law would allow the suit. Which state's law should apply? The traditional view is to apply the law of the place of the tort—Texas. But why would Texas courts care whether or not a New Mexico wife can recover from a New Mexico husband? Again, the strong modern trend is to move away from an automatic choice of the law of the place of the tort to an interest analysis. Modern courts often use the following factors in deciding which state has the "most significant relationship" to the occurrence and the parties: (a) the place where the injury occurred; (b) the place where the conduct causing the injury occurred; (c) the domicile, residence, nationality, place of incorporation and place of business of the parties; and (d) the place where the relationship, if any, between the parties is centered. In this case, New Mexico law was applied.[12]

## LAW, EQUITY, AND REMEDIES

In the next chapter we will examine the major steps in the process of adjudication, paying particular attention to the roles played by the trial and appellate courts in that process. We will see that in all legal controversies the plaintiff is asking for a **remedy**—an order addressed to the defendant, requiring that person to do (or not to do) a particular act. A remedy, then, is "the means by which a plaintiff's right is enforced, or the violation of a right is prevented, redressed, or compensated."[13] All remedies are either "legal" or "equitable" in nature, a fact that can be explained only by a brief glimpse at the development of the early court systems in England.

### *Courts of Law*

Some nine hundred years ago the first Norman kings of England established a system of courts by designating individuals throughout the country to be their per-

---

[11] *Wood Bros. Homes, Inc. v. Walker Adjustment Bureau,* 601 P.2d 1369 (Colo. 1979).

[12] *Robertson v. McKnight,* 609 S.W.2d 534 (Tex. 1980).

[13] *Black's Law Dictionary,* Fifth Edition, Copyright 1979 by West Publishing Co.

**Figure 2.3** Major Differences between Law and Equity

| Law | Method of resolving dispute | Equity |
|---|---|---|
| Application of existing rules of law | | Rules of law tempered by discretion—court of conscience |
| Jury | Trial | No jury |
| Legal remedy (usually damages, enforceable through execution) | Remedy | Decree, enforceable through contempt proceedings (e.g., injunction, decree of specific performance) |

sonal representatives in the settling of certain kinds of legal disputes. These representatives could grant only very limited types of relief: (1) money damages, (2) possession of real estate, or (3) possession of personal property.

In settling disputes, the courts made up their own rules as they went along, based largely on the customs and moral standards then prevailing, plus their own ideas of "justice" in particular situations. The formulation of rules in this manner, a process that continues today in some branches of law, gave birth to the *common law* (which we will study in more detail in Chapter 4). These royal courts ultimately became known as **courts of law** and the remedies which they granted were *remedies at law.*

## Courts of Equity

When plaintiffs needed relief other than what the courts of law could grant, they often petitioned the king. Such petitions were frequently decided by the king's chancellor, who granted relief when he thought the claim was a fair one. Out of the rulings of successive chancellors arose a new body of "chancery" rules and remedies for cases outside the jurisdiction of the courts of law. This developed eventually into a system of **courts of equity,** as distinct from the courts of law.

A plaintiff who wanted a legal remedy, such as money damages, would bring an **action at law** in a court of law. A plaintiff wanting some other relief, such as an **injunction** (e.g., an order forcing D to stop grazing cattle on land belonging to P) or a **decree of specific performance** (e.g., an order commanding D to live up to a contract to sell land to P) brought an **action in equity** in an equity court.[14]

## The Present Scene

While the distinction between legal and equitable remedies as diagrammed in Figure 2.3 persists today, there has been a fusion of law and equity courts in virtually all states. This means that separate courts of law and equity, as such, have been eliminated. Instead, the basic trial courts in the state and federal systems are empowered to hear both legal and equitable actions.

---

[14] Other common equitable actions, in addition to those asking for injunctions and decrees of specific performance, are (1) divorce actions, (2) mortgage foreclosure suits, and (3) actions for an accounting, brought by one member of a partnership against another.

Today, the basic distinctions between the two kinds of actions are these:

1. Whether an action is one at law or in equity depends solely upon the *nature of the remedy* that the plaintiff is seeking.

2. There is *no jury* in an equitable action. Questions of both fact and law are decided by the court, that is, the trial judge.

3. Proceedings in equitable actions are *less formal* than those at law, particularly in regard to the order in which witnesses' testimony can be presented and the determination of admissibility of their evidence.

## SUMMARY

Both the state and the federal court systems are organized similarly. At the first level are general trial courts, supplemented by specialized courts of limited jurisdiction. Appeals from the judgments of these courts are heard by appellate courts. In some states and in the federal system, there is an intermediate appellate court as well as a supreme court for a final appeal.

Federal courts can hear only the types of cases specified in the Constitution, primarily cases turning on federal questions and cases where a citizen of one state is suing the citizen of another for more than $50,000. State trial courts can hear just about any type of case, except for a few categories specifically limited for exclusive federal jurisdiction. However, if a case with federal subject matter jurisdiction potential is filed in state court, it might not stay there; the defendant may remove it to federal court.

Every court must have subject matter jurisdiction. Personal jurisdiction over the defendant is also a prerequisite to a valid judgment. Courts frequently use the long-arm statute of their state to establish personal jurisdiction over defendants from other states, consistent with due process, of course. The establishment of subject matter and personal jurisdiction does not end the inquiry as to where a case will be tried—matters of venue and *forum non conveniens* must also be considered. A court deciding a case that has contacts with many states will have to use choice of law rules to determine which state's law to apply.

Historically, common law courts were divided into courts of law, which rendered mostly damage judgments, and courts of equity, which could grant more varied forms of relief. Though there are no longer two separate court systems, the procedures in a court may vary depending on whether the plaintiff asks for damages or injunctive relief.

## KEY TERMS

**Adjudication**
**Courts of limited jurisdiction**
**General trial courts**
**Appellate courts**
**Jurisdiction**
**Federal question**
**Concurrent jurisdiction**
**Exclusive jurisdiction**
**Right of removal**
**Action** *in rem*
**Action** *in personam*
**Long-arm statutes**
**Venue**
*Forum non conveniens*
**Remedy**
**Courts of law**
**Courts of equity**
**Action at law**
**Injunction**
**Decree of specific performance**
**Action in equity**

## QUESTIONS AND PROBLEMS

**1.** A Michigan Department of Transportation rule required that all railroads have "adequate toilet facilities" for the health of their employees. About one-third of plaintiff CSXT's locomotives do not have toilets. CSXT protested, and a state administrative law judge upheld the rule. CSXT then filed suit in federal court, claiming that the state rule was inconsistent with federal regulations which do not require toilets. The Michigan Department of Transportation argued that the federal court should refuse to hear the case (abstain) because of the ongoing proceedings at the state level. The question arose as to whether a state court would have jurisdiction to decide a lawsuit involving federal statutes and regulations. Would it? (*CSXT, Inc. v. Pitz*, 883 F.2d 468, 6th Cir. 1989.)

**2.** Rate, a Georgia lawyer, is owed $55,000 in legal fees by Jackson, a Florida resident. Although Rate could have brought suit to recover the debt in a federal court in Florida on grounds of diversity of citizenship, he chose, instead, to file his suit in a Florida court in the county in which Jackson lives. If Jackson now asks that the suit be transferred to the federal courts, will his request have to be granted? Explain.

3. While walking across Gomez's property one evening, North is injured when he falls into an unguarded excavation. When North brings a negligence action against Gomez in the proper state court to recover damages, that court applies the rule that a trespasser cannot hold a landowner liable even if he is guilty of negligence, and dismisses the action. North appeals the decision to the state supreme court, which affirms the rule of nonliability. In this case, is the ruling of the state supreme court final? (If North were to appeal to the U.S. Supreme Court, would it refuse to consider the case?) Why or why not?

4. On December 21, 1985, an Arrow Air Corp. charter plane carrying 248 soldiers from active duty in the Middle East back to Fort Campbell, Kentucky, crashed in Newfoundland, killing all aboard. Relatives of the victims sued Arrow in Kentucky. Arrow moved to dismiss for lack of personal jurisdiction. Evidence showed that Arrow was incorporated in Delaware with its main office in Florida. Arrow hangared an aircraft in Kentucky in 1983, flying five cargo flights per week. It also made flights into Kentucky for the Military Airlift Command in 1984–85, earning over $2 million in charter revenue. The crash in question was Arrow's second flight into Fort Campbell. Arrow had no bank accounts or phone numbers in Kentucky. Does a Kentucky court have personal jurisdiction? (*In re Air Crash Disaster at Gander Newfoundland,* 660 F.Supp. 1202, W.D.Ky. 1987.)

5. Plaintiffs bought an Audi automobile in New York. Later, while moving to Arizona they were involved in a serious collision in Oklahoma when the Audi caught fire after being struck from behind. Filing in Oklahoma, plaintiffs sued the New York retailer from whom they had purchased the car and the wholesaler who had provided the car to the retailer. These defendants claimed that because they only sold cars in New York, an Oklahoma court had no personal jurisdiction over them. Does the Oklahoma long-arm statute reach this far? Discuss. (*World-Wide Volkswagen Corp. v. Woodson,* 444 U.S. 286, 1981.)

6. Dennis married Francie in West Virginia in 1976. They spent their married life in New Jersey, where their children were born. In July of 1987, they decided to separate. Francie moved herself and the children to San Francisco. Dennis visited Los Angeles on a business trip and then went to San Francisco to see the kids. When he arrived, Francie had him served with a summons and a divorce petition. Dennis went back to New Jersey and had his lawyer file a motion to dismiss the California suit for lack of personal jurisdiction. Should the motion be granted, given Dennis's lack of contacts with California? Discuss. (*Burnham v. Superior Court of California,* 110 S.Ct. 2105, 1990.)

7. Plaintiff corporation, incorporated in Michigan, hired defendant from Florida to operate a helicopter to spray agricultural chemicals on fields in Ohio. In a contract written and signed by plaintiff in Michigan and later signed by defendant in Florida, defendant agreed that if he left plaintiff's employ he would not enter into a competing business. After two years, defendant left plaintiff's employ and did begin a competing business in Ohio. Plaintiff sued in Ohio to enforce the covenant not to compete. Such a covenant is void under Michigan law, but enforceable if reasonable under the laws of Florida and Ohio. Which state's law should be applied by the Ohio court? Discuss. (*S&S Chopper Service, Inc. v. Scripter,* 394 N.E.2d 1011, Ohio App. 1977.)

8. Defendant airline, a Delaware corporation headquartered in New York, invited several Illinois travel agents to take an expense paid vacation to Mexico. While in Mexico, one of the travel agents was killed by unknown assailants. His wife, plaintiff, sued the airline in Illinois, claiming that its Illinois employees knew at the time of the invitation that portions of Mexico near the trip site were overrun with bands of armed guerrillas, yet they negligently failed to take precautions for the safety of her husband. Mexico's law would allow recovery on plaintiff's theory; Illinois law would not. Which law should apply? Discuss. (*Semmelroth v. American Airlines,* 448 F.Supp. 730, E.D.Ill. 1978.)

9. Durant was left paralyzed from the waist down when his tractor struck defendant's guide wire. Durant sued defendant on a theory of negligent maintenance, filing the suit in Lee County, South Carolina. Defendant filed a motion to change the suit's venue to Sumter County on grounds of convenience to witnesses. Nine of defendant's employees, who would also be witnesses, filed affidavits stating that they would have to travel 23 miles to the Lee County Courthouse. Plaintiff responded with an affidavit indicating that because of his paralysis he was difficult to move, and that the Lee County rescue squad had agreed to transport him to and from the Lee County Courthouse but no further. Should the court grant the motion to change venue on *forum non conveniens* grounds? Discuss. See *Durant v. Black River Electric Cooperative, Inc.*, 248 S.E.2d 264 (S.C. 1978).

# CHAPTER 3

# DISPUTE RESOLUTION

Many American novels, movies, and television programs feature courtroom scenes to produce dramatic tension for the readers and viewers. This is appropriate, because courtroom battles can produce high drama. Nothing quite matches the tension which litigants and attorneys feel when a jury verdict is about to be announced in open court.

This chapter will examine the litigation process, from the initiation of a civil suit through the trial process all the way to final appeal. After this examination, you will be better able to appreciate the context in which these few dramatic moments occur. You will also understand that litigation can be extremely complicated, expensive, and time-consuming. Indeed, litigation is usually something to be avoided. But when you cannot avoid litigation, it pays to understand the process.

## LITIGATION: PRETRIAL PROCEEDINGS

Pretrial proceedings consist of two stages, the **pleading stage** and the **discovery stage.** We will look at each of these steps briefly.

### *The Pleading Stage*

The typical suit is commenced by the plaintiff, through an attorney, filing a **complaint** (or petition) with the court having jurisdiction of the case. At the same time, the plaintiff asks the court to issue a summons to the defendant, notifying that person that a complaint is on file. In most instances, service of process is accomplished by a law officer hand-delivering the summons to the defendant. However, when this cannot be reasonably accomplished, most states provide for service by registered mail or by leaving the summons at the defendant's usual place of business or home. Even service by publication in local newspapers is sometimes allowed. Service on a corporate defendant must be in accordance with strict rules. All jurisdictions require every corporation doing business in a state to maintain a registered agent for purposes of receiving service of process. That agent's address is on file in the secretary of state's office. If a corporation fails to appoint a registered agent or if the agent cannot be found, service upon the secretary of state is effective against the corporation.

After receiving the summons, the defendant has a prescribed period of time in which to file a response of some sort, normally an **answer,** to the complaint. After that has been done, the plaintiff can file a **reply** to the answer. The complaint, answer, and reply make up the *pleadings* of a case, the main purpose of which is to permit the court and the parties to ascertain the actual points in issue.

**The Complaint:** The complaint briefly sets forth the plaintiff's version of the facts and ends with a "prayer" (request) for a certain remedy based on those facts. Its primary purpose is to notify the defendant that a claim is being asserted against him or her based on certain *allegations* of fact.

**The Answer:** The defendant usually responds to the complaint by filing an *answer* (or, in circumstances to be noted later, a "motion to dismiss"). In the typical case the defendant will disagree with one or more allegations of fact set forth in the complaint, and the answer will indicate the specific points of disagreement. For example, three allegations in a complaint growing out of an automobile accident may be (1) that the defendant was the driver of a car that collided with the plaintiff's on a certain date, (2) that defendant's car was to the left of the center line at the time of impact, and (3) that defendant was driving negligently at the time. Depending upon the particular circumstances, the defendant might deny the first allegation (on which the others are obviously based), claiming that he or she was merely a passenger in the car, which was being driven by someone else. Or the defendant might admit allegations (1) and (2) but deny allegation (3), claiming that he or she was directed to drive left of center by a police officer who was investigating a prior accident at the scene. In either event, the answer would raise *questions of fact,* which would have to be settled at the trial.

The answer also permits the defendant to raise *affirmative defenses*—legal points that will absolve the defendant of liability even if his or her version of the facts is proved wrong. For example, the defendant in the above case may deny that he or she was driving negligently, and, in addition, may allege that the accident was actually caused by *plaintiff's* careless driving. If proved at trial, carelessness by the plaintiff constitutes *comparative negligence,* a defense which can reduce or even bar the plaintiff's recovery.

Additionally, an answer may be accompanied by a **counterclaim** which, in an auto accident case, might contend that the plaintiff was the real cause of the accident and that the defendant was injured also. In the same proceeding the jury would decide whether plaintiff or defendant was at fault, and who could recover from whom. Many a plaintiff has regretted instigating litigation after a jury resolved all issues in favor of the defendant's counterclaim.

***Motion to Dismiss:*** If a defendant contends that he or she is not legally liable even if the plaintiff's allegations of fact are true, defendant will file a **motion to dismiss** instead of an answer. Technically this is called a "motion to dismiss" for the reason that the complaint states no cause of action: the complaint fails to state a legally recognizable claim. For example, if the D Company, a retailer, cut down two trees in front of its place of business in spite of protests from P, a neighboring retailer, and if P sued the D Company to recover damages, the D Company might well file such a motion in response to P's complaint. In such a case, assuming that the felling of the trees did not violate any municipal ordinance or rule of the local planning commission, the D Company had a perfect right to remove the trees; thus the motion to dismiss will be "sustained" by the court and the suit will be ended at that point. (A trial court's ruling on such a motion, however, may always be appealed to a higher court. If that court rules that a motion to dismiss should have been overruled rather than sustained, then the case will be sent back to the trial court for further proceedings.)[1]

By filing a motion to dismiss on the grounds that no cause of action is stated, the defendant does not admit that the plaintiff's version of the facts is correct. Rather, he or she is simply saying that even if the facts are as stated, plaintiff has no basis under the law for bringing the suit. Thus, if the motion is overruled, the defendant is permitted to raise questions of fact during the trial.

If the defendant files nothing within the prescribed time (20 days in the federal courts) after being served with a summons, the court may enter a **default judgment** against the defendant. In essence, a default judgment determines that the defendant has waived the right to contest liability. The court then proceeds to hold a hearing on damages to determine how much the plaintiff is entitled to recover.

***The Reply:*** If the defendant raises new matter—additional facts—in his or her answer, then the plaintiff must file a reply. In this pleading plaintiff will either deny or admit the new facts alleged in the answer.

## The Discovery Stage

In early years, cases moved directly from the pleading stage to the trial stage. This meant that each party, going into the trial, had little information as to the specific evidence that the other party would rely on in presenting his case. Trial proceedings, as a result, often became what was commonly described as a "cat and mouse" game, with the parties often bringing in evidence that surprised their opponents.

The undesirability of these proceedings was finally perceived by lawyers and judges, with the result that the Federal Rules of Civil Procedure, adopted in 1938, provided means (called "discovery proceedings") by which much of the evidence that each party was going to rely on in proving his or her version of

---

[1] The terminology used in referring to this particular type of "motion to dismiss" follows the rules of civil procedure that have, in recent years, been adopted by many states. The earlier name for this same pleading device—the "demurrer"—continues to be used in a number of states, however. In such states, what has been said here in regard to the motion to dismiss applies with equal force to the demurrer.

the facts would be fully disclosed to the other party before the case came on for trial. The most common discovery tools recognized by these federal rules, which have now been essentially adopted by the states, are *depositions, interrogatories,* and *requests for production of documents.*

A deposition is testimony of a witness that is taken outside of court. Such testimony is given under oath, and both parties to the case must be notified so that they can be present when the testimony is given, and thus have the opportunity to cross-examine the witness. Depositions are taken for these reasons: (1) to learn what the key witnesses know about the case; (2) to gain leads that will help obtain additional information; (3) to preserve the testimony of witnesses who might die or disappear; and (4) to set up cross-examination of witnesses who might later change their stories.

Interrogatories are written questions submitted by one party to the other, which must be answered under oath. Use of this device is a primary way by which the questioning party may gain access to evidence that otherwise would be solely in the possession of his or her adversary.

A demand for documents permits a party to gain access to those kinds of evidence—such as business records, letters, and hospital bills—which are in the possession of the other party. Under modern rules of civil procedure the party seeking the documents has the right to obtain them for purposes of inspection and copying.

A party that refuses to comply in good faith with legitimate discovery requests faces court sanctions up to and including default judgment. For example, in 1984 when a federal judge decided that Piper Aircraft Corp. had destroyed large amounts of evidence pertaining to the safety of its Cheyenne aircraft, one of which had crashed killing plaintiffs' relatives, he held that Piper had forfeited the right to defend the suit and entered judgment against it on the issue of liability. Piper was allowed to present evidence on the issue of damages.[2]

## Summary Judgment

At or near the end of discovery, one party or the other (and occasionally both) may file a motion for **summary judgment** as to one or more of the issues in the lawsuit. In filing such a motion a party is arguing to the judge, in essence, that the evidence produced by discovery makes it so clear that the moving party is legally entitled to prevail that a trial would be a waste of time. A judge should grant such a motion only if a thorough review of the evidence obtained through discovery indicates that there is "no genuine issue as to any material fact"—that is, that there is no real question as to any important factual matter.

Judges have traditionally been reluctant to grant summary judgment motions, especially when a party properly requests a jury trial. In recent years, however, the U.S. Supreme Court has encouraged use of the summary judgment device authorized by rule 56 in the Federal Rules of Civil Procedure, noting that "Summary judgment procedure is properly regarded not as a disfavored procedural shortcut, but rather as an integral part of the Federal Rules as a whole, which are designed to 'secure the just, speedy and inexpensive determination of every action.'" *Celotex Corp. v. Catrett,* 477 U.S. 317 (1986). The following case illustrates the struggle judges face in balancing a party's right to a jury trial against the need to preserve judicial resources for truly meritorious claims.

[2] *Carlucci v. Piper Aircraft Corp.,* 102 F.R.D. 472 (S.D. Fla. 1984).

---

### Donnelly v. Guion
U.S. Second Circuit Court of Appeals, 467 F.2d 290 (1972)

Plaintiff Donnelly's 16-year-old son David was a student in a boarding school in Connecticut. David suffered from Marfan's syndrome, a congenital condition affecting the connective tissues which often leads to formation of an aneurysm which may rupture and cause death. On January 31, 1969, David was found in his bed, apparently lifeless. McDonald, the school physician and city medical examiner, examined David and concluded that he was dead. McDonald knew from school records that David suffered from Marfan's syndrome, but concluded that an autopsy was necessary to determine with certainty the cause of David's death because there were no external indications of its cause. Subsequently an autopsy,

*(continued)*

performed by the county coroner, Dr. Guion, and his designated assistant, Dr. Izumi, revealed that death had indeed resulted from a ruptured aneurysm due to Marfan's syndrome.

Plaintiff filed this suit against McDonald, Izumi, and Guion, claiming damages for emotional and physical distress caused by wrongful performance of an autopsy. She also sued Dr. Izumi only for failure to return organs which had been removed from the body. Defendants moved for summary judgment. After all parties submitted affidavits to support their positions, the trial judge entered summary judgment for defendants on the wrongful autopsy claim, on grounds that they were not guilty of "wanton and willful" misconduct as is required for liability by Connecticut statute. However, he denied summary judgment on the claim regarding failure to return the organs, because of a conflict in testimony regarding whether such a return had been requested. Donnelly appealed as to the wrongful autopsy claim.

**Decision:** The trial judge's ruling was affirmed. Although "summary judgment is a drastic device [which] cuts off a party's right to present his case to the jury, . . . if the case is totally devoid of an issue of fact there is no reason why the curtain should rise on the trial." The medical defendants presented substantial, logical, and uncontradicted evidence in support of their decision to perform an autopsy. Although it was known that plaintiff's son suffered from Marfan's syndrome, the common indications of death from Marfan's were not present. Furthermore, his most recent X-rays, his recent general health, and the lack of external indications of the cause of death all indicated the need for an autopsy in order to determine the cause of death. Plaintiff's conclusory affidavit, containing only the bald assertion that she believed the fact that her son suffered Marfan's and was found dead in his bed "could lead only to a conclusion of a natural death," presents no reason whatsoever to conclude that defendants' determination that the cause of death was obscure was "wanton and willful" as required by statute. Summary judgment was clearly appropriate. ■

---

## LITIGATION: TRIAL PROCEEDINGS

### The Trial Stage

Unless a controversy is settled by a judgment on the pleadings (such as the granting of a motion to dismiss), or unless the parties settle out of court, a case will eventually come up for trial. In the **trial stage** a jury may be impaneled, evidence presented, a verdict returned, and a judgment entered in favor of one of the parties.

**Impaneling a Jury:** In any civil action in which the plaintiff is asking for a remedy at law, questions of fact are often resolved by a jury. However, a jury can be "waived" (dispensed with) if this is agreeable to both parties. In such instances the court decides questions of both fact and law. While waiver of a jury is increasingly common in civil actions today, there are still many actions where at least one of the parties demands a jury trial. The remainder of this discussion thus assumes the presence of a jury.

The names of prospective jurors are drawn from a list of those who have been selected for possible duty during the term. Each prospective juror is questioned in an effort to make sure that the jury will be as impartial as possible. If questioning indicates that a particular person would probably not be capable of such impartiality, he or she can be *challenged for cause*. Prospective jurors can be challenged, for example, if it is shown that they have a close friendship with one of the parties or the party's attorney, a financial interest in the case, or a bias resulting from any other aspect of the action. Any prospective juror disqualified for cause is excused, and another takes his or her place and is questioned in like fashion. This preliminary examination of prospective jurors is called the *voir dire* examination.[3]

When there are no more challenges for cause, the attorney for each party has a limited number of **peremptory challenges.** Such challenges permit the attorney to have a juror removed arbitrarily, without assigning a reason for doing so. Once the number of prospective jurors who have survived both kinds of challenges reaches the number required by law to hear the case, they are sworn in and the case proceeds. (Traditionally the number of jurors has been twelve, but in recent years many states have reduced the number to eight, or even fewer, in civil actions.)

**Order of Presentation of Proof:** After the opening statements, the case is presented by the plaintiff, who has the "burden of proof" (the duty to prove the facts alleged in the complaint). The plaintiff attempts

---

[3] "Voir dire," from the French, means "to speak the truth."

to meet this burden by calling witnesses whose testimony supports his or her version of the facts.

After each of the plaintiff's witnesses is examined by the plaintiff's attorney (direct examination), the defendant's attorney can cross-examine the witness for the purpose of discrediting the person's testimony on as many points as possible. For example, a cross-examination might divulge (1) that pertinent facts in the direct examination were omitted, (2) that a witness's powers of observation were poor, or (3) that the witness stood to benefit financially if the plaintiff won a judgment.

**The Rules of Evidence:** Before proceeding to the next steps in the trial of a case, a brief mention of *evidence* is necessary. As a practical matter, one of the most crucial steps in a lawsuit is the establishment of the facts—a final determination as to what actually happened. An early English judge said, "Without a known fact, it is impossible to know the law on that fact."[4] And unless a litigant can convince the jury that his or her version of the facts is correct, the case may very well collapse at the outset.

Because the findings of fact play such an important role in the outcome of a case, it is imperative that the jury determine the facts on the basis of the most reliable testimony possible—testimony that is relevant, factual, and based on direct observations of the witnesses. *The primary purpose of the rules of evidence is to exclude testimony that lacks these characteristics.* (With an exception to be noted later, the jury's findings of fact are conclusive. This means that an appellate court, in determining the propriety of a rule of law applied by a lower court, must normally accept the jury's version of the facts as being correct.)

While the **rules of evidence** are so numerous and so complex as to preclude any balanced survey of the subject here, it is possible to examine briefly three of the most common kinds of testimony that the rules ordinarily remove from the jury's consideration—assuming that timely objection to such testimony is made by counsel during the trial proceedings. That is, if improper testimony is elicited from a witness by the attorney for one of the parties, and the opposing counsel does *not* make a formal challenge by "objecting" to it at that time, such testimony is normally permitted to become part of the record.[5]

*Irrelevant Testimony:* If a witness is asked a question that can have no possible bearing on the facts in issue, the opposing counsel may enter an objection on the basis that the answer would be "irrelevant." In a personal injury suit, for example, such matters as the defendant's religious beliefs, or the fact that he was convicted of a charge of negligent driving several years earlier, would have no bearing on the instant case. Objections to such testimony would be "sustained" by the court.

*Hearsay:* It is essential that the jury have before it direct evidence—testimony based on the witnesses' *personal knowledge and observation* of facts and circumstances surrounding the issues being litigated. Evidence not of this type is called **hearsay** and is usually excluded. Thus if an issue in a particular case is whether a trucker delivered a shipment of goods to the X Company on a certain day, witness W (a jogger in the vicinity at the time) could testify that he saw packages being unloaded from a truck on the day in question. But neither W nor any other witness would be allowed to testify that he was *told by a third party* (Z) that Z saw goods being unloaded on the day in question.[6]

There are, however, many exceptions to the hearsay rule; that is, many admissions of out-of-court statements where experience has shown the statements to be generally reliable, and where there is a "necessity" for admission of the statement. For example, *business records* may usually be introduced in evidence by the person having custody of such records if the record was made "in the usual course of business," and if the record was made at or near the time of the act or transaction which it records.

*Opinion:* Sometimes a witness is asked for, or volunteers, information about a matter he or she believes to be true but of which the person actually has

---

[4] C. J. Vaughan, *Bushel's Case,* Jones (T.), 1670.
[5] Actions brought in the federal courts are governed by the Federal Rules of Evidence which Congress adopted in 1975. The rules of evidence that are applicable to actions in state courts are adopted by the various state supreme courts, and the rules vary somewhat from state to state. However, the federal rules are generally acknowledged as representing the most "modern view" of evidentiary rules and are increasingly being adopted by the state courts.
[6] Hearsay is essentially defined as any assertion (either orally or written) made by a person who is not in court and not subject to cross-examination when the said assertion is offered to prove the fact asserted. Thus the hearsay rule excludes many kinds of offered testimony in addition to what witnesses were told by others, such as statements in newspapers and books (unless they are "learned treatises") and those made by television newscasters.

no personal knowledge. Such testimony, calling for the **opinion** of the witness, is normally excluded. For example, a witness could testify that the defendant's car was weaving back and forth on a highway, but if he further testified—on the basis of that observation alone—that the defendant was "obviously drunk," a motion to strike that part of the testimony would be sustained. Not only does the witness lack personal knowledge as to the *cause* of the defendant's erratic behavior, but the statement also constitutes a "conclusion of fact"—an inference that the jury, rather than a witness, is to draw from the evidence presented.

Opinion testimony is not always excluded. On technical matters that lie outside the knowledge of ordinary jurors it is frequently necessary that qualified experts be permitted to state their opinions as an aid to the jury's determination of the probable facts. Thus a physician may give an opinion as to the cause of a death or an engineer as to the cause of a bridge collapsing. Additionally, courts have discretion to permit opinions of lay witnesses (nonexperts) on a number of issues—the speed of a car or a third party's emotions at a particular time, for instance.

**Motion for a Directed Verdict:** After all the plaintiff's evidence has been presented, it is likely that the defendant's attorney will make a *motion for a directed verdict.* By doing so, the attorney is contending that plaintiff has failed to prove his or her case—that is, either plaintiff has failed to introduce evidence tending to prove one or more allegations of fact necessary to the case, or the evidence on such points was too weak to present a jury question. Such a motion asks the judge to rule on a factual question *as a matter of law,* and can be granted only if the judge is convinced that the evidence is so clearly in defendant's favor that "reasonable minds could not differ" on the matter. As with summary judgment motions, judges are reluctant to terminate litigation through a directed verdict motion, especially because by this stage of the proceedings the jury has invested a lot of time and effort.

If the defendant's directed verdict motion is denied, the defendant will then present its case through witnesses, depositions, and documents. At the close of defendant's case, both parties will likely make motions for directed verdicts but, again, these are usually denied because the evidence is not that conclusive. Questions of fact usually remain and should be determined by the jury.

**Instructions:** When a case is submitted to the jury, the court instructs it about the law applicable to the various findings of fact which it might make. While the jurors are the "judges of the facts," they must make their determination within a legal framework provided by the judge. The **instructions** will cover such matters as the jury's responsibilities (e.g., "All parties are equal before the law; a corporation is entitled to the same fair treatment as an individual"); matters of evidence (e.g., "You must decide the case based on the weight of the evidence, not the number of witnesses each side presented; you are entitled to believe a single witness who, though outnumbered by contrary witnesses, appeared accurate and reliable in his testimony"); and substantive rules of law (e.g., "Negligence is the failure to use ordinary care a reasonable person would have exercised under like circumstances").

**After the Verdict:** After the jury has returned its verdict, the court enters a judgment in conformity with it. Thereafter, the party against whom the judgment was entered may make one of two common types of motions. The first is a **motion for a new trial,** which basically argues that a new trial is in order because of a serious legal error which the judge made during the first one. The second is a motion for **judgment notwithstanding the verdict** (also known by its Latin term judgment *non obstante veredicto,* or simply JNOV), which may challenge the jury's conclusion on the facts. Only if the judge concludes that, yes, he or she made a serious legal error, or that no reasonable mind could agree with the jury's factual findings, will such motions be granted. The process of litigation is illustrated in Figure 3.1.

# LITIGATION: THE APPELLATE COURTS

## An Overview

The work of the higher courts in ruling on appeals differs considerably from that of the trial courts.[7] In the first place, appellate courts are concerned only with *questions of law*—that is, whether the rulings of the trial court, of which the appellant complains,

---

[7] All appellate courts have *some* "original jurisdiction"; that is, certain exceptional cases can be properly commenced in them. However, we are not here concerned with the work of the appellate courts in such situations.

**Figure 3.1** Litigation Flow Chart

**Pretrial**
- Plaintiff's complaint (petition)
- Defendant's answer (counterclaims, denials, defenses, cross-claims against third parties) → Motion to dismiss (demurrer)
- Pretrial discovery → Summary judgment for one party or the other

**Trial**
- Jury selection
- Opening statements
- Plaintiff's case presented (direct examination of witnesses by plaintiff's attorney, cross-examination by defendant's attorney) → Motion for directed verdict by defendant
- Defendant's case presented (direct examination of witnesses by defendant's attorney, cross-examination by plaintiff's attorney) → Motion for directed verdict by plaintiff or defendant
- Closing arguments, instructions to jury (instructions include rules, definitions, the charge)
- Return of jury's verdict

**Post-trial**
- Post-trial motions for new trial or judgment notwithstanding the verdict
- Entry of judgment
- Appeals
- Collecting the judgment

---

were legally correct. Second, intermediate appellate courts are normally comprised of three judges, and the highest court in a state usually has five or seven justices. This obviously brings to bear *more judicial experience* on the points in issue than can be afforded by the single trial judge. Third, since only questions of law are in issue, there is *no reintroduction of evidence and thus no jury.* The questions of law are settled on the basis of the record in the lower court, together with consideration of the opposing parties' briefs (written arguments) and oral arguments as to the correctness of the rulings in question. As a result, unlike the rulings of the trial court, which must be made during "the heat of battle," the decisions of the appellate courts can be made in a detached and unhurried manner.

## Questions of Law

A great number of questions of law will be brought out by the cases in the remainder of this text. For now, suffice it to say that some of the most common of them arise where the appellant is claiming that errors were made by the trial court in (1) admitting or excluding testimony, (2) ruling on motions, particularly on motions for a directed verdict, (3) stating the law in instructions to the jury, and (4) interpreting state or federal statutes.

## Effect of Error

If the appellate court is of the opinion that an alleged error did occur and that it conceivably could have affected the outcome of the case, the lower court's judgment will be reversed (set aside), and normally the case will be *remanded* (sent back) to the trial court for a new trial. The reason for remanding is that most errors are of such a nature that the higher court cannot be positive the verdict or judgment would have gone for the other party had the error not occurred. For example, if it were determined that the trial court erred in admitting hearsay testimony of one witness, it is *possible* that the verdict and judgment would still have been entered for the same party who won in the lower court even if the testimony had been excluded.

Some judgments, however, are reversed outright, with no further proceedings being necessary. This is particularly true where the rule of law that the trial court has applied to the established facts is simply contrary to the law then existing in that state. In such a situation the appellate court will apply the correct rule of law and enter final judgment accordingly. Obviously, if the court finds that no error was committed or that any errors were minor and could not have affected the verdict, it will *affirm* the lower court's judgment.

## Setting Aside a Verdict

Appellate courts commonly set aside judgments on grounds that the trial judge made a critical *legal* error in admitting evidence, ruling on motions, or instructing the jury. Much less often will they set aside a judgment because the jury erred in finding the facts, though they are frequently asked to do so.

The jurors are the designated finders of fact. They heard the testimony in person. They had the opportunity to observe the witnesses while they testified and to observe important details (such as body language or coaching from the attorney) which the appellate court cannot discern from a cold transcript of testimony. The jurors are trusted to resolve conflicts of testimony. Their judgments as to credibility of witnesses will be accepted.

Even if the appellate judges disagree with the jury's factual conclusions, they will uphold the verdict if the record contains *any substantial evidence* to support it. Only in rare instances where the appellate court can confidently say that there is no substantial evidence to support the jury's verdict will it be set aside. The credible testimony of a single witness, even one of the parties, can provide the substantial evidence necessary to sustain a jury's verdict, as the following case illustrates.

---

### Batchoff v. Craney
Supreme Court of Montana,
172 P.2d 308 (1946)

D. A. (Jim) Batchoff was injured in November of 1940 when he was thrown from a car in which he was being driven from Billings to Butte, Montana. The car was owned by Craney, the defendant, and was being driven by Baily Stortz, a friend of the defendant.

Batchoff brought this action against Craney to recover damages, alleging (1) that Stortz was guilty of gross negligence in the operation of the vehicle, and (2) that Stortz was an agent of defendant Craney while making the drive to Butte. Defendant contended, on the other hand, that Stortz was acting as an agent of U.S. Senator Burton K. Wheeler at the time of the accident.

At the trial, plaintiff testified that he was at the Northern

*(continued)*

Pacific depot in Billings on the morning of November 2, waiting for the train to Butte, when he ran into the defendant, who said, "Oh, hell, Jim, stay here and miss this train. Senator and Mrs. Wheeler and Baily Stortz [Wheeler's secretary] are getting off of this train.... I am going to leave my automobile with Baily to drive it back to Butte and you can ride along with him." (Defendant himself was remaining in Billings.)

Later in the day plaintiff and Stortz set out for Butte in defendant's car, with Stortz driving. Plaintiff further testified that Stortz drove the car from seventy to seventy-five miles per hour; that he complained of the excessive speed but, instead of slowing down, the speed was increased to eighty-five miles per hour; there were wet spots in the road; the car hit a wet spot, skidded around several times; a door of the car swung open and plaintiff was thrown from the car into a borrow pit and the car followed and struck him, rendering him unconscious and causing the injuries complained of.

The jury accepted plaintiff's version of the facts and returned a verdict in his favor for $10,000. On appeal, the primary contention of the defendant was that the jury's verdict was unsupported by the evidence, and ought to be set aside for this reason.

In support of this contention, defendant argued that the jury should not have believed plaintiff's testimony that defendant offered plaintiff the ride, in view of the fact that defendant's witnesses testified that defendant had in fact *lent his car to Senator Wheeler* for the day, and in view of the fact that plaintiff, in an earlier proceeding before the State Industrial Accident Board, *had testified that it was Stortz, rather than the defendant, who had offered him the ride.*

**Decision:** The verdict was upheld. Whenever there is credible evidence to support the jury's verdict, it will be upheld by an appellate court. It was the jury's duty to decide whether to believe the testimony in support of Batchoff or that in support of Craney. Since the jury chose to accept Batchoff's version of the facts, the verdict (and judgment) in favor of plaintiff Batchoff will stand. ■

**Comment:** When the owner of an automobile permits another person to drive it, and the driver injures a third party as a result of operating it negligently, the owner is *not necessarily* liable to the injured party. Under the law of Montana and many other states, the injured party must ordinarily prove that the driver was an *agent* of the owner of the automobile at the time of the accident in order to recover a judgment against the owner.

That is why, in the instant case, defendant Craney would have escaped liability if the jury had accepted the testimony of his witnesses to the effect that Craney had actually lent his car to Senator Wheeler for the day (and that Stortz, without Craney's knowledge, offered plaintiff the ride). In such a situation, Stortz would have been Wheeler's agent, rather than Craney's. As we know now, the jury rejected this version of the facts in returning a verdict for plaintiff.

### Enforcement of Judgment

If a verdict for the plaintiff survives the appellate process (or if no appeal was ever taken), plaintiff may still have to worry about enforcing the judgment. If the defendant is wealthy, well-insured, or a large corporation, enforcement of the judgment will probably present no major obstacles.

If the defendant refuses to pay a valid judgment, the plaintiff will ask the court to issue a **writ of execution** by which a law enforcement official seizes defendant's nonexempt property and sells it at auction until enough money is raised to satisfy the judgment. Another procedure is a **writ of garnishment,** whereby the court orders a third party holding property belonging to the defendant (typically a bank with a savings account belonging to defendant) to deliver the property to the plaintiff in satisfaction of the judgment. Some states even allow garnishment of wages—a court order to defendant's employer to pay a specified percentage of defendant's wages to plaintiff every month until the judgment is satisfied. As we shall see in Chapter 50, there are legal limits on garnishment of wages.

## ANALYSIS OF THE ADJUDICATIVE PROCESS

A good many criticisms are made of the manner in which controversies are settled under our present legal system. Many of these have to do with the general nature of the "adversary system," the role of the jury, and the selection and performance of judges.

### The Adversary System

Most legal disputes are settled through *adversary proceedings,* where the parties meet face to face (legally speaking) with each permitted to contest the allegations of fact and points of law raised by the other. The attorney for each party determines how to prove that his or her client's version of the facts is correct, and each researches the law to find legal principles upon which to base the client's case. The parties themselves thus frame the issues, and the judge simply rules on the issues that are presented.

It is sometimes said that the adversary system puts an undue premium on the relative effectiveness of the competing attorneys and too greatly limits the trial judge's role in the outcome of the case. Overall, these criticisms are probably not as valid as they seem.

In the first place, the skill of the competing lawyers is usually equal enough for each party to be able to introduce the evidence and to present rules of law in support of his or her position. Additionally, the rules of procedure and evidence, and the normal desire of the trial judge to see that each party has a fair opportunity to "have a say," place certain limits on the practical advantage that one party might have in a case where his or her counsel is markedly more able than the other litigant's counsel.

## *The Role of the Jury*

Many weaknesses, real or imagined, are attributed to the jury's role in the adjudicative processes, including the following: (1) jurors cannot understand the complex issues that are presented; (2) jurors are too likely to be influenced by the personalities of the attorneys rather than by objective considerations; and (3) given the rules of law applying to the various alternative findings that they may return, juries frequently ignore (or overemphasize) evidence in order to bring in a verdict in favor of a party for whom they have sympathy or against a party for whom they have animosity. In recent years juries have received severe criticism for the large size of the monetary awards they have granted personal injury plaintiffs, especially in products liability cases.

Supporters of the jury system, on the other hand, feel that most of these criticisms are not, in general, supported by the facts. First, in many cases there are only one or two controlling issues, and these are quite understandable to the average person. Second, verdicts can be set aside if they are clearly based on "passion or prejudice," in addition to the other grounds mentioned earlier. Third, there is substantial evidence that most jurors take their duties seriously and try to perform them conscientiously.

## *Performance of the Judges*

The overall performance of a legal system obviously depends to a great extent upon the character and competence of its judges. For this reason, particularly, it is distressing to note that the judges of this country have, as a class, come in for rather heavy criticism over the years. While much of this criticism may be unjustified, there is cause for concern.

Three factors are chiefly responsible. First, judges' salaries are often lower than the income that can be earned in private practice by attorneys. Second, in the United States, persons who aspire to a career in the judiciary are not required to take special training or to go through an apprenticeship of a year or two on an appeals court, as is the case in many countries. Third, the judges of our state courts have traditionally been elected. This has frequently resulted in the nomination of candidates by the political parties on the basis of their party service and loyalty, rather than on ability and experience. And, once elected, incumbent judges have not easily been dislodged even when their performance has been mediocre or worse.

In recent years, in an effort to alleviate the shortcomings resulting from the election of judges, over thirty states and the District of Columbia have adopted some form of "merit plan" selection of judges. While these plans vary to some extent, they all are based on the idea that when a judicial vacancy occurs, a judicial nominating commission develops a list of three to five persons whom they feel to be the best qualified for the job. (These commissions are nonpartisan in nature, and are usually composed equally of lawyers and nonlawyers.) The list of names is submitted to the governor, who selects one person to fill the vacancy. Thereafter, appointees must indicate before their terms of office expire whether they wish to stand for another term. If so, the appointee runs unopposed in the next general election, with the voters simply indicating whether they are satisfied with the performance rendered during the first term of office. If the appointee loses on this vote, the appointive process then begins anew.

## ALTERNATIVE METHODS OF DISPUTE RESOLUTION

The American adversarial system of litigation has many benefits: it is an excellent truth-finding mechanism, and it helps control our heterogenous society by enforcing the rule of law. Lawyers are well-educated and plentiful; by working hard for individual rights, they help preserve the democratic ideal of rule by law.

A strong argument can be made, however, that this system that is laudable in some respects produces lawsuits that are too plentiful, too complex, too expensive, and too time-consuming. American corporations spend $20 billion a year on litigation attorneys, a good indication that formal "fight-to-the-death" litigation is not necessarily the best way to resolve some kinds of disputes. Considerations of expense and expediency have led to the rise of alternative methods of dispute resolution (ADR) in recent years. Businesses have been especially interested in finding ways to resolve disputes that involve less cost, delay, and disruption of commercial relationships than litigation. This section discusses some of those methods which, though they take different forms, have in common an attempt to lessen the "sharpness" that accompanies the adversarial system, replacing it with an increased emphasis on trust and respect between the parties and an honest effort to work out their differences fairly.

## *The Simple Out-of-Court Settlement*

Before we address specific methods of ADR, we should note that most disputes are settled either by compromise or by default. An example of a simple compromise would be where creditors accept smaller sums and debtors pay larger sums than either thinks is due. Or a contractor may agree to a modification in building plans in return for the building owner's agreement to an extension in the deadline for comtpletion. An example of default would be where one party chooses to forgo legal proceedings in order to preserve the other's goodwill, especially when the latter is a valued customer. Or one party may decide that pursuing any kind of remedy is not worth the wear, tear, and expense of litigation, and he or she simply accepts the loss.

## *Arbitration Agreements*

The essence of **arbitration** is that the parties agree to submit their dispute to a single arbitrator or panel of arbitrators whose decision will be binding. Although parties can agree to submit a dispute to arbitration after it has arisen, most arbitration agreements are of the "future disputes" variety, where the parties to a contract include a clause providing for binding arbitration of any disputes that may arise. The Federal Arbitration Act makes any written arbitration agreement relating to a transaction that affects interstate commerce valid and legally binding. The American Arbitration Association alone is now providing arbitrators to settle some 55,000 disputes each year.

Compared to litigation, voluntary arbitration has several advantages: (1) disputes can be settled more quickly; (2) arbitrators can be chosen who have special expertise in the particular business practices that are the subject of the controversy; (3) the proceedings are relatively informal; and (4) the cost is ordinarily less than if the cases go to court.

Arbitration has been so successful in the area of labor disputes and commercial contracts that the federal courts have begun experimenting with "court-annexed" arbitration panels of three volunteer lawyers who decide relatively small (e.g., under $75,000) civil cases.

## *Mediation*

**Mediation** is less formal than arbitration. Rather than imposing a binding solution, a neutral third party chosen by the disputants (the mediator) attempts to aid the parties in reaching their own solution. Depending on the attitudes of the parties, the type and size of the dispute, and numerous other variables, the mediator takes one or more of a range of less aggressive to more aggressive actions in order to facilitate resolution. The mediator might simply urge the parties to talk or offer to carry messages between them. He might help the parties agree upon an agenda for a meeting and provide an environment for negotiation. He might shoot down unrealistic proposals or help the parties formulate their own proposals for settlement. He might even pressure the parties to accept a settlement that he believes is reasonable.

Mediation has facilitated resolution of a wide range of disputes, from international political conflicts to labor disputes to landlord-tenant disagreements. For example, when IBM claimed that Fujitsu had illegally copied the former's mainframe operating-system software, a lengthy and expensive dispute arose. The parties reached certain settlement agreements in 1983, but disagreements continued to break out, largely because of the technical complexity of the area. The parties agreed to arbitration by a law professor and a retired computer industry executive. The arbitrators recognized that the controversy presented factual disputes about past copying that would be almost impossible to resolve. They focused primarily on the future, ordering Fujitsu to provide a complete accounting of its use of programs subject to the 1983 agreement and requiring the parties to participate in mediation regarding programs falling outside the earlier agreement. Through mediation, new agreements were produced, which the arbitrators incorporated into a binding arbitration order.

## Rent-a-Judge Programs

Several jurisdictions have developed a special form of arbitration which calls for the parties to select a retired judge to hear a case, much as an arbitrator would. Normal trial procedures are used, as modified by the parties. The decision of the "rent-a-judge" has the status of a trial court judgment without the necessity of any further proceedings. Because the parties pay the judge's fee and other expenses, this mechanism has been criticized as enabling only the wealthy to escape the delays existing in many court systems.

## Summary Jury Trial

Although 90–95 percent of civil lawsuits are settled before they reach trial, many complicated cases that will take weeks or months to try reach the trial phase with the litigants still poles apart. In the *summary jury trial* (SJT), a small jury is chosen from the regular jury panel. To ensure that the jurors take their responsibility seriously, they are not informed that their decision will not be binding. The parties are then given a few hours to summarize their positions and their evidence and to give closing arguments. Often the judge will require executives of the corporate parties to attend the trial. After the jury renders a verdict, the parties are urged to negotiate a settlement based on the additional guidance that the jury's reaction to the case provides.

The SJT is typically used in cases that have a below-average chance of settling before trial. Yet, in about 95 percent of the cases where the SJT has been used, the parties settled relatively quickly after the jury's advisory verdict. The SJT serves to puncture inflated expectations and induces the litigants to choose more realistic settlement positions.

## The Mini-Trial

This voluntary procedure, which may be initiated by the parties or suggested by the judge, is a highly-structured hybrid of mediation, traditional settlement negotiation, and arbitration. Typically, it involves the selection of a neutral advisor and an important executive from each party. The parties informally exchange key documents, summaries of witnesses' testimony, and short legal briefs. They also agree as to the format, timing, and procedures of a hearing.

Following the established format, each party will use its time as it chooses to present the strongest case it can to the panel consisting of the neutral party and the two executives. The panel members may ask questions and explore strengths and weaknesses. After the hearing, the executives may seek the neutral advisor's opinion as to likely trial outcome before they begin settlement talks, or they may do so only after their attempts at further negotiation fail.

The mini-trial has also had substantial success. Almost immediately after a mini-trial, Allied Corporation and Shell Oil settled a contract dispute that had been dragging on for almost ten years, including four years of expensive litigation.

## The Future of ADR

Given the time and expense associated with traditional litigation, use of one or more of these types of ADR (or some blend thereof) is likely to increase. In Texas, for example, a recent law states that "[i]t is the policy of the State to encourage the peaceable resolution of disputes . . . and the early settlement of pending litigation through voluntary settlement procedures." The law charges the courts of the state with the responsibility to carry out that policy by encouraging use of arbitration, mediation, mini-trials, and the like.

## SUMMARY

The basic phases of litigation are (1) the pleadings phase, in which the parties set forth their claims on paper; (2) the discovery phase, where investigation discloses evidence to support the parties' positions; (3) the trial phase, which includes the impaneling of a jury, presentation of proof by the parties in accordance with the rules of evidence, various motions made by the parties, instructions by the judge to the jury, and finally, deliberation by the jury. Often, there is (4) the appellate phase, where parties unhappy with the jury's verdict seek reversal or a new trial order from a higher court on the grounds of a legal error made by the trial judge or because the jury's verdict was not based on any substantial evidence.

This litigation system is as controversial as it is important. Reforms of the adversary system and our methods of selecting judges are continuously being debated.

Because of the time and expense involved in litigation, there has been a growing trend toward the use of alternative methods of dispute resolution, including arbitration, mediation, and mini-trials. That trend is likely to continue to accelerate.

## KEY TERMS

**Pleading stage**
**Discovery stage**
**Complaint**
**Answer**
**Reply**
**Counterclaim**
**Motion to dismiss**
**Default judgment**
**Summary judgment**
**Trial stage**
**Peremptory challenge**
**Rules of evidence**
**Hearsay**
**Opinion (testimony)**
**Instructions**
**Motion for a new trial**
**Judgment notwithstanding the verdict**
**Writ of execution**
**Writ of garnishment**
**Arbitration**
**Mediation**

## QUESTIONS AND PROBLEMS

**1.** After ten years of litigation, a federal antitrust case was submitted to a formally summoned jury. However, the attorneys were given only a half-day in which to present their case and the decision of the jury was not binding. Why would such a procedure be undertaken?

**2.** Wydel Associates, a partnership, sued Thermasol, Ltd. on a breach of contract claim. Thermasol moved to dismiss the lawsuit because the contract contained a clause stating that any dispute should be arbitrated in New York rather than litigated. Wydel argued that the arbitration clause was not binding because the law of the state in which its partnership was formed provided that any partnership agreement to submit a claim to arbitration must be signed by *all* the partners. This contract had been signed by only one Wydel partner. Should the court dismiss the suit? (*Wydel Associates v. Thermasol Ltd.,* 452 F.Supp. 739, W.D.Tex. 1978.)

**3.** The Brockton Bank sued First United, a broker-dealer, after defendant induced the bank to purchase a 90-day $1,000,000 CD from a bank (Penn Square) which failed. In discovery, Brockton sought to determine how much research First United had done before making the recommendation to purchase. Four times during discovery defendant made untimely and only partial responses to court orders to produce documents. After arguing unsuccessfully for months that certain documents should be protected from discovery, defendant claimed that the documents had been discarded long before. Suspecting the documents had been destroyed, the trial judge ordered defendant's president to appear in court. The president did not appear, his attorney stating, "My client chooses not to obey." What should the court do? (*Brockton Sav. Bank v. Peat, Marwick & Mitchell,* 771 F.2d 5, 1st Cir. 1985.)

**4.** In a report on plaintiff's business, defendant television station reported "[w]e spoke to Judge Rissman . . . he says they've [customers of plaintiff] got a good case." Plaintiff sued for defamation, claiming that this conversation never took place. Defendant moved to dismiss the suit on grounds that the conversation did take place and that it was just one man's opinion, anyway. Should the court dismiss? (*Action Repair, Inc. v. American Broadcasting Co.,* 776 F.2d 143, 7th Cir. 1985.)

**5.** Defendant company built a swimming pool for Denault. On January 9, 1978, defendant's president was served with a summons in a lawsuit filed by Denault. Denault claimed defendant's sloppy building of the pool forced her to make $2,000 in repairs. Under the court rules, an answer was due from defendant on January 29. Defendant tried to answer on January 31, but the court refused to accept the filing because it was untimely. The court entered a default judgment against defendant and set a hearing to establish damages. Defendant moved to set aside the default judgment on grounds of "excusable neglect," pointing out that its president had received two summons in the same week and thought Denault's had been served at the same time as the other summons, on January 13. Should the judge set aside the default judgment? (*Denault v. Holloway Builders, Inc.,* 248 S.E.2d 265, S.C. 1978.)

**6.** Under a kickback scheme devised by Moore, a purchasing agent, one of the bidders on a construction project submitted several price sheets; the purchasing agent read that bidder's price list last, choosing the highest one that was still low enough to get the bid. On discovering the extra sheets, Moore's secretary, Marren, exclaimed: "I've found the evidence I've been waiting for for a long time!"

Marszalek overheard this statement. At Moore's criminal trial, Marszalek was asked about this statement because Marren died before trial. Should Marszalek be allowed to testify about the statement? (*U.S. v. Moore,* 791 F.2d 566, 7th Cir. 1986.)

7. On behalf of her children who had heart valve problems, Fontenot sued Upjohn Company, claiming that a drug Upjohn manufactured caused the defects. During discovery, plaintiff was asked which experts she would call to testify that the drug had actually caused the defects. She responded "Unknown at the present time." After more time for discovery, Upjohn moved for summary judgment on grounds that plaintiff had produced no evidence to indicate that the drug had caused the heart defects. Plaintiff responded by pointing out that Upjohn had produced no evidence showing that the drug did *not* cause the defects and by arguing that the question of causation is inherently a jury question and inappropriate for resolution on a summary judgment motion. Should Upjohn's motion be granted? (*Fontenot v. Upjohn Co.,* 780 F.2d 1190, 5th Cir. 1986.)

8. A plane owned by Douglas landed at the Los Angeles airport and received permission from the tower to enter runway 22. Due to the shape of his plane, the Douglas pilot was not in a position to see clearly ahead, so he zigzagged the plane at 15° angles as he taxied to improve his forward vision. However, the plane collided with a P-51 owned by the government which was parked along the side of runway 22. The pilot of the government plane, which was painted a brown camouflaged, Army color, said after the accident: "I am sorry. I had no business being there. I have been here for about ten minutes. I called for a truck and they haven't come after me yet." The government sued Douglas for negligence; Douglas raised a contributory negligence defense. At the close of the evidence, the government moved for a directed verdict in its favor on the questions of respective negligence. The judge denied the motions, and the jury found for Douglas. On appeal, the government argued that the judge erred in failing to grant its directed verdict motions. Discuss. (*U.S. v. Douglas Aircraft Co.,* 169 F.2d 755, 9th Cir. 1948.)

9. According to one court: "Lawsuits have become particularly inappropriate devices for resolving minor disputes. They are clumsy, noisy, unwieldy and notoriously inefficient. Fueled by bad feelings, they generate much heat and friction, yet produce little that is of any use. Worst of all, once set in motion, they are well-nigh impossible to bring to a halt." Is this a fair assessment? Does it help explain the trend toward use of alternative methods of dispute resolution? (*Blackburn v. Goettel-Blanton,* 898 F.2d 95, 9th Cir. 1990.)

CHAPTER 4

# COMMON AND STATUTORY LAW

There are several basic processes by which law is made: (1) the formulation of rules by the courts—the judges—in deciding cases coming before them in those areas of law where no statutes apply; (2) the enactment and interpretation of statutes; (3) the interpretation and application of constitutional provisions; and (4) the promulgation of rules and regulations by administrative agencies. In this chapter we examine the first and second of these lawmaking processes. First, we show how *common law* (or *case law*) is formed by the courts. Then we turn our attention to the enactment and interpretation of statutory law.

## ORIGIN OF COMMON LAW

As we described in Chapter 2, the early king's courts in England largely made up the law on a case-by-case basis. If, for example, a plaintiff asked for damages for breach of contract in a situation where the defendant denied that a contract ever existed, the court had to spell out the nature of a contract—that is, specify the minimum elements which the court felt must exist in order for it to impose contractual liability on the defendant. Similarly, if a defendant admitted making the contract in question but sought to escape liability for reasons of illness or military service, the court had to decide what kinds of defenses ought to be legally recognizable—defenses that should free the defendant from his or her contractual obligations.

Over a period of time, then, as more and more cases were settled, a rudimentary body of contract law came into being. Thereafter, when other cases arose involving contractual matters, the courts quite naturally looked to the earlier cases to see what principles of law had been established. The same procedure was followed in many other branches of law, and the legal rules that arose in this manner constituted the common law, or **case law**, of England.

The common law rules that had developed in England became the law of our early colonies. And, when those colonies achieved statehood, they adopted those rules as a major part of their respective bodies of law. As the territories became states, they followed suit so that at one time the major portion of the law of all states (with the exception of Louisiana) was common law in nature.[1]

### *The Current Scene*

Gradually, the state legislatures began to pass increasing numbers of statutes, with the result that today most branches of the law are statutory in nature. For example, all states now have comprehensive statutes governing the areas of corporation law, criminal law, tax law, municipal corporations, and commercial law. Some of these statutes have been based largely on the common-law principles that were in effect earlier. Others, however, have been passed to create bodies of rules that did not exist previously, or that expressly overrule common-law principles.

Despite the ever increasing amount of statutory law in this country (which we examine in some detail later in this chapter), *several branches of law today are still essentially common-law in nature in forty-nine of our states*—particularly the subjects of *contracts, torts,* and *agency.* In these areas, where the legislatures have not seen fit to enact comprehensive statutes, the courts still settle controversies on the basis of judge-made or **case law**—the rules formulated by the courts in deciding earlier cases over the years, as illustrated in Figure 4.1. (While many of these rules had their origin in England, as has been

---

[1] Louisiana continues to be governed by the *civil-law* (as distinguished from common-law) system of law. Under such a system, adopted by most European countries, virtually all law is "codified"—that is, statutory.

41

**Figure 4.1** Common Law

Common Law
- Origin — Created by the judicial branch through decisions in cases decided by the courts
- Form — Diffuse—rules found in fact-patterns and decisions of prior cases
- Scope — Narrow—limited to actual cases
- Effect of social and political forces — Indirect—judges somewhat insulated from political pressures

law, as follows: (1) philosophy (logic); (2) history; (3) custom; and (4) social welfare (or sociology).

In his lecture on the role of philosophy in the law, Cardozo briefly commented on the special tasks of the judge in interpreting statutes and constitutions, and then continued:

> We reach the land of mystery when constitution and statute are silent, and the judge must look to the common law for the rule that fits the case.... The first thing he does is to compare the case before him with the precedents, whether stored in his mind or hidden in the books.... Back of precedents are the basic juridical conceptions which are the postulates of judicial reasoning, and farther back are the habits of life, the institutions of society, in which those conceptions had their origin, and which, by a process of interaction, they have modified in turn.... If [precedents] are plain and to the point, there may be need of nothing more. *Stare decisis* is at least the everyday working rule of the law....[2]

Early in that same lecture, however, Cardozo cautioned that the finding of **precedent** was only part of the judge's job, and indicated how the law must grow beyond the early precedents, in these words:

> The rules and principles of case law have never been treated as final truths, but as working hypotheses, continually retested in those great laboratories of the law, the courts of justice.... In [the] perpetual flux [of the law,] the problem which confronts the judge is in reality a twofold one: he first must extract from the precedents the underlying principle, the *ratio decidendi* [the ground of decision]; he must then determine the path or direction along which the principle is to move and develop, if it is not to wither and die....
>
> The directive force of a principle may be exerted along the line of logical progression; this I will call the rule of analogy or the method of philosophy; along the line of historical development; this I will call the method of evolution; along the line of the customs of the community; this I will call the method of tradition; along the lines of justice, morals and social welfare, the

indicated, our definition of common law also includes those additional rules that have originated in the state courts in this country.)

In deciding each case, judges bear the twin burden of attempting to provide "justice" for the case at hand while at the same time setting a precedent that will serve the greater interests of society when applied in future cases. The common law rules, like legislative statutes, must serve public policy interests—the "community common sense and common conscience." Therefore, courts have laid great stress on the customs, morals, and forms of conduct that are generally prevailing in the community at the time of decision. There is no doubt that occasionally the judge's personal feelings as to what kinds of conduct are just and fair, what rule would best serve societal interests, and simply what is "right or wrong" enter the picture.

## Role of the Judge

Benjamin N. Cardozo, an associate justice of the U.S. Supreme Court, contended that four "directive forces" shaped the law, and especially the common

---

[2] *Stare decisis* means, literally, "to stand by decisions." The concept is revisited later in this chapter.

*mores* of the day; and this I will call the method of sociology. . . .[3]

## COMMON LAW—THE DOCTRINE OF *STARE DECISIS*

The heart of the common-law process lies in the inclination of the courts generally to follow precedent—to stand by existing decisions. This policy, as we were told by Cardozo, is referred to as the doctrine of ***stare decisis.*** Under this approach, when the fact-pattern of a particular controversy is established, the attorneys for both parties search for earlier cases involving similar fact-patterns in an effort to determine whether applicable principles of law have been established. If this research produces a number of similar cases (or even one) within the state where a rule has been applied by the appellate courts, the trial court will ordinarily feel constrained to follow the same rule in settling the current controversy. (But, as we will see later, this does not mean that the courts are reluctant to abandon a precedent if it produces clear injustice under "contemporary conditions.")

---

[3]Benjamin N. Cardozo, *The Nature of the Judicial Process* (1921). Yale University Press.

## *Types of Precedent*

Authority originating in courts above the trial court in the appellate chain is called **mandatory authority.** The judge must follow it. Thus, a state trial judge in Ohio will follow the rulings of Ohio's intermediate appellate courts which will in turn follow the precedents established by the Ohio Supreme Court. In matters of federal law, the Ohio Supreme Court will follow the holdings of the United States Supreme Court. A judge who does not follow mandatory authority is not impeached or shot at dawn, but certainly runs a strong risk of reversal.

So strong is the hold of mandatory authority that judges will usually follow it even though they violently disagree with its reasoning and result. The following case illustrates this fact. The case involves a claim of *negligence,* which we shall study in detail in Chapter 8. It means simply that the defendant was more careless than a reasonable person would have been under the circumstances and should be liable for injuries which result. The case also involves a defense of governmental immunity, which stems from the ancient English doctrine that the King (or in this case the government) "can do no wrong" and therefore cannot be sued absent his consent. The decision is by a Michigan intermediate appellate court, sitting between the trial court and the Michigan Supreme Court in the appellate chain.

---

### Edwards v. Clinton Valley Center
Court of Appeals of Michigan, 360 N.W.2d 606 (1984)

Plaintiff is the estate of Jean Edwards, who was fatally stabbed by a former mental patient. Defendant is a government mental hospital that refused to admit the killer after she was brought to the facility by police when she threatened to "kill someone." Plaintiff alleges that defendant's refusal to admit the killer was negligent. The trial judge dismissed the suit on a purely legal ground—governmental immunity. Plaintiff appealed.

**Decision:** Under the doctrine of *stare decisis*, an intermediate appellate court is bound to follow the precedents established by a superior court. Because the Michigan Supreme Court had previously decided that governmental immunity for tort liability extended to public mental hospitals, the Michigan Court of Appeals felt bound by that decision and affirmed the summary judgment on grounds of governmental immunity. However, the court did express personal disapproval of the doctrine and called upon the Supreme Court of Michigan to reconsider it. The court of appeals felt that no public interest was served by relieving the hospital of all responsibility for its gross negligence. ■

What if a trial judge searches the law books and discovers that there is no precedent in the state on the legal question presented? In such a case, the judge may examine the decisions of courts of other states. For example, assume a state trial judge in Oregon is faced with the question of whether a landlord who did not attempt to lease an apartment after a tenant moved out in the middle of a lease should be barred from suing the tenant for damages. There are no Oregon cases addressing the issue, and the only case "on point" was rendered by the Alabama Supreme Court. Must the Oregon judge follow the Alabama precedent? No. Because the Oregon judge's decision cannot be appealed to the Alabama Supreme Court, the latter's rulings are not mandatory authority. The Alabama decision would constitute **persuasive authority.** That is, the Oregon judge can examine the Alabama decision and, upon finding it persuasive, may choose to follow it. However, if the judge finds the decision not to be persuasive, the judge need not apply its rationale in Oregon.

What if there are two existing precedents, that of the Alabama Supreme Court and one from the North Dakota Supreme Court, that reach diametrically opposed results on the same issue? Again, they are both only persuasive authority for the Oregon judge who can examine them and follow the one that seems more reasonable. Of course, the judge can also reject both persuasive precedents and create yet a third approach to the issue. Despite the importance of stability to the law, the majesty of the common law lies in its flexibility and adaptability. Though judges revere stability, they will change a rule when they become convinced that it was wrongly established and never served society's interests, or that while it was a good rule when established, changing social, moral, economic, or technological factors have rendered it outmoded. If no valid reason supports a common-law rule, no matter how long it has been established, the judges should and usually will change it.

Sometimes common law rules change slowly. Exceptions or qualifications to the rule will slowly appear in the case law. Most of the history of the common law is of a slow evolution as the law keeps pace with a changing society. Refer back to *Soldano v. O'Daniels* in Chapter 1. That case not only illustrates a minor change in the slow evolution of the law regarding our duties to our fellow man, it contains some eloquent language extolling the virtues of our flexible common law.

Sometimes the law will change dramatically, as when modern judges decide an established rule no longer serves society and must be scrapped, as the following case illustrates.

---

### Flagiello v. Pennsylvania Hospital
Supreme Court of Pennsylvania
208 A.2d 193 (1965)

**Mrs. Flagiello, a patient in the Pennsylvania Hospital in Philadelphia, fell and broke an ankle while being moved by two of its employees. She brought this action against the hospital to recover damages, alleging that the employees were guilty of negligence. The defendant hospital moved for a judgment on the pleadings, contending that under the case law of Pennsylvania, it was well established that a charitable institution was not responsible for the wrongs of its employees. The trial court sustained this motion and entered judgment for the defendant. The plaintiff appealed to the Supreme Court of Pennsylvania.**

**Decision:** Reversed and remanded for a new trial. The appellate court, while generally endorsing the rule of *stare decisis* because of the stability and predictability it gives our legal system, held that because the primary reason for the original rule of charitable immunity no longer existed, the rule should be changed. Charitable immunity arose from the idea that imposition of liability would be too great a financial burden for nonprofit institutions. In recent years, however, insurance has become available and patient fees provide 90 percent of the charitable hospitals' total income. When the justification for a rule changes, the rule itself must change. ■

## A PROFILE OF OUR FEDERAL AND STATE STATUTORY LAW

While a significant portion of our law is still common law in nature, most of our federal and state law today results from the enactment of **statutes** by legislative bodies. These are the formally adopted rules that constitute our *statutory law*, the second of the major sources of law.[4] All states, for example, have comprehensive statutes governing such subjects as banking law, criminal law, education, consumer sales, and motor vehicle law.

Similarly, at the federal level, sweeping statutes in the areas of antitrust law, labor law, food and drug regulation, and securities law have long been in effect. Newer (and usually narrower) statutes are added every year, including, for example, the Consumer Product Safety Act of 1972, the Bankruptcy Reform Act of 1978, and the Trademark Counterfeiting Act of 1984. Figure 4.2 summarizes the origin, form, scope, and effect of statutory law.

In this section our first objectives are to examine the reasons for the existence of statutory law, to become acquainted with the basic rules that delineate the jurisdictions of the federal and state governments, and to note the contrasts between statutory and common law. We then turn our attention to the closely related area of statutory interpretation—the process by which the courts spell out the precise meaning of statutes that are applicable to the particular cases coming before them—and conclude with a summary of selected state statutes that are of special significance to the business community.[5] As a backdrop for a better understanding of the issues that are addressed in this chapter, however, a brief description of the vast scope of our statutory law is first in order.

## STATUTORY LAW—THE RATIONALE

There are many reasons for the existence of statutory law, three of which deserve special mention.

**1.** One of the primary functions of any legislative body is to adopt measures having to do with the

---

[4] The term "statutory law," when broadly used in contrast to "common law," includes not only laws passed by legislative bodies but, additionally, U.S. treaties, the federal and state constitutions, and municipal ordinances. In this chapter, however, the term is used in its more customary sense, referring only to acts of the state legislatures and of Congress.

[5] Selected federal statutes are discussed in Chapters 41 and 48–50.

---

**Figure 4.2** Statutory Law

| | |
|---|---|
| Origin | Created by the legislative branch through a formal lawmaking process |
| Unified form | Official codified text |
| Scope | Broad—subject only to constitutional limitations |
| Effect of social and political forces | Direct—through the political process |

---

*structure and day-to-day operation* of the government of which it is a part. Thus many federal statutes are of the "nuts and bolts" variety relating to such matters as the operation of the federal court system, the Internal Revenue Service, and the administration and employment rules of the U.S. Civil Service Commission. In similar vein, many state statutes relate to such matters as the property tax laws, the operation of school systems, and the setting forth of powers of municipalities within their borders.

**2.** Many activities are of such a nature that *they can hardly be regulated by common-law principles* and the judicial processes. In the area of criminal law, for example, it is absolutely essential for the general populace to know what acts are punishable by fine and imprisonment; the only sure way to set forth the elements of specific crimes is through the enactment of federal and state criminal statutes. Similarly, the activities of corporations are so complex and so varied that they do not lend themselves to judicial regulation. Few judges, for example, have either the expertise to deal with such questions as the conditions under which the payment of corporate dividends should be permitted or the time to deal with the spelling out of such conditions on a case-by-case basis. Thus the only practical way to deal with these and other problems is by the drafting of detailed statutes which, in total, make up the comprehensive corporation laws of the states.

3. A third function of a legislature is to change expressly (or even overrule) common-law rules where it believes such modifications are necessary, and—even more commonly—to enact statutes to *remedy new problems* to which common-law rules do not apply. Thus a state legislature might pass a statute making nonprofit corporations (such as hospitals) liable for the wrongs of their employees to the same extent as are profit-making corporations, thereby reversing the early common-law rule of nonliability for such employers. Or a legislature, aware of increasing purchases of its farmlands by foreign citizens—a situation not covered by common-law rules—might react to this perceived evil by passing a statute placing limits on the number of acres aliens may own or inherit. (Over twenty states today have such statutes, and approximately ten have passed laws that prohibit aliens who live outside the U.S. from owning *any* farmlands within these states' borders.)

## LIMITATIONS ON LEGISLATIVE BODIES

### Procedural Requirements

All state constitutions (and, to a lesser extent, the federal Constitution) contain provisions about the manner in which statutes shall be enacted. As a general rule, acts that do not conform to these requirements are void. For example, virtually all state constitutions provide that revenue bills "shall originate in the House of Representatives," a requirement that also appears in the federal Constitution. Typical state constitutions also contain provisions (1) restricting the enactment of "special" or "local" laws that affect only a portion of the citizenry, (2) requiring that the subject of every act be set forth in its title, and (3) prohibiting a statute from embracing more than one subject. Additionally, all constitutions prescribe certain formalities in regard to the enactment processes themselves, such as specific limitations on the time and place of the introduction of bills, limitations on the amendment of bills, and the requirement that bills have three separate readings before final passage.

These kinds of provisions, while appearing to be unduly technical, actually serve meritorious purposes. For example, while legislatures normally strive to pass statutes of general application, it is necessary that some laws operate only upon certain classes of persons or in certain localities of a state. Such special or local laws are valid only if the basis of their classification is reasonable; two of the purposes of the constitutional provisions mentioned above are to insure such reasonableness and to guarantee that the classes of persons covered be given notice of the consideration of the bill prior to its passage. Similarly, the purpose of requiring that the subject of an act be expressed in its title is to insure that legislators voting on a bill are fully apprised as to its subject, thereby guarding against the enactment of "surprise" legislation. And the purpose of the requirement that a bill contain one subject is to prevent the passage of omnibus bills (those that bring together entirely unrelated, or incongruous, matters).

### Requirement of Certainty

All statutes are subject to the general principle of constitutional law that they be "reasonably definite and certain." While the Constitution itself does not expressly contain such a provision, the courts have long taken the view that if the wording of a statute is such that persons of ordinary intelligence cannot understand its meaning, then the statute violates the due process clause of the Constitution and is thus invalid.[6] In such instances, it is said that the statute is "unconstitutionally vague."

As a practical matter, the majority of statutes that are challenged on the ground of vagueness or uncertainty are upheld by the courts. This is because most statutes are, in fact, drafted carefully and because the courts are extremely reluctant to declare a statute unconstitutional if they can avoid doing so. Thus, if the wording of a statute is subject to two possible but conflicting interpretations, one of which satisfies constitutional requirements and the other of which does not, the former interpretation will be accepted by the courts if they can reasonably do so.

An application of the vagueness analysis in a criminal case occurred in *Kolender v. Lawson*, 461

---

[6]*State v. Jay J. Garfield Bldg. Co.,* 3 P.2d 983 (Ariz. 1931).

U.S. 352 (1983), where the U.S. Supreme Court struck down, on the ground of vagueness, a California statute that required persons who loitered or wandered on the streets to provide "credible and reliable" identification and to account for their presence when requested to do so by a peace officer. The court, speaking through Justice Sandra Day O'Connor, said "It is clear that the full discretion accorded to the police whether the suspect has provided a 'credible and reliable' identification necessarily entrusts lawmaking to the moment-to-moment judgment of the policeman on his beat," and "furnishes a convenient tool for harsh and discriminatory enforcement by local prosecuting officials against particular groups deemed to merit their displeasure."

In a case involving regulation of business, rather than criminal charges, the courts will not be as demanding in applying the vagueness test, as the next case illustrates.

## U.S. v. Sun and Sand Imports, Ltd., Inc.
U.S. Second Circuit Court of Appeals, 725 F.2d 184 (1984)

The Consumer Products Safety Commission (CPSC) issued an administrative complaint charging that Sun and Sand Imports had imported and transported in interstate commerce flammable children's sleepwear in violation of the Flammable Fabrics Act (FFA). The garments in question are sold in sizes which fit infants and toddlers, are made of soft stretchable fabric with no trim, have attached feet and a front zipper running from neck to crotch, and are, admittedly, made of flammable fabric. The trial judge enjoined importation of the garments pending conclusion of CPSC administrative proceedings.

Sun and Sand appealed, arguing that the regulatory definition of sleepwear is void for vagueness under the Due Process Clause of the Fifth Amendment.

**Decision:** The court of appeals affirmed the trial court's decision. The applicable regulation defines children's sleepwear as "any product of wearing apparel up to and including 6X, such as nightgowns, pajamas, or similar or related items, such as robes, intended to be worn primarily for sleeping or activities related to sleeping." In addition, the CPSC looks at such factors as the suitability of the product for sleeping, the manner in which it is distributed and promoted, and the likelihood that it will be used by children for sleeping.

The Supreme Court has held that a statute is void for vagueness under the Due Process Clause of the Constitution if "it is so vague that it gives no warning to the challenger that his conduct is prohibited." However, a relatively relaxed approach is taken to this standard where, as here, the law under scrutiny is a mere economic regulation which carries no criminal penalties and burdens no fundamental constitutional rights. Every regulation will have its close cases, but it is not unfair to require that "one who deliberately goes perilously close to an area of proscribed conduct shall take the risk that he may cross the line."

Sun and Sand's products were within the statute because, *inter alia,* (1) they had the same characteristics as infant sleepwear, especially the attached feet; (2) Sun and Sand does not promote them as playwear; (3) customers in several stores were shown Sun and Sand's garments when they asked for sleepwear; (4) Sun and Sand's garments were intermingled with sleepwear in many stores; and (5) the garments bore a "striking similarity" to classic sleepwear garments. ∎

## STATUTORY LAW AND COMMON LAW—A CONTRAST

Statutory law and common law differ in several significant respects. The most obvious of these are the *processes* by which each comes into being and the *form* of each after it becomes operative.

### Processes and Form

*Legislative acts* become law only after passing through certain formal steps in both houses of the state legislatures (or of Congress) and, normally, by subsequent approval of the governor (or the president). The usual steps are (1) introduction of a bill in the house or senate by one or more members of that body; (2) referral of the bill to the appropriate legislative committee, where hearings are held; (3) approval of the bill by that committee and perhaps others; (4) approval of the bill by the house and senate after full debate; and (5) signing of the bill by the executive (or overriding an executive veto). At each of these stages the opponents of the bill are given considerable opportunity to raise objections, with the result that the bill may be voted down or may pass only after being substantially amended. *Common-law rules,* by contrast, are creatures of the judicial branch of government; they are adopted by the courts for settling controversies in those areas of law where the legislature has not spoken.

In addition to these obvious contrasts between the two types of law, there are others that are equally significant. We note these briefly.

## Social and Political Forces

The social and political forces within a state have a greater and more evident impact on statutory law than on common law. Judges are somewhat more insulated from such pressures than are legislatures. Additionally, the steps required in the enactment of statutes enable representatives of vocal special-interest groups (who are frequently at odds with one another) to attract considerable publicity to their causes. And, of course, the raw political power that each is able to exert upon the legislators plays a significant, though not always controlling, part in the final disposition of a bill.

In addition to the political and financial pressures that have always been wielded by lobbyists, the past twenty years have seen an enormous increase in the activities of political action committees (PACs). Whereas lobbyists' activities are intended to sway the votes of lawmakers, PACs direct their efforts to raising funds for the election of candidates who will support their particular causes. A hint of the power of PACs can be gained from just three statistics: (1) over 4,000 PACs are registered with the Federal Elections Commission, representing virtually every business, union, and special interest group imaginable; (2) spending by PACs for the 1990 elections was estimated to be over $150 million, even though there was no presidential race that year; and (3) around 95 percent of the incumbents in the U.S. House of Representatives win reelection every term, a statistic that many attribute in large part to the fact that PACs tend to support incumbents.

## Legislative Options

While judges are required to settle controversies that come before them, legislatures generally have no duty to enact legislation. Thus legislatures have the option of refraining from the passage of laws where there is little public sentiment for them or where competing groups are so powerful that inaction is, politically, the better part of valor.

## Legislative Scope

Subject only to the relatively few constitutional limitations placed upon it, the legislative power to act is very broad. Thus legislatures are not only free to enact statutes where case law is nonexistent, but they also can pass statutes that expressly overrule common-law principles. Examples of the latter are those statutes involving the legality of married women's contracts. Under English and early American common law, it was firmly established that married women lacked the capacity—the legal ability—to contract, and thus any agreements they entered into while married had no effect. Today, all states have enacted statutes that generally confer upon married women the same rights to contract as those enjoyed by other citizens.

As for jurisdictional scope, legislatures have the power to pass broad statutes encompassing all aspects of a given subject, whereas the courts can "make law" only in deciding the cases that come before them. Every state, for example, has comprehensive corporation acts, in which virtually all aspects of corporate activities, from incorporation procedures to dissolution procedures, are specified in detail. Similarly, every state has an all-encompassing criminal code, within which the criminal offenses in the state are defined.

# STATUTORY INTERPRETATION

We have seen that legislative bodies make law whenever they enact statutes. By doing so, they formally state what kinds of conduct they are requiring or prohibiting in specified situations and what results they expect from the passage of these laws on the rights and duties of affected parties.

But the true scope and meaning of a particular statute is never known with precision until it is formally construed by the courts in settling actual disputes arising under it. This searching for legislative intent, which usually necessitates a *statutory interpretation,* is thus another major source of our law. **Interpretation** is the process by which a court determines the precise legal meaning of a statute as it applies to a particular controversy.

## *Interpretation: A Necessary Evil?*

Whenever a dispute arises where either of the parties is basing his or her case upon the wording of a particular statute, one might think that the court's job would be mechanical in nature; that is, once the facts were established, a careful reading of the statute would make it clear what result the legislature intended in such a situation. While this is often true, there are many instances in which it is not.

To bring the nature of the problem into sharper focus, consider the following situation. X flies a stolen airplane from one state to another and is convicted under a U.S. statute that makes the interstate movement of stolen motor vehicles a federal crime. In this statute, a motor vehicle is defined as "an automobile, automobile truck, automobile wagon, motorcycle, or any other self-propelled vehicle not designed for running on rails." Is an airplane a "motor vehicle" under this law? The problem is that the words of the statute are broad enough to embrace aircraft if they are given a literal interpretation; yet it is at least arguable that Congress did not really intend such a result. (The U.S. Supreme Court answered no to the question, with Justice Holmes saying that the term *vehicle* is "commonly understood as something that moves or runs on land, not something which flies in the air"—though he did admit that "etymologically the term might be considered broad enough to cover a conveyance propelled in the air.")[7]

## *The Plain-Meaning Rule*

The primary source of legislative intent is, of course, the language that makes up the statute itself. In the relatively rare case where a court feels that the wording of an act is so clear as to dictate but one result, and that the result is not "patently absurd," the consideration of other factors is unnecessary. If, for example, a state statute provides that "every applicant for examination and registration as a pharmacist shall be a citizen of the United States," a state pharmacy board would have to refuse to process the application of an alien even though he or she may have *applied for* U.S. citizenship as of the date of the pharmaceutical examination.[8] In cases of this sort (and occasionally in others where the language is somewhat less precise) the courts say that the statute possesses a **plain meaning** and that interpretation is thus unnecessary.

## *Aids to Interpretation*

Most statutes, however, do not easily lend themselves to the plain-meaning rule. This is true (1) because laws are usually drafted so as to contain an element of "deliberate imprecision," the legislature intending thereby to afford the courts some latitude in their application, and (2) because very few words (even in statutes that are highly restricted in scope) are susceptible to but one meaning. Thus in the majority of cases the courts recognize that some degree of *interpretation* is necessary and that a consideration of factors beyond the express language of a particular clause is advisable, if not mandatory, in determining the precise legislative intent. Even when purporting to apply the plainmeaning rule, most courts bolster their conclusion with various aids to interpretation.

For example, the court will examine the law's **textual context,** which involves reading the statute as a whole rather than concentrating solely upon the language of the disputed clause. The title of the act might give some indication of how the legislature meant a particular clause contained in it to be interpreted. Similarly, use of the same words in different sections of the act can indicate how the legislature meant them to be taken in the disputed clause. Rules of grammar and punctuation supplement this examination, and occasionally the dictionary is consulted to determine how the words are used in ordinary life.

The court will also examine the purpose for which the law was enacted. If, for example, the law was passed to fight organized crime, the courts will construe ambiguous portions to help achieve that purpose. This is sometimes called the **circumstantial context** or "purpose rule."

**Legislative history** can be particularly important. What did the legislators say as they debated the

---

[7] *McBoyle v. United States,* 283 U.S. 25 (1931).

[8] *State v. Dame,* Supreme Court of Wyoming, 249 P.2d 156 (1952).

bill that eventually was passed? Their comments, particularly those of its sponsors, may be enlightening.

Also, courts will give weight to prior *judicial interpretations* of the statute's meaning. This is appropriate simply on *stare decisis* grounds. More to the point, if a particular statute has been interpreted consistently by the courts for many years and Congress has never amended the provision in question although it has, perhaps, made changes in others in that statute, the courts sometimes assume Congress has implicitly approved the long-standing interpretation.

No matter which aids to interpretation the courts invoke, their guiding star in the process of interpretation is one thing only—*legislative intent.* The courts' task is not to interpret the statute to mean what they think it should say. It is not to interpret the statute to improve on what the legislature said. The courts' only duty is to discover the legislative intent and to interpret the law in a manner consistent with that intent. Sometimes this can be a distasteful task.

For example, the following case involves interpretation of the Racketeering Influenced and Corrupt Organizations Act (RICO). There is no doubt that the act was aimed primarily at the infiltration of legitimate business by organized crime. Yet, its civil provisions, studies showed, were used in over 90 percent of the cases not against "mobsters" but against ordinary businesses, including stock brokers such as Merrill Lynch and Dean Witter, CPA firms such as Arthur Andersen and Price Waterhouse, banks such as Citibank and Continental Illinois, and manufacturing companies such as Boeing and Miller Brewing. To slow down the spate of RICO lawsuits, some courts interpreted RICO's provisions to require that plaintiffs show that defendants had been *convicted* of certain specified "racketeering acts." The Supreme Court was called upon to resolve the meaning of the act. As you read the opinion, note which aids to interpretation the Court uses.

---

### Sedima v. Imrex Co., Inc.
U.S. Supreme Court, 105 S.Ct. 3275 (1985)

Plaintiff Sedima entered into a joint venture with defendant Imrex Co. to provide electronic components to a Belgian firm. The buyer was to order parts through Sedima; Imrex was to obtain the parts in America and ship them to Europe. Sedima and Imrex were to split the net proceeds. After Imrex filled $8,000,000 in orders, Sedima became convinced that Imrex was inflating bills, cheating Sedima out of a portion of its proceeds by collecting for nonexistent expenses.

Sedima sued Imrex and two of its officers under the Racketeering Influenced and Corrupt Organizations Act (RICO). It contains both criminal provisions and the civil provisions which Sedima invoked. Sedima claimed that Imrex had by its presentation of inflated, fraudulent bills committed mail and wire fraud, which are "racketeering" acts within the meaning of RICO.

The trial court dismissed the RICO claims, and the court of appeals affirmed for the reason, among others, that the complaint was defective for failing to allege that defendants had been convicted of mail and wire fraud. Sedima appealed.

**Decision:** Following a detailed search for legislative intent, the Supreme Court reversed, finding no strong evidence that Congress intended a *conviction* on racketeering charges to be a prerequisite to civil suit. The applicable section of RICO allows civil lawsuits to be brought by "[a]ny person injured in his business or property by reason of a violation" of another section that defines "racketeering activities."

Although RICO was aimed at organized crime, it was written broadly. Its legislative history demonstrates that it was patterned after the antitrust laws which also allow civil suits as a supplement to government enforcement. RICO's primary sponsor in the Senate deemed the provision for civil action by private citizens "a major new tool in extirpating the baneful influence of organized crime in our economic life."

The Court examined the wording of the statute, but found that the word "conviction" does not appear in any relevant portion of RICO. Instead, RICO speaks of acts that are "chargeable," "indictable," or "punishable" under various criminal statutes. So, as used in the statute, racketeering activity consists not of acts for which the defendant has been convicted, but of acts for which he could be. The court of appeals derived its requirement of a conviction from the term "violation." However, that term implies only a failure to adhere to legal standards, not a conviction. Indeed, the term "violation" is used elsewhere in RICO where its indisputable meaning does not include conviction.

*(continued)*

An examination of RICO's legislative history discloses that the only reference to a conviction requirement was one legislator's complaint that RICO did *not* contain one. To limit RICO's scope by imposing a conviction requirement would be inconsistent with Congress's underlying policy concerns. Congress wanted a broad "private attorney general" provision to supplement governmental efforts to stop mob infiltration into legitimate business.

The Supreme Court shared the Second Circuit's concern that, in practice, RICO had been used almost exclusively against "legitimate businessmen" rather than against classic organized crime figures. But the Court said that "this defect—if defect it is—is inherent in the statute as written, and its correction must lie with Congress. It is not for the judiciary to eliminate the private cause of action in situations where Congress has provided it simply because plaintiffs are not taking advantage of it in its more difficult applications."

---

## SELECTED STATE STATUTES

Before leaving the subject of statutory law, several widely adopted state statutes deserve brief mention.

### *The Uniform Commercial Code*

Discussed in detail in Chapters 20–29, the **Uniform Commercial Code** (UCC) is especially significant to businesspersons because (1) it is a dramatic illustration of one way changes in law can occur in response to shortcomings that exist in prior law; (2) it governs numerous commercial law subjects; and (3) it has been adopted with little variation by all states except Louisiana (which has adopted only Articles 1, 3, 4, and 5).

**Historical Background:** At the beginning of this century, the growth in interstate commercial activity was hobbled by great variation in the commercial laws of the various states. This caused substantial planning problems for merchants and raised legal expenses as a cost of doing business to unnecessarily high levels. In 1941, the National Conference of Commissioners on Uniform State Laws and the American Law Institute joined forces to draft a single "modern, comprehensive, commercial code, applicable through the country." Most states have adopted the official 1962 version of the UCC, along with some 1972 amendments.

**Coverage:** The UCC consists of eleven articles or chapters. The nine substantive areas of law covered by the code are found in Articles 2 through 9. (Articles 1 and 10 are merely introductory and procedural.)

Article 2, Sales, consists of 104 sections that govern virtually all aspects of the law of the sale of goods. Article 2A, the first new article added to the UCC since 1962, regulates leases of goods. As of this writing, about 15 states have adopted Article 2A. Wider adoption is expected to come in the near future.

Article 3, Commercial Paper, has 80 sections governing such matters as the rights and obligations of the makers of notes and the drawers of checks and drafts, and the rights and duties of holders and endorsers of all types of negotiable instruments.

Articles 4 through 8 deal with more specialized situations, such as the duties that exist between depositary and collecting banks and the resolution of problems resulting from the issuance and transfer of bills of lading and other documents of title. Article 9 covers all kinds of secured transactions, which arise when creditors seek to retain a security interest in goods physically in the possession of a debtor. These UCC subjects are treated in detail in Part III of this text.

### *Deceptive Trade Practices Acts*

Most states have **deceptive trade practices acts** which specifically forbid specified kinds of business misconduct. The typical act, for example, prohibits merchants from "passing off" (representing and selling) their goods or services as those of another; from representing used goods as being new; and from disparaging the goods or services of their competitors by false representations of fact. Additionally, the typical statute also prohibits such practices as advertising goods or services with the intent not to sell them as advertised, and the making of false statements concerning the reasons for, or the amounts of, price reductions. Such acts will be discussed in Chapters 9, 15, and 50.

## Business Organization Acts

All states have comprehensive statutes that control the formation, operation, and dissolution of various forms of business organizations. These will be studied in some detail in Parts IV and V of this text. For now it is sufficient to make just a few observations about these laws. In the area of general partnerships, there is substantial uniformity from state to state because virtually all states have adopted versions of the Uniform Partnership Act (UPA). The UPA has successfully accomplished the uniformity for partnership law which the UCC was meant to create for commercial transactions.

There is less uniformity for limited partnership law because some states' laws are based heavily on the Uniform Limited Partnership Act (ULPA) of 1916, others on the Revised Uniform Limited Partnership Act (RULPA) of 1976, and still others have adopted portions of a 1985 amended version of RULPA. Still, the states' laws are generally similar and moving in the same direction.

There is even less uniformity, however, in the states' laws governing corporations. Here, there is no *uniform* act, only two versions of a *model* act, the Model Business Corporation Act (MBCA) and the Revised Model Business Corporation Act (RMBCA). Many states pattern their laws after one of these two model acts, but most have felt free to introduce their own variations. Furthermore, many states pattern their corporate codes not on some version of the MBCA, but upon the Delaware Corporate Code. Delaware is the leading corporate law jurisdiction in the nation.

## SUMMARY

Judge-made or common law is not as pervasive in the American legal system as it once was, but it still dominates several important subject areas. As cases in these areas are decided over the years, a substantial body of precedent builds up. A judge who finds relevant decisions from courts above him or her in the appellate chain should follow that mandatory authority. If the only existing precedents come from courts that could not review the judge's decision, they need only be followed if the judge finds them persuasive.

The heart of the common law is the doctrine of *stare decisis*, which provides that relevant precedents from earlier cases should normally be followed so that the law will have stability and predictability. However, the common law is also flexible; it can be adapted to changing societal conditions. Therefore, if the policy reasons underlying a particular common law rule have evaporated, that rule can be changed. The need to correct an injustice outweighs the need for stability.

In recent years statutory law has become increasingly dominant in most areas of our legal system. The Constitution specifies the areas in which the federal Congress can legislate, and reserves the other areas for the states. If the proper procedures are followed and the laws passed are not so vague that citizens are unable to conform their actions to the law's requirements, the courts will enforce those laws. The courts may also be required to interpret the laws, for a legislature can never foresee all the circumstances that might arise. Then the courts must discover the legislative intent and construe the laws in such a way as to attain the legislative purpose. To achieve this the court will use various analytic techniques, including a close examination of the textual context, the stated purpose of the law, and its legislative history.

## KEY TERMS

**Case law**
**Precedent**
*Stare decisis*
**Mandatory authority**
**Persuasive authority**
**Statute**
**Interpretation**
**Plain-meaning rule**
**Textual context**
**Circumstantial context**
**Legislative history**
**Uniform Commercial Code**
**Deceptive trade practices acts**

## QUESTIONS AND PROBLEMS

**1.** Dissenting in *Taylor v. Allen*, 151 La. 82 (1921), Justice O'Neill wrote: "I have heard that lawyers in one of the Western states [say that a] precedent is a 'goose case.' The expression arose from the perplexity of a so-called 'case lawyer,' who was unprepared to advise his client whether he was liable in damages because his geese had trespassed on his neighbor's lawn. The lawyer said he had found several cases where the owners were held liable because their horses, cows, sheep, goats, or dogs had committed acts of trespass; but he could not find a 'goose case.' The distinction which he observed was that his 'goose case' was not 'on all fours.'" Explain what constitutes a "goose case." How does one avoid the problems of the perplexed lawyer in Justice O'Neill's story?

**2.** Maddux was injured when the car she was riding in was struck by a car driven by Donaldson, and, almost immediately thereafter, by a second car driven by Bryie. When Maddux sued the two negligent drivers, the facts of the case were such that it was impossible to determine which of her injuries were caused by the first collision and which by the second collision. At the time of the suit, the Michigan common-law rule was that, in such a case, neither defendant could be held liable for any damages; accordingly, the trial court dismissed Maddux's action. She then appealed to the Supreme Court of Michigan, claiming that the rule of non-recovery was too unfair to an injured plaintiff. Do you agree with this contention? If so, what do you think a better rule would be? (*Maddux v. Donaldson,* 108 N.W.2d 33, 1961.)

**3.** In a number of cases, the supreme court of State X had adopted the rule that a seller of land who overstated the *value of the land* to a prospective buyer was not guilty of fraud, even if he knew that the true market value of the land was much lower than the figure that he stated to the buyer. (In these cases, the reasoning of the court was that the value of any property is merely a matter of opinion, and that the buyer should realize this.) After this rule is adopted, a new case reaches the supreme court in which the buyer of land claims that the seller was guilty of fraud when he—the seller—intentionally misrepresented the *rental value* of the property (seller told buyer, an out-of-state resident who had never seen the land, that "it can readily be rented for $100 a month," a statement that proved to be false). If the supreme court felt that the seller in such a case should be made to pay damages on the theory that he *was* guilty of fraud, would the court have to overrule the prior decisions, or do you think the facts of the new case are sufficiently different to permit the court simply to apply a different rule to it? Explain your reasoning. (*Cahill v. Readon,* 273 P. 653, 1928.)

**4.** A student demonstrator and four labor pickets were convicted in the Hamilton County Municipal Court, Ohio, of violating a Cincinnati ordinance making it a criminal offense for three or more persons to assemble on a sidewalk "and there conduct themselves in a manner annoying to persons passing by." On appeal to the U.S. Supreme Court the five contended that the ordinance was unconstitutionally vague (that it was so vague that it violated the due process clause). Do you agree with this contention? Discuss. (*Coates v. Cincinnati,* 402 U.S. 611, 1971.)

**5.** The City of Petersburg had maintained a cemetery for over 100 years when it decided to move some of the bodies onto a 1.1 acre tract adjacent to the cemetery so that a road running in front of the cemetery could be widened. The Temples owned a home directly across the street from the 1.1 acre tract. They sued to prevent the bodies from being moved onto the tract, citing a state statute which said: "No cemetery shall be hereafter established within the corporate limits of any town; nor shall any cemetery be established within 250 yards of any residence without the consent of the owner of such residence." Does the City need the Temples' permission? Discuss. (*Temple v. City of Petersburg,* 29 S.E.2d 357, Va. 1944.)

**6.** Johnson, a teen-aged boy living in North Carolina, owned a motorcycle. After the motorcycle's original headlight became very weak, he and a friend taped a five-cell flashlight to the handlebars and that evening, with both boys on the motorcycle, they had a collision with an automobile. In ensuing litigation, the car owner pointed out that a North Carolina statute required every motorcycle to have a "headlamp," and he contended that the flashlight was not a headlamp. If you were a judge on the North Carolina Supreme Court hearing the case on appeal, what steps would you take in deciding whether the flashlight was a headlamp under the statute? What result? (*Bigelow v. Johnson,* 277 S.E.2d 347, 1981.)

**7.** In 1885 Congress passed a statute which provided: "[I]t shall be unlawful for any person, company, partnership, or corporation, in any manner whatsoever, to prepay the transportation, or in any way assist or encourage the importation or migration of any alien or aliens . . . into the United States . . . under contract or agreement . . . made previous to the importation or migration of such alien or aliens, . . . to perform labor or service of any kind in the United States." In 1887 the Holy Trinity Church of New York City made a contract with Warren, a pastor then living in England, under the terms of which he was employed to serve as its pastor. Pursuant to that contract, Warren immigrated to the United States and assumed his pastoral duties. The church was soon charged with violating the quoted statute. Did Congress intend the statute to cover this case? Discuss. (*Holy Trinity Church v. U.S.,* 143 U.S. 457, 1892.)

**8.** A city ordinance required that operators of coin-operated amusement machines be licensed, and provided that the chief of police was to determine whether an applicant has any "connections with criminal elements." The city manager, after receiving the report of the chief of police and reports from the building inspector and the city planner, would then decide whether to issue the license. (If the application were denied, the applicant could then petition the city council for a license.) In a legal case brought by a rejected applicant, the contention was made that the licensing ordinance was *unconstitutionally vague* because of the "connections with criminal elements" language. Do you think this contention is correct? Why or why not? (*City of Mesquite v. Aladdin's Castle, Inc.,* 102 S.Ct. 1070, 1982.)

CHAPTER 5

# CONSTITUTIONAL LAW

The most important document in the United States, and, arguably, in the world, is the United States Constitution. This wonderful document is the foundation of our democratic system of government and the basis of our many freedoms. Though drafted in a simpler time, the Constitution has evolved over the past 200 years to keep pace with changes in American society. Partly through amendment, more importantly through flexible Supreme Court interpretations, the Constitution has remained as vital and timely a document as it was when originally written.

Few areas of the law can be studied without reference to the Constitution. For example, Chapter 2 discussed the structure of the American court system, which is established in the Constitution, as well as the exercise of personal jurisdiction by courts, which is constrained by the Constitution's due process provisions. The Constitution governs the government's ability to search businesses (Chapter 6) and contains many protections for criminal defendants (Chapter 7). The Constitutional right to freedom of speech impacts defamation law (Chapter 8) and trademark and copyright law (Chapter 9).

The focus of this chapter will be on three major functions of the U.S. Constitution:

**1.** It prescribes the organization of the federal government, in addition to its jurisdiction.

**2.** It sets forth the authority of the legislative, executive, and judicial branches of that government.

**3.** It protects basic rights of individuals and businesses from certain governmental interference.

## ORGANIZATION AND JURISDICTION

One major function of the Constitution is to establish the organization and jurisdiction of the federal government. In so doing, the Constitution also establishes the role of state and local governments in our dual system of sovereignty. Fifty-one primary governments exist in America—the federal government and the fifty state governments. To prevent overlapping areas of authority, the Constitution enumerates many significant federal powers, which are referred to as **delegated powers** (or "enumerated powers"). All other powers (**reserved powers**) rest in the state governments.

Article I, Section 8 of the Constitution spells out the powers of the U.S. Congress, the most important of which include the power

> To lay and collect Taxes, Duties, Imposts and Excises, to pay the Debts and provide for the common Defense and general Welfare of the United States; . . .
>
> To borrow Money on the Credit of the United States;
>
> To regulate Commerce with foreign Nations, and among the several States, and with the Indian Tribes;
>
> To establish an uniform Rule of Naturalization, and uniform Laws on the subject of Bankruptcies throughout the United States;
>
> To coin Money, regulate the Value thereof, and of foreign Coin, and fix the Standard of Weights and Measures; . . .
>
> To establish Post Offices and post Roads;
>
> To promote the Progress of Science and useful Arts, by securing for limited Times to Authors and Inventors the exclusive right to their respective Writings and Discoveries;
>
> To constitute Tribunals inferior to the Supreme Court; . . .

To declare War, grant Letters of Marque and Reprisal, and make Rules concerning Captures on Land and Water;

To raise and support Armies, but no Appropriation of Money to that Use shall be for a longer Term than two Years;

To provide and maintain a Navy;

To make Rules for the Government and Regulation of the land and naval forces;

To provide for calling forth the Militia to execute the Laws of the Union, suppress Insurrections and repel Invasions;

To provide for organizing, arming, and disciplining the Militia, and . . .

To make all Laws which shall be necessary and proper for carrying into Execution the foregoing Powers, and all other Powers vested by this Constitution in the Government of the United States, or in any Department or Officer thereof.

## *State Police Power*

By and large, the lines of demarcation between the authority of the federal and state governments are quite clear. Most of the powers delegated to the federal government under Section 8—such as the power to operate post offices and to maintain the various armed forces—involve such clear-cut activities that no state could claim to possess any regulatory powers over them.

By the same token, the powers reserved to the states are also, in general, clearly established. Virtually all of the powers of a given state spring from the **state police power**—a term referring to the state's inherent authority to regulate the health, safety, morals, and general welfare of its people. Statutes relating to the operation of motor vehicles, the manufacture and sale of intoxicating liquors, and the regulation of crime obviously fall within the police power, since they are directly involved with matters of health, safety, and morals. Typical statutes based upon the "general welfare" component of the police power are those that regulate such matters as marriage and divorce, the inheritance of property, and the landlord-tenant relationship. (The power to enact zoning laws also falls within the police power category, but the legislatures normally delegate this power to their cities; thus most zoning regulations are, in fact, found in municipal ordinances and regulations of municipal zoning commissions.)

## *The Commerce Clause*

Although in most areas there is a clear delineation between the powers of the federal government on the one hand and the state governments on the other, one principal problem area exists—regulation of commerce. Federal regulation of commercial activity is nearly unlimited, yet the states also have a substantial role to play. Seldom does a year go by in which the Supreme Court does not decide an important case bearing on the respective spheres of authority to regulate commerce.

**Federal Regulation of Interstate Commerce:** Recent Supreme Court decisions have read Article I, Section 8's grant of power "to regulate Commerce with foreign Nations, and among the several States" very broadly. If Congress detects a problem, even a problem which is not primarily economic in nature such as racial discrimination, and legislates a solution under the commerce clause, the Supreme Court usually asks only two questions: (1) Did the regulated activity have "any appreciable effect" on interstate commerce? (2) Was the solution Congress selected reasonable and appropriate under the circumstances? The Court tends not to be too searching with either inquiry.

"Commerce" includes such activity as transportation, manufacturing, and sales efforts. Because Congress can reach any intrastate commercial activity which *affects* interstate commerce, few local businesses can escape the reach of the federal government. For example, in *Wickard v. Filburn,* 317 U.S. 111 (1942), an Ohio farmer was limited by federal law to raising 11.1 acres of wheat. Farmer Filburn ignored the limitation and planted 23 acres. He fought a penalty assessed by the government by arguing that because he used much of the wheat he grew right on his own farm and sold the rest at an elevator a few miles away, he was not engaged in interstate commerce. But the Supreme Court held that the power to regulate interstate commerce includes the power to regulate prices. The purpose of the law in question was to support agricultural prices by limiting production. If all small farmers such as Filburn were viewed as beyond the reach of the act, the supply of wheat would no doubt increase and appreciably *affect* the price of wheat selling in interstate commerce. Congressional authority extended to Filburn.

More recently, in *McLain v. Real Estate Board of New Orleans,* 444 U.S. 232 (1980), a question arose whether a number of New Orleans real estate firms and trade associations had violated the federal antitrust laws by entering into several price-fixing contracts. The lower courts dismissed the action, ruling that defendants' actions, which involved sales of land in New Orleans, were "purely local" in nature and thus not subject to federal law. The Supreme Court reversed, finding that the indirect effects of the defendants' activities were sufficiently related to interstate commerce to justify application of federal law. This finding of sufficient effect—a "not insubstantial effect"—was based primarily on the fact that (1) significant amounts of money lent by local banks to finance real estate purchases came from out-of-state banks, and (2) most of the mortgages taken by the local banks were "physically traded" by them to financial institutions in other states.

Although there are very few businesses today whose activities are so completely local (intrastate) in nature as to be outside the power of Congress to regulate, many federal statutes exempt certain companies from compliance—for example, those having assets of less than $5 million, or fewer than ten employees.

**State Regulation of Interstate Commerce:** Underlying the dominant federal role in regulation of commerce was the framers' "conviction that in order to succeed, the new Union would have to avoid tendencies toward economic Balkanization that had plagued relations among the Colonies and later among the States under the Articles of Confederation."[1] This does not mean, however, that the states have no role in regulating commerce. Obviously, their police powers give the states a very strong reason to protect the health, safety, and welfare of their citizens threatened by commercial activity originating both within and without the particular state's boundaries.

In fact, the states play a large role in the regulation of commercial activity, intrastate and interstate, in today's economy. However, because of the dominant federal role and the need for a smooth interstate flow of goods and services, there are three limitations on state regulation of commerce. First, a state cannot contradict a valid federal law regulating commerce. Second, a state cannot discriminate against interstate commerce. And, third, a state may not unduly burden the flow of interstate commerce.

***Preemption:*** The federal government's authority to regulate interstate commerce is paramount. Because the Constitution's "Supremacy Clause" found in Article VI, Section I makes the Constitution and federal laws "the supreme law of the land," any state law that on its face contradicts a federal law is automatically invalid. Any time it is impossible to comply with both a federal law and a state law, the state law must fall.

Furthermore, any time a state law undermines the objective of a federal law, it is invalid under the Supremacy Clause. For example, in *City of Burbank v. Lockheed Air Terminal, Inc.,* 411 U.S. 624 (1973), a city ordinance banned jet aircraft from taking off from a local airport between 11 p.m. and 7 a.m. Although the ordinance did not directly contradict a federal law, it conflicted with the purpose of the Federal Aeronautics Act by impeding the ability of the FAA to control air traffic flow.

On occasion, federal regulation of an area of commerce is so extensive that the courts conclude Congress has "occupied the field," leaving no room for state regulation. Sometimes Congress makes clear its intent to preempt state regulation, but many times the courts must decide whether such an intent should be inferred from congressional action. Obviously, the more comprehensive the federal scheme of regulation, the more likely it is that preemption will be inferred. To the extent that national uniformity is necessary for an effective regulatory scheme—as with air traffic control—the more likely preemption will be found. However, congressional *intent* to occupy the field, whether express or implied, is the key.

***Discrimination:*** Even in an area where there is no federal regulation or where existing federal regulation is not so extensive as to preempt concurrent state regulation, the states may not discriminate against interstate commerce. They may not, for example, shelter their own industries from competition emanating from other states. While they may act to preserve their own natural resources, they may not do so by discriminating against out-of-state buyers. Nor may

---

[1] *Wardair Canada, Inc. v. Florida Dept. of Revenue,* 477 U.S. 1 (1986), quoting *Hughes v. Oklahoma,* 441 U.S. 322 (1979).

they require that business operations that could be more efficiently conducted elsewhere take place in-state. For example, a state could not require that shellfish caught off its shores be processed in-state before being shipped elsewhere for sale.

It would be a rare case indeed where a state could produce a sufficiently important state interest to justify discrimination against interstate commerce. Almost always the interest could be attained by less restrictive means which do not discriminate in this way. A leading case in this area is *Hunt v. Washington State Apple Advertising Commission,* 432 U.S. 333 (1977), which involved a North Carolina regulation, unique in the fifty states, that required all closed containers of apples shipped into the state to display the applicable USDA grade; state grades were expressly prohibited. For many years, all apples shipped from the state of Washington had a state grade; these grades were in all cases equal or superior to comparable USDA grades. The North Carolina law would have required repackaging or obliteration of labels for Washington apples that happened to end up in North Carolina. The Supreme Court found that although matters of health and consumer protection are naturally of legitimate state concern, the superiority of the Washington grade made those concerns irrelevant in this case. Rather, it appeared that the state of North Carolina was attempting to advance its own apple industry at the expense of the Washington apple growers who had gained a competitive and economic advantage through an expensive inspection and grading system.

*Unduly Burdensome:* Even if a state regulation of commerce is applied in an even-handed fashion, governing in-state and out-of-state businesses alike, it may be invalid if it unduly burdens the flow of interstate commerce. To be sustained, such a regulation must advance a legitimate state interest, and that interest must outweigh the regulation's burden on interstate commerce. For example, a state requirement that cattle imported from other states be certified as free from certain types of diseases would be upheld so long as in-state cattle were required to meet the same standards in the interests of public health.

On the other hand, in *Kassell v. Consolidated Freightways Corp.,* 450 U.S. 662 (1981), the Supreme Court addressed an Iowa law which prohibited the use of 65-foot double-trailer trucks within its borders, while allowing 55-foot single trailers and 60-foot double trailers. States around Iowa all allowed 65-foot double trailers, but Iowa claimed the law was a safety measure. Statistics showed, however, that accidents were a function of mileage rather than truck size. Iowa's law actually worked against safety interests by requiring use of smaller trucks which would have to drive more miles to deliver the same load. It surely burdened the flow of interstate commerce by requiring 65-foot double trailers either to go around Iowa or unload onto smaller trucks when reaching the Iowa border. Exceptions in the law made it appear that Iowa was trying to gain the benefits of large trucks while shunting to neighboring states the costs associated with their use. The law was invalidated.

## *Other State Limitations*

At this point, two other constitutional limitations on the discretion of states are appropriately mentioned—the Full Faith and Credit Clause, and the Contract Clause.

**Full Faith and Credit:** Section 1 of Article IV of the Constitution provides in part that "Full faith and credit shall be given in each State to the public acts, records, and judicial proceedings of every other State." The import of the **Full Faith and Credit Clause** is quite clear: the courts of one state must recognize judgments and other public actions of its sister states. Thus a business firm that obtains a valid judgment against a debtor in one state may enforce that judgment in the courts of any other state in which that debtor's property may be located. The Full Faith and Credit Clause is, however, subject to a number of limitations. For example, if the court that entered the judgment originally did not have jurisdiction over the defendant, the courts of other states will not recognize the judgment. And the courts in a state in which a foreign judgment is sought to be enforced will not enforce that judgment if it violates the public policy of that state.

**Contract Clause:** Article I, Section 10 of the Constitution provides that "No State shall . . . pass any . . . Law impairing the Obligation of Contracts. . . ." This clause does not apply to the federal government, only to the acts of state legislatures. The thrust of the statute is to prevent states from changing the terms of *existing* contracts by passage of subsequent legislation.

The Contract Clause has undergone several vacillations in Supreme Court interpretation. At the moment, it appears that the proper application of the clause depends on whether a private contract or a public contract is at issue. If a private contract (one not involving the state as a party) is impaired by state legislation, the Contract Clause is violated unless the legislation (1) serves an important and legitimate public interest, (2) is necessary for the achievement of the public interest, and (3) is a reasonable impairment of the contract.

For example, in *Exxon Corporation v. Eagerton*, 462 U.S. 176 (1983), Exxon had for years paid a severance tax on oil and gas it drilled in Alabama. Under its sales contracts, it was able to pass on any tax increase to purchasers. When Alabama raised the severance tax and forbade producers of oil and gas from passing on the increase to purchasers, Exxon challenged the law as violative of the Contract Clause. The Supreme Court rejected Exxon's claim, stressing that the law was not aimed at impairing a specific, existing contract, but was instead a generally applicable rule of conduct designed to advance a broad societal interest (protecting consumers from excessive prices) that applied to all oil and gas producers regardless of whether they happened to be parties to contracts such as Exxon's.

The Supreme Court appears to give less deference to legislation which impairs public contracts, perhaps because the legislature's own self-interest is at stake. The key in such a case is whether the legislative modification is both reasonable and necessary to an important state purpose. For example, in *United States Trust Co. v. New Jersey*, 431 U.S. 1 (1977), the Court invalidated New York and New Jersey statutes whose sole effect was to repeal a covenant that the two states had entered into with the holders of bonds issued by The Port Authority of New York and New Jersey.

## LEGISLATIVE, EXECUTIVE, AND JUDICIAL AUTHORITY

The framers of the Constitution, drawing upon the ideas of Blackstone and Montesquieu, thought it imperative that the powers of the legislative, executive, and judicial branches be essentially separate from one another. This separation of powers is substantially brought about under the Constitution; and, by and large, the jurisdiction of each branch is clearly spelled out. Nonetheless, there are overlapping and gray areas. The executive branch has administrative law judges who perform essentially judicial functions. The legislature has numerous investigative powers typically considered executive in nature. The judiciary clearly makes "law" through its interpretation of constitutional and statutory provisions. These are but a few examples of the exceptions to the separation of powers doctrine. Some of the overlaps cause legal problems.

### *Legislative Branch*

Earlier in this chapter we saw that Article I, Section 8 of the Constitution enumerates the primary congressional powers. The ultimate source of congressional authority is in the specific provisions of the Constitution. Only in the realm of foreign affairs has the notion that the government has inherent power, independent of the Constitution, gained currency.

Congress is composed of but 535 members who must cope with the most difficult and complex of problems. As we shall see in the next chapter, the courts have long recognized that the complexities of modern society require that Congress be allowed to delegate its legislative power to administrative agencies. Although that power to delegate, for very practical reasons, is construed broadly, the doctrine of separation of powers does impose some limitations.

For example, in *Bowsher v. Synar*, 478 U.S. 714 (1986), the Supreme Court faced a legal challenge to the Balanced Budget and Emergency Deficit Control Act of 1985 ("Gramm-Rudman"), which established an automatic deficit reduction process. In the Act, Congress set a "maximum deficit amount" for each of the fiscal years 1986 through 1991. Each year the Directors of the Office of Management and Budget (OMB) and the Congressional Budget Office (CBO) were to estimate the amount of the deficit of the upcoming year. They then were to calculate program-by-program reductions necessary to achieve the target deficits and report to the Comptroller General who was required to issue his own report to the President who must issue a "sequestration" order containing the budget reductions specified by the

Comptroller General. The Court found that this delegation of power to the Comptroller General violated the constitutionally requisite separation of powers. The powers conferred on the Comptroller General, the Court held, cannot constitutionally be exercised by an officer removable by Congress because they are executive-type powers.

## *Judicial Branch*

Because there is very little federal "common law," the federal courts "make law" primarily through the interpretation of statutory and constitutional provisions. Atop the federal judiciary, of course, is the United States Supreme Court, the most powerful court in the world.

The Supreme Court's power to reverse the decisions of lower federal courts has always been accepted. What was not clear, at least early in the days of the Republic, was the question of which branch of government would reign supreme regarding Constitutional issues. The Constitution itself does not expressly grant authority to determine challenges to the constitutionality of actions of the legislature or the executive. However, in *Marbury v. Madison*, 5 U.S. 137 (1805), the Supreme Court assumed the power of **judicial review.** Under the doctrine of judicial review, the federal courts have the final say in whether the Constitution has been violated by a congressional law or an executive action.

Not long after *Marbury v. Madison,* the Supreme Court also assumed the power to review the decisions of state courts in both civil and criminal cases in which federal constitutional issues were at stake. The Supreme Court is truly the final arbiter of the meaning of the Constitution. It is no exaggeration to state that "the Constitution means what the Supreme Court says it means."

## *Executive Branch*

The Executive Branch of the federal government contains a plethora of powers. Enforcement of the laws passed by Congress is no doubt the executive branch's chief responsibility. A variety of investigative and even quasi-judicial powers are brought to bear in accomplishing the task. Through **executive orders** the executive branch makes law. Sometimes these orders only direct the manner in which acts of Congress shall be implemented; sometimes, when issued in the absence of congressional authority, they may be subject to court challenge.

Our constitutional system insists that any actions of the executive branch be authorized either by the Constitution or by congressional action. If unauthorized actions occur, the doctrine of judicial review may be invoked, as the following landmark case illustrates.

---

### Youngstown Sheet and Tube Co. v. Sawyer
U.S. Supreme Court,
343 U.S. 579 (1952)

In the latter part of 1951 a dispute arose between the nation's major steel mills and their employees over terms and conditions to be included in their new collective bargaining agreement. Lengthy negotiations proved fruitless, and the employees' representative, United Steelworkers of America, C.I.O., gave notice of an intent to strike when the existing bargaining agreements expired on December 31.

The Federal Mediation and Conciliation Service then intervened in an effort to get labor and management to agree. When this and other efforts were unsuccessful, President Truman issued Executive Order No. 10340, which directed the secretary of commerce to take possession of most of the country's steel mills and keep them running. The indispensability of steel as a component of substantially all weapons and other war materials then being used by the armed forces in Korea led the president to believe that the work stoppage would immediately jeopardize the nation's national defense and that government seizure of the mills was necessary in order to insure the continued availability of steel.

The secretary of commerce immediately issued his own orders, calling upon the presidents of the various seized companies to serve as operating managers for the United States. They were directed to carry on their activities in accordance with regulations and directions of the secretary. The next morning the president sent a message to Congress reporting

*(continued)*

his action. He sent another message twelve days later, and Congress took no action thereon.

Obeying the secretary's orders under protest, the companies brought proceedings against him in the U.S. district court. Their complaints charged that the seizure was not authorized by an act of Congress or by any constitutional provisions. The district court was asked to declare the orders of the president and the secretary invalid and to issue preliminary and permanent injunctions restraining their enforcement. Opposing the motion for preliminary injunction, the United States asserted that a strike disrupting steel production for even a brief period would so endanger the well-being and safety of the nation that the president had "inherent power" to do what he had done—power "supported by the Constitution, by historical precedent, and by court decisions."

The district court held against the government on all points and issued a preliminary injunction restraining the secretary from "continuing the seizure and possession of the plants . . . and from acting under the purported authority of Executive Order No. 10340." On the same day, April 30, the U.S. court of appeals stayed the injunction, and the U.S. Supreme Court "granted certiorari" (agreed to review the lower court's proceedings).

**Decision:** The president did not have the authority to seize the mills. Thus the district court's issuance of an injunction against the government was proper. A president's seizure power, like all others, must stem from either an act of Congress or the Constitution itself. While two federal acts authorize the president to take private property under certain conditions, they do not apply to this case. The Constitution also contains no provisions authorizing this particular act of the president.

While it is true that the president is commander in chief of the armed forces, his power is chiefly over military commanders engaged in day-to-day fighting in a theater of war. His position as commander in chief does not empower him to take possession of private property to prevent a labor dispute from stopping steel production. This would be a job for the nation's lawmakers, not its military authorities.

Despite the fact that the president has certain constitutional authority to issue executive orders, this authority can be exercised only for the purpose of implementing existing congressional policies—statutes or other actions approved by Congress. In this case, no such congressional policy exists. ∎

---

As much as anything else, the decision in *Youngstown Sheet and Tube Co. v. Sawyer* illustrates the widespread acceptance of the doctrine of judicial review. Although President Truman violently disagreed with the Supreme Court's interpretation of his authority in such a critical matter, he promptly and without question complied with the Court's decision.

A more recent illustration of the limitations of presidential power under the Constitution occurred in *United States v. Nixon,* 418 U.S. 683 (1974), which arose out of a criminal action against several of President Nixon's staff members as a result of their alleged obstruction of justice activities in the "Watergate coverup." When the U.S. district court hearing the criminal case demanded—at the request of the special prosecutor—that President Nixon produce tapes and documents involving specified communications between him and his staff members, he refused to do so on the ground that the doctrine of executive privilege immunized the office of the presidency against such orders from the judicial branch of government. When the case reached the Supreme Court, it unanimously held that the judiciary, not the president, was the constitutional arbiter authorized to determine the legitimate scope of executive privilege.

Turning to the specific question, the Court ruled that "neither the doctrine of separation of powers nor the need of confidentiality of high-level communications" could insulate the presidency from the demands for tapes and documents where (1) the communications did not involve diplomatic or national security matters, and (2) the demands were necessary to an important governmental process, in this case the prosecution of important criminal cases in the courts. Accordingly, the request for the materials was upheld, and Mr. Nixon acceded to it although he must have known that the incriminating evidence on the tapes would spell the end of his presidency.

## BASIC RIGHTS

The Constitution contains numerous limitations on the powers of the federal and state governments to restrict the freedoms of individuals and businesses.

Many of our basic rights are guaranteed in the Bill of Rights—the first ten amendments to the Constitution. Others are found in the body of the original Constitution itself or in subsequent amendments such as the post-Civil War amendments freeing the slaves and protecting all citizens from unequal treatment by state governments.

Before we examine some of the more important freedoms which the Constitution protects, a couple of preliminary observations should be made. First, the Bill of Rights applies only to the *federal* government, not to the state and local governments. Nothing in the Constitution specifically prohibits the states from infringing, for example, on freedom of speech. However, through the **doctrine of incorporation**—which is well established but nonetheless controversial—the Supreme Court has extended virtually all of the important provisions of the Bill of Rights (freedom of speech, freedom of press, freedom of religion, right to counsel, privilege against self-incrimination, right against unreasonable search and seizure, and others) to the states and their political subdivisions. The Fourteenth Amendment to the Constitution does apply to the states, and it provides that they may not deprive citizens of **due process of law.** The Supreme Court has broadly construed the concept of due process to include "principles of justice so rooted in the tradition and conscience of our people as to be ranked as fundamental" and thus "implicit in the concept of ordered liberty."[2] Most of the rights protected from federal infringement by the Bill of Rights have been deemed part of this "concept of ordered liberty" and therefore protected from infringement by state and local government.

Second, the prohibitions on infringements of individual rights in the Constitution apply to governmental bodies, but not to private individuals. On its face, nothing in the Constitution would prevent a private employer from denying its employees any or all constitutional rights. However, constitutional protections apply to any "state action," a concept that has been interpreted to cover the actions of private individuals and businesses where the state compelled or significantly participated in the private conduct. For example, in *Burton v. Wilmington Parking Authority,* 365 U.S. 715 (1961), the discriminatory actions of a restaurant which operated as an "integral part" of a public parking building in which it was located were held to be "state actions" and therefore prohibited by the Fourteenth Amendment's equal protection provisions. Further, as noted earlier, Congress has broad powers under the Commerce Clause to legislate civil rights protections.

## *Privileges and Immunities*

Section 2 of Article IV of the Constitution provides, in part, that "The citizens of each State shall be entitled to all privileges and immunities of the several states." The basic import of the **Privileges and Immunities Clause** is that, in general, a state cannot discriminate against citizens of another state solely because of their foreign citizenship. Thus a state cannot prohibit travel by nonresidents within its borders, nor can a state deny nonresident plaintiffs access to its court system.

The Privileges and Immunities Clause is, however, subject to many judicially imposed limitations. For example, a state law may—within reasonable limits—subject nonresidents to certain limitations if the law involves protection of a matter of "legitimate local interest." For example, because state universities are essentially supported by taxation of residents, and also because of the interest that residents have in such schools, the charging of higher tuition for nonresident students does not violate the Privileges and Immunities Clause.[3] And since corporations are *not* "citizens" within the meaning of this clause, nonresident corporations can be subject to higher tax rates than those applicable to domestic corporations. (Such rates cannot, however, be so high as to be "confiscatory" in nature—that is, enacted largely as a punishment for the privilege of doing business—or be so onerous as to effectively exclude nonresidents from doing business within the state, for such taxation would likely violate both the Due Process and Commerce Clauses of the Constitution.)

In the following case, the U.S. Supreme Court was called upon to determine whether an Alaskan statute violated the Privileges and Immunities Clause.

---

[2]*Palko v. Connecticut,* 302 U.S. 319 (1937).

[3]*Johns v. Redeker,* 406 F.2d 878 (1969). (The U.S. Supreme Court let this decision stand by denying certiorari.)

## Hicklin v. Orbeck
U.S. Supreme Court,
437 U.S. 518 (1978)

Alaska passed a statute in 1972 (known as "Alaska Hire") for the avowed purpose of reducing unemployment within the state. The key provision of the statute required all employers engaged in specific lines of work to hire qualified Alaskan residents in preference to nonresidents. The types of employment covered by the act were, for the most part, activities relating to "oil and gas leases, and easements or right-of-way permits for oil or gas pipeline purposes." To implement the act, persons who had resided in the state for a minimum period of one year were furnished "resident cards" as proof of their preferred status.

Hicklin and others, plaintiffs, were nonresidents who had worked on the Trans-Alaska pipeline for short periods until late 1975, when the act was first enforced. In 1976, when plaintiffs were refused employment on the pipeline, they brought this action against Orbeck, the state official charged with enforcement of Alaska Hire, contending that the act violated the Privileges and Immunities Clause. The Supreme Court of Alaska, by a vote of three to two, held that the law was constitutional. Plaintiffs appealed.

**Decision:** The Alaska Hire Law is unconstitutional. Accordingly, the U.S. Supreme Court reversed the judgment of the Supreme Court of Alaska.

The Privileges and Immunities Clause prohibits a state from discriminating against nonresidents unless it can show that there is a "substantial reason" for the discriminatory treatment. While it may be that the alleviation of unemployment is, in general, a substantial reason for the discrimination against nonresident job-seekers, Alaska Hire still violates the Privileges and Immunities Clause. The basic reason for this conclusion is the fact that the evidence shows that the "primary evil" that the law was meant to alleviate—i.e., Alaska's high unemployment rate—was not primarily caused by an influx of nonresidents. Rather, the high unemployment simply resulted from the fact that a substantial number of its residents—especially Eskimo and Indian residents—were unemployed because of their lack of education or geographical remoteness from job opportunities. Because Alaska Hire does not strike at the heart of the real causes of the unemployment, its discriminatory provisions against nonresidents cannot be justified under the "substantial reason" doctrine.

## *Freedom of Religion*

The First Amendment contains two clauses protecting freedom of religion. It provides that "Congress shall make no law [1] respecting an establishment of religion, or [2] prohibiting the free exercise thereof." Although the Establishment and Free Exercise Clauses overlap (and sometimes even conflict), they clearly create two separate guarantees. Both guarantees provide that the government's role is to be one of "benevolent neutrality," neither advancing nor inhibiting religion.

**Establishment Clause:** A large part of the metaphorical "wall" between church and state arises from the **Establishment Clause,** which prohibits the government from establishing a state religion and, according to the Supreme Court, from financially supporting religion, becoming actively involved in religion, or favoring one religion over another.

The most controversial manifestation of the Supreme Court's view of the Establishment Clause is probably the "school prayer" case, *Engel v. Vitale,* 370 U.S. 421 (1962). The New York State Board of Regents had written a nondenominational prayer to be recited by students in school on a voluntary basis. The Supreme Court found an Establishment Clause violation, saying, in part, that "the constitutional prohibition against laws respecting an establishment of a religion must at least mean that in this country it is no part of the business of government to compose official prayers for any group of the American people to recite as a part of a religious program carried on by any government."

An attempt to circumvent *Engel v. Vitale* by institution of a "moment of silence" in the public schools "for meditation or voluntary prayer" was declared unconstitutional in the recent case, *Wallace v. Jaffree,* 105 S.Ct. 2479 (1985). The legislative history of the law in question made it clear that its primary purpose was to promote religion.

When a state or federal law is challenged as violative of the Establishment Clause, it will be evaluated by a three-pronged test. First, the court will ask whether the law has a secular (nonreligious) purpose. If there is no such purpose, the law is invalid. Even if the law has a secular purpose, the court will ask, second, whether its *primary* purpose is to advance or inhibit religion. If the answer is in the affirmative, the law is unconstitutional. If the answer is in the negative, the court will ask, third, whether the law fosters excessive government entanglement with religion. Such entanglement might include government evaluation of religious practices, extensive government involvement in church finances and operations, or government attempts to classify what is religious and what is not. Presence of such entanglement obviously indicates an Establishment Clause violation.

A recent Establishment Clause case affecting business is *Estate of Thornton v. Caldor, Inc.,* 105 S.Ct. 2914 (1985), which involved a Connecticut statute guaranteeing every employee who "states that a particular day of the week is observed as his Sabbath," the right not to work on his chosen day. Because the law gave an absolute preference to the worker's religious practice, no matter how severe the hardship to the employer, the Court held that its primary purpose was to advance religion. Federal law validly requires that employers subject to Title VII, discussed in our later chapter on employment law, make "reasonable accommodations" for the religious practices of employees. But an absolute preference is invalid.

Finally, although the trend across the country is for states to repeal so-called **blue laws**—statutes and ordinances that limit or prohibit the carrying on of specified business activities on Sunday—such laws are generally upheld in the courts on the ground that the primary purpose of such statutes is the furtherance of legitimate social or economic ends, which affect religious beliefs and practices only incidentally.

**Free Exercise Clause:** The general thrust of this clause is to guarantee to all persons the right of religious belief and the freedom to practice their beliefs without governmental interference. The government may not single out any particular religion for discrimination. In order to claim the protection of the Free Exercise Clause, a plaintiff must normally prove that he is a sincere adherent of an established religion and that a fundamental tenet of that religion is at stake in the case. These requirements weed out spurious, insincere, and trivial claims.

Under the Free Exercise Clause, plaintiffs, frequently belonging to religious minorities, have paved the way for the religious freedoms we all enjoy. For example, in *West Virginia State Board of Education v. Barnette,* 319 U.S. 624 (1943), the Supreme Court held that a board of education requirement that students salute the flag and say the pledge of allegiance was unconstitutional as applied to plaintiff Jehovah's Witnesses. The court said: "If there is any fixed star in our constitutional constellation, it is that no official, high or petty, can prescribe what shall be orthodox in politics, nationalism, religion, or other matters of opinion, or force citizens to confess by word or act their faith therein. If there are any circumstances which permit an exception, they do not now occur to us."

In order to overcome the very important interest in free exercise of religious beliefs, the government must demonstrate that an unusually important interest is at stake (denominated in various cases "compelling," "of the highest order," or "overriding") and that granting an exemption to plaintiff will do substantial harm to that interest. The government has succeeded in cases requiring vaccinations for children against their parents' religious objections in furtherance of public health, in cases requiring medical treatment for children over their parents' objections where such treatment was necessary to save the child's life, and in cases banning the handling of poisonous snakes in religious services.

Recently, the Supreme Court reduced the government's burden where incidental effects of government programs interfere with religious practices but do not coerce individuals to act contrary to their religious beliefs. In such cases, the government need not show a "compelling justification" in order to prevail. Thus, in *Oregon v. Smith,* 58 U.S.L.W. 4433 (1990), the Supreme Court held that a state's interest in fighting drugs validated its decision to deny unemployment compensation on grounds of "misconduct" to two men who had been fired by a private employer because they ingested peyote, a hallucinogenic drug, for sacramental purposes at a ceremony of their native American church. The balancing test approach was held inapplicable to an across-the-board criminal prohibition on a particular form of conduct.

## Freedom of Speech

None of the many rights Americans enjoy is protected more than freedom of speech. The First Amendment provides that "Congress shall make no law . . . abridging the freedom of speech." Unlike citizens in so many other countries, we may freely criticize public officials and the laws of our government.

The **Free Speech Clause** protects messages that are both oral and written. It protects symbolic action, such as picketing and the wearing of black armbands (although conduct is frequently given slightly less protection than true speech). The First Amendment even protects the giving of money to political campaigns as a form of speech.

Implicit in the freedom to speak is the freedom not to speak in favor of causes we do not support. In the recent *Pacific Gas & Electric Co. v. Public Utilities Commission of California,* 475 U.S. 1 (1986), the Supreme Court overturned on free speech grounds a California Public Utilities Commission order which required a privately owned utility to include in its billing envelopes speech of a consumer group with which the utility disagreed. The court found that the order impermissibly burdened the utility's freedom not to speak which is protected because all speech inherently involves choices of what to say and what to leave unsaid.

**Scope of Protection:** Of course, like our other freedoms, the freedom of speech is not absolute. In the famous words of Justice Holmes, one is not free to yell "Fire" in a crowded theatre. Among the relatively few types of speech that are not protected by the First Amendment are obscenity, defamatory statements, and so-called "fighting words." Obscene speech is viewed as having no true value in a democratic society.

Defamatory statements, which by definition are untrue statements which injure another's reputation, similarly have nothing to contribute to a public debate of the issues in a free society. The impact of the freedom of speech on the tort of defamation is discussed in Chapter 8. "Fighting words" are epithets which by their nature are likely to lead to an outbreak of violence. Their minimal social value is viewed as outweighed by the danger to society. However, the "fighting words" exception is narrowly construed. As the Supreme Court said in *Cox v. Louisiana,* 379 U.S. 536 (1965), "Mere expression of unpopular views cannot be held to be a breach of peace." Sometimes the government has an obligation to provide protection for the speakers for unpopular positions.

Speech which is critical of the government, no matter how disrespectful or "unpatriotic," has generally been protected under the First Amendment. For example, the Supreme Court recently struck down a law making it a criminal act to "desecrate" the American flag. In *Texas v. Johnson,*[4] the Court invalidated the conviction of a communist protestor who had burned the flag at a Republican National Convention, saying, in part: "If there is a bedrock principle underlying the First Amendment, it is that the Government may not prohibit the expression of an idea simply because society finds the idea itself offensive or disagreeable." Indeed, in *Brandenburg v. Ohio,* 395 U.S. 444 (1969), the Court held that even speech calling for the overthrow of the government or other illegal action is protected unless it is "directed to inciting or producing *imminent* lawless action and is *likely* to incite or produce such action."

Although the government cannot regulate the content of our speech, it can impose reasonable **time, place, and manner** restrictions on that speech. A city cannot tell the Ku Klux Klan it can never hold a rally, but it can prohibit the Klan from holding a rally in a hospital zone at 2:00 a.m.

**Commercial Speech:** In recent years the Supreme Court has decided that **commercial speech**—speech intended primarily to propose a commercial transaction—is protected by the First Amendment, though not quite to the extent that political speech is protected. Thus, in *Virginia Board of Pharmacy v. Virginia Citizens Consumers Council,* 425 U.S. 748 (1976), the Supreme Court struck down a ban on advertising the prices of over-the-counter drugs. Absolute prohibitions on advertising by lawyers were invalidated in *Bates v. Arizona State Bar,* 433 U.S. 350 (1977). Prohibitions on the posting of "for sale" signs on real estate were found violative of the Free Speech Clause in *Linmark Associates, Inc. v. Township of Willingboro,* 431 U.S. 85 (1977), though they

---

[4] 109 S.Ct. 2533 (1989). The decision was so controversial that Congress debated passing a constitutional amendment to override it. Ultimately, Congress confined itself to a statute prohibiting flag desecration for any purpose. That statute was also declared unconstitutional by the Supreme Court.

had the purpose of preventing "white flight" from racially integrated neighborhoods.

According to the Supreme Court, commercial speech is protectable primarily because of the informational value it has for the listener (or reader). Drug consumers in the *Virginia Pharmacy* case could not learn, before the advertising ban was struck down, that variations of price of up to 600 percent existed commonly among competing stores. Information about the prices lawyers charge was viewed as valuable consumer information in *Bates*. Obviously, false advertising carries no informational value to the listener and is therefore unprotected by the First Amendment. The same may be said for speech proposing illegal transactions.

The Supreme Court recently has somewhat curtailed the protection accorded commercial speech. The current standards for such protection are discussed in the following case.

---

### Board of Trustees of the State University of New York v. Fox
U.S. Supreme Court,
109 S.Ct. 3028 (1989)

The State University of New York (SUNY) adopted a rule (66-156) for its dormitories which banned private commercial enterprises other than to provide food, legal beverages, books, vending, linen supply, laundry, and a few other specified services. American Future Systems, Inc. (AFS), sells housewares such as china and crystal to college students by demonstrating and offering products for sale to groups of ten or more prospective buyers at gatherings assembled and hosted by one of the buyers (for which the host or hostess receives some award). Fox, a student at SUNY's Cortland campus, was hosting one of these "Tupperware-type parties" when campus police asked the AFS representative to leave and arrested her when she refused to do so. Fox and other students sued, claiming that the rule violated the First Amendment. The trial court upheld the rule. The court of appeals reversed, noting that rule 66-156 was not the least restrictive means of advancing the state's interests. The Supreme Court granted certiorari and addressed the commercial speech issue in its opinion.

**Decision:** Reversed. The rule is upheld, as the Supreme Court eliminates the "least restrictive means" element from its test for commercial speech regulation. Instead, the Court asks three questions. First, does the commercial speech concern lawful activity and is it not misleading? If the answer is "yes," as it is in this case, the speech is entitled to some level of protection. Second, is the asserted government interest substantial? If the answer is "yes," as it is in this case (given the school's interest in promoting an educational rather than a commercial atmosphere, in preventing commercial exploitation of students, in preserving residential tranquility, and in promoting safety and security), then the Court must advance to step three to determine whether the regulation burdens substantially more speech than is necessary to further the government's legitimate interest. In this regard, the government need not prove that its regulation is the "least restrictive means" of accomplishing its goal, but only that there is a reasonable "fit" between the government's end and the means chosen to accomplish that end. The means should be narrowly tailored to achieve the desired object, but within that limitation it is left to governmental decisionmakers to judge what manner of regulation may best be employed. The school met that test in this case. The regulation is upheld. ■

---

**Corporate Speech:** The First Amendment does not protect only the speech of individuals. It also protects the speech of corporations, though perhaps not to as great a degree. Like commercial speech, corporate speech is protected because of the informational value it carries. Whether commercial or political in nature, the speech of a corporation adds to the public pool of information and to the public debate on issues of importance. Thus, in *First National Bank of Boston v. Bellotti,* 435 U.S. 765 (1978), the Supreme Court struck down a state criminal statute which prohibited expenditures by business corporations for the purpose of influencing the vote on state referendum proposals not "materially affecting" any of the business of the corporation, noting: "The inherent worth of the speech in terms of its capacity for informing the public does not depend upon the identity of its source, whether corporation, association, union, or individual."

## *Equal Protection*

The Fourteenth Amendment was passed in 1868, shortly after the Civil War. It states, in part, that "No State shall . . . deny to any person within its jurisdiction the equal protection of the laws." Although no provision of the Constitution explicitly mentions equal protection in connection with the *federal* government, the concept has been held to be implicit in the Fifth Amendment's Due Process Clause. Thus, no government, state or federal, may deny individuals or companies equal protection of the laws.

Because virtually every law and regulation involves distinctions and differences—e.g., applying to some industries, but not to others; applying to larger companies, but not to smaller ones; giving benefits to older people, but not to younger ones—many legal questions involving the **Equal Protection Clause** arise. The Supreme Court has used different formulations to gauge the legality of different types of distinctions. Three major types of distinctions that we shall discuss are (1) those involved in economic and social regulation, (2) those based on "suspect criteria," and (3) those involving gender discrimination.

**Economic and Social Regulations:** The Supreme Court realizes that legislatures must make distinctions in passing economic and social legislation. Only the poor need welfare; the rich do not. Some industries cause pollution; others do not. Some jobs imperil the safety of workers; others do not. Therefore, the Supreme Court uses a fairly lax standard for economic and social legislation when equal protection challenges are raised. If the distinction at issue bears a "rational relationship to a legitimate government interest," it will be sustained. Only if no reasonable state of facts can be conceived of to justify it, and it is clearly a display of arbitrary power and not a matter of judgment, will such a distinction be invalidated on equal protection grounds.

To decide that the "rational relationship" test applies is almost to decide the case. There is such a strong presumption of reasonableness that discriminations in economic and social legislation are almost always upheld. Distinctions need not be drawn with "mathematical nicety" nor must a legislature attack all aspects of a problem at once. Thus, a law requiring operators of "flea markets" who leased space to persons wishing to sell automobiles to have a type of license that persons who leased land to regular car dealers need not have, constituted permissible discrimination. The state has a legitimate interest in preventing fraud, and it is rational to presume that fraud will be a bigger problem in a "flea market" than in a stationary car dealership which will likely be there when a defrauded customer goes back to complain.[5] Similarly, in *Minnesota Clover Leaf Creamery Co.,* 449 U.S. 456 (1981), a Minnesota statute which banned the retail sale of milk in nonreturnable, nonrefillable plastic containers, but which permitted such sale in paperboard containers, was sustained. Whether or not elimination of the plastic milk jug would in fact encourage the use of environmentally superior containers was not the issue, the Supreme Court held. "The Equal Protection Clause is satisfied by our conclusion that the Minnesota legislature could rationally have decided" that it would.

However, this is not to say that challenges under the rational relationship test are never successful. In *City of Cleburne v. Cleburne Living Center,* 473 U.S. 432 (1985), for example, plaintiffs wished to establish a closely supervised and highly regulated home for the mentally retarded in Cleburne. The city required a special use permit for "homes for the lunatic" and denied plaintiff's request. The Court found that the denial was not based on any valid concern for public safety, but on an irrational prejudice against the retarded, and sustained plaintiffs' equal protection claim.

**Suspect Criteria:** If a law discriminates against "discrete and insular minorities," it utilizes "suspect criteria" under the Equal Protection Clause and is very much subject to challenge. Suspect criteria naturally include classifications based on race, but persons of Mexican ancestry and occasionally aliens have been protected also.

A law is also highly suspect if it discriminates among people regarding the exercise of certain "fundamental rights" (including freedom of association, right to travel interstate, right of privacy, right to vote, and freedom of speech).

Such laws undergo "strict scrutiny" and will be invalidated under the equal protection concept unless the challenged distinctions serve a *compelling*

---

[5]*North Dixie Theatre, Inc. v. McCullion,* 613 F.Supp. 1339 (S.D. Ohio 1985).

*state interest.* This is a very difficult test to meet, and almost always leads to invalidation of the discrimination. In *Korematsu v. United States,* 323 U.S. 214 (1944), the Supreme Court found a compelling government interest in the need for war-time national security, and therefore upheld discrimination against persons of Japanese ancestry in the form of relocation away from the West Coast and internment in prisonlike camps. History shows that this relocation was based on fear and prejudice rather than any real danger to security. The Supreme Court will henceforth be very careful before it finds that an interest justifies racial discrimination.

For example, in *Palmore v. Sidoti,* 466 U.S. 429 (1984), the Court invalidated the action of a trial judge who took a child away from its mother, who was white, because she married a black man. The Court held that the trial court's decision to shield the child from "the reality of private biases" was an insufficient justification for a racial classification. Only in the area of "affirmative action," which we discuss later in the chapter on employment law, has the Supreme Court found interests (e.g., remedying past intentional discrimination, achieving diversity in college admissions) sufficient to justify a race-based classification. Occasionally the courts find government interests sufficient to justify a classification that discriminates in matters of fundamental rights, but this is also relatively rare.

If a classification is neutral on its face and in its administration, yet unintentionally produces a racially disproportionate impact (e.g., a verbal job test is failed in disproportionately high percentages by blacks), **de facto discrimination** exists. However, *de facto* discrimination is judged by the relatively lax "rational relationship" test, rather than by the "strict scrutiny" applied to intentional racial classifications.

The following case involves strict scrutiny of a classification which discriminates against a fundamental right—the right to travel.

---

### Attorney General of New York v. Soto-Lopez
U.S. Supreme Court, 106 S.Ct. 2317 (1986)

The New York Constitution and Civil Service Law grant a civil service employment preference, in the form of points added to examination scores, to New York residents who are honorably discharged veterans of the Armed Forces, served during time of war, and were New York residents when they entered military service. Appellee Army veterans, long-time New York residents, passed the New York City civil service examinations but were denied the veterans' preference because they were not New York residents when they joined the Army. They then brought this action in federal district court, alleging that the requirement that they had to have been New York residents when they joined the military violated the Equal Protection Clause of the Fourteenth Amendment and their constitutional right to travel. The district court dismissed the suit. The court of appeals reversed. The New York Attorney General (appellant) appealed the case to the Supreme Court.

**Decision:** In affirming the appellate court's decision to strike down the statute, the Supreme Court noted that a state law which burdens a fundamental constitutional right will be subjected to strict scrutiny and cannot be upheld unless it serves a compelling state interest. The right to travel (migrate) from state to state is such a fundamental constitutional right.

New York's proffered justifications for the fixed point of residence requirement—the encouragement of New York residents to join the armed services, the compensation of residents for service in time of war by helping them reestablish themselves upon coming home, inducement of veterans to return to New York after wartime service, and the employment of a "uniquely valuable class of public servants" who possess useful experience acquired through their military service—could all be advanced by a law giving a veterans' preference to *all* otherwise qualified veterans regardless of original point of residence. ■

---

**Gender Discrimination:** Although the Supreme Court has not been completely consistent, it has tended to treat gender as a "quasi-suspect" classification. It has not required the demonstration of a compelling government interest to justify a gender-based classification. Instead, the government must prove that the classification bears a "*substantial* relationship to an *important* government interest." Thus, this is a middle-tier test, stricter than the mere rational relationship test, but not requiring the strict scrutiny of a racial classification.

In *Arizona v. Norris,* 463 U.S. 1073 (1983), the Supreme Court struck down an Arizona state employees' retirement plan which paid women smaller monthly benefits than men because actuarial tables predicted that the average woman would live longer than the average man. The plan was deemed unfair to the plaintiff who could not count on living as long as the "average" female.

One of the most controversial topics in the realm of gender discrimination law today is whether women doing jobs that are different than those done by men but of *comparable worth* to the employer should be paid the same as the men. This issue is addressed in our chapter on employment law.

## *Due Process of Law*

The Fifth Amendment, applicable to the federal government, provides in part that "No person shall . . . be deprived of life, liberty, or property without due process of law." The Fourteenth Amendment contains a clause imposing the same limitation upon state action. As interpreted by the courts, the concept of due process can be divided into two separate but related doctrines: substantive due process and procedural due process.

**Substantive Due Process:** At one time the doctrine of **substantive due process** was a strong bastion protecting businesses from government regulation in the form of social and economic reform. In one leading case, a law limiting the number of hours bakers could work was found violative of substantive due process because it unreasonably interfered with "the freedom of master and employee to contract in relation to their employment." Today, however, this doctrine which once invalidated an entire range of social legislation has a completely different status.

*Economic and Social Legislation:* In matters of economic and social legislation, the doctrine of substantive due process has been completely eviscerated as a protective device for business. When such a law is challenged today, the courts simply ask whether it can be viewed as "arbitrary or irrational." The courts presume such laws to be valid, and will uphold them unless no reasonable state of facts can be conceived to support them. Indeed, the courts virtually rubberstamp legislative judgments in this area.

In *Duke Power Co. v. Carolina Environmental Study Group, Inc.,* 438 U.S. 59 (1978), for example, the Supreme Court addressed a substantive due process challenge to the Price-Anderson Act, which placed a statutory limit of $560 million on the liability of nuclear power plant licensees. Although the trial court found the limitation unconstitutional, as not rationally related to potential losses and as tending to encourage irresponsibility in safety matters, the Supreme Court reversed because it deemed the act not "arbitrary or irrational." The Court found the risk of accident "exceedingly small" and noted that Congress had indicated a willingness to appropriate public funds if losses exceeded $560 million. This was a standard piece of economic legislation that should be presumed valid.

*Individual Rights:* In recent years the doctrine of substantive due process has been used increasingly to establish individual rights. Development in this area has been on a case-by-case basis, keyed to a rather vague standard—whether the right involved is of such a character that it cannot be denied without violating those "fundamental principles of liberty and justice which lie at the base of all our civil and political institutions."[6] Under this standard, substantive due process has been used to affirm a right to privacy in matters of birth control, to assert family rights when zoning restrictions have prohibited related persons from living together, and to promulgate rights to reasonably safe conditions, freedom from unnecessary bodily restraints, and minimally adequate training for the mentally ill. Most controversially, this doctrine played a part in the *Roe v. Wade* decision restricting the power of the states to regulate abortions.[7] In recent years the Supreme Court has begun giving the states increased latitude in restricting abortions,[8] underscoring the somewhat haphazard development of the law in this area.

**Procedural Due Process:** The primary purpose of the doctrine of **procedural due process** is to prevent the federal and state governments from depriving individuals of certain basic rights in an unfair or arbitrary manner. While life, liberty, and property can

---

[6] *Griswold v. Connecticut,* 381 U.S. 479 (1965) (Justice Goldberg, concurring).

[7] 410 U.S. 113 (1973).

[8] For example, *Webster v. Reproductive Health Services,* 109 S.Ct. 3040 (1989).

be taken in certain circumstances, the main thrust of the Due Process Clause—and the case law that has resulted under it—is that such deprivation should occur only by virtue of judicially acceptable proceedings. The underlying philosophy is aptly summed up in this statement:

> "Due process of law" implies at least a conformity with natural and inherent principles of justice, and forbids that one man's property, or right to property, shall be taken for the benefit of another, or for the benefit of the state, without compensation, and that no one shall be condemned in his person or property without an opportunity of being heard in his own defense.[9]

The guarantee springing from procedural due process extends to both criminal and civil proceedings. In criminal proceedings, the courts are especially solicitous of the rights of a defendant facing a deprivation of liberty. Key concerns include adequacy of notice of the charges, representation by counsel, fair selection of the jury, the ability to confront and cross-examine witnesses and to present evidence, and the impartiality of the judge. The statute under which a criminal charge is brought must also not be so vague as to fail to prescribe a "reasonable standard of guilt." In *City of Columbus v. Thompson*, 25 Ohio St.2d 25 (1971), the defendant was charged under a municipal "suspicious person" ordinance, which defined a suspicious person as one "who wanders about the streets or other public ways or who is found abroad at late or unusual hours of the night without any visible or lawful business and who does not give satisfactory account of himself." The Ohio Supreme Court held the ordinance violated procedural due process by leaving the public "uncertain as to the conduct it prohibits" and leaving "judges and jurors free to decide, without any legally fixed standards, what is prohibited and what is not in each particular case."

Standards need not be so stringent when property, rather than life or liberty is at stake. Still, in our civilized society the basic rights to notice, hearing,[10] and an impartial decisionmaker are valued. In a recent civil case, for example, the Supreme Court held that an insurance company's due process rights were violated by a decision of the Alabama Supreme Court which adopted a new theory of recovery at the same time that it sustained a very large punitive damages verdict against the company. The judge who wrote the opinion, it turned out, was a plaintiff in two similar cases and would directly benefit from the decision. The Supreme Court wrote that it violates the Due Process Clause "to subject [a person's] liberty or property to the judgment of a court the judge of which has a direct, personal, substantial, pecuniary interest in reaching a conclusion against him in his case."[11]

Many due process cases involve actions of government agencies which adversely affect the economic interests of individuals and companies. An illustrative case appears in the next chapter on administrative law. In these and other procedural due process cases, the proper approach is first to determine whether plaintiff has a protectable life, liberty, or property interest at stake. If so, then the court must ask how much "process is due" under all the circumstances. The more serious the potential deprivation, the more elaborate the protections the courts will require. The following case is a recent Supreme Court pronouncement on the matter.

---

[9] *Holden v. Hardy*, 169 U.S. 366 (1898).

[10] The matter of a fair opportunity to be heard under the Due Process Clause was the key issue in *Helicopteros Nacionales de Colombia v. Hall* in Chapter 2.

[11] *Aetna Life Ins. Co. v. Lavoie*, 475 U.S. 813 (1986).

---

## Cleveland Board of Education v. Loudermill
U.S. Supreme Court,
470 U.S. 532 (1985)

The Cleveland Board of Education informed Loudermill, a security guard, that his employment was being terminated because he had lied on his employment application about a 1968 grand larceny conviction. Loudermill was not afforded an opportunity to respond to the charge of dishonesty or to challenge his dismissal. He did file an appeal with the Cleveland Civil Service Commission which appointed a referee who eventually held a hearing. Loudermill argued that he didn't state on the employment application that he had been convicted of a felony because he thought the 1968 conviction was a misdemeanor. The referee recommended reinstatement. But, after oral argument, the Commission upheld the dismissal.

*(continued)*

The Cleveland Board also fired Donnelly, a bus mechanic, because he had failed an eye examination. He was offered a chance to retake the exam, but did not do so. Like Loudermill, Donnelly appealed to the Civil Service Commission, which ordered Donnelly reinstated, though without back pay. The procedures before the Civil Service Commission for both Loudermill and Donnelly took around a year to run their course.

Both Loudermill and Donnelly challenged the constitutionality of the dismissal procedures in federal district court. The trial court ruled against them. The court of appeals reversed, finding that both men had been denied due process. The Cleveland Board of Education (petitioner) brought the case before the Supreme Court.

---

**Decision:** In affirming the lower court's finding of a due process violation, the Supreme Court noted that a state cannot deprive an individual of a "property right" without due process of law. Respondents had a property right in their jobs because state civil service law gave them an expectation of continued employment "during good behavior and efficient service."

The question then became how much process was due the respondents. The formality required will vary with the circumstances. Where, as here, an employee faces the prospect of unemployment with its attendant difficulties, he should be given at least (1) notice of the charges against him, and (2) an opportunity to tell his side of the story before termination. Such minimal protection would avoid many erroneous terminations. The Court did not require more than this *before* termination, because it did not wish to intrude to an unwarranted extent on the government's interest in quickly removing an unsatisfactory employee. ■

---

**Takings Clause:** An integral part of due process is the Takings Clause of the Fifth Amendment, applicable to all levels of government, which provides that private property shall not "be taken for public use without just compensation." Thus, the government may take title to private land only when it seeks to use it for a public purpose and pays fair value. A classic example would be a state's use of its **eminent domain** power to seize lands (from owners unwilling to sell) for the building of a needed road or dam.

A difficult question that is of vital concern to business is whether a "taking" that requires the government to pay fair compensation can occur not only when the government takes title to private property, but also when the government so heavily regulates the use of private property as to deprive its owners of the use of their land. For example, in *Nollan v. California Coastal Commission,* 107 S.Ct. 3141 (1987), the Supreme Court held that a California Coastal Commission requirement that plaintiff landowners permit the public an easement to pass across a section of plaintiffs' beach as a condition of their being allowed to demolish a structure on their land and replace it with a house, was a compensable taking rather than a mere regulation. On the other hand, in *Keystone Bituminous Coal Assoc. v. DeBenedictis,* 107 S.Ct. 1232 (1987), the Court held that a law prohibiting underground mining that might cause subsidence damage to buildings above was a proper police power regulation rather than a taking of the mining companies' property.

Drawing the line between a mere regulation and a regulation that goes so far as to constitute a "taking" is difficult. If the regulation results in a long-term government occupation of land, it will probably be declared a taking. If there is no such occupation, the Supreme Court balances several factors, including whether the value of the owner's property (whether in terms of profitability or long-range investment potential) is significantly decreased, whether the regulated use constitutes a "nuisance," whether the law benefits many people in an important way, and whether the law benefits the property owner as well as the community.

## SUMMARY

Our magnificent Constitution performs many functions. It prevents the undue concentration of power by dividing the authority of the government both vertically and horizontally. Vertically, the federal government is supreme, but is limited to certain enumerated powers set out in the Constitution. All other powers are reserved to the states and their subordinate units of government.

Horizontally, the vast authority of the federal government is separated into the legislative, executive, and judicial branches of government. A system of checks and balances prevents undue influence of any one branch. Although the president of the United States is probably the most powerful person in the world, executive authority to act must be rooted in the Constitution or in congressional acts. If the president acts without authority, or if Congress passes acts inconsistent with the Constitution, the judiciary, pursuant to the doctrine of judicial review, will rein them in. The Constitution, after all, means what the Supreme Court says it means.

The Constitution also protects businesses and individuals from undue government encroachment. We enjoy more freedoms than citizens of any other country, including freedom of religion, freedom of speech, equal protection under the law, and due process of law.

## KEY TERMS

**Delegated powers**
**Reserved powers**
**State police power**
**Full Faith and Credit Clause**
**Judicial review**
**Executive orders**
**Doctrine of incorporation**
**Due process of law**
**Privileges and Immunities Clause**
**Establishment Clause**
**Blue laws**
**Free Speech Clause**
**Time, place, and manner restrictions**
**Commercial speech**
**Equal Protection Clause**
***De facto* discrimination**
**Substantive due process**
**Procedural due process**
**Eminent Domain**

## QUESTIONS AND PROBLEMS

**1.** Blanco was arrested at his apartment complex for disorderly conduct after he refused numerous requests by neighbors, the apartment manager, and police to turn down his stereo, which he had positioned in such a manner as to direct the sound of his rock music toward the swimming pool area of the complex. He had turned the stereo's volume up loud enough to cause vibrations in nearby apartments and to force his musical preferences on many neighbors who did not share them. What is the source, if any, of the city's authority to arrest Blanco? (*Blanco v. State*, 761 S.W.2d 38, Tex. App. 1988.)

**2.** The Heart of Atlanta Motel (P) was a 216-room motel in downtown Atlanta, Georgia. It was not located near a state line, though it was near two interstate highways and two state highways. It did extensive advertising in other states, and 75 percent of its guests were from outside Georgia. P refused to rent rooms to blacks, a practice which Congress outlawed by passage of Title II of the Civil Rights Act of 1964. P sued, claiming that the law was unconstitutional because Congress had no authority to regulate such a motel. Discuss. (*Heart of Atlanta Motel v. U.S.* 379 U.S. 241, 1964.)

**3.** New York passed a law requiring every drug prescription form to have two signature lines, one stating "dispense as written" and one stating "substitution permissible." If the latter line is signed, the doctor must tell the patient that the pharmacist will substitute a (generally cheaper) generic drug for the normal "name brand" drug if the FDA has determined the generic drug to be a bioequivalent substitute. Pharmacists who do not wish to dispense the generic drug challenge the law as unduly burdening interstate commerce. Should this claim prevail? (*Pharmaceutical Society of New York v. Lefkowitz,* 586 F.2d 953, 2d Cir. 1978.)

**4.** The Montana Fish and Game Commission adopted a regulation in 1976 that set the price of combination hunting licenses at $30 for residents and $225 for nonresidents. (A combination license permitted the taking of one elk, one deer, one black bear, and a specified number of game birds.) This regulation was challenged by nonresident hunters, who contended that it violated the Privileges and Immunities Clause of the U.S. Constitution. The State of Montana contended, among other things, that the interest of Montana residents in the wildlife within its borders was a matter of state protection, and that this interest was substantial enough to justify the regulation. Do you think the U.S. Supreme Court agreed with this defense? Why or why not? (*Baldwin v. Fish and Game Commission of Montana,* 436 U.S. 371, 1978.)

**5.** Lee, an Amish carpenter and farmer who employed other Amish in his business, had trouble with the IRS because he did not deduct for or contribute to Social Security. The IRS Code provides a religious exemption for self-employed individuals which Amish can take advantage of. However, there is no such exemption for employment of others. Lee claims that he should not be required to comply with the IRS Code because religious principles prevent him and his employees from claiming Social Security benefits. Discuss the validity of Lee's claim. (*U.S. v. Lee,* 455 U.S. 252, 1982.)

**6.** Puerto Rico allowed gambling. It also allowed advertising of the gambling in the mainland United States, but not in Puerto Rico. Casinos wishing to advertise in Puerto Rico challenged the ad ban on free speech grounds. Discuss. (*Posadas de Puerto Rico Assocs. v. Tourism Company of Puerto Rico,* 478 U.S. 328, 1986.)

7. Rock Against Racism (RAR), furnishing its own sound equipment and technicians, has sponsored yearly programs of rock music in a bandshell in New York City's Central Park. Because of complaints about excessive noise from neighbors, the city adopted new guidelines under which it provided the sound equipment and sound technicians for the bandshell. Although the technician generally accommodated any band's requests regarding mixing of sound, he controlled the mix and volume. RAR sued, claiming a free speech violation. RAR argued, in part, that it should be allowed to control the sound equipment, subject to an overall volume limit. Discuss. (*Ward v. Rock Against Racism,* 109 S.Ct. 2746, 1989.)

8. For the express purpose of providing a place where teenagers can socialize with each other but not be subjected to the potentially detrimental influence of older teenagers and adults (involving alcohol, drugs, and promiscuous sex), a Dallas ordinance was passed that authorizes the licensing of "Class E" dance halls, restricting admission to persons between the ages of 14 and 18 and limiting their hours of operation. Stanglin, whose roller-skating rink and Class E dance hall share a divided floor space, filed suit contending that the age and hour restrictions violated the minors' equal protection rights. Discuss. (*City of Dallas v. Stanglin,* 109 S.Ct. 1591, 1989.)

9. A motorist was convicted of two traffic offenses in a mayor's court, and the convictions were affirmed by the state's supreme court. He appealed this judgment to the U.S. Supreme Court. He contended that he had been denied a trial before "a disinterested and impartial judicial officer as guaranteed by the Due Process clause," in view of the fact that a major part of the village's income was derived from the fines, costs, and fees imposed by the mayor's court. Do you believe that the appellant's contention is valid? Explain. (*Ward v. Village of Monroeville,* 34 L.Ed.2d 265, 1972.)

10. Ewing enrolled in a 6-year program of study at the University of Michigan which awarded an undergraduate degree and a medical degree upon successful completion of the program. To qualify for the final two years of the program a student must pass an examination known as NBME Part I. Ewing, after an undistinguished academic career, was dismissed from the university when he failed this examination with the lowest score recorded in the history of the program. He sued, seeking readmission to the program and an opportunity to retake the exam on the ground, *inter alia,* that he had a property interest in the program and that his dismissal was arbitrary and capricious in violation of due process. Evidence showed that academic authorities had given careful consideration to their decision to dismiss Ewing, but that all other students in the program who had failed NMBE Part I had been allowed to retake it, some as many as four times. Should Ewing's due process claim prevail? Discuss. (*Regents of the University of Michigan v. Ewing,* 106 S.Ct. 507, 1986.)

CHAPTER 6

# LAWMAKING BY ADMINISTRATIVE AGENCIES

In the preceding chapters we have examined the major processes by which law is made—the formulation of common-law rules by the courts, the enactment of statutes by the legislative bodies, and the interpretation of statutes by the courts. But this examination does not present the total lawmaking picture. **Administrative agencies**—the hundreds of boards and commissions existing at all levels of government—also "make law" by their continual promulgation of rules and regulations.[1]

The number of administrative agencies has grown so rapidly in the last forty years that the practical impact of local, state, and federal agencies on the day-to-day activities of individuals and businesses is today probably at least as great as that of legislatures and courts. Every day, boards and commissions across the country engage in such traditional functions as assessing properties for tax purposes, granting licenses and business permits, and regulating rates charged in the transportation and public utility industries—actions that affect millions of Americans. And, more recently, newer agencies such as the Environmental Protection Agency (EPA), Occupational Safety and Health Administration (OSHA), and the National Highway Traffic and Safety Administration (NHTSA) have spawned regulations having broad impact on the nation's businesses. Justice Jackson was right when he wrote in *FTC v. Ruberoid Co.,* 343 U.S. 470 (1952):

> The rise of administrative bodies probably has been the most significant legal trend of the last century and perhaps more values today are affected by their decisions than by those of all the courts, review of administrative decisions apart.

They also have begun to have important consequences on personal rights. . . . They have become a veritable fourth branch of the Government, which has deranged our three-branch legal theories as much as the concept of a fourth dimension unsettles our three-dimensional thinking.

## RISE OF THE ADMINISTRATIVE AGENCY

At the risk of oversimplification, we can say that two major factors are responsible for the dramatic growth of the administrative agency in recent years. First was a change in attitude toward government regulation of business. Until about 1880 the basic attitude of the state and federal governments toward business firms was that of "hands-off"—a philosophy frequently characterized by the *laissez-faire* label. The theory was that trade and commerce could best thrive in an environment free of government controls. By the end of the nineteenth century, however, various monopolistic practices had begun to surface. The passage of the Sherman Act in 1890 reflected the growing idea that a certain amount of government regulation of business was necessary to preserve minimum levels of competition.

A second, and perhaps even more powerful, reason for the emergence of the modern administrative agency is that as our nation grew and became more industrialized, many complex problems sprang up that did not easily lend themselves to traditional types of regulation. Some were posed by technological advances such as the greatly increased generation and distribution of electrical power and the rapid growth of the airline industry. Others resulted from changes in social and economic conditions, particularly the rise of the giant manufacturers and the new

---
[1] The specific activities of certain federal agencies, such as the Federal Trade Commission, are examined in more detail in Part VII.

methods by which they marketed their products on a national basis. The solution of these problems required expertise and enormous amounts of time for continuous regulation, which the courts and the legislatures simply did not possess. Faced with this situation, the legislative bodies sought new ways to regulate business (and to implement nonbusiness government programs, such as social security) that would be more workable.

## THE AGENCY—AN OVERVIEW

In order to understand the basic workings of administrative agencies and the nature of the legal problems we will discuss later, it will be helpful to see how the typical agency is created and how it receives its powers. For this purpose, the Federal Trade Commission provides a good example.

By the turn of the century, it was apparent that some firms in interstate commerce were engaging in practices that, while not violating the Sherman Act, were nonetheless felt to be of an undesirable nature. While persons who were injured by these practices were sometimes able to obtain relief in the courts, the relief was sporadic and there was no single body that could maintain surveillance of these practices on a continuing basis.

Accordingly, in 1914 Congress passed the Federal Trade Commission Act, which created the *Federal Trade Commission (FTC)* and authorized it (among other things) to determine what constituted "unfair methods of competition" in interstate commerce. Not only could the commission issue regulations defining and prohibiting such practices but, additionally, it could take action against companies that it believed to be violating such regulations.

Several federal agencies are considered to be part of the executive branch, such as the Small Business Administration (SBA), the Occupational Safety and Health Administration (OSHA), and the Federal Aviation Administration (FAA). Others are structurally independent of the executive branch; once the president's appointment of the agency chief is confirmed by the Senate, the president has no direct control over the appointee and cannot remove him or her from office. Examples of independent regulatory agencies include the FTC, the Interstate Commerce Commission (ICC), the Securities and Exchange Commission (SEC), the National Labor Relations Board (NLRB), and the Federal Reserve Board (FRB).

## LEGISLATIVE DELEGATION OF LAWMAKING POWER

The administrative agency sits somewhat uncomfortably in our tripartite (legislative-executive-judicial) system of government. An agency which is technically part of the executive branch or perhaps an "independent regulatory agency" may exert powers which entail adjudication and rulemaking as well as traditional executive functions such as investigation and enforcement. A constitutional problem arises because the Constitution in Article I, Section 1 clearly vests all legislative powers in the Congress and does not provide for delegation of those powers. Therefore, rules and regulations that have been promulgated by agencies, and that have the force and effect of law, have been challenged as resulting from an unconstitutional delegation of legislative power.

Only in a couple of cases decided during the 1930s, in which the Supreme Court found "delegation running riot," have such challenges succeeded. The courts are well aware of the very practical need for administrative agencies which was described earlier in this chapter. Therefore, they will uphold any agency ruling, regulation, or act which is within standards set forth in an enabling act *if* that act contains "reasonable standards" to guide the agency. What are reasonable standards? Courts have upheld as constitutional delegations of power "to promulgate regulations fixing prices of commodities," to institute rent controls on real property anywhere in the nation under specified circumstances, even "to issue such orders and regulations as he [the President] deems appropriate to stabilize prices, rents, wages and salaries." Indeed, the doctrine of unconstitutional delegation of legislative power appears moribund at the federal level, though it still has some vitality in litigation involving state agencies.[2]

## FUNCTIONS AND POWERS

### Ministerial and Discretionary Powers

Before addressing the legal questions that are presented when agencies' rules or orders are appealed to the courts, we will briefly look at the nature of agency activities. The activities of these government boards and commissions vary widely. The functions and

---

[2] E.g., *State v. Marana Plantations, Inc.,* 252 P.2d 87 (1953) where the power to "regulate sanitary policies in the interests of public health" was deemed too vague.

powers of some agencies are only **ministerial**—concerned with routinely carrying out duties imposed by law. Boards that issue and renew drivers' licenses fall within this category, as do the many social security offices that give information or advice to persons filing for social security benefits.

But most agencies also possess broad **discretionary powers**—powers that require the exercise of judgment and discretion in carrying out their duties. Again there is variety in the specific powers of these agencies. Some agencies' discretionary power is largely **investigative** in nature. Two examples are the authority granted to the Internal Revenue Service to inquire into the legality of deductions on taxpayers' returns and the authority of some commissions to make investigations for the purpose of recommending needed statutes to legislatures. Other agencies have largely **rulemaking powers,** with perhaps some investigative but little **adjudicatory power** (enforcement power).

"Full-fledged" federal agencies, such as the Federal Trade Commission and the National Labor Relations Board, possess all three types of power—investigative, rulemaking, and adjudicative. Thus, typically, a board will conduct investigations to determine if conditions warrant the issuance of rules to require (or prohibit) certain kinds of conduct; then it will draw up the regulations and thereafter take action against individuals or firms showing evidence of violating them. In drawing up the rules the board acts quasi-legislatively, and in enforcing them it acts quasi-judicially.

## *The Investigative Power*

Agencies frequently hold hearings before drafting regulations, and the investigative powers they possess in connection with such hearings are largely determined by the statutes by which they are created.

Normally, agencies can order the production of accounts and records relative to the problem being studied and can **subpoena** witnesses and examine them under oath. More disruptive to businesses are the powers most major agencies have to investigate whether statutes they are charged with enforcing and rules they have promulgated are being violated. The two most intrusive forms of investigative power are the subpoena and the physical search and seizure.

**Subpoena Power:** In the exercise of its adjudicatory powers, which are soon to be discussed, agencies may issue subpoenas *ad testificandum,* which are writs ordering a witness into court (in this case before the Administrative Law Judge (ALJ)).

In any sort of investigation, agencies may issue subpoenas *duces tecum,* which are writs ordering the production of books, papers, records, and documents. Agency authority is construed very broadly in this area. According to *United States v. Powell,*[3] an agency must demonstrate that (1) the investigation will be conducted for a legitimate purpose, (2) the inquiry is relevant to the purpose, (3) the information sought is not already possessed by the agency, and (4) the administrative steps required by law have been followed. "Probable cause" in the criminal sense need not be shown.

Once the agency has established an apparently valid purpose for the investigation, the burden shifts to the company or individual being investigated to show that the purpose is illegitimate (e.g., undertaken for harassment). The following case illustrates the difficulty that the target of a federal agency's investigation can have in attempting to block enforcement of such a subpoena.

[3] 379 U.S. 48 (1964).

---

### EEOC v. Peat, Marwick, Mitchell and Co.
U.S. Eighth Circuit Court of Appeals, 775 F.2d 928 (1985)

In May of 1982, the Equal Employment Opportunity Commission (EEOC) began investigating the retirement practices and policies of Peat, Marwick, Mitchell & Co. (PM) in an effort to determine whether those policies violated the Age Discrimination in Employment Act (ADEA). In accordance with its statutory investigative powers, the EEOC subpoenaed from PM documents bearing upon the relationship of members to the firm and documents relating to PM's retirement practices and policies.

PM refused to comply with the subpoena, so the EEOC initiated this enforcement proceeding in the district court. The district court ordered enforcement of the subpoena, and PM appealed.

*(continued)*

**Decision:** Enforcement of the subpoena was affirmed, as will always be the case when the investigation is authorized by Congress, is for a purpose Congress can order, and the documents sought are relevant to the inquiry. Once those elements are established, the burden shifts to the subpoena's target to prove bad faith or abuse of the court's process by the agency. That was not done here. PM claimed that it was not covered by the ADEA because its partners are not "employees" within the meaning of the act. But that is exactly the question the EEOC sought to resolve with its subpoena. The authority to investigate violations of the ADEA, clearly granted by Congress to the EEOC, includes the authority to investigate coverage under the act. ∎

---

**Search and Seizure:** Many agencies carry out on-site searches when investigating matters under their jurisdiction. From city health inspectors checking a restaurant's kitchen to OSHA employees investigating trenches at a construction site to federal mine safety inspectors probing underground coal mines, such investigations are a frequent, and, for the investigated company, troublesome occurrence.

These searches have constitutional implications, because the Warrant Clause of the Fourth Amendment protects commercial buildings as well as private homes. As the Supreme Court pointed out in *Marshall v. Barlow's, Inc.,* 436 U.S. 307 (1978), the searching of businesses by the British immediately preceding the American Revolution was particularly offensive to the colonists and provided part of the rationale for the warrant requirement.

However, we are not accorded as great an expectation of privacy for our businesses as for our homes. For example, several types of businesses, including gun dealers, stone quarries, day care centers, fishing vessels, and others have been held to be so "pervasively regulated" that they can have little or no reasonable expectation of privacy. This doctrine appears to be shrinking the protection that businesses have from warrantless searches and seizures, as the following case illustrates.

---

### New York v. Burger
U.S. Supreme Court,
107 S.Ct. 2636 (1987)

Burger owned a junkyard which dismantled cars and sold their parts. Pursuant to a New York statute [Sec. 415-a] authorizing warrantless inspections of such junkyards, police officers entered Burger's junkyard and asked to see his license and records. He replied that he did not have such documents, though they are required by the statute. The officers then announced their intent to search the premises; Burger did not object. The officers found stolen vehicles and parts. Burger was charged in state court with possession of stolen property and unregistered operation of a vehicle dismantler. He moved to suppress the evidence, claiming that the administrative inspection statute was unconstitutional. The trial court denied the motion, but the New York Court of Appeals reversed. The Supreme Court granted the state's application for certiorari.

**Decision:** Reversed. The evidence should not be suppressed. The Fourth Amendment does protect commercial enterprises as well as private residences, but the expectation of privacy is less and so is the protection, especially where the commercial property is used in "closely regulated" industries. A three-part test governs such warrantless searches. First, there must be a "substantial government interest" that informs the regulatory scheme. The epidemic in stolen cars meets that requirement. Second, the warrantless inspections must be "necessary to further the regulatory scheme." This element is met by the fact that deterrence will be provided only by unannounced, frequent inspections which might be frustrated by the requirement of a warrant. Third, the statute's inspection program, in terms of the certainty and regularity of its application must provide a "consti-

*(continued)*

tutionally adequate substitute for a warrant." In other words, the law must (a) advise the owner of the commercial premises that the search is being made pursuant to the law and has a properly defined scope, and (b) it must limit the discretion of the inspecting officers. The New York law did this by stating that businesses such as Burger's are subject to inspection by policemen on a regular basis, and by allowing inspection only during regular and usual business hours and only of records and vehicles or parts subject to the record-keeping requirement. ■

---

Obviously, warrantless searches may occur in motel lobbies, bars, and other business premises open to the public. The business has no expectation of privacy there. Additionally, the "open field" doctrine allows warrantless searches of areas which are so open to plain view that no reasonable expectation of privacy can exist. For example, the Supreme Court approved a warrantless EPA search carried out by a commercial aerial photographer flying over a 2,000-acre chemical plant consisting of numerous covered buildings with outdoor manufacturing equipment and piping conduits. Though the company had substantial ground-level security, the Court concluded that the plant was more like an open field than it was like "curtilage"—open space in the immediate vicinity of a dwelling, such as a yard. The Court noted that a commercial property owner has to expect less privacy than a homeowner so that, correspondingly, the government's latitude to conduct warrantless searches is greater.[4]

## *Rulemaking*

Much of the legislative-type activity of federal agencies is carried out through their rulemaking function. Sometimes Congress spells out the procedures for rulemaking by a particular agency in that agency's enabling statute. Sometimes the agency is left to follow the Administrative Procedure Act (APA), which the more specific statutes normally follow anyway. The APA provides a comprehensive set of procedural guidelines for a variety of agency activities. In the rulemaking area, the APA provides for two basic types—informal and formal. A third type, called hybrid rulemaking, has also developed.

**Informal Rulemaking:** Sometimes Congress will authorize informal rulemaking. To properly promulgate a rule under these procedures, the agency usually publishes a notice of the proposed rule in the Federal Register. There follows a comment period, typically of 30 days, in which any interested citizen or company may send written comments to the agency regarding the rule. Such comments might argue that the rule is unnecessary, unduly burdensome to business, does not go far enough to remedy the problem, goes too far, and the like. The agency is then supposed to digest and react to the comments, perhaps by altering or even scrapping the proposed rule. Normally the rule is modestly altered, and then published in final form in the Federal Register. At that point, it becomes effective. Ultimately it will be codified in the Code of Federal Regulations along with the rules of all other federal administrative agencies.

**Formal Rulemaking:** Formal rulemaking also involves "notice and comment," but supplements these with formal hearings at which witnesses testify and are cross-examined by interested parties. Transcripts of the testimony are preserved and become part of the public record. Formal rulemaking can be very expensive and time-consuming, but theoretically leads to especially well-considered results.

**Hybrid Rulemaking:** Hybrid rulemaking closely resembles formal rulemaking, except that there is no right to cross-examine the agency's expert witnesses, and, as we shall soon see, a different standard of review is applied by the courts if the rulemaking procedure is challenged.

**Judicial Review of Rulemaking:** Naturally some parties are likely to be aggrieved by promulgation of rules that affect them adversely. Few important rules are issued without a subsequent court challenge. Courts will invalidate rules issued pursuant to an unconstitutional delegation of legislative power (as noted above, an extremely rare occurrence) and

---

[4]*Dow Chemical Co. v. U.S.,* 426 U.S. 227 (1986).

rules that are unconstitutional (perhaps because they discriminate on the basis of race in violation of equal protection principles).

Courts will also invalidate rules not issued in accordance with applicable procedural standards. For example, if an agency engaged in informal rulemaking fails to publish a proposed version of the rule in the Federal Register so that comments may be received, the rule will likely be invalidated if challenged. The courts will countenance minor deviations from APA procedures, but major ones are risky. In particularly sensitive areas, such as rules governing nuclear power plants, some courts have required more elaborate procedures than those specified in the APA's formal rulemaking sections. However, the Supreme Court, in *Vermont Yankee Nuclear Power Corp. v. Natural Resources Defense Council*,[5] held that courts could not legally require these extra procedures.

***Standards of Review:*** In issuing rules, an agency will have to make several types of decisions. One type of decision will likely turn on a pure **question of law** regarding its powers and the scope of its charge under a law passed by Congress. Courts are experts on the law. Therefore, they have the authority to substitute their interpretations for the meaning of laws passed by Congress for the interpretations made by the agency. Nonetheless, the Supreme Court has concluded that it makes sense to give deference to the expertise developed by the agency, noting:

> When a court reviews an agency's construction of the statute which it administers, it is confronted with two questions. First, always, is the question whether Congress has spoken to the precise question at issue. If the intent of Congress is clear, that is the end of the matter; for the court, as well as the agency, must give effect to the unambiguously expressed intent of Congress.

If, however, the court determines Congress has not directly addressed the precise question at issue, the court does not simply impose its own construction on the statute, as would be necessary in the absence of an administrative interpretation. Rather, if the statute is silent or ambiguous with respect to the specific issue, the question for the court is whether the agency's answer is based on a permissible construction of the statute. . . .

We have long recognized that considerable weight should be accorded to an executive department's construction of a statutory scheme it is entrusted to administer, and the principles of deference to administrative interpretations.[6]

An agency issuing rules must also make decisions as to facts and policy. Two tests predominate review of these types of decisions. The "arbitrary and capricious" test assumes the correctness of an agency's decision, placing the burden on any challenger to prove that the decision was not simply erroneous but so far off the mark as to be arbitrary and capricious. The "substantial evidence" test requires that an agency's decision be based not just on a scintilla of evidence, but on such relevant evidence as a reasonable mind might accept as adequate to support a conclusion.

The "arbitrary and capricious" test is usually used to judge any policy decision by an agency. Findings of fact made pursuant to formal rulemaking are judged by the "substantial evidence" test. Factual determinations made in informal rulemaking are gauged by the "arbitrary and capricious" test unless an agency's authorizing act calls for use of the "substantial evidence" test. Many courts have noted that there is little practical difference in how the two tests are usually applied. Both require court deference to agency decision making, but the following case shows that such deference is not unlimited.

---

[5] 435 U.S. 519 (1978).

[6] *Chevron U.S.A., Inc. v. Natural Resources Defense Council,* 467 U.S. 837 (1984).

## Motor Vehicle Manufacturers Ass'n v. State Farm Mutual Auto. Ins. Co.
U.S. Supreme Court,
463 U.S. 29 (1983)

To improve highway safety, Congress passed the National Traffic and Motor Vehicle Safety Act of 1966, which directs the secretary of transportation or a delegee to issue motor vehicle safety standards. In 1967, the secretary's delegee, the National Highway Traffic Safety Administration (NHTSA) issued Standard 208 which required installation of seatbelts in all new automobiles. Because usage by consumers was quite low, NHTSA studied passive restraints in the form of automatic seatbelts and airbags, which it estimated could prevent approximately 12,000 deaths and over 100,000 serious injuries annually. Deadlines for implementation of the passive restraint systems were repeatedly extended until, in 1977, the secretary promulgated Modified Standard 208, which ordered a phase-in on all new cars to take place between 1982 and 1984. The secretary assumed that 60 percent of new cars would have airbags and 40 percent would have automatic seatbelts.

However, it soon became apparent that 99 percent of American cars would have *detachable* seatbelts. In light of this fact and of economic difficulties in the auto industry, the secretary began in 1981 to reconsider the passive restraint requirement of Modified Standard 208 and ultimately rescinded it.

State Farm Mutual and other insurance companies sued for review of the rescission order. The federal district court and court of appeals held the rescission to be arbitrary and capricious in violation of law. The petitioner Motor Vehicle Manufacturers Association brought the case to the Supreme Court.

**Decision:** The Supreme Court agreed with the lower courts and remanded the case to the secretary of transportation for further proceedings. Because the rules were issued pursuant to the Administrative Procedure Act's informal rulemaking procedures of §553, the Court held that the decision to rescind could be overturned only if it was "arbitrary and capricious." Although a court is not to substitute its judgment for that of the agency, it may overturn an agency action if the agency has not examined the relevant data or it has not articulated a satisfactory explanation for its action including a rational connection between the facts found and the choice made.

NHTSA's decision regarding airbags was arbitrary and capricious because it simply never considered the "airbags only" option. The 1977 judgment that airbags are cost-effective was rejected here without a single sentence discussing an airbags only alternative.

NHTSA also failed to articulate a basis for rejecting automatic seatbelts as an alternative. "[A]n agency changing its course must supply a reasoned analysis." That was not done here. ■

## *Adjudication*

Most major federal agencies also exercise substantial powers of adjudication. That is, they not only issue rules and investigate to uncover violations, they may also charge alleged violators and try them to determine whether or not a violation has actually occurred.

Because the agency is acting as legislator, policeman, prosecutor *and* judge and jury, care must be taken to avoid abuse. For that reason, the APA and the courts demand that fairly formal procedural requirements be followed.

Over the years, procedures have evolved such that a person or company brought before an administrative agency for adjudication of a charged violation will usually have the right to notice, the right to counsel, the right to present evidence, and the right to confront and cross-examine adverse witnesses.

A jury trial is not allowed, but the case is heard by an Administrative Law Judge (ALJ), who is the finder of fact in the first instance. Although the 1000 plus ALJs in the federal system are employees of the agencies whose cases they hear, they cannot be disciplined except for good cause as determined by the federal Merit System Protection Board. Thus, the ALJs exercise substantial autonomy and are seldom puppets of the agency employing them.

Under the APA, all ALJ decisions are reviewable by the employing agency, which hears the case basi-

**Figure 6.1** The Administrative Law Process

```
┌─────────────────────────────────────────┐
│ Nature of violation or investigation    │
│ (complaint).                            │
└─────────────────────────────────────────┘
                    │
                    ▼
┌─────────────────────────────────────────┐
│ Informal discussion with agency.        │
│ Process may end if party complies or    │
│ ceases and desists.                     │
└─────────────────────────────────────────┘
                    │
                    ▼
┌─────────────────────────────────────────┐
│ Hearing before administrative law       │
│ judge. Decision rendered.               │
└─────────────────────────────────────────┘
                    │
                    ▼
┌─────────────────────────────────────────┐
│ Appeal to full board of agency. Agency  │
│ may overturn decision of administrative │
│ law judge.                              │
└─────────────────────────────────────────┘
                    │
                    ▼
┌─────────────────────────────────────────┐
│ Appeal to court of appeals or district  │
│ court. Case must fulfill three          │
│ requirements: standing, ripeness, and   │
│ exhaustion of administrative remedies.  │
│ Court must hear case if it meets these  │
│ requirements; no discretionary power.   │
└─────────────────────────────────────────┘
                    │
                    ▼
┌─────────────────────────────────────────┐
│ Appeal to Supreme Court if certiorari   │
│ is granted.                             │
└─────────────────────────────────────────┘
```

cally *de novo;* that is, the agency has full power to decide the case as if it had heard it first without the ALJ. Although agencies normally adopt the findings of the ALJ, they may utterly disregard the ALJ's findings. However, the ALJ's decision becomes part of the court record if the agency decision is challenged in litigation.

Adjudication is a very influential process. Not only are findings of fact required (e.g., Did the employer consult the union before deciding to move the plant?), but the ALJ and the agency must also interpret the applicable law (e.g., Is the employer required to consult the union before deciding to move the plant?). During the Reagan administration, the NLRB largely rewrote American labor policy through the process of adjudication. Though done piecemeal through several decisions involving unfair labor practice charges, the change in the law was as complete as if major rulemaking had been undertaken.

The quasi-judicial powers of major federal agencies are so significant that such decisions are normally reviewed directly by the Circuit Courts of Appeal. Other types of decisions—such as the decision to issue a subpoena or to promulgate a new rule—are normally reviewed in the first instance by federal district courts. (Figure 6.1 helps illustrate the adjudicatory process of a federal agency.)

## PROCEDURAL DUE PROCESS

Obviously a variety of agency actions can have an adverse impact on the status of individuals and companies. The Fifth Amendment to the Constitution prohibits the taking of life, liberty, or property, without due process of law. The right to due process protects us from the arbitrary actions of both state and federal agencies.

Exactly when we are entitled to due process, and how much process is due us are questions that the courts continually struggle to resolve. A leading due process case was discussed in the preceding chapter, *Cleveland Board of Education v. Loudermill.* Another very persuasive Supreme Court case, *Mathews v. Eldridge,* 424 U.S. 319 (1976), is discussed and applied in the following case involving a due process challenge to an agency action.

### Gun South, Inc. v. Brady
U.S. Eleventh Circuit Court of Appeals, 877 F.2d 858 (1989)

Gun South, Inc. (GSI), is a wholesale gun dealer licensed by the Treasury Department's Bureau of Alcohol, Tobacco, and Firearms. In late 1988 and again in early 1989, GSI applied for and was granted permits to import semiautomatic rifles for sporting purposes. On January 23, 1989, GSI ordered 800 AUG-SA semiautomatic rifles and obligated itself to pay $700,000 toward a larger total purchase price. On March 21, 1989, William Bennett, the "Drug Czar," speaking for the secretary of the treasury, announced a temporary 90-day suspension on the importation of five "assault-type" weapons, including those ordered by GSI, so that the bureau could review its conclusion that such rifles are "generally suitable for sporting purposes." Although the bureau assured GSI that the suspension did not apply to weapons purchased under pre-existing permits, the Customs Service intercepted GSI's shipment of the aforementioned rifles at the Birmingham Airport.

GSI brought this action to enjoin the government from interfering with the delivery of firearms imported under permits issued before the suspension. The district court issued such an injunction; Brady, secretary of the treasury, appealed. The appellate court's discussion of the due process issue follows.

**Decision:** Reversed; the government's action is upheld. Three factors must be considered in such procedural due process challenges. First is the nature of the private interest. Because the deprivation of GSI's property is only temporary (90 days), and because these weapons are only a small portion of GSI's inventory, this interest is not especially substantial. Second, the risk of an erroneous deprivation of such an interest must be considered. Normally, this means that the government should at least get the regulated party's side of the story before taking action. However, the determination in this case—whether these are "sporting" rifles or not—has nothing to do with any facts specific to GSI. The government had already undertaken substantial study of the issue before it took this action. Third, the government's interest in taking its action, including the burdens that any additional procedural requirement would entail, must be considered. The court concluded that protecting the public by ensuring that nearly 750,000 rifles do not improperly enter the country is a health and safety measure that justifies summary administrative action. ■

---

## ESTOPPEL

Often businesses that deal with the government seek advice from government officials, asking such questions as the right way to fill out tax returns, the correct interpretation of a zoning ordinance, or the legality of a securities sale. What all businesspersons must keep in mind is that government officials may from time to time give erroneous advice, but that does not relieve the businesses from culpability.

The legal doctrine of **estoppel** provides in many areas that an entity which takes a particular position that others rely upon cannot later change that original position when to do so would injure the party that relied upon it. Unfortunately, the general rule is that the doctrine of estoppel does not operate against the government. That is to say, if the government gives erroneous advice, it is not later "estopped to deny" its original position.

The leading case on this subject is *Federal Crop Insurance Corp. v. Merrill*,[7] where a government official told farmer Merrill that reseeded spring wheat would be covered by federal crop insurance. Unfortunately, the agency's regulations, printed in the *Federal Register*, stated that insurance would not be provided for reseeded crops. Merrill, not knowing of the regulation, relied on the advice. When the crop was destroyed, however, Merrill was unable to recover insurance. The government was not "estopped to deny" its original position. It was allowed to change its position in a way that the doctrine of estoppel would probably prevent a private insurance company from doing.

The reasoning behind the government exclusion lies, in part, in the notion that federal statutes are

[7] 332 U.S. 380 (1947).

contained in the *United States Code* and federal regulations are printed in the *Federal Register* and codified in the *Code of Federal Regulations* and therefore all citizens are "on notice" of these rules. Still, the exclusion seems unjust to many people, so some exceptions have developed. For example, some courts will invoke estoppel against the government when an official has intentionally misled someone. Others create an exception where the government is acting in a proprietary (businesslike) capacity. Today, for example, many courts might decide the 1947 *Merrill* case differently because in that case the agency was acting more in the role of a private insurance company than like a government agency.

The doctrine's impact when lower levels of government are involved is less clear, but cannot be ignored. This lesson was brought home recently when builders given the "go-ahead" by local government officials to build a 31-story building were, after substantial construction, forced to remove everything above the 19th floor because the officials had misread a zoning ordinance.[8] The court said that estoppel is not available "for the purpose of ratifying an administrative error."

## RECENT DEVELOPMENTS

The federal administrative process has been closely scrutinized from several angles in recent years. In order to make federal agencies more open to public view and more responsive to the needs of constituents and to fiscal and economic concerns, many changes have been made.

### *Freedom of Information Act*

The Freedom of Information Act of 1966, with significant amendments in 1974, is codified as section 552 of the Administrative Procedure Act. Prior to its enactment it was extremely difficult for a private citizen to obtain and examine government-held documents. The agency from which the information was requested could deny the applicant on the grounds that he or she was not properly and directly concerned or that the requested information should not be disclosed because to do so would not be in the public interest. Under FOIA, any person may reasonably describe what information is sought and the burden for withholding information is on the agency. A response is required of the agency within ten working days after receipt of a request, and denial by the agency may be appealed by means of an expeditable federal district court action. There are, of course, exemptions—nine specific areas to which the disclosure requirements do not apply. That is, if the information concerns certain matters, the agency is not required to comply with the request. The nine exemptions apply to matters that are:

1. Secret in the interest of national defense or foreign policy

2. Related solely to internal personnel rules and practices of an agency

3. Exempted from disclosure by statute

4. Trade secrets and commercial or financial information obtained from a person and privileged or confidential

5. Inter-agency or intra-agency memoranda or letters

6. Personnel and medical files, the disclosure of which would constitute an invasion of personal privacy

7. Certain investigatory records compiled for law enforcement purposes

8. Related to the regulation or supervision of financial institutions

9. Geological and geophysical information and data, including maps concerning wells

With regard to the exemptions, Chief Judge Bazelon had this to say in *Soucie v. David*, 448 F.2d 1067 (D.C.Cir. 1971):

> The touchstone of any proceedings under the Act must be the clear legislative intent to assure public access to all governmental records whose disclosure would not significantly harm specific governmental interests. The policy of the Act requires that the disclosure requirements be construed broadly, the exemptions narrowly.

Businesses have often complained that confidential information they were required to disclose to the government pursuant to regulatory programs might be vulnerable to disclosure to competitors through the FOIA. In 1987, regulations were issued that re-

---

[8] *Matter of Parkview Associates v. City of New York*, 513 N.Y.S.2d 342, *cert. denied*, 109 S.Ct. 30 (1988).

quire federal agencies to provide early notification to businesses whenever "arguably" confidential business data in government hands is about to be released under the FOIA. Those businesses are given an opportunity to object to the disclosure. Agencies are required to explain in writing if they choose to override such an objection.

## The Privacy Act

The Federal Privacy Act of 1974 seeks to protect individuals from unnecessary disclosures of facts about them from files held by federal agencies. Though the need of federal agencies for information is recognized through a large series of exceptions and qualifications, the general thrust of the Privacy Act is to prohibit federal agencies from disclosing information from their files about an individual without that individual's written consent. Federal agencies are specifically forbidden from selling or renting an individual's name and address, unless authorized by another law.

## The Government in the Sunshine Act

A further effort to open up the government is provided by the 1976 Government in the Sunshine Act, codified as section 552b of the Administrative Procedure Act. The purpose of the Act is to assure that ". . . every portion of every meeting of an agency shall be open to public observation." There are, however, exceptions to the open meeting requirement. If the meeting qualifies for one of ten specified exemptions and the agency by majority vote decides to do so, the meeting may be closed to the public. The exemptions of the Act are similar to the nine provided for in the FOIA but are not identical.

Most states have passed some form of open meetings laws. There is considerable diversity, but the common purpose is to permit the public to view the decision-making process at all stages.

## The Regulatory Flexibility Act

We are all presumed to know the law, and when final versions of rules are published in the Federal Register, legally speaking, we are all put on notice of their existence. Congress realized, however, that as a practical matter many persons, especially small businesses, do not closely follow proposed and final rules printed in the Federal Register. Therefore, Congress passed the Regulatory Flexibility Act in 1980. Among other provisions, the RFA requires most federal agencies to transmit to the Small Business Administration on a semiannual basis agendas briefly describing areas in which they may propose rules having a substantial impact on small entities (including small businesses, small governmental units, and nonprofit organizations). In this way the small businesses may be on the lookout for potential changes. Also, when any rule is promulgated which will have a significant economic impact on a substantial number of small entities, the agency proposing the rule must give notice not only through the Federal Register but also through publications of general notice likely to be obtained by small entities, such as trade journals.

## Deregulation

The economic efficiency of many programs of federal regulation is easily questioned. Furthermore, the paperwork burden on many companies attempting to comply with complex federal regulatory schemes can be overwhelming. For these and other reasons, recent administrations have attempted to "deregulate" the economy.

Congress has, at times, assisted the deregulation movement, as evidenced by the Airline Deregulation Act of 1978, the CAB Sunshine Act of 1984, and the Motor Carrier Act of 1980. Various executive orders and agency interpretations have supplemented the effort. During the Reagan administration, for example, there was a noticeably less aggressive enforcement attitude in such agencies as OSHA, the Consumer Products Safety Commission (CPSC), and the EPA.

The advantages and disadvantages of deregulation will be debated for years. Proponents point to the cost savings and the general fare reductions which have occurred in the airline industry through introduction of free competition and elimination of government rate-setting. Opponents point to a recent rise in injuries from products and in the workplace, the provinces of OSHA and the CPSC, and to alleged increases in various types of pollution due to EPA inactivity. Neither increases in regulation nor decreases in regulation (as the *Motor Vehicle Manufacturers Ass'n v. State Farm Mutual Auto Ins. Co.* case shows) come without cost. To a large extent, the positions taken on the deregulation debate are determined by political philosophies and "whose ox is being gored."

## SUMMARY

In terms of their influence on America's economy and society, administrative agencies truly constitute a "fourth branch of government."

Increased complexity in our economy and society means that our legislatures, state and federal, cannot give personal attention to even a fraction of the problems demanding government attention. Therefore, substantial legislative power is delegated to administrative agencies, sometimes under only the vaguest of guidelines.

Major federal agencies possess both ministerial and discretionary powers. The discretionary powers include those to investigate (as the executive branch does), to make rules (as the legislative branch does), and to adjudicate alleged violations (as the judicial branch does). The courts may review virtually all agency actions.

To be valid, agency rules must be promulgated in accordance with a constitutional delegation of authority, pursuant to proper procedures, in accordance with constitutional strictures—especially those of due process—and must not be arbitrary and capricious.

The power of administrative agencies is very controversial. In recent years the federal government especially has attempted to make administrative procedures more open to public scrutiny and to streamline them so they will be less burdensome for the regulated parties.

## KEY TERMS

**Administrative agency**
**Ministerial powers**
**Discretionary powers**
**Investigative powers**
**Rulemaking powers**
**Adjudicatory powers**
**Subpoena**
**Question of law**
**Estoppel**

## QUESTIONS AND PROBLEMS

1. Louisiana passed a statute to regulate commercial marine diving. Among other things, the statute created a Licensing Board, which thereafter promulgated rules and regulations relative to the qualifications of apprentice, journeyman, and master marine divers. One regulation provided that a person could be licensed as a master marine diver only if he had "continuously worked for a period of five years under supervision of a master marine diver." Under this regulation, the board refused to license a diver (as a master marine diver) who had had several years' diving experience in the U.S. Navy, and who had also had about eight years' commercial diving experience in Louisiana (but not under supervision of a master marine diver). The diver challenged the board's action, contending that the statute was an unconstitutional delegation of legislative authority in view of the fact that it permitted the board to set licensing qualifications without containing any statutory limitations on it, or any standards to which the board should look in setting its qualifications. Do you agree with this contention? Why or why not? (*Banjavich v. Louisiana Licensing Board of Marine Divers,* 111 So.2d 505, 1959.)

2. The U.S. Department of Energy (DOE) issued a subpoena for Phoenix Petroleum Company records during the course of an investigation to determine whether Phoenix had illegally sold crude oil. Phoenix moved to quash the subpoena, claiming DOE was on a "fishing expedition." DOE proved the subpoenaed items were reasonably relevant to the purpose of the investigation, but admitted that it could not establish probable cause to believe a violation had taken place. Should the subpoena be quashed by the court? Discuss. (*U.S. v. Phoenix Petroleum Co.,* 571 F.Supp. 16, S.D.Tex. 1982.)

3. Biswell, a pawnshop operator who was federally licensed to deal in sporting weapons, was visited one afternoon by a policeman and a Federal Treasury agent who requested entry into a locked gun storeroom. They had no search warrant, but showed Biswell a section of the Gun Control Act of 1968 which authorized warrantless entry of the premises of gun dealers. Biswell then allowed a search which turned up two sawed-off rifles and led to Biswell's conviction for dealing in firearms without having paid a required special occupational tax. On appeal, Biswell challenged the constitutionality of the warrantless search. Discuss. (*U.S. v. Biswell,* 406 U.S. 311, 1972.)

4. The Federal Trade Commission Act authorizes the Federal Trade Commission to determine what kinds of business practices constitute "unfair methods of competition, and deceptive or unfair practices," and to prohibit such practices. Traditionally, when such a practice has been found to exist, the FTC has simply ordered the offending company to stop the practice. In 1975, however, when the FTC ruled that Listerine ads had—for many years—falsely stated that Listerine was "effective in preventing and curing colds and sore throats," the FTC ordered the manufacturer to stop such advertising, and, in addition, it ordered the manufacturer to insert in *future* advertising the statement that Listerine would *not* prevent or cure colds and sore

throats. The manufacturer then asked the federal courts to rule that the FTC did not have the power, under the Federal Trade Commission Act, to issue such an order (known as "corrective advertising"). Do you think the manufacturer's argument is a good one? Why or why not? (*Warner-Lambert v. FTC,* 562 F.2d 749, 1977.)

5. A New Jersey statute provided that every taxicab owner who wished to operate in a city within the state had to obtain consent of the "governing body" of the municipality. The statute also provided that the governing body could "make and enforce" ordinances to "license and regulate" all vehicles used as taxis. Under this law a New Jersey city passed an ordinance that set a flat rate taxicab fare of $1.15 for all trips made within the city, regardless of the miles involved. A taxicab owner who wanted to charge $1.50 for some trips attacked this ordinance on the ground that the statute did *not,* expressly or impliedly, give to cities the power to set taxi fares (i.e., the gist of the attack was that legislatures could not delegate *ratemaking* powers to municipalities). What was the result? Discuss. (*Yellow Cab Corp. v. Clifton City Council,* 308 A.2d 60, 1973.)

6. One section of an Oklahoma law provided that no person shall "knowingly sell" alcoholic beverages to a minor. Certain penalties were provided for, in the event of violations. Another section of the law authorized the Oklahoma Beverage Control Board to promulgate rules and regulations to carry out the act. The board then adopted a rule that, in essence, provided that any liquor license could be revoked if the licensee sold liquor to a minor, even if he did *not* know the buyer was a minor. When the license of a liquor retailer, Wray, was revoked by the board as a result of his sale of liquor to a person who he did not know was a minor, he contended in the Oklahoma courts that the rule of the board was invalid because it conflicted with the quoted statute. Do you agree with this argument? Discuss. (*Wray v. Oklahoma Alcoholic Beverage Control Board,* 442 P.2d 309, 1968.)

7. Southern Ohio Coal Co. (SOCCO) sought review of an order compelling it to reinstate an employee it had fired for alleged excessive absenteeism. The employee had earlier complained about unsafe conditions in SOCCO's mines. The order was issued pursuant to rule 44, which was a Department of Labor rule implementing a statute prohibiting the discharge of employees for reporting unsafe mine conditions. In essence, the rule required the department to order reinstatement without a hearing if it found that the employee's complaint was "not frivolous." A full hearing followed reinstatement. SOCCO complained that rule 44 violated its procedural due process rights. Discuss. (*Southern Ohio Coal Co. v. Donovan,* 774 F.2d 693, 6th Cir. 1985.)

8. A Social Security Administration field representative erroneously told Hansen that she was not eligible for "mother's insurance benefits." Because of this advice, Hansen did not file a written application which, by the terms of the law, was a prerequisite to receiving benefits. Nor did the agent follow instructions to advise potential claimants of the written filing requirement and to encourage them to file in a close case. A year or so later, Hansen filed an application and received benefits. She then sued to recover the benefits that she had missed during the period that she had relied on the erroneous advice. Will she succeed? (*Schweiker v. Hansen,* 450 U.S. 785, 1981.)

# CHAPTER 7

# CRIMINAL LAW AND BUSINESS

Businesses are the victims of crime. Businesses commit crimes. This sad reality necessitates a general overview of the role of criminal law in the legal environment of business. Armed robberies, bad checks, employee pilfering, and other criminal acts cost businesses billions of dollars annually. Consumers suffer as well, because these losses are manifested either in the form of higher prices or, worse, failed businesses.

Criminal acts committed by businesses also cause enormous losses to our society. Though crimes committed *by* businesses received little attention in the criminal law until recently, that situation has changed dramatically as we have become aware of such wrongful acts as stifling competition by fixing prices, selling stock based on contrived financial statements, using false advertising to lure customers into buying inferior products, and the like.

The strong interrelationship between criminal law and the vital interests of business is highlighted by frequent references to criminal acts in other chapters of this text. For example, there is discussion of contracts calling for criminal acts in Chapter 14, of criminal securities law violations in Chapter 41, and of illegal competitive acts in Chapter 48.

## NATURE OF CRIMINAL LAW

A **crime** is a wrong committed against society. Indeed, that wrong is also defined by society, because the criminal law is one of a civilized society's primary tools for conforming the behavior of its citizens to societal norms. Even in a society with as many freedoms as America's, limits must be placed on individual and corporate actions. Today's drug epidemic is a vivid reminder of the damage that certain types of individual activity can inflict on society as a whole. Criminalizing activity is often far from the best way to address the causes of that activity or to solve the problems that arise from it. Nonetheless, criminal law is one of society's most important mechanisms for controlling individual behavior, and that will not change anytime soon.

### *Civil and Criminal Law Contrasted*

Most of this text discusses civil law matters. While there are many similarities between criminal law and civil law, there are also important distinctions. The civil law adjusts rights between or among individuals. The basis of the controversy may be a broken commercial promise, an injury caused by someone's careless driving, or a loss caused by a defective product. The focus is on adjusting the rights of the parties to the transaction. The criminal law, on the other hand, focuses on the individual's relationship to society. In enacting criminal statutes, a government is saying that there are certain activities so inherently contrary to the public good that they must be flatly prohibited *in the best interests of society.*

A civil lawsuit is brought by one individual or company (the plaintiff) against another (the defendant). A criminal action, on the other hand, is always brought by an agent of the government (the prosecutor or district attorney) against the alleged wrongdoer. The essence of the civil suit is an injury that the defendant's wrongful act caused to the individual plaintiff. The essence of a criminal prosecution is the injury that the defendant's wrongful act caused society. Of course, there are usually individual victims of criminal acts. The suffering of those victims is not ignored by the criminal law, but greater emphasis is placed on the implications that such conduct has for society at large.

A plaintiff in a civil suit usually requests money damages as compensation for injuries sustained by the defendant's wrongful conduct. In a criminal action, on the other hand, even a successful prosecution will not usually produce a dime for the plaintiff. Rather, the remedy sought by the prosecutor typically is punishment for the defendant, such as a fine (which usually goes to the state) and/or imprisonment.

Of course, many types of acts (such as battery) constitute both criminal wrongs and actionable torts. As illustrated in Figure 7.1, the same activity might be the subject of both a civil suit by the victim and a criminal action by the state. A critical difference in such actions lies in the burden of proof. A plaintiff in a civil action must prove the elements of recovery only by "a preponderance of the evidence." Because the consequences of a criminal conviction are generally considered much more severe, a higher standard of proof must be met by prosecutors. Jurors must be convinced of the defendant's guilt "beyond a reasonable doubt" before a guilty verdict is appropriate. Figure 7.2 outlines major differences between civil and criminal law.

## Classification of Crimes

**Degree of Seriousness:** Except for the most serious crime of treason, crimes are either *felonies* or *misdemeanors,* depending upon the severity of the penalty which the statute provides. The definition of **felony** varies from state to state, but it is usually defined as any crime where the punishment is either death or imprisonment for more than one year in a state penitentiary, as in the cases of murder, robbery, or rape. **Misdemeanors** are all crimes carrying lesser penalties (such as fines or confinement in county jails)—for example, petit larceny and disorderly conduct. In the federal system, felonies are crimes for which the designated penalty is more than one year in prison; misdemeanors are crimes with lesser designated penalties. Yet another category used in some states is *petty offenses,* covering such infractions as traffic and building code violations.

The distinction between felonies and misdemeanors can be important because of various penalties often imposed on persons convicted of the former, such as loss of the right to vote, to hold public office, or to pursue various careers.

**Degree of Moral Turpitude:** Crimes such as murder, rape, arson, or robbery are evil in and of themselves. Such acts are called *malum in se,* meaning that they are criminal because they are inherently wicked. Other acts, such as jaywalking or speeding are *malum prohibitum,* meaning that they are crimes merely because the legislature has said that they are wrong. Typically, greater punishments attach to crimes that involve moral turpitude.

**Jurisdiction:** As has already been noted, in America a federal criminal justice system is superimposed over state and local systems. These systems generally address different concerns. Murder is usually a concern only of the state in which it occurred unless, for example, it occurred on federal property, the victim was a federal official, or it occurred as part of an interstate kidnapping. Still, there are several areas of overlap and actions that might well violate both federal and state laws. For example, during the wave of bank robberies during the 1930s Depression, a federal law against bank robberies was passed so that the Federal

**Figure 7.1** A Single Act as Both Tort and Crime

```
A defrauds B using the U.S. mail and telephone to induce
a purchase of worthless stock.
        │                                │
        ▼                                ▼
  Fraud as a tort                 Fraud as a crime
                                  (mail fraud, wire
                                  fraud)
        │                                │
        ▼                                ▼
   A breaches                    Violation of statute
   duty to B
        │                                │
        ▼                                ▼
  Suit brought by B              Prosecution by state
        │                                │
        ▼                                ▼
  A pays B amount                A is punished by being
  paid for worthless             fined, imprisoned,
  stock and damages.             prohibited from
                                 trading securities.
```

**Figure 7.2** Major Differences between Civil and Criminal Law

| Civil | Nature | Criminal |
|---|---|---|
| Deals with rights and duties between individuals | Nature | Deals with offenses against society as a whole (the state) |
| Individual | Party bringing suit | The state |
| Causing harm to another individual | Wrongful act | Violating a statute prohibiting some type of activity |
| Damages to compensate for the loss sustained | Remedy sought | Punishment—fine and/or imprisonment |
| Preponderance of the evidence | Standard of proof | Beyond a reasonable doubt |

Bureau of Investigation and federal prosecutors could supplement the efforts of state police and judicial systems.

**Purpose of Punishment:** Perhaps the most salient feature of the criminal justice system is the punishment that it imposes on wrongdoers. As noted earlier, the punishment is not imposed in order to compensate the victim. That is the province of the civil tort system. Rather, there are four primary purposes of criminal punishment. First, there is *rehabilitation* or reformation. Although published rates of recidivism (relapse into crime) indicate that this is the most difficult of the punishment goals to attain, it is important that our system at least attempt to reform wrongdoers.

A second, less ambitious, purpose of punishment is simply *restraint* or incapacitation, on the theory that a robber cannot rob and a rapist cannot rape while they are locked up. A third purpose of punishment, and a somewhat controversial one, is that of *retribution*. The concept of retribution predates the Bible's admonition of "an eye for an eye," and society's infliction of retribution upon criminals still has strong popular support.

A final purpose of punishment is *deterrence*. The law seeks to persuade the wrongdoer being punished not to err again, and, at the same time, to provide an example that might generally deter other potential lawbreakers. The effectiveness of various types of criminal sanctions in deterring crime is not clear. One very controversial subject is the death penalty. Although most evidence makes it clear that a state will not reduce its murder rate by adopting a death penalty, advocates still justify the ultimate punishment on restraint and retribution grounds.

## CONSTITUTIONAL PROTECTIONS

Once arrested, a criminal defendant has the considerable power and resources of the government lined up against him. The potential for abuse of that power is considerable and one need not be a student of history to discover blatant examples of such abuses. Because our system operates on the theory that it is better that a guilty man go free than that an innocent man should suffer unjust punishment, we provide manifold protections for criminal defendants. Many of these protections are set forth in the Bill of Rights. Through the controversial process of "incorporation," most of these rights have been applied to the states as well. Additionally, many state constitutions contain parallel protections. The following discussion will help complete the examination of constitutional law begun in Chapter 5.

## *Fourth Amendment*

The Fourth Amendment protects people (and, as we saw in Chapter 6, businesses) against "unreasonable searches and seizures," requiring that search warrants not be issued absent "probable cause." A search warrant will be issued by a judge if the police have produced evidence that would lead a reasonably prudent person to believe there is a substantial likelihood that the defendant is guilty of the offense the police charge. The Fourth Amendment requires that the warrant "particularly describe" the place to be searched and the persons or things to be seized.

A controversial question regards enforcement of this prohibition. What happens to evidence that the police seize without a valid warrant? In *Mapp v. Ohio,* 367 U.S. 643 (1961), the Supreme Court held that "all evidence obtained by searches and seizures in violation of the Constitution is . . . inadmissible in a state court." This holding was very controversial, opponents arguing that "the crook should not go free just because the constable has erred." In recent years the increasingly conservative Supreme Court has fashioned a number of exceptions to this "exclusionary rule," weakening its impact substantially. For example, in *U.S. v. Leon,* 468 U.S. 189 (1984), the Court created a "good faith" exception for situations where the police searched pursuant to an apparently valid search warrant that was later determined to have been improperly issued. The Court reasoned, in part, that the exclusionary rule was meant to deter police abuses rather than to correct errors by judges.

## *Fifth Amendment*

The Fifth Amendment contains a number of provisions that protect criminal defendants from government abuse. For example, individuals cannot be held to answer for major criminal charges unless they have been indicted by a **grand jury.** A grand jury typically consists of 23 members of the community who hear evidence presented by the prosecution. If a majority concludes that there is probable cause to believe that the defendant has committed the crime alleged, the grand jury issues a "true bill." The right to indictment by grand jury is one of the few protections in the Bill of Rights that the Supreme Court has not applied to the states. However, many state constitutions have similar provisions.

The Fifth Amendment also protects defendants from **double jeopardy,** which is being tried twice for the same offense. This means that when a jury finds a defendant "not guilty," the government cannot simply reindict the defendant for the same crime and try again to convict him. However, it does not mean that a defendant acquitted of criminal assault and battery could not be sued civilly by his alleged victim. Because of the differential burden of proof, the same body of evidence that did not convince a criminal jury beyond a reasonable doubt might convince a civil jury applying a preponderance of evidence standard. The fact that a state prosecution will not bar a subsequent federal prosecution and vice versa constitutes another major exception to the double jeopardy prohibition. Thus, theoretically, a defendant who was acquitted of a federal bank robbery charge might be prosecuted by a state claiming that the same alleged robbery violated a state statute.

The Fifth Amendment mandates that no person be deprived of life, liberty, or property without due process of law. We know quite a bit about due process from previous chapters. One aspect of due process, for example, is that no one should be convicted of violating a statute that is unduly vague, so that a well-intentioned person could not conform his or her conduct to comply with the law. *Kolender v. Lawson,* mentioned in Chapter 4's discussion of the requirement of certainty, is a good example. In that case, a California criminal statute requiring persons on the street to provide "credible and reliable" identification and to account for their presence when requested to do so by a policeman was held to be unduly vague.

The concept of due process is very broad, touching almost every aspect of criminal law and procedure. The following case illustrates the Supreme Court's view of one interesting due process question.

### Arizona v. Youngblood
U.S. Supreme Court,
109 S.Ct. 885 (1989)

A doctor, treating a 10-year old boy who had been abducted and sodomized, used a "sexual assault kit" provided by the police to collect evidence of the attack from the boy's body. The doctor made slides from the samples he collected but did not examine them. The police placed the kit in a refrigerator at the police station and collected the boy's underwear and T-shirt but did not refrigerate them. Looking at photographs nine days after the attack, the boy identified Youngblood (respondent) as his assailant. Respondent was arrested four weeks later.

The first police criminologist to examine the kit did so ten days after the attack and did not use the P-30 protein molecule test, the most accurate test and one being used in slightly more than half of the crime laboratories in the country. Not until eighteen months after the crime did a police criminologist examine the victim's clothing. Tests from it were inconclusive.

Respondent's main defense at trial was that the boy had misidentified him. Expert witnesses testified that had the more advanced test been used on the samples collected or had the underwear been refrigerated and promptly tested, evidence from blood or semen samples might have exonerated him.

The jury found the respondent guilty, but the Arizona Court of Appeals reversed, holding that "when identity is an issue at trial and the police permit the destruction of evidence that could eliminate the defendant as the perpetrator, such loss is material to the defense and is a denial of due process." The Court did not find any bad faith by the police. The Arizona Supreme Court refused to review this decision, and the State of Arizona appealed.

**Decision:** Reversed. There was no denial of due process. The issue is the scope of the constitutionally guaranteed access to evidence. The prosecution may not suppress evidence favorable to the defense. However, in the absence of bad faith by the police (and none was found here), there is no denial of due process when the police fail to use the most advanced test or to preserve potentially useful evidence. ■

---

The most controversial part of the Fifth Amendment, as interpreted by the Supreme Court, is its protection against self-incrimination. No person "shall be compelled in any criminal case to be a witness against himself." This includes matters of document production as well as of oral testimony. The right is not available to corporations and is individual to the person charged. In a case of interest to all business persons, *U.S. v. Doe*, 104 S.Ct. 1237 (1984), the court held that the sole owner of a corporation could not claim the privilege against self-incrimination in order to avoid producing records that belonged *to the corporation*. Had the business been a sole proprietorship, the owner could have claimed the privilege because the records would have been his, not a separate entity's.

The most famous self-incrimination case is *Miranda v. Arizona*, 384 U.S. 436 (1966), which excluded from evidence any incriminating statements made by a defendant (and evidence to which those statements led police, called "fruit of the poisonous tree") who had not been fully warned of his constitutional right against self-incrimination (and his right to counsel). Thus, the famous "Miranda warning" was born.

As with the exclusionary rule, the current more conservative members of the Supreme Court have diluted the impact of *Miranda*. For example, in *Duckworth v. Eagan*, 109 S.Ct. 2875 (1989), the police told a criminal suspect that "we have no way of giving you a lawyer, but one will be appointed for you, if you wish, if and when you go to court." Dissenters felt that this statement might have misled the defendant into believing, inaccurately, that he did not have the right to consult an attorney then and there in the stationhouse before being interrogated by the police. But the majority said that "*Miranda* does not require that attorneys be producible on call . . ." and felt that the statement was not necessarily misleading given that the defendant had already been read the standard Miranda warning, which informs defendants that they have the right to speak to a lawyer before any questions are asked.

## Sixth Amendment

The Sixth Amendment contains a litany of constitutional protections for criminal defendants, including the important right to counsel that was mentioned in the previous discussion of the *Miranda* case. Generally speaking, any individual facing potential incarceration has the right to consult an attorney and to have one provided if he cannot afford one.

The right to counsel is made more meaningful by the defendant's Sixth Amendment rights to be informed of the nature of the accusation, to confront witnesses against him, and to call witnesses on his own behalf.

There is also the right to a "speedy and public trial." Court backlogs have threatened to make a mockery of the right to a "speedy" trial, but the federal government and most states have now passed "speedy trial" acts which place time limits on the government and give criminal cases priority over civil cases on crowded court dockets.

Importantly, there is also a right to trial by an impartial jury that applies in cases involving "serious" criminal charges. Juries, serving as the "conscience of the community," are a critical safeguard against the heavy hand of the government.

## Eighth Amendment

The Eighth Amendment contains important protections for criminal defendants. It states that "excessive bail" shall not be required. Thus, when a judge sets bail before trial, the aim should be not to punish the defendant who is presumed innocent, but simply to guarantee the defendant's appearance at trial. In recent years, Congress has increased the courts' authority to deny bail in situations where defendants pose special harm to the public.

The Eighth Amendment also bans "excessive fines" and "cruel and unusual punishment." The latter provision has been held not to bar the death penalty, even for juveniles or retarded defendants.

## Miscellaneous Protections

There are other protections for criminal defendants scattered throughout the Constitution. For example, there is a ban on *ex post facto* laws—laws that are passed to criminalize conduct *after* the conduct has occurred. Obviously, criminal laws must also be scrutinized to ensure that they do not violate basic freedoms, such as religion and speech. The government could not, for example, make it a crime to be a Baptist. Nor, the court has held, can a state criminalize the burning of the American flag when done as a form of political expression. *Texas v. Johnson,* 109 S.Ct. 2533 (1989) (see Chapter 5).

# GENERAL ELEMENTS OF CRIMINAL RESPONSIBILITY

As a general rule, the prosecutor in a criminal case must do three things to obtain a valid conviction: (1) show that the defendant's actions violated an existing criminal statute; (2) prove beyond a reasonable doubt that the defendant did do the *acts* alleged; and (3) prove that the defendant had the requisite *intent* to violate the law. The first element is important because though many of our crimes have strong common-law roots, today almost all crimes are statutory in nature. The other two elements of act and intent deserve separate consideration.

## Guilty Act

A basic element of a criminal conviction is the **actus reus,** a Latin term meaning "guilty act." This is a critical part of a criminal conviction because our legal system generally does not punish persons for their thoughts. Evil thoughts alone normally do not injure society and therefore do not justify bringing to bear the full power of the government's criminal justice system. This does not mean that a defendant must always successfully complete a criminal act in order to be guilty. Generally any act that clearly is a step in the commission of a crime will be sufficient for a conviction for *attempted* larceny, murder, etc., if the intent requirement is also present.

The guilty act must be voluntary and generally must be an act of commission rather than mere omission. However, there are exceptions. Failure to perform a legally imposed duty will constitute a sufficient *actus reus.* An example is failure to fulfill the legally required duty to file an income tax return.

## Guilty Mind

Generally, a defendant is not guilty unless his guilty act is coupled with a guilty mind, that is, unless the defendant had **mens rea,** an intent to do wrong. A murder conviction, for example, requires the act of killing the victim plus the evil intent to take a life.

Because a person's actual intent can rarely be known with absolute certainty, juries may often presume a criminal intent on the part of the defendant based on the established facts. Thus a jury may presume that an armed prowler apprehended at night entered the house "with the intention of committing a felony," one of the usual statutory elements of the crime of burglary. Intent is often a difficult element to prove beyond a reasonable doubt, but, as Justice Oliver Wendell Holmes once stated, "even a dog distinguishes between being stumbled over and being kicked."

Many crimes are called "specific intent" crimes, in that conviction is appropriate only if the defendant had the intent to commit the exact forbidden act charged. For other crimes, "general intent" will suffice, meaning that the defendant had the general intent to commit a wrongful act even though he did not intend to bring about the specific result. First degree murder is typically a specific intent crime; to be guilty the defendant must have intended to take a human life. However, if a defendant became very drunk and went on a rampage, killing a man with a gun, he may be found guilty of second degree murder even though he was so drunk he did not know he had a gun. This is an example of general intent.

There are a few crimes for which negligence will suffice and no intent need be proven. Negligent vehicular homicide is an example. There are even some *strict liability* crimes, where defendants can be found guilty absent intent or even careless behavior. These are typically misdemeanors. Examples include selling liquor to minors, violating traffic rules, and violating pure food and drug laws.

## GENERAL CRIMINAL DEFENSES

### Defenses Negating Intent

Many defenses raised in a criminal case are aimed at negating the *mens rea* element by showing that the defendant did not intend to commit a crime. Several such defenses exist. We will learn in Chapter 15 that many of these concepts also provide grounds for escaping contractual obligations.

**Infancy:** The common-law rule was that children under seven were *conclusively* presumed to be incapable of forming criminal intent. Children between seven and fourteen were accorded the same presumption, but in a *rebuttable* form. The presumption could be overcome by proof that the child understood the wrongful nature of his act. Many states still follow these basic notions in their criminal statutes. However, virtually all states have created juvenile courts which treat juveniles as delinquents rather than criminals with the purpose of reforming rather than punishing them. Therefore, infancy as a criminal defense is not as important as it once was, though prosecutors usually have the option of attempting to convince a court to try a juvenile as an adult where a particularly heinous crime has been committed.

**Insanity:** There are several approaches, none satisfactory, to handling defendants who "plead insanity." Some states use the *M'Naghten* test, which excuses a defendant whose mental defect renders him incapable of appreciating the difference between right and wrong. Others excuse defendants who may appreciate the difference between right and wrong but who suffer a mental defect causing an "irresistible impulse" to commit the crime. The District of Columbia courts developed the *Durham* rule, which simply asks whether the defendant was insane at the time of the crime and, if so, whether the crime was a product of that insanity. Finally, the Model Penal Code provides that a defendant "is not responsible for criminal conduct if at the time of such conduct as a result of mental disease or defect he lacks substantial capacity either to appreciate the wrongfulness of his conduct or to conform his conduct to the requirements of the law."

**Intoxication:** If a person *voluntarily* becomes intoxicated (or "high" on drugs), the general rule is that this may negate specific intent but will not negate general intent, as discussed above. Voluntary intoxication is generally no defense to crimes requiring mere negligence or recklessness.

*Involuntary* intoxication, on the other hand, is generally treated as equivalent to insanity. Thus, if a defendant unforeseeably became intoxicated because of an unusual reaction to prescribed medication, courts would be reluctant to hold him responsible for crimes he might commit under the influence of that medication.

**Duress:** Occasionally, persons will be forced to commit crimes against their will. When the wrongful threat of others causes a person to commit a crime, *mens rea* is negated. Duress is generally shown where an immediate and inescapable threat of serious bodily injury or death (that is greater than the harm to be caused by the crime) forces a person to commit a crime that he does not wish to commit. The threat must come through no fault of the defendant's. If, for example, a defendant voluntarily joins a criminal gang, he has no duress defense if the gang leader forces him to help in one of the gang's planned crimes.

**Mistake:** Because ignorance of the law is no excuse, a *mistake of law* is generally no defense to a criminal charge. Thus, a defendant who has intentionally done a specific act cannot usually defend by saying: "I didn't know that it was illegal," or even "My attorney told me that it was okay." The courts' refusal to hold an attorney's advice to be a valid defense discourages "attorney shopping." However, many courts will find that a mistake of law negates the intent element if (1) the law was not reasonably made known to the public, or (2) the defendant reasonably relied on an erroneous but official statement of the law (such as in a judicial opinion or administrative order).

A defense based on *mistake of fact* is more likely to succeed. Thus, a defendant charged with stealing a blue 12-speed bicycle might successfully defend by showing that he owned an identical blue 12-speed bicycle parked at the next rack and mistakenly rode off on the wrong one.

## *Other Defenses*

**Entrapment:** Police undercover work is often aimed at catching criminals "in the act." If the police not only create an opportunity for a criminal act but also persuade the defendant to commit a crime that he would not otherwise have committed, defendant may have a good **entrapment** defense. The entrapment defense presents difficult factual questions, for the court must draw the line between an unwary innocent and an unwary criminal. The key issue is whether the defendant was *predisposed* to commit the crime. That is, the criminal idea must originate with the defendant, not with the policeman. As the Supreme Court once said, "when the criminal design originates with the [police who] implant in the mind of an innocent person the disposition to commit the alleged offense and induce its commission in order that they may prosecute," entrapment results. *Sorrells v. U.S.,* 287 U.S. 435 (1932).

**Self-Defense:** Self-defense and defense of others may justify acts of violence that otherwise would be criminal. Though the courts do not require "detached reflection in the presence of an uplifted knife," *Brown v. U.S.,* 256 U.S. 335 (1921), the general rule permits only that degree of force reasonable under the circumstances. Deadly force can be used if the defendant has a reasonable belief that imminent death or grievous bodily injury will otherwise result. The law does not allow one to shoot an assailant in the back once that assailant is clearly fleeing and poses no further threat. In some cases, retreat might even be required as preferable to deadly force. Nondeadly force can be used in the degree reasonably believed necessary to protect persons or property from criminal acts, although obviously, a lesser degree of force will be viewed as "reasonable" in defense of property.

**Immunity:** Through the process of "plea bargaining," defendants often agree to testify against other criminals in return for consideration at time of sentencing and, perhaps, **immunity** from prosecution of certain potential charges. It is often said that such persons are "turning state's evidence" in order to help the prosecutor's case.

# STATE CRIMES AFFECTING BUSINESS

There are so many crimes against persons and property contained in state criminal codes that it would be impossible to list all of them. Furthermore, there is such variation from state to state that it is difficult to generalize about criminal law. Nonetheless, this section briefly describes a few of the more common crimes against businesses.

## *Theft*

Many state statutes criminalize the unlawful taking of another's property under a general statute which often terms the crime "theft." Such statutes consolidate a variety of related crimes that developed separately at the common law, such as larceny, burglary, false pretenses, and embezzlement.

**Larceny:** At common law, **larceny** was the trespassory taking away of the personal property of another with wrongful intent permanently to deprive that person of the use of the property. Larceny is viewed as an injury to the owner's interest in possessing the goods. Shoplifting is a good example. Promising to sell someone your car, taking the money, and then refusing to turn over the car is not larceny, because there is no wrongful taking. The concept of personal property generally does not include trees or personal services, but would include computer programs and trade secrets.

There are degrees of larceny. Petit larceny covers theft of smaller amounts (*e.g.,* under $500). Thefts of property worth more would be grand larceny. These statutory distinctions vary in amount from state to state.

**Burglary:** At common law, **burglary** was the trespassory breaking and entering of the dwelling house of another during the nighttime with intent to commit a felony. Over time, many of the technical requirements have been dropped. Now, most statutes would find burglary even though the building broken into was not a dwelling house and even though it occurred during the daytime. Burglary with use of a weapon is called aggravated burglary.

**False Pretenses:** Obtaining goods by **false pretenses** was defined by the common law as obtaining title to someone else's property by knowingly or recklessly making a false representation of existing material fact which is intended to and does defraud the victim into parting with his property. Technically, false pretenses is an injury to title, not mere possession. Title passes to the thief, quite unlike larceny. Examples of such conduct are the filing of false claims with insurance companies, the buying of a VCR with a check the purchaser knows will "bounce," and the taking of buyers' money for goods or services with no intent of delivering such goods or services.

**Embezzlement:** A wholly statutory offense, **embezzlement** is the fraudulent conversion of the property of another by one who has lawful possession of it. This crime somewhat overlaps with larceny, but the original possession by the wrongdoer is lawful. An example is an attorney who receives funds from his client for payment of a settlement, but later decides to spend the money on himself instead.

Some of the key elements of an embezzlement charge are discussed in the following case.

---

**State v. Joy**
Supreme Court of Vermont,
549 A.2d 1033 (1988)

Defendant Joy was president and sole shareholder of Credit Management Services (CMS), a debt collection agency that collected delinquent accounts for businesses in exchange for 40 percent of the amount collected. CMS was entitled to this percentage regardless of whether the debtor paid CMS or settled with the client directly. When CMS received a payment from a debtor, it would deposit the money with a Barre bank and within a month an invoice detailing the transaction would be sent to the client. If monies were due the client, a check would accompany the invoice. In addition, CMS maintained an account with a Montpelier bank from which it drew operating expenses.

In early 1981 CMS, suffering financial difficulties, began transferring funds from the Barre account to the Montpelier account to cover its operating expenses. In June 1981, CMS was hired by Stacey Fuel to collect several delinquent accounts. On August 14, CMS received a check from one of Stacey's debtors in the amount of $1,920.25. CMS never forwarded any of this money to Stacey, nor did it inform Stacey that the money had been received. Stacey ended its relationship with CMS in August, 1982, and only later learned that CMS had filed for bankruptcy and had listed Stacey as one of its creditors.

Joy was convicted of embezzlement and appealed.

---

**Decision:** Affirmed. Joy's defense is that he intended to repay the money as soon as he could, and therefore he was not guilty of embezzlement. However, intent to repay is not a defense to embezzlement under the Vermont statute. The crime is completed when the money is intentionally and wrongfully converted, temporarily or permanently, to the defendant's use. ∎

**Specialized Statutes:** The common-law classifications and general theft statutes have been supplemented by a variety of more specific laws aimed at the same types of conduct. For example, while obtaining money or property by the giving of a bad check would constitute false pretenses or general theft, all states have specific statutes relating to the issuance of bad checks, which impose criminal liability on persons who, with intent to defraud, issue or transfer checks or other negotiable instruments knowing that they will be dishonored. Such knowledge is presumed to exist, under the typical statute, if the drawer had no account with the drawee bank when the check was issued, or if the check was refused payment because of insufficient funds in the drawer's account when it was presented to the bank for payment. Similarly, most states have separate statutes relating to a number of special offenses, such as the setting back of automobile odometers with the intent to defraud and the knowing delivery of "short weights"—the charging of buyers for quantities of goods that are greater than the quantities that were actually delivered.

## Robbery

**Robbery** is stealing from a person or in his presence by use of force or threat of force. It is, essentially, a form of larceny but the extra element of force makes it a more serious offense. Removing someone's earring by stealth would be larceny; ripping it from the victim's earlobe would be robbery. Use of a weapon escalates the crime to aggravated robbery.

## Forgery

**Forgery** is the false making or altering of a legally significant instrument (such as a check, credit card, deed, passport, mortgage, or security) with the intent to defraud. Writing an insufficient fund check is not forgery, though it may constitute false pretenses or violate a state bad check law. But changing the true payee's name as written on a check to your own and cashing the check is certainly forgery.

Forgery is a crime with roots deep in the common law, but changing technologies can challenge traditional rules, as the following case illustrates.

---

### People v. Avila
Colorado Court of Appeals,
770 P.2d 1330 (1988)

For fees of between $1,500 and $3,000, Avila, a lawyer, altered the driver records of two of his clients whose driver's licenses were under revocation for alcohol-related offenses. Avila would instruct his contact in the Motor Vehicle Division (MVD) office, who had access to the data base where the driving records were maintained on computer disk, to delete the clients' records. The client would later apply for a driver's license, stating that he had no previous driver's license, which the altered computer records would verify. Avila was convicted of two counts of second degree forgery. He appealed, claiming that forgery cannot be committed on a computer.

**Decision:** Affirmed. The elements of second degree forgery under the Colorado statute are that a defendant with intent to defraud falsely alters a written instrument which is or purports to be a "written instrument officially issued or created by a public office, public servant, or government agency." Furthermore, under the statute, a "written instrument" means any paper, document, "or other instrument containing written or printed matter or the equivalent thereof." The court held that a computer disc is fairly included within that definition. Further, the term "alter" can be construed to cover deletion, because it is defined to include change "by means of erasure." ∎

---

## Arson

At common law, **arson** was the malicious burning of the dwelling house of another. Today, the building burned need not be a dwelling house. And, as all too commonly occurs, people who burn their own house (or other building or personal property) for purposes of defrauding an insurance company are almost certainly violating a state criminal statute prohibiting such fraud.

# FEDERAL CRIMES AFFECTING BUSINESS

As with state crimes, there are so many federal criminal statutes that it would be impossible to list them all. Many have been passed in response to perceived crises. In the era of the giant trusts in the late 1800s, Congress passed many antitrust laws, including some carrying criminal penalties (discussed in Chapter 48). As noted earlier, during the Depression Era epidemic of bank robberies, Congress passed a federal bank robbery law. In the wake of the Watergate scandal in the early 1970s, investigation disclosed widespread bribery of foreign officials by U.S. companies, leading to enactment of the Foreign Corrupt Practices Act (discussed in Chapter 41). Following the Ivan Boesky case and other insider trading scandals in the late 1980s, Congress increased the criminal penalties for that fraudulent activity (also discussed in Chapter 41). As this edition is being written, Congress has responded to the burgeoning savings and loan scandal by enacting criminal penalties to punish several types of fraudulent activity that required a multibillion dollar taxpayer bailout of savings and loans (see the Financial Institutions Reform, Recovery, and Enforcement Act of 1989). Instead of trying to list all such federal criminal statutes, we will briefly address a few of the more general ones.

## *Mail and Wire Fraud*

Two very general federal statutes punish **mail fraud** (use of the mails to defraud or swindle) and **wire fraud** (similar use of telephone, telegraph, radio, or television). The typical mail or wire fraud case would involve use of the mails or telephones to make false representations in order to sell products or securities. For example, the mail fraud law has been used to punish fraudulent representations in the use of the mails to advertise such articles as hair-growing products that proved to be worthless, to retrofit carburetors that totally failed to improve automobile fuel economy, and to issue false identification cards which the sellers knew were ordered by purchasers for the purpose of deceiving third parties. Similarly, schemes for the operation of "mail-order" schools, where degrees or diplomas are awarded "without requiring evidence of education or experience entitled thereto," and where the operators know such documents are likely to be used by purchasers to misrepresent their qualifications to prospective employers, violate these sections of the law. However, the statutes have been construed to cover a wide variety of factual situations.

For example, in *Carpenter v. U.S.,* 484 U.S. 19 (1987), a *Wall Street Journal* reporter tipped material nonpublic information (the contents of his columns that were about to be published) to confederates who profitably traded on it. Although the Supreme Court split 4-4 regarding the specific insider trading theory offered by the prosecution, it unanimously affirmed the defendant's conviction for mail and wire fraud. The fraudulent scheme's connection to the mails and wire services used to distribute the newspaper was deemed sufficient to support the conviction.

In the following case the Supreme Court dealt with a difficult mail fraud issue.

---

### Schmuck v. United States
U.S. Supreme Court,
109 S.Ct. 2091 (1989)

Petitioner Schmuck, a used-car distributor, purchased used cars, rolled back their odometers, and then sold the automobiles to Wisconsin retail dealers for prices artificially inflated because of the low-mileage readings. These unwitting car dealers, relying on the altered odometer figures, then resold the cars to customers, who in turn paid prices reflecting Schmuck's fraud. To complete the resale of each car, the dealer who bought it from Schmuck would submit a title-application form to the Wisconsin Department of Transportation on behalf of his retail customer. The receipt of a Wisconsin title was a legal prerequisite for transferring title and obtaining car tags.

Schmuck was convicted on 12 counts of mail fraud. He appealed, alleging that the mailings that were the crux of the indictment—the submissions of the title-application forms by the auto dealers—were not in furtherance of the fraudulent scheme and, thus, did not satisfy the mailing element of the crime of mail fraud. The circuit court rejected Schmuck's claim, but reversed on other grounds. The Supreme Court granted certiorari.

*(continued)*

**Decision:** Affirmed as to the mail fraud issue. The mail fraud statute does not reach all frauds, but only those where use of the mails is a part of the execution of the fraud. However, use of the mails need not be an essential element of the scheme; it may be only "incident to an essential part" or "a step in the plot." Even though the mailing here was done not by Schmuck, but by the innocent dealers, it was an essential step in his scheme. Absent the mailing, title could not have transferred. Absent transfer of title, none of these cars could have been resold by the dealers, so they would not have purchased them from Schmuck in the first place. Nor does it aid Schmuck that the mailings eventually provided the evidence that led to his conviction. ■

---

## Travel Act

Section 1952 of Title 18 of the *United States Code* is called the Travel Act. It punishes anyone who travels in interstate or foreign commerce or uses any facility in such commerce to (1) distribute the proceeds of illegal activity, (2) commit any crime of violence or further any unlawful activity, or (3) promote, manage, establish, carry on or facilitate any unlawful activity. Obviously, this is a very broad act which federalizes all sorts of traditionally state crimes. The "interstate commerce" element can be met by simply mailing a letter or using a telephone, for these are instrumentalities of interstate commerce. The Act has been used, for example, to convict a city electrical inspector who took bribes from private electrical contractors to overlook code violations and to facilitate departmental paperwork even though all the letters mailed by defendant stayed in one state. The mail is a facility of interstate commerce because it *can* be used to send letters from state to state.

## Hobbs Act

The Hobbs Act, 18 U.S.C. Sec. 951, punishes anyone who "in any way or degree obstructs, delays, or affects commerce or the movement of any article or commodity in commerce, by robbery or extortion. . . ." This law punishes extortion (obtaining money or something else of value by use of violence or threat of violence), but not merely accepting bribes. The distinction between the two can be difficult to draw, but has been characterized as the difference between "pay me and be assisted" (commercial bribery) and "pay me or be precluded" (extortion).

Because the law punishes those who "in any way" affect commerce, the reach of the federal statute is very broad. In one case, a county sheriff who extorted bribes to protect gamblers and prostitutes was convicted under the Hobbs Act after he solicited payments from an FBI undercover bookie operation. The court held that because the FBI operation bought furniture, paper, food, and natural gas, and could have bought more had it not given money to defendant, interstate commerce was affected. *U.S. v. Frasch*, 818 F.2d 631 (7th Cir. 1987).

## Racketeer Influenced and Corrupt Organizations Act

In 1970 Congress passed the Racketeer Influenced and Corrupt Organizations Act (RICO) to attack organized crime, especially its infiltration into legitimate business. RICO is an unusual criminal statute in that it expressly contains parallel civil provisions. In other words, it provides for both criminal penalties and private civil suits for damages. However, RICO neither included a definition of "organized crime" nor expressly required a link between a defendant's activities and organized crime. Therefore, about nine-tenths of the civil suits and many of the criminal prosecutions brought under RICO have had no connection with professional criminals (as thought of in the common sense), but have, instead, named as defendants accounting firms, banks, law firms, manufacturing corporations, anti-abortion protestors and a wide variety of others. Because of the importance of RICO *civil* actions to the area of securities law, RICO is examined in some detail in Chapter 41.

Fortunately, most of the criminal prosecutions brought under RICO have attacked the more traditional manifestations of organized crime. Prosecutors have secured RICO criminal convictions in cases involving marijuana smuggling, kickbacks to judges, extortion of "protection money" by police officers, loansharking, gambling, and the like. However, even in criminal prosecutions the government has occasionally pushed RICO to its limits by prosecuting actions in circumstances it is difficult to believe Congress had in mind when passing RICO. The following case is a classic RICO criminal action.

### United States v. LeRoy
U.S. Second Circuit Court of Appeals, 687 F.2d 610 (1982)

Defendant LeRoy was vice-president and later business manager of Local 214 of the Laborers International Union. During his terms, LeRoy was placed on the payroll of several contractors hiring Local 214's members. LeRoy did no work but received compensation so the contractors could "keep peace with the laborers." LeRoy also bought gasoline and had his brakes fixed and in so doing had the union pay the bills and then "reimburse" him as though he had paid them. LeRoy appealed his conviction of one count of conspiracy to violate §1962(c) of RICO, in violation of §1962(d).

**Decision:** The appellate court affirmed the conviction. RICO punishes patterns of racketeering activity in the operation of business enterprises. The union is an "enterprise" within the meaning of RICO, and LeRoy's actions occurred in the conduct of union business. His violation of two particular federal statutes, the Taft-Hartley Act and the Landrum-Griffin Act, were acts of racketeering sufficient to constitute a pattern of racketeering under RICO. ■

## COMPUTER CRIME

The explosive growth in the use of computers in the business world in the past few years has brought with it a corresponding increase in computer misuse. The *Avila* forgery case mentioned earlier in this chapter is a good example. Burgeoning computer crime and corresponding government responses justify separate discussion of the area of computer crime. Traditional (precomputer) state and federal laws applicable to such crimes as larceny are not necessarily appropriate for prosecution of cases of computer fraud and computer theft. For example, some cases held that an employee's unauthorized use of his employer's computer facilities in private ventures could not support a theft conviction because the employer had not been deprived of any part of value or use of the computer. Other cases have held that use of a computer is not "property" within traditional theft statutes.

Computer crimes fall mainly into three broad categories: unauthorized access, theft of information, and theft of funds. Among schemes that have been subject to prosecution are (1) stealing a competitor's computer program; (2) paying an accomplice to delete adverse information and insert favorable false information into the defendant's credit file; (3) a bank president's having his account computer coded so that his checks would be removed and held rather than posted so he could later remove the actual checks without their being debited; and (4) a disgruntled ex-employee's inserting a "virus" into his former employer's computer to destroy its records.

A recent survey found that 25 percent of businesses responding had recently experienced losses due to computer crime that averaged between $2 million and $10 million per year. Some estimate that losses due to computer misuse may be as high as $35 to $40 billion per year (including thefts of funds, losses of computer programs and data, losses of trade secrets, and damages done to computer hardware). These estimates may not be reliable, but it is clear that a substantial amount of computer crime is never discovered and a high percentage of that which is discovered is never reported because (1) companies do not want publicity about the inadequacy of their computer controls and (2) financial institutions such as banks and savings and loans fear that reports of large losses of funds, even when insured, are likely to cause customers to withdraw their deposits.

Whatever the actual loss due to computer misuse, both Congress and the state legislators have passed statutes to deal specifically with computer crime.

### *Federal Laws*

Although there have been convictions for computer crimes under general federal criminal statutes—such as those dealing with wire fraud, theft, and misappropriation—Congress has recently enacted laws specifically to deal with computer crime. The Counterfeit Access Device and Computer Fraud and Abuse Act of 1984, for example, outlaws (1) obtaining classified information from a computer without authorization and with intent or reason to believe that it is to be used to injure the United States; (2) obtaining from a computer without authorization information that is protected by the Right to Financial Privacy Act or contained in the consumer files of a credit reporting agency; and (3) interfering with the operation of a government computer.

The Comprehensive Crime Control Act of 1984 contained a section on the use of computers in credit card fraud, and established penalties for violation. In addition, the Computer Fraud and Abuse Act of 1986 established three federal crimes for computer fraud, destruction, and password trafficking.

## State Laws

At least 48 states have passed laws dealing with computer crime. Most of the statutes comprehensively address the problem, outlawing (1) computer trespass (unauthorized access); (2) damage to computers or software (e.g., use of "viruses"); (3) theft or misappropriation of computer services; and (4) obtaining or disseminating information via computer in an unauthorized manner.

# WHITE COLLAR CRIME

The term **white collar crime** generally encompasses nonviolent acts by individuals or corporations in order to obtain a personal or business advantage in a commercial context. Most of the crimes discussed earlier in this chapter are examples of white collar crime. White collar crime has become an extremely controversial subject in recent years for at least two reasons. First, there is evidence that the economic losses caused by white collar crime are at a staggering level (often estimated at well over $100 billion annually) and growing rapidly. Second, there is a perception, based on substantial fact, that criminal penalties for white collar crimes costing the public millions of dollars are often much less severe than criminal penalties imposed on the average street hood who steals a $75 pair of shoes.

Traditional criminal law did not punish corporations for crimes, reasoning that because a corporation is an artificial entity, it could not form the intent required to supply *mens rea*, and it could not be punished by incarceration. Also, American law was slow to punish corporate officials who committed crimes. One reason is illustrated by the oft-quoted sentiment of a federal judge who said that he would not "penalize a businessman trying to make a living when there are felons out on the street."

In recent years, however, the traditional views have changed rather dramatically. Potential criminal liability must now be a significant concern for both corporations and their officials.

## *Criminal Liability of Corporations*

Today, most criminal statutes include corporations in their definition of "persons" who may violate the statute. The traditional reluctance to impose criminal sanctions on corporations has been overcome by modern reasoning which suggests (1) that the *mens rea* necessary to convict a corporation can be supplied by imputing the intent of the corporation's agents who physically commit the crimes to the corporation (as has long been done in the area of tort law), and (2) that corporations can be punished by fines and by innovative punishments that might, for example, require a corporation that has been caught polluting to fund an environmental education course at a local high school.

The general rule today is that corporations can be held criminally liable for any acts performed by an employee if that employee is acting within the scope of his or her authority for the purpose of benefiting the corporation. The basic idea is that the corporation receives the benefit when the agent acts properly, and must bear the responsibility when the agent errs. This is simply an application of the *respondeat superior* doctrine (let the master answer for the wrongs of the agent) that will be discussed in more detail in Chapter 32. The corporation can even be held liable when the agent is violating company policy or disobeying a specific order from a superior. Some jurisdictions refuse to hold the corporation criminally liable for crimes committed by lower-level employees, but most states find the corporation responsible no matter how far down the ladder the actual wrongdoer is.

Corporations have been indicted for homicide and a wide variety of lesser offenses, including health and safety violations arising out of toxic waste disposal, failure to remove asbestos from buildings, and construction-site accidents.

## Criminal Liability of Corporate Officials

The increase in prosecutions of corporations has been matched by an increase in prosecutions of corporate officers as well. Corporate officers will definitely be held liable for criminal acts that they participate in or authorize. In addition, they will be held liable for acts that they aid and abet through any significant assistance or encouragement. Some courts find sufficient encouragement in mere acquiescence of a superior (which a subordinate may read as tacit approval) and even in failure to stop criminal activity that the official knows is occurring. In rare instances involving *strict liability* statutes, corporate officers have been held criminally liable because they failed to control the criminal acts of subordinates (even where they had no knowledge of the acts or had been assured that the acts had stopped). *U.S. v. Park*, 421 U.S. 658 (1975).

Indicative of the trend toward increased criminal liability are some recent cases in which corporate officials have been convicted of *murder* in cases arising out of the deaths of employees exposed to hazardous conditions in the workplace.

## SUMMARY

Crime is an unfortunate fact of life for businesses as well as individuals. Some acts of individuals in society are so inimical to the public good that remedy cannot be left to litigation between the victim and the wrongdoer. When that is true, the government initiates criminal actions to protect society at large.

The power of the government is great and potentially subject to abuse. The Bill of Rights contains a host of protections for criminal defendants, including protection from unreasonable searches and seizures, from self-incrimination, from excessive bail, and from cruel and unusual punishment. The Bill of Rights also contains a number of positive rights, including right to counsel, right to grand jury indictment, right to trial by jury, and right to a speedy and public trial.

The basic elements of any criminal conviction are a defendant's guilty act and guilty mind, both of which must be established beyond a reasonable doubt by the prosecutor.

A raft of states laws, such as those criminalizing larceny, embezzlement, forgery, and arson help to protect business interests. Congress has passed a host of federal criminal acts as well, including the Hobbs Act, the Travel Act, RICO, and the laws outlawing mail and wire fraud. Both federal and state governments have responded to technological innovations by passing new criminal laws dealing specifically with computer crime.

Today, criminal law is not a concern solely for the street criminal. Corporations and those staffing their boardrooms must also abide by society's laws. Criminal prosecutions for white collar crime are definitely increasing in number and severity of penalties meted out.

## KEY TERMS

**Crime**
**Felony**
**Misdemeanor**
**Grand Jury**
**Double Jeopardy**
*Actus reus*
*Mens Rea*
**Entrapment**
**Immunity**
**Larceny**
**Burglary**
**False Pretenses**
**Embezzlement**
**Robbery**
**Forgery**
**Arson**
**Mail fraud**
**Wire fraud**
**White collar crime**

## QUESTIONS AND PROBLEMS

1. Carella was convicted of grand theft for failure to return a rented car. Jurors were instructed that a California statute required them to presume intent to commit theft by one who had leased a car and failed to return it to its owner within 20 days after the owner had made written demand for its return following expiration of the lease. Is this presumption consistent with Carella's due process rights? Discuss. (*Carella v. California*, 109 S.Ct. 2419, 1989.)

2. Halper, manager of a company that provided medical services for patients eligible for federal Medicare benefits,

was convicted of submitting 65 false claims for Government reimbursement in violation of the federal criminal false-claims statute. He was sentenced to prison and fined $5,000. Based on the facts that led to the criminal conviction, the government sued Halper under the federal civil False Claims Act. The terms of that Act's remedial provision, as it then existed, would have rendered Halper liable for a civil fine of at least $130,000. Would imposition of this civil fine in addition to the criminal punishment already imposed violate the Double Jeopardy Clause of the Fifth Amendment? (*U.S. v. Halper,* 109 S.Ct. 1892, 1989.)

3. Speckman was an attorney for a partnership that financed a waterslide operation. In 1980, a partner, Schwab, indicated a desire to sell his interest. Speckman told Schwab that he had a buyer and later gave Schwab a check for around $5,000. In 1983, Speckman's client Young indicated an interest in investment opportunities. Speckman recommended the waterslide operation and Young gave Speckman a check for $7,500 to be used to buy Schwab's interest. However, Speckman never altered the partnership records to indicate that Schwab was no longer a partner. Neither Schwab nor Young received any monetary distribution from the partnership. In essence, Speckman bought Schwab's interest, resold it to Young, but then denied Young the benefit of his investment. A jury convicted Speckman of *both* embezzlement and larceny by false pretenses in the obtaining of Young's $7,500. Discuss the appropriateness of this verdict. (*State v. Speckman,* 374 S.E.2d 419, N.C. App. 1989.)

4. Using the name "Larry Grimes," Tolliver opened an account at Pioneer Savings & Loan with $50. He applied for a TYME card for use with Pioneer's automated tellers. He later used an automated teller to deposit a $2,500 check which had been stolen from Terry McCaughey. He then made several cash withdrawals with his TYME card before the McCaughey check was returned to Pioneer with the notation that the account was closed and the signature unauthorized. Tolliver was convicted of uttering a forged check. Under the statute, the forged writing must be "uttered" or offered as genuine. Tolliver appealed, claiming that it is impossible to offer a writing as genuine to a machine, and therefore the offering or uttering took place when the machines' owners presented the check for payment to the drawee. Is Tolliver's defense valid? (*State v. Tolliver,* 440 N.W.2d 571, Wis. App. 1989.)

5. Matt was a division manager in charge of sales promotion for a tobacco company. One promotion was to give cigarettes to retailers so they could engage in "buy one, get one free" promotions. Matt concocted a scheme that involved removing complimentary tobacco products and exchanging them through sales representatives for salable merchandise. Matt would sell the merchandise and keep the money. To hide the scheme, Matt forced sales representatives to file false reports with respect to the placement of complimentary goods, which he would then mail to the company. Matt was indicted for mail fraud. Should he be convicted? (*U.S. v. Matt,* 838 F.2d 1356, 5th Cir. 1988.)

6. Mulder was a commissioned salesman for Englehart's wholesale furniture business. He told Bateman, a furniture maker, that he "was in with a couple of new partners" who might have some work for him. Englehart and Mulder met Bateman; Englehart paid Bateman $8,750 to build 50 entertainment centers. A few days later, defendant told Bateman that Englehart had decided to get entertainment centers elsewhere and he would have to give the money back. Bateman, believing defendant to be Englehart's partner, gave him $6,250, retaining $2,500 per an agreement with defendant to stain units defendant falsely claimed were being bought elsewhere. Defendant used the $6,250 to pay personal debts. When charged with embezzlement, Mulder claimed that, unlike a bank teller for example, his job was not to handle Englehart's money, and therefore he had not committed embezzlement. Is this a reasonable defense? (*People v. Mulder,* 421 N.W.2d 605, Mich. App. 1988.)

7. Mathews, an administrator for the Small Business Administration, was taped by the FBI as he apparently accepted a bribe. Mathews was indicted for accepting a gratuity in exchange for an official act in violation of federal law. Mathews wished to raise an entrapment defense, but the trial judge refused to allow it unless Mathews first admitted all elements of the offense. In other words, Mathews could not plead in the alternative: "I didn't do it, but if I did I was entrapped." Should a defendant be required to admit the substantive elements of the offense or be barred from raising an entrapment defense? (*U.S. v. Mathews,* 485 U.S. 58, 1988.)

8. Being Director of Network Services for NYNEX Mobile Communications Co., Covino had substantial influence over selection of and compensation for construction companies working for NYNEX. Great Northeastern was a construction company that did a large proportion of its work for NYNEX. In May 1984, Covino told Brennan, Great Northeastern's president, that one of Brennan's employees had improperly billed $3,200 in phone calls to a NYNEX credit card and that it "wouldn't look good" if Covino showed the bill to his superiors. Brennan offered to pay the bill, but Covino said that he would take care of it. Not long thereafter, Covino asked Brennan to build a sun deck on Covino's home, telling him to keep "in mind the phone bill." The project evolved into a $20,000 addition. Covino asked Brennan to take a $15,000 check and then give him back that much in cash so that it would appear Covino had paid for the work. Brennan declined to assist in the coverup, but did not charge for the work. Because Brennan was afraid of losing the NYNEX work, he eventually paid over $85,000 in cash to Covino in addition to doing more work

on his house. Covino was discovered and indicted for a violation of the Hobbs Act. Discuss the appropriateness of this charge. (*U.S. v. Covino,* 837 F.2d 65, 2d Cir. 1988.)

9. Covino, from the preceding case, was also charged with a violation of the Travel Act. It was basically alleged that he had phoned Brennan to facilitate the commission of a state crime, specifically, bribery in violation of New York law. Discuss the appropriateness of this charge.

10. Covino was *also* accused of wire fraud. The indictment stated that he had used the wires to "violate his fiduciary duty to NYNEX Communications, by concealing information, to wit, his receipt of money and property . . . , which information was material to the conduct of the business of NYNEX," which was in furtherance of a scheme to defraud NYNEX by depriving it of defendant's "loyal and unbiased services." Discuss the validity of this charge.

# CHAPTER 8

# TORTS

Our primary concern in Part I of this text has been to familiarize the student with the aspects of our legal system that are common to all branches of law. Thus we have examined the nature and sources of law generally and the processes by which rules of law are formulated, paying little or no attention to such specific subjects as contracts, sales, or agency. However, we have also addressed two specific subjects of pervasive importance to the American legal system—constitutional law and criminal law. Now we turn to one other branch of law that merits special consideration—**torts** ("civil wrongs").

## A PREFACE

Two areas of law, criminal law and contract law, developed at an early time in England. While both were intended to eliminate, insofar as possible, various kinds of wrongful conduct, each was concerned with markedly different wrongs. The major purposes of criminal law were to define *wrongs against the state*—types of conduct so inherently undesirable that they were flatly prohibited—and to permit the state to punish those who committed such acts by the imposition of fines or imprisonment. The major purposes of contract law, on the other hand, were (1) to spell out the nature of the rights and duties springing from *private agreements between individuals,* and (2) in the event that one party failed to live up to these duties, to compensate the innocent party for the loss resulting from the other's breach of contract.

While criminal law and contract law were in their initial stages of development, it became apparent that neither one afforded protection to the large numbers of persons who suffered losses resulting from other kinds of conduct equally unjustifiable from a social standpoint—acts of carelessness, deception, and the like. Faced with this situation, the courts at an early time began to recognize and define other "legal wrongs" besides crimes and breaches of contract—and began to permit persons who were injured thereby to bring civil actions to recover damages against those who committed them. Acts that came to be recognized as wrongs under these rules, which were formulated by judges over the years on a case-by-case basis, acquired the name of *torts* (the French word for "*wrongs*").

Because tort law applies to such a wide range of activities, any introductory definition of tort must necessarily be framed in general terms—as, for example, "any wrong excluding breaches of contract and crimes," or "any noncontractual civil wrong committed upon the person or property of another." While such definitions are of little aid in illustrating the specific kinds of torts that are recognized, they do, at least, reflect the historical lines of demarcation between breaches of contract, crimes, and torts.[1]

## SCOPE AND COMPLEXITY OF TORT LAW

As our society has become increasingly industrialized and complex, with many relationships existing among individuals that were perhaps unthought of fifty years ago, the legal duties owed by one member of society to others have become considerably more numerous and varied. As a result, tort law encompasses such a wide range of human conduct that the breaches of some duties have little in common with others. For example, some actions are considered tortious

---

[1] As indicated by these definitions, torts and crimes are essentially two different kinds of wrongs—the first a wrong against the individual and the second a wrong against the state. However, as we will see, in many situations a single wrongful act can constitute both a tort and a crime.

(wrongful) only when the actor intended to cause an injury, while in other actions—especially those involving negligence—the actor's intentions are immaterial. Similarly, in some tort actions the plaintiff is required to show physical injury to his or her property as a result of the defendant's misconduct, while in other actions such a showing is not required. In the latter situations other kinds of legal injury are recognized, such as damages to reputation or mental suffering.

A somewhat clearer picture of the broad sweep of tort law can be gained from the realization that the rules making up this area of law must deal with such diverse matters as the care required of a surgeon in the operating room, the circumstances in which a contracting party has a legal obligation to inform the other party of facts which he or she knows that the other party does not possess, and the determination of the kinds of business information (trade secrets) that are entitled to protection against theft by competitors.

The courts clearly engage in some degree of social engineering as they shape the common law of torts. Common to all successful tort actions are the twin concepts of *interest* and *duty*. Each time a court allows tort recovery, it is saying that the plaintiff has an interest (for example, in bodily integrity, in enjoying the benefits of private property, in a good reputation) sufficiently important for the law to furnish protection, and that, correspondingly, in a civilized society the defendant has a duty (for example, not to strike the plaintiff, not to steal plaintiff's property, not to falsely injure plaintiff's reputation) that was breached. As society evolves technologically, morally, philosophically, and otherwise, tort law will evolve also. For example, one hundred years ago, Americans had very little privacy. However, as increased wealth has allowed us to purchase and enjoy privacy, most of us have come to value privacy very much. In recent years most courts have come to recognize privacy as an interest worth protecting and, as we shall see, have imposed a duty on others not to invade our privacy.

The law of torts is so broad and so pervasive that it cannot be treated in a single chapter. This chapter focuses on the law of negligence and on certain intentional torts. A number of torts of specific concern to business are discussed in Chapter 9. Lawsuits arising out of the sale of defective products are also primarily tort related; they are discussed in Chapter 22. While these three chapters are devoted almost solely to tort law, the subject will make appearances in several other chapters.[2]

This chapter begins with a treatment of negligence law, and then examines several important intentional torts.

# NEGLIGENCE

**Negligence,** to oversimplify, is carelessness. The courts long ago decided that our interests in economic well-being and personal safety are sufficiently important to be protected from the careless acts of others. Correspondingly, each of us has a duty as we live our lives and carry on our professions to exercise care so as not to carelessly injure others. Even though we may not intend to injure, the harm is just as real to the victim who is struck by the careless driver, burned by the carelessly designed product, crippled by the careless surgeon, or ruined financially by embezzlement that an accountant carelessly failed to detect.

The negligence cause of action is the most important method of redress existing today for persons injured accidentally. The newspapers are filled with accounts of negligence actions involving asbestos exposure, Agent Orange, the Exxon *Valdez* oil spill in Alaska, and the like. Whether a plaintiff was injured by a careless driver, a careless product designer, a careless surgeon, or a careless accountant, the same basic elements must be proved to establish a right of recovery: (1) that defendant owed plaintiff a *duty* of due care; (2) that defendant *breached* that duty of due care; (3) that defendant's breach *proximately caused* the injury; and (4) that plaintiff suffered *injury*.

## Duty

Few concepts are more fraught with difficulty than that of "duty" in the negligence cause of action. As a general rule, it may be said that we each owe a duty to every person whom we can *reasonably foresee* might be injured by our carelessness. If we drive down the street carelessly, pedestrians and other drivers are within the class of foreseeable plaintiffs whom we might injure. That we do not know the exact names of our prospective victims is unimportant.

To quickly illustrate, in *Burke v. Pan American World Airways, Inc.*,[3] plaintiff sued defendants al-

---

[2]For example, Chapter 32 (liability of parties in an agency relationship), Chapter 42 (legal liability of accountants), and Chapter 50 (consumer transactions and the law).

[3]484 F.Supp. 850 (S.D.N.Y. 1980).

legedly responsible for a terrible plane collision in the Canary Islands, claiming that she, though in California at the time, felt as though she were being "split in two" and felt an emptiness "like a black hole" at the exact instant of the crash. Plaintiff claimed that in that instant she knew that something terrible had happened to her identical twin sister who was, in fact, killed in the collision. Plaintiff was prepared to document the phenomenon of "extrasensory empathy" between some pairs of identical twins. Even assuming plaintiff could establish the point, the court dismissed the suit. When a plane crashes because of an airline's negligence, its passengers are certainly foreseeable plaintiffs, as are any persons on the ground hit by falling wreckage. However, Burke's injuries were too bizarre to be reasonably foreseeable, even if she did sustain them. The defendants owed no legal duty to plaintiff.

Though foreseeability is a very important consideration in establishing the parameters of a careless actor's duty, it is not the only one. The California courts, which have extended the notion of duty about as far as any jurisdiction, have taken into account such factors as:

. . . the foreseeability of harm to the plaintiff, the degree of certainty that the plaintiff suffered injury, the closeness of the connection between the defendant's conduct and the injury suffered, the moral blame attached to the defendant's conduct, the policy of preventing future harm, the extent of the burden to the defendant and consequences to the community of imposing a duty to exercise care with resulting liability, and the availability, cost, and prevalence of insurance for the risk involved.[4]

Indeed, these are the factors the court used in *Soldano v. O'Daniels,* a case discussed in Chapter 1, to impose a duty not to interfere with a Good Samaritan's attempt to aid a victim in distress.[5]

The following case is just one illustration of a court's struggle to meld foreseeability and public policy factors to produce a proper scope of duty.

---

[4]*Rowland v. Christian,* 70 Cal. Rptr. 97 (1968).
[5]Students should also consult *H. Rosenblum, Inc. v. Adler* in Chapter 42 regarding the duty accountants owe to foreseeable plaintiffs injured by the accountants' professional negligence.

---

## Otis Engineering Corp. v. Clark
Texas Supreme Court, 668 S.W.2d 307 (1983)

Matheson, an employee of defendant Otis Engineering Corporation, had a history of being intoxicated on the job. One night he was particularly intoxicated and his fellow employees believed he should be removed from the machines. Roy, Matheson's supervisor, suggested that Matheson go home, escorted him to the company parking lot, and asked him if he could make it home. Matheson answered that he could, but thirty minutes later and some three miles away he caused an accident killing the wives of plaintiffs Larry and Clifford Clark.

The Clarks sued Otis in a wrongful death action, but the trial court dismissed the suit holding that Otis could not be liable because Matheson was not acting within the scope of his employment at the time of the accident. The intermediate court of appeals reversed, and Otis appealed to the Texas Supreme Court.

**Decision:** The judgment of the appeals court was affirmed and the case remanded to the trial court for further proceedings. A plaintiff in a tort case must first prove that the defendant owed him a duty and breached that duty. Traditionally the courts have imposed a duty on us not to injure another by our affirmative act, but we have not been required to act to assist another in peril (*i.e.,* inaction is acceptable), nor have we been required to control the dangerous actions of others.

However, as human interrelationships become increasingly complex and social standards change, concepts of duty may evolve also. Professor Prosser has suggested that as between an entirely innocent plaintiff and a defendant who has admittedly departed from the appropriate standard of social conduct, the latter should bear the loss. "Therefore, the standard of duty that we now adopt . . . is: when, because of an employee's incapacity, an employer exercises control over the employee, the employer has a duty to take such actions as a reasonably prudent employer under the same or similar circumstances would take to prevent the employee from causing an unreasonable risk of harm to others."

The case was remanded for a determination as to whether Otis acted in compliance with this standard. ■

**Duty of Landowners:** A recurring problem in establishing the nature of a duty exists regarding the responsibility of owners or occupiers of land. How much of a duty they owe to visitors to their land has traditionally turned on whether the visitor was a trespasser (one who enters the land with no right to do so), a licensee (one who has a right to come onto the property for self-benefit, such as a door-to-door salesman or a neighbor dropping in uninvited), or an invitee (one invited by the owner or occupier or who enters for the benefit of the owner or occupier, such as a customer at a store). The following case discusses the duties owed under the traditional rule, and also examines a new trend toward breaking down the traditional categories and simply utilizing a foreseeability standard for all visitors to land. The traditional rule is still the majority rule, but cases such as this are eroding it.

---

**Ouellette v. Blanchard**
New Hampshire Supreme Court,
364 A.2d 631 (1976)

Defendant Blanchard, with a permit, was burning rubbish in an unsupervised fire on his premises. Plaintiff Jaye Ouellette, then ten years old, went onto the property with other children and with them threw sand on the fire. Jaye stepped on some hot coals and fell forward on her hands burning both her feet and hands. She and her father brought this negligence suit. At the close of plaintiffs' opening statement, defendant moved for judgment on grounds that Jaye was a trespasser to whom defendant owed no duty, or at best a licensee to whom he owed no duty of care regarding hazards known to her. The trial court denied the motion and transferred the question of law to the State Supreme Court.

**Decision:** The defendant's motion was overruled and the case remanded. The court felt that the traditional approach to landowner duty of dividing plaintiffs into the trespasser/licensee/invitee categories had become filled with exceptions and burdened with unneeded complexity. A test of reasonable care under all the circumstances, as used in other negligence cases, was simpler and preferable. The court held that the traditional tort test of foreseeability should determine the scope of duty in landowner cases as in other negligence cases. The trial court was asked to reconsider the case in light of this new standard. ∎

---

## Breach

To be liable for negligence, a defendant must have *breached* an existing duty. A breach occurs when defendant fails to exercise the same care as a "reasonable person under similar circumstances" would have exercised. This hypothetical "reasonable person" or "reasonable man" standard can be fairly strict because of a jury's tendency, confronted with a seriously injured plaintiff, to use 20-20 hindsight:

> [The reasonable man] is one who invariably looks where he is going and is careful to examine the immediate foreground before he executes a leap or bound; who neither star-gazes nor is lost in meditation when approaching trap doors or the margin of a dock; . . . who never mounts a moving omnibus, and does not alight from any car while the train is still in motion . . . and who informs himself of the history and habits of a dog before administering a caress.[6]

**All the Circumstances:** Whether or not a defendant's conduct met the "reasonable person" standard of care should be examined in light of all the circumstances of the case. Emergency conditions, for example, may be considered. Normally it would be a clear breach of due care to abandon a moving vehicle, but if a cab driver does so because a robber in his back seat has pulled a gun, a jury might determine

---

[6] A. P. Herbert, *Uncommon Law: Fardell v. Potts.*

that, under all the circumstances, there was no breach of due care so as to render the cab company liable to a pedestrian who was struck by the driverless cab.[7] An unexpected bee sting might cause a bus driver unavoidably to lose control of a bus, though he was a most careful driver.[8] The doctrine of "unavoidable accident" excuses liability in such cases.

The custom of others in the community or of other companies in the industry may also shed light on the proper standard of due care. If the defendant has acted in the same manner as most others in the same situation, it is difficult to conclude that a reasonable person standard was breached. However, custom is not always binding. In one famous case, barges were lost at sea because the tugs towing them had no radio sets to listen to weather reports that would have warned them to take shelter from an approaching storm. That few tug companies used the radio sets was not proof that the "reasonable person" standard was met, because "a whole calling may have unduly lagged in the adoption of new and available devices."[9]

**Conduct of Others:** Traditionally the courts allowed us to assume that other members of society would act carefully and lawfully. In other words, we had no duty to anticipate the negligent or criminal acts of others. However, increasingly courts and juries are concluding that such acts can and must be anticipated in certain circumstances. Thus, operators of a motel located in a high crime area that has itself been the scene of criminal acts in the past may be held to have breached a duty of due care by not providing adequate security for guests who are victimized by crime.[10] Though some courts refuse to impose a duty in such circumstances, providing adequate security is increasingly a concern for motel owners, common carriers, store owners, concert promoters, and even universities.

**Negligence *Per Se*:** Though the standard of care to which a defendant will be held in a negligence case is usually formulated by the jury's assessment of what a reasonable person would have done, in some cases the conduct is measured in accordance with legislatively-imposed standards. One example is a "dramshop" act which many states have passed making it illegal to sell liquor to an intoxicated person. Another is the 65-mile-per-hour speed limit.

Most courts have held that if a defendant violates such a statute, it is negligence *per se*.[11] That is, if the plaintiff can show that he or she is within the class of persons that the statute was meant to protect and the harm sustained was the type the statute was meant to prevent, then the issue of breach of due care is conclusively resolved against the defendant. The jury can be instructed that the defendant has breached the duty of due care. Lack of damages or proximate causation still might prevent recovery.

In one recent case, a small girl was abducted from the street in front of the building in which she lived, taken across the street to an open, vacant apartment, and assaulted. The girl sued the owners of the apartment building in which the assault occurred for not having locks on the doors, in violation of a city ordinance, and thereby providing a tempting location for the crime. Emphasizing that the ordinance was intended to provide security against crime by requiring all vacant apartments to be secured, the court found negligence *per se* in its violation.[12]

Many courts do not go quite so far, holding only that violation of a statute is one factor the jury can consider among all others in deciding whether defendant breached the duty of due care.

## *Proximate Cause*

After proving existence and breach of a duty of due care, the plaintiff in a negligence action must demonstrate that the breach proximately caused plaintiff's alleged injuries. There are many different labels and many different approaches to the proximate cause concept. Fundamentally, **proximate cause** means direct cause—that there is a direct causal connection between defendant's act of carelessness and plaintiff's injury—but it is more complicated than that.

Many courts speak in terms of two requirements being necessary to establish "legal cause" in each

---

[7] *Cordas v. Peerless Transp. Co.*, 27 N.Y.S.2d 198 (N.Y. 1941).
[8] *Schultz v. Cheney School District*, 371 P.2d 59 (Wash. 1962).
[9] *The T. J. Hooper*, 60 F.2d 737 (2d Cir. 1932).
[10] *Garzilli v. Howard Johnson's Motor Lodges, Inc.*, 419 F.Supp. 1210 (E.D.N.Y. 1976) (the "Connie Francis case").

[11] And, of course, if a plaintiff violates such a statute it is contributory negligence *per se*. This is a concept we shall address directly under the topic of "defenses."
[12] *Nixon v. Mr. Property Management Co.*, 690 S.W.2d 546 (Tex. 1985).

case. First, they require *causation in fact*. This is sometimes termed "but for" causation; that is, can we say that "but for" the defendant's act the injuries would not have taken place. For example, assume that Jill is driving her car at 40 miles per hour on a street where the speed limit is 30 miles per hour when a small child darts into the street from between two cars and is hit by Jill's car. Assume further that the child was so close to Jill's car when he darted into the street that even had Jill been driving 30 miles per hour, or even 20, she could not have avoided striking the child. In such a case we cannot say that "but for" Jill's speeding the accident would not have happened. Jill's careless speeding was not a proximate cause of the accident and Jill would not be liable.

"But for" causation is insufficient in and of itself, however. Almost every act has consequences which ripple through society, and every incident has several causes. Perhaps "but for" your carelessly running a stop sign, ambulance driver A would never have met nurse B and had child C who at the age of 14 murdered D. May D's family sue you? Obviously not. For policy reasons, we must limit the liability stemming from our actions in some fashion.

Most courts return to the notion of *foreseeability* in establishing the second element of legal causation. Factual causation ("but for") plus foreseeability will establish proximate or legal causation. Because foreseeability is an important factor in the establishment of both duty and proximate cause, court discussions of the two concepts tend to overlap.

The most famous tort case of all time is perhaps *Palsgraf v. Long Island R.R.*,[13] in which railway employees carelessly pushed a passenger who was trying to board a train. This caused him to drop a package he was carrying which, it turned out, contained fireworks which exploded beneath the wheels of the train. The force of the concussion knocked over a scale at the far end of the train station, injuring Mrs. Palsgraf. Injury to the boarding passenger and his property was a foreseeable result of the negligence of the railroad employees. They owed a duty of care to him and any injuries to him would have been proximately caused by their actions. However, the court found the injury to Mrs. Palsgraf unforeseeable. The duty owed to the boarding passenger did not protect her.

The *Palsgraf* dissent argued that every person owes to the world a duty to refrain from careless acts, and that we should be liable for all injuries flowing directly from our negligence, regardless of foreseeability. The dissenters felt the wrongdoer should be liable for all "proximate consequences," even where they consist of injuries to persons outside the foreseeable radius of danger.

Generally speaking, the "foreseeability" test of *Palsgraf* holds sway in our law today, but the "direct consequences" view of the dissent is frequently applied in various circumstances. For example, if we carelessly injure a person who turns out to be a hemophiliac, who then bleeds to death when most persons would not have, we are still liable for the death. Courts say that we must take our victims as we find them. Though it might not be reasonably foreseeable to us that our victim would be a hemophiliac, his death is a direct result of our carelessness.

**Independent Intervening Cause:** Especially in terms of foreseeability, the concept of **independent intervening cause** is important. Such a cause is one that emanates from a third party or source to disrupt the causal connection between the defendant's careless act and plaintiff's injury. Assume that Sue is driving down the street when she comes upon an intersection that is blocked by an accident caused by Joe's having run a stop sign. Sue turns her car around and while driving away is hit by a tree that is blown down by a strong breeze. Sue can argue that "but for" Joe's carelessness the intersection would not have been blocked and she would have been several miles away from the tree at the time it blew over. But should we hold Joe liable for Sue's injury? No, because the tree's falling is an independent, intervening cause that breaks up the causal chain between Joe's careless driving and Sue's injury. The key, again, is foreseeability. An intervening cause that can reasonably be foreseen by the defendant is usually insufficient to break the causal chain. The following case applies these principles of causation.

---

[13] 162 N.E. 99 (N.Y. 1928).

### Hoyem v. Manhattan Beach City School District
Supreme Court of California, 585 P.2d 851 (1978)

Michael Hoyem, a ten-year-old boy, attended a school in defendant Manhattan Beach City School District. One day during summer school he left early and was struck and seriously injured by a motorcycle at a public intersection nearby. Michael and his mother sued the school district for negligence, based on its alleged failure to properly supervise Michael. The trial court dismissed the suit, and plaintiffs appealed.

**Decision:** Reversed. Plaintiffs are entitled to a jury trial. The court first held that state law imposes on school authorities a *duty* to supervise students and to enforce rules necessary for their protection. Addressing the issue of *proximate cause,* the court held that it cannot be said *as a matter of law* that a school cannot be responsible for off-campus injuries. First, it may be said that "but for" defendant's alleged careless supervision the accident would not have happened because Michael would never have left the campus. The second key element of proximate causation is reasonable foreseeability. Since the days of Huck Finn and Tom Sawyer it has been foreseeable that children might play hooky. The school's duty to supervise recognizes this fact. The motorcyclist's action is an intervening act, but would break up the chain of causation only if it were unforeseeable. That is a jury question. ■

## *Injury*

As the final element of a negligence cause of action, the plaintiff must prove injury. Negligence recovery is allowed primarily for injury to person or property. Recovery for economic loss not related to personal injury or property damage is generally not allowed, although there are several exceptions for special situations. (See, for example, *H. Rosenblum, Inc. v. Adler* in Chapter 42.)

Courts have also been reluctant to allow recovery for emotional distress on grounds that such injuries are too intangible and too easily faked. Over the years, most courts have changed their views as psychiatric testimony regarding the actual existence of emotional distress has become more dependable.

At first, courts allowed recovery for negligently caused emotional distress where the plaintiff also sustained a physical injury in the accident. It was easier to believe that the plaintiff suffered emotional distress if there were accompanying physical injuries. Later courts also awarded recovery to plaintiffs who were not physically injured, but were in the "zone of danger." Thus, a pedestrian who was narrowly missed by an automobile which ran down a fellow pedestrian could sue the careless driver for emotional damages.

Because application of the "zone of danger" test leads sometimes to rather arbitrary distinctions, many courts have taken an additional step by allowing "bystander recovery." Thus, according to the leading case,[14] a parent who sees or hears an accident killing the parent's child can recover for emotional distress though not within the zone of danger. Three factors to be weighed in deciding whether to allow recovery are: (1) whether plaintiff was located near the scene of the accident; (2) whether the emotional shock resulted from a contemporaneous perception of the accident, as opposed to hearing about it later; and (3) whether the plaintiff and the victim were closely related. Many courts have rejected bystander recovery, which obviously entails an extension of the concept of duty. But the modern trend is to recognize that if an actor's carelessness causes an injury which kills or seriously injures someone, the victim's loved ones are almost certain to suffer emotional trauma.

Punitive damages, also known as exemplary damages, are not recoverable in mere negligence cases. These are monetary damages, over and above the sums necessary to compensate for plaintiff's injuries, which are assessed against the defendant to punish for wrongdoing and to deter defendant and others from engaging in such wrongful conduct. A defendant in a negligence action is guilty of mere carelessness, so punitive damages are viewed as inappropriate. However, punitive damages are available to plaintiffs injured by the intentional torts which we will discuss later in the chapter.

---

[14]*Dillon v. Legg,* 69 Cal. Rptr. 72 (1958).

## Defenses

Even if the plaintiff establishes all four elements of a negligence cause of action, the defendant may avert or reduce recovery by establishing certain defenses.

**Contributory Fault:** If the plaintiff is guilty of fault which contributed to the accident, a defense may exist. Under the old system of **contributory negligence,** a plaintiff who was guilty of carelessness which contributed in any material way to the accident was barred from recovery altogether. Even if the jury concluded that plaintiff was 1 percent at fault and defendant 99 percent, plaintiff could recover nothing, no matter how serious the injuries were.

Because of the harshness of the contributory negligence system, most jurisdictions have replaced it with a system of **comparative negligence.** Comparative negligence or comparative fault systems vary widely from jurisdiction to jurisdiction, so it is difficult to generalize. Some states have "pure" comparative negligence systems under which, no matter how great a share of the fault is attributable to plaintiff, plaintiff still is entitled to recover the portion of damages caused by defendant's carelessness. For example, let's assume that in a case arising out of an auto collision between P and D, a jury assesses P's damages at $100,000 and finds P 40 percent at fault and D 60 percent at fault. Rather than being barred from recovery as in a contributory negligence system, P would recover $60,000—that portion of the damages caused by D's fault. Indeed, in a pure system, even if P is found 99 percent at fault and D 1 percent, P would still recover $1,000. That P is many times more at fault than D does not bar recovery for that portion of the loss caused by D's carelessness.

Most jurisdictions have not adopted a pure comparative negligence system. Many allow a plaintiff to recover whatever percentage of damages were caused by defendant, unless plaintiff's share of the fault is assessed at 51 percent or higher. If plaintiff's fault exceeds 50 percent, recovery is barred altogether on the theory that plaintiff should recover nothing if he or she is more at fault than defendant. Other states set 49 percent as the cap, not allowing recovery to a plaintiff found 50 percent or more at fault.

**Statute of Limitations:** In negligence, as in other causes of action, every state has a **statute of limitations** within which the suit must be filed or forever barred. A typical tort statute of limitations is two years. Thus, a plaintiff injured by defendant's negligence must file suit within two years of the occurrence. Occasionally a plaintiff may not even know of the injury until more than two years after the occurrence, for example, when carelessly designed drugs with side effects which will not show up for years are sold. Most states have applied tolling devices which provide that in such a case the statute of limitations is tolled; that is, will not begin to run, until the plaintiff knows or should know of the injury. In response to the medical malpractice and products liability "crises," several states have passed statutes of "repose" which bar certain actions after, say 15 years, whether the injuries sustained were discoverable or not during that period.

## No Fault Systems

Negligence has been eliminated as a basis for lawsuits in at least two contexts which should be mentioned here. Every state has a *workers' compensation* system which allows injured employees to recover benefits from their employers when injured on the job. The employee can recover regardless of the presence of employer fault, but forfeits the right to sue the employer even if the employer has been careless. Most jurisdictions, however, allow an employee covered by workers' compensation to sue his or her employer in tort if injured by the employer's gross negligence (for example, if the employer has allowed several employees to be injured by the same defective machine without replacing it) or intentional tort. Workers' compensation plays a role in the *Caudle v. Betts* case in the next section, and is discussed in more detail in Chapter 49.

Several states have enacted "no fault" automobile statutes. The thrust of these statutes is to reduce litigation by allowing persons who suffer only minor injuries in car accidents to recover only from their own insurance company. Though these laws vary widely from jurisdiction to jurisdiction, in most the plaintiffs' losses must exceed a certain statutory threshold before resort to litigation is allowed.

## MAJOR INTENTIONAL TORTS
### Assault and Battery

Assault and battery are similar torts which may be treated together. Although modern courts and statutes frequently use the two terms interchangeably, technically a **battery** is a rude, inordinate contact with the person of another. An **assault,** basically, is any act which creates an apprehension of an imminent battery. That we can sue for assault and battery protects our personal dignity from intrusions of the mind (assault) and body (battery). The courts long ago concluded that we have a legitimate interest in being protected from offensive bodily contacts and fear of them. Indeed, assault and battery also constitute crimes.

**Elements:** One way to formulate the basic elements of the torts of assault and battery is to require plaintiff to prove (1) defendant's affirmative conduct, (2) intent, and (3) plaintiff's injury.

*Affirmative Conduct and Intent:* If Sue is carefully driving down the street and is hit by a car that runs a red light and as a result Sue's car is pushed into a pedestrian, Sue has not committed assault or battery. Though the pedestrian has sustained both apprehension (assuming she saw the accident as it happened) and rude contact, Sue committed no affirmative act which caused the injuries. The driver of the car that ran the red light did commit an affirmative act that was tortious, but that act was negligence, not assault or battery. On the other hand, if, while driving down the street, Sue spotted an enemy and deliberately ran down that person in a crosswalk, an assault and battery would have occurred.

The intent required for both assault and battery is the intent either to create an offensive contact to plaintiff's body or the apprehension of it in plaintiff. Furthermore, a person is presumed to intend the natural consequences of his or her actions. Thus, if A points an unloaded gun at B and utters threats to use it, an assault occurs if B did not know the gun was unloaded even if A's intent is simply to play a harmless prank. The natural consequences of A's act of pointing the gun is to create an apprehension in B.

Under the *doctrine of transferred intent,* if Sam shoots at Bill, but Bill ducks and the bullet hits Carlos, Carlos has an assault (assuming he saw the incident happening) and battery claim against Sam even if he is Sam's best friend and Sam wouldn't intentionally hurt him for the world. The law transfers the intent Sam had to injure Bill to Carlos.

*Injury:* If plaintiff seeks to establish an assault, the injury sustained must be in the nature of an apprehension of imminent bodily contact of an offensive nature. A threat of future contact or a threat by a defendant far away is insufficient. Threats or even attempts at violence which the intended victim does not know about until much later do not create the requisite apprehension, as where D shoots at and misses P from so far away that P never realizes the shot was fired. Usually plaintiff's reactions are judged by what would have caused apprehension in a reasonable person, but if defendant knows that plaintiff is an unusually sensitive person and threatens contacts which plaintiff finds offensive though most persons would not, an assault occurs.

If plaintiff sues for battery, the injury that must be demonstrated is an offensive contact. Being struck with a fist, a knife, or a bullet obviously satisfies the requirement. So does being spat upon, poisoned, and having one's clothes ripped or cane knocked away.

The following case illustrates the tort of battery in an employment context, thereby raising also some important workers' compensation issues.

---

### Caudle v. Betts
Supreme Court of Louisiana,
512 So.2d 389 (1987)

Plaintiff Ruben Caudle was a salesman at Betts Lincoln-Mercury, Inc. Shortly before an office Christmas party on December 23, 1983, other employees engaged in horseplay with an electric automobile condenser after discovering that it could be charged by touching one end to a car's spark plug wire and turning the engine over. Once charged, the condenser would deliver a slight electric shock when touched at both ends. Several employees played catch with the charged condenser. Peter Betts, president of the corporation, shocked the back of Caudle's neck with the charged condenser and chased Caudle with it until Caudle escaped by locking himself in an office. Following the incident, Caudle suffered headaches and passed out 30 to 40 times in the following months. The condition finally required occipital nerve surgery, leaving a slight numbness on the right side of plaintiff's head.

*(continued)*

Caudle sued Betts individually and Betts Lincoln-Mercury, Inc., for battery, seeking damages for, among other things, pain and suffering, past medical expenses, and loss of earnings. The trial court held that the injury to plaintiff was not an intentional injury and, therefore, that workers' compensation benefits were plaintiff's sole remedy. The appellate court affirmed the dismissal of plaintiff's tort suit, and plaintiff appealed to the Louisiana Supreme Court.

**Decision:** Judgment reversed. A harmful or offensive contact with a person, resulting from an act intended to cause the plaintiff to suffer such a contact, is a battery. It is undisputed that when the defendant shocked plaintiff, he intended the contact to be offensive. The defendant's liability for the resulting harm extends to consequences the defendant did not intend and could not reasonably have foreseen, because it is better for unexpected losses to fall upon the intentional wrongdoer than upon the innocent victim. ∎

---

**Defenses:** In addition to the statute of limitations, which typically is two years in such cases, the two primary defenses to assault and battery are **consent** and **self-defense.** A plaintiff who has consented to offensive contacts and the threat of them cannot sue for assault and battery. Thus, a boxer who steps into the ring or the quarterback who steps onto the football field consents to the normal contacts that go with the rules of the game. However, if a football player is forearmed from behind by an opposing player after the play is over, he might have a good battery claim because his consent does not extend to this contact outside the rules of the game any more than it would extend to being shot by an opponent.[15]

Consent cannot be procured by fraud, nor can it be ill-informed. Thus, if M procures F's consent to sexual intercourse by hiding the fact that he has herpes, her consent to the intercourse does not constitute consent to the harmful contact with the disease. She may sue for battery.[16] Doctors performing surgery must be very careful to fully inform their patients regarding the contacts that will take place during the surgery in order to avoid liability for battery. Consent to an appendectomy does not extend to removal of some of the reproductive organs even though it may be the doctor's best medical judgment that they should be removed.

Self-defense creates a well-recognized privilege to assault and battery. In Chapter 7 we described how the courts restrict one to that degree of force considered reasonable in the circumstances of a crime. The same rule applies in the circumstances of a tort.

## Defamation

Long ago the courts decided that we have a legitimate interest in preserving our good reputation in the community. Those who damage our reputation by spreading falsehoods commit the tort of **defamation** and may be liable in damages. Though defamation has historic common law roots, its development in recent years has been strongly influenced by a series of Supreme Court decisions which have molded the tort in accordance with First Amendment principles.

**Libel versus Slander:** Defamation takes two basic forms. **Libel** is written defamation; **slander** is oral. Television and radio broadcasts have generally been categorized as libel. The distinction is important because, traditionally, libel, perhaps because of its more permanent form, was considered more damaging than slander. At common law, a person who proved libel was able to recover damages without any proof of special damages; that is, the very proof that something potentially damaging to the reputation was circulated in public led the court to presume injury. The jury could assess damages without evidence of any specific loss.

Slander, on the other hand, required proof of special damages. Generally, a plaintiff had to prove some sort of economic loss stemming from the damage to reputation. Once that was proved, plaintiff could recover for all sorts of injuries, including humiliation, loss of friendship, and the like. However, in four special categories known as slander *per se,* no special damages needed to be proved. These categories were imputation of serious crime, of loathsome disease, of incompetence in plaintiff's profession, and of unchastity in women.

---

[15] *Hackbart v. Cincinnati Bengals,* 601 F.2d 516 (10th Cir. 1979).
[16] *Long v. Adams,* 333 S.E.2d 852 (Ga. App. 1985).

However, as we shall see, the Supreme Court's First Amendment decisions have had an impact on this traditional distinction.

**Elements:** In a defamation case, plaintiff must generally establish four elements in order to prevail: (1) that a matter defamatory of plaintiff, (2) and untrue, (3) was communicated by defendant, (4) to plaintiff's injury. Questions of defendant's fault, as we shall see, also arise.

***Matter Defamatory of Plaintiff:*** To be defamatory, a statement must be of such a nature as to tend to lower plaintiff's esteem in the eyes of others. An infinite variety of statements have been held defamatory, but if defendant falsely tells others that plaintiff is a thief, a bankrupt, a nazi, a communist, or a homosexual, it is likely that plaintiff's esteem in the eyes of others will be lowered. Though most defamation actions are brought by individuals, they can also be brought by corporations and other organizations.

The defamatory statement must be one that the readers or hearers will associate with plaintiff. Though not mentioned by name, a person who is obviously referred to in a disparaging way in a "novel" that is closely based on reality may have a claim against the author. So may a member of a small group when defendant defames the entire group (e.g., "All the male clerks at this store have AIDS") though plaintiff is not mentioned by name. When larger groups are referred to (e.g., "All Republicans are fascists"), the courts hesitate to allow recovery.

***Untrue:*** To be defamatory, a statement must not only tend to lower plaintiff's esteem in the eyes of others, it must be untrue. The question may be: Who has the burden of proving truthfulness or falsity? The common law presumed that everyone was a good person; therefore, if plaintiff proved that a statement tending to defame him had been published by defendant, the burden of proof was on defendant to prove the truthfulness of the statement. Truth, in other words, was an absolute *defense* to a defamation claim.

A recent Supreme Court case redistributed this burden of proof, at least in some cases, on First Amendment grounds. In *Philadelphia Newspapers, Inc. v. Hepps,*[17] the Court held that if the plaintiff is a public figure (such as a famous actress or athlete), a public official (such as a governor), or a "limited" public figure (a private citizen caught up in a public controversy, such as a businessman whose name appears in a newspaper article about the Mafia), free speech concerns require that the plaintiff be given the burden of proof to demonstrate falsity. The common law presumption that defamatory speech is false was rejected, at least when the defendant is a member of the media. The implications for a nonmedia defendant, or a case involving a private plaintiff not involved in any public controversy are unclear.

***Communication:*** To be defamatory, a statement must be "published" or communicated by the defendant—that is, overheard or read by a third party. If Joe and Kim are standing alone in a field miles from anyone else, Joe can say all the nasty things he wants to Kim without committing defamation. Kim's reputation in the community cannot be hurt if no one else hears the statements. If Kim goes back into town and repeats the statements for others, it is Kim doing the communicating, not Joe.[18]

***Injury:*** As noted earlier, the traditional common law rule presumed damages in libel and the four special types of slander. If a false statement tending to lower plaintiff's esteem in the eyes of others appeared in a local newspaper, it was sensible to presume that persons read it and that their impressions of plaintiff were adversely affected. Injury was presumed, and it made no difference that defendant did not intend to injure plaintiff.

Supreme Court interpretations of the First Amendment have had a big impact on this area. Injury can no longer be presumed unless, in some cases at least, plaintiff proves some fault on defendant's part. The law is still developing, but can be summarized by placing the cases into four categories.

**1.** A statement about a *public official or figure* involved in a *public* controversy. For example, assume a false statement is made concerning how a chief of police handles a significant law enforcement issue. To recover, plaintiff must prove actual malice on defendant's part. That is, plaintiff must prove that defendant knew or should have known that the statements were false. Good faith mistake is a defense. Plaintiff cannot recover punitive damages absent establishing malice.

---

[17] 475 U.S. 767 (1986).

[18] This is not to rule out a possible, but probably weak, claim for intentional infliction of emotional distress in this scenario.

2. A statement about a *public official or figure*, but involving a *private* matter. For example, assume a newspaper runs an untrue story about a famous actress being intoxicated in a restaurant. Again, plaintiff must prove malice to establish liability and, quite likely, to recover punitive damages.

3. A statement about a *private figure* involved in a *public* controversy. For example, assume a newspaper makes a false statement about a lawyer representing a client in a controversial case. In such a case, plaintiff need not prove actual malice to establish liability, but must do so to recover punitive damages.

4. A statement about a *private figure* involved in a *private* matter. For example, assume that a credit reporting agency falsely reports to its clients that plaintiff has taken bankruptcy. Because no public interest such as encouraging freedom of the press regarding matters of societal importance is involved, the state's interest in compensating for injured reputations is of paramount importance. Plaintiff need not prove actual malice to establish liability or to collect punitive damages.

**Defenses:** Several noteworthy defenses are available in defamation cases.

***Statute of Limitations:*** In most jurisdictions, the statute of limitations for defamation cases is one year, only half the two-year statute of limitations typically found for other types of tort claims.

***Absolute Privilege:*** To encourage certain types of activity, the courts have created an absolute privilege for the potential defendant in several contexts. That is, even if the plaintiff could prove all the elements of defamation discussed above, no liability would attach. The two most important of these are the privileges for judicial and legislative proceedings. To encourage judges to judge, witnesses to testify, lawyers to advocate, and legislators to aggressively debate the issues, all are protected absolutely when involved in their respective activities. Note, however, that the absolute privilege is narrow in scope. An attorney who wrote a book about a case after the trial was over or a legislator making statements not while debating a bill but while campaigning would not be protected.

***Qualified Privileges:*** There are also several qualified privileges where the defendant will be protected if he or she acted in *good faith*; that is, malice must be proved as a prerequisite for recovery. The primary example of this—when the plaintiff is a public figure or public official—has already been discussed. Others include, according to some jurisdictions, communications to those who can act in the public interest (for example, complaints to a school board about a teacher) and fair comment on matters of public interest by news commentators.

Many states have provided a business-related good faith privilege for those who traffic in commercially useful information such as credit reports and employee references. Thus, in many jurisdictions, a job applicant's former employer is protected if he tells the applicant's prospective employer that "We think she stole from us." Plaintiff would have to prove malice to prevail. Note, however, that *Dun & Bradstreet, Inc. v. Greenmoss Builders,* 472 U.S. 749 (1985) makes it clear that this privilege is not constitutionally mandated.

***Opinion:*** Under the First Amendment, there is no such thing as a false idea. We are all entitled to our opinions. Thus, "I think Joe is a jerk" is not actionable. Neither is: "I just don't trust Joe; he looks sneaky to me." On the other hand, when an editorial writer stated that a plaintiff had lied under oath, the Supreme Court rejected a defense of opinion because the statement was "sufficiently factual to be susceptible of being proved true or false." *Milkovich v. Loran Journal Co.,* 105 S.Ct. 2695 (1990).

***Injurious Falsehood:*** Closely allied to defamation (and perhaps equally as closely connected to the business torts discussed in Chapter 9) is the tort of **injurious falsehood,** also known as "disparagement," "slander of goods," and "trade libel." The elements are generally the same as for traditional defamation, but the subject matter relates not to an individual's reputation, but to plaintiff's title to property or to the quality or conduct of plaintiff's business. The tort is aimed at protecting economic interests and would allow suit against a defendant who, for example, falsely stated that plaintiff's business was no longer in existence.

## False Imprisonment

The privilege to come and go as we please is important in our society. The courts protect that interest by recognizing the right to sue for the tort of **false imprisonment** when persons are unlawfully confined or restrained without their consent. If the defendant purports to arrest plaintiff as well, the nearly identical claim of **false arrest** is applicable.

*Elements:* To prove a false imprisonment claim, plaintiff must usually prove that defendant: (1) confined or restrained plaintiff, (2) with intent, (3) without plaintiff's consent, (4) thereby injuring plaintiff.

*Confinement:* False imprisonment can occur when plaintiff is confined in a room, a building, a car, or even a boat. It can even occur in the wide open spaces if plaintiff is held in one spot against his or her will by force or threat. If defendant blocks one exit to a room, but another is available to plaintiff, the confinement requirement is not met.

*Intent:* If someone accidentally locks another in a room, perhaps negligence is involved, but not false imprisonment. False imprisonment requires a wrongful intent on the defendant's part. As with assault and battery, an intent to injure will suffice, as well as an intent to confine. If defendant stands outside plaintiff's house with a gun, issuing threats of bodily injury should plaintiff emerge, the intent requirement is met. Though defendant would like nothing better than for plaintiff to come out of the house, the natural consequence of defendant's actions is to force plaintiff to remain in the house.

*Against Consent:* The same force and threats of force that create an assault may force a person to remain in one place against his or her will. A large man could easily intimidate a small person into staying involuntarily in one place. However, if plaintiff stays in one place as an accommodation or to clear up an accusation with police, there is no involuntary confinement. If, for example, a store clerk told a customer only: "We believe you have stolen from the cash register and have called the police," and the customer voluntarily stayed in the store to give her side of the story—there would be no false imprisonment.

*Injury:* The injury necessary for a valid false imprisonment claim arises automatically from the confinement, even if it is brief. A restraint of hours or days is not required for the necessary injury to occur. However, since the injury is somewhat mental in nature, it will not occur if plaintiff is unaware of the confinement. Thus, if plaintiff sleeps through a confinement, there would be no cognizable injury. But if plaintiff knows of the confinement, actual and punitive damages are available.

*Defenses:* In addition to the statute of limitations (typically two years), the defendant's best chance in a false imprisonment case is to prove legal right. Obviously, police officers in possession of probable cause have the right to detain or confine suspects.

Many false imprisonment claims involve shopkeepers. Shoplifting, unfortunately, is a problem of epidemic proportions in the United States. When a shopkeeper detains a suspected shoplifter and presses charges, any number of things can prevent a conviction from being obtained, including prosecutorial or police error, or the failure of a witness to appear. At common law, even a well-founded belief by a shopkeeper that a theft had occurred frequently would not prevent the success of a later false imprisonment claim if, for whatever reason, no criminal conviction was obtained. However, many state legislatures have acted to protect shopkeepers with legislation such as that discussed in the following case.

---

**Jacques v. Sears, Roebuck & Company**
Court of Appeals of New York,
285 N.E.2d 871 (1972)

In May of 1966 the plaintiff, Jacques, a self-employed carpenter, entered a Sears store in Syracuse to purchase business supplies. He picked up 19 reflectorized letters and numbers costing ten cents apiece and put them in his pants pocket. He then selected a mailbox and had two extra keys made. He paid for the mailbox and keys, but left the store without paying for the letters and numbers. At the time he had over $600 in cash and a $400 check in his wallet.

A Sears security officer, Varisco, had observed Jacques putting the items in his pocket and leaving the store without paying for them. As Jacques approached his car in the store parking lot, Varisco stopped him and told him that he was under arrest. Varisco took Jacques back to a security office, where he filled out a questionnaire in which he admitted

*(continued)*

having taken the letters without paying for them. He said he wished then to pay for the letters; that he was "sorry about the whole thing"; and that he "would never do anything like this again."

Sears's security officers called the Syracuse police, who arrived soon after the detention began. With the security officers accompanying them, the police took Jacques to police headquarters, booked him, and later released him on bail. Two days later he appeared in police court and stated that he was guilty of petit larceny. The court, however, refused to accept the plea and advised him to get a lawyer. The charge of petit larceny was subsequently dismissed on recommendation of the district attorney because of "lack of proof of intent."

Jacques then brought this action for damages against Sears, alleging false imprisonment and false arrest. Sears contended that its detention of Jacques was "reasonable," and thus lawful under New York's "antishoplifting statute." The trial court disagreed with Sears's interpretation of the statute, and entered a judgment of $1600 in favor of Jacques, the amount of the jury's verdict.

Sears appealed to an intermediate court, which reversed the judgment and dismissed the action. Jacques appealed to New York's highest court, contending (1) that the statute afforded a defense against a reasonable detention, but not against any arrest; or, in the alternative, (2) that the statute afforded a defense only against arrests resulting in convictions.

**Decision:** Both of Jacques's contentions are wrong. Accordingly, the intermediate court was correct in dismissing his suit. Legal authorities view the terms "detention" and "arrest" as essentially interchangeable. Thus Jacques's first argument is erroneous.

Second, the statute expressly provides that a suspected shoplifter may be detained by a merchant if (1) the suspect was detained in a reasonable manner and for no more than a reasonable time and (2) the owner or agent of the mercantile establishment "had reasonable grounds to believe" that the suspect was shoplifting. If the belief is reasonable, the merchant has no liability whether or not the suspect is subsequently proven innocent of the theft charge. In this case Sears's belief was clearly reasonable, in view of the fact that its security officer saw Jacques put the merchandise in his pocket, leave without paying for it, and that Jacques immediately admitted upon being stopped that he had failed to pay for the merchandise. ∎

## Trespass

We work hard for our money, and when we spend it on property we should have the right to use that property without interference from others. When others infringe on our right to use real property—land and those things attached to it, such as houses—the tort of **trespass** to real property is committed. The tort has a convoluted common-law history that protects property owners from innocent as well as mean-spirited invasions of the right to use real property.

**Elements:** Generally speaking, to prevail in a trespass case plaintiff must establish the following elements: (1) affirmative conduct by defendant; (2) with intent to enter onto realty in the possession of another; and (3) resulting in actual entry.

**Affirmative Conduct:** If Joe is driving down the street when Alan runs a stop sign with his car, smashes into Joe, and pushes Joe up onto Ed's lawn, no trespass has been committed by Joe. He invaded Ed's real property, but not through any affirmative act of his own.

**Intent:** Unlike most other intentional torts, the intent element of a trespass cause of action requires only that plaintiff demonstrate that defendant intended to enter the place he did, which place belonged to plaintiff. No intent to do harm is required. Thus, if Cindy walks across Ann's land believing that she is walking across her own or across land belonging to her friend Sally who has given her permission to cross it, Cindy commits a trespass actionable by Ann. Cindy's good faith is no defense. On the other hand, if Mark has a heart attack and dies instantly while driving down the street, and his car runs onto Ed's lawn, the affirmative conduct element is arguably not met and certainly the intent element is missing. The same may be said of a person who, driving too fast on slick streets, loses control of the car and winds up on someone's lawn. The intent element is missing.

**Actual entry:** Entry is required for completion of the tort, but *usually* no real injury. Damage is presumed from the fact of entry, even if the only injury is trampled blades of grass. A judgment in the form of nominal damages of a dollar or so would still be warranted. According to most courts, the invasion need only be slight, including throwing a rock onto plaintiff's property, shooting a bullet over it, or tunnelling under it. Some courts refuse to recognize injury where the invasion is truly minor, such as where A's tree limb grows so far that it extends over B's property line.

The court must sometimes balance competing interests. For example, in *Bradley v. American Smelting and Refining Co.*, 709 P.2d 782 (Wash. 1985), defendant operated a copper smelter which emitted particulate matter, including arsenic, cadmium, and other metals. Though undetectable by human senses and not harmful to health, this matter did sometimes settle on plaintiff's property. The court felt constrained to create an exception to the general rule that any entry constitutes an injury, stating:

> When [airborne] particles or substance accumulates on the land and does not pass away, then a trespass has occurred. While at common law any trespass entitled a landowner to recover nominal and punitive damages for the invasion of his property, such a rule is not appropriate under the circumstances before us. No useful purpose would be served by sanctioning actions in trespass by every landowner within a hundred miles of a manufacturing plant. Manufacturers would be harassed and the litigious few would cause the escalation of costs to the detriment of the many.... The plaintiff who cannot show actual and substantial damages should be subject to dismissal.

The trespassory entry is an affront to the use of the property. Therefore, the cause of action is normally recognized as belonging to the possessor of the land. Thus, if T were renting a farm from L, and X trespassed on the farm, T would normally have the right to sue for trespass rather than L.

**Defenses:** In addition to the typical two-year statute of limitations (which is extended if the trespass is a continuing one, as where the trespasser has erected a small building on the plaintiff's property), the main defenses to a trespass cause of action are *consent* and *legal right.* Thus, a tenant has the landlord's consent, pursuant to a lease, to remain on the landlord's property. However, if the tenant stays beyond the term of the lease and refuses to leave, a trespass is committed because consent has expired.

A legal right might arise from, for example, an *easement,* which is a right to use someone's property for a limited purpose. Thus, if M's land is between N's land and a major highway, N might negotiate an easement from M, paying M a sum of money in exchange for the limited right to travel over M's land going to and from the highway.

## OTHER INTENTIONAL TORTS
### Invasion of Privacy

Slowly over the past 75 years or so, the courts have begun to recognize privacy as an interest worthy of legal protection. Today, many jurisdictions have recognized one or more of the following varieties of tort which come under the umbrella of **invasion of privacy.**

**Intrusion:** Intrusion occurs whenever a defendant intrudes into an area where a plaintiff has a reasonable expectation of privacy. Secretly placing a microphone under plaintiff's bed in order to overhear the goings on would be a classic example. A leading case involved an auto manufacturer's wiretapping and eavesdropping on Ralph Nader's activities.[19]

**Disclosure of Embarrassing Private Facts:** Where no justification exists, it may be actionable to disclose to the public facts which plaintiff finds embarrassing or offensive. Because they are "true," the disclosures do not constitute defamation; they may be more akin to blackmail. However, a newsworthiness defense exists, at least for the media. In one case, a woman sued for the embarrassment she was caused by a newspaper's disclosing that her husband was killed in a fire in a motel while accompanied by another woman. The court held that fires are newsworthy events and the newspaper could not be liable for accurately reporting the names of the victims.[20]

**False Light:** Very similar to the tort of defamation, the action for "false light" privacy renders liable a defendant who makes statements or does acts which place the plaintiff in a false light in the public eye. While usually these statements or actions would injure plaintiff's reputation and also be actionable as defamation, occasionally they might involve statements that plaintiff had done many wonderful things which in fact he had not. An attraction of this tort is that it frequently has a two-year statute of limitations, longer than the one-year statutes typical for defamation.

---

[19] *Nader v. General Motors Corp.*, 255 N.E.2d 765 (N.Y. 1970).
[20] *Fry v. Ionia Sentinel Standard,* 300 N.W.2d 687 (Mich. App. 1980).

**Appropriation of Name or Likeness:** This final type of privacy tort protects the economic interests that persons have in the potential exploitation of their names and faces. Thus, if a company uses the name or picture of a famous actress in its advertising campaign without her permission, it has appropriated her name or likeness to her economic detriment. The company should have acquired her consent and paid her for such use. After singer Bette Midler refused to sing for a company's TV commercial, it hired one of her back-up singers and asked her to sound as much like Midler as possible. Many listeners thought they were hearing the real Bette Midler, which formed the basis for a successful appropriation suit by Midler.[21]

## *Intentional Infliction of Mental Distress*

As noted earlier, because emotional injuries are difficult to prove and to value, courts have traditionally been reluctant to allow recovery for them. But just as they are now allowed in suitable cases of negligence, they are also allowed when intentionally caused. The turning point may have been cases like *Wilkinson v. Downtin*,[22] where, as a practical joke, defendant called plaintiff, a woman whose mental state was somewhat suspect anyway, and told her that her husband had been in a serious accident. This so upset plaintiff that she had to be hospitalized. Recovery for her emotional distress was allowed.

The requisite elements of proof for the tort of **intentional infliction of mental distress** are generally formulated as follows. First, that defendant is guilty of extreme and outrageous conduct. Mere insults are usually insufficient as are profanity and other abuses of a relatively minor nature. Second, defendant must have intended to cause plaintiff severe emotional distress. Again, defendant will be presumed to intend the natural consequences of his or her actions. And a defendant who is aware of a particular plaintiff's susceptibilities to mental distress will be judged accordingly. Finally, plaintiff must actually suffer such severe distress. Physical consequences are not required, but their presence does assist in establishing proof of severe emotional anguish.

Today, such suits frequently involve attempts by collection agencies to force debtors to pay bills. Thus, in *Turman v. Central Billing, Inc.*, 568 P.2d 1382 (1977), the collection agency was held liable to Turman, who was blind, when it badgered her in trying to collect a small debt assigned to it for collection, even after it knew that she and the creditor had come to a satisfactory settlement. This harassment, which resulted in plaintiff's hospitalization for anxiety and severe stress, was carried out by repeated phone calls—sometimes twice a day—in which defendant's agent "shouted" at her, used profanity, told her several times that her husband would lose his job and house if she didn't pay, and called her "scum" and a "deadbeat."

This tort cannot be used to evade First Amendment restrictions on recovery for defamation. When the Reverend Jerry Falwell sued *Hustler* magazine over an extremely rude parody, showing that it had caused him emotional distress, the Supreme Court held that freedom of expression considerations barred recovery.[23]

## *Fraud*

The essence of the tort of *fraud* is the intentional misleading of one person by another, which results in a loss to the deceived party. Because many kinds of fraudulent conduct occur where the sole purpose of the wrongdoer is to cause the innocent party to enter a contract which that person otherwise would not make, full consideration of this subject is undertaken in Chapter 15.

## *Conversion and Trespass to Personal Property*

The tort of **conversion** renders actionable certain invasions of personal property interests, just as trespass protects real property interests. Conversion remedies invasions so serious that they justify forcing defendant to compensate plaintiff for the reasonable value of the item involved. An example would be defendant's theft of plaintiff's automobile. A tort which generally covers more minor invasions of personal property rights is frequently called trespass to personal property. This tort would remedy, for example, defendant's minor vandalism of plaintiff's car.

---

[21] *Midler v. Ford Motor Co.*, 849 F.2d 460 (9th Cir. 1988).
[22] [1897] 2 Q.B.D. 57.

[23] 108 S.Ct. 876 (1988).

## Nuisance

Like trespass to real property, the tort of **nuisance** protects the enjoyment of such property. Frequently nuisance is used to compensate an intangible disruption of the enjoyment of property, as where plaintiff is injured by defendant's invasion through light (erection of tall light poles), vibrations (blasting with dynamite), or smells (pig farming). The courts will consider such factors as the type of neighborhood, the nature of the wrong, its proximity to the plaintiff, its frequency or continuity, and the nature and extent of the injury in deciding whether an actionable nuisance exists.

## SPECIAL PROBLEMS

### Business Torts

Some torts, such as the theft of trade secrets and the unjustified interference with business contracts, are so peculiarly related to the commercial world that they are called *business torts*. Because of the special issues that these kinds of torts present—and also because of their obvious importance to businesspersons—they will be considered at length in the next chapter.

### Employers' Liability

Ordinarily, the application of the principles of tort law results in the imposition of liability upon the wrongdoer alone. There is one major exception, however, which springs from the principles comprising our master-servant law and our law of agency.

Under these principles, an employer is uniformly held liable for the torts of employees if the employees are acting "within the scope of their employment" at the time of the injury. Thus, if T, a truckdriver employed by the D Furniture Company, negligently injures P while delivering a piece of furniture to a customer's home, P has a cause of action against both T and the D Company, as illustrated in Figure 8.1.

Ordinarily, in such a case, P brings just one action against both defendants; if he is successful in proving the facts as alleged, he obtains a "joint and several" judgment against T and the D Company. This means that if he is awarded a judgment of $4,000, he can enforce the judgment against the assets of either party, or of both, until that sum is recovered. (The "scope of employment" problem is covered further in Chapters 31 and 32.)

**Figure 8.1 Employer's Liability for Employee's Tort**

```
┌─────────────────────────────────────────┐
│ ABC employs John Doe to drive its       │
│ delivery truck.                         │
└─────────────────────────────────────────┘
                    │
                    ▼
┌─────────────────────────────────────────┐
│ Mr. Doe wrongfully causes an accident   │
│ in which Mr. Smith is injured.          │
└─────────────────────────────────────────┘
                    │
                    ▼
┌─────────────────────────────────────────┐
│             Mr. Smith sues              │
└─────────────────────────────────────────┘
           │                    │
           ▼                    ▼
┌──────────────────┐  ┌──────────────────────┐
│ John Doe for     │  │ ABC because John     │
│ causing the harm.│  │ Doe is ABC's         │
│                  │  │ employee *and* was   │
│                  │  │ within the scope of  │
│                  │  │ employment when      │
│                  │  │ the harm was done.   │
└──────────────────┘  └──────────────────────┘
```

### Joint and Several Liability

When two defendants' actions together contribute to a plaintiff's injury, they are frequently held jointly and severally liable. The "joint" portion of this liability means that each defendant may be held responsible for the entire loss caused to plaintiff. Thus, theoretically one defendant who is only 10 percent at fault might have to pay also for the 90 percent fault of another defendant, especially if the latter defendant is judgment-proof. The relatively harsh result which this can have for "deep pocket" defendants is a major cause of criticism of our present tort system.

### Statutory Reforms

Increases in the number of tort suits filed, the size of judgments and, consequently, insurance rates have become a major topic of discussion in both the federal and state legislatures. As this chapter is written both state and federal legislative reforms to limit tort recoveries are being debated and passed across the country. Though the ultimate impact of this wave of legislation cannot yet be gauged, it thus far has concentrated on such matters as medical malpractice and products liability suits, punitive damages, damages for emotional distress, joint and several liability, and statutes of limitation.

## SUMMARY

Tort law is, to a great extent, social engineering by the courts. As society evolves, the courts' concepts of what interests we have that are worth protecting also evolves. The courts impose duties on us not to injure the protectable interests of others.

The leading remedy for accidental injury in this country is the negligence cause of action. Existence of a duty and proximate causation, both of which turn largely on the notion of foreseeability, are the key elements for a plaintiff's recovery. A plaintiff's own carelessness can lead to reduction or a bar altogether on recovery.

Among intentional torts, assault and battery protect invasions of our mind and body, defamation protects our good reputation in the community, false imprisonment protects the right to come and go as we please, and trespass protects our right to enjoyment of our real property. To successfully pursue each tort, the plaintiff must prove a variety of specified elements. Each tort involves an intentional act by the defendant. Each has a variety of defenses ranging from self-defense for assault and battery, to absolute and qualified privileges for defamation, to consent and legal right for false imprisonment and trespass.

Intentional torts which are also worth noting include the four varieties of invasion of privacy tort, intentional infliction of emotional distress (which has been often used successfully against aggressive collection agencies), fraud, conversion, and nuisance (which involves lesser invasions of real property than does trespass).

Employers are liable for the torts of their employees committed within the scope of authority. And joint tortfeasors are each potentially liable for the entire judgment awarded plaintiff (though plaintiff cannot have a double recovery). Rapid change in the tort system and escalating monetary awards have led many legislatures to consider strong measures to reform American tort law. We are just now starting to see many of these changes.

## KEY TERMS

**Torts**
**Negligence**
**Proximate cause**
**Independent intervening cause**
**Contributory negligence**
**Comparative negligence**
**Statute of limitations**
**Battery**
**Assault**
**Consent**
**Self-defense**
**Defamation**
**Libel**
**Slander**
**Injurious falsehood**
**False imprisonment**
**False arrest**
**Trespass**
**Invasion of privacy**
**Intentional infliction of mental distress**
**Conversion**
**Nuisance**

## QUESTIONS AND PROBLEMS

1. For two years Lee was the patient of Milano, a psychiatrist. Lee was diagnosed as having an adjustment reaction to adolescence. He related many fantasies to Milano about being a hero or an important villain, or using a knife to threaten those who frightened him. At a session he showed a knife to Milano. Lee also related certain alleged sexual experiences with Kim, his next door neighbor. He was emotionally involved, possessive, and had fired a BB gun at a car occupied by Kim and her boyfriend as they drove away on a date. Later, Lee murdered Kim with a knife. Kim's family sued Milano in negligence for not having warned them of the danger from Lee. Should Milano be liable? Discuss. (*McIntosh v. Milano*, 403 A.2d 500, N.J. 1979.)

2. KHJ radio gave away money to listeners who could find deejay "The Real Don Steele" who traveled around town in a van. Two cars of teenagers arrived at one location to discover a prize had already been given away. Without knowledge of each other, they each decided to follow Steele to his next location in order to be the first to arrive. For the next few miles they jockeyed for position at speeds of up to 80 mph. The radio then announced that Steele was

headed for Thousand Oaks off a certain ramp. When Steele took that exit off the freeway, the teenagers followed. In so doing, one of their cars carelessly forced Weirum's car onto the center divider where it overturned and Weirum was killed. His family sued KHJ for negligence. Should they be allowed to recover? Discuss. (*Weirum v. RKO General, Inc.*, 539 P.2d 36, Cal. 1975.)

**3.** Charles and Carolyn needed to repair and clean a well on their property. Charles entered the well and placed a gasoline-powered pump directly above it to remove water. This was a bad idea because all of the carbon monoxide from the engine seeped into the well. When Charles did not respond to Carolyn's calls, she asked her neighbor Bob for help. Bob entered the well to help Charles, but was overcome by fumes himself and died. Bob's family sued Carolyn and Charles' estate for negligence. Should the family recover? Discuss. (*Lowrey v. Horvath*, 689 S.W.2d 625, Mo. 1985.)

**4.** Two children, Lisa and Deborah, were standing alongside a highway when Lisa was struck by Burd's carelessly driven car. Deborah was barely missed. JoAnne, the girls' mother, saw the whole incident from her front porch. When Lisa, Deborah, and JoAnne sue Burd for the emotional distress caused by his careless driving, who will be allowed to recover? (*Sinn v. Burd*, 404 A.2d 672, Pa. 1979.)

**5.** Mrs. Hill took a clock to defendant's office and there she found Sapp in charge, sitting behind a four-foot counter that separated him from the public. She handed him the clock. Having had a few drinks and feeling "good and amiable," Sapp said: "If you will come back here and let me love and pet you, I will fix your clock." He then reached forward in an effort to grasp Mrs. Hill's arm, but she jumped back out of the way, and no physical contact occurred. She later sued for assault. Should she prevail? (*Western Union Telegraph Co. v. Hill*, 150 So. 709, Ala. 1933.)

**6.** In a review of plaintiff's restaurant, defendant newspaper columnist referred to the sauce on the duck as "yellow death on duck" and the poached trout as something which should be renamed "trout à la green plague." Plaintiff sued for defamation, proving that most persons very much liked both dishes. Does plaintiff have a strong defamation claim? Discuss. (*Mashburn v. Collins*, 355 So.2d 879, La. 1977.)

**7.** National Bond Co. sent two of its employees to repossess Whithorn's car when Whithorn got behind in his payments. The two repossessors located Whithorn while he was driving his car. They asked him to stop, which he did, but he refused to abandon the car to them. They called a wrecker and ordered the driver to hook Whithorn's car and move it down the street while Whithorn was still in it. Whithorn started the car and tried to escape, but the wrecker lifted the car off the road and progressed 75 to 100 feet before Whithorn managed to stall the wrecker. Whithorn claimed that this incident amounted to a false imprisonment and sued National Bond Co. Does Whithorn have a valid claim? Discuss. (*National Bond Co. v. Whithorn*, 123 S.W.2d 263, Ky. 1939.)

**8.** Defendant is a crop duster who became confused and flew over plaintiff's land, spraying poison on plaintiff's crop. Defendant thought he was spraying the land he had been hired to spray, which was adjacent to plaintiff's land. Plaintiff sued defendant in trespass. Does plaintiff have a good claim? Discuss. (*Schronk v. Gilliam*, 380 S.W.2d 743, Tex. Civ. App. 1964.)

**9.** In 1955, plaintiff was 17 years old. He was convicted of being involved in a hit-and-run accident which killed a Las Vegas policeman. In 1978, in an article about police officers who had died in the line of duty, defendant newspaper mentioned plaintiff's 1955 conviction and his conviction two years later for possession of marijuana. Plaintiff sued the newspaper for disclosure of embarrassing private facts. Should plaintiff prevail? Discuss. (*Montesano v. Donrey Media Group*, 668 P.2d 1081, Nev. 1983.)

**10.** Defendant credit company called plaintiff and, in order to obtain the address of her son for collection purposes, told her that her grandchild had been in a car accident and defendant needed her son's address. When this turned out to be false, plaintiff sued for infliction of emotional distress. Does she have a good claim? Discuss. (*Ford Motor Credit Co. v. Sheehan*, 373 So.2d 956, Fla. App. 1979.)

# CHAPTER 9

# BUSINESS TORTS

Certain kinds of business interests and rights have been recognized and protected by common law rules since very early times. Many of these interests receive supplemental, and sometimes primary, protection from state, and especially federal, statutes. In this chapter we will examine some of the most common wrongful invasions of these interests, i.e., **business torts,** including (1) interference with existing and prospective contractual and business relationships, (2) trademark infringement, (3) misuse of trade secrets, (4) patent infringement, (5) copyright infringement, and (6) unfair competition.

## INTERFERENCE WITH BUSINESS CONDUCT

Beginning with the decision in an English case in 1853 in which an opera singer was induced by defendant theater owner to breach her contract to sing at plaintiff's theater and appear at defendant's instead,[1] the courts have recognized the general principle that a third party who wrongfully interferes with an existing contract has committed a tort. Indeed, the concept has been stretched to hold defendants liable for interfering with contracts which did not yet exist but were reasonably certain to be entered into, and with business relationships in general.

A typical example of **interference with business conduct** involved a salesman who followed customers away from his former employer's premises and convinced them to rescind their contracts with that business and purchase less expensive property from him.[2] Although his former employer's customers had the right under federal law to rescind their contracts within three days, the salesman was found civilly liable. Though there was no interference with an existing contract, there was interference with a prospective advantage flowing from an advantageous business relationship.

## *Elements of Tort*

In a tortious interference case, plaintiff must prove (1) the defendant acted intentionally to interfere with a known contract or business relationship or with one that was reasonably certain to occur; (2) defendant caused harm in so interfering; and (3) defendant acted in pursuit of an improper purpose or through improper means. No liability will attach if defendant's interference was not improper in the eyes of the law but was, instead, legally justified. Unfortunately, the law is somewhat muddled as to the line between acts that are justified and those that are unjustified and improper.

## *Defense of Justification*

A defendant using improper means to induce a breach of contract or to interfere with a business relationship will likely be held liable. For example, as part of a campaign to terrorize Vietnamese fishermen competing with American fishermen in Galveston Bay, the Ku Klux Klan told one man who leased his docks to the Vietnamese: "watch your boats—they're easy to burn," and sent a card to a woman who also leased her docks which said: "You have been paid a 'friendly visit' do you want the next one to be a 'real one.'" The court deemed this sufficient to establish an action for tortious interference with contractual relationships.[3]

Even if the means used are proper, such as simply opening up a competing business, the tort will be es-

---

[1] *Lumley v. Gye,* 2 E1 & B1 216.
[2] *Azar v. Lehigh Corp.,* 364 So.2d 860 (Fla. App. 1978).

[3] *Vietnamese Fishermen's Ass'n v. Knights of the Ku Klux Klan,* 518 F. Supp. 993 (N.D.Tex. 1981).

tablished if the purpose was improper. In one famous case,[4] the defendant opened up a competing barbershop not to make money, but as part of a malicious scheme to injure plaintiff by destroying his barbershop's business. "To call such conduct competition is a perversion of terms," the court said in allowing recovery for interference with business conduct.

**Justification** for a defendant's interference may be found if it is aimed at protecting a third person's legitimate interests, such as where an independent construction inspector hired by a city recommended that the city terminate the plaintiff's construction contract for poor workmanship,[5] or at protecting the public interest in general. Furthermore the defendant can claim justification for interference in order to protect its own existing contractual or property interest. Two examples can help illustrate the general kinds of interests that are often held to justify interference.

**Case 1:** P gets a new car franchise from D, an auto manufacturer. Later P makes a contract with X, a motorcycle wholesaler, under the terms of which X is permitted to sell motorcycles in a limited area in P's showroom. D subsequently causes P to break the contract with X because of complaints from new car buyers about dirt and noise associated with X's operation. Even if the contract between P and X did not violate any term of the franchise agreement, D's interest in the proper conduct of the new car dealership would probably justify its conduct (thus affording it a defense in any interference action brought either by P or X).

**Case 2:** A bank made a contract with a city, under which the city agreed to vacate (close) a street so that the bank could greatly expand its facilities. When a neighboring savings and loan company induced the city to cancel the contract, the bank sued the savings and loan for damages. The court ruled in favor of the savings and loan, finding that its primary purpose in preventing the closing was "to preserve an unimpaired visibility of its premises." Because it was found that the threatened impairment might substantially affect the savings and loan company's business, and the bank was still able to make a reasonable expansion despite the cancellation of the closing, the savings and loan company's interest was held to outweigh the contractual right of the bank.[6] Thus the bank's only cause of action would be against the city, on the breach of contract theory.

While the defendant may act to protect *existing* economic interests, it is usually improper to induce a third party to breach a contract with plaintiff solely to gain new customers. The right to engage in free competition does not go quite that far. However, the courts will grant a defendant more leeway in terms of seeking new customers or contracts if plaintiff's interest has not itself been reduced to a binding contract but is only prospective in nature. For example, where plaintiff's contract is terminable-at-will by both parties, some courts find that the privilege of competition allows defendant to vie for the plaintiff's business with the third party by fair means.

The competition privilege was raised as a defense in the following case.

[4]*Tuttle v. Buck,* 107 Minn. 145, 119 N.W. 946 (1909).
[5]*Solis v. City of Laredo,* 751 S.W.2d 132 (Tex. App. 1988).

[6]*Arlington Heights National Bank v. Arlington Heights Federal Savings and Loan Association,* 229 N.E. 2d 514 (1967).

---

## Leonard Duckworth, Inc. v. Michael L. Field & Co.
U.S. Fifth Circuit Court of Appeals
516 F.2d 952 (1975)

Plaintiff Leonard Duckworth, Inc., is a real estate sales corporation. It brought together a potential seller (Chase Manhattan Bank) and a potential buyer (Michael L. Field & Co.). During negotiations, there were two written drafts of a contract to be signed by all three parties. In each, the seller was required to pay a commission to plaintiff. In September of 1972 Chase rejected Field's offer, but stated that it might accept it if it were resubmitted at the first of the year after certain changes in Chase's personnel. Plaintiff did contact Chase in January 1973 to help secure financing.

In February 1973, Field initiated direct negotiations with Chase without going through plaintiff. These negotiations led to acceptance of Field's offer to buy. Before execution of the contract, plaintiff learned of the negotiations and asserted a right to a commission. Field denied this, and at Chase's urging, inserted a clause into the final contract in which Field

*(continued)*

agreed to indemnify Chase for any commission that plaintiff might assert against it.

Plaintiff sued Field for interfering with plaintiff's reasonable expectancy of a real estate commission. The jury found that Field induced Chase to circumvent plaintiff in order to avoid paying a commission. A judgment of $113,250 was entered against Field and this appeal followed.

**Decision:** The lower court's judgment was affirmed. Texas recognizes a cause of action for interference with contracts and business relationships—both those existing and those reasonably certain to be entered into. A plaintiff in an interference with a prospective contract case must prove: (1) there was a "reasonable probability" that plaintiff would enter into a contractual relationship; (2) defendant acted willfully and maliciously by intentionally preventing the relationship from occurring with the purpose of harming plaintiff; (3) the defendant was not privileged or justified; and (4) actual harm or damage occurred as a result.

All these elements are present in this case. The malice is apparent from Field's decision to enter into surreptitious negotiations with Chase despite its knowledge of plaintiff's involvement and reasonable expectation of a commission.

The privilege of fair competition is not available to Field, whose acts were sharp, overreaching, and beyond the pale of "fair play." ■

---

In one of the most controversial cases in recent legal history, Pennzoil sued Texaco for intentional interference with contract rights when Texaco bought control of Getty Oil after Pennzoil believed it had a contract to acquire Getty. A jury awarded Pennzoil the largest judgment in American legal history—$11.1 billion in compensatory and punitive damages. (That judgment was affirmed on appeal and later settled out of court when Texaco paid $3 billion to Pennzoil.)

## *Manager's Privilege*

When a corporation breaches a contract, the other party will frequently not only sue the corporation for breach of contract but also sue the corporate officers who made the decision to breach on a tortious interference claim. The corporate officers are usually protected from liability by a doctrine called the "manager's privilege" if their decision to have the corporation breach the contract was based solely or essentially on the best interests of the corporation. Such would be the case where it would be far more advisable for a corporation to pay damages resulting from a breach of contract than to live up to a contract that might be financially disastrous. On the other hand, if the officer is acting primarily to further his or her own personal interests, tort liability will be imposed.

## TRADEMARK INFRINGEMENT

A **trademark** is any distinctive word, symbol, device, or design adopted for the purpose of identifying the origin of goods being offered for sale. The tort of infringement, therefore, occurs when a competitor of the owner of the trademark uses a mark so similar to the owned trademark that purchasers of the competitor's goods are misled as to the origin of the goods which they are purchasing. In other words, a deception is accomplished that permits the competitor (typically a manufacturer) to "cash in" on the reputation and goodwill of the trademark owner (who is, typically, another manufacturer).

While the early trademark rules were exclusively common law in nature, the basis of most of our trademark law today is the Lanham Act—a federal statute passed in 1946. Nevertheless, case law remains a significant element of trademark law because certain aspects of this area of law are still governed by common-law principles, and also because a large body of case law has grown up as the courts have interpreted key provisions of the act on a case-by-case basis.

The act also governs other marks, such as **service marks**—used to identify the origin of services (for example "Budget," as applied to the car rental business) and certification marks—used by persons who do not own the marks, but who are authorized to indicate that their products are approved by the owner of such marks (for example, the "Good Housekeeping Seal of Approval"). We will limit our discussion here to consideration of only those principles of law having special applicability to the tort of trademark infringement.

## *Registration*

Under the Lanham Act, as amended in 1988, a person who owns a trademark that is affixed to or applies to his goods ("vendible commodities") may register that mark on the Principal Register either by showing that the mark has already been used in commerce, or indicating a "bona fide intent" to use the mark at a future date, followed by actual use within three years. Entry on the Principal Register is constructive notice, effective as of the date of filing, of the registrant's exclusive right to use the trademark throughout the entire country. This grant of a nationwide priority, with few exceptions, gives the registrant a right superior to everyone's except that of a person who used the mark before the filing date, a person who filed an application before that date, and foreign applicants who can claim a priority date under special rules.

The term of the registration is ten years, and it may be renewed in ten-year increments by registrants who show that they are still genuinely using the mark.

Certain kinds of marks are generally not registrable—the most important of which are those that are merely descriptive or geographic in nature, or are persons' surnames. Thus a term that merely describes a general kind of good, which is called a **generic term** (such as aspirin), cannot be registered under any circumstances. And other descriptive terms ("tender" steak), geographical terms ("Nebraska" butter), and surnames ("Henderson" hats) cannot be registered unless they have acquired a "secondary meaning" (a concept discussed later).

In *Zatrains, Inc., v. Oak Grove Smokehouse, Inc.*, 698 F.2d 786 (1983), where a primary question was whether Zatrains' trademark of "FISH FRI" batters was so descriptive of batters generally that it could not be protected against use of the mark "FISH FRY" batters by defendant Oak Grove, the higher court illustrated the applicable principles, as follows:

> Courts and commentators have traditionally divided potential trademarks into four categories. A potential trademark may be classified as (1) generic, (2) descriptive, (3) suggestive, or (4) arbitrary or fanciful. These categories, like the tones in a spectrum, tend to blur at the edges and merge together. . . .
>
> A *generic* term is the name of a particular genus or class of which an individual article or service is but a member. A generic term connotes the basic nature of articles or services rather than the more individualized characteristics of a particular product. Generic terms can never attain trademark protection. Furthermore, if at any time a registered trademark becomes generic as to a particular product or service, the mark's registration is subject to cancellation [under the Lanham Act]. Such terms as aspirin and cellophane have been held generic and therefore unprotectable as trademarks.
>
> A *descriptive* term identifies a characteristic or quality of an article or service, such as its color, odor, function, dimensions, or ingredients. Descriptive terms ordinarily are not protectable as trademarks; they may become valid marks, however, by acquiring a secondary meaning in the minds of the consuming public. . . . [An] example of a descriptive mark would be . . . "Vision Center" in reference to a business offering optical goods and services. . . .
>
> A *suggestive* term suggests, rather than describes, some particular characteristic of the goods or services to which it applies and requires the consumer to exercise the imagination in order to draw a conclusion as to the nature of the goods and services. A suggestive mark is protected without the necessity for proof of secondary meaning. The term "Coppertone" has been held suggestive in regard to sun tanning products.
>
> *Arbitrary* or *fanciful* terms bear no relationship to the products or services to which they are applied. Like suggestive terms, [these] marks are protectable without proof of secondary meaning. The term "Kodak" is properly classified as a fanciful term for photographic supplies, and "Ivory" is an arbitrary term as applied to soap.[7]

## Secondary Meaning Concept

If a trademark is unregistrable because it is essentially descriptive or geographic, or is a surname, the mark may still be registered if the owner can prove that an appreciable number of purchasers within the applicable market do, in fact, associate the mark with the owner (as distinguished from the term's more general meaning). In such a case the mark is said to have acquired a **secondary meaning**—a name that is a misnomer, in view of the fact that such proof indicates the mark has, in fact, a strong meaning.[8] Wal-

---

[7] On this aspect of the case, the court held that FISH FRI was essentially descriptive (but, on the basis of other evidence, nonetheless protectable under the secondary meaning concept).

[8] With the exception of generic marks, marks which do not acquire a secondary meaning (or which cannot be registered on the Principal Register for any other reason) can gain some protection by being registered on a Supplemental Register.

tham (watches) and Bavarian (beer) are examples of geographic names registered under the secondary meaning concept, and Safeway (food products) is a descriptive name that achieved registration under the same concept.

## Element of Confusion

In most infringement actions the plaintiff mark owner has the burden of proving that defendant's mark is so similar to plaintiff's that defendant's use will produce a "likelihood of confusion" in buyers' minds as to the true origin of the goods or services. Whether such likelihood exists is a question of fact in any particular case, and is determined by such factors as similarity of design of the marks, similarity of product, proof of confusion among actual buyers, and marketing surveys of prospective purchasers showing an appreciable misassociation of defendant's mark with plaintiff's product. On the basis of these factors, for example, Rotary De-Rooting was held to be a mark so similar to Roto-Rooter that the owner of Roto-Rooter was successful in recovering damages from the owner of Rotary De-Rooting.[9] But if the products are substantially dissimilar, even identical marks may not cause confusion. Thus, where a clothing manufacturer had purchased the right to use the mark "Here's Johnny," a court held that the use of that mark by a manufacturer of portable toilets was not likely to cause purchasers of the toilets to associate them with the producer of the suits.[10]

When the trademark at issue is a design on a book, difficult First Amendment questions may arise, as the next case demonstrates.

[9] *Roto-Rooter Corp. v. O'Neal,* 513 F.2d 44, 1975.
[10] *Carson v. Here's Johnny Portable Toilets, Inc.,* 698 F.2d 831 (1983). Although plaintiff suit manufacturer was unsuccessful in the infringement aspect of the case, plaintiff Johnny Carson was granted an injunction restraining defendant company from further use of the mark on the invasion of privacy theory.

---

### Cliffs Notes, Inc. v. Bantam Doubleday Dell Publishing Group
U.S. Second Circuit Court of Appeals, 886 F.2d 490 (1989)

Plaintiff-appellee publishes "Cliffs Notes," a series of study guides which are condensed versions, with brief analyses, of various short stories, plays and books. Defendant-appellant Bantam Doubleday Dell Publishing Group, working with the often satirical Spy magazine, publishes "Spy Notes," a onetime parody both of modern novels (such as Tama Janowitz's *Slaves of New York,* Bret Ellis's *Less Than Zero,* and Jay McInerney's *Bright Lights Big City*) and of Cliffs Notes.

Spy magazine's editors believed that a study guide would provide an ideal vehicle for a parody of modern novels, because the "flat, straightforward, academic style" of Cliffs Notes would contrast sharply with the "cool, ironic, sophisticated, urbane novels." Spy Notes, like Cliffs Notes, lists on the cover the works it condenses (i.e., the three aforementioned novels). It also replicates the distinctive yellow color, black diagonal stripes, and black lettering of Cliffs Notes, a design that is the subject of appellee's registered trademark.

On the other hand, Spy Notes contains: (1) humorous content rather than serious condensation and analysis; (2) the words "A Satire" in bright red lettering five times on the front and four times on the back; (3) colors (red, white and blue) not used on Cliffs Notes, (4) wry notations not found on Cliffs Notes (e.g., "Even funnier Than The Originals"). Spy Notes also is priced substantially higher than Cliffs Notes ($7.95 versus $3.50), and includes "The Spy Novel-O-Matic Fiction-Writing Device" which supposedly can be used by "young, world-weary urban authors" to create 16,765,056 different plot possibilities.

After Spy Notes had been bound but before it was shipped to bookstores, appellee sued for trademark infringement under the Lanham Act, claiming that Spy Notes would give consumers the false impression that it was appellee's product. The trial judge, applying the standards of *Polaroid Corp. v. Polarad Elec. Corp.,* 287 F.2d 492 (2d Cir.), cert. denied, 368 U.S. 820 (1961), found a "profound likelihood of confusion" and granted appellee's request for a preliminary injuction barring distribution of Spy Notes. Defendants appealed.

---

**Decision:** Reversed. The key to a trademark infringement case is whether there is a "likelihood of confusion" that would lead potential purchasers to believe that Cliffs Notes was the source of "Spy Notes." This decision must be reached keeping in mind that free speech principles and considerations of artistic expression require greater protection for parody and satire. Here, the likelihood of confusion is relatively slight for several reasons, including: (1) college age readers of Cliffs Notes are likely to be familiar with Spy Magazine; (2) the cover of "Spy Notes" contains several colors that are not on Cliffs Notes, shows a clay

*(continued)*

sculpture of New York City rather than of a bare cliff, states several times that it is "A Satire," and carries a cover price of twice that of Cliffs Notes; (3) purchasers of Cliffs Notes are not usually impulse buyers—they are looking for specific titles and Cliffs Notes does not produce any titles done by Spy; (4) the title page of the satire specifically states that it is produced by the editors of Spy magazine and its copyright notice page states that "Spy Notes" is a parody of Cliffs Notes; and (5) the satire contains a "Spy Novel-O-Matic Fiction-Writing Device," which is an immediate tip-off that something humorous is afoot. ∎

## *Remedies*

Where likelihood of confusion is established, the plaintiff's usual remedies under the Lanham Act or common-law principles are the *injunction* and *damages*. The injunction is an order prohibiting defendant's further use of the mark, and damages is a recovery of money to compensate plaintiff for the monetary injury (if any) which he or she has sustained as a result of the infringement.

Because of a tremendous increase in the trafficking of counterfeit designer goods, Congress passed the Trademark Counterfeiting Act of 1984 which provides escalating *criminal* penalties for multiple offenders. For example, a second offender, if an individual, can be fined up to $1,000,000 and/or imprisoned for up to 15 years.

## *Anti-Dilution Statutes*

Approximately half the states have extended trademark protection beyond situations where a "likelihood of confusion" exists by enacting **anti-dilution** statutes, which remedy dilution of the distinctive quality of a mark or injury to business reputation even where the parties do not compete and there is no real likelihood that consumers will believe that plaintiff (trademark owner) is the sponsor of defendant's products.

Consider the strong TIFFANY trademark, connoting luxury and excellence in products. If someone were to open a bar called TIFFANY, it is unlikely that the public would believe that the owners of the TIFFANY trademark were also responsible for the bar—there would be no likelihood of confusion. However, use of the name TIFFANY on the bar may injure the holder of the TIFFANY trademark in two ways: (1) it lessens the distinctiveness of the mark if it can be used on all manner of products and services (for bars, bicycles, feminine hygiene products, etc.) and (2) it undermines the positive image of the mark if it is no longer restricted to luxury-type products. *Tiffany v. Boston Club,* 231 F. Supp. 836 (D.Mass.

1964). State anti-dilution laws protect distinctive marks from these types of injuries.

## MISUSE OF TRADE SECRETS

It is an information age, and nothing is more important to most businesses than information. By means of industrial sabotage and the hiring of competitors' employees, companies annually acquire from competitors an estimated 20 billion dollars worth of confidential information. Patent law is often available to protect information, but trade secret law must be considered equally important. Trade secret law can protect a wider range of information at a cheaper cost and do so perpetually, which is preferable to the 17-year limit to patent protection. "The maintenance of commercial ethics and the encouragement of innovation are the broadly stated policies behind trade secret law."[11]

A **trade secret** is "any formula, pattern, device or compilation of information which is used in one's business, and which gives him an opportunity to obtain an advantage over competitors who do not know or use it."[12] Examples of protectable trade secrets include customer lists, manufacturing processes, chemical formulas, cookie recipes, operating and pricing policies, marketing techniques, raw materials sources, and computer software.

## *Elements of the Tort*

After Manville Corporation spent nine million dollars over seven years to perfect a new method of insulation, one of its competitors hired six key Manville employees and was able to enter the market in less than two years. Manville later prevailed in a lawsuit against the competitor because simple concepts of fairness suggest that a company that has acquired information or developed processes as a result of its own efforts—information or processes not generally

---

[11] *Kewanee Oil Co. v. Bicron Corp.*, 416 U.S. 460 (1973).
[12] *Restatement of Torts* §757 comment b (1939).

known to others—ought to be protected from the wrongful use of such information or processes by its competitors. The common law and the statutes of almost 20 states that have adopted the Uniform Trade Secrets Act provide such protection.

To successfully bring a misappropriation of trade secrets claim, a plaintiff must prove (1) existence and ownership of a trade secret; (2) defendant's acquisition of the trade secret by wrongful or improper means; and (3) use or disclosure of the trade secret to the injury of plaintiff.

In any trade secrets case, two issues are paramount: (1) whether the processes or information which the plaintiff is seeking to protect against the defendant's continued use are "secret" in the eyes of the law, and (2) if so, whether the defendant acquired the information by "wrongful means."

## *Secrecy Requirement*

A prototypical trade secret is the formula for Coca-Cola. A Coca-Cola company executive testified by affidavit in *Coca-Cola Bottling Co. v. Coca-Cola Co.,* 227 U.S.P.Q. 18 (D.Del. 1985) that

> The written version of the secret formula is kept in a security vault at the Trust Company Bank in Atlanta, and that vault can only be opened by a resolution from the Company's Board of Directors. It is the Company's policy that only two persons in the Company shall know the formula at any one time, and that only those persons may actually oversee the actual preparation of [the product]. The Company refuses to allow the identity of those persons to be disclosed or to allow those persons to fly on the same airplane at the same time.

Coca-Cola knows how to meet the "secrecy" requirement.

Perhaps the extreme measures adopted by Coca-Cola need not be exercised in every case. Nonetheless, to be protected, information must be kept reasonably (not absolutely) secret by its owner. In deciding whether specified information is, in fact, secret, courts generally consider (1) the extent to which the information is known outside the business; (2) the extent to which it is known by employees of the business; (3) the extent of security measures taken by the firm; (4) the value of the information to its owner; (5) the amount of effort or money expended to create the information; and (6) the ease or difficulty with which the information could be properly acquired or duplicated by others. *Restatement (Second) of Torts,* § 757, comment b. Thus, if a defendant has acquired information that was freely circulated by the plaintiff company among its employees, customers, or suppliers, the secrecy requirement is not met. In contrast, protection will be afforded where a company gives secret information only to a small number of employees on a "need to know" basis, under clear instructions not to disclose it to others. If an employee breaches this trust by passing it to a competitor, it remains a trade secret and the competitor's use of it subjects the competitor to tort liability.

## *The Wrongful Acquisition Requirement*

Even if information qualifies as a trade secret, its use by a competitor is normally lawful if the competitor has discovered the secret by means that are "not improper." Thus if X Company discovers a manufacturing process by independent research, or even by means of "reverse engineering"—disassembling a product of Y Company that it has lawfully purchased—the subsequent use of the process by X Company is generally lawful under trade secret rules (which is one reason that patent protection is usually desirable).

Historically, acquisition was considered to be improper only when it was illegal (e.g., acquisition by trespass, theft, or wiretapping) or involved breach of a confidential relationship (e.g., bribery of an employee of the owners). A recent high-profile example came to light in 1982 when the FBI arrested employees of Hitachi, Ltd., on the basis of evidence that it had paid over $600,000 for stolen data concerning a new IBM computer. More recently, courts have broadened the improper means concept to include methods which "fall below the generally accepted standards of commercial morality, even though not illegal."[13]

The following case illustrates a difficult trade secret question that should be of interest to any would-be inventors.

---

[13] *E.I. duPont de Nemours & Co., Inc. v. Christopher,* 431 F.2d 1012 (5th Cir. 1970), where duPont recovered damages from a company that had acquired its secret method of producing methanol by means of aerial photographs of a duPont plant under construction. Apparently companies need not use antiaircraft guns to keep their secrets; only "reasonable" efforts are required.

### Smith v. Snap-On Tools Corp.
U.S. Fifth Circuit Court of Appeals, 833 F.2d 578 (1987)

Smith made a ratchet by combining parts of two existing tools. Hoping to see his ratchet made available for sale, he brought it to the attention of Snap-On Tools, Inc., by showing the ratchet to an independent Snap-On dealer and then submitting a tool suggestion form to Snap-On's Wisconsin headquarters. Snap-On began making and selling the ratchet without paying anything to Smith. Smith sued, claiming that Snap-On had misappropriated a trade secret. The trial court, applying Wisconsin law, ruled for Smith, but did not give him as large a judgment as he desired. Both sides appealed.

**Decision:** Judgment reversed. Wisconsin law prescribes two essential elements in a cause of action for misappropriation of trade secrets: an actual trade secret and a breach of confidence. Even when a secret exists, a person who learns the secret legitimately, without any duty of confidentiality, is free to use it. Because the court found no confidential relationship between Smith and Snap-On, Snap-On violated no obligation to Smith by manufacturing the ratchet. Smith voluntarily disclosed the secret without asking Snap-On to keep it confidential or telling Snap-On that he wished to be compensated. ∎

## PATENT INFRINGEMENT

To encourage creation and disclosure of inventions, the Constitution authorizes the federal government to grant **patents** to inventors ("patentees"). In exchange for disclosing the invention, the inventor patentee receives a 17-year (14 years in the case of design patents) exclusive right to make, use, or sell the patented item. The 17-year patent is nonrenewable; after expiration of the period the item goes into the public domain and may be made, used, or sold by anyone.

### Subject Matter

Items that may be patented include (1) processes, (2) machines, (3) manufactures (e.g., products), (4) compositions of matter (e.g., new arrangements of elements as in metal alloys), and (5) any improvement upon the first four categories. In addition, design patents for ornamental designs have been granted, as have patents on new varieties of asexually reproducing plants which have been modified by humans and do not naturally occur in nature. In *Diamond v. Chakrabarty*,[14] the Supreme Court even found a new life form (a laboratory-created bacterium for "eating" oil spills) to be patentable.

On the other hand, one cannot patent (1) printed matter, (2) naturally occurring substances, (3) methods of doing business, (4) ideas (e.g., $E = MC^2$), or (5) scientific principles (e.g., chemical formulas). This list is nonexclusive, but the idea is that the patentee must create, not find; invent, not merely discover.

### Patentability

If it fits into a proper subject matter category, an item may be patented if it meets three main tests: utility, novelty, and nonobviousness. An item has *utility* if it produces a direct benefit to mankind. It does not if it is dangerous, immoral, or merely a matter of curiosity. The *novelty* test is met if the item is distinctive from what was present in the prior state of the art. Prior patents, public use or sale, and written descriptions of the item can destroy novelty. *Nonobviousness* is also decided in light of the prior state of the art. If the item could easily have been produced by someone with normal skill in the area, or if it is an obvious next step from prior inventions, the nonobviousness test is not met. If a product is immediately a tremendous success or if it fills a long-felt need in the marketplace, there is a presumption of nonobviousness.

In practice, these tests are somewhat vague. For that reason, although the Patent Office grants about 60 percent of the patent applications, when these applications are challenged by alleged infringers, about 60 percent of issued patents are invalidated by the courts.

---
[14] 447 U.S. 303 (1980).

## Patent Procedure

A patent application must be filed in the name of the inventor at the U.S. Patent and Trademark Office in Arlington, Virginia. The application must include a *specification* (a precise description of the item so that one skilled in the art could make use of it), and *claims* (a description of precisely what makes the item patentable—e.g., useful, novel, and nonobvious). The Patent Office will examine the application and search for previous patents on the same item. If the application is denied, it may be amended, and frequently substantial negotiation occurs between the applicant and the Patent Office. Decisions can be appealed administratively and, ultimately, to the courts.

Patent procedure is time consuming and expensive. It is also very complicated, and an inventor would be wise to hire an attorney who specializes in patent law.

Once the application is filed, the patentee can place "Patent Pending" on his products for which the patent is sought. This has no legal effect because the patent is not effective until issued by the Patent Office. However, it puts others on notice of the claim, and if the patent is ultimately granted they can be sued for infringements occurring during the patent pending stage.

## Ownership

The patentee can sell his title to the patent to a third party. The patentee can also retain the title, but grant a license under which a third party can use the patented item in exchange for payment of a royalty to the patentee. Assignments of title must be filed in the Patent Office.

Employees should be aware of the **shop right doctrine.** If an employee is hired for creative or inventive work, and invents something on company time while using company resources, the patent belongs to the company. The company will file the application in the employee's name, but the company will own it. Even if the employee was not hired for creative or inventive work, if he or she invents something on company time using company resources, the company will be granted a nonexclusive license to use the patented item without payment of a royalty. Of course, many employers have their employees sign agreements to assign title to all patents generated on company time to the employer.

## Infringement

A person infringes a valid patent by using a device which (1) literally meets each of the limitations of the patent's claim, or (2) under the "doctrine of equivalents," does the "same work in substantially the same way and accomplish[es] substantially the same result" as the patented device, even though the infringing device differs in name, form, or shape.[15]

## Defenses

An alleged misuser may raise a number of defenses. First, of course, the misuser may claim that his or her device did not meet the doctrine of equivalents. Second, the misuser may challenge the validity of the patent by arguing that it flunks one or more of the tests of novelty, utility, and nonobviousness or that it is not the type of subject matter that may be properly patented. Third, the misuser may claim that the patentee *forfeited* the patent by not filing an application within one year after the invention was in public use, or should have the patent revoked because he or she breached the *duty of candor,* a duty the law imposes to disclose everything the patentee knows about previous inventions and other facts which might bear on patentability. Finally, the infringer might argue that the patent should be revoked because of *patent misuse,* which occurs when the patentee abuses the patent, frequently in violation of antitrust laws, in order to gain more rights than the patent legally confers. This defense was watered down in 1988 when Congress passed the Patent Misuse Reform of the Patent and Trademark Office Authorization Act.

## Remedies

A patentee who successfully sues for infringement can obtain an injunction, damages of no less than a reasonable royalty rate (and perhaps trebled in the court's discretion where plaintiff was damaged to a greater extent than the demonstrated royalty rate), and in exceptional cases, attorneys' fees.

The following case contains a recent Supreme Court discussion of the basic philosophy underlying federal patent policy.

---

[15]*Autogyro Co. of America v. U.S.*, 384 F.2d 391 (Ct. Cl. 1967).

### Bonito Boats, Inc. v. Thunder Craft Boats, Inc.
U.S. Supreme Court,
109 S.Ct. 971 (1989)

In September 1976, Bonito Boats, Inc. (petitioner), a Florida corporation, developed a hull design for a fiberglass recreational boat which it marketed under the trade name Bonito Boat Model 5VBR. Designing the hull required substantial effort, including preparation of engineering drawings, creation of a hardwood model, and production of a fiberglass mold from the model. The 5VBR was favorably received by the boating public. Bonito never filed a patent application.

In May 1983, the Florida legislature enacted a statute that makes it "unlawful for any person to use the direct molding process to duplicate for the purpose of sale [or to sell] any manufactured vessel hull or component part of a vessel made by another without the written permission of that other person."

In 1984, Bonito filed this suit alleging that Thunder Craft Boats (respondent) had violated the Florida statute by using the direct molding process to duplicate the Bonito 5VBR fiberglass hull, and had sold such duplicates.

The trial court, the Florida Court of Appeals, and the Florida Supreme Court all concluded that the Florida law was invalid under the Supremacy Clause of the Constitution in that it impermissibly interfered with the scheme established by the federal patent laws. Bonito brought the matter to the U.S. Supreme Court.

**Decision:** Affirmed. The Florida law impermissibly interferes with the scheme established by the federal patent laws and therefore violates the Supremacy Clause. Patent law attempts to strike a balance between the interests of the public in having access to products and devices on the one hand, and, on the other hand, the right of inventors to exploit their ideas so that invention will be encouraged. Federal law has long struck this balance by allowing inventors to apply for patents. If an invention satisfies the requirements of novelty, nonobviousness, and utility, it may be patented. The inventor receives the exclusive right to exploit the patent economically for 17 years (14 years in the case of a design patent). In return, the inventor realizes that after the patent expires, the invention goes into the public domain and may be exploited by anyone. This is a carefully designed scheme, which Florida's law upset by protecting inventions that were not patented. For whatever reason, Bonito chose not to apply for a patent; therefore, it is not entitled to protection under the patent laws and Florida's attempt to provide that protection through state legislation must be invalidated. ∎

---

## COPYRIGHT INFRINGEMENT

To reward and stimulate intellectual endeavors, federal **copyright** law grants authors protection for the *expression* of their ideas, though not for the ideas themselves. Under the Copyright Act of 1976, all copyrightable works created after January 1, 1978, receive protection for the life of the author plus fifty years after his or her death. If the work is anonymous or a work for hire, the copyright lasts for the shorter of 75 years from its first publication or 100 years from its creation.

During that period, the owner of the copyright has the exclusive right to produce the work in any medium, to control derivative works, to distribute copies of the work, to perform the work in public, and to display the work in public.

### *Subject Matter*

Copyrights protect literary works (books, newspapers, magazines), works of a musical, dramatic, graphic, choreographic, or audiovisual nature, and sound recordings. This list is non-exclusive; the law is meant to protect any "original works of authorship." Computer software, jewelry designs, architectural designs, and speeches reduced to writing have been protected.

### *Copyrightability*

There are three basic elements of copyrightability. First, the work must be *fixed* in some *tangible medium of expression.* When a book is written, a song is recorded, a picture is painted, or a choreography is filmed, this requirement is met. Until tangibly fixed, a mere idea is unprotected.

The work must be *creative*, at least to some degree. This requirement is loosely applied in most cases. Some courts require a "modicum of creative work," while others only seek to insure that the author put some effort or "sweat" into the work. Photographs of real life scenes (such as the fortuitous Zapruder film of the Kennedy assassination) are clearly copyrightable, as are compilations of facts and directories, though little creative thought is involved.

Most important, the work must be *original*. This does not require novelty, only that the work not be copied from someone else. A person who had never seen the novel *Moby Dick* but wrote a nearly identical book independently could successfully copyright it.

A very controversial issue now facing the courts is the copyrightability of computer codes. Unfortunately, decisions have not been consistent. Most courts have held that the literal elements of a computer code, including its source and object code, may be copyrighted. Many courts have also found that the structure, sequence, and organization of software are copyrightable. However, it is not clear exactly how far operating instructions embedded in a microchip or added in a sequence of transistors may be protected.

## *Copyright Procedure*

Securing a copyright is much easier than securing a patent, and has recently become even easier. Copyright law has an important international dimension. Books, songs, movies, and other copyrightable material quickly travel from continent to continent in today's world. There are two major copyright treaties. Until 1989, the United States belonged only to the Universal Copyright Convention, administered by UNESCO. Effective in 1989, however, the United States also joined the Berne Convention, administered by the U.N. World Intellectual Property Organization.

The process of obtaining a copyright is virtually self-executing. Until 1989, copyright protection for a published work was obtained if each copy of the work contained (1) a copyright notice (e.g., the word "copyright," the abbreviation "Copr.," or the symbol ©), (2) the date of first publication, and (3) the name of the copyright holder. This relatively simple process is now even easier. For works first published after the March 1, 1989 effective date of the Berne Convention, the copyright notice is no longer a requirement. Including a copyright notice is still a good idea, because (1) it will protect the author in countries that have not signed the Berne Convention, and (2) the new law gives potentially important evidentiary weight to such a notice by eliminating any "innocent infringement" claim that a defendant might interpose to mitigate damages in a copyright infringement suit. Such a defense would be available if plaintiff's works did not include a copyright notice.

Before March 1989, a person who observed a published work that did not contain a copyright notice could feel assured that the work was in the public domain. For works published after that date, however, this is not necessarily the case.

## *Infringement*

If a plaintiff proves (even by circumstantial evidence) that a defendant had *access* to plaintiff's work, and that defendant's work bears a *substantial similarity* to plaintiff's copyrighted work (or a part of it), a claim for infringement is established. Plaintiff need not prove intent; an innocent infringement is actionable. For example, in *Bright Tunes Music Corp. v. Harrisongs Music, Ltd.*,[16] the judge did not believe that former Beatle George Harrison intentionally copied an earlier song, "He's So Fine," when he composed "My Sweet Lord." Nonetheless, Harrison had access to the earlier song (which was widely played on popular radio), and his song was substantially similar. Harrison was held to have infringed the owner's copyright.

## *Fair Use Doctrine*

An important, but rather vague, part of copyright law is the *Fair Use Doctrine*. Section 107 of the Copyright Act of 1976 states:

> [T]he fair use of a copyrighted work, including such use by reproduction in copies or phonorecords or by any other means specified by [§ 106], for purposes such as criticism, comment, newsreporting, teaching (including multiple copies for classroom use), scholarship, or re-

---

[16] 420 F. Supp. 177 (S.D.N.Y. 1977).

search, is not an infringement of copyright. In determining whether the use made of a work in any particular case is a fair use the factors to be considered shall include—

1. the purpose and character of the use, including whether such use is of a commercial nature or is for nonprofit educational purposes;

2. the nature of the copyrighted work;

3. the amount and substantiality of the portion used in relation to the copyrighted work as a whole; and

4. the effect of the use upon the potential market for or value of the copyrighted work.

Although the applications of this doctrine are shadowy at best, the Copyright Office has issued supplemental guidelines dealing with photocopies, and obviously copies used for literary criticism, classroom teaching, and parody fare better than those used for commercial purposes.

The following controversial case illustrates the fair use doctrine.

---

### Salinger v. Random House, Inc.
U.S. Second Circuit Court of Appeals, 811 F.2d 90 (1987)

The plaintiff, J. D. Salinger, is a famous author, best known for his novel *The Catcher in the Rye*. Defendant Ian Hamilton is a well-respected writer on literary topics who undertook a biography of Salinger despite the latter's opposition. An important source of material used by Hamilton was unpublished letters written by Salinger between 1939 and 1961. The letters were contained in collections in the libraries of Harvard, Princeton, and the University of Texas.

Salinger received a set of galley proofs (the "May galleys") of Hamilton's biography in May 1986. Noticing the many references to his letters, Salinger registered 79 of his unpublished letters for copyright protection and instructed his lawyer to object to publication of the biography until all of his unpublished materials were deleted.

Hamilton and his publisher, defendant Random House, revised the May galleys. The current version (the "October galleys") replaced many quotations of Salinger's letters with close paraphrasing. More than 200 quoted words remained and there are 59 instances of quotations or close paraphrasings from the unpublished letters.

Salinger sued, claiming, among other things, copyright infringement. The trial judge, Judge Leval, denied Salinger's request for a permanent injunction, finding that Hamilton's use of expressive materials was too minimal to have subjected Salinger to any serious harm and that it constituted "fair use" within the meaning of Section 107 of the 1976 Copyright Act. Salinger appealed.

**Decision:** Reversed. The "fair use" doctrine does not protect defendants' book. According to the Supreme Court, four factors must be examined. (1) *Purpose of the Use.* Because defendants' book may be considered "criticism," "scholarship," and "research," and is not an attempt to beat plaintiff to the marketplace, this factor weighs in their favor. (2) *Nature of the Copyrighted Work.* Unpublished works are entitled to special protection under the copyright laws. The defense of "fair use" is somewhat narrowed in this context, so this factor favors plaintiff. (3) *Amount and Substantiality of the Portion Used.* Given the substantial paraphrasing, as well as the occasional direct quote, it is clear that defendants' book substantially uses plaintiff's unpublished writings. Passages paraphrased or quoted contain a sufficient degree of creativity as to sequence of thoughts, choice of words, emphasis, and arrangement to satisfy the minimal threshold of required creativity. Letters are quoted or paraphrased on 40 percent of the book's pages. Therefore, this factor also favors plaintiff. (4) *Effect on the Market.* Though Salinger has not elected to publish his letters and has no plans to do so, he has the right to change his mind. He is entitled to the opportunity to sell his letters, which have an estimated market value of $500,000. Their marketability would most likely be impaired by publication of the quotes and paraphrases in defendants' book. Therefore, this factor also favors plaintiff, if only slightly. On balance, the claim of fair use fails. ■

## Remedies

A successful plaintiff in a copyright infringement action usually receives actual damages plus defendant's profits to the extent they were not calculated into the damage award. If plaintiffs have registered their copyright, they may waive actual damages and instead receive "statutory damages" in an amount the court finds "just," with the normal range being between $500 and $20,000 for any one work involved in the action, and up to $100,000 if the infringement was willful. In cases where the plaintiff has difficulty proving actual damages, the right to opt for statutory damages can be quite important. (An author who chooses to register a copyright may do so by sending a completed application form, a check for $10, and a copy of the work if it is unpublished or two copies if it is published to the Register of Copyrights in Washington, D.C.)

Copyright infringement can also constitute a federal misdemeanor punishable by fines of up to $10,000 and/or one year in jail.

## UNFAIR COMPETITION

The term **unfair competition** is an imprecise one. In its broadest sense, it covers all tortious business conduct. In its most common usage, however, the term refers only to those business practices that are based on *deception*. (Thus, of the torts discussed above, only trademark infringement would fall within the unfair competition category.)

In addition to trademark infringement, unfair competition includes any deceptive use by one person of the copyright or patent rights of another. It also embraces many other common-law torts, such as falsely inducing consumers to believe a product is endorsed by another, and "palming off." Palming off refers to any word or deed causing purchasers to be misled as to a product's source. It thus includes not only trademark infringement but all other means of source-deception as well.

## *State Deceptive Trade Practices Acts*

A consumer who is misled by false advertising or other deceptive practices may have the right to sue under a common-law fraud theory, or perhaps a breach of express warranty theory if the advertising involved a product. These theories are discussed in other chapters.[17] However, additional consumer protection legislation, passed at both the state and federal levels, also addresses such activity.

Misleading advertising is often prohibited by state **deceptive trade practices acts**.[18] Other types of unfair competition that are usually prohibited by such statutes are the advertising of goods or services with the intent not to sell them upon the advertised terms, representing goods as new when they are used or second-hand, and disparagement—making false statements of fact about competitors' goods or services.

## *The Lanham Act*

The federal government has also passed various acts that prohibit unfair competition, such as misleading advertising. In Chapter 50, for example, we will examine the Federal Trade Commission Act's ban on "unfair or deceptive acts or practices." In this chapter, our focus is on Section 43(a) of the Lanham Act, which outlaws "any false description or representation." While this section is frequently used to allow trademark owners to sue competitors for trademark infringement, it has also created a general federal law of unfair competition which is frequently applied to deceptive advertising. Designed in large part to protect consumers from being misled, the cause of action is given primarily to the competitors of the deceptive advertiser.

**Illicit Acts:** Section 43(a) of the Lanham Act has supported suits against companies that (1) used pictures of the plaintiff's product to advertise their own inferior brand; (2) used a confusingly similar color and shape of drug capsule which could mislead consumers into thinking that they were buying plaintiff's nontrademarked brand; (3) printed "$2.99 as advertised on TV" when only the plaintiff had run such ads; (4) claimed that their pain-reliever worked faster than the plaintiff's when it did not; and (5) displayed a rock star's picture on an album creating the impression that he was a featured performer when, in fact, he was not.

---

[17] Express warranties are discussed in Chapter 22. Fraud was mentioned in Chapter 8 and will be discussed in more detail in Chapter 15.

[18] In states having such statutes, the wrongs are thus statutory torts (rather than common-law torts).

As in all advertising, some "puffing" is permitted by the Lanham Act. For example, when a computerized chess game was advertised as "like having Karpov as your opponent," mere puffing was found.[19]

[19] *Data Cash Systems, Inc. v. JS&A Group, Inc.*, 223 U.S.P.Q. 865 (N.D.Ill. 1984).

**Enforcement:** Most courts have not allowed deceived consumers to bring Sec. 43(a) claims. Instead, suit is usually brought by competitors who, while redressing their own injuries, seek to end false advertising that also injures consumers. These competitors have been termed "vicarious avengers" of the consumer interest. A competitor's motive for bringing such a suit is easily seen in the following case.

### U-Haul International, Inc. v. Jartran, Inc.
U.S. District Court for Arizona, 601 F.Supp. 1140 (1984)

In 1979 plaintiff U-Haul International rented almost all of the "self-move" household goods trailers in the United States, and 60 percent of the "self-move" trucks. In that year defendant James A. Ryder entered the market by forming defendant Jartran, Inc. Jartran had limited financing, but bought a fleet of trucks and trailers with financing packages of 110 percent (i.e., equipment plus cash). However, these trucks and trailers were mostly in Detroit where they were manufactured, and it would cost $8,000,000 to move them to rental outlets.

Jartran decided to incorporate the distribution effort into an advertising campaign so that persons would rent the equipment at Detroit and move it throughout the United States. A massive advertising campaign had an immediate impact. Jartran's gross revenues rose from $3,000,000 in 1979 to $58,000,000 in 1980, and $95,000,000 in 1981. At the same time, U-Haul's gross revenue for 1981 was $49,000,000 less than it had predicted before it knew Jartran would be a competitor.

Jartran's ad campaign, on which it spent $6,000,000, featured comparisons of the one-way rental rates charged by U-Haul and Jartran. Most stated "U-Haul It to (City) . . . Jartran It to (City) . . ." with rates for U-Haul and Jartran stated after the name of the city. Jartran's advertised price to the advertised destination was a special promotional price relating to the nationwide distribution of the equipment, but was not advertised as such. It was meant to be perceived, and was perceived by the consuming public, as the price Jartran would normally charge.

Jartran's ads frequently included in the U-Haul price a basic rate and a distribution fee, without disclosing that the distribution fee was included. The self-move industry imposes distribution fees as a temporary device to regulate rentals to areas in which there is a build-up of equipment. Such fees are usually quoted separately to indicate their temporary nature. Distribution fees apply to less than 5 percent of U-Haul's yearly transactions.

Jartran's advertised prices were lower than rates reflected on Jartran's own rate sheet, and lower than the rates Jartran actually charged in most transactions. Jartran's company policy was to price above its competition; its rate structure was the same or slightly higher than U-Haul's. Jartran also published an ad showing a Jartran truck and a U-Haul truck with the comparative sizes of the vehicles adjusted to make the U-Haul truck appear smaller and less attractive.

After spending $13 million in advertising to combat Jartran's advertising campaign, U-Haul brought this § 43(a) suit under the Lanham Act.

**Decision:** The trial judge entered judgment against defendants in the sum of $40 million under § 43(a) of the Lanham Act after concluding that the advertisements at issue "contain false, misleading, deceptive, and incomplete statements of fact; (2) which statements are likely to deceive and actually did deceive a substantial segment of the buying public; (3) and which are material in that they are likely to and did influence the customer's choice of a self-move company; (4) because Jartran's goods and services travel in interstate commerce; and (5) the disputed advertisements actually injured U-Haul."

The First Amendment does not protect commercial speech if, as here, that speech is misleading. ∎

**Commercial Defamation:** On appeal, the previous case was affirmed as to all points discussed in the excerpt, but reversed as to some minor holdings. *U-Haul International, Inc. v. Jartran, Inc.,* 793 F.2d 1034 (9th Cir. 1986). The huge judgment recovered by the plaintiff is expected to increase the popularity of Section 43(a) suits. Additionally, a recent legislative development is also likely to boost the number of such suits.

Many courts had been allowing Lanham Act suits to be brought when companies ran ads that deceptively described their own products, but not when the ads deceptively described their competitors' products. Congress elected to bring deceptive "comparison advertisements" within the scope of the Lanham Act when it passed the Trademark Revision Act of 1988. In so doing, Congress established a clause of action for commercial defamation. The Act now bans false descriptions or representations about the "nature, characteristics [or] qualities of *any person's* goods, services or commercial activities" (emphasis added). Therefore, if Company A runs an ad comparing its products to those of Company B's, and in so doing misleadingly describes the characteristics of Company B's products, Company B will be able to recover treble damages such as those granted in the *U-Haul* case. For First Amendment reasons, the Act contains express protection for two broad types of activities: (1) political speech, consumer or editorial comment, and satire, and (2) "innocent infringement" (thereby insulating news media which innocently disseminate false advertising).

## SUMMARY

Businesses have a strong and legally protectable interest in free and fair competition, and in their intellectual property. The courts will protect against unfair interference not only with existing contractual and business relationships, but also, under proper circumstances, with prospective relationships. The key is frequently whether the defendant is acting with an improper purpose or in an improper manner.

The law protects properly registered trademarks so that producers can enjoy the reputations they have established and consumers are not misled as to the source of the products and services they purchase. To encourage creativity and inventiveness, the law protects intellectual property through patents and copyrights. And it prohibits the theft of trade secrets—the confidential bits of information that can give a business a competitive advantage.

The federal government and the states have also passed laws prohibiting various forms of unfair competition, including many forms of deceptive advertising.

## KEY TERMS

**Business torts**
**Interference with business conduct**
**Justification**
**Trademark**
**Service marks**
**Generic term**
**Secondary meaning**
**Anti-dilution**
**Trade secret**
**Patent**
**Shop right doctrine**
**Copyright**
**Unfair competition**
**Deceptive trade practices acts**

## QUESTIONS AND PROBLEMS

1. Perfect Subscription Co. (Perfect) solicited magazine subscriptions by phone. It had twenty to thirty supervisors who recruited large numbers of telephone sales representatives ("reps") to conduct the business. These supervisors and reps over the years had collected lists of magazine "expires"—names of persons whose subscriptions had expired, and who were contacted by phone to renew their subscriptions. These lists of expires were obtained by the supervisors, by requesting such information from magazine publishers, and by the reps, who kept updating the lists they were furnished.

Kavaler, a vice president of Perfect, quit his job and formed his own subscription company. After he began collecting lists of expires by contacting the supervisors and reps of his old company (Perfect), Perfect brought an action seeking an injunction barring Kavaler from such contacts on the theory that the lists were trade secrets.

   **a.** During the trial, Kavaler introduced evidence showing that magazines often gave lists of expires to any company asking for them, and also that lists were sometimes exchanged between sales reps of competing companies. Do you think this evidence should cause the court to reject Perfect's contention that the lists were trade secrets? Discuss.

**b.** If Kavaler had solicited these lists while still an officer of Perfect, do you think a court might be more likely to issue an injunction than in the instant fact-pattern? If so, on what theory might it be issued? (*Perfect Subscription Co. v. Kavaler,* 427 F. Supp. 1289, 1977.)

**2.** Plaintiff Walner purchased an ice cream parlor franchise from defendant Baskin-Robbins, Inc. The franchise agreement contained language requiring defendant's approval before the franchise could be sold. Two years later Walner contracted to sell the franchise to Garapet at a substantial profit, but Baskin-Robbins refused to grant permission for the sale. Walner sued for tortious interference with his right to contract with Garapet. Discuss. (*Walner v. Baskin-Robbins Ice Cream Co.*, 514 F. Supp. 1028, N.D.Tex. 1981.)

**3.** A trademark applicant wishes to mark the word "Bundt" in connection with one of its cake pans. Is this term suitable for trademark registration? Discuss. (*In re Northland Aluminum Products, Inc.,* 777 F.2d 1556, Fed. Cir. 1985.)

**4.** Miller Brewing Company purchased the trademark *Lite* and used this name on its labels for beer that was lower in calories than its regular beer. When a competitor, G. Heileman Brewing Company, started marketing a reduced-calorie beer that it labeled as "light beer," Miller brought a trademark infringement action against Heileman. At the trial, Heileman introduced evidence that the term "light" beer had been used for many years in the beer industry to refer to beers having certain flavors, bodies, or reduced alcoholic contents. On that basis, Heileman contended that "light" was, essentially, a generic term, and thus could not be the proper subject of a trademark. The trial court rejected this argument, and issued an injunction prohibiting further use of "light" by Heileman. On appeal, do you think the court should accept Heileman's argument? Discuss why, or why not. (*Miller Brewing Company v. G. Heileman Brewing Company,* 561 F.2d 75, 1977.)

**5.** Mead Data Central developed and trademarked LEXIS, a computerized legal research service. Toyota Motor Sales planned to begin selling cars trademarked LEXUS. Discuss Mead Data's possible theories for blocking sale of the cars. (*Mead Data Central, Inc. v. Toyota Motor Sales,* 875 F.2d 1026, 2d Cir. 1989.)

**6.** Plaintiff bakery filmed one of defendant bakery's delivery drivers in a grocery store taking plaintiff's fresh bread out of plaintiff's wrappers and replacing it with stale loaves. What theory should plaintiff pursue? Is this a good claim? (*Basque French Bakery v. Toscana Baking Co.,* No. 2937220-0, California Superior Court, Apr. 23, 1984.)

**7.** In response to complaints by customers of his sons' cycle shop, P developed a device to remedy a stall-out problem occurring when Yamaha racing cycles were run in mud or water. The device closed off the rear air intake, replacing it with an air snorkel located at a higher level under the seat cover. This device was used by P's sons when they raced and P installed it on the cycles his sons sold. When Yamaha representatives visited the business, P's sons showed them the device. Yamaha soon began using the device on all its cycles. At some point thereafter, P sued Yamaha for trade secret infringement. Will this claim succeed? (*Sheets v. Yamaha,* 657 F. Supp. 319, E.D.La. 1987.)

**8.** By combining plastic support blocks on pontoons, spaced I-beams, and separate bouyant chambers, Rivet reated a machine which could carry heavy loads across stump-filled marshes for extended periods. All three devices had been used before, but never in combination. Rivet's machine, which he patented, was significantly more efficient than any previous machine. Later, a former employee began making a similar machine. In a patent infringement suit, the defendant claimed Rivet's patent was invalid because the invention lacked novelty and nonobviousness. Discuss. (*Kori v. Wilco Marsh Buggies and Draglines, Inc.*, 708 F.2d 151, 5th Cir. 1983.)

**9.** Dr. Weissmann (P) and Dr. Freeman (D) collaborated for six years in research and publication of the results of that research. They produced a series of articles on radiopharmaceutical iminiodiacetic acid (IDA) scanning for diagnosing liver and biliary disorders. Then, P authored "Hepatobiliary Imaging," which was published as a chapter of a book. The chapter, listing P as sole author, clearly built upon the previous series of papers she had written with D. However, it contained a new selection of photo illustrations and captions, references to four recent reports in the pertinent literature, new textual material, and a reorganization of previous materials. When D was preparing to present a lecture on nuclear medicine at Mount Sinai hospital, he took P's chapter, removed her name, inserted his own, and added three words to the title. P sued for copyright infringement. Discuss the merits of P's claim and D's "fair use" defense. (*Weissmann v. Freeman,* 868 F.2d 1313, 2d Cir. 1989.)

**10.** Johnson Controls, Inc., developed a system of computer programs to control wastewater treatment plants. The "JC-5000S" program is customized for each location and carries a registered copyright. Former employees of Johnson, working for competitor Phoenix Control Systems, Inc., developed a similar program to do similar things. The Phoenix program did not copy the literal elements of Johnson's program (including the source and object code), however, it did copy the structure, sequence, and organization of the JC-5000S. Is such copying sufficient to constitute copyright infringement? (*Johnson Controls v. Phoenix Control Systems, Inc.,* 886 F.2d 1173, 9th Cir. 1989.)

CHAPTER 10

# BUSINESS ETHICS, CORPORATE SOCIAL RESPONSIVENESS, AND THE LAW

Jill is a regional sales manager for a nationwide chain of retail consumer electronics stores. She and her assistants at company headquarters design promotional programs for stores in the region, supervise store managers' implementation of company marketing strategies, and conduct sales seminars for salespeople at these stores. Questions continually arise about how far promotional materials and the statements of individual salespeople can go in pushing their products. These questions relate not only to what is legal, but also to what is "appropriate" or "ethical." If particular statements are legal, is there any reason at all to be concerned about them? Are there any other standards? Jill and her associates know that it usually will be illegal to brazenly lie about the quality of a product. But they also know that it is often very difficult for a buyer to prove that a seller made intentionally deceptive statements, so the legal risk is small even in such a case. Jill understands that a company's reputation, and ultimately its sales, may suffer if it becomes known for dealing dishonestly. She also knows, however, that if some forms of subtle deception are practiced with skill, most customers will never know. Although a few customers may discover the deception, the company does not depend on repeat business in most of its product lines.

Even if the legal or financial risks are not great, Jill feels that it is "wrong" to lie to a customer. When she receives a lot of pressure from her superiors to increase sales, however, she begins to ask herself various questions: "Why is it wrong, really?" "Who, after all, defines what is wrong if it isn't illegal?" "We're selling to adults; aren't they supposed to look after themselves?" "Isn't this just the free market at work, and doesn't the market operate impersonally on the assumption that all sellers and buyers pursue their own economic self-interests?" "Isn't it okay to do it if I *feel* okay about it?" "But what if I feel good about it only after some strained rationalizing?" "And . . . let's face it—I don't always feel good about what happens."

When Jill tries to define what is "wrong," she finds it difficult to come up with any standards or any systematic way to develop such standards. Not only that, but she cannot even decide whether there is a rational way to analyze problems of this nature. Assuming, again, that there are no significant legal risks, Jill wonders how much latitude a salesperson should have in extolling the virtues of a product. Must every shortcoming of the item be revealed? Surely not. But why not? May the sales pitch be couched in vague, laudatory terms or must all responses be absolutely factual, precise, and to-the-point? Should the salesperson be concerned about the customer's real need for the product, or is the customer's apparent willingness to purchase the only thing that matters? Should there be any regard for the customer's particular susceptibilities to advertising? What if the advertising campaign that brought the customer into the store was full of "subliminal" messages that subconsciously persuaded him that this product would improve his love life? Jill finally decides that she does not have the time or energy to worry about such things, and that she will just be guided by the opinion of the company's attorneys about the legal risks of particular strategies and statements. Over a period of time, however, she is increasingly bothered by some of the promotional strategies that she initiates or approves. After doing some reading, she realizes that she has been grappling with age-old questions and that there is an entire field of study concerned with questions of this nature. Jill has discovered "business ethics."

## WHAT IS ETHICS?

In a formal sense, the term **ethics** refers to the study of **morality** by systematically exploring moral values, moral standards and obligations, moral reasoning, and moral judgments. The terms morality and morals refer to the appropriate treatment of our fellow human beings. Although some people observe a technical distinction between "ethics" and "morals," these terms are often used interchangeably. When someone says, for example, that "Joe did not act ethically in that situation," the word "ethically" means the same thing as "morally." In this chapter, we are not very fussy about the use of these terms. Sometimes we will use them in their technical sense, and sometimes we will not. The context will make the meaning clear.

## *Is Business Ethics Different?*

Should a study of "business ethics" differ from a more general study of the subject? Questions about how we ought to interact with and treat others arise in all aspects of life. Moral issues arise in the realm of the family, social groups, neighborhoods, politics and government, interactions between nations, professional associations, and other relationships, as well as in business. The basic questions, arguments, and problem-solving methods remain the same for all these domains. The factual contexts will vary, of course, depending on the nature of the relationship. In studying "business" ethics, we focus on business relationships and use examples of business problems that raise ethical questions. In other words, business ethics consists of the application of moral principles to people in a business setting.

## THE RELATIONSHIP BETWEEN LAW AND ETHICS

One might legitimately ask why a study of business ethics should be included as a unit in a business course about law and the legal system. The material is admittedly somewhat different from the rest of the material in this book, and one could argue that the subject represents a digression from the main focus of the course. There are, however, a number of ways in which ethics and law fit together very naturally. As a result, there are several excellent reasons for dealing with the subject in the context of law. We will first recognize and discuss some of the differences between law and ethics, and then examine the close relationship between the two.

## *Differences between Legal and Moral Standards*

As we will see shortly, legal standards often have their counterparts in the ethical domain, and vice-versa. For example, lying not only may violate a fundamental moral standard but also may constitute fraud under the law of torts and under various criminal statutes. Similarly, breaking a promise not only may be unethical but also may constitute a legally impermissible breach of contract in some circumstances. There are, however, several basic differences between legal and moral standards.

First, legal standards have a different source than moral ones. Whether found in a constitution, statute, judicial decision, or administrative agency regulation, legal standards are defined and applied by governmental processes. It takes governmental power to adopt and enforce laws.

Moral standards, on the other hand, are internal; they are developed within each person. It is true that people develop their moral standards from input they receive from external sources, such as the tenets of their religion and instructions from parents, teachers, friends, and others under whose influence they fall during their formative years. People even pick up information about appropriate and inappropriate moral behavior by observing the conduct and speech of strangers. These moral perceptions are formed, modified, and reinforced over time as we go through the process of having to give rational support and justification for our conduct when it affects others. Despite external influences, people ultimately develop, apply, and modify *their own* moral standards. Legal authority may be complex, even murky, but it is always there. In the personal realm of morality, however, we simply cannot get off the hook by referring to outside authority. Our only human source of authority is our rational thought processes: clear and objective thinking about the dignity, worth, and integrity of people around us and our impact on their lives. Even when one derives his or her basic moral standards from religion, thus referring to a higher authority, conformity with those standards involves an individual choice—an exercise of the will.

Second, the consequences of violating legal and moral standards are different. Violations of the law, if detected, result in concrete sanctions. When lying violates the law against fraud, for example, the guilty person may have to pay damages to the victim in a civil action, and may even be prosecuted in a criminal action and forced to pay a fine to the state or serve a jail term. There are no externally imposed sanctions for violating moral standards, however. Although lying usually is clearly unethical even if it does not meet the legal definition of fraud, the violation of ethical norms by itself is not subject to any definite penalties. It is true that unethical conduct sometimes *can* result in tangible consequences such as lost business because of a damaged reputation. Mostly, however, the consequences are like the standards themselves, internal and difficult to define.

Third, even though legal standards sometimes need to be a bit vague in order to be flexible, they must be more clearly defined than moral standards. The obvious reason is that legal standards are imposed on us by society and we can be punished for violating them; because of this, legal standards must be expressed with enough clarity to give us reasonable notice of society's expectations.

Fourth, moral standards usually require more of us than legal standards. The law tends to seek out the average in human behavior, for at least three reasons: (1) Although people's ideas about what is appropriate behavior vary, the law attempts to prescribe and enforce norms for an entire society. (2) The enforcement of laws requires the use of scarce public resources to support courts, police, and so on. As a result, in order for legal standards to be effective, they must survive a rough cost/benefit analysis. In other words, we should generally allocate society's scarce resources to the enforcement of legal standards only if we feel that the costs of that enforcement are outweighed by the benefits to society of upholding those standards. This is one of the reasons why our legal system often does not do a very good job of providing remedies for small claims. (3) The law must be practical. It may be unethical to break a vaguely expressed promise, for example, but a court can require someone to pay monetary damages for breaking a promise only where the promise describes obligations with reasonable certainty.

Fifth, some laws have little or nothing to do with moral behavior because they exist for other purposes. Some laws, for instance, are adopted solely for the purpose of bringing order to our affairs. There is nothing inherently moral or immoral about driving on one side of the road rather than the other. To prevent chaos, however, a society must decide one way or the other.

## *The Legal/Ethical Overlap*

Despite their differences, law and ethics have much in common. First, as we will see shortly, sound moral reasoning is quite similar in methodology to sound legal reasoning. In other words, the method for rationally identifying and analyzing moral issues is very much like the method for dealing with legal issues.

Second, laws are intended to serve a variety of social purposes including, in some cases, promoting moral conduct. To again use fraud as an example, the laws that prohibit intentional misrepresentations of important facts in business transactions have at least two objectives: promoting adherence to the fundamental moral obligation of honesty in our dealings with others, and improving economic efficiency by improving the quality of information in the market.

Third, regardless of whether a given legal principle has a substantial moral content, evidence of ethical or unethical conduct can have significant effects on the outcome of a dispute. Judges, juries, arbitrators, and other decision makers in legal proceedings cannot help but take note of such behavior. Regardless of their own ethical level, they are likely to recoil when confronted with *your* unethical behavior. Most lawsuits or other dispute resolution procedures involve some close calls on factual and legal questions. When your behavior in the relevant events has been ethically questionable, these close calls are more likely to go against you.

The now-famous dispute between Texaco and Pennzoil illustrates how the ethical background of a transaction can affect the close decisions that often must be made when legal disputes are being resolved. Pennzoil claimed that it had reached an agreement to merge with Getty Oil Co. Even after the alleged agreement had been reached, Getty secretly shopped around for another merger partner. Within a matter of days, Texaco "pulled the rug out from under" Pennzoil and acquired Getty. Pennzoil sued, claiming that Texaco had committed the tort of intentionally interfering with its contract to buy Getty. As a foundation for its claim, Pennzoil had to show that there had actually been a contract between it and Getty. The facts relevant to this question were quite ambiguous, and the question was a close one. Although the way Texaco and Getty had behaved was not too unusual in the context of mergers and acquisitions, the jury was not favorably impressed by Getty's and Texaco's apparently cavalier attitude toward commitments. Even though the commitments were somewhat vague, and even though many observers thought that the decision was wrong on legal grounds, Pennzoil won a $10.5 billion judgment against Texaco. (Getty and its principals were not defendants because Texaco had agreed to indemnify these parties against any liability that might arise from Texaco's acquisition. The indemnities also did not look good to the jury; even though such clauses are common in merger transactions, the jury was persuaded that Texaco must have known that it and Getty were doing something wrong or it would not have granted the indemnities.)

## ARE THERE ANY MORAL STANDARDS?

There are those who believe that it is impossible to identify any concrete rules or standards to serve as a general foundation for evaluating the morality of behavior. The existence and content of particular ethical standards is too personal and individualized to formulate generally applicable rules. Moreover, they argue that what is "ethical" depends a great deal on what is viewed as acceptable behavior in a particular culture and that norms vary greatly from one culture to another. They assert that the formal study and practical application of ethics can consist only of defining and improving the *processes* by which moral issues are identified and analyzed.

Others argue that, although there are no overarching moral "rules" that can be applied to all human behavior, the general standard of **utilitarianism** can serve as a guide for moral behavior. Advanced by noted philosophers such as Jeremy Bentham and John Stuart Mill, utilitarianism is an ethical theory that is committed solely to the purpose of promoting "the greatest good for the greatest number." Utilitarianism essentially permits all conduct that will serve the objective of maximizing the social utility (i.e., the social "benefit" or "good"). As an abstract theory, utilitarianism makes a lot of sense. In actual practice, however, it can be all but impossible to predict, even roughly, which specific actions are likely to provide the greatest benefit to society. Moreover, even deciding how to define "benefit" to society can be an exercise in futility because of the many possible value judgments that may be involved. What one person views as a benefit to society may be quite different from the view of another person. In large part because of these difficulties, other ethicists view utilitarianism as being just one useful component in a rational process of ethical reasoning.

Some well-known philosophers do feel that certain threshhold standards of moral behavior can be identified and applied to real problems across various circumstances and cultures. The German philosopher Immanuel Kant wrote that every person's actions should be judged morally by asking the question: "Can this action be justified by reasons that are uniformly applicable to all other persons?" In other words, he suggested as an overarching standard of moral behavior the rule that people cannot make exceptions of themselves; one's behavior is morally defensible only if everyone else could do the same thing without interfering with the optimal functioning of an organized society. This means, among other things, that we should all treat others as we would wish to be treated, a wisdom embodied in the so-called Golden Rule. Each person should be treated as an end in himself, not as a means to an end.

We think there is merit in all of these positions, and that the best approach to questions about ethical behavior includes elements of each. Process is extremely important. It is essential to employ a rational process for analyzing these kinds of questions. (We will present such a process later in this chapter.) We also think, as did Kant, that there are certain fundamental moral standards that are virtually universal. As we discuss these principles, it will become apparent that some elements of utilitarianism are included; we recognize that costs and benefits of alternative courses of action may have to be taken into account when there are extenuating circumstances or conflicting moral obligations.

## THE "MORAL MINIMUM"

As we observe human interactions and learn more about human nature, examine and think deeply about the effects that our own actions have on others, and perhaps study the writings of those philosophers who have pondered moral questions over the years, we may begin to discover that certain basic values and standards of conduct are truly necessary for the existence of an advanced civilization. What form do these principles take? Lawrence Kohlberg writes that the morally mature individual bases his actions on "principles chosen because of their logical comprehensiveness, their universality, and their consistency." He then adds: "These ethical principles are not concrete like the Ten Commandments but abstract universal principles dealing with justice, society's welfare, the equality of human rights, respect for the dignity of individual human beings, and with the idea that persons are ends in themselves and must be treated as such."[1]

In our search for generally applicable moral standards, let us assume that we are looking only for those guideposts that are relatively comprehensive, universal, and consistent. We can also assume that the foundation for this search is a view of each human being as unique and as deserving to be treated as we ourselves would wish to be treated. Important questions remain, however: Exactly where do we find these standards? If they can be found, can they ever be expressed with enough certainty to provide meaningful guidance for our conduct?

The answer to the first question is that, in order to satisfy the requirements of comprehensiveness, universality, and consistency, we must rely on the rational human thought process as our source. Any other source is likely to produce results that are too variable across cultures, beliefs, circumstances, and even across time.

One approach to the second question is to determine whether there are any standards of behavior that do not need to be defended by a rational person. In other words, from the perspective of a rational mind, are there any general categories of behavior that stand on their own moral foundation, without any need for justification? If so, they could be identified as the **moral minimum**—a set of general standards that constitute the ethical minimum necessary for the functioning of civilization. Stated somewhat differently, violation of these standards is *prima facie* (on its face) wrong. Compliance with such standards requires no defense or justification. To the contrary, a rational person would expect a defense or justification for a *failure to comply* with them. The reason for expecting such a justification is that failure to comply with these standards tends to *destroy the social and economic relationships* that cause a society to function. We suggest the following as components of the moral minimum, fully recognizing that these components sometimes will overlap and that they could be organized and labeled in a variety of ways.

## *Honesty*

A rational person does not have to justify telling the truth. The notion that one should correctly represent the facts is so firmly ingrained in human relations that we expect a justification for not doing so. Without reasonable expectations of honesty, we cannot maintain the personal and business relationships that create order and economic well-being. As we have seen, there are also principles in the *legal* domain that are intended to encourage **honesty,** as with legal prohibitions against fraud. The moral obligation, however, is more encompassing.

## *Loyalty*

In any culture there are certain voluntary relationships in which one party places a higher degree of trust and confidence in the other than one would place in a stranger. These relationships are not forced upon us; we consent to them either explicitly or implicitly. Examples include an agent or employee's relationship with her principal, the corporate manager's relationship with the company's shareholders, a trustee's relationship with the beneficiary, and each partner's relationship with the others. A moral duty of **loyalty** is based on two facts: First, by virtue of the relationship, we have created in the other person a legitimate expectation that we will further his or her interests. Second, the relationship has placed us in a position where we have the ability to cause serious harm if we do not act in that person's interests. For example, these relationships often give one party some degree of control over information or assets that are valuable to the other person.

When we enter such relationships we take on an affirmative obligation to (1) fully disclose to the other person all material information that is relevant to our dealings; (2) keep confidential any information that the other party reasonably expects us to protect; (3) avoid undisclosed conflicts of interest, i.e., unless we obtain the other party's consent, stay out of situations that are likely to put pressure on us to act against the other party's best interests; and (4) generally act in the best interests of the other party, even if such action is not entirely in our own best interests. Relationships based on trust and confidence cannot exist without the observance of such behavioral standards, and these kinds of relationships contribute greatly to economic efficiency and social order. The moral duty of loyalty is one of those ethical obligations that has a very close analog in the legal domain.

---

[1] Lawrence Kohlberg, "Moral Stages and Moralization: The Cognitive-Developmental Approach," in Manuel Velasquez, *Business Ethics: Concepts and Cases* (Englewood Cliffs, N.J.: Prentice-Hall, Inc., 1982), 20–23.

The law identifies certain *fiduciary* relationships, such as agent-principal, in which there are legally enforceable obligations of loyalty. Again, the legal obligation is usually less demanding than the moral one.

## *Keeping Commitments*

Social and commercial relationships among people are quite difficult to maintain without accepting the notion that we should keep the promises we make to each other. For this reason, the rational person is not likely to feel it necessary to defend his actions in **keeping commitments.** Failing to keep them, however, normally requires justification. Sometimes there can be difficult questions about whether a commitment has been made, and if so, about its scope, but once these questions are resolved the rational mind will find little need to justify keeping a promise. Once again, we can find a narrower legal counterpart to this obligation—when a promise is part of a legally enforceable contract there are sanctions for breaking it.

## *Doing No Harm*

The rational person does not have to defend himself when he refrains from *intentional, reckless, or careless conduct that can cause reasonably foreseeable harm to others.* To the contrary, justification is usually expected for such conduct. Our actions have both expected and unexpected effects on others, and these effects can be positive or negative. Negative effects are those that damage some legitimate interest of another person. It is generally recognized that people have legitimate interests in their physical, economic, and emotional well-being, as well as in their property, privacy, and reputation. There obviously is overlap among these interests but, taken together, they include most of the things that are important to people. Sometimes our actions have negative consequences for others that we never could have foreseen. When, however, cautious concern for the welfare of others should lead us to anticipate that certain action or inaction may harm the legitimate interests of others, we should do what we can to avoid harm. Narrower legal counterparts for the obligation of **doing no harm** are found throughout the law of torts.

In the following case, the legal issue is whether the defendant committed the tort of fraud. After reading the case, carefully consider the following questions: (1) Aside from the legal principles involved, are there any basic moral obligations that are possibly relevant? If so, what are they? (2) Is this a situation in which the extent of any relevant moral obligation is basically the same as the legal obligation? If not the same, is the moral obligation broader or narrower than the legal one? (3) If the moral and legal obligations are somewhat different in scope, can you think of any reasons why this is so?

---

**Grendell v. Kiehl**
Supreme Court of Arkansas,
723 S.W.2d 830 (1987)

Don Grendell had served as an insurance agent for Loretta and Ferdinand Kiehl since 1971. The Kiehls also relied on Grendell for financial advice. One investment that Grendell promoted to the Kiehls was an oil and gas drilling venture. Grendell told the Kiehls that the investment was "a good thing" and would "make money" for them. On another occasion he "guaranteed that they would make lots of money," and "were going to get 50 barrels a day." No oil was discovered, and the Kiehls lost their investment. They sued Grendell, claiming that he had committed fraud, and they received a judgment against him for $11,329.60. Grendell appealed.

**Decision:** Judgment reversed. There was no fraud because Grendell's statements were expressions of opinion, not fact. The Kiehls also claimed that the relationship with Grendell was such that he owed them fiduciary obligations. The court said that even if the relationship was of such a nature, it did not make any difference because there was no allegation or evidence that he had knowingly failed to disclose relevant material information, which is the only legal obligation that a fiduciary relationship would have added to the situation. ■

# IS THERE A DUTY TO "DO GOOD"?

The components of the moral minimum relate only to preventing harm that we may cause, or correcting harm that we have actually caused. What about situations in which harm is being caused through no moral fault on our part? Do we also have a fundamental moral obligation to affirmatively "do good" by trying to prevent or correct harm that we had no part in causing?

Many people, of course, help others without even thinking about the moral implications. They give to charities, volunteer their time, and perform other altruistic acts for many complex reasons. They may do so for religious reasons, because they want to help create a better world for their children, because of the attention it brings them, or just because it makes them feel good. The question we are raising here is whether there is a rationally based moral obligation to do such things and, if so, what are its limits. In other words, is there something resembling the moral minimum for doing good, and can it be defined in any useful way?

Many people do seem to feel a strong sense of obligation to help others. Again, the reasons why they feel this way are varied and complex. It is therefore difficult to isolate the phenomenon's purely rational element. If we study the question solely from the perspective of rational analysis, we will find less general agreement than we did in the case of the moral minimum. At least part of the reasoning process that supports the moral minimum, however, can also be used to argue in favor of a moral obligation to do good. Most rational people would not feel it necessary to defend their actions in doing good. Similarly, they usually would not expect others to defend such actions. On the other hand, does the rational mind expect a justification for *not* doing good? The answer, which is not very helpful, is that some rational minds would and some would not.

If one tries to build an argument that there is a rationally based moral obligation to do good, the argument probably should contain the following elements:

**1.** In many cases it can be practically impossible to assign a specific moral responsibility for the existence of needs. A family may be desperate because the breadwinner has lost a job from bad health or an economic recession, and they have no family or friends who can help. A Boy Scout troop may need volunteer adult leadership in order to fulfill its goals of teaching, guiding, and nurturing a group of youths. The existence of such needs is really no one's "fault." Even if we can identify a responsible person or group, it may be totally unrealistic to expect them to take remedial action. The needy family's breadwinner may have lost the job because the company was recklessly or dishonestly managed and went bankrupt. In this case, we can trace moral fault but it is highly unlikely that the blameworthy person or group will correct the harm it has caused. Thus, in an organized society, the rational person should expect there to be unmet needs, and should understand that his efforts to meet these needs will improve the functioning of the society of which he is a member.

**2.** Although we should use government as one vehicle for meeting people's needs, government cannot serve effectively as our *only* social problem solver. For example, even though government programs can do much good in providing food and shelter for the poor, such programs will usually be inadequate by themselves. Resources will always be too scarce. Government agencies sometimes can be too impersonal, and too remote from the problem, to provide assistance as effectively as individuals or private groups. Moreover, government bureaucracy sometimes can make it a less efficient provider of assistance than individuals and private groups.

**3.** Helping others is clearly in harmony with the view that we generally should treat others as we would wish to be treated in similar circumstances.

**4.** In circumstances in which (1) a problem or need is brought to our attention, (2) we are in a good position to help, (3) we have the ability to help, and (4) taking positive action would not require an unreasonable risk or cost, our failure to do something positive is very similar to actually *doing harm by intentional, reckless, or careless conduct.*

If one argues that there is a moral obligation to do good, one must define some limits to the obligation. In item 4, we identified some possible limits which require a bit of further explanation. *First,* we can have no obligation to meet a need that we do not know about. This statement assumes, of course, that we have not consciously tried to avoid knowledge of the situation. If there is such an obligation, it cannot be avoided by intentional ignorance. *Second,* in a given situation we may not be the appropriate persons to take action. There are some cases in which our help is unwanted, or may actually do more harm than good. In addition, there may be some other person, organization or agency that is much better equipped to do the job than we are. This is not an excuse that one should look for, but sometimes good judgment suggests that we are inadequate to be useful. Of course, the fact that we are unable to solve the entire problem does not necessarily mean that we should do nothing at all. One person cannot solve the problem of world hunger, or even hunger in one city, but one person can do *something*. *Third,* any rational argument that there is a moral duty to do good must incorporate the concept of costs and benefits (or "risks and utility"). A rational person would not expect someone to take positive action that would entail far greater cost or risk to the provider than benefit to the recipient. One cannot be expected to impoverish oneself or one's family in order to give to a worthy cause. (Here, of course, a moral obligation to one's family would be violated at the same time.)

Although we have so far focused on personal situations, the preceding discussion serves as a necessary foundation for our later examination of corporate social responsiveness.

## EXCUSING CONDITIONS

There occasionally will be circumstances that may excuse one's violation of a basic moral obligation. The particular conditions surrounding a person's action or inaction may reduce the degree of moral responsibility or even completely remove it. Breaking a promise, for example, is *prima facie* wrong on moral grounds, but it may not always be absolutely wrong. **Excusing conditions** may be present. One must be careful about introducing this concept of excusing conditions into ethical analysis, however, because it so easily can be used improperly as a "cop-out." People are usually quite ready to offer "excuses" for their bad behavior, and they may have to be reminded that "reasons" are not necessarily moral excuses. When we speak of excusing conditions, we assume that they are not the result of carelessness, laziness, or conscious disregard of relevant information.

The kinds of circumstances likely to be viewed by a rational person as excusing conduct that otherwise would be morally blameworthy are those affecting a person's *knowledge* or *freedom of action*. Our status as fully responsible moral beings (or "moral agents") assumes that we act with knowledge of relevant and material information, and that our freedom of action is not substantially impaired by some external force. Suppose, for instance, that Joe promises to deliver 100 laser printers to Sam by December 1. We are not likely to view Joe as morally blameworthy if he fails to deliver on time because, through no fault of Joe's, one of his main suppliers suddenly cuts him off or his own factory has to shut down for several weeks because of a strike by a labor union. His freedom of action has been impaired. Morally he is still expected, of course, to do everything legally within his power to minimize the harm caused to Sam or to come as close as he can to fulfilling the commitment. His moral responsibility is diminished, however, to the extent that his freedom of action is diminished. In a similar fashion, Joe's moral culpability is reduced to the extent that, when he made the promise, he neither knew nor had reason to know of existing facts that would make it impossible to deliver on time.

As is true of many ethical concepts, the idea of excusing conditions has a roughly similar counterpart in the law. In some situations, evidence showing that a person did not have the knowledge or freedom to have acted differently can prevent liability for breach of contract, negligence, or some other *legal* wrong. Moral excuses and legal excuses are not necessarily equivalent, but the general concepts exist in both domains. Thus, the actions or failures of one of Joe's suppliers might excuse Joe from the *moral* obligation to carry out a promise to deliver printers, but in some circumstances the law may hold that Joe had assumed the risk of such an occurrence and is *legally* responsible. In other situations, extenuating circumstances may provide a legal excuse but not a moral one. In still other cases, both kinds of excuses may exist.

## MORAL DILEMMAS

On some occasions fundamental moral obligations may conflict. You know the familiar phrase for such a dilemma: "Caught between a rock and a hard place." Although **moral dilemmas** can arise in a wide variety of situations, *whistleblowing* presents a classic and often agonizing version of such an ethical conflict. The term whistleblowing normally refers to a situation in which an employee objects to or reports to the authorities the illegal or unethical activities of his employer. Because this kind of situation is frequently so rich in ethical questions, we will use the following hypothetical case for two purposes: as an illustration of how moral dilemmas arise and as a basis for our subsequent discussion of moral reasoning.

Suppose that Alexis works in the tax division of a large public accounting firm. One of the firm's major clients is Leviathan Corp. While working on one part of Leviathan's tax return, Alexis discovers that some expense items appear to have been overstated. No single item has been grossly inflated, and the total amount of expense overstatement is significant but not huge. Thus the risk of detection by the Internal Revenue Service probably is relatively small. Also, Alexis cannot tell for sure whether the overstatements are intentional or simply resulted from honest mistakes or incompetence. She speaks with her immediate supervisor about the matter, but the supervisor dismisses the evidence as a "nonproblem." When Alexis presses the issue a little harder, the supervisor says, "Just do your job and don't stick your nose in too far." Should Alexis take up the matter with a higher-level manager, perhaps even with the firm's top management? Suppose that she does so and receives the same kind of response at that level. What then?

Alexis owes a general moral duty of loyalty to her employer, an obligation that requires her to act in the firm's best interests. Moreover, in this case, she owes a duty of loyalty to the client. She also has made commitments, either explicitly or implicitly, to obey her superiors in the firm. Fulfilling these obligations, however, requires actions that are possibly dishonest and that may violate several conflicting moral obligations.

If Alexis refuses to overlook the problem, or if she reports it to the IRS, she stands an excellent chance of losing her job. How likely is it that she will be able to find a comparable job, especially if she cannot get a good reference from her current firm, a possibility that cannot be ignored? Does she have dependents who count on her for support? If so, she probably owes them a moral obligation that could be characterized as one of loyalty, or perhaps doing no harm. Is this duty strong enough to support a decision to keep quiet about something that is possibly dishonest?

Alexis owes a conflicting moral duty of honesty to the government, and to taxpayers who will have to pay more to make up for the underpayments by her firm's clients. It is true that the harm to any other single taxpayer will be extremely small, but the obligation exists nonetheless.

As an accountant, she also has made commitments to other members of her profession to uphold professional standards of honesty and competence. The failures of one member of a professional or trade group taint the reputation of the entire group and thus cause harm to every other member. To overlook the expense overstatements may violate this commitment and, if detected, harm the profession and its members.

Alexis faces a moral dilemma. Is there any way out of it? Of course, there are always ways out, but there may not be a painless way out. In the next section we will examine moral reasoning to see how ethical questions can be analyzed in a rational way. Part of this discussion will focus on moral dilemmas as a part of the overall process of moral reasoning. Clear, rational thinking about moral dilemmas does not necessarily eliminate the conflict or turn a difficult situation into an easy one. On the other hand, fuzzy or irrational thinking can certainly make matters worse. In the next section, we will explore the benefits that structured, rational thinking can bring to ethical problems, including moral dilemmas.

## MORAL REASONING AND DECISION MAKING

Ethical issues frequently are emotionally charged. Although it can be quite difficult to think rationally about emotional issues, it is in such situations that clear, organized thinking is most needed. One of the most important lessons one can learn from a study of ethics is that moral questions are capable of being analyzed rationally. The process of analyzing moral questions is essentially the same as rational problem solving or decision making in other situations.

### *Identifying Issues*

The necessary first step in problem solving is to figure out exactly what the problems are. In other words, one must identify the issues. If one is confronted with legal, financial, or marketing issues, for example, they first should be recognized and spelled out as clearly as possible. The same is true of ethical issues. In the hypothetical involving Alexis, the issue she must cope with immediately is *not* (1) whether it is wrong in general to cheat on one's taxes; (2) whether her superiors are bad people; (3) whether her accounting firm or Leviathan Corp. has developed an organizational structure that is insufficient to establish lines of individual accountability for wrongdoing; or (4) whether she can sue her employer for the tort of wrongful discharge if she is fired for objecting to the expense overstatements or reporting them to the IRS.

Problems have to be defined narrowly enough so that we have the ability both to analyze them adequately *and* exercise some degree of influence over the outcome. The issue that Alexis must confront at the present time is whether her most morally defensible course of action is to keep quiet and go along with her firm's possibly inappropriate behavior or to resist it by "blowing the whistle." Other issues may arise later, but for now this is all she needs to deal with from an ethical perspective.

## *Identifying the Governing Principles*

For every kind of issue there are governing principles or rules that guide or limit our decision. The source of these principles will vary, depending on the nature of the issue. There are legal rules, generally accepted accounting principles, marketing principles, generally accepted courses of medical treatment for particular illnesses, formulas for computing stress in the construction of bridges, and so on. In ethics we have the components of the moral minimum—the foundational moral obligations identified earlier in our discussion.

In some cases the principles will be relatively *specific,* but in others they may be quite *general.* Whether they are specific or general, different principles may be characterized by varying degrees of *certainty* or *acceptance.* In the case of some legal principles, for example, it can be difficult to determine precisely what the rule is. This uncertainty can result from conflicting court decisions, ambiguous statutory language, or other reasons. In addition, some principles are more generally accepted than others, whether the relevant field is law, medicine, accounting, engineering, ethics, or another discipline. These qualifying remarks do not diminish the importance of guiding principles. They represent the collective knowledge gained from experience and rational thought, and should serve as the foundation for rational problem solving.

In ethics, the principles are fairly general. As indicated earlier, however, we think that the *prima facie* duties that constitute the moral minimum are widely accepted across time, culture, and circumstance. Their relative degree of acceptance as societal norms has varied, no doubt, at different times and in different cultures, but in general they have remained intact.

When analyzing ethical issues, it is important to identify the pertinent moral obligations as precisely as possible. What is the *nature* of the obligation? Honesty? Loyalty? Keeping commitments? Doing no harm? After identifying the nature of each moral obligation, we must make sure we understand exactly *who* owes which obligation *to whom.* In Alexis's case we have already done a pretty good job of identifying the obligations that she owes to various parties. If we are doing a complete ethical analysis of the entire situation, we also would find it necessary to identify the moral obligations owed *to* Alexis by her superiors. One can argue persuasively that they are violating their duty of doing no harm by intentionally, recklessly, or negligently engaging in conduct that may cause reasonably foreseeable harm to Alexis. Acting in behalf of the firm, essentially what they have done is ask her to participate in conduct that may be dishonest and possibly even illegal. Even if she does not get into any legal trouble, emotional trauma also can be viewed as "harm" when it is a reasonably foreseeable result of their actions.

## *Collecting, Verifying, and Drawing Inferences from Information*

Issues of any kind always arise in a factual context—they do not exist in a vacuum. In our hypothetical case, the relevant information (i.e., "evidence" or "data") that initially caused Alexis to perceive a problem were the apparent inconsistencies between entries in Leviathan's general ledgers used to prepare its tax return and the figures in supporting documentation. When information raises potential ethical, legal, or other issues, we should first do what we can to verify the accuracy, reliability, and completeness of that information. If the issues are sensitive, we obviously must exercise great care in doing this. Caution and good judgment are essential.

We may find that the true facts are very different than we initially suspected, and that there is no problem at all. Of course, we may find that things are much worse than we thought. Frequently we may conclude after an initial inquiry that our information is incomplete and that we need further evidence to understand the situation. Again, in the subsequent search for additional evidence, caution is the watchword. It is usually impossible to acquire information that is so complete and so clearly accurate and reliable as to resolve all doubt. Decisions always have to be made on the basis of information that is less than perfect. When analyzing important issues and preparing to make important decisions, however, it is essential that our information be as complete and accurate as circumstances will allow.

As with any fact-finding process that serves as a foundation for problem solving, in ethical analysis we infer relevant facts from the evidence. In other words, we infer that certain things have happened. In addition to inferring facts, we use the evidence as a basis for making predictions about likely future events. Thus, from the evidence she has at her disposal, Alexis might infer that her firm condones or possibly even assists in tax cheating by clients, although more information is needed to support this inference. Alexis also may have enough information to predict that any further objection to superiors within the firm is likely to be fruitless, and that she may even be penalized in some way for making a fuss.

## *Applying the Facts to the Principles*

The remainder of the ethical problem-solving, or moral reasoning, process involves further application of the guiding principles to the facts that we have inferred from the evidence. In other words, we must determine how the identified moral obligations should apply to these particular facts. This determination should be relatively straightforward, of course, if there are no excusing conditions or moral dilemmas. Such complicating factors are present in many cases, however, and must be incorporated into the analysis.

In our hypothetical scenario, we already have identified the moral dilemmas created by several conflicting duties. The next step is to weigh and balance these obligations against one another. In doing so, we must keep in mind that this is not algebra. Despite being a rational analytical process, it is highly qualitative and involves a degree of subjectivity. The process of balancing conflicting obligations should incorporate at least the following factors.

**Excusing Conditions:** Are there any excusing conditions that might lessen the strength of one obligation relative to another? Remember that our moral accountability can be diminished or eliminated by genuine lack of knowledge or freedom. In Alexis's case, one can argue that her status as an employee who is acting under orders from her superiors causes her freedom of action to be considerably less than if she were in charge. No doubt this is true; the degree of her moral responsibility surely is not as great as it would be if she had more power over the firm's decisions. Is her freedom of action curtailed so much, however, that she has no moral duty at all? Certainly not—otherwise a person in a subordinate position could be morally answerable for his conduct only if he initiated and controlled the situation. In such a case, of course, either he would be acting outside his authority or else he really would not be acting as a subordinate at all. Completely relieving all subordinates of moral responsibility for their actions within the organization's chain of command has the potential to lower substantially the level of moral behavior within organizations and throughout society. Thus, Alexis should continue to have a moral duty of honesty with respect to her complicity in the firm's possible wrongdoing, although the strength of her obligation may be somewhat less than in other situations where she is not playing a subordinate role.

**Conflict Reduction:** Are there ways to minimize conflicts? As in this case, a *prima facie* moral duty usually is not eliminated by an excusing condition. Most of the time there either is no such condition or else the condition merely curtails the strength of a duty rather than doing away with it entirely. Thus, any moral dilemma that we previously identified still exists. Before getting to the point of having to make an all-or-nothing choice between conflicting duties, however, we should search for creative solutions that may diminish or remove the conflict.

Alexis might consider requesting reassignment within the firm, perhaps to another geographic location, so as to remove her from any direct role in the questionable activity. Reassignment may not be feasible, and even if it is feasible it may damage her future opportunities in the firm. Moreover, if the attitude of her current superiors is found throughout the organization, she may encounter similar problems in her new position. Assuming that she finds a higher level of ethical standards at her new location, Alexis still *knows* about the possible dishonesty at her previous one. If she remains silent about it, is she guilty of complicity in the questionable behavior even though she is no longer a participant? Many people would say yes. If we take the view that the duty of loyalty to her employer continues to exist, Alexis still owes the same basic duty because she has remained in the same organization. One can see that removing ourselves from direct involvement does not always eliminate a moral dilemma, although this course of action may reduce the acuteness of the conflict.

There remain other options for Alexis, which we will not pursue here.

In other situations, creative ideas for minimizing the degree of conflict between obligations will take other forms. For example, in some cases a person caught in a moral dilemma might be able to work out agreements with one or more of the parties to whom duties are owed so that the duties no longer conflict and all can be fulfilled. If we cannot make agreements that enable us to fulfill all moral duties, it may be possible to work out compromises that permit us to comply fully with one and partially with another. Such opportunities will not always exist, but it is important to give careful consideration to the possibilities.

**Prioritizing:** When we cannot eliminate a moral dilemma, we must choose between the obligations that we will attempt to satisfy. The choice should be made only after carefully weighing the strength and importance of the conflicting duties. In other words, we must prioritize the obligations. We already may have gone a long way toward weighing and prioritizing our duties as we considered whether excusing conditions were present and sought creative ways to minimize the conflict. We may have found that excusing conditions reduce the significance of one moral duty with respect to another. Similarly, we may have worked out agreements or discovered alternative courses of action that strengthen or weaken different obligations and, consequently, make our choice easier.

If the relative importance of particular obligations, and thus their proper place on our list of priorities, still remains unclear, we should next attempt to evaluate the *harm* that may result from violating the various moral duties. A careful evaluation of harm will take into account both *degree* and *probability*. Other factors being equal, the relative importance of a moral obligation increases proportionately with increases in (1) the degree of harm that is likely to be caused by violating the obligation and (2) the probability (or likelihood) that the harm actually will occur.

In the case of Alexis, for instance, the harm done to taxpayers by this instance of expense overstatement, or even by all similar actions by her employer's clients, is probably pretty small in relative terms. On the other hand, we should also consider cumulative effects. When one tax cheater is reported and gets caught, other cheaters may change their behavior. Thus the harm to taxpayers caused by her firm's conduct, and the harm that may be prevented by her reporting it, could be a lot greater than one might think. With regard to probability, the harm caused by even a single instance of cheating is certain to occur even if it is very small.

The potential harm that Alexis's silence may cause to her profession apparently has a very low probability of occurrence. This harm will occur only if real tax cheating actually happened, she gets into trouble for going along with it, and the profession receives bad publicity as a result. This harm not only has a low probability of occurring, but if limited to this one event, it will also be relatively minor. Again, however, we should consider whether there may be cumulative harmful effects.

If Alexis reports the expense overstatements to the IRS, there is no doubt that short-term harm will be caused to both her employer and Leviathan, especially if the overstatements are found to have been intentional. They will incur penalties, and perhaps substantial legal fees and court costs. These harms appear to be high in both degree and probability. In addition, the accounting firm and Leviathan may suffer long-term harm in the form of damaged company reputations and the various costs associated with an increased level of future oversight by the IRS. This kind of harm probably is somewhat less certain to occur, but if it does occur it could be even more substantial than the short-term damage. At the same time, we must not overlook the possibility that, if Alexis's firm and Leviathan are reported and get into legal trouble now, this event could lead them to clean up their general level of ethical behavior. Arguably, more ethical behavior in the future will reduce their chances of encountering costly legal problems. This leads us to the question of whether ethical behavior produces economic benefit to the ethical company or person. "Does ethics pay?" is an exceedingly difficult and complicated question. We will discuss it later, although we will not even pretend to answer it.

Finally, we need much more information before evaluating the degree or probability of harm that might be caused to others if Alexis loses her job after "blowing the whistle." How likely is it that she will actually lose her job? If she gets fired, how likely is it that she will be able to recover damages from her former employer in a lawsuit claiming the tort of wrongful discharge? Will she have a difficult time finding comparable employment? Do others depend on her for support?

**Making a Moral Decision:** Ultimately Alexis must make a decision that reflects a choice. Even inaction is a choice. There may be no choice that is totally satisfactory, and there almost certainly will not be one that is completely free of doubt or negative consequences. Whatever course she takes, her choice should be the *conscious* result of a rational process similar to the one we have described.

It is true that quick decisions sometimes have to be made. If so, we may not have the luxury to gather as much information or reflect on our choices as much as we would like. There is almost always *some* time, however, for reflection and rational thinking. When emotionally charged ethical questions arise, we are far more likely to work them out through a rational analytical process if we have already anticipated and carefully thought about general problems of this nature. This is especially true when decisions have to be made under pressure and in relatively short periods of time. If we have not already practiced rational thinking about ethical issues in our actual experiences, we should at least have taken the time to examine our own values and to think about how we would deal with particular moral questions should they arise. Without some preparation, we run a much greater risk of making rash responses under pressure.

It is true that decisions, moral or otherwise, may turn out all right even if not preceded by sound analytical reasoning. Such a result probably represents simple good fortune more than anything else. Conversely, rational thinking does not guarantee optimal results. Although carrying no guarantees, such a process can have the following benefits:

**1.** It increases our chances of having better and more complete information on which to base a decision.

**2.** It lowers the risk of completely overlooking an important issue.

**3.** It improves our chances of making a decision that best balances the various conflicting interests that may be present.

**4.** If we are later called upon to defend our decision, we will be better prepared to do so. Difficult decisions that affect others are often challenged, and a decision resulting from the type of process described here is more defensible. We have our facts straighter, and our reasons for making particular choices can be presented more clearly and forcefully because they have been thought through carefully. In addition, we are able to demonstrate a good faith effort to do the right thing. Evidence of good faith is no small matter, and often can make the difference when close judgment calls are at issue.

## ARE CORPORATIONS MORAL AGENTS?

There is nearly unanimous agreement that individuals are morally responsible for their actions within business organizations. Managers and employees in corporations, like other individuals in other settings, have moral obligations. These obligations can never be erased by joining anything, be it a club, fraternity, political party, or business organization. We do not, or at least should not, leave our values at the door when we enter the workplace.

There is less consensus, however, about whether a corporation itself can owe moral obligations independent of the individuals within the organization. A corporation is recognized as a **legal entity** that is capable of owning property, making contracts, being a party to legal proceedings, and so on. It can act, however, only through human beings. Thus, is a corporation a **moral agent** in addition to being a legal entity?

### *Does It Make Any Difference?*

Before examining this question, it is legitimate to ask, "So what?" Does it make any difference? It is no doubt true that in many cases, we can resolve relevant moral questions in business by focusing only on the moral duties of particular individuals within the company. There are situations, however, in which it is impossible to trace decisions or actions to any given individual. So the question about corporate moral status is not a purely abstract one. Even if we recognize the question as being a real one, does the answer to it have any impact? Suppose that we conclude that corporations themselves do have moral responsibilities. If a particular corporation's actions do not violate the *law,* however, are there any meaningful consequences of a conclusion that it has "acted unethically"?

We think there can be meaningful consequences. The consequences are not nearly as obvious or immediate as they may be when the law is violated, but they are there. The behavior of corporations is a frequent subject of discussion in the media, legislatures, regulatory agencies, classrooms, living rooms, and elsewhere. If there is a general perception in society that corporations are morally accountable for their actions, this perception will have an impact on the public debate over corporate behavior. It can alter the basic structure and direction of the debate, as well as the effect this debate has on people's attitudes about corporations. Feelings that a particular corporation, as an independent moral agent, has acted unethically can affect consumers' buying decisions. Similar feelings about an entire industry, or about corporations in general, can affect the decisions of legislatures and regulatory agencies as to the need for regulation. On the other hand, a company, industry, or the business community in general is much more likely to receive the benefit of the doubt in many different ways when there are no generally negative perceptions about its ethical standards.

## *The View That Corporations Are Not Moral Agents*

The most widely advanced view that corporations cannot have moral obligations is that of philosopher John Ladd, who regards corporations as purely formal organizations analogous to programmable robots or machines.[2] Machines have neither a will nor any freedom of action. Similarly, according to Ladd, a corporation is merely an aggregation of legally binding documents such as a state charter and the corporate bylaws, organizational charts, operating procedures, and customs. The human cogs in this machine are role-players. Moreover, they are replaceable and often virtually interchangeable. Rule-governed activities and impersonal operating procedures prevent the application, or even the hint, of moral responsibility. Support for Ladd's view may be found, among other places, in Chief Justice John Marshall's description of a corporation in the famous *Dartmouth College* case:

> A corporation is an artificial being, invisible, intangible, and existing only in contemplation of law. Being the mere creature of law, it possesses only those properties which the charter of creation confers upon it, either expressly, or as incidental to its very existence. These are such as are supposed best calculated to effect the object for which it was created.[3]

The fact that corporations are mere "artificial being(s)," or "creature(s) of law," does seem to support the argument that corporations cannot be moral agents with separate moral obligations. The lifeless pieces of paper that bring the corporation into existence and provide governing rules for its operation do not provide it with autonomy or reason. Therefore, we must look elsewhere for support if we are to argue that corporations are moral agents.

## *The View That Corporations Do Have Moral Responsibilities*

We mentioned that violations of moral obligations frequently cannot be traced to a particular individual within a corporation. As a rule, most actions and inactions of relatively large corporations cannot be tallied as the sum of individual actions—the whole is truly greater than the sum of its parts. As a result, individuals tend to escape moral accountability. This fact, in itself, provides considerable support for the argument that corporations should be viewed as separate moral agents.

Organization theory explains this phenomenon in terms of **group dynamics.** Groups often behave very differently than any member would have behaved, because the dynamics of the group transcend individual reason and autonomy. People sometimes just get "caught up in the spirit of things." Examples range all the way from the lynch mob to a corporate board that makes an ethically questionable decision despite the fact that each of its individual members has high personal moral standards. We find the phenomenon not only in groups of co-equal members, but also in chains of command. For example, managers at the top may set policies and give orders but deny any responsibility for conduct by their subordinates that they did not intend. Similarly, we often find those at the bottom denying responsibility because they did not make the policy and they themselves intended no harm; they were "just carrying out orders." Several complex factors seem to be responsible for the peculiarities of group dynamics in corporations:

---

[2] John Ladd, "Morality and the Ideal of Rationality in Formal Organizations," *Monist* 54 (1970): 488–516.

[3] 4 Wheat. (17 U.S.) 518 (1819).

1. Because the action is motivated by corporate purposes rather than personal reasons, participating individuals may not view their conduct as really their own. If they do not associate the action with themselves as human beings, they are not as likely to apply their own personal moral standards to it.

2. A member of a group may feel that there is "safety in numbers." As the number of individual participants in group action increases, each member's feeling of *anonymity* may also increase. Even if a person does recognize and feel somewhat responsible for the moral consequences of his group's proposed action, he nevertheless may go along with a plan because he doubts that he personally will ever be called upon to defend it.

3. Formal lines of authority and accountability within the organization may be fuzzy, thus increasing the chances that no single person really feels responsible. When people do not *feel* responsible, they are less likely to *act* responsibly.

4. Communication among individuals within the decision-making group may be less than perfect, and thus different individuals or subgroups may be acting on the basis of somewhat different facts and assumptions. One individual or subgroup within the organization may not be completely aware of the total picture, leading to the classic situation of the "right hand not knowing what the left hand is doing."

5. Peer pressure can cause a member of a group to be fearful of speaking up when he sees something wrong with the group's proposed action. Many of us do not want to be perceived as "different" or as a "prude." Peer pressure can produce some really strange results. One example is found in the actions preceding the so-called "Watergate cover-up" that ultimately led to President Nixon's resignation in 1974. Later interviews with the participants revealed that, when a group of Nixon's associates was planning to burglarize and plant microphones in Democratic Party headquarters in Washington, D.C.'s Watergate Hotel in the early 1970s, all of the major participants thought it was a dangerous, stupid thing to do. No one voiced this opinion at the time, however; each person thought that the others viewed the break-in as a good idea and no one wanted to risk being tagged as "not a team player." Similar things can happen in business when advertising campaigns, joint ventures, capital restructurings, mergers, new products, research and development programs, personnel policies, and countless other actions are being planned.

On balance, we believe that the arguments in favor of treating corporations as separate moral agents are stronger than those to the contrary. This conclusion is based upon three facts: (1) corporations can act only through the individuals they employ; (2) group dynamics is a reality, and often produces behavior very different than would have occurred had any individual in the group acted alone; and (3) it is frequently impossible to trace ethical failings to an individual in the organization and, consequently, there is no place to attach moral blame if we cannot attach it to the corporation.

## DOES ETHICS PAY?

Earlier we alluded to the question of whether ethical behavior by a corporation and the people within it actually produces economic benefit for the company. Ethical behavior ought to be our ideal regardless of the economic consequences. A corporation is, however, created for the primary purpose of operating a business profitably and providing a sufficient return on the shareholders' investment to justify their continuation of that investment. So the question about economic consequences of ethical behavior is a legitimate one.

"Does ethics pay?" is a complex question that is exceptionally difficult to answer. Although there can be no doubt that ethics does pay in some ways some of the time, there is no clear-cut answer that covers all situations. In trying to work toward a general answer, we find a few relevant facts that are based on fairly concrete evidence, but we must rely on intuition and even speculation for many others.

Several possible economic benefits of ethical behavior seem likely to occur, although they are of a long-term nature and are incapable of being measured with any precision. The following are some of these possible economic benefits.

1. It seems almost certain that the maintenance of high ethical standards in a company creates an environment in which very costly violations of the law are less likely to occur.

2. As mentioned earlier, such standards also may reduce the likelihood of new government regulations that are costly to comply with. Although this poten-

tial benefit is rather speculative, we do have evidence that *bad* ethical behavior can produce *more* regulation. The Foreign Corrupt Practices Act, for example, was passed by Congress primarily in response to revelations about widespread bribery by American companies in overseas transactions.

3. It also seems reasonable to assume that a high moral tone within a company will have a positive impact on employee morale and productivity. Intuitively, it would seem that, at least for most people, working in a company that observes and requires high ethical standards will be a much more pleasant experience than working in one with low standards. Employees and managers should experience less "cognitive dissonance," a disquieting and disruptive mental state caused by conflicting beliefs. Such a state can be created, for instance, when a manager or employee believes strongly that he should be loyal to the company, obey superiors, and work hard in pursuit of the company's interests, but where prevailing moral attitudes in the company are contrary to his personal moral standards. Since happier employees usually are more productive, the company should be more productive.

4. High ethical standards are likely to generate good will with suppliers and customers. The good reputation that results from ethical behavior does not substitute for quality products, good service, and competitive prices, but it can produce many intangible benefits over time. It makes it possible, for example, to develop long-lasting business relationships based on trust. These kinds of relationships are more economically efficient than those that are based solely on lengthy legal documents, legal threats, and keeping a close watch on the other party.

Balanced against these possible economic benefits is the fact that ethical behavior can sometimes be costly, and when these costs occur they are likely to be direct, immediate, and measurable. For example, it may be quite expensive to install better pollution control equipment than the law requires because of a strong moral commitment to those who drink the water and breathe the air. Competitors may not do the same thing, and their lower costs may enable them to undersell us. Or a company may lose business in the short term because it refuses to pay a bribe or kickback. And, unfortunately, an honest company can lose a business deal to a competitor who misrepresents the facts.

It takes a long-term view to properly assess the economic impact of ethical behavior. Whenever possible, of course, business firms should approach problems with a long-term perspective regardless of whether ethical questions are involved. We believe that the long-term economic benefits of high corporate ethical standards outweigh the more direct short-term economic benefits that low ethical standards sometimes produce. We cannot prove it, however. Studies indicate that very profitable companies *are* more likely to exhibit high standards of ethical behavior than less profitable ones. Although these studies may lend support to the argument that ethics pays, the results could also be interpreted as simply indicating that companies behave more ethically when they can *afford* to do so. Although we can engage in reasonable speculation that ethics pays, we are unable to prove that companies can become more profitable by behaving ethically.

## CORPORATE SOCIAL RESPONSIVENESS

If a person accepts the notion that corporations are moral agents and thus owe separate moral obligations, another question arises. Is it appropriate for a corporation to go beyond the moral minimum and correct problems it did not cause? Should a corporation expend corporate resources "doing good" by meeting societal needs? Such actions are sometimes described by the phrase "corporate social responsibility," but "responsiveness" describes the idea better than "responsibility." Going further, if it is *appropriate* for a corporation to do these kinds of things, is there actually an *obligation* to do them?

We first must recognize that questions about **corporate social responsiveness** do not necessarily arise every time a corporation's management considers spending corporate funds for a socially worthwhile cause such as helping a local elementary school offer enrichment programs for gifted students. Voluntarily responding to community needs often can be justified solely on economic grounds. Such actions can provide excellent promotional opportunities for the company and enhance its reputation and goodwill in a variety of ways. Also, improving the local community may improve the company's workforce and even its property values. Essentially, social responsiveness can provide some of the same economic benefits to a corporation that we mentioned earlier in our discussion of whether complying with the moral minimum can produce such benefits. Any attempt to justify socially responsive behavior on economic grounds must focus on long-term rather than short-term benefits, because the kind of benefit derived from such behavior is necessarily indirect and imprecise. Also, we should not put any less value on a corporation's voluntary contribution to society just because management was motivated by the company's self-interest. Indeed, the motives of the managers may have been very complex and indeterminate.

Our main question here, however, is how to deal with the question on moral grounds. Is socially responsive conduct appropriate regardless of whether it pays, and are there any circumstances in which it is morally required?

## *The Agents of Capital View*

One of the most well-known proponents of the view that corporations do not owe a moral duty to be socially responsive is Milton Friedman, a Nobel laureate in economics and an influential spokesman on the role of corporations in society. To begin with, Friedman does not view corporations as moral agents; only its managers and employees as individuals have moral status. In addition, he contends that there is no obligation to spend corporate resources correcting problems the company did not cause and, going even further, he asserts that it is not even *appropriate* for the company's managers to do so. They are **agents of capital,** that is, agents of the shareholders who own the corporation and provide its capital. As such, their only duty is to earn as much money as possible for the shareholders, within the limits of the law and customary ethical practices.

Unless specially approved by shareholder resolution, decisions concerning the use of corporate resources to do good necessarily are made by individual managers. According to Friedman, it is completely inappropriate for them to do so. Corporate managers are free to devote their own time and money to whatever pursuits they deem morally or socially appropriate, but when they divert corporate resources to such projects they breach their duty of loyalty to shareholders. Friedman finds the social responsiveness movement to be a "fundamentally subversive doctrine" that resembles theft—managers are using "someone else's money." The proper function of government is to attend to matters of the common good and social welfare. Corporate managers are not, by training or otherwise, equipped to do that, and even if they were, it would be intolerable in a democracy for unelected, unaccountable "civil servants" to be charged with the responsibility. While government might be slow and unresponsive in addressing current social problems, the insistence that this gap be filled by corporate action is just an acknowledgment of defeat by proponents of corporate social responsiveness who "have failed to persuade a majority of their fellow citizens to be of like mind and [who] are seeking to attain by undemocratic procedures what they cannot attain by democratic procedures."[4]

Another argument along the same lines is that when a social or religious organization or a government agency attempts to meet the needs of society, it usually does so with resources that were placed under the organization's control because of the merits of its social objectives. For example, grants from the American Cancer Society to researchers seeking a cure for cancer are made from funds that were donated to the Society because of the knowledge that the money would be used to fight the disease. Because of scarce resources, there is a "competition among good causes." Although it is unfortunate that all such needs cannot be fully met, this competition provides a method for roughly measuring the relative importance and value to the public of particular social needs. This prioritizing of needs by the marketplace is a very imperfect process that will always leave worthy needs unsatisfied. It does, however, introduce some necessary utilitarianism into the allocation of resources by reducing the chances that too much will go to causes that benefit too few. On the other hand, resources come into a corporation solely because of its business success, unless shareholders invest with the explicit understanding that certain corporate moneys will be spent on identified good causes. Thus, when managers use corporate funds to do good, the needs they meet have not withstood the test of this "market for donated funds."

## *The Agents of Society View*

There are those who argue that it is both appropriate and morally obligatory for corporations to contribute to the correction of problems they did not cause. They place this duty on the corporation as a moral

---

[4] *New York Times,* Sept. 12, 1962, sect. 6, 122.

agent, as well as on managers whose individual and group decisions energize the company. In a speech to the Harvard Business School in 1969, Henry Ford II stated: "The terms of the contract between industry and society are changing. . . . Now we are being asked to serve a wider range of human values and to accept an obligation to members of the public with whom we have no commercial transactions."[5] His words were foreshadowed by those of his grandfather some two generations earlier. "For a long time people believed that the only purpose of industry is to make a profit. They were wrong. Its purpose is to serve the general welfare."[6]

This notion of a "social contract" forms the foundation for many of the arguments that corporate social responsiveness is morally required. Under this view, a corporation is the result of a contract between those forming the corporation and the society that permits its creation. Thus, the corporation has a contract-like obligation to contribute positively to society, and the corporation's managers are not just agents of the shareholders but are also **agents of society.** One noted proponent of this view, philosopher Thomas Donaldson, hypothesized the existence of a society in which individuals always work and produce alone, and never in corporate form. A society such as this, composed of rational persons, would permit the legal creation of corporations only if the benefits to the public are great enough to justify the privileges granted to corporations and to outweigh the potential drawbacks. The privileges include limited liability—only the corporate entity and its assets are liable for corporate debts, not the individual shareholders or managers. This limited liability can come at a cost to other members of society. One potential drawback is that permitting corporations to exist generally leads to much larger aggregations of resources being under the effective control of a smaller number of people. Large resource accumulations in corporations can bring both economic and political power that few, if any, individuals could ever match. Such power can create risks for society.

Supporters of the agents of society view also would use the same basic line of reasoning that one would use to argue that *individuals* have a moral obligation to do good. These arguments were discussed earlier in the chapter. Similarly, for those wishing to build a rational argument in favor of morally required corporate social responsiveness, the same limits that were applied to the individual's obligation to do good would apply to the corporation's duty to be socially responsive.

## SUMMARY

In this chapter, we have shown, first, that business, like other human endeavors, is to be evaluated by the same moral standards that are applied throughout our society, and that these moral standards depend on the exercise of free will. Next, we explored the law-ethics relationship, including the differences and similarities between legal and moral standards. Our next step was to question whether there are any fundamental moral standards that are generally accepted across circumstances, cultures, and time. Using the rational human thought process as a foundation, we sought to determine whether there are any basic moral obligations that do not need to be defended by a rational person. From this perspective, we identified four obligations that we referred to as the "moral minimum": honesty, loyalty, keeping commitments, and doing no harm. Our discussion then turned to the question of whether there is anything resembling the moral minimum for "doing good," i.e., is there ever a basic moral obligation to take positive steps to correct harms and meet needs that we had no part in causing? In situations in which some basic moral obligation has possibly been violated, are there any "excusing conditions," and if so, what are their limits? In addition to dealing with this question, we also explored how a rational person should approach "moral dilemmas," i.e., situations in which moral obligations come into conflict.

The chapter then devoted considerable attention to the process of rationally analyzing ethical issues. Two major points made at the outset were that even emotionally charged issues like ethical ones can be analyzed in a rational way, and that this form of reasoning is essentially the same as rational problem solving or decision making in other situations. Next, we looked at the question of whether corporations can be held morally accountable, or whether the individuals within the firm are the only ones capable of having moral duties. In this regard, we discussed whether the concept makes any real difference, and concluded that it did. We then examined both sides

---

[5] Thomas Donaldson, *Corporations and Morality* (Englewood Cliffs, N.J.: Prentice-Hall, Inc., 1982), 36.
[6] Ibid.

of the issue, and expressed the view that the phenomenon of group dynamics strongly supports an argument that corporations are indeed "moral agents." We explored the difficult and complex question, "Does ethics pay?" without pretending to answer it in any definite way. Finally, we outlined the issues in the "corporate social responsiveness" debate; in other words, is it either appropriate or obligatory for managers to spend corporate funds "doing good"?

## KEY TERMS

**Ethics**
**Morality**
**Utilitarianism**
**Moral minimum**
**Honesty**
**Loyalty**
**Keeping commitments**
**Doing no harm**
**Excusing conditions**
**Moral dilemma**
**Legal entity**
**Moral agent**
**Group dynamics**
**Corporate social responsiveness**
**Agents of capital**
**Agents of society**

## QUESTIONS AND PROBLEMS

1. Robinson and Walters made an oral agreement for Walters to sell five acres of land to Robinson for $138,000. Walters definitely promised to sell and Robinson definitely promised to buy. Robinson wanted the land very badly so that he could build a home for his family in a place that provided them with a lot of space but was still relatively close to the city. Robinson felt that he had gotten a good price. Robinson made a down payment of $6,900. After they made the agreement Robinson prepared a brief written memorandum stating the basic terms of the deal. He signed it and gave a copy to Walters, but Walters never signed. Robinson paid an architect to draw plans for a new home. About this time, however, Walters called Robinson and said he had changed his mind and no longer wished to sell. Walters wanted to hold on to the land for another couple of years because he thought its value would increase substantially. Robinson was terribly upset, but Walters refused to speak with him any further about the matter. Robinson filed a lawsuit claiming breach of contract. Robinson lost in court, however. In most cases, an agreement for the sale of land is legally enforceable only if it is evidenced by a written document that is signed by the defendant and contains the agreement's essential terms, including an adequate legal description of the land. The memorandum Robinson had prepared was not sufficient for this purpose, because Walters had not signed it and there was not an adequate legal description of the property. Compare the applicable legal rules with any relevant moral standards. Are they different? If so, how are they different, and what are some likely reasons for the difference? Do the reasons make sense?

2. Sally worked as a state government relations specialist for Amalgamated Industries, a large and diversified corporation with operations in many states. She maintained contacts with members of state legislatures and their staffs, as well as with personnel in state regulatory agencies. Her job was to keep top management apprised of proposed legislation and regulations that might affect the company, and to put forth the company's positions on such proposals. The job required her to travel a great deal. Her company reimbursed her for all reasonable business-related travel expenses for which she had receipts. After she had been in the position for a few months, she discovered that many hotels did various things for certain business guests whose jobs would probably bring them to that city on a regular basis. At some hotels, for example, a business guest that the hotel hoped would become a "regular" would be given $20 or $30 cash as a "discount" on the room rate. The written receipt from the hotel, which the guest would submit to his or her employer for reimbursement, did not reflect this discount. What should Sally do if she is offered money in this way? Analyze any ethical questions that are raised by these facts.

3. Frenzoil Corporation is an American oil and gas company engaging in exploration, drilling, production, refining, and wholesale distribution. In addition to doing its own refining and distribution, it also sells crude oil to other refiners, especially smaller ones. One of its tanker ships was carrying a shipment of crude oil to a customer in an African coastal nation. The three-million-gallon shipment was worth $1.5 million and had to be delivered by March 29 in order to fulfill Frenzoil's commitment to its customer. The customer had to have the oil by this date so that it could meet commitments to its own customers for refined petroleum products. When Frenzoil's captain neared the port at his destination on March 28, he sought permission from the harbor master to dock and unload. The harbor master told the captain that many tankers and other ships were in the harbor and a lot of others were nearby awaiting entry. It would be very difficult for Frenzoil's tanker to dock and unload for at least the next two weeks, the harbor master said, "unless other arrangements were made." He said that one of his assistants would come aboard the tanker and talk to the captain about such arrangements. When the assistant arrived at the tanker, the captain found out that the "ar-

rangements" included substantial bribes to the harbor master and several other officials. If these arrangements were made, the tanker could dock and unload ahead of the many other ships that were waiting. Many of these other ships were operated by companies that were much smaller than Frenzoil, and which could not afford to pay a bribe of this size. The captain radioed his boss at Frenzoil, who took the matter to the company's management and attorneys. They concluded that, even though such bribes might violate federal law—the Foreign Corrupt Practices Act—the chances of the violation being detected were quite small. Some of Frenzoil's managers, however, were still bothered by the ethical implications of paying the bribes. Analyze these implications.

4. Tom Sayles worked as a deck hand on a merchant vessel, the *M.S. North Star*. While carrying cargo in the Atlantic Ocean near the north Florida coast, Tom's boss told him to dump the ship's bilge into the sea. The bilge of a ship is the place where foul water containing various wastes collects. At each port there are facilities for pumping out bilges for proper treatment and disposal of the wastes. Tom thought he remembered seeing a U.S. Coast Guard regulation prohibiting bilge-dumping in U.S. territorial waters. Even if the practice does not violate a legal regulation, Tom concluded, it obviously damages the environment. What should Tom do? Analyze the moral issues in this situation.

5. Judith Watson worked for Merritt Flynch & Co., a large New York securities firm with underwriting, brokerage, and investment advising operations throughout the United States and the world. Merritt had branches in many foreign countries. Although serving a stint at one of the foreign offices was not an absolute requirement for advancement, everyone understood that successfully handling a foreign assignment was viewed by top management as very important. Employees who aspired to be on the "fast track" for promotion through the ranks of management almost always had a foreign assignment relatively early in their careers. During her fours years at Merritt, Judith had received two significant promotions. Her work had been universally praised by her superiors, who viewed her as having tremendous potential for advancement into top management.

She was offered a position at the firm's office in Naphtali, an east Asian nation. This was considered a "plum" assignment, successful completion of which could mean a great deal to a person's career. Judith accepted the assignment and began work. She soon found, however, that the business culture in Naphtali was much different than in the United States. Women were generally not well accepted in management positions in that culture. Her immediate superior in the bank's Naphtali office, Dan Moseley, gave Judith much responsibility and always treated her as a co-equal professional, except when they were in the presence of Naphtali clients. In these situations, he referred to her as his "little helper," or his "lovely assistant." Viewed in this way, Merritt's clients felt comfortable dealing with her. On one occasion during discussions with Naphtali clients, Dan treated her as a manager with significant responsibility, and the clients became very uncomfortable, silent, and cold. The deal did not go through, and in all future situations Dan treated and referred to her in ways that made clients comfortable but that infuriated Judith. She discussed the situation with him, and he was very sympathetic and understanding but said he just could not see any other way to handle it. After feeling humiliated a few more times, Judith spoke with Dan's boss, who headed the Naphtali office. He responded in about the same way that Dan had. After continuing in these circumstances for several more months, Judith became irritable and uncooperative, and her performance suffered. The ratings she received on her quarterly performance reviews declined. She really did not know what to do. Analyze the ethical implications of this situation.

# PART II

# PRINCIPLES OF CONTRACT LAW

■ Part II is devoted entirely to the subject of contract law. Here we will be primarily focusing on the basic rules that make up this subject—an approach that is somewhat more traditional than the one taken in Part I. However, to preserve an analytical flavor to our treatment of the subject, the reasons underlying the rules are also given substantial attention.

Chapter 11 presents a brief description of the major classes of contracts recognized by the law. This presentation not only creates an awareness of the diversity of the subject, but also permits an identification of the conceptual principles applicable to all kinds of contracts.

Chapters 12 through 14 are devoted to the heart of contract law—examination of the basic elements that must generally be present in order for an agreement to rise to the level of an enforceable contract. In these chapters, then, we will examine the judicially imposed requirements applicable to the *agreement* (offer and acceptance); *consideration;* and the requirement of a *lawful objective.*

The next chapters deal with somewhat tangential matters, but ones of great significance in those situations where they apply. Thus Chapter 15 explores the circumstances in which the courts may free a person from his or her contractual obligations on the ground of minority, or upon proof of fraud, duress, or mistake of fact. Chapter 16 examines those kinds of contracts which are generally required by law to be in writing, and the rights of third parties are discussed in Chapter 17.

Chapter 18 is largely concerned with two subjects—performance and excuses for nonperformance. The first covers the level of performance that the law requires of a contracting party, while the second sets forth the circumstances in which a party may be legally freed of his or her contractual duties even in the absence of fraud, duress, or mistake of fact.

Chapter 19, the concluding chapter of Part II, discusses two important matters: (1) the rules of contractual interpretation that courts use to determine what the intent of the parties was at the time they entered into the contract, and (2) remedies that are available to parties injured when the promises they have received are not performed.

Throughout Part II, the focus is upon the common law of contracts, which governs, for example, contracts dealing with services and land. However, substantial attention will necessarily be given to sales law, which governs contracts dealing with tangible goods. Even though sales law as codified in the Uniform Commercial Code is treated separately in Chapters 20 through 23 of Part III, its interrelationship with the common law of contracts is so complete that neither subject can be treated on its own. ■

CHAPTER 11

# NATURE AND CLASSIFICATION OF CONTRACTS

## A PERSPECTIVE

In the preceding chapters we took a sweeping look at the aspects of our legal system that are common to all branches of law: the sources of our legal rules, the primary law-making processes, and the manner in which the rules of law are generally implemented by the courts. It is now time to move from the *environmental* approach to more *traditional*, i.e., rule-oriented, areas of the law. The various branches of law that directly control all the legal aspects of business transactions—such as contracts, sales, and corporate dealings—are composed primarily of substantive legal rules.

### *Contract Law—Special Characteristics*

Contract law, which is the subject of Part II, possesses several characteristics that make it the natural starting point for an examination of the other commercial law subjects. First, there is its pervasiveness in the average person's everyday activities. When a person buys a newspaper, leaves a car at a parking lot, or buys a ticket to a football game, a contract of some sort has been entered into. When someone borrows money, or hires someone to paint a house, or insures a car, a contract has again been made. And businesses—whether corner stores or large multinational corporations—must buy or lease office equipment, make agreements with employees, secure heat and light, buy materials from suppliers, and sell their goods and services to customers. All these transactions involve contracts.

Second, the basic principles of contract law are the underpinning of the more specialized business-related subjects, including sales and commercial paper, partnership and corporation law, and other areas.

Third, since the subject of contracts is essentially common-law in nature, the controversies that are presented usually require the courts to examine earlier decisions handed down in cases involving similar fact-patterns. Thus, the doctrine of *stare decisis* is illuminated; and an allied question—whether today's conditions have so changed as to justify a repudiation of earlier decisions—affords an opportunity to analyze more fully the process of judicial reasoning.

## NATURE OF A CONTRACT

A contract is a special sort of agreement—one that the law will enforce in some manner in the event that one party does not perform its promise. As will be seen in the next chapter, some agreements are not enforceable because their terms are too indefinite, or they are entered into in jest, or they involve obligations that are essentially social in nature (such as a date to go to a concert). Even seriously intended, definite business agreements, however, are generally not enforceable unless three additional elements are present—what the courts refer to as consideration, capacity, and legality. These concepts will be explored in later chapters also. Indeed, a comprehensive definition of *contract* cannot be attempted until these four elements have been examined in some detail. But for the limited purpose of this chapter, *a contract is an agreement that a court will enforce.*[1]

## CLASSIFICATION OF CONTRACTS

Contracts have many facets and, consequently, may be categorized in a variety of ways. Different aspects may be important in different contexts. In one case it

---

[1] A more technical definition is the following: "A contract is a promise or set of promises for the breach of which the law gives a remedy, or the performance of which the law in some way recognizes as a duty." *Restatement, Contracts 2d,* §1, The American Law Institute, 1979.

## Bilateral and Unilateral Contracts

Most contracts consist of the exchange of mutual promises, the actual performance of which is to occur at some later time. When a manufacturer enters into a contract in May with a supplier, calling for the supplier to deliver 10,000 steel wheels during September at a specified price, each party has promised the other to perform one or more acts at a subsequent time. Such contracts, consisting of "a promise for a promise," are **bilateral contracts.**

The same terminology applies to offers (proposals) that precede the making of a contract. If the terms of an offer indicate that all the offeror wants at the present time from the offeree is a return promise—rather than the immediate performance of an act—then the proposal can be called a **bilateral offer.**[2] Thus, if a professional football club sends a contract to one of its players in June, offering him $800,000 for the coming season, it is clear that all the club presently wants is the player's promise to render his services at a later time. Such an offer is bilateral; and if the player accepts it by signing and returning the contract, a bilateral contract has been formed.

Some offers, called **unilateral offers,** are phrased in such a way that they can be accepted only by the performance of a particular act. An example of such an offer would be the promise by a TV station to pay $5,000 to the first person who brings to its executive offices any piece of a fallen satellite, such as "Skylab." This offer can only be accepted by the actual physical production of a portion of the designated satellite, at which time a **unilateral contract** is formed; a promise by an offeree that he or she will bring in the item later does not result in the formation of a contract.[3]

True unilateral offers occur rather rarely. And, in cases where there is doubt as to the type of offer made, the courts generally construe them to be bilateral in nature—a view that is usually in keeping with the reasonable expectation of the offeree. One type of unilateral offer, however, *is* made frequently in the real world—the promise by a seller of property to pay a real estate agent a commission when the agent finds a buyer for it. The following case involves such a promise, which comes into being when the seller signs a "listing contract." In the court's decision, attention is focused upon the exact nature of the "act" that such an offer legally requires.

---

[2] The *offeror* is the person making the proposal; the *offeree* is the one to whom it is made.

[3] Under sales law, the distinction between bilateral and unilateral offers is blurred in one limited situation. Section 2-206 of the UCC is responsible for this result and will be discussed in the next chapter, where the primary focus is on offer/acceptance rules.

---

### Judd Realty, Inc. v. Tedesco
Supreme Court of Rhode Island,
400 A.2d 952 (1979)

Frank Tedesco, defendant, wanted to sell a lot that he owned in Johnston, Rhode Island. On November 18, 1973, he listed the property with Judd Realty, plaintiff, giving it the exclusive right to sell the property for a period of six months—i.e., until the following May 18th. The stated price was $25,000. The "listing contract" signed by Tedesco contained this standard provision: "Should a purchaser be found during the life of this agreement by me, or by you . . . I will pay you a commission of 8 percent of the price received."

About a week before the listing contract expired, plaintiff's president told defendant that she had a buyer for his property. A day or two later she had the prospective purchaser sign the customary "purchase and sale agreement," which was an offer by him to buy the property for $25,000. On May 15, two days before the listing contract expired, plaintiff's president took this offer and a $1,000 check drawn by the prospective purchaser to Tedesco. He told her then that he had decided not to sell. When he subsequently continued in his refusal to accept the offer to purchase, plaintiff brought this action to recover its commission.

The plaintiff claimed that it had produced a "purchaser" within the meaning of that term in the listing contract, even though no sale actually took place. Defendant, in support of the opposite view, contended that the term purchaser was an ambiguous one, in which case the court should follow the rule that the contract be construed against the drafter, the plaintiff. The trial court accepted defendant's contention, and thus ruled that the term "purchaser" meant "someone who actually pur-

*(continued)*

chases the property." On this basis it ruled there was no purchaser, and dismissed the complaint. Plaintiff appealed.

The higher court disagreed with the lower court's interpretation, saying that "It is well settled in Rhode Island that a broker has sufficiently performed, and is entitled to compensation under, a brokerage contract when the broker has produced a prospective purchaser who is ready, willing, and able to purchase at the price and terms of the seller." It thus reversed the judgment of the lower court and entered judgment for plaintiff. In that part of its decision summarized below, the higher court emphasized that the contract ultimately formed between plaintiff and defendant was *unilateral* in nature.

---

**Decision:** Prof. Corbin, a leading expert on contract law, contrasts unilateral contracts with bilateral contracts in respect to real estate listing contracts as follows:

*The most commonly recurring case is one in which the owner employs a broker to find a purchaser able and willing to buy, on terms stated in advance by the owner, and in which the owner promises to pay a specified commission for the service. This is an offer by the owner, the "acceptance of which occurs" by the actual rendition of the requested service "by the broker." Here the only contemplated contract between the owner and the broker is a unilateral contract—a promise to pay a commission for services rendered, "i.e., the production of a buyer."*

In regard to such contracts where the service requested by the owner is merely the production of a purchaser able and willing to buy on the stated terms, it is well settled that a unilateral contract is formed between the owner and broker the moment the broker has produced such a purchaser, and also that the broker has a right to his commission even though no sale actually takes place (i.e., even though the owner refuses to accept the purchaser's offer to buy the property). ∎

---

**Comment:** While the *broker* had a cause of action against Tedesco, the *prospective purchaser* in this case does not. As a general rule, a person who lists property for sale has a perfect legal right—insofar as prospective purchasers are concerned—to reject all purchase offers (as long as the rejection is not based on the purchaser's race, color, religion, or national origin).

## Express, Implied, and Quasi-Contracts

1. As has been indicated, the essence of a contract is an agreement (an understanding) that has been arrived at in some fashion. If the intentions of the parties are stated fully and in explicit terms, either orally or in writing, they constitute an **express contract.** The typical real estate lease and construction contract are examples of contracts normally falling within this category.

Express contracts are frequently in writing and of considerable length, but this is not necessarily so. If B orally offers to sell his used car to W for $450 cash, and W answers, "I accept," an express contract has been formed. The communications between B and W, while extremely brief, are themselves sufficient to indicate the obligations of each.

2. An **implied contract** is one in which the promises (intentions) of the parties have to be inferred in large part from the facts of their conduct and from the circumstances in which it took place. It is reasonable to infer, for example, that a person who is getting a haircut in a barbershop actually desires the service and is willing to pay for it. If the patron does not pay voluntarily, a court will have no hesitation in saying that by his conduct the patron had made an implied promise to pay a reasonable price, and will hold him liable on this obligation.

The words and conduct test is a good starting point in distinguishing between the two kinds of agreement, but it is also somewhat of an oversimplification. This is primarily so because some agreements are reached through the use of words and conduct both—especially in the case where one person requests a service from another without specifying a price that he or she is willing to pay for it. For example, if T asks J to keep his lawn mowed during the two months that T will be in Europe, and if J performs the requested service, T's request for the service carries with it in the eyes of the law an implied promise that he will pay J the "reasonable value" of his services. Thus the contract that has been formed upon J's completion of the work is an implied contract, even though T requested the service expressly.

3. A **quasi-contract,** in contrast to the express and implied contracts, exists only in those exceptional circumstances where a court feels compelled to impose an obligation upon one person even though he or she had no intention of making a contract at all. The classic illustration is that of a doctor who renders first aid to an unconscious man and later sends a bill

for his services. It is perfectly obvious that the patient neither expressly nor impliedly promised to pay for the services when they were rendered; yet to permit him to escape liability entirely on the grounds that a contract was not formed would be to let him get something for nothing—a result the law generally abhors. To solve this dilemma, the courts pretend that a contract was formed and impose a quasi-contractual obligation on the person receiving the service.[4]

A quasi-contractual obligation is imposed only in circumstances where the failure to impose such an obligation would result in one party receiving an "unjust enrichment"—a benefit which, on the grounds of fairness alone, he or she ought to pay for. Suppose, for example, that A plants and cultivates crops on land belonging to B, without B's knowledge. In such a case, B, upon learning the facts, is entitled to bring a *quantum meruit* action to recover from A the reasonable value of the benefit (the profit which A made as a result of the use of the land), for otherwise A would be unjustly enriched.[5]

Two limitations on the quasi-contractual principle should be noted.

**1.** It cannot be invoked by one who has conferred a benefit unnecessarily or as a result of negligence or other misconduct. Thus, suppose that the X Company contracts to blacktop Y's driveway at 540 Fox Lane for $900, and the company's employees instead mistakenly blacktop the driveway of Y's neighbor, Z, at 546 Fox Lane, in Z's absence. In such a situation Z has no liability to the X Company, since his retention of the blacktop, while a benefit to him, is not an unjust benefit or an unjust retention under the circumstances.

**2.** Quasi-contracts are contracts in fiction only, since they are not based upon a genuine agreement between the parties. Thus they are not "true" contracts. However, quasi-contractual remedies are often granted in contractual contexts. A combination of contractual rules and quasi-contractual remedies may be employed, for example, to divide losses between the parties where a contract is made and later avoided due to incapacity or fraud (see the discussion of voidable contracts in the next section) or where a contract is made but fails for indefiniteness.

**3.** A plaintiff generally will not be allowed quasi-contractual recovery from one person if he originally looked to another for compensation. Assume that C sells a house to B, and B hires A to plant shrubs around the house. A does so, but before he is paid, B dies and C generously allows B's widow to rescind the contract. If A sues C on quasi-contractual grounds, claiming that C was unjustly enriched by the planting of the shrubs, recovery will probably be denied because A originally looked to B for compensation and may still proceed against B's estate.

In the first of the following two cases, a state supreme court sets forth the general rules as to the nature and legal effects of implied contracts. The second presents a situation where a recovery of money by the plaintiffs under the quasi-contract principle might be proper.

---

[4]The technical name for implied contracts is *contracts implied in fact*, and for quasi-contracts *contracts implied in law*. We are using the less formal labels of "implied" and "quasi" for purposes of simplicity.

[5]*Quantum meruit* means, literally, "as much as is deserved."

---

### Carroll v. Lee
Supreme Court of Arizona,
712 P.2d 923 (1986)

Judy Carroll lived with Paul Lee for 14 years. Ultimately they settled in Ajo, Arizona, where Paul operated an automobile repair shop. Although Judy used the name Lee during this time, the couple did not marry or ever seriously consider marriage. In 1982 they "went their separate ways."

Prior to the relationship little personal property was owned by either party, and neither owned any real property (i.e., land). During the course of the relationship the couple jointly acquired three parcels of land, several antique or restored automobiles, a mobile home, and various other items of personal property. The real property was titled to the couple in one of three ways. Title was held either (1) as joint tenants with the right of survivorship, (2) as husband and wife, or (3) as husband and wife as joint tenants with the right of survivorship. (The mobile home and some of the automobiles were titled to Paul T. Lee and Judy Lee, with other automobiles titled to Paul T. Lee alone.)

*(continued)*

During the time the couple lived together Paul supplied virtually all of the money used to pay their living expenses, while Judy "kept the house" by cleaning, cooking, doing laundry, and working in the yard. After the couple split up Judy filed this partition action claiming a one-half interest in the jointly titled property listed above. (The fact that the properties were titled to both parties did not, in and of itself, convey a one-half interest to Judy. This was because Paul proved that the money used in purchasing them came from the operation of the repair shop, which he owned personally. In such a case, the rule in Arizona—and in most states—is that "where property is paid for by one party and title is taken in the name of that party and a second party who are not husband and wife, it is presumed that the property was taken for the benefit of the one paying for the property." Thus it was necessary for Judy to prove an agreement existed between them that they be co-owners, in order to rebut this presumption.)

The trial court ruled in favor of Judy, finding that an implied contract existed under which it was agreed that Paul and she would be co-owners of the property. (This finding was based on a 1984 case, *Cook v. Cook,* 691 P.2d 664, in which the Supreme Court of Arizona upheld an implied contract between an unmarried couple in circumstances similar to those presented by this case.) Paul appealed, and the court of appeals reversed the judgment. Judy petitioned the Supreme Court of Arizona for review.

**Decision:** The judgment of the court of appeals was reversed, and the trial court's judgment in favor of Judy was reinstated.

The court of appeals erred in ruling that *Cook v. Cook* was inapplicable to this case. (That ruling was based on the fact that in *Cook* both parties were earning income, while in this case Paul was the sole income producer.)

Arizona recognizes implied contracts, and there is no difference in legal effect between an express contract and an implied contract. An implied contract is one not created or evidenced by explicit agreement, but inferred by the law as a matter of reason and justice from the acts and conduct of the parties and circumstances surrounding their transaction. Furthermore, monetary consideration on the part of both parties is not required.

Judy clearly proved that the property was acquired through joint common effort and for a common purpose. This fact coupled with additional facts and circumstances established at the trial—especially Paul's testimony that he "supposed" they intended to be co-owners—sufficiently showed that the parties had an *implied joint enterprise agreement* that the two should be co-owners of the property. ∎

---

**Comment:** This case has been edited to emphasize the implied contract question. An additional question of equal importance was also presented: whether a finding that an implied contract existed even though the plaintiff's services were entirely of a "homemaking" nature, was contrary to public policy, on the ground that enforcement of such a contract might discourage marriage. The court of appeals, by refusing to apply the *Cook* rule, felt that the enforcement of such a contract would have that effect. The higher court, in a part of its decision omitted here, set forth reasons why enforcement of an implied contract in the circumstances presented here was *not* contrary to the public policy of the state.

---

### Deskovick et al. v. Porzio
Superior Court of New Jersey,
187 A.2d 610 (1963)

Plaintiffs in this action are brothers, Michael and Peter Deskovick, Jr. Their father, Peter Deskovick, Sr., was hospitalized in 1958 until his death in 1959. During this period Michael paid the hospital and medical bills as they came in, under the impression that the father was financially unable to do so. (This impression was based on statements made by the senior Deskovick in which he indicated an apparently genuine fear that he would not be able to pay the expenses of the hospitalization.) After the father's death it was discovered that, in fact, his estate was adequate to cover all of the payments made by Michael. The plaintiffs thereupon brought this action against the executor of their father's estate, Porzio, to recover the amounts paid out.

In the trial court, plaintiffs proceeded on the theory that an *implied contract* existed between them and their father in the foregoing fact-pattern. (No mention of quasi-contractual liability was made.) While the evidence was somewhat conflicting as to whether Michael intended to be repaid out of his father's estate at the time he made the payments, the trial judge

*(continued)*

ruled as a matter of law that no such intention was present, and, for that reason, no implied contract had been formed. Accordingly, the court directed a verdict for the defendant. On appeal, plaintiffs contended for the first time that the estate should be liable on the theory of *quasi-contract*. (As a general rule, the parties cannot raise new issues on appeal. It does not appear why this was permitted in this case.)

---

**Decision:** The plaintiffs' contention that a quasi-contract exists, or could exist, in this case is correct. If, upon retrial of the case, the plaintiffs' allegations of fact are found to be true, a judgment should be entered in their favor on the quasi-contract principle. A quasi-contractual obligation is one created by the law for reasons of justice only—especially to prevent one person from being unjustly enriched at the expense of another. In situations where this principle applies (unlike those where the express or implied contract allegedly exists), it is immaterial whether the parties actually intended to enter into a contract.

Here the plaintiffs allegedly paid their father's hospital and medical bills in the honest belief that he was financially unable to do so himself. When it turned out that their father's estate was, in fact, large enough to pay all the bills, the estate would be unjustly enriched if the plaintiffs were not permitted to recover the amount of their payments. Thus the quasi-contract principle can be invoked to permit this recovery, and it is immaterial that the plaintiffs had not intended to be repaid at the time they made the payments. ■

---

## Valid, Voidable, and Void Contracts

A **valid contract** is one in which all of the required elements are present. As a result, it is enforceable against both parties.

In some circumstances, one of the parties to a contract has the legal right to withdraw from it at a later time without liability. Such contracts are referred to as **voidable contracts.** Contracts in which fraud is present fall within this category, because the law permits the one who has been defrauded to set aside the contract. Minors' contracts are another common example of voidable contracts. (Because of their importance, voidable contracts are considered separately in Chapter 15.)

Courts occasionally designate a third type of contract as being *void.* Such contracts are those which, so far as the law is concerned, never existed at all. Contracts are usually void for either of two reasons: (1) one of the parties is wholly incompetent at the time of contracting (such as a person who has been legally declared insane) or (2) the purpose of the contract is totally illegal (such as an agreement calling for the commission of a crime). The designation **void contract** is admittedly self-contradictory—an improper combination of terms. Nevertheless, this label is used by the courts to distinguish such contracts from those which are merely voidable; and in that sense it is a useful term.

Another type of contract is referred to as being "unenforceable." An **unenforceable contract** was valid at the time it was made but was subsequently rendered unenforceable because of the application of some special rule of law. For example, if a debtor goes through bankruptcy proceedings, the debtor's nonexempt assets are distributed among creditors and the debtor ultimately receives a discharge in bankruptcy. Under bankruptcy law, this discharge prevents a creditor who was not paid in full from bringing legal action to recover the balance of the debt; thus the contract that created the indebtedness was rendered unenforceable by virtue of the discharge. Other examples of unenforceable contracts include those sued upon after the statute of limitations has expired, oral contracts that should have been in writing under the statute of frauds (see Chapter 16), and those calling for performance of personal services by a person who died after the agreement was made.

## Negotiated Contracts and Contracts of Adhesion

The terms of many contracts are agreed upon only after a certain amount of bargaining, or "dickering," takes place between the parties. After one party makes an offer to the other, for example, the latter—the offeree—may indicate that he or she will accept only if a specified change is made in the terms of the offer. Or the offeree may respond with a counteroffer, a substantially different proposal from that of the original offer. Contracts that result from these kinds of exchanges are "negotiated contracts."

**Contracts of adhesion,** by contrast, are formed where one party—usually having greatly superior bargaining power than the other—prepares the terms of a proposed contract and presents it to the other party on a *take-it-or-leave-it basis*. Examples of such "standard form" contracts are apartment leases, hospital admission forms, and sales contracts of new car dealers. While the terms of contracts of adhesion usually favor the parties who have prepared them, such contracts are generally enforceable unless the terms are so shockingly one-sided as to be, in the opinion of the courts, "unconscionable" in nature. (Unconscionable contracts are considered further in Chapter 14.)

### Hartland Computer Leasing Corp. v. The Insurance Man, Inc.
Missouri Court of Appeals, 770 S.W.2d 525 (1989)

Appellant Hartland (lessor) leases computers. Respondent The Insurance Man, Inc. (lessee), selected computer equipment sold by vendor Multitask. Hartland bought the equipment and in turn leased it to Insurance Man for $229.16 per month for 36 months. Respondents Saulsberry, the sole shareholder of Insurance Man, and Reese guaranteed that they would make the monthly payments if Insurance Man did not. The printed lease stated that the lessor Hartland made no warranties (promises that the computer equipment would perform properly) and that the lessee should look to the vendor for any needed repairs. Lease payments were due regardless of the condition of the machine. After problems arose with the equipment, respondents stopped making payments. When contacted by Hartland's agent, Hogan, they stated that they did not want the machine and that Hogan should sell it and they would settle the difference.

Hartland sued under the terms of the lease for the payments not made. The trial judge, concluding that the contract was an adhesion contract, disregarded the disclaimers of liability and ruled against Hartland, which appealed.

**Decision:** Reversed. In the modern business world, it would be impractical to rule that *all* adhesion or preprinted form contracts are sinister and automatically unenforceable. Only such provisions of standardized forms which fail to comport with the reasonable expectations of the parties and which are unexpected and unconscionably unfair should be held unenforceable. In this case, Insurance Man's sole shareholder, Saulsberry, being in the insurance business, was presumably familiar with form contracts. The testimony in the case made it clear that only Multitask made any warranties about the machines. Indeed, when problems first arose, Saulsberry looked to Multitask to remedy them. He had the right to pursue breach of warranty claims against Multitask, but chose not to pursue them. Insurance Man was fully protected, but sought relief from the wrong party. The form lease prepared by Hartland was enforceable. ■

## *Formal and Informal Contracts*

Some specialized types of contracts are referred to as **formal contracts.** The term usually is used to refer to sealed contracts—ones that the parties have formalized either by making a physical impression on the paper on which the agreement was written or, in some instances, simply by having the word *seal* or the letters *L.S.* appear at the end of the document.[6]

The great majority of ordinary business contracts are not sealed and are therefore **informal contracts** (or "simple contracts"). Thus any unsealed contract can be referred to as "simple," even though it may be several pages long and contain complex provisions.

## *Executory and Executed Contracts*

Once a contract is formed, it is an **executory contract** until both parties have fully performed their obligations. When performance has taken place, the contract is said to be an **executed contract.** If one party has fully performed his or her part of the bargain but the other party has not, the contract is executed as to the former and executory as to the latter.

## CONTRACT LAW AND SALES LAW— A SPECIAL RELATIONSHIP

The subjects of general contract law and sales law deserve separate treatment for at least two reasons:

**1.** Sales law is applicable only to those contracts calling for the sale of tangible articles of personal

[6] The letters stand for *Locus Sigilli,* meaning "the place for the seal."

property—goods such as automobiles, machine tools, grain, and items of clothing. Contract law, on the other hand, is applicable to virtually all other kinds of agreements—including leases, employment contracts, and real estate sales contracts.

2. Contract law is primarily composed of common-law rules, while sales law is a statutory subject, contained in Article 2 of the Uniform Commercial Code (see discussion in Chapter 4).

Therefore, Part II of this book, starting with this chapter and proceeding through Chapter 19, will address primarily contract law, and Chapters 20 through 23 of Part III will address sales law.

However, these two subjects cannot be discussed in isolation from each other. Of all the contracts that are entered into, a substantial number *are* sales contracts. Also, the drafters of the UCC Article 2 provisions on sales drew heavily from the common law of contracts, and common-law concepts continue to supplement the more specific UCC provisions. Furthermore, Article 2 of the UCC has been so successful in clarifying and modernizing sales law that judges deciding common-law cases often draw upon Article 2 principles, applying them by analogy. For all these reasons, the discussion of general contract law will refer frequently to Article 2 sales law. In particular, *major UCC modifications of well-established common-law principles will be discussed* in Part II. For example, this chapter has already noted that Section 2–206 blurs the distinction between bilateral and unilateral offers.

## SUMMARY

Contracts—agreements that courts will enforce—can be classified in several ways, depending upon the basis used. Sometimes the primary focus is upon the nature of the acceptance which the offeror wants; if the offeror merely wants a return promise from the offeree (and if the offeree makes the requested promise), a bilateral contract is formed. On the other hand, if the offer is phrased in such a way that acceptance can only take place by the performance of a particular act, the performance of that act results in the formation of a unilateral contract. (One significance of this classification is that if the offeror clearly requests performance of an act, a promise by the offeree to perform the act later does not result in the formation of a contract.)

A second basis for classification depends upon the extent to which the parties have manifested their agreement. If the intentions (and obligations) of the parties are set forth clearly in the language used, the agreement is an express contract. By contrast, if the intentions of the parties have to be inferred from their conduct, or where the language used shows an agreement, but requires inferences to be made as to the parties' precise duties, the agreement is an implied contract.

A third basis for classification depends upon the extent to which a contract is enforceable. An agreement that is enforceable by both parties is a valid contract. A contract that one of the parties has a legal right to withdraw from is a voidable contract. And a contract which is so defective that it never existed in the law is a void contract. Other classifications are based upon such factors as the extent to which the terms of the contract were mutually bargained for, and the extent to which a contract has been performed.

## KEY TERMS

**Bilateral contract**
**Bilateral offer**
**Unilateral offer**
**Unilateral contract**
**Express contract**
**Implied contract**
**Quasi-contract**
**Valid contract**
**Voidable contract**
**Void contract**
**Unenforceable contract**
**Formal contract**
**Informal contract**
**Executory contract**
**Executed contract**

## QUESTIONS AND PROBLEMS

1. A corporation employed a contractor to build a barn. Later the contractor quit the job, leaving the subcontractor unpaid. A corporation officer then told the subcontractor to finish the job, and promised that the corporation would pay him for his time and materials. Later the subcontractor finished the job, but the corporation refused to pay the amount that the subcontractor demanded. (It was, however, willing to pay a lesser sum.) In the ensuing lawsuit the corporation contended that no contract had ever been entered into here; the subcontractor, on the other hand, ar-

gued that the corporation had made a unilateral offer which he, the subcontractor, had accepted by the act of completing the barn. Do you agree with the corporation that no contract of any kind was entered into here? Why or why not? (*Redd v. Woodford County Swine Breeders, Inc.,* 370 N.E.2d 152, 1977.)

2. The law of Ohio required boards of education to furnish transportation to all children who lived more than four miles from the nearest high school. When one board refused to furnish such transportation to one of its eligible students, the student's father drove him to and from school for the school year. When the father then sued the board to recover his driving expenses, the board contended that no contract of any kind ever existed between it and him, and that it thus had no liability. Do you think an implied contract existed here, under which the board should be liable? If not, could the father recover on the quasi-contract theory? Why or why not? (*Sommers v. Board of Education,* 148 N.E. 682, 1925.)

3. Bio-Zyme (P) sold cattle feed on credit to Preston (D) for a period of 14 months. During this time, D received monthly statements of the amount due. Although sometimes he would be paid up, frequently D was behind in his payments, and P added interest on the unpaid amount to the next month's bill in accordance with a statement on each bill: "Accounts not paid within 30 days will be charged 1% each month." When P finally sued for unpaid amounts, D claimed that he should not have to pay the interest because he had never expressly agreed to pay interest on overdue accounts. Is D correct? Discuss. (*Preston Farm & Ranch Supply v. Bio-Zyme Enterprises,* 625 S.W.2d 295, Tex. 1981.)

4. A county grand jury investigating possible criminal activity in a school for problem children decided that it needed the services of a private investigator. The grand jury was informed that approval of the County Commissioner's Court was needed for such a contract. Upon being asked, the Commissioner's Court authorized the hiring of Stratton at $50/day, not to exceed 20 days. Stratton's services were very helpful, and with the approval of the grand jury foreman, he stayed on the job for 30 days. The Commissioner's Court refused to pay Stratton for the extra 10 days, so he sued in quasi-contract. Will he recover? Discuss. (*Stratton v. County of Liberty,* 582 S.W.2d 252, Tex. Civ. App. 1979.)

5. A schoolteacher owned some land on Lake Michigan. The land was eroding, and the teacher talked to a contractor about having a retaining wall built, but she never told him to go ahead with the job. Nevertheless, the contractor later built the wall without her knowledge. She refused to pay him for the job, whereupon he sued her—on the quasi-contract theory—to recover the reasonable value of the wall. Do you think she should be liable on this theory? What arguments can be made for, and against, recovery by the contractor on this theory? (*Dunnebacke Co. v. Pittman and Gilligan,* 257 N.W.30, 1934.)

6. Decedent Harold Lewis and plaintiff Helen Hall began dating and she eventually moved into his house at his request. They cohabited as "modern unmarrieds without benefit of portfolio" for a year, when Helen decided to move out. Harold begged her to stay and take care of him, promising that if she did so she would be "taken care of." She remained with Harold, taking care of him through his ill health until his death three years later. Several times, Harold asked Helen what she wanted him to leave her; she responded that it was up to him to decide. Perhaps she should have spoken up, for Harold left her nothing in his will. She sued his estate under an implied-in-fact contract theory for $15,840 as compensation for housekeeping and personal services. Should she recover? Discuss. (*Matter of Estate of Lewis,* 423 N.W.2d 600, Mich.App. 1988.)

7. Nye & Nissen Co. (D) bought Olwell's interest in an egg-packing company. Olwell (P) stored an egg-washing machine nearby. Without P's knowledge or permission, D took the egg-washing machine out of storage and used it. When P learned of this three years later, he offered to sell the machine to D for $600; D refused. P then sued in quasi-contract. Will he recover? Discuss. (*Olwell v. Nye & Nissen Co.,* 173 P.2d 652, Wash. 1946.)

8. John Deere Leasing (JDL) leased a tractor to Blubaugh with an option to buy. The lease agreement entitled Blubaugh to exercise an option to purchase at a predetermined price only at the end of the lease period. On the other hand, it gave JDL the right to claim as damages upon default not only the amount due on the lease but also the option-to-purchase price. These provisions were in light-colored fine print on the back of the lease and were nearly illegible because the darker print on the front of the lease showed through to the back. Blubaugh read the front of the lease but not the back, and testified that he assumed this was a typical lease which would not include liability for the purchase price upon default. Will JDL be able to enforce the contract's provisions if Blubaugh defaults? Discuss. (*John Deere Leasing v. Blubaugh,* 636 F.Supp. 1569, D.Kan. 1986.)

# CHAPTER 12

# THE AGREEMENT

The first and foremost element of any contract is an agreement—a reasonably definite understanding between two or more persons. It is for this reason that the liability or obligation resulting from the making of a contract (as distinguished from that imposed by the law of torts or the criminal law) is sometimes described as being "consensual" in nature.

The usual view taken by the law today is that if two or more persons, expressly or by implication, have reached a reasonably clear agreement as to what each party is to do, then that agreement shall be enforceable by the courts (assuming, of course, that the additional elements of consideration and legality are also present).[1] This means that if either party refuses to perform his or her part of the agreement without a lawful excuse, the other party is entitled to recover damages in a breach of contract action. On the other hand, if it is found that a legally sufficient agreement has *not* been formed, neither party has contractual liability to the other.

Because the word *agreement* encompasses a broad spectrum of situations where some kind of understanding has been reached (ranging from the extremely concise to the hopelessly vague), the courts are faced with the problem of deciding just what kinds of agreements are sufficiently definite to warrant judicial relief if they are breached. The universal approach to this problem is to break the agreement down into two parts—the offer and the acceptance. The inquiries then become whether either party made an *offer* to the other, and, if so, whether the offer was followed by an *acceptance*. Before considering the legal definitions of these terms, we will briefly mention the rules used by the courts to ascertain the intentions of the parties—with emphasis upon the applicability of these rules to the offer and acceptance.

## INTENTION OF THE PARTIES

In cases where the parties disagree as to whether their communications constituted an offer and an acceptance, the court will frequently emphasize the principle that the *intention of the parties* is controlling. If the court finds that their intentions were the same (that there was a "meeting of minds," as it is sometimes phrased), then there is a contract.

One caution about this principle, however, should be noted. When the courts view the parties' communications for the purpose of determining whether their intentions were one and the same, it is the parties' *manifested* (or apparent) intentions that control, rather than their actual intentions.[2] For example, if X writes a letter to Y containing a proposal which meets the legal requirements of an offer, and if Y promptly accepts the offer in a return letter, there is a contract—even if X later claims to have had some mental reservations about the proposal, or says that he really did not intend his letter to be an offer. Thus, when it is said that there must be a *meeting of minds* to have a contract, this usually means that there must only be a legal, or apparent, meeting of minds.

There are two compelling reasons for the frequent use of this objective view:

---

[1] Surprisingly, this has not always been the case. Several centuries ago, the English courts would not enforce agreements (even though the intentions of the parties were quite clear) unless the most rigid formalities had been adhered to—which included not only reducing the agreement to writing but affixing the parties' seals to the document. (See Chapter 13 for a discussion of consideration and Chapter 14 for one of legality.)

[2] A person's manifested or apparent intent is frequently referred to by the courts as "objective" intent, while actual or secret intent is called "subjective" intent. Thus the test used by the courts that is described here is referred to as the "objective test."

175

1. It is virtually impossible for a court to determine what a person's actual intent was at a specific moment.

2. It would be unfair to allow someone to indicate a particular intention to another person and then to come into court and claim that he or she did not mean what was apparently meant.

## REQUIREMENTS OF THE OFFER

Inherent in the many definitions of the word **offer** is the idea that it is a proposal made by one person, called the offeror, to another, the offeree, indicating what the offeror will give in return for a specified promise or act on the part of the offeree. That is, the offeror must manifest a willingness to enter into a contractual relationship with the other party. Sometimes the manifestation is referred to as a "conditional statement" of what the offeror will do for the offeree. Used in this manner, the term *statement* is broad enough to include both *words* and *conduct* by which the offeror indicates a willingness to contract. Thus, if a person in a drugstore shows a magazine to the cashier and deposits $2.50 (the stated price) on the counter, it is perfectly clear that he or she has made an *offer to purchase* the item without speaking a word. Similarly, when a company delivers an unordered article of merchandise under circumstances which indicate to the recipient that a charge will be made for the article if it is accepted, the company's act constitutes an *offer to sell* the product at the stated price. Of course, the recipient of such unsolicited merchandise does not incur a duty to pay for it unless he or she actually uses it or otherwise indicates acceptance of the sender's offer.[3]

The courts have never tried to specify the exact language or the particular kinds of conduct that must exist in order for one person to make an offer to another, for any attempt to do so would be quite unrealistic in the "real world." What the courts have done, instead, is to formulate several general requirements that must be met in order for a particular communication (or act) to achieve the legal status of an offer. These requirements are (1) a manifestation of an intent to contract; (2) a reasonably definite indication of what the offeror and the offeree are to do; and (3) a communication of the proposal to the intended offeree.

## *The Intent to Contract*

**Preliminary Negotiations:** Some language is so tentative or exploratory in nature that it should be apparent that an immediate contract is not contemplated. Such communications do not constitute offers; they are designated **preliminary negotiations,** or "dickering." For example, the statement "I'd like to get $4,000 for this car" would normally fall into this category, as would a letter indicating "I will not sell my home for less than $56,000." If the addressee in either of these instances were to reply, "I accept your offer," a contract would not result since no offer was made in either case. Along similar lines, it is usually held that requests for information—called inquiries—do not manifest a genuine intent to contract, and consequently such questions do not constitute offers in most circumstances. Thus, if A writes B, "Would you rent your summer home for the month of June for $900?" and B replies, "Yes, I accept your offer," there is no contract. (The most that can be said in this situation is that B has now made an offer to A, and it will ripen into a contract only if A subsequently accepts it.)

Difficult questions sometimes arise when there are multiple offerees. Suppose that A writes to B: "I hereby offer to sell my farm to you for $120,000." The letter informs B that A is simultaneously making the same offer to several other potential purchasers. B should know that although the language appears to be an offer, this letter is merely preliminary negotiation because A does not intend to be bound to sell the farm to several different persons. On the other hand, if the letter does not disclose that the offer is being made to others, B can make an effective acceptance. (If another offeree, not knowing of the offer to B, also effectively accepts, A faces certain liability in a breach of contract action.)

The decision in the well-known case below helps show how the courts try to draw the lines between preliminary negotiations and offers in several common situations.

---

[3] If the unsolicited goods are sent *by mail,* ordinarily no duty to pay arises even if the recipient uses the goods. Sec. 3009 of Title 39 of the U.S. Code, the Postal Reorganization Act of 1970, provides in part that, except for "merchandise mailed by a charitable organization soliciting contributions," the mailing of any unsolicited merchandise "may be treated as a gift by the recipient, who shall have the right to retain, use, discard, or dispose of it in any manner he sees fit without any obligations whatsoever to the sender."

### Richards v. Flowers et al.
District Court of Appeal, California, 14 Cal. Reptr. 228 (1961)

Mrs. Richards, plaintiff, wrote defendant Flowers on January 15, 1959, as follows: "We would be interested in buying your lot on Gravatt Drive in Oakland, California, if we can deal with you directly and not run through a realtor. If you are interested, please advise us by return mail the cash price you would expect to receive."

On January 19, 1959, Flowers replied: "Thank you for your inquiry regarding my lot on Gravatt Drive. As long as your offer would be in cash I see no reason why we could not deal directly on this matter. . . . Considering what I paid for the lot, and the taxes which I have paid I expect to receive $4,500 for this property. Please let me know what you decide."

On January 25, 1959, Mrs. Richards sent the following telegram to Flowers: "Have agreed to buy your lot on your terms will handle transactions through local title company who will contact you would greatly appreciate your sending us a copy of the contour map you referred to in your letter as we are desirous of building at once. . . ."

On February 5, 1959, Flowers entered into an agreement to sell the property to a third party, Mr. and Mrs. Sutton. Mrs. Richards, after learning of the Sutton transaction, called upon defendant to deliver his deed to her, claiming the above correspondence constituted a contract between him and her. Flowers refused to do so, denying that his letter of January 19 constituted an offer to sell, whereupon Mr. and Mrs. Richards commenced action, asking for specific performance of the alleged contract. (The Suttons intervened in this action to protect their interest by supporting Flowers' contention that a contract was not formed between him and plaintiffs.)

The trial court ruled that defendant's letter of January 19 did constitute an offer to sell, but it further ruled that plaintiff's telegram of January 25 was not a valid acceptance under a particular section of the California Code known as the "statute of frauds" (the provisions of which are not necessary to our consideration of this case). Accordingly the court entered judgment for the defendant. The Richardses appealed.

**Decision:** The judgment for Flowers is correct. The issue is whether Flowers's letter of January 19 constituted a legal offer to sell the property. It did not, for two reasons. First, the letter was simply a response to an inquiry initiated by the Richards. It is thus probable that Flowers considered his letter to be merely a communication that would lead to subsequent negotiations. Second, and more important, is Flowers's statement that he "would expect to receive $4,500 for the property"; this is merely a statement of the lowest price he was willing to consider. Based on prior cases where similar language was used, it is not the same as saying, "I offer you the property for $4,500." The letter was therefore merely a preliminary negotiation. That being the case, the Richards' telegram of January 25 could not constitute acceptance of an offer, for no offer had yet been made. ■

---

**Objective versus Subjective Considerations:** Up to this point, we have seen that the courts lay great stress on the actual language of a particular communication in determining whether it evidences an intent to contract. Another factor the courts have to consider is the background—the surrounding circumstances in which the communication was made. Examination of the background sometimes makes it quite clear that an intent to contract was not present, even though the language taken by itself meets the requirements of an offer, as where a statement is apparently made in jest, excitement, or anger. In *Higgins v. Lessig,* 49 Ill.App. 459 (1893), for example, a man who learned that his $15 harness had been stolen became so angry that he launched into a tirade in which he stated that he would "give $100 to any man who will find out who the thief is." The court held that this was not an enforceable offer, but merely the "extravagant exclamation of an excited man."

*Higgins* is consistent with the "objective theory" of contracts mentioned above, because a reasonable person hearing the owner's statement would have realized that once he calmed down he would not seriously wish to pay $100 for the return of a $15 harness. However, under this view parties are not required to read each others' minds. In *Lucy v. Zehmer,* 84 S.E.2d 516 (Va. 1954), for example, a man who claimed that he was only jesting when he offered to sell his farm to his neighbors was held to the bargain because the buyers reasonably believed that he was serious. Although the parties were drinking, they twice reduced their agreement to writing and its terms were reasonable.

This does not mean, however, that parties' intentions are always gauged totally objectively. Suppose, for example, that A promises to pay B $1,000,000 for his ranch. A stranger overhearing the promise might well believe that it was a serious offer because it outwardly appeared to be such. However, if B knows that A is a practical joker and nearly flat broke then B also knows that the statement is not a serious offer. If B attempted to accept the offer, no contract would result because of B's subjective knowledge. A's *apparently* serious offer does not bind him if B knows or should know that A is jesting.

**Advertisements:** Advertisements are usually considered to be preliminary negotiations, rather than offers to sell. The general rule is that a store advertisement that merely names the company, describes the article to be sold, and gives the price of the article "constitutes nothing more than an invitation to patronize the store." And this is usually true even if the terms "offer" or "special offer" appear in the advertisement.

The historic rationale for this rule is based (1) on the fact that most advertisements are silent on other material matters, such as the available quantity and credit terms, and (2) on the traditional principle that sellers of goods have the right to choose the parties with whom they deal and do not intend to commit themselves to sell to the potentially unlimited numbers of persons who might read advertisements. The rule also applies to catalogs, price quotations, and even articles displayed on a shelf with a price tag.

Thus, when a customer goes to the advertiser's store and tenders the advertised price, a contract is normally *not* formed. Rather, the customer is making an *offer* to purchase, which the store can accept or reject. Exceptions arise when the advertisement is worded so as to limit the number of persons who could reasonably accept the offer. Thus, when the advertisement limits the quantity of goods, *e.g.,* "Three 1990 Mazda Miatas at $20,000 each, on sale Saturday!", most courts hold that at least three buyers can promise to pay the advertised price and thereby create an enforceable contract. Quantity may also be limited by such phrases as "subject to prior sale" or "while they last." A similar exception arises when an advertisement creates a special method of sale (*e.g.,* "1 Black Lapin Stole, Beautiful, Worth $139.50 . . . $1.00, First-Come, First-Served" or "Any person entering our store on Christmas Day wearing a bathing suit can buy an XYZ CD Player for only $220").

An advertised reward for the return of a missing dog would also be an enforceable offer, since realistically only a limited number of people could accept it. Additionally, advertisements promising rewards for information leading to the apprehension of criminals are usually held to constitute offers, even though several people might be in a position to accept; these decisions apparently are based on public policy grounds.

**Consumer Protection:** The general rule on advertising creates the potential for abuse by unscrupulous merchants who might place advertisements, never intending to live up to their terms. Virtually all states have enacted **consumer protection statutes** which generally impose civil and/or criminal liability upon businesspersons who unfairly refuse to sell goods or services in conformity with the terms of their advertisements. For example, statutes in many states list *deceptive trade practices,* among which is the "advertising of goods or services with the intent not to sell them as advertised." Other states have special "bait and switch" advertising statutes which typically impose liability upon advertisers who lure readers into the store by offering fabulous deals on products, but then either have an insufficient quantity for an expected reasonable demand or focus all their sales efforts at convincing the shoppers to buy more expensive items that were not advertised.

**Auctions:** If conducted openly and fairly, auctions are an efficient way of determining a reasonable price in transactions between willing sellers and buyers. The UCC auction provision, Sec. 2-328, is generally consistent with common-law auction rules. In the typical *with reserve* auction, the act of putting a particular item up for auction indicates only a willingness to consider offers to purchase. A bidder's ensuing bid is treated as an offer which may be accepted when the auctioneer (the seller's agent) announces "sold" either verbally or through the fall of the hammer or some other customary means. Because no contract is formed until the hammer falls, the bidders are free to withdraw their bids prior to that event and, more importantly, the seller is free to withdraw the item from sale if no bids are as high as the seller desires.

Auctions are presumed to be with reserve unless they are explicitly represented as being *without reserve*. The act of putting an article up for sale in a without reserve auction is treated as a definite offer. The first bid creates a contract binding on the seller, unless a higher bid is made. The seller can no longer withdraw the item (though, surprisingly, bidders may withdraw their bids until the hammer falls). The highest bidder has a contract for sale that he can enforce.

## Reasonable Definiteness

The requirement that the offer be *reasonably definite* is largely a practical one. The terms of an agreement have to be definite enough that a court can determine whether both parties lived up to their promises, in the event that a question of breach of contract arises. If the offer is too indefinite, the court is unable to do this.

As a general rule, then, a communication must cover *all major matters* affecting the proposed transaction in order to constitute an offer. If one or more of these is missing, the communication is merely a preliminary negotiation. Thus if S makes a written proposal to sell his farm Blackacre to B upon specified terms and conditions, "at a mutually agreeable price," and if B promptly sends an acceptance, there is no contract for the reason that S's proposal was not an offer. In a similar case, a company told an injured employee that it would "take care of him" and offer him "light work" when his doctor certified that he was capable of doing such a job. The company later refused to rehire him, and he sued to recover damages, alleging that this was a breach of contract. In ruling against the employee, the court said that since no specific position was mentioned, and there was no discussion of rates of pay or hours of employment, it had no way of determining the amount of the employee's loss. The statement of the company, in other words, was held to be too indefinite to constitute an offer.[4] Similarly, if X writes Y, "I will sell you my car for $1,000, credit terms to be arranged," and Y replies, "I accept," there is no contract. X's statement does not constitute an offer, since there is no way of knowing what credit terms would be acceptable to her or whether any credit terms will ever be agreed on.

Despite the foregoing, the requirement of "reasonable definiteness" is, as the term itself indicates, relative rather than absolute. Thus it is not necessary that every detail be set forth in a contract, so long as there is agreement on major points. Where there is such agreement, missing terms about routine or mechanical matters may be supplied by the courts to "save" the contract; they may say in regard to such matters that there was *implied agreement.* For example, if X agrees to do certain clean-up work around a construction site for Y for $1,000, neither party can successfully contend that the agreement was too vague simply because no time of performance was specified. In this situation, it is implied that X will have a reasonable time in which to perform.

The case below presents a typical "definiteness" problem in a modern-day setting.

[4] *Laseter v. Pet Dairy Products Company,* 246 F.2d 747 (1957).

---

**Pyeatte v. Pyeatte**
Court of Appeals of Arizona, Division 1,
661 P.2d 196 (1983)

Charles Pyeatte and Margrethe May Pyeatte were married in Tucson, Arizona, in 1972. At the time of the marriage both had received bachelor's degrees. In early 1974 the couple reached an agreement concerning postgraduate education for both of them. The undisputed terms of the agreement were, in Mrs. Pyeatte's words, that she "would put him through three years of law school without his having to work, and when he finished he would put me through my master's degree without my having to work."

Thereafter she supported herself and her husband while he attended law school in Tucson. After his graduation Charles went to work for a law firm in Prescott, Arizona. Because they realized that his salary would not at that time be sufficient to support the marriage and pay for her graduate work simultaneously, she agreed to defer her plans for "a year or two" (during which time she obtained part-time employment as a teacher).

*(continued)*

In April, 1978, Charles told Margrethe he no longer wanted to be married, and in June she filed a petition for dissolution of the marriage. During the dissolution proceedings the trial court ruled that the above agreement constituted a reasonably definite and enforceable contract, and found that she had fully performed her part of the contract. The court also found that her husband had not performed his part of the contract, and that she had been damaged as a result of this failure to perform. Thus the court, in addition to granting a decree of dissolution, entered a judgment of $23,000 against Charles on the breach of contract theory (that amount based upon estimates of what her costs of obtaining a master's degree would be). Charles appealed this judgment.

On appeal, the primary questions were (1) whether the trial court was correct in ruling the agreement to be a valid contract, and (2) if not, whether the award of damages should be, nonetheless, affirmed "as an equitable award of restitution on the basis of unjust enrichment" (on the quasi-contract theory).

**Decision:** The judgment was reversed. The agreement did not constitute a contract because it was apparent that "certain critical provisions" of the agreement were lacking. Most important, the court said, was the fact that the agreement did not specify the *time* when Margrethe would commence her graduate studies, nor did it specify the length of time she would have in which to conclude those studies. Additionally, the agreement did not say anything about the *cost* of her graduate education. In that regard, the court noted that "there can be several thousand dollars' difference in tuition, fees, and other expenses between any two masters' programs, depending upon resident status, public versus private institutions, and other factors." Lastly, the agreement was silent as to the *place* where the graduate work would be undertaken.

After ruling that no express contract existed, the court agreed with the contention that Margrethe was entitled to the reasonable value of the services she rendered in putting Charles through law school, on the *quasi-contract* theory. The court then remanded the case to the trial court for the purpose of determining the amount of recovery to which Margrethe was entitled under this theory, such amount being based upon the "financial contributions" that Margrethe made to Charles's living expenses and "direct educational expenses." ∎

---

**Comment:** In a number of states, the ex-spouse's recovery is determined by statute. For example, in *O'Brien v. O'Brien*, 489 N.E.2d 712 (1985), the New York Court of Appeals held that a professional license held by the defendant spouse (the right to practice medicine, in this instance) constituted "marital property" under the state's Domestic Relations Law, the value of which must be considered by a court in making an equitable distribution of the spouses' property. In such states the ex-spouse's recovery does not depend upon proof of an express or implied contract, or upon quasi-contract principles.

## *Definiteness of the Agreement: Sales Law*

Among the most significant modifications of the common law achieved by the UCC is a general relaxation of the degree of definiteness required in the agreement. Several provisions indicate that the drafters of the UCC wanted to make the formation of binding contracts somewhat easier than under common law. They recognized that businesspersons frequently intend to enter into enforceable agreements in situations where it is impracticable to make those agreements as definite as required by common law.

A prime example of this approach is found in Sec. 2-204(3). This section broadly states that a sales contract is enforceable even if one or more terms are left open, so long as (1) the court feels that the parties *intended to make a binding contract* and (2) the agreement and the surrounding circumstances give the court a *reasonably certain basis for granting an appropriate remedy* (such as money damages). Of course, there is a line beyond which the courts will not go. For instance, the larger the number of undecided terms, the less likely it is that a court will find that the parties intended to be legally bound. For this reason, a seller and buyer who wish to make an agreement with one or more terms left for future determination would do well to state specifically whether they intend to be bound in the meantime.

In addition to Sec. 2-204, a number of other sections of the UCC deal with specific omissions or ambiguities often occurring in sales contracts. We will examine the most important of these "gap-fillers" here.

**Open Price Provisions:** In some circumstances a seller of goods may be primarily concerned with being assured of a market for the goods he or she is producing. Or perhaps a buyer wants a guaranteed supply of certain needed products. In either case, price may be of only secondary importance. Thus buyer and seller might draw up a contract for the sale and purchase of goods at a later date, with the contract providing that the price shall be agreed upon later. Or the contract may say nothing about price at all. (Open price terms may be especially desirable in a market where the going price is subject to daily or weekly fluctuation.)

At common law many courts refused to enforce either type of agreement because of its indefiniteness. Under Sec. 2-305 of the UCC, however, agreements of this nature are now enforceable if the court feels that the parties did intend to be bound by them. (Of course, if the evidence indicates that the agreement was merely tentative and the parties intended to be legally bound only if and when the price was ultimately set, there is no contract until that condition is met. The UCC cannot supply missing contractual intent.)

Whenever a court is called upon to enforce a contract in which the price (for one reason or another) was never actually set, and where it finds that the parties intended to be bound by the open price agreement, the court is faced with the task of providing a price term. Sec. 2-305 establishes a number of principles to guide the court in such a situation.

1. If the parties had expressly left the price *for later agreement* and then failed to agree, the price set by the court should be a "reasonable price at the time for delivery."

2. If the agreement had said *nothing at all about price,* and the price was never settled on, the method of determining it should depend on the circumstances. If the price had failed to be set through no fault of either party, the court should fix a "reasonable price at the time for delivery," as in item 1. But if the failure to set a price was caused by the fault of either party, the party not at fault can either treat the contract as cancelled or fix a "reasonable price" himself or herself. This price is binding and the court will uphold it, so long as it is found to be actually reasonable.

3. If the agreement had provided that the price was to be subsequently fixed *according to a definite standard set or recorded by a third party,* the rules for determining the unresolved price are exactly as they were in item 2. For example, the parties might have agreed that the contract price was to be the market price reported in a certain trade journal on a given date, but no such price was reported in the journal on that date. Or they might have agreed that an impartial third person was to set the price at a future date, but the third party later failed to do so. In either case, the price will be a "reasonable price at the time for delivery." This reasonable price will be set by the court if neither party was at fault; if one party caused the agreed upon method to fail, the other party may set a reasonable price.

4. If the parties had agreed that *one of them was to set the price* at a later time, the deciding party is obligated to set the price in good faith. Although *good faith* is defined differently for merchants and nonmerchants, the most compelling evidence of good or bad faith generally is whether the price fixed was a reasonable market price at that time.[5] If the party responsible for setting the price fails to do so or if he or she fixes a price in bad faith, the other party can either treat the contract as cancelled or set a reasonable price.

**Open Time Provisions:** The absence of a time provision does not cause a sales contract to be unenforceable. Sec. 2-309 states that, where a contract calls for some type of action by the *seller* (such as shipment or delivery) but does not specify the time for such action, a court may infer a "reasonable time" for performance. Of course, a reasonable time in a given case depends on all the circumstances known to the parties. For instance, suppose that the parties did not set a specific time for delivery but that the seller knew the reason for the buyer's purchase and the use to which the buyer intended to put the goods. A reasonable time for delivery would certainly be soon enough for the buyer to put the goods to their intended use.

**Open Delivery Provisions:** A sale of goods contract may also be enforceable even if certain delivery terms are to be decided at a later time. (We have already discussed the absence of a *delivery time.*) Another delivery term that might be absent is a provision for the *place of delivery.* Where the parties have

---

[5] *Good faith* is generally defined in Sec. 1-201(19) of the UCC as "honesty in fact." In the case of a merchant, it is defined in Sec. 2-103(1)(b) as "honesty in fact *and* the observance of reasonable commercial standards of fair dealing in the trade." (Emphasis added.) Generally, the merchant definition will prevail, since open price terms are rare among nonmerchants.

not included this provision in their contract, Sec. 2-308 sets forth the following rules to serve as "gap-fillers."

1. The goods should be delivered to the buyer at the *seller's place of business.*
2. If the seller has no place of business, they should be delivered to the buyer at the *seller's residence.*
3. Where the contract refers to specifically identified goods, and both parties knew when making the contract that the goods were located at *some other place,* that place is where delivery should be made.

The UCC also attempts to account for other omitted details relating to delivery. For example, if the agreement contemplates shipping the goods but does not mention *shipping arrangements,* the seller has the right under Sec. 2-311 to specify these arrangements. (His or her actions are subject only to the limitation that they be in good faith and within limits set by commercial reasonableness). Another example is the situation where the contract fails to indicate whether the goods are to be delivered *all at once, or in several lots.* In such a case Sec. 2-307 obligates the seller to deliver them all at one time. However, there is one exception to this duty. If both parties, when making the contract, know that the circumstances are such that delivery in a single lot is not practicable, then the seller can deliver in several lots. (This would apply, for instance, to a situation where the quantity involved is so large that both parties realize that a single shipment is not feasible).

**Open Payment Provisions:** UCC Sec. 2-310 is a "gap filler" for contracts that are silent as to the time of the buyer's performance—that is, the time of payment. The basic rule is that unless the parties have otherwise agreed, payment is due at the time and place at which the buyer is to receive the goods.[6]

## Communication of the Offer

Returning to the subject of contract law (i.e., the common-law principles applicable to the formation of contracts), it is a primary rule that an offer has no effect until it has legally reached the offeree. This requirement of **communication** is based on the obvious proposition that an offeree cannot agree to a proposal before knowing about it. To illustrate: A city council, via a public advertisement, offers to pay $200 to the person or persons who apprehend an escaped criminal. If X captures the fugitive on his farm, only to learn of the offer later, his act does not constitute an acceptance of the offer and he is not entitled to the reward under the principles of contract law. The relatively few cases that involve this kind of fact-pattern generally follow this view.[7]

The principle takes on broader scope—and is more difficult to apply—in situations where there has been clear-cut communication of some terms of the agreement but questionable communication of others. The so-called fine print cases illustrate the problem. For example, statements printed on the back of parking lot tickets frequently provide that "the company shall not be liable for loss of, or injury to, the automobile, regardless of cause," or words of similar import. The usual view is that such provisions have not been legally communicated to the owner of the car and that the owner is not bound by them unless they were actually brought to his or her attention when the contract was made.

One should not conclude, however, that an *actual* communication of terms is required in all cases. If a court feels that the offeror has made a reasonable effort, under the circumstances, to call the terms of the offer to the offeree's attention, then a legal communication has occurred. A subsequent acceptance of the offer would be binding on the offeree in such a case, even though he or she might not have been aware of all its terms.

The case of *Green's Executors v. Smith,* 131 S.E. 846 (1926) is particularly instructive. In that case Smith sent a folder to each of his garage patrons, which indicated on the cover, in large type, that "new storage rates" would be effective at a future date. Inside the folder various rates were set forth, followed by a "note" which provided, in effect, that commencing with the new rates, patrons would also accept all liability for injuries caused by Smith's drivers while taking the cars to and from patrons' homes. Subsequent litigation raised the question whether patrons were bound by the note even if they had not read it.

---

[6] As we shall see in Chapter 23, the buyer generally has the *right to inspect* the goods (and reject them if they do not conform to the contractual requirements) before making the payment—unless the contract provides otherwise—as in a collect on delivery (COD) contract.

[7] There are exceptions, however, where recovery has been allowed on noncontract grounds (for example, public policy, inherent fairness, and the like).

The court held that they were not. Quoting from an earlier decision, the court said: "When an offer contains various terms, some of which do not appear on the face of the offer, the question whether the acceptor is bound by the terms depends on the circumstances. . . . The question arises when a person accepts a railroad or steamboat ticket, bill of lading, warehouse receipt, or other document containing conditions. *He is bound* by all the conditions whether he reads them or not *if he knows that the document contains conditions.* But he is *not bound* by conditions of which he is ignorant . . . *unless he knows that the writing contains terms or unless he ought to know that it contains terms,* by reason of previous dealings, or by reason of the form, size, or character of the document." (Emphasis supplied by the court.) The court continued: "There was nothing on the face of the folder, nor in its form or character, to indicate that it contained [a liability change]. The paper only purported to contain a schedule of rates for services at plaintiff's garage, and defendant had no reason, on account of her previous dealings with plaintiff or otherwise, to know that plaintiff proposed . . . a new contract of such unusual terms."

The case below presents a communication of the offer problem in a much more modern setting.

## Newman v. Schiff
U.S. 8th Circuit Court of Appeals,
778 F.2d 460 (1985)

Irwin Schiff, defendant, is a self-styled "tax rebel" who has made a career (and substantial profits) out of his tax protest activities. On February 7, 1983, Schiff appeared on CBS News Nightwatch in New York, a program with a viewer participation format. During the program he repeated his long-standing position that "there is nothing in the Internal Revenue Code which I have here, which says anybody is legally required to pay the (federal income) tax." After a number of viewers called in questioning this position, Schiff stated on the air: "If anybody calls this show—I have the Code—and cites any section of this Code that says an individual is required to file a tax return, I will pay them $100,000." A two-minute segment of the program, in which the reward proposal was made, was rebroadcast early the next day on the CBS Morning News.

Newman, plaintiff, is a St. Louis lawyer who saw the rebroadcast (but not the original broadcast). On February 9, a day after viewing the rebroadcast, Newman called the CBS Morning News and cited six sections of the Internal Revenue Code as authority for his position that individuals *are* legally required to pay federal income taxes. The same day he wrote a letter to CBS Morning News citing the same sections, and stated that the letter represented "performance of the consideration requested by Mr. Schiff in exchange for his promise to pay $100,000."

Some additional correspondence ensued between CBS, Schiff, and Newman, which culminated in a letter from Schiff to Newman dated April 20, 1983. In that letter Schiff said, in part, "I did make an offer on the February 7, 1983, news." However, he went on to say that Newman had not properly accepted the offer, and was thus not entitled to the money. Newman then brought this action in federal district court to recover damages for breach of contract.

The court entered judgment for Schiff, ruling (1) that Schiff's offer remained open only until the conclusion of the live broadcast; (2) that the rebroadcast did not renew the offer, and (3) that Newman's acceptance was "untimely" (i.e., too late to result in the formation of a contract). Upon reconsideration of the case at Newman's request, the court ruled, in essence, that the offer *was* renewed when Schiff learned of the rebroadcast "and failed to object to it." The court concluded, however, that Newman's response to the renewed offer still was untimely. (While the court did not give a reason for this conclusion, it was apparently on the theory that Newman's phone call of February 9 was not an acceptance because it was directed to CBS rather than to Schiff, the offeror). Accordingly, the court affirmed its original judgment that no contract was formed; Newman appealed.

**Decision:** The result reached by the trial court—i.e., that no contract was formed—was correct, and its judgment was thus affirmed.

The *reasoning* of the trial court, however, was faulty. The rebroadcast did not constitute a renewal of the original offer but was, rather, only a news report. Accordingly, the only offer that was made was the original broadcast on February 7. And since Newman did not hear the broadcast, no offer was ever made to him. Thus Newman's phone call following the rebroadcast would not constitute an acceptance even if the call had been made directly to Schiff. ∎

# TERMINATION OF THE OFFER

Because of the rule that an offer can be accepted at any time before it is legally terminated, it becomes necessary to see what events will cause the offer to die. The rules in this area of the law are rather mechanical in their operation, and we need touch upon them but briefly.

## Termination by Act of the Parties

Most offers are terminated by the conduct of the parties themselves by (1) revocation, (2) rejection, or (3) lapse of time.

**Revocation:** A **revocation** is a withdrawal of the offer by the offeror. Like the offer itself, it is effective only when it has been communicated to the offeree. The mere mailing of a revocation, in other words, ordinarily does not terminate the offer.[8]

The ordinary offer can be revoked at any time—assuming, of course, that it is communicated to the offeree before an acceptance has occurred. This is generally true even if the offeror had promised to keep the offer open a certain length of time. Thus, if X makes an offer to Y, stating that the offer will remain open thirty days, X can revoke it the very next day if he wishes. While this may seem unfair to Y, the reason for this view lies in the fact that Y has not given "consideration" (something of value) in return for X's promise to keep the offer open.

There are two notable exceptions to the general rule that an offer may be revoked at any time prior to its acceptance.

*The Option:* In an option (or option contract, as it is frequently called) the offeree—either at the request of the offeror or acting on his or her own initiative—does give the offeror some consideration (usually a sum of money) in return for the offeror's promise to keep the offer open. Once the consideration is accepted by the offeror, the offer cannot be revoked during the specified period of time.

Thus, assume that X says to Y: "I offer to sell my farm to you for $100,000, this offer to remain open for 30 days." Y knows the general rule is that X may revoke this offer at any time before acceptance, yet Y truly wishes to buy the farm and needs time to line up his financing. Y may offer to pay X $50 in exchange for X's promise to keep the offer open for 30 days. If X accepts, an option contract is formed and X must keep the offer open. The amount paid for the option need not be a large sum, and a counteroffer will not terminate the offer.

*Sales Law—The Firm Offer:* The general rule and exception noted above apply with equal force to sales transactions. However, the UCC has added a second exception to the general rule by creating another type of irrevocable offer, referred to in Sec. 2-205 as a **firm offer.**

The following requirements must exist for an offer to be irrevocable under this section:

**1.** It must be an offer to buy or sell goods.

**2.** It must be made *by* a merchant—though not necessarily *to* a merchant. That is, only the offeror need be a merchant.

**3.** It must be written and signed by the offeror.

**4.** It must give assurance that it will be held open.

If all these requirements are met, the offer is irrevocable even if the offeree gives no consideration for the assurance that it will remain open.

The period of time during which the offeror cannot revoke the offer is the time stated in the offer so long as it does not exceed three months. If the offer contains an assurance that it will be held open but mentions no time period, it will be irrevocable for a reasonable time, again not exceeding three months. (The three-month limitation applies only where the offeree is relying on Sec. 2-205 to make the offer irrevocable. If he or she gives *consideration* for the offeror's assurance that the offer will remain open, an *option* exists, and the three-month limitation does not apply.)

**Rejection:** A **rejection** occurs when the offeree notifies the offeror that he or she does not intend to accept. Like the offer and the revocation, it takes effect only when it has been communicated (in this case, to the offeror). Thus, if an offeree mails a letter of rejection but changes his or her mind and telephones an acceptance before the letter arrives, there is a contract.

One form of rejection is the **counteroffer**—a proposal made by the offeree to the offeror that differs in any material respect from the terms of the

---

[8] However, one state—California—provides by statute that a revocation is effective when "dispatched" (when mailed, in this case).

original offer. Thus, if the price stated in an offer is $500, and the offeree replies, "I'll pay $400," the original offer is ended forever. A recent case, *Thurmond v. Weiser,* 699 S.W.2d 680 (1985), provides a further illustration. There the owner of a small Texas farm offered to sell it for $260,000. The buyer made a counter-offer of $250,000, which was rejected by the seller. Several negotiations ensued, which ended with the buyer sending a written "acceptance" of the $260,000 offer. The owner refused to convey the land, and in subsequent litigation it was held that there was no contract. The court ruled (1) that the original offer to sell for $260,000 was terminated by the buyer's counteroffer of $250,000, and (2) that because the seller did not renew her offer of $260,000 during the negotiations following the counteroffer, there was no outstanding offer capable of being accepted by the buyer.

A response in which the offeree deletes a term from, or adds a term to, the terms of the offer also constitutes a counteroffer. In the preceding case, for example, if the buyer had replied to the original offer, "Accept offer of $260,000; assume highway commission's proposed plan to relocate road on north side will be abandoned," the offer is again terminated.

**Lapse of Time:** If revocation and rejection were the only recognized means of terminating offers, many offers would remain open forever. To prevent such an unworkable result, a third method of termination is recognized—termination by the *passage of a reasonable length of time.*[9] What is reasonable depends on the circumstances of each case; thus it is virtually impossible to formulate general rules in this area of law.

What we will do instead is list the circumstances or factors that the courts consider in reaching an answer in a given case.

**1.** A circumstance of particular importance is the language used in the offer. Obviously, if an offeror states, "I must hear from you very soon," the time within which the offeree must accept is somewhat shorter than if such language were not used.

**2.** Another important circumstance is the means of communication used by the offeror. Sending the offer by telegram normally imports an urgency that the use of the mails does not.[10]

**3.** Yet another factor of special importance is based upon prevailing market conditions. If the price of a commodity is fluctuating rapidly, for example, a reasonable time might elapse within hours from the time the offer is received.

**4.** A final factor to be taken into consideration is the method by which the parties have done business in the past.

An offer in some circumstances may thus lapse soon after it has been made, while in other circumstances it may remain open weeks or even months. While there are surprisingly few cases in this area of law, *Ward v. Board of Education,* 173 N.E. 634 (1930) is one of them. In that case Ina Ward received an offer of employment for the following school year on June 18, and she mailed her acceptance on July 5. In subsequent litigation, the higher court stated the applicable rule as follows: "It is a primary rule that a party contracting by mail, as she did, when no time limit is made for the acceptance of the contract, shall have a reasonable time, acting with due diligence, within which to accept." Applying that rule, where Ms. Ward had no explanation for her delay other than the fact that she was hoping to hear from another school board, the court held that the offer had lapsed prior to July 5 and there was, therefore, no contract.

## *Termination by Operation of Law*

The rule that a revocation must be communicated to the offeree in order for it to take effect is based on the grounds of both fairness and logic. In ordinary circumstances, it seems reasonable that the offeree ought to be legally able to accept any offer until he or she has been put on notice that the offer has been terminated.

Certain exceptional events, however, will terminate an offer automatically—without notice to the offeree. These events fall into three categories: (1) death or adjudication of insanity of either party, (2) destruction of the subject matter of the contract, and (3) intervening illegality. The termination of an

---

[9] A different rule applies to offers in which the offeree is given a *specific* period, such as five days, in which to accept. In such offers, the lapse of the stated period terminates the offer.

[10] Some courts, for example, adopt the general rule that an offer made via telegram lapses at the close of business hours on the day it is received. (This rule is not applicable, obviously, to offers that by their language expressly or impliedly grant a longer period of time.)

**Figure 12.1 Methods of Terminating an Offer**

```
         Offeror makes offer to offeree.
          /                          \
Acceptance of offer         Termination of offer by:
                            revocation by offeror
                            rejection by offeree
                            lapse of time
                            operation of law
         |                          |
      Contract                  No contract
```

offer by any of these events is said to occur *by operation of law*.

To illustrate: On September 10, B offers a specific TV set to W for $525. On September 13, B dies. If W mails a letter of acceptance on September 14, there is no contract even if W is unaware of B's death. In the same example the result would be identical if, instead of B's death on September 13, the TV set were destroyed that day through no fault of B's. As another example, X offers to loan $1,000 to Y for one year with interest at the rate of 20 percent. Before the offer is accepted, a state statute takes effect which limits the rate of interest on that particular type of loan to 14 percent. The offer is terminated automatically. Figure 12.1 summarizes these methods of termination.

The various events that automatically terminate *unaccepted offers* generally do not terminate *existing contracts* (except those calling for the rendering of personal services, which we will discuss in Chapter 18). Thus, in the first example, if B's offer of September 10 had been accepted by W *before* B's death on September 13, B's estate would remain bound by the obligation to deliver the TV set.[11]

---

[11] Whether the destruction of the TV on September 13 (instead of B's death) would free B's estate from the duty to deliver another set or would free W from the obligation to pay for the set is controlled by the law of sales, especially sections 2-509 and 2-613 of the Uniform Commercial Code. These sections are discussed in the sales chapters in Part IV.

By the same token, the various terminations by operation of law do not generally apply to options (or option contracts). Thus, if B had promised on September 10 to keep his offer open for ten days, and if W had given B a sum of money in return for this promise, B's death on September 13 would *not* terminate the offer.

## PRELIMINARY CONSIDERATIONS OF THE ACCEPTANCE

An offer ripens into a contract if, and only if, it is accepted by the offeree. Remember that a bilateral offer is accepted by the offeree's making the return *promise* that the offeror has requested, while a unilateral offer is accepted only by the actual performance of the requested *act*.

In most situations the offeree's response to the offer is so clearly an acceptance or rejection of it that no misunderstanding between the parties arises. But in a few situations legal difficulties do crop up—as, for example, where the offeree "accepts" the offer but then adds new terms to it or where the offeree's response is vague or indecisive. Another difficulty is the determination of the precise moment at which the acceptance becomes effective—specifically, whether the acceptance has to be actually communicated to the offeror before it becomes legally effective.

In the following discussion, emphasis is given to the acceptance of bilateral offers—those in which the offeror merely wants a return promise on the part of the offeree. Special problems raised by the acceptance of unilateral offers are considered later in the chapter.

## REQUIREMENTS OF THE ACCEPTANCE

An acceptance is an expression on the part of the offeree by which he or she indicates a consent to be bound by the terms of the offer. Under general contract law, the acceptance must be a "mirror image" of the offer. Thus if a purported (intended) acceptance varies from the terms of the offer in any way—sometimes called a conditional acceptance—it ordinarily constitutes a counteroffer rather than an acceptance, as illustrated in Figure 12.2. (While an offeree usually states expressly that he or she is "accepting" the offer, it is not necessary that this particular term be used. Any language showing that the offeree is assenting to the proposal is sufficient.)

**Figure 12.2 Legal Ramifications of the Counteroffer**

```
Offeror A makes offer to offeree B.
            │
            ▼
Offeree B accepts offer with variance from original
terms (counteroffer). A's offer ends and B becomes offeror.
       │                              │
       ▼                              ▼
Acceptance of              Rejection of
counteroffer by A          counteroffer by A
       │                              │
       ▼                              ▼
   Contract                     No contract
```

Regardless of the particular words used by the offeree in his or her response to the offer, the response must meet certain requirements in order to constitute an acceptance. Generally, an acceptance must be (1) unconditional, (2) unequivocal, and (3) legally communicated to the offeror or to the offeror's agent.

## Requirement of an Unconditional Acceptance

We have already seen that when an attempted acceptance changes the terms of the offer, it becomes a *counteroffer* and a rejection rather than an acceptance. The same is true when the attempted acceptance adds new terms or conditions to those of the offer.

Thus, if S writes to B: "I hereby offer to sell my farm to you for $50,000," no acceptance would result if B responded: "I accept, if I can pay $2,000 for each of the next 25 years" or "I accept if you promise to repaint the barn before sale." The general common-law rule is that the acceptance must be a "mirror image" of the offer in order for a contract to result.

The following case presents an intriguing situation in which both parties originally assumed, quite understandably, that an agreement had clearly been reached—until the sharp-eyed bus driver began to compare the language of the school board's "acceptance" with the language of his offer. At that point, the fun began.

---

### Lucier v. Town of Norfolk
Supreme Court of Errors of Connecticut, 122 A. 711 (1923)

Lucier, plaintiff, operated a school bus for the defendant town for the school years of 1915, 1916, 1918, and 1919. In the summer of 1920 plaintiff and defendant began negotiating a contract for the coming year.

After several communications between the parties, plaintiff was asked by the Norfolk Town School Committee to submit a bid covering the transportation of students for the 1920–1921 school year. On August 12, plaintiff submitted his bid, offering to provide transportation at "$175 per week each school week" for that year.

On August 17 the board passed the following resolution: "Voted to award the contract for transporting children to and from Gilbert school and to and from various points in town to Mr. E. A. Lucier for the sum of $35 per day." The next day, a member of the committee, one Stevens, told plaintiff that the board "had voted to award him the contract" and requested plaintiff to have his buses ready.

On the first day of school, September 7, plaintiff transported the students as agreed. On the evening of September 7 the board presented plaintiff with a formal contract for him to sign, the contract embodying the wording of the August 17 resolution. Plaintiff refused to sign the contract, on the ground that it was not in accordance with his bid for compensation at the rate of $175 per week, but at the rate of $35 per day instead. Thereupon defendant refused to employ plaintiff and awarded the transportation contract to a third party.

Plaintiff brought action to recover damages for breach of contract, alleging that a contract was formed on his terms and was breached by defendant. (Specifically, plaintiff's argument was that his bid was accepted on August 18 when Stevens told him that the board "had voted to award him the contract.") Defendant contended that a contract was formed on *its* terms and that plaintiff was guilty of the breach. The trial court ruled that *no contract was formed in this situation* (but did award plaintiff $35 dollars, the reasonable value of his services performed on September 7). Plaintiff appealed.

*(continued)*

**Decision:** The judgment was affirmed. No contract existed. In determining whether an offer and an acceptance took place, the action of one of the school board members (Stevens) was of no legal consequence because he was not in any way authorized by the committee to communicate its actions to Lucier. Therefore, the situation presented was simply a case where Lucier offered to drive a school bus for $175 per week, and the board "accepted" by employing him at $35 per day. These two sums are not identical, because under Lucier's offer he would receive pay for a full week even if it contained a holiday, while under the board's resolution he would not. The board's resolution was a *counter-offer* rather than an acceptance of Lucier's offer; thus no contract was ever formed. ∎

---

**A Note of Caution:** In some situations the offeree's response does constitute an acceptance even though it contains one or more terms that were not set forth in the offer itself. This is true where a reasonable person, standing in the place of the offeree, would justifiably believe that the "new" terms were within the contemplation of, and were agreeable to, the offeror despite the failure to include them in the offer. Following are two illustrations.

**1.** For several years X has been performing maintenance work upon Y Company's assembly line equipment, and has always granted Y Company 90 days in which to pay for the work. If X writes to Y, offering to perform preventive maintenance on various equipment for $1,000, and Y responds, "We accept on condition that we will have 90 days in which to pay," Y's response very likely constitutes an acceptance. Under the circumstances—the manner in which they had been doing business in the past—Y could assume that it was *implied* that X would grant the usual credit. (Custom in the industry could give rise to a similar implication, if clearly proved by Y.)

**2.** F offers to sell certain land to D for $55,000 cash. D replies by telegram, "I accept, assuming you will convey good title." This is an acceptance, even though F did not mention the quality of his title, because it is *implied* (under real property law) that a seller of land guarantees good or marketable title unless he or she indicates a contrary intention.

The purpose of the foregoing is simply to warn the student that it is possible for a term or condition to be literally new without necessarily being new in the legal sense. Thus, while the responses of the offerees in the preceding examples appear at first glance to constitute counteroffers, in the eyes of the law they add nothing new and therefore constitute valid acceptances.

## *New Conditions: Sales Law*[12]

Under the UCC's provisions for the sale of goods contracts, an acceptance may be effective (under limited circumstances) even though it contains terms that conflict with, or add to, the terms of the offer. A major reason for rejection of the mirror-image rule by the drafters of the Code lies in the manner in which many sales contracts are entered into. Generally, such contracts are not fully negotiated. For example, commercial buyers often use their own printed forms in ordering goods from manufacturers or wholesalers, and the latter companies frequently use *their* forms in notifying buyers of their acceptance. Naturally, the terms and conditions of the two forms are rarely identical, because the order forms used by buyers contain buyer-oriented terms, while forms used by sellers to invite, acknowledge, or accept orders contain seller-oriented terms.

In the vast majority of situations, the parties do not pay much attention to the other's forms. The seller provides the goods, the buyer pays for them, and the forms are filed away and forgotten. However, in the occasional situation where problems result and one side or the other wishes to sue for breach of contract, strict adherence to the mirror-image rule would always allow the potential defendant to claim that there was no binding contract because of differences in the forms.

To illustrate: Suppose that on its purchase order form buyer B ordered a quantity of goods at a certain price from seller S, and that seller S sent a purchase

---

[12] Sec. 2-207 of the UCC, the basis of this discussion, is one of the most significant UCC sections relating to the acceptance of offers calling for the sale or purchase of goods. A limited number of other UCC provisions that also have application to the formation of sales contracts will, for ease of understanding, be considered together at the end of the chapter.

acknowledgment form to B indicating that the goods would be shipped. S's form, however, contained a clause stating that interest would be charged on late payments. Later B notified S that he did not want the goods and would not go through with the deal, whereupon S sued B to recover damages for breach of contract. Both parties look at the forms for the first time. In such a case the common law presumes that by responding with the varying term on interest rates, S intended to make a counteroffer, which B has not accepted. Thus no contract was ever formed, with the result that B has no liability to S.

In the modern era where so much commercial activity occurs through "form swapping," the mirror-image rule provides a haven for welshers, such as B in the foregoing example. The drafters of the UCC sought to eliminate such results in situations where the parties truly intended to contract. Section 2-207, which is often called the "Battle of the Forms" provision, addresses this problem. As our analysis will show, Sec. 2-207 reverses the common-law assumption, and presumes instead that an offeree who responds with varying terms intends to contract, unless he clearly indicates that he intends a counteroffer instead. Unfortunately, Sec. 2-207 is one of the most complicated, controversial, and inconsistently applied provisions of the entire Code.

**Text of Sec. 2-207:** This section reads, in material part, as follows (emphasis added):

**1.** A definite and seasonable expression of acceptance or a written confirmation which is sent within a reasonable time *operates as an acceptance* even though it states terms *additional to or different from* those offered or agreed upon unless acceptance is expressly made conditional on assent to the additional or different terms.

**2.** The additional terms are to be construed as proposals for addition to the contract. *Between merchants, such terms become part of the contract unless:*

 **a.** the offer expressly limits acceptance to the terms of the offer;

 **b.** they materially alter it; or

 **c.** notification of objection to them . . . is given within a reasonable time after notice of them is received.

**3.** Conduct by both parties which recognizes the existence of a contract is sufficient to establish a contract for sale although the writings of the parties do not otherwise establish a contract. . . . [T]he terms of the particular contract consist of those terms on which the writings of the parties agree [together with terms provided by UCC "gap-filler" rules].

**Written Confirmation of Informal Agreement:** Section 2-207 provides three routes to contract formation. The first involves *written confirmation of a previous informal agreement.* Often employees of two companies will reach an informal agreement by telephone. They then swap forms which contain terms not discussed. If the parties truly intended to contract, then there is a contract based on the informal understanding. That the terms of the forms do not match will not undo the oral agreement. The terms of the contract consist of those established in the informal agreement, the terms on which the confirmation forms agree, and terms provided by subsection (2) of Sec. 2-207 (which will be discussed in more detail presently).

**Exchange of Forms without Prior Agreement:** The second route to contract formation arises where there is an *exchange of forms without prior agreement* (though perhaps with prior negotiation). An understanding of this method of contract formation requires careful analysis of subsections (1) and (2) of Sec. 2-207.

***Subsection 1—Is There a Contract?*** The primary import of this provision is that a seller's response to a buyer's order for goods which clearly indicates that the seller is accepting *constitutes an acceptance* even if it contains terms additional to or different from those found in the offer. Thus Sec. 2-207 clearly rejects the mirror-image rule.

Assume that Buyer B orders 2,000 A-20 widgets from seller S for $9,000, the price appearing in S's catalog. S sends his acknowledgment form as follows: "Accept your sales order #1379; 2,000 A-20 widgets/$9,000"; but on the back of the form is the new term "seller makes no warranties, express or implied, as to goods sold." *A contract now exists,* despite the new term in S's response. In other words, under subsection 1, S's acknowledgment constitutes an acceptance rather than a counteroffer, resulting in a binding contract. If S did not wish to be bound unless the buyer accepted the warranty exclusion, S should have made the matter a subject of negotiation by clearly conditioning the acceptance upon B's approval of the exclusion. If S does not make this condition clear and if it appears that S's response is intended primarily as an acceptance, a contract results.

In situations where the offeree's form agrees with the offeror's as to key terms, such as price, quantity, and date of delivery, differing only as to nonbargained ancillary terms, courts are likely to hold that the offeree's primary purpose was to form a contract. On the other hand, if the offeror's form orders 100,000 pounds of plastic at $2.00 per pound and the offeree's form confirms the order of 100,000 pounds of plastic at $2.25 per pound, the second document is not an acceptance.

***Subsection 2—Is the New Term Included in the Agreement?*** If subsection 1 analysis leads to the conclusion that a contract has been formed, the remaining question is whether the warranty exclusion has become part of it. If B notices the clause and agrees to it, then it is, of course, included. If B notices the clause and objects to it, then it does *not* become part of the contract. But what about the usual case where B does not notice the clause, or, if he does notice it, simply ignores it? In this situation, a distinction is made between terms that are "different from" those of the offer, and those which are "additional to" those of the offer.

*Different Terms.* If the term in the acceptance is different from (i.e., conflicts with) a term of the offer, the term does not become a part of the contract. Thus, in the above example, if B's order form had contained a clause setting forth certain warranties that were to be made by the seller (e.g., "seller warrants the widgets to be in conformity with U.S. Department of Defense specification #497 dated 6-15-90"), S's warranty exclusion clause would clearly not be part of the contract.

*Additional Terms.* As to any term in the acceptance that is an additional term (i.e., regarding a matter not addressed in the offer), Sec. 2-207(2) provides that, *if both parties are merchants,* the term becomes a part of the contract without any further assent on the part of the offeree, unless (a) the offer stated that acceptance is limited to the terms of the offer itself; or (b) the term "materially alters" the contract; or (c) the offeror objects to the new term within a reasonable time after receiving the offeree's acceptance.[13] Thus, in our example involving the widget purchase, if both B and S were merchants, and if B's order form made no reference to warranties, S's warranty-exclusion clause would automatically become part of the contract, unless barred by a, b, or c.

In this case, most courts would hold that a warranty exclusion clause *does materially alter* an offer and therefore does *not* become part of the contract. The courts decide whether or not there was a material alteration on a case-by-case basis. The thrust of subsection 2(b) is that the offeree is not allowed to slip anything important past the offeror by simply including it in the acceptance form. Rather, the offeree should call the matter to the offeror's attention and make it a subject of negotiation. The case below is typical of those sales controversies in which the courts are called upon to apply the rules of Sec. 2-207.

---

[13] Therefore, in determining whether there is a contract (under subsection 1), it is not necessary that the parties be merchants. But their status as merchants *is* important in determining whether the additional term becomes part of the contract. The reason for this is that the drafters of the UCC felt that additional terms should be included in the contract without express agreement only where the transaction is between two professionals.

---

### St. Charles Cable TV v. Eagle Comtronics, Inc.
U.S. District Court, Southern District of New York,
687 F.Supp. 820 (1988)

St. Charles Cable TV (SCC) and its affiliate Cable Holdings, Inc., construct and operate cable television systems. SCC's representative Behrman had a series of meetings and telephone conversations with representatives of Eagle Comtronics, Inc., which makes addressable descramblers for use in the SCC cable system. On October 12, 1982, Behrman telephoned an order for 4,000 Eagle descramblers. The parties agree that the descramblers were warranted by Eagle for 18 months with an additional 18-month fixed-price replacement option. However, SCC contends that Eagle made various other warranties, which Eagle denies. Eagle sent a sales order acknowledgment to Cable Holdings after Behrman's telephone order. Each acknowledgment stated the price, the number of

*(continued)*

descramblers, the 18-month warranty period, and added conspicuously: "Subject to the Terms and Conditions on Reverse Side." Among the terms and conditions listed on the reverse side were provisions that (1) the buyer's remedy under Eagle's warranty is limited to repair or exchange of defective goods and all other warranties are excluded; (2) that buyer is responsible for freight charges and legal costs and interest arising out of any contract dispute; and (3) that the buyer must provide notice of defects within 15 days of delivery. Neither Cable Holdings nor SCC ever objected to the terms of the acknowledgment form; but they never signed it nor is there any evidence that their officers were aware of these terms.

Eagle began delivering descramblers in November of 1982. Over the next ten months, numerous problems arose with the operation of the descramblers. Eagle made numerous repairs and modifications in response to complaints by SCC. Ultimately, SCC and Cable Holdings sued Eagle for breach of warranty, based on a standard implied warranty of merchantability under the UCC rather than on Eagle's limited "replace or repair" warranty. Eagle counterclaimed for the amount due on the purchase price. The following summarizes the judge's ruling following a court trial.

---

**Decision:** There was a contract, and much of Eagle's form was part of it. The first question addressed by the court, governed by subsection 1 of UCC 2-207, is whether there was a contract. The evidence clearly shows that the parties reached an agreement through oral negotiation and informal correspondence. Given the level of performance, there can be little doubt that both parties intended a binding contract. The second question, governed by subsection 2 of 2-207, concerns the terms of the contract. Because SCC did not object to Eagle's additional terms (contained in the acknowledgment form) either before or after they were sent, they *automatically* become part of a contract between merchants *unless* they *materially alter* the agreed-upon terms. The key to "material alteration" is the *surprise or hardship* that would result if the terms are incorporated into the contract without the express awareness of the other party. Generally, disclaimers of warranties are deemed to be material alterations. Here, however, there was considerable evidence that negotiation between the parties was based on Eagle's limited warranty and that SCC had previously received other Eagle equipment with the limited warranty. Additionally, SCC repeatedly acted in accordance with Eagle's replace or repair warranty in this transaction. It therefore was not a surprise or hardship and thus became part of the contract. Interest on unpaid bills is customary in the industry, as is payment of freight charges by the buyer; therefore, those terms also became part of the contract. However, the provision for legal costs and the 15-day notice requirement were neither customary in the industry nor called to SCC's attention; therefore they did *not* become part of the contract. ∎

---

**Agreement Implied from Conduct:** To examine Sec. 2-207's third route to contract formation, assume that the parties have no prior informal agreement and even their forms do not produce a contract, perhaps because the offer explicitly limits acceptance to the terms of the offer and the purported acceptance just as clearly adds new terms. In such a case the documents do not appear to produce a contract, yet sellers often ship goods and buyers often pay for them in such instances. Here subsection 3 of 2-207 *implies a contract from the conduct* of the parties. The terms of the contract consist of those matters that the two forms do agree upon supplemented by the "gap-filler" provisions of the Code.

For example, in one case a buyer and seller exchanged a series of purchase orders, acknowledgments and letters regarding a purchase of aluminum. At no time did the buyer's forms and the seller's forms agree as to a date of delivery. Buyer committed itself to purchase on September 1 and demanded delivery within seven weeks. Seller immediately acknowledged the order, but set a delivery date of nine weeks, later changed to eleven. Buyer stated that this was not acceptable. Seller told buyer either to accept it or obtain the aluminum elsewhere. Nonetheless, seller delivered the aluminum after eleven weeks and buyer accepted and partially paid for the aluminum. Certain defects were found and litigation resulted. The court held that the parties' correspondence did not create a contract. Seller's response materially altered the buyer's offer. In short, the communications indicated that the parties "dickered" over a key term, but never reached agreement. Nonetheless, the *conduct* of the parties (the seller's shipping the goods and the buyer's partially paying for them) did establish formation of a contract under subsection 3 of 2-207. The court then used the UCC "gap-fillers" to establish a reasonable time of delivery in order to determine whether seller had breached.[14]

[14] *Alliance Wall Corp. v. Ampat Midwest Corp.,* 477 N.E.2d 1206 (Ohio App. 1984).

## Unequivocal Assent

Returning to common-law principles, an acceptance is an expression on the part of the offeree by which he or she indicates a consent to be bound by the terms of the offer. Under this definition, the courts require the "expression" be reasonably definite and unequivocal, and be manifested by some overt word or act. These requirements were developed, as a practical matter, to deal with the many situations where—from the language used by the offeree—his or her real intent is not at all clear; that is, the offeree's response is neither a clear-cut acceptance nor a flat rejection of the offer. At best, such responses cause initial delay and uncertainty between the parties as to whether a contract exists; at worst, litigation may ensue, with interpretation left to the courts.

To illustrate: X, in response to an advertisement placed by Y, sends a bid to Y offering to perform the described landscaping work for $23,000. Y replies by telegram: "Offer satisfies all requirements; will give it my prompt attention." Subsequently Y hires another landscaper to do the job, and, when X sues Y to recover damages for breach of contract, Y contends that his response did not constitute an acceptance of the offer. Applying the general rule to this case, Y's reply is too indefinite and tentative to satisfy the "unequivocal" requirement. Thus Y is correct in his contention that a contract was not formed.[15] On the other hand, each case has to be decided on its own merits, including consideration of the circumstances surrounding the communications. Thus a different result might be reached in the foregoing example if the evidence indicated that X and Y had in the past considered such language to be binding.

**Silence:** As a general rule, there is no duty on the offeree to reply to an offer. Silence on the part of the offeree, therefore, *does not usually constitute an acceptance.* This is true even when the offer states, "If you do not reply within ten days, I shall conclude that you have accepted," or contains language of similar import. The reasons underlying this view are fairly obvious: (1) the view is consistent with the basic idea that any willingness to contract must be manifested in some fashion, and (2) it substantially prevents an offeree from being forced into a contract against his or her will.

In exceptional circumstances, however, the courts may find that the general rule is unfair to the offeror—that under the facts of the particular case, the offeree owed the offeror a *duty to reject* if he or she did not wish to be bound. In such cases, silence on the part of the offeree does constitute an acceptance.

While it is difficult to generalize about these exceptional situations, two types of cases present little controversy.

1. If an *offeree* initially indicates that silence on his or her part can be taken as acceptance, there is no reason why that person should not be bound by the statement. For example: "If you do not hear from me by March 1, you can conclude that we have a contract."

2. If a series of *past dealings* between the parties indicates that the parties consider silence to be an acceptance, it can be assumed by the offeror that this understanding continues until it is expressly changed. For example: a retail jewelry store has, over the years, received periodic shipments of both ordered and unordered jewelry from a large supplier; during this time, the retailer-buyer has always paid for any unordered goods not returned within two weeks. A failure by the retailer to reject a particular shipment, or to give notice of such rejection, within two weeks would very likely operate as an acceptance under the circumstances.

In both the preceding kinds of cases, the courts are likely to say that the offeror "had reason to understand" that silence on the part of the offeree was to be taken as a manifestation of assent, and that the offeree should have been well aware of this fact.

There is another, smaller group of cases in which it has been held that the offeror is justified in believing silence to be a manifestation of assent. These are situations in which a retail buyer gives a salesperson an order (offer) for certain goods, which the salesperson forwards to his or her company. If a reasonable period of time elapses without the company taking action, some courts hold that the buyer can

---

[15] In a case of a similar nature, a school board advertised for bids for the construction of a school building. After fourteen bids were received, the board wired one contractor: "You are low bidder. Come on morning train." The board and the contractor were subsequently unable to agree to a formal contract, and litigation ensued. The Iowa Supreme Court ruled that the board's telegram did not of itself constitute an acceptance of the contractor's bid, saying that it indicated no more than a willingness on the part of the board to enter into contractual negotiations. (*Cedar Rapids Lumber Co. v. Fisher,* 105 N.W. 595, 1906.)

justifiably view such silence as an acceptance of the offer and can hold the company liable for damages if it refuses to deliver the goods. Such courts reason that a company which sends salespeople out to solicit offers owes a duty to buyers to reject their offers within a reasonable time if it does not intend to accept them. (The same rule has sometimes been applied to mail-order houses when they have failed to reject buyers' orders within a reasonable time.)

## When Does Acceptance Take Effect?

**Reasonable Medium or Mailbox Rule:** Offers, revocations, and rejections are effective when received. Acceptances are also effective upon receipt, *but* they may be effective even sooner. That is, under the "mailbox" or **reasonable medium rule,** an acceptance may be effective as soon as it is sent if the medium chosen is reasonable. Although there is variation from jurisdiction to jurisdiction in this area of the law, courts typically deem a chosen medium to be reasonable if (1) it is the same one used by the offeror; (2) it is one customarily used in prior dealings between the parties; (3) it is customarily used within the trade or industry in which the parties are doing business; or (4) it is one which is impliedly authorized by the language of the offer (for example, an acceptance by mail is probably reasonable in response to an offer by telegram if the offer indicated that there was no urgency about reaching an agreement).

If the offeree uses a medium that is not reasonable, the acceptance will be effective only when received. However, if the medium chosen by the offeree is reasonable, the acceptance will be effective *when dispatched* (out of the possession of the offeree). Assume that A mails an offer to B. If B mails an acceptance, there is a contract the minute the acceptance is dispatched even if the post office delays the acceptance or even loses it altogether. (Of course, if the acceptance is lost, the offeree will bear the burden of proving by other evidence that it was, in fact, mailed.) If A calls B to revoke the offer after B has mailed the acceptance, it is too late for the revocation to be effective. The offer, already accepted, has ripened into a binding contract.

**Exceptions:** There are at least three situations where the reasonable medium rule is generally inapplicable. First, the offeror is the master of his or her offer and may always require that an acceptance be made by a particular medium. If a particular medium (telegraph, for example) is *clearly* specified, then an acceptance sent by any other medium will not result in a contract being formed upon dispatch.

Similarly, the offeror may require that an acceptance be *actually received* in order to be effective. A company that has had difficulty with its mail service might well impose such a requirement, which will override the reasonable medium rule.

Third, if an offeree mails a rejection first, and only later changes his mind and sends an acceptance, the acceptance is not effective until received. Therefore, an offeror who receives the rejection first may assume that it is effective.

***Examples:*** The following examples will illustrate the sequence of events leading to the formation of a contract, given the use of a reasonable medium.

*Case 1:* June 1—Y receives an offer in the mail from X.
June 2—X mails letter of revocation.
June 3—Y mails acceptance at 5 p.m.
June 4—Y receives the revocation.
June 5—X receives Y's acceptance.

***Result:*** A contract was formed at 5 p.m. on June 3, since use of mail by Y was clearly reasonable. (Since a *revocation* is usually not effective until it is received, the letter that X mailed on June 2 had no effect until June 4, when Y received it. And by that time a contract had already been formed.)[16]

*Case 2:* June 1—Y receives an offer in the mail from X.
June 2—Y mails letter of rejection.
June 3—Y changes his mind and at 10 a.m. calls X on the telephone and accepts the offer, telling X to disregard his letter of rejection.
June 4—X receives letter of rejection.

***Result:*** A contract was formed at 10 a.m. on June 3, when Y gave X actual notice of acceptance. (Since a *rejection* is usually not effective until it is received, Y's letter of rejection had no effect on June 2. The offer was thus open on June 3, when Y accepted it.)

***Sales Law Changes:*** The Uniform Commercial Code generally adopts the reasonable medium rule of

---

[16] As noted earlier, in California (and perhaps a few other states) a revocation is effective when mailed—here, on June 2. In such states there would be no contract.

the common law, UCC Sec. 2-206(1)(a) providing that an offer may be accepted by "any medium reasonable in the circumstances." However, whereas the common law holds that if an *un*reasonable method of acceptance is utilized, it is not effective until received, UCC Sec. 1-201(38) provides that such an acceptance will be deemed effective as of the time it is sent *if* it is received within the time that a seasonably dispatched acceptance using a reasonable medium would normally arrive.

The following case applies the reasonable medium approach in a common-law context.

### Cushing v. Thomson
Supreme Court of New Hampshire, 386 A.2d 805 (1978)

An antinuclear protest group, the Clamshell Alliance, sent an application in March of 1978 to the New Hampshire Adjutant General's office, seeking permission to rent the national guard armory in Portsmouth the night of April 29. The alliance hoped to use the armory facilities for a dance it had scheduled on that date.

On March 31 the adjutant general mailed a "contract offer" to the alliance, agreeing to rent the armory upon specified terms. The offer required that a signed acceptance be returned to the adjutant general's office.

Cushing, a member of the alliance, received the offer at the alliance's office on Monday, April 3. That same day he signed it on behalf of the organization, put the acceptance in an envelope, and placed the letter in the office's "outbox."

At 6:30 in the evening of the next day, Tuesday, April 4, Cushing received a phone call from the adjutant general stating that he was withdrawing the offer on orders of Governor Meldrim Thomson. Cushing replied that he had already accepted the offer, but the adjutant general repeated the statement that the offer had been withdrawn. (The alliance's acceptance, postmarked April 5, reached the adjutant general's office on April 6.)

When the adjutant general continued in his refusal to give the alliance permission to use the armory, Cushing and other members of the organization brought suit against Governor Thomson and the adjutant general, seeking specific performance of the contract that had allegedly been formed. Defendants contended that there was no contract, claiming that they had revoked the offer prior to plaintiff's "acceptance." Although there was no direct evidence indicating the precise moment at which the outgoing mail was placed in the hands of the U.S. Postal Service, the trial court found that this had presumably occurred prior to the time of the attempted revocation on Tuesday evening. It thus ruled that a contract had been formed, and granted plaintiff a decree of specific performance. Defendants appealed.

**Decision:** The trial court was correct in ruling that a contract *was* formed prior to the time of the attempted revocation. When an offer is made by mail and an acceptance is made via the same medium, the contract is complete when the acceptance is mailed and "beyond the acceptor's control."

There was no direct evidence proving the exact time at which the Alliance's acceptance was deposited in the U.S. mail. However, Cushing stated in a sworn affidavit that he placed the acceptance in the Alliance's outbox, for mailing, on April 3, and other evidence clearly proved that it was "customary office practice" for such letters to be put in the U.S. mail the same day. Accordingly, the trial court's implied finding that the acceptance "presumably" was in the U.S. mail *prior* to the telephone call of April 4 was proper. ∎

## Acceptance of Unilateral Offers

*Unilateral offers* pose two unique problems insofar as offer and acceptance principles are concerned: (1) whether it is necessary for the offeree, having performed the requested act, to notify the offeror of that fact, and (2) whether the offeror has the right to revoke the offer after the offeree has commenced to perform but before the performance is completed.

**Is Notice Required?** The general rule is that a unilateral offer is accepted the moment the offeree performs the requested act; giving notice that the act has taken place is usually not required. This rule does not apply, obviously, to offers that expressly request notification. In such offers, a contract is not formed until the requisite notice is given.

Another type of case requiring notice involves those exceptional situations where the act is of such a nature that the offeror "has no adequate means of ascertaining with reasonable promptness and certainty" that the act has taken place.[17] The typical cases in this category are *contracts of guaranty*—those in which one person guarantees a loan made to another. For example: A, in Columbus, asks B, in Miami, to lend $1,000 to C, a Miami resident, A promising to pay the debt if C fails to do so. In this situation, most courts take the view that while a contract is formed between A and B the moment that B makes the loan, A's resulting obligation is discharged (terminated) if B fails to notify him within a reasonable time that the loan has been made.

**When Can Revocation Be Made?** Where the requested act will take a period of time for completion, the traditional rule has been that the offeror can revoke the offer at any time before full performance has taken place, even if the offeree has started to do the job. In such a case a contract is never formed. (However, under the quasi-contract theory, the offeree is ordinarily entitled to recover the reasonable value of his or her performance prior to the revocation. In the event that this partial performance is of no value to the offeror, the offeree will, of course, recover nothing.)

In recent years a growing number of courts have felt that the traditional view is unfair to the offeree in many circumstances, and they have abandoned it in favor of several other approaches. The most widely accepted of the newer views is that where the act is one that of necessity will take a period of time to complete, the *right of revocation is suspended* once the offeree starts to perform and remains suspended until the offeree has had a reasonable time to complete the act. This view is consistent with the traditional view to the extent that no contract is formed until the act has been completed, but it affords an interim protection to the offeree that the traditional view does not. Thus we have yet another illustration of the courts' freedom, within the framework of the common law, to modify those earlier principles whose application has brought about results of questionable merit.

## *Bilateral/Unilateral Contracts: Sales Law*

Many sales contracts are clearly bilateral in nature. For example, a buyer on September 10 sends an order for goods at a specified price for November shipment, and the seller accepts the offer—i.e., promises to ship the goods as ordered—by mailing his or her acknowledgment to the buyer on September 16. Because Sec. 2-206 provides that "an offer to make a contract shall be construed as inviting acceptance in any manner and *by any medium reasonable in the circumstances,*" a bilateral contract is formed the moment the acceptance is deposited in the mail on the 16th (assuming the mail was a reasonable medium).

**"Prompt Shipment" Offers:** Prior to adoption of the UCC, if a buyer ordered goods using such terms as "prompt shipment," "for current shipment," or "ship at once," the offer was usually construed as being an offer for a unilateral contract. Under this common-law view, *actual shipment* was the only way in which the offer could be accepted; a *promise to ship* would not cause a contract to come into existence (a result that sometimes came as a surprise to one or both of the parties). Sec. 2-206(1) of the UCC rejects that view by providing that an offer containing such language shall be construed as inviting acceptance *either* by prompt shipment *or* by a prompt promise to ship. Therefore, an offeree's sending of a return promise to ship forms a bilateral contract in such circumstances (although prompt shipment must follow or the contract will be breached).[18] Sec. 2-206 thus blurs the common-law distinction between bilateral and unilateral offers by permitting the offeree, in this limited instance, a choice as to how his or her acceptance shall be made. The differences between common law and the UCC on this point are illustrated in Figure 12.3.

---

[17] *Restatement, Contracts 2d,* §54. The American Law Institute, 1979.

[18] The buyer can still require acceptance of the offer only by the act of shipment itself, but he or she now must explicitly state this in the offer.

**Figure 12.3** Acceptance of a Unilateral Offer under Common-law and UCC Rules

**Common Law**

A → Offer requesting an act → B —— Performs act (no notice to A required) → Contract

B ---- Promises to perform ------→ No contract

**UCC 2-206**

A → Offer requesting "prompt shipment" of goods → B — either:
- Unilateral:
  - Promptly ships and notifies of shipment → Contract
  - Promptly ships (no notice to A) ---→ Contract in most circumstances
- Bilateral —— Promises to ship promptly → Contract

## SUMMARY

The first element of a contract (excluding quasi-contracts) is an agreement—an offer followed by an acceptance. In order for a communication to constitute an offer, the courts require it to (1) manifest a genuine intent to contract, (2) be reasonably definite, and (3) be legally communicated to the offeree. Communications failing to meet requirement 1 constitute mere "preliminary negotiations." Insofar as requirement 2 is concerned, the common-law rules require that the offer (and thus the ensuing agreement) include all major obligations of the parties. Sales contracts, however, are governed by more liberal rules. Under the UCC, such contracts are enforceable even if they fail to state some of the terms of the agreement. (In such circumstances, the missing terms are supplied by applicable provisions of Article 2 of the UCC.)

Once an offer is made, it remains open until terminated by act of the parties or by operation of law. The most common acts of termination by the parties are revocation and rejection. If a revocation or rejection occurs, any subsequent acceptance is too late and does not result in the formation of a contract. Termination by operation of law—an automatic termination—results where any of the following conditions occur: (1) death or adjudication of insanity of either party, (2) destruction of the subject-matter of the contract, or (3) intervening illegality.

In order for a communication of the offeree to constitute an acceptance, it must show an unequivocal intent to accept and must be in conformity with all of the terms of the offer. If a new term is added, or a term of the offer is deleted, the offeree's communication is a counteroffer (and a rejection of the offer). Under sales law, however (Sec. 2-207 of the UCC), if the offeree's communication is a "definite" acceptance, it constitutes an acceptance even if it contains an additional term. And, in such a case, if both parties are merchants the additional term automatically becomes a part of the contract (with limited exceptions).

When the parties are not dealing face-to-face (or by telephone), the modern rule is that the acceptance of a bilateral offer is effective *when sent* if the offeree uses a reasonable medium of communication. In most situations the U.S. mail is a reasonable medium, and thus, in such cases (under the "mailbox rule") a contract is formed when the acceptance is placed in the mail—even if it is delayed in transmission, or never reaches the offeror. As to unilateral offers, the traditional rule has been that an acceptance is not effective until the offeree has completed performance of the requested act; thus a revocation before completion is effective. However, an increasing number of courts are taking the view that once the offeree has commenced performance the offeror's right to revoke is suspended until the offeree has had a reasonable time in which to complete the requested performance.

## KEY TERMS

**Offer**
**Preliminary negotiations**
**Consumer protection statutes**
**Communication (of offer)**
**Revocation**
**Firm Offer**
**Rejection**
**Counteroffer**
**Reasonable medium rule**

## QUESTIONS AND PROBLEMS

1. Capital City Ford advertised that anyone who bought a 1954 model car could turn around and exchange it for a 1955 model at no additional cost. After reading the ad, P bought a 1954 model and then attempted to exchange it for a 1955 model. Capital City refused, pointing out that advertisements generally are not offers that consumers can turn into binding contracts. P sued to enforce an alleged contract. Will P prevail? Discuss. (*Johnson v. Capital City Ford,* 85 So.2d 75, La.App. 1955.)

2. In 1984 evangelist Jerry Falwell was on a TV show with homosexual activist Jerry Sloan. Sloan, who was also a baptist minister, contended that Falwell had said on his "Old-Time Gospel Hour" show that there would be "a celebration in heaven" when mostly gay metropolitan churches around the country were "annihilated." Fallwell responded: "That's an absolute lie, and I'll give you $5,000 if you can produce that tape." Sloan did. Falwell refused to pay. Sloan sued. Will he recover? (*Sloan v. Falwell,* Calif. Superior Court 1986.)

3. Blakeslee, who wished to buy some land owned by the Nelsons, wrote a letter to them asking if they would accept "$49,000 net" for the property. The Nelsons replied that they would "not sell for less than $56,000," whereupon Blakeslee wired back, "Accept your offer of $56,000 net." Does a contract now exist between the parties? Explain. (*Blakeslee v. Nelson,* 207 N.Y.S. 676, 1925.)

4. Condovest agreed "to use its utmost diligence and good faith" to obtain an FHA or VA loan to finance a condominium project. Upon production of the money, Street was to build the condos, "final plans and specifications to be agreed upon." Initially, Condovest could not secure the loan, so Street declared the agreement "void." A month later, however, Condovest tendered to Street $12,000 as a progress payment; this was the amount to be paid at the time the slab was poured. Condovest promised to make additional progress payments, but Street refused to perform. Condovest sued for breach of contract. Will it prevail? Discuss. (*Condovest Corp. v. John Street Builders,* 662 S.W.2d 138, Tex.App. 1983.)

5. The Jewish War Veterans, Post #58, offered a reward for the arrest and conviction of the killer of one of its members. Glover, not knowing of the offer, gave information to the police regarding the whereabouts of the killer. Glover subsequently learned of the reward and sued to recover it. Will he? Discuss. (*Glover v. Jewish War Veterans,* 68 A.2d 233, D.C. 1949.)

6. The Gator Company, a Florida firm, offered to buy 100 tons of scrap metal from the Sooner Company, located in Norman, Oklahoma, at a specified price. The Sooner Company accepted this offer using one of its own forms, which contained this new term: "It is agreed that any disputes arising out of the performance of this contract will be governed by Oklahoma law." Later the Gator Company wanted to get out of the deal, and contended that the Sooner Company's "acceptance" was legally a counteroffer, and that thus a contract was never formed. Under sales law, Sec. 2-207 of the UCC:

   **a.** Is the Gator Company correct? Why or why not?

   **b.** If a contract were formed, do you think the Sooner Company's new term became a part of that contract? Why or why not?

7. On January 1, 1985, P was injured in a car wreck caused by a person insured by West American Insurance

Co. (D). P hired attorney Murnane to negotiate on her behalf. D offered $25,000 in November of 1986. After continued telephonic negotiations, on December 1, 1986, D wrote to Murnane, stating that after further review, its "offer will remain $25,000." This letter did not specify a date on which the offer would terminate. On January 9, 1987, Murnane sent a mailgram to D unconditionally accepting the offer on P's behalf. D refused to pay, pointing out that the statute of limitations on P's right to sue expired on January 1, 1987, eight days before she accepted the offer. P sued to enforce the $25,000 settlement "agreement." Will she prevail? Discuss. (*Vaskie v. West American Insurance Co.,* 556 A.2d 436, 1989.)

**8.** P delivered eelskins to D four or five times. Each time D accepted delivery, waited a while, and then paid P. This time, D accepted delivery, waited several months, and then simply destroyed the eelskins without paying P. P sued. D claimed that there was no contract because it never expressly accepted any offer. Is this a good defense? Discuss. (*Hobbs v. Massasoit Whip Co.,* 33 N.E. 495, Mass. 1893.)

**9.** D hired an auctioneer to sell a piece of land for him. Together they prepared an advertisement stating that the land would be sold "without reserve." P started the bidding at $25,000, and it slowly rose to $41,000 (this also being P's bid) when D and his attorney ordered the auction stopped. They announced that they would not sell the land for less than $100,000 and would not allow any more bids to be made. P sued for specific performance, stating his willingness to pay $41,000. D claims that there is no contract. Is D correct? (*Zuhak v. Rose,* 58 N.W.2d 693, Wis. 1953.)

**10.** Tayloe applied to an insurance company for a fire insurance policy on his home. The company forwarded Tayloe's application to Minor, its agent in Tayloe's area, with a letter telling Minor that he could go ahead and negotiate a policy with Tayloe. Minor then wrote Tayloe, saying that if he desired to effect the insurance coverage for which he had applied, "send me your check for $57 and the business is concluded." Tayloe received this offer on December 20 and deposited his check in the mail on December 21. On December 22, while Tayloe's check was in the mail, his residence burned down. Was an insurance contract between Tayloe and the company in effect at the time of the fire? Explain. (*Tayloe v. The Merchants Fire Insurance Company,* U.S.S.Ct., 9 Howard 390, 1850.)

# CHAPTER 13

# CONSIDERATION

An elusive thing called **consideration** is the second element ordinarily required in a contract. Generally, if an agreement lacks consideration, neither party can enforce it, even if it is in writing. As a practical matter, consideration is present in most agreements; but since this is not always the case, we need a basic understanding of the *doctrine of consideration* in order to determine when an agreement is legally binding.

## HISTORICAL NOTE

Courts have long struggled with the question of what agreements ought to be enforced. No system of law has ever enforced all promises, nor could this feasibly be done. Present-day concepts of consideration have resulted from a mixture of logic and historical accident. At one time, contracts had to be "sealed" in order to be enforced. A **sealed contract** had to have a bit of wax affixed to it, on which the initials or other distinctive marks of each of the parties was imprinted. Today, sealed contracts are virtually unknown, though a few jurisdictions will enforce such a contract even in the absence of consideration. Most jurisdictions, however, will enforce no contract, sealed or unsealed, in the absence of consideration.

The present-day requirements of consideration centers in part on the notion that one party to an agreement should not be bound by it if the other party is not similarly bound. A's promise to give a present to B should not be binding on A because B is not bound to do anything. Promises to make gifts are generally unenforceable. Another important aspect of consideration is that it prevents one contracting party from exploiting another, as shall be illustrated later in this chapter in connection with a discussion of the "preexisting obligation" rule.

## THE BASIC CONCEPT OF CONSIDERATION

Courts agree substantially about the kinds of promises or acts constituting consideration in most situations. Although several definitions of and tests for consideration have been formulated over the years, most lead to the same conclusion when applied to agreements where the existence of consideration is questioned. Our discussion focuses on a popular approach that emphasizes the "bargain" element of a transaction, which helps distinguish a promise of a mere gift (which may not be enforced) from an enforceable commercial promise to do something that the other party has bargained for.

Assume that Company A promised to deliver 5,000 tires to Company B on July 1 in exchange for Company B's promise to pay $200,000. Assume further that Company B breached the promise; Company A sued for breach of contract; and Company B raised the defense that no consideration existed to support its promise. Many courts would analyze the agreement to determine if three essential elements were present, constituting consideration.[1]

The first determination is whether the promisee (Company A, the party that received the promise that was not performed) suffered a **legal detriment,** defined as (a) doing (or promising to do) something that it was not obligated to do, or (b) refraining from doing (or promising to refrain from doing) something that it had a right to do. Unless Company A had a preexisting legal or contractual obligation to deliver the 5,000 tires, it is clear that Company A did suffer a legal detriment in this transaction. It prom-

---

[1] *Allegheny College v. National Chautauqua County Bank,* 246 N.Y. 369, 159 N.E. 173 (1927).

ised to do something it did not otherwise have to do—to deliver 5,000 tires.

The second element of consideration is that the detriment (A's promise to deliver the 5,000 tires) must induce the promise that was not performed (B's promise to pay $200,000). Unless there is some other explanation for why Company B promised to pay $200,000 to Company A, it is clear that the detriment did induce the promise in this case. This is often called the "bargained for" element—B made its promise while bargaining to induce A to deliver the tires.

The third element of consideration is that the promise (B's promise to pay $200,000) must induce the detriment (A's promise to deliver the 5,000 tires). Again, unless some other reason appears to explain why A promised to deliver the 5,000 tires, it seems clear that it was in order to earn the $200,000 promised by B. All three elements of consideration are present, so the contract is enforceable.

Viewed in this light, consideration at a general level is easy to understand and, obviously, is present in most cases. Companies and individuals promise to deliver goods and services because they want the money that other companies and individuals are willing to pay for those goods and services.

Consider another example. Assume that X promises to install a home air-conditioning unit for Y, and Y promises to pay X $1,100 for the job. Consideration will become important if one of the parties, let us say X, breaches the promise, is sued by Y, and claims lack of consideration as a defense. A court will quickly find: (1) The promisee (Y) has suffered a legal detriment (promising to do something he did not have to do—pay $1,100). (2) The detriment (Y's promise to pay $1,100) induced the promise (X's promise to install the air-conditioning unit). Obviously X bargained for Y's promise of payment; that is how X makes his living. (3) The promise (X's promise to install the air-conditioning unit) induced the detriment (why else would Y have promised to pay $1,100?). Try to analyze the following cases using the three basic elements of consideration.

## Hamer v. Sidway
Court of Appeals of New York,
27 N.E. 256 (1891)

William E. Story, Sr., promised to pay his nephew, William E. Story, II, $5,000 if he would refrain from drinking, using tobacco, swearing, and playing cards or billiards for money until he became twenty-one years of age. The nephew refrained from all the specified activities as he was requested to do, and on his twenty-first birthday he wrote his uncle a letter asking him for the money.

The uncle, in reply, assured the nephew, "You shall have the $5,000 as I promised you." The uncle went on, however, to explain that he had worked very hard to accumulate that sum of money and would pay it "when you are capable of taking care of it, and the sooner that time comes the better it will suit me."

Two years later the uncle died, without having made payment. The administrator of the uncle's estate, Sidway, refused to pay the $5,000, and suit was brought to recover that sum. (The plaintiff is Hamer, rather than the nephew, for the reason that at some time before litigation was begun the nephew had assigned—that is, sold—his rights against the estate to Hamer. Thus Hamer's right to recover is entirely dependent upon whether the nephew had a valid contractual claim against his uncle.)

The trial court ruled that the uncle's promise to pay the $5,000 was not supported by consideration on the part of the nephew (the promisee) and entered judgment for the defendant. The plaintiff appealed.

**Decision:** The judgment was reversed and entered for the plaintiff. The nephew had the legal right to use tobacco and liquor in New York. Therefore, giving up those products for the specified period of time clearly constituted a legal detriment to him. The detriment (forgoing the right to smoke and drink) induced the uncle's promise to pay, because that is what the uncle was bargaining for. Finally, the promise of the uncle to pay induced the detriment, because we have no other explanation for why the nephew refrained from those activities. ■

**Comment:** Two consideration principles are underscored here, as a result of the higher court's rejection of the defenses raised by the uncle's estate. First, if a promisee incurs a detriment by waiving a legal right, the promisee has given consideration even though he or she may have received an incidental benefit at the same time. (Thus, the nephew gave consideration by giving up certain rights—such as the right to smoke—even though he may have also been physically benefited by this forbearance). Second, consideration exists if the promisee incurs a detriment. It is not a requirement that the promisor must also receive a benefit.

---

### Lampley v. Celebrity Homes, Inc.
Colorado Court of Appeals, Division II, 594 P.2d 605 (1979)

Linda Lampley, plaintiff, began work at Celebrity Homes in Denver in May of 1975. On July 29 of that year Celebrity announced the initiation of a profit-sharing plan. Under that plan all employees were to receive bonuses if a certain "profit goal" were reached for the 1975 fiscal year—April 1, 1975, to March 31, 1976. (Linda was working under an at-will agreement—that is, both she and Celebrity could terminate the relationship at any time.)

Plaintiff's employment was terminated in January of 1976. At the end of March, 1976, the company announced that the profit goal had been reached, and it made its first distribution of profits in May, 1976. When plaintiff was excluded from this distribution, she brought this suit for the share allegedly due her.

In the trial court Celebrity argued that its promise to pay the bonus was a mere "gratuity" on its part, on the ground that there was no consideration on the employee's part to support its promise. The trial court rejected this contention and entered judgment for plaintiff. Celebrity appealed.

**Decision:** The trial court was correct in ruling that consideration supported defendant's promise to pay. Plaintiff was employed for an indefinite term; that is, she was under no obligation to work until a fixed future date. Therefore, by voluntarily remaining on the job after the promise was made, plaintiff did something that she did not have to do, thus incurring a legal detriment. That detriment induced defendant's promise to pay a bonus, because plaintiff's staying on the job is precisely what defendant was bargaining for. Companies often offer profit bonuses to reduce employee turnover and to encourage employees to work harder. Finally, the court assumed that defendant's promise induced plaintiff's detriment. It is reasonable to assume that one of the reasons plaintiff stayed on the job as long as she did was the promise of this bonus, which she could consider as part of her compensation package as compared to compensation offered by other potential positions. ∎

---

Though consideration was found in both these cases and is usually present in commercial transactions, obviously it is not always present. Consider the following examples.

- Company A to Company B: "Because you are having such tough times, we will charge you 20 percent less for custodial services than our contract with you calls for." In most jurisdictions (but not all, as we shall see later in the chapter), a court would not hold A to this promise. It is basically a gift, since *B suffered no legal detriment.*

- Company A to Company B: "We have an old metal press that we are no longer using. If you would like to come over some time and pick it up, you may have it." If A reneges on this promise, it will not be deemed enforceable. Even if we assumed that B suffered a detriment in the transaction (making the effort to pick up the press), *that detriment did not induce A's promise.* A was not "bargaining for" that act. Rather, this is basically a promise to make a gift and is unenforceable.

- Wife attacks her husband (D) with an ax, knocking him down. As she is about to decapitate him, P intervenes, catching the ax on its downward flight. P's hand is badly mutilated. D jumps up and promises to pay P $1,000 for saving his life. P has clearly suffered a detriment, and it is exactly what D bargained for. However, the *promise did not induce the detriment.* That is, because D made his promise *after* P acted, we cannot say that his promise caused her to do what she did. Thus, most courts would not enforce this promise. *See Harrington v. Taylor,* 36 S.E.2d 227 (N.C. 1945). (Later in the chapter we shall learn that a minority of courts would enforce the contract to the extent of D's moral obligation.)

## Performance of Preexisting Obligations

As a general rule, a promisee does not incur a detriment by performing, or promising to perform, an act that he or she was under a preexisting duty to perform. One can be under a **preexisting obligation** because of the general law of a state or the federal government, or because a prior contract has not yet been carried out.

**Obligations Imposed by Law:** The following is a simple illustration of an obligation imposed by law. X's store has been burglarized, and X promises a local policeman $75 if he uncovers, and turns over to the authorities, evidence establishing the identity of the culprit. If the policeman furnishes the requested information, he is not entitled to the reward. Under city ordinances and department regulations he already has a duty to do this; therefore it does not constitute a detriment to him.

**Contractual Obligations:** Greater difficulty is presented in situations where the preexisting obligation exists (or may exist) as the result of a prior contract between the parties. While such situations involve varying fact-patterns, the starting point can be illustrated as follows. D contracts to drill a seventy-foot well for G for $200. After he commences work, D complains that he is going to lose money on the job and may not finish it unless he gets more money. G then says, "All right. Finish up and I'll pay you $100 extra," and D completes the job. G now refuses to pay the additional $100, and D brings suit to hold G to his promise. In this situation most courts would rule that D's act of completing the well was simply the performance of his original obligation—that he incurred no detriment thereby, and cannot enforce G's promise to pay the additional money. Thus, as a general rule, a **modification contract**—a contract that alters the terms of an existing contract—*requires some new consideration in order to be enforceable.* (Consideration would have been present in the above case for example, had the modification contract required something extra of D—such as drilling the well to a depth of eighty feet.)

The primary rationale for the rule that performance of one's preexisting obligations does not constitute consideration is the prevention of coerced modification contracts. In other words, referring to the original example, the purpose is to prevent D—by threatening to stop work, or by actually stopping it—from enforcing the new promise made by G to pay more, in these circumstances.

Application of the preexisting obligation rule in most instances makes sense and brings about reasonable results. The following case is typical of those in which the rule prevents the enforceability of the modification contract. Following this case, a number of exceptions to the rule (and the reasoning underlying them) will be noted.

---

### Quarture v. Allegheny County et al.
Superior Court of Pennsylvania, 14 A.2d 575 (1940)

Quarture, plaintiff, owned land in Pennsylvania. A portion of it was taken when the defendant county relocated and widened a state highway. Plaintiff needed legal help to recover damages from the county, and he employed a lawyer, Sniderman, to represent him in this effort.

A written contract was entered into, under the terms of which Sniderman was to "institute, conduct, superintend or prosecute to final determination, if necessary, a suit or suits, action or claim against the County of Allegheny on account of taking, injuring, and affecting (my, our) property in the relocation, widening, and opening of the State Highway known as Route No. 545." The contract further provided that Sniderman was to receive, as a fee for his services, "10 percent of all that might be recovered."

Sniderman represented plaintiff before the Board of Viewers of Allegheny County, and the board awarded plaintiff

*(continued)*

$1,650 damages. Plaintiff was dissatisfied with this amount and wished to appeal that award.

Subsequently, a new agreement was entered into between plaintiff and Sniderman. This agreement provided that Sniderman would appeal the case to the court of common pleas and that Quarture would pay him a fee of 33 percent of whatever recovery might be obtained on appeal.

Plaintiff, represented by Sniderman, then brought this action in the court of common pleas, appealing the award of the Board of Viewers, and the court awarded him a judgment of $2,961. At this point Sniderman filed a petition with the court, asking it to distribute to him 33 percent of the judgment—$987.

Quarture objected, contending that his promise to pay the larger percentage was not supported by consideration and that Sniderman was thus bound by his original contract (a fee of 10 percent). The court rejected this contention and awarded Sniderman $987. Plaintiff appealed.

**Decision:** The judgment of the lower court was reversed. Sniderman is entitled to receive only 10 percent of the total damages awarded to Quarture as provided by the first contract. Under that contract Sniderman agreed to prosecute Quarture's claim to "final determination" if necessary. This term obviously includes the handling of any appeal Quarture might subsequently want to make. Thus, when Quarture later made his promise to increase Sniderman's payment to 33⅓ percent of the total damages that might be recovered, Sniderman already had a *preexisting obligation* under the first contract to do the appeals work for 10 percent. Consequently, Sniderman's subsequent work in handling the appeal did *not* constitute a legal detriment. Therefore, Quarture's promise to pay 33⅓ percent was not binding upon him. ∎

## Exceptions to the Preexisting Obligation Rule

Generally, the preexisting obligation rule applies to both coerced promises and uncoerced promises. Thus if a party to a contract later makes a modification contract under which he or she agrees to pay a higher price for property or services to be received under the first contract, such party is not liable on the promise even if it was an entirely voluntary one on his or her part. Because the freeing of the promisor from liability on the second promise, when made voluntarily, is sometimes felt to be unfair to the promisee, the courts (or legislatures) of the various states have fashioned a number of exceptions that cause the voluntary modification contract to be enforceable. The exceptions noted below are often recognized (although the circumstances to which they apply are rather limited ones).

**The Unforeseen Difficulties Exception:** The **unforeseen difficulties rule** is most easily illustrated by reference to a leading case in which a builder, Schuck, contracted to dig a cellar under a portion of an existing house, to a depth of seven feet, for $1,500. (The contract was made after the parties examined an excavation across the street, where the soil appeared to be normal.) After commencing work, Schuck discovered that the ground below the three-foot level was "swamp-like, black muddy stuff," and that this condition would require the use of piling, which the parties did not contemplate under the contract. Thereupon the home owner, Linz, told Schuck to do whatever was necessary to dig a seven-foot cellar, adding that he would "pay him whatever additional cost" was involved. Schuck completed the job. In ensuing litigation, Linz denied that there was consideration on Schuck's part to support his promise to pay more than the $1,500. The court rejected this contention and permitted Schuck to recover his additional costs.[2]

In reaching this conclusion, the court stated that, in its opinion, *the preexisting obligation rule should not be applied to a situation of this sort.* To support its reasoning the court relied upon these statements from a prior decision:

> It is entirely competent [legally possible] for the parties to a contract to modify or waive their rights under it and ingraft new terms upon it, and in such a case the promise of one party is the consideration for that of the other; but, where the promise to the one is simply a repetition of a subsisting legal promise, there can be no consideration for the promise of the other party, and there is no warrant for inferring that the parties have voluntarily rescinded or modified their con-

---

[2]*Linz v. Schuck,* 67 Atl. 286 (1907). The facts of this case must be distinguished from those presented by the earlier well-drilling example. In that example, the well driller threatened to quit simply because he was losing money, not because of some unknown condition of the soil that required unanticipated efforts.

tract. But where the party refusing to complete his contract does so by reason of some *unforeseen and substantial difficulties in the performance of the contract, which were not known or anticipated by the parties when the contract was entered into, and which cast upon him an additional burden not contemplated by the parties, and the opposite party promises him extra pay or benefits if he will complete his contract, and he so promises, the promise to pay is supported by a valid consideration.* [Emphasis added.] (*Bryant v. Lord,* 19 Minn. 396, 1872.)

Situations where the rule is applied are admittedly exceptional; the courts of a few jurisdictions do not recognize it at all. And, among courts that do, they have historically taken the view that such circumstances as increased costs, unexpected labor difficulties, or loss of expected sources of materials do not fall within the unforeseen difficulties (or "unanticipated circumstances") rule. However, among such courts today there is a clear trend to recognize such circumstances as being within the rule if (1) the circumstance was truly unanticipated when the contract was made, and (2) the increased compensation is "fair and equitable under the circumstances"—i.e., the extra money promised is no more than a reasonable compensation to the promisee for the additional effort or costs he or she expended in finishing the job. To illustrate: C contracts to build a home for B for $95,000. After work is under way C is unable to get the Pella windows called for in the contract from his local supplier, because of a strike in the Pella plant. C learns, however, he can get the identical Pella windows from a distant supplier at a cost of $500 higher than he originally expected to pay for them. When C tells B this, B tells C to go ahead with the window installation and he will pay C the additional cost. If C completes the job, he is entitled to the extra $500.

**The Mutual Rescission Exception:** If the parties to the original contract expressly or impliedly rescind (cancel) it before it is fully performed, and enter into a new contract involving the same subject matter, the new contract is enforceable. To illustrate: C contracts to do certain work for B for $1,000. After C starts the job he complains on several occasions that he is going to lose money on the deal. B says that he will consider paying more, and suggests a new contract be made. C, with B's consent, then tears up the contract, and the parties make a new contract under which B agrees to pay C $1,200 for the job. When C finishes the work, he is entitled to the $1,200. The rationale is that the mutual cancellation of the first contract *freed* C of his preexisting duty to do the job, and when C later assumed the same obligation under the new agreement he thus incurred a new detriment sufficient to support B's promise to pay the larger sum. (While this view has been criticized by several authorities, it continues to be followed by most courts today.)

## *Modification Contracts: Sales Law*

The drafters of the UCC made several modifications of the common law aimed at preventing technical rules from impeding enforcement of the parties' factual bargain. As an example, the drafters believed that if the parties to a sales contract subsequently modified it voluntarily, that modification should be enforceable whether or not supported by consideration. Accordingly, UCC Sec. 2-209(1) rejects the general common-law rule by providing that "an agreement modifying a contract [for the sale of goods] needs no consideration to be binding." To illustrate: S and B have agreed that S will sell a certain quantity of goods (such as 10,000 gallons of fuel oil) to B at a certain price. S later finds that he is not going to be able to deliver by the agreed-upon date. He contacts B, *who agrees to an extension of the time for delivery.* B subsequently has a change of heart and demands the goods on the original date. Under the UCC, *B is bound by the agreed-upon modification* even though S gave no additional consideration for the extension of time. (The reasoning behind Sec. 2-209 has prompted several states, including California, New York, and Michigan to adopt a similar rule for common-law contracts.)

Although the modification agreement need not be supported by new consideration, it must still meet two requirements that the UCC imposes on all contracts falling within its scope. First, the modification must be made in good faith—that is, it must not be a coerced modification. And, second, the contract must not be "unconscionable"—i.e., shockingly one-sided. (The concepts of coercion [duress] and unconscionability are discussed in later chapters.)

To avoid difficulties caused by claims of subsequent modifications, many parties place in their written contracts clauses stating that subsequent modifications not evidenced by a writing shall have no effect. Such NOM ("no oral modification") clauses are expressly made enforceable by Sec. 2-209(2).

## *Adequacy of Consideration*

Whenever the enforceability of a promise is at issue, a finding that the promisee incurred a legally recognized detriment results in the promisor being bound by the contract. This is usually true even if the actual values of the promise and the detriment are unequal—as is reflected in the oft-repeated statement that "the law is not concerned with the **adequacy of consideration.**" To illustrate: X contracts to sell an acreage in Montana to Y for $60,000. Y later discovers that the actual value of the land is under $30,000. Y is liable on his promise to pay $60,000, even though what he received was worth much less. Under the usual test, X incurred a detriment when he promised to convey the land—the surrender of his right to retain the property. The presence of this detriment constituted a consideration sufficient to support Y's promise to pay; and Y's claim of inadequacy is therefore of no relevance. The legal sufficiency of an act or promise, rather than its adequacy, is controlling.[3]

---

[3] Adequacy of consideration is, however, inquired into by the courts in exceptional circumstances. They will, for example, refuse to issue a decree of specific performance against a promisor in a contract felt to be "unconscionable"—that is, where the value of the consideration given by the plaintiff-promisee is so grossly inadequate that enforcement of the contract would "shock the conscience and common sense of reasonable people." Additionally, the courts will refuse to enforce promises where the inadequacy of consideration suggests that the promisor has been the victim of fraud (a subject covered in some detail in Chapter 15).

## *Mutuality of Obligation*

The requirement of **mutuality of obligation** dictates that there must be consideration on the part of both parties to the contract. As we have indicated, in the typical bilateral contract each party's promise is supported by the promise of the other, and the requirement is met. If, however, in a particular case there is no mutuality because consideration is lacking on the part of one of the parties, neither party is bound by the agreement. Such an agreement is called an **illusory contract.** For example, A and B enter into a written agreement under the terms of which A promises to employ B as his foreman for one year at a salary of $22,000 and B promises to work in that capacity for the specified time. The last paragraph of the agreement provides that "A reserves the right to cancel this contract at any time." Because A has thus not absolutely bound himself to employ B for the year, A has incurred no detriment (no unconditional obligation) by such a promise, with the result that B's promise to work for the year is not binding upon him. Thus, he can quit work at any time without liability to A. In such a case the requirement of mutuality of obligation has not been met, since A is said to have a "free way out" of the contract.

In the next case the right of cancellation was a restricted one. See if you agree with the distinction which the higher court makes between this kind of a clause, on the one hand, and one where the right to cancel is absolute, on the other.

---

### Laclede Gas Company v. Amoco Oil Company
U.S. Eighth Circuit Court of Appeals,
522 F.2d 33 (1975)

In 1970 a number of mobile home parks were being built by developers in Jefferson County, Missouri. At this time there were no natural gas mains serving these areas, so that persons living in them needed propane gas until the mains would be built.

In order to meet this demand, the Laclede Gas Company (Laclede) entered into a written contract with the American Oil Company (Amoco), under the terms of which Amoco would supply Laclede with propane for its customers living in the parks for a minimum period of one year. The contract contained a clause giving Laclede the right to cancel the agreement after one year upon 30 days written notice to Amoco, but it did not give Amoco any corresponding right to cancel the contract.

For several months Amoco made the required deliveries of propane to Laclede, but thereafter Amoco sent a letter to Laclede saying that it was "terminating" the contract. When Laclede brought this action to recover damages for breach of contract, Amoco contended that it was not bound by the contract because it lacked mutuality (that is, Amoco claimed that its promise to supply the propane was not supported by con-

*(continued)*

sideration on the part of Laclede because of the cancellation clause.) The trial court agreed with this contention, and Laclede appealed.

**Decision:** There *was* consideration on Laclede's part, despite the right that it had to cancel the contract. It is true that if the contract had given Laclede the right to cancel the contract at any time and for any reason, then Amoco's argument that there was no consideration given by Laclede would have been correct.

Here, however, Laclede's right to cancel was limited in two basic respects. First, Laclede could not cancel until one year had passed after Amoco's first delivery of propane. Second, Laclede had to give Amoco 30 days notice of termination. Under prevailing case law, the existence of *either* of these limitations supports the conclusion that Laclede gave consideration to Amoco (i.e., when either of these limitations is present, a party in Laclede's position does *not* possess the unbridled right to cancel). Accordingly, the trial court was wrong in ruling that Laclede was not entitled to maintain this action to recover damages for breach of contract. ■

---

**Requirements Contracts:** Buyers and sellers of goods will sometimes enter into contracts where the quantity of the goods being sold—such as gasoline or coal—is not specified; rather, the quantity is to be determined by subsequent events. In some instances, the language of the contract is such that the buyer clearly has a "free way out"; that is, under the terms of the contract the buyer does not absolutely promise to buy any specific amount of goods. For example, S and B enter into a contract under the terms of which B promises to buy from S all the coal that he "might wish" over the next six months at a specified price per ton, with S promising to sell such quantity. Because of the language used, either intentionally or accidentally, B has not bound himself to buy *any* quantity of coal at all; thus the contract is illusory, since B has incurred no detriment. Because mutuality of obligation is lacking, the result is that if B later desires some coal, he is free to buy it from whomever he chooses. Conversely, if B orders coal from S, S has no duty to supply it.

Application of the mutuality of obligation requirement to cases such as the above soon began to cast doubt on the validity of all sales contracts in which buyers did not absolutely commit themselves to purchase some specified minimum quantity of goods. Many contracts, for example, were phrased in such a manner that the quantity of goods the buyer was committed to purchase depended on his or her subsequent needs (whatever they might prove to be) rather than on an obligation to take a fixed number of units at the outset. For example: An ice company contracts to sell to an ice cream manufacturer "all the ice you will need in your business for the next two years" at a specified price per ton.

The courts recognized the practicality of such **requirements contracts** and wanted to enforce them if they could; but the theoretical difficulty was that these contracts did not, by their terms, absolutely bind the buyer to take even a single unit of the product or commodity in question.[4] The courts therefore sought a theory by which many of these contracts could be upheld without demolishing the concept of mutuality.

They accomplished this, in large measure, by adopting the following view. If the parties, by the language of the contract, indicate that the quantity of goods is to be dependent upon the *requirements of the buyer's business,* then the contract is not void for want of mutuality and both parties are bound by it. (The determination of the exact quantity of goods is simply postponed, of necessity, until expiration of the period in question.)[5] Under this theory, while the buyer might not require any of the item or commodity in question, consideration on the part of the buyer exists as follows. In the event that the buyer subsequently requires the product, he or she is obligated to buy it solely from the seller. (That is, the

---

[4] Unlike the ice illustration, for example, it was often highly questionable whether the buyer would require any of the product at all, particularly where the period of time was a short one. (And even in the ice case it was possible that the buyer would go out of business the next day.)

[5] In other words, such contracts are to be distinguished from illusory contracts, in which the quantity is solely dependent upon the buyer's whim or will.

buyer *gives up the right to buy it from others.*) Thus contracts such as the one in the ice case are generally binding on both parties.[6]

**Output Contracts:** **Output contracts** are essentially similar to and governed by the same principles as requirements contracts. A seller contracts to sell his or her entire output of a particular article, or of a particular plant, for a specified period of time to the buyer at a designated unit price. The implied promise of the seller (in the event he or she does produce the articles) not to sell them to anyone other than the buyer constitutes a detriment to the seller. And the promise of the buyer to purchase the output, in the event there is any, constitutes a corresponding detriment to the buyer. As a result, such contracts are usually enforceable.[7]

## Settlement of Debts

After a debt becomes due, sometimes the creditor and debtor enter into a *settlement agreement.* This occurs when the creditor, either on his or her own initiative or that of the debtor, promises to release the debtor of all further liability if the debtor pays a specified sum of money. If, after the specified sum is paid, the creditor seeks to recover the balance of the debt on the ground that the agreement lacked consideration on the part of the debtor, the success of the suit usually depends on whether the original debt was "unliquidated" or "liquidated."

**Unliquidated Debts:** An **unliquidated debt** is one where a genuine dispute exists between the debtor and creditor as to the existence or amount of the indebtedness. *Compromise agreements as to such debts, if executed, are usually binding.* For example: C (creditor) claims that she is owed $150 by D (debtor) for work performed under a contract with D, and D contends that the job was to cost only $100. C then says, "I will settle for $120," and D pays her that sum in cash. If C later sues to recover the balance allegedly owing, *she will be unsuccessful* because her implied promise to release D is supported by D's payment of the $120. (The payment of $120 by D—a sum more than D admitted owing—constitutes consideration because D, by making the payment, thereby gave up the right to have a court rule on his contention that the debt was only $100. Since C's promise to release is thus supported by consideration, D has a good defense to C's suit to recover the balance.) In such a situation, the payment of the $120 by D and the acceptance of that sum by C is said to constitute an "accord and satisfaction"—a binding agreement of a type that will be discussed further in Chapter 18.

**Payment by Check:** The above rule—preventing a further recovery by the creditor—is also applicable to payments by check if the debtor indicates that the tendered payment is meant to be in full satisfaction of the indebtedness (rather than a partial payment.) For example: suppose that in the prior situation, before the parties had reached any agreement on the $120 figure, D simply mailed C a check for $120, bearing the inscription "payment in full." If C endorses the check in the usual manner by signing her name on the back of it, she is—because of D's inscription—impliedly promising to free D of any balance. *This promise is binding on C* because D, the promisee-debtor, by making the payment again gave up his right to contend in court that the debt was only

---

[6] This discussion simply sketches out the basic distinction between illusory and requirements contracts. There are many cases, however, where the courts have difficulty determining whether the contract falls into one category or the other. This is due largely to the fact that the language is frequently vague—terms much less rigid than *require* or *need* are commonly used. As one illustration, the courts by no means agree as to the effect of contracts in which the buyer promises to purchase all goods that he or she "wants" over a specified period. Many feel that this creates a requirements contract; others do not. Thus questions of interpretation arise. And in determining the effect of such terms, an examination of the surrounding circumstances—which differ from case to case—is always relevant. For these reasons, particularly, the results of some cases unquestionably conflict with others (and the student of the law just has to make the best of it).

[7] Sec. 2-306 of the UCC implicitly adopts the general principles stated above in regard to requirements and output contracts. It also tries to limit certain abuses that have occasionally cropped up. For example, a seller under an output contract might take advantage of the buyer by increasing his or her productive capacity far beyond anything the buyer could have anticipated on entering the contract. (A similar hardship can exist in a requirements contract when the buyer's requirements skyrocket far above what was reasonably contemplated by the seller or when the buyer shuts down operations solely for the purpose of escaping liability on the contract.) Sec. 2-306(1) tries to prevent such abuses by providing: *"A term which measures the quantity by the output of the seller or the requirements of the buyer means such actual output or requirements as may occur in good faith, except that no quantity unreasonably disproportionate to any stated estimate or in the absence of a stated estimate to any normal or otherwise comparable prior output or requirements may be tendered or demanded."*

$100. This common-law rule of "accord and satisfaction" is favored because it promotes out-of-court settlements of disputes. On the other hand, it may be viewed as unfair to creditors.

Suppose that a creditor such as C in the previous example attempts to protect herself by crossing out D's words "in full satisfaction" and adding her own inscription, such as "under protest" or "without prejudice," indicating an intent to collect the remainder of the asserted debt. The general common-law rule has been that this action has no effect—the act of cashing the check implies an acceptance that overrides the words written on the check.[8] *However,* UCC Sec. 1-207 provides that "[a]party who with explicit reservation of rights . . . assents to performance in a manner demanded . . . by the other party does not thereby prejudice the rights reserved." Thus, some courts read Sec. 1-207 to allow C to cash D's check while reserving rights, and then to attempt recovery of the rest of the alleged debt.

Unfortunately, the courts of the various jurisdictions are greatly split as to Sec. 1-207's effect. Some believe that Sec. 1-207 changes the common law only as to the sale of goods. Others hold that it changes the common-law rule in any contract where a check is written. Still others conclude that Sec. 1-207 does not change the common law at all.

**Liquidated Debts:** In **liquidated debts,** those in which there is *no dispute* as to the amount of the indebtedness, compromise agreements are less frequently binding. For example: A is owed $150 by B. The two parties agree about the amount of the debt and about its due date of June 1. On June 2, A agrees to accept $120 as payment in full, and B pays that sum in cash. A thereafter brings suit to recover the balance of $30, and B contends that A is bound by the implied promise he made on June 2 to release him.

The common-law view here is that A's promise to release is *not binding, and he can therefore recover the balance of $30.* The reasoning is that the payment of $120 by B did not constitute a detriment to him, since it was less than what he admittedly owed. This rule is followed by the courts of most states even where the promise to release is in writing. (It should be noted, however, that a growing number of states have rejected the latter view by enacting statutes providing that all settlement agreements, *if in writing,* are binding upon the creditor even though consideration is absent. Typical of such statutes is Sec. 1541 of the California Civil Code, which reads as follows: "An obligation is extinguished by a release therefrom given to the debtor by the creditor upon a new consideration, or in writing, with or without new consideration.")

***Payment by Check:*** The common-law view discussed above, permitting further recovery by the creditor in the liquidated debt situation, is also applied by the courts of most states where the compromise payment is made by check rather than in cash. Suppose, for example, that in the above case, where the debt was clearly $150, B sent A a check for $120 with the words "payment in full," and that A cashed it after endorsing it in blank. Even though A did not qualify his endorsement, the common-law view is that the payment of the $120 by B does not constitute the giving of consideration by B, and thus A is not bound by the implied promise to release which he made by cashing the check. Accordingly, A is *permitted to recover the balance,* just as in the case where payment was made in cash.[9] (Once more, a note of caution. In states having the "written release" statute referred to above, the blank endorsement of the check by the creditor is often held to constitute a release "in writing." In such states a recovery by the creditor is thus barred.)

**Composition Agreements:** A different situation is presented when a debtor makes an agreement with two or more creditors, under the terms of which he or she agrees to pay each creditor who joins in the agreement a stated percentage of that person's claim, with the creditors agreeing in return to accept that percentage as full satisfaction of their claims. Such agreements, called **composition agreements** (or *creditors' composition agreements*), are ordinarily

---

[8] If the payee of a check does not notice the "in full satisfaction" language, many courts hold that the act of cashing the check cannot support an inference that the creditor assented to the compromise. This is important for companies that may mechanically process thousands of checks a day. Thus, one court held that no inference of accord arose when a creditor's mailroom deposited a conditional check according to internal procedures without the matter coming to the attention of an authorized representative of the creditor. *Slavenburg Corp. v. Kinli Corp.,* 36 U.C.C.Rep. 8 (E.D.Pa. 1983).

[9] Since the blank endorser under the general rule applicable to liquidated debts is permitted to recover the balance allegedly due, presumably the "under protest" endorser is similarly protected by the rule.

held to be binding on the participating creditors even though each of them receives a sum less than what was originally owed.

To illustrate: X owes Y $1,000 and Z $600. The three parties agree that X will pay each creditor 60 percent of the amount owed and that Y and Z will accept the 60 percent as payment in full. X then pays Y the $600 and Z the $360. If either Y or Z brings suit to recover an additional sum on the theory that his promise to release was not supported by X's payment of the lesser sum, the usual view is that the composition is binding; therefore, the creditor's suit will be dismissed. To reach this result, the courts of many states find consideration to be present in that the promise of each creditor to accept the smaller sum supports the promise of the other creditors to do likewise. Other courts reach the same result by simply ruling that such agreements are binding on the ground of public policy, without trying to find consideration.

## *Consideration and Moral Obligation*

The law's traditional approach to consideration emphasizes the bargain element. As a general rule, the *moral obligation* that results from making a promise is not sufficient to cause it to be enforceable. Neither are the motives or feelings of the promisor. Thus, an uncle's promise to pay $500 to his niece "in consideration of the love and affection that I have for you" is not binding. Nor is a promise made "in consideration of your many acts of kindness over the years." These acts (commonly referred to as acts of past consideration), having been performed earlier and, presumably, without expectation of payment, have not been bargained for. Thus, under the traditional approach they do not make a promise enforceable.

However, a trend exists in the law today to modify the traditional approach by allowing recovery to the extent of the moral obligation involved, that is, by enforcing a promise which was no more than what the promisor ought to have done. So, if a millionaire without close relatives promised a woman who had already rendered household services to him without compensation for 20 years that upon his death he would leave $25,000 to her, this promise would, in the eyes of some courts, be enforceable against his estate even if the value of her services was much less.[10]

Similarly, if after P permanently injured himself while saving D's life, D gratefully promised to pay P $15 every two weeks for the rest of P's life, some courts would enforce the promise.[11]

## SPECIAL SITUATIONS

Up to this point, we have emphasized the usual situations where the courts require consideration to be present in order for promises to be enforced. (Occasional references to minority views were made only for purposes of completeness.) In the remainder of this chapter, we will focus on three exceptional situations where promises can be enforced by the same courts when consideration clearly is not present. The three are promissory estoppel, promises to charitable institutions, and promises made after the statute of limitations has run.

### *Promissory Estoppel*

While it is well established that a promise to make a gift is generally unenforceable by the promisee even where he or she has performed some act in reliance upon the promise, unusual circumstances exist where the application of this view brings about results that are grossly unfair to the promisee. In such circumstances, the courts occasionally will invoke the doctrine of **promissory estoppel** (or "justifiable reliance" theory, as it is often called) to enforce the promise.

The basic idea underlying this doctrine is that if the promisor makes a promise under circumstances in which he or she should realize that the promisee is almost certainly going to react to the promise in a particular way, and if the promisee does so react, thereby causing a substantial change in his or her position, *the promisor is bound by the promise even though consideration is lacking on the part of the promisee.* To illustrate: Tenant T leases a building from Landlord L from January 1, 1985, to December 31, 1986. In early December, 1986, T indicates that he is thinking of remodeling the premises and wants a renewal of the lease for another two years. L replies, "We'll get to work on a new lease soon. I don't know about two years, but you can count on one year for sure." T then spends $500 over the next few weeks in having the first-floor rooms painted, but the parties

---

[10] *See Restatement, Contracts 2d.*, Section 86 (1979).

[11] *See Webb v. McGowin*, 168 So. 196 (Ala. App. 1935).

never execute a new lease. If L seeks to evict T in March 1987 on the ground that his promise to renew was not supported by consideration, he will probably be unsuccessful—that is, he will be held to his promise regarding the year 1987. In this case, where L should have realized the likelihood of T's conduct in consequence of his promise, L is said to be "estopped by his promise"; that is, he is barred by his promise from contending that the lack of consideration on T's part caused his promise to be unenforceable.

To illustrate further: "A has been employed by B for forty years. B promises to pay A a pension of $200 per month when A retires. A retires and forbears to work elsewhere for several years while B pays the pension. B's promise is binding."[12]

The following case presents yet another situation where resort to the estoppel doctrine seemed appropriate to the court.

[12]*Restatement, Contracts 2d,* The American Law Institute Section 90, 1973. (The text of Section 90 itself appears in the decision in the next case.)

## Hoffman v. Red Owl Stores, Inc.
Supreme Court of Wisconsin, 133 N.W.2d 267 (1965)

In 1960 Hoffman, plaintiff, hoped to establish a Red Owl franchised grocery store in Wautoma, Wisconsin. During that year he and the divisional manager of Red Owl, Lukowitz, had numerous conversations in which general plans for Hoffman's becoming a franchisee were discussed. Early in 1961 Lukowitz advised Hoffman to buy a small grocery in order to gain experience in the grocery business before operating a Red Owl franchise in a larger community.

Acting on this suggestion, Hoffman bought a small grocery in Wautoma. Three months later Red Owl representatives found that the store was operating at a profit, at which time Hoffman told Lukowitz that he could raise $18,000 to invest in a franchise. Lukowitz then advised Hoffman to sell the store, assuring him that the company would find a larger store for him to operate elsewhere—that he would "be operating a Red Owl store in a new location by fall."

Relying on this promise, Hoffman sold the grocery and soon thereafter bought a lot in Chilton, Wisconsin (a site which the company had selected for a new store), making a $1,000 down payment on the lot. Hoffman then rented a home for his family in Chilton and, after being assured by Lukowitz that "everything was all set," made a second $1,000 payment on the lot.

In September 1961 Lukowitz told Hoffman that the only "hitch" in the plan was that he (Hoffman) would have to sell a bakery building he owned in Wautoma and that the proceeds of that sale would have to make up a part of the $18,000 he was to invest, thereby reducing the amount he would have to borrow. Hoffman sold the building for $10,000, incurring a loss thereon of $2,000.

About this time, Red Owl prepared a "Proposed Financing for an Agency Store" plan that required Hoffman to invest $24,100 rather than the original $18,000. After Hoffman came up with $24,100, by virtue of several new loans, Red Owl told him that another $2,000 would be necessary.

Hoffman refused to go along with this demand, negotiations were terminated, and the new store was never built. When Hoffman and his wife brought suit to recover damages for breach of contract, Red Owl defended on the ground that its promises were not supported by consideration on Hoffman's part (in view of the facts that no formal financing plan was ever agreed to by Hoffman and no franchise agreement obligations were undertaken by him). Hoffman contended that liability should nonetheless be imposed on the basis of promissory estoppel; the trial court agreed, entering judgment in his favor. Red Owl appealed.

**Decision:** The judgment for Hoffman was affirmed. The purpose of the doctrine of promissory estoppel is to permit a promisee to enforce a promise (even though consideration is lacking on the promisee's part) if a substantial injustice would otherwise result. In this case several promises were made by the defendant company to Hoffman, the promisee, and in each instance he took definite and substantial actions on the basis of these promises. Specifically, these actions consisted of the sale of his grocery, the purchase of a lot in Chilton, the renting of a home in Chilton, and the sale of his bakery building. As a result of these actions, Hoffman would obviously suffer great injustice if he were not awarded damages from the defendant company based on its refusal to live up to the promises made to him. ∎

**Applications of Promissory Estoppel:** Promissory estoppel is a doctrine of increasing importance and broadening application. We discuss promissory estoppel in this chapter because it is most commonly thought of as a method of enforcing a variety of promises that lack consideration. However, many courts invoke promissory estoppel in a variety of situations where they believe that contractual formalities are unnecessarily blocking attainment of the reasonable intentions and expectations of the parties. Consideration is one such formality; the requirement that some contracts be in writing in order to be enforceable is another. When the writing requirement is discussed in Chapter 16, we will see how promissory estoppel often provides an alternative means of enforcing oral promises that the parties intended to be enforceable, but did not put in writing.

Promissory estoppel doctrine is not completely consistent from jurisdiction to jurisdiction, but typical examples of the wide variety of uses of promissory estoppel include:

- X worries about floods and asks his insurance company whether his current policy protects his house from flood damage, indicating that he will procure a different policy if it does not. The company assures X that his current policy does cover flood damage. After X's house is damaged by a flood, examination of the policy clearly indicates that flood damage is excluded. The insurance company refuses to pay. Many courts would allow X to enforce the company's promise on grounds of promissory estoppel.[13]

- P interviews for a job with D Co., telling D that he has a good job with X Co. but would quit there if D offered him a job. D offers P a job, realizing that he will now resign his job with X. When P reports for work, D tells him that it no longer needs him and points out that his employment was "at-will" anyway (so that D is within its rights to terminate P at any time). Many courts would allow P to recover from D on promissory estoppel grounds.[14]

- Just before L, a general contractor, submits a bid on a construction project, M, a paving subcontractor, calls L and submits an $8,000 bid for the paving work. This is the lowest paving bid, so L reduces his overall bid, submits the bid, and is awarded the contract. Before L can inform M of the bid's success, M calls L to revoke its $8,000 offer, refusing to do the work for less than $15,000. M argues that it revoked its offer before L accepted it and that as of the time of revocation there was nothing to indicate to M that it had a contract it could enforce against L. Many courts would bind M to its promise through the doctrine of promissory estoppel.[15]

## Formal Promises to Charitable Institutions

The law generally looks favorably upon charitable institutions, such as churches, hospitals, and colleges. One result of this policy is that many courts enforce formal promises (e.g., charitable subscriptions) to make gifts to such institutions, even though technically there is no conventional consideration. Among the approaches that courts use to enforce promises to make such gifts are (1) invention of consideration, by finding that each donor's promise is made in consideration of the promises of the other donors (i.e., a donor's promise is supported by the detriment incurred by other donors who made similar promises); (2) promissory estoppel, by finding that donors should foresee that the donee institution will rely on the promised gift, for example, by drawing up plans and beginning construction; and (3) where all else fails, many courts will simply enforce the promise on grounds of public policy.

## Promises Made Subsequent to the Running of a Statute of Limitations

All states have **statutes of limitations** limiting the time a creditor has in which to bring suit against the debtor after the debt becomes due.[16] If the specified period of time elapses without the initiation of legal proceedings by the creditor, the statute is said to have "run." While the running of a statute does not extinguish the debt, it does cause the contract to be

---

[13] *See Travelers Indemnity Co. v. Holman,* 330 F.2d 142 (5th Cir. 1964).

[14] *See Roberts v. Geosource Drilling Co.,* 757 S.W.2d 48 (Tex.App. 1988).

[15] *See Drennan v. Star Paving Co.,* 333 P.2d 757 (Cal. 1958).

[16] These periods of time vary widely among the states, and there is no typical statute. As a general illustration, however, some states give the creditor three years on an oral contract and six years on a written one.

unenforceable—that is, it prevents the creditor from successfully maintaining an action in court to collect the debt.

**New Promise to Pay:** To what extent is the situation altered if the debtor, after the statute has run, makes a new promise to pay the debt? One might conclude that such a promise is unenforceable, since there is clearly no consideration given by the creditor in return. This, however, is not the case. *In all states, either by statute or by judicial decision, such a promise, if in writing, is enforceable despite the absence of consideration.*[17] In such a case, the debt is said to have been "revived," and the creditor now has a new statutory period in which to bring suit. (If the new promise was to pay only a portion of the original indebtedness, such as $200 of a $450 debt, the promise is binding only to the extent of that portion—in this case, $200.)

**Part Payment or Acknowledgment:** The debt is also revived if a part payment is made by the debtor after the statute has run. If, for example, a five-year statute had run on a $1,000 debt, and the debtor thereafter mailed a check for $50 to the creditor, the creditor now has an additional five years in which to commence legal action for the balance. A mere acknowledgment by the debtor that the debt exists will also revive the obligation to pay.

Imposition of liability in the above instances is based on the theory that the debtor has, by making the part payment or acknowledgment, *impliedly promised* to pay the remaining indebtedness. The debtor can escape the operation of this rule by advising the creditor, when making the payment or acknowledgment, that he or she *is not* making any promise as to payment of the balance.

## SUMMARY

As a general rule, a party is not bound by his or her promises unless "consideration" is present. If a defendant in a breach of contract suit claims there was no consideration for the promise he has refused to perform, courts will often ask three questions. First, did the promisee (plaintiff) incur a legal detriment by doing (or promising to do) something that he was not bound to do or by forgoing (or agreeing to forgo) something that he had the right to do? Second, did the promise that has been breached induce the promisee's detriment? Third, did the promisee's detriment induce the defendant's promise? If the answer to all three questions is "yes," as it almost always is in the commercial setting, consideration is present.

Note, however, that under the preexisting duty rule, the promisee generally suffers no detriment by merely promising to do something that he or she is already bound to do, either by statute or by contractual obligation. There are, however, several exceptions to this rule. Most importantly, the UCC allows modifications of contracts to be binding without consideration. (If the contract is for more than $500 either before or after the modification, the modification must be in writing.)

Applying the common-law rules to debt settlement agreements, a distinction is made between unliquidated and liquidated debts. If a debt is unliquidated (i.e., there is a genuine dispute as to the amount of debt), the acceptance by the creditor of the debtor's payment (under circumstances indicating it to be full payment) is binding upon the creditor. In such case, the creditor's express or implied promise to release is supported by consideration on the part of the debtor: the debtor's waiving of his or her right to contest the creditor's claim in court. If the debt is liquidated, however, the payment of a lesser sum than admittedly owing is not consideration, and thus the creditor is not bound by his or her promise to release. (In some states, however, the common-law rules have been modified by statute.)

In limited situations the courts have dispensed with the consideration requirement. The most common of these are situations where (1) the promisee has justifiably relied on the promisor's promise, resulting in the promisor being held liable under the doctrine of promissory estoppel; (2) the promise is made to a charitable institution; and (3) a debtor, after the statute of limitations has run, makes a new promise to pay his or her debt.

## KEY TERMS

**Consideration**
**Sealed contract**
**Legal detriment**

---

[17] This rule on the enforceability of promises to pay debts barred by the running of the statute of limitations was, at one time, generally applied to promises to repay debts that were made by debtors after they had gone through *bankruptcy proceedings*. However, under the federal Bankruptcy Reform Act of 1978, effective October 1, 1979, this is no longer true. Thus, today such a promise to repay a debt is not binding unless supported by consideration.

Preexisting obligation rule
Modification contract
Unforeseen difficulties rule
Adequacy of consideration
Mutuality of obligation
Illusory contract
Requirements contract
Output contract
Unliquidated debt
Liquidated debt
Composition agreement
Promissory estoppel
Statute of limitations

## QUESTIONS AND PROBLEMS

1. Dr. Browning made a contract with Dr. Johnson, under which he was to sell his practice and equipment to Johnson for a specified price. Before the time for performance, Browning changed his mind and asked Johnson to relieve him of his obligation to sell. Thereafter a new contract was made, under the terms of which Browning promised to pay Johnson $40,000 in return for Johnson's cancellation of the first contract. Later Browning refused to pay the $40,000, contending that this promise of his was not supported by consideration on Johnson's part. Is Browning correct? If not, where is the consideration on Johnson's part? (*Browning v. Johnson,* 422 P.2d 319, 1967.)

2. Hilda and Louis saw a movie, ate at a restaurant, and then had sexual intercourse in the back of Louis's car. Hilda later told Louis that she was pregnant and he was the father. He agreed to pay medical expenses and child support until the child reached the age of 21 if Hilda would promise not to institute bastardy proceedings against him. She agreed. After the child was born, blood tests proved that Louis was not the father, even though it appears that Hilda had believed in good faith that he was. Louis stopped making the child support payments. Hilda sued to enforce his promise. In defense, Louis claimed lack of consideration to support his promise. Is he correct? (*Fiege v. Boehm,* 123 A.2d 316, Md. 1956.)

3. Vinson agreed to do a certain construction job for Leggett, the owner, for $3,950. After work was commenced, Vinson found out that he was going to lose money on the job. Leggett examined Vinson's bills for materials to date and said, "Go ahead and complete the work like we said and I will pay you an additional $1,000." Vinson then completed the job. Is Leggett bound by his promise? Explain. (*Leggett v. Vinson,* 124 So. 427, 1929.)

4. Collins Corporation applied for a loan with the Gwinnett Bank. The bank was willing to loan the money to Collins, but only if its president, Sue, would agree to guarantee the loan in her individual capacity. She did so and the loan was made. When Collins Corp. failed to repay the loan, the bank sued Sue. She raised lack of consideration as a defense, arguing that because the loan went to the corporation, she received no benefit from the transaction. Is this a good defense? (*Collins v. Gwinnett Bank & Trust Co.,* 255 S.E.2d 122, Ga. 1979.)

5. A Pontiac dealer sold a new car to Knoebel under a contract that obligated him to make specified monthly payments. When Knoebel fell behind in his payments, the dealer repossessed the car, which he had a right to do. On July 26 the dealer told Knoebel that if he would pay off the amount then due ($498.99) by August 10, he—the dealer—would return the car to him at that time. On August 7 Knoebel went to the dealer with the money, but the dealer had sold the car to a third party. When Knoebel sued the dealer for damages for breach of contract (for failure to hold the car for him), the dealer argued that his promise to hold the car was not supported by consideration on Knoebel's part. Is this argument correct? Why or why not? (*Knoebel v. Chief Pontiac, Inc.,* 294 P.2d 625, 1956.)

6. Brian Construction hired Brighenti to perform "All Excavation, Grading, Site Work, Asphalt Pavement, Landscaping, and Concrete work" and "everything requisite and necessary to finish the entire work properly" at a construction site for $104,326. Before the contract was signed, Brian did test borings in the excavation area, finding nothing unusual. Brighenti relied on these borings in signing the contract, but they turned out to be very misleading. When Brighenti began excavation, he found that an old factory had been located on the site and Brighenti would have to remove concrete foundation walls, slab floors, twisted metals and other debris instead of just dirt. Upon this discovery, Brian agreed to pay Brighenti his costs of removing the material plus 10 percent. Brighenti agreed, but later refused to perform the work. Brian had the work done by someone else, then sued for breach of the second agreement. Brighenti claimed that the second agreement was unenforceable for a lack of consideration under the preexisting obligation rule since he was simply agreeing to perform work that he was already under contract to do. Is this a good defense? (*Brian Construction & Development Co. v. Brighenti,* 405 A.2d 72, Conn. 1978.)

7. Walquist was struck by a car driven by Christensen. The parties were in dispute as to whether or not the accident was Christensen's fault; they were also in disagreement as to the extent of Walquist's injuries. In this setting, they made an agreement: Christensen paid Walquist $500, and Walquist in turn released him from all liability. Later, when it turned out that Walquist's doctor bills alone came to $700, he sued Christensen to recover an additional sum. Christensen used the settlement agreement as a defense, but Walquist contended that Christensen's payment of $500 was not a sufficient consideration to support his promise to release, in view of the facts that his damages

were, in actuality, considerably greater than $500. Is Walquist right? Why or why not?

**8.** Mrs. Harmon was a long-time employee of the FoxLane Company. Her son's illness had caused her to consider retiring, but she was not sure she was financially able to do so. The president of the company told her, "Marie, I have tried to work something out for you. While I hope you can stay with us for two more years, I want you to know that upon your retirement—whenever it occurs—the company will pay you your present salary as long as you live." Two months later she retired, and the company made several monthly payments. When it then stopped the payments, she sued it for damages. The company contended that its promise was not supported by consideration on her part (i.e., the company did *not* say "Retire now and we will pay.") Was there consideration on Mrs. Harmon's part? If not, is there any principle under which she might recover? Explain.

**9.** In a dispute arising out of a contract to repair a leaking roof on debtor's building, debtor sent a "full payment" check for $500. The creditor payee indorsed the check below its notation, "Under Protest" and deposited the money into its account. Later, creditor sued debtor for $580 allegedly still due. If creditor can prove that $1,080 was the true amount of the debt, can creditor recover? (*Horn Waterproofing Corp. v. Bushwick Iron and Steel Co.,* 488 N.E.2d 56, N.Y. 1985.)

**10.** Fretz contracted to construct an office building for Stutts. However, when Stutts could not find financing, the contract was cancelled. A year later Stutts incorporated Aqua-Con, and it received a loan from Southern National Bank to build the building. Stutts again tried to hire Fretz as the builder, but Fretz was worried about being paid. He contacted the Bank, whose officer told him that two million dollars of the loan would not be paid to Stutts but would be held in reserve to insure payment to Fretz. Fretz then agreed to build the building, but when he finished and submitted his final bill of $275,000, he was paid only $50,000 which was all that was left of the loan. Fretz sued the bank for breaching its promise. The bank defended, arguing that its loan was to Aqua-Con and no consideration supported its promise to Fretz. Is this a good defense? (*Fretz Construction Co. v. Southern National Bank,* 626 S.W.2d 478, Tex. 1982.)

# CHAPTER 14

# ILLEGALITY

The third element of a contract is *legality of purpose*—the attainment of an objective that is not prohibited by state or federal law. In this chapter we will examine some of the most common kinds of contracts that are ordinarily illegal under state law.[1] Within a given state, a contract is illegal because it is either (1) contrary to that state's statutes (including the regulations of its administrative agencies) or (2) contrary to the public policy of that state, as defined by its courts.

All states have criminal statutes (many of which, as we saw in Chapter 7, are directed towards various kinds of misconduct in the business world). Such statutes not only prohibit certain acts but, additionally, provide for the imposition of fines or imprisonment on persons who violate them. Any contract calling for the commission of a crime is clearly illegal. Many other statutes simply prohibit the performance of specified acts without imposing criminal penalties for violations. Contracts that call for the performance of these acts are also illegal. (An example of the latter is lending money under an agreement that obligates the borrower to pay interest at a rate in excess of that permitted by statute.)

Still other contracts are illegal simply because they call for the performance of an act that the courts feel has an adverse effect on the general public. (Examples of contracts contrary to public policy are those under which a person promises never to get married or never to engage in a certain profession.)

As a general rule, contracts that are illegal on either statutory or public policy grounds are void. This means that (1) in cases where the contract is entirely executory, neither party is bound by the agreement, and (2) in cases where one of the parties has performed his or her part of the bargain, such party cannot recover the consideration, or the value of the consideration, that has passed to the other party. (Exceptions to this general rule will be discussed later in the chapter.) Furthermore, courts will not allow even quasi-contractual recovery where illegal action is involved. By denying recovery to the parties to an illegal transaction, courts reason that they will deter illegal activity.

## CONTRACTS CONTRARY TO STATUTE

### Wagering Agreements

All states have statutes relating to **wagering agreements,** or gambling contracts. Under the general language of most of these statutes, making bets and operating games of chance are prohibited. Any obligations arising from these activities are *void* (nonexistent) in the eyes of the law, and thus completely unenforceable by the "winner."

**Bets and Lotteries:** In most instances wagering agreements are easily recognized. Simple bets on the outcome of athletic events and lotteries such as bingo (when played for money) are the most common of them. On the other hand, merchants holding promotional schemes such as supermarket drawings sometimes have difficulty determining if they are holding an illegal **lottery,** especially because definitions vary widely from state to state. Courts tend to rule that a scheme that does not require a purchase of goods by the participant is not a lottery because consideration (which most courts view as an essential part of a lottery) is lacking. That is why so many contests state "no purchase necessary." The following case illustrates a common approach to the lottery issue.

---

[1] Certain federal statutes that have a bearing on the legality of contracts in interstate commerce will be covered in Part VII.

215

## Pepsi-Cola Bottling Co. of Luverne v. Coca-Cola Bottling Co., Andalusia

Supreme Court of Alabama,
534 So.2d 295 (1988)

Coca-Cola Bottling of Andalusia and Alabama Citizens Action Program sued, claiming that Pepsi-Cola Bottling Company of Luverne had violated a 1982 court order which permanently enjoined Coke and Pepsi "from operation of promotional campaigns whereby consumers of soft drink beverages are participants in 'under the crown' or 'on the tab' games of chance for which a purchase is necessary in all instances *except for the right to obtain free crowns, tabs, or chances at some place other than the point of purchase of the beverage.*" The injunction order found that a 1981 "Pepsi Spirit" campaign in which participants could win cash and "NFL Prizes" (football jerseys and gift certificates) was an illegal *lottery* that violated the Alabama Constitution. The court found that other than by buying the soft drink, the only way to participate was to request free bottle tops by mail or to visit the Pepsi bottling plant. Only 60 people had done so, and the trial court declared the free participation option to be a sham.

At issue in this case is Pepsi's 1987 "Instant Cash" promotion, in which certain caps were marked $0.25, $1.00, or $100.00, and others were marked with the letters needed to spell "Pepsi Instant Cash" (which could be worth $10,000 to a person with caps containing all the letters). For this campaign, Pepsi distributed 25,000 cards with a similar opportunity at participating stores, and advertised by means of store displays and radio that no purchase was required. Cards could also be obtained by telephone request and by writing the bottling plant.

The trial court found that Pepsi's "Instant Cash" promotion was a lottery that placed Pepsi in contempt of the 1982 injunction. Pepsi appealed.

**Decision:** Reversed. The three elements of a lottery are (1) a prize, (2) awarded by chance, and (3) for a consideration. The first two elements were present here, but not the third. The game was not a lottery because participants were not required to purchase anything in order to play. Unlike its 1981 promotion, here Pepsi provided ample opportunity for people to participate in the promotion without buying anything. People could obtain free cards at stores or could write to Pepsi to obtain them. Less than one month after the promotion began, 25,000 free cards had been distributed and 252 winning cards had been redeemed. By remedying the flaws of the 1981 promotion, Pepsi had complied in good faith with the injunction and was not operating an illegal lottery under Alabama law. ∎

---

In recent years a growing number of state statutes have been liberalized to permit wagering and lottery activities within narrow limits. For example, so-called "friendly bets"—those defined as not producing substantial sources of income—are frequently exempted from the basic wagering statutes, as are some lotteries operated by religious or charitable organizations. Additionally, a few states have sanctioned state-operated lotteries by special statutes.

**Insurance Contracts:** Many contracts whose performance is dependent upon an element of chance are clearly not wagers. This is particularly true of **risk-shifting contracts** (as distinguished from **risk-creating contracts**). If a person insures a home against loss by fire, for example, the contract is perfectly legal even though it is not known at the time the policy is issued whether the insurer will have liability under it. The contract is legal despite this uncertainty because the owner had an "insurable interest" in the home prior to taking out the policy—that is, a financial loss would have resulted if a fire had occurred. Thus an insurance policy is simply a contract by which an existing risk is shifted to an insurance company for a consideration paid by the owner. By contrast, an insurance policy on a building which the insured does not own and in which he or she has no other financial interest is clearly a wager and is unenforceable.

## Licensing Statutes

All states have **licensing statutes,** requiring that persons who engage in certain professions, trades, or businesses be licensed. Lawyers, physicians, real estate brokers, contractors, electricians, and vendors of milk and liquor are but a few examples of persons commonly subject to a wide variety of such statutes. In many instances, particularly those involving the professions, passing a comprehensive examination (along with proof of good moral character) is a condition of obtaining a license. In others, only proof of good moral character may be required.

To find out whether an unlicensed person can recover for services rendered under a contract, one must check the particular statute involved. Some licensing statutes expressly provide that recovery by unlicensed persons shall not be allowed (no matter how competent their work).[2] Others, however, are silent on the matter, in which case their underlying purposes must be determined. Most courts take the view in such instances that if the statute is *regulatory*—its purpose being the protection of the general public against unqualified persons—then the contract is illegal and recovery is denied. On the other hand, if the statute is felt to be merely *revenue-raising*, recovery is allowed.

The reasoning behind this distinction, of course, is that allowing recovery of a fee or commission by an unlicensed person in the first category would adversely affect public health and safety, while the enforcement of contracts in the second category does not have this result. Thus an unlicensed milk vendor who has sold and delivered a quantity of milk will ordinarily not be permitted to recover the purchase price from the buyer. Similarly, an unlicensed physician, real estate agent, or attorney will be denied his or her fee. On the other hand, a corporation that has merely failed to obtain a license to do business in a particular city is still permitted to enforce its contracts, because city licensing ordinances applicable to corporations are normally enacted for revenue-raising purposes.

The possibility that a regulatory statute might be passed for the protection of some persons, but not others, is presented in the case below.

---

[2] A provision that contracts made in violation of the statute shall be "void" usually, though not always, has this effect.

---

### Bremmeyer v. Peter Kiewit Sons Company
Supreme Court of Washington,
585 P.2d 1174 (1978)

The State of Washington awarded Peter Kiewit a prime contract to construct several miles of Interstate 90. The highway right-of-way was overgrown, and needed to have the trees and debris cleared before construction could begin. For this purpose, Peter Kiewit subcontracted the necessary clearing operation to Bremmeyer. Under the subcontract, Bremmeyer agreed to pay Peter Kiewit $35,000 for the right to fall, yard, buck, load and haul to a mill all the merchantable timber within the right-of-way. (Bremmeyer was to keep the proceeds of the sale of the timber as his compensation.)

Bremmeyer paid the $35,000 and began clearing the right-of-way, but before he had finished the job the state terminated Peter Kiewit's prime contract. Peter Kiewit, in turn, cancelled Bremmeyer's subcontract. Peter Kiewit received $1,729,050 from the state for "cancellation costs," but offered to pay Bremmeyer only $38 for cancellation of the contract. Bremmeyer refused the $38 and brought this action to recover the value of the merchantable timber that was still uncut at the time of termination.

In defense, Peter Kiewit's primary argument was that a state statute, RCW 18.27, required contractors to be registered with the state, and that Bremmeyer's failure to register barred his recovery. The trial court, citing a 1973 Washington State case, agreed with this contention and summarily dismissed the action. Bremmeyer appealed.

---

**Decision:** Bremmeyer was entitled to maintain this suit even though he was not registered with the state. The 1973 case was no longer controlling for two reasons. First, there were strong dissenting opinions when it was decided in the court, and it should be reviewed for that reason alone. More important, after the 1973 case was decided the Washington state legislature amended RCW 18.27 by adding this section:

It is the purpose of this chapter to afford protection *to the public* from unreliable, fraudulent, financially irresponsible, or incompetent contractors. [Emphasis supplied by the court.]

It is thus clear that the purpose of the statute was to provide protection to members of the *general public* against suits by unregistered contractors, rather than to provide protection to *prime contractors* (such as Peter Kiewit) against suits by unregistered subcontractors. The judgment of the lower court was, therefore, reversed and the case remanded to it for further proceedings.

## Sunday Contracts

Although the trend across the states is to eliminate or minimize the coverage of **Sunday statutes,** several jurisdictions still have some form of law prohibiting certain business transactions on Sunday. Often called "blue laws" (named for the color of paper they were originally printed on), these laws declare void and unenforceable certain contracts entered into on Sunday. Some laws forbid carrying on "all secular labor and business on the Sabbath," thus rendering void virtually all contracts made on a Sunday. Other laws are similar, but riddled with exceptions. Still others merely prohibit the sale of certain kinds of goods on Sunday. Such laws are disappearing, but a merchant moving into a new state should carefully check that jurisdiction's law.

## Usury

Partly as a result of religious views going back to early biblical statements, and partly because of the practical hardships resulting from high interest rates charged desperate borrowers, all states have statutes establishing the maximum rate of interest that can be charged on ordinary loans. Charging interest in excess of the permitted rate constitutes **usury.**

The interest ceilings that are imposed by the usury statutes vary from state to state. Traditionally the basic statutes have varied from 6 percent to 12 percent per annum. However, as a result of inflationary pressures in recent years, the basic statutes now generally range from 10 percent to 16 percent per annum.

More important, many kinds of loans are not governed by the basic state statutes. For example, most states put no limit on the rate of interest that can be charged on loans made to corporations. And, under federal regulations, national banks are permitted to charge interest rates that are usually in excess of those permitted by the state usury laws.

Additionally, all states in recent years—again, partly because of inflationary pressures—have adopted special statutes permitting higher rates of interest on other specified kinds of loans. For example, most state laws today provide that interest rates charged by issuers of bank credit cards (such as Visa and MasterCard), and by department stores on their revolving credit accounts, can be at an annual percentage rate of 18 percent. Similarly, home purchase and construction loans, car loans, and loans by credit unions may generally carry annual interest rates ranging from 18 to 25 percent.[3]

The basic statutes also vary widely insofar as the effect of usury is concerned. Many states permit the usurious lender to recover the principal and interest at the lawful rate, but not the excess interest. In such states the lender suffers no penalty. In others, the lender is permitted to recover the principal only, forfeiting all interest. And in three or four states, the lender forfeits both interest and principal.

It is thus clear that no determination can be made as to the legality or effect of a given loan without inspecting the statutes of the state in which the transaction took place.

# CONTRACTS CONTRARY TO PUBLIC POLICY

## Contracts in Restraint of Trade

Many contracts that unreasonably restrain trade or competition in interstate commerce are in violation of one or more federal statutes, such as the Sherman and Clayton acts.[4] Long before the enactment of these statutes, however, many other contracts in restraint of trade were illegal under the common law of the various states, and this continues to be the case today. Thus a contract that is not subject to the Sherman or Clayton acts may still result in such restraint of trade that courts will set it aside under common-law principles. These principles are briefly summarized here.

Contracts that contain **restrictive covenants**—promises by one party not to engage in a particular occupation or to operate a certain kind of business—compose one group of contracts that are in restraint of trade. However, such promises (sometimes called *covenants not to compete*) are not necessarily illegal.

Generally, covenants not to compete are lawful if two conditions are met. First, the covenant must be of an "ancillary" nature, and second, the restric-

---

[3] It should also be noted that most states have adopted special statutes that expressly permit small loan companies, such as "personal loan companies," to charge rates of interest that are considerably higher than those of the general interest statutes. For example, a loan company that qualifies under such statutes may be allowed to charge interest at the rate of 3 percent *per month* on the first $150 of a loan, 2 percent per month on the amount from $151 to $300, and 1 percent on the balance. These statutes usually provide that if interest is charged in excess of the specified rates, the loan is void. In such a case, neither principal nor interest can be recovered.

[4] These acts, and other federal statutes of a similar nature, are examined in Part VII.

tion (the covenant) must be reasonable under the circumstances.

**The Ancillary Requirement:** An **ancillary covenant** is one that is a subsidiary or auxiliary part of a larger agreement. A common example of an ancillary covenant is that found in a contract calling for the *sale of a business,* where the contract contains a promise by the seller of the business not to engage in the same type of business within a prescribed geographical area for a certain length of time after the sale. Equally common are covenants in *employment contracts,* under which the employee promises not to compete with the business of his or her employer for a specified period of time after the employment is terminated. (Nonancillary promises, on the other hand, stand alone; they do *not* protect any existing, legally recognized interest such as that in the prior examples. These covenants—such as a promise by a father to pay $10,000 for the son's promise not to engage in medical practice—are generally considered to be an unreasonable restraint of trade in all circumstances, and thus illegal and unenforceable on public policy grounds.)

**Reasonableness—Sale of Business Contracts:** When a business is being sold, the interest to be protected relates to the goodwill of the business. A restrictive covenant on the part of the seller, in a particular case, is thus enforceable if its space and time limitations are no broader than are reasonably necessary to afford such protection. For example, a promise by the seller of a retail grocery in Kalispell, Montana, that he will not engage in the retail grocery business "within the City of Kalispell for the period of one year after the sale" is probably reasonable and thus lawful. Similarly, in *Gann v. Morris,* 596 P.2d 43 (1979), a promise by the seller of a silk-screening business in Tucson, Arizona, that he would not operate a competing business within a hundred-mile radius of Tucson for a specified period of time was held to be reasonable in view of the fact that at least one of the business's customers was located that distance away. Thus, in the above instances, if the seller should violate his or her promise, the purchaser of the business is entitled to an injunction against him or her. (On the other hand, if the restraint is found to be excessive—as would be the case if the seller of the grocery in Kalispell was prohibited from engaging in the grocery business "anywhere within the state of Montana" for one year—the restraint is illegal, and thus unenforceable by the buyer.)

**Reasonableness—Employment Contracts:** Restrictive covenants in employment contracts are reasonable (1) if the restriction is reasonably necessary to protect the employer, and (2) if the restriction is "not unreasonably excessive" as to the employee. Because of this second requirement, **geographical restraints** in employment contracts are more likely to be set aside by the courts than those in contracts where businesses are being sold. In other words, because such restraints may operate with particular harshness upon the employee insofar as his or her ability to make a living is concerned, they are scrutinized with particular care.[5] The following case is illustrative of this approach by the courts.

---

[5] In contrast to geographical restraints are those covenants under which the employee promises not "to contact or deal with persons who are customers of the employer at the time the employment relationship is terminated" for a stated period of time. Where the time period is found to be reasonable, these kinds of covenants are more likely to be enforced.

---

**Bryceland v. Northey**
Court of Appeals of Arizona,
772 P.2d 36 (1989)

Bryceland, doing business as Johnny B's Disc Jockey Express, is in the mobile disc jockey business, providing recorded entertainment played by a "deejay" at parties, weddings, dances, and similar functions. He has numerous competitors in the Phoenix area.

Northey and Malvin applied to become deejays for Bryceland in 1985 and 1986, respectively. They received both classroom training and on-the-job help from Bryceland. After completing their training, they signed contracts in which they promised not to compete with Johnny B's for a period of two years within a 50-mile radius of Phoenix and such other areas where they might have performed.

In February 1987, Malvin and Northey both went to work for another mobile disc jockey service owned by Northey's father. Bryceland sued to enforce the covenant not to compete. The trial judge held for Bryceland on this issue, ordering de-

*(continued)*

fendants not to compete within a 50-mile radius of Phoenix for two years. Northey and Malvin appealed.

**Decision:** Reversed. Restrictive covenants in employment contracts are disfavored and construed against the employer, who has the burden to prove the extent of its protectable interest. Defendants received no trade secrets here. They did receive training, but a covenant not to compete should not be used to prevent a former employee from using the skills and talents he learned on the job. An employer does have a protectable interest in maintaining customer relationships when an employee leaves, but the law guards this interest only for as long as is needed to replace the employee and to give the replacement a chance to show that he or she can do the job . . . usually a relatively short amount of time. The two-year period at issue here is too long. Additionally, the covenant not to compete protects against employment by any *potential* customer or client, going beyond plaintiff's legitimate interest in preventing defendants from taking away customers they met while working for plaintiff. The clause is overly broad and therefore unenforceable. ■

---

**Will the Courts Rewrite the Contract?** The Arizona court in the previous case found that the unreasonably broad time restriction rendered the restrictive covenant completely unenforceable. The modern trend, however, is use of the "blue pencil" rule. Under this approach, courts finding that a contract's restrictions on competition serve an employer's legitimate interests but are unreasonably broad (either in terms of geography or time), will simply rewrite the covenant so that the restrictions are reasonable in scope and then will enforce them to that extent. Thus, a promise not to compete in the entire state of New York for three years might be rewritten to cover only a few counties in New York (where the promisor had worked) for one year.

## *Exculpatory Clauses*

The law of torts imposes certain duties on all persons, one of which is to carry out one's activities in a reasonably careful manner. If a person violates this duty by performing an act carelessly, he or she is guilty of the tort of negligence and is answerable in damages to anyone who was injured thereby.

Businesspersons, and others, often try to avoid this potential liability through the use of **exculpatory clauses** that purport to excuse them from liability resulting from their own negligence. Such clauses are generally—though not always—held to be contrary to public policy, and thus *unenforceable* against the injured party.[6]

[6]Some exculpatory clauses do *not* attempt to free a party from his or her negligence, but only from liability for injury caused by circumstances ouside his or her control; this kind of clause, not contravening public policy, is ordinarily lawful and binding. One example: a school district's form requiring parental permission for a student's attendance at a field day might provide "The district shall have no liability for injuries arising out of transportation of student to and from said location, other than those directly resulting from negligence of district-employed drivers."

**The Public Interest Inquiry:** The legality of the exculpatory clause depends almost entirely upon the relative strength of the bargaining powers of the contracting parties. Where the party utilizing the clause has *vastly superior bargaining power* over the other, the clause is clearly void. Such disparity is normally found only in those contracts that "substantially affect the public interest"—in other words, in contracts of parties who furnish goods or services that are routinely used by companies and individuals in the carrying on of their everyday business or personal activities. Several examples are listed in this chapter's next major case, *DeVito v. N.Y.U. College of Dentistry,* which addresses the question of whether the medical profession should be allowed to avoid liability for negligence by use of such clauses.

An early landmark case is instructive on the public policy aspects of exculpatory clauses.[7] A brakeman was hired by a railroad only after he promised not to sue the company for any injuries that resulted from the company's negligence. When the company raised the clause as a defense in a negligence suit filed by the brakeman's family after his death in an accident caused by a defective switch, the court stated that parties' contracts are normally enforceable as written. However, parties to contracts are not allowed to make agreements that violate express provisions of the law or injuriously affect public policy. If such clauses as that signed in this case were enforced, the court stated:

> [t]he consequence would be that every railroad company, and every owner of a factory, mill, or mine, would make it a condition precedent to the employment of labor, that the laborer should

[7]*Little Rock & Fort Smith Ry. Co. v. Eubanks,* 3 S.W. 808 (1886).

release all right for injuries sustained in the course of the service, whether by the employer's negligence or otherwise. The natural tendency of this would be to relax the employer's carefulness in those matters of which he has the ordering and control, such as the supplying of machinery and materials, and thus increase the perils of occupations which are hazardous even when well managed. And the final outcome would be to fill the country with disabled men and paupers whose support would become a charge upon the counties or upon public charity.

The recent trend has been to enforce exculpatory clauses where they involve only recreational activities, such as where people go rafting, sky-diving, or horseback riding. In such cases the courts are much more likely to give effect to an exculpatory clause than where the consumer is attempting to purchase needed services or to gain housing or employment.

In order to be given effect, even exculpatory clauses that are not declared outright to be against public policy because of the nature of the transaction must be (1) effectively called to the attention of the potential plaintiff, and (2) clearly written. An exculpatory clause buried in the fine print of a lengthy form-contract is unlikely to be given effect because the person against whom it is to operate probably will not notice it. Furthermore, even clauses that are carefully called to the potential plaintiff's attention will operate only to avoid the types of liability that they explicitly and clearly spell out. Any ambiguity in such a clause is construed against its drafter. The *DeVito* case also addresses this issue.

Finally, keep in mind that exculpatory clauses at best can relieve defendants of liability for simple negligence. Clauses that attempt to avoid liability for acts of intentional wrongdoing or even gross negligence are not enforceable.

---

**DeVito v. N.Y.U. College of Dentistry**
Supreme Court, New York County,
544 N.Y.S.2d 109 (1989)

**Plaintiff was injured. He sued NYU claiming negligence. Defendant moved for summary judgment based on the release. After noting that the New York courts have not always agreed on the effect of such releases, the trial judge entered the opinion summarized here.**

**Defendant New York University College of Dentistry (NYU) operates a dental clinic where, in exchange for reduced fees, patients agree to be treated by students working under faculty supervision. Plaintiff DeVito was treated at the clinic after signing a release which stated: "In consideration of the reduced rates given to me by New York University, I hereby release and agree to save harmless New York University, its doctors, and students, from any and all liability arising out of, or in connection with, any injuries or damages which I may sustain while on its premises, or as a result of any treatment in its infirmaries."**

**Decision:** Motion denied. Exculpatory clauses will generally not be enforced when the parties have a special relationship that makes enforcement of the clause against the public interest. This occurs where the party seeking exculpation is in a business or profession which is either publicly regulated or providing an essential service. The medical and dental profession should be included in that category. Additionally, the terms of an enforceable exculpatory clause must be very clear, explicit, and unambiguous. Open-ended terms like "any and all claims," such as those used here, are often simply disregarded. ∎

---

**Bailment Contracts: Bailment contracts** are similar to leases and employment contracts in that they, too, are so widely used as to substantially affect the public interest. Accordingly, the status of exculpatory clauses in such contracts is essentially the same as those in leases and employment contracts—that is, highly suspect in the eyes of the law.

A *bailment* occurs when the owner of an article of personal property temporarily relinquishes the possession and control of it to another. The person who has parted with the possession is the *bailor*, and the one receiving it is the *bailee*. Typical bailments result from checking a coat at a nightclub, leaving a car at a garage for repairs, and storing goods at a warehouse.

Under general bailment law, a bailee is liable for any damages to, or loss of, the property that is the result of his or her negligence—the failure to use reasonable care under the circumstances. Bailees frequently attempt to escape this liability by the use of an exculpatory clause in the bailment contract. Companies operating parking lots, for example, customarily print on the back of identification tickets something like the following: "The company will endeavor to protect the property of its patrons, but it is agreed that it will not be liable for loss or damage to cars, accessories, or contents, from whatever cause arising."[8]

As suggested earlier, such a clause is *contrary to public policy*—at least to the extent that it purports to free the bailee from liability for loss caused by his or her negligence. The reasoning, of course, is analogous to that applied in the illustration involving the employment contract—specifically, that if such a clause were given effect, all bailees would utilize it, with a consequent lessening of care on their part. As a result, such provisions do not prevent a bailor whose property is damaged while in the bailee's hands from bringing suit. If it is established that the loss was occasioned by negligence on the part of the bailee, the bailor can recover damages.[9]

## *Unconscionable Contracts*

As a general rule, the courts are not concerned with the fairness or unfairness of a particular contract. In other words, where competent parties have struck an agreement it will normally be enforced even if it proves much more advantageous to one party than to the other. However, occasionally the freedom to contract is abused so that the terms of a particular contract are so extremely unfair to one of the parties in light of common mores and business practices that they "shock one's conscience." Courts will not enforce such an **unconscionable contract** against the abused party.

A pre-UCC case vividly illustrating the common-law approach to unconscionability is *Williams v. Walker-Thomas Furniture Co.,* 350 F.2d 445 (D.D.C. 1965). There, a Mrs. Williams purchased some furniture in Washington, D.C., in 1957 on credit under a contract which contained the standard provision that the company would retain title to the goods until all monthly payments were made, and that the company could repossess in event of default. The contract also contained a clause that if Mrs. Williams purchased additional goods on credit, the company had the right to "credit pro-rata" her monthly payments against all such goods. She did, in fact, buy a number of additional items between 1957 and 1962, and the company, as permitted by the pro-rata clause, during that time had applied her payments so that a small balance remained due on all items, even those purchased in 1957 and 1958. In 1962, by which time Mrs. Williams had made payments of over $1,400, she was unable to make additional payments. When the company then sought to repossess all of the goods in her hands, the court refused repossession as to the first items that she had purchased. In part, the court said: "When a party of little bargaining power, and hence little real choice, signs a commercially unreasonable contract with little or no knowledge of its terms, it is hardly likely that his consent, or even an objective manifestation of consent, was ever given to all the terms. In such a case the usual rule that the terms of the agreement are not to be questioned should be abandoned, and the court should consider whether the terms of the contract are so unfair that enforcement should be withheld."

## *Unconscionability: Sales Law*

In most states the common law of unconscionability has been introduced to the sale of goods through UCC Sec. 2-302, which allows a court finding a sales contract or any clause of the contract to be unconscionable to: (1) refuse to enforce the contract, *or* (2) enforce the remainder of the contract without the unconscionable clause, *or* (3) limit the application of any unconscionable clause so as to avoid any unreasonable result.

Most courts require a showing of both procedural and substantive unfairness in order to find a

---

[8] While leaving a car at a parking lot creates a bailor-bailee relationship under ordinary circumstances, this is not always true. Many courts, for example, rule that such a relationship is not created if the patron is permitted to keep the car keys, on the theory that the lot operator in such a case is not given control of the car.

[9] Clauses that place a *limit* on the bailee's liability, in the event of a loss, are viewed more favorably by the courts. Such provisions, if reasonable, are usually not considered to be illegal. Additionally, some bailees are expressly permitted by statute to limit their liability by contract. Under federal law, for example, common carriers in interstate commerce are permitted to do so within limits approved by the Interstate Commerce Commission; thus the limitations commonly found in bills of lading and other transportation contracts are generally enforceable.

contract unconscionable. *Procedural unconscionability* exists when there is a lack of meaningful choice on the part of one of the parties. Courts must analyze the contract formation process, including such matters as the inability of one of the parties to bargain because of immaturity or old age, lack of sophistication, mental disability, inability to speak English, lack of education or business acumen, and the like; relative bargaining power; whether the party in the strongest economic position simply offered a printed form or boilerplate contract on a take-it-or-leave-it basis to the weaker party (adhesion contracts); whether the terms were explained to the weaker party; whether there were alternative sources for the goods or services; whether high-pressure or deceptive sales tactics were used; and whether important clauses were hidden in the fine print. Contracts entered into in a commercial context are generally presumed not to be unconscionable; businesspersons should be able to protect themselves. Courts are much more likely to find unconscionability in order to aid a consumer than to aid a business, but commercial transactions are not immune from such a finding.

In order to ascertain *substantive unconscionability,* the courts examine the terms of the contract itself to determine whether they are oppressive, perhaps because they involve unfair disclaimers of warranty, inflated prices, denial of basic rights and remedies to consumers, penalty clauses, and the like. The courts will decide whether or not a particular contract is unconscionable on a case-by-case basis in light of the overall commercial context in which it was made and as of the time it was made. Just because a bargain has turned out poorly for one party does not mean that the contract was unconscionable when made. Courts will not use the concept to reallocate the risks taken by the parties when they entered into the contract, as the following case demonstrates.

## Doughty v. Idaho Frozen Foods Corp.
Idaho Court of Appeals,
736 P.2d 460 (1987)

In 1983 Doughty contracted to sell a portion of his anticipated potato crop to Idaho Frozen Foods (IFF), a processor of potato products. The parties used a form contract developed through negotiations between IFF and the Potato Growers of Idaho (PGI), an independent bargaining organization which represented 1200 potato growers. Under the contract, Doughty was to receive a base price if the potato crop contained a certain percentage of potatoes weighing ten ounces or more. If the crop contained a higher percentage, the price would be increased; if it contained a lower percentage, the price would be decreased. Size was critical to IFF's processing needs. The contract provided that IFF could refuse any deliveries containing less than 10 percent ten-ounce or larger potatoes.

Unexpected weather conditions resulted in only 8 percent of Doughty's potatoes being ten-ounces or more, so he was entitled to only $2.57 per hundredweight under the IFF contract. After four days of delivery to IFF, Doughty breached the contract, delivering the remainder of his potatoes to the "fresh pack" market where he could receive $4.69 per hundredweight. Pursuant to an agreement with IFF, the proceeds of this sale were placed in a court-controlled bank account.

Doughty then filed this declaratory judgment action, asking the court to declare the contract unconscionable and therefore not binding on him. The trial judge ruled for IFF and Doughty appealed.

**Decision:** Affirmed. The contract is not unconscionable. Unconscionability has two aspects: (1) *Procedural unconscionability* is characterized by great disparity in the bargaining positions of the parties, by extreme need of one party to reach some agreement, or by threats short of duress. None of these factors was present in this case. The contract was one negotiated by a strong group of 1200 farmers, so Doughty cannot claim disparity of bargaining power. (2) *Substantive unconscionability* exists if, given the general commercial background in a particular case, the contract is so one-sided as to oppress or unfairly surprise one of the parties. That was not the case here either, even though the sliding scale was slanted slightly in favor of IFF and IFF had the right to refuse to receive shipments with less than 10 percent of the right size of potatoes. Had Doughty been able to produce the size of potatoes he had hoped, he would have had a very favorable contract. He cannot complain now, just because things did not turn out as he had planned. ∎

## Other Illegal Contracts

Many other contracts are generally held to be contrary to public policy. Of these, one broad class deserves comment—contracts that "injure the public service." Promises to pay legislators money in return for their votes and similar promises to judges in return for favorable rulings are clearly injurious to the public and therefore illegal. On the other hand, **lobbying contracts,** under which a person is employed by a third party to influence a legislator's vote or an administrator's decision in the awarding of a contract, are not necessarily illegal. The legality of such contracts largely depends on the propriety of the means used by the lobbyist. If, for example, an engineer simply agrees, for a fee, to present to a lawmaker or administrator factual information tending to show the superiority of one product or material over another, the means are proper and the agreement is not contrary to public policy. A contract, however, that contemplates influencing a government official essentially by reliance on the lobbyist's long personal friendship with that person would be illegal.

In regard to **contingent fee contracts,** under which payment of the fee is conditional upon passage of a particular bill or awarding of a contract, many courts flatly deny the lobbyist recovery of his or her fee under any circumstances—on the ground that the tendency of such contracts to induce improper activities is, by itself, sufficient to cause them to be contrary to public policy. Other courts, in such cases, permit the lobbyist to recover if he or she can prove proper conduct—that is, conduct free of deception, undue pressure, and the like.

## EFFECT OF ILLEGAL CONTRACTS

As noted early in the chapter, illegal contracts are generally void and unenforceable. This means that neither party to such a contract will be assisted by the courts in any way, regardless of the consequences to the parties involved. Thus, if S brings suit to recover the purchase price of a quantity of liquor that he has sold and delivered to B in violation of law, his action will be dismissed. Conversely, if B had paid the purchase price when the contract was made and S subsequently failed to deliver the liquor, any action brought by B to recover the price will also be unavailing.

Courts feel that such a hands-off policy is, in most cases, the best way to discourage the making of illegal contracts. There are exceptional situations, however, in which the courts feel that the results obtained under such a policy are so questionable as to warrant some measure of judicial relief. We will examine three of these situations.

## Rights of Protected Parties

Some statutes have as their clear purpose the protection of a certain class of persons. Any contract made in violation of such a statute is enforceable by persons within that class, despite its illegality. For example: a Nebraska insurance company, not licensed to sell insurance in Colorado, issues a fire insurance policy on K's home in Denver. The home is destroyed by fire, and the company refuses to pay on the ground that the contract was illegal. The company is liable on its policy. It would be a ludicrous result if K, a person for whose benefit the licensing statutes were enacted, were to be denied recovery on the ground of illegality.

## Parties Not Equally at Fault

In most illegal contracts the parties are equally at fault (or substantially equally at fault). In such instances when an action is brought to enforce the contract, the defendant may successfully assert the defense of *in pari delicto*—(literally, "at equal fault").

In some situations, however, the plaintiff may convince the court that he or she was *not* equally at fault with the defendant—i.e., that his or her guilt was substantially less than the defendant's. In such a case the plaintiff's action may be maintained. The exception applies particularly—but not exclusively— where the plaintiff was ignorant of essential facts when the contract was made, through no fault of his or her own. For example: X forges a warehouse receipt, which makes it appear that he is the owner of certain goods stored at a warehouse. X takes the receipt to a trucking company and employs it to pick up the goods at the warehouse and to deliver them to his place of business. The trucking company does so, not knowing that X is not the owner of the goods. The company is entitled to receive its transportation charge from X, even though it was a participant in an illegal transaction.

## Severable Contracts

Sometimes a single contract turns out on analysis to be two separate agreements. This can be illustrated by a contract under which a retiring restaurant owner agrees to sell to a former competitor his "ten pinball machines for $50 and one electric broiler for $75." In such a contract, called a **severable contract**, the fact that one of the agreements may be illegal does not prevent the other from being enforced. Thus, if the sale of the pinball machines is prohibited by law, the seller is still under an obligation, enforceable in court, to deliver the broiler. However, most contracts that contain several promises on the part of both parties are not severable. The promises of the two parties usually are so interdependent that the court must rule that they resulted in the creation of a single, indivisible contract. In such cases, if any part of the contract is illegal, the entire agreement is unenforceable.

## SUMMARY

A contract may be illegal either because it violates a statute (or administrative regulation), or because it is contrary to public policy. In either event such a contract is generally void and therefore unenforceable. Contracts that are often prohibited by state statute are wagers, those calling for the performance of work by unlicensed persons, contracts entered into (or to be performed) on Sundays, and usurious contracts (those in which a lender charges a rate of interest in excess of that permitted by law). Not all of these contracts, however, are illegal in all states. And even in states where a particular contract is contrary to the letter of a statute, the courts have, in limited circumstances, held the contract to be outside the statute. For example, they usually permit an unlicensed person to recover the contract price of his or her services if the licensing statute was primarily a revenue-raising one (as distinguished from a statute having as its purpose the protection of the health or safety of the citizenry).

The question of whether a particular contract, if enforced, would be injurious to the public at large is determined by the highest court in each state. If the contract is deemed injurious, enforceability is denied on the ground that the contract is contrary to public policy. Contracts that unreasonably restrain trade—being inimical to free and open competition—have long been held to fall within this category. Whether a particular restraint is unreasonable depends upon its purpose, and the scope of its time and space restrictions. Where the restraint is an ancillary part of a contract which itself is lawful, such as a promise by a seller of a business not to compete with the buyer, the restraint is lawful if the protection it affords the buyer is reasonable under the circumstances. Thus a promise by a seller of a single retail establishment not to engage in a similar business anywhere in the state would normally be unreasonably broad, and unenforceable. The test of reasonableness is also applied to restrictive covenants in employment contracts, but such restrictions are subject to closer scrutiny by the courts than are those in sale of business cases.

Exculpatory clauses in contracts that purport to free one party from liability for loss caused by his or her negligence are also viewed with disfavor by the courts, especially where the company utilizing the clause provides a service essential to the business world and which, therefore, possesses bargaining power superior to that of the other party. Unconscionable contracts are a third type of contract held to be contrary to public policy. Such contracts generally possess two characteristics: (1) terms that are shockingly one-sided, and (2) possession of greatly superior bargaining power by the party in whose favor the terms operate.

## KEY TERMS

**Wagering agreement**
**Lottery**
**Risk-shifting contract**
**Risk-creating contract**
**Futures contract**
**Licensing statutes**
**Sunday statutes**
**Usury**
**Restrictive covenant**
**Ancillary covenant**
**Geographical restraints**
**Exculpatory clause**
**Bailment contract**
**Unconscionable contract**
**Lobbying contract**
**Contingent fee contract**
**Severable contract**

## QUESTIONS AND PROBLEMS

1. Wilson was a licensed Hawaii architect who rendered extensive professional services for the owner of a ranch. When he sought his $33,900 fee, the owner refused to pay because Wilson had failed to pay a $15 state "annual registration fee." Does this failure to pay render Wilson's contract illegal, as the ranch owner contends? Explain. (*Wilson v. Kealakekua Ranch, Ltd.*, 551 P.2d 525, 1976.)

2. Bonasera brought an action against Roffe to recover a real estate commission due him for finding a buyer for Roffe's property. Bonasera was not a licensed broker, and Roffe's defense was an Arizona statute providing that only licensed brokers could recover real estate commissions in that state. Bonasera contended that the statute was not applicable to him since he was not in the real estate business, his activity in this instance being but a "single, isolated transaction." Is the statute applicable to Bonasera? Explain. (*Bonasera v. Roffe,* 442 P.2d 165, 1968.)

3. Diadrill, Inc., which makes drill bits for oil well production, sued Gillen, a former employee who had started in the summer of 1980 and was terminated in the spring of 1981. Gillen had signed a covenant not to compete for 12 months within Diadrill's marketing area, which covered several states. When Gillen left Diadrill, he took records, price lists, inventory lists, photos of Diadrill's drill bits, and customer lists. He went to work for a competitor and obtained the business of at least one of Diadrill's former customers for his new boss. Should the court enforce Diadrill's restrictive covenant? (*Gillen v. Diadrill, Inc.,* 624 S.W.2d 259, Tex.Civ.App. 1981.)

4. Lally sold a barbershop located in Rockville, Connecticut, "together with all good will," to Mattis. The bill of sale contained a clause providing that Lally would not engage in the barbering business in any capacity for a period of five years "anywhere in the City of Rockville, or within a radius of one mile" of the shop's location on Market Street in Rockville. (The one-mile alternative was included because the shop was located only a quarter of a mile from the Rockville city limits.) After the sale, Lally operated a restaurant; but when this became unprofitable a year or two later, he opened a one-chair barbershop in his own home, three hundred yards from the shop Mattis had purchased. When Mattis' business fell off thereafter, he brought an action asking the court to enforce the restrictive clause in the contract. Lally contended that the clause in question constituted an unreasonable restraint of trade and was therefore unlawful. Is Lally's contention correct? Explain. (*Mattis v. Lally,* 82 A.2d 155, 1951.)

5. Soble, a lawyer, represented a client in a condemnation suit—a suit in which the client's land was being taken by the state. Soble employed an expert real estate appraiser, Laos, to testify in the suit as to the value of the property. The contract between Soble and Laos provided that Laos was to receive a fee of $1,500 if the court found the value of the property to be $200,000 or less, and $2,500 if the valuation were set at any amount above $200,000. In subsequent litigation, the question arose as to whether this contingent fee contract was contrary to public policy and thus illegal. On what basis could it be argued that the contract *was* illegal? Discuss. (*Laos v. Soble,* 503 P.2d 978, 1972.)

6. When Bova left her car at a parking lot operated by Constantine, she was given an identification ticket upon which was printed matter, which she did not read, as follows: "This station will endeavor to protect the property of its patrons but it is agreed that it will not be liable for loss or damage of cars, accessories or contents from whatever cause arising." When Bova returned, the car was not in the lot. It had been stolen, and, when found, was in need of repairs totaling $154. In an action brought against Constantine to recover this amount, he contended that the clause on the identification ticket freed him of all liability. Was the clause lawful, and thus a good defense to the suit? Explain. (*Agricultural Insurance Co. v. Constantine,* 58 N.E.2d 658, 1944.)

7. Krazek hired D to take her on a white water rafting trip in West Virginia, signing a "Raft Trip Release and Assumption of Risk," which stated that she was aware of the "substantial risks and dangers" that may occur during white water rafting in remote terrain and that "in consideration of and as part payment for the right to participate," she agreed to assume all risks and to "release, and . . . hold [D] harmless from any and all liability of every kind and nature whatsoever" which might arise out of the trip. During the trip a severe hail storm occurred. D's guide ordered the rafters into the river to protect them from the hail. While in the river, Krazek was swept away by the current and injured. She sued D in negligence. Should the exculpatory clause prevent her from recovering? (*Krazek v. Mountain River Tours, Inc.,* 884 F.2d 163, 4th Cir. 1989.)

8. Plaintiff Michelle Triola Marvin alleged that she and defendant, actor Lee Marvin, orally agreed that they would "live together, hold themselves out to the public as husband and wife, and that she would render services as companion, homemaker, housekeeper and cook." She claimed further that she gave up her lucrative career as an entertainer in exchange for defendant's promise to "provide for all of plaintiff's financial support and needs for the rest of her life." After six years of living together, the parties split up. Plaintiff sued to enforce the agreement. Defendant moved to dismiss on grounds that the agreement was "immoral" and hence contrary to public policy because it involved a sexual relationship between nonmarital partners. Should a court refuse to enforce the agreement? (*Marvin v. Marvin,* 557 P.2d 106, Cal. 1976.)

9. The Crocker National Bank (D) imposed a charge for processing all checks drawn on accounts without sufficient funds (NSF checks). D requires each depositor to sign a signature card which states that depositors "agree with Crocker National Bank . . . that this account . . . shall be subject to the Bank's present and future rules, regulations, practices, and charges." The card does not identify the amount of the charge for NSF checks and the bank does not furnish the depositor with a copy of the applicable bank

rules and regulations. P sued on behalf of himself and all other depositors, claiming that the bank unilaterally and unjustifiably raised the NSF charge at will, eventually charging $6 for each check, though the actual cost incurred was only 30 cents. Is the charge unconscionable, as P claims? (*Perdue v. Crocker National Bank,* 702 P.2d 503, Cal. 1985.)

10. Plaintiffs alleged that D, their stockbroker, gave them a "tip" based on supposedly "inside information." Following the tip, plaintiffs invested, but lost substantial amounts of money when the tipped information turned out to be false. Ps sued D, who raised an "in pari delicto" defense. In essence, D argued that because Ps thought they were receiving secret inside information they knew that they were engaging in illegal "insider trading" violative of the federal securities laws and therefore should be barred from recovering. Is this a good defense? (*Bateman Eichler, Hill Richards, Inc. v. Berner,* 472 U.S. 299, 1985.)

# CHAPTER 15

# VOIDABLE CONTRACTS

A **voidable contract** is a contract which may be avoided—that is, may be legally set aside—by one of the parties, even though the contract consists of a definite agreement, is supported by consideration, and has a lawful purpose. In this chapter we will examine the most common grounds for the avoidance (disaffirmance) of a contract: *lack of capacity,* and *lack of reality of consent.*

## CAPACITY

The term **capacity** means the legal ability—the ability or "competence" in the eyes of the law—to perform a particular act. Within the context of this chapter, the particular act under consideration is the making of a binding contract.

A person's capacity to contract may be limited (or entirely lacking, in some instances) for any of three primary reasons: *minority, mental infirmity,* and *intoxication.* We will consider these subjects in order.[1]

## MINORS

Centuries ago, the English courts became aware of the fact that many of the contracts entered into by young persons displayed a shocking lack of judgment; such persons assumed obligations and made purchases that they probably would not have had they possessed greater maturity and experience. The courts, desirous of "protecting the young from the consequences of their own folly," began to wrestle with the question of how this protection could best be brought about.

They initially approached the problem by devising what came to be known as the *harm-benefit test.* Under this view, the courts permitted persons who had entered into contracts while under the age of twenty-one to disaffirm them if they were shown to be harmful to these individuals. This approach was followed for a time in the United States. Its application, however, produced such conflict and uncertainty in the law that a new solution became necessary.

### *The Common-Law Rule*

The U.S. courts finally adopted the sweeping rule that, virtually without exception, *all minors' contracts are voidable at their option.* The right thus given to minors to escape their contractual obligations is no longer dependent upon a showing that the contract is harmful or unwise, or that they have been taken advantage of in some way. To effect a disaffirmance of any contract, all the minor has to do is indicate to the other party his or her intention not to be bound by it. The disaffirmance can be express or implied, and the right to disaffirm continues until the minor reaches the age of majority, plus a "reasonable time thereafter."

Note that a minor's contract is enforceable against the minor *until* an effective disaffirmance occurs. Furthermore, only the minor has the right to disaffirm; the other party to the contract has no corresponding right to disaffirm. If the minor chooses, he or she may enforce the contract against the adult on the other side (assuming that adult's mental competence).

---

[1] Historically, there have been a number of additional classes of persons who possessed little or no capacity to contract: married women, convicted felons, aliens, American Indians, and unincorporated associations. Today, the legal capacity of some of these classes (e.g., married women, aliens, and felons) has generally been restored by statute or by judicial decision, and cases involving the others do not arise often. Thus we will not discuss these classes of persons in this chapter.

## Definition of Minority

In the past twenty years or so virtually every state has lowered the age of majority from the common law's 21 years to 18 years of age for most purposes, including the making of valid contracts.[2] Thus, a **minor** is a person who has not yet attained the age of 18. The agreements of minors of "tender years"—children so young that their minds have not matured sufficiently to understand the meaning of contractual obligations—are void rather than voidable. Because legal actions against this type of minor are virtually nonexistent, the rules considered below are those applicable to the contracts of "older minors"—typically, teenagers.[3]

We will now examine the results of the general rule permitting minors to disaffirm contracts at their option in three basic situations: (1) **ordinary contracts**—that is, contracts under which the goods or services being purchased are not necessities of life; (2) contracts for the purchase of "necessaries," and (3) contracts in which the minor has misrepresented his or her age.

## Minors' Liability on Ordinary Contracts

**Executory Contracts:** Few problems arise where the minor's repudiation occurs before either party has started to perform the obligations under the contract (that is, where the contract is still *executory*). Since the other party is caused little hardship in such a case, all states take the view that the disaffirmance entirely frees the minor of liability. For example, suppose that M, a minor, contracts on July 1 to buy a home stereo system from X for $1,200, the contract providing that the system will be delivered and the purchase price paid on July 15. If M notifies X on July 10 that he will not go through with the deal, the contract is at an end and X has no recourse against M. Similarly, if M contracts to paint Y's house for $400 and later refuses to do the job, the refusal absolves M of liability. If either X or Y were to bring suit against M to recover damages for breach of contract, the suit would be dismissed.

**Executed Contracts:** Surprising as it may seem, the same rule is also generally applied to executed contracts—those that have been fully performed before the repudiation takes place. Thus, in virtually all states, a minor can purchase a car for cash, drive it until he or she becomes an adult, and still disaffirm the contract (assuming, as is usually the case, that the car is not a necessity of life).[4]

While virtually all courts agree as to the minor's *right to disaffirm* a contract in a situation such as the above, they do not agree about the *extent of the relief* that should be given to the minor in some circumstances. This can be illustrated by amplifying the facts about the car purchase. Suppose that the purchase price of the car was $2,800 and that the minor brings suit to recover that amount. At the trial, the seller offers evidence establishing that the value of the car at the time the minor offered to return it was $1,500. In such a case the seller can make at least two contentions: (1) that the minor should be charged with the benefit received—that is, the reasonable value of the use of the car prior to disaffirmance or (2) if this contention is rejected, that the minor should at least be charged with the depreciation of the car while it was in the minor's hands.

***The Majority View:*** The courts of most states reject both contentions, permitting the minor to recover the full price of $2,800. Assuming that the automobile does not constitute a necessity, the majority rule is that the minor's only obligation is *to return the consideration if able to do so.* Under this view, the return of the car—even though it has greatly depreciated in value by reason of use or accident—entitles the minor to recover his or her *entire payment.* Furthermore, if the minor is unable to return the con-

---

[2] These statutes almost uniformly confer upon 18-year-olds the rights to sue and be sued in their own names, to make wills, to marry without parental consent, and to choose their own domiciles; but generally they do not sanction the right to buy alcoholic beverages until the age of 21 is reached.

[3] There are at least two unusual situations where minors may be treated as adults. First, a few states provide that married persons should be treated as adults for purposes of entering into contracts even if they are not yet 18. Second, several states have procedures where, under court supervision, minors may be treated as adults for purposes of making contracts. Such a procedure allows a child actor, for example, to contract with a movie studio. The studio is protected because the child is unable to disaffirm the contract. The child is protected because the funds he or she is paid under the contract typically go into a trust fund that is administered for the child's benefit.

[4] Standard forms of many car dealers contain a statement that the buyer "hereby certifies that he or she is eighteen years of age, or over." The minor's right to disaffirm this kind of contract is discussed later under the "misrepresentation of age" section.

sideration, as would be the case if the car were stolen, the minor is still permitted to recover the $2,800 from the unfortunate seller. And regardless of whether the consideration has depreciated in value or cannot be returned, the minor is not charged with the benefit received from the possession and use of the consideration.

Freedom from liability would also exist if the minor had purchased the car on credit rather than for cash. In that case, if the minor disaffirmed the contract before paying off the balance, and if the seller then brought action to recover that balance, the minor would again be freed of all liability (subject, again, only to the obligation to return the car if he or she is able to do so).[5]

[5] A procedural note: as the above examples illustrate, minority cases ordinarily arise in one of two ways. In the first (and most common) situation the minor has paid *cash* for the goods or services, and, upon disaffirmance, the minor is the plaintiff seeking return of his or her payment. In the second case, where the minor purchases goods or services *on credit* and then disaffirms, the unpaid seller is the plaintiff, seeking to recover the contract price. Regardless of how the cases arise, the applicable minority rules apply with equal force. (That is, if under the applicable rules the minor in the first case is permitted to recover the full purchase price, he or she in the second case will be entirely freed of the obligation to pay for the goods.)

*Some Other Views:* The courts of a growing number of states, feeling that the majority view imposes unreasonable hardship on the other party to the contract, *do* impose liability on the minor under one of two theories. Some states hold the minor liable for the *reasonable value of the benefit* received prior to the disaffirmance, while others reach a similar result by holding the minor liable for the depreciation that has occurred to the goods while in his or her possession. Going back to the original illustration, where the minor had paid cash for the car, the courts of these states would permit the minor to recover the purchase price *minus* the value of the benefit (or depreciation), whatever the jury finds this to be. Most of these minority jurisdictions would not require a disaffirming minor who had purchased on credit to produce the funds necessary to "make the adult whole" in order to disaffirm. Thus, these minority jurisdictions give less protection to adults who sell to minors on credit than to those who protect themselves by demanding the minors' money "up front."

The case below illustrates the broad protection the majority view affords the minor in a typical fact-pattern. (The rationale underlying this view follows the case.)

## Halbman v. Lemke
Supreme Court of Wisconsin,
298 N.W.2d 562 (1980)

James Halbman, a minor, worked at a gas station in Greenfield, Wisconsin. During his employment he contracted to buy a 1968 Oldsmobile from Michael Lemke, the station manager, for $1,250. At the time the contract was made Halbman paid Lemke $1,000 cash and took possession of the car. (Title to the vehicle was retained by Lemke.) Under the contract Halbman agreed to pay $25 per week until the balance was paid off.

A little more than a month later, at which time Halbman had paid $1,100 of the price, a connecting rod in the engine broke. He took the car to a garage, where it was repaired at a cost of $637. Halbman did not pay the repair bill. Shortly thereafter Lemke endorsed the car's title over to Halbman, even though the full purchase price had not been paid, in an effort to avoid any liability for the operation and maintenance of the vehicle (including the repair bill). Halbman returned the title to Lemke, with a letter saying he was disaffirming the contract and demanding the return of the $1,100 he had paid. Lemke did not return the money and did not pay the bill. (The car remained in possession of the repair shop). Five months later, with the repair bill still unpaid, the garage removed the car's engine and transmission in satisfaction of the debt. The garage then towed the vehicle to the home of Halbman's father. While there it was subjected to vandalism which made the car "unsalvageable."

Halbman then brought this action to recover the $1,100 he had paid, and Lemke counterclaimed for $150, the amount still owing on the contract. The trial court granted judgment for Halbman, ruling that when a minor disaffirms a contract for the purchase of an item, his or her only obligation is to return the property remaining in his hands. The court of appeals affirmed, and Lemke petitioned the Supreme Court of Wisconsin for review.

*(continued)*

**Decision:** Judgment for Halbman was affirmed. The rule applied by the lower courts—that when a minor disaffirms a contract for the purchase of an item, his or her only obligation is to return the remaining property—is the correct one. Under the well-established rule of Wisconsin and most states, a minor who is not guilty of misrepresentation or intentional damage who disaffirms a contract for the purchase of an item that is not a necessity may recover the full purchase price without liability for use, depreciation, damage or other diminution in value of the item. In fact, under this rule a full recovery is allowed even if the minor is unable to return the item at all. If any modifications of these rules are to be made, they should be made by the legislature rather than by the courts. ■

---

**Rationale:** There is no question but that the majority rule, as applied to specific situations, frequently results in a severe financial loss to the party who has dealt with the minor. It is also possible that some young people, aware of the rule, enter into contracts with the intention of getting something for nothing. Nevertheless, most courts justify the occasional hardships that result under the majority rule by noting that "the primary purpose of the common-law rule is to afford protection to minors by discouraging others from contracting with them," and this rule no doubt tends to bring about such a result. Thus we have once again a situation where the rights of some individuals, under certain circumstances, must give way to the rights of others because of public policy considerations.

A competent person can, of course, ordinarily escape such hardships by refusing to deal with minors.[6] All persons are presumed to know the law, so that (in theory at least) one who deals with a minor is on notice that it is at his or her peril. A second solution for someone who wishes to make a sale is to refuse to deal with the minor and to contract instead with one of the minor's parents. In such a case the possibility of a disaffirmance is eliminated, since both parties to the contract are competent. A third solution, in situations where the competent party does not know whether the person with whom he or she is dealing is a minor, is to have that person make a statement, preferably in writing, that he or she is over the age of eighteen. (The protection afforded to the competent party by such a representation is considered later in the chapter.)

**Ratification:** Once a minor reaches the age of majority, he or she has the ability to ratify any contracts made earlier. A **ratification** occurs when the minor indicates to the other party, expressly or impliedly, the intent to be bound by the agreement. Thus, if a minor, after reaching the age of 18, promises that he or she will go through with the contract, an express ratification has taken place and the right of disaffirmance is lost forever. Similarly, if a minor has received an article, such as a typewriter, under a contract and continues to use it for more than a "reasonable time" after reaching the age of 18, an implied ratification has occurred. Another situation in which a ratification can take place involves purchases made under installment contracts. Suppose, for example, that a minor has purchased a motorcycle, agreeing to pay the seller $25 a month until the purchase price has been paid in full. If he continues to make payments for any length of time after reaching the age of 18, it is probable that such payments will be held to constitute a ratification of the contract. (It is obvious, then, that any young person should review all of his or her contracts upon becoming an adult, and refrain from any conduct that would indicate to the other party an intent to be bound by them if he or she wishes to set any of them aside.)

## *Minors' Liability on Contracts to Purchase "Necessaries"*

When a minor purchases **necessaries** (goods that the law considers necessary to life or health), he or she incurs a greater liability than that imposed (by the majority rule) under contracts calling for the purchase of goods that are not necessities. The rule applicable to contracts calling for the purchase of "necessaries" is that the minor is liable to the other party for the *reasonable value of the goods actually used.* This is the quasi-contractual measure of recovery, because the minor is being held liable not on the con-

---

[6] Some persons, such as common carriers, have a legal duty to deal with everyone who requests (and is able to pay for) their services. Disaffirmance against such persons is generally not permitted once the contract has been executed. Thus, a 17-year-old who purchases and uses an airline ticket is not permitted to recover his or her fare.

tract but, instead, to avoid unjust enrichment. To illustrate: M, 17, buys a topcoat from C, contracting to pay the price of $150 one year later. At the end of that time, when the coat is completely worn out, C brings suit to recover the purchase price. If the court rules that the coat is a necessary, then it must determine what its reasonable value was at the time of the purchase, and M is liable to C in that amount. (In contrast, if the coat is held *not* to constitute a necessary, M is usually freed of all liability—as has been seen earlier.) This imposition of liability occurs only where the goods or services have been used by the minor; contracts calling for the purchase of necessaries can still be set aside as long as they are executory. Thus, if M contracts to purchase a coat from C, which is to be delivered one week later, he can set aside the contract without liability if he notifies C of his disaffirmance before the week is out—and indeed, even later as long as he does not use the coat.

**What Constitutes a Necessary?** In answering the question of what constitutes a necessary, it is possible to draw a clear line in most cases. Minimum amounts of food, clothing, and medical services are clearly necessary. So, too, is the rental of a house or apartment by a minor who is married. Many items, on the other hand, are clearly luxuries—such as TV sets, sporting goods, and dancing lessons, under most circumstances.[7] Other items held to be necessaries include legal services, taxes on real property owned by minors, and medical care for a minor's child.

A few states reason that items essential for a minor to earn a living (and therefore to have money to buy necessaries) should also be treated as necessaries. Thus, a minority of states would treat as necessaries such things as a car that a minor uses in his or her work or the services of an employment agency that the minor used to obtain a job.[8]

It should be noted that an item is a necessity only if it is actually needed at the time of purchase. Thus if a minor purchases an item that appears to be a necessity, such as an article of clothing, the minor still has no liability to the seller if he or she can prove that a parent or guardian was "willing and able" to furnish clothing of the type purchased under that particular contract.

**Rationale:** Why is it that under the majority rule, a minor who buys something frivolous may disaffirm the contract and recover the entire purchase price, whereas a minor who buys something truly needed can disaffirm only where the seller can retain the fair value of what the minor used? These rules seem paradoxical, but the clear rationale is, on the one hand, to discourage merchants from dealing with minors for the frivolous items (by allowing the minors to disaffirm even when it is unfair to the merchant), but on the other hand, to induce merchants to sell minors the things they need for survival (by ensuring that the minors will pay at least fair value).

## Minors' Liability on Contracts Involving Misrepresentation of Age

We have assumed so far that the minor has not led the other party to believe that he or she is an adult. If such misrepresentation does occur, the minor is guilty of a kind of fraud, and the courts of most jurisdictions will deny the protection that otherwise would be given that person.

Some states have provided by statute that a minor who has misrepresented his or her age is liable on the contract exactly as if he or she were an adult. Most states, however, have left the matter up to the courts, and a spate of rules has resulted. Without attempting to consider all of them, we can make one or two generalizations.

First, where the minor repudiates the contract while it is entirely executory, most courts permit the disaffirmance just as if there had been no misrepresentation. Although this does not penalize the minor for wrongdoing, it also does not cause particular hardship to the other party in most instances.

Second, where a contract calling for the purchase of a nonnecessary item has been fully or partially executed before the attempted disaffirmance, many courts allow the disaffirmance *only if it will not cause a loss to the other party.*[9] Under this approach, each case is analyzed separately to determine the effect of the disaffirmance. Two illustrations follow.

---

[7] In determining whether a doubtful item is a necessary, the courts take into account the "station in life" occupied by the particular minor. Thus a fourth sport coat might be ruled a necessary for a minor who is a member of high society, while it would not be so ruled in regard to others.

[8] *Gastonia Personnel Corp. v. Rogers,* 172 S.E.2d 19 (N.C. 1970).

[9] In cases of "necessary" contracts, the usual rule normally continues in effect—the minor is liable for the reasonable value of the articles actually used.

**Figure 15.1 Contract Liability of Minors**

|  | Ordinary contracts | Contracts for necessaries | Contracts involving misrepresentation of age |
|---|---|---|---|
| **Executory contracts** | Minor may disaffirm. | Minor may disaffirm. | Minor may disaffirm (most states). |
| **Executed contracts** | **Majority rule:** Minor may disaffirm. Minor may recover entire payment. Must return consideration if possible.<br><br>**Minority rule:** Minor may disaffirm but is liable for: 1) reasonable value of the benefit received, or 2) any depreciation. | Minor is liable for the reasonable value of any necessaries actually used. | Minor may disaffirm only if it will not cause a loss to the other party (most states). |

1. M, a minor, purchases a car from C, a competent party, for $2,500 cash, after telling C that she is 18. A year later, just before becoming 18, M wishes to disaffirm; at this time the market value of the car is $1,400. Despite the misrepresentation, disaffirmance will be permitted. C, however, will be allowed to withhold from the $2,500 the amount of the depreciation, $1,100, which—added to the $1,400 car—will restore him to his original position. M's recovery is thus only $1,400.

2. M purchases a car from C under a contract providing, "Buyer certifies that he or she is 18 years of age or older." The purchase price is $2,500, with $100 paid at the time of purchase and the balance of $2,400 payable in 24 monthly installments. Six months later, when the car is stolen, M notifies C that she wants to be relieved of the balance of the contract. Disaffirmance will probably not be allowed since this would cause a loss to C; thus a suit by C to recover the unpaid balance will be successful.[10]

The contract liability of minors regarding both executory and executed contracts is illustrated in Figure 15.1.

## Contracts That Cannot Be Disaffirmed

Not all contracts can be disaffirmed on the ground of minority. For example, disaffirmance of marriage contracts and contracts of enlistment in the armed forces is not permitted on the ground of public policy. For certain other contracts, such as those approved by a court or those made with banks or insurance com-

---

[10] This example is based on *Haydocy Pontiac, Inc. v. Lee*, 19 Ohio App.2d 217 (1969). The minor in this case was held to be "estopped" from disaffirming, in view of her misrepresentation; and she continued to be liable for the "fair value of the property."

panies, the same result is generally brought about by statute. For example, a North Carolina statute authorizes banks "in respect to deposit accounts and the rental of safe deposit boxes" to deal with minors as if they were adults. And another North Carolina statute authorizes minors of 15 and over to make life insurance contracts to the same extent as adults. Still other states have held that releases signed by minors to settle litigation are enforceable; otherwise, no suits involving minors could be effectively settled out of court.

## Torts and Crimes

The rules permitting minors to disaffirm most contracts do not apply to acts that are tortious or criminal in nature. Generally, minors are fully liable for any torts or crimes they commit (except, of course, minors of "tender years," such as two- or three-year-olds). Thus, if a minor drives a car negligently, anyone injured thereby can recover damages from him or her. Such liability cannot be disaffirmed. Similarly, if a minor operates a motor vehicle while intoxicated, the usual criminal penalties can be imposed (although in the criminal area, the penalties may be tempered under juvenile court procedures).

# MENTALLY IMPAIRED AND INTOXICATED PERSONS

## Mentally Impaired Persons

Persons with impaired mental capacity are, like minors, given substantial protection by the law insofar as their contractual obligations are concerned. We will briefly examine the general rules applicable to those falling within this broad category which includes the mentally retarded, the brain damaged, the senile, and persons suffering from mental illness. (In the law, the term "insane" is often broadly used to encompass all of the above classes, but sometimes is used more restrictively to refer only to the last class—persons of average intelligence who suffer periods of derangement that often vary widely as to intensity and duration.)[11]

**Adjudicated Insane:** Some mentally impaired persons are formally declared to be incompetent by a court after hearings and examination by psychologists or psychiatrists. After a person has been **adjudicated insane**, a guardian is appointed. Thereafter, any "contract" made by the insane person rather than by the guardian is absolutely void—that is, creates no liability whatever, even if it is never disaffirmed by the incompetent person or the guardian. (However, if any goods or services furnished under the contracts were *necessities* not being furnished by the guardian, the impaired person would be liable for their fair market value under a quasi-contract theory.)

**Insane in Fact:** Many mentally impaired persons have never been the subject of incompetency proceedings, but are nonetheless **insane in fact.** If at the time the contract was made, the person was so impaired that he or she was *incapable of understanding the nature and effect of the particular agreement,* then the contract is voidable. A court may order rescission of the contract at the request of the impaired party after he or she regains full mental capacity. (Again, if rescission is allowed, liability for the fair market value of any *necessities* furnished under the contract would exist under the quasi-contract principle.)

*Hanks v. McNeill Coal Corporation,* 168 P.2d 256 (1946), is typical of those controversies in which the evidence on the "understanding" issue was in sharp conflict. In that case Hanks, a farmer who had never been adjudicated insane, sold coal lands in Colorado to the coal company. At his death his executor sought to rescind the contract on the ground that Hanks was insane in fact—actually insane—at the time of the transaction. In support of this contention, the executor introduced evidence that in the months prior to the sale Hanks was increasingly interested in the "emotional type" of religion; was increasingly abusive to his family members; and manufactured a medicine for horses made of brick dust, burnt shoe leather, and pieces of ground glass. Despite this evidence, the court ruled Hanks to be sane with respect to the sale, on the basis of testimony by lawyers and a banker who had other dealings with him about the time of the sale, who testified that, as to business matters, he appeared to be "in grasp of his affairs" and "rational." In explaining its ruling, the court said: "One may have insane delusions regarding some

---

[11] In any event, the various terms or labels used in the law, such as those we mention here, are often somewhat different from, or less precise than, those used by the medical profession.

matters and be insane on some subjects, yet [be] capable of transacting business concerning matters wherein such matters are not concerned, and such insanity does not make one incompetent to contract unless the subject matter of the contract is so connected with an insane delusion as to render the afflicted party incapable of understanding the nature and effect of the agreement, or of acting rationally in the transaction."

## *Intoxicated Persons*

People occasionally seek to escape liability under a contract on the ground that they were intoxicated when it was made. Success in doing so depends primarily on the degree of intoxication found to exist at that time. Disaffirmance is allowed only if a person can establish that he or she was so intoxicated as not to understand the nature of the purported agreement. Thus a question of fact is presented, for a lesser degree of intoxication is not grounds for disaffirmance.

If the required degree of intoxication is found to have existed, the intoxicated person's right to disaffirm, upon regaining sobriety, also substantially parallels that of a minor—again, however, with one basic exception. While we have seen that minors may, as a general rule, disaffirm contracts even though unable to return the consideration that they received, intoxicated persons are required by most courts to return the full consideration as a condition of disaffirmance in all cases (unless they are able to show fraud on the part of the other contracting party). For apparent reasons, contracting parties who are intoxicated receive less protection from the law than do minors or the mentally impaired.

## REALITY OF CONSENT

A contract that has been entered into between two persons having full capacity to contract, and which appears to be valid in all other respects, may still be voidable if it turns out that the apparent consent of one or both of the parties was, in fact, not genuine. Contracts that are tainted with *fraud, innocent misrepresentation, mistake, duress, or undue influence* can ordinarily be voided (set aside) by the innocent parties. In such instances the courts will allow rescission on the ground that there was "no reality of consent." That is, although it *appears* from the form of the contract alone that the consent of both parties was genuine (or "real"), in fact it was not.

Many areas of law are essentially made up of rules that discourage conduct that is deceitful or otherwise injurious to individuals or to society in general. Some types of conduct are felt to be so detrimental to a stable society that they are flatly prohibited, and punishment for violators is prescribed. From hence have our bodies of criminal law been built up.

In other areas of law rules have come about that attempt to insure at least some degree of care and fairness when private citizens have dealings with one another, and which grant civil remedies against persons who violate them. We have seen, for example, that tortious conduct causes the wrongdoer to answer in damages to the injured party. This continuing filament of thought, to the effect that a person should not be allowed to profit by conduct that is patently offensive, is woven into the law of contracts. It is most apparent in that part of law having to do with fraud and duress and, to a lesser extent, mistake and undue influence.

## FRAUD

Leaving aside, for the moment, any attempt to define the term, the essence of **fraud** is deception—the intentional misleading of one person by another. Perhaps the most common type of fraud occurs when one person simply lies to another about a material fact, as a result of which a contract is made. Thus, if S, the owner of a current model car, tells B that he purchased it new six months ago, S knowing that it was in fact "second-hand" when he acquired it, S is guilty of fraud if B, believing this statement to be true, subsequently purchases the car. In this case, B—after learning the true facts—ordinarily can either rescind the contract and recover the purchase price or keep the car and recover damages from S.

## *Elements of Fraud*

One person can mislead another in so many ways that the courts have been reluctant to fashion a hard and fast definition of fraud; any precise definition almost certainly could be circumvented by persons intent on getting around it. Instead, the courts generally recognize that the various forms of deception they wish to forestall usually contain common elements.

When a court is called upon to decide in a given case whether the conduct of one of the parties was fraudulent, its usual approach is to see if the required elements are present. If so, fraud has been established and the victim will be afforded relief.

To be successful in a fraud action, the plaintiff is required to show all of the following:

1. That defendant made a *misrepresentation of a material fact.*
2. That the statement was made with the *intent to deceive* (i.e., defendant knew or should have known the statement was false).
3. That plaintiff *reasonably relied* on the misrepresentation.
4. That plaintiff suffered an *injury* as a result.

## *Misrepresentation of a Material Fact*

**Misrepresentation of a material fact** (or *misstatement*) is broadly interpreted to include any word or conduct that causes the innocent person to reach an erroneous conclusion of fact. Thus a seller of apples who selects the best ones in a basket and puts them on top of others of inferior quality has, in the eyes of the law, made a "statement" to a prospective buyer that all the apples are of the same quality as those which are visible.

In order for a misstatement to be fraudulent, it must be a **statement of fact**—an actual event, circumstance, or occurrence. Statements about the age of a horse, the number of acres in a tract of land, and the net profit made by a business during a given year are all statements of fact—that is, statements about a fact. And, the misstatement must be material (important). A statement that a 640-acre tract of land holds 642 acres would be false, but probably not materially so; a statement that it contained 670 acres probably would be materially false. If the innocent person can prove that a particular statement made to him or her was false in a material way, the first element of fraud has been established.

**Predictions:** Statements as to what will happen in the future are clearly not statements of fact and therefore are not fraudulent even if they turn out to be in error. Thus, if a seller of stock tells a buyer that the stock is "bound to double in value within six months," the buyer is not entitled to relief in the event the increase in value does not come about. The same is true when the seller of a motel states that "it will certainly net $14,000 in the coming year." The reason for the view that such statements do not constitute fraud, of course, is that no one can predict what will happen in the future, and a reasonable person would not put faith in such statements.[12]

**Opinion: Statements of opinion,** like predictions, are also distinguished from statements of fact. Contracts cannot be set aside on the ground of fraud simply because one of the parties, prior to making the contract, expressed an opinion that later turned out to be incorrect.

Most statements of opinion, in which the declarant is merely expressing personal feelings or judgments on a matter about which reasonable persons might have contrary views, are usually easy to recognize. For example, statements that "this is an excellent neighborhood in which to raise children" or that "this painting will harmonize beautifully with the colors of your living room" involve conclusions with which others might disagree; thus they cannot be the basis of an action of fraud brought by one who relied upon them.

Other statements, however, are not so easily placed in the "opinion" or "fact" categories. A statement by the seller of a boat that it is "perfectly safe" or a statement by a home owner that "the foundation is sound" are closer to being statements of fact than the previous representations about the neighborhood and the painting. But there are varying degrees of safety and soundness, so these statements too can be held in given situations to constitute only expressions of opinion—particularly if the declarant and

---

[12] One important type of statement about a present or future event or condition *does* impose a legal obligation on the one making it if it proves to be false: statements that are "warranties"—guarantees as to existing fact or assurances about future performance of a product by the seller. For example: A manufacturer of house paint states on the cans that "this paint, when applied according to the manufacturer's instructions above, will not crack, fade, or peel within two years of its application." If the statement proves to be false, a buyer who has purchased the paint in reliance on the statement can recover damages. The recovery in such a case would be on *breach of warranty* rather than on fraud, except in the rare situation where the buyer can prove that the seller knew the representation to be false when he or she made it. (Most, but not all, warranties are governed by the *law of sales.* Specific questions about the definition and application of express and implied warranties in regard to the sale of goods require reference to Secs. 2-312, 313, 314, 315, and 316 of the UCC, discussed in detail in Chapter 22.)

the innocent party were on a relatively equal basis insofar as their experience and general knowledge of the subject matter were concerned. (On the other hand, if the declarant is considerably more knowledgeable than the other party, such statements are likely to be viewed as statements of *fact,* and thus fraudulent if false. For example, in the case of *Groening v. Opsata,* 34 N.W.2d 560, 1948, it was held that a false statement by the seller of a summer home located on an eroding cliff on the shore of Lake Michigan that "it isn't too close [to the lake]" and that "there is nothing to fear, everything is all right" constituted fraud, in view of the fact that the seller was a builder of homes in the area.)

**Value:** Statements about an article's *value* have also caused difficulties. Nevertheless, the courts today adhere to the traditional view (in most circumstances) that the value of an article or piece of property is a matter of opinion rather than fact. Two practical reasons are the basis for this view: (1) an awareness that many types of property are prized by some people but are considered of little value by others, and (2) a recognition of the fact that sellers generally overvalue the things they are attempting to sell, and prospective buyers must accordingly place little or no reliance upon such statements.[13] Consequently, if a seller states that "this apartment building is easily worth $80,000," the buyer normally can not rescind the contract on the ground of fraud, even though he or she relied on the statement and can prove later that the actual market value of the building at the time of sale was nowhere near the stated figure and that the seller knew this at the time.

Again, the general rule is not followed when the declarant's experience and knowledge of the particular subject matter are *markedly superior* to those of the other party—especially if they are so great that the declarant is considered an "expert" in the eyes of the law. (In order to prevent such a person from taking grossly unfair advantage of those who are clearly less knowledgeable, his or her intentional misrepresentations *are* held to be fraudulent.)

The next case presents an allegation of fraud in a modern setting.

---

[13] Statements of gross overvaluation, like others that are grossly extravagant in nature ("this sport coat will wear like iron"), constitute mere "dealers' puffing."

---

### Steinberg v. Chicago Medical School
Supreme Court of Illinois,
371 N.E.2d 634 (1977)

The Chicago Medical School, defendant, issued a bulletin for the 1974–1975 school year which stated that applicants would be selected "on the basis of academic achievement, Medical College Admission Test results, personal appraisals by a pre-professional advisory committee or individual instructors, and the personal interview, if requested by the Committee on Admissions." Steinberg received a bulletin, applied for admission, and paid the required $15 application fee.

After his application was rejected, Steinberg learned that the defendant, in fact, used "nonacademic criteria" in admitting applicants, primarily the ability of the applicant or his family to pledge or make payments of large sums of money to the school. Steinberg then brought this action on behalf of all rejected applicants, claiming that defendant was guilty of fraud in failing to disclose such factors.

A number of issues were raised in the trial court. Two of these were (1) whether a contract was ever formed between the parties, and (2) if so, whether defendant's representations in its bulletin constituted fraud. The trial court ruled against plaintiff on all issues and dismissed the action. An intermediate court of appeals affirmed some rulings of the trial court but reversed others. Plaintiff appealed to the Supreme Court of Illinois. Those parts of the highest court's decision applicable to the two selected issues are summarized below.

---

**Decision:** The trial judge erred in dismissing the action. The defendant's brochure constituted an invitation for offers to apply to medical school. Steinberg's application constituted such an offer, and defendant's voluntary reception of the application and accompanying fee was an acceptance—i.e., a promise to evaluate Steinberg's qualifications. Thus a contract *was* formed, with its terms including the statement in the brochure regarding the criteria by which applications would be evaluated.

*(continued)*

In regard to the claim of fraud, Steinberg alleged that defendant gave strong preference to applicants whose families made substantial gifts (averaging $48,000 in 1973) to defendant, rather than using the criteria mentioned in the brochure. Although a fraud claim usually cannot be based on a false representation of intention or future conduct, "there is a recognized exception where the false promise or representation of future conduct is alleged to be the scheme employed to accomplish the fraud." That exception applies here. Steinberg has alleged facts which, if proved, would show that defendant did not intend to live up to its promise at the time it made it. The case is remanded to the trial court for determination of facts. ∎

---

**Law:** Under the early common-law rule of this country, *statements of law* made by lay persons were clearly held not to constitute statements of fact and thus could not be the basis for actions of fraud. If the seller of a vacant lot that carries a C-1 zoning classification assures the buyer that "this classification permits the erection of duplex rental units," a statement that the seller knows is not true, the buyer who purchases the property in reliance on the statement ordinarily cannot maintain an action for damages. The rule was based on two grounds: (1) the generally reasonable feeling that a statement made by a nonlawyer about a point of law should not be relied upon by the one to whom it is made, and (2) the somewhat more questionable maxim that "everyone is presumed to know the law."

While this is still the rule applied to most cases, it is subject to an increasing number of exceptions. One major exception comprises statements of law made by persons who—because of their professional or occupational status—can reasonably be expected to know the law relating to their specialty, even though they are not attorneys. Thus intentional misrepresentations of law by persons such as real estate brokers and bank cashiers as to legal matters within their particular specialties are frequently held to be fraudulent.

**Silence, Traditionally:** The traditional common-law rule was *caveat emptor* ("let the buyer beware"). Under this rule, buyers had the responsibility to look out for themselves in making a purchase. Thus, assume that a seller knew that a car had been involved in an accident that bent the car's frame. If the seller told the buyer: "This car has never been in an accident," a clear misstatement of material fact would have occurred. When the buyer learned the truth, he could rescind due to fraud. But what if the seller did not make such a statement, but simply kept silent about the accident? The traditional rule stated that mere silence (failure to disclose a material fact) does *not constitute fraud.* The reasoning was that in most instances the parties are dealing at arm's length,[14] possessing roughly the same amount of experience and knowledge relating to the subject matter of the contract. And, in many instances, the facts not disclosed could have been ascertained by the buyer with reasonable inspection or inquiry.

Today, however, *caveat emptor* has been so riddled with exceptions that in many jurisdictions it is difficult to speak of it as being the general rule. Court rulings and state consumer protection statutes have created so many situations where sellers must volunteer adverse information or be charged with fraud that many claim the new general rule is *caveat venditor* ("let the seller beware").

**Silence and the Duty to Speak:** The courts have found several types of situations where the withholding of information is so manifestly unfair that silence should be held to constitute fraud. To prevent unfairness of this degree, the courts say that, in such situations, a "duty to speak" exists. It is difficult to summarize the duty-to-speak categories with precision, because the silence cases involve such a wide variety of fact-patterns, and because the rules of the various states applicable to duty to speak situations are often couched in general terms (to give the courts substantial discretion in their application). Additionally, the law is continuing to evolve in this area, as the courts seek to raise moral standards in the marketplace by applying the rules to situations that were earlier outside their scope.

---

[14]Parties are said to deal at "arm's length" when their relationship is such that neither party owes a duty to divulge information to the other party (as distinguished from such exceptional relationships as attorney-client and guardian-ward relationships.)

Despite these factors, several fairly well-defined situations do exist in which the courts generally agree that a duty to speak exists. (In such instances the courts often speak of "intentionally withheld information," of "concealment," and of silence as part of a "plan" to deceive.)

The first of these instances is the sale of property that contains a **latent defect** (or *hidden defect*)—one that a simple or casual inspection by a prospective purchaser ordinarily would not disclose. Common examples are a cracked motor block in an automobile and a termite infestation in a house. A property owner who has knowledge of such conditions is guilty of fraud if he or she does not apprise the prospective purchaser of them—assuming, of course, that the innocent purchaser subsequently enters into a contract to buy the property.

While the latent defect rule, abstractly stated, is highly commendable, the practical protection it affords is less than one might hope for. Frequently it is difficult for the buyer to prove that the defect actually existed at the time of purchase—particularly if a long period of time has elapsed before its discovery. And even if this hurdle is cleared, the buyer has to establish that the seller knew, or should have known, of the defect when the sale occurred. The seller's contention that he or she was honestly unaware of the defective condition is frequently accepted by a jury.[15]

A second duty to speak situation occurs where a **fiduciary relationship** exists—that is, where one of the parties occupies a position of "trust and confidence" relative to the other. (This differs from the ordinary situation, where the parties are dealing "at arm's length.") For example, when a partnership is considering a land purchase, a partner who is part owner of the land under consideration has a duty to divulge his or her interest to the co-partner before the purchase is made. Similarly, a corporate officer who is purchasing stock from a shareholder has a duty to disclose any special facts of which he or she has knowledge, by virtue of that position, which would affect the value of the stock.

The third category comprises situations in which one party has **superior knowledge** about the subject matter of the contract as a result of his or her experience, training, or special relationship with the subject matter. In this type of circumstance the rule has obvious application where the silent party—the one possessing the superior knowledge—is an "expert" in the area, but it often applies to other parties as well. The rule commonly applied is that if one party has superior knowledge, *or* knowledge which is not within the reasonable reach of the other party (and which such party could not discover by the exercise of means open to both parties), there is a duty on the party possessing the knowledge to disclose it. Under this rule, for example, a buyer of Oklahoma land who, by virtue of his employment with an oil company, learns of an oil "strike" on an adjacent ranch would be guilty of fraud if he did not disclose this information to the seller, a rancher. On the other hand, if the buyer was simply another ranch owner in the area, his or her nondisclosure of this information would probably not be fraudulent.

Outside of these situations, most courts take the view that neither party has a duty to volunteer information to the other, even though it might bear materially on the other's decision of whether to contract. Thus the seller of a trash collection business probably has no duty to tell a prospective purchaser of indications that the city is going to institute a collection service of its own—especially if this information is as available to the buyer as it is to the seller.[16]

In the case below the California court applied a rule that was, in essence, the superior knowledge rule, although it did not specifically label it as such.

---

[15] Normally the rule on hidden defects does not work in reverse. Thus, if the buyer possesses information about the property that causes its value to be higher than the seller believes it to be, the buyer does not have a duty to divulge this information to the seller (unless the buyer is an expert in the field by reason of training or experience).

[16] *Jappe v. Mandt,* 278 P.2d 940 (1955). (Although the buyer's action for damages based upon fraud failed, an action for rescission might have succeeded on the ground of "unilateral mistake"—a subject discussed later in the chapter—*if* the buyer had been able to show that the seller was aware of his ignorance about the proposed city action.)

## Kallgren v. Steele
### District Court of Appeal, 2nd District, California, 279 P.2d 1027 (1955)

The Kallgrens, plaintiffs, bought a resort in the San Bernardino National Forest from the Steeles. After the purchase, the Kallgrens learned that some of the buildings encroached onto the state right-of-way through the forest, and for that reason the U.S. Forest Service was revoking their permit to maintain the resort. They brought action to recover damages, alleging that the Steeles were guilty of fraud in concealing the fact that the buildings were in part within the highway right-of-way.

As a defense, the Steeles contended that they had no duty to divulge any information to the Kallgrens about the encroachment of the buildings and that their silence thus could not constitute fraud. The trial court rejected this defense, and the Steeles appealed.

**Decision:** The trial court was correct in finding fraud on the part of the Steeles. The evidence was undisputed that they knew of the wrongful location of the buildings and were aware that the Kallgrens were ignorant of this fact. The Steeles therefore had a duty to speak, and their failure to do so constituted fraud. Under California case law, concealment constitutes fraud where a seller knows of facts which "materially affect the desirability of the property, and which he knows are unknown to the buyer." ∎

## *Intent to Deceive*

The second element of fraud is *knowledge of falsity* (or, as it is sometimes called, "scienter"). Thus the innocent party must ordinarily prove that the person making the statement knew, or should have known, that it was false at the time it was made. However, the knowledge of falsity requirement is also met if a person makes a statement "with a reckless disregard for the truth," even if the declarant did not actually know it was false. Thus, if the seller of a used car has no idea as to its mileage but nevertheless states that "it has not been driven more than 30,000 miles," the statement constitutes fraud if it is later proven that the true mileage materially exceeded that figure.

## *Reliance*

The victim of a misrepresentation must show that he or she reasonably relied on the misstatement at the time of contracting. Sometimes this is not difficult to establish. The innocent party does not have to prove that the fact in regard to which the misrepresentation was made was the primary factor in inducing him or her to make the contract. It is sufficient that the misrepresentation involved a matter tending to influence the decision.

Reliance does not exist, of course, if the one accused of fraud can prove that the other party actually knew the true facts before making the contract. Also, a charge of fraud will fail if the victim's reliance was not reasonable under the circumstances. While the old rule of *caveat emptor* is much less significant than formerly, a buyer still cannot blindly accept everything he or she is told. For example, a buyer given an opportunity to view the property is presumed to observe any patent (obvious) defects that might exist. To illustrate—the seller of a used television set tells the buyer it "produces an excellent picture on all channels." If the buyer viewed the set in operation prior to the sale and complained of reception on one channel, that person could hardly contend after the sale that he had reasonably relied on the seller's representation.

## *Injury*

The last element of a successful fraud action is a showing by the innocent party that he or she suffered an injury, usually an economic loss, as a result of the misrepresentation. In most cases proof of injury (or "damage") is the easiest of the fraud elements to prove. For example, in a typical case involving the sale of property, the buyer is able to show that the value of the property he or she received is substantially less than it would have been if the seller's representations had been true.

## Remedies for Fraud

Once fraud is established, the defrauded party always has the right to rescind the contract. When such a person chooses the remedy of *rescission,* he or she must ordinarily return the consideration, if any, that was received from the other party. Rescission, then, is designed to restore the parties to their original positions.

In some instances the defrauded party may wish to keep the consideration, for example, a parcel of land, even though it had been misrepresented by the seller. In such a case the buyer may keep the consideration (i.e., "affirm the contract") and bring suit for *damages*—which in the usual situation is, at the minimum, the difference between the actual value of the property the buyer received, and the value it would have had if the representations had been true. (Additionally, because fraud is a tort, the innocent party may be awarded punitive damages as well.)

As a general rule, the defrauded party must elect either to rescind the contract or to recover damages. However, where the fraud involves the making of a sales contract, such an election need not be made. Sec. 2-721 of the UCC provides, in part, that where fraud is established, "Neither rescission nor a claim for rescission of the contract . . . shall bar or be . . . inconsistent with a claim for damages or other remedy." Thus in circumstances where a buyer or seller seeking rescission can show that he or she will suffer a loss notwithstanding the rescission, damages may also be recovered.

## INNOCENT MISREPRESENTATION

If all the elements of fraud are present in a particular case, except that the person making the misstatement honestly (and reasonably) believed the statement to be true, that person is guilty of **innocent misrepresentation** rather than fraud. Under the rule of most states, the victim can rescind the contract on that ground, but is usually not given the alternative remedy of damages. Innocent misrepresentation and fraud are contrasted in Figure 15.2.

## MISTAKE

Cases are continually arising where one of the parties to a contract attempts to have it set aside by the court on the ground that he or she was mistaken in some respect at the time the contract was made. Often the mistake involves opinion or judgment rather than fact, in which case no relief will be granted. For example, a person contracts to buy land for $30,000 thinking this is its true value. If its actual value proves to be much less, he or she has shown bad judgment and will not be permitted to rescind the contract. Similarly, if a person purchases stock in the belief that it will greatly increase in value in a short time, he or she obviously cannot have the contract set aside in the event that it does not perform as hoped. If rescission were permitted on grounds such as these, the basic value of all contracts would be destroyed.

However, in certain limited situations a plea of mistake will afford grounds for rescission of a contract, if the mistake was one of *fact.* The general rule

**Figure 15.2 Fraud and Innocent Misrepresentation**

| | Innocent Misrepresentation | Fraud |
|---|---|---|
| Elements | The representation must:<br>1. Be false<br>2. Concern a fact<br>3. Be material<br>4. Be relied upon<br><br>5. Be made with reasonable belief that it is true | 5. Be made with knowledge of its falsity (or reckless disregard for truth)<br>6. Be made with the intent to deceive |
| Injury | None required | Financial loss as a result of the misrepresentation |
| Remedies | Rescission | Rescission, or retention of defective performance by fraud victim, *and* recovery of damages |

is that if both parties were mistaken as to a material fact at the time of contracting, either party can rescind the agreement. On the other hand, if only one of the parties was mistaken, rescission will not be granted unless that person can show that the other party knew, or should have known, of the mistake at the time the contract was made. When both parties are mistaken, the mistake is a **bilateral mistake;** when only one is mistaken, it is a **unilateral mistake.**

## Bilateral Mistake

The following examples illustrate the general principle that a contract can be set aside if there is a mutual mistake as to the *existence,* the *identity,* or the *character* of the subject matter of the contract.

**1.** B purchases S's summer home on April 10. Subsequently, B learns that, unknown to either party, the home was destroyed by fire on April 1. Since both parties entered into the contract under the mistaken assumption that the subject matter of the contract actually existed at that time, B can have the contract set aside.

**2.** P owns two properties outside Woodsfield, Ohio. G, after viewing both acreages, makes P a written offer to purchase one for $18,000. P accepts the offer. It later develops that G had one property in mind while P, after reading the description contained in G's offer, honestly and reasonably believed that G was referring to the other property. Either party can rescind the agreement, because there was a mutual mistake about the identity of the contract's subject matter.

**3.** C purchases a gemstone from D for $25. At the time of contracting, both parties believe the stone is a topaz. In fact, it turns out to be an uncut diamond worth $700. Since both parties were mistaken about the true character of the contract's subject matter, D can have the contract rescinded, thereby recovering the stone.

The principle is not applicable to situations where both parties realize that they are *in doubt* as to a particular matter, but enter into a contract nonetheless. Thus, in example 3 above, if neither C nor D had any idea what the stone was when they made the contract, D could not rescind the contract when the stone proved to be an uncut diamond (nor could C have rescinded had the stone turned out to be a worthless one). In such an instance both parties had, by contract, "assumed the risk" as to the stone's value.

With these general rules of law in mind let us examine the problem presented by the following case.

---

### Beachcomber Coins, Inc. v. Boskett
Superior Court of New Jersey, Appellate Division, 400 A.2d 78 (1979)

Boskett was a part-time dealer in coins in New Jersey. He owned a 1916 dime which bore the letter "D," indicating that it had been minted in Denver. Because of the rarity of such coins, their market value was greatly in excess of their monetary worth.

Beachcomber Coins, plaintiff, was interested in buying the coin, and one of its owners examined the coin to determine its genuineness. After an examination of 45 minutes he was satisfied that the coin was, in fact, minted in Denver, and he purchased it on behalf of plaintiff for $500. Later plaintiff was advised by the American Numismatic Society that the "D" was a counterfeit. When Boskett, the seller, refused to take back the coin and refund the purchase price, plaintiff brought this action asking rescission of the contract.

The trial judge, sitting without a jury, found that there was a mutual mistake of fact (a mistake as to the coin's genuineness) that would ordinarily justify rescission of the contract. However, he further found that under customary coin-dealing procedures a buyer of a coin who was permitted to examine it before purchase "assumed the risk" that it might be counterfeit. He therefore dismissed the action and plaintiff appealed.

---

**Decision:** The plaintiff was entitled to have the contract rescinded on the ground of mistake of fact. Both parties believed that the coin had been minted in Denver when in fact it was not. The finding of mutual mistake by the trial court, therefore, was correct.

However, the trial court's further finding, to the effect that the plaintiff assumed the risk of genuineness in this case, was not correct. It is true, under ordinary contract law, that if the parties to a sale know there is *doubt* as to a certain matter and

*(continued)*

contract on that basis, neither buyer nor seller can subsequently rescind the contract simply because the true fact turns out to be contrary to his or her belief. That rule is not applicable here, however, because both parties were "certain" that the coin was genuine. The trial court's finding that it was customary in the coin dealing business in New Jersey for the buyer of a coin to assume the risk of genuineness is also erroneous because the evidence produced by the defendant was too weak to support such a conclusion. Since the plaintiff did not, therefore, assume the risk under either theory, the case falls under the general rule that a contract entered into under a mutual mistake of fact may be set aside by either party. ■

## *Unilateral Mistake*

Where only one party to a contract is mistaken about a material fact, rescission is ordinarily not allowed unless the mistake was (or should have been) apparent to the other party. Two examples follow.

**1.** B purchases a painting from S for $300; B believes it was painted by a well-known artist. B does not, however, disclose this belief to S. In fact, the painting is the work of an amateur and consequently worth no more than $50. Since only B was mistaken as to the identity of the artist, the mistake is unilateral and the contract cannot be rescinded. On the other hand, B would have been permitted to rescind if S had been aware of B's mistake and had not corrected it.

**2.** X furnishes three contractors with specifications for a building project and asks them to submit construction bids. C submits a bid for $48,000 and D submits one for $46,500. E's bid, because of an error in addition, is $27,000 rather than the intended $47,000. If X accepts E's bid, E can have the contract set aside if the jury finds (as is likely to be the case) either that X actually knew of the mistake when he accepted the bid or that he should have been aware of the mistake because of the wide discrepancy in the bids.

## *Cautions*

The "bilateral-unilateral mistake" rule of thumb, while widely followed, by no means settles all cases that arise in the general area of mistake. In the first place, there is some disagreement as to what constitutes a bilateral mistake. Many courts, for example, take the view that such a mistake exists only where the parties have arrived at their erroneous conclusions independently of one another, rather than one party simply relying on information supplied by the other.

Second, a few states have statutes relating to contracts entered into under mistake of fact that sometimes permit rescission where common-law principles would not.

Third, the court will sometimes settle cases purely on "equitable principles"—the basis of overall fairness in particular situations—thereby giving little or no weight to the bilateral-unilateral factor. Many unilateral mistake cases arise in construction contracts when erroneous bids are made. A common approach allows rescission if three factors are present: (1) The mistake was one of mere negligence—for example, the misreading of plans or the erroneous adding of a column of figures due to exhaustion or haste. (2) Rescission would cause no injury to the nonmistaken party other than loss of the erroneous bargain—for example, if the mistake is discovered and called to the attention of the nonmistaken party before the contract is awarded or soon thereafter (i.e., before construction commences while the lowest nonmistaken bid could still be accepted). (3) Holding the mistaken party to his or her bid would be "unconscionable." Thus, a mistaken bidder in a school construction contract was allowed to rescind on the basis of unilateral mistake where the day after the contract was awarded he called the school district's attention to a simple error in addition that had led to a bid of $534,175 rather than the intended $634,175.[17]

## *Additional Types of Mistake*

Occasionally a mistake involves the provisions of the contract itself rather than the contract's subject matter. For example, an offeree might accept an offer that

---

[17] *Taylor v. Arlington ISD*, 335 S.W.2d 371 (Tex. 1960).

he or she has misread, only to learn later that the offer was in fact substantially different than it seemed. This is a unilateral mistake, and the offeree is bound by the resulting contract (unless the acceptance itself discloses the mistake to the offeror).

Mutual mistakes as to the value of an article being sold generally are held to constitute mistakes of opinion rather than fact, and rescission is not permitted in such cases. Thus, if B buys a painting from S for $10,000, both parties correctly believing that the artist was Andrew Wyeth, B obviously cannot have the contract set aside simply because he later learns that the painting's true value is only $5,000.

There is somewhat greater uncertainty insofar as mistakes of law are concerned. The courts at one time refused to permit rescission of contracts where a mistake of law existed, either bilateral or unilateral, on the theory that such a mistake was not a mistake of fact. (This idea was consistent with the view that a *misstatement of law* does not constitute a misstatement of fact, under the law of fraud.) Today, however, most courts treat *mistakes of law and fact* the same— that is, they will set aside contracts which both parties entered into under a mistake of law as well as those in which the mistake of one party was apparent to the other.

## DURESS

Occasionally a person will seek to escape liability under a contract on the ground that he or she was forced to enter into it. Often the courts find that the "force" is insignificant in the eyes of the law, and the complaining party is held to the contract. For example, if a person enters into a contract simply because he or she knows that failure to do so will incur the wrath of some third person, such as his or her employer or spouse, relief will not be granted. If, on the other hand, the degree of compulsion is so great as to totally rob the person of free will, duress exists, and the contract can be rescinded.

One early definition of **duress** that still remains authoritative is the following:

> (1) any wrongful act of one person that compels a manifestation of apparent assent by another to a transaction without his volition, or (2) any wrongful threat of one person by words or other conduct that induces another to enter into a transaction under the influence of such fear as precludes him from exercising free will and judgment, if the threat was intended or should reasonably have been expected to operate as an inducement.[18]

A necessary element of duress is fear—a genuine and reasonable fear on the part of the victim that he or she will be subjected to an injurious, unlawful act by not acceding to the other party's demands. Thus, if a person signs a contract at gunpoint or after being physically beaten, duress exists, and the victim can escape liability on that ground. Duress also exists when a person makes a contract as a consequence of another person's threat of harm (for instance, kidnapping a child) if the contract is refused.

Generally, the innocent party must show that the act actually committed or threatened was a wrongful one. For instance, a contract entered into between a striking union and an employer cannot be set aside by the latter on the ground of duress if the strike was a lawful one—as, for example, if the strike occurred after an existing "no-strike" contract between union and employer had expired.

The threat of a criminal suit is generally held to constitute duress. For example: X proposes a contract to Y and tells him that if he refuses to sign the agreement, X will turn over evidence to the prosecuting attorney's office tending to prove that Y had embezzled money from his employer six weeks earlier. To prevent this, Y signs the contract. Y can have the contract rescinded on the ground of duress, because a threat to use the criminal machinery of the state for such a purpose is clearly wrongful—regardless of whether or not Y had actually committed the crime in question. Threat of a civil suit, on the other hand, usually does not constitute duress.

While a contract cannot be set aside simply because there is a disparity of bargaining power between the parties, the courts are beginning to accept the idea that *economic duress* (or business compulsion) can be grounds for the rescission of a contract in exceptional situations. The decision in the next case sets forth three requirements that ordinarily must be met in order for a plaintiff to be successful in a suit asking rescission on this ground.

---

[18]*Restatement, Contracts,* §492. The American Law Institute, 1932.

### Totem Marine T. & B. v. Alyeska Pipeline
Supreme Court of Alaska,
584 P.2d 15 (1978)

Totem Marine Tug and Barge, Inc., entered into a contract with Alyeska Pipeline Services under which Totem was to transport large quantities of pipeline construction materials from Houston, Texas, to Alaska. After Totem began its performance, many problems arose. One major difficulty was the fact that the tonnages to be shipped were six times greater than Alyeska had indicated. Additionally, long delays occurred in getting Totem's vessels through the Panama Canal, which resulted from Alyeska's failure to furnish promised documents to Totem by specified dates. After these and other problems, Alyeska cancelled the contract without cause.

At the time of the wrongful termination, Alyeska owed Totem about $300,000. Officers of Alyeska at first promised that it would pay Totem invoices promptly, but later they told Totem that it would have its money "in six to eight months." (Totem alleged that the delay in payment occurred after Alyeska learned through negotiations with Totem lawyers that Totem's creditors were pressing it for their payments, and that without immediate cash it would go into bankruptcy—allegations that Alyeska did not deny.)

After further negotiations, a settlement agreement was made in 1975, under which Alyeska paid Totem $97,000 in return for surrender of all claims against it. In early 1976 Totem brought this action to rescind the settlement agreement on the ground of economic duress, and to recover the balance allegedly due under the original contract. The trial court ruled as a matter of law that the circumstances under which the settlement occurred did not constitute duress, and dismissed the complaint. Totem appealed.

**Decision:** The trial court should not have dismissed Totem's complaint. Economic duress exists where (1) one party involuntarily accepts the terms of another, (2) circumstances permit no other alternative, and (3) such circumstances are the result of coercive acts of the other party.

In this case, Totem's allegations, if proved, would support a finding that its settlement was executed under economic duress. Totem alleged that Alyeska withheld payment of an acknowledged debt because it knew that Totem had no choice but to accept an inadequate sum in settlement of that debt; that Totem was faced with bankruptcy; and that Totem was unable to meet its pressing debts other than by accepting the immediate cash payment. If, in fact, Totem's release of all claims against Alyeska was executed under these circumstances, the release may be set aside on the ground of economic duress. (The case was therefore remanded to the trial court for further proceedings.) ■

## UNDUE INFLUENCE

There are some circumstances in which a person can escape contractual liability by proving that his or her consent was brought about by the **undue influence** of the other party to the contract. While many kinds of influence are perfectly lawful, influence is undue (excessive) where one party so dominates the will of the other that the latter's volition actually is destroyed. A common example occurs where one person, as the result of advanced age and physical deterioration, begins to rely more and more upon a younger, more energetic acquaintance or relative for advice until the point is reached where the older person's willpower and judgment are almost totally controlled by the dominant party. If the older, weaker person can show (1) that he or she was induced to enter into a particular contract by virtue of the dominant party's power and influence, rather than as the result of exercising his or her own volition, and (2) that the dominant party used this power to take advantage of him or her, undue influence is established and he or she is freed of liability on this ground.

The same general rules for undue influence in the making of contracts also apply to the making of wills. Therefore, it may be helpful to read the *Casper v. McDowell* case in Chapter 46, which discusses wills and estate law.

### *Home Solicitation Statutes*

Several states have passed **home solicitation statutes** which protect persons who are subjected to high-pressure sales tactics by salespersons who come to their homes. These statutes supplement the common-law concepts discussed above. The general rule is that a buyer has an automatic three-day period in which to cancel a contract where: (1) the contract is for land, goods or services worth over $25; (2) the sale was initiated by the seller; and (3) the contract was completed at a place other than the seller's place of business (usually the buyer's home). The buyer need not show fraud, undue influence, or mistake. The three-day right to rescind is automatic. The federal government has passed a similar statute which applies to all sales affecting interstate commerce. Home solicitation statutes are discussed in more detail in Chapter 50.

## SUMMARY

A voidable contract is an agreement in which one of the parties possesses the legal right to have the contract set aside (i.e., avoided or disaffirmed). The two most common situations in which such a right exists are (1) where there is a lack of capacity, as in minors' contracts, and (2) where reality of consent is lacking, as in contracts tainted with fraud, mistake, or duress.

Minors generally have the right to disaffirm their contracts any time before reaching the age of majority—18 in most states—plus a reasonable time thereafter, even as to contracts that have been fully performed. In such a situation, the minor is required to return the consideration if able to do so. In situations where return of the consideration is not possible, disaffirmance is still generally allowed, in which case the entire loss is borne by the other party to the contract. Additionally, the right to disaffirm is a one-sided one, being possessed only by the minor.

Under the majority rule, where the minor is disaffirming an executed contract calling for the purchase of goods that are not a necessity of life, he or she can recover all of the contract price paid, without being charged with the reasonable value of the use of the goods while in his or her possession. However, where the contract is for the purchase of goods or services that qualify as necessities, the minor in all cases is liable for the reasonable value of the goods actually used, or the services received. And, in any case in which the minor, after reaching the age of majority, expressly or impliedly indicates that he or she will abide by it, the contract has been ratified and the right to disaffirm is lost. The rights of contracting parties who are under a mental disability, or who are intoxicated, generally parallel those of minors.

Even if both parties to a contract are competent, the contract can be set aside if tainted with fraud, innocent misrepresentation, or duress, and—in some circumstances—on the ground of mistake. The elements of fraud are (1) misrepresentation of a fact, (2) made with the intent to deceive (i.e., with knowledge of falsity), (3) reasonable reliance by the other party, and (4) injury to such party. A statement of opinion cannot normally be the basis for a fraud action unless the declarant—the one expressing the opinion—possesses a knowledge of the subject matter of the contract that is markedly superior to that of the other party. And silence does not constitute fraud, except in those limited circumstances in which the courts hold there was a "duty to speak." On the subject of mistake, the basic rule is that a contract can be rescinded only on the ground of mutual mistake of fact, or on the ground of unilateral mistake known to the other party. Duress—when one deprives a party of his or her free will to contract by committing (or threatening to commit) a wrongful act—is also a ground for the rescission of a contract.

## KEY TERMS

**Voidable contract**
**Capacity**
**Minor**
**Ordinary contract**
**Ratification**
**Necessaries**
**Adjudicated insane**
**Insane in fact**
**Fraud**
**Misrepresentation of a material fact**
**Statement of fact**
**Statement of opinion**
**Latent defect**
**Fiduciary relationship**
**Superior knowledge**
**Innocent misrepresentation**
**Bilateral mistake**
**Unilateral mistake**
**Duress**
**Undue influence**
**Home solicitation statutes**

## QUESTIONS AND PROBLEMS

1. McAllister, while a minor, purchased a car under circumstances in which it was clearly not a necessity, and gave the seller his promissory note in payment. The note obligated McAllister to make specified monthly payments beginning with the time of purchase. Just before reaching the age of majority, at which time McAllister had made no payments on the note, he lost possession of the car under circumstances which the trial court found to be "unknown." (It was clear, however, that the car was neither retained by McAllister nor returned to the seller.) Three years after McAllister reached the age of majority, at which time he had still made no payments, the seller sued him on the note, and McAllister then informed the seller that he was disaffirming the purchase and the note. The seller argued that McAllister's attempted disaffirmance was invalid since he waited so long to exercise this right. Is the seller correct? Explain. (*Warwick Municipal Employees Credit Union v. McAllister,* 293 A.2d 516, 1972.)

2. Ballinger and his wife, while minors, purchased a mobile home. In payment, they gave the seller of the home a promissory note which they signed as co-makers. Before reaching the age of majority they disaffirmed the contract and the note. The seller then brought suit against them to recover the reasonable value of the home, on the ground that it constituted a necessity of life. At the trial, the Ballingers introduced evidence showing that Ballinger's parents were more than willing to furnish them with living accommodations in their own home at the time they made the purchase, and thereafter. What bearing, if any, would this evidence have on the question whether the home constituted a necessity? Explain your reasoning. (*Ballinger v. Craig,* 121 N.E.2d 66, 1953.)

3. Robert Moore opened joint savings accounts in two banks, with the accounts listing a nephew and niece as co-depositors. These accounts, if valid, would result in the money in them passing to the nephew and niece as gifts upon Moore's death. After Moore died, other relatives brought a court action to set aside these joint accounts on the ground that Moore was incompetent to contract at the time that he established them. To support this contention, these relatives produced evidence that over a period of several weeks prior to the opening of the accounts Moore had often been found wandering on city streets late at night, not knowing where he was; that on one occasion he tried to extinguish the cooking units on his electric stove by pouring water on them; that a neighbor stopped transacting business with him "because he acted so queerly"; and that he was once stopped on a street by a police officer because of "insufficient clothing." Do you think this evidence is sufficient to support the relatives' claim that Moore was incompetent when he made the transactions with the banks? Can you think of other evidence that might contradict this claim? Discuss. (*In re Moore's Estate,* 188 N.E.2d 221, 1962.)

4. Several employees of Empiregas, Inc., plaintiffs, had signed one-year employment contracts with that company over a period of many years. Each time that the employees objected to noncompetition clauses in the contracts they were told by supervisors not to worry about them, just "to sign." At the time of signing their most recent contracts the employees were told by their supervisor that "you know what we have always told you. (These contracts) are not worth a damn; it is just a piece of paper." The employees signed, and after they had fulfilled their contracts they sought employment with a competing firm. Empiregas wrote the competing firm that the employees could not be hired by it because of the noncompetition clauses in their contracts. Empiregas also threatened to sue the firm and employees if it hired them. When the firm decided not to employ them, the employees brought this action against Empiregas alleging that it had "fraudulently induced" them to sign the contracts. Two of Empiregas's defenses were that the statements were not fraudulent because (1) they were merely statements of opinion and (2) they were statements of law rather than fact. Do you agree with either defense? Why or why not? (*Empiregas, Inc. v. Hardy,* 487 So. 2d 244, 1985.)

5. Midwest Supply, a company in the business of preparing income tax returns, advertised "guaranteed accurate tax preparation." Waters, after reading the ad, contacted Midwest and was induced to apply for refunds that he was not legally entitled to. After Waters received the improper refunds, the Internal Revenue Service recovered the payments from him in addition to substantial penalties. Waters then sued Midwest to recover damages on the basis of fraud, alleging that (1) the statement in its ad was false; (2) the employees of Midwest had little or no training in accounting or income tax preparation; and (3) Midwest told its employees not to correct newswriters who described the employees as "specialists and tax experts." On these facts, is Midwest guilty of fraud? Discuss. (*Midwest Supply, Inc. v. Waters,* 510 P.2d 876, 1973.)

6. Whale applied for the position of rabbi with the Jewish Center of Sussex County, New Jersey. The application listed information regarding his education, ordination as a rabbi, and job experience from 1956 to 1977, all of which was true. The Jewish Center employed Whale, but soon thereafter brought action to rescind the contract on the ground of fraud, alleging that Whale failed to disclose the fact that he had earlier been convicted of the crime of using the mails to defraud. Whale defended on the ground that in his resumé accompanying the application he indicated that further information and references would be furnished on re-

quest, but that the center did not avail itself of this opportunity. Is Whale's defense good? Why or why not? (*Jewish Center of Sussex County v. Whale,* 397 A.2d 712, 1978.)

**7.** The seller of a building in Lusk, Wyoming, told an out-of-state buyer who had not seen the property that "it could readily be rented for $100 per month." The buyer, after making the contract, learned that the building had no rental value and that the seller knew this when he made his statement. When the buyer brought a fraud action against him, the seller contended that his statement was merely an expression of value, and thus a statement of opinion rather than one of fact. Rule on this defense, with reasons to support your ruling. (*Cahill v. Readon,* 273 P. 653, 1928.)

**8.** Black purchased two violins from White for $8,000, the bill of sale describing them as "one Joseph Guarnerius violin and one Stradivarius violin dated 1717." Unknown to either party, neither violin was made by Guarnerius or Stradivarius. Upon discovery of this fact, can Black set aside the purchase and recover payment? Explain.

**9.** The federal government solicited bids for construction of a Veterans Administration Hospital. Peter Kiewit Sons Co. (D), a general contractor, contacted several subcontractors for purposes of compiling a bid. At the last minute, Heifetz Metal Crafts (P) called D and offered to do the kitchen-equipment part of the job for $99,500, which was $52,000 less than any other subcontractor had estimated. P asked D whether its bid was in accordance with all plans and specifications. P stated that it was and that the bid would remain firm. D then reduced its overall bid by $52,000 and submitted to the government a bid of $17,994,200, and was awarded the contract. After construction was underway, P discovered that it had made a unilateral mistake, believing that kitchen work was to be done in only one of the buildings in the complex, rather than several. P sued to rescind its bid. Should P succeed? (*Heifetz Metal Crafts. v. Peter Kiewit Sons Co.,* 264 F.2d 435, 8th Cir. 1959.)

**10.** IUC, a relatively small construction company, entered into a written contract with New England Telephone & Telegraph (NET) to assemble and install conduits under a river for $149,680. Delays caused by NET forced IUC to perform its work during the winter rather than the summer as originally contemplated. NET repeatedly told IUC that it would pay the extra cost if IUC would complete the work. The changes cost IUC over $800,000. However, it signed a release settling the claim for $575,000 because NET offered the amount on a "take-it-or-leave-it basis" at a time when IUC was in financial distress. Later IUC sought to invoke the theory of duress in order to disaffirm the release so it could sue for more money. Should IUC succeed? (*IUC v. New England Telephone & Telegraph Co.,* 393 N.E.2d 968, Mass.App. 1979.)

# CHAPTER 16

# CONTRACTS IN WRITING

Many people have the idea that contracts are never enforceable unless they are in writing; thus we hear movie magnate Sam Goldwyn's famous aphorism, "Oral contracts aren't worth the paper they're written on." Insofar as the law is concerned, however, most oral contracts are just as enforceable as written contracts *if their terms can be established in court.*[1] In this chapter we will examine the relatively few kinds of contracts that *are* required by law to be in writing; then we will consider general problems relating to written contracts. (In a situation where the law requires a contract to be in writing, any contract that does not meet that requirement—i.e., one that is entirely oral in nature, or that is written but ambiguous—is an "unenforceable" contract, rather than a "void" or "voidable" one. Thus, as the term indicates, neither party is bound by such a contract—with limited exceptions noted later.)

## THE STATUTE OF FRAUDS

In England, prior to the latter part of the seventeenth century, all oral contracts were enforceable as long as their existence and terms could be established. Under this approach, it became apparent that many unscrupulous plaintiffs were obtaining judgments against innocent defendants by the use of *perjured testimony*—false testimony given under oath. To illustrate: P claimed that D had breached a particular oral contract, a contract that D denied making. If P could induce his witnesses (usually by the payment of money) to falsely testify that they heard D agree to the alleged contract, and if D could neither refute such testimony by witnesses of his own nor otherwise prove that P's witnesses were lying, a judgment would ordinarily be granted in favor of P.[2] To eliminate this and other kinds of fraud, Parliament in 1677 passed "An Act for the Prevention of Frauds and Perjuries"—or, as it is commonly called, the **statute of frauds.**

The statute of frauds required certain types of contracts to be in writing in order to be enforceable. Virtually every American state has its own statute of frauds patterned after the original English version, which required the following types of contracts or promises to be in writing (or be evidenced by a written memorandum):

**1.** A contract calling for the sale of land or an interest therein.

**2.** A contract not to be performed within one year of its making.

**3.** A promise by one person to pay the debt of another.

**4.** A promise made in consideration of marriage.

**5.** A promise by the administrator or executor of an estate to pay a debt of the estate out of his or her own funds.

### Modern Rationale

Obviously, a continuing rationale for the statute of frauds is the hope that written agreements will ward off fraud.[3] It also represents a policy judgment that

---

[1] Many actions based on oral contracts that are otherwise valid are dismissed by the courts because their terms cannot be sufficiently established. For this reason, all contracts of any importance ought to be in writing, even when not required by law.

[2] D's situation was particularly difficult because, at the time we are speaking of, the parties to a civil suit were not permitted to testify in their own behalf; thus the testimony of their witnesses was all-important.

[3] Although we are dealing with something called the statute of frauds, whether or not *fraud* is present has no bearing on the requirement of a writing. The technical concept of fraud is only incidentally connected to the requirement of a writing.

written evidence is more reliable than fading memories. Additionally, the requirement of a writing serves the cautionary function of reminding the parties of the significance of their acts. On the other hand, the statute of frauds also allows some parties to evade obligations that they have willingly undertaken.[4] Indeed, it appears that it is used more often for this purpose than to defeat fraud. This concern has led England, where the statute of frauds originated, to virtually discard it.

## *Introduction to Exceptions*

Criticisms of the statute of frauds have also led courts in America to devise various rules which in certain circumstances will either take oral contracts out of the statute of frauds or grant relief to a party who has performed his or her half of an oral agreement. Thus, even before we address the types of contracts that generally must be in writing to be enforceable, we should mention that each rule has judicially created exceptions. Some courts enforce oral contracts only when there has been an *ancillary promise*—such as where the party against whom the oral promise is to be enforced not only made the promise but also promised to reduce it to writing or promised not to raise the statute of frauds as a defense.

A majority of jurisdictions, however, do not require such an ancillary promise. Rather, where mechanical application of the statute of frauds would cause injustice, these courts will enforce an oral promise to perform upon theories of promissory estoppel (if the promisee foreseeably relied on the oral promise in circumstances where injustice would result if it were not enforced), or part performance (if the promisee has completely or in some instances substantially performed his part of the bargain), or even quasi-contract (to avoid unjust enrichment of the promisor).

These exceptions vary substantially from jurisdiction to jurisdiction and even from category to category among the types of contracts that are supposed to be in writing. It is almost impossible to delineate exactly the scope of these exceptions. However, this chapter will give many examples and notes the strong trend among the courts to use promissory estoppel or related doctrines to enforce oral promises, notwithstanding the statute of frauds, where needed to avoid unfair results. The framers of the Uniform Commercial Code agreed with this trend. As we shall see when we address UCC Sec. 2-201, there are even more exceptions to the sales contract's writing requirement than to the traditional statute of frauds.

## CONTRACTS THAT MUST BE IN WRITING

### *Contracts Calling for the Sale of Land*

As a practical matter, the most important contracts required by the statute to be in writing are those calling for the sale of land—real estate. With an exception to be noted later, unwritten agreements of this kind are absolutely unenforceable. Thus, if X orally agrees to sell a farm to Y for a specified price, neither X nor Y can recover damages from the other if one of them refuses to go through with the deal. This is true even in the unlikely event that both parties admit in court that they made the contract.

In most cases it is easy to determine whether a contract does or does not involve the sale of land. Land, or *real property,* essentially consists of the earth's surface, vegetation, buildings, and other structures permanently attached to the soil. Growing crops, being physically attached to the ground, are also generally considered to be real property when sold in conjunction with the land. Thus, if S, by a written agreement, contracts to sell his farm to B for $50,000, B is entitled to receive any crops then growing on it, as well as the land itself—unless the contract provides otherwise. On the other hand, if S contracts merely to sell the crop to B, the crop is considered *personal property* and the contract does not have to be in writing under the statute of frauds. (If, however, the price of the crop were $500 or more, the contract would then be required to be in writing under a special section of the Uniform Commercial Code, which will be discussed later in the chapter.)

*Interests in land* include real estate mortgages and easements. A real estate **mortgage** is a convey-

---

[4]The parties to most oral business contracts do, in fact, perform their obligations in full, even though, because of the statute, they may not be obligated to. The statute is important, then, in those relatively few situations where one of the parties decides to stand on his or her legal rights by refusing to perform under an oral—but otherwise valid—contract.

ance of an interest in land by a debtor to a creditor as security for the debt. An **easement** is the right of one person to use or enjoy the land of another in a limited manner. Easements can be created in two general ways—expressly or by implication. If created in an express manner, the granting of the right must be evidenced by a writing—either specific language in a deed or a written contract in place of a deed. An easement created by implication, on the other hand, need not be evidenced by a writing. (One example of such an easement is an "implied easement of necessity." This is created when a landowner sells part of his or her property to another, the land being situated in such a way that the buyer has no access to it except by going across the seller's remaining land.) While real estate *leases* also convey interests in land and thus normally fall within the Statute of Frauds, most states have enacted special statutes providing that oral leases of a year's duration or less are valid.

**Effect of Part Performance—Estoppel:** As noted earlier, in some circumstances the courts have generally felt that oral contracts ought to be enforceable even though they are not in writing. Accordingly, they have recognized limited exceptions to the rules embodied in the statute of frauds.

One of these exceptions involves oral contracts calling for the sale of land. Such contracts are generally held to be enforceable if the buyer, in reliance upon the oral contract, has (1) paid part of the purchase price, (2) taken possession of the land, and (3) added substantial improvements to it.[5] In these circumstances the courts will permit the buyer to enforce the contract for either of two reasons. (In regard to oral *leases* of land of over one year, requirement 1 is, of course, dispensed with.)

First, the actions of the buyer, in and of themselves, may be felt to be "referable" to the oral contract that the buyer alleges has been formed—that is, the buyer's actions are fairly good evidence that an oral contract has, in fact, been entered into. These are actions that a person would normally take only if he or she expected to become the owner of the land. The second reason often cited for permitting the buyer to enforce the oral contract is the doctrine of *promissory estoppel* (discussed in Chapter 13). The reasoning here is that where the seller of the land has permitted the buyer to take such actions, it would be manifestly unfair to to permit the seller to evict the buyer on the ground that the contract was not in writing. In such a case, the courts are increasingly taking the view that the seller is estopped (i.e., prevented) from using the statute of frauds as a basis for having the oral contract set aside.

The case below presents two common questions: (1) Was a reasonably definite oral contract entered into? and (2) If so, was it saved by the part performance doctrine? (The second case in the chapter presents a situation in which the issue is whether the estoppel doctrine ought to be invoked.)

---

[5]Of course, if both parties have fully performed the contract, the statute is no longer relevant, and neither party can rescind it on the ground that it was originally required to be in writing.

---

## L.U. Cattle Company v. Wilson
Colorado Court of Appeals,
714 P.2d 1344 (1986)

Prior to September of 1980 the L.U. Cattle Company had been conducting farming operations on some Colorado land it was leasing from the land's owners, the Wilsons. Because the existing lease expired on November 1, 1980, a representative of the company, Kroeger, met with the Wilsons in September for the purpose of entering into a new lease. During the discussion the Wilsons told Kroeger that they wanted the company to plant alfalfa in the future, rather than corn, because this would produce more cash income out of which the company could make its rental payments. Kroeger said that if the acreage was to support alfalfa it had to be fertilized before planting, and, to maximize the efficiency of this plan, it would be necessary to plow and fertilize in the fall of 1980.

After a second meeting, Kroeger felt that as a result of these discussions an oral agreement had been reached for a lease that would be reduced to writing at a later date. Acting on this understanding, Kroeger prepared and mailed a memorandum to the Wilsons on October 4 expressing the terms of the parties' agreement. The last line of the memorandum read: "We will start plowing the last of the week." The

*(continued)*

Wilsons read and discussed the memorandum, but did not sign it or otherwise respond to it.

During the rest of October and early November the company plowed and fertilized the land, and Wilson was notified of this action. In late January of 1981 the company's owners were concerned that they had no written commitment from the Wilsons. On January 25 Kroeger expressed this concern to Wilson on the phone, who agreed to sign a lease. The next day Kroeger prepared a "Lease Agreement" which he signed on behalf of the company and mailed to the Wilsons. The Wilsons again did not respond to this document. Nothing further occurred until early March, when Wilson told Kroeger that he would not sign the agreement. Kroeger then removed certain equipment from the land and sent the Wilsons a bill for the cost of the fertilization. Wilson sent a check for the billed amount, but the company did not cash it. The cattle company then filed this suit asking for damages resulting from breach of the oral lease (including lost profits). The Wilsons defended on the ground that the contract was invalid under the statute of frauds.

The trial court found (1) that an oral lease had been entered into, and (2) that the company's actions in fertilizing the land constituted part performance of the agreement which "removed it from the statute of frauds"—i.e., which made the agreement enforceable. Accordingly, the court entered judgment for the company in the amount of $30,862. The Wilsons appealed, disputing both findings of fact.

---

**Decision:** The judgment of the trial court was affirmed. The evidence of the cattle company clearly proved that an oral contract was made, and that its terms were reasonably definite (such terms being set forth in the company's memorandum of the oral contract).

The only remaining question was the enforceability of the contract (since the Wilsons signed nothing). In that regard, the trial court was also correct in ruling that the doctrine of part performance applied. Under that doctrine, an oral contract is enforceable if "substantial part performance" has been given by the party seeking enforcement of the contract; if that performance is "fairly referable" to such contract; and if such performance is known to the other party. Here these conditions are met because (1) the company's planting and fertilizing of the alfalfa was substantial part performance; (2) these actions were referable to—i.e., consistent with—the terms of the oral agreement (rather than to an earlier contract, as alleged by the Wilsons); and (3) the actions of the cattle company were known to the Wilsons because the company's memorandum of October 4 notified them that it intended to take these actions. ∎

---

## Contracts Not to Be Performed within One Year

The section of the statute requiring that *agreements not to be performed within one year of the making thereof* be in writing is based on the fact that disputes over the terms of long-term oral contracts are particularly likely to occur; witnesses die, the parties' memories become hazy, and so on. Despite the logic underlying this provision, it has posed numerous problems in practice.

In deciding whether a particular agreement falls within this section, the usual (but not the only) approach taken by the courts is to determine whether it was *reasonably possible,* under its own terms, for the contract in question to have been performed within one year from the time it was made. If so, the contract is outside the statute and need not be in writing. The fact that performance *actually* may have taken more than one year is immaterial. Consider these examples.

1. A, on June 1, 1990, orally agrees to work for B as a personal secretary at a salary of $3,000 per month "as long as this arrangement is satisfactory to both parties." This is known as an "at-will" employment contract. It gives either party the right to terminate it at any time. It does not have to be in writing to be enforceable, because it can be fully performed *by its own terms* in less than a year. Assume that A worked for B for two years, and in the third year, B refused to pay wages for work A had performed. If A sued, most courts would hold that B could not successfully raise a statute of frauds defense. Even though performance actually took longer, the contract could have been fully performed in less than one year. (A minority of courts, rejecting the "reasonably possible" test, would hold that if performance longer than one year was *within the contemplation of the parties,* the contract would have to be in writing.)

2. On June 1, 1990, A promises to work for B "as long as you [B] shall live." Most courts, but not all,

would hold that this contract also need not be in writing to be enforceable. B might die in less than a year. If he did, the contract would have been fully performed in less than a year. Again, it is irrelevant if B actually did live longer than a year.

3. A promises on June 1, 1990, to work for B "for the next two years." This contract must be in writing to be enforceable, because it is not possible to work for two years in less than one year. True, it is again possible that B might die in less than a year, but the contract will not have been fully performed as written. (Instead, B's death would have *excused* performance under the doctrine of impossibility discussed later in Chapter 18.)

4. A promises on June 1, 1990, to sing a two-hour concert at XYZ University on August 12, 1991. This contract must be in writing to be enforceable. Even though the performance itself will take only two hours, by the contract's terms that performance must occur more than one year after the contract was made.

**Exceptions:** As with other categories of contracts that usually must be in writing, many courts have enforced oral contracts that would take more than one year from the making to perform where they believed that this was necessary to bring about just results. For instance, in example 1 above, even courts that choose the "contemplation of the parties" approach and conclude that the contract should be in writing would allow A to recover for *work performed* on a part performance basis. The case below is typical of those in which the exceptional result is largely based on the principle of promissory estoppel. This jurisdiction, however, appears to be one of the minority jurisdictions that also requires an ancillary promise (in this case, a promise to put the contract in writing) in order to invoke the exception.

## Harmon v. Tanner Motor Tours of Nevada, Ltd.
Supreme Court of Nevada,
377 P.2d 622 (1963)

This litigation came about as a result of a dispute over which one of two competing common carriers had the exclusive limousine ground transportation franchise for servicing the Las Vegas, Nevada, airport for a period of ten years. The carriers were Tanner Motor Lines, Ltd., plaintiff, and Las Vegas-Tonopah-Reno Stage Lines, Inc. (LTR), one of the defendants.

Five legal issues were involved, one of which had to do with the enforceability of an oral contract entered into between Tanner and the Board of Clark County Commissioners (Board), which was the governing authority of the Las Vegas airport. (Only that part of the fact-pattern and decision of the case relating to this issue is considered below.)

In late 1959 Tanner submitted a written bid for the limousine service, and that bid was *orally* accepted by the board members. Despite this acceptance, the board entered into a written contract in 1960 with the second carrier, LTR, giving it the exclusive transportation rights.

Tanner then brought this action against Harmon, a representative of the board, and LTR, defendants, asking for specific performance of its 1959 contract. The defendants contended, among other things, that that oral contract was unenforceable under the statute of frauds, because its performance was to take more than one year. The trial court ruled against the defendants on all points, and entered a decree of specific performance. (That is, the court ruled that Tanner's contract was valid and that he thus did possess the exclusive transportation rights, and it accordingly ordered the board to recognize these rights.) Defendants appealed.

**Decision:** The trial court was correct in ruling that the board was bound by its oral acceptance of Tanner's written offer. It is true that the ten-year contract could not be performed within one year, and thus it would normally have to be in writing in order to be binding upon the board. However, after the oral contract was made the board assured Tanner that it would prepare a formal written contract later. In reliance upon that assurance Tanner (1) continued to provide limousine service to the airport; (2) bought two limousines; and (3) paid the board $3,600 as a service "guarantee." While it is true that an assurance to reduce a contract to writing at a later date will not, itself, make the contract enforceable, such an assurance followed by *acts of reliance on the part of the other party* (here, Tanner) *does* cause the contract to be valid and fully enforceable. ■

## Promises to Pay Debts of Another

If A has received a benefit from B, then B's claim that A has made a promise to B is more plausible than if A has received no such benefit. To avoid perjury, the statute of frauds requires that if A has not received such a benefit, A's "promise to answer for the debt, default or miscarriage of another" must be in writing to be enforceable. The classic example is a "guaranty contract" in which A promises B that he will pay C's debt to B *if* C does not. Because A received no benefit in this transaction, the law is suspicious and demands that B provide written evidence of A's promise.

There are three standard elements of a guaranty contract. First, the guarantor promises to pay the debtor's obligation *if* the debtor does not. In other words, guaranty contracts occur in situations of "secondary liability." The creditor is to look primarily to the debtor for repayment, and only if the debtor does not pay is the creditor to look to the guarantor. If, on the other hand, A tells B: "Send C's bills to me," A is the primary debtor to whom B is to look first for payment. A is making the debt his own, not promising to pay the debt of another. Such a promise is not a guaranty and therefore need not be in writing to be enforceable.

Second, a guaranty promise is made for the benefit of the debtor. If the guarantor's "main purpose" in making the promise is to benefit himself, it is not a guaranty contract and need not be in writing to be enforceable. An aunt who, out of pity, promises a landlord that she will pay her niece's rent if the niece does not pay is making a guaranty promise that must be in writing to be enforceable. On the other hand, assume that Guarantor Company has a government contract to build a wind tunnel to test airplanes. Guarantor hires Joe Debtor to do the concrete work. Because Joe does not pay his bills, Creditor Concrete Supply stops delivering concrete, halting construction and endangering Guarantor's contract with the government. If an official of Guarantor called Creditor on the phone and said: "Please keep delivering concrete to Joe Debtor, and we'll pay the bills if he doesn't," the promise would be enforceable though never put in writing because Guarantor's main purpose in making the promise is obviously to benefit itself. Therefore, this is not a guaranty promise and need not be in writing to be enforceable.

Third, a guaranty promise is made to the creditor, not to the debtor. If in the previous example, Guarantor Company had told Joe Debtor: "Keep ordering concrete, and we'll pay the bill if you don't," such promise is not a guaranty and need not be in writing in order to be enforceable.

## Other Promises

Two other relatively insignificant categories of contracts—*promises made in consideration of marriage* and *executors' contracts*—fall within the statute. Thus, if A promises to pay B $5,000 when and if B marries C, A is liable only if his promise is in writing. The same is true in regard to prenuptial agreements, in which parties about to be married to each other expressly spell out their interests in the other's properties. (Indeed, some states have passed statutes requiring that "palimony" contracts—agreements for support or division of property between live-in lovers who are not married—be in writing to be enforceable.) Finally, if the administrator or executor of an estate promises personally to pay a debt of the deceased, the creditor can hold the promisor liable only if the promise is in writing.

In addition, recently many borrowers have sued banks claiming some form of breach of an oral promise to lend, to refinance an existing loan, or to refrain from enforcing remedies contained in a written loan agreement. In one case, for example, a jury awarded $28 million for breach of an alleged oral promise to extend an existing line of credit. In another, a jury awarded $69 million for breach of an alleged oral promise to make a loan. To protect banks and other lending institutions from such liability, many states have recently passed laws barring the enforcement of *oral lending agreements* without a signed agreement.

# CONTRACTS CALLING FOR SALE OF GOODS

## The UCC Statute of Frauds

Section 2-201 of the code, known as the **UCC statute of frauds,** states that a contract for the sale of goods for a price of $500 or more must be in writing to be enforceable (with exceptions noted subsequently). As is true of other statute of frauds provisions applicable to nongoods transactions, the requirement of

Sec. 2-201(1) can be satisfied either (1) by having the contract itself in writing, or (2) by having a subsequent written memorandum of the oral agreement. In either situation, *the writing must be signed by the party against whom enforcement is sought.*

**The UCC Confirmation:** The language of Sec. 2-201(1) in regard to enforceability parallels that of the basic statute of frauds. That is, if an oral sales contract is followed by a writing signed by only one of the parties, the signer is bound by the contract but the nonsigner is not. To eliminate this onesidedness in certain circumstances, subsection 2 of Sec. 2-201 provides another method (in addition to the two set forth above) for satisfying the writing requirement of subsection 1.

Suppose that two parties have orally agreed on a sale of goods. One of the parties then sends a signed letter or other written communication to the other party, saying: "This is to confirm that on June 20 we entered into an agreement for the sale of 175 men's suits on the following terms [the terms being stated in the letter]." If this is the only writing the parties make, the question is whether it can be used to satisfy the requirements of Sec. 2-201(1). If the sender breaches the contract, the letter can be used in a lawsuit by the recipient against the sender because the sender signed it. But if it is the recipient who breaches the contract, can the sender use the letter in his lawsuit to recover damages from the recipient, the nonsigner? In transactions not governed by the UCC, as we have seen, the answer is no. But as to sales of goods, however, (as in the above example), the answer sometimes is yes.

Under Sec. 2-201(2), the **UCC confirmation rule**, a confirmation such as the above can be used by the sender against a nonsigning recipient if the following requirements are met:

1. The writing must be "sufficient against the sender." In other words, the *sender* must have *signed* the confirmation, and its contents must meet the relatively lenient sufficiency requirements discussed later in the chapter.
2. Both parties must be *merchants.*
3. The recipient must have had reason to know of the contents of the confirmation *but had not objected to it in writing within ten days after receiving it.*

## UCC Exceptions:

Section 2-201(3) defines three situations in which an oral contract, if proved, will be enforceable despite the total absence of a writing, even when it involves a sale of goods for a price of $500 or more. The first exception can be used only by a seller; the other two can be used by either a seller or a buyer.

1. If the oral contract is for goods to be specifically manufactured for the particular buyer, it is enforceable against the buyer if two requirements are met:
   a. The goods must be of a type not suitable for sale to others in the ordinary course of the seller's business. For example: Suppose that C is an importer of small, foreign-made pickup trucks, and D is a manufacturer of campers that are mounted on pickups. C orally orders from D a number of campers made to fit the pickups imported by C (that is, they will fit no other pickups on the market). If C repudiates the bargain after the campers are made, D will be hard-pressed to sell them elsewhere. He might eventually be able to do so, but considerable effort would probably be required. Thus the goods cannot be sold in the ordinary course of his business.
   b. The seller must either have substantially started the manufacture of the goods, or have made commitments for procuring them, before he or she learned of the buyer's repudiation of the agreement.

2. If the defendant "admits in his pleading, testimony or otherwise in court that a contract for sale was made," it will be enforceable even though oral. (The common-law court decisions on this point are conflicting, most courts holding that such an admission does *not* remove the requirement of a writing. Thus the UCC exception represents a significant innovation in this regard.) Observe that not just any admission will suffice; the admission by the defendant must become part of official court records.

3. An oral agreement will be enforced to the extent that payment has been made and accepted or that the goods have been received and accepted. Suppose, for example, that X and Y have made an oral contract for Y to sell X twenty-five television sets at a price of $300 each. Before any of the sets are delivered, X makes a prepayment of $1,800, which Y accepts. Y then refuses to honor the contract. Even if Y were not

**Figure 16.1  Compliance with the Statute of Frauds in Contracts for the Sale of Goods, UCC 2-201**

A contract for sale of goods $500 or more satisfies the statute of frauds if:

- It is made in writing originally, or a later written memorandum of the agreement is made, and the contract or memorandum is signed by the party against whom enforcement is sought [UCC 2-201 (1)].
- It is made between merchants, and a written confirmation good against the sender is received and not objected to within ten days after receipt [UCC 2-201 (2)].
- It is made orally
  - If the goods are to be specially made for the buyer, are not suitable for sale in the ordinary course of the seller's business, and a substantial beginning has been made in their manufacture [UCC 2-201 (3) (a)].
  - To the extent a party admits a contract in pleadings or court [UCC 2-201 (3) (b)].
  - To the extent that goods have been delivered and accepted or payment has been made and accepted [UCC 2-201 (3) (c)].

---

bound by the contract, X could of course get her money back under the unjust enrichment theory (see Chapter 11). But under the UCC her part payment will make the contract partially enforceable, and she will be able to maintain a suit for breach of a contract obligation to deliver six of the twenty-five television sets. Similarly, if X has made no payment but Y has made a partial shipment which X has accepted, the oral contract is again partially enforceable. That is, if Y delivers and X accepts six television sets, and X then repudiates the agreement, Y can maintain a suit for breach of a contract obligation to pay $1,800.[6]

The rationale underlying these exceptions is entirely consistent with the purpose of the basic writing requirement of Sec. 2-201(1), which is to forestall the possibility of a party successfully maintaining a fabricated breach of contract suit by the use of perjured testimony. By providing these exceptions, the drafters of the UCC have recognized that, in cases falling within them, it is extremely unlikely that plaintiff's claim will be a complete fabrication. Therefore,

because the original purpose for the writing requirement no longer exists in such instances, the oral agreements ought to be binding. Compliance with the statute of frauds under UCC 2-201 is summarized in Figure 16.1.

## Modification Contracts

Under Section 2-209 of the UCC, agreements that modify existing sales contracts must be in writing in order to be enforceable in two situations:

1. The modification must be in writing if the original agreement had provided that it could be modified only by a writing.[7]

2. The modification must be in writing if the whole contract, *as modified*, is required to be in writing under the UCC statute of frauds (Sec. 2-201, discussed above).

## Other Statutes Requiring a Writing

In addition to the basic statute of frauds and Sections 2-201 and 2-209 of the UCC, all states have additional statutes—usually narrow in scope—that require still

---

[6] Prior to enactment of the UCC, part performance of this type made the *entire contract* enforceable. Also, the statutory language in this exception does not address the situation in which the buyer has made a partial repayment that cannot be allocated to a certain number of individual units of goods. For example, what if buyer makes and seller accepts a $1,000 down payment on a single $6,000 automobile? In the few cases involving this question since enactment of the UCC, most courts have applied the common-law rule and have held the entire contract to be enforceable despite the absence of a sufficient written document.

[7] Section 2-209(2) has an additional provision applicable to those sales contracts entered into between a merchant and a nonmerchant. In such a case, if the contract results from use of the *merchant's form* (with that form containing the requirement that any later modification had to be in writing), that requirement must itself be "separately signed" by the nonmerchant in order to be binding upon him or her.

other kinds of contracts to be in writing. For example, most states require real estate listing contracts and insurance contracts to be in writing. Additionally, Sec. 8-319 of the UCC requires, in general, that contracts calling for the sale of securities (i.e., stocks and bonds) must be in writing, and Sec. 9-203 of the UCC imposes the same requirement upon most "security agreements" governed by Article 9 (i.e., agreements that create security interests in favor of lenders of money or unpaid sellers of goods).

# WHEN IS THE WRITING SUFFICIENT?
## Contract Law

The original statute of frauds began: "No action shall be brought [upon the following kinds of contracts] unless the agreement upon which such action shall be brought, *or some memorandum or note thereof,* shall be in writing and signed by the party sought to be charged therewith or some other person thereunto by him lawfully authorized." Thus, even if the full contract is not in writing, a "sufficient written memorandum" may satisfy the statute of fraud's requirements. In such situations, the courts *generally require that the writing include at least the following:* (1) names of both parties, (2) the subject matter of the contract, (3) the consideration to be paid, and (4) any other terms that the court feels are material under the circumstances. Under this fairly strict approach, if any basic term is missing, the contract continues to be unenforceable.

This does not mean, however, that the writing must be in any particular form, or be complete in every detail. And because of the provision that a memorandum or note of the contract may satisfy the statute, it is entirely possible that an oral contract can be validated by the production in court of a confirming telegram, sales slip, check, invoice, or some other writing—assuming, of course, that it contains all the material terms of the agreement.

Additionally, it frequently happens that the contract is evidenced by two or more separate writings, none of which alone is sufficiently complete to satisfy the statute. In such cases the writings may be construed together, thus satisfying the memorandum requirement, if the writings clearly refer to one another (expressly or impliedly), or if they are physically attached to one another.

The requirement that the contract or written memorandum be signed by the party against whom the agreement is to be enforced (or a duly authorized representative) is somewhat loosely applied. It may be satisfied by a signature, by initials, by the letterhead on a sheet of paper, or even by a company's trademark appearing on the paper.

## Sales Law

Contracts calling for the sale of goods are often made in the business world under circumstances, because of the press of time or other factors, the parties put only the barest essentials of the agreement in writing. Recognizing this reality, Sec. 2-201 of the UCC has *greatly relaxed the requirements of the sufficiency of the writing.* For sales of goods, that section provides that the writing (whether the contract itself, or memorandum, or subsequent confirmation) merely has to be "sufficient to indicate that a contract for sale has been made between the parties." The only term that *must be included in the writing is the quantity.* Other terms that are orally agreed upon can be proved in court by oral testimony.[8] Terms that are not agreed upon at all can be supplied by Article 2 itself (as we saw in Chapter 12).

Cases have arisen presenting the question of whether a written "requirements contract" satisfies the quantity requirement of Sec. 2-201. For example, a seller might obligate himself or herself to sell and deliver "all of the 21 oz. plastic your plant can use" over a specified period of time at a specific unit price. In a case in which such language was utilized, *Fortune Furniture Co. v. Mid-South Plastic Co.*, 310 So.2d 725 (1975), the Supreme Court of Mississippi—following the majority rule—held that this type of provision satisfied the requirement that the writing state a quantity.

# THE PAROL EVIDENCE RULE

Whenever a contract (or a memorandum thereof) is reduced to writing, the writing out is to contain *all* the material terms of the agreement. This is true not only for contracts that fall within the statute of frauds,

---

[8] The oral testimony referred to here is intended to supplement an incomplete writing. If the writing does contain a particular term, oral testimony about anything supposedly agreed upon prior to execution of the writing is not admissible in court for the purpose of contradicting the clear terms of the writing. This is because of the UCC's "parol evidence rule," Sec. 2-202, which will be discussed subsequently.

but for all other contracts where a writing is utilized as well. One reason for this, as to statute of frauds contracts, is to make sure that the writing meets the sufficiency requirement under the statute. An equally powerful reason lies in the **parol evidence rule.** This rule provides, in general, that when any contract has been reduced to writing, neither party can introduce "parol" (outside) evidence in court for the purpose of modifying or changing the terms of that contract. More specifically, the rule prohibits a party to a written contract from unilaterally introducing either oral or written statements or agreements made at (or prior to) the time the written contract was made which either conflict with, or add to, the terms of the written contract.

Among the policy reasons for the existence of the parol evidence rule are (1) because a written contract is more reliable than oral testimony, it helps prevent perjury or fraud; (2) it encourages the parties to put their important agreements in writing, thus increasing the reliability of commercial transactions; and (3) it emphasizes a long-standing rule of contract interpretation to the effect that final expressions of intent should prevail over earlier tentative expressions of intent.

As to sales contracts, the UCC's parol evidence rule in Sec. 2-202 is essentially the same as the common-law parol rule, discussed above. However, its wording may increase the chances that extrinsic evidence will be allowed by narrowing the traditional view of what constitutes a *final* expression of the parties' agreement. Obviously, expressions of intent that are only preliminary are not protected by the rule from contradiction by parol sources.

### *Exceptions*

The courts feel that the parol evidence rule brings about clearly undesirable results in some circumstances; accordingly, they have recognized a number of exceptions to it. (In general, these exceptions apply both to cases governed by common-law principles and those governed by sales law.) Following are the most important situations in which a party to a written contract *is* permitted to introduce parol evidence in subsequent legal proceedings:

**1.** The written contract itself appears to be incomplete. The parol evidence rule applies only to final *and complete* expressions of intent.

**2.** The written contract is ambiguous, and the parol evidence tends to clear up the ambiguity. Such evidence does not contradict or add to the writing.

**3.** The written contract contains an obvious mistake, such as a typographical or clerical error, and the parol evidence tends to correct the error.

**4.** The parol evidence shows that the contract was not a valid one, as, for example, that it was induced by fraud or duress on the part of the other party, or was formed under mutual mistake of fact. Alleged fraud is the major exception under which parol evidence is admitted.

**5.** The evidence shows that the contract was subject to a condition precedent, i.e., that the parties had agreed that a specified event had to occur before the contract would be effective, and that the event had not occurred.

**6.** The evidence tends to prove that the parties made either an oral or written agreement that modified the written contract *after* the written contract had been entered into. Parties to written contracts often change their minds and later alter the agreements. Admission of such evidence does not contradict the basic reasoning behind the parol evidence rule which is that preliminary contract terms, which may vary substantially as the contract is negotiated, become merged into the final written contract.

A seventh exception, applicable only to sales contracts, allows evidence about the course of prior dealings of the parties or custom of the trade in which the parties are engaged to explain or supplement a writing, even when the evidence appears to contradict its unambiguous terms.

Cumulatively, these exceptions arm the courts with tools to avoid the operation of the parol evidence rule in instances where they believe its application would cause injustice. Thus, a substantial gap may exist between the theory underlying the formal rule on the one hand, and the rule's practical operation on the other.

## SUMMARY

Oral contracts are, as a general rule, enforceable if their terms can be proven in court. Under the typical state statute of frauds, however, five classes of contracts must generally be in writing (or be evidenced by a writing) in order to be enforceable. The most important of these are (1) contracts to sell land or an interest in land; (2) contracts not to be performed within one year from the time they were made; and (3) promises to pay debts of another. In all of these cases, however, the courts have recognized exceptions to the rules—thus enforcing the oral contracts—in circumstances where they feel a refusal to enforce would be extremely unfair to one of the parties. In cases where oral contracts have been entered into which clearly fall within the statute, followed by a written confirmation of the contract, the party who has signed the confirmation is bound by the contract, but the other party is not.

Article 2 of the UCC provides a sixth type of contract that must generally be evidenced by a writing: contracts calling for the sale of goods where the price is $500 or more. The UCC statute of frauds substantially removes, as to sales contracts, the one-sidedness that exists under the basic statute where one party has signed a written confirmation but the other party has not. This is achieved by Sec. 2-201(2), which provides that, if both parties are merchants, a written confirmation signed by one party and sent to the other party is binding upon the latter unless he or she objects to its terms within ten days of receiving it. Sec. 2-201(3) also specifies three exceptional situations in which oral contracts of $500 or more are valid even if not evidenced by a writing at all. If a contract falls within the basic statute, the written contract (or memorandum thereof) satisfies the statute only if it contains all the material terms of the agreement. By contrast, to satisfy the UCC requirement, the writing need only indicate that a sales contract has been entered into, and contain the quantity of the goods being sold.

Whenever a contract is in writing, whether or not it is required by law to be in writing, the *parol evidence rule* generally forbids either party from producing outside evidence in a later court action in an effort to change or add to the terms of the contract. The rule achieves this result by prohibiting the introduction of evidence showing that the parties, at or prior to the time of contracting, made oral or written promises in conflict with, or in addition to, the written terms. However, such evidence is allowed in some circumstances, as, for example, where the written contract is incomplete or ambiguous, or where the outside evidence shows that the contract itself was invalid.

## KEY TERMS

**Statute of frauds**
**Mortgage**
**Easement**
**UCC statute of frauds**
**UCC confirmation rule**
**Parol evidence rule**

## QUESTIONS AND PROBLEMS

1. Dr. Sahlin owned a summer cottage in New York. He told his nurse of many years that if she and her husband—the Strandbergs—would live at the cottage with him on the weekends, and care for him and keep the property in good repair, they would receive the property, when he died. The couple rendered the specified services until the time of his death, a period of several years. (Among other things, Mr. Strandberg reconstructed the cottage by shingling it, painting and rewiring it, and putting in new footings and plumbing throughout.) Dr. Sahlin died without a will, and the executor of his estate refused to convey the property to them since there was nothing in writing evidencing the agreement. Do you think the various services the Strandbergs performed caused the contract to be enforceable? Why or why not? (*Strandberg v. Lawrence,* 216 N.Y.S.2d 973, 1961.)

2. Warner wished to build a lumber mill, which would require construction of a railroad switch and spur line from the Texas and Pacific Railroad's main line in Texas. In 1874, he entered into an oral conract with the railroad, under the terms of which he was to supply the ties and grade the ground for the switch, with the railroad promising to construct and maintain the switch and spur line "for Warner's benefit as long as Warner needed it." Warner built the mill, and the railroad built the spur line and switch and maintained service for several years. In 1887, however, the railroad tore up the switch and ties, leaving Warner without transportation facilities. When Warner sued to recover damages for breach of contract, the railroad contended that the oral agreement "was a contract not to be performed within one year" and within the statute of frauds, and therefore was not enforceable against it. Is the railroad's contention correct? Explain. (*Warner v. Texas and Pacific Ry.,* 164 U.S. 418, 1896.)

3. After reviewing the financial records, Ogle and Melton (Ds) orally agreed to pay Trew (P) $145,000 for his woodshavings business. Under the agreement, they would pay $1,000 down and then $3,000 per month for 48 months. After two months of operating the business, Ds discovered that it was not as profitable as they had expected and refused to make any further payments. P sued for breach of contract and Ds raised a statute of frauds defense. P showed that Ds had acquired two of his trucks, his stockpile of shav-

ings and storage facilities, and all his existing customers. Additionally, P had made other special arrangements, such as helping Ds obtain insurance. Is the statute of frauds a good defense? (*Trew v. Ogle*, 767 S.W.2d 662, Tenn.App. 1988.)

4. In 1978, Moore, a major depositor in the First National Bank of Clarksville, told the bank to open up an account for his sons' trucking company and "I'll cover for them." In 1979, the sons bounced a check which Moore paid off when the bank called it to his attention. In 1980, the sons bounced two more checks simultaneously, totalling almost $500,000. When notified by the bank, Moore said he would cover the checks. However, that night he told his wife, who almost collapsed. The next day Moore told the bank that the deal was off. The bank sued; Moore raised a statute of frauds defense. Is this a good defense? (*First National Bank of Clarksville v. Moore*, 628 S.W.2d 488, Tex.Civ.App. 1982.)

5. Garland Co. sold almost $50,000 worth of materials to Roofco Co., for which Roofco failed to pay. In conversations between Rasor, president and principal shareholder of Roofco, and Garland, Rasor orally guaranteed that he would pay the debt out of personal funds if Roofco did not pay it. When Roofco did not pay, Garland sued to enforce the promise. Rasor raised a statute of frauds defense. Will the defense succeed? (*Garland Co., Inc. v. Roofco Co.*, 809 F.2d 546, 8th Cir. 1987.)

6. Pursuant to an oral contract for the sale of 2000 cattle, seller (P) delivered 222 cattle to buyer (D). Before any further delivery could occur, D breached the contract, claiming that it was unenforceable because it was oral. P sued to enforce the contract. Will P have any success? How much? (*Bagby Land & Cattle Co. v. California Livestock Comm'n Co.*, 439 F.2d 315, 5th Cir. 1971.)

7. After losing his race for the U.S. Senate, Collins did not wish to pay the $29,526.98 he owed for campaign posters that the Williamson Printing Corporation had printed for him and his supporters had spread around the state. So he didn't. Williamson sued for breach of contract. Collins defended by proving that there was no written contract. Is this a good defense? (*Collins v. Williamson Printing Corporation*, 746 S.W.2d 489, Tex.App. 1988.)

8. The owner of a dairy company orally contracted to sell certain land to the Hancock Construction Company, but later refused to go through with the deal. When the construction company brought an action for specific performance (an action seeking the property), the dairy company defended on the ground that the contract was not in writing. The construction company pointed out, however, that after the contract was made it had engineering studies made of the property, and also had made application for a loan of over $292,000 in order to finance the purchase. The construction company then contended that these acts on its part constituted "part performance" of the contract, and thus made the oral contract enforceable. Is this contention correct? Why or why not? (*Hancock Construction Co. v. Kempton & Snedigar Dairy*, 510 P.2d 752, 1973.)

9. In 1982, B&R Co. began buying doors from Lifetime Doors. In early 1983, a sales representative for Lifetime urged B&R to shift all its door purchases to Lifetime, making Lifetime its sole supplier. The sales representative provided literature which invited B&R to join Lifetime's "VIP Club." According to the literature, new purchasers would receive "continuous production availability in full proportion to monthly needs," which would allow them to "order flexible quantities" in shipments of a "desired number." B&R's president secured an oral commitment from Lifetime that Lifetime would supply B&R's requirements of four truckloads of six-panel doors each month in exchange for B&R's promise to purchase doors exclusively from Lifetime. Three months later, Lifetime began breaching the contract by allowing B&R to obtain the doors it needed only by agreeing to buy certain other types of doors as well. B&R sued for breach of contract. Lifetime raised a statute of frauds defense. Will this defense succeed? Can a "sufficient written memorandum" be found here? (*Barber & Ross Co. v. Lifetime Doors, Inc.*, 810 F.2d 1276, 4th Cir. 1987.)

10. Anderson hired Tri-State Home Improvement Co. to install siding on his home. Anderson claimed that as the contract was being negotiated, Tri-State's president promised that the siding would not rust and guaranteed this for at least 30 years. The written contract, however, did not contain such promises and stated: "The Company prohibits the making of any promises, or representations, unless it is inserted in writing in this agreement before signing." Within two years, extensive rust damage appeared. Anderson sued Tri-State for fraud and deceit. Is evidence as to the oral statements allegedly made by Tri-State's president admissible at trial? (*Anderson v. Tri-State Home Improvement Co.*, 68 N.W.2d 705, Wis. 1955.)

CHAPTER 17

# RIGHTS OF THIRD PARTIES

As a general rule, the rights created by the formation of a contract can be enforced only by the original parties to the agreement. A contract is essentially a private agreement affecting only the contracting parties themselves; both legal and practical difficulties would arise if a stranger to the contract (a **third party**) were permitted to enforce it. Suppose, for example, that X employed B to paint her house and that B subsequently refused to do the job. If Y, one of X's neighbors, were to bring suit against B to recover damages for breach of contract, it would be ludicrous if he were permitted to get a judgment. Since Y was not a party to the contract, he clearly had "no standing to sue," and his suit would be dismissed.

However, in certain exceptional circumstances a third party is permitted to enforce a contract made by others, particularly (1) where it appears, expressly or by necessary implication, that at the time the contract was made the parties to the contract intended that that person receive the benefit of the contract, or (2) where one of the parties, after making the contract, assigned (transferred) his or her rights to a third party. In the former situation the third party is called a *third-party beneficiary*, and in the latter he or she is designated an *assignee* of the contract.

## THIRD-PARTY BENEFICIARIES

The law recognizes three kinds of beneficiaries—creditor, donee, and incidental. Generally, creditor and donee beneficiaries (also known as "intended" beneficiaries) can enforce contracts made by others, while incidental beneficiaries cannot.

### Creditor Beneficiaries

When a contract is made between two parties for the express benefit of a third person, the latter is said to be a **creditor beneficiary** if he or she had earlier furnished consideration to one of the contracting parties. To illustrate: A owes X $500. A later sells a piano to B, on the understanding that B, in return, is to pay off A's indebtedness to X. Here X is a creditor beneficiary of the contract between A and B, inasmuch as she originally gave consideration to A, which created the debt in her (X's) favor. Once A has delivered the piano, X is entitled to recover the $500 from B—by suit, if necessary.[1]

**Assumption of Mortgage:** One typical situation involving a creditor beneficiary arises when mortgaged real estate is sold, with the purchaser agreeing to pay off the existing mortgage. For example: S owns a home subject to a $15,000 mortgage held by the Y Bank. S finds a buyer for the home, Z, who is willing to *assume the mortgage*. Thereupon S and Z enter into a contract, under the terms of which S agrees to convey the property to Z, and Z promises to pay S's existing indebtedness to the bank. The Y Bank now has become a creditor beneficiary of the contract between S and Z, since it originally gave consideration to S by making the loan, and it can hold Z liable on his promise to pay the indebtedness. (The assumption of the mortgage by Z does not by itself free S of his liability. Thus the bank can look to either party for payment in case Z defaults—unless it has expressly released S from his obligation.)[2]

---

[1] If A refused to deliver the piano to B, should B be required to pay X? Obviously, the answer is "no." The promisor (B) can raise the same defenses against an intended beneficiary (X) as he or she can raise against the promisee (A). In this case, the defense is A's failure to perform. Defenses such as lack of consideration, incapacity, fraud, mistake, or statute of frauds would also be effective. If B raises an effective defense to avoid paying X, clearly X could sue A on the original $500 debt.

[2] In most mortgages today, Z, even if willing, would not be allowed to assume the mortgages. "Due on sale clauses" (provisions in the mortgage which make the entire balance owed by S due immediately upon sale of the property) would render the loan "nonassumable."

263

## Donee Beneficiaries

Where a contract is made for the benefit of a third person who has not given consideration to either contracting party, that person is designated a **donee beneficiary** of the contract. To illustrate: P, an attorney, agrees to perform certain legal services for Q, with the understanding that Q will pay the $200 legal fee to R, P's son-in-law. Here P has made a gift of $200 to R, and R—the donee beneficiary of the contract—can enforce it against Q if Q refuses to pay him voluntarily.

**Life Insurance Contracts:** The most common type of contract involving donee beneficiaries is that of the ordinary life insurance policy. If A insures his life with the B Insurance Company, and the policy expressly designates C as the beneficiary of the proceeds of that policy, C—the donee beneficiary—can enforce the contract against the company. The fact that C has not furnished consideration to the company is immaterial; it is sufficient that A, the insured, has done so by making his premium payments.[3]

## Incidental Beneficiaries

An **incidental beneficiary** is a person whom the contracting parties did not intend to benefit by making the contract, but who nevertheless will benefit in some way if the contract is performed. Such a beneficiary, unlike a donee beneficiary, has no rights under the contract and thus is not entitled to enforce it. For example, a retail merchant in a college town would benefit from a contract between a construction firm and the university calling for the construction of a four-level parking facility on campus property just across the street from his (or her) store. However, if the builder breaches the contract with the university by refusing to go ahead with the project, the merchant cannot recover damages from the builder.

In determining whether a beneficiary is a donee beneficiary or an incidental beneficiary, the usual test is whether the contract was made primarily for his or her benefit. If so, the beneficiary is a donee beneficiary; if not, he or she is merely an incidental beneficiary. Strong evidence that a beneficiary is intended arises where the contract expressly designates the third party as such or where the promisor's performance is to be rendered directly to the third party.

Consider these illustrations:

1. A hires B Co. to construct a building. Soon after construction begins, A breaches the contract; as a result, B Co. lays off employee X. If X sued A for breach of contract, he would lose. His employment was an incidental benefit of the contract, but clearly A and B Co. did not make the contract for the purpose of benefitting X.

2. A promises to build an office building for B. The plans and specifications call for use of electrical wiring made by L Company. A uses wiring made by M Company instead. L could not sue A for breach of contract because the purpose of this requirement was not to provide business for L.

3. City hires ABC Water Co. to provide water for its citizens' needs at an agreed rate. If ABC charged more than the agreed rate, the citizens would probably be allowed to sue as intended beneficiaries for breach of contract. ABC's performance, after all, was to be directed to the citizens. (However, assume that citizen X's warehouse burns down, in part because ABC did not provide adequate water pressure for the fire fighters. Although the same reasoning would appear to apply, most courts would deny recovery by X against ABC on *public policy* grounds. For fear that allowing recovery in the latter instance would impose crushing financial burdens on entities with government contracts, such as public utilities, most courts would characterize X as a mere incidental beneficiary.)[4]

## ASSIGNMENTS

### Assignment of Rights

All contracts create certain rights and duties. With exceptions to be noted later, the *rights* a person has acquired under a contract can be transferred, or *assigned*, by that person to a third party.[5] Suppose, for example, that A agrees to add a family room to B's

---

[3] If A did not pay the premiums that the contract required, obviously B Insurance Co. would not have to pay C the proceeds of the policy, again illustrating that claims of intended beneficiaries against the promisor are subject to the same defenses that could be raised against the promisee.

[4] *H. R. Moch Co. v. Rensselaer Water Co.,* 159 N.E. 896, N.Y. 1928.)
[5] While a person's *duties* under a contract can also be transferred to a third party in some circumstances, such a transfer is a *delegation* rather than an *assignment.* The delegation of duties is discussed later in the chapter.

**Figure 17.1  Assignment of Rights**

Assignor A ←———— Contract ————→ B Obligor
  |                    ↗
Assignment        Performance
  |            ↗
  ↓      ↗
Assignee C

home for $13,500 and that A performs the required work. A thereafter assigns his right to collect the $13,500 to C, in which case A is the **assignor** and C the **assignee**. C can now recover the $13,500 from B, just as A could have done had there been no assignment. The relationship among the parties to an assignment is set forth in Figure 17.1.

## Status of the Assignee

Whenever an assignment takes place, the assignee acquires no greater rights than those possessed by the assignor. Putting it another way, the **obligor** (the person with a duty to perform) can assert the same defenses (if any) against the assignee that he or she had against the assignor.[6]

This can be easily illustrated by referring again to Figure 17.1. If B refuses to pay C and C brings suit against him on the contract, B can escape liability if he can prove that A breached his contract in some material way—by failing to complete the job, for example, or by using materials inferior to those required by the contract. In such a case C's only redress is the right to recover from A any consideration he had given to A in payment for the assignment.

---

[6] The rule that the assignee of a simple contract acquires no greater rights than those possessed by the assignor does not apply when a particular kind of contract—a *negotiable instrument*—is utilized by the parties. Under the law of commercial paper (which will be discussed in Part III) the purchaser of that special kind of instrument may qualify as a *holder in due course* of such instrument, in which case he or she can enforce the instrument against the obligor in certain situations where the seller of the instrument could not do so. In the above case, for example, if B's obligation were in the form of a negotiable promissory note, and if A negotiated the note to C, a holder in due course, *C is entitled to recover the amount of the note from B* even though A breached his contract with B. B's recourse is then to sue A for damages for breach of contract.

## What Rights Can Be Assigned?

Occasionally, when an assignee requests the obligor to perform his or her part of the bargain, the obligor refuses to do so on the ground that the assigned right was of such a nature that it could not be legally transferred without his or her consent. Usually, this contention is not accepted by the courts; most contractual rights can be assigned without the obligor's consent. This is especially true where the assigned right was that of *collecting a debt.* The reasoning is that it is ordinarily no more difficult for a debtor (obligor) to pay the assignee than to pay the assignor (the original creditor); hence the obligor has no cause to complain.

Some rights, however, *cannot* be assigned without the obligor's consent. Following are the most common of these situations:

**1.** The terms of the contract expressly prohibit assignment by one or both parties. (Such clauses are narrowly construed, however, often being interpreted to impose a duty on the assignor not to assign, but not to render invalid an assignment that does occur.)

**2.** The contract is "personal" in nature; specifically, the right in question involves a substantial *personal relationship* between the original parties to the contract. If X, for example, agrees to be Y's secretary for one year, any assignment by Y of the right to X's services would be invalid unless X consented to it. In fact, many (perhaps most) employment contracts fall within this category.

**3.** The assignment would materially alter the duties of the obligor. For example: S, of Columbus, Ohio, agrees to sell certain goods to B, also of Columbus, with the contract providing that "S will deliver the goods to the buyer's place of business." If B assigned this contract to the X Company of Cheyenne, Wyoming, S's obligation would be drastically increased and he would not be bound by the assignment unless he consented to it.

Additionally, the assignment of some rights is prohibited by statute. For example, a federal law (31 U.S.C.A. §203) generally prohibits the assignment of claims against the federal government, and some state statutes prohibit the assignment of future wages by wage earners. When the assignment of rights is prohibited by statute, such rights cannot be assigned even with the obligor's consent.

The following case poses a question of assignability in a modern business setting.

## Schupach v. McDonald's System, Inc.
Supreme Court of Nebraska,
264 N.W.2d 827 (1978)

McDonald's, defendant, is the corporation that grants all McDonald's fast food restaurant franchises. In 1959 defendant granted a franchise to a Mr. Copeland, giving him the right to own and operate McDonald's first store in the Omaha–Council Bluffs area. A few days later, in conformity with the negotiations leading up to the granting of the franchise, McDonald's sent a letter to Copeland giving him a "Right of First Refusal"—the right to be given first chance at owning any new stores that might subsequently be established in the area. In the next few years Copeland exercised this right and opened five additional stores in Omaha. In 1964 Copeland *sold and assigned all of his franchises* to Schupach, plaintiff, with McDonald's consent.

When McDonald's granted a franchise in the Omaha–Council Bluffs area in 1974 to a third party without first offering it to Schupach, he brought this action for damages resulting from establishment of the new franchise, claiming that the assignment of the franchises to him *also included the right of first refusal*.

A number of issues were raised in this litigation. Defendant contended, among other things, that the right it gave to Copeland was personal in nature, and thus was not transferable without its consent. Plaintiff alleged, on the other hand, that the right was not personal in nature, or, in the alternative, that its transfer was, in fact, agreed to by defendant.

On these issues the trial court ruled that the right was personal in nature. It also ruled, however, after analyzing voluminous correspondence between the parties, that defendant *had* consented to the transfer. It entered judgment for plaintiff, and defendant appealed.

**Decision:** The trial court was clearly correct in finding that the right was *personal in nature,* and thus could not be assigned without McDonald's permission. This finding was based on testimony of Mr. Ray Kroc, founder of McDonald's. He said that those to whom franchises were granted were selected with great care; they were people who had a great deal of pride, and who would create "an image of cleanliness, an image where parents would be glad to have their children come" as patrons or employees. The evidence overwhelmingly established the fact that the Right of First Refusal was personal in nature, and was separately a grant independent of the terms of the franchise itself.

(On the question as to whether McDonald's had given its permission to the assignment of the right to the plaintiff, the court reviewed the same correspondence that was examined by the trial court, and ruled that McDonald's had *not* given such permission. The judgment for plaintiff was therefore reversed.) ∎

## *Form of the Assignment*

As a general rule, no particular formalities need be observed in order for an assignment to be legally effective. Any words or conduct that indicate an intention on the part of the assignor to transfer his or her contractual rights are normally sufficient. Some assignments, however, are required by statute to be in writing. Thus the assignment of a contract that falls within the statute of frauds must be evidenced by a writing; similarly, under the statutes of most states, the assignment of one's rights to collect wages from an employer must also be in writing.

## *Absence of Consideration*

Once a valid assignment has occurred, the assignee is entitled to enforce the contract against the obligor even if the assignee did not give consideration for the assignment to the assignor. The absence of consideration on the part of the assignee does have one significant effect, however; the assignor in such a case has the right to *rescind the assignment* at any time before the contract has been performed by the obligor, without liability to the assignee. (It is assumed here that the assignment was not meant to be a *gift.* If it were, rescission of the assignment would not, of course, be permitted.)

## *Notice of Assignment*

A valid assignment takes effect the moment it is made, regardless of whether the obligor is aware that the assignment has occurred. However, the assignee should give *immediate notice* to the obligor whenever an assignment is made, in order to protect the rights received under it.

A primary reason for giving notice is that an obligor who does not have notice of an assignment is free to go ahead and render performance to the assignor, thereby discharging his or her contractual duties. Suppose, for example, that X is owed $500 by Y and that X assigns the right to collect the debt to Z. If Y, not knowing of the assignment, pays the debt to X (assignor), Z has lost her right to collect the indebtedness from Y. Any other result would be patently unfair to Y. Z's only redress in such a case is to recover payment from X, who clearly has no right to retain the money. On the other hand, if Y did pay the $500 to X *after* being informed of the assignment, Z could still collect from Y.

Notice of assignment can also be important in a case where successive assignments occur. To illustrate: R owes money to S. S assigns his right to collect the debt to A on June 10, then assigns the same right to B on June 15, B not knowing of the prior assignment. Suppose that the first assignee, A, does not give notice of assignment to R until June 25, while the second assignee, B, gives notice on June 20. In such a situation, a number of courts—though not a majority—would rule that B is entitled to payment of the debt, rather than A; in other words, the assignee who first gives notice prevails. (In states adopting this minority view, A's only redress is to recover the consideration, if any, that he gave to S in exchange for the assignment.) The majority view is that A, the first assignee, collects, even if he did not give notice first.

## *Sales Contracts*

The Uniform Commercial Code's provisions on assignments, primarily Sec. 2-210, are generally similar to the common-law rules discussed above, rendering ineffective only assignments that would (1) materially change the obligor's duties; (2) increase materially the burden or risk imposed on the obligor by contract, or (3) impair materially the obligor's chance of obtaining return performance. The Code is perhaps even more "pro-assignment" than the common law. For example, it contains numerous restrictions on anti-assignment clauses that are not present in the common law.

Most important, perhaps, several types of assignments come within the scope of Article 9's provisions relating to secured transactions. These rules are discussed in some detail in Chapter 29 and will not be repeated here. However, we emphasize that Article 9 does alter several of the common law's rules on assignments where secured transactions occur. For example, it may give priority to a second assignee over a first assignee if the second assignee was the first to file a proper financing statement covering the assignment (UCC 9-312(5)).

## DELEGATION OF DUTIES

Our discussion so far has been directed to those cases in which contractual rights alone have been transferred, or assigned—in other words, to those common situations in which it is reasonably clear that the parties understood that the assignor alone would be the party who would perform the contract, as he or she originally contracted to do. In many circumstances, however, a **delegation of duties**—the transfer of one party's contractual duties to another—*is* intended as part of the assignment of rights, and in other circumstances a delegation of duties may occur without an assignment of rights. We will briefly examine these situations.

### *Delegation in Conjunction with an Assignment*

If an assignment occurs in which the assigning party also delegates his or her contractual duties to the assignee, that party is the **delegator** (or assignor-delegator), and the party to whom the duties are transferred is the **delegatee** (or assignee-delegatee). The remaining party—the party to the original contract to whom the performance is owed—is the **obligee.** When a delegation occurs in conjunction with an assignment, the delegatee usually (but not necessarily) expressly or impliedly promises that he or she will perform the delegator's duties under the contract. Assuming such a promise, the relationships are diagrammed in Figure 17.2.[7]

**Obligations of the Parties:** Where a delegation occurs, and where the delegatee expressly or impliedly promises to perform the delegator's duties, the delegatee assumes the primary responsibility for performance of those duties. The delegator, however, remains secondarily liable for performance of those duties. To illustrate: X contracts to put in a driveway for Y, and X then delegates the duty to Z. If Z fails to do the job, X must either perform the job or be liable

---

[7]This discussion is based upon the assumption of a valid delegation—i.e., one in which the obligee has consented to the delegation, or in which the duty is of such nature that it can be delegated without the obligee's consent. (Non-delegable duties—those that cannot be assigned without the obligee's consent—will be examined later.)

**Figure 17.2  Delegation of Duties**

Delegator X ←— Contract —→ Y Obligee

Delegation ↓  ↘ Performance

Delegatee Z

to Y, the obligee, for damages for breach of contract. Thus, where the contract is never performed, the obligee has causes of action against both the delegatee and delegator. In other words, a delegation of duties—even when consented to by the obligee—does not in and of itself free the delegator of liability. (Thus, although a delegation is generally defined as a "transfer" of duties, this term is not entirely accurate in view of the retention of secondary liability by the delegator.)

The above discussion has assumed that the delegatee has promised, expressly or by clear implication, to perform the delegator's duties. In some situations, however, it is unclear whether the delegatee has made an implied promise to perform. Going back to the driveway illustration, for example, the assignment document might state that X hereby assigns to Z "all of my rights and obligations under my contract with Y," or it may simply say that X hereby assigns to Z the "entire contract" that he (X) has with Y. In either case, if Z accepts the assignment of rights but neither expressly promises to perform the contract nor commences performance, is he or she liable to Y if the driveway is never built? While there is disagreement on this point, the trend among the courts of most states *is* to find an implied assumption of duties by Z in both cases—with Z thus incurring liability in case he or she fails to perform.

**Novation:** As noted in the previous section, in the typical delegation, the delegator is secondarily liable on the contract if the delegatee assumes the duty but does not perform. An exception arises where the obligee agrees to substitute the delegatee for the delegator and to look no further to the delegator for performance in exchange for the delegatee's assumption of the duty. Such a consensual substitution of parties is called a **novation**. Mere approval by the obligee of a delegation does not constitute a novation, absent approval of the complete substitution of the delegatee for the delegator. The novation is discussed further in the next chapter.

## Delegation in Absence of Assignment—Subcontracts

A delegation of duties may be made without an assignment of the delegator's rights under his or her contract with the obligee. In such cases, where the delegatee by contract promises to perform the delegator's duties, the general rule is that the delegatee's only obligation is to the delegator. In the "real world" a delegation of duties in the absence of an assignment most often involves a partial delegation of duties. To illustrate: X, a builder, contracts to build a home for Y for $92,000. X then subcontracts the electrical work to the Z Company, an electrical firm. If the Z Company fails to do the work, or does it in an unacceptable manner, it is liable to X but not to Y. (Similarly, it should be noted in passing that if the Z Company *does* perform, it may look only to X, the delegator, for payment. In other words, in the usual situation, the subcontractor is neither an intended beneficiary nor an assignee of the contract between the prime contractor-delegator and the obligee.)

## What Duties Are Delegable?

In exceptional circumstances the obligee, upon learning of the delegation, will notify the parties that he or she will not accept performance by the delegatee. The general rule applicable to such a controversy is that any contractual duty may be delegated without the obligee's consent except (1) duties arising out of contracts which expressly prohibit delegation, and (2) contracts in which the obligee has a "substantial interest" in having the obligor-delegator perform personally.

Under the latter rule, contracts calling for the performance of *personal services*—such as those of a teacher, physician, or lawyer—are clearly nondelegable without the obligee's consent (even if the delegatee is as professionally competent as the delegator). Most other contracts call for the performance of duties that are described as essentially *routine* in nature, such as the repair of a building, the sale of goods, or the overhaul of machinery, and these duties are generally held to be delegable. (This result is not as unfair to the objecting obligee as it might appear, because, as we noted earlier, he or she may hold the delegator liable if the delegatee's performance is defective.)

The UCC's rules on delegation are virtually identical to those of the common law.

## SUMMARY

While contracts can normally be enforced only by the original contracting parties, some persons—called third parties—can enforce contracts made by others in certain circumstances. The major classes of third parties possessing this ability are beneficiaries and assignees. There are three types of beneficiaries: creditor, donee, and incidental beneficiaries. A creditor beneficiary is a third party to whom one of the contracting parties owes a debt, and who is to receive performance from the other contracting party as a means of extinguishing the debt. A donee beneficiary is a third party who, under the contract, is to receive performance from one of the contracting parties as a gift from the other contracting party. Creditor and donee beneficiaries are permitted to enforce the contracts because in both instances the contracts in question were made primarily for their benefit, i.e., the contracting parties had such beneficiaries in mind as persons who were to receive performance. By contrast, the incidental beneficiary is a person who might have some interest in seeing that the contract be performed, but was *not* a person for whose benefit the contract was made. Accordingly, incidental beneficiaries cannot enforce contracts made by others.

Assignees are persons to whom contractual rights have been assigned after the contract was entered into. As a general rule, one party to a contract may assign his or her rights under the contract without the consent of the other party, the "obligor." (There are, however, limited situations in which the obligor's consent is required.) Once an assignment has occurred, the assignee stands in the same position as the assignor; that is, if the assignor could have enforced the right against the obligor, the assignee has the same power. On the other hand, if the obligor had a valid defense against the assignor (such as breach of contract), the obligor can assert the same defense against the assignee.

In some situations a party to a contract may delegate his duties under the contract to a third party. (In such case, the person transferring his or her duties is the "delegator," the other party to the contract is the "obligee," and the person to whom the duties have been delegated is the "delegatee.") Delegation of duties requires consent of the obligee if the contract was made primarily upon the personal qualities or skill of the delegator, but is not required if the performance owed by the delegator to the obligee is "routine in nature." In any event, once a valid delegation occurs the delegator remains secondarily liable to the obligee in the event the delegatee fails to perform the contract (unless the obligee had expressly released the delegator).

## KEY TERMS

**Third party**
**Creditor beneficiary**
**Donee beneficiary**
**Incidental beneficiary**
**Assignor**
**Assignee**
**Obligor**
**Delegation of duties**
**Delegator**
**Delegatee**
**Obligee**
**Novation**

## QUESTIONS AND PROBLEMS

1. An agency of the State of Washington operated a ferry system providing service between the mainland and offshore islands. The ferry employees were unionized, and they worked under a contract between the union and the state. Just before a Labor Day weekend the union called a strike, which was a breach of its contract. As a result, tourist travel to the islands was substantially cut, and resort owners located on the islands sued the union to recover damages for breach of contract. Should they be able to recover on the theory they were donee beneficiaries? Why or why not? (*Burke and Thomas v. International Organization of Masters,* 585 P.2d 152, 1978.)

2. Rudolph bought a home from Ahlstrom. As a condition of the sale, Ahlstrom agreed to provide Rudolph with a written termite inspection report on the house. He hired ABC Pest Control which, after inspection, furnished Rudolph with a copy of its report which stated that there was no active infestation. Rudolph then bought the house, but less than a year later found a severe and active termite infestation that ABC had overlooked. Rudolph sued ABC for breach of contract. ABC defended by pointing out that it was hired by Ahlstrom and that Rudolph was not a party to the con-

tract. Is this a good defense? (*Rudolph v. ABC Pest Control, Inc.,* 763 S.W.2d 930, Tex. App. 1989.)

**3.** A labor union entered into a collective bargaining agreement with the Powder Power Tool Corporation, under which the company agreed to pay specified wages to various classes of its employees. When Springer, an employee and union member, was not paid the full wages to which he was entitled under the agreement, he brought action to recover the additional payments as specified. The company defended on the ground that Springer was not a party to the contract and thus could not maintain the action. Is the company correct? Explain. (*Springer v. Powder Power Tool Co.,* 348 P.2d 1112, 1960.)

**4.** A (franchisor) agreed to establish B (franchisee) as the holder of a Dairy Queen franchise. The agreement between the two prohibited B from assigning the franchise to a third party without A's permission. Later, B sought to make such an assignment without A's permission. A objected, claiming, in part, that the $90,000 price the third party had agreed to pay was too high and that inflated prices were bad for the business. Also, it appeared that the third party was young and inexperienced in business. The trial court held that the anti-assignment clause violated public policy and refused to give it effect. Did the trial judge rule correctly? (*Hanigan v. Wheeler,* 504 P.2d 972, Ariz.App. 1972.)

**5.** Abramov, when leaving the employment of a partnership, signed a contract promising not to compete with the partnership for five years. Soon thereafter the partnership incorporated. Abramov later started a business in competition with the corporation, whereupon it brought action for an injunction ordering him to live up to the terms of the contract not to compete. The issue was whether the contract could be assigned by the partnership to the corporation without Abramov's consent. Decide, with reasons. (*Abramov v. Royal Dallas, Inc.,* 536 S.W.2d 388, 1976.)

**6.** Cullins worked for an insurance agency under an employment contract that prevented him from competing with that agency for a period of three years after leaving its employment. Later, another company, Smith, Bell and Hauck, Inc., purchased the insurance agency. When Cullins quit the agency and formed a new insurance firm, Smith, Bell and Hauck brought an action for an injunction ordering Cullins to live up to his contract not to compete. When Cullins defended on the ground that Smith, Bell and Hauck were not parties to the contract, they contended that an implied assignment of the contract from the insurance agency had taken place and, as assignees, they were entitled to enforce that contract. Is this a good argument? Discuss. (*Smith, Bell and Hauck, Inc., v. Cullins,* 183 A.2d 528, 1962.)

**7.** Nexxus Products manufactures hair care products. After some negotiation with Mr. Reicheck, it contracted to have Reicheck's Best Barber & Beauty Supply Co. (Best) become the exclusive distributor of Nexxus hair care products throughout most of Texas. However, two years later, Sally Beauty Company bought all the stock of Best and merged Best into Sally Beauty, acquiring all Best's contracts. Because Sally Beauty was a wholly owned subsidiary of Alberto-Culver Co., one of Nexxus's major competitors in the national hair care products business, Nexxus cancelled the contract. Sally Beauty sued for breach of contract. The trial court held that because the contract was non-assignable, Nexxus had not acted improperly. Did the trial judge rule correctly? (*Sally Beauty Co. v. Nexxus Products Co., Inc.,* 801 F.2d 1001, 7th Cir. 1986.)

**8.** Coburn, a contractor, was building structures for the City of Boston, and was to be paid according to a certain schedule as jobs were completed. Coburn assigned his right to receive two payments under the contract to P. At the time of the assignment and notice to the City of the assignment, there were no complications. However, thereafter, Coburn defaulted on his contract with the City. The City refused to pay P, who sued. The City sought to raise Coburn's default as a defense against P's suit. Will the City succeed? (*American Bridge Co. v. Boston,* 88 N.E. 1089, Mass. 1909.)

**9.** Folquet was employed as a school bus driver by the Woodburn Public School District for a contract period of five years at a salary of $125 per school month. The contract required Folquet to furnish and maintain a bus at his own expense, to conduct himself in a proper and moral manner, and to be responsible for the conduct of the pupils while in the bus. Folquet died before the five years elapsed, and his son, an adult, was appointed administrator of his estate. When the son offered to drive the bus for the remainder of the contract, the district refused to let him do so. The son then brought suit to recover damages for breach of contract. The school district contended that the contract was of a personal nature and thus could not be delegated or assigned to any other driver without its consent. Is the school district's defense valid? Explain. (*Folquet v. Woodburn Public Schools,* 29 P.2d 554, 1934.)

**10.** A company assigned its accounts receivable to an insurance company and later assigned the same accounts to a bank. The bank gave notice of the assignment to the account debtors before the insurance company did. In subsequent litigation the issue was which of the two assignees was entitled to collect the accounts receivable. (*Boulevard National Bank of Miami v. Air Metals Industries, Inc.,* 176 So.2d 94, 1965.)

    **a.** If the majority rule were applied, who would win?

    **b.** If the minority rule were applied, who would win?

# CHAPTER 18

# DISCHARGE OF CONTRACTS

Sooner or later all contractual obligations come to an end. When this occurs in a particular case, the contract is said to be *discharged.* What is meant by this is that the *duties* of the contracting parties have been discharged.

There are many ways in which a discharge, or termination, can come about. Most of these result from the conduct of the parties themselves, while others involve events completely outside the control of either party. One leading treatise on contract law recognizes at least twenty separate and distinct ways in which a person's contractual obligations can be discharged.[1] The most important of these are discharge by (1) operation of conditions; (2) performance; (3) breach by the other party; (4) circumstances excusing performance (impossibility, impracticability, and frustration); (5) agreement of the parties; and (6) operation of law.

## DISCHARGE BY OPERATION OF CONDITIONS

### Conditions, Generally

In many contracts the parties simply exchange mutual promises to perform specified duties, with neither promise being conditioned or qualified in any way. Once such a contract is formed, each party is said to have incurred a "duty of immediate performance"—even though the performance of one or both parties may not be due until some specified time in the future.

In some situations, however, the performance of the contemplated contract is beneficial to one or both of the parties only if a certain event occurs in the future. And in other situations a contract may be mutually beneficial to the parties when entered into, but would be of little benefit if some event should occur before the stated time of performance arrives.

In these situations the parties can achieve substantial protection by the use of conditions in their contract. The term **condition,** in its broadest sense, can be defined as an express or implied provision in a contract which, upon the occurrence or nonoccurrence of a specified event, either creates, suspends, or terminates the rights and duties of the contracting parties. (While this definition refers to a provision or clause in a contract creating the condition, the terms may also be used to refer to the event itself that is designated in such provision.)

The law recognizes three kinds of conditions—*conditions precedent, conditions subsequent,* and *conditions concurrent.* Each type of condition can be further classified as *express* or *implied.* (Our discussion initially will focus on the nature of express conditions, with consideration of implied conditions precedent and implied conditions subsequent being delayed until we reach the subjects of performance and impossibility, respectively.)

### Conditions Precedent

A **condition precedent** is a clause in a contract which indicates that the promises made therein are not to be operative until a specified event occurs. For example, X makes this offer to Y: "If the city rezones your property at 540 Fox Lane from C-3 to C-1 within thirty days, I will pay you $18,000 cash for it." Y accepts the offer. While a contract has now been formed, it is clear that the specified event must occur before either party incurs "a duty of immediate performance." The act of rezoning, therefore, is a condition precedent. And, because the condition resulted from the language of the contract, rather than by im-

---

[1] *Restatement, Contracts 2d,* The American Law Institute, 1979.

plication, the rezoning constitutes an *express* condition precedent.[2]

**Discharge by Failure (or Nonoccurrence) of a Condition Precedent:** Where a contract clearly creates a condition precedent, no "duty of immediate performance" arises until the specified event occurs. In the above case, then, should the rezoning not occur within the specified time, the condition is said to have "failed" and both parties are accordingly discharged of their obligations. In other words, the parties' duties under the contract are terminated.

## Conditions Subsequent

Occasionally both parties to a contract are willing to incur a duty of immediate performance, but want to be freed of their obligations if a particular circumstance arises before the performance date. The parties can achieve this protection by use of an express **condition subsequent**—a clause in a contract providing that upon the happening of a specified event, the contract shall be inoperative (or void).[3] True conditions subsequent are rare, but consider this example: An insurance policy states "If written notice is given to the Company of Mr. A's death within 30 days of its occurrence, the Company will pay $100,000 to the beneficiaries. If the Company refuses to pay, and the beneficiaries do not file suit within one year of the death, any obligation of the Company under this contract shall be discharged."

**Discharge by Occurrence of Condition Subsequent:** In the above example, the death and the giving of written notice are conditions precedent which give rise to the Company's duty of immediate performance. However, that duty may be extinguished by the occurrence of a condition subsequent—the failure to file suit within one year. Conditions precedent are contrasted to conditions subsequent in Figure 18.1.

Most conditions subsequent (as is true of conditions generally) are express rather than implied. They can ordinarily be recognized by language providing that the contract is to be void, inoperative, or canceled if a certain event occurs in the future.

---

[2] Conditions precedent can usually be identified by clauses containing the words *if, in the event,* or *when.* Thus the following language creates a condition precedent: "If X is able to obtain a building permit from the city within sixty days" (or "In the event X is able to obtain a building permit . . ."), "it is agreed that Y will construct a swimming pool for her, according to the attached specifications, for $9,000."

[3] Thus the essential difference in legal effect between the two basic kinds of conditions is that the occurrence of a condition precedent *imposes* a duty of immediate performance, while the occurrence of a condition subsequent *removes* such a duty.

---

Figure 18.1  Conditions Precedent and Conditions Subsequent

**Condition precedent**

Agreement subject to condition precedent → Occurrence of condition → Duty to perform arises
Agreement subject to condition precedent → Nonoccurrence of condition → Discharge (no duty to perform arises)

**Condition subsequent**

Agreement subject to condition subsequent → Duty to perform → Occurrence of condition → Discharge
Agreement subject to condition subsequent → Duty to perform → Nonoccurrence of condition → Duty to perform continues

(The relatively few situations in which implied conditions subsequent exist will be discussed later in the chapter.)

## Conditions Concurrent

**Conditions concurrent** exist when a contract expressly provides (or if one can reasonably infer from its terms) that the performances of the parties are to occur at the same time. A common example is a land sale contract which provides that the seller is to deliver the deed on payment of the purchase price. The duty of each party is thus conditioned on performance by the other. The seller has no duty to deliver the deed until the buyer pays (or tenders) the purchase price, and the buyer has no duty to pay until the seller delivers (or tenders) the deed.[4]

The legal consequences that result from the use of express conditions precedent and subsequent are clear, once either condition is proven to exist. It is, however, often a more difficult question whether the parties conditioned their obligations at all, and, if so, whether the condition in the particular case fell in the precedent or subsequent category. The following case highlights the impact that such a determination might have on the outcome of a particular controversy.

[4] A tender is an *offer* to perform one's obligation.

---

### Rincones v. Windberg
Court of Appeals of Texas, Austin,
705 S.W.2d 846 (1986)

Rincones and Mena, plaintiffs, entered into a contract with Windberg, defendant, under which they were to "compile, research and edit material for academic and student services for a migrant program handbook." The contract was termed a "Consultant Agreement," and under it each plaintiff was to write specified chapters, for which Windberg would pay each $1,250 per chapter for their respective chapters.

The handbook was ultimately to be used by California authorities, and the parties were aware that the funds to pay plaintiffs would ultimately come from the State of California. *The consultant agreement, however, made no mention of Windberg's obligation to pay being contingent upon his receipt of funding by California.* Plaintiffs submitted the drafts of their respective chapters to Windberg, but he refused to pay for them because "the publication was not accepted by California," and no funding from that state, therefore, was available for the project.

Plaintiffs then brought this action to recover the monies promised them. The primary question was whether Windberg's receipt of funding from California was a condition precedent to his obligations under the contract, as Windberg contended. The trial court found (1) that the contract was partly written and partly oral; (2) that, under the oral agreement and the circumstances surrounding it, the parties had agreed that the contract was contingent upon California's funding of the project; and (3) that California refused to fund the project. The court concluded that a "condition precedent" existed; that proof of the condition was not barred by the parol evidence rule; that the condition precedent had not been met; that the contract was of no further force and effect, and that Windberg thus had no liability under it.[a] The plaintiffs appealed.

**Decision:** Judgment was reversed. The evidence does not support the trial court's conclusion that funding from California was a condition precedent, but shows, rather, that an effective and binding contract existed subject to a condition subsequent. This evidence shows that once the contract was made, all of the parties devoted substantial amounts of time and money attempting to perform their obligations. The plaintiffs submitted a draft of their manuscript to Windberg; one of his associates took it to California for review by California officials, and thereafter Windberg's associate took several trips to California attempting to get funding from the state.

Thus it is clear that the parties understood that they had a binding contract from the beginning. It follows, therefore, that the parties understood that a lack of funding from California was a condition subsequent which, if it occurred, *removed* the parties' obligations. As a result, the parol (oral) understanding that the parties had as to the effect that nonfunding by California would have is barred by the parol evidence rule, and should not have been admitted by the trial court. The case accordingly was remanded to the trial court for a new trial. ■

[a] As was noted in Chapter 16, parol evidence showing a condition precedent is admissible under one of the exceptions to the parol evidence rule.

# DISCHARGE BY PERFORMANCE

Most contracts are discharged by performance—by each party completely fulfilling his or her promises. In such cases, obviously, no legal problems exist. Nevertheless, the subject of performance merits special attention for several reasons.

In the first place, many cases arise in which the actual performance of a promisor is, to some extent, defective. Sometimes the performance falls far short of what was promised; other times it deviates from the terms of the contract in only minor respects. As one might expect, the legal consequences of a major breach of contract are more severe and far-reaching than those resulting from a minor breach.

Second, in some cases the courts must determine whether the defective performance constituted a breach of a condition or a mere breach of a promise. A breach of a condition, no matter how slight, usually frees the nondefaulting party, while a breach of a promise generally does not unless it is a material one.

## *Promises: Degree of Performance Required*

Many agreements consist simply of the exchange of mutual promises, with neither party's obligations expressly conditioned in any way. In most of these contracts, however, it is usually apparent from their nature that one of the parties is to perform his or her part of the bargain before the other is obligated to do so. For example: If X contracts to landscape Y's new home for $1,500, it can reasonably be inferred that the work is to be done by X before he can demand payment of Y.[5] Thus, in general, when a promisor seeks to recover the contract price, that person must show that he or she has *fully performed* the promise in some cases or *substantially performed it* in others—depending on the nature of the obligation involved. If it is determined that this performance has met the applicable minimum standard, the promisor is entitled to recover the contract price minus damages (if any) suffered by the promisee. However, if the performance falls short of this minimum, the promisor's obligation has not been discharged, and he or she will recover little or nothing. (The rules determining the extent of recovery in each of these situations will be discussed immediately after the next case in the chapter.)

**Total Performance:** Some promises are of such a nature that they can be discharged only by complete performance. If a promisor's performance falls short of that called for under such a contract, even though the breach is minor, his or her obligation is not discharged. Suppose, for example, that B contracts in May to buy a car from S for $2,000—the contract providing that the price is to be paid in full by B on June 1, at which time S is to assign the car title to her. If, on June 1, B tenders S a check for $1,950, S has no obligation to transfer the title. A contract under which a seller of land is obligated to convey "merchantable title" falls into the same category; delivery of a deed conveying any interest or title less than that specified will not discharge the seller's obligation.

**Substantial Performance:** Many obligations are of such a nature that it is unlikely (indeed, not even to be expected, given the frailties of mankind) that a 100 percent performance will actually occur. The typical example involves a construction contract under which a builder agrees to build a home according to detailed plans and specifications. It is quite possible that the finished building will deviate from the specifications in one or more respects no matter how conscientious and able the builder is. In contracts of this sort, if the promisee-owner seeks to escape liability on the ground of nonperformance of the promisor-builder, it is ordinarily held that the promisor has sufficiently fulfilled the obligation if his or her performance, though imperfect, conformed to the terms of the contract in all major respects. This rule is known as the doctrine of **substantial performance.**

In order for the doctrine to be applicable, two requirements must ordinarily be met:

**1.** Performance must be "substantial"—that is, the omissions and deviations must be so slight in nature that they do not materially affect the usefulness of the building for the purposes for which it was intended.

**2.** The omissions or deviations must not have been occasioned by bad faith on the part of the builder. (This is ordinarily interpreted to mean that the omissions or deviations must not have been made knowingly by the builder.)

Using the illustration involving the construction of a house, let us examine three cases where the

---

[5] In this regard, it is sometimes said that the actual performance of one's promises constitutes an *implied* condition precedent that must be met by that person.

builder is bringing suit against the owner to recover the last payment of $5,000 called for under the contract and where the owner is refusing to pay on the ground of inadequate performance.

1. The owner proves that the following defects exist: (a) the plaster in all rooms is considerably softer than expected, because the builder used one bag of adamant for each hod of mortar instead of the two bags called for by the contract, and (b) water seepage in the basement is so great as to make the game room virtually unusable, as a result of the builder's failure to put a required sealant on the exterior of the basement walls. Here the defects are so material, and so affect the enjoyment and value of the home, that the builder has *not substantially performed* his obligations. Thus recovery will be denied, even if the breaches on the part of the builder are shown to be accidental rather than intentional.

2. The owner proves that the following defects exist: (a) the detached garage was given but one coat of paint rather than the two required; (b) the water pipes in the walls were made by the Cohoes Company rather than the Reading Company as was specified (though otherwise the two types of pipe are virtually identical); and (c) the wallboard installed in the attic is ⅛ inch sheeting instead of the ¼ inch that was called for. Here the defects are so slight in nature, even when taken in total, that the builder has substantially performed the contract and can thus probably recover under the doctrine.

3. Same facts as case 2, but, in addition, the owner can show that one or more of the deviations were *intentional;* for example, he produces evidence tending to prove that the builder ordered the installation of the substitute pipe and wallboard knowing that they were not in conformity with the contract. Here the deviations are willful (rather than the result of simple negligence); therefore the builder is guilty of bad faith and the doctrine is not applicable.

Obviously, the requirement that performance be "substantial" is a somewhat elastic one, and necessitates a comparison of the promisor's actual performance with that which the terms of the contract really required of him. The following case is typical of those presenting substantial performance problems.

---

**Lane Wilson Company, Inc. v. Gregory**
Court of Appeal of Louisiana, Second Circuit,
322 So.2d 369 (1975)

Lane Wilson Company, plaintiff, contracted to build a swimming pool for Gregory, defendant, at Gregory's KOA Campground outside Monroe, Louisiana, for $12,000. Under the written agreement, the pool was to be 30 by 60 feet, with a depth varying from 3 feet to 6 feet. Later the parties orally modified their contract by agreeing that plaintiff would add a diving board and increase the depth of the pool to accommodate persons using the diving board. It was also orally agreed that a walkway around the pool would be enlarged, and a longer fence built than was originally contemplated. The cost of these modifications raised the contract price to $13,643.

During construction, defendant paid $8,400 on the contract. After the job was completed, however, he refused to pay the balance due because of various defects in the pool's construction (the most important of which are described in the appellate court's decision). Plaintiff then brought this action to recover the balance allegedly due. The trial court held that plaintiff had *substantially performed* the contract, and that plaintiff was thus entitled to the balance of the contract price minus a credit of $300 to remedy one of the defects (the installation of a chlorinator). Defendant appealed.

**Decision:** The judgment was affirmed. The major shortcomings in plaintiff's performance were these: As constructed, the pool's measurements fluctuated from 59 feet 3 inches to 59 feet 6 inches in length; the walls of the pool "sloped severely," instead of being vertical; and the pool was not 10 feet deep in the diving area.

In determining whether or not a promisor's performance is substantial, the court said that these factors are to be considered: (1) the extent of the defects or nonperformance; (2) the degree to which the purpose of the contract is defeated; (3) the ease of correction of the defects; and (4) the use or benefit to the promisee (defendant) of the work performed. In applying these factors to the instant case, the court said, plaintiff had

*(continued)*

substantially performed the contract. The minor deviations as to the length of the pool "did not in any way defeat the purpose of the contract." The same was true with regard to the shape of the walls; the sharply sloping walls were adequate for normal pool use. Moreover, the court said, while the pool was less than 10 feet deep in the diving area, it was shown to be deep enough to safely accommodate divers. In view of these facts, and the fact that the award of damages would enable the defendant to correct other minor deviations (such as failure to install the chlorinator), plaintiff's recovery under the doctrine of substantial performance was proper. ∎

---

**Substantial Performance—Amount of Recovery:** As noted earlier, if the rule of substantial performance is applicable to a particular case, the promisor-plaintiff is entitled to recover *the contract price minus damages* (that is, the promisor may recover the amount that the promisee agreed to pay under the contract, minus damages—if any—which the promisee sustained as a result of the deviations). Since the damages are typically inconsequential, the promisor usually recovers a high percentage of the contract price. By contrast, where the doctrine is not applicable, the recovery may be little or nothing. The general rules for such situations can be summarized as follows:

1. Where the performance falls short of being substantial and the breach is intentional, the promisor receives nothing. The rationale, of course, is that an intentional wrongdoer should not be rewarded—particularly where the promisee has not received the performance he or she was entitled to. (The rule of nonrecovery also has an affirmative aspect—it strongly "persuades" the promisor to actually finish the job, since he or she will receive nothing otherwise.)

2. In the somewhat rarer case where the performance is not substantial but the breach is unintentional, recovery is allowed on the basis of quasi-contract. For example, if the promisor is permanently injured when only halfway through the job, he or she is entitled to receive the reasonable value of the benefit received by the promisee as a result of the partial performance.

3. If the performance is clearly substantial but the breach is willful, there are conflicting views. Some courts deny any recovery, regardless of other circumstances, embracing the principle that aid should never be given to the intentional wrongdoer. Most courts, while endorsing this principle in the abstract, in practice allow the promisor to recover "the reasonable value of the benefit resulting from the performance, minus damages" (as distinguished from the "contract price, minus damages" recovery allowed in situations where the substantial performance requirements are met). Such a recovery is especially common where a failure to allow the promisor anything would result in the promisee being unjustly enriched—a result most likely to occur in cases where the performance is of such a nature that it cannot be returned by the promisee.

## Special Problems Relating to Performance

**Personal Satisfaction Contracts:** Under the ordinary contract, a person who has undertaken the performance of a job impliedly warrants only that he or she will perform in a "workmanlike manner," i.e., the performance will be free of material defect and of a quality ordinarily accepted in that line of work. If the performance meets this standard, he or she is entitled to recover the contract price even if the person for whom the work was done is not satisfied with it.

Some contracts, however, provide that "satisfaction is guaranteed," or contain other language of similar nature. In such cases, it is usually held that such satisfaction is a condition precedent that must be met in order for the promisor to recover under the contract; workmanlike performance alone will not suffice. In determining whether the condition has been met, the courts distinguish between two kinds of contracts: (1) those in which matters of personal taste, esthetics, or comfort are dominant considerations, and (2) those that entail work of mere "mechanical utility."

For contracts in the first category, the condition is fulfilled only if the *promisee is actually satisfied* with the performance that was rendered—no matter how peculiar or unreasonable that person's tastes may be. For example: X, an artist, contracts to paint a portrait of Y for $500 "that will meet with Y's complete satisfaction." When the portrait is completed, Y refuses to pay on the ground that he simply does not like it. If X brings suit to recover the $500, a question of fact is presented: Is Y's claim of dissatisfaction genuine? If the jury so finds, the condition has not been met and X is denied recovery. (Of course, if the jury finds that Y's claim of dissatisfaction is false—that is, he is actually satisfied and is simply using this claim as a ground to escape an otherwise valid contract—then the condition has been met and recovery is allowed.)

For contracts in the second category, where the performance involves work of mere mechanical fitness (or mechanical utility), an objective test is used. For example: M agrees to overhaul the diesel engine in T's tractor-trailer for $200, guaranteeing that T will be "fully satisfied" with the job. In this case, the condition precedent is met if the jury finds that *a reasonable person would have been satisfied* with M's job, even though T himself is dissatisfied.

**Performance by an Agreed Time:** If a contract does not provide a time by which performance is to be completed, the general rule is that each party has a reasonable time within which to perform his or her obligations. Whether the performance of a promisor in a given case took place within such a time is ordinarily a question for the jury. In practice this rule poses few problems and seems to produce acceptable results.

A more troublesome situation is presented by contracts that *do* contain a stated time of performance. For example: A printer agrees to print up 15,000 letterheads for a customer, with the contract specifying "delivery by April 10." If delivery is not made until April 14, and the customer refuses to accept the goods because of the late performance, the question for the jury is whether the stated time of performance legally constituted a condition precedent. If it did, the condition has obviously not been met and the customer has no obligation to accept the shipment.

The general rule is that such a provision, of and by itself, *does not create a condition precedent.* Under this view, it is sufficient if the performance occurs within a reasonable time after the date specified. Thus, in the preceding illustration, the customer is very likely obligated to accept the letterheads where delivery was only four days late. The customer may recover any damages caused by the delay in accordance with rules of recovery discussed in the next chapter.

*Time-of-the-Essence Clauses:* In some situations, however, the parties clearly intend that performance must actually take place by the specified time in order for the promisor to recover from the other party. In such situations, *performance by the agreed-upon time does constitute a condition precedent.* The intention can be manifested in two ways: (1) by the express wording of the agreement itself and (2) by implication (reasonable inference from the nature and subject matter of the contract alone).[6] Two examples may be helpful.

1. P agrees to print up and deliver 15,000 letterheads to Q by April 10, the contract further providing that *time is of the essence.* By this clause, the parties have made the stated time of performance an express condition precedent. Thus, if P fails to deliver the letterheads until April 11, Q can refuse to accept the belated performance. P's failure to meet the condition frees Q of her obligations under the contract. Additionally, Q can recover damages from P in a breach of contract suit. (An alternative open to Q is to accept the late performance and "reserve her rights" against P—in which case she is entitled to an allowance against the purchase price to the extent that she has suffered damages as a result of the late performance.)

2. A chamber of commerce purchases fireworks for a Fourth of July celebration it is sponsoring, with the contract providing that "delivery is to be made prior to July 4th." The fireworks arrive too late on July 4th to be used. From the nature of the *subject matter alone* it can be inferred that the stated time is a condition precedent, and the late delivery obviously did not meet that condition. In such a case it is said that time was made a condition "by operation of law" (that is, without regard to other factors).

The courts are reluctant to rule—from the subject matter of the contract or from the nature of the contract alone—that time is of the essence. Limited instances in which such a ruling *may* be made, however (in addition to the rare case typified in example 2), are option contracts—where, for example, a seller of land contracts to keep an offer open ninety days—and contracts in which the value of the subject matter is fluctuating rapidly.

At one time, many courts ruled that time was presumed to be of the essence in sales contracts. Today,

---

[6]The latter possibility is eliminated in some jurisdictions. A number of states provide by statute that time is never of the essence unless the contract expressly indicates that it is.

however, this is not the general rule. Thus, in most states, a late delivery does not free the buyer unless he or she can clearly prove that delivery by the date contained in the contract *was* material, and that the seller knew or should have been aware of the materiality.

## DISCHARGE BY BREACH

### *Actual Breach*

It would be contrary to common sense if a person who had materially breached a contract were nevertheless able to hold the other party liable on it, and the law does not tolerate such a result. As the preceding section on performance indicates, an **actual breach**—failure of the promisor to render performance that meets the minimum required by law (full performance in some cases and substantial performance in others)—ordinarily results in the other party's obligations being discharged. In such cases the promisor's breach operates as "an excuse for nonperformance" insofar as the other's obligation is concerned.

This principle has found its way into the law of sales. Thus, if Seller S on May 1 contracts to deliver a thousand gallons of crude oil to Buyer B on August 15, and on that date S delivers only two hundred gallons with no indication that the balance will be delivered shortly thereafter, B can cancel the entire contract, returning the oil already delivered (see Secs. 2-610 and 2-711 of the UCC).

### *Anticipatory Breach*

If one contracting party indicates to the other, before the time of performance arrives, that he or she is not going to perform his or her part of the bargain, an **anticipatory breach** has occurred; in most cases this has the same effect as an actual breach. For example: In March, X contracts to put in a sewer line for a city, with the contract providing that the work will be commenced by June 1. On April 10, X tells the city that he will not do the job. The city can immediately hire a new contractor to do the work and can institute a suit for damages against X as soon as the damages can be ascertained, without waiting until June to do so. (Such action is not mandatory; the city may ignore the repudiation in the hope that X will have a change of heart and actually commence the work on schedule.)

The doctrine of anticipatory breach does not apply to promises to pay money debts, such as those found in promissory notes and bonds. To illustrate: S borrows $500 from T on February 1, giving T a promissory note in that amount due September 1. If S tells T on August 6 that he will not pay the debt, T must nevertheless wait until September 2 before bringing suit to recover the $500. The UCC has detailed provisions addressing anticipatory breach that are discussed in detail in Chapter 23.

## DISCHARGE BY LEGAL IMPOSSIBILITY

Between the time of contracting and the time of performance, some event may occur that will make the performance of the contract—for one party, at least—considerably more difficult or costly than originally expected. When this happens, a promisor may contend that the occurrence legally discharged his or her obligations under the contract—that is, it created a **legal impossibility.**[7] For example: A, an accountant for a large corporation who "moonlights" in his spare time, contracts in May to perform certain auditing services for B during the first three weeks of August, A's regularly scheduled vacation. In June A is transferred to a city five hundred miles away; as a result, he does not perform the promised services. If B were to seek damages for breach of contract, the issue presented would be whether A's transfer discharged his obligations under the contract.

In such a case, the courts resort to a two-step process. The first question to be decided is whether one of the parties had assumed the risk in some manner. For example, in the case above, a court might conclude—from a reading of the entire contract, or from testimony regarding the negotiations leading up to the contract—that B had, in fact, agreed that A need not perform if he were located. If so, B had assumed the risk, and A need not perform.

If no assumption of risk is apparent (as is often the case), the court must proceed to the second question: whether it can rule, on the basis of the circumstances under which the contract was made, that the contract necessarily contained an *implied condition subsequent.* In other words, in the case above, A would be excused from performing the contract only

---

[7]A related subject, the doctrine of commercial impracticability, will be discussed subsequently.

if he could convince the court that *he and B agreed by implication* that the contract would be voided if he were transferred before the date of performance.

In most cases of this sort, the promisor's contention that an implied condition subsequent existed is rejected by the courts. The usual view is that such possibilities should have been guarded against by an express condition in the contract. Thus, when a corporation promises to manufacture engines by a certain date under a contract containing no express conditions, the fact that it is unable to do so because of a strike at one of its plants is no legal excuse for its nonperformance of the contract. And when a contractor agrees to construct a building by a certain date, with a monetary penalty imposed for late completion, the law normally does not excuse late performance simply because unexpectedly bad weather delayed the work. Nor will a court normally free a builder from his obligations, in the absence of an express condition, merely because unexpectedly high labor or materials costs will cause him to suffer a loss if he is held to the contract.

Notwithstanding these generalizations, there *are* limited situations in which the defense of legal impossibility is accepted by the courts. We will discuss them briefly.

## True Impossibility

Essentially, a contract is rendered impossible of performance only where the supervening event—the event occurring between the making of the contract and the time of performance—was unforeseeable at the time of contracting, and which creates an objective impossibility. An objective impossibility results in a situation where, as a result of the unanticipated occurrence, no one can perform the contract—that is, performance is physically impossible. By contrast, an occurrence that makes performance by the promisor, only, impossible (but does not make performance by others impossible) does not discharge the promisor's obligations. For example, the inability of a buyer of a condominium to make a cash payment of $10,000 at the time of closing, as required by the contract, is not excused because his or her business suffered a catastrophic loss just prior to that time. (The difference between the two types of impossibility is often summarized thus: where a promisor is claiming objective impossibility, he is saying "*No one can perform*," while in the subjective impossibility situation he is simply saying "*I cannot perform*.")

Up until recent years, implied conditions subsequent—i.e., conditions resulting in legal (objective) impossibility—have been recognized by the courts in only three situations: (1) in contracts calling for personal services, (2) where the subject matter of the contract is destroyed without the fault of either party, and (3) where the performance of the contract becomes illegal after the contract is formed.[8]

**Personal Services:** In contracts calling for the rendering of *personal services,* such as the ordinary employment contract, the death or incapacity of the promisor (employee) terminates the agreement. The same is true of contracts that contemplate a *personal relationship* between the promisor and the other party. In such cases the courts will accept the argument that the performer's promise was *subject to the implied condition* that his or her death prior to the time of performance (or illness at the time of performance) rendered the contract null and void.[9]

---

[8] The view is commonly held among lay persons, and sometimes finds its way into court decisions, that promisors are freed of their obligations by any "act of God," or "force majeure"—i.e., a force of nature of such degree that it could not be guarded against or prevented by any degree of care or diligence (such as an earthquake or unprecedented flood). This generalization is true when the subject matter of a contract is destroyed by such an occurrence, but it is not necessarily true in other cases. For example, the destruction of a partially completed building by a tornado may be accepted by a court as grounds for permitting the contractor additional time in which to complete the job, but, as a general rule, it does *not discharge* the contractor from the obligation to rebuild.

Because of this rule, and because of uncertainty as to application of the act-of-God defense to other contracts, construction contracts (and many others) typically contain *express* conditions subsequent excusing delays in performance, or completely excusing performance, in the event of adverse weather conditions, strikes, and so forth. The following clause, in a maritime shipping contract, is typical. "FORCE MAJEURE: In the event of any strike, fire or other event falling within the term 'Force Majeure' preventing or delaying shipment or delivery of the goods occurring prior to shipment or delivery and preventing or delaying reception of the goods by the buyer, then the contract period of shipment or delivery shall be extended by 30 days on telex request made within seven days of its occurrence. Should shipment or delivery of the goods continue to be prevented beyond 30 days, the unaffected party may cancel the unfulfilled balance of the contract. Should the contract thus be cancelled and/or performance be prevented during any extension to the shipment or delivery period *neither party shall have any claim against the other.*" [Emphasis added.]

[9] Note, however, that many obligations are not personal in nature. For example: If B contracts to sell his land to W for $30,000, and B thereafter dies, the agreement is not terminated. The reason is that B's estate, acting through the executor, is just as capable of delivering a deed to W as was B, had he lived. Nor would the contract be terminated if W rather than B had died. W's estate is just as capable of paying the $30,000 as W would have been, had he lived.

**Destruction of the Subject Matter:** The principle is well established that destruction of the subject matter of a contract without the fault of either party, before the time for performance, terminates the contract. Where such a situation occurs, the courts will accept the argument that the destruction *constituted an implied condition subsequent* and will rule, as in the personal service contracts, that a legal impossibility has occurred. For example: If C contracted in January to move D's house in March, the contract would be discharged if the house were destroyed by flood in February. In this regard, it can be said that the destruction of the subject matter of a contract by an act of God creates a legal impossibility. It should be noted, however, that it is the fact of destruction that discharges, rather than the cause (as long as the destruction is not attributable to neglect or misconduct of the parties). To illustrate: X contracts with an investors' syndicate to drive its race car at the next Indianapolis 500, and the night before the race the car is destroyed by a fire set by an arsonist. Both parties are discharged from their obligations, although the arsonist's act is not an act of God.

Beyond cases such as the above, it is often difficult to determine what is meant by the "subject matter" of a contract; the term is often used by the courts to include not only the precise subject matter involved, but any other "thing" or property that performance of the contract necessarily depends on. For example, the X Company in January agrees to manufacture and deliver five hundred widgets to the Y Company in March. In February the X Company's only plant is destroyed by fire, with the result that the widgets cannot be manufactured. In this case the courts will ordinarily rule that the existence of the plant is so necessary to the fulfillment of the contract that its destruction excuses the X Company from its obligations. (Such a ruling would not be made, however, if the X Company operated several plants and if there was no indication in the contract, expressly or impliedly, that the parties intended for the widgets to come from the particular plant that was destroyed.)[10]

**Subsequent Illegality:** If, after a contract is made, its performance becomes illegal because of a change in the law (including a promulgation of an administrative agency's regulation), a legal impossibility is created. Thus if B in September contracts to sell fifty pinball machines to G in December, the parties' obligations would be discharged if a state statute prohibiting such a transaction took effect in November.

The case below raises a "destruction of the subject matter" issue in regard to the performance of a construction contract that contained no express conditions subsequent. (However, as noted earlier, the general subject of impossibility should also be considered with a related view, the doctrine of "commercial impracticability," which is discussed immediately after this case.)

---

[10] Special problems arise in the "destruction" cases involving *sales of goods.* Specific "risk of loss" rules in Article 2 of the UCC govern situations of this sort, and are considered in Chapter 21.

---

**La Gasse Pool Construction Co. v. City of Fort Lauderdale**
Florida District Court of Appeal,
Fourth District,
288 So.2d 273 (1974)

The La Gasse Company, plaintiff, made a contract with the City of Fort Lauderdale under which it was to repair and renovate one of the city's swimming pools for a specified price. One night, when the job was almost completed, vandals damaged the pool so badly that most of the work had to be redone.

When the city refused to pay more than the contract price, plaintiff brought this action to recover compensation for the additional work. The primary contention of plaintiff was that the damage to its work constituted a destruction of the subject matter of the contract, and that it was consequently discharged from any obligation to redo the work. Accordingly, plaintiff argued, when it did do the work over again it was entitled to additional compensation for its services.

The trial court rejected this contention, holding that plaintiff had the responsibility under the original contract to redo the work, and it entered judgment for defendant. Plaintiff appealed.

---

**Decision:** The trial court was correct in ruling that plaintiff was not entitled to recover for the additional work. In the case of contracts to repair existing structures, the general rule is that *total*

*(continued)*

destruction of the structure, without fault of either the contractor or owner, excuses performance by the contractor and entitles him to recover the value of the work done. The reason for this rule is that the contract has an implied condition that the structure will remain in existence so that the contractor can render performance. Destruction of the structure makes this performance impossible.

But where the building or structure to be repaired is *not totally destroyed,* and the contractor's work is damaged so that it must be redone, performance is still possible. It is thus the contractor's responsibility to redo the work so as to complete the original repair contract. Any loss or damage to his work during the process of repairs which can be rectified is his responsibility. The reason for allowing recovery without full performance in the case of total destruction is that the destruction of the structure constitutes a legal impossibility; while in the partial destruction situation, the structure remains and simply requires a duplication of the repair work. ∎

## DISCHARGE BY COMMERCIAL IMPRACTICABILITY

Under the traditional views just discussed, most contracts did not present situations in which legal impossibility was recognized. Thus most contracting parties were not freed from their obligations even in cases where their performance was clearly made more difficult by events that occurred after the contracts were entered into. Today, however, courts are more likely to free contracting parties than was the case earlier, because of increasing recognition of the **doctrine of commercial impracticability.**

The drafters of the UCC felt that sellers of goods should be excused from their obligations not only where the strict conditions of impossibility existed, but also where performance was literally possible but would necessarily be so radically different from that originally contemplated by the parties that it was impracticable.

### *Commercial Impracticability under the UCC*

Section 2-615 of the UCC reads, in part, as follows: "Delay in delivery or nondelivery in whole or in part by a seller . . . is not a breach of his duty under a contract for sale if performance as agreed has been made impracticable by the occurrence of a contingency the non-occurrence of which was a basic assumption upon which the contract was made."

While a full discussion of the scope and ramifications of the commercial impracticability doctrine cannot be undertaken here, several of its basic characteristics can be noted. These characteristics are best explained in Comment 4 following Sec. 2-615, which reads as follows:

Increased cost alone does not excuse performance unless the rise is due to some unforeseen contingency which alters the essential nature of the performance. Neither is a rise or a collapse in the market in itself a justification, for that is exactly the type of business risk which business contracts made at fixed prices are intended to cover. But a severe shortage of raw materials or of supplies due to a contingency such as war, embargo, local crop failure, unforeseen shutdown of major sources of supply or the like, which either causes a *marked increase in cost* or *altogether prevents the seller* from securing supplies necessary to his performance, is within the contemplation of this section." [Emphasis added.]

Thus this section clearly recognizes certain kinds of contingencies *in addition to* those constituting true impossibilities that may free the seller of his or her obligations under the contract. (In that regard, however, under both Comment 1 to Sec. 2-615 and the case law that has developed with respect to this section, the seller must show that the contingency was not within the contemplation of the parties at the time of contracting.)

A second change brought about by the impracticability doctrine is its recognition that a "marked increase" in cost will free the seller, if caused by an unforeseen contingency. (By contrast, increased cost of performance alone is almost never recognized under the impossibility doctrine as a ground for excusing performance.) However, determination of what constitutes a marked increase in cost is left to the courts to decide on a case-by-case basis, and the courts have interpreted this term quite narrowly. That is, under the decisions, the courts have generally taken the view that the seller must prove that the cost of performance (as a result of the contingency) would at least be double or triple the original cost of performance. Thus the increased cost provision does not afford sellers relief in as many cases as would at first appear.

After adoption of the UCC, the courts generally recognized commercial impracticability as an excuse for nonperformance in sales contracts only, continuing to require a showing of strict impossibility where other types of contracts were involved. Today, however, *there is a growing tendency among the courts to apply the commercial impracticability yardstick to all kinds of contracts.*

## DISCHARGE BY FRUSTRATION OF PURPOSE

Occasionally, after a contract is entered into, some event or condition will occur that clearly does not fall within the impossibility or commercial impracticability doctrines, yet one of the parties will argue that it so *frustrated the purposes of the contract* that its occurrence ought to free him nonetheless. (In other words, such a party is contending that the happening of the event caused the contract to become worthless to him.) To illustrate: D, a car dealer embarking on an ambitious expansion program, makes a contract with C, a contractor, under the terms of which he is to pay C $250,000 for the construction of new showroom facilities. Shortly thereafter, because of an unanticipated national defense emergency, the federal government orders a 90 percent reduction in the production of new automobiles. D contends that this action constitutes grounds for cancelling its construction contract, since he will obviously have few new cars to sell.

Here the courts are on the horns of a dilemma. On the one hand, they understand that the virtual stoppage of new car production substantially eliminates the purpose for which the contract was made—and may even drive D into bankruptcy if he is held to its terms. On the other hand, the adoption of a general rule to the effect that contracts are discharged whenever the *purposes* of one of the parties cannot be attained as a result of unanticipated future occurrences would cast great uncertainty on the enforceability of almost all contracts.

While it is dangerous to generalize about the kinds of cases in which the doctrine of frustration may be accepted as grounds for avoiding contractual liability, it can safely be said that the courts—while giving the doctrine due consideration in their decisions—actually find it to be *inapplicable* in the great majority of cases. Thus, in the example above, D's contention that he was freed on the ground of frustration of purpose will probably (though not certainly) be rejected.

The following case discusses the entire bundle of doctrines—impossibility, commercial impracticability, and frustration of purpose—tracing their origins and rationale. (Another frustration of purpose case, *Waldinger Corp. v. CRS Group Engineers,* is presented in Chapter 23's discussion of the UCC.)

---

### Northern Indiana Public Service Co. v. Carbon County Coal Co.
U.S. Seventh Circuit Court of Appeals, 799 F.2d 265 (1986)

In 1978 Northern Indiana Public Service Company (NIPSCO), an electric utility in Indiana, contracted to buy 1.5 million tons of coal every year for 20 years, at a price of $24 a ton (subject to various provisions for escalation which by 1985 had driven the price up to $44 a ton) from Carbon County Coal Co., which operated a coal mine in Wyoming. NIPSCO's rates are regulated by the Indiana Public Service Commission which, because of complaints from consumers about higher rates, ordered NIPSCO to make a good faith effort to find and purchase electricity from other utilities who could produce it at prices lower than NIPSCO's internal generation ("the economy purchase orders"). NIPSCO was able to buy substantial amounts of electricity from other utilities at costs below the costs of generating its own electricity using Carbon County's coal. Therefore, NIPSCO stopped accepting coal deliveries from Carbon and brought suit seeking a declaration that it was excused from its obligations under the contract. The trial court ruled against NIPSCO and it appealed.

*(continued)*

**Decision:** Judgment affirmed. A fixed-price contract is an explicit assignment of the risk of market price increases to the seller and the risk of market price decreases to the buyer, and the assignment of the latter risk is even clearer where, as in this case, the contract places a floor under the price but allows for escalation. If, as is also the case here, the buyer forecasts the market incorrectly and therefore finds itself locked into a disadvantageous contract, it has only itself to blame and cannot shift the risk back to the seller by invoking impossibility, commercial impracticability, or related doctrines. ■

---

## DISCHARGE BY PARTIES' AGREEMENT

Once a contract has been formed, it is always possible for the parties to make a new agreement that will discharge or modify the obligations of one or both parties under the original contract. The new agreement can take any of several forms, the most common of which are rescission, novation, and accord and satisfaction.

### *Rescission*

A contract can always be canceled by mutual agreement. When this agreement occurs, the contract is *rescinded*, and the obligations of both parties are thereby discharged. An oral rescission agreement is generally valid and binding, even where the original contract was in writing—with one major exception. A rescission agreement must be in writing if it involves a retransfer of real property. (Additionally, under Sec. 2-209[2] of the UCC, modification or rescission of a written *sales contract* must be evidenced by a writing if the original contract so provides.)

### *Novation*

A **novation** occurs when the party entitled to receive performance under a contract agrees to release the party who "owes" the performance and to permit a third party to take that person's place. It is simply a three-sided agreement that results in the substitution of one party for another. For example: X and Y have a contract. Later, they and Z agree that Z will perform X's obligations, with Y expressly releasing X from the original contract. X's obligations are now discharged.

### *Accord and Satisfaction*

After a contract has been formed, the parties may agree that one of them will accept, and the other will render, a performance different from what was originally called for. Such an agreement is an *accord*. Thus, if B owes W $1,800, and they subsequently agree that B will air-condition W's home in satisfaction of the debt, an accord exists. The reaching of an accord does not, of and by itself, terminate the existing obligation. To effect a discharge, a *satisfaction* must take place—the actual performance of the substituted obligation. Thus B's indebtedness is discharged by **accord and satisfaction** only when he completes the air-conditioning job.

## DISCHARGE BY OPERATION OF LAW

In addition to the types of discharge already discussed, other events or conditions can bring about a *discharge by operation of law*. The most common of these are bankruptcy proceedings, the running of a statute of limitations, and the fraudulent alteration of a contract.

### *Bankruptcy Proceedings*[11]

Bankruptcy actions today are governed by the federal Bankruptcy Reform Act of 1978. If an individual has been adjudged bankrupt after proper bankruptcy proceedings have taken place, he or she receives a *discharge in bankruptcy* from a court which covers most—but not all—of his or her debts. While the discharge technically does not extinguish the debts that are subject to it, it does so as a practical matter by prohibiting creditors from thereafter bringing court action against the debtor to recover any unpaid balance.

### *Running of Statutes of Limitations*

All states have statutes providing that after a certain amount of time has elapsed, a contract claim is barred. The time limits vary widely from one jurisdiction to

---

[11] The subject of bankruptcy is treated in Chapter 30.

another. In some states, for example, claimants are given three years in which to bring suit on oral contracts and five years on written ones; in others, the times vary from two to eight years on oral contracts and from three to fifteen years on written ones.

In any event, if a contract claimant lets the applicable time elapse without initiating legal proceedings, the statute of limitations has run and subsequent court action by that person is barred. The period of time begins the day after the cause of action accrues. Thus, if X promises to pay Y $500 on June 10, 1987, in a state having a three-year statute, the statute begins to run on June 11, with the result that Y has until June 10, 1990, to institute suit. (As in the case of a discharge in bankruptcy, the running of the statute does not extinguish the debt or claim itself; it simply prevents the claimant from subsequently bringing a legal action to recover the indebtedness.)

## *Alteration*

The law generally strives to discourage dishonest conduct. Consistent with this policy is the rule that the fraudulent, material **alteration** of a written contract by one of the parties discharges the other party as a matter of law. Suppose, for example, that A makes a written contract with B under the terms of which he is to sell 1,000 gallons of paint to B at a specified price per gallon. If B subsequently changes the quantity to 1,200 gallons without A's knowledge, A is excused from delivering any paint at all, if that is his desire. (A also has the right to enforce the contract according to its original terms or as altered—that is, he can tender either 1,000 or 1,200 gallons to B and hold him liable for the quantity chosen.)

## SUMMARY

In some situations a contracting party does not want to be obligated by the contract unless and until a certain event occurs. This protection can be achieved by use of an express condition precedent—a clause in the contract providing that performance is to occur only if the specified event occurs. In other circumstances a party might want the contract to be performed unless a certain event occurs within a stated time. In the latter case he or she may achieve protection by use of an express condition subsequent—a clause providing that if the specified event occurs, the contract shall be null and void.

In addition to *express* conditions, in some circumstances the law will recognize that the contract was subject to various *implied* conditions. Most contracts are of such a nature that the parties understood that one party (X) was to perform his part of the bargain (e.g., the painting of Y's house) before the other party (Y) had a duty to pay. In such instances, performance by X constitutes an implied condition to his recovery of the price.

In cases where the promisor's performance falls short of complete performance, he or she may still be able to recover under the doctrine of substantial performance. Under this doctrine, the promisor is entitled to receive the contract price minus damages to the promisee if (1) the defects in his or her performance were slight, and (2) the failure to perform completely was not due to bad faith—i.e., the deviations from 100 percent performance were not intentional.

As seen above, one's contractual obligations may be discharged by the failure of an express condition precedent to occur, the occurrence of an express condition subsequent, or by complete or substantial performance on his or her part. One's contractual obligations are also discharged by breach by the other party, or where a legal impossibility exists. Such an impossibility exists in situations where the courts can rule that, under the circumstances, the contract was subject to an *implied* condition subsequent. Implied conditions are found to exist in only three limited situations: (1) in contracts calling for performance of personal services, and where the promisor dies prior to the time of performance (or is incapacitated at that time); (2) where the subject-matter of the contract is destroyed without fault of either party prior to the time of performance; and (3) where performance becomes illegal prior to the time of performance. Because the impossibility view excuses a promisor only in limited circumstances, most courts today are applying the more liberal doctrine of commercial impracticability, instead—a doctrine first recognized under sales law, and one which frees the promisor in more circumstances than does the impossibility view.

## KEY TERMS

**Condition**
**Condition precedent**
**Condition subsequent**
**Conditions concurrent**

Substantial performance
Actual breach
Anticipatory breach
Legal impossibility
Doctrine of commercial impracticability
Novation
Accord and satisfaction
Alteration

## QUESTIONS AND PROBLEMS

1. Roper contracted in writing to buy a Wyoming ranch from Lewis for a specified price. At the same time that this contract was made Roper and Lewis also orally agreed, in rather general terms, that Lewis would also sell his 400 head of cattle and some ranch machinery to Roper. Later, when the cattle and machinery deal fell through, Roper brought court action asking for rescission of the ranch contract. Roper's contention was that performance of the cattle and machinery agreement was a *condition precedent* to his obligations under the ranch-purchase contract. Lewis disagreed, pointing out that (a) the written ranch contract did not mention the oral agreement, and (b) that, in fact, the parties never did come to specific terms as to the cattle and machinery prices. Would these factors cause the court to rule that performance of the cattle and machinery contract was *not* a condition precedent? Discuss. (*Lewis v. Roper,* 579 P.2d 434, 1978.)

2. Western Commerce Bank (WCB) was a creditor of the Miller estate, but filed its claim late so that the trustee refused to pay it. WCB sued, claiming that the notice inviting claims published by the estate was defective. On February 10, 1988, the heirs tendered an offer of settlement that provided for the payment of $275,000, subject to the heirs obtaining the necessary financing. WCB accepted. On April 22, when the paperwork for the financing was almost (but not quite) completed, WCB repudiated the settlement agreement. The heirs completed the financing arrangements and asked the court to enforce the settlement. WCB argued that there was no contract because the heirs had not obtained the financing within a reasonable time. Discuss. (*Western Commerce Bank v. Gillespie,* 775 P.2d 737, N.M. 1989.)

3. Cayias owned a pool hall business, which he operated in a leased building. Wishing to sell the business, he listed it with the Associated Investment Company, a broker, under a contract providing that if the company found a buyer at a price agreeable to him, he would pay the company a commission of 10 percent of the purchase price. The company found a buyer willing to pay $3,000, and Cayias and the buyer entered into a contract calling for the sale of the business at that price. The contract provided, however, that if the buyer was not able to obtain a new lease on the building at a monthly rental of $150, "then and in that event the agreement shall become null and void." The purchaser thereafter was apparently not able to get a lease from the owner of the building at this figure, so the sale of the business fell through. The company now sued Cayias, the seller, to recover its commission of $300. Cayias defended on the ground that (a) the quoted clause in the purchase agreement constituted a condition subsequent, and (b) since the condition (the inability of the buyer to get a lease) occurred with the result that the buyer was released, he (Cayias) was released from his obligation to pay a commission on the "sale." Rule on the correctness of Cayias' contention. (*Associated Investment Co. v. Cayias,* 185 P. 778, 1920.)

4. A contractor who built a country home for Kent for $77,000 sought to recover the unpaid balance of $3,400. Kent refused to make the final payment because the building contract required that all pipe in the home be of "Reading manufacture," and the pipe actually installed was made by a different manufacturer, the Cohoes Company. The contractor proved that the Cohoes pipe met all the specifications of the Reading pipe and that he was not aware of the Reading requirement in the contract when he installed the other pipe. On these facts, does the doctrine of substantial performance apply to the plaintiff, the contractor? Explain. (*Jacobs and Young, Inc. v. Kent,* 129 N.E. 889, 1921.)

5. Waegemann leased commercial space to Montgomery Ward pursuant to an agreement which calculated rent according to the property tax index. During the term of the lease, voters of California passed Proposition 13, which slashed real estate taxes substantially, causing Waegemann to receive only one-third of the current fair market value in rent. In subsequent litigation, Waegeman claimed that the lease should be rescinded on grounds of commercial impracticability or frustration of purposes. Is Waegemann right? (*Waegemann v. Montgomery Ward & Co.,*) 713 F.2d 452, 9th Cir. 1983.)

6. A professional football player made a contract with Alabama Football, Inc. (Alabama), which at that time was a member of the World Football League. Under the contract Alabama agreed to pay the player a salary covering the years 1977, 1978, and 1979. Soon after the contract was made, the World Football League folded—ceased to exist. In subsequent litigation, Alabama contended that the failure of the league constituted a *legal impossibility* that freed Alabama of its obligations to the player. Should the court accept this argument? Discuss. (*Alabama Football, Inc. v. Wright,* 452 F.Supp. 182, 1977.)

7. The Republic Creosoting Company contracted to sell and deliver to the City of Minneapolis a quantity of paving blocks, with deliveries to be made in the first six months of 1920. The contract did not contain any clause excusing a

late delivery in the event of a strike, a boxcar shortage, or similar events beyond the company's control. Because of a nationwide boxcar shortage, the company was unable to deliver the blocks at the agreed upon time. The city considered this a breach of contract and purchased the blocks from another supplier at a higher price. The city then brought suit against the company to recover damages for breach of contract, and the company defended on the ground that the nationwide boxcar shortage constituted a legal impossibility. Rule on the validity of this defense (a) on the ground of impossibility, and (b) on the ground of commercial impracticability. (*Minneapolis v. Republic Creosoting Co.,* 201 N.W. 414, 1924.)

8. One railroad (the lessor) leased part of its depot facilities in Milwaukee to another railroad (the lessee) under a long-term contract. Thereafter, with several years on the contract remaining, Amtrak was formed by an act of Congress that resulted, among other things, in the lessee's passenger service in the Milwaukee area being very substantially reduced. As a result, the lessee would have very little use for the depot facilities. When the lessor sued the lessee to recover $2 million rental fees for subsequent years, the lessee contended that the formation of Amtrak (and the sharp curtailment of its services) freed it from its remaining obligations under the *frustration of purpose* doctrine. The lessor contested this argument, and offered evidence to show (a) that when the contract was made the lessee was aware that Amtrak might come into existence; (b) that both parties realized that their need for the depot might be substantially cut; and (c) that the lessee, by joining Amtrak—which it was not required by law to do—was itself partly responsible for its cutback of services. Should this evidence convince the court to rule that the frustration of purpose doctrine is *not* applicable? (That is, should this evidence cause the court to rule that the lessee is still bound by the contract?) Why or why not? (*Chicago, M., St.P.&P.R. Co. v. Chicago & N.W.,* 203 N.W.2d 189, 1978.)

# CHAPTER 19

# Contract Interpretation and Remedies for Breach

This chapter addresses two of the most practically important areas in all of contract law. Often a contract exists, in that all the basic elements of a binding contract (agreement, consideration, capacity, legality) are present, but its meaning is not clear. It expresses the general rights and obligations of the parties, but what it means *exactly* in relation to the events that have occurred since the contract was formed, cannot be agreed upon by the parties to the contract. Indeed, questions regarding the meaning of contracts generate more litigation than any other type of contract question. The first portion of this chapter discusses the basic rules which courts apply when resolving disputes as to the meaning of a contract's terms.

If a plaintiff convinces the court that a contract exists, and that the defendant has breached that contract as interpreted by the court, he has gained nothing unless the law provides him a full and appropriate remedy. The second half of this chapter explores the various avenues of remedy available to a party injured by a breach of contract.

## CONTRACT INTERPRETATION

It is told that the defenders of the bastion of Sebasta surrendered to Temures, their besieger, after he promised that "no blood would be shed" should they do so. Temures was good to the letter of his word. But, upon being buried alive, the defenders probably wished they had asked their lawyer to check the fine print. Most modern breach-of-contract lawsuits also involve, often among several issues, a dispute as to the meaning of the contract generally or some of its specific terms. It is a rare situation indeed when both parties to a contract agree as to the meaning of all of its provisions. Such difficulties are perhaps inevitable, a combination of the imprecision of human language, inattention to detail by the drafters of the agreement, and the inability of the parties to foresee events as they will eventually transpire. In Chapter 4, we discussed statutory law and learned that legislators face similar limitations in drafting statutes, giving rise to that "necessary evil"—judicial interpretation.

Similarly courts are often called upon to determine the meaning of contracts and their provisions. Courts do this through the processes of interpretation and construction. According to some sources, the process of **interpretation** focuses on determining the meaning of words as used in the contract while **construction** deals with the legal effect to be given those words. Generally, however, courts use the terms interchangeably because there is much disagreement as to their technical meaning and as to where one process ends and the other begins. No matter which term is used, the process is complicated.

### *Intent of the Parties*

The primary role of a court asked to interpret a contract is to determine the intent of the parties *at the time the contract was made* and to give effect to that intent. The court's job is not to improve the contract or to rewrite it to address matters that the parties should have considered but did not. As with the process of statutory interpretation, the parties' intent is the centerpiece of the process. The court's own evaluation as to how the contract *should* have been written is irrelevant.

There is disagreement as to the optimum approach to determining contract intent. Most courts speak of an "objective" test that gauges the meaning of a contract's words by how a hypothetical "reasonably intelligent person" would understand them. However, it is not at all rare to see courts strive to determine the common intent of the contracting parties at the time they made the contract.

Contractual interpretation generally raises questions of law to be resolved by the court. However, if a contract's wording is ambiguous, extrinsic evidence may be admitted to determine the parties' intent. Juries often play a role in resolving this question of fact.

While determination of the parties' intent is the overarching goal of contract interpretation, the courts, once they have determined that intent, are constrained by considerations of public policy. In other words, they cannot give effect to a contract where the intent is to produce illegal, unethical, or unconscionable activity.

## Plain Meaning Rule

We learned in Chapter 4 that the primary source of legislative intent is the wording of the statute itself. It should not be surprising, then, that in determining the intent of the parties to a contract, courts look first to the language of that contract. The parties' own words are the main evidence of their intentions at the time they made the contract.

Indeed, the words of the contract may be the *only* evidence of the parties' intentions that a court will consider. As in statutory interpretation, there is a well-recognized **plain meaning rule.** If the language of the contract appears clear and unambiguous, the plain meaning rule requires that the courts determine the intent of the parties solely from the face of the instrument. Absent ambiguity, the courts should not resort to extrinsic evidence (such as the actions of the parties, the testimony of the parties, or even the past practices of the parties) in their search for intent. Any attempt to alter the obvious meaning of the words with outside evidence would likely stray from the parties' intent at the time they made the agreement.

A few courts have rejected the plain meaning rule, concluding that it "asserts a semantic perfection which cannot hope to be achieved." *PG&E v. G.W. Thomas Drayage & Rigging Co.,* 442 P.2d 641 (Cal. 1968). Even in plain meaning rule jurisdictions, courts often conclude that the language of the parties, though it appears clear, is not in fact "plain and unambiguous." When that happens, courts resort to extrinsic evidence such as all relevant writings and oral statements, other conduct of the parties manifesting their intent, negotiations, prior course of dealing, and other relevant factors.

The following case examines these divergent approaches to the introduction of extrinsic evidence.

---

### Isbrandtsen v. North Branch Corporation
Supreme Court of Vermont,
556 A.2d 81 (1988)

Plaintiff (grantee) bought from defendant (grantor) a townhouse at a ski resort. Defendant operated recreational facilities, ski trails, parking areas, and assorted outbuildings. There were four townhouses and all adjoined a common area known as the "club" which contained a kitchen, restaurant, and sitting room. Defendant operated and maintained all these areas. Defendant's business depended in part upon rental income derived from lessees of owners of the townhouses who did not use them on a year-round basis. The development was designed so that the temporarily unoccupied townhouses could be rented out to paying guests. This benefitted the owners, who derived a percentage of income from the rentals, and it assured the defendant the income required to continue providing the maintenance services necessary to all occupants.

The deed through which defendant sold the townhouse to plaintiff contained this clause: *"The premises hereby conveyed shall be used only for private, single-family residence purposes, except that, under express agreement between Grantor and Grantee, the premises may be rented or used for paying guests in connection with Grantor's operations."*

Plaintiff asked the lower court to declare that she could rent her townhouse to paying guests without defendant's knowledge or consent. Defendant claimed that this clause prohibited plaintiff from any such rental except by and with defendant's express consent. The trial judge ruled for the defendant and the plaintiff appealed.

---

**Decision:** Affirmed. Plaintiff claims that extrinsic evidence supports her interpretation of the contract. The "four corners" or "plain meaning" rule states that if a writing appears to be plain and unambiguous on its face, its meaning must be determined from the four corners of the instrument without resort to extrinsic evidence. A different approach recognizes that "plain meaning" cannot exist in a vacuum, and may be supplemented by ad-

*(continued)*

mission of evidence as to the circumstances surrounding the making of the contract as well as its object, nature, and subject matter. In this case, the court chooses to consider the circumstances surrounding the making of an agreement if it is ambiguous, that is, if a writing in and of itself supports a different interpretation from that which appears when it is read in light of the surrounding circumstances, and both interpretations are reasonable. In view of the circumstances surrounding the making of this contract, and in light of the rule that an agreement must be viewed in the entirety with an eye toward giving effect to all its material parts, the agreement can be given but one reasonable interpretation, "that absent an express agreement between plaintiff and defendant, plaintiff is prohibited by the deed from renting her property to paying guests." ■

---

If courts decide to resort to evidence outside the language of the contract, the best evidence of the parties' intent may be their subsequent conduct in carrying it out. For example, in one case both Jewell and Thomas signed a promissory note. Jewell claimed that he had signed only to assist Thomas in getting the loan and that, therefore, Thomas should repay Jewell for the payments he made to the bank. Thomas claimed that Jewell was the primary obligor on the note. The evidence showed that as soon as the note was signed, Jewell treated the note as his own obligation, taking over complete responsibility for servicing the debt. Thomas never dealt with the bank. Thus, the court concluded, the intent of the parties appeared to be as asserted by Thomas. *Marvin E. Jewell & Co. v. Thomas,* 434 N.W.2d 532 (Neb. 1989).

## *Rules of Interpretation*

As in statutory interpretation, various rules of contract interpretation have developed over the years to assist the courts in determining the parties' intent from the words that they used. Courts should not apply the rules so conservatively as to obstruct the parties' true intentions, nor so liberally as to allow one of the parties to escape his obligations. As noted earlier, the courts are not at liberty to rewrite the contract while purporting to interpret it.

The first task in contract interpretation is to determine to the extent possible the parties' *principal objective* in forming the contract. This principal objective is accorded great weight, and all the contract's terms are construed in order to carry out that objective.

The parties' intentions are generally (though not exclusively) judged in an objective fashion from their expressed intent. Secret intentions are deemed irrelevant. Intentions expressed through either words or actions are given effect unless they conflict with law, morals, or public policy.

Contracts often contain conflicting and inconsistent terms. These will be interpreted, insofar as possible, to achieve the intentions of both parties. If possible, a contract will be construed so as to give effect to all of its provisions. The courts disfavor a construction which requires that a portion of the contract be ignored.

The courts also presume that the parties intended their agreement to be legal, reasonable, and effective. If alternative constructions are both plausible, the one that is preferred is the one least likely to render it illegal, unreasonable, or ineffective. Assume that a contract grants a patent licensee "exclusive use in the U.S.A." of the patented product. If the licensee argues that the right is to be perpetual and the licensor argues that it is to last only the life of the patent, the latter interpretation would be favored because the former would be inconsistent with antitrust laws.

Other aids to interpretation include the following:

**1.** Words and phrases are given their ordinary meaning, unless the parties indicate otherwise. Although the courts are not slaves to dictionaries, they do frequently consult them. Similarly, technical words are presumed to be used in their commonly accepted technical sense.

**2.** Specific language controls general language. For example, if a contract provided in one clause that a sole shareholder guaranteed payment for electrical service provided to his company, and another clause provided that the sole shareholder guaranteed electrical service provided to his company at a *specific* address, the court would likely conclude that the sole shareholder was not liable for electrical service provided to the company at other addresses.

**3.** When a contract is embodied in a printed form, any conflicting provisions added by the parties will prevail. Handwriting will prevail over typewriting. Thus, if a preprinted form contained a provision limiting liability to $1,000, but the figure $2,500 was handwritten into the relevant blank on the form, the latter would set the limit of liability.

4. Ambiguous language is construed against the party who prepares the agreement. This is especially true where the contract is a preprinted adhesion contract where there is little opportunity for negotiation. In *Comprehensive Health Ins. Ass'n v. Dye*, 531 N.E.2d 505 (Ind.App. 1988), for example, an insurance contract prepared by the insurance company contained two different definitions of "preexisting conditions" that would not be covered by the policy. One excluded any sickness that had been diagnosed or treated before the policy was issued; the other excluded any sickness for which a reasonable person would have sought diagnosis or treatment. The court chose to apply the first definition because it was narrower and therefore more favorable to the insured.

5. Where numbers are expressed, words prevail over figures where they are in conflict. For instance, if a typed contract indicated in one place that the purchase price was "four hundred dollars" but in another place indicated that it was "$405," the former would prevail.

6. In every contract, courts will imply a duty of good faith, fair dealing, and cooperation on the part of both parties. The law of the jurisdiction at the place and time the contract is made is also generally read into the contract. Courts will not imply any other terms, unless a contract is silent on a particular point. In such an instance, courts may occasionally imply terms. For example, a contract that is silent as to duration will generally be construed to last for a reasonable time. An obligation to pay money is construed to require that the money be paid in legal tender.

These rules of interpretation, when applied to a specific contract, will not always point in the same direction, as the following case illustrates.

### Innes v. Webb
Texas Court of Civil Appeals, 538 S.W.2d 237 (1976)

Appellee Webb wished to buy a house owned by Huller. Appellant Innes, a real estate broker, prepared an earnest money contract between Webb and Huller. Webb gave Innes a check for $2,000 as earnest money; Innes gave the money to Huller. Huller left town and never completed the contract. Webb seeks return of his $2,000, pointing to a provision in the standard preprinted form that was used for the earnest money contract which provided that if the seller did not comply with the contract for any reason, "Purchaser may demand back the earnest money. . . ." In essence, Webb alleged that Innes held the funds as stakeholder subject to Webb's demand for return of the funds should Huller breach.

Innes emphasized a provision that was *typed* onto the form which stated: "$2,000 escrow to be turned over to Seller for initial deposit on materials and administrative costs."

The trial court held for Webb in the sum of $2,000 and broker Innes appealed.

**Decision:** Reversed. The general rule is that the written or typewritten part of a contract controls in the event of any conflict thereof with the printed portion of the contract. This rule prevails over the rule advanced by plaintiff—that a contract should be strictly construed against the party who prepared it. ■

## Uniform Commercial Code

The UCC in Sec. 2-202 alters common-law practice by permitting more liberal use of extrinsic evidence in determining the parties' intent in sale-of-goods contracts. That is, the UCC backs away from the plain meaning rule, which focuses attention primarily on the language of the parties, by assuming that the parties considered matters such as (1) course of performance, (2) course of dealing, and (3) usage of trade. Thus, in construing a sales contract courts may resort to this extrinsic evidence without finding that the words of the contract are ambiguous.

A **course of performance,** according to UCC 2-208, arises out of "repeated occasions for performance by either party with knowledge of the nature of the performance and opportunity for objection to it by the other." Such performance which is accepted and acquiesced in without objection by the other party is a strong indication of what the parties intended.

A **course of dealing,** according to UCC 1-205, is "a sequence of previous conduct between the parties to a particular transaction which is fairly to be regarded as establishing a common basis of understanding for interpreting their expressions and other conduct." Thus, whereas course of performance arises out of the same contract the court is trying to interpret, course of dealing arises out of earlier transactions between the parties.

Finally, a **usage of trade,** according to UCC 1-205, is "any practice or method of dealing having such regularity of observance in a place, vocation, or trade as to justify an expectation that it will be observed with respect to the transaction in question."

It certainly makes sense to assume that the parties' conduct in performing the contract evidences their intentions and to assume that their intent at the time of making the contract took into account their prior dealings and the customs of their industry. UCC 1-205(4) establishes a priority for interpretation. Express terms of the agreement are the primary source for interpretation. Next in line is course of performance which, where conflicting, controls course of dealing. Course of dealing, in turn, prevails over a conflicting usage of trade. Use of this type of extrinsic evidence is, of course, consistent with the UCC's various "gap-filler" provisions that we studied in Chapter 12.

## REMEDIES FOR BREACH OF CONTRACT

Assuming that a valid contract exists and that one of the parties to that contract has breached its obligations (as those obligations were interpreted by the court), the matter of remedies arises.[1] The party who received the promises that were not performed will often look to the judicial system for a remedy (though, as we learned in Chapter 3, remedies may also be provided by alternative means of dispute resolution, such as arbitration). The form, availability, and extent of remedies will play a big part in a party's decision whether to litigate. If the law does not provide a remedy, or provides an inappropriate or inadequate remedy, the wronged party may never sue.

In our legal system, the freedom to contract entails the freedom to breach one's obligations. Our system of remedies aims not at coercing parties into performing their obligations, but at providing adequate remedies for the other party when breaches do occur. The distinction is subtle, but our free enterprise system's main goal is to encourage people to do business with those who make promises by assuring them that adequate remedies will be available to compensate them should the promisors not perform.

Our discussion is divided into two major sections because of the historical distinction (explored in the introductory chapters) between actions at law and actions in equity. Because the law/equity distinction has largely disappeared, virtually every court can grant remedies that traditionally were available in courts of law (i.e., money damages) *and* those traditionally available in courts of equity (e.g., orders of specific performance and injunction).

As with earlier contract-law chapters, we will note areas where the Uniform Commercial Code alters common-law rules because of the special needs of sale-of-goods transactions. However, these references will be brief, for the matter of Article 2 remedies is explored in detail in Chapter 23.

### *Money Damages*

The primary remedy available for breach of contract is money damages. Because this remedy originated in courts at law, a jury trial is available to plaintiffs seeking such damages. The main goal of an award of damages is to *compensate* the plaintiff for losses caused by the defendant's failure to perform as promised. We will emphasize **compensatory damages** in this discussion, but also explore other types of damages, including nominal damages and liquidated damages.

**Compensatory Damages:** The amount of money a jury might award depends upon which interest the law is attempting to compensate. There are three such interests that we must address.

**1.** *Expectation Interest.* The law usually seeks to compensate the plaintiff's *expectation* interest. That is, the law seeks to put the plaintiff in the position in

---

[1] We have already touched on the concept of remedies in several chapters. For example, in Chapter 15 we learned that rescission is available as a remedy where contracts were induced by fraud. In Chapter 18, we discussed remedies that are available where parties have only partially, but not completely, performed their contractual obligations.

which he expected to be after the defendant performed his promise. In other words, the law attempts to give the plaintiff the "benefit of his bargain."

2. *Reliance Interest.* In situations where it is not feasible or fair to award the plaintiff expectation damages, the law may seek to return the plaintiff to where he was before the contract was entered into. Because this frequently entails reimbursing the plaintiff for funds he spent (or other detriment incurred) in reliance on the defendant's promise, this is called the *reliance* interest.

3. *Restitution Interest.* Finally, a defendant who fails to perform a promise should not be allowed to keep a benefit conferred by a plaintiff who did perform his promise. Therefore, in a breach-of-contract action, the defendant is often ordered to compensate the plaintiff for such a benefit. This is called making restitution, and the law is compensating the plaintiff's *restitution* interest.

Illustration: Assume that D Company hired Ralph to build a storage shed for D for the sum of $10,000. Soon after the contract was made, D repudiated it. If Ralph sued for breach of contract, proving that he could have built the shed for $7,500, he will likely recover $2,500, the profit that he expected to receive from the transaction. This award gives Ralph the benefit of his bargain by placing him in the position he expected to occupy (a $2,500 profit in his pocket) if D performed its promise.

Assume, on the other hand, that sometime after Ralph began building the shed, D breached the contract, telling Ralph not to finish because D would pay nothing. If Ralph could not prove the profit he would have made had the shed been completed, but could show that he had spent $3,400 on labor and materials before the breach, the law would award Ralph that $3,400 to compensate his reliance interest. Ralph spent that amount in reliance on D's promise. (If Ralph could also establish the $2,500 expected profit, he would recover $5,900, because this is the sum required to place him in as good a position as he expected to be in when D performed.)

Assume, on the other hand, that on the day the contract was made, D paid Ralph $2,000 as an advance. Ralph told D the next day that he would not go through with the job, but was keeping the $2,000. If D sued Ralph, it would recover at least $2,000 to compensate its restitution interest.

**Expectation Measure:** The matter of expectation damages must be explored more thoroughly. Placing a plaintiff in the position he or she expected to be in had the defendant performed as promised is a complicated matter. The general term "expectation damages" can be broken down into at least three subcategories. "Direct" or "general" damages are those losses clearly and directly caused by the defendant's breach. "Consequential" or "special" damages include lost profits and injury to persons or property resulting from the defendant's defective performance. "Incidental" damages include such matters as costs incurred by the plaintiff in arranging for substitute performance.

Assume that D Corporation promised to repair a plastic-molding machine for P Corporation for $15,000 by June 1. D understood that time was of the essence, because P had a big contract to produce plastic cups that called for a June 1 start-up date. On May 20, D informed P that it would not perform its promise. P quickly but thoroughly investigated and found that X Company was willing to make the repairs for $17,000. Working quickly, X completed the repairs on June 15, but P lost $5,000 in profits because the machine was idled for two weeks. Because it cost P $2,000 more to have the machine repaired than it would have had D performed as promised, P can recover $2,000 in *direct damages.* P will also recover $5,000 in *consequential damages* to compensate for the lost profits. Finally, any costs incurred by P in finding X could be recovered as *incidental damages.*

Although this illustration gives a general idea as to calculation of compensatory damages to redress the expectation interest, remember that there are some very important limitations on the plaintiff's recovery:

1. *Causation.* Plaintiff must prove that the defendant's breach was a "substantial factor" in bringing about his or her injury. Assume that Pam proves that she runs a retail clothing store, that Dan promised to deliver winter coats to Pam by September 1, that the coats were not delivered until October 1, and that Pam's revenues for the month of September were down 40 percent from the previous year. Pam appears to have a strong case, but if evidence adduced at trial discloses that the street leading to Pam's store was under construction during the entire month of September so that it was very difficult for customers even to reach Pam's store, and that other stores in the area also sustained lost revenue, a jury might conclude that Dan's delay was not a "substantial factor" in bringing about the plaintiff's loss.

**2. *Reasonable Certainty.*** Judges and juries should not have to speculate as to the amount of damages the plaintiff sustained that were due to the defendant's breach. Therefore, the plaintiff must establish losses with "reasonable certainty," a higher standard of proof than is demanded for other issues. This is often a problem in consequential damages, such as lost profits at a sports event.

Assume, for example, that Pete, a candidate for governor in a primary election, contracted to have D Newspaper Co. run one of his ads on the Sunday before election day. The newspaper failed to run the ad, and Pete lost the election. If Pete sued for the salary he would have received as governor, it would be pure speculation to conclude that the missing ad caused Pete to lose the primary election or that Pete would have won the general election had he succeeded in the primary. Therefore, a court probably would deny Pete's claim for these consequential damages.

While the law does not wish to compensate the plaintiff for losses that did not occur, at the same time persons who have breached their promises should not escape liability simply because the plaintiff cannot prove the amount of damages to the penny. For that reason, the law requires reasonable, not absolute, certainty. The UCC reflects the trend in the common law by requiring the plaintiff to prove damages not with mathematical certainty, but with "whatever definiteness and accuracy the facts permit, but no more" (Sec. 1-106, comment 1).

Courts often are less demanding of a plaintiff's proof where the defendant's breach was willful and in situations where precision of proof is inherently impossible (such as in calculation of loss to "goodwill"). Similarly, where a defendant's wrong has caused the difficulty in proof of damages, many courts hold that the defendant "shall not be heard to complain." In short, where the courts are certain that a breach has occurred and that the plaintiff has suffered a loss, they hesitate to deny recovery on grounds that the plaintiff has failed to establish the amount of damages to a reasonable certainty. On the other hand, where the evidence is not clear that a loss even occurred, the reasonable certainty requirement is more likely to bar recovery. An interesting illustration of these general rules follows.

---

**Ericson v. Playgirl, Inc.**
California Court of Appeals,
140 Cal.Rptr. 921 (1977)

Plaintiff John Ericson, in an attempt to boost his career as an actor, agreed that defendant Playgirl, Inc., could publish without compensation as the centerfold of its January 1974 issue of *Playgirl* photographs of Ericson posing naked. No immediate career boost to Ericson resulted. In April 1974, defendant wished to use the pictures again for its annual edition entitled *Best of Playgirl*, a publication with half the circulation of *Playgirl* and without the advertising. Ericson agreed to a rerun of his pictures in *Best of Playgirl* on two conditions: that certain of them be cropped to more modest exposure, and that Ericson's photograph occupy a quarter of the front cover, which would contain photographs of five other persons on its remaining three-quarters. Defendant honored the first of these conditions but, due to an editorial mixup, Ericson's photograph did not appear on the cover of *Best of Playgirl*. Ericson sued for breach of contract, seeking to recover for the loss of publicity he would have received had his picture appeared on the cover as agreed.

The trial court entered a $12,500 judgment on behalf of Ericson, based in large part on the testimony of an advertising manager for *TV Guide* who placed the value to an entertainer of an appearance on the cover of a national magazine at $50,000. (¼ cover × $50,000 = $12,500.) *Playgirl* appealed.

---

**Decision:** Affirmed, but modified. Damages must be clearly ascertainable and reasonably certain, both in their nature and origin. Plaintiff did not prove that the failure to place his picture on the cover of *Best of Playgirl* injured him in any substantial way or in any specific amount. The trial judge's award was merely conjectural. As a matter of policy, there should be no recovery where denial of professional publicity bears no relation to the practice of one's art. However, a state statute allows recovery of a minimum of $300 in nominal damages in breach of contract cases. The judgment is therefore modified from $12,500 to $300. ∎

**3. *Foreseeability.*** Another important limitation on recovery of compensatory damages is that the loss sustained by the plaintiff should have been reasonably foreseeable to the defendant. Assume that Sam's Repair Shop promised to fix Al's car and deliver it to him on June 1. Sam was a day late, delivering the car on June 2. However, on June 1, Al had been bitten by a rabid dog and his injuries had been exacerbated because he had had no car with which to drive himself to the emergency room. The extra medical injuries (potential consequential damages) could not be compensated because the injury was not reasonably foreseeable to Sam.

The leading case in this area is *Hadley v. Baxendale*, 156 Eng.Rep. 145 (1854), where plaintiff's flour mill suffered a broken gear. Plaintiff hired defendant to transport the gear and its attached drive shaft to the manufacturer for repairs. Plaintiff told defendant that the gear was part of his milling machinery and that defendant should act promptly. Plaintiff did not, however, tell defendant that his entire mill would be shut down until the repairs were made. Defendant breached the contract by performing two days late. Plaintiff sued for the profits lost during this two-day period. The court held that it was not reasonably foreseeable to defendant that plaintiff's entire operation would be shut down for two days; therefore, the lost profits could not be recovered. In so ruling, the English court set forth two important rules. First, it held that a plaintiff can recover direct damages "as may fairly and reasonably be considered . . . arising naturally, i.e., according to the usual course of things" from the breach itself. Second, the court held that plaintiff may recover consequential damages "such as may reasonably be supposed to have been in the contemplation of both parties, at the time they made the contract, as the probable result of it." Thus, the court introduced reasonable foreseeability as an important aspect of recovery for consequential damages.

The following case applies these general rules of foreseeability.

---

### Kenford Company, Inc. v. County of Erie
Court of Appeals of New York,
540 N.Y.S.2d 1 (1989)

In May of 1968, the County of Erie adopted enabling legislation authorizing it to finance and construct a domed sports stadium in the vicinity of the City of Buffalo. Kenford Co., through its president and sole shareholder, Cottrell, had acquired options on various parcels of land. It offered to sell that land to the county for construction of the stadium; the county rejected the offer. Kenford then offered to donate to the county the land upon which the stadium was to be built, in exchange for which the county was to permit Cottrell and his associate Hofheinz (who together had formed the management company of Dome Stadium Inc. (DSI)) to lease or manage the proposed stadium.

In June 1969, the county adopted a resolution accepting this offer, after which the parties began contract negotiation. During this time, Kenford exercised the options to buy several parcels of land. The contract was signed requiring Kenford to donate 178 acres of land and the county to commence construction within 12 months. The county agreed to negotiate a 40-year lease with DSI under which the county was to receive revenues of not less than $63.75 million over the 40-year term, comprising (1) all tax revenues received by the county generated by operation of the stadium site; (2) rental payments from DSI; and (3) increased real property taxes resulting from increased assessments received from the "peripheral lands"—those lands near the stadium owned or to be acquired by Kenford.

When the county was unable to raise enough revenue to build the stadium, it adopted a resolution cancelling the contract with Kenford and DSI. DSI and Kenford sued for breach of contract and were awarded summary judgment on the issue of liability. A nine-month trial followed on the matter of damages. Appeals and a retrial followed. The matter then came before New York's highest court for review of a lower court judgment that Kenford was entitled to recover $6.5 million in lost appreciation in the value of its property located on the periphery of the stadium.

---

**Decision:** Reversed. Plaintiffs in breach of contract cases are entitled to recover general damages which are the natural and probable consequence of the breach. In order for recovery to be imposed for any further loss, the damages must flow naturally and directly from the breach and such extraordinary damages must have been brought within the contemplation of the parties as the probable result of a breach at the time of contracting. As

*(continued)*

in *Hadley v. Baxendale*, there is insufficient evidence that the parties contemplated at the time of contracting that defendant would assume liability for plaintiff's loss of anticipated appreciation in the value of peripheral lands. Defendant was no doubt aware that plaintiff had acquired such lands, but nothing in the contract required plaintiff to do so and nothing in the contract indicated that defendant assumed any legal responsibility for plaintiff's unfulfilled land appreciation expectations. ■

---

If the plaintiff establishes causation, reasonable certainty, and foreseeability of loss, recovery often will be calculated according to the following formula:

Damages = Direct Loss + Consequential Loss + Incidental Loss − Cost Avoided − Loss Avoided.

Assume that P had a contract to sell a tract of land to D for $50,000. In order to induce D to make the deal, P also agreed to do $500 worth of grading on the tract and to sell to D a smaller lot for $5,000. The fair market value of the two tracts was $40,000 and $6,000, respectively. D breached his promise and cancelled the deal after P had done half of the grading. P hired a real estate agent who sold the larger tract to X for $40,000, taking an 8 percent commission. P's direct loss is $10,000 ($50,000 − $40,000), his consequential loss is $250 (the cost of grading), and his incidental loss is $3,200 (the real estate commission). At the same time, P had avoided a cost of $250 (the remainder of the grading) and avoided a loss of $1,000 (for sale of the smaller tract). Therefore, P's recovery would be $10,000 + $250 + $3,200 − $250 − $1,000 = $12,200.

***Reliance Measure:*** If the law cannot compensate the plaintiff's expectation interest, perhaps because the plaintiff cannot establish with reasonable certainty the profit he would make on the transaction, the courts often protect the reliance interest instead. Other situations where the reliance interest is compensated include cases where a contract is frustrated by impossibility of performance or where there has been partial performance of an oral contract that the statute of frauds required to be in writing.

Plaintiffs suing for the reliance interest are allowed to recover such items as expenses incurred in preparing to perform their part of the contract, expenses incurred in actually performing, and losses incurred due to forgone opportunities that they would have pursued absent the contract with the defendant.

Assume that defendant promises to deliver a model stove to plaintiff at a trade fair. Plaintiff plans to demonstrate the stove and take orders from customers. Defendant fails to deliver the stove in time for the fair. If plaintiff could prove with reasonable certainty the profits he would have made from demonstrating the stove, he can recover them under the expectation interest. However, this is likely to be too speculative to establish with reasonable certainty. Therefore, at the very least, the court can compensate plaintiff's reliance interest by making defendant pay the costs, such as rental of the space at the trade fair and of materials to construct a booth, that plaintiff incurred in reliance on defendant's promise.

***Restitution Interest:*** Assume that in the trade fair case, the plaintiff had made an advance payment to the defendant of $400. Because the defendant did not perform, the plaintiff should recover that amount also. The defendant has received a benefit and the law requires the defendant to make restitution to the plaintiff. The key to restitution is "unjust enrichment"—the defendant should forfeit benefits he received from the plaintiff's performance in cases where the defendant did not do as he promised. The concept of restitution pervades the law of both legal and equitable remedies, and we shall return to it later in this chapter.

**Mitigation of Damages:** There is no reason for the law to compensate the plaintiff for losses arising from the defendant's breach that the plaintiff could reasonably have avoided. Therefore the **mitigation of damages doctrine** requires plaintiffs to take reasonable steps to minimize the accumulation of damages.

Once aware of the other party's breach, a potential plaintiff may not continue his activities so as to increase his damages. For example, assume that Deeco, Inc., hires Peeco, Inc., to build a parking garage. After Peeco has spent $10,000 in commencing performance, Deeco unequivocally tells Peeco that it no longer wants the parking garage built and will not pay for it. If Peeco continues to work on the garage, spending another $8,000, it clearly has failed to mitigate its damages. It may recover the first

$10,000, but not the subsequent $8,000, which was clearly avoidable.

A party may even be obliged to take positive steps to minimize damages. For example, assume that Juanita has a five-year contract to work for Acme Corporation as a research chemist. After one year, Acme fires Juanita without cause. Juanita should not sit home for the next four years. If she does, passing up several opportunities to obtain comparable jobs at comparable pay, the law will not compensate her for her lost salary. Instead, the law places on Juanita the obligation to make reasonable efforts to find comparable work. She need not take a job that does not utilize her education, nor need she move across the country in order to find a position. Reasonableness is the key. At the same time, any reasonable expenses Juanita incurs (e.g., hiring an employment agency) in attempting to mitigate her damages are compensable, even if ultimately unsuccessful.

The duty to mitigate is incorporated in Article 2 of the Uniform Commercial Code. We shall see in Chapter 23 that when a buyer of goods breaches a contract, the seller is often obliged to make conscientious efforts to find another buyer for those goods. If the second buyer pays less, the seller may recover from the breaching party not only the difference in purchase price but also the incidental expenses incurred in finding a new buyer.

Although almost every party in every situation has a duty to mitigate, a majority of jurisdictions make an exception for landlords where a lease has been executed. They do not require the landlord to search for a new tenant when the current tenant breaches its lease by moving out and refusing to pay rent. Many jurisdictions, on the other hand, do not recognize this exception.

Consider one other wrinkle. Assume that Acme has contracted to rent a truck from We-Haul Leasing, Inc. Acme breaches, but points out to We-Haul that it can mitigate its damages by leasing the truck to the next customer that comes in needing a truck. However, *if* We-Haul has a different truck that it would have rented to that next customer, then it cannot effectively mitigate its damages. It could have had *two* rentals if Acme had lived up to its part of the lease. Therefore, We-Haul may recover from Acme.

The following case illustrates some important mitigation principles in the employment context.

---

**Stewart v. Board of Education of Ritenour**
Missouri Court of Appeals,
630 S.W.2d 130 (1982)

In 1974, plaintiff Stewart was a "permanent teacher" under the Teacher Tenure Act, having taught for 15 years in defendant school district. The Board of Education terminated plaintiff in June, 1974. Plaintiff sued. After multiple trials and appeals, the termination was held to be wrongful and damages were assessed. However, the case was heard one more time by the trial court on the issue of mitigation of damages. Despite Stewart's statement that she had made no efforts to secure any type of teaching position during the five years that she was unemployed, the trial judge refused to reduce the damages it had assessed against the Board in the sum of $108,948.01. The board appealed.

**Decision:** Affirmed. Defendant has the burden to prove that plaintiff could have mitigated her damages. This entails proving that employment could have been secured. The evidence here indicates that there were three teaching jobs for which she was qualified available during plaintiff's period of unemployment. But the number of applicants for those jobs greatly exceeded the number of vacancies and no district hired a teacher in plaintiff's age bracket. In short, the board did not prove that there was a reasonable likelihood that plaintiff could have obtained a comparable job. Plaintiff's own expert judged the likelihood as "very poor." ∎

---

**Nominal Damages:** Nominal damages are a form of compensatory damages given in a trivial amount (such as six cents or one dollar). It is appropriate to grant nominal damages, for example, where the plaintiff establishes a breach of contract but cannot prove his or her damages with reasonable certainty. *Ericson* *v. Playgirl, Inc.* is an example (although a special statute established a minimum recovery of $300).

Nominal damages are also appropriate to remedy a technical breach of contract in situations where the plaintiff did not suffer any injury. Assume that P contracts to sell a tract of land to D for $50,000. D breaches, refusing to pay anything, and P sues. Before the suit progresses very far, a new buyer appears and pays P $70,000 for the land. P has not suffered any injury from D's breach. Still, D has breached a promise and the court will, as a matter of principle, allow P to recover nominal damages. In addition to the principle at stake, P is now the prevailing party in the lawsuit, making D responsible for paying court costs (but usually not attorney's fees) in many jurisdictions. (Other jurisdictions do not allow the plaintiff to recover court costs unless a specified minimum amount has been recovered. Such statutes are aimed at discouraging litigation over valid but trivial claims.)

**Punitive Damages:** The general rule in contract law is that punitive damages are *not* recoverable in breach-of-contract actions, even if the defendant intentionally refused to perform his promise. However, several jurisdictions do allow recovery of punitive damages when they find that the breach constitutes an independent intentional tort or an independent breach of fiduciary duty. These exceptions have been invoked increasingly in recent years to benefit consumers who have been mistreated by businesses. For example, many jurisdictions now recognize that an insurance company's intentional refusal to pay an insured's valid claim may constitute not only a breach of contract, but also an intentional tort often called the "bad faith" tort. Such jurisdictions allow plaintiffs to recover punitive damages in amounts that often dwarf the sum due under the policy.

Note that attempts to collect for "emotional distress" injuries caused by breach of contract are normally denied in accordance with rules similar to those applicable to punitive damages.

**Liquidated Damages:** A **liquidated damages** provision is a clause in a contract that stipulates the amount of damages that will be paid in the event of a breach. Such a clause has several purposes. It may avoid a protracted dispute and trial on the issue of damages. This will lower the parties' costs of proof and society's cost of providing a judge and jury. Such a clause may diminish the losses of the defaulting party or, conversely, establish a minimum level of recovery from the nondefaulting party in a case where losses may well be speculative. It allows both parties to better calculate their level of risk in a given transaction.

Courts generally wish to enforce contracts as made by the parties, but they do tend to be leery of liquidated damages clauses, mostly out of a fear that such clauses may be used as a "penalty" to unfairly punish or coerce one of the parties. Typically, courts set forth three criteria for an enforceable liquidated damages clause. First, the injury arising from the breach must be difficult or impossible to estimate accurately. If the amount of damages arising from a breach is easy to determine, a liquidated damages clause does not save trial time and expense and therefore loses much of its justification. Second, the parties must intend for the clause to provide a remedy for the injured party, not a penalty for the defaulting party. This relates back to the notion that part of the freedom of contract is the freedom to breach a contract.

In virtually every case involving the enforceability of a liquidated damages clause, the focus of the court becomes the third criterion—whether the amount established as liquidated damages is a *reasonable estimate* of the actual loss caused by the subsequent breach. The courts will not enforce a clause that sets an amount so far above the true damages sustained that it constitutes a "penalty" imposed on the defendant rather than legitimate compensation for the plaintiff's loss. The reasonableness of the estimate is judged as of the time the contract is entered into, although UCC 2-718(1) allows amounts that are reasonable considering anticipated *or* actual harm. (Indeed, even under the common law if the estimate turns out to be wildly inaccurate as a gauge of the actual damages, even if it seemed reasonable when the contract was made, the courts are unlikely to enforce it.)

Whether a liquidated damages clause is an unenforceable penalty provision is a matter of law for the judge to decide. The labels used by the parties in the contract do not control. In *U.S. v. Bethlehem Steel Co.,* 205 U.S. 105 (1907), because of a promise for early delivery, the government agreed to buy guns from defendant even though its bid was higher than those of competitors. The contract provided that for each day defendant's delivery was late, a "penalty" of $35 would be imposed. Because this sum represented the average difference in price between defendant's bid and those of the cheaper, but slower, suppliers, it was enforced as a genuine attempt to gauge the government's actual damages.

One form of liquidated damages clause that is almost always enforced is that calling for the breaching party to pay the attorney's fees of the nondefaulting party who is forced to bring a lawsuit.

## United Air Lines, Inc. v. Austin Travel Corp.
U.S. Second Circuit Court of Appeals, 867 F.2d 737 (1989)

Plaintiff United Air Lines owns and markets to travel agents the Apollo CRS, a computerized reservation system that provides subscribers access to a vast data bank through which they may make airline reservations, issue tickets, and reserve car rentals and hotel rooms. United is paid a monthly subscription fee and charges airlines a booking fee each time a travel agent uses Apollo to book a flight on another airline. United also markets its ABS, a back-office accounting and management system for travel agents.

Defendant Austin is a travel agency that formerly used a different CRS. However, in 1985 it acquired two small travel agencies (Karson and Fantasy) that subscribed to Apollo. Austin assumed their contracts with United and then executed a five-year Apollo contract to cover its Oceanside and Mitchell Field locations. The contract for Oceanside and Mitchell Field provided for liquidated damages consisting of (1) 80 percent of the remaining monthly fees due under the contract, (2) 80 percent of the variable charges accrued by generation of tickets and itineraries for the month preceding termination, multiplied by the number of months remaining on the contract, and (3) 50 percent of the average monthly booking fee revenues, using the first six months of the contract as a basis for calculation, multiplied by the number of months remaining on the contract. The Fantasy contract contained only the first two elements of liquidated damages.

Austin breached the agreement when one of United's rivals offered to indemnify Austin for any damages incurred for breach if it would terminate the Apollo contracts and buy the rival's system. United brought this breach of contract action. The trial judge held for United, ruling, most importantly, that the liquidated damages clauses were valid and enforceable. Austin appealed.

**Decision:** Affirmed. Liquidated damages clauses will generally be upheld unless they are penalties, plainly or grossly disproportionate to the probable loss anticipated when the contract was executed. Such clauses are not penalties if they bear a reasonable proportion to the probable loss and the amount of actual loss is difficult or impossible to determine. The evidence in this case fails to substantiate defendant Austin's claim that the 20 percent discount incorporated in the liquidated damages provision is not a "reasonable" estimate of the savings plaintiff United will realize in not having to provide services to defendant after the breach. Defendant claims that this discount is in fact a penalty, imposed on any breach, even if insignificant. However, the presumed intent of the parties is that a liquidated damages clause will apply only to material breaches, and there is no indication that the parties in this case had a different intention. ■

## *Equitable Remedies*

Courts of equity developed in England because the early courts at law could give only one form of remedy—money damages. In other words, they could award a landowner damages caused by a neighbor's trespassing, but could not order the neighbor not to trespass again in the future. Courts of equity developed in large part to provide more flexible forms of remedy in situations where fairness seemed to demand them. Several forms of equitable remedy are available to the party injured by breach of contract. Whereas damages are generally assessed by juries, equitable remedies are within the province of the court and are enforced through the court's authority to hold in contempt persons who violate its orders.

**Specific Performance:** When a plaintiff asks the court for an order of **specific performance,** he or she is asking the judge to order the defendant to perform the promise that was made. Obviously there may be many instances where specific performance is a remedy that a plaintiff would prefer. If the judge orders specific performance, the plaintiff receives exactly what was bargained for and need not worry about collecting a money judgment or searching for someone to provide substitute performance.

Nonetheless, the courts presume that an award of money damages is the primary remedy in breach-of-contract cases. Specific performance is reserved for the "extraordinary" cases where money damages are inadequate to fully compensate the plaintiff. Specific performance is most frequently ordered when "unique" property is at stake, so that an award of money damages would not fully compensate the plaintiff who could not take the money anywhere to buy the item originally contracted for. Assume, for example, that plaintiff contracted to buy a secret recipe from defendant. If defendant breached its promise to deliver the recipe, an award of damages to plaintiff would not enable plaintiff to obtain the recipe elsewhere, because it remains defendant's trade secret.

Other items often held to be "unique" include rare books and coins, family heirlooms, priceless works of art, items in extremely short supply, patents, copyrights, and shares of closely held corporations which cannot be bought through any market or stockbroker. For historical reasons, courts view every tract of land as unique (even though it may be the same size and have the same characteristics as a tract adjacent to it). Therefore, contracts to sell real property are always enforceable through orders of specific performance. The same may be said of contracts to sell businesses, for these are also presumed to be unique.

Courts will often specifically enforce contracts against *insolvent* defendants, because an award of money damages against a defendant who cannot pay is certainly not adequate compensation. (Conflicts with the priorities given creditors under the bankruptcy laws must be avoided, however.) Specific performance is often granted in cases where the plaintiff's monetary damages are difficult to measure with reasonable certainty; absent specific performance, the plaintiff might be relegated to mere nominal damages.

***Limitations:*** There are several factors that limit the availability of the specific performance remedy. First and foremost, specific performance is available only within the *discretion* of a court of equity. In attempting to achieve fairness and equity, courts must consider such factors as hardship to the defendant and impact on societal interests.

Additionally, courts consider traditional equitable rules such as the "clean hands" doctrine (no equitable remedy will be granted to a plaintiff who has breached his or her obligations in any material way), the doctrine of unconscionability (the courts will not be a party to enforcing an extremely one-sided bargain), and the doctrine of laches (no remedy for a party who has "slept on his rights" by unduly delaying the bringing of suit). Obviously courts will not order specific performance in contracts that involve illegality, mistake, or fraud.

Specific performance will not be granted in *personal service contracts*. Assume that Sally hires Waldo to paint her portrait because he is the best-known portrait artist in the state and Sally's personal favorite. If Waldo refuses to live up to his obligations the court might allow Sally to recover damages, but would not order specific performance. One reason often given is that it would violate the Thirteenth Amendment's proscription against involuntary servitude to force Waldo to paint against his will. A more plausible policy ground is the *difficulty of supervision* involved. How could a court effectively enforce Waldo's obligation? How could it supervise him to ensure that he did a "good job"? A court can transfer title to land, but it cannot paint for Waldo or sing for a reluctant rock star. For the same reason, courts often refuse to order specific performance in long-term contracts that might require them to undertake years of supervision.

Specific performance and damages are normally thought of as alternative forms of remedies. However, a plaintiff might be able to obtain both in the same case, especially if a court could feasibly order only partial performance by the defendant.

***UCC:*** If there has been any trend in the common law of specific performance in recent years, it has been to soften the "adequacy" of remedy test, thereby increasing the availability of specific performance. That trend is reflected in UCC 2-716, which authorizes specific performance in sale-of-goods contracts "where the goods are unique *or in other proper circumstances.*" [Emphasis added.] Still, even under the UCC, specific performance remains an "extraordinary" remedy.

***Injunction:*** Assume that Chuck, a football coach, has a five-year contract with the Armadillos, an NFL franchise. In the second year of the contract, Chuck is offered a much more lucrative deal by Big State University and announces that he is accepting it. Obviously the Armadillos will wish to force Chuck to live up to his contract. Just as obviously, no court would order Chuck to specifically perform that contract. In addition to the "involuntary servitude" consideration, there is the difficulty of supervision. How could a court ensure that Chuck hired the right assistants, kept the best players, or called the appropriate plays? However, while a court could not feasibly order Chuck to do what he had promised to do (coach the Armadillos), it could order him *not* to do what he had promised *not* to do (coach Big State U). By signing a full-time contract with the Armadillos, Chuck had implicitly promised not to take any conflicting obligations. Such an order is called an **injunction**.

As with orders of specific performance, injunctive orders are within the court's equitable discretion. Courts will consider factors of fairness, unconscionability, and the plaintiff's "clean hands" in deciding whether to issue such orders. Injunctions are often used in cases involving sports and entertainment, and in normal employment relationships when a party seeks to enforce a covenant not to compete signed by a former employee. We studied the enforceability of these covenants in Chapter 14.

**Reformation:** Assume that Sharon and Nick reach an oral agreement that Nick's attorney reduces to writing. After the contract is signed, Sharon realizes that because of the attorney's error, the writing does not accurately reflect the oral agreement. Sharon may ask a court for an order of **reformation**. In effect, Sharon is asking the court to rewrite the contract, but only for the limited purpose of enforcing its true terms. The court is not making a new contract, but simply enforcing the parties' agreement as made. Sharon should have read the contract before she signed it, but *if* she can prove that an error has caused a discrepancy between the oral agreement and the written contract, her negligence would not bar reformation in most courts.

The parol evidence rule (see Chapter 16), which prevents introduction of oral testimony to vary the terms of a written contract, would not block Sharon's efforts in this case. It applies only when the writing was intended to be the final and complete statement of the parties' agreement. Most courts conclude that such is not the case where an error in reducing the oral agreement to writing has occurred.

However, the statute of frauds (see Chapter 16, again) does pose serious problems. What if the agreement is the type that the statute of frauds requires to be in writing? Is Sharon asking the court to enforce an oral agreement in contravention of the statute of frauds? Some courts think that this is exactly what she is asking, and will refuse reformation. Other courts reason that they are simply correcting the mistaken written agreement, and will grant reformation.

In relatively rare instances, some courts will reform contracts not to enforce the parties' original agreement, but to modify that original agreement to conform to the law. For example, we learned in Chapter 14 that if a covenant not to compete is drawn too broadly, many courts will rewrite it to cover a smaller geographic area or a shorter time span and will then enforce the modified version.

**Rescission:** An order of **rescission** is a court order terminating the contractual duties of each party. Usually (but not always) such an order will also allow each party to obtain restitution for any performance rendered to the other party.

Rescission is granted as a remedy in a wide variety of contracts, including those involving voidable agreements (e.g., fraud, mistake, undue influence, innocent misrepresentation, or parties lacking capacity) and those involving illegal activity.

**Restitution:** An order of **restitution** seeks to place a party in the position he or she was in before the contract was entered into. As noted earlier in this chapter, sometimes such an order will take the form of a damages award telling the defendant to pay the plaintiff the monetary value of the benefit the plaintiff conferred on the defendant. But the notion of restitution is very broad. It can also include an equitable order for the defendant to return specific property that the plaintiff transferred to the defendant pursuant to the agreement that the defendant has breached or the court is rescinding (on grounds of mistake, indefiniteness, lack of capacity, statute of frauds violation, etc.).

Assume, for example, that plaintiff transferred a cow to defendant, both parties believing that the cow was barren but having since discovered that the cow was pregnant at the time of the contract (see mistake cases, Chapter 15). Plaintiff will ask the judge for rescission and for an order of specific restitution, requiring defendant to return the cow. Courts are generally willing to grant restitution in mistake cases (unless defendant has already transferred the cow to an innocent third party). However, had this been a breach case where no mistake was made but the defendant simply failed to pay the purchase price, most courts would refuse to issue an order of rescission, reasoning that money damages would adequately compensate the plaintiff.

Restitution, generally speaking, is used not to enforce promises, but to prevent unjust enrichment by returning the parties to their precontract positions following rescission or breach.

## SUMMARY

Judicial interpretation of contracts is, like judicial interpretation of statutes, a necessary evil. The courts' role is to determine the parties' common intent at the time the contract was formed, not to rewrite the contract. Courts will attempt to discover the parties' dominant purpose and construe the terms of the contract to give effect to that purpose.

Many courts apply the plain meaning rule, refusing to consider extrinsic evidence where the parties' intent as spelled out in the language of the contract seems plain and unambiguous. Even these courts will resort to extrinsic evidence of the parties' intentions where the contract is ambiguous. (And other courts will always do so, rejecting the plain meaning rule.) Several rules of interpretation—such as "specific language controls general language," and "unclear language is construed against its drafter"—assist the courts in determining the parties' intent.

The purpose of remedies for breach of contract is not to coerce all promisors into keeping their promises, but to redress injuries to promisees when the promisors fail to perform. Money damages are the main form of remedy for contractual breach. Courts award for damages caused directly by the breach, as well as for consequential and incidental damages under appropriate circumstances. Nominal damages and punitive damages are occasionally available.

The parties often set the amount of damages that should be paid in a liquidated damages clause. Like other contractual provisions, these are usually enforced. However, they are not enforced when they appear to be unreasonable in relation to the true damages sustained, thus constituting a "penalty."

In their discretion, courts may also, in appropriate circumstances (such as where money damages would be inadequate), invoke a raft of equitable remedies such as specific performance, injunction, reformation, rescission, and restitution.

## KEY TERMS

**Interpretation**
**Construction**
**Plain meaning rule**
**Course of performance**
**Course of dealing**
**Usage of trade**
**Compensatory damages**
**Mitigation of damages doctrine**
**Nominal damages**
**Liquidated damages**
**Specific performance**
**Injunction**
**Reformation**
**Rescission**
**Restitution**

## QUESTIONS AND PROBLEMS

1. Vole owned a parcel of land on which a lessee constructed a hotdog stand pursuant to a 24-year lease. The land was subleased by lessee McGrogan to sublessee Georgacopolous, who owned a restaurant and bar named "Fiddlesticks" next door. McGrogan sent a letter to Vole notifying Vole of his intention to erect a new sign on the leased property. The new sign advertised both the hot dog stand and Fiddlesticks. However, two-thirds of the sign was devoted to Fiddlesticks and indicated that it sold alcoholic beverages. After the sign was erected in this form, Vole objected and sued. Defendants claimed that they had the authority to erect the sign under a lease provision stating that the lessee "shall have the right . . . to make alterations and improvements within said building. . . ." Vole disagreed. Decide. (*Vole, Inc. v. Georgacopoulos,* 538 N.E.2d 205, Ill.App. 1989.)

2. The City of Spokane hired Keltch to construct storm sewers. The contract form, provided by the city, stated that "Sales tax on this Contract . . . will be added to the amount due. . . ." The city's bid form instructed bidders to omit sales taxes from their proposal. The final total read: "Total Bid Price (Not Including Sales Tax) $_____." Keltch claims that these documents indicate that he is entitled to be paid for the sales tax he paid on materials he purchased for installation. The city claims that the provisions simply reflect that the city is exempt from sales tax and that it does not have to reimburse Keltch for sales tax on materials. What rule of interpretation might help resolve this dispute? (*Universal/Land Construction Co. v. City of Spokane,* 745 P.2d 53, Wash.App. 1987.)

3. Tanya Niedbalski was a school teacher in Platte Center for five years. On March 12, 1985, she was offered a "Re-

newal Agreement" by the School Board. It was an offer to renew her contract and provided that "The failure to return a signed copy of the contract to the . . . Board of Education on or before March 19, 1985 shall constitute a rejection by the Teacher of the offer of employment." The date "March 19, 1985" was typewritten onto the printed form. Another paragraph in the "Renewal Agreement" provided that "Renewal Agreements must be executed by the Teacher and delivered to the . . . Board of Education within 15 calendar days of receipt thereof from the District." Tanya thought about returning the contract on March 19, but forgot to do so. At 11 P.M. she remembered it, but decided that it was too late to call the board members. Therefore, she delivered the contract on March 20. The board told her that she was too late. Was she? Discuss. (*Niedbalski v. Board of Education,* 418 N.W.2d 565, Neb. 1988.)

4. In 1984, defendant Keller hired plaintiff Cencula to build a home for Keller for $161,000. Plaintiff sued in 1985, alleging that he had completed the home, but defendant had failed to pay about $74,000 due under the contract and approximately $4,300 in claimed extras. The complaint sought as consequential damages interest the contractor had paid on a bank loan taken out by him in 1985 for the purpose of paying the subcontractors on the project. The jury found for plaintiff generally, awarding him $20,790 to compensate for the interest paid on the aforementioned loan. Discuss the appropriateness of this award. (*Cencula v. Keller,* 536 N.E.2d 93, Ill.App. 1989.)

5. Blumberg was president and a 50 percent shareholder of Meteor Industries, Inc. While still with Meteor, he formed a competing corporation, Metalloy Industries. He then resigned from Meteor and during the next three years did business with many of Meteor's customers. Meteor sued, alleging that Blumberg had breached a covenant not to compete, causing a decline in Meteor's profits. The court found that Blumberg had breached the covenant. Regarding damages, the evidence showed that before Blumberg left, 90–98 percent of Meteor's profits came from the sale of brass tubing. Because only Blumberg knew brass tubing, when he left Meteor changed its business "dramatically, completely, and totally" to sale of brass rods. What damages should Meteor recover? (*Meteor Industries, Inc. v. Metalloy Industries, Inc.,* 539 N.Y.S.2d 972, A.D. 1989.)

6. Plaintiff entered a beauty contest and out of 37 contestants was selected as "Miss Legs of Tulsa." The advertisement by the contest's sponsors stated: "And, the first-prize winner receives an all expenses paid Windjammer Cruise to the Caribbean for two." Plaintiff was given two tickets for the cruise, but no expenses for traveling to and from the point of embarkation. Plaintiff sued for breach of contract and fraud, claiming that the sponsors never intended to pay "all expenses." Plaintiff later dropped the breach-of-contract claim. A jury returned a verdict for plaintiff for $6,136 in actual damages and $20,000 in punitive damages. Defendants appealed, claiming that this was essentially a breach-of-contract action where punitive damages should be unavailable. Decide. (*LeFlore v. Reflections of Tulsa, Inc.,* 708 P.2d 1068, Okl. 1985.)

7. Plaintiff Shirley MacLaine Parker contracted to act in defendant Twentieth Century Fox's production of "Bloomer Girl." She was to be paid $750,000. Before production began, defendant wrote to plaintiff, announcing that it would not fulfill its obligations. The letter stated that "to avoid any damage to you," defendant was offering plaintiff a role in "Big Country, Big Man." The compensation offered was identical to that of the original contract, as were 31 of the 34 provisions. However, whereas "Bloomer Girl" was to have been a musical production filmed in California, "Big Country" was to be a dramatic "western type" movie filmed in Australia. Defendant gave plaintiff one week in which to accept the new deal. She did not do so. Rather, she sued for breach of contract. Defendant admitted the breach, but claimed that plaintiff did not mitigate her damages. Discuss. (*Parker v. Twentieth Century Fox Film Corporation,* 474 P.2d 689, Cal. 1970.)

8. Plaintiff H&M Driver Leasing agreed to lease truck drivers as needed to defendant Champion International. The written contract contained Champion's promise that it would not hire any of the drivers furnished by H&M for a period of one year following termination of the agreement. Champion later hired Clifton Sweezy in breach of this promise. H&M sued for breach of contract, invoking a liquidated damages clause under which Champion promised that if it breached the agreement, it would "pay $10,000.00 liquidated damages to H&M, plus any and all actual damages resulting to H&M." Champion admits the breach, but claims that the liquidated damages clause is unenforceable. Discuss. (*H&M Driver Leasing v. Champion International Corp.,* 536 N.E.2d 858, 1989.)

9. After his junior year in college, plaintiff Julius "Dr. J" Erving signed a four-year contract to play professional basketball with defendant Virginia Squires for $500,000 per year. After one year, he signed a contract to play for the Atlanta Hawks for $1,500,000 per year. Plaintiff brought this suit to set aside his contract with the Squires on grounds of fraud. The Squires counterclaimed, seeking arbitration pursuant to a contractual provision and an injunction to bar Erving from playing basketball for any team other than the Squires pending the arbitration. The trial judge granted the injunction and ordered arbitration. Erving appealed. Discuss. (*Erving v. Virginia Squires Basketball Club,* 468 F.2d 1064, 2d Cir. 1972.)

10. Susan Nylen, Elizabeth Lewis, and Julie Reed, students at Indiana University, executed a rental agreement with Park Doral Apartments (PDA) for a term from August 26, 1986 until August 19, 1987, paying a $420 deposit, repre-

senting the final month's rent. The lease contained a "savings clause" stating, "Eviction of tenant for breach of lease agreement shall not release tenant from liability for rent payment for the balance of the term of the lease." It also provided that a fee of $2.00 per day, per person, would be assessed for late payments. Julie moved out in December, refusing to pay any further rent. Susan and Elizabeth paid only two-thirds of the total rent due for February and March. PDA sued and the court preliminarily ordered Susan and Elizabeth to pay full rent or vacate. They vacated. After a trial, the lower court entered judgment in the amounts of $140 per month for February and March, $362 in late fees, $600 in attorney's fees, and $75.24 in consequential damages, offset by the $420 security deposit. Defendants appealed. Discuss the validity of the "savings clause" and of the late fee as a liquidated damages provision. (*Nylen v. Park Doral Apartments,* 535 N.E.2d 178, Ind.App. 1989.)

# PART III

# SALES, COMMERCIAL TRANSACTIONS, AND BANKRUPTCY

■ Part III begins by surveying the subjects of sales law and commercial paper. These areas of law govern two of the most important business activities that are carried on in our economic system—sales of personal property (such as television sets and machine tools) and the issuance of negotiable instruments (such as promissory notes and checks). Both of these subjects are governed by the Uniform Commercial Code (UCC); thus, unlike the common-law rules that make up the subject of contracts, the rules we will be considering throughout Part III are entirely statutory in nature.

Chapters 20 through 23 are devoted to *sales law*—the examination and application of the rules of Article 2 of the UCC. The first of these chapters is concerned with defining "goods" and highlighting the essential elements of a sale, so that sales transactions can be distinguished from other transactions in goods (such as bailments) and from contracts calling for the performance of services.

Chapter 21 deals with the rules that determine when title and risk of loss pass from seller to buyer—the latter being of special significance in cases where the goods are damaged or lost before reaching the buyer's hands. Of even more importance in many cases are the areas of warranties and products liability (covered in Chapter 22), which together impose the basic liability that sellers of goods have for injuries caused by defective products. Chapter 23 concludes the subject of sales law by summarizing the rights that a buyer or seller has when the other party breaches a sales contract.

*Commercial paper*—governed by Article 3 of the UCC—is covered in Chapters 24 through 28. The special characteristics of negotiable instruments and the rules applicable to the negotiation (transfer) of such instruments are summarized in Chapters 24 and 25. The next two chapters deal with the subjects of holders in due course and defenses, and liability of the parties (i.e., the liability of makers, drawers, and endorsers of negotiable instruments). Chapter 28 examines the special rules applicable to checks and to the bank-depositor relationship.

Chapter 29 focuses on the rights and responsibilities of the debtor and creditor when items of personal property (inventory, equipment, consumer goods, or intangibles) belonging to the debtor are used as security for the creditor's claim. Chapter 30, "Bankruptcy," concludes Part III by surveying the various methods for dealing with unpaid debts and then focusing on bankruptcy proceedings under federal law. ■

CHAPTER 20

# SALES

## INTRODUCTION TO THE LAW OF SALES

A college student purchases a stereo. A home owner buys several cans of house paint. A manufacturer of tires purchases raw rubber, sulphur, and other materials and ultimately sells tires to automobile owners. A mining company sells coal to an electric utility company. All of the above have at least two things in common. First, they are quite ordinary transactions, occurring countless numbers of times. Second, they involve sales of goods. Thus we can hardly question the relevance of studying the law of sales.

The principles governing sales of goods do not exist in a vacuum. Indeed, Article 2 of the UCC, which provides the legal rules for contracts selling goods, is closely related to the common law which governs other types of contracts. Thus, in Part II's discussion of general contract law (Chapters 11–19), we have already noted pertinent instances where the UCC altered the common law in order to facilitate commercial transactions in goods. (These concepts are briefly recapitulated later in this chapter.) In Chapters 20–23, we will explore in more detail the law governing the sale of goods. In so doing, we will also treat a few closely related matters, for example, the law regarding *leases* of goods and another subject known as *documents of title*.

## SCOPE OF ARTICLE 2 OF THE UCC

Article 2 of the UCC deals with the sale of goods.[1] It forms the basis for most of the following discussion of the law of sales.

### Sales

A **sale** is defined in Sec. 2-106 of the UCC as "the passing of title from the seller to the buyer for a price." Thus Article 2 does not apply to leases—such as the lease of an automobile—or to other types of bailments—such as the storage of furniture in a warehouse—because only temporary possession of the goods (rather than title) is transferred in these transactions.[2] Neither does Article 2 apply to gifts, because no price is paid. (The section on documents of title later in this chapter briefly discusses bailments, while Chapter 45 contains a more complete treatment of the subject. Gifts are also dealt with in Chapter 45.) A barter transaction (i.e, the trading of goods for other goods or services without the exchange of money) would be within the scope of Article 2.

### Goods

In the majority of cases there is no problem ascertaining whether the subject matter should be classified as **goods**. Occasionally, however, the term may present problems. Essentially, two requirements must be met before a particular item of property is classified as a good:

1. It must be *tangible*. In other words, it must have a physical existence. Thus intangible property such as a patent, copyright, trademark, investment security, or contract right would not come within the scope of Article 2.

2. It must be *movable*. This requirement obviously excludes real estate, which is tangible but not mov-

---

[1] Louisiana has adopted parts of the UCC, but not Article 2. Every other state has adopted all of the UCC (excepting the relatively new Article 2A, discussed later in this chapter, and the revised Article 6, discussed in Chapter 21).

[2] Many courts have in the past extended Article 2 sales principles to lease transactions by analogy. In the future, however, *leases* of goods are to be governed by the new Article 2A, discussed later in this chapter.

able. (Of course, almost anything, even real estate, is capable of being moved, shovel by shovel, if enough effort is expended. But the word is intended reasonably rather than literally.)

Using these two requirements we can easily envision the wide variety of products that are classified as goods, from airplanes to toothpaste.

Should things that are attached to real estate be considered goods? Because of the movability requirement this question would involve considerable conceptual difficulty were it not for Sec. 2-107 of the UCC, which sets forth the following basic rules:

1. A contract for the sale of *minerals or a structure* (such as a building or its materials) is a contract for the sale of goods if they are to be severed from the land by the *seller*. If, however, they are to be severed from the land by the *buyer*, the transaction is a sale of real estate and is governed by the principles of real estate law rather than by the UCC. Two examples may be of some help. First, suppose that S and B agree that S will sell to B a quantity of gravel to be taken from beneath the surface of land owned by S. If their agreement states that S will dig and remove the gravel, the transaction is a sale of goods. If, on the other hand, B is to dig and remove the gravel, the transaction is a sale of real estate. Second, suppose that S and B agree that S will sell to B a storage building (or perhaps the lumber from the building) located on land owned by S. If their agreement indicates that B will remove the building from the land, the transaction is a sale of real estate. If removal is to be by S, it is a sale of goods.

2. A contract for the sale of *growing crops* or *timber* is a contract for the sale of goods, regardless of who is to sever them from the land.

3. A contract for the sale of *anything else attached to real estate* is a sale of goods if it can be severed *without material harm* to the real estate. This rule is, perhaps, not as important as the two rules just discussed, simply because most of the problems regarding things attached to real estate have involved minerals, structures, timber, or growing crops. Situations might exist, however, where this third rule would be pertinent. For example: X and Y agree that X will sell to Y a window air conditioner that is now attached to X's home. (We are assuming it is attached, for otherwise the question would never arise—it would obviously be a sale of goods.) The air conditioner is bolted to a metal shelf supported by braces that are secured to the side of the house by bolts. It is fairly evident that the air conditioner can be removed without material harm to the real estate. Suppose, however, that the subject of the sale is a floor furnace. In this case a gaping hole in the floor would result. This might be a material harm, causing the sale to be treated as a sale of real estate rather than goods.

The rules regarding sales of goods attached to real estate apply to those contracts under which the items are being sold apart from the land. However, if two parties agree that one will sell a tract of land to the other, including a building or some timber located on the land, the sale is treated as a sale of real estate.

The UCC also gives special attention to three other potential problems of classification. It provides that (1) unborn animals are goods; (2) money treated as a commodity, such as a rare coin, is a good (though money used as a medium of exchange is not); and (3) things that are specially manufactured for the buyer are goods. Although item 3 seems clear-cut, the framers of Article 2 felt that such a sale might be seen as predominantly a sale of services rather than goods and therefore stated it definitely.

Sales of services (such as employment contracts) are obviously not within the scope of Article 2. However, as we saw in item 3, goods and services sometimes are so entwined that classification is no easy task. For example, when a hospital supplies blood to a patient, is the hospital selling a good or supplying a service? When a beautician applies hair dye to a customer in a beauty parlor, is it a contract for goods or services? In such contracts involving both goods and services, most courts attempt to determine whether the *predominant factor, thrust, and purpose* of the transaction as a whole is that of selling a good or supplying a service.[3] This determination often turns on the intent of the buyer, as gauged by several factors, including the relative dollar value involved.

For example, in *De Filippo v. Ford Motor Co.*, 516 F.2d 1313 (3d Cir. 1975), the court held that the sale of a car dealership, which included sales of items that were clearly goods (e.g., cars, parts, and accessories) as well as items that clearly were intangible and therefore not goods (e.g., goodwill, notes receivable,

---

[3] Although the UCC makes no statement regarding blood transfusions or hair treatments (and the courts are split on the matter), it does specifically provide in Sec. 2-314(1) that food sold in a restaurant is a sale of goods (at least as far as creation of the implied warranty of merchantability is concerned).

and used car warranties), was predominantly a sale of goods because the contract's terms assigned little dollar value to the intangible items. The court refused to split the contract into two parts, applying the UCC to one portion but not to the other.

And in *Grossman v. Aerial Farm Service, Inc.*, 384 N.W.2d 488 (Minn.App. 1986), the court held that a contract for the aerial spraying of a herbicide on a farm was predominantly a contract for services because the farmers could have applied the herbicide through several methods of ground spraying, but chose a method of application that could only be performed by a contractor equipped to handle their specific request. Thus, the farmers' selection of this type of service gave the contract its predominant character. A comparison of the reasoning in this case to that in the following case illustrates how sticky these issues can be.

---

### Micro-Managers, Inc. v. Gregory
Court of Appeals of Wisconsin, 434 N.W.2d 97 (1988)

Stanley Gregory was hired to develop a new programmable controller for a manufacturing firm. Gregory contacted Micro-Managers, Inc. (MMI), which indicated an interest in designing and developing the software required for the controller. After some negotiation, MMI drafted a letter incorporating what it believed to be its working arrangement with Gregory. The letter provided that "all MMI time will be billed by MMI at a rate of $40/hour for software, $50/hour for engineering, and $75/hour for supervision. Direct expenses will be billed as charged MMI."

After MMI delivered the software, Gregory complained that it was unsatisfactory. During litigation that resulted, the question arose as to whether MMI had breached an implied warranty which depended, in turn, upon whether this was a contract for "goods" governed by the UCC. The trial court held for MMI, ruling that Article 2 did not govern the contract and therefore there was no implied warranty to be breached. Gregory appealed.

**Decision:** Affirmed. Where, as here, a mixed contract for both goods and services exists, courts decide whether the contract is covered by the UCC by determining whether its "predominant factor, thrust, and purpose" is the rendition of services (with goods incidentally involved, such as a contract with an artist for a painting), or is a sale of goods (with labor incidentally involved, such as installation of a water heater). This contract emphasized MMI's *time*. Also, $55,968 of the contract price of $59,828 was for labor. The contract repeatedly spoke in terms of "man-days," "development," "design," etc., connoting the rendition of services. ■

---

## Merchants

For the most part, Article 2 applies to all sales contracts, even those in which neither the seller nor the buyer is a merchant. However, a few provisions of Article 2 do require one or both of the parties to be merchants in order for such provisions to be applicable. For this reason, we will now examine the UCC definition of a **merchant**.

Most people who see the word *merchant* probably think of someone engaged in the retail grocery business, the retail clothing business, or similar endeavors. While such people (or corporations) are indeed merchants, the UCC definition includes many others as well.

Sec. 2-104 of the UCC details three different ways in which a person or organization can be considered a merchant.

1. One who "deals in goods of the kind" that are involved under the particular contract in question is a merchant; thus, not only retailers but also wholesalers and probably even manufacturers are merchants. A party is considered a merchant, however, only for the types of goods dealt with regularly in his or her business. That is, a merchant in one type of goods is not a merchant for all purposes. Thus a retail shoe seller is a merchant with respect to transactions involving the purchase or sale of shoes. But if that person buys a new car or sells a secondhand lawn

mower, he or she is not a merchant in those transactions.

**2.** Even if a person does not regularly "deal" in a particular type of goods, he is nevertheless a merchant if he "by his occupation holds himself out as having knowledge or skill peculiar to the practices or goods involved in the transaction." While most persons who fall within this provision are also merchants under the first provision by dealing in the particular goods, there are a few who do not really deal in goods but who are merchants within this second category. For example, if we assume that the word *deal* means "to buy and sell goods," a building contractor does not actually deal in goods. He buys building materials but does not resell them; instead he uses them in the performance of a service—constructing a building. However, he does, by his occupation, hold himself out as having "knowledge or skill peculiar to the practices or goods" involved in certain transactions and thereby is a merchant by definition. Of course, his status is irrelevant in any agreement to construct a building, because that agreement is essentially for services and not within the scope of Article 2. But his status as a merchant can be important with respect to a dispute arising from the sale contract between him and his materials supplier.

**3.** If a party is not a merchant under either of the first two categories, he or she may nevertheless be treated as one by *employing a merchant* to act in his or her behalf in a particular transaction. The UCC states that one is a merchant if one employs "an agent or broker or other intermediary who by his occupation holds himself out" as having knowledge or skill peculiar to the goods or practices involved in the transaction. Suppose, for example, that Smith, who does not regularly deal in grain, hires a professional grain broker to procure a large quantity of feed for Smith's cattle. In this situation Smith is considered a merchant.

The common thread running through all the above categories of merchants is the possession of or access to a degree of commercial expertise not found in a member of the general public. The UCC occasionally treats merchants differently than nonmerchants. For example, it imposes a higher duty of "good faith" on them. Also, some provisions of the UCC apply only to merchants who are deemed such because they deal in goods, while others apply only to merchants who are deemed such because they hold themselves out as having skill peculiar to the practice. In most provisions, both types of merchants are treated in the same manner.

Courts in different states have taken various views as to whether a farmer or rancher is a "merchant" for UCC purposes. The following case represents a narrow approach that is commonly used in states with a strong agricultural sector, where it often appears that courts are attempting to protect farmers from burdens the UCC imposes on merchants.

---

**Chisolm v. Cleveland**
Court of Appeals of Texas,
741 S.W.2d 619 (1987)

Chisolm, a dairyman, bought $9,000 worth of "green chop" (a farm crop used as cattle feed) from Cleveland pursuant to an oral agreement. Cleveland wished to sell by volume; Chisolm wished to buy by weight. After the sale, Cleveland sent Chisolm a written confirmation of the contract, to which Chisolm did not respond within ten days. The terms stated by Cleveland called for price by volume. When the green chop was delivered and payment by volume was requested, Chisolm refused to accept the goods. Cleveland sued for breach of contract. Chisolm raised a statute of frauds defense. The trial court overruled the defense, because Chisolm had not objected within ten days to the written confirmation. This would be an exception to the writing requirement of UCC 2-201 statute of frauds *if* both parties were "merchants." Chisolm appealed.

---

**Decision:** Reversed. Chisolm was not a "merchant" simply because he had bought feed a few times for his cattle. Although he grew "green chop" for his own cattle, he was not an experienced buyer or seller of it. ∎

## Leases

Thousands of times a day, Americans rent cars, garden equipment, machines to clean rugs, and numerous other goods. Leasing is also quite common in industry. For example, assume that Company A needs to buy 100 new delivery trucks from Company C, but cannot afford them. Company B ("lessor") agrees to buy the 100 trucks and then to lease them to Company A ("lessee"). In 1986 alone, companies financed $90 billion in equipment such as airplanes, computers, and office equipment through such leases.

**Leases** of goods present many of the same legal issues that arise in sales of goods. Indeed, some courts have held that Article 2 applies to leases because UCC 2-102 states that it applies to "transactions in goods." Although most courts disagree, many have extended provisions of Article 2 to leases by analogy, reasoning that the rules governing sales could be helpful in resolving lease disputes. This has been unsatisfactory, however, because Article 2 was not designed to address leasing problems.

Therefore, Article 2A, the first new article to be added to the official text of the UCC in more than 35 years, was approved in 1987. Article 2A will probably be slightly revised soon to accommodate changes made by many of the first dozen or so states to adopt it. Thereafter, widespread adoption should quickly follow. Our discussion generally applies to both versions. Article 2A is designed to cover leases of goods in the same manner that Article 2 covers sales. It is intended to apply to virtually every type of lease of personal property, though it does not cover leases of intangible property, such as software rights.

Article 2A's provisions resemble the common law of bailment for hire (discussed in Chapter 45). This is the most-litigated pre-Article 2A issue related to the difference between a true lease (governed by bailment law) and a lease intended as security for a loan (subject to UCC Article 9). Return, for example, to the hypothetical involving the lease of 100 trucks. If Company A falls behind in its payments, the rights of Company B vis-à-vis Company A's other creditors will depend on whether the agreement is structured as a true lease or as a security interest. This is a matter that we will examine in detail in Chapter 29 which discusses Article 9's rules for secured transactions. For now, it is sufficient to highlight a few of Article 2A's provisions.

**Lessee's Remedies:** Remedies are usually set forth in the lease contract. The parties to the lease generally have the right to set their own terms and to vary any provision of Article 2A. However, when the lease does not establish remedies, Article 2A provides that in event of default by the lessor, the lessee has the right, among others, to cancel the lease, to recover paid-in rents and security deposits to the extent "just under the circumstances," to obtain substitute goods, and to recover damages.

**Lessor's Remedies:** If the lessee breaches the lease by wrongfully refusing delivery or failing to make payments when due, the remedies available to the lessor include cancellation of the lease, repossession and disposition, and damages. "Reasonable" liquidated damages clauses will be enforced. Mitigation of damages by re-leasing is not required, but if an item is released, the lessor is not entitled to recover double profits.

**Warranties:** Finance lessors (those who do not select, manufacture, or supply goods out of inventory, but simply serve as a financial conduit so that the lessee may obtain use of goods—such as Company B in the aforementioned truck example) are automatically exempted from implied warranties. For other lessors, Article 2A's warranty provisions generally track those of Article 2, which will be discussed in detail in the next chapter. Warranties not affecting third parties may be disclaimed by written and conspicuous provisions.

**Consumer Leases:** A consumer lease is one that a lessor regularly engaged in the business of leasing or selling makes to an individual lessee who takes primarily for a personal, family, or household purpose, providing total payments do not exceed $25,000. Article 2A contains several provisions to protect consumers in such leases, including one allowing a consumer to recover attorney's fees when a court finds a provision in the lessor's form lease to be "unconscionable."

## REVIEW OF BASIC PRINCIPLES OF SALES CONTRACTS

In explaining basic contract law, Chapters 11–19 of Part II focused on the common law of contracts, but highlighted changes that Article 2 makes for sales contracts. The first part of this chapter examined the scope of Article 2's coverage. The next three chapters will go into great detail regarding some very important features of Article 2. Before leaving this chapter, however, we will present a quick overview of some basic Article 2 rules on contract formation, enforcement, and interpretation.

## *Contract Formation*

The basic elements needed to form a contract at common law (agreement, consideration, capacity of the parties, legality of purpose) are also essential to formation of a sales contract under Article 2. However, the drafters of the Code meant it to be nontechnical and to operate fairly. For example, the common law says that even if an offeror promises to keep an offer open for a specified period of time, he may revoke the offer at any time before acceptance (unless he has been given consideration to keep it open). As explained in Chapter 12, Sec. 2-205's "firm offer rule" provides a fairer rule, holding merchants to their signed promises to keep offers open for a specified time less than three months' duration even in the absence of consideration.

Even more importantly, the Code's rules on formation of an agreement do not turn on whether there existed a detailed offer and a detailed acceptance, each containing all important elements of the contract. Rather, the drafters of the Code realized that parties often, perhaps pursuant to a quick telephone conversation, intend to form a contract but fail to agree as to a specific term such as price or date of delivery. Therefore, Sec. 2-204 provides that a contract is made if the parties clearly intend one to exist *and* there is a reasonably certain basis for giving an appropriate remedy. Resort may be had to the "gap-fillers" to provide terms the parties omit. For example, 2-305 will provide the price if that term has been omitted, 2-308 fills in the gap if the parties did not determine the place for delivery, 2-309 fills in the time of delivery, and 2-310 fills in the time of payment.

The common law also generally requires that an acceptance be the "mirror image" of the offer on all important terms before a contract exists. The framers of the UCC realized that this requirement was unduly technical, given the modern commercial world's reliance on form contracts that cannot feasibly be fully negotiated for each transaction. Therefore UCC 2-207, the "battle of the forms" provision, states that a contract is formed if the offeree's primary intent is to accept an offer even if the offeree's form does not match the offeror's form in all particulars. That section then gives rules to decide the content of that contract. The essence of 2-207 is that no party is allowed to unfairly surprise the other with contract provisions hidden in fine print.

The area of consideration also illustrates the Code's nontechnical approach. As noted in Chapter 13, Sec. 2-209 states that, unlike at the common law, an agreement modifying a sales contract *needs no consideration to be binding.* Parties are bound to their promises to modify an existing contract, and another technical defense is eliminated. (Somewhat surprisingly, perhaps, the doctrine of promissory estoppel plays almost no role in Article 2.)

## *Contract Enforcement*

No body of commercial law can be free of technical rules, of course. Like the common law, Article 2 carries a statute of frauds requirement that certain contracts for the sale of goods—those of $500 or more—must be in writing in order to be enforceable (Sec. 2-201). However, consistent with its overall approach, the Code makes several exceptions to this technical defense, providing that oral contracts of over $500 are enforceable where (1) the seller has already substantially begun producing specially made goods; (2) payment has been made and accepted or goods have been received and accepted; (3) between merchants there has been a confirmatory memorandum sent and the receiving party did not object to its terms in writing within 10 days; or (4) the party against whom the contract is to be enforced admitted in court proceedings that an oral agreement existed. The Code also has its own parol evidence rule, Sec. 2-202, which again is more generous than the common law, allowing unambiguous final written agreements to be explained or supplemented by course of dealing, usage of trade, or course of performance (see Chapter 16).

The Code also grants the parties the right to shape the contract's terms as they please. For example, they can establish their own remedies with very few limitations. However, in the interests of fairness, the Code does impose some limitations. As explained in Chapter 14, a contractual provision that is unconscionable will not be enforced. A party with superior bargaining power or sophistication will not be allowed to impose unfair terms on an inferior party (UCC 2-302). For example, we will see in Chapter 23 that if a seller with superior bargaining power contractually limits the remedies of the buyer of a defective product so severely that the remedy fails of its essential purpose depriving the buyer of the substantial value of the bargain, the limitation is unenforceable (UCC 2-719(2)).

## *Contract Interpretation*

The Code follows general rules of contract interpretation, but, as noted in Chapter 19, allows more liberal use of extrinsic evidence to determine the parties' intent in sale-of-goods contracts. The Code assumes that the parties considered three important concepts when they formed their agreement. First is *course of performance,* which arises out of "repeated occasions for performance by either party with knowledge of the nature of the performance and opportunity for objection to it by the other." Second is *course of dealing,* "a sequence of previous conduct between the parties to a particular transaction which is fairly regarded as establishing a common basis of understanding for interpreting their expressions and other conduct." Third is *usage of trade,* defined as "any practice or method of dealing having such regularity of observance in a place, vocation or trade as to justify an expectation that it will be observed with respect to the transaction in question." In essence, this means that in determining the meaning of the contract, the courts may consider, in order of importance, the previous course of performance of this particular contract, the past course of dealing between the parties in other contracts they have had, and, finally, the usage of the trade in general as established by contracts and performance of other persons in the industry.

## *Duty of Good Faith*

Finally, interpretation and enforcement of contracts for the sale of goods are flavored not only by Article 2's specific policies against surprise, unfairness, and unconscionability, but also by its "good faith" requirements. UCC 1-203 specifically states that "[e]very contract or duty within this Act imposes an obligation of good faith in its performance or enforcement." Section 2-103(1)(b) goes further, defining the "good faith duty of a merchant to mean acting with "honesty in fact and the observance of reasonable commercial standards of fair dealing in the trade." This again highlights that Article 2 is not a collection of dry rules, but an attempt to establish a framework promoting efficient, but also fair, commercial transactions in goods.

## DOCUMENTS OF TITLE

Before concluding this introductory chapter, we need to present some terms that will aid understanding of the subsequent sales chapters. When goods are shipped by a carrier or stored in a warehouse before sale, a *bailment* often occurs. The owner of the goods is the *bailor,* the warehouseman or carrier is the *bailee.* An owner of goods who sends them through a carrier receives a receipt called a **bill of lading**,[4] which contains instructions to the carrier regarding destination and the like, as well as the terms of the shipping agreement. If goods are stored with a bailee/warehouseman before sale, the owner will receive a *warehouse receipt,* which will also contain the terms of the storage agreement. Both instructions are sometimes referred to as *documents of title,* because they provide evidence of title to goods.

**Documents of title**—such as bills of lading, warehouse receipts, dock warrants, dock receipts, and other orders for delivery of goods which are treated in the regular course of business as adequate evidence that the holder is entitled to receive, hold, and dispose of the goods covered, are governed by Article 7 of the UCC. A **negotiable document of title** is one which by its terms specifies that the goods are to be delivered to "bearer" or to the "order" of a named person. Documents not meeting this requirement are **nonnegotiable documents of title**.[5] A negotiable document of title (e.g., "Deliver to bearer" or "Deliver to order of Dan Owens") entitles whoever is in legal possession of it (as bearer or as Dan Owens's endorsee) to possession of the underlying goods. A nonnegotiable document of title (e.g., "Delivery to Dan Owens"), on the other hand, is not equivalent to ownership of the goods. Regardless of who presents the document, the bailee is under a duty to deliver the goods only to the party who is supposed to receive them under the bailor's instruc-

---

[4] Technically, the bill of lading is called an *airbill* when air transportation is used.

[5] A negotiable bill of lading is sometimes called an *order bill* and a nonnegotiable one a *straight bill.*

tions. (The difference between a negotiable and a nonnegotiable document is somewhat akin to the difference between a five-dollar bill and a copy of a contract.)

But if the instrument is nonnegotiable in form, the possessor's rights in the goods are subject to the party who originally delivered them to the warehouse or carrier.

## SUMMARY

Sales law—Article 2 of the UCC—applies to sales of goods: items of tangible personal property, such as books, stereos, and structural steel plate. Contracts calling for the sale of land, or the transfer of intangible property (such as the assignment of contractual rights) are not, therefore, governed by Article 2. A sale is a transfer of title to goods from the seller to the buyer for a price. Contracts calling for the sale of growing crops and timber are sales of goods in all cases, but there are special rules for determining the status of sales of minerals, structures, and fixtures. If a sale contract is "mixed," covering goods and non-goods, the rule is that the contract is a sales contract if the bulk of the assets transferred qualify as goods, and is thus governed by Article 2.

As a general rule, sales law applies to sales by both merchants and nonmerchants. However, a few provisions of Article 2 apply only to sales by merchants, and others only to contracts where both parties are merchants. The courts of about half of the states take the view that a farmer is not a merchant, with the result that he or she is not subject to the special rules applicable to merchant sellers. An almost equal number of courts, however, hold the opposite view.

Leases of goods are now covered by Article 2A, which will likely be adopted in most states soon. Although the provisions of 2A are drawn heavily from Article 2's rules for sales, they do make many important modifications for specific problems that arise in the leasing context.

Article 2's rules for the formation, enforcement, and interpretation of contracts for the sale of goods are roughly similar to common-law rules that were discussed in Part II. However, Article 2 does make changes necessary to improve the efficiency of commercial transactions in goods and to eliminate some of the technicalities of the common law.

Sales of goods are frequently made by the transfer of a "document of title" from seller to buyer—e.g., a warehouse receipt or a bill of lading. If the document is "negotiable," the person who is in lawful possession of it is entitled to the goods; that is, such possession is tantamount to ownership of the goods.

## KEY TERMS

**Sale**
**Goods**
**Merchant**
**Lease**
**Bill of lading**
**Document of title**
**Negotiable document of title**
**Nonnegotiable document of title**

## QUESTIONS AND PROBLEMS

**1.** Helvey filed suit against Wabash County REMC for breach of a contract to supply electricity to Helvey's furniture factory. During the course of the lawsuit the issue arose as to whether Article 2 of the UCC applied to the dispute. Discuss whether the contract between Helvey and Wabash is covered by Article 2. (*Helvey v. Wabash County REMC,* 278 N.E.2d 608, 1972.)

**2.** Ernst and Williams agreed to trade an airplane owned by Ernst for an undeveloped residential lot owned by Williams. A dispute arose as to the time, place, and manner of delivering the airplane. Is this dispute governed by the provisions of Article 2? Explain.

**3.** Hauter agreed to sell 1,500 shares of General Manufacturing Co. common stock to Rogers for $15,000. Later, several terms of the contract became the subject of disagreement between Hauter and Rogers. Hauter filed suit. Does Article 2 govern the transaction? Explain.

**4.** The City of Twin Falls, Idaho was in trouble with the EPA for violating federal water pollution standards. It had hired Envirotech to design and construct its sewage treatment plant. Under the contract, Envirotech was to purchase and install equipment which would separate and dispose of sludge produced in the secondary treatment of waste water. Some of the contract documents referred to "construction" and "contractors." On the other hand, one contract provision noted: "Included shall be the percentage of the total selling price for which the supplier is furnishing and installing the particular piece of equipment, to include and cover piping, high pressure pumps and sludge grinders, heat exchangers, reactor boiler, vacuum filters and support equipment, etc., required for the complete installation." When Twin Falls was fined by the EPA, it filed a third-party indemnity action against Envirotech under a warranty theory. Did the UCC's warranty provisions apply?

Was this a contract for the sale of goods? Discuss. (*U.S. v. City of Twin Falls,* 806 F.2d 862, 9th Cir. 1986.)

**5.** Contractors Supply (CS) was contacted about a certain type of stucco by Acrylic Stucco Applicators (Acrylic), a subcontractor that had been hired to put stucco on an apartment building being built for Ashley Square. CS secured the stucco from the manufacturer and sold it to Acrylic. Defects began to appear in the stucco soon after it was applied to the building, and Ashley Square refused to pay. CS sued and Ashley counterclaimed for breach of the implied warranty of merchantability. CS proved that it does not regularly supply the special stucco involved and that Acrylic's order was the first and only time it had been asked to supply the special stucco. Therefore, CS claimed that it was not a "merchant" and that no implied warranty arose. Is CS correct? (*Ashley Square, Inc. v. Contractors Supply of Orlando,* 532 So.2d 710, Fla.App. 1988.)

**6.** Playboy Clubs International, Inc., operates a number of hotels and nightclubs. Playboy bought fabrics from Loomskill, Inc., which it was going to have made into costumes for its employees by a third party. A dispute arose between Playboy and Loomskill regarding the sale. Relevant to this dispute is a section in Article 2 which applies only if Playboy is considered a merchant. Does this section apply? Discuss. (*Playboy Clubs International, Inc., v. Loomskill,* 13 U.C.C. Rep. Serv. 765, 1974.)

**7.** Loeb & Co., Inc., marketed raw cotton; Schreiner was a farmer who had grown cotton and other crops for ten years. Although he had sold his own cotton, Schreiner had never sold cotton belonging to anyone else. The parties entered into a contract for Schreiner to sell 150 bales of cotton to Loeb & Co. But when the market price of cotton more than doubled, Schreiner refused to sell. The oral contract was for more than $500, but Loeb & Co. had sent a confirming memorandum to Schreiner that he had never objected to. If Schreiner is a "merchant," he has no statute of frauds defense under 2-201. Is he? (*Loeb & Co., Inc. v. Schreiner,* 320 So.2d 199, Ala. 1975.)

**8.** Are there any circumstances in which a university might be considered a merchant? Discuss.

**9.** What part can documents of title play in a sale of goods? Explain.

**10.** How can one tell whether a document of title is negotiable or nonnegotiable? What is the basic difference between the rights of a person in legal possession of a negotiable document of title and the rights of a person in legal possession of a nonnegotiable document of title?

CHAPTER 21

# SALES

TITLE, RISK OF LOSS, AND INSURABLE INTEREST

The ultimate objective of a sale of goods is to transfer from one party to another the rights and responsibilities that accompany ownership. After negotiation and formation of the sale contract, some amount of time will usually pass before this objective is realized. Time may be needed to produce, procure, or manufacture the goods, or simply to take them from inventory and ship them. And the buyer may not wish to receive the goods until some future date even if the seller is capable of immediate delivery.

Many events can occur during the lapse of time preceding the transfer of ownership. The goods may be destroyed by fire, flood, or other act of God. They may be lost or damaged in transit. The seller or buyer, or both, may attempt to obtain a casualty insurance policy on the goods. A government entity may levy a tax on them. During this lapse of time, then, the question often arises as to which of the contracting parties possesses various rights and is subject to various responsibilities regarding the goods. In this chapter we will examine the rules of Article 2 of the UCC that spell out these rights and responsibilities.

## TITLE TO GOODS

Prior to enactment of the UCC, all issues of rights and responsibilities were decided by answering a single question: Who had "title" to the goods at the relevant point in time? This procedure often produced fair and logical results, but sometimes it gave rise to poor ones. Different situations can involve different policy considerations and should therefore not be governed by a single standard. Moreover, the courts were never able to develop an objective method of determining the location of title. For these reasons the UCC has abandoned the concept that title determines all questions of rights and responsibilities, and has adopted the approach of identifying specific problems and establishing rules for their solution that do not depend on who had title to the goods at a given time. *The location of title is thus unimportant in resolving most legal issues arising under the UCC.*

However, in some situations title is still a relevant consideration. A few UCC provisions, for example, do make specific mention of title to the goods. Furthermore, application of various laws other than the UCC can depend on the location of title. (For instance, the issue of title can determine the party upon whom certain tax liabilities rest.) These situations make it desirable to discuss specific UCC rules for locating title and a few special problems relating to title. Later in the chapter we will consider the UCC's treatment of two important and related legal problems—who bears the risk in case of casualty to the goods and who has sufficient interest in the goods to obtain insurance coverage.

### *Passage of Title*

Under Sec. 2-105 of the UCC, goods must be *existing* before any interest in them can pass. Thus **future goods** (such as crops to be grown) can be the subject of a sale contract, but no title to them can pass to the buyer until they actually come into existence.

Other rules relating to passage of title are set forth in UCC 2-401:

**1.** Goods must be not only existing but also *identified* before title can pass to the buyer. Generally, identification occurs when specific goods are designated as being the subject of the sale contract. Thus, if a seller has an inventory of lumber and agrees to sell a certain described quantity, no title can pass to the buyer until the specific lumber to be sold is marked, segregated, or otherwise identified.

2. Subject to the requirement of identification, title can pass to the buyer in any manner and on any conditions expressly agreed on by the parties.

3. If the parties do not expressly agree as to passage of title, when and where this occurs depends on how the goods are to be delivered. If they are to be shipped to the buyer, title passes to the buyer when the seller "completes his performance with reference to the physical delivery of the goods." In this regard, two situations are possible:

  a. The parties may make a *shipment contract,* authorizing or requiring the seller to ship the goods to the buyer (but not obligating him to see that they actually reach that person). Title passes when the seller delivers the goods to a carrier, such as a trucking company.

  b. The parties may make a *destination contract,* obligating the seller to see that the goods are actually delivered to the buyer. Whether the seller personally delivers the goods or ships them through an independent carrier, title passes only when delivery occurs.[1]

4. Sometimes the parties will agree that delivery to the buyer is to be accomplished *without physically moving the goods.* For example, the contract may require the buyer to pick up the goods at the seller's place of business or at a warehouse owned by a third party. When title passes depends on whether a document of title is used.

  a. If the seller is required to deliver a document of title (such as a warehouse receipt) to the buyer, title passes *when the document is delivered.* Thus the buyer can have title to the goods even if they are left with the warehouseman for a time.

  b. If the seller is not required to furnish a document of title (e.g., where the buyer is to pick up the goods at the seller's premises), passage of title occurs *when the sale contract is made*—if the goods are identified. If the goods are not identified at that time, title passes when identification does occur. These rules are illustrated in Figure 21.1.

## Special Problems Regarding Title

**Sales by Persons with Imperfect Title:** A situation occasionally exists where a party with no title or with imperfect title sells goods to another. To illustrate: Suppose that S sells goods to B. O then appears on the scene and claims to be the true owner or to have some interest in the goods.[2] If O is correct, S will ultimately be responsible for any loss he has caused O or B. Often, however, the real dispute is between O and B over who has the greater right to the goods.

In attempting to resolve the conflict between O and B, UCC Sec. 2-403 focuses on the type of title held by S, distinguishing between a void and a voidable title. If S has a void title (which is actually no title at all), he cannot transfer any interest in the goods to B. The most common example of this situation is where S is a thief. If S has stolen goods from O and then sold them to B, O can reclaim the goods from B—even if B had no knowledge of the theft.

The result may be different if S has a **voidable title** at the time he sells to B. Here S actually has title, but O has the power to void S's title for some reason. Common examples are these:

1. S purchases the goods from O through fraud.

2. S purchases the goods from O in a "cash on delivery" transaction and pays with a check that bounces.

3. S is insolvent when he purchases the goods on credit from O. In this case, O's power to void S's title and reclaim the goods generally exists for only ten days after S receives the goods. However, under Sec. 2-702(2), if S has misrepresented his solvency to O in writing within three months before delivery, O's power to void S's title and reclaim the goods is not subject to the ten-day limitation.

4. S purchases the goods from O when O is a minor.

If O asserts his rights in any of the above situations while S still has the goods, no particular problems arise. Suppose, however, that S has already sold them to B. Can O reclaim the goods from B? The an-

---

[1] "FOB" terms usually determine which type of contract exists. Assume a contract is made between a seller in Dallas and a buyer in Miami. If the stated price is "$2,500 FOB Dallas," or "$2,500 FOB seller's plant," it is a shipment contract. On the other hand, if the price is "$2,500 FOB Miami" or "$2,500 FOB buyer's plant," it is a destination contract. Shipment contracts are more common than destination contracts. "FOB" and other commercial shipping terms are explained further in Chapter 23.

[2] If O is a creditor of S and claims that the goods are the agreed-upon security for the debt, his right to the goods is governed by Article 9 of the UCC, dealing with secured transactions, which is the subject of Chapter 29. At this point we are not dealing with that situation.

**Figure 21.1  Passage of Title under UCC 2-401**

```
Express agreement ──────▶ At time and place agreed (subject to 2-401 restrictions)

                            ┌── Shipment contract         ── When goods put in
                            │   [2-401 (2) (a)]              hands of carrier
              Transportation │   ↖ Seller's
              is contemplated┤     delivery
              [2-401 (2)]    │     obligation
                            │   ↙
                            └── Destination contract      ── When goods tendered
                                [2-401 (2) (b)]              at destination
No express agreement ──▶ Delivery
[2-401 (2) & (3)]        terms
                            ┌── Document of title required ── When document delivered
                            │   [2-401 (3) (a)]
              Transportation│
              is not        ┤
              contemplated  │                              ┌── When contract is made
              [2-401 (3)]   │                              │   (if goods identified at that time)
                            └── No document of ────────────┤
                                title required             │   When goods are identified
                                [2-401 (3) (b)]            └── (if not identified at the time
                                                               of contracting)
```

---

swer is yes, unless B is classified as a **bona fide purchaser** (BFP). Section 2-403(1) states that "a person with voidable title has power to transfer *good* title" to a BFP. (Emphasis added.) This represents an important exception to the general rule that a person can transfer no better title than he or she has.

A BFP is defined as a "good faith purchaser for value." Thus two requirements must be met before B can be considered a BFP.

**1.** B must have acted in "good faith." This essentially means that B purchased without notice of the facts that caused S's title to be voidable. ("Notice" means actual knowledge of such facts, or the possession of information that would have caused a reasonably prudent person to discover such facts.)

**2.** B must have given "value" for the goods, that is, "any consideration sufficient to support a simple contract." B meets the value requirement not only by giving S a usual form of consideration—such as payment in cash or by personal check—but also when B receives the goods in satisfaction of a preexisting claim against S. (However, an unreasonably small consideration might be evidence of bad faith on the part of the buyer.)[3]

A buyer cannot simply ignore suspicious circumstances and then claim to have purchased goods without notice that the seller's title was voidable. For example, in *Landshire Food Service, Inc. v. Coghill,* 709 S.W.2d 509 (1986), Bellman bought a Rolls Royce from Coghill with a forged cashier's check. Title was transferred to a phony company. Pretending to be Coghill, Bellman then sold the car to Hyken. After the forgery was discovered, a dispute arose as to whether Hyken was a BFP. The court held that he was not, holding that Hyken was put on notice of the irregularities in the title he received because (1) the certificate of title carried evidence of the previous transaction; (2) Bellman gave two contradictory addresses;

---

[3]The requirement of value is easier to satisfy for a BFP than for a holder in due course of a negotiable instrument (see Chapter 26 for details).

(3) the asking price was at the low end of fair market value; and (4) Hyken failed to verify the existence and status of a phony company listed as the prior transferee on the title.

**Entrustment to a Merchant:** One additional situation exists in which a seller can transfer a better title to a buyer than the seller actually has. Under Sec. 2-403(2), if an owner entrusts possession of goods to a merchant who deals in goods of that kind, the merchant has the power to transfer good title to a "buyer in the ordinary course of business." Suppose that Owner O leaves her typewriter to be repaired by M, who is in the business of both repairing and selling typewriters. M then sells O's typewriter to a customer, D. If D purchases the typewriter in an ordinary way from M, and if D has no knowledge that the typewriter actually belongs to O, D has good title. O's only remedy is to sue M for damages; she cannot reclaim the typewriter from D.[4] The "entrustment" necessary to bring this rule into effect can also occur if a buyer allows a merchant-seller to remain in possession of the goods after the sale. An obvious purpose of the rule is to facilitate the free flow of trade by relieving ordinary customers from the necessity of inquiring into the status of the merchant's title.[5]

The following case illustrates such a situation.

---

[4] D's purchase would not be in the "ordinary course of business," however, if he received the typewriter as security for or in satisfaction of a preexisting debt owed to him by M. D also would not be buying in the ordinary course of business if the typewriter was part of a bulk purchase of all or a substantial part of M's inventory.

[5] But even though D can acquire greater title in this situation than M had, D's title can be no better than O's.

---

### Canterra Petroleum, Inc. v. Western Drilling & Mining Supply
North Dakota Supreme Court,
418 N.W.2d 267 (1987)

Mitchell Energy Corporation entrusted oilfield pipe to Port Pipe Terminal, Inc., for storage. Through a paper transaction, two employees of Port Pipe fraudulently transferred apparent ownership of the pipe to Pharoah, Inc., a "dummy" corporation which they created to facilitate the fraudulent sale of merchandise stored at Port Pipe's facilities. In the next few days, Pharoah sold the pipe to Nickel Supply Co., which sold it to Yamin Oil Co., which sold it to NorthStar, which sold it to Western Drilling & Mining Supply, which sold it to Canterra Petroleum, Inc. During these paper transactions, the pipe never left Port Pipe's storage facility until Canterra had it delivered to a trucking company shortly after its purchase. The pipe was stored by the trucking company until law enforcement officers informed Canterra that it was owned by Mitchell. Canterra then surrendered possession to Mitchell and sued Western for breach of warranty of title. Western filed a third-party suit against NorthStar. Canterra received a summary judgment against Western and Western, in turn, received a summary judgment against NorthStar. NorthStar appealed.

**Decision:** Reversed. UCC 2-403 says that any entrusting of goods to a merchant who deals in goods of that kind gives him power to transfer all rights of the entruster to a buyer in the ordinary course of business. Here, it is arguable that Mitchell entrusted the pipe to Port Pipe, a merchant who dealt in pipe, and that through Pharoah the pipe was sold to Nickel, a buyer in the ordinary course of business. (There is a factual dispute as to whether Port Pipe was a merchant; that issue could not be resolved on summary judgment.) Though Western claims that the entrustment doctrine does not apply where the goods are fraudulently transferred to a dummy corporation by employees of the entruster, it misapprehends the policy behind 2-403, which is this: Between two innocent parties—the entruster and the purchaser from the fraudulent entrustee—the former should suffer because it had the best chance to avoid the fraud by carefully selecting its entrustee. This policy facilitates commercial transactions because purchasers in the ordinary course of business do not have to be unnecessarily leery of the title of goods they are offered. Thus, Nickel acquired the title of the entruster Mitchell, and that title was eventually passed to NorthStar. ∎

---

**Rights of Seller's Creditors against Goods Sold:** If a seller for some reason retains possession of the goods after they have been sold, his or her creditors can be misled by this fact. For example, a lender (a "new creditor") may make a loan to the seller, believing that the seller's assets are greater than they really are. Or a person who had a claim against the seller prior to the sale (an "existing creditor"), under the same erroneous belief, might fail to take timely protective measures that he or she would otherwise have taken.

Because of these possibilities, all states have **fraudulent conveyance statutes** which, while not entirely uniform, generally prescribe the circumstances in which the seller's retention of sold goods is fraudulent. When such retention in a particular case is found to be fraudulent, the applicable statute gives certain rights to the creditors insofar as the goods are concerned. The drafters of the UCC, wishing not to interfere with these rights that are created under the local law, achieved this purpose in Sec. 2-402. Section 2-402(2) provides, in essence, that if the seller's retention is "fraudulent under any rule of law of the state where the goods are situated," the seller's creditors *can treat the sale as being void* and the goods as being subject to their claims. Even "unsecured creditors" (those not having a lien on the specific goods) possess this power.[6]

The seller's retention of goods after the sale does not always constitute a fraud on creditors. Indeed, Sec. 2-402(2) states that *it is not fraud* for a seller to retain possession in good faith for a "commercially reasonable time." In other words, the retention must be for a legitimate purpose (such as making adjustments or repairs), and the seller must not keep the goods longer than is reasonably necessary to accomplish this purpose. If the criteria of good faith and a commercially reasonable time are met, the seller's unsecured creditors cannot void the sale.

Retention of possession is not the only way a seller can defraud his or her creditors. Sometimes the sale itself is fraudulent and can be voided by the creditors regardless of who has possession. For instance, a sale made for less than "fair consideration" (thereby depleting the seller's assets) is a fraud on the seller's creditors in either of the following two situations: (1) where the seller is *insolvent* (liabilities exceed assets) at the time of the sale or is made insolvent by the sale, or (2) where the evidence proves that the seller actually intended to hinder, delay, or defraud the creditors. These rules are intended to protect creditors from an attempt by the seller to conceal his or her assets through a sham transaction (usually with a friend or relative).

**Bulk Transfers:** Suppose that a merchant owing money to creditors sells his or her inventory to a third party. If the merchant uses the proceeds to pay the debts as they fall due, no problems arise. But what if he or she pockets the money and disappears, leaving the creditors unpaid? Can these creditors lay any claim to goods that are now in the buyer's hands? If the buyer has paid a fair consideration, the sale is probably not fraudulent under the rules just discussed.

In such a case, however, if the sale constitutes a "bulk transfer" (or bulk sale, as it is commonly called), the merchant's creditors may be protected by Article 6 of the UCC. The basic rules of that article are as follows:

**1.** A **bulk transfer** is any transfer (sale) "in bulk and not in the ordinary course of the transferor's business" of a major part of the inventory of an enterprise whose principal business is the sale of merchandise from inventory.

**2.** Before the bulk transfer takes place, the seller must furnish a list of his or her creditors to the buyer. Then the seller and buyer must prepare a list of the property to be sold. Finally, the buyer must notify the seller's creditors of the bulk sale at least *ten days* before taking possession of or paying for the goods (whichever occurs first). This notice enables creditors to take steps to protect themselves; for example, they can impound the proceeds of the sale if they deem it necessary.

**3.** If the buyer fails to comply with this advance notice requirement, the sale is ineffective against the seller's existing creditors. (Those who become creditors after the notice is given are not entitled to any notice.) That is, in seeking to obtain satisfaction of their claims, the seller's creditors can treat the goods as still belonging to the seller. For example, a creditor might obtain judgment against the seller and then levy execution on the goods (have them seized) even though they are in the buyer's hands. The creditor must do so, however, within *six months* after the buyer takes possession.

**4.** Even if a bulk transfer is ineffective because proper notice has not been given, the buyer can transfer good title to a BFP.

*The New Article 6:* Article 6 was obviously aimed at protecting creditors from debtors who sold their goods in bulk and then absconded. Since the original promulgation of Article 6, the law and the availability of credit information have both evolved to give sub-

---

[6]The rights of "secured" creditors will be discussed in Chapter 29.

stantially more protection to creditors. Today, many believe that Article 6 gives creditors too much protection, impeding normal business transactions. Dissatisfaction with Article 6 led the American Law Institute and National Conference of Commissioners on Uniform State Laws to recommend in 1988 that the states repeal it because it is no longer necessary. Those states believing that they still need a bulk sales statute are urged to replace the current Article 6 with a newer version which would make several changes, including the following:

**1.** The revised article will apply only when the buyer has notice that the seller will not continue to operate the same or a similar kind of business after the sale.

**2.** The revised article will not apply to sales in which the value of property otherwise available to creditors is less than $10,000 or greater than $25,000,000.

**3.** When the seller is indebted to a large number of persons, the buyer need not send individual notices to each, but may give notice by filing.

**4.** The notice period is increased from 10 days to 45 days and the statute of limitations is increased from six months to one year.

**5.** A buyer's noncompliance will not render the sale ineffective or adversely affect the buyer's title; rather, the noncomplying buyer will be liable for damages caused by the noncompliance.

**6.** There is no liability for a buyer who believed in good faith that Article 6 did not apply or who made a good faith attempt to comply with it.

This book's appendix contains a copy of the *original* version of Article 6, because at this writing it remains in effect in all jurisdictions.

## RISK OF LOSS

A warehouse fire damages thousands of dollars' worth of goods. A truck, train, ship, or airplane is involved in an accident that destroys a substantial quantity of goods. In these kinds of situations the question may arise as to who must bear the financial burden of the loss.

The **risk of loss** question is especially provocative when the goods are the subject of a sale contract at the time of damage or destruction. The risk that the goods will suffer some casualty initially rests on the seller, but ultimately it passes to the buyer. The crucial issue is whether the risk had passed from the seller to the buyer at the time of the loss. If it had not yet passed, the financial loss is borne by the seller. (Whether the seller in such a case also remains responsible to fulfill the contract with the buyer is a separate issue, to be discussed in Chapter 23.) If it had already passed, the buyer must bear the loss. This means that the buyer is obligated to pay for the goods if payment had not yet been made, and he or she is not entitled to a refund of any payment already made.

The existence of insurance coverage does not lessen the importance of this question; it simply means that the real issue is whose insurance company must bear the loss. Of course, insurance coverage may be inadequate or totally lacking in a given case. If the goods are damaged, lost, or destroyed while in possession of a bailee such as a carrier or warehouseman, the bailee will often be liable (see Chapter 43 for details). The risk of loss question in such a case is still important, however, because it determines whether the seller or buyer bears the burden of pursuing the bailee for a remedy.

As mentioned earlier in this chapter, risk of loss does not automatically pass with title. In resolving the problem of who bears the risk, the UCC differentiates between two situations: (1) where the contract has not been breached when the loss occurs, and (2) where there has been a breach at the time of the loss.

### *Risk of Loss Where the Contract Is Not Breached*

The rules for placing the risk of loss in the ordinary situation are found in Sec. 2-509, as follows:

**1.** As was the case with passage of title, the parties can make any agreement regarding the time at which risk of loss passes from seller to buyer.

**2.** Where there is no agreement as to when the risk passes, the issue is based on *how the goods are to be delivered.* Where the sale contract requires or authorizes the seller to ship the goods by carrier, the timing of the passage of risk depends on the seller's obligation.

   **a.** If the parties have made a *shipment contract,* in which the seller's obligation is completed upon shipment of the goods, the risk of loss passes to the buyer under Sec. 2-509(1)(a) when the goods are "duly delivered" to the carrier by the seller. In most cases, a due delivery occurs when the seller *puts the goods in the possession of the carrier.* Any loss occurring thereafter falls on the buyer. (The basic shipment section, Sec. 2-504, also requires the seller (1) to make a reasonable transportation contract with the carrier, including delivery to the buyer of any documents necessary for the buyer to take possession of the goods, and (2) to promptly notify the buyer of the shipment—actions that are, in fact, usually performed by the seller as a matter of routine. However, that section goes on to provide that if the seller fails to perform either of these additional acts, the buyer may reject the shipment only if "material loss ensues"—a clause that most courts interpret as meaning "ensues *as a result of* such failure." Because most cases of loss or damage during shipment are caused by factors unrelated to the seller's nonperformance of either of these duties, the usual result is that the buyer must accept and pay for goods damaged or lost in the carrier's possession even in those cases where the seller fails to perform either of these additional duties.)

**b.** If the parties have made a *destination contract,* in which the seller is obligated to see that the goods are actually delivered to the buyer, the risk of loss passes only upon fulfillment of that obligation *by the seller tendering the goods at their destination* under Sec. 2-509(1)(b).

Generally, in 2a and 2b situations, the rules governing risk of loss essentially correspond to those governing passage of title—though differences in wording between the two sections occasionally give rise to a situation where title and risk of loss do not pass at exactly the same time.

**3.** Sometimes the goods at the time of sale are being held by a **bailee** and are to be delivered *without being moved.* For example, they might be stored in a warehouse, the buyer intending to pick them up there or perhaps to leave them in storage until they are resold to someone else. In such a case, the placing of the risk of loss hinges primarily on whether the bailee has issued a document of title (warehouse receipt) and, if so, what type of document it is. Under Sec. 2-509(2):

**a.** If a *negotiable* document of title has been issued for the goods, the risk of loss passes to the buyer when he or she receives the document.

Since the holder of a negotiable document generally has an automatic right to receive the goods, it is logical to place the risk of loss on that person.

**b.** If a *nonnegotiable* document of title has been issued, the problem is different. A buyer with this kind of document is not as well protected as one who has a negotiable document. This person can, for example, lose his or her right to the goods to some third party, such as a creditor of the seller or a purchaser from the bailee. And the buyer does not actually have a right to the goods until he or she *notifies the bailee of the purchase.* (Indeed, the buyer does not have to accept a nonnegotiable document as performance by the seller; but if the buyer does not object, the seller can satisfy his or her performance requirements with such a document.) Logically, then, the buyer's receipt of a nonnegotiable document does not immediately shift the risk of loss to that person. In fact, the risk does not pass to the buyer until he or she has had a *reasonable amount of time* to present the document to the bailee and demand the goods; and, of course, the risk does not shift if the bailee refuses to honor the document.

**c.** When the bailee holds goods for which *no document of title* has been issued and the seller wishes to sell the goods without moving them, he or she can do so in either of two ways. First, the seller can give the buyer a writing that directs the bailee to deliver the goods to the buyer. Risk of loss in this instance is determined in the same way as if a nonnegotiable document of title had been issued. Second, the seller can obtain from the bailee an acknowledgment that the buyer is entitled to the goods. In this case, risk of loss passes to the buyer when the bailee acknowledges the buyer's right to possession.

**4.** Some situations are not covered by any of the foregoing rules. Two common examples are transactions in which the buyer picks up the goods at the seller's premises or in which the seller personally delivers the goods to the buyer (rather than shipping by independent carrier). In such cases, the time at which the risk of loss shifts to the buyer depends on whether the seller is a *merchant.* The rules set forth below are found in Sec. 2-509(3).

If the seller is a merchant, his or her responsibility is somewhat greater than that borne by the nonmerchant; thus the risk of loss does not pass from seller to buyer until the buyer *actually receives the goods.* If the seller is *not* a merchant, the risk of loss passes to the buyer when the seller "tenders" delivery. (The concept of *tender* is discussed in greater detail in Chapter 23, but it essentially means that the seller has placed at the buyer's disposal goods conforming to the contract requirements and has notified the buyer so as to enable that person to take possession.) Suppose, for example, that B purchases a new car from S, a dealer. S is supposed to install an AM-FM radio and speaker system before B takes possession of the car. S does the work and parks the car on his lot, then telephones B and informs her that the car is ready. Before B picks up the car, it is severely damaged by a hailstorm. S must bear the loss. *Since he is a merchant, the risk does not shift to B until the latter actually takes possession.* If S had been an individual selling his personal car, the loss would have been borne by B because risk of loss in that case would have passed to B *at the time of the tender*—the phone call from S prior to the storm.

The preceding points regarding risk of loss are capsulated in Figure 21.2.

The following case presents a typical situation in which determination of the time of passage of risk of loss becomes all important.

---

### Schock v. Ronderos
Supreme Court of North Dakota,
394 N.W.2d 697 (1986)

Schock (buyer) negotiated to buy a mobile home that was owned by the Ronderoses (sellers) and located on their property. On April 15, 1985, buyer went to sellers' home and paid them the agreed purchase price of $3,900. Buyer received a bill of sale and an assurance from sellers that title would be delivered soon. With sellers' permission, buyer prepared the mobile home for removal. Buyer intended to remove the home from sellers' property on the following Monday, April 22. Sellers had no objection to the mobile home remaining on their premises until that time. They agreed to remove a piano and davenport which were still in the home and to disconnect the electricity and natural gas.

On Friday, April 19, the mobile home was destroyed by high winds as it sat on sellers' property. Buyer received in the mail a clear certificate of title on April 23. Buyer later filed this suit for return of the purchase price, arguing that when the home was destroyed, the risk of loss was on the sellers. The trial judge ruled for sellers on this claim, and buyer appealed.

**Decision:** Affirmed. UCC 2-509(3) provides that in cases not within subsections (1) or (2), if, as here, the seller is not a merchant, "the risk passes to the buyer on tender of delivery." Tender of delivery occurred on April 15. Defendants had already disconnected the electricity and gas. They were prepared to remove the sofa and piano at any time, and were waiting only because plaintiff did not want to move the home until April 22. ■

---

## Effect of Breach on Risk of Loss

When one of the parties has breached the contract, that party sometimes is required to shoulder a risk that he or she otherwise would not have to bear. This risk is, of course, in addition to any damages that the party may have to pay. Section 2-510 sets forth three basic rules to cover such situations; rules 1 and 2 apply to breaches by the seller arising out of the delivery of nonconforming goods, while rule 3 applies to breaches by the buyer.

1. When a seller tenders or delivers goods that do not conform to the requirements of the contract, the buyer usually has a right to *reject* the goods. In such a case, the risk of loss does not pass to the buyer until the seller "cures" the defect or the buyer accepts the goods despite their nonconformity.[7] Suppose that S and B have made a shipment contract for the sale of some office furniture. The risk of loss in this situation

---

[7] The circumstances under which the buyer can reject goods are discussed in Chapter 23. And, in speaking of cure, we are assuming here that the seller has a right to do so—which may or may not be the case. If the seller does not have the right, he or she cannot cure the defect and then force the buyer to take the goods. (The subject of cure is also treated more fully in Chapter 23.)

# Figure 21.2 Risk of Loss

**If Contract provides—As agreed [2-509 (4)]**

**If Contract silent**

- **No breach [2-509]**
  - **Carrier shipment [2-509 (1)]**
    - Shipment contract [2-509 (1) (a)] —— Delivery to carrier
    - Destination contract [2-509 (1) (b)] —— Tender of delivery
  - **Bailee holds [2-509 (2)]**
    - Neg. doc. of title [2-509 (2) (a)] —— Receipt of document
    - No doc. of title [2-509 (2) (b)] —— Bailee acknowledgment
    - Nonneg. doc. of title [2-509 (2) (c)] —— By provision of 2-503 (4) (b)
  - **"Pick up" or noncarrier delivery [2-509 (3)]**
    - Merchant seller —— Receipt of goods
    - Nonmerchant seller —— Tender of delivery
  - **Sale on approval [2-509 (4)]** or **Sale or return**
    - Sale on approval [2-327 (1)] —— Buyer approval
    - Sale or return [2-327 (2)] —— According to shipment rules [2-509 (1)]

- **Breach [2-510]**
  - **By seller**
    - Delivery of nonconforming goods [2-510 (1)] —— At cure, or upon buyer acceptance
    - Buyer revokes acceptance [2-510 (2)] —— Stays with seller to extent of deficiency in buyer's insurance
  - **By buyer [2-510 (3)]** —— With buyer to extent of deficiency in seller's insurance

ordinarily passes to the buyer when the goods are duly delivered to the carrier. However, in this case some of the furniture is improperly upholstered. On receiving and inspecting the furniture, B rejects the shipment. The risk remains with S until he reupholsters the defective pieces of furniture or substitutes good pieces for the bad ones. However, if B had accepted the shipment despite its defects, the risk would have passed to him on acceptance. In other words, if the nonconforming shipment is destroyed or damaged (through no fault of the buyer) prior to cure or acceptance, the loss falls on S.

2. In some situations, a buyer who has accepted goods can *revoke the acceptance.* Suppose, for example, that B does not discover the defect until after he has accepted the shipment. (The circumstances in which B has a right to revoke his acceptance will be discussed in Chapter 23. Here, assume that B does have this right.) If B revokes his acceptance, the risk of loss is treated as having remained with S from the beginning. However, the risk borne by S is *only to the extent that B's insurance coverage is deficient.* Suppose, for example, that the value of the goods is $10,000 but that B has insurance coverage of only $5,000. If the goods are destroyed through no fault of either party (for example, by flood or fire), S will bear a loss of $5,000 and B's insurance company will bear the remaining $5,000 loss. If B had had no insurance, S would have borne the entire loss. If B's insurance had covered the entire loss, S would have borne none of it.

3. Situations 1 and 2 involved a breach by the *seller.* What effect does a breach by the *buyer* have on the risk of loss? Stated simply, a breach of the contract by the buyer immediately shifts the risk of loss to him or her. Of course, the risk shifts only if, before B's breach, specific goods had already been identified as the subject of the contract. For example, S might ship conforming goods and B might wrongfully reject them on their arrival. Or, after specific goods had been identified, but before shipment, B might notify S that he will not comply with the contract. In either case, the risk of loss immediately shifts to B even if it would not have passed until later had B not breached the contract. B must bear the risk, however, *only for a reasonable time thereafter* and *only to the extent that S's insurance coverage is deficient.*

In the case that follows, the issues are (a) whether the buyer breached, and (b) if so, how the rules summarized in 3 above would apply.

---

**Multiplastics, Inc. v. Arch Industries, Inc.**
Supreme Court of Connecticut,
348 A.2d 618 (1974)

The plaintiff, Multiplastics, Inc., brought this action to recover damages from the defendant, Arch Industries, Inc., for the breach of a contract to purchase 40,000 pounds of plastic pellets.

Plaintiff, a manufacturer of plastic resin pellets, agreed with defendant on June 30, 1971, to manufacture and deliver 40,000 pounds of brown polystyrene plastic pellets for nineteen cents a pound. The pellets were specially made for defendant, who agreed to accept delivery at the rate of 1,000 pounds per day after completion of production. Defendant's confirming order contained the notation, "Make and hold for release. Confirmation." Plaintiff produced the order of pellets within two weeks and requested release orders from defendant. Defendant refused to issue the release orders, citing labor difficulties and its vacation schedule. On August 18, 1971, plaintiff sent defendant the following letter:

*Against P.O. 0946, we produced 40,000 lbs. of brown high impact styrene, and you have issued no releases. You indicated to us that you would be using 1,000 lbs. of each per day. We have warehoused these products for more than forty days, as we agreed to do. However, we cannot warehouse these products indefinitely, and request that you send us shipping instructions. We have done everything we agreed to do.*

After August 18, 1971, plaintiff made numerous telephone calls to defendant to seek payment and delivery instructions. In response, beginning August 20, 1971, defendant agreed to release orders but in fact never did.

On September 22, 1971, plaintiff's plant, containing the pellets manufactured for defendant, was destroyed by fire. Plaintiff's fire insurance did not cover the loss of the pellets, and plaintiff brought action against defendant to recover the contract price.

The trial court concluded that (1) plaintiff had made a valid tender of delivery by its letter of August 18, 1971, and by its subsequent requests for delivery instructions; (2) defendant had repudiated and breached the contract by refusing to accept delivery on August 20, 1971; (3) the period from August 20, 1971, to September 22, 1971, was not a commer-

*(continued)*

cially unreasonable time for plaintiff to treat the risk of loss as resting on defendant under UCC Sec. 2-510(3); and (4) plaintiff was entitled to recover the contract price plus interest. Defendant appealed.

**Decision:** Judgment for plaintiff was affirmed. Sec. 2-510, entitled "Effect of Breach on Risk of Loss," reads in part as follows: "(3) Where the buyer as to conforming goods already identified to the contract for sale repudiates or is otherwise in breach before risk of loss has passed to him, the seller may to the extent of any deficiency in his effective insurance coverage treat the risk of loss as resting on the buyer for a commercially reasonable time." Defendant's contention that its failure to issue delivery instructions did not constitute a breach of contract is wrong. Under the contract defendant agreed to accept delivery of the pellets at the rate of 1,000 pounds per day after completion of production, and it failed to do so. It is true that in its confirming order defendant instructed plaintiff to "make and hold for release," but this order never became part of the contract between the parties.

Defendant was also wrong in contending that the period of time between August 20, 1971, the date of the breach, and September 22, 1971, the date of the fire, was not a "commercially reasonable" period of time within which to "treat the risk of loss as resulting on the buyer." During that time defendant repeatedly agreed to transmit delivery instructions, though it never did so. It was thus reasonable for plaintiff to believe that the goods would soon be taken off its hands and to forgo procuring the needed insurance. ■

## INSURABLE INTEREST

Parties often obtain insurance coverage to protect themselves against the possibility that property in which they have an interest might be lost, damaged, or destroyed. An insurance policy is valid only if the party purchasing the protection has an **insurable interest**. Whether a party has this in a given situation is primarily a matter of insurance law rather than sales law. Article 2 of the UCC does, however, contain certain rules regarding insurable interest in goods.

***Seller's Insurable Interest.*** So long as the seller has title to the goods, he or she obviously has an insurable interest. But even if title passes to the buyer, the seller continues to have an insurable interest—and can insure the goods—so long as he or she has a "security interest" (a lien or mortgage to secure payment) in the goods.

***Buyer's Insurable Interest.*** The buyer obtains an insurable interest and can insure the goods as soon as they have been identified as the subject of the sale contract.

Under these rules, seller and buyer can both have an insurable interest in the same goods at the same time. Of course, even if a party has an insurable interest and obtains insurance coverage, that person has no right to recover from the insurance company unless he or she actually sustains a loss.

An application of these rules can be seen in *Bowman v. American Home Assurance Co.,* 213 N.W.2d 446 (Neb. 1973), where Bowman contracted on December 12 to sell his plane to Hemmer. On December 18, before the paperwork was complete or a bill of sale transferred, Bowman loaned the plane to Hemmer so that Hemmer could make a short trip. Hemmer crashed the plane on the 18th. Bowman's insurance company refused to pay under a policy that apparently provided coverage until December 23, claiming that Bowman had no insurable interest in the plane at the time of the crash. The court ruled for Bowman, reasoning: (1) under UCC 2-501, a seller has an insurable interest until title passes to the buyer; (2) under UCC 2-401, title passes at the time the seller completes his performance with reference to physical delivery of the goods *or* at any other time explicitly agreed to by the parties; (3) Bowman had only loaned the plane to Hemmer and therefore had not completed physical delivery; and (4) in this case the parties agreed that title would not pass until the paperwork was completed, which had not yet occurred on December 18.

## SALE ON APPROVAL AND SALE OR RETURN

Occasionally a seller and buyer agree that the buyer is to have a *right to return the goods to the seller* even though the goods conform to the sale contract. Such transactions possess certain unique characteristics warranting a separate discussion.

A sale of this type is either a **sale on approval** or a **sale or return.** Which of the two forms the transaction takes can always be expressly agreed upon by the parties. If the contract provides for a return of conforming goods but does *not* designate which form is intended, the UCC provides specific rules for classifying the arrangement. Section 2-326 states: "Unless otherwise agreed, if delivered goods may be returned by the buyer even though they conform to the contract, the transaction is (a) a 'sale on approval' if the goods are delivered primarily for *use,* and (b) a 'sale or return' if the goods are delivered primarily for *resale.*" (Emphasis added.) This is a common sense test. The purpose of a *sale on approval* is to allow the buyer who will be using the goods an opportunity to try them out before committing himself or herself to pay for them. The purpose of a *sale or return* is to allow the buyer of goods who intends to resell them to others an opportunity to return the unsold items. Copying machines are often sold in a *sale on approval;* textbooks are often sold to bookstores in a *sale or return.*

In either type of transaction the sale contract can specify the period of time within which the buyer must make a decision. If no time is specified, the choice must be made within a *reasonable time.* Failure to decide within this time constitutes acceptance of the goods, and the buyer must pay for them.

In a sale on approval transaction, the buyer can express approval in several ways. For example, as we have already indicated, failure to express disapproval within the required time constitutes approval. Approval can also be given by any statements or actions signifying it. Of course, the buyer can make a *trial use* of the goods without implying approval—though the question sometimes arises as to whether a particular use is really just a trial. While this question must be answered on the basis of the facts of each case, the key is whether the use being made of the goods is consistent with the purpose of a trial.

## Consequences of Approval and Return Sales

Under Sec. 2-327, the legal consequences of a sale on approval and a sale or return differ in several significant respects. The most important of these are the following:

**1.** In a sale on approval, no sale exists until the buyer accepts the goods by giving approval. Up to that time the arrangement is a bailment (the buyer being the bailee), with title and risk of loss *remaining with the seller* until the buyer gives approval.[8] By contrast, in a sale or return a valid sale exists until the buyer returns the goods. Thus title and risk of loss *pass to the buyer* as in any other sale, and remain with him or her until the goods are actually returned to the seller.

**2.** In a sale on approval, if the goods are returned the seller bears the expense of such return (but if the buyer is a merchant, he or she must follow all reasonable instructions of the seller in making the return). On the other hand, under a sale or return the buyer bears the expense of returning the goods.

**3.** The rights of creditors also differ with the nature of the transaction. In a sale on approval, the buyer is not the "owner" of the goods in his or her possession prior to approval. Consequently, until an approval occurs, the goods are subject to the claims of the seller's creditors and, with one exception discussed below, not to the claim of the buyer's creditors. By contrast, in a sale or return the buyer *is* the owner of the goods in his or her possession. Therefore, such goods are subject to claims of the buyer's creditors rather than the seller's creditors.

**4.** We noted earlier that the parties can agree as they wish on whether a particular arrangement permitting the return of conforming goods is a sale on approval or a sale or return. One important exception to this rule places significant constraints on that freedom. Under Sec. 2-326(3), if the buyer maintains a place of business where he or she deals in goods of the kind involved, and if that place of business is conducted under any name other than that of the seller, then the goods in the buyer's possession "are deemed to be on sale or return." *In other words, in such a situation, the goods in the buyer's possession are subject to the claims of his or her creditors.*[9] This is true even though the parties had *agreed* that the arrangement was to be a consignment or a sale on approval, and even though the seller is still the owner of the goods. In order to protect creditors of the buyer,

---

[8] Of course, if the goods are damaged, lost, or destroyed due to the buyer's negligence or intentional wrong, he or she is responsible regardless of where the risk of loss rests.

[9] The exception does not apply if the buyer is an affiliate of the seller doing business under the seller's name. In this case the buyer's creditors should be aware of the seller's interest.

who might be misled by the buyer's possession, this section essentially provides that the agreement of the seller and buyer can simply be ignored. It will still be effective, however, in regard to the rights and obligations existing between the seller and buyer.

In this situation, certain measures are available to the seller to protect his or her ownership rights in the goods. In other words, even though the goods are reachable by the buyer's creditors, a cautious seller can take steps to see that his or her interest prevails. Section 2-326(3) spells out alternatives for the seller, the best of which is compliance with the provisions of Article 9 (secured transactions) with respect to obtaining a "security interest" in the goods and filing public notice of that interest with the appropriate state official. (See Chapter 29 for a detailed discussion of security interests.)

## *Sale on Consignment*

Somewhat akin to a sale on approval and a sale or return is the *sale on consignment*. In such a transaction, a seller (the consignor) delivers goods to another person (the consignee) for the purpose of having the consignee sell them on behalf of the consignor. The consignee is merely an agent of the consignor; both title and risk of loss *remain with the consignor* while the goods are in the consignee's hands. Any unsold goods are, of course, returned to the consignor. The sale on consignment differs from a sale on approval because the consignee does not have possession for the purpose of deciding whether he or she wishes to buy the goods. And it differs from a sale or return because in that transaction the buyer acquires title to the goods for the purpose of reselling them; by contrast, a consignee—being merely an agent of the consignor—does not acquire title to the goods.

## SUMMARY

In most circumstances it is immaterial at what moment title to the goods passed from seller to buyer. However, in cases where it is necessary to pinpoint the time of passage, Sec. 2-401 contains rules for making this determination.

There are four situations relevant to the transfer of title which are governed by special code rules, rather than those in Sec. 2-401. Two of these situations are (1) sales by persons having voidable title, and (2) sales by merchants of goods entrusted to them. In these situations an innocent purchaser may receive better title than that possessed by the seller.

Where goods are lost or damaged before receipt by the buyer, it is necessary to determine whether the risk of loss had, or had not, passed from seller to buyer prior to the time of loss or damage. Where neither party has breached the contract, the rules of Sec. 2-509 determine the time of passage of risk. If the parties had made a shipment contract, risk of loss passes when the seller delivers the goods to the carrier. In a destination contract, by contrast, the risk does not pass until the goods have reached their destination and the seller has made a due tender there.

In other situations, where transportation of the goods is not contemplated, the goods at the time of contracting are usually in the possession of a bailee (a warehouse) or in possession of the seller. In the first situation, if the warehouse receipt is negotiable, the risk of loss passes to the buyer when he or she receives the receipt. (If it is nonnegotiable, risk of loss does not pass until the buyer notifies the warehouse of the purchase). In the second situation, where possession is in the seller, the risk of loss does not pass to the buyer until he or she receives the goods *if* the seller is a merchant. If the seller is not a merchant, the risk of loss passes when the seller has tendered delivery (which is usually at some time before the buyer receives the goods).

If one of the parties has breached the contract prior to the time of the loss or damage, special rules set forth in Sec. 2-510 determine the time that risk of loss passes. When one of the parties is attempting to hold his or her insurance company liable for the loss or damage to the goods, such party must show that he or she possessed an insurable interest in the goods at the time of loss or damage. Section 2-501 sets forth the circumstances in which the buyer may have an insurable interest, and those in which the seller may have such an interest.

Sales on approval and sale or return transactions are those in which the buyer has the right to return the goods even though they conform to the terms of the contract. In a sale on approval title and risk of loss remain with the seller until the buyer expressly or impliedly approves; by contrast, in a sale or return title and risk of loss pass to the buyer when he or she receives the goods (but reverts to the seller if the buyer returns them).

## KEY TERMS

**Future goods**
**Voidable title**
**Bona fide purchaser**
**Fraudulent conveyance statutes**
**Bulk transfers**
**Risk of loss**
**Bailee**
**Insurable interest**
**Sale on approval**
**Sale or return**

## QUESTIONS AND PROBLEMS

1. In 1945, Lieber, then in the United States Army, was among the first soldiers to occupy Munich, Germany. There, he and some companions entered Adolph Hitler's apartment and removed various items of his personal belongings. Lieber brought his share, including Hitler's uniform jacket and cap and some of his decorations and personal jewelry, home to the U.S. after the war. In 1968 the collection was stolen by Lieber's chauffeur, who sold it to a New York dealer in historical Americana. The dealer sold it to the defendant, who purchased it in good faith. Through collectors' circles Lieber soon discovered the whereabouts of his stolen property. Lieber's demand for return of the property was refused, and he filed suit against defendant, seeking the return. Did Lieber or defendant prevail? Explain. (*Lieber v. Mohawk Arms, Inc.*, 64 Misc.2d 206, 1970.)

2. On January 9, 1985, Dartmouth Motor Sales sold a car to Wilcox who not only falsely represented himself to be a licensed car dealer but also paid for the car with a $6300 check that later bounced. The car's title was purportedly transferred by assignment. On January 10, Campbell, a licensed dealer, bought the car from Wilcox for $4300 and title was again transferred by assignment. At 2:00 P.M on January 15, Dartmouth's bookkeeper telephoned Campbell and told him that Dartmouth had a potential claim against the vehicle. Despite this and other communications, Campbell sold the car for $5,500 to Willis later that afternoon. Willis took possession of the car, but a dispute arose as to who was entitled to possession. Can you sort out the various rights of the parties? (*Dartmouth Motor Sales, Inc. v. Wilcox*, 517 A.2d 804, N.H. 1986.)

3. A entrusted goods to B, who was a merchant in the business of selling such goods. B was not authorized to sell A's goods, but he did in fact sell them in his regular manner to C, who thought they belonged to B. C paid for the goods by paying a debt that B owed to X. A filed suit to reclaim the goods from C. Was A successful? Explain.

4. Brown (D) bought five carloads of lumber from Lumber Sales (P). He admitted receiving four carloads but denied receiving the fifth, for which he refused to pay. The fifth carload was delivered to a railroad siding about one-half mile from D's business, as the parties had agreed. One of D's employees was notified of the delivery, but the lumber was not immediately unloaded, partly because the next day was Thanksgiving. The lumber then disappeared. P sued for the price of the fifth carload. Is P entitled to recover? (*Lumber Sales, Inc. v. Brown,* 469 S.W.2d 888, Tenn.App. 1971.)

5. Williams owned a motorboat, which he stored in a hobby shop. He agreed to sell the boat to Sanders. After making the agreement, Williams and Sanders went to the hobby shop, where Williams told the person in charge that Sanders would pick up the boat. Arrangements for the pickup were made between Sanders and the person in charge of the shop. When Sanders later returned to pick up the boat, it was gone. Sanders refused to pay for the boat, and Williams sued Sanders for the purchase price. Did he win his suit? Explain.

6. Lair Co. sold a TV antenna on credit to Crump. The contract provided that Crump could not remove the antenna from his premises while the price remained unpaid. The antenna was delivered and installed by Lair Co. Later it was destroyed by fire, and Crump refused to continue paying for it. When Lair Co. sued for the price, Crump claimed that risk of loss had not yet passed at the time of the fire. His reasoning was that, since the antenna was not shipped by carrier and not held by a bailee, risk would pass from Lair Co. (a merchant) to him only when he actually *received* the antenna. He argued that because of the restrictions placed upon his control of the antenna, Lair Co. technically had retained possession and he had not really received it. Who prevailed? Explain. (*Lair Distrib. Co. v. Crump,* 261 So.2d 904, 1972.)

7. X Company contracted to sell goods to Z Company. Both agreed that Z would pick up the goods at X's premises. The contract called for delivery "FOB purchaser's truck." X notified Z that the goods were ready for Z to pick up. Before Z called for them, however, they were destroyed. X Company sued for the purchase price. Did X win? Explain.

8. Fekkos (D) bought a tractor and various implements from Lykins Oil Co. (P) on April 27, 1985. The next day, while attempting to use the tractor, D discovered several defects, including a dead battery, overheating, missing safety shields, and a missing water pump. On that day D contacted P's employees who believed his objections to be valid and told him they would have the tractor picked up the next day. D stopped payment on the check he had written to P and placed the tractor with a tiller attached in his front yard because his garage was inaccessible and because P's employees would have to jump start the tractor when they

picked it up. P did not pick up the tractor on the 30th. On that day, D went to P's store and one of P's employees made the notation "cancelled 4-30-85" on the sale's invoice. The tractor was stolen sometime before 6:00 A.M. on May 1, 1985. The tiller had been removed and was still on the lawn. P later sued D for the purchase price of the tractor. Is D liable? (*Lykins Oil Co. v. Fekkos,* 507 N.E.2d 795, Ohio Ct.Comm.Pleas 1986.)

**9.** Shook bought electric cable from Graybar Electric Co. Shook was a contractor doing road work, and his place of operation continually changed. Graybar delivered the wrong cable to Shook, who promptly notified Graybar of the error and of the location where Graybar could pick up the cable. Graybar made no effort to take back the cable it had delivered, and after three months it was stolen. Graybar sued Shook to recover the purchase price for the cable. Did Graybar prevail? Explain. (*Graybar Elec. Co. v. Shook,* 195 S.E.2d 514, 1973.)

**10.** Scarola purchased goods from Pearsall, not knowing that Pearsall had stolen the goods. Scarola obtained an insurance policy on the goods, which were later destroyed by fire. When Scarola sought to recover their value from the insurance company, the company asserted that Scarola had no insurable interest in the goods. Scarola sued. Did he prevail against the insurance company? Discuss. (*Scarola v. Insurance Co. of North America,* 292 N.E.2d 776, 1972.)

# CHAPTER 22

# SALES

## WARRANTIES AND PRODUCTS LIABILITY

In recent years, courts have found themselves plagued with the problem of manufacturer liability, specifically the extent to which a manufacturer should be liable to a consumer who is injured by his product. To address this problem, various rules and legal theories for determining liability have been developed, and these make up the expanding area of law known as *products liability*. Since the 1960s, products liability has become one of the most rapidly changing areas in the history of English common law, its bias having undergone a dramatic shift away from the seller to favor, instead, the consumer. The pendulum has taken such a sudden swing that sellers' liability has emerged as one of the most controversial subjects in the business world today.

Under products liability law and sales law, three legal theories may be available to an injured consumer seeking redress: (1) warranty, (2) negligence, and (3) strict liability. The first is a contract theory and is governed by the UCC; the other two are tort theories. The elements of negligence have been discussed in Chapter 8 and will be applied here in the context of products liability. The principles of strict liability are taken from Section 402A of the American Law Institute's *Restatement (Second) of Torts*. Unlike the UCC, the *Restatement* is not a statute, but a model code of law whose recommendations have been adopted by courts of law in many states. Like the UCC, the strict liability theory applies primarily to transactions involving goods and not to those involving real estate or services.

## WARRANTY

A **warranty** is an assurance or guarantee that goods will conform to certain standards. If the standards are not met, the buyer can recover damages from the seller, under a breach of warranty theory.

Such has not always been the case, for though suits involving warranties date as far back as fourteenth century England, a recovery theory was slow in developing. *Caveat emptor* ("let the buyer beware") governed the state of law until recent times—here in America, until the beginning of the twentieth century. The concept of caveat emptor allowed the seller to escape liability altogether, in the absence of fraud.

With the growth of business and industry came a clear need to move away from laissez-faire values and to place legal strictures on sales transactions. Chains of distribution were widening the distance between manufacturers and ultimate consumers; and an increasing sophistication in product design made inspection for defects more difficult. As a result, courts came to recognize the existence of three types of warranties, discussed in the following pages: express warranties, implied warranties, and warranties of title.

### *Express Warranties*

**Express warranties** are those which originate from the words or actions of the seller. To create an express warranty, the seller does not have to use the word "warranty" or "guarantee," and the buyer does not have to show that the seller intended to make a warranty. Under Sec. 2-313 of the UCC, a seller can create an express warranty in three different ways: (1) by an affirmation of fact or a promise relating to the goods, (2) by a description of the goods, or (3) by providing a sample or model of the goods. Such representations by the seller create contractual obligations to the extent that they become "part of the basis of the bargain."

**Affirmation of Fact or Promise:** By making an affirmation of fact or a promise relating to the goods, the seller tactily guarantees that the goods will conform to the specifics he sets forth. For example, the seller might claim, "This boat is equipped with a two-year-old, 100 horsepower engine that was overhauled last month." The statement contains several affirmations of fact: (1) the boat is equipped with an engine, (2) the engine is two years old, (3) it generates 100 horsepower, and (4) it was overhauled last month. The seller might further state, "I assure you that this boat will not stall when run in choppy water." His affirmations concern past and present conditions; his promise, by contrast, relates to future events. Both affirmations and promises may create express warranties.

A seller's *commendation* or *expression of opinion* does not constitute an express warranty; neither does a statement that relates only to the *value* of the goods. Thus, the seller could claim that his boat was a "first class vessel, worth $25,000 at retail" without creating a warranty. The law is not so rigid as to disallow "puffing" of products; it assumes that a consumer can distinguish between sales talk and fact.

But at times the distinction between fact and opinion is not easy to make. Consider, for example, the following statement: "The steering mechanism on this boat has been thoroughly engineered." The claim is rather vague, and, as a descriptive phrase, "thoroughly engineered" may not be appreciably different from "first class." Yet the reference to engineering may create an impression of technological excellence in the mind of an unsophisticated buyer, and thus create a wrong impression.

In such cases, the courts tend to consider a number of factors, principally the buyer's frame of reference. If the buyer has limited knowledge of the goods involved, the statement from the seller is apt to be an affirmation of fact. If, however, the buyer is more knowledgeable than the seller, vague statements will be treated as mere expressions of opinion.

These additional generalizations can be made about the creation of express warranties: Statements which are specific and absolute are more readily construed as warranties than indefinite ones. Terms put in writing are more likely to create warranties than those given orally. A warranty is more likely to be found if the statement is objectively *verifiable* (e.g., "This machine is one year old."). The nature and seriousness of the defect may also have a bearing on the determination.

**Description of Goods:** A descriptive word or phrase used in a sale of goods may create an express warranty that the goods will conform to the description. The word "pitted" or "seedless" on a box of prunes or raisins warrants that the fruit will have no seeds. Recognized trade terms may also constitute descriptions. For example, the term "Scotchguard," used in connection with furniture upholstery, describes fabric which has been treated to make it water and stain resistant. Goods described by trade terms are warranted to possess those characteristics generally associated with the terms in the trade or business involved.

**Sample or Model:** If the seller provides to the buyer a sample or model of the goods to be sold, a warranty arises that the goods will conform to the sample or model. A sample is a single item taken from the mass to be sold, whereas a model is used to represent the goods. In a sale of wheat, a sample of one bushel might be drawn from the thousand bushels to be sold. But when the item being sold has not yet been manufactured or is too difficult to transport, a model might be used instead.

While the UCC makes no distinction between express warranties arising out of sales by sample or by model, a sample is more likely to create such a warranty than a model. Since a sample is actually taken from the inventory to be sold, it is usually easier for the buyer to prove that a sample was intended to establish a standard of quality for the sale.

**Basis of the Bargain:** Under Sec. 2-313, an express warranty is created only if the affirmation or promise, description, model, or sample is "part of the basis of the bargain." Courts have applied this phrase to two types of circumstances: First is the case where the seller makes a statement about the goods, and circumstances indicate that both parties intended the statement to be a part of the agreement. This would certainly be true if the statement appeared in the sales contract itself, and would apply also where it is reasonably clear that the statement played a material part in the buyer's decision to purchase the goods. The second type of case involves statements of fact contained in a brochure, provided to the buyer by the seller. Under pre-Code law, the burden of proof was generally on the buyer to show that he had read the statement and relied on it. If reliance could not be shown, the buyer could not recover on the breach of warranty theory. By contrast, under the "basis of the bargain" language, courts *assume* that the statement became a part of the contract unless the seller can show "good reason" for the contrary (Sec. 2-313, comment 8).

A different question arises when, *after* the sale has been made, the buyer requests a promise from the seller that the goods meet certain standards. If given, does this promise become "part of the basis of the bargain"? Prior to the enactment of the UCC, the answer probably would have been *no;* today it is probably *yes.* Under Sec. 2-209(1), the seller's post-sale promise is a modification of the contract and becomes an integral part of the agreement, even without additional consideration from the buyer.

A similar problem occurs sometimes in a sales negotiation, during which the seller makes statements that fail to appear in the written contract. Buyers who attempt to base a claim for breach of warranty on a recollection of oral statements are often thwarted by the *parol evidence rule* of UCC Sec. 2-202. Under this rule, if the court finds that the written form was intended as the final expression of the parties' agreement, any oral statement in contradiction of the written terms will not be admissible as evidence.

The following case illustrates how a company's advertising may expand the scope of an express warranty.

## Community Television Services, Inc. v. Dresser Industries, Inc.
U.S. Eighth Circuit Court of Appeals, 586 F.2d 637 (1978)

In 1965, two television stations in South Dakota created a separate corporation, Community Television Services, Inc. (Community), for the purpose of constructing and operating a 2,000-foot tower that would broadcast signals for both stations. Community contracted with Dresser Industries, Inc. (Dresser), who designed, manufactured, and erected the tower for a price of $385,000. The tower was completed in 1969 and Community used it until 1975. During this time, Community regularly inspected and properly maintained the tower. On January 10 and 11, 1975, a severe winter blizzard occurred in the area where the tower was located. During the early morning hours of January 11, as the storm reached its height with wind speeds of up to 80 miles per hour near the top of the tower, the structure collapsed.

Dresser denied responsibility and Community sued in federal district court for breach of an express warranty. The verdict and judgment in the trial court were in favor of Community, the plaintiff, for damages of $1,274,631.60, and Dresser, the defendant, appealed.

**Decision:** The judgment for plaintiff, Community, was affirmed. The advertising claims made by Dresser prior to the making of the contract with Community were "part of the basis of the bargain." These claims expanded the scope of the express warranty beyond the technical specifications in the contract. Since storms as severe as the one that blew over the tower did occur occasionally in South Dakota, the tower should have been able to withstand the wind and ice. ∎

## *Implied Warranties*

An implied warranty is created through the mere act of selling and is imposed upon the seller by law. Its purpose is to protect buyers who suffer economic and commercial losses when products fail to serve their needs. Unlike with express warranties, specific representations about a product have not actually been made. The consumer has been guided, instead, by the belief that his purchase is suitable for its intended use. In Sec. 2-314 and Sec. 2-315, the UCC names two types of implied warranties: the implied warranty of merchantability and the implied warranty of fitness for a particular purpose.

**Merchantability:** The law injects into the sales contract a warranty that the goods are "merchantable," if the seller is a *merchant with respect to the type of goods being sold.* (When a student sells her 1980 VW to a neighbor, no implied warranty of merchantability exists because she is not a merchant in automobiles.)

"Merchantable" means essentially that the goods are *fit for the ordinary purpose for which such goods are used.* The warranty of merchantability requires, for example, that shoes have their heels attached well enough that they will not break off under normal use. The warranty does not require, however, that ordinary walking shoes be suitable for mountain climbing. To be merchantable, goods must also serve their ordinary purpose *safely.* A refrigerator that keeps food cold but that gives an electric shock when the handle is touched is not merchantable. This is not to say that the seller becomes an insurer against accident or malfunction; the purchaser is expected to maintain his goods against the attrition of use.

The **implied warranty of merchantability** also does not guarantee that goods will be of the highest quality available. They are required to be only of *average or medium grade,* in addition to being adequately packaged and labeled. A growing minority of jurisdictions finds that the implied warranty of merchantability applies to sales of *used* goods; the majority limits the warranty to sale of new goods.

When applied to food, the implied warranty of merchantability can be related to *wholesomeness.* A tainted pork chop, for instance, is not merchantable. A number of cases decided prior to enactment of the UCC held that food purchased at a restaurant, hotel, or other such establishment carried no warranty because the sale involved a service rather than a product. The UCC, however, explicitly states that the implied warranty of merchantability extends to food sold at service establishments such as restaurants and hotels, whether the food is consumed on or off the premises.

Many cases alleging a breach of the implied warranty of merchantability have involved objects in food that caused harm to the consumer. Exceptional examples range from a mouse in a bottled soft drink to a screw in a slice of bread. In such cases the courts traditionally have distinguished between "foreign" and "natural" objects. They usually find that if the object is foreign to the mass (such as the mouse or screw mentioned above), the warranty of merchantability has been breached. If, on the other hand, the object is natural (such as a bone in a piece of fish), no breach of warranty has occurred.

A growing number of courts have rejected this approach and have based their decisions instead on the "reasonable expectation" of the consumer. The controlling factor in this approach is whether a consumer can reasonably expect the object in question to be in the food. A piece of chicken may be expected to contain a bone, but not when in a chicken sandwich; an olive may be expected to contain a pit, but not when a hole at the end indicates that it has been pitted. Bones and olive pits will not render food unmerchantable under the "foreign-natural object" test, *but may do so under the "reasonable expectation" test.* Thus, the results of a legal suit may vary considerably, depending on which approach is used. A famous case in this area follows.

---

**Webster v. Blue Ship Tea Room, Inc.**
Supreme Judicial Court
of Massachusetts,
198 N.E.2d 309 (1964)

**Plaintiff Webster, who was born and brought up in New England, ordered a cup of fish chowder while dining at defendant's "quaint" Boston restaurant. She choked on a fish bone contained in the soup, necessitating two esophagoscopies at the Massachusetts General Hospital. Plaintiff sued for breach of the implied warranty of merchantability. A jury returned a verdict for plaintiff. Defendant appealed the trial judge's refusal to direct a verdict for defendant.**

**Decision:** The judgment was for the defendant. A fish bone lurking in a bowl of fish chowder does not constitute a breach of the implied warranty of merchantability. Fish chowder is a traditional New England dish. Recipes call for head, tail, and backbone broken into pieces to be placed in a pot. "It is not too much to say that a person sitting down in New England to consume a good New England fish chowder embarks on a gustatory adventure which may entail the removal of some fish bones from the bowl as he proceeds." This is clearly distinguishable from the presence of tainted mackerel or the like which might constitute a breach of the implied warranty of merchantability. ∎

**Fitness for a Particular Purpose:** In Sec. 2-315, the UCC provides: "Where the seller at the time of contracting has reason to know any particular purpose for which the goods are required and that the buyer is relying on the seller's skill or judgment to furnish suitable goods, there is . . . an implied warranty that the goods shall be fit for such purpose" (hence the name **implied warranty of fitness for a particular purpose,** sometimes referred to as "warranty of fitness"). Note that the seller is not required to be a merchant, although merchants are defendants in the majority of cases.

Often the liability incurred by the seller under the implied warranty of fitness is greater than one incurred under the implied warranty of merchantability—a difference that can be best illustrated by a simple example: Suppose a buyer purchases an electric clock and discovers that its hands do not glow in the dark. The packaging carries no reference to visibility of the dial, neither does the instruction card. No breach of the implied warranty of merchantability exists here, for visibility of the dial under all conditions is not within the realm of a clock's "ordinary purpose." Yet, the seller *may* be liable to the buyer for breach of the implied warranty of fitness for a particular purpose if he or she knew that the buyer had a particular reason to need a clock with a lighted dial.[1]

A close examination of facts is required to ascertain whether a warranty of fitness exists, because such a warranty arises only if the following conditions exist:

**1.** The seller had "reason to know" of the particular purpose for which the goods were purchased. This requirement is obviously met if the seller was *actually informed* of the intended purpose; but such knowledge does not have to be proven. The requirement is also met if the circumstances dictate that the seller, as a reasonable person, *should have known* that the buyer was purchasing the goods for a particular purpose.

**2.** The seller also had reason to know that the buyer was relying on the seller's skill or judgment to furnish suitable goods. That is, the buyer must have relied on the seller's recommendation and the seller must have known or should have known of this dependence. If the buyer shows initiative by presenting brand names or introducing other specifications, recovery will be less likely.

**3.** Items 1 and 2 above must have existed at the time of contracting. If the seller learns the relevant facts only after the sale contract is made, a warranty does not exist.

These elements are applied in the following unique case.

---

[1] Some confusion exists because courts are split as to whether the "particular purpose" must be something other than the ordinary purpose for which the goods are used in order for the implied warranty of fitness to arise. Assume that Sally tells the salesman at the ABC Shoe Store that she wants some running shoes for jogging. He selects shoes clearly labeled as running shoes, which turn out to be unsuitable. Some courts would find that there was a breach of the implied warranty of fitness. Others would hold that since running was the ordinary purpose for which the shoes were intended, only an implied warranty of merchantability arose.

---

**Dempsey v. Rosenthal**
Civil Court, City of New York,
448 N.Y.S.2d 441 (1983)

Plaintiff bought a poodle, Mr. Dunphy, from defendant for $541.25. Five days later, an inspection by a veterinarian disclosed that Mr. Dunphy had one undescended testicle. Plaintiff returned the dog and demanded a refund. Defendant refused. Plaintiff brought this suit in small claims court, claiming breach of the implied warranties of merchantability and fitness.

---

**Decision:** Judgment was for plaintiff in the sum of $541.25. The elements of a breach of the implied warranty of *fitness* claim are (1) the seller must have reason to know the buyer's particular purpose; (2) the seller must have reason to know that the buyer is relying on the seller's skill or judgment to furnish appropriate goods; and (3) the buyer must, in fact, rely upon the seller's skill or judgment.

*(continued)*

Ms. Dempsey testified, and the judge believed, that she told defendant's salespeople that she wanted a dog suitable for breeding purposes. It is reasonable for the seller of a pedigreed dog to assume that the buyer intends to breed it. The dog was fertile, but would probably pass its condition on to its offspring, which would affect its stud value. All the elements of a fitness claim were present.

The court held that the implied warranty of merchantability was also breached because a dog with an undescended testicle would not pass without complaint in the trade. ■

---

## Warranties in Leases

As noted in Chapter 20, Article 2A contains warranty provisions for *leases* of goods. Except for "finance leases," Article 2A's rules regarding imposition and disclaimer of express and implied warranty liability are generally the same as those of Article 2 that we have just discussed.

## Warranties of Title

In most sales of goods, a warranty as to the validity of the seller's title automatically exists. Section 2-312 of the UCC imposes two basic types of **warranty of title**. The first is a warranty that *the title conveyed shall be good and its tranfer rightful.* This warranty is obviously breached if the seller has stolen the goods from some third party and therefore has no title at all. Other breaches, however, are not so obvious. Suppose that A buys goods from B and then is approached by C who claims to be the rightful owner. Inquiries reveal that there is some basis for C's claim and that the matter can be resolved only through a lawsuit. Will A have to become involved in a lawsuit initiated by C to determine if she bought a good title from B? Or has B breached his warranty of title by conveying a "questionable" title? The answer is that A has the option of returning the goods to B and getting her money back or defending against C's claim. If A takes the latter route and wins the lawsuit, she can recover her legal expenses from B. If A loses the lawsuit, she can recover from B not only her legal expenses, but also the value of the goods lost to C. A breach of the warranty of title exists if C's claim places a "substantial shadow" on the title, even if it ultimately might be proved invalid.

The second type of title warranty is that *the goods shall be delivered free from any security interest or other lien or encumbrance of which the buyer at the time of contracting has no knowledge.* This warranty will be breached, for instance, if B sells mortgaged goods to A without telling A of the mortgage.

Warranties of title accompany a sale of goods unless the seller indicates by specific language that no such assurances are being made, or unless the circumstances indicate as much (for example, in a public sale of goods seized by the sheriff to satisfy a debt, rightful transfers of title are generally not guaranteed).

An additional obligation—not, strictly speaking, a warranty of title—is imposed upon some sellers by Sec. 2-312: Unless otherwise agreed, a seller who is a merchant in the type of goods involved is deemed to warrant *that the goods sold do not infringe upon the patent, copyright, or trademark of a third party.* If a claim of infringement is made by a third party against the buyer, the seller is responsible—unless, of course, the goods were manufactured according to the *buyer's specifications.*

## Conflicting and Overlapping Warranties

Two or more warranties sometimes exist in a single sales transaction. For example, a machine might be warranted to perform certain functions and to last for a specified time. In addition to these express warranties, an implied warranty of merchantability or of fitness for a particular purpose, or both, might exist.

When more than one warranty is created in a given transaction, the buyer does not have to choose among them. The warranties are *cumulative,* such that the buyer can take advantage of *any* or *all* of them. According to Sec. 2-317, courts should interpret the warranties as being "consistent" whenever such an interpretation is reasonable. In the unusual event that two warranties are in conflict and cannot both be given effect, the court must attempt to determine the intent of the parties as to which warranty should prevail. Several rules offer guidance in determining intention:

1. Exact or technical specifications take precedence over inconsistent samples or models or general language of description.

2. A sample drawn from the goods to be sold takes precedence over inconsistent general language or description.

3. An express warranty, regardless of how it was created, takes precedence over the implied warranty of merchantability if the two are inconsistent. (An express warranty does not take precedence over the implied warranty of fitness for a particular purpose, although it is difficult to imagine a situation in which the two would be inconsistent.)

These rules are not absolute and can be disregarded by the court if they produce an unreasonable result. The following case illustrates a situation where a seller's express promise conflicted with a claimed implied warranty.

---

**Mohasco Industries, Inc. v. Anderson Halverson Corp.**
Supreme Court of Nevada,
520 P.2d 234 (1974)

Anderson Halverson Corp., owner of the Stardust Hotel in Las Vegas, Nevada, ordered carpeting to be manufactured by Mohasco and installed in the hotel lobby and casino showroom of the Stardust. After installation the buyer refused to pay, claiming that the carpet "shaded" excessively, giving it a mottled effect and the appearance of being water stained. Mohasco, plaintiff, sued Anderson Halverson, defendant, to recover the price of $18,242.50. The trial court held in favor of defendant, and plaintiff appealed.

**Decision:** The judgment for defendant was reversed. The trial court's finding that there was a "breach of the express warranty that the carpet would conform to the sample" was erroneous. The installed carpet conformed precisely to the sample the defendant/buyer had approved.

Since no breach of express warranty had occurred, the only remaining question involved defendant's argument that there was, nevertheless, a breach of the implied warranty of merchantability. This argument was not correct. When a buyer furnishes a seller with complete and minute specifications, the seller's only obligation is to deliver goods that meet those specifications. In other words, where an implied warranty of merchantability is limited by an express warranty of conformity to a precise description supplied by the buyer, if the latter warranty is not breached, neither is the former. Judgment was entered for plaintiff in the sum of $18,242.50, the contract price of the carpet. ■

---

## Disclaimers (Excluding and Limiting Warranties)

As we have seen, a sales transaction can give rise to three types of warranties: express warranties, implied warranties, and warranties of title. But the creation of these warranties is by no means automatic. The UCC allows a seller to disavow the existence of warranties or to limit the circumstances in which liability will apply by including a **disclaimer** in the sales contract. Theoretically, disclaimers can be justified on the grounds that their use advances freedom of contract, permitting parties to bargain over contract terms and to allocate the risk of loss. Yet in reality, the arrangement tends to be one-sided: consumers usually are in no bargaining position and often do not read disclaimers when making a purchase. For this reason, courts may find a particular disclaimer *unconscionable* under UCC Sec. 2-302.

**Disclaimers of Express Warranties:** A seller who wishes to avoid liability on an express warranty obviously should not do anything to create a warranty in the first place (a highly impractical measure to take in making sales!). An alternative would be to include a disclaimer in the contract. However, if a warranty has actually become part of the contract, an attempt to disclaim liability will usually not be effective. Section 2-316(1) states that a disclaimer will be disregarded if it is inconsistent with the words or conduct that created the express warranty. Suppose that an express warranty has been created by a statement of the seller, by the use of a sample, or by a written description of the goods. Liability could not then be disclaimed by specifying: "These goods are sold without warranties." Such a statement would almost always be inconsistent with the words or conduct that created the warranty. In short, *it is extremely diffi-*

cult for a seller to disclaim an express warranty which has become part of the contract.

**Disclaimers of Implied Warranties:** Because the existence of an implied warranty depends on circumstances rather than on the precise words used by the seller, such a warranty is relatively easy to disclaim. The UCC permits disclaimers of implied warranties through (1) the use of language specified in Sec. 2-316 of the Code, (2) the buyer's examination of the goods, or (3) custom and usage.

*Disclaimer by Language:* In the case of the *warranty of merchantability,* the language used by the seller to disclaim liability does not have to be in writing. If written, however, the disclaimer must be "conspicuous" enough to be noticed by any reasonable person involved in the purchase. (A disclaimer printed in larger type or in a different color than the remainder of the document will probably be considered conspicuous.) In addition, the word "merchantability" must be used—unless the seller employs a phrase such as "with all faults" or "as is," language which serves to disclaim *both* or *either* of the implied warranties.

In the case of the *warranty of fitness for a particular purpose,* the disclaimer must be in writing and must be conspicuous. Yet the statement itself can be a general one, such as, "There are no warranties extending beyond the description on the face hereof."

*Disclaimer by Examination:* If before making a contract, the buyer fully examines the goods (or a sample or model of them), or, on the other hand, deliberately refuses to examine them at all, no implied warranty exists for *reasonably apparent* defects. Yet if the buyer has no opportunity to examine the goods before contracting, the seller becomes liable for such defects.

When defects are hidden, the seller is always liable, unless it can be proved that the buyer had knowledge of the defects before contracting. It should be noted here that when deciding whether a defect is "reasonably apparent" or "hidden," a court will take into account the buyer's knowledge or skill. Such a factor obviously has a bearing on what an examination should have revealed to the buyer.

For example, in *Dempsey v. Rosenthal,* Mr. Dunphy's defective condition—the undescended testicle—was not readily observable. A manual manipulation of the scrotal area would have been the only means to verify the condition. The court found that Ms. Dempsey, the buyer, did not know this and should not be charged with knowledge of the fact. The type of examination that would be undertaken by the average buyer of a male puppy would not disclose the defective condition, so recovery was not barred by the inspection provisions of UCC 2-316.

*Disclaimer by Custom or Usage:* Implied warranties are sometimes excluded or modified by *trade usage* (industry-wide custom) or by a custom that has been established between the contracting parties. An industry-wide custom will have no effect, however, on a buyer who is not a member of the particular industry and is unaware of the custom.

*Limitation on Damages:* In contract cases, punitive damages traditionally have not been available to plaintiffs. For this reason, express and implied warranty suits usually involve two types of damages: basis-of-the-bargain damages (the value of the goods warranted less the value received) and consequential damages (personal and property damages proximately caused by the warranty breach, along with any indirect economic loss foreseeable by the defendant).[2] The buyer injured by a breached warranty also has the option to rescind the contract.

The Code allows limitations to be placed by the seller on damages that may be recovered by a breach of warranty. For example, recovery may be limited to *liquidated damages*—that is, a specified amount to be paid in the event of a breach. A limitation may also be placed on the type of remedy available, guaranteeing, for example, only the replacement of the product without charge.

However, such limitations will not be given effect if they are *unconscionable.* For example, UCC 2-719(3) provides that "[l]imitation of consequential damages for injury to the person in the case of consumer goods is prima facie unconscionable. . . ." Furthermore, comment #1 to 2-719 provides that "it is of the very essence of a sales contract that at least minimum adequate remedies be available. . . ." Even a clause that appears not to be unconscionable may be ignored if "because of circumstances [it] fails in its purpose or operates to deprive either party of the substantial value of the bargain."

A number of disclaimer of warranty and limitation of damage issues are discussed in the following case.

---

[2] In addition to damages, the buyer has an option to rescind the contract when a warranty has been breached, as we shall see in the next case, *Stream v. Sportscar Salon, Ltd.*

## Stream v. Sportscar Salon, Ltd.
Civil Court of the City of New York, 397 N.Y.S.2d 677 (1977)

Pursuant to a contract dated February 28, 1976, plaintiff Stream purchased from defendant Sportscar Salon, Ltd., an automobile which broke down on April 12, 1976, having been driven about 300 miles. Plaintiff had been adding oil, but the engine "seized" and was out of oil. The car was towed to defendant's premises. Defendant agreed to put another engine in the car. On April 20, plaintiff, after making reference to the defective engine and to other defects, notified defendant that he elected to "rescind" the sale and demanded return of the purchase price. The notice further stated that the plaintiff would consider "re-accepting" the car if it were repaired. Defendant worked on the car, and on May 1, 1976, plaintiff picked it up.

A few days later, the car broke down again. Plaintiff's mechanic examined the car and found its engine to be so defective as to be inoperable. The car was again towed to the defendant's premises. Plaintiff delivered the car's title to defendant and again notified defendant that he "elected to stand upon" the previous notice of rescission and demanded return of the purchase price. Defendant refused. The car, at time of trial, remained at defendant's lot. The following summarizes the trial judge's decision.

**Decision:** Judgment was entered for plaintiff for the requested relief—return of the purchase price. The judge first held that the car's engine was clearly defective. Then he addressed defendant's attempted warranty disclaimer and limitation on recovery.

The sales contract contained a number of warranties and also conflicting attempts to disclaim warranties. These conflicting provisions created an ambiguous situation. Ambiguous provisions should be construed against their drafter, the defendant in this case. Furthermore, defendant's attempts to disclaim the implied warranty of merchantability were ineffective because they did not use the word "merchantable" as required by UCC 2-316(2) or use the terms of art "as is" or "with all faults" as required by UCC 2-316(3).

Defendant also attempted to limit its remedial obligations to repair and replacement of defective parts, which it supposedly satisfied by replacing the car's engine. However, defendant's attempts to limit remedies failed because (a) the clauses were ambiguous and thus must be construed against defendant; (b) the clauses appeared to limit remedies only for breaches of express warranties and not to be applicable to implied warranties; (c) defendant did not follow the provisions of UCC 2-719 which are prerequisites to making "repair and replacement" exclusive remedies; and (d) if applied as requested by defendant, the limitation might well be unconscionable and therefore unenforceable. ■

## Defenses

**The Privity Defense:** Privity is a legal term for the direct relationship between buyer and seller. **Privity of contract** means relationship of contract: If Manufacturer A sells a yacht to Retailer B who in turn sells it to Consumer C, there is privity of contract between A and B and between B and C, but *not* between A and C. Because a warranty arises from the formation of a contract, privity of contract between plaintiff and defendant used to be required for the plaintiff suing for breach of warranty. Warranties did not "run with the goods" to subsequent purchasers and users. Thus, C could sue B, but not A.

The privity requirement was not a major hindrance in the early days of our country, when consumers bought most of their goods directly from artisans or local manufacturers. Today, however, when goods travel through chains of distribution, a privity requirement imposes an intolerable burden on consumers. Therefore, it has been greatly relaxed today *and is in the process of being eliminated.* All parties in the chain of distribution (manufacturers, wholesalers, and retailers) are now usually responsible to the last buyer for failure of the goods to live up to the standards of any warranties, especially for personal injuries.

***Innocent Bystanders:*** A final problem with the privity requirement is that defects in goods often injure persons other than the purchaser; yet the privity requirement prevented nonpurchasers (e.g., innocent bystanders or persons who borrowed the product from the buyer) from suing anyone in the chain of distribution for breached warranties.

Section 2-318 of the UCC has somewhat alleviated this problem by extending warranty protection to (1) members of the buyer's family, (2) members of the buyer's household, and (3) guests in the buyer's home, "if it is reasonable to expect that such person may use, consume or be affected by the goods, and [such person] is injured [physically] by the breach of the warranty." As the language indicates, the extended protection applies only when defective goods have caused a *physical injury to the individual.*

In recent years the drafters of the UCC have proposed alternative versions of Sec. 2-318 to further relax the privity requirement—primarily by granting protection to *any* injured person who could reasonably have been expected to use, consume, or be affected by the goods. While few states have enacted these versions of Sec. 2-318 to date, the trend in most jurisdictions is toward a loosening of the privity requirement in breach of warranty actions.

**Plaintiff Misconduct Defenses:** When a plaintiff's carelessness contributes to a products-related accident, the defendant can use that carelessness as a defense in most jurisdictions. However, there is a wide variety of approaches throughout the states regarding how to treat the plaintiff misconduct defense.

In negligence cases, of course, a plaintiff's carelessness is simply compared to the defendant's in most jurisdictions. The plaintiff's own carelessness can reduce or even bar recovery totally. In warranty cases, many jurisdictions do not deal simply with "plaintiff carelessness," as a single category. Instead, they recognize several types of such carelessness, with different categories having different effects on liability.

One category is *simple plaintiff carelessness*—frequently described as the failure to detect or guard against a defect in a product. In many jurisdictions this carelessness is compared to the defendant's fault under the comparative negligence statute.

Another category of plaintiff misconduct is **product misuse,** which occurs when a plaintiff uses a product for a purpose which was unforeseeable to the manufacturer. For example, the plaintiff might use a pop bottle as a hammer or a lawn mower as a hedge trimmer. Only when such misuse was not reasonably foreseeable to the defendants does a defense exist. When misuse is foreseeable, the law may impose on defendants a duty to warn against the misuse, or perhaps even to install safety devices to guard against the misuse. In some jurisdictions, unforeseeable product misuse constitutes a complete defense to a warranty claim; in other jurisdictions, it is merely evidence of plaintiff misconduct to be compared to defendants' fault.

A third category of plaintiff misconduct is **assumption of risk,** which occurs when a plaintiff, having discovered a defect in the product and fully appreciating its danger, uses the product anyway. Thus, assume that Sally purchases an airplane. The sellers promise Sally that the plane will fly six hours on a full tank of fuel. However, Sally is later told by several pilots who have experience with this type of plane that it will not fly more than five hours on a full tank. Nonetheless, Sally attempts to fly six hours and a crash ensues. Many courts would hold that Sally voluntarily and knowingly assumed the risk of the product's danger. In many jurisdictions, recovery is barred completely on a warranty theory. In other jurisdictions, the plaintiff's assumption of risk is compared to the defendant's fault under a comparative negligence statute, with the result that a plaintiff may still recover something.

Treatment of the plaintiff misconduct defense in the warranty area is similar to its treatment in a strict liability claim. Later in the chapter we will address these defenses in the strict liability context, and include a case illustrating one approach, *Smith v. Goodyear Tire & Rubber Co.*

**Statute of Limitations and Notice Requirements:** Under UCC 2-725, an action for breach of contract for sale of goods must be commenced within four years after the cause of action accrues. A traditional tort statute of limitations begins to run only when the right to sue is or should be discovered (and typically lasts two years). The UCC has a similar rule where a warranty *explicitly* extends to future performance of the goods and discovery of the breach must await the time of such performance. In such cases, the statute of limitations does not begin to run until the breach is or should be discovered. However, for all other suits under Article 2, the UCC statute of limitations begins to run when the goods are tendered for delivery. Thus, if the defect is not discovered for four years, the suit may well be time-barred before the defect is discovered. Many potential plaintiffs lose the right to sue by allowing the seller to attempt to effect repairs until after the four-year limit has expired. Furthermore, the Code provides that by agreement the parties may reduce the period of limitation to not less than one year, but may not extend it. Thus, the statute of limitations often bars warranty suits.

Some warranty actions are barred by a plaintiff's failure to comply with UCC 2-607(3) which imposes on the buyer a duty to notify the seller of a breach within a reasonable time after he or she discovers or should discover any breach, or be barred from remedy. The purpose of such a requirement is to minimize litigation by giving the seller a chance to effect repairs or otherwise satisfy the buyer. Courts have generally been reluctant to allow this provision to bar recovery by consumers who suffered personal injuries due to a breach of warranty. Courts are inclined to construe a "reasonable time" as being a longer period in a personal injury case than in a suit brought for economic loss by a commercial purchaser. The courts are split as to whether a person who bought an item from a retailer must give notice not only to that retailer but also to the manufacturer in order to be allowed to sue the manufacturer.

## NEGLIGENCE

Because the elements of negligence have been discussed at length in Chapter 8, our purpose here is simply to apply them to the area of products liability. Remember that in an action based on negligence, the defendant must have owed a duty to the plaintiff, and this duty must have been breached. Where a sales transaction is involved, the seller's duty to use reasonable care arises from the mere act of placing goods on the market. The economic benefit derived from a sale generates a responsibility to consumers; for the act of selling directly affects the interests of those who have no choice but to rely on the integrity of sellers. Privity of contract is no longer required in the usual negligence suit.

The manufacturer's liability for negligence is often predicated on negligent design or manufacture; in addition, *both* manufacturer and seller may be liable for failure to inspect or failure to adequately warn.

If the seller is a retailer, distributor, or wholesaler, he or she usually has no duty to inspect new goods, barring knowledge of defects. A duty to inspect does exist, however, when the seller is involved in the installation of goods (new or used) or in their preparation for eventual sale. Liability is imposed to the extent that defects are *reasonably apparent.* By the same token, a manufacturer is charged with taking reasonable measures to discover flaws created during the production process.

A *duty to warn* arises when a product's design (or its intended use) subjects the user to hazard or risk of injury. The danger in question need only be reasonably foreseeable—discoverable only within the limits of existing technology. Warnings given must be adequate in their specifics and must extend to all individuals whose harm is reasonably foreseeable. There is no duty to warn of obvious dangers—no duty, for example, to warn about fire on a box of matches.

*Negligent manufacture* is often cited in cases where defects are the result of oversight, human or mechanical error, or lack of judgment. For example, production line employees might not be properly trained, or materials selected for construction might not have sufficient strength to resist the stresses of normal use.

In contrast, actions based on charges of *negligent design* hold the manufacturer responsible for more than the exercise of care in production. In addition to warning about risks and hazards inherent in a design, the manufacturer is expected to design a product with optimal safety as the ideal, compromised only where the costs of improving design exceed the benefits derived therefrom. Under the rule adopted by most states, there is a duty to design products so that accidents are unlikely to occur and so that injuries suffered will be minimal if an accident does occur. To illustrate: Say X is driving a car which explodes when struck in the rear by Y, who has negligently maneuvered his truck. X may recover from Y for initial injuries, and may possibly recover from the car's manufacturer for additional injuries resulting from the impact if, for example, the gas tank were located vulnerably close to the rear bumper.

Of course, it would be unreasonable to expect cars to be accident-proof in all situations. (If this were the law, some courts have observed, manufacturers would produce nothing but tanks.) In evaluating the adequacy of design standards, courts have considered such factors as the state of existing technology, the expectation of the ordinary consumer, the danger of a product in relation to its social utility, and compliance with government safety standards.

To conclude, the negligence theory became viable as an avenue of recovery to injured plaintiffs when the privity requirement was finally abandoned.

This theory offers some advantages over the warranty theory, e.g., the buyer does not have to prove that a warranty existed, the buyer does not have to notify the seller within a reasonable time after discovering the defect, and disclaimers in the sales contract usually do not allow the seller to escape liability resulting from his or her negligence.

Yet certain disadvantages exist as well. A plaintiff must prove negligent conduct on the part of the manufacturer or seller, and proof of negligence is at times almost impossible to establish. Only in relatively rare cases have courts inferred negligence pursuant to the doctrine of **res ipsa loquitur** ("the thing speaks for itself").[3]

A second impediment to recovery under the negligence theory is that any type of plaintiff misconduct, even simple plaintiff carelessness will reduce or bar recovery.

Third, most jurisdictions hold that the UCC provides the only avenue for product liability recovery for mere *economic* loss (generally defined as all losses other than personal injury and tangible damage to property other than the product itself). For example, the majority rule is that if a piece of equipment contains an electrical defect that causes it to be destroyed in a fire resulting in no other loss, warranty provides the buyer's only avenue for recovery. Suit on a negligence theory (and, as we are about to see, a strict liability theory) is precluded in most states.

## STRICT LIABILITY

Most courts and legislatures have concluded in recent years that the warranty and negligence theories do not afford consumers as much protection as they ought, in fairness, to have. Many warranty claims are barred, for example, by disclaimers or because of the statute of limitations or failure to give notice of breach within a reasonable time. Many negligence suits fail because the plaintiff is not able to prove specific acts of negligence on the part of the manufacturer.

**Figure 22.1 Differences between Negligence and Strict Liability**

| | Negligence | Strict Liability |
|---|---|---|
| Principle | A test of whether reasonable care has been taken | A test of existence of defect |
| Application | Applies to virtually all goods and actions | Applies to products shown to have been dangerously defective in manufacture or design |
| Elements | Duty, breach, damages | Product defective in manufacture, design<br><br>Defect caused product to be unreasonably dangerous<br><br>Resulting injury |
| Defenses | Contributory or comparative negligence of plaintiff | Material alteration of product<br><br>Unforeseeable misuse of product<br><br>Unreasonable assumption of risk |

Recognizing these deficiencies, most jurisdictions have adopted the theory of **strict liability** by which manufacturers and sellers are held liable irrespective of fault. (See Figure 22.1 for a comparison of

---

[3] The doctrine of *res ipsa loquitur* may presume negligence from the fact that the accident did indeed occur. A plaintiff who can show that (a) the defendant controlled the product, and (b) the defect would not normally occur absent negligence can benefit from *res ipsa loquitur's* presumption of negligence. The presumption would be applicable, for example, if a product exploded immediately upon being removed from a container which was sealed at the defendant's factory.

strict liability with negligence.) Today, strict liability is the most common basis for imposition of product liability for personal injuries.

Justification for the strict liability theory lies in the notion that merchants and manufacturers are better able to bear losses than injured consumers, and that in many cases, losses will be transferred to the buying public in the form of higher prices on products. Thus, society at large assumes the cost of damages suffered by a few—an arrangement which is perhaps more equitable in that it offers relief for those injured by defective products.

Proponents of strict liability argue, in addition, that eliminating the need to prove negligence in a tort action will make manufacturers and sellers more mindful of accident prevention.

Finally, there is an economic basis for adopting this liability theory: Because negligence is often difficult to prove, litigation becomes excessively costly. From an overall economic standpoint, then, it can make sense to abandon proof of negligence in a products liability action.

## *Elements of Strict Liability*

The elements of strict liability are recorded in Section 402 of the American Law Institute's *Restatement (Second) of Torts*, a summary and clarification of American common-law principles. Section 402A reads:

1. One who sells any product in a defective condition unreasonably dangerous to the user or consumer or to his property is subject to liability for physical harm thereby caused to the ultimate user or consumer, or to his property, if
   a. the seller is engaged in the business of selling such a product, and
   b. it is expected to and does reach the user or consumer without substantial change in the condition in which it is sold.
2. The rule stated in Subsection (1) applies although
   a. the seller has exercised all possible care in the preparation and sale of his product, and
   b. the user or consumer has not bought the product from or entered into any contractual relation with the seller.

Two points regarding Section 402A merit special emphasis. First, Subsection (1)(a) limits application of the strict liability theory to those engaged in the business of selling the products in question. Second, Subsection (2) makes it clear that negligence and privity are not issues under the strict liability theory.

Thus in certain respects, strict liability may be viewed as an extension of the implied warranty of merchantability, where the warranty theory was applied to foreign objects in food and drink. (Recall our discussion of the "reasonable expectation" and "foreign-natural object" tests.) Taken further, strict liability is applied in cases involving virtually all kinds of goods. Though there is in fact some overlapping here with the warranty theory, actions based on strict liability are nevertheless considered to be actions in tort rather than under warranty.

The crux of a Section 402A action is the sale of a *defective product* which is *unreasonably dangerous* to the *user* or *consumer* or to his property. Section 402A covers only sales of products, not services. A product is defective if it is unreasonably dangerous because of a flaw in the product or a weakness in its design, or because adequate warning of risks and hazards related to the design has not been given.

A strict liability action differs from a negligence action in that the plaintiff need not prove the defect resulted from the defendant's failure to use reasonable care. Though in failure-to-warn cases the manufacturer will almost always be found negligent, the same cannot be said of resellers. New products packaged with inadequate warnings may be resold without subjecting middlemen and retailers to liability under the negligence theory; yet these very resellers could be held liable under Sec. 402A because no fault is required under the strict liability theory.

Defective conditions may result not only from flaws or harmful ingredients within the product, but also from foreign objects in its composition and defects in its container. In this regard, a product is not defective "when it is safe for normal handling or consumption." For example, beer consumed only occasionally and in moderate amounts is probably not harmful. If an adult drinks too much beer at a party and then becomes ill, the seller is probably not liable.

To be safe, a product should be properly packaged and otherwise treated so that it will not deteriorate or be rendered dangerous within a reasonable period of time under normal conditions.

The question of what constitutes an "unreasonably" dangerous product is taken up in Sec. 402A, comments i and k. Presumably, certain products are reasonably dangerous or "unavoidably unsafe"—that is to say, existing technology and scientific knowledge are insufficient to produce a completely safe result. An example often cited is that of the rabies vaccine, which has dangerous side-effects but which is the only existing treatment against a deadly disease. Drugs sold under prescription and experimental treatments also fall within this category. Unavoidably unsafe products must be accompanied by instructions and warnings, so that the user can decide whether to undergo the risks involved. If the harmful consequences of using a product generally exceed the benefits and if safer alternatives are available, a product will be considered unreasonably unsafe. In defining what is meant by "unreasonably unsafe," Sec. 402A also considers the expectations of the ordinary consumer, stating: "The articles sold must be dangerous to an extent beyond that which would be contemplated by the ordinary consumer who purchases it, with the ordinary knowledge common to the community as to its characteristics. . . . Good butter is not unreasonably dangerous merely because, if such be the case, it deposits cholesterol in the arteries and leads to heart attacks; but bad butter, contaminated with poisonous fish oil, is unreasonably dangerous."

Another stipulation in Sec. 402A is that products must be in a defective condition when they leave the seller. The burden of proof lies with the plaintiff to show that the product was defective at the time of sale. Subsequent alteration or further processing may operate to relieve the seller of liability.

In addition, the plaintiff's injury must occur as a result of a defect in the product itself, rather than from conditions surrounding its use or consumption. For example, if a killer bee stings a longshoreman unloading crates of tropical fruit, the fruit company is not necessarily liable under Sec. 402A—first, because there is no proof that the bee was a stowaway in the fruit, and second, because there is no defect inherent in the fruit itself.

In the following case, the strict liability theory was invoked by a plaintiff in an unusual situation. Among other points, the case illustrates that while most courts find a product "unreasonably dangerous" only if it is more dangerous than the average consumer would expect, some jurisdictions judge design defects by a "risk/utility" test.

---

### Patterson v. Rohm Gesellschaft
U.S. District Court,
Northern District of Texas,
608 F.Supp.1206 (1985)

**This strict liability action involves a Rohm .38 caliber revolver, a "Saturday Night Special" manufactured by the defendant. The gun functions as it was intended, by firing a bullet with deadly force when the trigger is intentionally pulled. Unfortunately, the gun was used in a robbery and caused the death of the clerk at the grocery store being robbed. The plaintiff in this action is the mother of the robbery victim. The following summarizes the trial judge's ruling on defendant's motion for summary judgment.**

---

**Decision:** The case was dismissed. Plaintiff presented a very strong case for the proposition that his handgun is unreasonably dangerous. In Texas, whether a design defect is unreasonably dangerous is judged by use of the risk/utility test. The risk from such handguns is very high—handgun use results in 22,000 deaths each year and medical care for gunshot victims exceeds $500 million annually. The utility of handguns is very small—a handgun purchased for self-protection is six times more likely to kill a friend or family member than to repel a burglar, and a person who uses a handgun in self-defense is eight times more likely to be killed than one who quietly acquiesces.

Nonetheless, strict liability is not a viable claim in Texas. Not only must a product be unreasonably dangerous, it must also be *defective*. The risk/utility test does not even come into the picture if the product is not defective. This handgun did just what handguns are designed to do. And plaintiff offered no alternative, safer design for a gun. If the design of this handgun were found to be a basis for strict liability despite its lack of a defect, rifles, Swiss Army knives, axes, whiskey, and automobiles might be similarly challenged.

Ultimately, whether handguns should be banned is a political question for the legislature, not a judicial matter.

## Limitations and Defenses

As we have already observed, the advantages of the strict liability theory are heavily stacked in favor of the consumer. The focus is no longer on the conduct of the defendant, but on the product itself—a far more tangible target. However, the strict liability theory is not an answer to every plaintiff's prayer. Various limitations and defenses operate against him, a number of which are effective in some states but not in others.

**Limitations:** First is the requirement that the product undergo no material change in condition after leaving the defendant's hands. To date, cases litigated have involved only products which are expected to reach the consumer without further processing. The Institute has not issued guidelines to cover circumstances where products are expected to undergo substantial change before reaching the ultimate user.

Second, the plaintiff may find it difficult to prove that a product left the hands of the seller in a defective condition. Where the technology involved in production is complex, witnesses who can testify to defective manufacture may not be available. For this reason, failure-to-warn cases are more common than those alleging errors in the production process.

While strict liability makes recovery easier in certain respects, the requirement that a defective product be "unreasonably dangerous" precludes recovery in many instances. Damages resulting from the failure of a product to perform its ordinary purpose, for example, would not be covered under Sec. 402A. As a result, some states have eliminated the "unreasonably dangerous" requirement.

In addition, Sec. 402A limits recovery to users and consumers (including family members, guests, and employees of the purchaser; and individuals who prepare a product for consumption, who repair a product, and who passively enjoy the benefit of a product, as in the case of passengers on an airplane). Recovery is not always allowed to injured bystanders or others who are brought into contact with the defective product; courts differ on this point, depending on the state. Most states have extended application of the theory to anyone suffering reasonably foreseeable injury because of the defect (such as the driver of a car struck from behind by another vehicle whose brakes were defectively manufactured).

Finally, damage limitations exist. Plaintiffs can usually recover only for property damages and personal injuries, but, as in negligence cases, not for basis-of-the-bargain damages. Recovery for mere economic losses is usually disallowed as inconsistent with the UCC's scheme for warranty recovery. Punitive damages are available in *some* jurisdictions if the defendant evinces utter disregard for the safety of consumers and users of the product. Finally, as we shall discuss in more detail later in the chapter, many states have recently imposed statutory limitations on recoveries in products liability cases in an attempt to stem the "products liability revolution."

**Defenses:** Most states, but not all, follow the Sec. 402A(2)(b) position abolishing the privity requirement. In some states the middleman is protected from Sec. 402A liability by requirements that the manufacturer be included in the plaintiff's suit wherever possible, or that the manufacturer be sued instead of the middleman.

Plaintiff misconduct defenses are generally rather limited in strict liability cases. While simple plaintiff carelessness may absolve the defendant in a negligence suit, it will not do so in a Sec. 402A case. Thus a buyer's failure to inspect the goods or to discover a defect will not prevent recovery of damages. Even misuse of the goods usually will not prevent recovery if the misuse is one which the seller could have reasonably foreseen. Thus, the only defense clearly appropriate to a strict liability claim is *assumption of risk*—the doctrine preventing suit by the buyer who knew of the defect and the resulting danger, but who used the goods anyway. Comparative fault has also been applied in 402A cases by many states adopting this defense.

There has been tremendous variation among the states regarding application of the defenses of simple contributory negligence, unforeseeable product misuse, and knowing assumption of risk in strict liability cases. The following case illustrates one court's thinking on the matter.

### Smith v. Goodyear Tire & Rubber Co.
U.S. District Court, District of Vermont, 600 F.Supp.1561 (1985)

Plaintiff Smith was injured in an automobile accident. He brought this action alleging negligence on the part of the driver, Young, in whose car Smith was riding at the time of the accident, and alleging a strict liability claim against defendant tire manufacturer, the Goodyear Tire & Rubber Company.

Defendants raised a "seat belt defense," asserting that their liability is reduced or completely erased by the fact that Smith was not wearing a seat belt although one was available to him, and that wearing it would have reduced, if not eliminated, his injuries. Plaintiff moved to strike this defense. The following summarizes the trial judge's ruling on the plaintiff's motion.

**Decision:** Although the courts are divided on the issue of the admissibility of evidence regarding the nonuse of seat belts, this court chose to admit it for the jury's consideration even though Vermont law did not require the use of seat belts.

The Restatement Sec. 402A, which is the basis for strict liability, suggests that knowing, voluntary assumption of the risk is a *complete* defense to a strict liability claim, but mere careless failure to discover or guard against a defect should be *no defense* at all. Some courts still follow this view, which was written before the advent of comparative negligence. Vermont, however, has comparative negligence, so the court saw no reason why a plaintiff who did not wear a seat belt should not have his or her recovery reduced (though not barred completely) when some of the injuries sustained could have been avoided by use of a seat belt.

Plaintiff argued that acceptance of this defense will lead defendants to argue that there are other things plaintiff could have done to minimize injury, such as install airbags, adjust the headrest, or drive a "Mack Truck." But allowing such evidence does not create a duty, it merely permits the jury to consider the information regarding the question of negligence. And the question is whether the plaintiff acted *reasonably* under the circumstances, not whether there was any possible means by which plaintiff could have reduced injuries. ■

---

In conclusion, the strict liability doctrine favors plaintiffs in that it possesses most of the advantages of the warranty and negligence theories, namely: (1) few defenses against liability can be raised by the defendant; (2) disclaimers are ineffectual; (3) privity is not required; and (4) buyers must prove only that goods were *dangerously defective* when they left the seller's hands and that this defect caused the buyer's injury.

On the other hand, disadvantages to the plaintiff include (1) applicability of Sec. 402A only against sellers who are merchants; and (2) availability of damages only for physical injuries to person and property, and not for economic injuries.

## FEDERAL CONSUMER LEGISLATION

Over the years Congress has enacted a number of federal regulatory laws dealing with the safety and quality of goods. For the most part these laws have focused solely on protecting ultimate consumers from physical harm, and until recently, they were enacted piecemeal and were rather narrow in scope. Examples include the Food, Drug, and Cosmetic Act (1938), the Flammable Fabrics Act (1953), the Refrigerator Safety Act (1956), the Hazardous Substances Act (1960), and the Poison Prevention Packaging Act (1970).

### *Consumer Product Safety Act*

In 1972 Congress enacted the Consumer Product Safety Act—the first law to deal with the safety of consumer products in general—and created a federal agency, the Consumer Product Safety Commission (CPSC), to administer it.[4]

This agency possesses broad powers and performs many functions, ranging from safety research and testing to preparing safety rules and standards for over 10,000 products. It has the power to ban or re-

---

[4] Some consumer products are not covered by the Consumer Product Safety Act because they come under the aegis of other federal laws. The most important of these are food, drugs, and cosmetics, which are regulated by the Food and Drug Administration under the Food, Drug, and Cosmetic Act. Automobiles are also excluded because of coverage by other legislation.

call products and to require special labeling in certain circumstances. It can levy civil penalties on those who violate the Act and criminal penalties on those who willfully violate it. Yet despite the extensive range of its power, the CPSC has been criticized for not issuing sufficient standards to ensure the integrity of consumer products. In 1990, Congress raised the civil penalties for CPSA violations from $2,000 to $5,000, required manufacturers to report repeated and serious problems with products to the agency, and made other changes to strengthen the CPSC.

## *Magnuson-Moss Warranty Act*

In 1975 Congress passed the **Magnuson-Moss Warranty Act.** Like the federal legislation discussed above, this statute is consumer-oriented. It applies only to purchases by ultimate consumers for personal, family, or household purposes, not to transactions in commercial or industrial settings. The Warranty Act, which is usually enforced by the Federal Trade Commission (FTC), does not regulate the safety or quality of consumer goods. Instead it prevents deceptive warranty practices, makes consumer warranties easier to understand, and provides an effective means of enforcing warranty obligations. The federal Warranty Act is limited to consumer transactions, and it modifies the UCC warranty rules in some respects; in nonconsumer transactions, the UCC rules continue in effect.

The type of warranty to which the Act applies is much more narrowly defined than is an express warranty under the UCC. Specifically, it is (1) any *written* affirmation of fact made by a supplier to a purchaser relating to the quality or performance of a product and affirming that the product is defect-free or that it will meet a specified level of performance over a period of time; or (2) a written undertaking to "refund, repair, replace, or take other action" if a product fails to meet written specifications. Obviously express warranties which are not in writing, such as those created by verbal description or by sample, will continue to be governed solely by the UCC, even though a consumer transaction is involved.

The Warranty Act does not *require* anyone to give a warranty on consumer goods. It applies only if the seller *voluntarily chooses* to make an express written warranty (perhaps in an effort to render a product more competitive). When a written warranty is provided for a product costing $10 or more, it must be labeled as either "full" or "limited." When the cost of goods exceeds $15, the warranty must be contained in a single document, must be written in clear language, and must make a number of disclosures, including (1) a description of items covered and those excluded, along with specific service guarantees; (2) instructions on how to proceed in the event of product failure; (3) the identity of those to whom the warranty is extended; and (4) limitations on the warranty period.

Under a full warranty, the warrantor must assume certain minimum duties and obligations.[5] For instance, he must agree to *repair or replace* any malfunctioning or defective product within a "reasonable" time and without charge. If the warrantor makes a reasonable number of attempts to remedy the defect and is unable to do so, the consumer can choose to receive a *cash refund* or *replacement* of the product without charge. No *time limitation* can be placed on a full warranty; and consequential damages (such as for personal injury or property damage) can be disclaimed only if the limitation is *conspicuous.*

A written warranty which does not meet the minimum requirements must be designated conspicuously as a *limited warranty.* It may cover, for example, parts but not labor, or it may levy shipping and handling fees. If a time limit (such as twenty-four months) is all that prevents the warranty from being a full one, it can be designated as a "full twenty-four month warranty."

Since its purpose is to regulate *written* warranties, the Warranty Act generally does not concern the implied warranties of merchantability and fitness for a particular purpose. These are governed by the UCC; and as we have seen, the UCC allows implied warranties to be disclaimed. However, drafters of the Warranty Act saw fit to limit the use of disclaimers where written warranties are involved, because of certain abusive practices prevalent at the time: Sellers were providing limited express warranties in bold print and then disclaiming implied warranties, thus leaving the consumer with few rights while appearing to offer substantial protection.

For this reason, the Magnuson-Moss Act *prohibits a disclaimer of implied warranties* (1) when an express written warranty is given, whether full or

---

[5] Only the person who actually makes the written warranty—no one else in the chain of distribution—is responsible under the Warranty Act.

limited, or (2) when a service contract is made with the consumer within ninety days after the sale.[6] If the written warranty specifies a *time* limitation, however, implied warranties may be suspended by a disclaimer effective *after* the written warranty expires.

The Warranty Act is usually enforced by the FTC, but the Attorney General or an injured consumer can also initiate an action if informal procedures for settling disputes prove ineffective. Sellers are authorized to dictate the informal procedures by which a particular dispute is to be settled. If these procedures follow FTC guidelines, the consumer cannot resort to court action until all established means have been exhausted.

## LEGISLATIVE LIMITATIONS ON PRODUCTS LIABILITY REVOLUTION

From 1960 until the mid-1980s, the general trend in products liability law was strongly pro-plaintiff. New theories allowed new classes of injured persons to sue defendants that had never before been vulnerable to suit. Injured consumers have been well served, and it is certainly arguable that products liability litigation has been the most influential factor in bringing about improved product designs and safety practices that have saved thousands of lives.

Recent years, however, have seen a countervailing pressure to reform products liability law in order to roll back the "products liability revolution." Damage awards have increased insurance premiums, raised the prices of some products, induced some companies to cease manufacturing certain products, and arguably, caused American business to suffer a competitive disadvantage abroad. The expense of designing eminently safe products, coupled with insurance rates 20 times higher than those in Europe, have added significantly to the costs of production. The apparent "explosion" of products liability has raised a storm of protest among manufacturers and sellers, and at present, almost every state has enacted or is considering tort reform.

Some states have already placed ceilings on damage awards in product liability suits. Others have enacted provisions which prohibit advances in technology from being used, with the benefit of hindsight, against manufacturers. More than one-third of the states have enacted **statutes of repose.** These provide a time period after which the manufacturer is not liable for injuries caused by a product, the statute of limitations notwithstanding. The periods range from 5 to 12 years and begin when a product is sold to an ultimate consumer (one who does not purchase for resale). The purpose of these provisions is to protect manufacturers from liability in situations where defects do not manifest themselves until many years after the product is sold.

## *Federal Products Liability Legislation*

There is substantial variation in the details of products liability law among the 50 state jurisdictions. A manufacturer seeking to market its products on a nationwide basis faces a formidable task in conforming its actions to these varying standards. While some maintain that optimal products liability law will eventually develop at the state level, the advantages of a comprehensive federal law are obvious.

Several products liability reform measures have been introduced in Congress in recent years, though none has passed. Most bills have sought not only to produce national uniformity, but also to limit product liability recoveries through a number of means. The leading bills have typically sought to (1) eliminate strict liability, returning to a negligence standard; (2) allow recoveries for manufacturing defects only when the manufacturer departs from *its own* standards or specifications; (3) place limits on recoveries for pain and suffering awards; (4) substantially limit the availability of punitive damages; and (5) introduce a 2-year statute of limitations and a 25-year statute of repose. While such a bill, if enacted into law, would not satisfy the interests of labor and consumer groups, it would bring uniformity to the area of products liability and afford some relief to manufacturers from the high costs they have come to bear under the strict liability theory.

## SUMMARY

A plaintiff injured by a defective product has several possible legal theories to pursue. If the defendant, be it retailer, wholesaler, or manufacturer, made any representations or affirmations of fact regarding the product's performance, an express warranty theory is available if the promises were breached. Although salespersons are allowed to "puff" their product, specific promises made orally or in written "guarantees" or in product advertising may form the basis for an express warranty claim.

---

[6] Under a *service contract* the seller agrees to service and repair a product for a set period of time in return for a fixed fee.

Even if the seller makes no representations about a product, the law implies a promise that the good is "merchantable"—of average quality acceptable in the trade of such goods—any time a merchant (one who makes a living selling such goods) sells a consumer a product. Additionally, if that merchant sells a good knowing that the purchaser needs it for a specific purpose and is relying on the seller's expertise to provide a product that can fulfill that purpose, a warranty of fitness for a particular purpose will be implied by the law.

Both implied warranties may be disclaimed, and recovery may be limited *if* UCC rules are strictly followed and the disclaimer or limitation is not "unconscionable."

A consumer injured by a defective product can recover against any parties the consumer can prove negligently designed, manufactured, tested, or marketed the product. Careless failure to warn of the unavoidable dangers of a product can also be grounds for suit.

Unlike the negligence theory, which focuses on the conduct of the defendant, the strict liability theory focuses only on the product. If the product is defective and unreasonably dangerous, defendants in the distribution chain (manufacturer-wholesaler-retailer) are liable for injuries caused by the defects, no matter how careful they were.

These remedies are supplemented by several federal statutes designed to protect the consumer, most importantly the Magnuson-Moss Act dealing with express warranties and the Consumer Product Safety Act.

Many believe the law of products liability has become so "pro-consumer" that drastic reforms are needed. Many state legislators have passed reform legislation which, for example, imposes "statutes of repose" to prevent recovery for injuries caused by old machines and limits on certain types of damage recoveries. As this chapter is written, Congress is considering federal legislation which would dramatically change the law that has evolved during the "consumer revolution" of the past 25 years.

## KEY TERMS

**Warranty**
**Express warranty**
**Implied warranty of merchantability**
**Implied warranty of fitness for a particular purpose**
**Warranty of title**
**Disclaimer**
**Privity of contract**
**Product misuse**
**Assumption of risk**
*Res ipsa loquitur*
**Strict liability**
**Magnuson-Moss Warranty Act**
**Statute of repose**

## QUESTIONS AND PROBLEMS

1. In August 1980, ITT loaned money to McGinn in return for a security interest in a Caterpillar hydraulic excavator. ITT properly perfected its security interest. In the summer of 1981, ITT learned that McGinn was having financial problems and had discussions with him, the contents of which are disputed. The excavator was sold by McGinn at auction through Vilsmeier in October 1981. Prior to the auction, Vilsmeier announced that the excavator was being sold free and clear of any liens or security interests. Arnold bought the equipment. In October 1983, however, Arnold surrendered the excavator to ITT on advice of counsel in light of ITT's security interest in the machine. Arnold sued Vilsmeier for breach of warranty of title. The trial judge directed a verdict for Arnold. Vilsmeier claimed that this was improper, for it prevented him from attempting to prove that ITT had waived its security interest in its conversation with McGinn. Did the trial judge err? (*Frank Arnold Contractors, Inc. v. Vilsmeier Auction Co.,* 806 F.2d 462, 3d Cir. 1986.)

2. Walcott & Steele, Inc., sold seed to Carpenter. State law required the package label to give the percentage of germination. The label on the seed bought by Carpenter carried the required statement, but the seed did not perform at the listed percentage. Carpenter sued for breach of an express warranty, which he claimed was created by the statement regarding percentage of germination. Did Carpenter prevail? Discuss. (*Walcott & Steele, Inc. v. Carpenter,* 436 S.W.2d 820, 1969.)

3. Kassab, a cattle breeder, purchased feed which had been manufactured by Central Soya. The feed was intended for breeding cattle, but Central had accidentally included an ingredient that should be used only for beef cattle. After eating the feed, Kassab's cattle grew and prospered. Kassab was upset, however, when he discovered that the mistakenly included ingredient had caused his entire herd of prize breeding cattle to become sterile. He sued Central for breach of the implied warranty of merchantability. Central claimed that there was no such breach because the feed had made the cattle gain weight exactly as it was supposed to do. Is Central's contention correct? Explain. (*Kassab v. Central Soya,* 246 A.2d 848, 1968.)

4. Henningsen bought a new automobile from Bloomfield Motors, Inc. Only ten days after the purchase, when the Chrysler had only 468 miles on the odometer, something under the hood cracked and the car veered 90 degrees into a brick wall. Henningsen's wife was seriously injured. When Henningsen sued Bloomfield and Chrysler on an implied warranty of merchantability theory, they raised as a defense a clause in the purchase contract which provided that the manufacturer's "obligation under this warranty [is] limited to making good at its factory any part or parts thereof which shall, within 90 days after delivery of such vehicle to the original purchaser or before such vehicle has been driven 4,000 miles, whichever event shall first occur, be returned to it with transportation charges prepaid and which its examination shall disclose to its satisfaction to have been thus defective; this warranty being expressly in lieu of all other warranties expressed or implied." Does this disclaimer bar plaintiff's suit? Discuss. (*Henningsen v. Bloomfield Motors, Inc.*, 161 A.2d 69, N.J. 1960.)

5. Johnson, plaintiff, raised hogs. He needed ventilating fans for his hog barn. He told the supplier's representative of his needs. When asked, plaintiff told the representative that there were no unusual humidity or dust problems in the hog barn, but this was not accurate. Plaintiff was advised to purchase certain fans with "open" motors not sealed off from outside air. He bought them but they malfunctioned because of clogging from humidity and feed dust. Many hogs died; plaintiff sued the supplier and the manufacturer, among others, for breach of the implied warranty of fitness for a particular purpose. Should plaintiff prevail? Discuss. (*Johnson v. Lappo Lumber Co.*, 181 N.W.2d 316, Mich.App. 1970.)

6. Marie, a college freshman, bought a bottle of tequila made by D. One evening she and some friends drank straight shots of the tequila, and she went to her room about 10 P.M. She was found dead the next morning, apparently as a direct result of acute alcohol intoxication. Marie's family sued on the basis of strict liability, claiming that the tequila contained a marketing defect because it was an unreasonably dangerous product in the absence of a warning and/or instructions for its safe use. Is this a good claim? (*Brune v. Brown Forman Corp.*, 758 S.W.2d 827, Tex.App. 1988.)

7. Daniell felt overburdened and wished to commit suicide. Seeking a place from which she could not escape, she climbed into the trunk of a 1973 Ford LTD and latched it. Later she changed her mind about suicide, but could not escape because the trunk contained no internal release mechanism. She was locked in the trunk for 9 days and suffered injuries before a passerby heard her cries for help. She sued Ford on the grounds of strict liability, claiming that the trunk was defective because it had no internal release mechanism. Is this a good claim? By what standard should the claim be judged? (*Daniell v. Ford Motor Corp.*, 581 F.Supp. 728, D.N.M. 1984.)

8. Laaperi bought a smoke detector from Sears and installed it in his bedroom. The detector was designed to be powered by AC (electrical) current. Six months later a fire broke out in the Laaperi home, killing three of Laaperi's children. The smoke detector did not sound an alarm on the night of the fire, because the fire started in a short circuit in an electrical cord. The smoke detector was connected to the circuit which shorted and cut off. Laaperi sued Sears claiming that it had breached a duty to warn him that the very short circuit which might ignite a fire in his home could, at the same time, incapacitate the smoke detector. Is this a viable theory? Discuss. (*Laaperi v. Sears, Roebuck & Co., Inc.*, 787 F.2d 726, 1st Cir. 1986.)

9. The Hauters, plaintiffs, purchased a "Golfing Gizmo" for their son from defendants. The device was designed to provide driving practice for novice golfers. On the package it said, "Completely safe ball will not hit player." But the Hauter's son, while using it as directed, was hit in the head by the ball and severely injured. Plaintiffs sued for breach of express and implied warranties, but defendants argued that their only obligation was to provide a device that was safe when the ball was hit "properly" and that a drawing on the package depicted a golfer hitting the ball "properly." Is this a good defense? Discuss. (*Hauter v. Zogarts,* 534 P.2d 377, Cal. 1975.)

10. Welch, plaintiff, bought a new Dodge station wagon from Fitzgerald-Hicks Dodge, Inc. (FHD). Over the next six months the car required a large number of repairs—"repairs too numerous to list," in the words of the higher court. While most repairs were satisfactory, the major continuing problem was a "shimmying" that could be felt when the car was driven. After many unsuccessful attempts by FHD to remedy that problem, plaintiff left the car with FHD with a letter stating that he was revoking his acceptance. Plaintiff then brought this action against FHD and Chrysler Corporation, the manufacturer, to recover the purchase price. Among the numerous issues at trial was the major question as to whether the shimmy caused the car to be unmerchantable. On that point plaintiff introduced evidence that the shimmy, while reduced, was still noticeable and bothersome; defendants, on the other hand, contended that, taken as a whole, the car was of such a nature that it would "pass without objection within the automobile industry." The jury found the car to be unmerchantable; on appeal, one of the questions was whether the jury's finding of unmerchantability was supported by the evidence (in view of evidence that all other aspects of the car were, by that time, satisfactory). Do you think the jury's verdict should be upheld? Discuss. (*Welch v. Fitzgerald-Hicks Dodge, Inc.*, 430 A.2d 144, 1981.)

CHAPTER 23

# SALES

## PERFORMANCE AND REMEDIES

In this final chapter on the law of sales we will discuss two subject areas: (1) performance of the sale contract (the obligations of both seller and buyer that are necessary to fulfill their agreement) and (2) remedies (the various avenues available to a seller or buyer if the other fails to live up to the contract obligations).

## PERFORMANCE OF THE SALE CONTRACT

Basically, the seller's obligation is to deliver goods that conform to the contract and to any applicable warranties, and the buyer's obligation is to accept and pay for them. However, *total performance* by the seller may involve a number of other aspects. In addition, several problem areas in the buyer's basic obligations of acceptance and payment require a closer look. The most important thing to remember is that the performance obligations of seller and buyer are ultimately controlled by the agreement of the parties themselves. The primary purposes of the UCC provisions in this area are to help in interpreting the agreement and to establish rules on matters not covered by the agreement.

### *Seller's Obligations*

**Tender of Delivery:** How does a seller deliver the goods? Must he or she actually put them into the buyer's hands? Has the seller performed the obligation if the buyer has changed his or her mind and refuses to take the goods? The answer to these questions is that the seller fully performs the delivery obligation by "tendering" delivery. According to Sec. 2-503(1), to make a **tender of delivery** the seller must "put and hold conforming goods at the buyer's disposition and give the buyer any notification reasonably necessary to enable him to take delivery." That is, the seller must keep the goods available for the period of time reasonably necessary to enable the buyer to take possession.

Tender must be made at a *reasonable hour.* Suppose, for example, that prices have risen since the making of the contract. The seller cannot perform by tendering delivery at three o'clock in the morning (unless the agreement so provided) in the hope that the buyer will reject the tender.

If the agreement makes no mention of the *place of delivery,* it should be at the seller's place of business or, if the seller has none, at his or her residence. However, if at the time the contract is made the goods are identified and both parties know that they are located at some other location, that place is the place of delivery.

Usually the parties will have agreed on the place of delivery, and most agreements fall within either of two categories:

**1.** The buyer agrees to pick up the goods at a particular place without the seller having any responsibility for moving them.

**2.** The seller undertakes responsibility for transporting the goods to the buyer.

The first category may involve an agreement that the buyer will call for the goods at the seller's premises. Or the goods may be in the possession of a bailee (such as a warehouseman), with the buyer being responsible for picking them up. Where the goods are held by a bailee, tender of delivery by the seller is a matter of paperwork. He or she must either deliver to the buyer a *negotiable document of title* (a warehouse receipt) or obtain the *bailee's acknowledgment* that the buyer is entitled to possession (see Chapter 20 for a discussion on documents of title). Delivery by the seller of a nonnegotiable document of title is a proper tender of delivery only if the buyer

353

does not object. Similarly, a mere written direction to the bailee to hand the goods over to the buyer (with no acknowledgment by the bailee of the buyer's rights) is a sufficient tender only if the buyer does not object.

The second category of agreement, in which the seller ships the goods, is further divided into shipment contracts and destination contracts. In a *shipment contract* the seller performs his or her obligations by tendering delivery at the point of shipment. Sec. 2-504 provides that, unless otherwise agreed:

**1.** The seller must put the goods in the possession of a carrier (such as a trucking or railway company), and the choice of carrier must be reasonable under the circumstances. Further, the seller's contract with the carrier for transporting the goods must also be reasonable under the circumstances. (For example, a contract with the carrier that understates the value of the goods for insurance purposes is not considered reasonable.)

**2.** The seller must obtain and promptly deliver in proper form any document (such as a bill of lading) necessary for the buyer to take possession of the goods.

**3.** The seller must promptly notify the buyer of shipment.

If the seller fails to meet the above requirements, the buyer can reject delivery only if a material loss or delay resulted—unless the parties have agreed differently. For instance, they might agree that failure to give prompt notification is a ground for rejection regardless of the consequences of the failure.

The seller's obligation in a *destination contract* is not fulfilled until delivery is tendered at the destination. Since the seller's required performance extends to the buyer's doorstep, so to speak, special provisions regarding selection of a carrier are not needed for the buyer's protection. The general tender requirements already set forth are sufficient. At the point of destination, the seller must put and hold the goods at the buyer's disposition at a reasonable hour, for a reasonable period of time, and with proper notice. And, of course, the seller must furnish any required documents. Figure 23.1 illustrates the above requirements.

**Commercial Shipping Terms:** Sales contracts frequently contain terms that have well-established meanings in the commercial world but that are somewhat mysterious to the newcomer. For example, the contract may include phrases such as *FOB Detroit* or *FAS vessel, New York*. These indicate the parties' agreement on particular terms of shipment and are treated as shipping terms even when they appear only in connection with the price ("2.00/lb. FOB seller's plant"). Some of the more common terms are defined below.

*FOB ("free on board")*. If the named location following the FOB designation is the point of shipment, the agreement is a *shipment contract*. If the vehicle of transportation at the point of shipment is also referred to, the seller must not only put the goods into the possession of a carrier but also bear the expense of loading them on board. An example is "FOB Car 235Y, Mo. Pac. R.R. Depot, Dallas." If the named location following the FOB designation is the destination, the agreement is a *destination contract*.

*FAS ("free alongside" vessel)*. FAS, frequently found in sale contracts where the goods are to be transported by seagoing vessel, indicates that a *shipment contract* has been made. The seller performs by delivering the goods alongside (on the dock next to) the vessel on which they are to be loaded, but does not bear the expense of loading.

*Ex-ship ("from the carrying vessel")*. The phrase *ex-ship*, also a maritime term, is actually the reverse of FAS. It denotes a *destination contract* and indicates that the seller's obligation extends to unloading the goods at the port of destination.

*CIF ("cost, insurance, and freight") and C & F ("cost and freight")*. CIF and C & F are also found almost exclusively in maritime agreements. CIF indicates that the price paid by the buyer includes the cost of the goods, insurance while they are in transit, and all freight charges. C & F means that the price includes the cost of the goods and freight charges but not insurance. Although the terms indicate that the agreement is a *shipment contract,* their inclusion means that the seller assumes obligations in addition to those of an ordinary shipment contract. The C & F term obligates the seller to see that the goods are loaded and to pay the freight charges. The CIF term further obligates the seller to obtain appropriate insurance coverage.

**The Perfect Tender Rule:** At common law there developed a doctrine known as the **perfect tender rule.** Under this rule, the seller's tender of delivery was required to conform in every detail to the terms

**Figure 23.1 Seller's Obligations**

- Seller to ship
  - Shipment contract → Seller must deliver goods to carrier. He must:
    1) deliver conforming goods to carrier.
    2) make reasonable contract for delivery.
    3) deliver any necessary documents to buyer.
    4) promptly notify buyer of shipment (but failure to notify is ground for rejection only if delay or loss results).
  - Destination contract → Seller must tender delivery to buyer. He must:
    1) deliver and hold conforming goods at destination.
    2) give notification necessary for buyer to take delivery.
    3) tender any required documents in proper form.
- Buyer to pick up
  - At seller's business → Seller must:
    1) notify buyer within a reasonable time that goods are ready.
    2) keep goods available for a reasonable time.
  - In bailee's hands → Seller must tender negotiable document of title to the buyer or obtain the bailee's acknowledgment of buyer's right to possession.

---

of the agreement. In other words, the doctrine of substantial performance (discussed in Chapter 18) did not apply to contracts for the sale of goods. An extreme illustration of the perfect tender rule is found in *Filley v. Pope,* 115 U.S. 213 (1885). The seller agreed to sell pig iron to the buyer, the contract calling for shipment to New Orleans from Glasgow, Scotland. When the time for shipment arrived, no ships were available at Glasgow. The seller's factory in Scotland was halfway between the ports of Glasgow and Leith; and since vessels were available at Leith, he sent the iron to Leith for shipment. The buyer rejected the goods when they arrived. The Supreme Court held that the buyer was entitled to do so, because a contract calling for shipment from Glasgow is not fulfilled by a shipment from Leith even though no delay results.

UCC Sec. 2-601 essentially restates the perfect tender rule by providing that "if the goods or the tender of delivery fail in *any respect* to conform to the contract," the buyer is not obligated to accept them. (Emphasis added.) Because the perfect tender rule has both limitations and exceptions, it is not absolute.

### Limitations of the Perfect Tender Rule:

***Parties' Agreement:*** The parties themselves can, of course, limit the perfect tender rule by agreement. For example, they might agree that a delivery of defective goods cannot be rejected if the seller repairs or replaces the defective parts.[1]

***Trade Usage, Etc.:*** Because the agreement of the parties to a sale of goods includes that part of their bargain found in usage of trade, course of dealing, and course of performance, sometimes these concepts limit the perfect tender rule. For example, if trade usage in a particular industry recognizes that a contract calling for 100 percent pure industrial plastic is satisfied by 99 percent purity, a buyer has no grounds to object when plastic of 99 percent purity is delivered. This is not an exception to the perfect tender rule; the trade usage simply helps define what constitutes a perfect tender in these circumstances.

***Cure:*** At common law the seller had only one chance to make a perfect tender. Section 2-508 of the UCC gives more latitude to the seller of goods, in an attempt to encourage the parties to mitigate losses by working out their differences. Subsection (1) provides that where the seller makes a tender of delivery that is rejected as nonconforming but the *time for performance has not yet expired,* if the seller promptly notifies the buyer of an intention to "cure," he or she can then make a conforming delivery (or perhaps repair the defective goods) *before* expiration of the time for performance.

Subsection (2) of 2-508 allows cure even *after* the agreed-upon time for performance, where the buyer rejects a nonconforming tender which the seller had *reasonable grounds to believe would be acceptable.* This can occur, for example, (1) where a prior course of dealing between the parties has led the seller to believe that the nonconforming goods would be acceptable because the buyer has accepted such goods before, or (2) where the seller delivers goods that he or she believes to be conforming but which contain a *latent* defect that is only discovered after delivery. Assume that a retailer delivered to a customer a television sealed in its factory crate. If, when uncrated in the customer's home, the set had a defective picture, a court would probably find that the retailer had the right to cure after promptly informing the customer of its intent to do so.

Note that the provisions allowing a seller to cure do not preclude a suit by the buyer for damages caused, for example, by the delay in delivering conforming goods.

***Good Faith:*** As noted before, UCC Sec. 1-203 imposes on all parties to the sale of goods a general obligation of good faith. Although this duty applies to all aspects of sales contracts, it has particular application to the perfect tender rule. Assume that a buyer contracts to pay a specified amount for delivery of one million widgets. Soon after the contract is entered into, the market price for widgets drops substantially, so that the buyer wishes to evade its contractual obligation. The good faith provision should prevent the buyer from rejecting the seller's goods on the basis of an insignificant deviation from contractual specifications where the buyer is receiving the true measure of what he bargained for and is attempting to reject the goods for reasons other than the deviation.

The "good faith" limitation is discussed in the following case.

---

[1] However, insofar as such a clause limits the application of an implied warranty, it must meet all the requirements of the UCC regarding disclaimers of warranty. In a consumer transaction it also must comply with the Magnuson-Moss Warranty Act.

---

**Printing Center of Texas, Inc. v. Supermind Publishing Co.**
Court of Appeals of Texas,
669 S.W.2d 779 (1984)

Appellee Supermind Publishing Co. sued appellant Printing Center of Texas for refund of a deposit made under a written contract to print 5,000 books. Appellee claimed that it rightfully rejected the books upon delivery under UCC 2-601, and that it had the right to cancel the contract and recover its deposit under 2-711. The trial court ruled for appellee, ordering refund of the $2,900 deposit. Appellant appealed.

---

**Decision:** Affirmed. The right to reject is governed by UCC 2-601, which states in part that "if the goods or tender of deliv-

*(continued)*

ery fail in any respect to conform to the contract, the buyer may (1) reject the whole. . . ." Of course, this right is qualified by UCC 1-203's good faith provision, but there is no evidence that Supermind rejected in bad faith (i.e., to escape the bargain, rather than to avoid acceptance of a tender which impairs the value of the bargain to him). There were many problems with the books, including wrinkled and crooked pages, off-center cover art, and inadequate perforations, that justified rejection. ■

---

**Exceptions to the Perfect Tender Rule:**

*Buyer Revocation of Acceptance:* Assume that a seller delivers nonconforming goods and a buyer, perhaps because of an inadequate inspection, accepts those goods. Only later does the buyer discover the nonconformity. At that point the buyer may well attempt to *revoke his acceptance,* as he is allowed to do under UCC 2-608. However, once the buyer has accepted delivery, the perfect tender rule no longer applies. While a buyer may reject an acceptance for *any* nonconformity, he may revoke an acceptance only by showing that the defect "substantially impaired" the value of the goods. This exception to the perfect tender rule makes sense because the longer buyers have the goods, the higher the likelihood that any defects were caused by them, the greater the benefit buyers may have derived from use of the goods, and the greater the loss to the sellers through depreciation or market fluctuations when the goods are thrown back on them.

*Rejection in Installment Contracts:* An **installment contract** is defined in Sec. 2-612 as one requiring or authorizing the delivery of goods in separate lots to be separately accepted. Under Sec. 2-612(2), a buyer can reject a particular installment only if the nonconformity *substantially impairs the value of that installment and cannot be cured.* If the seller gives adequate assurance of cure, the buyer must accept the installment. Under Sec. 2-612(3), the *entire* contract is breached if the nonconformity of the installment substantially impairs the value *of the whole contract.* Again, the "substantial impairment" standard clearly creates an exception to the perfect tender rule. However, in subsection (3) the buyer reinstates the contract if he or she accepts a nonconforming installment without seasonably notifying the seller of cancellation.

*Improper Shipping Arrangements:* Remember that in a shipping contract the seller must (1) act appropriately in selecting and making a transportation contract with the carrier, (2) provide any documents necessary for the buyer to take possession of the goods, and (3) promptly notify the buyer of the shipment. However, under Sec. 2-504, failure by the seller to fulfill obligations (1) (contract) or (3) (notification) entitles the buyer to reject the delivery only if *material loss or delay* has resulted. (If the UCC had existed at the time of *Filley v. Pope,* the outcome of that case would have been different.) There is no such exception to the perfect tender rule for the obligation to tender documents.

*Substitute Means of Delivery:* In some cases the parties specifically agree on the type of facilities to be used in loading, shipping, or unloading the goods. If, through no fault of either party, these agreed-upon facilities become unavailable or impracticable, but a *commercially reasonable substitute* is available, the seller and buyer are required to use the substitute.

**Effect of Unforeseen Occurrences:** The common-law rules applying to contracts in general also apply to sale of goods contracts unless they have been altered by the UCC. Thus, if the specific subject matter of the sale contract has been destroyed through no fault of either party, or if performance has become illegal because of a change in the law, both parties are excused from their contractual obligations.

Suppose that seller S and buyer B have contracted for the sale of one hundred head of cattle. If the cattle are damaged or destroyed after risk of loss has passed to B (as would be the case in a shipment contract if the carrier is involved in an accident while transporting the cattle), then obviously S has already performed and B will have to pay for the goods. On the other hand, if a flash flood on S's land destroys the cattle *before* risk of loss has passed to B, then the financial loss will have to be borne by S, and B will not have to pay for the cattle.

If the destruction occurs before the risk of loss has passed, a further question remains: Is S excused from performing his part of the bargain? If the contract was for the sale of one hundred head of cattle but not necessarily the specific cattle that were destroyed, the answer is no. Not only has S suffered the loss but he also must still perform the contract by delivering one hundred head of cattle. But if the contract was for the sale of the specific cattle that were subsequently destroyed, S is excused from his obligation and is under no further duty to perform. This common-law rule is restated in UCC Sec. 2-613. (In addition to the basic rule covering cases of *total* destruction, Sec. 2-613 also covers cases where the loss is only *partial.* In such a situation B has a choice. He can treat the contract as canceled, thereby excusing both parties from their obligations. Or he can accept the goods in their damaged condition with an allowance deducted from the contract price.)

***Commercial Impracticability:*** The UCC also contains a provision, Sec. 2-615, to deal with certain types of unforeseen occurrences that do not result in damage to the specifically identified subject matter of the contract. If, because of unforeseen circumstances, delivery of the goods becomes "commercially impracticable," the parties are excused from their obligations. Of course, an increase in costs or change in the market price alone is not enough to relieve the seller of his or her responsibility; the existence of such risks is one of the main reasons for making binding contracts. But where the difficulty is of an *extraordinary* nature, such as the destruction of a source of supply that had been agreed upon or contemplated by both parties, the seller is excused. In such a case, however, the seller must have taken *all reasonable steps* to assure himself or herself that the source would not fail. The seller also may be excused from delivering if a severe shortage of raw materials due to such events as war, embargo, or local crop failure causes a drastic increase in cost or completely prevents the seller from securing necessary supplies. A seller seeking to be excused because of commercial impracticability, however, must *promptly notify* the buyer of the problem.

Sometimes the commercial impracticability affects only *part* of the seller's capacity to perform. For instance, the unforeseen occurrence might result in a material delay or in a diminution of the quantity of available goods. Where the available quantity is diminished, Sec. 2-615 requires the seller to *allocate deliveries* among customers, including all customers then under contract and, if he or she chooses, regular customers not currently under contract. The seller must give *prompt notification* of either a delay or an allocation and, in the case of an allocation, must make an estimate of the quota available.

***Buyer's Choices:*** When the buyer is notified of a significant delay or an allocation justified by commercial impracticability, he or she has a choice of cancelling the contract or keeping it in effect. To cancel, the buyer can either notify the seller or merely remain silent. However, if the seller's inability relates only to a particular delivery in an installment contract, the buyer can cancel the contract only if the value of the *whole contract* is substantially impaired. If the buyer has a right to cancel but wishes to keep the contract alive, he or she must give written notice to the seller indicating agreement to the delay or allocation. This notice by the buyer actually amounts to a modification of the contract and must be made within a reasonable time, not exceeding 30 days.

The following case applies the rules of 2-615.[2]

---

[2] (Note that the doctrine of commercial impracticability, along with the related common-law concepts of impossibility and frustration of purpose, were discussed in detail in Chapter 18. It may be helpful to reread *Northern Indiana Public Service Co. v. Carbon County Coal Co.* in that chapter.)

---

**Waldinger Corporation v. CRS Group Engineers, Inc.**
U.S. Seventh Circuit Court of Appeals, 775 F.2d 781 (1985)

A city sanitation district hired Dietz as engineer to prepare specifications for two wastewater treatment facilities required by the EPA. The specifications for required belt-filter presses included both performance capabilities and mechanical components. Waldinger Corporation, a mechanical contractor preparing to bid on the mechanical portions, received a quotation for the belt presses from Ashbrook. Waldinger then bid successfully on the project. Ashbrook, however, was unable to supply the equipment described in the specifications set forth in its contract with Waldinger. Waldinger obtained the equipment from the Ralph B. Carter Company and sued Ashbrook for breach of contract.

*(continued)*

In defense, Ashbrook claimed impracticability of performance because of Dietz's intentional or negligent drafting of restrictive specifications. The trial judge found that Dietz had intentionally prepared exclusionary specifications that could be met only by equipment made by Carter, and insisted without justification that Ashbrook comply with them. Thus, he held that Ashbrook was excused from performing its contract with Waldinger because performance was impracticable. Waldinger appealed.

---

**Decision:** Affirmed. UCC 2-615 sets forth the requirements for excuse of performance: (1) a contingency has occurred; (2) the contingency has made performance impracticable; and (3) the nonoccurrence of that contingency was a basic assumption upon which the contract was made. The rationale of the defense of commercial impracticability is that circumstances causing the breach were "so vitally different from what was anticipated that the contract cannot be reasonably thought to govern." In this case, EPA regulations were expressly made part of the contract. Those regulations specifically prohibit exclusionary specifications. Yet, that is exactly what was provided, rendering Ashbrook's promised performance commercially impracticable. This was especially troublesome, since no Carter machine of this type was in operation, and the person who drew the specifications had done no independent study to determine if the Carter machine could even perform as promised. ∎

---

## Buyer's Obligations

When the seller has made a sufficient tender of delivery, the burden then falls on the buyer to perform his or her part of the contract.

**Providing Facilities:** Unless otherwise agreed, the buyer must furnish facilities that are reasonably suited for receipt of the goods.

**Right of Inspection:** Inspection of the goods by the buyer is a matter depending entirely upon the terms of the agreement. But if the parties have not limited inspection by their agreement, the buyer has a right to inspect the goods before accepting or paying for them—at any reasonable place and time and in any reasonable manner. When the goods are shipped to the buyer, inspection can occur after their arrival. Expenses of inspection must be borne by the buyer but can be recovered from the seller if the goods do not conform and are rejected.

Sometimes the parties' agreement obligates the buyer to make payment before inspecting the goods. For example, when a contract calls for COD ("collect on delivery"), there is no right of inspection before payment unless other terms of the contract expressly grant such a right. Contracts can also require "payment against documents," which means that, unless otherwise agreed, payment is due on receipt of the required documents of title regardless of when the goods themselves actually arrive. CIF and C & F contracts, for example, require payment on receipt of documents unless the parties have agreed to the contrary. Where a contract calls for payment before inspection, payment must be made unless the goods are so obviously nonconforming that inspection is not needed.

When payment is required before inspection, it does not constitute a final acceptance of the goods. Rejection of the goods can still occur if the buyer inspects after the required payment and finds that they are nonconforming.

**Acceptance:** When conforming goods have been properly tendered, the buyer's basic duty is to accept them, which means simply that the buyer takes the goods as his or her own. This **acceptance** can occur in three different ways:

**1.** The buyer can expressly indicate acceptance by words. For example, there is an acceptance if the buyer, after having had a reasonable opportunity to inspect, signifies to the seller either that the goods are conforming or that he or she will take them despite their nonconformity.

**2.** Acceptance also occurs if the buyer has had a reasonable opportunity to inspect the goods and has failed to reject them within a reasonable period of time.

**3.** The buyer accepts the goods by performing any act inconsistent with the seller's ownership. For example, using, consuming, or reselling the goods usually constitutes an acceptance. However, reasonable use or consumption for the sole purpose of testing is not an acceptance.

**Partial Acceptance:** If part of the goods are conforming and part are nonconforming, the buyer can make a partial acceptance; he or she cannot, however, accept less than a commercial unit. A *commercial unit* is defined in Sec. 2-105 as a unit of goods recognized in commercial practice as being a "single whole" for purposes of sale, the division of which materially impairs its value. It can be a single article (such as a machine), a set of articles (such as a suite of furniture or an assortment of suits in different sizes), a quantity (such as a bale, gross, or carload), or any other unit treated in use or in the relevant market as a single whole.

**Payment:** Seller and buyer can agree upon credit arrangements or agree that payment is due when the buyer receives a document of title, regardless of when the goods arrive. But if the parties do not expressly agree on a time for payment, *it is due when the buyer receives the goods.*

While the price is ordinarily payable in money, the parties can agree that some other medium of exchange (such as other commodities) will be used. In addition, the buyer can use any method of making payment that is generally acceptable in the commercial world (such as a check). But the seller can demand payment in *legal tender* (currency) if he or she desires. A seller who makes such a demand must allow the buyer a reasonable amount of time to obtain legal tender. If the buyer pays by check and the check is accepted by the seller, the buyer has performed the obligation of payment unless the check is dishonored (bounced) by the bank.

Some buyers pay with a *letter of credit* (used primarily in foreign commerce). The buyer obtains the letter of credit from his or her own bank, and the bank guarantees to the seller that payment will be made when the proper documents are tendered.

## INTRODUCTION TO REMEDIES

Thus far we have focused our discussion on the performance of the sale contract by both parties. But suppose the contract is instead breached by one of the parties. What avenues are open to the other party?

### *Options in the Event of Anticipatory Repudiation*

A breach of contract can occur at any stage in the transaction after the contract is made, even before the time for performance falls due. If, before time for performance, one party clearly communicates to the other the intention not to perform, that party has breached the contract by an **anticipatory repudiation.** In such an event, Sec. 2-610 provides that the "aggrieved party"—the party receiving the repudiation—has two options. First, the party may wait a reasonable length of time before resorting to any remedies, in the hope that the repudiating party will change his or her mind. In the alternative, the aggrieved party may treat the contract as having been breached, and immediately pursue the appropriate remedies. (And, in either case, the aggrieved party may suspend his or her performance.)

Sometimes there is not a clear-cut repudiation but the circumstances are such that one party has reasonable doubts about whether the other is going to perform. In such a case the party who has a reasonable basis for feeling insecure can demand in writing that the other party give *assurance of performance.* Adequate assurance of performance must then be given within a reasonable time (not exceeding thirty days) after receipt of the demand. Failure to give this assurance in response to a justified demand constitutes an anticipatory repudiation.

## SELLER'S REMEDIES

The seller's remedies are set forth in Secs. 2-703 to 710 of the UCC. Under these sections, the remedies that are available to a seller in a particular situation depend on the circumstances existing at the time of the buyer's breach.

### *Where Buyer Breaches before Receiving the Goods*

Following are the remedies for the seller where the buyer has repudiated or otherwise breached the contract before receiving the goods:

**1.** The seller can cancel the contract.

**2.** If the goods are in the seller's possession or control but have not yet been identified, he or she can take the steps necessary to identify them (separate them from inventory, tag or label them, and so on). If they are in an unfinished condition, the seller can complete their manufacture if it is reasonable to do so for the purpose of minimizing the loss—or cease manufacture and resell for scrap or salvage value.

3. The seller can *withhold delivery* of goods still in his or her hands, and in some cases even *stop delivery* where the goods have been shipped but have not yet been received by the buyer. Because of the burden to the carrier, seller can stop delivery only if a carload, truckload, planeload, or larger shipment is involved. (The only exception to this quantity requirement is where delivery is stopped because of the buyer's insolvency. In such a case, delivery can be stopped regardless of the quantity of goods involved.) Also, if the carrier has issued a *negotiable bill of lading* (see Chapter 20), the seller can stop delivery only by surrendering the document to the carrier. Thus stoppage in transit cannot occur if the seller has already sent a negotiable bill of lading to the buyer.

4. The seller can *resell* the goods in a commercially reasonable manner at either a private or public (auction) sale. If the resale is *private,* the buyer must be given prior notice of it; if it is *public,* the buyer must be given prior notice unless the goods are perishable or otherwise threaten to rapidly decline in value. A purchaser who buys in good faith at a resale takes the goods free of any rights of the original buyer even if the seller has not conducted the resale in a commercially reasonable manner. When the seller has resold the goods in a proper manner, the damages to which he or she is entitled include the amount by which the contract price exceeds the resale price plus incidental damages such as additional transportation and handling expenses.[3] Any expenses saved because of the buyer's breach are deducted from the seller's damages.

If the seller *does not resell,* the damages are computed in either of two ways, according to Sec. 2-708. The first measure is the amount by which the contract price exceeds the market price at the time and place for tender (rather than the actual resale price), plus incidental damages, minus expenses saved. If the first measure is inadequate to put the seller in as good a position as buyer's performance would have done, then a second measure is used, which is the profit the seller would have made had the contract been performed, plus incidental damages, minus expenses saved.

5. Under some circumstances the seller can sue to recover the *purchase price* from the buyer, even though the buyer did not receive the goods. This can occur, for example, where (a) the buyer legally accepted the goods while they were still in the seller's possession; (b) the seller shipped conforming goods that were lost or destroyed after risk of loss had passed to the buyer; or (c) the seller made reasonable but unsuccessful efforts to resell the goods at a reasonable price. If the seller receives a court judgment against the buyer for the purchase price, and then, because of changed conditions, is able to resell the goods before the buyer pays the judgment, the proceeds of the sale must be credited to the buyer. Payment of the judgment entitles the buyer to any of the goods not resold.

## Where Buyer Breaches after Receiving the Goods

The seller's remedies where buyer's breach occurs after he or she receives the goods are:

1. If the buyer accepts the goods and does not pay for them, the seller can recover the purchase price plus any incidental damages resulting from the breach.

2. If the buyer wrongfully rejects or revokes acceptance and does not pay, the seller's remedies depend on *whether he or she retakes possession* of the goods. If possession is retaken, the remedies are basically the same as if the buyer had breached *before* receiving the goods. In addition to canceling the contract, the seller can resell the goods, keep them and recover damages, or recover the purchase price plus incidental damages if resale is impossible. If the seller does not retake possession, the remedies are the same as if the buyer had accepted the goods. In other words, the seller can recover the purchase price plus incidental damages.

The issue raised in the following case, where the buyer breached the contract while the goods were still in the seller's hands, is typical of those which necessitate interpretation of the code sections applicable to sellers' (and buyers') remedies.

---

[3] The seller is not accountable to the buyer for any profit made on the resale.

**Luprofresh, Inc. v. Pabst Brewing Company**
Superior Court of Delaware, New Castle County, 505 A.2d 37 (1985)

Luprofresh, Inc., plaintiff, contracted to sell a quantity of hops to Pabst Brewing Company at a specified price. Luprofresh, after processing and storing the hops, notified Pabst that the hops were ready for delivery. Pabst replied with a letter saying it "accepted" the goods, but thereafter breached the contract by refusing to issue shipping orders. Luprofresh then brought this action to recover the purchase price of the hops from Pabst, defendant.

Defendant, in its pleadings, raised two defenses: (1) a claim that plaintiff's pricing policies (upon which the contract price was based) violated the federal antitrust laws, and (2) the contention that, under Article 2 of the UCC, plaintiff was entitled to recover the purchase price only after making a reasonable effort to resell the goods, and that plaintiff's pleadings did not allege such an effort was made.

The court ruled against defendant on both points. Accordingly, it entered a summary judgment (judgment on the pleadings) for plaintiff in the amount of the contract price. (A summary of that part of the trial court's decision relating to the UCC issue appears below.)

**Decision:** Sec. 2-709(1)(a) of the UCC provides that when the buyer fails to pay the price when it is due, the seller may recover the price in either of two situations: (1) where the buyer has accepted the goods, or (2) where conforming goods are lost or damaged after risk of loss has passed to the buyer. Sec. 2-709(1)(b) provides a third situation in which the purchase price may be recovered: where the goods are "identified to the contract and the seller is unable after reasonable effort to resell them at a reasonable price or the circumstances indicate that such effort will be unavailing."

Sec. 2-709(1)(b), on which the buyer relies, generally applies to the case where the goods have been identified to the contract but have *not* been accepted at the time of the buyer's breach. In this case, however, where seller had accepted the goods, he or she may choose to bring an action for the price immediately under Sec. 2-709(1)(a), *or* attempt to resell the goods at a reasonable price before proceeding further against the buyer. Since seller chose the first of these remedies, seller had no obligation to attempt to sell the goods prior to bringing this suit. Judgment, therefore, is for plaintiff/seller. ∎

## BUYER'S REMEDIES

The buyer's remedies are set forth in Secs. 2-711 to 2-718 of the UCC.

### *Where Seller Fails to Deliver*

When the seller breaches the contract by failing to deliver the goods according to the contract, the following remedies are available to the buyer:

1. The buyer can cancel the contract, which relieves him or her of any contractual obligations.

2. The buyer can recover any prepayments made to the seller.

3. The buyer can **cover** (buy the goods elsewhere in a commercially reasonable manner) and receive damages. The damages include (a) the amount by which the cover price exceeds the contract price; (b) any incidental expenses—out-of-pocket costs such as additional transportation and handling expenses; and (c) any consequential losses, such as the buyer's lost profits, that should have been foreseen by the seller as resulting from the breach. Deducted from the buyer's damages, however, are any expenses saved because of the seller's breach. If the buyer does not wish to cover or covers improperly, he or she can receive the amount by which the market price exceeds the contract price, plus any incidental and consequential damages, minus any expenses saved. The market price is determined as of the time when the buyer learned of the breach and as of the place where delivery should have been tendered.

4. In most cases the buyer will be unable to recover the goods themselves from the seller and will have to be content with money damages. In certain circumstances, however, the buyer can obtain a court decree entitling him or her to possession of the particular goods contracted for. If the goods are *unique*

(such as an heirloom) or in other proper circumstances, the buyer can recover them by obtaining a decree of *specific performance* (an order commanding the seller to live up to the agreement). Even if the goods are not unique, the buyer can recover them (a) where they have been specifically identified and (b) where the buyer has made reasonable but unsuccessful efforts to cover or where the circumstances reasonably indicate that such efforts would be fruitless (such as where the goods are in very short supply). The technical name for the buyer's recovery of goods in this type of situation is *replevin*.

## Where Seller Delivers Nonconforming Goods

If the seller delivers goods that are defective or in some other way do not conform to the contract, the buyer must notify the seller within a reasonable time after discovering the nonconformity in order to be able to pursue available remedies. The buyer's remedies in this situation are:

**1.** The buyer can cancel the contract.

**2.** The buyer can recover any prepayments made to the seller.

**3.** The buyer can *reject* the delivery. Under the perfect tender rule, the buyer can usually reject if the tender or the goods fail in any respect to conform to the contract. Where the defects are of a type that can be discovered by reasonable inspection, sometimes the buyer can reject only by specifying them in the notice to the seller. This duty to specify defects exists (a) where they can be cured if the seller learns of them promptly or (b) where the specification is requested by one merchant from another merchant.

**4.** If the buyer has already accepted delivery, however, he or she cannot thereafter reject it. Of course, acceptance is more than just receiving the goods; it means taking them as one's own. However, in a few circumstances the buyer can *revoke his or her acceptance*.

    **a.** An acceptance can be revoked only if the nonconformity *substantially impairs the value* to the buyer of the delivery or commercial unit in question. For example, a cracked engine block substantially impairs the value of a car, while a malfunctioning clock in the dashboard does not.

    **b.** Where the buyer *knew* of the nonconformity when accepting, he or she can revoke the acceptance only if it was made on the reasonable assumption that the nonconformity would be cured, but it has not been. On the other hand, where the buyer *did not know* of the nonconformity when accepting, he or she can revoke (1) if the acceptance had been made because of the difficulty of discovering the nonconformity at an earlier time or (2) because of the seller's assurances that there were no defects.

    **c.** Revocation of acceptance must occur within a reasonable time after the buyer discovers the basis for it and before any substantial change occurs in the condition of the goods (other than by their own defects).

**5.** The effect of a rejection or a revocation of acceptance is the same: the goods are not the buyer's and he or she does not have to pay for them. After a justified rejection or revocation the seller usually makes arrangements to take back the goods. The buyer must return the goods on request if the seller refunds any payments made on the price and reimburses the buyer for reasonable expenses incurred in inspecting, receiving, transporting, and caring for them. While in possession of the goods the buyer has certain rights and duties with respect to them:

    **a.** The first duty is to follow all reasonable instructions given by the seller regarding the goods. A seller's instructions are unreasonable if he or she does not guarantee payment of expenses after the buyer has demanded it.

    **b.** If the seller does not pick up the goods or give instructions as to their handling within a reasonable time, the buyer has three alternatives—storing the goods for the seller's account, reshipping them to the seller, or reselling them for the seller's account. (In unusual situations the buyer is actually under a *duty to try to resell the goods* for the seller when reasonable instructions are not given. This duty arises if the buyer is a merchant, the seller has no agent or place of business in the buyer's locality, and the goods are perishable or otherwise threaten to rapidly decline in value.) The buyer has a right to recover reasonable expenses in handling the goods in these situations, just as when following the seller's instructions. One note of caution: a buyer who resells goods without being entitled to do so has legally accepted them.

6. The buyer can cover if he or she wishes, and damages will be computed in the same manner as when the seller breaches by failing to deliver.

7. Finally, the buyer can *accept and keep the goods* despite their nonconformity and still recover all damages caused by the nonconformity. This is frequently the situation in *breach of warranty* cases where the product has already been used or consumed when the defect is discovered. The buyer's damages in such cases are the difference between the actual value of the goods and the value they would have had if they had conformed to the warranty, plus incidental and consequential damages. Consequential damages in a breach of warranty case include bodily injury and property damage caused by the breach and often constitute the largest portion of the buyer's damages. If the goods are not yet paid for, the purchase price is offset against the damages.

Both of the following cases have to do with buyers' remedies. In the first of these, the question is whether the buyer had the right to revoke her acceptance of the goods. The second case illustrates application of the rule that a plaintiff is allowed to recover those damages which are the reasonably direct and foreseeable consequence of the defendant's breach of contract.

## Alpert v. Thomas
U.S. District Court, District of Vermont, 643 F.Supp. 1406 (1986)

On March 15, 1984, defendant Thomas purchased from plaintiffs Alpert and Wolfman a Russian-Arabian stallion named Raxx. Plaintiffs knew that defendant was buying Raxx for breeding purposes and their agent, Mallory, expressly warranted Raxx's suitability for this purpose and promised to obtain the breeding soundness evaluation that is customary in the industry before sale occurred. Mallory did not procure such an evaluation, though a veterinarian's bill presented to Thomas when Raxx was delivered in May led her to believe that he had. During June and July, and again in September there were several attempts to breed Raxx, but none resulted in a pregnancy. Veterinarians who examined Raxx found that his breeding capability was questionable because of a "low number of morphologically normal, progressively motile sperm."

As late as November 1984, plaintiffs' agents were promising that they would "make things right" for defendant and were still warranting Raxx's breeding abilities. Further examinations in March 1985 again led to the conclusion that Raxx was an unsatisfactory candidate for breeding. On March 26, 1985, defendant sent a letter to plaintiffs revoking the entire contract. At that time, she had paid $94,879.28 of the $175,000 purchase price.

Plaintiffs sued for the balance of the purchase price. Defendant counterclaimed for rescission of the contract or, in the alternative, damages arising from breach of warranty. The following summarizes the trial judge's opinion.

**Decision:** Plaintiffs' summary judgment motion is denied; defendant's is granted. Defendant's revocation was entirely proper. Raxx clearly did not conform to express and implied warranties. UCC 2-608 provides four elements for proper revocation: (1) the goods' nonconformity with the contract substantially impairs the value to the buyer—there is no doubt that this was the case here; (2) the buyer's acceptance was either (a) forthcoming on the reasonable assumption that the nonconformity would be cured (discovery at the time of acceptance) or (b) reasonably induced by the difficulty of the discovery or by the seller's assurances (no discovery at the time of acceptance)—the requirements of alternative (b) were met here; (3) revocation occurred within a reasonable time after the nonconformity was or should have been discovered—given the assurances of remedy made by plaintiffs' agents, defendant did not wait too long before revoking; and (4) revocation took place before a substantial change occurred in the condition of the goods not caused by their own defects—there is no evidence of any change in Raxx's condition after his delivery to defendant. ∎

### Cricket Alley Corporation v. Data Terminal Systems, Inc.
Supreme Court of Kansas,
732 P.2d 719 (1987)

Desiring to modernize Cricket Alley's operations as a retail clothing store, its president contacted Data Terminal Systems (DTS) about buying a cash register system compatible with the Wang computer which Cricket Alley already owned. Through advertisements and statements of its employees, DTS seemed to warrant that its cash register system would work with the Wang computer. However, when installed, the system never worked. While DTS tried to remedy the problems, Cricket Alley's old cash registers began to break down. Replacement parts were unavailable. Finally, DTS's equipment was left in place to perform basic cash register functions, but it never did mesh with the Wang. Cricket Alley sued for breach of warranty.

A jury found that a warranty had been made and breached by DTS. It awarded Cricket Alley consequential and incidental damages in the form of additional labor costs incurred due to the absence of a working cash register system. DTS appealed.

**Decision:** Affirmed, including recovery of consequential and incidental damages in the form of additional labor costs incurred due to the absence of a working cash register system. UCC 2-715 codifies *Hadley v. Baxendale*'s rule that a breaching seller is liable for damage caused by all general requirements of the contract that are breached and liable for all specific needs of which he may be charged with knowledge. It was easily foreseeable to DTS that failure of a cash register to mesh with a computer system would create additional labor costs for a retail merchant. Cricket Alley carefully evidenced those extra costs for the jury, so DTS must pay for them. ■

## *Insolvency*

The insolvency of one party may affect the other's remedies. Suppose, for example, that the buyer has prepaid the purchase price and seller becomes insolvent before shipping the goods. If the goods have been identified to the contract, the buyer can compel the seller to turn them over to him or her in certain circumstances. (Sec. 2-502).

If the buyer becomes insolvent during the course of a transaction, under Sec. 2-702 the seller can refuse to deliver except for cash. Also—as noted earlier—if the goods have been shipped and are still in transit, the seller can usually stop delivery unless he or she has already forwarded a negotiable document of title to the buyer.

There are times, however, when the UCC, which is state law, will not prevail. A seller or buyer who becomes insolvent will often go into bankruptcy, a proceeding governed by federal law. Since the federal bankruptcy law prevails over state laws, the remedies granted in the UCC may have little practical significance in cases of insolvency.

## *Prior Agreement as to Remedies*

The parties to a sale contract can provide in their agreement for remedies to be available in the event of breach. Under Sec. 2-718, they can agree on liquidated damages (the measure of damages to be payable in case of breach). Their provision must be reasonable, taking into account the anticipated or actual harm caused by the breach, the difficulties of proof of loss, and the inconvenience of otherwise obtaining an adequate remedy. If the contract sets an unreasonably large amount of liquidated damages, the amount will simply be ignored by the court.

More generally, Sec. 2-719 states that "the agreement may provide for remedies in addition to or in substitution for" those provided in the UCC. For example, the parties might agree that the buyer's only remedy for breach of warranty will be to bring the goods back to the seller for repairs. However, Sec. 2-719 also provides that if the clause limiting remedies "fails of its essential purpose," it will be ignored by a court and the remedies normally available under the UCC will apply. A remedy limitation "fails of its essential purpose" if circumstances cause the limitation to substantially deprive one party of the value of his or her bargain. Thus, in the example above, if the seller does not repair the defective item within a reasonable period of time, the limitation clause will be ineffective and the buyer can resort to whatever remedies the UCC gives him in the circumstances. Furthermore, a limitation of remedies will be ignored by a court if it is so unfair and represents such a gross abuse of bargaining power that it is deemed *unconscionable.* Section 2-719 provides that, in a sale of *consumer goods,* a clause which limits the availability of damages for *bodily injury* is *presumed* to be unconscionable. Even though a remedy limitation clause is different from a warranty disclaimer (as explained in Chapter 22), such a clause in a consumer transaction must comply with the Magnuson-Moss Warranty Act when applicable.

## LEMON LAWS

The purchase of a new car is often part of the American dream. When the new car has repeated and serious problems, however, the dream can turn into a nightmare. Today, purchasers of such disappointing cars often obtain relief under special statutes applicable to motor vehicles known as **lemon laws.** At least 43 states have passed such laws, which represent a legislative judgment that the UCC remedies of rejection, revocation, and breach of warranty do not adequately protect the new car buyer. These laws impose a higher standard of quality and workmanship on the automobile manufacturer than does the UCC. While these laws vary in detail from state to state, in general they provide that (1) if a car under warranty possesses a defect which significantly affects its value or use, and (2) if the dealer is unable to fix the defect in four tries, the owner is entitled to a new car, a "buy-back" (an order requiring the manufacturer to refund the purchase price minus a per-mile depreciation charge), recovery of repair costs, or free replacement parts, depending upon the circumstances of the case.

Most lemon laws require that before the buyer is entitled to a buy-back, recovery of repair costs, or some other relief, he or she must go before an "appeal jury" which makes findings of fact relative to the buyer's claim, that is, as to the severity of the defects, and as to the extent of the dealer's correction of the defects. Arbitration is free to the buyer, and usually produces a decision within 40 to 60 days. (Among the major manufacturers, General Motors, American Motors, Honda, Nissan, Volkswagen, and Volvo have designated over 150 Better Business Bureaus to handle their disputes. Ford and Chrysler sponsor their own national mediation programs—Ford's panels are called Consumer Appeals Boards, and Chrysler's are Customer Satisfaction Boards. While mediation boards usually handle only warranty-related disputes, complaints involving out-of-warranty vehicles have sometimes been mediated.)

In general, appeal decisions are binding on the manufacturers but not on the car owners. Thus if a jury orders a buy-back, the manufacturer cannot appeal the decision to the courts, while a jury decision against the buyer is appealable. Although appeal juries have ordered manufacturers either to furnish new cars or make buy-backs in a number of cases, more often they have ordered manufacturers to make refunds of repair costs or to replace defective parts, such as transmissions and engines, with new components. (In a typical year, for example, Better Business Bureaus hear approximately 25,000 cases, but award fewer than 4,000 buy-backs.)

## SUMMARY

The basic obligation of the seller is to make a tender of delivery of the goods in conformity with the terms of the contract, and to keep the goods available for a period of time reasonably necessary for the buyer to take possession. If the seller has no responsibility for transporting the goods and they are in the possession of a bailee, the seller must deliver a negotiable document of title to the buyer or obtain the bailee's acknowledgment that the buyer is entitled to possession. If the seller does have responsibility for transporting the goods, under a shipment contract he or she must deliver the goods to a carrier, obtain and deliver any documents necessary for the buyer to take possession of the goods, and notify the buyer of the shipment. Under a destination contract, the seller is required to tender delivery of the goods at their destination.

Although Sec. 2-601 of the UCC adopts the common-law perfect tender rule, this rule is modified by other sections of the UCC. For example, if the seller's performance is deficient, he or she is permitted to "cure" by making a conforming delivery before expiration of the time for performance. (In some situations, cure may even be made after such time.) If, after a sales contract has been entered into, some unanticipated event occurs before the time of performance, the seller may be freed of his or her contractual obligations under the doctrine of commercial impracticability. Under that doctrine a late performance by the seller, or nondelivery in whole or in part, is excused if, because of an unforeseen circumstance, delivery of the goods becomes "commercially impracticable." While the determination of whether a contract has been rendered commercially impracticable is made on a case-by-case basis, in general delivery is impracticable if the unforeseen circumstance makes delivery impossible, or if it so alters the essential nature of the performance that it results in a very marked increase in the cost of performance (with the courts often requiring the seller to show that his or her costs of performance would be doubled or tripled before he or she is freed under this doctrine).

The buyer's basic obligation—to pay for the goods in conformity with the contract—is generally subject to the right of inspection. However, the right of inspection prior to payment is lost if the transaction is a COD one, or contains other terms extinguishing the right. If the buyer breaches the contract before receiving the goods, the *seller's* primary remedies are the right to cancel, to withhold or stop delivery, to resell the goods and recover resulting damages (or, in limited cases, to recover the price). If the buyer breaches after receiving the goods, the seller can recover the price. Also, if the seller reacquires possession, his or her remedies are the same as in the case where the buyer breaches before receiving the goods.

Turning to the *buyer's* remedies, if the seller breaches the contract by failing to deliver, the buyer's primary remedies are the right to cancel, to cover, and to recover damages if the cost of cover exceeds the contract price. If the seller breaches by delivering nonconforming goods, the buyer may cancel, and reject the delivery. And, if the buyer has accepted the goods prior to discovery of the nonconformity, the buyer may revoke his or her acceptance under limited conditions.

## KEY TERMS

**Tender of delivery**
**Perfect tender rule**
**Installment contract**
**Acceptance**
**Anticipatory repudiation**
**Cover**
**Lemon laws**

## QUESTIONS AND PROBLEMS

**1.** Smith purchased a new car. Almost immediately after taking delivery he discovered that the car had a defective transmission, and he promptly took the car back to the dealer. When he told the dealer that he wanted to return the car and cancel the sale, the dealer offered to replace the transmission. Smith refused the dealer's offer of "cure," left the car with the dealer, and made no further payments. The dealer fixed the car, resold it, and sued Smith for damages. Did the dealer prevail? Discuss. (*Zabriskie Chevrolet, Inc. v. Smith,* 240 A.2d 195, 1968.)

**2.** After Gulf and Sylvan carried on a series of negotiations, they made a contract providing for delivery in three separate lots, to be separately accepted and evidenced by three separate purchase orders sent on the same date. No problems arose in the first two deliveries, but the buyer noticed a minor defect in the third delivery and rejected it, citing the perfect tender rule as his authority. Moreover, he claimed that the seller had breached the entire contract. Is he correct? Explain. (*Gulf Chemical & Metallurgical Corp. v. Sylvan Chemical Corp.*, 12 U.C.C. Rep. Serv. 117, 1973.)

**3.** A dairy farm contracted with a public school district to supply the latter with half-pints of milk. Between the time of contracting and the time for performance, the price of raw milk rose 23 percent. Other increases in the market price had occurred in the past. The dairy filed suit for a declaratory judgment, asking the court to relieve it from its obligation to deliver the milk under Sec. 2-615. What was the result? Discuss. (*Maple Farms, Inc. v. City School Dist. of the City of Elmira,* 352 N.Y.S.2d 784, 1974.)

**4.** P advertised his used Triumph automobile for sale in July 1985. D drove the car on two separate occasions and had it inspected by a body shop and a mechanic (who listened to the engine and made a visual inspection). D negotiated the asking price from $2700 down to $2200 and then agreed to buy. The same day that title was signed over and D took possession, he called P and asked for a price adjustment on grounds that the engine was "worn out." P refused. D took the car to a mechanic who said that the car was "run down" and that engine repair work would cost between $1200 and $2000. Three days after the sale, D parked the car in front of P's house with the keys locked inside and placed the certificate of ownership in an envelope in P's mailbox. The car was ultimately towed away by the city. P sued D for $1700 unpaid on the purchase price. Should P recover? (*Herbert v. Harl,* 757 S.W.2d 585, Mo. 1988.)

**5.** Aubrey's R.V. Center bought a computer system from Tandy to perform certain functions, including most importantly, operating as a point-of-sale recorder of inventory for over 3,000 items. Tandy recommended Source Book software, helped Aubrey's procure it, and allegedly stated that it would "stand behind" the software. Because the software never recorded more than 600 items of inventory at once or performed as a point-of-sale recorder, Tandy made several efforts at correction. Unfortunately, they all failed. Almost a year after the system had been purchased, Aubrey's gave up and asked Tandy for rescission of the contract and return of the contract price. Tandy again sought an opportunity to remedy the problems, but soon turned the matter over to its legal department. Does Aubrey's have the right to rescind? (*Aubrey's R.V. Center v. Tandy Corporation*, 731 P.2d 1124, Wash.App. 1987.)

**6.** In the previous case, evidence showed that Tandy knew that Aubrey's was financing its purchase of the system through a leasing company on a lease-purchase contract. Assuming that Aubrey's *does* have the right to rescind, would Aubrey's also have the right to recover damages in the form of finance charges it incurred in purchasing the system?

**7.** Great Western Sugar Co. (P) contracted to sell refined beet sugar to Pennant Products (D) in two contracts. The first three-month contract called for purchase of 900,000 lbs. of sugar at $46 per hundred pounds. The second contract covering the next three months was for an additional 500,000 lbs. at $45 per hundred pounds. Both contracts called for periodic shipments to be made in accordance with shipping orders sent by D, and each allowed D to terminate by sending written notice. After receiving and paying for 371,500 lbs. under the first contract, D sent no more shipping orders. Nor did it send a written termination notice. Therefore, P sued for breach of contract. The trial court entered judgment for P. D appealed, arguing (a) that the subject of the contracts was not sufficiently identified for P to recover, and (b) that P had not resold the sugar to mitigate damages and therefore should be barred from recovery. Discuss. (*Great Western Sugar Co. v. Pennant Products, Inc.,* 748 P.2d 1359, Colo.App. 1987.)

**8.** Under their sale contract seller S was required to deliver goods to buyer B on October 25. On April 30, S called B and demanded more money for the goods. B refused, and S said, "Well, if that's the way you want it." On May 30, B filed suit against S for breach of contract. S contended that B was not entitled to file suit until after the date for performance, October 25. Is S correct? Explain.

**9.** Plymouth Chemical Co. used propane gas as an essential raw material in producing certain chemicals. It had a long-term supply contract for such gas with Commonwealth Gas Co. A shortage of propane gas occurred, and most suppliers were no longer committing themselves to long-term contracts. Commonwealth breached the contract, and Plymouth sued for specific performance. Commonwealth claimed that Plymouth should be allowed to sue for damages but not for specific performance. Is Commonwealth correct? Explain.

**10.** After Buyer's breach of contract, Seller resold the goods at a private sale but did not give prior notice of the sale. The resale netted Seller $1,000 less than he would have received under the contract with Buyer. Seller sued Buyer for the $1,000. Buyer claimed that Seller could not recover the $1,000 deficiency because he had not notified Buyer of the sale. Is Buyer correct? Explain.

CHAPTER 24

# Commercial Paper

## Types, Parties, and Basic Concepts

The term **commercial paper** refers to written promises or orders to pay sums of money and comprises such instruments as drafts, promissory notes, checks, and certificates of deposit. (The most common of these are notes and checks.) With the advent of "electronic banking" in recent years—such as the widespread use of automated teller machines and experimentation with point-of-sale terminals in retail stores—it has been predicted that some day we will live in an almost checkless society.[1] Because of such developments, the *rate of growth* of check usage has levelled off, or even slightly declined, in recent years. Americans continue to write 45 to 50 billion checks a year, however, and the checkless society seems far off. Thus the present use of commercial paper in our credit-oriented society is of enormous significance, and will remain so well into the foreseeable future. A knowledge of the basic rules for dealing with this subject thus continues to be important to the businessperson.

## DEVELOPMENT OF THE LAW

Commercial paper has been used for many centuries, probably as early as 1500 B.C., according to archeologists, who tell us that crude promissory notes existed in very early civilizations. By the thirteenth century, merchants in the Middle East were making significant use of both promissory notes and bills of exchange, and by the beginning of the seventeenth century both kinds of instruments were commonly used in England.

Because the early English courts refused to recognize commercial paper, the merchants created their own methods for enforcing rights arising from the use of these instruments. The rules they developed were enforced by traders at their "fair" or "borough" courts, and together they made up what is known as the *law merchant.*

During the eighteenth and nineteenth centuries these principles were substantially recognized by English and American courts and became part of the common law of both countries. In 1896 the American Bar Association drafted the Uniform Negotiable Instruments Law (NIL) for state consideration, and by the early 1920s this act was adopted by all the states. This caused our negotiable instruments law to be "codified."

### The Uniform Commercial Code

Today the old NIL has been superseded in all states by Article 3 of the Uniform Commercial Code, entitled "Commercial Paper." (Louisiana has not adopted the UCC in its entirety, but it has enacted Articles 1, 3, 4, 5, and 9.) While the adoption of the UCC resulted in a substantial updating of the earlier rules to conform to modern-day practices, the most important provisions of Article 3 are not much different from those of the original NIL. In any event, legal questions growing out of the use of negotiable instruments today are governed almost entirely by Article 3 of the UCC—although references to Article 4 are also necessary if problems arise that deal with the relationship existing between the drawer of a check and the bank upon which it is written.[2]

---

[1] More will be said about electronic banking in Chapter 28.

[2] A subcommittee of the Permanent Editorial Board of the UCC, a joint effort of the National Conference of Commissioners on Uniform State Laws and the American Law Institute, has just drafted substantial amendments to Articles 3 and 4 of the UCC. These amendments will be submitted to the state legislatures for adoption in the early 1990s. These chapters on Commercial Paper are based on Articles 3 and 4 of the UCC currently in effect. In addition, a new Article 4A of the UCC, dealing with electronic funds transfers between banks, has been completed and soon will be submitted to state legislatures.

## PURPOSES OF COMMERCIAL PAPER

During the early part of the Middle Ages, merchants and traders had to carry gold and silver to pay for the goods they purchased at the various international fairs. These precious metals were continually subject to loss or theft through the perils of travel.

To eliminate dangers of this sort, merchants began to deposit their gold and silver with bankers. When they needed funds to pay for goods they had purchased, they "drew" on them by giving the seller a written order addressed to the bank, telling it to deliver part of the gold or silver to the seller. These orders, called bills of exchange, were *substitutes for money.* Today, checks and the drafts and promissory notes that are payable on demand serve this same basic purpose.

The second major purpose of commercial paper is to serve as a *credit device;* this came about as a logical extension of its initial use as a money substitute. Soon after bills of exchange became established as substitutes for money, merchants who wished to purchase goods on credit discovered that sellers were sometimes willing to accept bills of exchange that were not payable until a stated time in the future—such as "ninety days after date." If the seller was satisfied as to the commercial reputation of the bill's drawer (the purchaser), he would take such an instrument (called a *time bill* or *draft*) and wait until the maturity date to collect it. In this way the seller-payee extended credit to the buyer-drawer.

Soon thereafter ways were devised by which payees could sell these instruments to third parties, usually banks, and receive immediate cash in return. Since the banks would then have to wait for the maturity dates before receiving payment, the payees would have to sell them the paper at a discount—that is, at perhaps 5 or 10 percent less than the face amount. This meant, in effect, that the purchasing banks were charging the sellers interest in advance as compensation for their role in the transaction.

Today, because of the widespread use of time notes and drafts, the credit aspect of commercial paper is as important to the business community as its "substitute for money" aspect.

## TYPES OF COMMERCIAL PAPER

There are numerous ways to classify the basic types of commercial paper. Of these, the classification specified by Article 3 of the UCC probably merits top billing.

### *The UCC Classification*

Section 3-104 specifies four types of instruments—drafts, checks, notes, and certificates of deposit.

**Drafts:** A **draft,** or bill of exchange, is an instrument whereby the party creating it (the *drawer*) orders another party (the *drawee*) to pay money to a third party (the *payee*). For example: X owes Y $100, and Y owes Z the same amount. Y signs a written

---

**Draft** A *draft* is an instrument by which the party creating it, the drawer (Kathi Erley in the example below) orders another party, the drawee (the bank) to pay money to a third party, the payee (Karen Shaw).

| | |
|---|---|
| $ 5,000.00 | January 2, 19XX |
| Ninety (90) days after the above date | PAY TO THE ORDER OF |
| Karen Shaw | |
| five thousand and no/100-------------------------------------- DOLLARS | |
| WITH EXCHANGE | |
| VALUE RECEIVED AND CHARGE TO ACCOUNT OF | |
| TO First National Bank of Chicago | *Kathi Erley* |
| NO. 02683    Chicago, Illinois | Kathi Erley |

STOCK FORM 990-8 BANKFORMS, INC.

**Sales Draft** A *sales draft* is a draft or bill of exchange drawn by the seller of goods on the purchaser of those goods and accepted (signed) by the purchaser. The purpose of the transaction is to enable the seller to raise money on the paper before the purchaser's obligation matures under the sales contract.

```
                                Draft
ACCEPTED: KMS Imports           Draft No. 1234                              Date  January 2, 19XX
  Karen Shaw                    At _____ ***90 Days From Date*** _____
                                Pay to the Order of _____ ***McNAMARA CORPORATION*** _____
                                the sum of  Five Thousand and no/100ths ****************  Dollars  $5,000.00
                                Value received and charge to the account of
                                       ┌   KMS Imports              The McNamara Corporation
                                   To ─┤                            Joanne McNamara
                                       └   Hinsdale, Illinois       Authorized Signature
                                1-32-0018 (6/78)
```

order directing X to pay the $100 to Z and gives it to Z. Z presents the instrument to X, who then pays him. Here Y is the drawer, X the drawee, and Z the payee.

In order for a draft to work, one of two general conditions must exist. Either the drawee must owe the drawer a debt (in which case the drawer is simply telling the drawee to pay the debt or a portion of it to a third party) or some kind of agreement or relationship must exist between the parties under which the drawee has consented to the drawing of the draft. If neither of these conditions existed, the drawee would not obey the order to pay the amount of the draft to the payee or to any subsequent holder of the instrument.

When a draft is used in connection with a sale of goods, it is called a **sales draft** (an instrument that has largely supplanted the "trade acceptance" of earlier years). A sales draft is a draft drawn by the seller of goods on the purchaser of those goods, which is subsequently accepted (signed) by the purchaser. The purpose of the transaction is to enable the seller to raise money on the paper before the purchaser's obligation matures under the sales contract.

We can illustrate this usage by referring to the specimen sales draft reproduced here. The McNamara Corporation has sold goods to KMS Imports. Because KMS Imports wishes to utilize a negotiable instrument rather than pay cash for the goods immediately, the McNamara Corporation (drawer) draws a draft on KMS Imports for the purchase price of the goods.

The instrument orders KMS Imports to pay the stated sum to the order of the McNamara Corporation at a stated time in the future—in this case, 90 days after January 2. (The McNamara Corporation is thus both the drawer and the payee of the instrument.) It is then presented to an officer of KMS Imports—Karen Shaw, in this instance—who accepts it by affixing that company's name to it in the space at the left hand margin. The acceptance, which constitutes a promise by KMS Imports (the drawee-acceptor) to pay the instrument when it becomes due, is then returned to the McNamara Corporation. It can now negotiate the draft to a third party, usually the McNamara Corporation's bank, and receive cash immediately. Use of the instrument in this manner—by sellers of goods—explains why it is called a *sales* draft. (Other kinds of drafts are also frequently accepted by their drawees; these are discussed in Chapter 27.) Another frequently used draft is the *bank draft,* which is utilized when one bank draws on its funds in another bank.

**Checks:** A **check** is a particular type of draft. Under Sec. 3-104(2), it is by definition a "draft drawn on a bank [and] payable on demand." It is thus distinguished from demand drafts drawn on individuals, or on corporations that are not banks. Similarly, it is also distinguished from drafts drawn on banks, but which are payable at specific future dates. As one might guess, checks are by far the most commonly used form of drafts. It should be noted that, today, the term

**Check** A *check* is the most common type of draft; it is an order (draft or bill of exchange) drawn on a bank and payable on demand.

```
KMS IMPORTS                              70-881
                      January 2  19 XX    719
PAY TO THE
ORDER OF  Scandinavian Export, Ltd.    $  5,878.00
ONLY Five Thousand Eight Hundred Seventy-Eight   DOLLARS
BANK OF HINSDALE
Subsidiary of Lake Shore Bancorp
400 E. Ogden Avenue Hinsdale, Illinois 60521
FOR  Invoice 0899                Karen M. Shaw
⑇0719088⑊⑇           BY: _____ DATE: _____
```

Source: Courtesy of Bank of Hinsdale, Hinsdale, Illinois.

"bank" also includes other financial institutions that are legally authorized to receive "demand deposits" and serve as drawees on checks. These include credit unions and savings institutions.

One particular form of check is the *cashier's check*, which is drawn by a bank on itself, payable on demand to a payee. Because this check is drawn by the bank ordering itself to pay, the bank must honor the check upon proper presentment. For this reason, in transactions involving the sale of property—where the owner-seller requires some form of guaranteed payment to accompany all offers to purchase—bidders commonly submit cashier's checks along with their bids.

**Notes:** A **note** is a promise by one party (the *maker*) to pay a sum of money to another party (the *payee*). Notes differ from drafts in two primary respects. They always contain promises to pay money (as distinguished from orders), and they have two parties—maker and payee—rather than three.

Because notes are used in a variety of transactions, they come in many different forms. For example, a note used in a real estate transaction secured by a mortgage on the property being purchased is a *real estate mortgage note*. A note containing a promise to make payments in specified installments, such as payments for a new car, is an *installment note*. And a note secured by personal property is a *collateral note*. While all of these are *promissory notes* in a general sense, that term when used alone usually refers to the simplest kind of notes, those merely containing promises by one person to pay money to another.

**Certificates of Deposit:** A **certificate of deposit** is an acknowledgment by a bank of receipt of money with a return "promise" on the bank's part to repay it at a fixed future date or, in some instances, on demand.

## Promises to Pay and Orders to Pay

A second method of classifying commercial paper uses only two categories. All instruments involving the payment of money, regardless of their specialized names within the business community, contain one of two elements—*promises* to pay money or *orders* to pay money. Instruments containing promises to pay can be broadly classified as *notes* and those containing orders to pay as *drafts*. As already indicated, the certificate of deposit is a special type of note, and the check is a special type of draft.

## Demand and Time Instruments

A third method of classifying commercial paper is based solely on the time at which the instrument is payable. Instruments that are payable whenever the holder chooses to present them to the maker (in the case of a note) or to the drawee (in the case of a draft) are called **demand instruments** (or *sight instruments*). Those payable at a specific future date

**Promissory Note** A *promissory note* is an instrument by which the maker promises to pay a sum of money to another party (the payee).

```
$ 5,000.00                                    ,  2 January        19 XX
    Ninety (90) days                  after date I    promise to pay to
the order of        James J. Walsh
Five thousand and no/100                                          Dollars
At twelve and one-half percent (12.5%) per annum
Value received.
No. 083153   Due                          Karen M. Shaw
```

are **time instruments.** Notes, drafts, and certificates of deposit can be either demand or time instruments, while checks—by definition—must be payable on demand.

## *Negotiable and Nonnegotiable Instruments*

The term *commercial paper,* used in its broadest sense, embraces both negotiable paper and nonnegotiable paper. **Negotiable instruments** are those whose terms meet the requirements of negotiability appearing in Sec. 3-104 of the UCC, while **nonnegotiable instruments** do not meet such requirements. Thus, whether a particular instrument falls into the one category or the other depends entirely on its form and content.

In many instances the negotiable-nonnegotiable classification of commercial paper transcends all others in importance, for two primary reasons:

**Certificate of Deposit** A *certificate of deposit* is an instrument by which a bank acknowledges receipt of money and promises to return it at a later date or on demand. Certificates of deposit may be negotiable or nonnegotiable, depending upon their terms.

```
CARB-OUT                    AUTOMATICALLY          BANK OF HINSDALE                      9010183
CERTIFICATE OF DEPOSIT      RENEWABLE              400 EAST OGDEN AVENUE • HINSDALE, ILLINOIS 60521
NOT SUBJECT TO CHECK                               SUBSIDIARY OF LAKE SHORE BANCORP
                                                                                January 2   19 XX
                            Karen M. Shaw                                         HAS DEPOSITED
                            Five thousand and no/100                  DOLLARS $   5,000.00
                            ADDRESS  One Oak Creek
                                     Buffalo Grove, IL 60089
                            SOCIAL SEC. NO.  000-00-0000           BY: Kelly L. Burkhart   DATE:
```

Source: Courtesy of Bank of Hinsdale, Hinsdale, Illinois.

1. The rules of Article 3 of the UCC apply (with rare exception) only to instruments that meet the tests of negotiability. By contrast, nonnegotiable instruments are governed by the ordinary principles of contract law. In other words, the rights and liabilities of makers, drawers, and indorsers of negotiable instruments are controlled by one body of law, while those of parties to nonnegotiable instruments are governed by another.

2. It is possible under the rules of Article 3 for a holder of a negotiable instrument to enjoy a special status, that of a *holder in due course (HDC)*. Such a holder takes the instrument free of many defenses that exist between its original parties. (*Defenses* are matters pleaded by defendants as a reason in law or fact why the plaintiff should not recover what he or she seeks.) The holder of a nonnegotiable instrument—such as a simple contract—on the other hand, can never qualify as an HDC. Such a holder takes it subject to these defenses.

While an examination of the precise rights of the HDC must await the subject of defenses in Chapter 26, the basic distinction between the status of such a holder and that of a mere assignee will be brought to light here.

## ASSIGNEE VERSUS HOLDER IN DUE COURSE

Under contract law, the assignee of a simple contract acquires no better rights under the contract than those possessed by the assignor. For example: X contracts to buy a bulldozer from Y for $25,000 under an installment contract. After delivery, Y assigns the contract (the right to collect the price) to a third party, Z. If the machine proves defective, X can successfully assert this fact as a defense against Z, just as he could have asserted it against Y had there been no assignment. This means that the assignee, Z, is not entitled to a judgment against X. The same would be true if X had simply given Y a nonnegotiable note or draft in payment for the bulldozer; Z's rights would be no better than those possessed by Y.

On the other hand, if X had given Y a *negotiable* note, draft, or check in payment for the machine, and if Y had then transferred the instrument to Z under circumstances that qualified Z as a holder in due course, then Z would be entitled to recover the full amount of the instrument from X, despite the fact that Y had breached his contract with X by delivering a defective machine.

The above is a simple illustration of one of the basic commercial paper concepts—*that it is possible for a third-party HDC to acquire greater rights under a negotiable instrument than those possessed by the payee-transferor.* This does not mean, however, that the HDC is always legally entitled to payment from the primary party. Sometimes the primary party has available a "real" or "universal" defense, which he or she can successfully assert against any holder, even the HDC. And the holder-in-due-course doctrine itself has been sharply limited in recent years. (These limitations will be explained more fully in Chapter 26.)

## PARTIES TO COMMERCIAL PAPER

We have already seen that notes have two original parties—the maker and the payee—while drafts and checks have three—the drawer, the drawee, and the payee. But after an instrument is issued, additional parties can become involved. (The liability incurred by each of these parties is spelled out in Chapter 27.)

### *The Acceptor*

Frequently, after a draft is issued, it is presented by the payee (or a subsequent holder) to the drawee (the person to whom the order is addressed) for that person's *acceptance*. Under the UCC some types of drafts require a presentment, while for others the presentment is at the option of the holder. In any event, the drawee who "accepts" the draft is called the **acceptor** (or *drawee-acceptor*), and he or she becomes a primary party to the instrument. (As we have seen, an acceptance occurs when the drawee signs his or her name somewhere on the face of the instrument.) In this capacity, the acceptor's liability is roughly akin to that of the maker of a note.

### *Indorsers*

Often the payee of a note or draft transfers it to a third party soon after acquiring it, instead of presenting it to the primary party for payment. When such a transfer occurs, the payee-transferor almost always "indorses" the instrument by signing his or her name on the back of it before delivering it to the third party; by so doing, the payee becomes an **indorser**.

For example, if P, the payee, receives a check from D, P can indorse it to a third party, Z, in payment of a debt that P owes to Z (or for any other reason).

## *Indorsees*

The **indorsee** is the person who receives an indorsed instrument; in the example above, the indorsee is Z. Z can indorse the instrument to another party, in which case Z also becomes an indorser.

## *The Bearer*

From both a legal and a practical standpoint, the term *bearer* is of limited (though well-defined) significance. A **bearer** is any person who has physical possession of an instrument that legally qualifies as a *bearer instrument*. For example, if a note is expressly made "payable to bearer" or is simply payable to "cash," whoever possesses it is the bearer.

Another type of bearer instrument comes into existence when an instrument is originally payable to the order of a named person, and the named person indorses it by signing his or her name on the back. An indorsement such as this, called a *blank indorsement*, converts the paper into a bearer instrument; therefore, the subsequent taker of the instrument also is a bearer. The blank indorsement is contrasted with a *special indorsement*, which specifies the person to whom, or to whose order, the instrument is payable. The different kinds of indorsements are discussed in Chapter 25.

## *Holders*

The term *holder* is broader in scope and of greater legal significance than the term *bearer*. Section 1-201(20) of the UCC defines a **holder** as a person who possesses a negotiable instrument which is either payable to the bearer or payable to such a person as the payee or indorsee. Thus the term includes not only persons possessing bearer instruments but also payees and indorsees possessing order instruments. To illustrate: X pays a utility bill by drawing a check "payable to the order of Columbia Gas of Ohio" and mailing it to that company. While Columbia Gas cannot be called a bearer (since the check is not payable to bearer), as payee it clearly qualifies as a holder.

**Holder in Due Course:** Under Sec. 3-302, a **holder in due course** is a holder who has given value for the instrument, has acquired it before it was overdue, and has taken it in good faith. As indicated earlier, it is the HDC who is afforded most-favored status under the code.[3]

**Ordinary Holder:** A person who qualifies as a holder but does not meet all the HDC requirements is called an **ordinary holder,** or sometimes a *mere holder, transferee* or *assignee*. Unlike the HDC, an ordinary holder cannot enforce the instrument against the primary party if the latter has a personal defense, such as fraud on the part of the payee. In other words, the ordinary holder takes the instrument subject to all defenses, much like the assignee of a nonnegotiable instrument or contract. However, also like the assignee, the ordinary holder can enforce the instrument against the primary party if the latter has no defense available.

**Holder through a Holder in Due Course:** If a holder fails to qualify as an HDC, he or she can still enjoy the special rights of a holder in due course by showing that any prior holder qualified as an HDC. Such a person is called a *holder through a holder in due course*.

## SUMMARY

The term commercial paper refers to written promises or orders to pay sums of money arising from the use of such instruments as drafts, checks, and promissory notes. These instruments may be either "negotiable" or "nonnegotiable," depending upon their terms. The question of negotiability is of primary concern to a purchaser of such an instrument, for if the instrument is negotiable the purchaser may qualify as a holder in due course. In such a case he or she takes the instrument free of many defenses that might exist between the maker (or drawer) and the payee.

For an instrument to qualify as a negotiable instrument, it must meet the requirements of Sec. 3-104 of the UCC (which are discussed in the next chapter). The UCC recognizes four kinds of commercial paper: drafts, checks, notes, and certificates of deposit. Drafts and checks contain orders to pay money. The person to whom the order is addressed is the drawee, the person to whom the order is payable is the payee, and the person issuing the instrument is the drawer.

---

[3] The precise rights of the holder in due course, ordinary holder, and holder through a holder in due course will be examined in Chapter 26.

In contrast to drafts, notes contain promises to pay, and have only two parties. The maker is the person making the promise to pay, and the payee is the person to whom the note is payable.

In many instances—usually after the instrument has been issued—two other classes of persons may become parties to it, the acceptor and the indorser. An acceptance occurs if the holder of a draft presents it to the drawee for his or her signature; by signing, the drawee becomes the acceptor (and is thus primarily liable on the instrument). The indorser, in most instances, is the owner of an instrument who signs his or her name on the back of it before delivering it to a third party, the indorsee.

Other persons recognized under Article 3 are the holder and the bearer. The holder is any person who possesses a negotiable instrument which is payable either to the bearer, to his or her order, or to the indorsee of such an instrument. A holder who meets certain requirements of Article 3 (also to be discussed in the next chapter) is a holder in due course; one not meeting these requirements is an ordinary holder.

## KEY TERMS

Commercial paper
Draft
Sales draft
Check
Note
Certificate of deposit
Demand instrument
Time instrument
Negotiable instrument
Nonnegotiable instrument
Acceptor
Indorser
Indorsee
Bearer
Holder
Holder in due course
Ordinary holder

## QUESTIONS AND PROBLEMS

**1.** X contracts to paint Y's house for $1,200 in June. On June 20, when X is half-way through with the job, Y is called to Europe on a business trip. Before leaving, Y makes out a promissory note for $1,200 that is payable July 15, and hands it to X. The next day X sells the note to a local bank for $1,100 (he "discounts" the note). In late July, when the bank demands payment from Y, Y refuses to pay the instrument because X never finished the job. If the note in question turns out to be nonnegotiable in form, what effect—if any—does this have upon Y's liability to the bank? Explain.

**2.** What were the major factors that were responsible for the creation of commercial paper in the Middle Ages?

**3.** Often the holder of a promissory note that is not due until some future date will "discount" it at a bank. What are the advantages to the holder, and to the bank, in doing this?

**4.** Tom is owed $1,000 by Dick, but he (Tom) in turn owes Harry $400. When Harry presses Tom for payment, Tom gives Harry this letter addressed to Dick: "Out of the $1,000 you owe me, please pay $400 of it to Harry as soon as he requests it." Does this letter look like a *draft,* or more like a *note?* What is the primary reason for your answer?

**5.** The Scarlet Corporation orders ten snowmobiles from the Gray Company at a total cost of $12,000. If a *sales draft* were to be used here (instead of a cash payment by the Scarlet Corporation), who would be (a) the drawer, (b) the drawee, and (c) the acceptor?

**6.** X sells a used car to Y and takes a promissory note from Y in payment. When the note comes due Y is financially unable to pay it. X then brings suit on the note, and Y's only defense is that the note is *nonnegotiable* in form. (That is, there was nothing wrong with the car that he received.) If Y can clearly prove that the note *is* nonnegotiable, is his defense good? (That is, will the court dismiss the action?) Why or why not?

**7.** You see this statement in a text: "As a general rule, bearer instruments are governed by contract law, and order instruments by Article 3 of the UCC." Is this statement essentially true? Why or why not?

**8.** B is the maker of a negotiable promissory note, and he issues it to C. C later negotiates it to D. In such a situation, D may qualify as a *holder in due course,* or he may be only an *ordinary holder.* If D were forced to bring suit against B in an effort to obtain payment of the note, under what circumstances might D's success depend entirely upon whether he was the one type of holder or the other? Explain.

CHAPTER 25

# Commercial Paper

Negotiability and Transfer

In many situations, whether an instrument is negotiable or nonnegotiable is of little importance. Suppose, for example, that P is willing to sell goods to M on credit, taking a promissory ninety-day note signed by M as evidence of the indebtedness. Suppose further that M's financial reputation is good, and that P is perfectly willing to hold the note himself until it matures. In these circumstances P might well be satisfied with a nonnegotiable note, for his chances of being paid on the due date, and his legal rights against M if payment is not made voluntarily, are about as good as those he would possess if the note were negotiable.

In many other circumstances, however, the negotiability or nonnegotiability of an instrument is of vital importance, for a number of reasons. First, as we briefly suggested in the preceding chapter, when legal problems arise as to the enforceability of the instrument, the rights and obligations of the parties are resolved under Article 3 of the UCC if the instrument is negotiable and under ordinary contract law if it is not. And since the holder-in-due-course concept is recognized only under Article 3, any person seeking to enforce the instrument under this concept must (among other things) show at the outset that the instrument meets the tests of negotiability.

In addition, as a practical matter, commercial paper cannot serve its "substitute for money" and "extension of credit" roles unless it is freely transferable (that is, unless prospective purchasers of the paper, especially financial institutions, are willing to accept it routinely). And, before such purchasers are willing to accept commercial paper, they not only want to be able to determine that the paper is negotiable in form but, additionally, that the seller/transferor has taken the steps necessary to insure that the transfer constitutes a "negotiation" of the paper as defined by Article 3 of the UCC.

In this chapter, then, we will discuss (1) the requirements of negotiability and (2) the rules applicable to the transfer of negotiable instruments.

## REQUIREMENTS OF NEGOTIABILITY

Today the requirements of negotiability are expressly set forth in Sec. 3-104 of the UCC. Subsection 1 reads as follows:

> Any writing to be a negotiable instrument within this Article must (a) be signed by the maker or drawer; and (b) contain an unconditional promise or order to pay a sum certain in money and [must contain] no other promise, order, obligation, or power given by the maker or drawer except as authorized by this Article; and (c) be payable on demand or at a definite time; and (d) be payable to order or to bearer.

As a result of these requirements, the negotiability or nonnegotiability of an instrument is entirely dependent upon its *form* and *content.* Each of these requirements, together with later sections that help in the interpretation of Sec. 3-104, will now be examined.

### The Writing and Signing Requirements

**The Writing:** Just as there is no such thing as "oral money," an oral promise or order to pay money obviously cannot serve as a substitute for it. Under contract law it is true that an oral promise to pay money can be enforced as long as its existence can be established in court. However, in the commercial world, where large numbers of promises and orders must be transferred daily, the need for such obligations to be evidenced in tangible written form becomes obvious.

Under Sec. 1-201(46), this "writing" can be handwritten, printed, or typewritten, or it can consist of "any other intentional [method of] reduction to tangible form."

Normally, of course, the substance on which the writing appears is paper, but the UCC does not require this. Thus we occasionally read in the newspaper about the holder of a "check" written on a watermelon or some similar object who was able to obtain payment at the drawee bank upon physical presentment of the object. These cases, of course, are rarities; they do, however, bring a welcome degree of humor and ingenuity to the subject of commercial paper (though the bank officials involved might not entirely share this view).

**The Signing:** A negotiable instrument must be signed by the maker in the case of a note or by the drawer in the case of a draft. Ordinarily there is little trouble with this requirement, since such a party almost invariably affixes his or her signature (in longhand) to the instrument at the outset.

In some instances, however, questions do arise. Section 1-201(39) is designed to alleviate these by stating that the term *signed* means "any symbol executed or adopted by a party with [the] present intention to authenticate a writing." Thus a signing can occur through the use of one's initials, a rubber stamp, or some other type of "signature," such as the mark X, so long as it is made with the intention of giving assent to the writing's terms. (Problems that relate to forgeries and the unauthorized signing of principals' names by their agents are examined in Chapter 27.)

## The Promise or Order Must Be Unconditional

In order for an instrument to be treated as a substitute for money or as a credit extension device, the holder wants assurance that no conditions will be imposed on the instrument's payment. Whether such conditions exist in a given case, thus causing the instrument to be nonnegotiable, depends on the totality of the terms and provisions that make up the instrument.

An almost infinite variety of clauses or notations find their way into some instruments and raise legitimate questions as to whether they condition the basic promise or order to pay. We will consider here the most common of these.

**Express Conditions:** A small percentage of notes and drafts contain clauses that *expressly condition* the primary promise or order to pay. Obviously these clauses destroy negotiability of the instrument at the outset. A note signed by M, maker, which is payable "upon the marriage of my daughter" or "on the date of the next Rose Bowl game," falls into this category, for it is expressly made payable upon an event that may never occur. Even if the event is very likely to occur (or does, in fact, occur subsequently), the instrument continues to be a nonnegotiable one.

**Permitted Provisions:** A more common situation is one where the basic obligation is itself unconditional but where the instrument contains language or clauses which will *possibly* condition the primary obligation—depending, of course, on how the clauses are legally interpreted.

Section 3-105 resolves many of these problems of interpretation. Subsection 1 contains eight express types of clauses or notations that may appear on the face of an instrument which do *not* condition the promise or order to pay. Thus any clause falling within this subsection does not destroy the negotiability of the instrument. For example, subsection 1 permits the maker or drawer to note on the face of the instrument its purpose ("January rent"), or the consideration received in exchange for the instrument ("Payment for 100 bushels wheat"). It also permits the maker or drawer to indicate that the instrument has arisen out of a separate agreement, if such is the case, or is secured by a mortgage on specified property. The UCC recognizes that these kinds of references should have no adverse legal or practical effect on the instrument's negotiability.

Subsections f and g under subsection 1 contain two "fund" provisions. Subsection f permits inclusion on the face of an instrument of a clause which merely "indicates a particular account to be debited or any other fund from which *reimbursement* is to be made." Two examples: (1) D draws a check on which he writes the words, "Charge to petty cash"; and (2) the X Corporation, a manufacturer holding several construction contracts with the U.S. Navy, writes on an obligation, "Charge to Navy Contract SX-102." In both instances it is clear that the instruments pledge the general credit of the parties issuing them, and that the extra notations merely refer to funds (or assets) out of which the parties will reimburse themselves after they have paid the instruments. The instruments, therefore, remain negotiable.

Subsection g further provides that two kinds of instruments are negotiable even though they are *payable* out of a specified fund. The more important of these consists of instruments issued by a government, a governmental unit, or a governmental agency. Thus a state-issued bond, payable out of the revenue of that state's turnpike commission, is a negotiable instrument. (In other words, under subsection g the commission's promise to pay is not conditioned upon the existence of a fund at maturity sufficient to permit payment of the full face value of the bonds.) Governmental obligations are given this special treatment because government funds are almost always adequate to honor the obligations, while this is less likely to be the case where the maker is an ordinary corporation or an individual.[1]

**Impermissible Provisions:** Subsection 2 of Sec. 3-105, in contrast to subsection 1, refers to two kinds of clauses or provisions that *do* destroy the negotiability of any note or draft.

*"Subject to" Clauses:* Instruments that contain language indicating that the promises or orders to pay are *subject to* some other agreement, such as a mortgage or a lease, are nonnegotiable. This results from subsection 2a, which provides that "A promise or order is not unconditional if the instrument states that it is subject to or governed by any other agreement." Prior to the adoption of the UCC, some courts took the view that the negotiability of an instrument that was subject to some other agreement depended upon the actual terms of that agreement. This meant that a prospective purchaser would have to search out that other agreement in order to know what the status of the instrument was—a most impractical requirement in the commercial world. Subsection 2a makes such instruments *nonnegotiable as a matter of law*—regardless of what the terms of the other agreement actually are. This subsection underscores the general idea that the negotiability or nonnegotiability of an instrument must be determinable from the face of the instrument alone.

*"Payable Out of Fund" Instruments:* The second kind of clause that destroys negotiability, found under subsection 2b, is that which makes the instrument *payable out of a specified fund* (with the two narrow exceptions noted in the discussion of Sec. 3-105(1)(g) above). Because the payment of such instruments is subject to the possibility that there may be no such fund in existence at maturity, the promise or order is obviously conditional in nature, and 2b expressly so provides. Thus if X in June promises to pay $5,000 to the order of Y on the following December 1 "out of the proceeds of the sale of my Ford Motor stock," the instrument is nonnegotiable when issued to Y, and remains nonnegotiable even if the stock is sold before December 1 for more than $5,000.[2]

The primary question in the first following case is whether the promise of the maker of a note was unconditional under the rules discussed above. In the second case, the issue is whether a notation on the face of a check causes it to be conditional, and thus not negotiable. As we will see, regardless of what the drawer intended such a notation prevents negotiability only if it makes the order to pay a conditional one.

---

[1] The second type of instrument that is negotiable, although payable out of a fund, consists of instruments payable out of the "entire assets of a partnership, unincorporated association, trust, or estate by or on behalf of which the instrument is issued."

[2] The "fund" rules of Sec. 3-105 can be summarized as follows: (1) An instrument that refers to a fund out of which reimbursement is to be made is negotiable. (2) An instrument that is payable out of a fund is nonnegotiable, except for instruments payable out of governmental funds and those payable out of the entire assets of a partnership, unincorporated association, trust, or estate.

---

**Calfo v. D. C. Stewart Co.**
Supreme Court of Utah,
717 P.2d 697 (1986)

D. C. Stewart Company (Stewart) owned the Astro Motel in Cedar City, Utah. It listed the motel for sale with C. J. Realty, and C. J. Realty obtained a Mr. and Mrs. Downward as potential buyers of the property. Stewart entered into a lease and purchase agreement with the Downwards on September 24, 1979, which gave the Downwards (lessees) an option to purchase the motel at a specified price until May 1, 1980.

Also, on September 24, Stewart executed a promissory note for $15,900 payable to C. J. Realty to secure the commission it would be entitled to if the lessees exercised their option to purchase. The note provided that it would be payable "upon final closing between . . . seller and . . . buyers,

*(continued)*

which shall be on or before May 1, 1980, when buyers exercise their option to purchase the Astro Motel. . . ."

On September 27 C. J. Realty sold the note to Calfo, plaintiff, for $12,720. After May 1, 1980, Calfo presented the note to Stewart for payment. Stewart refused to pay because the lessees did not exercise their option to purchase—i.e., the motel was never sold. Calfo then brought this action against Stewart, the maker, and C. J. Realty and an agent of C. J. Realty, the indorsers.

At the conclusion of the pleading stage, after a series of hearings, the trial court entered summary judgment in favor of Calfo, ruling (1) that the note was a negotiable instrument; (2) that Calfo was a holder in due course; and (3) that defendant Stewart, therefore, could not assert its defense of non-sale of the property against Calfo. Stewart appealed.

**Decision:** The judgment was reversed. The note is nonnegotiable because Stewart's promise to pay was not an "unconditional" one, as required by Sec. 3-104 of the UCC. Under the terms of the instrument, it is clear that Stewart's promise to pay is conditioned upon a contingency which might or might not occur—i.e., the exercise by the lessees, the Downwards, of their option to purchase the motel. Thus Calfo cannot qualify as a holder in due course, with the results that Stewart *can* assert its defense (non-sale of the property) against Calfo. Accordingly, the trial court's entry of judgment in favor of Calfo was improper. ■

---

### Carador v. Sana Travel Service, Ltd.
U.S. District Court for the Southern District of New York, 700 F. Supp. 787 (1988)

Sana Travel Service is a New York corporation, and Paracha is an officer and director of Sana. Paracha drew a check on Sana's account at the National Bank of Pakistan (NBP) for $33,000.00, payable to the order of Jamil Ahmed Kahn (Kahn), Al-Bark Turismo (Al-Bark). Kahn worked for Al-Bark, a travel and tourist service in Brazil. On the memorandum line on the lower left-hand portion of the check, Paracha wrote "Just to hold for the security of future business." Paracha then sent the check to Al-Bark's offices in Brazil.

At the direction of Al-Bark's owner, Kahn indorsed the check in blank and sold it to Carador for cash. Carador then sought to collect on the check by giving it to a firm specializing in foreign currency exchange, which then turned it over to a bank in the United States for collection. The U.S. bank sent it to the drawee bank, NBP, in Pakistan. When NBP received the check, it telephoned Sana, and Paracha directed that the check be dishonored. After the check was dishonored, Carador filed suit against Sana and Paracha. (Paracha is also a defendant because he signed the check without indicating on it that he was signing only in a representative capacity for Sana.) Sana and Paracha, the defendants, claimed that the check was rendered nonnegotiable by the notation on its face. If it was not negotiable, they argued, Carador could not be a holder in due course and would be subject to their defense that Al-Bark gave no consideration. Following is a summary of the federal district court's opinion on Carador's motion for summary judgment.

---

**Decision:** The U.S. district court ruled for Carador on its motion for summary judgment. The notation on the check does not prevent it from being negotiable: it does not indicate that the promise to pay is conditional, but merely indicates that Al-Bark and Sana had agreed that Sana would give Al-Bark a security deposit to insure future performance of another contract. Carador is an HDC and is not subject to the defense of no consideration. Paracha is liable along with Sana because he did not indicate he was signing only in a representative capacity. ■

---

**Definite Promise or Order to Pay:** Occasionally an instrument refers to the existence of a debt, but its language raises the question of whether the instrument really constitutes a promise or order that the debt be paid. For example, one person may hand to another a written IOU. A statement of this kind, or any other statement that merely acknowledges the existence of a debt, does not constitute a promise to pay, and the instrument thus fails to meet the requirements of negotiability.

## Amount to Be Paid Must Be a Sum Certain in Money

If an instrument is to be a substitute for money and have an equivalent degree of acceptability, the necessity that the amount be a *sum certain* is obvious. This requirement of certainty is met if the holder can determine from the terms of the instrument itself the amount he or she is entitled to receive at maturity.

The UCC recognizes that some instruments contain provisions that at least raise the question of whether they violate this requirement, and Sec. 3-106 is meant to "save" the negotiability of many of these instruments by providing that

> the sum payable is a sum certain even though it is to be paid (a) with stated interest or by stated installments; or (b) with stated different rates of interest before and after default or a specified date; or (c) with a stated discount or addition if paid before or after the date fixed for payment; or (d) with exchange or less exchange, whether at a fixed rate or at the current rate; or (e) with costs of collections or an attorney's fee or both upon default.

Subsections a, b, c, and e are self-explanatory. Subsection d refers to instruments that are payable in foreign currency. The holder of this kind of instrument may want payment in his or her own country's currency, which requires application of the exchange rate in effect between the two countries. Such instruments, whether payable at fixed exchange rates or at "current rates," are deemed by subsection d to meet the "sum certain" requirement.

**Payment to Be Made Only in Money:** Instruments must be payable only in *money*. Thus, any contract that requires the obligor to perform an act other than, or in addition to, the payment of money is non-negotiable (with exceptions noted later in the chapter).[3] Three examples of such contracts are: (1) M, in return for a loan, promises to deliver "sixty bushels of U.S. #1 blackeye peas ninety days after date"; (2) M signs a note that obligates him to pay at maturity $1,000 *and* to deliver to the holder at that time sixty bushels of U.S. #1 blackeye peas; and (3) M signs a note that obligates him to pay $1,000 *or* to deliver the peas at maturity.

Money is defined in Sec. 1-201(24) as a "medium of exchange authorized or adopted by a domestic or foreign government as a part of its currency." It thus follows that any instrument payable in the currency of a recognized government is payable in money regardless of where the instrument is to be paid. In that regard, Sec. 3-107(2) provides that an instrument payable in this country whose amount is stated in a foreign currency (such as 2,000 German marks) can be satisfied by the payment of an equivalent number of American dollars at the due date, unless the instrument *expressly* requires payment in marks. In either event the instrument is negotiable. In no case, however, can the instrument be payable in something other than money. To illustrate:

**1.** An instrument drafted in Mexico City and payable in Austin, Texas, expressly calls for payment in ten thousand Mexican pesos. The instrument is payable in money.

**2.** An instrument payable in U.S. government bonds is not negotiable, since government bonds are not a medium of exchange recognized by the U.S. government.

The next case deals with the question of whether a variable interest rate prevents a note from being negotiable.

---

[3] However, contracts that require the *delivery of goods* at a future date often do possess the quality of negotiability. While bills of lading and warehouse receipts fail to qualify as negotiable instruments under Article 3 of the UCC, because they do not contain promises to pay money, they do qualify as negotiable documents of title under Article 7 of the code.

---

### Centerre Bank of Branson v. Campbell
Court of Appeals of Missouri,
744 S.W.2d 490 (1988)

Curtis and Debbie Campbell purchased an interest in a limited partnership to be formed by Strand Investment Co. For this interest they executed a promissory note dated May 7, 1985, payable to the order of Strand in the amount of $11,250 together with interest at an annual rate of 14 percent. The note specified the amounts of principal and interest that would be due in three annual installments, and then concluded with several short clauses. One of these clauses stated, "Interest may vary with bank rates charged to Strand." Less than a week after the note was executed, Strand sold the note to Centerre Bank of Branson.

*(continued)*

The Campbells defaulted on the note, leaving an unpaid balance of $9,000 plus accrued interest. The bank, as holder of the note, filed suit against the Campbells to collect the unpaid balance. The Campbells defended on the ground that Strand had never formed the limited partnership, and that there was thus a complete failure of consideration for the note. They also claimed that the note was not negotiable because it stated a variable rate of interest. If the note was not a negotiable instrument, the bank could not be a holder in due course and would be subject to the Campbells' defense. The trial court ruled in favor of the bank, and the Campbells appealed.

**Decision:** Reversed and remanded for a new trial, at which the Campbells will have an opportunity to prove their defense. The variable interest rate prevented the note from being negotiable, because it was not payable in a "sum certain." The bank could not be an HDC. ■

## Payable on Demand or at a Definite Time

Under Sec. 3-108, to be negotiable an instrument must be either payable on demand or at a definite time. This requirement recognizes that the holder of an instrument wants to know with certainty when he or she will be entitled to payment. Any appreciable uncertainty as to time of payment makes the instrument commercially unacceptable and defeats the concept that a negotiable instrument is a substitute for money.

Instruments payable *on demand* (called **demand instruments**) include (1) those which are expressly so payable; (2) those whose terms make the instrument payable "at sight" or "on presentation" by the holder; or (3) those in which no time for payment is stated, as, for example, the following: "I promise to pay to the order of P one hundred dollars. (signed) M."

Instruments that are not payable on demand, called **time instruments,** must be payable at a definite time in order to be negotiable. When issuing this kind of note or draft, the maker or drawer usually wants assurance that there will be no obligation to pay until the specified time period has elapsed. The terms clearly indicate a definite future time for payment, such as "payable one year from date" or "payable July 1, 1990."

While no problems of negotiability are presented by these kinds of instruments, problems do arise when the note or draft contains additional terms that apparently conflict with the definite time requirement. Section 3-109 clears up most of these problem situations, as follows:

(1) An instrument is payable at a definite time if by its terms it is payable (a) on or before a stated date or at a fixed period after a stated date; or (b) at a fixed price after sight; or (c) at a definite time subject to any acceleration; or (d) at a definite time subject to extension at the option of the holder, or to extension to a further definite time at the option of the maker or acceptor or automatically upon or after a specified act or event.

(2) An instrument which by its terms is otherwise payable only upon an act or event uncertain as to time of occurrence is not payable at a definite time even though the act or event has occurred.

We will now briefly examine subsections a and b of Sec. 3-109(1), together with a case that involves an interpretation of these provisions. Following the case we will return to the "acceleration" and "extension" provisions of subsections c and d.

**Subsections 1a and 1b:** Subsections a and b of Sec. 3-109(1) are virtually self-explanatory. An instrument payable on or before a specified date gives the maker, drawer, or acceptor the option of paying before the stated maturity date if he or she wishes. Subsection 1a simply points out that such uncertainty does not violate the definite time requirement. Subsection 1b refers to a common provision in drafts that they are payable a specified time (frequently sixty or ninety days) "after sight." That is, the time period does not begin to run until "sight" (the moment the draft is accepted by the drawee) occurs. Although the time at which the acceptance will occur is unknown when the instrument is first issued, this subsection provides that the instrument nonetheless meets the definite time requirement.

In the following case the primary question is: "When is the instrument due?" rather than "Is the instrument negotiable?" The case is nonetheless useful, because in answering the primary question the higher court clearly implied that the note did qualify as a negotiable instrument under the code.

### Ferri v. Sylvia
Supreme Court of Rhode Island,
214 A.2d 470 (1965)

Mr. and Mrs. Sylvia, the defendants, signed a promissory note payable to Maria Ferri, plaintiff. Under the terms of the note, dated May 25, 1963, the Sylvias promised to pay plaintiff $3,000 "within ten (10) years after date." At some unspecified time thereafter, but long before the ten years had elapsed, plaintiff brought action to recover on the note. The Sylvias defended on the ground that the instrument had not yet matured.

The trial court ruled that the maturity date was "uncertain" and therefore admitted oral testimony by both parties "as to their intentions and prior agreements." On the basis of that testimony the court ruled that plaintiff had the right to demand payment at any time after May 25, 1963. Judgment was thus entered for plaintiff, and defendants appealed.

**Decision:** The judgment was reversed. Prior to adoption of the UCC, case law clearly ruled that the maturity date of a note payable "on or before" a stated date was the stated date itself—not any earlier date. Such clauses merely permitted makers to pay before that time if they so wished. The same rule, which now appears in Sec. 3-109(1) of the UCC, provides that "an instrument is payable at a *definite time* if by its terms it is payable . . . on or before a stated date." [Emphasis added.]

In principle there is no difference between a note payable on or before a fixed date and one that calls for payment "within" a stipulated period, as here. Thus the note signed by the Sylvias did have a fixed maturity date—ten years after May 25, 1963. Since, by that language, the parties agreed that plaintiff could not demand payment until expiration of the ten-year period, the trial court erred in ruling that the maturity date of the note was uncertain. ■

**Acceleration Clauses:** Instruments due at a fixed future date sometimes have **acceleration clauses** providing that the date of maturity shall be *moved ahead* if a specified event occurs prior to the stated due date. An instrument issued this year with a maturity date two years hence might contain, for example, either of these acceleration clauses: (1) "This instrument shall become immediately due and payable upon the maker's (or acceptor's) bankruptcy"; or (2) for a note payable in monthly installments, "If any installment is not paid when due, the entire instrument is due and payable."

Under Sec. 3-109(1)(c) all instruments with acceleration clauses meet the definite time test, even if the events upon which the acceleration is based are to some extent within the holder's control. To illustrate: "Should the holder deem himself insecure at any time prior to the maturity date, he can demand payment at such time and the entire instrument shall thereupon immediately become due and payable."

However, the right of the holder to accelerate an instrument containing a clause such as this is subject to the good faith requirement contained in Sec. 1-208—that the clause "shall be construed to mean that he shall have the power [to accelerate] only if he in good faith believes that the prospect of payment or performance is impaired."

**Extension Clauses:** **Extension clauses** are the reverse of acceleration clauses; that is, they appear in notes or drafts having a fixed future maturity date and provide that, under certain circumstances, the date shall be *extended further.* Before enactment of the UCC this kind of clause posed a number of questions for the courts about their effect on negotiability. Virtually all these questions have been eliminated by UCC Sec. 3-109(1)(d), which provides that an instrument is negotiable if by its terms it is payable "at a definite time subject to extension at the option of the holder, or to extension to a further definite time at the option of the maker or acceptor or automatically upon or after a specified event."

Thus extension clauses that give the *obligor* (maker or acceptor) the right to extend the time of payment meet the definite time test only if they contain a new fixed maturity date. (The same is true for clauses that extend the time of payment automatically on the occurrence of a specified event.) On the other hand, clauses giving the *holder* the right to extend the time of payment need not contain a new fixed maturity date.

This distinction is logical. If the obligor had the right to extend payment without limit, neither the holder nor any potential purchaser could determine with certainty when he or she would have the right to be paid. But when the holder has the option, he or she is free to demand payment at the maturity date or at any time thereafter. (Actually, the holder of any instrument is free to postpone the time of payment even if no extension clause appears.)

We can illustrate the primary effects of subsection d as follows:

**1.** "It is expressly agreed that the holder of this note at the date of maturity can extend the time of payment until the following Thanksgiving or even later if she wishes." *Result:* Negotiability is not destroyed, even though it is not known how long the extension will be, since the option is solely that of the holder.

**2.** "The maker has the unconditional right to postpone the time of payment of this note beyond its November 1, 1988, maturity date, but for no longer than a reasonable time after such date." *Result:* The definite time requirement is not met and the negotiability of the instrument is thus destroyed, since the right to extend is the maker's and since no further definite time is contained in the extension clause.

**Payable upon Happening of Specified Event:** An instrument that is payable upon the happening of an event that may never occur (such as "upon the marriage of my daughter") is nonnegotiable for the reason that the promise or order to pay is clearly *conditional* in nature. The instrument remains nonnegotiable even if the event subsequently does occur (although it would, of course, become *payable* at that time.)

Section 3-109(2) goes one step further by providing that "an instrument which by its terms is . . . payable only upon an act or event uncertain as to time of occurrence is not payable at a definite time even though the act or event has occurred." To illustrate: A draft is payable "upon the death of X." Even though X's death is an event that is certain to happen, the draft is nonnegotiable when issued, and remains nonnegotiable even after X's death. (As in the prior example, the draft would, however, become *payable* at that time.)

## *Payable to Order or to Bearer*

It is fundamental to the concept of negotiability that the instrument contain language clearly indicating that the maker or drawer intends it to be fully capable of being transferred to some person or persons other than the one to whom it was originally issued. This is why Sec. 3-104(1)(d) states that the instrument must "be payable to order or to bearer." *Order* and *bearer* are frequently referred to as the "words of negotiability" (although any other words indicating a similar intention will also meet this requirement of the code).[4]

**Order Instruments:** Section 3-110 defines **order instrument** and helps interpret Sec. 3-104(1)(d). Essentially Sec. 3-110(1) provides that "an instrument is payable to order when by its terms it is payable to the order or assigns of any person therein specified with reasonable certainty, or to him or his order."[5] Additionally, the instrument can be payable "to the order of (a) the maker or drawer; or (b) the drawee; or (c) a payee who is not maker, drawer, or drawee; or (d) two or more payees together or in the alternative; or (e) an estate, trust or funds . . . ; or (f) an office or an officer by his title as such . . . ; or (g) a partnership or unincorporated association. . . ."

The requirements of the order instrument are met by such language as "pay to the order of Jennifer Howell" and "pay to Melanie Howell or order." However, an instrument "payable to Carolyn Howell" is not an order instrument, and therefore is nonnegotiable.

---

[4] We are here concerned with the order-bearer requirement only as it affects *negotiability* of an instrument, but the requirement also affects the manner in which instruments are to be *transferred*. As we will see later in the chapter, a bearer instrument can be "negotiated" to a third party without being indorsed by the transferor, while an indorsement is essential for order instruments.

[5] *Assigns* simply means all third parties to whom the instrument might subsequently be transferred.

**Bearer Instruments:** A note or draft that fails to qualify as an order instrument is nonetheless negotiable if it is payable to the *bearer.* Section 3-111 provides that "an instrument is payable to bearer when by its terms it is payable to (a) bearer or the order of bearer; or (b) a specified person or bearer; or (c) 'cash' or the order of 'cash,' or any other indication which does not purport to designate a specific payee."

Under this section the following all qualify as **bearer instruments:** "payable to bearer," "payable to the order of bearer," and "payable to X or bearer." However, an instrument that is payable only to a specified person ("payable to X") is not payable to bearer and hence is nonnegotiable.

## *Terms and Omissions Not Affecting Negotiability*

The negotiability of most instruments is settled by reference to the basic sections we have examined. Occasionally, however, instruments present special problems—sometimes because they contain terms not covered by the preceding sections, sometimes because terms are omitted that normally are present, and sometimes because they contain provisions that are in apparent conflict. Sections 3-112 through 3-118 are designed to resolve most peripheral problems of this sort. We will discuss below the more important of these rules.

**Section 3-112—Omissions:** Section 3-112 provides in part that the negotiability of an instrument is not affected by "the omission of a statement of any consideration, or of the place where the instrument is drawn or payable." This provision rejects the possible view that such omissions cause an instrument to be incomplete and therefore nonnegotiable. (Along similar lines, Sec. 3-114 states that the negotiability of an instrument is not destroyed simply because the date of issue does not appear—unless, of course, the date of maturity is tied to the date of issue, as when an undated note is "payable sixty days after date.")

**Section 3-112—Additional Powers and Promises:** We have seen that under Sec. 3-104(1)(b) any instrument containing a promise or order *in addition to* the "promise or order to pay a sum certain in money" causes the instrument to be nonnegotiable "except as authorized by this Article." Several of these additional promises are expressly authorized by subsections b and c of Sec. 3-112.

Subsection b states that the negotiability of an instrument is not affected by a statement that collateral has been given as security for the obligation. Nor is it affected by a promise on the part of the maker, drawer, or acceptor to *maintain,* to *protect,* or to *give additional collateral* in specified circumstances. To illustrate: The maker of a time note has given the payee a warehouse receipt for six hundred bags of beans in the X Warehouse as security. The note further provides that "if a decline in the market value of this collateral should cause the holder of this instrument to deem himself insecure, the maker shall deliver additional collateral upon demand." This note is negotiable.

The reason why Sec. 3-112 provides that the stipulations noted above do not destroy negotiability lies in the fact that the stipulations actually *enhance* the value of the basic obligation, rather than limiting or conditioning it. Thus the instruments are more freely acceptable in commerce and even better able to fulfill their role as substitutes for money or as credit instruments than would be the case if the clauses were absent.

## TRANSFER

Commercial paper is designed primarily for the purpose of circulating freely in the business world, as was noted earlier. In the remainder of this chapter, then, we will look at the various ways such paper can be transferred from one holder to another, and at the basic UCC rules that apply to such transfers.

## ASSIGNMENT AND NEGOTIATION

A negotiable instrument has no legal significance of and by itself. In other words, its legal life does not begin until it is issued by the maker or drawer to the first holder.[6] After it has been issued to that person, it can be further transferred by him or her in one of two ways—by *negotiation* or by *assignment.*[7] While we shall be concerned in this chapter primarily with the legal requirements of a negotiation and the significant

---

[6] *Issue* is defined in Sec. 3-102(1)(a) as "the first delivery of an instrument to a holder."

[7] By contrast, the transfer of a nonnegotiable instrument *always* constitutes an assignment, no matter how the transfer is effected. This is because the negotiation provisions of Article 3 apply only to *negotiable instruments* (as is true of all other provisions of that article).

rights and duties that flow from it, it is first necessary to distinguish between the two kinds of transfers.

If a payee or other holder of an instrument transfers it to a third party in such a manner that the transfer qualifies as a negotiation under the UCC, the transferee is by definition a holder of the instrument. This makes it possible for the transferee to qualify as a holder in due course (HDC) if he or she meets the other HDC requirements of Article 3. As an HDC the person can acquire *greater rights* under the instrument than those possessed by the transferor, as indicated earlier.

## *Assignment*

If the transfer fails to qualify as a negotiation, it is merely an **assignment,** and the transferee is an *assignee* rather than a holder. As such, his or her status is governed by the common-law contract rules discussed in Chapter 16, under which the transferee's rights cannot be greater than those of the transferor. Obviously, then, the purchaser of a negotiable instrument will almost always want to be sure that the transfer qualifies as a negotiation rather than an assignment.

## *Negotiation*

The definition of **negotiation** and the requirements that must be met in order for the transfer of a particular instrument to qualify as a negotiation are found in Sec. 3-202(1): "Negotiation is the transfer of an instrument in such form that the transferee becomes a holder. If the instrument is payable to order it is negotiated by delivery with any necessary indorsement; if payable to bearer, it is negotiated by delivery [alone]."[8]

The requirements that must be met, then, in order for a particular transfer to qualify as a negotiation depend entirely upon the form of the instrument at the time of transfer. Before we examine the various kinds of indorsements that can be used, we will illustrate the basic delivery-indorsement requirements.

**1.** M issues two notes to X, one "payable to bearer" and the other "payable to cash." Because both notes are obviously bearer instruments, X can further negotiate either or both of them to a subsequent purchaser, Y, simply by handing them or mailing them to Y without an indorsement of any kind. (In practice, the purchaser of a bearer instrument normally requests the transferor to indorse it, but the indorsement is not required by the UCC.)

**2.** Same facts as for example 1, except that the two bearer notes are stolen from X's home by a thief, T. Because *delivery* means a voluntary delivery by the transferor, T's acquisition of the notes in this manner does not constitute a delivery; hence, no negotiation has occurred. However, a further delivery of either note by T to a third party does constitute a negotiation. This points up one of the dangers arising from the use of a bearer instrument. While a thief (or a finder) does not acquire title to the instrument by virtue of the theft (or finding), he or she can *transfer title* to a subsequent innocent purchaser. In such a case, the original owner, X, has lost all rights to the instrument itself.

**3.** D draws a check that is "payable to the order of P" and mails it to P. P writes her name on the back of the check (an indorsement) and transfers it to her grocer, G, in payment for groceries. The transfer from P to G constitutes a negotiation of this order instrument, since indorsement and delivery have both occurred. However, if P had delivered the instrument without indorsement, it would not constitute a negotiation. (G's rights in such a case will be discussed near the end of this chapter.)

**4.** B draws a check that is "payable to the order of C" and mails it to C. T, a thief, steals the check, signs C's name on the back, and delivers it to R, a retailer, in payment for liquor. The transfer from T to R is not a negotiation (nor is it even an assignment) because a forged "indorsement" is no indorsement. Nor would a further transfer by R constitute a negotiation; no one can qualify as a holder under a forged indorsement on an order instrument.

## BLANK, SPECIAL, QUALIFIED, AND RESTRICTIVE INDORSEMENTS

Essentially there are four kinds of indorsements: blank, special, qualified, and restrictive.

### *Blank Indorsements*

Under Sec. 3-204(1) a **blank indorsement** is one that specifies no particular indorsee; ordinarily it consists only of the name of the payee. If a check is pay-

---

[8] The issuance of an instrument to the payee technically constitutes a negotiation in view of the fact that the payee (as seen in Chapter 24) is one of the persons who qualifies as a holder under Sec. 1-201(20). However, in actual practice *negotiation* refers only to transfers that occur after an instrument has been issued.

able "to the order of Mary Glenn," she can indorse it *in blank* by simply writing or stamping her name on the back of the instrument.[9]

A blank indorsement converts an order instrument into a bearer instrument. If Mary Glenn delivers the check to Mark Rhee after indorsing it in blank, Rhee can further negotiate the check by delivery only. A blank indorsement makes the instrument virtually as transferable as cash, and for that reason the instrument should ordinarily be indorsed only at the time it is actually delivered to the transferee.

A person who receives an instrument bearing a blank indorsement can protect himself or herself against the possibility of loss of title through subsequent negotiation by a thief. Section 3-204(3) provides that a "holder may convert a blank indorsement into a special indorsement by writing over the signature of the indorser in blank any contract consistent with the character of the indorsement." Thus, where the instrument was indorsed "Mary Glenn" and delivered to Mark Rhee, he can write above the Glenn signature "pay to the order of Mark Rhee." The instrument is now "indorsed specially" and cannot be negotiated further without Rhee's indorsement. (Special indorsements will be discussed later in the chapter.)

**Effect of Indorsement:** A blank indorsement has three effects (in addition to converting the instrument into a bearer instrument):

**1.** It transfers title to the instrument to the indorsee on delivery.

**2.** It extends certain warranties to the indorsee and all subsequent holders.

**3.** It imposes a legal obligation on the indorser to pay the amount of the instrument to the person holding it at maturity if the maker, acceptor, or drawee does not pay (and if certain other conditions are met). This obligation is sometimes called the "conditional" or "secondary" liability of the blank indorser.[10]

## *Special Indorsements*

Under Sec. 3-204(1), a **special indorsement** "specifies the person to whom or to whose order it makes the instrument payable." To illustrate: A check is payable to the order of P, and he indorses it, "Pay to the order of X, (signed) P." An instrument indorsed in this manner remains an order instrument, and X's indorsement will be necessary for a further negotiation to occur. An indorsement need not, however, include words of negotiability; an indorsement "Pay to X (signed) P" has the same legal effect as "Pay to the order of X, (signed) P."

A special indorsement on a bearer instrument converts it into an order instrument. To illustrate: A note is "payable to bearer." The first holder, H, indorses it, "Pay to the order of X, (signed) H" and then delivers it to X. X's indorsement is now necessary for a further negotiation of the instrument. However, if X indorses it in blank, it is now reconverted to a bearer instrument.

The primary effect of a special indorsement, then, is that it requires the indorsement of the special indorsee before it can be negotiated further.

## *Qualified Indorsements*

Blank and special indorsements are "unqualified" indorsements for the reason that indorsers who use them incur what is called conditional liability on the instruments negotiated in this manner. Specifically, such indorsers are promising to pay the instruments themselves if the holder is unable to obtain payment from the maker, acceptor, or drawee at maturity. A blank or special indorser, then, is actually guaranteeing payment of the instrument in addition to transferring title to it.

A **qualified indorsement,** by contrast, is one whose wording indicates that the indorser is not guaranteeing payment of the instrument. The usual qualified indorsement is "without recourse, (signed) X," and the precise effect is illustrated as follows: P receives a check in the mail, drawn on an out-of-town bank and payable to his order. He indorses it "without recourse, (signed) P" and negotiates it to H. H deposits the check in his account at a local bank, but a week later the bank returns it to him because the drawer did not have sufficient funds in his account. Because P indorsed the instrument qualifiedly, H cannot recover the amount of the dishonored check from him.

---

[9] Indorsements are ordinarily written on the instrument itself. However, under Sec. 3-202(2), if there are so many indorsements on the back of an instrument that there is no room for more, subsequent indorsements can be written "on a paper so firmly affixed thereto as to become a part thereof." Such a paper, called an *allonge,* must be firmly pasted or stapled to the instrument; attachment by paper clip alone will not suffice.

[10] The warranty and conditional liabilities mentioned here arise from Secs. 3-417(1) and 3-414(1) respectively. Their nature and extent are covered in Chapter 27.

Except for eliminating the conditional liability of the indorser, a qualified indorsement has the same general effect as an unqualified (blank or special) indorsement. "Without recourse" indorsements thus transfer title to the indorsee, permitting further negotiation of the instrument. They also impose a warranty liability on the indorser that is quite similar to the liability of the blank and special indorsers (see Chapter 27 for details).

The effects of blank, special, and qualified indorsements are illustrated in Figure 25.1.

## Restrictive Indorsements

It is difficult to make broad generalizations about **restrictive indorsements,** because the UCC recognizes four distinctly separate kinds. Nonetheless, two observations do apply to all of them:

**1.** Under Sec. 3-206(1) restrictive indorsements are similar to the other indorsements discussed in this chapter in that they do not (despite their name) restrict the further negotiation of any instrument so indorsed.

**2.** They differ from the other indorsements by restricting the rights of the indorsee in order to give certain protection to the indorser.

According to Sec. 3-205:

> An indorsement is restrictive which either (a) is conditional; or (b) purports to prohibit further transfer of the instrument; or (c) includes the words "for collection," "for deposit," "pay any bank," or like terms signifying a purpose of deposit or collection; or (d) otherwise states that it is for the benefit or use of the indorser or of another person.

**Figure 25.1  Blank, Special, and Qualified Indorsements**

**Blank**

Peter Payee

Effects:
1. Transfers title
2. Extends warranties
3. Sets "conditional" liability

Also—converts order paper to bearer paper.

**Special**

Pay to John Doe
Peter Payee

Effect:
 Same as blank

But—allows order paper to remain order paper.

**Qualified**

Without recourse
Peter Payee

Effect:
1. Transfers title
2. Extends warranties

No conditional liability.

Before examining the specific kinds of restrictive indorsements, in the following case we will see an example of the fundamental differences between a blank indorsement and either a special or a restrictive one.

---

**Walcott v.
Manufacturers Hanover Trust**
Civil Court of New York City,
Kings County,
507 N.Y.S.2d 961 (1986)

Kenneth Walcott filed suit against Manufacturers Hanover Trust (MHT) and Bilko Check Cashing Corp. (Bilko). He claimed that on November 1, 1985, he sent his October 19, 1985 paycheck in the sum of $359.05 together with a Crossland Savings Bank money order in the sum of $251.54 to Midatlantic Mortgage Company in payment of his November 1985 mortgage. According to Walcott, he signed his name on the back of the check and also placed his mortgage number and the Midatlantic mailing sticker on the back with his signature. He asserted that he then put the check and money order in an envelope directed to Midatlantic Mortgage Company and mailed it.

The copy of the check, introduced into evidence, showed Walcott's indorsement and the mortgage number 603052, but no sign of the sticker. The check also showed that it was cashed by Bilko on November 4, 1985 and deposited into the Bilko account at defendant MHT on November 5, 1985.

In mid-November 1985, Mr. Walcott received a notice

*(continued)*

from Midatlantic that he was late in the November payment of his mortgage. He inquired and found that his paycheck had been cashed at Bilko, who then deposited the check in their account at MHT. The check ultimately cleared through Citibank, the drawee bank, and charged to the account of the payor, New York Transit Authority (Walcott's employer). The Crossland money order was never cashed; Walcott stopped it on November 22 and replaced it with a new one.

Walcott claimed that someone had stolen the check and cashed it at Bilko. The store manager of Bilko testified that in order for a government check to be cashed, two pieces of identification are required, usually an employee identification card containing an individual's Social Security number and a driver's license. She further testified that the person presenting the check in question must have had such identification since the notations as to the calculation of the check-cashing fees on the front of the check indicate that identification was shown. (The court stated: "This identification procedure creates doubt as to whether the check was actually stolen.)

Walcott claimed that his placing of the Midatlantic sticker by his signature caused his indorsement to be a special one, and his writing the mortgage number caused it to be a restrictive one. Thus, he claimed, Bilko and MHT improperly treated the check as a bearer instrument. Following is a summary of the trial court's decision.

**Decision:** Judgment was for defendants, dismissing Walcott's complaint. Even if the sticker had been attached, it obviously became easily detached and did not meet the UCC requirement that an indorsement must either be on the instrument itself or be on a paper "affixed so firmly thereto as to become a part thereof." Also, the numbers beneath Walcott's signature were not sufficient to make the indorsement restrictive. Walcott indorsed in blank, and the check became a bearer instrument. ■

---

**Conditional Indorsements:** As the name indicates, a **conditional indorsement** is an order to pay the instrument only if a specified event occurs. As such, the indorsement imposes a condition on the indorsee's right to collect the proceeds of the instrument. This kind of indorsement is not common, but it is useful in certain situations, particularly when combined with a special indorsement. To illustrate: "Pay to the order of Karen R. Jones upon her delivery to me of one hundred shares of AT&T stock as per our agreement of last November. (Signed) Paul Miller."

Such an indorsement has three basic effects:

**1.** It does not prohibit further negotiation of the instrument, regardless of whether the condition has or has not occurred.

**2.** Until the stated condition does occur, however, neither the restrictive indorsee nor any subsequent holder has the right to enforce the instrument.

**3.** In the event that a holder does receive payment from the maker (or drawee) when the condition has not yet occurred, both the maker (or drawee) and the holder remain liable to the restrictive indorser for the amount of the instrument.

***Special Bank Rules:*** Because of the large volume of commercial paper handled in the bank collection process, certain banks in that process are permitted to disregard any restrictive indorsements (including, of course, conditional indorsements). This result flows from Sec. 3-206(2), which provides that "an intermediary bank, or a payor bank which is not the depositary bank, is neither given notice nor otherwise affected by a restrictive indorsement of any person excepting the bank's immediate transferor or the person presenting for payment." To illustrate: D, in Worthington, Ohio, draws a check on his Worthington bank and mails it to P, payee, in Bozeman, Montana. P indorses it conditionally and cashes it at his Bozeman bank. The check, now in the bank collection process, is forwarded to a Billings bank, thence to a Chicago bank, and ultimately to the drawee bank in Worthington. Under Sec. 3-206, the Worthington bank may honor the instrument even if the condition specified in the indorsement has not occurred. Neither that bank nor the Billings or Chicago banks could be held liable to the restrictive indorser in such a situation.[11]

**Indorsements Purporting to Prohibit Further Negotiation:** Section 3-205(b) refers to indorsements that intend to prohibit further negotiation—for example, "Pay to the order of X only, (signed) P." Under pre-UCC law such an indorsement terminated negotiability of the instrument, and no subsequent purchaser could qualify as a holder. While this kind of indorsement is rarely used today, the drafters of

---

[11] Here the Bozeman bank is the "depositary bank"—the first bank to which an item is transferred for collection, under Sec. 4-105(a). The Billings and Chicago banks are "intermediary banks," and the Worthington bank the "payor" (and drawee) bank.

the UCC reversed the common-law view. Section 3-206(1) provides expressly that "no restrictive indorsement prevents further transfer or negotiation of the instrument." A "pay to X only" or "pay to the order of X only" indorsement thus has the same legal effect as a special indorsement, and an instrument indorsed in this manner can be further negotiated by X upon proper indorsement and delivery by him or her.

**"For Collection" and "For Deposit" Indorsements:** Indorsements for collection and for deposit are by far the most commonly used types of restrictive indorsements. Instruments indorsed in either way are almost always put directly into the bank collection process. Under Sec. 3-206(3), in such situations any depositary bank receiving the instrument is responsible for acting consistently with the terms of the indorsement, which ordinarily means that it must credit the restrictive indorser's account.

The protection afforded to the restrictive indorser is best illustrated by a situation where the transferee–depositary bank fails to live up to the duty imposed by Sec. 3-206: D draws and delivers a check payable to P. P indorses the check, "For deposit, (signed) P" and gives the check to his accountant, A, to deposit in P's bank. P's bank gives A cash for the check (or credits A's account), and the cash is not in fact turned over to P (or the funds in A's account are not subsequently made available to P). P can now maintain an *action of conversion* against the bank, and the bank will be liable because it clearly has acted inconsistently with the terms of the restrictive indorsement.

***Special Bank Rules:*** As indicated in the discussion of conditional indorsements, drawee and intermediary banks holding restrictively indorsed paper do not have the responsibility that is imposed on depositary banks. Thus, under Sec. 3-206(2), drawee and intermediary banks in possession of instruments indorsed "for collection" or "for deposit" are neither given notice of nor affected by such indorsements. In other words, these banks cannot be held liable to the restrictive indorser if the restrictive indorsee–depositary bank fails to act consistently with the terms of the indorsements.

A similar type of restrictive indorsement is the *pay any bank or banker indorsement.* This is expressly deemed a restrictive indorsement under Sec. 3-206(3), and the rules applicable to it are the same as those for the other types of restrictive indorsements discussed in this section.

**Trust Indorsements:** The fourth type of restrictive indorsement is one which by its terms shows an intent to benefit the indorser or some third party; it is frequently referred to as a **trust indorsement** or *agency indorsement.* For example: "Pay to A as agent of P, (signed) P," and "Pay to A in trust for B, (signed) P." In these situations, two results flow from the indorsements. (1) When the restrictive indorsee, A, receives payment of the instrument, he holds the proceeds in trust for the named beneficiary. (2) Any subsequent purchaser of the instrument takes it free of the restriction, and thus qualifies as an HDC unless he or she has actual knowledge that A's negotiation of the instrument is a breach of A's fiduciary duty.

The following case serves notice on bank officers of the unfortunate circumstances that may befall a bank when an employee takes an instrument without noticing that it has been restrictively indorsed.

---

***In re* Quantum Development Corp.; American Fidelity Fire Ins. Co. v. Joy; Lang v. Bank of Nova Scotia**
U.S. District Court, Virgin Islands, District of St. Croix,
397 F.Supp. 329 (1975)

American Fidelity Fire Insurance Company, plaintiff, was a surety of the Quantum Development Corporation. (A *surety* is a person or firm who has made himself or itself responsible for the debts or other obligations of another.)

Quantum Development went into bankruptcy in March of 1973. Soon thereafter American Fidelity, responding to its obligations as surety, delivered a certified check in the amount of $84,858 to the clerk of the bankruptcy court, who delivered the check to Charles Joy, the receiver of the bankrupt firm. The check was made payable to "Charles R. Joy, Receiver," and the bankruptcy judge ordered Joy to put the bulk of the money into certificates of deposit in Quantum Development's name, and the balance into a checking account for Quantum Development.

Joy took the check to Chandler, the manager of a branch of the Bank of Nova Scotia (BNS), and purchased $75,000

*(continued)*

worth of certificates of deposit with the check. The balance of approximately $9,000 was placed in a checking account in Joy's name. Although Joy indorsed the check "For Deposit in Quantum Acct. Quantum Bankruptcy, Charles R. Joy," the bank made out the CDs in the name of Joy personally.

Six months later, when the CDs matured, Joy cashed them at the bank and vanished with the money. Thereafter American Fidelity brought this action against BNS to recover the value of the CDs. (The trial court's decision is summarized below.)

**Decision:** Judgment was for plaintiff for the sum of $77,664 plus interest. Joy's indorsement of the $84,858 check "For deposit in Quantum Account" was clearly a restrictive indorsement under Sec. 3-205 of the UCC. Therefore, the Bank of Nova Scotia had the duty to apply the proceeds of the check as directed by the indorsement. It could have done this by depositing the check in Quantum Corporation's account or by issuing certificates of deposit in the corporation's name. When the bank issued certificates of deposit in *Joy's own name*, it clearly violated its duty to plaintiff under the indorsement. Since it was this breach that permitted Joy to abscond with the funds, the bank was liable to plaintiff for its resulting loss. ∎

# MISCELLANEOUS NEGOTIATION PROBLEMS

We conclude this chapter with a discussion of several peripheral problems not covered by the general rules of negotiation.

## *Multiple Payees*

Under Sec. 3-116(a), instruments are sometimes payable to two or more *alternative* persons ("pay to the order of A or B"). Negotiation of such an instrument requires only the indorsement of either of the payees. On the other hand, under Sec. 3-116(b), if the instrument is payable to the parties *jointly* ("pay to A and B"), then both indorsements are required for a further negotiation of the instrument.

## *Correction of Names*

Section 3-203 is self-explanatory; it provides that "where an instrument is made payable to a person under a misspelled name or [a name] other than his own, he may indorse in that name or his own or both; but signature in both names may be required by a person paying or giving value for the instrument."

## *Transfer of Unindorsed Order Paper*

If an order instrument is transferred without the indorsement of the payee, the transferee is not a holder of the instrument and therefore cannot negotiate it. He or she does, however, have the right (by legal action, if necessary) to require the transferor to indorse the instrument. Upon receiving the indorsement the transferee qualifies as a holder.

There is one exception to the rule that the transferee of an unindorsed order paper cannot negotiate the instrument further. Sec. 4-205 permits a depositary bank that received such a check either to supply its customer's indorsement or simply to note on the instrument that it has credited the check to its customer-depositor's account. In either case the bank is a holder and can negotiate the instrument further.

The following case shows how well this exception worked out for the defendant, the depositary bank.

---

**Cole v. First National Bank of Gillette**
Supreme Court of Wyoming,
433 P.2d 837 (1967)

Clarence and Wilma Cole, plaintiffs, purchased a home from Wyoming Homes of Gillette, Wyoming. As a down payment on the contract Mrs. Cole gave a Wyoming Homes salesman a $4,000 check. The check was drawn by Buffalo Auto Supply (a company owned by the Coles) on that company's account in the First National Bank of Buffalo, Wyoming, and it was payable to the order of Wyoming Homes.

The salesman took the check to the First National Bank of Gillette and, without indorsing it, deposited it in the Wyoming Homes account with that bank.

The Gillette bank stamped the check "First National Bank, Gillette, Wyoming, For Deposit Only" and put it into the bank collection process. The check reached the drawee bank

*(continued)*

in Buffalo, and the $4,000 was duly charged to the Buffalo Auto Supply account. Thereafter the Coles claimed that Wyoming Homes (1) had failed to give consideration and (2) was guilty of fraud in the sale of the home.

The Coles brought action against the First National Bank of Gillette to recover the $4,000 on the theory that it was merely a transferee of the check and had only the rights of the transferor, Wyoming Homes, in view of the fact Wyoming Homes did not indorse the check on depositing it in the Gillette bank. As a result, the Coles contended that the Gillette bank was not a holder in due course, or even a holder of the check as defined by the UCC, and that the bank thus took the check subject to the defenses of failure of consideration and fraud.

The trial court rejected plaintiffs' contentions and entered summary judgment for the defendant. The Coles appealed, claiming that the Supreme Court of Wyoming should, as a matter of law, reverse that judgment.

**Decision:** The judgment was affirmed. UCC Sec. 4-205 provides in material part that "a depository bank which has taken an item for collection may supply any indorsement of the customer which is necessary to title. . . . A statement placed on the item by the depository bank to the effect that the item was deposited by a customer or credited to his account is effective as the customer's indorsement." Under this section the Gillette bank, as the depository bank taking the check for collection, was authorized to indorse the instrument as it did. It thus became a holder of the instrument.

Furthermore, the Gillette bank qualified as a holder *in due course* once the amount of the check was credited to the account of the payee, Wyoming Homes, and once a final settlement of the item was made when the drawee bank honored the instrument. Therefore, the Gillette bank took the instrument free of any claims the Coles may have had against Wyoming Homes. ∎

---

## *Rescission of Indorsements*

Sometimes the indorsement and delivery of an instrument are made under circumstances in which the indorser, under ordinary contract law, has the right to rescind the transaction. The most common situations are those where: (1) the indorser is a minor, (2) the indorsement and subsequent delivery are brought about by fraud or duress on the part of the indorsee, and (3) the negotiation is part of an illegal transaction. Under Sec. 3-207:

**1.** Such negotiations are "effective" (that is, the indorsee qualifies as a holder and thus is capable of negotiating the instrument further).

**2.** However, until the instrument is negotiated to a party who qualifies as an HDC, the indorser can rescind the indorsement. To illustrate:

    **a.** P, a minor, indorses a note to H, the holder. As long as the note remains in H's hands, P can rescind the indorsement and recover the instrument.

    **b.** P indorses a note to H as a result of fraud practiced on him by H. After H negotiates the instrument to X (holder 2), P seeks to disaffirm the indorsement and recover the note from X. If X qualifies as an HDC of the instrument (under rules examined in the next chapter), P cannot set aside the negotiation.

## *The Fictitious Payee Problem*

The **fictitious payee** situation most often occurs where a dishonest employee, usually someone in charge of payrolls or payment of bills, draws a company check payable to the order of a nonexistent person or to the order of an actual person who is not entitled to payment. Following are three cases that illustrate situations to which the "fictitious payee" rule of Article 3 apply (with the results of that rule explained immediately thereafter).

*Case 1:* The D Company has fifty employees. B, the company's bookkeeper, has authority to issue checks in the corporate name to pay bills and the payroll for the firm's employees. B issues a check to P, who is neither a creditor nor an employee of the company. The check is drawn on the X Bank, where the company has its checking account. After drawing the check, *B indorses P's name on the back* and cashes it at some other local bank. The X Bank (drawee) receives the check through the collection process and charges the D Company's account.

*Case 2:* The same situation as for Case 1, except that B prepares checks for T, the company's treasurer, to sign. B drafts a check drawn on the X Bank payable to P (an accomplice of B) and puts the check, among others, on T's desk for his signature. T signs the check in the corporate name, believing P to be a creditor of the firm. B takes the check to P after T has signed it; P then indorses it and cashes it at a local bank. The X Bank (drawee) receives the check through the collection process and charges the D Company's account.

*Case 3:* The same situation as for Case 2, except that B, after receiving the signed check payable to the order of P, indorses P's name on the back and transfers it to a third party, H, instead of delivering it to P. H, an innocent purchaser, presents the check to the X Bank for payment but finds that payment has been stopped by the D Company, which had discovered what B had done.

Suppose, in Cases 1 and 2, that the D Company after learning the facts sues the X Bank to recover the amount of the checks on the theory that the indorsements were forgeries. And, in Case 3, suppose that H sues the D Company (drawer) on the check, and the D Company defends on the ground that the indorsement of P was a forgery. Under Sec. 3-405, *the D Company loses in all three of these situations.*

In Case 1, where B had the authority to sign checks in the corporate name and did so knowing that P was not entitled to payment, Sec. 3-405(1)(b) applies. It provides that "the indorsement by any person in the name of a named payee *is effective* if a person signing as or on behalf of a maker or drawer *intends the payee to have no interest in the instrument.*" (Emphasis added.) Thus the signing of P's name by B is an effective indorsement rather than a forgery. Consequently, the bank effectively obeyed the D Company's order to pay, and it was therefore entitled to charge the company's account.

The same is true in Case 2, where B supplied the D Company's treasurer with the checks payable to the order of P. This is because Sec. 3-405(1)(c) provides that "the indorsement by any person in the name of a named payee *is effective* if an agent or employee of the maker or drawer *has supplied him with* the name of the payee intending the latter to have no such interest." (Emphasis added). Thus the X Bank again had the right to charge the company's account with the check—assuming, of course, that the bank had no knowledge of B's misconduct.

In Case 3, for the same reason, the holder of the check, H, can enforce the check against the D Company. (As will be seen in Chapter 28, the fact that the D Company stopped payment on the check does not necessarily insulate it against liability to the holder of the check. A stop payment order simply prevents the holder from receiving payment on presenting the check to the drawee bank; a subsequent lawsuit by the holder against the drawee is what determines the liability or nonliability of the drawer.)

## SUMMARY

The negotiability or nonnegotiability of an instrument is determined entirely by its form and content. Under Sec. 3-104, to be negotiable an instrument must (1) be signed by the maker or drawer; (2) contain an unconditional order or promise to pay a sum certain in money; (3) be payable on demand or at a definite time; and (4) be payable to order or to bearer. Subsequent sections of Article 3 clarify these requirements. The "unconditional" requirement means that the promise or order must be absolute, rather than one payable only in certain circumstances. Two types of provisions generally condition an order or promise, and thus cause the instrument to be nonnegotiable: (1) provisions stating that payment is to be out of a specified fund, and (2) promises stating that the instrument is "subject to" another agreement. With respect to the time of payment requirements, an instrument is payable on demand if it so provides, or if it contains no time of payment. An instrument is payable at a definite time if payable at a specified future date, or at such a date with an acceleration clause providing for an earlier maturity date if a certain event occurs. Instruments payable "on or before" a specified date also meet the definite time requirement. An instrument payable "to X" is not negotiable, because it is neither a bearer nor an order instrument.

Turning to the question of transfer, a bearer instrument may be negotiated by delivery only, but an order instrument requires an indorsement in addition to delivery. If a transfer does not meet the "negotiation" requirements the transferee is merely an assignee of the transferor's rights, and the transferee cannot achieve the favored holder-in-due-course status.

There are four kinds of indorsements: blank, special, qualified, and restrictive. A blank indorsement converts an order instrument into a bearer instrument. Blank and special indorsements have three additional consequences. First, they transfer title to the indorsee when accompanied by delivery of the instrument. Second, such indorsers extend certain warranties, or guarantees, to the indorsee and to all subsequent holders. Third, such indorsers have the legal obligation to pay the instrument at maturity if the maker, acceptor, or drawee dishonors it. A qualified ("without recourse") indorsement has the same consequences as blank and special indorsements except that such an indorser does *not* have the legal obligation to pay the instrument if it is dishonored.

Restrictive indorsements are of four types. They do *not* prohibit further negotiation, but, in general, do restrict the rights of the indorsee in order to give certain protection to the indorser relative to the proceeds of the instrument upon its payment. A forged indorsement necessary to the negotiation of an order instrument is void. Thus if a payee's indorsement is forged and the instrument thereafter transferred, no negotiation has occurred and the transferee is neither a holder of the instrument nor entitled to payment of the instrument.

## KEY TERMS

**Demand instrument**
**Time instrument**
**Acceleration clause**
**Extension clause**
**Order instrument**
**Bearer instrument**
**Assignment**
**Negotiation**
**Blank indorsement**
**Special indorsement**
**Qualified indorsement**
**Restrictive indorsement**
**Conditional indorsement**
**Trust indorsement**
**Fictitious payee**

## QUESTIONS AND PROBLEMS

**1.** Sain Builders gave a $4,000 promissory note to Samuel Feinberg, with whom it had an existing contract. Feinberg later negotiated the note to D'Andrea. The note contained a clear-cut promise to pay, and was negotiable in all other respects, but in the lower left hand corner Sain Builders had written in the words "as per contract." Does this inscription destroy negotiability of the instrument? Why or why not? (*D'Andrea v. Feinberg*, 256 N.Y.S.2d 504, 1965.)

**2.** A law firm performed legal services for a client. Later the client wrote this letter: "I agree to pay to your firm as attorney's fees for representing me in obtaining property settlement agreement and tax advice, the sum of $2,760, payable at the rate of $230 per month for twelve (12) months beginning January 1, 1970. (Signed) Barbara Hall Lodge." Is this written promise a negotiable instrument? Why or why not? (*Hall v. Westmoreland et al.*, 182 S.E.2d 539, 1971.)

**3.** Following is a promissory note, written entirely in longhand: "I, the undersigned, hereby promise to pay to the order of Kevin Smith or bearer on January 2, 1987, one hundred dollars. Should I become bankrupt at any time, the entire sum shall be immediately due and payable upon demand of the holder. (Signed) Mark Gibson."

    **a.** Is this instrument payable to order or to bearer? Explain.
    **b.** Does the acceleration clause destroy negotiability of the instrument? Explain.

**4.** Holly Hill Acres, Ltd., executed a promissory note and a mortgage securing it and delivered both instruments to the payee, Rogers and Blythe. Part of the note read as follows: "This note with interest is secured by a mortgage on real estate . . . made by the maker hereof in favor of the said payee, and shall be construed and enforced according to the laws of the State of Florida. The terms of said mortgage are by this reference made a part hereof." Does this writing affect the negotiability of the note? Why or why not? (*Holly Hill Acres, Ltd. v. Charter Bank of Gainesville*, 17 UCC Rep. 144, 1975.)

**5.** M is the maker of a note "payable on or before June 1, 1987."

    **a.** Does this clause give the *maker* the right to pay the instrument before the due date, or does it give the *holder* the right to demand payment before the due date? What is the basis for your answer?
    **b.** Does the clause destroy the negotiability of the note? Explain.

**6.** The X Corporation issues a check "payable to the order of Ron St. Pierre." St. Pierre indorses the instrument in blank ("Ron St. Pierre") and negotiates it to the Y Company. Before the Y Company has time to indorse the check it is stolen by Z and transferred to H, who has no knowledge of the theft. The X Corporation then learns of the theft and stops payment on the check. In a subsequent suit brought by H against the X Corporation to recover the amount of the instrument, the X Corporation contends that H is not a holder of the instrument since the Y Company had not indorsed it. Is this contention correct? Why or why not?

**7.** D draws a draft payable to the order of P. P indorses it to A as follows: "Pay to A without recourse, (signed) P." A indorses the instrument to B as follows: "Pay to B upon her delivery of her 1980 Citation, (signed) A." B indorses the instrument, "Pay to the order of C, (signed) B," and gives it to C.

    **a.** Classify each of the above indorsements.

**b.** Since P indorsed the instrument "Pay to A . . ." instead of "Pay to the order of A . . . ," does this mean that A's subsequent transfer of it to B is not a negotiation? Explain.

**c.** Which of the transferees (A, B, or C)—if any—qualify as holders?

**8.** The D Company purchases its oil from a jobber, the P Company. In payment for its December purchases of oil the D Company sent a check to the P Company for $975, the check being payable "to the order of the P Company." An authorized employee of the P Company indorsed the check, by rubber stamp, "Pay to the order of Gulf Oil, the P Company." X, a janitor of the P Company, stole the check and forged this indorsement on it: "Gulf Oil, by John Andrews, assistant treasurer." If this instrument should later be cashed by a bank under circumstances in which it had no reason to suspect the forged indorsement, would the bank be a holder of it? Why or why not?

**9.** A check is drawn payable to the order of Chauncey Ricks, who is a minor. Chauncey indorses the check to X, and X in turn indorses it to Y. Y later learns that Chauncey is a minor, and also that he has disaffirmed the contract in payment for which he had negotiated the check to X. Does the fact that Chauncey disaffirmed his contract with X prevent Y from qualifying as a holder of the instrument? Why or why not?

**10.** The Soong Company of San Francisco draws a $1,500 check on its local bank payable to the order of the West Company of Baltimore, and mails it to the West Company. An officer of the West Company, which is in the process of liquidation, indorses the check under court order: "Pay to John Chandler, trustee of the X Company, (signed) the West Company." Chandler cashes the check at a Baltimore bank, which gives him cash for it. The bank then sends it to the San Francisco bank via a Chicago bank. If Chandler fails to turn the $1,500 over to the West Company, and if a new trustee is appointed, does the new trustee have any right to hold either the Baltimore bank or the Chicago bank liable for the amount of the instrument? Explain.

CHAPTER 26

# COMMERCIAL PAPER

HOLDERS IN DUE COURSE AND DEFENSES

Under ordinary contract law the assignment of a contractual (nonnegotiable) right passes to the assignee the same rights possessed by the assignor—no more and no less. The assignee thus takes the right or claim *subject to* all defenses that might exist between the original parties to the contract, regardless of whether the assignee knows of them at the time of acquiring the right. As a result, contractual claims are not transferred in large numbers in the business community, for most prospective assignees will purchase a claim only after satisfying themselves that the original obligor on the contract does not have a defense against it. This is usually a time-consuming process and often an impossible one.

The purchasers of negotiable instruments, by contrast, acquire them *free* of many defenses that exist between the original parties to the instrument if such purchasers qualify as "holders in due course" of the instruments. In fact, a major purpose of Article 3 of the UCC is to facilitate the negotiation of commercial paper by (1) spelling out the requirements that must be met by the purchaser of a negotiable instrument in order for that person to acquire the most favored status of a holder in due course (HDC), and (2) identifying the specific kinds of defenses that are cut off when a purchaser of the instrument attains this status.

In this chapter we will discuss, first, the holder in due course, and, second, the subject of defenses.

## HOLDERS IN DUE COURSE
### Holder in Due Course Status

It is helpful, at the outset, to understand the typical situation in which an HDC acquires greater rights than those possessed by his or her transferor. Suppose, for example, that M, a building contractor, has contracted to purchase certain plumbing fixtures from the P Company, a plumbing supply firm, for $2,250. M makes a negotiable promissory note for that amount, due sixty days later, and gives it to the P Company. After receiving the note, P Company negotiates it immediately to the B Bank, receiving cash in return (probably something less than $2,250). When the note comes due, M refuses to pay it because many of the fixtures delivered by the P Company are defective. In this situation the B Bank—if it qualifies as an HDC—*is entitled to a judgment against M for the full $2,250, even though its transferor, the P Company, probably would have recovered nothing from M had it held the instrument itself until maturity.*

The bank is entitled to a judgment in full because M's defense—breach of contract on the part of the payee—is one of the defenses that are cut off by negotiation of the instrument to an HDC. (Such defenses, often called "personal" defenses, will be discussed along with "real" defenses later in the chapter). Two further observations about HDCs and other holders should be made.

**Status of the Ordinary Holder:** In some situations a holder is entitled to payment of the instrument even though he or she is an ordinary holder (one who does *not* qualify as an HDC). In the above illustration, for example, if the plumbing fixtures that were delivered by the P Company to M were not defective in any way—in which case M possesses no defense against the P Company—the B Bank is entitled to recover the full $2,250 from M even if it did not meet the HDC requirements of the code. Thus the favored status of the HDC ordinarily is of significance only in those situations in which the primary party possesses a personal defense against the payee.

**Limitations on the Holder in Due Course:** Despite the favorable position that the HDC usually occupies, even holders in due course do not *always* prevail against the obligor. In the first place, if the obligor has a "real" defense—such as forgery—he or she may assert this defense against *all* holders. Second, and perhaps more important, *several recently enacted consumer protection statutes and orders of regulatory agencies have cut down the right of holders in due course by permitting obligors to assert personal defenses against them in certain situations.* (These limitations on the holder in due course doctrine will be discussed later in the chapter.)

## Holder in Due Course Requirements

Section 3-302 of the UCC is the definitive **holder in due course** section, containing the three basic requirements for HDC status. According to Sec. 3-302(1): "A holder in due course is a holder who takes the instrument (a) for value; and (b) in good faith; and (c) without notice that it is overdue or has been dishonored or of any defense against or claim to it on the part of any person." The major purpose of these requirements is to define the kind of person who deserves, as a matter of policy, to take the instrument free of certain defenses (such as breach of contract by the payee). Some purchasers of instruments are denied this favored treatment, for example, because they either knew or should have known of an existing defense at the time of purchase.

Before examining each of the requirements, we should remember that a person seeking HDC status must first qualify as a *holder,* defined by Sec. 1-201(20) as "a person who is in possession of . . . an instrument . . . drawn, issued or indorsed to him or to his order or to bearer or in blank." A transferee who acquires an instrument other than by issue or negotiation thus ordinarily fails to qualify as an HDC at the outset, regardless of the other circumstances under which the acquisition took place.

**Value:** The term **value** is defined in Sec. 3-303, which states that a holder (usually a purchaser) has given value (1) to the extent that the agreed-upon consideration has been performed (by him or her) or to the extent that he or she acquires a security interest in or a lien on the instrument other than by legal process, or (2) when he or she takes the instrument in payment of, or as security for, an antecedent claim against any person, whether or not the claim is due, or (3) when he or she gives a negotiable instrument in payment for it. The reasoning underlying the value requirement is that if a person receives a note or a check without having given value for it, he or she obviously will suffer no out-of-pocket loss by being unable to recover from the primary party in the event that the latter has a personal defense available.

The following examples most easily illustrate the basic import of Sec. 3-303.

1. P, the payee of an out-of-town check, cashes it at his own bank. The bank, by giving P cash, has obviously given value.

2. P, a retailer, is the payee of a $900 note issued by M. P makes a contract with a third party, H, under which H is to deliver thirty cameras to P in exchange for the note. Before the delivery date P runs into financial difficulties, and H, fearing that the note might be attached by P's creditors, demands that it be negotiated to him immediately. P delivers the note to H, and H later delivers the cameras. H is a holder for value, since he performed the agreed-upon consideration by delivering the cameras. H is entitled to enforce the instrument against the maker, M, at maturity even if M has a personal defense against P.

3. Same facts as 2, above, except that after H received the note, he delivered only twenty cameras, at which time H learned that M had a defense against P. Here H would be accorded HDC status only to the extent of $600 (the extent to which the "agreed-upon consideration has been performed").

4. Same facts as 2, above, except that after H received the note he failed to deliver any of the cameras before learning of M's defense against P. Here H has not given value for the instrument (that is, H's original *promise* to deliver the cameras does not constitute value). This illustration points up the fact that the term *value* in Article 3 of the UCC is not synonymous with *consideration* under contract law; that is, while a promise to perform an act constitutes consideration, it does *not* constitute value.

**Good Faith:** The requirement that one must take the instrument in good faith in order to qualify as an HDC is contained in Sec. 3-302(b). **Good faith** is defined (not too helpfully) in Sec. 1-201(19) as "honesty in fact in the conduct or transaction."

The wide-ranging circumstances in which a maker, acceptor, or drawer of an instrument can at least argue that the plaintiff-holder did not take the instrument in good faith make it difficult to accurately explain this term.[1] In some situations, for example, a purchaser might take an instrument under circumstances that are somewhat suspicious but of such a minor nature that he or she honestly does not believe the instrument is defective. Under these circumstances the purchaser might well satisfy the good faith requirement. At the other extreme, the circumstances under which a person acquires an instrument might be so unusual that it is quite clear he or she is not acting honestly in the transaction and hence is guilty of bad faith. An example of the latter is if a buyer of a $1,500 instrument purchases it from the payee for $500 in cash, a grossly inadequate consideration.

In most cases the good faith requirement and the requirement that a holder take an instrument "without notice of a defense" overlap. That is, if a court in a particular case finds the holder to be barred from holder in due course status because the instrument was acquired under circumstances in which he or she should have known of an existing defense, such holder also often has taken the instrument in bad faith. Conversely, if a court rules that the holder did *not* have reason to know of an existing defense when he or she acquired the instrument, such holder is also usually found to have taken the instrument in good faith.

Be that as it may, the UCC treats the two as separate requirements and, as the next case illustrates, so do many defendants when presenting reasons why the plaintiff is not an HDC. (This case also illustrates how a principle known as the "close connection" doctrine may lead to a finding that the holder of an instrument did not take it in good faith.)

---

[1] Partly as a result of this difficulty, the courts frequently attack the question from the other side by determining if the purchaser took the instrument in *bad faith*—a standard that is somewhat easier to apply. Either way, however, the test is subjective, asking, "Did the purchaser take the instrument honestly?" rather than "Did the purchaser act with the care of the reasonable, prudent person?" (This test is sometimes referred to as the "pure heart, empty head" concept.)

---

### Arcanum National Bank v. Hessler
Supreme Court of Ohio, 433 N.E.2d 204 (1982)

Hessler was in the hog raising business. For several years prior to 1977 he had an arrangement with John Smith Grain Co. under which either that company or J & J Farms, Inc., would sell hogs to Hessler, with the grain company requiring Hessler to sign promissory notes payable to the grain company to cover each delivery of hogs. The grain company would then sell the notes to Arcanum National Bank (the bank), plaintiff, which would credit the grain company with the amount of each note and open a commercial loan account for Hessler for said amount.

On January 4, 1977, Hessler signed a $16,800 promissory note payable to the grain company for hogs delivered on that date, and the grain company negotiated the note to the bank. Hessler then learned that the hogs delivered by J & J Farms, Inc., had previously been mortgaged to a third party. Therefore, because Hessler did not have clear title to the hogs, he refused to pay the note to the bank at maturity. (That is, Hessler had the defense of failure of consideration.)

In the bank's suit on the note, Hessler contended that the bank was not an HDC because the bank (1) took the note with notice of the defense, and (2) did not take the note in good faith. The trial court ruled against Hessler on both points because there was no proof that officers of the bank had actual knowledge of the mortgage, and entered judgment for the bank. Hessler appealed.

The Supreme Court of Ohio reversed, agreeing with Hessler that the bank did have notice of the defense, and did not take in good faith. (That part of the higher court's opinion dealing with the good faith issue is summarized below.)

---

**Decision:** Ohio courts have adopted the "close connectedness" doctrine. Under that doctrine a transferee does not take an instrument in good faith when the transferee is so closely connected with the transferor that the transferee may be charged with knowledge of an infirmity in the underlying transaction. That doctrine is applicable here for several reasons. First, the transferee (plaintiff bank) supplied the transferor (the grain company) with the forms it used in the transaction with Hessler (maker of the note), and the bank also ran an independent credit check of Hessler at that time. Second, there was a particularly heavy reliance by the grain company on the bank, with the grain company transferring virtually all of its commercial paper to that

*(continued)*

bank. Third, an officer of the grain company had actual knowledge at the time of the transaction with Hessler that the hogs were mortgaged, and this knowledge of the grain company was imputed to the bank, the transferee, because the president of the grain company was also a director of the bank. Thus, under the close connectedness doctrine, the bank in the eyes of the law had reason to know of the failure of consideration—the fact that defendant Hessler did not receive clear title to the hogs—and the bank did not, therefore, take in good faith. Accordingly, the trial court's judgment in favor of the bank was reversed. ∎

---

**The Taking "Without Notice" Requirement:** Section 3-302(1)(c) provides that, to be an HDC, a holder must take the instrument "without notice that it is overdue or has been dishonored [and without notice] of any defense against it or claim to it on the part of any person." The basic thrust of this section is that a holder should not receive the protection afforded an HDC if he or she acquires an instrument knowing that something is wrong with it.

Under Sec. 1-201(25) of the UCC, a person has notice of a fact when he or she has actual knowledge of it, or from the circumstances "has reason to know" of such fact. Thus if H acquires an instrument knowing that the payee has breached his or her contract with the maker or drawer, or under circumstances where a prudent person would reasonably suspect such a breach (although H did not have such suspicion), H is not an HDC.

Section 3-304 is an aid to the interpretation of the "without notice" requirement. Because of its length, the application of only a few of its salient provisions are summarized here. (The section can be read in its entirety in Appendix A.)

***Notice That Paper Is Overdue or Has Been Dishonored:*** As we saw in Chapter 24, all negotiable instruments are either time or demand instruments. Those bearing a fixed future date of maturity, such as "payable July 1, 1991," are time instruments; those stating that they are payable on demand or having no stated maturity date are demand instruments.

A person who purchases a *time instrument* even one day after its stated maturity date takes it with notice that it is overdue. Thus, if a note payable on September 1 is acquired by H on September 2, H does not qualify as an HDC. Section 3-304(3) provides in part that "the purchaser has notice that an instrument is overdue if he has reason to know (a) that any part of the principal amount is overdue or that there is an uncured default in payment of another instrument of the same series." And the purchaser has such notice here because the instrument carried its maturity date on its face.

The question as to when *demand* instruments are overdue has caused difficulties because such instruments do not, of course, contain a stated maturity date. The primary rule of Sec. 3-304(3)(c) is that a purchaser takes a demand instrument with notice that it is overdue if he or she acquires it more than a "reasonable time after its issue."

***What Is a Reasonable Time?*** The above section contains the only UCC provision that specifically defines a reasonable time, and it applies only to checks; as to checks drawn and payable in the United States, a reasonable time "is presumed to be 30 days." Thus if D draws and issues a check on June 1 payable to the order of P, and the check is negotiated to H on July 15, H is not an HDC in most circumstances. (The thirty-day limit is not absolute, however; rather, thirty days is "presumed" to be the deadline. In exceptional circumstances, then, a person might acquire a check beyond that limit and still qualify as an HDC.)

As to other instruments—demand notes and sight drafts—the question of reasonable time is left to the courts. Because these instruments are often held for longer periods of time than are checks, a person may well take such an instrument two or three months (or even longer) after its issue, and still qualify as an HDC. In determining what is a reasonable time in a given case, the courts take into account business and community customs, and other circumstances (e.g., interest-bearing notes circulate longer than noninterest-bearing ones, and a reasonable time is generally longer in rural areas than when the parties are residents of larger cities).

***Notice of Claim or Defense:*** Section 3-304(1) reads in part as follows:

> The purchaser has notice of a claim or defense if (a) the instrument is so incomplete, bears such visible evidence of forgery or alteration, or is

otherwise so irregular as to call into question its validity, terms or ownership or to create an ambiguity as to the party to pay; or (b) the purchaser has notice that the obligation of any party is voidable in whole or in part, or that all parties have been discharged.

Subsection a addresses itself to situations where some unusual aspect about the face of the instrument itself should indicate to a reasonable person that a defense very likely exists. Under this section, the fact that an instrument is incomplete to *some* extent or bears *some* evidence of a possible forgery or alteration does not necessarily prevent the holder from qualifying as an HDC. Rather, the disqualification occurs only where the irregularity is one that is so material as to call into question the instrument's validity, terms, or ownership.

*Missing Terms:* On the subject of incompleteness, it is well established that any third party who acquires an instrument so incomplete that one of the requirements of negotiability is missing is not an HDC. Thus, if H takes a check from P, payee, the amount of which is entirely blank, H does not qualify as an HDC since the instrument was not negotiable at the time she acquired it. Similarly, if H takes an instrument "payable twenty _____ after date," she is not an HDC.[2]

On the other hand, an instrument that is incomplete in only a minor respect is not considered so irregular as to prevent a purchaser from attaining HDC status. For example: A note is complete in all respects except that it contains this clause: "Payable at _____." Here the purchaser qualifies as an HDC because the place where an instrument is payable is not a required element of negotiability; thus the fact that this particular blank is not filled in does not of itself cause a reasonable person to question the instrument's validity. The same is true of a check that does not bear its date of issue; this alone is not a disqualifying irregularity.

*Altered Terms:* This approach also applies to altered terms in an instrument. Unexplained alterations that are both material and apparent (such as a line drawn through the original payee's name, with a second name substituted for it) will disqualify a taker from HDC status. But alterations so skillfully done that they are not readily apparent will not keep the instrument taker from qualifying as a HDC. Similarly, an instrument bearing some evidence of erasure and subsequent correction of a necessary element will not necessarily put a purchaser on notice of a defense; for example, the purchaser might have inquired about the erasure and received an adequate explanation of it. Thus any case arising under this section, like those dealing with the question of when a demand instrument is overdue, must also be settled on the basis of its own facts.

The gist of Sec. 3-304(1), then, is that a person who purchases an instrument knowing of a defense—or having reason to know of it because of the instrument's irregular, missing, or altered terms—is not a holder in due course.

In the next case it may be argued that the plaintiffs did not actually know that a defense (breach of contract) existed before they purchased the instrument. But let us see what other information the plaintiffs did possess at that time, and how the court viewed the effect of that information.

---

[2] If, in either of these cases, H completes the instrument and negotiates it to X, another holder, X probably will qualify as an HDC if he meets the other requirements. X's rights in these circumstances are discussed in the next chapter.

---

### Salter v. Vanotti
Colorado Court of Civil Appeals, Div. III, 599 P.2d 962 (1979)

Mr. and Mrs. Vanotti, defendants, signed an agreement to purchase a lot in an Arizona development from Cochise College Park, Inc. (Cochise), the developer of the area. As part of the transaction the Vanottis signed a negotiable promissory note (payable to Cochise) in the amount of $4,392, payable in monthly installments. Cochise thereafter negotiated the note to the Salters, plaintiffs.

The Vanottis made three monthly payments on the note, after which time they visited the property and found that it was not as Cochise had represented it to be. The Vanottis then demanded the return of their payments under a "money back

*(continued)*

guarantee" contained in the contract, but Cochise refused this demand.

In this action by the Salters to recover the unpaid balance of the note, the Vanottis alleged that they had several defenses against Cochise, and they further alleged that the Salters were not holders in due course of the note. On this basis the Vanottis claimed that they could assert their defenses against the Salters.

The trial court agreed that the Vanottis' defenses against Cochise were valid, and also agreed that the Salters were not holders in due course (for reasons appearing in the decision below). Accordingly, it dismissed the action. Plaintiffs appealed.

**Decision:** The judgment was affirmed. First, the trial court was correct in finding that defendants had three defenses: (1) that defendants had attempted to exercise their rights under the money back guarantee, as provided in the Property Report, and that the attempt was not honored by Cochise; (2) that defendants did not receive a copy of the Property Report, as required by federal law, and (3) that the contract had been breached by Cochise by failure to deliver a deed after three payments had been made.

Second, the court was correct in ruling that plaintiffs were not holders in due course. From the documents that were delivered with the note, plaintiffs knew that defendants had a right to rescind the contract within six months from the date of the contract, and that defendants were entitled to a deed after making three monthly payments. Plaintiffs also knew that Cochise was not able to deliver a deed, since only a photocopy was forwarded to them, yet plaintiffs took no steps to investigate these facts. The protection afforded a holder in due course cannot be invoked by a person who simply refuses to investigate when the facts known to him suggest an irregularity concerning the commercial paper that he purchases. Because the plaintiffs were not holders in due course, they took the instrument subject to all of defendants' defenses, and their suit was, therefore, properly dismissed. ■

## *Related Holder in Due Course Matters*

**Holder through a Holder in Due Course:** Any taker of an instrument who does not meet all the requirements for a holder in due course is called an *ordinary holder* (or sometimes a *mere holder, transferee,* or *assignee*). This person takes the instrument subject to all outstanding defenses—that is, like an assignee of a nonnegotiable instrument, the ordinary holder acquires only the rights of prior parties, no greater ones.

However, if an ordinary holder takes an instrument from someone who is an HDC, or takes an instrument where *any* prior party qualified as an HDC, he or she is now a "holder with all the rights of an HDC."[3] Thus if H purchases a note that is clearly overdue, or receives it as a gift, he can still enforce the instrument against the maker, even though the maker has a defense, if H can show that any prior holder met the requirements of an HDC.

One exception to the above does exist, however. If a purchaser of an instrument negotiates it to a subsequent holder and ultimately repurchases it from either that holder or a later holder, his or her status is determined at the time of first acquiring it. To illustrate: H purchases an instrument, failing to qualify as an HDC for some reason. Later she negotiates the instrument to a holder who does qualify as an HDC. If H reacquires the instrument subsequently, she is not accorded "holder with the rights of an HDC" status. In other words, H cannot improve (or "launder") her position by reacquiring from an HDC.

**The Payee as a Holder in Due Course:** Before adoption of the UCC, some courts took the view that the payee of an instrument was not a "holder," and thus could not qualify as an HDC even though he or she gave value for the instrument, purchased it before it was overdue, and took it without notice of any defense against, or claim to the instrument. Other courts disagreed. Section 3-302(2) of the UCC has resolved this conflict by flatly providing that "a payee may be a holder in due course" (assuming, of course that he or she meets the three basic HDC requirements).

As a practical matter, a payee who has fully performed his or her contract with the maker or drawer of an instrument ordinarily qualifies as an HDC, because in most such instances the payee has given value for the instrument, the maker or drawer pos-

---

[3] This results from Sec. 3-201(1), which provides that "the transfer of an instrument vests in the transferee such rights as the transferor has therein." This section, based on assignment law, is referred to as the *shelter provision* of the code.

sesses no defense, and the payee takes the instrument before it is overdue. In such cases the payee is clearly entitled to payment. On the other hand, if the maker or drawer *does* possess a defense, the payee ordinarily is not an HDC because a defense usually arises out of some default or misconduct on the part of the payee—such as breach of contract, or the perpetration of fraud upon the maker or drawer—of which the payee necessarily has notice. Thus, in an action by the payee in such a case, the maker or drawer may successfully assert the defense.

## DEFENSES

Earlier in the chapter we mentioned the two general classes of defenses, using the terms *personal* and *real*. While the UCC refers to these classes as *limited* and *universal*, we will use the older terms, personal and real, because they continue in widespread use today.

*Personal defenses*, under the UCC, can be asserted only against ordinary holders; generally they cannot be asserted against an HDC or against a holder with all the rights of an HDC. In fact, it is the cutting off of these defenses that gives the HDC his or her status as a favored holder.

*Real defenses* can be asserted against all holders, including HDCs and holders with all the rights of an HDC.[4] A defendant-maker who has available a real defense is under no liability to the plaintiff even if the latter is an HDC. This is why HDCs are not always entitled to judgments in actions brought against makers, acceptors, or drawers of negotiable instruments.

### Personal Defenses

Section 3-306 of the UCC lists all the **personal defenses** (or *limited defenses*)—those that are ordinarily assertable only against ordinary holders. The major part of that section follows:

> Unless he has the rights of a holder in due course, any person takes the instrument subject to (a) all valid claims to it on the part of any person; and (b) all defenses of any party which would be available in an action on a simple contract; and (c) the defenses of want or failure of consideration, nonperformance of any condition precedent, non-delivery, or delivery for a special purpose; and (d) the defense that he or a person through whom he holds the instrument acquired it by theft, or that payment or satisfaction to such holder would be inconsistent with the terms of a restrictive indorsement.

We will now examine the most common kinds of personal defenses under this section.

**Breach of Contract:** *Breach of contract* (or "failure of consideration") is the most common defense falling within the provision of Sec. 3-306(b). Many instruments are issued to payees in payment for goods (or services) that the payees are obligated to deliver (or perform) under contracts with the makers or drawers of the instruments. If the contract is breached by the payee, the maker of the note can refuse to pay it, and the drawer of a check can stop payment on it, claiming that the failure of the payee to perform the contract relieves him or her of liability.

The case of *Salter v. Vanotti*, earlier in the chapter, illustrates these rules. In that case the seller of land (Cochise) breached its contract with the buyers (the Vanottis) in at least two respects: (1) by failing to permit them to cancel the purchase, as the contract provided, if they were not satisfied with the land; and (2) by failing to deliver a deed to them after they had made three monthly payments. Those breaches afforded the Vanottis their personal defenses (which defeated the action brought by the Salters, who were not holders in due course).

*Breach of warranty*—a form of breach of contract—occurs when a seller of goods makes an express or implied statement or promise about the goods, and the goods do not conform to the statement or promise. For example, under sales law a merchant seller impliedly warrants that the goods are merchantable. If the buyer pays for the goods by giving the seller a negotiable note and later finds that the goods are not merchantable (do not perform in the expected manner), the buyer may assert the defense of breach of warranty against any holder of the note who is not an HDC.

A typical breach of warranty case is that of *United Securities Corp. v. Bruton*, 213 A.2d 892 (1965). Bruton purchased two wigs from a retailer, giving the retailer her promissory note in payment. The retailer-payee negotiated the note to United Securities. When

---

[4]Throughout this chapter, when we refer to the rights of an HDC, we will assume that whatever is said applies equally to holders with all the rights of an HDC.

United Securities presented the note to Bruton for payment, she refused to pay because the wigs were clearly defective—i.e., unmerchantable. In the ensuing lawsuit, Bruton was permitted to assert her defense of breach of warranty against United Securities (which did not qualify as an HDC of the note).

**Lack of Consideration:** *Lack* (or *want*) of consideration (as we saw in Chapter 13) exists in a commercial paper context where a maker or drawer of an instrument issues it to the payee in any case where the payee does not give consideration under ordinary contract law principles. In such situations "want of consideration" can be asserted by the maker or drawer against an ordinary holder. To illustrate: D, a distant relative of P, drafts a check and makes a gift of it to P so that P can attend college. P negotiates the check to H. P does not go to college, and D, in disgust, stops payment on the check. If H sues D on the instrument, D can successfully assert the defense of want of consideration—but only if H fails to qualify as an HDC.

**Fraud in the Inducement:** Two kinds of fraud are recognized in the area of commercial paper; one creates a personal defense and the other a real defense. **Fraud in the inducement** falls into the personal category. It arises where a person who signs a negotiable instrument (knowing it to be such) has been induced to sign by some intentional misrepresentation of the other party. For example: B agrees to purchase S's year-old car for $7,500 after being assured by S that the car is a demonstrator that S had purchased just six months earlier from a new car dealer. At the time of purchase B gives S $1,500 in cash and a promissory note for the balance of $6,000. Soon thereafter B learns that S had actually purchased the car from a private owner, a farmer, who in fact had driven it extensively before selling it to S. S's intentional misrepresentation constitutes fraud in the inducement, and B can assert this defense against S and against any subsequent holder who does not qualify as an HDC.

**Illegality:** Like the general defense of fraud, some types of *illegality* constitute personal defenses and others constitute real defenses. This is so because although certain transactions are illegal (prohibited) under state statutes or ordinances, the applicable statutes do not always provide that the prohibited transactions are void. If a statute voids the transaction, the defense is real; if it does not, the defense is merely personal. To illustrate: A retailer sells goods to D on a Sunday in violation of a state statute prohibiting the sale of goods by merchants on that day. However, the statute does not provide that such sales, or the contracts or papers connected with them, are void. The next day the retailer negotiates the check to H, who subsequently learns that D, the buyer-drawer, has stopped payment on it. Here D can assert the defense of illegality against H only if H is an ordinary holder. (Illegality as a real defense is discussed later in the chapter.)

**Unauthorized Completion:** Although it is ordinarily a bad practice, the maker or drawer of an instrument sometimes signs it while it is incomplete in some respect (for example, leaving blank the amount or the payee's name). He or she usually gives it to a third party—often an employee but sometimes the payee—with instructions as to how the blank should be filled in (such as, "fill in the amount for no more than $400"). The instrument is then completed contrary to instructions and later is acquired by a subsequent holder. If the latter fails to qualify as an HDC, the maker or drawer usually can assert the defense of **unauthorized completion** and avoid liability. However, under Sec. 3-407(3), if the subsequent holder does qualify as an HDC (by taking the instrument without knowledge of the wrongful completion and by meeting the other HDC requirements), he or she can enforce the instrument as completed. Thus, where the maximum authorized amount is $400, if the third party completes the instrument to read $1,000, a subsequent HDC can recover the full $1,000 from the maker or drawer. Therein lies the danger in signing an incomplete instrument.

**Nondelivery of an Instrument:** Sometimes an instrument finds its way into the hands of a subsequent holder through loss or theft. In such a case the maker or drawer of the instrument has available the defense of *nondelivery*. To illustrate: M is the maker of a bearer instrument that is stolen from her home by X and negotiated to H. If H is merely an ordinary holder, he takes the instrument subject to the defense of nondelivery and therefore cannot enforce it against M.

The case below involves a claim by the payee of a note against the maker's estate. The primary question was whether the estate's defense of nondelivery was a valid one.

### Matter of Estate of Balkus
Court of Appeals of Wisconsin,
381 N.W.2d 593 (1985)

James Balkus died on December 4, 1983, leaving no will. A few days after his death, his sister, Ann Vesely, examined his personal effects and found, among other things, two promissory notes in the amount of $6,000 each. The notes were payable to her order, and Balkus was the maker of both instruments.

When the administrator of Balkus's estate refused to pay the amount of the notes to Vesely, she filed a claim against Balkus's estate in the amount of $12,000. The circuit court ruled that Vesely was not a holder in due course of the notes, and thus held that the estate's defense of nondelivery was assertable against her. Judgment was accordingly entered for the estate, and Vesely appealed.

On appeal, Vesely's primary argument was that the estate did *not* possess the defense of nondelivery because there had been a "constructive delivery" of the instruments to her—that is, a delivery in the eyes of the law, although not a physical delivery. (If the estate did not possess such defense, Vesely contended that she, as payee, was entitled to payment even if she did not qualify as a holder in due course.)

**Decision:** The lower court was correct in ruling that the estate did possess the defense of nondelivery. Vesely admitted that there was no physical delivery of the notes to her, but contended that there was a constructive delivery to her because of a letter written by Balkus to her in 1974 in which he stated that he was leaving to her all his personal effects and the two notes "made out to you for the amount of money I borrowed from you in 1961 and 1962." Within the context of the facts of this case, a constructive delivery occurs only when the maker indicates an intention to make the instrument an enforceable obligation against him or her by surrendering control over it and intentionally placing it under the power of the payee or a third person. Because the notes were found in Balkus's possessions at his death, he had never placed them under the control of Vesely or any third party. The letter did not, therefore, serve as a constructive delivery of the notes. ■

---

**Prior Payment:** When a note or draft is paid by the maker or acceptor, it is routinely surrendered to that person, regardless of whether it is paid at or before maturity. Either way the instrument normally stops circulating. However, the maker or acceptor may neglect to ask for the return of the instrument, or, after its return, it may be stolen. If payment of the instrument occurred before maturity, and if the instrument bears no notation of payment, it is possible that it will get into the hands of an innocent third party. When that holder demands payment at maturity, the maker or acceptor has available the defense of *prior payment* or *payment before maturity* and is therefore not liable if the holder fails to qualify as an HDC. (If the holder is an HDC, the maker or acceptor must pay a second time.)

**Incapacity (except Minority):** As seen in Chapter 15, the law recognizes various types and degrees of incapacity. However, unless a maker's or drawer's incapacity is so extreme that under local law the contract or instrument is completely nullified, the defense of *incapacity* is only personal—except in the case of a minor (discussed later in the chapter).

**Duress:** Similarly, there are varying degrees of duress under the law, most of which are merely personal in nature. Thus if a person signs an instrument under a vague threat or through fear of economic-retaliation, the defense is only personal in nature. (Duress as a real defense is also discussed later in the chapter.)

### Real Defenses

**Real defenses** (or *universal defenses*) are defenses that can be successfully asserted against all holders, including holders in due course. We will now describe the more common types of real defenses, including the offshoots of some of the personal defenses already discussed.

**Forgery:** A fundamental legal principle of commercial paper, appearing in Sec. 3-401(1), is that a person cannot be held liable on an instrument unless his or her name appears on it. In the case of **forgery** the person's name does appear, probably as maker or drawer, but it is signed by another person who has no authority to do so. (An unauthorized signature of indorsement is defined in Sec. 1-201(43) as "one made without actual, implied, or apparent authority and includes a forgery.")

The "pure" forgery case occurs where a person who has no authority from (and usually no relationship with) the purported drawer or maker simply commits a criminal act by signing the latter's name to an instrument. For example: A thief steals a book of personalized checks belonging to D. The thief drafts a check and signs D's name as drawer. In this case D has no liability to any holder of the instrument. Section 3-404(1) provides that "any unauthorized signature is *wholly inoperative* as that of the person whose name is signed unless he ratifies it or is precluded from denying it." (Emphasis added.) *Ratification* consists of any conduct on the part of the person whose name has been signed without authority which indicates to third parties that he or she will assume liability on the instrument despite the unauthorized signing. It occurs rarely; and when it does, it is usually in a situation where a principal-agent relationship exists between the purported drawer and the forger.[5]

A situation related to forgery exists when an agent exceeds his or her authority by signing the principal's name on an instrument as drawer or maker. If the principal can show that the agent had no express, implied, or apparent authority to sign, and if the principal does not subsequently ratify the signature, he or she can assert the defense of *unauthorized signing* against any holder, even an HDC. (See Chapter 32 for a treatment of the rules which the courts use in determining whether express, implied, or apparent authority exists.)

**Fraud in the Execution:** Unlike fraud in the inducement, in the case of **fraud in the execution** a person is caused to sign a negotiable instrument under circumstances in which he or she honestly and reasonably believes it to be something other than a negotiable instrument, as, for example, a lease or receipt of some kind.

This commonly occurs when an experienced, high-pressure salesperson talks a home owner who has little education (or perhaps who is even illiterate) into signing a promissory note by telling him or her that it is only a request for an estimate or an application of some kind. The salesman's company then negotiates the instrument to a holder. Here the home owner-maker has a real defense, good against any holder, if the following conditions are met. The maker must show not only that he or she honestly believed the signing was for something other than a negotiable instrument but also that he or she was not guilty of negligence under the circumstances in failing to realize that the document was a negotiable instrument. The phrase *under the circumstances* takes into account such factors as the signer's age, experience, and schooling. Thus the maker who is very inexperienced in the business world, or is aged, or has failing eyesight may have a real defense, while such a defense would not exist if he or she were a businessperson who hurriedly signed the note after a cursory look (or perhaps without reading it at all) simply because in a rush to attend a meeting.

**Material Alteration:** Section 3-407, entitled "Alteration," covers two essentially different situations—alteration of a completed instrument and completion of a blank instrument contrary to instructions. (The latter topic was discussed earlier, under "Personal Defenses.")

***Alteration of a Completed Instrument:*** Sometimes, after a completed instrument is issued by the maker, one or more of the terms are changed without his or her knowledge by a holder, and the instrument is thereafter negotiated to a subsequent holder. The issue is thus raised whether the last holder can recover on the instrument—and, if so, to what extent. The answer to these questions depends on two factors: (1) whether the alteration was material and (2) whether the holder qualifies as an HDC.

Section 3-407 essentially defines a material alteration as one that changes the contract of the parties in any respect. A change in the amount of the instrument even by the addition of one cent, or an advance of the date of payment even by one day, is thus material. On the other hand, a correction of the spelling of the payee's name or the addition of the address of the maker would not be material. (If the alteration is not material, all holders are entitled to enforce the instrument as it was originally drawn.)

If the alteration *is* material, the holder's rights depend on whether he or she is an HDC. It is possible to be an HDC when the alteration is so skillfully done that it is not readily apparent to the subsequent purchaser.

---

[5]Under Sec. 3-404(1), the primary situation in which a drawer of an instrument may be precluded from asserting the defense of forgery is where he or she is guilty of negligence that contributed to the forgery. This topic will be discussed in Chapter 28.

Under Sec. 3-407(3), an HDC can enforce the instrument according to its "original tenor"—that is, as originally drawn. To illustrate: M is the maker of a note payable to the order of P in the amount of $1,000. P alters the amount to read $3,000 and negotiates the instrument to H, an HDC. At maturity, H is entitled to recover $1,000. (Since H cannot recover the balance of $2,000 from M, it is said that the defense of material alteration is a defense "to the extent of the alteration.") If, on the other hand, H is not an HDC, he recovers nothing. This is so because a material alteration that is also fraudulent—as is usually the case—is a complete defense against an ordinary holder. (See Figure 26.1.) In the unlikely event that the alteration is not fraudulent, the ordinary holder—like the HDC—is entitled to enforce the instrument according to its original tenor.

## Other Real Defenses:

*Illegality:* As we indicated in the section on personal defenses, some kinds of transactions are not only prohibited by statute but expressly made *void* or *void ab initio* (from the beginning). The defense of *illegality* in these situations is a real defense, assertable against both ordinary holders and HDCs. In a number of states, for example, checks and notes given in payment of gambling debts fall into this category.

The next case illustrates the fact that while crime does not pay, it frequently provides the innocent drawer of a check with a most welcome real defense.

**Figure 26.1  Material Alteration**

Alteration
- Not material → No defense: all holders can enforce instrument as originally drawn
- Material →
  - Non-HDC: complete defense (personal)—holder cannot enforce
  - HDC: partial real defense—HDC can enforce according to original tenor

---

### Commercial Bank & Trust Co. v. Middle Georgia Livestock Sales
Georgia Court of Appeals, 182 S.E.2d 533 (1971)

Middle Georgia Livestock Sales (MGLS) bought some cattle at an auction and gave the seller its check in payment. Soon thereafter MGLS discovered that the seller had stolen the cattle, and that it therefore had not acquired title to them. MGLS accordingly stopped payment on the check—that is, it ordered the drawee bank not to honor it when it was presented for payment.

Without knowledge of these facts another bank, the Commercial Bank and Trust Company, cashed the check for the seller-thief, and routinely presented it for collection to the drawee bank. That bank, because of the stop payment order, refused to pay it and returned the check to Commercial. Commercial then brought this action against MGLS, the drawer, who claimed that it possessed a real defense.

The trial court granted judgment for the plaintiff, and MGLS appealed.

**Decision:** The judgment was reversed. Plaintiff bank, a holder in due course, was entitled to judgment unless defendant's defense of illegality constituted a real defense. Whether the defense of illegality is a real defense or only a personal defense depends upon the nature of the particular act involved and the local (state) law relating to that act.

Under Georgia law the theft of cattle is a criminal offense. So, too, is the sale of stolen cattle, even to an innocent purchaser. Also, under Georgia case law, any contract or sale that constitutes a crime is "absolutely void" (rather than merely "voidable"). Thus the transaction for which Middle Georgia issued the check was absolutely void, and consequently Middle Georgia's defense was a *real* defense. Middle Georgia, therefore, was not liable on the check, even to a holder in due course. ∎

***Incapacity of a Minor or Insane Person:*** When the maker or drawer of an instrument is a minor, he or she may escape liability on the ground of *incapacity*. Whether this defense is real or personal depends upon applicable state law (and as we saw in Chapter 14, state laws differ in their treatment of minors' rights). Still, the defense of *minority* is in most states a real defense. Under this view, if it is asserted by the maker or drawer of an instrument—even against an HDC—the holder recovers nothing. Similarly, if a person signs a note or draft after having been adjudicated insane by a court, his or her defense is also real, the instrument being void *ab initio*.

***Extreme Duress:*** Most kinds of duress constitute only personal defenses. *Extreme duress*, however, is another matter; it exists where the force or threat of force is so overwhelming that the victim is entirely deprived of his or her will. A real defense exists, for example, if a person signs an instrument at gunpoint.

***Discharge in Bankruptcy:*** In some situations the general defense of *discharge* is available to one of the parties to an instrument; yet the instrument can still circulate, and an HDC can still take it free of the defense. One kind of discharge, however, is always a real defense: the *discharge in bankruptcy*. The person who has been discharged under bankruptcy proceedings has no further liability on any outstanding instrument, even if it is held by an HDC.

***Lack of Title:*** When a party to an instrument is being sued, he or she may be able to prove that the plaintiff is not even a holder. This defense obviously rules out any recovery by the plaintiff. Thus, if an instrument is payable to the order of P, and P's indorsement in blank is forged, no subsequent purchaser qualifies as a holder; nor can such a purchaser recover anything from the instrument's maker or drawer. Where lack of title is established, the plaintiff simply has no standing to sue; that is, the plaintiff is not the owner of the instrument that he or she is attempting to enforce.

## LIMITATIONS ON HOLDER IN DUE COURSE DOCTRINE

The basic holder in due course concept, which permits an HDC to take an instrument free of all personal defenses, is a necessity if commercial paper is to circulate freely. In certain situations, however, the HDC doctrine has brought about results that have been the subject of increasing scrutiny and dissatisfaction. A typical example is the situation where a person purchases a consumer good, such as a television set, from a retailer and gives the retailer an installment note in payment for it. The retailer then negotiates the instrument to a third party (usually a lending institution), who probably qualifies as an HDC. In such a case, if the television does not work properly (or even if it is never delivered), *the buyer remains fully liable to the HDC.* The buyer's only recourse is to harass the retailer until he or she delivers a workable set or to recover damages for breach of contract—certainly an unsatisfactory solution for the buyer. In recent years two general kinds of limitations on the HDC doctrine have come into existence in an effort to give the purchaser of consumer goods some relief.

### State Statutes

Some state legislatures have enacted statutes that give the consumer a measure of protection in situations such as the one described above. Because of their diversity, these statutes can only be summarized briefly.

A few states have adopted the Uniform Consumer Credit Code (not to be confused with the UCC), which prohibits a seller of consumer goods from taking a negotiable instrument—other than a check—as evidence of the buyer's obligation. Some other states have enacted legislation that flatly abolishes the HDC doctrine in many situations. And a number of states have legislation requiring instruments that evidence consumer indebtedness to bear the words "consumer paper," and providing further that such instruments are nonnegotiable.

### The Federal Trade Commission Rule

The statutes mentioned above have brought about consumer protection that varies from state to state, and in some states they give less protection than was originally expected. For that reason, the Federal Trade Commission (FTC) promulgated a "Rule to Preserve Buyers' Claims and Defenses in Consumer Installment Sales." This rule, usually referred to as the **FTC holder in due course rule,** took effect in 1976.

In general, the FTC rule applies to two situations: (1) where a buyer of consumer goods executes a sales contract that includes giving a promissory note to the seller, and (2) where a seller of consumer goods arranges for a direct loan by a third party—usually a bank or other commercial lending institution—to the customer in order for the sale to be made.

In regard to the first situation, the rule provides in part:

> In connection with any sale or lease of goods or services to consumers, in or affecting [interstate] commerce . . . it is an unfair or deceptive trade practice . . . for a seller, directly or indirectly to (a) *Take or receive a consumer credit contract which fails to contain* the following provisions in at least ten point, boldface type:
>
> NOTICE
> ANY HOLDER OF THIS CONSUMER CREDIT CONTRACT IS SUBJECT TO ALL CLAIMS AND DEFENSES WHICH THE DEBTOR COULD ASSERT AGAINST THE SELLER OF GOODS OR SERVICES OBTAINED PURSUANT HERETO OR WITH THE PROCEEDS HEREOF. RECOVERY HEREUNDER BY THE DEBTOR SHALL NOT EXCEED AMOUNTS PAID BY THE DEBTOR HEREUNDER.[6]

In regard to the direct loan by a third party situation, the rule provides in part:

> In connection with any sale or lease of goods or services to consumers, in or affecting [interstate] commerce . . . it is an unfair or deceptive trade practice . . . for a seller, directly or indirectly to (b) accept, as full or partial payment for such sale or lease, the proceeds of any purchase money loan . . . unless any consumer credit contract made in connection with such purchase money loan *contains the following provision* in at least ten point, boldface type:
>
> NOTICE
> ANY HOLDER OF THIS CONSUMER CREDIT CONTRACT IS SUBJECT TO ALL CLAIMS AND DEFENSES WHICH THE DEBTOR COULD ASSERT AGAINST THE SELLER OF GOODS AND SERVICES OBTAINED WITH THE PROCEEDS HEREOF. RECOVERY HEREUNDER BY THE DEBTOR SHALL NOT EXCEED AMOUNTS PAID BY THE DEBTOR HEREUNDER.

While the FTC rule permitting assertion of defense has widespread applicability, it does not, by any means, bring about the death of the HDC doctrine. For example, the rule does not apply to contracts of commercial buyers (as distinguished from consumer buyers), and commercial contracts account for a great deal of commercial paper activity. Additionally, the rule applies only to consumer purchases on credit; thus purchases in which checks are given in full payment are not subject to it. Finally, the rule permits the assertion of only those personal defenses which the purchaser could assert against the seller of the goods (such as fraud or breach of contract).

## SUMMARY

The primary attribute of the holder in due course (HDC) is that such a holder takes the instrument free of "personal" defenses existing between prior parties. (Ordinary holders, by contrast, take the instrument subject to such defenses.) A holder, to qualify as an HDC, must take the instrument (1) for value, (2) in good faith, and (3) without notice that it is overdue or has been dishonored, or that a defense against or a claim to the instrument exists. These requirements of Sec. 3-302 are explained in succeeding sections of Article 3.

The purpose of the value requirement is obvious; if a holder receives an instrument as a gift he or she does not need the protection given to a third party who has given value for it. Similarly, a holder should not be afforded HDC protection if he or she knows or should know of an existing claim to, or defense against, the instrument. This latter requirement essentially overlaps the good faith requirement, because a holder who knows or should know of a claim or defense would often also be a taker in bad faith.

In regard to the overdue requirement, there are three basic rules. (1) A note or draft with a fixed maturity date is overdue the day after such date. (2) Demand instruments become due a reasonable time after issue which (except for checks) varies from case to case. (3) Under Article 3, a reasonable time after issue is presumed to be no more than thirty days after issue.

An HDC, as indicated, takes an instrument free of personal ("limited") defenses. The most common of these are (1) breach of contract, (2) fraud in the inducement, and (3) unauthorized completion. Breach of contract exists where the payee of the instrument fails to perform the contract he or she had with the maker or drawer. Fraud in the inducement occurs where one person is induced to enter into a contract as a result of intentional misrepresentations by the other party, and as part of the transaction the victim

---

[6] The failure by a seller who is a "dealer" to include the required notice in each consumer credit contract subjects that person to a possible fine of up to $10,000 and to possible liability in a civil suit brought by the customer to recover damages incurred as a result of such failure.

of the fraud gives the defrauding party a note, draft or check in payment. The defense of unauthorized completion arises where a maker or drawer either entrusts an incomplete instrument to another, or issues such an instrument to the payee, and that party completes the instrument contrary to the instructions of the maker or drawer. While the maker or drawer cannot assert personal defenses against an HDC, he or she can assert them against ordinary holders.

Real ("universal") defenses are those possessed by the maker or drawer which free them of liability to HDCs as well as to ordinary holders. While real defenses are less common than personal defenses, the most representative of these are forgery, material alteration, and some types of illegality. Forgery is the signing of a maker or drawer's name by a party having no authority to do so. Such a signature is void. Material alteration occurs where a maker or drawer issues a completed instrument, and an essential term—usually the amount—is subsequently changed without his or her consent. (If a later purchaser qualifies as an HDC, such purchaser is entitled to payment according to the original terms of the instrument.) Illegality constitutes a real defense, rather than a personal defense, if an instrument is given in payment for the commission of a criminal act, or in connection with any other transaction which is not only prohibited by law but which is expressly made void under the law.

In recent years the holder in due course concept has been increasingly viewed as bringing about unfair results in some cases. This is especially true in the situation where a buyer of consumer goods gives a negotiable instrument in payment for them, and subsequently is obligated to pay a holder in due course the full amount of the instrument even if the goods prove to be defective, or are never received by the buyer. To provide the buyer protection in such a case, two major limitations on the HDC doctrine now exist. First, some states have adopted statutes prohibiting sellers of consumer goods from accepting negotiable instruments (except checks) in payment for such goods. And, second, the Federal Trade Commission has adopted a rule which provides, in general, that any credit contract received by a seller or lessor of consumer goods (or by a party supplying credit for such a sale or lease) must provide that any holder of the contract is subject to all claims and defenses which the buyer or lessee possesses against the seller or lessor.

# KEY TERMS

**Holder in due course**
**Value**
**Good faith**
**Personal defense**
**Fraud in the inducement**
**Unauthorized completion**
**Real defense**
**Forgery**
**Fraud in the execution**
**FTC holder in due course rule**

# QUESTIONS AND PROBLEMS

**1.** Willman was the maker of several notes payable to the order of a designated payee, and he issued them to the payee. Later the payee wanted to borrow money from Wood, and in order to get the loan the payee had to pledge the notes (deliver them) to Wood as security for the loan. The amount of the loan was substantially less than the total amount of the notes.

In subsequent litigation by Wood against Willman, the maker of the notes, the question arose whether Wood was a holder in due course to the full extent of the notes or only to the extent of the amount of the loan which Wood had made to the payee. How would you rule on this issue? What is your reason? (*Wood v. Willman,* 423 P.2d 82, 1967.)

**2.** On July 1, M signs a note, as maker, in the amount of $1,000, payable ninety days after date. He issues it to P, payee, in payment for the purchase of P's motorcycle. One month later P, needing cash to pay a debt, negotiates the note to H, who pays P $600 cash and agrees orally to pay an additional $400 within thirty days. Before the thirty days are up, H learns that M has rescinded the motorcycle purchase, claiming that the motorcycle has serious engine problems and that P knew this at the time of the sale.

    **a.** In this situation does H qualify as a holder in due course under the UCC? Explain.

    **b.** Assuming, for the sake of argument, that H is a holder in due course, to what extent (if any) can M assert as a defense his claim that the motorcycle was defective at the time of the sale? Explain.

**3.** A demand note, dated June 1, is issued to P on that date. On June 15, P demands payment from M, the maker, and payment is refused. On June 20, P negotiates the instrument to S. Later, S sues M on the note, and M proves that S knew, or had reason to know, of the dishonor at the time he acquired the instrument. S contends he still qualifies as an HDC since he clearly acquired the instrument within a reasonable time of its issue. Is S correct? Explain.

**4.** Cey makes out a promissory note payable to the order of the Griffey Corporation, and issues it to the corporation in payment for work to be done by it later. The Griffey Corporation negotiates the note for value to Concepcion, who qualifies as a holder in due course. Thereafter Concepcion becomes indebted to the Griffey Corporation, and in payment of this debt he negotiates the instrument back to the Griffey Corporation. When the note matures Cey (maker) refuses to pay the Griffey Corporation for the reason that the Griffey Corporation never did the work that it contracted to do for Cey in the first place.

**a.** Was the Griffey Corporation an HDC when it first received the note? Explain.

**b.** Does the Griffey Corporation have all the rights of an HDC in view of the fact that it acquired the note from Concepcion, who *was* an HDC? Why or why not?

**5.** A corporation borrowed $25,000 from a bank, with the corporation giving its promissory note to the bank as evidence of the debt. As a part of the deal, the bank demanded that four individuals—including Rochman—indorse the instrument as accommodation indorsers, who would thereby guarantee payment by the corporation. Rochman told the bank that he would indorse the note only if Raymond D'Onofrio would also indorse it, and the bank agreed to this condition. Rochman then indorsed the note, but the bank never did get D'Onofrio's indorsement. When the maker of the note (the corporation) later defaulted, the bank sued Rochman as indorser. Assuming that the bank is not an HDC, can Rochman successfully assert his defense against the bank that his liability was conditioned upon D'Onofrio's indorsement? Explain. (*Long Island Trust Company v. International Institute for Packaging Education, Ltd.*, 344 N.E.2d 377, 1976.)

**6.** A salesman for a corporation demonstrated a water softening device to the Hutchinsons. Before leaving, the salesman asked them to sign a form so that he could show it to his employer as proof that he had made the demonstration. The Hutchinsons signed, and later learned that they had actually signed a promissory note. The note was subsequently negotiated to a bank, which qualified as an HDC. When the bank sued the Hutchinsons after the note came due, they claimed that they had a real defense in view of the fact that they honestly did not think they were signing a promissory note. The bank sought to overcome that defense by producing evidence that showed the Hutchinsons were intelligent people, and could easily have discovered the true nature of the instrument if they had just read it. If this evidence is true, what effect—if any—does it have upon the Hutchinson's defense? Explain. (*Reading Trust Co. v. Hutchinson,* Court of Common Pleas of Pennsylvania, 1964.)

**7.** D, drawer, signs a check in blank for her son since she is going to be out of town for two weeks; she authorizes him to fill in an amount "not over $200." D's son loses the check before he has had a chance to complete it. F, finder, fills in his own name as payee and $400 as the amount. F then negotiates the instrument to H, who pays him $350 for it. D's son notifies D that he has lost the check, and D immediately stops payment. H now wishes to enforce the check against D.

**a.** What is the name of D's defense?

**b.** If H does not qualify as a holder in due course, is he entitled to recover $200, $400, or nothing from D? Explain.

**8.** M issues a promissory note to P for $500. P alters the amount of the note to $5,000 and negotiates it to H. At the date of maturity H demands payment of $5,000 from M, and M refuses to pay H anything. If H is a holder in due course, is he entitled to receive $500, $5,000, or nothing from M? Explain.

CHAPTER 27

# COMMERCIAL PAPER

LIABILITY OF THE PARTIES

All parties to commercial paper fall into one of two categories, as was noted in Chapter 24. Makers of notes and acceptors of drafts are **primary parties**, and all others are **secondary parties.**

As a general rule, a primary party is absolutely liable on the instrument, while a secondary party is only conditionally liable on it. Before we examine the ramifications of this rule, and its exceptions, it is necessary to see how a person may become a "party" in the first place.

## THE SIGNING REQUIREMENT

Section 3-401(1) of the UCC provides that "no person is liable on an instrument unless his signature appears thereon." (That section goes on to define a signature as "the use of any name . . . upon an instrument, or any word or mark used in lieu of a written signature.") A signature may be made personally, or by an authorized agent.

### *Signing by an Agent*

In most instances the maker, acceptor, drawer, or indorser does in fact personally sign the instrument, in which instances no problems arise under the above section. However, in cases where the instrument is signed by an agent or other representative, two related problems may arise. The first involves the liability of the principal (the person whom the agent is representing, and whose name is signed to the instrument), and the second involves the personal liability of the agent or representative himself. These problems—or potential problems—take on added significance when one realizes that all commercial paper issued by corporations necessarily involves corporate names being signed by agents, because all corporate activity can be carried on *only* through the actions of agents and employees.

**Signature by Authorized Agent:** Section 3-403 provides that the authority of the agent may be established "as in any other cases of representation"—i.e., under the ordinary principles of agency law.[1] Thus if the treasurer of the X Company has express or implied authority to issue promissory notes in the name of the corporation, the corporation alone would be liable as the maker of a note signed "The X Company, by R. J. Thomas, Treasurer."

***Liability of Agent—Improper Signature:***  Occasionally a signature on an instrument contains the name of both principal and agent, but fails to indicate that the agent signed in a representative capacity. (In the above example, the names of the makers may thus appear as "The X Company" and "R. J. Thomas.") Or the signature may not contain the name of the principal, but does show that the agent signed in a representative capacity ("R. J. Thomas, Treasurer").

Section 3-403(2)(b) applies to both of these situations. It provides that "except as otherwise established between the immediate parties, the representative (agent) is personally obligated on the instrument." Thus if the agent is being sued by a third-party holder—someone to whom the instrument has been negotiated—*the agent is personally liable.* (On the other hand, if the agent is being sued by the *payee,* the agent is permitted to introduce evidence showing that he or she actually signed in a rep-

---

[1] For a discussion of the different kinds of authority an agent might possess, see Chapters 31 and 32.

resentative capacity, and that the payee knew this to be the case. In such a case the agent is not liable.)

**Signature by Unauthorized Agent:** If an agent executes an instrument in the name of a principal that the agent has absolutely no authority to make, the named principal normally has no liability on the instrument. Section 3-304(1) provides, in part, that "Any unauthorized signature is wholly inoperative as that of the person whose name is signed. . . ." In effect, therefore, the unauthorized signature is a forgery. There is one exception, however. A principal is liable if its own negligence contributes substantially to the agent's unauthorized execution of the instrument in the principal's name. Such negligence may take the form, for example, of sloppy supervision and auditing of the agent's instrument-execution activities.

Whether the situation is the normal one in which the principal is not liable, or the unusual one in which the principal is liable because of its negligence, the *agent* is personally liable on the instrument. This results from additional language in that section which provides that an unauthorized signature *"operates as the signature of the unauthorized signer* in favor of any person who in good faith pays the instrument or takes it for value." (Emphasis added.)

The following case illustrates the critical need for an individual signing a negotiable instrument as an agent in behalf of a corporation or other principal to understand the legal consequences of signing in various ways.

---

### First Safety Fund National Bank v. Friel
Massachusetts Appeals Court,
504 N.E.2d 664 (1987)

Janet Friel became president of the New England Office Products Co. (the company) in 1981 after the death of her husband, who had founded the company in 1972. General management of daily operations was handled by Mrs. Friel's brother-in-law, David Friel, and her role was limited primarily to keeping the checkbook and signing all corporate checks. In 1982 and 1983, the company took out two loans in the amounts of $10,000 and $30,000, respectively, from First Safety Fund National Bank (the bank). On both occasions, Mrs. Friel signed promissory notes on behalf of the company payable to the order of the bank. On each note she signed twice: once, directly under the typed name of the corporate borrower, she wrote "Janet M. Friel, President"; on the line below that signature she wrote, without qualification, "Janet M. Friel."

Early in 1984, the company became insolvent and ceased operations. The bank filed suit against Mrs. Friel seeking to hold her personally liable on the two notes because, it claimed, her second signature on each note was in her personal capacity. The trial court ruled in Friel's favor, the appellate division of that court affirmed, and the bank appealed.

---

**Decision:** Reversed, and judgment entered for the bank against Janet Friel. The second signature on each note obligated her personally. The court said that she probably did not intend to be personally obligated, but that it did not matter what she intended. There was no evidence of any misrepresentation on the bank's part. ■

---

## LIABILITY OF PRIMARY PARTIES

For the remainder of this chapter we will make two assumptions: (1) that the party whose liability is being examined signed the instrument personally, and (2) that such party does not have an assertable defense against the holder. On this basis we will first examine the liability of *primary parties* (makers of notes and acceptors of drafts).

### Liability of the Maker

**Contractual Liability:** The maker of a note is *primarily* (absolutely) *liable* on it. That is, the party has the duty to pay the instrument at its maturity date even if the holder does not demand payment at that time. Section 3-413(1) provides that "the maker or acceptor engages [promises] that he will pay the instrument according to its tenor at the time of his engagement or as completed pursuant to Section 3-115 on incomplete instruments."

Furthermore, the maker—unlike the indorser—*is not discharged in any way by the fact that the instrument is presented for payment late;* even if a note is presented for payment many months or even years after its due date, the maker remains fully liable on it (until the statute of limitations has run).

There is, however, one limited exception to this rule. Under Sec. 3-502(1)(b), where a note is payable at a specified bank, and where presentment is not made at maturity, and where the bank becomes insolvent after the maturity date but before presentment for payment actually occurs—with the result that the maker is "deprived of funds" during the delay—the maker "may discharge his liability by written assignment to the holder of his rights against . . . the payor bank in respect [to] such funds." To illustrate: A note is made payable at the X Bank on March 1, at which time the maker has sufficient funds on deposit to meet the note. Presentment is not made on March 1 as required by the UCC.[2] On March 10 the bank fails. Presentment is finally made by the holder on March 11, at which time, of course, he does not obtain payment, because the bank has closed. In this case the maker can *assign his rights against the funds in the bank* (to the extent of the amount of the note) to the holder and *thereby be discharged* of further liability. Thus, if the bank does not pay out a hundred cents on the dollar and the account is not covered by federal deposit insurance, the loss falls on the holder because of the late presentment.

**Liability on Admissions:** By signing a promissory note, the maker *admits* (guarantees) certain facts. Section 3-413(3) provides in part that the maker "admits against all subsequent parties . . . the existence of the payee and his then capacity [capacity at the time of signing the note] to indorse." Thus, if a payee who is a minor negotiates an instrument to a holder and subsequently recovers the instrument by disaffirming his or her indorsement, the holder can recover from the maker any damages incurred as a result of the rescission.

## *Liability of the Acceptor*

As we saw in Chapter 24, time drafts are frequently presented to the drawee prior to maturity for his or her *acceptance.* Under the UCC, in some instances presentment for acceptance is mandatory while in others it is optional. In any event, when the drawee accepts the instrument he or she becomes liable on it for the first time.[3]

Once an acceptance occurs, the liability of the drawee-acceptor is virtually identical to that of the maker of a note. Under Sec. 3-413(3), by accepting, he or she admits the existence of the payee and that person's then capacity to indorse. More important, under Sec. 3-413(1) the drawee-acceptor promises to pay the instrument at its maturity date. Again the obligation to pay is not cut off or diminished by a late presentment for payment.[4] The only exception to this rule of continuing liability arises in the same circumstances as those connected with the liability of the maker of a note—where the draft is payable at a bank and where that bank becomes insolvent between the time presentment should have been made under the code and the time it actually was made. In such a situation, the drawer can discharge his or her liability to the holder by giving that person an assignment of funds, just as the maker of a note can do in similar circumstances.

Two further observations regarding acceptances are needed:

**1.** Until a draft is accepted, the drawee has no liability on the instrument to the payee or to any other holder. As we will see later in this chapter, the drawee usually owes the *drawer* a legal duty to accept the instrument, but does not owe such a duty to any *holder* of the draft. Thus if a holder presents the draft for acceptance and the drawee refuses to accept, the holder cannot bring action against the drawee (al-

---

[2] Presentment here is due on March 1 because, under a rule to be examined later, an instrument that is payable at a fixed future date must ordinarily be presented for payment *on that date.*

[3] While acceptance does not take place in the case of checks, they can be "certified," an act that is similar to acceptance (see Chapter 28 for details).

[4] The primary rules prescribing the various times at which presentments for acceptance or payment should be made are discussed later in the chapter.

though he or she can bring action against the drawer, who is a secondary party).

2. As a general rule, a refusal by the drawee to accept a draft that is properly presented constitutes a dishonor of the instrument, which triggers the liability of secondary parties on the instrument—the drawer and all indorsers except those indorsing "without recourse" (that is, without guaranteeing payment). The precise elements and ramifications of a dishonor will be examined later in this chapter.

## PROMISSORY LIABILITY OF SECONDARY PARTIES, GENERALLY

Secondary parties are *drawers* of drafts and checks and *indorsers* of all instruments. The liability of these parties is often significantly less than that of primary parties.

Primary parties *absolutely promise* to pay the instruments they have signed. Secondary parties promise to pay *only if certain conditions are met:* (1) due presentment, (2) dishonor, and (3) notice of dishonor. Essentially, the secondary party (except for the "without recourse" indorser) is saying, "I will pay this instrument to anyone holding it *if* it is presented to the primary party (or the drawee), and *if* he or she dishonors it (usually by failing to pay), and *if* I am given notice of the dishonor." These conditions, unless waived, must be met in order for the secondary party to be held on his or her **promissory liability**—or "contractual liability," as it is often called.[5] (These conditions need not be met, however, if a person is seeking to hold the secondary party liable on his or her *warranty* liability, an area we will examine later in this chapter.)

## PROMISSORY LIABILITY OF DRAWERS

All drawers, like makers and acceptors, admit the existence of the payee and his or her then capacity to indorse. Of more importance, however, is the drawer's promissory liability.

Under Sec. 3-413(2), a drawer promises that "upon dishonor of the draft and any necessary notice of dishonor . . . he will pay the amount of the draft to the holder or to any indorser who takes it up." Thus the drawer's contractual liability is conditioned upon the events of dishonor and the notice of dishonor. We will examine these conditions here.

### Dishonor of Drafts

While checks and promissory notes require only one kind of presentment, presentment for payment, drafts often involve two presentments—*presentment for acceptance* and, later, *presentment for payment.* Insofar as drafts are concerned, then, a dishonor can occur either by the refusal of the drawee to accept or the refusal to pay.

**Dishonor by Nonacceptance:** Under Sec. 3-501 (1)(a), presentment for acceptance is required in three situations. This section provides that, unless excused, presentment for acceptance is necessary to charge the drawer and indorsers (1) "where the draft so provides," (2) where it "is payable elsewhere than at the residence or place of business of the drawee," or (3) where its "date of payment depends upon such presentment." This section also provides that "the holder may *at his option* present for acceptance any other draft payable at a stated date"—that is, "time" drafts. Any refusal by the drawee to accept a draft that is properly presented for acceptance, regardless of whether presentment is required or optional, *constitutes a dishonor* that triggers the liability of the drawer and indorsers (assuming that any necessary notice of dishonor is also given).

**Dishonor by Nonpayment:** After an acceptance occurs, as well as in any case where an optional presentment for acceptance is dispensed with by the holder, a *presentment for payment,* at maturity, is required in order to fix the liability of the drawer—and indorsers, as well. (Until such presentment is made by the holder no dishonor has occurred, and the secondary parties' liability is not fixed.) Once a proper presentment for payment is made, however, a refusal by the drawee to make payment does constitute a dishonor.

**Effect of Late Presentment:** Section 3-503 brings together the rules that set the time limits within which presentment for acceptance and payment are to be made. Insofar as drafts are concerned, the rules for *presentment for payment* are as follows:

---

[5] Some drafts provide that the drawer waives presentment, dishonor, and notice of dishonor. This discussion, however, assumes that no such waiver exists. (Also, under Sec. 3-511, delay in presentment and notice of dishonor are excused in certain circumstances.)

1. Where a draft is payable at a fixed future date, presentment is due on that date.

2. As to other drafts, presentment must be made within a "reasonable time" after the secondary party became a party; in other words, where the drawer's liability is concerned, within a reasonable time after the draft is issued. Generally, under Sec. 3-503 a reasonable time in regard to such a draft is determined "by any usage of banking or trade, and the facts of the particular case." However, in the case of an uncertified check that section provides that it is "presumed" that 30 days after issuance is a reasonable time for presentment insofar as the drawer is concerned (but a shorter time applies to indorsers, as will be seen subsequently).

**Drawer's Liability Contrasted with Indorser's Liability:** While drawers and indorsers are both secondary parties, their liabilities differ in one significant respect. While a late presentment automatically frees indorsers of their secondary liability, such a presentment does not free the drawer except in the rare case where the drawee becomes insolvent during the delay in presentment. To illustrate, using the check as an example: D issues a check to P on June 10, and P indorses it to H on June 22. H presents the check to the drawee bank for payment on July 18, at which time the bank dishonors it because of a computer error showing insufficient funds in D's account. H gives immediate notice of dishonor to D. Although the presentment on July 18 was late—i.e., more than 30 days after its June 10 issuance—D remains liable on the instrument because the drawee bank did not fail after the 30 days had elapsed. (Because the "time of presentment" rules are thus of more significance to indorsers than to drawers, a fuller discussion of these rules appears in the "Liability of Indorsers" section later in this chapter.)

## *Notice of Dishonor*

When a dishonor occurs, notice of dishonor must generally be given to fix the drawer's liability. Section 3-508 provides that such notice may either be sent by mail or given orally. This section also provides that where the party giving notice is a bank, notice must be given "before its midnight deadline"—that is, by midnight of the day of dishonor. Where the party giving notice is not a bank, notice must be given by midnight of the third business day following dishonor.

(Under Sec. 3-511, however, notice of dishonor may be waived or excused; the most common situation in which notice is dispensed with is in the case where dishonor of a check occurs as a result of a stop-payment order issued to the drawee bank by the drawer; in such a case the drawer is obviously aware that the dishonor will be made.)

## PROMISSORY (CONDITIONAL) LIABILITY OF INDORSERS

Unqualified indorsers have two kinds of liability—*conditional liability* and *warranty liability.* Qualified ("without recourse") indorsers, on the other hand, incur warranty liability only. These two general kinds of liability will be discussed in order.

## *Conditions: Presentment, Dishonor, and Notice*

All unqualified indorsers promise that they will pay the instrument themselves if (1) the instrument is properly presented for acceptance or payment, (2) the instrument is dishonored, and (3) a proper notice of dishonor is given them. Thus the conditional liability of the indorser and drawer is the same in this respect: neither party incurs such liability until the specified conditions have occurred. There remains, however, the significant difference—noted earlier—that a *late* presentment frees the indorsers of their conditional liability in all cases, while this is not true of drawers.[6]

**How Presentments Are Made:** Under Sec. 3-504 (1), presentment is a demand for acceptance or payment made upon the maker, acceptor, drawee, or other payor by or on behalf of the holder. It can be made by mail (in which case the time of presentment is the time at which it is received); through a clearing house; at the place specified in the instrument; or, if no place is specified, at the place of business or at the residence of the maker. (In the latter case, if neither the maker "nor anyone authorized to act for him is accessible" at such place, then presentment is ex-

---

[6] Throughout this section it is assumed that the requirements of dishonor and notice of dishonor are not waived. In some situations, however, the purchaser of an instrument will not take it unless the transferor's indorsement provides that "presentment, dishonor, and notice of dishonor are hereby waived" (by the indorser). In such cases the discussion is inapplicable.

cused.) The importance of these rules is that if an attempted presentment is made in any manner other than these authorized ways, a refusal of the maker, acceptor, or drawee at that time does not constitute a dishonor.

**Time of Presentment:** As indicated, a required presentment must be made not only in a proper manner but also at a *proper time* if indorsers are to be held on their conditional liability. What is a proper time depends upon the type of presentment (presentment for acceptance or presentment for payment) and the time at which the instrument is payable.

Section 3-503(1) sets forth the rules for determining the times at which *all* presentments must be made. In the interest of brevity, we will concern ourselves only with those parts of this section that apply to presentments for payment. (This section appears in full in Article 3, Part Five of Appendix A.)

The two basic rules are provided by subsections c and e of Sec. 3-501(1). In essence, they are as follows:

**1.** If an instrument is payable at a specified time (for instance, "November 20, 1991"), presentment must be made *on that date* if secondary parties are to be held liable in the event of a dishonor.

**2.** As to all other instruments—demand notes, demand drafts, and checks—presentment must be made *within a reasonable time after the secondary party signed the instrument.*

As was indicated earlier, Sec. 3-503(2) goes on to indicate the factors to be taken into account in determining what is a reasonable time for various instruments, and provides that in regard to uncertified checks drawn and payable in the United States a reasonable time with respect to the *drawer* is presumed to be thirty days after its date or issue, whichever is later. Additionally, that section provides that with respect to the liability of an *indorser* of such a check a reasonable time is presumed to be "seven days after his indorsement."

We will now examine several of the more common fact-patterns to which these rules apply.

**1.** *Promissory note, payable at a fixed future date.* On March 3, M signs a note as maker and issues it to P, payee. The note is payable the following *September 5th.* P indorses the instrument in blank later in March and negotiates it to H. H presents the note to M for payment on September 10, and it is dishonored (that is, M simply does not pay it). Here H cannot hold the indorser, P, liable because presentment was five days late.

**2.** *Promissory note, payable on demand.* On February 2, M signs a note as maker and issues it to P, payee. The note is payable "on demand." On March 2, P indorses the instrument with a blank indorsement and negotiates it to H. On May 20, H presents the note to M for payment, and it is dishonored. H now brings action against P on her indorsement. Since the note is a demand note and thus governed by Sec. 3-503(1)(e), H—in order to hold P liable—must show that his presentment on May 20 was *within a reasonable time after P indorsed the instrument.* (As indicated earlier, a reasonable time as to demand notes and drafts "is determined by the nature of the instrument, any usage of banking or trade, and the facts of the particular case." Under this clause, for example, it is generally held that an interest-bearing demand note can be presented somewhat later than one bearing no interest, and that a reasonable time for presentment in rural communities is somewhat longer than when the parties are in urban areas.)

**3.** *Regular (uncertified) check.* D draws a check on his account in the B Bank payable to the order of P on April 6, and he issues it to P on that date. P, by a blank indorsement, negotiates the check to X on April 15, and X, by blank indorsement, negotiates it to H on April 20. On April 26, H presents the check to the drawee, the B Bank, and payment is refused for some reason; H then gives immediate notice of the dishonor to both indorsers, P and X. Under the "seven day" rule of Sec. 3-503(2) that applies to indorsers of ordinary checks, the last indorser (X) is liable to H, but the prior indorser, P, is not. Since P indorsed on April 15, he could be held on his conditional liability only if the check were presented to the drawee bank, or at least put into the bank collection process, within seven days—by April 22. In this case presentment on April 26 was late as to P but effective as to X, since the presentment *was* within seven days of X's becoming an indorser. (And if action were brought by H against D, drawer, as well, obviously the presentment *as to him* would be timely, since it would conform to the "within thirty days of issue" rule applicable to drawers.)

**Notice of Dishonor and Protest:** When a dishonor occurs, either by a refusal to accept or by nonpayment, any indorser is freed of conditional liability unless he or she is given a *notice of dishonor* within the time specified by Sec. 3-508. That section provides in part, as noted earlier, that "any necessary notice must be given by a bank before its midnight deadline, and *by any other person before midnight of the third business day after dishonor.*" (Emphasis added.)[7] The indorser receiving the notice then has the same prescribed time in which to give notice to his or her immediate indorser, if any.

Under Sec. 3-509, in some situations a *protest* (a formal, notarized notice of dishonor) can be made. Protest is required only where the dishonored instrument is drawn in or payable in a foreign country. As to other instruments, use of protest in lieu of ordinary notice of dishonor is optional.

**When Presentment Is Excused or Delay Permitted:** Section 3-511(1) provides: "Delay in presentment, protest or notice of dishonor is excused when the party is without notice that it is due or when the delay is caused by circumstances beyond his control and he exercises reasonable diligence after the cause of the delay ceases to operate." The phrase *without notice that it is due* has particular application to an instrument containing an acceleration clause. It is entirely possible that a holder will take an instrument *after* the time of payment has been accelerated but having no knowledge of the acceleration at the time of taking it. The phrase *circumstances beyond his control* excuses delay in presentment or in notice of dishonor when the delay is caused by such things as extreme weather conditions or the emergency closing of businesses in a certain area by act of the governor of the involved state.

Additionally, Sec. 3-511(2) provides that presentment or notice of dishonor is entirely excused if the party to be charged (1) has waived presentment or notice; (2) has personally dishonored or stopped payment on the instrument; or (3) "if by reasonable diligence the presentment . . . cannot be made, or the notice given."

The fact-pattern of the following case is typical of those in which the courts are required to determine whether or not the holder exercised "reasonable diligence" in trying to make presentment.

---

[7] The midnight deadline rule requires that if payment cannot be made because of insufficient funds or because a stop payment order has been issued, the drawee bank must give notice to its transferor no later than *midnight of the next business day.* If that transferor is also a bank, it must in turn give notice to *its* transferor by midnight of the day following its receipt of the original notice.

---

### Gaffin v. Heymann
Supreme Court of Rhode Island,
428 A.2d 1066 (1981)

In 1967 Gaffin (plaintiff) loaned $10,000 to Michael Heymann so he and a friend could open a travel agency. Later, the business failed and Gaffin told Heymann he wanted the loan repaid.

A series of negotiations between plaintiff, Michael Heymann, and Michael Heymann's father, Paul Heymann (defendant), then ensued. As a result of these discussions, plaintiff finally agreed to accept two promissory notes payable to his order in the amounts of $8,000 and $2,000 signed by Michael Heymann as maker, on condition that Paul Heymann would also be a party to the $8,000 note.

Accordingly, Michael Heymann delivered the notes to plaintiff in March 1968. The $8,000 note—the one involved in this litigation—had a maturity date of March 10, 1973. *Michael Heymann was the maker of this interest-bearing note, and the instrument bore the signature of Paul Heymann on the back.*

Over the next year or two several interest payments were missed. For reasons appearing in the decision below, plaintiff was unable to locate Michael Heymann in order to collect the payments, and he was also unable to present the note to Michael Heymann for payment on March 10, 1973. Plaintiff then brought this action to recover the amount of the note from defendant.

At the trial, defendant raised two primary issues: (1) whether he was a comaker of the note, as plaintiff contended, or an indorser; and (2) if he was an indorser, whether he was excused from liability because of plaintiff's failure to present the note to the maker at maturity. The trial court ruled that defendant was legally a *comaker* of the note, in view of plaintiff's refusal to accept the note unless signed by defendant. Accordingly, judgment was entered for plaintiff.

In the appellate court defendant raised the same issues as those presented in the trial court. As to the first issue, the

*(continued)*

appellate court accepted defendant's argument that he was an *indorser* of the instrument, rather than a comaker. This ruling was reached on the basis of Sec. 3-402 of the UCC, which provides that "unless the instrument clearly indicates that a signature is made in some other capacity, it is an indorsement."

The appellate court then turned to the second issue, whether defendant, as indorser, was released of liability by plaintiff's failure to present the note to the maker at maturity. The part of the opinion dealing with this issue is summarized below.

---

**Decision:** Defendant-indorser was *not* freed by plaintiff's failure to present the note to the maker (Michael) at maturity. While plaintiff's failure in this regard would ordinarily free the indorser, in some instances presentment by the holder is excused. The court here quoted Sec. 3-511 of the UCC as follows: "Presentment or notice of protest . . . is entirely excused when . . . by reasonable diligence, the presentment or notice of protest cannot be made or the notice given."

In this instance, the court said, Michael's whereabouts at the time of maturity were unknown. Plaintiff contacted Michael's father at that time. He told plaintiff that Michael, after traveling in Europe, had returned to the United States but that he did not know Michael's address or place of employment. The father also told plaintiff that Michael had not responded to mail sent to his last known address. Under these circumstances, the court said, the plaintiff had exercised due diligence in trying to find Michael. (In other words, plaintiff—upon receipt of the information appearing above—did not have a duty to make a further independent search for Michael, because the information indicated that such a search would probably be fruitless.) Accordingly, judgment was entered in favor of plaintiff. ∎

---

## WARRANTY LIABILITY OF INDORSERS

Every indorser makes certain warranties (or guarantees) about the instrument he or she is negotiating. This creates a **warranty liability,** which is sometimes called the unconditional liability of secondary parties, meaning that the liability is *not* conditioned upon proper presentment, dishonor, and notice of dishonor.

### Unqualified Indorsers

The warranties made by all unqualified indorsers are set forth below. (With an exception to be noted later, the same warranties are also made by qualified indorsers.)

Section 3-417(2) provides in part that a person who negotiates an instrument by indorsement and who receives consideration for it makes five warranties to the indorsee and subsequent holders.[8] Under this section the indorser essentially warrants that:

1. He or she has good title to the instrument.
2. All signatures are genuine or authorized.
3. The instrument has not been materially altered.
4. No defense of any party is good against him or her (the indorser).
5. He or she has no knowledge of any insolvency proceeding instituted against the maker, acceptor, or drawer of an unaccepted instrument.

The first four of these warranties are illustrated below. The fifth is rarely encountered.

A breach of *warranty of title* often involves a forged indorsement. For example: D draws and issues an instrument payable to the order of P. The instrument is stolen from P, and the thief forges P's indorsement on the back of it. He then sells the instrument to A, an innocent purchaser, who by blank indorsement, negotiates the instrument to B. B presents the instrument for payment, but payment is refused because the maker, acceptor, or drawee has learned that P's indorsement is a forgery. Because of the forged indorsement of P, B has not acquired title to the instrument and cannot hold the maker (or acceptor or drawee, in the case of a draft or check) liable on it. However, he can hold A liable on the warranty of title theory, because A did not have title either, because of the forged indorsement. A is liable on this warranty even if he had no reason to suspect the forgery and (as is true of all other warranties) even if the presentment for payment by B to the primary party was late.

The warranty that *all signatures are genuine or authorized* is almost self-explanatory. Suppose, for example, that P received a note of which M was the apparent maker. P later indorsed the note to H, and H recovered nothing from M because M was able to prove that her signature on the note was a forgery. (It

---

[8] The liability of a person who negotiates an instrument *by delivery only* (without indorsing it) is discussed later in the chapter.

may take a lawsuit against M to establish the fact of the forgery, or evidence of the forgery may be so convincing that H foregoes a lawsuit against M.) H can now hold P, the indorser, on his warranty that all signatures on the instrument at the time of the indorsement were genuine. Again, H need not show that P knew of the forgery when he indorsed; it is the fact of the forgery that is controlling.

We discussed the defense of *material alteration* in Chapter 26, where we saw that a maker or acceptor might escape liability on an instrument by showing that it was materially altered after he or she had made (or accepted) it. The ordinary holder who presents for payment in this situation will probably recover nothing from the maker or acceptor, and an HDC may make only a partial recovery (especially if the alteration involved a raising of the amount of the instrument.) However, either holder can hold any indorser liable on the breach of warranty theory and thereby recover whatever loss he or she sustained—assuming, of course, that the alteration occurred prior to the indorsement.

The warranty that *no defense is good against the indorser* refers to any kinds of defenses that do not fall within the first three subsections of Sec. 3-417(2)—as, for example, the defense of illegality. To illustrate: After a Saturday night poker game A ends up owing B $175; A gives B a check for that amount in payment. The following Monday A learns from a lawyer friend that gambling debts are totally unenforceable in his state, so he stops payment on the check. In the meantime B has indorsed the check to C. In this situation, after being refused payment by the drawee bank, C can hold B (the indorser) liable for breach of the warranty that no defense existed against him.

## *Qualified Indorsers*

The warranty liability of the person who indorses "without recourse" is exactly the same as that of the unqualified indorser—with one exception. While the unqualified indorser flatly guarantees that no defense of any party is good against him or her, the qualified indorser warrants only that he or she "has no knowledge of such a defense"—Sec. 3-417(3). Thus, if a check were given in payment of a totally illegal obligation and subsequently a party indorsed the instrument "without recourse," that indorser would not be liable upon dishonor unless it were established that he or she *knew of the defense* at the time of indorsement.

However, this warranty applies only to defenses falling within subsection d. Thus, if the qualified indorser were being sued for breach of the warranty that all signatures were genuine, for example, the indorser would be liable if the drawer's or maker's signature were a forgery, even if he or she did not know of the forgery.

The next case shows particularly well how the application of Sec. 3-417(3) works out in real life.

---

### Fair Finance Co. v. Fourco, Inc.
Court of Appeals of Ohio, 237 N.E.2d 406 (1968)

Fourco, defendant, sold goods to a buyer and had the buyer, in payment thereof, sign a promissory note payable to the order of Fourco. (For this reason, Fourco is usually referred to in the decision as the vendor-payee.)

Fourco indorsed the note "without recourse" and negotiated it to Fair Finance, plaintiff. When plaintiff sought payment from the maker (the buyer of the goods), it was discovered that the defendant (the payee and qualified indorser) had computed the interest at too high a rate in determining the face amount of the note. The maker was thus obligated to pay the plaintiff only the corrected amount due, and plaintiff then sought recovery of the balance from the defendant, the qualified indorser.

The lower court found that defendant had no notice of the fact that the interest provided for in its note was usurious (in excess of that permitted by Ohio law). In view of this fact, the court ruled that the defendant, having transferred the instrument by qualified indorsement, was not liable to plaintiff for the balance of the interest. Plaintiff appealed.

---

**Decision:** The judgment was reversed. Under Sec. 3-417 of the UCC, a qualified indorser, such as Fourco, warrants to subse-

*(continued)*

quent holders that he "has no knowledge" of any defense that might be asserted against him (the indorser). Since a defense did exist—the defense of usury—the question is whether Fourco had "knowledge" of it at the time of its indorsement.

Fourco had no actual knowledge of the usury when it prepared the note for its customer (the maker) to sign or when it indorsed the note to Fair Finance. However, in the eyes of the law, Fourco did have knowledge of the defense for two reasons.

First, Fourco used its own printed note in this transaction. Second, Fourco itself computed the interest provisions of the note incorrectly, that is, in excess of the rate permitted by Ohio law. In these circumstances Fourco could not be excused of liability on the ground of lack of knowledge. Accordingly, judgment was entered in favor of Fair Finance in the amount of the excess interest. ■

---

## SELECTED TRANSFEROR–INDORSER PROBLEMS

### Liability of Transferor without Indorsement

A person who negotiates a bearer instrument by mere delivery (that is, without indorsing it) has no conditional liability on the instrument. If the primary party is unable to pay the instrument at maturity, the transferor is not liable to the holder.

However, a transferor by mere delivery does have the same warranty liability as an unqualified indorser, with one important exception. While the warranties of indorsers run to all subsequent holders of the instrument, the warranties of the person who transfers without indorsement run only to his or her *immediate transferee*. To illustrate: P receives a bearer note of which M is apparently the maker. P negotiates the note to X by delivery only, and X in turn negotiates it by delivery only to H. If M's signature turns out to be a forgery, H can hold X, his immediate transferor, liable on his warranty that all signatures are genuine, but he cannot hold P, the prior transferor. (Of course, if X has to pay damages to H arising out of the breach of his warranty, X can then hold P because P's warranty did run to him.)

### Order of Indorsers' Liability

Where two or more indorsements appear on an instrument, it is presumed, under Sec. 3-414(2), that the indorsers are liable in the order in which their signatures appear. For instance, a note is indorsed by X, and the names of Y and Z appear successively below her indorsement. If Z is held liable to the holder, H, following a dishonor, Z can proceed against Y and Y against X. X will then be limited to an attempt to recover the amount of the instrument from the maker.[9]

While the holder of a dishonored instrument usually seeks to hold the last indorser liable, the holder is not limited to such a proceeding. For example, in the above case, if, upon dishonor, H *gives proper notice* to X, Y, and Z, he can then "skip" Y and Z if he wishes and bring suit directly against X, the first indorser.

### Liability of Accommodation Indorsers

Sometimes a person will indorse an instrument merely for the purpose of lending his or her credit to the instrument. Such a person is an **accommodation indorser**. To illustrate: P is the holder of a check of which she is the payee, and she wishes to cash it at a bank where she is unknown. At the bank's suggestion P asks A, an acquaintance who is a local merchant and depositor at the bank, to indorse the check along with her. A does so, becoming an accommodation indorser; the bank then cashes the check, giving the amount of the instrument to P in cash. (In this case, P is known as the *accommodated party*.)

In general, an accommodation indorser has the same liability to subsequent holders as does any other indorser. The accommodation indorser has both conditional and warranty liability to any subsequent holder (including a holder who knew that he or she was signing merely as an accommodation indorser). Once there is a dishonor of the instrument and proper notice is given to the accommodation indorser, that person is immediately liable to the holder. That is, the

---

[9] It is only *presumed* that the indorsers are liable in the order in which their signatures appear; a contrary agreement may exist among the indorsers. In the example above, X will not be liable to Y if she can prove that such an agreement existed between her and Y at the time of her indorsement.

holder does not have to bring suit against the primary party in an effort to obtain payment before initiating action against the accommodation indorser.

## DISCHARGE OF THE PARTIES

Examination of the rules regarding the liability of secondary parties has already presented several situations in which these parties are discharged—such as failure to make a required presentment or failure to give a notice of dishonor. Now we will briefly describe additional ways in which parties to commercial paper can be discharged.

### *Discharge by Payment*

The vast majority of negotiable instruments are discharged by payment. Under Secs. 3-601(1)(a) and 3-603, payment in good faith to the holder by a primary party or by the drawee of an unaccepted draft or check usually discharges all parties on the instrument. Payment by any other party, such as an indorser, only discharges the indorser and subsequent parties on the instrument. In such a case, the party making payment can still seek recovery from prior parties on the instrument.

If a payment is less than the amount owed, the party making the payment is discharged only to the extent of the payment, as determined by the rules of debt settlement (see Chapter 12). Under Sec. 3-604, if a party tenders payment, but it is refused, the party is not discharged from liability. However, the holder cannot later recover interest from the time of the tender; nor can he or she recover legal costs or attorney's fees.

### *Alteration*

Under Sec. 3-407, alteration of an instrument by a holder discharges any party whose obligation is affected by the alteration, except that a holder in due course can enforce the instrument according to its original terms.

### *Cancellation and Renunciation*

Section 3-605(1)(a) reads as follows: "(1) The holder of an instrument may even without consideration discharge any party (a) in any manner apparent on the face of the instrument or the indorsement, as by intentionally cancelling the instrument or the party's signature by destruction or mutilation, or by striking out the party's signature." To illustrate: Marking an instrument "paid" constitutes a cancellation of the instrument itself, as does intentional destruction or mutilation of it. Similarly, striking out a party's indorsement cancels that party's liability (but not the liability of prior parties). Under Sec. 3-605(1)(b), *renunciation* occurs when a holder gives up his or her rights against a party to the instrument in a particular way—either by renouncing them in a signed writing given to such party or by surrendering the instrument to that party.

### *Discharge of a Prior Party*

As a general rule, the intentional cancellation of an instrument discharges all parties to it. Additionally, the discharge of a *particular party* by cancellation or renunciation normally discharges that party and all subsequent parties. These results flow from Sec. 3-606, which provides in part that "the holder discharges any party to the instrument" when he or she "releases or agrees not to sue any person whom [that] party has a right of recourse against." To illustrate: A note bears three indorsements: X, Y, and Z, in that order. If the holder, H, gives a valid release to the first indorser, X, both subsequent indorsers, Y and Z, are thereby discharged. It is possible, however, for H in such a situation to release X but to expressly "reserve his rights" against Y and Z. If this occurs, and if H later collects the amount of the instrument from either Y or Z, then that party still retains the right of recourse against X, the first indorser. Thus H's release of X, where he reserves his rights against subsequent indorsers, does not insulate X from liability to the subsequent indorsers.

### *Discharge by Reacquisition*

If a person acquires an instrument that he or she had held at a prior time, all intervening indorsers are discharged as against the reacquiring party and as against subsequent holders who do not qualify as holders in due course. To illustrate: P indorses a note to A, and A indorses it to B. If P reacquires the note, indorsers A and B are freed of all liability to P. And if P thereafter recirculates the instrument, A and B will have liability to subsequent holders only if such holders are HDCs.

## SUMMARY

The primary parties to commercial paper are the makers of notes and acceptors of drafts. Both such parties admit (guarantee) the existence of the payee, and the payee's capacity to indorse. Of much more importance, however, is the promissory liability of makers and acceptors. Assuming they have no defenses against the holder of an instrument, their promises to pay are absolute—i.e., their liability is not extinguished by a late presentment for payment. To this there is one limited exception: if an instrument is payable at a designated bank, and if the bank fails between the time presentment should have been made and the time of the late presentment, the maker or acceptor may discharge his or her liability by giving the holder an assignment of his or her rights against the bank in respect to the funds held in the bank for payment.

Secondary parties are drawers of drafts and checks, and indorsers of all instruments. Such parties, like makers and acceptors, make certain guarantees about the instrument, and also have promissory liability. This promissory liability, however, unlike that of makers and acceptors, is conditional in nature; that is, they promise to pay the holder the amount of the instrument only upon the occurrence of three events: (1) a presentment for payment to the maker or drawee-acceptor; (2) a dishonor by such party; and (3) receipt of notice of dishonor. In that regard, however, the promissory liability of the drawer differs markedly from that of an indorser. While it is true that the drawer cannot be held liable until the three specified events occur, a late presentment—followed by dishonor and notice of dishonor—does not discharge the drawer from his or her promissory liability (except in the rare case where the drawee fails prior to the time of the late presentment). By contrast, assuming there is no waiver of presentment, dishonor, and notice, a late presentment automatically frees the indorser of his or her promissory liability.

Turning to the subject of warranty liability, the UCC provides that all persons who negotiate an instrument by indorsement (and who receive consideration for the indorsement) make four primary warranties to the indorsee and to all subsequent holders. Such indorsers warrant that (1) he or she has good title to the instrument; (2) all signatures and indorsements on the instrument at the time of indorsement are genuine or authorized; (3) the instrument has not been materially altered; and (4) no defense of any party is good against him or her (the indorser). If there is a breach of any of these guarantees resulting in failure of the indorsee or subsequent holder to obtain payment from the maker or drawee-acceptor, the indorser is liable in damages to such person. The warranty liability of the qualified ("without recourse") indorser is the same as that of the unqualified indorser, except that, as to warranty 4, the warranty is that he or she has *no knowledge* of any existing defenses. Finally, the warranty liability of an indorser, unlike his or her promissory liability, is not extinguished by a late presentment for payment.

## KEY TERMS

**Primary parties**
**Secondary parties**
**Promissory liability**
**Warranty liability**
**Accommodation indorser**

## QUESTIONS AND PROBLEMS

**1.** A promissory note was signed by three makers, as follows: "Leo Palmer; George Johnson, Secy; Hubert Alligood." All three men were officers of a corporation for whose benefit the note was issued, but the name of the corporation did not appear anywhere on the instrument. When the instrument was not paid at maturity, the payee-holder brought suit against Johnson personally. As a defense, Johnson offered evidence showing that the plaintiff knew, when he received the instrument, that Johnson was simply signing as a representative of the corporation. Should this evidence be allowed? Why or why not? (*Kramer v. Johnson,* 176 S.E.2d 108, 1970.)

**2.** A promissory note was issued by the Gold Company, payable to the order of X, and bears the following signatures as makers: (a) "The Gold Company, by George Blue, President," and (b) "Derek Vance." The note was subsequently negotiated by X to the Last National Bank. When the note was not paid at maturity, the bank sought to hold Vance personally liable on it. At the trial, Vance offered evidence showing that the payee, X, knew that he (Vance) was secretary-treasurer of the Gold Company, and that he also knew that Vance was simply signing as a representative of the company. Should this evidence be admitted? Explain why or why not.

**3.** As part of a real estate transaction, a $20,000 check was issued by Francis Kirby, of which he was the drawer. When difficulties about the transaction arose later, the holder of the check telephoned the drawee bank to find out whether Kirby had sufficient funds in his account to cover the check. A bookkeeper of the bank replied that the funds were insufficient. In subsequent litigation, the question arose as to whether the holder's inquiry to the bank constituted a valid "presentment for payment" under the UCC. Do you think the telephone call was a valid presentment? Why or why not? (*Kirby v. Bergfield,* 182 N.W.2d 205, 1970.)

4. Lucile Fisher was an accommodation indorser of a check that was drawn on a Missouri bank. The check was cashed by the payee at the Nevada State Bank (which was also Fisher's bank). The check was put in the channels of collection by the Nevada State Bank, but was "lost in transit" for almost three months before it finally reached the drawee bank in Missouri. At this time the instrument was dishonored by the drawee bank because of insufficient funds in the drawer's account. The drawee bank promptly returned the check to the Nevada State Bank, which gave Fisher notice of dishonor the next day. When the Nevada State Bank sought to hold Fisher liable as indorser, she contended that she was freed of liability in view of the fact that ninety days had elapsed between the time she indorsed the check and the time she was given notice of dishonor by the Nevada State Bank. Do you agree with this contention? Explain. (*Nevada State Bank v. Fisher,* 565 P.2d 332, 1977.)

5. M was the maker of a $5,000 note issued in 1985, due "June 1, 1987." The note was payable at the XYZ Bank. The holder of the note presented it for payment on June 1, 1987, only to learn for the first time that the bank had failed three months earlier. In a suit by the holder against M, M proved that he lost 50 percent of his money that was in the bank when it failed—assuming that for some reason federal deposit insurance did not cover the loss—and he argues that he is thus liable to the holder only in the amount of $2,500. Is M correct? Why or why not?

6. A corporation issues a note payable to the order of X. The note is stolen from X, and the thief forges X's indorsement on the back. The thief transfers the note to Y, an innocent purchaser, who indorses it "without recourse, Y" and transfers it to Z. The corporation refuses to pay the note after learning of the forgery of X's name, whereupon Z sues Y, the qualified indorser, claiming breach of warranty of title. Y claims he is not liable because he had no knowledge of the forgery whatever. Is this a good defense? Why or why not?

7. D draws a check "payable to bearer" and issues it to X. X negotiates it to H the next day by delivery only (without indorsing it) and H immediately presents the check to the drawee bank for payment. If the check is dishonored because of insufficient funds and if H gives X prompt notice of the dishonor, is X liable to H? Explain.

8. A note held by H bears the successive indorsements of Alpha (payee), Bravo, and Charlie. The note is not paid at maturity, whereupon H talks his old friend Bravo into taking up the instrument (Bravo pays the full amount of the note to H, who returns it to Bravo). What effect, if any, does this have on the liability of (a) the maker, (b) Alpha, and (c) Charlie?

CHAPTER 28

# COMMERCIAL PAPER

CHECKS AND THE BANK–DEPOSITOR RELATIONSHIP

While checks are simply one type of commercial paper, they do possess certain characteristics that set them apart from promissory notes and drafts. Although some of these special aspects have been discussed in prior chapters, others have not. In this chapter we will first summarize the special attributes of checks and then examine the legal relationship existing between the drawer of a check and the **drawee bank** (the bank on which the check is drawn).[1] A brief look at the subject of electronic banking and the basic federal law applicable to its various facets—the Electronic Funds Transfer Act—concludes the chapter.

## CHECKS

Under Sec. 3-104 of the UCC, a check is by definition "a draft drawn on a bank payable on demand." (The *demand* requirement thus means that a "postdated check"—for instance, one issued to the payee on March 10 but dated April 5—is, technically speaking, a draft rather than a check. The primary consequence of postdating is that the drawee bank should not honor the instrument until the specified date arrives.)

Checks generally have a shorter life than other instruments and thus circulate more quickly than ordinary drafts and promissory notes. This is reflected in Sec. 3-503, which provides that (1) for the drawer of a check, it is presumed that a reasonable time for presentment is to be no more than thirty days after issue, and (2) for an indorser, presumably only seven days after the indorsement.

In regard to the thirty-day provision, the general rule for drawers of drafts—that a late presentment excuses them of liability only if they have suffered a loss as a result of the delay—is illustrated as it specifically applies to checks: D draws and issues a check to P on March 1; after several negotiations the check is presented by H, the last holder, to the drawee bank on June 18. Payment is refused at that time (perhaps because D has insufficient funds in her account or because a creditor of D, through legal proceedings, has attached D's funds in the bank). In this case, though presentment has been made more than two months after the thirty-day deadline (March 31), D remains fully liable to H on the instrument *unless* the drawee bank failed after March 31 and before the late presentment on June 18. In that limited situation D can discharge her liability by giving an assignment of funds to H in the amount of the instrument, in the same manner that the maker of a note payable at a bank can—see Chapter 27.

### *A Check Is Not an Assignment of Funds*

As a practical matter, checks are drawn (and received by the payee and subsequent holders) on the assumption that the drawer has funds in his or her account at the drawee bank sufficient to pay the instrument when it is presented. In the great majority of instances this is, in fact, the case. Federal Reserve Board figures indicate that of every thousand checks drawn, only six or seven are dishonored because of insufficient funds.

Despite the likelihood that a given check will actually be honored, under Sec. 3-409 the issuance of a check does not constitute an "assignment of funds" in the drawee bank. Until final payment is made by the drawee bank, the issuance and circulation of the instrument have no effect on the funds in the drawer's account; nor do they discharge the underlying debt in payment for which it was issued.

Thus, while a check may be accepted by the payee in payment of a debt owed by the drawer, and

---

[1]As indicated in Chapter 24, proposed amendments to Articles 3 and 4 of the UCC which may effect some changes in the bank-depositor relationship are in the drafting stage. Because neither the final text nor ultimate disposition of these amendments can be predicted, this chapter is based on the present form of Articles 3 and 4.

while the payee may even give the drawer a receipt marked "paid in full," the receipt is conditional upon the check actually being honored by the drawee bank when presented. The same thing is true for bank credits. Thus where a payee deposits a check in his or her account in a bank (the depositary bank) and receives credit for the deposit, and that bank forwards the check to an intermediary bank which credits the depositary bank's account, the entire process is reversed if the drawee bank dishonors the check. That is, the check is returned to the payee through the same channels, each bank charging its transferor bank with the amount of the instrument. Ultimately the check is returned to the depositary bank, which charges the account of its depositor, the payee, with the amount of the check and returns it to him or her. The payee can then sue the drawer on the check or on the underlying debt itself.

## *Certification of Checks*

In our discussion of drafts we noted that checks (unlike many drafts) are not presented for acceptance. However, they are occasionally presented to the drawee bank for *certification;* if certification is made, the bank's liability is the same as that of the acceptor of a draft.

One of the most common uses of a **certified check** is where a seller of goods, such as a used car dealer, is selling to a buyer with whom he or she has had no business dealings. In such a case the seller will probably want the buyer to have his or her personal check certified before taking it in payment. From a practical standpoint the primary result of certification is that the seller no longer has to worry that the check will be dishonored because of insufficient funds. Frequently, certified checks are required by law from purchasers of real estate at sheriff's sales, and occasionally they are required from persons who are paying fees owed to a state or state agency.

**Mechanics and Effect:** In the absence of a special agreement, a bank has no legal duty to certify a check drawn on it; its only duty is to pay the holder in conformity with the terms of the instrument. A bank that accedes to a request for certification does so by stamping the word *certified* on the face of the check, together with the name of the bank and the date, and including the handwritten signature or initials of the officer making the certification. At that time the bank charges the drawer's account with the amount of the check and transfers the funds to its certified check account.

Certification has three basic effects:

**1.** The certifying bank is now primarily liable on the instrument (it absolutely promises to pay the instrument when it is presented for payment).

**2.** The certification of a check at the request of a holder discharges the drawer and any indorsers who indorsed prior to certification. To illustrate: A check drawn by D is issued to P; P indorses it to H, and H obtains certification from the drawee bank. At this point D (the drawer) and P (the indorser) are released of all liability on the instrument. On the other hand, if the *drawer* requests the certification, he or she remains secondarily liable; that is, in the unlikely event that the certifying bank subsequently cannot or will not honor the check when it is presented for payment, the drawer is liable to the holder. (While it is unlikely that any indorsements will appear on the instrument when certification is requested by the drawer, if there are any, the same rule applies to the indorsers; like the drawer, they are not released of secondary liability by the certification.)

**3.** Once a check is certified, the drawer no longer has the right to stop payment on it. This is true no matter who obtained the certification. (UCC Sec. 4-403, comment 5.)

**Revocation of Certification:** Under pre-UCC law a bank had the right to revoke a certification (sometimes called the right to "uncertify") if it could show that certification was obtained by fraud or made under a mistake of fact on its part—provided that the holder at the time of revocation had not substantially changed his or her position in reliance on the certification. This is still the general rule today, with one modification. Because Sec. 3-418 provides that "payment or acceptance of any instrument is final in favor of a holder in due course," it is probable that revocation cannot be made if the holder at the time of attempted revocation qualifies as an HDC, regardless of whether that person had changed his or her position subsequent to the certification.

## THE BANK–DEPOSITOR RELATIONSHIP

A bank may be liable to a depositor or a depositor liable to a bank solely through Article 3 of the UCC (dealing with commercial paper). However, the bank–depositor relationship is a broad one; thus many of the general rights and duties of the two parties spring from several sources in addition to that article. These sources include the following:

1. A *creditor-debtor relationship* exists between the depositor and the drawee bank, and sometimes the bank's obligations are essentially those of debtors generally.

2. In some transactions a *principal-agent relationship* exists between the depositor and the bank, and in these situations the bank has the same obligations as those imposed on all agents—for example, the duty to use reasonable care and the duty not to profit at the principal's expense.

3. In many situations involving controversies between the depositor and the bank, specific sections of Article 4 of the UCC (dealing with bank deposits and collections) enter the picture.

We begin our discussion by stating the primary duties of a bank. We will then examine some specific situations that commonly cause bank-depositor controversies.

## *The Bank's Duties*

**Duty to Honor Orders:** The drawee bank is generally obligated to honor checks drawn by the depositor so long as he or she has sufficient funds in the account and has not stopped payment.[2] The bank's failure to honor a check usually makes it liable to the depositor, under ordinary breach of contract principles, for damages resulting from the refusal to pay. (As we will see in more detail later, the bank also is obligated to obey the stop payment orders of its drawers.)

***Stale Checks:*** The duty to honor checks is not absolute, however. For example, the bank obviously does not have to honor checks if there are not sufficient funds in the drawer's account. The bank also does not have to honor **stale checks.** UCC Sec. 4-404 provides that "a bank is under no obligation to a customer having a checking account to pay a check, other than a certified check, which is presented more than six months after its date, but it may charge its customer's account for a payment made thereafter in good faith." This section suggests that a drawee bank presented with a check beyond the six-month time limit should secure a confirmation from the drawer before honoring it; failure to do so raises at least the possibility that the bank might not be able to show "good faith" in making the payment. (But see the *Granite Equipment Leasing Corp.* case later in the chapter for a fuller discussion of the good faith requirement.)

**Duty to Pay after Death of Drawer:** While the general rule under common law is that the death of a principal automatically terminates the authority of the agent to act on his or her behalf, the drafters of the UCC have taken a different position on checks. Section 4-405 provides in essence that the death of a customer (drawer) does not revoke the bank's authority to pay that customer's checks "until the bank knows of the fact of death . . . and has reasonable opportunity to act on it." Since the bank might not actually know of a customer's death for a long time after it has occurred (possibly weeks or even months), if it honors any of the customer's checks during this period, it is generally not liable to the drawer's estate for funds so paid out.

A second provision of Sec. 4-405 pertains to a different situation—where the bank does receive notice of the drawer's death soon after it has occurred. In this case the drawee bank still has the right to honor checks for a limited time. Section 4-405(2) provides: "Even with knowledge [of death] a bank may for ten days after the date of death pay or certify checks drawn on or prior to that date unless ordered to stop payment by a person claiming an interest in the account."

**Duty to Pay on Only Genuine or Authorized Signatures:** As we will see in more detail later in the chapter, a drawee bank that honors a check bearing a forged drawer's signature cannot legally charge the purported drawer's account even if the bank did not know of the forgery when it honored the instrument. Thus, if D's signature is forged to a check drawn on the X Bank, and that bank subsequently honors the instrument by paying a holder and charging D's account, D, upon discovery of the forgery, can require the bank to recredit her account in the amount of the instrument.

**Duty to Use Reasonable Care as Agent:** A bank has the duty to use reasonable care in handling com-

---

[2] A bank can, if it wishes, honor a drawer's check even if there are insufficient funds in the drawer's account. In such a case an *overdraft* is created, and the bank has the right to recover from the drawer the amount of the overdraft.

mercial paper when acting as an agent for a depositor. This relationship is usually created when a bank's customer deposits in his or her own account a check drawn by a third party (often on some other bank). In such a case, under Sec. 4-201(1), it is presumed that the bank receiving the check is taking it simply as agent for its depositor rather than purchasing it outright—and this presumption continues even if the bank permits the depositor to make immediate withdrawals against it. As a result of this relationship, the bank owes the depositor (among other things) the duty to use reasonable care in handling and forwarding the instrument through the bank collection process.

The following case invited a Pennsylvania appellate court to make forays into such varied but related matters as the law of bailments, the legality of "exculpatory clauses" in general, and the great public necessity for competent (nonnegligent) banking services.

---

### Phillips Home Furnishings, Inc. v. Continental Bank
Superior Court of Pennsylvania, 331 A.2d 845 (1974)

On the evening of June 16, 1973, Max Shectman prepared a bank deposit of $5,669 in receipts from his business, Phillips Home Furnishings, Inc. He then picked up his wife at her place of employment and proceeded to an office of Continental Bank, where he had done his banking for 30 years. Upon arriving at the bank, he placed his deposit in the bank's night depository safe in the wall of the bank building and returned home. Five days later, having received no confirmation of his deposit, Shectman phoned the bank, only to learn that it had no record of the deposit and no explanation of what might have happened to it. (At the subsequent trial, the two employees who had opened the safe the morning after the deposit was made filed affidavits in which they stated that no bag belonging to Shectman was found.)

When Shectman made further inquiries of the bank, one of its officers showed him a copy of the "night depository agreement" he had signed a year earlier. That agreement stated in part:

*Bank grants to the undersigned the privilege of using the Night Depository gratuitously and solely as an accommodation to the undersigned; and the exercise of the privilege by the undersigned will be at the sole risk of the undersigned. Bank will employ such safeguards . . . as it deems proper, [but] without any liability to the undersigned for their sufficiency. . . . Bank shall be under no liability with respect to anything placed in the Night Depository, except for the amount of cash and checks actually taken into its possession upon opening the Night Depository Safe.*

The bank, relying upon this agreement, refused to credit Shectman's account. He then brought action to recover damages for the bank's failure to credit the amount. The lower court found the night depository agreement to be legal and binding, and it entered judgment for the bank. Shectman appealed.

---

**Decision:** The judgment was reversed, and a trial on the question of negligence was ordered. An exculpatory clause such as this is invalid for two reasons. First, a bailor-bailee relationship was created when Shectman placed his deposit in the night depository. Under general bailment law, bailees cannot relieve themselves of liability arising out of their own negligence. Second, the Pennsylvania courts view exculpatory clauses as contrary to public policy in contracts formed between two parties of grossly unequal bargaining power, particularly where this inequality has grown out of public need for certain goods or services (here, banking services). Therefore, if Shectman were able to prove negligence on the part of the bank, the exculpatory clause would not free it of liability. (The court then ordered a new trial for the purpose of determining whether Shectman could prove his claim of negligence.) ■

---

## *The Depositor's Duties*

The depositor has the general obligation to keep sufficient funds in his or her checking account to permit the bank to honor all checks drawn on the account. In this respect the drawer of a check has a greater potential liability than the drawer of a draft. The drawer of a draft is liable only in a civil action to the holder of a draft where it is not paid by the drawee at maturity. The drawer of a check, however, has not only civil liability but also criminal liability for writing a "bad" check (if it is proved that the drawer issued the check with the intent to defraud). Under the statutes of many states there is a presumption of intent to defraud if the drawer does not "make good" to the holder of the check within a specified number of days after the dishonor occurs. Finally, as we will see in more detail later in the chapter, a depositor owes his or her bank the general duty to report forgeries and alterations within a reasonable length of time after he or she knows, or should know, of them.

## SELECTED BANK–DEPOSITOR PROBLEMS

### Stop Payment Orders

As we have indicated, it is possible for the drawer of a check to countermand the order contained in it by issuing the drawee bank a **stop payment order**. The purpose of this, of course, is to prevent the payee or other holder from receiving immediate payment from the bank. Usually the stop payment order is given only after the drawer discovers some default on the part of the payee (such as fraud or the delivery of defective goods under a sales contract) or after the check has been lost.[3] The order is binding for only a limited time period. Section 4-403(2) provides that "an oral order is binding upon the bank only for fourteen calendar days unless confirmed in writing within that period. A written order is effective for only six months unless renewed in writing."

1. What is the effect of such an order on the drawer?
2. What is the bank's liability in the event that it fails to obey the order?

**Effect of Stop Payment Order on Drawer:** Assuming that a stop payment order is given in time to permit the bank to act on it, the immediate effect is that the holder of the check fails to obtain payment when he or she presents it to the drawee bank. This does not necessarily mean, however, that the drawer is freed of liability on the instrument.

If the payee, after being refused payment, brings suit against the drawer, he or she may be able to prove that the drawer had no legal grounds for stopping payment; that is, the court may determine that the drawer had no assertable defense against the payee. In such case the payee is entitled to recover the amount of the instrument in full. The drawer also might have liability in a situation where he or she does in fact have a personal defense against the payee but where the holder who was refused payment qualifies as an HDC. In a suit against the drawer such a holder would also be entitled to full payment of the instrument.

Even in these instances the stop payment order is of some benefit to the drawer, for it at least assures him or her of the right to present, in a court proceeding, any reason for believing that the holder is not entitled to payment. And, of course, in many such proceedings the drawer can prove an assertable defense and escape all liability to the holder-plaintiff.

**Bank's Liability for Disobeying Stop Payment Order:** If the drawee bank honors a check after a valid stop payment order has been issued against it, the bank is liable to the drawer for any loss he or she suffers by reason of the wrongful payment. However, if the drawer has to bring legal action against the bank in order to have the account recredited in the amount of the check, he or she has the burden of proving the amount of loss.

Often it is not difficult for the drawer to prove that he or she suffered a loss. Such is the case where the payee obtained payment and the drawer is able to establish clearly that he or she had either a personal or real defense that could have been asserted against the payee. In this situation, if the stop payment order had been obeyed by the bank, it is obvious that the payee would never have been able to enforce the instrument against the drawer. The result is that the bank must recredit the drawer's account in the amount of the check.[4]

In some situations, however, the bank may be able to show that the drawer did *not* suffer a loss as a result of its failure to honor the stop payment order. Such is the case where, in the suit by the drawer against the bank, the facts are that the drawer did not have a defense of any kind against the payee. In this

---

[3] We are speaking throughout this section of *uncertified checks*. Once a check has been certified, at the request of either the drawer or a holder, no stop payment order can thereafter be effective.

[4] Written stop payment orders sometimes contain clauses to the effect that the drawer agrees not to hold the drawee bank liable if it should honor the check "through inadvertence or oversight." Such disclaimers are generally invalid. Section 4-103(1) provides in part that "no agreement can disclaim a bank's responsibility for its own lack of good faith or failure to exercise ordinary care" in a particular transaction.

## Figure 28.1 Bank's Liability for Disobeying Stop Order

**Example 1**

A (drawer) → Issues check as a result of fraud → B (payee) → Negotiation → C (HDC) → Drawee bank → Pays C in violation of A's stop order / Charges A's account

Bank need not recredit A's account. Fraud is a personal defense and not good against HDC; therefore, A has suffered no loss.

**Example 2**

A (drawer) → Issues check as a result of fraud → B (payee) → Drawee bank → Pays B in violation of A's stop order / Charges A's account

Bank must recredit A's account. A has a defense that is good against B; therefore A has suffered a loss. Bank would be subrogated to A's rights against B [UCC Sec. 4-407 (c)].

---

situation no loss was incurred by the drawer, because even if the stop payment order had been obeyed by the bank, the payee would still have been entitled to payment on the check (by legal action against the drawer, if necessary). The payee therefore had the right to the proceeds of the check in any event, and the drawer's suit against the bank will thus fail. The same result will occur (in the suit by the drawer against the bank) if it is determined that although the drawer had a personal defense against the payee, the person who obtained payment was a holder in due course—someone to whom the payee had negotiated the instrument and who met all the HDC requirements. These rules are illustrated in Figure 28.1.

The following case is particularly instructive in that it raises two important questions: (1) Is a bank generally free to honor a check after a stop payment order has expired, and (2) if so, does it have this right even when the check is presented several months after the expiration?

---

### Granite Equipment Leasing Corp. v. Hempstead Bank
New York Supreme Court, Nassau County, 326 N.Y.S.2d 881 (1971)

Granite Equipment Leasing Corp. kept a checking account with Hempstead Bank. On October 10, 1968, Granite drew a check payable to Overseas Equipment Co., Inc. After Overseas advised that the check had not been received, Granite wrote the bank on October 15, 1968, to *stop payment* on it. On that same day Granite authorized the bank to wire the funds to the payee in the same amount as the stopped check, and the bank did so. Granite did not renew its stop payment order. On November 10, 1969, without notice or inquiry to Granite, the bank accepted the check on which payment had been stopped the year before, paid the indicated funds to a collecting bank, and charged Granite's account.

*(continued)*

Granite then sought to recover the amount of the check from the defendant, Hempstead Bank. The bank defended on the ground that, under UCC Sec. 4-403, the stop payment order had expired for want of renewal and that, acting in good faith, it was entitled under UCC Sec. 4-404 to pay the stale check.

---

**Decision:** Judgment was for the defendant bank. Granite, plaintiff, makes two contentions: (1) that when the check was presented after the stop payment order had expired, the bank had the duty to query Granite before paying the check, and (2) that the bank was liable because the check was stale when the bank paid it. Both contentions were wrong.

UCC Sec. 4-403 provides merely that a stop payment order is effective for six months. It does not impose liability if the bank honors the check after that time. Similarly, the bank is not liable merely because the check was stale. UCC Sec. 4-404 permits a bank to refuse to honor a stale check, but it also provides that a bank can honor such a check as long as it does so in "good faith." There was no evidence in this case that the bank acted in bad faith (that is, dishonestly), recklessly, or carelessly. Therefore it was not liable under either of Granite's contentions. ■

---

## Payment on a Forged Indorsement

If a drawee bank honors a depositor's check that bears a *forged indorsement,* the bank must recredit the drawer's account upon his or her discovery and notification of the forgery. To illustrate: D draws a check on the X Bank payable to the order of P. The check is stolen from P by T, and T forges P's indorsement on the back of the instrument. Thereafter T negotiates the instrument to Y, and Y obtains payment from the X Bank, which has no knowledge of the forgery. The bank then charges D's account and returns the check to D at the end of the month along with D's other cancelled checks. If D later learns of the forged indorsement and notifies the bank within a reasonable time after this discovery, *the bank must recredit D's account in the amount of the check*; the bank in this case has obviously paid out the money to a person who was not the holder of the instrument. Usually the bank will recredit the account voluntarily; but if it does not, under Sec. 3-419(1) and (2) the drawer can bring an action of conversion against it to recover the amount of the check.

**Bank's Rights against Surrendering Party:** Since it is the bank rather than the drawer who initially suffers the loss in the case of a forged indorsement, the question arises whether the bank can recover payment from the person who surrendered the check to it for payment (Y in the above illustration). The general rule is that the bank can recover, even if the persons who surrendered the instrument for payment did not know of the forgery. Section 4-207(1)(a) provides that a customer "who obtains payment or acceptance of an item . . . warrants to the payor bank . . . that (a) he has good title to the item." Obviously, a person who surrenders an instrument for payment with a forged indorsement does not have title, so he or she is liable to the drawee bank in the amount of the check on the breach of warranty theory. (After making good to the bank, the person who surrendered the instrument can, of course, proceed against the forger, if that individual can be found.)

## Payment on a Forged Drawer's Signature

A somewhat different situation is presented when the drawee bank honors a check on which the *drawer's signature* is a forgery. To illustrate: F, forger, draws a check on the X Bank payable to the order of himself and forging the signature of G, one of the bank's depositors, as the drawer. F indorses the check to H, and H presents the check to the X Bank for payment. The X Bank, not knowing of the forgery, honors the instrument and charges G's account. At the end of the month the forged check is returned to G along with his other cancelled checks.

At this point, assuming that the forgery had occurred without any negligence on the part of G and that G has promptly notified the bank of the forgery, the bank must *recredit G's account in the amount of the check.* This is true because (1) a forged signature is wholly inoperative and (2) a drawee bank is presumed to know the signatures of its depositors. (The latter is based in part on the fact that when a depositor opens a checking account, he or she signs a signature card that is held by the bank and that can be used to determine whether the checks subsequently presented to the bank in the depositor's name are genuine.)

**Negligent Drawer:** The rule that the drawee bank is liable to its depositor in the case of forgery does not apply if the bank can show that the drawer was guilty of negligence that substantially contributed to the forgery.

Two primary situations exist in which negligence on the part of the drawer may be found to exist:

**1.** If the drawer (usually a corporation in this instance) signs its checks by means of a mechanical check writer, it may be shown that the drawer failed to use reasonable care in preventing unauthorized persons from gaining access to the machine. For example, if the device is left in an area where it is readily accessible to a large number of employees and the forgery is made by one of these employees, the drawer cannot require the bank to recredit its account.

**2.** It has long been established that a customer owes to the drawee bank the duty of examining his or her cancelled checks within a reasonable time after they have been returned to discover if any of the signatures are forgeries. If the person fails to do so, he or she may well be barred from holding the bank liable. This is especially true where a series of forgeries occurs after the initial one that went undetected.

Section 4-406(1) contains the basic provision requiring the drawer to "exercise reasonable care and promptness" in examining checks and statements. Section 4-406(2) sets forth specific rules that apply to various "failure to examine" situations. Because these subsections are difficult to understand in the abstract, we will present a hypothetical case along with the appropriate rules:

*February 2*—D, drawer, receives thirty cancelled checks from the drawee bank that have been charged against his account during the month of January. His signature has been forged on one check by E, an employee of D's who has access to D's printed check forms.

*February 10*—E forges another check and cashes it at the drawee bank.

*March 2*—this check is returned to D with others honored by the bank during February.

*March 3 to March 31*—E forges and cashes five more checks; these are also charged to D's account.

*April 2*—D receives all cancelled checks for the month of March, including the five forged checks.

On April 5, *D for the first time examines all the checks returned to him in February, March, and April.* He discovers the seven forgeries and immediately notifies the bank of them; later he asks the bank to recredit his account for all the forged checks. The bank refuses to do so, contending that it has no liability in view of D's failure to discover the first forgeries promptly.

In this situation D can probably hold the bank liable for the first two checks but not for the following five. Section 4-406(2)(b) states in essence that when a forged check is returned to the depositor and that person does not discover it within *fourteen days from the time of return,* he or she is "precluded from asserting" any *subsequent* forgeries against the bank that are forged "by the same wrongdoer." Thus, since the first forged check was returned to D on February 2, he had until February 16 to give the bank notice in order to protect himself against subsequent forgeries. Since he did not meet this deadline, the liability for the forged checks that were honored after that date is shifted from the bank to D.[5]

**Bank's Rights against Surrendering Party:** As seen earlier, if the drawer promptly examines his or her cancelled checks for forgeries and notifies the drawee bank of them, the bank rather than the drawer suffers the loss. The question then arises (as it did in the forged indorsement case) as to whether the bank can recover the amount of the check from the person who surrendered it for payment. The rule here (unlike that involving the forged indorsement) is that if the person did not know of the forged drawer's signature when receiving payment, the bank *cannot* hold him or her liable. Under Sec. 4-207(1)(b), a person who surrenders an instrument for payment guarantees to the drawee bank only that "he has *no knowledge* that the signature of the . . . drawer is unautho-

---

[5] As to the first two checks, since they had already been paid by the drawee bank before the February 16 deadline, it is probable that the bank could not shift its loss to the drawer—though Sec. 4-406(2)(a) keeps this possibility open in exceptional circumstances.

rized." (Emphasis added.) Thus, unless the bank can prove such knowledge, its only recourse is an action against the forger (if that person can be identified and located).

## *Payment on an Altered Check*

While it happens rather rarely, it is possible that the amount of a check will be raised and the instrument will be presented to the drawee bank and paid in its altered form. To illustrate: N draws a check for $75, and P (payee) or a subsequent holder alters the amount—both figures and words—to $175. If the bank charges N's account with the full $175, N can recover from the bank the amount of the alteration—$100. The general rule is that the drawee bank can charge the drawer's account only with the original amount of the check.

The exception to this rule is similar to that involving the forged drawer's signature. If the drawee bank can establish negligence on the part of the drawer that substantially contributed to the alteration, then the drawer is barred from recovering the difference. Two common kinds of negligence follow:

**1.** One kind of negligence occurs where a drawer drafts an instrument so carelessly that it invites alteration. For example, the amount might be written in such a way that there is ample space to insert a digit before (or after) it. Or the place where the amount is to appear in words is left entirely blank.

**2.** Another kind of negligence occurs where the drawer does not inspect his or her cancelled checks within a reasonable time after they are returned and thus fails to give the bank the notice of alteration that it is entitled to receive. Under Sec. 4-406(1), (2), and (3), the drawer in this situation is barred from asserting the fact of alteration against the drawee bank—in the same circumstances and to the same extent as the drawer who negligently failed to detect forged signatures on his or her cancelled checks.

**Bank's Rights against Surrendering Party:** We have seen that where no negligence exists on the part of the drawer, the loss (the amount of the alteration) is borne by the drawee bank. However, as a general rule, the bank is entitled to recover that loss from the person who surrendered the instrument for payment. Section 4-207(1)(c) provides that, with limited exceptions, a customer who obtains payment of an item warrants to the payor bank "that the item has not been materially altered." Thus the person who surrenders the check is usually liable on the breach of warranty theory even if he or she did not know of the alteration at the time of obtaining payment.

## INCREASED FEDERAL CONTROL OVER CHECKS AND THE BANK–DEPOSITOR RELATIONSHIP

The Federal Reserve Board (the board) traditionally has had significant control over the process by which checks move through the banking system. The rules governing the rights and duties among banks and between a depositor and his or her bank, however, have essentially been left to state law as spelled out in the UCC. For a variety of reasons, the degree of federal control is increasing.

## *Competitive Equality Banking Act*

In the Competitive Equality Banking Act of 1987, Congress gave the board broad new authority with respect to the payment system, which includes checks. Specifically, this new statute gives the board responsibility to regulate (1) any aspect of the payment system, including the receipt, payment, collection, or clearing of checks; and (2) any related function of the payment system with respect to checks. This legislation apparently grants the board almost unlimited authority to regulate the payment system, notwithstanding existing state laws or private agreements. It remains to be seen how completely this law will *federalize* the use of checks and other payment devices in this country.

## *Expedited Funds Availability Act and Regulation CC*

In 1988 Congress passed the Expedited Funds Availability Act (EFAA). In the same year, the Federal Reserve Board adopted Regulation CC, which implements EFAA. (Both EFAA and Regulation CC will be referred to as **Regulation CC.**) Regulation CC requires banks to (1) make funds deposited by customers available within specified time periods, (2) provide notices and disclosures describing the bank's funds availability practices, and (3) comply with certain check collection requirements, including the expedited processing and return of checks. The new law applies to U.S. commercial banks, savings banks, thrift institutions, and credit unions (all referred to as "banks").

**Funds Availability:** The availability requirements of Regulation CC are based on the type of deposit and the location of the bank in which a check is first deposited ("depositary bank") relative to the location of the bank by which the check is payable ("paying" or "payor" bank). Under the availability schedules of Regulation CC, banks generally must make deposited funds available on the business day after the day of deposit ("next-day availability") for the following deposits: (1) cash; (2) electronic payments, including wire transfers and automated credit transfers such as direct social security or payroll deposits; (3) certain government checks; (4) the first $100 of a day's check deposits to an account; (5) certain checks deposited at the bank upon which they were drawn ("on-us items"); and (6) certain cashier's, certified, and teller's checks.

For other types of deposits, primarily deposits of checks beyond $100 in a single day, funds must be made available by the second business day after the day of deposit when the paying bank is located in the same check-processing region as the depositary bank ("local checks"). If the paying bank is not located in the same check-processing region as the depositary bank ("nonlocal checks"), funds must be available by the fifth business day after the day of deposit. Under Regulation CC, funds must be made available at the *start* of the designated business day. The start of a business day for this purpose is the *later* of (a) 9:00 A.M. local time of the depositary bank, or (b) the time the depositary bank's teller facilities (including automated teller machines—"ATMs") are available for customer account withdrawals.

**Exceptions to Availability Requirements:** Regulation CC provides several exceptions to the funds availability requirements. Two of the most important exceptions apply to new accounts and large deposits.

*New Accounts:* The new account exception provides that most of the funds availability requirements do not apply during the first thirty days after a depositor establishes a new account. In the case of ordinary checks deposited to new accounts, the bank is not legally required to make those funds available for withdrawal for thirty days after establishment of the account. Deposits by cash or electronic transfer to new accounts still must be available on the next day after deposit, however. Also, in the case of government checks and other items that usually must be made available for withdrawal on the next day after deposit, when they are deposited to a new account the bank is required to make them available either five or nine days after deposit, depending on the item.

The new accounts exception was created because a substantial portion of bank losses from depositor fraud have traditionally involved new accounts. Many banks, however, might not use this exception to keep new account deposits from being available, because of (a) doubts about whether using the exception will really prevent fraud, and (b) competition among banks for new customers.

*Large Deposits:* Under this exception, only the first $5,000 of aggregate deposits to one or more accounts on any banking day must be made available to the depositor pursuant to Regulation CC's funds availability requirements. The bank can extend holds on the amount deposited on any banking day in excess of $5,000, but must give the customer written notice each time it uses this exception. This and several other exceptions permit a bank to delay making funds available to the depositor for a reasonable time beyond the period within which availability is normally required. The law provides that an additional delay of four days beyond the regular hold period is reasonable when an exception applies, and a longer extension may be reasonable in some instances. The large deposits exception is possibly the most important one, because it enables banks to use longer holding periods to avoid really large losses. Many banks probably will not use the exception to its fullest, however; for instance, some will use it only for deposits considerably larger than $5,000, and others may use it only on a case-by-case basis.

*Other Exceptions:* Several other exceptions also permit banks to hold funds for an additional reasonable time (i.e., usually four extra days) beyond the usual availability deadline. There is an exception for a check that has been *returned unpaid and then redeposited* by the customer or the depositary bank.

Another exception applies to an account that has been *repeatedly overdrawn.* An account is defined as repeatedly overdrawn if it had a negative balance (or would have had a negative balance if certain checks or charges had been paid) on at least six banking days during a six-month period. However, negative balances on only two separate days during that period are necessary if the amount of the negative balance was $5,000 or more. If an account meets the definition of repeatedly overdrawn, the exception then applies for six months after the last such overdraft. During operation of the exception, the bank may hold deposited funds for the additional period.

The bank must give written notice to the customer before using either the returned check or repeated overdraft exceptions. Again, the extent to which banks use these exceptions probably will vary widely from bank to bank.

Finally, there are exceptions for certain emergency circumstances and for any check that a bank has reasonable cause to believe is uncollectible. Written notice is also required before using these exceptions.

**Disclosure:** Regulation CC requires every bank to disclose its funds availability policy to its existing and potential customers. These policies must, of course, conform to the minimum availability requirements of Regulation CC. The written disclosure must reflect the policy that the bank actually follows in most cases. Thus, a bank cannot disclose that it will make funds available consistent with the maximum hold periods provided by Regulation CC if it actually makes funds available sooner in most cases. Similarly, a bank that usually makes funds available for withdrawal sooner than required by Regulation CC, but that imposes delays on a case-by-case basis up to the time limit allowed by law, must disclose that it may impose additional delays in some cases and that it will notify the customer if a longer delay will be imposed. A bank also has to disclose which exceptions it has determined to apply.

**Check Collection and Return Requirements:** The EFAA also gives the board broad authority to make improvements to the check collection and return system. In another part of Regulation CC, the board has (1) revised the manner in which banks must handle returned checks and (2) imposed new check indorsement standards.

Under the new rules, a payor bank that has determined not to pay a check must return the check "expeditiously." The same requirement applies to any other bank handling the check during the course of return. Although banks can choose either of two different standards for meeting the "expeditious return" requirement, most have chosen to use the "two-day/four-day standard." Under this rule, a *local check* is returned expeditiously if it is returned so that it will normally be received by the depositary bank *two business days* after it had been presented to the payor bank. For a *nonlocal check,* the requirement is four days.

The new check indorsement standards are aimed at making it easier to identify the name of the depositary bank and promoting the prompt return of checks. The board's indorsement standards specify the information each indorsement must contain, where on the back of the check it must be placed, and the color of ink that must be used. For example, the space on the back of the check beginning 1.5 inches from the left edge and ending three inches from the right edge is reserved for the endorsement of the depositary bank. Thus, a payee should not put any markings on the back of a check other than in the 1.5-inch space intended for the payee's indorsement. Merchants and other depositors who traditionally have stamped or otherwise marked the back of checks with information intended to identify the drawer or serve other purposes should no longer do so. The regulation permits banks to include provisions in their customer agreements shifting to the customer any loss resulting from customer markings in improper areas on the back of the check. Many banks have done so.

**Penalties:** A bank that violates the availability, disclosure, or other requirements of Regulation CC may be sued for any actual damages, plus an additional statutory penalty amount. In addition, any person may be able to recover penalties between $100 and $1,000 per violation regardless of whether he or she suffered any actual damages. In class actions, this automatic penalty amount may be as high as $500,000. A bank's failure to comply with the law's check and return requirements also may result in liability for resulting losses incurred by another bank or its customer. The board also may enforce the law's provisions.

## ELECTRONIC BANKING

Developments in computer technology have brought about a significant (and growing) phenomenon in recent years—the transfer of funds from one account to another electronically. As electronic fund transfers (**electronic banking**) increase in the years ahead, the use of checks will correspondingly decrease, and the rules applicable to electronic fund transfers will be of increasing importance insofar as the bank-depositor relationship is concerned. We will here note the most important developments in the area of electronic funds transfers and briefly summarize the basic federal law applicable to these transfers.

## Types of Transfers

**Automated Teller Machines:** It is estimated that roughly half of the adults in the larger cities of the United States today have coded bank cards that enable them to use automated teller machines (ATMs). In these cities—and smaller ones, too—bank customers are becoming increasingly accustomed to using ATMs for such routine tasks as making withdrawals from checking accounts, making deposits in checking accounts, and transferring funds between savings and checking accounts. The use of these "electronic branches" is not only a convenience to bank customers, but also constitutes an effort by banks to rein in their costs by reducing personnel and traditional branches.

**Point of Sale Terminals:** Point of sale transfers occur when a customer in a retail store, after making a purchase, gives a bank card to the sales clerk, who passes it through a "reading machine" attached to the cash register. The customer then punches in his or her personal identification number (the same number used for entry to ATMs) on a keyboard. The cash register electronically charges the customer's account at the bank with the amount of the purchase, and electronically credits the store's account in the same amount. The transaction is verified by a "processing center," thus enabling the store to give the customer a receipt. Point of sale transactions, if widely accepted, would be *the* single largest step towards our becoming a checkless society. However, point of sale purchasing has largely been carried on in only a few parts of the country since its introduction in 1984. And, on the basis of this use, customer acceptance of point of sale to date has been considerably less than originally expected.

**Home Shopping and Banking:** What is sometimes called the ultimate step in electronic banking is home shopping and banking. This development, involving a "home information service" consisting of a television set and a personal computer, permits customers to pay bills, make purchases from cooperating retailers, and conduct most of their banking transactions from their own homes. The relevant fund transfers in all of these transactions would, again, be done electronically. For example, in regard to home purchases, the amount of purchase is automatically charged to the buyer's bank account, and automatically credited to the seller's account. Consumer acceptance of home shopping and banking, like point of sale, has been slower than first anticipated. Because of such factors as cost and the "de-personalizing" of retail shopping, the ultimate impact of this development—like point of sale—remains to be seen.

## Electronic Funds Transfer Act

Electronic banking—even the simple use of ATMs—has carried with it a number of side effects. The stop payment order, for example, is eliminated (except for preauthorized transfers), and so is **float**—the period between the time a check is issued and the time it is charged to the drawer's account by the drawee bank.[6] More important, because electronic banking radically alters the way in which the bank and its customers have been doing business, it also creates potential new problems for both parties, including the unauthorized transfer of funds, the lack of documents (such as cancelled checks and deposit slips) in the customer's hands in order to prove alleged bank errors, and liabilities of the parties in case the customer's debit card is lost or stolen.

Anticipating these kinds of problems, Congress passed the **Electronic Funds Transfer Act** in 1978. First, the act defines an electronic transfer of funds as "any transfer of funds, other than by check, draft, or similar paper instrument, which is initiated through an electronic terminal, telephone instrument, computer, or magnetic tape so as to order, instruct or authorize a financial institution to debit or credit an account." The act then requires financial institutions to give disclosure statements to the "consumer" (the institution's customers) that describe the consumers' rights and duties; requires the institutions to keep written documentation of all electronic fund trans-

---

[6] A *preauthorized transfer* is a statement in writing by the customer authorizing in advance certain electronic transfers that the institution may automatically make in the future.

fers; provides methods of dispute resolution; and spells out the consumers' and institutions' liabilities. We will examine these matters briefly.

**Disclosure Statements:** The law requires the institution to provide a **disclosure statement** indicating to the consumer—in "readily understandable language"—such matters as the types of transfers that can be made through its transfer mechanisms; the telephone number and address of the person or office of the institution who should be contacted in the event that the consumer believes an error has been made; the consumer's right to stop payment of a preauthorized fund transfer; and the parties' rights, duties, and liabilities in the case of a breach of duty.

**Documentation:** The law obligates the institution to keep written documentation of all electronic funds transfers. This documentation must show the amount of the transfer, the number of the account being charged, the date of transfer, the identity of the party receiving the transfer, and the terminal location used in making the transfer. Additionally, the institution must send periodic statements to the customer summarizing the transfers made during the prior period.

**Dispute Resolution:** If a consumer believes that an error has been made by the institution, he or she must give notice of the alleged error to the person or office named in the periodic statement within 60 days of receipt of the institution's statement. The notice can be made either orally or in writing, but it must indicate the account number of the consumer (or information which will enable the institution to determine the number); indicate the consumer's belief that the account contains an error, and the amount of the error; and set forth (where applicable) the "reasons for the consumer's belief" that the error has occurred.

When a notice of error is received by a financial institution, it must "investigate the alleged error, determine whether an error has occurred, and report or mail the results of such investigation and determination within ten business days." If the institution determines that the error did occur, it must correct the error within one business day. If the institution determines that the error did not occur, it must deliver to the consumer an explanation of such determination within three business days after the conclusion of its investigation.

As an alternative to the above procedures, the institution, upon receipt of a notice of error, may within ten days "provisionally recredit" the consumer's account with the amount of the alleged error. In such case, it then has 45 days in which to make its investigation and determination. The act goes on to provide that the consumer may recover *treble damages* from the institution if it "knowingly and willfully" concluded that the consumer's account was not in error when such conclusion could not reasonably have been made, or, in regard to the alternative procedure, if the institution did not recredit the consumer's account within the ten day period and if (1) the institution did not make a good faith investigation of the alleged error, or (2) did not have a reasonable basis for believing that the account was not in error.

**Consumer Liability:** The act requires financial institutions to furnish to consumers wishing to make electronic transfers a "means of access"—usually a personal bank card—by which the consumer can request fund transfers. There are several rules as to the consumer's liability for unauthorized transfers made as a result of loss or theft of the card. The basic rule is that the consumer has the duty to notify the institution when he or she knows of the loss or theft of the card, in which case the consumer's liability is *limited to $50* (that is, $50 or the actual amount of the unauthorized transfers, whichever is less).

If the consumer fails to give notice to the institution within two business days after learning of the loss or theft, the ceiling on the consumer's liability is *raised to $500* (that is, $500 or the actual amount of the unauthorized transfers, whichever is less). And the consumer is liable for the *total amount* of the unauthorized transfers if he or she fails to give notice of such transfers within 60 days of receiving the institution's first periodic statement that reflects the transfers. In extenuating circumstances—for example, where the consumer is away on "extended travel" or is hospitalized—the 60-day provision is replaced by the duty to give notice "within a reasonable time, under the circumstances."

**The Institution's Liability:** The act has a number of provisions imposing *civil liability* upon financial institutions for damages the consumer suffers as a result of the institutions' breaches of duty, such as failure to make authorized transfers and failure to make a transfer on the erroneous ground that there were insufficient funds in the consumer's account to permit the transfer. Generally, the institutions' liability for breach of a duty is limited to actual damages incurred by the consumer; however, greater damages are sometimes allowed where bad faith on the part of the institution is shown. (The act also specifies situations in which class actions can be brought.)

*Criminal liability* is imposed by the act upon any person (including the consumer as well as the institution) who "knowingly and willfully" gives false information or fails to provide information required by the act. The liability for these violations is a fine of up to $5,000 or imprisonment for not more than a year, or both. And stiffer criminal penalties are provided for other specified wrongs affecting interstate commerce—such as knowingly using forged, fictitious, or lost **debit instruments** (usually personal bank cards); knowingly transporting such instruments in interstate commerce; and knowingly furnishing money, property, or services to another through the use of such instruments.

## *New Article 4A and Commercial Electronic Funds Transfers*

The Electronic Funds Transfer Act is a federal *consumer* protection law. As such, it does not apply to the billions of dollars that are transferred electronically from bank to bank on a daily basis. Articles 3 and 4 of the UCC also do not apply to these huge "commercial" electronic funds transfers. Thus, until recently there have been few settled legal guidelines for these largest of transfers, aside from basic contract law principles. To fill this void, a new Article 4A of the Uniform Commercial Code was very recently completed and presented to state legislatures for enactment. It is expected that 4A will be enacted by most states rather quickly.

Article 4A defines a "funds transfer" as a "payment order" or series of payment orders by which an "originator" accomplishes payment to the "beneficiary" of the originator's order. Such a transfer can be a very simple transaction in which a corporate originator orders its bank to debit one of its accounts and credit an account of another party at the same bank. Here, the payment order and funds transfer are coextensive. If the originator orders its bank to pay a beneficiary that is a customer of another bank, this payment order will require the originator's bank to then issue at least one other payment order. The additional payment order from the originator's bank may be to the beneficiary's bank directly, probably through a funds transfer system. In other situations, this additional order from the originator's bank may be made to an intermediary bank that will then issue yet another order to the beneficiary's bank.

Essentially, Article 4A creates a set of rules to govern the resolution of legal issues that may arise from commercial electronic funds transfers. Almost all of these rules, like most other UCC principles, can be varied by the agreements of the parties and the operating rules of a funds transfer system. Payment orders, unlike checks, do not establish independent rights and liabilities for the payment of money. Instead, the rights and liabilities of the parties to a payment order arise out of the contract formed when the receiving bank accepts the payment order, perhaps subject to the terms of a prior agreement or the rules of a funds transfer system.

## SUMMARY

Checks are governed in some instances by special rules of Article 3 of the UCC, and, additionally, the bank-depositor relationship is governed by special rules in both Articles 3 and 4. A check is, by definition, "a draft drawn on a bank payable on demand." The issuance of a check does not, in and of itself, result in an assignment of funds to the payee or to a subsequent holder; this occurs only after the instrument is honored by the drawee bank. A bank has no duty to certify a check, either at the request of the drawer or of a holder. If it does certify, however, the bank becomes primarily liable on the instrument (much like the acceptor of a draft). A certification at the request of a holder of the instrument discharges the drawer from liability, but a certification at the request of the drawer does not have this effect.

One of the primary duties owed by a bank to its depositor is to honor checks drawn by the depositor if there are sufficient funds in his or her account at presentment. If a check is stale—more than six months old at the time of presentment—the bank has no duty to honor it. It may, however, honor a stale check if it wishes, without liability to the drawer, unless its payment was made in bad faith.

There are limited situations where special bank-depositor rules apply; for example, the issuance of stop payment orders. A drawer may stop payment on his or her check by giving the drawee bank such an order. An oral order is effective for fourteen days, while a written one is effective for six months. If a bank disobeys a stop payment order by paying the instrument, it is liable to the drawer for any loss resulting from its failure to observe the order. A second example involves payment by a drawee bank of a check drawn by a depositor which—unknown to the bank at the time of payment—bore the forged indorsement of a party whose indorsement was necessary for the negotiation of the instrument. In such a case the bank, having made payment to a person who did not have title, must credit the drawer's account with the amount of the check. The bank—assuming it was not guilty of negligence in failing to know of the forged indorsement—may then recover the amount of the check from the surrendering party (the party to whom it made payment).

A different situation exists when a drawee bank honors an instrument bearing the forged signature of the drawer (its depositor). The bank must again credit the drawer's account, assuming the drawer was not negligent in the transaction, but in this situation the bank *cannot* recover from the surrendering party (unless he or she knew of the forgery when receiving payment).

A drawer may be negligent if a cancelled check bearing the drawer's forged signature is returned by the bank (together with all other cancelled checks for that period), and he or she does not notify the drawee bank of the forgery within fourteen days of the time the checks were returned. In such case, the drawer can *not* require the drawee bank to credit his account with the amount of any additional checks (forged by the same person) which the bank honors between the expiration of the fourteen-day period and the time that the drawer does ultimately give the bank notice of the first forgery.

Although the rules governing the rights and duties among banks and between a bank and its depositors have historically been found almost exclusively in *state law*, we are beginning to see an increase in *federal* control over these rules.

Transfers of funds via the use of electronic devices (i.e., "electronic banking") are governed by the federal Electronic Funds Transfer Act, rather than by Articles 3 and 4 of the UCC. New Article 4A of the UCC will govern "commercial" electronic funds transfers between banks.

# KEY TERMS

**Drawee bank**
**Certified check**
**Stale check**
**Stop payment order**
**Electronic banking**
**Point of sale transfers**
**Float**
**Regulation CC**
**Electronic Funds Transfer Act**
**Disclosure statement**
**Debit instruments**

## QUESTIONS AND PROBLEMS

**1.** On July 1, D draws a check payable to the order of P and issues it to P. P forgets about the check until August 10, at which time she presents it to the drawee bank for payment. Under what circumstances might D's liability be reduced as a result of the late presentment? What is D's only obligation in such circumstances?

**2.** What are the three basic effects of certifying a check?

**3.** You are manager of a branch bank, and one of your tellers comes to you with a check that an apparent holder wishes to have cashed. The check is drawn by one of your depositors, but it is seven months old. What are your bank's rights and duties in regard to this check?

**4.** On June 10, D (drawer) issues an oral stop payment order on a particular check to his drawee bank, just before leaving town for a short vacation. When he returns at noon on June 20, he goes to the bank and signs a written stop payment order. It turns out, however, that the bank had already honored the check at 10 A.M. that day. The bank now wishes to charge D's account with the amount of the check, in view of the fact that it had honored the check before the written order was issued. Can the bank charge D's account in these circumstances? Explain.

**5.** D issues a valid stop payment order, but the drawee bank, without excuse, fails to obey the order and charges D's account with the amount of the check. D sues the bank to force it to credit her account in the amount of the check. The bank can totally escape liability to D if it proves that she suffered no loss as a result of its failure to obey the stop payment order. What are the circumstances under which the bank can prove this?

**6.** D issues a check payable to the order of P. A few days later the drawee bank cashes the check at the request of H (who surrenders it to the bank). The instrument apparently bears the blank indorsement of P, the payee, at the time of surrender. The bank later learns, however, that P's indorsement is a forgery, so it credits D's account as required by law and now seeks to recover the amount of the check from H. H defends on the ground that he neither knew nor had reason to know that the indorsement was forged. Is H's defense valid? Explain.

**7.** D issues a check payable to the order of P. One week later the drawee bank cashes the check at the request of H, the surrenderer. At the time of the surrender the amount of the check was "$700," and that is the amount that the drawee bank gave to H when he cashed it. Later the bank learns that the original amount of the check was *$100,* and that P apparently was the party who made the alteration. The bank, having no reason to suspect the alteration, now seeks the $600 difference from H, while H contends that he, too, was innocent of the alteration. Is H's defense good? Why or why not?

**8.** The general rule is that a drawer's account cannot be charged with checks that are proved to be forgeries, unless the drawer has been guilty of negligence that contributed to the forgeries. Give examples of the two general types of misconduct on the part of the drawer that may constitute such negligence.

# CHAPTER 29

# SECURED TRANSACTIONS

A very large part of the business that is carried on in this country is done "on credit." While there are many types of transactions in which credit is extended by one person or firm to another, probably the two most common of these arise from sales of goods (in which the buyer promises to pay the purchase price in installments) and loans of money. In these transactions a *debtor-creditor* relationship results, with the buyer (or borrower) being the debtor, and the seller (or lender) being the creditor.

Sometimes a seller or lender is willing to extend credit without receiving any security from the debtor. Such transactions frequently occur at the retail sale level where, for example, a department store will sell a modestly priced article to a buyer who is permitted to charge it to his or her credit card account without executing a security agreement. Unsecured credit may also be extended by wholesalers and manufacturers, and by lenders, especially to debtors who have established a good credit record with the creditor as a result of past dealings.

In all unsecured credit cases, once the creditor delivers the goods or makes the loan to the debtor he or she has lost all rights to the goods or money. This means that if the debtor subsequently defaults, the creditor cannot immediately claim or attach any specific goods or money in the debtor's possession. Instead, he or she is initially limited to bringing an action to recover the amount of the indebtedness. After getting a judgment in such a suit the creditor has the right to have any unencumbered property then in the debtor's possession sold under court order to satisfy the debt.[1] However, it may be that these limited assets will have to be shared with other judgment creditors—or worse still, it may be that the debtor may not own any property at all by the time the judgment is obtained, or that the debtor has even become bankrupt by this time. *Thus an unsecured creditor runs a distinct risk that he or she may recover little or nothing from the debtor.*[2]

## SECURED CREDIT TRANSACTIONS

To minimize the above risks, many sellers and lenders routinely require the debtor to enter into a *security agreement* at the time credit is extended—an agreement by which the debtor conveys to the creditor a legally recognized interest in specific personal property owned by the debtor. Once such an interest is created, the creditor has the right to have the specific property sold if the debtor defaults on the payments, and to receive as much of the proceeds of the sale as is necessary to pay off the debt. (If the proceeds are not sufficient to pay the total indebtedness, the creditor then has an *unsecured* claim as to the unpaid balance.)

The dual purpose of a **secured transaction,** then, is to give to the creditor (1) a *specific interest* in the debtor's property that is covered by the security agreement, and (2) a *priority claim* in that property against other creditors who may seek to have the property sold in satisfaction of their claims. This priority, usually obtained by giving notice to all other creditors and third parties who may subsequently become creditors, is called "perfection." (The subject

---

[1] Unencumbered property is that which the debtor owns outright—that is, free of any security interest, mortgage, or other lien of a third party.

[2] By contrast, a secured creditor's interest in specific collateral, if "perfected," *is* protected against the claims of judgment creditors. And, if the debtor becomes bankrupt, the security interest survives bankruptcy proceedings—i.e., the collateral cannot be sold by the trustee in bankruptcy for the benefit of unsecured creditors.

443

of perfection will be discussed in more detail later in the chapter.)

To illustrate a secured transaction situation: R, an office supply retailer, needs to restock her inventory of electronic word processors, but does not want to pay cash for them. R finds a wholesaler, W, who is able to make immediate delivery of the kind of processor that R wants, and W is willing to sell the goods on credit. R and W therefore sign a security agreement under the terms of which W agrees to sell the word processors to R, with R paying 10 percent down and promising to pay the balance in monthly installments. The agreement describes the goods being sold, and further provides that W is retaining a security interest in them until the total price is paid. At this point a debtor-creditor relationship has been created. W, the secured party, has the inventory collateral of R as security for the debt. W now files a financing statement to give notice to all others of his security interest in the collateral. If R subsequently defaults, W can repossess the remaining inventory to satisfy the debt. Furthermore, assuming that W's filing has given him priority, the collateral will go first to pay off R's debt with W, with only the remaining collateral being available to other creditors.

## ARTICLE 9 TERMINOLOGY

Article 9 of the UCC substantially governs secured transactions law.[3] Following are the terms needed for an understanding of the basic concepts of secured transactions law. (These definitions come from Sec. 9-105, except where noted otherwise.)

- *Secured party.* A **secured party** is a lender, seller, or other person in whose favor a security interest exists—including a person to whom accounts or chattel paper have been sold.[4]

- *Debtor.* A **debtor** is a person who owes payment or other performance of the obligation that is secured, regardless of whether he or she owns or has rights in the collateral, and includes the seller of accounts or chattel paper.

- *Security interest.* Under Sec. 1-201(37), a **security interest** is an interest in personal property or fixtures that secures payment or performance of an obligation—that is, the interest granted the secured party.

   A recurrent problem has been distinguishing a security interest dressed up as a lease from a true lease. Promulgation of new UCC Article 2A for leasing transactions, which entails a significant amendment to the UCC's definition of "security interest," is aimed at clarifying this distinction. This is important, because Article 2A follows existing law in not requiring lessors to file a financing statement in connection with a true lease in order to protect their interests in leased property. Former case law concentrated on the intent of the parties in drawing a line between a lease (which does not require a filing to be protected) and a security interest (which usually does require filing for protection). The new amendment to Sec. 1-201(37) provides that for a transaction to be a security interest (and therefore governed by Article 9 rather than a lease governed by Article 2A), the obligation to pay rents must extend for the entire term of the lease and must not be subject to termination by the lessee. If this is the case, then a transaction framed as a lease will be treated as a security interest if it appears that the lessee will enjoy possession and use of the goods *for their entire economic life.* Various criteria are established to assist in this determination. Widespread adoption of an amended Article 2A is expected to occur soon.

- *Security agreement.* A **security agreement** is a security arrangement between the debtor and the secured party—the agreement that creates the security interest.

- *Collateral.* **Collateral** is the property subject to a security interest, and includes accounts and chattel paper that have been sold.

---

[3] Although secured transactions law stems primarily from state laws adopting the UCC, federal law has always exerted an influence through, for example, the Bankruptcy Code. In recent years, the federal government has increasingly superimposed its will in this area. An example, to be discussed later, is the Food Security Act of 1985, which effectively amended Sec. 9-307(1)'s priorities for purchasers of farm products. Another example is *Citicorp Indus. Credit, Inc. v. Brock,* 483 U.S. 27 (1987), in which the Supreme Court held that secured lenders at a foreclosure sale of inventory collateral get in line behind employees who claim that the debtor owed them money because of violations of the minimum wage or overtime provisions of the Fair Labor Standards Act.

[4] An "account" is "any right to payment for goods sold or leased or for services rendered which is not evidenced by an instrument or chattel paper . . ." Sec. 9-106.

"Chattel paper" is a writing which evidences both a monetary obligation and a security interest in specific goods. Sec. 9-105(1)(b).

- *Perfection.* **Perfection** is the taking, by a secured creditor, of those steps which are required under the UCC in order for his or her security interest to be valid as against other creditors.
- *Financing statement.* Under Secs. 9-401 and 9-402, the **financing statement** is the instrument filed to give public notice of the security interest in the collateral.

Following is an illustration of the basic concepts using this terminology. The *secured party* and *debtor* usually enter into a *security agreement* by which the secured party receives a *security interest* in one or more pieces of the debtor's collateral, to be available in the event of the debtor's default. To gain priority over others who may also want a security interest in this same collateral, the secured party files a *financing statement* as notice of his or her claim. The secured interest is now *perfected.* (While the usual security device is expressly labelled "security agreement" to conform to this terminology, older forms creating security interests—the chattel mortgage or conditional sale—are still used occasionally. In such cases these devices, too, are treated today as ordinary security agreements.)

## SCOPE OF ARTICLE 9

Article 9 covers agreements that create security interests in *personal* property. Therefore, security agreements applicable to interests in *real* property, such as those created by the mortgage of a farm or a home, are not governed by this article.[5]

Many times personal property that is subject to a security interest has a tangible existence as **goods.** Typical examples of goods are automobiles, cattle, grain, and television sets. In addition to goods, however, security interests are also commonly created in certain kinds of personal property that have no physical substance. These kinds of property, consisting of rights and interests, are properly termed "intangibles." A third category of personal property is called "indispensable paper." Because this category possesses some characteristics similar to those of goods, it is sometimes called "quasi-intangible." These three categories of property—goods, indispensable paper, and intangibles—may be further classified as indicated below.

### *Tangible Collateral ("Goods")*

Under Sec. 9-109, there are four kinds of goods, classified according to the buyer's primary intent at time of purchase:

- *Consumer goods.* Goods are consumer goods if they are used or bought for use primarily for personal, family, or household purposes.
- *Equipment.* Goods are equipment if they are used or bought for use primarily in business (including farming or a profession).
- *Farm products.* Goods are farm products if they are crops or livestock or supplies used or produced in farming operations, or products of crops or livestock in their unmanufactured state (such as eggs, milk, or sap used in the production of maple syrup), and if they are in the possession of a debtor engaged in raising, fattening, grazing, or other farm operations.
- *Inventory.* Goods are inventory if they are held by the debtor for the purpose of sale or lease to others in the ordinary course of the debtor's business. Also included in the inventory category are goods to be furnished by the debtor to others under service contracts, raw materials, work in process in the hands of a manufacturer, and materials used or consumed in a business. The last category is broad enough to include such items as duplication paper and related supplies of a bank.

A UCC drafters' comment to Sec. 9-109 states that the above classes of goods are "mutually exclusive"; a particular item of property cannot fall into two categories at the same time. However, a particular item of property may fall into different classes at different times. For example, a sofa on the floor of a furniture store is inventory, but is a consumer good when subsequently delivered to a buyer's home or equipment if sold for use in a dentist's office.

In addition to the four classifications of goods noted above, Article 9 also covers security interests in another kind of tangible property, *fixtures.* As we

---

[5] Some security interests in personal property fall outside the scope of Article 9. For example, under special statutes an auto mechanic usually obtains a lien on a car while it is in his or her possession, and under Article 2 of the UCC an unpaid seller of goods may have an interest in the goods while they are en route to the buyer. Such interests are governed by the special statutes that create them. Additionally, security interests in aircraft and maritime vessels are generally governed by specific federal statutes.

will see in Chapter 43, **fixtures** begin life as items of personal property but are subsequently attached to real estate—land and buildings—in such a manner that they become a part of that real estate.[6] To illustrate: M, a manufacturer, purchases an industrial electric motor on credit from the inventory of W, a wholesaler. The motor is delivered to M's factory, where it is permanently bolted to a concrete bed in the building. (Under special rules discussed later, a security interest in the motor given by M to W at the time of the purchase may continue to exist even though the motor has been converted from personal to real property.)

## Indispensable Paper Collateral

**Indispensable paper collateral** that may be the subject of a security interest can best be described as rights that are created by (in addition to being evidenced by) pieces of paper—written documents such as promissory notes or bills of lading. Under Sec. 9-102, the types of personal property falling within this category include:

- *Documents of Title.* Under UCC Sec. 1-201(15) **documents of title** include bills of lading, dock warrants, dock receipts, warehouse receipts, or any other orders for delivery of goods, and any other documents which in the regular course of business or financing are treated as adequate evidence that the person in possession is entitled to receive, hold, and dispose of them and the goods they cover. (See Chapter 20 for details.)
- *Instruments.* Under UCC Sec. 9-105(1)(i), the term **instrument** essentially refers to two interests: *negotiable instruments* and *securities.* A negotiable instrument is a promissory note, check, or any other written promise or order to pay money whose terms meet the requirements of negotiability set forth in Sec. 3-104 of the UCC. (See Chapter 25 for details.) Security refers to corporate stocks and bonds.
- *Chattel Paper.* An example of **chattel paper** is a promissory note which not only contains the usual promise to pay a sum of money at a stated future time, but, additionally, contains language that conveys to the holder of the note a security interest. Assume that F, a farmer, purchases a tractor from an implement dealer under a conditional sales contract. The contract (note) that F signs will contain a promise to pay the agreed purchase price in specified monthly installments. This is a negotiable instrument only. If the contract goes on to provide that the dealer-seller shall retain a security interest in the tractor until the note is paid in full, it is chattel paper. The chattel paper may serve as collateral for a later loan, if the implement dealer (debtor) assigns it to a bank (secured party).

## Intangible Collateral

Those types of personal property interests that do not possess the characteristics of goods or indispensable paper collateral are **intangible collateral.** Such interests are either *accounts* or *general intangibles.*

**Accounts:** Under Sec. 9-106, an **account** is any right to payment for goods sold or leased, or for services rendered, which is not evidenced by an instrument or chattel paper. Generally, the term refers to *accounts receivable.*

**General Intangibles:** **General intangibles** is a catch-all category, which is defined under Sec. 9-106 as consisting of any personal property ("including things in action"—rights to collect money or property) *other than* goods, accounts, chattel paper, documents, instruments, and money. Typical examples are literary rights, trademarks, patents, copyrights, and the like.

The case below presents one situation in which a determination of the type of collateral is necessary in order to decide the validity of a secured creditor's claim to the proceeds of that collateral.

---

[6]This is not true, however, in the case of ordinary building supplies, such as lumber that is used in building a house. In this case the lumber is not a fixture, and any security interest is lost when it becomes a part of the building.

## *In re* K. L. Smith Enterprises, Ltd.
U.S. Bankruptcy Court, D. Colo., 28 UCC Rep. 534 (1980)

K. L. Smith Enterprises operated a large-scale egg production business in Colorado. It housed thousands of laying hens in unique, semi-automated "egg production units" that permitted the efficient collection, sizing, and packaging of large quantities of eggs daily.

In November 1976 the United Bank of Denver loaned $2,400,000 to Smith Enterprises. In connection with the loan, Smith Enterprises executed two security agreements granting the bank security interests in all of its *inventory, accounts, contract rights, equipment, and machinery,* and in *"the proceeds therefrom"*—that is, in the money received by Smith Enterprises from the sale of any of the designated assets.[a]

In November 1979 Smith Enterprises sold $40,000 worth of eggs to Safeway Stores, Inc., its principal customer for many years. That same month it also sold a quantity of eggs to Gonzales, one of its occasional customers, and in December it sold 120,000 hens to the Campbell Soup Company. The sale to Safeway was "on account"—an account receivable was created on Smith Enterprises' books—and the sale of eggs to Gonzales was a cash transaction. It is not clear whether the sale of the hens to Campbell was on account or for cash.

Shortly thereafter Smith Enterprises went into bankruptcy. In those proceedings the United Bank of Denver claimed that it had a valid security interest in the eggs and chickens, and thus in the proceeds thereof. In response, Smith Enterprises (plaintiff in this action) filed a complaint disputing the bank's claim to the eggs, chickens, and the "cash collateral" in Smith Enterprises' possession at the time of bankruptcy.

[a] The subject of "proceeds" will be discussed further under the topic of perfection.

**Decision:** Judgment was for Smith Enterprises. The ultimate issue in the case was whether the eggs and chickens were "inventory," as contended by the bank, or "farm products," as contended by Smith Enterprises.

Farm products are defined in Sec. 9-109 of the UCC as "crops or livestock . . . produced in farming operations or . . . products of crops, or livestock in their unmanufactured states. . . ." Additionally, the court noted, the drafters of the code in the Official Comment to that section stated: "Products of crops or livestock . . . lose their status as farm products if they are subjected to a manufacturing process. . . ." Because the bank did not seriously contend that eggs were not products of livestock, the only question is whether the acts of Smith Enterprises in washing, candling, and packaging the eggs constituted a "manufacturing process," as claimed by the bank.

The court held that these actions did *not* constitute a manufacturing process, on the basis of further language in the Official Comment. In that comment, the drafters said, "At one end of the scale some processes are so closely connected with farming—such as pasteurizing milk or boiling sap to produce maple syrup or maple sugar—that they would not rank as manufacturing processes. On the other hand an extensive canning operation would be manufacturing. The line is one for the courts to draw." The court concluded that the washing, candling, and packaging of eggs was, like the pasteurization of milk, an insignificant treatment of the raw product, and could not be equated with a canning operation. Therefore, because the eggs were farm products at their inception and remained farm products to the time of their sale, the bank never had a security interest in them or in their proceeds. ■

**Note:** The bank in the previous case should have (1) included "farm products" in its security agreement description, or (2) emphasized terms like "chickens" and "eggs" in its description, rather than mere generic categories like "inventory." Here, the yolk was on the bank.

## ATTACHMENT (CREATION) OF A SECURITY INTEREST

Under Sec. 9-203, in order for the businessperson to be sure of having an **attachment,** i.e., an enforceable security interest that attaches to the collateral, three conditions must be met:

1. There must be a *security agreement* entered into which describes the collateral. This agreement must be in writing and signed by the debtor, with one exception: where the collateral is put in the possession of the secured party. Such delivery of possession, called a "pledge," can occur only where the collateral consists of goods (such as jewelry, cattle, or furniture) or quasi-tangibles (such as warehouse receipts or negotiable instruments). Because intangibles are incapable of physical delivery, security agreements creating interests in intangibles must always be in writing.

2. The secured party must give *value* to the debtor. In most instances this consists of a delivery of goods by the secured party to the debtor, or of the advancing of money by the secured party. However, under Sec. 1-201(44) of the UCC a person also gives value for rights in collateral if he or she acquires them (a) as security for a preexisting claim, or (b) in return for a binding commitment to extend credit in the future, or (c) in return for any consideration sufficient to support a simple contract.

3. The debtor must have *rights* (any current or future legally recognized interest) in the collateral. Obviously, if the debtor did not possess any such right, he or she could not convey a right to the secured party.

The following case illustrates the importance of these requirements and also gives a preview of the discussion regarding the priority of competing security interests.

---

**Crocker National Bank v. Ideco Division of Dresser Industries**
U.S. District Court, S.D. Texas,
660 F.Supp. 186 (1987)

TOS Industries, Inc., agreed to buy six drilling rigs from the Ideco Division of Dresser Industries. After Ideco began sending invoices to TOS, Crocker National Bank loaned money to TOS, receiving a security interest in all TOS after-acquired tubular goods, wellhead equipment, and oilfield supplies. After the rigs were ready for shipping, but before they were delivered, TOS told Ideco that it could not pay for the rigs. Ideco kept them.

This lawsuit was filed to determine the relative interests of the parties in the rigs. Crocker and TOS argue that TOS acquired title to the rigs when Ideco sent TOS invoices of the sale and that Crocker's security interest attached to the rigs.

Ideco argues that title to the rigs did not pass to TOS because Ideco kept possession and that Crocker's security interest does not encompass the rigs, even if title did pass. Both sides moved for summary judgment.

**Decision:** Summary judgment was granted to Ideco and denied to Crocker. Ideco prevails because it has a superior interest in the rigs. Crocker's security interest does not apply to the rigs unless TOS acquired "rights in the collateral." The key question is: Does a buyer who has not paid for goods and to whom they have not been delivered have sufficient rights in the goods to grant a security interest in them to another that takes precedence over the manufacturer's retained security interest perfected by possession? The answer is no. It would be very surprising to the sellers of the world to discover that a seller who has not parted with goods nor received payment for them has an interest in the goods inferior to the creditor of a holder of an executory contract to buy them. ∎

---

## PERFECTION OF THE SECURITY INTEREST

Under Sec. 9-201, the security agreement binds the debtor and secured party the moment that it attaches, without the taking of any additional steps by the secured party. In general, however, *the agreement does not protect the creditor against the rights of third parties until the agreement is perfected.* To illustrate: A loans B $500 and takes a security interest in a prize bull belonging to B. A does not perfect the security interest (that is, he neither files a financing statement nor takes possession of the bull). Later a third party, the X Bank, loans B $1,000, the bank also taking a security interest in the bull. The X Bank then perfects by duly filing its financing statement. If B thereafter defaults on both loans, under Sec. 9-312 X Bank's perfected security interest will prevail over A's unperfected interest even though A's security interest was created first.[7]

In order for the secured party to obtain *maximum protection against third parties* who may subsequently claim an interest in the collateral—such as the debtor's other secured and unsecured creditors, persons who may have purchased collateral from the debtor, and against a trustee in bankruptcy in case the debtor becomes bankrupt—*the secured party must perfect his or her interest.* Not only does perfection usually give the secured party a protected interest in the collateral, but it also usually gives him or her a protected interest in the *proceeds* of the collateral in case the debtor sells it. Under Sec. 9-306, proceeds is defined as "whatever is received when collateral . . . is sold . . . or otherwise disposed of," and usually consists of cash and checks which the debtor has received upon sale of the collateral. The right to proceeds is especially important in situations where the collateral cannot be traced, or is in the possession of a third party who, under special UCC provisions noted later, takes the collateral free from the secured party's interest even though perfection has occurred. (The security agreement and financing statement usually expressly provide that the agreement covers proceeds. However, the secured party's right to proceeds exists *even in the absence of such a provision* unless the security agreement—or a subsequent agreement between the secured party and the debtor—provides otherwise. Sec. 9-306(2).)

## *Methods of Perfection, Generally*

The secured party may perfect his or her interest in one of three ways, depending on the type of collateral that is involved. In many situations the secured party has a choice of means of perfection, while in others there is only one method that can be used. Except where the collateral consists of goods which are covered by certificates of title under state law (such as motor vehicles) and fixtures, the three methods of perfection are the following:[8]

1. *Perfection by filing.* As a general rule, perfection requires the creditor to file a financing statement at a designated location specified by the code. (As noted earlier, a financing statement is a document that evidences the secured party's interest and contains a description of the collateral covered by the security agreement.) **Filing** is the most commonly used method of perfection, and is the *only* way that perfection can occur where the collateral consists of intangibles. Because filing is the customary way of achieving perfection, it will be discussed more fully later in this chapter.

2. *Perfection by possession.* Section 9-305 provides, in part, that "a security interest in . . . goods, instruments . . . money, negotiable documents or chattel paper may be perfected by the secured party's taking possession of the collateral." In other words, such a transfer of possession of the collateral to the secured party (a transfer often called a "pledge") can occur only where the collateral consists of money, goods (such as jewelry) or quasi-tangibles (such as promissory notes or shares of stock).

Two special rules in regard to this kind of perfection of interests in quasi-tangible collateral should be noted. Both of these rules are found in Section 9-304(1).

A. If the collateral consists of negotiable instruments (or of money), possession is the *only* means of perfection; filing will not suffice.

B. If the collateral consists of chattel paper or negotiable documents of title, perfection by filing is permitted. However, Sections 9-308 and 9-309 provide, in general, that security interests in such types of collateral that have been perfected by filing *lose their priority* to good faith purchasers of the collateral. Thus, in order for a party who has a security interest in either chattel paper or negotiable documents of title to receive maximum protection—that is, to insure that the collateral will not be subsequently sold to a good faith purchaser—the secured party *should perfect by taking possession.*

While many kinds of collateral are too bulky for a transfer of possession, and others will not be transferred because the debtor needs to use them in his or her business—as in the case of plant machinery—the

---

[7] In addition to the priority gained under Sec. 9-312 by a subsequent third party who perfects his or her interest, as in the case of the X Bank above, there are a number of other third parties whose interests in the collateral also supersede those of the unperfected creditor under Sec. 9-301. (Additionally, as will be seen later, the rights of third parties in some situations even take precedence over perfected interests; obviously, the rights of these parties also prevail over unperfected interests.) As a result of these rules, it can be said that an unperfected interest generally affords *no protection against any third party* except a subsequent secured party who also fails to perfect his or her interest.

[8] The special rules applicable to motor vehicles and fixtures are discussed subsequently.

pledge, where feasible, does possess two significant advantages over the other kinds of perfection. First, it obviates the need for the security agreement to be in writing (though, in practice, a written agreement is still advisable). And, second, as indicated above, it reduces the possibility that third parties will subsequently acquire or claim interests in the collateral.

**3.** *Automatic perfection.* Occasionally an interest is perfected by mere attachment—that is, automatically—at the moment that the security interest is created. Such attachment, called **automatic perfection,** is applicable only where the collateral consists of *consumer goods* being purchased by the debtor. It exists in two common situations: (a) where the creditor (usually a retailer) sells the goods on credit and takes a security interest in return, or (b) where the creditor (usually a bank or finance company) loans money to the debtor for the purpose of buying the goods, and takes a security interest in return. To illustrate: B buys a washer and dryer on credit from the S Company under a conditional sale agreement (an agreement under which title to the goods is retained by the S Company until the price is paid in full). Under Sec. 9-302(1)(d) the interest of the S Company—called a **purchase money security interest**—is perfected even though it does not file a financing statement, and even though it does not have possession of the goods. Similarly, if B borrows the money to buy the appliances from a finance company, with that company taking a security interest in the goods when purchased, the finance company has a perfected, purchase money security interest in the washer and dryer when B buys them.[9] (The reason for the automatic perfection rule is one of practicality—the fact that secured sales of consumer goods are made in such large numbers by retailers that the filing requirement would place an undue burden upon such sellers.)

While automatic perfection does away with the necessity of filing a financing statement, it should be noted that the security agreement itself *must be in writing;* otherwise there is no attachment to which the perfection can relate.

## Perfection: Motor Vehicles and Fixtures

**Motor Vehicles:** Under Sec. 9-302(3), the usual methods of perfection are not applicable to security interests in collateral which are subject to state certificate of title laws—motor vehicles, boats, and motor homes. Security interests in such goods can be perfected only by compliance with the applicable state statute. In regard to automobiles (and to the other goods in this category), what this means is that—under the law of most states—a security interest can be perfected *only by the notation of such interest on the certificate of title covering the vehicle subject to the interest.* Generally, if such notation is not made, a good faith purchaser of the automobile takes it free of the interest. (In regard to the relatively few states that do not utilize title registration of such vehicles, an examination of the special statutes of such states must be made to determine the priority of conflicting interests.)

**Fixtures:** As noted above, a fixture is an item or good that becomes so firmly affixed to or so integrally connected to real estate that it is considered part of the real estate. How does the seller of a furnace, for example, obtain a security interest in the furnace that is superior to the interest of the lender who financed the house in which the furnace is to be installed? The rules here are very complicated. Generally, under Sec. 9-313(4)(a), the seller of the furnace who takes a purchase money security interest from the buyer-homeowner has priority over the holder of the mortgage on the real estate *if* the interest is properly filed

---

[9] An entirely different situation exists where a purchaser buys consumer goods (such as a washer or dryer) and pays cash for them, and subsequently uses such goods as collateral for a loan. Prior to 1984 these were very common transactions; typically, a person who wanted to borrow money from a lender—usually a small loan company, but sometimes a savings and loan association or a bank—would be asked to check a box in the lender's loan form which gave to the lender a blanket security interest in all of the borrower's household goods. In hearings before the Federal Trade Commission (FTC) in the early 1980s, voluminous testimony was given indicating that the use of such devices ("non purchase money interests") was attended by a variety of evils. Chief among these were (1) the fact that lenders often used these devices to continually threaten defaulting borrowers with repossession, causing borrowers "mental and psychological" injury; and (2) the fact that in cases where repossession actually occurred, the price of the goods obtained by the lender upon resale was usually so low that the borrower's obligation to the lender was actually reduced very little by the resale. Accordingly, the FTC included in Part VI of its Credit Practices Rule (adopted in 1984 and effective March 1, 1985) a rule that, in general, *prohibits lenders in interstate com-* *merce from taking non–purchase money security interests in household goods.* Two observations about the rule: (1) the term "household goods" excludes specified nonnecessities, such as jewelry and works of art; and (2) the rule does not, of course, have application to, or impose limitations upon the use of, *purchase money* security interests in household goods.

**Table 29.1** Permissible Types of Perfection for Various Kinds of Collateral

| TYPE OF COLLATERAL | FILING | POSSESSION | AUTOMATIC |
|---|---|---|---|
| **TANGIBLE COLLATERAL** | | | |
| Consumer Goods | X | X | X* |
| Equipment | X | X | |
| Farm Products | X | X | |
| Inventory | X | X | |
| Fixtures | X | | |
| **INDISPENSABLE PAPER COLLATERAL** | | | |
| Documents of Title | X** | X | |
| Instruments | X | X*** | |
| Chattel Paper | X | X | |
| **INTANGIBLE COLLATERAL** | | | |
| Accounts | X | | |
| General Intangibles | X | | |

*Automatic perfection arises if it is a purchase money security interest. Note also that special rules apply to motor vehicles.
**Temporary 21-day perfection exists without filing.
***Temporary 21-day perfection exists without possession.

before the furnace becomes attached to the property or within ten days thereafter. On the other hand, if the furnace is installed when the house is *under construction,* the seller's purchase money security interest will likely be subordinate to a construction mortgage recorded before the installation. The situation is further complicated by substantial variation in state law in this area. See Table 29.1 for clarification of the rules pertaining to perfection.

## *Filing Requirements, Generally*

**The Financing Statement:** Where perfection is made by the filing of a financing statement, as is usually the case, the requirements of Sec. 9-402 must be met. That section initially provides that "A financing statement is sufficient if it gives the names of the debtor and the secured party, is signed by the debtor, gives an address of the secured party from which information concerning the security interest may be obtained, gives a mailing address of the debtor and contains a statement indicating the types, or describing the items, of collateral." The section goes on to provide that additional information is needed for some types of collateral, so that a reading of the full section is necessary to determine the sufficiency of a financing statement in a given situation.

The following case illustrates one of many problems that commonly arise in determining whether a financing statement's description of collateral is adequate.

---

### Hixon v. Credit Alliance Corporation
Virginia Supreme Court
369 S.E.2d 169 (1988)

On April 29, 1982, Rodgers Brothers Construction Co. (Rodgers) bought a piece of equipment known as a "flusher." It was installed on Rodgers' truck in Illinois on May 28, 1982, on which date Rodgers executed a promissory note to Credit Alliance Corporation for $1,404,000. Rodgers also executed a security agreement giving Credit Alliance a security interest in all "the goods, chattels and property described in the annexed Schedule A and all other . . . machinery [and] equipment . . . now or hereafter belonging to [Rodgers]." On the attached schedule, 86 items of machinery and equipment were listed, but not the flusher, which was en route from Illinois to Virginia. Credit Alliance perfected the security interest by

*(continued)*

filing financing statements with the Virginia State Corporation Commission on June 3 and the County Clerk on June 7, 1982.

On December 1, 1982, Rodgers executed a promissory note payable to Virginia Tractor Company, Inc., for $44,000, together with a security agreement specifically naming the flusher as one of the items of equipment covered by the agreement. Virginia Tractor perfected its interest by filing financing statements with the State Corporation Commission and the County Clerk on December 7 and 9, 1982.

On October 5, 1983, Rodgers filed a petition for relief under Chapter 11 of the U.S. Bankruptcy Code. Credit Alliance then took possession of the flusher and sold it, despite Virginia Tractor's protest. Virginia Tractor filed this action, claiming that the sale was invalid and constituted a conversion because Credit Alliance had not perfected its security interest according to law. The trial court granted summary judgment to Credit Alliance and Virginia Tractor appealed.

**Decision:** The judgment for Credit Alliance was affirmed. Virginia Tractor challenged the description in Credit Alliance's security agreement. UCC 9-402 allows a creditor's financing statement to describe collateral by item or by type. Virginia Tractor argued that you cannot, as Credit Alliance did, describe by both means, but the court disagreed. It was proper for Credit Alliance to list specific items of collateral and then to add "and all other machinery and equipment." A reasonably diligent title searcher would not limit a search to the items listed on Schedule A, given the additional language. ∎

**Place of Filing:** In all cases where filing is utilized, the place for doing so depends on the classification of the collateral. In that regard, however, determination of the status of the debtor is not sufficient for a proper classification of the collateral. Rather, the determination in many jurisdictions may depend on how the collateral is used by the debtor. For example, a refrigerator is a *consumer good* if it is sold to a housekeeper, *inventory* if it is in the hands of a merchant selling appliances, *equipment* if it is used by a doctor for storing drugs in his or her office, and *farm equipment* if it is used to store eggs for resale.

Most states have two locations for filing—a *central* one (usually with the secretary of state) and a *local* one (usually with a county clerk). While the states have adopted somewhat varying location rules, most have adopted that version of Sec. 9-401(1) providing, essentially, that where the collateral is *farm equipment, farm products, or consumer goods,* filing is to be at a designated office in the county of the *debtor's residence* (or, if the debtor is not a resident of the state, then at a designated office in the county where the goods are kept). In other words, there is local filing for these kinds of security.

Where the collateral is *timber to be cut, minerals* (including oil and gas), *crops, or fixtures,* local filing is again usually proper—but, in these instances, "in the office where a mortgage on the real estate would be . . . recorded"—in such office in the county *where the land is located.*[10] Filings covering all other kinds of collateral, with minor exception, are to be made centrally—in the office of the secretary of state of the appropriate state. (That state is usually the state of the debtor's residence, or, in the case of a business firm, a state in which it has a place of business.) Additionally, several states have set up a central filing system for sales of farm product collateral, pursuant to the federal Food Security Act of 1985 (to be discussed presently).

**Duration of Filing:** Under Sec. 9-403(2), a filed financing statement is effective for five years from the date of filing. After this period, under Sec. 9-403(3), the security interest generally becomes unperfected unless the secured party files a *continuation statement* within six months prior to the expiration date. This continuation, good for five more years, can again be continued using the same procedure. Thus the secured party can continue the perfected interest indefinitely.

### Collateral Moved to Another State

There is always the possibility that collateral subject to a perfected security interest will be moved out of the state in which the perfection was made. Such movement may or may not have been contemplated by the parties, and it may or may not be a violation of the terms of the security agreement. In any event, the creditor needs to know what steps must be taken in order to keep his or her interest protected.

**General Rule:** The perfection of security interests in "multiple state transactions" is governed by

---

[10] Many states require an additional filing (dual filing) in the case of some of these kinds of collateral, especially fixtures.

Sec. 9-103. In regard to most kinds of collateral ("documents, instruments, and ordinary goods"), Sec. 9-103(1)(d) provides that the perfected creditor has *four months after the collateral has entered another state in which to reperfect.* If reperfection is made within that time, the security interest shall be "deemed to be perfected continuously" under Sec. 9-303(2). Thus if collateral is moved to a new state on March 1, and the creditor refiles there on May 10, his or her interest is generally protected as against any claimants in the state whose claim attached between those dates. On the other hand, if no reperfection is made within the four-month period, the creditor's interest is *unperfected beginning with the time that the collateral entered the state.* In other words, where there is no new perfection within the four-month period, the creditor is not protected by the four-month grace period.

**Special Rules—Motor Vehicles:** In cases where the collateral consists of accounts, general intangibles, chattel paper, and minerals, special rules apply. (Sec. 9-103[2][3][4] and [5].) Because of the complexity of these rules, the resolution of multistate disputes involving interests in these kinds of collateral can be achieved only by a careful reading of these express provisions and the case law developed under them.

Motor vehicles (and other goods covered by state certificate of title laws) are expressly exempted from the basic filing requirements of Article 9. As to security interests in such collateral as automobiles, then, perfection can be made only pursuant to the applicable state law. The rules here are complicated by the fact that while most states have certificate of title laws, some do not. Additionally, while the laws of most of the states having certificate of title laws provide that a notification of the security interest on the certificate of title is the only means of perfection, the laws of some title states do not so provide. Despite these variations, the rules applicable to two of the most common situations are clear:

**1.** Where a security interest exists in an automobile (or similar "certificate collateral") in a title state, and where the interest is duly noted on the certificate of title as required by the law of that state, the perfection continues after the automobile is removed to another title state *until it is registered* in the new state—the general four-month rule is inapplicable. Thus the secured party is protected against anyone who purchases the car in the new state prior to the new registration. Additionally, because a new registration normally requires the surrender of the old certificate of title, and the secured party is normally the holder of that certificate, the secured party usually can require that the security interest also be noted on the new certificate of title.

**2.** Where a security interest exists in an automobile in a non-certificate of title state, and where the interest is perfected by a filing of a financing statement under the basic filing section of Article 9, the security interest is generally protected when the automobile is moved to a new state *for four months* after it is brought into such state.

## LIMITATIONS ON PERFECTION

There are limited situations in which certain third parties acquire the collateral *free of* the security interest, even though the interest has been perfected. Following are the primary situations in which these third parties prevail.

### *Buyers in the Ordinary Course of Business*

Section 9-307(1) provides that "a buyer [of goods] in the ordinary course of business . . . takes free of a security interest created by his seller even though the security interest is perfected and even though the buyer knows of its existence." The rationale for this is that the ordinary person who purchases goods from a merchant should not be required to find out if there is an outstanding security interest covering the merchant's inventory. The key words identifying the buyer in this case, a **buyer in the ordinary course of business,** mean that he or she made the purchase in the ordinary course of the debtor's business—that is, that the collateral purchased was of a type which the debtor normally sold (customarily meaning inventory).

To illustrate: M, a merchant in the appliance business, seeks a loan from B Bank, putting up his inventory of refrigerators, stoves, freezers, and other appliances as security for the loan. B Bank perfects its security interest by filing a financing statement centrally with the secretary of state. A week later, C, a consumer, purchases a freezer from M for cash. Since C has purchased in the ordinary course of the seller's business, *he takes the property free of B Bank's security interest.* The ordinary course of business rule does not apply to the rare buyer who not only knows of the existence of the security interest, but also knows that the sale of the goods was a *violation* of the security agreement.

A second limitation on the course of business rule is contained in Sec. 9-307(1), under which ordinary course buyers of farm products (crops or livestock) take subject to a prior perfected security interest covering the products. However, Congress overrode this provision, which had been subject to conflicting court interpretations, in the Food Security Act of 1985. That act gives the same protection to ordinary course buyers of farm products as is accorded buyers of other products. However, the secured party can retain priority by (1) "prenotification," that is, giving *actual* notice to the buyer pursuant to strict guidelines, or (2) filing in a special central filing system for farm products independent of Article 9. Several states have created such a special filing system.

## Buyers Not in the Ordinary Course of Business

A second class of buyer who receives protection in some circumstances against a perfected security interest is the buyer who buys consumer goods not in the ordinary course of business, sometimes referred to as "the next-door neighbor buyer." This priority arises under Sec. 9-307(2), which applies to the situation where consumer goods are sold (usually by a retailer) subject to a purchase money security interest in favor of the seller, in which case—as we saw earlier—perfection is automatic. That section provides, in effect, that if the consumer-buyer (the debtor) resells the goods to a third party not in the ordinary course of business, the third party takes the goods *free of the perfected security interest* if the following conditions are met:

1. The buyer must buy without knowledge of the security interest.

2. He or she must give value for the goods.

3. The purchase must be for the buyer's own personal, family, or household purposes.

4. The purchase must take place before the secured party files a financing statement—a condition that is normally easy to meet, since the secured party in such a case usually does not file at all.

To illustrate: M, a merchant in the appliance business, sells a freezer out of his inventory to C, a consumer, under a conditional sales contract, because C cannot pay the full purchase price. Since this is a purchase money security interest in consumer goods, M makes no filing. C takes the freezer home but decides he does not like it and sells it to his friend, F, who purchases the freezer for his own use without knowledge of M's security interest. If C defaults, M will lose his security interest in the freezer and become a general creditor of C, since F has met the UCC requirements.

## Buyers of Chattel Paper, Negotiable Instruments, and Negotiable Documents

Under Article 3 of the UCC, "Commercial Paper," good faith purchasers of negotiable instruments who give value for such instruments generally take the instruments free of claims asserted by prior parties. This same general concept is recognized under Sections 9-308 and 9-309 of the UCC.

Section 9-308 provides, in part, that "a purchaser of chattel paper . . . who gives new value and takes possession of it in the ordinary course of his business *has priority over a security interest in the chattel paper* . . . which is perfected [by filing]." (Emphasis added.) Thus, if a perfected creditor does not take possession of the chattel paper, a person who buys the paper from the debtor in good faith generally takes it free of the perfected interest.

The most common situation (but by no means the only one) to which this section is applicable is the case where a dealer, usually a retailer, sells goods (for example, furniture) on credit to a consumer, the debtor, with the dealer taking a chattel paper (usually a promissory note coupled with a security interest in favor of the dealer) from the consumer-debtor. The dealer then subsequently assigns the paper to a financial institution, usually a bank, as security for a loan made by the bank to the dealer.[11] In such a case, if the

---

[11]In the general situation presented here (especially common in the furniture industry), the consumer-debtor is not notified of the assignment to the bank. Thus, in the usual case where the dealer retains possession of the paper *instead of selling it* to a third party, the consumer-debtor continues to make monthly payments to the dealer, and the dealer remits them to the bank. The transaction is referred to as *nonnotification* (or *indirect collection*), as distinguished from the case of *notification* (or *direct collection*), where the consumer-debtor is notified of the assignment and makes payments directly to the bank. In the case of direct notification, common in the automobile industry, possession of the paper is normally transferred to the bank, the secured party.

bank perfects by filing only, leaving possession of the paper in the dealer, a person who purchases the paper from the dealer in good faith—that is, without knowledge of the security interest of the bank—and for value takes the chattel paper free of the bank's perfected interest.

Along similar lines, Sec. 9-309 provides, in essence, that a holder in due course of a negotiable instrument, and a holder to whom a negotiable document of title has been duly negotiated, *takes priority over* an earlier security interest in such instrument or document even though the security interest is a perfected one. Further, that section provides that the filing of a security interest in a negotiable instrument or negotiable document (by the original secured party) does not constitute notice of the security interest to such holders.

## Other Protected Parties

In addition to buyers of collateral discussed above, there are other third parties whose interests in the collateral (usually arising under other statutes) are excluded from operation of Article 9 by Sec. 9-104. Such interests thus have priority over interests perfected under Article 9. Some of these interests, for example, are those arising under statutes of the United States, landlord liens, and liens "given by statute . . . for services or materials. . . ." To illustrate an interest in the latter category: M, a mechanic, repairs an automobile owned by O that is subject to a security interest in favor of a bank. Under the typical state statute M possesses an *artisan's lien*—the right to retain possession of the car until he or she is paid for the repair work. Generally, under such a lien the mechanic's right to retain possession may be successfully asserted against the bank.

# PERFECTION AND THE FLOATING LIEN CONCEPT

Section 9-204 of the UCC permits the security agreement to include a clause providing that the obligation covered by the agreement is also secured by any collateral that may subsequently be acquired by the debtor. Such a provision, called an **after-acquired property clause,** permits the secured creditor to have a **"floating lien"**—a lien on changing or shifting assets of the debtor. This clause is most often used to cover inventories of the debtor, where goods are continuously being sold and restocked by the debtor, but sometimes covers non-inventory assets of the debtor (such as plant machinery).

Section 9-204 also permits the security agreement to contain a **future advances clause,** which is a clause providing that the debtor's collateral shall also be security for any extensions of credit (advances) which the creditor may make in the future. The following example illustrates the extensive protection that is afforded a secured party who utilizes both the after-acquired property and future advances clauses.

*April 2*—D borrows money from X (creditor #1) under a security agreement that gives X a security interest in all of the equipment in D's plant. The agreement contains an after-acquired property clause and also a future advances clause. X perfects the same day by filing a financing statement centrally.

*June 1*—D purchases a new piece of equipment for $50,000, and pays cash for it.

*June 15*—D decides to replenish his raw material inventory. He does this by getting a loan from Y (creditor #2) for $25,000, putting up his new piece of equipment as security for the loan.

*June 16*—Y perfects by filing a financing statement centrally.

*June 30*—D needs additional funds to meet his payroll, and approaches X (creditor #1) for a $20,000 loan for this purpose. X makes the loan.

*September 1*—D's business is hit by a recession, with the result that D is in default to both X and Y.

In this situation, X's interest in the new piece of equipment has priority over Y's interest, for either of two reasons:

**1.** If D owes any balance on the original debt incurred April 2, X has a protected security interest in the new equipment by virtue of the after-acquired property clause. Thus, the new equipment can be acquired by X as satisfaction for that debt.[12]

**2.** If D's indebtedness arises out of the advance made to him by X on June 30, X again has priority

---

[12] The usual priority afforded by an after-acquired property clause may be lost in circumstances where the second creditor's interest is a "purchase money security interest." The special rules applicable to such interests are examined later in the chapter.

even though Y's security interest was perfected prior to that advance. This results from the future advances clause, which causes the June 30 advance *to date back to the April 2 perfection.*

## PROCEEDS AND COMMINGLING

The secured party's right to proceeds is extremely important when the debtor sells the collateral to a third party under circumstances in which the secured party loses his or her interest in the collateral. In such a case, any payments (or proceeds) made by the third party to the debtor can be claimed by the secured party in satisfaction of the debt. Under Secs. 9-203 and 306, this right of the secured party is automatic unless the parties agree otherwise, and it is usually continuous in duration until the debt is paid.

In certain business operations, goods under a perfected security interest are commingled with other goods and become part of the product or mass. What then happens to the security interest? Section 9-315(1) provides that the security interest *continues* in the product or mass if the goods lose their identity in processing or manufacturing, or if the financing statement covering the original goods also covers the product into which the goods have been manufactured or processed. Under Sec. 9-315(2), in the same situation, if more than one security interest attaches to the product or mass, they all rank equally according to the cost ratio of their contribution to the total.

The rules relating to after-acquired property, future advances, commingled or processed goods, and proceeds also make it possible for the lien to float on a *shifting stock* of goods. Under Sec. 9-205, the lien can start with raw materials and pass to work in process, to finished inventory, to accounts receivable or chattel paper, and to any cash proceeds under a single perfected security interest.

## PRIORITIES BETWEEN CREDITORS

Earlier, in the section entitled "Limitations on Perfection," we saw that certain *buyers of the collateral* took it free of a perfected security interest. In other words, in a contest between the perfected creditor and a buyer of the collateral, the buyer's interest (in limited circumstances) had priority over that of the creditor.

Here we will examine the rules applicable to even more common controversies—those in which both of the competing parties are *creditors of the debtor* (with both parties' interests arising under Article 9).

### *Unperfected Security Interests*

The basic priority section is Sec. 9-312, and most of the provisions found there deal with priorities between perfected creditors—situations in which both of the claimants to the collateral hold perfected security interests. Before we turn to an examination of these important rules, however, two introductory rules involving priorities relative to *unperfected* interests should be kept in mind.

First, in contests between two secured but unperfected creditors, under Sec. 9-312(5)(b) the creditor's interest that attached first—was created first—takes priority over the other.[13] (It should also be kept in mind, however, that should the debtor go into bankruptcy both unperfected interests are lost, with the unperfected creditors simply sharing in the bankrupt's assets along with his or her unsecured creditors.)

Second, in a contest between an unperfected creditor and a perfected creditor, the perfected creditor's interest, of course, has priority over the unperfected interest—Sec. 9-301(1)(a). And this priority exists even if the unperfected creditor's interest had attached first, and even if the perfected creditor knew of the unperfected interest before he or she perfected.

### *Perfected Security Interests*

Subject to special rules noted later, the basic priority rule applicable to controversies between perfected creditors is that *conflicting security interests rank according to priority in time of filing or perfection, whichever is earlier.* (Sec. 9-312(5)(a).) The following example illustrates the rule.

*June 1*—Bank A agrees to loan $4,000 to D, with the actual advance of the money to be made when subsequently requested by D. D signs a security agreement giving the bank a security interest in his Audemars Piguet watch, valued at $9,000. D retains possession of the watch.

*June 2*—Bank A files its financing statement.

---

[13] This situation does not get into the courts often, because in "real life" when it appears that there is going to be a controversy between two unperfected creditors, one or both of the creditors perfect before litigation begins.

*June 5*—D borrows $6,000 from bank B, signing a security agreement that gives the bank a security interest in the same watch. Bank B, after advancing the money, perfects by filing its financing statement immediately.

*June 7*—Bank A advances the $4,000 to D.

If D defaults on both loans, *bank A's interest has priority over that of bank B,* even though bank B's perfection occurred first.[14] The rationale for the rule, as applied to this situation, is that bank B would have known of bank A's agreement had it checked the appropriate filing system before making its loan.

Two words of caution about the basic rule must be made. First, the "first filing" part of the rule grants priority to such filer over a subsequently perfected interest only in those cases where a security agreement and filing occur at a given time, with the actual advance being made by the filing party at a later date (as in the example above). In the much more common case, where both the first and second creditors immediately advance funds upon the debtor's signing of their respective security agreements, the creditor who *perfects first* prevails. To illustrate: X borrows $1,000 from A on June 1, and signs a security agreement on that date giving A a security interest in certain collateral. X then borrows $2,000 from B on June 15, giving B a security interest in the same collateral. If B perfects by filing before A does, B's interest has priority over A's.

Second, the basic rule *does not always* give the party who files first or perfects first protection against subsequent creditors who possess purchase money security interests in the collateral (as indicated in the following discussion).

## SPECIAL RULES APPLICABLE TO PURCHASE MONEY SECURITY INTERESTS

Section 9-312 contains a number of special rules that bring about results different from those obtained under the general rule discussed above. Of these, two that grant special priority to holders of purchase money security interests in limited circumstances merit attention.

### Purchase Money Security Interests in Noninventory Collateral

Section 9-312(4) provides that "a purchase money security interest in collateral other than inventory has priority over a conflicting interest in the same collateral . . . if the purchase money security interest is perfected at the time the debtor receives possession of the collateral, or within ten days thereafter." This priority is sometimes referred to as the "super priority" of a purchase money security holder, because his or her interest takes precedence over the person who holds the conflicting interest in the collateral even if that person's interest was perfected prior to the creation of the purchase money interest.[15]

One situation (among several) to which this rule applies is the following: M, a manufacturer, borrows money from bank A, under a written agreement providing that the bank shall have a security interest in the M Company's present and future plant machinery. The bank duly files a financing statement that includes the after-acquired property clause. Thereafter, M buys additional machinery on credit from the XYZ Corporation (a tool and die company) under a security agreement conveying an interest in the additional machinery to the XYZ Corporation. The XYZ Corporation, the purchase money security interest holder, delivers the additional machinery to the M Company and files its financing statement within ten days of delivery. The XYZ Corporation's purchase money security interest in the additional machinery has priority over that of the bank's interest.

### Purchase Money Security Interests in Inventories

Purchase money security holders also have "super priority" over existing perfected holders of interests in inventory, but under more limited circumstances. Section 9-312(3)(b) provides, in part, that a perfected purchase money security interest *in inventory* has priority over a conflicting interest in the same inventory if two basic requirements are met: (1) the purchase money security interest must be perfected by the time that the debtor receives the inventory being purchased, and (2) if the holder of the conflicting interest in the inventory has perfected by filing only, the purchase money secured party must give written notification to such holder before the

---

[14]Bank B's perfection occurred on June 5, and bank A's perfection did not occur until June 7. Bank A's filing on June 2 did not constitute a perfection, because its interest had not even attached since it had not yet given value.

[15]Earlier in the chapter we saw one application of these rules in *Crocker National Bank v. Ideco Division of Dresser Industries.*

purchase money secured party files his or her financing statement, such notification stating that the purchase money secured party has or expects to acquire a purchase money interest in the debtor's inventory, describing such inventory by item or type. Once this notification is received by the holder of the conflicting interest, it is good for a period of five years.

*Again, a note of caution:* as to any priority controversies presenting facts that do not clearly fall within the general rule of Sec. 9-312(5) or within the special rules of Sec. 9-312(3)(b) applicable to purchase money security interests, other sections of Sec. 9-312 may apply. (Additionally, the status of perfected security interests in crops is governed by Sec. 9-312(2), a section whose complexity also precludes its treatment in an introductory chapter such as this.)

The next case presents priority issues in a controversy between perfected creditors.

### Kimbrell's Furniture Co., Inc. v. Friedman
Supreme Court of South Carolina, 198 S.E.2d 803 (1973)

This suit deals with two separate purchases made from the plaintiff, Kimbrell's Furniture Company—a new television set by Charlie O'Neal on July 11, 1972, and a tape player by his wife on July 15, 1972. Each purchase was on credit, and in each instance there was executed, as security, a conditional sale contract, designated a *purchase money security agreement*. On the same day of each purchase, O'Neal took the items to defendant, Friedman, a pawnbroker doing business as Bonded Loan, and *pledged* them as security for a loan—the television for a loan of $30 and the tape player for a loan of $25.

Kimbrell's did not record any financing statement or notice of these security agreements. O'Neal thereafter failed to make his required monthly payments to Kimbrell's, whereupon Kimbrell's brought this action to recover possession of the goods.

Bonded Loan, which held possession of the television set and tape player as security for its loan, contended that its lien had priority over Kimbrell's unrecorded security interest. The lower court sustained this contention, and Kimbrell's appealed.

The question to be decided is the following: Is a conditional seller of consumer goods required to file a financing statement in order to perfect his or her security interest as against a pawnbroker who subsequently takes possession of such goods as security for a loan?

**Decision:** The judgment of the trial court was reversed, and judgment was entered in favor of Kimbrell's. As a general rule, creditors are required to file a financing statement in order to protect their security interests against the claims of third parties.

However, several exceptions to the rule are found in Sec. 9-302(1)(d) of the UCC. That section provides in part that a financing statement need not be filed to perfect "a purchase money security interest in consumer goods." Since the television set and tape recorder were obviously consumer goods, no filing was necessary. Accordingly, Kimbrell's security interest attached and was perfected *when the debtors, the O'Neals, executed the purchase money security agreements and took possession of the property.* Kimbrell's security interest thus had priority over the security interest of Bonded Loan. ∎

## RIGHTS AND DUTIES PRIOR TO TERMINATION

The security agreement determines most of the rights and duties of the debtor and secured party. However, other rights and duties are imposed by the UCC, some of which are applied in the absence of a security agreement.

### Release, Assignment, and Amendment

Under Sec. 9-406, the secured party of record can release all or part of any collateral described in the filed financing statement, thereby ending his or her security interest in the described collateral. Under Sec. 9-405, the secured party can also assign all or part of the security interest to an assignee, who, in order to become the secured party of record, must file either by a disclosure method provided for in the code (such as a notation on the front or back of the financing statement) or by a separate written statement of assignment.

If the debtor and secured party so agree, under Sec. 9-402, the financing statement can be amended (for example, to add new collateral to the security interest). But the filed amendment must be signed by both the debtor and the secured party. This amendment does not extend the time period of the perfection unless collateral is added; in such a case, the perfection for the new collateral applies from the date of filing the amendment.

The debtor's signature is needed for (1) the security agreement, (2) the original financing statement, and (3) amendments to the financing statements. All other documents can be filed with only the signature of the secured party.

## Information Requests by Secured Parties

In most states the filing officer must furnish specified information on request to certain parties. For example, under Sec. 9-407(1), the person filing any of the above statements can furnish the filing officer with a duplicate and request that the officer note on such copy the file number, date, and hour of the original filing. The filing officer must send this copy to the person making the request, without charge.

Frequently, prospective secured parties request of the filing officer a certificate giving information on possible perfected financing statements with respect to a named debtor. Under Sec. 9-407(2), if so requested, the filing officer must furnish a copy of any filed financing statement or assignment. Given the priorities of secured interests and the attachment of security interest under the concept of the floating lien, businesspersons ought to request such information before advancing credit to debtors.

## Secured Party in Possession of the Collateral

Section 9-207 provides that generally a secured party in possession of the collateral must use reasonable care in the custody and preservation of it and is subject to liability by the debtor for any failure to do so (although he or she does not lose the security interest thereby). The secured party can use or operate the collateral as permitted in the security agreement or to preserve its value. Should the collateral increase in value or profits be derived from it, the secured party can hold these increases as additional security unless they are in the form of money. Any increase in money must be either remitted to the debtor or applied to reduction of the secured obligation.

Under the same section, the secured party must keep the collateral identifiable (except that when the collateral is fungible, it can be commingled with like goods). He or she can repledge the collateral, but this must be done on terms that do not impair the debtor's right to redeem it upon paying the debt.

Again under the same section, unless the security agreement provides to the contrary, the debtor is responsible for all reasonable charges incurred in the custody, preservation, and operation of the collateral possessed by the secured party. These charges include insurance, taxes, storage, and the like.

The following case presents an interesting application of Sec. 9-207's provisions.

---

**Citibank, N.A. v. Data Lease Financial Corp.**
U.S. Eleventh Circuit Court of Appeals, 828 F.2d 686 (1987)

On April 12, 1973, Citibank loaned $6.2 million to Data Lease. The collateral securing the loan included 870,000 shares (80.2 percent) of the capital stock of Miami National Bank. The pledge agreement expressly provided that, upon any default, Citibank had the absolute and exclusive right to vote the pledged shares. Data Lease defaulted by missing payments due July 12, 1974.

Miami National's financial soundness and competence of management were questioned by bank regulators in early 1975. Beginning in 1976, Citibank exercised its right under the pledge agreement to vote the Miami National stock it held as collateral. Indeed, Citibank elected the entire board. In De-

*(continued)*

cember 1978, Citibank brought this foreclosure action. On February 29, 1979, the court ordered an emergency judicial sale of the pledged stock, which was purchased by Citibank for $3 million. Data Lease then filed a counterclaim, alleging that Citibank's mismanagement of Miami National had dramatically reduced the value of the collateral, in violation of the UCC, among other provisions. The district court granted summary judgment on this counterclaim to Citibank, and Data Lease appealed.

**Decision:** The judgment for Citibank was reversed. UCC 9-207 provides that "[a] secured party must use reasonable care in the custody and preservation of collateral in its possession." Merely preserving the certificates physically is not enough. When a pledgee such as Citibank has a controlling interest and becomes involved in management of the company, it must act reasonably. A jury should decide whether Citibank's carelessness caused the precipitous decline in the value of Miami National stock, as Data Lease alleges. ∎

---

## *Debtor's Right to Request Status of Debt*

Under Sec. 9-208, the debtor can sign a statement indicating what he or she believes to be the aggregate amount of the unpaid indebtedness as of a specific date (and, under certain circumstances, including a list of collateral covered by the security agreement) with the request that the secured party approve or correct the statement. The secured party, unless he or she has a reasonable excuse, must comply with the request within two weeks of receipt or be liable for any loss caused to the debtor by such failure. Since the debtor could become a nuisance by making numerous and continuous requests to the secured party, he or she is entitled to make such a request without charge only once every six months. For each additional request made during this period, the secured party can require payment of a fee not exceeding $10.

## DEFAULT OF THE DEBTOR

In general, under Sec. 9-501, when the debtor is in default, the secured party can reduce his or her claim to judgment, foreclose, or otherwise enforce the security interest by any available judicial procedure. Under Sec. 9-503, unless otherwise agreed, the secured party also has the right to take possession of the collateral on default. This can be done without judicial process only if no breach of the peace occurs. Thus the creditor should not attempt to break into the debtor's home or take the collateral by force. If force is used, the debtor can file criminal charges against the secured party and can bring an action in tort for any damages he or she sustains. Although Section 9-503, the so-called "self-help" section on repossession, has been challenged by debtors in numerous cases on the ground that repossession without judicial process is a violation of the Due Process Clause of the U.S. Constitution, the highest courts of most states have ruled that the section is constitutional.

## *Duty to Assemble Collateral*

Under Sec. 9-503, if the security agreement so provides, the secured party can require the debtor to assemble the collateral upon default and to make it available at a location reasonably convenient to both. If it is impractical to move the collateral or it is too expensive to store, the secured party has the right to render the collateral unusable to the debtor and, following the proper procedure, to dispose of it on the debtor's premises.

## *Disposal of Collateral*

Under Sec. 9-504(1), once the secured party obtains possession, he or she generally has the right to sell, lease, or otherwise dispose of the collateral in its then existing condition or following any commercially reasonable preparation or process. Under 9-507(2), if the secured party sells the collateral, the sale must be handled in a "commercially reasonable manner." Although this is not expressly defined, the code does mention certain actions as being commercially reasonable. Sales made through such actions, or made otherwise and in good faith, are usually held to constitute compliance.

Under Sec. 9-504(3), the collateral can be disposed of at either a public or private sale if done in a commercially reasonable manner. Unless the collateral is perishable, threatens to decline quickly in value, or is of a type customarily sold in a recognized market, the secured party must give the debtor reasonable notice of the time and place of the sale (unless the debtor, after default, signed a statement renouncing or modifying this right to notification). No additional notification need be sent in the case of consumer goods, but in other cases notice must also be sent to any other secured creditor from whom the secured party has received written notice of a claim of an interest in the collateral. (Failure of the secured party to give such notice makes him or her liable for any ensuing loss.) The secured party can buy at *any* public sale—and at a private sale if the collateral customarily is sold in a recognized market or is of a type that is the subject of a widely distributed standard price quotation. (Under Sec. 9-501(3)(b), these provisions cannot be waived or varied.)

Under Sec. 9-504(4), when collateral is disposed of by a secured party after default of the debtor, a purchaser for value receives all the debtor's rights in the collateral free from the security interest and subordinate interests and liens. This is true even if the secured party failed to comply with the requirements of disposal under the code or under judicial proceedings, so long as the purchaser bought in good faith, and, at a public sale, had no knowledge of such interests or rights.

Section 9-505 provides that, except where the defaulting debtor has paid 60 percent of an obligation involving consumer goods, the secured party, upon obtaining possession of the goods, can *retain the collateral* in satisfaction of the secured obligation. However, to do so, the secured party must send written notice of such intention to the debtor and (except in the case of consumer goods) to any other secured party from whom written notice of a claim of an interest in the collateral has been received before such notification is sent to the debtor. If no objection is received from such parties within 21 days after notice is sent, the secured party can retain the collateral. But if any timely objection is received, the collateral must be disposed of in compliance with Sec. 9-504.

Section 9-505(1) provides that in the case of consumer goods, where the debtor has paid 60 percent or more of the obligation prior to default, the secured party must *dispose of the collateral* as previously discussed (in Sec. 9-504) within 90 days after taking possession—unless the debtor has signed a statement renouncing all rights in the collateral. Under Sec. 9-507(1), should the secured party fail to do so within this period, the debtor can recover an amount "not less than the credit service charge plus 10 percent of the principal amount of the debt or the time price differential plus 10 percent of the cash price." The secured party may thus suffer a loss by waiting too long to dispose of the collateral in this situation.

## Application of Proceeds

The proceeds of the sale are, under Sec. 9-504(1), applied first to the expenses incurred by the secured party in retaking, holding, and selling or leasing the collateral—including reasonable attorney's fees if the security agreement so provides. After these expenses are deducted, the remaining proceeds are applied to the indebtedness of the secured party. If any proceeds are then left, subordinate security interests, if any, are to be satisfied if the subordinate interest holders have made written demand for payment before the proceeds were distributed. (Of course, the secured party can demand that these holders give reasonable proof of their claims.) Thus, even if a businessperson's security interest is second in priority, it is still possible for that person to receive part of the proceeds in satisfaction of the claim by following the UCC procedure.

As a general rule, under Sec. 9-504(2), if any surplus is left after the expenses have been paid and the indebtedness and subordinate security interests have been satisfied, it goes to the debtor. Furthermore, under Sec. 9-501(3)(a), the duty to account to the debtor for this surplus cannot be waived or varied by agreement. Should the proceeds not cover the expenses and the indebtedness to the secured party, under Sec. 9-504(2), the debtor is liable for the deficiency unless otherwise agreed. If the collateral involves the sale of accounts or chattel paper, the rules regarding distribution of surplus and deficiency apply only if they are provided for in the security agreement.

## Redemption of Collateral

Section 9-506 provides that the debtor (or any other subordinate secured party) can redeem the collateral at any time before the primary secured party has disposed of (or contracted to dispose of) it, unless he or she has waived the right of redemption in writing after the default. The redemption is accomplished by tendering payment of all obligations secured by the collateral as well as all reasonable costs incurred by the secured party. Under Sec. 9-501(3)(d), a sale of part of the collateral does not remove the right of redemption for any collateral left in the hands of the secured party, and this right can be waived only in the manner indicated here.

## TERMINATION

The ultimate goal of the parties is to have the debt paid and the security interest terminated, particularly where it has been perfected by a filing. To accomplish this, when the debt is paid, the secured party files a *termination statement* with the officer with whom the financing statement was filed.

Under Sec. 9-404, if the financing statement covers consumer goods, the secured party must file the termination statement within one month after the secured obligation is no longer outstanding; however, if the debtor demands the statement in writing, it must be filed within ten days after the obligation is no longer outstanding. Thus filing of a termination statement in the case of consumer goods is required even if no demand is made for it by the debtor. In all other cases the secured party must file or furnish the debtor with a termination statement within ten days after written demand is made by the debtor. If the secured party fails to file or furnish the statement to the debtor, he or she is liable to that person for $100 and for any loss caused to the debtor by such failure.

## SUMMARY

The purposes of a secured transaction are twofold: (1) to give to a creditor a legally recognized interest in specific property of the debtor, and (2) to give such creditor a priority claim in that property against other creditors who may seek to have the debtor's assets sold in satisfaction of their claims. Secured transactions are governed by Article 9 of the UCC. Under the terminology of that article, the creditor is the secured party, the one owing the debt is the debtor, the interest of the creditor is a security interest, and the property subject to the interest is the collateral.

Secured transactions law applies only to secured interests in personal property. Such property may be classified as tangible collateral (consumer goods, equipment, farm products, and inventory); indispensable paper (documents of title, instruments, and chattel paper); and intangible collateral (accounts and general intangibles such as contractual and patent rights).

A security interest attaches (i.e., is created) by means of a security agreement between the secured party and the debtor. This agreement must be in writing unless the secured party takes possession of the collateral. (Since it is not possible for the creditor to take possession of an intangible, security agreements in intangibles must be in writing.) After a security agreement is made, the secured party will ordinarily "perfect" the interest so that it will have maximum protection against claims of other parties to the collateral. (If there is no perfection, the secured party loses his or her interest to a party having a perfected interest in the same collateral; the secured party also loses the interest if the debtor goes into bankruptcy.) Perfection is usually achieved by the filing of a financing statement by the creditor (at a designated office specified by the provisions of Article 9). Perfection may be achieved, however, by the secured creditor's taking possession of the collateral, and in some instances involving the sale of consumer goods on credit, perfection is automatic. There are special filing rules as to motor vehicles, fixtures, and to collateral moved to another state.

While a perfected interest is generally valid against all third parties, there are exceptions to this rule. A perfected creditor's interest, for example, is lost if the debtor sells the collateral to a buyer in the ordinary course of the debtor's business. Additionally, such interest is lost to a buyer *not* in the ordinary course of business under certain circumstances, and, where the collateral consists of negotiable instruments left in the debtor's possession, the creditor's interest is lost to a party who purchases them in good faith and for value.

A security agreement may cover a certain type of property (such as machinery or inventory) and such type of property as the debtor may acquire in the future. This protection can be achieved by use of an "after-acquired property" clause in the security agreement. However, this protection might be lost to the unpaid seller of such additional property who himself may have a purchase-money security in that property. A perfected security interest has priority over a nonperfected interest in the same property. Where there are two or more perfected interests in the same property, the rule is that the interests rank "according to priority in filing or perfection, whichever is earlier." The rights and duties of the parties prior to termination of the interest generally are spelled out in the security agreement. In the event of a default by the debtor, the creditor's remedies are set forth in Sec. 9-501 of the UCC.

## KEY TERMS

**Secured transaction**
**Secured party**
**Debtor**
**Security interest**
**Security agreement**
**Collateral**
**Perfection**
**Financing statement**
**Goods**
**Fixtures**
**Indispensable paper collateral**
**Documents of title**
**Instrument**
**Chattel paper**
**Intangible collateral**
**Account**
**General intangibles**
**Attachment**
**Filing**
**Automatic perfection**
**Purchase money security interest**
**Buyer in the ordinary course of business**
**After-acquired property clause**
**Floating lien**
**Future advances clause**

## QUESTIONS AND PROBLEMS

1. Rike-Kumler, a jeweler, sold a $1,237 diamond ring to Nicolosi which he was going to give to his fiancée. Nicolosi made a down payment and executed a purchase money security agreement to Rike-Kumler for the unpaid balance. Rike-Kumler did not file a financing statement. Nicolosi gave the ring to his fiancée, and later went into bankruptcy. His fiancée called off the engagement and delivered the ring to the trustee in bankruptcy. Rike-Kumler then claimed a protected purchase money security interest in the ring, as against the trustee's claim. At the trial, the trustee in bankruptcy contended that the ring was not a "consumer good," because Nicolosi did not intend to wear it himself. Do you think that the ring was a consumer good? Why or why not? In regard to Rike-Kumler's claim, what difference does it make whether the ring is or is not a consumer good? Explain. (*In re Nicolosi,* 4 UCC Rptr. 111, 1966.)

2. A, a furniture dealer, purchased a large number of sofas from W, a furniture wholesaler, signing a security agreement for the purchase price. A sold one of the sofas to B for $150, with B paying $100 down and signing a security agreement for the balance.
   a. How is an enforceable security interest created in this collateral by W? By A?
   b. What is the classification of collateral as between W and A? Between A and B? Where would each security interest be properly perfected?
   c. Suppose that, with both security interests in existence, A is in default to W. Assuming W's interest is properly perfected, does W have any rights in the sofa purchased by B? Why or why not?

3. A loan's collateral is a refrigerator. How would you, as the secured party, properly perfect your security interest in it under the following circumstances?
   a. You are a wholesaler and the refrigerator is part of a 250-appliance installment sale to a retailer.
   b. You are a retailer and sell the refrigerator, on an installment purchase plan, to a customer, for use in the customer's home.
   c. You are a retailer and sell the refrigerator, on an installment contract, to a farmer for use in storing eggs until they can be marketed.

4. Weiss and Bostron (W&B), engaged in a joint venture, borrowed money from a bank in Brush, Colorado, to buy some cattle. Weiss gave the bank a purchase money security interest in the cattle under a security agreement. After buying the cattle he bought feed on credit from the Colorado High Plains Agricultural Credit Corporation (CHPACC), giving that corporation a security interest in "all feed now or hereafter acquired," and in the "proceeds" of the feed. The cattle consumed the feed and were subsequently sold at a loss.

The sale of the cattle did not bring enough to pay off the full amount of the debt owed the bank, so the bank sued W&B for the balance due it. At this point the seller of the feed, CHPACC, intervened, claiming that any money the bank was able to recover from W&B was subject to its security under the proceeds clause of its security agreement. In other words, CHPACC claimed that since it would have priority in the proceeds of the feed if the feed were sold instead of being eaten by the cattle, it thus had a priority in the proceeds of the cattle sale, giving it priority over any money that might be recovered by the bank from W&B. The bank, by contrast, argued that once the feed was eaten, it lost its identity and that the proceeds sought to be recovered by CHPACC were also lost. Which of these arguments is the better? Explain. (*First National Bank of Brush v. Bostron,* 564 P.2d 964, 1977.)

5. CS, a college student, needed $5,000 to start up a small business. On October 10 the ABC Bank agreed to loan him

that amount, the advance of which would not occur until he notified the bank that the money was needed. On that same date CS signed a security agreement giving the bank a security interest in specified jewelry CS had just inherited. The bank perfected by filing a financing statement the same day.

On October 20 CS needed additional money for his project, so he borrowed another $5,000 from a second bank, the XYZ bank. CS signed a security agreement in favor of the XYZ Bank giving it a secured interest in the same jewelry. Because the bank had had difficulties with student loans before, it took possession of the jewelry with CS's permission and without knowledge of the ABC Bank's interest.

On November 1 the ABC Bank, at CS's request, advanced him the $5,000 it had earlier agreed to make available. Thereafter CS defaulted on both loans, and each bank claimed that its interest in the jewelry had priority over the interest of the other bank. Which bank wins? Explain.

**6.** A secured party has this problem: Four and a half years ago he properly created a security interest in the collateral of a debtor and filed a financing statement. The debtor now is unable to repay the loan. The secured party feels that, given more time, the debtor will be able to pay the balance due. However, another secured party whose filing came after his is in the same position. The collateral is sufficient to satisfy the remaining balance of either loan, but not both. What would you advise the first secured party to do to protect his interest in the collateral?

**7.** Rompon borrowed money from a bank in order to buy a mobile home. He gave a purchase money security interest in the mobile home to the bank, which perfected its interest by having a notation of such interest made on the Florida certificate of title covering the home, as required by the Florida certificate of title law. Thereafter Rompon moved the home to a trailer park, where its wheels were removed, the home was physically attached to the real estate, and hookups were made to underground facilities. Later the land to which the mobile home was attached was sold at a sheriff's sale to Langelier and Corbeil.

The bank then sought to foreclose on its lien (that is, to have the home sold) and to receive the proceeds of the sale free of any interest that Langelier and Corbeil might have in the home or its proceeds. The trial court ruled that the mobile home had become a "fixture" within the meaning of Article 9 of the UCC, and that since the bank's interest was not perfected as required by Sec. 9-401, the bank's interest was *subordinate to* the rights of Langelier and Corbeil. Was the judge correct? Why or why not? (*Barnett Bank of Clearwater N.A. v. Rompon,* 377 So.2d 981, 1979.)

**8.** On October 9, 1984, World Financial Services, Inc. (debtor) filed a Chapter 11 bankruptcy petition. Within 90 days before this filing, the debtor paid $18,347.82 to Sanyo Electric, Inc. The bankruptcy trustee claimed that this was an improper "preference" because Sanyo was an unsecured creditor, and sued to recover the funds from Sanyo. Sanyo produced a security agreement and financing statement, both naming "Margaret Howe dba Bargain Furn/World Finance" as debtor. Is this description sufficient? (*In re World Financial Services Center, Inc.,* 78 Bankr. 239, Bkrtcy.App. Panel, 9th Cir. 1987.)

**9.** Plaintiff, a trustee in bankruptcy, claims that defendant Salina Coffee House, Inc.'s security interest is unperfected because the financing statement and accompanying documents reflected the debtor's trade name "Hilton Inn" instead of its general partnership's legal name, "Beacon Realty Investment Co." Is the trustee correct? (*Pearson v. Salina Coffee House, Inc.,* 1 U.C.C.Rep.Serv.2d 584, D.Kan. 1986.)

**10.** Valley Bank had a general security interest in "all equipment" of a debtor, Curtis Press. Rockwell International Credit Corp. had a purchase money security interest in a particular item of equipment acquired by the debtor. Both security interests were duly perfected in Idaho, but the debtor moved the equipment to Wyoming and then defaulted on both obligations. Neither creditor reperfected its interest in Wyoming. Valley Bank eventually took possession of the equipment. Whose interest should have priority? (*Rockwell International Credit Corp. v. Valley Bank,* 707 P.2d 517, Idaho App. 1985.)

# CHAPTER 30

# BANKRUPTCY

## OVERVIEW OF DEBTOR–CREDITOR RELATIONS

The treatment of debtors has varied greatly over the years. During certain early periods, debtors were forced to become servants of their creditors, were thrown into prison, or even had body parts removed for failure to pay a debt. History finally demonstrated to both creditors and society that very little was accomplished by such methods. In seeking more humane solutions, the general problem has been how to balance the creditor's rights with the debtor's desire for relief from debts.

Numerous devices have been developed through the years for resolving debtor-creditor disputes. In this chapter we will deal primarily with one such procedure—*bankruptcy under federal law.* However, many of the other methods available under state common-law principles, state statutes, and private agreements may actually be preferable to bankruptcy when it is possible to use them. Bankruptcy has traditionally been viewed as an avenue of last resort. Before we turn to a detailed examination of the federal bankruptcy law, we first will survey some of the alternatives.

## *Alternatives to Bankruptcy*

Although time and space do not permit a detailed analysis of each method of debt resolution, the following methods are frequently used when a debtor cannot pay his or her obligation: (1) foreclosure on a real estate mortgage, (2) enforcement of a secured transaction (Article 9 of the UCC), (3) enforcement of an artisan's lien, (4) enforcement of a mechanic's lien, (5) writ of execution on a judgment, (6) garnishment, (7) attachment, (8) receivership, (9) cancelling a fraudulent conveyance, (10) composition of creditors, and (11) assignment for the benefit of creditors.

**Foreclosure on a Real Estate Mortgage:** When a mortgagor (debtor) defaults under the terms of a mortgage agreement, the mortgagee (creditor) has the right to declare the entire mortgage debt due and enforce his or her rights through a remedy called **foreclosure.** In most states the mortgagee is required to sell the mortgaged real estate (even if it is the person's homestead) under the direction of the court, using the proceeds to pay the foreclosure costs and the balance of the debt. If any proceeds are left over, the surplus goes to the mortgagor. If the proceeds are insufficient to cover the costs of foreclosure and the remaining indebtedness, the mortgagor is liable to the mortgagee for the unpaid balance of the debt. However, before the actual foreclosure sale and for a certain period of time thereafter (set by state statute), the mortgagor can *redeem* the property by full payment of costs, indebtedness, and interest.

**Enforcement of a Secured Transaction:** As we saw in the last chapter, under Article 9 of the UCC, when a debtor defaults on the security agreement made with a secured party (the creditor), the collateral (personal property) that is the subject of the security agreement can be used to satisfy the debt. The secured party can retain possession of the collateral or take it from the debtor, either by court order or without court action if it can be accomplished peaceably. He or she can then either (1) *keep the collateral* in satisfaction of the debt by giving proper notice to the debtor of such intention (assuming the debtor does not object), or (2) *sell the collateral* through a "commercially reasonable" process. The secured party must always sell the collateral if proper

465

objection is made by the debtor to the party keeping it or if the collateral is classified as "consumer goods" and the debtor has paid 60 percent or more of the debt.

If the collateral is kept by the secured party, the debt is discharged. If the collateral is sold and the proceeds are insufficient to pay the debt and the costs of enforcing the security interest, the secured party is usually entitled to seek a deficiency judgment for the balance. The debtor can redeem the collateral at any time until its sale or disposal.

**Enforcement of an Artisan's Lien:** The **artisan's lien,** a possessory lien given to creditors who perform services on personal property or take care of goods entrusted to them, was developed at common law. If the debtor does not pay for the services, the creditor is permitted to obtain a judgment and/or to foreclose and sell the property in satisfaction of the debt. Any proceeds remaining from the sale of the property after paying the debt and costs of sale must be returned to the debtor. In order to exercise this lien, the creditor must have retained possession of the property and must not have agreed to provide the services on credit. Many states have passed statutes governing the procedures to be followed in enforcing such a lien. If the creditor operates a warehouse and the claim arises from unpaid storage charges, the procedures which must be followed are set forth in Article 7 of the Uniform Commercial Code.

**Enforcement of a Mechanic's Lien:** Certain other liens have been made available to creditors by state statutes. One of the most common is the **mechanic's lien**—a lien against real estate for labor, services, or materials used in improving the realty. When the labor or materials are furnished, a debt is incurred. To make the real property itself security for the debt, the creditor must file a notice of lien in a manner provided by statute. To be effective, it usually must be filed within a specified period (usually 60 to 120 days) after the last materials or labor were furnished. If the notice is properly filed and the debt is not paid, the creditor can foreclose and sell the realty in satisfaction of the debt. (This is similar to a foreclosure of a real estate mortgage.)

**Writ of Execution on a Judgment:** Once a debt becomes overdue, a creditor can file suit for payment in a court of law and, if successful, be awarded a "judgment." If the judgment is not satisfied by the debtor, the creditor has the right to go back to court and obtain a **writ of execution.** The writ, issued by the clerk of the court, directs the sheriff or other officer to levy upon (seize) and sell any of the debtor's *nonexempt property* within the court's jurisdiction. The judgment is paid from the proceeds of the sale, and any balance is returned to the debtor. One limitation on the writ is that it can be levied only on nonexempt property. That is, exempt property, such as the debtor's homestead, cannot be taken to satisfy the judgment.

**Garnishment:** Another limitation of the writ of execution is that it usually cannot reach debts owed to the judgment debtor by third parties or the debtor's interests in personal property legally possessed by third parties. However, the law does permit the creditor (using the proper court procedure) to require these persons to turn over to the court or sheriff money owed or property belonging to the debtor. This method of satisfying a judgment is called **garnishment;** the third party, called the *garnishee,* is legally bound by the court order. The most common types of "property" garnished are wages and bank accounts. The federal Consumer Credit Protection Act limits garnishment of a debtor's current wages to 25 percent of take-home pay, and prohibits the debtor's employer from discharging him or her because of garnishment for "any one indebtedness." Some state laws place greater restrictions on garnishment of wages.

**Attachment:** The seizing of a debtor's property under a court order, known as *attachment,* is a statutory remedy and can be exercised only in strict accordance with the provisions of the particular state statutes. It is available to a creditor even *before* a judgment has been rendered, under some statutes. Statutory grounds for attachment prior to judgment are limited, usually including situations where the debtor is unavailable to be served with a summons or where there is a reasonable belief that the debtor may conceal or remove property from the jurisdiction of the court before the creditor can obtain a judgment.

To employ attachment as a remedy, the creditor must file with the court an affidavit attesting to the debtor's default and the legal reasons why attachment is sought. Additionally, the creditor must post a bond sufficient to cover at least the value of the debtor's property, the value of the loss of use of the goods suffered by the debtor (if any), and court costs in case the creditor loses the suit. Most states require the opportunity for some form of hearing before a judge. The court then issues a *writ of attachment,* directing the sheriff or other officer to seize nonexempt property sufficient to satisfy the creditor's claim. If the creditor's suit against the debtor is successful, the property seized can then be sold to satisfy the judgment.

**Receivership:** Attachment may prove inadequate to protect creditors while they pursue their claims if the debtor's property requires care (such as crops, livestock, etc.). In such cases, on essentially the same grounds as for attachment, the court may appoint a *receiver* to care for and preserve the property pending the outcome of the lawsuit in which one or more creditors are seeking to collect unpaid debts. It is then said that the debtor's property is placed in **receivership.** The object of receivership is to prevent a debtor from "wasting" assets while being pursued by creditors. Receivership may also be the appropriate protective device where the debtor has a going business and where creditors can convince the court that it is being grossly mismanaged.

**Cancelling a Fraudulent Conveyance:** A debtor may transfer property to a third party by gift or contract under circumstances in which his or her creditors are defrauded. If such fraud can be established, any creditor can have the conveyance (transfer) set aside and the property made subject to his or her claim—even if the property is in the hands of a third party.

The fraud necessary to have a conveyance set aside can be either fraud in fact or fraud implied in law. **Fraud in fact** occurs when a debtor transfers property with the specific intent of defrauding his or her creditors. A creditor will usually encounter difficulty in having a conveyance voided on this ground, simply because of the inherent problems in proving fraudulent intent. The creditor's chances of proving this intent will, however, be somewhat greater if the transfer was to the debtor's spouse or other relative. In addition, it is often the case that the debtor actually had no such fraudulent intent, but the creditor is harmed nevertheless.

To assist the creditor, most states have enacted laws (such as the Uniform Fraudulent Conveyance Act) which create a *presumption* of fraud under certain circumstances. This means that, in some situations, the burden of proof shifts to the debtor. If the debtor fails to prove the absence of fraud, there is **fraud implied in law** and the transfer is voided. Generally speaking, these statutes create a presumption of fraud whenever a debtor transfers property without receiving "fair consideration" in return and the debtor has insufficient assets remaining to satisfy creditors.

**Composition of Creditors:** Sometimes a debtor or his or her creditors recognize early (before bankruptcy) that the debtor is in financial difficulty. Instead of pursuing remedies under bankruptcy, the debtor and creditors make a *contract* to resolve the debts. The contract—referred to as a **composition of creditors**—calls for the debtor's immediate payment of a sum less than that owed and for the creditor's immediate discharge of the debt. This payment can be made from any of the debtor's assets, including exempt property. Such contracts are held to be binding by the courts. The advantage of an immediate payment and minimum costs makes the composition attractive to creditors. Whether the composition agreement is binding on nonparticipating creditors depends on state law. At common law the agreement was not binding on these creditors.

**Assignment for the Benefit of Creditors:** Under common-law principles and, in some states, under statute, an **assignment for the benefit of creditors** is available as an alternative to bankruptcy. In such an arrangement, the debtor voluntarily transfers title to some or all assets to a "trustee" or "assignee" for the creditors' benefit. By such a transfer, the debtor irrevocably gives up any claim to or control over the property. The trustee or assignee liquidates (sells) the property and makes payment to the creditors on a pro rata basis according to the debt amounts.

Creditors can either accept or reject the partial payment. One accepting such a payment may in effect be releasing the balance of his or her claim. In most states, creditors who do not participate in the assignment cannot reach the assets that have been so assigned. They do, however, have rights to any surplus remaining after participating creditors have been paid, any nonexempt property not assigned, and any nonexempt property acquired after the assignment. Nonparticipating creditors may also be able to force the debtor into bankruptcy.

# BANKRUPTCY PROCEEDINGS

## History of Bankruptcy Statutes

Bankruptcy as a legal device was initially applied only to commercial business failures. The first Bankruptcy Act in England was adopted in 1542 and applied only to traders or merchants who were unable to pay their debts. It was not until 1861 that bankruptcy was extended to other types of debtors.

The founders of the United States were well acquainted with the problems of debtors. In drafting the U.S. Constitution they stated in Article I, Section 8, clause 4: "The Congress shall have the power . . . to establish . . . uniform laws on the subject of bankruptcies throughout the United States."

## Bankruptcy Proceedings Today

Today's bankruptcy law comes primarily from the 1978 Bankruptcy Reform Act, also known as the Bankruptcy Code. The Code has been amended several times since 1978; our discussion will include those changes. Before 1978, federal district courts handled bankruptcy cases, often delegating the responsibility for hearing them to "bankruptcy referees" who were not federal judges but who performed many of the same functions. The 1978 Code established a set of bankruptcy courts, with one such court in each federal district. Bankruptcy judges are complemented by U.S. Trustees who, as we shall see, usually select the trustees who administer the debtors' estates.

Bankruptcy courts hear and decide all of the issues directly involving the bankruptcy proceeding itself, but related nonbankruptcy matters, such as a tort claim by or against the debtor, are decided by the federal district court. An appeal from a bankruptcy court decision is heard by a federal district court or, under certain conditions, by a bankruptcy appellate panel.

As we noted earlier, bankruptcy has traditionally been a solution of last resort. Despite this fact, thousands of cases are filed each year under the federal bankruptcy law. The large number of cases is not, however, the only reason for the importance of modern bankruptcy law. Many people have their only direct exposure to our legal system in bankruptcy proceedings. In bankruptcy court debtors and creditors alike find final, if not totally satisfactory, conclusions to disputes that may have seemed endless. In bankruptcy court businesses of all sizes are liquidated or rehabilitated, often affecting the livelihoods of many employees, the security of suppliers and customers, and even the economies of local communities.

The 1978 Code provides for three different kinds of proceedings: (1) liquidation; (2) reorganization; and (3) adjustment of the debts of an individual with regular income. The Family Farmer Bankruptcy Act of 1986 includes an additional kind of proceeding, a separate chapter in the Bankruptcy Code which provides adjustment of debts for family farmers. Our discussion focuses primarily on the liquidation proceeding, often referred to as "straight bankruptcy," because it is the most common type. We will, however, devote some attention to the other three types of proceedings at the end of this chapter. It should also be noted that current bankruptcy law contains a special section dealing with the rehabilitation of bankrupt *municipalities*, which is beyond the scope of our discussion.

# LIQUIDATION PROCEEDINGS

Stated very generally, the object of a **liquidation proceeding** under Chapter 7 of the Bankruptcy Act is to sell the debtor's assets, pay off creditors insofar as it is possible to do so, and legally discharge the debtor from further responsibility.

## Commencement of the Proceedings

A liquidation proceeding will be either a *voluntary case,* commenced by the debtor, or an *involuntary case,* commenced by creditors.

**Voluntary Case:** The filing of a **voluntary case** automatically subjects the debtor and its property to the jurisdiction and supervision of the Bankruptcy Court. Any debtor, whether an individual, a partnership, or a corporation, may file a petition for voluntary bankruptcy, with the following exceptions: (1) banks, (2) savings and loan associations, (3) credit unions, (4) insurance companies, (5) railroads, and (6) governmental bodies. These exempted organizations are covered by special statutes and their liquidation is supervised by particular regulatory agencies.

A debtor does *not* have to be insolvent in order to file a petition for voluntary bankruptcy, but as a practical matter it is usually insolvency that prompts such a petition.[1] In addition, a husband and wife may file a joint case if both consent.

**Involuntary Case:** The types of organizations which are not permitted to file a voluntary liquidation case also cannot be subjected to an **involuntary case.** In addition to these exemptions, creditors also cannot file an involuntary case against *farmers,*[2] *family farmers,*[3] or *nonprofit corporations.*

If the debtor has twelve or more creditors, at least three must join in filing the case. If there are fewer than twelve creditors, the involuntary case may be filed by one or more of them. Regardless of the number of creditors, those filing the petition must have noncontingent unsecured claims against the debtor totalling in the aggregate at least $5,000.

The debtor and its property automatically become subject to the jurisdiction and supervision of the bankruptcy court if the involuntary petition is not challenged. However, if the debtor contests the creditors' petition, they must prove either (1) that the debtor has not been paying debts as they became due or (2) that the debtor's property has been placed in a receivership or an assignment for the benefit of creditors within 120 days before the involuntary petition was filed. If the filing creditors prove either of the above, the debtor and its property are then under the supervision of the court. If no such proof is made, the petition is dismissed.

**Automatic Stay:** As soon as the petition is filed in either a voluntary or involuntary case, an automatic stay is in operation. The automatic stay puts creditors' claims "on hold" until they are dealt with in the bankruptcy proceeding, and prevents creditors from taking any judicial, administrative, or other action against the debtor. A *secured creditor,* however, may petition the bankruptcy court and receive protection against the loss of its security. The court-ordered protection for secured creditors may take the form of cash payments from the debtor, substitute collateral, or an express grant of relief from the automatic stay permitting foreclosure of the security interest.

## *The Trustee*

After the debtor becomes subject to the bankruptcy proceeding, the U.S. Trustee must appoint an **interim trustee** to take over the debtor's property or business. A U.S. Trustee is appointed in each of 29 regions (consisting of one or more judicial districts) to monitor certain aspects of bankruptcy cases and to appoint and supervise the standing and panel trustees. Within a relatively short time thereafter, a **permanent trustee** will take over. This trustee may be elected by the creditors, but if they do not do so, the interim trustee receives permanent status.

The trustee is an individual or corporation who, under the court's supervision, administers and represents the *debtor's estate.* (Which property is included within the debtor's estate is discussed later.) The basic duties of the trustee are to: (1) investigate the financial affairs of the debtor; (2) collect assets and claims owned by the debtor; (3) temporarily operate the debtor's business if necessary; (4) reduce the debtor's assets to cash; (5) receive and examine the claims of creditors, and challenge in bankruptcy court any claim which the trustee feels to be questionable; (6) oppose the debtor's discharge from its obligations when the trustee feels that there are legal reasons why the debtor should not be discharged; (7) render a detailed accounting to the court of all assets received and the disposition made of them; and (8) make a final report to the court when administration of the debtor's estate is completed. To fulfill these duties as representative of the debtor's estate, the trustee has the power to sue and be sued in that capacity, to use or sell property of the estate, and to employ accountants, attorneys, appraisers, auctioneers, and other professionals with court approval.

If they wish, unsecured creditors may elect a creditors' committee of three to eleven members for the purpose of consulting with the trustee. This com-

---

[1] Insolvency is defined in the federal bankruptcy law as the financial condition of a debtor whose debts exceed the fair market value of assets. The definition of insolvency under state law, as set forth in UCC Sec. 1-201(23), is broader. It states that a debtor is insolvent in the above situation *or* when the debtor "fails to pay his debts in the ordinary course of business or cannot pay his debts as they become due."

[2] Farmers other than in the term "family farmers" are defined as persons (which includes individuals, partnerships, or corporations) who received more than 80 percent of their gross income during the preceding taxable year from farming operations owned and operated by them. "Farming operations" includes growing crops, dairy farming, and raising livestock or poultry.

[3] The term "family farmers," important since the 1986 amendment to the Code, is defined later in this chapter.

mittee may make recommendations to the trustee or U.S. Trustee regarding the latter's duties and may submit questions to the court or U.S. Trustee concerning administration of the debtor's estate.

## Creditors' Meetings

Within a reasonable time after commencement of the case, the U.S. Trustee must call and preside at a meeting of unsecured creditors. The debtor will have already supplied the court with a list of creditors, so that they may be notified of the meeting. The judge of the bankruptcy court is not permitted to attend a creditors' meeting.

At the first meeting, creditors may elect the trustee. In order for such election to be possible, at least 20 percent of the total amount of unsecured claims which have been filed and allowed must be represented at the meeting. A trustee is elected by receiving the votes of creditors holding a majority, in amount, of unsecured claims represented at the meeting.

The other major item of business at the first creditors' meeting is an *examination of the debtor.* The debtor, under oath, will be questioned by the creditors and the trustee concerning (1) the debtor's assets, and (2) matters relevant to whether the debtor will be entitled to a discharge.

## Duties of the Debtor

The bankruptcy law imposes the following duties on the debtor: (1) within a reasonable time after commencement of the proceedings, file with the court a list of creditors, a schedule of assets and liabilities, a schedule of income and expenditures, and a statement of financial affairs; (2) file with the court a statement of intention with respect to the retention or surrender of any property of the estate which secures consumer debt, specifying that such property shall be claimed as exempt, redeemed, or the debt reaffirmed thereon, and perform these intentions within 45 days after filing the notice; (3) cooperate and respond truthfully during the examination conducted at the first creditors' meeting; (4) surrender to the trustee all property to be included in the debtor's estate, as well as all documents, books, and records pertaining to this property; (5) cooperate with the trustee in whatever way necessary to enable the trustee to perform his or her duties; and (6) appear at the hearing conducted by the court concerning whether the debtor should be discharged.

A debtor who fails to fulfill any of these duties may be denied a discharge from liabilities.

## The Debtor's Estate

**Types of Property:** The property owned by the debtor which becomes subject to the bankruptcy proceeding, ultimately to be sold by the trustee, is the **debtor's estate.** This includes all tangible and intangible property interests of any kind, unless specifically exempted. For example, the estate could consist of consumer goods, inventory, equipment, any of the various types of interests in real estate, patent rights, trademarks, copyrights, accounts receivable, and various contract rights.

**After-Acquired Property:** In addition to property owned at the time the bankruptcy petition (either voluntary or involuntary) was filed, the debtor's estate also includes after-acquired property under some circumstances. Specifically, the estate includes any type of property which the debtor acquires, or becomes entitled to acquire, within 180 days after the petition filing date (1) by inheritance, (2) as a beneficiary of a life insurance policy, or (3) as a result of a divorce decree or a property settlement agreement with the debtor's spouse. And, of course, if a particular item of property is part of the estate, any proceeds, income, production, or offspring from it will also be part of the estate. However, the debtor's earnings from his or her own labor or personal service after the filing date are *not* included in the estate.

**Exemptions:** A debtor who is an individual (rather than a partnership or corporation) may claim certain **exemptions.** This means that certain types of property are *exempt* and are not included in the debtor's estate. The debtor may keep such property and still receive a discharge from liabilities at the close of the proceedings. Every state has exemption statutes setting forth the types of property which are exempt from seizure under a writ of execution. Before passage of the 1978 Bankruptcy Code, the debtor's exempt property in a federal bankruptcy case was determined solely by the exemption statutes of the state where he or she lived. The 1978 Code, however, included for the first time a list of federal exemptions which are available to the debtor in bankruptcy regardless of the state of domicile.

Under the 1978 Code the debtor may claim the following exemptions (and *each* spouse may claim them in a joint case): (1) the debtor's interest in a homestead used as a residence, up to a value of $7,500; (2) the debtor's interest in a motor vehicle, up to $1,200; (3) the debtor's interest, up to $200 *per item,* in household furnishings, appliances, wearing apparel, animals, crops, or musical instruments which are owned primarily for personal, family, or household (nonbusiness) uses, subject to a total of $4,000 for all such items; (4) the debtor's interest in jewelry, up to a total of $500, which is owned primarily for personal, family, or household uses; (5) the debtor's interest in any kind of property, up to a limit of $400; (6) any unused portion of the $7,500 homestead exemption, subject to a limit of $3,750; (7) the debtor's interest in implements, tools, or professional books used in his or her trade, not to exceed $750 in value; (8) any unmatured life insurance policies owned by the debtor (except for credit life policies); (9) professionally prescribed health aids; (10) the debtor's right to receive various government benefits, such as unemployment compensation, social security, and veteran's benefits; (11) the debtor's right to receive various private benefits, such as alimony, child support, and pension payments, to the extent reasonably necessary for support of the debtor or the debtor's dependents; and (12) the right to receive damage awards for bodily injury.

Unfortunately, the 1978 Code has not brought about a great deal of national uniformity in the exemptions given to bankrupt debtors, for two reasons. First, the Code also includes a provision permitting the debtor to choose either the federal exemptions or those of the state where the debtor lives.[4] Because some state exemption laws are more advantageous than the federal exemptions for certain debtors, disparate state exemption laws continue to be important in federal bankruptcy cases. Second, Congress further stated in the 1978 Code that any state legislature can prohibit debtors in that state from using the federal exemptions in a bankruptcy case. The legislatures in a majority of states have done so; in these states, bankrupt debtors must use the state exemptions.

The debtor also has the power to avoid a lien on his exempt property if such lien is a judicial lien or a nonpossessory, nonpurchase-money security interest in personal-use goods, tools of the trade, or health aids. This preserves used, essential personal items for the debtor which were taken as collateral in order to threaten repossession rather than for their resale value.

Even though bankruptcy proceedings are governed by federal law, the ownership interests of a bankrupt debtor in particular items of property ordinarily are determined by *state* law. On the other hand, if a principle of state law conflicts with the overall purposes of the Bankruptcy Code, the state rule will not be applied.

---

[4]The debtor must choose one or the other, as a whole; there cannot be a selection of some exemptions from the federal law and some from a state law.

---

***In re* Atchison**
U.S. Bankruptcy Court, S.D. Ill.,
101 Bankr. Rptr. 556 (1989)

On April 16, 1987, less than three months before filing her bankruptcy petition, debtor Anola Atchison executed a disclaimer of inheritance of property given to her under the will of her deceased father. As a result of this disclaimer, the property passed to debtor's children, Darrell Atchison and Debra Bedard. On July 8, 1987, debtor and her husband filed a joint petition in bankruptcy under Chapter 7. The bankruptcy trustee sued the debtor and her children (defendants) asking the court to rule that the inheritance was part of the bankrupt debtor's estate.

**Decision:** Judgment was for the debtor; the property was not part of the estate. Prebankruptcy transfers may be set aside as fraudulent transfers under Sec. 548(a). However, under state law (which governs the disclaimer), disclaimers are retroactive,

*(continued)*

relating back to when the gift was made. Therefore, this property never vested in the debtor and her disclaimer was not a "transfer" under state law. The Illinois rule is that a person does not have to accept an estate against his or her will, and this policy overrides fairness to creditors. Note, however, that there is a specific Bankruptcy Code provision that would have led to a different result had the disclaimer occurred *after* the filing of the bankruptcy petition. ■

## Voidable Transfers

In a number of circumstances, the trustee has the power to sue and restore to the debtor's estate property or funds which the debtor (or someone acting in the debtor's behalf) had transferred to some third party. These situations, called **voidable transfers,** are as follows:

1. The trustee generally may cancel any transfer of property of the debtor's estate which was made *after* the debtor became subject to the bankruptcy proceeding. The trustee must exercise this power within two years after the transfer was made, or before the bankruptcy case is concluded, whichever occurs first.

2. The trustee may cancel any *fraudulent transfer* made by the debtor within one year prior to the filing of the bankruptcy petition. This power of the trustee applies to both *fraud in fact* and *fraud implied in law,* as discussed earlier in the chapter. It will be remembered that insolvency is an element of fraud implied in law. In determining the fair value of assets for this purpose under the bankruptcy law, exempt property and the property transferred in the particular transaction being challenged are not included.

3. The trustee has the power to cancel a property transfer on any ground that the debtor could have used, such as fraud, mistake, duress, undue influence, incapacity, or failure of consideration.

## Voidable Preferences

One of the fundamental objectives of the bankruptcy law is to insure equal treatment of most types of unsecured creditors. The primary reason why we are so concerned with equal treatment of creditors, of course, is that a bankrupt debtor's assets are usually sufficient to pay only a fraction of creditors' total claims. As a result of this concern, the trustee has the power to cancel any transfer by the debtor to a creditor which amounted to a **preference.** A preference is essentially a transfer of property or money, in payment of an existing debt, which causes that creditor to receive more of the debtor's estate than he or she would be entitled to receive in the bankruptcy proceeding had the transfer not occurred.

**General Rules for Cancelling Preferences:** In the ordinary situation, a preferential transfer to a creditor can be cancelled by the trustee, and the property or funds returned to the debtor's estate, if (1) it occurred within *90 days* prior to the filing of the bankruptcy petition, and (2) the debtor was *insolvent* at the time of the transfer. In this situation, however, insolvency is *presumed.* In other words, if a creditor has received a preferential transfer within the 90-day period prior to the filing of the bankruptcy petition, that creditor must prove that the debtor was *not* insolvent.

**Insiders:** If the creditor receiving the preference was an **insider,** the trustee's power of cancellation extends to any such transfer made within *one year* before the bankruptcy petition was filed. In general, an insider is an individual or business firm which had a close relationship with the debtor at the time of the transfer. Examples would include a relative or partner of the debtor, a corporation of which the debtor was a director or officer, or a director or officer of a corporate debtor. In such a case, however, the presumption of insolvency only applies to the 90 days prior to the petition filing. Therefore, if the preference being challenged by the trustee had taken place more than 90 days but less than a year before the petition filing, the trustee must prove that the debtor was insolvent. Figure 30.1 illustrates the rules for cancelling preferences to insiders and other creditors.

**Exceptions:** In certain circumstances, a payment or transfer to a creditor cannot be cancelled even though it meets the basic requirements of a voidable preference. Three of the most important exceptions are:

**Figure 30.1 Trustee's Recovery of Voidable Preference**

```
    ┌──────────────────┐
    │ Preferential transfer │
    │ to insider can be set │
    │ aside if it occurred │
    │ while the debtor     │
    │ was insolvent.       │
    └──────────────────┘

    ⎯⎯⎯⎯⎯⎯⎯⎯⎯⎯⎯⎯⎯⎯⎯⎯
        No presumption
         of insolvency          ⎯⎯ Presumption ⎯⎯
                                    of insolvency
    |⎯⎯⎯⎯⎯⎯⎯⎯⎯⎯⎯⎯⎯|⎯⎯⎯⎯⎯⎯⎯⎯⎯⎯⎯⎯⎯⎯⎯⎯|
    1 year              90 days              Petition
                                              filed

                      ┌──────────────────┐
                      │ Preferential transfer │
                      │ to any creditor      │
                      │ can be set aside if  │
                      │ it occurred while the│
                      │ debtor was insolvent.│
                      │                      │
                      │ Major exceptions:    │
                      │ 1. Contemporaneous   │
                      │    transaction       │
                      │ 2. Certain debts     │
                      │    incurred and      │
                      │    paid in the       │
                      │    ordinary course   │
                      │    of business       │
                      │ 3. Payment of        │
                      │    consumer debt     │
                      │    up to $600        │
                      └──────────────────┘
```

1. A transaction which involved a "contemporaneous" (that is, within a very short period of time) exchange between debtor and creditor cannot be cancelled by the trustee. For example, the debtor may have bought goods from the creditor and either paid for them immediately or within a few days. This type of transaction is treated differently than one in which the debtor was paying off a debt which had existed for some time. Such a contemporaneous exchange will be left standing even though it occurred during the 90-day period prior to the filing date.

2. Even though there is no contemporaneous exchange, a payment or transfer to a creditor within the 90-day period will not be cancelled if (1) the particular debt had been incurred by the debtor in the ordinary course of business, (2) the payment was made in the ordinary course of the debtor's business, and (3) the payment was made according to ordinary business terms. An example would be the debtor's payment, during the 90-day period, of the previous month's utility bill.

3. A debtor's repayment during the 90-day period of up to $600 in *consumer debt* is not treated as a voidable preference.

Voidable preferences can occur in an almost infinite variety of circumstances. The following case illustrates one such situation, and also shows one of the many reasons why it is so important for a creditor to obtain and perfect a security interest whenever possible.

---

*In re* **Fisher**
U.S. Bankruptcy Court, S.D. Ohio,
100 Bankr. Rptr. 351 (1989)

Defendant Almiro Fur Fashion Design ("Almiro") was a furrier who supplied furs to Kinston Lee Furriers when it was formerly owned and operated by debtor Julius Fisher under an arrangement giving Fisher the right to return unsold furs. As we saw in Chapter 21 concerning sales of goods, a "sale or return" is a sale transaction in which the buyer has a right to return the items to the seller within an agreed time period. A true sale or return actually transfers title to the buyer until a particular article is returned. In contrast, a "sale on approval" is a transaction in which the buyer has an agreed period of time to decide whether to keep the goods, with no title passing until the expiration of that time or until the buyer affirmatively indicates a desire to keep them. In other words, a sale on approval is a "consignment," the supplier being the "consignor" and the one holding them being the "consignee." A consignee is merely an agent for the purpose of selling the principal's goods, and owns no interest in them. When a right of return exists and the parties have not specified whether it is a sale or return or a sale on approval, the UCC provides that it usually is a "sale or return" if the goods are taken by the buyer for the

*(continued)*

purpose of resale, and a sale on approval if they are taken by the buyer for the purpose of use.

Under this arrangement with Almiro, Fisher received and held several mink coats ("Minks") having an approximate total wholesale value of $11,155. Almiro did not take a security interest in the Minks. Fisher returned the Minks to Almiro. Less than three months later, Fisher filed a voluntary petition under Chapter 7 of the Bankruptcy Code. The bankruptcy trustee (plaintiff) claimed that Fisher's return of the Minks to Almiro was a voidable preference and filed a complaint against Fisher (defendant) seeking to have the value of the Minks restored to the bankrupt debtor's estate.

---

**Decision:** Judgment was for the trustee; the transfers of the Minks are subject to avoidance. Under Sec. 547(b), the trustee may avoid any transfer of an interest of the debtor in property if several elements (benefit to creditor, on account of antecedent debt, made while debtor was insolvent, made within 90 days before filing of petition), such that creditor would receive more than if transfer had not been made, are present. All elements appear to be met here, but Almiro claims it was not a creditor of Fisher and that no transfer of the Minks occurred because Fisher had no property interest in the Minks. The essence of Almiro's claim is that the shipment of the Minks was "for the sole purpose of consigning the goods to [Fisher] for inspection only." Under UCC 2-326, because the Minks were delivered to Fisher primarily for resale and Fisher could return them to Almiro for credit even if they conformed to the contract, this transaction was a *sale or return*. Under 2-326(b), goods held on a sale or return basis are subject to the claims of the buyer's creditors while in the buyer's possession unless compliance with one of the provisions of subsection (c) of 2-326 is shown. Almiro did not comply with any of these. Most specifically, Almiro did not establish that Fisher was generally known by his creditors to be substantially engaged in the sale of goods belonging to others nor did Almiro file a security interest in accordance with Article 9. ■

---

## *Claims*

As a general rule, any legal obligation of the debtor existing pre-petition gives rise to a claim against the debtor's estate in the bankruptcy proceeding. There are, however, several special situations we should mention.

1. If the claim is *contingent* on the happening or nonhappening of some future event or, if its *amount is in dispute*, the bankruptcy court has the power to make an estimate of the claim's value.

2. If the claim against the debtor is for breach of contract, it will include any damages which accrued prior to the filing of the bankruptcy petition, and also those damages attributable to the debtor's failure to perform any future obligations under the contract. Of course, this is no different from an ordinary breach of contract claim when bankruptcy is not involved. However, under the bankruptcy law, if the claim arises out of an *employment contract* or a *real estate lease*, limits are placed on a claim for damages relating to future nonperformance. In the case of an employment contract, such damages are limited to a term of *one year* from the filing date or the date the contract was repudiated, whichever is earlier. In the case of a real estate lease, damages are limited to either *one year* or *15 percent* of the remaining term of the lease, whichever is greater, up to a maximum of *three years*. The starting point for measuring this time is the same as for employment contracts. One reason for these limits is that contracts of these two types are frequently long-term ones, and the farther in the future we try to compute damages, the more speculative they get.

3. A creditor who has received a voidable transfer or preference may not assert a claim of any kind until the wrongfully received property or funds are returned to the debtor's estate.

Subject to the above limitations, any claim filed with the bankruptcy court is allowed unless it is contested by an interested party, such as the trustee, debtor, or another creditor. If challenged, the court will rule on the claim's validity after pertinent evidence is presented at a hearing held for that purpose. In this regard, claims against the debtor's estate will be subject to any defenses that the debtor could have asserted had there been no bankruptcy. The fact that a claim is allowed, of course, does not mean that the particular creditor will be paid in full; it just means that the creditor has the hope of receiving *something*.

## *Distribution of Debtor's Estate*

A secured creditor—one having a security interest or lien in a specific item of property—can proceed directly against that property for satisfaction of his or her claim. This is true even though the debtor is or is about to become subject to a bankruptcy proceeding. In a sense, then, **secured creditors** have priority over all classes of unsecured creditors (usually referred to as **general creditors**). However, if a portion of a secured creditor's claim is not secured, that portion is treated like any other unsecured claim.

When the trustee has gathered all the assets of the debtor's estate and reduced them to cash, these proceeds will be distributed to unsecured creditors. There are certain unsecured claims which are given priority in this distribution. These claims are paid in full *in the order of their priority,* assuming there are sufficient proceeds available. The following seven classes of debts are listed in order of priority. Each class must be fully paid before the next is entitled to anything. If the available funds are insufficient to satisfy all creditors within a class, payment to creditors in that class is made in proportion to the amounts of their claims.

**1.** First to be paid are all costs and expenses involved in the administration of the bankruptcy proceeding, such as an auctioneer's commission, the trustee's fee, and accountants' and attorneys' fees.

**2.** If the proceeding is an *involuntary* one, the second priority is any expense incurred in the ordinary course of the debtor's business or financial affairs *after* commencement of the case but *before* appointment of the trustee.

**3.** Next is any claim for wages, salaries, or commissions, including vacation, severance, and sick leave pay earned by an individual within 90 days before the filing of the petition or the cessation of the debtor's business, whichever occurs first. This priority, however, is limited to $2,000 per individual.

**4.** The fourth priority is any claim for contributions to an employee benefit plan arising from services performed within 180 days before filing or business cessation. Again the limit is $2,000 per individual. However, a particular individual cannot receive more than $2,000 under the third and fourth priorities combined.

**5.** Fifth are claims of grain producers or U.S. fishermen against a debtor who owns or operates a grain or fish storage facility for the produce or its proceeds, limited to $2,000 for each such individual.

**6.** Next are claims of individuals, up to $900 per person, for deposits made on consumer goods or services that were not received.

**Figure 30.2 Distribution of Debtor's Estate**

**7.** Claims of governmental units for various kinds of taxes, subject to time limits that differ depending on the type of tax, are the last priority.

If all priority claims are paid and funds still remain, general creditors are paid in proportion to the amounts of their claims. Any portion of a priority claim that was beyond the limits of the priority is treated as a general claim. An example would be the amount by which an individual's wage claim exceeded $2,000. Figure 30.2 outlines the process of distributing the debtor's estate.

## *Discharge*

After the debtor's estate has been liquidated and distributed to creditors, the bankruptcy court may conduct a hearing to determine whether the debtor should be discharged from liability for remaining obligations.

**Grounds for Refusal of Discharge:** Under certain circumstances the court will refuse to grant the debtor a **discharge**. These are as follows:

1. Only an *individual* can receive a discharge in a liquidation proceeding. For a corporation to receive a discharge it must go through a reorganization proceeding (discussed later in the chapter), or be dissolved in accordance with state corporation statutes.

2. A debtor will be denied a discharge if he or she had previously received such a discharge within *six years* before the present bankruptcy petition was filed.

3. The debtor will be denied a discharge if he or she has committed any of the following acts: (a) intentionally concealed or transferred assets for the purpose of evading creditors, within one year before the filing of the petition or during the bankruptcy proceedings; (b) concealed, destroyed, falsified, or failed to keep business or financial records unless there was reasonable justification for such action or failure; (c) failed to adequately explain any loss of assets; (d) refused to obey a lawful court order or to answer a material court-approved question in connection with the bankruptcy case; or (e) made any fraudulent statement or claim in connection with the bankruptcy case.

4. If a discharge has been granted, the court may revoke it within one year if it is discovered that the debtor had not acted honestly in connection with the bankruptcy proceeding.

In the following case, creditors of the bankrupt debtor claimed that the debtor should not be discharged from his obligations because he had demonstrated an actual intent to defraud his creditors. The case demonstrates the importance of looking at a debtor's overall pattern of conduct when determining whether he or she has acted fraudulently.

---

### Norwest Bank Nebraska, N.A. v. Tveten
U.S. Eighth Circuit Court of Appeals, 848 F.2d 871 (1988)

Tveten was a 59-year-old physician and sole shareholder of Omar A. Tveten, P.A., a professional corporation. He began investing in real estate, initially quite successfully. Joined by other doctors, Tveten organized ventures that were highly leveraged. Debts were personally guaranteed by Tveten and the other doctors. In mid-1985, Tveten's investments began to sour. Appellees Norwest Bank and Business Development Corporation, and Harold Panuska became creditors of Tveten as a result of his various investment ventures.

Tveten filed a bankruptcy petition on January 7, 1986. Meanwhile, several creditors already had commenced lawsuits against him. Panuska had obtained a $139,657 judgment against him on October 9, 1985. Norwest Bank and Business Development had commenced an action against him but had not obtained a judgment when Tveten filed for bankruptcy. On the date the petition was filed, Tveten owed his creditors close to $19,000,000.

Before filing for bankruptcy, Tveten consulted a lawyer. As part of his prebankruptcy planning, he liquidated almost all of his nonexempt property, converting it into exempt property worth approximately $700,000. This was accomplished through some 17 separate transfers. The nonexempt property he liquidated included land sold to his parents and his brother, respectively, for $70,000 and $75,732 in cash; life insurance policies and annuities with a for-profit company with cash values totalling $96,307.58; his net salary and bonuses of $27,820.91; his KEOGH pension plan and individual retirement fund of $20,487.35; his corporation's profit-sharing plan worth $325,774.51; and a home sold for $50,000. All of the liquidated property was converted into life insurance or annuity contracts with the Lutheran Brotherhood, a fraternal benefit association, which, under Minnesota law, cannot be attached by creditors. Tveten concedes that the purpose of these transfers was to shield his assets from creditors. Minnesota law provides that creditors cannot attach *any* money or other benefits payable by a fraternal benefit association. Unlike most exemption provisions in other states, the Minnesota exemption has no monetary limit. Indeed, under this exemption, Tveten attempted to place $700,000 worth of his property out of his creditors' reach.

The bankruptcy court held that, even if the exemptions were permissible, Tveten had abused the protections permitted a debtor under the Bankruptcy Code. His awareness of Panuska's judgment against him and of several pending lawsuits, his rapidly deteriorating business investments, and his exposure to extensive liability well beyond his ability to pay, all led the court to find that Tveten intended to hinder and delay his creditors. Accordingly, the bankruptcy court denied

*(continued)*

**Tveten a discharge. The federal district court affirmed and Tveten appealed.**

---

**Decision:** The district court's judgment was affirmed. State law governs the right to claim exemptions. Tveten complied with state law. However, federal law governs the right to receive a discharge, and the Bankruptcy Code provides that discharge may be denied under Chapter 7 if the debtor has transferred property "with the intent to hinder, delay, or defraud a creditor" within one year before the date of the filing. Tveten so abused the state law exemptions that allowing a discharge would constitute a "perversion" of the bankruptcy laws. He wanted a "head start" rather than the "fresh start" that bankruptcy law provides. ■

---

**Nondischargeable Debts:** Even if the debtor is granted a general discharge from obligations, there nevertheless are a few types of claims for which he or she will continue to be liable. These **nondischargeable debts** are as follows:

1. Obligations for payment of taxes are not discharged if (a) the particular tax was entitled to a priority in the distribution of the debtor's estate, but was not paid; or (b) a tax return had been required but was not properly filed; or (c) the debtor had willfully attempted to evade the particular tax.

2. Claims arising out of the debtor's fraud, embezzlement, or larceny are not discharged.

3. The debtor is not excused from liability for a willful and malicious tort.

4. Claims for alimony and child support are not discharged.

5. The debtor is not discharged from a claim that he or she failed to list in the bankruptcy case if this failure caused the creditor not to assert the claim in time for it to be allowed.

6. A fine, penalty, or forfeiture payable to a governmental unit, which is neither compensation for actual pecuniary loss nor a tax penalty, is not discharged.

7. A student loan obligation is not dischargeable, unless (a) it is more than five years old, or (b) the debtor can demonstrate that failure to discharge would cause hardship.

8. Any judgments or awards of damages resulting from the debtor's operation of a motor vehicle while legally intoxicated are not dischargeable.

9. Primarily because of credit card abuse by debtors shortly before filing for bankruptcy, two types of *consumer debts* have been made nondischargeable: (a) debts of more than $500 to a particular creditor for *luxury goods or services*, if incurred within 40 days of the order for relief (i.e., the petition); and (b) cash advances totalling more than $1,000 obtained by using a credit card or other open-ended consumer credit arrangement, if incurred within 20 days of the order for relief.

## *Reaffirmation*

Prior to the 1978 Code, a debtor could renew his or her obligation on a debt that had been discharged in bankruptcy simply by expressing a willingness to be bound. This **reaffirmation** required no new consideration by the creditor, but some states did require it to be in writing.

During the course of revising the bankruptcy law, Congress found that many of these reaffirmations were obtained by creditors through the use of coercion or deception. As a result, the new law places significant constraints on the making of a reaffirmation. Specifically, a reaffirmation is not valid unless (1) the bankruptcy court conducted a hearing at which the debtor was fully informed of the consequences of his or her action or the debtor was represented by an attorney who filed an affidavit stating that debtor was fully informed and that the agreement was voluntarily made and does not impose hardship; and (2) the agreement to reaffirm was made *before* the debtor's discharge. In addition, the debtor can rescind the reaffirmation at any time prior to discharge or within 60 days after it is filed with the court.

## BUSINESS REORGANIZATION

If it is felt that reorganization and continuance of a business is feasible and is preferable to liquidation, a petition for reorganization may be filed under Chapter 11 of the 1978 Bankruptcy Code. The reorganization procedure is intended for use by *businesses,* but it does not matter whether the owner of the business is an individual, partnership, or corporation. A **reorganization case** can be either voluntary or involuntary, and the requirements for filing an involuntary case are the same as for a liquidation proceeding. In general, the types of debtors exempted from reorganization proceedings are the same as those exempted from liquidation proceedings. The major difference in coverage is that a railroad *can* be a debtor in a reorganization proceeding. The most important aspects of a reorganization case are summarized below.

**1.** As soon as the petition is filed, an *automatic stay* is in operation just as in a liquidation proceeding. The automatic stay is even more important in a reorganization proceeding, because without such a stay the debtor often would find it impossible to continue operating its business.

**2.** There may or may not be a trustee in a reorganization case. If a trustee is appointed, he or she will take over and will have basically the same duties and powers as in a liquidation case. Essentially, the court will appoint a trustee if requested by an interested party (such as a creditor) and if it appears that such an appointment would be in the best interests of all parties involved. Obviously a trustee will be appointed if the court feels there is a possibility of the debtor's business being mismanaged or assets being wasted or concealed. If a trustee is not appointed, the debtor remains in possession and control of the business. In this situation, the debtor is called the **debtor-in-possession,** and has all the powers of a trustee.

**3.** After commencement of the case, the U.S. Trustee must appoint a committee of unsecured creditors. If necessary, the court or the U.S. Trustee may appoint other creditors' committees to represent the special interests of particular types of creditors. A committee of shareholders may also be appointed to oversee the interests of that group, if the debtor is a corporation.

**4.** The creditors' and shareholders' committees, and the trustee, if one was appointed, will investigate the business and financial affairs of the debtor. A *reorganization plan* will then be prepared and filed with the bankruptcy court. This plan must divide creditors' claims and shareholders' interests into classes according to their type. For instance, claims of employees, secured creditors, bondholders, real estate mortgage holders, and government units might be segregated into different classes. The plan must indicate how claims within each class are going to be handled and to what extent each class will receive less than full payment, as well as provide adequate means for the plan's execution. Treatment of claims within each class must be equal.

**5.** The court will "confirm" (approve) the reorganization plan if (a) each class has approved the plan and (b) the court rules that the plan is "fair and equitable" to all classes. A plan is deemed to be accepted by a class of creditors if it received favorable votes from those representing at least two-thirds of the amount of claims and more than half of the number of creditors within that class. Acceptance by a class of shareholders requires an affirmative vote by those representing at least two-thirds of the shares in that class. If the parties are unable to produce an acceptable plan or if the plan subsequently does not work as expected, the court may either dismiss the case or convert it into a liquidation proceeding.

**6.** After the plan has been confirmed, the debtor is discharged from those claims not provided for in the plan. However, the types of claims that are not discharged in a liquidation case are also not discharged in a reorganization case.

## *Policy Issues in Reorganizations*

The attempt by bankruptcy laws to achieve equity among debtors and creditors has always raised questions of ethics and public policy. Indeed, the provisions of the Bankruptcy Code dealing with voidable preferences, refusal of discharge, and nondischargeable debts have ethical and policy questions at their core. The fact that the 1978 Code no longer requires that a debtor be insolvent to file a voluntary case has made these ethical questions even more important: If it is in the best interest of society to provide relief to an insolvent debtor, how far should public policy go in letting a debtor start afresh when that debtor is financially beleaguered but not insolvent?

Since the enactment of the 1978 Code, which increases the flexibility and acceptability of business reorganization cases, ethical and policy questions have arisen with increasing frequency under Chapter 11 of the Code. Again, there is no insolvency requirement, and the ultimate objective of a reorganization is to permit the debtor to continue as a viable entity. Although the reorganization provisions of Chapter 11 pursue worthwhile goals, the process of reorganization does present opportunities for abuse. As we mentioned previously, if a trustee is not appointed in a reorganization proceeding, the debtor becomes a so-called *debtor-in-possession*, with all the powers of a trustee. Although the exercise of such power obviously is under the supervision of the bankruptcy court, creditors, employee unions, and other groups often are understandably concerned about the actions of the debtor-in-possession. Bankruptcy reorganization is today being successfully utilized by major corporations to defer pre-petition debts in order to improve cash flow for post-petition operating costs, to alter obligations under burdensome labor contracts and underfunded pension plans, and to block products liability litigation.

One of the most important powers of the debtor-in-possession, like a trustee, is the power to *cancel executory contracts.* For a time, there was a question whether a debtor-in-possession could cancel a collective bargaining agreement covering its unionized employees. Unions claimed that a debtor-in-possession should not have the power to cancel collective bargaining agreements because an employer could then use a Chapter 11 reorganization as a "union busting" device. The Supreme Court ruled, however, in *NLRB v. Bildisco & Bildisco,* 465 U.S. 513 (1984), that collective bargaining agreements, like other contracts, can be cancelled by the debtor-in-possession when cancellation is in the best interests of a successful reorganization. Shortly thereafter, Congress amended the law so as to place restrictions on this power. Specifically, Congress provided that the debtor-in-possession (i.e., the employer) must first propose reasonable modifications to the existing union contract. If the union rejects these proposed modifications, the Bankruptcy Court then conducts a hearing to determine whether the union has "good cause" for the rejection. A union has good cause for rejecting the proposed modifications if the employer has failed to prove that the contract changes are "fair and equitable" to all parties and necessary for the company's survival. If it is found that the union does have good cause, the burden is then upon the employer to make further proposals. If the court finds that the union did not have good cause for rejecting a particular proposal for modifying the collective bargaining agreement, the employer then has the power to cancel the agreement and set new employment terms unilaterally. An example of the application of these new provisions is found in *Wheeling-Pittsburgh Steel Corp. v. United Steelworkers of America,* 791 F.2d 1074 (3d Cir. 1986), in which the court concluded that the union had good cause for rejection primarily because the employer based its proposals on a "worst case scenario" that required a one-third wage cut for five years and did not include a "snap back" provision that would increase workers' wages and benefits if the company performed better than expected.

One of the most important effects of the filing of a Chapter 11 bankruptcy is the imposition of the automatic stay. This prohibition of collection efforts with regard to pre-petition debts or any other action against the reorganizing debtor raises various ethical and policy questions. Suppose, for example, that a large, profitable company is faced with a great many claims for injuries allegedly arising from products made by the company. A large number of claims have already been filed, and many others are anticipated in the future, making it necessary for the company to set aside extremely large reserves to cover contingent liabilities. Can the company use a Chapter 11 reorganization proceeding to obtain settlements of these claims in an organized, hopefully uniform fashion? This is the question faced by the court in the following case.

---

### *In re* Johns-Manville Corporation
U.S. Bankruptcy Court, S.D. New York, 36 Bankr. Rptr. 727 (1984)

Johns-Manville Corp. (Manville) was a large, highly successful manufacturing enterprise. It and several other companies were major producers of several products, such as insulation, that contained asbestos. After many people who had been exposed to asbestos for lengthy periods of time developed very serious diseases such as asbestosis and lung cancer, large numbers of lawsuits began to be filed against asbestos producers.

Manville filed a petition for reorganization under Chapter 11 of the Bankruptcy Code, claiming that such filing was made necessary by the "uncontrolled proliferation" of asbestos-related lawsuits. At the time of the court's initial decision in

*(continued)*

the reorganization case, over 16,000 such suits had been filed against Manville. The company stated that its problems were compounded by the "crushing economic burden to be suffered by it over the next 20–30 years by the filing of an even more staggering number of suits by those who had been exposed but who will not manifest the asbestos-related diseases until some time during this future period." In addition, Manville showed that the insurance industry had generally disavowed coverage for asbestos-related claims under products liability insurance policies carried by the company. The question of insurance coverage had been tied up in state court litigation in California for several years.

Several different groups of creditors and asbestos-lawsuit plaintiffs challenged Manville's reorganization petition as inappropriate, and asked that it be dismissed. These groups contended that Manville was a healthy company and was misusing the Bankruptcy Code by attempting to use a reorganization proceeding to resolve products liability claims.

**Decision:** The bankruptcy court denied the motions to dismiss Manville's Chapter 11 petition. Manville was not misusing Chapter 11 by using it to resolve massive products liability claims, many of which were contingent. The objective of Chapter 11 of the Bankruptcy Code is to increase a firm's chances of remaining a viable company, with the benefits to many people that continuation of the business can bring. Manville was not required to wait until its economic picture had deteriorated beyond salvation before filing a Chapter 11 petition. ■

---

The Johns-Manville Corporation bankruptcy was described as "one of the most significant Chapter 11 bankruptcy proceedings" by the circuit court that affirmed confirmation of the reorganization plan on appeal. That plan, which resulted from more than four years of negotiations, is described in the ruling that follows.

### Kane v. Johns-Manville Corp.
U.S. Second Circuit Court of Appeals, 843 F.2d 636 (1988)

The bankruptcy court confirmed Johns-Manville's reorganization plan, and the district court affirmed. Kane, representing 765 "Class-4 creditors"—persons with asbestos-related disease who had filed personal injury suits against Manville prior to Manville's Chapter 11 status—appealed. Kane's primary argument is that the plan does not adequately protect the interests of asbestos victims.

**Decision:** The district court judgment was affirmed. The plan sets up a trust fund with the proceeds from Manville's settlements with insurers, certain cash, receivables, and stock of the reorganized company, long-term notes, and the right to receive 20 percent of Manville's yearly profits for as long as it takes to satisfy all health claims. Trials, arbitration, or mediation will be used to determine whether (and how much) compensatory damages are due the various creditors. Punitive damages are barred. The evidence presented at the confirmation hearing supported the conclusion that the plan provides compensation in a reasonable amount for the claims that are likely to occur. ■

---

## ADJUSTMENT OF DEBTS
### *Of an Individual with Regular Income*

Chapter 13 of the 1978 Code, "Adjustment of Debts of an Individual with Regular Income," provides a method by which an individual can pay his or her debts from future income over an extended period of time. It is intended for use by an individual whose primary income is from salary, wages, or commissions (that is, an employee). There is, however, nothing to prevent a self-employed individual, such as the owner of a business, from using this chapter of the bankruptcy law. But the debtor must be an *individual*; partnerships and corporations cannot institute this type of proceeding. The most important aspects of an **adjustment case** are summarized below.

1. There is no such thing as an involuntary adjustment case; only the debtor can file the petition. As in the other types of proceedings, an *automatic stay* exists upon filing. To be eligible to file an adjustment case, the debtor must have (a) "regular income," (b) less than $100,000 in noncontingent, undisputed debts which are *unsecured,* and (c) less than $350,000 in noncontingent, undisputed debts which are *secured.*

2. The U.S. Trustee will always appoint a trustee in an adjustment case. The primary function of the trustee in this type of proceeding is to receive and distribute the debtor's income on a periodic basis.

3. The debtor prepares and files an *adjustment plan* with the court. Neither the trustee, creditors, nor anyone else can file the plan. The essential functions of the plan are to designate the portion of the debtor's future income that will be turned over to the trustee for distribution to creditors, to describe how creditors are to be paid, and to indicate the period of time during which payment will be accomplished. If the plan segregates creditors into classes, each creditor within a class must be treated equally. As a general rule, the plan cannot extend the period for payment of debts more than three years. It can provide for less than full payment of many types of claims, but must call for full payment of the types of claims which are given priority in a liquidation case.

4. The court will confirm (approve) the plan if (a) the debtor proposed it in *good faith,* and (b) if all secured creditors have accepted it. It is not necessary for unsecured creditors to accept the plan; they are bound by it if the court confirms it, even if it modifies their claims. Furthermore, even if a secured creditor objects to the plan, the court may approve it if special provision is made to insure that the secured creditor is either fully paid or permitted to retain the lien or security interest protecting the claim.

5. At any time before or after confirmation of the plan, the debtor has the privilege of converting the adjustment proceeding to a liquidation case. The bankruptcy court may convert the adjustment proceeding to a liquidation case, or dismiss the case altogether, if the debtor fails to perform according to the plan. On the other hand, if the debtor does perform, he or she will ordinarily be granted a discharge upon completion of the payments provided for in the plan. There is no discharge, however, from the types of claims that cannot be discharged in a liquidation case. A discharge may be revoked within one year if it is discovered that the discharge was obtained through fraud.

## Of a Family Farmer with Regular Income

In 1986 in response to the farm economy crisis, Congress enacted Chapter 12, entitled "Adjustment of Debts of a Family Farmer with Regular Annual Income" to provide relief to family farmers who wished to retain and reorganize their farming operations. Most farmers are not eligible for such relief under Chapter 13 because their debts exceed statutory limits. Others are ineligible because they operate as a corporation or partnership. Chapter 11 reorganizations were considered by Congress to be excessively expensive, time-consuming, complicated, and unlikely to result in a confirmed plan for the family farmer.

Chapter 12 was generally modeled after Chapter 13 so that the procedures are basically the same as the Chapter 13 procedures outlined in paragraphs (1) through (5) above. The most striking distinctions found in Chapter 12 are set forth below.

1. The eligibility requirements of Chapter 12 are specifically aimed at the family farmer and exclude large agricultural operators. The debtor must be a **family farmer** defined as an individual engaged in farming whose aggregate debts do not exceed $1,500,000 and not less than 80 percent of whose debts (excluding debt on the principal residence) arise out of farming operations owned and operated by them and who received more than 50 percent of their gross income during the preceding taxable year from such farming operation. Only those partnerships and corporations are included in which more than 50 percent of the outstanding stock or equity is held by one family and its relatives who conduct the farming operation and more than 80 percent of the value of whose assets relate to the farming operation. In addition, the family farmer must have "regular income" defined as income sufficiently regular to enable the debtor to make payments under the Chapter 12 plan.

2. The family farmer's plan need not be filed for 90 days while the Chapter 13 plan must be filed within 15 days of filing the petition. Moreover, a Chapter 13 debtor must commence payments to the trustee within 30 days of filing his or her plan, while Chapter

12 has no provision requiring immediate payments so that a plan may be confirmed even though no payments are provided until the next harvest.

3. Congress has expressly provided that the adequate protection provision which applies in all other bankruptcy cases does not apply in Chapter 12 and has redefined the term more favorably for farmers. In Chapter 12 the customary, reasonable rental value of farmland constitutes adequate protection. Such rental payments should be significantly lower than adequate protection payments in a Chapter 11 case, where costs for lost opportunity to repossess may be included.

4. A Chapter 12 plan may provide for modification of the mortgage on a debtor's principal residence, which is prohibited in Chapter 13. It may also provide for the sale of farmland by parcels or farm equipment by items free and clear of blanket liens as long as the creditor's lien attaches to the proceeds. These modifications of creditors' liens, which would be objectionable in a Chapter 11 or 13 plan, are intended by Congress to permit the family farmer to scale down his operations by selling unnecessary property.

5. Chapter 12 was devised to provide extraordinary relief to eligible farmers during what was perceived by Congress as a temporary crisis and will automatically be repealed on October 1, 1993, unless extended.

## SUMMARY

When a debtor encounters difficulty in making repayment to creditors, many alternatives for attempting to resolve the problem exist under state statutory and common-law principles. Although bankruptcy under federal law traditionally has been viewed as a last resort, thousands of federal bankruptcy cases are filed each year. The 1978 Bankruptcy Code, as amended in 1984 and 1986, provides for four basic types of proceedings: liquidation, business reorganization, and adjustment of debts for individuals and for family farmers. Liquidation or reorganization proceedings can be either voluntary or involuntary, and can be instituted by or against either individuals, corporations, or partnerships. An adjustment proceeding can only be filed voluntarily by an individual.

The commencement of any type of proceeding causes an automatic stay of most other proceedings against the debtor. Contrary to prior law, under the 1978 Code a debtor does not have to be insolvent to file a voluntary petition, although insolvency is a requirement for the commencement of an involuntary case by creditors.

In a liquidation proceeding, a trustee is appointed by the bankruptcy court to administer the debtor's estate. The debtor's estate consists of practically all property interests of the debtor except for designated exempt items and is ultimately used to pay the claims of creditors according to a list of priorities contained in the Code. A debtor may select the property exemptions allowed by the law of the state where he or she resides, or the exemptions permitted by the Code; a particular state may, however, require debtors in that state to use only the state exemptions in a bankruptcy proceeding. The powers of the trustee include taking legal action to cancel (1) preferential transfers of property by the debtor to certain creditors and (2) other voidable transfers from the debtor. The trustee may also take legal action to collect claims owed to the debtor.

At the conclusion of a liquidation proceeding, a debtor is normally discharged from the unpaid portion of his or her obligations. Certain types of debts are not dischargeable, however. Moreover, proof of certain facts, such as concealment of assets or other fraudulent conduct by the debtor, may cause the court to deny the debtor a discharge.

A reorganization proceeding is intended to permit a financially overextended business to continue operating and work out a fair plan with creditors for repayment of its debts. A trustee may or may not be appointed in a reorganization proceeding; if one is not appointed, the debtor is called a debtor-in-possession and continues to control the business with all the powers of a trustee. An adjustment case is intended primarily to permit *employees* to work out repayment plans with creditors under court protection and supervision, but it can be used by self-employed individuals. Chapter 12 now provides similar adjustment procedures for family farmers.

## KEY TERMS

**Foreclosure**
**Artisan's lien**
**Mechanic's lien**
**Writ of execution**
**Garnishment**
**Receivership**

Fraud in fact
Fraud implied in law
Composition of creditors
Assignment for the benefit of creditors
Liquidation proceeding
Voluntary case
Involuntary case
Interim trustee
Permanent trustee
Debtor's estate
Exemptions
Voidable transfers
Preference
Insider
Secured creditors
General creditors
Discharge
Nondischargeable debts
Reaffirmation
Reorganization case
Debtor-in-possession
Adjustment case
Family farmer

## QUESTIONS AND PROBLEMS

**1.** Monroe, owner of a stereo equipment dealership, was several months behind on his obligations to an office supply store, a janitorial service, an advertising agency, and an accountant. After being unable to work out settlements with Monroe, these creditors joined in filing a petition for involuntary bankruptcy. Their claims totalled $6,200, all of which were unsecured. Monroe contested the petition, claiming that he was merely having "cash flow problems" and that his business was actually solvent. He said that lately all his cash receipts had been required to pay his landlord and inventory suppliers. Audited financial statements showed Monroe's total liabilities to be $184,000 and the fair value of his assets $202,000. Can these creditors force Monroe into bankruptcy? Discuss.

**2.** Mark and Patricia Maschhoff, in the year prior to the filing of their Chapter 12 bankruptcy petition, received income from the following sources: (a) $64,314 from the sale of farm products and from agricultural program payments; (b) income from wages and salaries totalling $53,479; and (c) $19,735 from rental of farmhouses located on their land to tenants who watched over farm buildings, stored grain, and assisted with handling farm implements. Creditor bank moved to dismiss the Maschhoff's petition on the basis that debtors were ineligible for Chapter 12 relief. Should the petition be dismissed? Discuss. (*In re Maschhoff*, 89 B.R. 768, Bkrtcy. S.D.Ill. 1988.)

**3.** James Taylor was the lead singer in a group known as "Kool and the Gang." In 1985 and 1986, the group executed three recording contracts which bound each member of the group to perform thereunder as a solo artist in the event of his departure from the group. In early 1988 Taylor terminated his relationship with Kool and the Gang, and in May 1988 he filed a Chapter 11 bankruptcy petition. He then filed a motion to reject the three personal service contracts under the general power of the trustee to reject or accept executory contracts. The recording companies holding the contracts argued that since earnings for services by a debtor after the commencement of a bankruptcy case are not considered property of the estate, the trustee had no power to accept or reject the contracts in question. Should Taylor be allowed to reject these contracts and be relieved of his obligations to perform thereunder as a part of his "fresh start"? (*Matter of Taylor*, 103 B.R. 511, D.N.J. 1989.)

**4.** Pennzoil was awarded a judgment against Texaco for more than $11.259 billion. Texaco then filed a Chapter 11 bankruptcy petition. Texaco and Pennzoil, its largest unsecured creditor, filed a Joint Plan of Reorganization which reduced Pennzoil's claim to a cash payment due upon confirmation of $3 billion. This payment was to be in full satisfaction and release of the judgment and all other possible litigation relating to the Getty Oil acquisition out of which the judgment had arisen. The plan also provided for payment of all other creditors in full. Texaco asserted that it was authorized to compromise and settle Pennzoil's claim in this manner under 11 U.S.C. Sec. 1123(b)(3) which provides for "the settlement or adjustment of any claim or interest belonging to the debtor or the estate. . . ." The court disagreed, stating that the Pennzoil claim did not belong to the debtor or the estate. Moreover, Pennzoil obviously was not being treated equally under the plan with all other creditors as required by Sec. 1123(a)(4). Could this plan be confirmed by the court? Discuss. (*In re Texaco, Inc.*, 84 B.R. 893, Bkrtcy. S.D.N.Y. 1988.)

**5.** Which of the following items of property would *not* be part of a debtor's estate in a bankruptcy case? Explain.
    **a.** A one-half interest in a patent on a machine the debtor had helped invent
    **b.** A fifty-acre tract of ranch land, used by the debtor to pasture cattle
    **c.** An easement which permitted the debtor to drive his pickup and run his cattle over another person's land to get to the public road
    **d.** The debtor's residence in the city
    **e.** One hundred head of cattle
    **f.** A diamond ring, as an inheritance from his father, which the debtor became entitled to receive 30 days after the petition filing date but which he actually received more than seven months later

g. The debtor's salary earned within 180 days after the petition filing date

h. Future payments under a veteran's pension, to which the debtor has a vested right

i. A claim by the debtor against a third party for breach of contract, whose claim could be worth anything from zero to $100,000

6. A Wyoming statute allowed an exemption from bankruptcy proceedings for motor vehicles "used and kept for the purpose of carrying on a trade or business." In his voluntary bankruptcy proceeding, Jerald Johnston claimed an exemption under this law for his 1967 half-ton pickup truck, which he used for transportation to and from his job as a waiter at a restaurant located several miles from his home. The trustee, Gary Barney, objected to the exemption, contending that the pickup did not meet the statute's requirements. Was the pickup exempt? (*Johnston v. Barney,* 842 F.2d 1221, 10th Cir. 1988.)

7. Greenway Plaza Investment Co. (Greenway) owned as its principal asset real property in Austin, Texas, known as the Greenway Plaza Apartments. Beneficial, a creditor with a lien on the apartments, foreclosed on the property. A foreclosure sale was conducted at which Beneficial purchased the apartments for a credit bid against their substantial lien. However, the fair market value of the property at the time of the sale was $2.5 million and the foreclosure price was only roughly 64 percent of that estimated value. Greenway filed a voluntary Chapter 11 bankruptcy petition within one year of the sale. The court found that debtor was insolvent at the time of the sale. A complaint was filed to set aside the foreclosure sale as a fraudulent transfer. What would be the result? (*In re Lindsay,* 98 B.R. 983, Bkrtcy. S.D.Cal. 1989.)

8. In 1986, Joe Henderson, while a manager at Economy Car Leasing (Economy), was discovered to have improperly diverted corporate funds for personal use. Henderson was fired, and on July 30, 1986, entered into an agreement with Economy to make certain restitution payments including $40,000 cash and a non-dischargeable note for $125,000 in exchange for Economy's agreement never to reveal the reasons for his termination. More than 90 days but less than one year later, Henderson filed a Chapter 7 bankruptcy petition. The trustee sought to avoid the payments made to Economy arguing that they constituted voidable preferences. It was stipulated that the debtor was insolvent at the time of the payments and that Economy received more than it would have in a Chapter 7 case. Were the payments voidable as preferences? Explain. (*In re Henderson,* 96 B.R. 820, Bkrtcy. E.D.Tenn. 1989.)

9. Jossee Dias owned and operated a cleaning business known as J.P. Cleaners prior to and after the filing of his Chapter 7 bankruptcy petition. Dias estimated that his annual income for the business was negligible. A creditor objected to discharge on the ground that Dias failed to keep adequate business records without justification. Dias kept no general ledgers of billings, receipts, expenses, or accounts payable. Instead, he kept only the cleaning ticket receipts, bank deposit slips, cancelled checks, and other miscellaneous documents including some cash register tapes from which he argued that a creditor could compile sufficient information to ascertain his financial condition. Dias testified that he did not have time to maintain additional financial records because the operation of his business required all his attention. Should discharge be denied? (*In re Dias,* 95 B.R. 419, Bkrtcy. N.D.Tex. 1988.)

# PART IV

# AGENCY AND PARTNERSHIPS

■ The law of agency deals with the various rights and responsibilities that exist when one person acts in a representative role for another. Because most of the world's work is done by persons acting as representatives of companies or of other individuals, the law of agency is among the most fundamental of subject areas. Moreover, an understanding of the law of agency is essential to the study of business organizations, including partnerships, which are discussed immediately following agency, and corporations, which are discussed in Part V.

The law of employment is also very closely related to the law of agency, because many agents are also employees. Most of our present laws governing employment, however, are statutory in nature, and most of them create legal rights for employees that were not recognized by the common law of agency. For this reason, we are deferring our discussion of employment law to Part VII, Government Regulation of Business.

Chapter 31 focuses on the basic nature of the agency relationship, the methods by which such a relationship is created and terminated, and the duties of the principal and agent to one another. Chapter 32 then examines the duties and liabilities of the principal and agent to third parties.

Following our discussion of agency, we will explore the partnership form of business organization. As you will see, the subject of partnerships ties in very closely with agency, because a business partnership is founded upon agency relationships. Chapter 33 looks primarily at the formation of partnerships, Chapter 34 at their daily operation, and Chapter 35 at their termination. Chapter 36 then discusses limited partnerships. ■

# CHAPTER 31

# AGENCY

## Nature, Creation, Duties, and Termination

## NATURE OF THE AGENCY RELATIONSHIP

In a legal context the term **agency** ordinarily describes a relationship in which two parties—the principal and the agent—agree that one will act as a representative of the other. The **principal** is the person who wishes to accomplish something, and the **agent** is the one employed to act in the principal's behalf to achieve it.

At one time or another, almost everyone has come into contact with the agency relationship. Anyone who has purchased merchandise at a retail store almost certainly has dealt with an agent—the salesclerk. Similarly, anyone who has ever held a job probably has served in some type of representative capacity for the employer.

The usefulness of the agency relationship in the business world is obvious. With few exceptions, no single individual is capable of performing every act required to run a business enterprise. Furthermore, many businesses are organized as corporations, which by definition can act only by employing agents. As a result, most business transactions throughout the world are handled by agents.

The term *agency* is often used loosely to describe many different types of relationships in which one party acts in a representative capacity for another. *Principal* and *agent* are also sometimes used loosely to denote the parties to various types of arrangements. However, throughout our discussion these terms are used narrowly to describe a particular type of relationship. The **principal-agent relationship,** as we use it, means a relationship in which the parties have agreed that the agent is to represent the principal in negotiating and transacting business; that is, the agent is employed to make contracts or enter similar business transactions in behalf of the principal. The term will ordinarily be used in discussions of contractual liability.

Two similar relationships are the **employer-employee relationship** (which is still sometimes referred to by the older term *master-servant relationship*), and the **employer-independent contractor relationship.** The distinction between an employee and an independent contractor is important to many different kinds of legal questions. For example, state workers' compensation laws, federal antidiscrimination statutes, and many other laws regulating employment are applicable only to employees and not to independent contractors. Similarly, federal tax laws requiring the employer to withhold income and social security taxes and to contribute to the worker's social security account are applicable only to employees and not to independent contractors. In the law of agency, the distinction is important when a third party tries to hold the employer legally responsible for a *tort* committed by the employee. As we will see toward the end of the next chapter, an employer often can be held liable for the job-related torts of its employees, but usually cannot be held liable for such torts committed by those working for it as independent contractors.

It also is important to note that the same worker can be both an agent and an employee or both an agent and an independent contractor. Which relationship is relevant depends on the nature of the legal issues in the dispute. When the legal question involves either (1) the rights and duties between the superior and subordinate or (2) the superior's liability to third parties for contracts or other transactions executed by the subordinate, the relevant question usually is whether the subordinate was an agent who acted with authority. On the other hand, if the legal question involves the superior's liability for a tort committed by the subordinate, the relevant ques-

487

tion usually is whether the subordinate was an employee who acted within the scope of his or her employment.

Sometimes, however, it is appropriate to use the term agent and to discuss the agent's authority when the legal issue is the superior's tort liability. This happens mainly in two situations: First, it is appropriate to use agent and authority concepts when the superior has directly authorized the agent to engage in the wrongful conduct. In such a case, the superior is liable to the third party for the subordinate's tort regardless of whether the latter is an employee or an independent contractor. Second, courts sometimes use agent and authority concepts when the subordinate's tort was *nonphysical* in nature, such as fraud, defamation, and so on.

Most of our discussion in these two chapters involves the principal-agent relationship; the employer-employee and employer-independent contractor relationships are dealt with in the latter part of the next chapter.

## CREATION OF THE AGENCY RELATIONSHIP

### *Necessary Elements*

The agency relationship is *consensual*—that is, based on the agreement of the parties. Many times it is created by a legally enforceable employment contract between the principal and the agent. A legally binding contract is not essential, however. An agency relationship that gives the agent authority to represent the principal and bind him or her by the agent's actions can generally be established by any words or actions that indicate the parties' consent to the arrangement. Consideration is not required.

In fact, no formalities are required for the creation of an agency relationship in most circumstances. For example, it is not usually necessary to spell out the agent's authority in writing; oral authority is ordinarily sufficient. Exceptions do exist, however. The most common one occurs when an agent is granted authority to sell real estate. In a majority of states an agent can make a contract for the sale of real estate that will bind the principal only if the agent's authority is stated in writing.

Even though formalities are usually not required for the creation of an agency, it is certainly wise to express the extent of an agent's authority and any other relevant matters in writing. This precaution often prevents misunderstandings between the principal and agent or between the agent and third parties with whom he or she is dealing. The formal written authorization given by a principal to an agent is frequently referred to as a **power of attorney.** When a formal power of attorney is used, the agent is sometimes referred to as an **attorney-in-fact.** This is simply another term for an agent, and should not be confused with attorney-at-law (a lawyer). Courts generally scrutinize powers of attorney very carefully and interpret their language strictly.

In the following case, an agent learned the hard way about the rule that powers of attorney are interpreted very strictly, and found that good intentions are no substitute for authority.

---

### King v. Bankerd
Court of Appeals of Maryland,
492 A.2d 608 (1985)

Howard R. Bankerd (Bankerd) and his wife Virginia owned, as "tenants by the entirety," a home in Montgomery County, Maryland. (A "tenancy by the entirety" is one type of joint ownership created by the marriage relationship in some states; see Chapter 43 for details.) They lived there until 1966 when Mrs. Bankerd moved out as a result of marital problems. Bankerd continued to live at the property until July, 1968, when he "left for the west." Mrs. Bankerd then resumed living on the property. For the next twelve years, Bankerd lived at various locations in Nevada, Colorado, and Washington, and made no payments on the mortgage, for taxes, or for the maintenance of the home.

Before Bankerd's departure, he executed a power of attorney to King, an attorney with whom he was acquainted. From 1971 to 1974, Bankerd did not communicate with King in any way. In 1975, however, King sent Bankerd a letter enclosing an updated power of attorney because the Washington Suburban Sanitary Commission was about to put a sewer adjacent to the property, and King believed the new power would be needed. This power of attorney, dated October 30, 1975, was executed by Bankerd and returned to King. It stated:

*(continued)*

**KNOW ALL MEN BY THESE PRESENTS,** that I, Howard R. Bankerd, hereby make, constitute and appoint ARTHUR V. KING, my attorney for me, and in my name to convey, grant, bargain and/or sell the property designated in the Montgomery County land record as Lot 9 of an unrecorded subdivision as recorded in Liber 3027 at folio 293, situated at 14026 Travilah Road, Rockville, Maryland on such terms as to him may seem best, and in my name, to make, execute, acknowledge and deliver, good and sufficient deeds and conveyances for the same with or without covenants and warranties and generally to do and perform all things necessary pertaining to the future transfer of said property, and generally to do everything whatsoever necessary pertaining to the said property.

After granting this power of attorney, Bankerd had no further communication with King until 1978.

Mrs. Bankerd, who had been living at and maintaining the property since 1968, requested King in September 1977 to exercise the power of attorney and to transfer Bankerd's interest in the property to her. King was aware that Mrs. Bankerd was nearing retirement and that she was "saddled" with a property she could neither sell nor mortgage because of her husband's legal interest in it. Consequently, King made several attempts to find and communicate with Bankerd, but was unsuccessful.

Mrs. Bankerd informed King that her husband had once attempted to give the property away to a neighbor on the condition that the neighbor assume the mortgage payments. As a result, King asserted that he believed Bankerd "didn't give a damn" about the property, and that given Bankerd's age (approximately sixty-nine years), King believed that Bankerd might even be deceased. King therefore conveyed Bankerd's interest in the property to Mrs. Bankerd by deed in 1978. Mrs. Bankerd paid no consideration for the transfer and King received no compensation for executing the deed. Mrs. Bankerd then sold the property to a third party for $62,500.

In 1981 Bankerd filed suit against King alleging that King had acted negligently and had exceeded his authority as Bankerd's agent. The trial court granted summary judgment to Bankerd against King and awarded $13,555.05 in damages. The intermediate appellate court affirmed, and King appealed to Maryland's highest court.

**Decision:** The judgment for plaintiff Bankerd was affirmed. A broad power of attorney authorizing the agent to "convey, grant, bargain and/or sell" the principal's property normally does not authorize the agent to give away that property, for several reasons: First, authority to give away the principal's property is a power that is potentially very hazardous to the principal's interests. Second, the main duty of an agent is to serve the principal's interests, and it would be uncommon for a gift of the principal's property to be in his or her interests. Third, if someone decides to give away property, that person usually does it personally rather than using an agent to accomplish the gift. Moreover, the general rule is that powers of attorney are construed very narrowly. Therefore, a broad power of attorney does not authorize the agent to make a gift of the principal's property unless that power is (1) expressly conferred, (2) arises as a necessary implication from the conferred powers, or (3) is clearly intended by the parties, as evidenced by the surrounding facts and circumstances. The first two situations clearly do not exist here. Regarding the third situation, there are no circumstances indicating that Bankerd had abandoned his interest in the property or wanted to give it away; in fact, on one occasion in a letter to the lawyer he indicated that the lawyer would "have a job" in connection with the property if Bankerd outlived his former wife. ■

---

## Capacity

If an agent, acting in behalf of a principal, makes a properly authorized contract with a third party, the contract is viewed legally as being one between the principal and the third party; that is, it is the *principal's* contract, not the agent's. For this reason the principal's capacity to make contracts may be important in determining the validity of the contract in question. The minority, insanity, or other incapacity of the principal has the same effect on contracts made through an agent as it does on contracts made personally.

On the other hand, the agent's capacity is usually immaterial. The reason is the same—the contract made by the agent for the principal is the principal's contract. A minor, for example, can serve as an agent; his or her lack of contractual capacity ordinarily has no effect on a contract made in behalf of the principal.[1]

---

[1] Of course, the agent's lack of contractual capacity has an effect on his or her own contract of employment with the principal, if one exists. The agent's capacity can also be important if for any reason the third party attempts to hold the agent personally responsible on a contract made with that party.

**Figure 31.1** Duties of Agents and Principals to Each Other

```
                  To comply with terms of
                  agreement (compensation),
                  reimbursement, indemnification
                  ┌─────────────────────────────┐
                  ▼                             │
Agent ─────── Agency agreement ─────────── Principal
        │                                     ▲
        └─── Fiduciary duties: ───────────────┘
                  Obedience
                  Reasonable care
                  Account for
                  funds and property
                  Notification
                  Loyalty
```

## DUTIES OF PRINCIPAL AND AGENT

The principal–agent relationship is a **fiduciary relationship**—one of trust. Each party owes the other a duty to act with the utmost good faith. Each should be entirely open with the other, not keeping any information from the other that has any bearing on their arrangement. Other duties, some of which are merely specific applications of the general fiduciary obligation, are discussed below and outlined in Fig. 31.1.

### Duties Owed by Principal to Agent

The primary duty owed by the principal to the agent is simply that of complying with the terms of their employment contract, if one exists. Failure of the principal to do so will render him or her liable to the agent for damages; if the breach is material, it will justify the agent in refusing to act for the principal any further. For example: P and A have agreed that A is to be paid a specified percentage of the sales she makes for P. If P refuses or fails to pay A, A can rightfully terminate their arrangement and hold P responsible for damages.

In addition, the principal is under a duty to reimburse the agent for any expenditures reasonably incurred by the agent in furthering the interests of the principal. For example, if P directs A to travel from Chicago to Los Angeles to transact business for P, but does not provide her with any funds for travel expenses, P will be under a duty when A returns to reimburse her for amounts she reasonably expended in making the trip, such as her round-trip air fare.

Similarly, the principal has an obligation to indemnify the agent for liabilities or losses the latter suffers while acting lawfully and within the scope of his or her authority.

### Duties Owed by Agent to Principal

**Obedience:** It is the duty of the agent to obey the clear instructions of the principal, so long as such instructions are legal. If the instructions are ambiguous, the agent cannot disregard them altogether, but he or she can fulfill the duty by acting in good faith and interpreting them in a manner that is reasonable under the circumstances.

Where the instructions are both legal and clear, the agent is justified in departing from them on only rare occasions. One such occasion is when an *emergency* occurs and following the principal's original instructions is not in that person's best interests. The agent should, of course, consult with the principal and obtain new instructions if possible. But if there is no opportunity to consult, the agent is justified in taking reasonable steps to protect the principal, even if it means deviating from prior instructions. Indeed, the agent may even be under a duty to depart from instructions if following them in the emergency can be considered so unreasonable as to be negligent. (The agent's authority to act in emergencies is discussed more fully in the next chapter.)

**Reasonable Care:** Unless special provisions in the agreement say otherwise, an agent is normally expected to exercise the degree of care and skill that is reasonable under the circumstances. In other words, the agent has a duty not to be negligent. For example, suppose that B has funds which he wishes to lend to borrowers at current interest rates. He employs C to act in his behalf in locating the borrowers. C lends B's money to T without investigating T's credit rating and without obtaining from T any security for the loan. T turns out to be a notoriously bad credit risk and is actually insolvent at the time of the loan. If B is later unable to collect from T, C will probably be liable to B, because he failed to exercise reasonable care in making the loan.

Under some circumstances, an agent may be under a special duty to exercise more than an ordinary degree of care and skill. For example, if a person undertakes to serve in a capacity that necessarily involves the possession and exercise of a special skill, such as that of a lawyer or stockbroker, he or she is required to exercise the skill ordinarily possessed by competent persons pursuing that particular calling.

In any agency relationship, the principal and agent can by agreement change the agent's duty of care and skill, making it either stricter or more lenient.

**Duty to Account:** Unless principal and agent agree otherwise, it is the agent's duty to keep and make available to the principal an account of all the money or property received or paid out in behalf of the principal. In this regard, an agent should never mix his or her own money or property with that of the principal. The agent should, for example, set up a separate bank account for the principal's money. If the agent commingles (mixes) his or her own money or property with the principal's in such a way that it cannot be separated or identified, the principal can legally claim all of it.

**Duty to Notify:** Another important duty of the agent is to notify the principal of all relevant facts—just about any information having a bearing on the interests of the principal—as soon as reasonably possible after learning of them. For example, if A (the agent) discovers that one of P's (the principal's) creditors is about to foreclose a lien on P's property, A should promptly notify P. Or if A learns that one of P's important customers, who owes P a substantial amount of money, has just filed for bankruptcy, A should contact P as soon as possible.

**Loyalty:** Perhaps the most important duty owed by the agent to the principal is that of loyalty. Violation of this duty can occur in numerous ways. A few of the more significant actions constituting a breach of the duty are discussed below.

Quite obviously, the agent should not *compete* with the principal in the type of business he or she is conducting for the principal, unless the principal expressly gives consent. To illustrate: X, who owns a textile manufacturing business, employs Y to act as his sales agent. Y will be violating his duty of loyalty if, without X's consent, he acquires a personal interest in a textile manufacturing business that competes with X's.

The law presumes that a principal hires an agent to serve the principal's interests and not the personal interests of the agent. Thus the agent should avoid any existing or potential conflict of interest. For example, if B is hired to sell goods for R, he should not sell to himself. Or if he is hired to buy goods for R, he should not buy them from himself. It is difficult, if not impossible, for the agent to completely serve the principal's interests when his or her own personal interests become involved. Of course, such things can be done if the principal is fully informed and gives consent.

In a similar fashion, the agent should not further the interests of any third party in his or her dealings for the principal. The agent also should not work for two parties on opposite sides in a transaction unless both parties agree to it.

If the agent, in working for the principal, acquires knowledge of any *confidential information,* he or she should not disclose this information to outsiders without the principal's consent. To illustrate: G hires H, a lawyer, to represent G in defending a lawsuit filed against G by T. T alleges that his factory was damaged in a fire caused by certain chemicals, purchased by T from G, that were highly flammable and not labeled with an adequate warning. In order to properly defend G, H must learn the secret formulas and processes for producing the chemicals. After learning them, he should not disclose them to anyone without G's consent, either at that time or at any time in the future.

The following case illustrates the strictness of the duty of loyalty owed by an agent to the principal.

## Girard v. Myers
Court of Appeals of Washington,
694 P.2d 678 (1985)

Michael Myers was a real estate developer and licensed salesman in the state of Washington. In 1974, he contracted to purchase a 290-acre tract of land known as the Pickering Farm. The purchase contract divided the land into seven parcels, and Myers then obtained groups of investors to purchase each parcel. Myers himself bought one 13.2-acre parcel out of the tract. As a condition of their participation, Myers required these investors to sign a document entitled "Trust and Resale Agreement." This agreement designated Myers as the exclusive sales agent for all of the investors in the event they later desired to resell their parcels, and also gave Myers a "right of first refusal." Under this right of first refusal, if a particular investor or group of investors owning a parcel subsequently desired to resell the land to a third party, they first had to give Myers the opportunity to purchase it at the price offered by the third party, less an 11 percent discount. If Myers chose not to buy the parcel, the investor was obligated to pay Myers an 11 percent commission on the sale to the third party.

In early 1977, two investors, Butler and Kline, decided to sell one-half of their parcel to Girard. Myers indicated that he would refrain from exercising his right of first refusal only if Girard signed a Trust and Resale Agreement identical to that signed by the original investors. This was done and Girard made the purchase, with Myers receiving a sales commission from Butler and Kline.

Myers controlled three limited partnerships that engaged in real estate investment and development. In late 1977 and 1978, these partnerships acquired 51 acres next to the parcel owned by Girard. In 1979 Girard informed Myers that Girard wanted to transfer his land to a partnership that was being formed between Girard and John Sato. Girard also told Myers that Girard considered the Trust and Resale Agreement to be void and that he did not intend to honor it. Girard filed suit asking the court to declare the agreement void and unenforceable. Myers asserted a counterclaim for an 11 percent sales commission on the transfer.

The court ruled that the right of first refusal was unenforceable because it placed no time limit on Myers' exercise of the right and because its terms were too vague, and then held that the sales commission and price discount provisions were void because Myers' ownership and financial interests in the 13.2-acre and 51-acre parcels created an impermissible conflict of interest. Thus the trial court held for Girard and dismissed Myers' counterclaim for the sales commission, and Myers appealed. A summary of that portion of the appellate court's opinion dealing with the conflict of interest is presented below.

**Decision:** The judgment for plaintiff Girard was affirmed; he did not have to pay Myers the commission. Although the evidence indicated that Girard probably knew of Myers's ownership of the 13.2 acres when Girard bought his land, Myers acquired the 51 acres through the three limited partnerships after Girard had acquired his property. Myers's property interests were potentially in competition with those of Girard; Myers was therefore under a duty to fully disclose his interest in the 51 acres to Girard and obtain Girard's consent to the continuation of the principal-agent relationship after the disclosure. Myers did not do this, and therefore breached his fiduciary duty of loyalty to Girard. (The court of appeals also agreed with the trial court that the right of first refusal was void because of its vagueness.) ∎

---

# TERMINATION OF THE AGENCY RELATIONSHIP

Like most private consensual arrangements, the agency relationship usually comes to an end at some point. Termination can occur because of something done by the parties themselves or by operation of law (something beyond their control). Our discussion focuses on the termination of the relationship between the principal and the agent, ignoring for the moment the effects of termination on third parties who might deal with the agent. (The circumstances under which third parties should be notified of the termination and the type of notice required are dealt with in the next chapter.)

## Termination by Act of the Parties

**Fulfillment of Purpose:** Many times an agent is employed to accomplish a particular object, such as the sale of a tract of land belonging to the principal.

When this object is accomplished and nothing else remains to be done, the agency relationship terminates.

**Lapse of Time:** If principal and agent have agreed originally that the arrangement will end at a certain time, the arrival of that time terminates their relationship. If nothing has been said as to the duration of the agency, and if nothing occurs to terminate it, the relationship is deemed to last for a period of time that is reasonable under the circumstances. This generally is a question of whether, after passage of a particular period of time, it is reasonable for the agent to believe that the principal still intends for him or her to act as earlier directed. Of course, if the principal *knows* that the agent is continuing to make efforts to perform, and if the principal does nothing about the situation, the agency relationship may remain alive for a period of time longer than would otherwise be held reasonable.

**Occurrence of Specified Event:** In a similar fashion, if the principal and agent have originally agreed that the agency, or some particular aspect of it, will continue until a specified event occurs, the occurrence of the event results in termination. For example: P authorizes A to attempt to sell P's farm, Blackacre, for him "only until P returns from New York." When P returns, A's authority to sell Blackacre as P's agent comes to an end. An analogous situation occurs when principal and agent have agreed that the agency, or some aspect of it, will remain in existence only during the continuance of a stated condition. If the condition ceases to exist, the agent's authority terminates. For instance: X directs Y, X's credit manager, to extend $10,000 in credit to T, so long as T's inventory of goods on hand and his accounts receivable amount to $50,000 and his accounts payable do not exceed $25,000. If T's combined inventory and accounts receivable drop below $50,000, the agency terminates insofar as it relates to Y's authority to grant credit to T.

**Mutual Agreement:** Regardless of what the principal and agent have agreed to originally, they can agree at any time to end their relationship. It makes no difference whether the relationship has been based on a binding employment contract or whether no enforceable employment contract exists; their mutual agreement terminates the agency in either case. It is a basic rule of contract law that the parties can rescind (cancel) the contract by mutual agreement.

**Act of One Party:** Since the agency relationship is consensual, it can usually be terminated by either the principal or the agent if that person no longer wants to be a party to the arrangement. In most circumstances termination occurs simply by one party indicating to the other that he or she no longer desires to continue the relationship. This is true even if the parties had originally agreed that the agency was to be irrevocable.

If no binding employment contract exists between the two of them, the party terminating the agency normally does not incur any liability to the other by this action. If an enforceable employment contract does exist, one party may be justified in terminating it if the other has violated any of the duties owed under it. Of course, if there are no facts justifying termination, the party taking such action may be responsible to the other for any damages caused by the breach of contract. But the agency relationship is ended nevertheless.

One major exception exists to the ability of either party to terminate the relationship. If the agency is not just a simple one but instead is an **agency coupled with an interest** (that is, the agent has an interest in the subject matter of the agency), the principal cannot terminate the agent's authority without the agent's consent. (Note, however, that an agent is not considered to have an interest in the subject matter simply because he or she expects to make a commission or profit from the activities as agent.) To illustrate: P borrows $5,000 from A. To secure the loan, P grants A a *security interest* (a property interest for the sole purpose of securing a debt) in P's inventory. As part of the agreement, P makes A his agent for the sale of the inventory in case P defaults on the loan. Since A has an interest in the subject matter of the agency (the inventory), the arrangement is an agency coupled with an interest, and P cannot terminate A's authority to sell without A's consent (unless, of course, P repays the loan, in which case A no longer has an interest in the subject matter).

The reason for the exception is that the agent is not really acting for the principal in this situation. By exercising this authority, the agent is acting in his or her own behalf to assert a personal interest.

## Termination by Operation of Law

**Death or Insanity:** The death or insanity of the *agent* immediately terminates an agency relationship. The death or insanity of the *principal* also terminates an agency relationship. In most cases the termination of an agency by the principal's death or insanity occurs immediately, regardless of whether the agent knows what has happened.

**Bankruptcy:** The insolvency or bankruptcy of the *agent* does not always terminate the agency, but will do so in those circumstances where it impairs the agent's ability to act for the principal. To illustrate: B is authorized by I, an investment house, to act as its agent in advising I's local clients about investments. If B becomes bankrupt, he will no longer be authorized to act for I. The reason is simple; the agent in this situation should realize that the principal probably would not want him to act in its behalf any longer if it knew the facts.

Suppose, however, that the *principal* becomes insolvent or bankrupt, and the agent knows about it. In this case the agent might no longer have authority to act for the principal—but only under circumstances where the agent ought to realize that the principal would no longer want such transactions to be conducted in his or her behalf. For example: P has authorized A to buy an expensive fur coat on credit for P. If P becomes bankrupt, this will probably terminate the agency when A learns of it. A should reasonably infer that under the circumstances P will no longer want him to make such a purchase. However, if A is P's housekeeper and has been authorized to buy groceries for P's household, P's bankruptcy probably will not extinguish that authority. The inference that A should reasonably draw when learning the facts is that P will want her to continue buying necessities such as food until informed otherwise. It is simply a matter of reasonableness.

**Change of Law:** If a change in the law makes the agency or the performance of the authorized act *illegal,* the agent's authority is ordinarily extinguished when he or she learns of the change. To illustrate: S is a salesperson for T, a toy manufacturer. If a federal agency determines that certain of T's toys are dangerous and bans them, S's authority to sell them to retailers probably will be terminated when she learns of the government ban. That is, upon learning the facts, S should reasonably assume that T will no longer want her to sell the banned items.

Even if the change in the law does not make the agency or the authorized act illegal, termination can still occur if the agent learns of the change and should reasonably expect that the principal will no longer want him or her to act in the manner previously authorized. For instance: A is authorized to purchase fabricated aluminum from a foreign supplier. The federal government imposes a new tariff on imported aluminum that results in substantially higher prices. It is likely that A's authority to buy foreign aluminum will be terminated when he learns of the change.

**Loss or Destruction of Subject Matter:** The loss or destruction of the subject matter of an agency relationship will terminate the agent's authority. If, for example, X employs Y to sell grain belonging to X that is being stored in a particular storage elevator, the destruction by fire of the elevator and the grain will ordinarily extinguish Y's authority.

Whether the agent's authority terminates automatically or only when he or she learns of the facts depends on the nature and terms of the original agreement between principal and agent. In the instant case, if, instead of a fire, X himself sells the grain to a buyer (which actually amounts to X revoking Y's authority), Y's authority may or may not be automatically terminated. If X has given Y *exclusive authority* to sell, that authority ends only if X notifies Y that he has sold the grain himself. On the other hand, if the authority is not exclusive and Y should realize that X may try to sell the grain himself, Y's authority will terminate when X sells the grain even if Y does not know of the sale.

If the subject matter of the agency (such as the grain) is not lost or destroyed but is merely damaged, Y's authority is terminated if the circumstances are such that Y ought to realize that X would not want the transaction to be carried out.

**Miscellaneous Changes of Conditions:** The various occurrences we have discussed that terminate an agency by operation of law are by no means an exclusive list. For instance, in some circumstances the outbreak of war, a sudden change in the market value of the subject matter of the agency, or an unexpected loss of some required qualification by the principal or the agent (such as a license) may terminate the agency. Again, if all the circumstances known to the agent are such that he or she, as a reasonable person, ought to realize that the principal would no longer wish him or her to continue in the endeavor, the authority is ended. The agent simply must act in a reasonable fashion until there is an opportunity to consult with the principal.

## SUMMARY

The law of agency governs the rights and responsibilities created when one person acts in a representative role for another. When the subordinate transacts business in behalf of the superior, the relationship is usually referred to as that of principal and agent. When the subordinate performs physical tasks for the superior, or when there is any question regarding the superior's tort liability for the actions of the subordinate, the relationship is usually referred to as that of either master and servant or employer and independent contractor. In general, an agency relationship of any type is created by agreement. The agreement may be a legally enforceable employment contract, but it does not have to be. The principal-agent relationship is a fiduciary relationship in which each party owes the other a duty to act in the utmost good faith. The principal owes to the agent the duty to compensate, reimburse for necessary expenses, and comply with any other terms of their agreement. The agent owes to the principal the duty to obey instructions, act with reasonable care, account for the principal's funds or property in the agent's possession, notify the principal of any facts relating to the interests of the principal, and always act with loyalty to the principal's interests. The principal-agent relationship may be terminated by various acts of the parties themselves, or by operation of law.

## KEY TERMS

Agency
Principal
Agent
Principal-agent relationship
Employer-employee relationship
Employer-independent
　contractor relationship
Power of attorney
Attorney-in-fact
Fiduciary relationship
Agency coupled with an interest

## QUESTIONS AND PROBLEMS

1. The Fiscal Court of Adair County, which is a governing body for the county, fills certain county job vacancies in the following way (although the procedure is not in writing):
   **a.** The Lake Cumberland Emergency Medical Systems, Inc. (LCEMSS) interviews job applicants to ensure minimum qualifications;
   **b.** If the position is initially to be funded under the federal Comprehensive Employment and Training Act (CETA), CETA representatives must certify the applicant as "eligible";
   **c.** The Fiscal Court then decides whom to hire.
   
   Carlyne Terbovitz applied for a position which was to be CETA funded. The CETA representatives refused to process Terbovitz's application because she was female. Thus, the Fiscal Court never even reviewed the application. Terbovitz filed suit claiming that the Fiscal Court was guilty of sex discrimination. In the trial, certain officials of LCEMSS testified that the Fiscal Court had told them not to hire a woman for this position. In light of the procedure that was used to screen applicants and make hiring decisions, as well as the statements made by the Fiscal Court to LCEMSS, is the Fiscal Court liable for CETA's discrimination? Discuss. (*Terbovitz v. Fiscal Court of Adair County*, 825 F.2d 111, 6th Cir. 1987.)

2. Lenhardt was the general partner in East Bay Investments, and Petersen was the limited partner. Thus, Lenhardt was the person with authority to manage the business. Lenhardt delegated some of this authority to Petersen by authorizing him to handle all of the financial transactions and sign all documents for East Bay. East Bay sold a piece of land to Barrasso, and there was no question about this transaction because Lenhardt signed the deed. Barrasso borrowed money to make the purchase and gave a mortgage on the property to the lending institution as security. The lender required additional security, however. In order for the sale to go through, East Bay also gave Barrasso's lender a mortgage on some other real estate owned by East Bay. This mortgage was executed and signed only by Petersen in behalf of East Bay. Lenhardt did not know the details of these financial arrangements. Later, Barrasso defaulted on his loan and the lender foreclosed on the mortgages. Lenhardt claimed that the additional mortgage on other East Bay property was void because he had not known of its details, and Petersen was not authorized to execute the mortgage. Is Lenhardt bound by the mortgage that Petersen executed? Discuss. (*Federal Deposit Insurance Corp. v. Barrasso*, 791 F.2d 1529, 11th Cir. 1986.)

3. Whisper Mills is required to bargain with an international union unless the international union authorizes a local union to act as its agent. A local union claims that it has the right to bargain with Whisper Mills even though the

international union has not given the local union permission to bind the international union to a collective bargaining contract with Whisper Mills. Is the local union the international union's agent? (*Whisper Soft Mills v. N.L.R.B.,* 754 F.2d 1381, 9th Cir. 1984.)

4. Treasure Salvors sought to recover the lost treasure of the Spanish ship, the Santa Margarita. Treasure Salvors signed a contract with Captain Jordan, granting him the privilege of working the wrecks, and providing him with pay, specialized supplies, and 5 percent of the recovery of treasures and artifacts. After having great success, Captain Jordan became dissatisfied with the terms of his contract and began to keep his many finds. Does Captain Jordan have any right to more than 5 percent of the treasure? (*Treasure Salvors, Inc. v. Unidentified, Wrecked and Abandoned Sailing Vessel,* 556 F.Supp. 1319, D.Fla. 1983.)

5. Billy Sims hired Argovitz to act as his agent for the purpose of negotiating a contract for Sims as a player in the U.S. Football League (USFL). Unknown to Sims, Argovitz had a very large financial interest in the Houston Gamblers, the USFL's Houston franchise. Argovitz negotiated a very favorable contract for Sims with the Gamblers. Later, Sims found out about Argovitz's interest in the Gamblers, and he wanted out of the contract so that he could play for the Detroit Lions of the National Football League. Is Sims bound by the contract? Discuss. (*Detroit Lions and Sims v. Argovitz,* 580 F.Supp. 542, E.D. Mich. 1984.)

6. St. Croix Homes promised to pay Wilcox management fees for managing St. Croix's housing development. In his seven years as manager, Wilcox did not render full and complete accounts of his service to St. Croix, and the physical and financial condition of the development declined dramatically. Is Wilcox entitled to management fees from St. Croix? (*Wilcox v. St. Croix Labor Union Mutual Homes,* 567 F.Supp. 924, D. Virgin Islands 1983.)

7. Clay was hired by Green to sell Green's boat for not less than $700, out of which Clay was to receive a 10 percent commission. Clay sold the boat for $800 and offered Green $630 in settlement ($700 less 10 percent). Green demanded an additional $90 as the amount due him. Was Green justified in claiming the additional money? Explain.

8. Harkins, a salesman for Watson, was paid a commission on sales made for Watson. Harkins took an order from Boswell for merchandise. Watson accepted the order and shipped the merchandise. In the meantime, Boswell changed his mind and repudiated the transaction, claiming he no longer needed the goods. When they arrived, he refused to accept or pay for them and shipped them back to Watson. Watson claimed that Harkins was not entitled to a commission because the sale had not been completed. Is Watson correct? Explain.

9. Enterprise Federal Savings & Loan Association hired Commonwealth Capital Corp. as its agent for the purpose of acquiring deposits for Enterprise. The parties' contract gave Commonwealth the right to collect commissions from Enterprise, but it did not give Commonwealth any right to the funds it acquired for Enterprise. Can Enterprise unilaterally terminate this agency relationship, and thus terminate Commonwealth's authority, despite the fact that the relationship was created by a legally enforceable contract? Discuss. (*Commonwealth Capital Corp. v. Enterprise Federal Savings & Loan Association,* 630 F.Supp. 1199, E.D. La. 1986.)

10. Wheeler was a sales representative for Burton Enterprises. During his employment—and without telling his employer—Wheeler became a 22 percent owner of a building to be equipped to manufacture and distribute products in direct competition with Burton Enterprises. At the same time, Wheeler lured another of Burton Enterprises' salespersons to join his new company. Wheeler then quit his job with Burton Enterprises and began employment with The Formula One Company. Is Wheeler entitled to commissions earned while employed by Burton Enterprises? (*Burton Enterprises v. Wheeler,* 643 F.Supp. 588, D. Kansas 1986.)

CHAPTER 32

# AGENCY

## LIABILITY OF THE PARTIES

We have already discussed the formation and termination of the agency relationship and the duties existing between the parties. Now we will focus our attention on the legal consequences of this relationship, primarily the *contractual liability* of those involved: principal, agent, and third parties. Near the end of the chapter we will deal with a superior's liability for the torts and crimes of his or her subordinates.

## LIABILITY OF THE PRINCIPAL

The principal is, of course, liable to the agent if he or she breaches a valid employment contract with the agent or violates any other duty owing to the agent. However, the most important questions in this area relate to the principal's liability to the third parties with whom the agent has dealt. If A, acting in behalf of P, makes a contract with T, what is P's legal responsibility to T? If P does not perform as required in the contract, is P required by law to compensate T for T's losses resulting from P's breach?

The answers to these questions usually depend on the court's decision on another question: Was the agent acting within the scope of his or her *authority* in making this particular contract? We will now examine the approach taken by the courts in arriving at an answer.

### The Agent's Authority to Act for the Principal

The fact that you have hired someone to act as your agent does not mean that the person can represent you in any way he or she sees fit. An agent ordinarily can act for the principal in such a way as to make the principal legally responsible only when he or she has **authority** to act that way. The agent's authority can be divided into two basic types: actual and apparent.

**Actual authority** is the authority that the agent does, in fact, have. For convenience it can be further divided into *express authority* and *implied authority*. On the other hand, *apparent authority* is something of a contradiction in terms. It describes a concept which, because of unusual circumstances giving rise to an appearance of authority, occasionally holds the principal responsible for certain of the agent's actions that were not really authorized at all.

**Express Authority:** Express authority is the most obvious and the most common type of authority—that which is directly granted by the principal to the agent. To illustrate: P authorizes A to sell P's farm for at least $25,000. If A sells the farm to T for $30,000, P is bound by the transaction and must honor it. The obvious reason is that A's actions are within the scope of his express authority. Conversely, under most circumstances, P will not be required to honor the transaction if A sells the farm for $20,000.

**Implied Authority:** As is the case with most business transactions, the principal and agent rarely, if ever, contemplate and provide for every possible event that might occur during the existence of their relationship. The law seeks to allow for this fact through the concept of implied authority. **Implied authority** is primarily a matter of what is *customary*. In other words, where the principal has said nothing about a particular aspect of the agent's authority, whether the agent has such authority normally depends on what type of authority a person in a similar position customarily has. Of course, the principal has the final word as to what authority the agent possesses and can grant more or less authority than such an agent usually has. The concept of implied authority serves only to fill in gaps where the principal has not spoken specifically on the subject but where it is reasonable to assume that the principal would have granted such authority if he or she had thought about it.

Many examples of implied authority can be found. For instance, unless the principal has given indications to the contrary, a traveling salesperson ordinarily has authority to take orders but not to make a binding contract to sell the principal's goods. He or she often will be in possession of samples but there usually is no implied authority to sell them. If, however, the salesperson is one who possesses goods *for immediate sale* (such as a salesclerk in a retail store or a door-to-door sales agent who actually carries the principal's merchandise), he or she ordinarily has authority to sell them and collect payment. But this type of agent still does not have implied authority to grant credit or accept payment from the customer for prior credit purchases. Such authority usually exists only if expressly given by the principal, because it is simply not customary for a salesperson to do these things.

Another common application of the concept of implied authority enables an agent to perform those acts which are merely incidental to the main purpose of the agency. (Some legal writers, in fact, use the term *incidental authority*.) Again, the key is what is customary. The rule regarding such authority is: *Unless the principal has indicated otherwise, his or her agent has implied authority to do those things which are reasonably and customarily necessary to enable that person to accomplish the overall purpose of the agency.*

To illustrate: O, the owner of a retail clothing store, hires M to act as manager of the store and gives M express authority to act in certain ways. For instance, M probably will be expressly authorized to purchase inventory and make sales. In addition, M will have implied authority to handle matters that are incidental to the main purpose of the agency. Thus, if the plumbing in the store begins to leak, M can hire a plumber, and O is bound to pay for the services. Similarly, unless instructed otherwise, M can hire an electrician to repair a short in the wiring or a janitorial service to clean the floors. He can also hire a salesclerk or other necessary assistants.

Of course, if the transaction is out of the ordinary or involves a substantial expenditure, the agent should first consult with the principal, because the agent's implied authority may not extend to such matters. Thus, if the electrician hired by M to repair a shorted wire informs him that the wiring in the building is badly worn and does not comply with city building code requirements, M should not act on his own to contract for the rewiring at a substantial cost. Instead he should consult with O before taking further action.

Interesting questions regarding an agent's authority are sometimes raised by the occurrence of an *emergency*. Although it is often said that the scope of an agent's implied authority is "expanded" in emergency situations, this is only sometimes true. If an emergency occurs and there is no opportunity to consult with the principal, the agent has implied authority to take steps that are reasonable and prudent under the circumstances—including actions that may be contrary to prior instructions by the principal.

To illustrate: A has been ordered by P to purchase badly needed raw materials from country X and to ship them through country Y, which has the nearest port facility where the goods can be loaded on vessels. A makes the purchase but then learns from a usually reliable source that a revolution is imminent in country Y and will probably break out while the goods are en route. Fearing that transportation may be impaired or that the goods may be seized by the revolutionaries, A attempts to contact P but is unable to do so. Since he knows that P needs the goods quickly, A arranges for shipment to another port through country Z. Shipment over the other route will be slightly more expensive and time-consuming but also presumably safe, and P will still receive the goods in time to meet his needs.

In this case, A was impliedly authorized to act as he did—even if no revolution actually occurred. What is important is that two elements were present: (1) A, the agent, was *unable to consult with his principal;* and (2) he acted *reasonably,* in light of all the knowledge available to him, to protect the interests of his principal.

**Apparent Authority:** Thus far we have dealt with situations where the agent has actual authority, either express or implied. Now we will examine the peculiar concept of **apparent authority** (sometimes called **ostensible authority**). As we mentioned earlier, speaking of apparent authority as a specific type of authority is something of a contradiction, because the phrase describes a situation where the agent actually has no authority. If the agent acts outside the scope of his or her actual (express or implied) authority, the principal is normally not responsible on the unauthorized transaction. However, if the principal, *by his or her own conduct,* has led reasonable third parties to believe that the agent actually has such authority, the principal may be responsible. In discussing implied authority, we were concerned with what appeared reasonable to the *agent.* But for apparent authority, our concern is with the viewpoint of reasonable *third parties.* Obviously, some situations can fall within the scope of either implied or apparent authority. In such cases we usually speak in terms of implied authority; apparent authority is used as a basis for holding the principal responsible only where no express or implied authority is present.

The importance of apparent authority can be illustrated by two examples:

**1.** S, a salesman for R, has in his possession R's goods (not just samples). It is customary for an agent in S's position who is handling this type of goods to have authority to actually sell and collect payment for them. While making his rounds, S calls the home office. R tells him that he is afraid some of the items S has are defective and instructs him not to sell the goods in his possession but merely to take orders for a period of time. Contrary to instructions, S sells the goods. R is bound by the transactions and will be responsible to T, the buyer, if the goods actually are defective. It appears that R has acted in a reasonable fashion under the circumstances. However, by allowing S to have possession of the goods, he has led T to believe that S is authorized to sell—because it is *customary.* T has no way of knowing that S's actual authority has been expressly limited to something less than what is customary. The basis of R's liability is *not* S's implied authority, because S *knew* that he had no authority and was acting contrary to express instructions. Instead, the basis for R's liability is apparent authority—arising out of the fact that T has been misled by the *appearance of authority.*

**2.** When the agency is terminated, the agent's *actual authority* is also terminated. But this does not automatically dispose of the problem of *apparent authority.* It is sometimes necessary to notify third parties of the termination in order to keep the principal from being liable under the concept of apparent authority. As a general rule, where termination has occurred *as a matter of law* (see Chapter 31 for details), all authority ceases automatically and the principal is not responsible for the agent's further actions regardless of whether the third party has been notified.[1] Most problems involving termination and apparent authority arise when the agency has been ended *by act of the parties* (such as the principal firing the agent). Where termination is by act of the parties, the principal may still be bound by the agent's actions (because of apparent authority) unless and until the third party is notified of the termination. The principal must notify third parties with whom the agent has dealt in the past by letter, telegram, telephone, or some other method of *direct communication* if their identities are reasonably easy to ascertain. Regarding all other third parties, the principal can protect himself simply by giving *public notice.* An advertisement in a local newspaper is the most common form of such notice, but other methods may be sufficient if they are reasonable under the circumstances.

## Ratification of Unauthorized Transactions

If an agent's action is not within the scope of his or her actual (express or implied) authority, and if the facts are such that no apparent authority is present, the principal generally is not liable to the third party for that action. Even in the absence of actual or apparent authority, however, the principal may become responsible if he or she *ratifies* (or *affirms*) the agent's unauthorized actions. An unauthorized act ratified by the principal is treated by the courts in the same manner as if it had been actually authorized from the beginning. The two forms of **ratification**—express and implied—are discussed below.

**Express Ratification:** If, upon learning of the agent's unauthorized dealings, the principal decides to honor the transaction, he or she can simply inform the agent, the third party, or someone else of that intention. In this situation an **express ratification** has obviously occurred.

**Implied Ratification:** Even if the principal has not expressly communicated the intent to ratify, the person can nevertheless be deemed to have done so if

---

[1] However, a few courts have held that where the agency is terminated by the principal's *death,* his or her estate can continue to be liable for the agent's actions, under the doctrine of apparent authority, until the third party learns of the death.

his or her words or conduct reasonably indicate that intent. *Inaction* and *silence* may even amount to ratification if, under the circumstances, a reasonable person would have voiced an objection to what the agent had done. The following five examples will help clarify the concept of **implied ratification.** For each example, no actual authority exists, and there are no facts present to indicate apparent authority.

***Example 1.*** A, who is a driver of a truck owned by P, enters into an unauthorized agreement with T, under which A is to haul T's goods on P's truck. Sometime later, while A is en route, T becomes concerned about the delay and calls P. Upon learning of the transaction, P does not repudiate it but instead assures T that "A is a good driver and the goods will be properly cared for." P has ratified the agreement.

***Example 2.*** Same facts as Example 1. This time, however, T does not call P. The goods arrive safely at their destination, and T sends a check for the shipping charges to P. This is when P first learns of the transaction. If P cashes or deposits the check and uses the money, he will be deemed to have ratified the agreement. Even if he simply retains the check for an appreciable period of time and says nothing, he will probably be held to have ratified.

***Example 3.*** A makes an unauthorized contract to sell P's goods to T. Upon learning of the contract, P says nothing to A or T but assigns the right to receive payment for the goods to X. P has ratified the agreement.

***Example 4.*** Same facts as Example 3. This time, however, P does not assign the right to receive payment. Instead he ships the goods to T. P has ratified the agreement.

***Example 5.*** Same facts as Example 4, but the goods are shipped to T without P's knowledge. P then learns of the transaction, and when T does not make payment by the due date, P files suit against T to collect the purchase price. P has ratified the transaction. (P would not have ratified if he had filed suit to rescind the sale and get his goods back.)

**Requirements for Ratification:** Certain requirements must be present for ratification to occur. Following are the most important of them:

1. The courts generally hold that a principal can ratify only if the agent, in dealing with the third party, has indicated that he or she is acting *for a principal* and not in his or her own behalf.

2. At the time of ratification, the principal must have *known* or *had reason to know* of the essential facts about the transaction. What this means is that the principal must have had either actual knowledge of the relevant facts or sufficient knowledge so that it would have been easy to find out what the essential facts were. The requirement of knowledge is usually important when the third party tries to hold the principal liable by claiming that some words or actions of the principal had amounted to ratification.

3. Ratification must occur within a *reasonable time* after the principal learned of the transaction. What constitutes a reasonable time will, of course, depend on the facts of the particular case. However, a court will automatically rule that a reasonable time period has already expired, and thus that there can be no ratification, if there has been a fundamental change in the facts that had formed the basis of the transaction. An example would be damage to or destruction of the subject matter of the transaction. Similarly, the principal will not be permitted to ratify if the third party has already indicated a desire to withdraw from the transaction. The third party has the right to withdraw prior to ratification and, when he or she does so, any later attempt by the principal to ratify will be treated as being too late.

4. If the principal ratifies, he or she must ratify the *entire transaction* rather than ratifying that part which is to his or her advantage and repudiating that which is to his or her disadvantage. For example, a principal ratifying a contract for the sale of goods to a third party is obligated on any warranties that accompany the goods.

5. The transaction obviously must be *legal,* and the principal must have the *capacity* required to be a party to the transaction.

6. If any *formalities* (such as a writing) would have been required for an original authorization, the same formalities must be met in ratifying the transaction. Of course, if formalities are required, the ratification will have to be express—it cannot be implied. Since most authorizations do not require any special formalities, this usually poses no problem.

The following two cases both deal with the question of apparent authority. The second case also involves the issue of ratification.

## Industrial Molded Plastic Products, Inc. v. J. Gross & Son, Inc.
Superior Court of Pennsylvania, 398 A.2d 695 (1979)

Industrial Molded Plastic Products (Industrial) is in the business of manufacturing custom injection molded plastics by specification for various manufacturers. Industrial also manufactures various "fill-in" items during slack periods, such as electronic parts, industrial components, mirror clips, and plastic clothing clips. J. Gross & Sons (Gross) is a wholesaler to the retail clothing industry, selling mostly sewing thread, but also other items such as zippers, snaps, and clips.

Sometime in the fall of 1970, Stanley Waxman (Gross's president and sole stockholder) and his son Peter (a 22-year-old salesman for Gross) appeared at the offices of Industrial's president, Judson T. Ulansey. They suggested to him that they might be able to market Industrial's plastic clothing clips in the retail clothing industry, in which they had an established sales force. At this initial meeting, there was no discussion of Peter Waxman's authority or lack thereof in the company. After this meeting, Stanley authorized Peter to purchase a "trial" amount of clips (not further specified) to test the market, but neither this authorization nor its limitation was communicated to Ulansey. All subsequent negotiations were between Ulansey and Peter Waxman only. Deceiving both his father and Ulansey, Peter held himself out as vice-president of Gross, and on December 10, 1970, signed an agreement obligating Gross to purchase from Industrial five million plastic clothing clips during the calendar year of 1971, at a price of $7.50 per thousand units, delivery at Industrial's plant in Blooming Glen, Pennsylvania. Before the execution of this agreement, Ulansey telephoned Stanley Waxman, who told Ulansey that Peter could act on behalf of Gross. There was no discussion of the specific terms of the agreement, such as the quantity purchased.

Industrial immediately began production of the five million clips during "fill-in" time. As they were manufactured, they were warehoused in Industrial's plant as specified in the contract. In February 1971, Peter Waxman picked up and paid for 772,000 clips. Stanley Waxman, who had to sign Gross's check for payment, thought that this was the "trial amount" he had authorized Peter to buy. These were the only clips which Gross ever took into its possession. On numerous occasions during the year Ulansey urged Peter to pick up more of the clips, which were taking up more and more storage space at Industrial's plant as they were being manufactured. Peter told Ulansey that he was having difficulty selling the clips and that Gross had no warehousing capacity for the inventory that was being accumulated. At no time, however, did Peter repudiate the contract or request Industrial to halt production. By the end of 1971, production was completed and Industrial was warehousing 4,228,000 clips at its plant.

On January 19, 1972, Industrial sent Gross an invoice for the remaining clips of $31,506.45. However, Gross did not honor the invoice or pick up any more of the clips. Ulansey wrote to Stanley Waxman on February 7, 1972, requesting him to pick up the clips. Receiving no response, Ulansey wrote to Stanley Waxman again on February 23, 1972, threatening legal action if shipping instructions were not received by March 1, 1972. Finally, on March 30, 1972, Peter Waxman responded with a letter to Ulansey, which stated that Gross's failure to move the clips was due to a substantial decline in the clothing industry in 1971 and competition with new lower-cost methods of hanging and shipping clothes. The letter asked for Industrial's patience and predicted that it would take at least the rest of the year to market the clips successfully. At this point, Industrial sued. Stanley Waxman learned of the five-million-clip contract for the first time when informed by his lawyer of the impending lawsuit. At this time, Peter began an extended (four years) leave of absence from Gross.

The trial court ruled in favor of Industrial, the plaintiff, but awarded damages of only $2,400. Both parties appealed, plaintiff claiming that it should be entitled to the entire contract price of over $31,000, and defendant claiming that it should not be liable at all.

**Decision:** The judgment for plaintiff was affirmed, but the appellate court ruled that plaintiff should receive the entire contract price of over $31,000. The defendant company was liable to plaintiff under the doctrine of apparent authority. Stanley Waxman's actions made it appear that his son Peter had the authority to do what he did, and plaintiff was misled by this appearance of authority. ■

## City Electric v. Dean Evans Chrysler-Plymouth
Supreme Court of Utah,
672 P.2d 89 (1983)

Dave Sturgill was a salesman for Dean Evans Chrysler-Plymouth, a retail automobile dealership. Dean Evans was president of the firm, and Mike Evans was assistant secretary. Mike Evans was also a partner with Johnny Rider in another business, Johnny Rider's Backstage Restaurant. On one occasion, Mike Evans and Johnny Rider were discussing the remodeling of their restaurant. Sturgill happened to be present during the discussion, and volunteered to contact City Electric, an electric materials supplier that Sturgill had previously worked for. Sturgill said that he might be able to get them a good price on the electrical materials they would need for the remodeling project. Sturgill called Don Hatch, a salesman for City Electric, and told Hatch that Sturgill was trying to do a favor for his boss (Mike Evans). Sturgill asked if City Electric would give Mike Evans a fair price, and if the restaurant could establish an account. Shortly after this conversation, and before City Electric had time to set up an account for the restaurant, Mike Evans told Sturgill that the materials should be purchased on the auto dealership's account with City Electric.

The next day, Sturgill again called Hatch and placed an order for materials, stating that the materials were to be charged to the account of Dean Evans Chrysler-Plymouth. Sturgill said that he was acting pursuant to Mike Evans's directions, but there was never any representation that the auto dealership owned or was affiliated with the restaurant. Hatch checked his firm's computer printouts of open accounts and found that the auto dealership did have such an account with City Electric. Hatch put this and several later orders on the account, and the materials were delivered to the restaurant. Several invoices were sent to the auto dealership, and two of them dated October 8 and 9, 1978, were paid in December, 1978. There was no evidence indicating who paid these two invoices in behalf of the auto dealership. Apparently, either Mike Evans or Sturgill paid the two invoices with company funds before the dealership's president, Dean Evans, discovered what had happened. Thereafter, the dealership refused to make any further payments, leaving an unpaid balance of $2,332.70. City Electric, plaintiff, filed suit against Dean Evans Chrysler-Plymouth, defendant, for this unpaid balance. The trial court held that both Mike Evans and Dave Sturgill had apparent authority to charge the orders to the dealerships account, and ruled in favor of plaintiff. Defendant appealed.

**Decision:** The judgment for plaintiff City Electric was reversed. The transactions in question obviously were not made with express or implied authority, and neither Mike Evans nor Dave Sturgill had any apparent authority to charge the materials to the auto dealership's account at City Electric. City Electric never spoke with Mike Evans or anyone else at the dealership; he relied solely on the statements of Sturgill that Mike Evans was behind the transaction. The dealership (i.e., Dean Evans) did nothing to cause City Electric to think that Sturgill or Mike Evans had such authority. Perhaps most important, as the transaction was far afield from the type of business that the dealership conducted, Sturgill had no cause to assume that it was authorized. Also, the fact that two invoices were paid does not amount to a ratification of the unauthorized transactions by the dealership. There was no evidence as to who actually wrote the checks, and there was no evidence indicating that Dean Evans or any other person in charge at the dealership knew the relevant facts pertaining to the transaction. ∎

---

## Importance of the Agent's Knowledge

In deciding the question of a principal's liability to a third party, sometimes a key issue is whether the principal has received notice of a particular fact. For example, P is obligated under a contract to make payment to T. T assigns her right to receive this payment to X, an assignee. Assuming that T's right is assignable, P is bound to honor the assignment and pay X instead of T only if he has received notice of the assignment. But what if P's agent, A, receives this notice rather than P himself? If A promptly relays the information to P, there is usually no problem. What happens, though, if A fails to do so and P, not knowing of the assignment, pays T instead of X? Is P liable to X because P's agent had received notice?

Ordinarily, in any case where notice to the principal is important, *notice to the agent is treated as notice to the principal if the agent's receipt of the notice is within the scope of his or her actual or apparent authority.* In other words, in such cases the law will treat the principal as if he or she had received notice even if the agent did not transmit it. Obviously, however, this does not apply where the third party who notifies the agent knows that the agent is acting adversely to the interests of the principal (as where the third party and the agent are conspiring to defraud the principal).

## LIABILITY OF THE AGENT

When the agent is acting for the principal, the agent ordinarily incurs no personal responsibility if he or she acts in a proper fashion. However, circumstances do exist where the agent can become liable.

### *Breach of Duty*

If the agent violates any of the duties owed to the principal, he or she naturally is liable for the damages caused by the breach. Where the duty which has been violated is that of loyalty, the penalties may be even more severe. A disloyal agent is not only responsible to the principal for any resulting loss sustained by the latter but also usually forfeits his or her right to be compensated for services rendered. Furthermore, the agent must turn over to the principal any profits made from his or her disloyal activity.

### *Exceeding Authority*

The agent who exceeds his or her actual authority is personally responsible unless the principal ratifies the unauthorized actions. Whether this responsibility is to the principal or to the third party depends on the circumstances. If the agent exceeds his or her actual authority, but the principal is liable to a third party on the ground of apparent authority, the agent's liability is to the *principal.* On the other hand, if the agent exceeds his or her actual authority and the facts are such that the principal is not liable to a third party under apparent authority, then the agent's liability is to the *third party.*

### *Assuming Liability*

If the agent personally assumes liability for a particular transaction, then he or she obviously is responsible. For instance: A is attempting to purchase goods for P on credit. T, the seller, is wary of P's credit rating and refuses to grant credit unless A also becomes obligated. A signs the agreement as P's agent and in his own individual capacity. A is in effect a *co-principal* and therefore personally liable to T if P defaults.

### *Nondisclosure of Principal*

If the agent, in dealing with a third party, fails to disclose that he or she is *acting for a principal* or fails to disclose the *principal's identity,* the agent is personally responsible to the third party. Additionally, the agent will sometimes be liable if he or she acts for a nonexistent principal or for one not having legal capacity. (These subjects are dealt with specifically later in the chapter.)

### *Commission of a Tort*

If the agent commits a *tort,* he or she is personally responsible to the injured party for the resulting harm. This is true regardless of whether the agent was working for the principal at the time. (Sometimes the principal also is responsible. This problem is discussed later in the chapter.)

## LIABILITY OF THE THIRD PARTY

Relatively little need be said about the liability of the third party. Since that party is acting in his or her own behalf, he or she is personally responsible to the other party to the transaction. This ordinarily means that:

**1.** If the third party fails to live up to his or her part of the bargain, that person will be liable to the principal.

**2.** The third party owes no responsibility to the agent unless the agent has personally become a party to the transaction.

**3.** The third party is liable for his or her torts to any party injured as a result.

## NONEXISTENT, PARTIALLY DISCLOSED, AND UNDISCLOSED PRINCIPALS

In discussing the principal-agent relationship we have thus far assumed that the principal exists when the agent executes the transaction in question and that both the existence and the identity of the principal are disclosed to the third party. This is usually, but not always, the case. The special problems that arise in connection with *nonexistent, partially disclosed,* and *undisclosed principals* are discussed below.

## Nonexistent Principals

If an agent purports to act for a principal who does not exist at the time, the agent is usually liable to the third party. Of course, since there is no principal, the agent is not really an agent at all; he or she merely *claims* to be one.

While this situation does not occur frequently, it is by no means rare. A common instance of the **nonexistent principal** is that of a person attempting to act for an organization that is not legally recognized as a separate entity. (A *legal entity* is an organization—such as a corporation—that is recognized by the law as having the rights and duties of a person, although it is not flesh and blood. It can, for example, make contracts, sue, and be sued in its own name.) Thus a member of an unincorporated association, such as a church, club, fraternity, or the like, may attempt to contract in behalf of the association. Since the "principal" is not legally recognized as one, the members who make the agreement are personally responsible. It is for this reason that many churches and other such organizations form corporations.

The contracts of *corporate promoters* (those who play a part in the initial organization of a corporation) have posed similar problems. Quite often, these people make various types of agreements before the proposed corporation is formed. They may, for example, enter contracts for the purpose of raising capital, purchasing a building site, or procuring the services of an attorney, an accountant, or other professionals. The liabilities of the promoter, of the corporation once it is formed, and of the third party are discussed in Chapter 36.

A similar situation occurs when a principal has existed but is now dead or lacks contractual capacity when the agent contracts with the third party. As we mentioned in Chapter 18, such an occurrence often terminates the agency, and the principal (or that person's estate) is not bound. If the agency is not terminated, the principal's status affects his or her own liability in the same way as if the principal had personally dealt with the third party.

Whether the *agent* is personally liable depends on the circumstances. If the principal is *dead* or has been *declared insane by a court* at the time of the transaction, the agent invariably is held personally liable to the third party. On the other hand, if, at the time the transaction is made, the principal is either a *minor* or *insane* (but not officially declared insane by a court), the agent is personally responsible to the third party in only two situations:

**1.** The agent is liable if he or she has made representations to the effect that the principal has contractual capacity. This is true even if the agent is honestly mistaken.

**2.** The agent who has made no such representations is still liable to the third party if he or she *knew or had reason to know* of the principal's lack of capacity *and* the third party's ignorance of the facts.

## Partially Disclosed Principals

As we indicated earlier, an agent usually is responsible to the third party if the agent discloses the fact that he or she is acting for a principal but does not *identify* that person. If the agent acts with authority, the principal is also responsible and may be held liable when the third party learns his or her identity.[2] Since the third party knows that the agent is acting for someone else, the third party is, in turn, liable to the principal. In sum, the liability of the principal and the third party is the same as in the case of a completely disclosed principal. The only difference is that in the case of a **partially disclosed principal,** *the agent is also liable,* unless the agent and the third party agree otherwise.

## Undisclosed Principals

Individuals and business organizations sometimes prefer not to have their connection with a transaction be known. If an agent acts in behalf of a principal but does not disclose to the third party the fact that he or she is representing another, it is said that the agent acts for an **undisclosed principal.** In other words, the third party, not knowing that a principal-

---

[2] There is conflict among the courts on whether the third party must make a choice (or *election*) between the agent and the principal in such a case or whether he or she can hold both of them responsible.

agent relationship exists, thinks that the agent is dealing solely for himself.

In a case such as this, the agent is personally liable to the third party. If and when the principal makes himself known, that person is also liable to the third party if the agent acted within the scope of his authority. In such an event, the third party must *elect* whether to hold the agent or the principal responsible.[3]

Thus far we have focused on the liability of the undisclosed principal and the agent. But what about the liability of the *third party?* Since the *agent* is a party to the contract, he or she can enforce the agreement against the third party. Once revealed, the *principal* ordinarily can also enforce the agreement. In three situations, however, the third party can refuse to perform for the undisclosed principal and can continue to treat the agent as the sole party to whom he or she is obligated.

**1.** If the third party has already performed for the agent before the principal is revealed, the third party is not required to render a second performance.

**2.** If, prior to the transaction, the third party has indicated that he or she will not deal with the one who is the undisclosed principal, the third party is not required to perform for that principal. Similarly, the third party is not responsible to the undisclosed principal if the former has indicated beforehand or in the agreement that he or she will not deal with *anyone* other than the agent.

**3.** In all other situations the undisclosed principal is treated in much the same way as an *assignee* from the agent (see Chapter 16 for a discussion of assignees). He or she can demand performance from the third party only if the contract is of a type that can be assigned. Thus, if the contract calls for personal service by the agent or if the agent's personal credit standing, judgment, or skill played an important part in the third party's decision to deal with that individual, the third party cannot be forced to accept the undisclosed principal as a substitute.

## TORT LIABILITY

Until now, our discussions of legal responsibility have focused almost exclusively on the parties' contractual liability. Now we will turn to their *tort liability.*

### *Circumstances in which the Superior Is Liable for the Subordinate's Torts*

Obviously, if either the superior, the subordinate, or the third party personally commits a tort, that person is liable to the one injured by the wrongful act. If the *subordinate* commits a tort, the additional question often arises whether his or her *superior* is also liable to the injured third party. This is often important because ordinarily the superior is insured or otherwise more financially capable of paying damages.

If the superior personally is at fault, that person obviously is liable because he or she has committed a tort. This can be seen in the following situations:

**1.** If the superior *directs* the subordinate to commit the tort (or even if the superior *intends* that the tort be committed), he or she is responsible.

**2.** If the superior carelessly allows the subordinate to operate potentially dangerous equipment (such as an automobile or truck), even though he or she knows or should know that the subordinate is unqualified or incapable of handling it safely, the superior is responsible for any resulting harm. The phrase *negligent entrustment* is often used to describe this situation.

**3.** Similarly, the superior is held liable if he or she is negligent in *failing to properly supervise a subordinate.*

Most often, however, the superior has not directed or intended the commission of a tort and has no reason to suppose that he or she is creating a dangerous situation. Therefore, the third party usually seeks to impose **vicarious liability** (liability imposed not because of one's own wrong but solely because of the wrong of one's subordinate) on the superior. The imposition of liability on the superior for a tort committed by a subordinate is based on the doctrine of **respondeat superior** ("let the master answer").

The theoretical justification for holding the superior responsible is that he or she can treat the loss—or the premiums for liability insurance—as a cost of

---

[3] Different jurisdictions apply different rules as to what constitutes an *election.* Demanding payment from the agent or the principal or even filing suit against one of them usually *is not* considered the third party's "point of no return." Obtaining satisfaction of the claim obviously *is* an election. However, courts differ on whether *obtaining a court judgment* (which has not yet been collected) constitutes an election. Of course, if the third party obtains a judgment against the agent before knowing the principal's identity, there is no binding election and the third party can still pursue the principal.

doing business. The cost is thus reflected in the price of his or her product, and the loss is ultimately spread over that segment of the population benefiting from that product.

When the superior is required to pay damages to a third party because of the tort of a subordinate, the superior usually has a legal right to recoup the loss from that subordinate. As a practical matter, this is an illusory right in many cases, because the subordinate frequently is unable to pay.

Of course, the superior is not always responsible for the torts of subordinates. In this regard, two issues must ordinarily be dealt with:

1. Was the relationship that of employer–employee (i.e., master-servant) or employer–independent contractor?

2. If an employer–employee relationship existed, was the employee acting within the scope of his or her employment at the time of committing the alleged tort?

## Employer–Employee or Employer–Independent Contractor

**Legal Significance of the Distinction:** The imposition of vicarious liability often depends on the nature of the relationship involved. If it is found to be that of employer–employee, the employer is liable for a tort committed by the employee if it was committed in the scope of the employee's employment for the employer.

On the other hand, if the relationship is found to be that of employer and independent contractor, the employer generally is not liable for a tort committed by the independent contractor. Those few instances in which the employer *is liable* for a tort are as follows.

1. If the task for which the independent contractor was hired is *inherently dangerous,* the employer will be responsible for harm to third parties caused by the dangerous character of the work. The employer's responsibility in such a case is based on the tort concept of *strict liability.* That is, the responsibility exists solely because of the nature of the activity, regardless of whether any negligence or other fault brought about the damage. Activities deemed to be inherently dangerous include blasting, using deadly chemicals, or working on buildings in populated areas where people must pass below the activity.

2. If the employer owes a *nondelegable duty,* he or she cannot escape ultimate responsibility for performing that duty by obtaining an independent contractor to perform it. Thus, if the independent contractor is negligent or commits some other tort in the performance of such a task, the employer is liable to the injured third party. Nondelegable duties are those duties owed to the public which courts feel to be of such importance that responsibility cannot be delegated. Examples are (a) a duty imposed by statute, such as the statutory duty of a railroad to keep highway crossings in a safe condition; (b) the duty of a city to keep its streets in a safe condition; (c) the duty of a landlord who has assumed responsibility for making repairs to the premises to see that those repairs are done safely; and (d) the duty of a business proprietor whose premises are open to the public to keep the premises in a reasonably safe condition.

3. As is usually the case regardless of the exact nature of the relationship between the superior and subordinate, an employer is liable for the independent contractor's tort if the employer specifically directed, authorized, or intended the wrongful conduct.

**Making the Distinction:** The determination of whether a particular subordinate is an employee or an independent contractor depends essentially on the issue of *control.* If the employer has hired the subordinate merely to achieve a result and has left decisions regarding the method and manner of achieving that result up to the subordinate, the latter is an independent contractor. On the other hand, if the superior actually controls or has the right to control the method and manner of achieving the result, then the subordinate is an employee. Thus a construction contractor hired to erect a building is usually an independent contractor, while a secretary hired to type and take dictation is usually an employee.

However, the delineation is not always easy, and sometimes it produces problems of extreme conceptual difficulty. The most important question, of course, is whether the employer *controls or has the right to control the method and manner of doing the work.* Where the matter of control is not so obvious as to make the determination readily apparent, other factors can be taken into account. Some facts which would increase the likelihood of a subordinate being viewed as an independent contractor are: (1) the subordinate has his own independent business or profession; (2) the subordinate uses his own tools, equipment, or workplace to perform the task; (3) the subordinate is paid by the job, not by the hour, week, or month; (4) the subordinate has irregular hours; and (5) the subordinate is performing a task that is not part of the employer's regular business. None of these facts automatically makes a subordinate an independent contractor; each is simply a factor to be weighed along with all the other evidence.

The following case illustrates the importance of the employer's right of control when there is a question about the subordinate's status as an employee or an independent contractor.

### Branco Wood Products, Inc. v. C.C. Huxford Trust
Court of Civil Appeals of Alabama, 521 So. 2d 73 (1988)

Branco, the defendant, is a corporation in the business of supplying wood to large purchasers such as Container Corp. of America (CCA), the buyer in this case. Branco has a number of individuals ("producers") who cut and deliver the timber which Branco supplies to its customers. CCA buys wood by means of a "ticket system." CCA provides tickets to suppliers (e.g., Branco) indicating the amount of wood ordered; the supplier selects producers and gives them CCA's tickets; the producers cut and deliver wood to CCA; CCA pays the supplier, and the supplier pays the producers. After Branco picks a producer, it leaves the details to him. The producer makes his own arrangements with a landowner for timber cutting, and controls his own hours and methods. Apparently, Branco also does not treat producers as employees in its payroll or other records.

In this case, Branco received CCA tickets and selected Bell as its producer. While cutting timber, Bell mistakenly crossed over the boundary line to another piece of property where he had no permission to cut. The property on which he trespassed and cut substantial timber was owned by the Huxford Trust, which sued Branco on the grounds that Bell was Branco's employee and was acting within the scope of his employment when he trespassed. The trial court ruled for the Trust, and Branco appealed.

**Decision:** The judgment for the trust was reversed. Bell was an independent contractor, and Branco was not liable for his wrongful conduct. ■

## Scope of Employment

If the subordinate is deemed to be an employee, the employer is liable to third parties for those torts committed by the employee in the *scope of his or her employment*. There exists no simple definition of the **scope of employment** (sometimes called *course of employment*) concept. Obviously, an employee is acting within the scope of employment while performing work that he or she has been *expressly directed to do by the employer*. To illustrate: X has directed Y to drive X's truck from New York to Albany via a certain route. While on that route, Y drives negligently and injures T. X is liable to T.

In the absence of a specific directive given by the employer, an act usually is in the scope of employment if it is *reasonably incidental to an activity that has been expressly directed*. Thus, in the above example, if Y had stopped to buy gasoline and had negligently struck a parked car belonging to T, X would have been liable to T.

**Deviations:** The employer sometimes can be held liable even though the employee has deviated from the authorized activity. The employer's liability in such cases depends on the *degree* and *foreseeability* of the deviation. If the deviation is great, the employer usually is not responsible. Suppose that Y, in driving X's truck from New York to Albany, decides to go a hundred miles off his authorized route to visit an old friend. On the way there, Y negligently collides with T. In this situation, X is not liable.

But what if Y has been to see his friend and was returning to his authorized route when the collision occurred? Three different viewpoints have been taken by various courts. Where there has been more than a slight deviation from the scope of employment, as in this case, some courts have held that the reentry into the scope of employment occurs only when the employee has *actually returned to the authorized route or activity.* Others have held that there is reentry the moment that the employee, with an intent to serve the employer's business, *begins to turn back toward the point of deviation.* However, a majority of courts have held that reentry occurs when the employee, with an intent to serve the employer's business, *has turned back toward and come reasonably close to the point of deviation.*

If the deviation from the authorized route or activity is only slight, many courts have held that the employee is still within the scope of employment if the type of deviation was *reasonably foreseeable* by the master. For example: While driving from New York to Albany, Y stops at a roadside establishment to get something to eat or buy a pack of cigarettes. While pulling off the road, he negligently strikes a parked car. In this situation X is liable. Although buying something to eat or smoke may not be necessary to drive a truck from New York to Albany (as is the purchase of gasoline) and although Y was not really serving his employer, the deviation was only slight and was of the type that any employer should reasonably expect.

Many examples of the scope of employment issue—such as the next two cases—involve auto accidents (though certainly the issue is not limited to them). These two cases illustrate some typical problems in this area.

---

### Lazar v. Thermal Equipment Corp.
Court of Appeals of California, 195 Cal. Rptr. 890 (1983)

Richard Lanno was employed as a project engineer for Thermal Equipment Co., which was a manufacturer of heating equipment and pressure vessels for the aerospace industry. In connection with his job, Lanno was sometimes required to proceed from his home directly to a job site in the mornings. In addition, he was constantly on call as a troubleshooter, and, consequently, Thermal's customers occasionally called him at his home after hours and on weekends. In order to answer these calls, Lanno needed the company truck, in which he sometimes carried tools; if the truck was not at his home, he would stop at Thermal to pick up needed tools on the way to answer the call. To facilitate these duties, Thermal allowed Lanno to take the company truck home with him on a daily basis. Thermal provided Lanno with gasoline for the truck, and allowed him to use it for personal purposes.

On one occasion, Lanno finished work and left Thermal's business premises. Driving the company truck, he headed in a direction away from both the workplace and his home; Lanno testified that he planned to stop at a store, purchase something, and then go home. Before reaching the store, Lanno was involved in an accident with Lazar, who suffered bodily injury and damage to his car. Lazar filed suit against Thermal, claiming that Lanno had driven the truck negligently and that Lanno was within the scope of his employment at the time of the accident. The jury found that Lanno was not acting within the scope of his employment at the time of the accident, but the trial court granted Lazar's motion for judgment notwithstanding the verdict, holding that Lanno was within the scope of employment as a matter of law. The jury had found Lazar's damages to be $81,000, and the trial court rendered judgment for Lazar against Thermal in this amount. Thermal appealed.

---

**Decision:** The judgment for plaintiff Lazar was affirmed. Lanno was acting within the scope of his employment at the time of the accident. The "coming and going" rule did not apply because Lanno used a vehicle (and it was his employer's vehicle, although this fact did not determine the outcome) in performing his work duties, and was "on call" to do repair work after normal business hours. His act of stopping by a store on the way home did not take him outside the scope of employment because the deviation from his normal route was minor and what he did was reasonably foreseeable by his employer. The fact that the store was in the opposite direction from his home does not matter. ■

**Comment:** If the deviation had been substantial and unforeseeable, such as a two-hour stop at a bar, Lanno would have been outside the scope of his employment during the deviation. However, because the "coming and going" rule did not apply to this case, Lanno would have *reentered* the scope of employment upon getting back into the truck and resuming the trip toward home.

---

### Dinkins v. Farley
New York Supreme Court, Monroe County, 434 N.Y.S.2d 325 (1980)

As part of its personnel policy, Xerox Corporation maintained a National Tuition Aid Program that provided financial assistance to employees taking advanced college courses. An employee's application to participate in the program had to be approved by the employee's immediate supervisor. The company provided tuition assistance only for those courses directly related to a present job or to a future job to which an employee might reasonably aspire at Xerox. Upon approval of the employee's application, Xerox advanced 100 percent of the tuition and lab fees and then deducted 35 percent of that amount from the employee's paychecks in installments. Thereafter, the employee was required to verify enrollment by submitting itemized receipts from the college, and later to verify successful completion of a course by submitting a grade report to Xerox within 30 days after the end of the semester. If a grade report for a course was not submitted to Xerox within 50 days after semester's end, the company initiated steps to collect the other 65 percent of course expenses from the employee. However, if the employee ultimately received an advanced degree as a result of his participation in the tuition aid program, Xerox would refund the 35 percent that had been paid by the employee. A course taken under the program was expected to be scheduled outside of working hours if possible; if this was not possible, the employee could have limited time off during the workday to attend classes, subject to approval by the employee's supervisor. Such time off had to be made up at another time decided by the supervisor. Xerox spent about $1,000,000 annually on the program, and at the time of this case over 6,000 of Xerox's employees had participated.

Victor Farley, an employee of Xerox, had a bachelor's degree in engineering and wished to take a linear systems course that would better prepare him for pursuing a master's degree in that field. His application for the tuition aid program was approved by Xerox and he enrolled in the course at the Rochester Institute of Technology. He usually got out of work at 4:20 or 4:30 p.m., and frequently was a few minutes late for the class, which began at 4:20. One afternoon as Victor was driving to class, he was involved in an automobile accident at an intersection on campus. The other driver, Diane Dinkins, sued both Victor and Xerox, claiming that Victor was guilty of negligence and that Xerox was also liable because Victor was acting within the scope of his employment at the time of the accident. Before trial, Xerox filed a motion for summary judgment on the ground that, as a matter of law, Victor was not acting within the scope of his employment when the accident occurred. Below is a summary of the trial court's opinion on this issue.

---

**Decision:** The trial court granted Xerox's motion for summary judgment. As a matter of law, Farley was not within the scope of his employment at the time of his accident with Dinkins on the college campus. It is true that Xerox encouraged and provided financial support for employees' efforts to further their education, and probably even benefitted from higher employee morale and a better educated workforce. But Farley's primary motive for taking the college courses, and consequently his primary motive for driving on the campus was to benefit himself personally. His education, with or without an additional degree, is something that will belong to him. ∎

---

**Intentional Torts:** Thus far we have assumed the tort to be that of *negligence* (simple carelessness). Most cases in fact are concerned with the employee's negligence. However, an employee's *intentional tort,* such as assault and battery, libel, slander, fraud, trespass, or the like, can also subject the employer to liability. The test is the same. The employer is liable if the employee was acting within the scope of his or her employment at the time. It should be emphasized, though, that an employer is *less likely* to be responsible if the employee's tort was *intentional* rather than merely negligent. The reason is that when an employee intentionally commits a wrongful act, he or she is more likely to be motivated by personal reasons rather than by a desire to serve the employer. Those cases where the employer *has* been held liable for his or her employee's intentional torts usually fall within one of four broad categories.

1. *Where the tort occurs in a job in which force is a natural incident.* An example is a bouncer in a saloon, who is naturally expected to use force occasionally. But if *excessive* force is used, the employer is liable.

2. *Where the employee is actually attempting to promote the employer's business but does it in a wrongful manner.* For example, two competing tow truck drivers are attempting to beat each other to the scene of an accident to get the business for their respective employers. One intentionally runs the other off the road. The employer of the one committing the tort is liable.

3. *Where the tort results from friction naturally brought about by the employer's business.* For instance, the employee, who works for a building contractor, argues with an employee of a subcontractor about the method for laying a floor. They become angry, and the building contractor's employee strikes the other party. The building contractor, as employer, is probably liable.

4. *Where the tort was directly authorized or clearly intended by the employer.* This situation usually, but not always, involves a nonphysical tort such as fraud or defamation. As mentioned at the beginning of this discussion of the employer's tort liability, an employer who authorizes or intends the subordinate's wrongful act is usually held liable regardless of the kind of tort or the type of relationship between superior and subordinate.

## Concluding Note on Tort Liability

Two additional problems regarding an employer's tort liability need to be discussed:

1. A minor is not necessarily the employee of his or her parents. Thus, in the absence of a special statute, the parent is not liable for the torts of a minor child unless the child was acting as an employee in the scope of employment for the parent. The parent can, of course, be held liable for his or her own wrongful act in negligently supervising the child. Also, several states have passed statutes making parents liable within set limits for intentional property damage caused by a minor child.

2. Although the subject of bailments is beyond the scope of this discussion, it should be mentioned that a bailee is not necessarily the employee of the bailor. A *bailment* occurs when the owner of an item of property (the bailor) turns over temporary custody (not ownership) of the item to the bailee for any reason. The bailor ordinarily is *not* liable to third parties for torts committed by the bailee while using the bailor's property. The bailor *is* liable, however, if he or she was negligent in entrusting the item to one whom he or she knew not to be qualified or capable of handling it safely. Otherwise, the bailor generally is liable only if the bailee was acting as the bailor's *employee* in the scope of employment at the time of the tort. Two exceptions exist with regard to *bailments of automobiles:*

   **a.** A few states follow the *family purpose doctrine.* Under that judge-made doctrine, a member of the family is treated as the employee of the head of the household when driving the family car, regardless of whether such a relationship actually existed.

   **b.** A few states have passed *owner-consent statutes,* which hold the owner of an automobile liable to a third party injured by the negligence of anyone who is driving it with the consent of the owner. This liability exists regardless of any employer-employee relationship and regardless of whether the owner was personally negligent.

## CRIMINAL LIABILITY

As a general rule, a superior cannot be *criminally* prosecuted for a subordinate's wrongful act unless the superior expressly authorized it. Thus, if Y, a subordinate, while acting within the scope of her employment, injures T, and T dies, Y's superior can be held liable in a civil suit for damages but cannot be subjected to criminal liability. Any criminal responsibility rests on the shoulders of the subordinate. The rule exists because crimes ordinarily require intent, and the superior in this situation has no criminal intent.

Exceptions to the rule usually fall within one of two categories:

1. The statute making the particular act a crime may specifically provide for placing criminal responsibility on the superior. For example, the federal antitrust laws provide for criminal penalties to be levied against

corporations, which can commit crimes only through their human agents.

2. A superior can sometimes be criminally prosecuted under statutes that do not require intent for a violation. A specific example is the offense of selling adulterated food under the federal Food, Drug, and Cosmetic Act. Other examples can be found in some state laws regulating liquor sales and the accuracy of weights of goods sold on that basis.

## SUMMARY

The contractual liability of the principal to third parties for transactions made by the agent is dependent on the agent's authority. If the agent acted within the scope of his or her authority when executing the transaction, the resulting contract is the principal's contract and the principal is bound by it. An agent's authority may be express—that which is directly granted by the principal to the agent. It may also be implied—that which is customary for an agent in such a position, or which is reasonably incidental to the agent's express authority. Even if the agent has no express or implied authority, it is possible for the principal to be liable for the agent's actions on the grounds of apparent authority. Apparent authority exists when the principal, by his or her conduct, has misled a reasonably acting third party to believe that the agent had authority. In addition, it is possible for a principal to become liable to the third party by subsequently ratifying the agent's unauthorized transaction. When a principal's liability to a third party depends on whether the principal had notice or knowledge of particular facts, notice to the agent is treated as notice to the principal if receipt of such information was within the scope of the agent's actual or apparent authority.

The agent usually does not incur personal liability when acting in behalf of the principal. The agent can become liable, however, by breaching a duty to the principal, exceeding his or her authority, personally assuming liability, not fully disclosing to the third party that the agent is acting for a particular principal, or committing a tort against a third party.

When a subordinate commits a tort harming a third party, the subordinate clearly is legally responsible to the third party. The superior also can be liable to the third party if it is found that the subordinate was an employee rather than an independent contractor, and if the subordinate was acting within the scope of his or her employment when the tort was committed. A subordinate is an employee if the superior had the right to exercise detailed control over the method and manner by which the subordinate was to accomplish the task. A subordinate is an independent contractor if he or she was hired to accomplish a particular result, and the details of how to do it were within the subordinate's discretion.

## KEY TERMS

**Authority**
**Actual authority**
**Express authority**
**Implied authority**
**Apparent authority (or ostensible authority)**
**Ratification**
**Express ratification**
**Implied ratification**
**Nonexistent principal**
**Partially disclosed principal**
**Undisclosed principal**
**Vicarious liability**
**Respondeat superior**
**Scope of employment**

## QUESTIONS AND PROBLEMS

1. Capital Dredge & Dock Corp. hired an attorney, Alteri, to represent the corporation. Capital Dredge held Alteri out to the City of Detroit as having authority to represent Capital Dredge in personal injury claims and "certain related claims against the City." However, Capital Dredge representatives specifically instructed Alteri not to compromise any of Capital Dredge's claims against the City of Detroit for extra work and delay. Alteri signed a document releasing all of Capital Dredge's claims against the City. Is the release valid? (*Capital Dredge & Dock Corp. v. City of Detroit,* 800 F.2d 525, 6th Cir. 1986.)

2. Consolidated Foods Corp. authorized Newman only to draft an agreement for David Chase to buy the Fuller Brush Company, a division of Consolidated Foods. The agreement was expressly to be subject to the approval of Consolidated Foods' board of directors. Upon drafting such an agreement, Newman sent a telegram to Chase stating that the board of directors had ratified the agreement to sell the Fuller Brush Company, even though the board had done no such thing. Is Consolidated bound by the terms of the agreement? (*Chase v. Consolidated Foods Corp.,* 744 F.2d 566, 7th Cir. 1984.)

3. Jerry Beck represented himself as acting on behalf of two partnerships investing in real estate in order to obtain

investment money from the Stolmeiers. The partnerships had not authorized Beck to be their agent, but they used the money solicited from the Stolmeiers to renovate partnership properties. The Stolmeiers became dissatisfied with their investment. When the members of the partnerships learned of this fact, they made no effort to repudiate Beck's authority to solicit funds on their behalf. Are the partnerships bound by Beck's guarantee to the Stolmeiers that they would receive a return on their investment? (*Stolmeier v. Beck,* 441 N.W.2d 889, Neb. 1989.)

**4.** Rodriguez was a salesman at a retail carpet outlet owned by Carpet World, Inc. He usually was the only employee in the store, and the company's sales manager only made occasional visits to the store. Although he had no hiring authority, Rodriguez hired Amy Schoonover on a salary and commission basis. Amy worked for two months, earning salary and commissions of $714, but was never paid. Rodriguez disappeared, and Amy sued Carpet World for her unpaid compensation. Is Carpet World liable? Discuss. (*Schoonover v. Carpet World, Inc.*, 588 P.2d 729, 1978.)

**5.** Bruton lent a D-8 Caterpillar rent-free to David Eckvall, who wanted to clear some land owned by Eckvall. It was agreed that Eckvall would provide an operator and pay for fuel and routine maintenance. Nothing was said about major repairs. While Eckvall was using the Cat, it broke down. Without contacting Bruton, he took it to Automatic Welding & Supply (AWS), where extensive repairs were made at a cost of $2,340. When the repairs were almost completed, Bruton happened to come into the AWS shop on other business and saw his Cat. He spoke to an AWS mechanic and learned of the scope of the repairs, but nothing was said about cost. After the repairs were completed, the Cat was returned to Eckvall's property, where he used it for some time thereafter. AWS billed Bruton for the repairs. Bruton denied liability, and AWS sued. Is Bruton responsible for the $2,340? Discuss. (*Bruton v. Automatic Welding & Supply,* 513 P.2d 1122, 1973.)

**6.** Chipman, an employee at Barrickman's service station, was towing a disabled car for Barrickman. Estell, Chipman's girlfriend, was a passenger in the tow truck. She was just along for the ride, without Barrickman's knowledge. The tow truck was involved in an accident and Estell, who was injured, sued Chipman and Barrickman. The trial court dismissed the suit against Barrickman, because he had an official "no rider" rule, even though he didn't always enforce it. Estell appealed. How should the appellate court rule? Discuss. (*Estell v. Barrickman,* 571 S.W.2d 650, 1978.)

**7.** Chambers was in the business of moving mobile homes. On previous occasions, Chambers had hired Ross and Bridges to help move mobile homes. Chambers had provided Ross with a truck that had on it magnetic signs bearing the name "Chambers Mobile Home Movers," but asked Ross to remove the signs after Ross damaged two mobile homes. Benny Tate hired Ross and Bridges to move Tate's mobile home based upon Ross's assurances that he was experienced and had insurance. When Tate met Ross and Bridges on the appointed day, both Ross and Bridges were wearing shirts with the name "Chambers Home Movers." The truck did not have the signs on it on that day, but it did on the second day. Tate overheard Ross tell a North Carolina Department of Transportation official that Chambers Home Movers was Ross's business. Tate's mobile home was damaged during the move. Ross told Tate that he worked for Chambers. Is Chambers responsible for the damaged mobile home? (*Tate v. Chambers,* 379 S.E.2d 681, N.C. App. 1989.)

**8.** Jimmy and Bonnie Gilkeson, husband and wife, jointly owned a farm. Dennis Holliday and a number of his friends gathered on the Gilkeson's property for the purpose of playing their radio and drinking beer. The Gilkesons heard the music. Mr. Gilkeson investigated the activity, and told Holiday and his friends that they were trespassing. In the altercation that followed, Mr. Gilkeson negligently shot Holiday. Holiday sued both Mr. and Mrs. Gilkeson for damages. Is Mrs. Gilkeson liable, based on the argument that she consented to her husband's role in investigating the activity, and that he was therefore representing her? Discuss. (*Holliday v. Gilkeson,* 363 S.E.2d 133, W.Va. 1987.)

**9.** Annie Brown was employed by Burlington Industries, Inc. For nearly two years, Ernest Whitmore, a manager at Burlington, made sexually suggestive remarks and gestures towards Brown. During this period of time, Brown complained on numerous occasions to her immediate supervisor and department head about the sexual harassment. (Burlington's open-door policy, as contained in its employee handbook, instructed employees to bring any complaints initially to their supervisor or department head.) Whitmore's sexual harassment of Brown continued despite Brown's complaints to her supervisor and department head. Is Burlington liable for Whitmore's intentional infliction of emotional distress upon Brown? (*Brown v. Burlington Industries, Inc.,* 378 S.E.2d 232, N.C. App. 1989.)

**10.** Supervisors at Church's Fried Chicken are authorized to engage in limited forms of disciplinary action. A particular supervisor attempted to reprimand one of the employees under his supervision for what he regarded as an instance of unsatisfactory job performance. The supervisor made several disparaging remarks about the employee's personal life, and then grabbed the employee by her collar, threw her to the ground, and kicked her in the back. Is Church's liable for this supervisor's actions? (*Hester v. Church's Fried Chicken,* 499 N.E.2d 923, Ohio App. 1986.)

CHAPTER 33

# PARTNERSHIPS
## Nature, Formation, and Property

## THE NATURE AND HISTORY OF PARTNERSHIPS

### Historical Background

The precise origin of the partnership form of business organization is unknown. It has been stated that "some form of partnership is probably as old as the first exhibition of the gregarious instinct of man."[1] We do know that the basic partnership concept of two or more persons combining their skills and property for mutual reward has existed in every organized society.

The English common law of partnership, from which the American law has developed, traces its derivations back to the Roman law and to the law merchant.[2] For several hundred years the rules of law regarding partnerships in England and America were developed almost solely by the courts. Shortly after the turn of the century, in 1914, work was completed on the Uniform Partnership Act (UPA). The UPA codified most of the common-law rules relating to partnerships and significantly altered a few of them. It has been adopted by 49 states, the exception being Louisiana.[3]

### Defining a Partnership

Section 6 of the UPA defines a *partnership* as "an association of two or more persons to carry on as coowners a business for profit." This definition can be broken into elements as follows.

[1] Walter Jaeger, "Partnership or Joint Adventure," *Notre Dame Lawyer* 37 (1961): 138.

[2] The law merchant, discussed earlier, was the body of rules created by English merchants that ultimately was absorbed into the English common law.

[3] The UPA, which appears in its entirety in Appendix B, and other "uniform" laws were created by the American Law Institute and the National Conference of Commissioners on Uniform State Laws. Since these groups possessed no legislative power, the laws were proposed to each of the state legislatures.

**Association:** The term *association* indicates that a partnership is a voluntary arrangement formed by agreement.

**Person:** Under the UPA the term *person* includes not only individuals but also corporations, other partnerships, and other types of associations. With regard to minors and insane persons, the same basic rules apply to partnership agreements as to other types of contracts. Thus a minor can treat the partnership agreement with the other partners as voidable. The minor usually can also repudiate personal liabilities to creditors beyond the amount of his or her investment in the business. But this investment *is* subject to the claims of partnership creditors, although it is the maximum liability that the minor ordinarily can incur.

**Co-owners:** The partners are defined as coowners of the business, which distinguishes them from those who are merely agents, servants, or other subordinates. Each partner has a voice in the management of the enterprise and a right to share in the profits.

**To carry on a business:** The term *business* has been defined in Section 2 of the UPA as including "every trade, occupation, or profession."

**For Profit:** An association cannot be a partnership unless the purpose of forming it is to make profits directly through its business activities. Associations for other purposes (including religious, patriotic, or public improvement purposes, or furtherance of the *separate* economic interests of members) are not partnerships, even if they engage in business transactions. Thus the local chapter of a fraternal lodge cannot be a partnership, and the rights and duties of partners cannot attach to its members. For example, individual members are not personally liable for debts incurred for the lodge by its officers unless an agency relationship has been expressly created.

## *The Entity Theory versus the Aggregate Theory*

For centuries there have been two theories of the nature of the partnership association. One theory, the **entity theory,** is that the partnership is a separate *legal entity*—in other words, a "legal person." Traditionally the viewpoint of those in the commercial world, it was the approach taken by the Roman civil law. A legal person can own and dispose of property, make contracts, commit wrongs, sue, and be sued. In our legal system most adults are considered legal persons. The English courts, however, found difficulty with the concept of a partnership as a legal person. They evidently felt that no one but the Crown could create a legal entity. Corporations, being creations of the Crown, were deemed to be separate legal entities. This remains true today; corporations are created by authority of the government, not simply by agreement, and are regarded as legal persons.

Partnerships, on the other hand, are formed simply by the express or implied agreement of the partners. And since the English courts would not allow private parties to create a legal person separate from their own identities, the traditional approach of the common law in both England and the United States was to treat the partnership as an aggregation of individuals. Under this approach, commonly called the **aggregate theory,** a partnership was not recognized as a separate legal entity. That is:

1. The partnership could not own property; the property of the business had to be owned individually by one partner or by two or more partners as co-owners.

2. The partnership could not sue or be sued in its own name, and a court could not render judgment separately against the partnership; such actions had to be in the name of one or more individual partners.

3. One partnership could not sue another where the two had a member in common, because a party cannot be both plaintiff and defendant in the same legal proceeding.

Although most American courts followed the aggregate theory, a few contrary decisions were rendered. In reality, the courts sometimes employed the different theories as rationalizations of results reached on other grounds. Professor Judson Crane, a leading authority on partnership law, has observed that "the entity may be recognized or disregarded according to the demands of justice in the particular situation."[4]

The UPA does not expressly adopt either the entity theory or the aggregate theory. In a sense it has retained the aggregate theory by defining a partnership as "an *association of two or more persons* to carry on a business for profit." (Emphasis added.) On the other hand, it has used the entity approach for selected purposes. For example, the UPA recognizes the concept of *partnership property* and allows a partnership to own and convey property in the partnership name. Also, it places liability for acts of the partners in conducting partnership business primarily on the partnership itself and the partnership property and only secondarily on individual partners and their individual property. The UPA says nothing of procedural matters such as lawsuits in the partnership name, but most states have enacted other statutes allowing suit to be brought by or against the partnership in the partnership name. In many instances, the procedural rules in federal courts also allow suits in the partnership name.

Many legal problems, such as those involving taxation, are not governed by the UPA. Depending on the particular problem presented, courts and certain other statutes sometimes treat the partnership as a separate legal entity, and sometimes as an aggregation of individuals.

# FORMATION OF A PARTNERSHIP

## *The Partnership Agreement*

As previously mentioned, the partnership is formed by agreement, either express or implied. It is not created by statute, as is a corporation. Few, if any, statutory requirements must be met in order to *form* a partnership. While the UPA governs many aspects of the *operation* of a partnership, it is intended primarily to fill in the gaps of the partnership agreement. Many UPA rules are applicable only if the partners do not agree otherwise.

The agreement obviously must have a *legal object,* but a partnership can be formed even if one or

---

[4] Judson Crane, *Handbook on the Law of Partnership,* 2d ed. (St. Paul, Minn.: West Publishing Co., 1952), Sec. 3.

more of the other elements of a valid contract is absent. A valid contract usually does exist as a practical matter, but it is not required. A partnership can be created without a written document, although any part of the agreement falling within the statute of frauds does require a writing for enforceability.

Despite the fact that a written partnership agreement is usually not required, it is highly desirable. Formation of a business is a substantial undertaking and should not be left to the oral declarations of the parties—for several reasons:

1. There are many inherent problems in proving the exact terms of an oral agreement.

2. Numerous problems (such as those relating to taxation) can be satisfactorily resolved only by a carefully drafted written instrument.

3. If the parties go through the process of drafting a formal document with the aid of an attorney, they are much more likely to foresee many problems they otherwise would not have thought about. For example, matters such as procedures for expulsion of a partner or for settlement of disputes between partners are easily overlooked because they seem so remote when the partnership is first formed.

## *Desirable Elements of a Partnership Agreement*

The formal partnership agreement, often referred to as the **articles of partnership,** should clearly reflect the intent of the partners as to the rights and obligations they wish to assume in the business. What is contained in these articles will depend on the nature of the business and the desires of the partners, but ordinarily the written instrument should include such items as the following:

1. Name of the firm. The partnership is not required to have a firm name, but it is usually a good idea to have one. The name can be that of one or more of the partners, or it can be fictitious. (But it cannot be deceptively similar to that of another business for the purpose of attracting its customers.) If the name is fictitious, it usually must be registered. Most states have **assumed name statutes** (sometimes called **fictitious name statutes**) that require any firm, including a partnership, to register with a state official the fictitious name under which the firm is doing business. The purpose of such statutes is to enable creditors of the firm to learn the identities of those responsible.

2. Nature and location of the business.

3. Date of commencement and duration of the partnership.

4. Amount of contributions in money or property each partner is to make (in other words, the amount of their investments in the business).

5. Time within which the contribution of each partner is to be made.

6. Salaries and drawing accounts of each partner, if such are desired.

7. Division of work and duties of each partner, including rights in management.

8. Admission requirements for new partners.

9. Each partner's proportionate share of net profits while the business is continuing to operate and upon dissolution.

10. Any proposed restrictions on the power of individual members to bind the firm.

11. Clear delineation of partnership assets as distinguished from individual partners' assets.

12. Bookkeeping and accounting methods to be used and location of and access to books.

13. Procedures for withdrawal or exclusion of a partner.

14. Indication of whether withdrawal or exclusion causes dissolution, and if not, rules for continuing the business after such an event.

15. Method for determining the value of a withdrawing or excluded partner's interest.

16. Requirements and procedures for notice to partners and partnership creditors in case of dissolution.

17. Which partner or partners will be in charge of winding up the business upon dissolution.

18. Procedures for settling disputes between partners, such as submitting them to arbitration.

The following case illustrates the value of a carefully planned and drafted partnership agreement. In this case a partnership of physicians was able to terminate an unsatisfactory relationship with one of their group who simply could not get along with the others. This would have been much more difficult had it not been for their well-planned partnership agreement.

## Gelder Medical Group v. Webber
**Court of Appeals of New York,**
**363 N.E.2d 573 (1977)**

The Gelder Medical Group, a partnership engaged in practicing medicine and surgery in Sidney, New York, was first formed in 1956. Some 17 years later, defendant Dr. Webber, then 61 years old and a newcomer to Sidney, was admitted to the partnership following a one-year trial period in which he was employed by the group as a surgeon.

Like the other members of the group who had joined since its inception, Dr. Webber agreed that he "will not for five years after any voluntary or involuntary termination of his association with said Gelder Medical Group, practice his profession within a radius of 30 miles of the Village of Sidney, as a physician or surgeon . . . without the consent, in writing, of said Gelder Medical Group." The partnership agreement also provided a procedure for the involuntary withdrawal of partners. It stated that "In the event that any member is requested to resign or withdraw from the group by a majority vote of the other members of the group, such notice shall be effective immediately and his share of the profits to the date of termination shall be computed and he shall be paid in full to the date of termination of his employment pursuant to his agreement with the association."

Dr. Webber's association turned out to be unsatisfactory to his partners. His conduct, both professional and personal, became abrasive and objectionable to his partners and their patients, a cause of "intolerable" embarrassment to the group. A psychiatrist who examined Dr. Webber a number of times on the referral of the partnership stated that Dr. Webber had "what would be termed an adjustment reaction of adult life with anxiety and depression." While the psychiatrist concluded that the adjustment reaction soon cleared, he summed up his description of Dr. Webber as a perfectionist who was a "rather idealistic, sincere, direct, frank individual who quite possibly could be perceived at times as being somewhat blunt."

Although the difficulties were from time to time discussed with Dr. Webber, the unhappy relationship persisted. In October, 1973, the discord culminated with the group's unanimous decision to terminate Dr. Webber's association with the partnership. After Dr. Webber refused to withdraw voluntarily, the group, in writing, formally notified him of the termination. It was effective immediately, and, on the basis of an accounting, Webber was paid $18,568.41 in full compliance with the partnership agreement.

In about two months, Dr. Webber, disregarding the restrictive covenant, resumed his surgical practice as a single practitioner in Sidney. The group, to protect its practice, promptly sued to enjoin Dr. Webber's violation of the restrictive covenant. Dr. Webber instituted his own lawsuit for damages resulting from his expulsion. The two lawsuits were consolidated. The trial court and the intermediate level appellate court both ruled in favor of the partnership, granting an injunction prohibiting Dr. Webber from violating the noncompetition clause and dismissing his claim for damages. Dr. Webber appealed.

**Decision:** The judgment for the partnership was affirmed for two reasons. First, although there is no common-law or statutory right to expel a member of a partnership, the partnership agreement may provide for dismissal with or without cause. Second, the covenant not to compete was reasonably limited in time and area, and, therefore, enforceable. ■

## Determining the Existence of a Partnership

When the parties have clearly expressed their intentions in a written instrument, there is ordinarily no difficulty in determining whether a partnership exists. But when the parties have not been explicit in declaring their intentions, problems frequently arise. The most fundamental, of course, is whether a partnership has even been *created*. This issue arises with surprising frequency, because of its importance in regard to the rights and obligations of the "partners" and third parties as well. For example, a creditor may seek to hold several persons liable for the transactions of one of them on the ground that they are partners. Or one party might claim that he and another are partners and that the other party has violated a resulting fiduciary duty by having a conflicting business interest.

When the existence of a partnership is disputed by an interested party, such existence becomes a question of fact to be decided on the basis of all the circumstances. No single factor usually is controlling, and the court's ultimate decision commonly is based on several considerations, the most important of which are (1) sharing of profits, (2) joint control of the business, and (3) joint ownership and control of capital or property.

**Sharing of Profits:** A distinction should be made between gross revenues and net profits. It has been consistently held by the courts, and reiterated in the UPA, that an agreement to share the *gross revenues* from a particular enterprise does not in itself indicate the existence of a partnership. Sharing of *net profits*, however, usually creates a very strong inference that the parties have formed a partnership. Indeed, where there has been no sharing of profits or agreement to share them, the court is very likely to find that no partnership exists.

In certain situations, profits are shared by persons who obviously never intended to become partners. Under such circumstances the fact that profits are shared or that the parties have agreed to share them will not by itself create a presumption that a partnership was intended. These situations are described below.

**Where the Profits Are Received by a Creditor in Payment of a Debt:** For example, O, the owner of a business in financial difficulty, owes debts to X, Y, and Z. In settlement of these debts, X, Y, and Z agree to accept a certain percentage of O's profits for a period of time. No inference of partnership is created by the sharing of profits, and no partnership exists between O, X, Y, and Z (unless, perhaps, X, Y, and Z take title to a portion of the business property and take part in managing the business).

**Where the Profits Are Received as Wages by an Employee:** Suppose that X is the owner of a business and A, B, and C are her employees. As an incentive to the employees, X establishes a plan whereby they share in the profits of the business. There is no presumption of a partnership so long as the evidence as a whole indicates an *employment* relationship; that is, X withholds federal taxes from the employees' salaries, exercises control over them, and does not allow them any management powers or co-ownership of business property.

**Where the Profits Are Received as Rent by a Landlord:** If the probable returns of a business being undertaken by a party are uncertain, that party may wish to avoid the burden of fixed charges as much as possible by leasing necessary equipment or real estate at a variable price. It is not uncommon, if the owner of the equipment or real estate is willing, for a rental agreement in such a case to provide that the rent will be based in whole or in part on the profitability of the business. Such an arrangement does not of itself make the owner a partner with the person carrying on the business. However, if the owner of the property also takes part in managing the business, this might be enough for a court to rule that a partnership has been formed.

**Where the Profits Are Received as an Annuity by the Spouse or Representative of a Deceased Partner:** If a successful partnership is dissolved by the death of a partner, it is often desirable to continue (rather than liquidate) the business because of the value of the goodwill it possesses as a going concern. Thus, it may be agreed, either in the original articles of partnership or by contract after a partner's death between the spouse, executor, or administrator and the surviving partners, that the dead partner's interest will not be liquidated. In consideration for allowing this interest to remain in the business, the spouse or representative might receive a share of the profits. Such facts do not by themselves make that person a partner. If, however, such a party exercises powers of control and management, a court might find that a partnership has been created.

**Where the Profits Are Received as Interest on a Loan:** If a creditor who has lent money to a person or persons carrying on a business agrees to receive a share of profits in lieu of interest, the courts generally have held that the lender has not become a partner unless he or she also participates in management. In a number of cases the courts also have held that no partnership exists even where the lender has been given a degree of control in the business, so long as the control is of a limited nature for the sole purpose of protecting the loan.

**Where the Profits Are Received as Consideration for the Sale of Property:** When an item of property having an uncertain value is sold to someone who expects to use it in carrying on a business, it is sometimes agreed that the price payable to the seller will include a share of the profits made from use of the property. Two common examples are *good-*

*will* and *trademarks*. The seller usually retains no ownership of the property or control over its use;[5] nor is he or she usually expected to share any losses incurred by the buyer. In many instances this is simply the best way of computing the value of a particular property right. No partnership is created by such an arrangement.

**Joint Control and Management:** Although sharing of profits is a cardinal element of the partnership, another factor often felt to be important by the courts is whether the parties have *joint control* over the operation of the business. For instance, where sharing of profits by itself is not sufficient to indicate existence of a partnership, the addition of the factor of joint control might well cause a court to hold that a partnership has been created. *Exercise of management powers* is obviously very strong evidence of control. But the fact that management powers have been expressly delegated to one or more of the partners does not mean that those who do not manage are not true partners if the other facts indicate that they are. In a sense, agreeing to relinquish control is itself an exercise of the right of control.

**Joint Ownership of Property:** Another factor that frequently finds its way into court opinions is *joint ownership of assets*. Of the three basic tests for existence of a partnership, this is the least important, although it certainly is taken into account by the court, along with all the other evidence. The UPA takes the position that co-ownership of property does not, of itself, establish a partnership. An inference of partnership is also not necessarily created by the fact that the co-owners share any profits made by the use of the property. This seems at first to be inconsistent with our earlier discussion of the presumption of partnership that is usually engendered by profit sharing. But there is no real inconsistency. In the case of co-owners of property, the sharing of profits made from the property is a basic part of co-ownership. In most cases the owner of property wishes to receive whatever income it generates; thus it is reasonable to assume that co-owners will want to share the income from their jointly owned property. A partnership should not be presumed simply because the owners act in a way totally consistent with simple co-ownership.

On the other hand, if the property and its use are only part of a larger enterprise, and the parties share profits from the whole enterprise, an inference of partnership is justified. For instance, co-ownership of a commercial building and sharing of its rental income by A and B does not necessarily make them partners. If, however, they use part of the building as premises for the operation of a going business of some type, sharing not only the rental income from the remainder of the building but also the profits and management of the business, they are quite likely to be considered partners.

The two cases below illustrate the type of evidence considered by courts in determining whether a partnership has been formed where no formal agreement has been made. In the first case there was no express agreement at all. In the second there was an express oral agreement to be partners, but the nature of the business venture changed over a period of time, thus prompting a question whether the original partnership agreement extended to the transformed enterprise.

---

[5] However, if there is no sale of the trademark but only a *license* (a permission to *use* the trademark), the licensor does retain ownership and, usually, a measure of control over how it is used. But the receipt of profits by the licensor as consideration for the license does not by itself make that person a partner in this case either.

---

### Lupien v. Malsbenden
Supreme Judicial Court of Maine,
477 A.2d 746 (1984)

York Motor Mart was in the business of assembling Bradley automobiles. The Bradley was a "kit car"; when a customer placed an order, York purchased from the manufacturer a kit that was used to build an automobile on a Volkswagen chassis. York Motor Mart was run by Stephen Cragin and Frederick Malsbenden, although they had no formal agreement as to the nature of their business relationship. As part of York Motor Mart, Cragin also operated a general automotive repair business. The repair shop was conducted on the same premises and under the same name as the Bradley business, but Malsbenden and Cragin apparently treated the two operations

*(continued)*

as separate and Malsbenden played no part in the repair business.

Robert Lupien placed an order with Cragin for a Bradley. The written contract was signed by Cragin but identified the seller as "York Motor Mart." Lupien made a deposit of $500 toward the purchase price of $8,020, and one week later made a further payment of $3,950. Lupien then made visits to York Motor Mart on the average of once or twice a week to check on the progress being made on his Bradley. During those visits Lupien generally dealt with Malsbenden, because Cragin was seldom present. On one such visit, Malsbenden told Lupien that he would have to transfer ownership of his pickup truck to York Motor Mart. It was agreed that this transfer would constitute the balance of Lupien's consideration under the contract and that York Motor Mart would sell the pickup and use the proceeds to complete construction of the Bradley. When Lupien complied, Malsbenden supplied him with a rental car, and later supplied him with a demonstrator model ("demo") of the Bradley for his use pending completion of the car he had ordered. When it was discovered that the "demo" actually belonged to a third party who had entrusted it to York Motor Mart for resale, Malsbenden purchased it for Lupien's use.

Lupien never received the Bradley he had ordered, and Cragin disappeared. Lupien filed suit against Malsbenden, claiming that Cragin and Malsbenden were partners in the operation of York Motor Mart and that Malsbenden was personally liable for the partnership's obligations. Malsbenden claimed that his interest in York Motor Mart was basically that of a "banker" rather than a partner. He testified that he had loaned $85,000 to Cragin, without interest, to finance the Bradley portion of York Motor Mart's business. The loan was to be repaid from the proceeds of each car sold. Malsbenden admitted that Bradley kits were purchased with his personal checks and that he had also purchased equipment for York Motor Mart. Malsbenden also admitted that after Cragin disappeared in May 1980, he had physical control of the York Motor Mart premises and that he continued to dispose of assets there even to the time of trial in 1983. The trial court held in favor of Lupien and Malsbenden appealed.

---

**Decision:** The judgment for plaintiff Lupien was affirmed. Malsbenden's total involvement in the business showed that he was a partner. The $85,000 "loan" was without interest; moreover, it was not made in the form of a fixed payment or payments, but took the form of Malsbenden's day-to-day purchase of kits, parts, and equipment, and the payment of wages. Furthermore, the "loan" was not to be repaid in fixed amounts or at fixed times. Therefore, the so-called loan was actually a contribution to capital. This fact, coupled with Malsbenden's continuing participation in managerial-type decisions, led to the conclusion that Malsbenden and Cragin were partners, and Malsbenden was thus personally responsible for the obligation. ■

---

## Shawn v. England
Court of Appeals of Oklahoma,
570 P.2d 628 (1977)

In the summer of 1973 Gary England was a weathercaster for television station KWTV Channel 9, Oklahoma City, and Bill Shawn was a stock market reporter and commentator for the same station.

For some time England had made occasional reference to what he called a "thunder lizard" while telecasting the weather. Usually he did so during thunderstorms as an interest provoker, particularly during his early morning reports. The make-believe creature engaged Shawn's imagination and eventually it occurred to him that it might be profitable to design and promote the sale of a stuffed thunder lizard which children could hold during thunderstorms as a comforter.

One day Shawn broached the idea to his friend England, who immediately saw merit in it. After some discussion the parties decided they needed a commercial artist to help design the mythical animal. Shawn thought of a longtime friend and artist, Larry May, with whom he had attended school. Shawn contacted May, told him of the idea, and learned that the commercial artist was interested and willing to help "poor boy" the project by contributing the art work.

The three individuals had their first meeting at May's office and at that time discussed ways to achieve maximum publicity for the fictional lizard. They accepted England's proposal that the three consider themselves equal partners in their venture and divide any profits realized three ways. During the next several months the threesome met frequently. At one early meeting they decided to have a drawing contest wherein they would ask youngsters and adults alike to send in drawings of what they envisioned the thunder lizard to be, with the promise of a prize to the winner. The contest had a good response and May, as judge, picked a nine-year-old boy's drawing for the prize. A little later the trio hit upon the idea of a weather fact cartoon book featuring thunder lizard drawings,

*(continued)*

which after further thought was transformed into a children's coloring book.

Gary England began gathering material for the coloring book, but after accumulating considerable weather data the three men concluded that the publication of a regular weather booklet about the weather in Oklahoma would have broader appeal and thus greater profit potential. They then turned their efforts to the development of a weather book.

By January of 1974, England had not only gathered considerable data for the booklet but had written the manuscript. Shawn was given the responsibility of having it typed and edited, which he accomplished promptly. England made additional changes in the text and added pictures in an effort to ready it for publication.

In the meantime, England met with the management of KWTV and discussed the possibility of the station's underwriting the booklet. He reported back that the station agreed to "bankroll" the project by buying enough copies to pay for the initial production of the work—estimated to be about 13,000 copies—and proceeds from sales exceeding this were to be the profit of the three-man partnership.

However, in April 1974, at one of their regular meetings, Shawn was abruptly informed he was no longer needed and the partnership was ended. He tried to get the other two to reconsider, but they insisted on terminating his relationship with them. England and May said there were too many people in the deal and that the partnership arrangement only applied to the "thunder lizard" idea.

Shawn, plaintiff, sued England and May, defendants, claiming that their original partnership agreement extended to the weather book. He sought to recover a one-third share of all profits to be made from the book. In the trial court a jury found that there was a partnership and that plaintiff should receive one-third of the profits, but the judge granted defendants' motion for judgment notwithstanding the verdict. Plaintiff appealed.

**Decision:** The trial court's judgment for defendants was reversed, and judgment rendered for plaintiff for one-third of the profits, in accordance with the jury's verdict. The enterprise evolved naturally, from the original idea to the final project, without any indication that the parties' relationship had changed. Until the end, both defendants continued to act as though there were still a three-member partnership. Their partnership extended to the production and sale of the weather booklet, and Shawn was entitled to a partner's share of the profits from that enterprise. ∎

## PARTNERSHIP PROPERTY

A partnership commonly requires various types of property for the operation of its business, including, for example, real estate, equipment, inventory, or intangibles such as cash or securities. The prevailing rule at common law was that a partnership, not being a separate legal entity, could not own real estate. Somewhat inconsistently, it was also generally held that a partnership *could own* other types of property. Under the UPA, a partnership is recognized as an entity insofar as property ownership is concerned and can own either real estate or other types of property. The UPA uses the phrase **tenants in partnership** to describe the status of individual partners with respect to the partnership property. (The rights that individual partners have regarding partnership property will be discussed in the next chapter.)

Although today a partnership can (and quite often does) own such property itself, it is not essential that it own *any property at all.* The partners themselves may wish to *individually* own the property needed for the operation of the business.

For a number of reasons it is sometimes important to determine whether an item of property belongs to the partnership or to an individual partner. Among them:

1. Creditors of the partnership must resort to partnership property for satisfaction of their claims before they can take property of individual partners.

2. The right of a partner to use partnership property is usually limited to purposes of furthering the partnership business.

3. The question of ownership can also be important with regard to taxation, distribution of assets upon dissolution of the partnership, and other matters.

### *Factors in Determining Ownership*

**Agreement:** The ownership of property is determined by *agreement* of the partners. Sound business practices dictate that the partners should explicitly agree on the matter and keep accurate records of their dealings with property. Unfortunately, partners often fail to indicate clearly their intentions as to whether ownership of particular items of property rests with the partnership or with one or more individual partners. In such cases, the courts consider all pertinent facts in an attempt to discover the partners' *intent.* Where it appears that the matter of property ownership never occurred to the partners, so that they actually had no definite intention, the court determines which of the possible alternatives—partnership or individual ownership—more closely accords with their general intentions and objectives for the business as a whole and which is fairer both to partners and to third parties.

**Legal Title:** In the absence of a clear agreement as to ownership, the strongest evidence of property ownership is the name in which the property is held, often referred to as the **legal title.** If an item of property is held in the name of the partnership, courts will hold it to be partnership property in almost every case. This principle most often plays a part where *real estate* is involved, because a deed has been executed in the name of some party and usually has been "recorded" (made part of official county records). Such formal evidence of ownership is frequently not available for property other than real estate, but if it is available, it will play the same important role. For example, this principle applies to motor vehicles, for which there is usually a state-issued certificate of title.

Problems regarding ownership seldom arise if title to the property in question is held in the partnership name. Those that do arise usually occur in either of two situations: (1) where the property is of a type for which there is no deed, certificate, or other formal evidence of ownership; or (2) where title is held in the name of one or more individual partners, but there is a claim that it is actually partnership property. In the first instance, evidence must be presented to establish just where ownership actually rests. In the second, evidence must be introduced to overcome the presumption of individual ownership and prove that the property actually belongs to the partnership. No single factor is controlling; the court's determination ordinarily is based on the cumulative weight of several factors. Discussion of some of the more important ones follows.

**Purchase with Partnership Funds:** The funds generated by the business operations of a partnership are partnership property. Additionally, the funds paid into the partnership by individual partners and used by the partnership as working capital are *presumed* to be partnership property. The courts will hold such funds to be individual property only if very strong evidence is produced to show that the payment was intended as a *loan* to the partnership by a partner, rather than a contribution to capital.

An item of property *purchased with partnership funds* is also presumed to be partnership property. The use of partnership funds in making a purchase often plays an important part in a court's decision that ownership resides in the partnership. Indeed, proof that partnership funds were used to buy the property is sufficient to establish the partnership as owner *even if this is the only evidence presented.* Moreover, the presumption created by use of partnership funds is very difficult to overcome. If property has been purchased with such funds, it will take a great deal of contrary evidence to establish that the property does not actually belong to the partnership—even if it is held in the name of an individual partner or other person.[6]

**The Way the Property Is Used:** Evidence indicating that the property has been used in the business of the partnership is considered by the courts, but by itself it is not sufficient to enable a court to hold that the property belongs to the partnership. For example, if the property is held in the name of an individual partner, the fact that it has been used for partnership purposes is not enough to make the partnership the owner. Courts realize that it is not uncommon for an individual partner to allow his or her property to be used in the partnership business without intending to surrender ownership of it.

**Treatment in the Partnership Records:** If the property is carried in the partnership books as an asset of the firm, this strongly tends to indicate that it is partnership property. The inference is even stronger

---

[6] On the other hand, if the fact that the property is held in the name of an individual has *misled an innocent third party,* such as a creditor, a different result may be reached. To illustrate: A tract of land was purchased with funds belonging to the B Company, a partnership; but title is held in the name of X, one of the partners. When X applies to C for credit, C innocently relies upon the fact that title to the land appears to rest with X, and C grants credit to X and obtains a lien on the land. If X defaults, C can reach the land for satisfaction of his claim. Even though it is really partnership property, it will be treated as X's individual property insofar as C is concerned. Of course, X will be held responsible to the partnership for the loss of its property.

if an unpaid balance on the property is carried in the records as a partnership liability.

**Other Factors:** Any number of other factors might influence a court's decision that an item is partnership property:

**1.** If property had been purchased with funds of an individual partner, the fact that partnership funds were later used to improve, repair, or maintain the property *tends* to show that it now belongs to the partnership. (But additional evidence usually is required, because most courts have been unwilling to infer that the property is owned by the partnership *solely* on the basis that partnership funds were later used to maintain it.)

**2.** The fact that *taxes* on the property have been paid by the partnership can be important.

**3.** The receipt by the partnership of *income* generated by the property is evidence that the partnership is the owner.

**4.** Any other conduct of those involved is considered if it tends to indicate their intent regarding property ownership.

The following case illustrates the strong presumption that property acquired with partnership funds or labor is partnership property, as well as some of the problems that may sometimes result from having partnership property in the name of one of the partners instead of the partnership.

---

**Eckert v. Eckert**
Supreme Court of North Dakota,
425 N.W. 2d 914 (1988)

Ben Eckert was Donovan Eckert's uncle. In 1959 the two formed a farming and ranching partnership called the "E-7 Ranch." No formal partnership agreement was ever executed. Donovan died in 1982, and Gaila Eckert, the representative of Donovan's estate, filed suit seeking dissolution and liquidation of the partnership.

Ben and Gaila agreed on the division of all partnership property except for cooperative patronage credits with the Minot Farmers Union Elevator, Minot Farmers Union Oil, and Harvest States Cooperative. Gaila asserted that these patronage credits are partnership property which should be equally split. Ben asserted that these credits were titled in his name individually and are not partnership property.

A portion of the cooperatives' profits each year are allocated to each member-patron and the cooperative is required to pay out at least 20 percent of this amount in cash to the member-patron. The remaining 80 percent is retained by the cooperative but shows on its books as a patronage credit to the member-patron. Although this portion is not distributed to the member-patron at the time it is earned, it must be reported as income by the member-patron. These unpaid distributions typically are retained by the cooperative until the member-patron reaches a certain age or the cooperative's board of directors votes to "retire" the credits for a specified past year.

In this case, patronage credits were earned on business generated by the partnership. The 20 percent annual cash distributions were paid to Ben Eckert, who placed them in the partnership account and included them as income to the partnership on the partnership tax return. The partnership return then allocated one-half of this income to Ben and one-half to Donovan. The 80 percent patronage credits were also included as partnership income each year, and again one-half of this income was allocated to each partner.

Upon reaching age 65 in 1978, Ben began receiving distributions of the retained patronage credits from Farmers Union Oil. Between 1978 and 1983, Ben received $28,612.28 of those credits. Ben kept all of these funds. None of the retained patronage credits earned on partnership business with Farmers Union Elevator and Harvest States had been distributed at the time of trial.

The trial court placed the burden on Gaila to prove that the patronage credits earned through partnership business were partnership property. In large part because the credits were held in Ben's name, the trial court concluded that Gaila had failed to meet her burden of proof and dismissed her claim. Gaila appealed.

---

**Decision:** The judgment was reversed. The credits were property derived from partnership funds, assets, labor, or materials, and thus were presumed to be partnership property. The trial court erred by placing the burden of proof on Gaila; Ben should have had the burden of proving that the credits were his individual property. ■

## SUMMARY

A partnership is defined as "an association of two or more persons to carry on as co-owners a business for profit." In some respects, a partnership is treated as a separate legal entity. For example, it is legally capable of owning property and making contracts, and partnership property is primarily liable for partnership debts. In other respects, however, the law treats a partnership as an aggregation of individuals rather than an entity. For example, individual partners are personally responsible for partnership debts after partnership assets are exhausted.

The partnership is created by agreement. Although this agreement does not have to be a formal written one, it ought to be. Partners should devote great care to the creation of a formal written partnership agreement, a document often called the articles of partnership.

Courts may examine a variety of factors to determine whether a partnership exists when there is no formal partnership agreement. The sharing of profits is an important indicator of partnership status, but there are several situations in which profit sharing does not mean that the parties intended to be partners. Showing that the parties each exercised control and management over the business is another important way of establishing the existence of a partnership. Joint ownership of property is a relevant factor, but it is not weighed as heavily in determining whether a partnership exists.

A partnership is legally capable of owning property, although it is not necessary that a partnership own property in order to operate its business. A partnership can use property that is owned by individual partners. It can be important to determine whether a particular item of property is owned by the partnership or by one or more individual partners, for several reasons. For example, partnership creditors must look first to partnership property for satisfaction of their claims, and an individual partner's right to use partnership property is restricted. The articles of partnership should specify which property is to be owned by the partnership. When a question of property ownership is not resolved by the articles of partnership, courts consider such things as the name in which legal title is held, whether the property was purchased with partnership funds, the way the property is used, and its treatment in the partnership records.

## KEY TERMS

**Entity theory**
**Aggregate theory**
**Articles of partnership**
**Assumed name statute (or fictitious name statute)**
**Tenants in partnership**
**Legal title**

## QUESTIONS AND PROBLEMS

1. The U.S. government filed suit against the "Bonanno Organized Crime Family of La Cosa Nostra," claiming that the family's activities violated the Racketeer Influenced and Corrupt Organizations Act (RICO). The government sought both monetary damages and forfeiture of property that allegedly had been used to carry out illegal purposes. In order to maintain the suit against the family as an organization, however, the government had to prove that the family was a legal "person," or entity. The government's argument was that the family operated as a partnership or a joint venture. The defendants filed a motion to dismiss the government's complaint, and the issue for the court at this point was whether the allegations in the complaint, if ultimately proved, would establish that the Bonanno family was a partnership.

The allegations in the government's complaint stated that the Bonanno family operates through groups known as "crews." Each crew has as its leader a person known as a "Capo," who is the captain or boss of a crew. A "Capo" of a crew is supervised by, reports to, and, where necessary, is supported by the head of the Bonanno Family, who is known as the "Boss." The Boss has a second-in-command, known as the "Underboss." The Bonanno Family also has a counselor or advisor, known as a "Consigliere," who advises about intra-Family disputes. The Bonanno Family rules dictate that a crew member cannot participate in illegal activities without the prior approval of the crew member's Capo. Likewise, a Capo can only undertake an illegal activity after the Boss or the Underboss has approved the activity. There is no indication that family members agree to share losses. Is the Bonanno family a partnership? Discuss. (*United States v. The Bonanno Organized Crime Family of La Cosa Nostra*, 879 F.2d 20, 2d Cir. 1989.)

2. Wishing to invest their money, Johnson and Watkins combined funds in equal portions and purchased a substantial amount of corporate stock as well as corporate and government bonds. They owned these securities jointly, shared equally in all dividends and other investment income, and jointly made all decisions relating to the management of their investments. Are they partners? Discuss.

3. Nelson was employed by Cox as an accountant for Cox's large chicken-raising business. Nelson contributed no capital to the business and followed Cox's orders in performing his duties. Nelson's pay, however, was to be one-third of each month's profits from the business. Does a partnership exist between Nelson and Cox? Explain.

4. X, Y, and Z were partners in an automobile dealership. Their partnership agreement provided for continuation of the business in the event of the death of any partner. X died, and Y and Z agreed with X's widow that she would receive a lump sum payment of $50,000 and a 25 percent share of the business's profits as compensation for X's share in the partnership. It was agreed, however, that she would not be required to perform any duties for the business and would take no part in management. Is X's widow a partner of Y and Z? Explain.

5. Shaw was the owner of a shopping center. He rented a store in the center to Winn and agreed to accept, as rent, 20 percent of the net profits of the business. Did this agreement make him a partner? Explain.

6. Wyman and Harvey, college students, each contributed $500 for the purchase of a refreshment stand near the beach of a summer resort. They spent the summer operating the stand and, at the end of the summer, divided the approximately $5,000 profit they had made. They had not entered into a written agreement at any time, and nothing had ever been said about their being partners. Did a partnership between them exist during the summer? Discuss.

7. Corley and Foster were partners in a grain brokerage business, Southwest Grain Brokers. They invested $10,000 of the profits from the business in the stock of Zeron Corp. The Zeron stock certificates were issued jointly to Corley and Foster in their individual names. Corley died, and his widow, as the sole heir of his estate, claimed a one-half interest in the Zeron stock. Will her claim be upheld? Discuss.

8. Dr. Citrin had the following oral agreement with Dr. Mehta: Dr. Mehta would perform medical services in Dr. Citrin's office while Dr. Citrin was away on vacation. Thirty percent of all fees collected from Medicare, Medicaid, and insurance companies were to be paid to Dr. Citrin, with such amounts characterized as rent and administrative services. Fees received directly from patients, however, were to be kept entirely by Dr. Mehta. In addition, while covering Dr. Citrin's office, Dr. Mehta had authority to use Dr. Citrin's prescription pads, and full use of equipment and staff. Does this relationship rise to the level of partnership? Discuss. (*Impastato v. De Girolamo*, 459 N.Y.S.2d 512, N.Y. Sup. Ct. 1983.)

# CHAPTER 34

# PARTNERSHIPS
## OPERATING THE BUSINESS

## RELATIONS AMONG PARTNERS
### Management Rights

One of the basic rights of a partner is to participate in the management of the enterprise. Unless the partnership agreement provides otherwise, all partners have equal rights in the conduct and management of the partnership business. This is true regardless of the amount of their capital contributions or services to the business.

Many partnership agreements expressly provide that a particular partner will be the "managing partner," exercising control over the daily operations of the business. Such agreements can also be implied from the conduct of the partners. For example: Ajax Co. is a partnership composed of partners A, B, C, D, and E. Over a substantial period of time, C, D, and E have left the management of the business to A and B, who possess recognized ability and experience as managers. If C, D, and E suddenly complain about a management decision made by A and B, the court probably will find that there was an implied agreement to give management powers completely to A and B and that they were therefore justified in acting without first consulting C, D, and E.

Unless it has been expressly or impliedly agreed otherwise, differences among the partners regarding management are usually settled by a *majority vote*. A few matters, however, such as admission of a new partner or amendment of the articles of partnership, require the consent of *all* the partners unless they have previously agreed that a less-than-unanimous vote will suffice.

### Individual Rights in Partnership Property

Although a partner does not actually *own*, as an individual, any part of the partnership property (the partnership is the owner), he or she does have *rights* in specific partnership assets. However, the interests of the partnership as a business entity are of greater importance than the rights of any of the individual partners. Let us assume that a partnership owns a piece of equipment and that this ownership is undisputed. If one of the partners wishes to make use of the property or otherwise control it, he or she is subject to a number of limitations.

**Limitations by Agreement:** The first limitation is that of the *partnership agreement.* If the agreement among the partners stipulates the rights each is to have with respect to partnership property, then the individual who wants to use or control the property is bound by the agreement. For example, the agreement might provide that one of the other partners has the exclusive right to possess or deal with the property.

**Equal Right to Possession:** Where there has been no agreement regarding partnership property, certain limitations are imposed by law on individual partners. Under the UPA, each partner has an *equal right to possess partnership property for partnership purposes.* Without the consent of all the other partners, an individual is not entitled to exclusive possession or control of partnership assets. Furthermore, the equal right of possession enjoyed by each partner is limited to purposes that further the partnership business, unless the other partners consent to a use for some different purpose.

**Nontransferability:** A partner's right to possess and control partnership property for partnership purposes *cannot be transferred by that person to a third party outside the partnership.* The reason is simple. In this situation the third party would be exercising a right that for all practical purposes would make him or her a new partner, and a new partner can be brought into the partnership only by the agreement of all the partners. For similar reasons, this right cannot be reached by a partner's personal creditors. Additionally, it does not pass to the executor or administrator of a partner's estate when he or she dies; instead it passes to the surviving partner or partners. A partner's rights with respect to specific partnership property should not be confused with his or her interest in the partnership. The **interest in the partnership** is each partner's share of the profits and surplus, and it is subject to different rules than the right to use partnership property. (This concept is more fully developed later in the chapter.)

The next case discusses and illustrates the principle that a partner does not actually own specific items of partnership property.

---

### Putnam v. Shoaf
Court of Appeals of Tennessee,
620 S.W.2d 510 (1981)

The Frog Jump Gin Company was a partnership in the business of running a cotton gin operation. Originally, the gin was operated as an equal partnership between E. C. Charlton, Louise Charlton, Lyle Putnam, and Carolyn Putnam. In 1974 Mr. Putnam died and his widow, Carolyn Putnam, received his interest. In 1976 Carolyn Putnam wished to sever her relationship with the other partners, and another couple, John and Maurine Shoaf, wanted to acquire Mrs. Putnam's one-half interest. The gin was heavily indebted to the Bank of Trenton, and had a $90,000 excess of liabilities over assets. The Shoafs agreed to take over Mrs. Putnam's interest if she and the Charltons would each pay $21,000 into the partnership account. The Shoafs agreed to assume personal liability for all partnership debts, including Putnam's share of any partnership debts made prior to their coming into the partnership. (It should be noted that if the Shoafs had not expressly agreed to assume liability for prior partnership debts, under the Uniform Partnership Act they would have been personally responsible only for debts incurred after their entry into the partnership.) In addition, Mrs. Putnam executed a deed purporting to convey to the Shoafs Mrs. Putnam's interest in specific assets of the partnership. These assets consisted of the cotton gin, its equipment, and the land on which it was located.

When the Shoafs assumed their positions as partners, the company's old bookkeeper was terminated and a new bookkeeper hired. Two months later, with the assistance of the new bookkeeper, it was learned that the old bookkeeper had engaged in a scheme of systematic embezzlement from the Frog Jump Gin Company from the time of Mr. Putnam's death until the bookkeeper's employment was terminated. The partnership filed suit against the old bookkeeper and the banks that had honored checks forged by the bookkeeper. The court allowed Mrs. Putnam to intervene and become a party to the lawsuit, as well. Judgment was rendered against the defendants, and $68,000 in damages was paid into court. By agreement, one-half of this amount was paid to the Charltons as owners of a one-half interest in the partnership. Ownership of the rest of the money was disputed by the Shoafs and Mrs. Putnam. The Shoafs asserted that the claim against the bookkeeper and banks was a partnership asset, Mrs. Putnam had transferred her interest in the partnership to the Shoafs, and, therefore, Mrs. Putnam had no right to any of the money. Mrs. Putnam asserted that she had only executed a deed transferring title to specific partnership assets, the claim against the bookkeeper and banks was unknown and unmentioned at the time of that transfer, and, therefore, Mrs. Putnam retained a one-half interest in the claim. The trial court agreed with the Shoafs and held that Mrs. Putnam had no right to any of the money.

---

**Decision:** The judgment in favor of the partnership and against Mrs. Putnam was affirmed. Because a partner does not actually own an interest in specific partnership assets, the only thing Mrs. Putnam had that she could transfer was her interest in the partnership. In addition, all the circumstances indicated that, at the time she sold out to the Shoafs, Mrs. Putnam wanted completely out of the partnership. Therefore, she intended to, and did, transfer to the Shoafs her interest in the partnership. Because she was no longer a partner, and the claim was a partnership asset, Mrs. Putnam had no legal interest in the claim. ∎

## Profits, Losses, and Other Compensation

As previously mentioned, a partner's *interest in the partnership* is his or her share in the profits of the business as well as a share of what the excess would be at a given time if all the partnership's debts were paid and all the accounts were tallied up and settled. The proportion of partnership profits to be received by each partner is ordinarily determined by an express provision in the articles of partnership. This proportion can be determined on the basis of each partner's contribution of capital, property, or services or by any other method the partners wish to use. If the agreement makes no provision for distributing profits, they will be divided *equally*. The rule requiring equal division in the absence of contrary agreement applies without regard to the amount of capital, property, or service contributed by each partner.

The agreement may also provide for the sharing of losses, although it is often silent on the matter, since few people enter a business expecting to lose money. If the agreement says nothing about losses, they are shared *in the same proportion as profits*. Thus, if nothing is agreed as to either profits or losses, both are shared equally.

The articles of partnership may provide for salaries or other compensation to be paid an individual partner or partners for services rendered in behalf of the partnership. If, however, the agreement does not so provide, a partner is *not entitled to any compensation for such services*. The law presumes in such cases that the parties' intent was that a share of the profits be each partner's only compensation. The sole exception to this rule occurs after the partnership has been dissolved. A partner who is in charge of winding up the affairs of the dissolved partnership is entitled to reasonable compensation for these services.

Unless otherwise agreed, a partner is *not entitled to interest on his or her contribution of capital* to the partnership (the partner's investment). But if the partners originally agreed upon a date for repayment to individual partners of their capital contributions, a partner has a right to receive interest on his or her contribution from that date if it remains unpaid. As we saw in the previous chapter, a partner's payment of money to the partnership is presumed to be a capital contribution rather than a *loan*. However, if a payment is clearly a loan, then the partner is entitled to receive interest computed from the date of the loan.

If an individual partner, acting reasonably in the ordinary and proper conduct of partnership business, makes a payment or incurs personal liability to a third party, the partner is entitled to be *reimbursed* or *indemnified* by the partnership. For example, suppose that the partnership has contracted to sell goods to a buyer. The buyer breaches the contract and refuses to accept the goods. While attempting to find another buyer, it is necessary for the partner handling the transaction to store the goods or to ship them elsewhere. If that partner personally pays such expenses, he or she is entitled to be reimbursed by the partnership.

## Basic Fiduciary Duties

Each partner maintains a *fiduciary* relationship with the partnership and with every other partner in matters pertaining to the partnership. This relationship is much the same as the one existing between principal and agent. (The analogy is particularly appropriate because each partner is an agent of the partnership.) Since such a relationship requires the highest standards of loyalty, good faith, and integrity, a partner who acts in his or her own self-interest and to the detriment of the partnership is accountable to it for any profits made from the endeavor. The seriousness with which courts view this fiduciary relationship is very well described in the following statement by Judge Benjamin Cardozo (who later became a member of the U.S. Supreme Court):

> [Partners] owe to one another, while the enterprise continues, the duty of the finest loyalty. Many forms of conduct permissible in a workaday world for those acting at arm's length, are forbidden to those bound by fiduciary ties. A [partner] is held to something stricter than the morals of the marketplace. Not honesty alone, but the punctilio of an honor the most sensitive, is then the standard of behavior. As to this there has developed a tradition that is unbending and inveterate. Uncompromising rigidity has been the attitude of courts of equity when petitioned to undermine the rule of undivided loyalty by the "disintegrating erosion" of particular exceptions.... Only thus has the level of conduct for fiduciaries been kept at a level higher than that

trodden by the crowd. It will not consciously be lowered by any judgment of this court.[1]

A partner may engage in his or her own enterprises outside the partnership, so long as the articles of partnership do not prohibit such activity and so long as the outside involvement does not cause the partner to neglect partnership affairs. But a partner cannot *compete* with the partnership. (For example, a partner in a grocery business obviously cannot legally run a competing store in the neighborhood.) Going one step farther, a partner cannot even *acquire* a business interest adverse to the interests of the partnership. Thus it has been held that a partner cannot acquire a partnership asset without the consent of the other partners. To illustrate: A lease on real estate held by the partnership is about to expire. One of the partners, acting on his own and for his own benefit, cannot secretly secure from the owner a renewal of the lease for himself. In a similar vein, if a partner in a partnership whose business is purchasing and selling real estate purchases and resells in his or her own name (or in the name of a relative) a lot that he or she should have purchased for the partnership, the partner is accountable to the partnership for the profit.

The fiduciary relationship also demands that each partner be utterly scrupulous when transacting business on his or her own behalf with the partnership or with another partner in matters pertaining to the partnership. To illustrate: If the partners decide to sell an item of partnership property to one of the partners, the purchasing partner is under a duty to disclose all material facts relevant to the transaction. If this partner has any information relating to the present or prospective value of the property, he or she must reveal it to the other partners. The same holds true where one partner is selling his or her interest in the partnership to another partner. Such transactions are not of an "arm's-length" nature, with each party looking after its own interests. They are, to the contrary, transactions in which individual self-interest must take a back seat to the requirements of complete disclosure and rigid fairness.

A partner can also be held responsible to the partnership for losses resulting from negligence. The partner is not liable simply because of bad judgment but is liable if the business is harmed because of carelessness or neglect.

## *Partnership Books*

All matters relating to record keeping should be dealt with in the articles of partnership. If the agreement is silent in this regard, the partnership books are required to be kept at the partnership's *principal place of business*. Every partner must at all times have access to the books and the opportunity to inspect or copy any of them.

If the partners have named one of themselves to be the managing partner or if they have given record-keeping duties to a particular partner, that partner must keep complete and accurate accounts and can be held liable for the failure to do so. He or she also has the burden of proving that the records are correct; and if an accurate account is not kept, any doubts that may arise when partnership affairs are being closed will usually be resolved against the responsible partner.

If in a particular situation the partnership agreement does not expressly resolve a question concerning the adequacy of partnership records, a court will consider the nature of the business, the experience and education of the partners, and other relevant circumstantial evidence when determining whether a partner has fulfilled his or her record-keeping responsibilities.

## *Right to an Account*

Under certain circumstances a partner can institute a legal proceeding called an **account** (or an **accounting**). In such a suit, all records of the partnership must formally be produced and all balances computed under court supervision. Since each partner ordinarily has free access to the books, this kind of lawsuit usually is filed only when the partnership has been dissolved.

There are circumstances, however, in which a partner may demand a formal account from his or her copartners without seeking the dissolution of the partnership. Then, if the copartners refuse or if the partner making the demand is dissatisfied with the accounting, he or she may institute legal action. Under Sec. 22 of the UPA, a partner has the right to a formal account as to partnership affairs under any of the following circumstances:

---

[1] *Meinhard v. Salmon*, 164 N.E. 545 (1928).

1. He or she has been *wrongfully excluded* by the other partners from the partnership business or from possession of partnership property.

2. The right to a formal account has been provided for in an *agreement* between the partners.

3. One of the other partners has, without consent, derived a *personal benefit* from a transaction related to partnership business.

4. Other circumstances render it "just and reasonable" (for example, if he or she has been traveling for a long period of time on partnership business and the other partners are in possession of the company's records).

The following case provides a practical example of the rule that partners owe fiduciary duties to each other, and that a partner who assumes responsibility for partnership records also assumes a correspondingly higher duty.

### Couri v. Couri
Supreme Court of Illinois,
447 N.E.2d 334 (1983)

In 1941, Joseph, Anthony, and Peter Couri orally agreed to operate as equal partners the "Couri Brothers Supermarket," a business which their father began in 1928. The brothers agreed that they would have equal control of the partnership, share equally in profits and losses, and have equal rights in the partnership property. The agreement was of indefinite duration. Later, Peter Couri withdrew from the partnership and his interest was purchased by Joseph and Anthony, who orally agreed that they would be equal partners. Over the years, Joseph had essentially worked in the supermarket at all times, as a clerk, butcher, and general supervisor of daily operations. Anthony worked full-time in the supermarket during World War II when Joseph was in the Army. After the war Anthony usually did not work at the supermarket itself, but had responsibility for the partnership's books, records, and investments. At times, Anthony also maintained other business interests separate from the partnership.

In September 1973, Joseph claimed that Anthony would not let him participate fully in the management of the business, and when the brothers were not able to reconcile their differences Joseph left the store permanently. Anthony claimed that Joseph unjustifiably abandoned the business and refused to participate. In November, Joseph visited Anthony at his home and requested and received some of the partnership records for the previous two years. They still were unable to resolve their dispute, and Joseph demanded that Anthony wind up the partnership's affairs. Instead, in July 1974 Anthony changed the locks on the store, closed out the partnership checking account, opened a new account which was in his exclusive control, and changed the name of the grocery store from "Couri Brothers Supermarket" to "Couri's Supermarket." Anthony continued to operate the store until Joseph, plaintiff, filed a lawsuit seeking an accounting and court-supervised winding up of the partnership's affairs.

The trial court ordered Anthony, the defendant, not to destroy, alter, or otherwise modify any of the partnership's records, and to render a complete accounting of revenues and expenses since 1957 (plaintiff and defendant agreed not to go back any further than 1957) and its current assets and liabilities. The records and tax returns of the partnership had been prepared and maintained by defendant since 1941. The records consisted of daily reports and monthly and yearly summaries. Tax returns were prepared from the summaries. Although the daily reports were theoretically restated in the monthly and yearly summaries, Anthony admitted that in several of the years of operation the summaries and tax returns did not accurately reflect actual income because the partnership's income was substantially understated. The daily reports themselves would provide the most accurate reflection of actual income, although these reports were often confusing and contradictory because defendant's bookkeeping practices were not in accord with generally accepted accounting principles. However, most of the daily reports were not available: some time after the plaintiff filed suit, the defendant's son cleaned his parents' attic while they were on vacation and destroyed several boxes of the partnership's daily reports. In court, the son testified that he was instructed to clean the garage and attic by his mother, who testified that she had acted without consulting the defendant.

Consequently, the evidence presented to the trial court was extremely incomplete. Both parties submitted sworn statements indicating how they thought the partnership's income should be computed from the available evidence. Defendant's computations produced a total net income figure for the period 1957–1980 ranging from $433,000 to $487,000, while plaintiff's computations produced a figure of over $1

*(continued)*

million. The income that had actually been reported to the Internal Revenue Service during the period was $424,000. The trial court held that defendant's accounting did not accurately reflect income, and that the partnership's total net income for the period was approximately $750,000. Based on this total income, the trial court computed plaintiff's share of the remaining surplus as $122,000 and rendered a judgment for plaintiff in that amount. Both parties appealed to the intermediate appellate court, which reversed the trial court's decision and dismissed plaintiff's suit on the ground that plaintiff had not proved any specific amount to which he was entitled. Plaintiff then appealed to the Illinois Supreme Court.

**Decision:** The judgment of the appellate court was reversed, and the judgment of the trial court for the plaintiff was affirmed. Anthony had control of the partnership's records and had a fiduciary duty to maintain them in a regular and accurate fashion. Any deficiencies in the records caused by his negligent failure to fulfill this duty would be resolved against him. In essence, a presumption was created in favor of Joseph's calculations, and the trial court's $750,000 estimate of partnership income for the relevant time period was a reasonable one under the existing evidence. In addition, the Supreme Court added $32,500 to the trial court's $122,000 judgment; this was half of the $65,000 that the trial court had awarded Anthony to compensate him for running the supermarket since Joseph had stopped participating. The court ruled that Anthony was not entitled to this amount, and added the $65,000 back into the partnership's surplus. ∎

## RELATIONS WITH THIRD PARTIES

### General Application of Agency Rules

In partnership transactions with third parties, the law of agency governs the liabilities of the partnership, the partners, and the third party. Technically, *the partnership is the principal and each partner an agent* with respect to partnership affairs. Statements are also found in many cases to the effect that each partner is an agent for the other partners (who are principals), as well as for the partnership as an entity. Of course, this is often the practical result anyway, since the other partners can be held personally liable if partnership assets are insufficient to satisfy the partnership liability.

The partnership is liable to third parties for a partner's transactions that are contractual in nature if the partner had actual or apparent authority. (Actual authority can, of course, be express or implied.) Partnership liability can also exist if the partnership, acting through the other partners, ratifies an unauthorized transaction of a partner. (More will be said later about partnership liability for a partner's contracts.)

As in agency law generally, the partnership is liable to third parties harmed by the tort or other wrongful act of a partner only if the tort was committed while the partner was acting in the ordinary course (or scope) of the partnership business. However, even if a partner's tort did not involve partnership business, any other partner participating in, directing, or authorizing the wrongful act is personally liable along with the one actually committing it.

The courts are somewhat more reluctant to impose *criminal liability* on a partnership or on the other partners for the act of one of them. Such liability is, of course, placed on any partner who participated in, directed, or expressly authorized the act of the other. However, the partnership as an entity (and other partners who did *not* participate in, direct, or expressly authorize the wrongful act) will be liable for the crime of a partner only if (1) it was committed in the ordinary course of the partnership business *and* (2) proof of criminal intent is *not* required for conviction. Examples include illegal liquor sales, mislabeling of goods, and unsafe transporting of explosives.

### Examples of a Partner's Implied Authority

Most questions concerning partnership liability for acts of individual partners stem from commercial dealings and other transactions of a contractual nature. The partnership, as principal, is usually liable for a partner's transaction only if it is *authorized*. Such authority can be expressly granted in the partnership agreement or by the other partners at a later time.

Even where no express authority has been given, under the UPA a partner can bind the partnership in transactions that are for the purpose of "carrying on the partnership business in the usual way." This *implied authority* exists with regard to those types of transactions that are *customary* in conducting the kind of business in which the partnership is engaged. In the articles of partnership or by other agreement the partners can expressly limit the authority of a partner to act for the partnership. If such a limitation restricts a partner's implied authority by prohibiting transactions that would otherwise be normal and customary, third parties are bound by the limitation only if they know of it. For example, suppose that a partnership is in the business of buying and selling real estate. It is customary in such a business for a partner to have authority to sell for the partnership real estate that is held for resale. Suppose, however, that the articles of partnership provide that such sales can be made only by two or more partners acting together. A third party who does not know of this restriction and who buys from a single partner is not affected by the limitation, and the partnership is bound by the transaction under the doctrine of *apparent authority.*

The following transactions are of such a usual and customary nature that a partner *ordinarily* is impliedly authorized to undertake them. These are only examples; other instances of implied authority exist, but they depend more on particular circumstances. Furthermore, these transactions might not be impliedly authorized in certain situations, particularly where the nature of the business is such that they are not usual and customary. Ultimately, the type of business conducted by the partnership and all the surrounding circumstances determine the extent of a partner's implied authority.

**Borrowing Money:** In determining whether a partner has implied authority to borrow money in behalf of the partnership, most courts have traditionally distinguished between *trading* and *nontrading* partnerships. Implied borrowing authority has been held to exist in trading partnerships but not in nontrading ones. A partner in a nontrading partnership usually has been held to have authority to borrow money only if this authority has been expressly granted by a majority of the other partners.

Essentially, a **trading partnership** is one that engages in the business of buying and selling goods. All others, ranging from professional partnerships such as those of lawyers and physicians to partnerships for the purpose of carrying on a real estate, insurance, or loan business, are classified as **nontrading partnerships.** In view of the increasing complexity of the business world, the simple division into trading and nontrading categories is of doubtful usefulness. Today many types of partnership require working capital, even though their business is not limited to merchandising.

The courts, perhaps sensing the inadequacies of the simple dichotomy between trading and nontrading partnerships, have expanded the trading category to include businesses such as those of tailors, plumbing and construction contractors, manufacturers, and dairy farmers. The courts will probably continue to use the terms *trading* and *nontrading,* but their importance will diminish. If a court holds a business to be a trading partnership, the authority of a partner to borrow money is automatically present unless the other partners expressly limit this authority and make such limitation known to third parties. In other types of partnerships, the courts will probably look at all the surrounding circumstances. If it is usual and customary for a partner in this particular partnership, or perhaps even in similar partnerships, to have borrowing authority, then such authority will probably be found to exist by many courts.

What has been said about implied authority to borrow money applies also to the execution of promissory notes and other types of instruments purporting to obligate the partnership to make a future payment of money. In fact, many of the cases decided on this point have involved such instruments.

**Selling Partnership Property:** A partner has implied authority to sell goods, real estate, or other property belonging to the partnership if sales of such items are within the ordinary course of the partnership's business. For example, suppose that a partnership engages in the wholesale grocery business and also owns real estate for investment purposes. In this case a partner has implied authority to sell groceries held for resale but usually does not have implied authority to sell the real estate. The latter authority will have to be expressly granted by a majority of the other partners. On the other hand, if the business of the partnership consists of buying and selling real estate, a partner *does have* implied authority to sell partnership real estate.

The addition of other facts might change the above example. For instance, if the other partners had in the past always allowed one partner to make all investment decisions individually, that partner might have implied authority to sell the grocery partnership's real estate.

Even if the sale of a certain type of property, such as goods, is part of the ordinary business of the partnership, a partner generally does not have implied authority to sell most or all of the items held in inventory if this will result in a suspension of the business.

**Hiring Employees:** A partner ordinarily has implied authority to hire employees whose services are necessary for carrying on the business of the partnership, to make reasonable agreements for their compensation, and to discharge them.

**Making Purchases:** A partner usually has implied authority to purchase items that are reasonably necessary to the operation of the partnership's business.

**Receiving and Enforcing Performance of Obligations:** If the partnership is entitled to some type of performance, such as a payment of money or delivery of goods, a partner ordinarily has implied authority to accept performance of the obligation in behalf of the partnership. In addition, a partner has implied authority to take legal action for the partnership if the other party defaults on the obligation.

In the case below, the court applies basic agency concepts contained in the UPA to the plaintiff's claim against a partnership on a real estate sale contract signed by a single partner.

---

**Owens v. Palos Verdes Monaco**
Court of Appeal of California,
191 Cal. Rptr. 381 (1983)

Seymour Owens, Albert Fink, and Manny Borinstein were in the business of acquiring, holding, and developing real estate on the Palos Verdes peninsula in California. They bought 250 acres, divided it into four tracts, and formed four separate partnerships to own and develop the tracts. Borinstein died, and the surviving partners agreed that Borinstein's widow, Pearl, would become a partner, but would hold the interests in the four partnerships in trust for her daughter Joan. Several years later, Kajima International, Inc., became interested in buying one of these tracts of land. The tract in question, 57 acres, was held by a partnership called Monaco Land Holders (MLH).

A representative of Kajima contacted a real estate brokerage firm in the Palos Verdes area. The brokerage firm contacted Owens, one of the three partners in MLH and the other partnerships. Owens told the broker to show the 57-acre tract to the Kajima representative, to "pursue the sale," and "keep him [Owens] informed." After Kajima's representative had seen the land and conferred with his superiors, Kajima made a written offer to buy. This offer was delivered by the broker to both Owens and Fink. They rejected the offer and Owens told the broker that "Al Fink will be handling this from now on; just keep me apprised of what's going on." A second offer was made and was again delivered to both Owens and Fink. Fink met with Owens and they decided to reject this offer, as well.

At this time, and later, Pearl Borinstein was kept informed about the negotiations and indicated that she would go along with any proposal that met with Owens's approval.

Over the next several months, the broker tried to put together a deal that would be agreeable to both sides. Three different meetings were held to negotiate the sale. Present at all three meetings were the broker and several representatives of Kajima, including a vice-president and another high-ranking officer. At the first two meetings, MLH was represented by Fink and Joan Borinstein (Pearl's daughter). Owens was informed about each of the meetings in advance, but each time he indicated that if Fink was going to be present, there was no need for him (Owens) to be there. At the third meeting, when the sale was finally concluded and the written contract was signed, only Fink was present in behalf of MLH, although Owens, Pearl, and Joan had all been notified of the meeting. Thus, Fink was the only partner signing the contract for the partnership. At this meeting, a question was raised about the fact that only one partner was signing, and Fink assured the buyers that he had authority to act for the partnership.

About two weeks after this third meeting, Owens indicated that he was unhappy with the terms of the sale contract and did not want the sale to go forward. The buyer insisted on completing the sale, and Owens filed suit against both the partnership and Kajima. In the suit, Owens sought a declaratory judgment that the contract was invalid and an injunction prohibiting the partnership from transferring title to the 57-acre tract to Kajima. Kajima filed a counterclaim against the partnership, Owens, and the other partners, seeking a decree of specific performance that would require the contract to be carried out by transferring title to Kajima. (Because initially

*(continued)*

there was some confusion as to whether the 57-acre tract was owned by MLH or by one of the other partnerships, Palos Verdes Monaco, both partnerships were named as parties to the lawsuit. Consequently, the name of Palos Verdes Monaco appears in the title of the case. After the suit was filed, it was determined that MLH owned this particular tract.) The trial court ruled that the contract was valid because Fink had authority to sign in behalf of the partnership, denied Owens's request for an injunction, and granted Kajima's request for specific performance of the contract. Owens, the partnership, and the other partners appealed.

**Decision:** The judgment for defendant Kajima was affirmed. The contract of sale was valid and bound the partnership. Although a contract to sell partnership real estate usually will not be valid if made by only one partner, in this case the business of the partnership was to buy, hold, and resell land. Therefore, a sale of one of the tracts was apparently for the carrying on of the partnership's business in the usual way, and a contract of sale by only one partner was binding on the partnership. ■

## *Examples of Authority Not Usually Implied*

The following actions are those for which implied authority usually does not exist. Again, these are only examples, and other actions also might not be impliedly authorized, depending on the nature of the business and the surrounding circumstances. Furthermore, the activities below might be impliedly authorized if the circumstances are such that the activity is usual and customary in the particular business involved. Remember, too, that any of these acts may be *expressly* authorized by the other partners if they so desire.

**Assumption of Debts:** In most cases, a partner does *not* have implied authority to assume, in the name of the partnership, liability for the debt of another. Such authority *may* exist, however, if the nature of the business includes this type of transaction. For instance, it might be customary for a partnership that sells stocks, bonds, and other securities to guarantee the securities it sells. This is, in effect, an assumption of the obligation of the company that originally issued the securities, but a partner can nevertheless have implied authority to make such a guarantee where it is a normal part of the partnership's business.

**Purchases of Corporate Stock:** The courts have generally held that a partner does not have implied authority to purchase or agree to purchase, for the partnership, stock in a corporation. Of course, such authority may exist if this type of transaction is within the usual scope of the business (for example, if the partnership's business is the sale of corporate stocks).

**Gratuitous Activities:** Since partnerships are formed for the purpose of operating a profit-making enterprise, a partner usually does not have implied authority to involve the partnership in a charitable undertaking or to give away partnership property. Such authority ordinarily has to be expressly given by the other partners. Exceptions might exist where it is customary for a business to provide certain free goods or services to customers in an effort to generate goodwill and enhance future business. Thus it might be customary for a brokerage firm to furnish free market information to prospective customers.

## *Actions Expressly Disallowed by the UPA*

In Sec. 9, the UPA specifically designates several types of actions that are completely unauthorized. In other words, a partner cannot bind the partnership by these acts regardless of the nature of the business or what is customary. Furthermore, even a *majority* of the partners do not have the power to bind the partnership by these acts; there must be express agreement by *all* the partners.[2]

**Confession of Judgment:** Action by all partners is required to confess judgment. A *confession of judgment* is the agreement of a debtor that allows the creditor to obtain a court judgment for a specified sum against the debtor without the necessity of legal proceedings. Agreement of all the partners is required because of the unusual and severe nature of a confession of judgment.[3]

---

[2] One exception exists. The consent of a partner who has abandoned the business need not be obtained.

[3] In some states a confession of judgment is not permitted at all. Also, a rule passed by the Federal Trade Commission in 1985 prohibits a creditor from including a confession of judgment clause in any *consumer credit transaction.*

**Arbitration:** Unanimous consent is also required to submit a claim by or against the partnership to *arbitration.* Although arbitration is now a common and accepted method of settling commercial disputes, this has not always been the case. Courts were not particularly receptive to the idea of arbitration at an earlier time, an antagonism reflected in the UPA when it was drafted in 1914.

**Acts Restricting Partnership Business:** The UPA also requires unanimous agreement by the partners to perform certain types of acts that restrict the operation of the partnership business. For example, consent of all partners is required before the partnership property can be placed in trust for the partnership's creditors. Such a transaction is commonly referred to as an *assignment for the benefit of creditors,* and it represents one way an insolvent business can settle with its creditors without formal bankruptcy proceedings.

Agreement of all partners is also necessary to dispose of the goodwill of the partnership. The courts have construed this provision as requiring unanimous consent to a covenant not to compete. For example, the partnership might sell part of its business and agree not to compete with the buyer. Such an agreement would bind the partnership only if it was made by all the partners.

The UPA also states that consent of all partners is required to "do any other act which would make it impossible to carry on the ordinary business" of the partnership. An example is an agreement to cancel the lease of the premises where the partnership conducts its business.

The following case illustrates (1) the importance of implied authority in partnership law and (2) how the concept of implied authority may be used to fulfill the UPA's requirement of unanimous consent for certain actions. It will be seen that, at least with respect to a partner's authority to commit the partnership to arbitrate a dispute, the requirement of unanimous consent may not be as difficult to satisfy as one might think.

### Eassa Properties v. Shearson Lehman Brothers
U.S. Eleventh Circuit Court of Appeals, 851 F.2d 1301 (1988)

Eassa Properties (Eassa), a Florida general partnership, is composed of four partners who are brothers. Alexander A. "Sandy" Simon, Jr., one of the partners, is the only brother to play a significant role in this case. Shearson Lehman Brothers (Shearson) is a Delaware corporation with its principal place of business in New York. During the relevant time period, Michael W. Swofford was a broker at Shearson. Bishop, a commodities specialist, assisted Swofford in trading for his commodity accounts at Shearson.

In 1982, Simon was hired by Burt Reynolds, a well-known actor and director, to handle his financial affairs. In order to facilitate this purpose, Simon held Reynolds's power-of-attorney. In mid-1983, Simon opened separate security accounts for himself and for Reynolds with Swofford at Shearson's Little Rock, Arkansas, office. In doing so, Simon and Reynolds signed Customer's Agreements. In August 1984, Simon opened separate commodity accounts for himself and for Reynolds with Swofford. Simon signed a Commodity Customer Agreement for his own account. Simon, as Reynolds's agent, executed a new Customer's Agreement for Reynolds's security account and a Commodity Customer Agreement for Reynolds's commodity account. In that same month, Simon also opened a security account and a commodity account with Swofford on behalf of Eassa.

On October 9, 1984, Swofford forged Simon's name to a purported letter of authorization, permitting the withdrawal of $700,000.00 from Reynolds's account. When confronted, Swofford eventually admitted that he had forged the signature on the letter. A subsequent investigation revealed that Swofford had stolen hundreds of thousands of dollars from Reynolds which he used to purchase a house, two expensive automobiles, a boat, and other items of personal property. It was also discovered that Swofford and Bishop apparently had transferred large sums of money without authorization from Eassa's security account to its commodity account and had begun to engage in high-volume discretionary trading of commodities in excess of the account limitations placed on Shearson by Eassa.

On October 4, 1984, Simon, having been told by Swofford that the Eassa accounts had generated substantial profits, elected to cease trading in Eassa's accounts and to collect its profits. Simon received a check for $100,000 payable to Eassa on October 5, 1984, but never received the balance of the money he claims is owed to Eassa. In November 1985, Eassa

*(continued)*

filed a complaint in federal district court against Shearson, Bishop, and Swofford, seeking damages for alleged violations of several laws, including the Racketeer Influenced and Corrupt Organizations Act (RICO), the antifraud provisions of the federal securities laws, various state securities laws, and several common-law principles. (Swofford was also named as a defendant in this lawsuit, but he never responded and a default judgment was entered against him. Separately, Swofford pleaded guilty to two counts of wire fraud and conspiracy in violation of federal criminal laws, and was sent to prison.)

Shearson and Bishop filed a motion to compel arbitration of Eassa's claims. Eassa opposed the motion because it wanted its claims to be litigated in federal court rather than decided in arbitration. The district court conducted a hearing and granted the motion. At the district court hearing, Shearson produced three documents that purported to require Eassa to arbitrate any claims against Shearson. These documents were a Customer's Agreement, a Commodity Customer Agreement, and a Commodity Option Agreement ("the Agreements"). The first two documents contained clauses by which the parties agreed to submit all future disputes arising out of the agreements to legally binding arbitration, while the third document incorporated by reference the arbitration provision in the second document.

Simon's name, what purported to be his signature, and an indication that he was signing in behalf of Eassa, were on all of the Agreements. Eassa contended that the signatures on these documents were forgeries, but that even if they were genuine, Simon did not intend, nor did he have the authority, to bind Eassa to arbitration.

Despite some expert testimony that some of the signatures may have been forgeries, the district court held that the signatures were genuine. The court also held that Simon intended to bind Eassa to these agreements when he signed them, and that by leaving blanks in them Simon authorized Shearson Lehman Brothers to fill in those blanks that were left in the Agreements. The district court also held that Simon did have authority to bind the partnership to the Agreements, including the arbitration clauses. Eassa appealed all of these rulings to the U.S. court of appeals.

**Decision:** The district court judgment was affirmed. Because Simon had been given broad authority to transact business in behalf of the partnership, he had implied authority to obligate the partnership to arbitrate. The UPA requirement of unanimous consent to arbitration can be fulfilled by evidence indicating that a single partner had implied authority to sign an agreement containing an arbitration clause. (The appellate court also affirmed the trial court's findings that Simon's signatures were genuine and that he had authorized Shearson to fill in certain blanks, holding that these findings were not clearly erroneous.) ∎

**Comment:** The UPA was drafted in 1914, when there was still much hostility by judges and lawyers toward arbitration as an alternative to lawsuits. The provision in the UPA that requires consent of all the partners to an arbitration agreement probably is explainable, at least in part, by this general hostility. The decision by this court that the general concept of implied authority can satisfy the UPA's unanimous consent requirement for arbitration agreements may be attributable partly to today's much more favorable attitude toward arbitration.

## Satisfaction of Creditors' Claims

One of the cardinal characteristics of the partnership form of business is that the individual partners are *personally liable* for the obligations of the partnership. This liability is secondary. A creditor having a claim against a partnership must first look to *partnership property* for satisfaction of the claim. The creditor can reach the assets of individual partners only after partnership assets are exhausted. Moreover, the assets of an individual partner must first be used to satisfy claims of his or her personal creditors before partnership creditors can assert their claims.

Quite naturally, then, creditors of an individual partner must first look to the personal assets of that partner for satisfaction of their claims. In fact, such creditors *cannot* reach specific items of partnership property. If some debt remains after a partner's personal assets have been exhausted, the creditor's only recourse with regard to the partnership is to obtain a **charging order** against the partner's *interest in the partnership* (that is, the partner's right to share in the profits and surplus of the partnership). A charging order issued by a court will order that partner's share of the profits to be paid to his or her creditor until the debt is fully discharged. If the debt has not been completely paid when the partnership is dissolved, the charging order will require payment to the creditor of that partner's share in the surplus, if any remains when all partnership affairs are settled.

## Special Rules Regarding Liability to Third Parties

**The Incoming Partner:** When a new partner is admitted into an existing partnership, he or she naturally becomes responsible along with the other partners for all partnership obligations that arise *after* the admittance. The new partner is also responsible for partnership obligations that arose *before* he or she became a partner, but this liability does not extend beyond his or her interest in the partnership. Partnership creditors whose claims against the partnership arose prior to admission of the new partner cannot reach his or her individual assets for satisfaction of the claims.

**Partner by Estoppel:** Even if a person is not a member of a particular partnership, under certain circumstances there may be personal liability to third parties as if the individual were a partner. If someone has represented himself or herself as a partner to a third party (or allowed such a representation to be made), that person is liable as a partner if the third party grants credit to the partnership because of the representation. This liability results because the individual is "estopped" (prohibited) from denying that he or she is a partner in a suit brought by the third party.

To illustrate: Regency Co., a partnership, wished to obtain credit. Fearful of being unable to do so, the partners in Regency Co., X and Y, appealed to Jones, a businessman whose name and financial capabilities were well known in the business community. Out of friendship, Jones agreed that X and Y could tell prospective creditors that he was a member of the partnership in order to obtain credit. Subsequently, X and Y represented to the First National Bank that Jones was a partner. Relying on the representation, the bank granted the loan to the partnership. Even though Jones is not actually a partner, he is liable to the bank as if he were one. However, he is not treated as a partner for any other purpose. No partnership relations have been created between Jones and X and Y, and he is not liable as a partner to third parties who have not relied on the representation.

## Assignment of a Partner's Interest

As previously discussed, a partner's right to possess and control partnership property cannot be assigned to a third party. However, a partner's interest in the partnership *can* be assigned to a third party without the consent of the other partners.

The assignee of a partner's interest is merely entitled to receive the profits to which the assigning partner would otherwise be entitled. If the partnership is subsequently dissolved, the assignee is entitled to receive whatever share of the surplus the assigning partner would have been entitled to receive. But the assignee acquires *nothing else*. He or she does not become a partner unless all the partners consent to the admission. Therefore, the assignee acquires no management powers, does not become an agent of the partnership, and, while the partnership exists, is not entitled to inspect the partnership books or to receive a formal account of partnership transactions.

Before enactment of the UPA, the assignment by a partner to a third party of his or her interest in the partnership was generally deemed to automatically *dissolve* the partnership, unless the partnership agreement provided otherwise. Under the UPA, this is not the case. The UPA recognizes that a partner may wish to assign the interest with absolutely no intention of bringing an end to the partnership. For example, a partner may wish to assign this interest to an individual creditor as security for a loan. On the other hand, in some circumstances a partner's assignment can be considered evidence of an intent to dissolve the partnership. For example, if, after the assignment, the assigning partner neglects partnership affairs and acts as if there is no longer any business relationship with the other partners, a court will be justified in holding the partnership to be dissolved. But the mere act of assignment, with nothing more, does not bring about dissolution. (The subject of dissolution will be treated more fully in the next chapter.)

## SUMMARY

One of the basic rights of a partner is to participate in the management of the business. It is possible, however, for partners to alter their management rights by agreement. If there is no agreement otherwise, most management decisions in a partnership are made by majority vote of the partners. A few unusual matters require consent of all the partners unless they had previously agreed to let such decisions be made by less-than-unanimous vote.

Unless the articles of partnership provide otherwise, an individual partner's right in partnership property is limited to the equal right (with other partners) to possess such property for partnership purposed. This right is not transferable. When the agreement does not provide otherwise, all partners share equally in profits and losses, regardless of the relative amounts of capital they contributed. A partner normally is not entitled to compensation other than a share of profits, unless the partnership agreement states otherwise.

Partners owe fiduciary duties to each other and must act with reasonable care and with the utmost good faith. Each partner has a right to have complete access to partnership records. Under certain circumstances, a partner has the right to an account, which is a court-supervised audit of all partnership records.

The partnership's relations with third parties are governed by the basic rules of the law of agency. Each partner is an agent of the partnership for the purposes of its business, and the partnership is bound by a partner's actions when they have the apparent purpose of operating the partnership's business in the usual manner.

## KEY TERMS

**Interest in the partnership**
**Account (or accounting)**
**Trading partnership**
**Nontrading partnership**
**Charging order**

## QUESTIONS AND PROBLEMS

1. X, Y, and Z were partners in Snappy Delivery Service Co. The partnership owned three delivery trucks. X borrowed one of the trucks to haul some of his personal belongings and never returned it to the business. Y and Z demanded the return of the truck, but X refused. X said that he owned a third of the partnership; and since the partnership owned three trucks, one of them naturally belonged to him personally. Is X correct? Explain.

2. Anderson, Richards, and Williams formed a partnership for the purpose of producing rock music concerts. The three partners initially contributed $2,000, $4,000, and $3,000, respectively, to the partnership for use as working capital. The partnership agreement made no provision for the division of profits. At the end of the first year, the partnership had made a profit of $4,500. What is each partner's share of the profits? Explain.

3. Suppose that in Question 2 the partnership agreement had provided that profits were to be divided equally but had made no provision for the division of losses. If the partnership loses $3,000 the first year, what proportion of this loss must each partner bear? Explain.

4. Wilkes, Watkins, and Weston formed a partnership for the express purpose, as provided in the partnership agreement, of engaging in the retail shoe business. Even though the business was relatively successful, Wilkes and Watkins wanted to change the nature of their business from a shoe store to a men's clothing store. Weston objected. Can Wilkes and Watkins take such action over Weston's objection? Discuss.

5. Oswald and Leckey, certified public accountants, executed a partnership agreement to conduct an accounting practice. After forming the partnership each partner continued to bill the clients that he personally served. The relationship between Oswald and Leckey was not harmonious and the partnership was dissolved about two years after it had been formed. Oswald filed suit for an accounting to determine each partner's share of a partnership bank account. In the lawsuit, Oswald claimed that Leckey had improperly "written down" several accounts while they were partners, and that Leckey should have to repay the partnership for the amount of the write-downs. An account is "written down" when the amount actually billed is less than the amount due as shown on the books. The evidence showed that part of Leckey's motive in writing down the accounts was to keep these clients as his own. Did Leckey violate his fiduciary duty of loyalty to Oswald? Discuss. (*Oswald v. Leckey,* 572 P.2d 1316, Sup. Ct. of Oregon 1977.)

6. Under the Nassau Queens Medical Group's partnership agreement, a partner could be terminated by a majority vote if the partner had reached the age of 70. Dr. Levy was expelled from the partnership on the ground that he was over 70 years old. Other partners over the age of 70, however, were not terminated. There was no evidence that the partnership acted out of a desire to gain a business or property advantage for the remaining partners. Was Dr. Levy's termination allowable under the partnership agreement? Discuss. (*Levy v. Nassau Queens Medical Group,* 102 A.2d 845, N.Y. App. Div. 1984.)

7. A, B, C, and D owned a used car business as partners. D sold a car to Johnson, guaranteeing in writing that any defects in the car would be repaired free of charge during the 90-day period following the sale. Johnson brought the car back a month later, claiming that the transmission was not operating properly. A, B, and C stated that the warranty was no good because D had not been given express authority to make warranties. Must the partnership honor the warranty made by D? Discuss.

8. Suppose that in Question 7 the partnership agreement had expressly provided that a partner does not have authority to make warranties in connection with the sale of cars. Would this fact make any difference? Would Johnson's knowledge of the provision be of any importance? Explain.

**9.** Jurgenson and Taylor were partners in an automobile repair business. Driver brought his car to Jurgenson and Taylor's garage to have the brakes repaired. Jurgenson repaired the brakes. Two days later Driver had a collision caused by failure of the brakes. The brake failure was due to Jurgenson's negligence in doing the repair work, so Driver sued the partnership. Is the partnership liable? Explain.

**10.** Suppose that in Question 9 Driver's suit against the partnership was successful. The assets of the partnership, however, were not sufficient to satisfy the judgment awarded to Driver by the court. Driver then sought to hold the individual partners personally liable for the unpaid portion of the judgment. Could he hold them personally responsible? Explain. Suppose that Jurgenson and Taylor had admitted Leonard as a new partner in the business. If Driver also tries to hold Leonard personally liable, what will be the importance of the time of Leonard's admission as a new partner? Discuss.

CHAPTER 35

# PARTNERSHIPS

TERMINATION

Complete termination of the partnership as a business organization is composed of two elements: *dissolution* and *winding up*. Dissolution does not of itself bring the partnership business to a close; it is, rather, the "beginning of the end." Essentially, the word **dissolution** designates that point in time when the object of the partners changes from continuing the organization in its present form to discontinuing it.[1] The partnership is not terminated at that time, but its object has become termination.

The second element of termination, commonly referred to as **winding up,** involves the actual process of settling partnership affairs after dissolution. After both dissolution and winding up have occurred, the partnership as an organization will have terminated.

## DISSOLUTION

### Causes of Dissolution

The events that cause dissolution can be divided into four categories: (1) act of one or more partners not in violation of their agreement, (2) act of one or more partners in violation of their agreement, (3) operation of law, and (4) court decree.

**Act of One or More Partners Not in Violation of Their Agreement:** As we have seen in the discussion of partnership formation and operation, the partnership is created by agreement. Thus, when the question becomes one of dissolution, the partnership agreement (articles of partnership) should be the first place to look for guidance.

The partnership agreement may provide, for example, that the partnership will exist for only a specified period of time. Upon expiration of this period, the partnership dissolves in accordance with the original agreement, unless all the partners agree to amend the articles of partnership and extend the prescribed duration.[2] The partnership agreement similarly could provide for automatic dissolution of the partnership upon the occurrence of some particular event. When this event takes place, the partnership dissolves unless the partners unanimously amend the agreement.

Where the partnership agreement makes no provision for a definite duration and places no other limitations on a partner's right to withdraw, a **partnership at will** exists. This means that any partner can withdraw at any time without violating the agreement and, therefore, without incurring contractual liability to the other partners. Such a withdrawal automatically dissolves the partnership unless the partnership agreement provides that withdrawal will not result in dissolution.

Similarly, as seen in Chapter 33 in *Gelder Medical Group v. Webber,* the partnership agreement may allow for exclusion of a partner by the other partners. Such a provision might permit exclusion of a partner

---

[1] Later in the chapter we will discuss the situation where certain of the partners wish to continue the *business,* even though the partnership as an organization is dissolved. It might be continued as a new partnership or in some other organizational form. In such a case, the termination of the partnership consists primarily of bookkeeping entries and purchase of the interests of noncontinuing partners.

[2] Continuance of the business by the partners after expiration of the agreed term constitutes an implied partnership agreement even in the absence of an express amendment of the articles of partnership. The partnership will then be one "at will," which means that the individual partners are legally free to withdraw at any time thereafter. So long as they actually continue, however, the partnership exists and the terms of the implied partnership agreement are those of the original agreement, insofar as they are applicable.

only for specified reasons, or it might even permit exclusion without cause by vote of a specified number of the other partners. In any event, the partners relying on the exclusion clause are not in violation of the agreement if they act in accordance with its terms. Moreover, an exclusion clause in the partnership agreement usually is interpreted by a court as an agreement among the partners that dissolution will not occur when a partner is excluded according to the clause.

Since a partnership is created by agreement, it can be dissolved by agreement. Regardless of the terms of the original partnership agreement, a partnership can be dissolved at any time without violating that agreement if all the partners consent to dissolution. A unanimous dissolution agreement overrides the original articles of partnership. A dissolution agreement that is not unanimous, however, constitutes a violation of the original partnership agreement by those causing dissolution unless their action is in accordance with a provision in the original agreement expressly permitting dissolution by a less-than-unanimous vote.[3]

The following case more fully explains the overriding nature of the partnership agreement in resolving questions relating to dissolution.

---

[3] However, if a partner has assigned his or her interest in the partnership to a third party, or if a partner's personal creditor has subjected the partner's interest in the partnership to a "charging order," the consent of that partner is not required for dissolution.

---

### Osborne v. Workman
Supreme Court of Arkansas,
621 S.W.2d 478 (1981)

In 1966 Merrill Osborne, a physician, joined with five other physicians in a partnership to operate a medical clinic. Their written partnership agreement specified no definite term, but only that it would continue "until said partnership is dissolved mutually or by law." The agreement also provided that if a doctor withdrew from the partnership he was to be paid his percentage share of the clinic's asset value at the time of withdrawal, *excluding* accounts receivable. When the partnership was formed, the clinic's accounts receivable were $105,000 and were treated as a partnership asset. The accounts gradually increased, and by 1979 totalled $513,000. Estimates of actual collectability of these accounts in 1979 varied from $100,000 to $400,000. Between 1966 and 1979 a number of new physicians were admitted to the partnership, and a total of seven withdrew. In six of the seven withdrawals, the withdrawing physicians received nothing from accounts receivable; one had received a portion of the accounts by unanimous vote of the remaining partners in 1968.

In 1978 Osborne announced his intention to withdraw from the partnership, and by 1979 he had relocated to a private medical practice. The remaining partners offered to pay him his percentage share of the partnership's present asset value, excluding accounts receivable, but Osborne insisted on receiving a share of those accounts. When the remaining partners refused, he filed suit seeking dissolution of the partnership and a winding up that would include liquidation of its assets. The trial court held for the partnership and remaining partners, and Osborne, appellant, appealed to the Supreme Court of Arkansas.

---

**Decision:** The judgment for defendant partnership was affirmed. Withdrawal of a partner causes dissolution, and requires winding up, unless the partners have agreed otherwise. By expressly providing for the computation and payment of a withdrawing partner's interest, the partnership agreement indicated an intent that withdrawal not cause dissolution. Osborne was not entitled to have the partnership dissolved, and he was bound by the partnership agreement's exclusion of accounts receivable from the computation of his interest. ∎

---

**Act of One or More Partners in Violation of Their Agreement:** Regardless of the terms of the partnership agreement, one or more partners can withdraw from the partnership at any time. Although the power to withdraw from a partnership always exists, any partner whose withdrawal violates the partnership agreement is liable to the nonwithdrawing partners for damages caused by the withdrawal. Such withdrawal causes a dissolution of the partnership unless the partnership agreement provided that dissolution would not result in these circumstances. Although withdrawal can cause dissolution without any formal court action, one or more of the withdrawing or non-withdrawing partners often will seek a court decree of dissolution if there is any disagreement about whether the withdrawal actually violated the partnership agreement or about the amount of damages.

**By Operation of Law:** The partnership automatically dissolves if an event occurs that makes it illegal to carry on the business. The *business itself* may become illegal, as where a partnership for the purpose of selling liquor loses its liquor license. Or it may become illegal for *these particular partners* to carry on the business together, as where an individual partner in a medical practice has his or her license revoked.

Unless otherwise agreed, dissolution also occurs automatically on the *death* of a partner or on the *bankruptcy* of either a partner or the partnership itself. The articles of partnership may, of course, provide that the death or bankruptcy of an individual partner will not cause a dissolution.

**By Court Decree:** Section 32 of the UPA specifically enumerates several situations in which dissolution of a partnership can be accomplished by seeking and obtaining a formal court decree. They can be divided into two broad categories: (1) situations in which a *partner* can obtain a decree of dissolution and (2) situations in which a *third party* can obtain such a decree.

*Decree Obtained by a Partner:* When a partner has become *insane,* either that person or another partner can obtain a court decree dissolving the partnership. In such a case dissolution does not occur automatically (as it does in the case of death or bankruptcy). A formal court decree is required in the instance of insanity because a person's mental competency is inherently subject to doubt and dispute, whereas death and bankruptcy are more certain events. The decree can be sought (1) when a partner has already been declared insane by a court in a sanity hearing or (2) when such a formal adjudication has not yet occurred. In the latter case, the court asked to dissolve the partnership will itself determine whether the partner is insane. The court will not dissolve the partnership in either case, however, unless it appears probable that the insanity will continue for a substantial part of the partnership's duration.

Dissolution also can be obtained by court decree if a partner becomes in any other way *incapable of performing his or her part of the partnership agreement.* This provision is usually applied to disabilities other than insanity (such as prolonged illness, a paralytic stroke, or a serious accident) when it appears that the disability will continue for a substantial period of time and will materially obstruct or negatively affect the objectives of the partnership. The court decree in this case can be sought by either the partner suffering the disability or any other partner.

A partner can obtain a decree of dissolution when one of the other partners has been guilty of *serious misconduct.* Breach of the partnership agreement is, of course, one example of such misconduct. Even if the partnership agreement has not been breached, under the UPA a decree of dissolution can be obtained if another partner has been "guilty of such conduct as tends to affect prejudicially the carrying on of the business" or if the other partner "so conducts himself in matters relating to the partnership business that it is not reasonably practicable to carry on the business in partnership with him." Examples of such conduct are fraud in dealing with partnership property or funds, substantial overdraft of a drawing account by a partner who has been temporarily left in charge of the business, and serious neglect of partnership affairs.

Where misconduct has occurred, the guilty partner cannot obtain dissolution by court decree; this right belongs solely to one or more of the other partners. Furthermore, if the other partner or partners so desire, they can simply withdraw and cause dissolution. A court decree is not essential, and the guilty partner cannot sue them for damages even if their withdrawal is contrary to the partnership agreement. Although formal court action is not essential in cases of misconduct, it is often desirable where any doubt exists as to whether the misconduct is serious enough to warrant dissolution or where disagreement exists regarding damages or the value of partners' interests.

Finally, any partner can obtain a decree of dissolution when it becomes evident that the business is *unprofitable* and will probably not be profitable in the future.

*Decree Obtained by a Third Party:* Two types of third parties are considered to have a sufficient interest in partnership affairs to obtain a decree of dissolution in certain circumstances: (1) an *assignee* of a partner's interest in the partnership and (2) a partner's *personal creditor* who has subjected that partner's interest to a charging order. Either of these third parties, however, can obtain a decree of dissolution in only two situations: (1) after expiration of the period of time or accomplishment of the purpose specified in the articles of partnership, in cases where the articles include such a provision, or (2) at any time, if the partnership is a partnership "at will" when the third party acquires his or her interest.

In the next case, a partner sought dissolution by court decree on the basis of a claim that one of the other partners had breached the partnership agreement. The question also arose whether the partner who violated the agreement forfeited all of his rights as a partner, or whether he was just liable for whatever monetary damage his breach caused to the other partners.

---

### Staszak v. Romanik
U.S. Sixth Circuit Court of Appeals, 690 F.2d 578 (1982)

Joseph Staszak and his cousin, Walter Romanik, formed a partnership in 1959 under the name North Star Tree Company for the purpose of growing and selling Christmas trees. Walter lived in Michigan, and Joseph in Maryland; both owned land in Michigan where the trees were to be grown. They made an oral agreement that Walter's 20 acres and Joseph's 80 acres both would be used in the business: Walter would supply labor and manage the operation, Joseph would supply the working capital, and profits and losses would be shared equally. In 1968 Walter and Joseph agreed that Walter should begin receiving a salary for his management services. Between 1959 and 1969 the partnership purchased and leased substantial additional land, so that by 1969 trees were being grown on 1,573 acres. Also by 1969, 94 full-time and part-time employees worked for the partnership.

In early 1969 Walter and Joseph purchased another Christmas tree business in Michigan, Sno Kist Tree Corporation, using as a down payment $134,000 that Joseph had personally borrowed and contributed to the partnership. The purchase included the Sno Kist trademark, a long-term lease on Sno Kist's land and equipment, and assignments of leases held by Sno Kist on several other tracts of land used for growing and harvesting trees. All of these leases included tree harvesting rights. Walter and Joseph agreed at the same time to admit Joseph's son Richard Staszak as an equal partner in the larger enterprise. Essentially, a new partnership was formed at this time, and the purchase of Sno Kist Tree Company was made in the names of all three partners. Thereafter, North Star and Sno Kist were operated as a single business, and in 1970 the three partners executed a written partnership agreement that formally adopted the Sno Kist name for the entire operation, and provided that the capital contributions of the partners were to be their interests in partnership real estate and other assets. The written agreement also stated that profits were to be shared equally, but that these profits were to be distributed in such a way as to eventually equalize the partners' capital contributions.

During the first year's harvest after formation of the three-way partnership, Richard Staszak went from Maryland to Michigan and stayed throughout the harvest season, overseeing the work on a portion of the operation. Richard spent part of each succeeding year, during the harvesting season, in Michigan. Beginning in 1972, Walter began complaining that Richard was not doing what was required by their agreement, because they had an unwritten understanding that Richard was to move to Michigan and work full time in the business. By 1975 relations between Walter and the Staszaks had completely deteriorated, and Joseph and Richard tried to buy out Walter's interest in the partnership. Walter refused to sell and filed suit claiming that the partnership should be dissolved because of Richard's breach of the partnership agreement. The trial court concluded that, even though the partnership agreement did not so state, there was an implied agreement that Richard Staszak would move to Michigan and work full time in the business, and that Richard had breached this agreement. Because the agreement had required Richard initially to contribute only services, and no capital, to the partnership, the trial court found that there was a complete failure of consideration on Richard's part. Consequently, the trial court held that Richard had never become a partner and had to return to the partnership over $80,000 in profit distributions he had received since 1969. Joseph and Richard appealed.

---

**Decision:** The judgment for the plaintiff Romanik was reversed. Richard Staszak did become a partner, because that was the intent of the parties. They had agreed that his contribution would

*(continued)*

take the form of services, and although he did not do all that was expected of him, he did in fact perform valuable services for the partnership. Richard did not forfeit his rights as a partner just by breaching the partnership agreement. Richard was liable for any damages to the partnership caused by his breach of contract, but he did not have to return his profit distributions. The case was remanded to the trial court for computation of damages caused to the partnership by Richard's breach. ■

## *Effect of Dissolution on Partners' Authority*

Despite the fact that dissolution does not sound the instantaneous death knell of the partnership, it is frequently important to ascertain the precise moment when it occurs. The reason is simple. When dissolution takes place, certain significant changes occur in the nature of the partners' relationships with one another and with outsiders. Of paramount significance is the effect dissolution has on the *authority of partners to bind the partnership.* In most cases, of course, a partner acting without authority must personally shoulder the burden of any liability resulting from such action.

Upon dissolution, the authority of individual partners to act in behalf of the partnership usually ceases, *except for acts necessary to complete unfinished transactions or those appropriate for winding up partnership affairs.* For example, suppose that a partnership, before dissolution, had made a contract to sell goods. After dissolution, a partner would have authority to arrange for shipping those goods in accordance with the existing contract. However, he or she would not have authority to make new contracts without the consent of the other partners, unless these contracts were in furtherance of liquidating the business. Thus the partner probably would be authorized to make contracts for the sale of existing inventory. Similarly, he or she usually would be able to do such things as hire an accountant to take inventory and perform an audit, pay partnership debts and receive payment of obligations owing to the partnership, and make reasonable compromise agreements with debtors and creditors. Obviously a partner's authority to borrow money would be severely restricted after dissolution. Borrowing in order to pay existing obligations would probably be authorized in many situations, but borrowing for any other reason probably would not.

If, instead of liquidating the business, some of the partners intend to continue it as a new partnership or other type of organization, these limitations on authority may cause short-term difficulties. During the changeover period, certain transactions not within the scope of this limited authority may be necessary to keep the business going. In such a case, the consent of *all* partners must be obtained to authorize this kind of transaction.

In the absence of a contrary agreement among the partners, the type of authority still existing after dissolution can be exercised by *any* of the partners. If they choose, however, they can agree that such authority rests only with a certain partner. The person delegated this type of responsibility is sometimes referred to as the **liquidating partner** (or **winding-up partner**). Then, if third parties are so notified, they can hold the partnership liable only if they deal with the designated partner.

**Special Situations:** Regarding the effect of dissolution, three exceptional situations must be mentioned.

*Partner's Knowledge:* Under some circumstances it is important to determine whether the partner transacting business for the partnership after dissolution has *knowledge* of certain facts. If dissolution is caused either by the *act* of any partner (whether in violation of the partnership agreement or not), the *death* of any partner, or the *bankruptcy* of any partner, the partnership will be bound by any transaction made by a partner who *did not know* the facts that caused dissolution.[4] This liability exists even if the transaction was not merely a completion of unfinished business and was not otherwise appropriate for winding up partnership affairs. (Of course, the transaction must be of a type that would have been

---

[4]Section 3 of the UPA makes a distinction between *knowledge* and *notice.* This distinction makes no difference in the majority of cases and its technicality is of too refined a nature for our discussion.

binding upon the partnership if dissolution had *not* occurred.)

***Notice to Third Parties:*** In some situations the *absence of notice to third parties* may result in partnership liability for unauthorized transactions entered into after dissolution. If the transaction is of a type that would have bound the partnership if dissolution had *not* taken place, the firm will be liable for it *after* dissolution if the third party being dealt with has not been properly notified of the dissolution. If, before dissolution, the third party has extended credit to the partnership, a transaction with this person after dissolution will bind the partnership unless he or she is proven to have had knowledge of the dissolution. The best way to prevent such a possibility is to directly notify all the partnership's creditors that dissolution has occurred. Since their names and addresses will almost certainly be in the partnership records, no undue inconvenience will result. If the third party had not extended credit to the partnership in the past but did know of its existence prior to dissolution, *the partnership is not liable for transactions with that party* made after dissolution if he or she either knows of the dissolution or if the fact of dissolution has been advertised in a newspaper of general circulation in those places where the partnership has regularly done business.[5] These rules regarding notice to third parties are simply an application of the principle of *apparent authority*.

***The Bankrupt Partner:*** Under the UPA, the partnership is not bound in any circumstances where the postdissolution transaction is made by a partner who is personally *bankrupt*. In such a case it does not matter whether the third party knows of the partner's bankruptcy or of the resulting dissolution; the UPA's view is that one should know the status of the person with whom one is dealing.

### Effect of Dissolution on Existing Liabilities

A cardinal rule of partnership law is that dissolution in and of itself does not alter the existing liabilities of the partnership or of individual partners. In some circumstances the event causing dissolution may also cause a discharge from certain liabilities, but it is not the dissolution itself that causes the discharge. Contracts in force at the time of the event that causes dissolution may or may not be discharged, depending upon the rules of contract law. For instance, the death of a partner might terminate an existing partnership contract if the contract had called for some type of personal service by the deceased partner. And bankruptcy of the partnership will not only result in dissolution but also will discharge partnership liabilities that are in excess of the combined assets of the partnership and all the partners. Whether existing liabilities in other situations will be discharged depends entirely on the circumstances.

## WINDING UP PARTNERSHIP AFFAIRS

*Winding up* is the second and final step after dissolution in the termination of a partnership.

### The Right to Wind Up

The question of which partners have the right to wind up partnership affairs can be determined by agreement of the partners.[6] In the absence of an agreement, all partners have an equal right to settle partnership affairs, with two notable exceptions. A partner who has *wrongfully caused dissolution* and a partner who is *personally bankrupt* do not have the right to exercise any control over the winding up process.

### Distribution of Assets

When dissolution has occurred and the business is to be terminated, the winding up process entails such activities as liquidating partnership property (turning it into cash), collecting outstanding accounts, paying outstanding debts, and any other actions required to bring partnership affairs to a close.

After all partnership assets have been liquidated, they are distributed to those having claims against the partnership. The order in which they are distributed is of little importance if the partnership has been profitable and all claims can be paid in full. Where partnership assets are insufficient to com-

---

[5] Before enactment of the UPA, some courts had recognized other methods of publicizing the dissolution, but the UPA speaks only of advertisement by newspaper.

[6] If the partners disagree as to who shall wind up, a court may appoint a qualified disinterested third party as a *receiver* to handle the winding up process.

pletely satisfy all claims, however, the issue obviously becomes quite significant.

As previously noted, when partnership assets are insufficient to pay partnership debts, assets of individual partners can be used insofar as necessary. Before this can happen, however, any claims of that partner's individual creditors must be satisfied.

Claims against the partnership are paid in the following order:

1. First to be paid are claims of outside creditors of the partnership.

2. Next are claims of individual partners for repayment of loans they have made to the partnership. Interest is ordinarily payable unless it had been agreed that the loan would be interest-free.

3. Claims of individual partners for return of contributions they have made to the partnership's working capital are third in line. Interest is not payable on contributions to capital unless the partners had agreed otherwise.

4. If any partnership assets remain after satisfying the other claims, these are distributed as profits to the partners in the proportion in which profits were to be shared.

To illustrate: Jones and Smith are partners in the retail clothing business. The partnership has not been profitable and is dissolved. The financial position of the partnership after all assets have been reduced to cash is summarized as follows (assuming no interest payable on partners' loans or capital contributions):

| Assets | | Liabilities and Partner's Equity | | |
|---|---|---|---|---|
| Cash | $200,000 | Liabilities | | |
| | $200,000 | Accounts payable | $225,000 | |
| | | Loans from partners | | |
| | | Jones | 25,000 | |
| | | Smith | 10,000 | $260,000 |
| | | Partners' equity | | |
| | | Jones (contribution to capital) | $ 50,000 | |
| | | Smith (contribution to capital) | 50,000 | 100,000 |
| | | | | $360,000 |

As we can see, the operations of the partnership have resulted in an overall loss of $160,000. Assuming that losses are to be divided equally, Jones and Smith will each have to personally bear an $80,000 loss. The following summary indicates the personal financial positions of Jones and Smith:

| | Jones | Smith |
|---|---|---|
| Assets | $150,000 | $200,000 |
| Liabilities | −75,000 | −250,000 |
| | $75,000 | ($50,000) |

Here we see that Smith is insolvent. Since his individual assets must first be used to pay his individual debts, he is financially unable to pay partnership obligations. As a result, Jones must use his personal assets to pay the remaining partnership debts to partnership creditors. This obligation amounts to $25,000, since partnership accounts payable were $225,000 and partnership assets were $200,000. The losses actually borne by each partner are summarized as follows:

| | Jones | Smith |
|---|---|---|
| Loans to partnership (unrepaid) | $ 25,000 | $10,000 |
| Contributions to partnership capital (unreturned) | 50,000 | 50,000 |
| Use of individual's assets to pay partnership creditors | 25,000 | — |
| | $100,000 | $60,000 |

Since each partner should have borne a loss of $80,000, Jones now has a claim against Smith for $20,000. Whether this claim will be collectible, as a practical matter, is a problem Jones must face.

## Continuing the Business

The business of a partnership is not always terminated after dissolution, even though the partnership as an organization comes to an end. Where the operations of the partnership have been profitable and customer goodwill has been built up, the business will be more valuable as a going concern than it will if it is liquidated. Thus some of the partners may wish to continue the business—and they can do so unless continuation would be illegal for some reason. If they decide to continue, the winding up process will consist primarily of bookkeeping entries and the purchase by continuing partners of the interests of withdrawing partners. Customers may never know there has been any change, unless some change is made in the firm name. And creditors of the dissolved partnership will continue to be creditors of the reorganized partnership.[7]

**According to Agreement:** If the articles of partnership provide for continuing the business after dissolution, these provisions dictate the procedures to be followed. For instance, the articles of partnership might specify procedures for continuing the business after the withdrawal, expulsion, or death of a partner, including methods for valuing that partner's interest and settling accounts between the continuing and noncontinuing partners. It also is possible for the partners to make a binding agreement concerning the continuation of the business at the time of dissolution.

**Without Agreement:** When there is no agreement for continuing the business, either in the articles of partnership or in a separate agreement made at the time of dissolution, the procedures for continuation are guided by the UPA. In this regard, the UPA makes a distinction between two situations: (1) where dissolution has occurred *without* a wrongful act by any partner, and (2) where it *has been caused* by such a wrongful act.

**Where Dissolution Occurred without a Wrongful Act:** The most common situations of no wrongful act are dissolution caused by death of a partner or by the withdrawal of a partner in a situation where he or she had the right to do so. In such a case, the continuing partners must immediately settle with the withdrawing partner or the estate of the deceased partner (the term *withdrawing partner* hereafter will also include the estate of a deceased partner) if the latter so desires. If settlement is made *immediately*, it consists only of a payment to the withdrawing partner of an amount equal to the value of that partner's interest in the partnership at the time of dissolution. This, of course, will be his or her share of any existing surplus of partnership asset value (including goodwill) over partnership liabilities. If settlement is *postponed*, the withdrawing partner receives not only the value of his or her interest in the partnership (computed as of the moment of dissolution) but also an additional amount to compensate for the delay. The additional amount is computed in one of two ways, depending on the choice of the withdrawing partner—either as *interest* on the amount due since dissolution or as an amount equal to that partner's proportionate share of partnership *profits* earned since dissolution.

**Where Dissolution Was Caused by a Partner's Wrongful Act:** In the second situation, where dissolution has been caused by a partner's wrongful act, somewhat different rules are applied. The wrongfully withdrawing partner is still entitled to receive the value of his or her interest in the partnership, but the value of partnership *goodwill* is not included in computing this value. Further, the damages caused by the wrongful dissolution are deducted from the total amount. If settlement is not made immediately, the rules for compensating the withdrawing partner for the delay are the same as in the first situation.

**Notice to Third Parties:** Notice of dissolution to third parties is as important when the business is continued as when it is terminated. Those continuing the business must take it upon themselves to provide proper notification (as explained earlier). If they do not, they may be bound by certain later acts of a former partner who has left the business. Also, if those continuing the business reorganize it as a *corporation* rather than as another partnership, they will need to notify their business creditors of the change in status. If this is not done, and new obligations to these creditors are incurred (the creditors still thinking they are dealing with a partnership), the former partners might find themselves personally liable for the new obligations as if they were still partners. If proper notice is given, of course, they will be able to claim the limited liability that is enjoyed by those who are officers, directors, or stockholders in a corporation.

---

[7] The situation may be different if the business is reorganized and continued in some form other than a partnership, such as a corporation. In such a case, all those who were partners in the dissolved partnership will be liable for debts incurred by the partnership before dissolution, unless the creditors release them. This is true for those persons continuing the business (who may now be officers, directors, and/or stockholders in the new corporation) and for those who have left it. The corporation itself is a separate legal entity not liable for these old debts unless it assumes them. This frequently occurs, however, because the new corporation ordinarily is controlled by at least some of the former partners, and it will often assume the old debts in return for a release by creditors of the former partners.

As we observed earlier, it is always best to deal thoroughly with the question of dissolution, continuation of the business, valuation of partners' interests, and similar matters in the original partnership agreement. In the first case that follows, the partners had done so in a comprehensive fashion. Later, several of the partners pulled out of the partnership and tried to get around some of the terms of the partnership agreement relating to dissolution.

If the original partnership agreement does not deal with dissolution and its many implications, or if the partners wish to modify the original agreement's dissolution provisions, they can make a separate agreement at the time of dissolution. This can be a risky proposition, however, because at such a time the partners are less likely to be in an agreeable frame of mind than they were when the partnership was formed. But if an agreement can be reached at this later time, it can resolve the various issues arising from dissolution. The second case below illustrates an agreement made by the partners when one of them withdrew from the partnership. When the withdrawing partner later had second thoughts about the agreement, he found out that courts take such agreements quite seriously, as they do all contracts.

### Curtin v. Glazier
Supreme Court of New York, Appellate Division,
464 N.Y.S.2d 899 (1983)

In 1968 Louis Glazier and Joseph Jackler formed a partnership, Glazier, Jackler & Company, for the practice of accounting. In 1972 Robert Nelkin was admitted as a partner with a 10 percent interest in the partnership. At that time, Articles of Partnership (the basic partnership agreement) and a Partnership Continuation Agreement were executed by the three partners. Thereafter, these agreements were executed in basically the same form each time a new partner was admitted. Paragraph 15 of the Articles of Partnership provided for removal of a partner without cause by the affirmative vote of partners representing a majority interest. In the event of such removal, the Articles also provided for the purchase by remaining partners of the removed partner's interest in accordance with the terms of the Partnership Continuation Agreement. The Partnership Continuation Agreement contained "Buy-Sell" provisions specifying the remaining partners' right to buy the removed partner's interest at a price to be computed according to a stated formula. The formula attempted to express the total value of the partnership as a going concern, with the removed partner receiving his or her pro rata share of that value. Under the agreed formula in the buy-sell provisions, this value was to be based on the net service receipts of the prior calendar year adjusted to account for future income from accounts receivable and work in progress, as well as for future expenses and accounts payable.

In the event of a dissolution of the partnership and actual termination of the business, the buy-sell provisions of the Continuation Agreement obviously would not apply. Instead, the dissolution provisions of the Articles would apply, which provided for payment to each partner of his or her share of the partnership's surplus. The going concern value of the partnership could not be taken into account in such a case, and a partner's share necessarily would be less than if the going concern value were included. Basically, these two methods of computing the values of partners' interests dealt with fundamentally different situations. However, the Articles also contemplated that the partners might remove one of the group and then attempt to circumvent the buy-sell provisions by dissolving the partnership and forming a new partnership to assume the business. In other words, the remaining partners might try to disguise a removal and continuation as a dissolution and liquidation, thus depriving the removed partner of his part of the going concern value computed under the buy-sell provisions. To prevent such a result, paragraph 10 of the Articles stated:

*The parties hereto are further in accord in their desire that under no circumstances are the obligations of the remaining partners who continue the business of this partnership to be circumvented by said remaining partners upon legal dissolution of the partnership caused by the termination of any partner by the formation of a "different" partnership, which would nevertheless take over the business of the present partnership without satisfying its obligations.*

The same idea was also expressed in paragraph 16, in which the partners had agreed that, in the case of a removal, if the remaining partners chose not to continue the partnership they should not attempt to accomplish a continuation in an indirect manner without giving the removed partner the benefit of the buy-sell provisions.

In May 1982 all of the partners except Thomas Curtin signed a written agreement to dissolve the partnership and

*(continued)*

distribute their shares of partnership surplus in accordance with the dissolution provisions of the original Articles of Partnership. The buy-sell provisions of the original Continuation Agreement were not used. These partners, minus Curtin, then split into two groups and formed two new partnerships. One of the new partnerships continued to do business at the offices previously used by Glazier, Jackler & Co., and served the same clients. Curtin, plaintiff, filed suit against the other partners, defendants, claiming that there had actually been a continuation of the business, and the buy-sell provisions of the Continuation Agreement should be enforced. The trial court granted summary judgment in favor of Curtin, and the other partners appealed.

**Decision:** The judgment for plaintiff Curtin was affirmed. This obviously was a continuation of the business under the guise of a phony dissolution, just as the partners had anticipated might happen and had provided for in the Articles of Partnership. Curtin was entitled to be compensated according to the buy-sell provisions, not the dissolution provisions. ■

## Dixon, Odom & Company v. Sledge
Court of Appeals of North Carolina, 296 S.E.2d 512 (1982)

In 1974 David Sledge signed a partnership agreement with the accounting firm of Dixon, Odom & Company. In 1977 Sledge withdrew from the partnership, and he and the other partners signed an agreement defining Sledge's and the partnership's rights and duties in connection with his withdrawal.

In the agreement, the partnership agreed to pay Sledge a salary through April 1977 and to cancel all debts due to the partnership from Sledge. The partnership also promised to pay Sledge a total of $12,000 by yearly payments of $1,200 through 1986, with 6 percent interest. The partnership also had the right at any time to prepay the balance due in whole or in part. Sledge agreed to provide the partnership with a list of clients anticipated to discontinue using the partnership's services and become Sledge's clients. As for Sledge's obligations, the agreement contained the following:

*The Withdrawing Partner agrees to pay to the Partnership fifty percent (50%) of all fees earned by him, either directly or indirectly as a partner or employee, from clients who were formerly clients of the Partnership at any time after January 17, 1975, subject to the following terms and conditions:*

*(a) The Withdrawing Partner shall not pay to the Partnership any part of fees earned by him after January 17, 1987, and*

*(b) With respect to each client served by the Withdrawing Partner, the Withdrawing Partner shall not pay any part of fees earned by him from that client after he has paid to the Partnership fifty percent (50%) of fees earned by him from that client for a period of three (3) years, and*

*(c) With respect to each client served by the Withdrawing Partner in a bookkeeping capacity, the Withdrawing Partner shall not pay any part of fees earned by him from that client after he has paid one hundred fifty percent (150%) of the amount of fees earned by the Partnership from that client during its last year of service to that client, and*

*(d) The Withdrawing Partner shall give to the Partnership on November 15, 1977 and annually thereafter until November 15, 1987 a list of former clients of the Partnership which he has served directly or indirectly since he ceased to be a partner of the Partnership and since his last similar report, together with a list of the amount of fees earned by him from each such client and the amount of fees received by him from each client, excluding any clients which sub-parts (a), (b) or (c) of this provision shall eliminate from the list, together with his payment of 50% of the fees received by him directly or indirectly, and. . . .*

*(g) The Withdrawing Partner shall maintain records adequate to provide the information required by this provision and shall allow his records to be examined by a representative of the Partnership for purposes of verification at any reasonable time and place.*

In 1980 Sledge completely repudiated the agreement, and the partnership, plaintiff, filed suit against Sledge and the new partnership he had formed with another accountant, defendants, seeking an accounting for the 1977–80 period and a decree of specific performance requiring Sledge to carry out the terms of the contract. The trial court granted summary judgment for the plaintiff, and defendants appealed.

**Decision:** The judgment for the plaintiff partnership was affirmed. Although Sledge tried to create some ambiguity regarding the term "former clients" as used in the withdrawal agreement, this term was adequately defined and the agreement was clear. Sledge had to comply with that agreement. ■

# SUMMARY

Termination of a partnership involves dissolution and winding up. Dissolution is the point when the object of the partners changes from continuing the organization in its present form to discontinuing it. Winding up is the actual process of settling partnership affairs after dissolution. The partnership agreement may specify the events that will or will not cause dissolution. In the absence of agreement to the contrary, withdrawal of a partner causes dissolution. Whether such withdrawal also amounts to a breach of the partnership agreement depends on the terms of that agreement.

Dissolution occurs by operation of law in the case of the death of a partner or the bankruptcy of either the partnership or an individual partner. Dissolution can be obtained by court decree when a partner becomes insane or otherwise incapable of performing his or her part of the partnership agreement. Dissolution by court decree also can be obtained when the partnership is unprofitable, or when a partner is found guilty of serious misconduct. Dissolution substantially restricts the authority of a partner to act as an agent for the partnership, but dissolution in and of itself has no effect on existing partnership liabilities.

In the winding up process, claims against the partnership by outside creditors are paid first, followed by repayment of loans from partners and repayment of partners' capital contributions; any remainder is distributed to partners as profits. When the business itself is continued after dissolution, winding up does not involve an asset liquidation but consists primarily of bookkeeping changes and payment to a withdrawing or excluded partner or to the estate of a deceased partner.

# KEY TERMS

Dissolution
Winding up
Partnership at will
Liquidating partner (or winding-up partner)

# QUESTIONS AND PROBLEMS

1. Discuss the difference between the terms *dissolution* and *winding up*.

2. Henderson and Alden were partners in a partnership that owned and operated a chain of movie theaters. Alden died, and his widow, who was his sole heir, informed Henderson that she would take her husband's place as a partner in the business. Henderson would not agree to this. Mrs. Alden stated that, as an alternative to becoming a partner, she would simply take half of the theaters in the chain, since her husband had owned a one-half interest in the partnership. Henderson refused to agree to this proposal and insisted on buying her interest even though the partnership agreement between Henderson and Alden had said nothing about the purchase of a deceased partner's interest. What is the effect of Alden's death on the partnership? Discuss.

3. In Question 2, what rights does Henderson have after Alden's death? Explain.

4. In Question 2, what rights does Alden's widow have regarding the partnership? Discuss.

5. What is the nature of a partner's authority to bind the partnership after dissolution? Give three examples of actions that might fall within the scope of this authority.

6. Does the fact that a partnership is dissolved necessarily mean that the business itself will cease to operate? Explain.

7. Parsons and Raymond were partners in the construction business. The business was not successful and the partnership was dissolved. After all the partnership's assets were liquidated, the partnership had a cash balance of $400,000 and accounts payable of $500,000. A $60,000 loan from Parsons to the partnership remained unpaid, and the unreturned capital contributions of Parsons and Raymond to the partnership were $75,000 and $50,000, respectively. Parsons had personal assets of $800,000 and liabilities of $400,000. Raymond had personal assets of $300,000 and liabilities of $200,000. Assuming that losses are to be divided equally, how much of each partner's assets should be used to pay partnership creditors? Explain.

8. In Question 7, how would your answer change if Raymond's liabilities were $250,000 instead of $200,000? Explain.

9. A partnership was created by Atkins, Benson, and Collier, who agreed to share profits equally. Nothing was agreed as to the sharing of losses. The partners decided to dissolve the partnership after a year of operation, at which time the partnership's books revealed the following: Atkins had loaned the partnership $10,000 and had made a capital contribution of $20,000; Benson had made a $10,000 capital contribution; Collier had made no capital contribution; the partnership had assets of $80,000 and owed outside creditors $55,000. Explain how distribution of assets should be made to the partnership's creditors and to the partners.

10. What is the proper basis for valuation of partnership assets after dissolution? Discuss.

# CHAPTER 36
# LIMITED PARTNERSHIPS

## THE NATURE AND HISTORY OF LIMITED PARTNERSHIPS

### The Nature of the Limited Partnership

The amount of capital required in a business often is greater than an individual is able to obtain or willing to risk. Meeting these capital requirements is one of the most important reasons for the formation of partnerships. In an ordinary partnership, however, each partner is personally liable for the partnership's obligations. The prospect of unlimited personal liability in the case of a partnership may create a major obstacle to capital raising efforts because many potential investors will be unwilling to accept such a risk.

As we will see in subsequent chapters, the creation of a corporation may provide the necessary means for meeting a firm's capital requirements. In many situations, however, the *limited partnership* is an attractive alternative for this purpose. A limited partnership is a partnership formed by two or more persons *and having at least one general partner and at least one limited partner.* The **general partners** essentially run the business as they would an ordinary partnership. The **limited partners,** on the other hand, are merely investors. Limited partners have little voice in the basic operation of the business, and their liability usually is limited to the amount of their investment in the enterprise.

### Historical Background

The type of organization we now call a limited partnership has existed since the Middle Ages. Legislation in France gave legal status to the limited partnership in the early eighteenth century. In the United States several states passed statutes governing limited partnerships in the nineteenth century. The need for uniformity and consistency in the way limited partnerships were treated in the various states led to the drafting of the Uniform Limited Partnership Act (ULPA) in 1916. The ULPA eventually was adopted in 49 states.

Because of several problems with the ULPA, the National Conference of Commissioners on Uniform State Laws drafted the Revised Uniform Limited Partnership Act (RULPA). The RULPA was completed in 1976 and made available to state legislatures for adoption in 1977.

Although the RULPA generally was hailed as a much-needed improvement, the position initially taken by the Internal Revenue Service toward taxation of limited partnerships under the RULPA caused most states to defer action. Traditionally, the IRS had treated most limited partnerships as partnerships for taxation purposes. When the RULPA was first proposed, however, the IRS indicated that limited partnerships under the new law might be taxed as corporations.

The tax treatment of these business organizations is important for several reasons. In a partnership, the income of the business passes directly to the partners and is treated as personal income to them. Perhaps more important, however, partnership losses are passed directly to the individual partners, who may offset these losses against personal income. Taxation of limited partnerships as partnerships is an especially attractive feature in businesses commonly showing low profits or "paper" losses despite positive cash flows. Such a phenomenon occurs frequently in enterprises having large depreciation or depletion deductions, substantial investment tax credits, and so forth. In addition, taxation as a partnership permits individual partners to take advantage of any tax exempt earnings the firm may have. If the firm is taxed as a corporation, these benefits do not pass directly to the investors, but go to the corporation as a separate entity.

The IRS ultimately decided to continue treating limited partnerships as partnerships in most situations, even in states adopting the RULPA. Since then, a majority of states have passed the RULPA, although several continue to use all or part of the ULPA.

## FORMING THE LIMITED PARTNERSHIP

The limited partnership is something of a hybrid between an ordinary partnership and a corporation. Like a partnership, the agreement of the partners determines the amount of capital contributions, the proportions in which profits and losses are shared, procedures for admitting new partners, procedures for the voluntary or involuntary withdrawal of partners, and many other matters concerning the operation of the business. However, the partners cannot confer limited liability on their members simply by agreeing to do so, because outsiders (creditors) are affected. Thus, like a corporation, the limited partnership can exist only if permitted by statute and the procedural requirements of the statute are met.

### *Filing the Certificate*

The agreement among the general and limited partners is embodied in the **certificate of limited partnership.** This certificate must be filed with the designated state official in order for the limited partnership to have legal status. Under the ULPA, designation of the official with whom the certificate must be filed was left up to the individual states. Although a few states permitted centralized filing with the secretary of state, many states required the certificate to be filed in the county where the firm was organized. This led to uncertainty as to whether the limited partnership would be legally recognized in other counties in which it might do business. As a result, many attorneys advised limited partnership clients to file a certificate in every county in which business was transacted. Under the RULPA, however, a limited partnership needs only to file one certificate with the secretary of state in the state where it operates.

Under both the ULPA and RULPA, technical defects in the certificate do not affect the status of a limited partnership. There simply must be "substantial compliance" with statutory requirements.

The ULPA and RULPA require essentially the same types of information to be included in the certificate. Section 201 of the RULPA requires the certificate to set forth:

1. The name of the limited partnership
2. The general character of its business
3. The address of the office of the firm's agent who is authorized to receive summonses or other legal notices
4. The name and business address of each partner, specifying which ones are general partners and which are limited partners
5. The amount of cash contributions actually made, and agreed to be made in the future, by each partner
6. A description and statement of value of noncash contributions made or to be made by each partner
7. The times at which additional contributions are to be made by any of the partners
8. Whether and under what conditions a limited partner has the right to grant limited partner status to an assignee of his or her interest in the partnership
9. If agreed upon, the time or the circumstances when a partner may withdraw from the firm
10. If agreed upon, the amount of, or the method for determining, the funds to be received by a withdrawing partner
11. Any right of a partner to receive distributions of cash or other property from the firm, and the times and circumstances for such distributions
12. The time or circumstances when the limited partnership is to be dissolved
13. The rights of the remaining general partners to continue the business after withdrawal of a general partner
14. Any other matters the partners wish to include.

### *The Name of the Business*

Both the ULPA and RULPA require that the surname of a limited partner *not* appear in the name of the business unless (1) that name is also the name of a general partner, or (2) the business had been carried on under this name before the limited partnership was formed. The purpose of this restriction is to prevent outsiders from thinking that a limited partner has managerial control or personal liability.

The RULPA imposes some restrictions, however, that the ULPA does not. Specifically, the RULPA provides that the name of the business (1) must contain, without abbreviation, the words "limited partnership," (2) may not contain any word or phrase indicating or implying that the firm is organized for any purpose other than that stated in its certificate, and (3) may not be the same as or deceptively similar to the name of any corporation or limited partnership already formed or registered in the state.

## Doing Business in Other States

The ULPA makes no provision for the conduct of business by a limited partnership in states other than that in which it was formed. Several states passed special legislation dealing with this situation, but many did not. In the absence of such legislation, a limited partnership formed in state X would have to re-form in state Y (and probably file the certificate in various counties in state Y) in order to do business there.

The RULPA resolves the problem by permitting a limited partnership formed in one state simply to *register* with the secretary of state in another state in which it wishes to do business. Registration is much simpler, and requires disclosure of less information, than the original certificate filing.

The following case provides a very practical example—tax liability—of the importance of fulfilling the requirements of the relevant state limited partnership law if one wants the protected status of a limited partner.

---

**United States v. Morton**
U.S. District Court for the Eastern District of Missouri,
682 F.Supp. 999 (1988)

Until his death in 1980, Cody Morton, deceased husband of Dormilee Morton, operated a commercial and residential construction business from his home in Salem. Upon Mr. Morton's death, Dormilee Morton succeeded to her husband's ownership interest in the business, including ownership of supplies, materials, and construction equipment. Steven Morton, the son, took over the operation and management of the construction company, with Mrs. Morton contributing the capital assets of business, which consisted of the construction equipment. The operation ceased in 1985.

From time to time Mrs. Morton would sign bank notes and supporting documents granting security interests in the equipment, designating the borrower as "Dormilee Morton and Steven Morton d/b/a Morton Construction Company." In addition, Mrs. Morton also provided funds for the operation of the business. The telephone listing for the business was situated in Mrs. Morton's home where she also received the business mail.

Partnership returns signed by Steven Morton and filed with the Internal Revenue Service for the taxable years 1980–82 listed Dormilee Morton as a partner in the Morton Construction Company. Mrs. Morton's individual tax returns for 1981 and 1984 reported her distributive shares of profits and losses from Morton Construction Company on attached Partner's Share of Income, Credits, Deductions, etc., schedules. Mrs. Morton did not protest taxes assessed against her, and IRS officials made frequent attempts to secure delinquent returns and taxes.

Between 1980 and 1984, the Morton Construction Company employed laborers and other persons to construct commercial and residential buildings and was required to withhold federal income taxes and Federal Insurance Contributions Act (FICA) taxes from the wages paid to its employees. Due to financial difficulties, during the 1980–84 period the company failed to pay the required withholding and FICA taxes to the federal government. The Internal Revenue Service made assessments against Dormilee and Steven Morton as partners for delinquent taxes, penalties, and interest in the amount of $44,460.52.

Notices of federal tax liens under the Internal Revenue Code for the assessments were filed properly with the recorder of deeds of Dent County, Missouri. The government then filed suit to obtain a judgment for the amount of the assessments. Steven Morton did not respond, and the court entered a default judgment against him. Dormilee Morton defended on the grounds that she was only a limited partner and therefore could not be held personally liable for the tax assessments. A summary of the district court's opinion follows.

---

**Decision:** The district court held that the business was a partnership and that Mrs. Morton was a general partner with personal liability. Although the evidence overall indicated a general partnership, the most important fact was that there was absolutely no compliance with the statutory formalities for creating a limited partnership. A limited partnership cannot exist for any purpose without compliance with state law. It makes no difference how inactive or "silent" she was in the business. ■

# FINANCING THE LIMITED PARTNERSHIP

## *Partners' Contributions*

The capital requirements of limited partnerships are met in the same way as those of ordinary partnerships—primarily by contributions from partners to the firm's capital. In addition to the investments of partners, borrowing may also be used to raise needed funds, although the availability of borrowed funds will depend on the amount and nature of the partnership's assets, its past and projected performance, and other factors.

For several reasons, the limited partnership usually provides greater capital raising opportunities than ordinary partnerships. First, a larger number of investors and larger amounts of individual investment may be attracted because prospective limited partners know they normally are shielded from personal liability. Second, the number of limited partners has no practical bounds because they do not participate in management. As we observed in Chapter 31, a large number of partners sometimes proves to be unwieldy in the case of an ordinary partnership.

The contributions of general partners can take any form—cash, property, or services. Under the ULPA the investments of limited partners are restricted to cash or property. A limited partner can provide services to the business, whether for compensation or not. But services of a limited partner cannot be considered as part of the initial contribution to the firm. Violation of this principle makes the limited partner liable as a general partner. The RULPA makes a major change in this regard by permitting the partners to place a value on services performed or promised by a limited partner and count that value as a contribution to capital.

## *Securities Laws*

Obtaining investments from limited partners is viewed as a sale of securities under state and federal securities regulation laws.[1] In most circumstances limited partnership interests are not advertised and sold publicly. As a result, the so-called "private placement" exemption for nonpublic offerings of securities is usually available. This exemption frees the general partners from having to comply with burdensome securities registration requirements. Care must be taken, however, to structure the capital raising effort to insure the availability of this or some other exemption. Even if the sale of limited partnership interests is exempt from registration, the antifraud provisions of state and federal securities laws will still apply.

# RIGHTS AND DUTIES OF GENERAL PARTNERS

With very few exceptions, the general partners in a limited partnership have the same rights and duties as partners in an ordinary partnership. For example, they have the right and authority to manage the business, use partnership property for partnership purposes, act as agents for the partnership in carrying on its normal business activities, and share profits. They also are personally liable for the obligations of the partnership. The rights and types of authority possessed by general partners can be modified by their agreement, as reflected in the certificate of limited partnership, but they obviously may not modify their liability to outsiders.

On unusual occasions, when one or more general partners are considering actions which will have a fundamental effect on the business, they must obtain the written consent of all general and limited partners. Such consent is required, for example, before one or more general partners may (1) admit a new general partner, (2) do any act which would make it impossible for the partnership to carry on its normal business, or (3) use partnership property for nonpartnership purposes. Several other kinds of action require *either* written consent of all general and limited partners *or* express authorization in the certificate. These actions include (1) admission of a new limited partner and (2) continuation of the business after the death, retirement, or insanity of a general partner.

# RIGHTS AND DUTIES OF LIMITED PARTNERS

Limited partners are essentially *investors*. They have no right to manage the business. They also have no right to use partnership property or conduct business in behalf of the partnership unless expressly authorized by the general partners or the certificate.

---

[1] Securities laws are discussed at several points in the chapters on corporations, and explored in depth in Chapter 41, "Securities Regulation."

Limited partners do, however, have certain rights which are necessary to protect their investments. Thus, they are entitled to inspect and copy partnership records and to receive full disclosure of any information affecting the partnership. Limited partners are entitled to a share of profits only as agreed upon and specified in the certificate.

As we have seen, a limited partner ordinarily can be held liable for partnership obligations only to the extent of his or her investment in the business. Thus, if the partnership's assets are insufficient to pay its debts, limited partners are not liable for the deficiency.

## Restrictions on Participation in Management

Limited partners lose their limited liability, and consequently are personally liable for partnership debts, if they participate in control of the business. Limited partners clearly must take part in some business decisions which may have a fundamental effect on their investments. Moreover, the general partners would be quite foolish in some cases not to take advantage of a limited partner's expertise. What limited partners must not do, however, is participate in the decision-making process on a continuing basis.

The ULPA provided that a limited partner becomes liable as a general partner if he or she "takes part in the control of the business." For decades, courts have had difficulty interpreting this provision. Almost all courts held that limited partners may provide services or advice to the partnership, with or without compensation, and still retain their limited liability. The line between permissible and impermissible activities is often blurred, however.

A question of particular difficulty was whether a specific creditor must have *relied* on the limited partner's apparent managerial status before the limited partner could be held personally liable to that creditor.

One group of courts employed the **control test.** These courts held the limited partner liable whenever control of the business was exercised, regardless of whether the particular creditor relied on the limited partner's actions. Another group of courts, however, applied the **reliance test,** and held the limited partner liable only where the evidence showed that the limited partner's conduct probably caused the third party to view the limited partner as a general partner.

## "Safe Harbor" Provisions of the RULPA

Providing clearer guidelines for determining the permissible extent of limited partners' participation in the business was one of the main goals of the RULPA.

The RULPA has achieved this increased clarity primarily by specifying certain "safe harbors" for limited partners. Section 303(b) states that limited partners do not become personally liable for partnership debts solely by doing one or more of the following:

1. Being a contractor for or an agent or employee of the limited partnership or of a general partner

2. Consulting with and advising a general partner regarding partnership business

3. Acting as a surety for the limited partnership

4. Approving or disapproving an amendment to the partnership agreement

5. Voting on one or more of the following matters:
   a. The dissolution and winding up of the limited partnership
   b. The sale, exchange, lease, mortgage, pledge, or other transfer of all or substantially all of the limited partnership's assets when such transfer is not in the ordinary course of business
   c. The incurrence of indebtedness by the limited partnership when it is not in the ordinary course of business
   d. A change in the nature of the business
   e. The removal of a general partner.

Thus, in the case of actions enumerated in Section 303(b), other evidence of managerial control must be present before a limited partner becomes liable.

When a limited partner participates in the business in some way that is not specifically protected by these safe harbor provisions, the RULPA's guidelines are less clear. Section 303(a) of the RULPA uses language identical to that of Section 7 of the ULPA and states that a limited partner is personally liable if he or she "takes part in the control of the business." Section 303(a) then continues, however, by providing that the limited partner is liable only to those creditors who had actual knowledge of the limited partner's participation in control, unless that participation was "substantially the same as the exercise of the powers of a general partner."

Thus the RULPA, like the ULPA, does not specifically define the phrase "takes part in the control of the business." The control concept cannot be defined with precision because of the almost infinite variety of circumstances in which the issue may arise. On the question of whether reliance by the outsider is a necessary element, the RULPA identifies two levels of participation by the limited partner. First, when the limited partner's participation in control is essentially the same as that of a general partner (i.e., on a continuing, not a sporadic, basis), the limited partner is personally liable regardless of an outsider's reliance. Second, when the limited partner's participation does not reach the level of a general partner's participation, the limited partner is personally liable only to those creditors who actually knew of his or her participation. In this second situation, the outsider's reliance on the limited partner's apparent managerial status does not have to be proved—it is conclusively presumed from the outsider's knowledge of the limited partner's participation in control.

In the following case, the court discusses the general problem of the extent to which a limited partner should be permitted to take part in the business, how the original UPA and the newer RULPA attempt to deal with it, and how the RULPA should be applied to the activities of a limited partner who was essentially the driving force behind the creation of the limited partnership.

## Mount Vernon Savings & Loan v. Partridge Associates
U.S. District Court for the District of Maryland, 679 F.Supp. 522 (1987)

MIW Investors sold an apartment project named Partridge Courts to Dreyfuss in 1971 for $4.8 million. During the next ten years Dreyfuss paid very little on the loan, and the note he had signed became an unproductive asset in MIW's portfolio. MIW then made an agreement to repurchase Partridge Courts by assuming the outstanding balance of the $4.8 million note plus certain other consideration. MIW planned to convert Partridge Courts into a condominium complex, and formed a limited partnership, Partridge Associates (Partridge), for that purpose. MIW was one of two limited partners and owned a 50 percent interest in Partridge. Friendship Services, Inc., a subsidiary of Friendship Savings & Loan Association, was the other limited partner and owned a 48 percent interest. American Housing, Inc., was the general partner and owned a 2 percent interest. MIW assigned its rights under the Dreyfuss repurchase agreement to Partridge. MIW also loaned $6 million to Partridge, $4.8 million of which was used by Partridge to buy the original 1971 Dreyfuss note from MIW.

The participants in Partridge put together a number of other complex financial arrangements. In one of these, representatives of Friendship (the other limited partner) and American Housing (the general partner) obtained for Partridge a $2.6 million loan from Mount Vernon Savings. The loan was on terms that were not very favorable to Mount Vernon, apparently because Mount Vernon's president, Russell, needed Friendship's help in an unrelated deal in which Mount Vernon had committed itself to a loan that was above its lending authority under federal regulations.

Several months later Partridge more or less fell apart. Mount Vernon never received any payments on its loan to the limited partnership. Later, Mount Vernon became insolvent and was taken over by the Federal Savings & Loan Insurance Corporation (FSLIC). In behalf of Mount Vernon, FSLIC sued Partridge Associates, American Housing (the general partner), and MIW. FSLIC's claim against MIW was based on the theory that, because MIW had been the driving force behind the organization of Partridge and had played an active role in helping it put together various financial arrangements, MIW should have the same unlimited liability for Partridge's obligations as a general partner. All parties filed motions for summary judgment. The federal district court held that there were disputed issues of fact regarding FSLIC's claims against Partridge and American Housing, so that a trial was necessary for these claims. The court's discussion of FSLIC's claim against MIW is summarized below.

**Decision:** Summary judgment was granted for MIW. All of the relevant documents clearly identified MIW as a limited partner, and there is no other evidence indicating that Mount Vernon reasonably relied on MIW having any status other than as a limited partner. Without such reliance, MIW would be personally liable for the debt only if its "participation in the control of [the limited partnership] was substantially the same as the exercise of the powers of a general partner." The court stated: "As is expressly recognized in the new ACT [RULPA], and as was implicit in the old [ULPA], a limited partner may be actively involved in the day-to-day operation of the partnership's affairs, provided that he does not have ultimate decision-making responsibility." FSLIC presented no evidence on this issue. ∎

## *Other Situations in which a Limited Partner May Be Liable*

A limited partner may be liable for partnership debts in a few other unusual situations.

1. If the name of the limited partnership contains the name of a limited partner, that limited partner is liable unless (a) the name is also the name of a general partner or (b) the business had been conducted under that name prior to becoming a limited partnership.

2. A limited partner who *knows* of a false statement in the certificate is liable to anyone who is harmed by relying on the false statement.[2]

## *Being a General Partner and a Limited Partner at the Same Time*

It is possible for a person to be both a general partner and a limited partner at the same time. Such a person is liable to outsiders as a general partner. His or her additional status as a limited partner is important only with respect to the dealings among the partners themselves. Thus, that portion of the person's investment designated as a limited partner contribution is treated as such for assignment, distribution, or other purposes.

## ASSIGNMENT OF AN INTEREST IN A LIMITED PARTNERSHIP

The rules regarding assignment of a partner's interests in a limited partnership are basically the same as for an ordinary partnership. The interests of both general and limited partners can be assigned, totally or partially, to third parties. An assignment by either a general or limited partner does not terminate the limited partnership.

Such an assignment also does not cause the assignee to become a partner—the assignee merely becomes entitled to receive the assigning partner's share of profits or other asset distributions.

The assignee of a *general partner's* interest can be admitted as a new general partner only by written consent of all the general and limited partners (other than the assigning partner), followed by formal amendment of the certificate. The assignee of a *limited partner's* interest can be admitted as a new limited partner by written consent of all general and limited partners (other than the assigning partner), *or* by a provision in the certificate permitting the assigning limited partner to designate an assignee as a new limited partner. In either case, the certificate must be amended formally to reflect admission of the new limited partner.

The provisions of the RULPA relating to assignments are substantially the same as those of the ULPA. There are two differences, however: (1) under the RULPA, the partnership agreement may specifically make the interests of general or limited partners *nonassignable*; and (2) the RULPA states that a general or limited partner ceases to be a partner upon assignment of *all* of his or her interest, unless the partnership agreement provides for a different result.

## DISSOLUTION AND WINDING UP OF THE LIMITED PARTNERSHIP

### *Dissolution*

A limited partnership dissolves at the time or under the circumstances specified in the certificate. It also can be dissolved at any time by written agreement of all the general and limited partners, followed by formal cancellation of the certificate.

Under both the ULPA and the RULPA, the death, insanity, or withdrawal[3] of a *general partner* causes dissolution of the limited partnership *unless* continuation of the business is provided for (1) in the certificate or (2) by written consent of all remaining general and limited partners. To continue the business as a limited partnership in any event, there must remain at least one general partner and one limited partner. To meet this requirement, new partners may be admitted.

Under the ULPA, a general partner's bankruptcy or involvement in some other insolvency proceeding is not treated as an automatic withdrawal from the limited partnership. The RULPA does, however, treat such an event as a withdrawal unless the certificate or unanimous written agreement of the partners provides otherwise.

The death, insanity, withdrawal, or bankruptcy of a *limited partner* does not cause dissolution of

---

[2] A general partner obviously would be liable under the same circumstances.

[3] Aside from the question of dissolution, the withdrawal of either a general or limited partner may subject him or her to liability for damages to the other partners if the withdrawal violates their partnership agreement.

the limited partnership. (This statement assumes, of course, that at least one limited partner remains.) When a limited partner dies, the executor or administrator of the person's estate exercises control over the interest in the limited partnership. In the case of insanity, such control is exercised by the limited partner's guardian. The interest of a bankrupt limited partner is controlled by the trustee in bankruptcy.

**Winding Up.** As is true of an ordinary partnership, a limited partnership continues to exist after dissolution for so long as necessary to wind up its affairs. Control of the winding up process is in the hands of the general partners. Their authority to act in behalf of the partnership is restricted to those activities necessary to bring the business to an end. Limited partners may supervise the process, however, if no general partners remain. Moreover, any general or limited partner, as well as the representative or assignee of any general or limited partner, may obtain court supervision of the winding up process.

After winding up, the assets of the limited partnership are liquidated and distributed. Under both the ULPA and RULPA, the claims of creditors must be satisfied first. The claims of *outside* creditors obviously are included in this priority group. The ULPA also includes the claims of limited partners who are creditors, but the claims of general partners who have lent money to the business are given a lower priority. The RULPA includes in the top priority the claims of both general and limited partners who are creditors of the partnership.

The certificate may specify the order in which the partners receive a return of their capital contributions and an allocation of any surplus. If not so specified, Section 23 of the ULPA or Section 804 of the RULPA governs the distribution. The most important difference between the asset distribution rules of the two statutes is that the ULPA gives priority to limited partners while the RULPA treats general and limited partners essentially the same.

A well-conceived and well-drafted agreement is as important to the participants in a limited partnership as it is in the case of a regular partnership. When beginning such a venture, the parties must realize that things may go wrong, and provide for such contingencies in the agreement. The importance of provisions dealing with removal of a general partner, election of a new one, and matters regarding dissolution is illustrated in the next case. The fact that the agreement in this case contained conflicting provisions made it somewhat more difficult for the limited partners to protect themselves from a bad general partner, but ultimately the agreement did provide them with sufficient protection.

---

**Obert v. Environmental Research & Development Corp.**
Supreme Court of Washington,
771 P.2d 340 (1989)

Plaintiffs are approximately 50 entities and individuals all of whom are limited partners of the Campus Park Associates Limited Partnership (Campus Park LP), a Washington limited partnership. The defendant, Environmental Research & Development Corp. (ERADCO), is a Washington corporation that served as the sole general partner of Campus Park LP from its inception in 1978 until May 1984.

The primary asset of the Campus Park LP is an 83-acre parcel of rural land located in Federal Way, Washington, which was purchased for $2,472,333 in December 1978. In 1978, ERADCO sold limited partnership units of the Campus Park LP to the plaintiffs through the use of a private placement memorandum. At the time of the purchase of the partnership units, each of the Campus Park LP limited partners and ERADCO entered into a limited partnership agreement.

In May 1984, 74.4 percent of the ownership of Campus Park LP amended the limited partnership agreement and voted to remove ERADCO as general partner, electing the Pace Corporation (Pace), a Washington corporation, as the new general partner. The limited partners' asserted reasons were ERADCO's alleged mismanagement and breach of fiduciary duty by failing to develop the Campus Park property, borrowing limited partnership funds for ERADCO's own unrelated purposes, commingling limited partnership funds with ERADCO's own funds, placing limited partnership funds in accounts earning less than half the interest rate that could have been earned, and being unable to substantiate about three-quarters of the management fees it had charged the limited partners.

The limited partners filed suit seeking a declaratory judgment that their action in replacing ERADCO with Pace was

*(continued)*

valid. ERADCO contended that its removal was not for good cause, and that even if the removal was valid, the election of Pace as a replacement general partner was void because a unanimous vote was required to do this. ERADCO based this contention on provisions in the limited partnership agreement. One provision authorized limited partners to remove or elect a general partner by a "majority vote," and defined "majority" as 66 percent. Another provision, however, indicated that electing a general partner required a unanimous vote. The district court ruled in favor of the limited partners. That court found that ERADCO had breached its fiduciary obligations to limited partners in a variety of ways and that its removal thus was based on good cause. The court also held that the vote by 74.4 percent of limited partners to remove ERADCO was valid because it exceeded the 66 percent required by the agreement. The court then ruled that the conflicting provisions relating to the vote necessary to elect Pace as a new general partner must be resolved in favor of the limited partners, because the law generally resolves a conflict or other ambiguity in the language of a contract against the drafter of that contract. ERADCO had been responsible for drafting the limited partnership agreement, so the court accepted as controlling the provision permitting election of a general partner by a 66 percent vote (rather than the conflicting provision requiring a unanimous vote). Finally, the district court held that ERADCO's breach of its fiduciary duties caused it to lose its right to receive 25 percent of the profits under a provision of the limited partnership agreement. ERADCO appealed.

The court of appeals affirmed the trial court's ruling that ERADCO was properly removed, but concluded that the election of Pace as the new general partner was void because a unanimous vote was required. The court agreed that contractual ambiguities should be resolved against the drafting party. It found, however, that a provision of the new Washington limited partnership law required a replacement general partner to be elected by unanimous vote within 90 days of the removal of the previous general partner, and that this law superseded everything else. Because a limited partnership cannot exist without at least one general partner, the court of appeals ordered the limited partnership to be dissolved (despite the fact that it had been operating smoothly and profitably under Pace for four years). The limited partners appealed to the Washington Supreme Court.

**Decision:** The judgment of the court of appeals was affirmed except for its dissolution of the limited partnership. The lower courts correctly resolved the conflicting contractual provisions in favor of the limited partners, so the removal of ERADCO by a 74 percent vote was valid. The court of appeals erred, however, in finding that a unanimous vote was required by statute to elect Pace. The legislature intended the statute in question to apply only when the agreement did not specify otherwise. Thus the limited partnership still exists and Pace is its general partner. (Also, the court agreed with the lower courts that ERADCO lost its right to a 25 percent share of profits because of its breach of fiduciary duty [commingling funds, not substantiating most of its management fees, etc.].) ■

## SUMMARY

A limited partnership is a partnership consisting of one or more general partners and one or more limited partners. The general partners have the same authority and liability as partners in an ordinary partnership. Limited partners, on the other hand, are merely investors who have little voice in the basic operation of the business and whose liability is limited to their investment in the partnership. Today, the law of limited partnerships is found primarily in the Revised Uniform Limited Partnership Act (RULPA) and in the original Uniform Limited Partnership Act (ULPA).

Because limited liability can be created only by statute, creation of a limited partnership involves compliance with statutory requirements in addition to a partnership agreement. The most important statutory requirement is the filing of a certificate of limited partnership. The capital requirements of a limited partnership are met in basically the same way as in an ordinary partnership, by contributions from partners. Although the general partners normally have the power to manage the partnership, they must have the written consent of all general and limited partners, or express authorization in the certificate, to perform certain actions that fundamentally affect the business. Limited partners lose their limited liability if they participate in the control of the business. Some courts have found the limited partner liable if such control has been exercised, regardless of whether the particular creditor has relied on the limited partner's actions. Other courts, however, have found the limited partner liable only if the evidence indicates that the limited partner's conduct probably caused the creditor to view the limited partner as a general partner. The RULPA does not specifically resolve this conflict, but does specify certain "safe harbors" in which particular types of conduct by a limited partner definitely will not cause a limited partner to be personally liable for partnership debts.

A limited partnership is dissolved by the death, insanity, or withdrawal of a general partner unless continuation is provided for by the certificate or written consent of all general and limited partners. The winding up of a limited partnership is very similar to that of an ordinary partnership. Outside creditors have first priority in the distribution of partnership assets. Remaining partnership assets are distributed as specified in the certificate of limited partnership; if the certificate does not so specify, the ULPA gives limited partners priority over general partners but the RULPA treats general and limited partners essentially the same.

## KEY TERMS

**General partner**
**Limited partner**
**Certificate of limited partnership**
**Control test**
**Reliance test**

## QUESTIONS AND PROBLEMS

1. An agreement for the creation of a limited partnership was signed in November. It named Dimentia Corporation and its president, Wilson, as general partners. Franklin and several others were named as limited partners. In December the limited partnership, acting through Wilson and Dimentia Corp., contracted to buy land from Rigg. The next April the limited partnership defaulted on the contractual obligation. It was not until shortly after this default that a certificate was filed to bring the limited partnership legally into existence. The limited partners then formally renounced (disclaimed) their interests in the limited partnership. Rigg sued and obtained a judgment against Dimentia Corp. and Wilson. Almost two years later, after discovering that the certificate had been filed late, Rigg also sued Franklin and the other limited partners to hold them personally liable. Should the limited partners be personally liable in this situation? Discuss. (*Franklin v. Rigg*, 237 S.E.2d 526, Ga. Ct. App. 1977.)

2. McRea owned an automobile dealership, and Rowlett operated an automobile repair business. The manufacturer for whom McRea was a dealer insisted that McRea have a repair shop as part of the dealership. As a result, McRea and Rowlett agreed to form a limited partnership with McRea as sole general partner and Rowlett as sole limited partner. Rowlett moved his equipment to the dealership premises, and also contributed cash to the limited partnership's capital. Rowlett served as foreman of the repair shop, while McRea continued to run the dealership as a whole. Although Rowlett supervised the repair shop, he was under the ultimate direction and control of McRea. McRea had to approve all extensions of credit in the repair shop, except in the case of customers personally known by Rowlett. If a credit customer known and approved by Rowlett did not pay, however, Rowlett had to make up the loss. The partnership's bank account was under the complete control of McRea, and he was the only person authorized to draw checks on the account. Some time later, the business ran into financial difficulties. Silvola, a creditor of the dealership, was unable to collect his claim from McRea or the partnership. Consequently, Silvola sued Rowlett on the debt, claiming that Rowlett's activities had made him liable as a general partner. Should Rowlett be held liable? Discuss. (*Silvola v. Rowlett*, 272 P.2d 287, Colo. Sup. Ct. 1954.)

3. Diversified Properties was a limited partnership engaged in buying, selling, and managing real estate. The limited partnership consisted of Weil as the sole general partner and a group of limited partners. About a year after its formation the business ran into severe cash flow problems and was on the verge of collapse. The limited partners had several meetings and hired two new employees to take over management of the business from Weil. During this time all of the limited partners also were personally involved in negotiations with creditors concerning the refinancing of Diversified's obligations. Weil was still formally the sole general partner, and creditors still recognized him as such. However, he no longer received a salary or occupied the partnership office, and exercised little authority. He subsequently went to work for another real estate firm. Weil then filed a lawsuit in which he sought a declaratory judgment that the limited partners had become liable as general partners because of their activities. Is Weil's contention correct? Discuss. (*Weil v. Diversified Properties*, 319 F.Supp. 778, D.D.C. 1970.)

4. Hacienda Farms, Limited, was organized as a limited partnership to engage in vegetable farming, with de Escamilla as the general partner and Russell and Andrews as limited partners. Most of Hacienda's vegetable crops were marketed through a separate produce company controlled by Andrews. Decisions as to which crops to plant were always made jointly by the three partners. Sometimes de Escamilla disagreed with Russell and Andrews on planting decisions; when this happened, de Escamilla was overruled by the limited partners. Checks could be drawn on the partnership account only with the signatures of at least two partners. Most of the checks were actually signed by Rus-

sell and Andrews, although a few were signed by de Escamilla and one of the limited partners. The firm went bankrupt, and Holzman, the trustee in bankruptcy, filed suit for the purpose of determining whether Russell and Andrews had become personally liable for partnership debts. Were the limited partners liable as general partners? Discuss. (*Holzman v. de Escamilla,* 195 P.2d 833, Cal. Dist. Ct. App. 1948.)

**5.** Westwood Place, Ltd., was a limited partnership with Dobbs Industries, Inc., and Oliver Dobbs as general partners. The partnership's only limited partner withdrew and transferred his interest to Leventhal, who then was formally admitted as the limited partner. One of the provisions in the limited partnership agreement stated that a limited partner would be liable for a proportionate share of any indebtedness secured by a mortgage "that may at any time or times in the future be placed on partnership property." The proportionate liability was stated as being the same as the limited partner's share of profits. Leventhal's specified share of profits was 30 percent. Leventhal became a limited partner on October 1. About three weeks prior to that time, on September 12, the limited partnership had borrowed money from a pension trust fund, and signed a promissory note for the indebtedness. The loan was secured by a fourth mortgage on partnership property. The loan was not paid when due, and Green, trustee for the pension trust fund, filed suit against the limited partnership, the two general partners, and Leventhal. After suit was filed, the two general partners withdrew from the partnership, and Leventhal became general partner. The limited partnership and the two former general partners were held liable for the debt. Should Leventhal also be liable for all or any part of the obligation? Discuss. (*Leventhal v. Green,* 271 S.E.2d 194, Ga. Sup. Ct. 1980.)

# PART V

# Corporations and Securities Regulation

■ After our discussion of the principal-agent relationship in Part IV we studied two closely related forms of business organization, the partnership and the limited partnership. We dealt with those kinds of organizations at that point because agency relationships serve as their basic building blocks. We now turn our attention to the form of organization that is the most important in terms of its overall contribution to business activity in this country—the corporation. Chapter 37 examines the nature and formation of corporations, and Chapter 38 discusses corporate powers and management. Chapter 39 looks at the basic rights and liabilities of corporate shareholders and managers, and Chapter 40 deals with mergers and other major structural changes in corporations.

Chapter 41 surveys the law of Securities Regulation, a subject which could logically be studied in Part VII along with other topics in Government Regulation of Business, but which is examined at this juncture because it places important limitations on the fundamental capital-raising activities of corporations. Although the federal and state laws that regulate securities can also apply to individuals and to organizations other than corporations, the heaviest impact is on corporations. Finally, Chapter 42 deals with the legal responsibilities of the certified public accountant (CPA). This subject is discussed here because most of a CPA's legal responsibilities arise from his or her relationship with corporations. ■

CHAPTER 37

# CORPORATIONS
## NATURE AND FORMATION

## THE NATURE AND HISTORY OF CORPORATIONS

### The Nature of the Corporation

Suppose for a moment that you have been given the authority to create a new organizational form for conducting a business enterprise. You probably would want to create an artificial being with a legally recognized identity of its own, so that it could make contracts, own property, sue and be sued, and do all the other things necessary for running a business. This artificial being, having existence only on paper but nevertheless recognized by law as a "person," could have perpetual existence. It would be completely unfettered by the limitations of a flesh-and-blood existence. There would be no worries about death and its effect upon the continuing vitality of the business. True, it would have to act through human agents, but these agents could be replaced with no effect on the artificial being.

You probably would want the ownership of this new organizational form to rest in the hands of investors who would have no management responsibilities. In this way, an investor's interest in the business could be sold to another investor with no effect on the operation of the enterprise. And management would be centralized, thus improving the efficiency of the business.

Investors could be attracted by making their ownership interests freely transferable and by shielding them from liability for business debts. The possibilities for raising capital would be practically endless. New shares in the ownership of the business could be issued as needed for capital requirements, and if the business had been successful, investors would buy them.

But despite the worthiness of your creation, it possesses one flaw: it is not new. It has already been conceived of and put into practice. *It is called a corporation.*

### Historical Background of Corporations

**Early History:** The concept of granting legal recognition to a group of individuals was developed to a very limited degree in Babylonian law as early as the twenty-first century B.C. More formal acceptance of the idea is found in ancient Roman law, although its application to commercial ventures was yet to come. At this time, the organizations acknowledged by the sovereign were formed primarily for religious, educational, governmental, and other noncommercial purposes.

Under canon law (the law of the Roman Catholic church), the corporation was employed by the church as a convenient vehicle for property ownership. Indeed, canon law made an extremely important theoretical contribution in the thirteenth century when Pope Innocent IV developed the concept of the corporation as an artificial person legally separate from the natural persons composing it.

Recognition of the corporation in English common law had become fairly sophisticated by the fourteenth century. However, the corporation had not yet been substantially utilized for commercial purposes; its use as an instrument of commerce did not become commonplace in England until the sixteenth century. Shortly thereafter, in the seventeenth century, the "concession theory" appeared in English law, treating the corporation as a concession of the government and thus justifying increased regulation and taxation.

The famous overseas trading companies of the sixteenth and seventeenth centuries, such as Hudson's Bay Company and the British East India Company, were chartered by the English government for purposes of exploration, colonization, and foreign trading. These companies, which were given substantial governmental powers and many trading privileges, became the models for our present-day business corporations.

**Sources of American Corporation Law:** During the first few decades after the Revolutionary War, corporations in the United States were formed only by special acts of state legislatures. In the nineteenth century, however, states began to enact "general incorporation" laws, under which persons could form corporations by following specified procedures and without special legislative action. By the end of that century general incorporation was the established rule.

The federal government can also charter corporations—insofar as it is "necessary and proper" for carrying out other express federal powers. Examples of federally chartered corporations are the national banks, the Tennessee Valley Authority, and the American Red Cross. Additionally, many of the federal regulatory statutes, such as the securities, antitrust, and labor laws, weigh heavily upon the operations of corporations.

However, despite increasing involvement by the federal government in the affairs of corporations, their organization and operation are still largely a matter of state law. Each state has its own corporation statutes, and they are not entirely uniform. The Model Business Corporation Act (the Model Act), drafted by the American Bar Association (ABA) in 1969, has provided a basic guideline for the modern corporation statutes of over half the states. In 1984 the ABA drafted the Revised Model Business Corporation Act (the Revised Model Act), which substantially changes many provisions of the Model Act. The Revised Model Act has not yet had a significant effect on state corporation laws and will not be mentioned further in these chapters.

The state of Delaware enacted an extremely flexible corporation statute at the end of the nineteenth century, when most state corporation laws were quite inflexible. Because the Delaware law permitted corporate management more alternatives in structuring and operating the business, and also because Delaware courts developed a relatively well-settled body of judicial precedent at an early time, many companies incorporated in Delaware even though their principal places of business were to be elsewhere. This trend has continued to the present, with many of the nation's largest companies being incorporated in Delaware. In recent years, several states have modeled their corporation statutes after those of Delaware.

## *Classification of Corporations*

**Domestic and Foreign Corporations:** A corporation that has been incorporated in a particular state is referred to as a **domestic corporation** in that particular state. One that has been incorporated in some other state or in another nation is called a **foreign corporation.**

**Private and Government Corporations:** A corporation formed by private parties is a **private corporation.** Almost all corporations, including those formed for business and nonprofit purposes, fall within this category. The **government corporation,** on the other hand, is one formed by the state or federal government. Incorporated cities and towns are examples of government corporations at the state level; the Tennessee Valley Authority and the United States Postal Service are examples at the federal level. (Government corporations are sometimes referred to as *public* corporations, but it is best to avoid this term because it tends to be confused with the *publicly held* corporation, discussed below.)

**Business and Nonprofit Corporations:** Private corporations are either of the business or the nonprofit variety. A **business corporation** is simply one that is formed to engage in a business activity for profit. A **nonprofit corporation** (sometimes called a *not-for-profit* corporation) is one formed for social, charitable, religious, or other nonprofit purposes.

**Publicly Held and Close Corporations:** A **publicly held corporation** is one whose shares of stock are offered for sale to the public. (Sometimes such a corporation is called a *public* corporation, a term that should be avoided because of potential confusion with the government corporation.) A **close corporation** is one whose shares of stock are not offered for sale to the public, but instead are owned by either a single shareholder or a small, closely knit group of shareholders. The shareholders themselves are usually active in managing the business of a close corporation. (The close corporation is sometimes referred to by a variety of other names, such as a *closed, closely held, one-person,* or *family corporation.*)

**Professional Corporations:** Until the early 1960s, state corporation laws usually did not allow persons to form corporations for the purpose of engaging in the practice of a profession such as medicine or law. Since that time, however, most states have enacted statutes permitting one or a group of professionals to form a **professional corporation.** Probably the most important result of these statutes is that physicians, attorneys, and members of other professions can now receive several federal tax advantages (such as tax-deductible insurance or pension plans) as "employees" of the corporation that they could not receive as sole proprietors or as members of a partnership.

## THE CORPORATION AS A LEGAL ENTITY

### Consequences

Perhaps the most important characteristic of the corporation is its recognition as a legal entity—an artificial being or person. This has many consequences, the most important of which are discussed below.

**Normal Business Operations:** The corporation can own property, make contracts, sue and be sued in court, and generally perform all legal functions that an individual can perform.

**Liability for Debts:** The individuals who own the corporation (the shareholders or stockholders) and those who manage it (the officers and members of the board of directors) generally are not personally liable for its debts. Conversely, the corporation is not liable for the personal debts of those who own and manage it. The legal identity of the corporation is thus distinct from the identities of its owners and managers. (Of course, these individuals can assume personal liability for corporate obligations if they so choose.)

**Income Taxation:** The income of the corporation is taxed under the federal income tax laws. And because the corporation and its shareholders have separate identities, the distribution of this income to shareholders as "dividends" is again taxed, this time as personal income to the individuals receiving it. A form of double taxation can result from the separate identities of the corporation and its owners. On the other hand, certain small corporations may elect to be taxed as partnerships in some circumstances. Those corporations making such a choice are referred to as "S corporations."

**Constitutional Rights:** As a "person," the corporation enjoys many of the same rights and privileges under the Constitution that are granted to individuals. For example, it has the right to be secure from "unreasonable searches and seizures"; the right to freedom of speech; the right not to be deprived of life, liberty, or property without "due process of law"; the right not to be tried twice for the same offense ("double jeopardy"); and the right not to be denied "equal protection of the laws." On the other hand, the corporation does *not* enjoy the privilege against "self-incrimination."

In the following case concerning the applicability to corporations of the Constitution's double jeopardy clause, the court discusses the rationale for recognizing the corporation as a "person" in the realm of constitutional protections.

---

### United States v. Hospital Monteflores
U.S. First Circuit Court of Appeals, 575 F.2d 332 (1978)

A corporation engaged in the business of operating a hospital, Hospital Monteflores, together with the director of the hospital, was charged with making false statements on Medicare reimbursement forms in violation of a federal criminal statute. The defendants were acquitted in federal district court, and the U.S. government, as prosecutor, sought to appeal the judgment of acquittal to a U.S. court of appeals. The double jeopardy clause of the Fifth Amendment to the U.S. Constitution prohibits a person from being tried twice for the same criminal offense. If a defendant in a criminal case is acquitted, the double jeopardy clause usually prevents the government from being able to appeal the acquittal to a higher court.

*(continued)*

In this case, the government did not attempt to appeal with regard to the hospital director because such an appeal clearly would not be permitted. However, the government claimed that the double jeopardy clause did not apply to corporations, and that it should be able to appeal the trial court's judgment of acquittal with respect to the corporation.

**Decision:** The government cannot appeal. The Fifth Amendment's Double Jeopardy Clause applies to corporations as it does to individuals. Although corporations do not suffer from criminal prosecutions (and from *multiple* prosecutions) in precisely the same ways as do individuals, they clearly are harmed substantially. Corporations can be fined, but more importantly, their business interests can suffer greatly from the adverse publicity and resulting loss of public confidence that often accompanies the criminal prosecution of companies. The rationale for the Double Jeopardy Clause thus extends to the case of corporations. ∎

## Disregarding the Corporate Entity

The general rule that a corporation possesses an identity separate from its owners and managers is almost always applied. For example, suppose that Beta Corporation becomes insolvent and goes into bankruptcy proceedings. Under most circumstances, the shareholders of Beta are not personally liable to Beta's creditors for its debts. These shareholders, whether they are individuals or other corporations, will lose their investments in Beta because their stock will be worthless, but Beta's creditors normally can reach only Beta's corporate assets to satisfy their claims.

In unusual situations, however, courts may ignore the separate status of the corporation and its owners. This disregard of the corporate identity is often referred to as **piercing the corporate veil.** Sometimes courts use different terminology for the concept; for instance, occasionally a court that disregards the separateness of the corporation and its owners will say that the corporation is the "alter ego" or the "mere instrumentality" of its owners. A court is most likely to pierce the corporate veil in the following circumstances:

1. When the corporation is used as a mere tool for accomplishing a fraud or some other illegal act, a court will disregard the separate identities of the corporation and its owners. For example, suppose that the sole or principal shareholder of the corporation sets fire to corporate property, and the corporation then sues to recover on its fire insurance policy. The court will disregard the separateness of the corporation and the shareholder and will not allow the corporation to recover from the insurance company.

2. When the corporation has been formed with insufficient capital to meet reasonably expectable business obligations *and* the shareholders themselves have intermingled and confused their personal identities with the corporation's identity, a court is likely to disregard the separateness of the corporation and its owners. This confusion of identities might, for instance, take the form of intermingling corporate and personal funds, failing to maintain corporate records separate from personal records, or failing to keep shareholder and corporate identities separate in dealings with outsiders. In such a case, an unpaid corporate creditor who is harmed by the inadequacy of corporate assets may be able to reach the personal assets of shareholders to satisfy its claims.

Corporations are sometimes formed by a single individual or by two or three persons (often family members) who own all the stock. This fact by itself will not cause a court to ignore the separateness of the corporation from its owners; one-person, family-owned, and similar close corporations are entirely permissible. However, those situations in which courts disregard the separateness of the corporation are much more likely to occur when a one-person, family-owned, or similar close corporation is involved. The reason is that the factors leading a court to pierce the corporate veil, such as undercapitalization and confusion of identities, are much more likely to exist in such a corporation.

**Subsidiary and Affiliated Corporations:** Often a corporation, as the "parent," forms or acquires another corporation as a "subsidiary" for some particular purpose. In such a case, the **parent corporation** owns all or a controlling portion of the stock of the **subsidiary corporation.** In the same manner as an individual shareholder, the parent corporation usually is treated as a separate entity from the subsidiary corporation. This is true even if some or all of the same people serve on the boards of directors of the two corporations. However, just as in the case of individual shareholders, in unusual situations a court will pierce the corporate veil and hold the parent liable for its subsidiary's debts or wrongful acts. The circumstances in which a court will take such action are essentially the same as in the case of an individual shareholder, although courts sometimes use different terminology to describe the concept in the parent-subsidiary context. For example, courts frequently say that a parent corporation is liable for the debts or wrongful acts of its subsidiary if the parent "dominates" or "controls" the subsidiary. However, the factors leading a court to reach such a conclusion are usually the same ones leading to this conclusion in the case of an individual shareholder, namely, (1) use of the subsidiary as a mere tool to accomplish a fraud or other illegal act, or (2) undercapitalization plus confusion of the parent's and subsidiary's identities.

Even if the two corporations technically do not have a parent-subsidiary relationship, a court may still disregard their separate identities if they are otherwise closely affiliated and one dominates the other. Such a situation might occur, for instance, where one person owns a controlling stock interest in two corporations, and one of these corporations dominates the other. The legal principles applied to determine whether the separate identities of the corporations should be disregarded are the same as in a situation where a plaintiff seeks to hold either a parent corporation or an individual shareholder liable for the debts or wrongful acts of the allegedly dominated corporation.

The following case involves two corporations affiliated through the stock ownership of a single individual, and provides an excellent illustration of the type of facts that will cause a court to pierce the corporate veil.

## Glenn v. Wagner
Supreme Court of North Carolina, 329 S.E.2d 326 (1985)

Salem Manor, an apartment complex in Winston-Salem, North Carolina, was owned by B-Bom, Inc. David Wagner and George Hill each owned 50 percent of B-Bom's stock, and David Wagner served as the corporation's president. David Wagner also formed another corporation, D&S Enterprises, Inc., in which he was the sole stockholder. B-Bom executed a lease on Salem Manor to D&S, and D&S managed the apartment complex through its agent Smilie Wagner, who was David Wagner's cousin.

Richard Glenn and other members of his family rented an apartment at Salem Manor. Under circumstances in which he had no legal right to take such action, Smilie Wagner evicted Glenn and his family from the apartment, padlocked it, removed and damaged Glenn's personal belongings, and had Glenn's mail returned to the post office. Glenn sued Smilie Wagner, D&S Enterprises, and B-Bom, Inc., claiming that Smilie had committed a trespass. D&S clearly was liable for Smilie's actions because he was acting within the scope of his employment for D&S. Because D&S had no assets, Glenn also attempted to hold B-Bom liable on the theory that B-Bom had completely dominated D&S and, therefore, that D&S was the "alter ego" or "instrumentality" of B-Bom.

In the trial, the evidence indicated that David Wagner had set up D&S mainly to benefit his cousin Smilie and to give the latter a source of income. The management of Salem Manor was D&S's only business. David Wagner testified that he and Smilie each owned 50 percent of D&S (although the articles of incorporation of D&S showed David to be the only stockholder). He stated that he "thought" that he was the president and treasurer of D&S and that Smilie "must be" the vice-president and secretary. He could not recall whether there had been an organizational meeting, when the by-laws were adopted, who was on the initial board of directors, or how many board meetings had been held. Although he and Smilie met regularly to deal with business matters, David could not recall having a formal shareholder meeting. According to David Wagner, Smilie managed Salem Manor for D&S on a daily basis, and David's own involvement in the operation of the apartment complex was "more of an advisory nature because that business was operated exclusively by Smilie . . . as a general rule he operated the business pretty much as he saw fit."

The only formal instrument executed on behalf of D&S was the agreement under which D&S leased Salem Manor from B-Bom. B-Bom established the amount of rent to be charged for each of the Salem Manor units, and most of D&S's

*(continued)*

rents and profits went to B-Bom as payment on the lease. David Wagner's office, from which he directed several business enterprises, served as the corporate office of both B-Bom and D&S. A few months after Smilie's wrongful eviction of Glenn, Smilie left D&S and went into business for himself, and Wagner terminated the lease between B-Bom and D&S. B-Bom then directly collected rent from Salem Manor for three months until an employee of another one of David Wagner's corporations, also located in the Salem Manor premises, was authorized to collect rent from the premises. D&S was never formally dissolved, but had no assets.

Based on this evidence, the trial court submitted to the jury the question whether B-Bom had so completely dominated D&S as to be its alter ego and to be liable for the trespass committed by D&S. The jury found that B-Bom was liable, and the court rendered judgment for Glenn for damages of approximately $10,000. The intermediate appellate court reversed, holding that there was insufficient evidence of B-Bom's control over D&S. Glenn appealed to the North Carolina Supreme Court.

**Decision:** The judgment of the appellate court was reversed, and the judgment of the trial court against B-Bom affirmed. David Wagner never observed corporate formalities regarding D&S Enterprises or otherwise treated D&S as a separate entity, and it was grossly undercapitalized. There was sufficient evidence to support the trial court's finding that B-Bom completely controlled D&S and was the alter ego of D&S. ■

## FORMATION OF THE CORPORATION

### *Promoters' Activities*

For various reasons the word *promoter* sometimes elicits unfavorable reactions from people. The negative connotations of the word are generally unwarranted, though, because promoters usually serve a legitimate and socially useful function. In essence, a **promoter** is the motivating force behind the creation of the corporation. He or she recognizes the business opportunity, analyzes it to determine its economic feasibility, and brings together the necessary resources and personnel.

In planning for the proposed corporation, the promoter often finds it necessary to employ the services of attorneys, accountants, architects, or other professionals. He or she may also have to borrow money or contract for the purchase of real estate, equipment, patent rights, or other property. And in some circumstances the promoter may find it desirable prior to incorporation to contract with persons to serve as officers and employees upon formation of the corporation. Several legal questions can arise in connection with such transactions. For example: Is the promoter personally liable on these contracts? Is the corporation liable once it is formed? What if the corporation is never actually formed? The approach taken by the courts is summarized as follows.

**Where Corporation Is Formed and Contract Adopted:** If the proposed corporation *is* later formed, it can adopt the promoter's contract and become a party to it. The corporation is not bound unless it adopts the transaction. Assuming that the corporation is formed and does adopt the contract, the question remains whether the promoter is still liable on the contract. If the promoter made the contract in his or her own name, with no reference to the proposed corporation, the promoter obviously continues to be liable unless released by the third party. On the other hand, if the promoter made the contract in the name of, or with reference to, the proposed corporation, there is a split of opinion among the various states: courts in several states have held that the promoter is automatically discharged from responsibility under the contract when the corporation adopts it, but in a majority of states courts have ruled that the promoter continues to be liable unless released by the third party.

**Where Corporation Is Not Formed or Contract Not Adopted:** If the proposed corporation is not ever formed, or if it is formed but does not adopt the contract, the promoter usually is personally liable on the contract. Under basic principles of contract law, however, the promoter is not liable if (1) the contract expressly provided that the promoter would be discharged from responsibility if the corporation was not formed or did not adopt the contract; (2) the third party later releases the promoter from liability; or (3) the court concludes that the promoter and the third party had originally intended only an informal agreement and that neither of them had intended to be bound unless the corporation ultimately was formed and became a party to the agreement.

Many times two or more promoters are involved. Prior to the actual creation of the corporation these promoters are viewed by the law as being engaged in a *joint venture*. As a result, they maintain the same kind of fiduciary relationship that exists among partners. In their dealings with one another they must exercise the highest standards of honesty and openness.

Once the corporation is formed, the promoters also owe the same type of fiduciary responsibility to the corporation itself and to all interested parties. Complete disclosure must be made, for example, to the board of directors and to all investors (shareholders). Promoters are not allowed to make secret profits on the promotional scheme.

In the two cases that follow, the courts deal with two difficult questions arising from the activities of corporate promoters. In the first case, the issue is whether a promoter is personally liable on a contract made prior to formation of the corporation. In the second, the issue is whether the promoters violated their fiduciary responsibilities to the other shareholders, and if so, whether the promoters' bank had participated in the wrongful conduct so as also to be liable.

### Goodman v. Darden, Doman, & Stafford Associates
Supreme Court of Washington, 670 P.2d 648 (1983)

John Goodman sold an apartment building to a partnership, Darden, Doman, & Stafford Associates (DDS) during August of 1979. The apartments needed extensive renovation, and Goodman contracted to perform the renovation for DDS, the work to be completed by October 15. While the renovation contract was being negotiated, Goodman told Don Doman, managing partner of DDS, that Goodman was going to form a corporation to limit his liability. Goodman signed the contract as "Building Design & Development, Inc. (In Formation), John A. Goodman, President." Between August and December 1979, DDS made five progress payments on the contract. The first payment was made to "Building Design & Development Inc.—John Goodman." Goodman struck out his name on the face of the check and endorsed it on the back "Bldg. Design & Dev. Inc., John A. Goodman, Pres." Goodman instructed DDS to make all further payments to the corporation only, which was done. Although Goodman had represented to Doman that Goodman was qualified to do the renovation, immediately after making the contract Goodman got a third party to do the work. On October 15, the work was not completed, and much of what had been done was allegedly of poor quality. On November 1 Goodman filed the articles of incorporation, and on November 2 the certificate bringing the corporation into existence was issued.

DDS then began arbitration proceedings in accordance with a clause in their contract providing that any disputes would be submitted to binding arbitration, and sought to hold Goodman personally liable for breach of the renovation agreement. Goodman filed suit, claiming that he should not be a party to the proceedings, because only the corporation was liable under the contract. The trial court agreed with Goodman that only the corporation was responsible, but the court of appeals reversed. Goodman appealed to the Washington Supreme Court.

**Decision:** The judgment of the appellate court was affirmed, and the judgment of the trial court reversed. The contract was made by Goodman before any corporation was formed, and there was insufficient evidence to conclude that DDS originally intended to look only to the corporation for satisfaction, or that DDS had subsequently intended to release Goodman. There is a strong presumption that one intends to contract with an existing party, and the mere signing of a contract with a corporation "in formation" does not suffice to show an agreement to look solely to the corporation. Regarding a subsequent release, it is not necessary that the agreement to release a promoter say "I agree to release," but that intent must be demonstrated very clearly by language or circumstances. Goodman's act of striking out his name on the front of a progress payment check and endorsing it as the corporation's president says nothing about the intent of DDS. The fact that DDS followed Goodman's instructions and made out the next four payments to the corporation also does not show an intent to release Goodman. ■

## First National Bank of Council Bluffs v. One Craig Place, Ltd.
Supreme Court of Iowa, 303 N.W.2d 688 (1981)

Midlands Corporation, a wholly-owned subsidiary of First National Bank of Council Bluffs (the Bank), was in the process of constructing a shopping mall and desired to lease space to tenants. Guy and Diane Craig, husband and wife, decided to open a clothing store in the mall and signed a lease with Midlands for this purpose. Each store premises in the mall was leased in an unfinished condition, and Midlands provided the tenant with an allowance to finish the interior to suit the particular type of store to be operated. Midlands agreed to furnish $57,600 for finishing the premises leased by the Craigs.

The Craigs calculated that a store such as they planned would require about $100,000 capital. They had only $3,000 cash, and a total net worth of about $31,000. They contacted Robert Emerine, senior vice-president of the Bank, who began to serve as their financial advisor. He helped them complete and file a loan application to the Small Business Administration, but the application was not approved. Realizing that they would not be able to borrow the necessary funds, the Craigs decided to form a corporation with a capitalization of $100,000. The corporation, One Craig Place, Ltd., was formed with the Craigs serving as promoters, officers, and directors. They persuaded four friends, Melvin Kvasnicka, Marvin Seibold, Carmen Craig, and John Williams, to invest $12,000 each—a total of $48,000 for 48,000 shares of stock.

Robert Emerine, who continued to advise the Craigs, then helped them put together a plan for raising the remaining $52,000. The plan consisted of two transactions: (1) In the first transaction, the Craigs paid their $3,000 to the corporation toward the purchase of 52,000 shares of stock. As part of this transaction, the Craigs then assigned their lease to the corporation, so that the $57,600 to be provided by Midlands for finishing the interior of the store was payable to the corporation. In behalf of the corporation, the Craigs agreed that $49,000 out of the $57,600 to be received from Midlands would be treated as payment by the Craigs for the remainder of their 52,000 shares of stock. (2) In the second transaction, the Bank (through Emerine) lent $49,000 *to the corporation* (not to the Craigs personally). In return for this loan, the Bank received a promissory note from the corporation, a security interest in all of the corporation's assets, an assignment from the corporation of the lease on the store premises, and a personal guaranty from the Craigs coupled with a security interest in all of the Craigs' personal assets.

As a result of these transactions, $100,000 ostensibly was paid to the corporation for 100,000 shares of stock, and the four minority shareholders thought that this was the case. In actuality, however, only the minority shareholders' $48,000 and the Craigs' $3,000 was paid to the corporation, because the remainder was offset by the corporation's secured $49,000 note to the bank.

During its first three months of operation the store did very little business, and was not able to meet its heavy rental obligation to Midlands or its other expenses. The four minority shareholders and Guy Craig each lent $5,000 to the corporation in return for the corporation's unsecured promissory notes, and the Craigs used this money to make back rental payments to Midlands. During the next two months the business fell further into debt, and the Craigs again called on the four minority shareholders. One of them, Williams, dropped out. The Bank lent the corporation an additional $36,000, the corporation gave the Bank another promissory note for $36,000, and the three remaining minority shareholders signed written guaranties of the note in the amount of $12,000 each. These three shareholders were not aware of the corporation's $49,000 obligation to the Bank and, consequently, thought the store's inventory and other assets were sufficient to justify the extension of further credit.

The store continued to lose money, the notes to the bank became due, and the three minority shareholders learned for the first time about the way the Craigs had financed their purchase of 52,000 shares of stock. Without the knowledge of the three minority shareholders, the Craigs, the Bank, and Midlands executed an agreement to close the business and liquidate its assets. The proceeds from the sale of the corporation's assets, and from foreclosure of a second mortgage on the Craigs' home, were paid to Midlands for back rent and to the Bank in partial satisfaction of the $49,000 note. The Bank then attempted to enforce the guaranties that had been executed by the three minority shareholders on the $36,000 note. They refused to pay, and the Bank filed suit against them, the Craigs, and the corporation. The trial court gave judgment for the Bank against the minority shareholders enforcing their guaranties and ordering them to pay the Bank $12,000 each plus interest. They appealed to the Iowa Supreme Court.

**Decision:** The judgment for the plaintiff was reversed. The Craigs, as promoters (and controlling shareholders), breached their fiduciary responsibilities to the minority shareholders by failing to disclose the sham financing arrangements. The bank participated in this breach through Emerine, one of its officers. The bank, therefore, was responsible for the consequences of this breach and could not enforce the guaranties. ■

## Incorporation

The word **incorporation** refers to the procedural mechanics of forming a corporation. Although the details of these procedures differ from state to state, substantial similarity exists with respect to their basic outline.

**Articles of Incorporation:** The first step in the formative process is preparation of **articles of incorporation,** a legal document that should be prepared by an attorney and that must be signed by the **incorporators.** A few states require the signature of only one incorporator, but most states follow the traditional requirement of three signatures. The incorporators are those individuals who *technically* apply to the state for incorporation. They must be adults, but they need not have any interest in the business enterprise itself. Often they are the persons actually forming the corporation, but they can be completely disinterested parties (such as secretaries in the office of the attorney who is preparing the articles).

The following is a summary of those matters which generally should be included in the articles of incorporation.

1. *The name of the corporation:* This name cannot be the same as, or deceptively similar to, that of any other corporation legally doing business within the state.

2. *The duration of the corporation:* In most states this can be perpetual. And in the few states that do place limitations on the number of years a corporation can exist, it is usually only a formality to renew the corporation's existence on expiration of the stated time period.

3. *The purpose or purposes for which the corporation is organized:* While most states allow the formation of a business corporation for any lawful purpose, a few still prohibit corporations from practicing medicine, law, or other professions. Also, many states do not allow banks, loan companies, insurance companies, public utilities, or railroads to be formed under the general incorporation statutes. These types of businesses are often required to incorporate under other, specialized statutes.

4. *The financial structure of the corporation:* Detailed information must usually be included about the methods by which the corporation will raise capital needed for its operations.

5. *Provisions for regulating the internal affairs of the corporation:* Examples of such provisions are the location of shareholders' meetings, quorum and voting requirements at shareholders' and board of directors' meetings, removal of directors, and filling director vacancies.

6. *The address of the corporation's registered office and the name of its registered agent at this address:* The registered office is simply the corporation's official office in the state, and the registered agent is its official representative. The purpose of requiring a corporation to have a registered office and registered agent is to insure that there will be an easily identifiable place and person for the receipt by the corporation of summonses, subpoenas, and other legal documents.

7. *Information relating to the first board of directors of the corporation:* The board of directors is the group of individuals who manage the affairs of the corporation. The number of directors constituting the initial board must be indicated in the articles. Additionally, the articles usually must include the names and addresses of those individuals who will serve as directors until the first annual shareholders' meeting or until another board of directors is otherwise selected.

8. *The name and address of each incorporator.*

**Certificate of Incorporation:** The articles of incorporation must be filed with the designated state official (usually the secretary of state). If they are in conformance with all legal requirements and if all required fees are paid, the state official will issue a **certificate of incorporation** (sometimes called a **charter**). This certificate represents the permission given by the state to conduct business in the corporate form. The corporation comes into existence when the certificate of incorporation is issued. After issuance, the certificate and an attached copy of the articles of incorporation are returned to the incorporators or their representatives.

**Initial Organization:** Under the laws of most states, the incorporators must hold an *organizational meeting* after issuance of the charter. In states where the first board of directors is not named in the articles of incorporation, the incorporators elect the directors at this meeting. In all states, authorization will usually be given to the board of directors to issue shares of stock. Perhaps the most important purpose of the meeting, however, is to adopt bylaws.[1]

**Bylaws** are the rules or "private laws" that regulate and govern the actions and affairs of the corporation. Although they ordinarily are *not* filed with a state official, the bylaws must not conflict in any way with the provisions of the articles of incorporation. The relationship between the articles and the bylaws is analogous to the relationship between the constitution and the statutes of a state. A corporation's bylaws sometimes amount to only a brief statement of rules for internal management of the corporation. Often, however, the bylaws are extremely detailed, sometimes even including a restatement of applicable statutes as well as provisions from the articles of incorporation. As an example of the type of details frequently included in the bylaws, many provisions relate to the specifics of conducting directors' and shareholders' meetings.

The board of directors also holds an organizational meeting, at which time it transacts whatever business is necessary to launch the operations of the enterprise. In some states the incorporators do *not* hold an organizational meeting, and in these states the board of directors adopts bylaws and performs the other tasks described earlier as functions of the incorporators. In the states in which incorporators *do* meet, the directors at their initial meeting usually approve all actions taken by the incorporators. In addition, the agenda of the first directors' meeting includes such matters as approval of the corporate seal, election of corporate officers, adoption of preincorporation agreements made by the promoters, selection of a bank for depositing corporate funds, and other pertinent items of business. Figure 37.1 outlines the steps in forming the corporation.

## *Effect of Improper Incorporation Procedures*

If all requirements for incorporation have been followed to the letter, it is said that a ***de jure* corporation** exists. The existence of such a corporation cannot be challenged by either the state or any other party so long as the corporation acts lawfully in the conduct of its business.

Figure 37.1  Basic Steps in Forming a Corporation

- Promotion (planning and structuring)
- Incorporation
- Prepare articles of incorporation
- File articles with state
- Certificate of incorporation (charter) issued by state
- Organizational meeting
- First board of directors meeting
- Corporation ready to do business

Occasionally there occurs some deviation from the procedures required for incorporation. If the deviation is relatively insignificant (in other words, if there is "substantial compliance" with procedures) and if no harm to the public interest results, the corporation still has *de jure* status. (An example of such

---

[1] In some states, however, formulation of the initial bylaws is a function of the shareholders, and in others it is a function of the board of directors.

an inconsequential procedural defect is a mistake in the address of one of the incorporators in the articles of incorporation.)

On the other hand, the defect may be sufficiently important that there is not substantial compliance with mandatory incorporation procedures. In such a case, there will not be a *de jure* corporation. There might, however, be what is commonly referred to as a **de facto corporation.** If the corporation has *de facto* status, the *state* can challenge the validity of its existence, but no other party can do so. (If it has neither *de jure* nor *de facto* status, the validity of its existence can be challenged by the state or by any other interested party, such as a creditor seeking to hold a shareholder personally liable for a corporate debt.) The requirements for the existence of a *de facto* corporation are:

1. There must be a state statute under which the corporation could have been validly incorporated.
2. There must have been a genuine, good-faith attempt by the incorporators to follow statutory requirements.
3. There must have been some type of business transacted by the enterprise *as a corporation.*

Historically, issues relating to *de facto* corporations have not arisen very frequently, and the importance of the concept in actual practice appears to be further diminishing.

Even if a corporation has neither *de jure* nor *de facto* status, particular situations exist where a party can be estopped (prohibited) from denying the validity of its existence. If, for example, the individuals operating a business represent their enterprise as being a corporation, they can be estopped from denying the corporate status in a particular lawsuit. (This concept is often denoted by the phrase *corporation by estoppel.*)

## Doing Business in Other States

A corporation that has been incorporated in one state may wish to do business in other states as well. Before doing so, the corporation must apply for and receive a **certificate of authority** in each state where it plans to do business. The process of obtaining the certificate is largely a formality, and the initial steps in applying for it often are taken at the organizational meeting of the board of directors. However, the corporation is also usually required to maintain a registered office and registered agent in each state where it does business.

The penalties levied by various states against foreign corporations that have not obtained a certificate of authority include fines, denial of the privilege of filing lawsuits in the courts of that state, and placement of personal liability for corporate obligations incurred in that state on the directors, officers, or agents involved.

## Financing the Corporation

After incorporation, the corporation must obtain the funds necessary to launch and initially operate the business. When the business has been in operation for a substantial period of time, a wider range of financing alternatives are available, including retained earnings, short-term borrowing, and accounts receivable financing. At the beginning, however, fewer alternatives exist.

The principal method of initially financing a corporation is by the issuance of **securities,** which are sold to investors. The board of directors usually authorizes their issuance during its initial organizational meeting. The most common types are equity securities and debt securities.

**Equity securities** are usually referred to as **shares of capital stock,** or simply as *shares.* Each share represents an interest in the ownership of the corporation. Therefore, the investors who purchase them (the **shareholders** or **stockholders**) are the owners of the corporation. (More is said about the various types of shares in Chapter 39.)

**Debt securities** are usually referred to as **bonds.** Corporate bonds do not represent ownership interests in the corporation, but are loans to the corporation from the investors who purchase them. The relationship between the investor who purchases bonds and the corporation which issues them is that of creditor and debtor.

## Registration of Securities

When a corporation issues securities to meet either its initial capital requirements or its later financial needs, it usually must comply with the securities laws of those states in which they are offered for sale.[2] The

---

[2] These state laws are often referred to as *blue-sky laws,* because they are largely antifraud statutes intended to prevent the sale of worthless securities ("pieces of the blue sky").

laws of some states simply prohibit fraud in the sale of securities. In many states, however, the issue of securities must be *registered* with the state agency empowered to administer the law. To register, the corporation must supply extremely detailed financial and other information about itself. These state agencies commonly have broad discretionary powers to pass judgment on the merits of a particular issue of securities—even to forbid such issuance—and penalties for failing to register with them can be quite severe.[3]

Many issues of securities, such as those sold in interstate commerce or through the mails, must also be registered under the **Securities Act of 1933**, a federal law. Here again, detailed financial and other information must be supplied. This information must be given both to the appropriate federal agency—the **Securities and Exchange Commission (SEC)**—and to the persons to whom the securities are offered for sale. The SEC does not pass judgment on the merits of a particular issue of securities but attempts only to insure full and complete disclosure of relevant information. The underlying rationale is that the light of publicity will serve to deter misconduct in the sale of securities. Under the Securities Act of 1933, failing to register or willfully making false statements in the registration is punishable by a fine of up to $10,000 and/or imprisonment of up to five years. Civil actions for damages can also be brought by injured private parties.

The purpose of both state and federal securities laws is protection of the investing public. Although compliance with these laws is costly and time-consuming, failure to comply can be even more costly. What is more, the protection afforded by these laws benefits not only the investors but also the corporations themselves by encouraging investment in corporate enterprises.

Securities laws are discussed in depth in Chapter 41, "Securities Regulation."

## SUMMARY

The concept of the corporation is of ancient origin, dating to the twenty-first century B.C. in Babylonian law. The famous overseas trading companies of the sixteenth and seventeenth century became the models for modern corporations. American corporation law today is found primarily in state statutes and the judicial interpretations of those statutes, although federal securities regulation law also plays an important role.

The most important characteristic of the corporation is its status as a legal entity with an identity separate from that of its owners and managers. In most situations the separateness of the corporate identity is recognized, but in unusual circumstances courts will disregard the corporate entity, or "pierce the corporate veil," in order to prevent the separateness of the corporation from being used as a mere tool to perpetrate fraud.

The promoter serves as the motivating force for the identification of a business opportunity, the marshalling of resources to exploit the opportunity, and the formation of the corporation as an operating format. The corporation, once formed, is liable for the promoter's preincorporation contracts only if the corporation adopts them. The promoter usually is liable on such contracts even if the corporation is later formed and adopts them. When two or more promoters act together, they are viewed prior to formation of the corporation as participants in a joint venture, and owe fiduciary duties to each other. A promoter also owes fiduciary duties to the corporation and its shareholders when the corporation is formed.

The actual procedure of forming a corporation is referred to as *incorporation,* and must strictly follow the statutory requirements of the state in which it is registered. The most important means for obtaining a corporation's necessary financing is the issuance of securities. The two most important types of securities are equity securities and debt securities. Equity securities are commonly called shares of capital stock. The purchasers of these securities, shareholders, are the owners of the corporation. Debt securities are commonly called bonds. The purchasers of these securities are creditors rather than owners of the corporation. New issues of securities usually must be registered with federal and state government agencies.

## KEY TERMS

**Domestic corporation**
**Foreign corporation**
**Private corporation**
**Government corporation**

---

[3] For example, the sale of unregistered securities in the state of Texas is a felony punishable by a fine of up to $10,000 and/or imprisonment for up to ten years.

Business corporation
Nonprofit corporation
Publicly held corporation
Close corporation
Professional corporation
Piercing the corporate veil
Parent corporation
Subsidiary corporation
Promoter
Incorporation
Articles of incorporation
Incorporators
Certificate of incorporation (charter)
Bylaws
*De jure* corporation
*De facto* corporation
Certificate of authority
Securities
Equity securities
Shares of capital stock
Shareholders (stockholders)
Debt securities
Bonds
Securities Act of 1933
Securities and Exchange Commission (SEC)

## QUESTIONS AND PROBLEMS

1. Progress Tailoring Co. advertised that it manufactured garments, although these garments actually were manufactured by its wholly owned subsidiary. The Federal Trade Commission instituted proceedings in which it sought to stop such advertising on the ground that it was deceptive. Did the FTC prevail? Discuss. (*Progress Tailoring Co. v. FTC*, 153 F.2d 103, 1946.)

2. A federal statute prohibited railroads from giving rebates to those using the railroad for shipping goods. X Corp. shipped substantial quantities of goods by rail. The officers and principal shareholders of X Corp. formed a separate corporation for the purpose of obtaining what were, in actuality, rebates. Did X Corp. violate the antirebate law by receiving rebates through the separate corporation? Explain.

3. Discuss why a nonprofit organization such as a church, fraternal club, or hospital might want to incorporate.

4. Boss, a promoter, signed a contract for architectural services as "agent for a Minnesota corporation to be formed which will be the obligor." The architectural drawings were prepared, but the proposed corporation was never formed, and the architects sued Boss for their fee. Will the architects recover from Boss? Discuss. (*Stanley J. How & Associates v. Boss*, 222 F.Supp. 936, 1963.)

5. Acting in his own behalf and not in behalf of any proposed corporation, Caparella purchased equipment subject to a debt, used it, then turned it over to a subsequently created corporation, of which he became president. The creditor sent bills to the corporation, but the corporation never responded. The creditor then sued the corporation. Will the creditor prevail? Explain.

6. Under what types of circumstances might it be useful to use "dummy" incorporators (those having no real interest in the corporation to be formed)?

7. Baum Holding Co. was formed in Nebraska in 1922, when there was no state statute authorizing the formation of holding companies (corporations whose operations consist only of the ownership of interests in other corporations). In 1941, a holding companies statute was enacted, but the company made no attempt to comply with its provisions. Sometime thereafter, several shareholders who were dissatisfied with the way the company was being run filed suit challenging the validity of the corporation's existence. Should they prevail? Discuss. (*Baum v. Baum Holding Co.*, 62 N.W.2d 864, 1954.)

8. Plaintiff entered the "corporation's" building on business and fell into an unlit, unguarded elevator shaft. Although the organizers of the "corporation" had filed its articles before the accident, no arrangements had been made for the issuance of shares of stock, no meeting of shareholders had been held, officers had not been elected, and the corporation had not done any business as a corporation. The plaintiff sued the individual organizers for his injuries. Should he recover? Explain.

9. What is a major difference between the authority of the SEC and the authority of many state securities agencies?

CHAPTER 38

# CORPORATIONS

## CORPORATE POWERS AND MANAGEMENT

## CORPORATE POWERS

As an "artificial person," a corporation possesses the power to do most of the things an individual can do in the operation of a business enterprise, such as own property, make contracts, borrow money, and hire employees. Corporate powers derive from several sources, traditionally classified as statutory, express, and implied powers. State corporation laws ordinarily contain a list of **statutory powers**—those activities in which corporations are permitted to engage. **Express powers** are those set forth in the articles of incorporation. The articles frequently restate the powers granted by the statutes of their jurisdiction and then enumerate other powers specifically related to the corporation's business. Of course, the powers stated in the articles must not conflict with the statutory powers, but this rarely happens, because most of the statutes are drafted in a rather broad fashion. With few exceptions, a corporation also has **implied powers** to do any other things reasonably necessary for carrying on its business. These powers simply serve to fill in gaps that exist in the statutory and express powers.

In past years, the law in many states denied corporations the implied power to engage in several types of activities, such as joining a partnership and making charitable donations. In modern times, however, corporations have implied power to do practically anything related to their business that individuals could do. Shareholders, of course, may place express limitations on management powers in the articles of incorporation.

### The Ultra Vires Doctrine

A corporation is organized for particular purposes. An important principle in the area of corporate powers is that *a corporation is empowered to act only insofar as necessary to further the purposes for which it was organized.* All that has been said regarding corporate powers must be qualified by this principle. Thus even such ordinary powers as making contracts and owning property can be exercised only within the limits of a corporation's expressed purposes.

Any act by a corporation that is beyond the scope of its business as defined in the articles of incorporation is said to be ***ultra vires***.[1] Many of the cases in which the *ultra vires* doctrine has been at issue have involved corporate contracts made for unauthorized purposes. The treatment accorded *ultra vires* contracts by the courts is summarized below.

**1.** In past years, some courts treated *ultra vires* contracts as absolutely void, with no rights or duties created on either side.

**2.** Most courts, however, did not apply an absolute rule of invalidity to *ultra vires* contracts unless they were illegal as well. Where the contracts were merely *ultra vires* but not otherwise illegal, these courts varied their treatment according to how far performance had progressed. For example, a fully executed *ultra vires* contract, where both parties had completely performed, was treated as valid and left undisturbed. On the other hand, where the contract was entirely executory, neither party having performed, the *ultra vires* nature of the agreement could be raised by either party; and this defense would prevent enforcement of the contract. Where the contract was partially executed, it would be enforceable under some circumstances. (For example, where one party had received benefits under the contract, that party would be estopped from asserting the defense of *ultra vires*.)

---

[1] *Ultra vires* acts should not be confused with illegal ones. All illegal corporate acts are inherently *ultra vires;* but not all *ultra vires* acts are illegal. In fact, most are not illegal but are merely beyond the scope of corporate powers.

3. Although some courts still take the approach discussed in item 2, a majority of states have passed statutes in recent years greatly diminishing the significance of the *ultra vires* doctrine. Most of these statutes follow the lead of the Model Act, which abolishes *ultra vires* as a contractual defense. In other words, in these states the *ultra vires* nature of the contract does not affect its validity as far as the parties themselves are concerned. However, other legal consequences continue to ensue from an *ultra vires* contract, including (a) a suit by shareholders for an injunction to prevent performance where it has not yet taken place, (b) a suit by the corporation itself or by shareholders acting in its behalf to recover damages from the directors and officers responsible for the action, and (c) a suit by the state either for an injunction or for dissolution of the corporation.

The diminishing importance of the *ultra vires* doctrine can be observed in other ways as well. For example, corporate attorneys have become increasingly adept at including within the statement of purpose in the articles of incorporation all remotely conceivable activities. This ordinarily is more convenient than amending the articles at a later time. In addition, some states' corporation laws permit incorporation for "any lawful purpose," with no requirement that the articles state specific purposes.

# CORPORATE MANAGEMENT

When one speaks of corporate "management" one is usually referring to the board of directors, officers, and managerial employees who oversee the details of corporate operation. Although shareholders generally do not take part in the daily running of the corporation, they do, as owners, have ultimate control over its policies.

The structure of corporate control can be viewed as pyramidal in nature, the shareholders forming the broad base of the pyramid. The shareholders exercise their control, for the most part, by selecting the individuals who serve on the board of directors. The board, in turn, usually selects corporate officers and other managerial employees at the top of the pyramid.

## *Shareholders' Functions*

The power to control the details of daily corporate operation resides with the board of directors, which often delegates much of the responsibility to officers and other employees. In most situations, the remedy for shareholder dissatisfaction with the manner in which corporate affairs are being handled is to elect a new board of directors. The most important shareholder functions are (1) election and removal of directors, (2) amendment of articles and bylaws, and (3) approval of certain extraordinary corporate matters.

**Election and Removal of Directors:** Although the initial board of directors is either named in the articles of incorporation or selected by the incorporators, its term ordinarily extends only until the first meeting of shareholders. The selection of directors then becomes a shareholder function.

Except for death or resignation, a director usually serves until the expiration of his or her term of office, and frequently is reelected to one or more subsequent terms. However, shareholders have always had the inherent power to remove directors at any time *for cause* (fraud, misconduct, neglect of duties, and so on)—subject, of course, to court review. On the other hand, the traditional common-law rule was that a director could not be removed *without cause* during his or her term unless the shareholders had expressly reserved that right at the time of election. Today, however, this rule has been changed by statute in a majority of states to permit shareholders to remove directors at any time *with or without cause*. Removal of a director in either case is accomplished by majority vote. However, if "cumulative voting" was used to elect the director, removing him or her may be somewhat more difficult. The concept of cumulative voting and its effects will be discussed shortly.

**Amendment of Articles and Bylaws:** Shareholders have the power to amend the articles of incorporation. Of course, since the corporation's articles must be filed with the secretary of state, any later amendments must also be filed.

In different states the bylaws are initially adopted by either the incorporators, the directors, or the shareholders. But regardless of which body possesses the power of original adoption, the shareholders are empowered to amend or even repeal them subsequently.

In many jurisdictions the directors have the power to amend or repeal the bylaws, but this power is really subordinate in nature. In other words, even when the directors are given such authority by statute, by the articles, or by the bylaws themselves, the ultimate power rests with the shareholders. Because they possess an inherent power with respect to bylaws, they can override the directors' actions even if such actions were authorized.

**Approval of Extraordinary Corporate Matters:** Although the authority to conduct most corporate affairs is held by the directors, certain matters are of such an unusual nature as to require shareholder approval. This approval is ordinarily given in the form of a "resolution" voted on at a shareholders' meeting. Extraordinary matters requiring shareholder approval include (1) sale or lease of corporate assets *not* in the regular course of the corporation's business, and (2) merger, consolidation, or dissolution of the corporation.

## *Exercise of Shareholders' Functions*

Shareholders as such are not agents of the corporation and therefore cannot bind the corporation by acting *individually;* their powers must be exercised *collectively.* The most common vehicle for the exercise of shareholder functions is the *shareholders' meeting.* In recent years, however, most states have amended their corporation laws to allow shareholders to take action by *written consent.* This consent must ordinarily be signed by all shareholders entitled to vote on the matter.[2] But the shareholders' meeting still remains the most common forum for shareholder action.

**Types of Meetings:** Shareholders' meetings are either *annual* or *special.* Corporations are usually required by state law to hold annual meetings; the most important item of business at these meetings is usually the election of some or all of the directors. Between annual meetings, special meetings may be called to transact business that cannot or should not wait until the next annual meeting.

**Time and Place of Meetings:** The time of annual meetings and the place for annual and special meetings may be set forth in the articles, but they are more commonly found in the bylaws. Most annual meetings are held in the spring. Older statutes often required shareholders' meetings to be held in the state of incorporation, but this generally is no longer a requirement.

**Notice of Meetings:** State laws usually require written notice of any shareholders' meeting to be sent to each shareholder a reasonable time prior to the meeting, although shareholders can waive this requirement by signing a waiver before or after the meeting. In some instances a shareholder's *conduct* may constitute a waiver of notice. For example, where a shareholder receives no formal notice but knows of the meeting and attends without protesting the lack of notice, he or she waives the requirement of notice.

The notice generally must state the place, day, and hour of the meeting; and in the case of a special meeting, the notice must state the purpose or purposes for which the meeting is being called. The business transacted at a special meeting must be limited to the purposes set forth in the notice.

**Quorum:** Before action can validly be taken at a shareholders' meeting, a **quorum** must be present. Quorum requirements are expressed in terms of either a specific portion of outstanding shares or a specific portion of shares entitled to vote. These requirements are usually set forth in the articles or the bylaws within limits defined by state statute. As an example, the Model Act allows the articles of incorporation to set the quorum requirement so long as it is not less than one-third of all outstanding shares. The Model Act further provides that, if the articles are silent on the matter, a majority of outstanding shares constitutes a quorum.

**Voting:** Action at a shareholders' meeting is taken by voting. The number of votes a shareholder has is determined by the number of shares he or she owns. Assuming that a quorum is present, the majority vote of the *shares represented at the meeting* (not the shares outstanding or entitled to vote) is usually sufficient for ordinary matters. More than a majority is sometimes required by state law or by the articles or bylaws for certain unusual matters such as mergers or consolidations. When a greater-than-majority vote is required, it is usually expressed in terms of all shares entitled to vote, not just those represented at the meeting.

---

[2] A few states allow shareholder action by a less-than-unanimous written consent.

State laws frequently require that a corporation keep a record of all its shareholders, listing their names and addresses as well as the number and type of shares held by each. Usually corporations are also required to prepare a *voting list* (a list of shareholders who can vote and the number of votes each is entitled to) prior to each shareholders' meeting. The record of shareholders and the voting list must be kept at a designated place (such as the principal corporate office) and must be available for inspection by shareholders.

Impartial individuals referred to as *tellers* (or sometimes as *judges* or *inspectors*) are usually present to supervise elections at shareholders' meetings. Although tellers are not generally required by law, many state statutes do require them if a shareholder so requests or if they are called for in the bylaws.

**Methods for Concentrating Voting Power:** Several methods exist by which a shareholder who owns a relatively small portion of the corporation's shares can increase his or her voting power.

*Cumulative Voting:* Practically every state provides for **cumulative voting** by shareholders. A few states *require* it, but most merely *permit* it if the articles of incorporation provide for it. Cumulative voting applies only to the *election of directors,* and it is designed to increase the likelihood of minority representation on the board. (*Minority* refers to the owner[s] of a less-than-controlling number of shares, not to an ethnic minority.) The following example illustrates the mechanics of cumulative voting: J is the owner of a hundred shares of stock in Gemini Corp. At the annual shareholders' meeting, three directors are to be elected. The slate of candidates includes A, B, C, D, E, and F. J wants to elect A, B, and C, or at least one of them. If "straight" voting is used, J can cast a hundred votes each for A, B, and C (that is, one vote per share for each directorship to be filled). But if cumulative voting is allowed, J can take the total three hundred votes that he is entitled to cast at the election and cast them *all* in favor of A or divide them in any manner he wishes.

We previously mentioned that a director may be removed from office by majority vote. This is true if the director is being removed *for cause,* even though he may have been elected by minority interests through cumulative voting. However, if a corporation uses cumulative voting and if the attempted removal is *without cause,* a director cannot be removed from office if the vote *against removal* would be sufficient to elect that director by cumulative voting.

*Shareholder Agreements:* Agreements in which a group of shareholders decide prior to a meeting to cast their votes in certain ways are sometimes employed to concentrate voting power. These agreements are usually valid and enforceable. Generally, such agreements must be in writing, deposited with the corporate secretary, and noted on all stock certificates.

*Voting Trusts:* Another method of concentrating voting power is the **voting trust.** This is formed by an agreement in which the "record ownership" of shares is transferred to trustees whose sole function is to vote the shares. "Voting trust certificates" are given by the trustees to the original shareholders, entitling them to all rights of share ownership other than voting rights. As a general rule, voting trusts must meet the same legal requirements as shareholder voting agreements.

*Proxies:* Shareholders can vote their shares at a meeting either in person or by proxy. A **proxy** is simply a signed, written document authorizing a person present at the meeting to vote the shares of a shareholder. Proxies (which create an agency relationship) are useful both to alleviate problems of distance between a shareholder's residence and the site of a meeting and to concentrate voting power. For example, one person might solicit and accumulate proxies authorizing him or her to vote in behalf of a number of shareholders. Proxies are usually solicited by corporate managers prior to each shareholder's meeting. (More is said later, particularly in Chapter 39, about the duties of one who solicits proxies.)

The two following cases involve shareholders' exercise of their voting rights. The first case illustrates an attempt to concentrate voting power by means of a shareholders' agreement. As we will see, the group was trying to oust the largest shareholder from his position as chairman of the board. The chairman responded with his own strategic moves which became the subject of this lawsuit. The second case deals with a claim that actions taken at a shareholders' meeting were void because the notice of the meeting was inadequate.

## Sanders v. McMullen
U.S. Fifth Circuit Court of Appeals,
868 F.2d 1465 (1989)

The Houston Sports Association (HSA) is a Texas corporation that owns and operates the Astrodome and the Houston Astros Baseball Club. In 1979, McMullen formed the Houston Astros Limited Partnership (HALP) to purchase the capital stock of HSA from its creditors. McMullen was a general partner of HALP and personally owned 25 percent of the partnership. His family owned an additional 8 percent. Sanders, as one of 25 other investors, owned a 2 percent interest in HALP. After the 1980 baseball season, investors sought to oust McMullen as a general partner of HALP, and the organization was dissolved. HSA, however, was recapitalized and the partners of HALP received HSA stock. The result was that McMullen controlled 34 percent of the stock and became chairman of the board. Sanders still owned 2 percent.

In 1984, minority shareholders tried to enter a voting agreement with 51 percent of the stockholders to remove McMullen from management of HSA. Sanders's 2 percent interest was included in the 51 percent, but he decided to withdraw from the agreement, leaving the shareholders with only 49 percent. Sanders claims he agreed to withdraw because of promises made by McMullen. McMullen was able to retain control of HSA, and even purchased more shares when the organization was restructured. McMullen then controlled 63 percent of the shares and Sanders increased his share to 13 percent with a $4 million stock purchase.

Sanders contended that McMullen promised him the following items in exchange for withdrawing from the voting trust: (1) He would participate in all management decisions involving the baseball team; (2) he would have access to all operational information; (3) the baseball manager and staff would be advised of his status; (4) he would participate in league meetings, World Series, and All Star Game activities; (5) he would have access to all baseball facilities; (6) his shares would be included in the control block for any sale; and (7) McMullen would vote his shares to keep Sanders on the board of directors.

Sanders contends that he purchased the additional stock and withdrew from the voting agreement that would have ousted McMullen in reliance on these promises. A continuing shareholder's agreement and a collateral agreement were both signed by the parties. The agreements reflected Sanders's additional investment of $4 million. The promises were not contained in the documents or mentioned on the stock certificates. In November 1986, Sanders was not reelected to the board of directors of HSA and McMullen sent him a letter stating that he was not entitled to any special privileges as a shareholder. Sanders sued McMullen for breaching the agreement and for fraudulent misrepresentation. He sought a decree of specific performance requiring McMullen to honor his agreement, or an order requiring McMullen to purchase Sanders's stock at the fair market price.

The trial court granted McMullen's motion for summary judgment, finding that there was no genuine issue of material fact, and Sanders appealed.

**Decision:** The trial court's judgment was reversed, and the case remanded for trial. The only promise that constituted a voting agreement was the one calling for McMullen to vote his shares to keep Sanders on the board. The trial court was correct that this promise did not constitute a valid contract because it did not meet statutory requirements; to have been valid under Texas law it must have been in writing, with a copy or duplicate original deposited at corporate headquarters and a reference to it on stock certificates. The other promises did not have to meet these formalities, however, and Sanders ought to have the opportunity to prove them in trial. In addition, there was enough evidence to create genuine fact issues requiring a trial on Sanders's fraud claim—the evidence indicated that McMullen may have made the promises without ever having had any intention of fulfilling them. ■

## Valerino v. Little
Court of Special Appeals of Maryland,
490 A.2d 756 (1985)

As of April 1, 1979, Frederick Valerino, Theresa Valerino, Gregory Hays, and Ann Hays owned, as a group, 195 shares of Electra-Mechanical of America, Inc. (EMA). Charles Little and Anna Little together owned 195 shares. The board of directors consisted of Charles Little, Anna Little, and Frederick Valerino. No shareholders meeting was held in 1980, and so this board was held over. On April 1, 1981, the shareholders were unable to elect a board of directors because a dispute over the operation of the company had resulted in a stalemate. At a board of directors meeting that same day, attended by all three directors, Charles and Anna Little voted to remove Frederick Valerino as vice-president of EMA. In addition the

*(continued)*

three agreed, as reflected in the minutes of the meeting, that Frederick Valerino would prepare a proposal offering to sell the Valerino/Hays block of shares to the corporation.

On April 10, 1981, a letter was sent to Frederick Valerino notifying him that a special meeting of the board of directors was called for April 17, "for the sale and purchase of the capital stock of EMA, Inc. No proposal will be considered unless it is reduced to writing, signed, witnessed, and notarized." Frederick Valerino responded with a telegram stating that the Valerino/Hays group was not yet prepared to make a proposal for the sale of their stock. Charles Little acknowledged receipt of the telegram by a letter dated April 13, and requested that Valerino "let us know when you have prepared proposals and we will have a special board of directors meeting at that time." Nevertheless, the special board meeting called for April 17 was held, with Frederick Valerino absent. At this meeting, the other two board members (the Littles) voted to issue an additional 520 shares of stock, 490 shares to be distributed to the Littles, and 10 shares each to be distributed to three other persons who previously had not been shareholders. As a result of this issuance of stock, the 50 percent interest of the Valerino/Hays group was reduced to less than 25 percent.

The Valerinos and the Hays then filed a lawsuit claiming that the notice of the April 17 meeting was insufficient because it spoke only of the sale and purchase of stock and not its issuance. Consequently, they argued, the action of the board at that meeting was void and they still owned 50 percent of EMA's stock. A Maryland statutory provision permitted the owners of at least 50 percent of the shares of a corporation to obtain a court-ordered dissolution on the grounds that the shareholders had failed to elect a board of directors for two consecutive years. On this basis, the plaintiffs sought dissolution of the corporation. (The subject of dissolution is discussed in Chapter 40.) The trial court ruled that the notice and the board's action were valid, and dismissed plaintiff's petition for dissolution. The plaintiffs appealed.

---

**Decision:** The judgment for defendants was reversed. The notice was not sufficient. A reasonable person under the circumstances probably would have interpreted the notice as referring only to the planned proposal to have the corporation buy the Valerino/Hays stock, and not to the issuance of new shares. The board's action was void, the Valerinos and Hays still owned 50 percent, and they could use a Maryland statute permitting the owners of 50 percent or more of a corporation's stock to obtain a court-ordered dissolution. ∎

---

## Board of Directors: Choice and Functions

**Number:** State statutes have traditionally required that there be at least *three* directors. In recent years, however, the laws in a majority of states have been changed to permit fewer directors in corporations that have fewer than three shareholders. Subject to these statutory limitations, the number of directors is usually set forth in either the articles or the bylaws.

**Qualifications:** In most states directors no longer have to meet minimum age requirements, although in a few states they do. Requirements that directors be residents of the state of incorporation, still found in a few states, are also becoming much less common. In the past, most states required that directors be shareholders. This requirement also is vanishing; statutes in a majority of states now provide that directors need not be shareholders unless they are so required by the articles or bylaws. In actual practice, most directors *are* shareholders; however, there is a growing trend toward obtaining the services of disinterested outsiders as "watchdogs" on the board of directors. Also, it is permissible for an individual to be both a director and a corporate officer, and this frequently occurs.

**Election and Term:** The initial board ordinarily serves until the first annual shareholders' meeting, when new directors are elected by majority vote of the shareholders.

The term of office for corporate directors is one year (that is, until the next annual shareholders' meeting) unless the board is "classified" (divided into classes, with only one class elected each year, the result being that the directors serve "staggered" terms). Today, most states permit a **classified board.** When this system is used, the most common practice is to have *three* classes, with one-third of the directors being elected each year for a three-year term. Classification prevents replacement of the entire board at the same time, thereby providing greater management continuity.

We mentioned earlier that removal of a director during his or her term is a shareholder function. The power to remove a director *for cause* can also be given, in the articles or bylaws, to the board of directors itself, although the shareholders have inherent power to review the action. But the board cannot be empowered to remove a director *without cause*.

When vacancies occur on the board (through death, resignation, or removal) or when an amendment to the articles or bylaws creates a new place on the board, filling of the opening generally is also a shareholder function. But several states now allow such openings to be filled by the board itself if it is so authorized by the articles or bylaws.

**Management Functions:** Even though the corporation generally is bound by the actions of the board, the directors are not agents of the corporation or of the shareholders who elect them. There are two reasons for this. First, their powers are conferred by the *state* rather than by the shareholders. And second, they do not have *individual* power to bind the corporation, as agents do; instead, they can only act *as a body*. Directors thus occupy a position unique in our legal system.

With the exception of certain extraordinary matters mentioned earlier, the board of directors is empowered to manage all the affairs of the corporation. It not only determines corporate policies but also supervises their execution. The management powers of the board of directors usually include the following:

1. Setting of basic corporation policy in such areas as product lines, services, prices, wages, and labor-management relations

2. Decisions relating to financing the corporation, such as the issuance of shares or bonds

3. Determination of whether (and how large) a dividend is to be paid to shareholders at a particular time

4. Selection, supervision, and removal of corporate officers and other managerial employees [3]

5. Decisions relating to compensation of managerial employees, pension plans, and similar matters.

## Exercise of Board's Functions

As we previously mentioned, most states now allow *shareholders* to act by unanimous written consent in addition to annual and special meetings. A majority of states (but not as many as allow shareholder action by written consent) also now allow the *board of directors* to act by unanimous written consent. The traditional, and still most uncommon, method for board action, however, is the board of directors' meeting.

**Time and Place of Board Meetings:** Board meetings are of two types—regular and special. The time and place of *regular meetings* is ordinarily established by the bylaws, by a standing resolution of the board, or simply by custom. Unless expressly required, notice of such meetings does not have to be given to directors. If the need arises, *special meetings* can be called between regular meetings. Prior notice is required in most cases, since special meetings by their very nature are not regularly scheduled.[4]

**Quorum:** Before action can validly be taken at a board of directors' meeting, a quorum must be present. Most state statutes are flexible on the matter of what constitutes a quorum. They usually provide that a quorum will be a majority of the authorized number of directors unless the articles or bylaws say otherwise. Some state statutes also place a maximum and a minimum on the quorum requirement.

**Voting:** As is true at shareholders' meetings, action at a board meeting is taken by voting. But a director's voting power is not determined by the size or nature of any financial interest he or she has in the corporation. Instead, each director has *only one vote*. Board action usually requires only a *majority vote*, although some states permit the articles or bylaws to require a greater-than-majority vote for certain actions. (The "majority" referred to here is a majority of the directors actually attending a meeting at which a quorum is present.) Unlike shareholders, directors cannot vote by proxy. However, a small number of states have recently changed their laws to permit a director to fully participate in a meeting by telephone. In such cases, a "conference call" must be used, so that the absent director and those present at the meeting can all speak and listen as a group.

In the next chapter, the fiduciary duties of directors are discussed in connection with their responsi-

---

[3] Several states now permit the shareholders to select corporate officers if so provided in the articles or bylaws.

[4] State laws usually provide, however, that a director waives any notice requirement if he or she actually attends the meeting, unless such attendance is limited to the express purpose of objecting that the meeting was not lawfully called.

bilities and resulting liabilities to the corporation. Although a director's conflict of interest can cause the director to be liable for resulting harm to the corporation, such a conflict also can affect the fundamental power of the board to manage the corporation. The next case illustrates such an effect.

## Weiss Medical Complex, Ltd. v. Kim
Appellate Court of Illinois,
408 N.E.2d 959 (1980)

Weiss Medical Complex, Ltd., a professional corporation, operated a medical clinic in Harvey, Illinois. Sun Kim and Chusak Ladpli, licensed physicians, entered into employment contracts with the corporation in 1972 and 1973, respectively. The contracts were for a term of one year, to be automatically renewed unless either party gave written notice of termination at least 90 days prior to the end of the year. Each contract contained a restrictive covenant in which the employee agreed not to practice medicine within a ten-mile radius of the corporation for a period of one year after termination of the employment.

In early 1977 the board of directors voted to cancel the restrictive covenants in physicians' contracts. At this time the corporation's bylaws provided for thirteen directors, but only seven directors had been elected. All seven directors attended the board meeting at which this action was taken. The minutes of this meeting were subsequently reviewed by the corporation's attorney, who indicated that the board's action was questionable because four of the directors had restrictive covenants in their own contracts, thus creating a possible conflict of interest. The attorney advised that the board should attempt to get shareholder approval of the action. At the shareholders' meeting that was held subsequently, the board's action was not ratified, mainly because the majority shareholder, Dr. Weiss, opposed the action.

In 1979 Dr. Kim and Dr. Ladpli terminated their employment with the corporation and opened their own medical practices within a ten-mile radius of the Weiss facility. At the insistence of Dr. Weiss, the corporation filed suit seeking an injunction enforcing the restrictive covenants in its former employees' contracts. The trial court held that the board's action had been valid, and dismissed the suit. The corporation appealed.

**Decision:** The judgment for the defendants was reversed. The action by the board of directors was void and, therefore, the noncompetition covenants were still valid and enforceable. Four of the seven directors had a personal interest in the action taken by the board, and were thus disqualified from voting. The bylaws call for a thirteen-member board, but only seven positions were filled. It took a majority of the thirteen to constitute a quorum, so all seven were necessary for a quorum. Four were disqualified, so there was no quorum and the action was invalid. In fact, under these particular circumstances there would have been no quorum if only one had been disqualified. ■

**Delegation of Board Powers to Officers and Employees:** We said earlier that all functions of the board of directors must be exercised by the board as a whole, usually by majority vote. This does not mean, however, that the board itself must carry out all the details of corporate management; it can, and quite often does, *delegate authority* to carry out its decisions. The most common instance of such delegation is the authority given by the board to corporate officers and other managerial employees. Not only is authority usually given to carry out board decisions, but managerial personnel also are generally given authority to make management decisions. The delegation of decision-making authority is usually a practical necessity, because daily business activities require too many decisions for each one to be made by the board. The powers delegated by the board, however, must not exceed two boundaries:

1. They must relate only to ordinary corporate affairs, not to matters of an unusual nature.

2. They must not be so broad as to give an officer or employee complete managerial discretion. In other words, the delegated authority must be either relatively limited in scope or accompanied by adequate guidelines.

Thus, even though certain management functions are often delegated to officers and other employees, the ultimate power to manage the corporation still rests with the board. And the authority delegated to managerial personnel is, of course, subject to board supervision.[5] The duties owed by the board of directors to the corporation and its shareholders are discussed in the next chapter, but we must emphasize here that a delegation of authority by the board does not relieve it of the responsibility to fulfill these duties.

**Other Delegations of Board Powers:** Most state corporation laws permit the board of directors to select a certain number of its members (usually two or more) to serve as the "executive committee." The rules governing delegation of authority to an executive committee are somewhat similar to those governing delegation to managerial personnel:

1. An executive committee is usually authorized to make management decisions relating only to ordinary business affairs. Power to make decisions on unusual matters generally cannot be delegated to the committee. Examples of unusual matters include: (a) amending corporate bylaws, (b) filling vacancies on the board, and (c) submitting to shareholders matters that require their approval.

2. The delegation of authority to an executive committee cannot be too broad in scope.

3. The committee can usually exercise its delegated powers only during the intervals between meetings of the whole board of directors.

## Officers and Other Managerial Employees

**Officers:** The officers of the corporation are usually selected by the board of directors, although in a few states they can be chosen by the shareholders. Most commonly, the corporate officers are the president, one or more vice-presidents, secretary, and treasurer. Some corporations also have other officers, such as chief executive officer, chairman of the board, general manager, comptroller (sometimes called "controller"), and general counsel.

*Qualifications:* In the past, many state laws required the president also to be a director. This requirement no longer exists in most states. In actual practice, however, the president almost always is a director as well. And when a corporation has a chairman of the board, he or she obviously must be a director. Other qualifications for the various officers can be included in the articles or bylaws if desired. In most states the same individual can hold more than one office. For example, it is not unusual for the offices of secretary and treasurer to be occupied by the same person. Limitations are frequently placed, however, on certain types of dual office holding. Most states, for instance, prohibit the same person from serving simultaneously as *president and secretary,* or as *president and vice-president.*

*Term of Office:* In a few states the term of office is limited by statute to a specific duration, such as one year. But in most states the only limitations are those expressed in the articles or bylaws. For the most part, officers hold their positions at the pleasure of the board and can be removed by the board either with or without cause and regardless of any enforceable employment contract. Of course, if the termination of an officer constitutes a breach of contract, the corporation can be held liable for damages to the discharged officer.

**Other Managerial Employees:** A corporation of almost any size requires the services of many employees to conduct its daily affairs. Some of these employees occupy supervisory positions and exercise certain managerial functions even though they are not officers. Selection of a few of the higher-ranking supervisory personnel is often done by the board of directors, but the task of hiring employees is generally delegated to the officers or even to other employees.

**Applicability of the Law of Agency:** Officers and other employees are agents of the corporation, and all the rules of agency law apply to the relationships created. Thus the corporation is bound by the actions of its officers and employees if they are acting within the scope of their authority—whether it is express, implied, or apparent. The express authority of *officers* comes only rarely from state laws or the articles of incorporation. It most frequently emanates from the corporate bylaws or from a resolution of the

---

[5] This is a statement of the *law*. However, in actual practice, because of personalities or financial interests, the boards of some corporations serve primarily as a "rubber stamp" for decisions initiated by high-ranking managers.

### Figure 38.1 Relationship of Shareholders, Directors, and Officers in a Corporation

**Shareholders**
Adopt and amend articles and bylaws.
Elect and remove directors.
Approve certain extraordinary corporate matters.

↓

**Board of directors**
Determines corporate policies and supervises their execution.

↓

**Officers and employees**
Carry out policies and make routine decisions.

---

board of directors. The express authority of *other employees* most commonly comes from the officers or from higher-ranking employees. Implied and apparent authority are created in essentially the same way as in any other principal-agent relationship.

Figure 38.1 illustrates the relationship of shareholders, directors, and officers.

In the following case, the court deals with several important issues regarding the role of both shareholders and directors in the management of a corporation.

---

### Rowland v. Rowland
Supreme Court of Idaho,
633 P.2d 599 (1981)

Rowland's, Inc., was a corporation engaged primarily in the dairy business in Power County, Idaho. The corporation's bylaws specified that the board of directors would consist of nine members, the presence of seven members would be necessary for a quorum at any board meeting, and a vote of three-fourths of the directors present at a meeting would be required for action by the board. At an annual shareholder meeting a proposal was introduced to amend the bylaws so that the presence of only five members would be required for a quorum at any board meeting, and a vote of only a majority of the directors present would be required for board action. Two shareholders, V. C. Rowland and Tom Rowland, strenuously objected to the consideration of this proposal because the notice of the shareholder meeting had not mentioned the matter. (At that time, Idaho law required notice of all shareholder meetings, including annual meetings; later, Idaho adopted a new corporation law based on the Model Business Corporation Act, which required notice of only special shareholder meetings. The prior law applied to this case.) Despite these objections, the proposal was passed by votes representing 60 percent of the corporation's outstanding shares. V. C. and Tom Rowland abstained from voting their shares on this proposal, but then participated along with the other shareholders in acting upon several other items of business at the meeting.

The annual board of directors meeting was held one week later and was attended by eight of the nine directors. By majority vote (but not three-fourths) the board elected officers of the corporation; V. C. and Tom Rowland were not reelected to officer positions. Later, V. C. and Tom Rowland filed suit claiming that the amendment of the bylaws at the shareholder meeting was void because it had not been mentioned in the notice of the meeting, and that the subsequent election of officers by the board was also void because this action was based on the amended bylaw. They also claimed that a series of management actions taken during the next year and a half were void because the actions were accomplished without approval of the board of directors acting as a body. The trial court ruled against V. C. and Tom Rowland on all their claims, and they appealed.

---

**Decision:** The judgment for the defendant corporation was affirmed. Although the meeting notice was deficient, V. C. and Tom waived the right to object by participating in other shareholder actions taken at the meeting. With regard to the other

*(continued)*

claim that management actions taken without formal approval by the board were void, it is true that management decisions normally must be approved formally by the board at one of its meetings. Informal board actions are sometimes legal, however, and those situations in which informal board action is permissible usually can occur only in the context of a close corporation, as was Rowland's, Inc. The prerequisites for permissible informal action are that (1) this method of informal managerial decision making must have become a well-established custom in the business, and (2) shareholders who did not participate in these informal decisions must have known the customary practice and acquiesced in it. Moreover, if those participating in informal board action own a majority of the corporation's shares, the informal actions will almost always be upheld in a close corporation unless there is evidence of an actual intent to harm minority shareholders. In this case, the two prerequisites were present, participants did hold a majority of the shares, and there was no evidence of an intent to harm minority shareholders. The court also made the observation that V. C. and Tom had been invited to participate in the informal board decisions, but had not done so, making it even more obvious that they knew about and acquiesced in the custom of informal decision making. ■

## MANAGEMENT OF CLOSE CORPORATIONS

As indicated in the previous chapter, a close corporation is one whose shares of stock are held by either a single shareholder or a small, closely knit group of shareholders. Since all these shareholders usually hold positions as directors and officers, the management of a close corporation in practice more closely resembles a sole proprietorship or partnership than a corporation. In fact, close corporations with more than one shareholder are frequently referred to as "incorporated partnerships."

However, the nature of a close corporation should not be misconstrued. In the eyes of the law, *it is still a corporation* and must meet the same legal requirements as other corporations. While this has sometimes caused practical problems for close corporations, the problems have usually been overcome by the exercise of organizational ingenuity. For example, the law traditionally required at least *three* directors. But what if only *two* individuals own shares of stock and are interested in the operation of the corporation? One method of resolving the problem has been to set the number of directors at three in the articles of incorporation but then to operate with a permanent vacancy on the board. Another method has been to persuade a disinterested party to serve as a director in name only, with authority delegated to an executive committee composed of the two interested directors. And if the delegation of powers is too broad, there is really no one to complain.

Given that the law recognizes the validity of close corporations, one might wonder why the parties are forced to resort to these clever devices. Modern corporation laws are beginning to recognize this dilemma. As indicated earlier, for example, a majority of states now require only one or two directors where there are only one or two shareholders. Furthermore, in recent years a few states have enacted special laws to deal with the unique nature of close corporations. The most striking of these is a provision found in a handful of states permitting the shareholders of a close corporation (as defined in the particular statute) to manage the enterprise *without a board of directors*. The primary purpose of these recent statutory innovations is to allow more internal flexibility in the management of a close corporation, thereby enabling the enterprise to operate with approximately the same degree of freedom and owner control that is found in partnerships while retaining the advantages of doing business as a corporation (such as limited shareholder liability for business debts).

Several of the cases in these chapters on corporations involve the application of the general rules of corporation law to close corporations. In most situations, the same basic principles apply to the close corporation as apply to those whose stock is publicly traded. Sometimes, however, the rules are modified somewhat to recognize the particular nature of a close corporation. For example, in the last case, *Rowland v. Rowland,* the court recognized that informal board action is more likely to be valid in a close corporation because there is a much greater likelihood that the directors involved have a majority stock interest and that informal board action has become customary. Moreover, as just mentioned, in recent years a substantial number of states have passed special legislation modifying some of the rules applicable to close corporations.

The following two cases each involve claims that majority shareholders violated fiduciary duties to a minority shareholder in a close corporation. The fiduciary responsibilities of those who manage and control a corporation are discussed in greater detail in the next chapter; at this point, however, we present these two cases because they illustrate some of the problems for managers and investors that are somewhat more likely to occur in the context of a close corporation. In each case, the court expressly discusses the special nature of the close corporation and the recognition given to it by courts and legislatures.

## Goode v. Ryan
Supreme Judicial Court of Massachusetts,
489 N.E.2d 1001 (1986)

Alice Marr owned 800 shares out of a total of 11,340 outstanding shares of the common stock of Gloucester Ice & Cold Storage Co. Gloucester engaged in the manufacture and sale of ice to fishing industry customers. Until 1980, Gloucester also operated a separate fish cold storage business. When Alice Marr died, the administrator of her estate, Thomas Goode, demanded that Gloucester purchase Marr's 800 shares. The demand was refused, and Goode filed suit against the officers, directors, and a controlling shareholder of Gloucester, seeking an order of the court requiring the corporation to purchase the 800 shares. The trial court granted the defendants' motion for summary judgment, and plaintiff appealed.

**Decision:** The judgment for the defendants was affirmed. Although a minority shareholder in a close corporation can be in the unfortunate position of holding unsaleable shares and having little voice in running the business, the corporation does not have a duty to purchase those shares. Such a shareholder is especially susceptible to oppression by the majority, and can obtain relief against such oppression, but there was no indication here that majority shareholders had acted unfairly to Alice Marr. ■

## Estate of Schroer v. Stamco Supply, Inc.
Court of Appeals of Ohio,
482 N.E.2d 975 (1984)

Since 1973, a controlling stock interest (approximately 84 percent of the voting power) in Stamco Supply, Inc., had been owned by Ralph Grimme and several members of his family. Ralph Grimme also was chief executive officer of the corporation. In 1974 the corporation repurchased all of the shares of Stamco stock owned by Ralph Grimme's mother for $208 per share. In 1976 the corporation repurchased all of the shares owned by Ralph Grimme's brother for $259 per share. The minority shareholders were not informed of either transaction.

One of these minority shareholders, Dorothy Schroer, later learned of the stock repurchases, and in 1980 demanded that the corporation repurchase her shares "on terms as favorable as those given to members of the controlling family group." The corporation refused, and she filed suit claiming that the controlling shareholders had breached their fiduciary duties to her and other minority shareholders. (The duties and liabilities of controlling shareholders to minority shareholders, as well as the duties and liabilities of officers and directors to the corporation and to all shareholders, are discussed in more detail in the next chapter.) The trial court ruled for Dorothy Schroer and granted her request for an order requiring the corporation to repurchase her shares on terms at least as favorable as those given to members of the Grimme family. The corporation and the controlling shareholder group appealed. During the litigation, Dorothy Schroer died, and the executor of her estate continued the lawsuit in her place.

**Decision:** The judgment for plaintiff Schroer was affirmed. The corporation must repurchase her shares on terms at least as favorable as those given to members of the Grimme family. Although a close corporation owes no absolute duty to repurchase a minority holder's shares, in this case the controlling shareholders violated their fiduciary duties to minority shareholders by discriminating in favor of members of the controlling group. ■

# SUMMARY

In modern times a corporation has the power to perform almost any legal act that an individual can perform. Under the *ultra vires* doctrine, a corporation has the power to engage only in those activities that are in furtherance of the stated purposes for which it is organized. In recent years, however, most state corporation statutes have been changed so as to (1) permit very broad statements of purpose in the articles of incorporation and (2) make *ultra vires* contracts legally enforceable; consequently, this doctrine does not limit a corporation's activities nearly as much as in earlier times.

In managing a modern corporation, the shareholders have ultimate control because they are the owners of the company. The power to make most business decisions, however, rests with the board of directors, and the shareholders usually exercise their ultimate control only through their election of directors. Shareholders do, however, have the right to act directly in the case of certain fundamental corporate changes such as amendment of the articles and bylaws and the approval of mergers.

Shareholders usually elect directors and take other action by voting at an annual shareholder meeting. Voting power corresponds to the number of shares owned; shareholders may, however, concentrate their voting power by a number of methods such as cumulative voting, shareholder agreements, voting trusts, and proxies. Special shareholder meetings may also be called by the board of directors upon the giving of adequate notice of the time, place, and purpose of the meeting.

The board of directors sets basic corporate policy and makes important business decisions; often it delegates to officers and other corporate employees the authority to make daily operational decisions. Directors take formal action only as a body; such action is usually taken at meetings, although some states permit board action by written consent or conference call in some situations. Each director has one vote, regardless of whether he or she owns shares in the corporation and regardless of the number of shares owned. Directors usually have regularly scheduled meetings, but special meetings may also be called upon the giving of adequate notice of the time, place, and purpose of the meeting.

Close corporations involve some special management problems because all or most of the shareholders themselves are usually intimately involved in managing the business; in actual operation, a close corporation resembles a partnership.

# KEY TERMS

**Statutory powers**
**Express powers**
**Implied powers**
*Ultra vires*
**Quorum**
**Cumulative voting**
**Voting trust**
**Proxy**
**Classified board**

# QUESTIONS AND PROBLEMS

1. Can a corporation be a partner? Explain.

2. Explain how the *ultra vires* doctrine has diminished in importance in recent years.

3. Charlestown Co. was dissolved, and its shareholders elected a committee to work with the board of directors in winding up the business. The laws of New Hampshire, where the case arose, provided that "the business of every such corporation shall be managed by the directors thereof, subject to the bylaws and votes of the corporation, and under their direction by such officers and agents as shall be duly appointed by the directors or by the corporation." The board ignored the committee. A shareholder filed suit challenging the board's failure to recognize the committee. Did the board act properly? Discuss. (*Charlestown Boot and Shoe Co. v. Dunsmore,* 60 N.H. 85, 1880.)

4. The directors of Omega Corp. proposed an amendment to the bylaws that would create a new class of shares with rights equal to an existing class. A special meeting was called to consider the amendment. The notice of the special meeting gave a brief statement about the amendment but did not mention the new class. The amendment was adopted at the meeting, but its validity was then challenged by a shareholder. Is the amendment valid? Discuss.

5. The bylaws of Thompson Co. set the quorum requirement for directors' meetings as a "majority of the directors." The number of directors provided for in the articles was eleven, but because of one death and one resignation, the board actually had only nine directors in office when it held a meeting in January 1976. Five directors attended. The action taken at the meeting was challenged by a shareholder on the ground that there had not been a quorum. Is the shareholder correct? Discuss.

6. Prince Co. owns a manufacturing plant, several trucks, and other items of equipment; it also owns two tracts of land of about 500 acres each, which it holds as an invest-

ment. Prince Co. was in need of cash, so Girard, who is both president and treasurer, sought to obtain a loan for the company from City National Bank. As security for the loan, the bank wanted a mortgage on one of the tracts of land. Can Girard execute the mortgage without express authority from the board of directors? Discuss.

7. The president of Hessler, Inc., made a contract with an employee, Farrell, in which retirement benefits were promised to him. In the past, the president had been allowed to manage the company's affairs more or less independently of the board; he also owned approximately 80 percent of the corporation's stock. When Farrell retired, the corporation refused to pay the benefits, and Farrell sued. The corporation claimed that the agreement made with Farrell by the president was invalid because it had not been approved by the board of directors. Is the corporation correct? Discuss. (*Hessler, Inc. v. Farrell,* 226 A.2d 708, 1967.)

8. Acting for the company, the executive committee of Ace Corp.'s board of directors made a contract with Henson, who was to perform services for Ace. The corporation's bylaws provided that all contracts must be approved "by the board of directors," but elsewhere in the bylaws it was stated that "the executive committee shall conduct the corporation's business." Is the contract valid? Discuss.

9. Plymouth Co. made an agreement with United National Bank in which Plymouth was to receive a substantial loan. In consideration of the loan, it was agreed that Plymouth's shareholders would elect two directors designated by United, one of whom would be comptroller and have complete charge of all the corporation's finances. Is the agreement valid? Explain.

10. Should a corporation's board of directors be permitted to hire an employee under a contract guaranteeing lifetime employment? Discuss.

# CHAPTER 39

# CORPORATIONS

## RIGHTS AND LIABILITIES OF SHAREHOLDERS AND MANAGERS

Successful operation of the corporate enterprise involves the concerted efforts of many people. Although success demands that their efforts be focused on essentially the same goals and objectives, their own *individual* interests inevitably come into play on some occasions. For this reason, we will now discuss the rights and liabilities of the parties to the corporate venture, with respect to one another, and with respect to the corporation as an entity.

## RIGHTS OF SHAREHOLDERS

### Voting Rights

As indicated in the previous chapter, shareholders exercise their ultimate control by voting. Unless otherwise provided in the articles of incorporation, a shareholder has one vote for each share. The right to vote does not have to be expressed in the articles; it is inherent in the ownership of shares. Of course, the articles can expressly exclude or limit the right to vote—for example, by providing for the issuance of a certain number of special shares without voting rights.

**Treasury stock** is made up of shares that have been issued and later repurchased by the corporation. They carry no voting rights, since a corporation cannot logically act as a shareholder of itself. If these shares are subsequently resold, however, they once again carry voting rights.

### Dividends

A person who purchases corporate shares is making an investment from which he or she obviously intends to receive a profit. Depending on the nature of the business and the type of shares purchased, the shareholder may expect such profit to arise either from increases in the market value of the shares, or from dividends, or perhaps from both.

**Dividends** are simply payments made by the corporation to its shareholders, representing income or profit on their investment. The payment is usually in the form of money, but it can consist of some type of property, such as the securities of another company that the corporation has been holding as an asset.

Sometimes the corporation pays a **stock dividend,** which is the issuance to shareholders of additional shares of the corporation's own stock. Such a distribution is *technically not a dividend,* because it does not represent a transfer of any property from the corporation to its shareholders. Instead, each shareholder simply becomes the owner of a larger number of shares. Although shareholders may not benefit immediately from a stock dividend, because the value of the preexisting shares is diluted, they usually do benefit in the long run because of the tendency of such shares to later increase in value.

The laws of the various states differ substantially with respect to the circumstances in which dividends can legally be paid. Generally, however, the following limitations are imposed:

**1.** Dividends cannot be paid if the corporation is insolvent or if the payment itself will cause the corporation to become insolvent. Depending on the particular state statute involved, *insolvency* is defined either as (a) the inability of the corporation to pay its debts as they become due, or (b) the possession of insufficient assets to meet all outstanding liabilities.

**2.** Dividends ordinarily can be paid only from a particular source. For example, some states allow dividends to be paid only from "current net earnings." This means that the source of funds for the payment must be the net profits of the corporation for the current year or the year just ended. Many states, however, permit dividends to be paid from any existing "surplus." In effect, this means that the payment must not be made out of the original capital investment in the corporation.

Shareholders do not have an absolute "right" to receive dividends. It is true that many corporations actually have long-established policies regarding payment of dividends. But whether a dividend is to be paid ("declared") in a given situation, and how large it is to be, are largely left to the discretion of the board of directors and usually cannot be challenged. A challenge to their decision ordinarily can be made only if (1) funds were not legally available for the dividend, (2) the division among shareholders was not fair and uniform, or (3) the special rights of any particular class of stock were not observed.

## *Preferences*

We have referred several times to different "classes" of corporate stock. The rights enjoyed by individual shareholders sometimes depend on the class of shares they own. In a given situation, a corporation might issue only one class of stock or it might issue several, depending upon the needs of the business.

Corporate stock is generally classified either as common or preferred. **Common stock,** the most basic and frequently issued type, enjoys no special privileges or preferences. **Preferred stock,** on the other hand, guarantees to its owner some type of special privilege or "preference" over the owners of common stock. The most frequently granted preferences relate to *dividends* and to *distribution of assets upon liquidation.*

**Dividend Preferences:** A preference as to dividends does not mean that the owners of the preferred shares are guaranteed the right to receive dividends. What it does mean is that, *if a dividend is declared,* owners of preferred stock have a priority over owners of common stock. For example: Zeta Corp. has issued one class of common stock and one class of preferred stock (the preferred stock being "$3 preferred"). In any given year, the owners of the common stock cannot be paid a dividend until the owners of the preferred stock have received a dividend of $3 per share. The preference can also be expressed as a percentage, such as "4 percent preferred." If this is the case, the owners of common stock cannot be paid a dividend until the preferred shareholders have received a dividend equal to 4 percent of the par value of their shares.

Shares that are preferred as to dividends may or may not be cumulative. The effect of a **cumulative dividend preference** is that if dividends are not paid in any year in the amount of the preference, they accumulate and must be paid in a future year before any dividend is paid to common shareholders. A majority of courts have held that preferred stock *is* cumulative unless there is an express statement in the articles of incorporation that it is not.

Furthermore, shares that are preferred as to dividends may or may not be participating. Holders of **participating preferred stock** are not only entitled to the original dividend, but, after the common shareholders receive a specified amount, they also share with the owners of common stock any additional dividends. Most of the time there is an express statement in the articles of incorporation that preferred stock is nonparticipating. But even without such a provision, a majority of courts have held preferred stock to be nonparticipating—in most states the only way for preferred stock to be participating is for the articles of incorporation to say that it is.

**Liquidation Preferences:** Owners of preferred stock sometimes are given a preference as to the distribution of corporate assets in the event that the corporation is dissolved. It is customary to limit this preference to the par value of the preferred shares plus any unpaid dividends. And, of course, a liquidation preference gives preferred shareholders a priority only over common shareholders, not over creditors of the corporation.

## *Preemptive Rights*

**Common-Law Treatment:** Suppose that Jupiter Corp. has a capitalization of $100,000 consisting of 1,000 shares of $100 par value common stock. X owns 100 shares of this stock. The corporation is in need of additional capital funds, so the shareholders authorize the issuance of another 1,000 shares. (This authorization is accomplished by a vote of the shareholders to amend the articles of incorporation.) If X is not given an opportunity to purchase shares of the new issue of stock, her proportionate interest in the corporation obviously will be reduced, and this will decrease her voting power and may result in her receiving a smaller amount of income from dividends.

For these reasons, the courts traditionally have recognized a concept known as the **preemptive right.** When a corporation issues new stock, the common-law preemptive right gives each shareholder an opportunity to purchase the number of new shares that will maintain his or her proportionate interest in the corporation. A shareholder possessing a preemptive right must be given notice and a reasonable amount of time to exercise the right by purchasing new shares. Anyone who fails to exercise this right within a reasonable time loses the right with respect to that particular issue of stock. A 30-day period for exercising the right has been frequently used and is generally deemed reasonable.

Preemptive rights are of vital importance in a *close corporation,* where each shareholder possesses a substantial interest in the enterprise and usually takes an active role in management. But the significance of preemptive rights diminishes when the corporation's stock is *publicly sold and traded* (i.e., when the company is a so-called "publicly held" corporation). In the latter case, the number of shareholders is often quite large and each shareholder usually owns a relatively small portion of the total outstanding shares.

Courts have not recognized preemptive rights in all circumstances. Following are two of the most important situations in which such rights have been held not to exist.

***Treasury Stock:*** If a corporation sells shares that it has been holding as treasury stock, it is obvious that this is not a "new issue" of shares and that there is no reduction in the proportionate interests of existing shareholders. Therefore, shareholders do not have preemptive rights with respect to sales of treasury stock.

***Shares Issued for Consideration Other than Money:*** A corporation may sometimes have a good reason for accepting something other than cash as the consideration for shares that it issues. This occurs very frequently in connection with a *merger.* As we will see in Chapter 40, the merger of two corporations can be achieved by various means. In some cases the acquiring corporation may issue new shares of its stock, which will then be exchanged for the assets or the shares of the acquired corporation. In other situations not involving a merger, a corporation might issue shares to be used in the purchase of patent rights, real estate, equipment, or other property. Or shares may be issued and used as part of a compensation package to recruit a top executive. In these examples and in other instances of noncash share issuances, the corporation is ordinarily pursuing legitimate objectives that may be hindered, if not completely defeated, by the exercise of preemptive rights on the part of existing shareholders. For this reason, courts have generally held that preemptive rights do not apply to noncash issuances.

***Statutory Treatment:*** In the earlier mentioned example of Jupiter Corp., the recognition of X's preemptive right was an easy matter. But the financial structure of many modern corporations is much more complex than that of Jupiter. This is particularly true of publicly held corporations, which often have several different classes of stock, each carrying different rights and preferences. This diversity of classes, coupled with the large number of shareholders, often makes it impractical to give complete recognition to preemptive rights. Furthermore, as previously mentioned, preemptive rights are often not of vital importance in publicly held corporations. For these reasons, most state statutes today permit the articles of incorporation to determine the matter of preemptive rights. The articles can limit the circumstances in which these rights exist or can abolish them altogether. In actual practice, most publicly held corporations have abolished preemptive rights in their articles.

## *Transferability of Shares*

Shares of corporate stock are recognized by the law as items of property. As is true of other kinds of property, shares ordinarily can be sold or otherwise transferred as the owner wishes. Thus a shareholder has the right to transfer his or her shares to someone else unless a valid restriction has been placed on such transferability.

***Restrictions:*** In some circumstances, it may be desirable for the corporation to restrict the shareholder's right to transfer his or her shares. Such restrictions are commonly employed by *close corporations,* because the shareholders themselves, who are few in number, actively manage the corporation and deal personally with one another on a daily basis. For example, assume that A, B, and C are the only shareholders of Prestige Corp. A and B will not want to wake up one morning and find that C has transferred his interest to D, a complete stranger with whom they will then have to share the management of the business.

Most restrictions on transferability take the form of *options to purchase,* which provide that a shareholder who wishes to sell his or her shares must first offer them to the corporation or to the other shareholders. Such restrictions are generally valid if a *reasonable time limit* is set for the exercise of the option. Provisions aimed at restricting transferability can be included in the articles or bylaws, but they are more often established by agreements among all the shareholders.

The existence of a transferability restriction should always be indicated explicitly on the **stock certificate.** The stock certificate is the formal document of particular shares. It also provides evidence of the *agreement between the corporation and the shareholder* as to preferences, voting rights, and other terms. If the certificate does not include a notice of transfer restrictions, a purchaser of the shares is not bound by the restriction unless it can be proved that he or she knew of it.

**Method of Transfer:** An agreement for the sale of stock in a close corporation normally is reached by individualized negotiation between the seller and buyer. (The other shareholders must also be involved in many cases, because contractual restrictions on transfer frequently exist in close corporations.) When shares of a publicly held corporation are traded, however, the sale is usually accomplished through a stock broker. The broker has access to the public market for corporate stock in two ways. First, with respect to the shares of a corporation that is listed on one of the national or regional stock exchanges, the broker has access through membership in the exchange where the company's stock is listed or through contact with another broker who is a member of that exchange. Second, with respect to the shares of a corporation whose shares are publicly traded but that is not listed on an exchange, the broker has computerized access to the so-called *over-the-counter (OTC)* market.

Performance of an agreement to sell shares is accomplished by the owner's endorsement and delivery of the stock certificate in return for payment.[1] Although the transfer of ownership technically requires no other formalities, as a practical matter it is extremely important that the buyer properly notify the corporation of the change in ownership so that the corporation's shareholder list can be changed. The corporation's records do not actually determine ownership, but they do determine who receives various information from the corporation, such as proxy materials, notice of shareholder meetings, and financial and operational reports. Corporate records of share ownership also determine where dividend checks are sent and who is permitted to vote at the shareholders' meeting.

## *Inspection Rights*

Unless limited by statute, every shareholder possesses the basic right of *access to corporate records.* This includes not only the right to inspect and copy corporate records personally but also the right to employ accountants, attorneys, stenographers, or other assistants as may reasonably be required to get the necessary information.

The right of inspection is one that possesses a definite potential for abuse. It could be used, for example, merely for harassment during a struggle for control of the corporation. Or a competitor could purchase a few shares and use the right to obtain trade secrets or other confidential information. Furthermore, even if the purposes for the inspection are legitimate, the existence of a large number of shareholders might cause unrestricted inspection rights to be impractical.

For these reasons, limitations are often placed on the inspection right. An illustration of the types of limitations that are frequently imposed is found in Sec. 52 of the Model Act:

> Any person who shall have been a holder of record of shares . . . at least six months immediately preceding his demand or shall be the holder of record of . . . at least five percent of all the outstanding shares of the corporation, upon written demand stating the purpose thereof, shall have the right to examine, in person, or by agent or attorney, at any reasonable time or times, for

---

[1] Under Sec. 8-319 of the UCC, an unperformed agreement for the sale of securities usually must be in writing to be legally enforceable.

any proper purpose its relevant books and records of accounts, minutes, and record of shareholders and to make extracts therefrom.

The following case presents an excellent illustration of a corporation's response to a rather wide-ranging request by a shareholder for inspection of corporate records, and of the court's review of both the request and the company's response.

## Riser v. Genuine Parts Co.
Court of Appeals of Georgia,
258 S.E.2d 184 (1979)

Riser, a shareholder and a former employee of Genuine Parts Co., made demand upon the corporation for copies of a lengthy list of corporate documents. The corporation responded by providing a variety of papers, including (1) shareholder lists; (2) minute books of directors' meetings; (3) minute books of the stock option committee's meetings; (4) corporate bylaws; (5) audited annual reports; (6) unaudited quarterly reports; (7) statements of attorneys' fees for 1974-76; and (8) the securities registration statements, prospectuses, and proxy statements filed by the corporation with the SEC.

On the other hand, the corporation refused to provide the following information: (1) Monthly profit and loss statements for the past five years of the corporation's 286 company-owned jobbing stores, 39 auto parts centers, and a wide range of other divisions and subsidiaries were not disclosed to Riser on the grounds that they were irrelevant and misleading because all intra-company sales reflected on such reports would be eliminated before preparation of the corporation's overall profit and loss statements. (2) Earnings projections for all divisions and subsidiaries were not given to Riser because, according to the corporation, the quarterly and annual financial reports furnish all the necessary information of this type. (3) Attorneys' work papers and other files relating to the investigation of the corporation by the Federal Trade Commission, were refused on the grounds that such information is legally privileged. (4) Records of investments of pension and retirement funds of the corporation, its divisions and its subsidiaries, were refused on the grounds that such information is confidential and not relevant to any proper purpose of Riser. (5) All data relating to a merger between the corporation and Motion Industries, including the statements and opinions of the attorneys, were refused on the grounds that such information is confidential. (6) All corporate tax returns and all reports submitted to the board of directors by the auditors were refused on the grounds that this information was already provided in the annual profit and loss statements. (7) All records relating to aircraft purchase and maintenance, plus the flight logs for such aircraft, were refused because, according to the corporation, it owns only one airplane and does not maintain a separate category for the airplane in its records of costs and maintenance.

Riser filed suit against the corporation asserting his rights under the Georgia statute permitting shareholder inspection of "books and records of account, minutes, and record of shareholders," and demanding disclosure of those documents that had been refused by the corporation. The trial court held that the corporation did not have to disclose any of the material that had been refused, and Riser, the plaintiff, appealed.

**Decision:** The judgment for defendant corporation was affirmed, with one exception: the corporation had to disclose one item it had previously refused—the material relating to the corporation's investment of plaintiff's retirement plan contributions. The plaintiff's reasons for the requests, determining whether adequate records were being kept and assessing the performance of management and the condition of the company, are proper motives in general. Basic records, such as the register of shareholders, will be provided to a requesting shareholder almost automatically if the requestor's motive is proper. The appellate court agreed with the trial court's statement that the requesting shareholder has the burden of showing a proper purpose as to specific materials and "this burden should become somewhat heavier as the information sought becomes increasingly remote from the statutory objects of 'books and records of account, minutes and record of shareholders.'" The relevant Georgia statute gives the trial court a great deal of discretion in determining whether a request for documents outside the normal meaning of "books and records of account, minutes and record of shareholders" is made for a proper purpose and can feasibly be complied with by the corporation. With the one exception, the corporation's reasons for refusing to supply several requested items were valid and the trial court acted properly in upholding the corporation's refusal. ∎

# LIABILITIES OF SHAREHOLDERS

As we saw earlier, one of the basic attributes of the corporate form of doing business is the limited liability of the owners. That is, shareholders are usually not personally liable for the debts of the corporation; they may lose their investment in the corporation if it is a failure, but usually their liability ends there. We also saw that in a few exceptional circumstances the separate identity of the corporation can be disregarded and liability imposed on the shareholders. We will now examine a few other situations in which the personal liability of shareholders can become an issue.

## *Liability on Stock Subscriptions*

A **stock subscription** is an offer by a prospective investor (a "subscriber") to buy shares of stock in a corporation. The ordinary rules of contract law apply to such offers, and they can thus be revoked prior to acceptance by the corporation—with two important exceptions:

**1.** Stock subscriptions are frequently made by the promoters before formation of the corporation. It is not uncommon for several promoters to agree that their subscriptions cannot be revoked for some period of time. In such a case, the subscriptions are irrevocable for the agreed time.

**2.** The statutes of a majority of states provide that a subscription is irrevocable for a certain time period, unless the subscription itself expressly provides that it can be revoked. For example, the Model Act provides for a six-month period of irrevocability.

A stock subscription can be made either before or after incorporation. Where it is made prior to formation of the corporation, some states hold that acceptance of the offer occurs automatically when the corporation comes into existence. In other states, the subscription must be formally accepted by the board after incorporation. Where the subscription is made for shares in an existing corporation, there obviously must be a formal acceptance by the board. (Of course, the sale of shares by an existing corporation often does not involve stock subscriptions at all. Instead, the corporation itself is frequently the offeror.)

In any event, an accepted stock subscription is a contract, and the subscriber is liable for damages to the corporation if he or she breaches that contract by refusing to pay the agreed price.

## *Liability for Watered Stock*

Corporate stock can be issued either as par value or no-par value stock. If the articles of incorporation assign a specific value to each share of stock, it is known as **par value stock.** The par value is a completely arbitrary figure and may be only nominal. It may or may not have any relation to the actual value of the stock as reflected by the financial condition of the corporation. If the articles do not state a value, the stock is called **no-par value stock.** In such a case, the board of directors normally places a value (called the "stated value") on the shares after they have been authorized but before they are actually issued.

Par value shares cannot lawfully be issued unless the corporation receives consideration at least equal to the par value. In the case of no-par value shares, the consideration must be at least equal to the stated value.

The consideration can be in the form of money, property, or services actually rendered (not just promised) to the corporation.[2] The board of directors generally determines the value of property or services received in return for shares, and this determination ordinarily will not be reviewed by a court so long as it appears to have been made in good faith.

Shares issued for less than the par or stated value are referred to as **watered stock.** A shareholder is personally liable for the deficiency (the "water"). This liability is usually to the corporation itself, but in some states an owner of watered stock is liable directly to the corporation's creditors when their claims cannot be satisfied out of corporate assets. Thus a shareholder can incur liability even if he or she has paid the agreed price for the shares, if that agreed price was less than the par or stated value. Of course, this rule applies only to the initial purchase of shares from the corporation upon their issuance, not to later purchases from the shareholder ("on the market") or to purchases of treasury shares.

## *Liability for Illegal Dividends*

Shareholders usually are liable for the return of any dividend that was improperly paid, as indicated below:

---

[2]In some states, the preincorporation services rendered by promoters or others can be treated as consideration for shares.

1. If the dividend is paid while the corporation is *insolvent,* shareholders are *always* liable for its return.

2. In the case of any other illegal dividend, a shareholder usually is required to account for its return only if he or she *knew* of the illegality when receiving payment. Examples of such illegal dividends are those that cause the corporation to become insolvent (as opposed to those made when the corporation is already insolvent) and those paid from an unauthorized source.

The liability of a shareholder for the return of an illegal dividend ordinarily is to the corporation itself. If the corporation is insolvent, however, the shareholder's liability often is to the corporation's creditors instead. Of course, those directors responsible for paying the illegal dividend also incur liability. When directors are subjected to such liability, however, they generally are allowed to recoup their loss from those shareholders who *knew* the dividend was illegal when they received it.

## RIGHTS OF CORPORATE MANAGERS

In the following discussion, the rights of directors will be dealt with separately from the rights of officers and other managerial employees. The reason for this is that some of the rights possessed by directors are unique to their position.

### *Directors*

**Recognition and Participation:** A director who has been properly elected possesses several rights of a very basic nature—for instance, the right to be recognized as a director by his or her associates, the right to receive notice of board meetings, and the right to attend and participate in them. A duly elected director who is excluded from recognition or participation by his or her associates can obtain a court order enforcing these rights.

**Inspection:** The right of directors to inspect all corporate records is somewhat similar to the inspection right possessed by shareholders. However, the reasons for allowing inspection by directors are even stronger than those for allowing shareholder inspection. Directors *must* have complete access to corporate records in order to fully discharge their decision-making responsibilities. It obviously would be unfair to hold them responsible for paying an illegal dividend, for example, if corporate financial records had not been completely at their disposal.

Because of this compelling need for access to corporate books, most states hold that a director's right of inspection is *absolute and unqualified* (that is, not subject to the various limitations that are often placed on a shareholder's inspection right). Of course, a director's abuse of this right can provide a basis for his or her removal from the board, as illustrated in *Campbell v. Loew's, Inc.*, in the previous chapter. And a director is liable for any damage to the corporation resulting from abuse of the right (such as its use for an improper purpose). But in the majority of states where the director's inspection right is absolute, *neither the other directors, the officers, nor the shareholders can restrict his or her examination of corporate records.*[3]

**Compensation:** The traditional rule was that directors were not entitled to compensation for their services to the corporation. This rule was predicated on the assumption that directors were usually shareholders and would receive their compensation in the form of dividends. It also took into account the fact that some directors also served as corporate officers and received compensation for their services in those positions.

The basis for this rule is not applicable to many modern corporations, however. It is not uncommon today for individuals having little or no stock ownership to serve as directors. Furthermore, a great many directors serve only as directors and do not hold other positions with the corporation.

For these reasons, there is a growing trend in modern corporations toward compensation of directors as such. The traditional rule provides no real obstacle to this trend, because it simply holds that directors have no inherent *right* to be compensated. They can in fact be paid if there is a valid authorization for such payment in the articles or bylaws. Indeed, the statutes of some states today go even farther, providing, for example, that the board of directors can fix the compensation of its own members unless the articles or bylaws state otherwise. Directors are, of course, responsible for any abuse of this power.

---

[3] The courts in a *few* states, however, have held that a director's inspection right can be denied where his or her motive is obviously hostile or otherwise improper.

**Indemnification:** The performance of their management responsibilities sometimes causes directors to become involved in legal proceedings. For example, the directors may be sued by a shareholder who claims that they acted negligently in managing the corporation. Or they may be charged by the government in a civil or criminal suit with a violation of the antitrust laws.

The costs of such lawsuits to the individual director, in terms of both expenses and potential liability for damages or fines, may be quite substantial. Under the common-law rule a director had no right to be indemnified (reimbursed) by the corporation for expenses or other losses. Today, however, the statutes of most states do permit indemnification of corporate directors in some circumstances. An excellent illustration of the modern statutory trend is found in Sec. 5 of the Model Act. Under this provision, a corporation generally is authorized (but not required) to indemnify a director regardless of whether he or she actually committed a wrongful act, "if he acted in good faith and in a manner he reasonably believed to be in . . . the best interests of the corporation." On the other hand, the Model Act applies special rules to a "shareholders derivative suit," which is discussed in detail later in this chapter. In such a suit, which is brought by a shareholder in behalf of the corporation (rather than in the shareholder's own behalf), indemnification usually is not permitted if the director is actually found guilty of negligence or misconduct in the performance of his or her duties.

## *Officers and Other Managerial Employees*

Corporate officers and other individuals who have managerial responsibilities are simply *employees* of the corporation.[4] It naturally follows, therefore, that the rights they have with respect to compensation and other matters are determined by their employment contracts.

Since their positions involve them in corporate decision making, officers and other managerial employees are subject to many of the same risks of litigation as are directors. Thus the rules regarding indemnification are the same for directors, officers, and managerial employees. That is, everything we have said about indemnification of directors applies with equal force to all others occupying management positions.

## LIABILITIES OF CORPORATE MANAGERS

Those who manage the corporate enterprise owe to the corporation and its shareholders a number of basic duties that can be classified under the headings of *obedience, due care,* and *loyalty.* A corporate manager incurs personal liability for the failure to fulfill any of these duties. In addition to these fundamental duties, certain special liabilities are imposed by federal securities laws. Unlike the previous section on the *rights* of corporate managers, our discussion of *liabilities* make no distinction between directors and other types of managers. The duties and liabilities of all who manage the corporation are essentially the same.

## *Obedience*

Corporate managers have a duty to see that the corporation obeys the law and confines its operations to those activities that are within the limits of its corporate powers. If they knowingly or carelessly involve the corporation in either an illegal or *ultra vires* act, they are personally liable for any resulting damage to the corporation.[5]

## *Due Care and the Business Judgment Rule*

The duty of due care is sometimes referred to as the duty of "diligence." It is, in effect, a duty "not to be negligent." In applying this standard, courts normally require a director, officer, or other manager to exercise the kind of care that an ordinarily prudent person would exercise in a similar position and under similar circumstances.

Although held to a standard of reasonable care, a manager is not liable for honest mistakes of judgment. Under normal circumstances, courts are ex-

---

[4] The word *employee* is used in a nontechnical sense. Managers and supervisors are not considered "employees" under some other specialized laws, such as those governing labor-management relations. But such laws are not our concern here.

[5] Of course, any manager who participates in the commission of an illegal act also may be personally subject to fines or other penalties imposed by the particular law.

tremely reluctant to interfere with the business decisions of a corporation's managers, and will not second-guess the wisdom of those decisions. Courts feel that if bad decisions are made, the proper remedy is for shareholders to exercise their voting power to bring in new management, and not to subject business decisions to judicial review. Under this so-called **business judgment rule,** a court will not hold a manager liable for the consequences of a decision, even if harm resulted to the corporation, so long as the manager made a reasonably informed decision and apparently acted in a good faith belief at the time that the decision was in the best interests of the corporation. The term "business judgment rule" is simply another way of referring to the manager's basic duty of due care.

Examples of those relatively unusual situations in which a manager might be liable despite the business judgment rule would include (1) the failure to review corporate records or to carefully consider other relevant evidence before making an important decision; (2) the failure to seek expert advice (such as that of an attorney, accountant, or engineer) about a technical matter that clearly called for input from such an expert; and (3) the complete reliance on someone else's opinion without making a reasonable inquiry, where the person giving the opinion clearly had a selfish interest in the matter, or where the opinion itself obviously was erroneous or baseless (such as relying totally on the opinion of another director who had a personal interest in the matter, or relying on the advice of an attorney that bid rigging or bribery was perfectly legitimate).

Although the business judgment rule, or duty of due care, is applied to all aspects of the manager's decision-making role, in recent years courts have been called upon with increasing frequency to apply the standard to managers' actions when the corporation is the target of an attempted takeover by another company. For this reason, in the discussion of mergers in the next chapter, a separate section deals with the responsibilities of corporate managers when responding to a takeover attempt.

In a non-takeover context, the next two cases each involve claims that corporate directors violated the duty of due care in their management of the business.

### Shlensky v. Wrigley
Appellate Court of Illinois,
237 N.E.2d 776 (1968)

Shlensky, the plaintiff, was a minority shareholder in Chicago National League Ball Club, Inc. The corporation owned and operated the major league professional baseball team known as the Chicago Cubs. The individual defendants were directors of the Cubs. Defendant Philip K. Wrigley was also president of the corporation and owner of approximately 80 percent of the corporation's shares.

Shlensky filed suit in behalf of the corporation (a derivative suit), claiming that it had been damaged by the failure of the directors to have lights installed in Wrigley Field, the Cubs' home park. No trial was held, however, because the trial court dismissed his complaint on the ground that it did not set forth a claim that the law would recognize even if his version of the facts were correct. Shlensky appealed.

**Decision:** The trial court's dismissal of the suit was affirmed. Plaintiff's argument that the directors were acting for reasons unrelated to the financial interest and welfare of the Cubs was highly questionable. The directors could well have concluded not only that the installation of lights would have a deleterious effect on the surrounding neighborhood, but that this in turn might have an adverse effect on patronage. In other words, they could have concluded that a substantial number of patrons would be unwilling to attend games at a park in a poor neighborhood. Furthermore, the corporation's long-run interest in the property value of Wrigley Field could require attention to the condition of the surrounding neighborhood.

Accordingly, plaintiff did not prove his claim—even if his allegations of fact were true—that Wrigley and the other directors had acted contrary to the best interests of the corporation and its shareholders. ■

### Francis v. United Jersey Bank
Superior Court of New Jersey, 392 A.2d 1233 (1978)

Pritchard & Baird Intermediaries Corp. (Pritchard & Baird) was engaged in the business of being a "reinsurance broker." (If an insurance company has a very large individual risk or a number of similar risks on which it has given coverage, it often protects itself from too heavy a loss by shifting the risk to another large insurer or group of insurers. It does this by "reinsuring," that is, by purchasing insurance on all or part of the underlying risk from one or more other insurers. A reinsurance broker brings the parties together in a reinsurance arrangement.) Charles Pritchard, Sr., the founder of the company, was for many years its principal shareholder and controlling force. In 1970 he took his sons, Charles, Jr., and William, into the business. Because of the father's advancing age, the two sons played an increasingly dominant role in the affairs of the corporation. After the father's death in 1973, the sons took complete control.

Pritchard & Baird had been a successful company under the control of Charles, Sr., even though he engaged in various questionable business practices. He commingled the funds of different clients, commingled the company's funds with his own personal funds, and kept incredibly poor records. However, his clients were always taken care of and his creditors were always paid. After his sons took over, they continued his sloppy business practices but did not continue taking care of clients and paying creditors. In essence, they "looted" the company of millions of dollars and by the end of 1975 had plunged it into bankruptcy.

Francis was appointed as trustee in bankruptcy for Pritchard & Baird. In this capacity he sought to recover for Pritchard & Baird's creditors several million dollars which had been wrongfully taken from the company. He brought suit against two defendants: (1) the father's estate, of which United Jersey Bank was administrator; and (2) the estate of Lillian Pritchard. Lillian Pritchard was the wife of Charles, Sr., and had served as a director of the corporation from its creation until its bankruptcy. She died after the bankruptcy proceedings began. Apparently because of the size of Lillian Pritchard's personal estate, the primary question in the case was whether she had acted negligently in her role as a director by not discovering and stopping the illegal actions of her sons. If so, her estate would be liable for that negligence. A summary of the trial court's opinion follows. (Note: There was no mention of the whereabouts of the two sons.)

**Decision:** The court held Lillian Pritchard's estate liable for over $10 million. Although Lillian Pritchard did not have actual knowledge that her sons were looting the corporation, she should have known. The company's financial statements, prepared by an accountant, showed an extremely rapid drop in its net worth for several successive years. Even a casual glance at these statements would have revealed that something was terribly wrong within the company. If Mrs. Pritchard had ever looked at one of the statements, she would have at least had the opportunity to make further inquiry. Her failure to pay the slightest attention to the corporation's affairs was negligence.

There really is no such thing as a "figurehead" director. All corporate directors have the responsibility to exercise some supervision over the corporate business. The allegation that Mrs. Pritchard was just a "simple housewife" is both irrelevant and insulting. She was a person who assumed a responsibility but who did not make the slightest effort to fulfill that responsibility. ∎

---

### Loyalty

Directors, officers, and other corporate managers are deemed to be *fiduciaries* of the corporation they serve. Their relationship to the corporation and its shareholders is one of trust. They must act in good faith and with the highest regard for the corporation's interests as opposed to their personal interests. Several problems that commonly arise in the context of the duty of loyalty are discussed below.

**Use of Corporate Funds:** Obviously, a director or other party who occupies a fiduciary position with respect to the corporation must not use corporate funds for his or her own purposes.

**Confidential Information:** A director or other manager sometimes possesses confidential information that is valuable to the corporation, such as secret formulas, product designs, marketing strategies, or customer lists. The manager is not allowed to appropriate such information for his or her own use.

**Contracts with the Corporation:** A corporate manager who enters into a contract with the corporation should realize that it is not an "arm's-length" transaction. That is, the manager must make a full disclosure of all material information he or she possesses regarding the transaction. Furthermore, if the contract is at all unfair to the corporation, it is *voidable* at the corporation's option.

For obvious reasons, courts have not looked kindly upon contracts in which a *director* has a personal interest. (The contract might be with the director personally or with another company in which he or she has a financial stake.) If a contract of this nature was authorized at a board meeting where the presence of the interested director was necessary for a quorum or where this director's vote was required for a majority, most states hold the contract to be voidable at the corporation's option *regardless of its fairness.*

**Corporate Opportunity:** The **corporate opportunity rule** prohibits corporate managers from personally taking advantage of business opportunities that, in all fairness, should belong to the corporation. An obvious violation of this rule occurs when a manager has been authorized to purchase land or other property for the corporation but instead purchases it for himself.

Application of the corporate opportunity rule is sometimes not so clear-cut, however. A much more difficult problem is presented, for instance, when a director or other manager is confronted with a business opportunity arising from an *outside source* rather than from direct corporate authorization. For example: C is a director of Ace Air Freight, a corporation engaged in the business of transporting freight by air. C learns that M, a third party, has a used airplane in excellent condition that he is offering for sale at a low price. Can C purchase the airplane for himself? If the plane is of a type suitable for the corporation's freight business, the answer probably is no. He is obligated to inform the corporation of the opportunity.

This example illustrates the so-called "line of business" test employed by most courts in resolving such problems. Under this approach, a corporate manager cannot take personal advantage of a business opportunity that is *closely associated with the corporation's line of business.* Furthermore, the rule includes opportunities not only in the area of current corporate business but also in areas where the corporation might naturally expand.

Of course, if the corporation is actually offered the opportunity and *rejects* it, an individual manager can then exploit it. Some courts also have held that if the corporation is financially *unable* to take a business opportunity, a manager can lawfully take personal advantage of it without first disclosing it to the corporation. Other courts, however, have held that the manager always must first disclose the opportunity and give the corporation a reasonable time to decide whether it is able and willing to exploit the opportunity before the manager can personally seize it.

The following case illustrates the type of double-dealing that the corporate opportunity doctrine is designed to prevent. In addition, the case involves the question whether a corporation's financial inability to take a business opportunity excuses a manager's failure to disclose the opportunity to the corporation.

---

**Klinicki v. Lundgren**
Supreme Court of Oregon,
695 P.2d 906 (1985)

In January 1977 Klinicki conceived the idea of engaging in the air transportation business in Berlin, West Germany. He discussed the idea with his friend Lundgren. At that time, both men were furloughed Pan American Airlines pilots stationed in West Germany. They decided to enter the air transportation business, planning to begin operations with an air taxi service and later to expand into other service, such as regularly scheduled or charter flights. In April 1977 they incorporated Berlinair, Inc., as an Oregon corporation. Lundgren was the corporation's president and a director; Klinicki was vice-president and a director. Each owned 33 percent of the corporation's stock. Lelco, Inc., a corporation owned by Lundgren

*(continued)*

and members of his family, also owned 33 percent, and the corporation's attorney owned the remaining 1 percent. Berlinair obtained the necessary government license, purchased an aircraft, and in November 1977 began passenger service.

As president, Lundgren was primarily responsible for developing and promoting Berlinair's transportation business. Klinicki was in charge of operations and maintenance. In November 1977 Klinicki and Lundgren, as representatives of Berlinair, met with representatives of the Berliner Flug Ring (BFR), a consortium of Berlin travel agents that contracts for charter flights to take German tourists to various vacation resorts. The BFR contract was considered a lucrative business opportunity by those familiar with the air transportation business, and Klinicki and Lundgren had contemplated pursuing the contract when they formed Berlinair. After the initial meeting, all subsequent contacts with BFR were made by Lundgren or other Berlinair employees acting under his direction.

During the early stages of negotiations, Lundgren believed that Berlinair could not obtain the contract because BFR was then satisfied with its existing carrier. In early June 1978, however, Lundgren learned that there was a good chance that the BFR contract might be available. He informed a BFR representative that he would make a proposal on behalf of a new company. On July 7, 1978, he incorporated Air Berlin Charter Co. (ABC) and was its sole owner. On August 20, 1978, ABC presented BFR with a contract proposal, and after a series of discussions it was awarded the contract on September 1, 1978. Lundgren effectively concealed from Klinicki his negotiations with BFR and his diversion of the BFR contract.

Klinicki, as a minority stockholder in Berlinair, filed suit against ABC and Lundgren for usurping a corporate opportunity of Berlinair. The trial court ruled in Klinicki's favor and imposed a constructive trust on ABC, which required ABC's profits to be turned over to Berlinair. The court of appeals affirmed, and Lundgren and ABC appealed.

---

**Decision:** The judgment for plaintiff Klinicki was affirmed. Lundgren violated his duty of loyalty to Berlinair by usurping the corporate opportunity. A director or officer must fully disclose a corporate opportunity and give the corporation a chance to take advantage of the opportunity. If the corporation is unable or unwilling to pursue the deal the director or officer may then do so personally. But disclosure is an absolute requirement. Lundgren did not disclose the opportunity to the corporation (Klinicki) before seizing it, and the court therefore made no inquiry into the question of whether Berlinair was financially able to pursue the BFR contract. ■

---

**Controlling Shareholders:** In some situations, **controlling shareholders** are placed under fiduciary duties similar to those owed by directors, officers, and other managers. If a single shareholder, or a group of shareholders acting in concert, owns a sufficient number of shares to control the direction of corporate affairs, the possibility exists that they will try to exercise this control so as to further their own personal interests at the expense of the corporation and the other shareholders. Corporate control must not be abused, however, and the controlling shareholders are required to act in the best interests of the corporation as a whole and with complete fairness to minority shareholders.

## Liability under Federal Securities Laws

The **Securities Act of 1933** and the **Securities Exchange Act of 1934** place a number of specific duties and liabilities upon corporate managers and others. In many cases, an activity that violates one of these federal regulatory provisions also amounts to a breach of duty under the state common-law rules previously discussed. Even in such instances, however, these federal statutes are of extreme importance because they (1) define some types of duties with greater precision than existed at common law, (2) provide for penalties that may not have existed under state law, and (3) provide for enforcement by a federal agency, the **Securities and Exchange Commission (SEC).** Several of the more important federal statutory provisions relating to duties and liabilities are discussed below. (These and other provisions of the securities laws are dealt with in much greater detail in Chapter 41, "Securities Regulation.")

**Registration Statements:** As indicated in Chapter 37, the 1933 Act requires corporations to file a registration statement with the SEC when nonexempt issues of securities are offered for sale in interstate commerce or through the mails. Under Secs. 5 and 11, if a violation occurs, either by filing a misleading registration statement or by failing to file one at all, the corporate managers involved in the securities issuance can be held personally responsible. Others involved, such as accountants, attorneys, and underwriters, may also be liable.

**Use of Inside Information:** Section 10b of the 1934 Act essentially prohibits *fraud* in the sale or purchase of securities.[6] Pursuant to this section, the SEC has promulgated Rule 10b-5, which makes the 10b prohibition more specific.

One of the most important features of Rule 10b-5 is that it effectively prohibits the use of **material inside information** in the sale or purchase of securities. The purpose of this rule is to maintain the fairness and integrity of securities markets and to protect investors who do not have the advantage of an "inside" connection. A person violating the prohibition against "inside trading" may be an actual insider such as a director, officer, manager, or employee who acquires valuable information about the company because of the person's position in the company. "Temporary insiders" also can be guilty; these are individuals such as attorneys, financial printers, and investment bankers who have a temporary fiduciary relationship with the company that brings them into possession of important corporate information.

In addition, a person who acquires such information as part of a fiduciary relationship with someone other than the corporation can be liable if he or she violates the confidentiality of that relationship by using the information for private gain. Such persons are called "misappropriators." One example would be an employee of a financial printing company that is employed by an "acquiring" company to print documents relating to a planned takeover of a "target" corporation. As part of her job, the employee of the printing company obtains information that, if divulged, would affect the price of the target company's stock. If she breaches the fiduciary relationship with her employer by "misappropriating" the information—i.e., by trading in the target's shares—she has committed illegal insider trading. This violation occurs even though the employee and her employer, the printing company, had no fiduciary relationship with the corporation whose shares were traded (i.e., the target company).

Either an actual or temporary insider, or a misappropriator, also can be held liable for intentionally "tipping" the information to someone else with the intent that the "tippee" use the information by trading on it. In such a case the "tipper" violates Section 10b even if he or she does not personally trade on the information. "Tippees" also are liable if they trade on the tipped information or tip it to someone else.

In any of these situations, a person can be found guilty of insider trading only if the information is *material*. Information is material if it probably would affect the investment decision of an average investor. Stated somewhat differently, information is material if making it public would probably affect the market price of the company's shares. Examples include earnings or earnings projections that are significantly different than had been expected, government investigations of wrongdoing in the company, merger proposals or negotiations, important discoveries of minerals or new technology, and so on.

In addition to being material, the information also must be *nonpublic* at the time it is improperly used. Information is public if an investor could find out about it by conducting a reasonable and proper investigation. Even if an average investor would have to go through a professional investment advisor or broker to discover the information, it is still public if the professional can get the information through proper means.

Finally, an actual or temporary insider or a misappropriator is guilty of inside trading only if it can be proved that the person *knew or had reason to know* that the information was nonpublic at the time it was misused. This requirement usually can be inferred from surrounding circumstances.

**Short-Swing Profits:** Under Sec. 16b of the 1934 Act, **short-swing profits** are defined as any profits made on either the sale and subsequent purchase or purchase and subsequent sale of equity securities where both purchase and sale take place within a six-month period. This section does not actually prohibit short-swing profits; it does, however, prevent certain insiders from keeping any short-swing profits made on transactions in the shares of their own corporation. Such profits made by these insiders must be turned over to the corporation. The **insiders** who are required to turn over their short-swing profits to the corporation are (1) directors, (2) officers, and

---

[6] This provision applies to fraud in the sale or purchase of securities *after* their initial issuance. Another provision, Sec. 17 of the 1933 Act, prohibits fraudulent practices with respect to the original issuance.

(3) owners of 10 percent or more of any type of shares issued by the corporation.[7]

Section 16b is essentially a preventive measure designed to discourage the misuse of inside information. It applies, however, without regard to whether the particular insider actually possessed material inside information. But it applies only to the types of insiders who are specifically listed. Short-swing profits made by others are not subject to the statute.

**Proxy Solicitation:** In the previous chapter we saw that corporate managers often solicit proxies from shareholders prior to a shareholders' meeting. In the "proxy statement" sent to shareholders, the managers request authority to cast votes in behalf of the shareholders for particular board candidates and for particular proposals the managers have made. The shareholders are, of course, under no obligation to grant this request; they can attend the meeting themselves or choose not to vote at all.

Section 14a of the 1934 Act prohibits making any false or misleading statements in the proxy material sent to shareholders. Furthermore, the proxy statement must disclose all material facts relating to the matters to be voted on. In other words, when corporate managers solicit proxies, they must reveal to the shareholders, in a clear and truthful manner, all facts that will probably affect the voting decision. Violation of this section subjects the responsible managers to personal liability.

## Shareholder Derivative Suits

As we saw in the previous chapter, the basic power to manage a corporation rests with the board of directors. Ordinarily, if a shareholder disagrees with a decision of the board to act or not act in a particular way, the shareholder's only recourse is to use his or her voting power, alone or in combination with the voting power of other shareholders, in an attempt to elect different directors at the next annual shareholders' meeting. Unless the shareholder can prove that directors have violated the duties of obedience, due care, or loyalty, the shareholder can obtain no assistance through the courts.

This fundamental principle of board control also applies to any decision regarding the filing of a lawsuit in behalf of the corporation. The board of directors has the power and the responsibility to determine whether the corporation's legal rights have been violated, and if so, whether it is in the best interests of the corporation to initiate legal action. Thus, if one or more shareholders feels that a wrong has been committed against the corporation and files a lawsuit *in behalf of the corporation,* the shareholder may find the courts less than totally receptive. Such a suit, called a **shareholder derivative suit** (or "stockholder" derivative suit) will be heard by the court only after the shareholder has fulfilled one of the following conditions.

**Demand and Refusal:** The shareholder must have formally demanded that the board of directors initiate legal action in behalf of the corporation but the board refused to do so. After the demand and refusal, the shareholder then files a derivative suit. When deciding whether to permit the shareholder to maintain the derivative suit, the court reviews the directors' decision not to take legal action under the same standards that are applied to other decisions by directors. Thus, the shareholder must prove that the directors' refusal violated the duties of obedience, due care, or loyalty to the corporation. The court's interpretation of the duty of due care is, of course, governed by the business judgment rule. As a result, courts are very reluctant to permit derivative suits when the shareholder claims that the corporation has been harmed by a person or firm totally unconnected with the corporation (such as a supplier, customer, or government agency). Whether to take legal action against such a party is a fundamental matter of business judgment within the directors' discretion, and the court will not second-guess that judgment so long as the directors apparently examined the facts and did not act in their own self-interest.

If the shareholder has demanded that the board take legal action against one or more of its own members, and the board refuses, the court applies the same standards in reviewing the board's refusal as it applies when an alleged wrong was committed by an outsider. If a majority of the board was not implicated in the alleged wrongdoing, there is no evidence that any members of this majority otherwise acted in their own self-interest, and the members of this majority apparently gave careful consideration to the charges and the relevant evidence, the decision not to take legal action usually will be upheld under the business

---

[7] Under Sec. 16a, these types of insiders are also required to make periodic reports to the SEC of *any* personal transaction in the shares of their corporation.

judgment rule and the court will dismiss the shareholder derivative suit. On the other hand, if a majority of the board was implicated in the alleged wrongdoing, the vote of a member with a personal interest in the decision was necessary for there to be a quorum or a majority decision not to take legal action, *or* the majority apparently did not give careful consideration to the charges and relevant evidence, the court probably will permit the derivative suit to continue. Once the derivative suit is allowed, the court then will fully review the merits of the charges to determine whether any of the directors violated their duties to the corporation.

When deciding whether to file a lawsuit, either on its own initiative or in response to a shareholder demand, the board may act as a whole or it may delegate the responsibility to a **special litigation committee** composed of several of the directors. Appointment of a special litigation committee is particularly desirable when improper action by one or more of the directors themselves has been alleged. In fact, in such a situation it is highly desirable that the committee consist of the board's *outside directors* (i.e., those not owning substantial amounts of shares or holding high management positions in the corporation). The decision of a special litigation committee that it would not be in the corporation's best interests to take legal action against one or more of the directors is far more likely to be upheld by a court when the committee consists of disinterested outside directors.

**Futility of Demand:** If the shareholder filing a derivative suit has not made a formal demand to the board that it take legal action, the court will permit the derivative suit to continue only if the shareholder convinces the court that such a demand would be futile. For example, if a shareholder produces plausible evidence that a majority of the board was guilty of wrongdoing or otherwise was acting in its own self-interest, the shareholder will be permitted to maintain the derivative suit without having first made a formal demand to the board. The court then will examine the merits of the charges against the directors.

It should be noted that a shareholder's lawsuit is characterized as a derivative one only if it asserts that harm has been done to the corporation as an entity or to shareholders as a group. If the shareholder has a plausible claim that action by directors or officers caused harm that is personal or unique to this particular shareholder, and not to the corporation as an entity or to its shareholders in general, the lawsuit is not a derivative one and the shareholder can pursue it as any other claim. Such a claim, that is not derivative in nature, is much more likely to arise in the context of a close corporation.

## SUMMARY

Although the various people involved in a corporation have many common objectives, their own individual interests can also be important. A substantial body of legal rules has been developed to achieve a workable balance among these interests. These rules, for example, provide shareholders with certain rights. Among the most important of these rights are those concerning voting, dividends, preferences, preemptive rights, transferability of shares, and inspection of corporate records. All of these rights are subject to limitations. Shareholders also are subject to liabilities in several situations, including contractual liability on stock subscriptions and liability for watered stock and illegal dividends.

A corporate director is given a number of rights necessary to the effective performance of his or her functions, including the right to be recognized as a director by associates, the right to receive notice of board meetings, and the right to attend and participate in those meetings. A director also has the right of inspection. Although there is no inherent right to compensation, the law normally permits corporations to compensate directors, and the trend is clearly toward the granting of substantial compensation. A director also has no inherent right to be indemnified for liabilities incurred while acting on corporate matters, but today the law usually does permit such indemnification. The rights of other managers, such as officers, are normally determined by their employment contracts with the corporation.

Directors, officers, and other corporate managers owe to the corporation and its shareholders the duties of obedience, due care, and loyalty. The business judgment rule is used by courts when interpreting and applying the duty of due care. Corporate managers may be held liable under federal securities laws in several situations, including those in which they either fail to file required registration statements or file statements that are misleading, buy or sell the company's securities on the basis of material inside information, make short-swing profits on the company's securities, and fail to reveal in a clear and truthful manner all relevant material information in a proxy solicitation. The general rule that the directors are charged with managing the corporation includes the filing of lawsuits in behalf of the corporation, and attempts by shareholders to sue in behalf of the corporation (shareholder derivative suits) are subject to very substantial limitations.

## KEY TERMS

**Treasury stock**
**Dividend**
**Stock dividend**
**Common stock**
**Preferred stock**
**Cumulative dividend preference**
**Participating preferred stock**
**Preemptive right**
**Stock certificate**
**Stock subscription**
**Par value stock**
**No-par value stock**
**Watered stock**
**Business judgment rule**
**Corporate opportunity rule**
**Controlling shareholders**
**Securities Act of 1933**
**Securities Exchange Act of 1934**
**Securities and Exchange Commission (SEC)**
**Material inside information**
**Short-swing profits**
**Insiders**
**Shareholder derivative suit**
**Special litigation committee**

## QUESTIONS AND PROBLEMS

1. Hanrahan, a shareholder of Puget Sound Corp., demanded the right to inspect corporate records prior to a shareholders' meeting. His purpose was to obtain the names and addresses of other shareholders so that he could urge them to elect directors who would seek a merger of Puget Sound with another corporation. Puget Sound refused the demand, and Hanrahan sued to enforce his right of inspection. Will Hanrahan win? Explain. (*Hanrahan v. Puget Sound Power & Light Co.*, 126 N.E.2d 499, 1955.)

2. Pioneer Savings & Loan Co. issued an additional 100,000 shares of common stock. The circumstances were such that Pioneer's existing shareholders should have been accorded preemptive rights. Because of a mistake, however, several of these shareholders had not been given an opportunity to exercise those rights. Upon discovering the situation, Pioneer sought to cancel the entire issue of stock. Can it do so? Discuss. (*Bursan v. Pioneer Savings & Loan Co.*, 121 N.E.2d 76, 1954.)

3. Explain the difference in the relative importance of preemptive rights in a close corporation and in a publicly held corporation.

4. An amendment to the articles of Constantin & Co. stated that "the holders of the preferred stock shall be entitled to receive, and the company shall be bound to pay thereon, but only out of the net profits of the company, a fixed yearly dividend of Fifty Cents (50¢) per share." The dividend was not paid in a particular year, and a preferred shareholder sued to compel its payment. Assuming that the company actually made a net profit that year, will the shareholder prevail? Discuss.

5. The articles of Apex Co. provide that, if preferred shareholders fail to receive a dividend in any given year, they "shall be entitled to the same voting power as the holders of the common stock." Except for this situation, the preferred shares of Apex carry no voting rights. One year the preferred shareholders did not receive a dividend. At the next shareholders' meeting, where the preferred shareholders were to exercise their newly acquired voting power, an issue arose as to the extent of this power. The preferred shareholders contended that the meaning of the quoted provision was that they *as a class* should have the same voting power as that possessed by the common shareholders *as a class*. Under this interpretation, each share of the preferred would be worth eighty-nine votes, rather than the ordinary one vote per share to which the common shareholders would be entitled. Are the preferred shareholders correct? Discuss.

6. The directors of Southwest State Bank were warned by the bank examiner that the bank was in a precarious condition. After the warning, the directors made no audit of the bank's affairs for the next year, did not check the cashier's statement as to loans made, and thus did not discover that the cashier was frequently using forged notes in the names of third parties to cover his embezzlements. The bank's directors were sued for negligence by a shareholder. What is the result? Explain.

7. Reese, a director of Lafleer, Inc., was seventy-five years old and in failing health. He was suspicious of the activities of the company's vice-president, but because of his poor health he no longer attended board meetings and did nothing about the matter. It was later discovered that the vice-president had involved the company in a number of prohibited activities, including illegal campaign contributions. The company was damaged by these activities, and a shareholder sued not only the vice-president but also Reese. Is Reese liable? Discuss.

8. Johnson, the president of Continental Co., badly mismanaged its affairs and caused the company to sustain heavy losses. The board of directors had allowed Johnson a free hand in running the company. A shareholder filed a derivative suit against Johnson and all the directors for negligence. One of the directors, Wembley, claimed that he should not be held responsible. His defense was that, because of the great distance between his home and Continental's headquarters (2,500 miles), he had not attended a board meeting in almost a year. Should Wembley's defense shield him from liability? Discuss.

9. Explain the rationale behind the corporate opportunity rule.

10. Carlton owned 1 percent of the shares of Zepco, Inc. He was not an officer or director. He sought to buy a piece of equipment worth $30,000 from Zepco for $25,000. Zepco's board of directors voted 9–2 to sell the equipment to him for $25,000. After the sale, another Zepco shareholder sued Carlton to force him either to return the equipment or to pay an additional $5,000. What was the result? Discuss.

CHAPTER 40

# CORPORATIONS

## MERGER, CONSOLIDATION, AND TERMINATION

In the preceding chapters we examined the nature and formation of the corporation, its basic operation, and the rights and liabilities of its individual participants. This final chapter focuses on more unusual aspects of corporate operation. Initially, we discuss changes in the fundamental structure of the corporation brought about by mergers and consolidations. Then we deal with the various circumstances in which the corporate existence can be terminated.

## MERGERS AND CONSOLIDATIONS

The terms *merger* and *consolidation* are often used interchangeably to describe any situation in which two or more independent businesses are combined under a single ownership. Technically, however, there is a difference in meaning between the two terms. A **merger** is the absorption of one existing corporation by another; the absorbing corporation continues to exist while the one being absorbed ceases to exist. A **consolidation,** on the other hand, is a union resulting in the creation of an entirely new corporation and the termination of the existing ones. Symbolically, a merger can be illustrated by the equation $A + B = A$, while a consolidation is represented by $A + B = C$.

The distinction between mergers and consolidations has very little practical significance. Whether a particular combination is a merger or consolidation, the rights and liabilities of the corporations and their shareholders and creditors are the same. For this reason, the popular term *merger* is sometimes used in the following discussion to describe both combinations.

### Reasons for Merging

The reasons for merging two corporations vary greatly, depending on the particular circumstances. The most common reasons are discussed below.

**General Advantages of Size:** In many cases the motive for a merger is the acquisition of some or all of the benefits that result from an increase in size. An ability to buy and produce in larger amounts, for example, may bring about greater efficiency and lower overhead costs.

Because the combination possesses greater resources than its constituent companies had possessed separately, it may be able to obtain capital more easily and to engage in more extensive advertising and research. Furthermore, the larger organization sometimes finds it easier to attract the best managers, technical advisers, and other personnel.

These advantages of size are usually legitimate. Occasionally, however, the motives of corporate managers in pursuing mergers may be less valid. Sometimes growth is sought merely for its own sake, without any resulting increase in efficiency. For instance, a merger might produce a much more impressive set of financial statements for the acquiring company, not through any improvement in its performance but simply because of the "larger numbers" brought about by the acquisition. And, of course, the personal rewards of the corporate managers may increase accordingly.

**Eliminating Competition:** Some mergers are motivated by the desire to lessen the rigors of competition. The most obvious example, of course, is the acquisition of a direct competitor for the purpose of suppressing competition between the two.[1] Mergers brought about solely for this purpose are less common than in the past, however, because of the enforcement of the antitrust laws.

---

[1] A merger between two competitors is called a *horizontal merger.*

**Acquisition of Know-how:** A large corporation might acquire a much smaller one in the same or a related line of business for the purpose of obtaining patents or other technological know-how owned by the smaller company. In addition, some of that company's employees might possess useful capabilities.

**Guaranteed Supplies or Outlets:** A company might seek to assure itself of an adequate supply of an essential item by acquiring a producer of that item. Conversely, a guaranteed outlet might be the motivating factor behind the acquisition of a company that purchases a product supplied by the acquiring firm.[2]

**Diversification:** One corporation sometimes wishes to acquire another in a totally unrelated line of business solely for the purpose of diversifying. Doing business in several diversified lines removes some of the economic risks that exist when a corporation commits all its resources to a single industry.[3]

**Defensive Mergers:** Occasionally a corporation actually seeks to be acquired by another. For example, suppose that X Corporation is attempting to acquire Y Corporation. However, the managers and shareholders of Y Corporation are opposed to the takeover because of differing business philosophies. Y Corporation thus arranges a merger with Z Corporation to avoid the takeover attempt by X. Such a merger is often called a **defensive merger.**

Another merger that might be classified as defensive is illustrated as follows. Jones, the founder of General Steel Corp. and its primary manager throughout its existence, now wishes to retire. Jones is afraid that "his" company will not be managed properly in his absence, so he arranges for General Steel to be acquired by a larger company whose management capabilities he trusts.[4]

**Tax Savings:** Although tax considerations are beyond the scope of this discussion, the lessening of federal income tax liability sometimes is an important reason for undertaking a particular merger. For example, a company facing a huge tax liability might acquire another company with large tax credits or loss carry-overs. Obviously, however, there should be good reasons for a merger other than just tax benefits, or the combination may later turn out to be problematic.

**Unused Capital:** Sometimes a merger may simply be an investment outlet for unused capital. For example, a corporation may have accumulated profits that it does not choose to pay out as dividends. The acquisition of another corporation may be an attractive investment opportunity for these funds.

## *Procedures*

The procedure for a merger or consolidation is governed by statute. Every state has a statute that authorizes the combination of two or more *domestic* corporations. In almost every state, the statutory procedures also allow the combination of a domestic and a *foreign* corporation. The procedures vary somewhat from state to state, but they can be outlined generally as follows:

1. The board of directors of each corporation must adopt a resolution approving the merger or consolidation. This resolution should set forth:

   a. The names of the combining corporations and the name of the corporation that will result from the combination.

   b. The terms and conditions of the proposed combination.

   c. The method and basis to be used in converting the securities of each corporation into securities of the resulting corporation.

   d. In the case of a merger, any changes caused thereby in the articles of incorporation of the surviving corporation. In the case of a consolidation, the resolutions of the respective boards should include the entire articles of incorporation for the resulting new corporation.

2. The plan must then be approved by the shareholders of each corporation, at either an annual or a special meeting. The vote required for approval varies among the states from a simple majority to four-fifths of the outstanding shares; a *two-thirds* vote is the most common requirement.

3. After shareholder approval, the plan for the combination must be submitted to the appropriate state official (usually the secretary of state) in a docu-

---

[2] A merger between firms in a supplier-customer relationship is called a *vertical merger.*

[3] A merger between firms in unrelated lines of business is called a *conglomerate merger.*

[4] In this case Jones is probably a controlling shareholder in General Steel Corp. and thus has the power to carry out his wish.

ment referred to as the **articles of merger or consolidation.**

4. If all documents are in the proper form, the state official issues a **certificate of merger or consolidation** to the surviving or new corporation.

## *Merger with a Subsidiary*

In a majority of states, the procedures have been greatly simplified for the merger of a subsidiary corporation into its parent. These streamlined procedures allow such a merger to be consummated *without shareholder approval.*

If the parent owns *all* the subsidiary's shares, the only requirements are that (1) the parent's board of directors adopt a resolution setting forth the plan for the merger, (2) articles of merger be filed, and (3) a certificate of merger be issued. If some of the subsidiary's shares are owned by others, there is an additional requirement that these minority shareholders be given prior notice of the merger. These simplified procedures can be used, however, only if the parent owns a *very large portion* of the subsidiary's shares (90 or 95 percent in most states).

## *Effects of Merger or Consolidation*

The effects of a merger or consolidation can be summarized as follows:

1. The corporations who are parties to the merger become a single corporation.

2. All of the corporate parties to the merger, other than the surviving or new corporation, cease to exist.

3. The surviving or new corporation possesses all the rights, privileges, and powers of the combining corporations.

4. The surviving or new corporation acquires all the property of the combining corporations without the necessity of a deed or other formal transfer.

5. The surviving or new corporation is liable for all the debts and obligations of the combining corporations.

6. In the case of a merger, the articles of incorporation of the surviving corporation are deemed to be amended to the extent, if any, that changes in these articles are stated in the articles of merger. In the case of a consolidation, the articles of consolidation serve as the articles of incorporation for the new corporation.

## *The Appraisal Right*

At common law a merger, consolidation, or other combination required the *unanimous* approval of the shareholders of each corporation. In an effort to lessen the severity of this restriction on corporate action, all the states at a fairly early time passed statutes providing for approval by less than unanimous vote.

One result of this change, however, was that any shareholders who disapproved of a merger might find themselves unwilling investors in a corporation different from the one whose shares they originally had purchased. Out of concern for fairness to these shareholders, provisions were included in the state laws giving them the right to sell their shares back to the corporation for cash. This right has generally become known as the **appraisal right.**

A dissenting shareholder must strictly follow the required procedures, or this appraisal right will be lost. The most important requirement is that the dissenting shareholder *object to the merger and demand payment within the designated time period.* For example, the Model Act provides that a dissenting shareholder must give the corporation written notice of objection to the proposed combination either prior to or at the meeting where the matter is voted upon. If the merger is approved at the meeting, the Model Act requires that the dissenting shareholder make written demand for payment from the corporation within the next ten days.

When the merger or consolidation takes place, the surviving or new corporation must make a written offer to each dissenting shareholder regarding the purchase of his or her shares. Under the Model Act, this offer must be made within ten days after the effective date of the combination and must be accompanied by the most recent balance sheet and income statement of the corporation whose stock is owned by the dissenting shareholder.

The overriding concern of the dissenting shareholder is, of course, the price to be paid for his or her shares. The requirement found in most state statutes is that the corporation pay the "fair value" of the shares, computed as of the date of the merger. If the dissenting shareholder feels that the offer does not reflect the fair value of the shares and refuses to accept it, the corporation can institute a court action to have the value determined. The shareholder can personally file such a suit only if the corporation fails to do so within a specified period of time (under the

**Figure 40.1  Steps in Merger or Consolidation**

Model Act, 60 days after the merger). In the court proceeding, the judge sometimes appoints an official "appraiser" to hear evidence and recommend a fair value.

Figure 40.1 illustrates the steps in a typical merger or consolidation.

## Asset and Stock Acquisitions

Thus far our discussion has been limited to "statutory" mergers and consolidations, in which all of the requisite formalities have been carried out. However, corporations can achieve the same practical results by less formal means, particularly through *asset acquisition* and *stock acquisition*. In legal circles these transactions are sometimes called *de facto* **mergers**, as contrasted with "statutory" mergers and consolidations. In everyday usage they are more frequently referred to simply as "mergers," or "takeovers."

**Asset Acquisitions:** Suppose that X Co. wishes to acquire all or most of the assets of Y Co. It may purchase these assets with cash or with a combination of cash and promissory notes. Or it may make the purchase by issuing shares of its stock to Y in return for Y's assets.

Although the practical effect of such an asset acquisition is to merge one company into the other, the *acquiring company* usually does not have to obtain shareholder approval. Ordinarily, the only situation in which the approval of the acquiring company's shareholders must be obtained is when the assets are to be bought with shares and there are not enough authorized but unissued shares to make the purchase. In such a case the shareholders will have to amend the articles of incorporation to authorize the issuance of additional shares.

The rules are substantially different, however, with respect to the *acquired company*. The sale of all or most of its assets puts its shareholders into a position very different from the one they previously occupied. Therefore, they must approve the sale. Indeed, in the past, the common-law rule required unanimous approval. This strict requirement was relaxed, however, along with the relaxation of the approval requirement for formal mergers and acquisitions. Today, the general rule is that the shareholders of the acquired company must approve the sale by the same vote required for a merger or consolidation. And the dissenting shareholders of the acquired company possess an appraisal right just as in a formal merger or consolidation.

After the sale, the corporation that has sold its assets may simply choose to dissolve. It may, however, decide to start its operations anew (either in the same or some other line of business). A third alternative is for the corporation to continue in existence as a **holding company** (or **investment company**). In the latter case, its sole (or at least primary) function will be to own and receive income from securities, such as those it may have received as the purchase price for its assets.

**Stock Acquisitions:** A frequently employed method for achieving a combination between two corporations is the purchase by one corporation of the shares of another. This generally is accomplished by action of the acquiring company's board of directors, without any need for approval by its shareholders. Unless the purchase is being made merely for investment purposes, the aim of the purchaser obviously is to obtain a sufficient number of shares so that it *controls* the company whose shares are acquired. Control usually requires ownership of over 50 percent of a corporation's voting shares. Although the present discussion assumes acquisition by one *corporation* of a controlling stock interest in another corporation, the same principles apply to such an acquisition by an *individual*.

**Open Market Purchases:** Although it is theoretically possible for the acquiring company to negotiate individually with the target company's shareholders for the purchase of their shares, this usually is not done. If the target company's shares are publicly traded, the large number of shareholders involved makes individual negotiation practically impossible; if the target company is a close corporation, transfer of the shares is usually restricted by a shareholder agreement that can be changed only by the shareholders as a group. Instead of individual negotiation, if the target company's shares are publicly traded the acquiring company can purchase the shares on the open market. Even if a sufficient number of shares can be obtained on the market, however, this method of acquiring control may be too slow if the target company's board opposes the change of control. Although the formal approval of the target company's board of directors is not a legal requirement for acquisition of the company's shares, the board is in a position to make acquisition of a controlling interest much more difficult. As we will see in a separate section on directors' responsibilities in a takeover situation, the target company's board often will take various steps either to persuade its shareholders not to sell their shares or to make the acquisition less attractive to the acquiring company. The slowness of open market purchases for the purpose of acquiring control gives the target company's board ample time to devise various strategies to defeat the attempted takeover.

*Tender Offers:* Because fast action is often necessary, it has become common for the acquiring company to make a **tender offer** for the target company's shares. A tender offer is a publicly advertised offer to the target company's shareholders to buy at a specified price those shares that are "tendered" (i.e., made available) to the acquiring company. The main advantage of a tender offer is speed—the acquiring company is more likely to obtain enough shares for control before the target company's board can erect effective barriers to the acquisition.

The price specified in a tender offer usually is substantially above the prevailing market price for the shares, because the market price does not reflect the value of having control over the corporation. Although this price often is in cash, it may consist of a stated number of the acquiring company's shares per share of the target company, or a combination of cash and a stated number of the acquiring company's shares. The specified price can even take the form of bonds or other property owned by the acquiring company, or a combination of such property with cash.

If the acquiring company's objective is to obtain control over the target company, the acquiring company may not want to purchase any shares unless it is assured of gaining control. Thus, the tender offer may provide that it will be valid only if accepted by the holders of a stated number of shares. On the other hand, the acquiring company may not want to buy any more shares than are necessary to achieve control. Thus, the tender offer may expressly limit the number of shares to be purchased and may provide that if more than this number are tendered, they will be purchased on a proportionate basis from all tendering shareholders.

The **Williams Act,** passed by Congress in 1968, amended the Securities Exchange Act of 1934 to regulate tender offers. One of the primary aspects of this law is the requirement that the individual or corporation making a tender offer supply a wide variety of detailed information to the target company's shareholders so that those shareholders can make a completely informed decision whether to tender their shares. (The Williams Act is discussed in more detail in Chapter 41, Securities Regulation.)

***Proxy Contests*** Sometimes a relatively small stock acquisition can provide a launching pad for a proxy contest that ultimately leads to a merger. Recall from previous chapters that shareholder voting power can be concentrated in several ways, including voting agreements, voting trusts, and proxies. In a publicly held corporation acquiring proxies from a large number of shareholders is the most common method of concentrating voting power to gain or keep control. Existing managers usually maintain control by acquiring proxies giving them the power to vote for themselves, or others they choose as directors. Occasionally one or more shareholders desiring a change in control may challenge existing management by attempting to persuade other shareholders to give their proxies to the challengers instead of current management.

An individual or company wishing to accomplish a merger sometimes will use a strategy that involves an initial stock acquisition followed by a proxy contest and then a formal merger. Suppose, for example, that X Corp. wishes to acquire and merge with Y Corp. X Corp. might acquire a significant (but much less than controlling) interest in Y Corp. by purchasing some of Y's shares in the open market. As a shareholder of Y Corp., X Corp. then launches a proxy contest prior to Y's next annual shareholders' meeting. In its communications with Y's other shareholders, X Corp. must reveal its true intentions. If X Corp.'s contest with Y Corp.'s management for proxies is successful, X Corp. will be able to elect its own candidates to Y Corp.'s board of directors. These directors will then vote to merge with X Corp. and again solicit proxies from Y's shareholders for formal approval of the merger.

## Management Responsibilities in a Takeover Attempt

In modern times, many of the court cases applying corporation law principles arise in the takeover context, and much of this litigation focuses on the response of the target company's board to a tender offer. When one corporation attempts to acquire a controlling stock interest in another corporation, the target company's board of directors occupies a central role, for two reasons. First, the board's recommendation to accept or reject a tender offer often will strongly influence the decision of the target company's shareholders. Second, as mentioned previously, the board has the ability to erect a number of obstacles to the takeover.

Sometimes the target company's board will view a tender offer favorably and will recommend to the shareholders that they sell their shares. It must be realized, however, that a formal merger probably would have been negotiated and presented to the target company's shareholders if that company's board had been favorably disposed toward the takeover. Consequently, in most situations the target company's board will resist the takeover attempt. A tender offer that is resisted by the target company's board is referred to as a "hostile" or "unfriendly" tender offer.

When responding to a tender offer, directors owe to the corporation and its shareholders the same fundamental duties of obedience, due care, and loyalty as they owe in other circumstances. Fulfilling these duties becomes especially demanding in the takeover setting, however, because the future ownership, control, and direction of the company are suddenly at stake, and tender offers do not permit a great deal of time for study and reflection.

**The Duty of Loyalty in the Takeover Setting:** Directors are fiduciaries of the corporation and its shareholders, and the duty of loyalty requires that directors act in the best interests of the shareholders. Inside directors, who also hold office or own significant numbers of shares, must be especially vigilant to fulfill the duty of loyalty because the takeover attempt presents them with an inherent conflict. Their position as directors requires them always to serve the interests of shareholders as a group, and sometimes a takeover by another company actually is in the best interests of those shareholders. On the other hand, inside directors face the probable loss of their management jobs if the takeover is successful. A court will conclude that directors have violated the duty of loyalty if it finds that they acted primarily for the purpose of maintaining their positions and control, or if they did not properly disclose relevant facts to shareholders. Directors must fully assess the tender offer and make a good faith decision whether the shareholders will receive the greatest benefit by accepting or rejecting it. If the directors make any recommendation to shareholders concerning a tender offer or other takeover attempt, they must fully disclose all material information relevant to that recommendation.

*Weinberger v. UOP, Inc.*, 457 A.2d 701 (Del. 1983), provides a good example of inadequate disclosure to shareholders during a takeover. In 1974 Signal Company acquired 50.5 percent of UOP's shares. Some of this stock was bought directly from UOP in the form of authorized but unissued shares, but most of it was acquired through a tender offer. In 1978 Signal sought to acquire the remainder of UOP's stock at $21 per share. This offer was presented to UOP's board, which included four members who also served on Signal's board. Two of these directors serving on both boards conducted a study and concluded that buying the remainder of UOP's stock would be a good investment for Signal at a price of up to $24 per share. However, the president of UOP, who was a former Signal officer, then commissioned another study by the Lehman Brothers investment banking firm. In commissioning this other study, UOP's president dealt with a partner of the Lehman Brothers firm who also served on UOP's board of directors. The study was performed very quickly and resulted in a conclusion that the $21 per share offer represented a fair price. UOP's board approved the offer from Signal to purchase UOP's remaining stock at $21 per share and formally recommended the sale to UOP's shareholders, who also approved it. Some of UOP's shareholders filed suit challenging the fairness of the transaction, however, primarily on the grounds that a complete disclosure of relevant information had not been made to the UOP shareholders. The Supreme Court of Delaware agreed with the plaintiffs and awarded damages to the UOP shareholders. The court's holding was based on its conclusion that UOP's board and Signal (as a controlling shareholder) had violated the fiduciary duty of loyalty to UOP's shareholders by failing to disclose the initial study indicating that any price up to $24 would be a good investment for Signal.

**Due Care and the Business Judgment Rule in the Takeover Setting:** Courts apply the business judgment rule when determining whether directors have fulfilled their duty of due care in responding to a takeover attempt. Directors are expected to give the matter the type of concentrated attention warranted by its great importance, but courts do take into account the fact that tender offers frequently do not give the target company's board a substantial amount of time for study. Essentially, the business judgment rule requires directors to make a decision that is as fully informed as the circumstances permit.

**Shark Repellants:** The boards of target companies have many methods at their disposal for resisting a takeover attempt. These methods sometimes are referred to generally as "shark repellants." Although some of these methods can be implemented without any change in the corporation's articles or bylaws, a few of them do require that the articles or bylaws be amended. It is increasingly common for boards of publicly held companies to anticipate possible future takeover attempts by persuading the shareholders to amend the articles or bylaws in advance. In addition, in some states directors have power to amend the bylaws themselves; this power sometimes is sufficient to enable the board to quickly adopt effective takeover defenses. Some of the more common shark repellants are described below.

***The Poison Pill:*** This maneuver involves granting existing shareholders special rights that are contingent upon the occurrence of a takeover. For instance, shareholders might be given the contingent right to purchase at a very low price shares in the new company that would result from a takeover. The exercise of this right after a takeover would greatly dilute the value of the new corporation, and thus makes the target company much less attractive to a prospective acquirer. Poison pills are usually upheld by the courts so long as the target company's board fully and completely disclosed to its shareholders all material information relating to the effect of the measure before it was adopted.

***Finding a White Knight:*** Sometimes the target company's board may resist a hostile tender offer by negotiating a merger with a third company (a "white knight"). Presumably, the white knight has a management philosophy more closely resembling that of the target company, or will permit the target company to continue operating independently after the merger. The target company's directors usually do not violate their duties to shareholders when negotiating a merger with a white knight, so long as (1) their recommendation that shareholders approve the merger is accompanied by complete factual disclosure, and (2) it does not deprive shareholders of a fair price for their shares by prematurely taking the company off the market. An example of the second situation is found in *Revlon v. MacAndrews & Forbes Holdings*, 506 A.2d 173 (Del. 1986). In that case, the target company's board resisted a hostile takeover attempt by negotiating a "lock-up option" with a third corporation. In this arrangement, the board of the target company (Revlon) gave the white knight (1) an option to acquire two valuable divisions of Revlon at a bargain price if another acquirer obtained as much as 40 percent of Revlon's shares, (2) a commitment that Revlon's board would not deal with any other prospective acquirer, (3) a promise to pay the white knight a $25 million cancellation fee if another acquirer obtained as much as 20 percent of Revlon's shares, and (4) access to Revlon's private financial data that was not available to any other potential acquirer. The Delaware Supreme Court held that Revlon's board violated its duty of due care to its shareholders by prematurely taking the company completely off the market and ending any possibility that the price of Revlon's shares might be "bid up" by a takeover contest between competing acquirers.[5]

***The Self-Tender:*** In the following case, the duty of due care is applied to the use of a "self-tender" as a shark repellant. In the decision, the Delaware Supreme Court provides an excellent discussion of the business judgment rule in the takeover setting, and establishes some important principles for evaluating the actions of a target board in defending against a hostile takeover.

---

[5] The white knight itself must also be careful not to intervene after an agreement between the initial acquirer and the target has already been made. For example, Pennzoil Corporation attempted to acquire Getty Oil Company. Getty then entered a formal merger agreement with Texaco, the white knight. After Getty and Texaco merged, Pennzoil sued Texaco. Pennzoil claimed that it had a contract of merger with Getty before Texaco entered the picture, and that Texaco had committed the tort of wrongful interference with a contractual relationship. The jury and trial judge agreed with Pennzoil and rendered a $10.5 billion judgment against Texaco. The state appellate court affirmed the trial court's decision but reduced the damages to $9 billion. The two companies ultimately settled for $3 billion and Texaco went through a reorganization proceeding under Chapter 11 of the Bankruptcy Code.

---

## Unocal Corporation v. Mesa Petroleum Co.
Supreme Court of Delaware,
493 A.2d 946 (1985)

Unocal and Mesa are oil companies incorporated in Delaware. Mesa had previously acquired 13 percent of Unocal's stock, and in 1985 commenced a "two-tiered, front loaded" tender offer for the remainder. This type of tender offer consists of two stages, the first being much more attractive than the second. In this instance, the first tier of the offer was $54 cash per share for 64 million shares, or about 37 percent of Unocal's stock. The second tier, or back end, offered other securities, claimed to be worth $54 per share, in exchange for the rest of Unocal's stock. The securities offered in the second tier were highly subordinated bonds, often referred to as "junk bonds." Such bonds may have relatively high returns, but also carry a very high risk because the assets securing them are subject to substantial secured claims of other creditors that are superior to the claims of the bondholders.

Unocal's board, which consisted of eight independent outside directors and six inside directors, met five days after the tender offer was made to consider it. All of the outside directors and five of the six inside directors were present, and the meeting lasted nine and one-half hours. Detailed presentations were given by legal counsel regarding the board's obligations under both Delaware corporate law and the federal securities laws. The board then received a presentation from an expert financial advisor who discussed the basis for the opinions of two large investment banking firms that the Mesa proposal was wholly inadequate. The advisor stated that the minimum cash value that could be expected from a sale or orderly liquidation of 100 percent of Unocal's stock was in excess of $60 per share. He also showed slides outlining the valuation techniques used by the two investment firms and others, depicting recent business combinations in the oil and gas industry. Finally, the financial advisor presented various defensive strategies available to the board if it concluded that Mesa's tender offer was inadequate and should be opposed. One of these devices was a self-tender by Unocal for its own stock with a reasonable price range of $70 to $75 per share. The cost of such a proposal would cause the company to incur $6.1–$6.5 billion of additional debt, and a part of the presentation discussed Unocal's ability to handle this debt. The directors were told that the primary effect of this debt would be to reduce exploratory drilling, but that the company would remain a viable entity.

*(continued)*

The eight outside directors, constituting a clear majority of the thirteen members present, then met separately with Unocal's financial advisors and attorneys. Thereafter, they unanimously agreed to advise the board that it should reject Mesa's tender offer as inadequate, and that Unocal should pursue a self-tender to provide the shareholders with a fairly priced alternative. The board then reconvened and voted unanimously to reject the tender offer as inadequate. Two days later the same thirteen directors met again, with four directors participating by telephone as permitted by Delaware law, and heard a detailed presentation from Unocal's top financial officer and its assistant general counsel regarding the proposed terms of the self-tender. The ultimately voted unanimously to make the self-tender in the form of secured, unsubordinated Unocal bonds worth an aggregate of $72 per share. The self-tender was to become effective if the first tier of Mesa's tender offer was successful, provided for the purchase of the remaining 49 percent of Unocal's shares, and expressly excluded Mesa from being able to accept Unocal's self-tender for the shares Mesa owned.

Mesa filed suit in Delaware seeking an injunction prohibiting Unocal's self-tender. Mesa claimed that Unocal's board owed a fiduciary duty to act in the best interest of all shareholders, including Mesa, and that treating shareholders selectively (i.e., excluding Mesa from the self-tender) was a violation of this duty. Mesa also claimed that Unocal's board had violated its duty of due care. The trial court ruled in favor of Mesa and granted a preliminary injunction against Unocal and its directors. Unocal appealed to the Delaware Supreme Court.

**Decision:** The judgment for plaintiff Mesa Petroleum was reversed. Unocal's board seriously considered the matter, used the services of expert financial and legal advisors, and apparently tried to act in the long-term best interests of shareholders. There was a reasonable basis for their expressed belief that Mesa's offer was both inadequate and coercive, and Mesa was a known "greenmailer." (The term greenmail refers to the situation in which the corporation attempting a takeover has already acquired a substantial number of the target company's shares when it moves to obtain control, and in return for abandonment of the takeover attempt the target company purchases these shares from the acquiring company at a premium price [i.e., the "greenmail"] that is not available to other shareholders. Mesa had made huge profits by this method in several "unsuccessful" takeover attempts in recent years.) Although its primary duty was to shareholders, Unocal's board also was entitled to give some consideration to the effect of Mesa's tender offer on employees, customers, suppliers, and the community. Unocal's board did not violate either the duty of loyalty or due care; their actions in defeating the tender offer by making a self-tender that excluded Mesa were within the protective scope of the business judgment rule. ∎

**Comment:** After the *Unocal* case was decided, the federal Securities and Exchange Commission (SEC) adopted an "all holders rule," which prohibits the making of a tender offer that excludes any shareholders. The rule applies to all tender offers, including a self-tender. Thus, this rule will now prevent a target company from using a discriminatory self-tender as Unocal did to defeat an attempted takeover. Although the precise result in the case would be different today, the court's excellent discussion of the business judgment rule in the takeover setting continues to be completely valid. In particular, the *Unocal* case established two important precedents that are still generally valid. First, if a target corporation's board has conducted a reasonable investigation of a takeover proposal, it is permissible for the board to take into consideration the welfare of several different groups in deciding whether the proposal is fair and adequate. The interests of the target company's shareholders are the most important, but the board can also consider the welfare of employees, creditors, customers, and possibly others. Second, if the board decides that the proposal is not in the best interests of the corporation and its various shareholders, the board's degree of freedom in using defensive tactics increases with the degree of threat to these interests. In addition, the new SEC rule will not prevent a target company from using a self-tender, so long as it is not discriminatory. A self-tender sometimes can be an effective defensive measure even if it is not discriminatory.

***Employee Stock Ownership Plans:*** An employee stock ownership plan (ESOP) provides a company's employees with opportunities to own stock in the company. Such plans serve to reward key employees and to create more loyalty and greater productivity among all employees by giving them a stake in the corporation's future profitability. Thus, ESOPs almost always are completely valid personnel policies. The ESOP also can place shares of the company's stock in the hands of a group that is much more likely to want the corporation to remain as it is, instead of being taken over by another firm. Consequently, one of management's goals in creating an ESOP may also be to provide some degree of protection against hostile takeovers. Normally, this is a perfectly lawful strategy. Almost anything can be abused, however, including an ESOP. In the following case, the question is whether a target corporation's board misused an ESOP in order to entrench the positions of the inside directors. There also is a question in the case about whether the board used another practice—transferring stock to a subsidiary—in an improper way.

## Norlin Corp. v. Rooney, Pace Inc.
U.S. Second Circuit Court of Appeals, 744 F.2d 255 (1984)

Norlin Corp. is a company whose shares are listed on the New York Stock Exchange. It is incorporated in Panama, but with its principal place of business in New York. Piezo Electric Products, Inc., on two trading days, January 6 and 12, 1984, in conjunction with the investment banking firm of Rooney, Pace Inc., purchased 32 percent of Norlin's common stock in a series of separate market transactions. Fearful of an imminent takeover, on January 20 Norlin transferred 28,295 shares of common stock to Andean Enterprises, Inc., a wholly owned subsidiary, incorporated in Panama, purportedly in consideration for Andean's cancellation of a Norlin promissory note of $965,454. On January 25, Norlin's board approved a transfer of 800,000 authorized but unissued shares of preferred stock to Andean in exchange for a $20 million promissory note. Also on January 25, Norlin created an ESOP and appointed three board members as trustees. The board immediately transferred 185,000 common shares to the ESOP in exchange for a promissory note of $6,824,945. In its filings of required disclosures with the SEC, Norlin admitted that its board was the beneficial owner of, and had voting control over, all transferred shares. As a result of these transactions, the Norlin board controlled 49 percent of the corporation's outstanding stock. Norlin's chairman, Stevens, and president, Simpkins, wrote the company's shareholders indicating that they were taking all necessary steps to oppose the Rooney, Pace–Piezo offer. The letter offered no justification for the transactions other than to defeat the potential takeover.

Norlin's attorneys warned Norlin that their actions might cause the New York Stock Exchange to delist Norlin stock, and on March 15, the NYSE suspended trading in Norlin stock and indicated an intent to delist because issuance of stock to Andean and the ESOP resulted in a change of control of the company, which, under NYSE rules, requires shareholder approval.

Norlin filed suit in federal district court seeking a preliminary injunction against Piezo that would prohibit it from acquiring any more Norlin shares and require it to sell those it had already acquired. Norlin's suit was based on a claim that Piezo had violated federal securities laws in making the acquisitions, but the district court found that Piezo's acquisitions had been completely lawful and denied Norlin's request. Norlin did not appeal this ruling. Piezo filed a counterclaim against Norlin in district court, alleging that Norlin had acted illegally in issuing the stock to the ESOP and the subsidiary. The district court ruled for Piezo on its counterclaim and issued a preliminary injunction barring Norlin from voting any of the transferred shares. Norlin appealed.

**Decision:** The lower court's judgment was affirmed. Under either Panamanian or New York law, it is illegal for a wholly owned subsidiary (or even a controlled but not wholly owned one) to vote the shares of its parent company. In addition, although ESOPs are perfectly legitimate and it is usually legal for an ESOP to hold the shares of the employer-corporation, in this case Norlin's board violated its fiduciary duty of loyalty to its shareholders by transferring the shares to the ESOP. The evidence indicated no reason for the action other than perpetuating the control of Norlin's incumbent management. ■

---

**Informed Decision:** As we have seen, the duty of due care requires that directors make an "informed" decision. Thus, despite the business judgment rule, directors violate the duty of due care if they do not give appropriate attention to an important matter and do not seek expert advice when it is clearly needed.

In the case that follows, the target company actually initiated a "friendly" takeover by another company. After the resulting merger, several of the target company's shareholders challenged the action of the target company's board as having been "uninformed."

## Smith v. Van Gorkom
Supreme Court of Delaware,
488 A.2d 858 (1985)

Trans Union was a widely diversified company, with its most substantial earnings coming from its railcar leasing business. Federal tax laws gave Trans Union a tremendous amount of investment tax credits (ITCs) to offset against income, but accelerated depreciation deductions were decreasing its taxable income to such an extent that it was unable to use all of its ITCs. By not using its ITCs, Trans Union was losing millions of dollars in tax benefits. Van Gorkom had been an officer of Trans Union for 24 years, its Chief Executive Officer for 17 years, and Chairman of the Board for two years. He was nearing retirement, and personally owned 75,000 shares of Trans Union stock. Trans Union's board consisted of five outside and five inside directors. In late August, 1980, the board, strongly led by Van Gorkom, concluded that it should seek a merger with a company having large amounts of taxable income so that the ITCs could be used. The type of merger they wished to pursue was a "leveraged buyout," in which the acquirer would borrow the funds necessary to purchase Trans Union's stock and then use the cash flow from Trans Union's operations to service the debt. Van Gorkom and two other Trans Union officers and directors, Romans and Chelberg, performed calculations indicating that such a leveraged buyout would be "easy" at $50 per share and "very difficult" at $60 per share. No independent financial advisors were consulted, and no study was done to determine what actually would be a fair price for Trans Union's shares. The only studies were aimed at determining what price would make a leveraged buyout feasible.

Van Gorkom then arranged meetings on September 13 and 15 with Jay Pritzker, a social acquaintance and well-known takeover specialist. At the first meeting, Van Gorkom proposed that Pritzker accomplish a leveraged buyout of Trans Union at $55 per share, and at the second meeting Pritzker indicated a definite interest in the proposal. Two other Van Gorkom–Pritzker meetings were held on the 16th and 17th, which were also attended by two other Trans Union officers (Chelberg and Peterson) and a paid consultant. At a final private meeting between Van Gorkom and Pritzker on September 18, Pritzker stated definitely that a corporation completely owned by Pritzker would offer to buy all of Trans Union's stock for $55 per share, that Trans Union's board would have only three days to act on the proposal, and that Trans Union would have to arrange the financing needed by Pritzker to make the acquisition.

Pritzker then had his attorney draft a formal merger agreement. In the meantime, Van Gorkom arranged for Trans Union's banks to finance Pritzker's purchase. On Friday, September 19, Van Gorkom called a special meeting of the Trans Union board for the next day. The directors were not given an agenda or told of the purpose of the meeting. At the meeting on September 20, which lasted two hours, presentations were made only by Van Gorkom and his personal attorney. Romans, one of the inside directors who had earlier performed the calculations concerning an appropriate price per share, told the board that his calculations did not deal with the question of a fair price but only with the question of a price that would make a leveraged buyout feasible. Copies of the formal merger agreement did not arrive until the end of the meeting, and were not examined by the directors. The board then voted to approve the merger and submit it to shareholders. That night at a social event hosted by Van Gorkom for the opening of the Chicago Lyric Opera, Van Gorkom and Pritzker signed the formal merger agreement. Neither Van Gorkom nor any other Trans Union board member read the agreement before it was executed.

The proposed merger between Trans Union and Pritzker's company was submitted to Trans Union's shareholders, and they voted to approve it. They were not informed about the basis for the $55 per share figure, however. Several shareholders then discovered how the transaction came about, and filed a class action in behalf of all Trans Union shareholders. The plaintiffs claimed that Trans Union's directors violated their duty of due care to the shareholders. The trial court ruled in favor of Trans Union's directors, and the shareholders appealed.

**Decision:** The judgment for the defendant directors was reversed. The directors breached their duty of due care. Several factors led to this conclusion, including the extreme haste with which the decision was made when haste was not really required, the absence of documentation, the total reliance by the directors on input from Van Gorkom, and the directors' failure to make any inquiry into Van Gorkom's methods or motives. ■

# TERMINATION

As we saw earlier, a primary characteristic of the corporation is that it can have a perpetual existence. (While a few states do place time limits on the duration of the certificate of incorporation, this is of no real consequence because renewal is usually only a formality.) This is not to say, however, that a corporation *must* exist forever. A number of different circumstances can bring about an end to its existence.

In discussing the termination of a corporation, a distinction must be made between liquidation and dissolution. **Liquidation** is the conversion of the corporation's assets to cash and the distribution of these funds to creditors and shareholders. **Dissolution** is the actual termination of the corporation's existence as an artificial person—its "legal death." A liquidation can occur without an actual dissolution, as where the corporation sells its assets to another company. The shareholders might then choose to dissolve the corporation, but it would not be required. On the other hand, dissolution sometimes takes place before liquidation. The remainder of our discussion is devoted primarily to the various circumstances that bring about dissolution, with a final mention of the process of winding up corporate affairs after dissolution.

## *Voluntary Dissolution*

A corporation can voluntarily terminate its own existence. Dissolution can be accomplished by the incorporators in some unusual circumstances, but the shareholders are ordinarily the only ones with such power. The board of directors does *not* have the power to dissolve the corporation.

**By Incorporators:** If the corporation has never gotten off the ground, it can be voluntarily dissolved by the incorporators. This can occur where the corporation has not done any business and no shares have been issued. In such a situation, the incorporators dissolve the corporation by filing "articles of dissolution" with the appropriate state official, who then issues a "certificate of dissolution."

**By Shareholders:** If the shareholders wish to discontinue the corporation's existence for any reason, they can do so. The most common reason for voluntary dissolution is that the enterprise has proved unprofitable.

The procedures for voluntary dissolution vary somewhat from state to state, but their general outline is basically the same. The process is usually initiated by resolution of the board of directors. A meeting of the shareholders is then called, at which time the matter is voted on. The vote required for approval varies among the states in the same manner as for mergers and consolidations, from a simple majority to four-fifths, with a *two-thirds* vote being the most common requirement. After shareholder approval, articles of dissolution are filed and the certificate of dissolution is issued.

Dissenting shareholders can challenge the dissolution in court. However, a court will issue an injunction prohibiting dissolution only if these shareholders are able to prove that the controlling shareholders dissolved the corporation in *bad faith,* with the intent of defrauding the minority.

## *Involuntary Dissolution*

In some circumstances, a court action can be instituted for the purpose of dissolving the corporation. A legal proceeding of this nature can be brought by a shareholder or by the state. Dissolution ordered by a court in such a proceeding is often referred to as an "involuntary" dissolution.

**By Shareholders:** The laws of the various states generally provide that one or more shareholders can file a lawsuit requesting that the court dissolve the corporation. Those situations in which a shareholder can obtain dissolution by court order are listed below.

***Oppression of Minority Shareholders:*** In most states, oppression of minority shareholders by those in control is a ground for judicial dissolution. Oppressive conduct generally includes any act by which controlling shareholders seek to take unfair advantage of the minority. One example is the purchase of corporate assets by controlling shareholders, who then lease them back to the corporation for exorbitant rental fees.

***Deadlock:*** Most states authorize dissolution by the court if it is proved that the corporation is unable to function because of a management deadlock. This is not a common occurrence and ordinarily could only happen in a closely held corporation. In order for there to be an unbreakable management deadlock, of course, there would have to be equal ownership interests by two separate factions and a board of directors with an even number of members split into equal, opposing groups.

***Mismanagement:*** Courts are generally reluctant to interfere with decisions made by corporate managers. However, a court may order dissolution of the corporation if it is being so grossly mismanaged that its assets are actually being wasted.

The following case illustrates the difficulty a shareholder may encounter in seeking to have the corporation involuntarily dissolved because of alleged mismanagement.

---

### Gruenberg v. Goldmine Plantation, Inc.
Court of Appeal of Louisiana, 360 So.2d 884 (1978)

Goldmine Corp's. principal asset was a 900-acre tract of land fronting on the Mississippi River in Louisiana. Acquired in 1941 for $65,000, the property was appraised at $3,000 per acre in 1975, giving it a value at that time of $2,700,000. Since its acquisition the land had been used solely for growing sugar cane, a business which in recent years had not been very profitable. However, since 1966 various industrial interests had expressed a desire to buy the land, the latest proposed price being $3,600 per acre.

Without even investigating the merits of these offers, Goldmine's directors voted to reject them. The directors apparently were motivated by a feeling that the land would probably continue to increase in value, but they made no effort to obtain information that would enable them to weigh the proposals intelligently and determine the best interests of the shareholders.

Ten of Goldmine's shareholders, who collectively owned 40 percent of its stock, filed suit seeking to have the corporation dissolved by court order. They were opposed by four shareholders who collectively owned the remaining 60 percent. These four also served as the company's directors. Louisiana law provided several grounds for involuntary dissolution, the following two of which were asserted by plaintiffs as applying to Goldmine's situation: (1) "The objects of the corporation have wholly failed, or are entirely abandoned, or their accomplishment is impracticable"; or (2) "It is beneficial to the interests of the shareholders that the corporation should be liquidated and dissolved."

The trial court dismissed the suit, and plaintiffs appealed.

---

**Decision:** The judgment for defendants was affirmed. Although the court sympathized with plaintiffs because their funds were locked up in an unprofitable enterprise, it could find no basis for dissolving the corporation. The company simply was not being so grossly mismanaged as to warrant dissolution.

The court held that the object of the corporation had not "wholly failed" or been "entirely abandoned," and had not become "impracticable." Although not very profitable, sugar cane farming was still going on. Low profits per se do not create a basis for dissolution. The court also refused to dissolve the corporation on the second ground. It concluded that dissolution and liquidation were not clearly "beneficial to the interests" of all the shareholders, because the land was in fact appreciating in value and in all likelihood would continue to do so in the foreseeable future. ∎

---

**By the State:** Since a corporation derives its right to exist from the state where it is incorporated, it seems natural that the state should also be able to take away that right. This power can be exercised, however, only in certain circumstances. The grounds for dissolution by the state (which are remarkably similar in the various jurisdictions) are discussed below.

***Failure to Comply with Administrative Requirements:*** All states insist that corporations comply with various administrative requirements. With respect to some of these duties, noncompliance may be cause for dissolution at the instance of the state. The most common examples are (1) failure to file required annual reports with the secretary of state, (2) failure to pay franchise fees or other state taxes, and (3) failure to appoint or maintain a registered agent. Many states acknowledge the relative insignificance of such omissions by providing for easy reinstatement upon compliance and payment of any penalties owed.

**Ultra Vires *Acts*:** The performance of acts that are beyond the corporation's powers constitutes a reason for dissolution. This principle is of little practical importance today, however, because most articles of incorporation now grant such broad powers that *ultra vires* acts are rather infrequent.

***Dormancy*:** If a corporation never commences business after it is formed or if it becomes dormant by abandoning its operations, the state can seek its dissolution in court. But the absence of corporate activity does not automatically bring about dissolution; it simply gives the state a basis for obtaining court-ordered dissolution.

***Antitrust Violations*:** In many jurisdictions, a corporation's violation of the state (not federal) antitrust laws is a cause for dissolution.

***Fraudulent Formation*:** Several states provide for dissolution where the corporation obtained its certificate of incorporation by misrepresenting material facts.

The attorney general of a state usually acts as its representative when a court action seeking dissolution is filed. But where the basis for dissolution is merely the failure to comply with an administrative requirement, some states authorize the secretary of state or other official to cancel the certificate of incorporation without court action.

## *Winding Up*

**Where Dissolution Is Voluntary:** When voluntary dissolution occurs, the corporation's directors become *trustees* who hold corporate assets for the benefit of creditors and shareholders. They usually are allowed to wind up corporate affairs without court supervision. The directors in this situation have four duties:

**1.** They must not undertake any new business. Their authority is limited to the fulfillment of existing corporate obligations.

**2.** They must make a reasonable attempt to collect debts owed to the corporation.

**3.** After liquidation of corporate assets, they must pay creditors insofar as these assets are sufficient to do so.

**4.** When the claims of corporate creditors have been satisfied, they must distribute any remaining funds to shareholders. This distribution is required to be in the proportion of shareholders' respective interests and in accordance with any special rights enjoyed by preferred shareholders.

The directors can be held personally responsible for the breach of any of these winding-up duties. However, if they are unwilling to serve as trustees in liquidating the corporation, a *receiver* will be appointed and supervised by a court for the purpose of winding up corporate affairs. The court can also take such action if a creditor or shareholder shows cause why the directors should not be allowed to perform this function.

**Where Dissolution Is Involuntary:** In any case where dissolution is involuntary, the liquidation of corporate assets and other winding-up activities are always performed by a court-appointed receiver.

## SUMMARY

Although there are technical differences between a merger and a consolidation, there really are no practical differences, and the two terms are often used interchangeably to describe a combination of independent corporations under common ownership. The term merger is usually used to describe both types of combinations, as well as a number of other variations.

The reasons for a merger between two corporations are many and varied. A merger begins with approval by the board of each company, and then must also be approved by a vote of each company's shareholders, usually by an extraordinary majority such as two-thirds. A dissenting shareholder, one who voted against an approved merger, usually has the right of appraisal. This right permits the shareholder to have his or her shares appraised and bought by the corporation at their fair value.

In addition to formal mergers and consolidations, corporations may be combined under common ownership by other means, such as asset or stock acquisitions. These variations often are also referred to as mergers in everyday usage. Stock acquisitions may be accomplished in different ways, including open market purchases and tender offers. When the target company's board resists an attempted takeover by stock acquisition, the acquiring company is likely to use a tender offer because it is faster and allows the target company's board less time to raise obstacles to the takeover. In responding to a takeover attempt, however, the target company's board must continue to fulfill its basic duties of obedience, due care, and loyalty. In the takeover setting, these duties require the board to act in good faith, make decisions that are as completely informed as possible under the circumstances, and seek the best interests of their company's shareholders.

A corporation can be dissolved in several different ways: there may be a voluntary dissolution by vote of an extraordinary majority (such as two-thirds) of the shareholders, or there may be an involuntary dissolution for prescribed reasons in a court action instituted by a shareholder or by the state.

## KEY TERMS

**Merger**
**Consolidation**
**Defensive merger**
**Articles of merger or consolidation**
**Certificate of merger or consolidation**
**Appraisal right**
***De facto* merger**
**Holding company (or investment company)**
**Tender offer**
**Williams Act**
**Liquidation**
**Dissolution**

## QUESTIONS AND PROBLEMS

1. X Co. manufactures casual and dress shoes of all types. It wishes to expand its product line by getting into the athletic shoe business. What factors should its board of directors consider in deciding whether to get into the new line by internal expansion or by acquiring an existing maker of athletic shoes?

2. Discuss the rationale behind the appraisal right.

3. Pierce Co. was merged into Rayex Co. One of Pierce's creditors was not paid before the merger took place. The creditor demanded payment from Rayex, but its directors refused, saying that Pierce no longer existed and Rayex had not agreed to take over Pierce's obligations. Is the position taken by Rayex correct? Explain.

4. Chemco, Inc., was merged into Atlas Industries according to a merger plan adopted by the controlling shareholders of both companies. Under the plan, Chemco's controlling shareholders received cash in return for their Chemco shares. Chemco's minority shareholders, on the other hand, were given Atlas shares in return for their Chemco shares. Although the amount of cash received by the controlling shareholders was reasonable and fair, several members of the minority filed suit, challenging the plan because of its different treatment of controlling and minority shareholders. Will their suit be successful? Discuss.

5. Tandem Corp. purchased all the assets of Kilmer Company for cash. After the sale, a creditor of Kilmer demanded payment from Tandem. The creditor asserted that by buying Kilmer's assets Tandem had automatically assumed Kilmer's obligations. Is the creditor correct? Discuss.

6. Portsmouth, Inc., had two classes of shares outstanding: common shares and nonvoting preferred shares. At the annual meeting, Portsmouth's shareholders voted to merge the company into International Conglomerate, Inc. Only the common shareholders, whose shares carried voting rights, were allowed to vote. As had been the case at past meetings, the preferred shareholders, who did not have voting rights, were not allowed to vote. The preferred shareholders challenged the validity of the merger, claiming that this situation was "different" than earlier ones and that they should have been allowed to vote. Will their challenge be successful? Explain.

7. What are the advantages of the tender offer as a method for obtaining control over another corporation?

8. What type of corporation seems the most susceptible to a deadlock? Explain.

9. National Equipment Rental Co. was dissolved, its assets liquidated, and all its liabilities paid. Remaining for distribution to shareholders was $5,000,000. Two classes of shares were outstanding: 150,000 shares of $35 par value common and 100,000 shares of $35 par value 8 percent preferred. National's articles of incorporation were silent on the matter of a preference as to assets on liquidation. What division will be made of the $5,000,000?

CHAPTER 41

# SECURITIES REGULATION

The great stock market crash of 1929 was one of the most dramatic turning points in American economic history. That event not only ushered in the Great Depression but also heralded the creation of modern securities regulation. Securities regulation is one of the most complicated areas of the law; attorneys who practice in the securities field are among the most specialized and well-paid of all lawyers. Although this vast, everchanging subject may be intimidating to the novice, few persons in business can afford to remain ignorant of its effects on the way business is done in this country.

Many aspects of securities regulation are highly visible. Most Americans are familiar with the hustle and bustle of the New York Stock Exchange. Over 30 million Americans own stock, many in major corporations such as General Motors and IBM. Through securities regulation the federal government, and to a lesser degree the states, regulate trading on the stock exchanges, protect the interests of shareholders, and attempt to insure that the collapse of 1929 is never repeated.

In this chapter, some of the more important aspects of the law of securities regulation are surveyed.

## INTRODUCTION TO SECURITIES REGULATION

As explained in Chapter 37, there are various forms of business organizations including partnerships and corporations. There are sufficient advantages to incorporating, especially for very large businesses, that three million corporations exist in the United States. The corporate form allows for accumulation of capital investment from many shareholders. These investors do not directly own the assets of the business; rather, they own part of the corporate entity, as evidenced by shares of stock. Shares of stock constitute the most familiar type of security regulated by federal and state governments.

A security such as a stock or a bond has no intrinsic value—its value lies in the ownership interest which it represents. The value of that ownership interest may be difficult to discover and easy to misrepresent. Securities may be produced in nearly limitless supply at virtually no cost by anyone with access to a printing press. For all these reasons, fraud, manipulation, and deceit have been frequent companions of the security. Government regulation of securities dates back to at least 1285, when King Edward I of England attempted to gain some control over the capital markets by licensing brokers located in London.

Securities regulation in the United States was almost nonexistent until 1911, when Kansas enacted securities laws. Other states soon followed suit, but without federal laws, companies could evade regulation by operating across state lines.

The 1920s were an especially active time for the issuance and trading of securities. The securities business was then characterized by price manipulation, deceitful practices, selling on excessive credit, and the abuse of secret information by corporate insiders. Of the $50 billion of new securities offered for sale in the United States in the 1920s, about one-half were worthless. The public and the national economy were devastated when stock market prices fell 89 percent between 1929 and 1933, a situation which finally produced federal action.

### *Federal Legislation*

The first federal securities law was the *Securities Act of 1933* (the 1933 Act), which regulated the initial issuance of securities by companies. Fraudulent and deceptive practices were outlawed, and registration was required before a new security could be offered or sold, unless that security was entitled to an exemption from registration.

A year later, Congress passed the *Securities Exchange Act of 1934* (the 1934 Act), which extended federal regulation to trading in securities already issued and outstanding, required registration of securities brokers and dealers, and created the Securities and Exchange Commission (SEC), the federal agency that enforces the federal securities laws through its extensive powers.

In 1935, Congress passed the *Public Utility Holding Company Act* in response to manipulative and monopolistic practices in the public utilities industry. The SEC in its early years was largely concerned with correcting abuses in the financing and operating of large public utilities. Because the commission has been very successful in this area, separate enforcement of the Public Utility Holding Company Act is no longer a major SEC priority.

The next securities law passed by Congress was the *Trust Indenture Act of 1939*, which helped protect persons investing in bonds, debentures, notes, and other debt securities by imposing qualification requirements on trustees of such instruments. A year later, the *Investment Company Act of 1940* imposed additional requirements on companies engaged primarily in the business of investing, reinvesting, and trading securities. For example, that Act prohibits anyone found guilty of securities fraud from being associated with investment companies and bans transactions between such companies and their officers without prior SEC approval. The *Investment Advisers Act of 1940* required persons or firms who engage in the business of advising others about investments for compensation to register with the SEC, as brokers and dealers are required to register under the 1934 Act.

The *Securities Investor Protection Act of 1970* amended the 1934 Act in response to a rash of failures in the late 1960s in the broker-dealer business. The Act creates the Securities Investor Protection Corporation (SIPC), which manages a fund to protect investors from the failure of broker-dealers in the same manner as the Federal Deposit Insurance Corporation protects the customers of banks.

In 1977 Congress passed the *Foreign Corrupt Practices Act* (FCPA) in response to questionable foreign political payments by U.S. companies that were disclosed in the wake of the Watergate scandal. This act has two aspects. First, it bans bribery of high foreign political officials for the purpose of obtaining or retaining business and attaches strong criminal penalties to violation. Concern that fear of violating the FCPA was hindering U.S. businesses in their attempts to compete internationally led to a 1988 amendment in which Congress emphasized an exception that allows so-called "grease payments" to lower-level officials to expedite the processing of permits, licenses, and the like. It also provides an affirmative defense for payments which are legal under the *written* law of the foreign country and allows the payment of legitimate expenses (e.g., travel expenses of a foreign official) associated with promotional activities.

The second part of the FCPA establishes stringent accounting requirements for bigger companies so that such illegal activities cannot be easily concealed. These accounting rules are not especially clear, and in 1988 Congress amended the FCPA to make it clear that penalties should not be imposed for insignificant or technical infractions or inadvertent conduct.

Of these acts, the 1933 Act and the 1934 Act remain the most important.

## What Is a Security?

**Securities** are commonly thought of as the stock issued by corporations. The shares of common and preferred stock issued by corporations constitute a major type of security. These are *equity securities* which evidence an ownership interest in the corporation. Holders of equity securities are normally entitled to vote on important corporate matters and to receive dividends as their share of the corporate profits. The other major type of security is the *debt security*, such as the bond, note, or debenture. Holders of debt securities are creditors rather than owners. They have no voice in corporate affairs but are entitled to receive regular interest payments according to the terms of the bond or note.

Because the inventive mind of man has devised an inordinate variety of investment interests, securities regulation goes beyond items that are clearly labeled "stocks" or "bonds." Section 2(1) of the 1933 Act broadly defines security to include

> any note, stock, treasury stock, bond, debenture, evidence of indebtedness, certificate of interest or participation in any profit-sharing agreement, . . . investment contract, voting-trust certificate, frac-

tional undivided interest in oil, gas or other mineral rights, or, in general, any interest or instrument commonly known as a 'security.' . . .

This broad definition has, of necessity, been liberally construed by the courts. Interest in limited partnerships, condominiums, farm animals with accompanying agreements for their care, franchises, whiskey warehouse receipts, and many other varied items have been deemed to be securities.

The inclusion of the term "investment contract" in the 1933 Act's definition of security has produced much litigation. Some very interesting investment opportunities have been held to constitute investment contracts, as the following case illustrates.

---

**Smith v. Gross**
U.S. Ninth Circuit Court of Appeals,
604 F.2d 292 (1979)

Gross used a promotional newsletter to solicit buyer-investors to raise earthworms in order to help him reach his quota of selling earthworms to fishermen. Buyers were promised that the seller's instructions would enable them to have a profitable worm farm, that the time required was similar to that of a garden, that the worms doubled in quantity every 60 days, and that Gross would buy back all bait-size worms produced by buyers at $2.25 per pound.

The Smiths invested, but later sued claiming that contrary to Gross's representations, the worms multiplied at a maximum of eight rather than sixty-four times per year, and that the promised profits could be achieved only if the multiplication rate were as fast as represented and Gross repurchased the Smiths' production at $2.25 per pound, which was much higher than the true market value. Gross could pay that amount only by selling the worms to new worm farmers at inflated prices.

The Smiths claimed that Gross made false representations which violated the federal securities laws. The federal district court dismissed the action for want of subject matter jurisdiction after concluding that no "security" was involved in the case. The Smiths appealed.

**Decision:** The judgment was reversed. The federal securities law lists investment contracts as a type of security. The Supreme Court defined "investment contract" in *SEC v. W. J. Howey Co.*, 328 U.S. 293 (1946), and its elements are all present here: (1) an investment of money, (2) in a common enterprise, (3) with profits to come solely (or primarily) from the efforts of others. This was a classic "pyramid scheme"; if Gross couldn't keep the base of the pyramid growing by finding more and more worm farmers to whom he could sell the production of investors like the Smiths, the whole scheme would collapse. A sale of securities was involved, and federal securities law applied. ■

---

## 1933 ACT: REGULATING THE ISSUANCE OF SECURITIES

A major portion of federal securities regulation concerns the issuance of securities by companies. Congressional investigations following the 1929 stock market crash disclosed that enthusiasm for investment opportunities in the 1920s was often so great that large offerings of stock would be gobbled up by an investing public that knew virtually nothing about the selling company.

The goal of the 1933 Act is to protect the investing public. The 1933 Act is a disclosure statute which is frequently called the "Truth in Securities" law. The Act requires full disclosure by companies wishing to issue and sell stock to the public. By requiring such companies to file a registration statement with the SEC and to use an offering circular called a **prospectus** when attempting to sell securities, the law attempts to enable the investor to make an informed decision. The SEC, which is charged with enforcement of the law, does not attempt to pass on the value of the securities offered nor to advise investors to purchase or not purchase the securities of particular companies.

The 1933 Act also protects investors by prohibiting fraud and deceit in the distribution of shares, even those which the law does not require to be registered.

## The Registration Process

**Elements of the Process:** Securities are distributed much like any product. The corporation selling securities to raise capital, the *issuer,* is analogous to the manufacturer of goods. *Underwriters* act as wholesalers, *dealers* act as retailers, and the *investor* is a consumer. By regulating the activities of the issuer, underwriter, and dealer, the 1933 Act seeks to insure that the investor has access to adequate information before purchasing a particular security.

The keystones to the disclosure process are the registration statement and the prospectus, the contents of which are discussed presently. Section 5(a) of the 1933 Act makes it unlawful to sell or deliver any security without first filing with the SEC a registration statement which has become effective. Section 5(b)(1) makes it unlawful to sell a security by means of a prospectus which does not meet statutory standards. Section 5(b)(2) makes it unlawful to sell securities which are not accompanied or preceded by a prospectus.

**SEC Approval:** The registration statement filed with the SEC is not automatically effective. Rather, the staff of the SEC may review the statement for omissions and inaccuracies. Some reviews may be more thorough than others. Because of budgetary cutbacks and staff reductions, the SEC in recent years has had to give cursory reviews to many registration statements, reserving the full review process primarily for statements filed by new issuers selling to the public for the first time. Indeed, today most registration statements are not reviewed at all.

Section 8(a) of the 1933 Act provides that if the SEC is silent, the registration statement automatically becomes effective on the twentieth day after its filing. The registration process may be analyzed in terms of its three major time periods. The first stage of the process is the period before the registration statement is filed (the "pre-filing" period). The second stage lasts from the filing of the statement until it becomes effective (the "waiting" period). The final stage is, of course, after the statement becomes effective (the "post-effective" period).

**The Pre-Filing Period:** To prevent circumvention of the provisions of Section 5, an issuer is strictly limited during the pre-filing period. The issuer may not sell or even offer to sell a security before the registration statement is filed. The term "offer" is broadly construed and encompasses not only formal sales campaigns, but any type of activity meant to "precondition" the market. A simple speech by a corporate executive or a press release about how well the company is doing may be improper if it "just happens" to be soon followed by the filing of a registration statement.

The only activities permitted during the pre-filing period, other than normal advertising and communications with shareholders by an issuer, are preliminary negotiations between the issuer and underwriters. This is necessary because a large distribution of securities may require that an entire syndicate of underwriters be assembled.

**The Waiting Period:** The purpose of the waiting period is to slow the distribution process so that the dealers and the public have time to familiarize themselves with the information disclosed in the registration process. Though no sales may be consummated during this period, certain types of offers are allowed, and underwriters may now make arrangements with dealers for their assistance in distribution.

In addition to oral offers, certain types of written offers are permissible during the waiting period. For example, an issuer may place in *The Wall Street Journal* a short announcement known as a tombstone ad because it is usually surrounded by a black border. Under SEC Rule 134, the announcement may contain only a few limited items, such as (1) the kind of security, (2) the amount, (3) by whom purchase orders will be executed, and (4) the location at which a prospectus may be obtained. The announcement must state that no offer to purchase can actually be accepted during the waiting period, and that an indication of interest is not binding on a prospective investor.

Offers may also be made by use of a preliminary prospectus, which contains information from the registration statement then under review. These are called "red herring" prospectuses, because SEC Rule 430 requires that a special legend be printed in red ink on each one labeling it a preliminary prospectus, stating that a registration statement has been filed but is not yet effective, that no final sale can be made during the waiting period, and that it does not constitute an offer to sell.

***Post-Effective Period:*** Once the registration statement becomes effective, sales of securities may be completed. However, the law still imposes requirements aimed at encouraging dissemination of information. With some exceptions, the issuer, underwriter, and dealer must provide a copy of the final prospectus with every written offer, supplemental sales literature, written confirmation of sale, or delivery of securities. The prospectus must be used as long as the distribution is taking place; if this period extends beyond nine months, Section 10(a)(3) requires that the prospectus be updated to reflect more recent information on the status of the issuer. In addition, the issuer must update the prospectus whenever important new developments occur; otherwise the information can become stale and misleading, resulting in liability for fraud under Section 17(a) of the 1933 Act.

***Shelf Registration:*** Traditionally, an issuer has been required to file a new registration statement every time it sought to initiate a new distribution of stock. However, the new Rule 415 establishes a system known as **shelf registration.** Under this system a company is allowed to file one registration statement announcing its long-term plans for sales of securities. Then, whenever the company thinks market conditions and its own financial needs require the sale of securities, it can issue the additional securities without going through the registration process described above to achieve SEC approval because it already has a registration statement and a prospectus "on the shelf." If periodically updated, the registration statement will remain continuously effective. Rule 415 enhances the ability of corporations to raise capital on short notice, but its use has been restricted primarily to the larger, more reliable corporations.

## *Disclosure Requirements*

The information disclosure requirements of the 1933 Act and the 1934 Act were for a long time separate, often overlapping, and sometimes conflicting. In recent years, the SEC has made an effort to coordinate the requirements for information disclosure contained in the two acts. The filing requirements of the 1934 Act must be mentioned here because they now bear significantly on the disclosure requirements of the 1933 Act regarding the registration statement and prospectus.

***Registration and Reporting:*** Section 12 of the 1934 Act requires all companies whose securities are traded on the national stock exchanges (such as the New York Stock Exchange) and any other companies with more than $5 million in assets and more than 500 shareholders to register their securities with the SEC. These companies are referred to as registered or reporting companies. There are about 10,000 such companies. The required registration statement must contain extensive information about such areas as the organization, financial structure, and nature of the business, the structure of present classes of stock, the directors and officers and their remuneration, important contracts, balance sheets, and profit-and-loss statements for the three preceding fiscal years.

Section 13 requires that the registration statement be continually updated with annual reports (called 10-Ks) and quarterly reports (10-Qs). In addition, if important facts change between quarterly reports, the company should amend the registration statement by use of an 8-K report.

***Integration of Registration Requirements:*** Despite all the information made public under the 1934 Act, even reporting companies traditionally had to go through the expensive registration process under the 1933 Act, which required disclosure of information already made public in the 1934 Act reports. Because of complaints about duplication and needless expense, the SEC changed the rules in 1982 to make disclosure requirements uniform under the 1933 and 1934 Acts and to utilize the periodic reports of the 1934 Act to satisfy many of the disclosure requirements of the 1933 Act registration statements by a process of incorporation by reference. The core of the new procedure is a three-tiered registration structure that creates three distinct categories of registration statement, depending upon the issuer's financial size and prior reporting history. The largest, most dependable companies can file very basic prospectuses that incorporate by reference all the information contained in previously filed 1934 Act reports. Medium-sized companies with less reliable reporting histories are allowed some incorporation by reference, and the remaining companies must file full-blown prospectuses with no incorporation by reference.

Section 10 of the 1933 Act, as supplemented by various rules issued by the SEC, controls the content of the prospectus. The most important information in the registration statement regarding the financial structure, organization, operations, and officers and directors of the issuer must be summarized in the prospectus (unless incorporation by reference is allowed under the new system).

**Materiality:** Exactly which details must be included in the registration statement and prospectus is a matter governed not only by statutes and rules, but also by the concept of **materiality**. The most important element in the disclosure provisions of both the 1933 and 1934 Acts is that all matters that are important or material to an investor's decision should be disclosed. Materiality is an elusive concept, but the Supreme Court has described information as material "if there is a substantial likelihood that a reasonable shareholder would consider it important" in making an investment decision.[1] This is usually limited to matters having a significant bearing on the economic and financial performance of the company.

Examples of material facts include an erratic pattern of earnings, an intention to enter into a new line of business, adverse competitive conditions, litigation with the government which might lead to imposition of a financially damaging fine, and a substantial disparity between the price at which the shares are being offered to the public and the cost of the shares owned by officers, directors, and promoters. The following case illustrates one application of the concept of materiality in the context of the 1933 Act disclosure requirements.

[1] *TSC Industries, Inc. v. Northway, Inc.,* 426 U.S. 438, 449 (1976).

---

*In re* **Doman Helicopters, Inc.**
Securities and Exchange Commission, 41 S.E.C. 431 (1963)

Doman Helicopters, Inc., was formed in 1945, but never was able to do business on a profitable basis. Except for one experimental model sold in 1950, two prototypes delivered to the Army in 1956 and 1957 (both subsequently repurchased by Doman), and one helicopter on loan to its Italian licensee, by 1962 Doman had never manufactured or sold any helicopters. Instead, it had continually flirted with bankruptcy. By September 30, 1961, its accumulated losses totalled over $5.7 million. On January 31, 1962, Doman's current liabilities were $292,446 while its assets were only $13,178.

On April 19, 1962, Doman filed a Form S-1 registration statement proposing to offer publicly 681,971 shares, some to current shareholders, some to creditors, and some to the public. The contemplated price was $1.50 per share. Doman's future plans were predicated on development of a proposed helicopter, the D-10B.

The SEC commenced a proceeding under Section 8(d) of the 1933 Act to determine whether a stop order should issue suspending the effectiveness of Doman's registration statement. The focus of the investigation was on deficiencies in the prospectus.

**Decision:** In this SEC proceeding, the Commission decided to issue a stop order to prevent Doman from selling any stock until the following misstatements and omissions in the prospectus were corrected: (1) The prospectus described the D-10B as though it were an existing and operational helicopter when, in fact, it had never been flown, tested, or even assembled in prototype form. (2) The prospectus made unqualified claims about the stability, long life, low initial cost and subsequent maintenance costs, and exceptional center of gravity characteristics of the "Doman Hingeless Rotor System." In actuality, this rotor system had only been used on a few converted or prototype models, and had never been used on a production model or subjected to normal day-to-day usage. (3) The prospectus made only a passing and ambiguous reference to Doman's unsuccessful efforts to secure military contracts for the helicopter; the Department of Defense had studied Doman's rotor system extensively and found that it offered no significant advantage over other systems. (4) The prospectus stated that the proceeds of the sale of stock would be used to develop the D-10B; it failed to disclose that a substantial portion of the proceeds would first have to be used to pay outstanding debts, current expenses, and accrued salaries to certain officers and directors. (5) The prospectus failed to disclose that Doman's currently outstanding shares had a book value of minus 30 cents per share; the proposed new issue of shares at $1.50 would change the book value of both currently outstanding shares and new shares to 55 cents per share. Thus, new shareholders would suffer an immediate dilution of the book value of their shares from $1.50 to 55 cents per share, and the corresponding benefit would inure entirely to existing shareholders. ■

## Exemptions

In certain situations where there is less need for regulation, Sections 3 and 4 of the 1933 Act provide exemptions from Section 5's registration requirements (though not from the anti-fraud provisions of the 1933 and 1934 Acts).

Perhaps the most important exemption is that for "transactions by any person other than an issuer, underwriter, or dealer" provided by Section 4(1). This simply means that once the issue is sold to the investing public, the public may trade, and the dealers may handle most transactions, without any worry about registration or prospectus delivery requirements. Thus, the 1933 Act does not apply to so-called "secondary trading," which is regulated by the 1934 Act.

Section 3(a) exempts from registration the securities of governments (state and federal), charitable organizations, banks, savings and loans, and common carriers, which are regulated under other federal laws.

**Small Issues:** There are also exemptions for small issues and small issuers. Section 4(2) exempts "transactions by an issuer not involving any public offering," an exemption used primarily in connection with (1) bank loans, (2) privately negotiated sales of securities to large institutional investors (private placements), and (3) the promotion of business ventures by a few closely related persons. Section 3(b) authorizes the SEC to exempt securities if it finds that registration "is not necessary in the public interest and for the protection of investors by reason of the small amount involved [a five-million-dollar ceiling] or the limited character of the public offering."

*Regulation D:* The SEC's Regulation D fleshes out the 3(b) exemption in Rules 504 and 505, and the 4(2) exemption in Rule 506. Rule 504 exempts from registration any offering in a 12-month period totalling less than $1,000,000 (reduced by amounts sold in reliance on other exemptions). This exemption is aimed at smaller businesses and is not available to 1934 Act reporting companies.

Rule 505 allows a company, including reporting companies, to sell up to $5,000,000 in securities (reduced by amounts sold in reliance on other exemptions) in any 12-month period without registering, provided the sales are to no more than 35 unaccredited investors. **Accredited investors** are persons and institutions—such as pension funds, banks, corporate insiders, and millionaires—who because of their very nature are unlikely to need government protection in making investment decisions. The number of sales to accredited investors is not limited, though no general advertising or soliciting is allowed.

Rule 506 allows all companies to sell an unlimited amount of securities in an issuance if sales are limited to 35 unaccredited investors, if the issuer makes a determination that all purchasers are "sophisticated" and therefore capable of protecting themselves without the assistance of a registration statement and prospectus. Accredited investors are assumed to be sophisticated, and an unsophisticated purchaser may act through a sophisticated purchaser representative. As with Rule 505, no general advertising or soliciting is allowed. The SEC recently added Rule 508, providing that a good faith attempt to comply with Regulation D would not be disqualified by technical, inadvertent violations of the rules.

A small issues partial exemption of decreasing importance is Regulation A, under which the SEC allows an issuer to sell up to $1.5 million of securities in a 12-month period with minimal disclosure requirements. An unaudited circular is permitted in place of the more detailed prospectus.

**Local Offerings:** A final important exemption is Section 3(a)(11)'s exemption for intrastate offerings, which applies where a selling company doing business in a state offers and sells securities only to residents of the same state and intends to use the proceeds there. An issuer, according to Rule 147, is doing business within a state if (1) it derives 80 percent or more of its revenue from operations within the state, (2) at least 80 percent of its assets are located within the state, (3) at least 80 percent of the net proceeds of the issuance will be used within the state, and (4) the issuer's principal office is located there. Offer of the shares for sale to a single nonresident will void the exemption. Federal regulation is deemed unnecessary because of the availability of state regulation and the close proximity of purchaser to seller.

## Enforcement and Civil Liabilities

**Government Action:** The SEC has numerous powers to enforce compliance with the provisions of the 1933 Act. For example, if the SEC believes that a registration statement is incomplete or inaccurate, Section 8(b) authorizes issuance of a "refusal order" which prevents the statement from becoming effective until SEC objections are satisfied. If inaccuracies are discovered after the effective date, the SEC may issue a "stop order" pursuant to Section 8(d), as was done in the *Doman Helicopters* case, to suspend the effectiveness of the statement. Section 8(e) authorizes the SEC to conduct an "examination" to fully investigate whether a stop order should be issued.

Section 8 was amended in 1990 by the Securities Enforcement Remedies and Penny Stock Act to allow the SEC to seek civil fines in court in order to punish persons who violate *any* provision of the Act, rule or regulation issued thereunder, or cease-and-desist order entered by the commission. The maximum potential fines are in three tiers ranging from $5,000 to $100,000 for individuals and from $50,000 to $500,000 for corporations and other artificial entities, with the heavier penalties reserved for serious violations involving fraud, deceit, manipulation, and the like. In addition, the 1990 Act authorized courts to prohibit persons from serving as officers and directors of certain corporations if their conduct demonstrates "substantial unfitness" to hold such positions.

The 1933 Act even contains criminal provisions. Section 24 provides that any person who willfully violates any provision of the Act or any SEC rule, or any person who willfully makes an untrue statement or omits a material fact in a registration statement, is subject to a fine of not more than $10,000, imprisonment of not more than five years, or both.

**Private Suit:** The 1933 Act provides remedies for violation of its provisions in the form of lawsuits that may be brought by injured investors.

***Section 11:*** An investor who is injured after buying securities with reliance on a rosy picture falsely painted in a prospectus will probably not be satisfied with the SEC's injunction remedy or even criminal prosecution. The investor will desire to recoup losses through a civil action for damages, and the 1933 Act has express provision for such lawsuits. Section 11 states that if "any part of the registration statement, when such part became effective, contained an untrue statement of a material fact or omitted to state a material fact required to be stated therein or necessary to make the statements therein not misleading, any person acquiring such security" may file a civil action. Potential defendants in such an action include every person who signed the registration statement (which includes the issuer, its principal executive officers, chief financial officer, principal accounting officers, and a majority of the board of directors), every person who was a director or identified as about to become a director, every accountant, every appraiser or other expert who is named as having helped prepare it, and every underwriter.

The Section 11 cause of action is loosely patterned after a common-law fraud action, but is modified so as to greatly ease a plaintiff's burdens in seeking recovery. For example, the common-law fraud elements of privity of contract and reliance are not necessary in a Section 11 claim so long as plaintiff can trace the purchased shares back to the defective offering and show they were not previously issued shares of the same company being publicly traded at the same time.

If plaintiff proves the registration statement contained misstatements or omissions of material facts, the law presumes that these caused plaintiff's damages, and the burden of proof shifts to defendants to prove that other factors were the true cause of plaintiff's losses.

Furthermore, Section 11 does not require proof of fraudulent intent. Proof of misstatement or omission shifts the burden of proof to defendants to establish that they were guilty of neither fraudulent intent nor negligence in preparing the registration statement. Individual defendants must establish that they used "due diligence" in preparing the registration statement. The amount of diligence that is due from a defendant depends on his or her position as an "insider" (with full access to key information) or an "outsider," and a defendant is generally allowed to rely on "expertised" portions of the statement—those portions prepared by experts such as independent auditors. The due diligence defense is not available to the issuing company, which is strictly liable for inaccuracies in the registration statement.

***Section 12:*** Complementing Section 11 are Section 12(1), which allows an investor to recover when offers or sales are made in violation of Section 5 (that is, without the filing of a registration statement, by use of a defective prospectus, or where securities are delivered without an accompanying prospectus), and Section 12(2), which allows recovery by investors injured by misrepresentations made outside a prospectus (such as in an oral sales pitch or in literature accompanying an unregistered offering). The elements of recovery and defenses in Section 12 suits are roughly the same as under Section 11, though the range of potential defendants is limited to "sellers" of securities—those who actually pass title or those who "solicit" transactions, such as brokers and dealers.

## 1934 ACT: REGULATING THE TRADING OF SECURITIES

While the 1933 Act regulates primarily the initial issuance of securities, the 1934 Act regulates the subsequent trading of those securities. An array of complex problems comes within the purview of the 1934 Act. The general registration and reporting requirements of the 1934 Act have already been discussed. Attention is now turned to several other major concerns of the Act.

### *Insider Trading*

Knowledge of the inner workings of a corporation can be very valuable in making investment decisions. For example, if a corporate vice-president learned that his company's scientists had just been granted an important patent which will open up a new sales field, he would have a distinct and arguably unfair trading advantage over the general investing public. Insider trading was a widespread phenomenon in the 1920s, yet the common law provided little protection from such abusive practices.

**Section 16(b):** One response to the insider trading problem is Section 16 of the 1934 Act. Subsection (a) is a reporting requirement which applies to three categories of persons: officers, directors, and owners of more than 10 percent of the shares of any one class of stock of a 1934 Act reporting company. These three categories of persons are deemed the corporation's "insiders." Section 16(a) requires that they file two types of reports with the stock exchanges and the SEC: an initial report revealing the holdings when a director or officer takes office or when a stockholder first obtains a 10 percent holding, and an additional report each month thereafter in which a change in holdings occurs.

Subsection (b) of Section 16 provides that any profits realized by such an insider in connection with a purchase and sale or sale and purchase within a six-month period is an illegal "short-swing" profit. Any such profit may be recaptured by the issuer.

The striking aspect of Section 16(b) liability is its near absolute nature. Because of the difficulty of proving that someone has improperly used inside information for personal gain, Congress elected to omit such actual use as a requirement for Section 16(b) liability. Instead, if someone fitting the definition of an insider does have a purchase and sale or sale and purchase within a six-month period which results in a profit, liability is automatic. There are no defenses. Even proof that inside information was not used is no defense in a standard transaction.

**Section 10(b):** Another provision of the 1934 Act which regulates insider trading, as well as many other facets of securities trading, is Section 10(b). This provision makes it unlawful to "use or employ, in connection with the purchase or sale of any security, . . . any manipulative or deceptive device or contrivance in contravention of such rules and regulations as the Commission may prescribe. . . ."

Pursuant to Section 10(b), the SEC has issued the most important of all its rules, Rule 10b-5, quoted in full:

> It shall be unlawful for any person, directly or indirectly, by the use of any means or instrumentality of interstate commerce, or of the mails, or of any facility of any national securities exchange,
>
> (1) to employ any device, scheme or artifice to defraud,
>
> (2) to make any untrue statement of a material fact or to omit to state a material fact necessary in order to make the statements made, in the light of the circumstances under which they were made, not misleading, or
>
> (3) to engage in any act, practice, or course of business which operates or would operate as a fraud or deceit upon any person, in connection with the purchase or sale of any security.

***General Provisions:*** One important category of Rule 10b-5 cases involves insider trading. Although a Section 10(b) case is more difficult to prove, its coverage is broader than Section 16(b)'s. The broad purpose of Section 10(b) and Rule 10b-5 is to protect the investing public by preventing fraud and equalizing access to material information. Section 10(b) applies to any purchase or sale by any person of any security—there are no exceptions. Thus, small close corporations (the shares of which are not offered to the public for sale but are typically held by just a few, perhaps members of a single family) are covered as well as the largest public corporations. Transactions covered include those occurring on the stock exchanges, in over-the-counter sales through stockbrokers, or even in privately negotiated sales. Any person connected with the transaction is regulated, not only insiders as in Section 16(b).

Unlike Section 16(b), Section 10(b) requires proof of actual use of inside information to establish a violation. There is no automatic presumption. Furthermore, the information must be material and it must be nonpublic.

***Disclose or Abstain:*** One key to insider trading liability is the "disclose or abstain" rule. A leading case, *SEC v. Texas Gulf Sulphur*,[2] which involved the purchase of stock of a company by its employees and their tippees who possessed nonpublic information about a massive ore strike by the company, held that a person possessing inside information with a duty to disclose "must either disclose it to the investing public or, if he is disabled from disclosing it in order to protect a corporate confidence, or he chooses not to do so, must abstain from trading in or recommending the securities concerned while such inside information remains undisclosed."

The disclose or abstain rule promotes fairness in securities trading by attempting to equalize *access* to important information affecting the value of securities. Equal information is not the goal; equal *access* is. Although the goal cannot be perfectly achieved, small investors will likely have more confidence in the market if they know the SEC is actively promoting equal access.

***Enforcement:*** On the civil side, the Securities Enforcement Remedies and Penny Stock Act of 1990, mentioned above in connection with the 1933 Act, similarly amended the 1934 Act. Therefore, a violator of *any* 1934 Act provision, rule or regulation is subject to sliding scale civil penalities ($5,000 to $100,000 for individuals, for example), and individuals may be barred from being an officer or director of large corporations if their conduct demonstrates "substantial unfitness" to hold such a position. A willful violation of any provision of the 1934 Act subjects the violator to the criminal provisions of Section 32, which carry penalties of imprisonment up to five years, a fine of $100,000, or both. Insider trading scandals in the 1980s prompted Congress to make the criminal penalties for that activity more severe than for other criminal violations of the 1934 Act. The maximum criminal penalty for insider trading is now ten years in jail and/or a fine of $1 million for individuals and $2.5 million for partnerships or corporations.

The SEC refers criminal cases to the Department of Justice for prosecution. But the SEC itself can take steps against inside traders. It can hold disciplinary proceedings if a regulated broker, dealer, or underwriter is involved. It can go to federal district court to obtain an injunction to halt illegal practices and perhaps an order rescinding the fraudulent sale. In 1988, the SEC was authorized to seek civil fines against securities firms that "knowingly and recklessly" fail to properly supervise their employees who engage in insider trading. Additionally, the SEC is authorized in civil insider trading cases to seek relief in the form of disgorgement of illicit profits and assessment of a civil penalty of up to three times the profit gained or loss avoided. Pursuant to these provisions, infamous arbitrageur Ivan Boesky consented to disgorge insider trading profits of $50 million and to pay a civil fine of $100 million.

In addition to government civil and criminal actions, a private civil lawsuit for damages may be brought by victims of fraud, such as insider trading, against the perpetrators. Although the 1934 Act does not explicitly provide for such a right of action, the courts have implied one since 1946.[3] Private lawsuits brought under Section 10(b) and Rule 10b-5 in the 1960s and 1970s dramatically altered the law of securities regulation in the United States.

***Potential Defendants:*** Those barred from insider trading have always included corporate "insiders," a term defined more broadly than in the §16(b) provisions, including any corporate employee with access to material inside information, not just officers and directors. Also barred are the "tippees" of these insiders. Unless tippees are covered, a corporate president could tip his or her spouse and then enjoy indi-

---

[2] 401 F.2d 833 (2d Cir. 1968).

[3] *Kardon v. National Gypsum Co.,* 69 F.Supp. 512 (E.D.Pa. 1946).

rectly the fruits of the spouse's trading. The Supreme Court made it clear in *Dirks v. SEC,* 436 U.S. 646 (1983), that a tippee could not be liable for insider trading unless the tipping insider had breached a duty to the corporation in passing along the information. Such a breach would occur if the information was passed for a personal benefit (whether monetary or otherwise).

A third major category of potential insider trading defendant are "temporary insiders." These are persons who receive confidential corporate information for a corporate purpose and with the expectation that it will be kept confidential, but then use it in insider trading. Classic examples are attorneys, accountants, and investment bankers hired temporarily by a corporation. For example, if an attorney is hired to help Corporation A merge with Corporation B, and the attorney realizes that this will be a very favorable arrangement for Corporation A, he may be tempted to trade in its stock. That would be illegal so long as the information is nonpublic.

A final category of potential insider trading defendant consists of "misappropriators"—noninsiders who steal confidential inside information. The "disclose or abstain" obligation must rest on a *duty* to someone. Insiders, their tippees, and temporary insiders all owe a duty to the corporation in whose shares they trade. It can be a little more elusive to determine the duty owed by a misappropriator. For that reason, some courts were cool to the misappropriation theory. It was used by the lower courts to criminally convict a *Wall Street Journal* reporter who secretly leaked information about articles the newspaper was about to publish to confederates who traded profitably on the information. In *Carpenter v. U.S.,* 108 S.Ct. 316 (1987), the Supreme Court addressed the misappropriation theory and split 4–4 in a vote on its validity, though the Court affirmed the conviction on the basis of the federal wire fraud statute.

In 1988 Congress expressly allowed civil suits by "contemporaneous traders" who were in the market at the time of illegal trading. Whether or not this indicates approval of the misappropriation theory is unclear, but the lower courts have clearly embraced it. The following case is a typical misappropriation action brought by the SEC.

---

### SEC v. Materia
U.S. Second Circuit Court of Appeals, 745 F.2d 197 (1984)

Materia was a proofreader for Bowne of New York City, Inc. (Bowne), a firm specializing in the printing of financial documents. Because even a hint of an upcoming tender offer may send the price of the target company's stock soaring, information regarding the target's identity is zealously guarded. The law firms which draft tender offer documents for Bowne to print omit identifying information until the last minute and use code names. Bowne scrupulously attempts to keep all such information confidential to serve its clients.

Nonetheless, Materia was able to divine the identities of at least four tender offer targets. Within hours of each discovery he purchased stock in the target and within days—after the offer had been made public—he sold all his holdings at substantial gains. The SEC filed a civil enforcement action against Materia, alleging that he was guilty of insider trading in violation of §10(b) and Rule 10b-5 because he had misappropriated information from his employer and its clients. The trial judge issued an order restraining Materia from further violations and ordering him to disgorge illegally obtained profits of $99,862.50. Materia appealed.

**Decision:** The judgment was affirmed. Materia admitted that he misappropriated confidential information from his employer and traded on it. His claim that such activity is permissible must be rejected in light of precedents declaring such actions to be a criminal violation of §10(b).

Materia's claim that he could not have defrauded his employer because he did not know the confidential nature of the information he handled is clearly inconsistent with the facts. His claim that his employer was not injured by his misappropriation is similarly unfounded. One of a financial printer's most valuable assets is its reputation as a safe repository for clients' secrets. Materia's actions undermined his employer's reputation in that regard. ∎

## False or Inadequate Corporate Disclosures

A second major category of Section 10(b) cases relates to disclosures of information about corporations. Already noted are the registration and reporting requirements of the 1934 Act. The registration forms—the 10-Ks, 10-Qs, and 8-Ks—are all designed to promote full disclosure of information important to the investing public. When a corporation or some person fraudulently misstates or fails to disclose material information, a Section 10(b) violation may occur.[4]

An investor who is injured because he or she bought or sold shares on the basis of inaccurate or incomplete corporate information may bring a private cause of action under the antifraud provisions of Section 10(b). The requirements of a valid claim in such a lawsuit are patterned after those of common-law fraud: (1) a misrepresentation of material fact, (2) made by defendant with knowledge of the falsity, (3) an intent to induce plaintiff to rely, (4) actual reliance by the plaintiff, (5) privity of contract between plaintiff and defendant, and (6) damage sustained. Modification of some of these common-law elements has been a source of controversy in this type of Section 10(b) case.

**Privity:** Privity of contract has been largely eliminated as a requirement of a Section 10(b) cause of action in the corporate disclosure setting. An injured shareholder is normally allowed to sue those persons responsible for false statements whether or not the stockholder purchased shares from or sold shares to the defendants.

**Intent:** Actual intent to defraud arising from knowledge of the falsity of a statement is a traditional element of common-law fraud. In order to advance the remedial purposes of the 1934 Act, many lower courts formerly interpreted Section 10(b) so as to virtually eliminate the requirement of intent by holding defendants liable though they were guilty of nothing more than simple negligence.

The Supreme Court overruled these cases, however, in *Ernst & Ernst v. Hochfelder,* a case excerpted in Chapter 42. There the Court held that the defendant accounting firm was not liable for a Section 10(b) violation "in the absence of any allegation of **scienter**—intent to deceive, manipulate, or defraud."

The question has subsequently arisen as to whether a defendant should be liable if guilty of "recklessness," which means being highly negligent or so careless as to exhibit a complete disregard for possible damage to others. Most lower courts have concluded that reckless conduct is sufficient for imposition of liability, although the Supreme Court has not spoken on the issue.

**Reliance:** In a common-law fraud case, plaintiff must normally prove that the defendant's fraudulent statement was relied on in making the sale or purchase. In order to advance the broadly remedial purposes of the 1934 Act, some adjustments have been made to the traditional reliance requirement.

A misleading corporate disclosure can occur either when a material fact is concealed or when it is misrepresented. Because it is impractical to require an investor to prove reliance on a fact that was concealed from him or her, the Supreme Court has eliminated the reliance requirement in concealment cases. In *Affiliated Ute Citizens v. United States,* 406 U.S. 128 (1972), plaintiffs, mixed-blood Ute Indians, sold shares in the Ute Development Corporation through defendants, bank officials. Defendants failed to disclose to plaintiffs their own interest in the transactions or the fact that shares were trading at higher prices among whites. The Court held:

> Under the circumstances of this case, involving primarily a failure to disclose, positive proof of reliance is not a prerequisite to recovery. All that is necessary is that the facts withheld be material in the sense that a reasonable investor might have considered them important in the making of this decision. This obligation to disclose and this withholding of a material fact establish the requisite element of causation in fact.

In cases of active misrepresentation, proof of reliance is practicable; nonetheless, there have been some important modifications of the reliance requirements even in misrepresentation cases, due partly to the impersonal nature of transactions that occur through the stock exchanges. The leading case follows.

---

[4] False or misleading statements in documents filed with the SEC may also lead to liability under Section 18(a) of the 1934 Act.

### Basic, Inc. v. Levinson
U.S. Supreme Court, 108 S.Ct. 978 (1988)

In 1965, Combustion Engineering, Inc. expressed an interest in acquiring Basic, Inc. That interest was reawakened by regulatory developments in late 1976. Beginning in September 1976, Combustion representatives had meetings and phone calls with Basic officers and directors about a possible merger. During 1977 and 1978, Basic made three public statements denying that it was engaged in merger negotiations. On December 18, 1978, Basic was asked by the New York Stock Exchange to suspend trading in its shares. It issued a press release stating that it had been "approached" about a merger. On December 19, Basic's board accepted Combustion's offer, and this was publicly announced on December 20.

Former Basic shareholders (respondents), who sold their stock after Basic's first denial that it was engaged in merger talks (October 21, 1977) and before the suspension of trading, sued Basic and its directors (petitioners). Respondents claim that petitioners' misleading statements caused them to miss the opportunity to sell at the higher merger price, in violation of Section 10(b) of the 1934 Securities Act.

The district court (1) granted class action status to respondents, adopting a presumption that they had relied upon petitioners' public statements thereby satisfying the "common question of fact or law" requirement of the Federal Rules of Civil Procedure; and (2) granted summary judgment to petitioners on the merits, holding that petitioners had no obligation to disclose the ongoing merger negotiations.

The circuit court affirmed on the class action issue, adopting the district court's "fraud on the market" theory, but reversed on the merits, finding that a duty to disclose the merger talks might have existed. Petitioners appealed.

**Decision:** The circuit court's judgment was vacated and the case remanded. Whether misleading statements about mergers are material depends upon a balancing of (a) the indicated probability that the merger will occur and (b) the anticipated magnitude of the merger in the totality of the company's activities. The circuit court applied the wrong standard in deciding the issue of materiality; therefore, the judgment was vacated.

Regarding the question of reliance and the fraud-on-the-market theory, requiring a plaintiff to show how he or she would have acted if omitted material had been disclosed is unnecessarily burdensome. In enacting the securities laws, Congress acted on the premise that information affects the markets, and recent studies have tended to confirm that the market price of shares traded on well-developed markets reflects all publicly available information, including that which is misleading. In other words, a misleading statement issued by a company will be read by market professionals whose actions and advice to clients will affect the market price of that stock. An individual investor who enters the market relying on its integrity will assume that the market price of the company's shares is a fair estimate of their true worth, and is thus indirectly misled, even though he or she never reads the specific misleading statement. Therefore, a presumption of reliance by such investors, such as that provided by the fraud-on-the-market theory, is permissible in a case such as this. A defendant could rebut the presumption by any showing that severs the link between the alleged misrepresentation and the price received or paid. For example, the defendant could show that the securities involved were not traded on an efficient market, or that the misstatement did not affect the market price. ∎

---

Although the outer limit of permissible 10b-5 actions is not completely settled, the Supreme Court has attempted to confine the actions to situations involving deceit and manipulation. Simple corporate mismanagement or breaches of fiduciary duty by corporate officials, not involving deceit, are not actionable under Rule 10b-5.[5]

[5] *Santa Fe Industries v. Green,* 430 U.S. 462 (1977).

## Proxy Regulation

Although most corporate decisions are made by the officers and directors, shareholders do occasionally vote on matters of importance. At the annual shareholders meeting, which state incorporation laws require be held, the shareholders elect directors to the board of directors. Their approval may also be required for certain extraordinary matters, such as amendments to corporate bylaws or articles of incorporation, mergers, or sales of major assets.

Valid shareholder approval requires at least a majority vote (and sometimes a two-thirds or three-fourths approval) of a quorum of shares eligible to vote. However, in a large corporation with thousands of shareholders, it is very unusual for more than a small percentage of shareholders to appear at the annual meeting. In order to obtain a quorum, corporate management is usually required to solicit *proxies* from the shareholders. A **proxy** is an authorization to vote shares owned by someone else. At a typical corporation's annual meeting, incumbent management will solicit and receive proxies from a sufficient number of shareholders to vote itself into control for another year.

Section 14(a) of the 1934 Act prohibits solicitation of proxies for any shares registered under the Act in contravention of rules promulgated by the SEC. The rules which the SEC has issued have three broad goals: full disclosure, fraud prevention, and increased shareholder participation.

**Full Disclosure:** State laws have not always required corporate management to be responsive to the informational needs and desires of shareholders. The SEC, knowing that most major corporations solicit proxies at least annually, requires in Rule 14a-3 that no soliciting occur unless each person solicited is furnished with a written proxy statement containing the information specified in Schedule 14A.

Schedule 14A contains over 20 items, some of which are applicable only if specified matters, such as merger approval, are involved. In the typical solicitation by management relating to election of directors, the proxy statement must be accompanied by an annual report to contain, *inter alia,* comparative financial statements for the last two fiscal years, a summary of operations, a brief description of the business done by the issuer and its subsidiaries, and identification of the issuer's directors and executive officers and their principal occupations. This information must be clearly presented.

**Proxy Contests:** Normally, incumbent management will face no organized opposition in the election of directors at the annual meeting. But if the corporation is floundering financially, perhaps a group of "insurgent" shareholders will attempt to elect its own slate of candidates to the board of directors. Or perhaps the insurgents have lined up a merger with or tendered their shares to another corporation, which intends to fire incumbent management, and incumbent management has negotiated a proposed defensive merger with yet another company, which would be willing to retain the incumbents in their present positions. In these and other situations, proxy contests arise over the control of the corporation. Incumbent management and insurgent shareholders vie for sufficient proxies to prevail in the shareholders' vote. Federal regulations specify the procedure for such contests and punish any fraud which may occur.

Prior to solicitation, Rule 14a-11 requires insurgents to file an informational statement with the SEC and exchanges disclosing the participants in the insurgent group—those persons soliciting the proxies, financing the effort, or serving as attorneys and accountants for the group. Schedule 14B sets out the information which must be disclosed about the participants, including their employment history, past criminal violations, and stock holdings. At the time of solicitation, the insurgents must provide the shareholders with their own proxy statement similar to that which management is required to provide.

*Anti-Fraud:* Proxy contests sometimes become quite heated. To prevent fraud, Rule 14a-9 prohibits the use of false or misleading statements to solicit proxies. The term "solicitation" is broadly defined to cover both statements seeking proxies and communications urging shareholders to refuse to give proxies. Thus, if incumbent management falsely states or omits to state a material fact in urging shareholders not to grant proxies to an insurgent group, a violation of Rule 14a-9 and Section 14(a) occurs. A private cause of action is available to remedy such a violation.

## Tender Offers

A final important area of federal securities law regulates a method of taking control of a corporation, called a **tender offer.** In a typical tender offer, one corporation (the "offeror") will publicly offer to purchase a controlling interest (over 50 percent of the shares) in another corporation (the "target"). The target's shareholders are invited to tender their shares to the offeror in return for cash or the offeror's equity or debt securities (or a combination) in an amount usually well above the prior market price of the target's stock. Two examples of large tender offers occurred in 1981—the Du Pont takeover of Conoco and the U.S. Steel Corporation's purchase of Marathon Oil Company. Both purchases involved sums exceeding $6 billion.

Because of the easy availability of credit then and lack of government regulation, the tender offer gained widespread usage in the 1960s. One variety, termed the "Saturday Night Special," featured a "take-it-or-leave-it" offer to the target's shareholders with a very short time for them to make up their minds. Afraid of losing an opportunity to sell their shares at above the market price, shareholders frequently would tender their shares without time to learn anything about the offeror or to evaluate the possibility of a higher offer from a different source.

**Federal Legislation:** Comprehensive federal regulation of tender offers began with the passage of the Williams Act in 1968. That act amended Sections 13 and 14 of the 1934 Act with the basic purpose of increasing both the amount of information flowing to target shareholders and the time available to utilize that information.

*Filing Requirements:* Section 13(d) of the 1934 Act requires that any person or group acquiring more than 5 percent of the shares of any corporation must file a Schedule 13D within ten days with the SEC. That schedule requires disclosure of the background of the person or group, their source of funds, their purpose, the number of shares owned, relevant contracts or other arrangements with the target, and any plans for change of the target's affairs.

*Procedural Rules:* Section 14(d) and Rule 14d-2 provide that a tender offer is commenced on the date of public announcement of the offer. On that date, Rule 14d-3 requires the offeror to file with the SEC a Schedule 14D-1, which requires informational disclosures similar to those of Schedule 13D.

The target's management may support a tender offer; perhaps the management even negotiated it. But tender offers frequently are "hostile," and the offeror intends to replace the target's management with its own people. Even if the target's management opposes the offer, Section 14(d) and Rule 14d-5 require the target's management to mail the tender offer to the target's shareholders or to promptly provide the offeror with a shareholder list so it can do the mailing itself.

Target management must file with the SEC a Schedule 14D-9. This document (1) discloses whether the officers and directors intend to hold their shares or to tender, (2) describes any contractual arrangements management may have with the offeror (for instance, the offeror sometimes can obtain management's support through monetary incentives), and (3) discloses any concrete negotiations with a "white knight"—a company willing to make a competing tender offer that is more advantageous to incumbent management.

*Substantive Rules:* Substantively, Section 14(d) and Rule 14e-1 provide that a tender offer must be held open for a minimum of 20 business days, so the target's shareholders will have an opportunity to fully evaluate the offer. No more Saturday Night Specials will occur. If more shares are tendered than the offeror wishes to purchase, the offeror must purchase from each shareholder on a *pro rata* basis. This requirement promotes equal treatment of shareholders.

What if an offeror initiates the tender offer at $40 per share, seeking to purchase 51 percent of the target's shares, but only 25 percent are tendered? The offeror may choose to extend the offering period and amend the offer to $50 per share. This higher price must be given to all tendering shareholders, including those who were willing to sell at the lower price.

The final important provision of the Williams Act is Section 14(e), the prohibition of fraud or manipulation in either supporting or opposing a tender offer.

*Remedies:* Violations of Sections 13(d), 14(d), and 14(e) may be remedied by civil actions for injunctive relief. Injured shareholders who, relying on fraudulent statements, either tendered when they would not have done so had they known the truth or failed to tender when they would have had they not been defrauded, also can sue for damages under Section 14(e).

**Defensive Tactics:** A recent controversy has focused on the latitude that should be accorded target management in opposing hostile tender offers. Normally, a court is hesitant to review the business judgments of a corporation's management. However, in recent years target managements have often taken extreme measures to fend off tender offers. For example, they have spent corporate cash and borrowed large sums of money in order to make the corporation less attractive and to prevent an offeror from using the target's own assets to help pay off debts incurred in the takeover. They have moved the corporation to states with laws that tend to make tender offers more difficult to consummate successfully. They have acquired competitors of the offeror in an attempt to create an antitrust impediment to the takeover. They have launched "Pac-Man" counter tender offers for control of the offeror. They have sold the corporation's "crown jewel" (the subsidiary that attracted the offer in the first place). They have granted "lock-up options" (opportunities to purchase part of the company at bargain prices) to "white knights" (friendly third-party bidders) to assure their victory over the hostile offerors. They have issued "poison pills" (shares of stock that carry the right, effective in the event of a change of control, to buy the corporation's shares for 50 cents on the dollar, thereby dramatically diluting the position of the offeror). They have even threatened "corporate suicide" (liquidation and dissolution).

Legal challenges to these defensive tactics have taken two major forms. One basis for attack is the argument that target managers are breaching their fiduciary duties to shareholders by using defensive tactics to save their jobs at the expense of the shareholders' opportunity to sell at a profit. For many years, such challenges were uniformly unsuccessful as the courts repeatedly held that defensive actions taken by target managements were protected by the "business judgment rule"—the courts' determination to defer to the expertise of the board of directors.

In recent years, however, the courts have been less willing to apply the business judgment rule automatically to protect target management, in light of the conflict-of-interest situation that exists when target managers face a hostile tender offer that has the potential for great profits for the shareholders but loss of jobs for the managers.

Two important rules have developed in Delaware, the leading corporate law jurisdiction. First, in *Unocal Corp. v. Mesa Petroleum Co.,* 493 A.2d 946 (Del. 1985), the Delaware Supreme Court held that a target management's defensive tactics must be reasonable in relation to the threat posed. If a hostile bidder's tender offer is coercive or clearly inadequate, target management will be given substantial leeway to defeat it. However, if the bid is not coercive and at a fair price that target shareholders can take or leave at their own discretion, target management "does not have unbridled discretion to defeat any perceived threat by any draconian means available."

Second, once target managers have decided that the corporation is for sale—e.g., they respond to a hostile bid by bringing in a "white knight" to make a competing bid or they make their own bid through a management-sponsored leveraged buy-out (an attempt by target management to buy out the public investors by using huge amounts of credit secured by the corporation's own assets)—they become "auctioneers" with a responsibility to obtain the highest possible price for the shareholders. *Revlon, Inc. v. MacAndrews & Forbes Holdings, Inc.,* 506 A.2d 173 (Del. 1986) holds that use of lock-up options to sell crown jewels to a white knight may unduly favor that white knight, thereby impermissibly stifling the bidding contest.

In *Paramount Communications, Inc. v. Time, Inc.,* 571 A.2d 1140 (Del. 1990), the Delaware Supreme Court's interpretation of these rules gave additional leeway to a target board by holding that directors "are not obliged to abandon a deliberately conceived corporate plan for a short-term shareholder profit [in the form of a tender offer] unless there is clearly no basis to sustain the corporate strategy." Time approved a target board's use of a poison pill to "just say no" to a hostile bid that would have disrupted the target's long-term strategic plan to merge with another corporation.

A second basis for attacking defensive tactics is to argue that they are "manipulative" in violation of Sec. 14(e) of the Williams Act. The Supreme Court dealt a serious blow to this argument in the following case.

### Schreiber v. Burlington Northern, Inc.
U.S. Supreme Court,
472 U.S. 1 (1985)

On December 21, 1982, Burlington Northern, Inc., made a hostile tender offer for 25 million shares of El Paso Gas Co. at $24 per share. Though El Paso's management initially opposed the offer, its shareholders fully subscribed to it. Burlington did not accept the tendered shares, however. Instead, after negotiations with El Paso's management, Burlington rescinded the December tender offer, purchased 4 million shares from El Paso, substituted a new tender offer for only 21 million shares at $24 each, and recognized certain contractual arrangements between El Paso and its management which guaranteed the managers substantial compensation upon a change of control ("golden parachutes"). Over 40 million shares were tendered in response to the second tender offer.

Rescission of the first offer diminished payment to those shareholders who had tendered during the first offer. Not only were fewer shares purchased, but the shareholders who retendered were subjected to substantial proration. Petitioner Schreiber sued on behalf of similarly situated shareholders, alleging that Burlington, El Paso, and members of El Paso's board violated §14(e). She claimed that withdrawal of the first tender offer coupled with substitution of the second was a "manipulative" distortion of the market for El Paso stock.

The trial court dismissed the suit for failure to state a claim. The U.S. Court of Appeals for the Third Circuit affirmed. Schreiber petitioned to the Supreme Court.

**Decision:** The judgment was affirmed. The term "manipulation" as used in §14(e) of the 1934 Act has the same meaning as when used in §10(b). According to an earlier Supreme Court case, "It is and was virtually a term of art when used in connection with the securities markets. It connotes intentional or willful conduct designed *to deceive or defraud* investors by controlling or artificially affecting the price of securities."

So, "manipulative" acts require misrepresentation or nondisclosure. That type of conduct was not present in this case. Defendants' challenged actions were fully disclosed, so they could not have been manipulative in violation of §14(e). Plaintiffs' real claim is that defendants' actions were unfair, but this type of a claim presents a *state law* issue as to whether defendants breached their fiduciary duty to plaintiffs. ∎

## STATE REGULATION

Because every state has its own system of securities regulation, corporations must always be cognizant of these rules also. The Commissioners on Uniform State Laws have produced the Uniform Securities Act, which has been used as a pattern for many states' laws. Still, because many large states have not followed this act and many have amended it to varying degrees, there is a lack of uniformity which complicates the marketing of securities. Perhaps the Revised Uniform Securities Act, promulgated in late 1985, will lead to more uniformity. It will likely change some of the present state practices described below.

### *Registration*

Most states have laws which, like the 1933 Securities Act, regulate the original distribution of securities. A corporation which intends to market its shares nationwide must comply with not only the 1933 Act but also approximately 40 separate state registration laws. There are three basic systems of state registration. Some states use *registration by notification,* which requires the filing of certain material and then a waiting period before the securities may be sold, similar to the procedure under the 1933 Act.

*Registration by qualification* is used by some states. This process goes beyond the simple disclosure philosophy of the 1933 Act and actually involves merit review of the securities by state officials. Typically, states using merit review refuse to allow sales of securities which do not meet a "fair, just and equitable" standard. The standard may not be met, for example, if the organizers and promoters of the corporation intend to sell to the public at per share prices much greater than they themselves paid.

The third type is *registration by coordination,* which results in automatic state approval whenever a security's registration has become effective under the 1933 Act at the federal level.

Some states allow registration by more than one method.

## Exemptions

State registration laws contain exemptions, as does the 1933 Act. There is an ongoing effort to coordinate state and federal exemptions to produce uniformity. A uniform system of exemptions would greatly simplify matters for a corporation planning a widespread distribution of securities, but the chances of achieving complete uniformity appear slim.

## Other Provisions

Many state securities laws also contain antifraud provisions similar to those in the 1933 and 1934 federal laws. In states without such laws, the courts have extended the common law of fraud to prohibit deceitful securities practices.

Some states also have qualification and registration provisions governing the activities of securities brokers and dealers, which are usually similar to federal registration provisions in the 1934 Act.

Many states also regulate tender offers. The constitutionality of one such state act was upheld recently in *CTS Corp. v. Dynamics Corp.*, 107 S.Ct. 1637 (1987).

# RICO

Although not a securities act in a strict sense, the Racketeer Influenced and Corrupt Organizations Act of 1970 (RICO) must be noted in this chapter. Congress passed RICO to attack organized crime, especially its infiltration into legitimate business. RICO provided both criminal penalties and private civil suits for damages. However, RICO neither included a definition of "organized crime" nor expressly required a link between a defendant's activities and organized crime. Therefore, about nine-tenths of the suits brought under RICO have had no connection with professional criminals, but have, instead, named as defendants accounting firms, banks, law firms, manufacturing corporations, and the like. The law has become very popular with plaintiffs because, unlike most civil causes of action, it provides a prevailing plaintiff with treble damages, attorneys' fees, and a very strong bargaining chip in settlement negotiations.

Generally speaking, a RICO plaintiff need prove only (1) a pattern of racketeering activity (commission of "predicate acts") by the defendant; (2) the existence of an enterprise affecting interstate commerce; (3) a nexus between the pattern of racketeering activity and the enterprise; and (4) an injury to the plaintiff's business or property by reason of the racketeering activity. Because racketeering activity is defined by means of a list of 34 offenses, including not only murder, kidnapping, gambling, arson, bribery, and extortion, but also mail, wire, and securities fraud, "legitimate" commercial businesses frequently find themselves named as defendants in RICO suits.

The lower courts realized that Congress probably did not intend the law to be such a harsh weapon for attacking otherwise legitimate businesses. Therefore, many of them began to require that a civil RICO plaintiff prove that a defendant had been criminally *convicted* of racketeering acts before recovering in civil suits. This slowed the pace of RICO litigation for a time, but the Supreme Court held in *Sedima v. Imrex, Inc.*, 473 U.S. 479 (1985),[6] that there was no support in the language of the statute for a conviction requirement. Though Congress had aimed the law at true organized crime, it had drafted the Act so broadly that the courts could limit it in this fashion only by improperly rewriting it. However, the *Sedima* opinion did give some hope for limiting RICO's impact by suggesting that the RICO "pattern" element (which had been construed by some courts to require simply two unrelated acts of racketeering within a 10-year period) required "continuity and relationship."

Congress has repeatedly considered amending RICO, but as of this writing, has failed to take any action. Therefore, the lower courts again took it upon themselves to narrow RICO's scope by use of the "pattern" requirement. The lower courts' holding that a "pattern" required multiple fraudulent schemes was rejected by the Supreme Court in *H.J., Inc. v. Northwestern Bell Telephone Co.*, 109 S.Ct. 2893 (1989), where the Court found a "pattern" to exist in a single criminal scheme to bribe members of a regulatory agency. Because the scheme contained numerous acts of bribery that were related to one another in terms of purpose, results, participants, victims, and methods of commission, the relationship requirement was met. Because the open-ended scheme lasted for over six years, the continuity requirement was met. The Supreme Court's refusal in *H.J., Inc.* to limit RICO caused critics to once again call for legislative reform.

---

[6] *Sedima* is a major case in Chapter 4.

# SUMMARY

Securities law is enmeshed in federal and state regulation. Securities, whether debt or equity, must upon initial issuance be registered with the SEC, unless an exemption is available. The goal of registration is to force disclosure of material facts regarding the issuing company so that potential investors can make an informed decision.

The registration process is burdensome and expensive. Companies are severely limited in terms of the publicity in which they can engage before and immediately after registration. To reduce the paperwork burden, the SEC has done its best in recent years to integrate the requirements of the 1933 Act, which govern the one-time registration of shares about to be issued, with those of the 1934 Act, which govern the continuous disclosures which larger corporations must make.

If errors of omission or misrepresentation appear in a registration statement, a battery of government and private actions are available to punish the wrongdoers.

The 1934 Act governs a number of important areas of trading in securities. Insider trading is an unfair practice of particular concern to the SEC these days. Both §16(b) which provides a form of strict liability for trading by officers, directors and 10 percent owners, and §10(b) which ranges more broadly but requires proof of actual use of material, nonpublic information, are available to punish such trading.

Section 10(b) is also available to remedy false or inadequate corporate disclosures in press releases, SEC filings, annual reports and the like. Private litigation under §10(b) for damages has reshaped securities law in the United States.

Two methods of gaining control of a corporation, proxy fights and tender offers, involve particularly high stakes. The opportunities for profit and abuse of shareholder interests are great. Both processes are subject to a web of federal regulation designed to protect shareholder interests. In the proxy realm, the key is full disclosure. In tender offers, it is disclosure plus fair treatment of all shareholders.

Though federal regulation tends to dominate the scene, no securities attorney may safely ignore the securities rules that most states have enacted to cover issuance of shares, fraud, tender offers, and other related matters.

Finally, the harsh RICO act carries severe penalties for any party engaging in wire, mail, or securities fraud. Although RICO may soon be amended, its present broad provisions pose great danger for accountants, lawyers, and securities professionals.

# KEY TERMS

**Securities**
**Prospectus**
**Shelf registration**
**Materiality**
**Accredited investor**
**Scienter**
**Proxy**
**Tender offer**

# QUESTIONS AND PROBLEMS

**1.** Co-op City was a massive, government-subsidized housing complex, operated as a nonprofit corporation. To acquire an apartment, eligible prospective tenants had to buy 18 shares of Co-op stock for each room at $25 per share. The purchase was in effect a recoverable deposit. The shares could not be transferred to a nontenant, did not carry votes as to management of the co-op, and had to be offered to the co-op for sale at the initial selling price whenever the tenant moved out. When rental rates went up, some tenants sued claiming inadequate disclosure under the federal securities law. Discuss whether these "shares of stock," as they were labeled, constituted securities under federal law. (*United Housing Foundation, Inc. v. Forman*, 421 U.S. 837, 1975.)

**2.** Holiday Inns' profits for the first quarter of 1975 were 20 cents per share. In the spring of 1976, Holiday Inns made a public offering. Straus purchased Holiday Inns stock on March 23, 1976, but its value declined soon thereafter when it was disclosed that Holiday Inns' profits for the first quarter of 1976 were only 7 cents per share. Plaintiff sued under Section 11 of the 1933 Act because the prospectus had not disclosed the drop in profits. Holiday Inns claimed that of the 13 cent decline, 12 cents occurred in March, and that could not have been known at the time Straus purchased. Discuss Holiday Inns' disclosure responsibilities in light of the concept of materiality. (*Straus v. Holiday Inns, Inc.*, 460 F.Supp. 729, S.D.N.Y. 1978.)

**3.** The SEC sued seeking to enjoin Schlitz Brewing Co. from further violations of the antifraud provisions of the 1933 and 1934 Acts. The suit was predicated on Schlitz's failure to disclose in its registration statements, prospectuses, and periodic reports that (1) it was involved in a nationwide scheme to induce retailers to purchase Schlitz's products by making kickback payments, and (2) it had violated Spanish tax and exchange laws. Schlitz claimed the omissions were nonmaterial, especially considering that the alleged kickbacks amounted to $3 million compared to Schlitz's annual sales of $1 billion. The SEC claimed they were material because they reflected on the integrity of management. Discuss. (*SEC v. Jos. Schlitz Brewing Co.*, 452 F.Supp. 824, E.D.Wis. 1978.)

**4.** Plaintiffs were worried about tax liability, so they consulted defendant, a tax adviser. Defendant recommended that plaintiffs look into a particular real estate deal which he described as the "best investment so far as tax shelter is concerned" he had ever seen. Plaintiffs invested in the deal, but did not get the tax break they wanted. Plaintiffs sued defendant under Section 12(2) of the 1933 Act because of alleged misrepresentations the sellers made regarding the property's taxable basis. Defendant was not a seller, so he raised the defense of lack of privity. Discuss. (*Croy v. Campbell*, 624 F.2d 709, 5th Cir. 1980.)

**5.** Claiming the intrastate exemption of Section 3(a)(11) of the 1933 Act, McDonald Investment Company did not register its offering of shares with the SEC. McDonald is a Minnesota corporation with its only offices in that state. It sold shares only to Minnesota residents. However, the funds were raised to lend to real estate developers in Arizona. Discuss the availability of the exemption. (*SEC v. McDonald Investment Co.*, 343 F.Supp. 343, D.Minn. 1972.)

**6.** Moore, a psychiatrist, was treating the wife of an officer of Posi-Seal. Another company was planning to acquire Posi-Seal. At a treatment session with the wife which the Posi-Seal officer attended in order to facilitate the treatment process, Moore learned of the planned acquisition. Before public announcement of the acquisition, Moore bought 9,000 shares of Posi-Seal stock. He sold them after the acquisition at a profit of $26,933.74. Discuss whether Moore has violated §10(b)'s ban on insider trading. (*SEC v. Morgan F. Moore*, No. N-86-88-PCD D.Conn. 1986.)

**7.** Lund was CEO of Verit Industries. Horowitz was on Verit's board, and was CEO of P&F Co. Lund and Horowitz were friends. P&F began negotiating a particular deal, and Horowitz called Lund to ask him if Verit would be interested in providing capital and being an investor in the acquisition. Lund said that Verit would not be interested. However, he soon bought 10,000 shares of P&F stock in his own name at $1.25/share—his only purchase of P&F stock in ten years. Soon the P&F deal was completed and announced to the public. Lund sold his shares for a $12,500 profit. The SEC charged that Lund had violated Rule 10b-5's insider trading prohibition. Did he? (*SEC v. Lund*, 570 F.Supp. 1397, C.D.Cal. 1983.)

**8.** A registered broker-dealer's sales force repeatedly made false and misleading statements in an effort to sell Lawn-A-Mat common stock. After several complaints were ignored, the SEC sought an injunction to halt the illicit practices. One respondent was the sales supervisor, who was informed of the misdeeds but did not take affirmative steps to prevent a recurrence of the deceit. One issue which arose was whether the SEC would have to prove scienter in order to obtain an injunction against practices which allegedly violated Rule 10b-5. Discuss. (*Aaron v. SEC*, 446 U.S. 680, 1980.)

**9.** Plaintiff purchased some industrial revenue bonds which turned out to be largely worthless. Later he sued under Rule 10b-5, claiming that the bonds' offering circular contained such fraudulent statements that the bonds could never have been placed on the market without the misrepresentations. However, plaintiff admitted that he had not read the circular before purchasing. Should this admission bar recovery? Discuss. (*Shores v. Sklar*, 647 F.2d 462, 5th Cir. 1981.)

**10.** VAC, a Delaware corporation, was the world's largest maker of cutting tools and quality hand tools. Its management and ownership were dominated by the Thomas family. Throughout its history, VAC pursued long-term profit maximization, often investing large amounts of capital at the expense of short-term profit. VAC has been quite successful. Newell Co. has also been successful, primarily by acquiring other companies. Ninety percent of Newell's sales and profits were generated by past acquisitions, often achieved through tender offers. Newell slowly accumulated 11 percent of VAC's stock and then made a tender offer for 10 percent more. The VAC board, dominated by outside directors, authorized a repurchase by VAC of its own shares that would increase the holdings of the Thomas family to over 50 percent, effectively blocking any attempted takeover. Is the repurchase consistent with the fiduciary duties of the VAC board? Discuss. (*Newell Co. v. Vermont American Corp.*, 725 F.Supp. 351, N.D.Ill. 1989.)

CHAPTER 42

# LEGAL LIABILITY OF ACCOUNTANTS

Modern economies are critically dependent on accurate, reliable financial information, which provides the basis by which investors and businesspersons value assets and enterprises. As accumulations of capital grow larger and economic transactions become more complex, the importance of this information grows ever greater.

Accountants provide much of this financial information. An accountant who audits a corporation's books is relied on not just by the corporation but also by investors, creditors, government agencies, and others to provide an accurate financial picture. Because the role of the accountant is so critical to our economy and the potential damage if the accountant errs is so great, all states regulate use of the title *certified public accountant* (*CPA*). All states require examinations for qualification, and many require additional experience and continuing education for CPAs. An extensive code of ethics promulgated by the American Institute of Certified Public Accountants (AICPA) sets out rules of conduct.

Despite a generally exemplary record, the accounting profession occasionally stubs its collective toe. A vast network of statutes and rules provides an arsenal of legal weapons for those who may be injured by the accountant's errors. Furthermore, when a company fails, its independent auditor may be one of the few potential defendants that is solvent. The auditor's assets and liability insurance policies present an attractive target for suit. Indeed, there have been more suits against accounting firms in the past 15 years than in the entire previous history of the profession. Between 1980 and 1988 major accounting firms paid out $300 million in audit-related litigation, and still had $2 billion worth of damage claims pending against them. It is no wonder liability insurance rates have skyrocketed for accountants in recent years.

It is important to be familiar with the legal obligations of accountants. This chapter surveys the many potential sources of an accountant's legal liability. Of the three major accounting functions—auditing, tax practice, and management advisory services—auditing is emphasized because it generates the most accounting revenue and gives rise to most of the lawsuits filed against accountants.

## COMMON-LAW LIABILITY TO CLIENTS
### *Contractual Liability*

An accountant hired to audit a company's books is an independent contractor who must perform the auditing responsibilities properly and with due care. Though not a guarantor of the accuracy of the client's financial records, the auditor must act diligently, independently, and honestly. The auditor's responsibilities are established by the contract with the client.

An audit is an independent critique of a business entity's financial statements in order to determine their accuracy and reliability. The audit consists of three phases: (1) collection of data, (2) analysis of data, and (3) report of data and conclusions in an appropriate form. The goal of the audit is an opinion by the auditor regarding the quality of the client's financial statements.

An auditor who is unable to form a valid opinion as to the accuracy of the company's records—perhaps because the company has allowed only a limited review, or the underlying financial records are incomplete, or the accuracy is dependent upon an event that has not yet transpired, such as the closing of a pending sale—uses a **disclaimer.** A disclaimer informs the reader that the auditor has had to

647

qualify the opinion and is therefore not vouching for the total accuracy of the company's financial statements. In one case an auditor was able to avoid legal liability by clearly noting that the auditors did not confirm the accounts receivable or review their collectability and that the balance sheet had not been adjusted for uncollectable receivables.[1] However, if the disclaimer is not sufficiently clear and definite to qualify a general impression of accuracy in the financial statements, the auditor may still be liable. Furthermore, an accountant who knows that statements compiled by the company are inaccurate cannot pass them along with a disclaimer and thereby avoid liability. A disclaimer does not relieve an accountant from the duty to refrain from knowingly being a party to fraud.[2]

The defensibility of the auditor's opinion is frequently the subject of litigation. Any number of auditing errors can produce an inaccurate opinion and constitute a breach of the auditing contract. The auditor may be inadequately trained or supervised or not sufficiently familiar with the client's business. Lapses in examination, such as the failure to verify inventory, or to discover that accounts receivable are uncollectable, may occur. Poor judgment in analyzing the data or a misleading manner of reporting conclusions are other errors. Such mistakes constitute a breach of the auditing contract and may result in liability on a breach of contract claim.

## Negligence Liability

The same auditing mistakes that constitute a breach of contract will normally also constitute a breach of the auditor's duty of due care and therefore provide a basis for a tort claim of negligence. An auditor who fails to observe professional standards is liable just like a doctor or lawyer who commits malpractice.

**Standard of Care in Auditing:** The duty of an auditor is to exercise the special care and skill that the typical professional auditor would exercise in the same circumstances. At trial, expert testimony will help establish that standard of care.

Where does the standard of care come from? The auditor may be guided by **Generally Accepted Accounting Standards (GAAS),** which establish the objectives to be obtained by an audit and set the quality of performance in terms of skill, independence, and care. **Generally Accepted Accounting Principles (GAAP)** address the theoretical aspects of how various transactions should be carried on the books. GAAS and GAAP are derived from such sources as (1) pronouncements of the AICPA, (2) pronouncements of the Financial Accounting Standards Board (FASB), (3) Securities and Exchange Commission accounting rules and releases, (4) rules of state boards of accounting and societies of CPAs, and (5) Internal Revenue Service rules of practice. These standards can be raised in a specific instance if more is promised by the auditor in a particular engagement contract.

A violation of GAAP or GAAS will be considered *prima facie* evidence of negligence by the auditor. On the other hand, compliance with GAAP and GAAS does not ensure an auditor of nonliability. Even if proper procedures and standards are used, poor judgment in analyzing the data collected can lead to liability. Furthermore, some courts demand more of auditors than mere mechanical application of GAAP and GAAS. For example, in *United States v. Simon*,[3] defendant auditors were convicted of conspiring to commit criminal fraud by knowingly certifying a false and misleading financial statement, despite their calling eight expert independent accountants who testified that defendants had complied with GAAP and GAAS. The court held such expert testimony to be "persuasive" but not "conclusive" and left to the jury the ultimate decision as to whether the financial statements as a whole did not fairly present the client's financial position. In most recent cases, however, courts have held that auditors fulfill their duty of due care by complying with GAAP and GAAS in good faith.[4]

**Standard of Care in Nonauditing Situations:** Sometimes accountants are hired to do less exacting work than a full audit. Traditionally, if the accountant did an unaudited financial statement or bookkeeping, he or she could avoid liability by marking each page as unaudited and accompanying all documents with a disclaimer to clearly indicate the auditor expressed no opinion on accuracy.

However, cases decided in the 1970s held accountants civilly and even criminally liable for their

---

[1] *Stephens Industries, Inc. v. Haskins & Sells*, 438 F.2d 357 (10th Cir. 1971).

[2] *Ashland Oil, Inc. v. Arnett*, 875 F.2d 1271 (7th Cir. 1989).

[3] 425 F.2d 796 (2d Cir. 1969), *cert. denied*, 397 U.S. 1006 (1970).

[4] *SEC v. Arthur Young & Co.*, 590 F.2d 785 (9th Cir. 1979).

"unauditor" activities. The courts clearly expected the auditors to take a more active role in detecting fraud and misstatements than did the accounting profession in these situations.

Because there was a lack of guidance as to what was expected of an accountant doing "unauditor" work, the AICPA issued Statements on Standards for Accounting and Review Services No. 1 (SSARS No. 1), which provides the heretofore missing standards. SSARS No. 1 divides nonaudit work into **compilation** (assembly and preparation of financial statements from records of the client) and **review** (limited review of financial statements prepared by the client), and provides specific guidelines as to what is expected of the accountant in both activities.

**Fraud Detection:** Auditors have often taken the position that it is not their job to detect fraud, but only to ensure that their clients prepare financial statements in accordance with GAAP and GAAS. They say that they are "watchdogs, not bloodhounds." Courts sometimes demand a higher standard than auditors desire, one stating: "general accounting standards . . . require the auditor to use his professional skill to follow up any signs of fraud that he discovers in the audit. . . . Auditors are not detectives hired to ferret out fraud, but if they chance on signs of fraud they may not avert their eyes—they must investigate."[5]

Numerous instances of "audit failure" (where firms took bankruptcy soon after their auditors had given them unqualified audit opinions attesting to the reliability of their financial reports) in the 1970s and 1980s led to pressure to increase the auditor's role as financial detective. In 1990, the Auditing Standards Board's SAS No. 53, dealing with an auditor's responsibility to detect fraud, became effective. Basically, SAS No. 53 states that an auditor should not only exercise due care in planning, performing, and evaluating the results of audit procedures, but also bring to bear the proper degree of "professional skepticism" to achieve reasonable assurance that material errors or irregularities will be discovered. (Under earlier standards, auditors were allowed to assume that management was honest, absent information to the contrary.)

Professional skepticism means assuming neither dishonest management nor unquestioned honesty. Auditors should certainly be alert to mistakes in gathering or processing accounting data, incorrect accounting estimates due to oversight or misrepresentation, and mistakes in application of accounting principles. It is important that auditors assess the integrity of management by considering circumstances that may indicate a tendency on management's part to distort financial statements, such as frequent disputes about aggressive application of accounting rules or evasive responses to audit inquiries. Accounting firms must keep a client's auditing committee informed as to any significant irregularities discovered.

Still, auditors are not required to be lawyers or criminal investigators. SAS No. 53 recognizes that auditors cannot *guarantee* the accuracy of their reports.

## Independence

The following guidelines serve to preserve the auditor's independence.

1. Accountants must not have any direct or material indirect financial interest in the client.
2. Auditors should not loan money to or accept loans from the client.
3. Auditors should not be officers or directors of the client.
4. Auditors should not work for a contingent fee.
5. Auditors should not allow clients to indemnify them for their professional liability exposure.

If independence is lacking, any issued reports should indicate it in an accompanying disclosure.

Because the client pays the auditor's fees, it is not always easy for the auditor to remain independent. In 1984, for example, approximately 450 public corporations changed auditors. Though most switches were supposedly motivated by an opportunity for lower fees, 20 percent of the changes followed issuance of a qualified opinion. This development has led both Congress and the SEC to scrutinize possible "opinion shopping"—a corporation's scouting about until it can find an accounting firm willing to support a favorable accounting treatment. As the SEC has stated: "If the manner in which the issuer changes its auditors restricts the independence of the new auditors or calls into question their objectivity, such conduct erodes the public's belief in the integrity of both the financial markets and the independent audit function."[6]

The SEC has adopted rules mandating prompt disclosure by large public companies of changes in

---

[5] *Cenco, Inc. v. Seidman & Seidman*, 686 F.2d 449 (7th Cir. 1982).

[6] *In re Broadview Financial Corp.*, Securities Exchange Act Release No. 21949.

auditors under circumstances indicating possible "opinion shopping." The disclosure must include the grounds of disagreement with the former auditor and any discussions the company had with the new auditor before the switch.

## Defenses

**Lack of Reliance:** Plaintiffs cannot recover on account of an auditor's careless mistake if they knew the true facts and therefore did not rely on the erroneous opinion of the auditor.

**Contributory Negligence:** Contributory negligence by the client has been asserted successfully as a defense by careless auditors, but the courts disagree as to the scope of the defense. If the client's contributory negligence consists of disregarding the auditor's recommendations or of activity which prevented the auditor from effectively performing his or her duties, most courts would either bar recovery or reduce it.

If, on the other hand, the auditor's negligence lies in failure to detect fraud by the client's employees, the courts are split. Some hold that careless supervision by client management contributing to the success of the fraud constitutes contributory negligence. Other courts hold that careless supervision is not the type of conduct which should block or reduce recovery.

The following case illustrates one school of thought.

---

### Lincoln Grain, Inc. v. Coopers & Lybrand
Nebraska Supreme Court,
345 N.W.2d 300 (1984)

Plaintiff Lincoln Grain, Inc., hired defendant Coopers & Lybrand to audit its financial statements. As part of that audit, defendant investigated the accuracy of the valuation placed upon the inventory of plaintiff's Iowa division. Its inventory consisted only of contracts to sell or purchase commodities. On June 30, 1975, Lincoln Grain valued the inventory of its Iowa division at nearly $2 million. Defendant certified that plaintiff's financial statements containing this figure fairly presented plaintiff's financial picture. In fact, because of embezzlement by the manager of the Iowa division, its inventory was worth only $143,000.

Lincoln Grain filed this suit contending that if the audit had been conducted in accordance with GAAS, the fraudulent activities of its employee would have been discovered earlier and that it was damaged by the delay. Plaintiff appealed from a jury verdict for defendant, raising several issues.

**Decision:** The judgment was reversed. The trial court first erred in instructing the jury that if Lincoln Grain knew and appreciated the danger of employee fraud it had assumed the risk, and the verdict must be for Coopers & Lybrand. The assumption of risk defense applies only where the plaintiff voluntarily assumes a risk arising from the careless conduct *of the defendant.* Lincoln Grain's employee is not the defendant, and "certainly it cannot be said that one who engages an accountant assumes the risk that the accountant will fail to adhere to proper professional standards."

The trial judge had also instructed the jury to compare Lincoln Grain's carelessness with that of Coopers & Lybrand if it found that Lincoln Grain had failed properly to monitor and review the Iowa division's financial data, failed properly to supervise that division, etc. To allow accountants to escape liability for their carelessness on grounds that those who hire them are careless "would render illusory the notion that an accountant is liable for the negligent performance of his duties." Therefore, the Supreme Court adopted the rule that a client's carelessness is a defense "only where it has contributed to the accountant's failure to perform the contract and to report the truth." Such had not been the case here. ∎

---

## COMMON LAW LIABILITY TO THIRD PARTIES

In recent years auditors have increasingly found themselves subject to suit by nonclient plaintiffs. As the defense of lack of privity has slowly eroded in many other areas of the law, so it has diminished as a shield for auditors. Increasing reliance by client creditors, investors, and others on the work of the auditors has led to their increasing liability.

## Fraud

An auditor is guilty of fraud whenever he or she intentionally assists a client in deceiving others with false financial statements. If an auditor makes a false statement which he or she does not know is false but does not have reasonable grounds to believe is true, the act is deemed constructive fraud or gross negligence and the result is the same—liability to injured parties. Many years ago, a court said:

> A representation certified as true to the knowledge of the accountants when knowledge there is none, reckless misstatement, or an opinion based on grounds so flimsy as to lead to the conclusion that there was no genuine belief in its truth, are all sufficient upon which to base liability. A refusal to see the obvious, a failure to investigate the doubtful, if sufficiently gross, may furnish evidence leading to an inference of fraud so as to impose liability for losses suffered by those who rely on the balance sheet. In other words, heedlessness and reckless disregard of consequence may take the place of deliberate intention.[7]

An auditor's liability to third parties in fraud cases was firmly established many years ago in *Ultramares Corp. v. Touche* wherein the defendants certified a firm's accounts knowing that banks and other lenders were relying on the audit. The certified balance sheet showed a net worth of a million dollars when, in reality, the company's capital had been wiped out. Justice Cardozo held that "To creditors and investors to whom the [auditor's] employer exhibited the certificate, the defendants owed a . . . duty to make it without fraud, since there was notice in the circumstances of its making that the employer did not intend to keep it to himself." Regarding fraud, constructive fraud, recklessness, or gross negligence, Justice Cardozo's statement remains the rule today.[8]

## Negligence

In the *Ultramares* opinion, Justice Cardozo drew a sharp distinction between fraudulent conduct and negligent conduct, holding that the auditor would not be liable to third parties for the latter:

> If liability for negligence exists, a thoughtless slip or blunder, the failure to detect a theft or forgery beneath the cover of deceptive entries, may expose accountants to a liability in an indeterminate amount for an indeterminate time to an indeterminate class. The hazards of a business conducted on these terms are so extreme as to enkindle doubt whether a flaw may not exist in the implication of a duty that exposes to these consequences.

Although the force of Justice Cardozo's reasoning protected auditors from negligent liability to third parties for many years, the modern trend is toward breaking down the privity barrier to recovery in negligence cases. The following case discusses the possible approaches.

---

[7] *State St. Trust Co. v. Ernst*, 15 N.E.2d 416 (N.Y. 1938).

[8] *Ultramares Corp. v. Touche*, 174 N.E. 441 (N.Y. 1931).

---

**H. Rosenblum, Inc. v. Adler**
New Jersey Supreme Court,
461 A.2d 138 (1983)

**Defendant Touche Ross & Co. (Touche) audited the financial statements of Giant Stores Corp. (Giant). Relying on the correctness of these statements, plaintiffs Harry and Barry Rosenblum sold their businesses in New Jersey to Giant in exchange for Giant stock. The stock turned out to be worthless because Touche had carelessly failed to discover that Giant had manipulated its books by listing assets it did not have and omitting substantial debts it owed. Plaintiffs sued Touche and its partners, including Adler, on a number of theories, including negligence. The trial court granted defendant's summary judgment motion. Plaintiff appealed.**

**Decision:** The judgment was reversed. The court eliminated the privity requirement for negligent actions just as it had previously

*(continued)*

been eliminated in fraud cases. Because accountants can frequently foresee that their work will be relied on by persons other than the client, their liability for negligence should extend to foreseeable third parties. The requirements of reliance and proximate cause, along with the defense of comparative negligence, will sufficiently limit the extent of the accountant's third-party liability. Therefore, the privity requirement is unnecessary. ■

---

Today, about seven jurisdictions still follow the limited privity *Ultramares* view, fifteen have adopted the more moderate Restatement view, and four have adopted the liberal "reasonably foreseeable" standard first adopted in *Adler*. Others are undecided.[9]

## MANAGEMENT ADVISORY SERVICES

A second basic function of accountants is to perform consulting or management advisory services (MAS). More and more accountants are expanding into management consulting, giving general advice on such matters as mergers and acquisitions, modernizing manufacturing plants, personnel training, office management, and choosing types of computers, methods of inventory control, and tax shelters. Some major accounting firms have earned more than a billion dollars a year in consulting fees.

Because the AICPA has promulgated few concrete standards to govern MAS and there have been few litigated cases, the accountant venturing into MAS has little guidance. Many predict litigation in this area will increase, especially because accountants are starting to give advice as to matters outside their traditional competence.

Potential liability in this area is high. In a case involving the band Creedence Clearwater Revival, a jury rendered an $8.6 million verdict against an accounting firm which placed $5 million of the band's money in a Bahamian bank which the firm should have known was in financial trouble.[10]

In the past the SEC discouraged accounting firms from expanding into MAS. For example, the SEC has banned direct business relationships between accountants and the companies they audit, reasoning that an accounting firm's auditors would have difficulty being objective about decisions the firm's consultants had played a part in making. However, in 1990 the SEC ruled that accounting firms could spin off separate entities to do consulting work for their audit clients. For its part, the AICPA has stated that CPAs performing consulting work for audit clients must not assume the role of employee or manager in audit client operations or exercise authority on behalf of audit clients (such as by consummating transactions or holding custody of assets).

## TAX PRACTICE

The tax practice in which many accountants engage is an increasingly big business. Heavy government regulation of the area exposes the accountant to a variety of legal constraints.

For example, the Tax Reform Act of 1976 requires a preparer of tax returns to furnish a complete copy of each return to the taxpayer at the time or before the taxpayer signs the return, and to retain copies of the returns for three years or retain lists of client names and taxpayer identification numbers for IRS inspection. All returns prepared by CPAs must be signed by them even if no fee is charged (however, they should be signed only if the accountant is satisfied that all relevant information has been provided and all questions answered).

The Internal Revenue Code penalizes accountants who prepare returns yet do not (1) furnish copies to the taxpayer; (2) retain copies of returns or

---

[9] California recently adopted the *Adler* "foreseeability" test in *International Mortgage Co. v. John P. Butler Accountancy Corp.*, 177 Cal. App.3d 806 (1986). However, New York recently reaffirmed its allegiance to the *Ultramares* rule, though modifying it slightly to allow liability to third parties relying on inaccurate financial reports only where: (1) the accountant was aware that the financial reports were to be used for a particular purpose; (2) in the furtherance of which a known party was intended to rely; and (3) some conduct on the part of the accountants *linking* them to that party evinced the accountants' understanding of that party's reliance. *Credit Alliance Corp. v. Arthur Andersen & Co.*, 493 N.Y.S.2d 435 (1985).

[10] *Clifford v. Kanter*, #778142 (San Francisco Superior Court, 1983).

lists of names and taxpayer identification numbers; or (3) correct incorrectly prepared returns. The law also imposes civil liability on accountants who aid and abet taxpayers in substantial underpayment of taxes, and criminal liability for aiding, abetting, or counseling the preparation of false tax returns. Penalties for violation are not insubstantial.

An accountant who carelessly advises a client on tax matters, miscalculates a client's tax liability, forgets to file a client's return on time, or loses a client's papers can be held liable for negligence. Liability can extend to fees and penalties incurred by the client in correcting the mistake, occasional punitive damages, and even loss on prospective transactions. In one case, for example, defendant accountants advised plaintiff she could sell certain stock at a loss to reduce her income tax liability by offsetting an earlier gain in selling North American Company stock. Unfortunately, defendants had erroneously calculated the North American sale which really resulted in a loss. Because there was no reason to sell the additional stock at a loss, plaintiff was entitled to recover the difference between the sale price and the cost of replacement after she learned of the mistake.[11]

The IRS has substantial powers to obtain the papers of an accountant in investigating the tax liability of the accountant's client. Failure to comply with IRS subpoenas can lead to a contempt citation.

## ACCOUNTANTS AND THE FEDERAL SECURITIES LAWS

In the wake of the great stock market crash of 1929, Congress passed several laws to regulate the sale of securities in this country. These acts protect the investing public by requiring companies to fully disclose information about themselves, by punishing fraudulent activity, and by promoting fair dealing.

The impact of these laws upon the accounting profession has been profound. Both Congress and the Securities Exchange Commission rely on auditors to play a major role in producing accurate financial information. Recently the SEC noted:

> During the past several years, public and Congressional attention has been focused to an unprecedented degree on the accounting profession and on its role in promoting public confidence in the integrity of financial reporting. The Federal securities laws, since their enactment in the aftermath of the economic crisis of the early 1930's, have authorized the Commission to require that independent accountants audit the financial statements of publicly-held corporations. Thus, those laws have placed upon the accountant unique and important responsibilities in facilitating the proper functioning of this nation's capital formation processes and, more broadly, of our economic system as a whole.[12]

Recognizing the importance of reliable accounting and auditing to the effectiveness of the securities law, Congress gave the SEC substantial powers to make and enforce rules for accounting. Although the SEC has let the accounting profession lead the way, it has retained final authority and issues several types of rules and pronouncements governing the accounting practices of companies and the proper form for information in financial statements which must be filed with the SEC. Any accountant who audits for a public company is vitally concerned with the rules that the SEC promulgates, and with those of the Financial Accounting Standards Board (FASB), which the SEC recognizes as the private sector's primary standard-setting entity. Although the SEC's express authority to regulate accounting practices extends only to those public companies which must file statements with it on a regular basis, its influence on the actions of the FASB and AICPA ultimately affects the work of all independent auditors no matter how small the client company.

So important is the quality of auditing of public companies that the AICPA voted in 1990 to require *peer reviews* for accounting firms auditing such large companies. Under this system, implemented under pressure from the SEC, a firm's audit procedures are scrutinized by outside accountants from other firms to ensure that proper standards are followed. Peer review will be expensive, but should raise the quality of audits.

---

[11] *Rassieur v. Charles*, 188 S.W.2d 817 (Mo. 1945).

[12] Report of the Securities and Exchange Commission on the Accounting Profession and the Commission's Oversight Role (1978). The Supreme Court's statements in *United States v. Arthur Young & Co.*, the last major case in this chapter, clearly indicate that the Supreme Court also believes in the public responsibilities of the accounting profession.

SEC Rule 2(e) provides for discipline of those who "practice" before the commission. An accountant who prepares any statement, opinion, or other paper filed with the SEC with the preparer's consent is deemed to be "practicing" before the commission. Under Rule 2(e), the SEC can punish those who are unqualified, unethical, or in violation of its rules, or who have lost their state license or been convicted of various crimes.

Though the audit failure rate among public corporations is less than 1 percent, SEC enforcement actions against accountants directly and against public corporations for their accounting activities have greatly increased in recent years. In 1983 and 1984 there were 23 SEC enforcement actions brought against accounting firms. Fifteen of these led to suspensions of one or more accountants. The suspensions ranged from thirty days to over five years. Typically, a suspended accountant may reapply for the right to practice before the SEC after taking additional coursework and joining the AICPA's SEC Practice Section (a peer review group).

Any accountant who undertakes to audit for a public corporation must also face the possibility of substantial liability in *civil lawsuits* filed under various provisions of the securities laws.[13]

## Securities Act of 1933

The Securities Act of 1933 regulates the initial sale of new stock by corporations to the public. It is frequently called the "truth in securities" law because its major goal is full disclosure to the investing public. If the financial statements required by the Securities Act of 1933 are inaccurate and investors are injured, lawsuits frequently follow. Accountants are often defendants in such lawsuits because of their role in preparing and auditing these statements.

**Section 11:** Section 11 of the Securities Act of 1933 expressly provides that if any part of a registration statement when it became effective contained an untrue statement of a material fact (or omitted a fact necessary to insure that the statements made were not misleading), any person who acquired such a security may sue for injuries sustained. Section 11 then expressly lists as among potential defendants the issuing company, directors, the underwriter who sold the stock, and "every accountant" who helped prepare any part of the registration statement or any financial statement used in it.

A plaintiff making a Section 11 claim need prove only that a false statement was made in the registration statement and that a loss was sustained. Section 11 plaintiffs need not prove that they relied on the false statements or that the false statements caused their loss; these are presumed. Significantly, plaintiffs need not prove that defendants acted fraudulently, nor do they have the burden of proving mere negligence. Negligence, which is a sufficient basis for liability, is presumed from the fact of the misleading statement.

An issuing company has virtually no defense under Section 11 if there has been a false statement and a loss. Individual defendants, such as accountants, can defend by proving (1) the false statements had no causal connection to plaintiff's loss; (2) plaintiff knew of the falsity of the statement at the time of the stock purchase; or (3) the defendant acted with "due diligence." The harsh negligence standard of Section 11 is made even more stringent by placing the burden of proof on defendants to prove they were not negligent, but subsection (b)(3)(B) provides that accountants may carry that burden by showing that both at the time of registration and at the time the statement became effective (after SEC review and approval) they "had after reasonable investigation, reasonable grounds to believe and did believe . . . that the statements were true and that there was no omission to state a material fact required to be stated therein or necessary to make the statements therein not misleading."

In a leading Section 11 case, *Escott v. Barchris Construction Corp.*, a company (Barchris) which constructed bowling alleys became insolvent soon after selling stock to the public pursuant to a registration statement. Among the many defendants in a Section 11 suit by investors was Peat, Marwick, the company's auditor. The registration statement contained reference to Peat, Marwick's 1960 audit of the company, which had several defects. The court noted that the accountant whom Peat, Marwick assigned to the task (Berardi) had little experience, was unfamiliar with the bowling industry, asked questions but did nothing to verify the answers, did not discover Barchris was listing sales that had not occurred, did not discover Barchris was holding up checks in substantial amounts because there was no money to pay

---

[13] A lengthier discussion of the substance of the U.S. securities laws is contained in Chapter 41. Here we only highlight those provisions most directly pertaining to accountants.

them, and did not learn about some major problems Barchris was having with delinquent notes. In summary, the court held:

> Accountants should not be held to a standard higher than that recognized in their profession. I do not do so here. Berardi's review did not come up to that standard. He did not take some of the steps which Peat, Marwick's written program prescribed. He did not spend an adequate amount of time on a task of this magnitude. Most important of all, he was too easily satisfied with glib answers to his inquiries.
>
> ... [T]here were enough danger signals in the materials which he did examine to require some further investigation on his part. Generally accepted accounting principles required such further investigation under these circumstances. It is not always sufficient merely to ask questions.... I conclude that Peat, Marwick has not established its due diligence defense.[14]

**Section 12(2):** In the past accountants were often sued under Section 12(2) of the Securities Act of 1933, which provides that any person who offers or sells a security by means of false statements, whether or not made in a prospectus, shall be liable to the purchaser for damages sustained. Only the "seller" was liable, but courts took a very broad view of the definition of "seller." Because the Supreme Court recently limited the definition of "seller" to those who actually pass title or those who "solicit" transactions (such as brokers or dealers), accountants who stick to traditional accounting functions should no longer be held liable under Section 12(2).[15]

[14] *Escott v. Barchris Construction Corp.*, 283 F.Supp. 643 (S.D.N.Y. 1968).

[15] *Pinter v. Dahl*, 108 S.Ct. 2063 (1988).

## Securities Exchange Act of 1934

The Securities Exchange Act of 1934 complements the Securities Act of 1933 by regulating the trading of securities after their initial issuance. The 1934 Act regulates such diverse matters as proxy solicitation, tender offers to purchase shares of other companies, and the activities of brokers and dealers who sell stock at the "retail" level. It contains numerous antifraud provisions and allows the SEC to keep tabs on major public companies by requiring them to file a registration statement with the Commission and to update that statement with annual reports, quarterly reports, and interim reports whenever material changes occur in the company's financial situation. The work of accountants in preparing and auditing the financial statements that go into the registration documents and supplemental reports is critical to the success of the Securities Exchange Act of 1934. If the accountant errs, liability may ensue.

**Section 10(b):** Perhaps the most litigated of all securities provisions are Section 10(b) of the 1934 Act and Rule 10b-5 which supplements it. The elements of a Section 10(b) violation are a manipulative or deceptive practice in connection with a purchase or sale of stock which results in a loss to plaintiff. Additionally, in most instances plaintiff must prove reliance on the deceptive statements or acts. Unlike in Section 11 of the Securities Act of 1933, the plaintiff carries the burden of proof under Section 10(b).

For many years it was unclear whether a defendant under Section 10(b) could be liable if guilty only of negligence in making a deceptive statement, or if plaintiff would have to prove fraudulent *intent* on defendant's part. The Supreme Court clarified the matter in the following case, which involved an accountant defendant.

---

### Ernst & Ernst v. Hochfelder
U.S. Supreme Court,
425 U.S. 185 (1976)

Defendant-petitioner Ernst & Ernst is an accounting firm which from 1946 through 1967 periodically audited the books of First Securities Company of Chicago, a small brokerage firm.

Plaintiffs-respondents, including Hochfelder, were induced by Nay, president of First Securities, to invest in "escrow" accounts which he said would yield a high return. In fact, there were no such accounts; Nay immediately converted these funds to his personal use. The accounts were not carried on First Securities' books, and were not discovered until after Nay committed suicide in 1968, leaving behind a note that described the escrow accounts as "spurious" and First Securities as bankrupt. Plaintiffs sued Ernst & Ernst under Sec-

*(continued)*

tion 10(b) and Rule 10b-5. Plaintiffs did not claim Ernst & Ernst knew of Nay's scheme or intentionally committed any wrong. Rather, plaintiffs claimed defendant's audits were negligently performed in that they failed to detect Nay's "mail rule"—that he was the only person in the office who could open mail. Had Ernst & Ernst discovered this unusual practice, it would have had to have been reported in the audit reports, leading to discovery of the fraud.

The trial court dismissed the action, and on appeal the Seventh Circuit held that negligence could be a proper basis for Section 10(b) liability. Ernst & Ernst petitioned for Supreme Court review.

**Decision:** The judgment of the court of appeals was reversed, and the judgment of the trial court dismissing the action was reinstated. Section 10(b) exists only for the purpose of remedying fraud or manipulation. Both the language of the statute and its legislative history indicate that Congress meant Section 10(b) to apply only to intentional conduct—in other words, conduct characterized by "scienter," the intent to deceive, manipulate, or defraud. The statute does not apply to conduct that is merely negligent. ∎

---

**Comment:** Although the Supreme Court has not spoken on the issue, a majority of lower courts have held that "recklessness" by a defendant is sufficient to satisfy the scienter requirement of Section 10(b), though mere negligence is not.

**Section 14:** Section 14 of the 1934 Act sets forth a comprehensive scheme governing solicitation of proxies. The SEC requires management to include an annual statement when it mails proxy solicitations to shareholders. The annual statement contains much useful information about the company, including financial statements which accountants helped compile and audit. If a group of shareholders (called insurgents) would like to oust incumbent management and gain control of the board of directors, a proxy fight may result in which insurgents and incumbents vie for shareholders' proxies to vote at the annual meeting. Proxy fights may also revolve around policy decisions which must be made by shareholders, such as whether to approve a merger. These elections frequently turn on the financial performance of the company, so the accuracy of the accountants' work is of vital importance.

Rule 14a-9, promulgated by the SEC, outlaws proxy solicitation by use of false statements or misleading omissions.

Individual causes of action are permitted under Section 14, and, although the courts are in disagreement, accountants have been held liable for both primary violations of Section 14 and for aiding and abetting violations by others. In one influential but controversial case, *Adams v. Standard Knitting Mills, Inc.,* Standard shareholders such as Adams were solicited to cast their proxies in favor of a merger with Chadbourn, Inc. The proxy statement was accompanied by Chadbourn's financial statements which had been prepared by its accountants, Peat, Marwick. Although Standard shareholders were convinced to approve the merger and exchange their Standard shares for Chadbourn shares of equal value and supposedly higher dividends, when Chadbourn's sales declined the following year it was unable to pay the promised dividends because of certain restrictions in its loan agreements with banks. These restrictions were not disclosed in the proxy statement, and the court held Peat, Marwick was negligent, but not guilty of scienter, in omitting them.[16]

Although it recognized other courts had held corporations liable for mere negligence under Section 14, the *Adams* court declined to do so, stating "we are influenced by the fact that the accountant here, unlike the corporate issuer, does not directly benefit from the proxy vote and is not in privity with the stockholder. Unlike the corporate issuer, the preparation of financial statements to be appended to proxies and other reports is the daily fare of accountants, and the accountant's potential liability for mistakes would be enormous under a negligence standard." Although Peat, Marwick, guilty only of negligence, was held not liable in this case, accountants guilty of scienter or recklessness may be held civilly liable for Section 14 violations. Even criminal liability may attach to intentional violations.

## Foreign Corrupt Practices Act of 1977

In the wake of Watergate and other political scandals of the 1970s, hundreds of American corporations were found to have been paying bribes to foreign po-

---

[16] 623 F.2d 422 (6th Cir. 1980), *cert. denied,* 449 U.S. 1067 (1980).

litical officials to obtain or keep business in foreign countries. Congress responded by passing the Foreign Corrupt Practices Act of 1977 (FCPA), which has broad implications for accountants.

The first part of the FCPA bans bribes to foreign officials by U.S. companies attempting to obtain or retain business in foreign countries. These rules were discussed in Chapter 41 and will not be repeated here.

The second part of the FCPA more directly involves accountants. Because bribes had been concealed by doctoring corporate records, Congress decided all public companies must (1) keep detailed records which "accurately and fairly" reflect the company's financial activities, and (2) devise a system of internal accounting controls sufficient to provide "reasonable assurance" that all transactions are authorized and accounted for. Though designed primarily to aid detection of foreign bribes, these accounting provisions are not limited to that function.

The FCPA has strengthened financial accounting of public corporations. The requirement of record-keeping and internal accounting controls are more stringent than the previous financial materiality standard that accountants had used.

Rule 13b2-1 prohibits any person from falsifying any book, record, or account subject to the FCPA. Rule 13b2-2 prohibits officers and directors of companies from making false statements to accountants. Penalties for violation of FCPA provisions are substantial and may include jail terms.

Because the accounting provisions of the FCPA are somewhat vague as to when records "accurately and fairly" reflect a company's financial picture or when an internal accounting control system allows "reasonable assurance" of accuracy, Congress in 1988 amended the FCPA to ensure that penalties will not be imposed for insignificant or technical infractions or inadvertent conduct. Additional guidance as to an auditor's evaluation of a company's internal accounting controls derives from the Accounting Standards Board's SAS No. 55, effective in 1990, which enlarges the auditor's traditional obligation to evaluate a client's internal control system by requiring him or her to focus not merely on the client's accounting controls but on its entire control structure, including the "control environment" (attitude of the board and management) and the control policies and procedures set up by management to ensure that the firm's specific objectives will be attained.

## RICO

The Racketeering Influenced and Corrupt Organizations Act (RICO) was passed in an attempt to blunt organized crime's infiltration into legitimate business. Perhaps unfortunately, Congress drafted the law in such broad terms that it has led to a plethora of suits against businesses having no connection to real mobsters. The elements of RICO civil liability are (1) the conduct, (2) of an enterprise, (3) through a pattern, (4) of racketeering activity. Because "racketeering activity" is defined to include several "garden varieties" of fraud (such as mail fraud and securities fraud), virtually all traditional securities cases can now include a RICO count.

The incentive to include a RICO count is simple—RICO provides for recovery of treble damages and attorneys' fees. Furthermore, RICO can provide a powerful bargaining chip—no mild-mannered accountant wants the neighbors reading in the morning paper that the accountant has been named in a "racketeering" lawsuit. Along with the nation's most respected corporations, banks, and insurance companies, virtually every major accounting firm has been sued in one or more RICO suits.

Because many people believe RICO has gotten out of hand, as this chapter is written, the AICPA has joined many other groups in lobbying Congress to amend RICO to end the flood of lawsuits against "legitimate" businesses.[17]

## CRIMINAL LIABILITY OF ACCOUNTANTS

Accountants face a number of criminal provisions which constrain their activities. Some accountants have gone to jail for violating these provisions.

### Federal Securities Acts

The two most important criminal provisions for accountants are those of the Securities Act of 1933 and the Securities Exchange Act of 1934. Section 24 of the 1933 Act makes it a crime to willfully violate any section or rule of the Act or to willfully make a false statement in any registration statement. Section 32 of the 1934 Act similarly makes it a crime to willfully violate any section or rule of the 1934 Act or to

---

[17] For more detail on RICO, consult Chapter 41 and see *Sedima v. Imrex* in Chapter 4.

willfully make a false statement in any document filed with the SEC. Because the accounting provisions of the FCPA amended the 1934 Act, willful violation of these provisions is also a crime.

Section 24 of the 1933 Act carries a potential penalty of up to five years in jail and/or a $10,000 fine. Section 32 of the 1934 Act is similar, except that the fine can be as high as $100,000 and even more for insider trading violations.

Because both provisions require violations be "willful" before they constitute crimes, scienter is an element of a criminal violation. Courts have held that negligence or mistake is insufficient for liability, but recklessness may be sufficient. For example, in *U.S. v. Natelli,* defendant auditors helped a company cover up the fact that previously reported sales had not really occurred by hiding a discrepancy in a footnote.[18] The appellate court approved the trial judge's instruction that "good faith, an honest belief in the truth of the data set forth in the footnote and entries in the proxy statement would constitute a complete defense here." On the other hand, the court quoted a holding that "Congress equally could not have intended that men holding themselves out as members of these ancient professions [law and accounting] should be able to escape criminal liability on a plea of ignorance when they shut their eyes to what was plainly to be seen or have represented a knowledge they knew they did not possess."

## *Other Criminal Provisions*

The most important additional criminal provision for accountants is the Federal Mail Fraud Statute, discussed in Chapter 7, which outlaws use of the federal mails to carry out fraudulent schemes. The penalty for violation is a fine up to $1,000, imprisonment of not more than five years, or both. Scienter is required for violation. In *U.S. v. Glick,* Chisolm, a con man with some flair, induced people to pay him nonrefundable front end fees to obtain loans for them. He represented himself as a man of great wealth who would guarantee the loans. Chisolm would show his victims financial statements prepared by his accountant, Glick. Glick knew the financial statements contained blatant violations of GAAP and that no lending institution would furnish a loan to Chisolm based on them.

Glick also knew of Chisolm's use of the statements. Although Glick professed his good faith belief that Chisolm really did possess substantial wealth, the appellate court affirmed his conviction under the mail fraud law, holding he could not deliberately close his eyes to what was obvious to him.[19]

Accountants must also be wary of the Federal False Filing Statement Statute, which attaches criminal penalties to the filing of knowingly false statements with any federal agency, including the SEC.

Furthermore, most state securities statutes, called "blue sky" laws, contain criminal provisions comparable to those of the 1933 and 1934 Acts.

As noted earlier, intentionally filing false income tax returns on behalf of a taxpayer-client is also a crime.

Finally, accountants must be aware of federal statutes which outlaw **conspiracy** (agreement) to violate, or aiding and abetting (taking action) violations of other federal laws, such as securities statutes. Again, these provisions require intentional wrongdoing. For example, the required elements of aiding and abetting a securities violation are "that [defendant-auditor] knew of the [securities law] violations and of its role in the scheme, and, with this knowledge, substantially assisted in the violation."[20]

## ACCOUNTANTS' PRIVILEGE AND CONFIDENTIALITY

Just as lawyers and doctors receive confidential, sensitive information from their clients and patients, so do accountants frequently receive extremely sensitive financial information from their clients. Indeed, AICPA ethics standards provide that accountants should not disclose confidential client information unless (1) the client consents; (2) it is necessary to avoid violation of GAAP or GAAS; (3) disclosure is in response to an enforceable subpoena; or (4) disclosure is necessitated by an inquiry made by the ethics division or trial board of the AICPA or a state CPA regulatory body.

To the chagrin of most accountants, the common law does not recognize an accountant-client privilege similar to that afforded to lawyers, doctors, or members of the clergy. A part of the rationale for this is

---

[18] *U.S. v. Natelli,* 527 F.2d 311 (2d Cir. 1975), *cert. denied,* 425 U.S. 934 (1976).

[19] 710 F.2d 639 (10th Cir. 1983).

[20] *Seiffer v. Topsy's Int'l, Inc.*, 487 F.Supp. 653 (D.Kan. 1980).

that much of what the accountant does is aimed at preparing forms and documents which will be disclosed publicly anyway.

The Federal Rules of Evidence do not provide for an accountant-client privilege, and traditionally there has been none at the federal level. Recently the Supreme Court confirmed the traditional federal approach by reversing a lower court decision which had created a limited confidential accountant-client privilege for tax accrual papers. The next case is a summary of that proceeding. (Note the opinion's emphasis on the *public* nature of an accountant's responsibilities.)

---

**United States v. Arthur Young & Co.**
U.S. Supreme Court,
465 U.S. 805 (1984)

**Respondent Arthur Young was the independent auditor of respondent Amerada Hess Corp., and therefore responsible for reviewing the corporation's financial statements as required by the federal securities laws. In so doing it verified Amerada's statement of contingent tax liabilities, preparing tax accrual workpapers relating to the evaluation of the corporation's reserves for such liabilities. In an IRS criminal investigation of Amerada's tax returns, the auditor's workpapers were summoned under §7602 of the IRS Code. Amerada instructed Arthur Young not to comply with the summons, so the IRS commenced an enforcement action in federal district court.**

**The district court ordered enforcement of the summons. On appeal, the court of appeals, while concluding that the papers were relevant to the IRS investigation, created a work-product immunity for independent auditors' work for public corporations. It found that the IRS had not made a sufficient showing to overcome the immunity and refused to enforce the summons. The government appealed.**

**Decision:** The Supreme Court reversed. The court of appeals' concern for the "chilling effect" that an accountant's disclosure of tax accrual workpapers might have on accountant-client communications created a remedy more closely resembling an accountant-client testimonial privilege than a work-product immunity. However, the Supreme Court had established in 1973 that federal law recognizes no confidential accountant-client privilege.

To the extent that this was viewed as a work-product immunity, the court of appeals had relied upon an earlier Supreme Court decision establishing such an immunity for attorneys in the attorney-client relationship. However, that reasoning did not apply here. The work-product immunity is crucial to the attorney, who is the client's confidential adviser and advocate and whose task is to present the client's case in the most favorable terms. But an independent public auditor performs a different task. By certifying public reports, the CPA "assumes a *public* responsibility transcending any employment relationship with the client. . . . To insulate from disclosure a certified public accountant's interpretations of the client's financial statements would be to ignore the significance of the accountant's role as a disinterested analyst charged with public obligations." ∎

---

At the state level, only about ten jurisdictions still recognize an accountant-client privilege. The scope of the privilege varies from state to state, with most having exceptions for criminal actions, bankruptcy proceedings, and the like.

The privilege, where it exists, belongs to the client, not to the accountant. The client waives the privilege by relying on the accountant's audits or opinions in litigation. Obviously clients cannot rely on the auditor's opinion and then prevent the opposing litigant from examining the procedures that the accountant used to reach the opinion.

## SUMMARY

Plaintiffs are reaching into the "deep pocket" of accountants with growing frequency. On a variety of fronts, litigation, the size of judgments, and liability insurance rates are all increasing.

Accountants can be held liable to their clients for both breach of contract and negligence when they fail to carefully and reasonably perform their agreed-upon services. At the same time, they must maintain independence from their clients, or the auditing function will be thwarted. If the client is also negligent, the courts are divided on how that fact should influence the liability of a negligent accountant.

There is also a trend to hold accountants liable to foreseeable third parties, such as creditors or investors, who rely on prepared financial statements for business decisions.

Accountants do extensive tax work and are expanding into management advisory services. There is likely to be an increase in litigation against them in these areas.

Numerous provisions in both the 1933 and 1934 securities acts give rise to potential liability for accountants. The standard of care imposed on the auditor varies from section to section; thus, each rule must be analyzed independently. In recent years the Foreign Corrupt Practices Act, and especially RICO, have expanded accountants' liability extensively.

In addition to being subject to civil penalties, accountants may have criminal penalties imposed on them if they are found to have intentionally violated any of a number of federal rules.

Unlike attorneys, at the federal level at least accountants have been denied an accountant-client privilege.

## KEY TERMS

**Disclaimer**
**Generally Accepted Accounting Standards (GAAS)**
**Generally Accepted Accounting Principles (GAAP)**
**Compilation**
**Review**
**Conspiracy**

## QUESTIONS AND PROBLEMS

1. The Professional Rodeo Cowboys Association (PRCA) hired the accounting firm of Wilch, Smith & Brock (WSB) to verify the prize money winnings of professional rodeo cowboys so that it could crown the World's Champion All-Around Cowboy on the basis of who had won the most prize money in sanctioned rodeos during the season. WSB determined that Camarillo was the top money winner, so he was crowned champion. Unfortunately, WSB had made two errors in its calculations; Ferguson was actually entitled to be champion. This led to a dispute which was settled by PRCA declaring the cowboys co-champions and awarding prizes and money to Ferguson equal to what had been awarded Camarillo. PRCA then sued the accountants, WSB. Are the accountants liable? Discuss. (*Professional Rodeo Cowboys Assoc. v. Wilch, Smith & Brock,* 589 P.2d 510, Colo. App. 1978.)

2. Shortly before a large corporation declared bankruptcy, three checks totalling $315,000 were drawn on the corporation's account and paid to the corporation's sole shareholder and to a corporate officer, to the detriment of corporate creditors. Birnie, who worked for Wilkes & Co., which had long been the corporation's outside auditor, helped conceal the transfers. Birnie then told the bankruptcy trustee that the corporate records were not complete, so the trustee hired Wilkes to compile complete records. Wilkes did so, and included false entries intended to conceal the fraudulent transfers. Later the fraud was discovered, and the trustee sued Wilkes for breach of contract. Wilkes argued the fraud occurred before the trustee had hired him. Is this a good defense? Discuss. (*In re F. W. Koenecke & Sons, Inc.*, 605 F.2d 310, 7th Cir. 1979.)

3. Timm, Schmidt & Co. (Timm) audited the financial statements of CFA, Inc., from 1973 to 1976. In November 1975, CFA obtained a $300,000 loan from Citizens State Bank (Citizens), which relied on the financial statements prepared by Timm. In early 1977, Timm discovered material errors totalling over $400,000 in the 1974 and 1975 statements of CFA. When Citizens learned of these errors, it called CFA's loan due, and CFA went into receivership. Citizens lost $150,000 on its loans and sued Timm for negligence. All Timm employees swore they did not know the financial statements would be used by CFA to obtain loans, but the senior partner stated "as a certified public accountant, I know that audited statements are used for many purposes and that it is common for them to be supplied to lenders and creditors, and other persons." Timm claimed its contract was with CFA and it had no liability to Citizens. Is Timm correct? Discuss. (*Citizens State Bank v. Timm, Schmidt & Co.*, 335 N.W.2d 361, Wis. 1983.)

4. Alexander Grant & Co. (AGC) was engaged by GHP Corp. to prepare an unaudited financial statement based on information provided by GHP. GHP submitted copies of the statement to Spherex, Inc., to obtain credit. Later Spherex sustained losses in its dealings with GHP, it appearing that the information in the unaudited statements was inaccurate. Spherex sued AGC, which argued that it should not be liable in negligence to a third party with whom it had no contract, especially on an *unaudited* statement. Does it matter that the statement was unaudited? Discuss. (*Spherex, Inc. v. Alexander Grant & Co.,* 451 A.2d 1308, N.H. 1982.)

5. Reid, a fashion designer, turned $1.4 million over to her accountant, Silver, who in effect became her business manager. Over the course of his employment, Silver paid himself $90,000 for services rendered and $72,500 for accounting fees, frequently made interest-free loans to himself from Reid's funds, and was reluctant to make full and

fair disclosure to Reid about the details of his activities. Reid sued for an accounting. Will Reid prevail? Discuss. (*Reid v. Silver,* 354 F.2d 600, 7th Cir. 1965.)

6. Beck Industries' trustee in bankruptcy sued Beck's auditors, Ernst & Ernst, alleging the auditors were guilty of negligence and breach of contract in failing to detect that Beck's earnings and overall financial condition had been much worse than publicly reported. The trustee alleged that the false statements caused Beck's board of directors to embark on an ill-advised acquisition program which led to ruin. Two of Beck's directors, including its president, knew of the overstatements; the other directors did not. Ernst & Ernst raised a contributory negligence defense. Is this defense valid? Discuss. (*Shapiro v. Glekel,* 380 F.Supp. 1053, S.D.N.Y. 1974.)

7. Early in 1964, PMM acted as independent auditor for Yale Express System. Later PMM was hired to do some "special studies" of Yale's past and current income and expenses. While engaged in these studies sometime in 1964, PMM discovered that the earlier financial statements it had audited were substantially misleading. PMM did not disclose this fact to the stock exchanges on which Yale stock was traded until May 1965. Investors who had traded in Yale stock during the interim sued PMM for common-law fraud and for a Section 10(b) violation. PMM claimed it had no duty to disclose the information since the original error was not its fault. Is PMM liable under Section 10(b)? Discuss. (*Fischer v. Kletz,* 266 F.Supp. 180, S.D.N.Y. 1967.)

8. Bunge, a merchandiser of grain, extended credit to county elevators throughout the northern Plains states. From 1963 until 1970, Bunge extended large sums to R. F. Gunkelman and Sons, Inc., in Fargo, North Dakota. In fact, the sums lent Gunkelman were much larger and less extensively secured than any other loans made by Bunge in the region. When Gunkelman went bankrupt in 1970, causing a $1.5 million loss to Bunge, Bunge sued Gunkelman's accountant. Bunge claimed the accountant's audit reports from 1963 to 1968 valued Gunkelman's sunflower seeds in the closing inventory as something more than cost in violation of AICPA guidelines, and sued for negligence. Is Bunge's negligence claim valid? Discuss. (*Bunge Corp. v. Eide,* 372 F.Supp. 1058, D.N.D. 1974.)

9. Al had Aberrant Fund, Inc. (AF), which he controlled, purchase substantial amounts of Dilly Modest Systems (DMS) shares. These purchases kept the market price of DMS stock high, allowing Al to sell his personal DMS stock holdings at a big profit. AF later sold at a big loss because, *inter alia,* DMS's registration statement had stated that DMS had over $12 million in back orders when in reality it had much less, and had not disclosed that the primary back order customer was in financial trouble, could not pay its debts, and was controlled by DMS. AF sued Etan & Etan (E&E), accountants who helped prepare the registration statement. E&E showed that although it knew of the overstatement of back orders, GAAP did not require that the back orders be audited or that the overreporting be noted in the audit. Does compliance with GAAP insulate E&E from liability? Discuss. (*Admiralty Fund v. Hugh Johnson & Co.,* 677 F.2d 1301, 9th Cir. 1982.)

10. Accountants Arthur Young & Co. (AY) prepared the financial information contained in the June 1971 prospectus of Land & Leisure, Inc. Several times during the next 18 months, Summer bought Land & Leisure stock, relying on the prospectus. Summer later sued AY for fraud under Sections 17(a) and 10(b) of the Securities Exchange Act of 1934, challenging the "clean" opinion which AY had given. The financial statements did not disclose that AY was to receive $50,000 in past due accounting fees from Land & Leisure out of the proceeds of the sale of stock under the prospectus. Summer claimed AY breached its duty of independence and committed fraud by not disclosing this fact. AY defended by claiming, among other things, that Summer could not rely on a prospectus which had become "stale" after 18 months. Should AY be liable? Discuss. (*Summer v. Land & Leisure, Inc.,* 571 F.Supp. 380, S.D. Fla. 1983.)

# PART VI

# Property: Ownership, Control, and Protection

All of the world's material wealth consists of *property* of one type or another. The acquisition of property has been and continues to be one of the primary goals of a major portion of the world's population. What is more, a substantial percentage of all the civil lawsuits ever commenced have arisen out of disputes over some sort of property. For these reasons, the rules of law governing the ownership of property are among the most fundamental in our legal system.

In a society without a system of laws, "ownership" of property would consist merely of physical possession plus the strength and wits to keep it. In an organized society, however, with rights and duties determined by law, the concept of ownership is considerably more sophisticated, in terms of both its complexity and the orderliness of its protection. In the modern sense, then, ownership comprises a group of rights (such as possession, use, enjoyment, and transfer) that are *protected and guaranteed by governmental authority.*

All property is divided into two basic categories: real property and personal property. Essentially, *real property* (often called "real estate" or "realty") is land and most things affixed to it. *Personal property,* on the other hand, consists of every item of tangible or intangible property not included within the definition of real property. Items of tangible personal property are usually called *goods.*

In Part VI we explore various legal aspects of owning, controlling, and protecting real and personal property. Chapter 43 surveys the law of real property. In Chapter 44 we examine the landlord-tenant relationship, which is created when real property is leased. Chapter 45 surveys the law of personal property, and then discusses the bailment relationship, which is created when the owner of an item of personal property transfers possession, but not title, to another. In Chapter 46, we deal with (1) the disposition of both real and personal property upon the death of the owner and (2) the transfer of real and personal property through the establishment of a trust. Finally, Chapter 47 discusses insurance—one of the most important means of protecting the value of all types of property. The chapter also examines other kinds of insurance, such as life insurance.

# CHAPTER 43

# REAL PROPERTY

In this chapter we survey the principles of law relating to the ownership and control of real property. After exploring the fundamental nature of real property, we examine the various types of ownership interests and the process of transferring these interests.

## THE NATURE OF REAL PROPERTY

The most important element of real property is, of course, the land itself. Things affixed to the land take the form of either vegetation or fixtures.

### *Land*

The definition of *land* includes not only the surface of the earth but also everything above and beneath it. Thus the ownership of a tract of land theoretically includes both the air space above it and the soil from its surface to the center of the earth.

**Air Rights:** A landowner's rights with respect to the air space above the surface are called **air rights.** In recent years, air rights have become an important part of land ownership in some areas. In densely populated metropolitan areas, for instance, air space is often quite valuable from a commercial standpoint. Thus the owner of an office building might sell a portion of its air space to a party who wishes to build and operate a restaurant or group of apartments atop the building. And railroad companies with tracks running through downtown areas, where building space is at a premium, sometimes sell the space above their tracks for office building construction.

For practical reasons, modern courts have held that a landowner's air rights are not violated by airplanes flying at reasonable heights. If, however, a flight is low enough to actually interfere with the owner's use of the land (such as when the plane is taking off or landing), there is a violation of these air rights.

**Subsurface Rights:** The most practical result of the rule extending a landowner's property rights to the center of the earth is that he or she owns the *minerals* beneath the surface. When the land is sold, the buyer acquires any existing minerals, such as coal, even if they are not expressly mentioned. These minerals in the ground can also be owned *separately*. Thus a landowner might sell only the minerals or sell the rest of the land and expressly retain the minerals.

In some states (such as Texas and Pennsylvania) oil and natural gas are treated like other minerals with respect to ownership. That is, they can be owned while they are still in the ground.[1] The courts in a few states (such as California) take a contrary view, holding that oil and gas are not owned by anyone until pumped out of the ground. Of course, regardless of the type of mineral or the particular jurisdiction, an owner who *first removes* the minerals and *then sells* them is making a sale of personal property (i.e., goods), not real property.

### *Vegetation*

Both natural vegetation, such as trees, and cultivated vegetation, such as corn, wheat, or other growing crops, are considered to be real property. Thus, in a land-sale transaction, the vegetation passes to the buyer along with the land unless expressly excluded from the sale.

When growing vegetation is sold by itself, and not with the land, the general rule today is that the transaction is a sale of personal property (goods). This rule holds true almost universally for growing

---

[1] Ownership of oil, gas, or other minerals while still in the ground is referred to as *ownership in place.*

crops.[2] The same rule is followed for growing timber in a majority of states, but several states treat a sale of growing timber as a sale of real property.

## *Fixtures*

A **fixture** is an item that was originally personal property but that has been attached to the land (or to another fixture) in a relatively permanent fashion. Fixtures are viewed by the law as *real property.* Thus title to them passes to the buyer of real property unless the seller expressly excludes them from the transaction. In other words, even if the documents employed in the transaction describe only the land and are silent with respect to fixtures, title to them nevertheless passes to the buyer. Items that are not fixtures, however, do not pass along with a sale of land unless they are expressly included in the terms of the transaction.

To illustrate: Jones contracts to sell his farm to Williams, and the contract describes only the boundaries of the land. Located on the farm are a house and a barn. These buildings are fixtures and will pass to Williams as part of the real property, as will the fence around the land. Inside the house, Jones's clothing and furniture are not fixtures, but the built-in cabinets and plumbing are. The hay stored in the barn is not a fixture, but the built-in feeding troughs are.

As is true of minerals, when a landowner removes a fixture from the soil or from the building to which it was attached and then sells the item *by itself,* it is considered a sale of *personal property* rather than real property. In fact, if a landowner removes a fixture with the intention that removal will be permanent, the item reverts back to its original status as personal property regardless of whether it is sold.

[2]See UCC Sec. 2-107.

**Determining Whether an Item Is a Fixture:** Although the decision on whether a particular article is a fixture is often obvious (as in the case of a house), many items are difficult to classify. In general, a court will hold that an item is a fixture if there was *an intent that it become a permanent part of the real property.* When the owner or occupier of land has not clearly expressed his or her intent, it must be determined from all the circumstances of the case. Following are three factors that are often considered in determining whether an item was intended to be a fixture.

*Attachment:* An item is usually classified as a fixture if it is attached to a building in such a manner that it cannot be removed without damage to the building. Examples include shingles on the roof, built-in cabinets or appliances, a floor furnace, or a floor covering that is cemented in place.

*Specialized Use:* An item is usually considered a fixture if it was specially made or altered for installation in a particular building. Examples include specially fitted window screens, drapes custom-made for an odd-sized window, and a neon sign created for particular business premises.

*Custom:* Sometimes local custom dictates whether an item is a fixture. For example, in some parts of the country it is customary for houses to be sold with refrigerators. Where this custom exists a landowner's intent when installing the refrigerator is probably that it be a permanent addition. Thus it is a fixture. (The same principle applies, of course, to any other "customary" item.)

The following case illustrates the analytical approach employed by courts when determining whether an item was intended to be a fixture.

---

### Johnson v. Hicks
Court of Appeals of Oregon,
626 P.2d 938 (1981)

Margaret and Hoy Johnson owned a tract of land in Klamath County, Oregon. Neil and Maxine Hicks (Hoy Johnson's sister) lived on an adjoining tract. In 1964, Hoy Johnson and Neil Hicks installed an irrigation system to serve both pieces of land. They shared both the labor and costs of installation. After installation, they also shared equally the maintenance and electricity costs for the system. The irrigation system contained approximately 700 feet of two-inch pipe that crossed the Johnson land and ran along the edge of the Hicks land. In addition, the system included 1,500 feet of aluminum pipe used to irrigate the pasture on the Johnson land, and a pump, motor, and pump house not located on the Johnson or Hicks

*(continued)*

land. About three-fourths of the system was underground. Later, in this lawsuit, Hoy Johnson testified that his purpose in installing the system was to irrigate the pastureland, on which he raised cattle and horses. He also testified that the installation was to be permanent and that when he sold the pastureland he "let the sprinkler system go with it." Neil Hicks wanted the system primarily to irrigate his yard.

In April 1967, when Margaret and Hoy Johnson were experiencing marital problems, Hoy Johnson and Neil Hicks entered into an agreement declaring the irrigation system to be their joint property and "upon the death or incapacity of either of the parties hereto the property shall be in the ownership and control of the surviving party." Hicks later testified in this lawsuit that their intent in drawing up the agreement was as follows:

*Well, at the time we made it up Hoy was the one—I told Hoy we were going to have trouble because—if something happened to him and she was involved in it. You know, we can't get along with her to begin with and he said that he can see our point and that we'll go to a lawyer and have him write this paper up, you know, in case something happened to him or to myself and there wouldn't be no women involved into it.*

In 1969 Margaret and Hoy Johnson were divorced. The divorce decree awarded to Margaret the family home and the one-third of an acre on which it was located, her personal property, and all furniture and fixtures in the home. Hoy was awarded two other parcels of land and all other personal property. The irrigation system was not mentioned in the decree. From 1969 until April 1979 a portion of the irrigation pipe remained on Margaret's land, and she continued to use the water from the system for watering her yard and trees. During this time she neither offered nor was asked to contribute to the expense of operating the system; Hoy Johnson and Neil Hicks continued to split all costs for the system. Margaret did, however, pay an annual assessment to the Klamath Basin Improvement District for the right to use the irrigation water.

In 1979 Neil suggested to Hoy that they "cut her off," but Hoy refused because the amount of water Margaret used was very small and he had no objection to it. On April 1, 1979, however, Neil moved 140 feet of irrigation pipe from Margaret's land and placed it on his land and on adjoining land owned by a brother of Hoy's. Margaret, plaintiff, filed suit against Neil Hicks, defendant, alleging that the irrigation system was a fixture and that the part of the system on her property passed to her in the divorce decree as part of the real estate. She sought an injunction requiring Neil to restore the pipe to its original position on her land and prohibiting him from further interference with it. Margaret also sought damages caused by the loss of water, and Neil asserted a counterclaim for the expenses of maintaining and operating the system. The trial court held that the part of the system on Margaret's property was not a fixture, and dismissed all claims. Margaret appealed.

**Decision:** The judgment for defendant Hicks was reversed. The irrigation system, including that part on Margaret's land, was a fixture. The intent of Neil and Hoy at the time of installation clearly was that the system become part of the land. Neil and Hoy's intent when installing the system determined its character; after its character had been determined, their later agreement had no effect on Margaret because she was not a party to the agreement and had no knowledge of it. Not having been mentioned in the divorce decree, the part of the system on the land received by Margaret automatically passed to her with the land. The case was remanded for determination of damages. The court pointed out that determination of water rights was not an issue in this case, and that the court was making no judgment on Neil's right to receive compensation for maintaining the system, since the issue had not been dealt with in the lower court because of the lower court's disposition of the case. ■

## INTERESTS IN REAL PROPERTY

Ownership of real property is not an "all or nothing" proposition. The total group of legal rights constituting complete ownership can be divided among several individuals. The particular set of rights owned in a given situation is referred to as an *estate* or an *interest* in real property. The common law developed a complex system of classifying and defining these various interests, a system which is described here in simplified form. Much of the terminology used to classify real property interests is of ancient origin. At the outset, the law distinguishes those interests that include the right of possession from those that do not. The so-called **possessory interests** are further subdivided into **freehold estates** and **nonfreehold estates.** The following discussion examines these types of possessory interests, and then outlines the different **nonpossessory interests.** It concludes by describing another classification, the so-called future interests in real property.

### *Freehold Estates*

A freehold estate is one that can legally exist for an indefinite period of time.

**Fee Simple:** When a person has complete ownership of real property, his or her interest is described as a **fee simple estate.**[3] This is the most important type of freehold estate. In everyday usage, when someone is spoken of as the "owner" or as "having title," it generally means that the individual owns a fee simple interest. The characteristics of a fee simple interest are: (1) ownership is of unlimited duration and (2) so long as the owner abides by the law and does not interfere with the rights of adjoining landowners, the owner is free to do whatever he or she chooses with the property.

If O, the owner of a fee simple interest in real property, conveys (transfers) the property to B, it is presumed that the entire fee simple is being conveyed. B will acquire a lesser interest only if the terms of the conveyance clearly so indicate. Thus a conveyance of the property "from O to B," with nothing said about the type of interest being conveyed, is deemed to transfer the entire fee simple interest to B.

**Fee Simple Defeasible:** Some interests in real property are classified as fee simple interests despite the fact that ownership is not absolute. Suppose, for example, that O conveys a fee simple interest to B, subject to the limitation that B's interest will cease upon the occurrence of a specified event. B's interest in this case is called a **fee simple defeasible.** It is a fee simple in every respect except that it is subject to the possibility of termination.

One of the most common limitations of this type relates to the *use* that is to be made of the land. For instance, the terms of the conveyance from O to B may state that B's ownership will continue only if the land is used for recreational purposes. The person entitled to the property if and when B's interest terminates is said to own a *future interest.* Future interests are discussed later in the chapter.

**Life Estate:** A **life estate** is an interest in real property, the duration of which is measured by the life of some designated person. For example, O, the fee simple owner, might convey the property to B "for B's lifetime." During his lifetime B would own a life estate. Similarly, if O's conveyance to B was "for the life of X," B would still own a life estate. (The latter is a much less common situation.) The person entitled to ownership after termination of a life estate owns a future interest.

Owning a life estate is not the equivalent of owning a fee simple for one's lifetime. It is true that the owner of the life estate (called the "life tenant") has the right to *normal use* of the property. For example, the life tenant can use it as a residence, farm it, conduct a business on it, allow another to use it in return for the payment of rent, or make any other reasonable use of it. However, the life tenant cannot do anything that will permanently damage the property and thus harm the owner of the future interest.

As an example of the limitations on a life tenant's use of the property, the right to cut timber on the land is somewhat restricted. The timber can be cut if it is required for fuel, fencing, or agricultural operations. But it cannot be cut for the purpose of *sale* unless (1) the life estate was conveyed to the life tenant specifically for that purpose, or (2) selling timber is the only profitable use that can be made of the land, or (3) the land was used for that purpose at the time the person became a life tenant, or (4) the owner of the future interest expressly permits the cutting.

Similarly, a life tenant can take oil and gas from existing wells and other minerals from existing mines if subsurface rights were not expressly excluded from the life estate. But this party cannot drill *new* wells or open *new* mines without authorization either in the document creating the life estate or at a later time from the owner of the future interest.

Although a life tenant is responsible to the owner of the future interest for any permanent damage he or she personally causes to the land, there is no such responsibility for damage caused by accidents, by third parties, or otherwise without the life tenant's fault.

A life tenant is also under a duty to pay taxes on the property. If this duty is neglected and the land is taken by the taxing authority, the life tenant is liable to the owner of the future interest.

## *Nonfreehold Estates*

The nonfreehold estates, sometimes called **leasehold estates,** are created by a *lease* of real property in which the owner grants to another the temporary right to possess the property in return for the payment of rent.[4] In such a case, the owner is called the *lessor,* or *landlord,* and the occupier is called the

---

[3] Various other phrases are also employed. It is sometimes said that the person is the *fee owner* or that he or she owns the land *in fee, in fee simple,* or *in fee simple absolute.*

[4] Although the granting of a *right to drill* for oil and gas is often called a *lease* in popular usage, it is not truly a lease because it does not convey a possessory interest in real property.

lessee, or *tenant*.[5] Several different types of nonfreehold, or leasehold, estates may be created, depending on the terms of the lease agreement. The next chapter discusses the landlord-tenant relationship in detail.

## *Nonpossessory Interests*

**Easements:** Essentially, an **easement** is the right to make some limited use of another's real property without taking possession of it. Stated another way, it is the right to do a specific thing on another's land. Sometimes an easement is referred to informally as a *right-of-way*. Examples of easements include the right to run a driveway or road across another's land, to run a power or telephone line above it, or to run a pipeline under it.

*Types of Easements:* Easements are either *appurtenant* or *in gross*. An **easement appurtenant** is one created specifically for use in connection with another tract of land. For example: A and B own adjoining tracts. A grants to B an easement to cross A's land to get to and from a highway. Here the easement on A's land is appurtenant, because it was created for use in connection with B's land. In this situation, A's land is called the **servient estate** and B's the **dominant estate.**

An **easement in gross,** on the other hand, is one *not* used in connection with another tract of land. For example, a telephone company has an easement in gross when it acquires the right to run poles and wires across A's land.

Whenever a tract of land subject to either type of easement is sold, the purchaser must continue to recognize the easement if he or she knew or should have known of its existence at the time of purchase. Even without such knowledge, the purchaser's ownership is subject to the easement if a document creating the interest was *recorded* (filed with the appropriate county official) prior to the purchase.

An easement appurtenant is said to "run with the land." This means that if the land being benefited by the easement (the dominant estate) is sold, the easement goes along with it. However, the owner of an easement appurtenant cannot sell or otherwise transfer it *by itself,* apart from the dominant estate. On the other hand, the owner of an easement in gross today is generally allowed to transfer it to another party.

*Creation of Easements:* An easement can be created in several ways. Creation of an **easement by express grant or reservation** is the most common method. An express grant occurs when a landowner expresses an intent to convey an easement to another party. An express reservation occurs when a landowner sells the land itself but expressly reserves, or keeps, an easement on the land being sold. Because an easement is an interest in real property, the expression of an intent to grant or reserve such an interest must be made in a written document containing a legally sufficient description of both the land and the scope of the easement. The document also must contain the names of the parties, the duration of the interest, and the signature of at least the party making the grant or reservation. The document could be either a *deed,* discussed later in the chapter, or a *will,* discussed in Chapter 46.

An **easement by implication** also can be created where surrounding circumstances reasonably indicate that the parties probably intended to create such an interest. An easement exists by implication only if the following facts are proved:

**1.** An easement will be implied only when land is subdivided into two or more segments. This would occur, for example, when A, who owns twenty acres of land, sells ten acres out of the tract to B.

**2.** Prior to the subdivision, the owner of the entire tract must have been making a particular use of the property, and continuance of this use after the subdivision would require recognition of an easement. Thus, suppose that prior to A's sale of ten acres to B, A had constructed and used a ditch to improve the drainage of one part of the property. The ditch went through the portion that A kept, but it benefited the part sold to B by improving the drainage of that portion.

**3.** The use that A was making of the property before the subdivision must have been apparent; in other words, it must have been observable to anyone conducting a reasonable inspection of the property.

**4.** Continuation of the use must be reasonably necessary to B's use of his ten acres. In this case, because the drainage improvement benefited the land purchased by B, the ditch across A's ten acres probably would be viewed as reasonably necessary.

In the circumstances just described, B would have an easement across A's land giving B the right to continue using the ditch to drain water from B's land.

---

[5] The "owner" in this situation might be the owner of a fee simple, of a fee simple defeasible, of a life estate, or even of a leasehold.

An **easement by necessity** also can be created in some circumstances. In contrast with an easement by implication, neither a subdivision of land nor a particular prior use is a prerequisite for the existence of an easement by necessity. However, the easement must be an absolute necessity, not just a reasonably necessary use. For example, a person leasing space in an office building has an easement by necessity that permits use of the stairs, elevators, hallways, and other common areas. Another example could be found in a situation similar to the one in which A sold a portion of his land to B. If B's ten acres had been at the back of the original tract, with no means of access to a public road other than by crossing A's ten acres, B would have an easement by necessity to cross A's land when going to and from B's land.

An **easement by prescription** (or **prescriptive easement**) may be created when someone actually does something on another's land for a period of time. Creation of an easement by prescription is similar to the acquisition of title by adverse possession, which is discussed later in the chapter. Such an easement is created if one party has actually exercised an easement (such as a driveway) on someone else's land continuously for a period of time specified by state statute, the use was made without the express consent of the landowner, and the use was an apparent one. The required period of time for creation of a prescriptive easement in a particular state is usually the same as for acquisition of title by adverse possession.

**Profits:** A **profit**, technically called a *profit à prendre*, is the right to go upon land and take something from it. Examples include the right to mine minerals, drill for oil, or take wild game or fish. A *right to take* minerals, which is a profit, must be distinguished from an actual *sale* of the fee simple interest in the minerals in the ground. The form the transaction takes depends on the intent of the parties, as evidenced primarily by the language used. Of course, in those states where oil and gas are not deemed capable of being owned while in the ground, any transaction in which the buyer is to drill for oil and gas is a profit.

The legal principles applicable to the creation, classification, transfer, and enforceability of profits are exactly the same as in the case of easements.

**Licenses:** In essence, a **license** is simply the landowner's permission for someone else to come upon his or her land. It does not create an interest in real property, because the landowner can revoke it at any time. But even though the grantee of the license does not have a legally enforceable *right* to go upon the land, the license (prior to its revocation) does keep the grantee from being considered a trespasser. Two examples of situations where licenses exist are:

**1.** The purchaser of a ticket to a movie or other amusement or sporting event has a license to enter the premises.

**2.** Sometimes a license is created when there is an ineffective attempt to create an easement or profit. For example, since these are required to be in writing, an oral easement or profit is merely a license.

**Mortgages and Liens:** A person who borrows money frequently has to grant the lender an interest in some item of property to secure payment of the debt. When the property to be used as security is real property, the landowner grants the lender an interest by executing a **mortgage.** The landowner-debtor is called the *mortgagor,* and the lender is called the *mortgagee.* In most states, the interest created by the mortgage is a **lien.**[6] If the mortgagor defaults on the obligation, the mortgagee has a right to *foreclose* the mortgage. This means that the real property can be seized and sold, usually at a public sale (auction), and the proceeds used to pay off the debt. The most common situation in which a mortgage is executed occurs when a buyer of real property borrows a portion of the purchase price and signs a mortgage giving the lender an interest in the property being purchased. Because a mortgage conveys an interest in real property, it must be expressed in a written document that is sufficient to satisfy the statute of frauds.

In some situations, real property may be subjected to a creditor's interest without the landowner's consent. Such an interest is referred to very generally as an **involuntary lien,** to contrast it with the voluntary lien created by a mortgage. Statutes or constitutional provisions in most states provide for the involuntary creation of a **mechanic's lien** to secure payment for work done on or materials added to real property. For example, the contractor who builds a house on the land or adds a new room to an existing house usually has a mechanic's lien on the real estate

---

[6] In several states, however, a mortgage actually transfers *legal title* to the property to the mortgagee. In such a state, the mortgage normally provides that the mortgagee does not have the right of possession unless the mortgagor defaults on the underlying obligation; but the mortgagor does not actually own the property until the debt is paid and the mortgage released.

that can be foreclosed if payment is not made. Many states require that, before any work is done or materials provided, the person claiming the lien give the landowner written notice that a mechanic's lien will be asserted. In addition, most states require that a written document in which the mechanic's lien is claimed be filed with the county clerk, recorder of deeds, or other designated county official.

Other types of involuntary liens also exist. When a plaintiff in a civil lawsuit receives a judgment for money damages against the defendant, and the defendant does not pay, in some states the plaintiff may create a **judgment lien** against the defendant's real property by filing a copy of the judgment with the appropriate county official.

It is important to note that, in the case of mechanic's liens, judgment liens, and other involuntary liens, the act of filing the written document with a public official actually *creates* the lien. As we will discuss later in the chapter, deeds, mortgages, and other documents creating *voluntary* interests in real property can be recorded to give greater protection to the person holding the interest, but the act of recording does not create the interest in such situations.

## *Future Interests*

A final category of real property interest is the **future interest,** which consists of the residue remaining when the owner of a fee simple estate transfers less than a fee simple to someone else. Despite its name, a future interest does have a present existence and can be transferred, mortgaged, and so on. It is the actual use and enjoyment of the interest that is unavailable until a future time.

The subject of future interests is quite complex, with its own system of classification. Very generally, there are two basic types of future interest: the reversion and the remainder. A **reversion** exists when the owner of a fee simple transfers a lesser interest and retains the residue. For example, suppose that O, the owner of a fee simple estate, conveys a fee simple defeasible or life estate to B. If no provision is made for ownership of the future interest, it is owned by O and is called a reversion. O can separately transfer the reversion to someone else, or let it pass to his or her heirs. Upon expiration of B's interest, the reversion becomes a present fee simple estate. On the other hand, a **remainder** exists when the owner of a fee simple transfers a lesser interest and expressly provides that ownership will pass to a third party upon expiration of the lesser interest. Suppose that when O conveys the fee simple defeasible or life estate to B, O expressly provides that ownership will pass to C upon expiration of B's interest. In this case, C's future interest is called a remainder. C can separately transfer the future interest or let it pass to his or her heirs. When B's interest terminates, the remainder becomes a fee simple estate.

## CONCURRENT OWNERSHIP

Any interest in real property that can be owned by one person can also be owned jointly by two or more persons. We will examine some of the more important types of concurrent ownership.

### *Tenancy in Common and Joint Tenancy*

**Characteristics:** The most frequently encountered types of concurrent ownership are the **tenancy in common** and the **joint tenancy.** In a tenancy in common, the co-owners are called *tenants in common* or *cotenants.* In a joint tenancy they are called *joint tenants.*

The most important distinction between these two types of concurrent ownership has to do with disposition of a co-owner's interest when he or she dies. The interest of a tenant in common passes to that person's heirs according to his or her will, or according to state statute if there was no will. The heirs and the surviving co-owner(s) then become tenants in common. The joint tenancy, on the other hand, is characterized by a *right of survivorship,* which means that the interest of a deceased joint tenant passes to the surviving joint tenant(s).

**Creation:** A tenancy in common can be created in several ways. For example, if O conveys a fee simple estate "to A and B," the real property will be owned by A and B as tenants in common. Similarly, if O dies and his land passes to his heirs, A and B, the property will be owned by A and B as tenants in common. Or if O conveys a fractional interest (such as one-half or one-third) to A, the property will be owned by O and A as tenants in common.

A joint tenancy is more difficult to create and, consequently, is not as frequently used or as important as a tenancy in common. In most states, concurrent ownership of real property is presumed to be a tenancy in common, and will be a joint tenancy only if explicitly created. Even the use of the terms "joint tenancy" or "joint tenants" is not a clear enough expression to create a joint tenancy in most states, because people often use such terms in a nontechnical sense to refer to a tenancy in common. Thus, if O wishes to create a joint tenancy between A and B, in most states O would have to refer expressly to the *right of survivorship* in addition to using the terms joint tenancy or joint tenants. Moreover, a joint tenancy traditionally could be created only if the joint tenants received their interests at the same time and in the same document, and only if their fractional interests were *equal*. In recent years, statutes in a few states have removed the requirement that a joint tenancy must be created at the same time by a single document. These requirements have never existed for the creation of a tenancy in common.

**Partition:** In either a tenancy in common or a joint tenancy, none of the co-owners owns any segregated portion of the land. Instead, each owns an undivided fractional interest in the entire tract of land. The tenants in common or joint tenants can agree in writing to *partition* the land; but if they do so, their relationship as co-owners ends, and each becomes the owner of a specifically designated section of the property. If one or more of the co-owners wants to partition the land but the parties are unable to reach unanimous agreement on the division, any one of them can initiate a lawsuit to have the land partitioned. In their decisions, courts commonly express a preference for a partition *in kind*, which is a physical division of the property into sections of equal value. As a practical matter, however, it is extremely difficult for a court to accomplish a physical division that gives each former co-owner a section of clearly equal value. Consequently, most court-ordered partitions ultimately involve a sale of the property and an equal division of the proceeds.

## Condominiums and Cooperatives

Although the **condominium** form of ownership was used in some European cities before and during the Middle Ages, only in recent years has it become popular in this country. Most buildings subject to condominium ownership today are physically similar to apartments, and may contain only a few units or as many as several hundred. Ordinarily, a person owns a fee simple estate in the living space of a particular unit, but not in the land on which the unit rests. The fee simple interest in the living space may be owned solely by an individual, or it may be subject to any of the various forms of concurrent ownership such as a tenancy in common. In addition, a tenancy in common among the owners of the living space units exists with respect to other areas such as common roofs and walls, parking lots, and recreation areas.

Although a building subject to **cooperative** ownership may also physically resemble an apartment building, this form of ownership is quite different than a condominium. A *cooperative corporation* is formed under special state statutory provisions, and the corporation owns the building. Each occupier of a living unit owns a share of stock in the corporation and leases the unit from the corporation. Because the corporate entity itself owns the real property, a cooperative is not technically a form of concurrent ownership.

## Marital Property

**Tenancy by the Entireties:** Under the English Common law, a conveyance of real property to husband and wife created a **tenancy by the entireties.** A tenancy by the entireties is essentially the same as a joint tenancy with right of survivorship, the surviving spouse taking complete ownership on the death of the other. Unlike a joint tenancy, a tenancy by the entireties cannot be severed by one party. A tenancy by the entireties also cannot be transferred by one spouse without the consent of the other, and the creditors of one spouse cannot reach the property without consent of the other.

The tenancy by the entireties has been abolished in several states and modified in others during recent years. Today, the tenancy by the entireties exists in about 20 states. In those states abolishing this form of ownership, a conveyance of real property to husband and wife will create either a joint tenancy or tenancy in common, depending on the language of conveyance.

Traditionally, the husband had the exclusive right to control and possession of property held in a tenancy by the entireties. Today, in those states still recognizing the tenancy by the entireties, statutory changes have given the spouses equal rights of control and possession.

**Community Property:** Another system of marital property ownership in this country is referred to as **community property.** The origin of the community property system can be traced directly to Spanish marital property law, which had borrowed the concept from medieval Germanic tribes in Europe. Nine American states presently employ the community property system. In five of these—Arizona, California, Louisiana, New Mexico, and Texas—the community property system was simply a continuation of Spanish law that had been in effect before statehood. Idaho, Nevada, and Washington voluntarily adopted the system early in their settlement, and Wisconsin adopted it in 1986.

The community property system recognizes two types of property: community property and separate property. Each spouse owns an undivided one-half interest in all community property, an interest which passes to his or her heirs upon death. Each has complete ownership of his or her separate property.

Because the community property system is based on the concept that the marital relationship itself is an entity, and that this entity benefits materially from the time and effort of both spouses, most property acquired by the husband or wife during marriage is community property. This includes the salary, wages, or other income earned by either spouse, income earned from community property, and property bought with the proceeds or income from community property. Money or property is the separate property of one of the spouses only if it was acquired by that person before marriage, or acquired after marriage by gift or inheritance. The income generated by one spouse's separate property is his or her separate property in a majority of the community property states. In any situation in which there is a question whether an item of property is community or separate, there is a strong legal presumption that it is community. The various community property states have their own specific rules for determining which spouse has management rights over particular types of community property.

**Other Marital Property Rights:** Various other property rights are created by marriage. The English common law gave the wife a right called **dower,** consisting of a life estate in one-third of her husband's real property after his death. The husband had a right called **curtesy,** consisting of a life estate in all of his wife's real property after her death. Almost all states have abolished or greatly altered these common-law rights in recent years. Most states, however, do provide a surviving spouse with some type of interest after the death of the other spouse to insure that the survivor will at least be able to continue living in their shared residence (i.e., the **homestead**).

## SALES OF REAL PROPERTY

Next to leases, sales are the most commonly occurring real estate transactions. Whether such sales involve a residential house and lot, a farm, or other real property, they are the most monetarily significant transactions many people ever experience.

Most real estate sales involve the transfer of a fee simple interest in the surface, minerals, or both. Transfer of other types of interests may be accomplished in much the same way, but the procedures are often modified to fit the particular circumstances. Leasehold interests are usually created simply by the signing of a lease contract. Throughout the following discussion we will assume that the transaction is of the most common type—the sale of a fee simple interest.

### *Brokers*

When a landowner wishes to sell property, the first step usually is to contact and employ a real estate broker (or "agent"). Although this is not required (the landowner can, of course, sell the land without help), it is usually desirable unless the owner already has a buyer lined up.

The function of the broker is to find a buyer. This is usually the extent of the broker's authority; he or she ordinarily is not given authority to actually sell or even to make a contract to sell. In return for finding a buyer the broker is entitled to be compensated by receiving an agreed-upon *commission,* which is usually a percentage of the selling price.

A formal employment contract setting out the terms of the arrangement should be made with the broker. Indeed, in many states a broker has no legally enforceable right to a commission unless the agreement to pay it is in writing.

The arrangement with the broker can be of several types, including an open listing, exclusive agency, or exclusive right to sell. In an **open listing,** the broker is entitled to a commission only if he or she is the *first one* to procure a buyer who is "ready, willing, and able" to buy at the stated selling price. The owner is free to sell the land personally or through another broker without incurring liability to the employed broker. Open listings are not extremely common today.

A second type, the **exclusive agency,** arises when the owner gives assurance that no other broker will be hired during the term of the agreement. If the owner does employ another broker who procures a buyer, the sale is valid but the original broker is still entitled to the agreed commission. However, the owner is entitled to sell the land *personally,* without the aid of the employed broker or any other broker. If the owner makes the sale without assistance, the employed broker is not entitled to a commission.

The type of arrangement most advantageous to the broker is an **exclusive right to sell,** in which the employed broker is entitled to the agreed commission if the property is sold during the agreement's duration by anyone, whether done with the aid of the employed broker or some other broker or by the owner acting alone.

**Multiple Listing Services:** In many localities today, real estate brokers have formed multiple listing services. A **multiple listing service (MLS)** is an arrangement whereby brokers in the area pool their listings, each member having access to the pool. A participating broker ordinarily obtains either an exclusive agency or exclusive right to sell agreement from the landowner, and then places that listing in the local MLS. If another broker who also is a member of the MLS finds a buyer for the property, the commission is split between the listing and selling brokers under the terms of the MLS membership agreement signed by each participating broker.

## *The Contract*

When a buyer is found, a contract for sale will ordinarily be made. When making an offer to buy, or when entering the contract itself, the buyer often makes a deposit referred to as **earnest money.** The real estate sale contract sometimes is called an *earnest money contract,* and normally provides that the buyer will forfeit the earnest money if he or she breaches the contract.

To be enforceable, a contract for the sale of land has to be in writing in almost all circumstances. Although the contract usually is evidenced by a detailed formal document signed by both seller and buyer, the requirement of written documentation can be satisfied by informal instruments such as letters or telegrams. The writing, whether formal or not, must contain *all the essential terms* of the agreement and must be signed by the party against whom enforcement is sought.[7] If any of the essential terms are missing, the writing is considered insufficient; oral testimony will not be allowed to fill in the gaps, and the contract is unenforceable.

Specifically, the terms that must be included in the written contract for sale are (1) the *names* of the seller and buyer and an indication of their intent to be bound, (2) a *description* of the property sufficient to identify it, and (3) the *price.*

More is said about the required description in the discussion of deeds later in this chapter. (Incidentally, if the seller does ultimately convey title by giving a deed, it is immaterial whether there was an enforceable contract. The contract simply prevents one party from reneging prior to transfer of title.)

## *Title Examination, Insurance, and Survey*

One of the main reasons for initially making a sale contract rather than immediately transferring ownership is to give the buyer an opportunity to investigate the seller's title (often called a **title examination**). This essentially involves an examination of all officially recorded documents concerning the property. The examination is usually made by an attorney employed either by the purchaser, by the lending institution from which the purchase price is being borrowed, or by a title insurance company.

The attorney may personally search the public records and on the basis of this investigation issue a "certificate of title" giving his or her opinion as to the validity of the seller's title. Or the attorney may examine an **abstract,** which is a compilation of the official records relating to a particular parcel of land. Privately owned *abstract companies* or *abstracters* produce such abstracts and keep them current.

The sale contract often requires the seller to provide evidence of a good title. The certificate of title is used as such evidence in some parts of the country, while in other areas the abstract and the attorney's opinion based thereon provide the required evidence. It is also becoming more frequent for the contract to require the seller to provide the buyer with "title insurance." This may be used as the sole evidence of

---

[7] The signature can be that of the party's authorized agent. However, in most states, a contract for the sale of real estate signed by an agent is enforceable only if the agent's authorization is also in writing. (The same is true for the signing of a deed, discussed later in this chapter.)

title, or it may be required in addition to other evidence. Title insurance, which is purchased from a company engaged in the business of selling such insurance (often called a *title company*), simply provides that the issuing company will compensate the buyer for any loss if the title ultimately proves defective. Of course, the title company will issue such a policy only if its own attorneys feel, after making a title examination, that the title is good.

Unless a survey has been made very recently, the seller is often required under the contract to have a new survey made. A licensed surveyor will be employed to make sure that the described boundaries are correct and that no buildings or other encroachments lie on the boundary line.

## *Financing and Closing the Sale*

Many times the buyer does not have sufficient funds available to pay the agreed price. In such cases, after the contract is made but before the transfer of title, the buyer must obtain the necessary financing. Savings and loan associations are one of the most frequently used sources of such funds, especially for the purchase of residential property. As we mentioned earlier, the buyer (mortgagor) normally executes a mortgage to the lender (mortgagee) as security for the loan.

Sometimes the seller provides the financing by permitting the buyer to pay the purchase price in installments. In such a case, the seller may immediately transfer title to the buyer and take a mortgage to secure payment, or the seller and buyer may agree that title will not be transferred to the buyer until the purchase price is completely paid. The latter type of arrangement is often called a **contract for deed.**

The actual transfer of ownership usually takes place at the **closing** (or **settlement**)—the meeting attended by the seller and buyer as well as other interested parties such as their attorneys, the broker, and a representative of the mortgagee. At the meeting the seller signs and delivers to the buyer a *deed* that transfers the ownership; and the buyer pays the purchase price. (As a practical matter, however, the representative of the mortgagee may actually pay the seller.) It is also common for the mortgage to be executed at the closing and for other incidental financial matters to be settled (such as apportionment of property taxes and insurance that the seller may have prepaid).

Sometimes a closing occurs in a different manner, by the use of an "escrow agent." The **escrow agent** is a disinterested third party to whom the seller has delivered the deed and to whom the buyer has made payment. It is fairly common for an institution such as a title insurance company to serve as escrow agent. This party's instructions generally are to close the deal by delivering the deed to the buyer and the payment to the seller on receipt of the required evidence of good title.

## *The Deed*

**Types of Deeds:** As we stated earlier, title to real property is conveyed by means of a written deed. Several types of deeds exist, each involving particular legal consequences.

*General Warranty Deed:* From the buyer's point of view, the **general warranty deed** is by far the most desirable kind to obtain, because it carries certain warranties, or covenants, that the title is good. These warranties may be expressed in the deed, but even if not expressed they are *implied* if the document is actually a general warranty deed. Whether a particular deed is one of general warranty depends on the language used in it. The wording necessary to create such a deed varies from state to state. In Illinois and Michigan, for example, the verb phrase *convey and warrant* makes it a general warranty deed. The warranties, which overlap somewhat, usually consist of the following: (1) **Covenant of seisin.** The seller (called *grantor* in the deed) guarantees that he or she has good title to the land conveyed. (2) **Covenant against encumbrances.** The grantor guarantees that there are no encumbrances on the land except as stated in the deed. (An *encumbrance* includes any type of lien or easement held by a third party.) The existence of such an encumbrance causes a breach of this warranty by the grantor, even if the grantee (the buyer) knows about it when receiving the deed, unless the deed states that the title is "subject to" the particular encumbrance. (3) **Covenant for quiet enjoyment.** The grantor guarantees that the grantee (or those to whom the grantee later conveys the property) will not be evicted or disturbed by a person having a better title or a lien.

*Special Warranty Deed:* In a **special warranty deed,** there is a warranty only that the title has not been diminished in any way by a personal act of the grantor. For example, suppose the grantor had previously executed a mortgage on the land that the deed does not mention. If the grantee later has to pay off the mortgage or if it is foreclosed and the grantee loses the property, the grantor will be liable to the grantee for damages. On the other hand, if the grantor has not personally encumbered the title but an outstanding title or interest in the land is later asserted by some third person, the grantor incurs no liability. This situation might arise, for instance, if the land is encumbered by a valid lien created by someone who owned the land prior to the grantor. The special warranty deed is a sufficient performance of the seller's obligations under the sale contract unless that contract specifically required a general warranty deed.

***Quitclaim Deed:*** In a **quitclaim deed,** the grantor does not really purport to convey any title at all to the grantee. The deed says, in essence, "If I have any present interest in this land, I hereby convey it to you." This deed is not a sufficient performance of the grantor's obligations under the sale contract unless the contract so provides. Quitclaim deeds are often used as a form of *release.* For example: A owns the land, but X arguably has some type of interest in it, and A negotiates with X for a release of X's claim. One way of accomplishing the release is for A to obtain a quitclaim deed from X. Quitclaim deeds are also frequently employed by government entities (such as cities and counties) when they sell land.

***Deed of Bargain and Sale:*** The **deed of bargain and sale** purports to convey title but does not contain any warranties. Even though differing in form, this deed conveys the same type of title as a quitclaim deed. It also is not a sufficient performance of the grantor's obligations under the sale contract unless the contract so provides.

**Requirements of a Valid Deed:** Because a deed accomplishes a present transfer of a property interest, *consideration* is not required. The owner can give away the property if he or she wishes. Of course, a *sale contract* must be supported by consideration, as must any other executory contract. A promise to make a gift of land or of anything else is generally not enforceable; but a completed gift by delivery of a deed is perfectly valid, assuming that there is no intent to defraud the grantor's creditors. Even though there is no requirement that a grantee give consideration for a deed or that consideration be stated in the deed, it is customary for the deed to contain a *recital of consideration*—a statement of what consideration is being given by the grantee. It is also customary for the recital to state merely a nominal consideration (such as $10) rather than the price actually paid.

There are several requirements that a deed must meet in order to transfer a real property interest. Although these requirements vary slightly among the states, they may be summarized as follows.

***Grantor and Grantee:*** The deed must name a grantor and grantee. The grantor must have legal capacity. If the grantor is married, it is generally desirable to have the grantor's spouse named as a grantor as well, for several reasons. In most states, if the property is occupied by husband and wife as their residence, or homestead, both must join in a conveyance of the property even if only one of them owns it. And as previously mentioned, the laws of many states give one spouse certain types of rights with respect to the property of the other regardless of whether the property is their homestead, and these rights are extinguished only if the grantor's spouse joins in the deed.

***Words of Conveyance:*** The deed must contain words of conveyance—words indicating a present intent to transfer ownership to the grantee, such as "I, Ruth Smith, do hereby grant, sell, and convey...."

***Description:*** The deed must contain an adequate description of the land being conveyed.

***Signature:*** The deed must be signed by the grantor. For the reasons already discussed, it is also usually desirable to obtain the signature of a married grantor's spouse.

***Delivery:*** The deed must be delivered to the grantee.

**Methods of Describing Land:** As previously mentioned, a valid deed must contain an adequate description of the property being conveyed. Although this description should be (and usually is) stated in the deed, it is permissible for the deed to refer to a sufficient description contained in another document.

Land can be adequately described in several ways, but regardless of the method employed the property must be identified in such a way that there can be no mistake about exactly which parcel of land is being conveyed. There is a general tendency for the courts to require a greater degree of precision in a deed than in a sale contract. For example, in the case of residential property, a sale contract usually is enforceable if the description is merely a street name and number in a particular city and state. In many states, however, such a description is not sufficient for a deed to be a valid conveyance of title to the property.

***Government Survey:*** In those states west of the Mississippi River (except Texas) and in Alabama, Mississippi, Florida, Illinois, Indiana, Ohio, and Michigan, land can be described by reference to the **United States Government Survey.** This survey was adopted by Congress in 1785 for the purpose of describing government-owned land that was to be transferred to states, railroads, and settlers. It uses meridians and parallels to divide the surveyed areas into quadrangles that are approximately 24 miles on each side. Each quadrangle is further divided into 16 tracts called **townships** that are approximately 6 miles on each side.

***Metes and Bounds:*** In those states not using the U.S. Government Survey (the eastern states and Texas), it is common for land to be described by **metes and bounds.** *Metes* means measures of length; *bounds* refers to the boundaries of the property. A metes and bounds description essentially just delineates the exterior lines of the land being conveyed. It may make use of a ***monument*** (a natural or artificial landmark such as a river or street) to constitute a boundary or to mark a corner of the tract. A metes and bounds description begins at a well-identified point and runs stated distances at stated angles, tracing the boundary until it returns to the starting point.

***Plat:*** The two methods just discussed, reference to the government survey and metes and bounds, are normally used to describe land in rural and semirural areas that have not been formally subdivided and platted. Most land in urban areas has been surveyed by private developers and subdivided into numbered blocks and lots on a **plat** (map) that is recorded (filed) with a designated county official. In almost all parts of the country, it is common to describe urban land by reference to the lot and block number in the recorded plat.

In the following case, we will see how problems can arise from "homemade" deeds. The case also illustrates that a court will, where it is possible to do so, attempt to make sense out of an imprecisely drafted deed.

---

**Baker v. Zingelman**
Superior Court of Pennsylvania,
393 A.2d 908 (1978)

Margaret and Carl DeBow owned a tract of land known as the Lakeland Allotment. There was a plat subdividing the land into lots, but no actual subdivision had occurred. The property was mostly farmland, and the DeBows lived in the farm house and operated an antique shop in the barn behind the house. There also were several other sheds and garages on their property. In 1968 they built and moved into a new home west of the land in question. They then asked Marie Baker (Margaret's sister) and her husband George to leave their home in Cleveland, Ohio, move to the farmhouse on the Lakeland Allotment, and operate the antique shop. They agreed to do so, and Margaret prepared a deed conveying the property to the Bakers.

Before preparing the deed, Margaret had "walked off" (measured) the land to be transferred, and asked the Bakers if they thought it was sufficient footage to include the buildings located on the land. Margaret stated that if the land she measured off was not sufficient to include the buildings, "we can clear it up later." The deed prepared by Margaret began "at a point where the east line of the proposed Michigan Avenue intersects the south line of West Erie Street" and then followed the directional and distance description matching a lot on the Lakeland Allotment plat. Michigan Avenue was an unopened street, and Margaret admitted that she did not know exactly where it began when she prepared the deed.

The Bakers moved into the farmhouse and reopened and operated the antique shop in 1971. During the same year Carl DeBow died. In 1973 Margaret married Zingelman, her present husband. It appears that this remarriage contributed in some way to the problems that later arose. Sometime in 1973 George Baker became upset with Margaret because she parked her truck in the garage which the Bakers claim is located on their property. There was a falling out between the families about this time. Margaret informed the Bakers that part of the barn, the garage, and sheds located on the land extended onto

*(continued)*

her adjacent land. By early 1975, Margaret's attorney informed the Bakers that the part of the barn which projected onto Margaret's property would be forcibly removed unless the Bakers chose to purchase for $10,000 the strip of property which would clear up the location problem of the buildings. The Bakers, plaintiffs, then sued to enjoin Margaret from parking her truck in the garage and from cutting off part of the barn.

At the trial, the testimony of two surveyors disclosed that all of one shed and garage and a portion of another shed and 13 feet of the barn extended onto Margaret's property. The lower court, however, enjoined Margaret from any further trespass and ordered her to convey to the Bakers the strip of land which would then place the buildings on the Baker property, in order to effectuate the original intent of the parties in their conveyance of 1971. Margaret, the defendant, appealed.

**Decision:** The judgment for the plaintiffs was affirmed. Although a deed ordinarily will be interpreted as including only what is described, in this case the court required Margaret to transfer without charge the strip of land that would place the buildings on the Baker property. There were essentially two reasons for the court's action. First, the evidence was overwhelmingly that the parties' original intent was to transfer enough land to include the buildings. Second, the circumstances under which the deed was prepared were such that an error in the description of the property was very likely. ■

---

**Acknowledgment:** An **acknowledgment** is a formal declaration before a designated public official, such as a notary public, by a person who has signed a document, that he or she executed the document as a voluntary act. The public official places his or her signature and seal after the declaration and the declarant's signature. The resulting instrument, referred to as a *certificate of acknowledgment,* is attached to the document to which it relates.

In most states an acknowledgment is not required for a deed to be valid, but it is required as a prerequisite to "recording."

**Recording:** **Recording** is the act of filing the deed with a public official, referred to in different states as the "recorder of deeds," "register of deeds," or any of several other titles. The official copies the deed into the record books, indexes it, and returns the original to the person who filed it.

As between the grantor and grantee, an otherwise valid deed is perfectly good even if it is not recorded. The purpose of recording procedures, which exist in every state, is to give notice to the world at large that the transfer of title has taken place. Frequently referred to as "constructive notice," this means that third parties are treated as having notice regardless of whether they actually do.

State recording statutes generally provide that an unrecorded deed, though valid between grantor and grantee, is void with respect to any subsequent bona fide purchaser. A **bona fide purchaser (BFP)** is a good faith purchaser for value. For example, suppose that O sells a tract of land to B, and B does not record her deed. O then sells the same land to C by executing another deed. If C pays for the land rather than receiving it as a gift, he is giving *value.* If C does not know of the earlier conveyance to B when he purchases, he is acting in *good faith.* Thus C qualifies as a BFP and has good title. In this situation B has no title. But if B has recorded her deed prior to C's purchase, B would have title even if C later gave value and acted in good faith. The reasoning is that C could have discovered B's interest if he had checked the records.

Although there is some conflict on the point, the courts in a majority of states hold that C qualifies as a BFP even if he does not record his own deed. (Of course, if he does not do so, he runs the risk of having the same thing happen to him that happened to B. If there was a "C," there could later be a "D.")

Regarding the status of C as a BFP, another point must be made. If B, the first grantee from O, is actually *in possession of the land* when C acquires his interest, this possession serves as notice to C. Thus, even if B did not record and C did not have actual knowledge of B's interest, C nevertheless is not a BFP.

Recording statutes apply not only to the sale of a fee simple interest but also to the conveyance of any other type of interest in land. For example, if O executes a mortgage to B, giving her a lien on the property, B should record her mortgage. If she does not, she risks losing her interest to a subsequent BFP.

Furthermore, the word *purchaser* actually means a grantee of any type of interest in the land, even such interests as liens or easements. Suppose, for instance, that O sells to B, who does not record her deed.

O later borrows money from C and executes a mortgage purporting to give C a lien on the land. By making the loan to O, C is giving value. If C receives the mortgage without knowledge of the earlier conveyance to B, he is acting in good faith and is treated as a BFP. Thus C's mortgage is valid, and B's ownership is subject to it. If B had been a mortgagee herself instead of an actual grantee of the title, the same rules would apply to the conflict between B and C, the two mortgagees.

# ADVERSE POSSESSION

Under some circumstances, a party can acquire ownership of land by taking possession of it and staying in possession for a certain number of years. The required time period is established by statute and varies from state to state, ranging from five years in California to thirty years in Louisiana.

Ownership acquired in this manner is frequently referred to as **title by adverse possession** or **title by limitation**.[8] Since it is not acquired by deed, there is nothing to record. Thus the recording statutes do not apply, and title by adverse possession, once acquired, cannot be lost to a subsequent BFP. Of course, even though such title is not *acquired* by deed, it can be *conveyed* by deed to someone else. Such a deed would be subject to all the rules applicable to deeds in general, including the recording statutes.

## Requirements for Title by Adverse Possession

Not all types of possession will ripen into ownership. The possession must be "adverse," which means, in effect, that it must be actual, hostile, open and notorious, and continuous.[9]

**Actual Possession:** The requirement that possession be *actual* simply means that the possessor must have exercised some type of *physical control* over the land that indicates a claim of ownership. The person need not actually live on the property, although this certainly constitutes actual possession. What is required is that the possessor act toward the land as an average owner probably would act, taking into account the nature of the land. For example, if it is farmland, the farming of it constitutes actual possession. Erecting buildings or other improvements may also be sufficient.

Construction of a fence or building that extends over the true boundary line and onto the land of an adjoining property owner generally constitutes actual possession of that part of the land encompassed by the fence or located under the building. Thus, if the other requirements of adverse possession are met, the party erecting the fence or building will become the owner of the area in question after the prescribed period of time.

**Hostile Possession:** The requirement that the possession be *hostile* does not mean that it must be accompanied by ill feelings. What it means is that possession must be *nonconsensual*; it is not adverse if it occurs with the consent of the true owner. Thus a tenant's possession of the landlord's property under a lease agreement is not hostile unless the tenant clearly communicated to the landlord that the tenant was claiming ownership.

Similarly, if two parties are co-owners of a tract of land, each of them has a right to possession. Therefore, possession by one co-owner is not hostile as to the other unless the possessor notifies the other that he or she is claiming sole ownership.

**Open and Notorious Possession:** The possession must be *open and notorious* rather than secretive. In other words, it must be a type of possession that will be easily noticeable by the true owner if a reasonable inspection is made.

**Continuous Possession:** In order for adverse possession to ultimately ripen into ownership, it must be *reasonably continuous* for the required period of time. The possessor does not have to be in possession every single day of the period. For instance, he or she could leave temporarily with an intent to return, and the law would treat the possession as not having been interrupted.

In answering the question of whether possession has been continuous, a court will take into account

---

[8] The latter phrase is explained by the fact that the prescribed time periods are, in essence, statutes of limitations setting forth the maximum length of time an owner has to sue someone who is wrongfully in possession of the owner's land.

[9] Some courts have also said that the possession must be "exclusive" and "under claim of right." These requirements will not be discussed because they overlap with the four listed here and really add nothing to what is required for adverse possession to exist.

the nature of the land and the type of use being made of it. Thus farming the land only during the growing season each year constitutes continuous possession.

Also, the uninterrupted possession by two or more successive possessors can sometimes be added together, or "tacked," to satisfy the statutory time requirement. For "tacking" to be permitted, there must have been *privity* between the successive possessors. This simply means that the possessions by different persons must not have been independent of each other; rather, there must have been a transaction between them which purported to transfer the property. To illustrate: In State X the required period for adverse possession is ten years. O is the true owner. B meets all the requirements for adverse possession except that he stays on the land only six years. B then purports to sell or otherwise transfer the land to C. If C stays in possession for four more years, continuing to meet all the requirements for obtaining title by adverse possession, C becomes the owner of the land.

The following case illustrates the applicability of the adverse possession doctrine to a common problem—a boundary dispute between "unneighborly" neighbors.

---

### Kline v. Kramer
Court of Appeals of Indiana,
386 N.E.2d 982 (1979)

The Klines and the Kramers were adjoining landowners who both claimed ownership of a strip of land 1 to 4 feet wide and 309 feet long. The disputed strip formed the northern boundary of the Kramer property and the southern boundary of the Kline property. Both claimed ownership through previous owners. The Klines, who acquired their property in 1972, based their claim to the strip on the legal description contained in their deed. The Kramers, who purchased their property in 1968, claimed the strip on the theory of adverse possession. The position of the Kramers was that the ten-year period of possession necessary to establish adverse possession had been satisfied by the previous owners of the Kramer property, Harry and Hazel Britt.

The Kramers, plaintiffs, filed suit against the Klines, defendants, seeking to establish ownership of the boundary strip. The trial court granted the plaintiffs' motion for summary judgment, ruling that they had title by adverse possession, and the defendants appealed.

**Decision:** The judgment for the plaintiffs was affirmed. A fence had been located in its present position since at least 1947, when the Britts purchased the property now owned by the Kramers. The Britts clearly had treated all the land up to the fence as their own. Thus, by 1957, the Britts had acquired the disputed strip of land by adverse possession. (The pertinent statute of limitations period in Indiana is ten years.) It is irrelevant whether the Britts intended to claim someone else's land. What is important is that they possessed what was enclosed by the fence, as if it were their own. When the Britts sold the land to the Kramers in 1968, the Kramers acquired the strip even though it was not part of the description in their deed. The Klines no longer owned the strip, despite the fact that it was part of the land described in their own deed. ∎

---

## REGULATION OF REAL PROPERTY OWNERSHIP, USE, AND SALE

### Eminent Domain

The power of the government to take private property for public purposes (such as a highway) is referred to as the power of **eminent domain**. The federal government derives the power of eminent domain from the Fifth Amendment to the U.S. Constitution. Individual states draw the power from their own constitutions. In addition, states have delegated the power of eminent domain by statute to local governments (such as counties, cities, and school districts) and to railroads and public utilities.

The power can be exercised without the owner's consent, but the government must pay *just compensation* (i.e., the fair value of the property) to the owner. In many cases, a governmental body seeking to acquire property for a public purpose will negotiate a purchase from the owner. If the owner does not consent, or if there is disagreement as to the fair value of the property, the government exercises the power of eminent domain by instituting a court action called **condemnation**. In a condemnation proceeding the court will set a fair value for the property based on the evidence of that value.

In some situations, a property owner may claim that an activity by a governmental body has so deprived the owner of the use of the property that a "taking" of the property has actually occurred. The property owner can institute a legal action known as **inverse condemnation**, in which a court will determine whether there has been a taking of the property and, if so, the fair value to be paid the owner. The mere fact that a governmental activity has diminished the use or value of property does not establish that there has been a "taking"; the evidence must demonstrate that the owner has been effectively deprived of any reasonable use of the land. For example, the taking off and landing of airplanes at a city-owned airport could constitute a taking of an adjoining property owner's land if the land was so close to the airport that the planes flew over it at extremely low altitude.

## Land Use Control

**Restrictive Covenants:** A deed may contain significant restrictions on the use of the property. For example, it might provide that only a single-family dwelling can be built on the land. Such **restrictive covenants** are usually valid and can be enforced by surrounding landowners. It also is common for a real estate developer to place restrictive covenants on all the residential lots in a subdivision and to specify those restrictions in the recorded plat. Such restrictions, such as those relating to the type and appearance of structures that can be built on the lots, are intended to preserve property values and can also be enforced by surrounding landowners in the subdivision.

**Zoning:** Pursuant to their constitutional police power, all states have passed legislation giving cities the power to enact zoning ordinances. In some states, similar powers have been given to counties. A **zoning ordinance** is essentially a law specifying the permissible uses of land in designated areas. Such an ordinance might specify zones for single-family dwellings, several categories of multiple-family dwellings, office buildings, various classifications of commercial structures, industrial facilities, and so on. Moreover, a zoning ordinance may impose even more detailed restrictions on use, such as minimum distances of structures from streets, lot sizes, and minimum parking accommodations for commercial buildings. The purposes of zoning laws are to permit the orderly planning of growth, protect against deterioration of surrounding property values by obnoxious uses, maintain the residential character of neighborhoods, and further other public purposes such as the prevention of overcrowding.

To prevent zoning from constituting a "taking" of property, zoning ordinances usually permit the continuance of a preexisting use even though it does not conform to the zoning restrictions for that area. In addition, a landowner may obtain a **variance**—permission from the city to make a use of the property that does not conform to the zoning ordinance—if he or she proves the following: (1) The zoning ordinance makes it impossible for the owner to receive a reasonable return on his or her investment in the land. (2) The negative effect of the zoning ordinance is unique to this owner's property; it is not an effect that is common to other landowners in the zone. (3) Granting the variance will not substantially alter the basic character of the surrounding neighborhood.

## The Implied Warranty of Habitability

In recent years courts in a majority of states have recognized an **implied warranty of habitability** in the sale of new residential housing. The warranty exists separately from, and in addition to, any express warranties made by the seller. The warranty of habitability does not apply to minor defects, but only to major defects that substantially interfere with the buyer's use of the property as a residence. Examples of defects that probably would be a breach of the warranty include a defective foundation, leaking roof, malfunctioning heating or cooling system, and unsafe electrical wiring. Breach of the warranty entitles the buyer to receive damages from the seller based on the cost of repairing defects that are reasonably correctable, or the amount by which the home's market value has been reduced in the case of noncorrectable defects.

The implied warranty of habitability generally has been applied only to sales by a builder or other seller who is in the housing business. Real estate brokers and agents normally have not been held responsible under this warranty. Although some courts have extended the builder's liability under the implied warranty of habitability to the subsequent sale of used homes, a majority of courts have restricted it to the first sale of new homes. In recent years most states also have imposed an implied warranty of habitability on the landlord who leases residential property; a detailed discussion of the warranty in that setting is included in the next chapter.

## SUMMARY

Real property includes (1) land, consisting of the surface, air rights, and subsurface rights, and (2) things affixed to the land, consisting of vegetation and fixtures. A fixture is an item that formerly was personal property and that has been attached to the land with an intent that it become a permanent part of the land.

The complete ownership of land can be divided in a number of ways. The particular set of rights owned in a given situation is an estate, or interest, in real property. These interests can be classified as freehold, nonfreehold, nonpossessory, and future. Any interest in real property that can be owned by one individual can also be owned concurrently by two or more individuals. There are several forms of co-ownership of real property.

Sales of real property commonly involve a transfer of complete ownership—the fee simple estate—but similar procedures may be employed to transfer lesser interests. In the typical sale of real property, the owner obtains the services of a broker, a buyer is found, a sale contract is executed, the buyer procures the necessary financing, various steps are taken to insure that the seller has a good title, and the closing or settlement occurs. The seller transfers title by executing and delivering a written deed. Although there are several types of deed, the general warranty deed is the best from the buyer's perspective. The deed must meet several requirements in order to transfer ownership effectively. Deeds should be acknowledged and recorded for the buyer's protection.

Title to real property can also be acquired by adverse possession, in which the taking of land must be actual, hostile, open and notorious, and the taking party must have continuous possession for a period of time specified by state statute. The ownership, use, and sale of real property is subject to several types of regulation, including the government's power of eminent domain, restrictive covenants, zoning ordinances, and the implied warranty of habitability.

## KEY TERMS

Air rights
Fixture
Possessory interests
Freehold estates
Nonfreehold estates
Nonpossessory interests
Fee simple estate
Fee simple defeasible
Life estate
Leasehold estates
Easement
Easement appurtenant
Servient estate
Dominant estate
Easement in gross
Easement by express grant or reservation
Easement by implication
Easement by necessity
Easement by prescription (or prescriptive easement)
Profit
License
Mortgage
Lien
Involuntary lien
Mechanic's lien
Judgment lien
Future interest
Reversion
Remainder
Tenancy in common
Joint tenancy
Condominium
Cooperative
Tenancy by the entireties
Community property
Dower
Curtesy
Homestead
Open listing
Exclusive agency
Exclusive right to sell
Multiple listing service (MLS)
Earnest money
Title examination
Abstract
Contract for deed
Closing (or settlement)

Escrow agent
General warranty deed
Covenant of seisin
Covenant against encumbrances
Covenant for quiet enjoyment
Special warranty deed
Quitclaim deed
Deed of bargain and sale
United States Government Survey
Townships
Metes and bounds
Plat
Acknowledgment
Recording
Bona fide purchaser (BFP)
Title by adverse possession (or title by limitation)
Eminent domain
Condemnation
Inverse condemnation
Restrictive covenants
Zoning ordinance
Variance
Implied warranty of habitability

## QUESTIONS AND PROBLEMS

**1.** Talley and Warren were adjoining landowners. Talley drilled a producing oil well on his land close to the boundary line between his and Warren's property. Warren sued Talley for trespass. Although the entire well was on Talley's property, Warren proved that the well was drawing oil not only from beneath Talley's land but also from beneath Warren's. Will Warren prevail? Discuss.

**2.** In the above situation, suppose that Talley had drilled a "slant well," which began on his land but ended beneath Warren's land because it had been drilled at an angle. What will be the result if Warren sues for trespass in this case? Discuss.

**3.** Jenkins sold a 10-acre tract of land to Watkins. In the past, Jenkins had engaged in the business of raising rabbits, and at the time of the sale a number of rabbit hutches were still on the land. They were not attached to the soil but merely rested upon it. Each hutch had a wire-covered wooden frame and a tin roof; each measured approximately 4 feet by 4 feet by 4 feet. These hutches were never mentioned in the transaction. When Jenkins moved from the premises after the sale, he claimed that the rabbit hutches were still his and that he was entitled to take them. Watkins disagreed. Who is correct? Discuss.

**4.** Discuss whether wall-to-wall carpeting should be considered a fixture.

**5.** What are some probable reasons for the rule that the owner of a fee simple interest is presumed to be selling the entire interest unless the terms of the conveyance clearly indicate transference of a lesser interest? Explain.

**6.** Kempin was the owner of a life estate in a 60-acre parcel of land. A valuable stand of growing timber was situated on the property, and substantial deposits of lignite were located beneath it. Kempin began cutting the timber, both for firewood and for the purpose of sale. He also undertook to mine the lignite, some of which he intended to use for fuel and some of which he intended to sell. Moskovitz, who was to become the fee simple owner on Kempin's death, sued Kempin to enjoin him from all of the above activities. Who will prevail? Explain.

**7.** Explain the difference between easements, profits, and licenses.

**8.** In connection with the employment of a real estate broker, what is the difference between an open listing, an exclusive agency, and an exclusive right to sell?

**9.** Poindexter sold his farm to Samuelson, who did not record his deed. Several weeks later, before Samuelson had taken possession of the land, Poindexter sold the same property to Rosser, who made a large down payment and knew nothing of the earlier sale to Samuelson. Does Samuelson or Rosser have title to the land? Explain. Would it matter whether Rosser recorded his deed? Explain. Would it make any difference if Samuelson had already taken possession of the land when Rosser bought it? Explain.

**10.** Arnold and Ross were adjoining landowners. The opening of a cave was located on Arnold's land, but the cave ran beneath Ross's land. Ross did not know of the cave's existence. For a continuous period of 25 years, Arnold used the entire cave for various purposes, including storage. On a number of occasions, doing business as the Marengo Cave Co., he also guided visitors through the cave for a fee. Ross finally learned of the cave and of the use Arnold had been making of it. He demanded that Arnold cease his use of the part of the cave beneath Ross's land. Arnold refused, claiming that he had acquired title to the cave by adverse possession. The pertinent state statute provided for acquisition of such title after 20 years. Ross filed suit to establish ownership of the cave. Who owned the portion of the cave located beneath Ross's land? Discuss. (*Marengo Cave Co. v. Ross,* 10 N.E.2d 917, 1937.)

# CHAPTER 44

# LANDLORD AND TENANT

## THE NATURE OF THE LANDLORD–TENANT RELATIONSHIP

The landlord-tenant relationship is created when the owner of real estate transfers temporary possession of the property to another person in return for the payment of rent.[1] The agreement providing for this transfer of possession and payment of rent is a **lease,** or *rental agreement.* The owner is referred to as the *landlord,* or *lessor,* and the one taking possession is the *tenant,* or *lessee.*

The identifying characteristic of a lease is the tenant's temporary acquisition of *exclusive possession* and *control* of the premises or the particular portion of it which he or she occupies. The tenant is distinguished from a *purchaser* because no title passes. On the other hand, the tenant is distinguished from a mere *licensee* who receives the temporary right to park a car in a space, occupy a seat in a theater, or make some other nonexclusive, revocable use of the premises. The tenant also is different from a *lodger* who occupies a room in a hotel but does not have legal control over the occupied area.

The law governing the landlord-tenant relationship consisted almost solely of common-law principles until recent times. Today many states have specific statutes concerning the rights and duties of landlords and tenants. A Uniform Residential Landlord and Tenant Act was proposed in 1972 by the National Conference of Commissioners on Uniform State Laws and, with some variations, has been adopted in one-third of the states. Common-law principles still control, however, in many situations not covered by specific statutes. This area of law is thus a mixture of statutory provisions and case precedents.

Landlord-tenant law developed in a basically agrarian economy when the focal point of the lease was the land itself. As a result, the transaction was viewed primarily as one for the transfer of an interest in real estate, and the principles of real estate law governed most aspects of the arrangement. In the great majority of leases today, however, the focal point of the transaction is the house, apartment, office, or other structure on the land. Consequently, the law has gradually changed so as to view the arrangement primarily as a contract, with the rules of contract law governing more and more aspects of the relationship. The movement in recent years toward greater legal protection for the consumer also has had a substantial impact on landlord-tenant law.

## CREATION AND TERMINATION OF THE LANDLORD–TENANT RELATIONSHIP

### The Lease

**The Importance of the Lease:** The landlord-tenant relationship is created by agreement. Therefore, the lease and its particular terms determine the rights and duties of the parties. Most of the relevant legal principles serve only to specify rights and duties when the lease is silent on a disputed matter. There are a few legal principles, however, which do take precedence over a conflicting lease term.

Because the specific terms of the lease are of such great importance, it is critical that the parties draft their agreement carefully to clearly reflect their intent and to provide for various contingencies that might arise. It is also important for one party to closely examine any lease form proposed by the other. There

---

[1] The "owner" might own a fee simple interest, life estate, or other type of possessory interest. See Chapter 43 for details.

685

is no standard form that must be used. Some groups, such as landlord associations, have developed their own standard form, but there is no law requiring it to be followed or preventing it from being changed.

**Form of the Lease:** A lease may be oral unless a state statute requires it to be written. Most states have statutes requiring a written document for any lease extending beyond a stated time period. In some states, leases for a term greater than one year must be written; in other states the period is three years.

Whether oral or written, a valid lease agreement must (1) indicate an intent to create the landlord-tenant relationship; (2) identify the parties, each of whom must have contractual capacity; (3) clearly identify the premises; and (4) state the amount of the rent and when it is to be paid.

**Covenants and Conditions:** A lease provision in which the landlord or the tenant promises to do something or not to do something is either a **covenant** or a **condition.** The difference lies in the consequences resulting from the breach of a promise. If one party fails to perform a *covenant,* the other party's recourse normally is to file suit for money damages. The innocent party is not relieved from his or her obligations, and the breaching party does not forfeit his or her rights under the lease.

On the other hand, the failure to perform a *condition* does cause a forfeiture of the lease and relieves the innocent party from further obligations. Because of the drastic nature of forfeiture, most lease provisions traditionally have been viewed as covenants unless the lease expressly provides for forfeiture as a consequence of breach.

For example, suppose that the tenant fails to make a rent payment within the agreed time. If the lease does not expressly provide for forfeiture of the lease as a result of nonpayment, the landlord's only remedy under the common-law rule is to sue for the unpaid rent. However, if the lease had expressly made rent payment a condition by providing for forfeiture in the event of nonpayment, the landlord could declare the lease terminated and evict the tenant. Today it is common for many lease clauses to provide for forfeiture as the penalty for breach of the clause. This is especially true of clauses spelling out tenants' duties in standard form leases prepared by landlords.

In recent years, statutes have been enacted in most states which make forfeiture the penalty for a tenant's failure to pay rent, even without an express lease clause to that effect.

## Types of Tenancies

The interest acquired by a tenant is called a **tenancy,** or **leasehold.** Several types of tenancies exist.

**Tenancy for Years:** The most common tenancy is one that is technically called a **tenancy for years.** The name of this tenancy is rather misleading because it actually is created whenever a lease provides for a specific duration, such as thirty days, six months, one year, or fifty years. Such a tenancy terminates automatically when the term expires.

**Periodic Tenancy:** A **periodic tenancy** exists when the parties have not agreed on a specific duration, but have agreed that rent is to be paid at particular intervals (such as monthly or yearly). In such a case, the tenancy exists from period to period and can be terminated by one party giving notice to the other. The parties may expressly agree on the form and timing of the notice. If the lease is silent on the question, the common-law rule required that such notice be given at least one full rental period prior to termination. An exception was made for leases having rental periods of one year or more—in such cases six months' notice was required. Most states now have statutes which modify the common-law rule. Many of these statutes shorten the notice requirement to thirty days for periodic tenancies having rental periods longer than one month.

**Tenancy at Will:** A **tenancy at will** is a landlord-tenant relationship which may be terminated at any time by either party without advance notice. It exists when the parties have not agreed on either an express duration or a particular interval for rental payment. A tenancy at will is an uncommon occurrence.

**Tenancy at Sufferance:** When a valid tenancy is terminated, but the tenant continues to occupy the premises after he or she no longer has the right to do so, a **tenancy at sufferance** is created. The landlord can choose to make another lease or force the tenant to leave. The phrase tenancy at sufferance merely distinguishes the tenant from a complete trespasser who never had permission to be on the premises in the first place.

## Termination for Reasons Other than Expiration of the Lease

We already have seen some of the ways in which tenancies can terminate: expiration of the term in a tenancy for years, advance notice in a periodic tenancy, and breach of a condition in the lease.

Although leases usually are *not* terminated by the death or disability of either party, there are several other ways in which leases may come to an end.[2] The parties may, for example, terminate the lease by mutual agreement. This is sometimes called **surrender and acceptance**—the tenant surrenders the lease, and the landlord accepts the surrender.

If the primary subject matter of a lease is a structure, such as a house or apartment, most courts hold that destruction of the structure through no fault of either party (such as fire or flood) will terminate the lease. As with other contracts, leases can also be terminated because of fraud, mistake, duress, undue influence, or minority.

## Sale of the Leased Property

The landlord continues to own an interest in the premises during the term of the lease. This interest is called a **reversion** and consists of the landlord's future right to possession after termination of the lease.

A landlord may sell the leased property during the term of the lease, but such a sale does not terminate the lease. In actuality, the landlord merely sells what he has—the reversion. The purchaser buys the property subject to the rights of the tenant.

There are a few limited exceptions to this principle. In some ways a modern-day lease is still considered to be a transfer of an interest in real estate, rather than a mere contract, and to be subject to some of the rules of real estate law. For example, real estate *recording statutes* (discussed in Chapter 43) generally do apply to leases. Therefore, a purchaser from the landlord does not have to honor the pre-existing lease if (1) the lease had not been recorded prior to the sale, *and* (2) the tenant was not in possession of the premises at the time of the sale. Either the recording or the tenant's possession will put the purchaser on notice of the tenant's rights, and the purchaser must honor the lease.

---

[2] In the event of death, the rights and duties under the lease are part of the estate of the deceased under the control of the executor or administrator. In the event of insanity, the insane person's guardian exercises the rights and duties existing under the lease.

## POSSESSION OF THE PREMISES

### Landlord's Obligation to Turn Over Possession

One of the most important obligations of the landlord is to give the tenant possession. However, the laws of the various states are in conflict as to the extent of this obligation. One group of states follows the so-called "English rule," which requires the landlord to give the tenant actual physical possession. Under this rule, for example, if a holdover tenant from a previous lease is still in possession when the new tenant becomes entitled to possession, the landlord breaches the obligation to the new tenant.

Another group of states follows the "American rule," which requires only that the landlord transfer the *legal right to possession* to the tenant. Under this rule, the presence of a holdover tenant who has no legal right to be there is really the new tenant's problem, not the landlord's. The new tenant must take the necessary steps to remove the holdover.

### Covenant of Quiet Enjoyment

During the term of the lease, the landlord owes to the tenant an obligation not to interfere with the tenant's lawful possession and use of the premises. This obligation, the **covenant of quiet enjoyment,** is expressly stated in most leases, but in most states is implied by law even if not stated in the lease. The covenant may be breached by the conduct of the landlord, someone acting under the landlord's authority, or someone having better title to the premises than the landlord has. It ordinarily may not be breached by other third parties—for example, in a majority of states the independent conduct of another tenant does not make the landlord liable for breach of this obligation. Therefore, if tenant X interferes with tenant Y's lawful possession and use, Y's remedy is against X and not against the landlord.

The most common actions of the landlord that breach this covenant are *eviction* and *constructive eviction.*

**Eviction:** An **eviction** occurs if the landlord padlocks the premises, changes the door lock and refuses to give the tenant a new key, or in some other way physically bars the tenant from entering the premises. A tenant who has a legal right to possession has a choice. He or she may (1) sue for damages or

(2) treat the eviction as a breach of *condition* and be relieved from further obligations under the lease.

**Constructive Eviction:** Even without physically barring the tenant from entry, the landlord's action or inaction may cause the property to be unsuitable for the purpose for which it was leased. An example would be the failure to provide heat in the winter as promised in the lease. In such a case, the tenant may remain on the premises and sue for damages. If the tenant remains, he or she usually continues to be liable for rent. The tenant may, however, choose to abandon the property and treat the landlord's conduct as a **constructive eviction.** The tenant then is under no further obligation to pay rent.

## USE OF THE PREMISES BY THE TENANT

### Restrictions on Use

The uses that can be made of the property by the tenant usually are specified by agreement. In fact, clauses detailing permissible and impermissible uses are among the most common and important parts of leases. Such provisions frequently concern matters such as number of occupants, whether pets are permitted, and so forth.

In the absence of a lease provision prohibiting a particular use, the tenant is entitled to make any use of the premises that is (1) legal and (2) reasonably in line with the basic purpose for which the property was leased.

**Damaging the Landlord's Reversionary Interest:** The tenant has no right to use the property in such a way as to cause permanent damage to it. The duty of a tenant not to damage the landlord's reversionary interest is sometimes referred to as the duty not to commit **waste.** For example, a tenant cannot take timber or minerals from the land unless the right to do so was (1) expressly permitted by the lease or by later agreement or (2) clearly implied from surrounding circumstances. The right may be implied, for instance, when the primary value of the leased property is its timber or minerals, so that the parties probably would not have executed the lease if these materials had not been there.[3]

A tenant can be held liable for either intentionally or negligently damaging the leased property. When determining whether a tenant was negligent, the courts apply general principles of tort law. Many cases of this type involve claims by landlords that fire damage was caused by the tenant's negligence. For the landlord to prevail in such a case, there must be evidence that the tenant failed to act with reasonable care, such as by smoking in bed or leaving the premises to go shopping while food was left cooking on the kitchen range. Many cases also involve assertions by the tenant that the provisions of the lease excused him or her from liability for negligent damage to the leased premises. The language of the lease itself is the starting point for resolving most disputes arising from the landlord-tenant relationship, including this type of dispute. In the following case, the question for the court is whether the provisions of the lease should be interpreted so as to excuse the tenant from liability for fire damage caused by the tenant's negligence.

---

[3] A point that was made in Chapter 43 must be reiterated. What is ordinarily called an oil and gas "lease" is not really a lease at all. It is either the sale of a fee simple interest in the minerals in the ground or it is the sale of a right to take the minerals from the ground (a so-called "profit").

---

### Acquisto v. Joe R. Hahn Enterprises, Inc.
Supreme Court of New Mexico,
619 P.2d 1237 (1980)

The defendant, Acquisto, leased a building from the plaintiff, Hahn Enterprises. During the term of the lease a fire broke out in the building, and the landlord sued Acquisto for damages caused by the fire. The landlord claimed that Acquisto had negligently caused the fire. Based upon a jury verdict, the trial court found that Acquisto had been guilty of negligence, and that there was no provision in the lease excusing Acquisto from responsibility for his negligence. The court of appeals reversed, holding that the lease did excuse Acquisto from such liability, and the landlord appealed to the New Mexico Supreme Court.

*(continued)*

**Decision:** The judgment of the court of appeals for defendant Acquisto was reversed, and the judgment of the trial court for plaintiff Hahn affirmed. There was no express clause excusing the tenant from responsibility for negligence, but an express clause is not required. When there is no express clause the court will examine the entire document to determine whether the parties apparently intended to excuse the tenant from liability for negligence. In this case, the lease agreement as a whole indicates that they did not intend to excuse the tenant. There was an express exculpatory clause, but it spoke only of events (including fire) that were either unavoidable accidents or acts of God. In addition, the form used by the parties to manifest their agreement included a provision for specifying which party would have responsibility for insuring the premises, but the space for identifying such party was left blank. There was a similar provision regarding taxes, and the parties filled this in. Thus, the court concluded that they specifically did not agree on responsibility for insurance coverage, and that they did not agree to relieve the tenant of liability for negligent harm to the property. ∎

---

## *Altering the Premises*

Suppose that a tenant in an apartment or house wants to add some built-in bookshelves or paint the interior walls. Or suppose that a business tenant wishes to build an additional storage area for inventory. Does the tenant have a right to alter the property?

Many leases expressly forbid the tenant from making alterations to the premises without specific consent of the landlord. Even if the lease contains no such clause, however, the tenant generally has no right to make alterations without consent.

In many states the law imposes an absolute requirement that the tenant return the premises to the landlord at the end of the lease in exactly the same condition they were in at the beginning, except for normal wear and tear. If the tenant has made any changes without the landlord's consent, the tenant is liable for the cost of putting the property back into the condition it was in at the beginning of the lease.

In a growing number of states, however, the tenant is not liable for the cost of "undoing" such alterations if (1) the alteration was consistent with and necessary for the tenant's reasonable use of the premises, and (2) the alteration did not diminish the value of the property.

**Fixtures:** We saw in Chapter 43 that an item of personal property becomes a *fixture* when it is affixed to real property. Even if not actually attached, the item is a fixture if circumstances indicate that it was intended to be part of the real estate.

If a tenant affixes an item to the leased property, the same basic rules are applied to determine whether the item is a fixture as are applied in other situations. Thus, a tenant who installs built-in bookshelves, new cabinets, or other such items probably has added fixtures to the property and cannot remove them when the lease expires.

However, many courts traditionally have drawn a distinction between fixtures added by a residential tenant and those added by a tenant who conducts a business on the leased property. Fixtures added by a business tenant are called **trade fixtures.** Courts generally have held that a business tenant probably did not intend for a trade fixture to become part of the real estate. Thus if an item such as a gasoline pump or neon sign can be removed without substantial damage to the real estate, the business tenant usually can remove it at the end of the lease.

This distinction between residential and business tenants has been frequently criticized as illogical.

## THE DUTY TO MAINTAIN THE PREMISES

The traditional common-law view was that the landlord was not responsible for the condition of the premises at the beginning of the lease or for making repairs during the lease. The tenant leased the premises "as is," and was responsible for making later repairs so that the premises were substantially in the same condition at the end of the lease as at the beginning.

The tenant's duty to repair has always been subject to certain important limits. The duty does not apply to major structural components such as the foundation and framework, but only to relatively minor items like windows, venetian blinds, and so forth. However, whether classified as major or minor, the tenant is responsible for making emergency repairs to protect the premises from the elements and thus prevent further damage. This responsibility is part of the tenant's overall duty not to commit waste by negligently or intentionally damaging the property.

The general rule that a landlord has no duty to maintain the premises still exists *in theory*. However, over the years the courts have recognized many exceptions to the rule. Today the exceptions are practically as broad as the general rule. We will examine the most important situations in which the landlord does have a duty to make repairs.

### *Express Covenant*

As with most other matters, the obligation to make repairs may be dealt with in a specific lease clause. If the landlord expressly promises to keep the premises in good repair, he or she is legally responsible for complying with the promise.[4] The extent of the obligation is determined by the language used.

A lease may sometimes place certain repair duties on the tenant. In such a situation, the language of the clause again determines the scope of the obligation.

### *Common Areas*

When a landlord leases several units of a multi-unit property to different tenants, the landlord is responsible for maintaining common areas in a reasonably safe condition. The most common example of a multi-unit property is an apartment complex. Common areas include swimming pools, stairs, halls, and similar places over which the landlord retains control. The duty of repair extends to defects that the landlord actually knows about and to those that he or she reasonably *should* know about. Thus, the landlord is obligated to make reasonable, periodic inspections of common areas.

Like any other individual or company, a landlord is responsible for the actions of its agents and employees when they are acting within the scope of their authority or employment. Thus, when an apartment manager is notified of an unsafe condition in a common area, the landlord is treated legally as knowing about the condition. Similarly, the manager or other agent's failure to inspect common areas is treated as the landlord's failure.

### *Building Codes*

Many state statutes and city ordinances specify certain standards for both the construction and maintenance of buildings. In the case of leased premises, the landlord, as owner, is ordinarily responsible for compliance with these codes. Provisions dealing with electrical wiring, heating, and other structural concerns usually apply to both commercial and residential structures. Some codes, however, impose a greater duty on the landlord in leases of residential property by requiring that the owner keep the premises in overall good repair. A few state legislatures have even adopted separate "housing codes" dealing especially with residential property.

### *Implied Warranty of Habitability*

Perhaps the most important development in landlord-tenant law in recent years has been the recognition of an **implied warranty of habitability** in leases of residential property.[5] Most courts that have considered the question recently have adopted the warranty. A few have based their decisions on particular language in state housing codes placing certain duties of repair on residential landlords. Most of them, however, have recognized the warranty as a matter of public policy regardless of the existence or wording of a housing code. In addition, several states have adopted the implied warranty of habitability by express legislative enactment.

The warranty of habitability requires landlords to maintain residential property, such as a house, apartment, or duplex, in a "habitable" or livable condition. Although this warranty is most commonly applied to physical defects in the property, it has also been applied to the provision of essential services such as garbage collection. The obligation of the landlord exists at the time the property is leased and throughout the term of the lease. Defects in the premises constitute a breach of the warranty only when the landlord knows or should know about them and has had a reasonable time to make repairs.

A dwelling can be habitable even though it has minor defects. Therefore, the warranty of habitability only applies to major deficiencies. Of course, in some cases a whole host of minor problems existing at the

---

[4] When such a promise is separately made *after* the lease has been agreed to, the new promise must be supported by new consideration.

[5] Judicial recognition of the implied warranty of habitability has also been a major development in the law relating to the *sale of new homes*, as was mentioned in the previous chapter.

same time may render a dwelling unlivable even though each defect alone is not major.

Some defects, such as a large hole in the ceiling or the lack of heat in a cold climate, obviously cause a dwelling to be unhabitable. Others, such as an occasional drip from the kitchen faucet, just as obviously do not cause the premises to be unhabitable. In many cases, however, the question is much closer. The courts in such situations must determine whether the particular defect involves an item which is truly essential or merely an amenity. One court observed:

> [I]n a modern society one cannot be expected to live in a multi-storied apartment building without heat, hot water, garbage disposal, or elevator service. Failure to supply such things is a breach of the implied covenant of habitability. Malfunction of venetian blinds, water leaks, wall cracks, lack of painting, at least of the magnitude presented here, go to what may be called "amenities." Living with lack of painting, water leaks and defective venetian blinds may be unpleasant, aesthetically unsatisfying, but does not come within the category of unhabitability.[6]

When determining whether defects are substantial enough to violate the warranty of habitability, the courts consider a variety of factors, including the following: (1) the impact of the defect on basic life functions—sleeping, eating, relaxing, and so on; (2) the actual or possible effect of the defect on the safety and health of tenants; (3) the length of time the defect has existed; (4) the age of the building—the newer the building, the higher are the tenant's reasonable expectations regarding its condition; and (5) whether the defect violates a building or housing code.

The next case discusses the public policy considerations underlying the implied warranty of habitability, and illustrates the standards used by courts in applying the warranty.

[6]*Academy Spires, Inc. v. Brown*, 111 N. J. 477, 268 A.2d 556, 559 (1970).

## Park West Management Corp. v. Mitchell
Court of Appeals of New York,
391 N.E.2d 1288 (1979)

Park West owned an apartment complex consisting of seven highrise buildings on the Upper West Side of Manhattan in New York City. Because of a strike by Employees' Union Local 32-B, the landlord's entire maintenance and janitorial staff did not report to work for a 17-day period. All of the incinerators were wired shut, thus requiring the tenants to dispose of garbage at the curbs in paper bags. Because employees of the New York Sanitation Department refused to cross the striking employees' picket lines, uncollected trash piled up to the height of the first floor windows. The garbage and the stench it produced led the Health Department to declare a health emergency at the complex.

Also during this period, regular exterminating service was not performed, which, together with the accumulated trash, created conditions in which rats, roaches, and vermin flourished. Routine maintenance and other service was not performed, and common areas were not cleaned.

A group of tenants withheld their rent payments during the period, and the landlord sued for the rent. About 400 tenants ultimately joined in the legal proceeding. The tenants defended against the landlord's suit by claiming a breach of the implied warranty of habitability. The trial court and intermediate appellate courts ruled that the warranty had been breached, and granted a 10 percent reduction in the tenants' June rent bill. The landlord appealed to the highest court in New York.

**Decision:** The judgment was affirmed. The traditional common-law rule that the landlord is not responsible for the physical condition of the premises developed in a rural, agrarian society. In such a society, the land was the most important part of the transaction, not the structures on it. Today, however, the needs and expectations of tenants are much different. In a more urbanized society, the structures on the land are usually the most important part of a lease; what the tenant normally seeks is shelter. Various vital systems, such as plumbing, heating, cooling, and electricity, are normally too complex for the average tenant to maintain, and are often located in areas where the landlord retains control. Thus, the old rule no longer makes sense; instead, an implied warranty of habitability should exist in residential leases.

*(continued)*

The warranty is not breached by minor inconveniences or by defects which are merely aesthetically unpleasing. To violate the implied warranty of habitability, defects or conditions must be of a substantial nature and must materially affect the health or safety of the tenant. The evidence in this case demonstrates that the warranty was breached. The evidence also supports the lower courts' determination that the value of the premises had been reduced by 10 percent during the strike. ■

---

## Tenant's Remedies for Landlord's Failure to Maintain the Premises

The instances in which a landlord has the duty to maintain the premises have been increasing in recent times. Along with the expansion of the landlord's obligation to maintain the premises, there has also been a general expansion of the tenant's remedies for breach of the obligation. The remedies available to the tenant will depend on the circumstances and on the law of the particular state.

**Suit for Damages:** Any time the landlord breaches a duty to repair, the tenant may sue for the damages caused by the landlord's failure. Damages in the case of relatively minor defects are based on the cost of repairing them. For major defects, damages usually are calculated as the difference between the rental value of the premises in unrepaired and repaired conditions. Because of the time and expense of pursuing a damage suit, it is a feasible remedy only for major defects. Even in the case of major defects, a damage lawsuit usually makes economic sense only if (1) the lease is a long-term one or (2) the tenant uses the premises for business purposes so that the attorney fees and other expenses of pursuing the claim can be treated as a business expense for tax purposes.

**Repair and Deduct:** In the past several years many states have enacted so-called **repair and deduct** statutes. This type of legislation permits the tenant to make repairs and then deduct the cost of such repairs from the rent. Courts in several states have recognized the right to repair and deduct even without a specific statute. The right of tenants to use this remedy is subject to several important limitations: (1) the defect must have been one that the landlord was legally obligated to repair; (2) the landlord must have been notified of the defect and failed to repair it within a prescribed period of time; (3) the amount that can be deducted by the tenant usually is limited—in some states the limitation is expressed as a specific maximum amount, such as $200; in other states it is based on a set formula, such as one month's rent; and (4) in several states, the tenant's right to repair and deduct applies only to defects that relate to essential services such as water and electricity.

The repair and deduct remedy has been applied most commonly to situations in which a landlord breached the implied warranty of habitability.

**Rent Withholding:** By statute or court decision, many states in recent years have authorized a reduction in the tenant's rent until the landlord makes required repairs. The amount of the reduction is computed in various ways, but generally must be proportionate to the diminishment of rental value caused by the defect. When the **rent withholding** right is created by statute, the statute usually requires the tenant to deposit the amount withheld with a court or other designated agency until the dispute is resolved.

Regardless of whether the right to reduce and withhold rent has been created by statute or judicial decision in a particular state, a tenant exercising the right always runs the risk of withholding too much. If a court ultimately determines that a tenant has withheld more than the law permits, the tenant is liable to the landlord for the amount that was impermissibly withheld.

Like the repair and deduct remedy, the rent withholding remedy also has usually been connected with the implied warranty of habitability. The *Park West* case provides an illustration of this remedy.

**Lease Cancellation:** The landlord's breach of a duty to repair ordinarily does not give the tenant a right to cancel the lease. However, when the defects are so major that the implied warranty of habitability is breached, most courts permit the tenant to cancel the lease, abandon the premises, and be relieved of any further rent payment obligation. When the tenant chooses this alternative, the implied warranty of habitability is essentially the same as the older principle of constructive eviction.

# INJURIES ON THE PREMISES

Suppose that a defect in the leased premises causes injury to the tenant, a member of the tenant's family, or someone else who is lawfully on the premises. Who is legally responsible for the damages caused by these injuries? Liability commonly depends upon whether the landlord or tenant has control over the particular area where the injury occurred. In a few situations, however, the existence of a duty to repair may create such liability regardless of control.

## *Liability of the Tenant*

The tenant has a general duty to maintain in a reasonably safe condition that part of the leased premises which is under his or her control. Thus, if a visitor on residential property or a customer on business property is injured by an unsafe condition, the tenant usually is responsible. Clearly, however, the tenant's responsibility does not extend to injuries occurring in those common areas controlled by the landlord.

The tenant's duty to maintain the premises in a safe condition exists even in situations where the landlord has a duty to make repairs. Consequently, in some situations both landlord and tenant may be legally responsible for injuries to a third party. Making both of them responsible increases the likelihood that the premises will be kept in a safe condition. Such a policy takes into account the fact that outsiders are less familiar with the property and less likely to be aware of potentially dangerous conditions than the landlord or tenant.

## *Liability of the Landlord*

The landlord's liability for injuries may be based on control, on an affirmative duty to make repairs, or on both factors.

**Public Purpose:** Ordinarily, the circumstances in which a landlord is liable for injuries are the same whether the injured person is a tenant or anyone else lawfully on the premises. There is, however, one major exception to this principle. When premises are leased for a purpose that involves admission of the public, such as a retail store, the landlord owes a continuing duty to the public to maintain the premises in a safe condition. This duty makes the landlord liable for injuries to members of the public even when there would have been no basis for landlord liability if the *tenant* had been the injured party.

When premises are leased for a public purpose, and a member of the public is injured by a defect in the property, the tenant also is responsible. The injured party could thus take action against both landlord and tenant.

**Common Areas:** The landlord is liable for injuries caused by defects in common areas over which the landlord has control. This liability to tenants or others lawfully on the premises is coextensive with the landlord's general duty to make repairs in common areas.

The following case presents a situation in which the landlord was held liable for injuries caused by defects in an outside porch.

---

**Cruz v. Drezek**
Supreme Court of Connecticut,
397 A.2d 1335 (1978)

The Cruz family rented a third-floor apartment in a three-family house in New Britain, Connecticut, from the owners, Edward and Jeanette Drezek. Outside the third-floor apartment was a porch. The evidence did not indicate whether other tenants also had access to the porch. Regardless of whether it was a true "common" area, the evidence did clearly show that the landlord retained control over this exterior porch.

Fourteen-year-old Hector Cruz was helping his family move in. A small mattress was being raised by ropes from the ground to the third-floor porch. Hector was on the porch pulling the mattress up. As he leaned on the railing surrounding the porch, it gave way and he fell to the ground. The Cruzes sued the Drezeks for damages resulting from Hector's injuries. Based on a jury verdict, the trial court awarded judgment in favor of Hector for $20,000 and Hector's parents for $1,952.40 to cover the medical bills they had paid. The Drezeks, defendants, appealed on the grounds that there was not enough evi-

*(continued)*

dence of negligence on their part to even create a jury question, and that the trial court should have ruled in their favor as a matter of law.

**Decision:** The judgment was affirmed. It was the defendants' duty to keep those portions of the premises over which they had control, including the third floor porch and railings, in reasonably safe condition. A police detective who investigated the accident and a nearby neighbor both testified that the railing was old and rotted. The evidence also showed that the defendants had bought the house about ten weeks before the accident. Before buying it, Edward Drezek had personally inspected the house and the porches. At the trial he claimed that they had been in good condition, but almost immediately after buying the house he had applied for a building permit to repair and enclose the three porches on the house. Thus, there was evidence to support the jury verdict that the porch was not reasonably safe and that the defendants knew or should have known of the defective condition. In addition, a moving company foreman with 50 years experience testified that raising mattresses up by ropes was a customary, accepted method for moving them because they were so hard to handle. ■

**Latent Defects:** A **latent defect** is one that is hidden to such an extent that the tenant is not likely to discover it during a normal initial inspection. If such a defect exists at the time a lease is made, and the landlord either knows or reasonably should know about it, the landlord has a duty to disclose the defect to the tenant. Failure to disclose makes the landlord liable for injuries subsequently caused by the defect. It is important to note that the landlord fulfills his or her duty by disclosing the existence of the defect—the landlord is not required to actually fix it unless there is some other legal basis for imposing a duty of repair.

The landlord's nondisclosure of hidden defects may bring about other consequences as well, such as giving the tenant a legal basis for cancelling the lease.

**Negligent Repairs:** Regardless of whether the landlord has a duty to make repairs, if he or she makes them and does so in a *negligent* manner, the landlord is liable for any injuries caused by the negligent repairs.

**Express Agreement, Statutory Duty, and Implied Warranty:** In the previous section we saw that, in modern times, the landlord has increasingly been placed under a duty to make repairs. This duty may exist because the landlord has agreed in an express lease provision to make repairs, or the duty may be imposed by a building or housing code or the implied warranty of habitability. In these situations, the landlord may have the duty to make repairs even with respect to those parts of the premises under the tenant's control.

Suppose that Thompson has leased an apartment from Leonard. Assume that, because of an express lease clause, an applicable code provision, or an implied warranty, Leonard has a duty to repair and maintain the apartment. Leonard then breaches this duty by failing to make certain repairs. If either Thompson or someone else lawfully on the premises is injured because of the defect, is Leonard liable for the injury?

The court decisions in the various states are somewhat evenly split on this issue. Some of them focus on the repair duty itself and conclude that liability for injuries is a logical component of the duty. Others focus on the factor of control and conclude that the landlord's liability for injuries should not extend to areas over which the landlord has very little daily control, even when the landlord has a duty to repair those areas.

Of course, when the injured person is an outsider who does not live on the leased premises, the tenant generally is liable for the injuries even though the landlord may also be liable.

## *Exculpatory and Indemnification Clauses*

Leases often contain **exculpatory clauses,** which state that the landlord is not liable for injuries on the premises. Such a clause cannot excuse the landlord from liability to outsiders who are not parties to the lease. However, it is also common for an **indemnification clause** to accompany the exculpatory clause. The indemnification clause states that the tenant must indemnify, or reimburse, the landlord for damages the landlord has to pay to outsiders.

The courts have reached different conclusions on the question of whether exculpatory and indemnification clauses are effective to shield the landlord. Some of these different results are based upon the language of the particular clause or the existence of a specific statute in the particular state. However, many of the decisions are simply in conflict with one another.

As a general proposition, courts are much more likely to throw out such clauses in residential leases than in commercial ones. Moreover, regardless of the type of lease, there is a gradual trend in the courts toward invalidating these clauses.

It should be emphasized that here we are speaking of exculpatory clauses that seek to excuse the *landlord* from liability. If the lease contains a clause purporting to excuse the *tenant* from liability, such a clause is normally valid. The question whether a lease expresses an intent to excuse the tenant was dealt with earlier in the chapter.

## LANDLORD'S RESPONSIBILITY TO PROTECT TENANTS FROM CRIMES

The landlord does not have an absolute duty to protect tenants from the criminal acts of outsiders. As part of the general expansion of the landlord's duties in recent years, however, several courts have found landlords responsible for providing such protection in certain circumstances. The situations in which the landlord has been found liable for crimes committed against tenants usually involve evidence that (1) the area around the leased premises has a high crime rate, (2) the landlord knew or should have known of the danger caused by criminal activity in the area, and (3) the landlord did not take precautions that were reasonably necessary to protect tenants under the circumstances.

When these facts are proved, the landlord is held responsible for criminal conduct occurring both in common areas and in the leased premises itself. The landlord's responsibility can take several forms. First, he or she may be held liable to a tenant for damages caused by the crime. Courts have based this liability on either the tort of negligence or the implied warranty of habitability. Second, a landlord's inadequate precautions in the face of known criminal activity could constitute a breach of the implied warranty of habitability or the covenant for quiet enjoyment even if the particular tenant making the claim has not actually been injured by a crime. In this situation, the tenant would be entitled to the normal remedies for breach of those obligations, including rent reduction, cancellation of the lease, and so on. The following case provides an illustration of the latter type of situation.

---

**Highview Associates v. Koferl**
District Court of Suffolk County,
477 N.Y.S.2d 585 (1984)

Jeanne Koferl, a single woman with an eight-year-old son, was a tenant in a large garden apartment complex owned by Highview in Selden, New York. Burglaries and robberies had become fairly common in the complex, and the landlord had done nothing to improve security. On one occasion, Koferl discovered a "peeping tom" looking through her window on the first floor, and she notified the apartment manager of the incident. Somewhat later, toward the end of January 1983, two unknown men attempted to burglarize Koferl's apartment at 3:00 a.m. She was awakened when one of the burglars started to rip the screen from the sliding glass door. She was able to ward off the criminals, and in terror she then grabbed her son and fled to her mother's home, never to return to the apartment. The lease did not expire until May 26, and the landlord was not able to rerent the apartment to another tenant until April 1.

The landlord sued Koferl, claiming that she breached the lease by moving out and paying no further rent. The landlord sought damages of $588, consisting of unpaid rent, painting and repairs, expenses involved in finding another tenant, and attorney fees, minus Koferl's $930 security deposit that the landlord had kept. Koferl defended by asserting that the landlord had breached the implied warranty of habitability and the covenant for quiet enjoyment by failing to provide adequate protection against criminals, thus relieving her of any responsibility under the lease. She did not seek damages or the return of her security deposit.

*(continued)*

**Decision:** The trial court rendered judgment for defendant Koferl dismissing the plaintiff's suit. The evidence of increased criminal activity was great enough to require more security measures. The apartment manager knew about the increased crime rate, and was negligent by failing to act. The implied warranty of habitability and the covenant for quiet enjoyment were both breached. (Because the tenant only sought to be excused from the lease and did not seek damages, the covenant for quiet enjoyment by itself would have provided her with the relief she sought.) ■

---

## RENT AND OTHER FINANCIAL OBLIGATIONS OF THE TENANT

### Rent

**Rent** is the compensation paid to the landlord for the tenant's possession and use of the leased premises. Leases almost always contain provisions expressly setting the rent. If this is omitted, the law of most states obligates the tenant to pay the reasonable rental value of the property. The right to receive rent can be *assigned,* or transferred, to a third party.

The time, method, and place for rent payment usually are specified in the lease. Most leases expressly require advance payment at the *beginning* of each rental period. If the parties do not agree on the time for payment, however, the general rule is that rent is due at the *end* of each rental period.

When the lease expressly requires payment of rent on or before a stated date, payment by this date usually is an absolute requirement. The tenant breaches his or her obligation by late payment. In a few states, however, statutes have been passed which provide a short "grace period" beyond the due date, such as five days. Until expiration of this grace period, the landlord may not terminate the lease for nonpayment. Also, if the landlord has customarily accepted late rental payments, he or she may have *waived* the right to prompt payment. In such a case, the landlord must continue to accept similarly late payments unless he or she expressly announces that late payments will not be accepted in the future.

Rent normally is not considered "paid" until actually received by the landlord or the landlord's agent. However, most courts do not permit lease termination because of relatively short, unexpected delays in mail delivery.

Rent is payable in money unless the parties agree on some other form of consideration. Payment by check is sufficient unless the landlord expressly requires cash.

The lease usually specifies the place for payment. If it does not, the leased property itself is the place where the rent is payable. In such a case, before the landlord can legally terminate the lease for nonpayment he or she must come onto the leased premises and demand the rent.

### Security Deposits

A **security deposit** of cash or property by the tenant is required only if the lease provides for it. Most leases do provide for security deposits. The purpose of a security deposit is to provide the landlord with a quick and sure remedy when the tenant damages the property, fails to pay rent, or breaks the lease.

Some landlords attempt to keep security deposits regardless of whether there is any justification for doing so. Legally, the landlord is entitled to keep only so much of the deposit as is necessary to compensate him or her for damages that actually can be proved. Today, many states have statutes specifically regulating the landlord's handling of the security deposit when a lease is terminated.

Typically, these statutes require that the landlord return the tenant's security deposit within a certain period of time, such as 30 days, and prohibit any deduction from the deposit that is not explained on an accompanying itemized list of damages and repairs.

### Other Payments

Unless the lease provides otherwise, the landlord is obligated to pay taxes on the leased property and the tenant is required to pay utility bills.

## THE LANDLORD'S REMEDIES

### Detainer

A lease legally may be terminated for several reasons, as we saw earlier in the chapter. For instance, expiration of the agreed duration terminates the lease. Also, in most states today, the landlord may terminate the lease for nonpayment of rent.

If the tenant wrongfully remains in possession after termination, the landlord may file a court action to have the tenant removed. This action, usually called **unlawful detainer, forcible entry and detainer,** or some similar name, is given special expedited treatment by the court and decided very quickly. If the landlord proves a right to possession, the sheriff or other officer removes the tenant from the property.[7]

## *Landlord's Lien*

At common law, the landlord had the right to seize, and hold or sell, the tenant's personal property for nonpayment of rent. The **landlord's lien** extended only to items actually located on the leased premises. Today in most states this remedy is regulated by statute. In some states the landlord must file a court action to exercise his or her lien. In these states, items of the tenant's property located on the leased premises are seized by a sheriff or other officer. Other states permit the landlord to seize the tenant's belongings, but a court proceeding normally is required before they can be sold.

Many leases, particularly residential ones, expressly grant the landlord a lien on the tenant's belongings located on the leased premises. The extent of the lien and method of enforcement are governed primarily by the language of the lease.

## *Damages*

When the tenant fails to pay rent or harms the property, the landlord is entitled to receive money damages to compensate for the loss. If the security deposit is inadequate to pay these damages, the landlord may file suit to collect the remainder.

**Duty to Mitigate Damages:** Suppose that T, the tenant, and L, the landlord, have agreed to the lease of a house for eighteen months at a monthly rental of $500. After six months T stops paying rent, and two months later she leaves (either voluntarily or involuntarily). T certainly is liable to L for $1,000—two months' unpaid rent. But is T also responsible for the $5,000 rent for the remaining ten months of the lease?

Traditionally, L could recover the $5,000 and was not obligated to *mitigate,* or lessen, his damages by seeking another tenant. He could simply leave the premises vacant. If L actually does find another tenant, the damages L can recover from T are reduced by the rent L receives from the substitute tenant during the remainder of the original lease term.

In a substantial minority of states, L is under a duty to mitigate his damages by making reasonable efforts to find a new tenant. Suppose that L finds a new tenant six months after T leaves (that is, with four months remaining in the original lease term). Obviously, L still could recover the $1,000 unpaid rent from T. But what about L's claim for $3,000 rent for the six months during which the house was vacant? In one of those states requiring L to mitigate his damages, the court will determine whether L had made a reasonable effort to find a new tenant after T left. If the court concludes that such an effort was made, and that the period of vacancy was not due to any lack of diligence on L's part, L can recover $3,000 in addition to the $1,000. On the other hand, if the court concludes that L did not make a reasonable effort and probably could have found a new tenant in *three months* had such an effort been made, L's recovery from T will be limited to $1,000 plus $1,500.

The requirement that L mitigate damages is being adopted by more and more courts and legislatures as they have an opportunity to consider the question, and probably will become the majority rule in the next few years.

## ASSIGNMENTS AND SUBLEASES

A tenant sometimes may want to transfer his or her rights and obligations under the lease to a third party. Such a transfer is either an assignment or a sublease.

### *Distinction between Assignment and Sublease*

An **assignment** of the lease occurs when the tenant transfers the entire remaining portion of the lease to a third party. A **sublease** occurs when the tenant transfers the lease for only part of its remaining duration. Suppose, for example, that two years remain on

---

[7] An older type of remedy, *ejectment,* still exists in many states. It is a much slower procedure for evicting tenants and has not often been used by landlords since statutes have created the quicker detainer procedure.

what was originally a three-year lease. If the tenant transfers the lease to another party for the remaining two years, the transfer is an assignment. If the tenant executes a transfer for less than two years, such as twelve or eighteen months, the transfer is a sublease.

When an assignment occurs, the third party (assignee) essentially takes the place of the original tenant. The landlord-tenant relationship, with all of its rights and responsibilities, then exists between the landlord and the assignee. The landlord and assignee each have the right to legally enforce the lease obligations of the other. However, the original tenant is not excused from his or her obligations unless expressly released by the landlord. Thus, if the assignee fails to pay rent, the landlord can proceed against the assignee, the original tenant, or both. If the original tenant has to pay, he or she is entitled to recoup the loss from the assignee.

In the case of a sublease, no legal relationship is created between the landlord and the third party (sublessee). Neither the landlord nor the sublessee has legally enforceable obligations to or rights against the other. The landlord-tenant relationship, with all its rights and duties, continues to exist between the landlord and the original tenant. Another landlord-tenant relationship is created between the original tenant and the sublessee.

## *The Tenant's Right to Transfer*

As a general rule, a tenant has the right to execute an assignment or sublease unless (1) the lease places express limitations on the right, or (2) a specific state statute modifies the right in some way. Today, most leases expressly prohibit assignments or subleases unless the landlord consents. Moreover, several states have statutes which regulate the execution of assignments and subleases. In some states, the transfer must be in writing to have any effect, and in some states recording statutes must be complied with to protect the interest of the assignee or sublessee.

## SUMMARY

The landlord-tenant relationship is created by an agreement commonly called a lease, which provides for the transfer of exclusive possession and control of real property in return for the payment of rent. The interest acquired by the tenant, or lessee, is called a tenancy, or leasehold, and takes different forms depending on the terms of the lease. The landlord, or lessor, is the owner of the reversionary fee simple interest, and owes the tenant the duty to allow possession and not to interfere with the lawful possession and use of the premises. The tenant, on the other hand, has a duty not to intentionally or negligently damage the premises, and usually has no right to add fixtures or otherwise alter the premises without the landlord's consent.

Although the traditional rule that a landlord has no duty to maintain the premises still exists theoretically, in modern times it has become subject to a great many important exceptions, including the duty to keep common areas in a reasonably safe condition and to observe the maintenance obligations imposed by building codes and the implied warranty of habitability. Both the tenant and the landlord can be held liable in some circumstances for injuries occurring on the premises. The tenant's liability is based on the duty to maintain in a reasonably safe condition that part of the premises under his or her control. The landlord can be held liable for injuries on premises that were leased for a purpose involving admission of the public and for those occurring in common areas, as well as for injuries resulting from latent defects or negligent repairs. In some states the landlord is liable for injuries caused by breach of an express lease provision, statutory duty, or implied warranty.

There is a modern trend for landlords to be held responsible for taking reasonable precautions to protect tenants from criminal activities. The landlord has a basic right to receive rent from the tenant, and may require the tenant to post a security deposit to cover possible damage to the property. The landlord has several remedies for the tenant's breach of the lease agreement, including detainer, exercise of the landlord's lien, and a suit for damages. As a general rule, a tenant has the right to transfer the right to possession by assignment or sublease unless such right is restricted by the lease or by statutory provision.

## KEY TERMS

**Lease**
**Covenant**
**Condition**
**Tenancy (or leasehold)**
**Tenancy for years**
**Periodic tenancy**
**Tenancy at will**
**Tenancy at sufferance**

**Surrender and acceptance**
**Reversion**
**Covenant of quiet enjoyment**
**Eviction**
**Constructive eviction**
**Waste**
**Trade fixtures**
**Implied warranty of habitability**
**Repair and deduct**
**Rent withholding**
**Latent defect**
**Exculpatory clause**
**Indemnification clause**
**Rent**
**Security deposit**
**Unlawful detainer (or forcible entry and detainer)**
**Landlord's lien**
**Assignment**
**Sublease**

## QUESTIONS AND PROBLEMS

**1.** Kolea rented a building from Greenfield for the purpose of storing automobiles. Approximately one year later, while the lease was still in effect, the building was destroyed by fire. The lease agreement was silent as to the effect of such an occurrence on the rental obligation. Thereafter, Kolea refused to continue paying rent, claiming that the destruction of the building excused him from any further obligation to pay rent. Greenfield sued for the unpaid rent under the remaining portion of the lease. Will Greenfield be successful? Discuss. (*Albert M. Greenfield & Co. v. Kolea,* 380 A.2d 758, Pa. 1977.)

**2.** Kilbourne rented an apartment from Forester for one year, beginning in June 1966. A provision in the lease stated that it was "renewable at the end of the year period." Kilbourne renewed the lease for an additional year in June 1967. Toward the end of the second year Kilbourne gave notice to Forester that she wished to renew the lease for a third one-year term. Forester refused to execute another lease, Kilbourne refused to leave, and Forester filed suit to have Kilbourne removed from the apartment. Who will prevail? Discuss. (*Kilbourne v. Forester,* 464 S.W.2d 770, Mo. Ct. App. 1971.)

**3.** Applegate and Turnquist leased an apartment from Inland for a one-year term. Before signing the lease agreement, Applegate inspected the apartment with the building manager. The apartment was very dirty and a couple of dead roaches could be seen. The manager said "it would be fixed" before Applegate moved in. At the time the lease was being signed, Applegate asked the manager if the apartment had any problem with roaches, because she didn't want to move in if it did. The manager replied that she hadn't heard anything about roaches. The next day, Applegate and Turnquist moved into the apartment and immediately saw roaches everywhere. They attempted for two days to exterminate the roaches, but were unsuccessful. The two tenants then moved out and refused to pay rent. Inland kept the security deposit. Applegate filed suit in which she sought to recover the security deposit, claiming that Inland had committed a constructive eviction. Inland asserted a counterclaim for damages, claiming that Applegate breached the lease agreement. Discuss whether a constructive eviction had occurred. (*Applegate v. Inland Real Estate Corporation,* 441 N.E.2d 379, Ill. App. Ct. 1982.)

**4.** The Norwoods rented a second-floor apartment from Lazarus. There were seven other apartments on the second floor, and a common hallway served all eight units. Children of various tenants, including the Norwoods' two-year-old daughter, regularly played in the hallway. Lazarus periodically inspected the building and saw the children playing. The paint on the walls and baseboards of the hallway was cracked and flaking. Flakes of paint were on the hall floor. On several occasions the Norwoods saw their daughter put paint flakes in her mouth. Each time they spanked her and told her to stop. Later she became ill and was diagnosed as having chronic lead poisoning. The paint in the hallway was tested by the Lead Poison Control Unit of the City of St. Louis, and was found to contain high levels of lead in violation of a city ordinance. The Norwoods sued Lazarus for damages, claiming that he was negligent in permitting an unsafe condition to exist. Are the Norwoods correct? Discuss. (*Norwood v. Lazarus,* 634 S.W.2d 584, Mo. Ct. App. 1982.)

**5.** Winslar rented an apartment from Bartlett. The police came to the apartment to arrest Winslar. When they knocked on the door, Winslar shot through the door with a gun, wounding one of the police officers. The police then threw tear gas canisters into the apartment and subsequently arrested Winslar. The tear gas caused substantial damage to the apartment, and Bartlett filed suit against Winslar. Should Winslar be held responsible to Bartlett for the damages to the apartment? Why or why not? (*Winslar v. Bartlett,* 573 S.W.2d 608, Tex. Ct. Civ. App. 1978.)

**6.** Williams worked for a company which conducted its business in offices leased from Koplin. To get to and from work, it was necessary for Williams to use an outside stairway. One day when Williams was leaving the building after work, she slipped on snow and ice which had accumulated on the stairs. She was injured in the resulting fall, and filed suit against Koplin, the owner of the building, and Hinsdale, who managed the building for Koplin. Should Williams win? Discuss. (*Williams v. Alfred N. Koplin & Co.,* 448 N.E.2d 1042, Ill. App. Ct. 1983.)

**7.** Crowell leased an apartment from the City of Dallas Housing Authority, a city government agency serving the purpose of providing safe and sanitary dwellings to persons of low income. In the standard lease agreement provided by the Housing Authority, a clause stipulated that the Authority would not be liable for any damages caused by the condition of the premises. A heater in Crowell's apartment was defective and caused the apartment to fill with carbon monoxide, killing Crowell. Crowell's son, in behalf of his father's estate, sued for damages resulting from medical expenses and his father's pain and suffering. The Housing Authority defended on the grounds that it was excused from liability by the clause in the lease. Is the Housing Authority's defense a good one? Discuss. (*Crowell v. Housing Authority of the City of Dallas,* 495 S.W.2d 887, Tex. 1973.)

**8.** In anticipation of his upcoming marriage, Kridel leased an apartment from Sommer for a two-year period. Shortly before the wedding, however, Kridel's fiancée broke the engagement. Kridel notified Sommer that he was breaking the lease. Sommer made no effort to rent the apartment to anyone else. In fact, another person wanted to rent it shortly thereafter, but Sommer refused, stating that the apartment was already leased to Kridel. Sommer finally put the apartment up for rent fifteen months later and immediately leased it to another tenant. Sommer sued Kridel for the unpaid rent during the time the apartment was vacant. Was Kridel responsible for the rent during this period? (*Sommer v. Kridel,* 378 A.2d 767, N. J. 1977.)

**9.** Trentacost was a 61-year-old widow who had rented an apartment from Brussel for more than ten years. The apartment was located in a building containing a total of eight units located over street-level stores. Access was provided by front and rear entrances. A padlock secured the back entrance, but there was no lock on the front entrance. One afternoon Trentacost was returning to her apartment from a shopping trip. After she had entered the building from the front and reached the top of a flight of stairs leading to her apartment, an assailant grabbed her ankles from behind and dragged her down the stairs. Her purse was stolen and she suffered severe injuries. She later filed suit against Brussel, claiming that he was negligent in not providing a lock or other adequate security for the front entrance. The evidence showed that during the past three years, police had investigated from 75 to 100 crimes in the neighborhood, mostly burglaries and street muggings. Two months before the attack, Trentacost herself had reported to Brussel an attempt by someone to break into the building's cellar. At other times she had notified him of the presence of unauthorized persons in the hallways. She claimed that Brussel had promised to put a lock on the front door, but he denied ever discussing the subject. Should the court hold Brussel liable for Trentacost's damages? Discuss. (*Trentacost v. Brussel,* 412 A.2d 436, N. J. 1980.)

# CHAPTER 45

# PERSONAL PROPERTY AND BAILMENTS

## OWNERSHIP OF PERSONAL PROPERTY

As we saw in the introduction to Part VI, all property is classified as either real or personal property. In some ways, the legal framework for personal property ownership is similar to that for real property. For example, personal property can be subject to many of the same categories of concurrent ownership as real property, including tenancy in common and joint tenancy, as well as marital co-ownership categories such as tenancy by the entireties and community property. The rules for creating and regulating these types of co-ownership are essentially the same for personal property as for real property.

In addition, a creditor can acquire a voluntary security interest in an item of personal property that is similar to the interest created by a real property mortgage. The debtor retains title to the property, but the creditor with such a security interest owns an interest that serves as security until the debt is paid. The creation, protection, and enforcement of security interests in personal property are governed by Article 9 of the Uniform Commercial Code, and are discussed separately in Chapter 29, "Secured Transactions."

In many ways, however, ownership of personal property is legally quite different than ownership of real property. Ownership of personal property is usually a simpler matter than ownership of real property, primarily because the law does not formally recognize the numerous types of interests that it does for real property. Ordinarily, a person either is the owner of an item of personal property or is not. There sometimes can be a difficult question regarding *who* is the owner of an item of personal property, but once that question is resolved, ownership usually is an all-or-nothing proposition. One example of this fact is found in the use of leases. As we saw in the previous chapter, a lease of real property actually creates another type of ownership interest. A lease of personal property, however, merely creates a *bailment;* the lessee has temporary possession but no ownership interest in the item of personal property.

This chapter deals with several basic topics concerning the ownership, possession, and use of personal property. It first discusses gifts of personal property, and then examines several other methods by which ownership of personal property can change. The chapter then provides a detailed discussion of bailments, an important form of personal property transaction in which possession but not ownership is transferred. It should be pointed out that several other topics related to personal property are sufficiently specialized and complex that they are dealt with in separate chapters. The subject of *sales of goods,* for instance, is thoroughly explored in Chapters 20 through 23. As already mentioned, the topic of secured transactions is covered in Chapter 29. In addition, transfers of both real and personal property by *will* are discussed in Chapter 46.

## GIFTS OF PERSONAL PROPERTY

A gift occurs when an owner of property (the **donor**) voluntarily transfers ownership of the property to another (the **donee**) without receiving any consideration in return. In order for the donor to accomplish a transfer of ownership by gift, two fundamental requirements must be met: (1) the donor must have a *present intent* to transfer ownership and (2) the donor must *deliver possession* to the donee.[1]

---

[1] There is also a requirement that the donee accept the gift, but acceptance is presumed unless the donee expressly rejects the gift. This issue arises only on rare occasions.

701

## Present Intent to Transfer Ownership

The language and conduct of the donor, considered in the light of all the surrounding circumstances, must indicate a present intent to transfer ownership. Thus, a promise or expression of intent to transfer ownership in the future is not sufficient. A promise to make a gift is not the same thing as an actual gift. By its very nature, such a promise is not made in return for consideration, as required by contract law. Accordingly, it usually confers no rights on the promisee and cannot be enforced.

It also is critical that the expression of present intent relate to *ownership*. If the evidence indicates that the current owner merely intends to transfer present custody or the right to use the property, there is no gift.

## Delivery of Possession

The donor also must actually carry out the expression of intent by delivering possession of the property to the donee. Once there has been an expression of present intent to transfer ownership coupled with actual delivery, the absence of consideration from the donee becomes irrelevant. Title to the property has passed. Many of the disputes involving gifts of personal property have centered on the question of whether there was delivery of possession to the donee. The most common problems relating to the question of delivery are outlined below.

**Retention of Control:** If the donor attempts to retain a degree of control over the property, there usually is not a legally effective gift. As one court stated, there must be "a complete stripping of the donor of dominion or control over the thing given."[2] To illustrate: X indicates he wants to give a diamond ring to Y. If X then places the ring in a safe-deposit box to which both X and Y have access, there is not a sufficient delivery. Another example is found in the case of *Lee v. Lee*, 5 F.2d 767 (1925): The widow of a grandson of General Robert E. Lee prepared a written document stating that she was giving to her two sons a trunk containing several items which had belonged to the general. She deposited the trunk with a storage company, with instructions to the company obligating it to deliver the trunk to either her or her sons. In holding that there had not been an adequate delivery, the court said, "[T]here was not that quality of completeness present in the transaction which distinguishes a mere intention to give from the completed act, and where this element is lacking the gift fails."

**Delivery to an Agent:** If delivery of the property is made to the donor's *own agent,* with instructions to deliver to the donee, there is not a completed gift until the donee actually receives the item. The reason, again, is that the donor does not part with sufficient control until the donee takes possession. If the donor delivers possession to the *donee's agent,* however, a valid gift has been made.

**Property Already in Possession of the Donee:** If the donee already possesses the property when the donor indicates an intent to presently make a gift, the gift is immediately effective. There is no need to make a formal delivery in this situation.

**Constructive Delivery:** In most cases, delivery of actual physical possession is required. In two types of circumstances, however, a **constructive delivery** (or **symbolic delivery**) will suffice.

*Impracticality:* If it is *impractical or inconvenient* to deliver actual physical possession because the item is too large or because it is located at too great a distance from the parties, constructive delivery is allowed. In such cases it ordinarily takes the form of a delivery of something that gives the donee *control* over the property. For example, if the item being given is a car, delivery of the car's key to the donee is sufficient. Similarly, delivery to the donee of a key to a building, room, or container in which an item is located constitutes a valid delivery if physical delivery of the property itself is impractical or inconvenient.

*Intangibles:* Constructive delivery is permissible for a gift of *intangible* personal property, for the obvious reason that there is nothing physical to deliver. Some types of intangible property rights are evidenced by written documents that by either law or business custom are accepted as representing the intangible right itself. Examples are bonds, promissory notes, corporate stock certificates, insurance policies, and savings account books. For these types of property rights, delivery of the written instrument evidencing the right is treated as delivery of the right it-

---

[2]*Allen v. Hendrick,* 206 Pac. 733 (1922).

self. If the property right is an ordinary contract right not represented by any commercially recognized document, most courts allow constructive delivery of it by delivery of a writing setting forth the *present intent* to assign the right to the donee.

**Grounds for Invalidating Gifts:** Of course, a gift will not be valid if the donor's action was induced by fraud, duress, mistake, or undue influence. In addition, the courts always examine very carefully any gift occurring between persons in a "fiduciary" relationship. Thus, if X owes a higher degree of trust to Y because of a fiduciary relationship, and X receives a gift from Y, the law places the burden upon X to prove that all was fair. The following case illustrates this important principle.

---

### Gordon v. Bialystoker Center & Bikur Cholim, Inc.
Court of Appeals of New York, 385 N.E.2d 285 (1978)

Ida Gorodetsky, who was 85 years old at the time, suffered a stroke and was admitted to Brookland-Cumberland Hospital in August 1972. Her closest relatives, two brothers and a niece, had not seen her for several years, and she had lived alone since 1962. From the time of her stroke until her death four months later, Ida remained partially paralyzed, confused, and sometimes semicomatose.

At the suggestion of one of Ida's acquaintances, the Bialystoker nursing home sent one of its social workers to visit the elderly lady in the hospital in October 1972. After learning that Ida had funds of her own, the director of the nursing home sent the social worker back to visit Ida on November 3 for the purpose of having her sign a withdrawal slip. A request had already been made for her admittance to the home, and the purpose of the withdrawal slip was to obtain funds for her care at the home. Using her withdrawal slip, the home obtained a $15,000 check from Ida's account payable to the home "for the benefit of Ida Gorodetsky."

On November 13 Ida was moved to the infirmary of the nursing home. That same day, within an hour and a half of admission, she was visited by a group consisting of the home's executive director, its fund raiser, one of its social workers, and a notary public. She was presented with a collection of instruments on each of which she placed her mark. These instruments included an application for admission to the home, an admission agreement, a withdrawal slip for the $12,864.46 remaining in her bank account, an assignment of that amount to the home, and a letter making a donation to the home of any part of the $27,864.46 remaining after paying expenses for her lifetime care.

Ida died on December 5 while still a resident of the nursing home. Her brother, Sam Gordon, administrator of her estate, filed suit against the nursing home to recover these funds, less the amount necessary to pay her expenses. The trial court ruled for the defendant nursing home on the ground that a valid gift had been made. The intermediate level appellate court reversed, ruling in favor of plaintiff administrator, and defendant appealed to New York's highest court.

**Decision:** The judgment of the intermediate level appellate court in favor of plaintiff was affirmed. By taking complete control of and responsibility for a person in a helpless condition, the nursing home occupied a fiduciary relationship with regard to Ida Gorodetsky. When someone owing a fiduciary duty receives a gift from the person to whom the duty is owed, the circumstances surrounding the gift will be carefully scrutinized. In contrast with a gift made under ordinary circumstances, the fiduciary in a situation such as this has the burden of proving that there was no fraud or undue influence, and that all was "fair, open, voluntary, and well understood." The nursing home did not meet that burden. The gift was invalid, and the nursing home had to return to Ida's estate all funds beyond what was necessary to pay her actual expenses. ■

---

## Special Treatment of Joint Bank Accounts

It is rather common for a bank account to be in the names of two persons, such as husband and wife. The phrase *joint account* is often used in a nontechnical sense to describe any bank account in the names of two people. These accounts are either a tenancy in common or a joint tenancy with survivorship rights, depending on the terms of the agreement with the bank.

In connection with the law of gifts, the requirement that the donor part with all control over the property is frequently an issue in cases involving a bank account jointly owned by the donor and the donee. For example, suppose that X deposits money belonging to him in a bank account that is in the name of X and Y. Both X and Y have the right to withdraw funds from the account. Obviously there is a completed gift from X to Y of all money actually taken from the account by Y. But because of the retention of control by X, money that is not withdrawn from the account by Y is not considered a gift.

Suppose, however, that the agreement between X and the bank provides that on the death of X or Y, the funds remaining in the account will go to the *survivor* (that is, a "joint tenancy" is created). If X dies first, the question will arise whether a valid gift of the remaining funds has been made by X to Y. A few courts have held that in such a situation there is not a sufficient relinquishment of control by X to create a gift. However, they also have usually held that Y is nevertheless entitled to the money as a *third party beneficiary* of an enforceable contract between X and the bank. On the other hand, a majority of courts have simply relaxed the delivery requirement in this type of case and have held that there is a valid gift to Y despite the retention of some control by X.

Of course, as is true of any other gift, X must have *intended* to make a gift to Y. In the case of a joint tenancy bank account (one with a right of survivorship), there is a *presumption* of intent on the part of X to make a gift to Y, and this presumption can be rebutted only by evidence clearly showing that X did *not* intend to make a gift. For instance, the evidence might show that the joint account was established solely to give Y access to X's funds so as to enable Y to help X handle his financial affairs.

## *Gifts* Inter Vivos *and* Causa Mortis

Gifts are classified as either *inter vivos* or *causa mortis*. A **gift *inter vivos*** is simply an ordinary gift between two living persons. A **gift *causa mortis*** is also between living persons, but it is made by the donor in contemplation of his or her death from some existing affliction or impending peril.

Although a gift *causa mortis* resembles a *will*, because both involve gifts in contemplation of death, it is important to emphasize their differences. As we will see in Chapter 44, a will must meet several formal statutory requirements such as written documentation and the signed attestation of a specified number of witnesses. A gift *causa mortis*, on the other hand, must meet the same requirements as a regular gift, intent and delivery. Execution of a formal will is the only way to make a gift conditional on the donor's death without an immediate transfer of possession.

Two special rules apply to the gift *causa mortis*, distinguishing it slightly from a regular gift: (1) The gift is revoked automatically if the donee dies before the donor, with the result that ownership reverts back to the donor. (2) The gift is also revoked automatically if the donor does not die from the current illness or peril.

## OTHER METHODS OF ACQUIRING OWNERSHIP

### *Ownership of Wild Game*

As a general rule, the law views wild animals, fish, and birds as being *unowned* property. The first person who takes possession with an intent to become an owner usually acquires legal ownership. The technical name for such acquisition is **occupation.** The one taking possession does not become the owner, however, if that person is a *trespasser* or is acting in violation of state or federal game and fish laws. A trespasser is one who is on land without the express or implied consent of the owner or tenant who has legal control of the land. Wild game taken by a trespasser belongs to the owner or the tenant of the land. In addition. no title is acquired to wild game taken in violation of state or federal laws.

### *Abandoned, Lost, and Mislaid Property*

The common law made a distinction between abandoned, lost, and mislaid property. An item was deemed to be **abandoned property** if found under circumstances indicating either that it was left by someone who did not want it anymore, or was left so long ago that the former owner almost certainly was no longer living. The nature of the property, its location, and other relevant factors can be taken into account in determining whether the property should be classified as abandoned. The common law characterized an item as **lost property** if it was discovered under circumstances indicating that it was *not* placed there voluntarily by the owner (such as a purse, billfold, or ring found on a street or sidewalk or on the floor of a hotel or theater lobby). **Mislaid property,** on the other hand, was property discovered under circumstances indicating that it was placed there voluntarily by the owner and then forgotten (such as a suitcase under the seat of an airplane or bus or a purse on a table in a restaurant).

The common law treated abandoned property in the same manner as wild game, the first person taking possession becoming the owner. If the acquirer was a trespasser on the land where the game was taken, however, the landowner or tenant became the owner. The finding of lost or mislaid property, on the other hand, did not change ownership of the item. Either the finder or the landowner (or tenant, if leased) acquired only a right to possession that was superior to the rights of everyone but the true owner. The finder or landowner taking possession was required to take reasonable steps to preserve the property and locate its owner. If the owner appeared to claim the property, he or she was obligated to pay the reasonable costs of storing and preserving it, but was not legally required to pay a reward. All of this assumes, of course, that the identity of the true owner was unknown; if known, the finder or landowner voluntarily taking possession had an absolute duty to deliver the property to its owner and was guilty of a crime for not doing so.

The distinction between lost and mislaid property was used to determine who was entitled to possession in the situation where the item was found by someone who did not own or control the premises. The owner or tenant of the land was entitled to possession if the item was characterized as mislaid property, because of the possibility that the true owner might remember where it was left and return to reclaim it. In the case of lost property, however, the finder was entitled to possession unless he or she was a trespasser, in which case the landowner or tenant had the possessory right.

**Finding Statutes:** In modern times, almost all jurisdictions have enacted legislation regulating the possession and ownership of found property. These laws are referred to as **finding statutes** (or **estray statutes**), and vary substantially from state to state. Several of these statutes, as interpreted by the courts, have retained the common-law distinctions between abandoned, lost, and mislaid property. Some of them apply only to lost property, not to mislaid or abandoned property. However, the courts in some of these states have applied a strong presumption that found property is lost and therefore subject to the statute. In other states, the finding statutes have completely preempted the common-law rules and apply to any found property regardless of its characterization as abandoned, mislaid, or lost.

State finding statutes typically require that the finder of an item of personal property turn it over to a designated governmental authority within a certain period of time, such as ten days. Some statutes designate a local authority for receipt and custody of the item, such as the city police, county sheriff, or county clerk. Others designate a state authority such as the state police. Depending on the provisions of the statute, either the finder or the custodial authority must then take specified steps to locate the true owner, such as by publishing newspaper notices a certain number of times during a particular time period. If the prior owner does not appear and establish ownership within a stated period of time, such as one year, most statutes provide that the finder acquires ownership (not just possession) of the property. A finder who does not comply with the finding statute in a particular state does not acquire ownership or a right to possession, and usually is guilty of a crime. Finding statutes normally place obligations and give rights to the *finder,* regardless of who owns or controls the land where the property is found. Some of these statutes, however, have been interpreted as incorporating the common-law rule that a finder who is a willful trespasser acquires no rights in found property; in such a case, the owner or tenant of the land where the item was found acquires the rights granted by the statute.

**Escheat Statutes:** All states also have enacted **escheat statutes,** which normally provide that intangible property such as money, corporate stock, or bonds is presumed abandoned if it has remained in the possession of a custodian, such as a bank or securities dealer, for a specified time period without any deposits, withdrawals, or other contact by the owner. The time period provided by these statutes is usually lengthy, seven years being a common term. After passage of this time period, a state governmental authority ordinarily is required to publish notices identifying the property; if the property still remains unclaimed for a shorter period, such as six months, the state becomes the owner. Escheat statutes generally apply also to unclaimed stolen property recovered by police, and to the unclaimed property of a person who dies without heirs or a will. Some escheat statutes include other abandoned property as well.

The following case illustrates the application of a finding statute to a hunter's unexpected discovery.

---

## Willsmore v. Township of Oceola
Michigan Court of Appeals, 308 N.W.2d 796 (1981)

While hunting on unposted (i.e., there were no signs prohibiting entry) and unoccupied land, Duane Willsmore's attention was drawn to a place on the ground where branches were arranged in a crisscross pattern. When he kicked aside the branches and some loose dirt, he found a watertight suitcase in a freshly dug hole. Inside the suitcase he found $383,400, which he immediately turned over to the state police. The police noted that some of the money had teller bands around it, indicating that it recently had been in a bank, but they were not able to trace the money to any particular source. The police placed the money in an interest-bearing account, and shortly thereafter Willsmore complied with the Michigan Lost Goods Act by notifying the clerk of the township where the money was found and properly publicizing the find. The statute provided that, one year after the required public notice, a finder who had complied with the law became owner of one-half of the property and the township in which it was found became owner of the other half.

After expiration of the one year, Willsmore filed suit against the township to determine ownership. The state of Michigan also asserted ownership of the money as abandoned property under the Code of Escheats—the Michigan escheat statute. The land on which the money was found was the subject of a sale contract at the time of the finding, although the landowner rightfully cancelled the transaction before the trial of this case because the buyer had breached the contract. The landowner expressly refused to assert any claim to the money.

However, the person who had been the buyer under the contract, Powell, alleged that he was the true owner of the money and asserted a claim in the lawsuit. At the trial, Powell offered his deposition into evidence, but it was not admitted because he was available to testify and he had refused to answer any questions on cross-examination at the taking of the deposition. Powell refused to testify at the trial, asserting his constitutional right to remain silent on the grounds that his statements might tend to incriminate him. The trial court granted a directed verdict awarding Willsmore and the township one-half of the money each according to the Lost Goods Act. Powell and the state of Michigan appealed.

---

**Decision:** The judgment giving Willsmore and the township each one-half of the money was affirmed. The escheat statute applies only where property has been left with holders who would not be considered "finders" in the usual sense (such as money left in a bank account). Therefore, the escheat statute does not apply to these facts and the state has no claim. Under the Michigan Lost Goods Act, Powell simply did not carry his burden of proof regarding his claim of ownership. Although Willsmore did not comply with the Lost Goods Act's strict (and short) time requirements for publishing notices, his failure is excused because of the unusual circumstances at the time of the find. After Willsmore notified the state police of his find, they took custody of the suitcase, advised him and his wife to keep silent because their lives might be in danger, suggested that leaving town for awhile might be a good idea, and even transported Willsmore and his wife, accompanied by officers, armed with rifles, in a state patrol car at speeds up to 100 m.p.h. Willsmore substantially complied with the statute and acted in good faith, and that was sufficient under these circumstances. ∎

---

## Accession

An **accession** is a change in or an addition to an item of personal property. If the change or addition occurs with the owner's knowledge or consent, there is no effect on ownership of the item of property, and the question of compensation to the one making the addition or change depends entirely on the express or implied contract between the parties.

If the change or addition occurs without the owner's knowledge or consent, however, it is possible for ownership to be affected. The person causing the change or addition might have acted with knowledge that the action was wrongful (in bad faith), or with the honestly mistaken belief that he or she owned the item or otherwise had the right to make the change or addition (in good faith). Good faith accessions frequently occur when someone buys an item such as a boat or automobile, makes substantial changes or additions, and then finds out that the title to the purchased item was void because the seller had stolen it. The rules regarding accessions are outlined below.

**Change in Personal Property by Labor:** If a change in an item of personal property is brought about entirely or almost entirely by a nonowner's *labor,* ownership passes to the person performing the labor only if (1) the *identity* of the property has been changed, or (2) the value of the property is *many times greater* than it was prior to the change. An example of a change in identity is shown in the situation where A makes B's grapes into wine without B's consent. An example of a sufficiently great increase in value is found in the case where A takes a piece of stone belonging to B and carves a statue from it without B's consent. There is a definite tendency on the part of courts to deal more harshly with someone who caused the accession while knowing that it was wrong. A greater magnitude of change is often required to pass title to such a party than to someone who acted in good faith.

**Addition of Other Property:** When one person permanently attaches something to another's personal property without the latter's consent, ownership of the resulting product goes to the owner of the "principal" item. For example, if A puts a new engine in a car owned by B, the car and the new engine belong to B. On the other hand, if A puts an engine owned by B in A's car, the car and engine are owned by A.

**Compensation to Owner:** In either of these situations, where an item is changed by a nonowner's labor or where other property has been added to the item, the party who caused the accession (the improver) is responsible for any loss to the other party. Thus, if the circumstances are such that the improver acquired title to the item as a result of the accession, that person must compensate the original owner. If the improver acted in good faith, he or she is required to pay the original owner only for the value of the property in its original condition. But if the improver acted in bad faith, he or she is required to pay to the original owner the value of the property in its improved state.

Where the accession itself does not cause title to pass to the improver, but the original owner simply chooses not to reclaim the property, the situation is treated the same as if the accession *had* caused title to pass. Where the accession does not cause title to pass to the improver, and the original owner *reclaims* the improved property, the improver usually is not entitled to any compensation at all, regardless of whether he or she acted in good faith.

## *Confusion of Goods*

A **confusion of goods** occurs where there has been an intermingling of the goods of different persons. It usually occurs in connection with **fungible goods** (i.e., each unit is identical), such as the same grade of grain, oil, or chemicals. It can, however, occur with nonfungible goods, such as cattle or quantities of packaged merchandise.

If the goods of A and B have been confused (1) by agreement between A and B, (2) by an honest mistake or accident, or (3) by the act of some third party, a tenancy in common is created. Here, A and B each owns an undivided interest in the mass according to the particular proportions they contributed to it.

Suppose, however, that A caused the confusion by deliberately wrongful or negligent conduct. In this case, if the goods of A and B are fungible, A can get his portion back if he proves with reasonable certainty how much that portion is. On the other hand, if the goods are not fungible, A must prove which specific items are his or else he gets nothing.

After there has been a confusion, the quantity of goods might be diminished by fire, theft, or other cause so that not enough is left to give each owner a complete share. If one owner caused the confusion by deliberately wrongful or negligent conduct, that person must bear the entire burden of the decrease. If the confusion came about by agreement, by accident or honest mistake, or by an act of a third party, the burden of the decrease is borne proportionately by both owners.

# BAILMENTS OF PERSONAL PROPERTY

The term *bailment* initially evokes a feeling of puzzlement in most people. Once it is described, however, it is immediately recognized as a simple and commonplace occurrence in everyday life. The taking of a dress to a dry cleaner, the lending of a car to a friend, and the delivering of goods to a railroad for shipment are all actions that result in the creation of bailments. A **bailment** can be defined as the delivery of possession of personal property from one person to another under an agreement by which the latter is obligated to return the property to the former or to deliver it to a third party. The person transferring possession is the **bailor,** and the one receiving it is the **bailee.**

The rules governing most ordinary bailment relationships are common-law in nature. Certain kinds of bailments, however, are subject to statutory enactments. As we will see later in this chapter, Article 7 of the Uniform Commercial Code governs many aspects of the bailment relationships created when one ships goods by common carrier or stores goods with a warehouseman. Also discussed later is the fact that special state statutes regulate some of the obligations of "innkeepers" (i.e., hotel owners) toward the property of guests. As discussed earlier in Chapter 20 (Introduction to the Law of Sales), a new Article 2A of the Uniform Commercial Code has recently been drafted and submitted to state legislatures for adoption. Article 2A covers *leases* of personal property, which are a form of bailment that occurs when one pays rent to the owner of an item such as a car, equipment, home appliance, etc., for the right to use the item for a designated time. Article 2A leaves most of the traditional common-law rules intact for this kind of bailment. One important step taken by Article 2A is that it applies the same basic warranty obligations to lessors in lease transactions that Article 2 applies to sellers in sales transactions. Although many courts had already adopted the sales warranty provisions for personal property leases, Article 2A attempts to do so formally and uniformly.

## *Elements of a Bailment*

By definition, the creation of a bailment requires that (1) one party must deliver possession (but not title) to the other, (2) the property delivered must be classified as personal property, and (3) the parties must agree that the recipient of the property will later return it, deliver it to a third party, or otherwise dispose of it in some specified manner.

**Delivery of Possession:** The requirement that possession of the property be delivered normally means that (1) the property must be transferred to the bailee, (2) the bailee must acquire control over the item, and (3) the bailee must knowingly accept the property.

Although actual physical possession of the bailed property is almost always transferred to the bailee, it is possible for a bailment to be created by delivery of something that gives the bailee effective control over the item, such as the keys or certificate of title to a boat or car.[3]

In addition to a transfer of the property, the circumstances must indicate that the recipient acquired control over it. For example, when a customer hangs his or her coat on a coatrack at a restaurant, and can get it back without notifying the restaurant's management or employees, there is no bailment of the coat because the restaurant did not acquire control over it. Similarly, if a waiter or other restaurant employee takes the coat and hangs it on a rack that is freely accessible to the customer, who may retrieve it without notice or assistance, there still is no bailment. On the other hand, if the coat is left with a coatroom attendant or other restaurant employee, who puts it in a place that is not accessible to the customer without assistance, a bailment has been created because the restaurant has control over the coat.

For the same reason, leaving a car at a parking lot or parking garage is generally held to constitute a bailment only if the car owner is required to leave the keys with an attendant. Otherwise, the parking lot company does not have sufficient control over the car. In a situation in which the car owner is permitted to lock the car and keep the keys, the transaction usually is not a bailment, but is merely a *license*—a contractual permission to use the parking space. The owner of the parking lot is a *licensor* and the car owner is a *licensee.*

Although the bailor normally is the owner of the bailed property, this is not always the case. What is required is that the bailor have a "superior right of

---

[3] This is another example of the concept of *constructive delivery,* which was discussed earlier in the chapter with regard to gifts of personal property.

possession" with regard to the bailee. Thus, if Joe lends his lawn mower to Robert for the summer and Robert takes it to a repair shop in September before returning it to Joe, a bailment exists between Robert and the repair shop while the mower is being repaired.

As we have seen, a physical delivery of property by one person to another does not create a bailment unless the recipient knowingly accepts the property. For example, suppose that Joan has several packages of merchandise in the trunk of her car when she leaves it at a parking lot under circumstances in which a bailment exists as to the car. There is no bailment of the packages unless Joan notifies the parking lot attendant of their presence.

**Personal Property:** As we previously observed, all property is either *real* or *personal.* By definition, bailments involve only transfers of personal property. Although owners of real property frequently transfer possession of it to others for limited periods of time, such transactions are not bailments.

Most bailments involve items of tangible personal property, such as automobiles or jewelry. It is possible, however, for intangible personal property to be the subject of a bailment. This occurs, for example, when a stock certificate representing ownership of corporate stock is delivered by a debtor to a creditor as security for the debt.

**The Agreement to Return:** A bailment necessarily involves an agreement that the property ultimately is to be returned by the bailee to the bailor or delivered to a designated third party. The bailment contract can be either express or implied, and in most cases is not legally required to be in writing. Obviously, however, it is advisable to have the bailment contract in writing if the value of the bailed property is substantial and particularly if a commercial bailor or bailee is involved. Most commercial bailors, such as car rental agencies, and commercial bailees, such as a company that is in the business of storing the property of others, customarily use detailed written contracts.

As a general rule, the bailee is required to return or deliver the *identical* goods at the end of the bailment. Thus, if a Buick dealer delivers a car to Joyce under a contract providing that in return she will deliver her used motor home to the dealer within a month, the transaction is a sale rather than a bailment. The arrangement also would be a sale if the contract gives Joyce the option of returning the car or delivering the motor home in a month.

The rule requiring delivery of the identical property is subject to two well-established exceptions, which are outlined below.

***Fungible Goods:*** If the subject matter of the transaction is *fungible goods,* each unit of which is interchangeable, with the contract obligating the recipient merely to later redeliver the same quantity of goods of the same description to the owner or to a third party, the transaction is still a bailment. This rule is especially important in grain storage situations, with the result that grain elevators taking in grain for storage are bailees even though the grain they later return to their customers or deliver to third parties is not the same grain they originally received.

***Options to Purchase:*** The second exception arises in a situation where the one receiving possession of the property has a specified period of time within which to decide whether to purchase or return it. This type of transaction, sometimes called a *bailment with the option to purchase,* is a bailment despite the fact that the bailee has the choice of turning it into a sale by giving the bailor the agreed price rather than the property itself. Bailments of this type can take several forms, e.g., a *lease with the option to purchase.* Another example is the *sale on approval,* which was discussed in Chapter 21 concerning sale transactions.

**Constructive Bailments:** There are a few cases in which the courts treat transactions as if they are bailments even though one of the ordinarily required elements is missing. One example of such a **constructive bailment** is found in the use of a bank safe-deposit box. When a customer places property in a safe-deposit box, the bank does not acquire *exclusive* control because access to the box requires both the customer's and the bank's key. In addition, the bank usually does not have actual knowledge of the contents of the box. Despite these differences from a traditional bailment, a majority of courts treat the arrangement as a bailment and hold the bank to the responsibilities of a bailee. In a few states, however, legislation has been passed declaring the use of a safe-deposit box to be only a rental of the space—that is, a *license* rather than a bailment.

The courts also usually treat a finder of personal property as a bailee even though the owner did not deliver the item to the finder. The bailment continues until the finder surrenders possession to a governmental authority or becomes the owner of the property by complying with a state finding statute.

## *Types of Bailments*

Bailments can be broadly classified as *ordinary bailments* and *special bailments*. As the name implies, ordinary bailments comprise the vast majority of bailment transactions. Special bailments are discussed briefly at the end of the chapter. Ordinary bailments may be further subdivided into (1) bailments for the sole benefit of the bailee, (2) bailments for the sole benefit of the bailor, and (3) mutual benefit bailments.

**Sole Benefit of the Bailee:** A bailment for the sole benefit of the bailee exists when the owner of an item permits another to use it without compensation or any other benefit. Examples include the loan of a car to a friend or a lawn mower to a neighbor.

**Sole Benefit of the Bailor:** A bailment for the sole benefit of the bailor exists when a person stores or takes care of someone else's property as a favor, without receiving any compensation or other benefit. Such a bailment would arise, for example, where Ruth permits George to store his furniture in her garage while he is away for the summer, with no benefit at all to Ruth.

**Mutual Benefit Bailments:** Because people ordinarily do not enter into bailments unless they receive some sort of gain from the transaction, mutual benefit bailments are by far the most common kind. Most mutual bailments involve a bailor or bailee who receives direct compensation, as in the case of an equipment rental firm or a company that is in the business of storing the property of others.

It is possible, however, for the benefit to be an indirect one. Suppose, for example, that an employer prohibits its employees from keeping their coats or other personal belongings in the immediate working area, and maintains a separate coatroom or other area where such items are left under the control of an attendant. Even though no direct compensation is paid, there is a mutual benefit bailment. The employees benefit by having a secure place to keep their property during working hours. The employer, on the other hand, benefits in several ways, including having an uncluttered working area with fewer distractions for employees, and with less potential for problems arising from theft among employees.

The example of the restaurant's provision of a coatroom where it takes control of customers' coats and hats, presented earlier in the discussion of bailments, also illustrates a mutual benefit bailment involving indirect compensation.

## *Rights of the Bailee*

The bailee's rights in a bailment transaction depend almost entirely on the express or implied terms of the parties' contract. These rights normally involve *possession, use,* and *compensation.*

If the contract provides that the bailee is to have possession for a specified period of time and if the bailor is receiving consideration in return, the bailee ordinarily has the right to retain possession for the entire time. And if the bailor wrongfully retakes possession before the agreed time has expired, the bailee is entitled to damages for breach of contract. The bailee also can enforce this possessory right against a third party who wrongly interferes with it. Thus, if the bailed property is stolen, destroyed, or damaged by a third party, the bailee has the right to initiate legal action to recover the property or receive money damages from the third party.

Whether the bailee has the right to use the bailed property depends on the express terms of the contract or, if there are no such terms, on the general purposes of the bailment. If the contract is for *storage,* for example, the bailee usually has no right to use the property while it is in his or her possession. On the other hand, if the bailee is *renting* the property, he or she obviously has the right to use it in a normal manner.

Except for bailments in which the bailee is renting property for the purpose of using it, or in situations where there is a clear understanding that he or she is not to receive any payment, the bailee normally has the right to some form of compensation for the safekeeping of the property. In the case of a bailee who is in the business of storing the property of others, the compensation is almost always spelled out in the contract. Where the amount of the compensation is not expressly agreed upon, the bailee is entitled to the reasonable value of his or her services. If the purpose of the bailment is to have the bailee perform a service, such as automobile repairs, the amount of the compensation again depends on the express or implied terms of the contract.

## Duties of the Bailee

A bailee has the fundamental duties of using and returning the bailed property in accordance with the bailment contract and exercising due care (or reasonable care) in handling the property.

**Use and Return:** If the bailee uses it in a way that is beyond the consent granted in the agreement, such use constitutes a breach of contract and the bailee is liable for any damages resulting from the unauthorized use regardless of whether he or she committed negligence or any other tort. For instance, Vance, a resident of Sacramento, California, borrows a pickup truck from his neighbor, Perez, to move some furniture from Stockton to Sacramento. After Vance reaches Stockton and loads the furniture, he decides to go on to Modesto, about 25 miles farther, to visit his brother. If the truck is damaged in an accident while Vance is in Modesto, he is fully liable to Perez for the damage even if the accident was not his fault in any respect.

A bailee who intentionally does not return the bailed property at the end of the bailment commits both a breach of contract and the tort of conversion, and is liable to the bailor for the value of the property.

**Due Care and the Presumption of Negligence:** When the bailed property is damaged, lost, stolen, or destroyed because the bailee has failed to exercise due care in handling the item, he or she is guilty of the torts of negligence and conversion and is responsible to the bailor for the amount of the damage or loss.

A variety of circumstances are taken into account to determine whether the bailee exercised due care, including the value of the bailed property, the susceptibility of this particular type of bailed property to damage or theft, and the amount of experience the bailee has had in dealing with similar types of property in the past. Thus, a bailee is expected to exercise greater care in handling a $2,000 diamond ring than a $100 chair. A bailee also would be expected to exercise more care in handling extremely flammable chemicals or a thoroughbred horse than a truckload of bricks.

Until recent years, most courts applied different degrees of care to the different categories of bailment. The bailee was required to exercise great care in a bailment for the sole benefit of the bailee, and only slight care in a bailment for the sole benefit of the bailor. In a mutual benefit bailment the bailee was required to exercise reasonable care, which was defined as the amount of care a reasonable person would exercise in protecting his or her own property. Although the courts in some states still make this rigid distinction, many of them have abandoned it as a strict basis for determining the bailee's required degree of care. These courts apply the general standard of reasonable care to all types of bailments, and simply treat the amount of benefit the bailee was receiving from the bailment as another one of the factors relevant to the question of whether he or she exercised such care.

Courts often emphasize that the bailee is ordinarily not an absolute insurer of the safety of the property, however, and is not liable unless the damage or loss results from his or her intentional or negligent act. Although true, this statement is somewhat misleading. The reason is that when a bailee fails to return the property in its former condition, there is a **presumption of negligence.** In other words, when the bailor proves that the property was not returned at all, or was returned in a damaged condition, the burden then shifts to the bailee to explain exactly what happened and to demonstrate how the loss occurred without his or her fault. Sometimes the courts use different terminology to refer to this presumption and say that the bailor's proof of damage or loss establishes a *prima facie* case of negligence. However it is stated, the rule makes it very difficult for a bailee to avoid liability once it is established that a bailment existed and the property was damaged or not returned.

The presumption of negligence greatly increases the importance of determining whether a bailment actually existed. A person who causes damage to or loss of another's property by failing to exercise due care is ordinarily liable for that damage or loss regardless of whether a bailment or any other particular relationship existed between the parties. In most situations, however, the property owner must prove specific acts on the part of the defendant that constituted negligence. In some cases, as where the item was stolen or destroyed by fire while on the defendant's premises, it can be almost impossible for the plaintiff to produce any specific evidence of what happened. Therefore, the question of whether a bailment existed frequently determines the outcome of such a case.

**Exculpatory Clauses:** Bailees frequently attempt to contractually excuse themselves from liability for harm to the bailed property. It is common, for example, for parking lots, automotive repair shops, or dry cleaners to post signs or give tickets or documents to bailors containing statements such as "The owner assumes all risk for damage to or loss of the property, and the proprietor is not responsible for such damage or loss resulting from fire, theft, flood, or negligence." Statements of this nature are referred to as **exculpatory clauses.**

In most situations exculpatory clauses are not effective to free the bailee from liability, for two reasons. First, as discussed in Chapter 11 regarding the formation of contracts, courts normally hold that such provisions are *not legally communicated* to the bailor unless specifically called to the bailor's attention. Second, even if the exculpatory clause is legally communicated and thus becomes part of the bailment contract, courts usually conclude that the clause *violates public policy* and is unenforceable on the grounds of illegality. This conclusion is almost always reached when the bailee is in the business of handling the property of others and the terms of the bailment contract are presented by the bailee to the bailor on a nonnegotiated "take it or leave it" basis. (In other words, the agreement is a *contract of adhesion,* a concept that was discussed at several points in the chapters on contracts.)

The following two cases illustrate the approach taken by courts to determine whether a bailment exists, and emphasize the critical importance of that question in situations where no one really knows exactly what happened to the bailed property. In addition, the second case provides an example of the courts' usual attitude toward exculpatory clauses in bailment contracts.

---

**Pinto v. Bridgeport Mack Trucks, Inc.**
Superior Court of Connecticut,
Appellate Session,
458 A.2d 696 (1983)

Alfred Pinto had worked as a diesel mechanic for Bridgeport Mack Trucks for nine years. As was the custom in the industry, the employer supplied all the larger tools and employees furnished their own hand tools. It also was customary for employees to leave their tools in the work area of the employer's premises after finishing a day's work. Pinto was hired with the understanding that he would provide his own hand tools, and he maintained a two-piece tool chest in the employer's work area. The top section of the chest loaded with his tools weighed approximately 500 pounds. There were about 25 other tool boxes scattered around the work area. This work area consisted of a 39,000 square foot space in the rear of the employer's building; a showroom area was in the front.

As often was the case, on the occasion in question the employer's volume of work required the services of two shifts of mechanics. The first shift worked from 8:00 a.m. to 4:30 p.m., and the second shift from 3:00 p.m. to 11:30 p.m. The employer was open for business until 11:00 p.m., but at the end of the first shift a chain link fence surrounding the sides and rear of the building was locked, leaving a front door leading into the showroom area as the only means of access to the work area. After finishing his work on the first shift, Pinto locked his tools in his box and left it beside the truck he was repairing. The second shift reported for work as usual and, as was their custom, the employees on the second shift took a meal break between 7:00 and 7:30 p.m. Some of the employees left the building during their break, while others ate in a lunchroom at the rear of the work area. During this half hour, McDonald, the foreman of the second shift, went back and forth between the lunchroom and work area answering the telephone and attending to other business matters. He was out of the work area a total of ten minutes during the entire break.

Upon returning from the break, an employee noticed that a battery charger was missing. The next morning Pinto discovered that the top section of his tool chest was also missing. The foreman had locked the building after the second shift the previous evening, and an investigation disclosed no signs of

*(continued)*

forced entry during the night. The employer refused to pay for Pinto's tools, so he filed suit against the employer seeking damages for their value. At the trial, evidence was presented showing that during the preceding year there had been discussions among employees and managers about storing the employees' tools to avoid their damaging or being damaged by the large trucks moving about the area. The employer's managers offered to provide a separate area where tool boxes could be wheeled and stored, and to obtain chains to secure them, but this action was never taken. The evidence also showed that, prior to the loss of the battery charger and Pinto's tools, there had been no thefts from the employer's building in nine years.

The trial court found that there was not a bailment of Pinto's tools, but held the employer liable because there was independent evidence of the employer's negligence. The employer appealed.

**Decision:** The judgment for plaintiff Pinto was reversed. As the trial court had held, there was no bailment of the tools because the employer had not assumed control over them. Contrary to the trial court's conclusion, however, there was not sufficient independent evidence of negligence to hold the employer liable in the absence of a bailment. There were no facts that would have put the employer on notice that theft of an employee's tool chest was a likely occurrence; the possibility was too remote to be reasonably foreseeable. The following factors lead to this conclusion: (1) the size and weight of the tool chest; (2) there had been no thefts from the building in nine years; (3) a chain link fence surrounding the sides and rear of the building was secured by the day shift; (4) the sole night access to the 39,000 square foot building was through a single door leading into the showroom; and (5) tool chests were in a maintenance area at the rear of the building and employees were in and out of this area constantly. ■

## Employers Insurance of Wausau v. Chemical Bank
Civil Court of New York,
459 N.Y.S.2d 238 (1983)

Suncrest Pharmacal Corp. claimed that Chemical Bank failed to credit one of Suncrest's deposits, resulting in a loss of over $11,000. Suncrest received $3,000 from its insurer, Employers Insurance of Wausau, and both Suncrest and the insurance company then filed suit against the bank to recover damages for the loss.

At the trial, Weintraub, president of Suncrest, testified that on a Friday evening about 7:00 p.m. he placed a paper bag containing two of the bank's cloth deposit bags in a night depository. Before leaving, he checked to see that the paper bag did in fact go down the chute. One of the deposit bags contained 850 one dollar bills, and the other contained cash and checks totalling $19,191.52. The deposit slip for both bags was in the one that contained $850. The following Monday the bank notified Weintraub that it had received only the bag containing the deposit slip and $850. Suncrest was able to have payment stopped on all of the checks in the missing bag on which it was the payee, but was unable to do so on any of the checks payable to others and endorsed over to Suncrest, because there was no record of the names of the makers of those checks. The lost cash and checks totalled $11,084.50.

An officer of the bank described the procedure used by the bank in opening the night deposit vault, and Suncrest conceded that it was unable to prove any specific acts of negligence relating to the bank's procedure in handling night deposits. Suncrest asserted, however, that the deposit had created a bailment, and that the bank had the burden of explaining exactly what happened to the lost bag. The bank claimed that there was no bailment, and that its liability was limited by the written deposit agreement between it and Suncrest, which provided that permission to use the night depository was a "privilege" and "gratuitous," and that "the exercise of that privilege [was] at the sole risk" of Suncrest. The following summarizes the opinion of the trial court.

**Decision:** The trial court rendered judgment for Suncrest and its insurer, the plaintiffs. A bailment was created, and the bank offered no evidence to show what actually happened to the other deposit bag. Although this type of situation is susceptible to the assertion of fraudulent claims by depositors, there was substantial evidence supporting Weintraub's testimony. Other customers commonly do what Weintraub did when making the deposit; Suncrest's foreman testified under oath that he saw Weintraub make the deposit; Suncrest was a long-time customer of the bank and frequent user of its night depository service; Suncrest had never before made any complaints about the facility or service; Suncrest had records of those checks in the missing bag on which Suncrest was the payee; and it is plausible that bank employees could have overlooked the second deposit bag within the paper bag. In addition, after Weintraub had gone through extensive direct and cross-examination the trial judge specifically concluded that he was a credible witness. ■

## Rights of the Bailor

Essentially, the rights of the bailor arise from the duties of the bailee. Thus, the bailor's most important rights are to have the bailed property returned at the end of the bailment period, to have the bailee use due care in protecting the property, and to have the bailee use the property (if use is contemplated at all) in conformity with the express or implied terms of the bailment contract. Additionally, if the bailor is having work performed on the property by the bailee, the bailor is entitled to have it done in a workmanlike fashion. If the purpose of the bailment is use of the property by the bailee, the bailor has the right to compensation under the express or implied terms of the contract.

## Duties of the Bailor

**Liability for Defects in the Bailed Property:** Obviously, the bailor has duties corresponding to the rights of the bailee discussed previously. In addition, the bailor has certain basic duties with respect to the condition of the bailed property.

*Negligence:* The bailor must not knowingly deliver property containing a hidden defect that is likely to cause injury. In either a mutual benefit bailment or one for the sole benefit of the bailee, the bailor is legally required to notify the bailee of any dangerous defect about which the bailor has *actual knowledge.* In a mutual benefit bailment, the bailor's duty regarding the condition of the bailed property is somewhat greater, and he or she can be held responsible for injury caused by hidden defects about which the bailor *either knew or should have known.*[4] Thus, in a mutual benefit bailment, the bailor's duty includes reasonably inspecting the property and maintaining it in a safe condition before delivery to a bailee.

In either of these situations, a violation of the bailor's duty constitutes negligence, and the bailor is liable for resulting harm to the bailee and to others coming into contact with the defective property in a reasonably foreseeable manner. For example, a bailor's liability for delivering a defective automobile to the bailee would include injuries to the bailee and his or her immediate family, as well as to innocent third parties such as the driver of another automobile involved in an accident because of the defect.

*Warranty and Strict Liability:* In addition to imposing liability for the bailor's negligence, most courts in recent years have placed additional liability on commercial bailors. In the case of bailors who are in the business of renting property, such as automobiles, construction equipment, and so on, a majority of courts have held the bailor responsible for dangerous defects in the bailed property on basis of the *implied warranty* and *strict products liability* theories. These courts have drawn an analogy from the liability imposed on merchants in *sales* transactions. The importance of this development, as we saw in Chapter 22, "Warranties and Products Liability," is that the supplier of a defective item can be held liable without any proof that the supplier knew or should have known of the defect. Moreover, the supplier's defenses are much more limited under the warranty and strict liability theories.

As mentioned earlier, new Article 2A of the Uniform Commercial Code formally adopts the same basic warranty obligations for lessors of personal property as exist under Article 2 for sellers of personal property.

**Bailor's Disclaimers:** We saw previously that commercial *bailees* frequently attempt to limit their liability contractually. It also is very common for commercial *bailors* to make similar attempts. This type of provision, whether it is called an exculpatory clause, disclaimer, or liability limitation, is given essentially the same treatment by the courts as bailees' exculpatory clauses. In fact, in the majority of states that have drawn an analogy between the bailor who is in the business of renting personal property and the merchant who is in the business of selling goods, a disclaimer by the bailor is given even harsher treatment by the courts. Such a provision violates public policy and thus is not allowed to shield a commercial bailor from liability for negligence, breach of warranty, or strict liability when a defect in the bailed property causes personal injury or property damage to either the bailee or someone else whose contact with the item was reasonably foreseeable.

---

[4] Questions concerning the condition of the bailed property almost never arise in a bailment for the sole benefit of the bailor, because the bailee does not *use* the property. If the bailed property was defective and harmed the bailee in such a case, however, the bailor's duty presumably would be the same as in a mutual benefit bailment.

# SPECIAL BAILMENTS

**Special bailments** are those involving common carriers, warehouse companies, and innkeepers (or hotelkeepers). Although bailments involving these types of bailees have most of the characteristics of ordinary bailments and are subject to most of the same rules, they are singled out because of certain unique aspects.

## *Common Carriers*

A **common carrier** is a company that is licensed by the state or federal government to provide transportation services to the general public. Most airlines, trucking companies, and railroad companies are common carriers. A company doing business as a common carrier must make its services available to the public on a nondiscriminatory basis. A common carrier can be contrasted with a **contract carrier,** which does not hold itself out as providing transportation services to the public and is not licensed to do so. A contract carrier provides service under contract only to a few selected customers.

Suppose that a furniture manufacturer in Pittsburgh, Pennsylvania, delivers a large quantity of furniture to a railroad company for shipment to a wholesale furniture distributor in St. Louis, Missouri. When the manufacturer, called the *shipper,* turns over possession of the furniture to the railroad company, called the *carrier,* a type of mutual benefit bailment has been created.

Bailments of this type are different from ordinary bailments in several important respects.

**Obligation to Transport:** Unlike most bailees, the carrier has a contractual obligation to transport the bailed property.

**Bills of Lading:** Also unlike other bailees, the carrier issues a **bill of lading** to the shipper. The bill of lading, the rules for which are set forth in Article 7 of the Uniform Commercial Code, serves as both a *contract of bailment* and a *document of title.* In other words, it sets forth the terms of the agreement between shipper and carrier and also serves as evidence of title to the goods.

As was discussed in Chapter 20 dealing with sales of goods, a bill of lading or other document of title can be either *negotiable* or *nonnegotiable.* A bill of lading ordering the carrier to "deliver to X" is a nonnegotiable document of title. The carrier's obligation in such a case is to deliver the goods only to X, and the nonnegotiable document does not confer the right to receive the goods to anyone else who might come into possession of the document.

On the other hand, a bill of lading ordering the carrier to "deliver to the order of X," or to "deliver to bearer," is a negotiable document of title. Lawful possession of a negotiable document is tantamount to ownership of the goods, and the carrier is obligated to deliver them to anyone having such possession. In the case of a bill of lading ordering the carrier to "deliver to the order of X," the carrier is required to surrender the goods to Y if X has endorsed and delivered the document to Y and Y presents it to the carrier. In the case of a bill of lading ordering the carrier to "deliver to bearer," the carrier is required to surrender the goods to anyone to whom the document has been delivered, even without the presence of an endorsement.

Bills of lading, especially negotiable ones, are often used to facilitate sales transactions by providing the seller (shipper) a document that can be sent to the buyer and then used by the buyer to take possession of the goods when they reach their destination. This document may be sent directly from the seller to the buyer, or it may be sent through banking channels with the seller's and buyer's banks acting as agents for delivery of the document and receipt of payment.

**Strict Liability:** Contrary to ordinary bailments, the carrier is absolutely liable to the shipper for damage to or loss of the goods. In other words, the carrier's liability is not based upon negligence or other fault.[5] There are, however, several narrow categories of circumstances in which the carrier is not liable. If the goods are damaged, stolen, lost, or destroyed during shipment, the carrier has the burden of proving that the situation falls within one of these categories. The categories are as follows.

---

[5] Frequently, one carrier will transport the goods for only part of the total trip, and other carriers will provide transportation for other portions of the journey. In such a situation, involving *connecting carriers,* the last carrier to have the goods is presumed to have received them in good condition, and is liable to the shipper for damage to the goods. If this carrier claims that the goods were damaged while in the hands of an earlier carrier, it must initiate legal action against the other carrier to recoup its loss.

***Act of God:*** The carrier is not liable if it can show that the loss was caused by an unexpected force of nature that was of such magnitude that damage to the goods could not have been prevented. The term Act of God is interpreted very strictly; evidence that the goods were damaged or destroyed by a flood, for example, will not suffice to excuse the carrier unless the flood was of such an unprecedented nature that no reasonable precautions could have forestalled the loss.

***Act of a Public Enemy:*** This term is also interpreted very narrowly, and is usually applied only to a situation in which the goods were damaged, destroyed, or seized by a foreign nation at war with the United States.

***Act of a Public Authority:*** The term public authority is much broader, and applies to actions by various local, state, or federal government officials. Examples would include the seizure of an illegal drug shipment by law enforcement officers, or the seizure of goods by a sheriff acting under a *writ of execution.* A writ of execution is a court order requiring an officer to seize property and sell it for the purpose of paying off a judgment against the owner.

***Act of the Shipper:*** The carrier is not responsible if the shipper's own actions are shown to have caused the loss. For example, the carrier is not liable for the death of the shipper's chickens if proved to have been caused by the shipper's improperly ventilated crates.

***The Inherent Nature of the Goods:*** The carrier is not liable if the loss is caused by an inherent characteristic of the goods themselves that the carrier had no control over. This category also is construed very strictly. For example, it would not be sufficient for the carrier to show that a shipment of fruit spoiled and that fruit is prone to spoilage. To escape liability, the carrier would have to prove that the fruit spoiled for a very specific reason, such as the fact that it was overripe at the time of shipment, and that the carrier could not have prevented the spoilage.

**Liability Limitations:** Despite the fact that carriers are liable for harm to the bailed property even without being at fault, they are permitted to limit their liability contractually to a greater extent than ordinary bailees. Under federal and state regulations, common carriers may obtain the shipper's agreement to place a dollar limit on the carrier's liability, and the limitation is valid if the shipper was given a choice of paying a higher transportation fee for a higher dollar limitation.

## Warehouse Companies

A **warehouse company** is in the business of storing other people's property for compensation. A *public* warehouse company is obligated to serve the general public without discrimination. Most of the principles applicable to warehouse companies are exactly the same as those for ordinary bailees. In fact, some of the illustrations presented in the discussion of ordinary bailments involved warehouses.

The most important characteristic that warehouse operators have in common with other bailees is the nature of the bailee's liability. A warehouse company is not absolutely liable like a common carrier, but is liable for damage to or loss of the bailed property only in those circumstances in which an ordinary bailee is liable, namely, where the damage or loss is caused by the bailee's negligence, conversion, or breach of contract. Warehouse companies, however, are also subject to the same presumption of negligence as ordinary bailees.

Thus, for most purposes a warehouse company is an ordinary bailee. It is often singled out as a special bailee, however, for three reasons: (1) Like a common carrier, and unlike other bailees, a warehouse operator may obtain the bailor's agreement to limit the warehouse's liability, and the limitation is valid if the bailor was given a choice of a higher dollar limitation in return for a higher fee. (2) Also like a common carrier, a warehouse company issues documents of title for the goods it receives. The document of title issued by a warehouse company is called a **warehouse receipt,** and is governed by the same rules as bills of lading under Article 7 of the UCC. (3) A warehouse company is subject to more extensive regulation by the state than most other bailees. For example, warehouses are usually subject to special building standards and fire prevention measures.

## Innkeepers

The taking of articles of personal property to a hotel or motel room by a guest does not create a bailment, for two reasons. First, the **innkeeper** (i.e., the hotel owner) normally does not have knowledge of the specific items that are brought into the room. Second, because the guest is free to remove the items from the room without notice to the innkeeper, the latter does not have exclusive possession of the items.

Despite the absence of a true bailment relationship, under common-law principles the innkeeper had exactly the same absolute liability as a common carrier for damage to or loss of guest's personal property. In modern times, however, all states have passed statutes diminishing the innkeeper's liability. The typical statute requires innkeepers to maintain a safe or other appropriate facility for the safekeeping of its guests' valuables. If a guest deposits property with the innkeeper, a bailment is created. Under most statutes, if the property then is damaged or lost, the innkeeper has the same absolute liability as a common carrier. Some statutes, however, place dollar limits on the innkeeper's liability.

With regard to property that is *not* turned over to the innkeeper for safekeeping, the statutes vary. Many provide that the innkeeper's common-law liability is reduced to that of an ordinary bailee. Other statutes do not remove the innkeeper's absolute responsibility, but place a dollar limit such as $50 on that liability.

## SUMMARY

Although the legal framework for personal property ownership bears a number of similarities to that for real property, there are also many differences. Primary among the differences is that ownership of personal property usually is an all-or-nothing proposition, and is not subdivided into the wide variety of interests that characterize real property ownership. Ownership of personal property can be acquired in a sale transaction or by will, subjects that are dealt with elsewhere in this book. Personal property ownership can be transferred by gift, which requires expression of a present intent to transfer ownership and delivery of possession. Other methods by which title to an article of personal property can be affected are occupation, finding, accession, and confusion.

A bailment of personal property arises when one party transfers temporary possession (but not title) to another under an agreement in which the recipient is required to return the property later or to deliver it to a designated third person. Bailments can be ordinary or special. Ordinary bailments can be further subdivided into those for the sole benefit of the bailee, sole benefit of the bailor, and mutual benefit of the parties. The most important duties of the bailee in an ordinary bailment are to use and return the property only in accordance with the bailment contract, and to exercise due care in protecting the property. When bailed property is not returned or is returned in a damaged condition, there is a presumption of negligence.

The most important duties of the bailor are to conform to the terms of the contract regarding the bailee's use and possession of the property, and not to deliver bailed property having a known dangerous defect. This duty is somewhat greater in a mutual benefit bailment than in one for the sole benefit of the bailee. In addition to this liability for negligence, in recent years liability under warranty and strict products liability theories has been imposed on commercial bailors.

Special bailments are those involving common carriers, warehouse companies, and innkeepers. A common carrier is absolutely liable for damage to or loss of the goods unless the carrier can prove that the damage or loss was caused by one of five narrowly interpreted events. A warehouse company has the liability of an ordinary bailee, but is different in that it issues warehouse receipts and is subject to greater regulation. An innkeeper, though not technically a bailee of the property its guests keep in their rooms, had the same absolute liability as a common carrier under common-law rules. All states have passed statutes modifying this liability in certain ways.

## KEY TERMS

**Donor**
**Donee**
**Constructive delivery (or symbolic delivery)**
**Gift *inter vivos***
**Gift *causa mortis***
**Occupation**
**Abandoned property**
**Lost property**
**Mislaid property**
**Finding statute (or estray statute)**
**Escheat statute**
**Accession**
**Confusion of goods**
**Fungible goods**
**Bailment**
**Bailor**
**Bailee**

Constructive bailment
Presumption of negligence
Exculpatory clause
Special bailments
Common carrier
Contract carrier
Bill of lading
Warehouse company
Warehouse receipt
Innkeeper

## QUESTIONS AND PROBLEMS

1. Closter was despondent and had decided to commit suicide. Before doing so, he inserted into an envelope a promissory note that he owned. On the note he wrote that he was giving it to Schutz. Closter then shot and killed himself. Schutz, who occupied another room in the same boardinghouse, heard the shot, rushed to his friend's room and found his body there. Schutz saw the envelope lying on the desk where Closter had placed it. Thinking that it might be a suicide note, Schutz opened it and found the promissory note containing Closter's expression of donative-intent. Schutz pocketed the envelope and note. The existence of the note later came to light, and Liebe, the administrator of Closter's estate, filed suit to collect on the note from Battman, who had originally executed it. Schutz claimed that *he* was the owner of the note and was entitled to collect on it from Battman. Who won? Discuss. (*Liebe v. Battman,* 54 Pac. 179, 1898.)

2. Walters suffered a heart attack. Fearful of impending death, he gave his diamond ring to his sister while he was still in the hospital. Walters' condition improved, and he was discharged from the hospital two months later. He asked his sister to return the ring, but she refused. Not wanting to cause a family quarrel, he said nothing more. Five years later he died from heart disease. Does the ring belong to his sister? Explain. Would it make any difference if he had never asked for the return of the ring? Discuss.

3. Hillebrant indicated to Brewer that he was making a gift to Brewer of a herd of cattle. Hillebrant then obtained Brewer's branding iron and branded the cattle with Brewer's registered brand. Before the cattle were delivered to Brewer, however, Hillebrant changed his mind. Brewer sued, claiming that a completed gift of the cattle had been made. Was Brewer correct? Discuss. (*Hillebrant v. Brewer,* 6 Tex. 45, 1851.)

4. Harkness was elderly and bedridden. So that his close friend Kuntz could pay his bills for him a joint account was established with money belonging to Harkness. The account was a joint tenancy with right of survivorship. It was used for its intended purpose until Harkness died two years later (that is, Kuntz never used the funds for any purpose other than to pay bills for Harkness). When Harkness died, Kuntz claimed the money remaining in the account, asserting that it was his as a gift. Harkness' heirs disagreed. What is the result? Explain.

5. X and Y consented to the mixing of their wheat in a grain storage elevator owned by Z. What is the status of the ownership of the wheat? Explain. Would the answer be different if Z had caused the confusion accidently? Explain. Would the answer be different if X had intentionally caused the confusion with knowledge that he had no right to do so? Explain.

6. Hanson agreed to loan $1,000 to Kristofferson only after Kristofferson agreed to *pledge* a ring valued at $3,000 with Hanson. A pledge involves transfer of possession of personal property to a creditor as security for the debt. Soon after the loan was made, the ring was stolen while in Hanson's possession. In subsequent litigation between the parties, Hanson contended that he was not a bailee in this situation because his obligation to return the ring was not absolute—he would not have to return it if Kristofferson defaulted on his loan. Is Hanson's contention correct? Why or why not?

7. X left her expensive leather handbag in a medical clinic waiting room when she was called into her doctor's office for her appointment. When she returned to the waiting room 45 minutes later, the handbag was gone. She later brought suit against the clinic to recover its value. At the trial the clinic receptionist and X's doctor testified that they did not see the handbag at any time during the day of her appointment. Assuming the receptionist and the doctor were telling the truth, would this testimony necessarily rule out a bailment relationship? Explain. If the receptionist had testified that she had noticed X placing the handbag in a corner of a couch before entering the doctor's office, would this fact clearly establish a bailment? Discuss.

8. Scarlet, a Ford dealer, delivered a new Taurus automobile to his neighbor, Gray, for ten days; the understanding between the two men was that at the end of that period Gray would have the option of (a) giving his 1913 Ford Model T to Scarlet in payment for the Taurus, or (b) paying Scarlet $15,000 in cash for the Taurus. During the ten-day period while Gray is in possession of the Taurus, is he a bailee of the car? Discuss. Would your answer be any different if the agreement had simply given Gray, at the end of the ten-day period, the option of either returning the Taurus or paying $15,000 cash for it? Explain.

9. X leaves his car at the Y Company's parking lot and returns an hour later to find that it has been badly damaged while in the Y Company's possession. In this situation, X's right to recover damages from the parking lot company might be seriously jeopardized if the legal relationship be-

tween X and the Y Company was merely that of licensee and licensor rather than bailor and bailee. Explain why this is so.

**10.** David Crystal, Inc., delivered goods to a trucking company for transportation. While in the trucking company's possession, the goods were lost when the truck carrying them was hijacked in New York City. In a legal action by David Crystal against the trucking firm, a common carrier, the trucking firm defended on the ground that truck hijackers are "public enemies," and that it thus was not liable for the loss. Is this contention correct? Why or why not? (*David Crystal, Inc. v. Ehrlich-Newmark Truck Co.*, 314 N.Y.S.2d 559, 1970.)

# CHAPTER 46

# WILLS, TRUSTS, AND ESTATE PLANNING

Although few people amass large fortunes in their lifetimes, most will not die penniless. Many people are surprised at the actual value of what they may have considered to be modest holdings. Real estate acquired early in life may appreciate dramatically; life insurance, both individual and group, may be owned in substantial amounts, and investment in the stock market through mutual funds is commonplace. One's personal property, slowly acquired over a period of years, may constitute a sizable asset. Some knowledge of wills, trusts, and other estate planning devices is essential to make informed decisions about one's personal situation.

The case of Pablo Picasso is a good example of what can happen when a person with a substantial estate fails to provide for its orderly disposition. When the famous artist died in 1973 he left a tremendous fortune—millions of dollars in assets. To whom did he leave it? As a matter of fact, Picasso died **intestate;** that is, at the time of his death he had not prepared a document—a will—to provide specific and detailed instructions about what to do with his property. A properly planned, drafted, and executed will might have eliminated most of the bitter controversy that arose among those close to him over the disposition of his wealth.

Picasso apparently felt that making a will was an act in contemplation of death and therefore an unpleasant subject to be avoided. He resisted all efforts by those who anticipated protracted legal proceedings to persuade him to make a will to provide for an orderly disposition of his property. When any person of considerable means refuses to provide for his or her estate's distribution on death, controversy is almost as certain as death itself.

## WILLS

A will transforms a person's wishes about the disposition of his or her property into a valid, legal instrument. This section covers formal, written wills in detail and mentions other types briefly. Following are some commonly used terms with which the student may be unfamiliar. A man who makes a will is a **testator,** a woman is a **testatrix.** A person who dies is a **decedent.** A decedent leaving a valid will is said to die *testate.* It is customary for a testator to designate a personal representative to carry out the provisions of the will. This person is an **executor** if male and an **executrix** if female. If there is no will or the will does not designate a personal representative, the court will appoint an **administrator** (or *administratrix*) to handle the decedent's estate. With regard to the testator's property, disposition of real estate is properly called a **devise,** money passing under a will is a **legacy,** and other property is disposed of by **bequest.**[1] (Today, lawyers use these terms interchangeably.)

### *Testamentary Capacity*

A will is valid only if the testator had **testamentary capacity** at the time of its making. In most states the testator must have attained a specific minimum age, usually 18. In all states the testator must possess the mental capacity to dispose of the property intelligently. Testamentary capacity is not identical to ca-

---

[1] The Uniform Probate Code, which has been largely adopted in about 15 states and partially in some others, uses the term "devise" to refer to any sort of testamentary gift whether of land, money, or personal property.

pacity to contract. In general, testators have the capacity to make wills if they have attained the statutory age, if they know what property they own, and if they reasonably understand how and to whom they want to leave their property. The following case illustrates this principle.

### Holladay v. Holladay
Court of Appeals of Kentucky,
172 S.W.2d 36 (1943)

This action was a will contest involving the will of Lewis Holladay. A college graduate, Holladay made his home on his mother's farm with her and a sister until his mother's death in 1929. He remained on the farm until he died in 1940 at age 66. He was survived by a brother, Joe, and three sisters. Joe was the sole beneficiary under Lewis's will. When he submitted the will for probate, the sisters opposed the proceeding on a number of grounds. The primary basis for the contest was the allegation by the sisters, the contestants, that Lewis did not possess sufficient mental capacity to execute a will.

Upon a verdict rendered in the Clark Circuit Court a judgment was entered adjudging that a paper executed by Lewis Holladay was his last will and testament. This appeal is prosecuted from that judgment.

**Decision:** The judgment was affirmed. Under the evidence presented, the question as to Holladay's testamentary capacity was clearly a question of fact rather than a question of law. The submission of this question to the jury, therefore, was proper. And since the verdict was clearly supported by credible (believable) evidence, it was not set aside. ∎

## Undue Influence

Even if a testator or testatrix has the legal capacity to make a will, that will should not be admitted to probate if it is the product of fraud, duress, or, more typically, undue influence. Many courts use a four-factor test to determine the existence of undue influence. That test is applied in the following case.

### Casper v. McDowell
Wisconsin Supreme Court,
205 N.W. 2d 753 (1973)

On April 2, 1970, 78-year-old Joseph Casper died. His will, drafted ten months before his death by a local attorney, provided for payment of debts and funeral expenses, bequeathed $1,500 to each of Casper's two sons (Alger and Richard), and left the residue and remainder of the estate to Wilma Jean McDowell, who had lived with Casper as housekeeper and friend from October 1964 to his death. Nothing was left to Joseph's brother, John. The will specified Wilma Jean's father or her brother as executor.

After the will was submitted for admission to probate, objections were filed by Alger and Richard. Later they also challenged, on undue influence grounds, transactions in which Joseph had named Wilma Jean a joint tenant on a bank account and two deposit certificates. A jury found no undue influence in the transactions, and the trial court admitted the will to probate. Alger and Richard appealed.

**Decision:** In affirming the trial court decision, the Wisconsin Supreme Court reiterated the four elements necessary to establish undue influence: (1) susceptibility of the testator; (2) opportunity to influence; (3) a disposition to influence; and (4) the desired result.

*Susceptibility.* There was evidence of susceptibility which included Joseph's deteriorating health, his strong attraction to the then 22-year-old Wilma, and some odd conduct, such as cutting off the tops of several of his trees and failure to recognize friends. However, the prevailing evidence was that Joseph was a

*(continued)*

strong-willed independent person. Several of his neighbors so testified.

*Disposition.* This court had previously held that "there is nothing wrong with aiding and comforting an ailing testator; indeed, such activity should be encouraged." So, no adverse inferences can be drawn from the attentions Wilma paid to Joseph. It was argued that Wilma poisoned Joseph's mind against his family. However, there was no direct evidence of this and it appeared that Joseph had not regarded his family members as potential beneficiaries even before he met Wilma.

*Result.* Where, as here, a testator leaves most of his assets to a nonrelative, a "red flag of warning" is raised, but all circumstances must be considered. The testator seldom saw his closest relatives—his two sons who lived in California. Wilma was his closest friend. Although Joseph may have deviated from socially acceptable conduct by considering his housekeeper, 50 years his junior, to be his best friend, no inference of impropriety need necessarily be drawn.

*Opportunity.* This element, alone, is not sufficient to establish undue influence. ■

---

## *The Formal Will*

The term *formal* indicates that the will has been prepared and executed in compliance with the state's law of wills ("probate code"). Although the right to make a will generally exists independent of statute, the procedures for drafting, executing, and witnessing the formal written document are governed by statute. Such statutory requirements, although basically similar, vary from state to state. Therefore the drafter must be thoroughly acquainted with the law of the state in which the testator's will is to be effective and must be sure to comply with its provisions. Noncompliance usually means that the will is declared invalid. If this happens, the decedent's property passes in accordance with the state's law of descent and distribution. (Such statutes and their application are discussed later in another section.)

**General Requirements:** A will must be written; it must be signed by the testator or testatrix or at his or her direction. In most states, the signing must be witnessed by two competent persons who themselves must sign as witnesses in the presence of each other and of the testator or testatrix.[2] Most states require an **attestation clause,** a paragraph beneath the testator's signature to the effect that the will was *published*—that is, declared by the testator to be the last will and testament, and signed in the presence of the witnesses, who themselves signed as attesting witnesses. These are the formalities required by statute, and they must be strictly observed. The witnesses do not need to read or know the contents of the will. The testator or testatrix simply announces to them that the document is the will and that he or she is going to sign it. The function of the attestation clause is to serve as a self-proving affidavit to relieve the witnesses of the burden of testifying when the will is submitted for admission to probate after the death of the testator or testatrix.

**Specific Provisions:** The main function of a will is to provide for the disposal of property. However, it can appoint an executor and cancel all previous wills if it so states. It can also provide for an alternative disposition of property in the event the primary beneficiary predeceases the testator. If the testator or testatrix is married, the surviving spouse is usually appointed as the executor or executrix; if unmarried, a close relative or friend may be designated.

A will can also cover the disposition of property in the event that husband and wife die nearly simultaneously. It is essential for the will to state that it revokes any and all prior wills. The existence of two or more wills can create insurmountable problems. Sometimes none are admitted to probate (the court proceedings whereby a will is proved and the estate of the decedent is disposed of), in which event the state's statutory provisions for the division of an estate are followed.

The will can also name a guardian for minor children. If both husband and wife die, the guardian they have appointed in their wills can be confirmed by the court if he or she is qualified and willing to serve in that capacity. This will obviate the necessity for a court-appointed guardian and a possible controversy between the two competing, though well-meaning, sides of the family.

**Modification:** While it is possible in some states to change one's will by erasure, by striking out portions, or by interlineation, such procedures are risky under-

---

[2] A few states require three witnesses.

takings at best. The proper method is to modify by means of a **codicil**. This is an addition to the will and must be executed with the same formalities as the original document. Consequently, if extensive modification is necessary, the testator would be well-advised to consider making a new will.

**Revocation:** A will becomes effective only at the death of the testator. The testator can revoke or amend the will at any time until death. Revocation can be accomplished in several ways, but usually must be done in strict compliance with statute by means evincing a clear intent to revoke. Executing a new will with a clause expressly revoking all prior wills and codicils is a customary method of revoking a will. The necessity for strict statutory compliance is illustrated in the following case.

---

*In re* **Estate of Haugk**
Wisconsin Supreme Court,
280 N.W.2d 684 (1979)

On January 6, 1965, Marie Haugk executed a will naming the Lutheran Children's Friend Society and the Easter Seal Society of Milwaukee County (appellants) as residual beneficiaries. On September 2, 1976, Marie's husband, Horst Haugk, burned the 1965 will in the family basement, while Marie, who was suffering from a heart condition and was thus unable to descend the stairs into the basement, stayed upstairs in the kitchen. Soon thereafter, Marie spoke to her attorney about execution of a new will which would have eliminated appellants as beneficiaries, purportedly because she had wearied of their repeated requests for funds. However, Marie died before the new will could be executed.

Haugk filed a petition with the probate court claiming his wife died intestate, leaving him as sole beneficiary of her $130,000 estate. Appellants then petitioned the court for admission of the 1965 will. The trial court found that the 1965 will was properly revoked and ruled for Haugk. Appellants challenged this ruling on appeal.

**Decision:** The judgment was reversed. The relevant statute states that a will is revoked in whole or in part by "Burning, tearing, canceling or obliterating the will or part, with the intent to revoke, by the testator or by some person *in the testator's presence* and by his direction." Horst burned the will in the basement while the testator, Marie, was upstairs in the kitchen. Although Horst argues that it was Marie's heart condition that kept her from descending the stairs, the fact remains that the will was not burned in her presence, as the statute requires for an effective revocation. The court further held that "[t]he requirement that a will must be destroyed in the 'testator's presence' must be strictly construed. This strict construction is necessary so as to prevent the inadvertent or more importantly the fraudulent destruction of a will contrary to the testator's intentions." ∎

---

Revocation can also be caused by operation of law. Marriage, divorce, or the birth of a child subsequent to making a will may affect its validity by revoking it completely or partially. State laws on wills are not uniform—the birth of a child may revoke a will completely in one state but only partially in another. Marriage and divorce also affect wills differently from state to state.

**Limitations:** There are a few limitations on a person's right to dispose of property through a will. For example, if a married person's will leaves no provision for inheritance by the spouse, many states allow the spouse to claim a share of the estate, typically one-third, under what is called a "forced share," "widow's share," or "elective share." If the spouse is left less than the statutory "forced share," the spouse has the right to renounce the actual devise and take the larger "forced share." In addition, many states provide the spouse a "homestead right" to a specific amount of land (for example, 1 acre in town or 160 acres in the country).

In community property states, each spouse owns one-half of the community property. In most of these states, the surviving spouse receives title to half the community property and the deceased spouse's share passes by will, if one exists, or by intestacy if no will exists. In no event can either spouse dispose of more than one-half the community property by will.

## *Holographic Wills*

Almost half the states allow testators to execute their own wills without formal attestation. These **holographic wills** must be entirely in the testator's own handwriting, including the signature. These wills differ from formal wills in that no attestation clause or witnesses are required. However, most states allowing holographic wills require that the testator's handwriting and signature be proved by two witnesses familiar with them during probate of the will. Competent witnesses would include persons who had received correspondence from the testator. A holographic will is purely statutory—that is, it must be made in accordance with the appropriate state's law and is subject to prescribed conditions and limitations. The principal requirement is that it be entirely in the testator's own handwriting. In *Estate of Thorn*, a testator in a holographic will used a rubber stamp to insert "Cragthorn" in the phrase "my country place Cragthorn." The will was held to be invalid since it was not entirely in the testator's handwriting.[3] In some jurisdictions the holographic will must be dated in the testator's handwriting. The requirements of testamentary capacity and intent are the same as those for formal wills, but a holographic will is otherwise informal and may even take the form of a letter if it conveys testamentary intent (the mental determination or intention of the testator that the document constitute the person's will).

## *Nuncupative Wills*

About half the states permit **nuncupative wills,** or *oral wills*. In general, statutes impose strict limitations on the disposal of property through a nuncupative will. Most states require that it be made during the testator's "last sickness"; that it be written down within a short period; that it be proved by two witnesses who were present at its making; and that the value of the estate bequeathed not exceed a certain amount, usually quite small. Some states also require that the decedent have been a soldier in the field or a sailor at sea in actual contemplation or fear of death.[4] Nuncupative wills, where recognized, usually effect distribution of personal property only, not real property.

Nuncupative wills are difficult to establish, and the restrictions placed on them are intended to discourage their use. There is always the possibility of mistake or fraud and, except on rare occasions, a testator can easily plan sufficiently ahead to use the more traditional and acceptable type of will.

## INTESTACY—STATUTES OF DESCENT AND DISTRIBUTION

State laws govern the disposition of a decedent's estate when the decedent has died without a will—intestate. Such laws are called statutes of descent and distribution. They provide for disposition of the decedent's property, both real and personal, in accordance with a prescribed statutory scheme. Real property descends; personal property is distributed. Consequently, the law of the state where the decedent's real estate is located will determine the heirs, by class, to whom it will descend. The decedent's personal property will be distributed in accordance with the law of the state in which he or she is domiciled. In addition to prescribing the persons who will inherit a decedent's property, statutes of descent and distribution also prescribe the order and proportions which they will take. The effect of this is that intestate decedents permit the state to select their heirs by default.

### *The Surviving Spouse*

Without exception, statutes of descent and distribution specify the portion of a decedent's estate that will be taken by his or her lawful, surviving spouse. Variation in this area is significant from state to state. Formerly, under common law, the surviving spouse was entitled only to a life estate (ownership for life) or *dower* (to the widow) or *curtesy* (to the widower) in the real property owned by the decedent. Personal property was divided among the surviving spouse and any children of the marriage. Today, the law of dower and curtesy has been either abolished or altered significantly by statute in all jurisdictions. Typically, if a husband or wife dies intestate, the stat-

---

[3] 183 Cal. 512, 192 P. 19 (1920).

[4] These are commonly known as soldiers' and sailors' wills.

utes provide that the surviving spouse takes one-half or one-third of the estate if there are children or grandchildren. If there are no children or grandchildren, in most jurisdictions the surviving spouse takes the entire estate. However, the states vary considerably in their treatment of this matter. In one jurisdiction, for example, children of the decedent take the real estate, to the exclusion of a surviving spouse, with the spouse taking one-third of the personal property. If there are no children or descendants of children the spouse takes the entire estate. In another, if there are children or representatives of deceased children, the surviving wife takes a child's share but not less than one-fifth of the estate.

In general, if there are children the surviving spouse must share the estate with them. The number of children or grandchildren will determine the share which is to pass to the surviving spouse. If there are no children or grandchildren, or none have survived the decedent, the surviving spouse takes everything.

As noted earlier, in a community property state, one-half of the community property is owned by the surviving spouse. The remaining half is subject to intestacy rules if no will exists.

## Descendants of the Decedent

There is little disparity in the statutes that govern the shares of an intestate's children or other lineal descendants (those in a direct line from the decedent—children and grandchildren). It is generally the case that, subject to the statutory share of a surviving spouse, children of the decedent share and share alike, with the children of a deceased child taking that child's share. This latter provision is known as a **per stirpes** distribution. For example, assume that a decedent dies after his spouse, leaving two children, a son and a daughter, who have two and three children of their own, respectively. If both son and daughter survive the decedent, each will take half the estate. However, if the son predeceases the decedent, his two children will take his share, each of them taking one-fourth of the estate with the daughter taking the other half. (If the decedent's spouse were still alive, the fractions described here would still apply, but only to that portion of the estate remaining after the spouse took her share.)

If the descendants are all of one class, that is, children or grandchildren, they will take **per capita**, each getting an equal share. Thus, if the intestate had a son and daughter who predeceased him, but those children left behind five living grandchildren, each grandchild would take one-fifth of what is left after the surviving spouse's share has been provided for. Figure 46.1 illustrates these differences.

Adopted children are generally treated the same as natural children; illegitimate children generally inherit only from their mother unless their father's paternity has been either acknowledged or established through legal proceedings.

## The Surviving Ascendants

There is general agreement that children of the decedent and subsequent generations of lineal descendants will take to the exclusion of other blood relatives such as parents or brothers and sisters. With regard to the ascendants of the intestate (parents and grandparents), there is much less uniformity in state law. In most states, where decedents leave no descendants, their parents will take the estate, with brothers and sisters (known as collaterals) taking if the parents are not living. In other jurisdictions, brothers and sisters share with the parents. Nephews and nieces may take the share of a predeceased parent if other brothers and sisters of the decedent are still living. If not, the nephews and nieces, as sole survivors, share and share alike in a *per capita* distribution. In any event, a distribution to ascendants and collaterals is made only if there are no surviving descendants or spouse.

Other than the surviving spouse, relatives by marriage have no claim on the decedent's estate. If the intestate has died leaving no heirs or next-of-kin whatsoever—no spouse, children, grandchildren, ascendants, or collaterals—the estate will pass to the state by a process known as **escheat**. This rarely happens, but it is provided for by law.

## ADMINISTRATION OF THE ESTATE

Administration of decedents' estates is accomplished by a proceeding in **probate** if they die leaving a will. The word derives from the Latin *probatio,* proof. In the law of wills it means the proof or establishment of a document as the valid last will and testament of the deceased. In most states, the court having jurisdiction is called the probate court, and the principal question to be decided by judicial determination is the validity or invalidity of the will. Once the will has

**Figure 46.1  Per Stirpes and Per Capita**

**Per Stirpes**

- Decedent — Predeceased spouse
  - Predeceased son
    - Grandchild A (takes 1/4)
    - Grandchild B (takes 1/4)
  - Predeceased daughter
    - Grandchild C (takes 1/6)
    - Grandchild D (takes 1/6)
    - Grandchild E (takes 1/6)

**Per Capita**

- Decedent — Predeceased spouse
  - Predeceased son
    - Grandchild A (takes 1/5)
    - Grandchild B (takes 1/5)
  - Predeceased daughter
    - Grandchild C (takes 1/5)
    - Grandchild D (takes 1/5)
    - Grandchild E (takes 1/5)

been admitted to probate—that is, determined to be valid—the probate court insures efficient distribution of the estate. Funeral expenses, debts to creditors and taxes are paid first. Then homestead rights and forced shares must be taken into account. Finally, the remaining assets are distributed impartially to heirs, devisees, legatees, and others, in accordance with the testator's wishes.

The *personal representative* of the decedent (called the executor if appointed by will and the administrator if appointed by the court) administers the estate under the supervision of the court—to collect decedent's assets, to pay or settle any lawful claims against the estate, and to distribute the remainder to those who will take under the will. If there is no will, the state's law of descent and distribution will determine how the estate is to be distributed.

Probate and the administration of decedents' estates are strictly regulated by statute and can be complex procedures when the estate is substantial and the interest in property of the deceased is not clear. Many parties may be affected by the administration process, so attention to detail and compliance with the state's probate law or code are essential. A personal representative who has effectively handled the estate and wound up its affairs may petition the court and be discharged from any further responsibilities.

## *Avoiding Administration*

Quite frequently, the formal administration of decedents' estates can be wholly or partially avoided. In fact, it is safe to say that fewer than half the deaths in this country result in administration proceedings.

Obviously, if the decedent died with no assets or a very small estate, there is no need for an involved administration. Most jurisdictions permit the handling of decedents' affairs without official administration in such cases.

There are, however, still other situations in which probate or formal administration can be avoided, at least for a portion of the decedent's assets. For example, if some or all of the property was co-owned with others as a "joint tenancy" with a right of survivorship, it passes to the surviving owners and not to the estate.[5] Joint tenancy bank accounts or securities or a residence owned as a joint tenancy or as a tenancy by the entirety all pass to the surviving owner. This method of owning property is sometimes referred to as the "poor man's will." It should be noted, however, that even though the decedent's interest in such property bypasses the estate, it can still be subject to an estate or inheritance tax.

If the decedent owned one or more life insurance policies, they will not be subject to administration if a beneficiary has been named. If one has not been named or if the one named has predeceased the decedent, the proceeds pass to the estate.

## TRUSTS

The trust is a versatile legal concept that is typically used to conserve family wealth from generation to generation, to provide for the support and education of children, and to minimize the tax burden on substantial estates. Trust law recognizes two types of property ownership, legal and equitable. One person can hold legal title to property while another can have the equitable title.

To establish a trust, the party intending to create a trust, called a **settlor** or *trustor*, transfers legal ownership of property to a *trustee* for the benefit of a third party, the **beneficiary.** The trustee is the legal owner of the property, called the *res* or *corpus,* but it is owned in trust to be used and managed solely for the benefit of others, who own the equitable title. A trust established and effective during the life of the settlor is known as an ***inter vivos*** or "living" **trust.** If it is created by the settlor's will, to be effective on that person's death, it is a **testamentary trust.** Trusts are also classified as *express, implied, private,* or *charitable,* depending on the purpose they serve and how they are created.

## *The Express Private Trust*

An express private trust is created when a settlor, with clear intent to do so, and observing certain formalities, sets up a fiduciary relationship involving a trustee, the beneficiaries, and management of the trust *res* for a lawful purpose. There is little uniformity in the statutes that govern trusts and their creation. It is a general requirement, however, that trusts be established by a writing or, if oral, subsequently proved by a writing. The writing need not be formal so long as it clearly identifies the trust property and the beneficiary and states the purpose for which the trust is created. The intent of the settlor to create a trust must be clear from the circumstances and the action taken. No particular language is required, but the settlor's instructions should be direct and unambiguous. If the purpose of the trust is to put children through college, this should be stated clearly. Language that "requests," or "hopes," or "desires" that the trustee do certain things is considered to be precatory in nature (a mere request and not an order or command) and may not be binding on the trustee. Further, words or phrases that fall short of appointing a trustee or imposing positive responsibilities should be avoided. For example, when a husband left his estate to his wife, stating in the will that it was his "request" that upon her death his wife "shall give my interest to each of my brothers," the language was viewed as purely **precatory.** The brothers had no legal right to object when the wife gave the land to her nephew instead.[6]

## *The Trust Property*

The subject matter of a trust may be any property of value. Money, interests in real estate, securities, and insurance are commonly used. However, settlors must own the property at the time they create the trust. They cannot transfer in trust property they expect to acquire and own at a later date. When the property is transferred to the trustee it becomes his or hers to manage for the benefit of the beneficiaries and in accordance with the terms of the trust. If the

---

[5] See Chapter 45 for a discussion of concurrent ownership and the right of survivorship.

[6] *Comford v. Cantrell,* 151 S.W.2d 1076 (Tenn. 1941).

essential elements of a valid trust are missing or if the trust fails, the property will revert to the settlor, if living, or to that person's estate, if deceased.

### The Trustee

A **trustee** is, of course, essential; a trust without one cannot be effective. However, the courts will not let an otherwise valid trust fail for want of a trustee. If the named trustee dies or declines to serve or is removed for cause, the court will appoint a replacement. The court will also appoint a trustee when the settlor fails to name one in the trust. No special qualifications are necessary. Since trustees take title to property and manage it, they must be capable of owning property. Minors and incompetents can own property, but they are under a disability in regard to contractual capacity. Consequently, since their contracts are voidable, they cannot function as trustees. Settlors can appoint themselves trustees and, in fact, designate themselves as beneficiaries. The settlor cannot, however, be the sole trustee and the sole beneficiary of a single trust. This relationship would merge both legal and equitable titles to the trust property in the trustee, and he or she would hold it free of any trust.

If a corporation (an artificial person) is not prohibited by its charter from doing so, it can act as a trustee. Trust companies and banks, for example, frequently serve as trustees for both large and small trusts. They typically charge fees amounting to 1 percent of the value of the *res* per year.

### Beneficiaries

The express private trust is ordinarily created for the benefit of identified, or identifiable, beneficiaries. A father can establish a trust for the care and education of his minor children—and can name them in the trust instrument. However, a settlor can also simply specify as the beneficiaries a class of persons, such as "my minor children" or "my brothers and sisters." In either case, the persons who are to benefit are readily identifiable. Trusts have also been held to be valid when established for domestic animals, household pets, and even inanimate objects. Such trusts present problems, since nonhuman and inanimate beneficiaries are incapable of holding title to property. Additionally, there will be no beneficiary with the capacity to enforce the provisions of the trust against the trustee. This is not to say that a charitable trust for animals in general or a trust for humane purposes will fail. (The charitable trust is discussed in a following section.)

The beneficiary does not have to agree to accept the benefits of the trust. It is presumed that beneficiaries accept the trust unless they make a specific rejection. Their interest in the trust can, in general, be reached by creditors, and they can sell or otherwise dispose of their interests. However, beneficiaries can transfer only the interests they hold—the equitable title. If a beneficiary holds more than a life estate, and the trust does not make other provisions, this interest can be disposed of in a will or can pass to the beneficiary's estate after death.

### Managing the Trust

The administration of a trust is highly regulated by statute. Trustees must know the law of their jurisdictions. In general, they must make every effort to carry out the purpose of the trust. They must act with care and prudence and use their best judgment, and at all times they must exercise an extraordinary degree of loyalty to the beneficiary—the degree of loyalty required of those in a fiduciary position.

In carrying out the purposes of a trust, the trustees ordinarily have broad powers that are usually described in the trust instrument. In addition, they may have implied powers that are necessary to carry out their express duties. For example, trustees can have express authority to invest the trust property and pay the beneficiary the income from such investments. They can also have the implied power to incur reasonable expenses in administering the trust.

Insofar as it is possible trustees should exercise the care and skill of a "prudent person" in managing the trust. A reasonable goal for a trustee is to exercise the diligence necessary to preserve the corpus and realize a reasonable return on income from "prudent" investments at the same time. State laws often specify the types of investments a trustee can make. In Georgia, for example, trust law authorizes investment in bonds or securities issued by the state and by the U.S. government and certain of its agencies and in certain banks or trust companies insured by the Federal Deposit Insurance Corporation. With certain exceptions, any other investment of trust funds must be under an order of the superior court or at the risk of the trustee. If the trust instrument gives the trustee wide discretion to invest in "other" securities, many jurisdictions allow this. Statutes often indicate that prudent persons should diversify their investments. However, the trustee can still be held accountable for a failure to exercise proper care. In other words, the law discourages bad investments.

The relationship between the trustee and the beneficiary is fiduciary in nature. Consequently, in managing trusts, trustees must act solely for the benefit of the beneficiaries. For example, trustees cannot borrow any portion of the trust funds or sell their own property to the trust. Neither can they purchase trust property for themselves. Even though the trustee's personal dealings with the trust may prove to be advantageous to the beneficiary, the duty of loyalty is breached and the trustee can be charged with such breach. If there are multiple trustees, an innocent trustee may well be held liable for not preventing a co-trustee's breach of fiduciary duty.

The duties of a trustee are highlighted in the following case.

### Witmer v. Blair
Missouri Court of Appeals,
588 S.W.2d 222 (1979)

At his death in 1960, Henry Nussbaum's will created a trust for the education of his grandchildren. Defendant Jane Ann Blair, Nussbaum's niece, was named trustee. Nussbaum's daughter, Dorothy Janice Witmer (defendant's cousin) was given a reversionary interest in the residue of the trust should none of the grandchildren survive to inherit the estate. Marguerite Janice Witmer (Dorothy's daughter) became the only beneficiary of the trust.

Defendant Blair received the trust estate in 1961. It consisted of $1,905 in checking and savings accounts, $5,700 in certificates of deposit, and a house valued at $6,000. The house was sold in 1962, netting $4,467 to the trust estate, which amount was deposited in a trust checking account. For the next several years, the trustee kept funds in checking and savings accounts and in certificates of deposit. As of December 31, 1975, the trust assets consisted of $2,741 checking account, $5,474 in savings, and $8,200 in certificates of deposit.

Marguerite was 23 years old at the time of trial. She had not attended college, but various sums of money had been expended from the trust for her benefit, including a typewriter, clothes, glasses, modeling school tuition and expenses, and a tonsillectomy, all totalling some $1,250. The trust also spent $350 for dentures for Dorothy.

Marguerite and Dorothy brought this suit against Blair for breach of trust for failure to properly invest the funds of the trust. The trial judge removed the trustee and surcharged her account for $309 in unexplained expenditures, but refused to assess actual or punitive damages for breach of trust. Plaintiffs appealed.

**Decision:** The appellate court reversed and ordered entry of judgment for plaintiffs in the sum of $2,840. A trustee has a duty to the beneficiary to use reasonable skill and care to make trust property productive, and is liable to the beneficiary for a breach of that duty. Trust funds should not be allowed to lie dormant; they should be invested carefully. Defendant handled this trust informally. She kept too much of the money in a checking account where it drew no interest. Had she kept only $800 (the maximum disbursement in any single year) in the checking account and invested the rest, the trust would have earned $9,138 more. The defendant's inexperience and good faith are not a defense to a breach of the duty of due care. ∎

## The Spendthrift Trust

Settlors may be concerned that beneficiaries may be incapable of managing their own affairs either because of inexperience and immaturity or simply because they are "spendthrifts." Settlors can therefore determine that beneficiaries will not sell, mortgage, or otherwise transfer their rights to receive principal and income and that the beneficiaries' creditors will not reach the income or principal while it is in the hands of the trustee. Such a provision no longer applies after the income or principal has been paid over to the beneficiary. Further, some modern statutes limit the **spendthrift trust.** They either limit the income that is protected from creditors or they permit creditors to reach amounts in excess of what the beneficiary is considered to need.

## Trust Termination

In most states, settlors can revoke a trust at any time if they have reserved that power. However, most trusts are terminated when the stated period has elapsed or when the trust purpose has been served. In a trust for the care of minor children, it logically ends when the beneficiaries have reached their majority. In a trust for the college education of the beneficiary, it will terminate when that goal has been attained. In any event, upon termination of a trust, any balance of funds remaining reverts to the settlor or is disposed of in accordance with the instructions contained in the trust.

## Charitable Trusts

The purpose of a charitable trust is the general benefit of humanity. Its beneficiaries can be education, science, religion, hospitals, homes for the aged or handicapped, and a host of other charitable or public entities. Charitable trusts are much like private trusts. Furthermore, the courts of most jurisdictions will find another suitable purpose for a charitable trust when the settlor's stated purpose is impossible or difficult to achieve. The courts do so under the doctrine of *cy pres,* meaning so near or as near. The doctrine is used to prevent a charitable trust from failing for want of a beneficiary. To illustrate: a testator establishes a testamentary trust for the support and maintenance of orphans in a specified orphanage. If the specified orphanage ceased to exist before the testator's death, the court could use the *cy pres* doctrine, find that the trustor's intent was to benefit orphans generally, and apply the trust to some other orphanage in the area. The *cy pres* doctrine applies only where there is definite charitable intent, never to private trusts.

## Implied Trusts

An implied trust, constructive or resulting, is created by law. While the distinction is not always clear, a **constructive trust** is usually imposed upon property by the courts to correct or rectify fraud or to prevent one party from being unjustly enriched at the expense of another. In reality, it is a fiction or remedy to which a court of equity will resort to prevent injustice. Suppose that A and B have agreed to purchase a tract of land jointly with the deed to list both of them as grantees. If, despite the agreement, A secretly buys the land alone, and the deed fails to list B as grantee, the court will impose a constructive trust on the property to the extent of the half interest B should have. This procedure assumes that B is ready and willing to pay half the purchase price. In another case, directors of corporations who take advantage of their positions to make secret profits from corporate opportunities will be constructive trustees for the corporations to the extent of the profits they make. Constructive trusts commonly arise out of the breach of a fiduciary relationship where no trust intent is present or required.

The **resulting trust** arises out of, or is created by, the conduct of the parties. It is imposed in order to carry out the apparent intentions of the parties at the time they entered into the transaction that gave rise to the trust. The most frequent use of the resulting trust occurs when one party purchases property but records the title in the name of another. For example, A wants to purchase a tract of real estate but does not want it subjected to the hazards of his business ventures. He therefore buys the land but has the deed made out in the name of a friend, B. There is no problem if B conveys the real estate to A on demand in accordance with their understanding of the nature of the transaction. However, if B refuses to convey the land, the courts can impose a resulting trust on B for A's benefit. Some difficulty can arise if, in the situation above, A has title taken in the name of his wife or a close relative, because it could be valid to presume that A intended the land as a gift. And if A had purchased in the name of another to defraud his creditors, it is likely that the courts would refuse to impose the resulting trust, being reluctant to afford relief to a wrongdoer.

## ESTATE PLANNING

"*Estate Planning* is applying the law of property, trusts, wills, future interests, insurance, and taxation to the ordering of one's affairs, keeping in mind the possibility of retirement and the certainty of death."[7] Wills and trusts are the most commonly used estate planning devices. This final section briefly explores other aspects of the estate planning process, touching first on the philosophy that has previously guided or misguided many in the disposition of their property—a disposition that usually occurs after death,

---

[7] R. J. Lynn, *An Introduction to Estate Planning* (St. Paul, Minn.: West Publishing, 1975), 1.

with dire results for the surviving heirs. The general public equates estate planning with death; lifetime planning is more important than death planning. The aim is not merely to dispose of one's estate at death but to organize resources during life in order to provide for the present and future well-being of one's family.

The major consideration in preserving estate integrity today is the impact taxes may have if little thought is given to methods for reducing estate shrinkage. In fact, it is quite likely for the decedent's survivors to find on settling the estate that the principal heir is the government. It is, of course, unlawful to evade taxes, but there is nothing illegal about doing everything possible to avoid paying unnecessary taxes. Various planning devices can keep unwanted heirs, in the form of estate and inheritance taxes, and the expense of probate and administration to a minimum.

## *Gifts*

One of the keys to cutting estate taxes is to give away some assets before death. The gifts shift income to children or perhaps retired parents who may be in lower tax brackets. Giving, as an estate planning device, may be hard to accept for the donor who has spent a lifetime slowly accumulating an estate. Nevertheless, it is something to consider, keeping in mind one's personal situation. Amateur philanthropy, however, can be dangerous. Property given outright to a poor manager can be wasted away; a gift with too many strings attached can be something less than useful to the donee. Gift taxes must also be considered. Under current tax law, each parent may transfer $10,000 each year to any recipient, including children, without any gift tax liability.

## *Life Insurance*

Life insurance, in its various forms, can serve many purposes in estate planning. Ownership can be so arranged that the proceeds will not become part of the insured's estate to be taxed. It is a good means of providing liquid funds so that forced sales of other property to pay estate charges or debts can be avoided. In general, life insurance is not subject to probate and administration expenses and is a good way to make *inter vivos* (during lifetime) gifts to children, to grandchildren, or, if the donor is so inclined, to charity. Many kinds of policies are available—term, whole life, and endowment, for example—and there may be a place for one or more types in an estate plan. For the average wage earner life insurance is the major, perhaps the only, means of providing security for the family. Indeed, it may be all that is necessary, other than a valid will. With regard to business ventures, the members of a partnership often enter into buy and sell agreements with a view to continuing the partnership after the death of a partner. The partnership agreement sometimes provides that the estates of deceased partners will sell their interests to surviving partners and that the partners will buy such interests. Insurance is frequently used by the partnership to fund the agreement.

## *The Marital Deduction*

For federal estate tax purposes the **marital deduction** is a useful device in estate planning involving substantial assets. It reflects the social concept that property accumulated during marriage should be treated as community property, disregarding the fact that differing amounts could have been contributed by the husband and wife. The marital deduction was designed to more nearly equate tax treatment between residents of states that have community property laws and those of states which do not. No matter what amount a decedent spouse passes to a surviving spouse, that amount will not be taxed in the decedent spouse's estate. This allows the surviving spouse to continue to have the use of up to all of the "community" assets for the rest of his or her life. The amount passing to the surviving spouse is included in his or her estate and will be taxed at the surviving spouse's death. The amount passing to the surviving spouse under the marital deduction must be determined through careful planning to maximize tax savings and meet the objectives of a particular family. Competent legal counsel and financial advice should be sought early in the estate planning process.

## SUMMARY

The inevitability of death makes proper estate planning a very wise idea. A basic method of distributing property upon death is through an instrument known as a will. A testator must have testamentary capacity, that is, the mental ability to understand the property owned and the persons to whom he or she would like to give it, and not be under the undue influence of any particular person. A formal will must meet several statutory requirements, including being signed in the presence of witnesses. Modifications and even revocations must similarly follow a proper statutory pattern; for example, a will burned at the direction of a testatrix may not be effectively revoked if the destruction does not take place in her presence.

Many states allow handwritten wills, and even oral wills may be effective in limited circumstances. Should no valid will exist, a decedent's possessions will pass to relatives under state laws of descent and distribution, which impose a standardized division of the property.

Use of a trust is another method of estate planning. The settlor of a trust places property in the control of a trustee who administers the property for the advantage of beneficiaries. There are several types of trusts, and tax laws have traditionally had a significant impact on their numbers and use. The trustee owes a fiduciary duty to the beneficiaries, and may be liable in damages for wrongful or negligent administration of the assets.

Intelligent estate planning frequently uses gifts and life insurance in addition to wills and, where appropriate, trusts.

## KEY TERMS

**Intestate**
**Testator**
**Testatrix**
**Decedent**
**Executor**
**Executrix**
**Administrator**
**Devise**
**Legacy**
**Bequest**
**Testamentary capacity**
**Attestation clause**
**Codicil**
**Holographic will**
**Nuncupative will**
***Per stirpes***
***Per capita***
**Escheat**
**Probate**
**Settlor**
**Beneficiary**
***Inter vivos* trust**
**Testamentary trust**
**Precatory**
**Trustee**
***Res***
**Spendthrift trust**
***Cy pres***
**Constructive trust**
**Resulting trust**
**Marital deduction**

## QUESTIONS AND PROBLEMS

**1.** Decedent, Matilda Manchester, prepared the following document, wholly in her own handwriting:

*I, Matilda Manchester, leave and bequeath all my estate and effects, after payment of legal, funeral and certain foreign shipment expenses (as directed) to the following legatees, viz.*

Then followed a statement of devises and bequests to divers persons. It ended as follows:

*Whereunto I hereby set my hand this fourteenth day of January, 1914.*

Decedent did not sign the document, her name appearing only in the opening clause as shown above. The paper was folded and sealed in an envelope which was endorsed by the decedent: "My Will, Ida Matilda Manchester." Should the document be admitted to probate as a valid holographic will? (*Estate of Manchester,* 163 P. 358, Cal. 1917.)

**2.** A father purchased 100 shares of stock for each of his two children, using money he had withdrawn from their savings accounts. The shares of stock were issued to the mother and registered in her name. When the mother died, a question arose as to ownership of the stock. What are the children's rights in this matter? (*Markert v. Bosley,* 207 N.E.2d 414, 1965.)

**3.** A state's law required that all formal wills must be "subscribed at the end thereof by the testator" and that attesting witnesses must "sign the instrument as a witness, at the end of the will." The will in question consisted of three pages. The first page was a printed form entitled "Last Will and Testament." Typed on the form were two testamentary provisions and the appointment of executors. On the same form, in the spaces provided, appeared the signature of the testatrix and an attestation clause signed by three witnesses. There were two additional typewritten pages containing testamentary clauses, each of the two pages being signed at the bottom by only the testatrix. The attesting witnesses had not signed the additional pages, their signatures appearing only on the first, "form" page. Does the document qualify as a will? (*Estate of Howell,* 324 P.2d 578, Cal. 1958.)

**4.** A testator wanted to revoke his will by having his wife burn it. In his presence she burned an envelope which she fraudulently represented to him to contain his will. (*Brazil v. Silva,* 185 P. 174, 1919.)

   **a.** If she was the sole legatee under his will, is she likely to take his estate?

   **b.** If the testator had two children, are they, in effect, disinherited?

**5.** A widow died intestate. There had been four children; but one, who had two children, predeceased his mother. How will the estate be divided among the widow's descendants?

**6.** Edward Muder died on March 15, 1984, leaving behind an unwitnessed "will form" that, in addition to the preprinted words, contained the following handwritten statement: "My wife Retha F. Muder, our home and property in Shumway, Navajo County, car-pick up, travel trailer, and all other earthly possessions belonging to me, livestock, cattle, sheep, etc. Tools, savings accounts, checking accounts, retirement benefits, etc." Retha submitted the will to probate as either a proper formal will, or as a valid holographic will. Should the will be admitted to probate? (*Matter of Estate of Muder,* 751 P.2d 986, Ariz. App. 1987.)

**7.** The will of Lauren M. Townsend, after a statement of several specific bequests, provided: ". . . that the remainder be made into a fund, the interest of which shall be used to help defray the expense of educating some girl or boy in music or art. I appoint Paul Gill to have charge of selecting the recipient of this last bequest." Is the quoted language sufficiently specific to create a charitable trust? (*Estate of Huebner,* 15 P.2d 758, Cal. 1932.)

**8.** Reed died on March 2, 1982, leaving behind a tape recording in a sealed envelope on which was handwritten "Robert Reed To be played in the event of my death only! (signed) Robert G. Reed." Buckley sought to have the tape recording admitted to probate as a holographic will. Should the tape be admitted? (*Matter of Estate of Reed,* 672 P.2d 829, Wyo. 1983.)

**9.** McGurrin signed his will when no one else was present. An intermediary then took the will to other persons who added their signatures to the document. The testator's only contact with these persons was by telephone after all signatures had been affixed. He thanked them for "witnessing" his will. Should this will be accepted in probate? (*Matter of Estate of McGurrin,* 743 P.2d 994, Idaho App. 1987.)

**10.** In 1960, Leonard Garver executed a will which created a trust. The trust instrument named the Baker Boyer National Bank (Bank) as trustee and included certain farmland. After Leonard's wife and son had enjoyed a life estate in the farmland, it was to be held in trust until Leonard's grandsons, Russell and Gregory (beneficiaries) reached the age of 25. After Leonard and his wife died, his son Richard, as executor of the estates, sold some of the land and invested the $194,000 proceeds in tax-free municipal bonds. For the next nine years the bank, as trustee, continued to invest the funds in tax-free municipal bonds at the recommendation of Richard's attorney and his broker. After a dispute between the bank as trustee and Russell and Gregory as beneficiaries, the portfolio of bonds was liquidated at a loss of $63,750. Russell and Gregory sued the bank for breach of its duty as trustee, claiming that the bank should have diversified the investment portfolio. Discuss the merits of this claim. (*Baker Boyer National Bank v. Garver,* 719 P.2d 583, Wash. App. 1986.)

# CHAPTER 47

# INSURANCE LAW

## NATURE AND FUNCTIONS OF INSURANCE

Almost every type of endeavor or venture, individual or business, involves risk or uncertainty concerning financial loss. Insurance is a means of transferring or shifting risk from the individual or business to a group whose members agree to share losses on some equitable basis. Suppose that a manufacturer produces and markets a line of products the use of which poses considerable risk, such as bicycles, swings and slides, and power lawnmowers. An injury or death caused by such products may result in a lawsuit and a substantial damages award to the injured user or, if the product has caused death, to his or her surviving family. Such awards may be in the millions of dollars, causing extreme economic hardship to an individual manufacturer. The design, manufacture, and marketing of a potentially dangerous product may pose a risk too great for a single business to assume.

Manufacturers can collectively share products liability losses by transferring the risk to a professional risk bearer, the insurer, through the purchase of an insurance contract. The group of manufacturers share the cost of losses as they occur so that no one of them will be forced to bear the entire cost of a substantial judgment awarded as the result of a products liability lawsuit.

The exact cost of insurance is established statistically based upon the loss costs and expenses of insurers writing the coverage involved. The premium paid by the insured is an expense of doing business.

This chapter examines briefly the general types of insurance, placing major emphasis on the coverages that are relevant for business: *life, health, property,* and *liability.* In addition, the concept of risk management is presented.

## *The Insurance Contract*

An insurance contract is often called a *policy*. The person or company purchasing insurance coverage is called the *insured,* or the *policyholder.* The company issuing the insurance policy is called the *insurer,* or the *insurance company.* To be an enforceable agreement, a contract of insurance must contain the essential elements of contract: *offer and acceptance, consideration, legal purpose, competent parties,* and *legal form.*

**Offer and Acceptance:** The offer is customarily made by the prospective insured when he or she makes application for the desired coverage. The acceptance occurs when the agent or broker issues a **binder** (a temporary contract) or when the policy itself is issued by the insurance company. A binder can be either written or oral and is used to bind the company immediately prior to the receipt of the application and issuance of the policy.

**Consideration:** The considerations exchanged in an insurance transaction are the payment of the **premium** by the insured or other responsible party (such as the parents of an insured minor), and the promise of the insurer to pay if the covered contingency occurs.

**Legal Purpose:** A contract made for an illegal purpose, or containing an illegal provision, is usually void and cannot be enforced by either party. This general principle is equally applicable to contracts of insurance. If the insurance company violates state law by failing to include a required provision that was intended to protect policyholders, however, the policyholder can still enforce the contract under a well-

735

established exception to the illegality doctrine. The most important application of the requirement of a legal purpose is the *insurable interest* rule, which is discussed separately in the following section.

**Insurable Interest:** A fundamental requirement of a legally valid insurance contract is that an insured must have an **insurable interest** in the subject matter of the insurance, that is, a benefit to be derived from the continued existence of the person or property insured. Without the existence of an insurable interest, the policyholder is simply wagering on the occurrence of death, in the case of life insurance, or property damage, in the case of property insurance. Because gambling contracts are void, an insurance policy issued to an insured not having an insurable interest is unenforceable. In addition to furthering the general prohibition against gambling agreements, the requirement of insurable interest also helps protect against murder or property destruction for the purpose of collecting insurance proceeds. The rationale for the insurable interest requirement in the life insurance context was expressed as follows by the court in *New England Mutual Life Insurance Co. v. Null*, 605 F.2d 421 (1979):

> It is contrary to sound public policy to permit one, having no interest in the continuance of the life of another, to speculate upon that other's life—and it should be added that to permit the same might tend to incite the crime of murder—and the rule is enforced, and the defense permitted, not in the interest of the defendant insurer, but solely for the sake of the law, and in the interest of a sound public policy.

The absence of an insurable interest causes the contract to be void, and no benefits are payable under the policy. In such a case the insured is entitled to a refund of premiums paid, however. Other legal consequences can also result from the issuance of a policy to someone without an insurable interest. For instance, if an insurance company issues a life insurance policy to someone who does not have an insurable interest, and the insured then murders the subject of the life insurance, the insurance company can be held liable for negligence to the estate of the murder victim. Similarly, if an insurance company issues a policy covering property to someone not having an insurable interest, and the insured then intentionally destroys the property, the insurance company can be held liable for negligence to the owner of the property.

***Insurable Interest Distinguished from Other Concepts:*** It is important to distinguish the insurable interest requirement from other related concepts. For example, life insurance policies normally contain a provision expressly excluding liability if the person whose life is insured commits suicide. This provision applies even if the person taking out the policy had an insurable interest. Also, courts do not permit a beneficiary named in a life insurance policy to recover under the policy if the beneficiary murders the person whose life is insured. Again, this rule applies even if the person taking out the insurance had an insurable interest in the life being insured, and the policy itself is valid. In such a case, since the policy is valid, the proceeds are payable either to a secondary beneficiary specified in the policy or to the estate of the deceased if there is no secondary beneficiary. Similarly, a person who intentionally damages or destroys property is not permitted to collect under an insurance policy covering the property, even if the insured had an insurable interest.

***Insurable Interest in Life:*** A person obviously may obtain a policy of insurance on his or her own life. If one person takes out life insurance on someone else's life, however, it is required that the policyholder have an insurable interest in the life of the person who is the subject of the insurance. In the case of life insurance, the insurable interest must exist at the time the policy is issued, but does not have to exist at the time of death. Thus, if a wife takes out life insurance on her husband, there is an insurable interest at the time the policy is issued; the policy remains valid even after divorce unless a specific provision calls for termination upon divorce.

As a general rule, an insurable interest exists when the policyholder and the person whose life is being insured have a relationship such that the policyholder will benefit from the continuance of the person's life or suffer financial loss from the person's death. State laws usually specify the types of relationships that create insurable interests, and these laws vary somewhat. In all states, husband and wife have an insurable interest in each other's life. In some states, other relationships within the immediate family, such as parent-child or brother-sister, also create an insurable interest. The relationship between a nephew or niece and an aunt or uncle usually does not create an insurable interest. Except for husband and wife, relationships through marriage do not create insurable interests. For example, a person does not have an insurable interest in the life of his or her mother-in-law.

An employer has an insurable interest in the life of a *key employee,* that is, an employee whose death would cause substantial hardship to the employer. An employee with significant managerial or supervisory responsibilities, or especially valuable knowledge or skills would, for example, be a key employee. In addition, an unsecured creditor usually has an insurable interest in the life of the debtor up to the amount of the indebtedness. The following case presents an illustration and discussion of the insurable interest requirement in life insurance.

---

### New York Life Insurance Co. v. Baum
U.S. Fifth Circuit Court of Appeals, 700 F.2d 928 (1983)

Baum and Cook made preliminary plans for the formation of a media advertising business in Louisiana. It was agreed that Baum would provide capital and Cook would furnish the experience necessary to launch the venture. Their understanding was that a corporation would be formed to carry on the business. Over the next several months, Baum lent Cook $16,500 for getting the business started. Shortly after Baum and Cook had made their agreement, however, Cook made a separate agreement with Cutler to form a partnership in Texas under the name of Media Sales. The Cook-Cutler partnership, also engaged in the media advertising business, was unknown to Baum.

After Baum had lent money to Cook, Baum decided to obtain "key man" life insurance coverage on Cook to protect Baum's investment, and a policy was purchased from New York Life Insurance Company. At first, Baum listed himself as the beneficiary; upon the insistence of the insurance company, however, the named beneficiary was changed to Media Sales & Marketing, Inc., the planned name of the corporation Baum and Cook were to form. The name of the prospective corporation was used because Baum was an agent of New York Life, and the insurance company would not permit one of its agents to be named as a beneficiary except in a policy issued on the life of one of the agent's family members. A few days after Baum obtained this policy, Cook and Cutler incorporated their business in Texas as Media Sales Corporation, and totally excluded Baum. Baum paid premiums on the life insurance policy until Cook died one year later. After Cook's death, Baum filed suit in federal district court asserting a claim to the life insurance proceeds because his money had provided the primary capital for the business and he was actually the intended beneficiary. Media Sales Corporation also asserted a claim because it claimed to be the same corporation as the one that was expressly named as beneficiary. (Presumably, Cutler was behind the assertion of a claim by Media Sales.)

The trial court held that neither Baum nor Media Sales Corporation had an insurable interest in Cook's life, and that the policy was completely void. Both parties appealed to the U.S. court of appeals.

**Decision:** The judgment for the defendant life insurance company was reversed. Baum did have an insurance interest in Cook's life because Baum was Cook's creditor. However, the court remanded the case to the trial court for resolution of several remaining issues, including whether it was possible under the facts for Media Sales (the Texas corporation) also to have an insurable interest and to have been intended as a beneficiary. Although a corporation normally has an insurable interest in the lives of its key employees, Media Sales (Texas) was nothing more than a nonfunctioning corporate shell, and the creation of a Texas corporation was apparently never contemplated by the parties. Despite remanding the case to the trial court for a decision as to whether the Texas corporation had an insurable interest and had been an intended beneficiary, the appeals court's directions to the lower court made it highly likely that Baum ultimately would receive all of the insurance proceeds. ■

---

*Insurable Interest in Property:* The underlying rationale for the requirement of an insurable interest in property is essentially the same as the requirement of an insurable interest in life: one should be permitted to obtain insurance coverage on property only if that person would suffer a financial loss as a result of damage to or destruction of the property. While an insurable interest in life must be present when the policy is issued, the rule is different for property. An insurable interest in property must exist at the time the loss occurs, and is not required to have existed when the policy was issued. An owner of property obviously has an insurable interest in it, but others also may have such an interest. Thus, the mortgagee has an insurable interest in the mortgaged real estate, and a secured creditor has an insurable interest in the specific item of personal property (such as an automobile) that serves as collateral to secure the debt. In cases in which a nonowner has an insurable interest in property, the owner continues to have such an interest as well. Both parties may obtain insurance coverage on the value of their respective interests in the property.

The next case provides a further example of one of the many types of situations in which a person may have an insurable interest in property.

---

**Motorists Mutual Insurance Co. v. Richmond**
Court of Appeals of Kentucky,
676 S.W.2d 478 (1984)

After 13 years of marriage and two children, Linda Richmond and Eddie Durham were divorced in 1977. The divorce decree called for their house to be sold within six months, but no sale ever took place. Instead, the couple attempted to reconcile their differences until March 1981 when Richmond and the two children moved out. During this four-year period between the divorce and Richmond's departure, the couple made extensive improvements in the house, including interior remodeling and the addition of exterior walkways and a porch. Each of them contributed equally to the labor and expense of the improvements. In February 1980, while they were still living together, Richmond executed a deed transferring her interest in the house and lot to Durham. In March 1980, Durham executed a second mortgage on the property to secure a loan of almost $5,000. In June 1981, three months after Richmond moved out, Durham died of chronic heart disease.

Richmond immediately moved back into the house with her two children and made it their residence. She assumed liability on the second mortgage and made the payments. In January 1982 Richmond took out a fire insurance policy on the home and its contents from Motorists Mutual Insurance Co. When making application for the insurance policy, Richmond was asked by the insurance company's agent whether there was a lien on the property. She replied that there was, and stated that the lien was in her name. Although this statement was technically in error because the mortgage was still in Durham's name, Richmond's reply was based on a good faith belief that her assumption of liability on the mortgage meant that the lien was in her name. Nothing was said about legal title to the property, but the agent checked a box on the application form indicating that Richmond was the sole owner of the property. In actuality, her two children owned legal title as the only heirs of Durham, who died without a will.

In October 1982 the property was totally destroyed by fire. In response to Richmond's claim under the policy, the insurance company paid her $11,740 for the value of the contents, but refused to pay anything for the value of the house on the grounds that she had no insurable interest in the real estate. Richmond, her two children, and her mortgagee, Farmers National Bank (which was entitled to a portion of the insurance proceeds to satisfy the mortgage), sued the insurance company to recover the policy amount for the house. The trial court held that she had an insurable interest, and awarded her and the mortgagee a judgment of $29,000. The insurance company appealed.

---

**Decision:** The judgment for the plaintiffs was affirmed. Although she had no legal title, Linda Richmond had an insurable interest because of (1) her position as legal guardian of her children, who owned legal title, and (2) her substantial investment in the house. Richmond, her children, and the mortgagee all had an insurable interest. ■

---

**Competent Parties:** As is the case with other contracts, the parties to an insurance contract must have contractual capacity. Certain persons (minors and mental incompetents, for example) lack capacity or are under a disability. Minors, defined by statute in most states as anyone under the age of eighteen, may disaffirm a contract. In the absence of a statute regulating insurance for minors, a minor could purchase insurance, pay premiums until nearly eighteen, and then disaffirm and demand the refund of premiums paid. However, most states have conferred capacity on minors to contract for annuities, endowments, life insurance, accident and health insurance, and other forms of insurance in which the minor has an insurable interest. The minor may cancel the policy, as may an adult, but he or she may not demand return of the premiums paid. The age at which a minor may contract for insurance varies from state to state.

**Legal Form:** The form and content of insurance contracts are highly regulated by state law. Certain standard provisions relating to the specific type of insurance must be included in the policy and are spelled out in detail by statute in most states. Consequently, the proper form of insurance contracts is prescribed by law.

An agreement as complex as an insurance policy obviously should be in writing. Some states require that all insurance contracts be in writing, but several states merely prohibit oral agreements for certain types of insurance. Even in those states that do not prohibit all oral insurance contracts, it is exceedingly rare for an insurance agreement to be oral because of its inherently complex nature.

## Other Aspects of the Insurance Contract

**Unilateral in Nature:** Most commercial contracts are *bilateral:* each of the parties makes a legally enforceable promise and each is therefore obligated to perform as promised. An insurance contract, however, is *unilateral.* Only one party, the insurer, makes an enforceable promise. After the insurance is in effect, the insured having paid the first premium, he or she is under no obligation to pay further premiums or to comply with other policy provisions. Payment must be made to continue the coverage, but only the insurer is legally required to perform.

**Contract of Adhesion:** Even though state laws prescribe the form and provisions of insurance contracts, the insurer prepares the contract, and it can be accepted or rejected by the other party, the insured. There is little negotiation as to terms; if the insured wishes to accept the contract it must be taken "as is" (this type of contract is called a **contract of adhesion**). Because the insurer prepares the contract, questions of construction or interpretation are construed most strictly against the insurer. Ambiguity in the wording of the contract is interpreted by the courts in favor of the insured.

**Aleatory in Nature:** The ultimate discharge of the parties to an insurance contract is governed by chance. The profit and loss involved usually depend upon an uncertain event or contingency; the values exchanged by the contracting parties will quite likely be unequal. For example, a motorist may pay automobile insurance premiums for years and never have reason to make a claim against the insurance company. In this case, the insured pays a substantial sum and the insurer pays nothing to that particular insured.

## TYPES OF INSURANCE

### Life Insurance

A contract of life insurance typically provides that the insurer will pay a specified sum of money—the face amount of the policy—upon the death of the insured if the premiums have been paid in accordance with the terms of the contract. There are basically three types of life insurance policies, *whole life, term insurance,* and *endowment insurance.*

**Whole Life:** The key characteristic of **whole life insurance** is that it provides protection for the whole of life (or to age 100, the end of the mortality table on which premiums are based). There are two primary types of whole life coverage: ordinary life and limited payment whole life. Under *ordinary life* contracts, premiums are payable for the entire lifetime of the insured or until he or she reaches age 100. Under *limited payment whole life* policies (examples are twenty payment, thirty payment, or paid-up at age sixty-five), premiums are payable until death or until the end of the predetermined premium paying period, whichever occurs first. Under both ordinary and limited payment whole life policies, payment of the specified sum of money is made upon the death of the insured to a named beneficiary or to the estate of the deceased. Payment to a named beneficiary may be a lump sum or periodic payments, as elected by the insured or the beneficiary. After the policy has been in effect for a specified number of years, the insured can discontinue paying premiums and receive a paid-up policy to the extent that his or her premiums have purchased such coverage.

During the life of the policy the insured has a right to borrow from the insurer an amount approximately equal to the cash surrender value of the policy. Should the insured die with all or part of such a loan unpaid the unpaid loan or balance would be deducted from the proceeds paid to the beneficiary.

**Term Insurance:** Term insurance is written for a specified period of time. It is relatively inexpensive but provides protection for death occurring only during the period of the policy. Term insurance can be written for any number of years. The insured may, in most cases, renew the policy for additional terms at increased premiums as age increases, and may have the option to convert the policy to some form of permanent insurance without a medical examination.

Because it is temporary protection, term insurance does not build cash values, nor may the insured borrow on the policy. Because of its low cost for younger ages, it is useful for those who cannot afford the higher cost of whole life. This might be the case for a young person with a family who wants to provide protection but is not yet in a position to purchase insurance as part of his or her estate plan.

**Endowment Insurance:** Endowment insurance provides that the insurer will pay the policy face amount to the insured when he or she reaches the end of the policy period (such as at age 65) or, should the insured die before the end of the period, to a designated beneficiary. Since maturity of the policy is ordinarily prior to the death of the insured, the cost of the endowment policy is substantially higher than that of whole life or term insurance.

**Universal Life:** Universal life insurance is a new form that combines some features of both whole life and term life. Payments are often called "contributions." One portion of each payment is a charge for term life coverage, and another portion is for the insurance company's overhead and profit. The remaining part of each payment goes into an account that earns interest at a variable rate that is set periodically by the company. The amount in this account is similar to the cash surrender value of whole life insurance.

**State Regulation of Life Insurance:** The states exercise extensive regulatory control over the insurance industry within their jurisdictions. State insurance laws require that certain provisions be included in each policy delivered or issued within the state. Examples of typical required provisions include:

1. *Grace period:* A period of not less than 30 days within which the payment of any premium after the first may be made without the policy lapsing.

2. *Incontestability:* After a policy has been in force for a period of two years from its date of issue, the policy shall become incontestable during the lifetime of the insured.

3. *Misstatement of age:* Where the age of the insured has been misstated, the benefit accruing under the policy shall be that which the premium would have purchased at the correct age.

## Health Insurance

Many types of health insurance are available both to individuals and to employees as a group under a company-sponsored health plan. Health insurance can be divided into two basic types, *income replacement* and *medical expense* insurance.

**Income Replacement:** Income replacement policies provide for the payment of a stated periodic sum in the event the insured becomes disabled through sickness or injury and is unable to work. Eligibility for benefits is usually based on the fact that the insured is so sick or severely injured that he or she is unable to pursue the usual line of work.

The benefit period purchased under income replacement policies can be either short-term or long-term. A period longer than two years is considered long-term; the majority of policies are short-term.

**Medical Expense:** Medical expense insurance pays the cost of medical care required as a result of injury or sickness. Included are payments for physicians, hospital, nursing, and medicines and medical supplies. The insured is reimbursed for medical expenses within certain limits; the payments may be made either to the facility providing the medical service or to the insured.

***The Health Maintenance Organization:*** A **health maintenance organization (HMO)** is a formal organization of physicians who provide medical care to their subscriber patients on an as-needed basis. HMOs provide benefits that are in many respects broader than those offered by other plans. For example, the typical HMO stresses prevention of sickness by offering preventive medical care. The Health Maintenance Organization Act of 1973 requires employers of more than 25 employees to offer enrollment in an HMO as an option to existing health care plans.

An HMO subscriber pays a fixed fee in exchange for all the medical care that may be required. In addition to the fee, the subscriber may pay a nominal fee, $1 or $2, for each visit to the facility, but the charge is the same regardless of the nature of the service or treatment rendered by the physician.

## Social Insurance

While the normal expectation is that individuals and families should be able to care for themselves, economic security is beyond the reach of part of society. The concept of **social insurance** involves the notion that a certain segment of society is unable to fully care for itself and is thus subject to the risk of existing without an adequate standard of living. Social insurance, as defined by the Committee on Social Insurance of the Commission on Insurance Terminology of the American Risk and Insurance Association, is a device for pooling risks by transfer to a governmental service organization.

Various governmental programs have been enacted into law to assure each member of society at least a minimum standard of living. These include far-reaching social insurance programs.

**Old-Age, Survivors', Disability, and Health Insurance:** Known as Social Security, old-age, survivors', disability, and health insurance is an extremely comprehensive social insurance program that affects almost every individual in the country. As enacted in 1935 and extensively amended over the years, it provides a measure of security for eligible workers and their families against the risks associated with old age and the loss of ability to provide for themselves (although the benefits were never intended to provide full financial support). Its chief features are *old-age benefits, survivors' benefits, disability benefits,* and *medicare benefits.* Many claims may be controversial with regard to eligibility. An administrative hearing is frequently required to resolve a disputed claim for benefits. To illustrate the scope of the problem, there are approximately 1,100 administrative law judges assigned to federal agencies to conduct administrative hearings. Of that number, about 700 are assigned to the Social Security Administration alone.

**Unemployment Compensation:** **Unemployment compensation** is intended for workers who have been laid off and are unable to find other work through no fault of their own. Individual states operate the system, with each state levying a tax on employers to finance benefits. Each state has its own rules for determining eligibility. Benefit amounts are usually based on a fraction of average wages during a recent period, subject to minimum and maximum amounts, and are paid for a prescribed period. (When the general level of unemployment reaches a certain level, benefits may be paid for an additional period, usually 13 weeks. One-half of the benefits paid during this extended period are financed by the federal government.)

**State Workers' Compensation Laws:** As discussed in Chapter 49, Employment Law, the basic thrust of **workers' compensation** legislation is to provide medical care expense, income replacement, and rehabilitation benefits to employees suffering from work-related injury or occupational disease. The costs of these benefits, or the premiums for insurance to pay them, are borne by the employer and reflected in the cost of producing the employer's product or service. Although most employment is covered by workers' compensation, many states exclude farm laborers, domestic servants, and casual employees because their work is often of a sporadic or multi-employer nature. Workers' compensation is a no-fault system. If the agency (or the court) decides that the injury was job-related, compensation is awarded regardless of whether the employer, employee, or anyone else was at fault in causing the injury.

## Property Insurance

*Property insurance* protects against financial loss because of damage to or destruction of the covered property. It is available in many forms and can be written to protect against a variety of perils. The basic kinds of coverage and a few of the important principles that apply are examined here.

**Standard Fire Policy:** Fire is the most common type of peril to which buildings and other structures are susceptible. Consequently, insurance coverage to protect against the risk of fire loss is the oldest, and still the most important, form of property insurance. A standard fire insurance policy was adopted by the state of New York in 1943 and has served as a model for standard fire policies in most states. Even though the standard fire policies in most states still retain the basic provisions of the New York Standard Fire Policy, much of the language has been changed by many states in recent years in an effort to make policies more easily understood by policyholders.

**Homeowner's Policy:** The **homeowner's policy** is a package agreement covering (1) damage to the dwelling, (2) damage to or loss of the policyholder's personal property located either on or off the premises, and (3) legal liability of the homeowner for injury to others. Each type of coverage is subject to dollar limitations specified in the policy. Because of its broad coverage, the homeowner's policy has become very popular in modern times.

The typical homeowner's policy covers damage to the home, its contents, and many other items of personal property caused by fire, lightning, wind, hail, vandalism, and other specified perils. Coverage against theft of items of personal property is also frequently included. The coverage for personal property normally excludes motor vehicles, farm equipment, and airplanes, as well as boats while they are in the water. Such items are the subject of separate insurance policies. In addition, coverage is often excluded or limited for several other types of personal property, such as money, securities, and jewelry unless additional coverage is obtained in return for a higher premium.

One of the most attractive features of the typical homeowner's policy is its provision of coverage on a **replacement cost basis.** In other words, subject to the policy's dollar limits, and sometimes subject to other restrictions, the insurance company pays the amount required to repair or replace the structure without deduction for depreciation or obsolescence.

**Interpretation of Fire Coverage:** Most property insurance policies cover fire losses only from so-called *hostile* fires, and do not cover losses from *friendly* fires. If a fire is characterized as hostile, covered losses include those from fire and smoke as well as from water or other efforts to save the property. A hostile fire is one that begins in a place that was not intended or escapes from its originally intended place; a friendly fire is one that is confined to the place where it should be. The lighted burner of a gas cooking stove is a friendly fire, as is the fire in a fireplace or a backyard incinerator, because these fires are confined to their intended places. Consequently, damage caused by smoke from the fireplace or incinerator is normally not covered by insurance. Similarly, the loss is not covered when someone accidently throws a ring or other valuable property into the incinerator. On the other hand, a fire started by an electrical short in the attic is a hostile fire, as is a fire started when furniture or clothing catches fire from a fireplace or heater. In addition, if the flame from a cooking stove flares up because of spilled or overheated grease and spreads to the kitchen window curtains, the fire has become a hostile one within the meaning of fire insurance coverage.

**Coinsurance Requirement:** Today, most property insurance policies include a **coinsurance clause.** The basic purpose of such a clause is to encourage policyholders to insure their property for an amount that is at least close to its full value. If a policyholder does not insure the property for an amount that is sufficiently close to its full replacement cost, the policyholder must bear a proportionate part of any loss from fire or other covered peril. The coinsurance requirement applies only to partial losses. Coinsurance clauses do not apply to cases of total destruction.

In most policies, the coinsurance clause requires that the amount of the coverage be at least 80 percent of the property's replacement cost. If the coverage amount is less than 80 percent, the insurance company pays a fraction of the replacement cost, the fraction derived by dividing the policy amount by the amount that would have satisfied the coinsurance clause. Suppose, for example, that Otto owns a home with a current replacement cost of $100,000. To satisfy the usual coinsurance clause, he must obtain and pay for insurance in an amount of at least $80,000. If he insures the home for $80,000 or more and it is damaged by fire or other covered peril, he will receive the replacement cost for the damage. Thus, if it will cost $15,000 to repair the damage, he will receive the full $15,000 (minus, of course, any deductible the parties have agreed upon and specified in the policy). If he insures the home for only $60,000, however, the insurance company will pay only $12,000 (again, minus any agreed deductible). This amount is calculated as follows: Otto's policy amount ($60,000) divided by the amount of coverage that would have been necessary to satisfy the coinsurance clause ($80,000) is 3/4. The $15,000 replacement cost multiplied by this fraction equals $12,000.

In times of inflation, it is particularly important for the policyholder to review the amount of coverage periodically and increase it as necessary to continue meeting the coinsurance requirement. Today, many insurance companies offer an *inflation guard endorsement,* an optional provision in homeowner's policies that periodically increases the coverage automatically by predetermined amounts.

**Pro rata Coverage:** An owner who obtains two or more policies from different insurance companies covering the same property could potentially profit by receiving more than the replacement cost. Today, most property insurance policies (as well as other types of insurance, such as health insurance) contain a **pro rata clause,** which specifies that each insurance company is responsible only for a proportionate share of the loss. Thus, if Ruth obtains two homeowner's policies on her house, one from X insurance company for $100,000 and the other from Y insurance company for $50,000, the prorata clauses in the policies would result in X being responsible for 2/3 and Y for 1/3 of any covered loss.

## Liability Insurance

**Liability insurance** provides protection against the risk of a legal action for damages that may be brought against the policyholder. Liability insurance may be written to meet a variety of needs.

Each year individuals and businesses are exposed to legal liability resulting in the payment of millions of dollars to compensate plaintiffs for injury to their persons or property. A homeowner may fail to remove ice from a sidewalk, and a caller falls and is injured. A bottle of cooking oil has been broken on the floor of a supermarket, and a patron is injured. A manufacturer produces and markets a consumer product that proves to be dangerously defective, and a user is injured. Lawsuits by injured parties against the property owner or manufacturer are being filed with increasing frequency as our society has become more consumer-protection oriented. And the judgments awarded by juries, both of actual damages, to compensate the plaintiff, and punitive damages, to punish the defendant, are sometimes staggering. The possibility that accidents will occur on residential or commercial premises presents another form of risk that can be transferred to an insurer. General liability exposure can be classified as *personal liability, business liability,* and *professional liability.*

**Personal Liability—Coverage by the Homeowner's Policy:** Personal liability coverage is an integral part of the homeowner's policy. In essence, it protects the policyholder against the financial risk of injuries or property damage to others. This coverage usually applies to damage caused to others by the unsafe condition of the policyholder's premises, or by the negligence of the policyholder. As in other types of insurance, the coverage limits are specified in the policy. A typical homeowner's policy might limit personal liability coverage, for example, to $100,000, with higher limits available upon payment of a higher premium.

Liability coverage in the homeowner's policy normally applies only to personal activities, not to business or professional activities. In addition, liability resulting from the operation of a motor vehicle or airplane usually is not covered. The risks associated with these excluded activities are the subject of separate insurance policies.

The basic thrust of liability coverage is to insure against the policyholder's *negligence* or carelessness. Consequently, most liability insurance provisions do not cover damage claims against the policyholder resulting from his or her *intentionally wrongful acts.* As is true of most other issues, the question whether someone has been harmed by the policyholder's negligence, or by his or her intentional conduct, is not always easy to resolve. In the following case, these principles are applied to a situation in which harm certainly was intended, but the policyholder made a mistake in his choice of a target.

---

**Peters v. Trousclair**
District Court of Appeal of Florida,
431 So.2d 296 (1983)

James Trousclair was a riverboat pilot whose occupation required extended absences from his wife and home. During one of those absences, Peters, Mrs. Trousclair's cousin, had been residing at Trousclair's home for several days. The record reflects that although Trousclair had extended the invitation, he had only met Peters on two prior occasions, was not familiar with him, and was unaware that Peters had begun residing in the home. In the meantime, one Humphreys, not at Trousclair's invitation, was also residing at the home, having become amorously involved with Mrs. Trousclair. On the occasion that led to this lawsuit, Trousclair returned home without forewarning to find his wife and the two men lounging in

*(continued)*

the living room in the early morning hours. In a fit of jealous rage, Trousclair burst into the room, grabbed Peters, whom he did not recognize, and repeatedly stabbed him, causing serious injury. He then pursued Humphreys.

Upon venting the remainder of his frustration on Humphreys, Trousclair suddenly realized that Peters was his wife's cousin and promptly took him to a hospital. Peters initiated a civil lawsuit alleging that Trousclair had committed the tort of either assault and battery or negligence, in the alternative. Trousclair held a homeowner's insurance policy with American Liberty Insurance Company that included personal liability coverage. His request that the company defend him was denied. Judgment was rendered for Peters against Trousclair for compensatory and punitive damages totalling $105,606.55. Peters then sought to have the court hold the insurance company responsible for this amount under the personal liability provision of Trousclair's policy. The trial court found no coverage because the insurance policy expressly excluded liability for intentional harm, and Peters appealed.

**Decision:** The judgment for the defendant insurance company was affirmed. The personal liability provisions of Trousclair's homeowner's policy expressly excluded liability for intentionally caused harm. Despite the fact that Trousclair was mistaken about the identity of Peters, Trousclair did intend to do harm. As this was a case of intentionally caused harm, the exclusion clause applies. ■

---

**Business Liability Coverage:** Businesses that need broad, all-risk coverage against the perils of doing business may obtain what is known as the comprehensive general liability form of insurance. This form covers a variety of risks and, with appropriate endorsements, can be tailored to fit specific business needs. The broad form comprehensive general liability endorsement adds coverage for a wide range of liability exposures that are otherwise excluded from the basic coverage. Included are such items as blanket contractual liability, personal injury and advertising injury, premises medical payments, host liquor liability (this covers the selling or serving of liquor at social events), and other coverages that a business may need but has overlooked.

There are special policies to cover storekeepers, the owners and operators of small shops, and so-called dram shop (bar or saloon) owners or operators. In some states owners of dram shops may be liable for injury or damage caused by their patrons to third parties. For example, a saloon keeper who permits a patron to overimbibe may be guilty of negligence and therefore liable for the injury or damage caused by the patron who, while driving, is involved in an auto accident.

**Products Liability Coverage:** Manufacturers of consumer and other products face special risks. In the Federal District Courts, there were over 10,000 products liability cases commenced between July 1, 1984, and June 30, 1985. This number, of course, does not include the many products liability suits filed in *state* courts. Products liability and the risks faced by the manufacturer whose product may injure a user are discussed in the risk management section of this chapter.

**Professional Malpractice Liability Coverage:** The term *malpractice* is often used to refer to negligence by a professional. The proliferation of lawsuits alleging malpractice against physicians and hospitals in recent years has generated a heavy demand for medical **malpractice insurance.** Moreover, the number and size of damage awards and settlements against insurance companies providing malpractice coverage have increased dramatically. As a result, premium rates for such insurance have skyrocketed.

While malpractice insurance is generally thought of as needed only by physicians and hospitals, others who render specialized services to the public also find themselves increasingly liable for malpractice. Attorneys, engineers, pharmacists, and architects, for example, have experienced greater exposure to damage claims and much higher liability insurance premiums in the last few years. Similarly, the demand and the premiums for liability insurance covering the activities of corporate managers have grown. Today, so-called "D & O" (directors and officers) insurance is frequently demanded by executives as part of their compensation packages, although it is becoming extremely expensive and much more difficult to obtain.

## *Automobile Insurance*

Ownership of an automobile poses risks that are too great for most individuals to assume on their own. Consequently, the automobile owner must transfer the risk to a professional risk bearer by purchasing automobile insurance of the various kinds and in the amounts of coverage that fit his or her needs. These needs may be dictated by statute.

**Types of Coverage:** The typical automobile insurance policy includes several types of coverage which are discussed below.

*Liability Coverage:* The liability coverage in the automobile policy protects the insured, the insured's family members, and certain others against loss that may arise as a result of legal liability when the insured's auto is involved in an accident and causes personal injury or property damage. The policy is written subject to limits and is expressed in terms such as $25/$50/$5. In this example, coverage is provided for up to $50,000 for all persons injured in a single accident, with a limit of $25,000 for any one individual; the $5 figure indicates that up to $5,000 will be paid for property damage resulting from a single accident. Larger amounts can be purchased and, as the limits are increased, the cost is proportionately greater.

Most states have enacted **financial responsibility laws** that, in effect, require a driver to have at least a specified amount of coverage or risk the imposition of some form of state sanction. State requirements vary, ranging from $5/$10/$1 to $25/$50/$10 (numbers expressed in thousands). And more than half the states have "compulsory" insurance laws requiring some form of state-approved security.

Under the automobile insurance policy the insurer is obligated to pay for injuries "arising out of the ownership, maintenance, or use" of the insured vehicle. In litigation involving the insurer's obligation to pay, the issue is frequently "use," that is, was there a causal relationship or connection between the injury and the use of the vehicle. Obviously, if the vehicle is being driven for some legitimate purpose it is being "used" and resulting injuries would be covered. But suppose that a plaintiff slips and falls while pushing an insured auto, with a dead battery, on an icy driveway. Did the injury from the fall arise out of the use of the vehicle? The court in *Union Mutual Fires Ins. Co. v. King,* 300 A.2d 335 (N.H. 1973), said yes and the insurer paid. The following case also confronts the "use" question.

---

### McNeill v. Maryland Insurance Guaranty Association
Court of Special Appeals of Maryland, 427 A.2d 1056 (1981)

When Charlie McNeill could not start his car, he asked his friend, Evelyn Watkins, to bring her car to where McNeill's was located so that he could use her car's battery to "jump start" his own. Watkins got a third person, Edwin Hill, to drive her car and keep it running during the operation. McNeill correctly attached the jumper cables to the battery posts of both cars while the engine of the Watkins car was running, and removed one or more of the caps from his battery to check its fluid level. (These caps were removable for the addition of water to the battery; at the time of these events, car batteries were not of the sealed, maintenance-free variety.) While Hill was operating Watkins's car, Hill lit a match, presumably to light a cigarette, and tossed it out the window. The match evidently landed close to the battery, and the flame caused McNeill's battery to explode. McNeill, who was standing beside and leaning over his battery, was seriously injured.

Watkins had an insurance policy covering her car, and it included provisions making the insurance company liable for any bodily injury or property damage to others that Watkins would be responsible for. These provisions expressly applied, however, only to such injuries or damages "arising out of the ownership, maintenance, or use" of Watkins's car. McNeill filed suit against the insurance company that had issued the policy on Watkins's car. Attorneys for both parties stipulated that the accident was caused by the negligence of Hill, acting as Watkins's agent, and that McNeill was not contributorily negligent. The trial court ruled that McNeill's injuries did not arise out of the ownership, maintenance, or use of Watkins's car, and held that the insurance company was not liable. McNeill appealed.

---

**Decision:** The judgment for the defendant insurance company was reversed. The injury did arise out of the ownership, maintenance, or use of Watkins's car, and the insurance company is liable. Where a dangerous situation causing injury is one which arises out of or has its source in the use or operation of the auto-

*(continued)*

mobile, the insurance company's chain of responsibility continues until broken by some event which has no relation to the use or operation of the car. In this case, the chain was not so broken. There was a causal relationship between the use of the Watkins vehicle to start McNeil's car and the explosion. Hill's negligent act of tossing the match after lighting a cigarette was not so unusual and remote as to be viewed as an unforeseeable act. ■

---

*Medical Payments Coverage:* The medical payments coverage provides that the insurer will pay reasonable expenses for necessary medical and funeral services rendered because of bodily injury or death caused by an accident and suffered by a person covered by the policy. Included would be any occupant of the insured's automobile. There are limitations on the medical payments, usually ranging from $500 to $5,000 per person per accident.

*Uninsured Motorist Coverage:* Another part of the automobile policy covers the driver and passengers in the event of bodily injury caused by a hit-and-run driver or by a negligent driver who is financially irresponsible (unable to pay). Under the coverage the insurer will pay up to a specified amount to compensate for the insured's being unable to collect from the negligent driver. Uninsured motorist coverage usually has the same limits as the bodily injury limits of the liability coverage.

Additionally, if an insured purchases increased uninsured motorist coverage he or she may also purchase *underinsured* motorist coverage. This endorsement to the policy covers the situation in which the other driver, at fault, has some insurance but the limits of his or her policy are less than those of the insured's uninsured motorist coverage.

*Physical Damage—Collision and Comprehensive Coverage:* Physical damage coverage protects the insured against the loss of or damage to his or her automobile. There are two basic forms, *collision* and *comprehensive* (other than collision). As the term implies, collision coverage protects the insured against the perils of upset of the covered automobile or its impact with some object. Many perils are not covered by the collision insurance. These include damage or loss caused by thrown or falling objects, explosion, windstorm, earthquake, hail, flood, vandalism, and glass breakage. For example, suppose that the insured's car is severely pitted by large hailstones or dented by a tree limb blown down in a storm. There has been impact, but the collision insurance would not cover the damage.

To protect against the perils not covered by collision insurance the insured can purchase comprehensive coverage. The items noted above as being excluded would thus be covered.

Both types of physical damage coverage are less costly if there is a deductible provision. That is, the insured agrees to pay for any damages that do not exceed the amount of the deductible, perhaps $100 or $200. If the insured with $200 deductible collision coverage suffers collision damage of $500, the insurer would pay $300 and the balance, $200, would be paid by the insured.

**Duties after an Accident or Loss:** An insured involved in an auto accident is under a contractual agreement to promptly notify his or her insurer of all the details of the accident together with the names and addresses of any injured persons and any witnesses. The policy further provides for the insured to cooperate fully with the insurance company in its conduct of an investigation, settlement, or defense of a claim or suit. In its handling of a claim or lawsuit, the insurer will settle, or defend the insured, as it deems appropriate and will pay all defense costs. However, the insurer's duty to settle or defend ends when the limits of its liability have been reached.

**Subrogation:** *Subrogation* may be defined as the substitution of one person in another's place, allowing the party substituted the same rights and claims as the party being substituted. The subrogation clause in the automobile policy provides:

A. If we make a payment under this policy and the person to or for whom payment was made has a right to recover damages from another we shall be subrogated to that right. That person shall do:

1. Whatever is necessary to enable us to exercise our rights; and

2. Nothing after loss to prejudice them.

To illustrate, suppose that the insured's car is totally demolished in an accident, the other driver being at fault. The insurance company would pay the insured in accordance with the terms of the policy. However, the insured has the right to proceed against the negligent driver but, having been paid by his or her own insurance company, relinquishes that right to the company. The insurer may now proceed against the negligent driver to recover the amount it had paid the insured. In other words, the insurer is subrogated to the rights of the insured.

**Cancellation of the Automobile Policy:** By state law, after the insured has had the policy for a specified number of days, from 30 to 90 depending upon the state, it may be terminated by the insurer only for certain reasons. Typical of these reasons are:

1. Nonpayment of required premiums.
2. Material misrepresentations by the insured in the policy application.
3. Making of a fraudulent claim by the insured.
4. Suspension or revocation of the insured's driver's license.
5. The insured's addiction to drugs.
6. The insured or other customary operator has been convicted or forfeited bail during the 36 months preceding cancellation for any felony, criminal negligence while operating a motor vehicle, driving under the influence, leaving the scene of an accident, theft of a motor vehicle, or making false statements in an application for a driver's license.

**No-Fault Insurance:** Under traditional tort law a party who drives negligently and causes personal injury or property damage may be held liable and forced to pay damages. Traditionally, it must be determined which insured is at fault with his or her insurer then paying the damages. Under certain states' *no-fault* systems the determination of fault is unnecessary; each insured collects for injuries and damages from his or her own insurer. Both negligent and nonnegligent parties are covered.

A strict **no-fault insurance** system would do away with tort actions for bodily injuries caused by automobile accidents. There would be no recovery for damages other than bodily injury, and recovery for "pain and suffering" would not be allowed. However, in most of the 23 states having no-fault laws, modification of the pure no-fault concept permits tort suits subject to specific restrictions and limitations on the right to sue. There is considerable variation from state to state, with no state having a pure no-fault law.

Since the first no-fault insurance law, enacted by Massachusetts in 1970, considerable dissatisfaction with the concept has been expressed by those with a vested interest in automobile insurance. American trial lawyers and certain segments of the insurance industry have voiced objections on grounds ranging from unconstitutionality to claims that under no-fault the allocation of the costs of accidents will be unfair and incentives for careful driving will be reduced.

On the other hand, proponents of the system argue that the long-run effect will be to cut costs and reduce premiums for motorists. Whether or not this will happen remains to be seen. The many factors to be taken into account in determining costs in those states having no-fault systems have made it difficult to ascertain how much is being saved if indeed lower premiums are being realized.

***Proposals for Federal No-Fault Legislation:*** Because there is little or no uniformity among the states in their approach to no-fault laws, many proponents of the concept feel that federal regulation is a necessity. Several no-fault proposals have been introduced in Congress but none have been received with much enthusiasm. They have been opposed by a large segment of the insurance industry, the American Bar Association, and the American Trial Lawyers Association. Consequently, passage of a federal no-fault bill, at least for the immediate future, seems a remote possibility. A more likely solution may be federal legislation that prescribes standards for the states to follow in developing their own no-fault laws. There has been some movement in this direction.

## SUMMARY

An insurance contract, or policy, must possess the same essential elements as other contracts. The person purchasing the insurance makes an offer by submitting the application; the offer is accepted either by the agent's issuance of a binder or the insurance company's issuance of the policy itself. One of the most important elements in the case of insurance is that the insured, or policyholder, must possess an insurable interest in the subject matter of the policy. Insurance issued to one without an insurable interest amounts to an illegal gambling contract, and is void. The policyholder also must be of sufficient age, and most insurance contracts are required by state law to be in writing.

Insurance contracts are usually contracts of adhesion and are therefore construed in the insured's favor when an ambiguity arises. They also are unilateral and aleatory in nature.

The major types of insurance are life, health, social, property, liability, and automobile. Several subcategories exist within each type, and many aspects of the different types are overlapping. Homeowner's insurance, for example, includes both property and liability coverage. Automobile insurance is a specialized type of property and liability insurance. The typical property insurance policy includes a coinsurance clause that encourages the owner to insure his or her property for at least close to its full value by requiring the owner to bear a proportionate part of any loss if coverage is not maintained for a specified percentage of the property's replacement cost. Most types of liability insurance cover the policyholder's liability only for negligence, and not for intentionally wrongful acts.

## KEY TERMS

**Binder**
**Premium**
**Insurable interest**
**Contract of adhesion**
**Whole life insurance**
**Term insurance**
**Endowment insurance**
**Health maintenance organization (HMO)**
**Social insurance**
**Unemployment compensation**
**Workers' compensation**
**Homeowner's policy**
**Replacement cost basis**
**Coinsurance clause**
**Pro rata clause**
**Liability insurance**
**Malpractice insurance**
**Financial responsibility laws**
**No-fault insurance**

## QUESTIONS AND PROBLEMS

1. Kludt and his family live on a farm that is entirely owned by his wife. The deed to the farm names only his wife as the owner. However Kludt operates the farm and applies any profit he makes to improvements and the support of himself and his family. He has insured the property naming himself as the insured. When the farm was damaged by fire the insurance company refused to pay Kludt's claim, alleging that the policy was void because Kludt has no insurable interest in the property. Is the insurer correct? (*Kludt v. German Mutual Fire Ins. Co.*, 140 N.W. 321, Wis. 1913.)

2. John Smith and Jane Doe have been close to each other since childhood and made plans to marry in June 1984. With this in mind, and to take advantage of the lower premiums for younger persons, in February 1984 Jane purchased a policy of life insurance on John naming herself as beneficiary. Should John die after they are married will Jane be paid the proceeds of the policy?

3. The X, Y, Z partnership has been in business for twenty years and has been profitable. It is estimated that each partner's interest in the firm amounts to approximately $120,000. Partner X died suddenly, and his surviving spouse wants to be paid her deceased husband's share of partnership assets as soon as the amount has been determined. What problems might this pose for the surviving partners if they want to continue the business? How could these problems have been avoided?

4. Plaintiff was the insured under an accidental death and dismemberment policy that provided full coverage for, among other things, the "total and irrecoverable loss of entire sight of an eye." After a cataract operation on his right eye the plaintiff was fitted with a contact lens that permitted him very limited vision in the eye. However, he could not tolerate the contact lens and without it the eye was practically sightless with no medical assurance that it would ever be any better. When the insurer denied coverage plaintiff filed an action against it claiming the total and irrecoverable loss of entire sight of an eye. A major issue in the case was the meaning of the phrase "irrecoverable loss of sight." In deciding this case what rule of construction will the court apply? (*Roy v. Allstate Ins. Co.*, 383 A.2d 637, Conn. 1978.)

5. A bakery oven was badly damaged in the amount of $2,160 when its thermostatic control failed and caused it to overheat to 650° and become red hot on the outside. This charred the wooden floor, which was damaged to the extent of $800. On what grounds might the insurer attempt to deny coverage? Will it be successful? (*L. L. Freeberg Pie Co. v. St. Paul Mut. Ins. Co.*, 100 N.W.2d 753, Minn. 1960.)

6. A home has a market value of $80,000. To replace the home in the event of total destruction would cost $120,000. The owner has a homeowner's policy with $90,000 of coverage. If a fire damages the house in the amount of $20,000, at replacement cost, how much will the insurer pay?

7. A woman operates a beauty salon in a building she owns that in 1980 was valued at $85,000. She has a policy

of fire insurance for $85,000 with a 90 percent coinsurance clause. In 1982 a hair dryer overheated and resulted in a fire that caused $25,000 in damages. After the fire it was determined that the building, in its pre-fire state, was worth $130,000. How much will the owner collect from her insurer?

8. The phrase "arising out of the . . . use" of the insured automobile frequently raises questions as to the kinds of things that constitute "use" so that the injured insured, or others, are covered by the insured's policy. A truckdriver, while fueling the truck for a trip, is injured when the fuel tank explodes. The driver was not in the truck at the time of the explosion. Did this accident result from "use" of the truck so that there was coverage? (*Red Ball Motor Freight, Inc. v. Employers Mut. Liab. Ins. Co.*, 189 F.2d 374, 1951.)

# PART VII

# Government Regulation of Business

Today, for better or for worse, the major business activities that are carried on in this country are subject to a substantial amount of federal and state regulation. This fact of life was mentioned in Chapter 6 (Lawmaking by Administrative Agencies), because much of the regulation is, in fact, carried on by government boards and commissions.

In that chapter, however, our primary mission was to see how administrative agencies—whether regulatory or not—actually "make law." We did not attempt to cover the entire subject of government regulation itself. In these final chapters we will make several excursions into this highly complex area of law. It is important to note, also, that several state and federal regulatory laws have been examined elsewhere in the text. For example, in Chapter 22, Warranties and Products Liability, the Magnusson-Moss and Consumer Product Safety Acts are discussed along with other aspects of products liability law. In Chapter 41, we examined the federal and state laws that regulate the issuance and trading of stocks, bonds, and other securities.

The subject of government regulation of business is so broad, far-reaching, and varied that a balanced treatment of it, in any degree of depth, would require a work of several volumes. Obviously, that is not our purpose here.

Instead, our goals will be more modest. In Chapter 48, we provide an overview of the federal antitrust laws, which are aimed at promoting competition in American markets. Then, in Chapter 49, we focus on a variety of federal and state laws that regulate the employment relationship. Chapter 50 is devoted to a survey of federal and state regulatory provisions aimed at protecting the consumer. Finally, Chapter 51 surveys some of the regulations imposed by the United States and other nations on international business transactions.

# CHAPTER 48
# ANTITRUST LAW

## INTRODUCTION

### The Objectives of Antitrust Law

An economy such as that of the United States, which depends primarily on the operation of market forces, cannot function properly without competition. Although the word "competition" is subject to various shades of meaning, it most often refers to a condition of economic rivalry among firms. That is, firms should be engaged in a contest for customers, the outcome of that contest depending on each firm's ability to satisfy customer wants.

The primary purpose of antitrust law is to promote competition. In the various types of markets, competition can take somewhat different forms. In the case of many kinds of products, for example, price is a very important factor in customers' buying decisions (that is, "price elasticity" is high), and much of the competitive rivalry among sellers may focus on price. On the other hand, in some markets price may not be quite as important to most customers as good service, availability of many product options, convenience, or other factors. In such markets, competition among sellers is likely to emphasize these nonprice attributes to a greater extent. Not only does the form of competition vary somewhat among markets, but the intensity of competition also is less in some markets than in others. The job of antitrust law is to encourage competition in its various forms and to preserve it to the extent feasible in a given market.

Most economists feel that a competitive, market-based economy produces a number of beneficial results such as efficient allocation of scarce resources, lower prices, higher quality, greater innovation, and economic freedom. In the view of some authorities, there is another reason for having a strong antitrust policy in the United States—more competition in an economic sense may diminish the amount of power that large firms have over the political process and over the lives of large numbers of people.

Has antitrust law achieved its goals? This question cannot be answered with certainty because it is practically impossible to measure the effects of antitrust law on the American economy. There are many markets (so-called **oligopolies**) in which most of the sales are made by a few large companies. Many of these firms are very efficient; some are not. Many do not abuse their power; some do. In some of these markets, competition appears to be quite vigorous, but in others it is rather stagnant. Moreover, in many of these markets concentration of power in a few firms is an inevitable result of extremely large capital requirements and economies of scale. On the other hand, the *degree* of economic concentration is clearly not always inevitable.

Thus, it is not surprising to find substantial disagreement among authorities concerning the wisdom and effect of antitrust law. Some say the law has not been enforced aggressively enough, while others say that it has been applied too aggressively to the wrong things. Many points of criticism and support have been raised over the years. Only two conclusions are relatively certain: (1) although the interpretation of some of the antitrust rules will vary over time, the fundamental principles are probably going to remain with us; and (2) antitrust law will always be controversial. With that, we will examine the law itself.

### The Federal Antitrust Statutes

The first, and still the most important, of the federal antitrust laws is the Sherman Act, passed by Congress in 1890. Section 1 of this Act prohibits "contracts, combinations, and conspiracies in restraint of trade."

The focus of Section 1 is collusion among firms that are supposed to be acting independently when making basic business decisions. Section 2 prohibits "monopolization, attempts to monopolize, and conspiracies to monopolize." The prohibition of monopolization, which is the most important part of Section 2, focuses on single-firm domination of a market.

In 1914, Congress enacted the Clayton Act with two main purposes in mind: (1) to make the prohibitions against certain anticompetitive practices more specific, and (2) to make it easier to challenge certain practices, such as mergers, when the evidence shows only probable future anticompetitive effects and not actual present effects. Section 2 of the Act prohibits price discrimination; Section 3 prohibits some tying and exclusive dealing agreements; and Section 7 forbids anticompetitive mergers. In any of these cases, the law is violated only if the evidence demonstrates an actual or highly probable anticompetitive effect of a substantial nature. Section 8 of the Clayton Act prohibits *interlocking directorates* between certain large corporations that are in direct competition with each other. An interlocking directorate occurs when the same individual serves on the boards of directors of two corporations.

Also in 1914, Congress passed the Federal Trade Commission Act (FTC Act). In addition to creating the Federal Trade Commission (FTC) as an enforcement agency, the Act also prohibited "unfair methods of competition" in Section 5. Any conduct that violates one of the other antitrust laws, plus a few other types of conduct, constitutes an unfair method of competition. In 1938, Congress added another phrase to Section 5 prohibiting "unfair or deceptive acts or practices." Thus the first part of the statute deals with antitrust matters, and the second part deals with various forms of consumer deception such as false advertising.

In 1936 Congress passed the Robinson-Patman Act, which amended Section 2 of the Clayton Act in an effort to make the law against price discrimination more effective.

Even though antitrust law is based on statutory enactments, most of the language in those statutes is so broad that court interpretations account for most of the lawmaking process. Also, our attention in this chapter is focused only on *federal* antitrust law. Most states have their own antitrust laws, which usually apply to the same basic practices that are forbidden by federal law.

## Coverage and Exemptions

**Coverage:** Like many other federal statutes that are based on the Commerce Clause of the U.S. Constitution, the federal antitrust laws apply to business activities that either directly involve or substantially affect interstate commerce. Business activities occurring in foreign commerce, such as imports and exports, are also covered by U.S. antitrust law if there is a substantial effect on an American market.

**Exemptions:** The actions of the federal government are exempt from the antitrust laws, as are most actions of state governments so long as they are acting pursuant to legitimate and clearly expressed state regulatory interests. In this regard, actions of cities and other local governments are treated as state action if the local government is essentially just carrying out some aspect of state regulatory policy. Actions by foreign governments also are not within the scope of the antitrust laws.

If particular activities of a firm are subject to special regulation by a federal agency, such as the Securities Exchange Commission or the Commodity Futures Trading Commission, any possible anticompetitive consequences of those activities will usually not be scrutinized under the antitrust laws if the responsible agency has approved the activities after carefully considering the impact on competition.

In addition, the formation and ordinary activities (collective bargaining and strikes, for instance) of labor unions are exempt. Similarly, the actions of firms are exempt to the extent that they form a legitimate part of the union-company collective bargaining agreement and do not affect parties outside the union-company relationship. Finally, the joint activities of two kinds of selling cooperatives are exempt from the antitrust laws: (1) those formed by agricultural or livestock producers, and (2) export groups, so long as the limitation on export competition among members of the group does not adversely affect a domestic U.S. market.

## Enforcement

Enforcement of the federal antitrust laws can take one or more of several different forms. The Antitrust Division of the U.S. Department of Justice, which operates under the attorney general as part of the executive branch, can institute civil lawsuits and criminal prosecutions in federal district court. In a civil suit, if the Justice Department proves a violation of the Sherman, Clayton, or Robinson-Patman Acts, the remedy it normally obtains from the court is an injunction. The injunction will order the cessation of particular illegal actions, and may even require substantial modification of a firm's everyday business practices so as to lessen the likelihood of future violations. Many times the terms of an injunction are the result of an agreed settlement between the Justice Department and the defendant. In such cases, the injunction issued by the court after approving the terms of the settlement is called a *consent decree*. A firm or individual violating the terms of an injunction will be held in contempt of court.

If the case falls under the Sherman Act and involves a flagrant violation, such as blatant price fixing among competitors, the Justice Department may file a criminal prosecution in federal court. Upon conviction (which is a felony), the maximum penalty in a criminal case is a $1 million fine for corporations, and a $100,000 fine and three years' imprisonment for individuals.

The FTC also has authority to enforce the Clayton, Robinson-Patman, and FTC Acts. Even though it technically has no power to enforce the Sherman Act, any conduct that would violate the Sherman Act will also constitute an "unfair method of competition" under Section 5 of the FTC Act. FTC enforcement, which is civil in nature, consists of a hearing before an administrative law judge of the agency, with subsequent review by the five-member FTC. If a violation is found, the FTC will issue a "cease and desist order," which is essentially the same as an injunction. Violation of an FTC order is punishable by a penalty of up to $10,000 for each day of noncompliance.

A private party can file a civil lawsuit in federal court claiming a violation of the Sherman, Clayton, or Robinson-Patman Acts. The plaintiff sometimes can obtain an injunction in such a suit, but the remedy normally sought is *treble damages*. This means that if the plaintiff proves it was damaged by the defendant's violation, the law automatically multiplies the plaintiff's money damages by three.

In the following pages, we look first at that portion of the law concerned primarily with industry structure, namely the law of *monopolization* and *mergers*. We then turn to the antitrust laws that focus on particular kinds of conduct in our discussion of *horizontal restraints of trade*, *vertical restraints of trade*, and *price discrimination*.

# MONOPOLIZATION

In trying to formulate a working definition of **monopoly** under Section 2 of the Sherman Act, as a practical matter the courts could not simply adopt the classical economic model of monopoly: one seller, very high entry barriers to the market, and no close substitutes for the product. Instead, they defined a monopoly in more pragmatic terms as "a firm having such an overwhelming degree of market power that it is able to control prices or exclude competition."

The center of this definition is *market power*. Essentially, market power is the ability of a firm to behave differently than it could behave in a perfectly competitive market. Stated differently, market power is the ability to exercise some degree of control over the price of its product, that is, to raise its price without losing most of its customers. In virtually every market, there will be firms with *some* control over the price they charge, although the degree of control varies greatly from case to case.

The concept of market power is critical to any examination of competition under the antitrust laws, because competition usually cannot be harmed unless one firm, or a group of firms acting together, possesses some degree of market power. With respect to other issues in antitrust law, degrees of market power that are less than monopolistic can be very important. However, in deciding whether there is a monopoly under Section 2 of the Sherman Act, courts look for an *overwhelming* degree of market power. This exists when one firm dominates a market to such an extent that it does not have to worry much about the response of competitors.

## *Measuring Market Power*

Traditionally, the enforcement agencies and courts have looked primarily at the *structure* of a market when trying to draw inferences about degrees of market power. The most important structural factor is usually the firm's **market share.** In other words, what percentage share of the relevant market does the firm have? The courts have not developed hard and fast rules as to what market share definitely does or does not demonstrate overwhelming market power. However, the cases indicate that a market share of less than 50 percent will never be enough, and a share of 75 percent will frequently (but not always) be enough. Although other indicators of market power are always important, they become critical when the share is below or above this range.

Other structural factors include the following:

1. The *relative size of other firms* in the market can be important. If M has, say, 60 percent of the market, M generally will have less market power if there are at least one or two other very large firms with perhaps 20 or 30 percent shares than if the remainder of the market is occupied by a large number of very small firms. The reason is that if the other firms are themselves quite large, even though smaller than M, they are more likely to have economies of scale and costs similar to M. Thus, although oligopoly may not be the most desirable market structure, it is usually much better than monopoly.

2. The *size and power of customers* is also relevant, because the existence of large, powerful buyers can put a damper on the market power of a potentially monopolistic seller.

3. The market's **entry barriers** are quite important. Entry barriers are conditions that make entry into the market by a new competitor significantly more costly and risky. If a market has low entry barriers, and a powerful firm in the market earns very high returns by using its power to charge high prices, the high returns will attract new competition to the market that will diminish the dominant firm's power. High entry barriers, on the other hand, provide substantial insulation for the powerful firm so that it can fully exploit its market power. Examples of entry barriers include excess production capacity in the market, higher costs of capital for potential competitors than for the dominant firm, strong customer preferences for brands produced by the dominant firm, important technology or know-how that is protected by patents or by trade secret law, complex distribution channels, and so forth. Entry barriers are not necessarily good or bad; they are just conditions that may be relevant. It also should be noted that some entry barriers are inevitable, whereas some can be intentionally erected by a dominant firm. Although the importance of entry barriers has long been recognized, in recent years some authorities have come to view them as even more important to the question of market power than the internal composition of the market.

4. In addition to market share and other structural factors, the *dynamics* of the market can also be relevant to the question of how much power a firm has. For instance, if the market is characterized by rapidly developing technology, or if total market demand is expanding rapidly, it will be much harder for a firm to hold on to its dominant position for very long.

## Defining the Relevant Market

Before seeking to determine whether a firm has overwhelming power, it is necessary to define the relevant market. Essentially, the process of market definition involves an attempt to identify a category of business transactions that accurately reflects the operation of competitive forces. A market can be thought of as the context within which competitive forces can be measured with reasonable accuracy. Any market must be defined in terms of two elements: (1) a particular product or service, or some grouping of products or services, and (2) a geographic area.

**Product Market:** Suppose that M Company is charged with monopolizing the market for the sale of zippers in the United States. Most of M's zippers are sold to clothing manufacturers, but some are sold to fabric stores and other retail outlets for resale to consumers. M produces 90 percent of the zippers sold in the United States. If "zippers" is the proper market definition, M's market share almost certainly demonstrates overwhelming market power. M argues, however, that zippers actually face stiff competition from buttons, snaps, hooks, and Velcro, and that the 90 percent figure does not accurately portray M's power. If buttons, snaps, hooks, and Velcro are included in the market definition, let us suppose that M's share of this larger "clothing fastener" market will be only 23 percent, a figure that certainly does not indicate overwhelming power.

The approach that most courts have taken to such a problem is to look first at the **cross elasticity of demand** among the products in question. The term describes the concept of interchangeability. If there is a substantial degree of cross elasticity of demand between two or more products, they usually will be treated as occupying the same product market. In other words, if the evidence indicates that a substantial portion of customers view two products as being reasonable substitutes for one another, a court is likely to treat the products as being part of a single market.

The evidence in such a case, like so many others, will usually not be very "neat." It probably will show that zippers are preferred by most customers for particular uses, and that these customers are willing to pay significantly more for zippers than other fasteners for these uses. Buttons are probably preferred for certain other uses, snaps for others, and Velcro for still others. For some uses, two or more types of fasteners may be viewed as basically equivalent, and customers may choose solely on the basis of price. Courts necessarily must employ some fairly rough approximations in such cases. Thus, if the evidence convinces a court that a substantial body of customers views two or more products as reasonably interchangeable for a substantial number of important uses, they probably will be included in a single product market. It is also possible, of course, that the evidence will justify a conclusion that fasteners for one particular use constitute a separate market, and that one or more other markets exist for other uses. This conclusion is likely only if the use is quite distinctive from other uses and the volume of business for this use is very substantial.

Another factor that sometimes is relevant to the process of product market definition is **cross elasticity of supply.** This refers to the relative ease or difficulty with which producers of related products may respond to increases in demand. Suppose, for example, that many customers view buttons and zippers as basically interchangeable for certain important uses. Thus, there may be a high degree of cross elasticity of *demand*. However, all button manufacturers are operating at close to their production capacity, and the building of additional button-making facilities is very costly and time-consuming. Therefore, if M raises the price of zippers substantially and many customers would consider switching to buttons, button manufacturers cannot absorb the additional demand. These zipper customers will have to keep buying zippers at a higher cost. Button makers will not build additional capacity unless they think that zipper prices will remain high for the foreseeable future, so they could count on the additional demand for buttons for a long enough time to justify the investment in new button-making capacity. Thus, even though *demand* cross elasticity may be relatively high, there is low *supply* cross elasticity, and courts will probably treat zippers and buttons as two separate markets. It is also true that high cross elasticity of supply can support a conclusion that two products should be in the same market even though there is currently a low degree of demand cross elasticity. Suppose, for example, that most customers view zippers and Velcro as not being interchangeable for a particular use. However, if a price increase for zippers causes many customers to look for a substitute, and if Velcro manufacturers could modify their product easily and inexpensively so that it would be a reasonable zipper substitute for this particular use, zippers and Velcro may be treated as one market.

**Geographic Market:** Depending on the situation, the relevant geographic market can be local, regional, national, or international. It represents the area within which buyers can reasonably be expected to seek alternative sources of supply. Retail geographic markets tend to be smaller than wholesale markets, which tend to be smaller than manufacturing markets, although there are many exceptions to this generalization. The factor that usually determines the size of a geographic market is the relative cost of searching for and shipping products from more distant geographic locations. When we speak of relative cost, we mean relative to the cost of the product itself. Buyers obviously will spend more time and money searching for better deals and shipping from more distant places when the desired purchase is 100 million computer chips than when it is a loaf of bread.

## *Intent to Monopolize*

If a firm has overwhelming market power and thus is a monopolist, is there automatically a violation of Section 2 of the Sherman Act? Or must something else be proved? The answer is that the evidence must also demonstrate that the dominant firm had an intent to monopolize, that is, that it willfully acquired or maintained its monopoly power. This obviously means that there can be legal monopolies. For example, a monopoly is legal if it exists solely because of lawful patents or trade secrets, or because economies of scale are so large that the market will support only one profitable firm.

As in other areas of law, intent is inferred from conduct. In the case of monopolization, courts usually will infer an intent to monopolize only if the dominant firm has engaged in *predatory* conduct, that is, conduct which is aimed at inflicting economic harm on one or more other firms for reasons that are not related to greater efficiency or better performance. There are two very general categories of predatory behavior: predatory pricing and nonprice predation.

**Predatory pricing** is usually found where the dominant firm has persistently sold at prices below its average variable cost. Such pricing is viewed as predatory because it cannot be justified by a legitimate profit motive; while these prices are being charged, it is a money-losing proposition for the dominant firm.

Instead, predatory pricing can only pay off for the dominant firm if it permits that firm to maintain its monopoly position so that it can later recover its losses by charging very high prices and earning monopoly profits. Predatory pricing can be used to drive another firm out of the market, although this is so costly for the dominant firm and has such uncertain long-term payoffs for that firm that it may not happen very often. Strategic predatory pricing can also be used on a periodic basic to discourage other firms from entering the market, or to send a clear signal to smaller firms in the market that they had better not engage in aggressive price competition. Predatory pricing for these purposes is probably more common than for the purpose of actually driving a competitor out.

**Nonprice predation** is probably more common than any kind of predatory pricing because it does not cost the dominant firm as much. Most forms of nonprice predation are aimed at increasing the costs of competitors or increasing entry barriers for potential competitors. A few examples are (1) tying up customers with long-term contracts that are not justified by cost savings, so that it is much more difficult for existing and potential competitors to engage in a fair contest for those customers; (2) taking away key employees from a smaller competitor; (3) falsely disparaging the products of smaller competitors; (4) forcing smaller firms into completely unjustified lawsuits and administrative proceedings because the costs of such proceedings hurt the smaller firms more than the dominant firm; and (5) various forms of sabotage. Some kinds of nonprice predation may violate other laws as well, but many kinds do not.

The following case illustrates a form of nonprice predation that the U.S. Supreme Court found sufficient to fulfill the intent requirement of Section 2.

---

### Aspen Skiing Co. v. Aspen Highlands Skiing Corp.
U.S. Supreme Court,
105 S.Ct. 2847 (1985)

The plaintiff, Aspen Highlands Skiing Corp. (Highlands), and the defendant, Aspen Skiing Co. (Ski Co.), were involved in the business of operating downhill skiing facilities in the Aspen, Colorado, area. There are four major mountain facilities in the area, and most customers prefer a ticket that permits them to use all four facilities. Because of this customer preference, the companies operating the facilities at the four mountains had for several years cooperated in offering an "all-Aspen" ticket that would permit customers to use any of the four facilities. Although the four facilities were originally developed by separate firms, over a period of years Ski Co. acquired ownership of three of these facilities. The fourth was owned and operated by Highlands. After several years of cooperating to the extent necessary to offer an all-Aspen ticket because of strong customer demand for such a ticket, Ski Co. stopped the practice and began offering only a ticket that permitted access to its three facilities. Highlands suffered substantial economic damage as a result, because there was not a great demand for a ticket to just its one mountain. The skiing school operated by Highlands, which was generally recognized as the best in the area, also lost a great deal of business because of the termination of the all-Aspen ticket program.

Highlands sued Ski Co., alleging illegal monopolization in violation of Section 2 of the Sherman Act. Based upon a jury verdict, the trial court found that Aspen Ski Co. had a monopoly in the market for downhill skiing facilities in the Aspen area, and that its refusal to deal with Highlands demonstrated the requisite intent to monopolize. Highlands was awarded a judgment of $7.5 million (after trebling). The court of appeals affirmed. The only issue presented to the Supreme Court was whether the evidence was sufficient for an inference of intent to monopolize.

---

**Decision:** Judgment for the plaintiff, Highlands, was affirmed. The lower courts' conclusion that Ski Co. had a monopoly was not challenged, and the evidence supported the conclusion that Ski Co. also had an intent to monopolize. Although a monopolist does not have an absolute duty to deal with others or to cooperate with rivals, in these circumstances the discontinuance of the "all-Aspen" ticket does support a finding of monopolistic intent. Customers apparently preferred the all-Aspen ticket, its use was a long-standing practice, and Ski Co. was unable to produce plausible evidence of a legitimate business justification for the discontinuance. ∎

**Comment:** Although the all-Aspen 4-mountain ticket program had been a legitimate joint venture because it resulted in a product for which there was strong demand and which could not have been offered by a single firm, the participants in such an arrangement would have to maintain independent control of their own pricing and be careful not to let the joint venture limit competition any more than necessary to achieve its legitimate goals. If the participants cooperated in pricing more than necessary to make the joint venture work, they could be guilty of violating the prohibition in Section 1 of the Sherman Act against "contracts, combinations, or conspiracies in restraint of trade."

# MERGERS

## Basic Principles

A **merger** between two companies clearly is a "combination" that could be scrutinized under Section 1 of the Sherman Act, which prohibits "contracts, combinations, and conspiracies in restraint of trade." In the early years after Congress passed the Sherman Act, however, the Supreme Court interpreted Section 1 in such a narrow way, at least as applied to mergers, that a merger could be illegal only if it occurred between two direct competitors with very large market shares. Because Congress intended antitrust law to reach some other mergers as well, in 1914 it enacted Section 7 of the Clayton Act. The statute was amended substantially by the Cellar-Kefauver Act of 1950, further demonstrating an intent to prevent mergers when the evidence indicates either actual harm to competition or a substantial probability of such harm in the future. Another amendment in 1976 requires the participants in most mergers of any significant size to give both the Justice Department and the FTC advance notice of a merger so that these agencies can assess its possible effects before it occurs.

Section 7 prohibits one company from acquiring the stock or assets of another company if the acquisition is likely to diminish competition in a substantial way. Total or partial acquisitions are covered. Obviously, however, a stock acquisition cannot raise any concerns about harming competition unless the acquiring company obtains a large enough stake in the acquired company either to control it or at least to have substantial influence over its board of directors. Similarly, an acquisition of assets cannot harm competition unless the assets are very important to competition in the particular market, such as major manufacturing facilities, airline routes, critical patented technology, and so on.

So long as there is an acquisition of assets or shares of stock, the exact form of the transaction does not matter. It may be a "friendly" merger or consolidation negotiated between the boards of the two firms and then approved by shareholders, a "hostile" stock acquisition by means of a public tender offer, a series of stock purchases either on the open market or through negotiations with individual shareholders, or any other form.

In attempting to assess a merger's actual or probable effects on competition, a court will first define the relevant market or markets. This is done in exactly the same way as in a monopoly case. As we will see in our discussion of the different types of mergers, the question of market power is also very important in merger cases. It is important to note, however, that a merger does not have to result in market power that is even close to being monopolistic in order to be ruled illegal. Although substantial market power is necessary for substantial anticompetitive effects, that power does not have to be overwhelming for such effects to occur.

Another important point about the law in this area is that periodic political changes in Washington affect the enforcement and interpretation of Section 7 to a greater extent than the other antitrust laws. Although such changes affect antitrust law in general, private lawsuits are much less important as an enforcement tool in the case of mergers than in other areas of antitrust. Most challenges to mergers are made by either the Justice Department or the FTC, rather than by private plaintiffs. Thus, when the current political climate is relatively conservative and probusiness, the enforcement attitude toward mergers is likely to be quite lenient. On the other hand, when an administration is in power that distrusts large concentrations of economic power and does not really believe that most mergers contribute to economic efficiency, more mergers are usually challenged under Section 7. In recent times, the attitude toward mergers was rather strict between the mid-1950s and early 1970s. It was somewhat less strict during the remainder of the 1970s, and was quite lenient during the 1980s.

## Types of Mergers

Mergers traditionally have been classified as horizontal, vertical, or conglomerate. A *horizontal merger* occurs if the two firms are competitors, and a *vertical merger* occurs if one of the firms sells something that the other firm buys. Any other is a *conglomerate merger.* Although these classifications are useful to describe very broadly some relevant differences in the various factual settings in which mergers occur, the same basic test applies to all mergers: does the merger substantially diminish competition, or is it quite likely to do so in the future? Moreover, a merger may sometimes fit more than one category. For instance, in *Brown Shoe Co. v. United States,* 370 U.S. 294 (1962), the challenged merger had both horizontal and vertical aspects because each of the merging firms, Brown Shoe Co. and Kinney Shoe Co., was both a manufacturer *and* a retailer of shoes.

**Horizontal Mergers:** A merger between competitors poses the greatest danger to competition because the market has one less competitor. In assessing the impact of a **horizontal merger,** the courts usually emphasize the same general kinds of evidence that are important in measuring market power in a monopoly case.

*Market Share:* The *combined market share* of the merging firms is often the first thing the courts look at. During earlier periods when the attitude toward mergers was very strict, a number of them were challenged and ruled illegal when the combined market shares were under 10 percent and other evidence indicated a definite trend toward concentration of economic power in the relevant market. Today, however, a horizontal merger is not likely to get much attention under Section 7 unless the combined market share exceeds 30 percent.

*Market Concentration:* The *overall concentration of the market* is also important. In general, the more concentrated the market is at the time of the merger, the more likely it is that a questionable merger will be held illegal. Suppose, for example, that a merger occurs between two firms having market shares of 20 percent and 15 percent, and the remainder of the market consists of three other firms with shares of 25 percent, 20 percent, and 20 percent. This merger would be somewhat more likely to violate Section 7 than it would if the remainder of the market consisted of, say, six other firms with shares of approximately 11 percent each.

*Acquisition by Leading Firm:* In addition, if a single firm already dominates a market rather completely and there are no other firms that can come close to its resources and scale economies, *any* acquisition of a competitor by the *dominant firm* runs a great risk of being held illegal.

*Entry Barriers:* If the market is characterized by high entry barriers, a borderline merger is much more likely to be ruled illegal, and vice versa. Indeed, as we mentioned in the discussion of monopoly, an increasing number of authorities have begun to view a market's entry barriers as being at least as important to the market power question as the market's internal composition. One practical difficulty with this view, however, is that entry barriers usually are much more difficult to measure with any kind of precision than the market's internal structure.

*Increased Risk of Collusion:* Another relevant factor could be the existence of evidence indicating that collusion among competitors had been a problem in this market in the past, and that by further reducing the number of competitors this merger could make collusion even easier in the future. In general, the lower the number of competitors, the easier it is for them to put together and maintain a price-fixing conspiracy or other collusive anticompetitive arrangement.

*Other Factors:* Other factors can also be important to the evaluation of horizontal mergers. For example, a firm with 15 or 20 percent of a market ordinarily could acquire a firm with a 2 or 3 percent share without much fear of legal challenge. Suppose, however, that the smaller firm had recently developed patented technology of major significance to future competition in the market, or that it had traditionally been a very efficient "maverick" and frequently had led the way in vigorous price competition. In such a case, the acquisition would run a significantly higher risk of being challenged successfully under Section 7.

**Vertical Mergers:** Although a **vertical merger** is much less likely to harm competition than a horizontal one, it is possible for such a merger to diminish competition. Essentially, a vertical merger creates **vertical integration,** which occurs when one firm operates at more than one level of the distribution chain for a product. (Obviously, a firm can also become vertically integrated, without a merger, by creating new facilities to operate at another level.) Suppose that S Company is an important producer of a key component or ingredient used by B Company in manufacturing an end product, and that S acquires

B. S would be using the merger to vertically integrate "downstream." If B had acquired S, B would be vertically integrating "upstream."

***The Debate:*** There has been a long-standing debate about the merits of vertical integration. Some experts have viewed vertical integration as being primarily a vehicle for greater efficiency. Others have viewed it as being primarily a tool for locking up markets and supply sources, raising entry barriers, and making collusion easier. Still others have viewed vertical integration as something of a "mixed bag" of economic effects that is exceptionally difficult to sort out. Currently, the prevailing attitude among a majority of economists and enforcement officials toward vertical integration is basically a favorable one. Not everyone shares that view, however, and the pendulum of expert opinion could swing in the other direction at some point in the future.

***Efficiency Argument:*** Undoubtedly, vertical integration can create efficiencies, primarily by saving transaction costs. If the vertically integrated firm ("S-B") is managed properly, it usually should be able to transfer goods and services from one level to another more cheaply than if it were two separate firms operating at the two levels. Being part of one company ideally should permit better coordination and planning. Having an assured source of supply for B and an assured market for S should permit better inventory control. This, in turn, should produce lower carrying costs by avoiding excess inventory and lower delay-related costs by reducing instances of shortage. Vertical integration also can reduce the various kinds of selling costs between S and B, such as those associated with promotion, sales personnel, and contract drafting and monitoring. Opponents of vertical integration reply that, even if these efficiencies are created, the cost savings are not going to be passed along to consumers unless competition in the downstream market is vigorous. They also argue that many of the same efficiencies can be achieved through relatively long-term contracts without creating the same degree of risk for competition.

***Entry Barriers:*** Some observers argue that vertical integration can increase entry barriers and thus insulate firms in the market from new competition. The reason, they say, is that a firm thinking about entering a market in which the major competitors are vertically integrated will have to come into the market at two levels simultaneously, which is more costly and difficult. Those favoring vertical integration, however, reply that new entry into such a market is more difficult simply because the vertically integrated firms in the market are more efficient, and that it is more difficult to compete against efficient firms with low costs.

***Making Collusion Easier:*** Some critics of vertical integration also claim that it can make collusion easier for the vertically integrated firms, especially those at the "upstream" level (in our example, S's level). This can happen, they claim, because removing the layer of independent buyers from the downstream level does away with an important set of "watchdogs" on the upstream firms. Those with a favorable view of vertical integration often admit that this is a possibility, but point out that it is likely to happen only if there are very few firms at both levels and if most of these large firms are already vertically integrated. Besides, they say, antitrust enforcers can just watch out for the collusion and take action if they find it.

***Current Law:*** Because of today's generally favorable attitude toward vertical integration, a vertical merger will usually be legal. A successful challenge to such a merger is likely only if most of the firms in the market are already vertically integrated, this vertically combined market is a highly concentrated oligopoly, and both S and B have large market shares. It is mainly the fear of collusion being made easier in this kind of situation that creates the risk of a successful legal challenge.

**Conglomerate Mergers:** Mergers without horizontal or vertical characteristics are usually called **conglomerate mergers.** Although several grounds for striking down conglomerate mergers have been employed in the past, such a merger creates very little legal risk today. About the only situation where such a risk exists now is in the following circumstances: (1) X enters the widget market in the western U.S. by acquiring Y, a major producer of widgets in that area. (2) That market was already a highly concentrated oligopoly. (3) For a substantial period of time before the merger, X had a special incentive to enter the market and the resources to do it. Other potential new entrants did not have similar incentives. This special incentive may have existed because the widget market was an unusually attractive extension of X's product line, or perhaps because X already sold widgets elsewhere and this was an ideal geographic expansion. In either case, X could get into the market and compete more easily and cheaply than other new firms because of the product or geographic relationship. (4) The western widget market had high entry barriers that discouraged other firms from entering, but that were not so high as to discourage X because of its large resources and special incentive. (5) Prior to the merger, the major firms in the western widget market knew that X was a probable future entrant.

In this situation, the presence of X "on the edge" of the western widget market prior to the merger was probably having a beneficial effect by causing widget makers in the market to keep their prices lower than they would have otherwise, in the hope of discouraging X from actually entering. When X enters, this beneficial "edge effect" is removed. If X had entered by building new facilities, or by acquiring a very small firm in the market and expanding it into a major competitor, X's entry would have positive effects that would offset the removal of its former "edge effect." But when X enters by acquiring a firm that is already a major player, there is nothing positive to counteract the negative, and the merger may be illegal.

## *Failing Company Defense*

Even if a merger is one that normally would violate Section 7 of the Clayton Act, proof of the *failing company defense* prevents a violation. This defense exists if one of the merging firms probably will not be able to meet its financial obligations in the near future; (2) it appears unlikely that the failing firm will be able to reorganize successfully under Chapter 11 of the Bankruptcy Code and emerge as a viable company; and (3) the failing firm has made a good faith, but unsuccessful, effort to obtain a merger offer from another firm that would pose less danger to competition than does the merger being challenged.

## *Merger Guidelines*

The Justice Department's Antitrust Division first issued Merger Guidelines in 1968. The guidelines, which are also followed by the FTC, were completely rewritten in 1982, and again revised slightly in 1984. These guidelines are not binding law but do provide business with a valuable planning tool by specifying the circumstances in which the two agencies can ordinarily be expected to challenge a merger.

One of the key innovations of the current guidelines is the use of the Herfindahl-Hirschman Index (HHI) for measuring the relative level of economic concentration in a market. This index involves squaring the market share of each firm in the market and then adding the squares. Thus, a market with 10 firms of equal size would have an HHI of 1,000. The guidelines consider a market with an HHI under 1,000 to be unconcentrated, between 1,000 and 1,800 to be moderately concentrated, and over 1,800 to be concentrated. The greater the level of concentration in the relevant market, the more likely it is that a merger will be challenged and that it will be ruled illegal.

The following Supreme Court decision is from a case involving a horizontal merger between two relatively large competitors. It is an important decision because, among other things, it illustrates how evidence of surrounding economic circumstances may convince a court that such a merger is legal.

---

### United States v. General Dynamics Corp.
U.S. Supreme Court,
415 U.S. 486 (1974)

Material Service Corp. owned Freeman Coal Mining Co. In 1954 Material Service began purchasing the stock of United Electric Coal Co., and by 1959 had acquired effective control of United. General Dynamics Corp. then acquired Material Service Corp. Subsequently, the government sued General Dynamics, claiming that the merger of Freeman and United violated Section 7 of the Clayton Act.

Freeman and United together accounted for about 23 percent of total coal production in the state of Illinois. If the geographic market was defined more broadly as the Eastern Interior Coal Province, one of the country's four major coal distribution areas, the combined share would have been about 12 percent. Over the past several decades, however, the electric utility industry had become the main consumer. Electric utilities usually do not contract to buy coal in individual transactions as they need fuel. Instead, they enter into long-term

*(continued)*

requirements contracts with coal producers. The ability of a coal company to compete for these long-term supply contracts does not depend on its current production or even its production capacity. A coal company's viability as a strong competitor depends, instead, on the amount of *uncommitted* coal reserves it has in the ground. Thus, the production statistics relied on by the government to indicate that Freeman and United had substantial market shares are not as meaningful as they would be in many other markets where competition takes a different form. In this case, despite the fact that United was a large and profitable company, the evidence indicated that its uncommitted reserves were very small and that its chances of increasing those reserves were quite low. Because of this evidence, the district court found that the merger did not violate Section 7, and the government appealed to the Supreme Court.

**Decision:** The judgment in favor of defendant, General Dynamics, was affirmed. The merger of the two coal companies under the ownership umbrella of Material Service Corp., and later under General Dynamics, was not likely to lessen competition substantially. Although the market share figures in this case might indicate a substantial lessening of competition in some situations, the particular dynamics of competition in this market caused the market shares of Freeman and United to be less meaningful. ■

## HORIZONTAL RESTRAINTS OF TRADE

In examining the law pertaining to monopolies and mergers, we were concerned primarily with market structure and only secondarily with specific instances of conduct. We now turn our attention to particular types of business behavior. Market structure continues to be relevant here, but its role is a secondary one.

Our first inquiry into the behavioral side of antitrust is **horizontal restraints of trade**—arrangements between two or more competitors that suppress or limit competition. The applicable statute is Section 1 of the Sherman Act which, as stated earlier, prohibits "contracts, combinations, or conspiracies in restraint of trade."

### The Requirement of Collusion

Section 1 of the Sherman Act can be applied only if there was **collusion** between two or more independent entities. Many different terms are used to describe the concept: joint action, concerted action, agreement, combination, conspiracy, and others. As is true of all things that must be proved in the law, the collusion requirement is sometimes obvious and sometimes not. An example of a case in which the requirement obviously was present is *National Society of Professional Engineers v. United States,* 435 U.S. 679 (1978), in which the Court held illegal an ethical rule of the society that prohibited competitive bidding by its 69,000 members. The collusion requirement was so obviously satisfied that it was not even an issue. In such a case, even if the association has been incorporated and thus is a single independent entity, its rules and other actions are in reality the collective actions of its members who explicitly or implicitly granted their approval.

If collusion is not obvious, courts normally have to rely on circumstantial evidence to decide the question. Evidence of any *communications* among the parties can be very important, but such evidence may or may not be strong enough to permit the fact finder to conclude that collusion has taken place. If there is no such evidence, or if it is not sufficient to prove collusion, there must at least be evidence demonstrating that the parties had an *opportunity to conspire*. To establish a circumstantial case of collusion, it usually is also necessary to prove *uniformity of action* among the defendants. Thus, a court is quite unlikely to find that collusion occurred unless the defendants acted in a very similar fashion in pricing, refusing to deal with another party such as a customer or supplier, or other important matter.

It is not enough, however, merely to prove that the firms did about the same thing, because there can be many legitimate reasons for such an occurrence. This is especially true in a market with a relatively small number of firms. In an oligopoly, for example, it sometimes is inevitable that several companies will make similar pricing moves within a relatively short time span, primarily because they all know what the others are doing and the actions of each one are quite important. In other situations, there also may be reasonable explanations for uniformity; for instance, the same external factor such as a supply shortage may have affected all firms simultaneously. If there is substantial uniformity, however, without any legitimate explanation, the situation is suspicious and the firms' parallel conduct is fairly strong evidence of collusion. Also, the greater the *degree* of uniformity, the more strongly this evidence points toward collusion.

## *The Rule of Reason*

Assuming that collusion has been proved, the defendants' action violates Section 1 only if it "restrains trade." What this means is that their conduct must have suppressed or limited competition. Relatively early in the history of the Sherman Act, in *Standard Oil Co. v. United States,* 221 U.S. 1 (1911), the Supreme Court held that Section 1 does not forbid *all* arrangements that limit competition. If the statute had been interpreted in a literal, all-inclusive fashion, it could have produced strange and inefficient results such as prohibiting the formation of partnerships, corporations, and other business organizations because they involve the combination of individuals who might otherwise be competitors. Instead, the Court adopted the so-called **rule of reason,** under which arrangements are illegal only if they "unreasonably" restrict competition.

The next question, of course, is how do the courts decide whether a particular arrangement is reasonable or unreasonable? In essence, the rule of reason involves an examination of the *purpose* and the *effect* of the conduct being challenged.

**Purpose:** The firms will always claim that their purpose was legitimate—i.e., not anticompetitive. They may insist, for example, that their motive was to promote ethical conduct in their industry, prevent fraudulent practices by their suppliers or customers, encourage product standardization or safety, or any one of many other lawful purposes. The court will examine all pertinent evidence before deciding whether the defendants are to be believed, or whether their predominant motive was to restrict competition. If the court concludes that their primary motive was to limit competition, the arrangement is illegal if there is a likelihood of even a small restriction on competition. If, on the other hand, the court decides that their primary motive was a legitimate one, the court will find a violation of Section 1 only if the evidence indicates that competition will be diminished in a substantial way. There is actually something of a rough sliding scale. The greater the apparent bad effect on competition, the less weight the court will give to any legitimate motive.

**Effect on Competition:** Perhaps the most important factor in the analysis of an arrangement's effect on competition is the collective *market power* of the group. Market power is evaluated in the same way here as in the more structurally oriented situations of monopoly and merger. A group's aggregate market power does not have to be huge for an arrangement to violate the rule of reason, but if the group's purpose was apparently all right, its power must be substantial enough to convince a court that serious anticompetitive effects are likely to result.

Another factor that often plays a part in the court's analysis is the existence of a *less restrictive alternative.* Thus, if the evidence establishes that the firms could have achieved their claimed objectives by using some other arrangement that would have posed less danger to competition, a court is somewhat more likely to find a violation of Section 1. The existence of a less restrictive alternative does not automatically cause their arrangement to be illegal, but it does tip the scales a bit in that direction, for two reasons. First, it demonstrates that the firms caused a greater negative effect on competition than they really had to. Second, such evidence may even cause a court to view their alleged motive with more suspicion.

If evidence of market power and other relevant factors indicates that a substantial negative effect on competition is possible, the legality of the arrangement sometimes can be saved by clear evidence that it also will have *offsetting procompetitive effects.* These are just positives to offset the negatives, and usually involve some aspect of the arrangement that will improve the efficiency of the market. The court will engage in a rough balancing of these effects against the anticompetitive ones and decide which seem to predominate. Examples of procompetitive effects include creating a new kind of market that otherwise would not exist, stimulating competition by bringing more transactions into the market, improving the quality or quantity of information available to buyers and sellers, and so on.

The following landmark Supreme Court case illustrates most of these aspects of rule-of-reason analysis. You will be able to see the Court examining (1) motives; (2) market power (although it does not use this term); (3) the fact that the scope of the arrangement seemed to be limited so that it was not any more restrictive than it had to be; and (4) what the judges viewed as offsetting procompetitive effects brought about by taking quite a few transactions from a few large dealers and bringing them into the organized market where information was more accurate and up-to-date and trading more open and competitive.

## Chicago Board of Trade v. United States
U.S. Supreme Court, 246 U.S. 231 (1918)

In the late 1800s and early 1900s Chicago was the leading grain market in the world, and the Board of Trade was the commercial center through which most of the trading in grain was done. Its 1,600 members included brokers, commission merchants, dealers, millers, manufacturers of corn products, and grain elevator owners. Grain transactions usually took one of three forms: (1) spot sales—sales of grain already in Chicago in railroad cars or elevators ready for immediate delivery; (2) future sales—agreements for delivery of grain at a later time; (3) sales "to arrive"—agreements for delivery of grain which was already in transit to Chicago or which was to be shipped almost immediately from other parts of the Midwest.

On each business day, sessions of the Board of Trade were held at which all bids and sales were publicly made. Spot sales and future sales were made during the regular session between 9:30 A.M. and 1:15 P.M. Special sessions, referred to as the "Call," were held immediately after the close of the regular session. During the Call, which usually lasted about 30 minutes, members of the Board of Trade engaged only in "to arrive" transactions. These transactions usually involved purchases from farmers or small dealers in one of the Midwestern states. Participation in the Call session was limited to members, but they could trade on behalf of nonmembers if they wished. Members also could make any of the three types of transaction privately with each other at any place, either during or after board sessions. Members could engage privately in any type of transaction at any time with nonmembers, but not on the board's premises.

With respect to "to arrive" transactions, a particular market price would be established by the public trading during the short Call session. Until 1906, however, members were not bound by that price during the remainder of the day. In that year the Board of Trade adopted what was known as the "Call rule." The rule, which applied only to "to arrive" transactions, required members to use the market price established at the public Call session when they bought grain in private transactions between the end of that session and 9:30 the next morning.

The government filed suit in federal district court, claiming that the Call rule violated Section 1 of the Sherman Act. The board contended that the purpose and effect of the rule was to bring more of the "to arrive" transactions into the public market at the Call session. By bringing more of these transactions into the public market, the board felt that four or five large grain warehouse owners in Chicago would no longer have such a controlling grip over "to arrive" transactions. The district court, however, ruled that evidence relating to the history and purpose of the rule was irrelevant and issued an injunction against the operation of the rule. The Board of Trade then appealed to the U.S. Supreme Court.

**Decision:** The judgment was reversed and the government's complaint dismissed. This was not an obvious case of price fixing, and the purpose and effect of the "Call rule" should be considered. The court concluded that the real purpose of the rule was essentially to bring more grain transactions into the public market and thus to stimulate the functioning of that market. The court also felt that this would be the major effect of the rule. Any potential anticompetitive effects were offset by the fact that the Board of Trade was only one of several public grain markets available in the Midwest and that the rule applied to only one relatively minor type of transaction. ■

## *The Per Se Rule*

Also relatively early in the history of the Sherman Act, the Supreme Court recognized that certain types of practices are obviously anticompetitive and do not really have any redeeming social virtues. In such a case, the **per se rule** applies. This means that, once the particular type of activity is identified as one that falls within a per se category, it is automatically illegal and the inquiry ends. Of the various horizontal restraints of trade, price fixing, market division, and boycotts are per se illegal. It is very important to understand, however, that the per se rule has its greatest impact in situations where the challenged activity can be easily labeled as price fixing, market division, or a boycott. If there is a close question whether the arrangement should be characterized in this way, the court must analyze its purpose and effect in order to decide how to label it. This analysis is basically the same as in a rule-of-reason case.

**Price Fixing:** Price fixing among competitors is per se illegal. This activity occurs when two or more competitors agree explicitly to charge a specific price, or to set a price floor, but many other arrangements can also constitute price fixing because they substantially interfere with the price-setting function of the market. Some examples include agreements or understandings among competitors to (1) not submit competitive bids; (2) rotate the privilege of being low bidder on contracts; (3) artificially manipulate supply or demand in a way that affects price substantially; (4) not advertise prices; (5) not grant certain discounts; (6) maintain uniformity on a particular term that constitutes a component of price, such as shipping or credit charges; (7) keep prices within a particular range; and even (8) maintain a *ceiling* on prices.

Many other joint arrangements may have an arguable effect on the market's pricing mechanism. If the court is convinced that the parties' main purpose is to suppress price competition, it will probably call the arrangement price fixing and find it illegal. As mentioned earlier, however, if there is significant doubt about the question, a court will probably engage in a rule-of-reason type analysis, regardless of whether it uses that phrase.

**Market Division:** Market division among competitors is also per se illegal, assuming that such division is found to be the primary objective of a particular arrangement. The same rule can be applied to market division agreements involving *potential* competitors making decisions about entering new markets. Market division arrangements can take at least three forms: (1) in a *territorial* market division, the firms agree to refrain from competing with each other in designated geographic areas; (2) in a *customer allocation* arrangement, the firms assign particular customers or classes of customers to each seller and agree not to solicit customers of another seller; (3) in a *product line* division, the firms agree to limit their activities to particular types of products or services so as to avoid competing with each other.

**Boycotts:** A firm ordinarily has freedom to choose those with whom it will transact business. However, when two or more parties agree not to deal with some other party, antitrust problems arise. When the agreeing parties are competitors and their primary purpose apparently is to curtail competition, the resulting **boycott** is per se illegal. Two or more firms will violate Section 1, for example, if they agree to quit selling to a customer because the latter is trying to integrate upstream and become their competitor. Likewise, a group of firms would be engaged in an illegal boycott if they agreed to stop selling to certain customers unless those customers quit buying from a competitor of those in the agreeing group. A similar violation would occur if the group agreed not to buy from a supplier unless that supplier refrained from selling to a competitor or potential competitor of the group. Boycotts are sometimes used to drive a firm out of a market, keep it from entering in the first place, or discipline a firm by "showing it who's boss" and thus convincing it to stop competing so aggressively.

Although labeling problems occur with respect to all of the per se categories, they seem to be especially troublesome in the case of boycotts. The reason is that there are many group activities that have legitimate reasons for existing, but that also may have the tendency to *exclude* other firms. Suppose for example, that many of the automotive repair businesses in Missouri, Kansas, and Oklahoma form an organization called the Midwest Auto Repair Association (MARA). The stated purposes of the group are to promote the auto repair business in various ways and encourage high ethical standards in the industry. Like any organization, MARA establishes rules for membership that might require such things as full-time participation in the auto repair business, a fee to cover the organization's costs, fewer than a specified number of verified customer complaints during a given period of time, and so on. Jones does not meet one of the requirements and is either denied membership initially or is forced out later. He claims that he has been the victim of a boycott.

There are many other examples. Similar problems can arise if a group of firms in the same industry tries to establish uniform product standards for the purpose of either safety or reducing customer confusion and dissatisfaction. One firm's product does not meet the standard and thus does not receive the approval of the group. The firm claims a boycott.

Yet another example arises where a group of firms pool their resources to develop a facility such as a research lab. This can be legitimate where the great cost, risk, and uncertainty of constructing a major facility or engaging in a particular undertaking is too much for a single firm. (This last example describes a "joint venture," which will be discussed shortly.) A competitor is not permitted to join the venture and claims a boycott.

When confronted with such claims, courts first look at the group's apparent *purpose*. If the primary purpose was to exclude others and achieve some restriction on competition, it will be per se illegal as a boycott. If the main purpose appears to have been a legitimate one, the court engages in a rule-of-reason type of analysis. The court will try to determine just how important it is for a firm to participate. (This is just another kind of inquiry into a group's collective market power.) If exclusion really does *not* harm a firm's ability to compete in the relevant market, the arrangement is legal. On the other hand, if participation *is* very important to a firm's ability to compete, the rules or restrictions that have the result of excluding others must be *reasonable*. To be reasonable, they must (1) have a logical relationship to the group's legitimate objectives, and (2) not exclude others any more than is necessary to accomplish those objectives.

## Trade Associations

A trade association is a loosely knit organization of firms with mutual interests. Its membership usually includes firms within the same industry, but sometimes also includes suppliers or customers of these firms, and perhaps others with an interest in the field, such as consultants. The mere existence of a trade association presents no antitrust problems—most industries have some type of trade association. Moreover, the activities of these associations usually are legitimate and socially useful. Associations in some industries have been instrumental, for example, in setting product safety standards, maintaining ethical norms, providing arbitration or other procedures for resolving disputes between members, forming group self-insurance pools, and so on.

The problem with trade associations is that they can present very tempting opportunities for illegal group activities such as price fixing, market divisions, boycotts, or other arrangements that stifle competition. Members must be vigilant to ensure that the association's activities do not harm competition, and have all proposals reviewed by attorneys with antitrust expertise. If a firm believes that action about to be taken by the group is legally questionable, the firm should voice its dissent and not participate.

## *Joint Ventures*

Although the term **joint venture** has no precise meaning, it has been likened to a partnership for a limited purpose. The joint research lab used earlier as an illustration is a type of joint venture. When two or more firms collaborate for some reason, their joint undertaking may or may not be a joint venture. The basic characteristics of a legitimate joint venture are (1) a partial pooling of resources by two or more firms, (2) a limited degree of integration of some aspect of the firms' operations, and (3) an intent to accomplish a defined business objective that could not be accomplished as efficiently (or at all) by a single firm. Situations in which joint ventures are commonly accepted as legitimate include those in which extremely large economies of scale, very high risks, or unusually extended long-term payoffs are involved, or where the nature of the product is such that it cannot be produced or marketed efficiently without collaboration between two or more firms.

Joint ventures usually do not violate the antitrust laws, but they can do so on occasion. Section 1 of the Sherman Act is the primarily applicable statute, and joint ventures are normally judged under the rule of reason. If formation of the joint venture involves an asset or stock acquisition, Section 7 of the Clayton Act also can be applied, although the legal standards for joint ventures are basically the same under both statutes.

The risk of illegality obviously is greater when actual or potential competitors are involved. In addition, certain kinds of activities are more likely to limit competition than those involving other kinds of activities. A joint venture might involve matters ranging along a continuum from basic research to applied research, product development, production, promotion and other marketing activities, selling, and finally, distribution. The risk of harm to competition, and thus the degree of scrutiny under the antitrust laws, increases as the activity moves along the continuum away from research. Joint ventures involving activities farther along the continuum, such as production, can be valid, but their justification must be stronger.

Assuming that the basic objectives of the joint venture are legitimate, three basic types of antitrust questions can still be raised. First, the formation of a joint venture occasionally may create dangers to competition that probably will not be outweighed by increased efficiency or other positive effects. This may happen if the venture is just *too big*—that is, if it is larger than really necessary to accomplish its legitimate objectives. Second, even if the venture is not too large, it may include some *ancillary restriction* that limits competition among the participants more than necessary. For example, participants might agree to exchange certain kinds of information which, if misused, could make it fairly easy to engage in horizontal price fixing. This restriction would require a very strong justification. Third, the joint venture may harm outsiders who are excluded from participation. This situation is analyzed as described earlier in the discussion of various group activities that tend to exclude others.

## VERTICAL RESTRAINTS OF TRADE

When firms operating at different levels of the distribution chain enter some arrangement that may harm competition, we call it a **vertical restraint of trade.**

### *Resale Price Maintenance*

**Nature and Effects:** Resale price maintenance **(RPM),** which is also called vertical price fixing, occurs when a seller and buyer agree on the price at which the buyer will resell to its own customers. RPM usually is a method by which a manufacturer or other supplier limits price competition among its dealers or distributors in the market for resale of the product. Competition among such dealers for sales of the manufacturer's product is called **intrabrand competition,** in contrast with the **interbrand competition** that occurs between different manufacturers' brands.

RPM has always been controversial. Many economists and legal scholars believe that RPM and other forms of restriction on intrabrand competition are usually employed to increase efficiency. They claim that these limits on intrabrand competition can be used by a manufacturer to make sure that its dealers invest in the facilities, trained personnel, and promotional activities necessary to stimulate sales and properly serve customers. If one dealer makes such an investment and thereby stimulates demand for the manufacturer's product, but another dealer does not, the latter has lower costs and can underprice the former. The first dealer will then be discouraged and will stop making such investments. Because of some dealers' **free riding,** the argument goes, many (or most) of the manufacturer's dealers will not do those things necessary to compete vigorously with other brands. If the manufacturer uses RPM to put a floor below its dealers' resale prices, however, some argue that this will solve the problem by reducing dealers' incentives to take a free ride on the investment of other dealers. The incentive is gone because they cannot use their lower costs to underprice and take customers from another dealer. Those arguing that the law should treat RPM very leniently also claim that, because any potential harm to competition is only intrabrand, customers are protected so long as competition among different brands remains active.

Other experts have serious doubts about the "free rider" justification for RPM. They argue that free rider problems are really not that common, and that many cases of resale price maintenance have involved products like toothpaste or blue jeans, for which there is not much need for the kinds of costly facilities or services that are susceptible to free riding. They also claim that, even if free rider problems are common, other means are available for solving them that do not cause similar harm to price competition. Such means include contractual commitments from dealers to provide the necessary facilities, personnel, promotion, and services. Opponents of RPM claim that the true reason for the practice often may be the manufacturer's desire to keep dealers' prices up and relieve them from intrabrand competition so that they do not pressure the manufacturer to lower its prices to them. They also sometimes argue that RPM can be used as a device to carry out a horizontal price-fixing conspiracy among dealers.

**Legal Standards:** The statute applicable to RPM is Section 1 of the Sherman Act. From the early days of the Sherman Act, RPM was viewed as per se illegal. In 1937, Congress passed legislation that delegated to state legislatures the power to determine the status of RPM in their particular states. Most states passed so-called Fair Trade laws that permitted RPM on branded merchandise within their borders if meaningful competition existed among different brands of the same product. Congress strengthened the power of the states to permit this practice in 1945. Gradually, however, the notion of permitting RPM fell out of favor. Many states repealed their Fair Trade laws, and many state supreme courts held that the statutes violated provisions in their state constitutions. Most of the remaining Fair Trade statutes fell into disuse, either because ambiguous interpretations created uncertainty, or simply because it was difficult for an interstate seller to use RPM legally when it was illegal in so many places. In 1975, Congress repealed the federal law that permitted states to enact Fair Trade laws. Thus, RPM became per se illegal everywhere in the nation once again.

Although resale price maintenance is per se illegal, there continues to be a vigorous debate about whether it should be. Until the early 1980s, the U.S. Justice Department aggressively prosecuted cases of RPM and the federal courts generally took a very harsh view of the practice. (Until 1975, the Justice Department and courts dealt with RPM only if it occurred in a state where it was illegal.) Since the early 1980s, the law against RPM has not been enforced as aggressively, and the courts have begun to interpret the law so as to make it somewhat more difficult for either the Justice Department or private parties to prove RPM. These attitudes and interpretations could easily change again in the future, as they have several times in the past.

**Proving a Vertical Agreement:** Most of the difficult issues in RPM cases have involved the question of whether there actually has been an "agreement" to set resale prices. "Suggested" resale prices at the retail level are quite common. They do not constitute RPM unless there is evidence that there really has been an agreement (either voluntary or coerced) that gives the manufacturer or other supplier effective control over the dealer's resale prices. This point also illustrates the fact that there can be an illegal RPM "agreement" even if one party has coerced the other into participating; Section 1 of the Sherman Act does not require that the agreement be completely voluntary.

One of the most difficult issues in this area involves the extent to which a seller lawfully may use a *refusal to deal* in an attempt to control buyers' resale prices. In *United States v. Colgate & Co.,* 250 U.S. 300 (1919), the Supreme Court stated that a "unilateral refusal to deal" cannot violate Section 1 of the Sherman Act even if controlling resale prices is the seller's ultimate goal. In other words, so long as a seller acts entirely on its own ("unilaterally") it can refuse to sell to anyone it chooses, regardless of the motive. The problem, of course, is distinguishing between unilateral action by the seller and action that is part of an RPM arrangement between the seller and others. Suppose that M, a manufacturer, either initially refuses to sell to R, a retailer, or later terminates an existing supplier-customer relationship with R. (When RPM is claimed, the second situation is the most common.) To create a genuine fact issue for the jury, R must present evidence indicating that (1) there was an agreement to fix resale prices at R's level, and (2) M refused to deal with R because R would not go along with the arrangement. The agreement to limit price competition at R's level could be between M and wholesalers who act as intermediaries between M and R, between M and other retailers who compete with R, or even between M and R if the evidence shows that R previously had been part of an RPM arrangement with M and then tried to get out of it.

## Vertical Nonprice Restrictions

**Nature and Effects:** Vertical restrictions may relate to matters other than price. The **vertical nonprice restrictions (VNRs)** that can cause some concern under Section 1 of the Sherman Act generally are those involving some type of market division. VNRs take many forms, depending on several factors. These factors include the relative bargaining power of the manufacturer and its dealers or distributors, and the nature of the product and the markets in which it sells.

One type of VNR is the *territorial exclusive,* in which M, the manufacturer, guarantees its dealers that they will have the exclusive right to market M's product in their respective geographic areas. In order to honor this arrangement with each dealer, M obviously must keep all dealers from reselling outside their own areas. Because this restriction places a contractual limitation on M's freedom, M will not use exclusive territories in its distribution system unless it has relatively less bargaining power than its dealers. More often, M will use **territorial and customer restrictions,** without any promise of exclusive territories. Such an arrangement requires dealers or distributors to resell only within their respective territories or only to particular customers, but does not guarantee them exclusive rights to sell in those areas or to those customers. A similar provision that restricts dealers somewhat less is the *area of primary responsibility,* which does not absolutely prohibit a dealer from reselling outside its designated territory but requires only that the territory be thoroughly served before sales can be made outside the area. Another fairly common provision is the *location requirement,* which requires a dealer to sell only from a specified location. In most cases, a location requirement has the same effect as a territorial restriction.

Like RPM, all forms of VNRs have the common characteristic of limiting *intrabrand* competition. Also like RPM, there is a long-standing debate about the competitive benefits and dangers of VNRs. Today, and commonly during the past, the prevailing attitude toward these restrictions has been more favorable than the attitude toward RPM. Generally, the feeling has been that VNRs are more likely than RPM (1) to be based on legitimate motives and (2) to help *intrabrand* competition more than they hurt *intrabrand* competition. A significant number of authorities think, however, that the law should not treat VNRs and RPM any differently because they are usually employed for the same purposes, have basically the same effects, and can be difficult to distinguish in practice.

**Legal Standards:** The legal status of VNRs has varied over the years. Until 1967, they were analyzed under the rule of reason. In that year, a decision of the U.S. Supreme Court caused some kinds of nonprice restriction on dealers to be per se illegal. This decision was overruled by the Court in 1977, and since then the rule of reason has been applied to all forms of VNRs.

In the case of VNRs, the question of motive is usually not as important as it can be when the rule of reason is applied to horizontal restrictions. Courts generally accept as legitimate M's objective of using a VNR to limit intrabrand competition, so long as there apparently is some business justification for the limitation. Under the rule of reason, M's market share will be the most important factor. If it is below approximately 10 percent, the restriction usually will be legal without further inquiry. If the share is at or above this level, courts normally will look at other factors. Other factors that could increase the chances of illegality in a close case include (1) evidence that *interbrand* competition in this particular market is not very strong, and that *intrabrand* competition is especially important; (2) evidence that most other manufacturers in this market also use such restrictions to limit intrabrand competition among their dealers; and (3) evidence that M selected a form of VNR that limits intrabrand competition much more than is really necessary under the circumstances.

The following case is the one in which the U.S. Supreme Court switched from the per se rule back to the rule of reason for judging VNRs. The Court's discussion outlines and adopts some of the arguments made by those who feel that VNRs usually produce more economic benefits than harms.

---

**Continental T.V., Inc. v. G.T.E. Sylvania, Inc.**
U.S. Supreme Court,
433 U.S. 36 (1977)

Sylvania manufactured and sold television sets through its Home Entertainment Products Division. Prior to 1962, like most other television manufacturers, Sylvania sold televisions to independent or company-owned wholesale distributors who then resold them to a large and diverse group of retailers. Prompted by a decline in its market share to a relatively insignificant 1 to 2 percent of national television sales, Sylvania conducted an intensive reassessment of its marketing strategy and in 1962 adopted the franchise plan challenged here. Sylvania phased out its wholesale distributors and began to sell its televisions directly to a smaller and more select group of franchised retailers. The main purpose of the change was to decrease the number of competing Sylvania retailers in the hope of attracting the more aggressive and competent retailers, which Sylvania felt was necessary to improve its market position.

Thus, Sylvania limited the number of franchises granted for any given area and required each retail dealer to sell Sylvania products only from the location or locations specified in the franchise agreement. These retailers were not prohibited from selling the products of competing manufacturers. A franchise did not constitute an exclusive territory, and Sylvania retained sole discretion to increase the number of retailers in an area in light of the success or failure of existing retailers in developing their market. The revised marketing strategy apparently was successful, and by 1965 Sylvania's share of national television sales increased to 5 percent, making it the eighth largest manufacturer of televisions.

In 1965 Sylvania proposed to franchise an additional retailer in San Francisco. This proposal upset Continental T.V., an existing Sylvania dealer in the city. Continental then proposed to open a new store in Sacramento. Sylvania denied Continental's request because it felt that Sacramento presently was being adequately served. Continental then began selling Sylvania televisions in Sacramento in defiance of Sylvania, and the manufacturer stopped selling to Continental.

Continental filed a treble damage suit against Sylvania, claiming that the restrictions on dealer location violated Section 1 of the Sherman Act. In federal district court Continental received a jury verdict against Sylvania for approximately $600,000 and a judgment for $1.8 million. In ruling for Continental, the district court applied the Supreme Court's 1967 decision in *United States v. Arnold, Schwinn & Co.*, which had held vertical nonprice restrictions to be per se illegal. When Sylvania appealed to the court of appeals, that court reversed and ordered a retrial because it thought that the *Schwinn* case was inapplicable to the present situation. Continental then appealed to the U.S. Supreme Court. The Supreme Court felt that the *Schwinn* case was indeed applicable to the facts of the present case, but wished to decide whether *Schwinn* should still be the law. Thus, the issue for the Supreme Court was whether to follow its earlier decision in the *Schwinn* case and apply the per se rule, or to overrule that case and apply the rule of reason to vertical nonprice restrictions.

**Decision:** The judgment of the court of appeals was affirmed and the case remanded to the district court. The rule of the *Schwinn* case that vertical nonprice restrictions are per se illegal was overruled. Vertical nonprice restrictions can be used to prevent a dealer from free riding on the investment another dealer has made in better facilities and service, better trained personnel, and other things that stimulate overall demand for the product. Thus, even though VNRs limit intrabrand competition among a manufacturer's dealers, by helping to eliminate free riding these restrictions can encourage dealer investments that make this brand a stronger competitor against other brands. Thus, the limitation on intrabrand competition may actually increase interbrand competition. Because positive effects on competition are possible, VNRs should not be treated as automatically illegal, but should be illegal only where the evidence proves an actual anticompetitive effect in the circumstances. The Supreme Court held that the rule of reason should be applied by the district court when the case was retried. (On retrial, the district court found that Sylvania's system of location clauses was legal under the rule of reason.) ■

**Comment:** On retrial, the district court found that Sylvania's vertical restrictions were valid under the rule of reason. This holding was based primarily on (1) Sylvania's legitimate business justification, (2) Sylvania's small market share, and (3) the court's feeling that Sylvania had chosen the "least restrictive alternative"—in other words, that the location clause was less restrictive of competition than other methods Sylvania might have used to accomplish its objectives.

## Tying Agreements

**Nature and Effects:** When one party agrees to supply (sell, lease, etc.) a product or service only on the condition that the customer also take another product or service, a **tying agreement** has been made. The desired item is the *tying* product, and the item the customer is required to take is the *tied* product. Tying agreements are scrutinized under both Section 1 of the Sherman Act and Section 3 of the Clayton Act. Section 3 of the Clayton Act applies only to the tying of two tangible commodities. Section 1 of the Sherman Act applies to all tying arrangements, including those in which either or both products is not a tangible commodity (such as a service, an intangible property right, or land). Today tying agreements are analyzed the same way under the two statutes, so Section 3 of the Clayton Act is largely redundant.

An early landmark case provides a clear example of tying. In *IBM v. United States*, 298 U.S. 131 (1936), IBM was found guilty of illegal tying by requiring all customers leasing its tabulating machines to also purchase their tabulating cards from IBM.

The main concern about tying is that a supplier may use power in one market (the market for the *tying* product) to distort competition in another market (the market for the *tied* product). Such distortion can occur, it is argued, because the supplier's sales of the tied product are not based on the independent competitive merits of that product.

Several different motivations may lead a supplier to use tying arrangements. In some cases, the supplier may be trying to use the power it has in the tying market to expand its power in the tied market. Such a practice is sometimes referred to as *leveraging*. There is quite a bit of debate among experts as to the extent to which power actually can be leveraged from one market to another.

A supplier also might use tying in an attempt to *protect its goodwill*. This could be the motive, for example, where the supplier sells or leases product X, and where product Y must be used in conjunction with X. The supplier may be concerned that some customers might use inferior versions of Y that will cause X to perform poorly, and thus hurt the reputation of X. In such a case, the supplier might require buyers to buy the supplier's own version of Y along with X. The general feeling under the antitrust laws, however, has been that the supplier should accomplish its objective by requiring the customer to use any version of Y that meets specifications set by the supplier, unless the use of specifications is very difficult.

Another possible motive for tying is to *discriminate among customers* according to the intensity with which they use the supplier's product. Suppose that M manufactures a machine used by food processing companies to inject salt into foods during processing. If M feels that customers who use the machine more may be willing to pay more for it, M may try to charge them based on intensity of use so as to maximize its total revenues. Direct metering may be very difficult. Sometimes, however, intensity of use is directly proportional to the amount of a second product the customer uses in connection with M's product. In the case of the salt-dispensing machine, intensity of use can be measured by the amount of salt used by the customer. Thus, M may try to measure intensity by requiring customers of its machines also to buy its salt. Through the salt sales, M's total revenue will be greater in transactions with high-intensity users.

**Legal Standards:** Tying can occur only if two separate products are involved. Often this is obvious, but sometimes it is not, as for example in the case of various options on new automobiles. Generally, a transaction will be viewed as including two separate products if the evidence demonstrates that there really are two separate markets in which the different items are commonly demanded. However, even if there are two separate markets, courts usually will treat a transaction as involving only one product if packaging two items is significantly more efficient than selling them separately.

If there are two separate products, tying is illegal only if the supplier has *substantial power in the market for the tying product.* The reason for this requirement is the generally accepted proposition that tying cannot cause any substantial harm in the *tied* market unless the supplier has quite a bit of power in the *tying* market. Market power is measured in the same way here as in other cases. Today, a supplier probably has to have at least a 30 percent share of the tying market to be viewed as having substantial power in that market. Other factors, such as entry barriers, are also very important. According to the courts, there is a second requirement for tying to be illegal, namely, that the supplier's tying arrangements must generate a substantial amount of business in the *tied* market. This requirement is so easy to establish, however, that it is practically always present.

## *Exclusive Dealing*

**Nature and Effects:** The most common form of **exclusive dealing** agreement is one in which the customer makes a commitment that it will purchase a particular product or service only from the supplier (and, implicitly or explicitly, *not* from the supplier's competitors). Many times these arrangements are called "requirements contracts" because the parties often speak in terms of the buyer's commitment to purchase its "requirements" of a product from the seller. The primary concern caused by this type of arrangement is that there may be fewer and less frequent opportunities for the seller's competitors to compete for those customers who are parties to the exclusive dealing. Widespread use of such agreements in a market may also increase entry barriers for potential competitors.

Another kind of exclusive dealing that occurs less often is one in which the seller agrees to sell only to a particular buyer (and, thus, not sell to the buyer's competitors). This is sometimes called an "output" contract, because the seller obligates itself to sell all of its output of a product to the buyer. Output contracts usually raise no competitive concerns, but occasionally might unreasonably prevent the buyer's competitors from acquiring products needed to compete.

**Legal Standards:** Today, exclusive dealing is likely to be illegal under Section 1 of the Sherman Act or Section 3 of the Clayton Act only if a dominant share—probably more than 30 percent—of the relevant market is locked away from competitors. Thus, the practice creates a real legal risk only when a leading or dominant firm in a market makes widespread use of it.

## *Price Discrimination*

Although the original version of Section 2 of the Clayton Act contained a prohibition of **price discrimination,** it proved ineffective because of certain major loopholes. In 1936 Congress enacted the Robinson-Patman Act in an effort to make the law against price discrimination more effective. Congress's main purpose in passing this law was to protect small businesses from having to pay higher prices than larger companies.

**Basic Elements:** The interstate commerce requirement in the Robinson-Patman Act is more difficult to prove than in any other of the antitrust laws. It is not enough that the seller or buyer is an interstate company or that the transaction affects interstate commerce—at least one of the relevant sales must actually cross state lines. Only a few states have laws prohibiting intrastate price discrimination within their borders. It should also be noted that many nations, including the United States, have *antidumping laws* that prohibit a foreign producer from selling goods in the country at a lower price than in that producer's home country.

Assuming that the interstate commerce requirement is met, the following must be proved to establish a violation of the Robinson-Patman Act. (1) The seller must have charged *different prices* to two or more different customers. (2) The transaction must have involved *tangible commodities,* not services, land, or intangibles. (3) The transactions must have been *sales,* rather than consignments, leases, or some other form of transaction. (4) The goods sold in the transactions being compared must have been *of like grade and quality,* which means that the products sold to different customers at different prices must have been essentially the same. Trivial differences are ignored. (5) The evidence must demonstrate a likelihood of *substantial harm to competition.* Generally speaking, isolated or sporadic instances of price discrimination will not violate the Act because it usually will be impossible to prove competitive injury. Such injury often can be proved only where the discrimination was recurring and systematic. To prove injury to one of the seller's competitors, it is usually necessary to show that the discriminatorily lower prices to favored customers were *predatory* (below cost). To prove injury to one of the favored customer's competitors, it is usually necessary to show that the disfavored buyer actually lost substantial business to the favored buyer because of the discrimination.

**Defenses:** When the basic elements of a Robinson-Patman Act violation are proved, the seller is guilty unless it can prove one of three available defenses. The first is *cost justification.* There is no violation if the seller's different prices are simply a reflection of differences in the costs of "manufacture, sale, or delivery." Thus the seller wins if it proves that the higher prices to one buyer or group of buyers are directly attributable to the higher costs of providing the goods to that buyer or group. The second defense is *meeting competition.* A seller does not violate the Act if a lower price to one buyer "was made in good faith to meet an equally low price of a competitor." Suppose S generally charges $10 for a product, but learns that its competitor is offering the product to a certain customer for $9. S can legally meet the $9 price to that customer even while keeping its price to other buyers at $10. Another version of the meeting competition defense permits a seller to charge different prices in different geographic markets in order to meet different prevailing market prices in those different areas. The third defense is *changing conditions.* The seller is permitted to change prices in response to changing conditions that affect the marketability of the goods, such as imminent deterioration of perishable commodities or obsolescence of seasonal goods.

## SUMMARY

The primary objective of antitrust law is to promote competition in markets. The various antitrust laws generally apply to activities occurring in or affecting interstate commerce. The laws are subject to a few limited exemptions, and are enforced by the U.S. Justice Department, Federal Trade Commission, and private parties. Section 2 of the Sherman Act prohibits monopolization, which occurs when one firm dominates a market so completely that it really does not have to worry about the responses of competitors. In addition to proving that a firm has overwhelming market power, it also must be shown that the monopolist willfully acquired or maintained its power by predatory conduct. Mergers—acquisitions of stock or assets—are prohibited by Section 7 of the Clayton Act if the evidence indicates that they are likely to diminish competition in a substantial way. Mergers are usually classified as horizontal (between competitors), vertical (where one of the merging firms buys something that the other sells), and conglomerate. Horizontal mergers pose the greatest risk to competition and thus are more likely to violate Section 7.

Horizontal restraints of trade—arrangements between competitors that restrict competition—are covered by Section 1 of the Sherman Act, which prohibits "contracts, combinations, or conspiracies in restraint of trade." Horizontal price fixing, market divisions, and boycotts are per se illegal, which means that these arrangements are automatically illegal once they are identified. Other arrangements between competitors are judged under the rule of reason, and are illegal only if they are likely to cause substantial restrictions on competition.

Vertical restraints of trade occur between firms at different levels of the distribution chain. Resale price maintenance involves arrangements by which a seller and buyer agree on the price at which the buyer will resell the products to its own customers. Despite substantial controversy, the practice is per se illegal under Section 1 of the Sherman Act. Vertical nonprice restrictions, on the other hand, are judged under Section 1's rule of reason. These restrictions normally relate to the area within which or the customers to whom the buyer can resell.

A tying arrangement occurs where the supplier provides a product only on the condition that the customer take another product. Tying agreements violate Section 1 of the Sherman Act or Section 3 of the Clayton Act when the supplier has substantial power in the market for the tying product. An exclusive dealing agreement occurs where the buyer agrees to buy all of its requirements of a product from the seller (and not from the seller's competitors), or where the seller agrees to sell all of its output to the buyer (and not to the buyer's competitors). The requirements type of exclusive dealing is much more common. Exclusive dealing violates Section 1 of the Sherman Act or Section 3 of the Clayton Act only if the arrangements lock up a substantial portion of the relevant market, probably at least 30 percent today.

Price discrimination violates the Robinson-Patman Act when the seller sells the same tangible product to two or more different purchasers at different prices, state lines are crossed, and competitive injury results. There are three defenses to a Robinson-Patman Act violation.

## KEY TERMS

**Oligopoly**
**Monopoly**
**Market share**
**Entry barriers**
**Cross elasticity of demand**
**Cross elasticity of supply**
**Predatory pricing**
**Nonprice predation**
**Merger**
**Horizontal merger**
**Vertical merger**
**Vertical integration**
**Conglomerate merger**
**Horizontal restraint of trade**
**Collusion**
**Rule of reason**
**Per se rule**
**Price fixing**
**Market division**
**Boycott**
**Joint venture**
**Vertical restraint of trade**
**Resale price maintenance (RPM)**
**Intrabrand competition**

Interbrand competition
Free riding
Vertical nonprice restriction (VNR)
Tying agreement
Exclusive dealing
Price discrimination

## QUESTIONS AND PROBLEMS

**1.** Alcoa was charged with monopolizing the U.S. market for aluminum ingot. Aluminum ingot is sold in blocks or bars to fabricators, who use it to make aluminum sheets, conduit, wiring, and other end products. Alcoa produced 90 percent of the "virgin" aluminum ingot sold in the United States. Some of its ingot production, however, was actually fabricated by Alcoa into end products before being sold. Another factor in the market was "secondary" ingot, or aluminum ingot made from recycled aluminum. Secondary ingot was acceptable for many of the same uses as virgin ingot, but not for all of them. If the product market was defined to include all of Alcoa's virgin ingot production, including that part which Alcoa itself fabricated before selling, but not to include secondary ingot, Alcoa's market share would be about 90 percent. If the market definition also included secondary ingot, Alcoa's share would be 64 percent. If the market definition included secondary ingot, but did not include that part of Alcoa's ingot which it fabricated before selling, Alcoa's share would be 33 percent. Discuss how the product market should be defined. (*United States v. Aluminum Co. of America,* 148 F.2d 416, 2d Cir. 1945.)

**2.** Suppose that in a particular three-state region there are only two granite quarries from which granite suitable for cemetery monuments can be obtained. This type of granite is not available anywhere else in this region, and transportation costs are too high for granite to be shipped in from outside the region. Ace owns one quarry and Beta owns the other. Ace produces 60 percent of the region's total granite production from its quarry, and Beta produces the other 40 percent. Ace does not fabricate any of its granite but sells it in large blocks to firms who make cemetery monuments. Beta is also a cemetery monument maker and uses all of its granite production to manufacture monuments. It sells none to other monument manufacturers. Ace is charged by the Justice Department with monopolizing the sale of granite in this three-state region. Discuss how the product and geographic market should be defined and whether Ace is likely to be found in violation of Section 2 of the Sherman Act.

**3.** Martex Co. produces a special type of scalpel used by surgeons. The scalpel effectively cauterizes the incision as the surgeon operates, thus eliminating much of the bleeding problem in surgery. Although Martex was not able to obtain a patent on the scalpel when it was developed several years ago, there still is only one other manufacturer of this type of scalpel. Of the total sales of the cauterizing scalpel, Martex accounts for 85 percent. The scalpel is used by most surgeons for major surgical procedures, and Martex sales represent 70 percent of the total sales of all types of scalpels. Whenever Martex sells these scalpels to surgeons or hospitals, it does so under a contract requiring the buyer to return the scalpel to Martex when it is worn out. Martex uses the worn-out scalpels in its research lab for experimentation, with the objective of improving the product.

Discuss whether Martex may have violated Section 2 of the Sherman Act.

**4.** The nation's second largest can producer acquired the nation's third largest producer of glass containers. Cans and bottles did not compete for all end uses, but for some uses they did compete. For example, there was clear rivalry between cans and bottles for the business of soft drink and beer producers. Both industries were relatively concentrated: the top two can manufacturers had 70 percent of can sales; the top three bottle manufacturers had 55 percent of bottle sales. If cans and bottles were viewed as a single market, the two firms would have, respectively, 22 percent and 3 percent of that market. Discuss whether this merger would violate Section 7 of the Clayton Act. (*United States v. Continental Can Co.,* 378 U.S. 441, 1964.)

**5.** General Motors, Ford, and Chrysler, in that order, were the largest automobile producers in America. Together they accounted for 90 percent of domestic production. The domestic spark plug market was dominated by Champion (40 percent), AC (30 percent—wholly owned by General Motors), and Autolite (15 percent). The remainder of the spark plug market was accounted for by very small producers.

The independent spark plug makers (primarily Champion and Autolite) sold spark plugs to the automakers (primarily Ford and Chrysler) at cost or below. These original equipment (OE) plugs were sold so cheaply because auto mechanics almost always replace worn out plugs with the same brand that had been original equipment (called the OE tie). Thus, it was essential to get into the OE market in order to get into the market for replacement plugs—the aftermarket. Large profits were made in this aftermarket.

Ford, whose purchases of OE plugs from the independent spark plug makers amounted to 10 percent of all the spark plugs produced domestically, wanted to gain entry into the profitable spark plug aftermarket. It did so by purchasing Autolite's only spark plug factory, as well as its trademark and distribution facilities. Discuss whether this merger might violate Section 7 of the Clayton Act. (*Ford Motor Co. v. United States,* 405 U.S. 562, 1972.)

**6.** Theatre Enterprises, Inc., owned and operated the Crest Theatre in a suburban shopping center located about six miles from downtown Baltimore. At that time, the downtown area was still the most important shopping district. As a result, a downtown movie theatre generally had about 10 times the drawing power of a suburban theatre like the Crest. Before and after the opening of the Crest, Theatre Enterprises sought to obtain first-run films from several major film distributors. It approached each distributor individually, and was turned down on every occasion. As a result, the Crest was able to show first-run films only after the downtown theatres had shown them. Other than these delayed first-runs, Crest was left with "subsequent runs" (films that had been re-released). Theatre Enterprises sued the distributors, claiming that they had violated Section 1 of the Sherman Act by engaging in a group refusal to deal. There was no direct evidence of agreement among the distributors. Discuss whether and under what circumstances Theatre Enterprises could prevail. (*Theatre Enterprises, Inc. v. Paramount Film Distributing Corp.*, 346 U.S. 537, 1954.)

7. During a period of time in which demand for refined sugar was falling because of increasing consumer preferences for artificial sweeteners, several sugar refiners began offering price discounts to some of their larger customers in an effort to stimulate sales and decrease inventories. These discounts were generally in the form of secret rebates. Before long, most other sugar refiners and their customers learned about these rebates. Claiming that these discriminatory rebates were "demoralizing the industry at a time when market conditions were already bad" and that customers were "losing faith in the integrity of the sugar industry," these other refiners urged those granting rebates to stop the practice. The rebating refiners argued, however, that their practices were completely legitimate because "everybody knows it's cheaper to sell to large customers." The nonrebating refiners then put pressure on sugar cane and sugar beet growers and within a short time the rebating refiners were unable to buy cane and beets for making sugar. Within a month the rebating refiners all stopped the practice of favoring certain customers. The Justice Department filed suit in federal district court, claiming that the "nonrebating" sugar refiners and the growers had violated Section 1 of the Sherman Act. Discuss whether Section 1 has been violated.

8. Many retail department stores provide delivery service for large items purchased by their customers. In the New York City area, the presidents of three stores were talking privately about delivery problems at a Chamber of Commerce luncheon. One of them mentioned that the costs involved in maintaining delivery trucks, forklifts, and other equipment and employees were becoming too great to justify the service. The other two agreed, but all of them were concerned about the business they might lose if they discontinued delivery service. They decided to contact other department stores in the metropolitan area to find out what their feelings were. After a series of discussions among the presidents of 18 of the 20 largest department stores in the area, they came up with the following alternative proposals:

**a.** They could all simultaneously stop providing delivery service.

**b.** They could jointly select and deal with an existing independent delivery service. The group would investigate existing services, invite them to submit bids, and ultimately select one and jointly contract with it.

Upon hearing of these proposals, the U.S. Department of Justice initiated an investigation. The department was interested in whether any of these proposals might violate Section 1 of the Sherman Act. Discuss the legality of proposals a and b.

9. Chemco is a manufacturer of various agricultural chemicals such as herbicides and insecticides. Most of these products were sold to wholesale distributors who then resold either to retail dealers or directly to farmers. During a 20-day period in late 1980, Chemco received individual complaints from five of its distributors in the Pacific Coast region of the country. These distributors complained that a sixth distributor, Ace, had been significantly undercutting their prices and hurting their sales. Chemco made no promises to them, but a month later it announced to all of its distributors across the nation that it was implementing a new policy. Chemco's new policy was that, in the future, it would sell only to those distributors who would indicate in advance their intent to abide by Chemco's schedule of suggested resale prices. Most distributors responded affirmatively to Chemco's new policy. Those few who did not respond affirmatively were discontinued as Chemco distributors. One of those who did not respond affirmatively and who was discontinued was Ace. Discuss whether Chemco and its distributors may have violated Section 1 of the Sherman Act.

10. Sarco, Inc., a manufacturer of various types of electronic equipment and devices used for industrial and medical purposes, sold its products to franchised dealers who then resold to their customers. Many of the products were complicated and relatively expensive. As a result, dealers needed to be carefully selected and trained so that they would be knowledgeable about the products and could offer essential consultation and demonstration services to potential customers. In addition, it was necessary that dealers be able to expertly perform repairs on the products. Sarco, which accounted for between 10 and 18 percent of national sales in its various product lines, granted each dealer an exclusive territory and required each to sell only in that territory. Sarco's distribution system was challenged under Section 1 of the Sherman Act. Discuss whether the system is likely to be legal or illegal under Section 1 of the Sherman Act.

# CHAPTER 49

# EMPLOYMENT LAW

The law of employment relations has undergone a fundamental transformation within recent years and change continues even today. For much of our nation's history, the legal relationship between employer and employee was governed by general traditional principles of common law, which in practice typically tilted in the direction of the employer's authority. For example, employers lawfully could discharge their workers for any (or no) reason, including the individual employee's race, union membership, or job-related injury.

The growth of unions was the working person's first response to this legal regime, which seemingly favored employers to an inordinate degree. Unionization was frustrated at first by a series of judicial decisions, but once Congress provided statutory protection in the 1930s, the new labor organizations were able to thrive and provided considerable benefits to member workers.

Notwithstanding the advantages provided the majority of employees, unions had some serious shortcomings, especially when it came to protecting small groups of employees and dealing with noneconomic issues. In the 1960s Congress once again intervened to expand the protection of workers in areas where unions had contributed little. A number of antidiscrimination laws were enacted, the most significant being the Civil Rights Act of 1964. The Occupational Safety and Health Act of 1968 established a new agency and granted it considerable power to guard against workplace hazards. Legislation expanded worker rights in other areas as well. Perhaps prodded by this congressional activity, the courts also began to reexamine old precedents and initiate new common-law protections for employees. This chapter exlores these developments in the law of employment relations and the complications the changes create for employers.

## LABOR RELATIONS LAW

In the early nineteenth century, attempts to unionize were stymied by the doctrine that they represented unlawful criminal conspiracies at common law. This theory gradually fell into disfavor and by the end of the century unions began to achieve some success, especially with the advent of industrialization and a rise in perceived employer abuse of power. Even in the early twentieth century, however, the courts continued to frustrate union development by enjoining critical functions of such organizations, such as striking and picketing. This was an era of much labor strife and periodic outbreaks of violence associated with labor/management disputes.

Recognizing the existence of a serious national problem, Congress passed several laws in an attempt to resolve labor/management difficulties, including the Railway Labor Act and the Norris–La Guardia Act, which prohibited, among other provisions, the use of injunctions against many union activities. Although these statutes eased the situation somewhat, it soon became clear that more extensive legislation was necessary. In 1935 Congress created a comprehensive framework for labor relations law by passing the National Labor Relations Act (NLRA). While this act has been amended, the basic rules established by the original NLRA survive today as the foundation of current law.

The NLRA unambiguously recognized an employee's right to organize by forming unions and authorized these labor organizations to bargain collectively with employers. Certain practices were declared to be **unfair labor practices,** and these were prohibited. Unfair labor practices were defined to include employer domination of unions, interference with employee organizing, discrimination against union members, and refusal to bargain collectively.

In order to enforce these requirements, the NLRA established a new agency, the National Labor Relations Board (NLRB). The NLRB consists of the General Counsel and the Board itself. The General Counsel investigates charges of unfair labor practices and, if they are found meritworthy, initiates an action against the responsible party. These actions are heard by an administrative law judge and may be appealed to the entire Board. If the Board finds a violation, it can seek enforcement of a number of sanctions, including cease-and-desist orders and back pay awards. Board decisions may be appealed to the U.S. Courts of Appeals.

## Coverage

The NLRA applies generally to all employers involved in or affecting interstate commerce. As discussed in Chapter 5 (Constitutional Law), this language is quite broad in scope. The act is limited to protection of employees, however, and does not cover independent contractors, a distinction explained in Chapter 19. In addition, some categories of employees are specifically excluded from the act's coverage. Government employees, as well as workers for railways and airlines (protected under a different statute) are outside the NLRA's coverage. Significantly, managerial and supervisory employees are not covered by the act, as they are considered to be part of "management" rather than "labor."

## Right to Organize

Central to the NLRA is its guarantee of a right to form unions. Once a group of employees determines that it desires to form an organization for collective bargaining, the group seeks out other workers for support. Once 30 percent of the eligible employees in an appropriate job category sign authorization cards, the employee group may petition for an election to certify a union as the employees' bargaining representative. Conduct of such elections is carefully scrutinized by the NLRB to ensure "laboratory conditions" of fairness. Employers opposing unionization must take special care in their actions and statements lest they be found to have committed an unfair labor practice, in which case the union may be automatically certified by the Board, regardless of the election's outcome. The following case illustrates the care that an employer must take to avoid disturbing the laboratory conditions required for a unionization election.

---

### NLRB v. Exchange Parts Co.
U.S. Supreme Court,
375 U.S. 405 (1964)

Exchange Parts Co. is in the automobile parts rebuilding business. On November 9, 1959, the International Brotherhood of Boilermakers, Iron Shipbuilders, Blacksmiths, Forgers and Helpers informed the company that a majority of workers favored unionization and on February 19 the Board granted an election petition.

On February 25, the company held a dinner for employees, at which a vice-president announced that a previously granted extra vacation day could be either a floating holiday or could be taken on the individual employee's birthday. The workers chose the latter. The vice-president also mentioned the upcoming election as an opportunity for employees to "determine whether they wished to hand over their right to speak and act for themselves."

On March 4, the company sent its employees a letter that spoke of the "Empty Promises of the Union" and "the fact that it is the Company that puts things in your envelope. . . ." After mentioning a number of benefits, the letter stated: "The Union can't put any of those things in your envelope—only the Company can do that." The letter also went on to state that "it didn't take a Union to get any of those things and . . . it won't take a Union to get additional improvements in the future." Past company benefits were summarized and new benefits were announced, including the new birthday holiday, a new system for computing overtime that had the effect of increasing wages, and a new vacation schedule that enabled employees to take more time off per year.

The election was held on March 18, and the union lost. The union promptly filed a charge with the Board, which held that the company actions had the intent to induce employees

*(continued)*

to vote against the union, thereby disrupting laboratory conditions and amounting to an unfair labor practice. The Board sought enforcement of its ruling in the court of appeals, which held against the Board. The Board then appealed this decision to the Supreme Court.

---

**Decision:** The Supreme Court reversed, ordering that the Board's order be enforced. The NLRA makes it an unfair labor practice for an employer "to interfere with, restrain, or coerce employees in the exercise of [their rights to form labor unions]." The Court had earlier held that "[t]he action of employees with respect to the choice of their bargaining agents may be induced by favors bestowed by the employer as well as by his threats or domination." The employees are unlikely to miss the suggestion of "a fist inside the velvet glove" that comes from well-timed increases in employee benefits. ■

---

In addition to benefits, employers must be careful not to say anything that may be interpreted as a "threat." An employer's statement that a plant shutdown was possible because the union would make company survival impossible was held to be unlawful.

## Collective Bargaining

**Collective bargaining** is the term for negotiations between an employer and the union representative. Once a union has been certified as an official bargaining representative of a category of employees, the NLRA imposes a duty to bargain in good faith on both employer and union. Mandatory subjects of bargaining include wages and most working conditions. The good faith provision requires the parties to make a sincere effort to reach agreement. Approaches such as "take it or leave it" proposals may support an inference of bad faith and hence an unfair labor practice finding. An employer also must be willing to furnish certain information to the union and cannot delay unduly in doing so.

## Strikes

The most powerful device possessed by unions under the NLRA is the right to strike. This right is available when collective bargaining has reached an impasse. For a strike to be legal it must be supported by a majority of members and cannot be a "wildcat" strike by a disgruntled minority. The NLRA also restricts strikes to those against the primary employer and prohibits strikes against third parties in an attempt to coerce that third party to pressure the primary employer. Even primary strikes are unlawful if they are violent or designed to compel "featherbedding" (the hiring of unnecessary employees) or other illegal contract terms.

The NLRA imposes other conditions on the conduct of strikes. For example, if workers are on strike against one employer at a multi-employer location (such as a construction site), the employees may not picket the entire site, as this applies unlawful secondary pressure against the other employers. Workers may picket a portion of the site that is used largely by their primary employer. If a strike is legal, the employer may be restricted in dealing with his striking employees. If the workers are engaged in an authorized strike protesting the employer's unfair labor practices, the strikers are automatically entitled to reinstatement after the strike is resolved. In the more traditional economic wage strike, the employer need not necessarily rehire strikers but never can discriminate against strikers, who have a right to seek reemployment on terms equal to those offered other prospective employees.

## Nonunion Employees

Although the NLRA was designed primarily to protect unionization, it extends certain rights to nonunion workers as well. Where nonunion employees engage in concerted activity, such as a walkout in response to perceived unsafe working conditions, they are protected much like strikers on behalf of a union. In general, however, employers have a relatively free hand in dealing with nonunion workers. This situation gives rise to one potentially serious pitfall, however. If an employer sets up "employee committees" or other groups to address grievances in the absence of a union, the committee's independence from management must be carefully ensured. Otherwise, the employer may be found to have created a company-dominated labor organization, which is an unfair labor practice under the NLRA.

The above discussion represents an exceedingly brief review of labor relations law. There is a huge body of precedent under the NLRA elaborating on the above principles. Many of the legal rules in this field have become quite picayune. Consequently, employers must take special care in any controversy involving an organization of employees.

# EMPLOYMENT DISCRIMINATION LAW

For much of America's history, employers had the legal right to discriminate among employees on any basis other than union membership. Recently, however, antidiscrimination laws have been enacted that affect all phases of the employment process and that prohibit discrimination based on race, color, religion, sex, age, national origin, or perceived handicap. Worker use of these laws has grown to the point where they may exceed the NLRA as a source of litigation and potential employer liability.

## *Title VII*

**Coverage:** The Civil Rights Act of 1964 is a comprehensive federal enactment prohibiting discrimination in various settings, including housing, public accommodations, and education. Title VII of the Act deals specifically with discrimination in employment. Title VII prohibits discrimination against individuals because of their *race, color, religion, sex, or national origin*. Although Title VII was one of the earliest laws prohibiting employment discrimination, it remains the most significant.

The provisions of Title VII apply to employers, employment agencies, and labor unions. An employer is subject to Title VII if it (1) has 15 or more employees *and* (2) is engaged in business that affects interstate or foreign commerce. State and local governments are also within the definition of employer, and their employment practices are covered by Title VII. In most instances, the federal government's employment practices are also covered.

**Scope of Protection:** Title VII's prohibition against discrimination on the basis of race or color is very broad. It obviously protects blacks, but it also protects many other classes from unequal treatment, including Hispanics, American Indians, and Asian-Americans. Even whites are protected against racial discrimination.

The prohibition against national origin discrimination is violated if an employer discriminates on the basis of a person's country of origin. It is not illegal, however, for an employer to require employees to be U.S. citizens. (However, a *government* employer must have a very good reason for requiring its employees to be U.S. citizens, or the requirement will violate the equal protection clause of the U.S. Constitution.) Title VII also protects individuals against discrimination based on the race, color, or national origin of their family members or friends.

Title VII's prohibition against sex discrimination, which forbids unequal treatment based on *gender,* is aimed primarily at discrimination against females, but it also protects males against gender-based discrimination. The law makes it illegal to use sex as a factor in employment decisions, and also to engage in sexual harassment. Title VII protects women from discrimination because of pregnancy or childbirth, as well. It does not apply to discrimination based on sexual practices, preferences, or lifestyles, so long as the employer treats employees of both sexes equally.

Although religious organizations can lawfully hire employees based on their religious beliefs, other employers cannot make distinctions for religious reasons. The term religion not only includes well-recognized religious faiths, but also unorthodox ones. For Title VII purposes, the courts use the same broad definition of religion that they use in freedom-of-religion cases under the first amendment to the Constitution: "a sincere and meaningful belief occupying in the life of its possessor a place parallel to that filled by the God of those admittedly qualified."

In addition to forbidding discrimination based on religion, the law also requires an employer to make "reasonable accommodation" for employees' religious beliefs and practices. Employers do not have to go to great lengths or incur significant expense in order to make reasonable accommodation, however. For example, in *TWA v. Hardison,* 432 U.S. 63 (1977), Hardison worked in a department of TWA that had to operate 7 days a week, 24 hours a day. He became an adherent of a religious denomination that observed a Saturday sabbath, and tried to get Saturdays off. The collective bargaining agreement between TWA and the labor union included a seniority system that controlled many aspects of employment, including priorities in getting particular days off. Hardison did not have enough seniority to get Saturdays off most of the time. TWA tried unsuccessfully to find other employees who would voluntarily switch days with him so that he would not have to work Saturdays. Hardison requested that TWA use supervisors to fill in for him, hire additional personnel, or require other employees to switch with him regardless of seniority. TWA declined, Hardison refused to work on Saturday, and the employer fired him. When Hardison claimed a Title VII violation, the Supreme Court ruled that TWA had acted properly. The company fulfilled its obligation to make reasonable accommodation by reducing weekend shifts to minimum crews and trying to find volunteers to trade shifts.

**Procedures and Remedies:** Title VII establishes special procedures for enforcing its dictates. An individual who believes him- or herself to be the victim of unlawful discrimination cannot simply take an employer to court. Rather, the Civil Rights Act created the Equal Employment Opportunity Commission (EEOC) to receive complaints of violations. The EEOC investigates these complaints and, when they are adequately supported by facts, the Commission attempts conciliation measures between the employer and employees. If conciliation efforts fail, the EEOC may file suit in federal district court. Individuals may sue to enforce Title VII only after EEOC and the particular state equal employment opportunity agency has had the opportunity to take action.

Once a court finds that Title VII has been violated, the court is empowered to grant an injunction prohibiting future violations and correcting past actions. Retroactive back pay or seniority may be ordered for employees who have suffered from unlawful discrimination. In addition, a court may compel an offending company to implement an "affirmative action" program to recruit and retain minority employees.

## What Constitutes Discrimination Under Title VII?

Illegal discrimination can be proved in either of two ways. First, the plaintiff may show that the defendant had engaged in *intentional* discrimination—sometimes referred to as "disparate treatment." Second, the plaintiff may show that some employment practice or policy of the defendant has had a discriminatory *effect,* or impact—sometimes referred to as "disparate impact." The following discussion explains the use of these terms.

**Intentional Discrimination:** In general, any employment decision or practice which treats individuals unequally *because of* race, color, religion, sex, or national origin violates Title VII. Illegal discrimination might occur, for example, in connection with firing, refusing to hire, refusing to train or promote, granting unequal compensation or fringe benefits, or practicing any type of segregation or classification of employees or applicants that tends to deprive them of employment opportunities.

A violation of Title VII may be proved by showing that an employer *intended* to discriminate for a prohibited reason. There obviously would be a violation, for instance, if an employer maintained an express policy of "whites only" for admission of employees to a management training program.

**Prima Facie *Case*:** Express discrimination such as this became much less common after employers became fully aware of Title VII and its requirements. Intentional discrimination still occurs, but that intent usually is not expressed so openly as before. Recognizing this fact, the courts have ruled that an inference of discriminatory intent may be drawn in certain circumstances. When the EEOC or an individual plaintiff proves facts which make it logical to conclude that intentional discrimination probably has occurred, the courts hold that a ***prima facie*** **case** of discrimination exists.

Suppose, for example, that an individual job applicant is rejected and has reason to believe that the employer's refusal to hire was motivated by unlawful discrimination. Even though there was no explicit discriminatory motive on the employer's part, a *prima facie* violation of Title VII can be established by showing that (1) the applicant is within a protected class (racial or ethnic minority or female); (2) the applicant applied for a job for which the employer was seeking applicants; (3) the applicant was qualified to perform the job; (4) the applicant was not hired for the job; and (5) the employer either filled the position with a nonminority person or continued trying to fill it. If the claim of discrimination is based on a discharge rather than a refusal to hire, a *prima facie* case can be established by showing that

(1) the plaintiff is within a protected class; (2) the plaintiff was performing the job satisfactorily; (3) the plaintiff was discharged, and (4) the plaintiff's work was then assigned to someone who was not within a protected class. In other employment decisions, the requirements of a *prima facie* case would similarly have to be modified to fit the circumstances. (It should be noted that when courts speak of "protected class," they are referring to the usual situation in which a female or nonwhite person is the plaintiff; it is possible, however, for a male or white to be the plaintiff.)

***Employer's Rebuttal:*** When the plaintiff in such a case introduces evidence sufficient to create a *prima facie* case, the burden then shifts to the employer to bring forth evidence of a *legitimate, nondiscriminatory reason* for plaintiff's rejection. To overcome plaintiff's *prima facie* case, the employer can introduce evidence relating to matters such as the applicant's past experience and work record, letters of recommendation, or the superior qualifications of the person actually hired. An example is found in *Peters v. Jefferson Chemical Co.,* 516 F.2d 447 (5th Cir. 1975), in which the employer successfully rebutted the female plaintiff's *prima facie* case by showing that she had not been hired as a laboratory chemist because she had not done laboratory work for several years. The court did not require the employer to prove that her skills were actually inadequate, but accepted the employer's assumption that laboratory skills diminish from nonuse over a substantial period of time. In another case, *Boyd v. Madison County Mutual Insurance Co.,* 653 F.2d 1173 (7th Cir. 1981), a male employee established a *prima facie* case of sex discrimination against the employer by showing that the employer had a policy of awarding attendance bonuses only to clerical employees, all of whom were women. The employer was able to rebut the *prima facie* case successfully by demonstrating that there had been a serious absenteeism problem with clerical staff and that the bonus policy was aimed at correcting that problem.

In a case based on an allegedly discriminatory discharge, the employer might overcome the plaintiff's *prima facie* case by showing evidence of the plaintiff's poor performance, absenteeism, insubordination, and so on.

The types of reasons that are sufficient to rebut a plaintiff's *prima facie* case may vary from one kind of job to another. For instance, some jobs require skills that are quite subjective and extremely difficult to measure. Many executive and professional jobs are of such a nature, requiring traits such as creativity, initiative, ability to delegate and supervise, communicative skills, and a facility for persuasion. With regard to jobs that are inherently subjective, an employer usually will be permitted to use subjective justifications for the action taken. Thus, an attorney could be rejected because of "poor reputation," so long as the employer actually had some evidence of this fact. On the other hand, a court ordinarily will not accept an employer's purely subjective evaluation of an individual when the job in question requires little skill or responsibility or when it requires skills that can be objectively measured.

***Pretext:*** If the plaintiff establishes a *prima facie* Title VII violation and the employer fails to come forth with acceptable evidence of a legitimate, nondiscriminatory reason, the plaintiff wins. If the employer does produce such evidence, the plaintiff will lose unless he or she can then convince the court that the employer's asserted reason was really just a "pretext"—that is, a cover-up for intentional discrimination. Plaintiff might be able to show, for example, that the employer's "legitimate reason" was applied discriminatorily. In *Corley v. Jackson Police Dept.,* 566 F.2d 994 (5th Cir. 1978), the employer proved that the plaintiffs, black police officers, had been fired for accepting bribes. Although this clearly was a legitimate reason for firing them, the plaintiffs proved that white officers who also had been accused of the same conduct by an informant were not investigated as thoroughly and were not fired. The court held that the employer's reason was a pretext for racial discrimination and that Title VII had been violated.

***Mixed Motive Cases:*** Let us assume that the employee has established a *prima facie* case of intentional discrimination, the employer has produced plausible evidence of a legitimate nondiscriminatory reason, and the employee has produced some evidence of pretext. In most cases, after weighing the evidence, the trial judge will then find that the employer's action was based on either an illegal reason or a legitimate one and will rule accordingly. Suppose, however, that the court finds that the employer acted on the basis of a dual motive. In other words, the evidence convinces the court that the employer treated the employee in a particular way because of *both* illegitimate discrimination *and* a legitimate reason.

In *Price Waterhouse v. Hopkins,* 109 S.Ct. 1775 (1989), the U.S. Supreme Court held that a somewhat different method should be used for deciding so-called "mixed motive" cases. In that case, the district court found that Hopkins, an accountant for Price Waterhouse, was denied partnership status for both legitimate and illegitimate reasons. The legitimate reason was Hopkins's abrasive personality and inability to get along well with staff employees in the firm. The illegitimate reason was "sexual stereotyping"; in other words, she was also turned down because many of the male partners thought she did not act in certain ways that they thought women should act. The Supreme Court said that, in such a case, the employer must prove, by a preponderance of the evidence, that it would have made the same decision regarding the employee even if it had not taken gender (or race) into account. Thus, when the district court analyzes all the evidence that has been presented and determines that the case is of the mixed motive type, the court then must decide whether the employer's evidence has met this burden of proof.

**Discriminatory Impact:** We have seen that a violation of Title VII can be proved by showing that the employer intended to discriminate. This proof is accomplished either by presenting direct evidence of discriminatory motive or by establishing a *prima facie* case from which discriminatory intent can be inferred.

Another way to prove that an employer has violated Title VII is to show that a particular employment rule or practice, although apparently neutral on its face, actually has an unequal impact on a protected group. Examples include height and weight requirements having the effect of excluding a disproportionate number of females, or a standardized test or educational requirement having the effect of excluding a disproportionate number of persons from a particular ethnic group. In such a case, the plaintiff is not required to show that the defendant had an intent to discriminate. The procedure for establishing a Title VII violation in this way, however, is similar to the procedure for establishing a *prima facie* case of discriminatory intent.

**Prima Facie *Case*:** The individual plaintiff, or the EEOC acting in the individual's behalf, must initially prove that the employment practice in question has an adverse impact on the protected group of which the individual is a member. This can be accomplished by the use of several different types of evidence. It could be shown, for example, that the employment practice has caused the employer to hire 40 percent of the whites who had applied, but only 20 percent of black applicants. Or, in another situation, discriminatory impact might be proved by showing that some action of the employer had the effect of eliminating 75 percent of all women from possible consideration even though women comprise approximately one-half of the total population. Still other types of evidence might be used in other cases.

It is important to realize, however, that the method used to prove discriminatory impact must be tailored to fit the particular employment practice being challenged and the particular group allegedly being affected. Thus, a court usually would not accept a comparison of the employer's minority hiring rate with general population statistics where the job in question required special qualifications. For example, if the job required a degree in mechanical engineering, the employer's experience in filling that job would need to be compared with the available population of mechanical engineers. The geographic area in which the statistical comparison should be made will also differ from one case to another. Suppose, for instance, that a plaintiff is trying to establish discriminatory impact in the case of an employer in San Francisco. If the job in question involves unskilled or semiskilled labor, general population statistics for the San Francisco–Oakland Bay area would probably be appropriate for comparison. On the other hand, if the job requires such special training and qualifications that the employer normally would have to recruit over a wider geographic area, the appropriate base for statistical comparison would be the population of qualified individuals in that larger area, such as the United States.

If the plaintiff proves discriminatory impact, a *prima facie* case of illegal discrimination has been established. The burden then shifts to the employer.

***Employer's Rebuttal:*** As we have seen, an employer may successfully overcome a *prima facie* case of discriminatory intent by showing that the challenged action was prompted by a legitimate, nondiscriminatory reason. When the plaintiff has established a *prima facie* case by proving discriminatory *impact,* the employer's rebuttal today is essentially the same as it is in an intent case. This was not true until recently, however. Formerly, the employer had to prove "business necessity" in order to rebut the employee's *prima facie* case of discriminatory impact, which was considerably more difficult than just showing a legitimate reason. To prove business necessity, the employer had to establish that (1) the challenged employment practice was necessary to achieve an important business objective, (2) the practice actually achieved this objective, and (3) there was no other reasonably available method for accomplishing the objective without discriminatory impact. In 1989, the U.S. Supreme Court made things somewhat easier for the employer in an impact case. In the *Wards Cove* case, which is presented below, the Court held that the employer could rebut a *prima facie* case of discriminatory impact merely by introducing plausible evidence of a legitimate justification for the challenged practice or policy.

***Alternatives:*** In the *Wards Cove* case the Court also held that, if the employer successfully rebuts an impact case by showing a legitimate business reason, the employee can win only if he or she then proves that the employer could have accomplished its legitimate objectives just as efficiently and effectively by using some other method that did not have such a discriminatory impact.

In the *Wards Cove* case that follows, the Supreme Court not only changed the rules for an employer's rebuttal of an impact case, but also discussed the statistical methods that can be used by the employee to establish a *prima facie* case of discriminatory impact in the first place.

---

**Wards Cove Packing Co. v. Atonio**
U.S. Supreme Court,
109 S.Ct. 2115 (1989)

The defendants are two companies that operate salmon canneries in Alaska. The canneries operate only during the salmon runs in the summer months. In May or June of each year, a few weeks before the salmon runs begin, workers arrive and prepare the equipment and facilities for the canning operation. Most of these workers possess a variety of skills. When salmon runs are about to begin, the workers who will operate the cannery lines arrive, remain as long as there are fish to can, and then depart. The canneries are then closed down, winterized, and left vacant until the next spring. Because the length and size of salmon runs vary from year to year, the number of employees needed at each cannery also varies. Estimates are made as early in the winter as possible; the necessary employees are hired, and when the time comes, they are transported to the canneries, where they both work and live until the end of the salmon runs.

Jobs at the canneries are of two general types: "cannery jobs" and "noncannery jobs." Cannery jobs are unskilled positions on the cannery line, and are filled predominantly by nonwhites—Filipinos and Alaska Natives. The Filipinos are hired through and dispatched by a local branch of the Longshoremen's Union under a hiring hall agreement. The Alaska Natives primarily reside in villages near the remote cannery locations. Noncannery jobs fall into a variety of categories, most of which are classified as skilled positions. Examples include machinists, engineers, quality control personnel, "tenders" who operate the boats that bring salmon from the independent fishing vessels to the canneries, cooks, carpenters, storekeepers, bookkeepers, dock workers, and construction workers. Noncannery jobs are filled predominantly with white workers, who are hired during the winter months from the companies' offices in Washington and Oregon. Virtually all of the noncannery jobs pay more than cannery jobs.

Several present and former nonwhite cannery workers filed a class action against the companies alleging that various employment practices violated Title VII by effectively barring them from noncannery positions. The practices included failure to post noncannery openings, nepotism, an English language requirement, a rehiring preference, and a practice of not promoting from within. The cannery workers claimed both intentional and impact discrimination. The district court found no intentional discrimination, and the court of appeals agreed. The finding of no intentional discrimination was not appealed further to the U.S. Supreme Court.

The district court also found no discriminatory impact, but the court of appeals disagreed. The court of appeals found that the employees had established a *prima facie* case of discriminatory impact because there was a high percentage of nonwhite workers in cannery jobs and a low percentage of nonwhite workers in noncannery jobs. That court also held that the canneries then had the burden of proof to demonstrate business necessity. The canneries appealed to the Supreme Court on the grounds that the employees' statistics were inadequate and that the court of appeals placed an improper burden of rebuttal on the canneries.

*(continued)*

**Decision:** The Supreme Court reversed the decision of the court of appeals for three reasons. First, the plaintiffs' statistics were inadequate to establish a *prima facie* case of impact. The comparison between the percentage of nonwhites in cannery and noncannery positions is irrelevant because it provides no information about the available labor pool. Statistics must be presented that compare the racial composition of the qualified persons in the relevant labor market and the persons holding the jobs in question. (If labor market statistics are impossible to get, statistics showing the racial composition of "otherwise-qualified applicants" may be substituted.) Second, it is necessary for plaintiffs to show a cause-and-effect relationship between particular employment practices and the statistical disparity. Third, the court of appeals erred by placing the burden of proving business necessity on defendants. If, on remand, plaintiffs are able to establish a *prima facie* case of discriminatory impact, the defendants' burden is simply to show a business justification for the practices. The plaintiffs then must prove that other employment practices, without a similarly undesirable racial effect, would also serve the employer's legitimate hiring interests. ■

---

**Bona Fide Occupational Qualification:** Once discrimination has been proved, the employer has few defenses. One such defense in Title VII provides that it is not illegal to discriminate on the basis of religion, sex, or national origin in situations where religion, sex, or national origin is a **bona fide occupational qualification (BFOQ).** Race or color cannot be a BFOQ. Congress intended the BFOQ defense to be a very limited exception that would apply only to rare situations. The EEOC and the courts have followed this intent by recognizing the exception very infrequently.

Most of the situations in which BFOQ has been an issue have involved sex discrimination. Stereotypes or traditional assumptions about which jobs are appropriate for males or females do not establish the BFOQ exception. A basic principle of Title VII is that the individual should decide whether the job is appropriate, assuming that person is qualified to perform it. Thus, males cannot automatically be barred from jobs such as airline flight attendant or secretary, and females cannot be barred from mining, construction, or other jobs requiring lifting, night work, and so forth. Even the fact that the employer's customers strongly prefer employees to be of one sex or the other does not create the BFOQ exception.

In a few circumstances, however, gender is an essential element of the job. For example, the BFOQ defense has been permitted where one sex or the other is necessary for authenticity, as in the case of models or actors. In addition, being a woman has been held to be a BFOQ for employment as a salesperson in the ladies' undergarments department of a department store, and as a nurse in the labor and delivery section of an obstretrical hospital. Being a man has been held to be a BFOQ for employment as a security guard, where the job involved searching male employees, and also as an attendant in a men's restroom.

**Seniority Systems:** Seniority refers to the length of time an employee has worked for a company, or perhaps the time worked within a particular department or other division of the company. Many companies, especially those having collective bargaining agreements with unions, have seniority systems. These systems provide that many kinds of employment rights and privileges are to be determined on the basis of seniority. For example, the right to bid for another job or another shift within the company, or the right to be protected from lay-off, may be determined by seniority. Although far from perfect, seniority systems are generally recognized as one of the few truly objective means for making many kinds of employment decisions. Such systems, however, can sometimes have a discriminatory impact on women and minorities, because these employees on the average are likely to have less seniority than white males. Because of their positive aspects, seniority systems are partially exempted from Title VII. A "bona fide" (good faith) seniority system does not violate Title VII just because it has a discriminatory impact; the system is illegal only if it is intentionally used to discriminate.

## Other Issues under Title VII

**Sexual Harassment:** Harassment or intimidation of an employee violates Title VII when it is based on that person's sex just as it does when based on race, color, religion, or national origin. **Sexual harassment** may take the same form that other illegal harassment normally takes, namely, slurs, taunts, epithets, or other abuses that create a hostile, intimidating, or offensive working environment. In some situations, however, sexual harassment may be quite different from harassment for racial or other reasons. Sexual harassment may take the form of unwelcome requests for sexual favors. Indeed, it probably takes the form of unwelcome requests more often than slurs, taunts, and so on.

The courts and EEOC have recognized two general kinds of situations in which such unwelcome requests constitute illegal sexual harassment. These two varieties, which may sometimes overlap, are referred to as "*quid pro quo*" and "hostile environment" sexual harassment.

**Quid Pro Quo *Harassment*:** The term *quid pro quo* means "something for something," and refers to the situation in which continued employment, a favorable review, promotion, or some other tangible job benefit is explicitly or implicitly conditioned upon an employee's positive response to a requested sexual favor. To prove this kind of illegal sexual harassment, the following facts must be established:

**1.** The employer, or someone for whose actions the employer is responsible, requested sexual favors from an employee, and the request was *unwelcome*.

**2.** The request was a term or condition of employment, or was reasonably seen by the employee as such a term or condition. This means that the request either (a) was actually part of the employment and would have an effect on the employee's status or opportunity, or (b) the employee reasonably interpreted the request as being part of the employment and having such an effect.

*Hostile Environment Harassment:* This form of sexual harassment can occur where there are requests for sexual favors, but the evidence does not prove that the requests were tied to tangible job benefits. To prove **hostile environment** sexual harassment, the following facts must be established:

**1.** Like the *quid pro quo* variety, the employer, or someone for whose actions the employer is responsible, requested sexual favors from an employee, and the request or requests must have been *unwelcome*.

**2.** The request or requests must have been of such a nature as to create an intimidating, hostile, or offensive working environment. Although it is conceivable that a single unwelcome request could seriously infect the working environment, in most cases it will be difficult to prove that the hostile environment form of sexual harassment has occurred unless the unwelcome requests and accompanying conduct were repeated over a period of time.

**Affirmative Action:** The primary strategy in the legal battle against employment discrimination has been simply to prohibit discriminatory practices and to strike them down when they are discovered. Another important weapon, however, has been **affirmative action**—actually giving preferences to minorities and women in the hiring process. In many cases, affirmative action programs include goals and timetables for increasing the percentage of minorities and women in the employer's work force. The basic purpose of affirmative action is to rectify previous discrimination.

Affirmative action has been used by some courts as a remedy in specific cases of discrimination. In other words, after concluding that an employer had practiced discrimination, some courts have both ordered the cessation of the practice and required the employer to implement an affirmative action program. In addition, some employers, either on their own or in connection with union collective bargaining agreements, have instituted voluntary affirmative action programs.

Since their inception, affirmative action programs have raised difficult legal questions. By granting preferences to minorities and women, these programs discriminate in some degree against white males. White males are protected against race and sex discrimination by Title VII; does so-called reverse discrimination, brought about by affirmative action programs, violate Title VII or other discrimination laws?

In *United Steelworkers of America v. Weber,* 443 U.S. 193 (1979), the Supreme Court ruled that *voluntary* affirmative action programs are permissible under Title VII in certain circumstances. In several other cases, lower courts have upheld *mandatory* affirmative action programs in similar circumstances. As a limited exception to the basic prohibition against discrimination, reverse discrimination brought about by affirmative action programs is legal under the following conditions.

**1.** There must be a formal, systematic program—the employer cannot discriminate against nonminorities on an isolated, ad hoc basis.

2. Any such program must be temporary—it must operate only until its reasonable minority hiring goals are reached.

3. The program cannot completely bar the hiring or promotion of nonminority workers.

4. The program cannot result in the actual firing of nonminority workers.

5. The program cannot force the employer to hire or promote unqualified workers.

6. If the program is court-ordered, it must be based on evidence that there actually had been discrimination by the employer in the past. If the program is voluntary, it can be based either on evidence of past discrimination or merely on evidence that there has been a substantial underutilization of minorities or women by the employer.

7. In general, an affirmative action plan cannot override preexisting employee rights that have been established by a valid seniority system. The following case illustrates this additional limitation on the operation of an affirmative action program.

---

**Firefighters Local Union No. 1784 v. Stotts**
U.S. Supreme Court,
467 U.S. 561 (1984)

In 1977, Carl Stotts brought a Title VII action alleging that the Memphis Fire Department was engaged in unlawful racial discrimination. In 1980, the case was settled by consent decree between the parties. To increase black participation in the department, the consent decree established the goal of 50 percent black hiring and 20 percent black promotions for a designated time. In 1981, budget constraints in Memphis necessitated the layoff of numerous firefighters. Under the "last hired, first fired" protection of the Fire Department's seniority system, the laid off workers were predominantly blacks hired under the terms of the consent decree.

Mr. Stotts went back to court seeking an injunction that would prevent layoffs from obstructing the goal of the consent decree to increase the number of black firefighters. The union intervened to oppose this request and protect the terms of their seniority system. The district court held for Stotts and entered an injunction that effectively required the department to fire white firefighters with seniority protection rather than the more recently hired black firefighters. This injunction was upheld on appeal, and the union appealed to the U.S. Supreme Court.

**Decision:** The judgment was reversed. During the debate on Title VII, Sen. Hubert Humphrey said that "there is nothing in it that will give any power to any court to require firing of employees in order to meet a racial quota or to achieve a certain racial balance." Thus, a bona fide seniority system must be respected. The decision to lay off workers in accordance with the seniority system was not discriminatory.

If individual plaintiffs demonstrate that they have been actual victims of past discriminatory practices, they may be given their rightful place on the seniority roster. But mere membership in a disadvantaged class is not enough to merit a seniority award. There was no finding in this case that any of the blacks protected from the layoff had been victims of discrimination. ∎

---

**Comparable Worth:** As we will see shortly, a separate federal statute, the Equal Pay Act of 1963, prohibits sex-based discrimination in rates of pay. This law applies only when a male and a female are doing jobs that are substantially the same. Therefore, the Equal Pay Act does not apply to a situation in which a male and a female receive different pay for jobs that are different, even if the evidence indicates that the two jobs are of equal economic value to the employer. Although the doctrine of **comparable worth** does not provide a basis for a claim under the Equal Pay Act, the fact that men and women receive different pay for jobs that are of comparable worth to the employer might be relevant in a Title VII case in some circumstances. Suppose, for example, that a female employee claims that her employer violated Title VII by intentionally placing males and females in different categories of job because of their sex, or by setting different rates of pay for different jobs because one category of job was held primarily by men and the other primarily by women. In such a situation, evidence that the two categories of job were of comparable economic value to the employer would be a relevant factor to be considered by a court when it decides whether an inference of discriminatory intent is warranted.

Although evidence of different pay for jobs of comparable worth may in some circumstances be relevant to a possible inference of discriminatory intent, the courts thus far have held that evidence of comparable worth, by itself, does not establish a violation of Title VII. In other words, the fact that an employer has different pay rates for two different jobs of comparable worth, one type of job being held primarily by males and the other primarily by females, does not establish a violation of Title VII. Other evidence of gender-based discrimination would have to be present.

It is quite common for employers to base pay rates for different jobs on prevailing market rates for such jobs in the area. If such dependence on the market creates a situation in which women and men are paid differently for jobs of comparable worth, has the employer violated Title VII? In the leading case on this question, *American Federation of State, County, and Municipal Employees v. State of Washington*, 770 F.2d 1401 (9th Cir. 1985), the court of appeals concluded that an employer does not violate Title VII merely by basing pay scales on prevailing market rates even if the result is a differential between men and women. After this case and some others, the doctrine of comparable worth probably is of limited value in challenging a compensation system under Title VII. It should be noted, however, that several state legislatures have adopted comparable worth systems for state government employees. Because government jobs usually are classified in a systematic fashion, with substantial uniformity within a classification, the concept of comparable worth may have its greatest utility in government employment.

## *Equal Pay Act*

The first antidiscrimination in employment act, predating even Title VII, is the Equal Pay Act. This statute prohibits an employer from paying an employee of one sex less than an employee of the opposite sex, when the two are performing jobs that require "equal skill, effort, and responsibility" and "under similar working conditions." Proof that the pay differential is due to the workers' varying merit or pursuant to a legitimate seniority system are available defenses under the Act. The Equal Pay Act is limited to sex discrimination in the form of wages and overlaps considerably with Title VII. There are slight differences in employers covered by the two Acts, however, and the Equal Pay Act may be a worker's only recourse for wage discrimination in some companies with fewer than 15 employees.

## *Age Discrimination in Employment Act*

Title VII expanded the scope of employment discrimination protection in 1967, when it passed the Age Discrimination in Employment Act (ADEA). The coverage of this Act is quite similar to Title VII, except that it applies only to situations where there is a minimum of 20 employees. The ADEA prohibits discrimination based on age against anyone over age 40. Prohibited discrimination may take the form of disparate individual treatment, when an individual is penalized for being part of the protected age range, or disparate impact, when an employer's general policy needlessly discriminates against those aged 40 and over. Only the age of the victim of discrimination is relevant. Thus, an employer automatically favoring a 45-year-old over a 60-year-old, or vice versa, has violated the ADEA just as surely as if the employer had favored a 25-year-old.

The ADEA provides several statutory defenses for employers. An employee may always be discharged or otherwise penalized for good cause other than age. A bona fide occupational qualification defense also exists and closely resembles that under Title VII. Bona fide seniority systems or employee benefit plans are also exempted from ADEA violation. Courts have interpreted these defenses somewhat more expansively, in the employer's favor, than in most cases decided under Title VII.

## *Rehabilitation Act*

The Rehabilitation Act of 1973 was enacted to protect handicapped individuals from employment discrimination. This legislation has narrower focus than the previous acts, and is limited to federal agencies, employers having contracts with the federal government in excess of $2,500, and employers receiving any form of federal financial assistance. Given the federal government's prevalence in many aspects of our economy, the Rehabilitation Act has relatively broad reach.

The Rehabilitation Act protects individuals who have "a physical or mental impairment, which substantially limits one or more of such person's major life activities." Also protected are individuals "regarded as having such an impairment." "Major life activities" are defined broadly and the Act encompasses virtually any disease or disability that might be the subject of discrimination.

To be protected, an individual must be "qualified" for the job. While this is somewhat difficult to define, the Act requires employers to make reasonable accommodations for a handicap, where an individual is otherwise qualified. Thus an employer may be required to provide, for example, wheelchair access or telephone amplifiers, so long as the expense of accommodation is not unreasonable. The Rehabilitation Act prohibits discrimination against the protected class, and government contractors must undertake affirmative action programs to encourage the hiring of the handicapped.

# PROTECTION OF SAFETY AND WELFARE

Although unions undoubtedly have improved the safety and welfare of individual employees, they have failed to provide full protection, at least in the judgment of Congress and the states. Numerous laws have been passed to protect workers from on-the-job injuries and the financial consequences of such injuries. Congress also has legislated to preserve the financial welfare of workers, especially in the context of pension and other employee benefit plans.

## *Workers' Compensation*

In the 19th century, workers were frequently injured on the job and often without legal recourse to compensate them for their injuries. In response, state legislatures passed workers' compensation statutes. All fifty states have such laws and while they vary somewhat, the laws all share certain common features. Workers' compensation is paid without regard to employer negligence and workers receive a predetermined amount, based on the injury suffered. Benefits payable include medical costs, income replacement, death benefits, and rehabilitation costs.

Levels of compensation are typically lower than a worker might receive in a lawsuit, but the statutory system avoids much of the attorney and other costs of litigation, while eliminating most employer defenses to payment of the lesser sum.

The main restriction on recovery under workers' compensation statutes is the requirement that the injury must have arisen "out of and in the course of employment." Although the majority of injuries are clearly job-related, a large number of cases lie on the disputed borderline of work. For example, an employee whose job requires travel will ordinarily be able to receive benefits for injuries incurred in the course of such travel. By contrast, a mere commuter will not be compensated if injured on the way to work.

Employees typically are also covered while engaging in activities reasonably incidental to job duties. Thus, an employee on a lunch break who slips and falls in the employer's cafeteria would be covered. State laws also cover diseases arising out of employment, but proof of the source of disease is much more complicated to obtain than is proof of work injuries, and such cases are more often disputed.

## *Occupational Safety and Health Act*

In 1970, Congress passed the Occupational Safety and Health Act to help prevent workplace disease and injuries. The Act creates the Occupational Safety and Health Administration (OSHA), part of the U.S. Department of Labor, to administer its provisions. This statute applies to virtually every United States employer.

Central to OSHA's powers is its standard-setting authority. The agency promulgates regulations compelling employers to make their workplaces safer in a variety of ways. Most of the early standards were intended to prevent job injuries, and OSHA suffered considerable ridicule because of the highly detailed nature of its rules. For example, the agency devoted considerable effort to regulating the number of toilets to be available and the allowable design of such facilities. As the agency has gained experience, its standards have allowed more flexibility for employers, and the regulatory focus has shifted toward prevention of occupational diseases.

Unlike some agencies that have been largely co-opted by the industries they regulate, OSHA has maintained standards that are often quite strict. These rules have given rise to litigation that has helped define the extent of the agency's powers. In an attempt to prevent a cancer associated with the inhalation of benzene, a petroleum byproduct, OSHA promulgated a stringent standard without attempting to specify the magnitude of the harm created by existing levels. The agency believed that it was simply fulfilling its mandate to create the healthiest workplace feasible, but the Supreme Court overturned the regulation in *Industrial Union Department v. American Petroleum Institute,* 448 U.S. 607 (1980). The Court held that OSHA could regulate only "significant risks" and generally should quantitatively measure a risk before promulgating rules. Shortly after this decision, industry challenged an OSHA regulation limiting exposure to cotton dust, which causes several lung diseases. Industry contended that OSHA had to base regulation on a cost/benefit analysis, but the Supreme Court upheld the agency's regulation in *American Textile Manufacturers Inst. v. Donovan,* 452 U.S. 490 (1981). This decision held that OSHA possessed authority to require any health protection "feasible" for industry and was not required to weigh the costs of a rule against its benefits before acting.

While OSHA has broad standard-setting authority, the task of establishing rules against all workplace hazards is beyond the capabilities of any agency. In recognition of this limit, Congress created a "general duty clause" in the Safety Act. This provision requires all employers to provide a place of employment free from recognized hazards of death or serious harm, regardless of whether a federal standard applies to the particular situation. As an example of the application of this clause, one employer was found in violation for permitting untrained employees to attempt electrical repairs on a wet floor without any protective equipment.

Beyond standards development, OSHA is also responsible for enforcing the Act, and considerable controversy has circulated around these enforcement powers. The agency's compliance officers make unannounced inspections. While search warrants are required for the inspections, they are liberally granted. When violations are found, OSHA may issue citations to an employer that include penalties of up to $1,000 per violation. An employer may contest these penalties before a separate, independent organization known as the Occupational Safety and Health Review Commission.

## *Fair Labor Standards Act*

The Fair Labor Standards Act (FLSA) was among the federal government's first employment law statutes. Passed in response to the Great Depression, the FLSA regulates the hours that employees may be required to work and the wages they must be paid. As was the case in the statutes discussed above, the coverage of the FLSA is extremely broad. An employer involved in any way in interstate commerce falls under the Act's purview. An exception is made for managerial employees, as well as those employed in the professions, such as lawyers and accountants.

Among the most controversial provisions of FLSA immediately after its passage was the Act's prohibition of certain forms of child labor. Employees under 18 years of age are excluded from occupations designated as hazardous, such as mining, logging, and excavation work. Hours are strictly regulated for employees who are less than 16 years old.

The FLSA is also the source of the federal minimum wage requirements. This wage level is currently set at $3.80 per hour for each of the first 40 hours worked in a week. Any work in excess of 40 hours per week must be paid at a "time-and-a-half" rate, 50 percent greater than the employee's normal wage. If employees are not paid on an hourly basis, the FLSA requires at least as much compensation as a per hour minimum wage rate would require for the hours they actually worked. Employers must maintain complete employment and payroll records for review by the Department of Labor. Substantial penalties are imposed for violations. With the exception of the above provisions, the Act imposes no other requirements on the employment relationship, such as mandatory vacations or rest periods.

## EMPLOYER'S RIGHT TO DISCHARGE EMPLOYEES

An employer must have considerable freedom to discipline or fire employees in order to manage its work force effectively and efficiently. If an employer is unable to discharge disgruntled or shirking workers, we all pay. On the other hand, many feel that employees deserve protection from unjustified dismissals. (Incidentally, when we speak of an employee being fired or discharged, we are referring not only to actual firing but also to "constructive discharges," where the employer creates such an intolerable situation for the employee that he or she is forced to quit.)

An employee who has a legally enforceable employment contract obviously has whatever job security the contract specifies. Most employees, however, do not have such a contract. An employee who is covered by a labor-management collective bargaining agreement usually enjoys considerable protection from improper discharge. Most such contracts provide that employees can be fired or otherwise disciplined only for "good cause." Approximately 30 percent of the American work force is covered by collective bargaining agreements. Public employees, i.e., those who work for a federal, state, or local government agency, also enjoy significant job security under federal and state "civil service" laws. In general, after a designated probationary period, these employees can be fired only for good cause and only after specified procedures have been followed. Public employees account for about 17 percent of the American work force.

## Employment at Will

All other employees (over half of the work force) are covered by the so-called **employment-at-will** doctrine. This traditional common-law rule provides that, in the absence of a contract, either the employer or employee can terminate the relationship at any time, for any reason or no reason. In recent years, however, many people have come to view this rule as overly harsh toward employees and, consequently, a number of exceptions have been created.

**Statutory Exceptions:** A few federal and state statutes provide protection for employees in specific situations. For example, federal employment laws like Title VII, FLSA, and OSHA include provisions making it illegal for an employer to punish an employee for filing a complaint or cooperating with an investigation or proceeding under the particular law. In some states, employees are protected from being penalized for filing a workers' compensation claim or taking time off to serve on a jury. Also, several states now have statutes giving an employee a right to sue an employer for damages if the employer fired the employee for "whistle-blowing." Whistle-blowing occurs when a worker objects to or reports the employer's suspected illegal activities. Even if the employee turned out to be wrong, and the employer was not actually doing anything illegal, these statutes apply so long as the employee was sincere and had a solid factual basis for believing that illegal practices were occurring.

**The Public Policy Exception:** Although a number of statutes such as these have been enacted during recent times, the most important developments in the area have been judicial ones. On their own, the courts in a majority of states have carved out several important exceptions to employment at will. The most notable of these exceptions can be grouped together under the idea of "public policy." In other words, these courts have ruled that an employee should be able to recover damages for the tort of "wrongful discharge" (or "retaliatory discharge") when the employer's conduct is contrary to a clearly established public policy. Defining public policy is not always an easy task, however. Most courts are fully aware that a vague, expansive public policy concept will provide very little guidance to employers or employees. Without reasonable guidance, employers will find it very difficult to maintain an effective personnel management system because of the fear that every discharge might lead to an expensive lawsuit.

As a result, most courts have concluded that the public policy claimed to have been violated by the employer must be clearly stated in a federal or state statute, constitutional provision, or widely recognized and accepted judicial decision. In those states permitting an employee to assert a claim for wrongful discharge based on public policy, a fired employee is likely to have a good claim in the following situations:

**1.** The employer may not discharge a worker for refusing to commit an act that is *illegal* under a statute, constitutional provision, or prior judicial decision. For example, courts have found employers liable for firing employees who refused to participate in an illegal price-fixing scheme, commit perjury, mislabel food products, falsify a pollution control test, sign a false defamatory statement about a co-employee, perform a medical procedure for which the nurse-employee was not licensed, or pump a ship's bilges into the water.

**2.** Generally, an employee has a good wrongful discharge claim if he or she has been fired for *exercising* *a statutory right.* For example, an employer has been held liable for damages to an employee who was fired for exercising the right to sign a union authorization card. Similarly, employers have been held liable for discharging employees because they filed workers' compensation claims or served on juries, even if there was no specific antiretaliation statute in that state covering the situation.

3. An employer often will be held liable to an employee who was fired for *whistleblowing*—objecting to or disclosing the employer's violations of the law. The employee normally has a valid claim if he or she (a) acted in good faith and (b) had reasonable cause to believe that the employer was violating the law, even if later investigation reveals that the employer actually did not act illegally. On the question of whether an employee must first give company management an opportunity to correct the problem before complaining to the authorities, the courts are split. A majority of them, however, recognize the wrongful discharge claim regardless of where the employee first lodged an objection.

Courts usually have stressed that an employee is not protected from discharge just because he or she acted out of strong, and even admirable, convictions if a purely private matter is involved that does not affect the public interest. For example, one court concluded that there was no wrongful discharge claim where the employee was fired for refusing to follow a particular research program. As a matter of personal conscience, the employee felt that the research was not proper, but there was nothing illegal, immoral, or hazardous about it. Two Illinois cases also provide an illustrative contrast. In one, the court found that no violation of public policy had occurred when a company's chief financial officer was fired for a continuing disagreement with the company's president about accounting methods. There was no plausible claim that the president's methods were deceptive or violated securities or tax laws or generally accepted accounting principles. In the other case, the court held that the employee did have a claim for wrongful discharge where he had been fired for complaining about the company's use of accounting methods that substantially overstated income and assets in a way that very likely would violate tax laws and the disclosure provisions of federal securities laws.

The following case illustrates an unfortunate situation that led one state supreme court to consider and adopt the public policy exception to employment at will.

## Wagenseller v. Scottsdale Memorial Hospital
Arizona Supreme Court,
710 P.2d 1025 (1985)

Catherine Wagenseller worked as an emergency room nurse for the Scottsdale Memorial Hospital. She had originally been recruited personally by the emergency department's manager, Kay Smith, and for four years maintained a superior work record and enjoyed excellent professional and personal relationships with Smith and others in the department. She was an "at-will" employee, with no contractual or other job guarantees.

Wagenseller, Smith, and several others from the emergency department, as well as a number of employees from other area hospitals, went on an eight-day camping and rafting trip down the Colorado River. While on the trip, Wagenseller became very uncomfortable because of the behavior of Smith and a few others. This behavior included heavy drinking, group nude bathing and other public nudity, and a lot of unnecessary closeness while rafting. In addition, Smith and others staged a parody of the song "Moon River," which ended with members of the group "mooning" the audience. Wagenseller declined to participate in any of these activities. Smith and others also performed the "Moon River" skit twice at the hospital after the group's return from the river, but Wagenseller declined to participate there as well.

After the trip, relations between Wagenseller and Smith deteriorated. Smith began harassing Wagenseller, using abusive language and embarrassing her in the presence of other staff. These problems continued, and Wagenseller was fired about five months after the camping trip. Wagenseller appealed her dismissal to the hospital's administrative and personnel department, but the dismissal was upheld. She then filed suit for damages against Smith, the hospital, and several of its personnel administrators. In the suit, she alleged that her termination violated public policy and therefore constituted the tort of wrongful discharge. Although Wagenseller's claims had been substantiated by the pretrial statements of several others, the trial court refused to recognize any exception to the employment-at-will doctrine and granted the defendants' motions for summary judgment. The appeals court reversed part of the judgment, but still did not grant Wagenseller the relief she sought, so she appealed to the Arizona Supreme Court.

**Decision:** The judgment was reversed and the case remanded for a trial where Wagenseller would have a full opportunity to prove her allegations. The Arizona Supreme Court adopts the public policy exception to the traditional employment-at-will termination rule. An employer may fire for a good cause or for no cause but may not fire for bad cause—that which violates public policy. The court here concludes that termination of employment for refusal to participate in indecent exposure is a termination contrary to the policy of the state, a policy expressed clearly in a state statute making indecent exposure a crime. ■

## PROTECTION OF EMPLOYEE PRIVACY

### Lie Detector Testing

Employers have extremely important interests in learning certain kinds of background information about people who are applying for jobs. Incompetent, dishonest, or violent employees can cause untold harm to an employer. A company may need to know about a job applicant's past work record, criminal record, and general character when legitimately attempting to protect itself against lawsuits and against a damaged reputation, as well as to protect its customers and its other employees from physical harm. Employers also have a valid interest in obtaining information from existing employees when theft or other wrongdoing has occurred at the workplace.

During the past several decades, more and more employers used the lie detector (polygraph) examination in an effort to get accurate information from employees and job applicants. Because of mounting evidence that these examinations are not very reliable, and that thousands of employees and applicants were being harmed each year by erroneous results, Congress passed the Employee Polygraph Protection Act of 1988. This law prohibits most uses of the polygraph by private employers, subject only to a few limited exceptions. The most important exception permits a private employer to require an employee to take a lie detector test as part of an ongoing investigation of theft, sabotage, or other property loss, if this employee had custody of the property and if there is other independent evidence creating a reasonable suspicion that this employee was involved in the incident. The law also does not prohibit federal, state, or local government agencies from requiring their employees and job applicants to take lie detector tests, mainly because the Constitution applies to government employers. The constitutional right of privacy protects against many unreasonable uses of the polygraph by government employers, but clearly does not protect employees to the extent that the federal polygraph statute does.

### Employee Drug Testing

Employees who are impaired by drugs or alcohol endanger the public and their fellow workers, and cost their employers millions of dollars annually as a result of accidents, absenteeism, higher health insurance claims, low productivity, and poor workmanship. Employers have legitimate interests in minimizing these costs; maintaining a safe, secure, and productive workplace; and protecting themselves against liability to those injured by the actions of impaired employees. Both co-workers and members of the public have a legitimate claim to protection against the unsafe conduct or defective products resulting from employees' drug or alcohol use.

Employees subjected to drug testing, on the other hand, have important interests in preventing harm to their reputations and economic security resulting from inaccurate test results and avoiding unwarranted intrusions into their personal lives. Drug tests are not always accurate, and the analysis of urine, blood, or hair specimens often reveals a lot of private information about the subject that has nothing to do with the use of illicit drugs. It is certainly true that alcohol use causes the same kinds of workplace problems as drug use, but alcohol-impaired employees often can be identified more easily without the risk of erroneous test results or the disclosure of irrelevant private information that may be revealed in drug testing. Most of the difficult legal issues, therefore, have involved employers testing for controlled substances other than alcohol.

Most employers take some kind of action against an employee who refuses a test or who tests positive for illicit drugs. This action can range from required enrollment in a rehabilitation program to immediate discharge. Similarly, job applicants who refuse testing or test positive are virtually assured of not getting the job. As a result, legal action by employees challenging drug-testing programs is becoming increasingly common. The legal system has not yet had sufficient time, however, to develop a coherent, uniform set of principles to balance the various interests that are involved. Although the law pertaining to employee drug testing is still in a formative stage, it is possible to make some generalizations.

If the employer is a federal, state, or local government agency, the Constitution provides a measure of protection for the legitimate privacy interests of employees. The Constitution also applies if the government requires a private employer to do drug testing. The most obviously applicable constitutional provision is the Fourth Amendment prohibition of *unreasonable searches and seizures.* The taking of a urine, blood, or hair specimen is a "search and seizure." Generally, people and their belongings can be searched only if there is "probable cause" to believe that they possess evidence of a violation of the law. Recently, in *National Treasury Employees Union v. Von Raab,* 109 S.Ct. 1384 (1989) (involving testing by a government agency), and *Skinner v. Railway Labor Executives Ass'n,* 109 S.Ct. 1402 (1989) (involving government-required testing by private employers), the U.S. Supreme Court held that drug testing sometimes is constitutionally permissible even without any evidence that a particular employee is a drug user. The Court said that, in the case of employees whose work creates significant safety, health, or security risks, testing may be done on a random or mass basis so long as the testing program is conducted in a reasonable manner overall. To be reasonable, the program must include ample safeguards to ensure accuracy and privacy.

The Constitution does not apply to drug testing by private employers unless the testing is required by the government. Tort law does apply, however, if an employer conducts a test or uses the results in such a way that a tort is committed. If the employer intentionally reveals private information from the test to others who have no legitimate interest in receiving it, the employer may be liable to the employee for the tort of invasion of privacy. If the test produces a false positive result, and the employer reveals it to others without a legitimate interest in knowing it, the employer may be liable for defamation. In some cases, carelessness in the administration of the test or use of the results may cause the employer to be liable for the tort of negligence.

A few states have passed statutes specifically regulating the design and implementation of drug testing programs by private employers. The objective of these statutes is to increase the likelihood that results will be accurate and that employee privacy will be protected to the fullest extent possible.

In the case of unionized workers, the implementation of a drug testing program is a so-called "mandatory subject of collective bargaining." This means that the employer cannot make such a decision on its own, but must submit the question to the process of collective bargaining with the union. If the company and the union cannot agree, either or both may use economic weapons such as lockouts or strikes to put pressure on the other side.

## SUMMARY

The law of employment relationships has undergone a series of fundamental changes in recent decades. For much of our nation's history, employment was governed by traditional common-law rules of contracts, with little government involvement. Today's employer, however, must be cognizant of numerous government requirements in the areas of health and safety, discrimination, wages, employee benefits, and labor organization.

The first inroads in the common law came in the National Labor Relations Act. This legislation facilitated unionization of the workplace by protecting organizing campaigns, compelling collective bargaining between management and lawfully recognized employee representatives, prohibiting discrimination against union members, and guaranteeing the right to strike, among other provisions. A long list of employer activities may be considered unfair labor practices, for which the employer may be penalized. This labor law also provides some benefits to employers in terms of prohibiting certain types of actions by union and nonunion employees.

The most significant recent labor laws are those against employment discrimination. Under Title VII of the Civil Rights Act, employers are prohibited from intentionally discriminating against employees because of their race, sex, color, religion, or national origin. Moreover, even seemingly neutral employment practices may be found illegal if they have the effect of discriminating against one or more of the protected classes. This statute has given rise to the controversial social issue of affirmative action, in which protected classes are granted special benefits, often at the expense of other workers. While some forms of affirmative action are legal, courts have placed limits on many programs. Other related legislation proscribes discrimination because of age or handicap and compels equal pay for equal work.

Another significant area of employment law regulation deals with worker safety and welfare. The Occupational Safety and Health Act enables the federal government to set standards for workplace safety. When accidents do occur, state workers' compensation statutes ensure that employees are compensated for their injuries. The Fair Labor Standards Act regulates pay levels for workers.

Yet another employment law issue involves standards for firing workers. Recent statutes and court decisions are placing important limits upon an employer's discretion in discharging employees. Such a decision may be unlawful if it violates public policy principles.

Finally, a number of legal developments in recent years have focused on the privacy rights of employees. An important federal law now restricts employers' use of the lie detector, and provisions of constitutional and tort law are being applied to workplace drug testing.

## KEY TERMS

**Unfair labor practice**
**Collective bargaining**
***Prima facie* case**
**Bona fide occupational qualification (BFOQ)**
**Sexual harassment**
***Quid pro quo***
**Hostile environment**
**Affirmative action**
**Comparable worth**
**Employment at will**

## QUESTIONS AND PROBLEMS

**1.** Republic Aviation Corp. operated a large military aircraft manufacturing plant that was not unionized. Republic had a rule against soliciting union membership within the plant. A worker ignored the rule and passed out application cards on his own time during lunch periods. Republic fired the worker for violating company rules, and the worker filed a complaint with the NLRB. Has the company committed an unfair labor practice? (*Republic Aviation Corp. v. NLRB,* 324 U.S. 793, 1945.)

**2.** A building stone supplier and its union were involved in a labor dispute and a strike was called. The company's customers at construction sites rented independent trucking companies to deliver the company's stones during the strike and deducted the rental cost from their payments to the supplier. The stone supplier's union picketed the construction site customers and the rental trucking companies. Has the union committed an unfair labor practice? (*Laborers Local 859 v. NLRB (Thomas S. Byrne, Inc.),* 446 F.2d 1319, D.C. Cir. 1971.)

**3.** As a protest against the Russian invasion of Afghanistan, members of the International Longshoremen's Association refused to handle cargoes arriving from or departing to the Soviet Union. An American company that imports Russian wood products for sale in the United States complained to the NLRB that the union action was illegal. Has the union committed an unfair labor practice? (*Int'l Longshoremen's Assn. v. Allied Int'l Inc.,* 102 S.Ct. 1656, 1982.)

**4.** The Los Angeles Dept. of Water & Power provided retirement and death benefits for its employees. Because, statistically speaking, the women employees would outlive the male employees by a number of years, the total retirement benefits paid out would be greater. Consequently, the Department required female employees to pay more toward the retirement fund. A female employee claimed that this was unlawful sex discrimination and sued. Should she win? (*L.A. Dept. of Water & Power v. Manhart,* 435 U.S. 702, 1978.)

**5.** A male airline pilot decided that he would be more comfortable as a woman and underwent a sex change operation. The pilot's employment record as a man was very good. After the operation, however, the airline fired the pilot, expressing a variety of medical and psychological concerns for safety. The pilot claimed that she was discriminated against as a transsexual in a way "based on sex" and that her firing therefore constituted illegal discrimination. Should she win?

**6.** Employee X has been exposed to the AIDS virus. After admitting this fact on a questionnaire, he was fired by the employer. Assume that the employer receives federal funds. Can the employee successfully sue for unlawful discrimination under the Rehabilitation Act?

**7.** A railroad had an absolute policy of refusing consideration for employment to any person convicted of a crime other than a minor traffic offense. Green, a prospective employee, had been convicted for refusing military induction in 1967. Statistics showed that in urban areas between 37 and 78 percent of all blacks would be excluded by this policy, while 11 to 17 percent of whites would be so excluded. Green, refused employment as a consequence of the policy, sued the railroad under Title VII of the Civil Rights Act. Should Green win? (*Green v. Missouri Pacific Railroad Co.,* 523 F.2d 1290, 8th Cir. 1975.)

**8.** McKeever worked as an attorney of New Jersey Bell Telephone Co. While driving home from work one day he was killed in an auto accident. His family claimed for workers' compensation death benefits, noting that at-home work was a regular part of McKeever's job, that the employer encouraged and benefitted from this at-home work, and that he had work in his briefcase in the car at the time he was killed. Is this a valid workers' compensation claim? (*McKeever v. New Jersey Bell Telephone Co.,* Workmen's Comp. Law Rep. (CCH) Sec. 2566, N.J. Super. Ct. App. Div. 1981.)

**9.** An employee of Sanders Roofing Co. fell from the flat roof where he was working. Because there was no catch platform around the roof the Labor Department issued a citation to Sanders for violating the "general duty" clause of OSHA. Sanders argued in defense that OSHA had a specific standard requiring catch platforms around sloped roofs but not flat ones. Should Sanders be found guilty of violating OSHA? (*R. L. Sanders Roofing Co. v. OSHRC,* 620 F.2d 97, 5th Cir. 1980.)

**10.** Cleary worked for American Airlines for 20 years as a payroll clerk and an airport operations agent. American fired Cleary for being absent from his work area and threatening another employee, but provided him no hearing to answer these charges. Cleary alleged that the real reason for his firing was his union activities and sued American Airlines for unlawful discharge, claiming that the company violated an implied covenant of good faith. Should Cleary prevail? (*Cleary v. American Airlines, Inc.,* 168 Cal. Rptr. 722, 2nd Ct. App. 1980.)

CHAPTER 50

# Consumer Transactions and the Law

During recent years the creditor-debtor relationship has undergone a significant shift in emphasis from protection of the creditor to protection of the debtor in the **consumer transaction,** in which a consumer borrows to purchase a product or purchases on credit. Consumer protection law is designed to protect the buyer-debtor from such things as **usury** (lending money at interest rates higher than the law allows), excessive **garnishments,** and hidden costs in credit transactions. This is not to say that the creditor, or seller, is completely at the mercy of the buyer, or debtor. However, the rights of the seller-creditor are defined by the numerous laws on the subject. Therefore, a knowledge of the basic provisions of consumer protection statutes is essential to the businessperson of today to operate a commercially successful venture and, at the same time, conduct consumer transactions within the law.

The law of consumer transactions is primarily statutory. Consumers derive their rights and incur their obligations from the many state and federal statutes available for their benefit. Some laws protect consumers from false advertising and other deceptive practices. A number of statutes protect consumers in the financial dealings associated with borrowing or buying. Others afford protection in the purchasing process and set guidelines for the degree of performance and satisfaction it is reasonable to expect from a purchase. Finally, some statutes and a large body of case law relate to product safety. They provide a measure of protection against unsafe products and allow recovery for damages or injury caused by such products. Table 50.1 is a guide to some of the more important statutes.

## DECEPTIVE TRADE PRACTICES

A consumer who is misled by false advertising or other deceptive practices may have the right to sue under a common-law fraud theory, or perhaps a breach of express warranty theory if the advertising involved a product. These theories have been discussed in earlier chapters.[1] However, two federal statutes help protect consumers from such deceptive practices without involving the consumers as plaintiffs. These are §5 of the Federal Trade Commission Act and §43(a) of the Lanham Act.

### *Federal Trade Commission Act*

Section 5(a)(1) of the FTC Act declares invalid (1) unfair methods of competition, and (2) unfair or deceptive acts or practices. Both must at least "affect" interstate commerce for federal jurisdiction to exist. Unfair methods of competition substantially duplicate the antitrust violations that were covered earlier in Part VIII.[2] Our major concern in this chapter on consumer protection relates to the prohibition against "unfair or deceptive acts or practices."

**Illicit Acts:** Deceptive advertising is the main target of FTC concern in the realm of "unfair or deceptive acts or practices." With assistance from the courts, the FTC has prohibited and often punished: (1) deceptive price advertising (e.g., advertising a sale as 20 percent off a "suggested retail price" when in fact the goods are hardly ever sold at that price); (2) affirmative product claims which cannot be substantiated (e.g., claiming without evidence that a

---

[1] Fraud is covered in Chapter 8; products liability warranty claims are discussed in Chapter 22.

[2] Antitrust law is discussed in Chapter 48.

**Table 50.1 Current Consumer Protection Statutes**

| POPULAR NAME | PURPOSE | REFERENCES |
| --- | --- | --- |
| Child Protection and Toy Safety | Requires special labeling and child-proof devices | 15 U.S.C.A. §§1261 et seq. |
| Cigarette Labeling and Ad | Surgeon general's warning of possible health hazard | 15 U.S.C.A. §§1331 et seq. |
| Consumer Credit Protection | Comprehensive protection, all phases of credit transactions | 15 U.S.C.A. §§1601 et seq. |
| Consumer Leasing Act | Improves disclosure of true costs in leasing transactions | 15 U.S.C.A. §§1667 |
| Consumer Product Safety | Protects consumer against defective or dangerous products | 15 U.S.C.A. §§2051 et seq. |
| Equal Credit Opportunity | Prohibits discrimination in extending credit | 15 U.S.C.A. §1691 |
| Fair Credit and Charge Card Disclosure | Allows consumers to comparison shop for credit | 15 U.S.C.A. §1610 |
| Fair Credit Reporting | Protects consumer's credit reputation | 15 U.S.C.A. §1681 |
| Fair Debt Collection Practices | Prohibits abuses by debt collectors | 15 U.S.C.A. §1692 |
| Fair Packaging and Labeling | Requires accurate name, weight, quantity | 15 U.S.C.A. §§1451 et seq. |
| Federal Trade Commission | Prohibits unfair or deceptive trade practices | 15 U.S.C.A. §45 |
| Flammable Fabrics | Eliminates or controls manufacture and marketing of dangerous fabrics | 15 U.S.C.A. §§1191 et seq. |
| Food, Drug, and Cosmetic | Prohibits marketing of impure, adulterated products | 21 U.S.C.A. §§301 et seq. |
| Fur Products Labeling | Prohibits misbranding of fur products | 15 U.S.C.A. §69 |
| Home Equity Loan Consumer Protection Act | Protects consumers who use homes as collateral | 15 U.S.C.A. §1637a |
| Interstate Land Sales Act | Protects against land sale abuses | 15 U.S.C.A. §1701 |
| Lanham Act | Prohibits deceptive acts or practices in product sales | 15 U.S.C.A. §43(a) |
| Magnuson-Moss Warranty | Governs content of warranties | 15 U.S.C.A. §§2301 et seq. |
| National Traffic and Motor Vehicle Safety | Promotes traffic and auto safety | 15 U.S.C.A. §§1381 et seq. |
| Real Estate Settlement Procedures | Requires disclosure of home buying costs | HUD Reg. X |
| Truth in Lending | Requires complete disclosure of credit terms | 15 U.S.C.A. §§1601 et seq. |
| Uniform Commercial Code | Law of sales—unconscionable contracts | §2-302 |
| Uniform Consumer Credit Code | Similar to federal Truth in Lending | 9 states have adopted[a] |

[a] Colorado, Idaho, Indiana, Iowa, Kansas, Maine, Oklahoma, Utah, and Wyoming have adopted substantial parts of some version of the Uniform Consumer Credit Code (UCCC).

mouthwash helps fight the common cold); (3) deceptive advertising demonstrations (e.g., claiming that a shaving cream moisturizes so well that sandpaper can easily be shaved, yet demonstrating this by passing a razor through loose sand scattered on plexiglass); (4) product endorsements by celebrities who do not really use the product; (5) failure to indicate the origin of foreign goods; (6) misleading product comparisons (e.g., claiming that a cigarette contains only 1 mg. of tar, when the mechanical device normally used to establish the tar content of cigarettes did not accurately measure the impact of the advertiser's special filter which allowed humans to receive 3–7 mg. of tar, a higher amount than contained in many competitors' "low-tar" cigarettes); and (7) product claims which "tend to deceive" (e.g., selling a facial cream under the name "Rejuvenescence," although it did not truly rejuvenate the skin).

The FTC's reach under §5 extends beyond deceptive advertising to other deceptive practices, including: (1) "bait and switch" tactics (e.g., advertising a low-quality good at a low price to induce consumers to come to the store and then pressuring them to buy a higher-priced model); (2) deceptive debt collection practices (e.g., sending letters to delinquent creditors which promised that a suit would be filed if no payments were made when, in fact, a determination to sue had not been made); and (3) unfair door-to-door selling—the FTC has promulgated a rule allowing consumers three days to rescind purchases made in their homes from door-to-door salesmen.[3]

**Enforcement:** The FTC issues various rules, regulations and guidelines regarding deceptive or unfair acts and practices. If the FTC discovers a potential violation, it can institute proceedings by filing a formal administrative complaint against the offender. The charge is normally heard before an FTC administrative law judge (ALJ) whose decision is reviewed by the FTC. The FTC's decisions may be reviewed by the courts.

Normally the FTC issues a "cease and desist" order to recalcitrant violators, ordering them to stop the deceptive acts or practices. Violation of such an order can precipitate fines of up to $10,000 per day. If the FTC has a strong case, an offender may agree to a "consent" order in which the FTC promises no further prosecution if the offender agrees to "go and sin no more."

In addition to obtaining injunctive orders from courts to support its cease and desist orders, the FTC is empowered to seek redress for consumers, perhaps in the form of refunds or cancellation of unfair contracts.

In the advertising cases, the FTC has occasionally ordered "corrective advertising" by a company which has long deceived the public. In such a case, the company must spend its own money to inform the public that its prior claims were untrue. "Multiproduct orders" are more frequently issued. Such an order is typically used for a company that has flagrantly engaged in falsely advertising a few of its products, and is aimed at *all* of the company's products. The rationale for such an order is that a company that has engaged flagrantly in the false advertising of some of its products is likely to do the same with others of its products.

Although the FTC Act is aimed primarily at false advertising, it has been applied to other types of behavior, as the following case illustrates.

---

[3] A similar provision under the Uniform Consumer Credit Code is discussed later in this chapter. The subject was earlier addressed near the end of Chapter 15.

---

### Orkin Exterminating Co., Inc. v. FTC
U.S. Eleventh Circuit Court of Appeals, 849 F.2d 1354 (1988)

In a series of promotions between 1968 and 1975, defendant Orkin made guarantees of *lifetime* termite control in exchange for timely payment of an annual fee that *would not be raised* unless the homeowner structurally modified the covered house. In 1978, Orkin decided that it could no longer afford to live up to this guarantee, so it substantially raised the annual fee on 207,000 contracts, pleading "inflation" as an excuse. Many customers complained, leading Orkin to roll back increases on 21,500 contracts. Those who did not complain or who did not have the documentation that Orkin required did not receive a rollback, however. Pursuant to its Section 5 authority to block behavior constituting "unfair or deceptive" acts, the FTC ordered Orkin to rescind the price increases as to all of the contracts. Orkin sought review of this order.

**Decision:** The FTC's order was affirmed. The appeals court rejected Orkin's contention that a "mere breach of contract" cannot be unfair or deceptive. The FTC policy focuses on consumer injury and defines unfairness by reference to three tests: it must be substantial; it must not be outweighed by any countervailing benefits to consumer or competition; and it must be an injury that consumers themselves could not reasonably have avoided.

*(continued)*

Here, the injury was substantial, because there was increased cost to over 200,000 consumers. Because no improvement in service accompanied the rate increase, the second factor also weighed in favor of a finding of unfairness. Finally, there was no feasible way for consumers to avoid the harm caused by Orkin's price increase. Although the finding set a new precedent, it was justified by the extraordinary level of consumer injury which Orkin caused. The court added in response to Orkin's final argument, that a good faith reliance upon advice of counsel is no defense. ■

---

## *The Lanham Act*

The Lanham Act is another important federal act that outlaws "any false description or representation" in connection with any person's goods, services, or commercial activities. The pertinent provisions of Section 43(a) of the Lanham Act have been discussed in Chapter 9 and will not be repeated here.

## THE CONSUMER CREDIT PROTECTION ACT

It is a fairly easy matter for the average householder to obtain and use any number of credit cards. The cash purchase of major appliances and automobiles is now a rare occurrence. Even the smallest supermarket purchases are paid for by check. The proliferation of credit has required legislation to define the rights and obligations of those who deal in it.

Congress enacted the Consumer Credit Protection Act (CCPA) in 1968 in response to unscrupulous and predatory practices on the part of creditors extending credit in consumer transactions. Congress was concerned with consumer credit disclosure methods, credit advertising, garnishment methods, questionable procedures used by some credit reporting agencies, and certain debt collection practices (a problem recognized in a 1977 amendment to the act).

## *Truth in Lending*

Before the **truth-in-lending** portion of the CCPA was passed in 1969, it was very difficult for consumers to understand what they were being charged for borrowing money or buying on time. Some lenders or sellers on credit would quote a "discount," others would refer to an "add on," and still others to various fees plus "simple interest." Some would quote monthly rates, while others quoted annual rates. The purpose of the Truth in Lending Act (TILA) is not to limit interest rates but to mandate disclosure of the true cost of credit so consumers borrowing money or buying on time can comparison shop.

Unfortunately, TILA, as originally passed, was quite complicated and burdensome. Indeed, it was virtually impossible for creditors to comply with. Over 14,000 lawsuits were filed by consumers under TILA in federal courts alone in the ten years following its passage. There were thousands more of these suits in state courts. This led to passage of the Truth in Lending Simplification and Reform Act of 1980 which simplified disclosure requirements, and limited the creditor liability in civil suits by debtors.

**Coverage:** TILA now applies to credit transactions involving personal, family, or household purposes. Loans for commercial or agricultural purposes are not covered. And, because Congress assumed that borrowers of large sums can protect themselves, TILA only applies to consumer loans not exceeding $25,000. Unlike many other consumer protection statutes, however, TILA also applies to credit secured by real property or a dwelling, such as a mortgage loan. There is no ceiling amount for this type of transaction; TILA applies even if the amount involved exceeds $25,000.

Only natural persons are protected by TILA's provisions. Debtors such as corporations or other organizations are not protected. All creditors who in the ordinary course of business lend money or sell on credit must comply with TILA provisions. TILA would not, however, apply to one consumer's loan to another.

**Disclosure:** TILA is primarily a disclosure act. It is clarified by Regulation Z, a set of rules promulgated by the Federal Reserve Board. TILA's two key disclosure requirements relate to the **annualized percentage rate (APR),** which is the yearly cost of credit calculated on a uniform basis, and the *finance charge,* which is any additional amount the consumer pays as a result of buying on credit instead of paying cash. Examples of a finance charge would include application and processing charges such as a loan origination fee charged by mortgage lenders, investigation or credit reporting fees, and premiums for required credit insurance.

All disclosures must be written, clear, and conspicuous. The APR and finance charge must be more conspicuous than the other required disclosures.

Specific disclosure requirements are keyed to the type of transaction. On the one hand is an *open-end* (revolving) transaction, such as a gasoline credit card or VISA and MasterCard. On the other hand are all transactions other than open-end, usually characterized as closed-end (installment) sales or loans with a fixed number of payments. If repeated transactions are reasonably expected by the creditor, the open-end requirements apply.

In an open-end transaction, there are two types of required disclosure—an initial disclosure and periodic supplementary disclosures. The initial disclosure, which should be made prior to the first transaction, is general in nature, covering important terms of the credit plan rather than specific transactions. Required initial disclosures include: (1) a statement of when finance charges begin to accrue, including any "free ride" period; (2) the APR; (3) in a variable rate plan, conditions under which the interest rate may increase; (4) an explanation of the method used to determine the balance on which the finance charge may be computed and of how the amount of finance charge will be determined; (5) conditions under which the creditor may acquire a security interest in the debtor's property; and (6) a statement of the debtor's billing rights.

Creditors in open-end transactions must also make periodic disclosures at the end of each billing cycle. These disclosures are geared to the specific transactions which have occurred, and include such things as: (1) the account balance at the beginning of the cycle; (2) identification of each transaction with descriptions of date, amount, and creditor; (3) the periodic rates that may be used to compute the finance charge and corresponding APR; (4) amounts of other charges; (5) account balance as of the closing date of the cycle; (6) any free ride period; and (7) an address to be used for notice of billing errors. These disclosures are contained in the monthly statements credit card holders receive.

Disclosures in a closed-end transaction are somewhat different. They must be made before consummation of the transaction in question. An important concept is the "federal box." The written disclosures should, by use of lines, a separate sheet of paper, boldface type or the like call attention to the required TILA disclosures. If the creditor puts too much information in the "federal box", thus detracting from attention given the required federal disclosures, a TILA violation occurs just the same as if insufficient information is disclosed.

Among the required disclosures in a closed-end transaction are: (1) the creditor's identity; (2) the amount financed and how it is computed; (3) the finance charge and APR (and circumstances under which it may be increased); (4) number, amounts, and timing of payments; (5) total dollar value of all payments; and (6) effect of prepayment.

**Substantive Provisions:** Although TILA is primarily a disclosure statute, it does shape some credit practices through substantive provisions. For example, it provides a three-day right of rescission for consumers who use their residence to secure credit in a nonpurchase money transaction. The rule does not apply to the first mortgage, issued when a house is purchased. But assume a homeowner contracts to buy a new air conditioner on credit. If the credit purchase is secured by the retailer's receiving a second mortgage on the residence, the right of rescission would apply. Absent an emergency, the seller should not deliver goods or perform services during that three-day period.

TILA also contains certain rules regarding how credit may be advertised. Again, the purpose is to create uniform, clear statements that will allow for comparison shopping. Furthermore, TILA contains numerous provisions regarding use of credit cards, even where no finance charge exists. One such provision is the $50 maximum ceiling for credit card holder liability which is discussed later in this chapter.

**Enforcement:** Various federal agencies, most importantly the FTC, enforce the civil provisions of TILA, and the Department of Justice can bring criminal charges for TILA violations. The maximum criminal penalty is one year in jail and/or a $5,000 fine for *each* violation.

Consumers are accorded a private right of action under TILA, and may recover their actual damages *plus* two times the finance charge (not to be less than $100 nor more than $1,000) and attorneys' fees. Suit should be brought within one year of a disclosure violation. The statute of limitations in a case involving a house being used as collateral is three years from the date of violation. TILA also contains a limited good-faith defense, which is applied in the following case.

### Hendley v. Cameron-Brown Co.
U.S. Eleventh Circuit Court of Appeals, 840 F.2d 831 (1988)

On April 1, 1984, the Hendleys and the Blacks (appellants) obtained discounted variable rate mortgage loans from Cameron-Brown Co. (appellee) to finance the purchase of their homes. The loans featured an annual adjustment of the interest rate. The annual interest rate was based on an "index plus margin" formula that was determined by adding to the margin, then at 2.79 percent, the current index (subject to a 2 percent annual cap and an overall cap of 5.75 percent for the lifetime of the loan). Appellants claim they were told that the interest rate would adjust annually in the same direction as the index.

At the end of the first year, appellee informed appellants that the interest rate for the second year would increase from 9.875 percent to 11.875 percent. Appellee claims that this increase was based on the "index plus margin" formula checked by the 2 percent cap. Objecting to this increase, appellants filed this suit claiming that appellee had violated TILA's disclosure requirements. Because the index actually declined in the second year from 10.53 percent to 9.61 percent, appellants maintain that the increase is inconsistent with the disclosure statement's language that the interest rate would be adjusted annually in the same direction as the index. Appellants argue that appellee failed to disclose the initial index and that the initial interest rate was discounted (lower than it would have been if it had been calculated by using the "index plus margin" formula).

The trial court granted summary judgment to appellee, finding that it had "technically complied" with TILA and that any deficiencies were protected by its "good faith" effort at complying with relatively new rules. Appellants appealed.

**Decision:** The trial court's judgment was reversed. Appellee did not comply with the first requirement for disclosure regarding variable rate loans in that it did not fully disclose the "circumstances under which the rate may increase." Honest and reasonable but mistaken attempts to comply with TILA rules and regulations are not protected. As a matter of law, good faith is no defense. ■

## Home Equity Loan Consumer Protection Act

Consumers occasionally use their homes as security when applying for open-end credit. The consequences for the homeowner who defaults on such a loan are obviously quite significant. Therefore, in an amendment to TILA, Congress passed the Home Equity Loan Consumer Protection Act of 1988 (HELCPA). Basically, this act requires lenders to provide an application-stage disclosure statement in addition to a consumer education pamphlet whenever a consumer puts up his or her "principal dwelling" (defined, unusually, to include second or vacation homes) as security for open-end credit. In addition to a broad range of disclosure requirements, HELCPA also contains several substantive provisions, including (1) restrictions on the creditor's ability to change unilaterally the plan's terms; (2) limitations on grounds for terminating the loan and requiring immediate repayment of the balance ("acceleration"); and (3) requirements that an external, publicly available index or formula be used if the home equity plan allows for rate changes.

## Restrictions on Garnishment

*Garnishment* can be defined as the legal proceedings of a judgment creditor to require a third person owing money to the debtor or holding property belonging to the debtor to turn over to the court or sheriff the property or money for the satisfaction of the judgment.[4] Congressional hearings leading to the enactment of the CCPA revealed that the unrestricted garnishment of wages encouraged predatory extension of credit, that employers were often quick to discharge an employee whose wages were garnished, and that the laws of the states on the subject were so different they effectively destroyed the uniformity of the bankruptcy laws and defeated their purpose. Consequently, the CCPA section on garnishment set limits on the extent to which the wages of an individual could be garnished. In general, wages cannot be garnished in any workweek in excess of 25 percent of the individual's disposable (after-tax) earnings or the amount by which the disposable earnings for that workweek exceed 30 times the federal minimum hourly wage, whichever is less. Such restrictions do not apply in the case of a court order for the support of any person (wife or child, for example), any order of a court of bankruptcy under Chapter 13, Adjustment of Debts of an Individual with Regular Income, of the Federal Bankruptcy Act, or any debt due for state or federal taxes.

## *The Fair Credit Reporting Act*

The section of the CCPA known as the Fair Credit Reporting Act is directed at consumer reporting agencies. It is an effort by Congress to ensure that the elaborate mechanism developed for investigating and evaluating the credit-worthiness, credit standing, credit capacity, character, and general reputation of consumers is fair with respect to the confidentiality, accuracy, relevance, and proper utilization of the reported information. Too often in the past, the consumer was denied credit because of misleading or inaccurate information supplied to a prospective creditor by a consumer reporting agency.[5] The effect could be devastating, particularly as it affected the consumer's credit standing and general reputation in the business community.

The information on individual consumers is derived from many sources, including creditors, court and other official records, and, in many cases, from facts consumers supply themselves. Information accumulated in a **consumer report** and disseminated to users can and often does include such items as judgments, liens, bankruptcies, arrest records, and employment history. In addition, the Fair Credit Reporting Act covers the **investigative reports** made by credit reporting agencies. Often used by prospective employers or by insurance companies, investigative reports are more personal in nature than consumer reports and can contain information on the subject's personal habits, marital status (past and present), education, political affiliation, and so on.

With regard to both consumer reports and investigative reports, the law requires that, upon request and proper identification, consumers are entitled to know the nature and substance of all information about them (except medical information) in the agency's file, the sources of the information, and the identity of those who have received the report from the credit reporting agency. Those entitled to receive consumer reports include businesses that may want to extend credit to the consumer, prospective employers or insurers, and government licensing agencies that may be concerned with the financial responsibility of the consumer. Access to the information can also be gained by court order. In addition, an investigative report cannot be prepared on an individual consumer unless that person is first notified and given the right to request information on the nature and scope of the pending investigation.

An important provision of the act requires that all information in consumer reports be current and that consumer reporting agencies maintain reasonable procedures designed to avoid violations of certain other provisions. This is an obvious effort to reduce the incidence of carelessly prepared reports having inaccurate information.

Finally, civil penalties for a *negligent* violation of the act include the actual damages to the consumer and, in a successful action, court costs and reasonable attorneys' fees. In case of *willful* noncompliance, punitive damages may also be awarded to the successful plaintiff-consumer. It is interesting to note that administrative enforcement of the act and compliance with its provisions is a function of the Federal Trade Commission because violations are considered unfair or deceptive acts or practices.

---

[4] See the discussion on garnishment in Chapter 30.

[5] This is not an agency of the government. Such agencies are persons or businesses that regularly assemble credit information and provide it to others for a fee.

## Zamora v. Valley Federal Savings & Loan Association of Grand Junction
U.S. Tenth Circuit Court of Appeals, 811 F.2d 1368 (1987)

Plaintiff Zamora's wife was employed by Valley Federal (defendant) as a loan officer. When she married plaintiff, a Valley Federal vice-president, Inscho, obtained a credit report on plaintiff from the Mesa County Credit Bureau by representing that the report was to be used for "employment purposes." At the time the report was requested, plaintiff's wife was being considered for a promotion. When plaintiff discovered that the credit report had been obtained, he sued, alleging that defendant had knowingly and willfully obtained a credit report on plaintiff under false pretenses in violation of the Fair Credit Reporting Act (FCRA). The jury found for plaintiff in the sum of $61,500, and defendant appealed.

**Decision:** The trial court's judgment was affirmed. The appellate court held that it was reasonable for the jury to have found that Valley Federal obtained the credit report under false pretenses. The FCRA sets forth an exclusive list of permissible purposes for which a consumer credit report can be obtained. "Employment purposes" is included, but only for the actual person being considered. To allow a user of consumer reports to obtain information on the *spouse* of such a person "would violate the right to privacy that Congress intended to protect." ∎

## Credit Cards

The widespread use of credit cards, issued by all manner of companies, created much legal controversy when a card fell into the wrong hands through loss or theft. Many companies provided their credit cards indiscriminately to any person who might want one and to many who had not requested them. It became a major problem to determine who was to assume the liability for unauthorized credit card purchases: the person to whom the card was issued, the unauthorized user, the merchant who made the sale, or the credit card issuer. Congress addressed the problem in CCPA provisions that prohibit the issuance of credit cards except in response to a request or application and that place limits on the liability of a cardholder for its unauthorized use. In general, if a cardholder loses a credit card and it is used by someone without authority to do so, the cardholder is liable if: (1) the liability does not exceed $50; (2) the card is an accepted card; (3) the issuer has given notice to the cardholder as to the potential liability; (4) the issuer has provided the cardholder with a self-addressed, prestamped notification to be mailed by the cardholder in the event of loss or theft; (5) the unauthorized use occurs before the cardholder has notified the issuer that an unauthorized use of the card has occurred; and (6) the card issuer has provided a method whereby the user of the card can be identified by the merchant, either by photograph or signature, as the authorized user.

The above provisions are for the protection of a lawful cardholder. Unauthorized use of a credit card can result in severe penalties. If the unauthorized transaction involves goods or services, or both, having a retail value of $5,000 or more, the penalty can be a fine of up to $10,000 or imprisonment for up to five years, or both. These provisions are at issue in the following case.

## Transamerica Insurance Co. v. Standard Oil Co.
North Dakota Supreme Court, 325 N.W.2d 210 (1982)

Smith was office manager of MBS. In March 1967 he obtained Amoco credit cards for employees; charges were paid by MBS. In May 1975, Smith made a written request to Amoco for a Torch Club credit card that could be used to purchase consumer goods. The application contained Smith's signature as office manager, and Switzer's signature as general manager of MBS. However, Smith had forged Switzer's signature. Amoco issued the card after checking MBS's payment record, without contacting credit references or inquiring into Smith's authority.

*(continued)*

Between May 1975 and July 1978, Smith fraudulently used the Torch Club card to obtain goods and services worth $26,376.53. Smith again used forgery to cause MBS to pay these bills. Neither MBS nor its auditors detected the fraud until July 1978 when Smith was fired. Plaintiff Transamerica, MBS's fidelity-bond carrier, paid MBS its claim in full for the loss. Transamerica now sues defendant, which does business as Amoco, as a subrogee under MBS's claim, alleging that it was not liable for the charges under TILA provisions dealing with credit card liability.

The trial court entered judgment for Transamerica in the amount of $26,376.53. Amoco appealed.

---

**Decision:** The judgment was reversed in part. A credit card holder's liability for misuse of a credit card by another is limited to $50 if certain conditions are met and if use of the card was unauthorized. Amoco is responsible for negligently *issuing* this card to Smith. Smith had no apparent authority to secure this credit card and Amoco did not inquire as to whether he had actual authority. Also, to impose limited cardholder liability, the card must be an "accepted card," one that the cardholder has requested, signed, used, or authorized another to use. MBS did none of these things. Therefore, MBS (and its subrogee Transamerica) were not liable for the initial charges by Smith on the credit card.

However, after monthly statements were first sent to MBS, it was negligent in not discovering the fraud and reporting it to Amoco. MBS could be held liable for this type of carelessness, because, as the court stated, "otherwise, an unscrupulous cardholder could allow another to charge hundreds of dollars in goods and services and then attempt to limit its liability to 50 dollars." Amoco is liable for Smith's charges from the time it issued the card until it sent a monthly statement to MBS plus a reasonable time to examine the statement. Thereafter, MBS is liable. When MBS should have discovered the fraud is a question for a jury to decide. The case was remanded for that determination. ■

---

## *Fair Credit and Charge Card Disclosure Act:*

Concerned over high interest rates charged credit card borrowers, Congress considered enacting a ceiling on such charges, but ultimately decided that competition was the best regulation. Therefore, to enable consumers to better comparison shop, Congress enacted the Fair Credit and Charge Card Disclosure Act of 1988 (an amendment to TILA), which requires disclosure of certain key items of information at the solicitation and application stages for credit and charge card accounts.

The amount of disclosure required varies with the type of solicitation. Direct mail applications and solicitations must disclose more information, for example, than solicitations made by telephone or through ads contained in magazines. A complete catalogue of the required disclosures would be too lengthy to repeat here. However, among the key disclosures that must be made in connection with a direct mail solicitation for a *credit card* are: (1) each periodic rate of finance charge expressed as an annual percentage rate; (2) if the plan includes a variable rate of interest, the fact that the rate may vary, how the rate is determined, and the APR in effect within 30 days before the time of the mailing; (3) any annual or other periodic fee imposed for issuance of the credit card; (4) any transaction fee imposed in connection with purchase transactions; and (5) any minimum or fixed finance charge that could be imposed during a billing cycle. These and other "core disclosures" must be placed in a prominent location either on or with the application or solicitation.

Less onerous disclosures are required for applications or solicitations for a "charge card," defined as "a card, plate, or other single credit device that may be used from time to time to obtain credit which is *not* subject to a finance charge." The act also requires disclosure of any fees charged to renew a credit or charge card account. Atypically, it preempts rather than supplements state laws in the area.

## *The Fair Debt Collection Practices Act*

A 1977 amendment to the CCPA, the Fair Debt Collection Practices Act, became effective March 20, 1978. It has as its purpose the elimination of abusive debt collection practices by debt collectors and the protection of individual debtors against debt collection abuses. The following excerpt from *Duty v. General Finance Co.*, 273 S.W.2d 64 (Tex. 1954), illustrates some of the tactics employed by an overzealous debt collector. It is important to note that each and every tactic employed by the General Finance Company debt collector is now prohibited by the Fair Debt Collection Practices Act.

> The harassment alleged may be summarized as follows: Daily telephone calls to both Mr. & Mrs.

Duty which extended to great length; threatening to blacklist them with the Merchants' Retail Credit Association; accusing them of being deadbeats; talking to them in a harsh, insinuating, loud voice; stating to their neighbors and employers that they were deadbeats; asking Mrs. Duty what she was doing with her money; accusing her of spending money in other ways than in payments on the loan transaction; threatening to cause both plaintiffs to lose their jobs unless they made the payments demanded; calling each of the plaintiffs at the respective places of their employment several times daily; threatening to garnish their wages; berating plaintiffs to their fellow employees; requesting their employers to require them to pay; calling on them at their work; flooding them with a barrage of demand letters, dun cards, special delivery letters, and telegrams both at their homes and their places of work; sending them cards bearing this opening statement: "Dear Customer: We made you a loan because we thought that you were honest."; sending telegrams and special delivery letters to them at approximately midnight, causing them to be awakened from their sleep; calling a neighbor in the disguise of a sick brother of one of the plaintiffs, and on another occasion as a stepson; calling Mr. Duty's mother at her place of employment in Wichita Falls long distance, collect; leaving red cards in their door, with insulting notes on the back and thinly-veiled threats; calling Mr. Duty's brother long distance, collect, in Albuquerque, New Mexico, at his residence at a cost to him in excess of $11, and haranguing him about the alleged balance owed by plaintiffs.

The debt collector's communications with others and with the debtor in an effort to locate the debtor are governed by a provision of the act. The debt collector is prohibited from making false representations or misleading the debtor about the nature of the collection process. The collector cannot solicit or take from any person a check postdated by more than five days without notice of the intent to deposit the check. On occasion, debt collectors have encouraged the debtor to write a postdated check for the amount of the debt knowing that the debtor had insufficient funds to cover the check. A threat to deposit the postdated check was often enough to compel the debtor to seek the funds necessary to pay the collector and thereby avoid criminal prosecution for issuing a bad check. The act further provides that written notice of the amount of the debt and the name of the creditor be sent to the consumer together with a statement that, unless the consumer disputes the validity of the debt within 30 days, the debt collector can assume it is a valid obligation. If the consumer owes multiple debts and makes a single payment, the debt collector cannot apply the payment to any debt that is disputed by the consumer.[6]

The Fair Debt Collection Practices Act protects the consumer-debtor and places significant burdens on the debt collector. Compliance with the act is enforced by the Federal Trade Commission, since violations are considered to be unfair or deceptive trade practices. A debt collector who fails to comply with the provisions of the act may incur civil liability to the extent of actual damages sustained by the plaintiff, additional punitive damages not to exceed $1,000, and court costs and reasonable attorneys' fees.

## *Fair Credit Billing*

Prior to the Fair Credit Billing Act, the burden of resolving a billing dispute rested mainly on the customer-debtor. This is no longer true. The Fair Credit Billing Act requires that creditors maintain procedures whereby consumers can complain about billing errors and obtain satisfaction within a specified period, not later than two billing cycles or ninety days. The consumer must give the creditor notice of the billing error with a statement explaining the reasons for questioning the item or items felt to be in error. The creditor must then either make appropriate corrections in the consumer's account or conduct an investigation into the matter. If, after the investigation, the creditor feels that the statement is accurate, it must so notify the debtor and explain why it believes the original statement of account to be correct. The act also requires that payments be credited promptly and that any overpayment be refunded (on request by the debtor) or credited to the debtor's account.

## *Equal Credit Opportunity*

The Equal Credit Opportunity Act (ECOA), as amended, quite simply prohibits discrimination based on race, color, religion, national origin, sex, marital

---

[6] This provision may be contrary to a commonly accepted principle of contract law: Where a debtor owes multiple debts and fails to specify to which debt the payment is to be applied, the creditor can make the choice.

status, or age in connection with extensions of credit. The applicant must, however, have contractual capacity; minors, for example, cannot insist on credit under the act. The enactment is the result of complaints by married persons that credit frequently was denied unless both parties to the marriage obligated themselves. Each party can now separately and voluntarily apply for and obtain credit accounts, and state laws prohibiting separate credit no longer apply. The act also directs the Board of Governors of the Federal Reserve System to establish a Consumer Advisory Council to provide advice and consultation on consumer credit and other matters. The following case offers an interesting application of the ECOA.

### United States v. American Future Systems, Inc.
U.S. Third Circuit Court of Appeals, 743 F.2d 169 (1984)

American Future Systems, Inc. (AFS), sells china, cookware, crystal, and tableware, 95 percent of the time on credit. AFS markets its wares through three separate programs. Its summer program targets as preferred customers single white females between the ages of 18 and 21 who live at home. AFS hopes parents will co-sign the order, but will extend credit and automatically ship goods to the buyer even without a co-signature. Nonpreferred customers, almost always young black females, are extended credit only after a satisfactory credit check. If the buyer does not pass the check, goods will not be shipped. AFS sales employees are urged to sell only in areas believed to be all or predominantly white, and work under commission arrangements which encourage sales to whites.

AFS's winter program has two aspects. Its preferred sales targets are single white females in their final three years of college. They are given immediate credit and the ordered goods are shipped to them immediately, regardless of age, prior credit histories, or any other normal indicia of creditworthiness. Nonpreferred customers for the winter program include all minorities, males, married persons, and freshmen in college. AFS will not ship goods to these customers until they have made three successive monthly payments. Although these customers are led to believe they are being treated the same as other AFS customers, AFS has made a marketing judgment to prefer white females.

The Department of Justice sued AFS, its president and an affiliated company, claiming violation of the ECOA. AFS defended, claiming that minority customers are, as a group, less creditworthy than their white counterparts. AFS could produce no reliable evidence to support this position, so the trial court found both the winter and summer programs to violate the ECOA. AFS appealed as to the winter program only.

**Decision:** The judgment was affirmed. The ECOA prohibits racial and other types of discrimination in the extension of credit. It is true that the ECOA does allow special credit programs that serve special social needs of a class of persons. Here the defendant claimed that its program catered to the 18–21 group, which has special credit needs. The evidence showed that all individuals in that age bracket share the same credit disability, yet defendant's plan assisted only white females. Black and Hispanic women have the credit door slammed in their faces by defendant. The court stated that it did "not believe that it was the intention of Congress to accentuate the disparities among disadvantaged groups by helping those women who have been the *least* deprived while denying equal opportunity to those women who have been the *most* deprived." ∎

## THE UNIFORM CONSUMER CREDIT CODE

Federal legislation does not necessarily preclude similar state legislation. For example, Section 1610 of the Consumer Credit Protection Act generally preempts only state laws that are *less* protective of debtors. State laws that are *more* protective probably are not precluded.[7] This principle—that state laws are enforceable even though they may regulate an area already covered by federal statutes—is illustrated by the Uniform Consumer Credit Code (UCCC).

---

[7] For example, state laws that prohibit garnishments or provide for more limited garnishments than are allowed under the federal statute are effective and enforceable despite the federal regulations on the same subject.

The Uniform Consumer Credit Code has been promulgated by the National Conference of Commissioners on Uniform State Laws in two versions—one in 1968 and one in 1974. Nine states have adopted substantial parts of one form or another of the UCCC. Many other states have similar provisions. However, there is great variation from state to state, even among the UCCC adopters. Therefore, our discussion of the UCCC's features must be somewhat general.

The UCCC is much like the Federal Consumer Credit Protection Act. It covers consumer credit sales, loans, garnishment, and insurance provided in relation to a consumer credit sale. Its truth-in-lending provisions require full disclosure to the consumer of all aspects of the credit transaction and further require that charges to the consumer be computed and disclosed as an annual percentage rate. The code does not prescribe any specific rates for credit service charges, but it sets maximums based on unpaid balances—36 percent per year on $300 or less in non-open-end accounts, 21 percent per year for balances of $300 to $1,000, and 15 percent for unpaid balances in excess of $1,000. Since the law permits higher charges for smaller transactions, it forbids creditors from breaking large transactions down into smaller ones to take advantage of higher credit charges.

## Home Solicitation Sales

The UCCC covers door-to-door solicitation in some detail, since this is a troublesome area for consumers. Consumers tend to be more vulnerable to high-pressure selling tactics in their homes; after signing an agreement to purchase, they often regret the decision. The UCCC therefore permits the rescission of a credit sale solicited and finalized in the customer's home if the customer gives written notice to the seller within 72 hours after signing the agreement to purchase.[8] The cancellation notice is effective when deposited in a mailbox and can take any form so long as it clearly expresses the buyer's intention to void the home solicitation sale. Sellers are required to provide a statement informing buyers of their right to cancel, including the mailing address for the written cancellation notice.

---

[8] Many of the states that have not adopted the UCCC do have statutes governing door-to-door solicitation, and many municipalities have ordinances regulating solicitors, peddlers, and transient merchants. The latter regulations are known as Green River ordinances. See *Green River v. Fuller Brush Co.*, 65 F.2d 112 (1933).

---

### Cole v. Lovett
U.S. District Court, Southern District of Mississippi,
672 F.Supp. 947 (1987)

On Tuesday, November 9, 1982, at approximately 6:00 P.M., plaintiffs Norman and Judy Cole were visited by two representatives of Capitol Roofing, Tony Stepp and Ken Smith. That same evening plaintiffs signed a contract for the installation of vinyl siding on their home. At that time, Stepp provided several documents for the Coles to sign, but did not allow them to read them, representing that they were work papers, credit applications, and insurance papers. The Coles received only a single carbon copy of the work order contract and a copy of a disclosure statement. Shortly after Stepp and Smith left, plaintiffs changed their minds and decided to obtain more estimates. The next morning Judy called Stepp and informed him of this decision, but Stepp replied that the papers had already been processed, the workers would be out at the end of the week, and there was nothing he could do.

When she returned home from work that day, Judy discovered Capitol's workers installing siding. She did not tell them to leave, because she thought she had no choice. As soon as the work was done, Capitol Roofing assigned the contract to defendant UCM. Problems resulted with the siding, but repeated calls to Capitol brought no satisfaction. After having made 11 monthly payments to UCM on the $4900 bill, plaintiffs consulted a lawyer who, by letter of December 19, 1984, informed both Capitol and UCM that the Coles desired to exercise their right of rescission under both the Truth in Lending Act (TILA) and the Mississippi Home Sales Solicitation Act (MHSSA). Upon receiving no response, plaintiffs sued J. L. Lovett d/b/a Capitol Roofing to rescind. UCM counterclaimed for the remaining sum due on the contract. The trial judge's opinion is summarized below.

*(continued)*

**Decision:** The Coles are entitled to cancellation of the finance charges on the transaction and to have the security interest in their home voided because of TILA violations. They are relieved of any further obligation to make payment because of the MHSSA violations. UCM must cancel the deed of trust and return the payments made by the Coles. The siding becomes the property of the Coles. These are the harsh consequences of a violation of the MHSSA, which was intended as a warning to merchants to deal fairly in contracts entered into outside their usual place of business. ∎

---

## *Debtor Default*

Generally, if a consumer defaults on payments, creditors can repossess the property the consumer has purchased and sell it to satisfy the unpaid debt. If the sale earns too little to discharge the debt, the creditor can normally sue the debtor and obtain a deficiency judgment. However, the 1968 UCCC distinguishes between debts incurred in the purchase of goods for $1,000 or less and debts exceeding $1,000. If the goods purchased were worth $1,000 or less, the creditor must *either* repossess the goods *or* sue the debtor for the unpaid balance. If the creditor chooses to repossess, the debtor is not personally liable for the unpaid balance. Only if the original sale exceeded $1,000 can the creditor repossess *and* seek a deficiency judgment if repossession fails to cover the unpaid balance.

With regard to garnishment, the UCCC prevents any prejudgment attachment of the debtor's unpaid earnings and limits the garnishment to 25 percent of net income or to that portion of the income in excess of 40 times the federal minimum hourly wage. The UCCC also prohibits an employer from discharging an employee whose wages are garnished to pay a judgment arising from a consumer credit sale, lease, or loan.

Although the UCCC has been adopted by nine states, the law as adopted can vary considerably from state to state. It is generally true of the so-called uniform laws that a state can make significant changes so the law reflects local attitudes or conforms to local policy in the particular matter covered.

## THE REAL ESTATE SETTLEMENT PROCEDURES ACT

The purchase of a residence is the largest single transaction most consumers ever make. It can be a traumatic experience for the novice who finds that, in addition to the down payment, substantial sums of money will be required on settlement, or closing day. Items to be paid for may include attorney's fees; title insurance; various inspections, surveys, and appraisals; agent's or broker's services; taxes and insurance; and many other miscellaneous items. Congress found that because of the variation in the kinds of items included in the settlement costs and the amount charged for each, significant reforms were needed in the real estate settlement process. The purpose of the Real Estate Settlement Procedures Act (RESPA), enacted in 1974 and subsequently amended, is to insure that buyers of residential property are given timely information on the nature and costs of the settlement process and that they are protected against obvious abuses. The Act requires that effective advance disclosure be made to home buyers and sellers. It prohibits kickbacks or referral fees and, in general, affords considerable protection by letting the home buyer know what it is going to cost to buy a given home.

RESPA applies to all federally related mortgage loans and is administered and enforced by the Secretary of Housing and Urban Development.[9] The secretary has issued comprehensive regulations, known as Regulation X, to prescribe procedures for curbing questionable practices in real estate transactions. Various forms have been devised and are in use, and a special information booklet has been developed for the lender to distribute to the borrower at the time a loan application is made. The lender is also required to provide the borrower with "good faith estimates" of the dollar amount or range of each settlement service charge that the borrower is likely to incur. Generally speaking, RESPA places the burden on the lender to provide the borrower good advance information about the costs of purchasing a home—the

---

[9] Most, if not all, mortgage loans on residential property are federally related. The deposits or accounts of the lending institution may be insured by an agency of the federal government or the lender may be regulated by a federal agency.

basic cost and the substantial sums needed on settlement day.

# ADDITIONAL CONSUMER PROTECTION MEASURES

Federal legislation primarily insures fair treatment for consumers seeking credit, borrowing money, or contemplating the purchase of a residence or automobile. For the most part, the statutes examined in this chapter have been remedial in nature. Their purpose is to correct what Congress has determined to be persistent abuses. Many other statutes, however, are designed to protect the consumer's safety and well-being. These laws concern general health and welfare and alert the consumer to the possibility of harm from the use or misuse of certain products.

## *Packaging and Labeling*

The Public Health Cigarette Smoking Act of 1969, popularly known as the Cigarette Labeling and Advertising Act, establishes a comprehensive federal program to deal with labeling and advertising the ill effects of smoking on health. The Act bans completely advertising of cigarettes and little cigars on any medium of electronic communication subject to the jurisdiction of the Federal Communications Commission. It also requires that every cigarette package, every cigarette advertisement, and every billboard carrying such an advertisement carry one of four warning labels. These labels warn consumers about the various adverse health effects of smoking.

The courts have split over the issue of whether compliance with federal labeling laws preempts state law products liability claims by smokers or their families against cigarette makers. Most courts hold that such compliance preempts any claims based on a failure-to-warn theory, but so far the courts are about evenly divided on whether compliance preempts claims based on a design defect theory.

The Wholesome Poultry Products Act and the Wholesome Meat Act are also examples of the protective statute. Each establishes procedures to insure that only wholesome products are distributed to consumers and that they are properly labeled and packaged.

The Federal Food, Drug, and Cosmetic Act establishes extensive controls over various products and regulates their development, premarketing testing, labeling, and packaging.

In the Fair Packaging and Labeling Act, Congress has stated that informed consumers are essential to the fair and efficient functioning of a free market economy and that packages and labels should enable consumers to obtain accurate information about the quantity of the contents and should facilitate value comparisons. The act therefore establishes comprehensive requirements for the identification of commodities and provides that net quantities must be conspicuously displayed in a uniform location on the principal panel of the product. The main purpose of the act, set forth in some detail, is the prevention of unfair or deceptive packaging and labeling and general misbranding of consumer commodities.

An important amendment, the Poison Prevention Packaging Act of 1970, resulted in the mandatory development and use of child-proof devices on household substances that could harm young children if mishandled or ingested. Other statutes for children are the Flammable Fabrics Act and the Child Protection and Toy Safety Act. The Consumer Product Safety Commission is responsible for administering many of the statutes relating to product safety.

In Chapter 22 we also discussed the work of the CPSC and the Magnuson-Moss Act which help assure that consumers receive what they bargain for when they purchase products.

# SUMMARY

Many state and federal consumer protection laws now create an atmosphere in which many believe *caveat venditor* ("let the seller beware") has replaced the traditional *caveat emptor.*

Consumers are protected from deceptive practices, including deceptive advertising, by §5 of the Federal Trade Commission Act and §43(a) of the Lanham Act. These laws authorize the FTC, as well as competitors of the misleading advertiser, to bring suit to correct deceptive ads.

The Consumer Credit Protection Act creates an arsenal of weapons which protect the borrower or purchaser on credit. The Truth in Lending Act mandates extensive disclosures whenever a consumer borrows money or buys on credit. The purpose is to ensure that the consumer knows the true cost of the borrowing and can comparison shop. The Fair Credit Reporting Act protects consumers from the serious damage that misleading credit reports can have on consumers' economic status. The Fair Debt Collection Practices Act protects debtors from abusive collection practices by professional collection agencies. Also, in this nonexclusive listing of protective statutes, the Equal Credit Opportunity Act promotes equality in the extension of credit by outlawing discrimination on the basis of sex, age, race, and other grounds.

The Uniform Consumer Credit Code, which has been adopted by nine states, and copied in many others, also contains credit disclosure requirements and home solicitation provisions protecting vulnerable consumers from unfair practices by door-to-door salesmen.

Packaging and labeling laws and the Real Estate Settlement Procedures Act are just two of an extensive battery of proconsumer statutes that every businessperson must understand and comply with.

## KEY TERMS

**Consumer transaction**
**Usury**
**Garnishment**
**Truth in lending**
**Annual percentage rate (APR)**
**Consumer report**
**Investigative report**

## QUESTIONS AND PROBLEMS

1. Removatron International makes and sells an epilator machine designed to remove unwanted hair permanently without the side effects associated with electrolysis. The machine uses a pair of tweezers to remove the hair; while the tweezers grasp the hair but before it is removed, the machine emits radio frequency energy that travels down the tweezers and along the hair. Removatron advertises in beauty industry trade magazines. Removatron's ads state that hair removal can be "permanent" and that unwanted hair will no longer be a problem, that the machine has been "clinically tested and endorsed," and that it is approved by the FCC. When the FTC challenged these ads, evidence showed that the machines cost $4,000 and treatment costs $35/hour. During the sales process, purchasers are informed that the machine will not work for everyone and that permanent removal will be obtained only after several treatments. The FCC does not approve the product, but only approved the machine to emit radio waves at a particular frequency. No controlled scientific studies have been performed to test the effectiveness and safety of the machine. Should the FTC be allowed to block Removatron's ads in their current form? How should a cease and desist order be structured? (*Removatron International Corp. v. FTC*, 884 F.2d 1489, 1st Cir. 1989.)

2. A husband and wife signed an agreement to subscribe to several magazines with a door-to-door salesperson who had called on them one evening during the dinner hour. What are the rights of both seller and buyer if the husband and wife decide the next morning that they have been high-pressured and want to void the transaction?

3. Litton Industries advertised that a survey of "independent microwave oven service technicians" indicated that 76 percent of the surveyed population "recommend Litton." Evidence showed that in conducting its survey, Litton used only its own service agency lists, though it had lists of its competitors; Litton knew at least 100 agencies were excluded from the survey; Litton surveyed only one technician at each agency; Litton knew its list contained some dealers who sold Litton microwaves and therefore had reason to favor them and certainly were not "independent"; Litton knew many of those surveyed had insufficient experience with other brands to respond accurately. In a §5 action, the FTC entered a "multiproducts" order, prohibiting Litton from misusing survey information with all of its products, not just microwaves. Should the court uphold this order? (*Litton Industries, Inc. v. FTC*, 676 F.2d 364, 9th Cir. 1982.)

4. An ambulance company charges its customers an additional $5.00 when they do not pay by cash or check at the time services are rendered. Does this arrangement constitute a "finance charge" that must be disclosed under the Truth in Lending Act? Discuss. (*Hahn v. Hank's Ambulance Service, Inc.*, 787 F.2d 543, 11th Cir. 1986.)

5. Maurice had an American Express card. Later, his wife Virginia was granted a supplementary card. When Maurice died, Virginia's card was cancelled under American Express's general policy of automatically terminating supplemental cards upon the death of the basic cardholder. The cancellation had nothing to do with Virginia's creditworthiness or ability to pay. Virginia did reapply for a card and was granted it. Still, she sued American Express for violation of the ECOA. Discuss. (*Miller v. American Express Co.*, 688 F.2d 1235, 9th Cir. 1982.)

6. John Smith is the sole proprietor of a small restaurant. Desiring to renovate and extend his premises he borrowed $30,000 from a local bank. Does the Truth in Lending Act have any applicability to this transaction?

7. The odometer of a motorcycle purchased by plaintiff indicated that it had been driven 875 miles. The actual mileage was 14,000. Plaintiff sought damages claiming that defendant failed to disclose the actual mileage or that the true mileage was unknown; that defendant altered the odometer intending to defraud; or that defendant repaired the odometer, failed to adjust it to zero, and failed to so notify the purchaser of the repair. Such allegations, if proven, would constitute violations of the Motor Vehicle Information and Cost Savings Act. Defendant moved to dismiss claiming that the act did not apply to motorcycles, and if it

did, it was unconstitutionally vague. The act provided that notice of any alteration in mileage must be attached to the left door frame of the vehicle. Motorcycles, claimed defendant, do not have door frames. Is this a good defense? Discuss. (*Grambo v. Loomis Cycle Sales, Inc.,* 404 F.Supp. 1073, N.D.Ind. 1975.)

**8.** In October 1974, Sheehan purchased a Ford automobile which was financed by Ford Credit on a retail installment contract. Later Sheehan moved to various locations and became delinquent on his account. When Ford Credit was unable to locate Sheehan it assigned the delinquent account to a central recovery office for collection or repossession. A short time later Sheehan's mother, who resided in Rhode Island, received a phone call from a woman who identified herself as an employee of the Mercy Hospital in San Francisco. (The call actually emanated from Ford Credit's office in Dearborn, Michigan.) She advised Sheehan's mother that one or both of Sheehan's children had been involved in a serious automobile accident and that she, the caller, was attempting to locate Sheehan. The mother supplied the caller with Sheehan's home and business addresses and phone numbers. The following day Sheehan's car was repossessed and subsequent inquiry revealed that the call referred to above was a ruse and that Sheehan's children had not been injured. Are consumers protected against such practices? (*Ford Motor Credit Company v. Frances C. Sheehan,* 373 So.2d 956, Fla. 1979.)

**9.** A consumer who tried to obtain information from a credit reporting agency on the nature and substance of items in his file was denied such information and forced to return to the credit reporting agency's office several times. The consumer was finally given some of the information held by the agency, but several items were withheld. Discuss this situation with regard to the Fair Credit Reporting Act. (*Millstone v. O'Hanlon Reports, Inc.*, 383 F.Supp. 269, 1974.)

**10.** Betty Jones had a VISA and Master Charge account with defendant Bank. Upon her request, the Bank issued cards on those accounts to her husband also. On November 11, 1977, Jones informed the Bank by two separate letters that she would no longer honor charges made by her husband on the two accounts, whereupon the Bank immediately revoked both accounts and requested the return of the cards. Despite numerous notices and requests for surrender of the cards, both Jones and her husband retained the cards and continued to make charges against the accounts. Not until March 9, 1978 did Jones relinquish her credit cards. Is Jones responsible for the balance owing on the account, which includes sums charged by her husband after November 11, 1977? Discuss. (*Walker Bank & Trust Co. v. Jones,* 672 P.2d 73, Utah 1983.)

# CHAPTER 51

# THE LEGAL ENVIRONMENT OF INTERNATIONAL BUSINESS

## INTRODUCTION

As early as 1816 in *The Schooner Exchange v. McFadden*,[1] Chief Justice Marshall wrote: "The world [is] composed of distinct sovereignties . . . whose mutual benefit is promoted by intercourse with each other, and by an exchange of those good offices which humanity dictates and its wants require." As long as nations have existed, there has been commercial activity among them. That activity is generally very beneficial to all the parties involved, and in our modern world the amount of international commercial activity is exploding.

For example, worldwide exports of goods exceed $2 trillion annually. The United States alone exports more than $200 billion in goods per year. (Unfortunately for our trade balance, we import a substantially greater amount annually than that.) Many of the largest U.S. corporations derive more than half their profits from sales outside the country. On the flip side of the coin, more than 70 percent of U.S. manufacturers face direct foreign competition for sales in the United States.

Direct U.S. investment[2] in foreign countries exceeds $475 billion. In turn, foreigners have directly invested around $300 billion in the United States. More than three million Americans are employed by companies directly owned by foreign investors. This is only one aspect of the situation, because foreign entities also own over a trillion dollars of U.S. securities.[3] Increasingly, U.S. companies are forming joint ventures with foreign companies to do business overseas. Conversely, many foreign companies are entering U.S. markets through similar means.

All in all, an already small world is growing smaller. Every day, investors in the United States watch the Tokyo stock market, for its fluctuations will affect the U.S. stock markets. The tearing down of the Berlin Wall in early 1990 is cause for celebration in the United States not only because it portends democracy but also because of the commercial opportunities opening for U.S. businesses in Eastern Europe. Just as dramatically, the events of Tiananmen Square in China in 1989 quickly put a damper on the interests of foreign investors.

Just as each company or investor hoping to do business abroad must be concerned with the events occurring in other countries, so must they be concerned with the *legal* aspects of international transactions. The laws of the countries in which they intend to do business, as well as **international law**, must be considered in each and every transaction.

Legal problems are pervasive and inescapable. Can a U.S. company selling its goods in South Korea expect protection from trademark infringement by local companies?[4] Must a Japanese company operating its plant on American soil comply with U.S. laws when making its employment decisions?[5] Does a European company wishing to purchase an American company face any barriers that a potential U.S. purchaser would not face?[6] An endless variety of legal questions shape international commerce.

---

[1] 7 Cranch 116 (1812).

[2] "Direct investment" means that the investor not only invests money but also takes an active role in the foreign enterprise.

[3] The purchasing of securities of a foreign business (but not actively taking a part in its operation) is often called "portfolio investment."

[4] Under American pressure, South Korea has strengthened its trademark laws, but these laws often are underenforced.

[5] Generally, Japanese companies must follow U.S. antidiscrimination laws, but they are allowed to prefer Japanese nationals for top management positions. U.S. courts have not been completely consistent in interpreting laws in this area.

[6] In 1988, the Omnibus Trade and Competitiveness Act authorized the president to block purchases of U.S. firms by foreign buyers when the takeover would threaten national security.

This chapter provides an introduction to the basic aspects of international legal rules as they bear most directly on persons and business organizations engaged in commercial transactions across national borders. It does not pursue in any detail many related and very important fields such as *public* international law, which regulates legal and political relationships among sovereign states.

## *Classifying International Trade*

Today we classify within the term "international trade" any movement of goods, services, or capital across national boundaries. In its normal use, the term includes three major components:

1. The *export* of goods, services, or commodities from one country to another

2. The *import* of goods, services, or commodities into one country from another

3. Of increasing importance since the end of the Second World War, *foreign direct investment,* such as the acquisition of interests in capital facilities in one country by investors from another

Each of these components of international trade is distinct from the other; each raises particular legal and business issues; and each has been met with a distinct legal response intended to facilitate, harmonize, and regulate this aspect of global commercial and economic relations. With the growth in complexity of modern trade, the competition among nations as expressed in trade policy, and the growing presence of centrally planned economies in socialist bloc and Third World countries, the three main facets of international trade noted above have come to demonstrate, to varying degrees, three different sources of regulations:

1. Procedures developed by the *international trading community,* intended to ease trading relations and foster the resolution of disputes

2. Regulations developed by *national governments* designed to protect national trading interests and to make them more competitive in international markets

3. Laws and standards for international trade relations established by *international governmental organizations* such as the United Nations and the Organization for Economic Cooperation and Development, intended to harmonize trading community and national principles, to eliminate trade abuses, and to develop a greater participation in world trade, especially on the part of those nations which form the Third World

This chapter will examine some of the major features of each of these components of the international trade framework.

## THE INTERNATIONAL SALES CONTRACT

Although foreign direct investment has become an increasingly important factor in world trade in the last 30 years, most international business transactions still relate to the transfer of goods across national frontiers. This type of transaction—an export from the seller's perspective and an import from the buyer's point of view—is fundamentally a contract of sale, much like its domestic cousin in its essential features. However, special factors such as the great distances involved, accompanying insurance considerations, and differences in legal systems present special problems. An overriding factor in the formation of the international sales contract is that the parties do not, in the normal situation, know each other; this ignorance can lead to uneasiness over the creditworthiness of the buyer and the dependability of the seller, and anxiety about the enforcement of the obligations of the parties if there should be a breach of contract.

In response to these and other concerns, international private sector traders have over time devised a series of specialized but fairly standard techniques and legal devices which take the form of a series of "side" contracts that supplement the basic sales contract.

## *Financing the Transaction: The Letter of Credit*

Because of the presumed lack of knowledge on the part of the seller as to the creditworthiness of the buyer, the export trade has developed a reliance on the **letter of credit** financing device.[7] Basically, the letter of credit is an irrevocable assurance by the bank of the importer/buyer that funds for the payment for the goods sold by the exporter/seller are available beyond the control of the buyer and that these can be obtained by the seller upon provision of documentary proof that the goods have been shipped and that other contractual obligations of the seller

---

[7]Standardization in the use and implications of the letter of credit device has been advanced by the publication of *Uniform Customs and Practice for Documentary Credits,* Publication No. 400, (Paris: The International Chamber of Commerce, 1984).

have been fulfilled and are thus beyond the arbitrary control of the seller.

The documents which the seller must produce in order to be paid can include: (1) inland and ocean **bills of lading** to establish receipt of the goods by the shipper and to serve as "documents of title" for the merchandise; (2) commercial invoices and packing lists to attest to the contents of bulk and packaged materials; (3) an **export license** and shipper's export declaration to show compliance with any applicable export controls; and (4) any **import licenses,** consular invoices, or **certificates of origin** necessary to comply with the import laws of the receiving country.

Because the buyer's bank is typically a foreign bank, the seller may have no more confidence in it than in the buyer itself. It is not unusual, then, for the seller to involve its own bank in the transactions to transmit the funds or to confirm or guarantee the performance of the buyer's bank which is issuing the letter of credit. In these circumstances, the seller's bank may undertake only to accept the transfer of funds from the buyer's bank and to credit these to the account of the seller (an "advising" bank); it may go further, however, and contract to guarantee this payment to the seller (a "standby" or "confirming" bank). In either event, an additional layer of contractual obligation will appear, this time between the seller and its bank and, further, between the seller's bank and the buyer's bank.

The letter of credit is essentially a means to make the seller comfortable that the goods will be paid for and to assure the buyer that the purchase money will not be released to the seller until proper, conforming goods are suitably shipped. Strict compliance with the letter of credit is generally required, as the following case illustrates.

---

**Board of Trade of San Francisco v. Swiss Credit Bank**
U.S. Ninth Circuit Court of Appeals,
728 F.2d 1241 (1984)

Swiss Credit Bank (SCB) refused to honor a letter of credit issued in favor of the plaintiff's assignor (Antex Industries) for the sale of 92,000 microchips to Electronic Arrays for use in electronic computers. When the letter was presented to the bank, it was accompanied by an air waybill showing that the goods had been airfreighted to their destination. The letter of credit stipulated that a "full set clean on board bills of lading," evidencing ocean shipment of the microchips, was to have been presented. The trial court refused to order SCB to honor the letter of credit, and Antex appealed.

**Decision:** The lower court's judgment was affirmed. The appellate court refused to put the issuer of a letter of credit in the position of having to determine whether an unauthorized method of shipment is material. Whether air shipment was considered hazardous by the parties or apt to damage sensitive electronic equipment is not the type of decision that the issuer should be required to make in a transaction where promptness and certainty are of the essence. Absent a waiver, an issuer may insist on strict compliance with the letter of credit. ∎

---

The complexity of these multilayered arrangements is greatly reduced by the frequency with which they are used and their corresponding familiarity in the international trading community. It may help to chart the usual financing techniques of a typical international sales transaction in goods (left).

## Trade Terms

Financing is, of course, only a means to an end, and a myriad of other factors—almost all of them bearing directly on the ultimate price paid for the goods—will be resolved in the terms of the international sales contract. The parties may wish to provide for a fixed rate of currency exchange or to specify the currency of payment for the contract; they may elect to identify the "official" language of the sales contract, or to provide that two or more languages each represent the agreed terms of the transaction; they may choose the applicable law and identify the court that will have jurisdiction in the event of a subsequent disagreement; or they may decide to refer any contract disputes to binding or nonbinding arbitration. Clauses such as these, while very important, may or may not appear in the final contract, depending upon a host of subtle factors, including the current economic and political climate, the degree of mutual trust and familiarity between the parties, the extent to which they share common linguistic, cultural, business, or legal traditions, and others. For instance, an American exporter will have, in most cases, fewer questions about the conditions of commerce with a long-time Canadian business associate than, for instance, with a first-time trading partner in Sri Lanka or Liechtenstein.

Various commonly accepted **trade terms**, addressing matters of universal concern such as factors of distance, language barriers, and general unfamiliarity between the parties, have evolved over time within the international trading community.[8] These terms are often used to allocate responsibility between the parties. For example, "CIF" stands for "cost, insurance, and freight," meaning that the seller's quoted price is inclusive of the cost of goods, shipping charges, and a marine insurance policy providing at least minimum coverage. This implies that the seller will bear the risk of loss during transit from the factory to the port of shipment; thereafter the risk shifts to the buyer who pays for the marine insurance policy that is usually arranged by the seller.

The term "FAS" (Free Alongside) implies that the risk of loss will pass from the seller/exporter when the goods are delivered alongside a vessel, usually designated by the buyer. Risk of damage in the onloading operation rests on the buyer. "FOB" (Free On Board) contemplates delivery of the goods by seller, usually on a designated vessel where shipment has been arranged by the buyer; risk of loss passes at the ship's rail. "CAF" (Cost and Freight) is similar to CIF, but the buyer arranges for insurance during carriage. "Ex" terms (e.g., "ex-factory") can be used to designate a place of delivery from seller to buyer that is other than the location of the carrier—for instance, at the factory, or perhaps, at the ultimate destination of the goods.

## Convention on Contracts

In an attempt to add uniformity and certainty to the terms of international sales of goods contracts, several countries have ratified the 1980 United Nations Convention on Contracts for the International Sale of Goods (CISG). The CISG became part of American law on January 1, 1988, and has been ratified by China, Finland, France, Italy, Mexico, and several other countries. It is predicted that most of America's major trading partners will soon ratify the CISG.

Assume that Country A and Country B have both ratified the CISG. If a purchaser with a place of business in A makes a contract to buy goods from a company with a place of business in B, the CISG's provisions will automatically govern the contract unless the parties "opt out" of its coverage. The CISG does not apply to consumer sales and has no provisions governing the validity of contracts, ownership claims of third parties, or liability claims for death or personal injury. However, it does have provisions governing most other issues that could arise in a contractual setting. The parties may provide their own variations, but the CISG augments contractual terms and provides the rules for situations the parties did not contemplate or address in their agreement.

The CISG could be loosely termed an international Uniform Commercial Code. It addresses most of the same subjects as Article II of the UCC, such as definiteness and revocability of offers, timeliness of acceptances, risk of loss, excuse from performance, and remedies. However, the CISG differs from the UCC in several respects. For example, Article 11 of the Convention largely abolishes the statute of frauds requirement of a written contract. Article 16 states that an offer cannot be revoked if it was reasonable

---

[8] Attempts have been made to further standardize these trade terms by the publication of uniform trade term definitions. This work was undertaken in the Revised American Foreign Trade Definitions (RAFTD) of 1941 and subsequently by the International Chamber of Commerce (ICC) in the 1953 publication of "International Commercial Terms" (Incoterms) which has been periodically revised since that time. The Uniform Commercial Code also sets forth definitions of some of these terms and these are, in states which have adopted the UCC, binding as law although subject to express modification by agreement of the parties. The 1980 U.N. Convention on the International Sale of Goods will displace inconsistent UCC provisions in circumstances where the Convention applies.

for the offeree to rely on it as being irrevocable and the offeree has acted in reliance thereon. Article 35 alters the UCC's "perfect tender" rule. A seller must deliver goods fit for ordinary use or the buyer's particular purpose that is known to the seller. A buyer may reject goods only if there is a "fundamental breach." Article 50 addresses buyers' remedies, providing that a buyer may require a seller to perform in accordance with the promise or fix an additional time for the seller to perform. This latter option is not contained in the UCC, but is derived from German law. A complete discussion of the CISG's provisions is beyond the scope of this chapter, but be assured that lawyers who specialize in international law are acquainting themselves with them. A single set of rules should greatly assist businesspersons in planning and executing international sales transactions.

## *Convention on Notes*

The CISG's attempt to add uniformity to international sales law may soon be supplemented by the U.N. Convention on International Bills of Exchange and International Promissory Notes. Approved by the U.N. General Assembly on December 9, 1988, and now open for ratification, the Convention creates a new type of international negotiable instrument and represents an attempt to provide the same uniformity for international commercial paper transactions that Article 3 of the UCC provides for interstate transactions.

## RESOLVING INTERNATIONAL TRADE DISPUTES

No contract—including one for an international business transaction—can be so tightly drawn that it is totally impervious to later disagreement; similarly, unforeseen changes in circumstances may make performance of the contract impossible or, perhaps, more difficult or expensive than originally contemplated by the parties. An international trader should, therefore, have a clear understanding of the means available to resolve such disputes if they should arise.

Judicial litigation is rarely the best means to resolve any business dispute: the costs associated with it (attorney's fees, court costs, and general expenses) will often offset any profit expected from the transaction. These factors are compounded in transnational litigation.

Difficulties often arise, in the first instance, in identifying a court with proper jurisdiction over the subject matter of the action or the parties to the transaction. In many types of litigation the question will arise as to which state has the authority to assert its law over the transaction and the parties.

## *Domestic Court Jurisdiction*

In business litigation, and in other types of litigation touching the international sphere, the rules of jurisdiction are evolving, but are as yet unclear. The as yet unadopted American Law Institute *Restatement of the Foreign Relations Law of the United States (Revised)* may be a good indicator of the direction in which the law is heading. Rather than using the traditional categories of subject matter jurisdiction and personal jurisdiction, the proposed revision to this Restatement establishes three categories: (1) *jurisdiction to prescribe,* i.e., the authority of a state to make its law applicable to persons or activities; (2) *jurisdiction to adjudicate,* i.e., the authority of a state to subject particular persons or things to its judicial process; and (3) *jurisdiction to enforce,* i.e., the authority to use the resources of government to induce or compel compliance with its law.

Attempts by the United States to impose its legal regulations on activities occurring abroad has caused substantial resentment in foes and allies alike in recent years. The revised Restatement's Sec. 402 would recognize a nation's *jurisdiction to prescribe* with respect to:

(1) (a) conduct, a substantial part of which takes place within its territory;
  (b) the status of persons, or interests in things, present within its territory;
  (c) conduct outside its territory which has or is intended to have a substantial effect within its territory;
(2) the activities, status, interests or relations of its nationals outside as well as within its territory; or
(3) certain conduct outside its territory by persons not its nationals which is directed against the security of the state [example: terrorism] or a limited class of other state interests.

Thus, links of territoriality and nationality are ordinarily necessary to the power to prescribe law, though they are not sufficient in all cases. Furthermore, these criteria are expressly limited by Sec. 403 which states that even when they are present, jurisdiction to prescribe should not be exercised when it would be "unreasonable" as determined by an evaluation of all relevant factors, including: (1) the extent to which the activity takes place in the regulating state and has a substantial, direct, and foreseeable effect there; (2) the connections, such as nationality, residence, or economic activity, between the regulating state and the persons responsible for the activity to be regulated or between the state and those whom the law is designed to protect; (3) the character of the activity to be regulated, the extent to which other states regulate it, and its general acceptability; (4) the existence of justified expectations that might be injured; (5) the importance of the regulation to the international political, legal, or economic system; (6) the extent to which such regulation is consistent with the traditions of the international system; (7) the extent to which another state may have an interest in regulating the activity; and (8) the likelihood of conflict with regulation by other states. A state should defer to another state whose interest in regulating the same conduct is clearly greater.

The *Timberlane* case, which soon follows, illustrates a court's independent formulation of a "reasonableness" approach.

Reasonableness also is the hallmark of the revised Restatement's approach to *jurisdiction to adjudicate*. According to proposed Sec. 421, personal jurisdiction is to be exercised only if reasonable. Such exercise will generally be deemed reasonable if an individual defendant is present (other than transitorily) in the territory of the state, *or* is a domiciliary, resident, or national of the state, *or* regularly carries on business there, *or* has consented to the exercise of jurisdiction. Additionally, exercise of jurisdiction to adjudicate will be reasonable if the person had carried on activity in the state that created the liability in question or had carried on outside the state an activity having a substantial, direct, or foreseeable effect within the state that created the liability in question.

Finally, under Sec. 431 of the proposed revised Restatement, *jurisdiction to enforce* will be present only where a state had the power to prescribe, in accordance with Secs. 402 and 403, and the power to adjudicate as to the particular defendant. Enforcement measures must be proportional to the gravity of the violation, and may be employed against persons located outside the territory of the enforcing state only if such persons are given fair notice and an opportunity to be heard.

The following case illustrates one court's approach to the thorny jurisdictional problems that arise in the international setting.

## Timberlane Lumber Co. v. Bank of America
U.S. Ninth Circuit Court of Appeals, 549 F.2d 597 (1976)

Timberlane Lumber Company, an American corporation with subsidiary corporations in Honduras, brought a Sherman Act antitrust suit against the Bank of America and several Honduran citizens alleging that the defendants had conspired to shut down the plaintiff's milling operations in Honduras so that the Bank (and its Honduran affiliates and customers) could monopolize Honduran lumber exports to the United States. Timberlane filed suit in a federal court in California, arguing that the illegal activities of the defendants in Honduras had effects in the United States sufficient to vest the American court with personal jurisdiction over the foreign defendants. The district court dismissed the action for lack of jurisdiction, and the plaintiff appealed.

**Decision:** There is no doubt that American antitrust laws extend over some conduct in other nations, but determining how far it extends is difficult and not fully defined by international law. The district court's use of the "effects" test, requiring that a "direct and substantial effect" on United States foreign commerce occur, was not completely satisfactory. Preferable is a weighing test, a "jurisdictional rule of reason," that would consider such matters as "the degree of conflict with foreign law or policy, the nationality or allegiance of the parties and the locations or principal places of business of corporations, the extent to which enforcement by either state can be expected to achieve compliance, the relative significance of effects on the United States as compared with those elsewhere, the extent to which there is

*(continued)*

explicit purpose to harm or affect American commerce, the foreseeability of such effect, and the relative importance to the violation charged of conduct within the United States as compared with conduct abroad."

Here, most of the activity took place in Honduras, though the conspiracy may have been directed from San Francisco. Most direct economic effects were on Honduras. However, there was no indication of any conflict with the law or policy of the Honduran government, nor any comprehensive weighing of the relative connections and interests of Honduras and of the United States. The case was thus remanded to the district court for a consideration of the various factors listed above. ∎

## *Foreign Sovereign Immunities Act*

Even in circumstances where the court would be willing to assert its jurisdiction over the defendant under the effects or the reasonableness tests, it may be barred from doing so because of a personal immunity of the defendant. This bar is most often encountered where the defendant is a foreign state or state agency, a circumstance more frequently present today when many nations—especially those with centrally planned economies—are engaging directly in trading activities. The Foreign Sovereign Immunities Act (FSIA), passed by Congress in 1976, modifies the absolute sovereign immunity which the common law had recognized but continues to limit a plaintiff's ability to recover a judgment from a foreign state or state agency. The Act basically permits suits against foreign sovereigns where the claim arises from:

1. commercial activity of the foreign sovereign in the United States;

2. activities in the United States related to the sovereign's commercial undertakings outside this country; or

3. commercial actions of the foreign sovereign outside the United States which have direct effects within this nation.

The Act imposes additional limitations on the seizure of property of a foreign sovereign to satisfy any judgment which the plaintiff might ultimately obtain. The following case is one of the Supreme Court's most recent applications of the FSIA.

---

**Argentine Republic v. Amerada Hess Shipping Corporation**
U.S. Supreme Court,
488 U.S. 428 (1989)

A crude oil tanker chartered by one Liberian corporation to another (respondents United Carriers, Inc., and Amerada Hess Corp.) was severely damaged when it was attacked in international waters by Argentine military aircraft during the war between Great Britain and Argentina over the Falkland Islands (Malvinas).

Respondents brought this suit in federal district court, claiming subject matter jurisdiction under (1) the Alien Tort Statute (ATS) (which grants district courts jurisdiction in civil actions by an alien for a tort committed in violation of the law of nations or a treaty of the United States), (2) general admiralty and maritime jurisdiction of the federal courts, and (3) "the principle of universal jurisdiction recognized under international law."

The district court dismissed the suit for lack of subject matter jurisdiction, holding that the action was barred by the Foreign Sovereign Immunity Act (FSIA). The court of appeals reversed. Petitioner brought the suit to the Supreme Court.

**Decision:** The judgment of the court of appeals was reversed. Subject matter jurisdiction in district court depends on the existence of one of the specified exceptions to the FSIA. In Sec. 1605, several exceptions are listed, including cases involving the waiver of immunity, commercial activities occurring in the United States or causing a direct effect in this country, property expropriated in violation of international law, real estate located in the United States, and maritime liens. None of the exceptions applies in this case. The exception for noncommercial torts applies only when damage to or loss of property occurs *in the United States*. The provision's purpose was to eliminate a foreign state's immunity for traffic accidents and other torts occurring in the United States. This injury occurred 5,000 miles from the nearest shore. ∎

## Act of State Doctrine

Closely related in effect to the doctrine of sovereign immunity is the **act of state doctrine.** This doctrine is based on the concept that it is beyond the sensible exercise of judicial powers for a court in this country to sit in judgment on the actions of another sovereign nation taken in its own territory. Any redress of grievances caused by such actions should be obtained by the United States government dealing directly with the other sovereign. Thus, in *Banco Nacional de Cuba v. Sabbatino,* 376 U.S. 398 (1964), a case challenging Cuba's expropriation of a Cuban corporation that was largely owned by U.S. residents, the Supreme Court held:

> [T]he Judicial Branch will not examine the validity of a taking of property within its own territory by a foreign sovereign government, extant and recognized by this country at the time of the suit, in the absence of treaty or other unambiguous agreement regarding controlling legal principles, even if the complaint alleges that the taking violates customary international law.

Also related to sovereign immunity is the doctrine of **sovereign compulsion,** under which American courts will refuse to hold a defendant liable for actions that it was compelled to take under the law of a recognized foreign sovereign.

The following case illustrates some of the difficult questions that can arise in application of the act of state doctrine.

### W. S. Kirkpatrick & Co. v. Environmental Tectonics Corporation
U.S. Supreme Court,
110 S.Ct. 701 (1990)

Petitioner W. S. Kirkpatrick & Co. pleaded guilty to a violation of the Foreign Corrupt Practices Act for having paid a bribe to a Nigerian official in order to obtain a contract with the Republic of Nigeria. Respondent Environmental Tectonics Corporation, an unsuccessful bidder on the contract, then brought this suit claiming that petitioner had violated the Racketeer Influenced Corrupt Organizations Act (RICO) among others. Despite having received a letter from the Department of State indicating its view that this case posed no "unique embarrassment" to execution of American foreign policy, the trial court granted summary judgment to petitioner on grounds that the act of state doctrine barred the claim. The court of appeals reversed, concluding that no embarrassment of the executive in its conduct of foreign affairs was evident. Petitioner appealed.

**Decision:** The decision of the court of appeals was affirmed. The act of state doctrine is based on "'the strong sense of the Judicial Branch that its engagement in the task of passing on the validity of foreign acts of state may hinder' the conduct of foreign affairs. . . . In every case in which the doctrine has been applied, the relief sought or the defense interposed would have required a court to declare invalid the official act of a foreign sovereign performed within its own territory." In this case, there is no need for such a determination because the act of a foreign sovereign is not at issue. ∎

## International Litigation: Other Concerns

In the domestic setting, it can be quite troublesome to obtain service of summons over a proper defendant, obtain evidence to support the claim through oral depositions, written interrogatories, and document production, and, ultimately to enforce the judgment against a recalcitrant defendant. In the international context, such tasks can be overwhelming. To reduce these barriers to the civil prosecution of a valid claim, several international agreements have been reached that are intended generally to increase international cooperation in these respects.

The Hague Convention on Service Abroad of Judicial and Extrajudicial Documents in Civil or Commercial Matters provides that each signatory state will maintain a Central Authority to process judicial documents, such as complaints, and expedite their transmission. The Hague Convention on the Taking of Evidence Abroad in Civil or Commercial Matters of 1970 seeks to reduce the barriers raised by national laws to obtaining evidence for use in court and to streamline the discovery process in international litigation. The Convention creates Central Authorities in each signatory nation through which discovery requests ("Letters of Request") are channeled; it permits consuls to conduct some discovery procedures regarding their own nationals; and, finally, it allows the use of court-appointed commissioners for discovery purposes in limited circumstances. The United States is a signatory of both Conventions.

The task of enforcing local judgments against parties in other nations has been eased considerably by a number of national statutes and international agreements that afford recognition to foreign court orders. Federal courts in the United States will generally enforce foreign judgments by the doctrine of **comity** where it is shown that the foreign court had competent jurisdiction and acted in a fair and impartial fashion, that no fraud was committed against the defendant, and that due notice of the proceedings was provided. Many state legislatures in the United States have adopted the Uniform Foreign Money-Judgments Recognition Act which permits the enforcement of final foreign money-judgments in civil matters. This Act also provides for denial of recognition of the foreign judgment when it was rendered "under a system which does not provide impartial tribunals or procedures compatible with the requirements of due process of law."

## *Arbitration*

In view of the special difficulties encountered in international court litigation, it is not surprising that the international business community has actively sought alternative methods of commercial dispute resolution.

Arbitration is a process whereby parties to a transaction agree (either within the terms of their basic agreement or subsequently) to submit any future disagreements and disputes to an impartial third party (which may consist of a single individual or a panel) for nonjudicial resolution. The decision of the arbitrator—termed an "award"—may, depending upon the agreement of the parties, be binding or nonbinding.

Arbitration within the international trading context has a long and colorful history. In a real sense, the commercial courts established by the *lex mercatoria*[9] in medieval times had much of the flavor of arbitration, consisting as they did of a board of commercial experts who would hear and decide disputes in accordance with commercial custom, usage, and practice. Arbitration gained renewed popularity in the latter part of the nineteenth century when it was used in the public international law sphere to settle claims of the United States against the United Kingdom arising from the activities of Confederate men-of-war on the high seas, notably the *CSS Alabama*. So great was its appeal that a Permanent Court of Arbitration was established at the Hague in 1899. Arbitration is still used in international commercial circles as the preferred alternative to litigation in the national courts.

The advantages of arbitration are many. It is usually less expensive than court procedures and offers the parties the opportunity to select knowledgeable experts to decide the matter rather than turning it over to unknown judges who are typically "generalists." The use of arbitration provides a means to avoid overcrowded courts with their high costs, technical delays, and formalities. Perhaps a primary reason why commercial traders frequently resort to arbitration is the privacy that it affords and the assurance that the award will be based on commercial realities rather than theoretical legal concepts.

Arbitration is not, however, without some disadvantages. Arbitral panels generally do not have the power to compel the attendance of witnesses or the production of other information relevant to the case; the familiar institution of the jury trial is absent; the informality of the procedure can lead to an undesired degree of "looseness" in the process; and, because the arbitrators are generally not bound by the strict letter of the law, the final terms of the award may be somewhat difficult to forecast.

---

[9] *Lex mercatoria*, also known as the law merchant, was a set of truly international commercial principles cutting across national boundaries that was established and observed by commercial people throughout medieval Europe. The *lex mercatoria* was the forerunner of the commercial codes now in force in Europe and the United States.

One of the major disadvantages of the arbitral process is the fact that the award is "unofficial" and presents special problems in enforcement. Traditionally, arbitral awards were enforced through a subsequent court judgment which upheld the award as a matter of contract between the parties. The use of the court to enforce arbitral awards deprived the procedure of many of its apparent advantages.

This concern has been greatly reduced through the widespread adoption of the United Nations Convention on the Recognition and Enforcement of Foreign Arbitral Awards, concluded at New York in 1958 and effective in the United States in 1970. This Convention provides, in essence, that arbitral awards issued in one country can be enforced in another upon the presentation of a duly authenticated original award, together with a copy of the agreement upon which it was based. The Convention reserves the right of the receiving state to refuse to recognize a foreign arbitral award in certain circumstances, such as the incapacity of the parties to the agreement, defects in the composition of the arbitral panel, or cases in which the terms of the award either exceed the scope of authority of the arbitral panel or violate the public policy of the receiving country. A similar multilateral agreement was concluded by the Organization of American States in 1975 with the adoption of the Inter-American Convention on International Commercial Arbitration and the Inter-American Convention on Extraterritorial Validity of Foreign Judgments and Arbitral Awards.

So frequent has been the resort to commercial arbitration by the international trading community in this century that several international organizations have sought to facilitate this means of dispute resolution by providing standard arbitral rules and procedures. Chief among these organizations have been the International Chamber of Commerce (headquartered in Paris), the United Nations Commission on International Trade Law (UNCITRAL), the American Arbitration Association, the International Centre for Settlement of Investment Disputes (ICSID—created by the 1965 Convention on the Settlement of Investment Disputes Between States and Nationals of Other States), the Inter-American Commercial Arbitration Commission, and the London Court of Arbitration.

For years, U.S. courts resisted arbitration on the international scene, just as they did on the domestic scene. More recently, courts have been more receptive to arbitration in both spheres. The following Supreme Court decision is illustrative in the international arena.

## Mitsubishi Motors Corp. v. Soler Chrysler-Plymouth, Inc.
U.S. Supreme Court,
105 S.Ct. 3346 (1985)

Petitioner Mitsubishi, a Japanese corporation that manufactures automobiles, is the product of a joint venture between Chrysler International, S.A. (CISA), a Swiss corporation, and another Japanese corporation, aimed at distributing automobiles manufactured by the petitioner through Chrysler dealers outside the continental United States. Respondent Soler, a Puerto Rican corporation, entered into distribution and sales agreements with CISA. These agreements contained a clause providing for arbitration by the Japan Commercial Arbitration Association of all disputes arising out of certain articles of the agreement or for the breach thereof. Disagreements did arise, and petitioner filed suit in federal district court in Puerto Rico under the federal Arbitration Act and the Convention on the Recognition and Enforcement of Foreign Arbitral Awards, seeking an order to compel arbitration of the dispute in accordance with the arbitration clause. Respondent filed a counterclaim alleging antitrust violations by petitioner and CISA. The district court ordered arbitration of almost all issues. On appeal, the circuit court affirmed, except as to the antitrust issues, which it held to be inappropriate for arbitration.

**Decision:** All issues should be arbitrated. Previous precedents indicating that antitrust issues are not suitable for arbitration should be disregarded in this case. There is a federal policy favoring arbitration of claims. Concerns of international comity, respect for the capacities of foreign and transnational tribunals, and sensitivity to the need of the international commercial system for predictability in the resolution of disputes, all require enforcement of the arbitration clause in question, even assuming that a contrary result regarding the antitrust issues might be forthcoming in a domestic context. ∎

# NATIONAL REGULATION OF THE EXPORT/IMPORT PROCESS

The impact of export trade transcends, of course, the private interests of the parties to the international sales contract. Concerns at the national level touch upon defense and security matters (especially in the export of high technology with military applications) and the depletion of national stocks of critical materials. Moreover, the volume and direction of flow of export sales are inextricably bound up in the general economic posture of a nation and thus bear directly on its overall pattern of foreign relations. Not surprisingly, almost all nations have responded to these factors by adopting broad regulatory schemes to control exports. The implementation of these programs will directly affect the international trader and the methods used in that trade.

In the United States, the power to regulate international trade is vested in the Congress under the provisions of the Commerce Clause of the federal Constitution. Congress has used this power repeatedly since the early days of the Republic and the trail of congressional legislation dealing with import and export matters continues into the present day. The Export Administration Act of 1979 is perhaps the most important piece of federal legislation impacting American export traders today.

## *Export Administration Act*

This Act is a comprehensive scheme to regulate exports from the United States and, together with the regulations adopted pursuant to it, extends its controls in some instances to the re-export of certain American goods to third countries. The Act grants discretionary authority to the Office of Export Administration (OEA) of the Department of Commerce to impose export controls for three basic reasons: (1) national security (to prevent "dual use" products which might have military applications from reaching the Soviet Union and its allies); (2) foreign policy (for example, to prevent goods from reaching countries that practice terrorism or apartheid); and (3) short supply of the goods in the United States.

In general terms, the Act provides for three broad types of required export licenses:

1. A general license authorizing exports—this type of license covers the vast bulk of American exports and is normally issued by the OEA without a formal application by the exporter. (There is also a qualified general license authorizing multiple imports.)

2. A validated license relating to a specific export

3. A distribution license permitting export of unlimited quantities of certain commodities under an international marketing program without additional approval from OEA

The Export Administration Regulations (found in the *Code of Federal Regulations*) round out, define, and implement the provisions of the 1979 act. They contain a Commodity Control List which will assist the exporter in identifying circumstances where a validated export license must be obtained and where a general license will not suffice. In most instances, this decision is a function of what commodity is going to which country. Some few nations (North Korea, Cuba, and Vietnam, among others) are virtually closed to American exports. These regulations also contain provisions relating to the export of technical data (as opposed to commodities, which are treated as a separate and distinct category for licensing purposes). The general license "GTDR" controls the export of technical data both in terms of destination and the degree of "public accessibility" to the information; a more liberal license, the general license "GTDA," allows technical data exports to virtually any destination if the data meets the regulations' standard of public availability. A 1985 amendment to the Export Administration Act also provides for a comprehensive operations license to govern exports from American corporations to offshore affiliates and subsidiaries. This type of license will have frequent use within transnational corporate systems.

The 1979 Act has provisions which are directly related to defense and national security interests of the United States. Any new technology developed through research funding by the Department of Defense requires the consent of that department before it can be exported; moreover, a 1985 amendment to the act calls upon the Commerce Department and the Department of Defense to merge the Militarily Critical Technologies List (maintained by the Department of Defense) with the Commodities Control List provided for in the Export Administration Regulations to make export control over such materials more efficient and less subject to gaps. In the foreign policy field, recent amendments to the Export Administration Act prohibit export controls on shipments of donated goods relating to basic human needs.

Although the Export Administration Act is the major source of export regulation in the United States, it is by no means the only one.[10] Export control provisions are also found in the Nuclear Non-Proliferation Act (1978) and Atomic Energy Act (1954) which govern the export of nuclear materials. The Arms Export Control Act, the Trading with the Enemy Act, and the International Emergency Economic Power Act also contain important export restrictions.

In addition, the United States is a member of the Coordinating Committee for Multilateral Export Controls (COCOM) along with Japan and most NATO members. This is an international group that cooperates in the control of exports of strategic goods to sensitive destinations. COCOM has no authority to enforce its own policies, but relies on regulations of its member states. During the Reagan administration, the United States was much more sensitive to export of technology than were the other COCOM members. The Commodities Control List of the United States was much longer than that of COCOM, whose other members resented U.S. attempts to extend its regulations to its allies. Continued leaks of technology to the Soviet Union and its allies are of major concern. But after a 1987 National Academy of Sciences panel found that U.S. controls covered too many products and technologies and were "not generally perceived as rational, credible, and predictable by many" of our allies, Congress, in 1988, instructed the Departments of Commerce and Defense to reduce their lists of controlled goods in order to build higher fences around fewer goods.

## Export Incentives

United States export policy and legislation is not, however, totally negative. Important legislation has long been on the books to encourage increased export trade by manufacturers and suppliers in this country.

As early as 1918, Congress adopted the Webb-Pomerene Act to promote American export trade by granting limited exemptions to exporters from the application of U.S. antitrust laws, principally the Sherman and Clayton Acts. Congress acted in the belief that American traders could better compete in foreign markets if they were permitted to form associations capturing the benefits of economies of scale and greater efficiency; such associations, however, involved a danger of criminal or civil liability under American antitrust laws. The Webb-Pomerene Act, therefore, relieved export associations of this risk, but conditioned the exemption in important respects. Principally, such an association is prohibited by the act from entering into any agreement that "artificially or intentionally" depresses commodity prices within the United States or that "substantially lessens competition within the United States, or otherwise restrains trade therein." Further, the benefits of the Act (obtained by registration of the association with the Federal Trade Commission) are limited to associations formed for the export of commodities; transactions for services or technology are not protected. As a result of these limitations and lingering anxiety about possible antitrust liability, comparatively few Webb-Pomerene associations are registered with the FTC.

**Export Trading Company Act.** The failure of the 1918 legislation to promote greater American export trade, coupled with increasing U.S. trade deficits in the mid- and late 1970s,[11] created a sense of urgency in Congress to devise new and more effective means to encourage increased exports from this country, especially by small- and medium-sized companies historically underrepresented in international trade transactions. The legislative response was the Export Trading Company Act of 1982.

At the heart of this Act is the provision that

> no criminal civil action may be brought under the antitrust laws [of the United States] against a person to whom a certificate of review is issued [by the Secretary of Commerce] which is based on conduct which is specified in, and complies with the terms of, a certificate . . . which . . . was in effect when the conduct occurred.

This exemption is available to individual persons resident in the United States; partnerships or corpo-

---

[10] Note, too, the impact of other federal legislation on the conduct of international business. For instance, the Foreign Corrupt Practices Act controls bribery and other undesirable acts abroad. This Act is considered separately in Chapter 41.

[11] The United States never experienced a trade deficit—an excess of imports over exports—until 1971. Between 1971 and 1976, however, the American trade deficit rose to $5 billion, largely because of massive oil imports which amounted to $77 billion in 1981 alone. The deficit then exploded, reaching $170 billion in 1986. (U.S. Bureau of the Census, *Highlights of U.S. Export and Import Trade,* FT1990, Feb. 1987.)

rations created under state or federal law; and, significantly for antitrust purposes, "any association or combination, by contract or other arrangement" between or among any of these.

The Act's scope is comprehensive. It extends its antitrust protection to activities related to the export of goods and merchandise and (going beyond the reach of the Webb-Pomerene Act) to services. This latter category is defined to include services which are the subject of the transaction (as in transborder management agreements) and includes accounting, architectural, data processing, business, communications, consulting, and legal services, among many others. Also eligible for exemption from possible antitrust liabilities are "export trade services," i.e., international market research, product research and design, transportation, warehousing, insurance, and the like.

The Export Trading Company Act also contains important provisions that modify statutory impediments that separate the banking community from participation in international trade. Title II of the Act (termed the Bank Export Services Act) permits banks to invest in export trading companies up to the statutory limit of 5 percent of their consolidated capital and surplus; further, they are also allowed to own such companies outright. These provisions are intended to marshal substantial capital to promote international trade. The absence of such funding has hobbled export trade in the past since many small- and medium-sized banks were reluctant to finance "speculative foreign ventures" over which they had little or no control.

## Regulating Imports

Compared with the elaborate nature of export controls and incentives, the regulation of imports into the United States is relatively straightforward. The application of these import control laws can, however, be quite complex.

Under the Import-Export Clause of the federal Constitution, the power to levy import customs and duties rests exclusively with the federal government. Using federal power in this regard, the government has established a comprehensive system of tariff schedules that apply to goods entering the United States—the Tariff Schedules of the United States (TSUS). The TSUS will be applied by federal customs officials first, to classify the entering goods and then, to determine the applicable tariff rate to the goods so classified. The actual rate is, of course, set by the federal government, but it may do so subject to bilateral or multilateral restraints that it has assumed. For example, a treaty with another nation may stipulate the tariff level or, more generally, the applicable tariff may have been negotiated within the framework of a multinational commitment, e.g., the General Agreement on Tariffs and Trade (GATT). In either event, the tariff generally must be paid before the goods are admitted into this country.

An important exception to this principle is the use of a Foreign Trade Zone. Established by federal law, these Zones (FTZs) are fenced-off, policed warehouses and industrial parks usually located near American ports of entry. Goods entering the port from abroad may be taken into the FTZ and stored there without paying any applicable tariff and with a minimum of formality and procedure. As long as the goods are warehoused within the FTZ, no duty is payable and the goods may be further processed, assembled, or finished. Only when the merchandise leaves the confines of the FTZ will the duty be imposed, frequently at a reduced rate. The FTZ has shown itself to be an effective device for encouraging additional international trade in the United States.

While import licenses are generally not required for imports into the United States, certain goods may be denied entry altogether. Bans on importation may be applied against undesirable imports such as narcotics, pornographic material, or printed materials advocating the violent overthrow of the United States. Import bans may be applied to prevent entry of automobiles that do not meet vehicle safety regulations or against other products not meeting standards established to protect public health and safety. Products violating the patent, trademark, and copyright laws of the United States may also be excluded. Moreover, certain goods may be subjected to tariff increases to offset foreign government subsidies which unfairly reduce their U.S. market price, or to counteract a foreign producer's deliberate attempt to destabilize or destroy the product's domestic production in the United States. These "countervailing" and "antidumping" measures are considered again in this chapter with regard to the General Agreement on Tariffs and Trade (GATT).

**Trade and Tariff Act:** One method of increasing the access of U.S. companies to foreign markets is retaliation against countries that treat U.S. companies unfairly. A series of Acts over the years have authorized and encouraged the president to take such retaliatory action. The most recent, but likely not the last, in this series of escalating measures is Sec. 301 of the Trade and Tariff Act of 1984. Aimed especially at nontariff barriers, Sec. 301 provides a mechanism for relief to U.S. exporters of goods, services, and investments that have been denied access to foreign markets in violation of trade agreements the United States has entered, (such as denial of "most favored nation" status under GATT), or who have been the victims of unreasonable, unjustifiable, or discriminatory trade practices whether or not violative of international agreements.

As amended in 1988, the Act (now called "Super 301") requires the White House trade representatives to identify patterns of supposedly unfair trading practices involving specific countries. The trade representative is then to attempt to eliminate the unfair practices through bilateral negotiations. If this is unsuccessful, however, the law *mandates* that trade retaliation occur within 12 months. This retaliation may take the form of higher tariffs, import quotas, or withdrawal from existing trade agreements with the offending country. "Super 301" may serve to pry open new markets for U.S. companies, but it may also unnecessarily antagonize existing trading partners and undermine cooperative bilateral and multilateral attempts to negotiate trade freedom (which we are about to discuss).

**Protection from Unfair Competition:** Various provisions of federal law protect U.S. companies from unfair practices by foreign competitors selling in this country. The primary protective provision is Sec. 337 of the Tariff Act of 1930, which protects "domestic industries" from "substantial injury" stemming from "unfair methods of competition and unfair acts in the importation of articles into the United States, or in their sale. . . ." Sec. 337 has been invoked most often in cases of alleged patent infringement, but it also protects U.S. businesses from copyright and trademark infringement, false advertising, trade secret misappropriation, palming off (misleading consumers into thinking they are buying another company's goods), and even "dumping."

Sec. 337 is activated by a domestic company's complaint to the U.S. International Trade Commission, an independent federal regulatory commission. The commission follows the Administrative Procedure Act in investigating the complaint and determining whether there has been a violation. The president has 60 days to review the commission's decision. Remedies can include cease and desist orders, temporary exclusion orders, and even permanent exclusion orders.

Because American businesses were losing as much as $20 billion annually from foreign infringement of U.S. patents and other intellectual property rights, in 1988 Congress directed the president to identify countries that do not protect copyrights and patents and to initiate expedited unfair trade investigations in egregious cases unless to do so would harm national economic interests.

## ORGANIZING FOR INTERNATIONAL TRADE

The massive devastation of the Second World War had among its many casualties the international trade infrastructure which had been growing slowly but perceptibly since the middle of the nineteenth century. One of the major tasks of reconstruction following 1945 was the recreation of a framework for international trade. Negotiations focusing on trade, money, and finance led to establishment of the current international economic institutions, including the General Agreement on Tariffs and Trade (GATT), the International Monetary Fund, and the International Bank for Reconstruction and Development. More recently, regional trade agreements have become a prominent means of facilitating international trade.

### *The GATT*

The United Nations Conference on Trade and Employment met in Havana in late 1947 and was attended by more than 50 countries (though boycotted by the Soviet Union and its satellite states). Although the conference was unsuccessful in creating a proposed International Trade Organization, it led almost two dozen countries to conclude a General Agreement on Tariffs and Trade (GATT), the essential purpose of which was to achieve a significant reduction of the general level of national tariffs and, further, to provide an institutional framework within which future tariff conflicts could be resolved. The GATT has, since its creation, shown itself to be of enduring significance in international economic and trade relations. According to its supporters, the GATT trading system has achieved unprecedented trade expansion and world prosperity. (Its detractors note that GATT provisions are often breached by participating countries.)

The GATT achieves its overall objective of liberalized international trade by addressing a series of key issues regarding import restrictions. It requires that each signatory state extend "most favored nation" tariff rates to goods from other signatory nations and, further, obligates participating nations to afford "national treatment" to the imported goods from other signatory countries. Article III of the agreement provides:

> The products of the territory of any contracting party imported into the territory of any other contracting party shall be accorded treatment no less favorable than that accorded to like products of national origin in respect of all laws, regulations and requirements affecting their internal sale, offering for sale, purchase, transportation, distribution or use.

The GATT prohibits discrimination by participating states through quantitative trade restrictions by providing that import quotas, if adopted at all by a state, shall be applied equally to all nations which are parties to the agreement. An even more ambitious objective of the GATT is the elimination of all prohibitions or restrictions (other than duties, taxes, or other charges) on imports and exports among the member nations.

In large measure, the GATT implements its goals of free trade through a series of published tariff schedules which are developed through an intricate negotiation process within the framework of the organization and which, once published, are binding on each of the participating states. In recognition of inevitable trade anomalies and in order to secure the willing participation and cooperation of member states in its tariff reduction program, the GATT provides special circumstances where unilateral exceptions to the schedules of tariffs may be made. The most well known of these relate to antidumping duties and countervailing subsidies.

If the products of one country are "dumped" into another at prices below their fair market value in the exporting country in an effort to disrupt or destroy the domestic production of those goods in the receiving nation, the GATT contemplates that the government of the receiving country may impose an "antidumping duty" in an effort to equalize the domestic price in those goods with the prevailing fair market price in the exporting country. Similarly, where the production of certain goods in the exporting state is heavily subsidized by the government of that nation (leading to a reduced export price for that product), the GATT permits the receiving state to impose a "countervailing duty" to bring the market price up to a competitive level.[12]

In its formative years, the GATT concentrated almost exclusively on measures to reduce tariff barriers to increase international trade. More recently, it has turned its attention to the reduction of nontariff barriers, such as unreasonably restrictive local standards and inaccessible national distribution systems, to further increase the volume of trade among nations.

GATT negotiations occur in "rounds" that may last several years. As this edition is written, the Uruguay Round is under way, focusing substantial attention on methods to enhance free trade in agricultural products.

## The IMF and the IBRD

The International Monetary Fund (IMF), like the GATT, is intended to coordinate the activities of governments regarding international trade functions and does not primarily address the individual international trader. Growing out of discussions held at Bretton Woods, New Hampshire, late in the Second World War, the IMF was designed to speed international financial and economic reconstruction by providing an institutional structure within which intergovern-

---

[12] Both of these GATT "escape clauses"—permitting the imposition of additional customs payments above the published tariff schedules to offset foreign governmental subsidies and private "dumping" activities—are codified in U.S. trade law. The U.S. Trade Agreements Act of 1979 permits the secretary of the treasury to impose antidumping and countervailing duties to correct the price imbalances flowing from such unfair practices. In both instances, however, the U.S. International Trade Commission must first investigate the matter and determine that the practice is materially injuring an American industry or is threatening it with harm that is not inconsequential, immaterial, or unimportant. Such an investigation can lead to very sophisticated economic analyses of the foreign practice. The definition of a governmental "subsidy" for purposes of imposing a countervailing duty can be troublesome. A direct cash subsidy is, perhaps, the clearest case, but what about whole or partial exemptions on property taxes for the warehouses where the goods are kept prior to export to the United States? What about government participation in the research and development of the exported product? Government support for labor relocation programs for the employees of the foreign company that produces the exported product? These were considered recently by the U.S. Court of International Trade in *Agrexco Agricultural Export Co., Ltd. v. United States*, 604 Fed. Sup. 1238 (1985).

mental loans would be used to stabilize currency exchange rates and, through a system of credits (termed "Special Drawing Rights" or "SDRs"), to enable member countries to borrow from the fund or from each other as a means of stabilizing their national currencies within the international monetary system.

Affiliated with the International Monetary Fund is the International Bank for Reconstruction and Development (IBRD) which was founded to "assist in the reconstruction and development of territories of members by facilitating the investment of capital for productive purposes" and to "promote private foreign investment by means of guarantees or participations in loans and other investments made by private investors." The IBRD, located in Washington, D.C., is permitted under its charter to guarantee, participate in, or make loans to member states and to any business, industrial, or agricultural enterprise in the territories of a member state. The availability through the IMF and IBRD of massive amounts of financial credit was particularly significant in Western Europe during the immediate postwar years and has had, in addition, a very significant role in the industrial development of Asia and Africa in the last several decades.

## Regional Trade Agreements

The multilateral approach to trade negotiation embodied in GATT is complemented by various regional trading arrangements. Latin American countries, Pacific Rim countries, and various other regional groupings have acted in concerted fashion to enhance trade and investment among their members. Two such regional agreements are of particular importance to American businesses.

**U.S.-Canada Free Trade Act:** The United States and Canada have the world's largest trading partnership. Trade between the two countries rose from $74 billion in 1980 to over $150 billion by 1988. In order to further enhance this already productive relationship, the two countries entered into the Free Trade Act (FTA), which took effect on January 1, 1989 and, over a 10-year period, is intended to phase out virtually all remaining tariffs.

The FTA will not result in the complete integration that exists among American states or Canadian provinces. However, it will curtail trade barriers and ensure that any still existing serve legitimate purposes, such as protection of health, environment, or national security. Approximately 80 percent of all goods were already crossing the border between the two countries duty-free. The FTA will reduce tariffs on most other items and will significantly relax foreign investment restrictions (especially those existing in Canada) to facilitate direct investment between businesses of the two nations. The FTA also aims to facilitate fair competition, to establish effective dispute-resolution procedures, and to lay the foundation for further bilateral and multilateral trade cooperation.

**European Economic Community:** By the Treaty of Rome in 1958, six European countries (Belgium, France, Italy, Luxembourg, The Netherlands, and West Germany) formed the European Economic Community (EEC). Eventually joined by six other nations (Denmark, Ireland, the United Kingdom, Greece, Portugal, and Spain), the EEC seeks economic integration and the creation of a single internal European market.[13] The Single European Act of 1987 set December 31, 1992, as the target date for completion of implementing legislation.

EEC members are motivated not only by the hope of gaining an economic advantage by combining their markets, but also by a desire to bind Western Europe more tightly in a political and social sense. A basic principle of the EEC is creation of a Community Law which will preempt national law wherever national law might conflict. The EEC is not likely to create a "United States of Europe." After all, there are still twelve separate governments and nine different languages. However, by harmonizing economic regulations in the various states and breaking down trade barriers, the EEC will probably become a very strong economic entity that all trading competitors, including U.S. businesses, will have to reckon with.

As of this writing, the EEC has already transferred to Community institutions the power to set tariff policies and abolish customs duties among member states, harmonized the system for designation and codification of goods, empowered the Community to counteract anticompetitive practices and to defend itself politically, and issued 300 very precise directives concerning industrial products, metrology, textiles, electricity, labeling, advertising, sale of hazard-

---

[13] Greenland joined the EEC, but later withdrew. Turkey has asked to become a member, and it is expected that Austria will also apply for membership.

ous materials, and the like—all aimed at expediting trade among Community members.

## OTHER WAYS OF DOING BUSINESS

Thus far, we have spoken of international trade mainly in terms of direct sales from a seller in one country to a buyer in another. However, there are many other forms of international transactions. Take the case of an American corporation wishing to export its goods. Rather than sending its own employees to the foreign markets to drum up business at the retail or wholesale level, it might hire an **agent** in that foreign country to act on its behalf. Such agents would typically have authority to contract on behalf of the American sellers. Complications would likely arise from the differences between agency law and customs in the United States and those of the foreign country.

Or the American company might choose to do business through a **licensee** in the foreign country. That licensee would pay a fee to the American company for the right to sell the company's goods. Such licensees, of course, will want exclusive rights to sell the American company's products, if possible. Legal problems here may result from the antitrust laws of the United States and the foreign country. An increasingly popular form of such licensing arrangement is the franchising of trademarks, tradenames, and copyrights. Many American service industries, such as fast food chains and convenience store chains, are expanding to foreign markets through use of this device.

Or, an American seller may wish to have a foreign subsidiary corporation formed in the foreign nations in which it seeks to do business. This process is complicated by the many restrictions that most countries, especially in the underdeveloped world, place upon such corporations. Such restrictions may take the form of **currency controls** which make it difficult to take profits out of the country. Or the host country may require a certain percentage of host country ownership of the American company's subsidiary, or require that it enter into a joint venture with the host government or a local company.

India, for example, has endeavored to "Indianize" foreign companies operating there. In the wake of the terrible 1984 Bhopal, India, gas leak which killed 2,700 and injured perhaps 200,000, the Union Carbide Corporation has *claimed* that its subsidiary—Union Carbide India Ltd.—was so "Indianized" that Union Carbide could not have shut the plant down out of safety concerns had it wanted to. All 9,000 employees of the company were Indian, and quasi-governmental Indian financial institutions owned 25 percent of its stock. Union Carbide itself retained only 50.9 percent of the subsidiary's stock. In many lesser developed countries, foreign corporations are limited to 49 percent ownership; local entities must retain control.

The following case illustrates legal issues that may arise with use of one of these methods of doing business abroad—the franchise.

---

### Dayan v. McDonald's Corporation
Illinois Court of Appeals, 466 N.E.2d 948 (1984)

In 1971, Dayan and McDonald's Corporation signed a master license agreement (MLA) granting Dayan a 30-year franchise right to use the McDonald's patents, trademarks, and tradenames in Paris. The agreement bound Dayan to meet McDonald's Quality, Service, and Cleanliness (QSC) standards, because his departure from them would impede the successful operation of McDonald's restaurants in other parts of the world. If Dayan defaulted, McDonald's had the right to terminate the agreement. McDonald's issued operating licenses to Dayan for 14 restaurants. However, McDonald's was never satisfied with Dayan's compliance with QSC standards. In 1976, McDonald's told Dayan that his substandard operation could no longer be tolerated and that he would have six months to bring his restaurants into compliance with the QSC standards. When Dayan failed to do so, McDonald's sued in Paris to terminate the MLA. Dayan then brought suit in Illinois to enjoin termination.

The trial judge, after 65 days of testimony, refused to issue the injunction, ruling that McDonald's properly terminated the MLA. Dayan appealed.

**Decision:** The trial court's decision was affirmed. The trial judge applied the proper legal standard, which requires McDonald's,

*(continued)*

as franchisor with the discretion to terminate the MLA, to exercise that discretion reasonably and with proper motive, and not arbitrarily, capriciously, or in a manner inconsistent with the reasonable expectations of the parties. The trial judge's factual finding that McDonald's was justified in terminating the MLA because of Dayan's failure to comply with the QSC standards was supported by substantial evidence regarding the filthy conditions of Dayan's restaurants. Dayan complained that McDonald's was tardy in sending him a French-speaking operations man to help rescue his restaurants. However, as the trial judge stated, "It does not take a McDonald's trained French-speaking operational man to know that grease dripping from the vents must be stopped and not merely collected in a cup hung from the ceiling, that dogs are not permitted to defecate where food is stored, that insecticide is not blended with chicken breading, that past-dated products should be discarded, that a potato peeler should be somewhat cleaner than a tire-vulcanizer and that shortening should not look like crankcase oil." ■

---

## REGULATING THE TRANSNATIONAL CORPORATION

In the early 1970s, a series of economic, political, and legal factors focused international attention on the role and impact of the **transnational corporation** (TNC) in global economic relationships.[14] Third World countries had experienced renewed political and economic strength as a result of the oil crisis of 1973–1974 and seized the opportunity to assert with increased vigor international programs to eliminate neocolonialist economic policies and practices in their relationships with industrialized states. International sensitivity to political abuses in developing countries became fixed on the TNC after the revelation of the roles of the Central Intelligence Agency and American TNCs in the downfall of socialist President Salvadore Allende of Chile. A conceptual framework for these growing concerns was provided when Jean-Jacques Servan-Schreiber published his influential study, *The American Challenge*,[15] which documented the management expertise and worldwide economic influence of American transnational corporations.

### Codes of Conduct for Transnational Corporations

The international response to these developments was swift. The United Nations began to draft a (still uncompleted) code of conduct for transnational corporations. Latin American members of the Andean Pact adopted Decision 24, which aimed at reducing TNC control of businesses in South America, replacing it with greater local control. Even the nations of Western Europe, the United States, Japan, and Canada, as members of the Organization for Economic Cooperation and Development (OECD), have adopted "Guidelines for Multinational Enterprises." The provisions of this instrument address virtually every aspect of transnational corporate relations with host nations. For example, they require that TNCs conduct their operations in harmony with the general policy objectives of their host countries, giving "due consideration" to the economic and social policies of

---

[14] International usage differs regarding the proper terminology for the TNC. Most United Nations organs seem to prefer "transnational corporations" but the International Labour Organization (ILO) and the Organization for Economic Cooperation and Development (OECD) have opted for "multinational enterprise." Other variations include multinational corporation and transnational enterprise. These distinctions are not merely semantic: they mask deep disagreements about a legal definition of the TNC. A final, legal statement in this respect has not yet been achieved and the attempt to reach one has led to much delay in the formulation of the various international codes which address the TNC. The OECD Guidelines take this interesting approach to the matter:

> *A precise legal definition of multinational enterprises is not required for the purposes of the guidelines. These usually comprise companies or other entities whose ownership is private, state or mixed, established in different countries and so linked that one or more of them may be able to exercise a significant influence over the activities of others and, in particular, to share knowledge and resources with the others. The degree of autonomy of each entity in relation to the others varies widely from one multinational enterprise to another, depending on the nature of the links between such entities and the fields of activity concerned. For these reasons, the guidelines are addressed to the various entities within the multinational enterprise (parent companies and/or local entities) according to the actual distribution of responsibilities among them on the understanding that they will co-operate and provide assistance to one another as necessary to facilitate observance of the guidelines. The word "enterprise" as used in these guidelines refers to these various entities in accordance with their responsibilities.*

Many of the codes considered in this chapter appear, with their texts, in *Legal Problems of Codes of Conduct for Multinational Enterprises,* Norbert Horn, ed. (Deventer, The Netherlands: Kluwer, B.V., 1980).

[15] J.-J. Servan-Schreiber, *The American Challenge* (New York: Atheneum, 1968).

those nations regarding industrial development, environmental protection, the development of employment opportunities, and transfers of technology.

These various international codes serve to provide TNCs with better defined environmental and public interest objectives and standards with which to formulate policies and procedures in pursuit of their corporate purposes. In general terms, the codes oblige the TNC to adhere to national standards and policies and to cooperate with host countries by considering the impact of their activities on the welfare of the local population and environment. Most of these codes attempt to achieve this result by host-country monitoring of transnational corporate activities through the required disclosure of relevant information. Thus, the basic duty of TNCs under these codes is to respect and adhere to the laws and regulations of the host country and to use reasonable measures to blunt any detrimental effects on the local citizenry that arise from their profit-seeking activities.

## *The New International Economic Order*

These multilateral efforts to harness TNCs and harmonize their activities with social and economic aspirations of the countries where they operate should be seen in a larger context of global economic adjustments to accommodate the emerging interests of less developed countries. A number of initiatives—collectively known as the New International Economic Order (NIEO)—have asserted Third World views in economic, political, and legal matters; these are treated with increasing sensitivity on the international level. U.N. General Assembly Resolutions 3201 (Declaration on the Establishment of a New International Economic Order) and 3202 (Programme of Action on the Establishment of a New International Economic Order), adopted on May 1, 1974, both address strategies to correct perceived imbalances in global economic relationships. Specific recommendations in these instruments address the core of traditional international business linkages:

- Permanent local sovereignty over natural resources should be ensured; these resources should be available to serve the national interests of developing countries.
- The operation of producers' associations to control primary commodities should be encouraged and enhanced.
- Access to markets in developed countries should be improved.
- The costs of insurance and reinsurance should be reduced through the growth of institutions in developing countries to service these markets.
- Indigenous transportation networks should be improved in developing countries to raise their capability to support export/import trade.

These instruments also direct attention to Third World needs relative to development finance, special measures to increase industrialization, improved access to technology, and TNC regulation. Many of these principles were reinforced when, in December of 1974, the General Assembly adopted its Resolution 3281, the Charter of Economic Rights and Duties of States, providing that every nation has the right:

- to choose its own economic, social, and political system;
- to regulate foreign investment in its territory;
- to nationalize and expropriate foreign property within its borders, subject to a duty to pay "appropriate compensation."

These rights, with others set forth in the Charter, are the fundamentals of the economic platform of the NIEO.

The principles of the NIEO have not been universally accepted; nor has their articulation through U.N. Resolutions been afforded the status of binding international law on a wide basis. Whether these initiatives—and particularly their efforts to control the TNC—will prove economically sound or politically wise in the long run lies in the realm of speculation. It is beyond debate, however, that these measures are impacting on the methods of international business. They are perhaps the most dramatic development of this century in the evolution of international trade law.

## SUMMARY

International commercial relations is a growing field. Each year an increasing volume of diverse goods are traded among an expanding number of nations. Both direct and indirect investment in foreign economies are also expanding. Such commercial relations are governed by a network of rules arising from multiple sources, including the domestic rules of the trading partners, the rules established by the international trading community, and the rules promulgated by regional organizations, such as the European Economic Community, and by international organizations, such as the United Nations and its various organs.

The international community has developed various uniform trade terms, financing devices (such as the letter of credit), and even trade rules such as those embodied in the Convention on Contracts for the International Sale of Goods in order to facilitate international trade. The Convention on Notes will probably be the next development.

When disputes over international agreements arise, the difficulties of domestic litigation are multiplied many times. U.S. courts must juggle such doctrines as the act of state doctrine and the doctrine of sovereign compulsion, as well as examine domestic legislation such as the Foreign Sovereign Immunities Act in order to determine which cases they can and cannot hear. These difficulties make arbitration a natural answer and, indeed, many international disputes are settled through arbitration.

Every nation is concerned with its export and import process. Like other nations, the United States has passed legislation to encourage the overall level of exports, while at the same time controlling the items that are exported in the interest of national security. Imports are also regulated to protect U.S. industry from unfair competition.

The international trade scene features not only bilateral trade agreements between nations, but also the multinational approach of GATT, and regional trade agreements such as that embodied in the European Economic Community. By 1992 the EEC, if things develop as its member nations envision, may be an increasingly formidable commercial entity on the international scene.

Investment by developed nations in lesser developed nations can stimulate the latter's economies. At the same time, if not properly handled, that investment can lead to charges of exploitation. Both international organizations and the lesser developed nations themselves have worked on investment codes designed to facilitate beneficial investment, while limiting the adverse side effects that sometimes arise.

# KEY TERMS

**International law**
**Letter of credit**
**Bill of lading**
**Import license**
**Export license**
**Certificate of origin**
**Trade terms**
**Act of state doctrine**
**Sovereign compulsion**
**Comity**
**Agent**
**License**
**Currency controls**
**Transnational corporation**

# QUESTIONS AND PROBLEMS

**1.** Schlunk, an American whose parents were killed in an accident, filed suit in the United States against a German company, Volkswagen AG (VWAG), and its wholly owned U.S. subsidiary, Volkswagen of America (VWOA). Schlunk did not attempt to serve VWAG in West Germany. Instead, he argued that service on VWOA in the United States constituted adequate service on VWAG. VWAG took the view that it could be served only at its West German headquarters pursuant to the provisions of the Hague Convention on the Service of Process. Which view seems to be the better one? (*Volkswagenwerk Aktiengesellschaft v. Schlunk*, 108 S.Ct. 2104, 1988.)

**2.** Defendants are two corporations owned by the Republic of France. They design, manufacture, and market aircraft, including the "Rallye." Plaintiffs were injured when a Rallye crashed in Iowa; they filed a breach of warranty suit in federal court in Iowa. Plaintiffs made various discovery requests under the Federal Rules of Civil Procedure. Defendants complied with initial requests, but later took the position that because they were French corporations, "and the discovery sought can only be found in a foreign state, namely France," the Hague Convention on the Taking of Evidence Abroad in Civil or Commercial Matters provided the exclusive means of pretrial discovery. Should this be the case? (*Societe Nationale Industrielle Aerospacetiale v. U.S. District Court*, 482 U.S. 522, 1987.)

**3.** In *Board of Trade of San Francisco v. Swiss Credit Bank*, the court held that the shipper's use of aircraft to transport goods did not strictly comply with the provision of the letter of credit stipulating ocean shipment. Does the manner of shipment make any difference if, in fact, they arrive on time and undamaged? What if the commercial invoices presented to the bank by the seller do not use the same unit of measurement for the goods as used in the letter of credit? The court in *Atari, Inc. v. Harris Trust and Savings Bank*, 599 F. Supp. 592 (N.D. Ill. 1984) said that this was not a basis on which to dishonor the letter of credit. How strict, then, is the doctrine of strict compliance?

**4.** It is normally important to an exporter that the letter of credit issued in payment for the goods be "irrevocable" so that the buyer/importer cannot cancel the letter after the seller has shipped under the contract. Must the term "irrevocable" be used in the letter of credit to make it so? Will words having the same significance make the letter "irrevocable"? If the letter of credit states that it "shall remain in force for a period of six (6) months," is it an irrevocable letter of credit for that period of time? *Conoco, Inc. v. Norwest Bank Mason City,* 767 F.2d 470 (8th Cir. 1985) held that such language made the letter of credit an irrevocable one.

5. Segni, a citizen of Argentina, was hired in 1984 to develop a market for Spanish wines in the United States. His employer was the Commercial Office of Spain and the term of his contract was to be three years. However, he was fired just six months later, so he sued the Commercial Office for breach of contract. Suit was filed in the United States. The Commercial Office moved to dismiss, claiming immunity under the FSIA. Segni claimed that the "commercial activity" exception applied. Discuss. (*Segni v. Commercial Office of Spain,* 835 F.2d 160, 7th Cir. 1987.)

6. American courts will enforce foreign court money-judgments by comity if, in the terms of *Hilton v. Guyot,* 159 U.S. 113 (1895), the foreign legal system is "likely to secure an impartial administration of justice between the citizens of its own country and those of other countries." By what standard is the "impartiality" test of *Hilton v. Guyot* to be measured? What legal system will define "justice"? Do international standards exist by which these concepts can be defined? Does the rule of this case open the door to racial or cultural prejudice through the selective enforcement of foreign money-judgments?

7. Geosource, Inc. of Houston, Texas, owned Sensor, a Netherland business organization. Sensor made a contract, governed by the law of The Netherlands, to deliver 2,400 strings of geophones to C.E.P. by September 1982, with the ultimate destination identified as the U.S.S.R. In June 1982, pursuant to the Export Administration Act of 1979, President Reagan prohibited the shipment to the U.S.S.R. of equipment manufactured in foreign countries under license from U.S. firms. The purpose of the embargo was to sanction the imposition of martial law in Poland. Sensor notified C.E.P. that as a subsidiary of a U.S. company, it was bound to follow this ban and could therefore not fulfill its contract. C.E.P. sued in District Court at The Hague, Netherlands. To what extent should the court be bound to follow U.S. political policies? (*Compagnie Europeenne Des Petroles v. Sensor Nederland,* 22 ILM 66, District Court at The Hague, 1983.)

8. The possibility of damage is not the only risk that passes to the buyer at ship's rail in a C.I.F. contract. In *Badhwar v. Colorado Fuel & Iron Corp.,* 138 F. Supp. 595 (S.D.N.Y. 1955), goods shipped under a C.I.F. contract from California to Bombay were delayed en route almost six months because of a labor strike on the West Coast, causing damage to the Indian buyer. Neither buyer nor seller was responsible for the delay or the consequent loss to the buyer. The court nonetheless held that the risk of this loss had passed to the buyer when the goods cleared ship's rail in California. Does fault play no role in allocating the risk of loss? What if a seller is responsible for delay or damage after the goods are unloaded? Will this make any difference in a C.I.F. contract?

# APPENDIX A

# THE UNIFORM COMMERCIAL CODE

## ARTICLE 1/GENERAL PROVISIONS

### Part 1/Short Title, Construction, Application and Subject Matter of the Act

**§ 1—101**
**Short Title**

This Act shall be known and may be cited as Uniform Commercial Code.

**§ 1—102**
**Purposes; Rules of Construction; Variation by Agreement**

(1) This Act shall be liberally construed and applied to promote its underlying purposes and policies.

(2) Underlying purposes and policies of this Act are
 (a) to simplify, clarify and modernize the law governing commercial transactions;
 (b) to permit the continued expansion of commercial practices through custom, usage and agreement of the parties;
 (c) to make uniform the law among the various jurisdictions.

(3) The effect of provisions of this Act may be varied by agreement, except as otherwise provided in this Act and except that the obligations of good faith, diligence, reasonableness and care prescribed by this Act may not be disclaimed by agreement but the parties may by agreement determine the standards by which the performance of such obligations is to be measured if such standards are not manifestly unreasonable.

(4) The presence in certain provisions of this Act of the words "unless otherwise agreed" or words of similar import does not imply that the effect of other provisions may not be varied by agreement under subsection (3).

(5) In this Act unless the context otherwise requires
 (a) words in the singular number include the plural, and in the plural include the singular;
 (b) words of the masculine gender include the feminine and the neuter, and when the sense so indicates words of the neuter gender may refer to any gender.

**§ 1—103**
**Supplementary General Principles of Law Applicable**

Unless displaced by the particular provisions of this Act, the principles of law and equity, including the law merchant and the law relative to capacity to contract, principal and agent, estoppel, fraud, misrepresentation, duress, coercion, mistake, bankruptcy, or other validating or invalidating cause shall supplement its provisions.

**§ 1—104**
**Construction Against Implicit Repeal**

This Act being a general act intended as a unified coverage of its subject matter, no part of it shall be deemed to be impliedly repealed by subsequent legislation if such construction can reasonably be avoided.

**§ 1—105**
**Territorial Application of the Act;**
**Parties' Power to Choose Applicable Law**

(1) Except as provided hereafter in this section, when a transaction bears a reasonable relation to this state and also to another state or nation the parties may agree that the law either of this state or of such other state or nation shall govern their rights and duties. Failing such agreement this Act applies to transactions bearing an appropriate relation to this state.

(2) Where one of the following provisions of this Act specifies the applicable law, that provision governs and a contrary agreement is effective only to the extent permitted by the law (including the conflict of laws rules) so specified:

Rights of creditors against sold goods. Section 2—402.

Applicability of the Article on Bank Deposits and Collections. Section 4—102.

Bulk transfers subject to the Article on Bulk Transfers. Section 6—102.

Applicability of the Article on Investment Securities. Section 8—106.

Perfection provisions of the Article on Secured Transactions. Section 9—103.

**§ 1—106**
**Remedies to Be Liberally Administered**

(1) The remedies provided by this Act shall be liberally administered to the end that the aggrieved party may be put in as good a position as if the other party had fully performed but neither consequential or special nor penal damages may be had except as specifically provided in this Act or by other rule of law.

(2) Any right or obligation declared by this Act is enforceable by action unless the provision declaring it specifies a different and limited effect.

### § 1—107
**Waiver or Renunciation of Claim or Right After Breach**

Any claim or right arising out of an alleged breach can be discharged in whole or in part without consideration by a written waiver or renunciation signed and delivered by the aggrieved party.

### § 1—108
**Severability**

If any provision or clause of this Act or application thereof to any person or circumstances is held invalid, such invalidity shall not affect other provisions or applications of the Act which can be given effect without the invalid provision or application, and to this end the provisions of this Act are declared to be severable.

### § 1—109
**Section Captions**

Section captions are parts of this Act.

## Part 2/General Definitions and Principles of Interpretation

### § 1—201
**General Definitions**

Subject to additional definitions contained in the subsequent Articles of this Act which are applicable to specific Articles or Parts thereof, and unless the context otherwise requires, in this Act:

(1) "Action" in the sense of a judicial proceeding includes recoupment, counterclaim, set-off, suit in equity and any other proceedings in which rights are determined.

(2) "Aggrieved party" means a party entitled to resort to a remedy.

(3) "Agreement" means the bargain of the parties in fact as found in their language or by implication from other circumstances including course of dealing or usage of trade or course of performance as provided in this Act (Sections 1—205 and 2—208). Whether an agreement has legal consequences is determined by the provisions of this Act, if applicable; otherwise by the law of contracts (Section 1—103). (Compare "Contract".)

(4) "Bank" means any person engaged in the business of banking.

(5) "Bearer" means the person in possession of an instrument, document of title, or certified security payable to bearer or indorsed in blank.

(6) "Bill of lading" means a document evidencing the receipt of goods for shipment issued by a person engaged in the business of transporting or forwarding goods, and includes an airbill. "Airbill" means a document serving for air transportation as a bill of lading does for marine or rail transportation, and includes an air consignment note or air waybill.

(7) "Branch" includes a separately incorporated foreign branch of a bank.

(8) "Burden of establishing" a fact means the burden of persuading the triers of fact that the existence of the fact is more probable than its non-existence.

(9) "Buyer in ordinary course of business" means a person who in good faith and without knowledge that the sale to him is in violation of the ownership rights or security interest of a third party in the goods buys in ordinary course from a person in the business of selling goods of that kind but does not include a pawnbroker. All persons who sell minerals or the like (including oil and gas) at wellhead or minehead shall be deemed to be persons in the business of selling goods of that kind. "Buying" may be for cash or by exchange of other property or on secured or unsecured credit and includes receiving goods or documents of title under a pre-existing contract for sale but does not include a transfer in bulk or as security for or in total or partial satisfaction of a money debt.

(10) "Conspicuous": A term or clause is conspicuous when it is so written that a reasonable person against whom it is to operate ought to have noticed it. A printed heading in capitals (as: NON-NEGOTIABLE BILL OF LADING) is conspicuous. Language in the body of a form is "conspicuous" if it is in larger or other contrasting type or color. But in a telegram any stated term is "conspicuous". Whether a term or clause is "conspicuous" or not is for decision by the court.

(11) "Contract" means the total legal obligation which results from the parties' agreement as affected by this Act and any other applicable rules of law. (Compare "Agreement".)

(12) "Creditor" includes a general creditor, a secured creditor, a lien creditor and any representative of creditors, including an assignee for the benefit of creditors, a trustee in bankruptcy, a receiver in equity and an executor or administrator of an insolvent debtor's or assignor's estate.

(13) "Defendant" includes a person in the position of defendant in a cross-action or counterclaim.

(14) "Delivery" with respect to instruments, documents of title, chattel paper or securities means voluntary transfer of possession.

(15) "Document of title" includes bill of lading, dock warrant, dock receipt, warehouse receipt or order for the delivery of goods, and also any other document which in the regular course of business or financing is treated as adequately evidencing that the person in possession of it is entitled to receive, hold and dispose of the document and the goods it covers. To be a document of title a document must purport to be issued by or addressed to a bailee and purport to cover goods in the bailee's possession which are either identified or are fungible portions of an identified mass.

(16) "Fault" means wrongful act, omission or breach.

(17) "Fungible" with respect to goods or securities means goods or securities of which any unit is, by nature or usage of trade, the equivalent of any other like unit. Goods which are not fungible shall be deemed fungible for the purposes of this Act to the extent that under a particular agreement or document unlike units are treated as equivalents.

(18) "Genuine" means free of forgery or counterfeiting.

(19) "Good faith" means honesty in fact in the conduct or transaction concerned.

(20) "Holder" means a person who is in possession of a document of title or an instrument or a certificated investment security drawn, issued or indorsed to him or to his order or to bearer or in blank.

(21) To "honor" is to pay or to accept and pay, or where a credit so engages to purchase or discount a draft complying with the terms of the credit.

**(22)** "Insolvency proceedings" includes any assignment for the benefit of creditors or other proceedings intended to liquidate or rehabilitate the estate of the person involved.

**(23)** A person is "insolvent" who either has ceased to pay his debts in the ordinary course of business or cannot pay his debts as they become due or is insolvent within the meaning of the federal bankruptcy law.

**(24)** "Money" means a medium of exchange authorized or adopted by a domestic or foreign government as a part of its currency.

**(25)** A person has "notice" of a fact when
  (a) he has actual knowledge of it; or
  (b) he has received a notice or notification of it; or
  (c) from all the facts and circumstances known to him at the time in question he has reason to know that it exists.

A person "knows" or has "knowledge" of a fact when he has actual knowledge of it. "Discover" or "learn" or a word or phrase of similar import refers to knowledge rather than to reason to know. The time and circumstances under which a notice or notification may cease to be effective are not determined by this Act.

**(26)** A person "notifies" or "gives" a notice or notification to another by taking such steps as may be reasonably required to inform the other in ordinary course whether or not such other actually comes to know of it. A person "receives" a notice or notification when
  (a) it comes to his attention; or
  (b) it is duly delivered at the place of business through which the contract was made or at any other place held out by him as the place for receipt of such communications.

**(27)** Notice, knowledge or a notice or notification received by an organization is effective for a particular transaction from the time when it is brought to the attention of the individual conducting that transaction, and in any event from the time when it would have been brought to his attention if the organization had exercised due diligence. An organization exercises due diligence if it maintains reasonable routines for communicating significant information to the person conducting the transaction and there is reasonable compliance with the routines. Due diligence does not require an individual acting for the organization to communicate information unless such communication is part of his regular duties or unless he has reason to know of the transaction and that the transaction would be materially affected by the information.

**(28)** "Organization" includes a corporation, government or governmental subdivision or agency, business trust, estate, trust, partnership or association, two or more persons having a joint or common interest, or any other legal or commercial entity.

**(29)** "Party," as distinct from "third party", means a person who has engaged in a transaction or made an agreement within this Act.

**(30)** "Person" includes an individual or an organization (See Section 1—102).

**(31)** "Presumption" or "presumed" means that the trier of fact must find the existence of the fact presumed unless and until evidence is introduced which would support a finding of its nonexistence.

**(32)** "Purchase" includes taking by sale, discount, negotiation, mortgage, pledge, lien, issue or re-issue, gift or any other voluntary transaction creating an interest in property.

**(33)** "Purchaser" means a person who takes by purchase.

**(34)** "Remedy" means any remedial right to which an aggrieved party is entitled with or without resort to a tribunal.

**(35)** "Representative" includes an agent, an officer of a corporation or association, and a trustee, executor or administrator of an estate, or any other person empowered to act for another.

**(36)** "Rights" includes remedies.

**(37)** "Security interest" means an interest in personal property or fixtures which secures payment or performance of an obligation. The retention or reservation of title by a seller of goods notwithstanding shipment or delivery to the buyer (Section 2—401) is limited in effect to a reservation of a "security interest". The term also includes any interest of a buyer of accounts or chattel paper which is subject to Article 9. The special property interest of a buyer of goods on identification of those goods to a contract for sale under Section 2—401 is not a "security interest", but a buyer may also acquire a "security interest" by complying with Article 9. Unless a consignment is intended as security, reservation of title thereunder is not a "security interest", but a consignment is in any event subject to the provisions on consignment sales (Section 2—326).

Whether a transaction creates a lease or security interest is determined by the facts of each case; however, a transaction creates a security interest if the consideration the lessee is to pay the lessor for the right to possession and use of the goods is an obligation for the term of the lease not subject to termination by the lessee, and
  (a) the original term of the lease is equal to or greater than the remaining economic life of the goods,
  (b) the lessee is bound to renew the lease for the remaining economic life of the goods or is bound to become the owner of the goods,
  (c) the lessee has an option to renew the lease for the remaining economic life of the goods for no additional consideration or nominal additional consideration upon compliance with the lease agreement, or
  (d) the lessee has an option to become the owner of the goods for no additional consideration or nominal additional consideration upon compliance with the lease agreement.

A transaction does not create a security interest merely because it provides that
  (a) the present value of the consideration the lessee is obligated to pay the lessor for the right to possession and use of the goods is substantially equal to or is greater than the fair market value of the goods at the time the lease is entered into,
  (b) the lessee assumes risk of loss of the goods, or agrees to pay taxes, insurance, filing, recording, or registration fees, or service or maintenance costs with respect to the goods,
  (c) the lessee has an option to renew the lease or to become the owner of the goods,
  (d) the lessee has an option to renew the lease for a fixed rent that is equal to or greater than the reasonably predictable fair market rent for the use of the goods for the term of the renewal at the time the option is to be performed, or
  (e) the lessee has an option to become the owner of the goods for a fixed price that is equal to or greater than the reasonably predictable fair market value of the goods at the time the option is to be performed.

For purposes of this subsection (37):
  (x) Additional consideration is not nominal if (i) when the option to renew the lease is granted to the lessee the rent is

stated to be the fair market rent for the use of the goods for the term of the renewal determined at the time the option is to be performed, or (ii) when the option to become the owner of the goods is granted to the lessee the price is stated to be the fair market value of the goods determined at the time the option is to be performed. Additional consideration is nominal if it is less than the lessee's reasonably predictable cost of performing under the lease agreement if the option is not exercised;

(y) "Reasonably predictable" and "remaining economic life of the goods" are to be determined with reference to the facts and circumstances at the time the transaction is entered into; and

(z) "Present value" means the amount as of a date certain of one or more sums payable in the future, discounted to the date certain. The discount is determined by the interest rate specified by the parties if the rate is not manifestly unreasonable at the time the transaction is entered into; otherwise, the discount is determined by a commercially reasonable rate that takes into account the facts and circumstances of each case at the time the transaction was entered into.

(38) "Send" in connection with any writing or notice means to deposit in the mail or deliver for transmission by any other usual means of communication with postage or cost of transmission provided for and properly addressed and in the case of an instrument to an address specified thereon or otherwise agreed, or if there be none to any address reasonable under the circumstances. The receipt of any writing or notice within the time at which it would have arrived if properly sent has the effect of a proper sending.

(39) "Signed" includes any symbol executed or adopted by a party with present intention to authenticate a writing.

(40) "Surety" includes guarantor.

(41) "Telegram" includes a message transmitted by radio, teletype, cable, any mechanical method of transmission, or the like.

(42) "Term" means that portion of an agreement which relates to a particular matter.

(43) "Unauthorized" signature or indorsement means one made without actual, implied or apparent authority and includes a forgery.

(44) "Value". Except as otherwise provided with respect to negotiable instruments and bank collections (Sections 3—303, 4—208 and 4—209) a person gives "value" for rights if he acquires them

    (a) in return for a binding commitment to extend credit or for the extension of immediately available credit whether or not drawn upon and whether or not a chargeback is provided for in the event of difficulties in collection; or

    (b) as security for or in total or partial satisfaction of a pre-existing claim; or

    (c) by accepting delivery pursuant to a pre-existing contract for purchase; or

    (d) generally, in return for any consideration sufficient to support a simple contract.

(45) "Warehouse receipt" means a receipt issued by a person engaged in the business of storing goods for hire.

(46) "Written" or "writing" includes printing, typewriting or any other intentional reduction to tangible form.

Amended in 1962, 1972 and 1977.

## § 1—202
### Prima Facie Evidence by Third Party Documents

A document in due form purporting to be a bill of lading, policy or certificate of insurance, official weigher's or inspector's certificate, consular invoice, or any other document authorized or required by the contract to be issued by a third party shall be prima facie evidence of its own authenticity and genuineness and of the facts stated in the document by the third party.

## § 1—203
### Obligation of Good Faith

Every contract or duty within this Act imposes an obligation of good faith in its performance or enforcement.

## § 1—204
### Time; Reasonable Time; "Seasonably"

(1) Whenever this Act requires any action to be taken within a reasonable time, any time which is not manifestly unreasonable may be fixed by agreement.

(2) What is a reasonable time for taking any action depends on the nature, purpose and circumstances of such action.

(3) An action is taken "seasonably" when it is taken at or within the time agreed or if no time is agreed at or within a reasonable time.

## § 1—205
### Course of Dealing and Usage of Trade

(1) A course of dealing is a sequence of previous conduct between the parties to a particular transaction which is fairly to be regarded as establishing a common basis of understanding for interpreting their expressions and other conduct.

(2) A usage of trade is any practice or method of dealing having such regularity of observance in a place, vocation or trade as to justify an expectation that it will be observed with respect to the transaction in question. The existence and scope of such a usage are to be proved as facts. If it is established that such a usage is embodied in a written trade code or similar writing the interpretation of the writing is for the court.

(3) A course of dealing between parties and any usage of trade in the vocation or trade in which they are engaged or of which they are or should be aware give particular meaning to and supplement or qualify terms of an agreement.

(4) The express terms of an agreement and an applicable course of dealing or usage of trade shall be construed wherever reasonable as consistent with each other; but when such construction is unreasonable express terms control both course of dealing and usage of trade and course of dealing controls usage trade.

(5) An applicable usage of trade in the place where any part of performance is to occur shall be used in interpreting the agreement as to that part of the performance.

(6) Evidence of a relevant usage of trade offered by one party is not admissible unless and until he has given the other party such notice as the court finds sufficient to prevent unfair surprise to the latter.

## § 1—206
### Statute of Frauds for Kinds of Personal Property Not Otherwise Covered

**(1)** Except in the cases described in subsection (2) of this section a contract for the sale of personal property is not enforceable by way of action or defense beyond five thousand dollars in amount or value of remedy unless there is some writing which indicates that a contract for sale has been made between the parties at a defined or stated price, reasonably identifies the subject matter, and is signed by the party against whom enforcement is sought or by his authorized agent.

**(2)** Subsection (1) of this section does not apply to contracts for the sale of goods (Section 2—201) nor of securities (Section 8—319) nor to security agreements (Section 9—203).

## § 1—207
### Performance or Acceptance Under Reservation of Rights

A party who with explicit reservation of rights performs or promises performance or assents to performance in the manner demanded or offered by the other party does not thereby prejudice the rights reserved. Such words as "without prejudice", "under protest" or the like are sufficient.

## § 1—208
### Option to Accelerate at Will

A term providing that one party or his successor in interest may accelerate payment or performance or require collateral or additional collateral "at will" or "when he deems himself insecure" or in words of similar import shall be construed to mean that he shall have power to do so only if he in good faith believes that the prospect of payment or performance is impaired. The burden of establishing lack of good faith is on the party against whom the power has been exercised.

## § 1—209
### Subordinated Obligations

An obligation may be issued as subordinated to payment of another obligation of the person obligated, or a creditor may subordinate his right to payment of an obligation by agreement with either the person obligated or another creditor of the person obligated. Such a subordination does not create a security interest as against either the common debtor or a subordinated creditor. This section shall be construed as declaring the law as it existed prior to the enactment of this section and not as modifying it. Added 1966.

Note: *This new section is proposed as an optional provision to make it clear that a subordination agreement does not create a security interest unless so intended.*

# ARTICLE 2/SALES
## *Part 1/Short Title, General Construction and Subject Matter*

### § 2—101
### Short Title

This Article shall be known and may be cited as Uniform Commercial Code—Sales.

### § 2—102
### Scope; Certain Security and Other Transactions Excluded From This Article

Unless the context otherwise requires, this Article applies to transactions in goods; it does not apply to any transaction which although in the form of an unconditional contract to sell or present sale is intended to operate only as a security transaction nor does this Article impair or repeal any statute regulating sales to consumers, farmers or other specified classes of buyers.

### § 2—103
### Definitions and Index of Definitions

**(1)** In this Article unless the context otherwise requires
  **(a)** "Buyer" means a person who buys or contracts to buy goods.
  **(b)** "Good faith" in the case of a merchant means honesty in fact and the observance of reasonable commercial standards of fair dealing in the trade.
  **(c)** "Receipt" of goods means taking physical possession of them.
  **(d)** "Seller" means a person who sells or contracts to sell goods.

**(2)** Other definitions applying to this Article or to specified Parts thereof, and the sections in which they appear are:

"Acceptance". Section 2—606.
"Banker's credit". Section 2—325.
"Between merchants". Section 2—104.
"Cancellation". Section 2—106(4).
"Commercial unit". Section 2—105.
"Confirmed credit". Section 2—325.
"Conforming to contract". Section 2—106.
"Contract for sale". Section 2—106.
"Cover". Section 2—712.
"Entrusting". Section 2—403.
"Financing agency". Section 2—104.
"Future goods". Section 2—105.
"Goods". Section 2—105.
"Identification". Section 2—501.
"Installment contract". Section 2—612.
"Letter of Credit". Section 2—325.
"Lot". Section 2—105.
"Merchant". Section 2—104.
"Overseas". Section 2—323.
"Person in position of seller". Section 2—707.
"Present sale". Section 2—106.
"Sale". Section 2—106.
"Sale on approval". Section 2—326.
"Sale or return". Section 2—326.
"Termination". Section 2—106.

**(3)** The following definitions in other Articles apply to this Article:

"Check". Section 3—104.
"Consignee". Section 7—102.
"Consignor". Section 7—102.
"Consumer goods". Section 9—109.
"Dishonor". Section 3—507.
"Draft". Section 3—104.

(4) In addition Article 1 contains general definitions and principles of construction and interpretation applicable throughout this Article.

## § 2—104
### Definitions: "Merchant"; "Between Merchants"; "Financing Agency"

(1) "Merchant" means a person who deals in goods of the kind or otherwise by his occupation holds himself out as having knowledge or skill peculiar to the practices or goods involved in the transaction or to whom such knowledge or skill may be attributed by his employment of an agent or broker or other intermediary who by his occupation holds himself out as having such knowledge or skill.

(2) "Financing agency" means a bank, finance company or other person who in the ordinary course of business makes advances against goods or documents of title or who by arrangement with either the seller or the buyer intervenes in ordinary course to make or collect payment due or claimed under the contract for sale, as by purchasing or paying the seller's draft or making advances against it or by merely taking it for collection whether or not documents of title accompany the draft. "Financing agency" includes also a bank or other person who similarly intervenes between persons who are in the position of seller and buyer in respect to the goods (Section 2—707).

(3) "Between merchants" means in any transaction with respect to which both parties are chargeable with the knowledge or skill of merchants.

## § 2—105
### Definitions: Transferability; "Goods"; "Future" Goods; "Lot"; "Commercial Unit"

(1) "Goods" means all things (including specially manufactured goods) which are movable at the time of identification to the contract for sale other than the money in which the price is to be paid, investment securities (Article 8) and things in action. "Goods" also includes the unborn young of animals and growing crops and other identified things attached to realty as described in the section on goods to be severed from realty (Section 2—107).

(2) Goods must be both existing and identified before any interest in them can pass. Goods which are not both existing and identified are "future" goods. A purported present sale of future goods or of any interest therein operates as a contract to sell.

(3) There may be a sale of a part interest in existing identified goods.

(4) An undivided share in an identified bulk of fungible goods is sufficiently identified to be sold although the quantity of the bulk is not determined. Any agreed proportion of such a bulk or any quantity thereof agreed upon by number, weight or other measure may to the extent of the seller's interest in the bulk be sold to the buyer who then becomes an owner in common.

(5) "Lot" means a parcel or a single article which is the subject matter of a separate sale or delivery, whether or not it is sufficient to perform the contract.

(6) "Commercial unit" means such a unit of goods as by commercial usage is a single whole for purposes of sale and division of which materially impairs its character or value on the market or in use. A commercial unit may be a single article (as a machine) or a set of articles (as a suite of furniture or an assortment of sizes) or a quantity (as a bale, gross, or carload) or any other unit treated in use or in the relevant market as a single whole.

## § 2—106
### Definitions: "Contract"; "Agreement"; "Contract for Sale"; "Sale"; "Present Sale"; "Conforming" to Contract; "Termination"; "Cancellation"

(1) In this Article unless the context otherwise requires "contract" and "agreement" are limited to those relating to the present or future sale of goods. "Contract for sale" includes both a present sale of goods and a contract to sell goods at a future time. A "sale" consists in the passing of title from the seller to the buyer for a price (Section 2—401). A "present sale" means a sale which is accomplished by the making of the contract.

(2) Goods or conduct including any part of a performance are "conforming" or conform to the contract when they are in accordance with the obligations under the contract.

(3) "Termination" occurs when either party pursuant to a power created by agreement or law puts an end to the contract otherwise than for its breach. On "termination" all obligations which are still executory on both sides are discharged but any right based on prior breach or performance survives.

(4) "Cancellation" occurs when either party puts an end to the contract for breach by the other and its effect is the same as that of "termination" except that the cancelling party also retains any remedy for breach of the whole contract or any unperformed balance.

## § 2—107
### Goods to Be Severed From Realty: Recording

(1) A contract for the sale of minerals or the like (including oil and gas) or a structure or its materials to be removed from realty is a contract for the sale of goods within this Article if they are to be severed by the seller but until severance a purported present sale thereof which is not effective as a transfer of an interest in land is effective only as a contract to sell.

(2) A contract for the sale apart from the land of growing crops or other things attached to realty and capable of severance without material harm thereto but not described in subsection (1) or of timber to be cut is a contract for the sale of goods within this Article whether the subject matter is to be severed by the buyer or by the seller even though it forms part of the realty at the time of contracting, and the parties can by identification effect a present sale before severance.

(3) The provisions of this section are subject to any third party rights provided by the law relating to realty records, and the contract for sale may be executed and recorded as a document transferring an interest in land and shall then constitute notice to third parties of the buyer's rights under the contract for sale.

## Part 2/Form, Formation and Readjustment of Contract

### § 2—201
### Formal Requirements; Statute of Frauds

(1) Except as otherwise provided in this section a contract for the sale of goods for the price of $500 or more is not enforceable

by way of action or defense unless there is some writing sufficient to indicate that a contract for sale has been made between the parties and signed by the party against whom enforcement is sought or by his authorized agent or broker. A writing is not insufficient because it omits or incorrectly states a term agreed upon but the contract is not enforceable under this paragraph beyond the quantity of goods shown in such writing.

(2) Between merchants if within a reasonable time a writing in confirmation of the contract and sufficient against the sender is received and the party receiving it has reason to know its contents, it satisfies the requirements of subsection (1) against such party unless written notice of objection to its contents is given within ten days after it is received.

(3) A contract which does not satisfy the requirements of subsection (1) but which is valid in other respects is enforceable
    (a) if the goods are to be specially manufactured for the buyer and are not suitable for sale to others in the ordinary course of the seller's business and the seller, before notice of repudiation is received and under circumstances which reasonably indicate that the goods are for the buyer, has made either a substantial beginning of their manufacture or commitments for their procurement; or
    (b) if the party against whom enforcement is sought admits in his pleading, testimony or otherwise in court that a contract for sale was made, but the contract is not enforceable under this provision beyond the quantity of goods admitted; or
    (c) with respect to goods for which payment has been made and accepted or which have been received and accepted (Sec. 2—606).

§ 2—202
**Final Written Expression: Parol or Extrinsic Evidence**

Terms with respect to which the confirmatory memoranda of the parties agree or which are otherwise set forth in a writing intended by the parties as a final expression of their agreement with respect to such terms as are included therein may not be contradicted by evidence of any prior agreement or of a contemporaneous oral agreement but may be explained or supplemented
    (a) by course of dealing or usage of trade (Section 1—205) or by course of performance (Section 2—208); and
    (b) by evidence of consistent additional terms unless the court finds the writing to have been intended also as a complete and exclusive statement of the terms of the agreement.

§ 2—203
**Seals Inoperative**

The affixing of a seal to a writing evidencing a contract for sale or an offer to buy or sell goods does not constitute the writing a sealed instrument and the law with respect to sealed instruments does not apply to such a contract or offer.

§ 2—204
**Formation in General**

(1) A contract for sale of goods may be made in any manner sufficient to show agreement, including conduct by both parties which recognizes the existence of such a contract.

(2) An agreement sufficient to constitute a contract for sale may be found even though the moment of its making is undetermined.

(3) Even though one or more terms are left open a contract for sale does not fail for indefiniteness if the parties have intended to make a contract and there is a reasonably certain basis for giving an appropriate remedy.

§ 2—205
**Firm Offers**

An offer by a merchant to buy or sell goods in a signed writing which by its terms gives assurance that it will be held open is not revocable, for lack of consideration, during the time stated or if no time is stated for a reasonable time, but in no event may such period of irrevocability exceed three months; but any such term of assurance on a form supplied by the offeree must be separately signed by the offeror.

§ 2—206
**Offer and Acceptance Formation of Contract**

(1) Unless otherwise unambiguously indicated by the language or circumstances
    (a) an offer to make a contract shall be construed as inviting acceptance in any manner and by any medium reasonable in the circumstances;
    (b) an order or other offer to buy goods for prompt or current shipment shall be construed as inviting acceptance either by a prompt promise to ship or by the prompt or current shipment of conforming or nonconforming goods, but such a shipment of nonconforming goods does not constitute an acceptance if the seller seasonably notifies the buyer that the shipment is offered only as an accommodation to the buyer.

(2) Where the beginning of a requested performance is a reasonable mode of acceptance an offeror who is not notified of acceptance within a reasonable time may treat the offer as having lapsed before acceptance.

§ 2—207
**Additional Terms in Acceptance or Confirmation**

(1) A definite and seasonable expression of acceptance or a written confirmation which is sent within a reasonable time operates as an acceptance even though it states terms additional to or different from those offered or agreed upon, unless acceptance is expressly made conditional on assent to the additional or different terms.

(2) The additional terms are to be construed as proposals for addition to the contract. Between merchants such terms become part of the contract unless:
    (a) the offer expressly limits acceptance to the terms of the offer;
    (b) they materially alter it; or
    (c) notification of objection to them has already been given or is given within a reasonable time after notice of them is received.

(3) Conduct by both parties which recognizes the existence of a contract is sufficient to establish a contract for sale although the writings of the parties do not otherwise establish a contract. In such case the terms of the particular contract consist of those terms on which the writings of the parties agree, together with any supplementary terms incorporated under any other provisions of this Act.

## § 2—208
### Course of Performance or Practical Construction

(1) Where the contract for sale involves repeated occasions for performance by either party with knowledge of the nature of the performance and opportunity for objection to it by the other, any course of performance accepted or acquiesced in without objection shall be relevant to determine the meaning of the agreement.

(2) The express terms of the agreement and any such course of performance, as well as any course of dealing and usage of trade, shall be construed whenever reasonable as consistent with each other; but when such construction is unreasonable, express terms shall control course of performance and course of performance shall control both course of dealing and usage of trade (Section 1—205).

(3) Subject to the provisions of the next section on modification and waiver, such course of performance shall be relevant to show a waiver or modification of any term inconsistent with such course of performance.

## § 2—209
### Modification, Rescission and Waiver

(1) An agreement modifying a contract within this Article needs no consideration to be binding.

(2) A signed agreement which excludes modification or rescission except by a signed writing cannot be otherwise modified or rescinded, but except as between merchants such a requirement on a form supplied by the merchant must be separately signed by the other party.

(3) The requirements of the statute of frauds section of this Article (Section 2—201) must be satisfied if the contract as modified is within its provisions.

(4) Although an attempt at modification or rescission does not satisfy the requirements of subsection (2) or (3) it can operate as a waiver.

(5) A party who has made a waiver affecting an executory portion of the contract may retract the waiver by reasonable notification received by the other party that strict performance will be required of any term waived, unless the retraction would be unjust in view of a material change of position in reliance on the waiver.

## § 2—210
### Delegation of Performance; Assignment of Rights

(1) A party may perform his duty through a delegate unless otherwise agreed or unless the other party has a substantial interest in having his original promisor perform or control the acts required by the contract. No delegation of performance relieves the party delegating of any duty to perform or any liability for breach.

(2) Unless otherwise agreed all rights of either seller or buyer can be assigned except where the assignment would materially change the duty of the other party, or increase materially the burden or risk imposed on him by his contract, or impair materially his chance of obtaining return performance. A right to damages for breach of the whole contract or a right arising out of the assignor's due performance of his entire obligation can be assigned despite agreement otherwise.

(3) Unless the circumstances indicate the contrary a prohibition of assignment of "the contract" is to be construed as barring only the delegation to the assignee of the assignor's performance.

(4) An assignment of "the contract" or of "all my rights under the contract" or an assignment in similar general terms is an assignment of rights and unless the language or the circumstances (as in an assignment for security) indicate the contrary, it is a delegation of performance of the duties of the assignor and its acceptance by the assignee constitutes a promise by him to perform those duties. This promise is enforceable by either the assignor or the other party to the original contract.

(5) The other party may treat any assignment which delegates performance as creating reasonable grounds for insecurity and may without prejudice to his rights against the assignor demand assurances from the assignee (Section 2—609).

## Part 3/General Obligation and Construction of Contract

### § 2—301
### General Obligations of Parties

The obligation of the seller is to transfer and deliver and that of the buyer is to accept and pay in accordance with the contract.

### § 2—302
### Unconscionable Contract or Clause

(1) If the court as a matter of law finds the contract or any clause of the contract to have been unconscionable at the time it was made the court may refuse to enforce the contract, or it may enforce the remainder of the contract without the unconscionable clause, or it may so limit the application of any unconscionable clause as to avoid any unconscionable result.

(2) When it is claimed or appears to the court that the contract or any clause thereof may be unconscionable the parties shall be afforded a reasonable opportunity to present evidence as to its commercial setting, purpose and effect to aid the court in making the determination.

### § 2—303
### Allocations or Division of Risks

Where this Article allocates a risk or a burden as between the parties "unless otherwise agreed," the agreement may not only shift the allocation but may also divide the risk or burden.

### § 2—304
### Price Payable in Money, Goods, Realty, or Otherwise

(1) The price can be made payable in money or otherwise. If it is payable in whole or in part in goods each party is a seller of the goods which he is to transfer.

(2) Even though all or part of the price is payable in an interest in realty the transfer of the goods and the seller's obligations with reference to them are subject to this Article, but not the transfer of the interest in realty or the transferor's obligations in connection therewith.

## § 2—305
### Open Price Term

**(1)** The parties if they so intend can conclude a contract for sale even though the price is not settled. In such a case the price is a reasonable price at the time for delivery if
    **(a)** nothing is said as to price; or
    **(b)** the price is left to be agreed by the parties and they fail to agree; or
    **(c)** the price is to be fixed in terms of some agreed market or other standard as set or recorded by a third person or agency and it is not so set or recorded.

**(2)** A price to be fixed by the seller or by the buyer means a price for him to fix in good faith.

**(3)** When a price left to be fixed otherwise than by agreement of the parties fails to be fixed through fault of one party the other may at his option treat the contract as cancelled or himself fix a reasonable price.

**(4)** Where, however, the parties intend not to be bound unless the price be fixed or agreed and it is not fixed or agreed there is no contract. In such a case the buyer must return any goods already received or if unable so to do must pay their reasonable value at the time of delivery and the seller must return any portion of the price paid on account.

## § 2—306
### Output, Requirements and Exclusive Dealings

**(1)** A term which measures the quantity by the output of the seller or the requirements of the buyer means such actual output or requirements as may occur in good faith, except that no quantity unreasonably disproportionate to any stated estimate or in the absence of a stated estimate to any normal or otherwise comparable prior output or requirements may be tendered or demanded.

**(2)** A lawful agreement by either the seller or the buyer for exclusive dealing in the kind of goods concerned imposes unless otherwise agreed an obligation by the seller to use best efforts to supply the goods and by the buyer to use best efforts to promote their sale.

## § 2—307
### Delivery in Single Lot or Several Lots

Unless otherwise agreed all goods called for by a contract for sale must be tendered in a single delivery and payment is due only on such tender but where the circumstances give either party the right to make or demand delivery in lots the price if it can be apportioned may be demanded for each lot.

## § 2—308
### Absence of Specified Place for Delivery

Unless otherwise agreed
    **(a)** the place for delivery of goods is the seller's place of business or if he has none his residence; but
    **(b)** in a contract for sale of identified goods which to the knowledge of the parties at the time of contracting are in some other place, that place is the place for their delivery; and
    **(c)** documents of title may be delivered through customary banking channels.

## § 2—309
### Absence of Specific Time Provisions; Notice of Termination

**(1)** The time for shipment or delivery or any other action under a contract if not provided in this Article or agreed upon shall be a reasonable time.

**(2)** Where the contract provides for successive performances but is indefinite in duration it is valid for a reasonable time but unless otherwise agreed may be terminated at any time by either party.

**(3)** Termination of a contract by one party except on the happening of an agreed event requires that reasonable notification be received by the other party and an agreement dispensing with notification is invalid if its operation would be unconscionable.

## § 2—310
### Open Time for Payment or Running of Credit; Authority to Ship Under Reservation

Unless otherwise agreed
    **(a)** payment is due at the time and place at which the buyer is to receive the goods even though the place of shipment is the place of delivery; and
    **(b)** if the seller is authorized to send the goods he may ship them under reservation, and may tender the documents of title, but the buyer may inspect the goods after their arrival before payment is due unless such inspection is inconsistent with the terms of the contract (Section 2—513); and
    **(c)** if delivery is authorized and made by way of documents of title otherwise than by subsection (b) then payment is due at the time and place at which the buyer is to receive the documents regardless of where the goods are to be received; and
    **(d)** where the seller is required or authorized to ship the goods on credit the credit period runs from the time of shipment but post-dating the invoice or delaying its dispatch will correspondingly delay the starting of the credit period.

## § 2—311
### Options and Cooperation Respecting Performance

**(1)** An agreement for sale which is otherwise sufficiently definite (subsection (3) of Section 2—204) to be a contract is not made invalid by the fact that it leaves particulars of performance to be specified by one of the parties. Any such specification must be made in good faith and within limits set by commercial reasonableness.

**(2)** Unless otherwise agreed specifications relating to assortment of the goods are at the buyer's option and except as otherwise provided in subsections (1)(c) and (3) of Section 2—319 specifications or arrangements relating to shipment are at the seller's option.

**(3)** Where such specification would materially affect the other party's performance but is not seasonably made or where one party's cooperation is necessary to the agreed performance of the other but is not seasonably forthcoming, the other party in addition to all other remedies
    **(a)** is excused for any resulting delay in his own performance; and
    **(b)** may also either proceed to perform in any reasonable manner or after the time for a material part of his own performance treat the failure to specify or to cooperate as a breach by failure to deliver or accept the goods.

## § 2—312
### Warranty of Title and Against Infringement; Buyer's Obligation Against Infringement

(1) Subject to subsection (2) there is in a contract for sale a warranty by the seller that
   (a) the title conveyed shall be good, and its transfer rightful; and
   (b) the goods shall be delivered free from any security interest or other lien or encumbrance of which the buyer at the time of contracting has no knowledge.

(2) A warranty under subsection (1) will be excluded or modified only by specific language or by circumstances which give the buyer reason to know that the person selling does not claim title in himself or that he is purporting to sell only such right or title as he or a third person may have.

(3) Unless otherwise agreed a seller who is a merchant regularly dealing in goods of the kind warrants that the goods shall be delivered free of the rightful claim of any third person by way of infringement or the like but a buyer who furnishes specifications to the seller must hold the seller harmless against any such claim which arises out of compliance with the specifications.

## § 2—313
### Express Warranties by Affirmation, Promise, Description, Sample

(1) Express warranties by the seller are created as follows:
   (a) Any affirmation of fact or promise made by the seller to the buyer which relates to the goods and becomes part of the basis of the bargain creates an express warranty that the goods shall conform to the affirmation or promise.
   (b) Any description of the goods which is made part of the basis of the bargain creates an express warranty that the goods shall conform to the description.
   (c) Any sample or model which is made part of the basis of the bargain creates an express warranty that the whole of the goods shall conform to the sample or model.

(2) It is not necessary to the creation of an express warranty that the seller use formal words such as "warrant" or "guarantee" or that he have a specific intention to make a warranty, but an affirmation merely of the value of the goods or a statement purporting to be merely the seller's opinion or commendation of the goods does not create a warranty.

## § 2—314
### Implied Warranty: Merchantability; Usage of Trade

(1) Unless excluded or modified (Section 2—316), a warranty that the goods shall be merchantable is implied in a contract for their sale if the seller is a merchant with respect to goods of that kind. Under this section the serving for value of food or drink to be consumed either on the premises or elsewhere is a sale.

(2) Goods to be merchantable must be at least such as
   (a) pass without objection in the trade under the contract description; and
   (b) in the case of fungible goods, are of fair average quality within the description; and
   (c) are fit for the ordinary purposes for which such goods are used; and
   (d) run, within the variations permitted by the agreement, of even kind, quality and quantity within each unit and among all units involved; and
   (e) are adequately contained, packaged, and labeled as the agreement may require; and
   (f) conform to the promises or affirmations of fact made on the container or label if any.

(3) Unless excluded or modified (Section 2—316) other implied warranties may arise from course of dealing or usage of trade.

## § 2—315
### Implied Warranty: Fitness for Particular Purpose

Where the seller at the time of contracting has reason to know any particular purpose for which the goods are required and that the buyer is relying on the seller's skill or judgment to select or furnish suitable goods, there is unless excluded or modified under the next section an implied warranty that the goods shall be fit for such purpose.

## § 2—316
### Exclusion or Modification of Warranties

(1) Words or conduct relevant to the creation of an express warranty and words or conduct tending to negate or limit warranty shall be construed wherever reasonable as consistent with each other; but subject to the provisions of this Article on parol or extrinsic evidence (Section 2—202) negation or limitation is inoperative to the extent that such construction is unreasonable.

(2) Subject to subsection (3), to exclude or modify the implied warranty of merchantability or any part of it the language must mention merchantability and in case of a writing must be conspicuous, and to exclude or modify any implied warranty of fitness the exclusion must be by a writing and conspicuous. Language to exclude all implied warranties of fitness is sufficient if it states, for example, that "There are no warranties which extend beyond the description on the face hereof."

(3) Notwithstanding subsection (2)
   (a) unless the circumstances indicate otherwise, all implied warranties are excluded by expressions like "as is", "with all faults" or other language which in common understanding calls the buyer's attention to the exclusion of warranties and makes plain that there is no implied warranty; and
   (b) when the buyer before entering into the contract has examined the goods or the sample or model as fully as he desired or has refused to examine the goods there is no implied warranty with regard to defects which an examination ought in the circumstances to have revealed to him; and
   (c) an implied warranty can also be excluded or modified by course of dealing or course of performance or usage of trade.

(4) Remedies for breach of warranty can be limited in accordance with the provisions of this Article on liquidation or limitation of damages and on contractual modification of remedy (Sections 2—718 and 2—719).

## § 2—317
### Cumulation and Conflict of Warranties Express or Implied

Warranties whether express or implied shall be construed as consistent with each other and as cumulative, but if such construction is unreasonable the intention of the parties shall determine which warranty is dominant. In ascertaining that intention the following rules apply:

(a) Exact or technical specifications displace an inconsistent sample or model or general language of description.

(b) A sample from an existing bulk displaces inconsistent general language of description.

(c) Express warranties displace inconsistent implied warranties other than an implied warranty of fitness for a particular purpose.

§ 2—318
**Third Party Beneficiaries of Warranties Express or Implied**

Note: *If this Act is introduced in the Congress of the United States this section should be omitted. (States to select one alternative.)*

*Alternative A*

A seller's warranty whether express or implied extends to any natural person who is in the family or household of his buyer or who is a guest in his home if it is reasonable to expect that such person may use, consume or be affected by the goods and who is injured in person by breach of the warranty. A seller may not exclude or limit the operation of this section.

*Alternative B*

A seller's warranty whether express or implied extends to any natural person who may reasonably be expected to use, consume or be affected by the goods and who is injured in person by breach of the warranty. A seller may not exclude or limit the operation of this section.

*Alternative C*

A seller's warranty whether express or implied extends to any person who may reasonably be expected to use, consume or be affected by the goods and who is injured by breach of the warranty. A seller may not exclude or limit the operation of this section with respect to injury to the person of an individual to whom the warranty extends. As amended 1966.

§ 2—319
**F.O.B. and F.A.S. Terms**

(1) Unless otherwise agreed the term F.O.B. (which means "free on board") at a named place, even though used only in connection with the stated price, is a delivery term under which

(a) when the term is F.O.B. the place of shipment, the seller must at that place ship the goods in the manner provided in this Article (Section 2—504) and bear the expense and risk of putting them into the possession of the carrier; or

(b) when the term is F.O.B. the place of destination, the seller must at his own expense and risk transport the goods to that place and there tender delivery of them in the manner provided in this Article (Section 2—503);

(c) when under either (a) or (b) the term is also F.O.B. vessel, car or other vehicle, the seller must in addition at his own expense and risk load the goods on board. If the term is F.O.B. vessel the buyer must name the vessel and in an appropriate case the seller must comply with the provisions of this Article on the form of bill of lading (Section 2—323).

(2) Unless otherwise agreed the term F.A.S. vessel (which means "free alongside") at a named port, even though used only in connection with the stated price, is a delivery term under which the seller must

(a) at his own expense and risk deliver the goods alongside the vessel in the manner usual in that port or on a dock designated and provided by the buyer; and

(b) obtain and tender a receipt for the goods in exchange for which the carrier is under a duty to issue a bill of lading.

(3) Unless otherwise agreed in any case falling within subsection (1)(a) or (c) or subsection (2) the buyer must seasonably give any needed instructions for making delivery, including when the term is F.A.S. or F.O.B. the loading berth of the vessel and in an appropriate case its name and sailing date. The seller may treat the failure of needed instructions as a failure of cooperation under this Article (Section 2—311). He may also at his option move the goods in any reasonable manner preparatory to delivery or shipment.

(4) Under the term F.O.B. vessel or F.A.S. unless otherwise agreed the buyer must make payment against tender of the required documents and the seller may not tender nor the buyer demand delivery of the goods in substitution for the documents.

§ 2—320
**C.I.F. and C. & F. Terms**

(1) The term C.I.F. means that the price includes in a lump sum the cost of the goods and the insurance and freight to the named destination. The term C. & F. or C.F. means that the price so includes cost and freight to the named destination.

(2) Unless otherwise agreed and even though used only in connection with the stated price and destination, the term C.I.F. destination or its equivalent requires the seller at his own expense and risk to

(a) put the goods into the possession of a carrier at the port for shipment and obtain a negotiable bill or bills of lading covering the entire transportation to the named destination; and

(b) load the goods and obtain a receipt from the carrier (which may be contained in the bill of lading) showing that the freight has been paid or provided for; and

(c) obtain a policy or certificate of insurance, including any war risk insurance, of a kind and on terms then current at the port of shipment in the usual amount, in the currency of the contract, shown to cover the same goods covered by the bill of lading and providing for payment of loss to the order of the buyer or for the account of whom it may concern; but the seller may add to the price the amount of the premium for any such war risk insurance; and

(d) prepare an invoice of the goods and procure any other documents required to effect shipment or to comply with the contract; and

(e) forward and tender with commercial promptness all the documents in due form and with any indorsement necessary to perfect the buyer's rights.

(3) Unless otherwise agreed the term C. & F. or its equivalent has the same effect and imposes upon the seller the same obligations and risks as a C.I.F. term except the obligation as to insurance.

(4) Under the term C.I.F. or C. & F. unless otherwise agreed the buyer must make payment against tender of the required documents and the seller may not tender nor the buyer demand delivery of the goods in substitution for the documents.

## § 2—321
### C.I.F. or C. & F.: "Net Landed Weights"; "Payment on Arrival"; Warranty of Condition on Arrival

Under a contract containing a term C.I.F. or C. & F.

**(1)** Where the price is based on or is to be adjusted according to "net landed weights", "delivered weights", "out turn" quantity or quality or the like, unless otherwise agreed the seller must reasonably estimate the price. The payment due on tender of the documents called for by the contract is the amount so estimated, but after final adjustment of the price a settlement must be made with commercial promptness.

**(2)** An agreement described in subsection (1) or any warranty of quality or condition of the goods on arrival places upon the seller the risk of ordinary deterioration, shrinkage and the like in transportation but has no effect on the place or time of identification to the contract for sale or delivery or on the passing of the risk of loss.

**(3)** Unless otherwise agreed where the contract provides for payment on or after arrival of the goods the seller must before payment allow such preliminary inspection as is feasible; but if the goods are lost delivery of the documents and payment are due when the goods should have arrived.

## § 2—322
### Delivery "Ex-Ship"

**(1)** Unless otherwise agreed a term for delivery of goods "ex-ship" (which means from the carrying vessel) or in equivalent language is not restricted to a particular ship and requires delivery from a ship which has reached a place at the named port of destination where goods of the kind are usually discharged.

**(2)** Under such a term unless otherwise agreed
  (a) the seller must discharge all liens arising out of the carriage and furnish the buyer with a direction which puts the carrier under a duty to deliver the goods; and
  (b) the risk of loss does not pass to the buyer until the goods leave the ship's tackle or are otherwise properly unloaded.

## § 2—323
### Form of Bill of Lading Required in Overseas Shipment; "Overseas"

**(1)** Where the contract contemplates overseas shipment and contains a term C.I.F. or C. & F. or F.O.B. vessel, the seller unless otherwise agreed must obtain a negotiable bill of lading stating that the goods have been loaded on board or, in the case of a term C.I.F. or C. & F., received for shipment.

**(2)** Where in a case within subsection (1) a bill of lading has been issued in a set of parts, unless otherwise agreed if the documents are not to be sent from abroad the buyer may demand tender of the full set; otherwise only one part of the bill of lading need be tendered. Even if the agreement expressly requires a full set
  (a) due tender of a single part is acceptable within the provisions of this Article on cure of improper delivery (subsection (1) of Section 2—508); and
  (b) even though the full set is demanded, if the documents are sent from abroad the person tendering an incomplete set may nevertheless require payment upon furnishing an indemnity which the buyer in good faith deems adequate.

**(3)** A shipment by water or by air or a contract contemplating such shipment is "overseas" insofar as by usage of trade or agreement it is subject to the commercial, financing or shipping practices characteristic of international deep water commerce.

## § 2—324
### "No Arrival, No Sale" Term

Under a term "no arrival, no sale" or terms of like meaning, unless otherwise agreed,
  (a) the seller must properly ship conforming goods and if they arrive by any means he must tender them on arrival but he assumes no obligation that the goods will arrive unless he has caused the non-arrival; and
  (b) where without fault of the seller the goods are in part lost or have so deteriorated as no longer to conform to the contract or arrive after the contract time, the buyer may proceed as if there had been casualty to identified goods (Section 2—613).

## § 2—325
### "Letter of Credit" Term; "Confirmed Credit"

**(1)** Failure of the buyer seasonably to furnish an agreed letter of credit is a breach of the contract for sale.

**(2)** The delivery to seller of a proper letter of credit suspends the buyer's obligation to pay. If the letter of credit is dishonored, the seller may on seasonable notification to the buyer require payment directly from him.

**(3)** Unless otherwise agreed the term "letter of credit" or "banker's credit" in a contract for sale means an irrevocable credit issued by a financing agency of good repute and, where the shipment is overseas, of good international repute. The term "confirmed credit" means that the credit must also carry the direct obligation of such an agency which does business in the seller's financial market.

## § 2—326
### Sale on Approval and Sale or Return; Consignment Sales and Rights of Creditors

**(1)** Unless otherwise agreed, if delivered goods may be returned by the buyer even though they conform to the contract, the transaction is
  (a) a "sale on approval" if the goods are delivered primarily for use, and
  (b) a "sale or return" if the goods are delivered primarily for resale.

**(2)** Except as provided in subsection (3), goods held on approval are not subject to the claims of the buyer's creditors until acceptance; goods held on sale or return are subject to such claims while in the buyer's possession.

**(3)** Where goods are delivered to a person for sale and such person maintains a place of business at which he deals in goods of the kind involved, under a name other than the name of the person making delivery, then with respect to claims of creditors of the person conducting the business the goods are deemed to be on sale or return. The provisions of this subsection are applicable even though an agreement purports to reserve title to the person making delivery until payment or resale or uses such words as "on consignment" or "on memorandum". However, this subsection is not applicable if the person making delivery

    (a) complies with an applicable law providing for a consignor's interest or the like to be evidenced by a sign, or

    (b) establishes that the person conducting the business is generally known by his creditors to be substantially engaged in selling the goods of others, or

    (c) complies with the filing provisions of the Article on Secured Transactions (Article 9).

(4) Any "or return" term of a contract for sale is to be treated as a separate contract for sale within the statute of frauds section of this Article (Section 2—201) and as contradicting the sale aspect of the contract within the provisions of this Article on parol or extrinsic evidence (Section 2—202).

§ 2—327
**Special Incidents of Sale on Approval and Sale or Return**

(1) Under a sale on approval unless otherwise agreed

    (a) although the goods are identified to the contract the risk of loss and the title do not pass to the buyer until acceptance; and

    (b) use of the goods consistent with the purpose of trial is not acceptance but failure seasonably to notify the seller of election to return the goods is acceptance, and if the goods conform to the contract acceptance of any part is acceptance of the whole; and

    (c) after due notification of election to return, the return is at the seller's risk and expense but a merchant buyer must follow any reasonable instructions.

(2) Under a sale or return unless otherwise agreed

    (a) the option to return extends to the whole or any commercial unit of the goods while in substantially their original condition, but must be exercised seasonably; and

    (b) the return is at the buyer's risk and expense.

§ 2—328
**Sale by Auction**

(1) In a sale by auction if goods are put up in lots each lot is the subject of a separate sale.

(2) A sale by auction is complete when the auctioneer so announces by the fall of the hammer or in other customary manner. Where a bid is made while the hammer is falling in acceptance of a prior bid the auctioneer may in his discretion reopen the bidding or declare the goods sold under the bid on which the hammer was falling.

(3) Such a sale is with reserve unless the goods are in explicit terms put up without reserve. In an auction with reserve the auctioneer may withdraw the goods at any time until he announces completion of the sale. In an auction without reserve, after the auctioneer calls for bids on an article or lot, that article or lot cannot be withdrawn unless no bid is made within a reasonable time. In either case a bidder may retract his bid until the auctioneer's announcement of completion of the sale, but a bidder's retraction does not revive any previous bid.

(4) If the auctioneer knowingly receives a bid on the seller's behalf or the seller makes or procures such a bid, and notice has not been given that liberty for such bidding is reserved, the buyer may at his option avoid the sale or take the goods at the price of the last good faith bid prior to the completion of the sale. This subsection shall not apply to any bid at a forced sale.

## Part 4/Title, Creditors and Good Faith Purchasers

§ 2—401
**Passing of Title; Reservation for Security; Limited Application of This Section**

Each provision of this Article with regard to the rights, obligations and remedies of the seller, the buyer, purchasers or other third parties applies irrespective of title to the goods except where the provision refers to such title. Insofar as situations are not covered by the other provisions of this Article and matters concerning title become material the following rules apply:

(1) Title to goods cannot pass under a contract for sale prior to their identification to the contract (Section 2—501), and unless otherwise explicitly agreed the buyer acquires by their identification a special property as limited by this Act. Any retention or reservation by the seller of the title (property) in goods shipped or delivered to the buyer is limited in effect to a reservation of a security interest. Subject to these provisions and to the provisions of the Article on Secured Transactions (Article 9), title to goods passes from the seller to the buyer in any manner and on any conditions explicitly agreed on by the parties.

(2) Unless otherwise explicitly agreed title passes to the buyer at the time and place at which the seller completes his performance with reference to the physical delivery of the goods, despite any reservation of a security interest and even though a document of title is to be delivered at a different time or place; and in particular and despite any reservation of a security interest by the bill of lading

    (a) if the contract requires or authorizes the seller to send the goods to the buyer but does not require him to deliver them at destination, title passes to the buyer at the time and place of shipment; but

    (b) if the contract requires delivery at destination, title passes on tender there.

(3) Unless otherwise explicitly agreed where delivery is to be made without moving the goods,

    (a) if the seller is to deliver a document of title, title passes at the time when and the place where he delivers such documents; or

    (b) if the goods are at the time of contracting already identified and no documents are to be delivered, title passes at the time and place of contracting.

(4) A rejection or other refusal by the buyer to receive or retain the goods, whether or not justified, or a justified revocation of acceptance revests title to the goods in the seller. Such revesting occurs by operation of law and is not a "sale".

§ 2—402
**Rights of Seller's Creditors Against Sold Goods**

(1) Except as provided in subsections (2) and (3), rights of unsecured creditors of the seller with respect to goods which have been identified to a contract for sale are subject to the buyer's

rights to recover the goods under this Article (Sections 2—502 and 2—716).

(2) A creditor of the seller may treat a sale or an identification of goods to a contract for sale as void if as against him a retention of possession by the seller is fraudulent under any rule of law of the state where the goods are situated, except that retention of possession in good faith and current course of trade by a merchant-seller for a commercially reasonable time after a sale or identification is not fraudulent.

(3) Nothing in this Article shall be deemed to impair the rights of creditors of the seller

(a) under the provisions of the Article on Secured Transactions (Article 9); or
(b) where identification to the contract or delivery is made not in current course of trade but in satisfaction of or as security for a pre-existing claim for money, security or the like and is made under circumstances which under any rule of law of the state where the goods are situated would apart from this Article constitute the transaction a fraudulent transfer or voidable preference.

## § 2—403
### Power to Transfer; Good Faith Purchase of Goods; "Entrusting"

(1) A purchaser of goods acquires all title which his transferor had or had power to transfer except that a purchaser of a limited interest acquires rights only to the extent of the interest purchased. A person with voidable title has power to transfer a good title to a good faith purchaser for value. When goods have been delivered under a transaction of purchase the purchaser has such power even though

(a) the transferor was deceived as to the identity of the purchaser, or
(b) the delivery was in exchange for a check which is later dishonored, or
(c) it was agreed that the transaction was to be a "cash sale", or
(d) the delivery was procured through fraud punishable as larcenous under the criminal law.

(2) Any entrusting of possession of goods to a merchant who deals in goods of that kind gives him power to transfer all rights of the entruster to a buyer in ordinary course of business.

(3) "Entrusting" includes any delivery and any acquiescence in retention of possession regardless of any condition expressed between the parties to the delivery or acquiescence and regardless of whether the procurement of the entrusting or the possessor's disposition of the goods have been such as to be larcenous under the criminal law.

(4) The rights of other purchasers of goods and of lien creditors are governed by the Articles on Secured Transactions (Article 9), Bulk Transfers (Article 6) and Documents of Title (Article 7).

## Part 5/Performance

### § 2—501
### Insurable Interest in Goods; Manner of Identification of Goods

(1) The buyer obtains a special property and an insurable interest in goods by identification of existing goods as goods to which the contract refers even though the goods so identified are nonconforming and he has an option to return or reject them. Such identification can be made at any time and in any manner explicitly agreed to by the parties. In the absence of explicit agreement identification occurs

(a) when the contract is made if it is for the sale of goods already existing and identified;
(b) if the contract is for the sale of future goods other than those described in paragraph (c), when goods are shipped, marked or otherwise designated by the seller as goods to which the contract refers;
(c) when the crops are planted or otherwise become growing crops or the young are conceived if the contract is for the sale of unborn young to be born within twelve months after contracting or for the sale of crops to be harvested within twelve months or the next normal harvest season after contracting whichever is longer.

(2) The seller retains an insurable interest in goods so long as title to or any security interest in the goods remains in him and where the identification is by the seller alone he may until default or insolvency or notification to the buyer that the identification is final substitute other goods for those identified.

(3) Nothing in this section impairs any insurable interest recognized under any other statute or rule of law.

### § 2—502
### Buyer's Right to Goods on Seller's Insolvency

(1) Subject to subsection (2) and even though the goods have not been shipped a buyer who has paid a part or all of the price of goods in which he has a special property under the provisions of the immediately preceding section may on making and keeping good a tender of any unpaid portion of their price recover them from the seller if the seller becomes insolvent within ten days after receipt of the first installment on their price.

(2) If the identification creating his special property has been made by the buyer he acquires the right to recover the goods only if they conform to the contract for sale.

### § 2—503
### Manner of Seller's Tender of Delivery

(1) Tender of delivery requires that the seller put and hold conforming goods at the buyer's disposition and give the buyer any notification reasonably necessary to enable him to take delivery. The manner, time and place for tender are determined by the agreement and this Article, and in particular

(a) tender must be at a reasonable hour, and if it is of goods they must be kept available for the period reasonably necessary to enable the buyer to take possession; but
(b) unless otherwise agreed the buyer must furnish facilities reasonably suited to the receipt of the goods.

(2) Where the case is within the next section respecting shipment tender requires that the seller comply with its provisions.

(3) Where the seller is required to deliver at a particular destination tender requires that he comply with subsection (1) and also in any appropriate case tender documents as described in subsections (4) and (5) of this section.

(4) Where goods are in the possession of a bailee and are to be delivered without being moved

(a) tender requires that the seller either tender a negotiable document of title covering such goods or procure acknowledgment by the bailee of the buyer's right to possession of the goods; but

(b) tender to the buyer of a non-negotiable document of title or of a written direction to the bailee to deliver is sufficient tender unless the buyer seasonably objects, and receipt by the bailee of notification of the buyer's rights fixes those rights as against the bailee and all third persons; but risk of loss of the goods and of any failure by the bailee to honor the non-negotiable document of title or to obey the direction remains on the seller until the buyer has had a reasonable time to present the document or direction, and a refusal by the bailee to honor the document or to obey the direction defeats the tender.

(5) Where the contract requires the seller to deliver documents
(a) he must tender all such documents in correct form, except as provided in this Article with respect to bills of lading in a set (subsection (2) of Section 2—323); and
(b) tender through customary banking channels is sufficient and dishonor of a draft accompanying the documents constitutes non-acceptance or rejection.

§ 2—504
**Shipment by Seller**

Where the seller is required or authorized to send the goods to the buyer and the contract does not require him to deliver them at a particular destination, then unless otherwise agreed he must
(a) put the goods in the possession of such a carrier and make such a contract for their transportation as may be reasonable having regard to the nature of the goods and other circumstances of the case; and
(b) obtain and promptly deliver or tender in due form any document necessary to enable the buyer to obtain possession of the goods or otherwise required by the agreement or by usage of trade; and
(c) promptly notify the buyer of the shipment.

Failure to notify the buyer under paragraph (c) or to make a proper contract under paragraph (a) is a ground for rejection only if material delay or loss ensues.

§ 2—505
**Seller's Shipment Under Reservation**

(1) Where the seller has identified goods to the contract by or before shipment:
(a) his procurement of a negotiable bill of lading to his own order or otherwise reserves in him a security interest in the goods. His procurement of the bill to the order of a financing agency or of the buyer indicates in addition only the seller's expectation of transferring that interest to the person named.
(b) a non-negotiable bill of lading to himself or his nominee reserves possession of the goods as security but except in a case of conditional delivery (subsection (2) of Section 2—507) a non-negotiable bill of lading naming the buyer as consignee reserves no security interest even though the seller retains possession of the bill of lading.

(2) When shipment by the seller with reservation of a security interest is in violation of the contract for sale it constitutes an improper contract for transportation within the preceding section but impairs neither the rights given to the buyer by shipment and identification of the goods to the contract nor the seller's powers as a holder of a negotiable document.

§ 2—506
**Rights of Financing Agency**

(1) A financing agency by paying or purchasing for value a draft which relates to a shipment of goods acquires to the extent of the payment or purchase and in addition to its own rights under the draft and any document of title securing it any rights of the shipper in the goods including the right to stop delivery and the shipper's right to have the draft honored by the buyer.

(2) The right to reimbursement of a financing agency which has in good faith honored or purchased the draft under commitment to or authority from the buyer is not impaired by subsequent discovery of defects with reference to any relevant document which was apparently regular on its face.

§ 2—507
**Effect of Seller's Tender; Delivery on Condition**

(1) Tender of delivery is a condition to the buyer's duty to accept the goods and, unless otherwise agreed, to his duty to pay for them. Tender entitles the seller to acceptance of the goods and to payment according to the contract.

(2) Where payment is due and demanded on the delivery to the buyer of goods or documents of title, his right as against the seller to retain or dispose of them is conditional upon his making the payment due.

§ 2—508
**Cure by Seller of Improper Tender or Delivery; Replacement**

(1) Where any tender or delivery by the seller is rejected because non-conforming and the time for performance has not yet expired, the seller may seasonably notify the buyer of his intention to cure and may then within the contract time make a conforming delivery.

(2) Where the buyer rejects a non-conforming tender which the seller had reasonable grounds to believe would be acceptable with or without money allowance the seller may if he seasonably notifies the buyer have a further reasonable time to substitute a conforming tender.

§ 2—509
**Risk of Loss in the Absence of Breach**

(1) Where the contract requires or authorizes the seller to ship the goods by carrier
(a) if it does not require him to deliver them at a particular destination, the risk of loss passes to the buyer when the goods are duly delivered to the carrier even though the shipment is under reservation (Section 2—505); but
(b) if it does require him to deliver them at a particular destination and the goods are there duly tendered while in the possession of the carrier, the risk of loss passes to the buyer when the goods are there duly so tendered as to enable the buyer to take delivery.

**(2)** Where the goods are held by a bailee to be delivered without being moved, the risk of loss passes to the buyer

    **(a)** on his receipt of a negotiable document of title covering the goods; or

    **(b)** on acknowledgment by the bailee of the buyer's right to possession of the goods; or

    **(c)** after his receipt of a non-negotiable document of title or other written direction to deliver, as provided in subsection (4)(b) of Section 2—503.

**(3)** In any case not within subsection (1) or (2), the risk of loss passes to the buyer on his receipt of the goods if the seller is a merchant; otherwise the risk passes to the buyer on tender of delivery.

**(4)** The provisions of this section are subject to contrary agreement of the parties and to the provisions of this Article on sale on approval (Section 2—327) and on effect of breach on risk of loss (Section 2—510).

### § 2—510
### Effect of Breach on Risk of Loss

**(1)** Where a tender or delivery of goods so fails to conform to the contract as to give a right of rejection the risk of their loss remains on the seller until cure or acceptance.

**(2)** Where the buyer rightfully revokes acceptance he may to the extent of any deficiency in his effective insurance coverage treat the risk of loss as having rested on the seller from the beginning.

**(3)** Where the buyer as to conforming goods already identified to the contract for sale repudiates or is otherwise in breach before risk of their loss has passed to him, the seller may to the extent of any deficiency in his effective insurance coverage treat the risk of loss as resting on the buyer for a commercially reasonable time.

### § 2—511
### Tender of Payment by Buyer; Payment by Check

**(1)** Unless otherwise agreed tender of payment is a condition to the seller's duty to tender and complete any delivery.

**(2)** Tender of payment is sufficient when made by any means or in any manner current in the ordinary course of business unless the seller demands payment in legal tender and gives any extension of time reasonably necessary to procure it.

**(3)** Subject to the provisions of this Act on the effect of an instrument on an obligation (Section 3—802), payment by check is conditional and is defeated as between the parties by dishonor of the check on due presentment.

### § 2—512
### Payment by Buyer Before Inspection

**(1)** Where the contract requires payment before inspection non-conformity of the goods does not excuse the buyer from so making payment unless

    **(a)** the non-conformity appears without inspection; or

    **(b)** despite tender of the required documents the circumstances would justify injunction against honor under the provisions of this Act (Section 5—114).

**(2)** Payment pursuant to subsection (1) does not constitute an acceptance of goods or impair the buyer's right to inspect or any of his remedies.

### § 2—513
### Buyer's Right to Inspection of Goods

**(1)** Unless otherwise agreed and subject to subsection (3), where goods are tendered or delivered or identified to the contract for sale, the buyer has a right before payment or acceptance to inspect them at any reasonable place and time and in any reasonable manner. When the seller is required or authorized to send the goods to the buyer, the inspection may be after their arrival.

**(2)** Expenses of inspection must be borne by the buyer but may be recovered from the seller if the goods do not conform and are rejected.

**(3)** Unless otherwise agreed and subject to the provisions of this Article on C.I.F. contracts (subsection (3) of Section 2—321), the buyer is not entitled to inspect the goods before payment of the price when the contract provides

    **(a)** for delivery "C.O.D." or on other like terms; or

    **(b)** for payment against documents of title, except where such payment is due only after the goods are to become available for inspection.

**(4)** A place or method of inspection fixed by the parties is presumed to be exclusive but unless otherwise expressly agreed it does not postpone identification or shift the place for delivery or for passing the risk of loss. If compliance becomes impossible, inspection shall be as provided in this section unless the place or method fixed was clearly intended as an indispensable condition failure of which voids the contract.

### § 2—514
### When Documents Deliverable on Acceptance; When on Payment

Unless otherwise agreed documents against which a draft is drawn are to be delivered to the drawee on acceptance of the draft if it is payable more than three days after presentment; otherwise, only on payment.

### § 2—515
### Preserving Evidence of Goods in Dispute

In furtherance of the adjustment of any claim or dispute

    **(a)** either party on reasonable notification to the other and for the purpose of ascertaining the facts and preserving evidence has the right to inspect, test and sample the goods including such of them as may be in the possession or control of the other; and

    **(b)** the parties may agree to a third party inspection or survey to determine the conformity or condition of the goods and may agree that the findings shall be binding upon them in any subsequent litigation or adjustment.

## Part 6/Breach, Repudiation and Excuse

### § 2—601
### Buyer's Rights on Improper Delivery

Subject to the provisions of this Article on breach in installment contracts (Section 2—612) and unless otherwise agreed under the sections on contractual limitations of remedy (Sections 2—718 and 2—719), if the goods or the tender of delivery fail in any respect to conform to the contract, the buyer may

(a) reject the whole; or
(b) accept the whole; or
(c) accept any commercial unit or units and reject the rest.

## § 2—602
### Manner and Effect of Rightful Rejection

(1) Rejection of goods must be within a reasonable time after their delivery or tender. It is ineffective unless the buyer seasonably notifies the seller.

(2) Subject to the provisions of the two following sections on rejected goods (Sections 2—603 and 2—604),
   (a) after rejection any exercise of ownership by the buyer with respect to any commercial unit is wrongful as against the seller; and
   (b) if the buyer has before rejection taken physical possession of goods in which he does not have a security interest under the provisions of this Article (subsection (3) of Section 2—711), he is under a duty after rejection to hold them with reasonable care at the seller's disposition for a time sufficient to permit the seller to remove them; but
   (c) the buyer has no further obligations with regard to goods rightfully rejected.

(3) The seller's rights with respect to goods wrongfully rejected are governed by the provisions of this Article on seller's remedies in general (Section 2—703).

## § 2—603
### Merchant Buyer's Duties as to Rightfully Rejected Goods

(1) Subject to any security interest in the buyer (subsection (3) of Section 2—711), when the seller has no agent or place of business at the market of rejection a merchant buyer is under a duty after rejection of goods in his possession or control to follow any reasonable instructions received from the seller with respect to the goods and in the absence of such instructions to make reasonable efforts to sell them for the seller's account if they are perishable or threaten to decline in value speedily. Instructions are not reasonable if on demand indemnity for expenses is not forthcoming.

(2) When the buyer sells goods under subsection (1), he is entitled to reimbursement from the seller or out of the proceeds for reasonable expenses of caring for and selling them, and if the expenses include no selling commission then to such commission as is usual in the trade or if there is none to a reasonable sum not exceeding ten per cent on the gross proceeds.

(3) In complying with this section the buyer is held only to good faith and good faith conduct hereunder is neither acceptance nor conversion nor the basis of an action for damages.

## § 2—604
### Buyer's Options as to Salvage of Rightfully Rejected Goods

Subject to the provisions of the immediately preceding section on perishables if the seller gives no instructions within a reasonable time after notification of rejection the buyer may store the rejected goods for the seller's account or reship them to him or resell them for the seller's account with reimbursement as provided in the preceding section. Such action is not acceptance or conversion.

## § 2—605
### Waiver of Buyer's Objections by Failure to Particularize

(1) The buyer's failure to state in connection with rejection a particular defect which is ascertainable by reasonable inspection precludes him from relying on the unstated defect to justify rejection or to establish breach
   (a) where the seller could have cured it if stated seasonably; or
   (b) between merchants when the seller has after rejection made a request in writing for a full and final written statement of all defects on which the buyer proposes to rely.

(2) Payment against documents made without reservation of rights precludes recovery of the payment for defects apparent on the face of the documents.

## § 2—606
### What Constitutes Acceptance of Goods

(1) Acceptance of goods occurs when the buyer
   (a) after a reasonable opportunity to inspect the goods signifies to the seller that the goods are conforming or that he will take or retain them in spite of their non-conformity; or
   (b) fails to make an effective rejection (subsection (1) of Section 2—602), but such acceptance does not occur until the buyer has had a reasonable opportunity to inspect them; or
   (c) does any act inconsistent with the seller's ownership; but if such act is wrongful as against the seller it is an acceptance only if ratified by him.

(2) Acceptance of a part of any commercial unit is acceptance of that entire unit.

## § 2—607
### Effect of Acceptance; Notice of Breach; Burden of Establishing Breach After Acceptance; Notice of Claim or Litigation to Person Answerable Over

(1) The buyer must pay at the contract rate for any goods accepted.

(2) Acceptance of goods by the buyer precludes rejection of the goods accepted and if made with knowledge of a non-conformity cannot be revoked because of it unless the acceptance was on the reasonable assumption that the non-conformity would be seasonably cured but acceptance does not of itself impair any other remedy provided by this Article for non-conformity.

(3) Where a tender has been accepted
   (a) the buyer must within a reasonable time after he discovers or should have discovered any breach notify the seller of breach or be barred from any remedy; and
   (b) if the claim is one for infringement or the like (subsection (3) of Section 2—312) and the buyer is sued as a result of such a breach he must so notify the seller within a reasonable time after he receives notice of the litigation or be barred from any remedy over for liability established by the litigation.

(4) The burden is on the buyer to establish any breach with respect to the goods accepted.

(5) Where the buyer is sued for breach of a warranty or other obligation for which the seller is answerable over
   (a) he may give his seller written notice of the litigation. If the notice states that the seller may come in and defend and

that if the seller does not do so he will be bound in any action against him by his buyer by any determination of fact common to the two litigations, then unless the seller after seasonable receipt of the notice does come in and defend he is so bound.

(b) if the claim is one for infringement or the like (subsection (3) of Section 2—312) the original seller may demand in writing that his buyer turn over to him control of the litigation including settlement or else be barred from any remedy over and if he also agrees to bear all expense and to satisfy any adverse judgment, then unless the buyer after seasonable receipt of the demand does turn over control the buyer is so barred.

(6) The provisions of subsections (3), (4) and (5) apply to any obligation of a buyer to hold the seller harmless against infringement or the like (subsection (3) of Section 2—312).

## § 2—608
### Revocation of Acceptance in Whole or in Part

(1) The buyer may revoke his acceptance of a lot or commercial unit whose non-conformity substantially impairs its value to him if he has accepted it

(a) on the reasonable assumption that its non-conformity would be cured and it has not been seasonably cured; or

(b) without discovery of such non-conformity if his acceptance was reasonably induced either by the difficulty of discovery before acceptance or by the seller's assurances.

(2) Revocation of acceptance must occur within a reasonable time after the buyer discovers or should have discovered the ground for it and before any substantial change in condition of the goods which is not caused by their own defects. It is not effective until the buyer notifies the seller of it.

(3) A buyer who so revokes has the same rights and duties with regard to the goods involved as if he had rejected them.

## § 2—609
### Right to Adequate Assurance of Performance

(1) A contract for sale imposes an obligation on each party that the other's expectation of receiving due performance will not be impaired. When reasonable grounds for insecurity arise with respect to the performance of either party the other may in writing demand adequate assurance of due performance and until he receives such assurance may if commercially reasonable suspend any performance for which he has not already received the agreed return.

(2) Between merchants the reasonableness of grounds for insecurity and the adequacy of any assurance offered shall be determined according to commercial standards.

(3) Acceptance of any improper delivery or payment does not prejudice the aggrieved party's right to demand adequate assurance of future performance.

(4) After receipt of a justified demand failure to provide within a reasonable time not exceeding thirty days such assurance of due performance as is adequate under the circumstances of the particular case is a repudiation of the contract.

## § 2—610
### Anticipatory Repudiation

When either party repudiates the contract with respect to a performance not yet due the loss of which will substantially impair the value of the contract to the other, the aggrieved party may

(a) for a commercially reasonable time await performance by the repudiating party; or

(b) resort to any remedy for breach (Section 2—703 or Section 2—711), even though he has notified the repudiating party that he would await the latter's performance and has urged retraction; and

(c) in either case suspend his own performance or proceed in accordance with the provisions of this Article on the seller's right to identify goods to the contract notwithstanding breach or to salvage unfinished goods (Section 2—704).

## § 2—611
### Retraction of Anticipatory Repudiation

(1) Until the repudiating party's next performance is due he can retract his repudiation unless the aggrieved party has since the repudiation cancelled or materially changed his position or otherwise indicated that he considers the repudiation final.

(2) Retraction may be by any method which clearly indicates to the aggrieved party that the repudiating party intends to perform, but must include any assurance justifiably demanded under the provisions of this Article (Section 2—609).

(3) Retraction reinstates the repudiating party's rights under the contract with due excuse and allowance to the aggrieved party for any delay occasioned by the repudiation.

## § 2—612
### "Installment Contract"; Breach

(1) An "installment contract" is one which requires or authorizes the delivery of goods in separate lots to be separately accepted, even though the contract contains a clause "each delivery is a separate contract" or its equivalent.

(2) The buyer may reject any installment which is non-conforming if the non-conformity substantially impairs the value of that installment and cannot be cured or if the non-conformity is a defect in the required documents; but if the non-conformity does not fall within subsection (3) and the seller gives adequate assurance of its cure the buyer must accept that installment.

(3) Whenever non-conformity or default with respect to one or more installments substantially impairs the value of the whole contract there is a breach of the whole. But the aggrieved party reinstates the contract if he accepts a non-conforming installment without seasonably notifying of cancellation or if he brings an action with respect only to past installments or demands performance as to future installments.

## § 2—613
### Casualty to Identified Goods

Where the contract requires for its performance goods identified when the contract is made, and the goods suffer casualty without fault of either party before the risk of loss passes to the buyer, or in a proper case under a "no arrival, no sale" term (Section 2—324) then

(a) if the loss is total the contract is voided; and

(b) if the loss is partial or the goods have so deteriorated as no longer to conform to the contract the buyer may nevertheless demand inspection and at his option either treat the contract as voided or accept the goods with due allowance from the contract price for the deterioration or the deficiency in quantity but without further right against the seller.

## § 2—614
### Substituted Performance

(1) Where without fault of either party the agreed berthing, loading, or unloading facilities fail or an agreed type of carrier becomes unavailable or the agreed manner of delivery otherwise becomes commercially impracticable but a commercially reasonable substitute is available, such substitute performance must be tendered and accepted.

(2) If the agreed means or manner of payment fails because of domestic or foreign governmental regulation, the seller may withhold or stop delivery unless the buyer provides a means or manner of payment which is commercially a substantial equivalent. If delivery has already been taken, payment by the means or in the manner provided by the regulation discharges the buyer's obligation unless the regulation is discriminatory, oppressive or predatory.

## § 2—615
### Excuse by Failure of Presupposed Conditions

Except so far as a seller may have assumed a greater obligation and subject to the preceding section on substituted performance:

(a) Delay in delivery or non-delivery in whole or in part by a seller who complies with paragraphs (b) and (c) is not a breach of his duty under a contract for sale if performance as agreed has been made impracticable by the occurrence of a contingency the non-occurrence of which was a basic assumption on which the contract was made or by compliance in good faith with any applicable foreign or domestic governmental regulation or order whether or not it later proves to be invalid.

(b) Where the causes mentioned in paragraph (a) affect only a part of the seller's capacity to perform, he must allocate production and deliveries among his customers but may at his option include regular customers not then under contract as well as his own requirements for further manufacture. He may so allocate in any manner which is fair and reasonable.

(c) The seller must notify the buyer seasonably that there will be delay or non-delivery and, when allocation is required under paragraph (b), of the estimated quota thus made available for the buyer.

## § 2—616
### Procedure on Notice Claiming Excuse

(1) Where the buyer receives notification of a material or indefinite delay or an allocation justified under the preceding section he may by written notification to the seller as to any delivery concerned, and where the prospective deficiency substantially impairs the value of the whole contract under the provisions of this Article relating to breach of installment contracts (Section 2—612), then also as to the whole,

(a) terminate and thereby discharge any unexecuted portion of the contract; or

(b) modify the contract by agreeing to take his available quota in substitution.

(2) If after receipt of such notification from the seller the buyer fails so to modify the contract within a reasonable time not exceeding thirty days the contract lapses with respect to any deliveries affected.

(3) The provisions of this section may not be negated by agreement except in so far as the seller has assumed a greater obligation under the preceding section.

## Part 7/Remedies

### § 2—701
### Remedies for Breach of Collateral Contracts Not Impaired

Remedies for breach of any obligation or promise collateral or ancillary to a contract for sale are not impaired by the provisions of this Article.

### § 2—702
### Seller's Remedies on Discovery of Buyer's Insolvency

(1) Where the seller discovers the buyer to be insolvent he may refuse delivery except for cash including payment for all goods theretofore delivered under the contract, and stop delivery under this Article (Section 2—705).

(2) Where the seller discovers that the buyer has received goods on credit while insolvent he may reclaim the goods upon demand made within ten days after the receipt, but if misrepresentation of solvency has been made to the particular seller in writing within three months before delivery the ten day limitation does not apply. Except as provided in this subsection the seller may not base a right to reclaim goods on the buyer's fraudulent or innocent misrepresentation of solvency or of intent to pay.

(3) The seller's right to reclaim under subsection (2) is subject to the rights of a buyer in ordinary course or other good faith purchaser under this Article (Section 2—403). Successful reclamation of goods excludes all other remedies with respect to them.

### § 2—703
### Seller's Remedies in General

Where the buyer wrongfully rejects or revokes acceptance of goods or fails to make a payment due on or before delivery or repudiates with respect to a part or the whole, then with respect to any goods directly affected and, if the breach is of the whole contract (Section 2—612), then also with respect to the whole undelivered balance, the aggrieved seller may

(a) withhold delivery of such goods;

(b) stop delivery by any bailee as hereafter provided (Section 2—705);

(c) proceed under the next section respecting goods still unidentified to the contract;

(d) resell and recover damages as hereafter provided (Section 2—706);

(e) recover damages for non-acceptance (Section 2—708) or in a proper case the price (Section 2—709);

(f) cancel.

## § 2—704
### Seller's Right to Identify Goods to the Contract Notwithstanding Breach or to Salvage Unfinished Goods

(1) An aggrieved seller under the preceding section may
    (a) identify to the contract conforming goods not already identified if at the time he learned of the breach they are in his possession or control;
    (b) treat as the subject of resale goods which have demonstrably been intended for the particular contract even though those goods are unfinished.

(2) Where the goods are unfinished an aggrieved seller may in the exercise of reasonable commercial judgment for the purposes of avoiding loss and of effective realization either complete the manufacture and wholly identify the goods to the contract or cease manufacture and resell for scrap or salvage value or proceed in any other reasonable manner.

## § 2—705
### Seller's Stoppage of Delivery in Transit or Otherwise

(1) The seller may stop delivery of goods in the possession of a carrier or other bailee when he discovers the buyer to be insolvent (Section 2—702) and may stop delivery of carload, truckload, planeload or larger shipments of express or freight when the buyer repudiates or fails to make a payment due before delivery or if for any other reason the seller has a right to withhold or reclaim the goods.

(2) As against such buyer the seller may stop delivery until
    (a) receipt of the goods by the buyer; or
    (b) acknowledgment to the buyer by any bailee of the goods except a carrier that the bailee holds the goods for the buyer; or
    (c) such acknowledgment to the buyer by a carrier by reshipment or as warehouseman; or
    (d) negotiation to the buyer of any negotiable document of title covering the goods.

(3) (a) To stop delivery the seller must so notify as to enable the bailee by reasonable diligence to prevent delivery of the goods.
    (b) After such notification the bailee must hold and deliver the goods according to the directions of the seller but the seller is liable to the bailee for any ensuing charges or damages.
    (c) If a negotiable document of title has been issued for goods the bailee is not obliged to obey a notification to stop until surrender of the document.
    (d) A carrier who has issued a non-negotiable bill of lading is not obliged to obey a notification to stop received from a person other than the consignor.

## § 2—706
### Seller's Resale Including Contract for Resale

(1) Under the conditions stated in Section 2—703 on seller's remedies, the seller may resell the goods concerned or the undelivered balance thereof. Where the resale is made in good faith and in a commercially reasonable manner the seller may recover the difference between the resale price and the contract price together with any incidental damages allowed under the provisions of this Article (Section 2—710), but less expenses saved in consequence of the buyer's breach.

(2) Except as otherwise provided in subsection (3) or unless otherwise agreed resale may be at public or private sale including sale by way of one or more contracts to sell or of identification to an existing contract of the seller. Sale may be as a unit or in parcels and at any time and place and on any terms but every aspect of the sale including the method, manner, time, place and terms must be commercially reasonable. The resale must be reasonably identified as referring to the broken contract, but it is not necessary that the goods be in existence or that any or all of them have been identified to the contract before the breach.

(3) Where the resale is at private sale the seller must give the buyer reasonable notification of his intention to resell.

(4) Where the resale is at public sale
    (a) only identified goods can be sold except where there is a recognized market for a public sale of futures in goods of the kind; and
    (b) it must be made at a usual place or market for public sale if one is reasonably available and except in the case of goods which are perishable or threaten to decline in value speedily the seller must give the buyer reasonable notice of the time and place of the resale; and
    (c) if the goods are not to be within the view of those attending the sale the notification of sale must state the place where the goods are located and provide for their reasonable inspection by prospective bidders; and
    (d) the seller may buy.

(5) A purchaser who buys in good faith at a resale takes the goods free of any rights of the original buyer even though the seller fails to comply with one or more of the requirements of this section.

(6) The seller is not accountable to the buyer for any profit made on any resale. A person in the position of a seller (Section 2—707) or a buyer who has rightfully rejected or justifiably revoked acceptance must account for any excess over the amount of his security interest, as hereinafter defined (subsection (3) of Section 2—711).

## § 2—707
### "Person in the Position of a Seller"

(1) A "person in the position of a seller" includes as against a principal an agent who has paid or become responsible for the price of goods on behalf of his principal or anyone who otherwise holds a security interest or other right in goods similar to that of a seller.

(2) A person in the position of a seller may as provided in this Article withhold or stop delivery (Section 2—705) and resell (Section 2—706) and recover incidental damages (Section 2—710).

## § 2—708
### Seller's Damages for Non-Acceptance or Repudiation

(1) Subject to subsection (2) and to the provisions of this Article with respect to proof of market price (Section 2—723), the measure of damages for non-acceptance or repudiation by the buyer is the difference between the market price at the time and place for tender and the unpaid contract price together with any incidental damages provided in this Article (Section 2—710), but less expenses saved in consequence of the buyer's breach.

(2) If the measure of damages provided in subsection (1) is inadequate to put the seller in as good a position as performance would

have done then the measure of damages is the profit (including reasonable overhead) which the seller would have made from full performance by the buyer, together with any incidental damages provided in this Article (Section 2—710), due allowance for costs reasonably incurred and due credit for payments or proceeds of resale.

§ 2—709
**Action for the Price**

**(1)** When the buyer fails to pay the price as it becomes due the seller may recover, together with any incidental damages under the next section, the price

(a) of goods accepted or of conforming goods lost or damaged within a commercially reasonable time after risk of their loss has passed to the buyer; and

(b) of goods identified to the contract if the seller is unable after reasonable effort to resell them at a reasonable price or the circumstances reasonably indicate that such effort will be unavailing.

**(2)** Where the seller sues for the price he must hold for the buyer any goods which have been identified to the contract and are still in his control except that if resale becomes possible he may resell them at any time prior to the collection of the judgment. The net proceeds of any such resale must be credited to the buyer and payment of the judgment entitles him to any goods not resold.

**(3)** After the buyer has wrongfully rejected or revoked acceptance of the goods or has failed to make a payment due or has repudiated (Section 2—610), a seller who is held not entitled to the price under this section shall nevertheless be awarded damages for non-acceptance under the preceding section.

§ 2—710
**Seller's Incidental Damages**

Incidental damages to an aggrieved seller include any commercially reasonable charges, expenses or commissions incurred in stopping delivery, in the transportation, care and custody of goods after the buyer's breach, in connection with return or resale of the goods or otherwise resulting from the breach.

§ 2—711
**Buyer's Remedies in General; Buyer's Security Interest in Rejected Goods**

**(1)** Where the seller fails to make delivery or repudiates or the buyer rightfully rejects or justifiably revokes acceptance then with respect to any goods involved, and with respect to the whole if the breach goes to the whole contract (Section 2—612), the buyer may cancel and whether or not he has done so may in addition to recovering so much of the price as has been paid

(a) "cover" and have damages under the next section as to all the goods affected whether or not they have been identified to the contract; or

(b) recover damages for non-delivery as provided in this Article (Section 2—713).

**(2)** Where the seller fails to deliver or repudiates the buyer may also

(a) if the goods have been identified recover them as provided in this Article (Section 2—502); or

(b) in a proper case obtain specific performance or replevy the goods as provided in this Article (Section 2—716).

**(3)** On rightful rejection or justifiable revocation of acceptance a buyer has a security interest in goods in his possession or control for any payments made on their price and any expenses reasonably incurred in their inspection, receipt, transportation, care and custody and may hold such goods and resell them in like manner as an aggrieved seller (Section 2—706).

§ 2—712
**"Cover"; Buyer's Procurement of Substitute Goods**

**(1)** After a breach within the preceding section the buyer may "cover" by making in good faith and without unreasonable delay any reasonable purchase of or contract to purchase goods in substitution for those due from the seller.

**(2)** The buyer may recover from the seller as damages the difference between the cost of cover and the contract price together with any incidental or consequential damages as hereinafter defined (Section 2—715), but less expenses saved in consequence of the seller's breach.

**(3)** Failure of the buyer to effect cover within this section does not bar him from any other remedy.

§ 2—713
**Buyer's Damages for Non-Delivery or Repudiation**

**(1)** Subject to the provisions of this Article with respect to proof of market price (Section 2—723), the measure of damages for non-delivery or repudiation by the seller is the difference between the market price at the time when the buyer learned of the breach and the contract price together with any incidental and consequential damages provided in this Article (Section 2—715), but less expenses saved in consequence of the seller's breach.

**(2)** Market price is to be determined as of the place for tender or, in cases of rejection after arrival or revocation of acceptance, as of the place of arrival.

§ 2—714
**Buyer's Damages for Breach in Regard to Accepted Goods**

**(1)** Where the buyer has accepted goods and given notification (subsection (3) of Section 2—607) he may recover as damages for any non-conformity of tender the loss resulting in the ordinary course of events from the seller's breach as determined in any manner which is reasonable.

**(2)** The measure of damages for breach of warranty is the difference at the time and place of acceptance between the value of the goods accepted and the value they would have had if they had been as warranted, unless special circumstances show proximate damages of a different amount.

**(3)** In a proper case any incidental and consequential damages under the next section may also be recovered.

§ 2—715
**Buyer's Incidental and Consequential Damages**

**(1)** Incidental damages resulting from the seller's breach include expenses reasonably incurred in inspection, receipt, transportation and care and custody of goods rightfully rejected, any commercially reasonable charges, expenses or commissions in connection with effecting cover and any other reasonable expense incident to the delay or other breach.

(2) Consequential damages resulting from the seller's breach include

(a) any loss resulting from general or particular requirements and needs of which the seller at the time of contracting had reason to know and which could not reasonably be prevented by cover or otherwise; and

(b) injury to person or property proximately resulting from any breach of warranty.

### § 2—716
**Buyer's Right to Specific Performance or Replevin**

(1) Specific performance may be decreed where the goods are unique or in other proper circumstances.

(2) The decree for specific performance may include such terms and conditions as to payment of the price, damages, or other relief as the court may deem just.

(3) The buyer has a right of replevin for goods identified to the contract if after reasonable effort he is unable to effect cover for such goods or the circumstances reasonably indicate that such effort will be unavailing or if the goods have been shipped under reservation and satisfaction of the security interest in them has been made or tendered.

### § 2—717
**Deduction of Damages From the Price**

The buyer on notifying the seller of his intention to do so may deduct all or any part of the damages resulting from any breach of the contract from any part of the price still due under the same contract.

### § 2—718
**Liquidation or Limitation of Damages; Deposits**

(1) Damages for breach by either party may be liquidated in the agreement but only at an amount which is reasonable in the light of the anticipated or actual harm caused by the breach, the difficulties of proof of loss, and the inconvenience or nonfeasibility of otherwise obtaining an adequate remedy. A term fixing unreasonably large liquidated damages is void as a penalty.

(2) Where the seller justifiably withholds delivery of goods because of the buyer's breach, the buyer is entitled to restitution of any amount by which the sum of his payments exceeds

(a) the amount to which the seller is entitled by virtue of terms liquidating the seller's damages in accordance with subsection (1), or

(b) in the absence of such terms, twenty per cent of the value of the total performance for which the buyer is obligated under the contract or $500, whichever is smaller.

(3) The buyer's right to restitution under subsection (2) is subject to offset to the extent that the seller establishes

(a) a right to recover damages under the provisions of this Article other than subsection (1), and

(b) the amount or value of any benefits received by the buyer directly or indirectly by reason of the contract.

(4) Where a seller has received payment in goods their reasonable value or the proceeds of their resale shall be treated as payments for the purposes of subsection (2); but if the seller has notice of the buyer's breach before reselling goods received in part performance, his resale is subject to the conditions laid down in this Article on resale by an aggrieved seller (Section 2—706).

### § 2—719
**Contractual Modification or Limitation of Remedy**

(1) Subject to the provisions of subsections (2) and (3) of this section and of the preceding section on liquidation and limitation of damages,

(a) the agreement may provide for remedies in addition to or in substitution for those provided in this Article and may limit or alter the measure of damages recoverable under this Article, as by limiting the buyer's remedies to return of the goods and repayment of the price or to repair and replacement of non-conforming goods or parts; and

(b) resort to a remedy as provided is optional unless the remedy is expressly agreed to be exclusive, in which case it is the sole remedy.

(2) Where circumstances cause an exclusive or limited remedy to fail of its essential purpose, remedy may be had as provided in this Act.

(3) Consequential damages may be limited or excluded unless the limitation or exclusion is unconscionable. Limitation of consequential damages for injury to the person in the case of consumer goods is prima facie unconscionable but limitation of damages where the loss is commercial is not.

### § 2—720
**Effect of "Cancellation" or "Rescission" on Claims for Antecedent Breach**

Unless the contrary intention clearly appears, expressions of "cancellation" or "rescission" of the contract or the like shall not be construed as a renunciation or discharge of any claim in damages for an antecedent breach.

### § 2—721
**Remedies for Fraud**

Remedies for material misrepresentation or fraud include all remedies available under this Article for non-fraudulent breach. Neither rescission or a claim for rescission of the contract for sale nor rejection or return of the goods shall bar or be deemed inconsistent with a claim for damages or other remedy.

### § 2—722
**Who Can Sue Third Parties for Injury to Goods**

Where a third party so deals with goods which have been identified to a contract for sale as to cause actionable injury to a party to that contract

(a) a right of action against the third party is in either party to the contract for sale who has title to or a security interest or a special property or an insurable interest in the goods; and if the goods have been destroyed or converted a right of action is also in the party who either bore the risk of loss under the contract for sale or has since the injury assumed that risk as against the other;

**(b)** if at the time of the injury the party plaintiff did not bear the risk of loss as against the other party to the contract for sale and there is no arrangement between them for disposition of the recovery, his suit or settlement is, subject to his own interest, as a fiduciary for the other party to the contract;

**(c)** either party may with the consent of the other sue for the benefit of whom it may concern.

### § 2—723
**Proof of Market Price: Time and Place**

**(1)** If an action based on anticipatory repudiation comes to trial before the time for performance with respect to some or all of the goods, any damages based on market price (Section 2—708 or Section 2—713) shall be determined according to the price of such goods prevailing at the time when the aggrieved party learned of the repudiation.

**(2)** If evidence of a price prevailing at the times or places described in this Article is not readily available the price prevailing within any reasonable time before or after the time described or at any other place which in commercial judgment or under usage of trade would serve as a reasonable substitute for the one described may be used, making any proper allowance for the cost of transporting the goods to or from such other place.

**(3)** Evidence of a relevant price prevailing at a time or place other than the one described in this Article offered by one party is not admissible unless and until he has given the other party such notice as the court finds sufficient to prevent unfair surprise.

### § 2—724
**Admissibility of Market Quotations**

Whenever the prevailing price or value of any goods regularly bought and sold in any established commodity market is in issue, reports in official publications or trade journals or in newspapers or periodicals of general circulation published as the reports of such market shall be admissible in evidence. The circumstances of the preparation of such a report may be shown to affect its weight but not its admissibility.

### § 2—725
**Statute of Limitations in Contracts for Sale**

**(1)** An action for breach of any contract for sale must be commenced within four years after the cause of action has accrued. By the original agreement the parties may reduce the period of limitation to not less than one year but may not extend it.

**(2)** A cause of action accrues when the breach occurs, regardless of the aggrieved party's lack of knowledge of the breach. A breach of warranty occurs when tender of delivery is made, except that where a warranty explicitly extends to future performance of the goods and discovery of the breach must await the time of such performance the cause of action accrues when the breach is or should have been discovered.

**(3)** Where an action commenced within the time limited by subsection (1) is so terminated as to leave available a remedy by another action for the same breach such other action may be commenced after the expiration of the time limited and within six months after the termination of the first action unless the termination resulted from voluntary discontinuance or from dismissal for failure or neglect to prosecute.

**(4)** This section does not alter the law on tolling of the statute of limitations nor does it apply to causes of action which have accrued before this Act becomes effective.

## ARTICLE 2A/LEASES

### *Part 1/General Provisions*

### § 2A—101
**Short Title**

This Article shall be known and may be cited as the Uniform Commercial Code—Leases.

### § 2A—102
**Scope**

This Article applies to any transaction, regardless of form, that creates a lease.

### § 2A—103
**Definitions and Index of Definitions**

**(1)** In this Article unless the context otherwise requires:

**(a)** "Buyer in ordinary course of business" means a person who in good faith and without knowledge that the sale to him [or her] is in violation of the ownership rights or security interest or leasehold interest of a third party in the goods buys in ordinary course from a person in the business of selling goods of that kind but does not include a pawnbroker. "Buying" may be for cash or by exchange of other property or on secured or unsecured credit and includes receiving goods or documents of title under a pre-existing contract for sale but does not include a transfer in bulk or as security for or in total or partial satisfaction of a money debt.

**(b)** "Cancellation" occurs when either party puts an end to the lease contract for default by the other party.

**(c)** "Commercial unit" means such a unit of goods as by commercial usage is a single whole for purposes of lease and division of which materially impairs its character or value on the market or in use. A commercial unit may be a single article, as a machine, or a set of articles, as a suite of furniture or a line of machinery, or a quantity, as a gross or carload, or any other unit treated in use or in the relevant market as a single whole.

**(d)** "Conforming" goods or performance under a lease contract means goods or performance that are in accordance with the obligations under the lease contract.

**(e)** "Consumer lease" means a lease that a lessor regularly engaged in the business of leasing or selling makes to a lessee, except an organization, who takes under the lease primarily for a personal, family, or household purpose, if the total payments to be made under the lease contract, excluding payments for options to renew or buy, do not exceed $25,000.

**(f)** "Fault" means wrongful act, omission, breach, or default.

**(g)** "Finance lease" means a lease in which (i) the lessor does not select, manufacture or supply the goods, (ii) the lessor acquires the goods or the right to possession and use of the goods in connection with the lease, and (iii) either the lessee receives a copy of the contract evidencing the lessor's purchase of the goods on or before signing the lease contract, or the lessee's approval of the contract evidencing the lessor's purchase of the goods is a condition to effectiveness of the lease contract.

(h) "Goods" means all things that are movable at the time of identification to the lease contract, or are fixtures (Section 2A—309), but the term does not include money, documents, instruments, accounts, chattel paper, general intangibles, or minerals or the like, including oil and gas, before extraction. The term also includes the unborn young of animals.

(i) "Installment lease contract" means a lease contract that authorizes or requires the delivery of goods in separate lots to be separately accepted, even though the lease contract contains a clause "each delivery is a separate lease" or its equivalent.

(j) "Lease" means a transfer of the right to possession and use of goods for a term in return for consideration, but a sale, including a sale on approval or a sale or return, or retention or creation of a security interest is not a lease. Unless the context clearly indicates otherwise, the term includes a sublease.

(k) "Lease agreement" means the bargain, with respect to the lease, of the lessor and the lessee in fact as found in their language or by implication from other circumstances including course of dealing or usage of trade or course of performance as provided in this Article. Unless the context clearly indicates otherwise, the term includes a sublease agreement.

(l) "Lease contract" means the total legal obligation that results from the lease agreement as affected by this Article and any other applicable rules of law. Unless the context clearly indicates otherwise, the term includes a sublease contract.

(m) "Leasehold interest" means the interest of the lessor or the lessee under a lease contract.

(n) "Lessee" means a person who acquires the right to possession and use of goods under a lease. Unless the context clearly indicates otherwise, the term includes a sublessee.

(o) "Lessee in ordinary course of business" means a person who in good faith and without knowledge that the lease to him [or her] is in violation of the ownership rights or security interest or leasehold interest of a third party in the goods, leases in ordinary course from a person in the business of selling or leasing goods of that kind but does not include a pawnbroker. "Leasing" may be for cash or by exchange of other property or on secured or unsecured credit and includes receiving goods or documents of title under a pre-existing lease contract but does not include a transfer in bulk or as security for or in total or partial satisfaction of a money debt.

(p) "Lessor" means a person who transfers the right to possession and use of goods under a lease. Unless the context clearly indicates otherwise, the term includes a sublessor.

(q) "Lessor's residual interest" means the lessor's interest in the goods after expiration, termination, or cancellation of the lease contract.

(r) "Lien" means a charge against or interest in goods to secure payment of a debt or performance of an obligation, but the term does not include a security interest.

(s) "Lot" means a parcel or a single article that is the subject matter of a separate lease or delivery, whether or not it is sufficient to perform the lease contract.

(t) "Merchant lessee" means a lessee that is a merchant with respect to goods of the kind subject to the lease.

(u) "Present value" means the amount as of a date certain of one or more sums payable in the future, discounted to the date certain. The discount is determined by the interest rate specified by the parties if the rate was not manifestly unreasonable at the time the transaction was entered into; otherwise, the discount is determined by a commercially reasonable rate that takes into account the facts and circumstances of each case at the time the transaction was entered into.

(v) "Purchase" includes taking by sale, lease, mortgage, security interest, pledge, gift, or any other voluntary transaction creating an interest in goods.

(w) "Sublease" means a lease of goods the right to possession and use of which was acquired by the lessor as a lessee under an existing lease.

(x) "Supplier" means a person from whom a lessor buys or leases goods to be leased under a finance lease.

(y) "Supply contract" means a contract under which a lessor buys or leases goods to be leased.

(z) "Termination" occurs when either party pursuant to a power created by agreement or law puts an end to the lease contract otherwise than for default.

(2) Other definitions applying to this Article and the sections in which they appear are:

"Accessions". Section 2A—310(1).
"Construction mortgage". Section 2A—309(1)(d).
"Encumbrance". Section 2A—309(1)(e).
"Fixtures". Section 2A—309(1)(a).
"Fixture filing". Section 2A—309(1)(b).
"Purchase money lease". Section 2A—309(1)(c).

(3) The following definitions in other Articles apply to this Article:

"Accounts". Section 9—106.
"Between merchants". Section 2—104(3).
"Buyer". Section 2—103(1)(a).
"Chattel paper". Section 9—105(1)(b).
"Consumer goods". Section 9—109(1).
"Documents". Section 9—105(1)(f).
"Entrusting". Section 2—403(3).
"General intangibles". Section 9—106.
"Good faith". Section 2—103(1)(b).
"Instruments". Section 9—105(1)(i).
"Merchant". Section 2—104(1).
"Mortgage". Section 9—105(1)(j).
"Pursuant to commitment". Section 9—105(1)(k).
"Receipt". Section 2—103(1)(c).
"Sale". Section 2—106(1).
"Sale on Approval". Section 2—326.
"Sale or Return". Section 2—326.
"Seller". Section 2—103(1)(d).

(4) In addition Article 1 contains general definitions and principles of construction and interpretation applicable throughout this Article.

§ 2A—104
**Leases Subject to Other Statutes**

(1) A lease, although subject to this Article, is also subject to any applicable:

(a) statute of the United States;
(b) certificate of title statute of this State: (list any certificate of title statutes covering automobiles, trailers, mobile homes, boats, farm tractors, and the like);
(c) certificate of title statute of another jurisdiction (Section 2A—105); or
(d) consumer protection statute of this State.

(2) In case of conflict between the provisions of this Article, other than Sections 2A—105, 2A—304(3) and 2A—305(3), and any statute referred to in subsection (1), the provisions of that statute control.

(3) Failure to comply with any applicable statute has only the effect specified therein.

### § 2A—105
**Territorial Application of Article to Goods Covered by Certificate of Title**

Subject to the provisions of Sections 2A—304(3) and 2A—305(3), with respect to goods covered by a certificate of title issued under a statute of this State or of another jurisdiction, compliance and the effect of compliance or noncompliance with a certificate of title statute are governed by the law (including the conflict of laws rules) of the jurisdiction issuing the certificate until the earlier of (a) surrender of the certificate, or (b) four months after the goods are removed from that jurisdiction and thereafter until a new certificate of title is issued by another jurisdiction.

### § 2A—106
**Limitation on Power of Parties to Consumer Lease to Choose Applicable Law and Judicial Forum**

(1) If the law chosen by the parties to a consumer lease is that of a jurisdiction other than a jurisdiction in which the lessee resides at the time the lease agreement becomes enforceable or within 30 days thereafter or in which the goods are to be used, the choice is not enforceable.

(2) If the judicial forum chosen by the parties to a consumer lease is a forum that would not otherwise have jurisdiction over the lessee, the choice is not enforceable.

### § 2A—107
**Waiver or Renunciation of Claim or Right After Default**

Any claim or right arising out of an alleged default or breach of warranty may be discharged in whole or in part without consideration by a written waiver or renunciation signed and delivered by the aggrieved party.

### § 2A—108
**Unconscionability**

(1) If the court as a matter of law finds a lease contract or any clause of a lease contract to have been unconscionable at the time it may enforce the remainder of the lease contract without the unconscionable clause, or it may so limit the application of any unconscionable clause as to avoid any unconscionable result.

(2) With respect to a consumer lease, if the court as a matter of law finds that a lease contract or any clause of a lease contract has been induced by unconscionable conduct or that unconscionable conduct has occurred in the collection of a claim arising from a lease contract, the court may grant appropriate relief.

(3) Before making a finding of unconscionability under subsection (1) or (2), the court, on its own motion or that of a party, shall afford the parties a reasonable opportunity to present evidence as to the setting, purpose, and effect of the lease contract or clause thereof, or of the conduct.

(4) In an action in which the lessee claims unconscionability with respect to a consumer lease:
(a) If the court finds unconscionability under subsection (1) or (2), the court shall award reasonable attorney's fees to the lessee.
(b) If the court does not find unconscionability and the lessee claiming unconscionability has brought or maintained an action he [or she] knew to be groundless, the court shall award reasonable attorney's fees to the party against whom the claim is made.
(c) In determining attorney's fees, the amount of the recovery on behalf of the claimant under subsections (1) and (2) is not controlling.

### § 2A—109
**Option to Accelerate at Will**

(1) A term providing that one party or his [or her] successor in interest may accelerate payment or performance or require collateral or additional collateral "at will" or "when he [or she] deems himself [or herself] insecure" or in words of similar import must be construed to mean that he [or she] has power to do so only if he [or she] in good faith believes that the prospect of payment or performance is impaired.

(2) With respect to a consumer lease, the burden of establishing good faith under subsection (1) is on the party who exercised the power; otherwise the burden of establishing lack of good faith is on the party against whom the power has been exercised.

## Part 2/Formation and Construction of Lease Contract

### § 2A—201
**Statute of Frauds**

(1) A lease contract is not enforceable by way of action or defense unless:
(a) the total payments to be made under the lease contract, excluding payments for options to renew or buy, are less than $1,000; or
(b) there is a writing, signed by the party against whom enforcement is sought or by that party's authorized agent, sufficient to indicate that a lease contract has been made between the parties and to describe the goods leased and the lease term.

(2) Any description of leased goods or of the lease term is sufficient and satisfies subsection (1)(b), whether or not it is specific, if it reasonably identifies what is described.

(3) A writing is not insufficient because it omits or incorrectly states a term agreed upon, but the lease contract is not enforceable under subsection (1)(b) beyond the lease term and the quantity of goods shown in this writing.

(4) A lease contract that does not satisfy the requirements of subsection (1), but which is valid in other respects, is enforceable:

(a) if the goods are to be specially manufactured or obtained for the lessee and are not suitable for lease or sale to others in the ordinary course of the lessor's business, and the lessor, before notice of repudiation is received and under circumstances that reasonably indicate that the goods are for the lessee, has made either a substantial beginning of their manufacture or commitments for their procurement;

(b) if the party against whom enforcement is sought admits in that party's pleading, testimony or otherwise in court that a lease contract was made, but the lease contract is not enforceable under this provision beyond the quantity of goods admitted; or

(c) with respect to goods that have been received and accepted by the lessee.

(5) The lease term under a lease contract referred to in subsection (4) is:

(a) if there is a writing signed by the party against whom enforcement is sought or by that party's authorized agent specifying the lease term, the term so specified;

(b) if the party against whom enforcement is sought admits in that party's pleading, testimony, or otherwise in court a lease term, the term so admitted; or

(c) a reasonable lease term.

## § 2A—202
### Final Written Expression: Parol or Extrinsic Evidence

Terms with respect to which the confirmatory memoranda of the parties agree or which are otherwise set forth in a writing intended by the parties as a final expression of their agreement with respect to such terms as are included therein may not be contradicted by evidence of any prior agreement or of a contemporaneous oral agreement but may be explained or supplemented:

(a) by course of dealing or usage of trade or by course of performance; and

(b) by evidence of consistent additional terms unless the court finds the writing to have been intended also as a complete and exclusive statement of the terms of the agreement.

## § 2A—203
### Seals Inoperative

The affixing of a seal to a writing evidencing a lease contract or an offer to enter into a lease contract does not render the writing a sealed instrument and the law with respect to sealed instruments does not apply to the lease contract or offer.

## § 2A—204
### Formation in General

(1) A lease contract may be made in any manner sufficient to show agreement, including conduct by both parties which recognizes the existence of a lease contract.

(2) An agreement sufficient to constitute a lease contract may be found although the moment of its making is undetermined.

(3) Although one or more terms are left open, a lease contract does not fail for indefiniteness if the parties have intended to make a lease contract and there is a reasonably certain basis for giving an appropriate remedy.

## § 2A—205
### Firm Offers

An offer by a merchant to lease goods to or from another person in a signed writing that by its terms gives assurance it will be held open is not revocable, for lack of consideration, during the time stated or, if no time is stated, for a reasonable time, but in no event may the period of irrevocability exceed 3 months. Any such term of assurance on a form supplied by the offeree must be separately signed by the offeror.

## § 2A—206
### Offer and Acceptance in Formation of Lease Contract

(1) Unless otherwise unambiguously indicated by the language or circumstances, an offer to make a lease contract must be construed as inviting acceptance in any manner and by any medium reasonable in the circumstances.

(2) If the beginning of a requested performance is a reasonable mode of acceptance, an offeror who is not notified of acceptance within a reasonable time may treat the offer as having lapsed before acceptance.

## § 2A—207
### Course of Performance or Practical Construction

(1) If a lease contract involves repeated occasions for performance by either party with knowledge of the nature of the performance and opportunity for objection to it by the other, any course of performance accepted or acquiesced in without objection is relevant to determine the meaning of the lease agreement.

(2) The express terms of a lease agreement and any course of performance, as well as any course of dealing and usage of trade, must be construed whenever reasonable as consistent with each other; but if that construction is unreasonable, express terms control course of performance, course of performance controls both course of dealing and usage of trade, and course of dealing controls usage of trade.

(3) Subject to the provisions of Section 2A—208 on modification and waiver, course of performance is relevant to show a waiver or modification of any term inconsistent with the course of performance.

## § 2A—208
### Modification, Rescission and Waiver

(1) An agreement modifying a lease contract needs no consideration to be binding.

(2) A signed lease agreement that excludes modification or rescission except by a signed writing may not be otherwise modified or rescinded, but, except as between merchants, such a requirement on a form supplied by a merchant must be separately signed by the other party.

(3) Although an attempt at modification or rescission does not satisfy the requirements of subsection (2), it may operate as a waiver.

(4) A party who has made a waiver affecting an executory portion of a lease contract may retract the waiver by reasonable notification received by the other party that strict performance will be

required of any term waived, unless the retraction would be unjust in view of a material change of position in reliance on the waiver.

### § 2A—209
**Lessee under Finance Lease as Beneficiary of Supply Contract**

**(1)** The benefit of the supplier's promises to the lessor under the supply contract and of all warranties, whether express or implied, under the supply contract, extends to the lessee to the extent of the lessee's leasehold interest under a finance lease related to the supply contract, but subject to the terms of the supply contract and all of the supplier's defenses or claims arising therefrom.

**(2)** The extension of the benefit of the supplier's promises to the lessee does not: (a) modify the rights and obligations of the parties to the supply contract, whether arising therefrom or otherwise, or (b) impose any duty or liability under the supply contract on the lessee.

**(3)** Any modification or rescission of the supply contract by the supplier and the lessor is effective against the lessee unless, prior to the modification or rescission, the supplier has received notice that the lessee has entered into a finance lease related to the supply contract. If the supply contract is modified or rescinded after the lessee enters the finance lease, the lessee has a cause of action against the lessor, and against the supplier if the supplier has notice of the lessee's entering the finance lease when the supply contract is modified or rescinded. The lessee's recovery from such action shall put the lessee in as good a position as if the modification or rescission had not occurred.

### § 2A—210
**Express Warranties**

**(1)** Express warranties by the lessor are created as follows:
(a) Any affirmation of fact or promise made by the lessor to the lessee which relates to the goods and becomes part of the basis of the bargain creates an express warranty that the goods will conform to the affirmation or promise.
(b) Any description of the goods which is made part of the basis of the bargain creates an express warranty that the goods will conform to the description.
(c) Any sample or model that is made part of the basis of the bargain creates an express warranty that the whole of the goods will conform to the sample or model.

**(2)** It is not necessary to the creation of an express warranty that the lessor use formal words, such as "warrant" or "guarantee," or that the lessor have a specific intention to make a warranty, but an affirmation merely of the value of the goods or a statement purporting to be merely the lessor's opinion or commendation of the goods does not create a warranty.

### § 2A—211
**Warranties Against Interference and Against Infringement; Lessee's Obligation Against Infringement**

**(1)** There is in a lease contract a warranty that for the lease term no person holds a claim to or interest in the goods that arose from an act or omission of the lessor, other than a claim by way of infringement or the like, which will interfere with the lessee's enjoyment of its leasehold interest.

**(2)** Except in a finance lease there is in a lease contract by a lessor who is a merchant regularly dealing in goods of the kind a warranty that the goods are delivered free of the rightful claim of any person by way of infringement or the like.

**(3)** A lessee who furnishes specifications to a lessor or a supplier shall hold the lessor and the supplier harmless against any claim by way of infringement or the like that arises out of compliance with the specifications.

### § 2A—212
**Implied Warranty of Merchantability**

**(1)** Except in a finance lease, a warranty that the goods will be merchantable is implied in a lease contract if the lessor is a merchant with respect to goods of that kind.

**(2)** Goods to be merchantable must be at least such as
(a) pass without objection in the trade under the description in the lease agreement;
(b) in the case of fungible goods, are of fair average quality within the description;
(c) are fit for the ordinary purposes for which goods of that type are used;
(d) run, within the variation permitted by the lease agreement, of even kind, quality, and quantity within each unit and among all units involved;
(e) are adequately contained, packaged, and labeled as the lease agreement may require; and
(f) conform to any promises or affirmations of fact made on the container or label.

**(3)** Other implied warranties may arise from course of dealing or usage of trade.

### § 2A—213
**Implied Warranty of Fitness for Particular Purpose**

Except in a finance of lease, if the lessor at the time the lease contract is made has reason to know of any particular purpose for which the goods are required and that the lessee is relying on the lessor's skill or judgment to select or furnish suitable goods, there is in the lease contract an implied warranty that the goods will be fit for that purpose.

### § 2A—214
**Exclusion or Modification of Warranties**

**(1)** Words or conduct relevant to the creation of an express warranty and words or conduct tending to negate or limit a warranty must be construed wherever reasonable as consistent with each other; but, subject to the provisions of Section 2A—202 on parol or extrinsic evidence, negation or limitation is inoperative to the extent that the construction is unreasonable.

**(2)** Subject to subsection (3), to exclude or modify the implied warranty of merchantability or any part of it the language must mention "merchantability", be by a writing, and be conspicuous. Subject to subsection (3), to exclude or modify any implied warranty of fitness the exclusion must be by a writing and be conspicuous. Language to exclude all implied warranties of fitness is sufficient if it is conspicuous and states, for example, "There is no warranty that the goods will be fit for a particular purpose".

(3) Notwithstanding subsection (2), but subject to subsection (4),

(a) unless the circumstances indicate otherwise, all implied warranties are excluded by expressions like "as is" or "with all faults" or by other language that in common understanding calls the lessee's attention to the exclusion of warranties and makes plain that there is no implied warranty, and is conspicuous;

(b) if the lessee before entering into the lease contract has examined the goods or the sample or model as fully as desired or has refused to examine the goods, there is no implied warranty with regard to defects that an examination ought in the circumstances to have revealed; and

(c) an implied warranty may also be excluded or modified by course of dealing, course of performance, or usage of trade.

(4) To exclude or modify a warranty against interference or against infringement (Section 2A—211) or any part of it, the language must be specific, be by a writing, and be conspicuous, unless the circumstances, including course of performance, course of dealing, or usage of trade, give the lessee reason to know that the goods are being leased subject to a claim or interest of any person.

### § 2A—215
### Cumulation and Conflict of Warranties Express or Implied

Warranties, whether express or implied, must be construed as consistent with each other and as cumulative, but if that construction is unreasonable, the intention of the parties determines which warranty is dominant. In ascertaining that intention the following rules apply:

(a) Exact or technical specifications displace an inconsistent sample or model or general language of description.

(b) A sample from an existing bulk displaces inconsistent general language of description.

(c) Express warranties displace inconsistent implied warranties other than an implied warranty of fitness for a particular purpose.

### § 2A—216
### Third-Party Beneficiaries of Express and Implied Warranties

*Alternative A*

A warranty to or for the benefit of a lessee under this Article, whether express or implied, extends to any natural person who is in the family or household of the lessee or who is a guest in the lessee's home if it is reasonable to expect that such person may use, consume, or be affected by the goods and who is injured in person by breach of the warranty. This section does not displace principles of law and equity that extend a warranty to or for the benefit of a lessee to other persons. The operation of this section may not be excluded, modified, or limited, but an exclusion, modification, or limitation of the warranty, including any with respect to rights and remedies, effective against the lessee is also effective against any beneficiary designated under this section.

*Alternative B*

A warranty to or for the benefit of a lessee under this Article, whether express or implied, extends to any natural person who may reasonably be expected to use, consume, or be affected by the goods and who is injured in person by breach of the warranty. This section does not displace principles of law and equity that extend a warranty to or for the benefit of a lessee to other persons. The operation of this section may not be excluded, modified, or limited, but an exclusion, modification, or limitation of the warranty, including any with respect to rights and remedies, effective against the lessee is also effective against the beneficiary designated under this section.

*Alternative C*

A warranty to or for the benefit of a lessee under this Article, whether express or implied, extends to any person who may reasonably be expected to use, consume, or be affected by the goods and who is injured by breach of the warranty. The operation of this section may not be excluded, modified, or limited with respect to injury to the person of an individual to whom the warranty extends, but an exclusion, modification, or limitation of the warranty, including any with respect to rights and remedies, effective against the lessee is also effective against the beneficiary designated under this section.

### § 2A—217
### Identification

Identification of goods to which a lease contract refers may be made at any time and in any manner explicitly agreed to by the parties. In the absence of explicit agreement, identification occurs:

(a) when the lease contract is made if the lease contract is for a lease of goods that are existing and identified;

(b) when the goods are shipped, marked, or otherwise designated by the lessor as goods to which the lease contract refers, if the lease contract is for a lease of goods that are not existing and identified; or

(c) when the young are conceived, if the lease contract is for a lease of unborn young of animals.

### § 2A—218
### Insurance and Proceeds

(1) A lessee obtains an insurable interest when existing goods are identified to the lease contract even though the goods identified are nonconforming and the lessee has an option to reject them.

(2) If a lessee has an insurable interest only by reason of the lessor's identification of the goods, the lessor, until default or insolvency or notification to the lessee that identification is final, may substitute other goods for those identified.

(3) Notwithstanding a lessee's insurable interest under subsections (1) and (2), the lessor retains an insurable interest until an option to buy has been exercised by the lessee and risk of loss has passed to the lessee.

(4) Nothing in this section impairs any insurable interest recognized under any other statute or rule of law.

(5) The parties by agreement may determine that one or more parties have an obligation to obtain and pay for insurance covering the goods and by agreement may determine the beneficiary of the proceeds of the insurance.

### § 2A—219
### Risk of Loss

(1) Except in the case of a finance lease, risk of loss is retained by the lessor and does not pass to the lessee. In the case of a finance lease, risk of loss passes to the lessee.

(2) Subject to the provisions of this Article on the effect of default on risk of loss (Section 2A—220), if risk of loss is to pass to the lessee and the time of passage is not stated, the following rules apply:
    (a) If the lease contract requires or authorizes the goods to be shipped by carrier.
        (i) and it does not require delivery at a particular destination, the risk of loss passes to the lessee when the goods are duly delivered to the carrier; but
        (ii) if it does require delivery at a particular destination and the goods are there duly tendered while in the possession of the carrier, the risk of loss passes to the lessee when the goods are there duly so tendered as to enable the lessee to take delivery.
    (b) If the goods are held by a bailee to be delivered without being moved, the risk of loss passes to the lessee on acknowledgment by the bailee of the lessee's right to possession of the goods.
    (c) In any case not within subsection (a) or (b), the risk of loss passes to the lessee on the lessee's receipt of the goods if the lessor, or, in the case of a finance lease, the supplier, is a merchant; otherwise the risk passes to the lessee on tender of delivery.

### § 2A—220
### Effect of Default on Risk of Loss

(1) Where risk of loss is to pass to the lessee and the time of passage is not stated:
    (a) If a tender or delivery of goods so fails to conform to the lease contract as to give a right of rejection, the risk of their loss remains with the lessor, or, in the case of a finance lease, the supplier, until cure or acceptance.
    (b) If the lessee rightfully revokes acceptance, he [or she], to the extent of any deficiency in his [or her] effective insurance coverage, may treat the risk of loss as having remained with the lessor from the beginning.

(2) Whether or not risk of loss is to pass to the lessee, if the lessee as to conforming goods already identified to a lease contract repudiates or is otherwise in default under the lease contract, the lessor, or, in the case of a finance lease, the supplier, to the extent of any deficiency in his [or her] effective insurance coverage may treat the risk of loss as resting on the lessee for a commercially reasonable time.

### § 2A—221
### Casualty to Identified Goods

If a lease contract requires goods identified when the lease contract is made, and the goods suffer casualty without fault of the lessee, the lessor or the supplier before delivery, or the goods suffer casualty before risk of loss passes to the lessee pursuant to the lease agreement or Section 2A—219, then:
    (a) if the loss is total, the lease contract is avoided; and
    (b) if the loss is partial or the goods have so deteriorated as to no longer conform to the lease contract, the lessee may nevertheless demand inspection and at his [or her] option either treat the lease contract as avoided or, except in a finance lease that is not a consumer lease, accept the goods with due allowance from the rent payable for the balance of the lease term for the deterioration or the deficiency in quantity but without further right against the lessor.

## Part 3/Effect Of Lease Contract

### § 2A—301
### Enforceability of Lease Contract

Except as otherwise provided in this Article, a lease contract is effective and enforceable according to its terms between the parties, against purchasers of the goods and against creditors of the parties.

### § 2A—302
### Title to and Possession of Goods

Except as otherwise provided in this Article, each provision of this Article applies whether the lessor or a third party has title to the goods, and whether the lessor, the lessee, or a third party has possession of the goods, notwithstanding any statute or rule of law that possession or the absence of possession is fraudulent.

### § 2A—303
### Alienability of Party's Interest Under Lease Contract or of Lessor's Residual Interest in Goods; Delegation of Performance; Assignment of Rights

(1) Any interest of a party under a lease contract and the lessor's residual interest in the goods may be transferred unless
    (a) the transfer is voluntary and the lease contract prohibits the transfer; or
    (b) the transfer materially changes the duty of or materially increases the burden or risk imposed on the other party to the lease contract, and within a reasonable time after notice of the transfer the other party demands that the transferee comply with subsection (2) and the transferee fails to comply.

(2) Within a reasonable time after demand pursuant to subsection (1)(b), the transferee shall:
    (a) cure or provide adequate assurance that he [or she] will promptly cure any default other than one arising from the transfer;
    (b) compensate or provide adequate assurance that he [or she] will promptly compensate the other party to the lease contract and any other person holding an interest in the lease contract, except the party whose interest is being transferred, for any loss to that party resulting from the transfer;
    (c) provide adequate assurance of future due performance under the lease contract; and
    (d) assume the lease contract.

(3) Demand pursuant to subsection (1)(b) is without prejudice to the other party's rights against the transferee and the party whose interest is transferred.

(4) An assignment of "the lease" or of "all my rights under the lease" or an assignment in similar general terms is a transfer of rights, and unless the language or the circumstances, as in an assignment for security, indicate the contrary, the assignment is a

delegation of duties by the assignor to the assignee and acceptance by the assignee constitutes a promise by him [or her] to perform those duties. This promise is enforceable by either the assignor or the other party to the lease contract.

(5) Unless otherwise agreed by the lessor and the lessee, no delegation of performance relieves the assignor as against the other party of any duty to perform or any liability for default.

(6) A right to damages for default with respect to the whole lease contract or a right arising out of the assignor's due performance of his [or her] entire obligation can be assigned despite agreement otherwise.

(7) To prohibit the transfer of an interest of a party under a lease contract, the language of prohibition must be specific, by a writing, and conspicuous.

## § 2A—304
### Subsequent Lease of Goods by Lessor

(1) Subject to the provisions of Section 2A—303, a subsequent lessee from a lessor of goods under an existing lease contract obtains, to the extent of the leasehold interest transferred, the leasehold interest in the goods that the lessor had or had power to transfer, and except as provided in subsection (2) and Section 2A—527(4), takes subject to the existing lease contract. A lessor with voidable title has power to transfer a good leasehold interest to a good faith subsequent lessee for value, but only to the extent set forth in the preceding sentence. When goods have been delivered under a transaction of purchase the lessor has that power even though:

(a) the lessor's transferor was deceived as to the identity of the lessor;
(b) the delivery was in exchange for a check which is later dishonored;
(c) it was agreed that the transaction was to be a "cash sale"; or
(d) the delivery was procured through fraud punishable as larcenous under the criminal law.

(2) A subsequent lessee in the ordinary course of business from a lessor who is a merchant dealing in goods of that kind to whom the goods were entrusted by the existing lessee before the interest of the subsequent lessee became enforceable against the lessor obtains, to the extent of the leasehold interest transferred, all of the lessor's and the existing lessee's rights to the goods, and takes free of the existing lease contract.

(3) A subsequent lessee from the lessor of goods that are subject to an existing lease contract and are covered by a certificate of title issued under a statute of this State or of another jurisdiction takes no greater rights than those provided both by this section and by the certificate of title statute.

## § 2A—305
### Sale or Sublease of Goods by Lessee

(1) Subject to the provisions of Section 2A—303, a buyer or sublessee from the lessee of goods under an existing lease contract obtains, to the extent of the interest transferred, the leasehold interest in the goods that the lessee had or had power to transfer, and except as provided in subsection (2) and Section 2A—511(4), takes subject to the existing lease contract. A lessee with a voidable leasehold interest has power to transfer a good leasehold interest to a good faith buyer for value or a good faith sublessee for value, but only to the extent set forth in the preceding sentence. When goods have been delivered under a transaction of lease the lessee has that power even though:

(a) the lessor was deceived as to the identify of the lessee;
(b) the delivery was in exchange for a check which is later dishonored; or
(c) the delivery was procured through fraud punishable as larcenous under the criminal law.

(2) A buyer in the ordinary course of business or a sublessee in the ordinary course of business from a lessee who is a merchant dealing in goods of that kind to whom the goods were entrusted by the lessor obtains, to the extent of the interest transferred, all of the lessor's and lessee's rights to the goods, and takes free of the existing lease contract.

(3) A buyer or sublessee from the lessee of goods that are subject to an existing lease contract and are covered by a certificate of title issued under a statute of this State or of another jurisdiction takes no greater rights than those provided both by this section and by the certificate of title statute.

## § 2A—306
### Priority of Certain Liens Arising by Operation of Law

If a person in the ordinary course of his [or her] business furnishes services or materials with respect to goods subject to a lease contract, a lien upon those goods in the possession of that person given by statute or rule of law for those materials or services takes priority over any interest of the lessor or lessee under the lease contract or this Article unless the lien is created by statute and the statute provides otherwise or unless the lien is created by rule of law and the rule of law provides otherwise.

## § 2A—307.
### Priority of Liens Arising by Attachment or Levy on, Security Interests in, and Other Claims to Goods

(1) Except as otherwise provided in Section 2A—306, a creditor of a lessee takes subject to the lease contract.

(2) Except as otherwise provided in subsections (3) and (4) of this section and in Sections 2A—306 and 2A—308, a creditor of a lessor takes subject to the lease contract:

(a) unless the creditor holds a lien that attached to the goods before the lease contract became enforceable, or
(b) unless the creditor holds a security interest in the goods that under the Article on Secured Transactions (Article 9) would have priority over any other security interest in the goods perfected by a filing covering the goods and made at the time the lease contract became enforceable, whether or not any other security interest existed.

(3) A lessee in the ordinary course of business takes the leasehold interest free of a security interest in the goods created by the lessor even though the security interest is perfected and the lessee knows of its existence.

(4) A lessee other than a lessee in the ordinary course of business takes the leasehold interest free of a security interest to the extent that it secures future advances made after the secured party acquires knowledge of the lease or more than 45 days after the lease contract becomes enforceable, whichever first occurs, unless the future advances are made pursuant to a commitment entered into

without knowledge of the lease and before the expiration of the 45-day period.

## § 2A—308
### Special Rights of Creditors

**(1)** A creditor of a lessor in possession of goods subject to a lease contract may treat the lease contract as void if as against the creditor retention of possession by the lessor is fraudulent under any statute or rule of law, but retention of possession in good faith and current course of trade by the lessor for a commercially reasonable time after the lease contract becomes enforceable is not fraudulent.

**(2)** Nothing in this Article impairs the rights of creditors of a lessor if the lease contract (a) becomes enforceable, not in current course of trade but in satisfaction of or as security for a pre-existing claim for money, security, or the like, and (b) is made under circumstances which under any statute or rule of law apart from this Article would constitute the transaction a fraudulent transfer or voidable preference.

**(3)** A creditor of a seller may treat a sale or an identification of goods to a contract for sale as void if as against the creditor retention of possession by the seller is fraudulent under any statute or rule of law, but retention of possession of the goods pursuant to a lease contract entered into by the seller as lessee and the buyer as lessor in connection with the sale or identification of the goods is not fraudulent if the buyer bought for value and in good faith.

## § 2A—309
### Lessor's and Lessee's Rights When Goods Become Fixtures

**(1)** In this section:
  **(a)** goods are "fixtures" when they become so related to particular real estate that an interest in them arises under real estate law;
  **(b)** a "fixture filing" is the filing, in the office where a mortgage on the real estate would be recorded or registered, of a financing statement concerning goods that are or are to become fixtures and conforming to the requirements of subsection (5) of Section 9—402;
  **(c)** a lease is a "purchase money lease" unless the lessee has possession or use of the goods or the right to possession or use of the goods before the lease agreement is enforceable;
  **(d)** a mortgage is a "construction mortgage" to the extent it secures an obligation incurred for the construction of an improvement on land including the acquisition cost of the land, if the recorded writing so indicates; and
  **(e)** "encumbrance" includes real estate mortgages and other liens on real estate and all other rights in real estate that are not ownership interests.

**(2)** Under this Article a lease may be of goods that are fixtures or may continue in goods that become fixtures, but no lease exists under this Article of ordinary building materials incorporated into an improvement on land.

**(3)** This Article does not prevent creation of a lease of fixtures pursuant to real estate law.

**(4)** The perfected interest of a lessor of fixtures has priority over a conflicting interest of an encumbrancer or owner of the real estate if:
  **(a)** the lease is a purchase money lease, the conflicting interest of the encumbrancer or owner arises before the goods become fixtures, the interest of the lessor is perfected by a fixture filing before the goods become fixtures or within ten days thereafter, and the lessee has an interest of record in the real estate or is in possession of the real estate; or
  **(b)** the interest of the lessor is perfected by a fixture filing before the interest of the encumbrancer or owner is of record, the lessor's interest has priority over any conflicting interest of a predecessor in title of the encumbrancer or owner, and the lessee has an interest of record in the real estate or is in possession of the real estate.

**(5)** The interest of a lessor of fixtures, whether or not perfected, has priority over the conflicting interest of an encumbrancer or owner of the real estate if:
  **(a)** the fixtures are readily removable factory or office machines, readily removable equipment that is not primarily used or leased for use in the operation of the real estate, or readily removable replacements of domestic appliances that are goods subject to a consumer lease, and before the goods become fixtures the lease contract is enforceable; or
  **(b)** the conflicting interest is a lien on the real estate obtained by legal or equitable proceedings after the lease contract is enforceable; or
  **(c)** the encumbrancer or owner has consented in writing to the lease or has disclaimed an interest in the goods as fixtures; or
  **(d)** the lessee has a right to remove the goods as against the encumbrancer or owner. If the lessee's right to remove terminates, the priority of the interest of the lessor continues for a reasonable time.

**(6)** Notwithstanding paragraph (a) of subsection (4) but otherwise subject to subsections (4) and (5), the interest of a lessor of fixtures is subordinate to the conflicting interest of an encumbrancer of the real estate under a construction mortgage recorded before the goods become fixtures if the goods become fixtures before the completion of the construction. To the extent given to refinance a construction mortgage, the conflicting interest of an encumbrancer of the real estate under a mortgage has this priority to the same extent as the encumbrancer of the real estate under the construction mortgage.

**(7)** In cases not within the preceding subsections, priority between the interest of a lessor of fixtures and the conflicting interest of an encumbrancer or owner of the real estate who is not the lessee is determined by the priority rules governing conflicting interests in real estate.

**(8)** If the interest of a lessor has priority over all conflicting interests of all owners and encumbrancers of the real estate, the lessor or the lessee may (a) on default, expiration, termination, or cancellation of the lease agreement by the other party but subject to the provisions of the lease agreement and this Article, or (b) if necessary to enforce his [or her] other rights and remedies under this Article, remove the goods from the real estate, free and clear of all conflicting interests of all owners and encumbrancers of the real estate, but he [or she] must reimburse any encumbrancer or owner of the real estate who is not the lessee and who has not otherwise agreed for the cost of repair of any physical injury, but not for any diminution in value of the real estate caused by the absence of the goods removed or by any necessity of replacing them. A person entitled to reimbursement may refuse permission to remove until the party seeking removal gives adequate security for the performance of this obligation.

(9) Even though the lease agreement does not create a security interest, the interest of a lessor of fixtures is perfected by filing a financing statement as a fixture filing for leased goods that are or are to become fixtures in accordance with the relevant provisions of the Article on Secured Transactions (Article 9).

## § 2A—310
### Lessor's and Lessee's Rights When Goods Become Accessions

(1) Goods are "accessions" when they are installed in or affixed to other goods.

(2) The interest of a lessor or a lessee under a lease contract entered into before the goods became accessions is superior to all interests in the whole except as stated in subsection (4).

(3) The interest of a lessor or a lessee under a lease contract entered into at the time or after the goods became accessions is superior to all subsequently acquired interests in the whole except as stated in subsection (4) but is subordinate to interests in the whole existing at the time the lease contract was made unless the holders of such interests in the whole have in writing consented to the lease or disclaimed an interest in the goods as part of the whole.

(4) The interest of a lessor or a lessee under a lease contract described in subsection (2) or (3) is subordinate to the interest of
   (a) a buyer in the ordinary course of business or a lessee in the ordinary course of business of any interest in the whole acquired after the goods became accessions; or
   (b) a creditor with a security interest in the whole perfected before the lease contract was made to the extent that the creditor makes subsequent advances without knowledge of the lease contract.

(5) When under subsections (2) or (3) and (4) a lessor or a lessee of accessions holds an interest that is superior to all interests in the whole, the lessor or the lessee may
   (a) on default, expiration, termination, or cancellation of the lease contract by the other party but subject to the provisions of the lease contract and this Article, or
   (b) if necessary to enforce his [or her] other rights and remedies under this Article, remove the goods from the whole, free and clear of all interests in the whole, but he [or she] must reimburse any holder of an interest in the whole who is not the lessee and who has not otherwise agreed for the cost of repair of any physical injury but not for any diminution in value of the whole caused by the absence of the goods removed or by any necessity for replacing them. A person entitled to reimbursement may refuse permission to remove until the party seeking removal gives adequate security for the performance of this obligation.

## Part 4/Performance Of Lease Contract: Repudiated, Substituted And Excused

### § 2A—401
### Insecurity: Adequate Assurance of Performance

(1) A lease contract imposes an obligation on each party that the other's expectation of receiving due performance will not be impaired.

(2) If reasonable grounds for insecurity arise with respect to the performance of either party, the insecure party may demand in writing adequate assurance of due performance. Until the insecure party receives that assurance, if commercially reasonable the insecure party may suspend any performance for which he [or she] has not already received the agreed return.

(3) A repudiation of the lease contract occurs if assurance of due performance adequate under the circumstances of the particular case is not provided to the insecure party within a reasonable time, not to exceed 30 days after receipt of a demand by the other party.

(4) Between merchants, the reasonableness of grounds for insecurity and the adequacy of any assurance offered must be determined according to commercial standards.

(5) Acceptance of any nonconforming delivery or payment does not prejudice the aggrieved party's right to demand adequate assurance of future performance.

### § 2A—402
### Anticipatory Repudiation

If either party repudiates a lease contract with respect to a performance not yet due under the lease contract, the loss of which performance will substantially impair the value of the lease contract to the other, the aggrieved party may:
   (a) for a commercially reasonable time, await retraction of repudiation and peformance by the repudiating party;
   (b) make demand pursuant to Section 2A—401 and await assurance of future performance adequate under the circumstances of the particular case; or
   (c) resort to any right or remedy upon default under the lease contract or this Article, even though the aggrieved party has notified the repudiating party that the aggrieved party would await the repudiating party's performance and assurance and has urged retraction. In addition, whether or not the aggrieved party is pursuing one of the foregoing remedies, the aggrieved party may suspend performance or, if the aggrieved party is the lessor, proceed in accordance with the provisions of this Article on the lessor's right to identify goods to the lease contract notwithstanding default or to salvage unfinished goods (Section 2A—524).

### § 2A—403
### Retraction of Anticipatory Repudiation

(1) Until the repudiating party's next performance is due, the repudiating party can retract the repudiation unless, since the repudiation, the aggrieved party has cancelled the lease contract or materially changed the aggrieved party's position or otherwise indicated that the aggrieved party considers the repudiation final.

(2) Retraction may be by any method that clearly indicates to the aggrieved party that the repudiating party intends to perform under the lease contract and includes any assurance demanded under Section 2A—401.

(3) Retraction reinstates a repudiating party's rights under a lease contract with due excuse and allowance to the aggrieved party for any delay occasioned by the repudiation.

### § 2A—404
### Substituted Performance

(1) If without fault of the lessee, the lessor and the supplier, the agreed berthing, loading, or unloading facilities fail or the agreed type of carrier becomes unavailable or the agreed manner of delivery otherwise becomes commercially impracticable, but a com-

mercially reasonable substitute is available, the substitute performance must be tendered and accepted.

(2) If the agreed means or manner of payment fails because of domestic or foreign governmental regulation:

(a) the lessor may withhold or stop delivery or cause the supplier to withhold or stop delivery unless the lessee provides a means or manner of payment that is commercially a substantial equivalent; and

(b) if delivery has already been taken, payment by the means or in the manner provided by the regulation discharges the lessee's obligation unless the regulation is discriminatory, oppressive, or predatory.

### § 2A—405
### Excused Performance

Subject to Section 2A—404 on substituted performance, the following rules apply:

(a) Delay in delivery or nondelivery in whole or in part by a lessor or a supplier who complies with paragraphs (b) and (c) is not a default under the lease contract if performance as agreed has been made impracticable by the occurrence of a contingency the nonoccurrence of which was a basic assumption on which the lease contract was made or by compliance in good faith with any applicable foreign or domestic governmental regulation or order, whether or not the regulation or order later proves to be invalid.

(b) If the causes mentioned in paragraph (a) affect only part of the lessor's or the supplier's capacity to perform, he [or she] shall allocate production and deliveries among his [or her] customers but at his [or her] option may include regular customers not then under contract for sale or lease as well as his [or her] own requirements for further manufacture. He [or she] may so allocate in any manner that is fair and reasonable.

(c) The lessor seasonably shall notify the lessee and in the case of a finance lease the supplier seasonably shall notify the lessor and the lessee, if known, that there will be delay or nondelivery and, if allocation is required under paragraph (b), of the estimated quota thus made available for the lessee.

### § 2A—406
### Procedure on Excused Performance

(1) If the lessee receives notification of a material or indefinite delay or an allocation justified under Section 2A—405, the lessee may by written notification to the lessor as to any goods involved, and with respect to all of the goods if under an installment lease contract the value of the whole lease contract is substantially impaired (Section 2A—510):

(a) terminate the lease contract (Section 2A—505(2)); or

(b) except in a finance lease that is not a consumer lease, modify the lease contract by accepting the available quota in substitution, with due allowance from the rent payable for the balance of the lease term for the deficiency but without further right against the lessor.

(2) If, after receipt of a notification from the lessor under Section 2A—405, the lessee fails so to modify the lease agreement within a reasonable time not exceeding 30 days, the lease contract lapses with respect to any deliveries affected.

### § 2A—407
### Irrevocable Promises: Finance Leases

(1) In the case of a finance lease that is not a consumer lease the lessee's promises under the lease contract become irrevocable and independent upon the lessee's acceptance of the goods.

(2) A promise that has become irrevocable and independent under subsection (1):

(a) is effective and enforceable between the parties or against third parties including assignees of the parties, and

(b) is not subject to cancellation, termination, modification, repudiation, excuse, or substitution without the consent of the party to whom the promise runs.

## Part 5/Default
## A. In General

### § 2A—501
### Default: Procedure

(1) Whether the lessor or the lessee is in default under a lease contract is determined by the lease agreement and this Article.

(2) If the lessor or the lessee is in default under the lease contract, the party seeking enforcement has rights and remedies as provided in this Article and, except as limited by this Article, as provided in the lease agreement.

(3) If the lessor or the lessee is in default under the lease contract, the party seeking enforcement may reduce the party's claim to judgment, or otherwise enforce the lease contract by self-help or any available judicial procedure or nonjudicial procedure, including administrative proceeding, arbitration, or the like, in accordance with this Article.

(4) Except as otherwise provided in this Article or the lease agreement, the rights and remedies referred to in subsections (2) and (3) are cumulative.

(5) If the lease agreement covers both real property and goods, the party seeking enforcement may proceed under this Part as to the goods, or under other applicable law as to both the real property and the goods in accordance with his [or her] rights and remedies in respect of the real property, in which case this Part does not apply.

### § 2A—502
### Notice After Default

Except as otherwise provided in this Article or the lease agreement, the lessor or lessee in default under the lease contract is not entitled to notice of default or notice of enforcement from the other party to the lease agreement.

### § 2A—503
### Modification or Impairment of Rights and Remedies

(1) Except as otherwise provided in this Article, the lease agreement may include rights and remedies for default in addition to or in substitution for those provided in this Article and may limit or alter the measure of damages recoverable under this Article.

(2) Resort to a remedy provided under this Article or in the lease agreement is optional unless the remedy is expressly agreed to be exclusive. If circumstances cause an exclusive or limited remedy

to fail of its essential purpose, or provision for an exclusive remedy is unconscionable, remedy may be had as provided in this Article.

(3) Consequential damages may be liquidated under Section 2A—504, or may otherwise be limited, altered, or excluded unless the limitation, alteration, or exclusion is unconscionable. Limitation of consequential damages for injury to the person in the case of consumer goods is prima facie unconscionable but limitation of damages where the loss is commercial is not.

(4) Rights and remedies on default by the lessor or the lessee with respect to any obligation or promise collateral or ancillary to the lease contract are not impaired by this Article.

## § 2A—504
### Liquidation of Damages

(1) Damages payable by either party for default, or any other act or omission, including indemnity for loss or diminution of anticipated tax benefits or loss or damage to lessor's residual interest, may be liquidated in the lease agreement but only at an amount or by a formula that is reasonable in light of the then anticipated harm caused by the default or other act or omission.

(2) If the lease agreement provides for liquidation of damages, and such provision does not comply with subsection (1), or such provision is an exclusive or limited remedy that circumstances cause to fail of its essential purpose, remedy may be had as provided in this Article.

(3) If the lessor justifiably withholds or stops delivery of goods because of the lessee's default or insolvency (Section 2A—525 or 2A—526), the lessee is entitled to restitution of any amount by which the sum of his [or her] payments exceeds:

  (a) the amount to which the lessor is entitled by virtue of terms liquidating the lessor's damages in accordance with subsection (1); or
  (b) in the absence of those terms, 20 percent of the then present value of the total rent the lessee was obligated to pay for the balance of the lease term, or, in the case of a consumer lease, the lesser of such amount or $500.

(4) A lessee's right to restitution under subsection (3) is subject to offset to the extent the lessor establishes:

  (a) a right to recover damages under the provisions of this Article other than subsection (1); and
  (b) the amount or value of any benefits received by the lessee directly or indirectly by reason of the lease contract.

## § 2A—505
### Cancellation and Termination and Effect of Cancellation, Termination, Rescission, or Fraud on Rights and Remedies

(1) On cancellation of the lease contract, all obligations that are still executory on both sides are discharged, but any right based on prior default or performance survives, and the cancelling party also retains any remedy for default of the whole lease contract or any unperformed balance.

(2) On termination of the lease contract, all obligations that are still executory on both sides are discharged but any right based on prior default or performance survives.

(3) Unless the contrary intention clearly appears, expressions of "cancellation," "rescission," or the like of the lease contract may not be construed as a renunciation or discharge of any claim in damages for an antecedent default.

(4) Rights and remedies for material misrepresentation or fraud include all rights and remedies available under this Article for default.

(5) Neither rescission nor a claim for rescission of the lease contract nor rejection or return of the goods may bar or be deemed inconsistent with a claim for damages or other right or remedy.

## § 2A—506
### Statute of Limitations

(1) An action for default under a lease contract, including breach of warranty or indemnity, must be commenced within 4 years after the cause of action accrued. By the original lease contract the parties may reduce the period of limitation to not less than one year.

(2) A cause of action for default accrues when the act or omission on which the default or breach of warranty is based is or should have been discovered by the aggrieved party, or when the default occurs, whichever is later. A cause of action for indemnity accrues when the act or omission on which the claim for indemnity is based is or should have been discovered by the indemnified party, whichever is later.

(3) If an action commenced within the time limited by subsection (1) is so terminated as to leave available a remedy by another action for the same default or breach of warranty or indemnity, the other action may be commenced after the expiration of the time limited within 6 months after the termination of the first action unless the termination resulted from voluntary discontinuance or from dismissal for failure or neglect to prosecute.

(4) This section does not alter the law on tolling of the statute of limitations nor does it apply to causes of action that have accrued before this Article becomes effective.

## § 2A—507
### Proof of Market Rent: Time and Place

(1) Damages based on market rent (Section 2A—519 or 2A—528) are determined according to the rent for the use of the goods concerned for a lease term identical to the remaining lease term of the original lease agreement and prevailing at the time of the default.

(2) If evidence of rent for the use of the goods concerned for a lease term identical to the remaining lease term of the original lease agreement and prevailing at the times or places described in this Article is not readily available, the rent prevailing within any reasonable time before or after the time described or at any other place or for a different lease term which in commercial judgment or under usage of trade would serve as a reasonable substitute for the one described may be used, making any proper allowance for the difference, including the cost of transporting the goods to or from the other place.

(3) Evidence of a relevant rent prevailing at a time or place or for a lease term other than the one described in this Article offered by one party is not admissible unless and until he [or she] has given the other party notice the court finds sufficient to prevent unfair surprise.

(4) If the prevailing rent or value of any goods regularly leased in any established market is in issue, reports in official publications or

trade journals or in newspapers or periodicals of general circulation published as the reports of that market are admissible in evidence. The circumstances of the preparation of the report may be shown to affect its weight but not its admissibility.

## B. Default by Lessor

### § 2A—508
### Lessee's Remedies

(1) If a lessor fails to deliver the goods in conformity to the lease contract (Section 2A—509) or repudiates the lease contract (Section 2A—402), or a lessee rightfully rejects the goods (Section 2A—509) or justifiably revokes acceptance of the goods (Section 2A—517), then with respect to any goods involved, and with respect to all of the goods if under an installment lease contract the value of the whole lease contract is substantially impaired (Section 2A—510), the lessor is in default under the lease contract and the lessee may:
    (a) cancel the lease contract (Section 2A—505(1));
    (b) recover so much of the rent and security as has been paid, but in the case of an installment lease contract the recovery is that which is just under the circumstances;
    (c) cover and recover damages as to all goods affected whether or not they have been identified to the lease contract (Sections 2A—518 and 2A—520), or recover damages for nondelivery (Sections 2A—519 and 2A—520).

(2) If a lessor fails to deliver the goods in conformity to the lease contract or repudiates the lease contract, the lessee may also:
    (a) if the goods have been identified, recover them (Section 2A—522); or
    (b) in a proper case, obtain specific performance or replevy the goods (Section 2A—521).

(3) If a lessor is otherwise in default under a lease contract, the lessee may exercise the rights and remedies provided in the lease contract and this Article.

(4) If a lessor has breached a warranty, whether express or implied, the lessee may recover damages (Section 2A—519(4)).

(5) On rightful rejection or justifiable revocation of acceptance, a lessee has a security interest in goods in the lessee's possession or control for any rent and security that has been paid and any expenses reasonably incurred in their inspection, receipt, transportation, and care and custody and may hold those goods and dispose of them in good faith and in a commercially reasonable manner, subject to the provisions of Section 2A—527(5).

(6) Subject to the provisions of Section 2A—407, a lessee, on notifying the lessor of the lessee's intention to do so, may deduct all or any part of the damages resulting from any default under the lease contract from any part of the rent still due under the same lease contract.

### § 2A—509
### Lessee's Rights on Improper Delivery; Rightful Rejection

(1) If a lessee elects not to cover or a lessee elects to cover and the cover does not qualify for treatment under Section 2A—518(2), the measure of damages for non-delivery or repudiation by the lessor is Subject or accept the goods or accept any commercial unit or units and reject the rest of the goods.

(2) Rejection of goods is ineffective unless it is within a reasonable time after tender or delivery of the goods and the lessee seasonably notifies the lessor.

### § 2A—510
### Installment Lease Contracts: Rejection and Default

(1) Under an installment lease contract a lessee may reject any delivery that is nonconforming if the nonconformity substantially impairs the value of that delivery and cannot be cured or the nonconformity is a defect in the required documents; but if the nonconformity does not fall within subsection (2) and the lessor or the supplier gives adequate assurance of its cure, the lessee must accept that delivery.

(2) Whenever nonconformity or default with respect to one or more deliveries substantially impairs the value of the installment lease contract as a whole there is a default with respect to the whole. But, the aggrieved party reinstates the installment lease contract as a whole if the aggrieved party accepts a nonconforming delivery without seasonably notifying of cancellation or brings an action with respect only to past deliveries or demands performance as to future deliveries.

### § 2A—511
### Merchant Lessee's Duties as to Rightfully Rejected Goods

(1) Subject to any security interest of a lessee (Section 2A—508(5)), if a lessor or a supplier has no agent or place of business at the market of rejection, a merchant lessee, after rejection of goods in his [or her] possession or control, shall follow any reasonable instructions received from the lessor or the supplier with respect to the goods. In the absence of those instructions, a merchant lessee shall make reasonable efforts to sell, lease, or otherwise dispose of the goods for the lessor's account if they threaten to decline in value speedily. Instructions are not reasonable if on demand indemnity for expenses is not forthcoming.

(2) If a merchant lessee (subsection (1)) or any other lessee (Section 2A—512) disposes of goods, he [or she] is entitled to reimbursement either from the lessor or the supplier or out of the proceeds for reasonable expenses of caring for and disposing of the goods and, if the expenses include no disposition commission, to such commission as is usual in the trade, or if there is none, to a reasonable sum not exceeding 10 percent of the gross proceeds.

(3) In complying with this section or Section 2A—512, the lessee is held only to good faith. Good faith conduct hereunder is neither acceptance or conversion nor the basis of an action for damages.

(4) A purchaser who purchases in good faith from a lessee pursuant to this section or Section 2A—512 takes the goods free of any rights of the lessor and the supplier even though the lessee fails to comply with one or more of the requirements of this Article.

### § 2A—512
### Lessee's Duties as to Rightfully Rejected Goods

(1) Except as otherwise provided with respect to goods that threaten to decline in value speedily (Section 2A—511) and subject to any security interest of a lessee (Section 2A—508(5)):
    (a) the lessee, after rejection of goods in the lessee's possession, shall hold them with reasonable care at the lessor's or

the supplier's disposition for a reasonable time after the lessee's seasonable notification of rejection;

(b) if the lessor or the supplier gives no instructions within a reasonable time after notification of rejection, the lessee may store the rejected goods for the lessor's or the supplier's account or ship them to the lessor or the supplier or dispose of them for the lessor's or the supplier's account with reimbursement in the manner provided in Section 2A—511; but

(c) the lessee has no further obligations with regard to goods rightfully rejected.

(2) Action by the lessee pursuant to subsection (1) is not acceptance or conversion.

§ 2A—513
### Cure by Lessor of Improper Tender or Delivery; Replacement

(1) If any tender or delivery by the lessor or the supplier is rejected because nonconforming and the time for performance has not yet expired, the lessor or the supplier may seasonably notify the lessee of the lessor's or the supplier's intention to cure and may then make a conforming delivery within the time provided in the lease contract.

(2) If the lessee rejects a nonconforming tender that the lessor or the supplier had reasonable grounds to believe would be acceptable with or without money allowance, the lessor or the supplier may have a further reasonable time to substitute a conforming tender if he [or she] seasonably notifies the lessee.

§ 2A—514
### Waiver of Lessee's Objections

(1) In rejecting goods, a lessee's failure to state a particular defect that is ascertainable by reasonable inspection precludes the lessee from relying on the defect to justify rejection or to establish default:

(a) if, stated seasonably, the lessor or the supplier could have cured it (Section 2A—513); or

(b) between merchants if the lessor or the supplier after rejection has made a request in writing for a full and final written statement of all defects on which the lessee proposes to rely.

(2) A lessee's failure to reserve rights when paying rent or other consideration against documents precludes recovery of the payment for defects apparent on the face of the documents.

§ 2A—515
### Acceptance of Goods

(1) Acceptance of goods occurs after the lessee has had a reasonable opportunity to inspect the goods and

(a) the lessee signifies or acts with respect to the goods in a manner that signifies to the lessor or the supplier that the goods are conforming or that the lessee will take or retain them in spite of their nonconformity; or

(b) the lessee fails to make an effective rejection of the goods (Section 2A—509(2)).

(2) Acceptance of a part of any commercial unit is acceptance of that entire unit.

§ 2A—516
### Effect of Acceptance of Goods; Notice of Default; Burden of Establishing Default after Acceptance; Notice of Claim or Litigation to Person Answerable Over

(1) A lessee must pay rent for any goods accepted in accordance with the lease contract, with due allowance for goods rightfully rejected or not delivered.

(2) A lessee's acceptance of goods precludes rejection of the goods accepted. In the case of a finance lease, if made with knowledge of a nonconformity, acceptance cannot be revoked because of it. In any other case, if made with knowledge of a nonconformity, acceptance cannot be revoked because of it unless the acceptance was on the reasonable assumption that the nonconformity would be seasonably cured. Acceptance does not of itself impair any other remedy provided by this Article or the lease agreement for nonconformity.

(3) If a tender has been accepted:

(a) within a reasonable time after the lessee discovers or should have discovered any default, the lessee shall notify the lessor and the supplier, or be barred from any remedy;

(b) except in the case of a consumer lease, within a reasonable time after the lessee receives notice of litigation for infringement or the like (Section 2A—211) the lessee shall notify the lessor or be barred from any remedy over for liability established by the litigation; and

(c) the burden is on the lessee to establish any default.

(4) If a lessee is sued for breach of a warranty or other obligation for which a lessor or a supplier is answerable over:

(a) The lessee may give the lessor or the supplier written notice of the litigation. If the notice states that the lessor or the supplier may come in and defend and that if the lessor or the supplier does not do so he [or she] will be bound in any action against him [or her] by the lessee by any determination of fact common to the two litigations, then unless the lessor or the supplier after seasonable receipt of the notice does come in and defend he [or she] is so bound.

(b) The lessor or the supplier may demand in writing that the lessee turn over control of the litigation including settlement if the claim is one for infringement or the like (Section 2A—211) or else be barred from any remedy over. If the demand states that the lessor or the supplier agrees to bear all expense and to satisfy any adverse judgment, then unless the lessee after seasonable receipt of the demand does turn over control the lessee is so barred.

(5) The provisions of subsections (3) and (4) apply to any obligation of a lessee to hold the lessor or the supplier harmless against infringement or the like (Section 2A—211).

§ 2A—517
### Revocation of Acceptance of Goods

(1) A lessee may revoke acceptance of a lot or commercial unit whose nonconformity substantially impairs its value to the lessee if he [or she] has accepted it:

(a) except in the case of a finance lease, on the reasonable assumption that its nonconformity would be cured and it has not been seasonably cured; or

(b) without discovery of the nonconformity if the lessee's acceptance was reasonably induced either by the lessor's assurances or, except in the case of a finance lease, by the difficulty of discovery before acceptance.

**(2)** Revocation of acceptance must occur within a reasonable time after the lessee discovers or should have discovered the ground for it and before any substantial change in condition of the goods which is not caused by the nonconformity. Revocation is not effective until the lessee notifies the lessor.

**(3)** A lessee who so revokes has the same rights and duties with regard to the goods involved as if the lessee had rejected them.

### § 2A—518
**Cover; Substitute Goods**

**(1)** After default by a lessor under the lease contract (Section 2A—508(1)), the lessee may cover by making in good faith and without unreasonable delay any purchase or lease of or contract to purchase or lease goods in substitution for those due from the lessor.

**(2)** Except as otherwise provided with respect to damages liquidated in the lease agreement (Section 2A—504) or determined by agreement of the parties (Section 1—102(3)), if a lessee's cover is by lease agreement substantially similar to the original lease agreement and the lease agreement is made in good faith and in a commercially reasonable manner, the lessee may recover from the lessor as damages (a) the present value, as of the date of defaut, of the difference between the total rent for the lease term of the new lease agreement and the total rent for the remaining lease term of the original lease agreement and (b) any incidental or consequential damages less expenses saved in consequence of the lessor's default.

**(3)** If a lessee's cover does not qualify for treatment under subsection (2), the lessee may recover from the lessor as if the lessee had elected not to cover and Section 2A—519 governs.

### § 2A—519
**Lessee's Damages for Non-Delivery, Repudiation, Default and Breach of Warranty in Regard to Accepted Goods**

**(1)** If a lessee elects not to cover or a lessee elects to cover and the cover does not qualify for treatment under Section 2A—518(2), the measure of damages for non-delivery or repudiation by the lessor or for rejection or revocation of acceptance by the lessee is the present value as of the date of the default of the difference between the then market rent and the original rent, computed for the remaining lease term of the original lease agreement together with incidental and consequential damages, less expenses saved in consequence of the lessor's default.

**(2)** Market rent is to be determined as of the place for tender or, in cases of rejection after arrival or revocation of acceptance, as of the place of arrival.

**(3)** If the lessee has accepted goods and given notification (Section 2A—516(3)), the measure of damages for non-conforming tender or delivery by a lessor is the loss resulting in the ordinary course of events from the lessor's default as determined in any manner that is reasonable together with incidental and consequential damages, less expenses saved in consequence of the lessor's default.

**(4)** The measure of damages for breach of warranty is the present value at the time and place of acceptance of the difference between the value of the use of the goods accepted and the value if they had been as warranted for the lease term, unless special circumstances show proximate damages of a different amount, together with incidental and consequential damages, less expenses saved in consequence of the lessor's default or breach of warranty.

### § 2A—520
**Lessee's Incidental and Consequential Damages**

**(1)** Incidental damages resulting from a lessor's default include expenses reasonably incurred in inspection, receipt, transportation, and care and custody of goods rightfully rejected or goods the acceptance of which is justifiably revoked, any commercially reasonable charges, expenses or commissions in connection with effecting cover, and any other reasonable expense incident to the default.

**(2)** Consequential damages resulting from a lessor's default include:
   **(a)** any loss resulting from general or particular requirements and needs of which the lessor at the time of contracting had reason to know and which could not reasonably be prevented by cover or otherwise; and
   **(b)** injury to person or property proximately resulting from any breach of warranty.

### § 2A—521
**Lessee's Right to Specific Performance or Replevin**

**(1)** Specific performance may be decreed if the goods are unique or in other proper circumstances.

**(2)** A decree for specific performance may include any terms and conditions as to payment of the rent, damages, or other relief that the court deems just.

**(3)** A lessee has a right of replevin, detinue, sequestration, claim and delivery, or the like for goods identified to the lease contract if after reasonable effort the lessee is unable to effect cover for those goods or the circumstances reasonably indicate that the effort will be unavailing.

### § 2A—522
**Lessee's Right to Goods on Lessor's Insolvency**

**(1)** Subject to subsection (2) and even though the goods have not been shipped, a lessee who has paid a part or all of the rent and security for goods identified to a lease contract (Section 2A—217) on making and keeping good a tender of any unpaid portion of the rent and security due under the lease contract may recover the goods identified from the lessor if the lessor becomes insolvent within 10 days after receipt of the first installment of rent and security.

**(2)** A lessee acquires the right to recover goods identified to a lease contract only if they conform to the lease contract.

## C. Default by Lessee

### § 2A—523
**Lessor's Remedies**

**(1)** If a lessee wrongfully rejects or revokes acceptance of goods or fails to make a payment when due or repudiates with respect to a part or the whole, then, with respect to any goods involved, and with respect to all of the goods if under an installment lease contract the value of the whole lease contract is substantially impaired (Section 2A—510), the lessee is in default under the lease contract and the lessor may:

(a) cancel the lease contract (Section 2A—505(1));

(b) proceed respecting goods not identified to the lease contract (Section 2A—524);

(c) withhold delivery of the goods and take possession of goods previously delivered (Section 2A—525);

(d) stop delivery of the goods by any bailee (Section 2A—526);

(e) dispose of the goods and recover damages (Section 2A—527), or retain the goods and recover damages (Section 2A—528), or in a proper case recover rent (Section 2A—529).

(2) If a lessee is otherwise in default under a lease contract, the lessor may exercise the rights and remedies provided in the lease contract and this Article.

§ 2A—524
**Lessor's Right to Identify Goods to Lease Contract**

(1) A lessor aggrieved under Section 2A—523(1) may:

(a) identify to the lease contract conforming goods not already identified if at the time the lessor learned of the default they were in the lessor's or the supplier's possession or control; and

(b) dispose of goods (Section 2A—527(1)) that demonstrably have been intended for the particular lease contract even though those goods are unfinished.

(2) If the goods are unfinished, in the exercise of reasonable commercial judgment for the purposes of avoiding loss and of effective realization, an aggrieved lessor or the supplier may either complete manufacture and wholly identify the goods to the lease contract or cease manufacture and lease, sell, or otherwise dispose of the goods for scrap or salvage value or proceed in any other reasonable manner.

§ 2A—525
**Lessor's Right to Possession of Goods**

(1) If a lessor discovers the lessee to be insolvent, the lessor may refuse to deliver the goods.

(2) The lessor has on default by the lessee under the lease contract the right to take possession of the goods. If the lease contract so provides, the lessor may require the lessee to assemble the goods and make them available to the lessor at a place to be designated by the lessor which is reasonably convenient to both parties. Without removal, the lessor may render unusable any goods employed in trade or business, and may dispose of goods on the lessee's premises (Section 2A—527).

(3) The lessor may proceed under subsection (2) without judicial process if that can be done without breach of the peace or the lessor may proceed by action.

§ 2A—526
**Lessor's Stoppage of Delivery in Transit or Otherwise**

(1) A lessor may stop delivery of goods in the possession of a carrier or other bailee if the lessor discovers the lessee to be insolvent and may stop delivery of carload, truckload, planeload, or larger shipments of express or freight if the lessee repudiates or fails to make a payment due before delivery, whether for rent, security or otherwise under the lease contract, or for any other reason the lessor has a right to withhold or take possession of the goods.

(2) In pursuing its remedies under subsection (1) the lessor may stop delivery until

(a) receipt of the goods by the lessee;

(b) acknowledgment to the lessee by any bailee of the goods, except a carrier, that the bailee holds the goods for the lessee; or

(c) such an acknowledgment to the lessee by a carrier via reshipment or as warehouseman.

(3) (a) To stop delivery, a lessor shall so notify as to enable the bailee by reasonable diligence to prevent delivery of the goods.

(b) After notification, the bailee shall hold and deliver the goods according to the directions of the lessor, but the lessor is liable to the bailee for any ensuing charges or damages.

(c) A carrier who has issued a nonnegotiable bill of lading is not obliged to obey a notification to stop received from a person other than the consignor.

§ 2A—527
**Lessor's Rights to Dispose of Goods**

(1) After a default by a lessee under the lease contract (Section 2A—523(1)) or after the lessor refuses to deliver or take possession of goods (Section 2A—525 or 2A—526), the lessor may dispose of the goods concerned or the undelivered balance thereof in good faith and without unreasonable delay by lease, sale or otherwise.

(2) If the disposition is by lease contract substantially similar to the original lease contract and the lease contract is made in good faith and in a commercially reasonable manner, the lessor may recover from the lessee as damages (a) accrued and unpaid rent as of the date of default, (b) the present value as of the date of default of the difference between the total rent for the remaining lease term of the original lease contract and the total rent for the lease term of the new lease contract, and (c) any incidental damages allowed under Section 2A—530, less expenses saved in consequence of the lessee's default.

(3) If the lessor's disposition is by lease contract that for any reason does not qualify for treatment under subsection (2), or is by sale or otherwise, the lessor may recover from the lessee as if the lessor had elected not to dispose of the goods and Section 2A—528 governs.

(4) A subsequent buyer or lessee who buys or leases from the lessor in good faith for value as a result of a disposition under this section takes the goods free of the original lease contract and any rights of the original lessee even though the lessor fails to comply with one or more of the requirements of this Article.

(5) The lessor is not accountable to the lessee for any profit made on any disposition. A lessee who has rightfully rejected or justifiably revoked acceptance shall account to the lessor for any excess over the amount of the lessee's security interest (Section 2A—508(5)).

### § 2A—528
**Lessor's Damages for Non-Acceptance or Repudiation**

(1) Except as otherwise provided with respect to damages liquidated in the lease agreement (Section 2A—504) or determined by agreement of the parties (Section 1—102(3)), if a lessor elects to retain the goods or a lessor elects to dispose of the goods and disposition is by lease agreement that for any reason does not qualify for treatment under Section 2A—527(2), or is by sale or otherwise, the lessor may recover from the lessee as damages for non-acceptance or repudiation by the lessee (a) accrued and unpaid rent as of the date of default, (b) the present value as of the date of default of the difference between the total rent for the remaining lease term of the original lease agreement and the market rent at the time and place for tender computed for the same lease term, and (c) any incidental damages allowed under Section 2A—530, less expenses saved in consequence of the lessee's default.

(2) If the measure of damages provided in subsection (1) is inadequate to put a lessor in as good a position as performance would have, the measure of damages is the profit, including reasonable overhead, the lessor would have made from full performance by the lessee, together with any incidental damages allowed under Section 2A—530, due allowance for costs reasonably incurred and due credit for payments or proceeds of disposition.

### § 2A—529
**Lessor's Action for the Rent**

(1) After default by the lessee under the lease contract (Section 2A—523(1)), if the lessor complies with subsection (2), the lessor may recover from the lessee as damages:

(a) for goods accepted by the lessee and for conforming goods lost or damaged within a commercially reasonable time after risk of loss passes to the lessee (Section 2A—219), (i) accrued and unpaid rent as of the date of default, (ii) the present value as of the date of default of the rent for the remaining lease term of the lease agreement, and (iii) any incidental damages allowed under Section 2A—530, less expenses saved in consequence of the lessee's default; and

(b) for goods identified to the lease contract if the lessor is unable after reasonable effort to dispose of them at a reasonable price or the circumstances reasonably indicate that effort will be unavailing, (i) accrued and unpaid rent as of the date of default, (ii) the present value as of the date of default of the rent for the remaining lease term of the lease agreement, and (iii) any incidental damages allowed under Section 2A—530, less expenses saved in consequence of the lessee's default.

(2) Except as provided in subsection (3), the lessor shall hold for the lessee for the remaining lease term of the lease agreement any goods that have been identified to the lease contract and are in the lessor's control.

(3) The lessor may dispose of the goods at any time before collection of the judgment for damages obtained pursuant to subsection (1) and the lessor may proceed against the lessee for damages pursuant to Section 2A—527 or Section 2A—528.

(4) Payment of the judgment for damages obtained pursuant to subsection (1) entitles the lessee to use and possession of the goods not then disposed of for the remaining lease term of the lease agreement.

(5) After a lessee has wrongfully rejected or revoked acceptance of goods, has failed to pay rent then due, or has repudiated (Section 2A—402), a lessor who is held not entitled to rent under this section must nevertheless be awarded damages for non-acceptance under Sections 2A—527 and 2A—528.

### § 2A—530
**Lessor's Incidental Damages**

Incidental damages to an aggrieved lessor include any commercially reasonable charges, expenses, or commissions incurred in stopping delivery, in the transportation, care and custody of goods after the lessee's default, in connection with return or disposition of the goods, or otherwise resulting from the default.

### § 2A—531
**Standing to Sue Third Parties for Injury to Goods**

(1) If a third party so deals with goods that have been identified to a lease contract as to cause actionable injury to a party to the lease contract (a) the lessor has a right of action against the third party, and (b) the lessee also has a right of action against the third party if the lessee:

(i) has a security interest in the goods;
(ii) has an insurable interest in the goods; or
(iii) bears the risk of loss under the lease contract or has since the injury assumed that risk as against the lessor and the goods have been converted or destroyed.

(2) If at the time of the injury the party plaintiff did not bear the risk of loss as against the other party to the lease contract and there is no arrangement between them for disposition of the recovery, his [or her] suit or settlement, subject to his [or her] own interest, is as a fiduciary for the other party to the lease contract.

(3) Either party with the consent of the other may sue for the benefit of whom it may concern.

## ARTICLE 3/COMMERCIAL PAPER
### *Part 1/Short Title, Form and Interpretation*

### § 3—101
**Short Title**

This Article shall be known and may be cited as Uniform Commercial Code—Commercial Paper.

### § 3—102
**Definitions and Index of Definitions**

(1) In this Article unless the context otherwise requires
(a) "Issue" means the first delivery of an instrument to a holder or a remitter.
(b) An "order" is a direction to pay and must be more than an authorization or request. It must identify the person to pay with reasonable certainty. It may be addressed to one or more such persons jointly or in the alternative but not in succession.
(c) A "promise" is an undertaking to pay and must be more than an acknowledgment of an obligation.
(d) "Secondary party" means a drawer or endorser.
(e) "Instrument" means a negotiable instrument.

**(2)** Other definitions applying to this Article and the sections in which they appear are:

"Acceptance". Section 3—410.
"Accommodation party". Section 3—415.
"Alteration". Section 3—407.
"Certificate of deposit". Section 3—104.
"Certification". Section 3—411.
"Check". Section 3—104.
"Definite time". Section 3—109.
"Dishonor". Section 3—507.
"Draft". Section 3—104.
"Holder in due course". Section 3—302.
"Negotiation". Section 3—202.
"Note". Section 3—104.
"Notice of dishonor". Section 3—508.
"On demand". Section 3—108.
"Presentment". Section 3—504.
"Protest". Section 3—509.
"Restrictive Indorsement". Section 3—205.
"Signature". Section 3—401.

**(3)** The following definitions in other Articles apply to this Article:

"Account". Section 4—104.
"Banking Day". Section 4—104.
"Clearing House". Section 4—104.
"Collecting Bank". Section 4—105.
"Customer". Section 4—104.
"Depositary Bank". Section 4—105.
"Documentary Draft". Section 4—104.
"Intermediary Bank". Section 4—105.
"Item". Section 4—104.
"Midnight deadline". Section 4—104.
"Payor Bank". Section 4—105.

**(4)** In addition Article 1 contains general definitions and principles of construction and interpretation applicable throughout this Article.

## § 3—103
### Limitations on Scope of Article

**(1)** This Article does not apply to money, documents of title or investment securities.

**(2)** The provisions of this Article are subject to the provisions of the Article on Bank Deposits and Collections (Article 4) and Secured Transactions (Article 9).

## § 3—104
### Form of Negotiable Instruments; "Draft"; "Check"; "Certificate of Deposit"; "Note"

**(1)** Any writing to be a negotiable instrument within this Article must
    **(a)** be signed by the maker or drawer; and
    **(b)** contain an unconditional promise or order to pay a sum certain in money and no other promise, order, obligation or power given by the maker or drawer except as authorized by this Article; and
    **(c)** be payable on demand or at a definite time; and
    **(d)** be payable to order or to bearer.

**(2)** A writing which complies with the requirements of this section is
    **(a)** a "draft" ("bill of exchange") if it is an order;
    **(b)** a "check" if it is a draft drawn on a bank and payable on demand;
    **(c)** a "certificate of deposit" if it is an acknowledgment by a bank of receipt of money with an engagement to repay it;
    **(d)** a "note" if it is a promise other than a certificate of deposit.

**(3)** As used in other Articles of this Act, and as the context may require, the terms "draft", "check", "certificate of deposit" and "note" may refer to instruments which are not negotiable within this Article as well as to instruments which are so negotiable.

## § 3—105
### When Promise or Order Unconditional

**(1)** A promise or order otherwise unconditional is not made conditional by the fact that the instrument
    **(a)** is subject to implied or constructive conditions; or
    **(b)** states its consideration, whether performed or promised, or the transaction which gave rise to the instrument, or that the promise or order is made or the instrument matures in accordance with or "as per" such transaction; or
    **(c)** refers to or states that it arises out of a separate agreement or refers to a separate agreement for rights as to prepayment or acceleration; or
    **(d)** states that it is drawn under a letter of credit; or
    **(e)** states that it is secured, whether by mortgage, reservation of title or otherwise; or
    **(f)** indicates a particular account to be debited or any other fund or source from which reimbursement is expected; or
    **(g)** is limited to payment out of a particular fund or the proceeds of a particular source, if the instrument is issued by a government or governmental agency or unit; or
    **(h)** is limited to payment out of the entire assets of a partnership, unincorporated association, trust or estate by or on behalf of which the instrument is issued.

**(2)** A promise or order is not unconditional if the instrument
    **(a)** states that it is subject to or governed by any other agreement; or
    **(b)** states that it is to be paid only out of a particular fund or source except as provided in this section.

## § 3—106
### Sum Certain

**(1)** The sum payable is a sum certain even though it is to be paid
    **(a)** with stated interest or by stated installments; or
    **(b)** with stated different rates of interest before and after default or a specified date; or
    **(c)** with a stated discount or addition if paid before or after the date fixed for payment; or
    **(d)** with exchange or less exchange, whether at a fixed rate or at the current rate; or
    **(e)** with costs of collection or an attorney's fee or both upon default.

**(2)** Nothing in this section shall validate any term which is otherwise illegal.

## § 3—107
### Money

**(1)** An instrument is payable in money if the medium of exchange in which it is payable is money at the time the instrument is made. An instrument payable in "currency" or "current funds" is payable in money.

**(2)** A promise or order to pay a sum stated in a foreign currency is for a sum certain in money and, unless a different medium of payment is specified in the instrument, may be satisfied by payment of that number of dollars which the stated foreign currency will purchase at the buying sight rate for that currency on the day on which the instrument is payable or, if payable on demand, on the day of demand. If such an instrument specifies a foreign currency as the medium of payment the instrument is payable in that currency.

## § 3—108
### Payable on Demand

Instruments payable on demand include those payable at sight or on presentation and those in which no time for payment is stated.

## § 3—109
### Definite Time

**(1)** An instrument is payable at a definite time if by its terms it is payable
  **(a)** on or before a stated date or at a fixed period after a stated date; or
  **(b)** at a fixed period after sight; or
  **(c)** at a definite time subject to any acceleration; or
  **(d)** at a definite time subject to extension at the option of the holder, or to extension to a further definite time at the option of the maker or acceptor or automatically upon or after a specified act or event.

**(2)** An instrument which by its terms is otherwise payable only upon an act or event uncertain as to time of occurrence is not payable at a definite time even though the act or event has occurred.

## § 3—110
### Payable to Order

**(1)** An instrument is payable to order when by its terms it is payable to the order or assigns of any person therein specified with reasonable certainty, or to him or his order, or when it is conspicuously designated on its face as "exchange" or the like and names a payee. It may be payable to the order of
  **(a)** the maker or drawer; or
  **(b)** the drawee; or
  **(c)** a payee who is not maker, drawer or drawee; or
  **(d)** two or more payees together or in the alternative; or
  **(e)** an estate, trust or fund, in which case it is payable to the order of the representative of such estate, trust or fund or his successors; or
  **(f)** an office, or an officer by his title as such in which case it is payable to the principal but the incumbent of the office or his successors may act as if he or they were the holder; or
  **(g)** a partnership or unincorporated association, in which case it is payable to the partnership or association and may be indorsed or transferred by any person thereto authorized.

**(2)** An instrument not payable to order is not made so payable by such words as "payable upon return of this instrument properly indorsed."

**(3)** An instrument made payable both to order and to bearer is payable to order unless the bearer words are handwritten or typewritten.

## § 3—111
### Payable to Bearer

An instrument is payable to bearer when by its terms it is payable to
  **(a)** bearer or the order of bearer; or
  **(b)** a specified person or bearer; or
  **(c)** "cash" or the order of "cash", or any other indication which does not purport to designate a specific payee.

## § 3—112
### Terms and Omissions Not Affecting Negotiability

**(1)** The negotiability of an instrument is not affected by
  **(a)** the omission of a statement of any consideration or of the place where the instrument is drawn or payable; or
  **(b)** a statement that collateral has been given to secure obligations either on the instrument or otherwise of an obligor on the instrument or that in case of default on those obligations the holder may realize on or dispose of the collateral; or
  **(c)** a promise or power to maintain or protect collateral or to give additional collateral; or
  **(d)** a term authorizing a confession of judgment on the instrument if it is not paid when due; or
  **(e)** a term purporting to waive the benefit of any law intended for the advantage or protection of any obligor; or
  **(f)** a term in a draft providing that the payee by indorsing or cashing it acknowledges full satisfaction of an obligation of the drawer; or
  **(g)** a statement in a draft drawn in a set of parts (Section 3—801) to the effect that the order is effective only if no other part has been honored.

**(2)** Nothing in this section shall validate any term which is otherwise illegal.

## § 3—113
### Seal

An instrument otherwise negotiable is within this Article even though it is under a seal.

## § 3—114
### Date, Antedating, Postdating

**(1)** The negotiability of an instrument is not affected by the fact that it is undated, antedated or postdated.

**(2)** Where an instrument is antedated or postdated the time when it is payable is determined by the stated date if the instrument is payable on demand or at a fixed period after date.

**(3)** Where the instrument or any signature thereon is dated, the date is presumed to be correct.

## § 3—115
### Incomplete Instruments

**(1)** When a paper whose contents at the time of signing show that it is intended to become an instrument is signed while still incomplete in any necessary respect it cannot be enforced until completed, but when it is completed in accordance with authority given it is effective as completed.

**(2)** If the completion is unauthorized the rules as to material alteration apply (Section 3—407), even though the paper was not delivered by the maker or drawer; but the burden of establishing that any completion is unauthorized is on the party so asserting.

## § 3—116
### Instruments Payable to Two or More Persons

An instrument payable to the order of two or more persons
  (a) if in the alternative is payable to any one of them and may be negotiated, discharged or enforced by any of them who has possession of it;
  (b) if not in the alternative is payable to all of them and may be negotiated, discharged or enforced only by all of them.

## § 3—117
### Instruments Payable With Words of Description

An instrument made payable to a named person with the addition of words describing him
  (a) as agent or officer of a specified person is payable to his principal but the agent or officer may act as if he were the holder;
  (b) as any other fiduciary for a specified person or purpose is payable to the payee and may be negotiated, discharged or enforced by him;
  (c) in any other manner is payable to the payee unconditionally and the additional words are without effect on subsequent parties.

## § 3—118
### Ambiguous Terms and Rules of Construction

The following rules apply to every instrument:
  (a) Where there is doubt whether the instrument is a draft or a note the holder may treat it as either. A draft drawn on the drawer is effective as a note.
  (b) Handwritten terms control typewritten and printed terms, and typewritten control printed.
  (c) Words control figures except that if the words are ambiguous figures control.
  (d) Unless otherwise specified a provision for interest means interest at the judgment rate at the place of payment from the date of the instrument, or if it is undated from the date of issue.
  (e) Unless the instrument otherwise specifies two or more persons who sign as maker, acceptor or drawer or indorser and as a part of the same transaction are jointly and severally liable even though the instrument contains such words as "I promise to pay."
  (f) Unless otherwise specified consent to extension authorizes a single extension for not longer than the original period. A consent to extension, expressed in the instrument, is binding on secondary parties and accommodation makers. A holder may not exercise his option to extend an instrument over the objection of a maker or acceptor or other party who in accordance with Section 3—604 tenders full payment when the instrument is due.

## § 3—119
### Other Writings Affecting Instrument

**(1)** As between the obligor and his immediate obligee or any transferee the terms of an instrument may be modified or affected by any other written agreement executed as a part of the same transaction, except that a holder in due course is not affected by any limitation of his rights arising out of the separate written agreement if he had no notice of the limitation when he took the instrument.

**(2)** A separate agreement does not affect the negotiability of an instrument.

## § 3—120
### Instruments "Payable Through" Bank

An instrument which states that it is "payable through" a bank or the like designates that bank as a collecting bank to make presentment but does not of itself authorize the bank to pay the instrument.

## § 3—121
### Instruments Payable at Bank

Note: *If this Act is introduced in the Congress of the United States this section should be omitted.*
*(States to select either alternative)*

### Alternative A

A note or acceptance which states that it is payable at a bank is the equivalent of a draft drawn on the bank payable when it falls due out of any funds of the maker or acceptor in current account or otherwise available for such payment.

### Alternative B

A note or acceptance which states that it is payable at a bank is not of itself an order or authorization to the bank to pay it.

## § 3—122
### Accrual of Cause of Action

**(1)** A cause of action against a maker or an acceptor accrues
  (a) in the case of a time instrument on the day after maturity;
  (b) in the case of a demand instrument upon its date or, if no date is stated, on the date of issue.

**(2)** A cause of action against the obligor of a demand or time certificate of deposit accrues upon demand, but demand on a time certificate may not be made until on or after the date of maturity.

**(3)** A cause of action against a drawer of a draft or an indorser of any instrument accrues upon demand following dishonor of the instrument. Notice of dishonor is a demand.

**(4)** Unless an instrument provides otherwise, interest runs at the rate provided by law for a judgment
  (a) in the case of a maker, acceptor or other primary obligor of a demand instrument, from the date of demand;

(b) in all other cases from the date of accrual of the cause of action.

## Part 2/Transfer and Negotiation

### § 3—201
### Transfer: Right to Indorsement

(1) Transfer of an instrument vests in the transferee such rights as the transferor has therein, except that a transferee who has himself been a party to any fraud or illegality affecting the instrument or who as a prior holder had notice of a defense or claim against it cannot improve his position by taking from a later holder in due course.

(2) A transfer of a security interest in an instrument vests the foregoing rights in the transferee to the extent of the interest transferred.

(3) Unless otherwise agreed any transfer for value of an instrument not then payable to bearer gives the transferee the specifically enforceable right to have the unqualified indorsement of the transferor. Negotiation takes effect only when the indorsement is made and until that time there is no presumption that the transferee is the owner.

### § 3—202
### Negotiation

(1) Negotiation is the transfer of an instrument in such form that the transferee becomes a holder. If the instrument is payable to order it is negotiated by delivery with any necessary indorsement; if payable to bearer it is negotiated by delivery.

(2) An indorsement must be written by or on behalf of the holder and on the instrument or on a paper so firmly affixed thereto as to become a part thereof.

(3) An indorsement is effective for negotiation only when it conveys the entire instrument or any unpaid residue. If it purports to be of less it operates only as a partial assignment.

(4) Words of assignment, condition, waiver, guaranty, limitation or disclaimer of liability and the like accompanying an indorsement do not affect its character as an indorsement.

### § 3—203
### Wrong or Misspelled Name

Where an instrument is made payable to a person under a misspelled name or one other than his own he may indorse in that name or his own or both; but signature in both names may be required by a person paying or giving value for the instrument.

### § 3—204
### Special Indorsement; Blank Indorsement

(1) A special indorsement specifies the person to whom or to whose order it makes the instrument payable. Any instrument specially indorsed becomes payable to the order of the special indorsee and may be further negotiated only by his indorsement.

(2) An indorsement in blank specifies no particular indorsee and may consist of a mere signature. An instrument payable to order and indorsed in blank becomes payable to bearer and may be negotiated by delivery alone until specially indorsed.

(3) The holder may convert a blank indorsement into a special indorsement by writing over the signature of the indorser in blank any contract consistent with the character of the indorsement.

### § 3—205
### Restrictive Indorsements

An indorsement is restrictive which either
    (a) is conditional; or
    (b) purports to prohibit further transfer of the instrument; or
    (c) includes the words "for collection", "for deposit", "pay any bank", or like terms signifying a purpose of deposit or collection; or
    (d) otherwise states that it is for the benefit or use of the indorser or of another person.

### § 3—206
### Effect of Restrictive Indorsement

(1) No restrictive indorsement prevents further transfer or negotiation of the instrument.

(2) An intermediary bank, or a payor bank which is not the depositary bank, is neither given notice nor otherwise affected by a restrictive indorsement of any person except the bank's immediate transferor or the person presenting for payment.

(3) Except for an intermediary bank, any transferee under an indorsement which is conditional or includes the words "for collection", "for deposit", "pay any bank", or like terms (subparagraphs (a) and (c) of Section 3—205) must pay or apply any value given by him for or on the security of the instrument consistently with the indorsement and to the extent that he does so he becomes a holder for value. In addition such transferee is a holder in due course if he otherwise complies with the requirements of Section 3—302 on what constitutes a holder in due course.

(4) The first taker under an indorsement for the benefit of the indorser or another person (subparagraph (d) of Section 3—205) must pay or apply any value given by him for or on the security of the instrument consistently with the indorsement and to the extent that he does so he becomes a holder for value. In addition such taker is a holder in due course if he otherwise complies with the requirements of Section 3—302 on what constitutes a holder in due course. A later holder for value is neither given notice nor otherwise affected by such restrictive indorsement unless he has knowledge that a fiduciary or other person has negotiated the instrument in any transaction for his own benefit or otherwise in breach of duty (subsection (2) of Section 3—304).

### § 3—207
### Negotiation Effective Although It May Be Rescinded

(1) Negotiation is effective to transfer the instrument although the negotiation is
    (a) made by an infant, a corporation exceeding its powers, or any other person without capacity; or
    (b) obtained by fraud, duress or mistake of any kind; or
    (c) part of an illegal transaction; or
    (d) made in breach of duty.

(2) Except as against a subsequent holder in due course such negotiation is in an appropriate case subject to rescission, the declaration of a constructive trust or any other remedy permitted by law.

## § 3—208
### Reacquisition

Where an instrument is returned to or reacquired by a prior party he may cancel any indorsement which is not necessary to his title and reissue or further negotiate the instrument, but any intervening party is discharged as against the reacquiring party and subsequent holders not in due course and if his indorsement has been cancelled is discharged as against subsequent holders in due course as well.

## Part 3/Rights of a Holder

### § 3—301
### Rights of a Holder

The holder of an instrument whether or not he is the owner may transfer or negotiate it and, except as otherwise provided in Section 3—603 on payment or satisfaction, discharge it or enforce payment in his own name.

### § 3—302
### Holder in Due Course

(1) A holder in due course is a holder who takes the instrument
  (a) for value; and
  (b) in good faith; and
  (c) without notice that it is overdue or has been dishonored or of any defense against or claim to it on the part of any person.

(2) A payee may be a holder in due course.

(3) A holder does not become a holder in due course of an instrument:
  (a) by purchase of it at judicial sale or by taking it under legal process; or
  (b) by acquiring it in taking over an estate; or
  (c) by purchasing it as part of a bulk transaction not in regular course of business of the transferor.

(4) A purchase of a limited interest can be a holder in due course only to the extent of the interest purchased.

### § 3—303
### Taking for Value

A holder takes the instrument for value
  (a) to the extent that the agreed consideration has been performed or that he acquires a security interest in or a lien on the instrument otherwise than by legal process; or
  (b) when he takes the instrument in payment of or as security for an antecedent claim against any person whether or not the claim is due; or
  (c) when he gives a negotiable instrument for it or makes an irrevocable commitment to a third person.

### § 3—304
### Notice to Purchaser

(1) The purchaser has notice of a claim or defense if
  (a) the instrument is so incomplete, bears such visible evidence of forgery or alteration, or is otherwise so irregular as to call into question its validity, terms or ownership or to create an ambiguity as to the party to pay; or
  (b) the purchaser has notice that the obligation of any party is voidable in whole or in part, or that all parties have been discharged.

(2) The purchaser has notice of a claim against the instrument when he has knowledge that a fiduciary has negotiated the instrument in payment of or as security for his own debt or in any transaction for his own benefit or otherwise in breach of duty.

(3) The purchaser has notice that an instrument is overdue if he has reason to know
  (a) that any part of the principal amount is overdue or that there is an uncured default in payment of another instrument of the same series; or
  (b) that acceleration of the instrument has been made; or
  (c) that he is taking a demand instrument after demand has been made or more than a reasonable length of time after its issue. A reasonable time for a check drawn and payable within the states and territories of the United States and the District of Columbia is presumed to be thirty days.

(4) Knowledge of the following facts does not of itself give the purchaser notice of a defense or claim
  (a) that the instrument is antedated or postdated;
  (b) that it was issued or negotiated in return for an executory promise or accompanied by a separate agreement, unless the purchaser has notice that a defense or claim has arisen from the terms thereof;
  (c) that any party has signed for accommodation;
  (d) that an incomplete instrument has been completed, unless the purchaser has notice of any improper completion;
  (e) that any person negotiating the instrument is or was a fiduciary;
  (f) that there has been default in payment of interest on the instrument or in payment of any other instrument, except one of the same series.

(5) The filing or recording of a document does not of itself constitute notice within the provisions of this Article to a person who would otherwise be a holder in due course.

(6) To be effective notice must be received at such time and in such manner as to give a reasonable opportunity to act on it.

### § 3—305
### Rights of a Holder in Due Course

To the extent that a holder is a holder in due course he takes the instrument free from

(1) all claims to it on the part of any person; and

(2) all defenses of any party to the instrument with whom the holder has not dealt except
  (a) infancy, to the extent that it is a defense to a simple contract; and
  (b) such other incapacity, or duress, or illegality of the transaction, as renders the obligation of the party a nullity; and
  (c) such misrepresentation as has induced the party to sign the instrument with neither knowledge nor reasonable opportunity to obtain knowledge of its character or its essential terms; and
  (d) discharge in insolvency proceedings; and
  (e) any other discharge of which the holder has notice when he takes the instrument.

## § 3—306
### Rights of One Not Holder in Due Course

Unless he has the rights of a holder in due course any person takes the instrument subject to

(a) all valid claims to it on the part of any person; and

(b) all defenses of any party which would be available in an action on a simple contract; and

(c) the defenses of want or failure of consideration, non-performance of any condition precedent, non-delivery, or delivery for a special purpose (Section 3—408); and

(d) the defense that he or a person through whom he holds the instrument acquired it by theft, or that payment or satisfaction to such holder would be inconsistent with the terms of a restrictive indorsement. The claim of any third person to the instrument is not otherwise available as a defense to any party liable thereon unless the third person himself defends the action for such party.

## § 3—307
### Burden of Establishing Signatures, Defenses and Due Course

(1) Unless specifically denied in the pleadings each signature on an instrument is admitted. When the effectiveness of a signature is put in issue

(a) the burden of establishing it is on the party claiming under the signature; but

(b) the signature is presumed to be genuine or authorized except where the action is to enforce the obligation of a purported signer who has died or become incompetent before proof is required.

(2) When signatures are admitted or established, production of the instrument entitles a holder to recover on it unless the defendant establishes a defense.

(3) After it is shown that a defense exists a person claiming the rights of a holder in due course has the burden of establishing that he or some person under whom he claims is in all respects a holder in due course.

## Part 4/Liability of Parties

### § 3—401
### Signature

(1) No person is liable on an instrument unless his signature appears thereon.

(2) A signature is made by use of any name, including any trade or assumed name, upon an instrument, or by any word or mark used in lieu of a written signature.

### § 3—402
### Signature in Ambiguous Capacity

Unless the instrument clearly indicates that a signature is made in some other capacity it is an indorsement.

### § 3—403
### Signature by Authorized Representative

(1) A signature may be made by an agent or other representative, and his authority to make it may be established as in other cases of representation. No particular form of appointment is necessary to establish such authority.

(2) An authorized representative who signs his own name to an instrument

(a) is personally obligated if the instrument neither names the person represented nor shows that the representative signed in a representative capacity;

(b) except as otherwise established between the immediate parties, is personally obligated if the instrument names the person represented but does not show that the representative signed in a representative capacity, or if the instrument does not name the person represented but does show that the representative signed in a representative capacity.

(3) Except as otherwise established the name of an organization preceded or followed by the name and office of an authorized individual is a signature made in a representative capacity.

### § 3—404
### Unauthorized Signatures

(1) Any unauthorized signature is wholly inoperative as that of the person whose name is signed unless he ratifies it or is precluded from denying it; but it operates as the signature of the unauthorized signer in favor of any person who in good faith pays the instrument or takes it for value.

(2) Any unauthorized signature may be ratified for all purposes of this Article. Such ratification does not of itself affect any rights of the person ratifying against the actual signer.

### § 3—405
### Impostors; Signature in Name of Payee

(1) An indorsement by any person in the name of a named payee is effective if

(a) an impostor by use of the mails or otherwise has induced the maker or drawer to issue the instrument to him or his confederate in the name of the payee; or

(b) a person signing as or on behalf of a maker or drawer intends the payee to have no interest in the instrument; or

(c) an agent or employee of the maker or drawer has supplied him with the name of the payee intending the latter to have no such interest.

(2) Nothing in this section shall affect the criminal or civil liability of the person so indorsing.

### § 3—406
### Negligence Contributing to Alteration or Unauthorized Signature

Any person who by his negligence substantially contributes to a material alteration of the instrument or to the making of an unauthorized signature is precluded from asserting the alteration or lack of authority against a holder in due course or against a drawee or other payor who pays the instrument in good faith and in accordance with the reasonable commercial standards of the drawee's or payor's business.

## § 3—407
### Alteration

**(1)** Any alteration of an instrument is material which changes the contract of any party thereto in any respect, including any such change in
- (a) the number or relations of the parties; or
- (b) an incomplete instrument, by completing it otherwise than as authorized; or
- (c) the writing as signed, by adding to it or by removing any part of it.

**(2)** As against any person other than a subsequent holder in due course
- (a) alteration by the holder which is both fraudulent and material discharges any party whose contract is thereby changed unless that party assents or is precluded from asserting the defense;
- (b) no other alteration discharges any party and the instrument may be enforced according to its original tenor, or as to incomplete instruments according to the authority given.

**(3)** A subsequent holder in due course may in all cases enforce the instrument according to its original tenor, and when an incomplete instrument has been completed, he may enforce it as completed.

## § 3—408
### Consideration

Want or failure of consideration is a defense as against any person not having the rights of a holder in due course (Section 3—305), except that no consideration is necessary for an instrument or obligation thereon given in payment of or as security for an antecedent obligation of any kind. Nothing in this section shall be taken to displace any statute outside this Act under which a promise is enforceable notwithstanding lack or failure of consideration. Partial failure of consideration is a defense pro tanto whether or not the failure is in an ascertained or liquidated amount.

## § 3—409
### Draft Not an Assignment

**(1)** A check or other draft does not of itself operate as an assignment of any funds in the hands of the drawee available for its payment, and the drawee is not liable on the instrument until he accepts it.

**(2)** Nothing in this section shall affect any liability in contract, tort, or otherwise arising from any letter of credit or other obligation or representation which is not an acceptance.

## § 3—410
### Definition and Operation of Acceptance

**(1)** Acceptance is the drawee's signed engagement to honor the draft as presented. It must be written on the draft, and may consist of his signature alone. It becomes operative when completed by delivery or notification.

**(2)** A draft may be accepted although it has not been signed by the drawer or is otherwise incomplete or is overdue or has been dishonored.

**(3)** Where the draft is payable at a fixed period after sight and the acceptor fails to date his acceptance the holder may complete it by supplying a date in good faith.

## § 3—411
### Certification of a Check

**(1)** Certification of a check is acceptance. Where a holder procures certification the drawer and all prior indorsers are discharged.

**(2)** Unless otherwise agreed a bank has no obligation to certify a check.

**(3)** A bank may certify a check before returning it for lack of proper indorsement. If it does so the drawer is discharged.

## § 3—412
### Acceptance Varying Draft

**(1)** Where the drawee's proffered acceptance in any manner varies the draft as presented the holder may refuse the acceptance and treat the draft as dishonored in which case the drawee is entitled to have his acceptance cancelled.

**(2)** The terms of the draft are not varied by an acceptance to pay at any particular bank or place in the United States, unless the acceptance states that the draft is to be paid only at such bank or place.

**(3)** Where the holder assents to an acceptance varying the terms of the draft each drawer and indorser who does not affirmatively assent is discharged.

## § 3—413
### Contract of Maker, Drawer and Acceptor

**(1)** The maker or acceptor engages that he will pay the instrument according to its tenor at the time of his engagement or as completed pursuant to Section 3—115 on incomplete instruments.

**(2)** The drawer engages that upon dishonor of the draft and any necessary notice of dishonor or protest he will pay the amount of the draft to the holder or to any indorser who takes it up. The drawer may disclaim this liability by drawing without recourse.

**(3)** By making, drawing or accepting the party admits as against all subsequent parties including the drawee the existence of the payee and his then capacity to indorse.

## § 3—414
### Contract of Indorser; Order of Liability

**(1)** Unless the indorsement otherwise specifies (as by such words as "without recourse") every indorser engages that upon dishonor and any necessary notice of dishonor and protest he will pay the instrument according to its tenor at the time of his indorsement to the holder or to any subsequent indorser who takes it up, even though the indorser who takes it up was not obligated to do so.

**(2)** Unless they otherwise agree indorsers are liable to one another in the order in which they indorse, which is presumed to be the order in which their signatures appear on the instrument.

## § 3—415
### Contract of Accommodation Party

**(1)** An accommodation party is one who signs the instrument in any capacity for the purpose of lending his name to another party to it.

(2) When the instrument has been taken for value before it is due the accommodation party is liable in the capacity in which he has signed even though the taker knows of the accommodation.

(3) As against a holder in due course and without notice of the accommodation oral proof of the accommodation is not admissible to give the accommodation party the benefit of discharges dependent on his character as such. In other cases the accommodation character may be shown by oral proof.

(4) An indorsement which shows that it is not in the chain of title is notice of its accommodation character.

(5) An accommodation party is not liable to the party accommodated, and if he pays the instrument has a right of recourse on the instrument against such party.

## § 3—416
### Contract of Guarantor

(1) "Payment guaranteed" or equivalent words added to a signature mean that the signer engages that if the instrument is not paid when due he will pay it according to its tenor without resort by the holder to any other party.

(2) "Collection guaranteed" or equivalent words added to a signature mean that the signer engages that if the instrument is not paid when due he will pay it according to its tenor, but only after the holder has reduced his claim against the maker or acceptor to judgment and execution has been returned unsatisfied, or after the maker or acceptor has become insolvent or it is otherwise apparent that it is useless to proceed against him.

(3) Words of guaranty which do not otherwise specify guarantee payment.

(4) No words of guaranty added to the signature of a sole maker or acceptor affect his liability on the instrument. Such words added to the signature of one or two or more makers or acceptors create a presumption that the signature is for the accommodation of the others.

(5) When words of guaranty are used presentment, notice of dishonor and protest are not necessary to charge the user.

(6) Any guaranty written on the instrument is enforceable notwithstanding any statute of frauds.

## § 3—417
### Warranties on Presentment and Transfer

(1) Any person who obtains payment or acceptance and any prior transferor warrants to a person who in good faith pays or accepts that
    (a) he has a good title to the instrument or is authorized to obtain payment or acceptance on behalf of one who has a good title; and
    (b) he has no knowledge that the signature of the maker or drawer is unauthorized, except that this warranty is not given by a holder in due course acting in good faith
        (i) to a maker with respect to the maker's own signature; or
        (ii) to a drawer with respect to the drawer's own signature, whether or not the drawer is also the drawee; or
        (iii) to an acceptor of a draft if the holder in due course took the draft after the acceptance or obtained the acceptance without knowledge that the drawer's signature was unauthorized; and
    (c) the instrument has not been materially altered, except that this warranty is not given by a holder in due course acting in good faith
        (i) to the maker of a note; or
        (ii) to the drawer of a draft whether or not the drawer is also the drawee; or
        (iii) to the acceptor of a draft with respect to an alteration made prior to the acceptance if the holder in due course took the draft after the acceptance, even though the acceptance provided "payable as originally drawn" or equivalent terms; or
        (iv) to the acceptor of a draft with respect to an alteration made after the acceptance.

(2) Any person who transfers an instrument and receives consideration warrants to his transferee and if the transfer is by indorsement to any subsequent holder who takes the instrument in good faith that
    (a) he has a good title to the instrument or is authorized to obtain payment or acceptance on behalf of one who has a good title and the transfer is otherwise rightful; and
    (b) all signatures are genuine or authorized; and
    (c) the instrument has not been materially altered; and
    (d) no defense of any party is good against him; and
    (e) he has no knowledge of any insolvency proceeding instituted with respect to the maker or acceptor or the drawer of an unaccepted instrument.

(3) By transferring "without recourse" the transferor limits the obligation stated in subsection (2)(d) to a warranty that he has no knowledge of such a defense.

(4) A selling agent or broker who does not disclose the fact that he is acting only as such gives the warranties provided in this section, but if he makes such disclosure warrants only his good faith and authority.

## § 3—418
### Finality of Payment or Acceptance

Except for recovery of bank payments as provided in the Article on Bank Deposits and Collections (Article 4) and except for liability for breach of warranty on presentment under the preceding section, payment or acceptance of any instrument is final in favor of a holder in due course, or a person who has in good faith changed his position in reliance on the payment.

## § 3—419
### Conversion of Instrument; Innocent Representative

(1) An instrument is converted when
    (a) a drawee to whom it is delivered for acceptance refuses to return it on demand; or
    (b) any person to whom it is delivered for payment refuses on demand either to pay or to return it; or
    (c) it is paid on a forged indorsement.

(2) In an action against a drawee under subsection (1) the measure of the drawee's liability is the face amount of the instrument. In any other action under subsection (1) the measure of liability is presumed to be the face amount of the instrument.

(3) Subject to the provisions of this Act concerning restrictive indorsements a representative, including a depositary or collecting bank, who has in good faith and in accordance with the reasonable commercial standards applicable to the business of such representative dealt with an instrument or its proceeds on behalf of one who was not the true owner is not liable in conversion or otherwise to the true owner beyond the amount of any proceeds remaining in his hands.

(4) An intermediary bank or payor bank which is not a depositary bank is not liable in conversion solely by reason of the fact that proceeds of an item indorsed restrictively (Sections 3—205 and 3—206) are not paid or applied consistently with the restrictive indorsement of an indorser other than its immediate transferor.

## Part 5/Presentment, Notice of Dishonor and Protest

### § 3—501
**When Presentment, Notice of Dishonor, and Protest Necessary or Permissible**

(1) Unless excused (Section 3—511) presentment is necessary to charge secondary parties as follows:
   (a) presentment for acceptance is necessary to charge the drawer and indorsers of a draft where the draft so provides, or is payable elsewhere than at the residence or place of business of the drawee, or its date of payment depends upon such presentment. The holder may at his option present for acceptance any other draft payable at a stated date;
   (b) presentment for payment is necessary to charge any indorser;
   (c) in the case of any drawer, the acceptor of a draft payable at a bank or the maker of a note payable at a bank, presentment for payment is necessary, but failure to make presentment discharges such drawer, acceptor or maker only as stated in Section 3—502(1)(b).

(2) Unless excused (Section 3—511)
   (a) notice of any dishonor is necessary to charge any indorser;
   (b) in the case of any drawer, the acceptor of a draft payable at a bank or the maker of a note payable at a bank, notice of any dishonor is necessary, but failure to give such notice discharges such drawer, acceptor or maker only as stated in Section 3—502(1)(b).

(3) Unless excused (Section 3—511) protest of any dishonor is necessary to charge the drawer and indorsers of any draft which on its face appears to be drawn or payable outside of the states, territories, dependencies and possessions of the United States, the District of Columbia and the Commonwealth of Puerto Rico. The holder may at his option make protest of any dishonor of any other instrument and in the case of a foreign draft may on insolvency of the acceptor before maturity make protest for better security.

(4) Notwithstanding any provision of this section, neither presentment nor notice of dishonor nor protest is necessary to charge an indorser who has indorsed an instrument after maturity.

### § 3—502
**Unexcused Delay; Discharge**

(1) Where without excuse any necessary presentment or notice of dishonor is delayed beyond the time when it is due
   (a) any indorser is discharged; and
   (b) any drawer or the acceptor of a draft payable at a bank or the maker of a note payable at a bank who because the drawee or payor bank becomes insolvent during the delay is deprived of funds maintained with the drawee or payor bank to cover the instrument may discharge his liability by written assignment to the holder of his rights against the drawee or payor bank in respect of such funds, but such drawer, acceptor or maker is not otherwise discharged.

(2) Where without excuse a necessary protest is delayed beyond the time when it is due any drawer or indorser is discharged.

### § 3—503
**Time of Presentment**

(1) Unless a different time is expressed in the instrument the time for any presentment is determined as follows:
   (a) where an instrument is payable at or a fixed period after a stated date any presentment for acceptance must be made on or before the date it is payable;
   (b) where an instrument is payable after sight it must either be presented for acceptance or negotiated within a reasonable time after date or issue whichever is later;
   (c) where an instrument shows the date on which it is payable presentment for payment is due on that date;
   (d) where an instrument is accelerated presentment for payment is due within a reasonable time after the acceleration;
   (e) with respect to the liability of any secondary party presentment for acceptance or payment of any other instrument is due within a reasonable time after such party becomes liable thereon.

(2) A reasonable time for presentment is determined by the nature of the instrument, any usage of banking or trade and the facts of the particular case. In the case of an uncertified check which is drawn and payable within the United States and which is not a draft drawn by a bank the following are presumed to be reasonable periods within which to present for payment or to initiate bank collection:
   (a) with respect to the liability of the drawer, thirty days after date or issue whichever is later; and
   (b) with respect to the liability of an indorser, seven days after his indorsement.

(3) Where any presentment is due on a day which is not a full business day for either the person making presentment or the party to pay or accept, presentment is due on the next following day which is a full business day for both parties.

(4) Presentment to be sufficient must be made at a reasonable hour, and if at a bank during its banking day.

### § 3—504
**How Presentment Is Made**

(1) Presentment is a demand for acceptance or payment made upon the maker, acceptor, drawee or other payor by or on behalf of the holder.

(2) Presentment may be made
   (a) by mail, in which event the time of presentment is determined by the time of receipt of the mail; or
   (b) through a clearing house; or

(c) at the place of acceptance or payment specified in the instrument or if there be none at the place of business or residence of the party to accept or pay. If neither the party to accept or pay nor anyone authorized to act for him is present or accessible at such place presentment is excused.

(3) It may be made
   (a) to any one of two or more makers, acceptors, drawees or other payors; or
   (b) to any person who has authority to make or refuse the acceptance or payment.

(4) A draft accepted or a note made payable at a bank in the United States must be presented at such bank.

(5) In the cases described in Section 4—210 presentment may be made in the manner and with the result stated in that section.

## § 3—505
### Rights of Party to Whom Presentment Is Made

(1) The party to whom presentment is made may without dishonor require
   (a) exhibition of the instrument; and
   (b) reasonable identification of the person making presentment and evidence of his authority to make it if made for another; and
   (c) that the instrument be produced for acceptance or payment at a place specified in it, or if there be none at any place reasonable in the circumstances; and
   (d) a signed receipt on the instrument for any partial or full payment and its surrender upon full payment.

(2) Failure to comply with any such requirement invalidates the presentment but the person presenting has a reasonable time in which to comply and the time for acceptance or payment runs from the time of compliance.

## § 3—506
### Time Allowed for Acceptance or Payment

(1) Acceptance may be deferred without dishonor until the close of the next business day following presentment. The holder may also in a good faith effort to obtain acceptance and without either dishonor of the instrument or discharge of secondary parties allow postponement of acceptance for an additional business day.

(2) Except as a longer time is allowed in the case of documentary drafts drawn under a letter of credit, and unless an earlier time is agreed to by the party to pay, payment of an instrument may be deferred without dishonor pending reasonable examination to determine whether it is properly payable, but payment must be made in any event before the close of business on the day of presentment.

## § 3—507
### Dishonor; Holder's Right of Recourse; Term Allowing Re-Presentment

(1) An instrument is dishonored when
   (a) a necessary or optional presentment is duly made and due acceptance or payment is refused or cannot be obtained within the prescribed time or in case of bank collections the instrument is seasonably returned by the midnight deadline (Section 4—301); or
   (b) presentment is excused and the instrument is not duly accepted or paid.

(2) Subject to any necessary notice of dishonor and protest, the holder has upon dishonor an immediate right of recourse against the drawers and indorsers.

(3) Return of an instrument for lack of proper indorsement is not dishonor.

(4) A term in a draft or an indorsement thereof allowing a stated time for re-presentment in the event of any dishonor of the draft by nonacceptance if a time draft or by nonpayment if a sight draft gives the holder as against any secondary party bound by the term an option to waive the dishonor without affecting the liability of the secondary party and he may present again up to the end of the stated time.

## § 3—508
### Notice of Dishonor

(1) Notice of dishonor may be given to any person who may be liable on the instrument by or on behalf of the holder or any party who has himself received notice, or any other party who can be compelled to pay the instrument. In addition an agent or bank in whose hands the instrument is dishonored may give notice to his principal or customer or to another agent or bank from which the instrument was received.

(2) Any necessary notice must be given by a bank before its midnight deadline and by any other person before midnight of the third business day after dishonor or receipt of notice of dishonor.

(3) Notice may be given in any reasonable manner. It may be oral or written and in any terms which identify the instrument and state that it has been dishonored. A misdescription which does not mislead the party notified does not vitiate the notice. Sending the instrument bearing a stamp, ticket or writing stating that acceptance or payment has been refused or sending a notice of debit with respect to the instrument is sufficient.

(4) Written notice is given when sent although it is not received.

(5) Notice to one partner is notice to each although the firm has been dissolved.

(6) When any party is in insolvency proceedings instituted after the issue of the instrument notice may be given either to the party or to the representative of his estate.

(7) When any party is dead or incompetent notice may be sent to his last known address or given to his personal representative.

(8) Notice operates for the benefit of all parties who have rights on the instrument against the party notified.

## § 3—509
### Protest; Noting for Protest

(1) A protest is a certificate of dishonor made under the hand and seal of a United States consul or vice consul or a notary public or other person authorized to certify dishonor by the law of the place where dishonor occurs. It may be made upon information satisfactory to such person.

(2) The protest must identify the instrument and certify either that due presentment has been made or the reason why it is excused and that the instrument has been dishonored by non-acceptance or nonpayment.

(3) The protest may also certify that notice of dishonor has been given to all parties or to specified parties.

(4) Subject to subsection (5) any necessary protest is due by the time that notice of dishonor is due.

(5) If, before protest is due, an instrument has been noted for protest by the officer to make protest, the protest may be made at any time thereafter as of the date of the noting.

§ 3—510
**Evidence of Dishonor and Notice of Dishonor**

The following are admissible as evidence and create a presumption of dishonor and of any notice of dishonor therein shown:

    (a) a document regular in form as provided in the preceding section which purports to be a protest;

    (b) the purported stamp or writing of the drawee, payor bank or presenting bank on the instrument or accompanying it stating that acceptance or payment has been refused for reasons consistent with dishonor.

    (c) any book or record of the drawee, payor bank, or any collecting bank kept in the usual course of business which shows dishonor, even though there is no evidence of who made the entry.

§ 3—511
**Waived or Excused Presentment, Protest or Notice of Dishonor or Delay Therein**

(1) Delay in presentment, protest or notice of dishonor is excused when the party is without notice that it is due or when the delay is caused by circumstances beyond his control and he exercises reasonable diligence after the cause of the delay ceases to operate.

(2) Presentment or notice or protest as the case may be is entirely excused when

    (a) the party to be charged has waived it expressly or by implication either before or after it is due; or

    (b) such party has himself dishonored the instrument or has countermanded payment or otherwise has no reason to expect or right to require that the instrument be accepted or paid; or

    (c) by reasonable diligence the presentment or protest cannot be made or the notice given.

(3) Presentment is also entirely excused when

    (a) the maker, acceptor or drawee of any instrument except a documentary draft is dead or in insolvency proceedings instituted after the issue of the instrument; or

    (b) acceptance or payment is refused but not for want of proper presentment.

(4) Where a draft has been dishonored by nonacceptance a later presentment for payment and any notice of dishonor and protest for nonpayment are excused unless in the meantime the instrument has been accepted.

(5) A waiver of protest is also a waiver of presentment and of notice of dishonor even though protest is not required.

(6) Where a waiver of presentment or notice or protest is embodied in the instrument itself it is binding upon all parties; but where it is written above the signature of an indorser it binds him only.

## Part 6/Discharge

§ 3—601
**Discharge of Parties**

(1) The extent of the discharge of any party from liability on an instrument is governed by the sections on

    (a) payment or satisfaction (Section 3—603); or

    (b) tender of payment (Section 3—604); or

    (c) cancellation or renunciation (Section 3—605); or

    (d) impairment of right of recourse or of collateral (Section 3—606); or

    (e) reacquisition of the instrument by a prior party (Section 3—208); or

    (f) fraudulent and material alteration (Section 3—407); or

    (g) certification of a check (Section 3—411); or

    (h) acceptance varying a draft (Section 3—412); or

    (i) unexcused delay in presentment or notice of dishonor or protest (Section 3—502).

(2) Any party is also discharged from his liability on an instrument to another party by any other act or agreement with such party which would discharge his simple contract for the payment of money.

(3) The liability of all parties is discharged when any party who has himself no right of action or recourse on the instrument

    (a) reacquires the instrument in his own right; or

    (b) is discharged under any provision of this Article, except as otherwise provided with respect to discharge for impairment of recourse or of collateral (Section 3—606).

§ 3—602
**Effect of Discharge Against Holder in Due Course**

No discharge of any party provided by this Article is effective against a subsequent holder in due course unless he has notice thereof when he takes the instrument.

§ 3—603
**Payment or Satisfaction**

(1) The liability of any party is discharged to the extent of his payment or satisfaction to the holder even though it is made with knowledge of a claim of another person to the instrument unless prior to such payment or satisfaction the person making the claim either supplies indemnity deemed adequate by the party seeking the discharge or enjoins payment or satisfaction by order of a court of competent jurisdiction in an action in which the adverse claimant and the holder are parties. This subsection does not, however, result in the discharge of the liability

    (a) of a party who in bad faith pays or satisfies a holder who acquired the instrument by theft or who (unless having the rights of a holder in due course) holds through one who so acquired it; or

    (b) of a party (other than an intermediary bank or a payor bank which is not a depositary bank) who pays or satisfies the holder of an instrument which has been restrictively indorsed in a manner not consistent with the terms of such restrictive indorsement.

(2) Payment or satisfaction may be made with the consent of the holder by any person including a stranger to the instrument. Sur-

render of the instrument to such a person gives him the rights of a transferee (Section 3—201).

## § 3—604
### Tender of Payment

**(1)** Any party making tender of full payment to a holder when or after it is due is discharged to the extent of all subsequent liability for interest, costs and attorney's fees.

**(2)** The holder's refusal of such tender wholly discharges any party who has a right of recourse against the party making the tender.

**(3)** Where the maker or acceptor of an instrument payable otherwise than on demand is able and ready to pay at every place of payment specified in the instrument when it is due, it is equivalent to tender.

## § 3—605
### Cancellation and Renunciation

**(1)** The holder of an instrument may even without consideration discharge any party
  (a) in any manner apparent on the face of the instrument or the indorsement, as by intentionally cancelling the instrument or the party's signature by destruction or mutilation, or by striking out the party's signature; or
  (b) by renouncing his rights by a writing signed and delivered or by surrender of the instrument to the party to be discharged.

**(2)** Neither cancellation nor renunciation without surrender of the instrument affects the title thereto.

## § 3—606
### Impairment of Recourse or of Collateral

**(1)** The holder discharges any party to the instrument to the extent that without such party's consent the holder
  (a) without express reservation of rights releases or agrees not to sue any person against whom the party has to the knowledge of the holder a right of recourse or agrees to suspend the right to enforce against such person the instrument or collateral or otherwise discharges such person, except that failure or delay in effecting any required presentment, protest or notice of dishonor with respect to any such person does not discharge any party as to whom presentment, protest or notice of dishonor is effective or unnecessary; or
  (b) unjustifiably impairs any collateral for the instrument given by or on behalf of the party or any person against whom he has a right of recourse.

**(2)** By express reservation of rights against a party with a right of recourse the holder preserves
  (a) all his rights against such party as of the time when the instrument was originally due; and
  (b) the right of the party to pay the instrument as of that time; and
  (c) all rights of such party to recourse against others.

# Part 7/Advice of International Sight Draft

## § 3—701
### Letter of Advice of International Sight Draft

**(1)** A "letter of advice" is a drawer's communication to the drawee that a described draft has been drawn.

**(2)** Unless otherwise agreed when a bank receives from another bank a letter of advice of an international sight draft the drawee bank may immediately debit the drawer's account and stop the running of interest pro tanto. Such a debit and any resulting credit to any account covering outstanding drafts leaves in the drawer full power to stop payment or otherwise dispose of the amount and creates no trust or interest in favor of the holder.

**(3)** Unless otherwise agreed and except where a draft is drawn under a credit issued by the drawee, the drawee of an international sight draft owes the drawer no duty to pay an unadvised draft but if it does so and the draft is genuine, may appropriately debit the drawer's account.

# Part 8/Miscellaneous

## § 3—801
### Drafts in a Set

**(1)** Where a draft is drawn in a set of parts, each of which is numbered and expressed to be an order only if no other part has been honored, the whole of the parts constitutes one draft but a taker of any part may become a holder in due course of the draft.

**(2)** Any person who negotiates, indorses or accepts a single part of a draft drawn in a set thereby becomes liable to any holder in due course of that part as if it were the whole set, but as between different holders in due course to whom different parts have been negotiated the holder whose title first accrues has all rights to the draft and its proceeds.

**(3)** As against the drawee the first presented part of a draft drawn in a set is the part entitled to payment, or if a time draft to acceptance and payment. Acceptance of any subsequently presented part renders the drawee liable thereon under subsection (2). With respect both to a holder and to the drawer payment of a subsequently presented part of a draft payable at sight has the same effect as payment of a check notwithstanding an effective stop order (Section 4—407).

**(4)** Except as otherwise provided in this section, where any part of a draft in a set is discharged by payment or otherwise the whole draft is discharged.

## § 3—802
### Effect of Instrument on Obligation for Which It Is Given

**(1)** Unless otherwise agreed where an instrument is taken for an underlying obligation
  (a) the obligation is pro tanto discharged if a bank is drawer, maker or acceptor of the instrument and there is no recourse on the instrument against the underlying obligor; and
  (b) in any other case the obligation is suspended pro tanto until the instrument is due or if it is payable on demand until its presentment. If the instrument is dishonored action may be maintained on either the instrument or the obligation; dis-

charge of the underlying obligor on the instrument also discharges him on the obligation.

(2) The taking in good faith of a check which is not post-dated does not of itself so extend the time on the original obligation as to discharge a surety.

### § 3—803
### Notice to Third Party

Where a defendant is sued for breach of an obligation for which a third person is answerable over under this Article he may give the third person written notice of the litigation, and the person notified may then give similar notice to any other person who is answerable over to him under this Article. If the notice states that the person notified may come in and defend and that if the person notified does not do so he will in any action against him by the person giving the notice be bound by any determination of fact common to the two litigations, then unless after seasonable receipt of the notice the person notified does come in and defend he is so bound.

### § 3—804
### Lost, Destroyed or Stolen Instruments

The owner of an instrument which is lost, whether by destruction, theft or otherwise, may maintain an action in his own name and recover from any party liable thereon upon due proof of his ownership, the facts which prevent his production of the instrument and its terms. The court may require security indemnifying the defendant against loss by reason of further claims on the instrument.

### § 3—805
### Instruments Not Payable to Order or to Bearer

This Article applies to any instrument whose terms do not preclude transfer and which is otherwise negotiable within this Article but which is not payable to order or to bearer, except that there can be no holder in due course of such an instrument.

## ARTICLE 4/BANK DEPOSITS AND COLLECTIONS

### Part 1/General Provisions and Definitions

### § 4—101
### Short Title

This Article shall be known and may be cited as Uniform Commercial Code—Bank Deposits and Collections.

### § 4—102
### Applicability

(1) To the extent that items within this Article are also within the scope of Articles 3 and 8, they are subject to the provisions of those Articles. In the event of conflict the provisions of this Article govern those of Article 3 but the provisions of Article 8 govern those of this Article.

(2) The liability of a bank for action or non-action with respect to any item handled by it for purposes of presentment, payment or collection is governed by the law of the place where the bank is located. In the case of action or non-action by or at a branch or separate office of a bank, its liability is governed by the law of the place where the branch or separate office is located.

### § 4—103
### Variation by Agreement; Measure of Damages; Certain Action Constituting Ordinary Care

(1) The effect of the provisions of this Article may be varied by agreement except that no agreement can disclaim a bank's responsibility for its own lack of good faith or failure to exercise ordinary care or can limit the measure of damages for such lack or failure; but the parties may by agreement determine the standards by which such responsibility is to be measured if such standards are not manifestly unreasonable.

(2) Federal Reserve regulations and operating letters, clearing house rules, and the like, have the effect of agreements under subsection (1), whether or not specifically assented to by all parties interested in items handled.

(3) Action or non-action approved by this Article or pursuant to Federal Reserve regulations or operating letters constitutes the exercise of ordinary care and, in the absence of special instructions, action or non-action consistent with clearing house rules and the like or with a general banking usage not disapproved by this Article, prima facie constitutes the exercise of ordinary care.

(4) The specification or approval of certain procedures by this Article does not constitute disapproval of other procedures which may be reasonable under the circumstances.

(5) The measure of damages for failure to exercise ordinary care in handling an item is the amount of the item reduced by an amount which could not have been realized by the use of ordinary care, and where there is bad faith it includes other damages, if any, suffered by the party as a proximate consequence.

### § 4—104
### Definitions and Index of Definitions

(1) In this Article unless the context otherwise requires
  (a) "Account" means any account with a bank and includes a checking, time, interest or savings account;
  (b) "Afternoon" means the period of a day between noon and midnight;
  (c) "Banking day" means that part of any day on which a bank is open to the public for carrying on substantially all of its banking functions;
  (d) "Clearing house" means any association of banks or other payors regularly clearing items;
  (e) "Customer" means any person having an account with a bank or for whom a bank has agreed to collect items and includes a bank carrying an account with another bank;
  (f) "Documentary draft" means any negotiable or non-negotiable draft with accompanying documents, securities or other papers to be delivered against honor of the draft;
  (g) "Item" means any instrument for the payment of money even though it is not negotiable but does not include money;
  (h) "Midnight deadline" with respect to a bank is midnight on its next banking day following the banking day on which it receives the relevant item or notice or from which the time for taking action commences to run, whichever is later;
  (i) "Properly payable" includes the availability of funds for payment at the time of decision to pay or dishonor;
  (j) "Settle" means to pay in cash, by clearing house settlement, in a charge or credit or by remittance, or otherwise as instructed. A settlement may be either provisional or final;

(k) "Suspends payments" with respect to a bank means that it has been closed by order of the supervisory authorities, that a public officer has been appointed to take it over or that it ceases or refuses to make payments in the ordinary course of business.

(2) Other definitions applying to this Article and the sections in which they appear are:

"Collecting bank" Section 4—105.
"Depositary bank" Section 4—105.
"Intermediary bank" Section 4—105.
"Payor bank" Section 4—105.
"Presenting bank" Section 4—105.
"Remitting bank" Section 4—105.

(3) The following definitions in other Articles apply to this Article:

"Acceptance" Section 3—410.
"Certificate of deposit" Section 3—104.
"Certification" Section 3—411.
"Check" Section 3—104.
"Draft" Section 3—104.
"Holder in due course" Section 3—302.
"Notice of dishonor" Section 3—508.
"Presentment" Section 3—504.
"Protest" Section 3—509.
"Secondary party" Section 3—102.

(4) In addition Article 1 contains general definitions and principles of construction and interpretation applicable throughout this Article.

## § 4—105
### "Depositary Bank"; "Intermediary Bank"; "Collecting Bank"; "Payor Bank"; "Presenting Bank"; "Remitting Bank"

In this Article unless the context otherwise requires:

(a) "Depositary bank" means the first bank to which an item is transferred for collection even though it is also the payor bank

(b) "Payor bank" means a bank by which an item is payable as drawn or accepted;

(c) "Intermediary bank" means any bank to which an item is transferred in course of collection except the depositary or payor bank;

(d) "Collecting bank" means any bank handling the item for collection except the payor bank;

(e) "Presenting bank" means any bank presenting an item except a payor bank;

(f) "Remitting bank" means any payor or intermediary bank remitting for an item.

## § 4—106
### Separate Office of a Bank

A branch or separate office of a bank [maintaining its own deposit ledgers] is a separate bank for the purpose of computing the time within which and determining the place at or to which action may be taken or notices or orders shall be given under this Article and under Article 3.

Note: *The brackets are to make it optional with the several states whether to require a branch to maintain its own deposit ledgers in order to be considered to be a separate bank for certain purposes under Article 4. In some states "maintaining its own deposit ledgers" is a satisfactory test. In others branch banking practices are such that this test would not be suitable.*

## § 4—107
### Time of Receipt of Items

(1) For the purpose of allowing time to process items, prove balances and make the necessary entries on its books to determine its position for the day, a bank may fix an afternoon hour of two P.M. or later as a cut-off hour for the handling of money and items and the making of entries on its books.

(2) Any item or deposit of money received on any day after a cut-off hour so fixed or after the close of the banking day may be treated as being received at the opening of the next banking day.

## § 4—108
### Delays

(1) Unless otherwise instructed, a collecting bank in a good faith effort to secure payment may, in the case of specific items and with or without the approval of any person involved, waive, modify or extend time limits imposed or permitted by this Act for a period not in excess of an additional banking day without discharge of secondary parties and without liability to its transferor or any prior party.

(2) Delay by a collecting bank or payor bank beyond time limits prescribed or permitted by this Act or by instructions is excused if caused by interruption of communication facilities, suspension of payments by another bank, war, emergency conditions or other circumstances beyond the control of the bank provided it exercises such diligence as the circumstances require.

## § 4—109
### Process of Posting

The "process of posting" means the usual procedure followed by a payor bank in determining to pay an item and in recording the payment including one or more of the following or other steps as determined by the bank:

(a) verification of any signature;
(b) ascertaining that sufficient funds are available;
(c) affixing a "paid" or other stamp;
(d) entering a charge or entry to a customer's account;
(e) correcting or reversing an entry or erroneous action with respect to the item.

## *Part 2/Collection of Items: Depositary and Collecting Banks*

### § 4—201
#### Presumption and Duration of Agency Status of Collecting Banks and Provisional Status of Credits; Applicability of Article; Item Indorsed "Pay Any Bank"

(1) Unless a contrary intent clearly appears and prior to the time that a settlement given by a collecting bank for an item is or becomes final (subsection (3) of Section 4—211 and Sections 4—212 and 4—213) the bank is an agent or sub-agent of the owner of the item and any settlement given for the item is provisional. This provision applies regardless of the form of indorsement or lack of

indorsement and even though credit given for the item is subject to immediate withdrawal as of right or is in fact withdrawn; but the continuance of ownership of an item by its owner and any rights of the owner to proceeds of the item are subject to rights of a collecting bank such as those resulting from outstanding advances on the item and valid rights of setoff. When an item is handled by banks for purposes of presentment, payment and collection, the relevant provisions of this Article apply even though action of parties clearly establishes that a particular bank has purchased the item and is the owner of it.

(2) After an item has been indorsed with the words "pay any bank" or the like, only a bank may acquire the rights of a holder

    (a) until the item has been returned to the customer initiating collection; or

    (b) until the item has been specially indorsed by a bank to a person who is not a bank.

## § 4—202
### Responsibility for Collection; When Action Seasonable

(1) A collecting bank must use ordinary care in

    (a) presenting an item or sending it for presentment; and

    (b) sending notice of dishonor or non-payment or returning an item other than a documentary draft to the bank's transferor [or directly to the depositary bank under subsection (2) of Section 4—212] (*see note to Section 4—212*) after learning that the item has not been paid or accepted, as the case may be; and

    (c) settling for an item when the bank receives final settlement; and

    (d) making or providing for any necessary protest; and

    (e) notifying its transferor of any loss or delay in transit within a reasonable time after discovery thereof.

(2) A collecting bank taking proper action before its midnight deadline following receipt of an item, notice or payment acts seasonably; taking proper action within a reasonably longer time may be seasonable but the bank has the burden of so establishing.

(3) Subject to subsection (1)(a), a bank is not liable for the insolvency, neglect, misconduct, mistake or default of another bank or person or for loss or destruction of an item in transit or in the possession of others.

## § 4—203
### Effect of Instructions

Subject to the provisions of Article 3 concerning conversion of instruments (Section 3—419) and the provisions of both Article 3 and this Article concerning restrictive indorsements only a collecting bank's transferor can give instructions which affect the bank or constitute notice to it and a collecting bank is not liable to prior parties for any action taken pursuant to such instructions or in accordance with any agreement with its transferor.

## § 4—204
### Methods of Sending and Presenting; Sending Direct to Payor Bank

(1) A collecting bank must send items by reasonably prompt method taking into consideration any relevant instructions, the nature of the item, the number of such items on hand, and the cost of collection involved and the method generally used by it or others to present such items.

(2) A collecting bank may send

    (a) any item direct to the payor bank;

    (b) any item to any non-bank payor if authorized by its transferor; and

    (c) any item other than documentary drafts to any non-bank payor, if authorized by Federal Reserve regulation or operating letter, clearing house rule or the like.

(3) Presentment may be made by a presenting bank at a place where the payor bank has requested that presentment be made.

## § 4—205
### Supplying Missing Indorsement; No Notice from Prior Indorsement

(1) A depositary bank which has taken an item for collection may supply any indorsement of the customer which is necessary to title unless the item contains the words "payee's indorsement required" or the like. In the absence of such a requirement a statement placed on the item by the depositary bank to the effect that the item was deposited by a customer or credited to his account is effective as the customer's indorsement.

(2) An intermediary bank, or payor bank which is not a depositary bank, is neither given notice nor otherwise affected by a restrictive indorsement of any person except the bank's immediate transferor.

## § 4—206
### Transfer Between Banks

Any agreed method which identifies the transferor bank is sufficient for the item's further transfer to another bank.

## § 4—207
### Warranties of Customer and Collecting Bank on Transfer or Presentment of Items; Time for Claims

(1) Each customer or collecting bank who obtains payment or acceptance of an item and each prior customer and collecting bank warrants to the payor bank or other payor who in good faith pays or accepts the item that

    (a) he has a good title to the item or is authorized to obtain payment or acceptance on behalf of one who has a good title; and

    (b) he has no knowledge that the signature of the maker or drawer is unauthorized, except that this warranty is not given by any customer or collecting bank that is a holder in due course and acts in good faith

        (i) to a maker with respect to the maker's own signature; or

        (ii) to a drawer with respect to the drawer's own signature, whether or not the drawer is also the drawee; or

        (iii) to an acceptor of an item if the holder in due course took the item after the acceptance or obtained the acceptance without knowledge that the drawer's signature was unauthorized; and

    (c) the item has not been materially altered, except that this warranty is not given by any customer or collecting bank that is a holder in due course and acts in good faith

(i) to the maker of a note; or
(ii) to the drawer of a draft whether or not the drawer is also the drawee; or
(iii) to the acceptor of an item with respect to an alteration made prior to the acceptance if the holder in due course took the item after the acceptance, even though the acceptance provided "payable as originally drawn" or equivalent terms; or
(iv) to the acceptor of an item with respect to an alteration made after the acceptance.

(2) Each customer and collecting bank who transfers an item and receives a settlement or other consideration for it warrants to his transferee and to any subsequent collecting bank who takes the item in good faith that
(a) he has a good title to the item or is authorized to obtain payment or acceptance on behalf of one who has a good title and the transfer is otherwise rightful; and
(b) all signatures are genuine or authorized; and
(c) the item has not been materially altered; and
(d) no defense of any party is good against him; and
(e) he has no knowledge of any insolvency proceeding instituted with respect to the maker or acceptor or the drawer of an unaccepted item.

In addition each customer and collecting bank so transferring an item and receiving a settlement or other consideration engages that upon dishonor and any necessary notice of dishonor and protest he will take up the item.

(3) The warranties and the engagement to honor set forth in the two preceding subsections arise notwithstanding the absence of indorsement or words of guaranty or warranty in the transfer or presentment and a collecting bank remains liable for their breach despite remittance to its transferor. Damages for breach of such warranties or engagement to honor shall not exceed the consideration received by the customer or collecting bank responsible plus finance charges and expenses related to the item, if any.

(4) Unless a claim for breach of warranty under this section is made within a reasonable time after the person claiming learns of the breach, the person liable is discharged to the extent of any loss caused by the delay in making claim.

## § 4—208
### Security Interest of Collecting Bank in Items, Accompanying Documents and Proceeds

(1) A bank has a security interest in an item and any accompanying documents or the proceeds of either
(a) in case of an item deposited in an account to the extent to which credit given for the item has been withdrawn or applied;
(b) in case of an item for which it has given credit available for withdrawal as of right, to the extent of the credit given whether or not the credit is drawn upon and whether or not there is a right of charge-back; or
(c) if it makes an advance on or against the item.

(2) When credit which has been given for several items received at one time or pursuant to a single agreement is withdrawn or applied in part the security interest remains upon all the items, any accompanying documents or the proceeds of either. For the purpose of this section, credits first given are first withdrawn.

(3) Receipt by a collecting bank of a final settlement for an item is a realization on its security interest in the item, accompanying documents and proceeds. To the extent and so long as the bank does not receive final settlement for the item or give up possession of the item or accompanying documents for purposes other than collection, the security interest continues and is subject to the provisions of Article 9 except that
(a) no security agreement is necessary to make the security interest enforceable (subsection (1)(b) of Section 9—203); and
(b) no filing is required to perfect the security interest; and
(c) the security interest has priority over conflicting perfected security interests in the item, accompanying documents or proceeds.

## § 4—209
### When Bank Gives Value for Purposes of Holder in Due Course

For purposes of determining its status as a holder in due course, the bank has given value to the extent that it has a security interest in an item provided that the bank otherwise complies with the requirements of Section 3—302 on what constitutes a holder in due course.

## § 4—210
### Presentment by Notice of Item Not Payable by, Through or at a Bank; Liability of Secondary Parties

(1) Unless otherwise instructed, a collecting bank may present an item not payable by, through or at a bank by sending to the party to accept or pay a written notice that the bank holds the item for acceptance or payment. The notice must be sent in time to be received on or before the day when presentment is due and the bank must meet any requirement of the party to accept or pay under Section 3—505 by the close of the bank's next banking day after it knows of the requirement.

(2) Where presentment is made by notice and neither honor nor request for compliance with a requirement under Section 3—505 is received by the close of business on the day after maturity or in the case of demand items by the close of business on the third banking day after notice was sent, the presenting bank may treat the item as dishonored and charge any secondary party by sending him notice of the facts.

## § 4—211
### Media of Remittance; Provisional and Final Settlement in Remittance Cases

(1) A collecting bank may take in settlement of an item
(a) a check of the remitting bank or of another bank on any bank except the remitting bank; or
(b) a cashier's check or similar primary obligation of a remitting bank which is a member of or clears through a member of the same clearing house or group as the collecting bank; or
(c) appropriate authority to charge an account of the remitting bank or of another bank with the collecting bank; or
(d) if the item is drawn upon or payable by a person other than a bank, a cashier's check, certified check or other bank check or obligation.

(2) If before its midnight deadline the collecting bank properly dishonors a remittance check or authorization to charge on itself or presents or forwards for collection a remittance instrument of or on another bank which is of a kind approved by subsection (1) or has not been authorized by it, the collecting bank is not liable to prior parties in the event of the dishonor of such check, instrument or authorization.

(3) A settlement for an item by means of a remittance instrument or authorization to charge is or becomes a final settlement as to both the person making and the person receiving the settlement
    (a) if the remittance instrument or authorization to charge is of a kind approved by subsection (1) or has not been authorized by the person receiving the settlement and in either case the person receiving the settlement acts seasonably before its midnight deadline in presenting, forwarding for collection or paying the instrument or authorization,—at the time the remittance instrument or authorization is finally paid by the payor by which it is payable;
    (b) if the person receiving the settlement has authorized remittance by a non-bank check or obligation or by a cashier's check or similar primary obligation of or a check upon the payor or other remitting bank which is not of a kind approved by subsection (1)(b),—at the time of the receipt of such remittance check or obligation; or
    (c) if in a case not covered by sub-paragraphs (a) or (b) the person receiving the settlement fails to seasonably present, forward for collection, pay or return a remittance instrument or authorization to it to charge before its midnight deadline,—at such midnight deadline.

## § 4—212
### Right of Charge-Back or Refund

(1) If a collecting bank has made provisional settlement with its customer for an item and itself fails by reason of dishonor, suspension of payments by a bank or otherwise to receive a settlement for the item which is or becomes final, the bank may revoke the settlement given by it, charge back the amount of any credit given for the item to its customer's account or obtain refund from its customer whether or not it is able to return the items if by its midnight deadline or within a longer reasonable time after it learns the facts it returns the item or sends notification of the facts. These rights to revoke, charge-back and obtain refund terminate if and when a settlement for the item received by the bank is or becomes final (subsection (3) of Section 4—211 and subsections (2) and (3) of Section 4—213).

[(2) Within the time and manner prescribed by this section and Section 4—301, an intermediary or payor bank, as the case may be, may return an unpaid item directly to the depositary bank and may send for collection a draft on the depositary bank and obtain reimbursement. In such case, if the depositary bank has received provisional settlement for the item, it must reimburse the bank drawing the draft and any provisional credits for the item between banks shall become and remain final.]

Note: *Direct returns are recognized as an innovation that is not yet established bank practice, and therefore, Paragraph 2 has been bracketed. Some lawyers have doubts whether it should be included in legislation or left to development by agreement.*

(3) A depositary bank which is also the payor may chargeback the amount of an item to its customer's account or obtain refund in accordance with the section governing return of an item received by a payor bank for credit on its books (Section 4—301).

(4) The right to charge-back is not affected by
    (a) prior use of the credit given for the item; or
    (b) failure by any bank to exercise ordinary care with respect to the item but any bank so failing remains liable.

(5) A failure to charge-back or claim refund does not affect other rights of the bank against the customer or any other party.

(6) If credit is given in dollars as the equivalent of the value of an item payable in a foreign currency the dollar amount of any charge-back or refund shall be calculated on the basis of the buying sight rate for the foreign currency prevailing on the day when the person entitled to the charge-back or refund learns that it will not receive payment in ordinary course.

## § 4—213
### Final Payment of Item by Payor Bank; When Provisional Debits and Credits Become Final; When Certain Credits Become Available for Withdrawal

(1) An item is finally paid by a payor bank when the bank has done any of the following, whichever happens first:
    (a) paid the item in cash; or
    (b) settled for the item without reserving a right to revoke the settlement and without having such right under statute, clearing house rule or agreement; or
    (c) completed the process of posting the item to the indicated account of the drawer, maker or other person to be charged therewith; or
    (d) made a provisional settlement for the item and failed to revoke the settlement in the time and manner permitted by statute, clearing house rule or agreement.

Upon a final payment under subparagraphs (b), (c) or (d) the payor bank shall be accountable for the amount of the item.

(2) If provisional settlement for an item between the presenting and payor banks is made through a clearing house or by debits or credits in an account between them, then to the extent that provisional debits or credits for the item are entered in accounts between the presenting and payor banks or between the presenting and successive prior collecting banks seriatim, they become final upon final payment of the item by the payor bank.

(3) If a collecting bank receives a settlement for an item which is or becomes final (subsection (3) of Section 4—211, subsection (2) of Section 4—213) the bank is accountable to its customer for the amount of the item and any provisional credit given for the item in an account with its customer becomes final.

(4) Subject to any right of the bank to apply the credit to an obligation of the customer, credit given by a bank for an item in an account with its customer becomes available for withdrawal as of right
    (a) in any case where the bank has received a provisional settlement for the item,—when such settlement becomes final and the bank has had a reasonable time to learn that the settlement is final;
    (b) in any case where the bank is both a depositary bank and a payor bank and the item is finally paid,—at the opening of the bank's second banking day following receipt of the item.

**(5)** A deposit of money in a bank is final when made but, subject to any right of the bank to apply the deposit to an obligation of the customer, the deposit becomes available for withdrawal as of right at the opening of the bank's next banking day following receipt of the deposit.

§ 4—214
**Insolvency and Preference**

**(1)** Any item in or coming into the possession of a payor or collecting bank which suspends payment and which item is not finally paid shall be returned by the receiver, trustee or agent in charge of the closed bank to the presenting bank or the closed bank's customer.

**(2)** If a payor bank finally pays an item and suspends payments without making a settlement for the item with its customer or the presenting bank which settlement is or becomes final, the owner of the item has a preferred claim against the payor bank.

**(3)** If a payor bank gives or a collecting bank gives or receives a provisional settlement for an item and thereafter suspends payments, the suspension does not prevent or interfere with the settlement becoming final if such finality occurs automatically upon the lapse of certain time or the happening of certain events (subsection (3) of Section 4—211, subsections (1)(d), (2) and (3) of Section 4—213).

**(4)** If a collecting bank receives from subsequent parties settlement for an item which settlement is or becomes final and suspends payments without making a settlement for the item with its customer which is or becomes final, the owner of the item has a preferred claim against such collecting bank.

## Part 3/Collection of Items: Payor Banks

§ 4—301
**Deferred Posting; Recovery of Payment by Return of Items; Time of Dishonor**

**(1)** Where an authorized settlement for a demand item (other than a documentary draft) received by a payor bank otherwise than for immediate payment over the counter has been made before midnight of the banking day of receipt the payor bank may revoke the settlement and recover any payment if before it has made final payment (subsection (1) of Section 4—213) and before its midnight deadline it
  **(a)** returns the item; or
  **(b)** sends written notice of dishonor or nonpayment if the item is held for protest or is otherwise unavailable for return.

**(2)** If a demand item is received by a payor bank for credit on its books it may return such item or send notice of dishonor and may revoke any credit given or recover the amount thereof withdrawn by its customer, if it acts within the time limit and in the manner specified in the preceding subsection.

**(3)** Unless previous notice of dishonor has been sent an item is dishonored at the time when for purposes of dishonor it is returned or notice sent in accordance with this section.

**(4)** An item is returned:
  **(a)** as to an item received through a clearing house, when it is delivered to the presenting or last collecting bank or to the clearing house or is sent or delivered in accordance with its rules; or

  **(b)** in all other cases, when it is sent or delivered to the bank's customer or transferor or pursuant to his instructions.

§ 4—302
**Payor Bank's Responsibility for Late Return of Item**

In the absence of a valid defense such as breach of a presentment warranty (subsection (1) of Section 4—207), settlement effected or the like, if an item is presented on and received by a payor bank the bank is accountable for the amount of
  **(a)** a demand item other than a documentary draft whether properly payable or not if the bank, in any case where it is not also the depositary bank, retains the item beyond midnight of the banking day of receipt without settling for it or, regardless of whether it is also the depositary bank, does not pay or return the item or send notice of dishonor until after its midnight deadline; or
  **(b)** any other properly payable item unless within the time allowed for acceptance or payment of that item the bank either accepts or pays the item or returns it and accompanying documents.

§ 4—303
**When Items Subject to Notice, Stop-Order, Legal Process or Setoff; Order in Which Items May Be Charged or Certified**

**(1)** Any knowledge, notice or stop-order received by, legal process served upon or setoff exercised by a payor bank, whether or not effective under other rules of law to terminate, suspend or modify the bank's right or duty to pay an item or to charge its customer's account for the item, comes too late to so terminate, suspend or modify such right or duty if the knowledge, notice, stop-order or legal process is received or served and a reasonable time for the bank to act thereon expires or the setoff is exercised after the bank has done any of the following:
  **(a)** accepted or certified the item;
  **(b)** paid the item in cash;
  **(c)** settled for the item without reserving a right to revoke the settlement and without having such right under statute, clearing house rule or agreement;
  **(d)** completed the process of posting the item to the indicated account of the drawer, maker or other person to be charged therewith or otherwise has evidenced by examination of such indicated account and by action its decision to pay the item; or
  **(e)** become accountable for the amount of the item under subsection (1)(d) of Section 4—213 and Section 4—302 dealing with the payor bank's responsibility for late return of items.

**(2)** Subject to the provisions of subsection (1) items may be accepted, paid, certified or charged to the indicated account of its customer in any order convenient to the bank.

## Part 4/Relationship Between Payor Bank and Its Customer

§ 4—401
**When Bank May Charge Customer's Account**

**(1)** As against its customer, a bank may charge against his account any item which is otherwise properly payable from that account even though the charge creates an overdraft.

(2) A bank which in good faith makes payment to a holder may charge the indicated account of its customer according to
- (a) the original tenor of his altered item; or
- (b) the tenor of his completed item, even though the bank knows the item has been completed unless the bank has notice that the completion was improper.

## § 4—402
### Bank's Liability to Customer for Wrongful Dishonor

A payor bank is liable to its customer for damages proximately caused by the wrongful dishonor of an item. When the dishonor occurs through mistake liability is limited to actual damages proved. If so proximately caused and proved damages may include damages for an arrest or prosecution of the customer or other consequential damages. Whether any consequential damages are proximately caused by the wrongful dishonor is a question of fact to be determined in each case.

## § 4—403
### Customer's Right to Stop Payment; Burden of Proof of Loss

(1) A customer may by order to his bank stop payment of any item payable for his account but the order must be received at such time and in such manner as to afford the bank a reasonable opportunity to act on it prior to any action by the bank with respect to the item described in Section 4—303.

(2) An oral order is binding upon the bank only for fourteen calendar days unless confirmed in writing within that period. A written order is effective for only six months unless renewed in writing.

(3) The burden of establishing the fact and amount of loss resulting from the payment of an item contrary to a binding stop payment order is on the customer.

## § 4—404
### Bank Not Obligated to Pay Check More Than Six Months Old

A bank is under no obligation to a customer having a checking account to pay a check, other than a certified check, which is presented more than six months after its date, but it may charge its customer's account for a payment made thereafter in good faith.

## § 4—405
### Death or Incompetence of Customer

(1) A payor or collecting bank's authority to accept, pay or collect an item or to account for proceeds of its collection if otherwise effective is not rendered ineffective by incompetence of a customer of either bank existing at the time the item is issued or its collection is undertaken if the bank does not know of an adjudication of incompetence. Neither death nor incompetence of a customer revokes such authority to accept, pay, collect or account until the bank knows of the fact of death or of an adjudication of incompetence and has reasonable opportunity to act on it.

(2) Even with knowledge a bank may for ten days after the date of death pay or certify checks drawn on or prior to that date unless ordered to stop payment by a person claiming an interest in the account.

## § 4—406
### Customer's Duty to Discover and Report Unauthorized Signature or Alteration

(1) When a bank sends to its customer a statement of account accompanied by items paid in good faith in support of the debit entries or holds the statement and items pursuant to a request or instructions of its customer or otherwise in a reasonable manner makes the statement and items available to the customer, the customer must exercise reasonable care and promptness to examine the statement and items to discover his unauthorized signature or any alteration on an item and must notify the bank promptly after discovery thereof.

(2) If the bank establishes that the customer failed with respect to an item to comply with the duties imposed on the customer by subsection (1) the customer is precluded from asserting against the bank
- (a) his unauthorized signature or any alteration on the item if the bank also establishes that it suffered a loss by reason of such failure; and
- (b) an unauthorized signature or alteration by the same wrongdoer on any other item paid in good faith by the bank after the first item and statement was available to the customer for a reasonable period not exceeding fourteen calendar days and before the bank receives notification from the customer of any such unauthorized signature or alteration.

(3) The preclusion under subsection (2) does not apply if the customer establishes lack of ordinary care on the part of the bank in paying the item(s).

(4) Without regard to care or lack of care of either the customer or the bank a customer who does not within one year from the time the statement and items are made available to the customer (subsection (1)) discover and report his unauthorized signature or any alteration on the face or back of the item or does not within three years from that time discover and report any unauthorized indorsement is precluded from asserting against the bank such unauthorized signature or indorsement or such alteration.

(5) If under this section a payor bank has a valid defense against a claim of a customer upon or resulting from payment of an item and waives or fails upon request to assert the defense the bank may not assert against any collecting bank or other prior party presenting or transferring the item a claim based upon the unauthorized signature or alteration giving rise to the customer's claim.

## § 4—407
### Payor Bank's Right to Subrogation on Improper Payment

If a payor bank has paid an item over the stop payment order of the drawer or maker or otherwise under circumstances giving a basis for objection by the drawer or maker, to prevent unjust enrichment and only to the extent necessary to prevent loss to the bank by reason of its payment of the item, the payor bank shall be subrogated to the rights
- (a) of any holder in due course on the item against the drawer or maker; and
- (b) of the payee or any other holder of the item against the drawer or maker either on the item or under the transaction out of which the item arose; and
- (c) of the drawer or maker against the payee or any other

holder of the item with respect to the transaction out of which the item arose.

## Part 5/Collection of Documentary Drafts

### § 4—501
**Handling of Documentary Drafts; Duty to Send for Presentment and to Notify Customer of Dishonor**

A bank which takes a documentary draft for collection must present or send the draft and accompanying documents for presentment and upon learning that the draft has not been paid or accepted in due course must seasonably notify its customer of such fact even though it may have discounted or bought the draft or extended credit available for withdrawal as of right.

### § 4—502
**Presentment of "On Arrival" Drafts**

When a draft or the relevant instructions require presentment "on arrival", "when goods arrive" or the like, the collecting bank need not present until in its judgment a reasonable time for arrival of the goods has expired. Refusal to pay or accept because the goods have not arrived is not dishonor; the bank must notify its transferor of such refusal but need not present the draft again until it is instructed to do so or learns of the arrival of the goods.

### § 4—503
**Responsibility of Presenting Bank for Documents and Goods; Report of Reasons for Dishonor; Referee in Case of Need**

Unless otherwise instructed and except as provided in Article 5 a bank presenting a documentary draft

(a) must deliver the documents to the drawee on acceptance of the draft if it is payable more than three days after presentment; otherwise, only on payment; and

(b) upon dishonor, either in the case of presentment for acceptance or presentment for payment, may seek and follow instructions from any referee in case of need designated in the draft or if the presenting bank does not choose to utilize his services it must use diligence and good faith to ascertain the reason for dishonor, must notify its transferor of the dishonor and of the results of its effort to ascertain the reasons therefor and must request instructions.

But the presenting bank is under no obligation with respect to goods represented by the documents except to follow any reasonable instructions seasonably received; it has a right to reimbursement for any expense incurred in following instructions and to prepayment of or indemnity for such expenses.

### § 4—504
**Privilege of Presenting Bank to Deal With Goods; Security Interest for Expenses**

(1) A presenting bank which, following the dishonor of a documentary draft, has seasonably requested instructions but does not receive them within a reasonable time may store, sell, or otherwise deal with the goods in any reasonable manner.

(2) For its reasonable expenses incurred by action under subsection (1) the presenting bank has a lien upon the goods or their proceeds, which may be foreclosed in the same manner as an unpaid seller's lien.

## ARTICLE 5/LETTERS OF CREDIT

### § 5—101
**Short Title**

This Article shall be known and may be cited as Uniform Commercial Code—Letters of Credit.

### § 5—102
**Scope**

(1) This Article applies

(a) to a credit issued by a bank if the credit requires a documentary draft or a documentary demand for payment; and

(b) to a credit issued by a person other than a bank if the credit requires that the draft or demand for payment be accompanied by a document of title; and

(c) to a credit issued by a bank or other person if the credit is not within subparagraphs (a) or (b) but conspicuously states that it is a letter of credit or is conspicuously so entitled.

(2) Unless the engagement meets the requirements of subsection (1), this Article does not apply to engagements to make advances or to honor drafts or demands for payment, to authorities to pay or purchase, to guarantees or to general agreements.

(3) This Article deals with some but not all of the rules and concepts of letters of credit as such rules or concepts have developed prior to this act or may hereafter develop. The fact that this Article states a rule does not by itself require, imply or negate application of the same or a converse rule to a situation not provided for or to a person not specified by this Article.

### § 5—103
**Definitions**

(1) In this Article unless the context otherwise requires

(a) "Credit" or "letter of credit" means an engagement by a bank or other person made at the request of a customer and of a kind within the scope of this Article (Section 5—102) that the issuer will honor drafts or other demands for payment upon compliance with the conditions specified in the credit. A credit may be either revocable or irrevocable. The engagement may be either an agreement to honor or a statement that the bank or other person is authorized to honor.

(b) A "documentary draft" or a "documentary demand for payment" is one honor of which is conditioned upon the presentation of a document or documents. "Document" means any paper including document of title, security, invoice, certificate, notice of default and the like.

(c) An "issuer" is a bank or other person issuing a credit.

(d) A "beneficiary" of a credit is a person who is entitled under its terms to draw or demand payment.

(e) An "advising bank" is a bank which gives notification of the issuance of a credit by another bank.

(f) A "conforming bank" is a bank which engages either that it will itself honor a credit already issued by another bank or that such a credit will be honored by the issuer or a third bank.

(g) A "customer" is a buyer or other person who causes an

issuer to issue a credit. The term also includes a bank which procures issuance or confirmation on behalf of that bank's customer.

(2) Other definitions applying to this Article and the sections in which they appear are:

"Notation of Credit". Section 5—108.
"Presenter". Section 5—112(3).

(3) Definitions in other Articles applying to this Article and the sections in which they appear are:

"Accept" or "Acceptance". Section 3—410.
"Contract for sale". Section 2—106.
"Draft". Section 3—104.
"Holder in due course". Section 3—302.
"Midnight deadline". Section 4—104.
"Security". Section 8—102.

(4) In addition, Article 1 contains general definitions and principles of construction and interpretation applicable throughout this Article.

## § 5—104
### Formal Requirements; Signing

(1) Except as otherwise required in subsection (1)(c) of Section 5—102 on scope, no particular form of phrasing is required for a credit. A credit must be in writing and signed by the issuer and a confirmation must be in writing and signed by the confirming bank. A modification of the terms of a credit or confirmation must be signed by the issuer or confirming bank.

(2) A telegram may be a sufficient signed writing if it identifies its sender by an authorized authentication. The authentication may be in code and the authorized naming of the issuer in an advice of credit is a sufficient signing.

## § 5—105
### Consideration

No consideration is necessary to establish a credit or to enlarge or otherwise modify its terms.

## § 5—106
### Time and Effect of Establishment of Credit

(1) Unless otherwise agreed a credit is established
  (a) as regards the customer as soon as a letter of credit is sent to him or the letter of credit or an authorized written advice of its issuance is sent to the beneficiary; and
  (b) as regards the beneficiary when he receives a letter of credit or an authorized written advice of its issuance.

(2) Unless otherwise agreed once an irrevocable credit is established as regards the customer it can be modified or revoked only with the consent of the customer and once it is established as regards the beneficiary it can be modified or revoked only with his consent.

(3) Unless otherwise agreed after a revocable credit is established it may be modified or revoked by the issuer without notice to or consent from the customer or beneficiary.

(4) Notwithstanding any modification or revocation of a revocable credit any person authorized to honor or negotiate under the terms of the original credit is entitled to reimbursement for or honor of any draft or demand for payment duly honored or negotiated before receipt of notice of the modification or revocation and the issuer in turn is entitled to reimbursement from its customer.

## § 5—107
### Advice of Credit; Confirmation; Error in Statement of Terms

(1) Unless otherwise specified an advising bank by advising a credit issued by another bank does not assume any obligation to honor drafts drawn or demands for payment made under the credit but it does assume obligation for the accuracy of its own statement.

(2) A confirming bank by confirming a credit becomes directly obligated on the credit to the extent of its confirmation as though it were its issuer and acquires the rights of an issuer.

(3) Even though an advising bank incorrectly advises the terms of a credit it has been authorized to advise the credit is established as against the issuer to the extent of its original terms.

(4) Unless otherwise specified the customer bears as against the issuer all risk of transmission and reasonable translation or interpretation of any message relating to a credit.

## § 5—108
### "Notation Credit"; Exhaustion of Credit

(1) A credit which specifies that any person purchasing or paying drafts drawn or demands for payment made under it must note the amount of the draft or demand on the letter or advice of credit is a "notation credit".

(2) Under a notation credit
  (a) a person paying the beneficiary or purchasing a draft or demand for payment from him acquires a right to honor only if the appropriate notation is made and by transferring or forwarding for honor the documents under the credit such a person warrants to the issuer that the notation has been made; and
  (b) unless the credit or a signed statement that an appropriate notation has been made accompanies the draft or demand for payment the issuer may delay honor until evidence of notation has been procured which is satisfactory to it but its obligation and that of its customer continue for a reasonable time not exceeding thirty days to obtain such evidence.

(3) If the credit is not a notation credit
  (a) the issuer may honor complying drafts or demands for payment presented to it in the order in which they are presented and is discharged pro tanto by honor of any such draft or demand;
  (b) as between competing good faith purchasers of complying drafts or demands the person first purchasing has priority over a subsequent purchaser even though the later purchased draft or demand has been first honored.

## § 5—109
### Issuer's Obligation to Its Customer

(1) An issuer's obligation to its customer includes good faith and observance of any general banking usage but unless otherwise agreed does not include liability or responsibility
  (a) for performance of the underlying contract for sale or other transaction between the customer and the beneficiary; or

(b) for any act or omission of any person other than itself or its own branch or for loss or destruction of a draft, demand or document in transit or in the possession of others; or

(c) based on knowledge or lack of knowledge of any usage of any particular trade.

(2) An issuer must examine documents with care so as to ascertain that on their face they appear to comply with the terms of the credit but unless otherwise agreed assumes no liability or responsibility for the genuineness, falsification or effect of any document which appears on such examination to be regular on its face.

(3) A non-bank issuer is not bound by any banking usage of which it has no knowledge.

## § 5—110
**Availability of Credit in Portions; Presenter's Reservation of Lien or Claim**

(1) Unless otherwise specified a credit may be used in portions in the discretion of the beneficiary.

(2) Unless otherwise specified a person by presenting a documentary draft or demand for payment under a credit relinquishes upon its honor all claims to the documents and a person by transferring such draft or demand or causing such presentment authorizes such relinquishment. An explicit reservation of claim makes the draft or demand non-complying.

## § 5—111
**Warranties on Transfer and Presentment**

(1) Unless otherwise agreed the beneficiary by transferring or presenting a documentary draft or demand for payment warrants to all interested parties that the necessary conditions of the credit have been complied with. This is in addition to any warranties arising under Articles 3, 4, 7 and 8.

(2) Unless otherwise agreed a negotiating, advising, confirming, collecting or issuing bank presenting or transferring a draft or demand for payment under a credit warrants only the matters warranted by a collecting bank under Article 4 and any such bank transferring a document warrants only the matters warranted by an intermediary under Articles 7 and 8.

## § 5—112
**Time Allowed for Honor or Rejection; Withholding Honor or Rejection by Consent; "Presenter"**

(1) A bank to which a documentary draft or demand for payment is presented under a credit may without dishonor of the draft, demand or credit

(a) defer honor until the close of the third banking day following receipt of the documents; and

(b) further defer honor if the presenter has expressly or impliedly consented thereto.

Failure to honor within the time here specified constitutes dishonor of the draft or demand and of the credit [except as otherwise provided in subsection (4) of Section 5—114 on conditional payment].

Note: *The bracketed language in the last sentence of subsection (1) should be included only if the optional provisions of Section 5—114(4) and (5) are included.*

(2) Upon dishonor the bank may unless otherwise instructed fulfill its duty to return the draft or demand and the documents by holding them at the disposal of the presenter and sending him an advice to that effect.

(3) "Presenter" means any person presenting a draft or demand for payment for honor under a credit even though that person is a confirming bank or other correspondent which is acting under an issuer's authorization.

## § 5—113
**Indemnities**

(1) A bank seeking to obtain (whether for itself or another) honor, negotiation or reimbursement under a credit may give an indemnity to induce such honor, negotiation or reimbursement.

(2) An indemnity agreement inducing honor, negotiation or reimbursement

(a) unless otherwise explicitly agreed applies to defects in the documents but not in the goods; and

(b) unless a longer time is explicitly agreed expires at the end of ten business days following receipt of the documents by the ultimate customer unless notice of objection is sent before such expiration date. The ultimate customer may send notice of objection to the person from whom he received the documents and any bank receiving such notice is under a duty to send notice to its transferor before its midnight deadline.

## § 5—114
**Issuer's Duty and Privilege to Honor; Right to Reimbursement**

(1) An issuer must honor a draft or demand for payment which complies with the terms of the relevant credit regardless of whether the goods or documents conform to the underlying contract for sale or other contract between the customer and the beneficiary. The issuer is not excused from honor of such a draft or demand by reason of an additional general term that all documents must be satisfactory to the issuer, but an issuer may require that specified documents must be satisfactory to it.

(2) Unless otherwise agreed when documents appear on their face to comply with the terms of a credit but a required document does not in fact conform to the warranties made on negotiation or transfer of a document of title (Section 7—507) or of a certificated security (Section 8—306) or is forged or fraudulent or there is fraud in the transaction:

(a) the issuer must honor the draft or demand for payment if honor is demanded by a negotiating bank or other holder of the draft or demand which has taken the draft or demand under the credit and under circumstances which would make it a holder in due course (Section 3—302) and in an appropriate case would make it a person to whom a document of title has been duly negotiated (Section 7—502) or a bona fide purchaser of a certificated security (Section 8—302); and

(b) in all other cases as against its customer, an issuer acting in good faith may honor the draft or demand for payment despite notification from the customer of fraud, forgery or other defect not apparent on the face of the documents but a court of appropriate jurisdiction may enjoin such honor.

(3) Unless otherwise agreed an issuer which has duly honored a draft or demand for payment is entitled to immediate reimbursement of any payment made under the credit and to be put in effectively available funds not later than the day before maturity of any acceptance made under the credit.

[(4) When a credit provides for payment by the issuer on receipt of notice that the required documents are in the possession of a correspondent or other agent of the issuer

(a) any payment made on receipt of such notice is conditional; and

(b) the issuer may reject documents which do not comply with the credit if it does so within three banking days following its receipt of the documents; and

(c) in the event of such rejection, the issuer is entitled by charge back or otherwise to return of the payment made.]

[(5) In the case covered by subsection (4) failure to reject documents within the time specified in subparagraph (b) constitutes acceptance of the documents and makes the payment final in favor of the beneficiary.]

Amended in 1977.

Note: *Subsections (4) and (5) are bracketed as optional. If they are included the bracketed language in the last sentence of Section 5—112(1) should also be included.*

## § 5—115
### Remedy for Improper Dishonor or Anticipatory Repudiation

(1) When an issuer wrongfully dishonors a draft or demand for payment presented under a credit the person entitled to honor has with respect to any documents the rights of a person in the position of a seller (Section 2—707) and may recover from the issuer the face amount of the draft or demand together with incidental damages under Section 2—710 on seller's incidental damages and interest but less any amount realized by resale or other use or disposition of the subject matter of the transaction. In the event no resale or other utilization is made the documents, goods or other subject matter involved in the transaction must be turned over to the issuer on payment of judgment.

(2) When an issuer wrongfully cancels or otherwise repudiates a credit before presentment of a draft or demand for payment drawn under it the beneficiary has the rights of a seller after anticipatory repudiation by the buyer under Section 2—610 if he learns of the repudiation in time reasonably to avoid procurement of the required documents. Otherwise the beneficiary has an immediate right of action for wrongful dishonor.

## § 5—116
### Transfer and Assignment

(1) The right to draw under a credit can be transferred or assigned only when the credit is expressly designated as transferable or assignable.

(2) Even though the credit specifically states that it is non-transferable or nonassignable the beneficiary may before performance of the conditions of the credit assign his right to proceeds. Such an assignment is an assignment of an account under Article 9 on Secured Transactions and is governed by that Article except that

(a) the assignment is ineffective until the letter of credit or advice of credit is delivered to the assignee which delivery constitutes perfection of the security interest under Article 9; and

(b) the issuer may honor drafts or demands for payment drawn under the credit until it receives a notification of the assignment signed by the beneficiary which reasonably identifies the credit involved in the assignment and contains a request to pay the assignee; and

(c) after what reasonably appears to be such a notification has been received the issuer may without dishonor refuse to accept or pay even to a person otherwise entitled to honor until the letter of credit or advice of credit is exhibited to the issuer.

(3) Except where the beneficiary has effectively assigned his right to draw or his right to proceeds, nothing in this section limits his right to transfer or negotiate drafts or demands drawn under the credit.

## § 5—117
### Insolvency of Bank Holding Funds for Documentary Credit

(1) Where an issuer or an advising or confirming bank or a bank which has for a customer procured issuance of a credit by another bank becomes insolvent before final payment under the credit and the credit is one to which this Article is made applicable by paragraphs (a) or (b) of Section 5—102 (1) on scope, the receipt or allocation of funds or collateral to secure or meet obligations under the credit shall have the following results:

(a) to the extent of any funds or collateral turned over after or before the insolvency as indemnity against or specifically for the purpose of payment of drafts or demands for payment drawn under the designated credit, the drafts or demands are entitled to payment in preference over depositors or other general creditors of the issuer or bank; and

(b) on expiration of the credit or surrender of the beneficiary's rights under it unused any person who has given such funds or collateral is similarly entitled to return thereof; and

(c) a charge to a general or current account with a bank if specifically consented to for the purpose of indemnity against or payment of drafts or demands for payment drawn under the designated credit falls under the same rules as if the funds had been drawn out in cash and then turned over with specific instructions.

(2) After honor or reimbursement under this section the customer or other person for whose account the insolvent bank has acted is entitled to receive the documents involved.

# ARTICLE 6/BULK TRANSFERS

## § 6—101
### Short Title

This Article shall be known and may be cited as Uniform Commercial Code—Bulk Transfers.

## § 6—102
### "Bulk Transfers"; Transfers of Equipment; Enterprises Subject to This Article; Bulk Transfers Subject to This Article

(1) A "bulk transfer" is any transfer in bulk and not in the ordinary course of the transferor's business of a major part of the mate-

rials, supplies, merchandise or other inventory (Section 9—109) of an enterprise subject to this Article.

(2) A transfer of a substantial part of the equipment (Section 9—109) of such an enterprise is a bulk transfer if it is made in connection with a bulk transfer of inventory, but not otherwise.

(3) The enterprises subject to this Article are all those whose principal business is the sale of merchandise from stock, including those who manufacture what they sell.

(4) Except as limited by the following section all bulk transfers of goods located within this state are subject to this Article.

## § 6—103
### Transfers Excepted From This Article

The following transfers are not subject to this Article:

(1) Those made to give security for the performance of an obligation;

(2) General assignments for the benefit of all the creditors of the transferor, and subsequent transfers by the assignee thereunder;

(3) Transfers in settlement or realization of a lien or other security interest;

(4) Sales by executors, administrators, receivers, trustees in bankruptcy, or any public officer under judicial process;

(5) Sales made in the course of judicial or administrative proceedings for the dissolution or reorganization of a corporation and of which notice is sent to the creditors of the corporation pursuant to order of the court or administrative agency;

(6) Transfers to a person maintaining a known place of business in this State who becomes bound to pay the debts of the transferor in full and gives public notice of that fact, and who is solvent after becoming so bound;

(7) A transfer to a new business enterprise organized to take over and continue the business, if public notice of the transaction is given and the new enterprise assumes the debts of the transferor and he receives nothing from the transaction except an interest in the new enterprise junior to the claims of creditors;

(8) Transfers of property which is exempt from execution.

Public notice under subsection (6) or subsection (7) may be given by publishing once a week for two consecutive weeks in a newspaper of general circulation where the transferor had its principal place of business in this state an advertisement including the names and addresses of the transferor and transferee and the effective date of the transfer.

## § 6—104
### Schedule of Property; List of Creditors

(1) Except as provided with respect to auction sales (Section 6—108), a bulk transfer subject to this Article is ineffective against any creditor of the transferor unless:

 (a) the transferee requires the transferor to furnish a list of his existing creditors prepared as stated in this section; and
 (b) the parties prepare a schedule of the property transferred sufficient to identify it; and
 (c) the transferee preserves the list and schedule for six months next following the transfer and permits inspection of either or both and copying therefrom at all reasonable hours by any creditor of the transferor, or files the list and schedule in (*a public office to be here identified*).

(2) The list of creditors must be signed and sworn to or affirmed by the transferor or his agent. It must contain the names and business addresses of all creditors of the transferor, with the amounts when known, and also the names of all persons who are known to the transferor to assert claims against him even though such claims are disputed. If the transferor is the obligor of an outstanding issue of bonds, debentures or the like as to which there is an indenture trustee, the list of creditors need include only the name and address of the indenture trustee and the aggregate outstanding principal amount of the issue.

(3) Responsibility for the completeness and accuracy of the list of creditors rests on the transferor, and the transfer is not rendered ineffective by errors or omissions therein unless the transferee is shown to have had knowledge.

## § 6—105
### Notice to Creditors

In addition to the requirements of the preceding section, any bulk transfer subject to this Article except one made by auction sale (Section 6—108) is ineffective against any creditor of the transferor unless at least ten days before he takes possession of the goods or pays for them, whichever happens first, the transferee gives notice of the transfer in the manner and to the persons hereafter provided (Section 6—107).

## [§ 6—106
### Application of the Proceeds

In addition to the requirements of the two preceding sections:

(1) Upon every bulk transfer subject to this Article for which new consideration becomes payable except those made by sale at auction it is the duty of the transferee to assure that such consideration is applied so far as necessary to pay those debts of the transferor which are either shown on the list furnished by the transferor (Section 6—104) or filed in writing in the place stated in the notice (Section 6—107) within thirty days after the mailing of such notice. This duty of the transferee runs to all the holders of such debts, and may be enforced by any of them for the benefit of all.

(2) If any of said debts are in dispute the necessary sum may be withheld from distribution until the dispute is settled or adjudicated.

(3) If the consideration payable is not enough to pay all of the said debts in full distribution shall be made pro rata.]

Note: *This section is bracketed to indicate division of opinion as to whether or not it is a wise provision, and to suggest that this is a point on which State enactments may differ without serious damage to the principle of uniformity. In any State where this section is omitted, the following parts of sections, also bracketed in the text, should also be omitted, namely:*

 Section *6—107(2)(c).*
  *6—108(3)(c).*
  *6—109(2).*

 *In any State where this section is enacted, these other provisions should be also.*

*Optional Subsection (4)*

[(4) The transferee may within ten days after he takes possession of the goods pay the consideration into the (specify court) in the county where the transferor had its principal place of business in this state and thereafter may discharge his duty under this section by giving notice by registered or certified mail to all the persons to whom the duty runs that the consideration has been paid into that court and that they should file their claims there. On motion of any interested party, the court may order the distribution of the consideration to the persons entitled to it.]

Note: *Optional subsection (4) is recommended for those states which do not have a general statute providing for payment of money into court.*

## § 6—107
### The Notice

(1) The notice to creditors (Section 6—105) shall state:
   (a) that a bulk transfer is about to be made; and
   (b) the names and business addresses of the transferor and transferee, and all other business names and addresses used by the transferor within three years last past so far as known to the transferee; and
   (c) whether or not all the debts of the transferor are to be paid in full as they fall due as a result of the transaction, and if so, the address to which creditors should send their bills.

(2) If the debts of the transferor are not to be paid in full as they fall due or if the transferee is in doubt on that point then the notice shall state further:
   (a) the location and general description of the property to be transferred and the estimated total of the transferor's debts;
   (b) the address where the schedule of property and list of creditors (Section 6—104) may be inspected;
   (c) whether the transfer is to pay existing debts and if so the amount of such debts and to whom owing;
   (d) whether the transfer is for new consideration and if so the amount of such consideration and the time and place of payment; [and]
   [(e) if for new consideration the time and place where creditors of the transferor are to file their claims.]

(3) The notice in any case shall be delivered personally or sent by registered or certified mail to all the persons shown on the list of creditors furnished by the transferor (Section 6—104) and to all other persons who are known to the transferee to hold or assert claims against the transferor.

## § 6—108
### Auction Sales; "Auctioneer"

(1) A bulk transfer is subject to this Article even though it is by sale at auction, but only in the manner and with the results stated in this section.

(2) The transferor shall furnish a list of his creditors and assist in the preparation of a schedule of the property to be sold, both prepared as before stated (Section 6—104).

(3) The person or persons other than the transferor who direct, control or are responsible for the auction are collectively called the "auctioneer". The auctioneer shall:

   (a) receive and retain the list of creditors and prepare and retain the schedule of property for the period stated in this Article (Section 6—104);
   (b) give notice of the auction personally or by registered or certified mail at least ten days before it occurs to all persons shown on the list of creditors and to all other persons who are known to him to hold or assert claims against the transferor; [and]
   [(c) assure that the net proceeds of the auction are applied as provided in this Article (Section 6—106).]

(4) Failure of the auctioneer to perform any of these duties does not affect the validity of the sale or the title of the purchasers, but if the auctioneer knows that the auction constitutes a bulk transfer such failure renders the auctioneer liable to the creditors of the transferor as a class for the sums owing to them from the transferor up to but not exceeding the net proceeds of the auction. If the auctioneer consists of several persons their liability is joint and several.

## § 6—109
### What Creditors Protected; [Credit for Payment to Particular Creditors]

(1) The creditors of the transferor mentioned in this Article are those holding claims based on transactions or events occurring before the bulk transfer, but creditors who become such after notice to creditors is given (Sections 6—105 and 6—107) are not entitled to notice.

[(2) Against the aggregate obligation imposed by the provisions of this Article concerning the application of the proceeds (Section 6—106 and subsection (3)(c) of 6—108) the transferee or auctioneer is entitled to credit for sums paid to particular creditors of the transferor, not exceeding the sums believed in good faith at the time of the payment to be properly payable to such creditors.]

## § 6—110
### Subsequent Transfers

When the title of a transferee to property is subject to a defect by reason of his non-compliance with the requirements of this Article, then:

(1) a purchaser of any of such property from such transferee who pays no value or who takes with notice of such non-compliance takes subject to such defect, but

(2) a purchaser for value in good faith and without such notice takes free of such defect.

## § 6—111
### Limitation of Actions and Levies

No action under this Article shall be brought nor levy made more than six months after the date on which the transferee took possession of the goods unless the transfer has been concealed. If the transfer has been concealed, actions may be brought or levies made within six months after its discovery.

Note to Article 6: *Section 6—106 is bracketed to indicate division of opinion as to whether or not it is a wise provision, and to suggest that this is a point on which State enactments may differ without serious damage to the principle of uniformity. In any State where Section 6—106 is not enacted, the following parts of sections, also bracketed in the text, should also be omitted, namely:*

*Sec. 6—107(2)(e).*
*6—108(3)(c).*
*6—109(2).*

*In any State where Section 6—106 is enacted, these other provisions should be also.*

## ARTICLE 7/WAREHOUSE RECEIPTS, BILLS OF LADING AND OTHER DOCUMENTS OF TITLE

### Part 1/General

§ 7—101
**Short Title**

This Article shall be known and may be cited as Uniform Commercial Code—Documents of Title.

§ 7—102
**Definitions and Index of Definitions**

(1) In this Article, unless the context otherwise requires:
   (a) "Bailee" means the person who by a warehouse receipt, bill of lading or other document of title acknowledges possession of goods and contracts to deliver them.
   (b) "Consignee" means the person named in a bill to whom or to whose order the bill promises delivery.
   (c) "Consignor" means the person named in a bill as the person from whom the goods have been received for shipment.
   (d) "Delivery order" means a written order to deliver goods directed to a warehouseman, carrier or other person who in the ordinary course of business issues warehouse receipts or bills of lading.
   (e) "Document" means document of title as defined in the general definitions in Article 1 (Section 1—201).
   (f) "Goods" means all things which are treated as movable for the purposes of a contract of storage or transportation.
   (g) "Issuer" means a bailee who issues a document except that in relation to an unaccepted delivery order it means the person who orders the possessor of goods to deliver. Issuer includes any person for whom an agent or employee purports to act in issuing a document if the agent or employee has real or apparent authority to issue documents, notwithstanding that the issuer received no goods or that the goods were misdescribed or that in any other respect the agent or employee violated his instructions.
   (h) "Warehouseman" is a person engaged in the business of storing goods for hire.

(2) Other definitions applying to this Article or to specified Parts thereof, and the sections in which they appear are:

   "Duly negotiate". Section 7—501.
   "Person entitled under the document". Section 7—403(4).

(3) Definitions in other Articles applying to this Article and the sections in which they appear are:

   "Contract for sale". Section 2—106.
   "Overseas". Section 2—323.
   "Receipt" of goods. Section 2—103.

(4) In addition Article 1 contains general definitions and principles of construction and interpretation applicable throughout this Article.

§ 7—103
**Relation of Article to Treaty, Statute, Tariff, Classification or Regulation**

To the extent that any treaty or statute of the United States, regulatory statute of this State or tariff, classification or regulation filed or issued pursuant thereto is applicable, the provisions of this Article are subject thereto.

§ 7—104
**Negotiable and Non-Negotiable Warehouse Receipt, Bill of Lading or Other Document of Title**

(1) A warehouse receipt, bill of lading or other document of title is negotiable
   (a) if by its terms the goods are to be delivered to bearer or to the order of a named person; or
   (b) where recognized in overseas trade, if it runs to a named person or assigns.

(2) Any other document is non-negotiable. A bill of lading in which it is stated that the goods are consigned to a named person is not made negotiable by a provision that the goods are to be delivered only against a written order signed by the same or another named person.

§ 7—105
**Construction Against Negative Implication**

The omission from either Part 2 or Part 3 of this Article of a provision corresponding to a provision made in the other Part does not imply that a corresponding rule of law is not applicable.

### Part 2/Warehouse Receipts: Special Provisions

§ 7—201
**Who May Issue a Warehouse Receipt; Storage Under Government Bond**

(1) A warehouse receipt may be issued by any warehouseman.

(2) Where goods including distilled spirits and agricultural commodities are stored under a statute requiring a bond against withdrawal or a license for the issuance of receipts in the nature of warehouse receipts, a receipt issued for the goods has like effect as a warehouse receipt even though issued by a person who is the owner of the goods and is not a warehouseman.

§ 7—202
**Form of Warehouse Receipt; Essential Terms; Optional Terms**

(1) A warehouse receipt need not be in any particular form.

(2) Unless a warehouse receipt embodies within its written or printed terms each of the following, the warehouseman is liable for damages caused by the omission to a person injured thereby:
   (a) the location of the warehouse where the goods are stored;
   (b) the date of issue of the receipt;

(c) the consecutive number of the receipt;

(d) a statement whether the goods received will be delivered to the bearer, to a specified person, or to a specified person or his order;

(e) the rate of storage and handling charges, except that where goods are stored under a field warehousing arrangement a statement of that fact is sufficient on a non-negotiable receipt;

(f) a description of the goods or of the packages containing them;

(g) the signature of the warehouseman, which may be made by his authorized agent;

(h) if the receipt is issued for goods of which the warehouseman is owner, either solely or jointly or in common with others, the fact of such ownership; and

(i) a statement of the amount of advances made and of liabilities incurred for which the warehouseman claims a lien or security interest (Section 7—209). If the precise amount of such advances made or of such liabilities incurred is, at the time of the issue of the receipt, unknown to the warehouseman or to his agent who issues it, a statement of the fact that advances have been made or liabilities incurred and the purpose thereof is sufficient.

(3) A warehouseman may insert in his receipt any other terms which are not contrary to the provisions of this Act and do not impair his obligation of delivery (Section 7—403) or his duty of care (Section 7—204). Any contrary provisions shall be ineffective.

## § 7—203
### Liability for Non-Receipt or Misdescription

A party to or purchaser for value in good faith of a document of title other than a bill of lading relying in either case upon the description therein of the goods may recover from the issuer damages caused by the non-receipt or misdescription of the goods, except to the extent that the document conspicuously indicates that the issuer does not know whether any part or all of the goods in fact were received or conform to the description, as where the description is in terms of marks or labels or kind, quantity or condition, or the receipt or description is qualified by "contents, condition and quality unknown", "said to contain" or the like, if such indication be true, or the party or purchaser otherwise has notice.

## § 7—204
### Duty of Care; Contractual Limitation of Warehouseman's Liability

(1) A warehouseman is liable for damages for loss of or injury to the goods caused by his failure to exercise such care in regard to them as a reasonably careful man would exercise under like circumstances but unless otherwise agreed he is not liable for damages which could not have been avoided by the exercise of such care.

(2) Damages may be limited by a term in the warehouse receipt or storage agreement limiting the amount of liability in case of loss or damage, and setting forth a specific liability per article or item, or value per unit of weight, beyond which the warehouseman shall not be liable; provided, however, that such liability may on written request of the bailor at the time of signing such storage agreement or within a reasonable time after receipt of the warehouse receipt be increased on part or all of the goods thereunder, in which event increased rates may be charged based on such increased valuation, but that no such increase shall be permitted contrary to a lawful limitation of liability contained in the warehouseman's tariff, if any. No such limitation is effective with respect to the warehouseman's liability for conversion to his own use.

(3) Reasonable provisions as to the time and manner of presenting claims and instituting actions based on the bailment may be included in the warehouse receipt or tariff.

(4) This section does not impair or repeal . . .

Note: *Insert in subsection (4) a reference to any statute which imposes a higher responsibility upon the warehouseman or invalidates contractual limitations which would be permissible under this Article.*

## § 7—205
### Title Under Warehouse Receipt Defeated in Certain Cases

A buyer in the ordinary course of business of fungible goods sold and delivered by a warehouseman who is also in the business of buying and selling such goods takes free of any claim under a warehouse receipt even though it has been duly negotiated.

## § 7—206
### Termination of Storage at Warehouseman's Option

(1) A warehouseman may on notifying the person on whose account the goods are held and any other person known to claim an interest in the goods require payment of any charges and removal of the goods from the warehouse at the termination of the period of storage fixed by the document, or, if no period is fixed, within a stated period not less than thirty days after the notification. If the goods are not removed before the date specified in the notification, the warehouseman may sell them in accordance with the provisions of the section on enforcement of a warehouseman's lien (Section 7—210).

(2) If a warehouseman in good faith believes that the goods are about to deteriorate or decline in value to less than the amount of his lien within the time prescribed in subsection (1) for notification, advertisement and sale, the warehouseman may specify in the notification any reasonable shorter time for removal of the goods and in case the goods are not removed, may sell them at public sale held not less than one week after a single advertisement or posting.

(3) If as a result of a quality or condition of the goods of which the warehouseman had no notice at the time of deposit the goods are a hazard to other property or to the warehouse or to persons, the warehouseman may sell the goods at public or private sale without advertisement on reasonable notification to all persons known to claim an interest in the goods. If the warehouseman after a reasonable effort is unable to sell the goods he may dispose of them in any lawful manner and shall incur no liability by reason of such disposition.

(4) The warehouseman must deliver the goods to any person entitled to them under this Article upon due demand made at any time prior to sale or other disposition under this section.

(5) The warehouseman may satisfy his lien from the proceeds of any sale or disposition under this section but must hold the balance for delivery on the demand of any person to whom he would have been bound to deliver the goods.

## § 7—207
### Goods Must Be Kept Separate; Fungible Goods

**(1)** Unless the warehouse receipt otherwise provides, a warehouseman must keep separate the goods covered by each receipt so as to permit at all times identification and delivery of those goods except that different lots of fungible goods may be commingled.

**(2)** Fungible goods so commingled are owned in common by the persons entitled thereto and the warehouseman is severally liable to each owner for that owner's share. Where because of overissue a mass of fungible goods is insufficient to meet all the receipts which the warehouseman has issued against it, the persons entitled include all holders to whom overissued receipts have been duly negotiated.

## § 7—208
### Altered Warehouse Receipts

Where a blank in a negotiable warehouse receipt has been filled in without authority, a purchaser for value and without notice of the want of authority may treat the insertion as authorized. Any other unauthorized alteration leaves any receipt enforceable against the issuer according to its original tenor.

## § 7—209
### Lien of Warehouseman

**(1)** A warehouseman has a lien against the bailor on the goods covered by a warehouse receipt or on the proceeds thereof in his possession for charges for storage or transportation (including demurrage and terminal charges), insurance, labor, or charges present or future in relation to the goods, and for expenses necessary for preservation of the goods or reasonably incurred in their sale pursuant to law. If the person on whose account the goods are held is liable for like charges or expenses in relation to other goods whenever deposited and it is stated in the receipt that a lien is claimed for charges and expenses in relation to other goods, the warehouseman also has a lien against him for such charges and expenses whether or not the other goods have been delivered by the warehouseman. But against a person to whom a negotiable warehouse receipt is duly negotiated a warehouseman's lien is limited to charges in an amount or at a rate specified on the receipt or if no charges are so specified then to a reasonable charge for storage of the goods covered by the receipt subsequent to the date of the receipt.

**(2)** The warehouseman may also reserve a security interest against the bailor for a maximum amount specified on the receipt for charges other than those specified in subsection (1), such as for money advanced and interest. Such a security interest is governed by the Article on Secured Transactions (Article 9).

**(3) (a)** A warehouseman's lien for charges and expenses under subsection (1) or a security interest under subsection (2) is also effective against any person who so entrusted the bailor with possession of the goods that a pledge of them by him to a good faith purchaser for value would have been valid but is not effective against a person as to whom the document confers no right in the goods covered by it under Section 7—503.

**(b)** A warehouseman's lien on household goods for charges and expenses in relation to the goods under subsection (1) is also effective against all persons if the depositor was the legal possessor of the goods at the time of deposit. "Household goods" means furniture, furnishings and personal effects used by the depositor in a dwelling.

**(4)** A warehouseman loses his lien on any goods which he voluntarily delivers or which he unjustifiably refuses to deliver.

## § 7—210
### Enforcement of Warehouseman's Lien

**(1)** Except as provided in subsection (2), a warehouseman's lien may be enforced by public or private sale of the goods in block or in parcels, at any time or place and on any terms which are commercially reasonable, after notifying all persons known to claim an interest in the goods. Such notification must include a statement of the amount due, the nature of the proposed sale and the time and place of any public sale. The fact that a better price could have been obtained by a sale at a different time or in a different method from that selected by the warehouseman is not of itself sufficient to establish that the sale was not made in a commercially reasonable manner. If the warehouseman either sells the goods in the usual manner in any recognized market therefor, or if he sells at the price current in such market at the time of his sale, or if he has otherwise sold in conformity with commercially reasonable practices among dealers in the type of goods sold, he has sold in a commercially reasonable manner. A sale of more goods than apparently necessary to be offered to insure satisfaction of the obligation is not commercially reasonable except in cases covered by the preceding sentence.

**(2)** A warehouseman's lien on goods other than goods stored by a merchant in the course of his business may be enforced only as follows:

**(a)** All persons known to claim an interest in the goods must be notified.

**(b)** The notification must be delivered in person or sent by registered or certified letter to the last known address of any person to be notified.

**(c)** The notification must include an itemized statement of the claim, a description of the goods subject to the lien, a demand for payment within a specified time not less than ten days after receipt of the notification, and a conspicuous statement that unless the claim is paid within the time the goods will be advertised for sale and sold by auction at a specified time and place.

**(d)** The sale must conform to the terms of the notification.

**(e)** The sale must be held at the nearest suitable place to that where the goods are held or stored.

**(f)** After the expiration of the time given in the notification, an advertisement of the sale must be published once a week for two weeks consecutively in a newspaper of general circulation where the sale is to be held. The advertisement must include a description of the goods, the name of the person on whose account they are being held, and the time and place of the sale. The sale must take place at least fifteen days after the first publication. If there is no newspaper of general circulation where the sale is to be held, the advertisement must be posted at least ten days before the sale in not less than six conspicuous places in the neighborhood of the proposed sale.

**(3)** Before any sale pursuant to this section any person claiming a right in the goods may pay the amount necessary to satisfy the lien and the reasonable expenses incurred under this section. In that event the goods must not be sold, but must be retained by the warehouseman subject to the terms of the receipt and this Article.

(4) The warehouseman may buy at any public sale pursuant to this section.

(5) A purchaser in good faith of goods sold to enforce a warehouseman's lien takes the goods free of any rights of persons against whom the lien was valid, despite noncompliance by the warehouseman with the requirements of this section.

(6) The warehouseman may satisfy his lien from the proceeds of any sale pursuant to this section but must hold the balance, if any, for delivery on demand to any person to whom he would have been bound to deliver the goods.

(7) The rights provided by this section shall be in addition to all other rights allowed by law to a creditor against his debtor.

(8) Where a lien is on goods stored by a merchant in the course of his business the lien may be enforced in accordance with either subsection (1) or (2).

(9) The warehouseman is liable for damages caused by failure to comply with the requirements for sale under this section and in case of willful violation is liable for conversion.

## Part 3/Bills of Lading: Special Provisions

### § 7—301
**Liability for Non-Receipt or Misdescription; "Said to Contain"; "Shipper's Load and Count"; Improper Handling**

(1) A consignee of a non-negotiable bill who has given value in good faith or a holder to whom a negotiable bill has been duly negotiated relying in either case upon the description therein of the goods, or upon the date therein shown, may recover from the issuer damages caused by the misdating of the bill or the non-receipt or misdescription of the goods, except to the extent that the document indicates that the issuer does not know whether any part or all of the goods in fact were received or conform to the description, as where the description is in terms of marks or labels or kind, quantity, or condition or the receipt or description is qualified by "contents or condition of contents of packages unknown", "said to contain", "shipper's weight, load and count" or the like, if such indication be true.

(2) When goods are loaded by an issuer who is a common carrier, the issuer must count the packages of goods if package freight and ascertain the kind and quantity if bulk freight. In such cases "shipper's weight, load and count" or other words indicating that the description was made by the shipper are ineffective except as to freight concealed by packages.

(3) When bulk freight is loaded by a shipper who makes available to the issuer adequate facilities for weighing such freight, an issuer who is a common carrier must ascertain the kind and quantity within a reasonable time after receiving the written request of the shipper to do so. In such cases "shipper's weight" or other words of like purport are ineffective.

(4) The issuer may by inserting in the bill the words "shipper's weight, load and count" or other words of like purport indicate that the goods were loaded by the shipper; and if such statement be true the issuer shall not be liable for damages caused by the improper loading. But their omission does not imply liability for such damages.

(5) The shipper shall be deemed to have guaranteed to the issuer the accuracy at the time of shipment of the description, marks, labels, number, kind, quantity, condition and weight, as furnished by him; and the shipper shall indemnify the issuer against damage caused by inaccuracies in such particulars. The right of the issuer to such indemnity shall in no way limit his responsibility and liability under the contract of carriage to any person other than the shipper.

### § 7—302
**Through Bills of Lading and Similar Documents**

(1) The issuer of a through bill of lading or other document embodying an undertaking to be performed in part by persons acting as its agents or by connecting carriers is liable to anyone entitled to recover on the document for any breach by such other persons or by a connecting carrier of its obligation under the document but to the extent that the bill covers an undertaking to be performed overseas or in territory not contiguous to the continental United States or an undertaking including matters other than transportation this liability may be varied by agreement of the parties.

(2) Where goods covered by a through bill of lading or other document embodying an undertaking to be performed in part by persons other than the issuer are received by any such person, he is subject with respect to his own performance while the goods are in his possession to the obligation of the issuer. His obligation is discharged by delivery of the goods to another such person pursuant to the document and does not include liability for breach by any other such persons or by the issuer.

(3) The issuer of such through bill of lading or other document shall be entitled to recover from the connecting carrier or such other person in possession of the goods when the breach of the obligation under the document occurred, the amount it may be required to pay to anyone entitled to recover on the document therefor, as may be evidenced by any receipt, judgment, or transcript thereof, and the amount of any expense reasonably incurred by it in defending any action brought by anyone entitled to recover on the document therefor.

### § 7—303
**Diversion; Reconsignment; Change of Instructions**

(1) Unless the bill of lading otherwise provides, the carrier may deliver the goods to a person or destination other than that stated in the bill or may otherwise dispose of the goods on instructions from
  (a) the holder of a negotiable bill; or
  (b) the consignor on a non-negotiable bill notwithstanding contrary instructions from the consignee; or
  (c) the consignee on a non-negotiable bill in the absence of contrary instructions from the consignor, if the goods have arrived at the billed destination or if the consignee is in possession of the bill; or
  (d) the consignee on a non-negotiable bill if he is entitled as against the consignor to dispose of them.

(2) Unless such instructions are noted on a negotiable bill of lading, a person to whom the bill is duly negotiated can hold the bailee according to the original terms.

## § 7—304
### Bills of Lading in a Set

**(1)** Except where customary in overseas transportation, a bill of lading must not be issued in a set of parts. The issuer is liable for damages caused by violation of this subsection.

**(2)** Where a bill of lading is lawfully drawn in a set of parts, each of which is numbered and expressed to be valid only if the goods have not been delivered against any other part, the whole of the parts constitute one bill.

**(3)** Where a bill of lading is lawfully issued in a set of parts and different parts are negotiated to different persons, the title of the holder to whom the first due negotiation is made prevails as to both the document and the goods even though any later holder may have received the goods from the carrier in good faith and discharged the carrier's obligation by surrender of his part.

**(4)** Any person who negotiates or transfers a single part of a bill of lading drawn in a set is liable to holders of that part as if it were the whole set.

**(5)** The bailee is obliged to deliver in accordance with Part 4 of this Article against the first presented part of a bill of lading lawfully drawn in a set. Such delivery discharges the bailee's obligation on the whole bill.

## § 7—305
### Destination Bills

**(1)** Instead of issuing a bill of lading to the consignor at the place of shipment a carrier may at the request of the consignor procure the bill to be issued at destination or at any other place designated in the request.

**(2)** Upon request of anyone entitled as against the carrier to control the goods while in transit and on surrender of any outstanding bill of lading or other receipt covering such goods, the issuer may procure a substitute bill to be issued at any place designated in the request.

## § 7—306
### Altered Bills of Lading

An unauthorized alteration or filling in of a blank in a bill of lading leaves the bill enforceable according to its original tenor.

## § 7—307
### Lien of Carrier

**(1)** A carrier has a lien on the goods covered by a bill of lading for charges subsequent to the date of its receipt of the goods for storage or transportation (including demurrage and terminal charges) and for expenses necessary for preservation of the goods incident to their transportation or reasonably incurred in their sale pursuant to law. But against a purchaser for value of a negotiable bill of lading a carrier's lien is limited to charges stated in the bill or the applicable tariffs, or if no charges are stated then to a reasonable charge.

**(2)** A lien for charges and expenses under subsection (1) on goods which the carrier was required by law to receive for transportation is effective against the consignor or any person entitled to the goods unless the carrier had notice that the consignor lacked authority to subject the goods to such charges and expenses. Any other lien under subsection (1) is effective against the consignor and any person who permitted the bailor to have control or possession of the goods unless the carrier had notice that the bailor lacked such authority.

**(3)** A carrier loses his lien on any goods which he voluntarily delivers or which he unjustifiably refuses to deliver.

## § 7—308
### Enforcement of Carrier's Lien

**(1)** A carrier's lien may be enforced by public or private sale of the goods, in block or in parcels, at any time or place and on any terms which are commercially reasonable, after notifying all persons known to claim an interest in the goods. Such notification must include a statement of the amount due, the nature of the proposed sale and the time and place of any public sale. The fact that a better price could have been obtained by a sale at a different time or in a different method from that selected by the carrier is not of itself sufficient to establish that the sale was not made in a commercially reasonable manner. If the carrier either sells the goods in the usual manner in any recognized market therefor or if he sells at the price current in such market at the time of his sale or if he has otherwise sold in conformity with commercially reasonable practices among dealers in the type of goods sold he has sold in a commercially reasonable manner. A sale of more goods than apparently necessary to be offered to ensure satisfaction of the obligation is not commercially reasonable except in cases covered by the preceding sentence.

**(2)** Before any sale pursuant to this section any person claiming a right in the goods may pay the amount necessary to satisfy the lien and the reasonable expenses incurred under this section. In that event the goods must not be sold, but must be retained by the carrier subject to the terms of the bill and this Article.

**(3)** The carrier may buy at any public sale pursuant to this section.

**(4)** A purchaser in good faith of goods sold to enforce a carrier's lien takes the goods free of any rights of persons against whom the lien was valid, despite noncompliance by the carrier with the requirements of this section.

**(5)** The carrier may satisfy his lien from the proceeds of any sale pursuant to this section but must hold the balance, if any, for delivery on demand to any person to whom he would have been bound to deliver the goods.

**(6)** The rights provided by this section shall be in addition to all other rights allowed by law to a creditor against his debtor.

**(7)** A carrier's lien may be enforced in accordance with either subsection (1) or the procedure set forth in subsection (2) of Section 7—210.

**(8)** The carrier is liable for damages caused by failure to comply with the requirements for sale under this section and in case of willful violation is liable for conversion.

## § 7—309
### Duty of Care; Contractual Limitation of Carrier's Liability

**(1)** A carrier who issues a bill of lading whether negotiable or non-negotiable must exercise the degree of care in relation to the goods which a reasonably careful man would exercise under like circumstances. This subsection does not repeal or change any law or rule of law which imposes liability upon a common carrier for damages not caused by its negligence.

**(2)** Damages may be limited by a provision that the carrier's liability shall not exceed a value stated in the document if the carrier's rates are dependent upon value and the consignor by the carrier's tariff is afforded an opportunity to declare a higher value or a value as lawfully provided in the tariff, or where no tariff is filed he is otherwise advised of such opportunity; but no such limitation is effective with respect to the carrier's liability for conversion to its own use.

**(3)** Reasonable provisions as to the time and manner of presenting claims and instituting actions based on the shipment may be included in a bill of lading or tariff.

## Part 4/Warehouse Receipts and Bills of Lading: General Obligations

§ 7—401
**Irregularities in Issue of Receipt or Bill or Conduct of Issuer**

The obligations imposed by this Article on an issuer apply to a document of title regardless of the fact that

(a) the document may not comply with the requirements of this Article or of any other law or regulation regarding its issue, form or content; or
(b) the issuer may have violated laws regulating the conduct of his business; or
(c) the goods covered by the document were owned by the bailee at the time the document was issued; or
(d) the person issuing the document does not come within the definition of warehouseman if it purports to be a warehouse receipt.

§ 7—402
**Duplicate Receipt or Bill; Overissue**

Neither a duplicate nor any other document of title purporting to cover goods already represented by an outstanding document of the same issuer confers any right in the goods, except as provided in the case of bills in a set, overissue of documents for fungible goods and substitutes for lost, stolen or destroyed documents. But the issuer is liable for damages caused by his overissue or failure to identify a duplicate document as such by conspicuous notation on its face.

§ 7—403
**Obligation of Warehouseman or Carrier to Deliver; Excuse**

**(1)** The bailee must deliver the goods to a person entitled under the document who complies with subsections (2) and (3), unless and to the extent that the bailee establishes any of the following:
(a) delivery of the goods to a person whose receipt was rightful as against the claimant;
(b) damage to or to delay, loss or destruction of the goods for which the bailee is not liable [but the burden of establishing negligence in such cases is on the person entitled under the document];

Note: *The brackets in (1)(b) indicate that State enactments may differ on this point without serious damage to the principle of uniformity.*

(c) previous sale or other disposition of the goods in lawful enforcement of a lien or on warehouseman's lawful termination of storage;
(d) the exercise by a seller of his right to stop delivery pursuant to the provisions of the Article on Sales (Section 2—705);
(e) a diversion, reconsignment or other disposition pursuant to the provisions of this Article (Section 7—303) or tariff regulating such right;
(f) release, satisfaction or any other fact affording a personal defense against the claimant;
(g) any other lawful excuse.

**(2)** A person claiming goods covered by a document of title must satisfy the bailee's lien where the bailee so requests or where the bailee is prohibited by law from delivering the goods until the charges are paid.

**(3)** Unless the person claiming is one against whom the document confers no right under Section 7—503(1), he must surrender for cancellation or notation of partial deliveries any outstanding negotiable document covering the goods, and the bailee must cancel the document or conspicuously note the partial delivery thereon or be liable to any person to whom the document is duly negotiated.

**(4)** "Person entitled under the document" means holder in the case of a negotiable document, or the person to whom delivery is to be made by the terms of or pursuant to written instructions under a non-negotiable document.

§ 7—404
**No Liability for Good Faith Delivery Pursuant to Receipt or Bill**

A bailee who in good faith including observance of reasonable commercial standards has received goods and delivered or otherwise disposed of them according to the terms of the document of title or pursuant to this Article is not liable therefor. This rule applies even though the person from whom he received the goods had no authority to procure the document or to dispose of the goods and even though the person to whom he delivered the goods had no authority to receive them.

## Part 5/Warehouse Receipts and Bills of Lading: Negotiation and Transfer

§ 7—501
**Form of Negotiation and Requirements of "Due Negotiation"**

**(1)** A negotiable document of title running to the order of a named person is negotiated by his indorsement and delivery. After his indorsement in blank or to bearer any person can negotiate it by delivery alone.

**(2) (a)** A negotiable document of title is also negotiated by delivery alone when by its original terms it runs to bearer.
**(b)** When a document running to the order of a named person is delivered to him the effect is the same as if the document had been negotiated.

**(3)** Negotiation of a negotiable document of title after it has been indorsed to a specified person requires indorsement by the special indorsee as well as delivery.

(4) A negotiable document of title is "duly negotiated" when it is negotiated in the manner stated in this section to a holder who purchases it in good faith without notice of any defense against or claim to it on the part of any person and for value, unless it is established that the negotiation is not in the regular course of business or financing or involves receiving the document in settlement or payment of a money obligation.

(5) Indorsement of a non-negotiable document neither makes it negotiable nor adds to the transferee's rights.

(6) The naming in a negotiable bill of a person to be notified of the arrival of the goods does not limit the negotiability of the bill nor constitute notice to a purchaser thereof of any interest of such person in the goods.

## § 7—502
### Rights Acquired by Due Negotiation

(1) Subject to the following section and to the provisions of Section 7—205 on fungible goods, a holder to whom a negotiable document of title has been duly negotiated acquires thereby:
    (a) title to the document;
    (b) title to the goods;
    (c) all rights accruing under the law of agency or estoppel, including rights to goods delivered to the bailee after the document was issued; and
    (d) the direct obligation of the issuer to hold or deliver the goods according to the terms of the document free of any defense or claim by him except those arising under the terms of the document or under this Article. In the case of a delivery order the bailee's obligation accrues only upon acceptance and the obligation acquired by the holder is that the issuer and any indorser will procure the acceptance of the bailee.

(2) Subject to the following section, title and rights so acquired are not defeated by any stoppage of the goods represented by the document or by surrender of such goods by the bailee, and are not impaired even though the negotiation or any prior negotiation constituted a breach of duty or even though any person has been deprived of possession of the document by misrepresentation, fraud, accident, mistake, duress, loss, theft, or conversion, or even though a previous sale or other transfer of the goods or document has been made to a third person.

## § 7—503
### Document of Title to Goods Defeated in Certain Cases

(1) A document of title confers no right in goods against a person who before issuance of the document had a legal interest or a perfected security interest in them and who neither
    (a) delivered or entrusted them or any document of title covering them to the bailor or his nominee with actual or apparent authority to ship, store or sell or with power to obtain delivery under this Article (Section 7—403) or with power of disposition under this Act (Sections 2—403 and 9—307) or other statute or rule of law; nor
    (b) acquiesced in the procurement by the bailor or his nominee of any document of title.

(2) Title to goods based upon an unaccepted delivery order is subject to the rights of anyone to whom a negotiable warehouse receipt or bill of lading covering the goods has been duly negotiated. Such a title may be defeated under the next section to the same extent as the rights of the issuer or a transferee from the issuer.

(3) Title to goods based upon a bill of lading issued to a freight forwarder is subject to the rights of anyone to whom a bill issued by the freight forwarder is duly negotiated; but delivery by the carrier in accordance with Part 4 of this Article pursuant to its own bill of lading discharges the carrier's obligation to deliver.

## § 7—504
### Rights Acquired in the Absence of Due Negotiation; Effect of Diversion; Seller's Stoppage of Delivery

(1) A transferee of a document, whether negotiable or non-negotiable, to whom the document has been delivered but not duly negotiated, acquires the title and rights which his transferor had or had actual authority to convey.

(2) In the case of a non-negotiable document, until but not after the bailee receives notification of the transfer, the rights of the transferee may be defeated
    (a) by those creditors of the transferor who could treat the sale as void under Section 2—402; or
    (b) by a buyer from the transferor in ordinary course of business if the bailee has delivered the goods to the buyer or received notification of his rights; or
    (c) as against the bailee by good faith dealings of the bailee with the transferor.

(3) A diversion or other change of shipping instructions by the consignor in a non-negotiable bill of lading which causes the bailee not to deliver to the consignee defeats the consignee's title to the goods if they have been delivered to a buyer in ordinary course of business and in any event defeats the consignee's rights against the bailee.

(4) Delivery pursuant to a non-negotiable document may be stopped by a seller under Section 2—705, and subject to the requirement of due notification there provided. A bailee honoring the seller's instructions is entitled to be indemnified by the seller against any resulting loss or expense.

## § 7—505
### Indorser Not a Guarantor for Other Parties

The indorsement of a document of title issued by a bailee does not make the indorser liable for any default by the bailee or by previous indorsers.

## § 7—506
### Delivery Without Indorsement: Right to Compel Indorsement

The transferee of a negotiable document of title has a specifically enforceable right to have his transferor supply any necessary indorsement but the transfer becomes a negotiation only as of the time the indorsement is supplied.

## § 7—507
### Warranties on Negotiation or Transfer of Receipt or Bill

Where a person negotiates or transfers a document of title for value otherwise than as a mere intermediary under the next following section, then unless otherwise agreed he warrants to his

immediate purchaser only in addition to any warranty made in selling the goods
    (a) that the document is genuine; and
    (b) that he has no knowledge of any fact which would impair its validity or worth; and
    (c) that his negotiation or transfer is rightful and fully effective with respect to the title to the document and the goods it represents.

### § 7—508
**Warranties of Collecting Bank as to Documents**

A collecting bank or other intermediary known to be entrusted with documents on behalf of another or with collection of a draft or other claim against delivery of documents warrants by such delivery of the documents only its own good faith and authority. This rule applies even though the intermediary has purchased or made advances against the claim or draft to be collected.

### § 7—509
**Receipt or Bill: When Adequate Compliance With Commercial Contract**

The question whether a document is adequate to fulfill the obligations of a contract for sale or the conditions of a credit is governed by the Articles on Sales (Article 2) and on Letters of Credit (Article 5).

## Part 6/Warehouse Receipts and Bills of Lading: Miscellaneous Provisions

### § 7—601
**Lost and Missing Documents**

(1) If a document has been lost, stolen or destroyed, a court may order delivery of the goods or issuance of a substitute document and the bailee may without liability to any person comply with such order. If the document was negotiable the claimant must post security approved by the court to indemnify any person who may suffer loss as a result of non-surrender of the document. If the document was not negotiable, such security may be required at the discretion of the court. The court may also in its discretion order payment of the bailee's reasonable costs and counsel fees.

(2) A bailee who without court order delivers goods to a person claiming under a missing negotiable document is liable to any person injured thereby, and if the delivery is not in good faith becomes liable for conversion. Delivery in good faith is not conversion if made in accordance with a filed classification or tariff or, where no classification or tariff is filed, if the claimant posts security with the bailee in an amount at least double the value of the goods at the time of posting to indemnify any person injured by the delivery who files a notice of claim within one year after the delivery.

### § 7—602
**Attachment of Goods Covered by a Negotiable Document**

Except where the document was originally issued upon delivery of the goods by a person who had no power to dispose of them, no lien attaches by virtue of any judicial process to goods in the possession of a bailee for which a negotiable document of title is outstanding unless the document be first surrendered to the bailee or its negotiation enjoined, and the bailee shall not be compelled to deliver the goods pursuant to process until the document is surrendered to him or impounded by the court. One who purchases the document for value without notice of the process or injunction takes free of the lien imposed by judicial process.

### § 7—603
**Conflicting Claims; Interpleader**

If more than one person claims title or possession of the goods, the bailee is excused from delivery until he has had a reasonable time to ascertain the validity of the adverse claims or to bring an action to compel all claimants to interplead and may compel such interpleader, either in defending an action for non-delivery of the goods, or by original action, whichever is appropriate.

# ARTICLE 8/INVESTMENT SECURITIES

## Part 1/Short Title and General Matters

### § 8—101
**Short Title**

This Article shall be known and may be cited as Uniform Commercial Code—Investment Securities.

### § 8—102
**Definitions and Index of Definitions**

(1) In this Article unless the context otherwise requires
    (a) A "certificated security" is a share, participation, or other interest in property of or an enterprise of the issuer or an obligation of the issuer which is
        (i) represented by an instrument issued in bearer or registered form;
        (ii) of a type commonly dealt in on securities exchanges or markets or commonly recognized in any area in which it is issued or dealt in as a medium for investment; and
        (iii) either one of a class or series or by its terms divisible into a class or series of shares, participations, interests, or obligations.
    (b) An "uncertificated security" is a share, participation, or other interest in property or an enterprise of the issuer or an obligation of the issuer which is
        (i) not represented by an instrument and the transfer of which is registered upon books maintained for that purpose by or on behalf of the issuer;
        (ii) of a type commonly dealt in on securities exchanges or markets; and
        (iii) either one of a class or series or by its terms divisible into a class or series of shares, participations, interests, or obligations.
    (c) A "security" is either a certificated or an uncertificated security. If a security is certificated, the terms "security" and "certificated security" may mean either the intangible interest, the instrument representing that interest, or both, as the context requires. A writing that is a certificated security is governed by this Article and not by Article 3, even though it also meets the requirements of that Article. This Article does not apply to money. If a certificated security has been retained by or surrendered to the issuer or its transfer agent for

reasons other than registration of transfer, other temporary purpose, payment, exchange, or acquisition by the issuer, that security shall be treated as an uncertificated security for purposes of this Article.

(d) A certificated security is in "registered form" if
  (i) it specifies a person entitled to the security or the rights it represents; and
  (ii) its transfer may be registered upon books maintained for that purpose by or on behalf of the issuer, or the security so states.

(e) A certificated security is in "bearer form" if it runs to bearer according to its terms and not by reason of any indorsement.

(2) A "subsequent purchaser" is a person who takes other than by original issue.

(3) A "clearing corporation" is a corporation registered as a "clearing agency" under the federal securities laws or a corporation:
  (a) at least 90 percent of whose capital stock is held by or for one or more organizations, none of which, other than a national securities exchange or association, holds in excess of 20 percent of the capital stock of the corporation, and each of which is
    (i) subject to supervision or regulation pursuant to the provisions of federal or state banking laws or state insurance laws,
    (ii) a broker or dealer or investment company registered under the federal securities laws, or
    (iii) a national securities exchange or association registered under the federal securities laws; and
  (b) any remaining capital stock of which is held by individuals who have purchased it at or prior to the time of their taking office as directors of the corporation and who have purchased only so much of the capital stock as is necessary to permit them to qualify as directors.

(4) A "custodian bank" is a bank or trust company that is supervised and examined by state or federal authority having supervision over banks and is acting as custodian for a clearing corporation.

(5) Other definitions applying to this Article or to specified Parts thereof and the sections in which they appear are:

"Adverse claim". Section 8—302.
"Bona fide purchaser". Section 8—302.
"Broker". Section 8—303.
"Debtor". Section 9—105.
"Financial intermediary". Section 8—313.
"Guarantee of the signature". Section 8—402.
"Initial transaction statement". Section 8—408.
"Instruction". Section 8—308.
"Intermediary bank". Section 4—105.
"Issuer". Section 8—201.
"Overissue". Section 8—104.
"Secured Party". Section 9—105.
"Security Agreement". Section 9—105.

(6) In addition, Article 1 contains general definitions and principles of construction and interpretation applicable throughout this Article.

Amended in 1962, 1973 and 1977.

### § 8—103
### Issuer's Lien

A lien upon a security in favor of an issuer thereof is valid against a purchaser only if:

(a) the security is certificated and the right of the issuer to the lien is noted conspicuously thereon; or

(b) the security is uncertificated and a notation of the right of the issuer to the lien is contained in the initial transaction statement sent to the purchaser or, if his interest is transferred to him other than by registration of transfer, pledge, or release, the initial transaction statement sent to the registered owner or the registered pledgee.

Amended in 1977.

### § 8—104
### Effect of Overissue; "Overissue"

(1) The provisions of this Article which validate a security or compel its issue or reissue do not apply to the extent that validation, issue, or reissue would result in overissue; but if:

(a) an identical security which does not constitute an overissue is reasonably available for purchase, the person entitled to issue or validation may compel the issuer to purchase the security for him and either to deliver a certificated security or to register the transfer of an uncertificated security to him, against surrender of any certificated security he holds; or

(b) a security is not so available for purchase, the person entitled to issue or validation may recover from the issuer the price he or the last purchaser for value paid for it with interest from the date of his demand.

(2) "Overissue" means the issue of securities in excess of the amount the issuer has corporate power to issue.

Amended in 1977.

### § 8—105
### Certificated Securities Negotiable; Statements and Instructions Not Negotiable; Presumptions

(1) Certificated securities governed by this Article are negotiable instruments.

(2) Statements (Section 8—408), notices, or the like, sent by the issuer of uncertificated securities and instructions (Section 8—308) are neither negotiable instruments nor certificated securities.

(3) In any action on a security:

(a) unless specifically denied in the pleadings, each signature on a certificated security, in a necessary indorsement, on an initial transaction statement, or on an instruction, is admitted;

(b) If the effectiveness of a signature is put in issue, the burden of establishing it is on the party claiming under the signature, but the signature is presumed to be genuine or authorized;

(c) if signatures on a certificated security are admitted or established, production of the security entitles a holder to recover on it unless the defendant establishes a defense or a defect going to the validity of the security;

(d) if signatures on an initial transaction statement are admitted or established, the facts stated in the statement are presumed to be true as of the time of its issuance; and

(e) after it is shown that a defense or defect exists, the plaintiff has the burden of establishing that he or some person under whom he claims is a person against whom the defense or defect is ineffective (Section 8—202).

Amended in 1977.

## § 8—106
**Applicability**

The law (including the conflict of laws rules) of the jurisdiction of organization of the issuer governs the validity of a security, the effectiveness of registration by the issuer, and the rights and duties of the issuer with respect to:

(a) registration of transfer of a certificated security;

(b) registration of transfer, pledge, or release of an uncertificated security; and

(c) sending of statements of uncertificated securities.

Amended in 1977.

## § 8—107
**Securities Transferable; Action for Price**

(1) Unless otherwise agreed and subject to any applicable law or regulation respecting short sales, a person obligated to transfer securities may transfer any certificated security of the specified issue in bearer form or registered in the name of the transferee, or indorsed to him or in blank, or he may transfer an equivalent uncertificated security to the transferee or a person designated by the transferee.

(2) If the buyer fails to pay the price as it comes due under a contract of sale, the seller may recover the price of:

(a) certificated securities accepted by the buyer;

(b) uncertificated securities that have been transferred to the buyer or a person designated by the buyer; and

(c) other securities if efforts at their resale would be unduly burdensome or if there is no readily available market for their resale.

Amended in 1977.

## § 8—108
**Registration of Pledge and Release of Uncertificated Securities**

A security interest in an uncertificated security may be evidenced by the registration of pledge to the secured party or a person designated by him. There can be no more than one registered pledge of an uncertificated security at any time. The registered owner of an uncertificated security is the person in whose name the security is registered, even if the security is subject to a registered pledge. The rights of a registered pledgee of an uncertificated security under this Article are terminated by the registration of release.

Added in 1977.

# Part 2/Issue—Issuer

## § 8—201
**"Issuer"**

(1) With respect to obligations on or defenses to a security, "issuer" includes a person who:

(a) places or authorizes the placing of his name on a certificated security (otherwise than as authenticating trustee, registrar, transfer agent, or the like) to evidence that it represents a share, participation, or other interest in his property or in an enterprise, or to evidence his duty to perform an obligation represented by the certificated security;

(b) creates shares, participations, or other interests in his property or in an enterprise or undertakes obligations, which shares, participations, interests, or obligations are uncertificated securities;

(c) directly or indirectly creates fractional interests in his rights or property, which fractional interests are represented by certificated securities; or

(d) becomes responsible for or in place of any other person described as an issuer in this section.

(2) With respect to obligations on or defenses to a security, a guarantor is an issuer to the extent of his guaranty, whether or not his obligation is noted on a certificated security or on statements of uncertificated securities sent pursuant to Section 8—408.

(3) With respect to registration of transfer, pledge, or release (Part 4 of this Article), "issuer" means a person on whose behalf transfer books are maintained.

Amended in 1977.

## § 8—202
**Issuer's Responsibility and Defenses; Notice of Defect or Defense**

(1) Even against a purchaser for value and without notice, the terms of a security include:

(a) if the security is certificated, those stated on the security;

(b) if the security is uncertificated, those contained in the initial transaction statement sent to such purchaser or, if his interest is transferred to him other than by registration of transfer, pledge, or release, the initial transaction statement sent to the registered owner or registered pledgee; and

(c) those made part of the security by reference, on the certificated security or in the initial transaction statement, to another instrument, indenture, or document or to a constitution, statute, ordinance, rule, regulation, order or the like, to the extent that the terms referred to do not conflict with the terms stated on the certificated security or contained in the statement. A reference under this paragraph does not of itself charge a purchaser for value with notice of a defect going to the validity of the security, even though the certificated security or statement expressly states that a person accepting it admits notice.

(2) A certificated security in the hands of a purchaser for value or an uncertificated security as to which an initial transaction statement has been sent to a purchaser for value, other than a security issued by a government or governmental agency or unit, even though issued with a defect going to its validity, is valid with respect to the purchaser if he is without notice of the particular defect unless the defect involves a violation of constitutional provisions, in which case the security is valid with respect to a subsequent purchaser for value and without notice of the defect. This subsection applies to an issuer that is a government or governmental agency or unit only if either there has been substantial compliance with the legal requirements governing the issue or the

issuer has received a substantial consideration for the issue as a whole or for the particular security and a stated purpose of the issue is one for which the issuer has power to borrow money or issue the security.

(3) Except as provided in the case of certain unauthorized signatures (Section 8—205), lack of genuineness of a certificated security or an initial transaction statement is a complete defense, even against a purchaser for value and without notice.

(4) All other defenses of the issuer of a certificated or uncertificated security, including nondelivery and conditional delivery of a certificated security, are ineffective against a purchaser for value who has taken without notice of the particular defense.

(5) Nothing in this section shall be construed to affect the right of a party to a "when, as and if issued" or a "when distributed" contract to cancel the contract in the event of a material change in the character of the security that is the subject of the contract or in the plan or arrangement pursuant to which the security is to be issued or distributed.

Amended in 1977.

## § 8—203
### Staleness as Notice of Defects or Defenses

(1) After an act or event creating a right to immediate performance of the principal obligation represented by a certificated security or that sets a date on or after which the security is to be presented or surrendered for redemption or exchange, a purchaser is charged with notice of any defect in its issue or defense of the issuer if:

(a) the act or event is one requiring the payment of money, the delivery of certificated securities, the registration of transfer of uncertificated securities, or any of these on presentation or surrender of the certificated security, the funds or securities are available on the date set for payment or exchange, and he takes the security more than one year after that date; and

(b) the act or event is not covered by paragraph (a) and he takes the security more than 2 years after the date set for surrender or presentation or the date on which performance became due.

(2) A call that has been revoked is not within subsection (1).

Amended in 1977.

## § 8—204
### Effect of Issuer's Restrictions on Transfer

A restriction on transfer of a security imposed by the issuer, even if otherwise lawful, is ineffective against any person without actual knowledge of it unless:

(a) the security is certificated and the restriction is noted conspicuously thereon; or

(b) the security is uncertificated and a notation of the restriction is contained in the initial transaction statement sent to the person or, if his interest is transferred to him other than by registration of transfer, pledge, or release, the initial transaction statement sent to the registered owner or the registered pledgee.

Amended in 1977.

## § 8—205
### Effect of Unauthorized Signature on Certificated Security or Initial Transaction Statement

An unauthorized signature placed on a certificated security prior to or in the course of issue or placed on an initial transaction statement is ineffective, but the signature is effective in favor of a purchaser for value of the certificated security or a purchaser for value of an uncertificated security to whom the initial transaction statement has been sent, if the purchaser is without notice of the lack of authority and the signing has been done by:

(a) an authenticating trustee, registrar, transfer agent, or other person entrusted by the issuer with the signing of the security, of similar securities, or of initial transaction statements or the immediate preparation for signing of any of them; or

(b) an employee of the issuer, or of any of the foregoing, entrusted with responsible handling of the security or initial transaction statement.

Amended in 1977.

## § 8—206
### Completion or Alteration of Certificated Security or Initial Transaction Statement

(1) If a certificated security contains the signatures necessary to its issue or transfer but is incomplete in any other respect:

(a) any person may complete it by filling in the blanks as authorized; and

(b) even though the blanks are incorrectly filled in, the security as completed is enforceable by a purchaser who took it for value and without notice of the incorrectness.

(2) A complete certificated security that has been improperly altered, even though fraudulently, remains enforceable, but only according to its original terms.

(3) If an initial transaction statement contains the signatures necessary to its validity, but is incomplete in any other respect:

(a) any person may complete it by filling in the blanks as authorized; and

(b) even though the blanks are incorrectly filled in, the statement as completed is effective in favor of the person to whom it is sent if he purchased the security referred to therein for value and without notice of the incorrectness.

(4) A complete initial transaction statement that has been improperly altered, even though fraudulently, is effective in favor of a purchaser to whom it has been sent, but only according to its original terms.

Amended in 1977.

## § 8—207
### Rights and Duties of Issuer With Respect to Registered Owners and Registered Pledgees

(1) Prior to due presentment for registration of transfer of a certificated security in registered form, the issuer or indenture trustee may treat the registered owner as the person exclusively entitled to vote, to receive notifications, and otherwise to exercise all the rights and powers of an owner.

(2) Subject to the provisions of subsections (3), (4), and (6), the issuer or indenture trustee may treat the registered owner of an

uncertificated security as the person exclusively entitled to vote, to receive notifications, and otherwise to exercise all the rights and powers of an owner.

(3) The registered owner of an uncertificated security that is subject to a registered pledge is not entitled to registration of transfer prior to the due presentment to the issuer of a release instruction. The exercise of conversion rights with respect to a convertible uncertificated security is a transfer within the meaning of this section.

(4) Upon due presentment of a transfer instruction from the registered pledgee of an uncertificated security, the issuer shall:
  (a) register the transfer of the security to the new owner free of pledge, if the instruction specifies a new owner (who may be the registered pledgee) and does not specify a pledgee;
  (b) register the transfer of the security to the new owner subject to the interest of the existing pledgee, if the instruction specifies a new owner and the existing pledgee; or
  (c) register the release of the security from the existing pledge and register the pledge of the security to the other pledgee, if the instruction specifies the existing owner and another pledgee.

(5) Continuity of perfection of a security interest is not broken by registration of transfer under subsection (4)(b) or by registration of release and pledge under subsection (4)(c), if the security interest is assigned.

(6) If an uncertificated security is subject to a registered pledge:
  (a) any uncertificated securities issued in exchange for or distributed with respect to the pledged security shall be registered subject to the pledge;
  (b) any certificated securities issued in exchange for or distributed with respect to the pledged security shall be delivered to the registered pledgee; and
  (c) any money paid in exchange for or in redemption of part or all of the security shall be paid to the registered pledgee.

(7) Nothing in this Article shall be construed to affect the liability of the registered owner of a security for calls, assessments, or the like.

Amended in 1977.

### § 8—208
### Effect of Signature of Authenticating Trustee, Registrar, or Transfer Agent

(1) A person placing his signature upon a certificated security or an initial transaction statement as authenticating trustee, registrar, transfer agent, or the like, warrants to a purchaser for value of the certificated security or a purchaser for value of an uncertificated security to whom the initial transaction statement has been sent, if the purchaser is without notice of the particular defect, that:
  (a) the certificated security or initial transaction statement is genuine;
  (b) his own participation in the issue or registration of the transfer, pledge, or release of the security is within his capacity and within the scope of the authority received by him from the issuer; and
  (c) he has reasonable grounds to believe the security is in the form and within the amount the issuer is authorized to issue.

(2) Unless otherwise agreed, a person by so placing his signature does not assume responsibility for the validity of the security in other respects.

Amended in 1962 and 1977.

## Part 3/Transfer

### § 8—301
### Rights Acquired by Purchaser

(1) Upon transfer of a security to a purchaser (Section 8—313), the purchaser acquires the rights in the security which his transferor had or had actual authority to convey unless the purchaser's rights are limited by Section 8—302(4).

(2) A transferee of a limited interest acquires rights only to the extent of the interest transferred. The creation or release of a security interest in a security is the transfer of a limited interest in that security.

Amended in 1977.

### § 8—302
### "Bona Fide Purchaser"; "Adverse Claim"; Title Acquired by Bona Fide Purchaser

(1) A "bona fide purchaser" is a purchaser for value in good faith and without notice of any adverse claim:
  (a) who takes delivery of a certificated security in bearer form or in registered form, issued or indorsed to him or in blank;
  (b) to whom the transfer, pledge, or release of an uncertificated security is registered on the books of the issuer; or
  (c) to whom a security is transferred under the provisions of paragraph (c), (d)(i), or (g) of Section 8—313(1).

(2) "Adverse claim" includes a claim that a transfer was or would be wrongful or that a particular adverse person is the owner of or has an interest in the security.

(3) A bona fide purchaser in addition to acquiring the rights of a purchaser (Section 8—301) also acquires his interest in the security free of any adverse claim.

(4) Notwithstanding Section 8—301(1), the transferee of a particular certificated security who has been a party to any fraud or illegality affecting the security, or who as a prior holder of that certificated security had notice of an adverse claim, cannot improve his position by taking from a bona fide purchaser.

Amended in 1977.

### § 8—303
### "Broker"

"Broker" means a person engaged for all or part of his time in the business of buying and selling securities, who in the transaction concerned acts for, buys a security from, or sells a security to, a customer. Nothing in this Article determines the capacity in which a person acts for purposes of any other statute or rule to which the person is subject.

### § 8—304
### Notice to Purchaser of Adverse Claims

(1) A purchaser (including a broker for the seller or buyer, but excluding an intermediary bank) of a certificated security is charged with notice of adverse claims if:

(a) the security, whether in bearer or registered form, has been indorsed "for collection" or "for surrender" or for some other purpose not involving transfer; or

(b) the security is in bearer form and has on it an unambiguous statement that it is the property of a person other than the transferor. The mere writing of a name on a security is not such a statement.

(2) A purchaser (including a broker for the seller or buyer, but excluding an intermediary bank) to whom the transfer, pledge, or release of an uncertificated security is registered is charged with notice of adverse claims as to which the issuer has a duty under Section 8—403(4) at the time of registration and which are noted in the initial transaction statement sent to the purchaser or, if his interest is transferred to him other than by registration of transfer, pledge, or release, the initial transaction statement sent to the registered owner or the registered pledgee.

(3) The fact that the purchaser (including a broker for the seller or buyer) of a certificated or uncertificated security has notice that the security is held for a third person or is registered in the name of or indorsed by a fiduciary does not create a duty of inquiry into the rightfulness of the transfer or constitute constructive notice of adverse claims. However, if the purchaser (excluding an intermediary bank) has knowledge that the proceeds are being used or the transaction is for the individual benefit of the fiduciary or otherwise in breach of duty, the purchaser is charged with notice of adverse claims.

Amended in 1977.

## § 8—305
**Staleness as Notice of Adverse Claims**

An act or event that creates a right to immediate performance of the principal obligation represented by a certificated security or sets a date on or after which a certificated security is to be presented or surrendered for redemption or exchange does not itself constitute any notice of adverse claims except in the case of a transfer:

(a) after one year from any date set for presentment or surrender for redemption or exchange; or

(b) after 6 months from any date set for payment of money against presentation or surrender of the security if funds are available for payment on that date.

Amended in 1977.

## § 8—306
**Warranties on Presentment and Transfer of Certificated Securities; Warranties of Originators of Instructions**

(1) A person who presents a certificated security for registration of transfer or for payment or exchange warrants to the issuer that he is entitled to the registration, payment, or exchange. But, a purchaser for value and without notice of adverse claims who receives a new, reissued, or re-registered certificated security on registration of transfer or receives an initial transaction statement confirming the registration of transfer of an equivalent uncertificated security to him warrants only that he has no knowledge of any unauthorized signature (Section 8—311) in a necessary indorsement.

(2) A person by transferring a certificated security to a purchaser for value warrants only that:

(a) his transfer is effective and rightful;

(b) the security is genuine and has not been materially altered; and

(c) he knows of no fact which might impair the validity of the security.

(3) If a certificated security is delivered by an intermediary known to be entrusted with delivery of the security on behalf of another or with collection of a draft or other claim against delivery, the intermediary by delivery warrants only his own good faith and authority, even though he has purchased or made advances against the claim to be collected against the delivery.

(4) A pledgee or other holder for security who redelivers a certificated security received, or after payment and on order of the debtor delivers that security to a third person, makes only the warranties of an intermediary under subsection (3).

(5) A person who originates an instruction warrants to the issuer that:

(a) he is an appropriate person to originate the instruction; and

(b) at the time the instruction is presented to the issuer he will be entitled to the registration of transfer, pledge, or release.

(6) A person who originates an instruction warrants to any person specially guaranteeing his signature (subsection 8—312(3)) that:

(a) he is an appropriate person to originate the instruction; and

(b) at the time the instruction is presented to the issuer

(i) he will be entitled to the registration of transfer, pledge, or release; and

(ii) the transfer, pledge, or release requested in the instruction will be registered by the issuer free from all liens, security interests, restrictions, and claims other than those specified in the instruction.

(7) A person who originates an instruction warrants to a purchaser for value and to any person guaranteeing the instruction (Section 8—312(6)) that:

(a) he is an appropriate person to originate the instruction;

(b) the uncertificated security referred to therein is valid; and

(c) at the time the instruction is presented to the issuer

(i) the transferor will be entitled to the registration of transfer, pledge, or release;

(ii) the transfer, pledge, or release requested in the instruction will be registered by the issuer free from all liens, security interests, restrictions, and claims other than those specified in the instruction; and

(iii) the requested transfer, pledge, or release will be rightful.

(8) If a secured party is the registered pledgee or the registered owner of an uncertificated security, a person who originates an instruction of release or transfer to the debtor or, after payment and on order of the debtor, a transfer instruction to a third person, warrants to the debtor or the third person only that he is an appropriate person to originate the instruction and, at the time the instruction is presented to the issuer, the transferor will be entitled to the registration of release or transfer. If a transfer instruction to a third person who is a purchaser for value is originated on order of the debtor, the debtor makes to the purchaser the warranties of paragraphs (b), (c)(ii) and (c)(iii) of subsection (7).

**(9)** A person who transfers an uncertificated security to a purchaser for value and does not originate an instruction in connection with the transfer warrants only that:
   **(a)** his transfer is effective and rightful; and
   **(b)** the uncertificated security is valid.

**(10)** A broker gives to his customer and to the issuer and a purchaser the applicable warranties provided in this section and has the rights and privileges of a purchaser under this section. The warranties of and in favor of the broker, acting as an agent are in addition to applicable warranties given by and in favor of his customer.

Amended in 1962 and 1977.

## § 8—307
### Effect of Delivery Without Indorsement; Right to Compel Indorsement

If a certificated security in registered form has been delivered to a purchaser without a necessary indorsement he may become a bona fide purchaser only as of the time the indorsement is supplied; but against the transferor, the transfer is complete upon delivery and the purchaser has a specifically enforceable right to have any necessary indorsement supplied.

Amended in 1977.

## § 8—308
### Indorsements; Instructions

**(1)** An indorsement of a certificated security in registered form is made when an appropriate person signs on it or on a separate document an assignment or transfer of the security or a power to assign or transfer it or his signature is written without more upon the back of the security.

**(2)** An indorsement may be in blank or special. An indorsement in blank includes an indorsement to bearer. A special indorsement specifies to whom the security is to be transferred, or who has power to transfer it. A holder may convert a blank indorsement into a special indorsement.

**(3)** An indorsement purporting to be only of part of a certificated security representing units intended by the issuer to be separately transferable is effective to the extent of the indorsement.

**(4)** An "instruction" is an order to the issuer of an uncertificated security requesting that the transfer, pledge, or release from pledge of the uncertificated security specified therein be registered.

**(5)** An instruction originated by an appropriate person is:
   **(a)** a writing signed by an appropriate person; or
   **(b)** a communication to the issuer in any form agreed upon in a writing signed by the issuer and an appropriate person.

If an instruction has been originated by an appropriate person but is incomplete in any other respect, any person may complete it as authorized and the issuer may rely on it as completed even though it has been completed incorrectly.

**(6)** "An appropriate person" in subsection (1) means the person specified by the certificated security or by special indorsement to be entitled to the security.

**(7)** "An appropriate person" in subsection (5) means:
   **(a)** for an instruction to transfer or pledge an uncertificated security which is then not subject to a registered pledge, the registered owner; or
   **(b)** for an instruction to transfer or release an uncertificated security which is then subject to a registered pledge, the registered pledgee.

**(8)** In addition to the persons designated in subsections (6) and (7), "an appropriate person" in subsections (1) and (5) includes:
   **(a)** if the person designated is described as a fiduciary but is no longer serving in the described capacity, either that person or his successor;
   **(b)** if the persons designated are described as more than one person as fiduciaries and one or more are no longer serving in the described capacity, the remaining fiduciary or fiduciaries, whether or not a successor has been appointed or qualified;
   **(c)** if the person designated is an individual and is without capacity to act by virtue of death, incompetence, infancy, or otherwise, his executor, administrator, guardian, or like fiduciary;
   **(d)** if the persons designated are described as more than one person as tenants by the entirety or with right of survivorship and by reason of death all cannot sign, the survivor or survivors;
   **(e)** a person having power to sign under applicable law or controlling instrument; and
   **(f)** to the extent that the person designated or any of the foregoing persons may act through an agent, his authorized agent.

**(9)** Unless otherwise agreed, the indorser of a certificated security by his indorsement or the originator of an instruction by his origination assumes no obligation that the security will be honored by the issuer but only the obligations provided in Section 8—306.

**(10)** Whether the person signing is appropriate is determined as of the date of signing and an indorsement made by or an instruction originated by him does not become unauthorized for the purposes of this Article by virtue of any subsequent change of circumstances.

**(11)** Failure of a fiduciary to comply with a controlling instrument or with the law of the state having jurisdiction of the fiduciary relationship, including any law requiring the fiduciary to obtain court approval of the transfer, pledge, or release, does not render his indorsement or an instruction originated by him unauthorized for the purposes of this Article.

Amended in 1962 and 1977.

## § 8—309
### Effect of Indorsement Without Delivery

An indorsement of a certificated security, whether special or in blank, does not constitute a transfer until delivery of the certificated security on which it appears or, if the indorsement is on a separate document, until delivery of both the document and the certificated security.

Amended in 1977.

## § 8—310
### Indorsement of Certificated Security in Bearer Form

An indorsement of a certificated security in bearer form may give notice of adverse claims (Section 8—304) but does not otherwise affect any right to registration the holder possesses.

Amended in 1977.

## §8—311
### Effect of Unauthorized Indorsement or Instruction

Unless the owner or pledgee has ratified an unauthorized indorsement or instruction or is otherwise precluded from asserting its ineffectiveness:

(a) he may assert its ineffectiveness against the issuer or any purchaser, other than a purchaser for value and without notice of adverse claims, who has in good faith received a new, reissued, or re-registered certificated security on registration of transfer or received an initial transaction statement confirming the registration of transfer, pledge, or release of an equivalent uncertificated security to him; and

(b) an issuer who registers the transfer of a certificated security upon the unauthorized indorsement or who registers the transfer, pledge, or release of an uncertificated security upon the unauthorized instruction is subject to liability for improper registration (Section 8–404).

Amended in 1977.

## §8—312
### Effect of Guaranteeing Signature, Indorsement or Instruction

(1) Any person guaranteeing a signature of an indorser of a certificated security warrants that at the time of signing:
   (a) the signature was genuine;
   (b) the signer was an appropriate person to indorse (Section 8—308); and
   (c) the signer had legal capacity to sign.

(2) Any person guaranteeing a signature of the originator of an instruction warrants that at the time of signing:
   (a) the signature was genuine;
   (b) the signer was an appropriate person to originate the instruction (Section 8—308) if the person specified in the instruction as the registered owner or registered pledgee of the uncertificated security was, in fact, the registered owner or registered pledgee of the security, as to which fact the signature guarantor makes no warranty;
   (c) the signer had legal capacity to sign; and
   (d) the taxpayer identification number, if any, appearing on the instruction as that of the registered owner or registered pledgee was the taxpayer identification number of the signer or of the owner or pledgee for whom the signer was acting.

(3) Any person specially guaranteeing the signature of the originator of an instruction makes not only the warranties of a signature guarantor (subsection (2)) but also warrants that at the time the instruction is presented to the issuer:
   (a) the person specified in the instruction as the registered owner or registered pledgee of the uncertificated security will be the registered owner or registered pledgee; and
   (b) the transfer, pledge, or release of the uncertificated security requested in the instruction will be registered by the issuer free from all liens, security interests, restrictions, and claims other than those specified in the instruction.

(4) The guarantor under subsections (1) and (2) or the special guarantor under subsection (3) does not otherwise warrant the rightfulness of the particular transfer, pledge, or release.

(5) Any person guaranteeing an indorsement of a certificated security makes not only the warranties of a signature guarantor under subsection (1) but also warrants the rightfulness of the particular transfer in all respects.

(6) Any person guaranteeing an instruction requesting the transfer, pledge, or release of an uncertificated security makes not only the warranties of a special signature guarantor under subsection (3) but also warrants the rightfulness of the particular transfer, pledge, or release in all respects.

(7) No issuer may require a special guarantee of signature (subsection (3)), a guarantee of indorsement (subsection (5)), or a guarantee of instruction (subsection (6)) as a condition to registration of transfer, pledge, or release.

(8) The foregoing warranties are made to any person taking or dealing with the security in reliance on the guarantee, and the guarantor is liable to the person for any loss resulting from breach of the warranties.

Amended in 1977.

## §8—313
### When Transfer to Purchaser Occurs; Financial Intermediary as Bona Fide Purchaser; "Financial Intermediary"

(1) Transfer of a security or a limited interest (including a security interest) therein to a purchaser occurs only:
   (a) at the time he or a person designated by him acquires possession of a certificated security;
   (b) at the time the transfer, pledge, or release of an uncertificated security is registered to him or a person designated by him;
   (c) at the time his financial intermediary acquires possession of a certificated security specially indorsed to or issued in the name of the purchaser;
   (d) at the time a financial intermediary, not a clearing corporation, sends him confirmation of the purchase and also by book entry or otherwise identifies as belonging to the purchaser
      (i) a specific certificated security in the financial intermediary's possession;
      (ii) a quantity of securities that constitute or are part of a fungible bulk of certificated securities in the financial intermediary's possession or of uncertificated securities registered in the name of the financial intermediary; or
      (iii) a quantity of securities that constitute or are part of a fungible bulk of securities shown on the account of the financial intermediary on the books of another financial intermediary;
   (e) with respect to an identified certificated security to be delivered while still in the possession of a third person, not a financial intermediary, at the time that person acknowledges that he holds for the purchaser;
   (f) with respect to a specific uncertificated security the pledge or transfer of which has been registered to a third person, not a financial intermediary, at the time that person acknowledges that he holds for the purchaser;
   (g) at the time appropriate entries to the account of the purchaser or a person designated by him on the books of a clearing corporation are made under Section 8—320;
   (h) with respect to the transfer of a security interest where the debtor has signed a security agreement containing a de-

scription of the security, at the time a written notification, which, in the case of the creation of the security interest, is signed by the debtor (which may be a copy of the security agreement) or which, in the case of the release or assignment of the security interest created pursuant to this paragraph, is signed by the secured party, is received by

> (i) a financial intermediary on whose books the interest of the transferor in the security appears;
> (ii) a third person, not a financial intermediary, in possession of the security, if it is certificated;
> (iii) a third person, not a financial intermediary, who is the registered owner of the security, if it is uncertificated and not subject to a registered pledge; or
> (iv) a third person, not a financial intermediary, who is the registered pledgee of the security, if it is uncertificated and subject to a registered pledge;

(i) with respect to the transfer of a security interest where the transferor has signed a security agreement containing a description of the security, at the time new value is given by the secured party; or

(j) with respect to the transfer of a security interest where the secured party is a financial intermediary and the security has already been transferred to the financial intermediary under paragraphs (a), (b), (c), (d), or (g), at the time the transferor has signed a security agreement containing a description of the security and value is given by the secured party.

(2) The purchaser is the owner of a security held for him by a financial intermediary, but cannot be a bona fide purchaser of a security so held except in the circumstances specified in paragraphs (c), (d)(i), and (g) of subsection (1). If a security so held is part of a fungible bulk, as in the circumstances specified in paragraphs (d)(ii) and (d)(iii) of subsection (1), the purchaser is the owner of a proportionate property interest in the fungible bulk.

(3) Notice of an adverse claim received by the financial intermediary or by the purchaser after the financial intermediary takes delivery of a certificated security as a holder for value or after the transfer, pledge, or release of an uncertificated security has been registered free of the claim to a financial intermediary who has given value is not effective either as to the financial intermediary or as to the purchaser. However, as between the financial intermediary and the purchaser the purchaser may demand transfer of an equivalent security as to which no notice of adverse claim has been received.

(4) A "financial intermediary" is a bank, broker, clearing corporation, or other person (or the nominee of any of them) which in the ordinary course of its business maintains security accounts for its customers and is acting in that capacity. A financial intermediary may have a security interest in securities held in account for its customer.

Amended in 1962 and 1977.

## §8—314
### Duty to Transfer, When Completed

(1) Unless otherwise agreed, if a sale of a security is made on an exchange or otherwise through brokers:

> (a) the selling customer fulfills his duty to transfer at the time he:
>> (i) places a certificated security in the possession of the selling broker or a person designated by the broker;
>> (ii) causes an uncertificated security to be registered in the name of the selling broker or a person designated by the broker;
>> (iii) if requested, causes an acknowledgment to be made to the selling broker that a certificated or uncertificated security is held for the broker; or
>> (iv) places in the possession of the selling broker or of a person designated by the broker a transfer instruction for an uncertificated security, providing the issuer does not refuse to register the requested transfer if the instruction is presented to the issuer for registration within 30 days thereafter; and
>
> (b) the selling broker, including a correspondent broker acting for a selling customer, fulfills his duty to transfer at the time he:
>> (i) places a certificated security in the possession of the buying broker or a person designated by the buying broker;
>> (ii) causes an uncertificated security to be registered in the name of the buying broker or a person designated by the buying broker;
>> (iii) places in the possession of the buying broker or of a person designated by the buying broker a transfer instruction for an uncertificated security, providing the issuer does not refuse to register the requested transfer if the instruction is presented to the issuer for registration within 30 days thereafter; or
>> (iv) effects clearance of the sale in accordance with the rules of the exchange on which the transaction took place.

(2) Except as provided in this section or unless otherwise agreed, a transferor's duty to transfer a security under a contract of purchase is not fulfilled until he:

> (a) places a certificated security in form to be negotiated by the purchaser in the possession of the purchaser or of a person designated by the purchaser;
> (b) causes an uncertificated security to be registered in the name of the purchaser or a person designated by the purchaser; or
> (c) if the purchaser requests, causes an acknowledgment to be made to the purchaser that a certificated or uncertificated security is held for the purchaser.

(3) Unless made on an exchange, a sale to a broker purchasing for his own account is within subsection (2) and not within subsection (1).

Amended in 1977.

## §8—315
### Action Against Transferee Based Upon Wrongful Transfer

(1) Any person against whom the transfer of a security is wrongful for any reason, including his incapacity, as against anyone except a bona fide purchaser, may:

> (a) reclaim possession of the certificated security wrongfully transferred;
> (b) obtain possession of any new certificated security representing all or part of the same rights;

(c) compel the origination of an instruction to transfer to him or a person designated by him an uncertificated security constituting all or part of the same rights; or

(d) have damages.

(2) If the transfer is wrongful because of an unauthorized indorsement of a certificated security, the owner may also reclaim or obtain possession of the security or a new certificated security, even from a bona fide purchaser, if the ineffectiveness of the purported indorsement can be asserted against him under the provisions of this Article on unauthorized indorsements (Section 8—311).

(3) The right to obtain or reclaim possession of a certificated security or to compel the origination of a transfer instruction may be specifically enforced and the transfer of a certificated or uncertificated security enjoined and a certificated security impounded pending the litigation.

Amended in 1977.

§8—316
**Purchaser's Right to Requisites for Registration of Transfer, Pledge, or Release on Books**

Unless otherwise agreed, the transferor of a certificated security or the transferor, pledgor, or pledgee of an uncertificated security on due demand must supply his purchaser with any proof of his authority to transfer, pledge, or release or with any other requisite necessary to obtain registration of the transfer, pledge, or release of the security; but if the transfer, pledge, or release is not for value, a transferor, pledgor, or pledgee need not do so unless the purchaser furnishes the necessary expenses. Failure within a reasonable time to comply with a demand made gives the purchaser the right to reject or rescind the transfer, pledge, or release.

Amended in 1977.

§8—317
**Creditors' Rights**

(1) Subject to the exceptions in subsections (3) and (4), no attachment or levy upon a certificated security or any share or other interest represented thereby which is outstanding is valid until the security is actually seized by the officer making the attachment or levy, but a certificated security which has been surrendered to the issuer may be reached by a creditor by legal process at the issuer's chief executive office in the United States.

(2) An uncertificated security registered in the name of the debtor may not be reached by a creditor except by legal process at the issuer's chief executive office in the United States.

(3) The interest of a debtor in a certificated security that is in the possession of a secured party not a financial intermediary or in an uncertificated security registered in the name of a secured party not a financial intermediary (or in the name of a nominee of the secured party) may be reached by a creditor by legal process upon the secured party.

(4) The interest of a debtor in a certificated security that is in the possession of or registered in the name of a financial intermediary or in an uncertificated security registered in the name of a financial intermediary may be reached by a creditor by legal process upon the financial intermediary on whose books the interest of the debtor appears.

(5) Unless otherwise provided by law, a creditor's lien upon the interest of a debtor in a security obtained pursuant to subsection (3) or (4) is not a restraint on the transfer of the security, free of the lien, to a third party for new value; but in the event of a transfer, the lien applies to the proceeds of the transfer in the hands of the secured party or financial intermediary, subject to any claims having priority.

(6) A creditor whose debtor is the owner of a security is entitled to aid from courts of appropriate jurisdiction, by injunction or otherwise, in reaching the security or in satisfying the claim by means allowed at law or in equity in regard to property that cannot readily be reached by ordinary legal process.

Amended in 1977.

§8—318
**No Conversion by Good Faith Conduct**

An agent or bailee who in good faith (including observance of reasonable commercial standards if he is in the business of buying, selling, or otherwise dealing with securities) has received certificated securities and sold, pledged, or delivered them or has sold or caused the transfer or pledge of uncertificated securities over which he had control according to the instructions of his principal, is not liable for conversion or for participation in breach of fiduciary duty although the principal had no right so to deal with the securities.

Amended in 1977.

§8—319
**Statute of Frauds**

A contract for the sale of securities is not enforceable by way of action or defense unless:

(a) there is some writing signed by the party against whom enforcement is sought or by his authorized agent or broker, sufficient to indicate that a contract has been made for sale of a stated quantity of described securities at a defined or stated price;

(b) delivery of a certificated security or transfer instruction has been accepted, or transfer of an uncertificated security has been registered and the transferee has failed to send written objection to the issuer within 10 days after receipt of the initial transaction statement confirming the registration, or payment has been made, but the contract is enforceable under this provision only to the extent of the delivery, registration, or payment;

(c) within a reasonable time a writing in confirmation of the sale or purchase and sufficient against the sender under paragraph (a) has been received by the party against whom enforcement is sought and he has failed to send written objection to its contents within 10 days after its receipt; or

(d) the party against whom enforcement is sought admits in his pleading, testimony, or otherwise in court that a contract was made for the sale of a stated quantity of described securities at a defined or stated price.

Amended in 1977.

§8—320
**Transfer or Pledge Within Central Depository System**

(1) In addition to other methods, a transfer, pledge, or release of a security or any interest therein may be effected by the making of

appropriate entries on the books of a clearing corporation reducing the account of the transferor, pledgor, or pledgee and increasing the account of the transferee, pledgee, or pledgor by the amount of the obligation or the number of shares or rights transferred, pledged, or released, if the security is shown on the account of a transferor, pledgor, or pledgee on the books of the clearing corporation; is subject to the control of the clearing corporation; and

    **(a)** if certificated,

        **(i)** is in the custody of the clearing corporation, another clearing corporation, a custodian bank, or a nominee of any of them; and

        **(ii)** is in bearer form or indorsed in blank by an appropriate person or registered in the name of the clearing corporation, a custodian bank, or a nominee of any of them; or

    **(b)** if uncertificated, is registered in the name of the clearing corporation, another clearing corporation, a custodian bank, or a nominee of any of them.

**(2)** Under this section entries may be made with respect to like securities or interests therein as a part of a fungible bulk and may refer merely to a quantity of a particular security without reference to the name of the registered owner, certificate or bond number, or the like, and, in appropriate cases, may be on a net basis taking into account other transfers, pledges, or releases of the same security.

**(3)** A transfer under this section is effective (Section 8—313) and the purchaser acquires the rights of the transferor (Section 8—301). A pledge or release under this section is the transfer of a limited interest. If a pledge or the creation of a security interest is intended, the security interest is perfected at the time when both value is given by the pledgee and the appropriate entries are made (Section 8—321). A transferee or pledgee under this section may be a bona fide purchaser (Section 8—302).

**(4)** A transfer or pledge under this section is not a registration of transfer under Part 4.

**(5)** That entries made on the books of the clearing corporation as provided in subsection (1) are not appropriate does not affect the validity or effect of the entries or the liabilities or obligations of the clearing corporation to any person adversely affected thereby.

Added in 1962; amended in 1977.

## §8—321
### Enforceability, Attachment, Perfection and Termination of Security Interests

**(1)** A security interest in a security is enforceable and can attach only if it is transferred to the secured party or a person designated by him pursuant to a provision of Section 8—313(1).

**(2)** A security interest so transferred pursuant to agreement by a transferor who has rights in the security to a transferee who has given value is a perfected security interest, but a security interest that has been transferred solely under paragraph (i) of Section 8—313(1) becomes unperfected after 21 days unless, within that time, the requirements for transfer under any other provision of Section 8—313(1) are satisfied.

**(3)** A security interest in a security is subject to the provisions of Article 9, but:

    **(a)** no filing is required to perfect the security interest; and

    **(b)** no written security agreement signed by the debtor is necessary to make the security interest enforceable, except as provided in paragraph (h), (i), or (j) of Section 8—313(1). The secured party has the rights and duties provided under Section 9—207, to the extent they are applicable, whether or not the security is certificated, and, if certificated, whether or not it is in his possession.

**(4)** Unless otherwise agreed, a security interest in a security is terminated by transfer to the debtor or a person designated by him pursuant to a provision of Section 8—313(1). If a security is thus transferred, the security interest, if not terminated, becomes unperfected unless the security is certificated and is delivered to the debtor for the purpose of ultimate sale or exchange or presentation, collection, renewal, or registration of transfer. In that case, the security interest becomes unperfected after 21 days unless, within that time, the security (or securities for which it has been exchanged) is transferred to the secured party or a person designated by him pursuant to a provision of Section 8—313(1).

Added in 1977.

## Part 4/Registration

### § 8—401
### Duty of Issuer to Register Transfer, Pledge, or Release

**(1)** If a certificated security in registered form is presented to the issuer with a request to register transfer or an instruction is presented to the issuer with a request to register transfer, pledge, or release, the issuer shall register the transfer, pledge, or release as requested if:

    **(a)** the security is indorsed or the instruction was originated by the appropriate person or persons (Section 8—308);

    **(b)** reasonable assurance is given that those indorsements or instructions are genuine and effective (Section 8—402);

    **(c)** the issuer has no duty as to adverse claims or has discharged the duty (Section 8—403);

    **(d)** any applicable law related to the collection of taxes has been complied with; and

    **(e)** the transfer, pledge, or release is in fact rightful or is to a bona fide purchaser.

**(2)** If an issuer is under a duty to register a transfer, pledge, or release of a security, the issuer is also liable to the person presenting a certificated security or an instruction for registration or his principal for loss resulting from any unreasonable delay in registration or from failure or refusal to register the transfer, pledge, or release.

Amended in 1977.

### §8—402
### Assurance that Indorsements and Instructions Are Effective

**(1)** The issuer may require the following assurance that each necessary indorsement of a certificated security or each instruction (Section 8—308) is genuine and effective:

    **(a)** in all cases, a guarantee of the signature (Section 8—312(1) or (2)) of the person indorsing a certificated security or originating an instruction including, in the case of an instruction, a warranty of the taxpayer identification number or, in the absence thereof, other reasonable assurance of identity;

    **(b)** if the indorsement is made or the instruction is originated by an agent, appropriate assurance of authority to sign;

(c) if the indorsement is made or the instruction is originated by a fiduciary, appropriate evidence of appointment or incumbency;

(d) if there is more than one fiduciary, reasonable assurance that all who are required to sign have done so; and

(e) if the indorsement is made or the instruction is originated by a person not covered by any of the foregoing, assurance appropriate to the case corresponding as nearly as may be to the foregoing.

(2) A "guarantee of the signature" in subsection (1) means a guarantee signed by or on behalf of a person reasonably believed by the issuer to be responsible. The issuer may adopt standards with respect to responsibility if they are not manifestly unreasonable.

(3) "Appropriate evidence of appointment or incumbency" in subsection (1) means:

(a) in the case of a fiduciary appointed or qualified by a court, a certificate issued by or under the direction or supervision of that court or an officer thereof and dated within 60 days before the date of presentation for transfer, pledge, or release; or

(b) in any other case, a copy of a document showing the appointment or a certificate issued by or on behalf of a person reasonably believed by the issuer to be responsible or, in the absence of that document or certificate, other evidence reasonably deemed by the issuer to be appropriate. The issuer may adopt standards with respect to the evidence if they are not manifestly unreasonable. The issuer is not charged with notice of the contents of any document obtained pursuant to this paragraph

(c) except to the extent that the contents relate directly to the appointment or incumbency.

(4) The issuer may elect to require reasonable assurance beyond that specified in this section, but if it does so and, for a purpose other than that specified in subsection (3)(b), both requires and obtains a copy of a will, trust, indenture, articles of co-partnership, bylaws, or other controlling instrument, it is charged with notice of all matters contained therein affecting the transfer, pledge, or release.

Amended in 1977.

## § 8—403
### Issuer's Duty as to Adverse Claims

(1) An issuer to whom a certificated security is presented for registration shall inquire into adverse claims if:

(a) a written notification of an adverse claim is received at a time and in a manner affording the issuer a reasonable opportunity to act on it prior to the issuance of a new, reissued, or re-registered certificated security, and the notification identifies the claimant, the registered owner, and the issue of which the security is a part, and provides an address for communications directed to the claimant; or

(b) the issuer is charged with notice of an adverse claim from a controlling instrument it has elected to require under Section 8—402(4).

(2) The issuer may discharge any duty of inquiry by any reasonable means, including notifying an adverse claimant by registered or certified mail at the address furnished by him or, if there be no such address, at his residence or regular place of business that the certificated security has been presented for registration of transfer by a named person, and that the transfer will be registered unless within 30 days from the date of mailing the notification, either:

(a) an appropriate restraining order, injunction, or other process issues from a court of competent jurisdiction; or

(b) there is filed with the issuer an indemnity bond, sufficient in the issuer's judgment to protect the issuer and any transfer agent, registrar, or other agent of the issuer involved from any loss it or they may suffer by complying with the adverse claim.

(3) Unless an issuer is charged with notice of an adverse claim from a controlling instrument which it has elected to require under Section 8—402(4) or receives notification of an adverse claim under subsection (1), if a certificated security presented for registration is indorsed by the appropriate person or persons the issuer is under no duty to inquire into adverse claims. In particular:

(a) an issuer registering a certificated security in the name of a person who is a fiduciary or who is described as a fiduciary is not bound to inquire into the existence, extent, or correct description of the fiduciary relationship; and thereafter the issuer may assume without inquiry that the newly registered owner continues to be the fiduciary until the issuer receives written notice that the fiduciary is no longer acting as such with respect to the particular security;

(b) an issuer registering transfer on an indorsement by a fiduciary is not bound to inquire whether the transfer is made in compliance with a controlling instrument or with the law of the state having jurisdiction of the fiduciary relationship, including any law requiring the fiduciary to obtain court approval of the transfer; and

(c) the issuer is not charged with notice of the contents of any court record or file or other recorded or unrecorded document even though the document is in its possession and even though the transfer is made on the indorsement of a fiduciary to the fiduciary himself or to his nominee.

(4) An issuer is under no duty as to adverse claims with respect to an uncertificated security except:

(a) claims embodied in a restraining order, injunction, or other legal process served upon the issuer if the process was served at a time and in a manner affording the issuer a reasonable opportunity to act on it in accordance with the requirements of subsection (5);

(b) claims of which the issuer has received a written notification from the registered owner or the registered pledgee if the notification was received at a time and in a manner affording the issuer a reasonable opportunity to act on it in accordance with the requirements of subsection (5);

(c) claims (including restrictions on transfer not imposed by the issuer) to which the registration of transfer to the present registered owner was subject and were so noted in the initial transaction statement sent to him; and

(d) claims as to which an issuer is charged with notice from a controlling instrument it has elected to require under Section 8—402(4).

(5) If the issuer of an uncertificated security is under a duty as to an adverse claim, he discharges that duty by:

(a) including a notation of the claim in any statements sent with respect to the security under Sections 8—408(3), (6), and (7); and

(b) refusing to register the transfer or pledge of the security unless the nature of the claim does not preclude transfer or pledge subject thereto.

(6) If the transfer or pledge of the security is registered subject to an adverse claim, a notation of the claim must be included in the initial transaction statement and all subsequent statements sent to the transferee and pledgee under Section 8—408.

(7) Notwithstanding subsections (4) and (5), if an uncertificated security was subject to a registered pledge at the time the issuer first came under a duty as to a particular adverse claim, the issuer has no duty as to that claim if transfer of the security is requested by the registered pledgee or an appropriate person acting for the registered pledgee unless:

(a) the claim was embodied in legal process which expressly provides otherwise;

(b) the claim was asserted in a written notification from the registered pledgee;

(c) the claim was one as to which the issuer was charged with notice from a controlling instrument it required under Section 8—402(4) in connection with the pledgee's request for transfer; or

(d) the transfer requested is to the registered owner.

Amended in 1977.

## § 8—404
### Liability and Non-Liability for Registration

(1) Except as provided in any law relating to the collection of taxes, the issuer is not liable to the owner, pledgee, or any other person suffering loss as a result of the registration of a transfer, pledge, or release of a security if:

(a) there were on or with a certificated security the necessary indorsements or the issuer had received an instruction originated by an appropriate person (Section 8—308); and

(b) the issuer had no duty as to adverse claims or has discharged the duty (Section 8—403).

(2) If an issuer has registered a transfer of a certificated security to a person not entitled to it, the issuer on demand shall deliver a like security to the true owner unless:

(a) the registration was pursuant to subsection (1);

(b) the owner is precluded from asserting any claim for registering the transfer under Section 8—405(1); or

(c) the delivery would result in overissue, in which case the issuer's liability is governed by Section 8—104.

(3) If an issuer has improperly registered a transfer, pledge, or release of an uncertificated security, the issuer on demand from the injured party shall restore the records as to the injured party to the condition that would have obtained if the improper registration had not been made unless:

(a) the registration was pursuant to subsection (1); or

(b) the registration would result in overissue, in which case the issuer's liability is governed by Section 8—104.

Amended in 1977.

## § 8—405
### Lost, Destroyed, and Stolen Certificated Securities

(1) If a certificated security has been lost, apparently destroyed, or wrongfully taken, and the owner fails to notify the issuer of that fact within a reasonable time after he has notice of it and the issuer registers a transfer of the security before receiving notification, the owner is precluded from asserting against the issuer any claim for registering the transfer under Section 8—404 or any claim to a new security under this section.

(2) If the owner of a certificated security claims that the security has been lost, destroyed, or wrongfully taken, the issuer shall issue a new certificated security or, at the option of the issuer, an equivalent uncertificated security in place of the original security if the owner:

(a) so requests before the issuer has notice that the security has been acquired by a bona fide purchaser;

(b) files with the issuer a sufficient indemnity bond; and

(c) satisfies any other reasonable requirements imposed by the issuer.

(3) If, after the issue of a new certificated or uncertificated security, a bona fide purchaser of the original certificated security presents it for registration of transfer, the issuer shall register the transfer unless registration would result in overissue, in which event the issuer's liability is governed by Section 8—104. In addition to any rights on the indemnity bond, the issuer may recover the new certificated security from the person to whom it was issued or any person taking under him except a bona fide purchaser or may cancel the uncertificated security unless a bona fide purchaser or any person taking under a bona fide purchaser is then the registered owner or registered pledgee thereof.

Amended in 1977.

## § 8—406
### Duty of Authenticating Trustee, Transfer Agent, or Registrar

(1) If a person acts as authenticating trustee, transfer agent, registrar, or other agent for an issuer in the registration of transfers of its certificated securities or in the registration of transfers, pledges, and releases of its uncertificated securities, in the issue of new securities, or in the cancellation of surrendered securities:

(a) he is under a duty to the issuer to exercise good faith and due diligence in performing his functions; and

(b) with regard to the particular functions he performs, he has the same obligation to the holder or owner of a certificated security or to the owner or pledgee of an uncertificated security and has the same rights and privileges as the issuer has in regard to those functions.

(2) Notice to an authenticating trustee, transfer agent, registrar or other agent is notice to the issuer with respect to the functions performed by the agent.

Amended in 1977.

## § 8—407
### Exchangeability of Securities

(1) No issuer is subject to the requirements of this section unless it regularly maintains a system for issuing the class of securities involved under which both certificated and uncertificated securities are regularly issued to the category of owners, which includes the person in whose name the new security is to be registered.

(2) Upon surrender of a certificated security with all necessary indorsements and presentation of a written request by the person

surrendering the security, the issuer, if he has no duty as to adverse claims or has discharged the duty (Section 8—403), shall issue to the person or a person designated by him an equivalent uncertificated security subject to all liens, restrictions, and claims that were noted on the certificated security.

(3) Upon receipt of a transfer instruction originated by an appropriate person who so requests, the issuer of an uncertificated security shall cancel the uncertificated security and issue an equivalent certificated security on which must be noted conspicuously any liens and restrictions of the issuer and any adverse claims (as to which the issuer has a duty under Section 8—403(4)) to which the uncertificated security was subject. The certificated security shall be registered in the name of and delivered to:

(a) the registered owner, if the uncertificated security was not subject to a registered pledge; or

(b) the registered pledgee, if the uncertificated security was subject to a registered pledge.

Added in 1977.

§ 8—408
**Statements of Uncertificated Securities**

(1) Within 2 business days after the transfer of an uncertificated security has been registered, the issuer shall send to the new registered owner and, if the security has been transferred subject to a registered pledge, to the registered pledgee a written statement containing:

(a) a description of the issue of which the uncertificated security is a part;

(b) the number of shares or units transferred;

(c) the name and address and any taxpayer identification number of the new registered owner and, if the security has been transferred subject to a registered pledge, the name and address and any taxpayer identification number of the registered pledgee;

(d) a notation of any liens and restrictions of the issuer and any adverse claims (as to which the issuer has a duty under Section 8—403(4)) to which the uncertificated security is or may be subject at the time of registration or a statement that there are none of those liens, restrictions, or adverse claims; and

(e) the date the transfer was registered.

(2) Within 2 business days after the pledge of an uncertificated security has been registered, the issuer shall send to the registered owner and the registered pledgee a written statement containing:

(a) a description of the issue of which the uncertificated security is a part;

(b) the number of shares or units pledged;

(c) the name and address and any taxpayer identification number of the registered owner and the registered pledgee;

(d) a notation of any liens and restrictions of the issuer and any adverse claims (as to which the issuer has a duty under Section 8—403(4)) to which the uncertificated security is or may be subject at the time of registration or a statement that there are none of those liens, restrictions, or adverse claims; and

(e) the date the pledge was registered.

(3) Within 2 business days after the release from pledge of an uncertificated security has been registered, the issuer shall send to the registered owner and the pledgee whose interest was released a written statement containing:

(a) a description of the issue of which the uncertificated security is a part;

(b) the number of shares or units released from pledge;

(c) the name and address and any taxpayer identification number of the registered owner and the pledgee whose interest was released;

(d) a notation of any liens and restrictions of the issuer and any adverse claims (as to which the issuer has a duty under Section 8—403(4)) to which the uncertificated security is or may be subject at the time of registration or a statement that there are none of those liens, restrictions, or adverse claims; and

(e) the date the release was registered.

(4) An "initial transaction statement" is the statement sent to:

(a) the new registered owner and, if applicable, to the registered pledgee pursuant to subsection (1);

(b) the registered pledgee pursuant to subsection (2); or

(c) the registered owner pursuant to subsection (3).

Each initial transaction statement shall be signed by or on behalf of the issuer and must be identified as "Initial Transaction Statement."

(5) Within 2 business days after the transfer of an uncertificated security has been registered, the issuer shall send to the former registered owner and the former registered pledgee, if any, a written statement containing:

(a) a description of the issue of which the uncertificated security is a part;

(b) the number of shares or units transferred;

(c) the name and address and any taxpayer identification number of the former registered owner and of any former registered pledgee; and

(d) the date the transfer was registered.

(6) At periodic intervals, no less frequent than annually and at any time upon the reasonable written request of the registered owner, the issuer shall send to the registered owner of each uncertificated security a dated written statement containing:

(a) a description of the issue of which the uncertificated security is a part;

(b) the name and address and any taxpayer identification number of the registered owner;

(c) the number of shares or units of the uncertificated security registered in the name of the registered owner on the date of the statement;

(d) the name and address and any taxpayer identification number of any registered pledgee and the number of shares or units subject to the pledge; and

(e) a notation of any liens and restrictions of the issuer and any adverse claims (as to which the issuer has a duty under Section 8—403(4)) to which the uncertificated security is or may be subject or a statement that there are none of those liens, restrictions, or adverse claims.

(7) At periodic intervals no less frequent than annually and at any time upon the reasonable written request of the registered pledgee, the issuer shall send to the registered pledgee of each uncertificated security a dated written statement containing:

(a) a description of the issue of which the uncertificated security is a part;

(b) the name and address and any taxpayer identification number of the registered owner;
(c) the name and address and any taxpayer identification number of the registered pledgee;
(d) the number of shares or units subject to the pledge; and
(e) a notation of any liens and restrictions of the issuer and any adverse claims (as to which the issuer has a duty under Section 8—403(4)) to which the uncertificated security is or may be subject or a statement that there are none of those liens, restrictions, or adverse claims.

(8) If the issuer sends the statements described in subsections (6) and (7) at periodic intervals no less frequent than quarterly, the issuer is not obligated to send additional statements upon request unless the owner or pledgee requesting them pays to the issuer the reasonable cost of furnishing them.

(9) Each statement sent pursuant to this section must bear a conspicuous legend reading substantially as follows: "This statement is merely a record of the rights of the addressee as of the time of its issuance. Delivery of this statement, of itself, confers no rights on the recipient. This statement is neither a negotiable instrument nor a security."

Added in 1977.

## ARTICLE 9/SECURED TRANSACTIONS; SALES OF ACCOUNTS AND CHATTEL PAPER

Note: *The adoption of this Article should be accompanied by the repeal of existing statutes dealing with conditional sales, trust receipts, factor's liens where the factor is given a non-possessory lien, chattel mortgages, crop mortgages, mortgages on railroad equipment, assignment of accounts and generally statutes regulating security interests in personal property.*

*Where the state has a retail installment selling act or small loan act, that legislation should be carefully examined to determine what changes in those acts are needed to conform them to this Article. This Article primarily sets out rules defining rights of a secured party against persons dealing with the debtor; it does not prescribe regulations and controls which may be necessary to curb abuses arising in the small loan business or in the financing of consumer purchases on credit. Accordingly there is no intention to repeal existing regulatory acts in those fields by enactment or re-enactment of Article 9. See Section 9—203(4) and the Note thereto.*

### Part 1/Short Title, Applicability and Definitions

§ 9—101
**Short Title**

This Article shall be known and may be cited as Uniform Commercial Code—Secured Transactions.

§ 9—102
**Policy and Subject Matter of Article**

(1) Except as otherwise provided in Section 9—104 on excluded transactions, this Article applies
(a) to any transaction (regardless of its form) which is intended to create a security interest in personal property or fixtures including goods, documents, instruments, general intangibles, chattel paper or accounts; and also
(b) to any sale of accounts or chattel paper.

(2) This Article applies to security interests created by contract including pledge, assignment, chattel mortgage, chattel trust, trust deed, factor's lien, equipment trust, conditional sale, trust receipt, other lien or title retention contract and lease or consignment intended as security. This Article does not apply to statutory liens except as provided in Section 9—310.

(3) The application of this Article to a security interest in a secured obligation is not affected by the fact that the obligation is itself secured by a transaction or interest to which this Article does not apply. Amended in 1972.

§ 9—103
**Perfection of Security Interest in Multiple State Transactions**

(1) Documents, instruments and ordinary goods.
(a) This subsection applies to documents and instruments and to goods other than those covered by a certificate of title described in subsection (2), mobile goods described in subsection (3), and minerals described in subsection (5).
(b) Except as otherwise provided in this subsection, perfection and the effect of perfection or non-perfection of a security interest in collateral are governed by the law of the jurisdiction where the collateral is when the last event occurs on which is based the assertion that the security interest is perfected or unperfected.
(c) If the parties to a transaction creating a purchase money security interest in goods in one jurisdiction understand at the time that the security interest attaches that the goods will be kept in another jurisdiction, then the law of the other jurisdiction governs the perfection and the effect of perfection or non-perfection of the security interest from the time it attaches until thirty days after the debtor receives possession of the goods and thereafter if the goods are taken to the other jurisdiction before the end of the thirty-day period.
(d) When collateral is brought into and kept in this state while subject to a security interest perfected under the law of the jurisdiction from which the collateral was removed, the security interest remains perfected, but if action is required by Part 3 of this Article to perfect the security interest,
(i) if the action is not taken before the expiration of the period of perfection in the other jurisdiction or the end of four months after the collateral is brought into this state, whichever period first expires, the security interest becomes unperfected at the end of that period and is thereafter deemed to have been unperfected as against a person who became a purchaser after removal;
(ii) if the action is taken before the expiration of the period specified in subparagraph (i), the security interest continues perfected thereafter;
(iii) for the purpose of priority over a buyer of consumer goods (subsection (2) of Section 9—307), the period of the effectiveness of a filing in the jurisdiction from which the collateral is removed is governed by the rules with respect to perfection in subparagraphs (i) and (ii).

(2) Certificate of title.
   (a) This subsection applies to goods covered by a certificate of title issued under a statute of this state or of another jurisdiction under the law of which indication of a security interest on the certificate is required as a condition of perfection.
   (b) Except as otherwise provided in this subsection, perfection and the effect of perfection or non-perfection of the security interest are governed by the law (including the conflict of laws rules) of the jurisdiction issuing the certificate until four months after the goods are removed from that jurisdiction and thereafter until the goods are registered in another jurisdiction, but in any event not beyond surrender of the certificate. After the expiration of that period, the goods are not covered by the certificate of title within the meaning of this section.
   (c) Except with respect to the rights of a buyer described in the next paragraph, a security interest, perfected in another jurisdiction otherwise than by notation on a certificate of title, in goods brought into this state and thereafter covered by a certificate of title issued by this state is subject to the rules stated in paragraph (d) of subsection (1).
   (d) If goods are brought into this state while a security interest therein is perfected in any manner under the law of the jurisdiction from which the goods are removed and a certificate of title is issued by this state and the certificate does not show that the goods are subject to the security interest or that they may be subject to security interests not shown on the certificate, the security interest is subordinate to the rights of a buyer of the goods who is not in the business of selling goods of that kind to the extent that he gives value and receives delivery of the goods after issuance of the certificate and without knowledge of the security interest.

(3) Accounts, general intangibles and mobile goods.
   (a) This subsection applies to accounts (other than an account described in subsection (5) on minerals) and general intangibles (other than uncertificated securities) and to goods which are mobile and which are of a type normally used in more than one jurisdiction, such as motor vehicles, trailers, rolling stock, airplanes, shipping containers, road building and construction machinery and commercial harvesting machinery and the like, if the goods are equipment or are inventory leased or held for lease by the debtor to others, and are not covered by a certificate of title described in subsection (2).
   (b) The law (including the conflict of laws rules) of the jurisdiction in which the debtor is located governs the perfection and the effect of perfection or non-perfection of the security interest.
   (c) If, however, the debtor is located in a jurisdiction which is not a part of the United States, and which does not provide for perfection of the security interest by filing or recording in that jurisdiction, the law of the jurisdiction in the United States in which the debtor has its major executive office in the United States governs the perfection and the effect of perfection or non-perfection of the security interest through filing. In the alternative, if the debtor is located in a jurisdiction which is not a part of the United States or Canada and the collateral is accounts or general intangibles for money due or to become due, the security interest may be perfected by notification to the account debtor. As used in this paragraph, "United States" includes its territories and possessions and the Commonwealth of Puerto Rico.
   (d) A debtor shall be deemed located at his place of business if he has one, at his chief executive office if he has more than one place of business, otherwise at his residence. If, however, the debtor is a foreign air carrier under the Federal Aviation Act of 1958, as amended, it shall be deemed located at the designated office of the agent upon whom service of process may be made on behalf of the foreign air carrier.
   (e) A security interest perfected under the law of the jurisdiction of the location of the debtor is perfected until the expiration of four months after a change of the debtor's location to another jurisdiction, or until perfection would have ceased by the law of the first jurisdiction, whichever period first expires. Unless perfected in the new jurisdiction before the end of that period, it becomes unperfected thereafter and is deemed to have been unperfected as against a person who became a purchaser after the change.

(4) Chattel paper.
The rules stated for goods in subsection (1) apply to a possessory security interest in chattel paper. The rules stated for accounts in subsection (3) apply to a non-possessory security interest in chattel paper, but the security interest may not be perfected by notification to the account debtor.

(5) Minerals.
Perfection and the effect of perfection or non-perfection of a security interest which is created by a debtor who has an interest in minerals or the like (including oil and gas) before extraction and which attaches thereto as extracted, or which attaches to an account resulting from the sale thereof at the wellhead or minehead are governed by the law (including the conflict of laws rules) of the jurisdiction wherein the wellhead or minehead is located.

(6) Uncertificated securities.
The law (including the conflict of laws rules) of the jurisdiction of organization of the issuer governs the perfection and the effect of perfection or non-perfection of a security interest in uncertificated securities.

Amended in 1972 and 1977.

§ 9—104
**Transactions Excluded From Article**

This Article does not apply
   (a) to a security interest subject to any statute of the United States, to the extent that such statute governs the rights of parties to and third parties affected by transactions in particular types of property; or
   (b) to a landlord's lien; or
   (c) to a lien given by statute or other rule of law for services or materials except as provided in Section 9—310 on priority of such liens; or
   (d) to a transfer of a claim for wages, salary or other compensation of an employee; or
   (e) to a transfer by a government or governmental subdivision or agency; or
   (f) to a sale of accounts or chattel paper as part of a sale of the business out of which they arose, or an assignment of accounts or chattel paper which is for the purpose of collection

only, or a transfer of a right to payment under a contract to an assignee who is also to do the performance under the contract or a transfer of a single account to an assignee in whole or partial satisfaction of a preexisting indebtedness; or

(g) to a transfer of an interest in or claim in or under any policy of insurance, except as provided with respect to proceeds (Section 9—306) and priorities in proceeds (Section 9—312); or

(h) to a right represented by a judgment (other than a judgment taken on a right to payment which was collateral); or

(i) to any right of set-off; or

(j) except to the extent that provision is made for fixtures in Section 9—313, to the creation or transfer of an interest in or lien on real estate, including a lease or rents thereunder; or

(k) to a transfer in whole or in part of any claim arising out of tort; or

(l) to a transfer of an interest in any deposit account (subsection (1) of Section 9—105) except as provided with respect to proceeds (Section 9—306) and priorities in proceeds (Section 9—312).

Amended in 1972.

§ 9—105
**Definitions and Index of Definitions**

(1) In this Article unless the context otherwise requires:

(a) "Account debtor" means the person who is obligated on an account, chattel paper or general intangible;

(b) "Chattel paper" means a writing or writings which evidence both a monetary obligation and a security interest in or a lease of specific goods, but a charter or other contract involving the use or hire of a vessel is not chattel paper. When a transaction is evidenced both by such a security agreement or a lease and by an instrument or a series of instruments, the group of writings taken together constitutes chattel paper;

(c) "Collateral" means the property subject to a security interest, and includes accounts and chattel paper which have been sold;

(d) "Debtor" means the person who owes payment or other performance of the obligation secured, whether or not he owns or has rights in the collateral, and includes the seller of accounts or chattel paper. Where the debtor and the owner of the collateral are not the same person, the term "debtor" means the owner of the collateral in any provision of the Article dealing with the obligation, and may include both where the context so requires;

(e) "Deposit account" means a demand, time, savings, passbook or like account maintained with a bank, savings and loan association, credit union or like organization, other than an account evidenced by a certificate of deposit;

(f) "Document" means document of title as defined in the general definitions of Article 1 (Section 1—201), and a receipt of the kind described in subsection (2) of Section 7—201;

(g) "Encumbrance" includes real estate mortgages and other liens on real estate and all other rights in real estate that are not ownership interests;

(h) "Goods" includes all things which are movable at the time the security interest attaches or which are fixtures (Section 9—313), but does not include money, documents, instruments, accounts, chattel paper, general intangibles, or minerals or the like (including oil and gas) before extraction. "Goods" also includes standing timber which is to be cut and removed under a conveyance or contract for sale, the unborn young of animals, and growing crops;

(i) "Instrument" means a negotiable instrument (defined in Section 3—104), or a security (defined in Section 8—102) or any other writing which evidences a right to the payment of money and is not itself a security agreement or lease and is of a type which is in ordinary course of business transferred by delivery with any necessary indorsement or assignment;

(j) "Mortgage" means a consensual interest created by a real estate mortgage, a trust deed on real estate, or the like;

(k) An advance is made "pursuant to commitment" if the secured party has bound himself to make it, whether or not a subsequent event of default or other event not within his control has relieved or may relieve him from his obligation;

(l) "Security agreement" means an agreement which creates or provides for a security interest;

(m) "Secured party" means a lender, seller or other person in whose favor there is a security interest, including a person to whom accounts or chattel paper have been sold. When the holders of obligations issued under an indenture of trust, equipment trust agreement or the like are represented by a trustee or other person, the representative is the secured party;

(n) "Transmitting utility" means any person primarily engaged in the railroad, street railway or trolley bus business, the electric or electronics communications transmission business, the transmission of goods by pipeline, or the transmission or the production and transmission of electricity, steam, gas or water, or the provision of sewer service.

(2) Other definitions applying to this Article and the sections in which they appear are:

"Account". Section 9—106.
"Attach". Section 9—203.
"Construction mortgage". Section 9—313(1).
"Consumer goods". Section 9—109(1).
"Equipment". Section 9—109(2).
"Farm products". Section 9—109(3).
"Fixture". Section 9—313(1).
"Fixture filing". Section 9—313(1).
"General intangibles". Section 9—106.
"Inventory". Section 9—109(4).
"Lien creditor". Section 9—301(3).
"Proceeds". Section 9—306(1).
"Purchase money security interest". Section 9—107.
"United States". Section 9—103.

(3) The following defintions in other Articles apply to this Article:

"Check". Section 3—104.
"Contract for sale". Section 2—106.
"Holder in due course". Section 3—302.
"Note". Section 3—104.
"Sale". Section 2—106.

(4) In addition Article 1 contains general definitions and principles of construction and interpretation applicable throughout this Article.

Amended in 1966, 1972, and 1977.

## § 9—106
### Definitions: "Account"; "General Intangibles"

"Account" means any right to payment for goods sold or leased or for services rendered which is not evidenced by an instrument or chattel paper, whether or not it has been earned by performance. "General intangibles" means any personal property (including things in action) other than goods, accounts, chattel paper, documents, instruments, and money. All rights to payment earned or unearned under a charter or other contract involving the use or hire of a vessel and all rights incident to the charter or contract are accounts.

Amended in 1966, 1972.

## § 9—107
### Definitions: "Purchase Money Security Interest"

A security interest is a "purchase money security interest" to the extent that it is

(a) taken or retained by the seller of the collateral to secure all or part of its price; or

(b) taken by a person who by making advances or incurring an obligation gives value to enable the debtor to acquire rights in or the use of collateral if such value is in fact so used.

## § 9—108
### When After-Acquired Collateral Not Security for Antecedent Debt

Where a secured party makes an advance, incurs an obligation, releases a perfected security interest, or otherwise gives new value which is to be secured in whole or in part by after-acquired property his security interest in the after-acquired collateral shall be deemed to be taken for new value and not as security for an antecedent debt if the debtor acquires his rights in such collateral either in the ordinary course of his business or under a contract of purchase made pursuant to the security agreement within a reasonable time after new value is given.

## § 9—109
### Classification of Goods; "Consumer Goods"; "Equipment"; "Farm Products"; "Inventory"

Goods are

(1) "consumer goods" if they are used or bought for use primarily for personal, family or household purposes;

(2) "equipment" if they are used or bought for use primarily in business (including farming or a profession) or by a debtor who is a non-profit organization or a governmental subdivision or agency or if the goods are not included in the definitions of inventory, farm products or consumer goods;

(3) "farm products" if they are crops or livestock or supplies used or produced in farming operations or if they are products of crops or livestock in their unmanufactured states (such as ginned cotton, woolclip, maple syrup, milk and eggs), and if they are in the possession of a debtor engaged in raising, fattening, grazing or other farming operations. If goods are farm products they are neither equipment nor inventory;

(4) "inventory" if they are held by a person who holds them for sale or lease or to be furnished under contracts of service or if he has so furnished them, or if they are raw materials, work in process or materials used or consumed in a business. Inventory of a person is not to be classified as his equipment.

## § 9—110
### Sufficiency of Description

For the purposes of this Article any description of personal property or real estate is sufficient whether or not it is specific if it reasonably identifies what is described.

## § 9—111
### Applicability of Bulk Transfer Laws

The creation of a security interest is not a bulk transfer under Article 6 (see Section 6—103).

## § 9—112
### Where Collateral Is Not Owned by Debtor

Unless otherwise agreed, when a secured party knows that collateral is owned by a person who is not the debtor, the owner of the collateral is entitled to receive from the secured party any surplus under Section 9—502(2) or under Section 9—504(1), and is not liable for the debt or for any deficiency after resale, and he has the same right as the debtor

(a) to receive statements under Section 9—208;

(b) to receive notice of and to object to a secured party's proposal to retain the collateral in satisfaction of the indebtedness under Section 9—505;

(c) to redeem the collateral under Section 9—506;

(d) to obtain injunctive or other relief under Section 9—507(1); and

(e) to recover losses caused to him under Section 9—208(2).

## § 9—113
### Security Interests Arising Under Article on Sales

A security interest arising solely under the Article on Sales (Article 2) is subject to the provisions of this Article except that to the extent that and so long as the debtor does not have or does not lawfully obtain possession of the goods

(a) no security agreement is necessary to make the security interest enforceable; and

(b) no filing is required to perfect the security interest; and

(c) the rights of the secured party on default by the debtor are governed by the Article on Sales (Article 2).

## § 9—114
### Consignment

(1) A person who delivers goods under a consignment which is not a security interest and who would be required to file under this Article by paragraph (3)(c) of Section 2—326 has priority over a secured party who is or becomes a creditor of the consignee and who would have a perfected security interest in the goods if they were the property of the consignee, and also has priority with respect to identifiable cash proceeds received on or before delivery of the goods to a buyer, if

(a) the consignor complies with the filing provision of the Article on Sales with respect to consignments (paragraph (3)(c) of Section 2—326) before the consignee receives possession of the goods; and

(b) the consignor gives notification in writing to the holder of the security interest if the holder has filed a financing statement covering the same types of goods before the date of the filing made by the consignor; and

(c) the holder of the security interest receives the notification within five years before the consignee receives possession of the goods; and

(d) the notification states that the consignor expects to deliver goods on consignment to the consignee, describing the goods by item or type.

(2) In the case of a consignment which is not a security interest and in which the requirements of the preceding subsection have not been met, a person who delivers goods to another is subordinate to a person who would have a perfected security interest in the goods if they were the property of the debtor.

Added in 1972.

## Part 2/Validity of Security Agreement and Rights of Parties Thereto

### § 9—201
### General Validity of Security Agreement

Except as otherwise provided by this Act a security agreement is effective according to its terms between the parties, against purchasers of the collateral and against creditors. Nothing in this Article validates any charge or practice illegal under any statute or regulation thereunder governing usury, small loans, retail installment sales, or the like, or extends the application of any such statute or regulation to any transaction not otherwise subject thereto.

### § 9—202
### Title to Collateral Immaterial

Each provision of this Article with regard to rights, obligations and remedies applies whether title to collateral is in the secured party or in the debtor.

### § 9—203
### Attachment and Enforceability of Security Interest; Proceeds; Formal Requisites

(1) Subject to the provisions of Section 4—208 on the security interest of a collecting bank, Section 8—321 on security interests in securities and Section 9—113 on a security interest arising under the Article on Sales, a security interest is not enforceable against the debtor or third parties with respect to the collateral and does not attach unless:

(a) the collateral is in the possession of the secured party pursuant to agreement, or the debtor has signed a security agreement which contains a description of the collateral and in addition, when the security interest covers crops growing or to be grown or timber to be cut, a description of the land concerned;

(b) value has been given; and

(c) the debtor has rights in the collateral.

(2) A security interest attaches when it becomes enforceable against the debtor with respect to the collateral. Attachment occurs as soon as all of the events specified in subsection (1) have taken place unless explicit agreement postpones the time of attaching.

(3) Unless otherwise agreed a security agreement gives the secured party the rights to proceeds provided by Section 9—306.

(4) A transaction, although subject to this Article, is also subject to . . . . . . . . . . .*, and in the case of conflict between the provisions of this Article and any such statute, the provisions of such statute control. Failure to comply with any applicable statute has only the effect which is specified therein.

Amended in 1972 and 1977.

Note: *At * in subsection (4) insert reference to any local statute regulating small loans, retail installment sales and the like.*

*The foregoing subsection (4) is designed to make it clear that certain transactions, although subject to this Article, must also comply with other applicable legislation.*

*This Article is designed to regulate all the "security" aspects of transactions within its scope. There is, however, much regulatory legislation, particularly in the consumer field, which supplements this Article and should not be repealed by its enactment. Examples are small loan acts, retail installment selling acts and the like. Such acts may provide for licensing and rate regulation and may prescribe particular forms of contract. Such provisions should remain in force despite the enactment of this Article. On the other hand if a retail installment selling act contains provisions on filing, rights on default, etc., such provisions should be repealed as inconsistent with this Article except that inconsistent provisions as to deficiencies, penalties, etc., in the Uniform Consumer Credit Code and other recent related legislation should remain because those statutes were drafted after the substantial enactment of the Article and with the intention of modifying certain provisions of this Article as to consumer credit.*

### § 9—204
### After-Acquired Property; Future Advances

(1) Except as provided in subsection (2), a security agreement may provide that any or all obligations covered by the security agreement are to be secured by after-acquired collateral.

(2) No security interest attaches under an after-acquired property clause to consumer goods other than accessions (Section 9—314) when given as additional security unless the debtor acquires rights in them within ten days after the secured party gives value.

(3) Obligations covered by a security agreement may include future advances or other value whether or not the advances or value are given pursuant to commitment (subsection (1) of Section 9—105).

Amended in 1972.

### § 9—205
### Use or Disposition of Collateral Without Accounting Permissible

A security interest is not invalid or fraudulent against creditors by reason of liberty in the debtor to use, commingle or dispose of all or part of the collateral (including returned or repossessed goods) or to collect or compromise accounts or chattel paper, or to accept the return of goods or make repossessions, or to use, commingle or dispose of proceeds, or by reason of the failure of the secured party to require the debtor to account for proceeds or replace collateral. This section does not relax the requirements of possession where perfection of a security interest depends upon possession of the collateral by the secured party or by a bailee.

Amended in 1972.

### § 9—206
**Agreement Not to Assert Defenses Against Assignee; Modification of Sales Warranties Where Security Agreement Exists**

(1) Subject to any statute or decision which establishes a different rule for buyers or lessees of consumer goods, an agreement by a buyer or lessee that he will not assert against an assignee any claim or defense which he may have against the seller or lessor is enforceable by an assignee who takes his assignment for value, in good faith and without notice of a claim or defense, except as to defenses of a type which may be asserted against a holder in due course of a negotiable instrument under the Article on Commercial Paper (Article 3). A buyer who as part of one transaction signs both a negotiable instrument and a security agreement makes such an agreement.

(2) When a seller retains a purchase money security interest in goods the Article on Sales (Article 2) governs the sale and any disclaimer, limitation or modification of the seller's warranties.

Amended in 1962.

### § 9—207
**Rights and Duties When Collateral is in Secured Party's Possession**

(1) A secured party must use reasonable care in the custody and preservation of collateral in his possession. In the case of an instrument or chattel paper reasonable care includes taking necessary steps to preserve rights against prior parties unless otherwise agreed.

(2) Unless otherwise agreed, when collateral is in the secured party's possession

    (a) reasonable expenses (including the cost of any insurance and payment of taxes or other charges) incurred in the custody, preservation, use or operation of the collateral are chargeable to the debtor and are secured by the collateral;

    (b) the risk of accidental loss or damage is on the debtor to the extent of any deficiency in any effective insurance coverage;

    (c) the secured party may hold as additional security any increase or profits (except money) received from the collateral, but money so received, unless remitted to the debtor, shall be applied in reduction of the secured obligation;

    (d) the secured party must keep the collateral identifiable but fungible collateral may be commingled;

    (e) the secured party may repledge the collateral upon terms which do not impair the debtor's right to redeem it.

(3) A secured party is liable for any loss caused by his failure to meet any obligation imposed by the preceding subsections but does not lose his security interest.

(4) A secured party may use or operate the collateral for the purpose of preserving the collateral or its value or pursuant to the order of a court of appropriate jurisdiction or, except in the case of consumer goods, in the manner and to the extent provided in the security agreement.

### § 9—208
**Request for Statement of Account or List of Collateral**

(1) A debtor may sign a statement indicating what he believes to be the aggregate amount of unpaid indebtedness as of a specified date and may send it to the secured party with a request that the statement be approved or corrected and returned to the debtor. When the security agreement or any other record kept by the secured party identifies the collateral a debtor may similarly request the secured party to approve or correct a list of the collateral.

(2) The secured party must comply with such a request within two weeks after receipt by sending a written correction or approval. If the secured party claims a security interest in all of a particular type of collateral owned by the debtor he may indicate that fact in his reply and need not approve or correct an itemized list of such collateral. If the secured party without reasonable excuse fails to comply he is liable for any loss caused to the debtor thereby; and if the debtor has properly included in his request a good faith statement of the obligation or a list of the collateral or both the secured party may claim a security interest only as shown in the statement against persons misled by his failure to comply. If he no longer has an interest in the obligation or collateral at the time the request is received he must disclose the name and address of any successor in interest known to him and he is liable for any loss caused to the debtor as a result of failure to disclose. A successor in interest is not subject to this section until a request is received by him.

(3) A debtor is entitled to such a statement once every six months without charge. The secured party may require payment of a charge not exceeding $10 for each additional statement furnished.

## Part 3/Rights of Third Parties; Perfected and Unperfected Security Interests; Rules of Priority

### § 9—301
**Persons Who Take Priority Over Unperfected Security Interests; Rights of "Lien Creditor"**

(1) Except as otherwise provided in subsection (2), an unperfected security interest is subordinate to the rights of

    (a) persons entitled to priority under Section 9—312;

    (b) a person who becomes a lien creditor before the security interest is perfected;

    (c) in the case of goods, instruments, documents, and chattel paper, a person who is not a secured party and who is a transferee in bulk or other buyer not in ordinary course of business or is a buyer of farm products in ordinary course of business, to the extent that he gives value and receives delivery of the collateral without knowledge of the security interest and before it is perfected;

    (d) in the case of accounts and general intangibles, a person who is not a secured party and who is a transferee to the extent that he gives value without knowledge of the security interest and before it is perfected.

(2) If the secured party files with respect to a purchase money security interest before or within ten days after the debtor receives possession of the collateral, he takes priority over the rights of a transferee in bulk or of a lien creditor which arise between the time the security interest attaches and the time of filing.

(3) A "lien creditor" means a creditor who has acquired a lien on the property involved by attachment, levy or the like and includes an assignee for benefit of creditors from the time of assignment, and a trustee in bankruptcy from the date of the filing of the petition or a receiver in equity from the time of appointment.

(4) A person who becomes a lien creditor while a security interest is perfected takes subject to the security interest only to the extent that it secures advances made before he becomes a lien credit or within 45 days thereafter or made without knowledge of the lien or pursuant to a commitment entered into without knowledge of the lien.

Amended in 1972.

## § 9—302
### When Filing Is Required to Perfect Security Interest; Security Interests to Which Filing Provisions of This Article Do Not Apply

(1) A financing statement must be filed to perfect all security interests except the following:

(a) a security interest in collateral in possession of the secured party under Section 9—305;

(b) a security interest temporarily perfected in instruments or documents without delivery under Section 9—304 or in proceeds for a 10 day period under Section 9—306;

(c) a security interest created by an assignment of a beneficial interest in a trust or a decedent's estate;

(d) a purchase money security interest in consumer goods; but filing is required for a motor vehicle required to be registered; and fixture filing is required for priority over conflicting interests in fixtures to the extent provided in Section 9—313;

(e) an assignment of accounts which does not alone or in conjunction with other assignments to the same assignee transfer a significant part of the outstanding accounts of the assignor;

(f) a security interest of a collecting bank (Section 4—208) or in securities (Section 8—321) or arising under the Article on Sales (see Section 9—113) or covered in subsection (3) of this section;

(g) an assignment for the benefit of all the creditors of the transferor, and subsequent transfers by the assignee thereunder.

(2) If a secured party assigns a perfected security interest, no filing under this Article is required in order to continue the perfected status of the security interest against creditors of and transferees from the original debtor.

(3) The filing of a financing statement otherwise required by this Article is not necessary or effective to perfect a security interest in property subject to

(a) a statute or treaty of the United States which provides for a national or international registration or a national or international certificate of title or which specifies a place of filing different from that specified in this Article for filing of the security interest; or

(b) the following statutes of this state; [list any certificate of title statute covering automobiles, trailers, mobile homes, boats, farm tractors, or the like, and any central filing statute]; but during any period in which collateral is inventory held for sale by a person who is in the business of selling goods of that kind, the filing provisions of this Article (Part 4) apply to a security interest in that collateral created by him as debtor; or

(c) a certificate of title statute of another jurisdiction under the law of which indication of a security interest on the certificate is required as a condition of perfection (subsection (2) of Section 9—103).

(4) Compliance with a statute or treaty described in subsection (3) is equivalent to the filing of a financing statement under this Article, and a security interest in property subject to the statute or treaty can be perfected only by compliance therewith except as provided in Section 9—103 on multiple state transactions. Duration and renewal of perfection of a security interest perfected by compliance with the statute or treaty are governed by the provisions of the statute or treaty; in other respects the security interest is subject to this Article.

Amended in 1972 and 1977.

## § 9—303
### When Security Interest Is Perfected; Continuity of Perfection

(1) A security interest is perfected when it has attached and when all of the applicable steps required for perfection have been taken. Such steps are specified in Sections 9—302, 9—304, 9—305 and 9—306. If such steps are taken before the security interest attaches, it is perfected at the time when it attaches.

(2) If a security interest is originally perfected in any way permitted under this Article and is subsequently perfected in some other way under this Article, without an intermediate period when it was unperfected, the security interest shall be deemed to be perfected continuously for the purposes of this Article.

## § 9—304
### Perfection of Security Interest in Instruments, Documents, and Goods Covered by Documents; Perfection by Permissive Filing; Temporary Perfection Without Filing or Transfer of Possession

(1) A security interest in chattel paper or negotiable documents may be perfected by filing. A security interest in money or instruments (other than certificated securities or instruments which constitute part of chattel paper) can be perfected only by the secured party's taking possession, except as provided in subsections (4) and (5) of this section and subsections (2) and (3) of Section 9—306 on proceeds.

(2) During the period that goods are in the possession of the issuer of a negotiable document therefor, a security interest in the goods is perfected by perfecting a security interest in the document, and any security interest in the goods otherwise perfected during such period is subject thereto.

(3) A security interest in goods in the possession of a bailee other than one who has issued a negotiable document therefor is perfected by issuance of a document in the name of the secured party or by the bailee's receipt of notification of the secured party's interest or by filing as to the goods.

(4) A security interest in instruments (other than certificated securities) or negotiable documents is perfected without filing or the taking of possession for a period of 21 days from the time it attaches to the extent that it arises for new value given under a written security agreement.

(5) A security interest remains perfected for a period of 21 days without filing where a secured party having a perfected security interest in an instrument (other than a certificated security), a negotiable document or goods in possession of a bailee other than one who has issued a negotiable document therefor

    (a) makes available to the debtor the goods or documents representing the goods for the purpose of ultimate sale or exchange or for the purpose of loading, unloading, storing, shipping, transshipping, manufacturing, processing or otherwise dealing with them in a manner preliminary to their sale or exchange, but priority between conflicting security interests in the goods is subject to subsection (3) of Section 9—312; or

    (b) delivers the instrument to the debtor for the purpose of ultimate sale or exchange or of presentation, collection, renewal or registration of transfer.

(6) After the 21 day period in subsections (4) and (5) perfection depends upon compliance with applicable provisions of this Article.

Amended in 1972 and 1977.

## § 9—305
### When Possession by Secured Party Perfects Security Interest Without Filing

A security interest in letters of credit and advices of credit (subsection (2)(a) of Section 5—116), goods, instruments (other than certificated securities), money, negotiable documents or chattel paper may be perfected by the secured party's taking possession of the collateral. If such collateral other than goods covered by a negotiable document is held by a bailee, the secured party is deemed to have possession from the time the bailee receives notification of the secured party's interest. A security interest is perfected by possession from the time possession is taken without a relation back and continues only so long as possession is retained, unless otherwise specified in this Article. The security interest may be otherwise perfected as provided in this Article before or after the period of possession by the secured party.

Amended in 1972.

## § 9—306
### "Proceeds"; Secured Party's Rights on Disposition of Collateral

(1) "Proceeds" includes whatever is received upon the sale, exchange, collection or other disposition of collateral or proceeds. Insurance payable by reason of loss or damage to the collateral is proceeds, except to the extent that it is payable to a person other than a party to the security agreement. Money, checks, deposit accounts, and the like are "cash proceeds". All other proceeds are "non-cash proceeds".

(2) Except where this Article otherwise provides, a security interest continues in collateral notwithstanding sale, exchange or other disposition thereof unless the disposition was authorized by the secured party in the security agreement or otherwise, and also continues in any identifiable proceeds including collections received by the debtor.

(3) The security interest in proceeds is a continuously perfected security interest if the interest in the original collateral was perfected but it ceases to be a perfected security interest and becomes unperfected ten days after receipt of the proceeds by the debtor unless

    (a) a filed financing statement covers the original collateral and the proceeds are collateral in which a security interest may be perfected by filing in the office or offices where the financing statement has been filed and, if the proceeds are acquired with cash proceeds, the description of collateral in the financing statement indicates the types of property constituting the proceeds; or

    (b) a filed financing statement covers the original collateral and the proceeds are identifiable cash proceeds; or

    (c) the security interest in the proceeds is perfected before the expiration of the ten day period.

Except as provided in this section, a security interest in proceeds can be perfected only by the methods or under the circumstances permitted in this Article for original collateral of the same type.

(4) In the event of insolvency proceedings instituted by or against a debtor, a secured party with a perfected security interest in proceeds has a perfected security interest only in the following proceeds:

    (a) in identifiable non-cash proceeds and in separate deposit accounts containing only proceeds;

    (b) in identifiable cash proceeds in the form of money which is neither commingled with other money nor deposited in a deposit account prior to the insolvency proceedings;

    (c) in identifiable cash proceeds in the form of checks and the like which are not deposited in a deposit account prior to the insolvency proceedings; and

    (d) in all cash and deposit accounts of the debtor in which proceeds have been commingled with other funds, but the perfected security interest under this paragraph (d) is

        (i) subject to any right to set-off; and

        (ii) limited to an amount not greater than the amount of any cash proceeds received by the debtor within ten days before the institution of the insolvency proceedings less the sum of (I) the payments to the secured party on account of cash proceeds received by the debtor during such period and (II) the cash proceeds received by the debtor during such period to which the secured party is entitled under paragraphs (a) through (c) of this subsection (4).

(5) If a sale of goods results in an account or chattel paper which is transferred by the seller to a secured party, and if the goods are returned to or are repossessed by the seller or the secured party, the following rules determine priorities:

    (a) If the goods were collateral at the time of sale, for an indebtedness of the seller which is still unpaid, the original security interest attaches again to the goods and continues as a perfected security interest if it was perfected at the time when the goods were sold. If the security interest was originally perfected by a filing which is still effective, nothing further is required to continue the perfected status; in any other case, the secured party must take possession of the returned or repossessed goods or must file.

    (b) An unpaid transferee of the chattel paper has a security interest in the goods against the transferor. Such security interest is prior to a security interest asserted under paragraph (a) to the extent that the transferee of the chattel paper was entitled to priority under Section 9—308.

    (c) An unpaid transferee of the account has a security interest in the goods against the transferor. Such security interest is subordinate to a security interest asserted under paragraph (a).

(d) A security interest of an unpaid transferee asserted under paragraph (b) or (c) must be perfected for protection against creditors of the transferor and purchasers of the returned or repossessed goods.

Amended in 1972.

## § 9—307
### Protection of Buyers of Goods

(1) A buyer in ordinary course of business (subsection (9) of Section 1—201) other than a person buying farm products from a person engaged in farming operations takes free of a security interest created by his seller even though the security interest is perfected and even though the buyer knows of its existence.

(2) In the case of consumer goods, a buyer takes free of a security interest even though perfected if he buys without knowledge of the security interest, for value and for his own personal, family or household purposes unless prior to the purchase the secured party has filed a financing statement covering such goods.

(3) A buyer other than a buyer in ordinary course of business (subsection (1) of this section) takes free of a security interest to the extent that it secures future advances made after the secured party acquires knowledge of the purchase, or more than 45 days after the purchase, whichever first occurs, unless made pursuant to a commitment entered into without knowledge of the purchase and before the expiration of the 45 day period.

Amended in 1972.

## § 9—308
### Purchase of Chattel Paper and Instruments

A purchaser of chattel paper or an instrument who gives new value and takes possession of it in the ordinary course of his business has priority over a security interest in the chattel paper or instrument

    (a) which is perfected under Section 9—304 (permissive filing and temporary perfection) or under Section 9—306 (perfection as to proceeds) if he acts without knowledge that the specific paper or instrument is subject to a security interest; or

    (b) which is claimed merely as proceeds of inventory subject to a security interest (Section 9—306) even though he knows that the specific paper or instrument is subject to the security interest.

Amended in 1972.

## § 9—309
### Protection of Purchasers of Instruments, Documents and Securities

Nothing in this Article limits the rights of a holder in due course of a negotiable instrument (Section 3—302) or a holder to whom a negotiable document of title has been duly negotiated (Section 7—501) or a bona fide purchaser of a security (Section 8—302) and the holders or purchasers take priority over an earlier security interest even though perfected. Filing under this Article does not constitute notice of the security interest to such holders or purchasers.

Amended in 1977.

## § 9—310
### Priority of Certain Liens Arising by Operation of Law

When a person in the ordinary course of his business furnishes services or materials with respect to goods subject to a security interest, a lien upon goods in the possession of such person given by statute or rule of law for such materials or services takes priority over a perfected security interest unless the lien is statutory and the statute expressly provides otherwise.

## § 9—311
### Alienability of Debtor's Rights: Judicial Process

The debtor's rights in collateral may be voluntarily or involuntarily transferred (by way of sale, creation of a security interest, attachment, levy, garnishment or other judicial process) notwithstanding a provision in the security agreement prohibiting any transfer or making the transfer constitute a default.

## § 9—312
### Priorities Among Conflicting Security Interests in the Same Collateral

(1) The rules of priority stated in other sections of this Part and in the following sections shall govern when applicable: Section 4—208 with respect to the security interests of collecting banks in items being collected, accompanying documents and proceeds; Section 9—103 on security interests related to other jurisdictions; Section 9—114 on consignments.

(2) A perfected security interest in crops for new value given to enable the debtor to produce the crops during the production season and given not more than three months before the crops become growing crops by planting or otherwise takes priority over an earlier perfected security interest to the extent that such earlier interest secures obligations due more than six months before the crops become growing crops by planting or otherwise, even though the person giving new value had knowledge of the earlier security interest.

(3) A perfected purchase money security interest in inventory has priority over a conflicting security interest in the same inventory and also has priority in identifiable cash proceeds received on or before the delivery of the inventory to a buyer if

    (a) the purchase money security interest is perfected at the time the debtor receives possession of the inventory; and

    (b) the purchase money secured party gives notification in writing to the holder of the conflicting security interest if the holder had filed a financing statement covering the same types of inventory (i) before the date of the filing made by the purchase money secured party, or (ii) before the beginning of the 21 day period where the purchase money security interest is temporarily perfected without filing or possession (subsection (5) of Section 9—304); and

    (c) the holder of the conflicting security interest receives the notification within five years before the debtor receives possession of the inventory; and

    (d) the notification states that the person giving the notice has or expects to acquire a purchase money security interest in inventory of the debtor, describing such inventory by item or type.

(4) A purchase money security interest in collateral other than inventory has priority over a conflicting security interest in the

same collateral or its proceeds if the purchase money security interest is perfected at the time the debtor receives possession of the collateral or within ten days thereafter.

**(5)** In all cases not governed by other rules stated in this section (including cases of purchase money security interests which do not qualify for the special priorities set forth in subsections (3) and (4) of this section), priority between conflicting security interests in the same collateral shall be determined according to the following rules:

    **(a)** Conflicting security interests rank according to priority in time of filing or perfection. Priority dates from the time a filing is first made covering the collateral or the time the security interest is first perfected, whichever is earlier, provided that there is no period thereafter when there is neither filing nor perfection.

    **(b)** So long as conflicting security interests are unperfected, the first to attach has priority.

**(6)** For the purposes of subsection (5) a date of filing or perfection as to collateral is also a date of filing or perfection as to proceeds.

**(7)** If future advances are made while a security interest is perfected by filing, the taking of possession, or under Section 8—321 on securities, the security interest has the same priority for the purposes of subsection (5) with respect to the future advances as it does with respect to the first advance. If a commitment is made before or while the security interest is so perfected, the security interest has the same priority with respect to advances made pursuant thereto. In other cases a perfected security interest has priority from the date the advance is made.

Amended in 1972 and 1977.

## § 9—313
### Priority of Security Interests in Fixtures

**(1)** In this section and in the provisions of Part 4 of this Article referring to fixture filing, unless the context otherwise requires

    **(a)** goods are "fixtures" when they become so related to particular real estate that an interest in them arises under real estate law

    **(b)** a "fixture filing" is the filing in the office where a mortgage on the real estate would be filed or recorded of a financing statement covering goods which are or are to become fixtures and conforming to the requirements of subsection (5) of Section 9—402

    **(c)** a mortgage is a "construction mortgage" to the extent that it secures an obligation incurred for the construction of an improvement on land including the acquisition cost of the land, if the recorded writing so indicates.

**(2)** A security interest under this Article may be created in goods which are fixtures or may continue in goods which become fixtures, but no security interest exists under this Article in ordinary building materials incorporated into an improvement on land.

**(3)** This Article does not prevent creation of an encumbrance upon fixtures pursuant to real estate law.

**(4)** A perfected security interest in fixtures has priority over the conflicting interest of an encumbrancer or owner of the real estate where

    **(a)** the security interest is a purchase money security interest, the interest of the encumbrancer or owner arises before the goods become fixtures, the security interest is perfected by a fixture filing before the goods become fixtures or within ten days thereafter, and the debtor has an interest of record in the real estate or is in possession of the real estate; or

    **(b)** the security interest is perfected by a fixture filing before the interest of the encumbrancer or owner is of record, the security interest has priority over any conflicting interest of a predecessor in title of the encumbrancer or owner, and the debtor has an interest of record in the real estate or is in possession of the real estate; or

    **(c)** the fixtures are readily removable factory or office machines or readily removable replacements of domestic appliances which are consumer goods, and before the goods become fixtures the security interest is perfected by any method permitted by this Article; or

    **(d)** the conflicting interest is a lien on the real estate obtained by legal or equitable proceedings after the security interest was perfected by any method permitted by this Article.

**(5)** A security interest in fixtures, whether or not perfected, has priority over the conflicting interest of an encumbrancer or owner of the real estate where

    **(a)** the encumbrancer or owner has consented in writing to the security interest or has disclaimed an interest in the goods as fixtures; or

    **(b)** the debtor has a right to remove the goods as against the encumbrancer or owner. If the debtor's right terminates, the priority of the security interest continues for a reasonable time.

**(6)** Notwithstanding paragraph (a) of subsection (4) but otherwise subject to subsections (4) and (5), a security interest in fixtures is subordinate to a construction mortgage recorded before the goods become fixtures if the goods become fixtures before the completion of the construction. To the extent that it is given to refinance a construction mortgage, a mortgage has this priority to the same extent as the construction mortgage.

**(7)** In cases not within the preceding subsections, a security interest in fixtures is subordinate to the conflicting interest of an encumbrancer or owner of the related real estate who is not the debtor.

**(8)** When the secured party has priority over all owners and encumbrancers of the real estate, he may, on default, subject to the provisions of Part 5, remove his collateral from the real estate but he must reimburse any encumbrancer or owner of the real estate who is not the debtor and who has not otherwise agreed for the cost of repair of any physical injury, but not for any diminution in value of the real estate caused by the absence of the goods removed or by any necessity of replacing them. A person entitled to reimbursement may refuse permission to remove until the secured party gives adequate security for the performance of this obligation.

Amended in 1972.

## § 9—314
### Accessions

**(1)** A security interest in goods which attaches before they are installed in or affixed to other goods takes priority as to the goods installed or affixed (called in this section "accessions") over the claims of all persons to the whole except as stated in subsection (3) and subject to Section 9—315(1).

**(2)** A security interest which attaches to goods after they become part of a whole is valid against all persons subsequently acquiring interests in the whole except as stated in subsection (3) but is invalid against any person with an interest in the whole at the time the security interest attaches to the goods who has not in writing consented to the security interest or disclaimed an interest in the goods as part of the whole.

**(3)** The security interests described in subsections (1) and (2) do not take priority over
  **(a)** a subsequent purchaser for value of any interest in the whole; or
  **(b)** a creditor with a lien on the whole subsequently obtained by judicial proceedings; or
  **(c)** a creditor with a prior perfected security interest in the whole to the extent that he makes subsequent advances.

If the subsequent purchase is made, the lien by judicial proceedings obtained or the subsequent advance under the prior perfected security interest is made or contracted for without knowledge of the security interest and before it is perfected. A purchaser of the whole at a foreclosure sale other than the holder of a perfected security interest purchasing at his own foreclosure sale is a subsequent purchaser within this section.

**(4)** When under subsections (1) or (2) and (3) a secured party has an interest in accessions which has priority over the claims of all persons who have interests in the whole, he may on default subject to the provisions of Part 5 remove his collateral from the whole but he must reimburse any encumbrancer or owner of the whole who is not the debtor and who has not otherwise agreed for the cost of repair of any physical injury but not for any diminution in value of the whole caused by the absence of the goods removed or by any necessity for replacing them. A person entitled to reimbursement may refuse permission to remove until the secured party gives adequate security for the performance of this obligation.

### § 9—315
### Priority When Goods Are Commingled or Processed

**(1)** If a security interest in goods was perfected and subsequently the goods or a part thereof have become part of a product or mass, the security interest continues in the product or mass if
  **(a)** the goods are so manufactured, processed, assembled or commingled that their identity is lost in the product or mass; or
  **(b)** a financing statement covering the original goods also covers the product into which the goods have been manufactured, processed or assembled.

In a case to which paragraph (b) applies, no separate security interest in that part of the original goods which has been manufactured, processed or assembled into the product may be claimed under Section 9—314.

**(2)** When under subsection (1) more than one security interest attaches to the product or mass, they rank equally according to the ratio that the cost of the goods to which each interest originally attached bears to the cost of the total product or mass.

### § 9—316
### Priority Subject to Subordination

Nothing in this Article prevents subordination by agreement by any person entitled to priority.

### § 9—317
### Secured Party Not Obligated on Contract of Debtor

The mere existence of a security interest or authority given to the debtor to dispose of or use collateral does not impose contract or tort liability upon the secured party for the debtor's acts or omissions.

### § 9—318
### Defenses Against Assignee; Modification of Contract After Notification of Assignment; Term Prohibiting Assignment Ineffective; Identification and Proof of Assignment

**(1)** Unless an account debtor has made an enforceable agreement not to assert defenses or claims arising out of a sale as provided in Section 9—206 the rights of an assignee are subject to
  **(a)** all the terms of the contract between the account debtor and assignor and any defense or claim arising therefrom; and
  **(b)** any other defense or claim of the account debtor against the assignor which accrues before the account debtor receives notification of the assignment.

**(2)** So far as the right to payment or a part thereof under an assigned contract has not been fully earned by performance, and notwithstanding notification of the assignment, any modification of or substitution for the contract made in good faith and in accordance with reasonable commercial standards is effective against an assignee unless the account debtor has otherwise agreed but the assignee acquires corresponding rights under the modified or substituted contract. The assignment may provide that such modification or substitution is a breach by the assignor.

**(3)** The account debtor is authorized to pay the assignor until the account debtor receives notification that the amount due or to become due has been assigned and that payment is to be made to the assignee. A notification which does not reasonably identify the rights assigned is ineffective. If requested by the account debtor, the assignee must seasonably furnish reasonable proof that the assignment has been made and unless he does so the account debtor may pay the assignor.

**(4)** A term in any contract between an account debtor and an assignor is ineffective if it prohibits assignment of an account or prohibits creation of a security interest in a general intangible for money due or to become due or requires the account debtor's consent to such assignment or security interest.

Amended in 1972.

## Part 4/Filing

### § 9—401
### Place of Filing; Erroneous Filing; Removal of Collateral

*First Alternative Subsection (1)*

**(1)** The proper place to file in order to perfect a security interest is as follows:
  **(a)** when the collateral is timber to be cut or is minerals or the like (including oil and gas) or accounts subject to subsection (5) of Section 9—103, or when the financing statement is filed as a fixture filing (Section 9—313) and the collateral is goods which are or are to become fixtures, then in the office where a mortgage on the real estate would be filed or recorded;
  **(b)** in all other cases, in the office of the [Secretary of State].

*Second Alternative Subsection (1)*

(1) The proper place to file in order to perfect a security interest is as follows:

    (a) when the collateral is equipment used in farming operations, or farm products, or accounts or general intangibles arising from or relating to the sale of farm products by a farmer, or consumer goods, then in the office of the ............ in the county of the debtor's residence or if the debtor is not a resident of this state then in the office of the ............ in the county where the goods are kept, and in addition when the collateral is crops growing or to be grown in the office of the ............ in the county where the land is located;

    (b) when the collateral is timber to be cut or is minerals or the like (including oil and gas) or accounts subject to subsection (5) of Section 9—103, or when the financing statement is filed as a fixture filing (Section 9—313) and the collateral is goods which are or are to become fixtures, then in the office where a mortgage on the real estate would be filed or recorded;

    (c) in all other cases, in the office of the [Secretary of State].

*Third Alternative Subsection (1)*

(1) The proper place to file in order to perfect a security interest is as follows:

    (a) when the collateral is equipment used in farming operations, or farm products, or accounts or general intangibles arising from or relating to the sale of farm products by a farmer, or consumer goods, then in the office of the ............ in the county of the debtor's residence or if the debtor is not a resident of this state then in the office of the ............ in the county where the goods are kept, and in addition when the collateral is crops growing or to be grown in the office of the ............ in the county where the land is located;

    (b) when the collateral is timber to be cut or is minerals or the like (including oil and gas) or accounts subject to subsection (5) of Section 9—103, or when the financing statement is filed as a fixture filing (Section 9—313) and the collateral is goods which are or are to become fixtures, then in the office where a mortgage on the real estate would be filed or recorded;

    (c) in all other cases, in the office of the [Secretary of State] and in addition, if the debtor has a place of business in only one county of this state, also in the office of ............ of such county, or, if the debtor has no place of business in this state, but resides in the state, also in the office of ............ of the county in which he resides.

Note: *One of the three alternatives should be selected as subsection (1).*

(2) A filing which is made in good faith in an improper place or not in all of the places required by this section is nevertheless effective with regard to any collateral as to which the filing complied with the requirements of this Article and is also effective with regard to collateral covered by the financing statement against any person who has knowledge of the contents of such financing statement.

(3) A filing which is made in the proper place in this state continues effective even though the debtor's residence or place of business or the location of the collateral or its use, whichever controlled the original filing, is thereafter changed.

*Alternative Subsection (3)*

[(3) A filing which is made in the proper county continues effective for four months after a change to another county of the debtor's residence or place of business or the location of the collateral, whichever controlled the original filing. It becomes ineffective thereafter unless a copy of the financing statement signed by the secured party is filed in the new county within said period. The security interest may also be perfected in the new county after the expiration of the four-month period; in such case perfection dates from the time of perfection in the new county. A change in the use of the collateral does not impair the effectiveness of the original filing.]

(4) The rules stated in Section 9—103 determine whether filing is necessary in this state.

(5) Notwithstanding the preceding subsections, and subject to subsection (3) of Section 9—302, the proper place to file in order to perfect a security interest in collateral, including fixtures, of a transmitting utility is the office of the [Secretary of State]. This filing constitutes a fixture filing (Section 9—313) as to the collateral described therein which is or is to become fixtures.

(6) For the purposes of this section, the residence of an organization is its place of business if it has one or its chief executive office if it has more than one place of business.

Amended in 1962 and 1972.

Note: *Subsection (6) should be used only if the state chooses the Second or Third Alternative Subsection (1).*

### § 9—402
### Formal Requisites of Financing Statement; Amendments; Mortgage as Financing Statement

(1) A financing statement is sufficient if it gives the names of the debtor and the secured party, is signed by the debtor, gives an address of the secured party from which information concerning the security interest may be obtained, gives a mailing address of the debtor and contains a statement indicating the types, or describing the items, of collateral. A financing statement may be filed before a security agreement is made or a security interest otherwise attaches. When the financing statement covers crops growing or to be grown, the statement must also contain a description of the real estate concerned. When the financing statement covers timber to be cut or covers minerals or the like (including oil and gas) or accounts subject to subsection (5) of Section 9—103, or when the financing statement is filed as a fixture filing (Section 9—313) and the collateral is goods which are or are to become fixtures, the statement must also comply with subsection (5). A copy of the security agreement is sufficient as a financing statement if it contains the above information and is signed by the debtor. A carbon, photographic or other reproduction of a security agreement or a financing statement is sufficient as a financing statement if the security agreement so provides or if the original has been filed in this state.

(2) A financing statement which otherwise complies with subsection (1) is sufficient when it is signed by the secured party instead of the debtor if it is filed to perfect a security interest in

    (a) collateral already subject to a security interest in another jurisdiction when it is brought into this state, or when the debtor's location is changed to this state. Such a financing statement must state that the collateral was brought into this state or that the debtor's location was changed to this state under such circumstances; or

(b) proceeds under Section 9—306 if the security interest in the original collateral was perfected. Such a financing statement must describe the original collateral; or

(c) collateral as to which the filing has lapsed; or

(d) collateral acquired after a change of name, identity or corporate structure of the debtor (subsection (7)).

(3) A form substantially as follows is sufficient to comply with subsection (1):

Name of debtor (or assignor) ........................
Address ..........................................
Name of secured party (or assignee) ..................
Address ..........................................
1. This financing statement covers the following types (or items) of property:
  (Describe) .......................................
2. (If collateral is crops) The above described crops are growing or are to be grown on:
  (Describe Real Estate) ...........................
3. (If applicable) The above goods are to become fixtures on *

*Where appropriate substitute either "The above timber is standing on . . . ." or "The above minerals or the like (including oil and gas) or accounts will be financed at the wellhead or minehead of the well or mine located on . . . ."

  (Describe Real Estate) ...........................
and this financing statement is to be filed [for record] in the real estate records. (If the debtor does not have an interest of record) The name of a record owner is ..................
4. (If products of collateral are claimed) Products of the collateral are also covered.

  (use whichever signature is applicable)
  ...............................................
  Signature of Debtor (or Assignor)
  ...............................................
  Signature of Secured Party (or Assignee)

(4) A financing statement may be amended by filing a writing signed by both the debtor and the secured party. An amendment does not extend the period of effectiveness of a financing statement. If any amendment adds collateral, it is effective as to the added collateral only from the filing date of the amendment. In this Article, unless the context otherwise requires, the term "financing statement" means the original financing statement and any amendments.

(5) A financing statement covering timber to be cut or covering minerals or the like (including oil and gas) or accounts subject to subsection (5) of Section 9—103, or a financing statement filed as a fixture filing (Section 9—313) where the debtor is not a transmitting utility, must show that it covers this type of collateral, must recite that it is to be filed [for record] in the real estate records, and the financing statement must contain a description of the real estate [sufficient if it were contained in a mortgage of the real estate to give constructive notice of the mortgage under the law of this state]. If the debtor does not have an interest of record in the real estate, the financing statement must show the name of a record owner.

(6) A mortgage is effective as a financing statement filed as a fixture filing from the date of its recording if

(a) the goods are described in the mortgage by item or type; and

(b) the goods are or are to become fixtures related to the real estate described in the mortgage; and

(c) the mortgage complies with the requirements for a financing statement in this section other than a recital that it is to be filed in the real estate records; and

(d) the mortgage is duly recorded.

No fee with reference to the financing statement is required other than the regular recording and satisfaction fees with respect to the mortgage.

(7) A financing statement sufficiently shows the name of the debtor if it gives the individual, partnership or corporate name of the debtor, whether or not it adds other trade names or names of partners. Where the debtor so changes his name or in the case of an organization its name, identity or corporate structure that a filed financing statement becomes seriously misleading, the filing is not effective to perfect a security interest in collateral acquired by the debtor more than four months after the change, unless a new appropriate financing statement is filed before the expiration of that time. A filed financing statement remains effective with respect to collateral transferred by the debtor even though the secured party knows of or consents to the transfer.

(8) A financing statement substantially complying with the requirements of this section is effective even though it contains minor errors which are not seriously misleading.

Amended in 1972.

Note: *Language in brackets is optional.*

Note: *Where the state has any special recording system for real estate other than the usual grantor-grantee index (as, for instance, a tract system or a title registration or Torrens system) local adaptations of subsection (5) and Section 9—403(7) may be necessary. See Mass.Gen.Laws Chapter 106, Section 9—409.*

§ 9—403
**What Constitutes Filing; Duration of Filing;
Effect of Lapsed Filing; Duties of Filing Officer**

(1) Presentation for filing of a financing statement and tender of the filing fee or acceptance of the statement by the filing officer constitutes filing under this Article.

(2) Except as provided in subsection (6) a filed financing statement is effective for a period of five years from the date of filing. The effectiveness of a filed financing statement lapses on the expiration of the five year period unless a continuation statement is filed prior to the lapse. If a security interest perfected by filing exists at the time insolvency proceedings are commenced by or against the debtor, the security interest remains perfected until termination of the insolvency proceedings and thereafter for a period of sixty days or until expiration of the five year period, whichever occurs later. Upon lapse the security interest becomes unperfected, unless it is perfected without filing. If the security interest becomes unperfected upon lapse, it is deemed to have been unperfected as against a person who became a purchaser or lien creditor before lapse.

(3) A continuation statement may be filed by the secured party within six months prior to the expiration of the five year period specified in subsection (2). Any such continuation statement must be signed by the secured party, identify the original statement by file number and state that the original statement is still effective. A continuation statement signed by a person other than the secured party of record must be accompanied by a separate written statement of assignment signed by the secured party of record and complying with subsection (2) of Section 9—405, including payment of the required fee. Upon timely filing of the continuation statement, the effectiveness of the original statement is continued for five years after the last date to which the filing was effective whereupon it lapses in the same manner as provided in subsection (2) unless another continuation statement is filed prior to such lapse. Succeeding continuation statements may be filed in the same manner to continue the effectiveness of the original statement. Unless a statute on disposition of public records provides otherwise, the filing officer may remove a lapsed statement from the files and destroy it immediately if he has retained a microfilm or other photographic record, or in other cases after one year after the lapse. The filing officer shall so arrange matters by physical annexation of financing statements to continuation statements or other related filings, or by other means, that if he physically destroys the financing statements of a period more than five years past, those which have been continued by a continuation statement or which are still effective under subsection (6) shall be retained.

(4) Except as provided in subsection (7) a filing officer shall mark each statement with a file number and with the date and hour of filing and shall hold the statement or a microfilm or other photographic copy thereof for public inspection. In addition the filing officer shall index the statement according to the name of the debtor and shall note in the index the file number and the address of the debtor given in the statement.

(5) The uniform fee for filing and indexing and for stamping a copy furnished by the secured party to show the date and place of filing for an original financing statement or for a continuation statement shall be $ . . . . . . . . . . . if the statement is in the standard form prescribed by the [Secretary of State] and otherwise shall be $ . . . . . . . . . . . , plus in each case, if the financing statement is subject to subsection (5) of Section 9—402, $ . . . . . . . . . . . The uniform fee for each name more than one required to be indexed shall be $ . . . . . . . . . . . The secured party may at his option show a trade name for any person and an extra uniform indexing fee of $ . . . . . . . . . . . shall be paid with respect thereto.

(6) If the debtor is a transmitting utility (subsection (5) of Section 9—401) and a filed financing statement so states, it is effective until a termination statement is filed. A real estate mortgage which is effective as a fixture filing under subsection (6) of Section 9—402 remains effective as a fixture filing until the mortgage is released or satisfied of record or its effectiveness otherwise terminates as to the real estate.

(7) When a financing statement covers timber to be cut or covers minerals or the like (including oil and gas) or accounts subject to subsection (5) of Section 9—103, or is filed as a fixture filing, [it shall be filed for record and] the filing officer shall index it under the names of the debtor and any owner of record shown on the financing statement in the same fashion as if they were the mortgagors in a mortgage of the real estate described, and, to the extent that the law of this state provides for indexing of mortgages under the name of the mortgagee, under the name of the secured party as if he were the mortgagee thereunder, or where indexing is by description in the same fashion as if the financing statement were a mortgage of the real estate described.

Amended in 1972.

Note: *In states in which writings will not appear in the real estate records and indices unless actually recorded the bracketed language in subsection (7) should be used.*

### § 9—404
### Termination Statement

(1) If a financing statement covering consumer goods is filed on or after . . . . . . . . . . . , then within one month or within ten days following written demand by the debtor after there is no outstanding secured obligation and no commitment to make advances, incur obligations or otherwise give value, the secured party must file with each filing officer with whom the financing statement was filed, a termination statement to the effect that he no longer claims a security interest under the financing statement, which shall be identified by file number. In other cases whenever there is no outstanding secured obligation and no commitment to make advances, incur obligations or otherwise give value, the secured party must on written demand by the debtor send the debtor, for each filing officer with whom the financing statement was filed, a termination statement to the effect that he no longer claims a security interest under the financing statement, which shall be identified by file number. A termination statement signed by a person other than the secured party of record must be accompanied by a separate written statement of assignment signed by the secured party of record complying with subsection (2) of Section 9—405, including payment of the required fee. If the affected secured party fails to file such a termination statement as required by this subsection, or to send such a termination statement within ten days after proper demand therefor, he shall be liable to the debtor for one hundred dollars, and in addition for any loss caused to the debtor by such failure.

(2) On presentation to the filing officer of such a termination statement he must note it in the index. If he has received the termination statement in duplicate, he shall return one copy of the termination statement to the secured party stamped to show the time of receipt thereof. If the filing officer has a microfilm or other photographic record of the financing statement, and of any related continuation statement, statement of assignment and statement of release, he may remove the originals from the files at any time after receipt of the termination statement, or if he has no such record, he may remove them from the files at any time after one year after receipt of the termination statement.

(3) If the termination statement is in the standard form prescribed by the [Secretary of State], the uniform fee for filing and indexing the termination statement shall be $ . . . . . . . . . . . , and otherwise shall be $ . . . . . . . . . . . , plus in each case an additional fee of $ . . . . . . . . . . . for each name more than one against which the termination statement is required to be indexed.

Amended in 1972.

Note: *The date to be inserted should be the effective date of the revised Article 9.*

## § 9—405
### Assignment of Security Interest; Duties of Filing Officer; Fees

**(1)** A financing statement may disclose an assignment of a security interest in the collateral described in the financing statement by indication in the financing statement of the name and address of the assignee or by an assignment itself or a copy thereof on the face or back of the statement. On presentation to the filing officer of such a financing statement the filing officer shall mark the same as provided in Section 9—403(4). The uniform fee for filing, indexing and furnishing filing data for a financing statement so indicating an assignment shall be $ . . . . . . . . . . . . if the statement is in the standard form prescribed by the [Secretary of State] and otherwise shall be $ . . . . . . . . . . . . , plus in each case an additional fee of $ . . . . . . . . . . . . for each name more than one against which the financing statement is required to be indexed.

**(2)** A secured party may assign of record all or part of his rights under a financing statement by the filing in the place where the original financing statement was filed of a separate written statement of assignment signed by the secured party of record and setting forth the name of the secured party of record and the debtor, the file number and the date of filing of the financing statement and the name and address of the assignee and containing a description of the collateral assigned. A copy of the assignment is sufficient as a separate statement if it complies with the preceding sentence. On presentation to the filing officer of such a separate statement, the filing officer shall mark such separate statement with the date and hour of the filing. He shall note the assignment on the index of the financing statement, or in the case of a fixture filing, or a filing covering timber to be cut, or covering minerals or the like (including oil and gas) or accounts subject to subsection (5) of Section 9—103, he shall index the assignment under the name of the assignor as grantor and, to the extent that the law of this state provides for indexing the assignment of a mortgage under the name of the assignee, he shall index the assignment of the financing statement under the name of the assignee. The uniform fee for filing, indexing and furnishing filing data about such a separate statement of assignment shall be $ . . . . . . . . . . . . if the statement is in the standard form prescribed by the [Secretary of State] and otherwise shall be $ . . . . . . . . . . . . , plus in each case an additional fee of $ . . . . . . . . . . . . for each name more than one against which the statement of assignment is required to be indexed. Notwithstanding the provisions of this subsection, an assignment of record of a security interest in a fixture contained in a mortgage effective as a fixture filing (subsection (6) of Section 9—402) may be made only by an assignment of the mortgage in the manner provided by the law of this state other than this Act.

**(3)** After the disclosure or filing of an assignment under this section, the assignee is the secured party of record.

Amended in 1972.

## § 9—406
### Release of Collateral; Duties of Filing Officer; Fees

A secured party of record may by his signed statement release all or a part of any collateral described in a filed financing statement. The statement of release is sufficient if it contains a description of the collateral being released, the name and address of the debtor, the name and address of the secured party, and the file number of the financing statement. A statement of release signed by a person other than the secured party of record must be accompanied by a separate written statement of assignment signed by the secured party of record and complying with subsection (2) of Section 9—405, including payment of the required fee. Upon presentation of such a statement of release to the filing officer he shall mark the statement with the hour and date of filing and shall note the same upon the margin of the index of the filing of the financing statement. The uniform fee for filing and noting such a statement of release shall be $ . . . . . . . . . . . . if the statement is in the standard form prescribed by the [Secretary of State] and otherwise shall be $ . . . . . . . . . . . . , plus in each case an additional fee of $ . . . . . . . . . . . . for each name more than one against which the statement of release is required to be indexed.

Amended in 1972.

## [§ 9—407
### Information From Filing Officer

**[(1)** If the person filing any financing statement, termination statement, statement of assignment, or statement of release, furnishes the filing officer a copy thereof, the filing officer shall upon request note upon the copy the file number and date and hour of the filing of the original and deliver or send the copy to such person.]

**[(2)** Upon request of any person, the filing officer shall issue his certificate showing whether there is on file on the date and hour stated therein, any presently effective financing statement naming a particular debtor and any statement of assignment thereof and if there is, giving the date and hour of filing of each such statement and the names and addresses of each secured party therein. The uniform fee for such a certificate shall be $ . . . . . . . . . . . . if the request for the certificate is in the standard form prescribed by the [Secretary of State] and otherwise shall be $ . . . . . . . . . . . . Upon request the filing officer shall furnish a copy of any filed financing statement or statement of assignment for a uniform fee of $ . . . . . . . . . . . . per page.]

Amended in 1972.

Note: *This section is proposed as an optional provision to require filing officers to furnish certificates. Local law and practices should be consulted with regard to the advisability of adoption.*

## § 9—408
### Financing Statements Covering Consigned or Leased Goods

A consignor or lessor of goods may file a financing statement using the terms "consignor," "consignee," "lessor," "lessee" or the like instead of the terms specified in Section 9—402. The provisions of this Part shall apply as appropriate to such a financing statement but its filing shall not of itself be a factor in determining whether or not the consignment or lease is intended as security (Section 1—201(37)). However, if it is determined for other reasons that the consignment or lease is so intended, a security interest of the consignor or lessor which attaches to the consigned or leased goods is perfected by such filing.

Added in 1972.

## Part 5/Default

### § 9—501
### Default; Procedure When Security Agreement Covers Both Real and Personal Property

**(1)** When a debtor is in default under a security agreement, a secured party has the rights and remedies provided in this Part and except as limited by subsection (3) those provided in the security agreement. He may reduce his claim to judgment, foreclose or otherwise enforce the security interest by any available judicial procedure. If the collateral is documents the secured party may proceed either as to the documents or as to the goods covered thereby. A secured party in possession has the rights, remedies and duties provided in Section 9—207. The rights and remedies referred to in this subsection are cumulative.

**(2)** After default, the debtor has the rights and remedies provided in this Part, those provided in the security agreement and those provided in Section 9—207.

**(3)** To the extent that they give rights to the debtor and impose duties on the secured party, the rules stated in the subsections referred to below may not be waived or varied except as provided with respect to compulsory disposition of collateral (subsection (3) of Section 9—504 and Section 9—505) and with respect to redemption of collateral (Section 9—506) but the parties may by agreement determine the standards by which the fulfillment of these rights and duties is to be measured if such standards are not manifestly unreasonable:

    **(a)** subsection (2) of Section 9—502 and subsection (2) of Section 9—504 insofar as they require accounting for surplus proceeds of collateral;

    **(b)** subsection (3) of Section 9—504 with subsection (1) of Section 9—505 which deal with disposition of collateral;

    **(c)** subsection (2) of Section 9—505 which deals with acceptance of collateral as discharge of obligation;

    **(d)** Section 9—506 which deals with redemption of collateral; and

    **(e)** subsection (1) of Section 9—507 which deals with the secured party's liability for failure to comply with this Part.

**(4)** If the security agreement covers both real and personal property, the secured party may proceed under this Part as to the personal property or he may proceed as to both the real and the personal property in accordance with his rights and remedies in respect of the real property in which case the provisions of this Part do not apply.

**(5)** When a secured party has reduced his claim to judgment the lien of any levy which may be made upon his collateral by virtue of any execution based upon the judgment shall relate back to the date of the perfection of the security interest in such collateral. A judicial sale, pursuant to such execution, is a foreclosure of the security interest by judicial procedure within the meaning of this section, and the secured party may purchase at the sale and thereafter hold the collateral free of any other requirements of this Article.

Amended in 1972.

### § 9—502
### Collection Rights of Secured Party

**(1)** When so agreed and in any event on default the secured party is entitled to notify an account debtor or the obligor on an instrument to make payment to him whether or not the assignor was theretofore making collections on the collateral, and also to take control of any proceeds to which he is entitled under Section 9—306.

**(2)** A secured party who by agreement is entitled to charge back uncollected collateral or otherwise to full or limited recourse against the debtor and who undertakes to collect from the account debtors or obligors must proceed in a commercially reasonable manner and may deduct his reasonable expenses of realization from the collections. If the security agreement secures an indebtedness, the secured party must account to the debtor for any surplus, and unless otherwise agreed, the debtor is liable for any deficiency. But, if the underlying transaction was a sale of accounts or chattel paper, the debtor is entitled to any surplus or is liable for any deficiency only if the security agreement so provides.

Amended in 1972.

### § 9—503
### Secured Party's Right to Take Possession After Default

Unless otherwise agreed a secured party has on default the right to take possession of the collateral. In taking possession a secured party may proceed without judicial process if this can be done without breach of the peace or may proceed by action. If the security agreement so provides the secured party may require the debtor to assemble the collateral and make it available to the secured party at a place to be designated by the secured party which is reasonably convenient to both parties. Without removal a secured party may render equipment unusable, and may dispose of collateral on the debtor's premises under Section 9—504.

### § 9—504
### Secured Party's Right to Dispose of Collateral After Default; Effect of Disposition

**(1)** A secured party after default may sell, lease or otherwise dispose of any or all of the collateral in its then condition or following any commercially reasonable preparation or processing. Any sale of goods is subject to the Article on Sales (Article 2). The proceeds of disposition shall be applied in the order following to

    **(a)** the reasonable expenses of retaking, holding, preparing for sale or lease, selling, leasing and the like and, to the extent provided for in the agreement and not prohibited by law, the reasonable attorneys' fees and legal expenses incurred by the secured party;

    **(b)** the satisfaction of indebtedness secured by the security interest under which the disposition is made;

    **(c)** the satisfaction of indebtedness secured by any subordinate security interest in the collateral if written notification of demand therefor is received before distribution of the proceeds is completed. If requested by the secured party, the holder of a subordinate security interest must seasonably furnish reasonable proof of his interest, and unless he does so, the secured party need not comply with his demand.

**(2)** If the security interest secures an indebtedness, the secured party must account to the debtor for any surplus, and, unless otherwise agreed, the debtor is liable for any deficiency. But if the underlying transaction was a sale of accounts or chattel paper, the debtor is entitled to any surplus or is liable for any deficiency only if the security agreement so provides.

(3) Disposition of the collateral may be by public or private proceedings and may be made by way of one or more contracts. Sale or other disposition may be as a unit or in parcels and at any time and place and on any terms but every aspect of the disposition including the method, manner, time, place and terms must be commercially reasonable. Unless collateral is perishable or threatens to decline speedily in value or is of a type customarily sold on a recognized market, reasonable notification of the time and place of any public sale or reasonable notification of the time after which any private sale or other intended disposition is to be made shall be sent by the secured party to the debtor, if he has not signed after default a statement renouncing or modifying his right to notification of sale. In the case of consumer goods no other notification need be sent. In other cases notification shall be sent to any other secured party from whom the secured party has received (before sending his notification to the debtor or before the debtor's renunciation of his rights) written notice of a claim of an interest in the collateral. The secured party may buy at any public sale and if the collateral is of a type customarily sold in a recognized market or is of a type which is the subject of widely distributed standard price quotations he may buy at private sale.

(4) When collateral is disposed of by a secured party after default, the disposition transfers to a purchaser for value all of the debtor's rights therein, discharges the security interest under which it is made and any security interest or lien subordinate thereto. The purchaser takes free of all such rights and interests even though the secured party fails to comply with the requirements of this Part or of any judicial proceedings

    (a) in the case of a public sale, if the purchaser has no knowledge of any defects in the sale and if he does not buy in collusion with the secured party, other bidders or the person conducting the sale; or

    (b) in any other case, if the purchaser acts in good faith.

(5) A person who is liable to a secured party under a guaranty, indorsement, repurchase agreement or the like and who receives a transfer of collateral from the secured party or is subrogated to his rights has thereafter the rights and duties of the secured party. Such a transfer of collateral is not a sale or disposition of the collateral under this Article.

Amended in 1972.

## § 9—505
### Compulsory Disposition of Collateral; Acceptance of the Collateral as Discharge of Obligation

(1) If the debtor has paid sixty per cent of the cash price in the case of a purchase money security interest in consumer goods or sixty per cent of the loan in the case of another security interest in consumer goods, and has not signed after default a statement renouncing or modifying his rights under this Part a secured party who has taken possession of collateral must dispose of it under Section 9—504 and if he fails to do so within ninety days after he takes possession the debtor at his option may recover in conversion or under Section 9—507(1) on secured party's liability.

(2) In any other case involving consumer goods or any other collateral a secured party in possession may, after default, propose to retain the collateral in satisfaction of the obligation. Written notice of such proposal shall be sent to the debtor if he has not signed after default a statement renouncing or modifying his rights under this subsection. In the case of consumer goods no other notice need be given. In other cases notice shall be sent to any other secured party from whom the secured party has received (before sending his notice to the debtor or before the debtor's renunciation of his rights) written notice of a claim of an interest in the collateral. If the secured party receives objection in writing from a person entitled to receive notification within twenty-one days after the notice was sent, the secured party must dispose of the collateral under Section 9—504. In the absence of such written objection the secured party may retain the collateral in satisfaction of the debtor's obligation.

Amended in 1972.

## § 9—506
### Debtor's Right to Redeem Collateral

At any time before the secured party has disposed of collateral or entered into a contract for its disposition under Section 9—504 or before the obligation has been discharged under Section 9—505(2) the debtor or any other secured party may unless otherwise agreed in writing after default redeem the collateral by tendering fulfillment of all obligations secured by the collateral as well as the expenses reasonably incurred by the secured party in retaking, holding and preparing the collateral for disposition, in arranging for the sale, and to the extent provided in the agreement and not prohibited by law, his reasonable attorneys' fees and legal expenses.

## § 9—507
### Secured Party's Liability for Failure to Comply With This Part

(1) If it is established that the secured party is not proceeding in accordance with the provisions of this Part disposition may be ordered or restrained on appropriate terms and conditions. If the disposition has occurred the debtor or any person entitled to notification or whose security interest has been made known to the secured party prior to the disposition has a right to recover from the secured party any loss caused by a failure to comply with the provisions of this Part. If the collateral is consumer goods, the debtor has a right to recover in any event an amount not less than the credit service charge plus ten per cent of the principal amount of the debt or the time price differential plus 10 percent of the cash price.

(2) The fact that a better price could have been obtained by a sale at a different time or in a different method from that selected by the secured party is not of itself sufficient to establish that the sale was not made in a commercially reasonable manner. If the secured party either sells the collateral in the usual manner in any recognized market therefor or if he sells at the price current in such market at the time of his sale or if he has otherwise sold in conformity with reasonable commercial practices among dealers in the type of property sold he has sold in a commercially reasonable manner. The principles stated in the two preceding sentences with respect to sales also apply as may be appropriate to other types of disposition. A disposition which has been approved in any judicial proceeding or by any bona fide creditors' committee or representative of creditors shall conclusively be deemed to be commercially reasonable, but this sentence does not indicate that any such approval must be obtained in any case nor does it indi-

cate that any disposition not so approved is not commercially reasonable.

## ARTICLE 10/EFFECTIVE DATE AND REPEALER

### § 10—101
**Effective Date**

This Act shall become effective at midnight on December 31st following its enactment. It applies to transactions entered into and events occurring after that date.

### § 10—102
**Specific Repealer; Provision for Transition**

(1) The following acts and all other acts and parts of acts inconsistent herewith are hereby repealed:
(Here should follow the acts to be specifically repealed including the following:

    Uniform Negotiable Instruments Act
    Uniform Warehouse Receipts Act
    Uniform Sales Act
    Uniform Bills of Lading Act
    Uniform Stock Transfer Act
    Uniform Conditional Sales Act
    Uniform Trust Receipts Act

Also any acts regulating:

    Bank collections
    Bulk sales
    Chattel mortgages
    Conditional sales
    Factor's lien acts
    Farm storage of grain and similar acts
    Assignment of accounts receivable)

(2) Transactions validly entered into before the effective date specified in Section 10—101 and the rights, duties and interests flowing from them remain valid thereafter and may be terminated, completed, consummated or enforced as required or permitted by any statute or other law amended or repealed by this Act as though such repeal or amendment had not occurred.

Note: *Subsection (1) should be separately prepared for each state. The foregoing is a list of statutes to be checked.*

### § 10—103
**General Repealer**

Except as provided in the following section, all acts and parts of acts inconsistent with this Act are hereby repealed.

### § 10—104
**Laws Not Repealed**

(1) The Article on Documents of Title (Article 7) does not repeal or modify any laws prescribing the form or contents of documents of title or the services or facilities to be afforded by bailees, or otherwise regulating bailees' businesses in respects not specifically dealt with herein; but the fact that such laws are violated does not affect the status of a document of title which otherwise complies with the definition of a document of title (Section 1—201).

[(2) This Act does not repeal . . . . . . . . . . .*, cited as the Uniform Act for the Simplification of Fiduciary Security Transfers, and if in any respect there is any inconsistency between that Act and the Article of this Act on investment securities (Article B) the provisions of the former Act shall control.]

Note: *At * in subsection (2) insert the statutory reference to the Uniform Act for the Simplification of Fiduciary Security Transfers if such Act has previously been enacted. If it has not been enacted, omit subsection (2).*

# APPENDIX B

# THE UNIFORM PARTNERSHIP ACT

## Part I/Preliminary Provisions

§ 1
**Name of Act**

This act may be cited as Uniform Partnership Act.

§ 2
**Definition of Terms**

In this act, "Court" includes every court and judge having jurisdiction in the case.

"Business" includes every trade, occupation, or profession.

"Person" includes individuals, partnerships, corporations, and other associations.

"Bankrupt" includes bankrupt under the Federal Bankruptcy Act or insolvent under any state insolvent act.

"Conveyance" includes every assignment, lease, mortgage, or encumbrance.

"Real property" includes land and any interest or estate in land.

§ 3
**Interpretation of Knowledge and Notice**

**(1)** A person has "knowledge" of a fact within the meaning of this act not only when he has actual knowledge thereof, but also when he has knowledge of such other facts as in the circumstances shows bad faith.

**(2)** A person has "notice" of a fact within the meaning of this act when the person who claims the benefit of the notice:

(a) States the fact to such person, or

(b) Delivers through the mail, or by other means of communication, a written statement of the fact to such person or to a proper person at his place of business or residence.

§ 4
**Rules of Construction**

**(1)** The rule that statutes in derogation of the common law are to be strictly construed shall have no application to this act.

**(2)** The law of estoppel shall apply under this act.

**(3)** The law of agency shall apply under this act.

**(4)** This act shall be so interpreted and construed as to effect its general purpose to make uniform the law of those states which enact it.

**(5)** This act shall not be construed so as to impair the obligations of any contract existing when the act goes into effect, nor to affect any action or proceedings begun or right accrued before this act takes effect.

§ 5
**Rules for Cases Not Provided for in This Act**

In any case not provided for in this act the rules of law and equity, including the law merchant, shall govern.

## Part II/Nature of Partnership

§ 6
**Partnership Defined**

**(1)** A partnership is an association of two or more persons to carry on as co-owners a business for profit.

**(2)** But any associaton formed under any other statute of this state, or any statute adopted by authority, other than the authority of this state, is not a partnership under this act, unless such association would have been a partnership in this state prior to the adoption of this act; but this act shall apply to limited partnerships except in so far as the statutes relating to such partnerships are inconsistent herewith.

§ 7
**Rules for Determining the Existence of a Partnership**

In determining whether a partnership exists, these rules shall apply:

**(1)** Except as provided by section 16 persons who are not partners as to each other are not partners as to third persons.

**(2)** Joint tenancy, tenancy in common, tenancy by the entireties, joint property, common property, or part ownership does not of itself establish a partnership, whether such co-owners do or do not share any profits made by the use of the property.

**(3)** The sharing of gross returns does not of itself establish a partnership, whether or not the persons sharing them have a joint or common right or interest in any property from which the returns are derived.

**(4)** The receipt by a person of a share of the profits of a business is prima facie evidence that he is a partner in the business, but no such inference shall be drawn if such profits were received in payment:

(a) As a debt by installments or otherwise,

(b) As wages of an employee or rent to a landlord,

(c) As an annuity to a widow or representative of a deceased partner,
(d) As interest on a loan, though the amount of payment vary with the profits of the business,
(e) As the consideration for the sale of a good-will of a business or other property by installments or otherwise.

## § 8
### Partnership Property

(1) All property originally brought into the partnership stock or subsequently acquired by purchase or otherwise, on account of the partnership, is partnership property.

(2) Unless the contrary intention appears, property acquired with partnership funds is partnership property.

(3) Any estate in real property may be acquired in the partnership name. Title so acquired can be conveyed only in the partnership name.

(4) A conveyance to a partnership in the partnership name, though without words of inheritance, passes the entire estate of the grantor unless a contrary intent appears.

## Part III/Relations of Partners to Persons Dealing with the Partnership

## § 9
### Partner Agent of Partnership as to Partnership Business

(1) Every partner is an agent of the partnership for the purpose of its business, and the act of every partner, including the execution in the partnership name of any instrument, for apparently carrying on in the usual way the business of the partnership of which he is a member binds the partnership, unless the partner so acting has in fact no authority to act for the partnership in the particular matter, and the person with whom he is dealing has knowledge of the fact that he has no such authority.

(2) An act of a partner which is not apparently for the carrying on of the business of the partnership in the usual way does not bind the partnership unless authorized by the other partners.

(3) Unless authorized by the other partners or unless they have abandoned the business, one or more but less than all the partners have no authority to:
(a) Assign the partnership property in trust for creditors or on the assignee's promise to pay the debts of the partnership,
(b) Dispose of the good-will of the business,
(c) Do any other act which would make it impossible to carry on the ordinary business of a partnership,
(d) Confess a judgment,
(e) Submit a partnership claim or liability to arbitration or reference.

(4) No act of a partner in contravention of a restriction on authority shall bind the partnership to persons having knowledge of the restriction.

## § 10
### Conveyance of Real Property of the Partnership

(1) Where title to real property is in the partnership name, any partner may convey title to such property by a conveyance executed in the partnership name; but the partnership may recover such property unless the partner's act binds the partnership under the provisions of paragraph (1) of section 9, or unless such property has been conveyed by the grantee or a person claiming through such grantee to a holder for value without knowledge that the partner, in making the conveyance, has exceeded his authority.

(2) Where title to real property is in the name of the partnership, a conveyance executed by a partner, in his own name, passes the equitable interest of the partnership, provided the act is one within the authority of the partner under the provisions of paragraph (1) of section 9.

(3) Where title to real property is in the name of one or more but not all the partners, and the record does not disclose the right of the partnership, the partners in whose name the title stands may convey title to such property, but the partnership may recover such property if the partners' act does not bind the partnership under the provisions of paragraph (1) of section 9, unless the purchaser or his assignee, is a holder for value, without knowledge.

(4) Where the title to real property is in the name of one or more or all the partners, or in a third person in trust for the partnership, a conveyance executed by a partner in the partnership name, or in his own name, passes the equitable interest of the partnership, provided the act is one within the authority of the partner under the provisions of paragraph (1) of section 9.

(5) Where the title to real property is in the names of all the partners a conveyance executed by all the partners passes all their rights in such property.

## § 11
### Partnership Bound by Admission of Partner

An admission or representation made by any partner concerning partnership affairs within the scope of his authority as conferred by this act is evidence against the partnership.

## § 12
### Partnership Charged with Knowledge of or Notice to Partner

Notice to any partner of any matter relating to partnership affairs, and the knowledge of the partner acting in the particular matter, acquired while a partner or then present to his mind, and the knowledge of any other partner who reasonably could and should have communicated it to the acting partner, operate as notice to or knowledge of the partnership, except in the case of a fraud on the partnership committed by or with the consent of that partner.

## § 13
### Partnership Bound by Partner's Wrongful Act

Where, by any wrongful act or omission of any partner acting in the ordinary course of the business of the partnership or with the authority of his co-partners, loss or injury is caused to any person, not being a partner in the partnership, or any penalty is incurred, the partnership is liable therefor to the same extent as the partner so acting or omitting to act.

## § 14
### Partnership Bound by Partner's Breach of Trust

The partnership is bound to make good the loss:

(a) Where one partner acting within the scope of his apparent authority receives money or property of a third person and misapplies it; and

(b) Where the partnership in the course of its business receives money or property of a third person and the money or property so received is misapplied by any partner while it is in the custody of the partnership.

## § 15
### Nature of Partner's Liability

All partners are liable

(a) Jointly and severally for everything chargeable to the partnership under sections 13 and 14.

(b) Jointly for all other debts and obligations of the partnership; but any partner may enter into a separate obligation to perform a partnership contract.

## § 16
### Partner by Estoppel

(1) When a person, by words spoken or written or by conduct, represents himself, or consents to another representing him to any one, as a partner in an existing partnership or with one or more persons not actual partners, he is liable to any such person to whom such representation has been made, who has, on the faith of such representation, given credit to the actual or apparent partnership, and if he has made such representation or consented to its being made in a public manner he is liable to such person, whether the representation has or has not been made or communicated to such person so giving credit by or with the knowledge of the apparent partner making the representation or consenting to its being made.

(a) When a partnership liability results, he is liable as though he were an actual member of the partnership.

(b) When no partnership liability results, he is liable jointly with the other persons, if any, so consenting to the contract or representation as to incur liability, otherwise separately.

(2) When a person has been thus represented to be a partner in an existing partnership, or with one or more persons not actual partners, he is an agent of the persons consenting to such representation to bind them to the same extent and in the same manner as though he were a partner in fact, with respect to persons who rely upon the representation. Where all the members of the existing partnership consent to the representation, a partnership act or obligation results; but in all other cases it is the joint act or obligation of the person acting and the persons consenting to the representation.

## § 17
### Liability of Incoming Partner

A person admitted as a partner into an existing partnership is liable for all the obligations of the partnership arising before his admission as though he had been a partner when such obligations were incurred, except that this liability shall be satisfied only out of partnership property.

## Part IV/Relations of Partners to One Another

## § 18
### Rules Determining Rights and Duties of Partners

The rights and duties of the partners in relation to the partnership shall be determined, subject to any agreement between them, by the following rules:

(a) Each partner shall be repaid his contributions, whether by way of capital or advances to the partnership property and share equally in the profits and surplus remaining after all liabilities, including those to partners, are satisfied; and must contribute towards the losses, whether of capital or otherwise, sustained by the partnership according to his share in the profits.

(b) The partnership must indemnify every partner in respect of payments made and personal liabilities reasonably incurred by him in the ordinary and proper conduct of its business, or for the preservation of its business or property.

(c) A partner, who in aid of the partnership makes any payment or advance beyond the amount of capital which he agreed to contribute, shall be paid interest from the date of the payment or advance.

(d) A partner shall receive interest on the capital contributed by him only from the date when repayment should be made.

(e) All partners have equal rights in the management and conduct of the partnership business.

(f) No partner is entitled to remuneration for acting in the partnership business, except that a surviving partner is entitled to reasonable compensation for his services in winding up the partnership affairs.

(g) No person can become a member of a partnership without the consent of all the partners.

(h) Any difference arising as to ordinary matters connected with the partnership business may be decided by a majority of the partners; but no act in contravention of any agreement between the partners may be done rightfully without the consent of all the partners.

## § 19
### Partnership Books

The partnership books shall be kept, subject to any agreement between the partners, at the principal place of business of the partnership, and every partner shall at all times have access to and may inspect and copy any of them.

## § 20
### Duty of Partners to Render Information

Partners shall render on demand true and full information of all things affecting the partnership to any partner or the legal representative of any deceased partner or partner under legal disability.

## § 21
### Partner Accountable as a Fiduciary

(1) Every partner must account to the partnership for any benefit, and hold as trustee for it any profits derived by him without the consent of the other partners from any transaction connected with the formation, conduct, or liquidation of the partnership or from any use by him of its property.

(2) This section applies also to the representatives of a deceased partner engaged in the liquidation of the affairs of the partnership as the personal representatives of the last surviving partner.

## § 22
### Right to an Account

Any partner shall have the right to a formal account as to partnership affairs:
(a) If he is wrongfully excluded from the partnership business or possession of its property by his co-partners,
(b) If the right exists under the terms of any agreement,
(c) As provided by section 21,
(d) Whenever other circumstances render it just and reasonable.

## § 23
### Continuation of Partnership Beyond Fixed Term

(1) When a partnership for a fixed term or particular undertaking is continued after the termination of such term or particular undertaking without any express agreement, the rights and duties of the partners remain the same as they were at such termination, so far as is consistent with a partnership at will.

(2) A continuation of the business by the partners or such of them as habitually acted therein during the term, without any settlement or liquidation of the partnership affairs, is prima facie evidence of a continuation of the partnership.

## *Part V/Property Rights of a Partner*

### § 24
#### Extent of Property Rights of a Partner

The property rights of a partner are (1) his rights in specific partnership property, (2) his interest in the partnership, and (3) his right to participate in the management.

### § 25
#### Nature of a Partner's Right in Specific Partnership Property

(1) A partner is co-owner with his partners of specific partnership property holding as a tenant in partnership.

(2) The incidents of this tenancy are such that:
(a) A partner, subject to the provisions of this act and to any agreement between the partners, has an equal right with his partners to possess specific partnership property for partnership purposes; but he has no right to possess such property for any other purpose without the consent of his partners.
(b) A partner's right in specific partnership property is not assignable except in connection with the assignment of rights of all the partners in the same property.
(c) A partner's right in specific partnership property is not subject to attachment or execution, except on a claim against the partnership. When partnership property is attached for a partnership debt the partners, or any of them, or the representatives of a deceased partner, cannot claim any right under the homestead or exemption laws.
(d) On the death of a partner his right in specific partnership property vests in the surviving partner or partners, except where the deceased was the last surviving partner, when his right in such property vests in his legal representative.

Such surviving partner or partners, or the legal representative of the last surviving partner, has no right to possess the partnership property for any but a partnership purpose.
(e) A partner's right in specific partnership property is not subject to dower, curtesy, or allowances to widows, heirs, or next of kin.

### § 26
#### Nature of Partner's Interest in the Partnership

A partner's interest in the partnership is his share of the profits and surplus, and the same is personal property.

### § 27
#### Assignment of Partner's Interest

(1) A conveyance by a partner of his interest in the partnership does not of itself dissolve the partnership, nor, as against the other partners in the absence of agreement, entitle the assignee, during the continuance of the partnership, to interfere in the management or administration of the partnership business or affairs, or to require any information or account of partnership transactions, or to inspect the partnership books; but it merely entitles the assignee to receive in accordance with his contract the profits to which the assigning partner would otherwise be entitled.

(2) In case of a dissolution of the partnership, the assignee is entitled to receive his assignor's interest and may require an account from the date only of the last account agreed to by all the partners.

### § 28
#### Partner's Interest Subject to Charging Order

(1) On due application to a competent court by any judgment creditor of a partner, the court which entered the judgment, order, or decree, or any other court, may charge the interest of the debtor partner with payment of the unsatisfied amount of such judgment debt with interest thereon; and may then or later appoint a receiver of his share of the profits, and of any other money due or to fall due to him in respect of the partnership, and make all other orders, directions, accounts and inquiries which the debtor partner might have made, or which the circumstances of the case may require.

(2) The interest charged may be redeemed at any time before foreclosure, or in case of a sale being directed by the court may be purchased without thereby causing a dissolution:
(a) With separate property, by any one or more of the partners, or
(b) With partnership property, by any one or more of the partners with the consent of all the partners whose interests are not so charged or sold.

(3) Nothing in this act shall be held to deprive a partner of his right, if any, under the exemption laws, as regards his interest in the partnership.

## *Part VI/Dissolution and Winding Up*

### § 29
#### Dissolution Defined

The dissolution of a partnership is the change in the relation of the partners caused by any partner ceasing to be associated in the carrying on as distinguished from the winding up of the business.

## § 30
### Partnership not Terminated by Dissolution

On dissolution the partnership is not terminated, but continues until the winding up of partnership affairs is completed.

## § 31
### Causes of Dissolution

Dissolution is caused:

(1) Without violation of the agreement between the partners,
   (a) By the termination of the definite term or particular undertaking specified in the agreement,
   (b) By the express will of any partner when no definite term or particular undertaking is specified,
   (c) By the express will of all the partners who have not assigned their interests or suffered them to be charged for their separate debts, either before or after the termination of any specified term or particular undertaking,
   (d) By the expulsion of any partner from the business bona fide in accordance with such a power conferred by the agreement between the partners;

(2) In contravention of the agreement between the partners, where the circumstances do not permit a dissolution under any other provision of this section, by the express will of any partner at any time;

(3) By any event which makes it unlawful for the business of the partnership to be carried on or for the members to carry it on in partnership;

(4) By the death of any partner;

(5) By the bankruptcy of any partner or the partnership;

(6) By decree of court under section 32.

## § 32
### Dissolution by Decree of Court

(1) On application by or for a partner the court shall decree a dissolution whenever:
   (a) A partner has been declared a lunatic in any judicial proceeding or is shown to be of unsound mind,
   (b) A partner becomes in any other way incapable of performing his part of the partnership contract,
   (c) A partner has been guilty of such conduct as tends to affect prejudicially the carrying on of the business,
   (d) A partner wilfully or persistently commits a breach of the partnership agreement, or otherwise so conducts himself in matters relating to the partnership business that it is not reasonably practicable to carry on the business in partnership with him,
   (e) The business of the partnership can only be carried on at a loss,
   (f) Other circumstances render a dissolution equitable.

(2) On the application of the purchaser of a partner's interest under sections 28 or 29:
   (a) After the termination of the specified term or particular undertaking,
   (b) At any time if the partnership was a partnership at will when the interest was assigned or when the charging order was issued.

## § 33
### General Effect of Dissolution on Authority of Partner

Except so far as may be necessary to wind up partnership affairs or to complete transactions begun but not then finished, dissolution terminates all authority of any partner to act for the partnership,

(1) With respect to the partners,
   (a) When the dissolution is not by the act, bankruptcy or death of a partner; or
   (b) When the dissolution is by such act, bankruptcy or death of a partner, in cases where section 34 so requires.

(2) With respect to persons not partners, as declared in section 35.

## § 34
### Right of Partner to Contribution from Co-partners after Dissolution

Where the dissolution is caused by the act, death or bankruptcy of a partner, each partner is liable to his co-partners for his share of any liability created by any partner acting for the partnership as if the partnership had not been dissolved unless
   (a) The dissolution being by act of any partner, the partner acting for the partnership had knowledge of the dissolution, or
   (b) The dissolution being by the death or bankruptcy of a partner, the partner acting for the partnership had knowledge or notice of the death or bankruptcy.

## § 35
### Power of Partner to Bind Partnership to Third Persons after Dissolution

(1) After dissolution a partner can bind the partnership except as provided in Paragraph (3)
   (a) By any act appropriate for winding up partnership affairs or completing transactions unfinished at dissolution;
   (b) By any transaction which would bind the partnership if dissolution had not taken place, provided the other party to the transaction
      (I) Had extended credit to the partnership prior to dissolution and had no knowledge or notice of the dissolution; or
      (II) Though he had not so extended credit, had nevertheless known of the partnership prior to dissolution, and, having no knowledge or notice of dissolution, the fact of dissolution had not been advertised in a newspaper of general circulation in the place (or in each place if more than one) at which the partnership business was regularly carried on.

(2) The liability of a partner under Paragraph (1b) shall be satisfied out of partnership assets alone when such partner had been prior to dissolution
   (a) Unknown as a partner to the person with whom the contract is made; and
   (b) So far unknown and inactive in partnership affairs that the business reputation of the partnership could not be said to have been in any degree due to his connection with it.

(3) The partnership is in no case bound by any act of a partner after dissolution

(a) Where the partnership is dissolved because it is unlawful to carry on the business, unless the act is appropriate for winding up partnership affairs; or
(b) Where the partner has become bankrupt; or
(c) Where the partner has no authority to wind up partnership affairs; except by a transaction with one who
  (I) Had extended credit to the partnership prior to dissolution and had no knowledge or notice of his want of authority; or
  (II) Had not extended credit to the partnership prior to dissolution, and, having no knowledge or notice of his want of authority, the fact of his want of authority has not been advertised in the manner provided for advertising the fact of dissolution in Paragraph (1bII).

(4) Nothing in this section shall affect the liability under Section 16 of any person who after dissolution represents himself or consents to another representing him as a partner in a partnership engaged in carrying on business.

## § 36
### Effect of Dissolution on Partner's Existing Liability

(1) The dissolution of the partnership does not of itself discharge the existing liability of any partner.

(2) A partner is discharged from any existing liability upon dissolution of the partnership by an agreement to that effect between himself, the partnership creditor and the person or partnership continuing the business; and such agreement may be inferred from the course of dealing between the creditor having knowledge of the dissolution and the person or partnership continuing the business.

(3) Where a person agrees to assume the existing obligations of a dissolved partnership, the partners whose obligations have been assumed shall be discharged from any liability to any creditor of the partnership who, knowing of the agreement, consents to a material alteration in the nature or time of payment of such obligations.

(4) The individual property of a deceased partner shall be liable for all obligations of the partnership incurred while he was a partner but subject to the prior payment of his separate debts.

## § 37
### Right to Wind Up

Unless otherwise agreed the partners who have not wrongfully dissolved the partnership or the legal representative of the last surviving partner, not bankrupt, has the right to wind up the partnership affairs; provided, however, that any partner, his legal representative or his assignee, upon cause shown, may obtain winding up by the court.

## § 38
### Rights of Partners to Application of Partnership Property

(1) When dissolution is caused in any way, except in contravention of the partnership agreement, each partner, as against his co-partners and all persons claiming through them in respect of their interests in the partnership, unless otherwise agreed, may have the partnership property applied to discharge its liabilities, and the surplus applied to pay in cash the net amount owing to the respective partners. But if dissolution is caused by expulsion of a partner, bona fide under the partnership agreement and if the expelled partner is discharged from all partnership liabilities, either by payment or agreement under section 36(2), he shall receive in cash only the net amount due him from the partnership.

(2) When dissolution is caused in contravention of the partnership agreement the rights of the partners shall be as follows:
(a) Each partner who has not caused dissolution wrongfully shall have,
  (I) All the rights specified in paragraph (1) of this section, and
  (II) The right, as against each partner who has caused the dissolution wrongfully, to damages for breach of the agreement.
(b) The partners who have not caused the dissolution wrongfully, if they all desire to continue the business in the same name, either by themselves or jointly with others, may do so, during the agreed term for the partnership and for that purpose may possess the partnership property, provided they secure the payment by bond approved by the court, or pay to any partner who has caused the dissolution wrongfully, the value of his interest in the partnership at the dissolution, less any damages recoverable under clause (2aII) of this section, and in like manner indemnify him against all present or future partnership liabilities.
(c) A partner who has caused the dissolution wrongfully shall have:
  (I) If the business is not continued under the provisions of paragraph (2b) all the rights of a partner under paragraph (1), subject to clause (2aII), of this section,
  (II) If the business is continued under paragraph (2b) of this section the right as against his co-partners and all claiming through them in respect of their interests in the partnership, to have the value of his interest in the partnership, less any damages caused to his co-partners by the dissolution, ascertained and paid to him in cash, or the payment secured by bond approved by the court, and to be released from all existing liabilities of the partnership; but in ascertaining the value of the partner's interest the value of the good-will of the business shall not be considered.

## § 39
### Rights Where Partnership Is Dissolved for Fraud or Misrepresentation

Where a partnership contract is rescinded on the ground of the fraud or misrepresentation of one of the parties thereto, the party entitled to rescind is, without prejudice to any other right, entitled,
(a) To a lien on, or a right of retention of, the surplus of the partnership property after satisfying the partnership liabilities to third persons for any sum of money paid by him for the purchase of an interest in the partnership and for any capital or advances contributed by him; and
(b) To stand, after all liabilities to third persons have been satisfied, in the place of the creditors of the partnership for any payments made by him in respect of the partnership liabilities; and
(c) To be indemnified by the person guilty of the fraud or making the representation against all debts and liabilities of the partnership.

## § 40
### Rules for Distribution

In settling accounts between the partners after dissolution, the following rules shall be observed, subject to any agreement to the contrary:

(a) The assets of the partnership are:
   (I) The partnership property,
   (II) The contributions of the partners necessary for the payment of all the liabilities specified in clause (b) of this paragraph.

(b) The liabilities of the partnership shall rank in order of payment, as follows:
   (I) Those owing to creditors other than partners,
   (II) Those owing to partners other than for capital and profits,
   (III) Those owing to partners in respect of capital,
   (IV) Those owing to partners in respect of profits.

(c) The assets shall be applied in order of their declaration in clause (a) of this paragraph to the satisfaction of the liabilities.

(d) The partners shall contribute, as provided by section 18 (a) the amount necessary to satisfy the liabilities; but if any, but not all, of the partners are insolvent, or, not being subject to process, refuse to contribute, the other partners shall contribute their share of the liabilities, and, in the relative proportions in which they share the profits, the additional amount necessary to pay the liabilities.

(e) An assignee for the benefit of creditors or any person appointed by the court shall have the right to enforce the contributions specified in clause (d) of this paragraph.

(f) Any partner or his legal representative shall have the right to enforce the contributions specified in clause (d) of this paragraph, to the extent of the amount which he has paid in excess of his share of the liability.

(g) The individual property of a deceased partner shall be liable for the contributions specified in clause (d) of this paragraph.

(h) When partnership property and the individual properties of the partners are in possession of a court for distribution, partnership creditors shall have priority on partnership property and separate creditors on individual property, saving the rights of lien or secured creditors as heretofore.

(i) Where a partner has become bankrupt or his estate is insolvent the claims against his separate property shall rank in the following order:
   (I) Those owing to separate creditors,
   (II) Those owing to partnership creditors,
   (III) Those owing to partners by way of contribution.

## § 41
### Liability of Persons Continuing the Business in Certain Cases

(1) When any new partner is admitted into an existing partnership, or when any partner retires and assigns (or the representative of the deceased partner assigns) his rights in partnership property to two or more of the partners, or to one or more of the partners and one or more third persons, if the business is continued without liquidation of the partnership affairs, creditors of the first or dissolved partnership are also creditors of the partnership so continuing the business.

(2) When all but one partner retire and assign (or the representative of a deceased partner assigns) their rights in partnership property to the remaining partner, who continues the business without liquidation of partnership affairs, either alone or with others, creditors of the dissolved partnership are also creditors of the person or partnership so continuing the business.

(3) When any partner retires or dies and the business of the dissolved partnership is continued as set forth in paragraphs (1) and (2) of this section, with the consent of the retired partners or the representative of the deceased partner, but without any assignment of his right in partnership property, rights of creditors of the dissolved partnership and of the creditors of the person or partnership continuing the business shall be as if such assignment had been made.

(4) When all the partners or their representatives assign their rights in partnership property to one or more third persons who promise to pay the debts and who continue the business of the dissolved partnership, creditors of the dissolved partnership are also creditors of the person or partnership continuing the business.

(5) When any partner wrongfully causes a dissolution and the remaining partners continue the business under the provisions of section 38(2b), either alone or with others, and without liquidation of the partnership affairs, creditors of the dissolved partnership are also creditors of the person or partnership continuing the business.

(6) When a partner is expelled and the remaining partners continue the business either alone or with others, without liquidation of the partnership affairs, creditors of the dissolved partnership are also creditors of the person or partnership continuing the business.

(7) The liability of a third person becoming a partner in the partnership continuing the business, under this section, to the creditors of the dissolved partnership shall be satisfied out of partnership property only.

(8) When the business of a partnership after dissolution is continued under any conditions set forth in this section the creditors of the dissolved partnership, as against the separate creditors of the retiring or deceased partner or the representative of the deceased partner, have a prior right to any claim of the retired partner or the representative of the deceased partner against the person or partnership continuing the business, on account of the retired or deceased partner's interest in the dissolved partnership or on account of any consideration promised for such interest or for his right in partnership property.

(9) Nothing in this section shall be held to modify any right of creditors to set aside any assignment on the ground of fraud.

(10) The use by the person or partnership continuing the business of the partnership name, or the name of a deceased partner as part thereof, shall not of itself make the individual property of the deceased partner liable for any debts contracted by such person or partnership.

## § 42
### Rights of Retiring or Estate of Deceased Partner When the Business Is Continued

When any partner retires or dies, and the business is continued under any of the conditions set forth in section 41(1, 2, 3, 5, 6), or section 38(2b) without any settlement of accounts as between him or his estate and the person or partnership continuing the business, unless otherwise agreed, he or his legal representative as against such persons or partnership may have the value of his interest at the date of dissolution ascertained, and shall receive as an ordinary creditor an amount equal to the value of his interest in the dissolved partnership with interest, or, at his option or at the option of his legal representative, in lieu of interest, the profits attributable to the use of his right in the property of the dissolved partnership; provided that the creditors of the dissolved partnership as against the separate creditors, or the representative of the retired or deceased partner, shall have priority on any claim arising under this section, as provided by section 41(8) of this act.

### § 43
**Accrual of Actions**

The right to an account of his interest shall accrue to any partner, or his legal representative, as against the winding up partners or the surviving partners or the person or partnership continuing the business, at the date of dissolution, in the absence of any agreement to the contrary.

## Part VII/Miscellaneous Provisions

### § 44
**When Act Takes Effect**

This act shall take effect on the . . . . . . . . . . . day of . . . . . . . . . . . . one thousand nine-hundred and . . . . . . . . . . .

### § 45
**Legislation Repealed**

All acts or parts of acts inconsistent with this act are hereby repealed.

# APPENDIX C

# Uniform Limited Partnership Act

## § 1
### Limited Partnership Defined

A limited partnership is a partnership formed by two or more persons under the provisions of Section 2, having as members one or more general partners and one or more limited partners. The limited partners as such shall not be bound by the obligations of the partnership.

## § 2
### Formation

(1) Two or more persons desiring to form a limited partnership shall
    (a) Sign and swear to a certificate, which shall state
        (I) The name of the partnership,
        (II) The character of the business,
        (III) The location of the principal place of business,
        (IV) The name and place of residence of each member; general and limited partners being respectively designated,
        (V) The term for which the partnership is to exist,
        (VI) The amount of cash and a description of and the agreed value of the other property contributed by each limited partner,
        (VII) The additional contributions, if any, agreed to be made by each limited partner and the times at which or events on the happening of which they shall be made,
        (VIII) The time, if agreed upon, when the contribution of each limited partner is to be returned,
        (IX) The share of the profits or the other compensation by way of income which each limited partner shall receive by reason of his contribution,
        (X) The right, if given, of a limited partner to substitute an assignee as contributor in his place, and the terms and conditions of the substitution,
        (XI) The right, if given, of the partners to admit additional limited partners,
        (XII) The right, if given, of one or more of the limited partners to priority over other limited partners, as to contributions or as to compensation by way of income, and the nature of such priority,
        (XIII) The right, if given, of the remaining general partner or partners to continue the business on the death, retirement or insanity of a general partner, and
        (XIV) The right, if given, of a limited partner to demand and receive property other than cash in return for his contribution.
    (b) File for record the certificate in the office of [here designate the proper office].

(2) A limited partnership is formed if there has been substantial compliance in good faith with the requirements of paragraph (1).

## § 3
### Business Which May Be Carried On

A limited partnership may carry on any business which a partnership without limited partners may carry on, except [here designate the business to be prohibited].

## § 4
### Character of Limited Partner's Contribution

The contributions of a limited partner may be cash or other property, but not services.

## § 5
### A Name Not to Contain Surname of Limited Partner; Exceptions

(1) The surname of a limited partner shall not appear in the partnership name, unless
    (a) It is also the surname of a general partner, or
    (b) Prior to the time when the limited partner became such the business had been carried on under a name in which his surname appeared.

(2) A limited partner whose name appears in a partnership name contrary to the provisions of paragraph (1) is liable as a general partner to partnership creditors who extend credit to the partnership without actual knowledge that he is not a general partner.

## § 6
### Liability for False Statements in Certificate

If the certificate contains a false statement, one who suffers loss by reliance on such statement may hold liable any party to the certificate who knew the statement to be false.
    (a) At the time he signed the certificate, or
    (b) Subsequently, but within a sufficient time before the statement was relied upon to enable him to cancel or amend the certificate, or to file a petition for its cancellation or amendment as provided in Section 25(3).

## § 7
### Limited Partner Not Liable to Creditors

A limited partner shall not become liable as a general partner unless, in addition to the exercise of his rights and powers as a limited partner, he takes part in the control of the business.

## § 8
### Admission of Additional Limited Partners

After the formation of a limited partnership, additional limited partners may be admitted upon filing an amendment to the original certificate in accordance with the requirements of Section 25.

## § 9
### Rights, Powers and Liabilities of a General Partner

**(1)** A general partner shall have all the rights and powers and be subject to all the restrictions and liabilities of a partner in a partnership without limited partners, except that without the written consent or ratification of the specific act by all the limited partners, a general partner or all of the general partners have no authority to

    **(a)** Do any act in contravention of the certificate,

    **(b)** Do any act which would make it impossible to carry on the ordinary business of the partnership,

    **(c)** Confess a judgment against the partnership,

    **(d)** Possess partnership property, or assign their rights in specific partnership property, for other than a partnership purpose.

    **(e)** Admit a person as a general partner,

    **(f)** Admit a person as a limited partner, unless the right so to do is given in the certificate,

    **(g)** Continue the business with partnership property on the death, retirement or insanity of a general partner, unless the right so to do is given in the certificate.

## § 10
### Rights of a Limited Partner

**(1)** A limited partner shall have the same rights as a general partner to

    **(a)** Have the partnership books kept at the principal place of business of the partnership, and at all times to inspect and copy any of them

    **(b)** Have on demand true and full information of all things affecting the partnership, and a formal account of partnership affairs whenever circumstances render it just and reasonable, and

    **(c)** Have dissolution and winding up by decree of court.

**(2)** A limited partner shall have the right to receive a share of the profits or other compensation by way of income, and to the return of his contribution as provided in Sections 15 and 16.

## § 11
### Status of Person Erroneously Believing Himself a Limited Partner

A person who has contributed to the capital of a business conducted by a person or partnership erroneously believing that he has become a limited partner in a limited partnership, is not, by reason of his exercise of the rights of a limited partner, a general partner with the person or in the partnership carrying on the business, or bound by the obligations of such person or partnership; provided that on ascertaining the mistake he promptly renounces his interest in the profits of the business, or other compensation by way of income.

## § 12
### One Person Both General and Limited Partner

**(1)** A person may be a general partner and a limited partner in the same partnership at the same time.

**(2)** A person who is a general, and also at the same time a limited partner, shall have all the rights and powers and be subject to all the restrictions of a general partner; except that, in respect to his contribution, he shall have the rights against the other members which he would have had if he were not also a general partner.

## § 13
### Loans and Other Business Transactions with Limited Partner

**(1)** A limited partner also may loan money to and transact other business with the partnership, and, unless he is also a general partner, receive on account of resulting claims against the partnership, with general creditors, a pro rata share of the assets. No limited partner shall in respect to any such claim

    **(a)** Receive or hold as collateral security any partnership property, or

    **(b)** Receive from a general partner of the partnership any payment, conveyance, or release from liability, if at the time the assets of the partnership are not sufficient to discharge partnership liabilities to persons not claiming as general or limited partners,

**(2)** The receiving of collateral security, or a payment, conveyance, or release in violation of the provisions of paragraph (1) is a fraud on the creditors of the partnership.

## § 14
### Relation of Limited Partners Inter Se

Where there are several limited partners the members may agree that one or more of the limited partners shall have a priority over other limited partners as to the return of their contributions, as to their compensation by way of income, or as to any other matter. If such an agreement is made it shall be stated in the certificate, and in the absence of such a statement all the limited partners shall stand upon equal footing.

## § 15
### Compensation of Limited Partner

A limited partner may receive from the partnership the share of the profits or the compensation by way of income stipulated for in the certificate; provided, that after such payment is made, whether from the property of the partnership or that of a general partner, the partnership assets are in excess of all liabilities of the partnership except liabilities to limited partners on account of their contributions and to general partners.

## § 16
### Withdrawal or Reduction of Limited Partner's Contribution

**(1)** A limited partner shall not receive from a general partner or out of partnership property any part of his contribution until

(a) All liabilities of the partnership, except liabilities to general partners and to limited partners on account of their contributions, have been paid or there remains property of the partnership sufficient to pay them,
(b) The consent of all members is had, unless the return of the contribution may be rightfully demanded under the provisions of paragraph (2), and
(c) The certificate is cancelled or so amended as to set forth the withdrawal or reduction.

(2) Subject to the provisions of paragraph (1) a limited partner may rightfully demand the return of his contribution
(a) On the dissolution of a partnership, or
(b) When the date specified in the certificate for its return has arrived, or
(c) After he has given six months' notice in writing to all other members, if no time is specified in the certificate either for the return of the contribution or for the dissolution of the partnership,

(3) In the absence of any statement in the certificate to the contrary or the consent of all members, a limited partner, irrespective of the nature of his contribution, has only the right to demand and receive cash in return for his contribution.

(4) A limited partner may have the partnership dissolved and its affairs wound up when
(a) He rightfully but unsuccessfully demands the return of his contribution, or
(b) The other liabilities of the partnership have not been paid, or the partnership property is insufficient for their payment as required by paragraph (1a) and the limited partner would otherwise be entitled to the return of his contribution.

## § 17
### Liability of Limited Partner to Partnership

(1) A limited partner is liable to the partnership
(a) For the difference between his contribution as actually made and that stated in the certificate as having been made, and
(b) For any unpaid contribution which he agreed in the certificate to make in the future at the time and on the conditions stated in the certificate.

(2) A limited partner holds as trustee for the partnership
(a) Specific property stated in the certificate as contributed by him, but which was not contributed or which has been wrongfully returned, and
(b) Money or other property wrongfully paid or conveyed to him on account of his contribution.

(3) The liabilities of a limited partner as set forth in this section can be waived or compromised only by the consent of all members; but a waiver or compromise shall not affect the right of a creditor of a partnership who extended credit or whose claim arose after the filing and before a cancellation or amendment of the certificate, to enforce such liabilities.

(4) When a contributor has rightfully received the return in whole or in part of the capital of his contribution, he is nevertheless liable to the partnership for any sum, not in excess of such return with interest, necessary to discharge its liabilities to all creditors who extended credit or whose claims arose before such return.

## § 18
### Nature of Limited Partner's Interest in Partnership

A limited partner's interest in the partnership is personal property.

## § 19
### Assignment of Limited Partner's Interest

(1) A limited partner's interest is assignable.

(2) A substituted limited partner is a person admitted to all the rights of a limited partner who has died or has assigned his interest in a partnership.

(3) An assignee, who does not become a substituted limited partner, has no right to require any information or account of the partnership transactions or to inspect the partnership books; he is only entitled to receive the share of the profits or other compensation by way of income, or the return of his contribution, to which his assignor would otherwise be entitled.

(4) An assignee shall have the right to become a substituted limited partner if all the members (except the assignor) consent thereto or if the assignor, being thereunto empowered by the certificate, gives the assignee that right.

(5) An assignee becomes a substituted limited partner when the certificate is appropriately amended in accordance with Section 25.

(6) The substituted limited partner has all the rights and powers, and is subject to all the restrictions and liabilities of his assignor, except those liabilities of which he was ignorant at the time he became a limited partner and which could not be ascertained from the certificate.

(7) The substitution of the assignee as a limited partner does not release the assignor from liability to the partnership under Sections 6 and 17.

## § 20
### Effect of Retirement, Death or Insanity of a General Partner

The retirement, death or insanity of a general partner dissolves the partnership, unless the business is continued by the remaining general partners
(a) Under a right so to do stated in the certificate, or
(b) With the consent of all members.

## § 21
### Death of Limited Partner

(1) On the death of a limited partner his executor or administrator shall have all the rights of a limited partner for the purpose of settling his estate, and such power as the deceased had to constitute his assignee a substituted limited partner.

(2) The estate of a deceased limited partner shall be liable for all his liabilities as a limited partner.

## § 22
### Rights of Creditors of Limited Partner

(1) On due application to a court of competent jurisdiction by any judgment creditor of a limited partner, the court may charge the interest of the indebted limited partner with payment of the unsatisfied amount of the judgment debt; and may appoint a receiver, and make all other orders, directions, and inquiries which the circumstances of the case may require.

In those states where a creditor on beginning an action can attach debts due the defendant before he has obtained a judgment against the defendant it is recommended that paragraph (1) of this section read as follows:

On due application to a court of competent jurisdiction by any creditor of a limited partner, the court may charge the interest of the indebted limited partner with payment of the unsatisfied amount of such claim; and may appoint a receiver, and make all other orders, directions, and inquiries which the circumstances of the case may require.

(2) The interest may be redeemed with the separate property of any general partner, but may not be redeemed with partnership property.

(3) The remedies conferred by paragraph (1) shall not be deemed exclusive of others which may exist.

(4) Nothing in this act shall be held to deprive a limited partner of his statutory exemption.

## § 23
### Distribution of Assets

(1) In settling accounts after dissolution the liabilities of the partnership shall be entitled to payment in the following order:
   (a) Those to creditors, in the order of priority as provided by law, except those to limited partners on account of their contributions, and to general partners,
   (b) Those to limited partners in respect to their share of the profits and other compensation by way of income on their contributions,
   (c) Those to limited partners in respect to the capital of their contributions,
   (d) Those to general partners other than for capital and profits,
   (e) Those to general partners in respect to profits,
   (f) Those to general partners in respect to capital.

(2) Subject to any statement in the certificate or to subsequent agreement, limited partners share in the partnership assets in respect to their claims for capital, and in respect to their claims for profits or for compensation by way of income on their contributions respectively, in proportion to the respective amounts of such claims.

## § 24
### When Certificate Shall Be Cancelled or Amended

(1) The certificate shall be cancelled when the partnership is dissolved or all limited partners cease to be such.

(2) A certificate shall be amended when
   (a) There is a change in the name of the partnership or in the amount or character of the contribution of any limited partner,
   (b) A person is substituted as a limited partner,
   (c) An additional limited partner is admitted,
   (d) A person is admitted as a general partner,
   (e) A general partner retires, dies or becomes insane, and the business is continued under Section 20,
   (f) There is a change in the character of the business of the partnership,
   (g) There is a false or erroneous statement in the certificate,
   (h) There is a change in the time as stated in the certificate for the dissolution of the partnership or for the return of a contribution,
   (i) A time is fixed for the dissolution of the partnership, or the return of a contribution, no time having been specified in the certificate, or
   (j) The members desire to make a change in any other statement in the certificate in order that it shall accurately represent the agreement between them.

## § 25
### Requirements for Amendment and for Cancellation of Certificate

(1) The writing to amend a certificate shall
   (a) Conform to the requirements of Section 2(1a) as far as necessary to set forth clearly the change in the certificate which it is desired to make, and
   (b) Be signed and sworn to by all members, and an amendment substituting a limited partner or adding a limited or general partner shall be signed also by the member to be substituted or added, and when a limited partner is to be substituted, the amendment shall also be signed by the assigning limited partner.

(2) The writing to cancel a certificate shall be signed by all members.

(3) A person desiring the cancellation or amendment of a certificate, if any person designated in paragraphs (1) and (2) as a person who must execute the writing refuses to do so, may petition the [here designate the proper court] to direct a cancellation or amendment thereof.

(4) If the court finds that the petitioner has a right to have the writing executed by a person who refuses to do so, it shall order the [here designate the responsible official in the office designated in Section 2] in the office where the certificate is recorded to record the cancellation or amendment of the certificate; and where the certificate is to be amended, the court shall also cause to be filed for record in said office a certified copy of its decree setting forth the amendment.

(5) A certificate is amended or cancelled when there is filed for record in the office [here designate the office designated in Section 2] where the certificate is recorded
   (a) A writing in accordance with the provisions of paragraph (1), or (2) or
   (b) A certified copy of the order of court in accordance with the provisions of paragraph (4).

(6) After the certificate is duly amended in accordance with this section, the amended certificate shall thereafter be for all purposes the certificate provided for by this act.

## § 26
### Parties to Actions

A contributor, unless he is a general partner, is not a proper party to proceedings by or against a partnership, except where the object is to enforce a limited partner's right against or liability to the partnership.

## § 27
### Name of Act

This act may be cited as The Uniform Limited Partnership Act.

## § 28
### Rules of Construction

**(1)** The rule that statutes in derogation of the common law are to be strictly construed shall have no application to this act.

**(2)** This act shall be so interpreted and construed as to effect its general purpose to make uniform the law of those states which enact it.

**(3)** This act shall not be so construed as to impair the obligations of any contract existing when the act goes into effect, nor to affect any action or proceedings begun or right accrued before this act takes effect.

## § 29
### Rules for Cases Not Provided for in This Act

In any case not provided for in this act the rules of law and equity, including the law merchant, shall govern.

## § 30
### Provisions for Existing Limited Partnerships

**(1)** A limited partnership formed under any statute of this state prior to the adoption of this act, may become a limited partnership under this act by complying with the provisions of Section 2; provided the certificate sets forth

    **(a)** The amount of the original contribution of each limited partner, and the time when the contribution was made, and

    **(b)** That the property of the partnership exceeds the amount sufficient to discharge its liabilities to persons not claiming as general or limited partners by an amount greater than the sum of the contributions of its limited partners.

**(2)** A limited partnership formed under any statute of this state prior to the adoption of this act, until or unless it becomes a limited partnership under this act, shall continue to be governed by the provisions of [here insert proper reference to the existing limited partnership act or acts], except that such partnership shall not be renewed unless so provided in the original agreement.

## § 31
### Act [Acts] Repealed

Except as affecting limited partnerships to the extent set forth in Section 30, the act (acts) of [here designate the existing limited partnership act or acts] is (are) hereby repealed.

# APPENDIX D

# REVISED UNIFORM LIMITED PARTNERSHIP ACT

The Act consists of 11 Articles as follows:
1. General Provisions
2. Formation; Certificate of Limited Partnership
3. Limited Partners
4. General Partners
5. Finance
6. Distribution and Withdrawal
7. Assignment of Partnership Interests
8. Dissolution
9. Foreign Limited Partnerships
10. Derivative Actions
11. Miscellaneous

## ARTICLE 1/GENERAL PROVISIONS

### § 101
**Definitions**

As used in this Act, unless the context otherwise requires:

**(1)** "Certificate of limited partnership" means the certificate referred to in Section 201, as that certificate is amended from time to time.

**(2)** "Contribution" means any cash, property, or services rendered, or a promissory note or other binding obligation to contribute cash or property or to perform services, which a partner contributes to a limited partnership in his capacity as a partner.

**(3)** "Event of withdrawal of a general partner" means an event that causes a person to cease to be a general partner as provided in Section 402.

**(4)** "Foreign limited partnership" means a partnership formed under the laws of any State other than this State and having as partners one or more general partners and one or more limited partners.

**(5)** "General partner" means a person who has been admitted to a limited partnership as a general partner in accordance with the partnership agreement and named in the certificate of limited partnership as a general partner.

**(6)** "Limited partner" means a person who has been admitted to a limited partnership as a limited partner in accordance with the partnership agreement and named in the certificate of limited partnership as a limited partner.

**(7)** "Limited partnership" and "domestic limited partnership" mean a partnership formed by 2 or more persons under the laws of this State and having one or more general partners and one or more limited partners.

**(8)** "Partner" means any limited partner or general partner.

**(9)** "Partnership agreement" means any valid agreement, written or oral, of the partners as to the affairs of a limited partnership and the conduct of its business.

**(10)** "Partnership interest" means a partner's share of the profits and losses of a limited partnership and the right to receive distributions of partnership assets.

**(11)** "Person" means a natural person, partnership, limited partnership (domestic or foreign), trust, estate, association, or corporation.

**(12)** "State" means a state, territory, or possession of the United States, the District of Columbia, or the Commonwealth of Puerto Rico.

### § 102
**Name**

The name of each limited partnership as set forth in its certificate of limited partnership:

**(1)** shall contain without abbreviation the words "limited partnership";

**(2)** may not contain the name of a limited partner unless (i) it is also the name of a general partner or the corporate name of a corporate general partner, or (ii) the business of the limited partnership had been carried on under that name before the admission of that limited partner;

**(3)** may not contain any word or phrase indicating or implying that it is organized other than for a purpose stated in its certificate of limited partnership;

**(4)** may not be the same as, or deceptively similar to, the name of any corporation or limited partnership organized under the laws of this State or licensed or registered as a foreign corporation or limited partnership in this State; and

**(5)** may not contain the following words [here insert prohibited words].

### § 103
**Reservation of Name**

**(a)** The exclusive right to the use of a name may be reserved by:
    **(1)** any person intending to organize a limited partnership under this Act and to adopt that name;
    **(2)** any domestic limited partnership or any foreign limited

partnership registered in this State which, in either case, intends to adopt that name;

(3) any foreign limited partnership intending to register in this State and to adopt that name; and

(4) any person intending to organize a foreign limited partnership and intending to have it registered in this State and to adopt that name.

(b) The reservation shall be made by filing with the Secretary of State an application, executed by the applicant, to reserve a specified name. If the Secretary of State finds that the name is available for use by a domestic or foreign limited partnership, he shall reserve the name for the exclusive use of the applicant for a period of 120 days. Once having reserved a name, the same applicant may not again reserve the same name until more than 60 days after the expiration of the last 120-day period for which that applicant reserved that name. The right to the exclusive use of a reserved name may be transferred to any other person by filing in the office of the Secretary of State a notice of the transfer, executed by the applicant for whom the name was reserved and specifying the name and address of the transferee.

§ 104
**Specified Office and Agent**

Each limited partnership shall continuously maintain in this State:

(1) an office, which may but need not be a place of its business in this State, at which shall be kept the records required by Section 105 to be maintained; and

(2) an agent for service of process on the limited partnership, which agent must be an individual resident of this State, a domestic corporation, or a foreign corporation authorized to do business in this State.

§ 105
**Records to be Kept**

Each limited partnership shall keep at the office referred to in Section 104(1) the following: (1) a current list of the full name and last known business address of each partner set forth in alphabetical order, (2) a copy of the certificate of limited partnership and all certificates of amendment thereto, together with executed copies of any powers of attorney pursuant to which any certificate has been executed, (3) copies of the limited partnership's federal, state, and local income tax returns and reports, if any, for the 3 most recent years, and (4) copies of any then effective written partnership agreements and of any financial statements of the limited partnership for the 3 most recent years. These records are subject to inspection and copying at the reasonable request, and at the expense, of any partner during ordinary business hours.

§ 106
**Nature of Business**

A limited partnership may carry on any business that a partnership without limited partners may carry on except [here designate prohibited activities].

§ 107
**Business Transactions of Partner With the Partnership**

Except as provided in the partnership agreement, a partner may lend money to and transact other business with the limited partnership and, subject to other applicable law, has the same rights and obligations with respect thereto as a person who is not a partner.

# ARTICLE 2/FORMATION; CERTIFICATE OF LIMITED PARTNERSHIP

§ 201
**Certificate of Limited Partnership**

(a) In order to form a limited partnership two or more persons must execute a certificate of limited partnership. The certificate shall be filed in the office of the Secretary of State and set forth:

(1) the name of the limited partnership;

(2) the general character of its business;

(3) the address of the office and the name and address of the agent for service of process required to be maintained by Section 104;

(4) the name and the business address of each partner (specifying separately the general partners and limited partners);

(5) the amount of cash and a description and statement of the agreed value of the other property or services contributed by each partner and which each partner has agreed to contribute in the future;

(6) the times at which or events on the happening of which any additional contributions agreed to be made by each partner are to be made;

(7) any power of a limited partner to grant the right to become a limited partner to an assignee of any part of his partnership interest and the terms and conditions of the power;

(8) if agreed upon, the time at which or the events on the happening of which a partner may terminate his membership in the limited partnership and the amount of, or the method of determining, the distribution to which he may be entitled respecting his partnership interest, and the terms and conditions of the termination and distribution;

(9) any right of a partner to receive distributions of property, including cash from the limited partnership;

(10) any right of a partner to receive, or of a general partner to make, distributions to a partner which include a return of all or any part of the partner's contribution;

(11) any time at which or events upon the happening of which the limited partnership is to be dissolved and its affairs wound up;

(12) any right of the remaining general partners to continue the business on the happening of an event of withdrawal of a general partner; and

(13) any other matters the partners determine to include therein.

(b) A limited partnership is formed at the time of the filing of the certificate of limited partnership in the office of the Secretary of State or at any later time specified in the certificate of limited partnership if, in each case, there has been substantial compliance with the requirements of this section.

§ 202
**Amendment to Certificate**

(a) A certificate of limited partnership is amended by filing a certificate of amendment thereto in the office of the Secretary of State. The certificate shall set forth:

(1) the name of the limited partnership;
(2) the date of filing of the certificate; and
(3) the amendments to the certificate.

**(b)** Within 30 days after the happening of any of the following events an amendment to a certificate of limited partnership reflecting the occurrence of the event or events shall be filed:
(1) a change in the amount or character of the contribution of any partner, or in any partner's obligation to make a contribution;
(2) the admission of a new partner;
(3) the withdrawal of a partner; or
(4) the continuation of the business under Section 801 after an event of withdrawal of a general partner.

**(c)** A general partner who becomes aware that any statement in a certificate of limited partnership was false when made or that any arrangements or other facts described have changed, making the certificate inaccurate in any respect, shall promptly amend the certificate, but an amendment to show a change of address of a limited partner need be filed only once every 12 months.

**(d)** A certificate of limited partnership may be amended at any time for any other proper purpose the general partners may determine.

**(e)** No person has any liability because an amendment to a certificate of limited partnership has not been filed to reflect the occurrence of any event referred to in subsection (b) of this Section if the amendment is filed within the 30-day period specified in subsection (b).

§ 203
**Cancellation of Certificate**

A certificate of limited partnership shall be cancelled upon the dissolution and the commencement of winding up of the partnership and at any other time there are no remaining limited partners. A certificate of cancellation shall be filed in the office of the Secretary of State and Shall set forth:

(1) the name of the limited partnership;
(2) the date of filing of its certificate of limited partnership;
(3) the reason for filing the certificate of cancellation;
(4) the effective date (which shall be a date certain) of cancellation if it is not to be effective upon the filing of the certificate; and
(5) any other information the general partners filing the certificate may determine.

§ 204
**Execution of Certificates**

**(a)** Each certificate required by this Article to be filed in the office of the Secretary of State shall be executed in the following manner:
(1) each original certificate of limited partnership must be signed by each partner named therein;
(2) each certificate of amendment must be signed by at least one general partner and by each other partner designated in the certificate as a new partner or whose contribution is described as having been increased; and
(3) each certificate of cancellation must be signed by all general partners.

**(b)** Any person may sign a certificate by an attorney-in-fact, but a power of attorney to sign a certificate relating to the admission, or increased contribution, of a partner must specifically describe the admission or increase.

**(c)** The execution of a certificate by a general partner constitutes an affirmation under the penalties of perjury that the facts stated therein are true.

§ 205
**Amendment or Cancellation by Judicial Act**

If a person required by Section 204 to execute a certificate of amendment or cancellation fail or refuse to do so, any other partner, and any assignee of a partnership interest, who is adversely affected by the failure or refusal, may petition the [here designate the proper court] to direct the amendment or cancellation. If the court finds that the amendment or cancellation is proper and that the person so designated has failed or refused to execute the certificate, it shall order the Secretary of State to record an appropriate certificate of amendment or cancellation.

§ 206
**Filing in the Office of the Secretary of State**

**(a)** Two signed copies of the certificate of limited partnership and of any certificates of amendment or cancellation (or of any judicial decree of amendment or cancellation) shall be delivered to the Secretary of State. A person who executes a certificate as an agent or fiduciary need not exhibit evidence of his authority as a prerequisite to filing. Unless the Secretary of State finds that any certificate does not conform to law, upon receipt of all filing fees required by law he shall:
(1) endorse on each duplicate original the word "Filed" and the day, month, and year of the filing thereof;
(2) file one duplicate original in his office; and
(3) return the other duplicate original to the person who filed it or his representative.

**(b)** Upon the filing of a certificate of amendment (or judicial decree of amendment) in the office of the Secretary of State, the certificate of limited partnership shall be amended as set forth therein, and upon the effective date of a certificate of cancellation (or a judicial decree thereof), the certificate of limited partnership is cancelled.

§ 207
**Liability for False Statement in Certificate**

If any certificate of limited partnership or certificate of amendment or cancellation contains a false statement, one who suffers loss by reliance on the statement may recover damages for the loss from:

(1) any person who executes the certificate, or causes another to execute it on his behalf, and knew, and any general partner who knew or should have known, the statement to be false at the time the certificate was executed; and

(2) any general partner who thereafter knows or should have known that any arrangement or other fact described in the certificate have changed, making the statement inaccurate in any respect within a sufficient time before the statement was relied upon reasonably to have enabled that general partner to cancel or amend the certificate, or to file a petition for its cancellation or amendment under Section 205.

## § 208
### Notice

The fact that a certificate of limited partnership is on file in the office of the Secretary of State is notice that the partnership is a limited partnership and the persons designated therein as limited partners are limited partners, but is not notice of any other fact.

## § 209
### Delivery of Certificates to Limited Partners

Upon the return by the Secretary of State pursuant to Section 206 of a certificate marked "Filed," the general partners shall promptly deliver or mail a copy of the certificate of limited partnership and each certificate to each limited partner unless the partnership agreement provides otherwise.

# ARTICLE 3/LIMITED PARTNERS

## § 301
### Admission of Additional Limited Partners

(a) After the filing of a limited partnership's original certificate of limited partnership, a person may be admitted as a new limited partner:

(1) in the case of a person acquiring a partnership interest directly from the limited partnership, upon the compliance with the partnership agreement or, if the partnership agreement does not so provide, upon the written consent of all partners; and

(2) in the case of an assignee of a partnership interest of a partner who has the power, as provided in Section 704, to grant the assignee the right to become a limited partner, upon the exercise of that power and compliance with any conditions limiting the grant or exercise of the power.

(b) In each case under subsection (a), the person acquiring the partnership interest becomes a limited partner only upon amendment of the certificate of limited partnership reflecting that fact.

## § 302
### Voting

Subject to Section 303, the partnership agreement may grant to all or a specified group of the limited partners the right to vote (on a per capita or any other basis) upon any matter.

## § 303
### Liability to Third Parties

(a) Except as provided in subsection (d), a limited partner is not liable for the obligations of a limited partnership unless he is also a general partner or, in addition to the exercise of his rights and powers as a limited partner, he takes part in the control of the business. However, if the limited partner's participation in the control of the business is not substantially the same as the exercise of the powers of a general partner, he is liable only to persons who transact business with the limited partnership with actual knowledge of his participation in control.

(b) A limited partner does not participate in the control of the business within the meaning of subsection (a) solely by doing one or more of the following:

(1) being a contractor for or an agent or employee of the limited partnership or of a general partner;

(2) consulting with and advising a general partner with respect to the business of the limited partnership;

(3) acting as surety for the limited partnership;

(4) approving or disapproving an amendment to the partnership agreement; or

(5) voting on one or more of the following matters:

(i) the dissolution and winding up of the limited partnership;

(ii) the sale, exchange, lease, mortgage, pledge, or other transfer of all or substantially all of the assets of the limited partnership other than in the ordinary course of its business;

(iii) the incurrence of indebtedness by the limited partnership other than in the ordinary course of its business;

(iv) a change in the nature of the business; or

(v) the removal of a general partner.

(c) The enumeration in subsection (b) does not mean that the possession or exercise of any other powers by a limited partner constitutes participation by him in the business of the limited partnership.

(d) A limited partner who knowingly permits his name to be used in the name of the limited partnership, except under circumstances permitted by Section 102(2)(i), is liable to creditors who extend credit to the limited partnership without actual knowledge that the limited partner is not a general partner.

## § 304
### Person Erroneously Believing Himself a Limited Partner

(a) Except as provided in subsection (b), a person who makes a contribution to a business enterprise and erroneously but in good faith believes that he has become a limited partner in the enterprise is not a general partner in the enterprise and is not bound by its obligations by reason of making the contribution, receiving distributions from the enterprise, or exercising any rights of a limited partner, if, on ascertaining the mistake; he:

(1) causes an appropriate certificate of limited partnership or a certificate of amendment to be executed and filed; or

(2) withdraws from future equity participation in the enterprise.

(b) Any person who makes a contribution of the kind described in subsection (a) is liable as a general partner to any third party who transacts business with the enterprise (i) before the person withdraws and an appropriate certificate is filed to show withdrawal, or (ii) before an appropriate certificate is filed to show his status as a limited partner and, in the case of an amendment, after expiration of the 30-day period for filing an amendment relating to the person as a limited partner under Section 202, but in either case only if the third party actually believed in good faith that the person was a general partner at the time of the transaction.

## § 305
### Information

Each limited partner has the right to:

(1) inspect and copy any of the partnership records required to be maintained by Section 105; and

(2) obtain from the general partners from time to time upon reasonable demand (i) true and full information regarding the state of the business and financial condition of the limited partnership, (ii) promptly after becoming available, a copy of the limited partnership's federal, state, and local income tax returns for each year, and (iii) other information regarding the affairs of the limited partnership as is just and reasonable.

## ARTICLE 4/GENERAL PARTNERS

### § 401
### Admission of Additional General Partners

After the filing of a limited partnership's original certificate of limited partnership, additional general partners may be admitted only with the specific written consent of each partner.

### § 402
### Events of Withdrawal

Except as approved by the specific written consent of all partners at the time, a person ceases to be a general partner of a limited partnership upon the happening of any of the following events:

(1) the general partner withdraws from the limited partnership as provided in Section 602;

(2) the general partner ceases to be a member of the limited partnership as provided in Section 702;

(3) the general partner is removed as a general partner in accordance with the partnership agreement;

(4) unless otherwise provided in the certificate of limited partnership, the general partner: (i) makes an assignment for the benefit of creditors; (ii) files a voluntary petition in bankruptcy; (iii) is adjudicated a bankrupt or insolvent; (iv) files a petition or answer seeking for himself any reorganization, arrangement, composition, readjustment, liquidation, dissolution, or similar relief under any statute, law, or regulation; (v) files an answer or other pleading admitting or failing to contest the material allegations of a petition filed against him in any proceeding of this nature; or (vi) seeks, consents to, or acquiesces in the appointment of a trustee, receiver, or liquidator of the general partner or of all or any substantial part of his properties;

(5) unless otherwise provided in the certificate of limited partnership, [120] days after the commencement of any proceeding against the general partner seeking any reorganization, arrangement, composition, readjustment, liquidation, dissolution, or similar relief under any statute, law, or regulation, the proceeding has not been dismissed, or if within [90] days after the appointment without his consent or acquiescence of any trustee, receiver, or liquidator of the general partner or of all or any substantial part of his properties, the appointment is not vacated or stayed, or within [90] days after the expiration of any such stay, the appointment is not vacated;

(6) in the case of a general partner who is a natural person
   (i) his death; or
   (ii) the entry by a court of competent jurisdiction adjudicating him incompetent to manage his person or his property;

(7) in the case of a general partner who is acting as a general partner by virtue of being a trustee of a trust, the termination of the trust (but not merely the substitution of a new trustee);

(8) in the case of a general partner that is a separate partnership, the dissolution and commencement of winding up of the partnership;

(9) in the case of a general partner that is a corporation, the filing of a certificate of dissolution, or its equivalent, for the corporation or the revocation of its charter; and

(10) in the case of an estate, the distribution by the fiduciary of all the estate's entire interest in the partnership.

### § 403
### General Powers and Liabilities

Except as otherwise provided in this Act and in the partnership agreement, a general partner of a limited partnership has the rights and powers and is subject to the restrictions and liabilities of a partner in a partnership without limited partners.

### § 404
### Contributions by a General Partner

A general partner of a limited partnership may make contribution to the partnership and share in the profits and losses of, and in distributions from, the limited partnership as a general partner. A general partner also may make contributions to and share in profits, losses, and distributions as a limited partner. A person who is both a general partner and a limited partner has the rights and powers, and is subject to the restrictions and liabilities, of a general partner and, except as provided in the partnership agreement, also has the powers, and is subject to the restrictions, of a limited partner to the extent of his participation in the partnership as a limited partner.

### § 405
### Voting

The partnership agreement may grant to all or certain identified general partners the right to vote (on a per capita or any other basis), separately or with all or any class of the limited partners, on any matter.

## ARTICLE 5/FINANCE

### § 501
### Form of Contributions

The contribution of a partner may be in cash, property, or services rendered, or a promissory note or other obligation to contribute cash or property or to perform services.

### § 502
### Liability for Contributions

(a) Except as otherwise provided in the certificate of limited partnership, a partner is obligated to the limited partnership to perform any promise to contribute cash or property or to perform services even if he is unable to perform because of death, disability or any other reason. If a partner does not make the required contribution of property or services, he is obligated at the option of the limited partnership to contribute cash equal to that portion of the value (as stated in the certificate of limited partnership) of the stated contribution that has not been made.

**(b)** Unless otherwise provided in the partnership agreement, the obligation of a partner to make a contribution or return money or other property paid or distributed in violation of this Act may be compromised only by consent of all of the partners. Notwithstanding the compromise, a creditor of a limited partnership who extends credit, or whose claim arises, after the filing of the certificate of limited partnership or an amendment thereto which, in either case, reflects the obligation and before the amendment or cancellation thereof to reflect the compromise, may enforce the obligation.

### § 503
### Sharing of Profits and Losses

The profits and losses of a limited partnership shall be allocated among the partners, and among classes of partners, in the manner provided in the partnership agreement. If the partnership agreement does not so provide, profits and losses shall be allocated on the basis of the value (as stated in the certificate of limited partnership) of the contributions made by each partner to the extent they have been received by the partnership and have not been returned.

### § 504
### Sharing of Distributions

Distributions of cash or other assets of a limited partnership shall be allocated among the partners, and among classes of partners, in the manner provided in the partnership agreement. If the partnership agreement does not so provide, distributions shall be made on the basis of the value (as stated in the certificate of limited partnership) of the contributions made by each partner to the extent they have not been received by the partnership and have not been returned.

## ARTICLE 6/DISTRIBUTIONS AND WITHDRAWAL

### § 601
### Interim Distributions

Except as provided in this Article, a partner is entitled to receive distributions from a limited partnership before his withdrawal from the limited partnership and before the dissolution and winding up thereof:

**(1)** to the extent and at the times or upon the happening of the events specified in the partnership agreement; and

**(2)** if any distribution constitutes a return of any part of his contribution under Section 608(c), to the extent and at the times or upon the happening of the events specified in the certificate of limited partnership.

### § 602
### Withdrawal of General Partner

A general partner may withdraw from a limited partnership at any time by giving written notice to the other partners, but if the withdrawal violates the partnership agreement, the limited partnership may recover from the withdrawing general partner damages for breach of the partnership agreement and offset the damages against the amount otherwise distributable to him.

### § 603
### Withdrawal of Limited Partner

A limited partner may withdraw from a limited partnership at the time or upon the happening of the events specified in the certificate of limited partnership and in accordance with the partnership agreement. If the certificate does not specify the time or the events upon the happening of which a limited partner may withdraw or a definite time for the dissolution and winding up of the limited partnership, a limited partner may withdraw upon not less than 6 months' prior written notice to each general partner at his address on the books of the limited partnership at its office in this State.

### § 604
### Distribution Upon Withdrawal

Except as provided in this Article, upon withdrawal any withdrawing partner is entitled to receive any distribution to which he is entitled under the partnership agreement and, if not otherwise provided in the agreement, he is entitled to receive, within a reasonable time after withdrawal, the fair value of his interest in the limited partnership as of the date of withdrawal based upon his right to share in distributions from the limited partnership.

### § 605
### Distribution in Kind

Except as provided in the certificate of limited partnership, a partner, regardless of the nature of his contribution, has no right to demand and receive any distribution from a limited partnership in any form other than cash. Except as provided in the partnership agreement, a partner may not be compelled to accept a distribution of any asset in kind from a limited partnership to the extent that the percentage of the asset distributed to him exceeds a percentage of that asset which is equal to the percentage in which he shares in distributions from the limited partnership.

### § 606
### Right to Distribution

At the time a partner becomes entitled to receive a distribution, he has the status of, and is entitled to all remedies available to, a creditor of the limited partnership with respect to the distribution.

### § 607
### Limitations on Distribution

A partner may not receive a distribution from a limited partnership to the extent that, after giving effect to the distribution, all liabilities of the limited partnership, other than liabilities to partners on account of their partnership interests, exceed the fair value of the partnership assets.

### § 608
### Liability Upon Return of Contributions

**(a)** If a partner has received the return of any part of his contribution without violation of the partnership agreement or this Act, he is liable to the limited partnership for a period of one year thereafter for the amount of the returned contribution, but only to the extent necessary to discharge the limited partnership's liabilities to creditors who extended credit to the limited partnership during the period the contribution was held by the partnership.

**(b)** If a partner has received the return of any part of his contribution in violation of the partnership agreement or this Act, he is liable to the limited partnership for a period of 6 years thereafter for the amount of the contribution wrongfully returned.

**(c)** A partner receives a return of his contribution to the extent that a distribution to him reduces his share of the fair value of the net assets of the limited partnership below the value (as set forth in the certificate of limited partnership) of his contributions which has not been distributed to him.

## ARTICLE 7/ASSIGNMENT OF PARTNERSHIP INTERESTS

### § 701
**Nature of Partnership Interest**

A partnership interest is personal property.

### § 702
**Assignment of Partnership Interest**

Except as provided in the partnership agreement, a partnership interest is assignable in whole or in part. An assignment of a partnership interest does not dissolve a limited partnership or entitle the assignee to become or to exercise any rights of a partner. An assignment entitles the assignee to receive, to the extent assigned, only the distribution to which the assignor would be entitled. Except as provided in the partnership agreement, a partner ceases to be a partner upon assignment of all his partnership interest.

### § 703
**Rights of Creditor**

On application to a court of competent jurisdiction by any judgment creditor of a partner, the court may charge the partnership interest of the partner with payment of the unsatisfied amount of the judgment with interest. To the extent so charged, the judgment creditor has only the rights of an assignee of the partnership interest. This Act does not deprive any partner of the benefit of any exemption laws applicable to his partnership interest.

### § 704
**Right of Assignee to Become Limited Partner**

**(a)** An assignee of a partnership interest, including an assignee of a general partner, may become a limited partner if and to the extent that (1) the assignor gives the assignee that right in accordance with authority described in the certificate of limited partnership, or (2) all other partners consent.

**(b)** An assignee who has become a limited partner has, to the extent assigned, the rights and powers, and is subject to the restrictions and liabilities, of a limited partner under the partnership agreement and this Act. An assignee who becomes a limited partner also is liable for the obligations of his assignor to make and return contributions as provided in Article 6. However, the assignee is not obligated for liabilities unknown to the assignee at the time he became a limited partner and which could not be ascertained from the certificate of limited partnership.

**(c)** If an assignee of a partnership interest becomes a limited partner, the assignor is not released from his liability to the limited partnership under Sections 207 and 502.

### § 705
**Power of Estate of Deceased or Incompetent Partner**

If a partner who is an individual dies or a court of competent jurisdiction adjudges him to be incompetent to manage his person or his property, the partner's executor, administrator, guardian, conservator, or other legal representative may exercise all of the partner's rights for the purpose of settling his estate or administering his property, including any power the partner had to give an assignee the right to become a limited partner. If a partner is a corporation, trust, or other entity and is dissolved or terminated, the powers of that partner may be exercised by its legal representative or successor.

## ARTICLE 8/DISSOLUTION

### § 801
**Nonjudicial Dissolution**

A limited partnership is dissolved and its affairs shall be wound up upon the happening of the first to occur of the following:

**(1)** at the time or upon the happening of events specified in the certificate of limited partnership;

**(2)** written consent of all partners;

**(3)** an event of withdrawal of a general partner unless at the time there is at least one other general partner and the certificate of limited partnership permits the business of the limited partnership to be carried on by the remaining general partner and that partner does so, but the limited partnership is not dissolved and is not required to be wound up by reason of any event of withdrawal if, within 90 days after the withdrawal, all partners agree in writing to continue the business of the limited partnership and to the appointment of one or more additional general partners if necessary or desired; or

**(4)** entry of a decree of judicial dissolution under Section 802.

### § 802
**Judicial Dissolution**

On application by or for a partner the [here designate the proper court] court may decree a dissolution of a limited partnership whenever it is not reasonably practicable to carry on the business in conformity with the partnership agreement.

### § 803
**Winding Up**

Except as provided in the partnership agreement, the general partners who have not wrongfully dissolved a limited partnership or, if none, the limited partners, may wind up the limited partnership's affairs; but the [here designate the proper court] court may wind up the limited partnership's affairs upon application of any partner, his legal representative, or assignee.

### § 804
**Distribution of Assets**

Upon the winding up of a limited partnership, the assets shall be distributed as follows:

**(1)** to creditors, including partners who are creditors, to the extent otherwise permitted by law, in satisfaction of liabilities of the limited partnership other than liabilities for distributions to partners under Section 601 or 604:

**(2)** except as provided in the partnership agreement, to partners and former partners in satisfaction of liabilities for distributions under Section 601 or 604; and

**(3)** except as provided in the partnership agreement, to partners *first* for the return of their contributions and *secondly* respecting their partnership interests, in the proportions in which the partners share in distributions.

## ARTICLE 9/FOREIGN LIMITED PARTNERSHIPS

### § 901
### Law Governing

Subject to the Constitution of this State, (1) the laws of the state under which a foreign limited partnership is organized govern its organization and internal affairs and the liability of its limited partners, and (2) a foreign limited partnership may not be denied registration by reason of any difference between those laws and the laws of this State.

### § 902
### Registration

Before transacting business in this State, a foreign limited partnership shall register with the Secretary of State. In order to register, a foreign limited partnership shall submit to the Secretary of State, in duplicate, an application for registration as a foreign limited partnership, signed and sworn to by a general partner and setting forth:

**(1)** the name of the foreign limited partnership and, if different, the name under which it proposes to register and transact business in this State;

**(2)** the state and date of its formation;

**(3)** the general character of the business it proposes to transact in this State;

**(4)** the name and address of any agent for service of process on the foreign limited partnership whom the foreign limited partnership elects to appoint, the agent must be an individual resident of this State, a domestic corporation, or a foreign corporation having a place of business in, and authorized to do business in this State;

**(5)** a statement that the Secretary of State is appointed the agent of the foreign limited partnership for service of process if no agent has been appointed under paragraph (4) or, if appointed, the agent's authority has been revoked or if the agent cannot be found or served with the exercise of reasonable diligence;

**(6)** the address of the office required to be maintained in the State of its organization by the laws of that State or, if not so required, of the principal office of the foreign limited partnership; and

**(7)** If the certificate of limited partnership filed in the foreign limited partnership's state of organization is not required to include the names and business addresses of the partners, a list of the names and addresses.

### § 903
### Issuance of Registration

**(a)** If the Secretary of State finds that an application for registration conforms to law and all requisite fees have been paid, he shall:
  **(1)** endorse on the application the word "Filed," and the month, day, and year of the filing thereof;
  **(2)** file in his office a duplicate original of the application; and
  **(3)** issue a certificate of registration to transact business in this State.

**(b)** The certificate of registration, together with a duplicate original of the application, shall be returned to the person who filed the application or his representative.

### § 904
### Name

A foreign limited partnership may register with the Secretary of State under any name (whether or not it is the name under which it is registered in its state of organization) that includes without abbreviation the words "limited partnership" and that could be registered by a domestic limited partnership.

### § 905
### Changes and Amendments

If any statement in a foreign limited partnership's application for registration was false when made or any arrangements or other facts described have changed, making the application inaccurate in any respect, the foreign limited partnership shall promptly file in the office of the Secretary of State a certificate, signed and sworn to by a general partner, correcting the statement.

### § 906
### Cancellation of Registration

A foreign limited partnership may cancel its registration by filing with the Secretary of State a certificate of cancellation signed and sworn to by a general partner. A cancellation does not terminate the authority of the Secretary of State to accept service of process on the foreign limited partnership with respect to [claims for relief] [causes of action] arising out of the transaction of business in this State.

### § 907
### Transaction of Business Without Registration

**(a)** A foreign limited partnership transacting business in this State may not maintain any action, suit, or proceeding in any court of this State until it has registered in this State.

**(b)** The failure of a foreign limited partnership to register in this State does not impair the validity of any contract or act of the foreign limited partnership or prevent the foreign limited partnership from defending any action, suit, or proceeding in any court of this State.

**(c)** A limited partner of a foreign limited partnership is not liable as a general partner of the foreign limited partnership solely by reason of having transacted business in this State without registration.

**(d)** A foreign limited partnership, by transacting business in this State without registration, appoints the Secretary of State as its agent for service of process with respect to [claims for relief] [causes of action] arising out of the transaction of business in this State.

### § 908
### Action by [Appropriate Official]

The [appropriate official] may bring an action to restrain a foreign limited partnership from transacting business in this State in violation of this Article.

## ARTICLE 10/DERIVATIVE ACTIONS

### § 1001
### Right of Action

A limited partner may bring an action in the right of a limited partnership to recover a judgment in its favor if general partners with authority to do so have refused to bring the action or if an effort to cause those general partners to bring the action is not likely to succeed.

### § 1002
### Proper Plaintiff

In a derivative action, the plaintiff must be a partner at the time of bringing the action and (1) at the time of the transaction of which he complains or (2) his status as a partner had devolved upon him by operation of law or pursuant to the terms of the partnership agreement from a person who was a partner at the time of the transaction.

### § 1003
### Pleading

In any derivative action, the complaint shall set forth with particularity the effort of the plaintiff to secure initiation of the action by a general partner or the reasons for not making the effort.

### § 1004
### Expenses

If a derivative action is successful, in whole or in part, or if anything is received by the plaintiff as a result of a judgment, compromise, or settlement of an action or claim, the court may award the plaintiff reasonable expenses, including reasonable attorney's fees, and shall direct him to remit to the limited partnership the remainder of those proceeds received by him.

## ARTICLE 11/MISCELLANEOUS

### § 1101
### Construction and Application

This Act shall be so applied and construed to effectuate its general purpose to make uniform the law with respect to the subject of this Act among states enacting it.

### § 1102
### Short Title

This Act may be cited as the Uniform Limited Partnership Act.

### § 1103
### Severability

If any provision of this Act or its application to any person or circumstance is held invalid, the invalidity does not affect other provisions or applications of the Act which can be given effect without the invalid provision or application, and to this end the provisions of this Act are severable.

### § 1104
### Effective Date, Extended Effective Date and Repeal

Except as set forth below, the effective date of this Act is _____ and the following Acts [list prior limited partnership acts] are hereby repealed:

(1) The existing provisions for execution and filing of certificates of limited partnerships and amendments thereunder and cancellations thereof continue in effect until [specify time required to create central filing system], the extended effective date, and Sections 102, 103, 104, 105, 201, 202, 203, 204 and 206 are not effective until the extended effective date.

(2) Section 402, specifying the conditions under which a general partner ceases to be a member of a limited partnership, is not effective until the extended effective date, and the applicable provisions of existing law continue to govern until the extended effective date.

(3) Sections 501, 502 and 608 apply only to contributions and distributions made after the effective date of this Act.

(4) Section 704 applies only to assignments made after the effective date of this Act.

(5) Article 9, dealing with registration of foreign limited partnerships, is not effective until the extended effective date.

### § 1105
### Rules for Cases Not Provided for in This Act

In any case not provided for in this Act the provisions of the Uniform Partnership Act govern.

# APPENDIX E

# THE MODEL BUSINESS CORPORATION ACT

## § 1
### Short Title

This Act shall be known and may be cited as the "............*Business Corporation Act."

## § 2
### Definitions

As used in this Act, unless the context otherwise requires, the term:

**(a)** "Corporation" or "domestic corporation" means a corporation for profit subject to the provisions of this Act, except a foreign corporation.

**(b)** "Foreign corporation" means a corporation for profit organized under laws other than the laws of this State for a purpose or purposes for which a corporation may be organized under this Act.

**(c)** "Articles of incorporation" means the original or restated articles of incorporation or articles of consolidation and all amendments thereto including articles of merger.

**(d)** "Shares" means the units into which the proprietary interests in a corporation are divided.

**(e)** "Subscriber" means one who subscribes for shares in a corporation, whether before or after incorporation.

**(f)** "Shareholder" means one who is a holder of record of shares in a corporation. If the articles of incorporation or the by-laws so provide, the board of directors may adopt by resolution a procedure whereby a shareholder of the corporation may certify in writing to the corporation that all or a portion of the shares registered in the name of such shareholder are held for the account of a specified person or persons. The resolution shall set forth (1) the classification of shareholder who may certify, (2) the purpose or purposes for which the certification may be made, (3) the form of certification and information to be contained therein, (4) if the certification is with respect to a record date or closing of the stock transfer books within which the certification must be received by the corporation and (5) such other provisions with respect to the procedure as are deemed necessary or desirable. Upon receipt by the corporation of a certification complying with the procedure, the persons specified in the certification shall be deemed, for the purpose or purposes set forth in the certification, to be the holders of record of the number of shares specified in place of the shareholder making the certification.

*Insert name of State.

**(g)** "Authorized shares" means the shares of all classes which the corporation is authorized to issue.

**(h)** "Employee" includes officers but not directors. A director may accept duties which make him also an employee.

**(i)** "Distribution" means a direct or indirect transfer of money or other property (except its own shares) or incurrence of indebtedness, by a corporation to or for the benefit of any of its shareholders in respect of any of its shares, whether by dividend or by purchase, redemption or other acquisition of its shares, or otherwise.

## § 3
### Purposes

Corporations may be organized under this Act for any lawful purpose or purposes, except for the purpose of banking or insurance.

## § 4
### General Powers

Each corporation shall have power:

**(a)** To have perpetual succession by its corporate name unless a limited period of duration is stated in its articles of incorporation.

**(b)** To sue and be sued, complain and defend, in its corporate name.

**(c)** To have a corporate seal which may be altered at pleasure, and to use the same by causing it, or a facsimile thereof, to be impressed or affixed or in any other manner reproduced.

**(d)** To purchase, take, receive, lease, or otherwise acquire, own, hold, improve, use and otherwise deal in and with, real or personal property, or any interest therein wherever situated.

**(e)** To sell, convey, mortgage, pledge, lease, exchange, tranfer and otherwise dispose of all or any part of its property and assets.

**(f)** To lend money and use its credit to assist its employees.

**(g)** To purchase, take, receive, subscribe for, or otherwise acquire, own, hold, vote, use, employ, sell, mortgage, lend, pledge, or otherwise dispose of, and otherwise use and deal in and with, shares or other interests in, or obligations of, other domestic or foreign corporations, associations, partnerships or individuals, or direct or indirect obligations of the United States or of any other government, state, territory, governmental district or municipality or of any instrumentality thereof.

**(h)** To make contracts and guarantees and incur liabilities, borrow money at such rates of interest as the corporation may determine, issue its notes, bonds, and other obligations, and secure any of its obligations by mortgage or pledge of all or any of its property, franchises and income.

**(i)** To lend money for its corporate purposes, invest and reinvest its funds, and take and hold real and personal property as security for the payment of funds so loaned or invested.

**(j)** To conduct its business, carry on its operations and have offices and exercise the powers granted by this Act, within or without this State.

**(k)** To elect or appoint officers and agents of the corporation, and define their duties and fix their compensation.

**(l)** To make and alter by-laws, not inconsistent with its articles of incorporation or with the laws of this State, for the administration and regulation of the affairs of the corporation.

**(m)** To make donations for the public welfare or for charitable, scientific or educational purposes.

**(n)** To transact any lawful business which the board of directors shall find will be in aid of governmental policy.

**(o)** To pay pensions and establish pension plans, pension trusts, profit sharing plans, stock bonus plans, stock option plans and other incentive plans for any or all of its directors, officers and employees.

**(p)** To be a promoter, partner, member, associate, or manager of any partnership, joint venture, trust or other enterprise.

**(q)** To have and exercise all powers necessary or convenient to effect its purposes.

## § 5
### Indemnification of Directors and Officers

**(a)** As used in this section:

**(1)** "Director" means any person who is or was a director of the corporation and any person who, while a director of the corporation, is or was serving at the request of the corporation as a director, officer, partner, trustee, employee or agent of another foreign or domestic corporation, partnership, joint venture, trust, other enterprise or employee benefit plan.

**(2)** "Corporation" includes any domestic or foreign predecessor entity of the corporation in a merger, consolidation or other transaction in which the predecessor's existence ceased upon consummation of such transaction.

**(3)** "Expenses" include attorneys' fees.

**(4)** "Official capacity" means

(A) when used with respect to a director, the office of director in the corporation, and

(B) when used with respect to a person other than a director, as contemplated in subsection (i), the elective or appointive office in the corporation held by the officer or the employment or agency relationship undertaken by the employee or agent in behalf of the corporation.

but in each case does not include service for any other foreign or domestic corporation or any partnership, joint venture, trust, other enterprise, or employee benefit plan.

**(5)** "Party" includes a person who was, is, or is threatened to be made, a named defendant or respondent in a proceeding.

**(6)** "Proceeding" means any threatened, pending or completed action, suit or proceeding, whether civil, criminal, administrative or investigative.

**(b)** A corporation shall have power to indemnify any person made a party to any proceeding by reason of the fact that he is or was a director if

**(1)** he conducted himself in good faith; and

**(2)** he reasonably believed

(A) in the case of conduct in his official capacity with the corporation, that his conduct was in its best interests, and

(B) in all other cases, that his conduct was at least not opposed to its best interests; and

**(3)** in the case of any criminal proceeding, he had no reasonable cause to believe his conduct was unlawful.

Indemnification may be made against judgments, penalties, fines, settlements and reasonable expenses, actually incurred by the person in connection with the proceeding; except that if the proceeding was by or in the right of the corporation, indemnification may be made only against such reasonable expenses and shall not be made in respect of any proceeding in which the person shall have been adjudged to be liable to the corporation. The termination of any proceeding by judgment, order, settlement, conviction, or upon a plea of nolo contendere or its equivalent, shall not, of itself, be determinative that the person did not meet the requisite standard of conduct set forth in this subsection (b).

**(c)** A director shall not be indemnified under subsection (b) in respect of any proceeding charging improper personal benefit to him, whether or not involving action in his official capacity, in which he shall have been adjudged to be liable on the basis that personal benefit was improperly received by him.

**(d)** Unless limited by the articles of incorporation,

**(1)** a director who has been wholly successful, on the merits or otherwise, in the defense of any proceeding referred to in subsection (b) shall be indemnified against reasonable expenses incurred by him in connection with the proceeding; and

**(2)** a court of appropriate jurisdiction, upon application of a director and such notice as the court shall require, shall have authority to order indemnification in the following circumstances:

(A) if it determines a director is entitled to reimbursement under clause (1), the court shall order indemnification, in which case the director shall also be entitled to recover the expenses of securing such reimbursement; or

(B) if it determines that the director is fairly and reasonably entitled to indemnification in view of all the relevant circumstances, whether or not he has met the standard of conduct set forth in subsection (b) or has been adjudged liable in the circumstances described in subsection (c), the court may order such indemnification as the court shall deem proper, except that indemnification with respect to any proceeding by or in the right of the corporation or in which liability shall have been adjudged in the circumstances described in subsection (c) shall be limited to expenses.

A court of appropriate jurisdiction may be the same court in which the proceeding involving the director's liability took place.

**(e)** No indemnification under subsection (b) shall be made by the corporation unless authorized in the specific case after a determination has been made that indemnification of the director is permissible in the circumstances because he has met the standard of conduct set forth in subsection (b). Such determination shall be made:

(1) by the board of directors by a majority vote of a quorum consisting of directors not at the time parties to the proceeding; or

(2) if such a quorum cannot be obtained, then by a majority vote of a committee of the board, duly designated to act in the matter by a majority vote of the full board (in which designation directors who are parties may participate), consisting solely of two or more directors not at the time parties to the proceeding; or

(3) by special legal counsel, selected by the board of directors or a committee thereof by vote as set forth in clauses (1) or (2) of this subsection (e), or, if the requisite quorum of the full board cannot be obtained therefor and such committee cannot be established, by a majority vote of the full board (in which selection directors who are parties may participate); or

(4) by the shareholders.

Authorization of indemnification and determination as to reasonableness of expenses shall be made in the same manner as the determination that indemnification is permissible, except that if the determination that indemnification is permissible is made by special legal counsel, authorization of indemnification and determination as to reasonableness of expenses shall be made in a manner specified in clause (3) in the preceding sentence for the selection of such counsel. Shares held by directors who are parties to the proceeding shall not be voted on the subject matter under this subsection (e).

(f) Reasonable expenses incurred by a director who is a party to a proceeding may be paid or reimbursed by the corporation in advance of the final disposition of such proceeding upon receipt by the corporation of

(1) a written affirmation by the director of his good faith belief that he has met the standard of conduct necessary for indemnification by the corporation as authorized in this section, and

(2) a written undertaking by or on behalf of the director to repay such amount if it shall ultimately be determined that he has not met such standard of conduct, and after a determination that the facts then known to those making the determination would not preclude indemnification under this section. The undertaking required by clause (2) shall be an unlimited general obligation of the director but need not be secured and may be accepted without reference to financial ability to make repayment. Determinations and authorizations of payments under this subsection (f) shall be made in the manner specified in subsection (e).

(g) No provision for the corporation to indemnify or to advance expenses to a director who is made a party to a proceeding, whether contained in the articles of incorporation, the by-laws, a resolution of shareholders or directors, an agreement or otherwise (except as contemplated by subsection (j)), shall be valid unless consistent with this section or, to the extent that indemnity hereunder is limited by the articles of incorporation, consistent therewith. Nothing contained in this section shall limit the corporation's power to pay or reimburse expenses incurred by a director in connection with his appearance as a witness in a proceeding at a time when he has not been made a named defendant or respondent in the proceeding.

(h) For purposes of this section, the corporation shall be deemed to have requested a director to serve an employee benefit plan whenever the performance by him of his duties to the corporation also imposes duties on, or otherwise involves services by, him to the plan or participants or beneficiaries of the plan; excise taxes assessed on a director with respect to an employee benefit plan pursuant to applicable law shall be deemed "fines"; and action taken or omitted by him with respect to an employee benefit plan in the performance of his duties for a purpose reasonably believed by him to be in the interest of the participants and beneficiaries of the plan shall be deemed to be for a purpose which is not opposed to the best interests of the corporation.

(i) Unless limited by the articles of incorporation,

(1) an officer of the corporation shall be indemnified as and to the same extent provided in subsection (d) for a director and shall be entitled to the same extent as a director to seek indemnification pursuant to the provisions of subsection (d);

(2) a corporation shall have the power to indemnify and to advance expenses to an officer, employee or agent of the corporation to the same extent that it may indemnify and advance expenses to directors pursuant to this section; and

(3) a corporation, in addition, shall have the power to indemnify and to advance expenses to an officer, employee or agent who is not a director to such further extent, consistent with law, as may be provided by its articles of incorporation, by-laws, general or specific action of its board of directors, or contract.

(j) A corporation shall have power to purchase and maintain insurance on behalf of any person who is or was a director, officer, employee or agent of the corporation, or who, while a director, officer, employee or agent of the corporation, is or was serving at the request of the corporation as a director, officer, partner, trustee, employee or agent of another foreign or domestic corporation, partnership, joint venture, trust, other enterprise or employee benefit plan, against any liability asserted against him and incurred by him in any such capacity or arising out of his status as such, whether or not the corporation would have the power to indemnify him against such liability under the provisions of this section.

(k) Any indemnification of, or advance of expenses to, a director in accordance with this section, if arising out of a proceeding by or in the right of the corporation, shall be reported in writing to the shareholders with or before the notice of the next shareholders' meeting.

## § 6
**Power of Corporation to Acquire Its Own Shares**

A corporation shall have the power to acquire its own shares. All of its own shares acquired by a corporation shall, upon acquisition, constitute authorized but unissued shares, unless the articles of incorporation provide that they shall not be reissued, in which case the authorized shares shall be reduced by the number of shares acquired.

If the number of authorized shares is reduced by an acquisition, the corporation shall, not later than the time it files its next annual report under this Act with the Secretary of State, file a statement of cancellation showing the reduction in the authorized shares. The statement of cancellation shall be executed in duplicate by the corporation by its president or a vice president and by its secretary or an assistant secretary, and verified by one of the officers signing such statement, and shall set forth:

(a) The name of the corporation.

(b) The number of acquired shares cancelled, itemized by classes and series.

(c) The aggregate number of authorized shares, itemized by classes and series, after giving effect to such cancellation.

Duplicate originals of such statement shall be delivered to the Secretary of State. If the Secretary of State finds that such statement conforms to law, he shall, when all fees and franchise taxes have been paid as in this Act prescribed:

(1) Endorse on each of such duplicate originals the word "Filed," and the month, day, and year of the filing thereof.

(2) File one of such duplicate originals in his office.

(3) Return the other duplicate original to the corporation or its representative.

## § 7
### Defense of Ultra Vires

No act of a corporation and no conveyance or transfer of real or personal property to or by a corporation shall be invalid by reason of the fact that the corporation was without capacity or power to do such act or to make or receive such conveyance or transfer, but such lack of capacity or power may be asserted:

(a) In a proceeding by a shareholder against the corporation to enjoin the doing of any act or the transfer of real or personal property by or to the corporation. If the unauthorized act or transfer sought to be enjoined is being, or is to be, performed or made pursuant to a contract to which the corporation is a party, the court may, if all of the parties to the contract are parties to the proceeding and if it deems the same to be equitable, set aside and enjoin the performance of such contract, and in so doing may allow to the corporation or to the other parties to the contract, as the case may be, compensation for the loss or damage sustained by either of them which may result from the action of the court in setting aside and enjoining the performance of such contract, but anticipated profits to be derived from the performance of the contract shall not be awarded by the court as a loss or damage sustained.

(b) In a proceeding by the corporation, whether acting directly or through a receiver, trustee, or other legal representative, or through shareholders in a representative suit, against the incumbent or former officers or directors of the corporation.

(c) In a proceeding by the Attorney General, as provided in this Act, to dissolve the corporation, or in a proceeding by the Attorney General to enjoin the corporation from the transaction of unauthorized business.

## § 8
### Corporate Name

The corporate name:

(a) Shall contain the word "corporation," "company," "incorporated" or "limited," or shall contain an abbreviation of one of such words.

(b) Shall not contain any word or phrase which indicates or implies that it is organized for any purpose other than one or more of the purposes contained in its articles of incorporation.

(c) Shall not be the same as, or deceptively similar to, the name of any domestic corporation existing under the laws of this State or any foreign corporation authorized to transact business in this State, or a name the exclusive right to which is, at the time, reserved in the manner provided in this Act, or the name of a corporation which has in effect a registration of its corporate name as provided in this Act, except that this provision shall not apply if the applicant files with the Secretary of State either of the following: (1) the written consent of such other corporation or holder of a reserved or registered name to use the same or deceptively similar name and one or more words are added to make such name distinguishable from such other name, or (2) a certified copy of a final decree of a court of competent jurisdiction establishing the prior right of the applicant to the use of such name in this State.

A corporation with which another corporation, domestic or foreign, is merged, or which is formed by the reorganization or consolidation of one or more domestic or foreign corporations or upon a sale, lease or other disposition to or exchange with, a domestic corporation of all or substantially all the assets of another corporation, domestic or foreign, including its name, may have the same name as that used in this State by any of such corporations if such other corporation was organized under the laws of, or is authorized to transact business in, this State.

## § 9
### Reserved Name

The exclusive right to the use of a corporate name may be reserved by:

(a) Any person intending to organize a corporation under this Act.

(b) Any domestic corporation intending to change its name.

(c) Any foreign corporation intending to make application for a certificate of authority to transact business in this State.

(d) Any foreign corporation authorized to transact business in this State and intending to change its name.

(e) Any person intending to organize a foreign corporation and intending to have such corporation make application for a certificate of authority to transact business in this State.

The reservation shall be made by filing with the Secretary of State an application to reserve a specified corporate name, executed by the applicant. If the Secretary of State finds that the name is available for corporate use, he shall reserve the same for the exclusive use of the applicant for a period of one hundred and twenty days.

The right to the exclusive use of a specified corporate name so reserved may be transferred to any other person or corporation by filing in the office of the Secretary of State a notice of such transfer, executed by the applicant for whom the name was reserved, and specifying the name and address of the transferee.

## § 10
### Registered Name

Any corporation organized and existing under the laws of any state or territory of the United States may register its corporate name under this Act, provided its corporate name is not the same as, or deceptively similar to, the name of any domestic corporation existing under the laws of this State, or the name of any foreign corporation authorized to transact business in this State, or any corporate name reserved or registered under this Act.

Such registration shall be made by:

**(a)** Filing with the Secretary of State (1) an application for registration executed by the corporation by an officer thereof, setting forth the name of the corporation, the state or territory under the laws of which it is incorporated, the date of its incorporation, a statement that it is carrying on or doing business, and a brief statement of the business in which it is engaged, and (2) a certificate setting forth that such corporation is in good standing under the laws of the state or territory wherein it is organized, executed by the Secretary of State of such state or territory or by such other official as may have custody of the records pertaining to corporations, and

**(b)** Paying to the Secretary of State a registration fee in the amount of . . . . . . . . . . . for each month, or fraction thereof, between the date of filing such application and December 31st of the calendar year in which such application is filed.

Such registration shall be effective until the close of the calendar year in which the application for registration is filed.

## § 11
### Renewal of Registered Name

A corporation which has in effect a registration of its corporate name, may renew such registration from year to year by annually filing an application for renewal setting forth the facts required to be set forth in an original application for registration and a certificate of good standing as required for the original registration and by paying a fee of . . . . . . . . . . . A renewal application may be filed between the first day of October and the thirty-first day of December in each year, and shall extend the registration for the following calendar year.

## § 12
### Registered Office and Registered Agent

Each corporation shall have and continuously maintain in this State:

**(a)** A registered office which may be, but need not be, the same as its place of business.

**(b)** A registered agent, which agent may be either an individual resident in this State whose business office is identical with such registered office, or a domestic corporation, or a foreign corporation authorized to transact business in this State, having a business office identical with such registered office.

## § 13
### Change of Registered Office or Registered Agent

A corporation may change its registered office or change its registered agent, or both, upon filing in the office of the Secretary of State a statement setting forth:

**(a)** The name of the corporation.

**(b)** The address of its then registered office.

**(c)** If the address of its registered office is to be changed, the address to which the registered office is to be changed.

**(d)** The name of its then registered agent.

**(e)** If its registered agent is to be changed, the name of its successor registered agent.

**(f)** That the address of its registered office and the address of the business office of its registered agent, as changed, will be identical.

**(g)** That such change was authorized by resolution duly adopted by its board of directors.

Such statement shall be executed by the corporation by its president, or a vice president, and verified by him, and delivered to the Secretary of State. If the Secretary of State finds that such statement conforms to the provisions of this Act, he shall file such statement in his office, and upon such filing the change of address of the registered office, or the appointment of a new registered agent, or both, as the case may be, shall become effective.

Any registered agent of a corporation may resign as such agent upon filing a written notice thereof, executed in duplicate, with the Secretary of State, who shall forthwith mail a copy thereof to the corporation at its registered office. The appointment of such agent shall terminate upon the expiration of thirty days after receipt of such notice by the Secretary of State.

If a registered agent changes his or its business address to another place within the same . . . . . . . . . . . ,* he or it may change such address and the address of the registered office of any corporation of which he or it is registered agent by filing a statement as required above except that it need be signed only by the registered agent and need not be responsive to (e) or (g) and must recite that a copy of the statement has been mailed to the corporation.

## § 14
### Service of Process on Corporation

The registered agent so appointed by a corporation shall be an agent of such corporation upon whom any process, notice or demand required or permitted by law to be served upon the corporation may be served.

Whenever a corporation shall fail to appoint or maintain a registered agent in this State, or whenever its registered agent cannot with reasonable diligence be found at the registered office, then the Secretary of State shall be an agent of such corporation upon whom any such process, notice, or demand may be served. Service on the Secretary of State of any such process, notice, or demand shall be made by delivering to and leaving with him, or with any clerk having charge of the corporation department of his office, duplicate copies of such process, notice or demand. In the event any such process, notice or demand is served on the Secretary of State, he shall immediately cause one of the copies thereof to be forwarded by registered mail, addressed to the corporation at its registered office. Any service so had on the Secretary of State shall be returnable in not less than thirty days.

The Secretary of State shall keep a record of all processes, notices and demands served upon him under this section, and shall record therein the time of such service and his action with reference thereto.

Nothing herein contained shall limit or affect the right to serve any process, notice or demand required or permitted by law to be served upon a corporation in any other manner now or hereafter permitted by law.

## § 15
### Authorized Shares

Each corporation shall have power to create and issue the number of shares stated in its articles of incorporation. Such shares may be

---

*Supply designation of jurisdiction, such as country, etc., in accordance with local practice.

divided into one or more classes with such designations, preferences, limitations, and relative rights as shall be stated in the articles of incorporation. The articles of incorporation may limit or deny the voting rights of or provide special voting rights for the shares of any class to the extent not inconsistent with the provisions of this Act.

Without limiting the authority herein contained, a corporation, when so provided in its articles of incorporation, may issue shares of preferred or special classes:

**(a)** Subject to the right of the corporation to redeem any of such shares at the price fixed by the articles of incorporation for the redemption thereof.

**(b)** Entitling the holders thereof to cumulative, noncumulative or partially cumulative dividends.

**(c)** Having preference over any other class or classes of shares as to the payment of dividends.

**(d)** Having preference in the assets of the corporation over any other class or classes of shares upon the voluntary or involuntary liquidation of the corporation.

**(e)** Convertible into shares of any other class or into shares of any series of the same or any other class, except a class having prior or superior rights and preferences as to dividends or distribution of assets upon liquidation.

## § 16
**Issuance of Shares of Preferred or Special Classes in Series**

If the articles of incorporation so provide, the shares of any preferred or special class may be divided into and issued in series. If the shares of any such class are to be issued in series, then each series shall be so designated as to distinguish the shares thereof from the shares of all other series and classes. Any or all of the series of any such class and the variations in the relative rights and preferences as between different series may be fixed and determined by the articles of incorporation, but all shares of the same class shall be identical except as to the following relative rights and preferences, as to which there may be variations between different series:

**(a)** The rate of dividend.

**(b)** Whether shares may be redeemed and, if so, the redemption price and the terms and conditions of redemption.

**(c)** The amount payable upon shares in the event of voluntary and involuntary liquidation.

**(d)** Sinking fund provisions, if any, for the redemption or purchase of shares.

**(e)** The terms and conditions, if any, on which shares may be converted.

**(f)** Voting rights, if any.

If the articles of incorporation shall expressly vest authority in the board of directors, then, to the extent that the articles of incorporation shall not have established series and fixed and determined the variations in the relative rights and preferences as between series, the board of directors shall have authority to divide any or all of such classes into series and, within the limitations set forth in this section and in the articles of incorporation, fix and determine the relative rights and preferences of the shares of any series so established.

In order for the board of directors to establish a series, where authority so to do is contained in the articles of incorporation, the board of directors shall adopt a resolution setting forth the designation of the series and fixing and determining the relative rights and preferences thereof, or so much thereof as shall not be fixed and determined by the articles of incorporation.

Prior to the issue of any shares of a series established by resolution adopted by the board of directors, the corporation shall file in the office of the Secretary of State a statement setting forth:

**(1)** The name of the corporation.

**(2)** A copy of the resolution establishing and designating the series, and fixing and determining the relative rights and preferences thereof.

**(3)** The date of adoption of such resolution.

**(4)** That such resolution was duly adopted by the board of directors.

Such statement shall be executed in duplicate by the corporation by its president or a vice president and by its secretary or an assistant secretary, and verified by one of the officers signing such statement, and shall be delivered to the Secretary of State. If the Secretary of State finds that such statement conforms to law, he shall, when all franchise taxes and fees have been paid as in this Act prescribed:

**(A)** Endorse on each of such duplicate originals the word "Filed," and the month, day, and year of the filing thereof.

**(B)** File one of such duplicate originals in his office.

**(C)** Return the other duplicate original to the corporation or its representative.

Upon the filing of such statement by the Secretary of State, the resolution establishing and designating the series and fixing and determining the relative rights and preferences thereof shall become effective and shall constitute an amendment of the articles of incorporation.

## § 17
**Subscriptions for Shares**

A subscription for shares of a corporation to be organized shall be irrevocable for a period of six months, unless otherwise provided by the terms of the subscription agreement or unless all of the subscribers consent to the revocation of such subscription.

Unless otherwise provided in the subscription agreement, subscriptions for shares, whether made before or after the organization of a corporation, shall be paid in full at such time, or in such installments and at such times, as shall be determined by the board of directors. Any call made by the board of directors for payment on subscriptions shall be uniform as to all shares of the same class or as to all shares of the same series, as the case may be. In case of default in the payment of any installment or call when such payment is due, the corporation may proceed to collect the amount due in the same manner as any debt due the corporation. The bylaws may prescribe other penalties for failure to pay installments or calls that may become due, but no penalty working a forfeiture of a subscription, or of the amounts paid thereon, shall be declared as against any subscriber unless the amount due thereon shall remain unpaid for a period of twenty days after written demand has been made therefor. If mailed, such written demand shall be deemed to be made when deposited in the United States mail in a sealed envelope addressed to the subscriber at his last post-office address known to the corporation, with postage thereon prepaid.

In the event of the sale of any shares by reason of any forfeiture, the excess of proceeds realized over the amount due and unpaid on such shares shall be paid to the delinquent subscriber or to his legal representative.

## § 18
### Issuance of Shares

Subject to any restrictions in the articles of incorporation:

**(a)** Shares may be issued for such consideration as shall be authorized by the board of directors establishing a price (in money or other consideration) or a minimum price or general formula or method by which the price will be determined; and

**(b)** Upon authorization by the board of directors, the corporation may issue its own shares in exchange for or in conversion of its outstanding shares, or distribute its own shares, pro rata to its shareholders or the shareholders of one or more classes or series, to effectuate stock dividends or splits, and any such transaction shall not require consideration; provided, that no such issuance of shares of any class or series shall be made to the holders of shares of any other class or series unless it is either expressly provided for in the articles of incorporation, or is authorized by an affirmative vote or the written consent of the holders of at least a majority of the outstanding shares of the class or series in which the distribution is to be made.

## § 19
### Payment for Shares

The consideration for the issuance of shares may be paid, in whole or in part, in money, in other property, tangible or intangible, or in labor or services actually performed for the corporation. When payment of the consideration for which shares are to be issued shall have been received by the corporation, such shares shall be nonassessable.

Neither promissory notes nor future services shall constitute payment or part payment for the issuance of shares of a corporation.

In the absence of fraud in the transaction, the judgment of the board of directors or the shareholders, as the case may be, as to the value of the consideration received for shares shall be conclusive.

## § 20
### Stock Rights and Options

Subject to any provisions in respect thereof set forth in its articles of incorporation, a corporation may create and issue, whether or not in connection with the issuance and sale of any of its shares or other securities, rights or options entitling the holders thereof to purchase from the corporation shares of any class or classes. Such rights or options shall be evidenced in such manner as the board of directors shall approve and, subject to the provisions of the articles of incorporation, shall set forth the terms upon which, the time or times within which and the price or prices at which such shares may be purchased from the corporation upon the exercise of any such right or option. If such rights or options are to be issued to directors, officers or employees as such of the corporation or of any subsidiary thereof, and not to the shareholders generally, their issuance shall be approved by the affirmative vote of the holders of a majority of the shares entitled to vote thereon or shall be authorized by and consistent with a plan approved or ratified by such a vote of shareholders. In the absence of fraud in the transaction, the judgment of the board of directors as to the adequacy of the consideration received for such rights or options shall be conclusive.

## § 21
### Determination of Amount of Stated Capital

[Repealed in 1979.]

## § 22
### Expenses of Organization, Reorganization and Financing

The reasonable charges and expenses of organization or reorganization of a corporation, and the reasonable expenses of and compensation for the sale or underwriting of its shares, may be paid or allowed by such corporation out of the consideration received by it in payment for its shares without thereby rendering such shares assessable.

## § 23
### Shares Represented by Certificates and Uncertified Shares

The shares of a corporation shall be represented by certificates or shall be uncertificated shares. Certificates shall be signed by the chairman or vice-chairman of the board of directors or the president or a vice president and by the treasurer or an assistant treasurer or the secretary or an assistant secretary of the corporation, and may be sealed with the seal of the corporation or a facsimile thereof. Any of or all the signatures upon a certificate may be a facsimile. In case any officer, transfer agent or registrar who has signed or whose facsimile signature has been placed upon such certificate shall have ceased to be such officer, transfer agent or registrar before such certificate is issued, it may be issued by the corporation with the same effect as if he were such officer, transfer agent or registrar at the date of its issue.

Every certificate representing shares issued by a corporation which is authorized to issue shares of more than one class shall set forth upon the face or back of the certificate, or shall state that the corporation will furnish to any shareholder upon request and without charge, a full statement of the designations, preferences, limitations, and relative rights of the shares of each class authorized to be issued, and if the corporation is authorized to issue any preferred or special class in series, the variations in the relative rights and preferences between the shares of each such series so far as the same have been fixed and determined and the authority of the board of directors to fix and determine the relative rights and preferences of subsequent series.

Each certificate representing shares shall state upon the face thereof:

**(a)** That the corporation is organized under the laws of this State.

**(b)** The name of the person to whom issued.

**(c)** The number and class of shares, and the designation of the series, if any, which such certificate represents.

**(d)** The par value of each share represented by such certificate, or a statement that the shares are without par value.

No certificate shall be issued for any share until such share is fully paid.

Unless otherwise provided by the articles of incorporation or by-laws, the board of directors of a corporation may provide by resolution that some or all of any or all classes and series of its shares shall be uncertificated shares, provided that such resolution shall not apply to shares represented by a certificate until such certificate is surrendered to the corporation. Within a reasonable time after the issuance or transfer of uncertificated shares, the corporation shall send to the registered owner thereof a written notice containing the information required to be set forth or stated on certificates pursuant to the second and third paragraphs of this section. Except as otherwise expressly provided by law, the rights and obligations of the holders of uncertificated shares and the rights and obligations of the holders of certificates representing shares of the same class and series shall be identical.

## § 24
### Fractional Shares

A corporation may (1) issue fractions of a share, either represented by a certificate or uncertificated, (2) arrange for the disposition of fractional interests by those entitled thereto, (3) pay in money the fair value of fractions of a share as of a time when those entitled to receive such fractions are determined, or (4) issue scrip in registered or bearer form which shall entitle the holder to receive a certificate for a full share or an uncertificated full share upon the surrender of such scrip aggregating a full share. A certificate for a fractional share or an uncertificated fractional share shall, but scrip shall not unless otherwise provided therein, entitle the holder to exercise voting rights, to receive dividends thereon, and to participate in any of the assets of the corporation in the event of liquidation. The board of directors may cause scrip to be issued subject to the condition that it shall become void if not exchanged for certificates representing full shares or uncertificated full shares before a specified date, or subject to the condition that the shares for which scrip is exchangeable may be sold by the corporation and the proceeds thereof distributed to the holders of scrip, or subject to any other conditions which the board of directors may deem advisable.

## § 25
### Liability of Subscribers and Shareholders

A holder of or subscriber to shares of a corporation shall be under no obligation to the corporation or its creditors with respect to such shares other than the obligation to pay to the corporation the full consideration for which such shares were issued or to be issued.

Any person becoming an assignee or transferee of shares or of a subscription for shares in good faith and without knowledge or notice that the full consideration therefor has not been paid shall not be personally liable to the corporation or its creditors for any unpaid portion of such consideration.

An executor, administrator, conservator, guardian, trustee, assignee for the benefit of creditors, or receiver shall not be personally liable to the corporation as a holder of or subscriber to shares of a corporation but the estate and funds in his hands shall be so liable.

No pledgee or other holder of shares as collateral security shall be personally liable as a shareholder.

## § 26
### Shareholders' Preemptive Rights

The shareholders of a corporation shall have no preemptive right to acquire unissued shares of the corporation, or securities of the corporation convertible into or carrying a right to subscribe to or acquire shares, except to the extent, if any, that such right is provided in the articles of incorporation.

## § 26A
### Shareholders' Preemptive Rights [Alternative]

Except to the extent limited or denied by this section or by the articles of incorporation, shareholders shall have a preemptive right to acquire unissued shares or securities convertible into such shares or carrying a right to subscribe to or acquire shares.

Unless otherwise provided in the articles of incorporation,

**(a)** No preemptive right shall exist

(1) to acquire any shares issued to directors, officers or employees pursuant to approval by the affirmative vote of the holders of a majority of the shares entitled to vote thereon or when authorized by and consistent with a plan theretofore approved by such a vote of shareholders; or

(2) to acquire any shares sold otherwise than for money.

**(b)** Holders of shares of any class that is preferred or limited as to dividends or assets shall not be entitled to any preemptive right.

**(c)** Holders of shares of common stock shall not be entitled to any preemptive right to shares of any class that is preferred or limited as to dividends or assets or to any obligations, unless convertible into shares of common stock or carrying a right to subscribe to or acquire shares of common stock.

**(d)** Holders of common stock without voting power shall have no preemptive right to shares of common stock with voting power.

**(e)** The preemptive right shall be only an opportunity to acquire shares or other securities under such terms and conditions as the board of directors may fix for the purpose of providing a fair and reasonable opportunity for the exercise of such right.

## § 27
### By-Laws

The initial by-laws of a corporation shall be adopted by its board of directors. The power to alter, amend or repeal the by-laws or adopt new by-laws, subject to repeal or change by action of the shareholders, shall be vested in the board of directors unless reserved to the shareholders by the articles of incorporation. The by-laws may contain any provisions for the regulation and management of the affairs of the corporation not inconsistent with law or the articles of incorporation.

## § 27A
### By-Laws and Other Powers in Emergency [Optional]

The board of directors of any corporation may adopt emergency by-laws, subject to repeal or change by action of the shareholders, which shall, notwithstanding any different provision elsewhere in this Act or in the articles of incorporation or by-laws, be operative during any emergency in the conduct of the business of the corporation resulting from an attack on the United States or any nuclear or atomic disaster. The emergency by-laws may make any provision that may be practical and necessary for the circumstances of the emergency, including provisions that:

**(a)** A meeting of the board of directors may be called by any officer or director in such manner and under such conditions as shall be prescribed in the emergency by-laws;

---

*Supply designation of jurisdiction, such as country, etc., in accordance with local practice.

**(b)** The director or directors in attendance at the meeting, or any greater number fixed by the emergency by-laws, shall constitute a quorum; and

**(c)** The officers or other persons designated on a list approved by the board of directors before the emergency, all in such order of priority and subject to such conditions, and for such period of time (not longer than reasonably necessary after the termination of the emergency) as may be provided in the emergency by-laws or in the resolution approving the list shall, to the extent required to provide a quorum at any meeting of the board of directors, be deemed directors for such meeting.

The board of directors, either before or during any such emergency, may provide, and from time to time modify, lines of succession in the event that during such an emergency any or all officers or agents of the corporation shall for any reason be rendered incapable of discharging their duties.

The board of directors, either before or during any such emergency, may, effective in the emergency, change the head office or designate several alternative head offices or regional offices, or authorize the officers so to do.

To the extent not inconsistent with any emergency by-laws so adopted, the by-laws of the corporation shall remain in effect during any such emergency and upon its termination the emergency by-laws shall cease to be operative.

Unless otherwise provided in emergency by-laws, notice of any meeting of the board of directors during any such emergency may be given only to such of the directors as it may be feasible to reach at the time and by such means as may be feasible at the time, including publication or radio.

To the extent required to constitute a quorum at any meeting of the board of directors during any such emergency, the officers of the corporation who are present shall, unless otherwise provided in emergency by-laws, be deemed, in order of rank and within the same rank in order of seniority, directors for such meeting.

No officer, director or employee acting in accordance with any emergency by-laws shall be liable except for willful misconduct. No officer, director or employee shall be liable for any action taken by him in good faith in such an emergency in furtherance of the ordinary business affairs of the corporation even though not authorized by the by-laws then in effect.

## § 28
### Meetings of Shareholders

Meetings of shareholders may be held at such place within or without this State as may be stated in or fixed in accordance with the by-laws. If no other place is stated or so fixed, meetings shall be held at the registered office of the corporation.

An annual meeting of the shareholders shall be held at such time as may be stated in or fixed in accordance with the by-laws. If the annual meeting is not held within any thirteen-month period the Court of ............ may, on the application of any shareholder, summarily order a meeting to be held.

Special meetings of the shareholders may be called by the board of directors, the holders of not less than one-tenth of all the shares entitled to vote at the meeting, or such other persons as may be authorized in the articles of incorporation or the by-laws.

## § 29
### Notice of Shareholders' Meetings

Written notice stating the place, day, and hour of the meeting and, in case of a special meeting, the purpose or purposes for which the meeting is called, shall be delivered not less than ten nor more than fifty days before the date of the meeting, either personally or by mail, by or at the direction of the president, the secretary, or the officer or persons calling the meeting, to each shareholder of record entitled to vote at such meeting. If mailed, such notice shall be deemed to be delivered when deposited in the United States mail addressed to the shareholder at his address as it appears on the stock transfer books of the corporation, with postage thereon prepaid.

## § 30
### Closing of Transfer Books and Fixing Record Date

For the purpose of determining shareholders entitled to notice of or to vote at any meeting of shareholders or any adjournment thereof, or entitled to receive payment of any dividend, or in order to make a determination of shareholders for any other proper purpose, the board of directors of a corporation may provide that the stock transfer books shall be closed for a stated period but not to exceed, in any case, fifty days. If the stock transfer books shall be closed for the purpose of determining shareholders entitled to notice of or to vote at a meeting of shareholders, such books shall be closed for at least ten days immediately preceding such meeting. In lieu of closing the stock transfer books, the by-laws, or in the absence of an applicable by-law the board of directors, may fix in advance a date as the record date for any such determination of shareholders, such date in any case to be not more than fifty days and, in case of a meeting of shareholders, not less than ten days prior to the date on which the particular action, requiring such determination of shareholders, is to be taken. If the stock transfer books are not closed and no record date is fixed for the determination of shareholders entitled to notice of or to vote at a meeting of shareholders, or shareholders entitled to receive payment of a dividend, the date on which notice of the meeting is mailed or the date on which the resolution of the board of directors declaring such dividend is adopted, as the case may be, shall be the record date for such determination of shareholders. When a determination of shareholders entitled to vote at any meeting of shareholders has been made as provided in this section, such determination shall apply to any adjournment thereof.

## § 31
### Voting Record

The officer or agent having charge of the stock transfer books for shares of a corporation shall make a complete record of the shareholders entitled to vote at such meeting or any adjournment thereof, arranged in alphabetical order, with the address of and the number of shares held by each. Such record shall be produced and kept open at the time and place of the meeting and shall be subject to the inspection of any shareholder during the whole time of the meeting for the purposes thereof.

Failure to comply with the requirements of this section shall not affect the validity of any action taken at such meeting.

An officer or agent having charge of the stock transfer books who shall fail to prepare the record of shareholders, or produce and keep it open for inspection at the meeting, as provided in this section, shall be liable to any shareholder suffering damage on account of such failure, to the extent of such damage.

## § 32
### Quorum of Shareholders

Unless otherwise provided in the articles of incorporation, a majority of the shares entitled to vote, represented in person or by proxy, shall constitute a quorum at a meeting of shareholders, but in no event shall a quorum consist of less than one-third of the shares entitled to vote at the meeting. If a quorum is present, the affirmative vote of the majority of the shares represented at the meeting and entitled to vote on the subject matter shall be the act of the shareholders, unless the vote of a greater number or voting by classes is required by this Act or the articles of incorporation or by-laws.

## § 33
### Voting of Shares

Each outstanding share, regardless of class, shall be entitled to one vote on each matter submitted to a vote at a meeting of shareholders, except as may be otherwise provided in the articles of incorporation. If the articles of incorporation provide for more or less than one vote for any share, on any matter, every reference in this Act to a majority or other proportion of shares shall refer to such a majority or other proportion of votes entitled to be cast.

Shares held by another corporation if a majority of the shares entitled to vote for the election of directors of such other corporation is held by the corporation, shall not be voted at any meeting or counted in determining the total number of outstanding shares at any given time.

A shareholder may vote either in person or by proxy executed in writing by the shareholder or by his duly authorized attorney-in-fact. No proxy shall be valid after eleven months from the date of its execution, unless otherwise provided in the proxy.

[Either of the following prefatory phrases may be inserted here: "The articles of incorporation may provide that" or "Unless the articles of incorporation otherwise provide"] at each election for directors every shareholder entitled to vote at such election shall have the right to vote, in person or by proxy, the number of shares owned by him for as many persons as there are directors to be elected and for whose election he has a right to vote, or to cumulate his votes by giving one candidate as many votes as the number of such directors multiplied by the number of his shares shall equal, or by distributing such votes on the same principle among any number of such candidates.

Shares standing in the name of another corporation, domestic or foreign, may be voted by such officer, agent or proxy as the by-laws of such other corporation may prescribe, or, in the absence of such provision, as the board of directors of such other corporation may determine.

Shares held by an administrator, executor, guardian or conservator may be voted by him, either in person or by proxy, without a transfer of such shares into his name. Shares standing in the name of a trustee may be voted by him, either in person or by proxy, but no trustee shall be entitled to vote shares held by him without a transfer of such shares into his name.

Shares standing in the name of a receiver may be voted by such receiver, and shares held by or under the control of a receiver may be voted by such receiver without the transfer thereof into his name if authority so to do be contained in an appropriate order of the court by which such receiver was appointed.

A shareholder whose shares are pledged shall be entitled to vote such shares until the shares have been transferred into the name of the pledgee, and thereafter the pledgee shall be entitled to vote the shares so transferred.

On and after the date on which written notice of redemption of redeemable shares has been mailed to the holders thereof and a sum sufficient to redeem such shares has been deposited with a bank or trust company with irrevocable instruction and authority to pay the redemption price to the holders thereof upon surrender of certificates therefor, such shares shall not be entitled to vote on any matter and shall not be deemed to be outstanding shares.

## § 34
### Voting Trusts and Agreements Among Shareholders

Any number of shareholders of a corporation may create a voting trust for the purpose of conferring upon a trustee or trustees the right to vote or otherwise represent their shares, for a period of not to exceed ten years, by entering into a written voting trust agreement specifying the terms and conditions of the voting trust, by depositing a counterpart of the agreement with the corporation at its registered office, and by transferring their shares to such trustee or trustees for the purposes of the agreement. Such trustee or trustees shall keep a record of the holders of voting trust certificates evidencing a beneficial interest in the voting trust, giving the names and addresses of all such holders and the number and class of the shares in respect of which the voting trust certificates held by each are issued, and shall deposit a copy of such record with the corporation at its registered office. The counterpart of the voting trust agreement and the copy of such record so deposited with the corporation shall be subject to the same right of examination by a shareholder of the corporation, in person or by agent or attorney, as are the books and records of the corporation, and such counterpart and such copy of such record shall be subject to examination by any holder of record of voting trust certificates, either in person or by agent or attorney, at any reasonable time for any proper purpose.

Agreements among shareholders regarding the voting of their shares shall be valid and enforceable in accordance with their terms. Such agreements shall not be subject to the provisions of this section regarding voting trusts.

## § 35
### Board of Directors

All corporate powers shall be exercised by or under authority of, and the business and affairs of a corporation shall be managed under the direction of, a board of directors except as may be otherwise provided in this Act or the articles of incorporation. If any such provision is made in the articles of incorporation, the powers and duties conferred or imposed upon the board of directors by this Act shall be exercised or performed to such extent and by such person or persons as shall be provided in the articles of incorporation. Directors need not be residents of this State or shareholders of the corporation unless the articles of incorporation or by-laws so require. The articles of incorporation or by-laws may prescribe other qualifications for directors. The board of directors shall have authority to fix the compensation of directors unless otherwise provided in the articles of incorporation.

A director shall perform his duties as a director, including his duties as a member of any committee of the board upon which he may serve, in good faith, in a manner he reasonably believes to be in the best interests of the corporation, and with such care as an ordinarily prudent person in a like position would use under similar circumstances. In performing his duties, a director shall be entitled to rely on information, opinions, reports or statements, including financial statements and other financial data, in each case prepared or presented by:

(a) one or more officers or employees of the corporation whom the director reasonably believes to be reliable and competent in the matters presented;

(b) counsel, public accountants or other persons as to matters which the director reasonably believes to be within such person's professional or expert competence; or

(c) a committee of the board upon which he does not serve, duly designated in accordance with a provision of the articles of incorporation or the by-laws, as to matters within its designated authority, which committee the director reasonably believes to merit confidence; but he shall not be considered to be acting in good faith if he has knowledge concerning the matter in question that would cause such reliance to be unwarranted. A person who so performs his duties shall have no liability by reason of being or having been a director of the corporation.

A director of a corporation who is present at a meeting of its board of directors at which action on any corporate matter is taken shall be presumed to have assented to the action taken unless his dissent shall be entered in the minutes of the meeting or unless he shall file his written dissent to such action with the secretary of the meeting before the adjournment thereof or shall forward such dissent by registered mail to the secretary of the corporation immediately after the adjournment of the meeting. Such right to dissent shall not apply to a director who voted in favor of such action.

## § 36
### Number and Election of Directors

The board of directors of a corporation shall consist of one or more members. The number of directors shall be fixed by, or in the manner provided in, the articles of incorporation or the by-laws, except as to the number constituting the initial board of directors, which number shall be fixed by the articles of incorporation. The number of directors may be increased or decreased from time to time by amendment to, or in the manner provided in, the articles of incorporation or the by-laws, but no decrease shall have the effect of shortening the term of any incumbent director. In the absence of a by-law providing for the number of directors, the number shall be the same as that provided for in the articles of incorporation. The names and addresses of the members of the first board of directors shall be stated in the articles of incorporation. Such persons shall hold office until the first annual meeting of shareholders, and until their successors shall have been elected and qualified. At the first annual meeting of shareholders and at each annual meeting thereafter the shareholders shall elect directors to hold office until the next succeeding annual meeting, except in case of the classification of directors as permitted by this Act. Each director shall hold office for the term for which he is elected and until his successor shall have been elected and qualified.

## § 37
### Classification of Directors

When the board of directors shall consist of nine or more members, in lieu of electing the whole number of directors annually, the articles of incorporation may provide that the directors be divided into either two or three classes, each class to be as nearly equal in number as possible, the term of office of directors of the first class to expire at the first annual meeting of shareholders after their election, that of the second class to expire at the second annual meeting after their election, and that of the third class, if any, to expire at the third annual meeting after their election. At each annual meeting after such classification the number of directors equal to the number of the class whose term expires at the time of such meeting shall be elected to hold office until the second succeeding annual meeting, if there be two classes, or until the third succeeding annual meeting, if there be three classes. No classification of directors shall be effective prior to the first annual meeting of shareholders.

## § 38
### Vacancies

Any vacancy occurring in the board of directors may be filled by the affirmative vote of a majority of the remaining directors though less than a quorum of the board of directors. A director elected to fill a vacancy shall be elected for the unexpired term of his predecessor in office. Any directorship to be filled by reason of an increase in the number of directors may be filled by the board of directors for a term of office continuing only until the next election of directors by the shareholders.

## § 39
### Removal of Directors

At a meeting of shareholders called expressly for that purpose, directors may be removed in the manner provided in this section. Any director or the entire board of directors may be removed, with or without cause, by a vote of the holders of a majority of the shares then entitled to vote at an election of directors.

In the case of a corporation having cumulative voting, if less than the entire board is to be removed, no one of the directors may be removed if the votes cast against his removal would be sufficient to elect him if then cumulatively voted at an election of the entire board of directors, or, if there be classes of directors, at an election of the class of directors of which he is a part.

Whenever the holders of the shares of any class are entitled to elect one or more directors by the provisions of the articles of incorporation, the provisions of this section shall apply, in respect to the removal of a director or directors so elected, to the vote of the holders of the outstanding shares of that class and not to the vote of the outstanding shares as a whole.

## § 40
### Quorum of Directors

A majority of the number of directors fixed by or in the manner provided in the by-laws or in the absence of a by-law fixing or providing for the number of directors, then of the number stated in the articles of incorporation, shall constitute a quorum for the transaction of business unless a greater number is required by the articles of incorporation or the by-laws. The act of the majority of the directors present at a meeting at which a quorum is present shall be the act of the board of directors, unless the act of a greater number is required by the articles of incorporation or the by-laws.

## § 41
### Director Conflicts of Interest

No contract or other transaction between a corporation and one or more of its directors or any other corporation, firm, association or entity in which one or more of its directors are directors or officers or are financially interested, shall be either void or voidable because of such relationship or interest or because such director or directors are present at the meeting of the board of directors or a committee thereof which authorizes, approves or ratifies such contract or transaction or because his or their votes are counted for such purpose, if:

**(a)** the fact of such relationship or interest is disclosed or known to the board of directors or committee which authorizes, approves or ratifies the contract or transaction by a vote or consent sufficient for the purpose without counting the votes or consents of such interested directors; or

**(b)** the fact of such relationship or interest is disclosed or known to the shareholders entitled to vote and they authorize, approve or ratify such contract or transaction by vote or written consent; or

**(c)** the contract or transaction is fair and reasonable to the corporation.

Common or interested directors may be counted in determining the presence of a quorum at a meeting of the board of directors or a committee thereof which authorizes, approves or ratifies such contract or transaction.

## § 42
### Executive and Other Committees

If the articles of incorporation or the by-laws so provide, the board of directors, by resolution adopted by a majority of the full board of directors, may designate from among its members an executive committee and one or more other committees each of which, to the extent provided in such resolution or in the articles of incorporation or the by-laws of the corporation, shall have and may exercise all the authority of the board of directors, except that no such committee shall have authority to (1) authorize distributions, (2) approve or recommend to shareholders actions or proposals required by this Act to be approved by shareholders, (3) designate candidates for the office of director, for purposes of proxy solicitation or otherwise, or fill vacancies on the board of directors or any committee thereof, (4) amend the by-laws, (5) approve a plan of merger not requiring shareholder approval, (6) authorize or approve the reacquisition of shares unless pursuant to a general formula or method specified by the board of directors, or (7) authorize or approve the issuance or sale of, or any contract to issue or sell, shares or designate the terms of a series of a class of shares, provided that the board of directors, having acted regarding general authorization for the issuance or sale of shares, or any contract therefor, and, in the case of a series, the designation thereof, may, pursuant to a general formula or method specified by the board by resolution or by adoption of a stock option or other plan, authorize a committee to fix the terms of any contract for the sale of the shares and to fix the terms upon which such shares may be issued or sold, including, without limitation, the price, the dividend rate, provisions for redemption, sinking fund, conversion, voting or preferential rights, and provisions for other features of a class of shares, or a series of a class of shares, with full power in such committee to adopt any final resolution setting forth all the terms thereof and to authorize the statement of the terms of a series for filing with the Secretary of State under this Act.

Neither the designation of any such committee, the delegation thereto of authority, nor action by such committee pursuant to such authority shall alone constitute compliance by any member of the board of directors, not a member of the committee in question, with his responsibility to act in good faith, in a manner he reasonably believes to be in the best interests of the corporation, and with such care as an ordinarily prudent person in a like position would use under similar circumstances.

## § 43
### Place and Notice of Directors' Meetings; Committee Meetings

Meetings of the board of directors, regular or special, may be held either within or without this State.

Regular meetings of the board of directors or any committee designated thereby may be held with or without notice as prescribed in the by-laws. Special meetings of the board of directors or any committee designated thereby shall be held upon such notice as is prescribed in the by-laws. Attendance of a director at a meeting shall constitute a waiver of notice of such meeting, except where a director attends a meeting for the express purpose of objecting to the transaction of any business because the meeting is not lawfully called or convened. Neither the business to be transacted at, nor the purpose of, any regular or special meeting of the board of directors or any committee designated thereby need be specified in the notice or waiver of notice of such meeting unless required by the by-laws.

Except as may be otherwise restricted by the articles of incorporation or by-laws, members of the board of directors or any committee designated thereby may participate in a meeting of such board or committee by means of a conference telephone or similar communications equipment by means of which all persons participating in the meeting can hear each other at the same time and participation by such means shall constitute presence in person at a meeting.

## § 44
### Action by Directors Without a Meeting

Unless otherwise provided by the articles of incorporation or bylaws, any action required by this Act to be taken at a meeting of the directors of a corporation, or any action which may be taken at a meeting of the directors or of a committee, may be taken without a meeting if a consent in writing, setting forth the action so taken, shall be signed by all of the directors, or all of the members of the committee, as the case may be. Such consent shall have the same effect as a unanimous vote.

## § 45
### Distributions to Shareholders

Subject to any restrictions in the articles of incorporation, the board of directors may authorize and the corporation may make distributions, except that no distribution may be made if, after giving effect thereto, either:

**(a)** the corporation would be unable to pay its debts as they become due in the usual course of its business; or

**(b)** the corporation's total assets would be less than the sum of its total liabilities and (unless the articles of incorporation otherwise permit) the maximum amount that then would be payable, in any liquidation, in respect of all outstanding shares having preferential rights in liquidation.

Determinations under subparagraph (b) may be based upon (1) financial statements prepared on the basis of accounting practices and principles that are reasonable in the circumstances, or (2) a fair valuation or other method that is reasonable in the circumstances.

In the case of a purchase, redemption or other acquisition of a corporation's shares, the effect of a distribution shall be measured as of the date money or other property is tranferred or debt is incurred by the corporation, or as of the date the shareholder ceases to be a shareholder of the corporation with respect to such shares, whichever is earlier. In all other cases, the effect of a distribution shall be measured as of the date of its authorization if payment occurs 120 days or less following the date of authorization, or as of the date of payment if payment occurs more than 120 days following the date of authorization.

Indebtedness of a corporation incurred or issued to a shareholder in a distribution in accordance with this Section shall be on a parity with the indebtedness of the corporation to its general unsecured creditors except to the extent subordinated by agreement.

## § 46
### Distributions from Capital Surplus

[Repealed in 1979.]

## § 47
### Loans to Employees and Directors

A corporation shall not lend money to or use its credit to assist its directors without authorization in the particular case by its shareholders, but may lend money to and use its credit to assist any employee of the corporation or of a subsidiary, including any such employee who is a director of the corporation, if the board of directors decides that such loan or assistance may benefit the corporation.

## § 48
### Liability of Directors in Certain Cases

In addition to any other liabilities, a director who votes for or assents to any distribution contrary to the provisions of this Act or contrary to any restrictions contained in the articles of incorporation, shall, unless he complies with the standard provided in this Act for the performance of the duties of directors, be liable to the corporation, jointly and severally with all other directors so voting or assenting, for the amount of such dividend which is paid or the value of such distribution in excess of the amount of such distribution which could have been made without a violation of the provisions of this Act or the restrictions in the articles of incorporation.

Any director against whom a claim shall be asserted under or pursuant to this section for the making of a distribution and who shall be held liable thereon, shall be entitled to contribution from the shareholders who accepted or received any such distribution, knowing such distribution to have been made in violation of this Act, in proportion to the amounts received by them.

Any director against whom a claim shall be asserted under or pursuant to this section shall be entitled to contribution from any other director who voted for or assented to the action upon which the claim is asserted and who did not comply with the standard provided in this Act for the performance of the duties of directors.

## § 49
### Provisions Relating to Actions by Shareholders

No action shall be brought in this State by a shareholder in the right of a domestic or foreign corporation unless the plaintiff was a holder of record of shares or of voting trust certificates therefor at the time of the transaction of which he complains, or his shares or voting trust certificates thereafter devolved upon him by operation of law from a person who was a holder of record at such time.

In any action hereafter instituted in the right of any domestic or foreign corporation by the holder or holders of record of shares of such corporation or of voting trust certificates therefor, the court having jurisdiction, upon final judgment and a finding that the action was brought without reasonable cause, may require the plaintiff or plaintiffs to pay to the parties named as defendant the reasonable expenses, including fees of attorneys, incurred by them in the defense of such action.

In any action now pending or hereafter instituted or maintained in the right of any domestic or foreign corporation by the holder or holders of record of less than five per cent of the outstanding shares of any class of such corporation or of voting trust certificates therefor, unless the shares or voting trust certificates so held have a market value in excess of twenty-five thousand dollars, the corporation in whose right such action is brought shall be entitled at any time before final judgment to require the plaintiff or plaintiffs to give security for the reasonable expenses, including fees of attorneys, that may be incurred by it in connection with such action or may be incurred by other parties named as defendant for which it may become legally liable. Market value shall be determined as of the date that the plaintiff institutes the action or, in the case of an intervenor, as of the date that he becomes a party to the action. The amount of such security may from time to time be increased or decreased, in the discretion of the court, upon showing that the security provided has or may become inadequate or is excessive. The corporation shall have recourse to such security in such amount as the court having jurisdiction shall determine upon the termination of such action, whether or not the court finds the action was brought without reasonable cause.

## § 50
### Officers

The officers of a corporation shall consist of a president, one or more vice presidents as may be prescribed by the by-laws, a secretary, and a treasurer, each of whom shall be elected by the board of directors at such time and in such manner as may be prescribed by the by-laws. Such other officers and assistant officers and agents as may be deemed necessary may be elected or appointed by the board of directors or chosen in such other manner as may be prescribed by the by-laws. Any two or more offices may be held by the same person, except the offices of president and secretary.

All officers and agents of the corporation, as between themselves and the corporation, shall have such authority and perform such duties in the management of the corporation as may be provided in the by-laws, or as may be determined by resolution of the board of directors not inconsistent with the by-laws.

## § 51
### Removal of Officers

Any officer or agent may be removed by the board of directors whenever in its judgment the best interests of the corporation will be served thereby, but such removal shall be without prejudice to the contract rights, if any, of the person so removed. Election or appointment of an officer or agent shall not of itself create contract rights.

## § 52
### Books and Records: Financial Reports to Shareholders, Examination of Records

Each corporation shall keep correct and complete books and records of account and shall keep minutes of the proceedings of its shareholders and board of directors and shall keep at its registered office or principal place of business, or at the office of its transfer agent or registrar, a record of its shareholders, giving the names and addresses of all shareholders and the number and class of the shares held by each. Any books, records and minutes may be in written form or in any other form capable of being converted into written form within a reasonable time.

Any person who shall have been a holder of record of shares or of voting trust certificates therefor at least six months immediately preceding his demand or shall be the holder of record of, or the holder of record of voting trust certificates for, at least five percent of all the outstanding shares of the corporation, upon written demand stating the purpose thereof, shall have the right to examine, in person, or by agent or attorney, at any reasonable time or times, for any proper purpose its relevant books and records of account, minutes, and record of shareholders and to make extracts therefrom.

Any officer or agent who, or a corporation which, shall refuse to allow any such shareholder or holder of voting trust certificates, or his agent or attorney, so to examine and make extracts from its books and records of account, minutes, and record of shareholders, for any proper purpose, shall be liable to such shareholder or holder of voting trust certificates in a penalty of ten percent of the value of the shares owned by such shareholder, or in respect of which such voting trust certificates are issued, in addition to any other damages or remedy afforded him by law. It shall be a defense to any action for penalties under this section that the person suing therefor has within two years sold or offered for sale any list of shareholders or of holders of voting trust certificates for shares of such corporation or any other corporation or has aided or abetted any person in procuring any list of shareholders or of holders of voting trust certificates for any such purpose, or has improperly used any information secured through any prior examination of the books and records of account, or minutes, or record of shareholders or of holders of voting trust certificates for shares of such corporation or any other corporation, or was not acting in good faith or for a proper purpose in making his demand.

Nothing herein contained shall impair the power of any court of competent jurisdiction, upon proof by a shareholder or holder of voting trust certificates of proper purpose, irrespective of the period of time during which such shareholder or holder of voting trust certificates shall have been a shareholder of record or a holder of record of voting trust certificates, and irrespective of the number of shares held by him or represented by voting trust certificates held by him, to compel the production for examination by such shareholder or holder of voting trust certificates of the books and records of account, minutes and record of shareholders of a corporation.

Each corporation shall furnish to its shareholders annual financial statements, including at least a balance sheet as of the end of each fiscal year and a statement of income for such fiscal year, which shall be prepared on the basis of generally accepted accounting principles, if the corporation prepares financial statements for such fiscal year on that basis for any purpose, and may be consolidated statements of the corporation and one or more of its subsidiaries. The financial statements shall be mailed by the corporation to each of its shareholders within 120 days after the close of each fiscal year and, after such mailing and upon written request, shall be mailed by the corporation to any shareholder (or holder of a voting trust certificate for its shares) to whom a copy of the most recent annual financial statements has not previously been mailed. In the case of statements audited by a public accountant, each copy shall be accompanied by a report setting forth his opinion thereon; in other cases, each copy shall be accompanied by a statement of the president or the person in charge of the corporation's financial accounting records (1) stating his reasonable belief as to whether or not the financial statements were prepared in accordance with generally accepted accounting principles and, if not, describing the basis of presentation, and (2) describing any respects in which the financial statements were not prepared on a basis consistent with those prepared for the previous year.

## § 53
### Incorporators

One or more persons, or a domestic or foreign corporation, may act as incorporator or incorporators of a corporation by signing and delivering in duplicate to the Secretary of State articles of incorporation for such corporation.

## § 54
### Articles of Incorporation

The articles of incorporation shall set forth:

(a) The name of the corporation.

(b) The period of duration, which may be perpetual.

(c) The purpose or purposes for which the corporation is organized which may be stated to be, or to include, the transaction of any or all lawful business for which corporations may be incorporated under this Act.

(d) The aggregate number of shares which the corporation shall have authority to issue and, if such shares are to be divided into classes, the number of shares of each class.

(e) If the shares are to be divided into classes, the designation of each class and a statement of the preferences, limitations and relative rights in respect of the shares of each class.

(f) If the corporation is to issue the shares of any preferred or special class in series, then the designation of each series and a statement of the variations in the relative rights and preferences as between series insofar as the same are to be fixed in the articles of incorporation, and a statement of any authority to be vested in the board of directors to establish series and fix and determine the variations in the relative rights and preferences as between series.

**(g)** If any preemptive right is to be granted to shareholders, the provisions therefor.

**(h)** The address of its initial registered office, and the name of its initial registered agent at such address.

**(i)** The number of directors constituting the initial board of directors and the names and addresses of the persons who are to serve as directors until the first annual meeting of shareholders or until their successors be elected and qualify.

**(j)** The name and address of each incorporator.

In addition to provisions required therein, the articles of incorporation may also contain provisions not inconsistent with law regarding:

**(1)** the direction of the management of the business and the regulation of the affairs of the corporation;

**(2)** the definition, limitation and regulation of the powers of the corporation, the directors, and the shareholders, or any class of the shareholders, including restrictions on the transfer of shares;

**(3)** the par value of any authorized shares or class of shares;

**(4)** any provision which under this Act is required or permitted to be set forth in the by-laws.

It shall not be necessary to set forth in the articles of incorporation any of the corporate powers enumerated in this Act.

## § 55
### Filing of Articles of Incorporation

Duplicate originals of the articles of incorporation shall be delivered to the Secretary of State. If the Secretary of State finds that the articles of incorporation conform to law, he shall, when all fees have been paid as in this Act prescribed:

**(a)** Endorse on each of such duplicate originals the word "Filed," and the month, day and year of the filing thereof.

**(b)** File one of such duplicate originals in his office.

**(c)** Issue a certificate of incorporation to which he shall affix the other duplicate original.

The certificate of incorporation, together with the duplicate original of the articles of incorporation affixed thereto by the Secretary of State, shall be returned to the incorporators or their representative.

## § 56
### Effect of Issuance of Certificate of Incorporation

Upon the issuance of the certificate of incorporation, the corporate existence shall begin, and such certificate of incorporation shall be conclusive evidence that all conditions precedent required to be performed by the incorporators have been complied with and that the corporation has been incorporated under this Act, except as against this State in a proceeding to cancel or revoke the certificate of incorporation or for involuntary dissolution of the corporation.

## § 57
### Organization Meeting of Directors

After the issuance of the certificate of incorporation an organization meeting of the board of directors named in the articles of incorporation shall be held, either within or without this State, at the call of a majority of the directors named in the articles of incorporation, for the purpose of adopting by-laws, electing officers and transacting such other business as may come before the meeting. The directors calling the meeting shall give at least three days' notice thereof by mail to each director so named, stating the time and place of the meeting.

## § 58
### Right to Amend Articles of Incorporation

A corporation may amend its articles of incorporation, from time to time, in any and as many respects as may be desired, so long as its articles of incorporation as amended contain only such provisions as might be lawfully contained in original articles of incorporation at the time of making such amendment, and, if a change in shares or the rights of shareholders, or an exchange, reclassification or cancellation of shares or rights of shareholders is to be made, such provisions as may be necessary to effect such change, exchange, reclassification or cancellation.

In particular, and without limitation upon such general power of amendment, a corporation may amend its articles of incorporation, from time to time, so as:

**(a)** To change its corporate name.

**(b)** To change its period of duration.

**(c)** To change, enlarge or diminish its corporate purposes.

**(d)** To increase or decrease the aggregate number of shares, or shares of any class, which the corporation has authority to issue.

**(e)** To provide, change or eliminate any provision with respect to the par value of any shares or class of shares.

**(f)** To exchange, classify, reclassify or cancel all or any part of its shares, whether issued or unissued.

**(g)** To change the designation of all or any part of its shares, whether issued or unissued, and to change the preferences, limitations, and the relative rights in respect of all or any part of its shares, whether issued or unissued.

**(h)** To change the shares of any class, whether issued or unissued, into a different number of shares of the same class or into the same or a different number of shares of other classes.

**(i)** To create new classes of shares having rights and preferences either prior and superior or subordinate and inferior to the shares of any class then authorized, whether issued or unissued.

**(j)** To cancel or otherwise affect the right of the holders of the shares of any class to receive dividends which have accrued but have not been declared.

**(k)** To divide any preferred or special class of shares, whether issued or unissued, into series and fix and determine the designations of such series and the variations in the relative rights and preferences as between the shares of such series.

**(l)** To authorize the board of directors to establish, out of authorized but unissued shares, series of any preferred or special class of shares and fix and determine the relative rights and preferences of the shares of any series so established.

**(m)** To authorize the board of directors to fix and determine the relative rights and preferences of the authorized but unissued shares of series theretofore established in respect of which either the relative rights and preferences have not been fixed and determined or the relative rights and preferences theretofore fixed and determined are to be changed.

**(n)** To revoke, diminish, or enlarge the authority of the board of directors to establish series out of authorized but unissued shares of any preferred or special class and fix and determine the relative rights and preferences of the shares of any series so established.

**(o)** To limit, deny or grant to shareholders of any class the preemptive right to acquire additional shares of the corporation, whether then or thereafter authorized.

## § 59
### Procedure to Amend Articles of Incorporation

Amendments to the articles of incorporation shall be made in the following manner:

**(a)** The board of directors shall adopt a resolution setting forth the proposed amendment and, if shares have been issued, directing that it be submitted to a vote at a meeting of shareholders, which may be either the annual or a special meeting. If no shares have been issued, the amendment shall be adopted by resolution of the board of directors and the provisions for adoption by shareholders shall not apply. If the corporation has only one class of shares outstanding, an amendment solely to change the number of authorized shares to effectuate a split of, or stock dividend in, the corporation's own shares, or solely to do so and to change the number of authorized shares in proportion thereto, may be adopted by the board of directors; and the provisions for adoption by shareholders shall not apply, unless otherwise provided by the articles of incorporation. The resolution may incorporate the proposed amendment in restated articles of incorporation which contain a statement that except for the designated amendment the restated articles of incorporation correctly set forth without change the corresponding provisions of the articles of incorporation as theretofore amended, and that the restated articles of incorporation together with the designated amendment supersede the original articles of incorporation and all amendments thereto.

**(b)** Written notice setting forth the proposed amendment or a summary of the changes to be effected thereby shall be given to each shareholder of record entitled to vote thereon within the time and in the manner provided in this Act for the giving of notice of meetings of shareholders. If the meeting be an annual meeting, the proposed amendment of such summary may be included in the notice of such annual meeting.

**(c)** At such meeting a vote of the shareholders entitled to vote thereon shall be taken on the proposed amendment. The proposed amendment shall be adopted upon receiving the affirmative vote of the holders of a majority of the shares entitled to vote thereon, unless any class of shares is entitled to vote thereon as a class, in which event the proposed amendment shall be adopted upon receiving the affirmative vote of the holders of a majority of the shares of each class of shares entitled to vote thereon as a class and of the total shares entitled to vote thereon.

Any number of amendments may be submitted to the shareholders, and voted upon by them, at one meeting.

## § 60
### Class Voting on Amendments

The holders of the outstanding shares of a class shall be entitled to vote as a class upon a proposed amendment, whether or not entitled to vote thereon by the provisions of the articles of incorporation, if the amendment would:

**(a)** Increase or decrease the aggregate number of authorized shares of such class.

**(b)** Effect an exchange, reclassification or cancellation of all or part of the shares of such class.

**(c)** Effect an exchange, or create a right of exchange, of all or any part of the shares of another class into the shares of such class.

**(d)** Change the designations, preferences, limitations or relative rights of the shares of such class.

**(e)** Change the shares of such class into the same or a different number of shares of the same class or another class or classes.

**(f)** Create a new class of shares having rights and preferences prior and superior to the shares of such class, or increase the rights and preferences or the number of authorized shares, of any class having rights and preferences prior or superior to the shares of such class.

**(g)** In the case of a preferred or special class of shares, divide the shares of such class into series and fix and determine the designation of such series and the variations in the relative rights and preferences between the shares of such series, or authorize the board of directors to do so.

**(h)** Limit or deny any existing preemptive rights of the shares of such class.

**(i)** Cancel or otherwise affect dividends on the shares of such class which have accrued but have not been declared.

## § 61
### Articles of Amendment

The articles of amendment shall be executed in duplicate by the corporation by its president or a vice president and by its secretary or an assistant secretary, and verified by one of the officers signing such articles, and shall set forth:

**(a)** The name of the corporation.

**(b)** The amendments so adopted.

**(c)** The date of the adoption of the amendment by the shareholders, or by the board of directors where no shares have been issued.

**(d)** The number of shares outstanding, and the number of shares entitled to vote thereon, and if the shares of any class are entitled to vote thereon as a class, the designation and number of outstanding shares entitled to vote thereon of each such class.

**(e)** The number of shares voted for and against such amendment, respectively, and, if the shares of any class are entitled to vote thereon as a class, the number of shares of each such class voted for and against such amendment, respectively, or if no shares have been issued, a statement to that effect.

**(f)** If such amendment provides for an exchange, reclassification or cancellation of issued shares, and if the manner in which the same shall be effected is not set forth in the amendment, then a statement of the manner in which the same shall be effected.

## § 62
### Filing of Articles of Amendment

Duplicate originals of the articles of amendment shall be delivered to the Secretary of State. If the Secretary of State finds that the articles of amendment conform to law, he shall, when all fees and franchise taxes have been paid as in this Act prescribed:

**(a)** Endorse on each of such duplicate originals the word "Filed," and the month, day and year of the filing thereof.

**(b)** File one of such duplicate originals in his office.

**(c)** Issue a certificate of amendment to which he shall affix the other duplicate original.

The certificate of amendment, together with the duplicate original of the articles of amendment affixed thereto by the Secretary of State, shall be returned to the corporation or its representative.

## § 63
### Effect of Certificate of Amendment

Upon the issuance of the certificate of amendment by the Secretary of State, the amendment shall become effective and the articles of incorporation shall be deemed to be amended accordingly.

No amendment shall affect any existing cause of action in favor of or against such corporation, or any pending suit to which such corporation shall be a party, or the existing rights of persons other than shareholders; and, in the event the corporate name shall be changed by amendment, no suit brought by or against such corporation under its former name shall abate for that reason.

## § 64
### Restated Articles of Incorporation

A domestic corporation may at any time restate its articles of incorporation as theretofore amended, by a resolution adopted by the board of directors.

Upon the adoption of such resolution, restated articles of incorporation shall be executed in duplicate by the corporation by its president or a vice president and by its secretary or assistant secretary and verified by one of the officers signing such articles and shall set forth all of the operative provisions of the articles of incorporation as theretofore amended together with a statement that the restated articles of incorporation correctly set forth without change the corresponding provisions of the articles of incorporation as theretofore amended and that the restated articles of incorporation supersede the original articles of incorporation and all amendments thereto.

Duplicate originals of the restated articles of incorporation shall be delivered to the Secretary of State. If the Secretary of State finds that such restated articles of incorporation conform to law, he shall, when all fees and franchise taxes have been paid as in this Act prescribed:

**(1)** Endorse on each of such duplicate originals the word "Filed," and the month, day and year of the filing thereof.

**(2)** File one of such duplicate originals in his office.

**(3)** Issue a restated certificate of incorporation, to which he shall affix the other duplicate original.

The restated certificate of incorporation, together with the duplicate original of the restated articles of incorporation affixed thereto by the Secretary of State, shall be returned to the corporation or its representative.

Upon the issuance of the restated certificate of incorporation by the Secretary of State, the restated articles of incorporation shall become effective and shall supersede the original articles of incorporation and all amendments thereto.

## § 65
### Amendment of Articles of Incorporation in Reorganization Proceedings

Whenever a plan of reorganization of a corporation has been confirmed by decree or order of a court of competent jurisdiction in proceedings for the reorganization of such corporation, pursuant to the provisions of any applicable statute of the United States relating to reorganizations of corporations, the articles of incorporation of the corporation may be amended, in the manner provided in this section, in as many respects as may be necessary to carry out the plan and put it into effect, so long as the articles of incorporation as amended contain only such provisions as might be lawfully contained in original articles of incorporation at the time of making such amendment.

In particular and without limitation upon such general power of amendment, the articles of incorporation may be amended for such purpose so as to:

**(a)** Change the corporate name, period of duration or corporate purposes of the corporation;

**(b)** Repeal, alter or amend the by-laws of the corporation;

**(c)** Change the aggregate number of shares or shares of any class, which the corporation has authority to issue;

**(d)** Change the preferences, limitations and relative rights in respect of all or any part of the shares of the corporation, and classify, reclassify or cancel all or any part thereof, whether issued or unissued;

**(e)** Authorize the issuance of bonds, debentures or other obligations of the corporation, whether or not convertible into shares of any class or bearing warrants or other evidences of optional rights to purchase or subscribe for shares of any class, and fix the terms and conditions thereof; and

**(f)** Constitute or reconstitute and classify or reclassify the board of directors of the corporation, and appoint directors and officers in place of or in addition to all or any of the directors or officers then in office.

Amendments to the articles of incorporation pursuant to this section shall be made in the following manner:

**(1)** Articles of amendment approved by decree or order of such court shall be executed and verified in duplicate by such person or persons as the court shall designate or appoint for the purpose, and shall set forth the name of the corporation, the amendments of the articles of incorporation approved by the court, the date of the decree or order approving the articles of amendment, the title of the proceedings in which the decree or order was entered, and a statement that such decree or order was entered by a court having jurisdiction of the proceedings for the reorganization of the corporation pursuant to the provisions of an applicable statute of the United States.

(2) Duplicate originals of the articles of amendment shall be delivered to the Secretary of State. If the Secretary of State finds that the articles of amendment conform to law, he shall, when all fees and franchise taxes have been paid as in this Act prescribed:

(A) Endorse on each of such duplicate originals the word "Filed," and the month, day and year of the filing thereof.

(B) File one of such duplicate originals in his office.

(C) Issue a certificate of amendment to which he shall affix the other duplicate original.

The certificate of amendment, together with the duplicate original of the articles of amendment affixed thereto by the Secretary of State, shall be returned to the corporation or its representative.

Upon the issuance of the certificate of amendment by the Secretary of State, the amendment shall become effective and the articles of incorporation shall be deemed to be amended accordingly, without any action thereon by the directors or shareholders of the corporation and with the same effect as if the amendments had been adopted by unanimous action of the directors and shareholders of the corporation.

## § 66
### Restriction on Redemption or Purchase of Redeemable Shares

[Repealed in 1979.]

## § 67
### Cancellation of Redeemable Shares by Redemption or Purchase

[Repealed in 1979.]

## § 68
### Cancellation of Other Reacquired Shares

[Repealed in 1979.]

## § 69
### Reduction of Stated Capital in Certain Cases

[Repealed in 1979.]

## § 70
### Special Provisions Relating to Surplus and Reserves

[Repealed in 1979.]

## § 71
### Procedure for Merger

Any two or more domestic corporations may merge into one of such corporations pursuant to a plan of merger approved in the manner provided in this Act.

The board of directors of each corporation shall, by resolution adopted by each such board, approve a plan of merger setting forth:

(a) The names of the corporations proposing to merge, and the name of the corporation into which they propose to merge, which is hereinafter designated as the surviving corporation.

(b) The terms and conditions of the proposed merger.

(c) The manner and basis of converting the shares of each corporation into shares, obligations or other securities of the surviving corporation or of any other corporation or, in whole or in part, into cash or other property.

(d) A statement of any changes in the articles of incorporation of the surviving corporation to be effected by such merger.

(e) Such other provisions with respect to the proposed merger as are deemed necessary or desirable.

## § 72
### Procedure for Consolidation

Any two or more domestic corporations may consolidate into a new corporation pursuant to a plan of consolidation approved in the manner provided in this Act.

The board of directors of each corporation shall, by a resolution adopted by each such board, approve a plan of consolidation setting forth:

(a) The names of the corporations proposing to consolidate, and the name of the new corporation into which they propose to consolidate, which is hereinafter designated as the new corporation.

(b) The terms and conditions of the proposed consolidation.

(c) The manner and basis of converting the shares of each corporation into shares, obligations or other securities of the new corporation or of any other corporation or, in whole or in part, into cash or other property.

(d) With respect to the new corporation, all of the statements required to be set forth in articles of incorporation for corporations organized under this Act.

(e) Such other provisions with respect to the proposed consolidation as are deemed necessary or desirable.

## § 72A
### Procedure for Share Exchange

All the issued or all the outstanding shares of one or more classes of any domestic corporation may be acquired through the exchange of all such shares of such class or classes by another domestic or foreign corporation pursuant to a plan of exchange approved in the manner provided in this Act.

The board of directors of each corporation shall, by resolution adopted by each such board, approve a plan of exchange setting forth:

(a) The name of the corporation the shares of which are proposed to be acquired by exchange and the name of the corporation to acquire the shares of such corporation in the exchange, which is hereinafter designated as the acquiring corporation.

(b) The terms and conditions of the proposed exchange.

(c) The manner and basis of exchanging the shares to be acquired for shares, obligations or other securities of the acquiring corporation or any other corporation, or, in whole or in part, for cash or other property.

(d) Such other provisions with respect to the proposed exchange as are deemed necessary or desirable.

The procedure authorized by this section shall not be deemed to limit the power of a corporation to acquire all or part of the shares of any class or classes of a corporation through a voluntary exchange or otherwise by agreement with the shareholders.

## § 73
### Approval by Shareholders

(a) The board of directors of each corporation in the case of a merger or consolidation, and the board of directors of the corporation the shares of which are to be acquired in the case of an exchange, upon approving such plan of merger, consolidation or exchange, shall, by resolution, direct that the plan be submitted to a vote at a meeting of its shareholders, which may be either an annual or a special meeting. Written notice shall be given to each shareholder of record, whether or not entitled to vote at such meeting, not less than twenty days before such meeting, in the manner provided in this Act for the giving of notice of meetings of shareholders, and, whether the meeting be an annual or a special meeting, shall state that the purpose or one of the purposes is to consider the proposed plan of merger, consolidation or exchange. A copy or a summary of the plan of merger, consolidation or exchange, as the case may be, shall be included in or enclosed with such notice.

(b) At each such meeting, a vote of the shareholders shall be taken on the proposed plan. The plan shall be approved upon receiving the affirmative vote of the holders of a majority of the shares entitled to vote thereon of each such corporation, unless any class of shares of any such corporation is entitled to vote thereon as a class, in which event, as to such corporation, the plan shall be approved upon receiving the affirmative vote of the holders of a majority of the shares of each class of shares entitled to vote thereon as a class and of the total shares entitled to vote thereon. Any class of shares of any such corporation shall be entitled to vote as a class if any such plan contains any provision which, if contained in a proposed amendment to articles of incorporation, would entitle such class of shares to vote as a class and, in the case of an exchange, if the class is included in the exchange.

(c) After such approval by a vote of the shareholders of each such corporation, and at any time prior to the filing of the articles of merger, consolidation or exchange, the merger, consolidation or exchange may be abandoned pursuant to provisions therefor, if any, set forth in the plan.

(d) (1) Notwithstanding the provisions of subsections (a) and (b), submission of a plan of merger to a vote at a meeting of shareholders of a surviving corporation shall not be required if:
 (A) the articles of incorporation of the surviving corporation do not differ except in name from those of the corporation before the merger,
 (B) each holder of shares of the surviving corporation which were outstanding immediately before the effective date of the merger is to hold the same number of shares with identical rights immediately after,
 (C) the number of voting shares outstanding immediately after the merger, plus the number of voting shares issuable on conversion of other securities issued by virtue of the terms of the merger and on exercise of rights and warrants so issued, will not exceed by more than twenty percent the number of voting shares outstanding immediately before the merger, and
 (D) the number of participating shares outstanding immediately after the merger, plus the number of participating shares issuable on conversion of other securities issued by virtue of the terms of the merger and on exercise of rights and warrants so issued, will not exceed by more than twenty percent the number of participating shares outstanding immediately before the merger.

(2) As used in this subsection:
 (A) "voting shares" means shares which entitle their holders to vote unconditionally in elections of directors;
 (B) "participating shares" means shares which entitle their holders to participate without limitation in distribution of earnings or surplus.

## § 74
### Articles of Merger, Consolidation or Exchange

(a) Upon receiving the approvals required by Sections 71, 72 and 73, articles of merger or articles of consolidation shall be executed in duplicate by each corporation by its president or a vice president and by its secretary or an assistant secretary, and verified by one of the officers of each corporation signing such articles, and shall set forth:

(1) The plan of merger or the plan of consolidation;

(2) As to each corporation, either (A) the number of shares outstanding, and, if the shares of any class are entitled to vote as a class, the designation and number of outstanding shares of each such class, or (B) a statement that the vote of shareholders is not required by virtue of subsection 73(d);

(3) As to each corporation the approval of whose shareholders is required, the number of shares voted for and against such plan, respectively, and, if the shares of any class are entitled to vote as a class, the number of shares of each such class voted for and against such plan, respectively.

(b) Duplicate originals of the articles of merger, consolidation or exchange shall be delivered to the Secretary of State. If the Secretary of State finds that such articles conform to law, he shall, when all fees and franchise taxes have been paid as in this Act prescribed:

(1) Endorse on each of such duplicate originals the word "Filed," and the month, day and year of the filing thereof.

(2) File one of such duplicate originals in his office.

(3) Issue a certificate of merger, consolidation or exchange to which he shall affix the other duplicate original.

(c) The certificate of merger, consolidation or exchange together with the duplicate original of the articles affixed thereto by the Secretary of State, shall be returned to the surviving, new or acquiring corporation, as the case may be, or its representative.

## § 75
### Merger of Subsidiary Corporation

Any corporation owning at least ninety per cent of the outstanding shares of each class of another corporation may merge such other corporation into itself without approval by a vote of the shareholders of either corporation. Its board of directors shall, by resolution, approve a plan of merger setting forth:

**(a)** The name of the subsidiary corporation and the name of the corporation owning at least ninety per cent of its shares, which is hereinafter designated as the surviving corporation.

**(b)** The manner and basis of converting the shares of the subsidiary corporation into shares, obligations or other securities of the surviving corporation or of any other corporation or, in whole or in part, into cash or other property.

A copy of such plan of merger shall be mailed to each shareholder of record of the subsidiary corporation.

Articles of merger shall be executed in duplicate by the surviving corporation by its president or a vice president and by its secretary or an assistant secretary, and verified by one of its officers signing such articles, and shall set forth:

**(1)** The plan of merger;

**(2)** The number of outstanding shares of each class of the subsidiary corporation and the number of such shares of each class owned by the surviving corporation; and

**(3)** The date of the mailing to shareholders of the subsidiary corporation of a copy of the plan of merger.

On and after the thirtieth day after the mailing of a copy of the plan of merger to shareholders of the subsidiary corporation or upon the waiver thereof by the holders of all outstanding shares duplicate originals of the articles of merger shall be delivered to the Secretary of State. If the Secretary of State finds that such articles conform to law, he shall, when all fees and franchise taxes have been paid as in this Act prescribed:

**(A)** Endorse on each of such duplicate originals the word "Filed," and the month, day and year of the filing thereof,

**(B)** File one of such duplicate originals in his office, and

**(C)** Issue a certificate of merger to which he shall affix the other duplicate original.

The certificate of merger, together with the duplicate original of the articles of merger affixed thereto by the Secretary of State, shall be returned to the surviving corporation or its representative.

## § 76
### Effect of Merger, Consolidation or Exchange

Upon the issuance of the certificate of merger or the certificate of consolidation by the Secretary of State, the merger or consolidation shall be effected.

When such merger or consolidation has been effective:

**(a)** The several corporations parties to the plan of merger or consolidation shall be a single corporation, which, in the case of a merger, shall be that corporation designated in the plan of merger as the surviving corporation, and, in the case of a consolidation, shall be the new corporation provided for in the plan of consolidation.

**(b)** The separate existence of all corporations parties to the plan of merger or consolidation, except the surviving or new corporation, shall cease.

**(c)** Such surviving or new corporation shall have all the rights, privileges, immunities and powers and shall be subject to all the duties and liabilities of a corporation organized under this Act.

**(d)** Such surviving or new corporation shall thereupon and thereafter possess all the rights, privileges, immunities, and franchises, of a public as well as of a private nature, of each of the merging or consolidating corporations; and all property, real, personal and mixed, and all debts due on whatever account, including subscriptions to shares, and all other choses in action, and all and every other interest of or belonging to or due to each of the corporations so merged or consolidated, shall be taken and deemed to be transferred to and vested in such single corporation without further act or deed; and the title to any real estate, or any interest therein, vested in any of such corporations shall not revert or be in any way impaired by reason of such merger or consolidation.

**(e)** Such surviving or new corporation shall thenceforth be responsible and liable for all the liabilities and obligations of each of the corporations so merged or consolidated; and any claim existing or action or proceeding pending by or against any of such corporations may be prosecuted as if such merger or consolidation had not taken place, or such surviving or new corporation may be substituted in its place. Neither the rights of creditors nor any liens upon the property of any such corporation shall be impaired by such merger or consolidation.

**(f)** In the case of a merger, the articles of incorporation of the surviving corporation shall be deemed to be amended to the extent, if any, that changes in its articles of incorporation are stated in the plan of merger; and, in the case of a consolidation, the statements set forth in the articles of consolidation and which are required or permitted to be set forth in the articles of incorporation of corporations organized under this Act shall be deemed to be the original articles of incorporation of the new corporation.

## § 77
### Merger, Consolidation or Exchange of Shares Between Domestic and Foreign Corporations

One or more foreign corporations and one or more domestic corporations may be merged or consolidated in the following manner, if such merger or consolidation is permitted by the laws of the state under which each such foreign corporation is organized:

**(a)** Each domestic corporation shall comply with the provisions of this Act with respect to the merger or consolidation, as the case may be, of domestic corporations and each foreign corporation shall comply with the applicable provisions of the laws of the state under which it is organized.

**(b)** If the surviving or new corporation, as the case may be, is to be governed by the laws of any state other than this State, it shall comply with the provisions of this Act with respect to foreign corporations if it is to transact business in this State, and in every case it shall file with the Secretary of State of this State:

**(1)** An agreement that it may be served with process in this State in any proceeding for the enforcement of any obligation of any domestic corporation which is a party to such merger or consolidation and in any proceeding for the enforcement of the rights of a dissenting shareholder of any such domestic corporation against the surviving or new corporation;

**(2)** An irrevocable appointment of the Secretary of State of this State as its agent to accept service of process in any such proceeding; and

**(3)** An agreement that it will promptly pay to the dissenting shareholders of any such domestic corporation the amount, if any, to which they shall be entitled under the provisions of this Act with respect to the rights of dissenting shareholders.

The effect of such merger or consolidation shall be the same as in the case of the merger or consolidation of domestic corporations, if the surviving or new corporation is to be governed by the laws of this State. If the surviving or new corporation is to be governed by the laws of any state other than this State, the effect of such merger or consolidation shall be the same as in the case of the merger or consolidation of domestic corporations except insofar as the laws of such other state provide otherwise.

At any time prior to the filing of the articles of merger or consolidation, the merger or consolidation may be abandoned pursuant to provisions therefor, if any, set forth in the plan of merger or consolidation.

## § 78
### Sale of Assets in Regular Course of Business and Mortgage or Pledge of Assets

The sale, lease, exchange, or other disposition of all, or substantially all, the property and assets of a corporation in the usual and regular course of its business and the mortgage or pledge of any or all property and assets of a corporation whether or not in the usual and regular course of business may be made upon such terms and conditions and for such consideration, which may consist in whole or in part of cash or other property, including shares, obligations or other securities of any other corporation, domestic or foreign, as shall be authorized by its board of directors; and in any such case no authorization or consent of the shareholders shall be required.

## § 79
### Sale of Assets Other Than in Regular Course of Business

A sale, lease, exchange, or other disposition of all, or substantially all, the property and assets, with or without the good will, of a corporation, if not in the usual and regular course of its business, may be made upon such terms and conditions and for such consideration, which may consist in whole or in part of cash or other property, including shares, obligations or other securities of any other corporation, domestic or foreign, as may be authorized in the following manner:

(a) The board of directors shall adopt a resolution recommending such sale, lease, exchange, or other disposition and directing the submission thereof to a vote at a meeting of shareholders, which may be either an annual or a special meeting.

(b) Written notice shall be given to each shareholder of record, whether or not entitled to vote at such meeting, not less than twenty days before such meeting, in the manner provided in this Act for the giving of notice of meetings of shareholders, and, whether the meeting be an annual or a special meeting, shall state that the purpose, or one of the purposes is to consider the proposed sale, lease, exchange, or other disposition.

(c) At such meeting the shareholders may authorize such sale, lease, exchange, or other disposition and may fix, or may authorize the board of directors to fix, any or all of the terms and conditions thereof and the consideration to be received by the corporation therefor. Such authorization shall require the affirmative vote of the holders of a majority of the shares of the corporation entitled to vote thereon, unless any class of shares is entitled to vote thereon as a class, in which event such authorization shall require the affirmative vote of the holders of a majority of the shares of each class of shares entitled to vote as a class thereon and of the total shares entitled to vote thereon.

(d) After such authorization by a vote of shareholders, the board of directors nevertheless, in its discretion, may abandon such sale, lease, exchange, or other disposition of assets, subject to the rights of third parties under any contracts relating thereto, without further action or approval by shareholders.

## § 80
### Right of Shareholders to Dissent and Obtain Payment for Shares

(a) Any shareholder of a corporation shall have the right to dissent from, and to obtain payment for his shares in the event of, any of the following corporate actions:

(1) Any plan of merger or consolidation to which the corporation is a party, except as provided in subsection (c);

(2) Any sale or exchange of all or substantially all of the property and assets of the corporation not made in the usual or regular course of its business, including a sale in dissolution, but not including a sale pursuant to an order of a court having jurisdiction in the premises or a sale for cash on terms requiring that all or substantially all of the net proceeds of sale be distributed to the shareholders in accordance with their respective interests within one year after the date of sale;

(3) Any plan of exchange to which the corporation is a party as the corporation the shares of which are to be acquired;

(4) Any amendment of the articles of incorporation which materially and adversely affects the rights appurtenant to the shares of the dissenting shareholder in that it:

(A) alters or abolishes a preferential right of such shares;

(B) creates, alters or abolishes a right in respect of the redemption of such shares, including a provision respecting a sinking fund for the redemption or repurchase of such shares;

(C) alters or abolishes a preemptive right of the holder of such shares to acquire shares or other securities;

(D) excludes or limits the right of the holder of such shares to vote on any matter, or to cumulate his votes, except as such right may be limited by dilution through the issuance of shares or other securities with similar voting rights; or

(5) Any other corporate action taken pursuant to a shareholder vote with respect to which the articles of incorporation, the by-laws, or a resolution of the board of directors directs that dissenting shareholders shall have a right to obtain payment for their shares.

(b) (1) A record holder of shares may assert dissenters' rights as to less than all of the shares registered in his name only if he dissents with respect to all the shares beneficially owned by any one person, and discloses the name and address of the person or persons on whose behalf he dissents. In that event, his rights shall be determined as if the shares as to which he has dissented and his other shares were registered in the names of different shareholders.

(2) A beneficial owner of shares who is not the record holder may assert dissenters' rights with respect to shares held on his behalf, and shall be treated as a dissenting shareholder under the terms of this section and section 81 if he submits to the corporation at the time of or before the assertion of these rights a written consent of the record holder.

(c) The right to obtain payment under this section shall not apply to the shareholders of the surviving corporation in a merger if a vote of the shareholders of such corporation is not necessary to authorize such merger.

(d) A shareholder of a corporation who has a right under this section to obtain payment for his shares shall have no right at law or in equity to attack the validity of the corporate action that gives rise to his right to obtain payment, nor to have the action set aside or rescinded, except when the corporate action is unlawful or fraudulent with regard to the complaining shareholder or to the corporation.

§ 81
**Procedures for Protection of Dissenters' Rights**

(a) As used in this section:

(1) "Dissenter" means a shareholder or beneficial owner who is entitled to and does assert dissenters' rights under section 80, and who has performed every act required up to the time involved for the assertion of such rights.

(2) "Corporation" means the issuer of the shares held by the dissenter before the corporate action, or the successor by merger or consolidation of that issuer.

(3) "Fair value" of shares means their value immediately before the effectuation of the corporate action to which the dissenter objects, excluding any appreciation or depreciation in anticipation of such corporate action unless such exclusion would be inequitable.

(4) "Interest" means interest from the effective date of the corporate action until the date of payment, at the average rate currently paid by the corporation on its principal bank loans, or, if none, at such rate as is fair and equitable under all the circumstances.

(b) If a proposed corporate action which would give rise to dissenters' rights under section 80(a) is submitted to a vote at a meeting of shareholders, the notice of meeting shall notify all shareholders that they have or may have a right to dissent and obtain payment for their shares by complying with the terms of this section, and shall be accompanied by a copy of sections 80 and 81 of this Act.

(c) If the proposed corporate action is submitted to a vote at a meeting of shareholders, any shareholder who wishes to dissent and obtain payment for his shares must file with the corporation, prior to the vote, a written notice of intention to demand that he be paid fair compensation for his shares if the proposed action is effectuated, and shall refrain from voting his shares in approval of such action. A shareholder who fails in either respect shall acquire no right to payment for his shares under this section or section 80.

(d) If the proposed corporate action is approved by the required vote at a meeting of shareholders, the corporation shall mail a further notice to all shareholders who gave due notice of intention to demand payment and who refrained from voting in favor of the proposed action. If the proposed corporate action is to be taken without a vote of shareholders, the corporation shall send to all shareholders who are entitled to dissent and demand payment for their shares a notice of the adoption of the plan of corporate action. The notice shall (1) state where and when a demand for payment must be sent and certificates of certificated shares must be deposited in order to obtain payment, (2) inform holders of uncertificated shares to what extent transfer of shares will be restricted from the time that demand for payment is received, (3) supply a form for demanding payment which includes a request for certification of the date on which the shareholder, or the person on whose behalf the shareholder dissents, acquired beneficial ownership of the shares, and (4) be accompanied by a copy of sections 80 and 81 of this Act. The time set for the demand and deposit shall be not less than 30 days from the mailing of the notice.

(e) A shareholder who fails to demand payment, or fails (in the case of certificated shares) to deposit certificates, as required by a notice pursuant to subsection (d) shall have no right under this section or section 80 to receive payment for his shares. If the shares are not represented by certificates, the corporation may restrict their transfer from the time of receipt of demand for payment until effectuation of the proposed corporate action, or the release of restrictions under the terms of subsection (f). The dissenter shall retain all other rights of a shareholder until these rights are modified by effectuation of the proposed corporate action.

(f) (1) Within 60 days after the date set for demanding payment and depositing certificates, if the corporation has not effectuated the proposed corporate action and remitted payment for shares pursuant to paragraph (3), it shall return any certificates that have been deposited, and release uncertificated shares from any transfer restrictions imposed by reason of the demand for payment.

(2) When uncertificated shares have been released from transfer restrictions, and deposited certificates have been returned, the corporation may at any later time send a new notice conforming to the requirements of subsection (d), with like effect.

(3) Immediately upon effectuation of the proposed corporate action, or upon receipt of demand for payment if the corporate action has already been effectuated, the corporation shall remit to dissenters who have made demand and (if their shares are certificated) have deposited their certificates the amount which the corporation estimates to be the fair value of the shares, with interest if any has accrued. The remittance shall be accompanied by:

(A) the corporation's closing balance sheet and statement of income for a fiscal year ending not more than 16 months before the date of remittance, together with the latest available interim financial statements;

(B) a statement of the corporation's estimate of fair value of the shares; and

(C) a notice of the dissenter's right to demand supplemental payment, accompanied by a copy of sections 80 and 81 of this Act.

(g) (1) If the corporation fails to remit as required by subsection (f), or if the dissenter believes that the amount remitted is less than the fair value of his shares, or that the interest is not correctly determined, he may send the corporation his own estimate of the value of the shares or of the interest, and demand payment of the deficiency.

(2) If the dissenter does not file such an estimate within thirty days after the corporation's mailing of its remittance, he shall be entitled to no more than the amount remitted.

(h) (1) Within sixty days after receiving a demand for payment pursuant to subsection (g), if any such demands for payment remain unsettled, the corporation shall file in an appropriate court a petition requesting that the fair value of the shares and interest thereon be determined by the court.

(2) An appropriate court shall be a court of competent jurisdiction in the county of this state where the registered office of the corporation is located. If, in the case of a merger or consolidation or exchange of shares, the corporation is a foreign corporation without a registered office in this state, the petition shall be filed in the county where the registered office of the domestic corporation was last located.

(3) All dissenters, wherever residing, whose demands have not been settled shall be made parties to the proceeding as in an action against their shares. A copy of the petition shall be served on each such dissenter; if a dissenter is a nonresident, the copy may be served on him by registered or certified mail or by publication as provided by law.

(4) The jurisdiction of the court shall be plenary and exclusive. The court may appoint one or more persons as appraisers to receive evidence and recommend a decision on the question of fair value. The appraisers shall have such power and authority as shall be specified in the order of their appointment or in any amendment thereof. The dissenters shall be entitled to discovery in the same manner as parties in other civil suits.

(5) All dissenters who are made parties shall be entitled to judgment for the amount by which the fair value of their shares is found to exceed the amount previously remitted, with interest.

(6) If the corporation fails to file a petition as provided in paragraph (1) of this subsection, each dissenter who made a demand and who has not already settled his claim against the corporation shall be paid by the corporation the amount demanded by him, with interest, and may sue therefor in an appropriate court.

(i) (1) The costs and expenses of any proceeding under subsection (h), including the reasonable compensation and expenses of appraisers appointed by the court, shall be determined by the court and assessed against the corporation, except that any part of the costs and expenses may be apportioned and assessed as the court may deem equitable against all or some of the dissenters who are parties and whose action in demanding supplemental payment the court finds to be arbitrary, vexatious, or not in good faith.

(2) Fees and expenses of counsel and of experts for the respective parties may be assessed as the court may deem equitable against the corporation and in favor of any or all dissenters if the corporation failed to comply substantially with the requirements of this section, and may be assessed against either the corporation or a dissenter, in favor of any other party, if the court finds that the party against whom the fees and expenses are assessed acted arbitrarily, vexatiously, or not in good faith in respect to the rights provided by this Section and Section 80.

(3) If the court finds that the services of counsel for any dissenter were of substantial benefit to other dissenters similarly situated, and should not be assessed against the corporation, it may award to these counsel reasonable fees to be paid out of the amounts awarded to the dissenters who were benefitted.

(j) (1) Notwithstanding the foregoing provisions of this section, the corporation may elect to withhold the remittance required by subsection (f) from any dissenter with respect to shares of which the dissenter (or the person on whose behalf the dissenter acts) was not the beneficial owner on the date of the first announcement to news media or to shareholders of the terms of the proposed corporate action. With respect to such shares, the corporation shall, upon effectuating the corporate action, state to each dissenter its estimate of the fair value of the shares, state the rate of interest to be used (explaining the basis thereof), and offer to pay the resulting amounts on receiving the dissenter's agreement to accept them in full satisfaction.

(2) If the dissenter believes that the amount offered is less than the fair value of the shares and interest determined according to this section, he may within thirty days after the date of mailing of the corporation's offer, mail the corporation his own estimate of fair value and interest, and demand their payment. If the dissenter fails to do so, he shall be entitled to no more than the corporation's offer.

. . . .

## § 82
### Voluntary Dissolution by Incorporators

A corporation which has not commenced business and which has not issued any shares, may be voluntarily dissolved by its incorporators at any time in the following manner:

(a) Articles of dissolution shall be executed in duplicate by a majority of the incorporators, and verified by them, and shall set forth:

(1) The name of the corporation.

(2) The date of issuance of its certificate of incorporation.

(3) That none of its shares has been issued.

(4) That the corporation has not commenced business.

(5) That the amount, if any, actually paid in on subscriptions for its shares, less any part thereof disbursed for necessary expenses, has been returned to those entitled thereto.

(6) That no debts of the corporation remain unpaid.

(7) That a majority of the incorporators elect that the corporation be dissolved.

(b) Duplicate originals of the articles of dissolution shall be delivered to the Secretary of State. If the Secretary of State finds that the articles of dissolution conform to law, he shall, when all fees and franchise taxes have been paid as in this Act prescribed:

(1) Endorse on each of such duplicate originals the word "Filed," and the month, day and year of the filing thereof.

(2) File one of such duplicate originals in his office.

(3) Issue a certificate of dissolution to which he shall affix the other duplicate original.

The certificate of dissolution, together with the duplicate original of the articles of dissolution affixed thereto by the Secretary of State, shall be returned to the incorporators or their representative. Upon the issuance of such certificate of dissolution by the Secretary of State, the existence of the corporation shall cease.

## § 83
### Voluntary Dissolution by Consent of Shareholders

A corporation may be voluntarily dissolved by the written consent of all of its shareholders.

Upon the execution of such written consent, a statement of intent to dissolve shall be executed in duplicate by the corporation by its president or a vice president and by its secretary or an assistant secretary, and verified by one of the officers signing such statement, which statement shall set forth:

(a) The name of the corporation.

(b) The names and respective addresses of its officers.

(c) The names and respective addresses of its directors.

(d) A copy of the written consent signed by all shareholders of the corporation.

(e) A statement that such written consent has been signed by all shareholders of the corporation or signed in their names by their attorneys thereunto duly authorized.

## § 84
### Voluntary Dissolution by Act of Corporation

A corporation may be dissolved by the act of the corporation, when authorized in the following manner:

(a) The board of directors shall adopt a resolution recommending that the corporation be dissolved, and directing that the question of such dissolution be submitted to a vote at a meeting of shareholders, which may be either an annual or a special meeting.

(b) Written notice shall be given to each shareholder of record entitled to vote at such meeting within the time and in the manner provided in this Act for the giving of notice of meetings of shareholders, and, whether the meeting be an annual or special meeting, shall state that the purpose, or one of the purposes, of such meeting is to consider the advisability of dissolving the corporation.

(c) At such meeting a vote of shareholders entitled to vote thereat shall be taken on a resolution to dissolve the corporation. Such resolution shall be adopted upon receiving the affirmative vote of the holders of a majority of the shares of the corporation entitled to vote thereon, unless any class of shares is entitled to vote theron as a class, in which event the resolution shall be adopted upon receiving the affirmative vote of the holders of a majority of the shares of each class of shares entitled to vote thereon as a class and of the total shares entitled to vote thereon.

(d) Upon the adoption of such resolution, a statement of intent to dissolve shall be executed in duplicate by the corporation by its president or a vice president and by its secretary or an assistsant secretary, and verified by one of the officers signing such statement, which statement shall set forth:

(1) The name of the corporation.

(2) The names and respective addresses of its officers.

(3) The names and respective addresses of its directors.

(4) A copy of the resolution adopted by the shareholders authorizing the dissolution of the corporation.

(5) The number of shares outstanding, and, if the shares of any class are entitled to vote as a class, the designation and number of outstanding shares of each such class.

(6) The number of shares voted for and against the resolution, respectively, and, if the shares of any class are entitled to vote as a class, the number of shares of each such class voted for and against the resolution, respectively.

## § 85
### Filing of Statement of Intent to Dissolve

Duplicate originals of the statement of intent to dissolve, whether by consent of shareholders or by act of the corporation, shall be delivered to the Secretary of State. . . .

## § 86
### Effect of Statement of Intent to Dissolve

Upon the filing by the Secretary of State of a statement of intent to dissolve, whether by consent of shareholders or by act of the corporation, the corporation shall cease to carry on its business, except insofar as may be necessary for the winding up thereof, but its corporate existence shall continue until a certificate of dissolution has been issued by the Secretary of State or until a decree dissolving the corporation has been entered by a court of competent jurisdiction as in this Act provided.

## § 87
### Procedure after Filing of Statement of Intent to Dissolve

After the filing by the Secretary of State of a statement of intent to dissolve:

(a) The corporation shall immediately cause notice thereof to be mailed to each known creditor of the corporation.

(b) The corporation shall proceed to collect its assets, convey and dispose of such of its properties as are not to be distributed in kind to its shareholders, pay, satisfy and discharge its liabilities and obligations and do all other acts required to liquidate its business and affairs, and, after paying or adequately providing for the payment of all its obligations, distribute the remainder of its assets, either in cash or in kind, among its shareholders according to their respective rights and interests.

(c) The corporation, at any time during the liquidation of its business and affairs, may make application to a court of competent jurisdiction with the state and judicial subdivision in which the registered office or principal place of business of the corporation is situated, to have the liquidation continued under the supervision of the court as provided in this Act.

## § 88
### Revocation of Voluntary Dissolution Proceedings by Consent of Shareholders

. . . .

## § 89
### Revocation of Voluntary Dissolution Proceedings by Act of Corporation

. . . .

(d) Upon the adoption of such resolution, a statement of revocation of voluntary dissolution proceedings shall be executed in duplicate by the corporation by its president or a vice president and by its secretary or an assistant secretary, and verified by one of the officers signing such statement, which statement shall set forth:

(1) The name of the corporation.

(2) The names and respective addresses of its officers.

(3) The names and respective addresses of its directors.

(4) A copy of the resolution adopted by the shareholders revoking the voluntary dissolution proceedings.

(5) The number of shares outstanding.

(6) The number of shares voted for and against the resolution, respectively.

## § 90
### Filing of Statement of Revocation of Voluntary Dissolution Proceedings

....

## § 91
### Effect of Statement of Revocation of Voluntary Dissolution Proceedings

....

## § 92
### Articles of Dissolution

If voluntary dissolution proceedings have not been revoked, then when all debts, liabilities and obligations of the corporation have been paid and discharged, or adequate provision has been made therefor, and all of the remaining property and assets of the corporation have been distributed to its shareholders, articles of dissolution shall be executed in duplicate by the corporation by its president or a vice president and by its secretary or an assistant secretary, and verified by one of the officers signing such statement, which statement shall set forth:

(a) The name of the corporation.

(b) That the Secretary of State has theretofore filed a statement of intent to dissolve the corporation, and the date on which such statement was filed.

(c) That all debts, obligations and liabilities of the corporation have been paid and discharged or that adequate provision has been made therefor.

(d) That all the remaining property and assets of the corporation have been distributed among its shareholders in accordance with their respective rights and interests.

(e) That there are no suits pending against the corporation in any court, or that adequate provision has been made for the satisfaction of any judgment, order or decree which may be entered against it in any pending suit.

## § 93
### Filing of Articles of Dissolution

Duplicate originals of such articles of dissolution shall be delivered to the Secretary of State. If the Secretary of State finds that such articles of dissolution conform to law, he shall, when all fees and franchise taxes have been paid as in this Act prescribed: ...

(c) Issue a certificate of dissolution to which he shall affix the other duplicate original. ...

## § 94
### Involuntary Dissolution

A corporation may be dissolved involuntarily by a decree of the ............ court in an action filed by the Attorney General when it is established that:

(a) The corporation has failed to file its annual report within the time required by this Act, or has failed to pay its franchise tax on or before the first day of August of the year in which such franchise tax becomes due and payable; or

(b) The corporation procured its articles of incorporation through fraud; or

(c) The corporation has continued to exceed or abuse the authority conferred upon it by law; or

(d) The corporation has failed for thirty days to appoint and maintain a registered agent in this State; or

(e) The corporation has failed for thirty days after change of its registered office or registered agent to file in the office of the Secretary of State a statement of such change.

## § 95
### Notification to Attorney General

The Secretary of State, on or before the last day of December of each year, shall certify to the Attorney General the names of all corporations which have failed to file their annual reports or to pay franchise taxes in accordance with the provisions of this Act, together with the facts pertinent thereto. He shall also certify, from time to time, the names of all corporations which have given other cause for dissolution as provided in this Act, together with the facts pertinent thereto. Whenever the Secretary of State shall certify the name of a corporation to the Attorney General as having given any cause for dissolution, the Secretary of State shall concurrently mail to the corporation at its registered office a notice that such certification has been made. Upon the receipt of such certification, the Attorney General shall file an action in the name of the State against such corporation for its dissolution. ...

## § 96
### Venue and Process

....

## § 97
### Jurisdiction of Court to Liquidate Assets and Business of Corporation

The ............ courts shall have full power to liquidate the assets and business of a corporation:

(a) In an action by a shareholder when it is established:

(1) That the directors are deadlocked on the management of the corporate affairs and the shareholders are unable to break the deadlock, and that irreparable injury to the corporation is being suffered or is threatened by reason thereof; or

(2) That the acts of the directors or those in control of the corporation are illegal, oppressive or fraudulent; or

(3) That the shareholders are deadlocked in voting power, and have failed, for a period which includes at least two consecutive annual meeting dates, to elect successors to directors whose terms have expired or would have expired upon the election of their successors; or

(4) That the corporate assets are being misapplied or wasted.

(b) In an action by a creditor:

(1) When the claim of the creditor has been reduced to judgment and an execution thereon returned unsatisfied and it is established that the corporation is insolvent; or

(2) When the corporation has admitted in writing that the claim

of the creditor is due and owing and it is established that the corporation is insolvent.

(c) Upon application by a corporation which has filed a statement of intent to dissolve, as provided in this Act, to have its liquidation continued under the supervision of the court.

(d) When an action has been filed by the Attorney General to dissolve a corporation and it is established that liquidation of its business and affairs should precede the entry of a decree of dissolution.

Proceedings under clause (a), (b) or (c) of this section shall be brought in the county in which the registered office or the principal office of the corporation is situated.

It shall not be necessary to make shareholders parties to any such action or proceeding unless relief is sought against them personally.

## § 98
### Procedure in Liquidation of Corporation by Court

In proceedings to liquidate the assets and business of a corporation the court shall have the power to issue injunctions, to appoint a receiver or receivers pendente lite, with such powers and duties as the court, from time to time, may direct, and to take such other proceedings as may be requisite to preserve the corporate assets wherever situated, and carry on the business of the corporation until a full hearing can be had.

After a hearing had upon such notice as the court may direct to be given to all parties to the proceedings and to any other parties in interest designated by the court, the court may appoint a liquidating receiver or receivers with authority to collect the assets of the corporation, including all amounts owing to the corporation by subscribers on account of any unpaid portion of the consideration for the issuance of shares. Such liquidating receiver or receivers shall have authority, subject to the order of the court, to sell, convey and dispose of all or any part of the assets of the corporation wherever situated, either at public or private sale. The assets of the corporation or the proceeds resulting from a sale, conveyance or other disposition thereof shall be applied to the expenses of such liquidation and to the payment of the liabilities and obligations of the corporation, and any remaining assets or proceeds shall be distributed among its shareholders according to their respective rights and interests. The order appointing such liquidating receiver or receivers shall state their powers and duties. Such powers and duties may be increased or diminished at any time during the proceedings.

The court shall have power to allow from time to time as expenses of the liquidation compensation to the receiver or receivers and to attorneys in the proceeding, and to direct the payment thereof out of the assets of the corporation or the proceeds of any sale or disposition of such assets.

A receiver of a corporation appointed under the provisions of this section shall have authority to sue and defend in all courts in his own name as receiver of such corporation. The court appointing such receiver shall have exclusive jurisdiction of the corporation and its property, wherever situated.

## § 99
### Qualifications of Receivers

. . . .

## § 100
### Filing of Claims in Liquidation Proceedings

. . . .

## § 101
### Discontinuance of Liquidation Proceedings

. . . .

## § 102
### Decree of Involuntary Dissolution

In proceedings to liquidate the assets and business of a corporation, when the costs and expenses of such proceedings and all debts, obligations and liabilities of the corporation shall have been paid and discharged and all of its remaining property and assets distributed to its shareholders, or in case its property and assets are not sufficient to satisfy and discharge such costs, expenses, debts, and obligations, all the property and assets have been applied so far as they will go to their payment, the court shall enter a decree dissolving the corporation, whereupon the existence of the corporation shall cease.

## § 103
### Filing of Decree of Dissolution

. . . .

## § 104
### Deposit with State Treasurer of Amount Due Certain Shareholders

Upon the voluntary or involuntary dissolution of a corporation, the portion of the assets distributable to a creditor or shareholder who is unknown or cannot be found, or who is under disability and there is no person legally competent to receive such distributive portion, shall be reduced to cash and deposited with the State Treasurer and shall be paid over to such creditor or shareholder or to his legal representative upon proof satisfactory to the State Treasurer of his right thereto.

## § 105
### Survival of Remedy after Dissolution

The dissolution of a corporation either (1) by the issuance of a certificate of dissolution by the Seretary of State, or (2) by a decree of court when the court has not liquidated the assets and business of the corporation as provided in this Act, or (3) by expiration of its period of duration, shall not take away or impair any remedy available to or against such corporation, its directors, officers, or shareholders, for any right or claim existing, or any liability incurred, prior to such dissolution if action or other proceeding thereon is commenced within two years after the date of such dissolution. Any such action or proceeding by or against the corporation may be prosecuted or defended by the corporation in its corporate name. The shareholders, directors and officers shall have power to take such corporate or other action as shall be appropriate to protect such remedy, right or claim. If such corporation was dissolved by the expiration of its period of duration, such corporation may amend its articles of incorporation at any time during such period of two years so as to extend its period of duration.

## § 106
### Admission of Foreign Corporation

No foreign corporation shall have the right to transact business in this State until it shall have procured a certificate of authority so to do from the Secretary of State. No foreign corporation shall be entitled to procure a certificate of authority under this Act to transact in this State any business which a corporation organized under this Act is not permitted to transact. A foreign corporation shall not be denied a certificate of authority by reason of the fact that the laws of the state or county under which such corporation is organized governing its organization and internal affairs differ from the laws of this State, and nothing in this Act contained shall be construed to authorize this State to regulate the organization or the internal affairs of such corporation.

Without excluding other activities which may not constitute transacting business in this State, a foreign corporation shall not be considered to be transacting business in this State, for the purposes of this Act, by reason of carrying on in this State any one or more of the following activities:

(a) Maintaining or defending any action or suit or any administrative or arbitration proceeding, or effecting the settlement thereof or the settlement of claims or disputes.

(b) Holding meetings of its directors or shareholders or carrying on other activities concerning its internal affairs.

(c) Maintaining bank accounts.

(d) Maintaining offices or agencies for the transfer, exchange and registration of its securities, or appointing and maintaining trustees or depositaries with relation to its securities.

(e) Effecting sales through independent contractors.

(f) Soliciting or procuring orders, whether by mail or through employees or agents or otherwise, where such orders require acceptance without this State before becoming binding contracts.

(g) Creating as borrower or lender, or acquiring, indebtedness or mortgages or other security interests in real or personal property.

(h) Securing or collecting debts or enforcing any rights in property securing the same.

(i) Transacting any business in interstate commerce.

(j) Conducting an isolated transaction completed within a period of thirty days and not in the course of a number of repeated transactions of like nature.

## § 107
### Powers of Foreign Corporation

A foreign corporation which shall have received a certificate of authority under this Act shall, until a certificate of revocation or of withdrawal shall have been issued as provided in this Act, enjoy the same, but no greater, rights and privileges as a domestic corporation organized for the purposes set forth in the application pursuant to which such certificate of authority is issued; and, except as in this Act otherwise provided, shall be subject to the same duties, restrictions, penalties and liabilities now or hereafter imposed upon a domestic corporation of like character.

## § 108
### Corporate Name of Foreign Corporation

No certificate of authority shall be issued to a foreign corporation unless the corporate name of such corporation:

(a) Shall contain the word "corporation," "company," "incorporated," or "limited," or shall contain an abbreviation of one of such words, or such corporation shall, for use in this State, add at the end of its name one of such words or an abbreviation thereof.

(b) Shall not contain any word or phrase which indicates or implies that it is organized for any purpose other than one or more of the purposes contained in its articles of incorporation or that it is authorized or empowered to conduct the business of banking or insurance.

(c) Shall not be the same as, or deceptively similar to, the name of any domestic corporation existing under the laws of this State or any foreign corporation authorized to transact business in this State, or a name the exclusive right to which is, at the time, reserved in the manner provided in this Act, or the name of a corporation which has in effect a registration of its name as provided in this Act except that this provision shall not apply if the foreign corporation applying for a certificate of authority files with the Secretary of State any one of the following:

(1) a resolution of its board of directors adopting a fictitious name for use in transacting business in this State which fictitious name is not deceptively similar to the name of any domestic corporation or of any foreign corporation authorized to transact business in this State or to any name reserved or registered as provided in this Act, or

(2) the written consent of such other corporation or holder of a reserved or registered name to use the same or deceptively similar name and one or more words are added to make such name distinguishable from such other name, or

(3) a certified copy of a final decree of a court of competent jurisdiction establishing the prior right of such foreign corporation to the use of such name in this State.

## § 109
### Change of Name by Foreign Corporation

Whenever a foreign corporation which is authorized to transact business in this State shall change its name to one under which a certificate of authority would not be granted to it on application therefor, the certificate of authority of such corporation shall be suspended and it shall not thereafter transact any business in this State until it has changed its name to a name which is available to it under the laws of this State or has otherwise complied with the provisions of this Act.

## § 110
### Application for Certificate of Authority

A foreign corporation, in order to procure a certificate of authority to transact business in this State, shall make application therefor to the Secretary of State, which application shall set forth:

(a) The name of the corporation and the state or county under the laws of which it is incorporated.

(b) If the name of the corporation does not contain the word "corporation," "company," "incorporated," or "limited," or does not contain an abbreviation of one of such words, then the name of the corporation with the word or abbreviation which it elects to add thereto for use in this State.

(c) The date of incorporation and the period of duration of the corporation.

**(d)** The address of the principal office of the corporation in the state or country under the laws of which it is incorporated.

**(e)** The address of the proposed registered office of the corporation in this State, and the name of its proposed registered agent in this State at such address.

**(f)** The purpose or purposes of the corporation which it proposes to pursue in the transaction of business in this State.

**(g)** The names and respective addresses of the directors and officers of the corporation.

**(h)** A statement of the aggregate number of shares which the corporation has authority to issue, itemized by classes and series, if any, within a class.

**(i)** A statement of the aggregate number of issued shares, itemized by class and by series, if any, within each class.

**(j)** An estimate, expressed in dollars, of the value of all property to be owned by the corporation for the following year, wherever located, and an estimate of the value of the property of the corporation to be located within this State during such year, and an estimate, expressed in dollars of the gross amount of business which will be transacted by the corporation during such year, and an estimate of the gross amount thereof which will be transacted by the corporation at or from places of business in this State during such year.

**(k)** Such additional information as may be necessary or appropriate in order to enable the Secretary of State to determine whether such corporation is entitled to a certificate of authority to transact business in this State and to determine and assess the fees and franchise taxes payable as in this Act prescribed.

Such application shall be made on forms prescribed and furnished by the Secretary of State and shall be executed in duplicate by the corporation by its president or a vice president and by its secretary or an assistant secretary, and verified by one of the officers signing such application.

## § 111
### Filing of Application for Certificate of Authority

Duplicate originals of the application of the corporation for a certificate of authority shall be delivered to the Secretary of State, together with a copy of its articles of incorporation and all amendments thereto, duly authenticated by the proper officer of the state or country under the laws of which it is incorporated.

If the Secretary of State finds that such application conforms to law, he shall, when all fees and franchise taxes have been paid as in this Act prescribed: . . .

**(c)** Issue a certificate of authority to transact business in this State to which he shall affix the other duplicate original application. . . .

## § 112
### Effect of Certificate of Authority

Upon the issuance of a certificate of authority by the Secretary of State, the corporation shall be authorized to transact business in this State for those purposes set forth in its application, subject, however, to the right of this State to suspend or to revoke such authority as provided in this Act.

## § 113
### Registered Office and Registered Agent of Foreign Corporation

Each foreign corporation authorized to transact business in this State shall have and continuously maintain in this State:

**(a)** A registered office which may be, but need not be, the same as its place of business in this State.

**(b)** A registered agent, which agent may be either an individual resident in this State whose business office is identical with such registered office, or a domestic corporation, or a foreign corporation authorized to transact business in this State, having a business office identical with such registered office.

## § 114
### Change of Registered Office or Registered Agent of Foreign Corporation

A foreign corporation authorized to transact business in this State may change its registered office or change its registered agent, or both, upon filing in the office of the Secretary of State a statement setting forth:

**(a)** The name of the corporation.

**(b)** The address of its then registered office.

**(c)** If the address of its registered office be changed, the address to which the registered office is to be changed.

**(d)** The name of its then registered agent.

**(e)** If its registered agent be changed, the name of its successor registered agent.

**(f)** That the address of its registered office and the address of the business office of its registered agent, as changed, will be identical.

**(g)** That such change was authorized by resolution duly adopted by its board of directors.

Such statement shall be executed by the corporation by its president or a vice president, and verified by him, and delivered to the Secretary of State. If the Secretary of State finds that such statement conforms to the provisions of this Act, he shall file such statement in his office, and upon such filing the change of address of the registered office, or the appointment of a new registered agent, or both, as the case may be, shall become effective.

Any registered agent of a foreign corporation may resign as such agent upon filing a written notice thereof, executed in duplicate, with the Secretary of State, who shall forthwith mail a copy thereof to the corporation at its principal office in the state or country under the laws of which it is incorporated. The appointment of such agent shall terminate upon the expiration of thirty days after receipt of such notice by the Secretary of State.

If a registered agent changes his or its business address to another place within the same . . . . . . . . . . . . ,* he or it may change such address and the address of the registered office of any corporation of which he or it is registered agent by filing a statement as required above except that it need be signed only by the registered agent and need not be responsive to (e) or (g) and must recite that a copy of the statement has been mailed to the corporation.

---

*Supply designation of jurisdiction, such as country, etc., in accordance with local practice.

## § 115
### Service of Process on Foreign Corporation

The registered agent so appointed by a foreign corporation authorized to transact business in this State shall be an agent of such corporation upon whom any process, notice or demand required or permitted by law to be served upon the corporation may be served.

Whenever a foreign corporation authorized to transact business in this State shall fail to appoint or maintain a registered agent in this State, or whenever any such registered agent cannot with reasonable diligence be found at the registered office, or whenever the certificate of authority of a foreign corporation shall be suspended or revoked, then the Secretary of State shall be an agent of such corporation upon whom any such process, notice, or demand may be served. Service on the Secretary of State of any such process, notice or demand shall be made by delivering to and leaving with him, or with any clerk having charge of the corporation department of his office, duplicate copies of such process, notice or demand. In the event any such process, notice or demand is served on the Secretary of State, he shall immediately cause one of such copies thereof to be forwarded by registered mail, addressed to the corporation at its principal office in the state or country under the laws of which it is incorporated. Any service so had on the Secretary of State shall be returnable in not less than thirty days.

The Secretary of State shall keep a record of all processes, notices and demands served upon him under this section, and shall record therein the time of such service and his action with reference thereto.

Nothing herein contained shall limit or affect the right to serve any process, notice or demand, required or permitted by law to be served upon a foreign corporation in any other manner now or hereafter permitted by law.

## § 116
### Amendment to Articles of Incorporation of Foreign Corporation

Whenever the articles of incorporation of a foreign corporation authorized to transact business in this State are amended, such foreign corporation shall, within thirty days after such amendment becomes effective, file in the office of the Secretary of State a copy of such amendment duly authenticated by the proper officer of the state or country under the laws of which it is incorporated; but the filing thereof shall not of itself enlarge or alter the purpose or purposes which such corporation is authorized to pursue in the transaction of business in this State, nor authorize such corporation to transact business in this State under any other name than the name set forth in its certificate of authority.

## § 117
### Merger of Foreign Corporation Authorized to Transact Business in This State

Whenever a foreign corporation authorized to transact business in this State shall be a party to a statutory merger permitted by the laws of the state or country under the laws of which it is incorporated, and such corporation shall be the surviving corporation, it shall, within thirty days after such merger becomes effective, file with the Secretary of State a copy of the articles of merger duly authenticated by the proper officer of the state or country under the laws of which such statutory merger was effected; and it shall not be necessary for such corporation to procure either a new or amended certificate of authority to transact business in this State unless the name of such corporation be changed thereby or unless the corporation desires to pursue in this State other or additional purposes than those which it is then authorized to transact in this State.

## § 118
### Amended Certificate of Authority

A foreign corporation authorized to transact business in this State shall procure an amended certificate of authority in the event it changes its corporate name, or desires to pursue in this State other or additional purposes than those set forth in its prior application for a certificate of authority, by making application therefor to the Secretary of State.

The requirements in respect to the form and contents of such application, the manner of its execution, the filing of duplicate originals thereof with the Secretary of State, the issuance of an amended certificate of authority and the effect thereof, shall be the same as in the case of an original application for a certificate of authority.

## § 119
### Withdrawal of Foreign Corporation

A foreign corporation authorized to transact business in this State may withdraw from this State upon procuring from the Secretary of State a certificate of withdrawal. In order to procure such certificate of withdrawal, such foreign corporation shall deliver to the Secretary of State an application for withdrawal, which shall set forth:

**(a)** The name of the corporation and the state or country under the laws of which it is incorporated.

**(b)** That the corporation is not transacting business in this State.

**(c)** That the corporation surrenders its authority to transact business in this State.

**(d)** That the corporation revokes the authority of its registered agent in this State to accept service of process and consents that service of process in any action, suit or proceeding based upon any cause of action arising in this State during the time the corporation was authorized to transact business in this State may thereafter be made on such corporation by service thereof on the Secretary of State.

**(e)** A post-office address to which the Secretary of State may mail a copy of any process against the corporation that may be served on him.

**(f)** A statement of the aggregate number of shares which the corporation has authority to issue, itemized by class and series, if any, within each class, as of the date of such application.

**(g)** A statement of the aggregate number of issued shares, itemized by class and series, if any, within each class, as of the date of such application.

**(h)** Such additional information as may be necessary or appropriate in order to enable the Secretary of State to determine and assess any unpaid fees or franchise taxes payable by such foreign corporation as in this Act prescribed.

The application for withdrawal shall be made on forms prescribed and furnished by the Secretary of State and shall be executed by the corporation by its president or a vice president and by its secretary or an assistant secretary, and verified by one of the officers signing the application, or, if the corporation is in the hands of a receiver or trustee, shall be executed on behalf of the corporation by such receiver or trustee and verified by him.

## § 120
**Filing of Application for Withdrawal**

. . . .

## § 121
**Revocation of Certificate of Authority**

The certificate of authority of a foreign corporation to transact business in this State may be revoked by the Secretary of State upon the conditions prescribed in this section when:

**(a)** The corporation has failed to file its annual report within the time required by this Act, or has failed to pay any fees, franchise taxes or penalties prescribed by this Act when they have become due and payable; or

**(b)** The corporation has failed to appoint and maintain a registered agent in this State as required by this Act; or

**(c)** The corporation has failed, after change of its registered office or registered agent, to file in the office of the Secretary of State a statement of such change as required by this Act; or

**(d)** The corporation has failed to file in the office of the Secretary of State any amendment to its articles of incorporation or any articles of merger within the time prescribed by this Act; or

**(e)** A misrepresentation has been made of any material matter in any application, report, affidavit, or other document submitted by such corporation pursuant to this Act.

No certificate of authority of a foreign corporation shall be revoked by the Secretary of State unless (1) he shall have given the corporation not less than sixty days' notice thereof by mail addressed to its registered office in this State, and (2) the corporation shall fail prior to revocation to file such annual report, or pay such fees, franchise taxes or penalties, or file the required statement of change of registered agent or registered office, or file such articles of amendment or articles of merger, or correct such misrepresentation.

## § 122
**Issuance of Certificate of Revocation**

. . . .

## § 123
**Application to Corporations Heretofore Authorized to Transact Business in This State**

. . . .

## § 124
**Transacting Business Without Certificate of Authority**

No foreign corporation transacting business in this State without a certificate of authority shall be permitted to maintain any action, suit or proceeding in any court of this State, until such corporation shall have obtained a certificate of authority. Nor shall any action, suit or proceeding be maintained in any court of this State by any successor or assignee of such corporation on any right, claim or demand arising out of the transaction of business by such corporation in this State, until a certificate of authority shall have been obtained by such corporation or by a corporation which has acquired all or substantially all of its assets.

The failure of a foreign corporation to obtain a certificate of authority to transact business in this State shall not impair the validity of any contract or act of such corporation, and shall not prevent such corporation from defending any action, suit or proceeding in any court of this State.

A foreign corporation which transacts business in this State without a certificate of authority shall be liable to this State, for the years or parts thereof during which it transacted business in this State without a certificate of authority, in an amount equal to all fees and franchise taxes which would have been imposed by this Act upon such corporation had it duly applied for and received a certificate of authority to transact business in this State as required by this Act and thereafter filed all reports required by this Act, plus all penalties imposed by this Act for failure to pay such fees and franchise taxes. The Attorney General shall bring proceedings to recover all amounts due this State under the provisions of this Section.

## § 125
**Annual Report of Domestic and Foreign Corporations**

Each domestic corporation, and each foreign corporation authorized to transact business in this State, shall file, within the time prescribed by this Act, an annual report setting forth:

**(a)** The name of the corporation and the state or country under the laws of which it is incorporated.

**(b)** The address of the registered office of the corporation in this State, and the name of its registered agent in this State at such address, and, in case of a foreign corporation, the address of its principal office in the state or country under the laws of which it is incorporated.

**(c)** A brief statement of the character of the business in which the corporation is actually engaged in this State.

**(d)** The names and respective addresses of the directors and officers of the corporation.

**(e)** A statement of the aggregate number of shares which the corporation has authority to issue, itemized by class and series, if any, within each class.

**(f)** A statement of the aggregate number of issued shares, itemized by class and series, if any, within each class.

**(g)** A statement, expressed in dollars, of the value of all the property owned by the corporation, wherever located, and the value of the property of the corporation located within this State, and a statement, expressed in dollars, of the gross amount of business transacted by the corporation for the twelve months ended on the thirty-first day of December preceding the date herein provided for the filing of such report and the gross amount thereof transacted by the corporation at or from places of business in this State. If, on the thirty-first day of December preceding the time herein provided for the filing of such report, the corporation had not been in existence for a period of twelve months, or in the case of a foreign corporation had not been authorized to transact business in this State for a period of twelve months, the statement with respect to business transacted shall be furnished for the period between the date of incorporation or the date of its authorization to transact business in this State, as the case may be, and such thirty-first day of December. If all the property of the corporation is located in this State and all of its business is transacted at or from places of business in this State, then the information required by this subparagraph need not be set forth in such report.

**(h)** Such additional information as may be necessary or appropriate in order to enable the Secretary of State to determine and assess the proper amount of franchise taxes payable by such corporation.

Such annual report shall be made on forms prescribed and furnished by the Secretary of State, and the information therein contained shall be given as of the date of the execution of the report, except as to the information required by subparagraphs (g) and (h) which shall be given as of the close of business on the thirty-first day of December next preceding the date herein provided for the filing of such report. It shall be executed by the corporation by its president, a vice president, secretary, an assistant secretary, or treasurer, and verified by the officer executing the report, or, if the corporation is in the hands of a receiver or trustee, it shall be executed on behalf of the corporation and verified by such receiver or trustee.

### § 126
**Filing of Annual Report of Domestic and Foreign Corporations**

. . . .

### § 127
**Fees, Franchise Taxes and Charges to be Collected by Secretary of State**

. . . .

### § 128
**Fees for Filing Documents and Issuing Certificates**

. . . .

### § 129
**Miscellaneous Charges**

. . . .

### § 130
**License Fees Payable by Domestic Corporations**

. . . .

### § 131
**License Fees Payable by Foreign Corporations**

. . . .

### § 132
**Franchise Taxes Payable by Domestic Corporations**

. . . .

### § 133
**Franchise Taxes Payable by Foreign Corporations**

. . . .

### § 134
**Assessment and Collection of Annual Franchise Taxes**

. . . .

### § 135
**Penalties Imposed Upon Corporations**

Each corporation, domestic or foreign, that fails or refuses to file its annual report for any year within the time prescribed by this Act shall be subject to a penalty of ten percent of the amount of the franchise tax assessed against it for the period beginning July 1 of the year in which such report should have been filed. Such penalty shall be assessed by the Secretary of State at the time of the assessment of the franchise tax. If the amount of the franchise tax as originally assessed against such corporation be thereafter adjusted in accordance with the provisions of this Act, the amount of the penalty shall be likewise adjusted to ten percent of the amount of the adjusted franchise tax. The amount of the franchise tax and the amount of the penalty shall be separately stated in any notice to the corporation with respect thereto.

If the franchise tax assessed in accordance with the provisions of this Act shall not be paid on or before the thirty-first day of July, it shall be deemed to be delinquent, and there shall be added a penalty of one percent for each month or part of month that the same is delinquent, commencing with the month of August.

Each corporation, domestic or foreign, that fails or refuses to answer truthfully and fully within the time prescribed by this Act interrogatories propounded by the Secretary of State in accordance with the provisions of this Act, shall be deemed to be guilty of a misdemeanor and upon conviction thereof may be fined in any amount not exceeding five hundred dollars.

### § 136
**Penalties Imposed Upon Officers and Directors**

Each officer and director of a corporation, domestic or foreign, who fails or refuses within the time prescribed by this Act to answer truthfully and fully interrogatories propounded to him by the Secretary of State in accordance with the provisions of this Act, or who signs any articles, statement, report, application or other document filed with the Secretary of State which is known to such officer or director to be false in any material respect, shall be deemed to be guilty of a misdemeanor, and upon conviction thereof may be fined in any amount not exceeding . . . . . . . . . . . . dollars.

### § 137
**Interrogatories by Secretary of State**

The Secretary of State may propound to any corporation, domestic or foreign, subject to the provisions of this Act, and to any officer or director thereof, such interrogatories as may be reasonably necessary and proper to enable him to ascertain whether such corporation has complied with all the provisions of this Act applicable to such corporation. Such interrogatories shall be answered within thirty days after the mailing thereof, or within such additional time as shall be fixed by the Secretary of State, and the answers thereto shall be full and complete and shall be made in writing and under oath. If such interrogatories be directed to an individual they shall be answered by him, and if directed to a corporation they shall be answered by the president, vice president, secretary or assistant secretary thereof. The Secretary of State need not file any document to which such interrogatories relate until such interrogatories be answered as herein provided, and not then if the answers thereto disclose that such document is not in conformity with the provisions of this Act. The Secretary of State shall certify to the Attorney General, for such action as the Attorney General may deem appropriate, all interrogatories and answers thereto which disclose a violation of any of the provisions of this Act.

## § 138
### Information Disclosed by Interrogatories

. . . .

## § 139
### Powers of Secretary of State

. . . .

## § 140
### Appeal from Secretary of State

If the Secretary of State shall fail to approve any articles of incorporation, amendment, merger, consolidation or dissolution, or any other document required by this Act to be approved by the Secretary of State before the same shall be filed in his office, he shall, within ten days after the delivery thereof to him, give written notice of his disapproval to the person or corporation, domestic or foreign, delivering the same, specifying the reasons therefor. From such disapproval such person or corporation may appeal to the . . . . . . . . . . . court of the county in which the registered office of such corporation is, or is proposed to be, situated by filing with the clerk of such court a petition setting forth a copy of the articles or other document sought to be filed and a copy of the written disapproval thereof by the Secretary of State; whereupon the matter shall be tried de novo by the court, and the court shall either sustain the action of the Secretary of State or direct him to take such action as the court may deem proper.

If the Secretary of State shall revoke the certificate of authority to transact business in this State of any foreign corporation, pursuant to the provisions of this Act, such foreign corporation may likewise appeal to the . . . . . . . . . . . court of the county where the registered office of such corporation in this State is situated, by filing with the clerk of such court a petition setting forth a copy of its certificate of authority to transact business in this State and a copy of the notice of revocation given by the Secretary of State; whereupon the matter shall be tried de novo by the court, and the court shall either sustain the action of the Secretary of State or direct him to take such action as the court may deem proper.

Appeals from all final orders and judgments entered by the . . . . . . . . . . . court under this section in review of any ruling or decision of the Secretary of State may be taken as in other civil actions.

## § 141
### Certificates and Certified Copies to be Received in Evidence

All certificates issued by the Secretary of State in accordance with the provisions of this Act, and all copies of documents filed in his office in accordance with the provisions of this Act when certified by him, shall be taken and received in all courts, public offices, and official bodies as prima facie evidence of the facts therein stated. A certificate by the Secretary of State under the great seal of this State, as to the existence or nonexistence of the facts relating to corporations shall be taken and received in all courts, public offices, and official bodies as prima facie evidence of the existence or nonexistence of the facts therein stated.

## § 142
### Forms to be Furnished by Secretary of State

. . . .

## § 143
### Greater Voting Requirements

Whenever, with respect to any action to be taken by the shareholders of a corporation, the articles of incorporation require the vote or concurrence of the holders of a greater proportion of the shares, or of any class or series thereof, than required by this Act with respect to such action, the provisions of the articles of incorporation shall control.

## § 144
### Waiver of Notice

Whenever any notice is required to be given to any shareholder or director of a corporation under the provisions of this Act or under the provisions of the articles of incorporation or by-laws of the corporation, a waiver thereof in writing signed by the person or persons entitled to such notice, whether before or after the time stated therein, shall be equivalent to the giving of such notice.

## § 145
### Action by Shareholders Without a Meeting

Any action required by this Act to be taken at a meeting of the shareholders of a corporation, or any action which may be taken at a meeting of the shareholders, may be taken without a meeting if a consent in writing, setting forth the action so taken, shall be signed by all of the shareholders entitled to vote with respect to the subject matter thereof.

Such consent shall have the same effect as a unanimous vote of shareholders, and may be stated as such in any articles or document filed with the Secretary of State under this Act.

## § 146
### Unauthorized Assumption of Corporate Powers

All persons who assume to act as a corporation without authority so to do shall be jointly and severally liable for all debts and liabilities incurred or arising as a result thereof.

## § 147
### Application to Existing Corporations

. . . .

# APPENDIX F

# THE CONSTITUTION OF THE UNITED STATES OF AMERICA

We the People of the United States, in Order to form a more perfect Union, establish Justice, insure domestic Tranquility, provide for the common defence, promote the general Welfare, and secure the Blessings of Liberty to ourselves and our Posterity, do ordain and establish this Constitution for the United States of America.

## ARTICLE I

### Section 1

All legislative Powers herein granted shall be vested in a Congress of the United States, which shall consist of a Senate and House of Representatives.

### Section 2

The House of Representatives shall be composed of Members chosen every second Year by the People of the several States, and the Electors in each State shall have the Qualifications requisite for Electors of the most numerous Branch of the State Legislature.

No Person shall be a Representative who shall not have attained to the Age of twenty five Years, and been seven Years a Citizen of the United States, and who shall not, when elected, be an Inhabitant of that State in which he shall be chosen.

Representatives and direct Taxes shall be apportioned among the several States which may be included within this Union, according to their respective Numbers, which shall be determined by adding to the whole Number of free Persons, including those bound to Service for a Term of Years, and excluding Indians not taxed, three fifths of all other Persons. The actual Enumeration shall be made within three Years after the first Meeting of the Congress of the United States, and within every subsequent Term of ten Years, in such Manner as they shall by Law direct. The number of Representatives shall not exceed one for every thirty Thousand, but each State shall have at Least one Representative; and until such enumeration shall be made, the State of New Hampshire shall be entitled to chuse three, Massachusetts eight, Rhode Island and Providence Plantations one, Connecticut five, New-York six, New Jersey four, Pennsylvania eight, Delaware one, Maryland six, Virginia ten, North Carolina five, South Carolina five, and Georgia three.

When vacancies happen in the Representation from any State, the Executive Authority thereof shall issue Writs of Election to fill such vacancies.

The House of Representatives shall chuse their Speaker and other Officers; and shall have the sole Power of Impeachment.

### Section 3

The Senate of the United States shall be composed of two Senators from each State, chosen by the Legislature thereof, for six Years; and each Senator shall have one Vote.

Immediately after they shall be assembled in Consequence of the first Election, they shall be divided as equally as may be into three Classes. The Seats of the Senators of the first Class shall be vacated at the Expiration of the second Year, of the second Class at the Expiration of the fourth Year, and of the third Class at the Expiration of the sixth Year, so that one third may be chosen every second Year; and if Vacancies happen by Resignation, or otherwise, during the Recess of the Legislature of any State, the Executive thereof may make temporary Appointments until the next Meeting of the Legislature, which shall then fill such Vacancies.

No Person shall be a Senator who shall not have attained to the Age of thirty Years, and been nine Years a Citizen of the United States, and who shall not, when elected, be an Inhabitant of that State for which he shall be chosen.

The Vice President of the United States shall be President of the Senate, but shall have no Vote, unless they be equally divided.

The Senate shall chuse their other Officers, and also a President pro tempore, in the Absence of the Vice President, or when he shall exercise the Office of President of the United States.

The Senate shall have the sole power to try all Impeachments. When sitting for that Purpose, they shall be on Oath or Affirmation. When the President of the United States is tried, the Chief Justice shall preside: And no Person shall be convicted without the Concurrence of two thirds of the Members present.

Judgment in Cases of Impeachment shall not extend further than to removal from Office, and disqualification to hold and enjoy any Office of honor, Trust or Profit under the United States: but the Party convicted shall nevertheless be liable and subject to Indictment, Trial, Judgment and Punishment, according to Law.

### Section 4

The Times, Places and Manner of holding Elections for Senators and Representatives, shall be prescribed in each State by the Legislature thereof: but the Congress may at any time by Law make or alter such Regulations, except as to the Places of chusing Senators.

The Congress shall assemble at least once in every Year, and such Meeting shall be on the first Monday in December, unless they shall by Law appoint a different Day.

## Section 5

Each House shall be the Judge of the Elections, Returns and Qualifications of its own Members, and a Majority of each shall constitute a Quorum to do Business; but a smaller Number may adjourn from day to day, and may be authorized to compel the Attendance of absent Members, in such Manner, and under such Penalties as each House may provide.

Each House may determine the Rules of its Proceedings, punish its Members for disorderly Behaviour, and, with the Concurrence of two thirds, expel a Member.

Each House shall keep a Journal of its Proceedings, and from time to time publish the same, excepting such Parts as may in their Judgment require Secrecy; and the Yeas and Nays of the Members of either House on any question shall, at the Desire of one fifth of those Present, be entered on the Journal.

Neither House, during the Session of Congress, shall, without the Consent of the other, adjourn for more than three days, nor to any other Place than that in which the two Houses shall be sitting.

## Section 6

The Senators and Representatives shall receive a Compensation for their Services, to be ascertained by Law, and paid out of the Treasury of the United States. They shall in all Cases, except Treason, Felony and Breach of the Peace, be privileged from Arrest during their Attendance at the Session of their respective Houses, and in going to and returning from the same; and for any Speech or Debate in either House, they shall not be questioned in any other Place.

No Senator or Representative shall, during the Time for which he was elected, be appointed to any civil Office under the Authority of the United States, which shall have been created, or the Emoluments whereof shall have been encreased during such time; and no Person holding any Office under the United States, shall be a Member of either House during his Continuance in Office.

## Section 7

All Bills for raising Revenue shall originate in the House of Representatives; but the Senate may propose or concur with Amendments as on other Bills.

Every Bill which shall have passed the House of Representatives and the Senate, shall, before it become a Law, be presented to the President of the United States; If he approve he shall sign it, but if not he shall return it, with his Objections to that House in which it shall have originated, who shall enter the Objections at large on their Journal, and proceed to reconsider it. If after such Reconsideration two thirds of that House shall agree to pass the Bill, it shall be sent, together with the Objections, to the other House, by which it shall likewise be reconsidered, and if approved by two thirds of that House, it shall become a Law. But in all such Cases the Votes of both Houses shall be determined by Yeas and Nays, and the Names of the Persons voting for and against the Bill shall be entered on the Journal of each House respectively. If any Bill shall not be returned by the President within ten Days (Sundays excepted) after it shall have been presented to him, the Same shall be a Law, in like Manner as if he had signed it, unless the Congress by their Adjournment prevent its Return, in which Case it shall not be a Law.

Every Order, Resolution, or Vote to which the Concurrence of the Senate and House of Representatives may be necessary (except on a question of Adjournment) shall be presented to the President of the United States; and before the Same shall take Effect, shall be approved by him, or being disapproved by him, shall be repassed by two thirds of the Senate and House of Representatives, according to the Rules and Limitations prescribed in the Case of a Bill.

## Section 8

The Congress shall have Power to lay and collect Taxes, Duties, Imposts and Excises, to pay the Debts and provide for the common Defence and general Welfare of the United States; but all Duties, Imposts and Excises shall be uniform throughout the United States;

To borrow Money on the credit of the United States;

To regulate Commerce with foreign Nations, and among the several States, and with the Indian Tribes;

To establish an uniform Rule of Naturalization, and uniform Laws on the subject of Bankruptcies throughout the United States;

To coin Money, regulate the Value thereof, and of foreign Coin, and fix the Standard of Weights and Measures;

To provide for the Punishment of counterfeiting the Securities and current Coin of the United States;

To establish Post Offices and post Roads;

To promote the Progress of Science and useful Arts, by securing for limited Times to Authors and Inventors the exclusive Right to their respective Writings and Discoveries;

To constitute Tribunals inferior to the supreme Court;

To define and punish Piracies and Felonies committed on the high Seas, and Offenses against the Law of Nations;

To declare War, grant Letters of Marque and Reprisal, and make Rules concerning Captures on Land and Water;

To raise and support Armies, but no Appropriation of Money to that Use shall be for a longer Term than two Years;

To provide and maintain a Navy;

To make Rules for the Government and Regulation of the land and naval Forces;

To provide for calling forth the Militia to execute the Laws of the Union, suppress Insurrections and repel Invasions;

To provide for organizing, arming, and disciplining, the Militia, and for governing such Part of them as may be employed in the Service of the United States, reserving to the States respectively, the Appointment of the Officers, and the Authority of training the Militia according to the discipline prescribed by Congress;

To exercise exclusive Legislation in all Cases whatsoever, over such District (not exceeding ten Miles square) as may, by Cession of particular States, and the Acceptance of Congress, become the Seat of the Government of the United States, and to exercise like Authority over all Places purchased by the Consent of the Legislature of the State in which the Same shall be, for the Erection of Forts, Magazines, Arsenals, dock-Yards, and other needful Buildings;—And

To make all Laws which shall be necessary and proper for carrying into Execution the foregoing Powers, and all other Powers vested by this Constitution in the Government of the United States, or in any Department or Officer thereof.

## Section 9

The Migration or Importation of such Persons as any of the States now existing shall think proper to admit, shall not be prohibited by the Congress prior to the Year one thousand eight hundred and eight, but a Tax or Duty may be imposed on such Importation, not exceeding ten dollars for each Person.

The Privilege of the Writ of Habeas Corpus shall not be suspended, unless when in Cases of Rebellion or Invasion the public Safety may require it.

No Bill of Attainder or ex post facto Law shall be passed.

No Capitation, or other direct, Tax shall be laid, unless in Proportion to the Census or Enumeration herein before directed to be taken.

No Tax or Duty shall be laid on Articles exported from any State.

No Preference shall be given by any Regulation of Commerce or Revenue to the Ports of one State over those of another: nor shall Vessels bound to, or from, one State, be obliged to enter, clear, or pay Duties in another.

No Money shall be drawn from the Treasury, but in Consequence of Appropriations made by Laws; and a regular Statement and Account of the Receipts and Expenditures of all public Money shall be published from time to time.

No Title of Nobility shall be granted by the United States: And no Person holding any Office of Profit or Trust under them, shall, without the Consent of the Congress, accept of any present, Emolument, Office, or Title, of any kind whatever, from any King, Prince, or foreign State.

## Section 10

No State shall enter into any Treaty, Alliance, or Confederation; grant Letters of Marque and Reprisal; coin Money; emit Bills of Credit; make any Thing but gold and silver Coin a Tender in Payment of Debts; pass any Bill of Attainder, ex post facto Law, or Law impairing the Obligation of Contracts, or grant any Title of Nobility.

No State shall, without the Consent of the Congress, lay any Imposts or Duties on Imports or Exports, except what may be absolutely necessary for executing its inspection Laws: and the net Produce of all Duties and Imposts, laid by any State on Imports or Exports, shall be for the Use of the Treasury of the United States; and all such Laws shall be subject to the Revision and Controul of the Congress.

No State shall, without the Consent of Congress, lay any Duty of Tonnage, keep Troops, or Ships of War in time of Peace, enter into any Agreement or Compact with another State, or with a foreign Power, or engage in War, unless actually invaded, or in such imminent Danger as will not admit of delay.

# ARTICLE II

## Section 1

The executive Power shall be vested in a President of the United States of America. He shall hold his Office during the Term of four Years, and, together with the Vice President, chosen for the same Term, be elected, as follows:

Each State shall appoint, in such Manner as the Legislature thereof may direct, a Number of Electors, equal to the whole Number of Senators and Representatives to which the State may be entitled in the Congress: but no Senator or Representative, or Person holding an Office of Trust or Profit under the United States, shall be appointed an Elector.

The Electors shall meet in their respective States, and vote by Ballot for two Persons, of whom one at least shall not be an Inhabitant of the same State with themselves. And they shall make a List of all the Persons voted for, and of the Number of Votes for each; which List they shall sign and certify, and transmit sealed to the Seat of the Government of the United States, directed to the President of the Senate. The President of the Senate shall, in the Presence of the Senate and House of Representatives, open all the Certificates, and the Votes shall then be counted. The Person having the greatest Number of Votes shall be the President, if such Number be a Majority of the whole Number of Electors appointed; and if there be more than one who have such Majority, and have an equal Number of Votes, then the House of Representatives shall immediately chuse by Ballot one of them for President; and if no Person have a Majority, then from the five highest on the List the said House shall in like Manner chuse the President. But in chusing the President, the Votes shall be taken by States, the Representation from each State having one Vote; A quorum for this Purpose shall consist of a Member or Members from two thirds of the States, and a Majority of all the States shall be necessary to a Choice. In every Case, after the Choice of the President, the Person having the greatest Number of Votes of the Electors shall be the Vice President. But if there should remain two or more who have equal Votes, the Senate shall chuse from them by Ballot the Vice President.

The Congress may determine the Time of chusing the Electors, and the Day on which they shall give their Votes; which Day shall be the same throughout the United States.

No Person except a natural born Citizen, or a Citizen of the United States, at the time of the Adoption of this Constitution, shall be eligible to the Office of President; neither shall any Person be eligible to that Office who shall not have attained to the Age of thirty five Years, and been fourteen Years a Resident within the United States.

In Case of the Removal of the President from Office, or of his Death, Resignation, or Inability to discharge the Powers and Duties of the said Office, the Same shall devolve on the Vice President, and the Congress may by Law provide for the Case of Removal, Death, Resignation or Inability, both of the President and Vice President, declaring what Officer shall then act as President, and such Officer shall act accordingly, until the Disability be removed, or a President shall be elected.

The President shall, at stated Times, receive for his Services, a Compensation, which shall neither be encreased nor diminished during the Period for which he shall have been elected, and he shall not receive within that Period any other Emolument from the United States, or any of them.

Before he enter on the Execution of his Office, he shall take the following Oath or Affirmation:—"I do solemnly swear (or affirm) that I will faithfully execute the Office of President of the United States, and will to the best of my Ability, preserve, protect and defend the Constitution of the United States."

## Section 2

The President shall be Commander in Chief of the Army and Navy of the United States, and of the Militia of the several States, when called into the actual Service of the United States; he may require the Opinion, in writing, of the principal Officer in each of the executive Departments, upon any Subject relating to the Duties of their respective Offices, and he shall have Power to grant Reprieves and Pardons for Offences against the United States, except in Cases of Impeachment.

He shall have Power, by and with the Advice and Consent of the Senate, to make Treaties, providing two thirds of the Senators present concur; and he shall nominate, and by and with the Advice and Consent of the Senate, shall appoint Ambassadors, other public Ministers and Consuls, Judges of the supreme Court, and all other Officers of the United States, whose Appointments are not herein otherwise provided for, and which shall be established by Law: but the Congress may by Law vest the Appointment of such inferior Officers, as they think proper, in the President alone, in the Courts of Law, or in the Heads of Departments.

The President shall have Power to fill up all Vacancies that may happen during the Recess of the Senate, by granting Commissions which shall expire at the End of their next Session.

## Section 3

He shall from time to time give to the Congress Information of the State of the Union, and recommend to their Consideration such Measures as he shall judge necessary and expedient; he may, on extraordinary Occasions, convene both Houses, or either of them, and in Case of Disagreement between them, with Respect to the Time of Adjournment, he may adjourn them to such Time as he shall think proper, he shall receive Ambassadors and other public Ministers; he shall take Care that the Laws be faithfully executed, and shall Commission all the Officers of the United States.

## Section 4

The President, Vice President and all civil Officers of the United States, shall be removed from Office on Impeachment for, and Conviction of, Treason, Bribery, or other high Crimes and Misdemeanors.

# ARTICLE III

## Section 1

The judicial Power of the United States, shall be vested in one supreme Court, and in such inferior Courts as the Congress may from time to time ordain and establish. The Judges, both of the supreme and inferior Courts, shall hold their Offices during good Behaviour, and shall, at stated Times, receive for their Services, a Compensation, which shall not be diminished during their Continuance in Office.

## Section 2

The judicial Power shall extend to all Cases, in Law and Equity, arising under this Constitution, the Laws of the United States, and Treaties made, or which shall be made, under their Authority;—to all Cases affecting Ambassadors, other public Ministers and Consuls;—to all Cases of admirality and maritime Jurisdiction;—to Controversies to which the United States shall be a Party;—to Controversies between two or more States;—between a State and Citizens of another State;—between Citizens of different States;—between Citizens of the same State claiming Lands under Grants of different States, and between a State, or the Citizens thereof, and foreign States, Citizens or Subjects.

In all Cases affecting Ambassadors, other public Ministers and Consuls, and those in which a State shall be Party, the supreme Court shall have original Jurisdiction. In all the other Cases before mentioned, the supreme Court shall have appellate Jurisdiction, both as to Law and Fact, with such Exceptions, and under such Regulations as the Congress shall make.

The Trial of all Crimes, except in Cases of Impeachment, shall be by Jury; and such Trial shall be held in the State where the said Crimes shall have been committed; but when not committed within any State, the Trial shall be at such Place or Places as the Congress may by Law have directed.

## Section 3

Treason against the United States, shall consist only in levying War against them, or in adhering to their Enemies, giving them Aid and Comfort. No Person shall be convicted of Treason unless on the Testimony of two Witnesses to the same overt Act, or on Confession in open Court.

The Congress shall have Power to declare the Punishment of Treason, but no Attainder of Treason shall work Corruption of Blood, or Forfeiture except during the Life of the Person attainted.

# ARTICLE IV

## Section 1

Full Faith and Credit shall be given in each State to the public Acts, Records, and judicial Proceedings of every other State. And the Congress may by general Laws prescribe the Manner in which such Acts, Records and Proceedings shall be proved, and the Effect thereof.

## Section 2

The Citizens of each State shall be entitled to all Privileges and Immunities of Citizens in the several States.

A Person charged in any State with Treason, Felony, or other Crime, who shall flee from Justice, and be found in another State, shall on Demand of the executive Authority of the State from which he fled, be delivered up, to be removed to the State having Jurisdiction of the Crime.

No Person held to Service or Labour in one State, under the Laws thereof, escaping into another, shall, in Consequence of any Law or Regulation therein, be discharged from such Service or Labour, but shall be delivered up on Claim of the Party to whom such Service or Labour may be due.

## Section 3

New States may be admitted by the Congress into this Union; but no new State shall be formed or erected within the Jurisdiction of any other State; nor any State be formed by the Junction of two or more States, or Parts of States, without the Consent of the Legislatures of the States concerned as well as of the Congress.

The Congress shall have Power to dispose of and make all needful Rules and Regulations respecting the Territory or other Property belonging to the United States; and nothing in this Constitution shall be so construed as to Prejudice any Claims of the United States, or of any particular State.

## Section 4

The United States shall guarantee to every State in this Union a Republican Form of Government, and shall protect each of them against Invasion; and on Application of the Legislature, or of the

Executive (when the Legislature cannot be convened) against domestic Violence.

## ARTICLE V

The Congress, whenever two thirds of both Houses shall deem it necessary, shall propose Amendments to this Constitution, or, on the Application of the Legislatures of two thirds of the several States, shall call a Convention for proposing Amendments, which, in either Case, shall be valid to all Intents and Purposes, as Part of this Constitution, when ratified by the Legislatures of three fourths of the several States, or by Conventions in three fourths thereof, as the one or the other Mode of Ratification may be proposed by the Congress; Provided that no Amendment which may be made prior to the Year One thousand eight hundred and eight shall in any Manner affect the first and fourth Clauses in the Ninth Section of the first Article; and that no State, without its Consent, shall be deprived of its equal Suffrage in the Senate.

## ARTICLE VI

All Debts contracted and Engagements entered into, before the Adoption of this Constitution, shall be as valid against the United States under this Constitution, as under the Confederation.

This Constitution, and the Laws of the United States which shall be made in Pursuance thereof; and all Treaties made, or which shall be made, under the Authority of the United States, shall be the supreme Law of the Land; and the Judges in every State shall be bound thereby, any Thing in the Constitution or Laws of any State to the Contrary notwithstanding.

The Senators and Representatives before mentioned, and the Members of the several State Legislatures, and all executive and judicial Officers, both of the United States and of the several States, shall be bound by Oath or Affirmation, to support this Constitution; but no religious Test shall ever be required as a Qualification to any Office or public Trust under the United States.

## ARTICLE VII

The Ratification of the Conventions of nine States, shall be sufficient for the Establishment of this Constitution between the States so ratifying the Same.

## AMENDMENT I [1791]

Congress shall make no law respecting an establishment of religion, or prohibiting the free exercise thereof; or abridging the freedom of speech, or of the press; or the right of the people peaceably to assemble, and to petition the Government for a redress of grievances.

## AMENDMENT II [1791]

A well regulated Militia, being necessary to the security for a free State, the right of the people to keep and bear Arms, shall not be infringed.

## AMENDMENT III [1791]

No Soldier shall, in time of peace be quartered in any house, without the consent of the Owner, nor in time of war, but in a manner to be prescribed by law.

## AMENDMENT IV [1791]

The right of the people to be secure in their persons, houses, papers, and effects, against unreasonable searches and seizures, shall not be violated, and no Warrants shall issue, but upon probable cause, supported by Oath or affirmation, and particularly describing the place to be searched, and the persons or things to be seized.

## AMENDMENT V [1791]

No person shall be held to answer for a capital, or otherwise infamous crime, unless on a presentment or indictment of a Grand Jury, except in cases arising in the land or naval forces, or in the Militia, when in actual service in time of War or public danger; nor shall any person be subject for the same offense to be twice put in jeopardy of life or limb; nor shall be compelled in any criminal case to be a witness against himself, nor be deprived of life, liberty, or property, without due process of law; nor shall private property be taken for public use, without just compensation.

## AMENDMENT VI [1791]

In all criminal prosecutions, the accused shall enjoy the right to a speedy and public trial, by an impartial jury of the State and district wherein the crime shall have been committed, which district shall have been previously ascertained by law, and to be informed of the nature and cause of the accusation; to be confronted with the Witnesses against him; to have compulsory process for obtaining witnesses in his favor, and to have the Assistance of counsel for his defence.

## AMENDMENT VII [1791]

In Suits at common law, where the value in controversy shall exceed twenty dollars, the right of trial by jury shall be preserved, and no fact tried by a jury, shall be otherwise reexamined in any Court of the United States, than according to the rules of the common law.

## AMENDMENT VIII [1791]

Excessive bail shall not be required, no excessive fines imposed, nor cruel and unusual punishments inflicted.

## AMENDMENT IX [1791]

The enumeration in the Constitution, of certain rights, shall not be construed to deny or disparage others retained by the people.

## AMENDMENT X [1791]

The powers not delegated to the United States by the Constitution, nor prohibited by it to the States, are reserved to the States respectively, or to the people.

## AMENDMENT XI [1798]

The Judicial power of the United States shall not be construed to extend to any suit in law or equity, commenced or prosecuted against one of the United States by Citizens of another State, or by Citizens or Subjects of any Foreign State.

## AMENDMENT XII [1804]

The Electors shall meet in their respective states and vote by ballot for President and Vice-President, one of whom, at least, shall not be an inhabitant of the same state with themselves; they shall name in their ballots the person voted for as President, and in distinct ballots the person voted for as Vice-President, and they shall make distinct lists of all persons voted for as President, and of all persons voted for as Vice-President, and of the number of votes for each, which lists they shall sign and certify, and transmit sealed to the seat of the government of the United States, directed to the President of the Senate;—The President of the Senate shall, in the presence of the Senate and House of Representatives, open all the certificates and the votes shall then be counted;—The person having the greatest number of votes for President, shall be the President, if such number be a majority of the whole number of Electors appointed; and if no person have such majority, then from the persons having the highest numbers not exceeding three on the list of those voted for as President, the House of Representatives shall choose immediately, by ballot, the President. But in choosing the President, the votes shall be taken by states, the representation from each state having one vote; a quorum for this purpose shall consist of a member or members from two-thirds of the states, and a majority of all the states shall be necessary to a choice. And if the House of Representatives shall not choose a President whenever the right of choice shall devolve upon them, before the fourth day of March next following, then the Vice-President shall act as President, as in the case of the death or other constitutional disability of the President. The person having the greatest number of votes as Vice-President, shall be the Vice-President, if such number be a majority of the whole number of Electors appointed, and if no person have a majority, then from the two highest numbers on the list, the Senate shall choose the Vice-President; a quorum for the purpose shall consist of two-thirds of the whole number of Senators, and a majority of the whole number shall be necessary to a choice. But no person constitutionally ineligible to the office of President shall be eligible to that of the Vice-President of the United States.

## AMENDMENT XIII [1865]

### Section 1

Neither slavery nor involuntary servitude, except as a punishment for crime whereof the party shall have been duly convicted, shall exist within the United States, or any place subject to their jurisdiction.

### Section 2

Congress shall have power to enforce this article by appropriate legislation.

## AMENDMENT XIV [1868]

### Section 1

All persons born or naturalized in the United States, and subject to the jurisdiction thereof, are citizens of the United States and of the State wherein they reside. No State shall make or enforce any law which shall abridge the privileges or immunities of citizens of the United States; nor shall any State deprive any person of life, liberty, or property, without due process of law; nor deny to any person within its jurisdiction the equal protection of the laws.

### Section 2

Representatives shall be appointed among the several States according to their respective numbers, counting the whole number of persons in each State, excluding Indians not taxed. But when the right to vote at any election for the choice of electors for President and Vice President of the United States, Representatives in Congress, the Executive and Judicial officers of a State, or the members of the Legislature thereof, is denied to any of the male inhabitants of such State, being twenty-one years of age, and citizens of the United States, or in any way abridged, except for participation in rebellion, or other crime, the basis of representation therein shall be reduced in the proportion which the number of such male citizens shall bear to the whole number of male citizens twenty-one years of age in such State.

### Section 3

No person shall be a Senator or Representative in Congress, or elector of President and Vice President, or hold any office, civil or military, under the United States, or under any State, who, having previously taken an oath, as a member of Congress, or as an officer of the United States, or as a member of any State legislature, or as an executive or judicial officer of any State, to support the Constitution of the United States, shall have engaged in insurrection or rebellion against the same, or given aid or comfort to the enemies thereof. But Congress may by a vote of two-thirds of each House, remove such disability.

### Section 4

The validity of the public debt of the United States, authorized by law, including debts incurred for payment of pensions and bounties for services in suppressing insurrection or rebellion, shall not be questioned. But neither the United States nor any State shall assume or pay any debt or obligation incurred in aid of insurrection or rebellion against the United States, or any claim for the loss or emancipation of any slave; but all such debts, obligations and claims shall be held illegal and void.

### Section 5

The Congress shall have power to enforce, by appropriate legislation, the provisions of this article.

## AMENDMENT XV [1870]

### Section 1

The right of citizens of the United States to vote shall not be denied or abridged by the United States or by any State on account of race, color, or previous condition of servitude.

### Section 2

The Congress shall have power to enforce this article by appropriate legislation.

## AMENDMENT XVI [1913]

The Congress shall have power to lay and collect taxes on incomes, from whatever source derived, without apportionment among the several States, and without regard to any census or enumeration.

## AMENDMENT XVII [1913]

The Senate of the United States shall be composed of two Senators from each State, elected by the people thereof, for six years; and each Senator shall have one vote. The electors in each State shall have the qualifications requisite for electors of the most numerous branch of the State legislatures.

When vacancies happen in the representation of any State in the Senate, the executive authority of each State shall issue writs of election to fill such vacancies; *Provided*, That the legislature of any State may empower the executive thereof to make temporary appointments until the people fill the vacancies by election as the legislature may direct.

This amendment shall not be so construed as to affect the election or term of any Senator chosen before it becomes valid as part of the Constitution.

## AMENDMENT XVIII [1919]

### Section 1

After one year from the ratification of this article the manufacture, sale, or transportation of intoxicating liquors within, the importation thereof into, or the exportation thereof from the United States and all territory subject to the jurisdiction thereof for beverage purposes is hereby prohibited.

### Section 2

The Congress and the several States shall have concurrent power to enforce this article by appropriate legislation.

### Section 3

This article shall be inoperative unless it shall have been ratified as an amendment to the Constitution by the legislatures of the several States, as provided in the Constitution, within seven years from the date of the submission hereof to the States by the Congress.

## AMENDMENT XIX [1920]

The right of citizens of the United States to vote shall not be denied or abridged by the United States or by any State on account of sex.

Congress shall have power to enforce this article by appropriate legislation.

## AMENDMENT XX [1933]

### Section 1

The terms of the President and Vice President shall end at noon on the 20th day of January, and the terms of Senators and Representatives at noon on the 3d day of January, of the years in which such terms would have ended if this article had not been ratified; and the terms of their successors shall then begin.

### Section 2

The Congress shall assemble at least once in every year, and such meeting shall begin at noon on the 3d day of January, unless they shall by law appoint a different day.

### Section 3

If, at the time fixed for the beginning of the term of the President, the President elect shall have died, the Vice President elect shall become President. If a President shall not have been chosen before the time fixed for the beginning of his term, or if the President elect shall have failed to qualify, then the Vice President elect shall act as President until a President shall have qualified; and the Congress may by law provide for the case wherein neither a President elect nor a Vice President elect shall have qualified, declaring who shall then act as President, or the manner in which one who is to act shall be selected, and such person shall act accordingly until a President or Vice President shall have qualified.

### Section 4

The Congress may by law provide for the case of the death of any of the persons from whom the House of Representatives may choose a President whenever the right of choice shall have devolved upon them, and for the case of the death of any of the persons from whom the Senate may choose a Vice President whenever the right of choice shall have devolved upon them.

### Section 5

Sections 1 and 2 shall take effect on the 15th day of October following the ratification of this article.

### Section 6

This article shall be inoperative unless it shall have been ratified as an amendment to the Constitution by the legislatures of three-fourths of the several States within seven years from the date of its submission.

## AMENDMENT XXI [1933]

### Section 1

The eighteenth article of amendment to the Constitution of the United States is hereby repealed.

### Section 2

The transportation or importation into any State, Territory, or possession of the United States for delivery or use therein of intoxicating liquors, in violation of the laws thereof, is hereby prohibited.

### Section 3

This article shall be inoperative unless it shall have been ratified as an amendment to the Constitution by conventions in the several States, as provided in the Constitution, within seven years from the date of the submission hereof to the States by the Congress.

## AMENDMENT XXII [1951]

### Section 1

No person shall be elected to the office of the President more than twice, and no person who has held the office of President, or acted as President, for more than two years of a term to which some other person was elected President shall be elected to the office of the President more than once. But this Article shall not apply to any person holding the office of President when this Article was proposed by the Congress, and shall not prevent any person who may be holding the office of President, or acting as President, during the term within which this Article becomes operative from holding the office of President or acting as President during the remainder of such term.

### Section 2

This article shall be inoperative unless it shall have been ratified as an amendment to the Constitution by the legislatures of three-fourths of the several States within seven years from the date of its submission to the States by the Congress.

## AMENDMENT XXIII [1961]

### Section 1

The District constituting the seat of Government of the United States shall appoint in such manner as the Congress may direct:

A number of electors of President and Vice President equal to the whole number of Senators and Representatives in Congress to which the District would be entitled if it were a State, but in no event more than the least populous State; they shall be in addition to those appointed by the States, but they shall be considered, for the purposes of the election of President and Vice President, to be electors appointed by a State; and they shall meet in the District and perform such duties as provided by the twelfth article of amendment.

### Section 2

The Congress shall have power to enforce this article by appropriate legislation.

## AMENDMENT XXIV [1964]

### Section 1

The right of citizens of the United States to vote in any primary or other election for President or Vice President, for electors for President or Vice President, or for Senator or Representative in Congress, shall not be denied or abridged by the United States or any State by reason of failure to pay any poll tax or other tax.

### Section 2

The Congress shall have power to enforce this article by appropriate legislation.

## AMENDMENT XXV [1967]

### Section 1

In case of the removal of the President from office or of his death or resignation, the Vice President shall become President.

### Section 2

Whenever there is a vacancy in the office of the Vice President, the President shall nominate a Vice President who shall take office upon confirmation by a majority vote of both Houses of Congress.

### Section 3

Whenever the President transmits to the President pro tempore of the Senate and the Speaker of the House of Representatives his written declaration that he is unable to discharge the powers and duties of his office, and until he transmits to them a written declaration to the contrary, such powers and duties shall be discharged by the Vice President as Acting President.

### Section 4

Whenever the Vice President and a majority of either the principal officers of the executive departments or of such other body as Congress may by law provide, transmit to the President pro tempore of the Senate and the Speaker of the House of Representatives their written declaration that the President is unable to discharge the powers and duties of his office, the Vice President shall immediately assume the powers and duties of the office as Acting President.

Thereafter, when the President transmits to the President pro tempore of the Senate and the Speaker of the House of Representatives his written declaration that no inability exists, he shall resume the powers and duties of his office unless the Vice President and a majority of either the principal officers of the executive department or of such other body as Congress may by law provide, transmit within four days to the President pro tempore of the Senate and the Speaker of the House of Representatives their written declaration that the President is unable to discharge the powers and duties of his office. Thereupon Congress shall decide the issue, assembling within forty-eight hours for that purpose if not in session. If the Congress, within twenty-one days after receipt of the latter written declaration, or, if Congress is not in session, within twenty-one days after Congress is required to assemble, determines by two-thirds vote of both Houses that the President is unable to discharge the powers and duties of his office, the Vice President shall continue to discharge the same as Acting President; otherwise, the President shall resume the powers and duties of his office.

## AMENDMENT XXVI [1971]

### Section 1

The right of citizens of the United States, who are eighteen years of age or older, to vote shall not be denied or abridged by the United States or by any State on account of age.

### Section 2

The Congress shall have power to enforce this article by appropriate legislation.

# Glossary

**abandoned property** Property that is unowned because the owner has given up dominion and control with the intent to relinquish all claim or rights to it.

***ab initio*** From the very beginning (Latin).

**abstract** In real property law, a summary compilation of the official records relating to a particular parcel of land.

**abuse of discretion** The failure of a judge or administrator to use sound or reasonable judgment in arriving at a decision.

**acceleration clause** In commercial paper, a statement in a time instrument (where payment is to be made at a prescribed time or times) that permits the entire debt to become due immediately upon the occurrence of some event, such as failure to pay one installment when due.

**acceptance** In contract law, the agreement of the offeree to the proposal or offer of the offeror.

**acceptor** In commercial paper, a drawee who agrees by his or her signature to honor a draft as presented.

**accession** An addition to, product of, or change in personal property; depending on the circumstances, either the owner of the original property or another person responsible for the accession might be the owner of the altered property.

**accommodated party** The person who benefits by having another party lend his or her name (credit) on an instrument.

**accommodation party** A person who signs an instrument for the purpose of lending his or her name (credit) to another party on that instrument.

**accord and satisfaction** A form of discharge in contract law by which an agreement between the parties of a contract permits a substituted performance in lieu of the required obligation under the existing contract. The contract can be effectively terminated (satisfied) by performance as originally agreed upon or by the substitute performance.

**account receivable** A record of a debt owed to a person but not yet paid.

**accredited investor** An investor who is deemed not to need protection and, thus, can be sold securities exempt from SEC regulation.

**accretion** The gradual adding of land by natural causes, such as a deposit of soil by the action of a river.

**acknowledgment** A formal declaration or admission before a designated public official, such as a notary public, that something is genuine or that a particular act has taken place.

**action at law** A suit in which the plaintiff is seeking a legal remedy (such as damages), as distinguished from an equitable remedy (such as an injunction).

**action in equity** A civil suit in which the plaintiff is seeking an equitable remedy, such as an injunction or decree of specific performance.

**action *in personam*** A suit to hold a defendant personally liable for a wrong committed.

**action *in rem*** A suit to enforce a right against property of the defendant.

**act of state doctrine** In international law, a rule that a foreign government's public acts committed in its territory are beyond review or inquiry by a domestic court.

**actual authority** The express and implied authority of an agent.

**actus reus** An act or conduct which the law seeks to prohibit or preclude.

**adhesion contract** A form contract prepared by a dominant party (such as a retailer) and then presented to a weaker party (such as a customer) on a take-it-or-leave-it basis.

**adjudication** The legal process of resolving a dispute.

**adjudicatory power** In administrative agency law, the right of an administrative agency to initiate actions as both prosecutor and judge against those thought to be in violation of the law (including agency rules and regulations) under the jurisdiction of the administrative agency—referred to as the quasi-judicial function of an agency.

**adjustment case** A procedure under Chapter 13 of the Bankruptcy Act which allows an individual to pay his or her debts from future income over an extended period of time.

**administrative agency** A board, commission, agency, or service authorized by a legislative enactment to implement specific laws on either the local, state, or national level.

**administrative law** Public law administered and/or formulated by a government unit such as a board, agency, or commission to govern the conduct of an individual, association, or corporation.

**administrator** In probate law, a person appointed by a probate court to supervise the distribution of a deceased person's property. This title is usually given when there is no will or when the person named as executor or executrix in the will cannot serve.

**adverse possession** The acquisition of title to real property by actually taking possession of the land without the owner's consent and retaining such possession openly for a prescribed statutory period.

**affidavit**  A written sworn statement made before a person officially authorized to administer an oath.

**affirmative action**  The granting of preferences based on race or gender to minority or women employees.

**affirmative defense**  A defendant's claim to dissolve himself or herself of liability even if the plaintiff's claim is true.

**after-acquired property**  Property received or added after a specific event has taken place. For example, in secured transactions law, an after-acquired property clause in a security agreement means that property received by the debtor after the security agreement is made will be subject to the same security interest as the existing property referred to therein.

**agency**  A relationship created by contract, agreement, or law between a principal and an agent whereby the principal is bound by the authorized actions of the agent.

**agency coupled with an interest**  A relationship in which an agent, with consideration, has the right to exercise authority or is given an interest in the property of the principal subject to the agency.

**agent**  One who is authorized to act for another, called a principal, whose acts bind the principal to his or her actions.

**aggregate theory**  An approach under which associations or organizations are treated as a collection of persons, each with individual rights and liabilities.

**agreement**  A meeting of the minds between two or more parties, which may or may not constitute a contract.

**air rights**  A landowner's rights to the air space above his or her real property.

**alien corporation**  A corporation chartered or incorporated in another country but doing business in the United States.

**alteration (material)**  In commercial paper, the modification of the terms of an instrument that results in a change of the contract of any party on that instrument.

**amendment**  The changing of a law, right, or interest that usually becomes binding upon fulfillment of a required act or action.

**ancillary covenant**  A covenant that is a subsidiary or auxiliary part of a larger agreement; to be valid, a covenant not to compete must be ancillary as well as reasonably limited in time and area.

**annual percentage rate**  The total of the items making up the finance charge, or cost of borrowing money or buying on credit, expressed as a yearly percentage rate that the consumer can use to "shop around" for the best credit terms.

**answer**  In pleadings, the defendant's response to the plaintiff's complaint or petition.

**anticipatory breach**  The repudiation of a contract by a party before the time of performance has arrived, allowing the nonbreaching party the opportunity to seek a remedy.

**anticipatory repudiation**  Breaching a contract by refusing to perform before it is actually time to perform.

**apparent authority**  Authority created by the words or conduct of the principal that leads a third person to believe the agent has such authority.

**apparent intent**  The establishment of a person's motive from his or her actions and/or words as interpreted by a reasonable person.

**appellant**  The party who appeals a decision of a lower court, usually that of a trial court.

**appellee**  The party against whom an appeal is made (sometimes referred to as a respondent—a person who defends on an appeal).

**appraisal right**  The right of a dissenting shareholder to sell back his or her shares to the corporation for cash.

**arbitration**  The submission of a dispute to a third party or parties for settlement.

**arson**  At common law, the act of willfully and maliciously burning the dwelling of another.

**articles of incorporation**  A legal document, meeting the legal requirements of a given state, filed with a designated state official as an application for a certificate of incorporation.

**articles of partnership**  The agreement of the partners that forms and governs the operation of the partnership.

**artisan's lien**  A possessory lien held by one who has expended labor upon or added value to another's personal property as security for the work performed (labor and/or value added).

**ascendants**  The heirs of a decedent in the ascending line—parents or grandparents.

**assault**  The intentional movement or exhibition of force that would place a reasonable person in fear of physical attack or harm.

**assault and battery**  Any intentional physical contact by a person on another without consent or privilege.

**assignee**  The one to whom an assignment has been made.

**assignment**  The transfer of rights or a property interest to a third person, who can receive no greater rights than those possessed by the transferor.

**assignment for the benefit of creditors**  The voluntary transfer by a debtor of some or all of his or her property to an assignee or trustee, who sells or liquidates the debtor's assets and tenders to the creditors (on a pro rata basis) payment in satisfaction of the debt.

**assignor**  The one who makes an assignment.

**association**  The voluntary act or agreement by which two or more persons unite together for some special purpose or business.

**assumed name statute**  A law in most states which requires any firm, including a partnership, to register with a state official the fictitious name under which the firm is doing business; also called fictitious name statute.

**attachment**  (1) A legal proceeding provided by statute that permits a plaintiff in an existing court action to have nonexempt property of the defendant seized and a lien placed on the property as security of a judgment that may be rendered in the plaintiff's favor (this action being independent of plaintiff's suit and exercisable only on grounds provided by statute). (2) In secured transactions law, a method of perfecting a security interest without the secured party taking possession of the collateral or making a proper filing (which in most states applies only to a purchase money security interest in consumer goods).

**attestation** The act of witnessing a document, such as a will, and signing to that effect.

**attorney-at-law** A lawyer.

**attorney-in-fact** An agent.

**auction with reserve** An auction in which the auctioneer, as agent for the owner of the goods, has the right to withdraw the goods from sale at any time prior to accepting a particular bid (such acceptance usually being signified by the fall of the hammer).

**auction without reserve** An auction where once the goods are placed on the auction block (for sale) they must be sold to the highest bidder.

**award** In arbitration proceedings, the decision or determination rendered by an arbitrator on a controversy submitted for settlement. For example, the arbitrator's award was unfair. In general usage, to grant some type of remedy. For example, the court awards an injunction.

**bailee** The person to whom a bailor has entrusted or transferred personal property without transferring title.

**bailee's lien** Usually a possessory lien held by a bailee on bailed property for which the bailee is entitled to compensation or reimbursement.

**bailment** The creation of a legal relationship through delivery or transfer of personal property (but not title) by one person, called the bailor, to another person, called the bailee, usually for a specific purpose as directed by the bailor.

**bailor** A person who entrusts or transfers personal property (but not title) to another, called the bailee, usually for the accomplishment of a specific purpose.

**bank draft** A draft by one bank on funds held by another bank.

**bankruptcy** A court procedure by which a person who is unable to pay his or her debts may be declared bankrupt, have nonexempt assets distributed to his or her creditors, and thereupon be given a release from any further payment of the balance due on most of these debts.

**battery** The wrongful intentional physical contact by a person (or object under control of that person) on another.

**bearer** In commercial paper, the person possessing an instrument either payable to anyone without specific designation or one indorsed in blank.

**bearer instrument** An instrument either payable to anyone without specific designation or one indorsed in blank.

**beneficiary** A person for whose benefit a will, trust, insurance policy, or contract is made.

**benefit test** A test through which the law determines whether a promise has consideration by seeing if the promisor has received an advantage, profit, or privilege in return for his or her promise.

**bequest** In a will a gift by the testator of specific personal property other than money.

**bilateral contract** A contract formed by the mutual exchange of promises of the offeror and the offeree.

**bilateral mistake** A mistake in which both parties to a contract are in error as to the terms of or performance expected under the contract. Also called mutual mistake.

**bill of lading** A negotiable or nonnegotiable document of title evidencing the receipt of goods for shipment, with shipping instructions to the carrier. A negotiable bill of lading is both a receipt and evidence of title to the goods shipped.

**binder** A temporary insurance contract formed when the insurance agent or broker accepts a prospective policyholder's application.

**blank indorsement** An indorsement that specifies no particular indorsee and that usually consists of a mere signature of the indorser.

**blue sky laws** Laws enacted for the protection of investors that regulate the sales of stocks and bonds, and that also regulate other activities of investment companies related to such sales.

**board of directors** A body composed of persons elected by the corporation's shareholders and entrusted with the responsibility of managing the corporation.

**bona fide occupational qualification (BFOQ)** A defense in Title VII discrimination suits in which an employer must demonstrate a connection between the protected classification and job performance, and must prove that the performance affected is of the "essence" of the job and not merely tangential to the fundamental job function.

**bona fide purchaser** A purchaser who acts in good faith and gives something of value for the goods received.

**bonds** In corporate financing, secured or unsecured debt obligations of a corporation in the form of securities (instruments).

**boycott** In antitrust law, an agreement between two or more parties not to deal with a third party. When the purpose is to exclude a firm or firms from a market, such an agreement is per se illegal under Section 1 of the Sherman Act. In labor law, action by a union to prevent others from doing business with the employer. A primary boycott, directed at the employer with whom the union has a labor dispute, is usually legal. A secondary boycott, aimed at an employer with whom the union does not have a labor dispute, is usually an unfair labor practice.

**breach of duty** Failure to fulfill a legal obligation.

**broker** In real property law, an agent employed by a landowner to find an acceptable buyer for his or her real property or employed by a prospective buyer to find a landowner willing to sell such property.

**bulk transfer** A transfer of goods—such as materials, supplies, merchandise, or inventory (including equipment)—in such quantity or under such circumstances that the transfer is considered not to be in the ordinary course of the transferor's business.

**burden of proof** The duty of a party to prove or disprove certain facts.

**burglary** The act of entering, with or without force, in daytime or nighttime, any dwelling or other building with the intent to commit a felony or larceny.

**business judgment rule** A rule which protects corporate managers from responsibility for honest errors of judgment.

**business trust** A business association created by agreement in which legal ownership and management of property is transferred, in return for trust certificates, to trustees who have the power to operate the business for the benefit of the original owners or certificate holders. It is usually treated in the same manner as a corporation if certificate holders do not control the management activities of the trustees.

**bylaws** The internal rules made to regulate and govern the actions and affairs of a corporation.

**capacity** The legal ability to perform an act—especially an act from which legal consequences flow, such as the making of a contract.

**case law** Essentially synonymous with "common law."

**cashier's check** A check drawn by a bank on itself.

**cause of action** A person's right to seek a remedy when his or her rights have been breached or violated.

*caveat emptor* In sales law, "let the buyer beware."

**Celler-Kefauver Act** A 1950 congressional enactment amending Section 7 of the Clayton Act. The act prohibits a firm from acquiring all or part of the stock or assets of another firm where, in any line of commerce in any section of the country, the effect of such acquisition may be substantially to lessen competition.

**certificate of authority** A foreign corporation's permission to do business in the state of issuance.

**certificate of deposit** An instrument (essentially a note) that is an acknowledgment by a bank that it has received money and promises to repay the amount upon presentment when due.

**certificate of incorporation** A document of a state that grants permission to do business in that state in the corporate form—sometimes called a charter.

**certificate of origin** A document that designates the country from which goods originate.

**certificate of title** A written opinion by an attorney as to the validity of a title.

**certified check** A bank's guaranty (acceptance) by an appropriate signature that it will pay the check upon presentment.

**challenge for cause** In jury selection, an objection to a prospective juror hearing a particular case, stating a reason that questions the impartiality of the juror.

**charging order** An action by a creditor which requires that a partner's share of partnership profits be paid to the creditor until the debt is fully discharged.

**chattel** Any property or interest therein other than real property. The more modern term is "personal property."

**chattel paper** Any writing or writings that evidence both a monetary obligation for and a security interest in (or a lease of) specific goods.

**check** A draft drawn on a bank (drawee) payable on demand.

**CIF** Cost, insurance, and freight; that is, the price charged by the seller includes not only the cost of the goods but also the cost of freight and insurance charges on the goods to the named destination.

**circumstantial context** In the process of statutory interpretation, a court's examination of the problem or problems that caused the enactment of the statute.

**civil law** As compared to criminal law, rules for establishing rights and duties between individuals whereby an individual can seek personal redress for a wrong committed by another individual. As compared to common law, codified rules reduced to formal written propositions as the law of a state or country. The written code serves as the basis of all decisions.

**Civil Rights Act** A comprehensive 1964 congressional enactment that prohibits discrimination in housing, public accommodations, education, and employment.

**civil rights law** The body of statutory and constitutional law defining and enforcing the privileges and freedoms belonging to every person in the United States. The objective of civil rights law is to secure equality of opportunity for all persons.

**class action** A legal proceeding initiated by one or more members of a similarly situated group or class of persons on behalf of themselves and other group members.

**classified board** A board of directors divided into classes with only one class elected each year; the result is directors who serve staggered terms.

**Clayton Act** A 1914 congressional enactment to generally prohibit price discrimination by a seller of goods, exclusive dealing and tying of a seller's products, mergers and consolidations of corporations that result in a substantial lessening of competition or tend to create a monopoly, and certain interlocking directorates. The act also provides an exemption from the antitrust laws for the organization and normal activities of labor unions.

**close corporation** A corporation that has a limited number of outstanding shares of stock, usually held by a single person or small group of persons, with restrictions on the right to transfer those shares to others.

**closing** In real property law, a meeting between the seller and buyer and any other interested parties at which passage of title and matters relating thereto are executed.

**COD** Collect on delivery; that is, the buyer must pay for the goods before he or she can inspect or receive possession of them.

**codicil** An addition to or change in a will executed with the same formalities as the will itself.

**coinsurance clause** A provision in a property insurance policy specifying that the property owner must bear a proportionate part of a casualty loss if he or she does not insure the property in an amount equal to a stated percentage of the property's value.

**collateral** In secured transactions law, the property subject to a security interest.

**collateral note** A note secured by personal property.

**collective bargaining** The term for negotiations between an employer and the union representative.

**collusion** Joint conduct by two or more independent entities for a common purpose. A prerequisite to finding a violation of Section 1 of the Sherman Act.

**co-makers** Two or more persons who create or execute a note or certificate of deposit.

**comity** In international law, the recognition that one nation or sovereign gives to the judicial or legislative acts of another nation or sovereign.

**Commerce Clause** A clause contained in Article I, Section 8, of the U.S. Constitution, which permits Congress to control trade among the several states (and with foreign nations).

**commercial contract** A contract between two or more persons (merchants) engaged in trade or commerce.

**commercial impracticability** A legal doctrine which excuses a seller of goods from performance because an unforeseen occurrence has caused performance to be extremely burdensome.

**commercial paper** Instruments that are written promises or obligations to pay sums of money (called drafts, checks, certificates of deposit, or notes). When used in Article 3 of the UCC, the term refers only to negotiable instruments; when used elsewhere, to negotiable and nonnegotiable instruments.

**commercial speech** Expressions that primarily convey a commercial message (i.e., advertising); recently recognized by the Supreme Court as being protected by the First Amendment to the U.S. Constitution.

**commingle** To blend or mix together.

**common carrier** A carrier that holds itself out for hire to the general public to transport goods.

**common law** Rules that have been developed from custom or judicial decisions without the aid of written legislation, and subsequently used as a basis for later decisions by a court—also referred to as judge-made or case law.

**common stock** A class of stock that carries no rights or priorities over other classes of stock as to payment of dividends or distribution of corporate assets upon dissolution.

**community property** A system of marital property ownership recognized in eight states under which property acquired after marriage (except by gift or inheritance) is co-owned by the husband and wife, regardless of which person acquired it.

**comparable worth** The theory that jobs having comparable worth should receive comparable pay.

**comparative negligence** The rule used in negligence cases in many states that provides for computing both the plaintiff's and the defendant's negligence, with the plaintiff's damages being reduced by a percentage representing the degree of his or her contributing fault. If the plaintiff's negligence is found to be greater than the defendant's, the plaintiff will receive nothing and will be subject to a counterclaim by the defendant.

**compensatory damages** A monetary sum awarded for the actual loss a person has sustained for a wrong committed by another person.

**complaint** In an action at law, the initial pleading filed by the plaintiff in a court with proper jurisdiction. In an action in equity, it is frequently referred to as a *petition*.

**composition of creditors** An agreement between a debtor and his or her creditors that each creditor will accept a lesser amount than the debt owed as full satisfaction of that debt.

**conclusions of law** Answers derived by applying law to facts.

**concurrent jurisdiction** Where more than one court of a different name or classification has the right to hear a particular controversy.

**condemnation** The process by which the government either exercises its power of eminent domain to take private property or officially declares property unfit for use.

**condition** In contract law, a provision or clause in a contract which, upon the occurrence or nonoccurrence of a specified event, either creates, suspends, or terminates the rights and duties of the contracting parties.

**condition concurrent** A condition in a contract that both parties' performances are to take place at the same time.

**condition precedent** A condition that must take place before the parties are bound to their contractual obligations.

**condition subsequent** A condition that terminates the rights and obligations of the parties under an existing contract.

**conditional indorsement** An indorsement whereby the indorser agrees to be liable on the instrument only if a specified event takes place.

**confession of judgment** An agreement whereby a debtor allows a creditor to obtain a court judgment without legal proceedings in the event of nonpayment or other breach by the debtor. Usually not permissible today.

**conflict of laws** The body of rules specifying the circumstances in which a state or federal court sitting in one state shall, in deciding a case before it, apply the rules of another state (rather than the rules of the state in which the court is sitting).

**confusion of goods** An intermingling of the goods of different persons such that the property of each can no longer be distinguished.

**conglomerate merger** A merger between two companies which are not competitors and do not occupy a supplier-customer relationship.

**consent** A defense in an assault and battery action where it is alleged that the plaintiff expressly or implicitly agreed to expose himself to certain physical dangers.

**consent decree** A court injunction, the terms of which are arrived at by agreement of the parties.

**consent order** An administrative agency order, the terms of which are arrived at by agreement between the agency and the charged party.

**consideration** In contract law, a detriment to the promisee or benefit to the promisor, bargained for and given in exchange for a promise.

**consolidation** A transaction in which two corporations combine to form an entirely new corporation, thereby losing their former identities.

**construction (of contracts)** The use of considerations outside of the expressed or stated language of a contract to ascertain the true intent and purpose of the parties at the time they entered into the agreement.

**constructive annexation** The situation existing when personal property not physically attached to real property is adapted to the use to which the realty is designed so that the law considers it a fixture.

**constructive bailment** A bailment created when a bailee comes into possession of personal property without the consent of the owner. (An example is lost property found by a person—a bailee.)

**constructive delivery** A legal substitute for actual delivery of property which is the subject of a gift; consists of delivery of something which represents an item of intangible property or which gives control over an item of tangible property; also called symbolic delivery.

**constructive eviction** Legally justified abandonment of leased property by a tenant because of a landlord's action which has caused the property to be unsuitable for the purpose for which it was leased.

**constructive trust** A trust imposed by law to correct or rectify a fraud or to prevent one party from being unjustly enriched at the expense of another.

**consumer goods** Goods that are used or bought primarily for personal, family, or household purposes.

**Consumer Product Safety Act** A congressional enactment that created the Consumer Product Safety Commission, which has the responsibility of establishing and enforcing rules and standards to insure that products covered under the Act are safe for consumers' use.

**continuation statement** In secured transactions law, a document filed with a proper public official to continue public notice of the priority of an existing security interest in collateral upon the expiration of a previous filing.

**contract** An agreement that establishes enforceable legal relationships between two or more persons.

**contract, combination, or conspiracy** Express or tacit agreement required for a violation of the Sherman Act.

**contract carrier** A carrier who transports goods only for those under individual contract.

**contributory negligence** The fault (negligence) of a plaintiff, the result of which contributed to or added to his or her injury (used as a defense by a defendant against whom the plaintiff has filed a negligence action).

**controlling shareholders** Usually the majority shareholders or those with sufficient voting power to elect a majority of the directors, pass motions, or make binding decisions.

**conversion** An action which unlawfully injures the personal property of another or unlawfully interferes with the owner's right to possess and enjoy such property.

**conveyance** A transfer of an interest in property.

**corporate opportunity** A doctrine that prohibits directors, officers, or any other corporate managers from personally taking advantage of business situations that belong solely to or should be given to the corporation.

**corporate stock** Shares of stock, each representing an ownership interest in the business, issued by a corporation for the purpose of raising capital.

**corporation** An association of persons created by statute as a legal entity (artificial person) with authority to act and to have liability separate and apart from its owners.

**counterclaim** A pleading by the defendant in a civil suit against the plaintiff, the purpose being to defeat or sue the plaintiff so as to gain a judgment favorable to the defendant.

**counteroffer** A proposal made by an offeree in response to the offer extended him or her, the terms varying appreciably from the terms of the offer. Such a proposal by the offeree usually constitutes a rejection of the offer.

**course of dealing** The situation in which past conduct between two parties in performing a prior contract is used as a basis for interpreting their present conduct or agreement.

**course of performance** When a contract for the sale of goods involves repeated occasions for performance known by both parties and not objected to by either, the performance is considered interpretive of the remaining obligations of the contract.

**covenant against encumbrances** A guaranty by a grantor that there are no outstanding liens, easements, or liabilities held by a third party on the real property he or she is conveying, except as stated in the deed.

**covenant not to compete** A clause within a contract legally permitting a restraint of trade where such is a legitimate protection of a property interest and the restraint as to area and time is reasonable under the circumstances. An example is a clause in a sale of business contract where the seller agrees not to start up a competing business within a reasonable time and within the area where the said business has been operating.

**covenant of quiet enjoyment** A guaranty by a grantor of real property that the grantee or those who hold the property in the future will not be evicted or disturbed by a person having a better title or a right of foreclosure of a lien. Also, a guaranty by a landlord to a tenant that the tenant's right to possession will not be disturbed substantially.

**covenant of seisin** A guaranty by a grantor that he or she has good title to the real property being conveyed.

**covenants of title** The guarantees given by the grantor in a warranty deed.

**cover** In response to a seller's failure to deliver goods, the buyer's purchase of the goods from someone else in a commercially reasonable manner; the buyer's basic measure of damages for breach of contract in such a case is the difference between the contract price and the cover price.

**creditor beneficiary** A creditor who has rights in a contract (of which he or she is not a party) made by the debtor and a third person, where the terms of said contract expressly benefit the creditor.

**crime** Any wrongful action by an individual or persons for which a statute prescribes redress in the form of a death penalty, imprisonment, fine, or removal from an office of public trust.

**cross-elasticity of demand** The extent to which the quantity of a commodity demanded responds to changes in price of a related commodity. Used to help define a relevant market.

**cross-elasticity of supply** The extent to which the quantity of a product supplied responds to changes in price of a related commodity. Used to help define a relevant market.

**cumulative dividend preference** A characteristic of most preferred stock whereby all dividends in arrears must be paid to the preferred shareholders before any dividends can be paid to owners of common stock.

**cumulative preferred stock** A type of preferred stock on which dividends not paid in any given year are accumulated to the next succeeding year. The total amount accumulated must be paid before common shareholders can receive a dividend.

**cumulative voting** Where permitted, the procedure by which a shareholder is entitled to take his or her total number of shares, multiply that total by the number of directors to be elected, and cast the multiplied total for any director or directors to be elected.

**currency control** In international law, restrictions by a government on the transfer of currency from one country to another.

**curtesy** The common-law right of a surviving husband to a life estate in a portion of his deceased wife's real property.

*cy pres* So near or as near. The doctrine by which the courts will find a substitute purpose when the stated purpose of a charitable trust is not possible to accomplish.

**damages** The monetary loss suffered by a party as a result of a wrong.

**deadlock** A situation in a corporation where two equally divided factions exist in opposition to each other, thus bringing the affairs of the corporation to a virtual standstill.

**debenture** In securities regulation law, a debt security; a written promise by a corporation to repay borrowed money. Usually refers to a corporate bond or promissory note that is not secured by specific assets of the firm (i.e., is not secured by a mortgage on corporate assets).

**debit** A charge of indebtedness to an account (for example, a charge against a bank deposit account).

**debt securities** Instruments representing the bonded indebtedness of a corporation (they may be secured by corporate property or simply by a general obligation debt of the corporation).

**debtor** A person who owes payment of a debt and/or performance on an obligation.

**decedent** A person who has died.

**deceit** A false statement, usually intentional, that causes another person harm.

**deed** The document representing ownership of real property.

**deed of bargain and sale** A deed without warranties.

**de facto corporation** A corporation not formed in substantial compliance with the laws of a given state but which has sufficiently complied to be a corporation in fact, not right. Only the state can challenge the corporation's existence.

**de facto merger** A less formal means of merger where the results are achieved through asset or stock acquisition. Also called a practical merger.

**defamation** Injury of a person's character or reputation, usually by publication of a false statement about that person.

**default** The failure to perform a legal obligation.

**defendant** The party against whom a civil lawsuit has been instituted by a plaintiff, or against whom a criminal prosecution has been instituted by the government.

**defense** Any matter which is advanced or put forth by a defendant as a reason in law or fact why the plaintiff is not entitled to recover the relief he seeks.

**defensive merger** A merger sought by management in order to avoid consequences it does not feel will be in its best interests.

**deficiency judgment** A personal judgment given by a court against a debtor in default where the value of the property placed as security for the debt is less than the debt owed.

**de jure corporation** A corporation formed in substantial compliance with the laws of a given state; a corporation by right.

**delegated powers** The constitutional right of the federal government to pass laws concerning certain subjects and fields, thereby keeping the states from passing laws in these areas (sometimes referred to as enumerated powers).

**delegation** In contract law, the transfer of the power or right to represent or act for another; usually referred to as the delegation of duties to a third party, as compared to the assignment of rights to a third party.

**delegation of authority** In administrative law, a grant of authority from a legislative body to an administrative agency.

**demand instrument** An instrument which is payable immediately when the holder decides to present it.

**demurrer** A pleading by a defendant in the form of a motion denying that plaintiff's complaint or petition states a cause of action.

*de novo* To start completely new. A trial *de novo* is a completely new trial requiring the same degree of proof as if the case were being heard for the first time.

**depositary bank** The first bank to which an instrument is transferred for collection.

**deposition** Testimony of a witness, under oath and subject to cross examination, which is taken outside of court; an important discovery procedure.

**descendants** The lineal heirs of a decedent in a descending line—children and grandchildren.

**destination contract** In sales law, a contract whereby the seller is required to tender goods to the buyer at a place designated by the buyer.

**detriment test** A test to determine whether a promise is supported by consideration. The law requires the promisee to have done something not otherwise legally required or to have refrained from doing something he or she had a right to do.

**devise** A term of conveyance in real estate transactions. In a will, a gift of real estate by the testator is a devise.

**direct collection** The collection by the assignee (of an assignor-creditor) of a debt originally owed the creditor.

**directed verdict** A verdict that is directed by the court because reasonable persons could not differ as to the result.

**disaffirmance** The legal avoidance, or setting aside, of an obligation.

**discharge in bankruptcy** A release granted by a bankruptcy court to a debtor who has gone through proper bankruptcy proceedings; the release frees the person from any further liability on provable claims filed during the proceedings.

**disclaimer** A provision in a sales contract which attempts to prevent the creation of a warranty.

**discovery** Full disclosure of the evidence in a particular case before it comes to trial; various procedures are available to accomplish this disclosure.

**dishonor** In commercial paper, a refusal to pay or accept an instrument upon proper presentment.

**disparagement of goods** Making malicious and false statements of fact as to the quality or performance of another's goods.

**dissolution** The termination of a partnership's or corporation's right to exist as a going concern.

**diversity of citizenship** The condition that exists when the plaintiff and defendant are citizens of different states.

**dividend** A payment made by a corporation in cash or property from the income or profit of the corporation to a shareholder on the basis of his or her investment.

**documents of title** Bills of lading, dock warrants, dock receipts, warehouse receipts, and any other paper that, in the regular course of business or financing, is evidence of the holder's right to obtain possession of the goods covered.

**domestic corporation** A corporation chartered or incorporated in the state in which the corporation is doing business.

**dominant estate** The land that benefits from an easement appurtenant.

**donee** The person to whom a gift is made or a power is given.

**donee beneficiary** A person who has rights in a contract (to which he or she is not a party) made between two or more parties for his or her express benefit.

**donor** The person making a gift or giving another the power to do something.

**double jeopardy** A constitutional prohibition against trying a person a second time for the same crime for which he or she was convicted or acquitted at an earlier trial.

**dower** The common-law right of a widow to a life estate in a specific portion of her deceased husband's real property.

**draft** An instrument created by a party (the drawer) that orders another (the drawee) to pay the instrument to a third party (the payee); also called a bill of exchange.

**drawee** The person on whom a draft or check is drawn and who is requested (ordered) to pay the instrument.

**drawee bank** A bank on which a draft or check is drawn, such bank being ordered to pay the instrument when it is duly presented.

**drawer** The person creating (drafting) a draft or check.

**due process** The right of every person not to be deprived of life, liberty, or property without a fair hearing and/or just compensation.

**duress** The overcoming of a person's free will through the use of threat, force, or actions whereby the person is forced to do something he or she otherwise would not do.

**earnest money** A deposit paid by a buyer to hold a seller to a contractual obligation. Frequently this amount also serves as liquidated damages in the event of the buyer's breach. Historically, the deposit was said to show the buyer's good faith in entering into the contract with the seller.

**easement** A nonpossessory interest in real property that gives the holder the right to use another's land in a particular way.

**easement appurtenant** An easement created specifically for use in connection with an adjoining tract of land.

**easement in gross** An easement that is not used in connection with another tract of land.

**economic duress** The overcoming of a person's free will by means of a threat or other action involving the wrongful use of economic pressure, whereby the person is forced to do something he or she otherwise would not do.

**election** A principle of law whereby a third person who learns of the identity of the undisclosed principal prior to receiving a judgment must choose to receive the judgment against either the agent or the undisclosed principal. Election of one releases the other from liability to the third party.

**embezzlement** The act of expropriating from the true

owner property entrusted to the wrongdoer through a fiduciary relationship.

**eminent domain** The power of the government to take private property for public use by paying just compensation.

**employment at will** A common-law doctrine under which workers are hired for an indefinite period of time. Either party can terminate the employment contract at any time, with no reason being given. In recent years, courts and legislatures have created a number of exceptions to the employer's absolute right to terminate an employment-at-will relationship.

**endowment insurance** Life insurance which is payable either to the insured when he or she reaches a specified age or to the named beneficiary if the insured dies before reaching the specified age.

**entity theory** The view that a partnership is a legal entity separate from the individual partners.

**entrapment** The act by a government official of encouraging or inducing a person to commit a crime that he or she would not otherwise commit for the sole purpose of instituting a criminal prosecution against him or her.

**entry barrier** A condition that makes entry into a market by a new competitor more costly and risky.

**environmental impact statement** The statement required by federal law that describes the effect of proposed major federal action on the quality of the human environment.

**Environmental Protection Agency** The federal agency charged with the responsibility for establishing and enforcing environmental standards and for continuing research on pollution and measures to eliminate or control it.

**equal protection clause** A provision in the Fourteenth Amendment to the U.S. Constitution that prohibits states from making distinctions among persons or firms without a reasonable, rational basis.

**equipment** Goods that are used or bought for use primarily in business.

**equitable action** An action brought in a court seeking an equitable remedy, such as an injunction or decree of specific performance.

**equity securities** Shares of capital stock representing an ownership interest in the corporation.

**escheat** The process by which a decedent's property passes to the state when he or she did not leave a valid will and there are no legal heirs.

**escrow agent** An agent who, by agreement, holds property, documents, or money of one party with the authority to transfer such property to a designated person upon the occurrence of a specified event.

**establishment of religion clause** The clause in the First Amendment to the U.S. Constitution which prohibits the federal government from "establishing" a religion. This restriction has also been applied to the states under the due process clause.

**ethics** The study and application of moral principles.

**eviction** Action by the landlord which physically bars the tenant from entering the leased premises.

**exclusive agency** In real property law, the arrangement by a seller of real property with a broker whereby only that broker is entitled to a commission if a sale of the real property is made through the efforts of anyone other than the seller.

**exclusive dealing agreement** An agreement which commits a buyer to purchase a certain product only from one seller, or a seller to sell only to one buyer.

**exclusive right to sell** In real property law, the arrangement by a seller of real property with a broker whereby the broker is entitled to his or her commission if a sale of the real property is made through the effort of anyone, including the seller.

**exculpatory clause** A contract clause providing that one party agrees to free the other of all liability in the event he or she suffers a physical or monetary injury in a particular situation, even if the loss is caused by the negligence of the other party to the contract.

**excusing conditions** Conditions affecting a person's knowledge or freedom of action and eliminating or reducing a moral obligation.

**executed contract** A contract wholly performed by both parties to the contract, as opposed to an executory contract, which is wholly unperformed by both parties.

**execution of a judgment** The process by which a judgment creditor obtains a writ directing the sheriff or other officer to seize nonexempt property of the debtor and sell it to satisfy the judgment.

**executive committee** In a corporation, a certain number of the members of the board of directors appointed by the board as a committee with the delegated authority to make decisions concerning ordinary business matters that come up during intervals between regular board meetings.

**executive order** An order by the president of the United States or governor of a state that has the force of law.

**executor (female, executrix)** The personal representative in a testator's will to dispose of an estate as the will has directed.

**executory contract** A contract wholly unperformed by both parties to the contract, as opposed to an executed contract, where both parties have fully performed their obligations under the contract.

**executory interest** A future interest held by a third party.

**exempt property** Real or personal property of a debtor that cannot by law be seized to satisfy a debt owed to an unsecured creditor.

***ex parte*** On one side only. For example, an *ex parte* proceeding is held on the application of one party only, without notice to the other party; and an *ex parte* order is made at the request of one party when the other party fails to show up in court, when the other party's presence is not needed, or when there is no other party.

**export license** A license to ship goods or articles of commerce from a particular country.

**express authority** Authority specifically given by the principal to the agent.

**express contract** A contract formed from the words (oral and/or in writing) of the parties, as opposed to an implied contract, which is formed from the conduct of the parties.

**express warranty** In sales law, a guarantee or assurance as to the quality or performance of goods that arises from the words or conduct of the seller.

**ex-ship** From the carrying vessel; a delivery term indicating that the seller's risk and expense for shipment of goods by vessel extends until the goods are unloaded at the port of destination.

**extension clause** A clause in a time instrument providing that under certain circumstances the maturity date can be extended.

**extraordinary bailment** A bailment in which the bailee is given by law greater duties and liabilities than an ordinary bailee. Common carriers and innkeepers are the most common examples of extraordinary bailees.

**Fair Labor Standards Act (FLSA)** A 1938 congressional enactment regulating minimum wages, overtime, and child labor.

**false imprisonment** The wrongful detention or restraint of one person by another.

**false pretenses** A material misrepresentation of a fact or circumstance calculated to mislead.

**family purpose doctrine** The doctrine under which (in a few states) the head of a household is liable for the negligent acts of any members of his or her family that occur while they are driving the family car.

**farm products** Goods that are crops, livestock, or supplies used or produced in farming operations, or goods that are products or livestock in their unmanufactured state (such as ginned cotton, maple syrup, milk, and eggs). For secured transactions law these goods must be in the possession of a debtor engaged in raising, fattening, grazing, or other farm operations.

**FAS** Free alongside ship; a delivery term indicating that the seller must deliver goods to the designated dock alongside the vessel on which the goods are to be loaded and must bear the expenses of delivery to the dock site.

**fault** Breach of a legal duty.

**Federal Communications Commission (FCC)** A seven-member commission established in 1934 by congressional enactment of the Federal Communications Act. The commission is empowered to regulate all interstate communication by telephone, telegraph, radio, and television.

**federal preemption** A legal principle which grants the Congress, the federal courts, and federal agencies exclusive authority in certain matters of law where the need for a uniform national body of law is great. Labor relations law, for example, is almost exclusively the domain of the federal government.

**federal question** A question presented by a case in which one party, usually the plaintiff, is asserting a right (or counterclaim, in the case of the defendant) which is based upon a federal rule of law—e.g., a provision of the U.S. Constitution, an act of Congress, or a U.S. treaty.

**Federal Trade Commission (FTC)** A five-member commission established in 1914 by congressional enactment of the Federal Trade Commission Act. The commission enforces prohibitions against unfair methods of competition and unfair or deceptive acts or practices in commerce; it also enforces numerous federal laws (particularly federal consumer protection acts, such as "Truth in Lending" and "Fair Packaging and Labeling").

**fee simple** The absolute ownership of real property.

**fee simple defeasible** An ownership interest in real property subject to termination by the occurrence of a specific event.

**felony** A criminal offense punishable by death or imprisonment for a period exceeding one year.

**fictitious payee** A payee on an instrument who is either nonexistent or an actual person not entitled to payment. (Usually the fraud is perpetrated by a dishonest employee in charge of payroll or payment of accounts who drafts an instrument with intent to defraud his or her employer.)

**fiduciary** A position of trust in relation to another person or his or her property.

**financing statement** An instrument filed with a proper public official that gives notice of an outstanding security interest in collateral.

**finding of fact** The process whereby from testimony and evidence a judge, agency, or examiner determines that certain matters, events, or acts took place upon which conclusions of law can be based.

**firm offer** In sales law, an irrevocable offer dealing with the sale of goods made by a merchant offeror in a signed writing and giving assurance to the offeree that the offer will remain open. This offer is irrevocable without consideration for the stated period of time or, if no period is stated, for a reasonable period, neither period to exceed three months.

**fixture** A piece of personal property that is attached to real property in such a manner that the law deems the item to be part of the real property.

**floating lien concept** In secured transactions law, the concept whereby a security interest is permitted to be retained in collateral even though the collateral changes in character and classification. For example, a security interest in raw materials is retained even if the raw materials change character in the manufacturing process and end up as inventory.

**FOB** Free on board; a delivery term indicating that the seller must ship the goods and bear the expenses of shipment to the FOB point of designation (which can be either the seller's or the buyer's place of business).

**forbearance** The refraining from doing something that a person has a legal right to do.

**foreclosure** The procedure or action taken by a mortgagee, upon default of the mortgagor, whereby the mortgagee satisfies his or her claim by some action (usually by selling off the mortgaged property).

**foreign corporation** A corporation chartered or incorporated in one state but doing business in a different state.

**forgery** The act of making a false instrument and/or passing an instrument known to be false with the intent to perpetrate a fraud or injury to another. Also, the false instrument itself. Also, a signature of another made without authorization.

**formal contract** A contract that derives its validity only from compliance with a specific form or format required by law. Examples are contracts under seal (where a seal is required), negotiable instruments, and recognizances (formal acknowledgments of indebtedness made in a court of law).

**franchise** (1) A business conducted under someone else's trademark or tradename. The owner of the business, which may be a sole proprietorship, partnership, corporation, or other form of organization, is usually referred to as the *franchisee*. The owner of the trademark or tradename, who contractually permits use of the mark or name, in return for a fee and usually subject to various restrictions, is ordinarily referred to as the *franchisor*. The permission to use the mark or name, which is part of the franchising agreement, is called a *trademark license*. (2) The term can also be used to refer to a privilege granted by a governmental body, such as the exclusive right granted to someone by a city to provide cable TV service in that city.

**fraud** An intentional or reckless misrepresentation of a material fact that causes anyone relying on it injury or damage.

**fraud implied in law** A presumption of fraud which exists when a debtor transfers property without receiving fair consideration in return and the debtor has insufficient assets remaining to satisfy creditors; burden of proof falls to debtor to show absence of fraud.

**fraud in fact** An action by a debtor in which he transfers property with the specific intent of defrauding creditors.

**fraud in the execution** In commercial paper, inducing a person to sign an instrument, the party signing being deceived as to the nature or essential terms of the instrument.

**fraud in the inducement** In commercial paper, the use of deceit in inducing a person to sign an instrument, although the deceived party knows what he or she is signing and the essential terms of the instrument. This knowledge is what distinguishes fraud in inducement from fraud in the execution.

**fraudulent conveyance** The transfer of property in such a manner that the conveyance is deemed either in fact or by law to defraud creditors.

**free speech clause** The clause in the First Amendment to the U.S. Constitution which prohibits the federal government from abridging the freedom of speech. This restriction has also been applied to the states under the Due Process Clause.

**frustration of purpose doctrine** A legal doctrine followed in many states which excuses a party from a contract because of an occurrence which undermines the basic purpose of the contract.

**FTC holder in due course rule** An FTC rule which states that it is illegal for a seller to execute a sales contract or arrange a direct loan unless the contract includes a clause which informs the holder of the contract that he or she is subject to all claims and defenses against such contract.

**full faith and credit clause** The provision in the U.S. Constitution which requires the courts of one state to recognize judgments and other public actions of its sister states.

**fungible** In sales or securities law, goods or securities of which any unit is, by nature or usage of trade, the equivalent of any other like unit.

**future advance** In secured transactions law, the concept whereby an outstanding security interest applies to future loans made by the secured party. If the security interest is properly perfected, the future loan, for priority purposes, dates back to the time the original security interest was created.

**future interest** An interest in real property, the use or enjoyment of which is postponed until a later date or the occurrence of a designated event.

**futures contract** A contract to buy or sell standard commodities (such as rice, coffee, or wheat) at a future date and a specified price. (The seller is agreeing to sell goods he or she does not own at the time of making the contract.)

**garnishee** A person who holds money owed to or property of a debtor subject to a garnishment action.

**garnishment** The legal proceeding of a judgment creditor to require a third person owing money to the debtor or holding property belonging to the debtor to turn over to the court or sheriff the property or money owed for the satisfaction of the judgment. State and federal laws generally permit only a limited amount of a debtor's wages to be garnished.

**general warranty deed** A deed to real property which guarantees that the title is a good, marketable one.

**gift** A voluntary transfer of property to another without consideration.

**gift *causa mortis*** A gift made by a donor in contemplation of his or her death from some existing affliction or impending peril.

**gift *inter vivos*** A gift made during the lifetime of a donor and not in contemplation of his or her death.

**Golden Rule, The** A rule of ethical conduct stating that one should do to others as one would have others do to oneself.

**good faith** Honesty in fact on the part of a person in negotiating a contract, or in the carrying on of some other transaction.

**goods** Tangible and movable personal property except for money used as medium of exchange.

**grand jury** An inquisitional body of citizens charged with the duty of conducting its own investigation into a crime to determine if sufficient evidence exists to warrant the issuance of an indictment against an alleged offender.

**grantee** The person to whom an interest in real property is conveyed by deed.

**grantor** The person conveying an interest in real property by deed.

**Green River ordinances** State and municipal laws that regulate door-to-door sales on private premises. So called after the Green River, Wyoming, case in which such laws were held to be valid and enforceable.

**guaranty** A promise to pay an obligation of a debtor if the debtor is in default.

**holder** Any person in possession of a document, security, or instrument that is drawn, issued, or indorsed to him or her.

**holder in due course (HDC)** A holder who takes an instrument for value, in good faith, and without notice that the instrument is overdue or has been dishonored or that any defense or claim by any person exists against it.

**holder through a holder in due course** A holder who fails to qualify as a holder in due course but has the rights of one (by law of assignment) if he or she can show that a prior holder of the instrument qualified as a holder in due course. This is referred to as the "shelter provision."

**holding company** A company whose main function is to own other companies through control of their stock. Also called an investment company.

**holographic will** A will entirely in the handwriting of the testator. Witnesses are not required for its execution but are necessary at probate to prove the handwriting of the testator.

**horizontal merger** A merger of two competing firms at the same level in the production or distribution of a product.

**horizontal price fixing** Price fixing among competitors. *Per se* illegal under Section 1 of the Sherman Act.

**horizontal restraint of trade** An arrangement between two or more competitors that suppresses or limits competition.

**hostile environment harassment** In employment discrimination law, unwelcome requests for sexual favors made to an employee by the employer or by someone for whose actions the employer is responsible, under circumstances in which the requests have created an intimidating, hostile, or offensive environment.

**illusory contract** An agreement of the parties that, on examination, lacks mutuality of obligation—i.e., one in which consideration is found to be lacking on the part of one party. The result is that neither party is bound by the agreement.

**immunity** The right of a witness to be free from indictment or arrest in exchange for particular or general testimony offered to a court.

**implied authority** Authority inferred for an agent to carry out his or her express authority and/or authority inferred from the position held by the agent to fulfill his or her agency duties.

**implied contract** A contract in which the parties' manifestation of assent or agreement is inferred, in whole or in part, from their conduct, as opposed to an express contract formed by the parties' words.

**implied warranties** Assurances or guarantees of certain standards or actions imposed by law.

**implied warranty of habitability** An obligation imposed on the landlord to keep residential property in a liveable condition.

**import license** A license allowing the importation of goods or articles of commerce into a particular country.

**incidental beneficiary** One who benefits from a contract between others but who cannot legally enforce the contract because his or her benefit is a secondary effect, not an intended result of the contract.

**incorporated partnership** A close corporation with more than one shareholder.

**incorporation** The act or process of forming or creating a corporation.

**indemnification** Where allowed, the right to reimbursement for expenses, losses, or costs incurred.

**independent contractor** One who is hired by another to perform a given task in a manner and method independent from the control of employer.

**indirect collection** The creditor's collection of payment(s) of a debt, even though the debt has been assigned by the creditor to an assignee.

**indorsee** The person who receives an indorsed instrument.

**indorsement** The signature of the indorser (usually on the back of an instrument) for the purpose of transferring an instrument and establishing the limits of his or her liability.

**indorsement for deposit** A type of restrictive indorsement that requires the depositary bank to place into the account of the restrictive indorser the amount of the instrument.

**indorsement in trust** A type of restrictive indorsement whereby the amount on the instrument is to be paid to the indorsee, who in turn is to use or hold the funds for the benefit of the indorser or a third party.

**indorser** The person who indorses an instrument, usually for the purpose of transferring it to a third person.

**informal contract** Any contract that does not depend on a specified form or formality for its validity.

**injunction** A decree issued by a court hearing an equity action either prohibiting a person from performing a certain act or acts or requiring the person to perform a certain act or acts.

**innocent misrepresentation** A false statement of fact, not known to be false, that causes another harm or damage.

**insider trading** The buying or selling of corporate securities of a particular firm by persons having business knowledge about such firm that is not available to the general public, with the expectation of making a personal profit in such transactions.

**insolvency** In bankruptcy law, the financial condition of a debtor when his or her assets at fair market value are less than his or her debts and liabilities.

**installment contract** In sales law, a contract that authorizes or requires the delivery and acceptance of goods in separate lots.

**installment note** An instrument (note) in which the principal (plus interest usually) is payable in specified partial amounts at specified times until the full amount is paid.

**insurable interest** The rights of a person who will be directly or financially affected by the death of a person or the loss of property. Only these rights can be protected by an insurance policy.

**intermediary bank** Any bank to which an instrument is transferred in the course of collection and which is not the depositary or payor bank.

**interpretation (of statutes)** An analysis of the expressed words of a statute to ascertain their meaning and significance.

**interrogatories** In a lawsuit, a discovery procedure involving the submission of written questions by one party to the other, which the other party must answer under oath.

**interstate commerce** The carrying on of commercial activities or the commercial transportation of persons or property between points lying in different states.

**Interstate Commerce Commission (ICC)** An administrative agency established in 1887 by congressional enactment of the Interstate Commerce Act regulating the licensing and rates of common carriers in interstate commerce.

*inter vivos* "Between the living," as an *inter vivos* gift (one made during the life of the donor) or an *inter vivos* trust.

*inter vivos* **trust** A trust established and effective during the life of the settlor.

**intestate** The situation in which a person dies without leaving a valid will.

**inventory** Goods held by a person or firm for sale or lease in the ordinary course of business; also refers to raw materials (and work in process on them) where held by a manufacturing company.

**investment company** Any corporation organized for the purpose of owning and holding the stock of other corporations.

**involuntary case** In bankruptcy, a liquidation proceeding that is brought about by the unpaid creditors.

**irrevocable offer** An offer or proposal that by law cannot be withdrawn by an offeror without liability.

**issue** The first delivery of an instrument to a holder.

**joint stock company** An unincorporated association that closely resembles a corporation but for most purposes is treated as a partnership.

**joint tenancy** A co-ownership of property by two or more parties in which each owns an undivided interest that passes to the other co-owners on his or her death (known as the "right of survivorship").

**joint tortfeasors** Two or more persons who in concert commit a tort; also two or more persons whose independent torts are so linked to an injury that a court will hold either or both liable.

**joint venture** Collaboration by two or more firms involving a pooling of resources, integration of some aspect of the firms' operations, and an intent to accomplish a defined business objective that could not be accomplished as efficiently (or at all) by a single firm.

**judgment notwithstanding the verdict (judgment n.o.v.)** The entry of a judgment by a trial judge in favor of one party even though the jury returned a verdict in favor of the other party.

**judicial review** The process by which the courts oversee and determine the legitimacy or validity of executive, legislative, or administrative agency action.

**junior security interest** A security interest or right that is subordinate to another security interest or right.

**jurisdiction of a court** The power of a court to hear and decide a particular dispute and to issue a judgment that is legally binding on the parties in the dispute.

**justice** The application of rules to arrive at what is recognized as a fair and reasonable result; also a title given to a judge.

**landlord's lien** The right held by the landlord to seize, hold, or sell a tenant's personal property for nonpayment of rent.

**Landrum-Griffin Act** A 1959 congressional amendment of the 1935 NLRA which established a bill of rights for union members, required public financial disclosures by unions and union leaders, and regulated election procedures for union officials by union members.

**larceny** The unlawful taking and carrying away of property of another with the intent to permanently deprive the owner of its use.

**latent defect** In sales law, an imperfection in a good that cannot be discovered by ordinary observation or inspection.

**law** Enforceable rules governing the relationship of individuals and persons, their relationship to one another, and their relationship to an organized society.

**lease** A conveyance to another of the right to possess property in return for a payment called rent.

**leasehold** The interest acquired by the lessee under a lease.

**leasehold estate** The real property held by the lessee who has been given temporary possession in return for payment of rent.

**legacy** In a will, a specific gift of money.

**legal detriment** A required element of contractual consideration; exists when the promisee does or promises to do something he or she is not legally obligated to do, or refrains or promises to refrain from doing something he or she has a legal right to do.

**legal entity** An association recognized by law as having the legal rights and duties of a person.

**legal impossibility of performance** An event that takes place after a contract is made, rendering performance under the contract, in the eyes of the law, something that cannot be done. Also referred to as objective impossibility, it legally discharges a party's obligation; it can be compared to subjective impossibility, which makes the contractual obligation more difficult to perform but does not discharge it.

**legal rate of interest** The rate of interest applied by statute where there is an agreement for interest to be paid but none is stated, or where the law implies a duty to pay interest irrespective of agreement. In the latter case, this may be referred to as a *judgment rate*, a rate of interest applied to judgments until paid by the defendant.

**legal tender** Any currency recognized by law as the medium of exchange that must be accepted by a creditor in satisfaction of a debtor's debt.

**legal title** That which represents ownership of property.

**legislative history** The history of the legislative enactment used by the court as a means of interpreting the terms of a statute. It consists primarily of legislative committee reports and the transcripts of committee hearings and floor debates.

**lessee** The person who leases or rents property from a lessor. If the lease involves an interest in real property, the lessee is frequently referred to as the tenant.

**lessor** The person who leases property to the lessee. If the lease involves an interest in real property, the lessor is frequently referred to as the landlord.

**letter of credit** A letter authorizing one person to pay money, to extend credit, or to supply a commodity to a third person on the credit of the writer.

**libel** Written defamation of one's character or reputation.

**license** In real property law, the landowner's permission for another to come upon his or her land. In intellectual property law, a contract by which the owner grants permission to another to use a patent, copyright, trademark, or trade secret, usually in return for payment of a royalty.

**licensee** In real property and tort law, a person who enters upon the property of another for his or her own convenience, pleasure, or benefit with the knowledge or consent of the owner. In other contexts, such as intellectual property law, one to whom a license is granted.

**lien** An interest held by a creditor in property of the debtor for the purpose of securing payment of the debt.

**lien creditor** In secured transactions law, any creditor who is able to legally attach the property of the debtor. This includes an assignee for the benefit of creditors, a trustee in bankruptcy, or an appointed receiver in equity.

**life estate** An interest in real property for the duration of the life of some designated person, who may be the life tenant or a third person.

**life tenant** The person holding (owning) a life estate in designated property.

**limitation of remedies** A provision in a sales contract which attempts to limit the remedies available to a party; usually employed by a seller to limit a buyer's remedies for breach of warranty.

**limited defense** See *personal defense*.

**limited partnership** A partnership created under statute with at least one limited and one general partner. The limited partner's liability to third persons is restricted to his or her capital contributions.

**liquidated damages** An amount of, or a method for computing, breach of contract damages that is agreed upon by the parties to a contract before a dispute actually arises.

**liquidated debt** An undisputed debt; that is, a debt about which there is no reasonable basis for dispute as to its existence or amount.

**liquidating partner** After an act of dissolution of the partnership, any partner who has authority to wind up the partnership, thereby terminating it.

**liquidation** Conversion of the assets of a corporation to cash and the subsequent distribution of the cash to creditors and shareholders.

**liquidation preference** Preferred shareholders' priority over common shareholders to the distribution of corporate assets upon the corporation's dissolution.

**liquidation proceeding** Under the Bankruptcy Act, a proceeding in which the debtor's assets are sold to pay off creditors insofar as it is possible to do so and the debtor is discharged from further responsibility.

**lobbying contract** A contract made by one person with another under the terms of which the former agrees to represent the latter's interest before legislative or administrative bodies by attempting to influence their votes or decisions on legislative, quasi-legislative, or related proceedings.

**long-arm statutes** Laws that permit a plaintiff to bring a certain action and recover a judgment in a court in his or her home state against a defendant who resides in another state.

**lost property** Property located at a place where it was not put by its owner, which place is unknown by the owner.

**Magnuson-Moss Warranty Act** A congressional enactment designed to prevent deceptive warranty practices, make warranties easier to understand, and create procedures for consumer enforcement of warranties. The act applies only to written warranties given in a consumer sales transaction and can be enforced by the Federal Trade Commission, attorney general, or an aggrieved party.

**mail fraud** The use of the mails for the purpose of executing a fraudulent scheme.

**maker** The person who creates or executes a promissory note or certificate of deposit.

**marital deduction** An estate planning device that can be used by the surviving husband or wife to effect substantial estate tax savings.

**market** (1) An area over which buyers and sellers negotiate the exchange of a well-defined commodity. (2) From the point of view of the consumer, the firms from which he or she can buy a well-defined product. (3) From the point of view of a producer, the buyers to whom it can sell a well-defined product. Market definition is crucial in determining the market shares of firms under antitrust scrutiny.

**market division arrangements** Any concerted action among actual or potential competitors to divide *geographic* markets, to assign particular *customers*, or to market particular *products* among themselves so as to avoid or limit competition. Such market divisions are treated as *per se* violations of Section 1 of the Sherman Act.

**market power** The ability of a firm to raise its price without losing most of its customers.

**market share** A firm's percentage of the production or sales in a relevant market; an important measure of market power.

**maturity** In commercial paper, the time when a debt or obligation is due.

**maximum rate of interest** A statutory limit on the amount of interest that can be charged on a given transaction.

**mechanic's lien** A statutory lien against real property for labor, services, or materials used in improving the real property.

***mens rea*** The evil mental state required to attach criminal liability to a person for his or her conduct.

**merchant** In sales law, a person who customarily deals in goods of the kind that are involved in a transaction, or who otherwise by occupation holds himself or herself out as having knowledge or skill peculiar to the goods involved in the transaction.

**merger** The purchase of either the physical assets or the controlling share ownership of one company by another. As a business combination, a merger can come under antitrust review if the Justice Department or the FTC have reason to believe it might lessen competition.

**metes and bounds** A term used to describe the exterior lines of a parcel of land where metes means measure of length and bounds refers to the boundaries of the property.

**ministerial power** In administrative agency law, the routine day-to-day administration of the law, as opposed to discretionary powers, which involve the power to exercise judgment in the rendering of decisions.

**minor** Any person under the age of majority. In most states the age of majority is eighteen years; in some it is 21.

**minority shareholders** Those shareholders whose voting power is not sufficient to elect a majority of the directors, pass motions, or make binding decisions.

**mirror image rule** A principle used in contract law where the acceptance must adhere exactly to the offer in order for it to be valid.

**misdemeanor** Any crime or offense which is punishable by fine or imprisonment for less than a year. Less serious than a felony.

**mislaid property** Property located at a place where it was put by the owner, who has now forgotten the location.

**mistake** An unintentional error.

**mitigation of damages** A duty imposed on an injured party to minimize his or her losses or injuries through the exercise of reasonable diligence and ordinary care after the injury has been inflicted.

**Model Business Corporation Act** Uniform rules governing the incorporation and operation of corporations for profit recommended by the American Bar Association for enactment by the various states.

**money** In commercial paper, any medium of exchange authorized or adopted by a domestic or foreign government as part of its currency.

**monopoly** According to the economic model, a market having only one seller, high barriers to entry, and no close substitutes for the product being sold. The courts generally define a monopolist as a firm possessing such an overwhelming degree of market power that it is able to control prices or exclude competition.

**moral agent** A person or organization capable of having moral obligations.

**moral dilemmas** Situations involving two distinct moral obligations that are in conflict.

**moral minimum** The minimum obligations of moral responsibility.

**mortgage** The agreement by which a lien on a debtor's property is conveyed to a creditor.

**mortgagee** The creditor in a mortgage agreement.

**mortgagor** The debtor in a mortgage agreement.

**motion to dismiss** Motion filed by the defendant in which he alleges that the complaint does not state a cause of action, in other words, that the complaint fails to state a legally recognizable claim.

**mutual-benefit bailment** A nongratuitous bailment frequently formed by contract through which both parties benefit.

**mutuality of obligation** The principle in contract law that both parties must obligate themselves in order for either to be obligated.

**National Labor Relations Act (NLRA)** A 1935 congressional enactment regulating labor-management relations. This act (1) established methods for selecting a labor union that would represent a particular group of employees, (2) required the employer to bargain with that union, (3) prescribed certain fundamental employee rights, (4) prohibited several "unfair labor practices" by employers, and (5) created the National Labor Relations Board to administer and enforce the NLRA. Also known as the Wagner Act.

**natural monopoly** Unusual market structure resulting from unique characteristics of the product or service offered. Some goods (e.g., electricity) or services (e.g., local telephone system) require large capital outlays and/or require uniformity in delivery systems so that only one firm can efficiently provide them at a profit.

**necessaries** In contract law, items contracted for which the law deems essential to a person's life or health (usually such items as food, clothing, shelter, medical services, and primary and secondary education).

**negligence** The failure to exercise reasonable care required under the circumstances, which failure is the proximate or direct cause of damage or injury to another.

**negotiability** The status of an instrument that meets the requirements under the UCC for an instrument to be negotiable.

**negotiable document of title** A document of title in which the terms state the goods are to be delivered to "bearer" or to the "order" of a named person. The person who is in legal possession of the document is entitled to the goods described therein.

**negotiable instrument** A signed written document that contains an unconditional promise or order to pay a sum certain in money on demand or at a definite time to the order of a specific person or to bearer. The document can be either a draft, a check, a certificate of deposit, or a note.

**negotiation** The transfer of an instrument in such form that the transferee becomes a holder.

**nominal damages** A monetary award by a court where there is a breach of duty or contract but where no financial loss has occurred or been proven.

**nonexempt property** The property of a debtor subject to the claims of unsecured creditors.

**nonexistent principal** A principal not recognized by law.

**nonnegotiable document of title** A document of title which states that the goods are to be delivered to a specific person or entity. Legal possession of this document is not tantamount to ownership of the goods.

**nonnegotiable instrument** An instrument that does not meet the requirements of negotiability under the UCC.

**nonprice predation** Conduct by a dominant firm that is aimed at increasing the costs of competitors or increasing entry barriers for potential competitors.

**nonprofit corporation** A private corporation formed to perform a religious, charitable, educational, or benevolent purpose without a profit-oriented goal.

**nonstock corporation** A corporation in which capital stock is not issued; usually occurs only in the case of a nonprofit corporation.

**nontrading partnership** A partnership formed primarily for the production (but not sale) of commodities or for the providing of services.

**no-par value stock** Stock issued by a corporation with no amount stated in the certificate. The amount a subscriber pays is determined by the board of directors.

**note** In commercial paper, an instrument whereby one party (the maker) promises to pay another (the payee or bearer) a sum of money on demand or at a stated date.

**notice** A fact that a person actually knows, or one he or she should know exists based on all facts and circumstances.

**novation** The substitution, by agreement, of a new contract for an existing one, thereby terminating the old contract. This is usually accomplished by a three-sided agreement of the parties that a third person's performance be substituted for that of one of the original parties to the contract.

**nuisance** Action by a defendant that impinges upon or interferes with the rights of others. The remedy for plaintiff is an injunction compelling abatement.

**nuncupative will** An oral will permitted by some states but on which significant restrictions and conditions are imposed by statute.

**obligee** The person to whom a duty is owed.

**obligor** A person who owes a duty to another.

**occupation** In personal property law, the acquisition of unowned property by the first person to take possession with an intent to become the owner.

**Occupational Safety and Health Act (OSHA)** A 1970 congressional enactment creating the Occupational Safety and Health Administration as part of the Labor Department, and requiring that agency to develop and enforce occupational safety and health standards for American industries.

**offer** In contract law, a proposal made by an offeror which manifests a present intent to be legally bound and expresses the proposed terms with reasonable definiteness.

**offeree** The person to whom an offer is made.

**offeror** A person who makes a proposal to another, with the view in mind that if it is accepted, it will create a legally enforceable agreement between the parties.

**oligopoly** A market structure in which a small number of firms dominate the industry.

**open listing** The arrangement by a seller of real property whereby the seller's obligation to pay a commission to a broker arises only if he or she is the first broker to procure an acceptable buyer (a buyer who is ready, willing, and able to buy at the stated price).

**option** An irrevocable offer formed by contract and supported by consideration.

**option contract** A contract in which consideration is given to the offeror from the offeree in return for the promise to keep the offer open.

**order instrument** An instrument payable to a designated payee or payees, or whomever they so direct, and requiring for its negotiation the indorsement of those persons.

**ordinary bailment** Any bailment not classified as an extraordinary bailment.

**output contract** An enforceable agreement for the sale of all the goods produced by a seller (the exact amount of which is not set or known at the time of the agreement) or all those produced at a given plant of the seller during the term of the contract; a contract in which the seller agrees to sell and the buyer agrees to buy all or up to a stated amount that the seller produces.

**owner-consent statute** A legislative enactment in a few states whereby the owner is liable for the negligence of any person driving the owner's car with his or her permission.

**ownership in place** The rights to oil, gas, and other minerals while they are still in the ground.

***pari delicto*** Parties equally at fault.

**parol evidence rule** A rule that in some instances prohibits the introduction of evidence, oral or written, that would, if admitted, vary, change, alter, or modify any terms or provisions of a complete and unambiguous written contract.

**partially-disclosed principal** In agency law, a principal who is known to exist but whose identity is unknown by third persons dealing with the agent.

**participating preferred stock** A type of preferred stock giving its holders the right to share with common shareholders in any dividends remaining after the preferred shareholders have received their preferred dividend and common shareholders have received their specified dividend.

**partition** The dividing of land co-owned by several persons into specific designated pieces (sections) of property.

**partnership** An association of two or more persons who by agreement as co-owners carry on a business for profit.

**par value stock** Stock that has been assigned a specific value by the board of directors; the amount is stated in the certificate, and the subscriber to the corporation must pay at least this amount.

**payee** The person to whom an instrument is made payable.

**payment against documents** A term in a contract that requires payment for goods upon receipt of their documents of title, even though the goods have not as yet arrived.

**payor bank** The bank (drawee) on which an instrument is drawn (payable).

***per capita*** "By heads," in descent and distribution of a decedent's estate where the heirs are of one class (such as children) and take equal shares.

**peremptory challenge** The right to exclude a prospective juror without having to state a reason or cause.

**perfection** In secured transactions law, the concept whereby a secured party obtains a priority claim on the collateral of his or her debtor as against other interested parties by giving some form of notice of his or her outstanding security interest.

**perfect tender rule** In sales law, a rule of law providing that it is a seller's obligation to deliver or tender delivery of goods that are in strict conformance with the terms of the sales contract.

**performance** Carrying out of an obligation or promise according to the terms agreed to or specified. In contract law, complete performance by both parties discharges the contract.

**periodic tenancy** The interest created by a lease for an indefinite duration where rent is paid at specified intervals and a prescribed time for giving notice of termination is required.

**per se rule** Antitrust doctrine wherein certain types of group business behavior are inherently anticompetitive and are therefore automatically illegal. Horizontal price fixing and boycotts are examples of per se illegal activities.

**personal defense** In commercial paper, any defense by a party that cannot be asserted against a holder in due course or against a holder through a holder in due course. A personal defense (often referred to as a limited defense) is effective only against ordinary holders.

**personal property** All property not classified as real property; "movables." May be tangible (e.g., cars and gasoline) or intangible (e.g., shares of corporate stock and other contractual rights).

***per stirpes*** "By roots or stocks," in descent and distribution of a decedent's estate, where a class of heirs take the share their predeceased ancestor would have taken.

**piercing the corporate veil** The action of a court in disregarding the separate legal entity (identity) of the corporation, thereby subjecting the owners to possible personal liability.

**plain meaning rule** The rule under which a court applies a particular statute literally, where it feels the wording of the statute is so clear as to require no interpretation (that is, no resort to outside factors).

**plaintiff** The party who initiates a civil lawsuit.

**plat** A map showing how pieces of real property are subdivided.

**pledge** In secured transactions law, a transfer of personal property from the debtor to the creditor, as security for a debt owed.

**pledgee** A person to whom personal property is pledged by a pledgor.

**pledgor** A person who makes a pledge of personal property to a pledgee.

**police power** The inherent power of a government to regulate matters affecting the health, safety, morals, and general welfare of its citizens; usually used to refer to such power possessed by the state governments, as distinguished from the federal police power.

**possibility of reverter** A future interest retained by the grantor when he or she conveys real property subject to a condition that upon the occurrence of a designated event the title will automatically be returned to the grantor or his or her heirs.

**power of attorney** An instrument or document authorizing one person to act as an agent for another (the principal), who is issuing the instrument or document. The agent does not have to be an attorney-at-law.

**precatory** Expressive of a wish or desire, as in a devise by a testator of real estate expressing the "hope" that the devisee will pass it on to another named party. Such language may not be legally binding.

**precedent** A rule of a previously decided case that serves as authority for a decision in a current controversy—the basis of the principle of *stare decisis*.

**predatory pricing** Below-cost pricing by a dominant firm for the purpose of suppressing competition.

**preemption** The federal regulation of an area of law which is so complete that any state statutes or other regulations affecting that area are, as to such area, completely void.

**preemptive right** The right of a shareholder to purchase shares of new stock issues of a corporation equal in number to enable the shareholder to maintain his or her proportionate interest in the corporation.

**preexisting obligation** A legal duty for performance previously contracted or imposed by statute. A later promise to perform an existing contractual obligation or a promise to perform a duty imposed by law is a promise without consideration and therefore unenforceable.

**preference** The transfer of property or payment of money by a debtor to one or more creditors in a manner that results in favoring those creditors over others. This is an act of bankruptcy, and the trustee can set aside the transfer if the creditors knew or had reason to know that the debtor was insolvent and if the transfer took place within four months of filing the petition in bankruptcy.

**preferred stock** A class of stock that has a priority or right over common stock as to payment of dividends and/or distribution of corporate assets upon dissolution.

**preliminary negotiations** In contract law, usually an invitation to a party to make an offer—not the offer itself but only an inquiry.

**preponderance of the evidence** The greater weight and degree of the credible evidence; this is the burden of proof in most civil lawsuits.

**prescriptive easement** An easement acquired without consent of the owner by continuous and open use for a prescribed statutory period.

**presentment** In commercial paper, the demand by a holder for payment or acceptance of an instrument.

**presumption** Upon introduction of certain proof, a fact that is assumed even though direct proof is lacking. Presumptions of fact usually are rebuttable while presumptions of law usually are not.

**price discrimination** Under the Robinson-Patman Act, the practice of charging different prices to different buyers for goods of like grade and quality.

**price fixing** Any action or agreement which tampers with the free market pricing mechanism of a product or service.

*prima facie* At first sight (Latin); on the face of it; a fact that will be considered as true unless disproved.

*prima facie* **case** In employment discrimination law, the situation that exists when the plaintiff has proved facts which make it logical to infer that intentional discrimination probably has occurred.

**primary party** The maker of a note or the acceptor of a draft or check.

**principal** One who agrees with another (called an *agent*) that that person will act on his or her behalf.

**prior restraint** Government action which prevents a rally, assembly, or expressive activity from taking place because of the probability of violence or other unlawful conduct. A prior restraint usually is unconstitutional.

**private corporation** A corporation formed by individuals, as compared to one formed by the government.

**private law** Rules of laws that determine rights and duties between private parties, that is, between individuals, associations, and corporations.

**privilege** An advantage or right granted by law. Using it as a defense, a person is permitted to perform an act that is not ordinarily permitted to others without liability. In some cases the defense of privilege is absolute, resulting in complete immunity from liability, while in other cases it is qualified, resulting in immunity only if certain factors are proven.

**privileges and immunities clause** A provision in the U.S. Constitution which usually prohibits a state from discriminating against the citizens of another state because of their out-of-state residency.

**privity of contract** Relationship of contract; a relationship that exists between two parties by virtue of their having entered into a contract.

**probate** The legal procedure by which a deceased person's property is inventoried and appraised, claims against the estate are paid, and remaining property is distributed to the heirs under the will or according to state law if there is no will.

**procedural due process** The constitutional requirement that government action be preceded by fair procedures, including notice and an opportunity to be heard.

**procedural law** The rules for carrying on a lawsuit (pleading, evidence, jurisdiction), as opposed to substantive law.

**proceeds** The money or property received from a sale.

**professional corporation** Where permitted, the formation of a corporation by persons engaged in a particular profession, such as medicine, law, or architecture.

**profit** Under real property law, a nonpossessory right to go upon the land of another and take something from it—sometimes referred to as "profit à prendre" (French), particularly when the interest involves the right to take growing crops from another's land.

**promise** In commercial paper, an undertaking to pay an instrument. The promise must be more than a mere acknowledgment of an obligation, such as an IOU.

**promisee** The person who has the legal right to demand performance of the promisor's obligation. In a bilateral contract both the offeror and the offeree are promisees. In a unilateral contract only the offeree is the promisee.

**promisor** The person who obligates himself or herself to do something. In a bilateral contract both offeror and offeree are promisors. In a unilateral contract only the offeror is the promisor.

**promissory estoppel** A doctrine whereby a promise made by a promisor will be enforced, although not supported by consideration, if such promise would reasonably induce the promisee to rely on that promise and thereby so change his or her position that injustice can be avoided only by enforcement of the promise.

**promissory note** A note containing the promise of the maker to pay the instrument upon presentment when due.

**promoter** A person who makes necessary arrangements and/or contracts for the formation of a corporation. Promoters are the planners for the creation of a corporation.

**prospectus** A document provided by a corporation that sets forth the nature and purposes of an issue of stock, bonds, or other securities being offered for sale, usually including additional financial data about the issuing corporation.

**protest** A formal certification of an instrument's notice of dishonor, under the seal of an authorized person or a notary public (required only for notice of dishonor of foreign drafts).

**proximate cause** The foreseeable or direct connection between the breach of duty and an injury resulting from that breach.

**proxy** An authorization by one person to act for another; usually refers to the exercise of a shareholder's voting rights by another person or group.

**public corporation** A corporation formed by the government, as distinguished from one formed by private parties.

**public law** Rules that deal with either the opinion of government or the relationship between a government and its people.

**public policy** Any conduct, act, or objective that the law recognizes as being in the best interest of society at a given time. Any act or conduct contrary to the recognized standard is illegal, even if there is no statute expressly governing such act or conduct.

**punitive damages** A monetary sum awarded as a punishment for certain wrongs committed by one person against another. The plaintiff must prove his or her actual out-of-pocket losses directly flowing from the wrong before punitive damages will be awarded.

**purchase money security interest** A security interest taken or retained by a seller to secure all or part of the price of the collateral; also a security interest taken by a secured party who lends money specifically to allow the debtor to acquire the collateral (where the acquisition does subsequently take place).

**qualified indorsement** An indorsement whereby the indorser does not guarantee payment but does extend warranties to subsequent holders; usually a blank or special indorsement accompanied by the words *without recourse*.

**qualified indorser** An indorser who only guarantees that he or she has no knowledge of any defense against him or her.

**quasi-contract** A contract imposed upon the parties by law to prevent unjust enrichment, even though the parties did not intend to enter into a contract (sometimes referred to as an *implied-in-law contract*).

**quasi-judicial** The case-hearing function of an administrative agency.

**quasi-legislative** The rule-making power of an administrative agency.

*quid pro quo* Something given or received for something else.

*quid pro quo* **harassment** In employment discrimination law, unwelcome requests for sexual favors made to an employee by the employer or by someone for whose actions the employer is responsible, under circumstances indicating that the request is tied to tangible job benefits.

**quitclaim deed** A deed by a grantor that passes to the grantee only those rights and interests (if any) the grantor has in the real property. This deed does not purport to convey any particular interest.

**quorum** The number of qualified persons whose presence is required at a meeting for any action taken at the meeting to be valid. Unless otherwise specified, a majority.

**ratification** The affirmance of a previous act.

**rational basis test** The usual test applied by the courts in determining the constitutionality of a statute that is challenged on the ground that it violates the equal protection clause; under this test, if the classification of subject-matter in the statute is found to be reasonably related to the purposes of the statute, the statute is not a violation of the equal protection clause.

**real defenses** In commercial paper, certain defenses listed in the UCC that can be asserted against any holder, including a holder in due course (sometimes referred to as universal defenses).

**real estate mortgage note** A note secured by a parcel or parcels of the maker's real property.

**real property** Land and most things attached to the land, such as buildings and vegetation.

**reasonable definiteness** In contract law, the requirement that a contract possess sufficient certainty to enable a court to determine the rights and obligations of the parties (especially to determine whether a breach has occurred).

**receiver** A person appointed and supervised by the court to temporarily manage a business or other assets for the benefit of creditors or others who ultimately may be entitled to the assets. The business or other property is said to be placed in *receivership*.

**recording** The filing of a document with a proper public official, which serves as notice to the public of a person's interest.

**redemption** The exercise of the right to buy back or reclaim property upon the performance of a specified act.

**reformation (of contract)** An equitable remedy that modifies the actual words of the existing contract to reflect the true intentions or agreement of the contracting parties at the time of the making of the contract.

**registration statement** A document setting forth certain corporate financial and ownership data, including a prospectus, that is generally required by the SEC to be filed with it before the corporation can offer its securities for sale.

**rejection** In contract law, a refusal by the offeree of proposal or offer of the offeror, such refusal being known to the offeror.

**release** The voluntary relinquishing of a right, lien, interest, or any other obligation.

**relevant market** In antitrust law, the geographic area and/or product or products determined by a court or government agency to measure whether an antitrust violation has taken place.

**remand** To send back a case from an appellate court to the lower court with instructions (usually to hold a new trial).

**remedy** Generally, the means by which a right is enforced or a wrong is prevented; in a narrower sense, a court order addressed to the defendant, in proper circumstances, requiring the defendant to do a particular act requested by plaintiff (e.g., payment of damages) or to refrain from a particular act (e.g., prohibition of specified conduct on the part of defendant by the issuance of an injunction).

**renunciation** In commercial paper, the action of a holder who gives up his or her rights against a party to an instrument either by giving a signed writing or by surrendering the instrument to that party.

**reorganization case** A procedure under Chapter 11 of the Bankruptcy Act which reorganizes a company and restructures its debt in order to allow for the continuance of a business.

**replevin** A legal remedy that permits recovery of possession of personal property.

**repossession** The taking back or regaining of possession of property, usually on the default of a debtor. Repossession can take place peaceably (without breach of the peace) or by judicial process.

**requirements contract** An enforceable agreement for a supply of goods, the exact amount of which is not set or known at the time of the agreement but which is intended to satisfy the needs of a buyer during the term of the contract; a contract in which the seller agrees to sell and the buyer agrees to buy all (or up to a stated amount) of the goods that the buyer needs.

**res** In law a thing or things; property (corpus) made subject to a trust.

**resale price maintenance** An agreement by which a seller and buyer agree on the price at which the buyer will resell to others. The agreement may be explicit or implicit and may be completely voluntary or forced upon one party by the other. Also called vertical price fixing.

**rescission** In contract law, the cancellation of a contract by a court, the effect being as if the contract had never been made.

**reserved powers** The constitutional rights of states to pass laws under powers that are not specifically delegated to the federal government.

**respondeat superior** The doctrine under which a master or employer can be held liable for the actions of his or her subordinate.

**restitution** An equitable remedy that places the nonbreach or injured party in his pre-contracting position or returns him or her to the status quo.

**restraint of trade** Any contract, agreement, or combination which eliminates or restricts competition (usually held to be against public policy and therefore illegal).

**restrictive indorsement** An indorsement that either is conditional or purports to prohibit the further transfer of an instrument, or an indorsement that states a particular purpose to be fulfilled before the restrictive indorser can be held liable on the instrument.

**resulting trust** A trust created by law, when none was intended, to carry out the intentions of the parties to a transaction where one of the parties is guilty of wrongdoing.

**reversion** A future right to possession kept by a person who has transferred land; an example is the landlord's right to possession after termination of a lease.

**revocation** In contract law, the withdrawing of an offer by the offeror.

**risk of loss** The financial burden for damage or destruction of property.

**robbery** The felonious taking of things of value from the person of another or in his or her presence, by force or intimidation.

**Robinson-Patman Act** A 1936 congressional enactment that substantially amended Section 2 of the Clayton Act, basically making it illegal for a seller in interstate commerce to so discriminate in price that the likely result would be competitive injury.

**rule-making power** The statutory right of an administrative agency to issue rules and regulations governing both the conduct and the activities of those within the agency's jurisdiction (referred to as an agency's *quasi-legislative function*).

**sale** Passage of a title from a seller to a buyer for a price.

**sale of control** A transfer by sale of a sufficient number of a corporation's shares of stock to allow the purchaser to control the corporation.

**sale on approval** A bailment of goods coupled with an offer to sell the goods to the bailee.

**sale or return** A sale of goods with possession and title passing to the buyer but with the buyer given the right, by agreement, to retransfer both possession and title to the seller without liability for doing so.

**sanction** A penalty used as a means of coercing obedience with the law or with rules and regulations.

**scienter** The intent to deceive, manipulate, or defraud.

**scope of employment** The range of activities of a servant for which the master is liable to third persons. These actions may be expressly directed by the master or incidental to or foreseeable in the performance of employment duties.

**secondary party** The drawer or indorser of an instrument.

**secured party** The lender, seller, or other person in whose favor there is a security interest.

**securities** In securities regulation law, primarily stocks and bonds; also includes such items as debentures, investment contracts, and certificates of interest or participation in profit-sharing agreements.

**Securities Act of 1933** A federal statute establishing requirements for the registration of securities sold in interstate commerce or through the mails (prior to sale). The statute basically requires that pertinent financial information be disclosed to both the Securities and Exchange Commission and to the prospective purchaser. A misleading failure to make such disclosure renders directors, officers, accountants, and underwriters severally and jointly liable.

**Securities and Exchange Commission** A federal agency given the responsibility to administer and enforce federal securities laws.

**Securities Exchange Act of 1934** A federal statute designed to strengthen the Securities Act of 1933 and expand regulation in the securities business. This Act deals with regulation of national stock exchanges and over-the-counter markets. Numerous provisions were enacted to prevent unfair practices in trading of stock, to control bank credit used for speculation, to compel publicity as to the affairs of corporations listed on these exchanges, and to prohibit the use of inside information. This Act created the Securities and Exchange Commission (SEC).

**security agreement** The contractual arrangement made between a debtor and a secured party.

**security interest** The right or interest in property held by a secured party to guarantee the payment or performance of an obligation.

**separation of powers** The result of the U.S. Constitution, which created and balanced the powers of three branches of government (executive, legislative, and judicial) by giving each separate duties and jurisdictions.

**servient estate** The land that gives up or is subject to an easement.

**settlor** The party who establishes a trust by transferring property to a trustee to be managed for the benefit of another.

**severable** In contract law, the portion of a contract that, in the eyes of the law, is capable of possessing an independent legal existence separate from other parts of the same contract. Thus certain obligations of a severable contract may be construed as legally valid even though a clause or part of the contract purporting to create other obligations is declared illegal.

**sexual harassment** Harassment or intimidation of an employee based on the employee's sex.

**shareholder** The owner of one or more shares of capital stock in a corporation.

**shareholder agreement** A binding agreement made prior to a meeting by a group of shareholders as to the manner in which they will cast their votes on certain issues.

**shares of capital stock** Instruments in the form of equity securities representing an ownership interest in a corporation.

**shelf registration** A SEC rule which allows a company to file one registration statement for the future sale of securities and, thus, enables the company to react quickly to favorable market conditions and raise capital on short notice.

**Sherman Antitrust Act** An 1890 congressional enactment that (1) made illegal every contract, combination in the form of trust or otherwise, or conspiracy in restraint of trade or commerce among the several states, and (2) made it illegal for any person to monopolize, or attempt to monopolize, or combine or conspire with any other person or persons to monopolize any part of the trade or commerce among the several states.

**shipment contract** In sales law, a contract whereby the seller is authorized or required to ship goods to the buyer by delivery to a carrier.

**short-swing profits** In securities law, any profits made on a sale and purchase or purchase and sale of securities where both took place within a six-month period.

**sight draft** A draft payable on demand; that is, upon presentment to the drawee.

**slander** Oral defamation of one's character or reputation.

**sole proprietorship** A person engaged in business for himself or herself without creating any form of business organization.

**sovereign compulsion** The doctrine under which a domestic court will refuse to hold a defendant liable for actions that it was required to take by the law of a recognized foreign sovereign.

**sovereign immunity** The doctrine that bars a person from suing a government body without its consent.

**special indorsement** An indorsement that specifies the person to whom or to whose order the instrument is payable and that requires a proper indorsement of the indorsee for further negotiation.

**special warranty deed** A deed containing a warranty by the grantor that the title being conveyed has not been impaired by the grantor's own act; in other words, the grantor's liability is limited to his or her own actions.

**specific performance** A decree issued by a court of equity that compels a person to perform his or her part of the contract where damages are inadequate as a remedy and the subject matter of the contract is unique.

**spendthrift trust** A provision in a private, express trust to prevent the beneficiary from squandering the principal or income of the trust.

**stale check** Any noncertified check that is over six months old.

**standing** The right to sue.

*stare decisis* Literally "stand by the decision"—a principle by which once a decision has been made by a court, it serves as a precedent or a basis for future decisions of similar cases.

**statute of frauds** The requirement that certain types of contracts be in writing (or that there be written evidence of the existence of the oral contract) in order for the contract to be enforceable in a lawsuit.

**statute of limitations** A law that sets forth a maximum time period, from the happening of an event, for a legal action to be properly filed in or taken to court. The statute bars the use of the courts for recovery if such action is not filed during the specified time.

**statutes of descent and distribution** State laws that specify to whom and in what proportions the estate of an intestate decedent will be distributed.

**statutory law** Enforceable rules enacted by a legislative body.

**stock** Equity securities that evidence an ownership interest in a corporation; shares of ownership in a corporation.

**stock certificate** A formal document that provides evidence of the ownership of particular shares of stock.

**stock dividend** A dividend which consists of the issuance of additional shares of the corporation's own stock to be given to the current shareholders.

**stock subscription** An offer by a prospective investor to buy shares in a corporation.

**stop payment order** A bank customer's direction (order) to his or her bank to refuse to honor (pay) a check drawn by him or her upon presentment.

**strict liability** A legal theory under which a person can be held liable for damage or injury even if not at fault or negligent. Basically, any seller of a defective product that is unreasonably dangerous is liable for any damage or injury caused by the product, provided that the seller is a merchant and the product has not been modified or substantially changed since leaving the seller's possession. This rule applies even if there is no sale of the product and even if the seller exercised due care.

**strike** A cessation of work by employees for the purpose of coercing their employer to accede to some demand. A strike is legal only if it consists of a complete work stoppage by a participating majority of employees for a legally recognized labor objective.

**S corporation** A corporation with only one class of stock held by thirty-five or fewer individual stockholders who all agree in writing that the corporation will be taxed in the same manner as a partnership.

**sublease** The transfer by the lessee (tenant) of a portion of the leasehold to a third party, as compared to an assignment of a lease, where the lessee transfers the entire unexpired term of the leasehold to a third party.

**subrogation** The substitution of one person in another's place, allowing the party substituted the same rights and claims as the party being substituted.

**subsidiary corporation** A corporation that is controlled by another corporation (called a *parent corporation*) through the ownership of a controlling amount of voting stock.

**substantial performance** The doctrine that a person who performs his or her contract in all major respects and in good faith, with only slight deviation, has adequately performed the contract and can therefore recover the contract price less any damages resulting from the slight deviation.

**substantive due process** The constitutional requirement that government action must be fair and reasonable in substance.

**substantive law** The basic rights and duties of parties as provided for in any field of law, as opposed to procedural law, under which these rights and duties are determined in a lawsuit.

**subsurface rights** The right of a landowner to use or own minerals, oil, gas, and the like beneath the land's surface.

**summary judgment** A court's judgment for one party in a lawsuit, before trial, on the ground that there are no disputed issues of fact which would necessitate a trial. The court's conclusion is based upon the motion of that party, the pleadings, affidavits, depositions, and other documentary evidence.

**summons** A writ by a court that is served on the defendant, notifying that person of the cause of action claimed by the plaintiff and of the requirement to answer.

**surety** A person or business entity that insures or guarantees the debt of another by becoming legally liable for the debt upon default.

**symbolic delivery** The delivery of something that represents ownership of or control over an item of property in a case where actual physical delivery of the property itself is not feasible because of its bulk or because it is intangible (often referred to as constructive delivery).

**Taft-Hartley Act** A 1947 congressional amendment of the 1935 NLRA which (1) prohibited certain "unfair labor practices" by unions, (2) outlawed closed shop agreements, (3) established the Federal Mediation and Conciliation Service for the purpose of assisting employers and unions in reaching compromises, (4) granted employers and unions the power to file lawsuits to enforce collective bargaining agreements, and (5) gave the president authority to intervene in industry-wide disputes when, in the president's opinion, the occurrence or continuance of the dispute would "imperil the national health or safety." This Act is also known as the Labor-Management Relations Act.

**tellers** Impartial individuals used to supervise an election (sometimes referred to as judges or inspectors).

**tenancy at sufferance** The interest held by a tenant who remains on the land beyond the period of his or her rightful tenancy and without permission of the landlord.

**tenancy at will** The interest created by a lease for an indefinite duration that either party can terminate at any time.

**tenancy by the entirety** A joint tenancy between husband and wife. In some states neither of the spouses can convey their interest without the consent of the other.

**tenancy for years** The interest created by a lease for a specific period of time.

**tenancy in common** A co-ownership of property by two or more parties in which each owns an undivided interest that passes to his or her heirs at death.

**tenants in partnership** The legal interest of partners in partnership property.

**tender** An offer by a contracting party to pay money, or deliver goods, or perform any other act required of him or her under the contract.

**tender of delivery** In sales law, where the seller places or holds conforming goods at the buyer's disposition and gives the buyer notification sufficient to enable that person to take possession of the goods.

**tender offer** In securities regulation law, an offer to buy a certain amount of a corporation's stock at a specified price per share; usually made with the intention of obtaining the controlling interest in the corporation.

**tenor** In commercial paper, the exact copy of an instrument. If the amount of an instrument has been altered, the holder in due course can recover only the original amount on the instrument, called the original tenor.

**termination** The ending of an offer, contract, or legal relationship (usually an ending without liability).

**term insurance** Life insurance which is effective only for a specified period of time, and which does not build up a cash surrender value or include a borrowing privilege.

**testamentary capacity** The state of mind of a testator in knowing what property is owned and how he or she wants to dispose of it.

**testamentary trust** A trust created by the settlor's will, to be effective on his or her death.

**testate** The situation in which a person dies leaving a valid will.

**testator (female, testatrix)** A person who makes a will.

**textual context** The court's reading of a statute in its entirety rather than a single section or part; a principle of statutory interpretation.

**time instrument** An instrument which is payable at a specific future date.

**time is of the essence** In contract law, a phrase in a contract that requires performance within a specified time as a condition precedent to liability.

**title** A person's right of ownership in property. The extent of this right is dependent on the type of title held.

**title examination** The buyer's investigation of a seller's title to real property.

**title insurance** A policy issued by an insurance company to compensate a buyer of real property for any loss he or she will suffer if the title proves to be defective.

**Title VII** That portion of the Civil Rights Act of 1964 that prohibits discrimination in employment on the basis of race, color, religion, sex, or national origin.

**title warranty** In sales law, an assurance or guarantee given by the seller, expressly or impliedly, to the buyer that he or she has good title and the right to transfer that title, and that the goods are free from undisclosed security interests.

**tort** A noncontractual wrong committed by one against another. To be considered a tort, the wrong must be a breach of a legal duty directly resulting in harm.

**tortfeasor** A person who commits a noncontractual wrong (sometimes referred to as a *wrongdoer*).

**tort of conversion** One's unlawful interference with the right of another to possess or use his or her personal property.

**trade acceptance** A draft or bill of exchange drawn by a seller of goods on the purchaser and obligating the purchaser to pay the instrument upon acceptance.

**trade fixture** A piece of personal property affixed by a tenant to the real property that is necessary for carrying on the tenant's business.

**trademark** A distinctive mark, sign, or motto that a business can reserve by law for its exclusive use in identifying itself or its product.

**trade secret** Valuable, confidential data or know-how developed and possessed by a business firm; can be legally protected.

**trading partnership** A partnership formed primarily for the purpose of buying and selling commodities.

**transferee** A person to whom a transfer is made.

**transferor** A person who makes a transfer.

**treasury stock** Shares of stock that were originally issued by a corporation and that subsequently were reacquired by it.

**trespass** In realty and personalty, the wrongful invasion of the property rights of another.

**trust** Two or more companies that have a monopoly. In the law of property, a relationship whereby a settlor transfers legal ownership of property to a trustee to be held and managed for a beneficiary who has equitable title to the property.

**trustee** One who administers a trust.

**trustee in bankruptcy** A person elected or appointed to administer the estate of the bankrupt person.

**trust indorsement** A restrictive indorsement that by its terms shows an intent to benefit the indorser or some third party.

**tying agreement** Any arrangement in which one party agrees to supply a product or service only on the condition that the customer also take another product or service.

***ultra vires*** Any acts or actions of a corporation that are held to be unauthorized and beyond the scope of the corporate business as determined by law or by the articles of incorporation.

**unconscionable contract** A contract or a clause within a contract which is so grossly unfair that a court will refuse to enforce it.

**underwriter** The person or entity who markets a security offering from the issuer to dealers; analogous to a wholesaler.

**undisclosed principal** In agency law, a principal whose identity and existence are unknown by third parties, leading them to believe that the agent is acting solely for himself or herself.

**undue influence** The overcoming of a person's free will by misusing a position of confidence or relationship, thereby taking advantage of that person to affect his or her decisions or actions.

**unenforceable contract** Generally a valid contract that cannot be enforced in a court of law because of a special rule of law or a failure to meet an additional legal requirement (such as a writing).

**unfair labor practices** Certain practices, including employer domination of unions, interference with employee organizing, discrimination against union members, and refusal to bargain collectively, which were prohibited by the National Labor Relations Act (NLRA).

**Uniform Commercial Code (UCC)** Uniform rules dealing with the sale of goods, commercial paper, secured transactions in personal property, and certain aspects of banking, documents of title, and investment securities. Recommended by the National Conference of Commissioners on Uniform State Laws for enactment by the various states, it has been adopted by forty-nine states (and Louisiana has adopted parts of it).

**Uniform Limited Partnership Act (ULPA)** Uniform rules governing the organization and operation of limited partnerships recommended by the National Conference of Commissioners on Uniform State Laws for enactment by the various states. The ULPA was substantially modified in 1976 by the Revised Uniform Limited Partnership Act (RULPA).

**Uniform Partnership Act (UPA)** Uniform rules governing the partnership operation, particularly in the absence of an agreement, recommended by the National Conference of Commissioners on Uniform State Laws for enactment by the various states.

**unilateral contract** An offer or promise of the offeror which can become binding only by the completed performance of the offeree; an act for a promise, whereby the offeree's act is not only his or her acceptance but also the completed performance under the contract.

**unilateral mistake** A mistake in which only one party to a contract is in error as to the terms or performance expected under the contract.

**universal defenses** See *real defenses*.

**unliquidated debt** A disputed debt; a debt about which there is a reasonable basis for dispute as to its existence or amount.

**unqualified indorsement** A special or blank indorsement that guarantees payment upon proper presentment, dishonor, and notice of dishonor.

**unqualified indorser** An indorser who guarantees that no defense of any party is good against him or her.

**usage of trade** Any practice or method repeated with such regularity in a vocation or business that it becomes the legal basis for expected performance in future events within that vocation or business.

**usury** An interest charge exceeding the maximum amount permitted by statute.

**U.S. Code** The full and complete compilation of all federal statutes.

**Utilitarianism** An ethical theory that is committed solely to the purpose of promoting "the greatest good for the greatest number."

**valid contract** A contract that meets the four basic requirements for enforceability by the parties to it.

**venue** A designation of the right of the defendant to be tried in a proper court within a specific geographic area.

**vertical integration** A condition that exists when one firm operates at more than one level of the distribution chain for a product.

**vertical merger** A merger of two firms, one of which is a supplier or customer of the other.

**vertical nonprice restriction** An arrangement between a seller and buyer that places limitations on the area within which, location from which, or customers to whom the buyer can resell.

**vertical price fixing** See *resale price maintenance*.

**vertical restraint of trade** An arrangement among firms at different levels of the distribution chain that suppresses or limits intrabrand competition.

**vicarious liability** The liability of a person, not himself or herself at fault, for the actions of others.

**voidable contract** A contract from which one or both parties can, if they choose, legally withdraw without liability.

**voidable transfer** In bankruptcy law, a transfer by a bankrupt debtor that can be set aside by a trustee in bankruptcy.

**void contract** A contract without legal effect.

*voir dire* The examination of prospective jurors by lawyers in a particular case to determine their fitness (i.e., to discover whether they have an interest in the outcome of the suit, a bias or prejudice against a party, or are otherwise unlikely to exercise the objectivity necessary in jury deliberations).

**voluntary case** Under the Bankruptcy Act, a proceeding that is instituted by the debtor, not the creditors.

**voting trust** A trust whereby shareholders transfer their shares of stock to a trustee for the sole purpose of voting those shares. The shareholders, through trust certificates, retain all other rights as they pertain to the transferred shares.

**wagering agreement** Any agreement, bet, or lottery arrangement the performance of which is dependent primarily upon chance, such agreement usually being prohibited by statute. These agreements are in contrast to risk-shifting (insurance) contracts and speculative bargaining (commodity market) transactions, which are usually legal by statute.

**waiver** The voluntary giving up of a legal right.

**warehouseman** A person engaged in the business of storing the property of others for compensation.

**warehouse receipt** A document of title issued by a person engaged in the business of storing goods for hire and containing the terms of the storage agreement. A negotiable warehouse receipt acts as both receipt and evidence of title to the goods stored.

**warranty** An assurance or guaranty, expressly or impliedly made, that certain actions or rights can take place, that information given is correct, or that performance will conform to certain standards.

**warranty deed** A deed with covenants, express or implied, that the title to real property is good and complete.

**warranty of fitness for a particular purpose** In sales law, an implied warranty imposed by law on a seller, who has reason to know of the buyer's intended use of the goods (where the buyer relies on the seller's skill and judgment), that the goods are suitable for the buyer's intended use.

**warranty of merchantability** In sales law, an implied warranty imposed by law upon a merchant seller of goods that the goods are fit for the ordinary purposes for which goods of that kind are used.

**waste** A term used to describe a tenant's duty not to damage a landlord's reversionary interest.

**watered stock** Shares of stock issued by a corporation for a consideration less than the par value or stated value of the stock.

**whole life insurance** Life insurance which continues in effect during the entire life of the insured; this type of life insurance also builds up a cash surrender value over time, and often includes the privilege of borrowing money from the insurance company.

**will** A document by which a person directs the disposition of his or her property (estate) upon his or her death.

**winding up** The actual process of settling the affairs of a partnership or corporation after dissolution.

**wire fraud** Fraud committed by use of telephone or telegraph or other such electronic means.

**workers' compensation laws** State statutory provisions calling for payments to employees for accidental injuries or diseases arising out of and in the course of employment. These payments, for medical expenses and lost income, are made regardless of whether anyone is at fault.

**writ of certiorari** An order issued by an appellate court directing a lower court to remit to it the record and proceedings of a particular case so that the actions of the lower court may be reviewed.

**writ of execution** In a civil lawsuit in which the plaintiff has won, a court order directing an enforcement agent to sell the defendant's nonexempt property in order to pay the judgment against him or her.

# Case Index*

Aaron v. SEC, 646
Abramov v. Royal Dallas, Inc., 270
**Acquisto v. Joe R. Hahn Enterprises, Inc., 688–689**
Action Repair, Inc. v. American Broadcasting Co., 39
Adams v. Standard Knitting Mills, Inc., 656
Admiralty Fund v. Hugh Johnson & Co., 661
Affiliated Ute Citizens v. United States, 638
Agricultural Insurance Co. v. Constantine, 226
Air Crash Disaster at Gander New Foundland, in re, 26
Alabama Football, Inc. v. Wright, 285
Albert M. Greenfield & Co. v. Kolea, 699
**Alpert v. Thomas, 364**
American Bridge Co. v. Boston, 270
American Federation of State, County, and Municipal Employees v. State of Washington, 788
American Textile Manufacturers Inst. v. Donovan, 790
Anderson v. Tri-State Home Improvement Co., 262
Applegate v. Inland Real Estate Corporation, 699
**Arcanum National Bank v. Hessler, 399–400**
**Argentine Republic v. Amerada Hess Shipping Corporation, 819**
Arizona v. Norris, 69
**Arizona v. Youngblood, 93**
Ashley Square, Inc. v. Contractors Supply of Orlando, 315
**Aspen Skiing Co. v. Aspen Highlands Skiing Corp., 758**
Associated Investment Co. v. Caylas, 285
Atari, Inc. v. Harris Trust and Savings Bank, 832
**Atchison, in re, 471–472**
**Attorney General of New York v. Soto-Lopez, 68**
Aubrey's R. V. Center v. Tandy Corporation, 368

Badhwar v. Colorado Fuel & Iron Corp., 833
Bagby Land & Cattle Co. v. California Livestock Comm'n Co., 262
**Baker v. Zingelman, 677–678**
Baker Boyer National Bank v. Garver, 734
Baldwin v. Fish and Game Commission of Montana, 72
**Balkus, Matter of Estate of, 405**
Ballinger v. Craig, 248
Banco Nacional de Cuba v. Sabbatino, 820
Banjavich v. Louisiana Licensing Board of Marine Divers, 86
Barber & Ross Co. v. Lifetime Doors, Inc., 262
Barnett Bank of Clearwater N.A. v. Rompon, 464
Barsan v. Pioneer Savings & Loan Co., 608
**Basic, Inc. v. Levinson, 639**
Basque French Bakery v. Toscana Baking Co., 142
**Batchoff v. Craney, 34–35**

Bateman Eichler, Hill Richards, Inc. v. Berner, 227
Bates v. Arizona State Bar, 65
Baum v. Baum Holding Co., 577
**Beachcomber Coins, Inc. v. Boskett, 243–244**
Bigelow v. Johnson, 53
Blakeslee v. Nelson, 197
Blanco v. State, 72
**Board of Trade of San Francisco v. Swiss Credit Bank, 815, 832**
**Board of Trustees of the State University of New York v. Fox, 66**
Bonasera v. Roffe, 226
**Bonito Boats, Inc. v. Thunder Craft Boats, Inc., 136**
Boulevard National Bank of Miami v. Air Metals Industries, Inc., 270
Bowman v. American Home Assurance Co., 327
Bowsher v. Synar, 59
Boyd v. Madison County Mutual Insurance Co., 782
Bradley v. American Smelting and Refining Company, 139
**Branco Wood Products, Inc. v. C.C. Huxford Trust, 507**
Brandenburg v. Ohio, 65
Brazil v. Silva, 734
**Bremmeyer v. Peter Klewlt Sons Company, 217**
Brian Construction & Development Co. v. Brighenti, 213
Bright Tunes Music Corp. v. Harrisongs Music, Ltd., 137
Brockton Sav. Bank v. Peat, Marwick & Mitchell, 39
Brown v. Burlington Industries, Inc., 512
Brown v. United States, 96
Browning v. Johnson, 213
Brown Shoe Co. v. United States, 760
Brune v. Brown Forman Corp., 352
Bruton v. Automatic Welding & Supply, 512
Bryant v. Lord, 204
**Bryceland v. Northey, 219–220**
Bunge Corp. v. Eide, 661
Burke v. Pan American World Airways, Inc., 108–109
Burke and Thomas v. International Organization of Masters, 269
Burton v. Wilmington Parking Authority, 62
Burton Enterprises v. Wheeler, 496

Cahill v. Readon, 53, 249
**Calfo v. D.C. Stewart Co., 379–380**
Campbell v. Loew's, Inc., 599
**Canterra Petroleum, Inc. v. Western Drilling & Mining Supply, 320**
Capital Dredge & Dock Corp. v. City of Detroit, 511
**Carador v. Sana Travel Service, Ltd., 380**
Carella v. California, 103
Carpenter v. United States, 99, 637
**Carroll v. Lee, 168–169**
**Casper v. McDowell, 246, 722–723**
**Caudle v. Betts, 114, 115–116**

Celotex Corp. v. Catrett, 29
Cencula v. Keller, 302
**Centerre Bank of Branson v. Campbell, 381–382**
Charlestown Boot and Shoe Co. v. Dunsmore, 591
Chase v. Consolidated Foods Corp., 511
**Chicago Board of Trade v. United States, 765**
Chicago, M., St.P. & P.R. Co. v. Chicago & N.W., 286
Chisolm v. Cleveland, 310
**Citibank, N.A. v. Data Lease Financial Corp., 459–460**
Citizens State Bank v. Timm, Schmidt & Co., 660
**City Electric v. Dean Evans Chrysler-Plymouth, 502**
City of Burbank v. Lockheed Air Terminal, Inc., 57
City of Cleburne v. Cleburne Living Center, 67
City of Columbus v. Thompson, 70
City of Dallas v. Stanglin, 73
City of Mesquite v. Aladdin's Castle, Inc., 53
Cleary v. American Airlines, Inc., 796
**Cleveland Board of Education v. Loudermill, 70–71, 82**
**Cliffs Notes, Inc. v. Bantam Doubleday Dell Publishing Group, 131–132**
Coates v. Cincinnati, 53
Coca-Cola Bottling Co. v. Coca-Cola Co., 133
**Cole v. First National Bank of Gillette, 391–392**
**Cole v. Lovett, 808–809**
Collins v. Gwinnett Bank & Trust Co., 213
Collins v. Williamson Printing Corporation, 262
**Commercial Bank & Trust Co. v. Middle Georgia Livestock Sales, 407**
Commonwealth Capital Corp. v. Enterprise Federal Savings & Loan Association, 496
**Community Television Services, Inc. v. Dresser Industries, Inc., 335**
Compagnie Europeenne Des Petroles v. Sensor Nederland, 833
Comprehensive Health Ins. Ass'n v. Dye, 290
Condovest Corp. v. John Street Builders, 197
Conoco, Inc. v. Norwest Bank Mason City, 833
**Continental T.V., Inc. v. G.T.E. Sylvania, Inc., 770–771**
Cook v. Cook, 169
Corley v. Jackson Police Dept., 782
**Couri v. Couri, 529–530**
Cox v. Louisiana, 65
**Cricket Alley Corporation v. Data Terminal Systems, Inc., 365**
**Crocker National Bank v. Ideco Division of Dresser Industries, 448**
Crowell v. Housing Authority of the City of Dallas, 700
Croy v. Campbell, 646
**Cruz v. Drezek, 693–694**

1027

*Cases appearing in bold face are excerpted in the text.

**1028    CASE INDEX**

CSXT, Inc. v. Pitz, 25
**Curtin v. Glazier, 547–548**
Cushing v. Thomson, **194**

D'Andrea v. Feinberg, 394
Daniell v. Ford Motor Corp., 352
Darrin v. Gould, 13
Dartmouth College case, 156
Dartmouth Motor Sales, Inc. v. Wilcox, 330
David Crystal, Inc. v. Ehrlich-Newmark Truck Co., 718
**Dayan v. McDonald's Corporation, 829–830**
De Filippo v. Ford Motor Co., 308
**Dempsey v. Rosenthal, 337–338,** 340
Denault v. Holloway Builders, Inc., 39
**Deskovick et al. v. Porzio, 169–170**
Detroit Lions and Sims v. Argovitz, 496
**Devito v. N.Y.U. College of Dentistry, 221**
Diamond v. Chakrabarty, 134
Dias, *in re,* 484
**Dinkins v. Farley, 509**
Dirks v. SEC, 637
**Dixon, Odom & Company v. Sledge, 548**
Doman Helicopters, Inc., *in re,* **632,** 634
**Donnelly v. Guion, 29–30**
**Doughty v. Idaho Frozen Foods Corp., 223**
Duckworth v. Eagan, 93
Duke Power Co. v. Carolina Environmental Study Group, Inc., 69
Dun & Bradstreet, Inc. v. Greenmoss Builders, 118
Dunnebacke Co. v. Pittman and Gilligan, 173
Durant v. Black River Electric Cooperative, Inc., 26
Duty v. General Finance Co., 805

**Eassa Properties v. Shearson Lehman Brothers, 534–535**
**Eckert v. Eckert, 522**
**Edwards v. Clinton Valley Center, 43**
**EEOC v. Peat, Marwick, Mitchell and Co., 77–78**
Empiregas, Inc. v. Hardy, 248
**Employers Insurance of Wausau v. Chemical Bank, 713**
Engel v. Vitale, 63
**Ericson v. Playgirl, Inc., 293**
**Ernst & Ernst v. Hochfelder,** 638, **655–656**
Erving v. Virginia Squires Basketball Club, 302
Escott v. Barchris Construction Corp., 654
Estate. *See* name of principals involved
Estell v. Barrickman, 512
Exxon Corporation v. Eagerton, 59

**Fair Finance Co. v. Fourco, Inc., 421–422**
Federal Crop Insurance Corp. v. Merrill, 83
Federal Deposit Insurance Corp. v. Barrasso, 495
Federal Trade Commission. *See* FTC cases
**Ferri v. Sylvia,** 383
Fiege v. Boehm, 213
Filley v. Pope, 355
**Firefighters Local Union No. 1784 v. Stotts, 787**
First National Bank of Boston v. Bellotti, 66
First National Bank of Brush v. Bostron, 463
First National Bank of Clarksville v. Moore, 262
**First National Bank of Council Bluffs v. One Craig Place, Ltd., 572**
**First Safety Fund National Bank v. Friel, 414**
Fischer v. Kletz, 661
**Fisher,** *in re,* **473–474**

**Flagiello v. Pennsylvania Hospital, 44**
Folquet v. Woodburn Public Schools, 270
Fontenot v. Upjohn Co., 40
Ford Motor Credit Company v. Frances C. Sheehan, 125, 812
Ford Motor Co. v. United States, 775
Fortune Furniture Co. v. Mid-South Plastic Co., 259
**Francis v. United Jersey Bank, 602**
Frank Arnold Contractors, Inc. v. Vilsmeier Auction Co., 351
Franklin v. Rigg, 560
Freeberg, L.L., Pie Co. v. St. Paul Mut. Ins. Co., 748
Fretz Construction Co. v. Southern National Bank, 214
FTC v. Ruberoid Co., 75

**Gaffin v. Heymann, 419–420**
Gann v. Morris, 219
Garland Co., Inc. v. Roofco Co., 262
**Gelder Medical Group v. Webber, 516,** 539
Gillen v. Diadrill, Inc., 226
**Girard v. Myers,** 492
**Glenn v. Wagner, 569–570**
Glover v. Jewish War Veterans, 197
**Goode v. Ryan,** 590
**Goodman v. Darden, Doman, & Stafford Associates, 571**
**Gordon v. Bialystoker Center & Bikur Cholim, Inc., 703**
Grambo v. Loomis Cycle Sales, Inc., 812
**Granite Equipment Leasing Corp. v. Hempstead Bank,** 429, **432–433**
Graybar Elec. Co. v. Shook, 331
Great Western Sugar Co. v. Pennant Products, Inc., 368
Green v. Missouri Pacific Railroad Co., 796
Green's Executors v. Smith, 182
**Grendell v. Kiehl,** 148
Groening v. Opsata, 238
Grossman v. Aerial Farm Services, Inc., 309
**Gruenberg v. Goldmine Plantation, Inc., 623**
Gulf Chemical & Metallurgical Corp. v. Sylvan Chemical Corp., 367
**Gun South, Inc. v. Brady, 83**

Hadley v. Baxendale, 294, 295, 365
Hahn v. Hank's Ambulance Service, Inc., 811
**Halbman v. Lemke, 231–232**
Hall v. Westmoreland et al., 394
**Hamer v. Sidway, 200**
Hancock Construction Co. v. Kempton & Snedigar Dairy, 262
H&M Driver Leasing v. Champion International Corp., 302
Hanrahan v. Puget Sound Power & Light Co., 608
Hanigan v. Wheeler, 270
Hanks v. NcNeill Coal Corporation, 235–236
**Harmon v. Tanner Motor Tours of Nevada, Ltd., 255**
Harrington v. Taylor, 202
**Hartland Computer Leasing Corp. v. The Insurance Man, Inc., 171**
**Haugk, Estate of,** *in re,* **724**
Hauter v. Zogarts, 352
Heart of Atlanta Motel v. U.S., 72
Heifetz Metal Crafts v. Peter Kiewit Sons Co., 249
**Helicopteros Nacionales de Colombia v. Hall, 21**
Helvey v. Wabash County REMC, 314
Henderson, *in re,* **512**
**Hendley v. Cameron-Brown Co., 802**
Henningsen v. Bloomfield Motors, Inc., 352

Herbert v. Harl, 367
Hessler, Inc. v. Farrell, 592
Hester v. Church's Fried Chicken, 512
**Hicklin v. Orbeck, 63**
Higgins v. Lessig, 177
**Highview Associates v. Koferl, 695–696**
Hillebrant v. Brewer, 718
Hilton v. Guyot, 833
**Hixon v. Credit Alliance Corporation, 451–452**
H.J. Inc. v. Northwestern Bell Telephone Co., 644
Hobbs v. Massasoit Whip Co., 198
**Hoffman v. Red Owl Stores, Inc., 210**
**Holladay v. Holladay, 722**
Holliday v. Gilkeson, 512
Holly Hill Acres, Ltd. v. Charter Bank of Gainesville, 394
Holy Trinity Church v. U.S., 53
Holzman v. de Escamilla, 561
Horn Waterproofing Corp. v. Bushwick Iron and Steel Co., 214
Howell, Estate of, 733
**Hoyem v. Manhattan Beach City School District, 113**
Huebner, Estate of, 734
Hunt v. Washington State Apple Advertising Commission, 58

IBM v. United States, 771–772
Impastato v. De Girolamo, 524
**Industrial Molded Plastic Products, Inc., v. J. Gross & Sons, Inc., 501**
Industrial Union Department v. American Petroleum Institute, 790
**Innes v. Webb, 290**
Int'l Longshoremen's Assn. v. Allied Int'l Inc., 795
**Isbrandtsen v. North Branch Corporation, 288–289**
IUC v. New England Telephone & Telegraph Co., 249

Jacobs and Young, Inc. v. Kent, 285
**Jacques v. Sears, Roebuck & Company, 119–120**
Jewish Center of Sussex County v. Whale, 249
John Deere Leasing v. Blubaugh, 173
**Johns-Manville Corporation,** *in re,* **479–480**
Johnson v. Capital City Ford, 197
**Johnson v. Hicks, 666–667**
Johnson v. Lappo Lumber Co., 352
Johnson Controls v. Phoenix Control Systems, Inc., 142
Johnston v. Barney, 484
**Judd Realty, Inc. v. Tedesco, 166–167**

**Kallgren v. Steele, 241**
**Kane v. Johns-Manville Corp., 480**
Kassab v. Central Soya, 351
Kassell v. Consolidated Freightways Corp., 58
**Kenford Company, Inc. v. County of Erie, 294–295**
Keystone Bituminous Coal Assoc. v. DeBenedictis, 71
Kilbourne v. Forester, 699
**Kimbrell's Furniture Co., Inc. v. Friedman, 458**
Kirby v. Bergfield, 425
**King v. Bankerd, 488–489**
**Kirkpatrick, W.S., & Co. v. Environmental Tectonics Corporation, 820**
**Kline v. Kramer,** 680
**Klinicki v. Lundgren, 603–604**

## CASE INDEX

Kludt v. German Mutual Fire Ins. Co., 748
Knoebel v. Chief Pontiac, Inc., 213
Koenecke F.W., & Sons, Inc., *in re,* 660
Kolender v. Lawson, 46–47, 92
Korematsu v. United States, 68
Kori v. Wilco Marsh Buggies and Draglines, Inc., 142
Kramer v. Johnson, 424
Krazek v. Mountain River Tours, Inc., 226

Laaperi v. Sears, Roebuck & Co., Inc., 352
Laborers Local 859 v. NLRB, 795
**Laclede Gas Company v. Amoco Oil Company, 205–206**
**La Gasse Pool Construction Co. v. City of Fort Lauderdale, 280–281**
Lair Distrib. Co. v. Crump, 330
**Lampley v. Celebrity Homes, Inc., 201**
Landshire Food Service, Inc. v. Coghill, 319
**Lane Wilson Company, Inc. v. Gregory, 275–276**
Laos v. Soble, 226
Lasher v. Kleinberg, 14
**Lazar v. Thermal Equipment Corp., 508**
Lee v. Lee, 702
LeFlore v. Reflections of Tulsa, Inc., 302
Leggett v. Vinson, 213
**Leonard Duckworth, Inc. v. Michael L. Field & Co., 128–129**
Lewis, Matter of Estate of, 173
Lewis v. Roper, 285
Leventhal v. Green, 561
Levy v. Nassau Queens Medical Group, 537
Liebe v. Battman, 718
Lieber v. Mohawk Arms, Inc., 330
**Lincoln Grain, Inc. v. Coopers & Lybrand, 650**
Lindsay, *in re,* 484
Linmark Associates, Inc. v. Township of Willingboro, 65
Litton Industries, Inc. v. FTC, 811
Loeb & Co., Inc. v. Schreiner, 315
Long Island Trust Company v. International Institute for Packaging Education, Ltd., 411
Los Angeles Dept. of Water & Power v. Manhart, 795
Lowrey v. Horvath, 125
**L.U. Cattle Company v. Wilson, 253–254**
**Lucier v. Town of Norfolk, 187–188**
Lucy v. Zehmer, 177–178
Lumber Sales, Inc. v. Brown, 330
**Lupien v. Malsbenden, 518–519**
**Luprofresh, Inc. v. Pabst Brewing Company, 362**
Lykins Oil Co. v. Fekkos, 331

Maddux v. Donaldson, 53
Manchester, Estate of, 733
Maple Farms, Inc. v. City School Dist. of the City of Elmira, 367
Mapp v. Ohio, 92
Marbury v. Madison, 60
Marengo Cave Co. v. Ross, 683
Market v. Bosley, 733
Marshall v. Barlow's, Inc., 78
Marvin v. Marvin, 226
Marvin E. Jewell & Co. v. Thomas, 289
Maschhoff, *in re,* 483
Mashburn v. Collins, 125
Mathews v. Eldridge, 82
Mattis v. Lally, 226
McGurrin, Matter of Estate of, 734
McIntosh v. Milano, 124
McKeever v. New Jersey Bell Telephone Co., 796
McLain v. Real Estate Board of New Orleans, 57

**McNeill v. Maryland Insurance Guaranty Association, 745–746**
Mead Data Central, Inc. v. Toyota Motor Sales, 142
Meteor Industries, Inc. v. Metalloy Industries, Inc., 302
**Micro-Managers, Inc. v. Gregory, 309**
Midwest Supply, Inc. v. Waters, 248
Milkovich v. Loran Journal Co., 118
Miller v. American Express Co., 811
Miller Brewing Company v. G. Heileman Brewing Company, 142
Millstone v. O'Hanlon Reports, Inc., 812
Minneapolis v. Republic Creosoting Co., 286
Miranda v. Arizona, 93
**Mitsubishi Motors Corp. v. Soler Chrysler-Plymouth, Inc., 822**
**Mohasco Industries, Inc. v. Anderson Halverson Corp., 339**
Montesano v. Donrey Media, 125
Moore's Estate, *in re,* 248
**Motorists Mutual Insurance Co. v. Richmond, 738**
**Motor Vehicle Manufacturers Ass'n v. State Farm Mutual Auto. Ins. Co., 81,** 85
**Mount Vernon Savings & Loan v. Partridge Associates, 556**
Muder, Matter of Estate of, 734
**Multiplastics, Inc. v. Arch Industries, Inc., 326–327**

National Bond Co. v. Whithorn, 125
National Society of Professional Engineers v. United States, 763
National Treasury Employees Union v. Von Raab, 794
Nevada State Bank v. Fisher, 425
Newell Co. v. Vermont American Corp., 646
New England Mutual Life Insurance Co. v. Null, 736
**Newman v. Schiff, 183**
**New York v. Burger, 78–79**
**New York Life Insurance Co. v. Baum, 737**
Nicolosi, *in re,* 463
Niedbalski v. Board of Education, 302
NLRB v. Bildisco & Bildisco, 479
**NLRB v. Exchange Parts Co., 708–709**
Nollan v. California Coastal Commission, 71
**Norlin Corp. v. Rooney, Pace Inc., 620**
**Northern Indiana Public Service Co. v. Carbon County Coal Co., 282–283**
Northland Aluminum Products, Inc., *in re,* 142
**Norwest Bank Nebraska, N.A. v. Tveten, 476–477**
Norwood v. Lazarus, 699
Nylen v. Park Doral Apartments, 303

**Obert v. Environmental Research & Development Corp., 558–559**
O'Brien v. O'Brien, 180
Olwell v. Nye & Nissen Co., 173
*Oregon v. Smith,* 64
**Orkin Exterminating Co., Inc. v. FTC, 799–800**
**Osborne v. Workman, 540**
Oswald v. Leckey, 537
**Otis Engineering Corp. v. Clark, 109**
**Ouellette v. Blanchard, 110**
**Owens v. Palos Verdes Monaco, 532–533**

Pacific Gas & Electric Co. v. Public Utilities Commission of California, 65
Palmore v. Sidoti, 68
Palsgraf v. Long Island R.R., 112
Paramount Communications, Inc. v. Time, Inc., 642

Parker v. Twentieth Century Fox Film Corporation, 302
**Park West Management Corp. v. Mitchell, 691–692**
**Patterson v. Rohm Gesellschaft, 346**
Pearson v. Salina Coffee House, Inc., 464
**People v. Avila, 98**
People v. Mulder, 104
**Pepsi-Cola Bottling Co. of Luverne v. Coca-Cola Bottling Co., Andalusia, 216**
Perdue v. Crocker National Bank, 227
Perfect Subscription Co. v. Kavater, 142
Peters v. Jefferson Chemical Co., 782
**Peters v. Trousclair, 743–744**
PG&E v. G.W. Thomas Drayage & Rigging Co., 288
Pharmaceutical Society of New York v. Lefkowitz, 72
Philadelphia Newspapers, Inc. v. Hepps, 117
**Phillips Home Furnishings, Inc. v. Continental Bank, 430**
**Pinto v. Bridgeport Mack Trucks, Inc., 712–713**
Playboy Clubs International, Inc. v. Loomskill, 315
Polaroid Corp. v. Polarad Elec. Corp., 131
Preston Farm & Ranch Supply v. Bio-Zyme Enterprises, 173
Price Waterhouse v. Hopkins, 783
**Printing Center of Texas, Inc. v. Supermind Publishing Co., 356–357**
Professional Rodeo Cowboys Assoc. v. Wilch, Smith & Brock, 660
Progress Tailoring Co. v. FTC, 577
**Putnam v. Shoaf, 526**
**Pyeatte v. Pyeatte, 179–180**

**Quantum Development Corp.; American Fidelity Fire Ins. Co. v. Joy; Lang v. Bank of Nova Scotia,** *in re,* **390–391**
**Quarture v. Allegheny County et al., 202–203**

Reading Trust Co. v. Hutchinson, 411
Red Ball Motor Freight, Inc. v. Employers Mut. Liab. Ins. Co., 749
Redd v. Woodford County Swine Breeders, Inc., 173
Reed, Matter of Estate of, 734
Regents of the University of Michigan v. Ewing, 73
Regina v. Dudley & Stephens, 13–14
Reid v. Silver, 661
Removatron International Corp. v. FTC, 811
Republic Aviation Corp. v. NLRB, 795
Revlon, Inc. v. MacAndrews & Forbes Holdings, Inc., 618, 642
**Richards v. Flowers et al., 177**
**Rincones v. Windberg, 273**
**Riser v. Genuine Parts Co., 597**
Roberson v. McCarthy, 14
Rockwell International Credit Corp. v. Valley Bank, 464
Roe v. Wade, 13, 69
**Rosenblum, H., Inc. v. Adler, 113, 651–652**
**Rowland v. Rowland, 588–589,** 589
Roy v. Allstate Ins. Co., 748
Rudolph v. ABC Pest Control, Inc., 270

**St. Charles Cable TV v. Eagle Comtronics, Inc., 190–191**
Salinger v. Random House, Inc., 138
Sally Beauty Co. v. Nexxus Products Co., Inc., 270
**Salter v. Vanotti, 401–402,** 403
**Sanders v. McMullen, 583**
Sanders, R.L., Roofing Co. v. OSHRC, 796

## CASE INDEX

S & S Chopper Service, Inc. v. Scripter, 26
Scarola v. Insurance Co. of North America, 331
**Schmuck v. United States, 99–100**
**Schock v. Ronderos, 324**
Schooner Exchange, The, v. McFadden, 813
Schoonover v. Carpet World, Inc., 512
**Schreiber v. Burlington Northern, Inc., 643**
**Schroer, Estate of, v. Stamco Supply, Inc., 590**
Schronk v. Gilliam, 125
**Schupach v. McDonald's System, Inc., 266**
Schweiker v. Hansen, 87
SEC v. Jos. Schlitz Brewing Co., 645–646
SEC v. Lund, 646
**SEC v. Materia, 637**
SEC v. McDonald Investment Co., 646
SEC v. Morgan F. Moore, 646
SEC v. Texas Gulf Sulphur, 636
SEC v. W.J. Howey Co., 629
Securities and Exchange Commission. *See* SEC cases
**Sedima v. Imrex Co., Inc., 50–51**, 644
Segni v. Commercial Office of Spain, 833
Semmelroth v. American Airlines, 26
Shapiro v. Glekel, 743, 661
**Shawn v. England, 519–520**
Sheets v. Yamaha, 142
**Shlensky v. Wrigley, 601**
Shores v. Sklar, 646
Silvola v. Rowlett, 560
Sinn v. Burd, 125
Skinner v. Railway Labor Executives Ass'n, 794
Sloan v. Falwell, 197
**Smith v. Goodyear Tire & Rubber Co., 342, 348**
**Smith v. Gross, 629**
**Smith v. Snap-On Tools Corp., 134**
**Smith v. Van Gorkom, 621**
Smith, Bell and Hauck, Inc. v. Cullins, 270
**Smith, K.L., Enterprises, Ltd., *in re*, 447**
Societe Nationale Industrielle Aerospaceitale v. U.S. District Court, 832
**Soldano v. O'Daniels, 5, 10**, 44, 109
Sommer v. Kridel, 700
Sommers v. Board of Education, 173
Soucie v. David, 84
Southern Ohio Coal Co. v. Donovan, 87
Spherex, Inc. v. Alexander Grant & Co., 660
Springer v. Powder Power Tool Co., 270
Standard Oil Co. v. United States, 764
Stanley J. How & Associates v. Boss, 577
**Staszak v. Romanik, 542–543**
**State v. Joy, 97**
State v. Speckman, 104
State v. Tolliver, 104
**Steinberg v. Chicago Medical School, 238–239**
**Stewart v. Board of Education of Ritenour, 296**
Stolmeier v. Beck, 512
Strandberg v. Lawrence, 261
Stratton v. County of Liberty, 173
Straus v. Holiday Inns, Inc., 645
**Stream v. Sportscar Salon, Ltd., 341**
Summer v. Land & Leisure, Inc., 661

Tate v. Chambers, 512
Tayloe v. The Merchants Fire Insurance Company, 198
Taylor, Matter of, 483
Taylor v. Allen, 52
Temple v. City of Petersburg, 53
Terbovitz v. Fiscal Court of Adair County, 495

Texaco, Inc., *in re*, 483
Texas v. Johnson, 65, 94
Theatre Enterprises, Inc. v. Paramount Film Distributing Corp. 776
Thorn, Estate of, 725
Thornton, Estate of, v. Caldor, Inc., 64
Thurmond v. Weiser, 185
Tiffany v. Boston Club, 132
**Timberlane Lumber Co. v. Bank of America, 818–819**, 932
**Totem Marine T. & B. v. Alyeska Pipeline, 246**
**Transamerica Insurance Co. v. Standard Oil Co., 804–805**
Treasure Salvors, Inc. v. Unidentified, Wrecked and Abandoned Sailing Vessel, 496
Trentacost v. Brussel, 700
Trew v. Ogle, 262
Turman v. Central Billing, Inc., 122
TWA v. Hardison, 780

**U-Haul International, Inc. v. Jartran, Inc., 140**, 141
Ultramares Corp. v. Touche, 651, 652
Union Mutual Fires Ins. Co. v. King, 745
**United Air Lines, Inc. v. Austin Travel Corp., 298**
United Housing Foundation, Inc. v. Forman, 645
United Securities Corp. v. Bruton, 403–404
United States v. Aluminum Co. of America, 775
**United States v. American Future Systems, Inc., 807**
United States v. Arnold, Schwinn & Co., 771
**United States v. Arthur Young & Co., 659**
United States v. Bethlehem Steel Co., 297–298
United States v. Biswell, 86
United States v. The Bonanno Organized Crime Family of La Cosa Nostra, 523
United States v. City of Twin Falls, 314–315
United States v. Colgate & Co., 769
United States v. Continental Can Co., 775
United States v. Covino, 105
United States v. Doe, 93
United States v. Douglas Aircraft Co., 40
United States v. Frasch, 100
**United States v. General Dynamics Corp., 762–763**
United States v. Glick, 658
United States v. Halper, 104
**United States v. Hospital Montefiores, 567–568**
United States v. Lee, 72
United States v. Leon, 92
United States v. LeRoy, **101**
United States v. Mathews, 104
United States v. Matt, 104
United States v. Moore, 39–40
**United States v. Morton, 553**
United States v. Natelli, 658
United States v. Nixon, 61
United States v. Park, 103
United States v. Phoenix Petroleum Co., 86
United States v. Powell, 77
United States v. Simon, 648
**United States v. Sun and Sand Imports, Ltd., Inc., 47**
United States Trust Co. v. New Jersey, 59
United Steelworkers of America v. Weber, 786
Universal/Land Construction Co. v. City of Spokane, 301
**Unocal Corporation v. Mesa Petroleum Co., 618–619**, 642

**Valerino v. Little, 583–584**
Vaskie v. West American Insurance Co., 198
Vermont Yankee Nuclear Power Corp. v. Natural Resources Defense Council, 80
Virginia Board of Pharmacy v. Virginia Citizens Consumers Council, 65
Vole, Inc. v. Georgacopoulos, 301
Volkswagenwerk Aktiengesellschaft v. Schlunk, 832

Waegemann v. Montgomery Ward & Co., 285
**Wagenseller v. Scottsdale Memorial Hospital, 792–793**
**Walcott v. Manufacturers Hanover Trust, 388–389**
Walcott & Steele, Inc. v. Carpenter, 351
**Waldinger Corporation v. CRS Group Engineers, Inc., 282, 358–359**
Walker Bank & Trust Co. v. Jones, 812
Wallace v. Jaffree, 63
Walner v. Baskin-Robbins Ice Cream Co., 142
Ward v. Board of Education, 185
Ward v. Village of Monroeville, 73
**Wards Cove Packing Co. v. Atonio, 784–785**
Warner v. Texas and Pacific Ry., 261
Warner-Lambert v. FTC, 87
Warwick Municipal Employees Credit Union v. McAllister, 248
**Webster v. Blue Ship Tea Room, Inc., 336**
Weil v. Diversified Properties, 560
Weinberger v. UOP, Inc., 617
Weirum v. RKO General, Inc., 125
Weissmann v. Freeman, 142
**Weiss Medical Complex, Ltd. v. Kim, 586**
Welch v. Fitzgerald-Hicks Dodge, Inc., 352
Western Commerce Bank v. Gillespie, 285
Western Union Telegraph Co. v. Hill, 125
West Virginia State Board of Education v. Barnette, 64
Wheeling-Pittsburgh Steel Corp. v. United Steelworkers of America, 479
Whisper Soft Mills v. N.L.R.B., 495–496
Wickard v. Filburn, 56
Wilcox v. St. Croix Labor Union Mutual Homes, 496
Wilkinson v. Downtin, 122
Williams v. Alfred N. Koplin & Co., 699
Williams v. Walker-Thomas Furniture Co., 222
**Willsmore v. Township of Oceola, 706**
Wilson v. Kealakekua Ranch, Ltd., 225
Winslar v. Bartlett, 699
**Witmer v. Blair, 730**
Wood v. Willman, 410
World Financial Services Center, Inc., *in re*, 464
World-Wide Volkswagen Corp. v. Woodson, 26
Wray v. Oklahoma Alcoholic Beverage Control Board, 87
Wydel Associates v. Thermasol Ltd., 39

Yellow Cab Corp. v. Clifton City Council, 87
**Youngstown Sheet and Tube Co. v. Sawyer, 60–61**

Zabriskie Chevrolet, Inc. v. Smith, 367
**Zamora v. Valley Federal Savings & Loan Association of Grand Junction, 804**
Zatrains, Inc. v. Oak Grove Smokehouse, Inc., 130
Zubak v. Rose, 198

# Subject Index

Abandoned property, 704
Abstract, 674
Acceleration clauses, 383
Acceptance
 and contract, 175, 189
  case, 190–191
 of contract offer, 186–195, 196
 taking effect of, 193
 unconditional, 187–188
 unequivocal assent as, 192–193
 of unilateral offers, 194–195
Acceptance of good, revocation of, 363
 case, 364
Accession, 706–707
Accommodation indorser, 422–423
Accord and satisfaction, 283
Account
 duty to, 491
 proceeding, 528–529
  case, 529–530
Accountant-client privilege, 658–659
Accountants
 criminal liability of, 657–658
 legal liability of, 647–661
  case, 650
 management advisory services of, 652
 privilege and confidentiality of, 658–659
  case, 659
 and securities regulation, 653–658
  case, 655–656
 tax practice of, 652–653
Accounts
 as intangible collateral, 446
Accredited investors, 633
Acknowledgment, 678
Action at law, 24
Action of conversion, 390
Actions
 *in personam,* 20
 *in rem,* 20
Act of God, 279n, 716
Act of state doctrine, 820
 case, 820
Actual authority, 497, 499
Actual breach discharge of contracts, 278
*Actus reus,* 94
Adequacy of consideration, 205
Adhesion
 contracts of, 170–171, 739
  case, 171
Adjudication, 15, 16
Adjudicative system, analysis of, 35–36
Adjudicatory power, of federal agencies, 77, 81–82
Adler foreseeability test, 652n
Administrative agencies, lawmaking by, 75–87
Administrative law, 8
Administrative Law Judge (ALJ), 77, 81–82
Administrative Procedure Act (APA), 79, 84–85
Administrator/administratix, 721
Adopted children, and estate, 726
Adversary system, 35–36
Adverse possession, 679–680
 case, 680

Advertisements, as preliminary negotiations, 178
Advertising, 797–799
 case, 799–800
Affirmative action, 781, 786–787
 case, 787
Age Discrimination in Employment Act (ADEA), 788
Age misrepresentations, minors' liability and, 233–234
Agency
 creation of relationship, 488–489
  case, 488–489
 liability of parties, 497–512
 termination of relationship, 492–495
Agency law, 11
Agency rules, and partnership, 530
Agent(s), 487, 490–491, 494
 of capital, 159
 and commercial paper, 413–414
 in foreign trade, 829
 liability of, 503
 real estate, 673
 of society, 159–160
Aggregate theory of partnerships, 514
Agreement(s), 175–198
 exchange of forms without, 189–190
 informal, 189
 and partnership dissolution, 539–540
  case, 540
Airbill, 313n
Air rights, 665
Alcohol. *See* Intoxication
Allegations of fact, 27–28
Allonge, 387n
Alteration defense, 406–407
Alteration of contract, 284
Alternative methods of dispute resolution (ADR), 36–38
Amendments. *See also* amendments by number
 First, 63
 Fifth, 71
 Fourteenth, 62, 67
American Arbitration Association, 822
American Bar Association
 and corporations, 566
 and no-fault insurance, 747
*American Challenge, The,* 830
American Institute of Certified Public Accountants (AICPA), 647
American Law Institute, 4, 322, 369n, 513n
American Trial Lawyers' Association, 747
Ancillary covenant, 219
Ancillary promise, and oral contracts, 252
Annualized percentage rate (APR), 800–801
Annual reports, 631
Answer, 27–28
Anticipatory breach discharge, of contracts, 278
Anticipatory repudiation, 360
Anti-dilution statutes, and trademarks, 132
Antidiscrimination laws, 777
Antidumping laws, 773
Antitrust acts, and corporate dissolution, 624
Antitrust law, 753–776

Apparent authority, 498–499, 531
 case, 501, 502
Appellate courts, 16–17
 litigation in, 32–35
Appraisal right, 613–614
Approval sales, 327–329
Arbitrary and capricious test, of agency rulemaking, 80
 case, 81
Arbitration, 37, 534
 and international trade, 821–822
 case, 822
Arms Export Control Act, 824
Arms' length dealing, 239n
Arson, 98
Articles of Confederation, 57
Articles of incorporation, 573
Articles of merger or consolidation, 613
Articles of partnership, 515
Artisan's lien, 455, 466
Ascendants, 726
Assault and battery, 114–115
Asset acquisitions, 614–616
Assets, partnership, 544–545
Assignee, 265
 of contract, 374, 375
Assignment
 of interest in limited partnership, 557
 of lease, 697–698
 of negotiable instrument, 385n, 386
 of partner's interest, 536
 of rights, 264–265
  case, 266
Assignor, 265
Association, UPA definition of, 513
Assumed name statutes, 515
Assumption of risk, and strict liability, 347
 case, 348
Atomic Energy Act (1954), 824
Attachment, 447, 466–467
 case, 448
Attestation clause, 723
Attorney-in-fact, 488
Attorneys, 11–12
At-will employment contract, 254
Auctions, 178–179
Audit, 647
Audit failure, 649
Auditing Standards Board, 649
Auditor, independence of, 649–650
Authority. *See also* Ratification
 of agent, 497–499
 exceeding, 503
 in partnership, 530–532, 533
  case, 534–535
 and partnership dissolution, 543–544
Auto insurance, no-fault, 747
Automated teller machines (ATMs), 436, 438
Automatic perfection, 450
Automobile insurance, 744–747
 case, 745–746
Automobiles, and lemon laws, 366. *See also* Motor vehicles

Bad checks, 430–431
Bad faith, 399n

1031

## SUBJECT INDEX

Bad faith tort, 297
Bail, 94
Bailee, 221, 313, 323
   duties of, 711–712
      case, 712–713
   rights of, 710
Bailee's acknowledgment, 353
Bailment contracts, 221–222
Bailments, 313, 510, 701, 708–717
   and common carriers, 715–716
   constructive, 709–710
   types of, 710
Bailor, 313, 708
   duties of, 714
   rights of, 714
Bait and switch, 799
Balanced Budget and Emergency Deficit Control Act (1985) (Gramm-Rudman Act), 59
Bank accounts, joint, 703–704
Bank credit cards, 218
Bank-depositor relationship, 429–431
   federal control of, 435–437
   problems in, 431–435
Bank draft, 371
Bank Export Services Act, 825
Banking, electronic, 437–440
Bank robbery law, 99
Bankruptcy, 408, 465–484, 803
   and agent, 494
   alternatives to, 465–468
   business reorganization and, 477–480
   discharge in, 283
   proceedings, 468
Bankruptcy code (1978), 470–471
   Chapter 11 and, 477, 478–479
      case, 479–480
   Chapter 12, 481–482
   Chapter 13, 481–482
Bankruptcy law, and contracts, 170
Bankruptcy Reform Act (1978), 212n, 283
Banks
   and conditional indorsements, 389
   drawee, 427
   duties of, 429–430
      case, 430
   funds availability, 435–436
   and letter of credit, 814–816
Battery, 114–115
   case, 115–116
Bearer, 375
Bearer instrument, 375, 385
Beneficiaries, 263–264, 704
   of trust, 728, 729
Bentham, Jeremy, 146
Bequest, 721
Berne Convention, and copyrights, 137
Bets, 215–216
Bilateral contract, 166–167, 739
Bilateral mistake, 243
   case, 243–244
Bilateral offer, 166
Bill of lading, 313, 815, 818
Bill of Rights, 62
Binder, 735
Blank indorsement, 375, 386–387, 388
   case, 388–389
Blue laws, 64, 218
Blue-sky laws, 575n
Board of directors, 584–587, 588
   cases, 586, 588–589
Boesky, Ivan, 99, 636
Bona fide occupational qualification (BFOQ), 785
Bona fide purchaser (BFP), 319, 678
Bonds, 575, 628

Books (financial). *See* Record keeping
Boycotts, 766–767
Breach, and negligence, 111–112
Breach discharge of contracts, 278
Breach of contract, 342–343, 403–404
   equitable remedies for, 298–301
   lawsuits, 287
   and money damages, 291–298
      case, 293, 294–295, 296–297, 298
   remedies for, 360–361
      case, 362, 365
   and risk of loss, 324–326
      case, 326–327
Breach of duty, by agent, 503
Breach of warranty, 237n, 403–404
Bretton Woods, 827
Broker, 673–674
   real estate, 167
Building codes, 690
Bulk transfers, 321
Burden of proof, 30–31
Burglary, 97
Business
   continuation of partnership, 539
   criminal law and, 89–105
   federal crimes affecting, 99–101
   government regulation of, 751. *See also* Antitrust law; Consumer transactions; Employment law; International business
   sale of, 219
   state crimes affecting, 96–98
   UPA definition of, 513
Business conduct, interference with, 127–129
Business corporation, 566
Business insurance coverage, 744
Business judgment rule, 600–601
   case, 601, 602
   and takeovers, 617
Business organization acts, 52
Business records, 31
Business reorganization, and bankruptcy, 477–479
Business torts, 123, 127–142
Buyer, 453–455
   in ordinary course of business, 453–454
   revocation of acceptance by, 357
Buyer's obligations, 359–360
Buyer's remedies, 362–366
Bylaws, of incorporation, 574

California Civil Code, 208
Cancellation rights, case, 205–206
C&F (cost and freight), 354
Canon law, 565
Capacity
   and agency, 489
   and contracts, 229
Capital, agents of, 159
Capital stock, shares of, 575
Cardozo, Benjamin N., 5, 42–43, 527–528, 651
Carson, Johnny, 131n
Case law, 41–42
Cashier's check, 372
Causation in fact, 112
*Caveat emptor*, 239, 333
*Caveat venditor*, 239
Cellar-Kefauver Act (1950), 759
Certainty, 46–47
   case, 47
Certificate of deposit, 372, 373
Certificate of incorporation (charter), 573
Certificate of limited partnership, 552
Certificate of merger or consolidation, 613

Certificates of origin, 815
Certified check, 428
Certified public accountant (CPA), 647
Charge card, 805. *See also* Credit card
Changing order, 535
Charitable gifts, promises of, 211
Charitable trusts, 731
Charter, 573
Chattel paper, 444n, 446
   case, 447
Checks, 369, 371–372, 427–428. *See also* Negotiable instruments
   altered, 435
   bad, 430–431
   certification of, 428
   federal control over, 435–437
   federalization of, 435
   local and nonlocal, 437
   signing of, 378
   stale, 429–430
   time of presentment of, 418
   writing of, 377–378
Child labor, 790
Child Protection and Toy Safety Act, 810
Children
   and criminal defense, 95
   and estate, 725–726
CIF (cost, insurance, and freight), 354, 816
Cigarette Labeling and Advertising Act (1969), 810
Circumstantial context, of law, 49
Citizenship, 19
Civil law, 7, 41n, 89–90, 91
Civil rights, of U.S. citizens, 61–71
Civil Rights Act (1964), 777
   Title VII, 780
Claims, 474
Classified board of directors, 584
Clayton Act (1914), 218, 754, 759
Close connection doctrine, 399
   case, 399–400
Close corporation, 566, 589–590, 595–596
   case, 590
Close-end transactions, 801
Closing (settlement), real estate, 675
*Code of Federal Regulations*, 84, 823
Codicil, 724
Coinsurance, 742
Collateral, 444, 449–450, 465–466
   indispensable paper, 446
      case, 447
   intangible, 446
   movement out of state, 452–453
   secured transactions and, 459, 460–461
      case, 459–460
   tangible (goods), 445–446
Collateral note, 372
Collective bargaining, 779, 791
Collusion, 760, 761, 763–764
Comity, 821
Commerce, 100
Commerce Clause, of U.S. Constitution, 56–58, 823
Commercial impracticability doctrine, 281–282, 358
   case, 358–359
Commercial paper, 369–376. *See also* Bank
   checks, 427–428
   defenses and, 403–408
   and holders in due course, 397–403
   liability of the parties, 413–425
   negotiability, 377–385
   parties to, 374–375

## SUBJECT INDEX

transfer of, 385
types of, 370–374
UCC classification of, 370–372
Commercial speech, 65–66
   case, 66
Commercial shipping, 354
Commercial unit, 360
Commingling, 456
Commissioners on Uniform State Laws, 643
Commitments, 148
Commodity Control List, 823
Common carriers
   and bailments, 715–716
   and minors, 232n
Common law (case law), 6, 7, 41–44
   and corporation, 565
   and minors' contracts, 229–235
   and *stare decisis* doctrine, 43–44
   and statutory law, 47–48
   unilateral offer, acceptance under, 195, 196
Common pleas courts, 16
Common stock, 594
Communication, of offer, 182–183
   case, 183
Community property, 672–673
Comparable worth, 787–788
Comparative negligence, 114
Compensation
   of corporate directors, 599
   in partnership, 527
Compensatory damages, 291–295
   case, 293, 294–295
   and mitigation of damages, 295–296
      case, 296
   and nominal damages, 296–297
Competence, and contracts, 229
Competition
   and horizontal restraints of trade, 764–765
   and international trade, 825–826
   unfair, 139–141
Competition privilege, 127–129
   case, 128–129
Competitive Equality Banking Act (1987), 435
Compilation, by accountant, 649
Complaint, 27
Composition agreements, 208–209
Comprehensive Crime Control Act (1984), 102
Compromise agreements, for debt settlement, 207
Comptroller General, 59–60
Computer codes, copyright of, 137
Computer crime, 101–102
Computer Fraud and Abuse Act (1986), 102
Concurrent state jurisdiction, 19
Condemnation, 681
Conditional indorsements, 389
Conditions
   concurrent, 273
      case, 273
   in contract, 271
   and leases, 686
   precedent, 271–272
      case, 273
   subsequent, 272–273
      case, 273
Condominiums, 672
Confession of judgment, 533
Confidentiality, and accountants, 658–659
   case, 659
Conflict of interest, of corporate directors, 586
   case, 586

Conflicts, moral duty and, 153–154
Conglomerate merger, 760, 761–762
Congressional Budget Office (CBO), 59
Consent
   and battery, 116
   reality of, 236
Consent decree, 755
Consideration
   absence of, 266
   adequacy of, 205
   and assignment of rights, 266–267
   and holders in due course, 398
   insurance, 839
   and moral obligation, 209
Consideration doctrine, 199–214
   case, 200, 201, 202–203, 205–206, 210
Consignee, 329
Consignment, sale on, 329
Consignor, 329
Consolidation. *See also* Mergers
   and appraisal right, 613–614
   effects of, 613
   steps in, 614
Constitutional law, 8, 55–73
Constitutional rights. *See* Rights
Constitutions, and statutory law, 46–47. *See also* United States Constitution
Construction, of contracts, 287
Constructive bailments, 709–710
Constructive eviction, 688
Constructive trust, 731
Consumer Credit Protection Act (CCPA) (1968), 466, 800–807
Consumer credit transaction, 533n
Consumer goods, 445
Consumer leases, 311
Consumer legislation, federal, 348–350
Consumer Product Safety Act (1972), 348–349
Consumer protection laws, 178, 348–350. *See also* Consumer Credit Protection Act
Consumers, banking transfer liability of, 439
Consumer transactions, 797–812
   statutes regulating, 798
Contemporaneous traders, 637
Contingency fee, 11
Contingent fee contracts, 224
Contract carrier, 715
Contract Clause, 58–59
Contract for deed, 675
Contract law, 107, 259
   and sales law, 171–172
Contract rights, 129
   and manager's privilege, 129
Contracts, 165–173
   acceptance of, 186–195, 196
   of adhesion, 170–171, 712, 739
      case, 171
   agreement and, 175–198
   assignee of, 374
   bailment, 221–222
   bilateral, 166–167
   breach of, 324–326, 342–343, 403–404
      case, 326–327
   breach of discharge, 278
   for business sale, 219
   cancellation of, case, 205–206
   classification of, 165–173
   commercial impracticability and, 281–282
   contingent fee, 224
   contrary to public policy, 218–224
   destination, 318, 323, 354
   discharge of, 271–286, 354
   employment, 219

executed, 177, 230
executory, 177, 230
express, 167
formal, 171
of guaranty, 195
illegal, 224–225
illegality of, 215–227
illusory, 205
implied, 167, 168n
   case, 168–169
informal, 171
installment, 357
insurance, 216, 735–739
intent to, 176–179
international convention on, 816–817
international sales, 814–817
interpretation of, 287–291
liability of minors, 234. *See also* Liability; Minority
life insurance, 264
lobbying, 224
modification, 202, 204–205, 258
nature of, 165
negotiable instrument as, 265n
negotiated, 170–171
objective theory of, 177–178
open provisions of, 181–182
option, 184
oral, 170, 251, 254–255
ordinary, 230
output, 207
privity of, 341–342
quasi-, 167–168, 195
   case, 168–169
real estate, 166–167, 673–679
remedies for breach of, 291–301
   cases, 290, 293, 294–295, 296, 298
requirements, 260–261
revocation of, 195
risk-creating and risk-shifting, 216
for sale of goods, 256–259
sales, 267, 311–313, 353–360. *See also* Sales contracts
sealed, 199
severable, 224–225
shipment, 318, 322–323, 353
and state law, 22–23
and subcontracts, 268
subjective considerations and, 177–178
Sunday, 218
termination of, 184–186
unconscionable, 171, 222
unenforceable, 170–171
unilateral, 166
   case, 166–167
valid, 170
void, 170
voidable, 170, 229–249
written, 251–262
Contractual liability, 414–416. *See also* Promissory liability
   and auditor, 647–648
   of indorsers, 417–420
Contributory negligence, 114
Control test, 555
Conversion, 122
Cooperatives, 672
Coordinating Committee for Multilateral Export Controls (COCOM), 824
Co-owners, partners as, 513
Copyright infringement, 136–139
   and *Fair Use Doctrine*, 137–138
Corporate disclosures, regulation of, 638
Corporate opportunity rule, 603
   case, 603–604

# 1034 · SUBJECT INDEX

Corporate suicide, 642
Corporate veil, piercing, 568
  case, 569–570
Corporation law, in U.S., 566
Corporations, 565–625
  attorneys and, 12
  board of directors, 584–588
    case, 586
  classification of, 566–567
  close, 589–590, 595–596
  criminal liability of, 102–103
  financing, 575
  formation of, 570–576
    case, 571, 572
  incorporation and, 573–574
  as legal entities, 567–569
    case, 567–568, 569–570
  liability of, 567
  management of, 580–588
  managerial employees of, 587–588
  managers' liabilities, 600–607
  managers' rights, 599–600
  mergers and consolidations, 611–621
  as moral agents, 155–157
  nature and history of, 565–569
    case, 569–570
  nonprofit, 469
  officers of, 587–588
  parent, 569
  powers of, 579–580
  publicly held, 595
  shareholders, 580–582, 587–588
    rights of, 593–597
  social responsiveness of, 158–160
  subsidiary, 568–569
  termination of, 622–624
Cotenants, 671
Counsel, right to, 94
Counterclaim, 28
Counterfeit Access Device and Computer Fraud and Abuse Act (1984), 102
Counteroffer, 184–185, 187
  legal ramifications of, 187
Course of dealing, 291
Course of performance, 290–291
Court decree, dissolution by, 541
  case, 542–543
Courts
  appellate, 16
  of equity, 24, 298
  federal, 16–18
  general trial, 16, 17–18
  and international trade, 817–818
  jurisdiction of, 18–23
  of law, 23–24
  of limited jurisdiction, 15–16
  state, 15–16, 17–18
  systems, 15–18
Covenants
  ancillary, 218
  and general warranty deeds, 675
  and leases, 686
  not to compete, 218–219
  of quiet enjoyment, 687–688
  restrictive, 218–219, 681
Credit, 443–444. See also Secured transactions
  commercial paper as, 370
  and consumer protection, 800–802
  letter of, 360
  and usury, 218
Credit cards, 804
  case, 804–805
Creditor beneficiary, 263–264

Creditors, 469–470
  assignment for the benefit of, 467–468
  composition of, 467
  general, 475
  and partnership, 535
  rights of seller's, 320–321
  secured, 475
Creditors' composition agreements, 208–209
Credit Practices Rule (FTC), 450n
Crime(s), 89
  classification of, 90–91
  and landlord's responsibility, 695
    case, 695–696
  of minors, 235
  tort and, 90
Criminal law, 7–8, 107
  and business, 89–105
  and civil law, 89–90, 91
  and crimes affecting business, 96–98
  defenses, 95–96
  and white collar crime, 102–103
Criminal liability
  of accountants, 657–658
  and partnership, 530
Cross elasticity of demand, 756–757
Cross elasticity of supply, 757
Crown jewel, 642
Cumulative dividend preference, 594
Currency controls, 829
Curtesy, 673, 829
Curtilage, 79
Cy pres doctrine, 731

Damages, 7, 132, 241–242, 697
  compensatory, for breach of contract, 291–293
  limitation on, 340
    case, 341
  liquidated, 297–298
    case, 298
  mitigation of, 295–296
    case, 296
  nominal, 296–297
  punitive, 297
Dealers, and securities, 630
Death, and partnership dissolution, 541
Debit instruments, 440
Debtor, 444, 465–468, 470–471. See also Bankruptcy
  case, 471–472
  -creditor relationship, 443, 465–468
  default, 809
  estate of, 474–475
  -in-possession, 478
  and secured transactions, 460–461
Debts
  adjustment of, 480–482
  collecting, 265
  liquidated, 208
  nondischargeable, 477
  of partnership, 533
  payment of another's, 256
  revival of, 212
  settlement of, 207–209
  unliquidated, 207
Debt securities, 575, 628
Decedent, 721, 726
Deception, 139
Deceptive trade practices, 178, 797–800
  acts, 51, 139–140
Decree of specific performance, 24
Deeds, 669, 675–679
  case, 677–678

De facto corporation, 575
De facto mergers, 614
Defamation, 65, 116–118
Default, 460–462
Default judgment, 28
Defendant, 7, 27, 89
  person of, 19–20, 22
Defenses. See also specific topics and holders in due course, 403–408
  and negligence, 114
  plaintiff misconduct, 342
  privity, 341
Defensive mergers, 612
Deficit, maximum, 59
Definiteness problem, 179–180
  case, 179–180
  in sales law, 180–182
De jure corporation, 574–575
Delaware, corporations in, 566. See also Delaware Corporate Code
Delaware Corporate Code, 52
Delegated powers, 55–56
Delegatee, 267
Delegation of duties, and assignment of rights, 267–269
Delegator, 267
Delivery
  and contracts, 181–182
  of possession, 702–703, 708–709
Demand instruments, 372–373, 382, 400
Depositary banks, 389–390
Deposition, 29
Deposits, regulation of, 436
Deregulation, 85
Descendants, and estate, 726
Descent statutes, 725–726
Destination contract, 318, 323, 354
Detainer, 696–697
Devise, 721
Directors
  board of, 584–588
    case, 586
  corporate, 580, 584–588
  rights of, 599–600
Disability benefits, 741
Discharge
  in bankruptcy, 408
  of debtor, 475–477
    case, 476–477
  of contracts, 271–286
    by breach, 278–280
      case, 280–281
    and commercial impracticability, 281–282
    by failure, 272
    and frustration of, 282
    by legal impossibility, 278–280
    by operation of conditions, 271–273
    by operation of law, 283–284
    by parties' agreement, 283
    by performance, 274–278
  of parties, 423–424
Disclaimers
  of auditor, 647–648
  of warranty, 339–340
    case, 341
Disclosure
  of bank funds availability policy, 437
  and securities regulation, 640
Discovery stage, 28–29
Discretionary powers, 77
Discrimination
  de facto, 68
    case, 68

# SUBJECT INDEX

employment, 780–789
   case, 784–785
   gender, 68–69
Dishonor notice, 418–419
Dishonor of drafts, 416–417
Dispute resolution, 27–40
Dissolution
   of corporation, 622–624
     case, 623
   of limited partnership, 557–558
     case, 558–559
   of partnership, 539–544
     case, 540
Distribution, of estate, 725–726
District courts, 16
Dividends, 567, 593–594
   liability for illegal, 598–599
Doctrine of incorporation, 62
Documents of title, 313–314
Doing no harm, 148
   case, 148
Domestic corporation, 566
Domestic courts, and international trade, 817–818
   case, 818–819
Dominant estate, 669
Donee, 701
Donee beneficiary, 264
Donor, 701
Door-to-door solicitation sales, 808
   case, 808–809
Double jeopardy, 92, 567
   case, 567–568
Dower, 725
Dower right, 673
Draft, 370–371
Drawee, 370
Drawers
   and forged signature, 432
   promissory liability of, 417–419
Drug testing, 793–794
*Duces tecum* subpoenas, 77
Due care, 600–601
   and bailee, 711–712
   case, 601, 602
   and takeovers, 617
Due on sale clauses, 263n
Due process, 62, 92
   procedural, 82
   case, 83
Due Process Clause, 69–70
   case, 70–71
Dumping, 826, 827
Duress, 95–96
   defense, 405, 408
   and voidable contracts, 245
     case, 246
Durham rule, 95
Duties
   delegation of, 267–269
   non-delegable, 267n
Duty. *See also* Breach of duty
   of agent, 490–491
     case, 492
     negligence and, 108–109
   of principal, 490–491
Duty of good faith, 313

Earnest money, 674
Earnings, current net, 593–594
Easement, 253, 669
   appurtenant, 669
   by express grant or reservation, 669
   in gross, 669
   by implication, 669–670
   by necessity, 670
   by prescription, 670
Economic duress, 245
Economic regulations, 67
Eighth Amendment, 94
8-Ks, 631
Electronic banking, 369
Electronic Funds Transfer Act (1978), 437–440
Embezzlement, 97
   case, 97
Eminent domain, 71
Employee Polygraph Protection Act (1988), 793
Employees
   corporate, 600
   drug testing of, 793–794
   key, 737
   of partnership, 532
   privacy of, 793–794
Employee stock ownership plan (ESOP), 619–620
   case, 620
Employer-employee relationship, 487, 506–507
   case, 507
Employer-independent contractor relationship, 487, 506–507
   case, 507
Employers' liability, 123
Employment
   contracts, covenants in, 218–219
   discrimination law, 780–789
     case, 784–785
   and employee discharge, 790–792
   scope of, 507–510
     case, 508, 509
   at will, 254, 791–792
     case, 792–793
Employment law, 777–796
Encumbrance, 675
Endowment insurance, 740
Enforcement power, 77
English common law, 565
English rule of possession, 687
Entity theory of partnerships, 514
Entrapment, 96
Entrustment, to merchant, 320–321
   case, 320
Entry barriers, 756, 761
Equal Credit Opportunity Act (ECOA), 806–807
   case, 807
Equal Employment Opportunity Commission (EEOC), 781
Equal Pay Act, 788
Equal Protection Clause, 67–69
Equipment, 445
Equitable actions, 24–25
Equity
   action in, 24
   courts of, 24
Equity securities, 628
Error, effect of, 34
Escheat, 726
   statutes, 705–706
     case, 706
Escrow agent, 675
Establishment Clause, 63–64
Estate
   administration of, 726–731
   of debtor, 474–475
   debtor's, 470–471

Estate planning, 731–732
Estates, 667–669. *See also* Wills
Estoppel, 83–84
   corporation by, 575
   partnership and, 536
   promissory, 209–211
     case, 210
Estray statutes, 705
Ethics, 143–162. *See also* Morality
European Economic Community (EEC), 828–829
Eviction, 687–688
Evidence, rules of, 31
Exclusive dealing, 772–773
Exclusive jurisdiction, 19
Exculpatory clauses, 220–222, 694
   and bailments, 711–712
   case, 221
Excusing conditions, 150
Executed contracts, 171, 230
Executive branch, 60
   federal agencies in, 76
Executive orders, 60
   case, 60–61
Executor/executrix, 721
Executors' contracts, 256
Executory contracts, 171, 230
Exemptions, and bankruptcy, 470–471
   case, 471–472
Expedited Funds Availability Act (EFAA) (1988), 435–436
Export Administration Act (1979), 823–824
Export Administration Regulations, 823–824
Export/import process, national regulation of, 823–826
Export incentives, 824–825
Export license, 815, 823
Export Trading Company Act (1982), 824–825
*Ex post facto* laws, 94
Express authority, 497
Express condition precedent, 272
Express contracts, 167
Express covenant, 690
Express powers, of corporations, 579
Express private trust, 728
Express ratification, 499
Express warranties, 333–335
   case, 335
   disclaimers of, 339–340
Ex-ship (from the carrying vessel), 354
Extension clauses, 383–384
Ex terms, 816
Extrinsic evidence, 288, 290
   case, 288–289

Fact
   allegations of, 27
   conclusion of, 32
   questions of, 28
Failing company defense, 762
Failure of consideration, 404
Fair Credit and Charge Card Disclosure Act (1988), 805
Fair Credit Billing Act, 806
Fair Credit Reporting Act, 803
   case, 804
Fair Debt Collection Practices Act (1978), 805–806
Fair Labor Standards Act (FLSA), 790
Fair Packaging and Labeling Act, 810
Fair Use Doctrine, 137–138
   case, 138
False arrest, 119

# 1036 SUBJECT INDEX

False imprisonment, 118–119
  case, 119–120
False light, 121
False pretenses, 97
Falsity, knowledge of, 241
Family purpose doctrine, 510
Farmers
  and bankruptcy, 469
  and bankruptcy code, 481–482
  as merchants, case, 310
Farm products, 445
FAS (free alongside), 354
Federal agencies, lawmaking by, 75–87
Federal consumer legislation, 348–350
Federal courts, 16–17
  appellate, 16–17
Federal crimes, 99–101
Federal Deposit Insurance Corporation, 628
Federal government
  Constitutional organization of, 55–59
  and corporations, 566–567
  jurisdiction of, 61–71
Federal law, 6
Federal legislation, and checks and bank-depositor relationship, 435–437
Federal Privacy Act (1974), 85
Federal questions, in suit, 19
*Federal Register,* 84, 85
Federal regulation
  antitrust statutes as, 753–754
  of securities, 627–643
Federal rules of evidence, 31n, 659
Federal Trade Commission (FTC), 15n, 77, 349, 450n, 533n, 754
  holder in due course rule, 408–409
Federal Trade Commission Act (FTC Act), 754
  and consumer transactions, 797–800
Fee simple estate, 668
Fees, contingency and hourly, 11–12
Felony, 90
Fictitious name statutes, 515
Fiduciary relationships, 148, 490
  and fraud, 240
  in partnership, 527–528
  case, 529–530
Fifth Amendment, 67, 69–71, 92–93
  case, 93
Filing, 449
Finance charge, 800–801
Financial Accounting Standards Board (FASB), 653
Financial Institutions Reform, Recovery, and Enforcement Act (1989), 99
Financial responsibility laws, 745
Financing, of real estate sale, 675
Financing statement, 445
Finding statutes, 705
Fines, 7, 94
Fire insurance, 741–743
Firm offer, 184–185
First Amendment, 63–64
  and defamation, 117, 118
  and trademarks, 131–132
Fixtures, 445–446, 450–451, 666, 689
  case, 666–667
Flammable Fabrics Act, 810
Float, 438
Floating lien, 455
FOB (free on board), 354, 816
  terms, 318n
Food and Drug Administration, 348n
Food Security Act (1985), 452, 454
Force. *See* Duress

Force majeure, 279n
Ford, Henry, II, 160
Foreclose, 670
Foreclosure, 465
Foreign corporation, 566
Foreign Corrupt Practices Act (FCPA) (1977), 99, 158, 657, 824n
Foreign Sovereign Immunities Act (FSIA) (1976), 819
  case, 819
Foreign Trade Zone (FTZ), 825
Foreseeability, 108–109, 112
  case, 109
  of loss, and compensatory damages, 294
  case, 294–295
Forgery, 98
  case, 98
  of check indorsement, 420–421, 433
  of check signatures, 429
  defense, 405–406
  of drawer's signature, 433–435
Formal contracts, 171
Form swapping, 189
*Forum non conveniens,* 22
Fourteenth Amendment, 62, 67–69
Fourth Amendment, 92
  Warrant Clause of, 78
Fraud(s), 9, 122
  and accounting, 649, 651
  case, 148, 238–239
  elements of, 236–237
  in fact, 237–238, 529
  implied in law, 467
  and innocent misrepresentation, 242
  mail, 99
  case, 99–100
  remedies for, 242
  and securities regulation, 638
  statute of, 251–252
  in transfers, 472
  and voidable contracts, 472–473
  wire, 99
Fraud in the execution defense, 406
Fraud in the inducement, 404
Fraudulent conveyance statutes, 321
Freedom of Information Act (1966), 84–85
Freedom of religion, 63–64
Free Exercise Clause, 64
Freehold estates, 667–668
Free Speech Clause, 65–66
Free Trade Act (FTA), 828
Friedman, Milton, 159
Friendly takeover, 620
  case, 621
Full Faith and Credit Clause, 58
Funds, availability of, 436
Fungible goods, 707, 709
Future goods, 317
Future interest, 668, 671

Garnishment, 466, 797, 802–803
GDTA license, 823
General Agreement on Tariffs and Trade (GATT), 825, 826–827
Generally Accepted Accounting Principles (GAAP), 648, 649
Generally Accepted Accounting Standards (GAAS), 648, 649
General partners, 551, 557
  rights and duties of, 554
General trial courts, 16, 18
Generic term, 130
Geographical restraints, as restrictive covenants, 219
  case, 219–220

Geographic market, 757
Getty Oil Company, 129, 145–146
Gifts
  *causa mortis,* 704
  and estate planning, 731–732
  *inter vivos,* 704
  invalidating, 703
  case, 703
  of personal property, 701–704
  case, 703
Good, and morality, 149–150
Good faith, 181, 398–399
  case, 399–400
  and defamation, 118
  duty of, 313
Good faith limitation, 356
  case, 356–357
Goods, 445–446
  acceptance of, 358–359
  confusion of, 707
  leases of, 311
  movable, 307–308
  sale of, 307–311
  tangible, 307
  title to, 317–322
Goodwill, 517–518
  and partnership, 546
Government corporations, 566
Government regulation, 753–776. *See also* Antitrust law
Gramm-Rudman Act, 59
Grand jury, 92
Great Depression, 627
Greenmail, case, 619
Group dynamics, 156–157
GTDR license, 823
Guarantee, 333
Guaranty promise, 256
Guilty act, 94
Guilty mind, 94–95

Habitability, 681–682
  implied warranty of, 681–682
  case, 691–692
Hague Convention on the Service Abroad of Judicial and Extrajudicial Documents in Civil or Commercial Matters, 820–821
Harassment, 785–786
Harm, 148
Harm-benefit test, and minors, 229
Harrison, George, 137
Health insurance, 740–741
Health maintenance organization (HMO), 740–741
Hearsay, 31
Hobbs Act, 100
Holder, 375, 383
  ordinary, 375
Holder in due course, 374, 397–403
  and defense, case, 401–402
  holder through, 402
  limitations on, 408–409
  payee as, 402–403
  requirements of, 398–401
Holding (investment) company, 615
Holmes, Oliver Wendell, 65
Holographic wills, 725
Home Equity Loan Consumer Protection Act (HECPA) (1988), 802
Homeowner's insurance, 742
  liability coverage of, 743–744
Home shopping/banking, 438
Home solicitation sales, 808–809

## SUBJECT INDEX

Home solicitation statutes, 246–247
Honesty, 147
Horizontal merger, 611n, 759–760
   case, 762–763
Horizontal restraints of trade, 763–768
Hostile environment harassment, 786
Hostile tender offer, 616
Hourly fees, 11–12

Illegality
   of contracts, 215–227
   as defenses, 404, 407
      case, 407
Illusory contract, 205
Immunity, from prosecution, 96
Implied agreement, 179
Implied authority, 497–498
   in partnership, 530–532, 533
      case, 534–535
Implied condition subsequent, 280
Implied contracts, 167–168
   case, 168–169
Impliedly promised, 212
Implied powers, of corporations, 579
Implied ratification, 499–500
Implied trusts, 731
Implied warranties, 335–337
   and bailor, 714
   case, 337–338
   disclaimers of, 339–340
   of fitness, 337
      case, 337–338
   of habitability, 690–691
      case, 691–692
   of merchantability, 335–336
Import-Export Clause, 825
Import licenses, 815
Imports, regulating, 825–826
Imprisonment, 7
Incapacity defense, 405
Incidental authority, 498
Incidental beneficiary, 264
Income replacement insurance, 740
Income taxes, and corporations, 567
Incompetency proceedings, 235
Incorporation, 573–574
Indemnification, of corporate directors, 600
Indemnification clause, 694–695
Independent intervening cause, 112
Individual rights, 69
Indorsee, 375
Indorsements, 375
   blank, 386–387, 388
   conditional, 389
   forged, 433
   and negotiable instruments, 386–390
   qualified, 387–388
   rescission of, 392
   restrictive, 388–390
   special, 387, 388
   and unindorsed order paper, 391
      case, 391–392
Indorsers, 374–375
   accommodation, 422
   promissory liability of, 417–419
   warranty liability of, 420–421
      case, 421–422
Infancy, and criminal defense, 95
Informal agreement, written confirmation of, 189
Informal contracts, 171
Injunction, 7, 24, 132, 299–300
Injuries, liability for, 693–695
Injurious falsehood, 118

Injury, 113
Injury (damage), and fraud, 241
Innkeepers, and personal property, 716–717
Innocent misrepresentation, and voidable contracts, 242
*In pari delicto*, 224
Insane in fact,
Insanity
   and contracts, 235–236
   and criminal defense, 95
   and partnership dissolution, 541
Inside information, 605
Insiders, and bankruptcy, 472
Insider trading, regulation of, 635–637
   case, 639
Insolvency, 299, 365, 472, 593
Inspection of goods, 359
Installment contract, 357
Installment note, 372
Instructions, to jury, 32
Instruments, negotiable, 446. *See also* Negotiable instruments
   securities, 446
Insurable interest, 736–738
   case, 737
Insurance
   automobile, 744–747
   contract, 735–739
   health, 740–741
   liability, 743–744
      case, 743–744
   life, 732, 739–740
   property, 741–743
   social, 741
   title, 674–675
Insurance contracts, 216
Insurance law, 735–749
Intangible collateral, 446–447
Intangible personal property, 702–703
Intent, 175n, 176–179
Intention of parties, 175–176, 287–288
Inter-American Convention on Extra-territorial Validity of Foreign Judgments and Arbitral Awards, 822
Inter-American Convention on International Commercial Arbitration Commission, 822
Interests in real property, 667–671
Interests in land, 252–253
Interference, with business conduct, 127–129
Interlocking directorates, 754
Internal Revenue Code, and accountants, 652–653
International business, legal environment of, 813–833
International Centre for Settlement of Investment Disputes (ICSID), 822
International Chamber of Commerce, 816n, 822
International Commercial Terms (Incoterms), 816n
International Emergency Economic Power Act, 824
International Labour Organization (ILO), 830n
International Monetary Fund (IMF), 827–828
International sales contract, 814–817
International trade
   classifying, 814
   conducting transactions, 829
   organizations for, 825–826
International trade disputes, 817–822
Interpretation
   of contracts, 287–291

   rules of, 289–290
      case, 290
   statutory, 48–51
Interrogatories, 29
Interstate commerce, 100
   federal and state regulation of, 56–58
Interstate Commerce Commission, 222n
Intervening cause, 112
   case, 113
*Inter vivos* gifts, 732
*Inter vivos* trust, 728
Intestacy, 725–726
Intestate, 721
Intoxication, 95–96
   and contracts, 229, 236
Intrabrand and interbrand competition, 768, 770
Intrusion, 121
Invasion of privacy, 121–122
Inventories, 445
   purchase money security interests in, 457–458
      case, 458
Inverse condemnation, 681
Investigative powers, of federal agencies, 77–79
Investment Advisers Act (1940), 628
Investment Company Act (1940), 628
Investors
   accredited, 633
   and corporations, 565
   in securities, 629–630
Involuntary dissolution, of corporation, 622–623
   case, 623
Involuntary lien, 670
Issue, 385n
Issuer, of securities, 630

Jackson, Robert, 75
Joint accounts, 703–704
Joint tenancy, 671
Joint venture, 571, 767–768
Judges, 36
   in common law system, 42–43
Judgment
   enforcement of, 35
   lien, 671
Judicial branch, of U.S. government, 60
Judicial interpretation, 287
Judicial review, 60
Jurisdiction, 18–23
   original, 32n
Jury
   and equitable action, 25
   impaneling, 30
   role of, 36
Jury trial
   case, 29–30
   summary, 38
Justice, 9
Justification, defense of, 127–129

Kant, Immanuel, 146
Kohlberg, Lawrence, 146–147

Labeling, 810
Labor, and personal property, 707
Labor policy, and adjudication process, 82
Labor relations law, 777–796
Lack (want) of consideration, 404
Ladd, John, 156
Land, 665
   descriptions of, 676–677

# 1038 SUBJECT INDEX

Landlord, 668
  and crimes, 695
    case, 695–696
  lease termination by, 696–697
  liability for injuries, 693–695
    case, 693–694
  premise maintenance by, 689–692
Landlord's lien, 697
Landlord-tenant relationship, 685–687
Landowners, duty of, 110
  case, 110
Lanham Act, 129, 130, 132, 139–140, 800
  case, 140
Larceny, 96–97
Latent defect, 356, 792
  and fraud, 240
Later agreement, 181
Law
  classifications of, 6–8
  common, 41–44, 47–48
  and computer crime, 101–102
  conflict of, 22–23
  contract, 107, 165–173
  courts of, 23–24, 25
  criminal, 107
  and ethics, 144–146. *See also* Ethics
  and justice, 9
  misconceptions about, 8
  and morals, 9–10
    case, 10
  nature of, 3–14
  question of, 32–33, 80
  sales, 171–172
  statutory, 45–52
  study of, 3
Lawmaking, by administrative agencies, 75–87
Law merchant, 369
Law of sales, 307–315
  and warranties, 237n
Law statements, and fraud, 239
Lawyers. *See* Attorneys
Lease, 685–687
  cancellation of, 692
  of goods, 311
  of land, 253
  landlord termination of, 696–697
  oil and gas, 688n
  warranties in, 338
Leasehold estates, 668–669
Legacy, 721
Legal detriment, 199–200
Legal entity, 504
  corporation as, 155
Legal impossibility, and discharge of contracts, 278–280
  case, 280–281
Legality of purpose, 215
Legal system, requisites of, 4–6
Legal tender, 360
Legal title, 521
Legislation, consumer, 348–351. *See also* Federal legislation
Legislative acts, 47–48
Legislative bodies, limits on, 46–47
Legislative branch, of U.S. government, 59–60
Legislative history, 49–50
Legislative intent, 50
Legislatures, and statutory law, 45–47, 48
Lemon laws, 366
Lessee, 669
Lessor, 668
Letter of credit, 360, 814–816
  case, 815

Letters of Request, 821
Leveraging, 772
*Lex mercatoria,* 821
Liabilities
  of corporate managers, 600–601
  and partnership dissolution, 544
  and securities regulation, 633–635
  of shareholders, 598–599
Liability. *See also* Promissory liability
  of acceptor, 415–416
  of accountants, 647–661
  on admissions, 415
  of agent, 503
  business insurance coverage, 744
  and commercial paper, 413–425
  and common carriers, 715–716
  contractual, of accountants, 647–650
  contractual, of minors, 230–234
    case, 231–232
  of corporations, 567
  criminal, of accountants, 657–659
  and electronic banking, 439–440
  employers', 123
  federal products legislation, 350
  under federal securities laws, 605–607
  for illegal dividends, 598–599
  of indorsers, 417–419
  for injuries, 693–695
  joint and several, 123
  of limited partners, 554–557
  of minors, 230–234
  negligence, 648–649
    case, 693–694
  in partnership, 530–532, 535–536
  of primary parties, 413–414
  of principal, 497–503
  products, 342
  strict, 95, 344–348
  and third parties, 503, 651
    case, 651–652
  tort, 505–510
  of transferor, 422–423
  warranty, 420–421
    case, 421–422
Liability insurance, 743–744
  case, 743–744
  malpractice, 744
Libel, 116
License, 518n, 670, 708
  export, 823
  and foreign trade, 829
Licensing statutes, 216–217
  case, 217
Lie detector testing, 793
Liens, 670–671
  artisan's, 466
  floating, 455–456
  mechanic's, 466
Life estate, 668
Life insurance, 732, 739–740
  contracts, beneficiary of, 264
Limited partners, 551, 557
  rights and duties of, 554
    case, 556
Limited partnership, 551–561. *See also* General partners; Limited partners
  assignment of interest in, 557
  dissolution of, 556–557
    case, 558–559
  financing, 554
  formation of, 552–553
Line of business test, 603
Liquidated damages, 298–299
  case, 298
Liquidated debts, 208

Liquidating (winding up) partner, 543
Liquidation, 468–477
  of corporation, 622
  of preferred stock, 594
  proceedings, 468–477
Listings, real estate, 673–674
Litigation
  appellate courts, 32–35
  flow chart of, 33
  international, 820–821
  pretrial proceedings, 27–30
  trial proceedings, 30–32
Litigation committee, 607
Loans, 218
  nonassumable, 201n
Lobbying contracts, 224
Lock-up options, 642
London Court of Arbitration, 822
Long-arm statutes, 20
  case, 21
Loss
  in partnership, 527
  risk of, 322–327
    case, 324
Lost Goods Act, case, 706
Lost property, 704–705
Lotteries, 215–216
  case, 216
Louisiana
  common law and, 41
  and UCC, 369
Loyalty, 147–148
  of agent, 491
    case, 492
  of corporate managers, 602–603
    case, 603–604
  and takeovers, 616–617
L.S., 171n

Magnuson-Moss Warranty Act (1975), 349–350, 356n, 924
  and insolvency, 365
Mailbox rule, and acceptance, 193
Mail fraud, 99
  case, 99–100
Majority rule, and minors, 232–233
Malpractice liability insurance coverage, 744
*Malum in se* acts, 90
*Malum prohibitum* acts, 90
Management, limited partnership limitations on, 555
Management advisory services, of accountants, 652
Manager's privilege, 129
Mandatory authority, 43
  case, 43
Manifested (apparent) intentions, 175
Marital deduction, and estate planning, 732
Marital property, 672–673
Market
  concentration, 759
  division, 766
  geographic, 757
  power, 755–756
  product, 756–757
  share, 755–756
  and mergers, 759–760
Marriage, promises and, 256
Marshall, John, 156, 813
*Martindale-Hubbell Law Directory,* 11
Material alteration defense, 421
Materiality, 632
  case, 632
Maturity date, of negotiable instrument, 384
Mechanic's lien, 466, 670–671

## SUBJECT INDEX

Mediation, 37–38
Medical expense insurance, 740
Meeting of minds, 175
*Mens rea,* 94–95
Mental distress, intentional infliction of, 122
Mental infirmity, and contracts, 229, 235–236
Merchantability, 335–336
   disclaimers of warranty of, 340
Merchants
   entrustment to, 320–321
      cases, 320
   farmers as, case, 310
   sales and, 309–310
Merchant's form, 258n
Mergers, 595, 611–621, 759–762
   and appraisal rights, 613–614
   effects of, 613
   guidelines for, 762
      case, 762–763
   steps in, 614
   with subsidiary, 613
Merit System Protection Board, 81
Metes and bounds, 677
Military Critical Technologies List, 823
Mill, John Stuart, 146
Mineral rights, 665
Minimum wage, 790
Ministerial powers, 77
Mini-trial, 38
Minority. *See also* Minors
   and contracts, 229–235
   as defense, 408
   definition of, 230
   and disaffirming contracts, 234–235
   and liability, 230–232, 233–234
      case, 231–232
Minors. *See also* Minority
   and insurance contracts, 738–739
   and tort liability, 510
Miranda warning, 93
Misappropriations, and insider trading, 636–637
   case, 637
Misconduct, and partnership dissolution, 541
Misdemeanor, 7, 90
Mislaid property, 705
Misrepresentation
   innocent, 242
   of a material fact, 237–240
Mistakes
   bilateral, 243
      case, 243–244
   as criminal defense, 96
   unilateral, 244
   and voidable contracts, 242–245
Mitigation of damages doctrine, 295–296
   case, 296
M'Naghten test, 95
Model Act, 566, 596–597
   and idemnification of directors, 600
Model Business Corporation Act (MBCA) (Model Act), 52, 566
Model Penal Code, 95
Modification contract, 202, 204–205, 258
Money
   commercial paper as, 370–371
   negotiable instruments and, 380–381
      case, 381–382
Monopoly, 755–759
   case, 758
Moral agent, corporation as, 155–156
Morality, 9–11, 143–144. *See also* Ethics
   case, 10
   corporations and, 155–157
   and decision making, 151–155
   dilemmas of, 150–151
   and information, 152–153
   and obligations, 152
   standards of, 144–149
Moral minimum, 146–149
Moral obligation, consideration and, 209
Moral turpitude, 90
Mortgage, 252–253, 674, 809n
   assumption of, 263
   creditor beneficiary and, 263
Most favored nation status, 826
Motion to dismiss, 28
Motor vehicles, 450–451
   perfection and, 453
Multinational enterprise, 830n
Multiple listing service (MLS), 674
Mutual benefit bailments, 710
Mutual rescission exception, and contracts, 204

Name
   of limited partnership, 552–553
   and negotiable instruments, 391
   of partnership firm, 515
National Conference of Commissioners on Uniform State Laws, 322, 369n, 513n
   and Uniform Consumer Credit Code, 808
National Highway Traffic Safety Administration (NHTSA), 81
National Labor Relations Act (NLRA), 777
   and collective bargaining, 779
   coverage of, 778
   and nonunion employees, 779–780
   and right to organize, 778
   and strikes, 779
National Labor Relations Board (NLRB), 778
National Traffic and Motor Vehicle Safety Act (1966), 81
Necessaries, minors and, 232–233
Negligence, 43, 95, 108–114
   of accountant, 648–649, 650, 651–652
      case, 650, 651–652
   and bailee, 711–712
   and bailor, 714
   comparative, 114
   contributory, 114
   and forged signatures, 434
   and injuries, 695
   and mistakes, 244
   *per se,* 111
   and personal liability insurance, 743
   and products liability insurance, 743
   and products liability, 343–344
   and strict liability, 344
      case, 346
Negotiability, words of, 385
Negotiable bill of lading, 361
Negotiable document of title, 313
Negotiable instruments, 265n, 373–374, 377–385
   case, 379–380, 381–382
   demand instruments, 382
   defenses and, 403–409
   and holder in due course, 397–403
   time instruments, 382–383
      case, 381–382
   transfer of, 385
Negotiated contracts, 170–171
Negotiation
   of negotiable instrument, 385–386
   preliminary, 176
      case, 177
Net earnings, 593–594
New International Economic Order (NIEO), 831
Net York Standard Fire Policy, 741
New York Stock Exchange, 627
Nixon, Richard, 157
No-fault auto insurance, 747
No fault systems, 114
NOM (no oral modification) clauses, 205
Nominal damages, 296–297
Noncupative wills, 725
Non-delegable duties, 267n
Nondelivery defense, 404
   case, 405
Nonfreehold estates, 667, 668–669
Nonnegotiable documents of title, 313–314
Nonnegotiable instruments, 373–374
Nonprice predation, 758
   case, 758
Nonprofit corporation, 566
Nontrading partnership, 531
Nontransferability, of partnership property, 526
   case, 526
Nonunion employees, 779–780
No-par value stock, 598
Norris-La Guardia Act, 777
Notes, 369, 372, 373
Notify, duty to, 491
Novation, 268, 283
Nuclear Non-Proliferation Act (1978), 824
Nuisance, 123

Obedience, 490, 600
Obligations
   buyer's, 359–360
   contractual, 202
   and delegation of duties, 267–269
   mutuality of, 205–207
   of partnership, 532
      case, 532–533
   preexisting, 202, 203–204
      case, 202–203
   seller's, 353–358
Obligee, 267
Obligor, 384
O'Connor, Sandra Day, 47
Occupation, and unowned property, 704
Occupational Safety and Health Act (1968), 777, 789–790
Occupational Safety and Health Administration (OSHA), 789–790
Offer and acceptance, of insurance, 735
Offeree, 166n, 176
Offeror, 166n, 176
Offers
   communication of, 182–183
      case, 183
   and contracts, 176–179
   firm, 184–185
   to purchase, 176
   to sell, 176
   shipment, 195
   termination of, 184–186
   unilateral, 194–195
Office of Export Administration (OEA), 823
Office of Management and Budget (OMB), 59
Oil and gas lease, 688n
Oligopolies, 753
Omnibus Trade and Competitiveness Act, 813n
Open delivery provisions, of contracts, 181–182
Open-end (revolving) credit, 801
Open market purchases, 615
Open payment provisions, of contracts, 182
Open price provisions, of contracts, 180–181

## SUBJECT INDEX

Open time provisions, of contracts, 181
Operation of law
  agency termination by, 494–495
  discharge of contract by, 283–284
Opinion, 31–32
Opinion shopping, 649–650
Option contract, 184
Options, 596
Option to purchase, 709
Oral contracts, 170, 251
  performance of, 254–255
Order instruments, 384
Ordinary contracts, 230
  minors' liability on, 230–232
Organization for Economic Cooperation and Development (OECD), 830
Organization of American States, 822
Organized crime, 100
Ostensible authority, 498
Out-of-court settlement, 37
Output contracts, 207
Over-the-counter (OTC) market, 596
Owner-consent statutes, 510
Ownership, 663
  concurrent, 671–673
  intent to transfer, 702–703
  of partnership property, 520–522
    case, 522
  in place, 665
  of wild game, 704

Packaging, 810
Pac-Man counter tender offers, 642
Parent corporation, 568
Parol evidence rule, 259–260, 335
Participating preferred stock, 594
Partnership, 513–549
  aggregate theory of, 514
  agreement for, 514–515, 525
    case, 516
  articles of, 515
  business continuation after dissolution, 545–547
    case, 547–548
  business operation of, 525–529
  and compensation, 527
  determining existence of, 516–518
    case, 518–520
  dissolution and authority, 543–544
  employees of, 532
  entity theory of, 514
  fiduciary duties in, 527–528
    case, 529–530
  interest in, 526, 527, 535
    case, 526
  liabilities and, 536, 544
  limited, 551–561
  management rights in, 525
    case, 526, 529–530
  property of, 514, 520–522, 531–532
    case, 522
  restrictions on business, 534
    case, 534–535
  termination of, 539–549
  and third parties, 530–536
  trading and nontrading, 531
  UPA-dissallowed actions, 533–535
    case, 534–535
  winding up affairs of, 544–547
Partnership at will, 539
Partition, 672
Par value stock, 598
Patent infringement, 134–135
  case, 136
Patent law, 132

Patent Misuse Reform, of Patent and Trademark Office Authorization Act, 135
Patent pending, 135
Payable out of fund instruments, 379
Payable to order or bearer, 384–385
Payee, 370
  fictitious, 392–393
  and negotiable instruments, 391
Payment defense, 405
Payment for goods, 360
Pennzoil, 129, 145–146, 618n
Per capita distribution, 726, 727
Peremptory challenges, 30
Perfection, 445, 448–456
  filing and, 452
  of fixtures, 450–451
  and floating lien, 455–456
  limitations on, 453–455
  of motor vehicles, 450–451
Perfect tender rule, 354–355
  exceptions to, 357–358
    case, 358–359
  limitations of, 355–356
    case, 356–357
Performance, and sales interpretation, 313
Performance of contracts
  by agreed time, 277–278
  discharge of contracts by, 274–278
    case, 275–276
  frustration of, 282
    case, 282–283
  legal impossibility and, 278–280
  and personal satisfaction contracts, 276–277
Periodic tenancy, 686
Perjured testimony, 251
Permanent Court of Arbitration, 821
Per se rule, 765–767
Person
  jurisdiction of, 19–22
  UPA definition of, 513
Personal liability insurance, 743
  case, 743–744
Personal (limited) defenses, 403–405
Personal property, 252, 445, 666. See also Real property
  accession and, 706–707
  bailments of, 708–717
  conversion and trespass to, 122
  and innkeepers, 716–717
  ownership of, 701
Personal service contracts, 299
Personal services
  and delegable duties, 268–269
  performance of, 279
Per stirpes distribution, 726
Persuasive authority, 44
  case, 44
Petty offenses, 90
Picasso, Pablo, estate of, 721
Piercing the corporate veil, 568
  case, 569–570
Plain meaning rule, 49, 288
Plaintiff, 7, 27, 89
Plaintiff misconduct defense, 342
Plat (map), 677
Pleading stage, 27–28
Point of sale transfers, 438
Poison pill, 617, 642
Poison Prevention Packaging Act (1970), 810
Police power, of state governments, 56
Policy (insurance), 735
Possession
  delivery of, 702–703, 708–709
  of leased property, 687
  by perfection, 449–450

Possessory interests, 667
Power of attorney, 488
  case, 488–489
Powers, of federal agencies, 76–82
Precatory language, 728
Precedent, 42, 43–44
Predatory conduct, 757
Predatory pricing, 757–758
Preemptive rights, 595
Preexisting obligation, 202
  case, 202–203
  exceptions to rule, 203–204
Preferences, voidable, 472–473
  case, 473–474
Preferred stock, 594
Preliminary negotiations, 176
  advertisements as, 178
  case, 177
Premium, 735
Prescriptive easement, 670
Presentment, 416–419
  case, 419–420
Pretrial litigation proceedings, 27–30
Price discrimination, 773–774
Price fixing, 766
*Prima facie* case, 781–782, 783
Primary parties
  to commercial paper, 413
  liability of, 414–416
Principal (person), 487, 490–491, 493
  death of, 499n
  liability of, 497–503
  nondisclosure of, 503
  nonexistent, 504
  partially disclosed, 504
  undisclosed, 504–505
Principal Register, 129–130
Prior payment defense, 405
Privacy
  invasion of, 121–122
  and search and seizure, 78
Privacy Act (1974), 85
Private corporation, 566
Private law, 8
Privilege, of accountants, 658–659
  case, 659
Privileges and Immunities Clause, 62
  case, 63
Privity, 638
  defense, 341–342
Probate, 726–727
Procedural due process, 69–70, 82
  case, 83
Procedural unconscionability, 223
Product market, 756–757
Product misuse, 342
Product liability, 714. See also Warranties
  legislative limitations on, 350
  insurance, 744
  and negligence, 343–344
  strict liability, 344–348
Professional corporation, 567
*Profit à prendre,* 670
Profits, 670
  in partnership, 517–518, 527
  short-swing, 605–606
Prohibition Amendment, 6
Promises, 211–212
  as contracts, 256
Promissory estoppel, 209–211
  case, 210
  and land sale, 253
  case, 255
  and oral contracts, 253
Promissory liability
  of drawers, 416–417

## SUBJECT INDEX 1041

of indorsers, 417–419
of secondary parties, 416
Promissory note, 372, 373, 415, 418
Promoter, and corporate creation, 570–571
  case, 571, 572
Property. *See also* Landlord-tenant relationship
  abandoned, lost, and mislaid, 704–706
    case, 706
  after-acquired, 455
  insurance interest in, 737–738
    case, 738
  and land sale contracts, 252–253
  of partnership, 521
    case, 522
  partnership ownership of, 518
    cases, 518–520
  and partnership rights, 525–526
    case, 526
  personal, 445
  real, 445, 665–683
  sale of leased, 687
  unencumbered, 443
  unowned, 704
Property insurance, 741–743
Pro rata insurance coverage, 743
Prospectus, 629
Proximate cause, and negligence, 111–112
Proxy, 639–640
  contests, 616
Public Health Cigarette Smoking Act (1969), 810
Public law, 7–8
Publicly held corporation, 566, 595
Public policy, contracts contrary to, 218–224
Public Utility Holding Company Act (1935), 628
Punishment, for criminal acts, 91
Punitive damages, 297
Purchase money security interests, 450, 457–458
  case, 458

Qualified indorsements, 387–388
*Quantum meruit* action, 168
Quasi-contracts, 167–168, 195
  case, 168–169
Question of law, 80
Quid pro quo harassment, 786
Quitclaim deed, 676
Quorum
  and corporate board of directors, 585
  at shareholders' meeting, 581

Racketeer Influenced and Corrupt Organizations Act (RICO) (1970), 58, 100, 644
  and accountants, 657
  case, 50–51
Railway Labor Act, 777
Ratification, 406
  and minors, 232
  of unauthorized transactions, 499–500
    case, 502
*Ratio decidendi*, 42
Reaffirmation, 477
Real defenses, 405–408
Real estate, 663
  goods attached to, 308
  and injuries, 693–695
  and partnerships, 520–521
  as real property, 665–683
  sales of, 673–679
  and unilateral contracts, 166
    case, 166–167
Real estate mortgage note, 372

Real Estate Settlement Procedures Act (RESPA), 809–810
Real property, 252, 445, 663, 665–671. *See also* Personal property
  interest in, 667–671
  marital, 672–673
  sales of, 673–679
Reasonable definiteness
  of offer, 179–180
    case, 179–180
  in sales law, 180–182
Reasonable estimate of loss, 297
Reasonable expectation test, 336
  case, 336
Reasonable medium rule of acceptance, 193–194
  case, 194
Reasonable person standard, 111
Receiver, 544
Receivership, 467
Record keeping, in partnership, 528–529
  case, 529–530
Reformation order, 300
Reforms, statutory, 123–124
Registration
  of limited partnerships, 553
    case, 553
  of securities, 576, 743
  of trademark, 129–130
Regulation
  of export/import process, 823–826
  of insurance, by state, 740
Regulation A, 633
Regulation CC, 435–437
Regulation D, 633
Regulation Z, 800
Regulatory agencies, 76
Regulatory Flexibility Act (1980), 85
Regulatory statutes, 216–217
  case, 217
Rehabilitation Act (1973), 788–789
Rejection, of offer, 184–185
Reliance, 638
  case, 639
  and fraud, 241
Reliance test, 555
Religion, freedom of, 63–64
Remainder, 671
Remedies, 23–24, 25
  for breached contract, 360–366
Rent
  tenant responsibility for, 696
  withholding, 692
Rent-a-judge programs, 38
Repair and deduct, 692
*Replevin*, 363
Reply, 27
Requirements contracts, 206
Resale, 361
Resale price maintenance (RPM), 768–769
Rescission, 242, 244
  and breach of contract, 300
  of contract, 283
Reserved powers, 55
*Res ipsa loquitur* doctrine, 344
*Respondeat superior* doctrine, 102
Restatement of the Foreign Relations Law of the United States (Revised), 817
Restatement (Second) of Torts, 345
Restitution, and breach of contract, 300–301
Restraints of trade
  horizontal, 763–768
  vertical, 768–774
Restrictive covenants, 218–219, 681
  case, 219–220

Restrictive indorsements, 388–390
  case, 388–389, 390–391
Resulting trust, 731
Return sales, 327–329
Revenue-raising statutes, 217
Reversion, 671
Review, in accounting, 649
Revised American Foreign Trade Definitions (RAFTD) (1941), 816n
Revised Model Business Corporation Act (Revised Model Act) (RMBCA), 52, 566
Revised Uniform Limited Partnership Act (RULPA) (1977), 52, 551–552
  dissolution and, 557–558
  safe harbor provisions of, 555–556
    case, 556
Revised Uniform Securities Act, 643
Revocation
  of acceptance, 357
  of offer, 184
  timing of, 195
Revolving credit accounts, 218
RICO, 644
Rights
  of corporations, 567
    case, 567–568
  to counsel, 94
  individual, 69, 70
  to inspect goods, 182n
  in partnership property, 525–526
  of removal, 19
  of survivorship, 672
  of third parties, 263–270
  third party assignment of, 264–267
    case, 266
  of U.S. citizens, 61–71
Right to Financial Privacy Act, 102
Risk
  assumption of, 342
  pooling of, and social insurance, 741
Risk-creating contracts, 216
Risk of loss, 322–326
  breach of contract and, 324–326
    case, 326–327
  and documents of title, 323
Risk-shifting contracts, 216
Robbery, 98
Robinson-Patman Act (1936), 755
  violation of, 773–774
Rotary D-Rooting, 131
Roto-Rooter, 131
Rule 147, of Securities Act, 633
Rules 505, 506, 508, of Securities Act, 633
Rulemaking powers, 77
  of federal agencies, 79–80
Rule of reason, 764–765
  case, 765
Rules of evidence, 31

Safe harbor provisions, of RULPA, 555–556
  case, 556
Sale on consignment, 329
Sales, 307. *See also* Federal consumer legislation; Sales contracts; Sales law
  on approval, 327–329
  basic contract principles, 311–313
  breached contract remedies, 362–366
    case, 362, 364, 365
  law of, 307–315
  and product liability, 344–348
  and returns, 327–329
  and title to goods, 317–322
  and warranties, 333–343
Sales contracts
  enforcing, 312–313

## 1042  SUBJECT INDEX

Sales contracts (continued)
  formation of, 312
  international, 814–817
  interpretation of, 313
  performance of, 353–360
Sales draft, 371
Sales law, 166n, 259
  contract law and, 171–172
  contracts and, 188–191
    case, 190–191
  firm offer in, 184–185
  modification contracts, 204–205
  reasonable definiteness problem in, 180–182
  unconscionability and, 222–223
School prayer, 63
Scienter, 241
Scope of employment, 507–510
  case, 508, 509
S corporations, 567
Seal (word), 171
Sealed contract, 199
Search and seizure, 78, 92
  case, 78–79
Secondary meaning concept, and trademark, 130–131
Secondary parties
  to commercial paper, 413
  liability of, 416
Secrecy. See Trade secrets
Secured creditors, 469, 475
Secured party, 444
Secured transactions, 443–464, 465–466
Securities, 446, 813n
  accountants and, 653–657
  registration of, 575–576
  regulation of, 627–646
  state regulation of, 643–644
  types of, 575, 628–629
    case, 629
Securities Act (1933), 576, 604, 627–628, 629–635
  and accountants, 654–655
  disclosure requirements, 631
    case, 632
  enforcement, 633–635
  registration exemptions, 633
Securities Enforcement Remedies and Penny Stock Act (1990), 634
Securities and Exchange Commission (SEC), 576, 604, 628
  and auditors, 653
  Regulation D, 633
Securities Exchange Act (1934), 604, 605, 628, 635–642, 644
  and accountants, 655–656, 657, 658
    case, 655–656
  and corporate disclosures, 638
  and insider trading,
    case, 635–637
  proxy regulation, 639–640
  and tender offers, 640–642
    case, 643
Securities Investor Protection Act (1970), 628
Securities Investor Protection Corporation (SIPC), 628
Securities laws
  liability under, 604–606
  and limited partnership, 554
Security deposit, 696
Security interest, 444
  attachment of, 447–448
    case, 448
  money, 457–458
    case, 458

  perfected and unperfected, 448–453, 456–457
Self-defense, 96
  and battery, 116
Self-incrimination, 93, 567
Self-tender, 618–619
  case, 618–619
Seller's obligations, 353–358
Seller's remedies, 360–361
Seniority system, and employment, 785
Separate property, 673
Servan-Schreiber, Jean-Jacques, 830
Service contract, 349n
Services, sale of, 309
  case, 309
Servient estate, 669
Settlement agreement, 207
Settlements. See Dispute resolution
Settlor (trustor), 728
Severable contracts, 224–225
Sexual harassment, 785–786
Shareholder derivative suit, 606
Shareholders, 567, 575, 580–582
  controlling, 604
  liabilities of, 598–599
  minority, 622
  rights of, 593–597
  and tender offers, 619
  voting rights of, 582
    case, 583–584
Shares, 575
  and mergers, 595
  transferability of, 595–596
Shark repellants, 617
  case, 618–619
Shelf registration, 631
Shelter provision, 402n
Sherman Act (1890), 75, 218
  and joint ventures, 767
  and RPM, 768
Shipment contract, 318, 322–323, 354, 357
Shipment offers, 195
Shop right doctrine, 135
Short-swing profits, 605–606
Signatures
  check payment and, 429
  and commercial paper, 413–414
    case, 414
  forged, 433–435
  and indorser liability, 420–421
    case, 421–422
Silence
  as contract acceptance, 192–193
  and fraud, 239–240
Silent partner, case, 553
Single European Act (1987), 828
Sixth Amendment, 94
Slander, 116
Social benefit or good, 146
Social insurance, 741
Social legislation, 67
Social responsiveness, of corporations, 158–160
Social Security, 741
Society, agents of, 159–160
Sole benefit bailments, 710
Sovereign compulsion, 820
Special Drawing Rights (SDRs), 828
Special indorsement, 375
Specific performance, and breach of contract, 298–299
Speech, commercial, 65–66
Spendthrift trust, 730
Spouse, surviving, 725–726
Stale checks, 429

Standards, legal and moral, 144–145
Stare decisis doctrine, 43–44
State crimes, and business, 96–98
Statement of fact, and fraud, 237
States, 6
  and bankruptcy, 471
  and commercial paper, 369
  and computer crimes, 102
  conflict of laws between, 22–23
  corporate business in, 575
  and corporations, 566
  court systems of, 15–16, 17–18
  and deceptive trade practices, 139
  governments, authority and powers of, 55–71. See also United States Constitution
  and holder in due course, 408
  jurisdictions, 19
  life insurance regulation by, 740
  limited partnership registration in, 553
    case, 553
  securities regulation by, 643–644
  selected statutes of, 52
  and tort liability, 510
  workers' compensation laws in, 741
Statute of frauds, 170, 251–252
Statute of limitations, 114, 211–212
  and breach of contract, 342–343
  running of, 283–284
Statutes, 7, 45
  consumer protection, 798
  licensing, 216–217
  long-arm, 20
  of repose, 350
  selected state, 52
  Sunday, 218
Statutory law, 7, 45–53
  and common law, 47–48
  interpretation of, 48–51
Statutory powers, of corporations, 579
Statutory reforms, and torts, 123–124
Stock, 594, 628
  acquisitions, 615–616
  certificate, 596
  dividend, 593–594
  employee ownership plans, 619–620
    case, 620
  of partnership, 533
  subscriptions, 598
  watered, 598
Stockholders, 575
Stop payment, 393, 431–432
  case, 432–433
Strict liability, 344–352
  case, 346, 348
Strikes, 779
Subcontracts, 268
Subject matter destruction, and contract performance, 280
  case, 280–281
Subject matter jurisdiction, 18–19
Sublease, 697–698
Subpoena, 77
  case, 77–78
Subrogation, 746–747
Subsidiary corporation, 568–569
Substantial evidence test, of agency rulemaking, 80
  case, 81
Substantial performance doctrine, 8, 274–276
  case, 275–276
Substantive unconscionability, 223
  case, 223
Subsurface rights, 665

# SUBJECT INDEX  1043

Sum certain, 380–381
Summary judgment, 29
Summary jury trial (SJT), 38
Summons, 20, 27
Sunday statutes, 218
Sunshine Act, 85
Superior courts, 16
Superior knowledge, and fraud, 240
   case, 241
Super 301, 826
Supplemental Register, 130n
Supremacy clause, 57
Supreme court, state, 16, 17, 18
Supreme court of the U.S., 16, 17, 18
Surrender and acceptance, 687
Survivors' benefits, 741

Takeovers, 616–620
Tariff Act (1930), 825–826
Tariff Schedules of the U.S. (TSUS), 825
Taxation
   of corporations, 567
   of limited partnerships, 551–552
      case, 553
   and mergers, 612
Taxes, and estate planning, 731–732
Tax practice, of accountants, 652–653
Tax Reform Act (1976), 652
Tenancy
   in common, 671–672
   by the entireties, 672
   at sufferance, 686
   types of, 686
   at will, 686
   for years, 686
Tenant, 669
   financial obligations of, 696–697
   landlord relationship with, 685–700
   liability for injuries, 693
   premise maintenance and, 689–692
   property use by, 688–689
      case, 688–689
   and right to transfer, 698
Tenants in partnership, 520
Tender, 324
   of delivery, 353
Tender offer, 273, 615–616, 640–641
   case, 643
   and shareholders, 619–620
   state regulation of, 644
10-Ks, 631
10-Qs, 631
Termination of offer, 184–186
   by operation of law, 185–186
Term insurance, 740
Territorial and custom restrictions, 770
Testamentary capacity, 721–722
   case, 722
Testamentary trust, 728
Testate/testator/testatrix, 721
Testimony, 32
Texaco, 129, 145–146, 618n
Textual context, of law, 49
Theft, 96–98
Third party, 31, 449
   as beneficiaries, 263–264
   liability of, 503
   and partnership dissolution, 541–542, 543, 546–547
      case, 547–548
   partnership liability to, 536
   and partnerships, 530–536
   rights of, 263–270
Third world, 831
Time, lapse of, and contracts, 185
Time bill, 370

Time instruments, 373–374, 382–384, 400
   case, 383
Time-is-of-the-essence clauses, 277
Tipping of information, 605
Title
   assignment of, 135
   documents of, 313–314, 446
   lack of, 408
   negotiable document of, 353
   and risk of loss, 324–326
   warranties of, 338
Title by adverse possession (title by limitation), 679
Title examination, 674–675
Title VII, of Civil Rights Act, 780
Title to goods, 317–322
   passage of, 317–318
   problems regarding, 318–322
Tortious act, 20
Tort liability, and agency, 505–510
   case, 507, 508, 509
Torts, 11, 107–125, 139
   agency and, 487
   and agent, 503
   bad faith, 297
   business, 123, 127–142
   and crime, 90
   and exculpatory clauses, 220–222
   intentional, 114–121, 509–510
   liability. *See* Tort liability
   of minors, 235
   and state law, 23
   and trade secrets, 132–133
Trade, usage of, 313
Trade agreements, regional, 828
Trade and Tariff Act (1984), 825–826
Trade associations, 767
Trade disputes, 817–822
Trade fixtures, 689
Trademark, 518
   infringement, 129–132
      case, 131–132
Trademark Counterfeiting Act (1984), 132
Trademark Revision Act (1988), 141
Trade secrets, 132–133
   case, 134
Trade terms, 815–816
Trading partnership, 531
Trading with the Enemy Act, 824
Transfer
   of commercial paper, 385
   voidable, 472
Transferability, of stock, 596
Transferee, and contracts, 375
Transferors, liability of, 422
Transferred intent doctrine, 115
Transnational corporation, 830–831
Travel Act, 100
Treasury stock, 593, 595
Trespass, 5, 120–121
   conversion and, 122
Trespasser, 704
Trial
   mini-, 38
   proceedings of, 30–32
   right to, 94
   summary jury, 38
Trial courts, 16, 17, 18
Trial stage, 30–32
True bill, 92
Trust, 728–731
   charitable, 731
   implied, 731
   property in, 728–729
   termination of, 731

Trustee, 469–470, 729
   case, 730
Trust Indenture Act (1939), 628
Trust indorsements, 390
Truth in lending, 800–802
Truth in Lending Act (TILA), 800–802
   case, 802
Tying agreements, 771–772

*Ultramares* opinion, 651, 652
   case, 651–652
*Ultra vires* doctrine, 579–580, 600, 624
Unauthorized completion, 404
Unavoidable accident doctrine, 111
Unconscionable contracts, 171, 222
   and sales law, 222–223
   case, 223
Underwriters, 630
Undue influence
   over estate, 722
      case, 722–723
   and voidable contracts, 246–247
Unemployment compensation, 741
Unenforceable contracts, 170
Unfair labor practices, 777–778
Unforeseen difficulties rule, and contracts, 203–204
Uniform Commercial Code (UCC), 51
   Article 1
      course of dealing, 291
      extrinsic evidence, 291
      good faith, 356
      security interest, 444
      usage of trade, 291
      without notice, 400
   Article 2
      acceptance of offers, 188n
      anticipatory repudiation, 360
      assignments, 266–267
      auction provision, 178
      battle of forms provision, 189–190, 312
         case, 190–191
      breach of contract, 342–343
      commercial impracticability, 281–282, 358
      commercial unit, 360
      confirmation rule, 257
      contracts, 312–313
      course of performance, 290–291
      defective property, 313
      destruction of goods, 358
      express warranty, 333–335
      extrinsic evidence, 290
      fraudulent sales, 321
      imperfect title, 318–320
      insolvency, 365
      leasing transactions, 311, 444
      mitigation of damages, 295–296
      modification contracts, 204–205
      NOM clauses, 205
      oral clauses, 257–258
      parol evidence rule, 259–260, 312, 335
      passage of title, 317–318
      perfect tender rule, 354–356
      and privity defense, 341–342
      reasonable medium rule, 193–194
         case, 194
      requirements and output contracts, 207n
      sale of goods contracts, 188, 307–311, 317. *See also* Sales; Title to goods
      sales contracts, 171–172, 180–182, 311–313
      seller's obligations, 353–358
      shipment offers, 195
      specific performance, 298–299
      statute of frauds, 252, 256–258

Article 2 (continued)
  unilateral offer of acceptance, 194–195, 196
  voidable title, 319
  written contracts, 258, 259
  written sales contracts, 284, 312
Article 3, 305, 369
  alteration, 406–407
  bank-depositor relationship, 428–429
  bearer instrument, 384–385
  certification of checks, 428
  checks, 427–428
  commercial paper, 305, 369–374, 454
  discharge by payment, 423
  drawers, 416–417
  extension clauses, 383–384
  forgery, 405–406
  holder in due course, 398–409
  indorsements, 389–390
  indorsers, 420–421
    case, 421–422
  liability, 413–424
  negotiable instruments, 377, 378–379, 382, 384–385, 386, 400–401, 418
  order instruments, 384
  personal defenses, 403–405
  presentments, 418, 419
  restrictive indorsements, 388, 389
    case, 388–389
  shelter provision, 402n
  special indorsements, 387
  time instruments, 383–384
  unauthorized completion, 404
  value, 398
  without notice, 400–401
Article 4, 369
  bank customer death, 429
  checks, 428–430, 434–435
  funds transfer, 440
  stop payment orders, 431–432
Article 6, creditors, 321–322
Article 8, sale of securities, 259, 596n
Article 9, 259, 465–466
  attachment, 447–448
  commingling, 456
  creditors' priorities, 456–457
  debtor default, 460–462
  and floating lien, 455–456
  perfection, 448–453
  purchase money security, 457–458
  scope of, 445–447
  secured transactions, 318n
  security agreements, 259
  termination, 458–459, 462
  terminology, 444–445
Uniform Consumer Credit Code, (UCCC), 408, 807–809
*Uniform Customs and Practice for Documentary Credits,* 814n
Uniform Fraudulent Conveyance Act, 467
Uniform Limited Partnership Act (ULPA), 52, 551, 552, 555. *See also* Revised Uniform Limited Partnership Act
  dissolution and, 557–558
Uniform Negotiable Instruments Law (NIL), 369
Uniform Partnership Act (UPA), 52, 513–514. *See also* Partnerships
  and arbitration, 534–535
  disallowed actions, 533–535
    case, 534–535
  and dissolution by court decree, 541
    case, 542–543
Uniform Probate Code, 721n

Uniform Residential Landlord and Tenant Act, 685
Uniform Securities Act, 643–644
Unfriendly tender offer, 616
Unilateral contract, 166–167, 739
  case, 166–167
Unilateral mistake, 244
Unilateral offer, 166
  acceptance of, 194–195, 196
Union busting, 479
Unions, 777–780
  case, 778–779
United Nations Commission on International Trade Law (UNCITRAL), 822
United Nations Convention on Contracts for the International Sale of Goods (CISG), 816–817
United Nations Convention on International Bills of Exchange and International Promissory Notes, 817
United Nations Convention on the International Sale of Goods, 816n
United Nations Convention on the Recognition and Enforcement of Foreign Arbitral Awards, 822
United Nations General Assembly Resolutions 3201 and 3202, 831
United States-Canada trade, 828
*United States Code,* 84
United States Constitution. *See also* Amendments
  Article I
    Contract Clause, 58–59
  Article III
    and court system, 16
    legislative powers, 76
    powers of Congress, 55–58
  Article IV
    Full Faith and Credit Clause, 58
    Privileges and Immunities Clause, 62
  criminal protections in, 91–94
  Fifth Amendment, 67, 69–71
  and statutory law, 45–46
United States Court of Appeals, 17
United States Department of Justice, Antitrust Division, 754
United States government, branches of, 59–60
United States Patent and Trademark Office, 135
United States Trade Agreement Act (1979), 827n
Universal Copyright Convention, 137
Universal life insurance, 740
Unliquidated debts, 207
Usage of trade, 291
Usury, 218, 797
Utilitarianism, 146

Vagueness, 46–47
  case, 47
Valid contracts, 170
Value, 398
  and fraud, 238
Variance, 681
Vegetation, as property, 665–666
Venue, 22
Verdict, 32
  judgment notwithstanding the, 32
  motion for directed, 32
  setting aside, 34–35
    case, 34–35
Vertical integration, 760–761
Vertical merger, 760–761
Vertical nonprice restrictions (VNRs), 769–770

  case, 770–771
Vertical restraints of trade, 768–774
Voidable contracts, 170, 229–249
Voidable preferences, 472–473
  case, 473–474
Voidable title, 318
Voidable transfers, 472
Void contracts, 170, 215
*Voir dire* examination, 30
Voluntary dissolution, of corporation, 622
Voting
  by corporate shareholders, 582
    case, 583–584
  trusts, 582
Voting rights, of shareholders, 593–594

Wagering agreements, 215–216
Warehouse companies, 716
Warehouse receipt, 313
Warrant Clause, 78
Warranty, 237n, 333. *See also* Implied warranty
  breach of, 364, 403–404
  conflicting and overlapping, 338–339
    case, 339
  disclaimers of, 339–340
    case, 341
  express, 333–335
    case, 335
  implied, 335–337
    case, 337–338
  in leases, 338
  of title, 338
Warranty liability, of indorsers, 420–421
  case, 421–422
Watchdogs, corporate, 584
Watered stock, 598
Watergate coverup, 157
Webb-Pomerene Act, 825
Whistleblowing, 150–151, 900
White collar crime, 102–103
White knight, 617–618, 642
Whole life insurance, 739–740
Wholesome Meat Act, 810
Wholesome Poultry Products Act, 810
Will, 669, 721–725. *See also* Estates
  formal, 723
  holographic, 725
  noncupative, 725
  revocation of, 724
    case, 724
Williams Act (1968), 616, 641, 642
Winding up
  and corporate termination, 624
  of limited partnership, 558
  of partnership, 544–547
Wire fraud, 99
Women, 68–69
Workers' compensation, 741, 789
  system, 114
Writ
  of execution, 35
  of garnishment, 35
Written contracts, 251–262
  case, 255
  land sale, 252–253
    case, 253–254
  performance and, 254–255
Written release statute, 208
*Writ of certiorari,* 17
Writ of execution, 716
Wrongful acquisition, and trade secrets, 133

Zoning ordinance, 681